THE GOOD SCHOOLS GUIDE

Eleventh Edition

www.goodschoolsguide.co.uk

LUCAS
PUBLICATIONS

The Good Schools Guide is a registered trademark

Eleventh Edition published 2006

by Lucas Publications Ltd

Bowland House, West Street, Alresford SO24 9AT

ISBN 09532 659 86

A CIP catalogue record for this book is available from the British Library.

Every care has been taken that all information was correct at the time of going to press. The publishers accept no responsibility for any error in detail, inaccuracy or judgement whatsoever.

Publishing Project Management by Pencil-Sharp Editors

Designed and typeset by Optima Information Design

Print management by Susan Sutterby

Printed and bound in Great Britain by Polestar Wheatons Ltd

Writers:
Simon Arbuthnott
Lindsey Aspinall
John Richard Badham
Ellen Baylis
Godfrey Bishop
Susannah Camps Harris
Elizabeth Coatman
Charles Cowling
Sarah Crabb
Sarah Drummond
Arabella Dymoke
Sue Fieldman
Sara Freakley
Lisa Freedman
Pippa Goedkoop
Elizabeth Grahamslaw
Debra Hamblin
Susan Hamlyn
Bernadette Henniker
Sandra Hutchinson
Ali Hutchison

Sophie Irwin
Christine Jefferson
Caroline Karwowska
Emma Lee-Potter
Priscilla McCall
Victoria McKee
Elizabeth Moody-Stuart
Patrea More Nisbett
Beth Noakes
Suzie Oweiss
Stephanie Page
Jill Parsons
Harriet Plyler
Anne Prendergast
Catriona Prest
Angela Pullin
Rosemary Taylor
Carolyn Thomas
Anthony Verity
Janette Wallis
Sue Wood

Thanks to:
Annie Finn
Shari Lord

Editorial review: Susan Hamlyn

Everything organised by Anthea Palmer

Acknowledgements

We should also like to thank the countless friends, pupils,
parents, staff (not to mention moles because they would rather
we didn't) who have contributed enormously valuable information
and to whom we are deeply indebted.

The delightful illustrations in the text have been contributed by
pupils of Manor House School (junior department), Leatherhead,
Surrey. We are grateful for their permission to reproduce them in
this edition.

Contents

The Good Schools Guide Advisory Service

The **Good Schools Guide Advisory Service**® is a consultancy run by The Good Schools Guide® to advise parents, on a one-to-one basis, on choosing the best schools for their children.

The Good Schools Guide is in a unique position to do this because its advisors have visited hundreds of schools over the past twenty years, and have gathered an enormous reservoir of information and experience. The *Guide* is only a glimpse of this. We would be happy to put our knowledge and our wide network of personal contacts to work for you.

The advisory service is provided by our most experienced editors, most of whom are parents like you, although some have been professionally involved with education. We offer access to advice on that basis.

Not even the best school is perfect. Good schools differ enormously in what they offer and in the kind of child they suit best. Our service can help you with:

■ Finding schools which are likely to suit your child

■ Inside information on what a particular school is really like

■ Suggesting good schools that you may not know about

■ Checking out specific schools for you

■ Information on strong specialist departments and unusual features

■ Suggestions on how to improve your chances of getting your child accepted by a school.

Tell us what you need, and we will tell you if we are able to help. All information is treated in the strictest confidence. We act as agent for our advisers, and, if we can help, the next step is for us to put you in touch directly with an appropriate adviser who will agree directly with you about a consultation in person or by e-mail, fax or telephone. If we cannot refer you to an appropriate adviser, we may be able to suggest someone else who can meet your needs.

Our standard fee is £250. The adviser may suggest a higher or lower fee, which is between you and the adviser to agree in particular cases.

The Good Schools Guide on the Web

www.goodschoolsguide.co.uk

Half price for owners of this book

There's a lot more now to *The Good Schools Guide* than we can fit in this book.

There's all the advice, information and write-ups in *The Good Schools Guide for Special Educational Needs*, for a start. This new guide sets out to provide everything that a parent requires when they are first confronted with the possibility that their child has a special educational need: hundreds of pages of advice and information, write-ups on hundreds of schools which do superbly by children with special educational needs, and hundreds of links to other sources of advice and information.

We carry a small but fast increasing number of short reviews that are only on the web, not in the printed guide.

Then (for English schools) there is the A level data: results analysed at the level of subject and grade, so that you can see exactly how popular each subject is and how well pupils do. You can use our search program to look for schools which are particularly good at individual subjects, or at least have enough pupils doing them for you to be sure that they are really on offer.

Then (again for English schools) there's the five-year history of performance table data, which you can use to track how a school has been improving (or not), and how it rates in comparison with other schools (we provide performance tables based on a total of 10 different measures).

(We are doing our best, too, to provide data on Scottish, Welsh and Northern Irish schools: we have made some progress in negotiations, so with luck it will find its way onto the website during 2006.)

In addition, there is a summary of where pupils go after GCSE, and (as we are able to obtain data under the Freedom of information act) doubtless we will be adding other fascinating analyses over the course of the year.

And there's the facilities that have always been there for our online subscribers: searches based on geography and on school characteristics; searches of the *Good Schools Guide* text and of our links pages; links to school websites and to Ofsted and other inspection reports; links to hundreds of other websites that contain information that we think will be useful to parents who are looking for schools.

You will also find that the Good Schools Guide online is updated regularly as rewrites and new schools are added, and as we make thousands of minor alterations throughout the year.

All this is yours for a year if you subscribe to the Good Schools Guide online. And, because you have already paid to purchase the book, we will only charge you half price (for as long as this eleventh edition is in print). Go to www.goodschoolsguide.co.uk, click on 'buy the guide' and, book in hand, answer a question to prove your ownership. When, later in the year, we introduce an updated version of our Good Schools Guide online shop, you may also be asked for a reference code. Use 'Apple'.

When our Good Schools Guide for Special Educational Needs comes out in April, that too will be available on our website to owners of this book at a discounted price.

Introduction

Education in the UK is in good shape, at least for those of us who are able to choose which school we send our children to – and since you're looking at this guide, that probably includes you. There are a lot of good schools out there, and it is my continuing pleasure to read the reviews of them coming in from our team of editors. As ever, we base our choice of schools on what you, as parents, are telling us; as ever, we try not to impose any judgement on what kind of schools you should like, but aim to respond to your preferences and then to visit each school so that we can paint a detailed portrait of them.

The range of good schools is extraordinary, from the furiously academic to schools which are focused on educating ordinary children; from the disciplinarian to the gentle; from the sporting to the laid-back; from the monocultural to the Babylonian. Our favourites, and I expect it shows, are the schools which set out to look after ordinary kids, and do it well. Every year they and their governors have to face the ignominy of appearing way down the league tables; every year parents have their doubts about their choice refreshed. Head teachers, brought up to be academics, find it terribly hard to love looking after a school where an Oxbridge success is a rarity, is indeed not perhaps what the school is aiming at. So we salute you educators of our ordinary children. For all the bankers and lawyers who come rolling out of the great academic machines, it is to their less celebrated brethren that we should look for the next Branson or Churchill.

We are taking a step further in that direction this year, by taking a serious and separate look at special needs. *The Good Schools Guide for Special Educational Needs* will appear in April, full of advice and information, articles by experienced parents and professionals, and of course reviews of hundreds of schools both special and mainstream. I can confidently say that it will be the essential and invaluable guide for anyone setting out to look after the education of a child with special needs, however mild or transitory – and if statistics are any guide, that means about half of you at one time or another. And, as an owner of this book, you will be able to buy it at a discount: see The Good Schools Guide on the Web.

We have added to the introduction to this guide too. Admissions seem to be becoming ever more fraught, so we have added an article on interviews and how to navigate them. Inspection reports are, when they are up-to-date, full of interesting information about a school: we have added articles on how to interpret Ofsted and (for those of you using boarding schools) CSCI inspection reports. And we have added to our information on boarding, principally to help our overseas and expat readers.

We are also adding considerably to our website, in particular data gathered under the Freedom of Information Act. Already you can use our website to delve into the A level results of your chosen schools, throwing a fascinating light on just how good the teaching is in each individual subject. You can use the website, too, to search for schools that do well in the subject that you care about, and to avoid ones where it is a backwater. We will continue our efforts to add data to the site: as a purchaser of *The Good Schools Guide* you can have free access to all this data during the currency of the 11th edition.

One of the points of choosing a good school for your children is to get them into good universities. This result is becoming less and less certain as universities strive to meet the government's targets for admitting the disadvantaged. Years of underspending on universities means that finding yourself at a lesser university can be a very thin experience academically (though perhaps just as much fun) , with only a few hours tuition a week, leading to an unrewarding experience when it comes to looking for a job. When the Warden of New College Oxford, writing in *The Times Higher Educational Supplement*, can say of undergraduates at Oxford: 'As to finding out the limits of their own abilities, learning how to contradict their teachers and leading an intellectual life that is genuinely their own, that is something they will have to do somewhere else', intellectual life lower down the pecking order must be pretty grim. So, besides writing a book on American universities as an additional arrow in your quiver, we are paying more attention to how well schools educate their pupils for the world outside. Do they know what's what? How well will they perform at interview? Are they the sort of young people that you would like to employ yourself? These are the sort of things which will count when the three inebriated years at de Montfort are forgotten.

Schools, of course, used to be famous for teaching this sort of thing; it was what going to a great school was all about. And we always expected to find a great list of oversubscribed extracurricular activities, lectures from seriously interesting people, optional classes in uplifting subjects, all helping to stretch and to civilise our young. The examination culture has buried much of that. Not only have the gaps between lessons (and associated homework) shrunk, but the content of those lessons has been stripped of the challenging and delightful. For many, that is making the later years of school life extremely challenging in quite the wrong way. We see all sorts of reasons why this needs to change. Fortunately, so do other people.

The whole 14 to 19 curriculum is in a ferment. Don't mistake me: it's not that the courses and examinations that are worthless, very much not so, but they are worth a good deal less than they might be. The government is vacillating, and into the gap made by its hesitation is trooping a host of proposals for curriculum reform. So here's mine:

Redesigning the curriculum to meet the needs of the people who are actually taking the courses has potentially extraordinary benefits.

Let's take maths as an example.

The place to start, it seems to me, is with the majority. For GCSE maths – and indeed for every other GCSE, A level and university examination – the vast majority of

pupils taking it will never take another examination in the subject in their lives. What they need to get out of their GCSE maths experience are the mathematical skills that they will need in life – not just for mundane tasks, but to appreciate fully what is going on around them: mental maths, money, risk/chance, the sort of basic geometry that is needed for DIY and a general sense of being at ease with numbers is about the limit. Having taken my children through this examination recently, and from reading the wisdom of a number of mathematical experts, I would say that about 20 per cent of the current curriculum would remain, to which you would need to add a further 20 per cent of mathematics that has practical use but which is not included in the current curriculum.

What a wonderful conclusion! Suddenly we have some space in the curriculum! Actually, an immense amount of space when this dictum is applied to all subjects. What shall we do with it? Well, let's put some of the joy back into teaching and learning. We want stuff that is a pleasure to do, but which teaches at the same time, and perhaps most importantly may inspire pupils to take the subject further. For mathematics, I suspect that it is things like code breaking, and other logic-based exercises: you can understand it without knowing the mathematics, but there's an enormous incentive to learn the maths because then you understand it so much better. Perhaps we allow this to amount to another 20 per cent of the current workload.

For those splendid few who wish to take mathematics on to a higher level (and for them only) we will need a separate part of the course: a test of the students' abilities to tackle higher things.

So, the reformed GCSE would consist of three parts: mathematics for life, which would be rigorously examined and graded so that employers and others could have a certificate of the pupil's grasp of useful mathematics; mathematics for fun, which would be lightly examined (say through a project) so that those who really made progress with it would have something to show for their efforts; and mathematics for mathematicians, which would be a rigorously examined academic exercise, the results of which are generally of no interest to anybody except an academic, because either they would be an effective fail (in which case the mathematics for life grade would be the one that counted) or they would be superseded by a mathematical qualification at a higher level. So students might emerge with say A*1:- on her way to Oxford, B2: let's settle for Economics at A level, or C*: just about manages his day-to-day mathematics, but there's a spark in there somewhere (or perhaps just a sparky parent).

A recipe, I think, for happy and motivated pupils, and for teachers who again have the time to teach as they would wish. Plus lots of time freed up from the current curriculum for all the other things that education ought to mean.

Let me know what you think. Although I enjoy my annual visit to the soap box, for the rest of the year what I like to do is listen to you. It is your views and experiences that make *The Good Schools Guide* as varied and as interesting as it is, and help us to see schools as they really are.

Ralph Lucas
editor@goodschoolsguide.co.uk

How to read this book

This is a GOOD schools guide, but what's good for one child may be useless for another, what is one parent's dream may turn another sick with horror. We try not to impose our own views of what a school should be like, but try rather to be guided by what the parents who like a school like about it, and to write our descriptions from their point of view. So read between the lines.

Our write-ups are intended to be portraits of the schools, not inventories of their assets and achievements. The school's prospectus or (for independent schools) the encyclopaedic A&C Black's *The Independent Schools' Yearbook* are the best sources of the factual background – or would be if the schools' marketing departments had not got at so many of them. If you are a subscriber to the *Guide* online, you can click straight through to the schools' websites – some of them are excellent.

If a school is not included in the *Guide* this does not necessarily mean it is not a good school – our selection is a personal one. In any event, we are in the process of gently expanding our coverage to include more good local schools. If you know of one that we have missed, or have got wrong, please tell us: it's parents like you who have made the *Guide* as good as it is.

Thoughts for parents

First and most importantly, what is your child really like? This is your starting point for finding the school to suit him/her rather than you.

Secondly, what do you want for your child? It helps to have a game plan, even if you change it at a later date— state or fee-paying? Day or boarding? Single sex or co-ed?

Thirdly, what do you want from the school? Make an honest list for yourself of everything that occurs to you, however ambitious, frivolous or peripheral it may seem. You must both do this. Your list may include, for example: happiness, safety, beauty of architecture, a stepping stone to university, social status, very local, very convenient, exeats that fit in with your career, offers Japanese, doesn't cost too much (if anything). Are you looking for a traditional approach, or something totally different? What do you really feel and think about co-education?

Beware the danger of judging a school exclusively by the bottom end because your child is young – look at the end product. How and where do you want your child to end up? Is there a member of staff at the school who is on the same wavelength as you? There must be someone you can turn to (particularly true of boarding).

See several schools – it's a process of elimination, and comparisons are vital to make. Go by your gut reaction. Were you impressed with the head? You don't have to like him/her, but it helps. Did he/she appear in control of the situation? The head really does make or break a school.

Finally, did you come out feeling good?

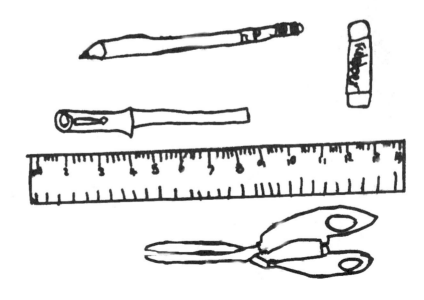

Sussing out a school and horses for courses

Every single reference book on schools indulges in advice on this. Lists of questions tend to make head teachers bristle, but going in as a parent can be daunting. The following is a list of guidelines we drew up as we went around. Obviously not all are applicable to every school: ask even half these questions and you will probably never be invited back again, but it does no harm to take them along for prompting.

Action

Send for the prospectus, a copy of the school magazine, a list of governors, and ask for the last three years' results (for senior schools) and leavers' destinations (for junior schools), the latest Ofsted or ISC inspection report (and the school's reply to it), and any other bumf – and read it. This saves time on crucial matters such as registration, subjects offered, exeats, although some of the information may be out of date.

NB: Ofsted reports, good as they are, are written in obscure language by educationalists, can be hard to penetrate, and may entirely fail to see the school from a parental point of view. ISC reports can be too cosy by half, although we have seen some excellent ones recently.

Make an appointment to see the head, and to see round the school (being shown round by pupils is best). You may find you are fobbed off with an open day or registrars, and for big schools with large numbers of applicants this is an understandable way to start. It is, however, time-consuming for you: remember you have to meet the head – no amount of wonderful buildings make up for a rotten one. Make a note of how the receptionist or secretary who answers your telephone call or greets you on arrival seems to you – they often absorb the underlying character of the school and play it back amplified.

What to wear? Projecting the right image – not too smart (particularly if you are looking for a cut-price offer), but not dowdy either. No school wants to feel it is attracting dull people, and if you have something to offer, however humble, say so.

On the day of your visit, get to the school early in order to sniff around. Approach children/staff and ask them anything ('where is the main school notice board?'). It's amazing how telling their replies can be.

What to look out for
Atmosphere and attitudes
■ What are the pupils like? Do you want your child to be like that?

■ Bearing of pupils – politeness, neatness. Bearing of staff, ditto. Do they look clean, bright-eyed and bushy-tailed (or whatever you like)?

■ Attitude of pupils to staff and vice versa. Does the head know who they all are (not often practicable in big or house-based schools)? Do pupils flatten themselves against the wall as the head passes? Do they flatten him/her against the wall as they pass. (If so, do they stop and say sorry?)

■ Watch the interaction of staff and pupils: it should be easy and unforced, but respectful.

■ Is self-confidence universal, or confined to just some kids (and if so, which ones?) Is the atmosphere happy? Fraught? Coerced or co-opted?

■ Do you fall over pupils smoking in corners? How many are slumped in front of the television (key question when visiting around 1.30pm especially)?

■ What does the school smell like? What is the state of the paintwork – a glance at the ceiling will usually tell (not that it matters per se).

Classes and teaching

■ Grab an exercise book or three in passing and look at the standard of work and the standard of marking – this can tell you an enormous amount. Check the size of teaching groups – it's amazing how often numbers do not tally with the official version.

■ What is the average age of the staff? All old can mean not enough dynamic new ideas or energy; all young can mean too inexperienced and also, possibly, too transitory.

■ Ask if you can pop in to a class, or have a good long look through the peep holes, and see what is really happening. Are the children dozing? Is the teacher dozing? Is there rapport between the teacher and the taught?

■ What's on the walls – look for evidence of creativity and the celebration of pupils' achievements.

■ Look at notice boards for signs of plenty going on, and names you know (for grilling later).

■ And, incidentally, where is the head's study: in the thick of things, indicating a finger on the pulse, or still in an ivory tower? (For some heads unbreakable precedent governs where they reign from.)

Resources

■ Observe the state of the library: rows of dusty tomes look impressive but bright, new and dog-eared is healthier. Where is the library – is it in a useful position, do the troops use it? What is the annual book budget?

■ What are the computer facilities like? Are there enough for all the kids all the time? According to the school? According to the kids?

■ Go-ahead schools are starting to use a laptop each. (Alternative view: image-conscious schools are using a laptop each. Laptops are a pain in the fundament to most schools, parents and even pupils who have to worry about losing them and – if their parents are buying them rather than the school supplying them – have to worry about whether their model is sufficiently cool.)

■ Are keyboarding/typing skills universal? Is good use made of the internet, and is the internet access fast? Do all teachers use computers/interactive white boards in class as an integral part of lessons, or just some of them? Is the school proud of its imaginative use of computers?

Finally, do you like the look of the parents, and would you be happy for your children to mix with theirs?

Questions to have up your sleeve

1. What are the results like?
This is one for the head. Watch the whites of their eyes as they give you the answer – and see 'What the league tables don't tell you'.

2. What are the 'value-added' scores like?
Most schools now use one system or another of monitoring value added – the improvement in pupils' performance over the years. Very few publish it (yet), but you should be allowed a look. What's the overall value added compared with the national average? Is this consistent over all subjects, or is the good news all in one or two areas?

3. How does the school monitor progress (pupils and, indeed, staff?) School reports? Point systems? Incentives? Regular tests?
The best will be integrated with the value-added system. Expect systems that pick up underperformance quickly (within a term), and are equally good for teachers as for pupils.

4. How much does the school spend on staff training, and what does it train them to do? Do any of the staff write school books or work as chief examiners?

5. What are the sizes of the classes – biggest and smallest? NB: a good teacher teaches any class size competently; bad teachers do not become good teachers by reducing class size.

6. What is the ratio of full-time teaching staff to pupils? How many part-timers are there? How part-time are they?

7. What is the turnover of staff – do too many stay too long? You are unlikely to get a straight answer on this.

8. Which exam boards are taken? (This doesn't help, but shows you are on the ball.)

9. What is the size of the library budget? What arrangements are there for getting hold of new books, papers?

10. What special projects are currently on the go?

11. Does the school have special help on tap for learning difficulties? If so, how much help, in what form, and is it going to cost you extra?
If this is of particular interest to you, look at *The Good Schools Guide for Special Educational Needs*. NB: mainstream schools that do well by children with SENs are often excellent places for all sorts too – the systems of individual attention and understanding that support SEN pupils mean that any child in any trouble is picked up quickly and dealt with sympathetically. Such an approach also nurtures 'diagnostic teaching' – not 'it's wrong' but 'what's wrong'.

12. Does the school feel responsible for pupils once they are accepted – or will it fire misfits/slow learners if they don't shape up quickly? If pupils are encouraged to leave, how well are they supported in this decision: are they given lots of notice, and experienced help in finding somewhere else?

13. How many are imported into the sixth form from outside?
This probably will affect the school's results and needs to be looked at with a beady eye – it may be reaping the benefits of another school's hard work.

14. How is the school coping with the AS/A2 system? Is it managing to fit in a full range of extras? Are pupils taking an interesting spread of courses – or have they relapsed to 3AS, 3A2s and the rest not taken seriously? Could this be justified by the general lack of interest in A2s from top universities? Talk to some sixth-formers about how they are finding it.

15. What is the pressure of work? Amount of work? Homework? Setting? Streaming?

16. How involved are parents with the school? Can parents talk to (or e-mail) teachers when they want to? Is there special provision for parents on the school website? How does the school report to parents? How often are school reports issued? Monthly? Termly? You would be surprised how many fee-paying schools only provide one written report a year.

17. What emphasis is there (if any) on religious teaching? Daily chapel? Daily assembly? Weekly chapel? Are special arrangements made for any other faiths – and what are they?
Some schools claiming to cater for Roman Catholics, for example, make it quite hard for them to get to Mass. How many of each faith are in the school?

18. How are pupils selected? What is the school looking for in the pupils it takes?

19. Is there automatic promotion from the junior school to the senior? If not, in what circumstances are pupils rejected, and how many each year? How much notice should you expect to be given that your child is not among the chosen (look for a minimum of two years).

20. Who are the pupils and where do they come from, both geographically and socially? How many Brits and, in particular, how many non-Brits whose first language is not English? Too many of the latter can grind teaching to a halt – very few schools can afford to cater for them separately.

21. Where do pupils go on to?

22. What is the careers advice like? Ask a sixth-former if you can; otherwise it may be a deficiency that you discover only when it's too late to do anything about it.

23. What scholarships are available and won? What bursaries and funding are available when finances come adrift?

24. What about cost: fees, plus real cost, i.e. the size of the bill?
Some schools quote an 'all-in' fee, others quote tuition fees only and charge massively for extras (such as lunch!) 'Extras' are usually listed on a separate sheet of paper (because they constantly rise) and tucked into the back of the prospectus.

25. What languages are genuinely on offer (without having to import the local Chinese take-away man)?

26. How many pupils learn a musical instrument, and for how long? Are practice sessions timetabled? What proportion of these are taught privately outside the school? This can be quite telling if you are trying to suss out the strength of a school's music department. Also: what does music tuition cost? The price of a half-hour piano lesson can vary by 100 per cent from school to school.

27. Who owns the school? If privately owned – though few are – are there any checks and balances, such as governors, PTA, and to whom do you make out your cheque? Who takes over when the current owner calls it a day?

28. How does the head run the school? Are staff and pupils happy with the result?

29. What are the head's ambitions, for the school and personally? What is his/her history? What does he/she regard as most important? What does the head really want for the pupils in the long run?

30. Until when is the head 'contracted'? (is he/she about to leave?) Is he/she married, with children (i.e. hands-on experience)? How old are the children, and where are they at school?

31. What is the head's attitude to discipline? Drugs? Sex? Alcohol? Homosexuality? Stealing? Bad language? Breaking the more petty school rules? What form do punishments take? Are prefects allowed to mete it out? Ask for a copy of the school rules – this can be illuminating – and ask how they have been established (from on high? with pupils?) Be conscious as you ask these questions that the answer you want to hear for your sheltered 10-year-old may not be the answer that you want when she is sinful and 16.

32. What does the school do about bullying?
Bullying is universal, so 'we don't have it here' probably means they don't look, and there's lots of it. A good sign is frequent examples of dealing well with it. Who chooses the prefects? 'The boys alone' is an invitation to bullying, 'the staff alone choose the nicest boys' the kindest.

33. How many people have been expelled, asked to leave, suspended in the last two years? (This could pinpoint specific major problems.)

34. Who would not be happy at the school?

35. What is the pastoral care like and who is responsible to whom and are problems spotted early? Is there a tutorial system (moral or academic)? Does it work? (Ask the pupils).

36. How good is the health care? Do they notice if pupils skip meals? How aware is the school of the dangers and signs of anorexia? Is there a cafeteria system or a table laid and 'table talk'? How much fresh raw food is there? Who oversees the tables: the staff at each end? or prefects? or is it a free-for-all?

37. What are the present numbers in the school? What has the trend been like over the last five years, and why? You need to look at the trend within age groups to see which bits of the school are popular, and also factor in any change to co-ed. What is the school's capacity?

38. What is the structure of the school? What houses are there, if any? What is the school hierarchy?

39. Every school says it has plenty of extracurricular activities, but don't take its word for it. Ask for a timetable of what happens when and who is eligible. Are the choir and the dance club by audition only? Is your talented flautist unlikely to get into the orchestra for years because they have plenty of flutes already? Does the trampolining club actually happen, or is the teacher off on maternity leave for a year?

40. If your child is keen on sport but unlikely to make the first XI, find out the school's attitude. Are there house teams, fourth and fifth teams, sports clubs open to everyone? Or does the school concentrate all its efforts on the top performers, with no opportunities for those who just like to play for fun? How much choice is there – many boys' schools insist on rugby? Are there options for the boy who refuses to play rugby or the girl who loathes hockey/lacrosse or wants to avoid team games altogether?

41. If there's an extracurricular activity that matters to you – sport, drama, riding etc. – check it out in detail, and talk to current participants. Just because something features in the literature does not mean it is taken seriously and is well provided for.

42. If you think school trips are important, find out what actually happens. How many times a term will the average class get a trip? Is the German exchange trip open to everyone, or is it first come first served? Does the head think that outings broaden the education or disrupt the timetable?

43. Is there a shadowing system for new pupils? Any special arrangements in place to welcome a pupil who comes in at an odd moment, such as the middle of term?

44. How much pocket money is suggested? A vital question, this.

45. What is the temperature at the school in the winter? A question for Scottish and seaside schools particularly.

46. Is there a holiday reading list, and is there holiday homework? Ever? Never?

47. What are the strengths of this school – and its weaknesses?

48. For boys' schools which have gone co-ed in the last 20 years: how many female academic staff are there? How many girls are there? What provision is there for the girls to play games (small numbers mean no hope of making up teams)? What facilities are there for them? What is the school's policy on boy/girl relationships?

49. At prep/junior schools: do staff sit with pupils at meal times and supervise table manners and behaviour or is lunchtime intended to be a break for the teachers?

50. Is food prepared from scratch with fresh ingredients. Is fruit easily available around the school. Does the tuck shop sell good food or junk?

51. For boarding schools: what time is supper? Is there nutritious food (containing protein) available after supper? Is the food different at weekends? (For further thoughts see the Good Food and Board Initiative: www.goodfoodandboard.org).

52. Is there a designated member of staff with a special responsibility for food at the school? What is the school's policy on attending or missing meals?

53. Are drinking water fountains placed conveniently around the school? Are pupils allowed to take water into classes?

For more questions, see the section on Boarding.

Questions for pupils
1. What is the food like?

2. What subjects do you like best? (This often reveals the most popular members of staff.)

3. What do you like best about the school?

4. What do pupils value/care about/look up to pupils for being good at (in rank order) – work, sport (which sports?), social life, drama, art?

5. What changes would you make if you were in charge?

6. Where is the head's office?

7. Are you happy here? What sort of kid would not fit in here?

8. Are you allowed to get on with your own thing without teasing or bullying? (This might flush out peer group pressure to conform.)

9. Boarding school question: what do you do at weekends? Does this correspond with what the school says happens?

10. Have you got a brother or sister in the school, what does he/she think?

11. Why did you choose this school, and what do you think of the others that you might have chosen?

12. How difficult is it to get selected for a school sports team?

Question for the local shop/taxi driver/estate agent
What is the school like? This can produce a flood of enlightening comment.

What the league tables don't tell you

League tables have caused a lot of agony and misunderstanding. As we have said elsewhere, as raw statistics, they are more or less meaningless. You will observe, for a start, that results swing wildly according to which newspaper you happen to look at. Among other things they don't tell you:

■ The pupils' IQ: two Ds for some pupils is a triumph of wonderful teaching.

■ The pupils' background: how much help/support are they getting at home?

■ The school's background: is it academically selective or mixed ability?

■ The school's policy towards A levels: does it allow pupils to 'have a go' or to take an extra A level (for stretching/breadth). Does it operate a policy of dissuading borderline candidates from taking a subject? We are hearing some disturbing stories these days of schools chucking out pupils who have not done well enough at AS level, to keep them from polluting the school's A level results.

■ The school's policy at sixth form? Is it pinching, for example, bright girls from neighbouring girls' schools? Or is it turfing out the less able pupils? Does it insist on very high (A grade) GCSEs in proposed A level subjects for those coming into the school at sixth form?

■ Good years and bad years: is this a blip, a one-off? There may be exceptional circumstances, such as the death of a teacher six months before the exam.

■ What subjects are taken. Some, e.g. business studies, classical civilisation, are considered easier than others. The league tables do not tell you which schools are taking general studies at A level: A level general studies can push league table ratings up no end.

■ The spread of subjects at A level. Which are popular? Which neglected? Does that profile fit your child – it may reflect the relative quality of teaching, or just the spirit of the school.

■ Whether a large enough number of children are doing really well, especially in subjects that you are interested in. A cohort of excellence will give leadership and confidence to the rest of the school Are sufficiently few pupils failing altogether to avoid the reverse effect?

■ The quality of education overall: depth, breadth, all-round, music, debating... things that help pupils learn to think for themselves By sheer swotting, exams can be successfully passed – but at the expense of what?

■ The reliability of the figures. The more pupils there are, the more statistically significant the results are.

■ The results of children who took the exam late. Schools that encourage pupils to polish off GCSEs as and when the kids feel ready may come off looking worse than they should – the separate year 11 column in the tables may be a better indication of their quality. NB: it is expected that the 2005 results (to be published after this guide has gone to press) will show the results for the year cohort (i.e. what used to be known as year 11) as the main measure, so that this difficulty will no longer apply.

■ Also, watch out for Scottish schools lurking in among the English league tables. Many Scottish schools offer two systems: Scottish Highers (usually for the weaker brethren) and A levels. Only the A levels show up in the league tables. Ditto the International Baccalaureate (IB) system, which is now offered by a fair number of English schools: again, only A levels show up in the league tables, but with the IB it's usually the weaker candidates who are left doing A levels.

■ And while we are on the subject of statistics, treat class size figures with care too. How you teach, what you teach and to whom all govern the size that a class can be before performance deteriorates. Other intangible factors (quality of management and teachers, the spirit of the school) are usually much more important. If the children are excited about learning, and there's lots going on after school, then it's clear that there are enough good teachers about and that they are not over-stretched. The only certain thing about small class sizes is that they mean large bills.

Interpreting results (as best you can)

This is what you need to ask the schools you are interested in:

1. Have they anything to declare – any special circumstances?

2. Ask for a complete breakdown of exam results for the last three years. This means a complete list of subjects taken, showing the number of pupils taking each subject and the number achieving each grade from A to U. If you are fobbed off with a 'summary' of results, be indignant and suspicious – they are asking you to trust them with your child, so why won't they trust you to react sensibly to the results? Ask also which year group took the exams – make sure that re-takes and early examinations are listed separately.

3. With all this in front of you and a cold towel wrapped around your head, look to see where the weaknesses and strengths are to be found. Which are the popular and successful subjects? Is one subject pulling the overall results up? Or down? Or is a 100 per cent A grade pass in Norwegian translated as one pupil (with a Norwegian mother)? Is it pure coincidence that the best two subjects at A level are Chinese and mathematics?

4. How many pupils are taking exams over all? A school with a sixth form of 40 (three children doing each subject) should find it considerably easier to come up high on the league tables than larger schools. The larger the number taking any one subject, the more commendable when the results are strong, and the wider the scope for failure. Watch out for sudden improvements, particularly in mainstream subjects, and look warily at the numbers of candidates: if the number has halved from one year to the next, could it be that the school policy has been to force out the weaker candidates and so manipulate the results?

5. You might also take a look at the A level results displayed on the relevant school's page on our website. This table will help you see quickly which are the more successful subjects, and which are unusually popular. You will also be able to see (from the figures at the foot of the table) how well girls do compared to boys, what percentage of pupils gained three A grades, and so on.

6. This will give you some idea of what is going on and where the weak teaching might be (or perhaps it is just that the less academic children tend to take that subject – there is no way of knowing without asking). Now you are in a position to ask the head to explain those appalling geography results, and to explain what is being done about the situation. Listen carefully, because all schools have weaknesses, and the important thing is what is being done to remedy them.

7. Ask for the ALIS/MIDYIS/YELLIS (systems covering the A level, middle and primary years respectively, managed by the University of Durham) or other value-added data, which should show how good the results really are, allowing for the quality of individual pupils. Government value-added tables are now published (though not for all ages, or for many independent schools). Do they show the school in a better light, or a worse one? Ask why.

But at the end of the day, remember that league tables are only one often unreliable indicator of how a school performs. And, of course, this still won't tell you which is the right school for your child.

Inspection reports from Ofsted and others

There's no longer any great secrecy surrounding school inspections. For some years now, reports have been published and available to view on the web, warts and all. So it should be easy to find a good or even great school. Log on to Ofsted, ISI (for independent schools), HMIe (for Scottish schools), DENI (in Northern Ireland) or Estyn (for Wales). Read the report, make a decision and bingo, found! The erudite institution where little Johnny will spend at least five years questioning, discovering, reasoning, having fun, joining the intelligentsia all prior to his appointment as a prefect, head boy and sailing gallantly into the sunset… No need for *The Good Schools Guide* then?

Well, not quite. As with most reports there's a code to decipher and a few questions to ask. The local school gets a glowing report, yet you know half the population are banned from the shopping centre; mothers with young children dodge the area, avoiding it altogether at dropping off and kicking out times. Oh, and then there are the rumours about teachers being attacked, drugs, knives – just rumours, yet last year's local primary 6 all opted for a school a tricky bus ride away. Puzzling?

So just what do inspection reports tell us and have they any value? The answers are lots and yes – if you know how to read the reports and understand what happens (or rather happened until very recently) when the notice of inspection drops through the letterbox.

The odd pupil or ten are siphoned to some cobwebbed corner of the school, long since Tippexed from the map. Classes suddenly find the deluge of supply teachers replaced with the most senior and, without doubt, strictest teachers in the school. Ed Double-Trouble is excluded along with his sidekicks. Local colleges are implored to run a special course, preferably in the Outer Hebrides, for a bunch of recalcitrant reprobates. Trips are planned; classes become smaller and more manageable. Teachers suddenly discover the switch for the interactive whiteboard; lessons have a zing (must be the three months' planning). Work from last term isn't only marked, it's graded, with targets written in, ticked off and achieved all in one go (wow!). The graffiti disappears overnight. Oh, and there's a team of important-looking people parading round in suits. (So that's why they said in assembly that if we were on our best behaviour this week, we'd not only get Friday afternoon off next week but a trip to Alton Towers, at least one effort grade higher on subject reports, a disco, plus cuddly toy, ride in a space ship…)

It happened. Not everywhere. Indeed, we hope, not in too many places and certainly not for much longer. There's a new Ofsted system in place. Instead of months of notice, followed by blood, sweat, tears, tantrums, exhaustion, depression (and that's just the head); there's a mere two minutes (well, as little as two days) before the inspectors scrutinise every last policy document, using only the finest-toothed nit-comb ever wielded by even the starchiest of school nurses. It's now a short, sharp, shock! Followed by a couple of days under the magnifying glass before the painful process is gone; quicker than a molar extraction and certainly too quick for the long-term sick to be dragged from beds or malingerers sent to theirs.

So what happens? They look at the data to hand: the Performance AND Assessment Report (PANDA –something that eats, shoots and leaves?), school improvement plan (SIP) and the self-evaluation form (SEF), trickier than the latest England team selection. Can't work out why this wasn't invented by mediaeval torturers: put yourself on the rack, turn the screws, and we'll turn up to see if you are screaming loudly enough. Say all the teaching is fantastic and everything hunky-dory? Seeing is believing! Say all hopeless, they'll definitely observe. Something in the middle? Does this mean wishy-washy and in need of a kick? Things have to be kept up to date: no more last-minute marking of books. Setting targets and monitoring them is now part of the daily grind; writing lesson plans no longer something waved goodbye to at the end of teaching practice; there's even an expectation they'll be delivered to support assistants before, not after lessons! Observations are shorter – as little as five minutes (because teaching was so impressive… or boring?) and feedback faster.

The new reports are slimmer (so you can print them out without using an entire ink cartridge). Each section is headed and graded. Grade 1, outstanding (and we've seen several of these), grade 4, inadequate with good and satisfactory in between. Where a section isn't grade 1, helpful comments will be made about what the school should do to improve. They grade overall effectiveness, achievements and standards, including how well learners with disabilities or learning difficulties progress, personal development and well-being of pupils including behaviour and healthy lifestyles (so the cola and chocolate machines are a no-no then, drat) and how well learners develop workplace skills (no, not how to have a sneaky fag break). As you'd expect, the quality of provision is reported on. This isn't so much about how pretty the corridors are (though undoubtedly these will make an impression), it's how effective teaching and learning is, in meeting the full range of learners' needs (teaching to the middle no longer an option). A key part of the leadership and management section refers to how effectively management raises achievement and supports learners (but not really about how they support staff in doing so); governors can expect to be grilled (and they don't even get paid for the privilege of doing their job!) plus a comment on what pupils and parents think of the school (although the parent and student questionnaires have gone).

After the inspection, not only do the schools receive the report, with an opportunity to reply to it, but a delightful letter is sent to the children of the school. The one to secondary age is quite formal, though in pupil-friendly language, beginning: 'Dear pupils and students.' Primary ones we've seen have pretty graphics in colour and start 'Dear children.' Both thank the children for letting the inspection team visit (as if they had a choice). Ticks (primary) or bullet points (secondary), indicate what the inspectors liked best about the school and an arrow (not a cross) or further bullet points mark out what they've asked the head to think about, so the school can improve (retirement?). Both end with a 'thank you for all your help.'

If you are looking through older inspection reports, or non-Ofsted (some of the others are well below Ofsted standard), the key bits are usually under headings along the lines of 'what the school does well and what the school could do better'. This provides a useful summary. If the school still looks interesting, some reports have grading, comparing the school with all schools, similar schools etc.

Beware, inspection reports can date very quickly – that can be a plus or a minus. In smaller schools, a change of head can alter the whole dynamics of the school. In large schools a previously outstanding report for Spanish may well be down to one member of staff.

Individual subject reports have disappeared from the new reports…and don't be fooled into thinking specialist status means the school really is the best in the area for a subject – only one school can have the status. If another school nabbed maths and science first, schools may be left with limited options to grab the extra cash that goes with the status.

Read reports with care, and use your imagination – inspectors have seen too many schools and tend to think everyone knows what's meant by, e.g., 'low-level disruption' Does this mean 'Nothing much' then? No! It actually means the most annoying kind, where the teacher can't nail the kid but would love to throttle him. Where lessons are constantly spoiled and marred by a handful who know how to play the system, throw bits of paper while the teacher writes on the board, make silly noises, call out inappropriately. The sort that's much worse for other pupils than the occasional spectacular blow-out followed by a quick expulsion.

So read the reports, they're intended for the parents of the school and are a valuable part of the picture. But you will be lucky if the report is recent enough to be decisive. And always take a critical look yourself, before you entrust your child to a school.

The Commission for Social Care Inspection: CSCI

Boarding schools often used to conjure up images of freezing showers, inedible food, Flashman-type bullies and terrible homesickness. Not any more. Today's boarders are more likely to live in cosy houses equipped with TVs, washing machines, hair-dryers – you name it. Parents often remark that they'd move in like a shot given half a chance!

But now that boarders are so well cared for and comfortable, the powers that be have invented an inspection regime to keep them up to the mark. The CSCI, the lead inspectorate for social care in England, has been given responsibility to inspect 'welfare arrangements' at state and independent boarding schools and to check they meet national minimum standards.

CSCI inspectors usually visit schools in teams of four, spending three days questioning staff and talking to small groups of boarders in private to ascertain whether their welfare is being 'adequately safeguarded and promoted'. They then write a detailed report, which is sent to the school head to sign and confirm as 'fair and accurate'.

Each school is judged on 52 standards. These cover a wide range of issues, including bullying, relationships between staff and boarders, racial and sexual discrimination, intrusions into privacy, accommodation, food and access to information about events in the world outside.

So far, inspectors have concluded that most boarding schools look after children well. But they have found areas of concern in some schools. A handful have been criticised for the quality of accommodation and furnishings on offer to boarders, while others have been taken to task over the quality of food served up or for allowing raunchy posters on bedroom walls.

Eton, for instance, received high praise for providing 'a positive boarding experience for its pupils'. But inspectors also drew attention to the fact that rules on posters in boys' rooms varied considerably among the 25 boarding houses. 'In one house domestic staff reported that they were uncomfortable with some of the posters on display in the boys' rooms,' they said. 'It is advised that school-wide guidance on posters be developed and implemented.'

At other schools boarders complained they found it difficult to sleep at night and didn't have enough privacy and space. Some pupils at Clifton College said their dorms were noisy when they were trying to get to sleep. And although girls, parents and staff were 'very complimentary' about the boarding provision at Cheltenham Ladies' College, a few complained about the morning waking-up procedure. 'The pupils felt that they were woken up rather harshly, with loud greetings and bright lights, and on occasions staff knocked on doors whilst simultaneously opening the door,' said the inspectors. Oh, the poor darlings.

But despite these quibbles, boarding schools are perceived as doing a good job. In 2004, Dr Roger Morgan, the children's rights directors for England – based within the CSCI – questioned 2,000 boarders and their parents and found they were generally positive about boarding schools. 'They are seen as offering a positive social life, with plenty of friends and activities – often across cultures – and with strong benefits of learning social skills and independence,' reported Dr Morgan. 'The public caricature of boarding is very negative, with people imagining lots of bullying, poor care and extreme homesickness. These are not major issues for today's boarders or their parents.'

Indeed not. Parents' memories may stray back to the days when they were lads and lasses at boarding school; some of their schools would have had to have been transformed into the penal institutions that they resembled to accommodate those who had been convicted of crimes that, these days, would keep the *Daily Mail* fulminating for a week.

Bear in mind, though, that there is a long tradition in many schools of not talking to anybody about what's really going on. If, when you go around a school, the pupils are open and talk to you easily about how the little miseries of school life are dealt with, then they probably talked to the CSCI too.

Further information about the CSCI and its work can be found at www.csci.org.uk.

Entrance

Fee-paying schools

As a rule of thumb this is what you do:

1. Visit the schools you have shortlisted, take a tour round them and talk with the head and/or housemaster or whoever is appropriate. V time-consuming, but infinitely less so than making the wrong choice.

2. Register your child's name in the school(s) you have chosen. Telephone the school and it will send you an application/registration form. If your child is still in the cradle, and the schools you have your eye on are v oversubscribed, you may decide to register before visiting.

3. Filling in the form has to be done at the right moment or the 'list' may be 'full'. Embryos are acceptable at some schools; the lists for many successful schools will close several years before the date of entry. It will usually cost a registration fee (usually non-returnable) ranging from £25 to £200 or more.

4. The school will then contact you and your child's current school about the next stage (it doesn't hurt to telephone and check, though, if you think it may have forgotten you – and don't forget to tell the school if you change your address). They will usually get a report from the head of your child's current school and attention is paid to that.

5. Your child is usually, though not always, put through their paces, which might (at a young age) mean an exam, a test or two, or 'meaningful' play' or whatever. (NB: you might also – openly or surreptitiously – be put through your paces as well: are you a good parent? Is there discipline in the home? Are you educated? Are you a complainer or a worrier? Have you some wonderful attribute the school might be able to use?). For entry to senior schools there may be a scholarship/entrance exam or, in the private sector, 'Common Entrance' – a standard exam taken by applicants to a wide range of schools, but marked by the school of first choice.

6. All being well, the school will then offer a firm place. You must write and confirm acceptance of this place or it may be offered to someone else. NB: you will probably be asked for a large non-returnable deposit at this stage, which can be many hundreds of pounds. Those public schools that require prospective pupils to attend an exam/assessment when they are 10 or 11 may require a massive cheque when the child is still years away from leaving prep school.

7. Pay school fees – in advance of the term is normal practice, alas.

8. Read any contract you have to sign carefully: if in any doubt – such as what do they mean by 'a term's notice' – a little legal advice at this stage can save you a lot of agony later.

There are a few variations on this theme. For example, grammar schools will often accept entries up to the last minute, though there will be an official date for closing the 'list', from about three weeks to three terms before the entrance exam.

> **TIP:** All things being equal, always have a go at the school you think is right for your child. Even those schools you have been told are jam-packed may have a place. Don't restrict yourself to trying at the 'normal' entry periods. Dare to try mid-term, and mid-academic year, or even the day before term starts. If you get a no, don't be afraid to try again. NB: Many schools (especially now, when it's a provider's market) simply refuse to consider non-standard entries. Play the rules as far as you can.

State schools in England

The state schools admissions system is a complicated mess and needs to be understood in the light of the particular admissions criteria of each school. Key factors are usually:

■ Geographical location. This is often particularly important though defined in many different ways – distance as the crow flies, distance by a safe route, catchment area, previous school attended etc. – and liable to change each year as applications vary. Parents have been known to rent houses within the requisite area of the school in order to establish residence there, or 'borrow' an address, or invent one. Some schools also operate a 'banding' system to ensure that their intake is a fair reflection of the ability spectrum of their applicants or neighbourhood – this can lead to different geographical limits for each ability band.

■ Religion. Some of the best UK schools have a religious foundation, and are more or less devoted to education children of that religion. You need to start attending church weekly at least a year before conception to have a chance at some schools. You may also need to engage in voluntary work or prove your social worth in other ways.

■ Attainments. There are still almost 200 academically selective schools in England, and many more that have special admissions arrangements for particular talents – they may specialise in languages, science or sports, or they may admit a few talented musicians. Understand how the criteria work, and consider some targeted coaching. Ask those whose children succeeded last year and who have no younger children – they have nothing to lose by letting you in on their secrets.

■ Medical grounds. If this might apply to your child (even cleaner air for an asthmatic) get your case documented – it can be an overriding criterion. See below

■ An expressed preference by parents for some special character of the school, e.g. single-sex education or boarding.

■ Preference for siblings. But, if that applies to you, you are there already and in no need of our advice.

Getting into the nursery class at a primary school does not guarantee admission to the main school and, vice versa, you do not have a lesser chance of getting into the main school if you choose another nursery school. You may be able to secure a place in the main school by applying for a place in the reception class – but you do not then need to take that place up.

Start looking early – you may need to move house. Get the admissions booklets from your local education authority, and any neighbouring LEA whose schools you might consider – they should give you a good idea of what you will have to do to get in. Apply for your chosen schools a good year before the likely date of entry if they are not part of a 'co-ordinated admissions policy' (see below).

For all England, there is a system of co-ordinated admissions arrangements, and applications are all (or almost all) made through the local education authority. You are likely to be faced with arrangements that require you to state your preferences in order of priority. At that point you need to know one vital fact: do the schools get told what your order of priority is?

If the schools are told, you may need to do some careful research to decide which schools to put on your list and in which order. Top comprehensives in areas that have grammar schools may refuse to consider your child if you have also applied to a grammar school; you may not be considered by your local school if you have put another as your first choice. The threat you are faced with is that if you aim for the best and miss, you may only be offered a sink school miles away. London examples include schools that have said that they will compare applications and disregard pupils who have applied to more than one, and some that say that if you also apply to a selective school they will not offer you a place (whether or not you put them first).

We think that this is entirely the wrong way round. It makes life easy for schools and difficult for parents. It is essential that you find out exactly how the rules work in practice, and that you are realistic about your first choice.

If the schools are not told – as in the system in Kent – you are in a much better position. You put the schools that you like (up to three, usually) in order of preference; the LEA passes these choices on to the schools concerned but does not tell them if they are your 1, 2 or 3. Each school then assesses its applicants against its admissions criteria and tells the LEA who it will accept. The LEA looks to see what acceptances you have received, and passes on to you the acceptance that you gave the highest priority to – let's say that it is number 2 on your list – and that is where, barring appeals, you go.

Or is it? Because schools will have had some of their acceptances disregarded by the LEA (because parents have put another acceptance higher up their list) they will have some unfilled places, for which they will issue acceptances to children who just missed the cut on the first round. If your child gets offered a place by your number 1 choice in this way, then you can choose to go there and rescind your place at number 2. Up to a dozen rounds may be required to sort everyone out. Complicated for the LEA? – certainly. Uncertain for schools? – indeed so. But wonderful for parents and something to be grateful to this government for. If you do not have this in your patch, campaign for it. There are bound to be teething troubles, especially where cross-border applications are concerned, but there's no reason why it should not all work out well in the end.

If you get what appears to be a 'No' on any count you have the right of appeal, stating to an appeal committee why you think little Edna should go to Grunts and not St Dumps. One of the most successful reasons seems to be health: if you can get a doctor's letter stating that your ewe lamb gets asthma and will only flourish in the pure air of Grunts, you are half-way there. Like any other appeal you need to lobby like mad – the head, the governors, the doctor, the local authority, your MP, the lollipop man – whoever seems good to you. The parents' section of the DfES website www.dfes.gov.uk is a good place to bone up on appeals procedures. Don't get your hopes up too high – 90 per cent of appeals fail.

State schools in Scotland

The system in Scotland is pretty much catchment-area based, though with a right for a parent to ask for another school. As the government website says: 'If you have a child who is due to start primary school or who will be transferring to secondary school soon, you have a right to express a preference for a particular school. Your Council will probably suggest that you should use the local school designated by them, and of course you may be happy to do so, but the Council must also tell you of your right to choose a different school, and give you an address where you can get help in making up your mind.' Some councils are more helpful than others.

State schools in Wales

You have a right to attend your local school but can apply for another. Your choice will be respected if (as far as we can see) the school and the LEA feel so inclined.

Interviews

'I'll always be grateful to Gordon Brown. Not because of his macro-management of the economy, but because his name was the correct answer to my son's 11-plus interview question: 'Who is the Chancellor of the Exchequer?' It was the possession of this crucial piece of information that, in my view, tipped the balance in my son's search for a secondary school place.'

The school interview is one which tends to send the applicant's parents rather than the actual applicant into a spin. Parents feel considerably more responsible for their child's social presentation than for his or her ability to do long division or conjugate French verbs. And, while a school may breezily describe the interview as 'just a chance to get to know the child better', this hardly overcomes concerns about sending young Daniel or Daniella into the lion's den.

The London day-school interview is perhaps the most straightforward. Over-subscribed at every point, the selective urban independent tends to concentrate on the academic. The majority usually only meet the child after a written exam (generally used as a first edit), and the interview itself will contain a significant component of maths, comprehension or reasoning. The aim here is to probe intellectual strengths and weaknesses in order to select from the central bulk of candidates or to pick scholarship material. Finding out a little about a child's character is only of secondary importance.

Even the most academic schools, however, are not necessarily just looking for those guaranteed to deliver a stream of A*s. Jane Sullivan – for many years the headmistress of one of the country's top selective prep schools – used her 7 plus interview as an opportunity to create as balanced a community as possible.

'I didn't want 50 extroverts or 50 eggheads. Most children who sat our exam scored between 40 and 65 per cent in the written paper, so I was looking for an individual spark. At the age of 7, too, the interview is a crucial counter-balance to the exam. Those born between September and December always scored higher marks in the written paper. At interview we would go back to the list and bring in some younger children.'

Concerned parents often do their best to control the outcome of the interview, but professional preparation is universally descried, both by those who interview and by teachers who send children to be interviewed. 'I always tell parents if they're paying to coach 3-year-olds, they might as well burn £20 notes,' says Jo Newman, headmistress of North London Collegiate Junior School, who has the daunting task of selecting 40 4-year-olds from 200 applicants in a two-tier interview. 'The only useful preparation is to talk to them, play with them and read them stories.'

Further up the system, the advice is equally non-prescriptive. Jenny Aviss, head of Wetherby School in west London, does her best to relax the 7-year-olds she sends to prep-school interviews by providing them with as much factual information as she can beforehand. 'I try to prepare them for what they'll find. I usually describe the head – because I'm a smallish woman they might expect all heads to be like me – and I'll tell them what the school looks like. Beyond that I just say, "Look them in the eye, answer carefully and be honest." Children sell themselves.'

Some pre-preps and prep schools provide mock interviews, some will carefully guide children on what books or hobbies that might show to best advantage, but most interviewers say they always know when a child has been coached, and honesty – at least in theory – is the quality they're looking for. 'I tell children,' says one private tutor who prepares children for 11-plus, 'to say what's in their heart, not what their teacher told them to say.'

Those moving from state to private will undoubtedly have to take any preparation into their own hands. Some particularly pro-active parents of my acquaintance have used job manuals and professional coaching techniques to ready their child. One parent videoed his daughter to give her positive feedback on her strengths and weaknesses; another asked a friend unknown to the child to conduct a mock interview.

Personality, of course, will always be the most variable aspect of any interview and all interviewers have a personal bias. They may hate boastful children, or those who say their favourite leisure activity is computer games; they may prefer Arsenal fans to Tottenham supporters, but some schools do make a strenuous attempt to counteract the sense of one adult sitting in judgement on one child. City of London School, for example, sees candidates individually before sending them off to a lesson where they can be observed by another teacher as they work in a group. At Rugby, every child is interviewed by at least two people.

The best interviewers can and do overcome the limitations both of the written examination and of the child. 'Children, even very shy ones, like to talk about themselves, their friends, their families and their pets. I'd get them to describe what they did on Sunday, or I'd turn my back and ask them to describe something in the room,' says Jane Sullivan. 'Sometimes I'd even get a child to sing or dance. I was looking for sparkly eyes and interest. If child just sat there like a pudding, you usually didn't take them.'

Some schools get over the 'what to talk about' dilemma by asking children to bring along a favourite object. Rugby sensibly provides a questionnaire about hobbies and interests to fill in in advance, which not only provides a talking point, but also allows parents to feel they've done what they can. If, however, the child pitches up with a copy of Proust or boasts a collection of Roman ceramics, parents shouldn't be surprised if the interviewer is somewhat sceptical.

Children themselves tend to be annoyingly honest. The headmaster of one highly selective north London school dealing with 7-year-old entrants always used to ask what the Roman numerals on his clock stood for. One carefully prepared child answered correctly, and then added, 'My parents told me you were going to ask that.' Another

parent regrets that he didn't bother overly with his son's interview when he discovered that the boy had answered the Harrow housemaster's: 'What is your worst subject?' with: 'I don't really have one.'

Although a number of leading boarding schools – Marlborough, for example – still rely solely on the prep-school report and Common Entrance papers, most now feel that the interview can identify serious pastoral concerns. 'We sometimes discover that a child really doesn't want to come to boarding school,' says Hilary Morrish, registrar of Rugby. 'The interview is also very helpful in establishing the academic level the prep-school is working at. We ask children to bring in their exercise books. Some London prep schools are so geared up at that point that all the child is doing is practice papers. Country prep schools tend to be more relaxed.'

Although most heads are honest in their report about a child – after all, their reputation depends on it – the interview can also benefit them. 'Occasionally, a prep-school head knows perfectly well that a child is not suited to our school, but the parents just won't listen,' say Hilary Morrish. 'Coming from us it doesn't sour the relationship with the school.'

Boarding schools, of course, tend to have another layer to their selection process and interview when they match boys and girls to an appropriate house. Here the parent, even more than the child, can be in the spotlight.

Dr Andrew Gailey, housemaster of Manor House, Prince William's house at Eton, always tries to strike a balance of the sporty and industrious, the musical and the generally decent in his annual selection of ten boys, but, for him, the parental part of the equation plays an even greater role. 'The boy is going to change, but you have shared management of the child's adolescence with the parents and you have to have some common bond for that to work.'

However anxiety-making interviews are, I would be wary of a school that didn't at least wish to meet your child. An interview can fire a prospective candidate's enthusiasm for a school, make teachers more committed to teaching the child and give parents a clearer notion of the school's pastoral style. Although arranged marriages may have a successful history elsewhere, a meeting of true minds is a far more desirable approach in education.

The System

It helps, when planning your child's journey through the maze of state and private schools, to know the main stages of jumping from one to another.

Advantages of state education are usually that it's close by and part of the community; a free school bus operates in country areas (often but by no means always avoiding the need to become full-time driver); a broad social mix; no school fees; a slight edge on the private sector when it comes to Oxbridge entrance (if your child has the determination and confidence to get straight As in the state school); often greater understanding of the wide world at the end of it.

Advantages of the private system are usually a greater chance of doing well in public exams, especially for an average child (although there are many exceptions); often better academic (as opposed to pastoral) care; a wider range of extras and often at a higher standard; smaller classes; the opportunity to study elite subjects such as Greek and start modern languages earlier; the opportunity to board and all that that implies.

Many parents play the system, moving between the state and independent sectors. See 'Finessing the System', below.

Age -1. Start looking at schools – you may need to book a place soon after birth in the private sector; for the best state schools you have three or four years to move into the catchment area. If you are after a religious school, start going to church every week.

Age 2+ to 4+. Nursery/kindergarten, particularly in the private sector.

Age 4. 'Pre-prep' starts in the private sector.

Age 5. Education is compulsory for everyone in the UK. Year 1, in the English state system, is the year beginning in the September following the child's fifth birthday.

NB: this places children born late in the school year at a disadvantage – on average they will do less well throughout their school careers, and the latest research suggests that they are 20 per cent less likely to make it to university. So, avoid getting pregnant between July and November inclusive. The obvious remedy for this disadvantage is to allow those younger children who seem to be falling behind to drop back a year. This practice has never been popular in the UK, and was made particularly difficult by the Government's former practice (only abolished in 2005) of reporting schools' GCSE and A level results as if children who had been held back had failed all their exams, so that senior schools (conscious of their position in the league tables) became extremely reluctant to accept them. Government policy seems at last to have turned around, and finally to have accepted that what should come first is the interests of the child rather than the league tables: so if it seems right to you that your child should drop back a year, this is a battle that you ought now to be able to win.

Age 7-8. 'Prep' school starts in the private sector.

Age 11. State secondary schools and grammar schools usually start, i.e. in year 7.

Age 13 (or thereabouts). Move to most private secondary schools (known as 'public schools' for reasons of history, a source of confusion to all but the Brits) for boys, and to private co-educational establishments, although some have lowered their entry age to 11.

Age 16. Once GCSEs are over, all change is possible: boys and girls may move from state schools to private ones (almost all now have entry at 16+, sometimes with scholarships), or from private schools to, say, state sixth-form colleges as petty restrictions begin to irk. You may want to leave for a school that offers the International Baccalaureate (IB).

Entry at sixth-form level increasingly depends on GCSE results. Check with the school when applications need to be made. Girls applying to the sixth form of boys' or co-ed schools may expect toughish competition.

If it looks as though A levels may be a struggle for your child and he/she is set on university, it is possible (though the logistics may defeat you, and it will almost certainly mean going to school in Scotland) to change from the English exam system to the Scottish one of Highers (see below). This is much more broadly based – more subjects at a slightly lower level – and is now accepted by most English as well as all Scottish universities.

Another possibility for the less academic is to find a school or college that offers the more vocational GNVQs (now renamed AVCEs), a blend of the academic and practical delivered in a much more practical style than A levels. Many universities are now happy to admit students with AVCEs (particularly business).

The International Baccalaureate
Developed 40 years ago by teachers in Geneva who were faced with teaching children of many different nationalities, the IB is now established worldwide. In the UK there are about 70 schools that offer it (both state and private), and it is accepted as a means of entry by all universities. Most offer the sixth-form curriculum, where students study six subjects: two languages, a humanities subject, a science, maths, and a free choice that might be anything from drama to another science. Pupils are also required to engage in non-academic activities embracing creativity, action and service. A few schools offer the IB programme for earlier years too. There's an underlying international flavour to the IB – an avowed aim to build good citizens of the world. To succeed at the IB you need to be of an academic (as opposed to vocational) turn of mind, and to have a breadth of ability; pure scientists or budding architects may be better suited by A levels. You don't, though, need to be especially brilliant.

The Scottish system
The Scots do things differently. Better too, they say.

First things first: in the state system, nursery is followed by primary at 5, followed by senior school at 11. The fee-paying sector often has entry ages of 8 for the prep schools and 13 for the senior schools. If you are after switching systems at 11 most of the big Scottish independent schools run junior schools, where your little darling may transfer automatically to senior school without having to take the Common Entrance exam; and most prep schools are quite used to an influx of numbers at that age.

The Scottish examination system consists of:

Standard Grades (Lowers as they used to be called), taken in the fifth year (i.e. aged 16, the same age as GCSEs in the rest of the UK). Each pupil is expected to take seven or eight (or more).

Highers, taken a year later in the sixth year. Three or more is the norm (with exceptional schools such as Hutcheson's Grammar knocking up sixes and sevens). Pupils can – and many do – leave school after taking Highers and are then qualified for university entrance (which can be a problem as a bright student may then hit university at 16, which is a bit young). This is why Scottish university courses are a year longer than English ones.

Advanced Highers, occasionally called Higher Stills. These equate to the A2. Not all Scottish schools stick rigorously to the Scottish system, and we have found some state schools preferring the English qualification, particularly in geography, music and art.

However, in their wisdom the Scottish Qualifications Authority have introduced Intermediate 1 and 2, which are intended to supplement or extend Standard Grades. It is not clear to us where this is intended to lead: at the moment they just duplicate Standard Grades.

A good collection of Advanced Highers may (and the jury is still out on this) allow students to go straight into the second year of a four-year course at a Scottish university (as may good A levels).

And if you are looking at independent schools, remember that quite a lot also do the English system in a sort of wobbly tandem – traditionally with the less academic doing the Scottish system. This makes it almost impossible to judge by exam results.

Finessing the state and independent sectors

All those scary newspapers statistics about the long-term costs of keeping your child in nappies and birthday presents pale into insignificance when set beside the £100,000+ you'll need to educate a child privately from nursery to university.

But paying for a private education from finger painting to Freshers' Week is no longer the necessity it was once. There may be more people than ever before opting for the independent sector, but those without private means or surplus wealth are often choosing to pay selectively.

If mix and match is what you're after, how you do it will very much depend on where you live (are there good local primaries, excellent comprehensives, grammar schools?); the sex of your child (in general pay for boys before girls, they need all the help they can get); the religion you practise (convert to Catholicism and go straight to education heaven); and, of course, upon your child's personality and ability.

Primary v prep

Financially, obviously the longer you defer paying the longer you'll have to save.

A good primary school – particularly since the introduction of the national curriculum and the competitive energy now put into SATs – should ensure that your child will read and write fluently and achieve a high level of verbal and numerical understanding by the age of 11. Some primaries will also provide excellent music, drama and sport, although these are often catered for in out-of-school clubs and with the support of parents.

If you want to check how a primary school matches up to the private sector, one of the best indicators is the percentage of year 6 children (10–11-year-olds) who achieve level 5 in their Key Stage 2 SATs – the level that would be expected from the majority of children in a good prep school. These figures are now included in the performance tables and you will find them on our website if you click on the 'performance table data' link.

State primary school works particularly well if you have an able child who finds little difficulty with the three Rs – particularly since the government is now putting considerable energy into programmes for the 'gifted and talented'. At the other extreme, those with serious learning difficulties, particularly if they are 'statemented' (i.e. officially recognised as needing support) will be given one-on-one extra help at no extra charge to you.

Those in the middle may be the ones who thrive least well in a busy primary school – as much psychologically as academically. A hard-pressed teacher with a mixed-ability class of 30 children often simply doesn't have the energy to focus on this unexciting middle group, and a parent with an under-confident, just-getting-by child may decide it's worth pinching pennies for the extra attention that a private school can provide at this stage.

Some parents choose to use the state system for the early years only (nursery to year 2), intending to move to a prep school at 7 or 8. In many ways this is one of the most difficult leaps to execute. Prep schools, particularly in central London, make little allowance for a child who cannot read and write as fluently as candidates from more results-driven pre-preps. So, unless you have an exceptionally able child, or live in an area where prep school entry is not so competitive, it's probably wise to get some coaching in at home.

Secondary choices

Moving from state to private at 11 is becoming increasingly widespread and many leading days schools – for boys as well as girls – now have their largest intake at this age.

The 11-plus entry works particularly well for boys moving from the state sector, since, unlike their less fortunate sisters competing against prep-school educated girls (who also change schools at 11), the prep-school educated boys don't change schools until they are 13.

Many independent schools, too – ever mindful of those A level league tables – are increasingly keen to attract the brightest and the best, so much of the emphasis of the 11-plus entrance test is now put on raw IQ, which is generally gauged by verbal and non-verbal reasoning tests. English and maths are also on the menu at many schools.

The high-flying City of London School for Boys, for example – which has always had a broad intake in terms of means and social class – take two-thirds of their 11-plus entrants from the state sector and adjust their marking according to the provenance of their candidates, giving leeway to those from state primary schools. Even academically and socially elite public schools such as Westminster and Eton are now eager to attract the ablest 11-year-olds from the state sector, and are prepared to educate them in the years between 11 and 13 at their own or allied prep schools.

IQ alone, however, is not the only factor. Parents keen to make the transition at this point would be advised to hire a tutor (or tutor them yourself) from the middle of year 5 (year 6 is too late!) to solidify their child's literacy and numeracy and prepare their child for the unfamiliar and idiosyncratic verbal and non-verbal reasoning tests. You can find some help for this at our www.11plusEnglish.com website.

Alternatively, many prep schools welcome pupils aged 10 or 11 to train them up for senior school entrance at 13 – although this mostly applies to boys' or co-ed schools.

Don't be too concerned about how your son or daughter will cope with the change from state to private; most schools say that pupils have entirely integrated by the end of their first year.

Grammar school v public school

If you live in an area such as Kent or Buckinghamshire, still primarily served by grammar or selective state schools, the approach is often to concentrate expenditure at primary level, hoping to ensure a child will be ahead in the race for a grammar-school place.

If this is your intended strategy, bear in mind that the grammar schools – which are not allowed to interview candidates – are even more dependent on IQ testing than the independent sector. So, if you feel your child doesn't have the raw material to compete in these immensely cut-throat exams (a top grammar school may be as much as ten times over-subscribed, compared to three or four times at a leading independent school), be prepared to go private all the way.

The more difficult debate – admittedly only a conflict for a small number – is the choice between, say, a scholarship to City of London, a place at Westminster and a place at one of London's leading grammar schools. Thinking of all the other things you can do with the money solves that for most people, but you lose out on the breadth and quality and social cachet that the fees buy.

Public schools, A levels and universities

Social issues are, of course, as important for many parents of children at independent schools as the education itself, but some of the benefits conferred by attending a leading public school are now under attack from the government's attempt to widen access to university.

It may now be slightly more difficult for some public school-educated candidates to study some subjects at some universities, but Oxbridge – despite all its best efforts – still takes 50 per cent of its candidates from the independent sector. A good independent school should add an extra grade more to a marginal candidate's chances than the government deducts – in attitude as much as results.

If financial constraints are paramount, then this is a reasonable time to return to the state, since there's far greater choice than at 11. Catchments areas become more flexible, older students can travel greater distances, and a well-prepared candidate from an independent school may well achieve the clutch of As and A*s at GCSE needed to gain a place at a highly selective state sixth form. Your son or daughter will need to have strong foundations and good motivations – it can be easy to go astray unobserved in a big state sixth form, let alone a college.

From state to private at A level

For those with a gifted or able child – in music, art, sports or academia – transferring to the private sector for A levels can also be a wise choice. There is far greater scholarship funding for students with ability at this stage than there is at any other time in the independent education cycle. For those with an idiosyncratic choice of A level subjects, there can be considerably more flexibility and some really superb teaching. Or you may wish to do the IB.

Conclusion

However you choose to play the education game, you should bear in mind – something often neglected by parents transfixed by a system as complex as Grand Master chess – that no decision is final. If something is not working out for you or your child at any point, it's almost always possible to change, and often much easier to do at a stage when not everyone else is making the same decision.

Money Matters

Schools in this country are mostly state funded, that, is, they're paid for by the government and local authorities from taxes. A small proportion are private, funded mostly from fees paid by parents, but also indirectly by the state, given that most private schools enjoy charitable status. Approximately 7 per cent of children in education are at fee-paying schools. Fees range from under £1,000 per term to £4,000 and above per term for a day pupil, with wide variations depending on the age of the child, the staff/pupil ratio and so on – and £1,500 (if you're v lucky) to £6,000++ per term for boarding.

Fee-paying schools: bargain hunting

Scholarships
These are to attract the academically bright or specifically talented child (art, music, science, sports, all-round and one or two amazing ones – for chess, for example) and they vary in amount. Girls' schools, alas, offer fewer and less valuable scholarships. As a rule of thumb, the old famous foundations are the richest: they may well disclaim this, but all is relative. The largest scholarships awarded by HMC and GSA (the top schools' trade organisations) schools are now normally 50 per cent of the full fees, which was a policy decision made a few years ago to spread the bunce around. However, we note that almost all schools are now breaking ranks on this and offering to 'top up' your 'scholarship' with a means-tested 'bursary'. There are also schools offering scholarships which hardly cover the cost of extras. Some schools (e.g. Eton, Westminster, St Paul's) also have a statutory number of full scholarships to offer – and from them 'full' may include the cost of uniforms and travel to school. An increasing number of schools, wary of the Labour government's threat to their charitable status, are actively seeking pupils from seriously underprivileged backgrounds.

Look out for esoteric scholarships for, for example, sons and daughters of clergy, medics, single mothers. If your name is West and you live in the parish of Twickenham there could be bursary waiting for you (at Christ's Hospital). Scholarships to choir schools are worth thinking about, but they will not cover full fees and the children work incredibly hard for them (and it is worth asking what happens when their voices break). But this could well be the beginning of a music scholarship into public school. If you are after a musical scholarship then *Music Awards at Independent Schools* from the Music Masters and Mistresses Association, by Jonathan Varcoe, may be just what you need.

Keep your eyes open for internal scholarships which run at various stages, sixth form especially. Of course, there are also increasing numbers of schools luring pupils in at sixth form with generous scholarships: might be worth moving schools for.

Useless scholarships: don't fall for them. It is a false economy to be flattered into going to the wrong school for £200 off the bill. You may be much better off with a school with slightly lower fees to start with but no scholarship on offer.

By the way, it is well worth lobbying for 10 per cent off in any case – if you have three children you should be able to negotiate a job lot. Heads are used to this, wary of it – but take courage: this is the way the world now is. Of course, you may get a raspberry.

Bursaries
Usually for helping out the impoverished but deserving and those fallen on hard times. We have listed them as far as possible under each school, but a more complete collection will be found in *The Independent Schools' Yearbook* (see 'Useful names and addresses').

Charitable trusts

Charitable grant-making trusts can help in cases of genuine need. ISCis (the Independent Schools Council information service) warns parents considering this route: 'Do not apply for an education grant for your child unless the circumstances are exceptional. The grant-giving trust will reject applications unless their requirements are satisfied.' The genuine needs recognised by the grant-making trusts are:

■ boarding need, where the home environment is unsuitable because of the disability or illness of the parents or of siblings

■ unforeseen family disaster, such as the sudden death of the breadwinner when a child is already at school

■ need for continuity when a pupil is in the middle of a GCSE or A level course and a change in parental circumstances threatens withdrawal from school

■ need for special education where there is a genuine recognised learning handicap which cannot be catered for at a state school.

If you want to explore this road, the key books are *The Educational Grants Directory* (specifically directed at funding for schoolchildren and students in need), *The Guide to the Major Trusts* (in three volumes). *The Directory of Grant Making Trusts* and the *Charities Digest*. Most come out annually with a year suffix to the title, and you should be able to find one or more in your local library.

Other cheapos

Certain schools are relatively cheap. The Livery Companies, such as Haberdashers and Mercers, fund various schools, e.g. 'Haberdashers' Monmouth, Gresham's. Such schools are usually excellent value – not only cheap(er), but with good facilities.

Also cheap, but with fewer frills, are The Girls' Day Schools Trust (GDST) schools.

It may well be worth considering sending your child as a day pupil to a big strong boarding school. This way you will reap the benefits at a lesser price (although sometimes the day fees are ridiculous).

Fees

Take great care in comparing fees between schools. Some quote an all-in fee, others seem cheaper but have a load of unavoidable 'extras' that can add up to 25 per cent to the bill.

Things that you may have to add in include:

■ lunches – many day schools charge for these on top

■ uniform. Many schools have a flourishing second hand shop – Eton has several

■ books: an extra in some schools

■ trips: at some schools almost all included (bar holiday expeditions); at others you will pay even for ones that are part of the curriculum. The greater likelihood, though, is that trips that are nominally optional will be socially compulsory.

■ transport to and from school: can be very steep indeed at some day schools.

■ capital levy: usually a large once-off impost, supposedly to pay for new building

■ special education (such as one-on-one aid in classroom, dyslexia support or tutoring) or EFL

■ insurance

■ unusual subjects: e.g. languages, where there are less than, say, four in a class

■ seriously hefty deposit on a firm offer of a place

■ keeping up with the Joneses: in a money- or status-conscious school, all sorts of possessions or expenditure may be required for a child to remain one of the in-crowd.

Paying the fees

There are any number of wizard wheezes on the market. The schools offer 'composition fees', which means, in a nutshell, you put a sum of money down one year and get a sum of money back later. The 'school fee specialists' offer endowment-backed, mortgage-backed schemes and so on, which, in effect, do the same thing. Either way, you are stepping into deep waters. Unless you totally understand what you are doing and all the implications – how the money is being invested, what the returns are, how it compares with any other investment, what the charges are, hidden and otherwise etc. – we think it might be safest to avoid such schemes.

This does not mean you should not save and invest. The earlier you start, the better – obviously enough. We have commissioned a survey of the options: see 'Finance for fees' on our website.

Given the astronomical sums involved, it is worth looking very carefully at what you are actually buying. Most good schools have viable numbers, but there are still those that are struggling, and you need to know that the school you are interested in is in good financial health. This is easier said than done. A good indicator is to compare the number of pupils this year with last year and indeed the year before that. The numbers should not show too marked a dip (though watch out for schools whose numbers are now topped up with their new nursery/pre-prep).

Other indicators of financial problems are not sacking troublemakers – one sacking can mean the loss of £15,000 a year ('This can be the difference between profit and loss,' said a bursar); cutting corners in the curriculum (such as offering German one year, Spanish the next); the head being away too much drumming up business; cheap labour – gap year students can be wonderful, but they are inexperienced and they don't last. Also look out for dilapidated buildings, dirty decor, unkempt grounds, teeny libraries and scarcity of computers.

If possible, pick a blue chip school with a rich foundation: these are better positioned to ride out any storms. Look at the Money Matters sections of individual entries in this guide.

Scrutinise your bill carefully. We have noticed an increasing tendency to pop in items with a footnote (inertia selling) saying that 'unless you notify the school and deduct the amounts mentioned, it will automatically be charged to you'. for example, the Old Boys/Girls society; the ISIS membership, your 'contribution' to charities. Do not be shy about deducting these sums from your cheque.

Insurance needs particular care. Often policies are taken out automatically unless you say otherwise – and we know of sickness policies on offer, for example, that only pay up once the child has been ill for at least eight days, but don't pay up for illnesses lasting longer than a term.

Getting in and out of financial difficulties

If you do get into financial difficulties, you will not be alone, and schools are very used to this. Their attitude to bill-paying and money varies hugely. The best schools are wonderful and increasingly flexible over payment, allowing arrangements such as monthly instalments. Bursars are expecting this request – no shame attached. Indeed the bursar has changed from the enemy to being the father confessor (with some notable exceptions – best description received: 'the bursar is a most evil toad').

A lot will depend on how well funded the school is: it is worth investigating this before you go any further. A few well-funded rich schools will pick up the tab until further notice if you fall on hard times and your child is a good egg. Most of them will do their very best to see you through exam periods, but most poor schools simply cannot afford to do this for long, however much they may wish too.

Don't assume that because they are called 'charities' that they will be charitable to you. Some may send out the debt collectors. They will hold you to the small print –one term's payment or one term's notice to quit really means it. They may well threaten to take you to court – although of course it will be an extremely different matter if your child is especially bright (see 'What the league tables don't tell you').

Action

1. Speak to the head. Mothers and New Fathers may burst into tears at this point.

2. The head will immediately direct you to the bursar.

3. Explain your position – as optimistically, positively and realistically as possible.

4. Hope for flexible arrangements: monthly payments or deferred payment.

5. Have all the scholarships gone? Is there a spare bursary?

6. Assess the situation. How vital is it to keep your child in this school? Will the world fall apart if he/she leaves now?

7. If you really feel it is vital the child stays put, try touching a relation for a loan/gift. Grandparents are still the number one source of school fees. Investigate the possibility of an extra mortgage.

8. And if it is not vital, start looking for state alternatives. See: The System.

Boarding schools

To board or not to board… that is the question.

Traditionally, heartless British parents sent their little darlings off to school at seven or eight and didn't think about them again until it was time for university. Think Tom Brown's schooldays … and go to the bottom of the class. Cold showers, initiation ceremonies and enforced runs are more or less a thing of the past – the CSCI (see 'The Inspectors'), would hastily intervene.

So why board? It depends on where you live. If you happily live near a seriously good state or independent day school, and that is the most rewarding solution either morally or financially, then don't even think about it. If you live in the depths of the country or overseas, or in that educational desert central London, then boarding may well be your answer.

But beware, boarding schools are not a universal panacea. Putting your child in boarding school implies partnership and trust between school and parent. It is no use sending your utterly revolting child away to school and assuming you will get an angel back at half term: boarding schools can, and will, dis your child for a variety of reasons (drugs, serious bad behaviour, bullying etc) and – following a recent ruling which involved Marlborough – you will have no recourse. So think carefully before you embark on what is a seriously expensive process. (This can often be ameliorated by scholarships, bursaries, kindly grandparents, employment benefits or Services bursaries – although in the case of the last you can't just chop and change schools at will but must stick with the one you first thought of).

So, how to choose?

Do not be taken in by charming heads or their marketing genies entertaining you with PowerPoint presentations and handing out videos (always taken on sunny days and always displaying the best of everything).

Give some thought to what sort of character you want your child to turn out to be. Boarding schools, because they enfold your child for so much of the year, will make a substantial contribution to their character, and different boarding schools mould character in very different ways. You will never pick this up from the school's marketing material: they all want to appear blandly wonderful. *The Good Schools Guide* does its best to draw this character out, and you should be able to get a taste of it when you go round the school. Having your child end up at Freedom Hall when what you wanted was a traditional British public school education is seriously careless.

Have a clear view, too, of where you want your child to go on to next. It is easier to get a guide to whether a school is the right place for this ambition: all schools publish lists of where their pupils go on to, and if the education that they provide and the spirit that they inculcate is capable of taking your child where you want them to go, then other children will have gone that way before, probably in some numbers.

Remember that not all boarding schools are in the UK. Most European countries have one or two, Switzerland has some which follow the English academic syllabus, and so do many of the Middle and Far Eastern countries. Some follow the trad British A level syllabus and some the IB. Ditto Australia and New Zealand (which have several really great boarding schools). There's less boarding in the Americas, though the US has one or two and so does Canada and some of the countries in South America, particularly those which came under British influence in the past. And then there's Africa. There are schools in South Africa that are so exactly British that the only real difference is the minuscule fees.

For families from outside the UK, one of the first things that you have to look at is the weekend arrangements ('exeats'). Most schools (prep schools in particular) now work on a formula where the whole school is expected to close down for the weekend every other week. If there are no handy grandparents, godparents or accommodating family friends you must find a guardian. Many schools have a list of wonderful tried and trusted guardians who have taken dozens of tinies under their wing, turn up for speech days and school performances and really provide a second home. But we have heard of a number of distinctly commercial guardians who charge the earth, restrict their input to the barest minimum, and bill for each expense and extra hour. See 'Finding a guardian' for more advice.

Most of the bigger schools have staff available to keep the school open during exeats and will, at no extra cost (or very little), take their charges on jollies to local theme parks, cinemas and the like during closed weekends. But ask. Of course children form friendships (and this, for the lonely child, is the most important part of school life) but don't count on it. If your child is likely to find itself at school on weekends when many have departed, be sure to enquire closely how many other children will be in the same position, and how they will be occupied.

And what happens (perish the thought) if your little darling errs and is sent home to cool their heels? Doting relatives may quite like the idea of having them round the house, but your commercial guardian now, that is a problem. Some are fine, and some, well...

If you are not an expat you will want to know how many other pupils from your country there are, and whether arrangements are made for children from the same country to be in different dormitories (otherwise they form cliques, never learn English, and might as well have stayed at home). And while on the subject of dormitories, will your child have any real privacy at all?

Look at travelling logistics, particularly if you want to turn up for the school play. Cheapo air fares have done wonders for the UK boarding system. Think Stansted, think East Midlands, think Edinburgh or Glasgow – long- and short-haul flights land at these places regularly, so you are not restricted to Heathrow and the M4 corridor.

And see Notes for Foreign Parents for some more general questions on British schools.

All parents should be sure to meet the head, your child's houseparents and the matron. These last three are the ones who really make a difference to the day-to-day happiness of a boarder. And if your child is to have a tutor who stays with them throughout their time at school, meet them too. Get the home phone number of whoever has charge of your child's welfare, and ask if you can call at any time.

Ask how parent and child communicate. Weekly letter? A phone for each fifty pupils? Or nightly e-mails and a mobile phone? This is definitely something to talk to pupils about when you visit.

Be relentlessly questioning about any requirements which are particular to you. If your child has special educational needs (and there are many boarding schools in the UK which make superb provision for these) you will need to know exactly what is on offer, and how the school proposes to make you part of the decision-making process on such questions as whether to include or exclude your child from particular lessons. How good are the EFL lessons, and how much extra do they cost? What provision do they make for your faith? Don't just take this on trust, talk to a co-religionist who is already at the school and find out what really happens.

Some problems that are easily tackled by local parents become much harder to deal with when a parent is distant. Discover whether matron will replenish (and mend) school (and home) clothes and if she can do it out of the secondhand shop (and all the while you are sussing up whether matron, and the under matrons, are cuddly or moustachioed dragons who grump). Find out if boarders are allowed into town at weekends. How does the school control what they get up to? How can parents ditto? It helps a lot if a child has a bolt hole in town where they can go rather than be dragged into some den of iniquity by their friends because they have no alternative. Do you have a friend or relative who is willing to let them have a key?

The same problem of distance applies to bullying. Being able to recharge courage and self-confidence at home makes a child much more resilient in the face of low-level bullying than is the case for a child who has no such resort. Don't be satisfied with the mere absence of stories about bullying; look for stories (particularly from gentler pupils) about how well bullying is dealt with.

All these problems become considerably easier if you leave boarding until your child has done their GCSEs or equivalent, and has developed a reasonable degree of maturity and independence. Many schools now have expanded sixth forms and happily take children either from the UK (state or other independent schools) or from further afield for a two-year sixth-form course leading to A levels or an IB and university entrance globally. Take care to suit the school to the student: the range of styles is particularly broad at this age, from the disciplinarian academic to the 'almost-university'.

Our editors have experienced boarding schools as expats and as locals, as members of families who have used boarding schools for generations and as parents who are tackling boarding for the first time. All of them confirm that, in the words of one editor, 'boarding schools are brilliant, children make friends for life, share the experiences and cultures, and learn tolerance for their fellow man.' That editor remembers finding her eldest son in tears during his first half-term from prep school: 'Mummy, there's no one to play with at home.' That said, there are still many children who end up miserable: you need to take care to match the child to the school, and to watch how things develop thereafter. It should be totally obvious if things are going well.

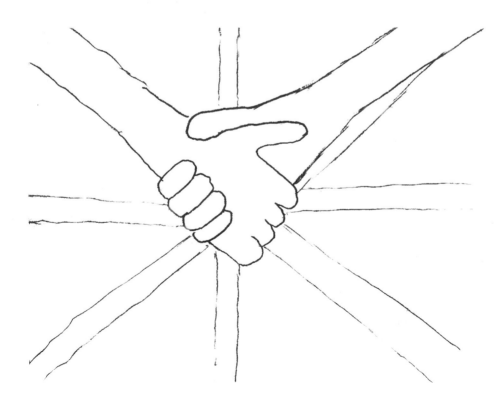

Notes for foreign parents

Most UK schools are now genuinely thrilled to welcome in foreign students, and no longer regard a cosmopolitan mix as a matter for shame (that they cannot fill the school with home-grown products). Foreign students are perceived to add breadth, excitement, new horizons, not to mention fantastic exam results in exotic languages (Turkish, Norwegian, Polish, Mandarin, Japanese, Gujerati, Urdu among the most common), high intelligence (often), motivation and – last but not least – cash.

The best schools in this country are outstanding by any standards. Beware, though, of being fobbed off with second-rate places.

Here are a few thoughts from overseas parents who are already in the UK system.

1. Be on the look out for academic schools which pay lip service to 'potential' but in reality are only interested in performance on the day of the entrance exam. It's no use explaining your child is trilingual and English is their fourth language – they do not want to take the risk or have the bother.

2. The majority of schools in this country are not geared to teaching the English language to pupils who don't know it. Beware of schools which have a high proportion of foreigners, but no real way of teaching them English. Schools which have very few foreigners in the school are another matter – being immersed in a language without the option is the quickest way to learn, particularly for younger children.

3. If a school says it has got 'provision' for teaching English as a Foreign Language (EFL) ask exactly what that provision consists of, and whether it will cost extra. EFL teachers need to have a proper teaching degree/diploma as well as an EFL qualification: the latter means very little.

4. Don't ask the impossible. Do not, for example, expect an English academic secondary school to cater at public exam level for a pupil whose English is almost non-existent. However quick at learning your child is, he/she will certainly struggle at this stage – the pressure of work is just too high.

5. Be prepared to 'sell' yourself a bit to the school. Private schools in this country have a tendency to ask what you can do for them, rather than what they can do for you. This shocks parents from other countries, but it is a fact.

6. Ask what arrangements a boarding school has for exeats (weekends when the pupils are allowed away from the school premises). There is an increasing tendency in the UK towards 'weekly' and 'flexi' boarding where pupils can go home any weekend they want. If you live overseas, this is obviously bad news. It is best, if you can, to opt for a 'full' boarding school, which has a proper programme of activities at weekends, and one or two pre-arranged exeats per term.

7. You will usually be asked to appoint a UK guardian for your child – someone whom the school can deal with on day-to-day matters, and whom your child can turn to for help, outings and so on. If you have no contacts in Britain, will the school find guardians for your child or children, to collect them at the airport, take them to school, care for them at exeats and take them back to the airport again? Is there a charge for this? Some schools and agencies thrive merrily on these extras.

8. Ask what the school would do if your child were to be found guilty of a serious misdemeanour (drugs etc). You do not want to find him/her ejected from the school at a moment's notice.

9. Ask what arrangements are made at the end of public exam terms. There is an increasing tendency to send pupils home early once they have finished their exams – sometimes weeks early. Again, not good news for overseas parents. You need to know that the school has a proper programme of activities to keep pupils occupied until the last official day of term.

10. Various 'international centres' have sprung up, most attached to solid private schools. The best of these do a good job in preparing children with little English for entry to British boarding schools. Beware those that are too newly established, and make sure to ask for a full list of the schools that pupils move on to.

11. Do not assume a school is good simply because it is famous: an obvious point, but you would be surprised how many people believe famous equals good.

12. If – once your child is in a school – he or she tells you about being miserable/homesick/ bullied – believe them. Act at once by telephoning the school and explaining the problem. If the problem persists, consider taking your child out of the school and finding another, more compatible one. Better a temporary disruption to your child's schooling than permanent damage.

13. Consider doing a summer/holiday course before opting for mainstream schooling. There are courses which take place in British public schools, for example, which will give your child a 'feel' for what's in store – and get the English up to scratch. The British Council vets most such courses, and lists the ones that it approves of.

14. Always go and see a school you are interested in yourself – or at least send someone whose judgement you trust (and who knows your child). You will be surprised how much you can learn about a place from even a brief look.

15. Look for a school that is popular with the British as well as with foreigners – talk to personal contacts if possible. British Embassies Abroad (www2.tagish.co.uk/Links/embassy1b.nsf) and The British Council (www.britcoun.org) are often useful initial points of contact, but don't rely on their advice over particular schools.

16. Placement agencies will give you a list of schools in the UK which have places available when you ask – beware, though, as these are usually no more than lists, and do not differentiate between the good, the bad and the ugly. Such agencies are usually paid fat commissions by the schools they recommend, and may be reluctant to mention those schools that do not pay them a commission (this includes many of the more famous ones).

17. Ask what the school does by way of cross-cultural training, especially if you come from a culture that has a different set of attitudes and assumptions from the British (e.g. the East, or France). How do staff help your child fit in? How do they help the British children understand your child? Such training is common in business, but not yet in schools. Organisations such as Farnham Castle (www.farnhamcastle.com) run courses which your child can attend as an individual should the school have nothing on offer.

See the section on 'Boarding schools' for other things that you will need to keep in mind.

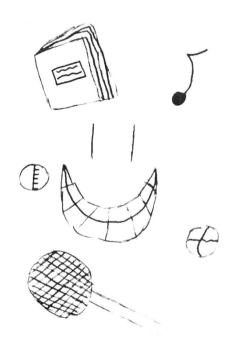

Finding a Guardian

British boarding schools will not admit an overseas pupil under the age of 18 unless he or she has a local guardian. It can seem an unnecessary annoyance, especially for older children, but most schools have had enough grim experiences (such as children left unclaimed on day one of the Christmas holidays) that they have learned to demand it.

Guardians do three main things. They provide a place for your child to stay during the – sometimes numerous – school holidays (and many schools also have compulsory exeats half-term breaks when all pupils have to vamoose). Guardians also need to serve as your representatives, making some decisions for your child, signing forms, attending parents' evenings and being available in an emergency – for instance, if your child falls ill or is temporarily or permanently excluded from school (it happens more often than you think). Finally, guardians may need to assist with transport to and from school or from airports, etc. In addition, guardians are sometimes required to act as a sort of bank, doling out pocket money, funds for school trips, etc. In general, the younger the pupil, the more comprehensive the service will need to be.

How do you find a guardian? Start by asking friends in your own country who have used one. If they had a good experience with a firm, there is a good chance you will too.

If you don't know anyone who has used a guardian, then ask the school your child will be attending. Most schools will be reluctant to recommend one guardianship firm – they don't want to be responsible if you end up with a duff one. But if you ask them to name a few companies that have supplied guardians for their pupils in the past schools, schools will often give you good leads. Schools have a lot of experience with guardians and will be likely to know of the smaller, more local (and perhaps less expensive) firms that may be just what you need. Be on guard, however, if a school is tied to one particular firm. There may be a financial relationship between the two that can lead to a conflict of interest – do you really want your guardian in cahoots with the school when Johnny and his housemaster have a conflict that you would like the guardian to help resolve?

Many schools will point you towards one of two accredited associations of guardians. The largest of these is the Association of Educational Guardianship of International Students (Aegis) (www.aegisuk.net e-mail; aegisuk@btopenworld.com). Aegis members include such giants in the field as Gabbitas and Sutherland Education. The Association of Guardianship Services (TAGS) (www.tags-uk.org; e-mail: chairman@tags-uk.org) is a similar accrediting organisation with seven current members and others waiting to join. Members of both organisations are vetted and insured and all their host families are carefully checked.

There are, of course, alternatives to using a professional guardianship agency. The first choice for most expat Brits, and for foreign families who have relatives in the UK, is to house children with British relatives. The benefits are that it is cheap and the guardian is likely to have a genuine interest in the welfare of the child. On the downside, relatives may be working people who will find a long journey to fetch their cousin's wife's niece a bind, not to mention looking after her for a week or more, or even between terms. Financial arrangements with relatives can also become a strain, as they will need to pay out in advance for your child's travel expenses, entertainment, clothes etc. Occasionally, schools will not accept relatives as guardians if they live very far away from the school.

Language schools and tutorial colleges will sometimes have families on their books who can take in older teenagers, thereby sidestepping guardianship firms. You will need to find out how carefully the families have been checked and whether there is any back-up from the school if the family can no longer fulfil its role. You should also ask for references on the families (ideally from pupils who have previously lodged with them) and check them rigorously.

Some parents try to dispense with formal guardians all together, looking to house their child with the local exile community in exchange for some light work. Parents of older teenagers often ask if they can billet their young-sters in a bed and breakfast during school holidays rather than fuss with the expense of guardians. While we admire the ingenuity of these sorts of parents, they are leaving themselves open to trouble if anything goes wrong. And you would be amazed how things can go wrong. Schools sometimes find themselves on the phone to guardianship agencies at the last minute asking for help with a student whose guardian has proved to be non-existent.

Ideally you will want to meet the family your child will be staying with. If that is impossible, you can cover a lot of ground on the telephone or via e-mail.

Questions for guardianship firms

1. What exactly will I be paying for? Go through this with a fine-toothed comb. You do not want to pay for more than you will need, nor do you want to be caught short.

2. Will my child be able to stay with the same family throughout the time they are educated in the UK?

3. Can my child move to a different host family if things don't work out?

4. Do you offer 24-hour cover in case of an emergency?

5. Are you fully insured?

6. Who will be the legal guardian – the host family or the director of the guardianship firm? Who should my child contact if he or she is having a problem? It is key that you establish this because in many firms the appointed guardian is actually the director of the firm, not the host family.

7. How do you choose and inspect your guardians? Are they CRB (Criminal Record Bureau) checked?

8. Will my child's host family have other overseas pupils stay-ing with them? Most, but not all, parents from abroad prefer their child to be the only overseas pupil in a household.

Questions for the host family

1. Do you have children of your own? What ages?

2. Have you been a guardian before?

3. What are your rules on television viewing, homework, going out with friends, use of telephone and computer, drinking (for older teenagers) etc? What will the arrange-ments be for pocket money and my child's other financial needs? Emergencies can arise when you least expect them. Quest Guardians in Dorset remembers the SARS outbreak in 2003 when scores of Southeast Asian pupils were stranded after returning from their Easter holidays. Some British schools, including Eton, had made sudden decisions not to readmit them until they had been quaran-tined for ten days. Host families were also reluctant to har-bour the potentially contagious pariahs in their homes. It is testing times like that when a guardianship firm (hopefully) proves its commitment and its value.

The Good Schools Guide for Special Educational Needs

www.goodschoolsguide.co.uk/?SEN

This April, for the first time, we will be publishing a separate book on special educational needs and schools.

If you're coming across special needs for the first time, or suspect that that your child might need help, then this will be a book well worth your while looking at. Special educational needs are common: about 20 per cent of children at any one time, the majority of children at some time or another. Diagnosis, though, is not easy. Symptoms to look out for are a lack of pleasure in reading, problems with writing, clumsiness, not enjoying school, disorganisation, being easily distracted and generating distraction, reluctance to do homework, not getting on with other children, not thriving at school – and having parents with these symptoms. In the case of hearing loss, symptoms to look out for include tiredness, lack of concentration, apparent forgetfulness. But all are also symptoms of normal childhood – which is why SENs can be hard to spot. Our new guide will give you a real insight into what to look out for, and how to set about confirming (or allaying) your suspicions.

If you are setting out to battle for your child's education, then *The Good Schools Guide for Special Educational Needs* should be the book for you too. With comprehensive coverage of the SEN system, articles by parents and professionals who have been through it all, reviews of hundreds of schools that handle SEN well, and pointers to hundreds of sources of specialist advice, *The Good Schools Guide for Special Educational Needs* is the right place to start.

If you have conquered the system, and found a perfect place for your child, then it's we who need you: go to the page for your perfect school on www.goodschoolsguide.co.uk, enter a comment about the school, and we will make a donation to the SEN charity of your choice.

If you have subscribed to the Good Schools Guide online (and as an owner of this book, you are entitled to do that at half price) you will find that you also get access to our new guide for no additional cost.

Some basic advice on choosing a school for a child with SEN

■ Be honest with yourself. Neither over-emphasise your child's problems nor underplay them. Be honest with the school too.

■ Get as good a professional assessment as possible. For a child who has a physical problem it is likely you will have much useful information from the clinicians who have worked with him or her. For the child who has a learning difficulty, be it specific or global, get as much up-to-date advice as you can. The more a school knows about your child, the more easily the staff can be sure of their ability to do well by him or her.

■ Make use of an appropriate support group, such as those listed on our website, who will be able to recommend professional people who can give you a frank description of your child's needs.

■ Think of the end point. What would you realistically expect your son or daughter to be doing in twenty years' time? Education must be challenging, bringing out a child's full potential, and, if possible, going beyond what that potential is currently perceived to be. Look for schools that are excellent in areas where your child can shine despite their disability. Parent support groups may also prove helpful.

If you are looking at mainstream schools, for a child with a relatively mild degree of need:

■ Ask if the school tests all children on entry – there are lots of ways of doing this, and most will do as long as the assessor is SEN-aware. If a school is really switched on to SEN it will be testing.

■ Ask if the school's special needs support is an integral part of the school, with a two-way flow of information between specialist teachers and subject teachers. Schools where SEN support is an 'add on', with help found when needed and specialist teachers having little contact with the school, are really only suitable for very mild cases. Ask a teacher or two where they turn to for advice, and how often, and how good it has been.

■ Ask how many pupils in the school have special needs like your child's and how many teachers offer specialist support. A sizeable peer group will ensure that support is there in depth, and that your child's difficulties are not misunderstood, underestimated or looked down on by staff or pupils.

■ Are teaching methods appropriate for SEN children – worksheets always provided, lessons in relatively short sections? Or are there long periods of dictation/copying off the board, or half an hour's chat and then 'now make notes of what I have said?'

■ What do pupils miss in order to receive extra help? Do you mind?

■ What is the head's attitude to special needs? Does he or she have high expectations of them, celebrate their successes? A head who is not enthusiastic about helping SEN children may mean that staff are not as supportive or understanding as they should be. Be sure that your child will never be asked 'Is this the best you can do?' For some children with SENs the level of pastoral care may be as important as specialist understanding of a particular disability.

■ Do the school make use of concessions for public exams, such as providing a laptop, or an amanuensis (push for the legitimate use of these via an educational psychologist's report)? Is a full degree of training available for your child in how to make best use of these aids?

■ Talk to some pupils with the same diagnosis as your child – are they bubbling with pride and confidence?

■ How much extra will you have to pay for the support that you want?

If you are looking for a school for a child who needs a high level of support, or specialist facilities:

■ When it comes to choosing a specialist school beware of those schools that offer all things to all men.

■ Remember that head teachers of specialist schools, like their mainstream counterparts, need to fill places in order to balance the books. Be wary of those schools who say they will take special measures for a child who is obviously going to be treated differently from the other children in the school.

■ If a child has a substantial learning difficulty, exam results may not be particularly useful to measure the success of a school (though they will give an indication of how well it is possible to do in that school). Try to find another baseline from which to work. See if you can discover what the typical child has in terms of both emotional and educational status on arriving at the school, and see if you can determine what value has been added to that child when he/she leaves. What success does the school have in getting students into further education, or employment, and how well do they keep up a relationship with ex-students to see if they are successful in their chosen field of work? Look for signs of confidence in the older children, and see what help they are given with 'life skills', either formally through programmes in the curriculum, or informally in the way the pastoral side of the school is run. Ask for contacts with existing parents of children like yours, and make your telephone calls to three or four across the age range.

And again, what is the head's attitude, and what are the kids like? There is simply no excuse for a school with low expectations and dulled kids.

Tutorial Colleges

Tutorial colleges – 'crammers' as they are unkindly known – offer intensive teaching in small groups to 'cram' knowledge into your child's head. They may be the answer if your mainstream school has let you down in the results (failed to get those 3 Bs at A level you needed to get into wherever), or you think it is going to let you down and a little extra pre-exam tuition might make all the difference.

They may also be the answer if your child can't stand the pressure in her hot-shot school, or if he has been expelled and you are at your wits' end to know what to do next.

Crammers are (or were) basically aimed at post-GCSE pupils coming in to do A level re-takes, or possibly to do a complete A level course, maybe doing a couple of GCSE re-takes at the same time. Some of them have moved beyond this, and are more like schools or sixth-form colleges – there for the child who needs that extra measure of independence and responsibility, with much less emphasis on rescue work.

The great plus of a crammer is that it is there, and it takes in the good, the bad and the ugly – though some have a policy of not taking in children expelled for drug-taking. The good ones are also very successful in bumping up exam grades. Minuses are the cost, which is unbelievable (almost as much as boarding school for day students, and considerably more if accommodation is needed too), the lack of 'extras' and the often dodgy pastoral care (crammers are simply not geared to provide a nanny service).

The all-important thing here is the work, and providing this is done, and the (relatively few) classes are attended on time, then pupils are usually left very much to their own devices. This can cause problems if the crammer is in a big city (and most of them are) away from your home. Tales of hanging out in pubs by day, staying out all night and/or not getting up until the afternoon are very common.

The crammers, tutorial colleges or just schools with a crammerish aspect which we cover in this guide include: Ashbourne Independent School, London; Basil Paterson Tutorial College, Edinburgh; Collingham, London; D'Overbroek's College, Oxford; Mander Portman Woodward, London; St Clare's, Oxford; Wallace College, Edinburgh.

Questions for crammers

1. How big is the maximum class size? For A levels, seven is fine, ten is moving into a different ball game.

2. Which subjects do they teach? If it is science, have they an in-house lab? Ask to see it. Ditto art, and the art room. You would be surprised at how many practical subjects take place elsewhere.

3. How many taught periods are there a week for each subject?

4. Which exam boards does the place offer? (Don't get stuck with a board that only examines in summer if you want a re-take in winter.)

5. Where do students work in their (bags of) free time?

6. Can I have a copy of your latest value-added data for A levels? This really means something in crammers, as points scored are based on what students are expected to get as a result of their GCSEs, so if students are doing better than expected, then the crammer is doing something right.

7. What proportion of students starting an A level course actually take the exam with the crammer in question?

Useful contacts

The British Accreditation Council
42 Manchester Street, London W1U 7LW
Tel: 020 7224 5474
Fax: 020 7224 5475
Web: www.the-bac.org
E-mail: info@the-bac.org.

CIFE (Conference for Independent Further Education)
75 Foxbourne Road, London SW17 8EN
Web: ww.getthegrade.co.uk
Tel: 020 8767 8666.

The crammers' professional association and your first
point of call for information such as: what colleges are in
your area, and which, for example, might be persuaded
to take little Johnny if he's been sacked from school for
drug-taking.

We would love to hear your views

The Good Schools Guide is written by parents for parents. We do not take money from the schools in the guide in any shape or form, either directly or indirectly – no fees, no commissions for 'introducing' pupils to particular establishments, no retainers. We do not take advertising from schools. We are therefore in a position to be outspoken, to write and to advise you impartially, without fear of being biased or having a conflict of loyalties.

We visit all the schools ourselves and – since we were first published in 1986 – have visited most of them several times over, both formally and informally. We can compare the strengths and weaknesses of one school with another – to put them into context. We have a team of local editors who bring us news and views from all over Britain, and help us find the good schools that only their neighbours know about.

Visiting is, of course, only a start. We also spend many happy hours talking to pupils, staff, heads, educationalists of all sorts, matrons – even the school dog. Most importantly, we listen to you, the consumer.

We would like to know what you think of the schools that you know. All information will be gratefully (and confidentially) received – no detail too slight to mention. Suggestions for schools to be included in the next edition would also be welcome. Send your opinions and experiences to us through the website (there's a comments button on each school's page) if that suits you – it makes life easier for us – but we welcome your views by e-mail, fax, letter or telephone.

You can reach us via the website:
www.goodschoolsguide.co.uk

or at:

E-mail: editor@goodschoolsguide.co.uk
Fax: +44 (0)870 052 067
Tel: +44 (0)20 7801 0191

3 Craven Mews,
London SW11 5PW.

Other Good Schools Guide publications

11 Plus English: a Parent's Toolkit

www.11PlusEnglish.com

Help your child get up to speed in English for secondary school.

Is this your child?:

'Her class teacher just doesn't have time to help her with the basics.'

'He just can't seem to get started with story writing.'

'Her stories are lovely but she can't manage a time limit!'

'I would like him to go to a selective school, but I'm worried that his English is not good enough.'

'She hasn't a clue about comprehensions.'

If you share any of these concerns then this is the book for you. It has been written to help parents and children work together on all aspects of English around the transition to senior schools, and specifically for children who are going to take entrance examinations for grammar schools or selective independent schools.

11 Plus English: a Parent's Toolkit has been distilled from Katherine Hamlyn's 25 years of experience of teaching at this level. The highly readable guide pinpoints common problems and, using child-centred techniques and games concentrating on relaxed child/parent collaboration, takes you through essential English with common sense, clarity and humour.

Uni in the USA
The UK Guide to US Universities

www.UniintheUSA.com

Britain has some magnificent universities, but they are getting desperately hard to get into. You may be giving Oxbridge or London your best shot, but however well you do you may find yourself among the two-thirds of candidates who have had to accept a lesser institution. Yes, sure, you'll have great fun there. If you find it easy to work hard on your own, and don't get tempted, you will end up with a worthwhile degree. But is a course that only offers you a few hours a week of lectures or tutorials really value for all that money that you are having to invest in it?

Look at the USA too. Not only does this give you an extra chance of getting to a top-ranking university, but once you start looking at what is on offer over the Atlantic you will realise how much damage years of financial deprivation have done to UK undergraduate courses. At any of the better US universities you should expect to get 18 hours a week of lectures and tutorials, to have them quickly marked and returned to you, and to find that you are frequently in conversation with the first-rate intellectuals who are teaching you. And if you want to keep your education broad, and are not ready to narrow your range of subjects or to declare yourself set on a firm career path, American liberal arts degree courses may have a particular attraction for you.

Uni in the USA is written by an Englishwoman at Harvard, with the help of fellow exiles at the top two dozen US universities. She describes with great clarity and humour the experiences that you should expect if you venture west, and the qualities of the universities that you might consider. She answers all the questions that you might have about the American university system: who to see, what to ask and when to do it by. Anthony Nemecek, director of the educational advisory service of the US–UK Fulbright Commission, contributes to the general advice sections of the book, so that you can rely on it for accurate advice about all the hurdles which you need to leap to make it to the USA.

Thousands of us make it to US universities every year and, as Stephen Baldock (formerly High Master of St Paul's) says in his introduction, he has known few, if any, pupils who have regretted it. And don't think that you have to be rich: the excellent financial aid and bursary programs at most American universities ensure that many British students can afford to go, regardless of their educational background or economic status.

Useful names and addresses

Our extensive links section on our website, www.goodschoolsguide.co.uk, is a useful supplement to this page.

Government

The Department for Education and Skills
Sanctuary Buildings, Great Smith Street,
London SW1T 3BT
Web: www.dfes.gov.uk
Tel: 0870 000 2288
Fax: 01928 794 248
E-mail: info@dfes.gsi.gov.uk

A very helpful site, but use the menus not the inadequate search engine. Has an information division which will give you the names of schools, pressure groups and leaflets, Tel: 0870 001 2345. There is also a publications division on Tel: 0845 6022260.

The Scottish Executive Education Department
Victoria Quay, Edinburgh EH6 6QQ.
Web: www.scotland.gov.uk
Tel: 08457 741 741
Fax: 0131 244 8240
E-mail: ceu@scotland.gov.uk

Not an easy site to navigate, but if you persevere the information's there.

The Public Information and Education Service
The National Assembly for Wales
Cardiff Bay, Cardiff CF99 1NA
Web: www.wales.gov.uk

For School Performance Division contact:
Tel: 02920 825 111
Fax: 02920 826 016

DENI – the Northern Ireland Department of Education
Rathgael House, 43 Balloo Road, Bangor,
County Down BT19 7PR
Web: www.deni.gov.uk
Tel: 02891 279 279   Fax: 02891 279 100

Information

The Advisory Centre for Education
Department A, Unit 1C Aberdeen Studios,
22 Highbury Grove, London N5 2DQ
Advice line (2–5pm, Monday to Friday):
0800 800 5793
Web: www.ace-ed.org.uk
Office tel: 020 7354 8318
Fax: 020 7354 9069
A charity founded in 1960. Publishes guides on such subjects as how to approach primary schooling, UK school law and how to deal with the bureaucrats on special educational needs, school choice and appeals, home education, bullying and so on.

Aegis: The Association of Educational Guardians for International Students

The industry association for guardianship accredits guardianship companies and offers a complaints service. Easiest to find on the web at www.aegisuk.net. Their secretary can be reached at:

66 Humphreys Close, Randwick, Stroud GL5 4NY
Tel/Fax: 01453 755 160
E-mail: aegis@btopenworld.com

CIFE: the Conference for Independent Further Education

The crammers' professional association and your first port of call for advice on which school might, for instance, be persuaded to take on little Johnny when he's been sacked from school for drug taking. Also covers summer schools and revision courses. Easiest to deal with on the web: www.getthegrade.co.uk.

75 Foxbourne Road, London SW17 8EN
Tel: 020 8767 8666

The National Association for Gifted Children

Suite 14, Challenge House, Sherwood Drive, Bletchley MK3 6DP
Web: www.nagcbritain.org.uk
Tel: 0870 770 3217
Fax: 0870770 3219
E-mail: amazingchildren@nagcbritain.org.uk

Independent Schools Council information service (ISCis)

35 Grosvenor Gardens, London SW1W 0BS
Web: www.iscis.uk.net
Tel: 020 7798 1500
Fax: 020 7798 1501

The site formerly known as ISIS – the Independent Schools Information Service – now trendily renamed and slipping into lower case. The 'official' site for schools belonging to the Independent Schools Joint Council, about 1,300 of the 2,000 plus independent schools in the UK. ISJC members would regard themselves as being the best 1,300. An excellent and very helpful site. Good search facility. Inspection reports are now beginning to be available on the Independent Schools Inspectorate site. Contact ISCis for information on charities for parents who wish to send their children to fee-paying schools but cannot afford the fees.

For lists of all schools registered in your area (state and private) telephone the county or borough concerned (e.g. Westminster City Council, Suffolk Education Authority). Local authority contact details can be traced though our website, www.goodschoolsguide.co.uk

Lawyers with expertise in educational matters

Woodroffes

36 Ebury Street, London SW1W 0LU
Tel: 020 7730 0001   Fax: 020 7730 7900

Peter Woodroffe specialises, among other things, in advising parents about legal matters to do with fee-paying schools.

Levenes

Ashley House, 235–239 High Rd, Wood Green, London N22 8HF
Web: www.levenes.co.uk
Tel: 020 8881 7777   Fax: 020 8889 6395
E-mail: info@ levenes.co.uk

David Ruebain has developed particular expertise in the field of special educational needs law.

The Education Law Association

39 Oakleigh Avenue, London N20 9JE
Tel/Fax: 0130 3211570

Network of solicitors who are experts on educational law.

And for home study, *Independent Schools Law Custom and Practice* by Robert Boyd. Written by a partner at Veale Wasbrough (a firm with much schools experience, but which acts mostly for schools rather than against them) in magnificently plain English. Intended as a guide for schools and their governors, but so clearly and readably set out that it should prove an invaluable aid to parents brewing up for a dispute with a school, or just wanting to know where they stand.

Books

The private schools' 'bible' is *The Independent Schools' Yearbook* (A & C Black). Covers around 1,500 schools for children between the ages of 3 and 18. Like a huge collection of prospectuses. Beware in general of books with advertorial entries written by the schools themselves.

Much comfort may be had from *Molesworth* by Geoffrey Willans with illustrations by Ronald Searle. A timeless companion for little mites sent off to boarding school, and for their parents.

Glossary and abbreviations

A level General Certificate of Education, second public exam in the UK, taken at age 18

AS level Advanced Supplementary level public exam equivalent to half an A level, formerly taken as a supplement to A levels but now forming the first year of a standard A level course

A2 The examinations at the end of the second year of an A level course

ALIS A system of value-added measurement used by many schools to compare their GCSE and A level results

Amanuensis Someone who sits with a special needs student to help them put their thoughts on paper

ARCM Associate of the Royal College of Music

Assistant A young person from abroad, usually French or German, who helps teach the language (not to mention taking rugby, etc)

AVCE Advanced Vocational Certificate of Education. A system of vocational qualifications, formerly GNVQ

BA Bachelor of Arts. University first degree

Bands Different academic levels for students. Some comprehensive schools divide their intake according to bands

BD Bachelor of Divinity

Beacon schools Exemplary state secondary and primary schools that have been identified as amongst the best performing in the country in some stated way(s), e.g. teaching French, training new teachers

etc. They are expected to work in partnership with other schools to pass on their particular areas of expertise

BEcon Bachelor of Economics

BEd Bachelor of Education. A teaching qualification

BHSAI British Horse Society Assistant Instructor – the lowest qualification needed to be a riding instructor

BLit Bachelor of Literature. University qualification

Brill Slang for brilliant

BSc Bachelor of Science

BTEC A vocational qualification – alternative to A level – awarded by the Business and Technology Education Council

Bursary Contribution to the school fees, usually given to those who are poor

C of E Church of England

C of S Church of Scotland

CAD Computer-aided design

CAE Computer-aided engineering

Cantab Cambridge (from the Latin)

CAT Cognitive ability test

CCF Combined Cadet Force. Para-military training corps for the young (boys and girls)

CDT Craft, design and technology

CE Common Entrance. Qualifying exam taken usually at 11, 12 or 13 in the private sector for entry to senior schools

CertEd Certificate of Education. A teaching qualification

CLAIT Computer literacy and information technology

Combined sciences GCSE exam covering biology, chemistry and physics, counts as one GCSE

Comprehensive school Takes all pupils, regardless of their ability or aptitude. Some are fully comprehensive (no entrance exam whatsoever) and others have some selective measures

Crammers Schools that cram knowledge into the reluctant child, especially those having to re-take A levels because of low grades; not a term that the schools use of themselves – 'independent sixth form colleges', 'tutorial colleges' or 'independent further education' is more to their taste

CReSTeD Council for the Registration of Schools Teaching Dyslexic Pupils, a charity that assesses and certifies the quality of teaching for dyslexic pupils

CSYS Certificate of Sixth Year Studies (used occasionally in Scotland)

CTC City technology college – a quasi-independent state school

D of E Duke of Edinburgh Award Scheme. A combination of various different activities, including demanding physical exercise, culminating in a medal

DfES (Government) Department for Education and Skills (formerly the DfEE)

DipEd A teaching qualification

DPhil Doctor of Philosophy

DT Design Technology

Dual Award (Science) GCSE exam covering biology, chemistry and physics – counts as two GCSEs

EAL English as an Additional Language – the latest and PC acronym

EFL English as a Foreign Language

ESL English as a Second Language

Fab Slang for fabulous

Forces The Army, Navy or Air Force, and adjuncts thereto

Foundation school A state school owned by a foundation (generally religious) which appoints some – but not most – of the governing body

FP Former pupil (Scottish expression)

FRS Fellow of the Royal Society (v grand)

FRSA Fellow of the Royal Society of Arts (not grand)

Gap Work experience projects, expeditions etc. in year between school and university. Also (when in capitals) name of organisation specialising in this

Gappies Foreign (usually Aus, NZ, SA) students in their gap year working in UK independent schools

GCSE General Certificate of Secondary Education. First public exam in the UK

GDST Girls' Day School Trust (Formerly called the Girls' Public Day School Trust) A foundation of private schools

GNVQ General National Vocational Qualification. A system of vocational qualifications, now renamed AVCE

Grammar school A type of school which selects pupils on academic merit and provides a rigorous academic education (and sometimes not much else)

GSA Girls' Schools' Association. Female equivalent of HMC. *See below*

Highers/Higher Grades Scottish public exam, usually taken one or two years after Standard Grade (qv)

HMC Headmasters' Conference. A sort of headmasters' (and now one or two headmistresses) trade union, mostly for public schools, whose heads belong and are considered 'top' by those in it

HND Higher National Diploma, a well-respected vocational qualification usually taken after A levels or AVCEs

IAPS Incorporated Association of Preparatory Schools. Organisation of prep schools. Again, generally considered the 'top' ones by those in it

IB International Baccalaureate. A public exam at secondary level, increasingly recognised for entry to university in the UK

ICT Information communications technology

IGCSE International GCSE

ILEA Inner London Education Authority – local administration of state schools, now defunct

Inclusion The concept that all children with special educational needs should be educated, if at all possible, in mainstream schools

Independent Word used by fee-paying schools to describe themselves – erroneously

Inter-denom Inter-denominational (refers to religious affiliation, supports more than one brand of Christianity)

IQ Intelligence Quotient

ISC Independent Schools Council – inspects independent schools (but not itself independent; owned and run by the schools)

ISCis information service of the above

ISCO Independent Schools Careers Organisation

IT Information technology

JMB Joint Matriculation Board

KS (Key Stage) The national curriculum is divided into four Key Stages according to pupils' ages: KS1 for 5–7-year-olds, KS2 for 7–11, KS3 for 11–14, KS4 for 14–16

LesL Licencié ès Lettres. French university degree

Lab Laboratory

LAMDA London Academy of Music and the Dramatic Arts

LTA Lawn Tennis Association

MA Master of Arts. University degree

MEd Master of Education. Teaching qualification

MIDYIS *See ALIS*, but this measure's value-added up to GCSE

MoD Ministry of Defence

MSc Master of Science. University qualification

NFER National Foundation for Educational Research

NNEB Nursery nurses official qualification

Non-denom Non-denominational (refers to religious affiliation, generally means pretty low-key)

NQT Newly qualified teacher

NVR(Q) Non-verbal reasoning (quotient), a test of ability used by some selective schools

OB Old Boy (i.e. former pupil of a school)

OED Oxford English Dictionary

Ofsted Office for Standards in Education. Officially the Office of Her Majesty's Chief Inspector of Schools. Inspects schools and publishes reports on them

OG Old Girl (i.e. former pupil of a school)

OSB Order of St Benedict

OTT Over the top, as in unacceptable behaviour

Oxbridge Short for Oxford and/or Cambridge universities

Oxon Oxford

Pastoral care Care of pupil on matters not related to their work, e.g. personal and social ones

PE Physical education

PFI Private finance initiative: off-balance-sheet funding for the government, with private firms providing finance and facilities management

PGCE Postgraduate Certificate of Education. A teaching qualification

PhD Doctor of Philosophy (postgraduate degree)

PPP Public private partnership. *See PFI*

PSD Personal and Social Development

PS(H)E Personal, social (and health) education (courses)

PTA Parent-teacher association

qv quod vide – for which see, i.e. it has its own entry in this book

RC Roman Catholic

RCSLT Royal College of Speech and Language Therapists

QCA Qualifications and Curriculum Authority, a government agency operating in England only

RE Religious education – learn about beliefs

RI Religious instruction – learn to believe

RS Religious studies – learn about beliefs

RSA Royal Society of Arts

RSA CLAIT The RSA's computer literacy and information technology qualification

RYA Royal Yachting Association

San Sanatorium, sick bay

SATs Tests sat by English state (and some private) school kids at 7, 11 and 14

SATS Test sat by American kids to get into US universities

Scotvec A Scottish vocational qualification

SEN Special educational needs - having disabilities (e.g. dyslexia, deafness) which require special provision to be made for a child's education

Services The Army, Navy or Air Force, and adjuncts thereto

Set A group of children of similar ability within a subject and year (children can be in the top set for one subject and the bottom for others, and may move between sets)

Six-inch rule Rule applied at some co-educational schools whereby boys and girls may not come closer to each other than six inches (in case they get over-excited)

SpLD Specific learning difficulties, a portmanteau phrase covering dyslexia, dyspraxia etc

SSSI Site of special scientific interest – designated as such by the government and, as such, protected

Standard Grades The Scottish equivalent of GCSEs

Stooge A foreign gap year student employed by a school

Streaming The practice of dividing a year group into streams of similar ability – if you are in the top stream you are in the top stream for all subjects

Suss Slang for find out, get to the bottom of, investigate, sniff out

TLC Tender loving care

Twoccer One who Takes a car Without the Owner's Consent

V very

Vibes Slang for vibrations

VIP Very important person

VR(Q) Verbal reasoning (quotient), a test of ability used by many selective schools

WASP White Anglo-Saxon Protestant

YE Young Enterprise. A hands-on business studies course

YELLIS *See ALIS,* but this measures value-added at primary level

YMCA Young Men's Christian Association (Youth Hostel organisation)

SENIOR SCHOOLS

THE ABBEY SCHOOL READING

Linked to Abbey Junior School (The) in the Junior section

Kendrick Road, Reading, Berkshire, RG1 5DZ

Tel: 0118 987 2256
Fax: 0118 987 1478
E-mail: schooloffice@theabbey.co.uk
Website: www.theabbey.co.uk

• Pupils: 685 girls, all day • Ages: 11-18 • Size of sixth form: 155 • Non-denom • Fees: £2,980 • Independent • Open days: Early October; sixth form late October

Head: Since 2002, Mrs Barbara Stanley BA PGCE FRGS (mid fifties). Educated at Glenlola Collegiate School, County Down, and universities of Belfast and Leicester. A geographer. Headed up Bedford High and Alexandra College Dublin before coming to the Abbey, where her predecessor left big shoes to fill. Her first year had its scrunchy moments and, through earnest dialectic with some miffed girls, staff and parents, she won affection and admiration. Direct, 'calls a spade a spade'. Humane. Approachable. Listens. Knows all the girls by name and levels with them – they like that. 'An educationist, a thinker, just right for the Abbey in these fast-moving times.' A quietly impressive person who blends strong purpose with open-minded curiosity. Her mission is to urge these exam-clever girls to try their hands at everything. Strong commitment to social responsibility, she is a member back home of the inter-faith Corrymeela Community (www.corrymeela.org), which reconciles riven communities post-Troubles.

Academic Matters: To have a daughter at the Abbey is to elicit the response 'Oh – ah' followed by a reverential nod. This is a premiership school with more about it of Chelsea than West Brom. At A level you're looking at 87 per cent A/B, 99 per cent A/C. Sciences very strong – a benefit of single sex – so we find 29 biologists, 24 chemists and 20 mathematicians compared with 17 Eng literati and 17 psychologists. Close to 20 per cent go on to med/vet degree courses. Art and des tech are straight-A subjects, history (difficult) exceptional. Few if any weak links (psychology could do better). Low numbers in IT ought to be boosted by recent investment. At GCSE it's 99.9 per cent A*-C (pity the one poor girl who got a D). Girls know the moment they get their results if they can step up to the sixth form.

Not an exam factory, 'no!' they emphatically say, though a visitor's first impressions are mostly of statistics glistening on noticeboards and even on classroom doors – everywhere you go you're up against last year's results. Parents – some crossly – assert that there's more, much more, going on than meets the untutored eye. 'Marvellous teachers', 'they respond to parental queries within 24 hours' – and get pretty good reviews from the girls, too. They want to know about problems and, said one mum, 'we wish we'd spoken out earlier'. Teachers' work ethic, the need to pack every day, imposes a focus which, for us as visitors, came over too frequently as blinkers. There were warm, well-mannered exceptions. Girls invariably jolly nice. Trad flavour – not much evidence of rebs or boundary pushers – this is the sort of place where attitude would probably come over as, like, so irrelevant. Tutors urge girls to wander outside the curriculum and follow their own intellectual curiosity – good results are not enough. Progress minutely, scientifically monitored, non-thrivers, 'coasters and sliders' chivvied and egged on by mentors abetted by parents.

Parents praise the way the school bends over backwards to accommodate unconventional A level choices – 'the timetabler is a genius'. They laud savvy university application advice and the way they back you to the hilt however you opt. They also praise teachers' expert understanding of their daughters, the way they set apt expectations. Marvellous drama and art, inspirationally led music, terrific sport, all examinable. Sumptuous LRC. Attractively grown-up routines for sixth formers. Own clothes, own classrooms, damn fine common room constitute a counter-lure to local excellent sixth form colleges.

SEN provision not high profile given the requirement to pass the entry exam and cope with the subsequently sprightly pace of life here notwithstanding an SpLD. Around 50 girls come to the attention of the SENCO, who also runs the gifted and talented programme. Most are mildly dyslexic, some dyspraxic. ADHD is not unknown. Around half of these get just 30 mins a week 1 to 1.

Games, Options, The Arts: Sports England's Sportsmark Gold says it all. It means they coax the reluctant kindly and make it fun – parents agree – and they regale the very best and catapult them as high as they can go. Hockey, netball and cricket are tops, but it's all top notch – regular county and UK representation. Rowing growing: one GB oarsgirl and others coming through. Links with borough council brings in the local community. Fine swimming pool. Music very strong – 45+ per cent learn an instrument. Ensembles of all kinds from swing to Stravinsky, thrash metal in your own time, please. Drama is adventurous, art well resourced, well done. Considering they're all off the campus by 4 it's amazing what product they get. Good breadth of extra-curricular activities – plus D of E, Young Enterprise, the usual suspects. Trips and expeds in the hols.

Background and Atmosphere: School began in 1887 as Reading High School then, in 1914, after divorcing the Church Schools Company, took their present name in commemoration of a school which had conked out years before having, for two years, had Jane Austen on its books (she reckons they taught her nothing). Buildings turn-of-the-century, typical school brick, gloomy exterior but bright enough inside with some classy add-ons. Spacious playing fields and no sense of the crampedness you get at so many of these off-street city schools.

Pastoral Care and Discipline: Careful attention to best emotional health – this a particular preoccupation of the head. Teachers are appraised 50 per cent on their teaching skills, 50 per cent on their pastoral value. Compared with schools with similar pressures to succeed, it's amazing what a sunny lot they are. Sixth formers are buddies to younger girls and talk them through stuff as it happens. No matter how hard we peered, no evidence of anorexia or drugs – parents concurred, praised the PSHE and general caring vigilance. A striking feature, this. Community values and 'spiritual awareness' instilled by hymn and prayers each morning. They look beyond, too. Every year group must raise money for charity using their own initiative. Discipline is strict but reasonable. When a girl gets baleful they normally bring her round. Expulsion rare.

Pupils and Parents: Parents are professionals who want a powerhouse. Not all by any means awash with money – 20 to 30 per cent dropout after GCSE a symptom, though the growing excellence of local sixth form colleges encourages a fee holiday. Evident ethnic mix enriched by BBC monitoring station at nearby Caversham. No way snobby, too meritocratic. Not a school for a daffy lass, these are sorted girls all going for it. Pleasant social atmosphere, sense of pace, but we were charmed to see a little catching game happening in a corridor. They come also from Maidenhead (1/2 hr) and Windsor (3/4). Fleets of buses. Busy-bee PTA with own website – www.theabbeypa.org.uk.

Entrance: Own entry exam in maths, English and verbal reasoning. Interview picks up on any other desirable attribute. Around 45 per cent come up from the juniors, joined by girls from more than 60 other schools including sizeable wodges from Eton End, Highfield and St Joseph's. New sixth formers need min 7 GCSEs at A*-C plus glowing reference.

Exit: Around 10 per cent to Oxbridge. They like London, Birmingham and Nottingham especially. Proper subjects at proper places – as you'd expect. Good range, preponder-antly scientific. Heard-of high-fliers include the late Baroness Brigstocke, Sally Taylor (BBC South Today) and Helen Ganly, artist and social reformer. They lay no claim to Miss Austen but cherish Elizabeth Taylor, 'one of the great neglected voices of English fiction.' We know how she felt.

Money Matters: Fees decidedly competitive. Scholarships at age 11 up to 20 per cent for the best 10 per cent. Reverse these numbers in the sixth form, where 20 per cent get 10 per cent – another inducement to stay. Music awards win free instrumental tuition. Some bursaries for those in financial peril, esp in sixth form.

Remarks: It's an anxious business being and staying this good. League table place matters because parents obsess about it (they deny it, of course, and blame politicians). Defection to free sixth form colls post-GCSE has stimulated both a more young adult-friendly sixth form regime and greater efforts in all areas. This is a school which does the biz examwise, no doubt, but also tries with sincerity and enlightenment of purpose, especially under this humane head, to turn out girls who are in touch with everything they can do well and who will go on to be good citizens.

ABBOTS BROMLEY SCHOOL FOR GIRLS

Linked to Abbots Bromley School for Girls Junior School in the Junior section

Abbots Bromley, Nr Rugeley, Staffordshire, WS15 3BW

Tel: 01283 840 232
Fax: 01283 840 988
E-mail: registrar@abbotsbromley.net
Website: www.abbotsbromley.staffs.sch.uk

• Pupils: 285 girls in senior and junior schools; 70 boarders, also occasional overnight and flexi-boarders • Ages: 4-18 • Size of sixth form: 60 • Anglican • Fees: Day £1,650- £3,620; boarding £4,850 - £6,195 • Independent • Open days: March and October

Headmistress: Since 2005, Mrs Trish Woodhouse BMus Hons. Educated locally at Stafford Girls' High and graduated in music from London University. Been involved in the education of girls for 20 years ('I only 'do' girls!), – a career which includes being director of music at Wimbledon High and sixth form housemistress at Queenswood School before her previous post as deputy head at St Mary's Wantage.

Academic Matters: Solidly good results, especially as it's non-selective, with all academic abilities welcomed. Definitely not a league table chaser – won't be found in top 100. Focus is very much on individual effort and achievement. Girls encouraged to do their best in whatever subject/area. Head describes results as 'superb' and with 95 per cent plus getting A*-C at GCSE, and 75 per cent plus A/B at A level, they're certainly on the high side of acceptable. Choice of 18 subjects at A/AS level. Maths is popular (over 40 per cent of sixth formers study it). Science taught as three separate subjects in well-equipped labs. Other subjects like history, geography and modern languages also have their own dedicated teaching areas with impressive student work much in evidence.

Small classes (maximum 18 but most just 15) with traditional eyes front teaching methods in most lessons. Streaming for maths and English. Supervised daytime prep but also an hour in the evening for boarders. No Saturday morning school any more due to clash with other activities. SEN support for learning difficulties like dyslexia and extra English for overseas students (currently 20 girls getting tuition). Sixth formers also help younger pupils with their study skills. Large, airy, well-stocked library offers internet access and computers in library, sixth form study room and ICT department linked up to school network. Plenty of surfing going on at time of visit – even youngest girls seemed to know exactly what they were doing.

Games, Options, The Arts: In a word – dance! To be fair, there's lots more on offer than that – like the equestrian centre, offering stabling for pupils' ponies plus indoor and outdoor arenas. Also art – much space is devoted to this and work on show is of an extremely high standard, a fact reflected in selection of higher education. But dance is the area in which, in recent years, the school has excelled. Over a third (around 100) take dance lessons – of those, up to 20 on vocational courses fit in two to three classes a day around their other curricular demands. Staff of five headed by director of dance Russell Alkins teach in two fully equipped studios. Modern and tap also on the agenda but core discipline is ballet. High success rate in Royal Academy of Dance grades as GCSE and AS equivalents. Four years ago started vocational courses for girls wishing to pursue dancing career. But dance director stresses, 'we are not trying to be another specialist or vocational school. We think we can do better than that.' Number of parents choose to send daughters here because of its dancing excellence. Some students members of National Youth Ballet (Wayne Sleep sometimes choreographs).

Music also a major part of school life with orchestras, junior and senior choirs (they've a number of CDs to their credit) and an entire school wing devoted to musical activities. Music compulsory to year 9 then an option for GCSE. Two thirds of girls from prep school upwards learn at least one instrument, many two or three. Prep school classes offered half-term's free tuition in strings or brass to see if they like it. Choirs sing regularly in school chapel and nearby Lichfield Cathedral, as well as trips abroad (Disneyland Paris in 2002). As befits the 21st century, the music department has a music computer suite and electronic keyboard studio.

Indoor and outdoor sports played to high competitive level (several girls in county teams) and covered heated pool used all year round, as is the all-weather hockey pitch. (Locals and other schools nearby also welcome to swim or use sports hall facilities.) But some parents say there could be more athletics.

Background and Atmosphere: A strongly C of E Woodard Foundation school with 130-year history. School more commonly known by village name Abbots Bromley (home of the horn dance, a unique pagan ritual a bit like Morris dancing only with antlers) or more fondly, by past and present pupils, simply as AB. Dominates centre of pretty redbrick Staffordshire village. Bulk of school situated at St Anne's on one side of main road (includes all classrooms and study areas, boarding houses, dining room, school halls, stables and some playing fields) with junior department (Roch House), sports hall, swimming pool and more playing fields plus Astroturf on opposite side in St Mary's. Despite spread of buildings and activities, a very close-knit community.

Strong religious tradition which still pervades all areas though in a more 21st century way. Regular services and assemblies in exquisite school chapel. All faiths welcome and studied in religious teachings. Heartfelt messages on chapel prayer boards show as clearly as anything what a nice bunch they are! Head undertook much restructuring when she arrived – moving boarders under one roof, reorganising school week – but now 'in a period of relative calm'. School uniform was updated two years ago but traditional (and apparently much-loved) straw boaters ('boards') will stay. Loads going on for all ages, both in school and trips away. Real 'buzz' to the place. 'That's what attracted me to AB,' says head. 'It's a 'can-do' environment.' Same noticed by school inspectors who reported, 'it's not magic but there's something that happens here.' One mum reports strong rapport between staff and girls in sixth form. 'They are treated as young adults, not kids,' she says. 'Teachers often come in in extra time to help their pupils with their course work.'

Pastoral Care and Discipline: Girls know where to turn for help, advice or comfort. Older girls ('they're very supportive of each other'), housemistresses and form teachers, not to mention school chaplain who's there for general as well as spiritual guidance. 'My daughter felt so at home at AB,' says one parent. 'In fact it was her decision to board because she felt she was missing out.' Classrooms and dorms are all being refurbished and furnished. Girls can put up posters and bring in toys and extra comfort comes from being with their friends. Bath and shower rooms may not be that new but they're in good condition and everything was clean. Zero tolerance of bullying, theft, rule breaking and antisocial behaviour. Head has only had to suspend one girl in her time (parents chose not to send her back) and a disciplinary matter was being dealt with at time of visit. Even so, it's not seen as a major problem (this was supported by parents and pupils alike). There are notices up all round the school. 'We have a clearly defined system for dealing promptly with incidents by form tutors, housemistresses and deputy head. I'm seen as the last resort,' says head.

Pupils and Parents: Wide variety of backgrounds, majority from midlands but some Hong Kong and Far East. No particular social grouping – a healthy mix, refreshingly classless. Pupils come across as smart, confident, and well mannered. 'That our daughters may be as the polished corners of the temple' as the school motto has it. Famous old girls include Sue Nicholls, long-standing character in Coronation Street.

Entrance: Non-selective. Entry to Roch House after day's assessment. Staff want to see what girls can do. Senior school entry slightly more academic – tests in maths and English, 'just to make sure we're not admitting someone with difficulties we can't help' – plus other day-long activities to see if they'll blend in. Says head, 'we attract all sorts but the girls who thrive best are the ones who want to have a go.' School still has spare capacity and is not oversubscribed – well worth bearing in mind.

Exit: Some Oxbridge success, great spread of degree courses and colleges, law and art prominent.

Money Matters: Up to 50 per cent of boarding and tuition fees can be covered by number of scholarships/exhibitions including academic, music, art, sports, and dance. Others available in sixth form. All open to internal and external candidates.

Remarks: A large, well organised and well equipped school for relatively few pupils. Beautiful surroundings and enough diversity to satisfy all tastes, whether academic or arty. Current swing away from boarding left something of a void in this very traditional boarding school which staff have worked hard to fill with other activities. Certainly the girls we spoke to seemed wonderfully content. 'I adore it,' said one. 'I never thought I'd say that about school, but it's true.' Produces young women confident and qualified to take on outside world. It will be of some importance to local families to see which way the new regime steers the school.

ABINGDON SCHOOL

Linked to Josca's School in the Junior section

Park Road, Abingdon, Oxfordshire, OX14 1DE

Tel: 01235 849041
Fax: 01235 849 085
E-mail: admissions@abingdon.org.uk
Website: www.abingdon.org.uk

• Pupils: 800 boys, 140 board • Ages: 11-18 • Size of sixth form: 260 • C of E • Fees: Weekly boarding £6,334; Full boarding £6,548; Day £3,589. Josca's £2,937 • Independent • Open days: October. Mini open morning in Lent term

Headmaster: Since 2002, Mr Mark Turner MA PGCE (fortyish). Educated Rossall, Mansfield College, Oxford (read geography), then four years in the Army. Previously at Oundle, where he was a housemaster, then head of Kelly College, Devon. Married with two boys. A keen traveller and fly fisher, Mr Turner follows a distinguished, long-serving head, Michael St John Parker who 'put school on the map'. Intense, vigorous and committed, Mr Turner has tightened up discipline in a way that seems to be appreciated by both boys and parents; the increased numbers of applicants bear witness to this. Very conscious of the school's history, he has ambitious plans for a school which is already undergoing considerable redevelopment. Sits on the Navy's Admiralty Interview Board and runs, it seems, a tight ship but with a light touch.

Academic Matters: Good across the board results and outstanding in a few subjects especially maths and sciences, assisted by excellent staff, often spouses of Oxford academics or scientists at local research institutions eg Rutherford Appleton Laboratory. Results have improved consistently over recent years. Some less popular subjects, principally the arts, taught at sixth form level in collaboration with local girls' school, St Helen's and St Katharine's. A good library in very attractive surroundings. Saturday school for all but years 1 and 2.

Games, Options, The Arts: Outstanding games especially rowing, cricket and rugby. Rowers won a grand triple in 2002 – Schools' Head, National Schools' Regatta and Princess Elizabeth Cup at Henley. Playing fields extensive. Good sports facilities in all areas and boys can have a go at a huge variety of competitive and individual sports including golf, basketball, fencing, athletics, fives, canoeing, wargaming. A new £3.2 million arts centre and a spectacular boathouse were both opened in 2003. Ambitious plans to refurbish the indoor sports facilities. Good range of options and activities in what school calls 'The Other Half' includes brewing, shooting and very popular boat club. CCF and Duke of Edinburgh Awards well-supported. Music is strong and has been further strengthened, as have art and drama, by new arts block designed around existing excellent Amey Hall, built in 1980. Drama already enthusiastically supported – and assisted by girls from St Helen's and St Katharine's. Academic options a traditional mix and good to see classical Greek still holding its own. Good results in Latin too. Languages not overly popular in later years but results good.

Background and Atmosphere: Ancient monastery foundation (it is known to have existed in 1256), endowed in the 16th century by a mercer and supported thereafter by the Mercers' Company. School occupies a large and attractive, landscaped site in the centre of Abingdon. Buildings of various dates but all merge pleasantly around extensive playing fields and carefully tended gardens. Splendid 1990s Mercers' Court at heart of school and space for new buildings when required. Atmosphere is purposeful and relaxed. Boarding – though taken up by minority – seen as central to school's ethos and future and boarding staff are accessible and popular. Boarders' rooms in the three houses are for 3s and 4s for younger boys and for 1s and 2s in the sixth. Most rooms snug, light and freely adorned by residents. As few boarders spend weekends in school, local friends/family are valuable for those who do.

Pastoral Care and Discipline: Pastoral care is carefully structured and depends on interaction in houses and tutor groups. Boys feel that their individual needs are catered for in the main. Discipline, tightened up under the head, appears strong and effective. Changes to the, hitherto bizarrely inconsistent, school uniform were fully implemented in September 2004 – navy blue blazers and grey flannels for all except the sixth form who wear dark suits. Head has clear policy on dress code/drink/drugs/smoking and enforces it effectively if need be.

Pupils and Parents: About 17 per cent board; some from abroad, although half are locally based weekly boarders, numbers which head is keen to build on. Changing social mix, now far more professional families, two working

parents, keen to be involved with school. 50 per cent first-time buyers of independent education. Parents increasingly seeing the point of a traditional, academic, public school education but keeping boys at home or weekly boarding. Head, who has expanded traditional catchment limits, feels school fills social and geographical niche between Marlborough and Radley – schools with higher profiles and fees! Also stresses that 'one of the school's greatest strengths is its wide social mix.'

Entrance: At 11 via the Abingdon School exam, current head's report and interview. At 13 via pre-test at 11, CE and/or the school's own scholarship exam or 13+ examination. Overseas candidates may sit assessment paper in home countries. Sixth form entrants need 7 GCSEs at C or above, including at least 3 As and 2 Bs. Pupils come from many local preps at 13 and from various local primary schools at 11, as well as preps further afield. Increasing competition for places, currently more than 2:1.

Exit: Almost all to good degree courses at good universities and an impressive 20 per cent heading to Oxbridge. Strong on science, technological and engineering subjects.

Money Matters: Good number of scholarships at 11 and 13; all are means-tested to some extent and require academic aptitude. Music, art, all-rounder and sixth form scholarships have special criteria. Scholars given special consideration and opportunities including exclusive Roysse Society, a discussion group, as well as links with Pembroke College, Oxford. Bursaries also available to help and encourage those on lower incomes.

Remarks: An impressive school which does what it sets out to do well. Likely to increase in popularity because of its location and increasingly sparkly achievements. A serious contender for new pupils against some of its better-known but less academically successful competitors. Developing interestingly under Mark Turner.

ACKWORTH SCHOOL

Linked to Coram House in the Junior section

Ackworth, Pontefract, West Yorkshire, WF7 7LT

Tel: 01977 611 401
Fax: 01977 616 225
E-mail: admissions@ackworthschool.com
Website: www.ackworthschool.com

- Pupils: 180 boys and 190, girls of whom 100 board • Ages: 11-18 • Size of sixth form: 90 • Quaker (but other faiths welcome) • Fees: Senior: day £3,118; boarding £5,166. Coram House: day £1,890 • Independent • Open days: A Saturday in early October

Head: Since 2004, Mr Peter J Simpson MA (early forties) educated at Dartford Grammar, read history at Oxford and got his MA in education management from Keele. Was deputy head at Kimbolton and head of humanities at The Grange School in Cheshire. Loves singing and has two passions – opera, especially Wagner, and outdoor pursuits. Spent 5 years running an outdoor pursuits unit, and behind the thick-rimmed spectacles his face lights with enthusiasm as he tells of the range of activities available at Ackworth, everything from caving through mountaineering to cross-country skiing. He thinks the school is a real gem and should celebrate achievements more overtly. Pupils say the head understands, is in tune and in touch, 'it's the small things he does that make a difference,' he's keen to please, completely at ease with them and always has a quip or witticism. All this about a head who expelled a couple of youngsters shortly after his arrival – surprisingly, pupils sympathised with him.

Academic Matters: Not an academic hothouse, majority of pupils study for 9 GCSEs with a creditable 90 per cent A*-C. At A level A/B grades fluctuate between 43 and 63 per cent. Class sizes average 18 in the senior school and 8 in the sixth form. Science and maths are ever popular but it is in the creative subjects where the real strengths lie. Plenty of IT facilities including a new ICT suite, next step is to improve the integration of IT into all areas of teaching. Pupils say that lessons are interesting, lively and fun and that they are encouraged to think for themselves and to question.

The school identifies fifteen per cent of pupils as having special educational needs, mainly dyslexia and dyspraxia, though the school can cater for those with dyscalculia, behavioural difficulties and autism. For more than one in

seven pupils English is not their first language, of these more than half receive EAL support. School has a newly opened International Language School – doesn't guarantee admission to sixth form but is a step in the right direction.

Not a school for special needs – but a school that caters outstandingly well for children who have them. Pupils display a broad range of aptitudes, characters and academic ability. Head proudly tells of a recent star autistic pupil who got 7A*s and 3As at GCSE – talented teaching and a genuine understanding of the needs of the individual child. Special needs children thrive in part because the Quaker ethos – 'that of God is in each of us' – is reinforced by school's motto – non sibi sed omnibus (not for oneself but for everybody.)

The school houses a fantastic, heart-warming and deservedly highly regarded autism resource where four statemented pupils are educated. Expert and compassionate resource head, develops confidence and self-esteem. Attention is paid to developing social and communication skills at all levels including specialist speech and language therapy, computer conversations and using interests such as snooker to promote conversation. Teaching is painstakingly geared to the individual. Each child has an individually designed curriculum, and with the help of dedicated learning support assistants pupils are integrated into a range of classes. Inclusion is a two-way process: children in the main school welcome the pupils from the resource and clamour to spend break and lunchtimes at the resource's Shed Court Club. Two major drawbacks – what lies ahead after Ackworth for those lucky enough to have spent time here and, with only four places available, it's likely to be 'no room at the inn'.

Games, Options, The Arts: Oodles of clubs and societies; those old enough can learn to drive, others take up jewellery, silversmithing, join Amnesty International, relax with yoga, philosophise, fence, play golf – you name it they offer it (well maybe not CCF, rugby or wargaming but pretty much everything else). Students must participate in at least two activities. All pupils play sport, and the school offers outreach support to local physically disabled through Sports Ability, which is modelled on the Paralympics. Music, music technology and drama very popular with plenty of opportunities to participate. Technology and design including HE and textiles are sought after options – over the years school has boasted several Arkwright scholars. There is a fabulous DT department – school full of desks, chairs, cupboards etc made by them ... who needs IKEA with these chaps around?

Background and Atmosphere: One of the first Quaker schools, founded by John Fothergill in 1779. Set among undulating fields and pastures, the school was a Foundling

Hospital until the magnificent site and elegant sandstone Georgian buildings were purchased by a group of eminent Friends to provide a place to educate Quakers 'not in affluence.' Recent sympathetic additions blend into the Georgian splendour with the little changed rural landscape providing a contrast to the nearby earthy industrial heartlands. A magnificent setting, it's no wonder an overwhelming sense of joy pervades. Indeed this is such a friendly, welcoming school you probably need to allow two days for a visit instead of the usual one. We were constantly hijacked, not just by staff (who in some schools sprint faster than Kelly Holmes when they see us beckoning) but also by enthusiastic youngsters with a refreshing openness. They had no idea who we were but nonetheless were keen (and determined) to relate the many joys of being at the school and the fun they have, whether we wanted to know or not! We tried desperately hard to ease out a few negatives but all were either too canny to fall for our wily ways or genuinely too enthused by everything.

Pastoral Care and Discipline: There's a great family feel to this school and, as you might expect, discipline errs on the side of tolerance and understanding but that doesn't mean those who push the boundaries don't get punished. Tutors oversee pastoral care but others are involved. Boarding is an integral part of the school and accommodation is very good, some rooms even have en-suite facilities. Day pupils are always welcome to stay for both tea and supervised prep at no extra cost; the weekend activity programme set up for boarders is open to day pupils too. A full(ish) programme is rounded off on Sunday evenings with a Quaker meeting followed by a special tea and activity perhaps a talk, lecture or musical event.

Pupils and Parents: Mostly from professional and business families living in Ackworth and Pontefract with some travelling from Sheffield and Doncaster. Of the 100 boarders, two thirds live abroad, half of these are Chinese. School takes students who will both benefit from the education provided and are willing to make the most of the opportunities offered.

Entrance: Half the pupils come from Coram House, the rest in equal numbers from local state and prep schools. Entry is based on tests in maths and English together with a non-verbal reasoning test. For sixth form entry a minimum of five GCSEs at grade C or above are required.

Exit: Almost half leave at the end of y11 mostly for local colleges but are replaced by new entrants, mainly boarders. Majority (97 per cent) of sixth form goes on to university, a couple a year to Oxbridge, some overseas, rest to a range of destinations with Leeds, Nottingham and Newcastle perennially popular.

Money Matters: Over 15 per cent of pupils receive help with fees either through scholarships (academic, art, music), bursaries or staff concessions. Discounts for second and subsequent children.

Remarks: If you want to be miserable or bored, go somewhere else. Rule breakers and those easily fatigued would find this school hard to cope with, but anyone wanting to experience and enjoy life will have a lot of fun.

ACLAND BURGHLEY SCHOOL

Burghley Road, London, NW5 1UJ

Tel: 020 7485 8515
Fax: 020 7284 3462
E-mail: genadmin@aclandburghley.camden.sch.uk
Website: www.aclandburghley.camden.sch.uk

• Pupils: 790 boys and 465 girls, all day • Ages: 11 – 19 • Size of sixth form: 355 boys and girls • Non-denom • State • Open days: October

Head: Since 2002, Mr Michael Shew (fifties), previously head of Wembley High School. Taught at Parliament Hill School (qv) in the 1980s, before a stint as an education inspector and then a deputy headship in Fulham. He is married with a daughter at primary school in Haringey. Keen on travelling, sailing and family life (when time). Informal, friendly but a strong leader.

Academic Matters: A genuinely comprehensive school, with no selection by ability or specialist places. Wide ability range, including more than its fair share of students with statements of special education need, and a strong cohort of dedicated teachers. 60-ish per cent 5+ A*-C grades at GCSE – well above the inner-London average. Specialist arts college status is evident in the stupendous artwork adorning the walls and its particularly successful subjects mostly have an arts bias – 40 per cent A grades for art at GCSE and at A level.

The head has been working hard to raise standards in the lower part of the school. One of his first actions was to ditch the SMILE system of individualised maths teaching, a relic of ILEA, 'which could result in students meandering along for five years without achieving too much.' A recent Ofsted report commented that mixed-ability teaching in maths and languages did not always produce appropriate work for all abilities and the school now sets in these subjects from year 8 and science from year 9. 'We will evaluate whether this is benefiting everyone.' Students learn French or Spanish but not both, in years 7 – 9.

Teaching and learning improve higher up the school and are particularly good in the sixth form. Sociology is one of the most popular and successful A level choices, with half A or B grades. History, psychology, business studies and media studies are all strong. A good range of vocational courses, including skills for life, art and design and business studies.

Good learning support department with effective SEN and EAL teaching, and enrichment opportunities for gifted and talented students.

Games, Options, The Arts: As previously mentioned, exceptional art teaching, especially in the sixth form. 'It's the best school for art in the world,' said a pupil. Extensive programme of visiting artists; the head talks of 'visual literacy as a learning style.' Music is now improving rapidly under a new head of department. Excellent drama. Offers an AVCE in performing arts, as well as drama GCSE and A level.

PE is good. No grassy acres, but a large sports hall and a gym – soon to be refurbished courtesy of a £1.3 million lottery grant – and a rooftop tarmac football pitch. Students also use Tufnell Park playing fields, the Michael Sobell sports centre and Leaside canoeing centre. Everyone does dance and drama in the first three years. Lots of extracurricular activities, some open to the local community, such as fencing, life drawing and classical civilisations classes.

Background and Atmosphere: A very urban school in the side-streets of Tufnell Park. 1960s concrete exterior gives on to bright and cheerful class-rooms, including a £900,000 learning resource centre stocked with computers, CD-ROMs and books, and staffed from 8am – 5.30pm. Two thirds of pupils are boys – there's a girls' co-ordinator to make sure girls are not overwhelmed, and girls have their own den where they can gather at lunchtimes and their own clubs and projects. Girls comment, 'it makes us stick together more. And we have boys as friends, which really surprises girls from single-sex schools.' Older students in particular enjoy the equal relationship they have with teachers. 'There's a feeling of co-operation and mutual respect here,' said a sixth former. 'I expect my views to be valued.'

Pastoral Care and Discipline: The school is renowned for its peer counselling and anti-bullying service, ABC. Pupils from year 8 upwards are trained to support others who are having difficulties and to run drama workshops in local primary schools. Pupils feel that this affects the whole atmosphere of the school. 'You get to know so many people you wouldn't usually meet and there's a real sense of community. It makes the school feel safer and more friendly.'

Some pupils are less interested than others in arriving on time, sitting down and learning. 'We will always have students with challenging behaviour and there will always be a period of adjustment in year 7 as so many different cohorts from so many different primary schools come together,' says the head. The school is concentrating on honing its behaviour strategies. Year 7s now have a three-day residential course in Surrey, 'where we focus on listening skills and on working together – on the right attitudes to learning.' The school has significant government funding for reducing truancy and exclusions. Skilled at supporting pupils with emotional and behavioural difficulties, and learning mentors work with pupils in the lower years. The school's focus on these areas has improved behaviour and academic performance at key stage 3.

Pupils and Parents: A huge social mix, with plenty of children from the tough local estates and those from liberal middle-class families, who have often chosen Acland Burghley for its relaxed co-ed atmosphere over the single sex comprehensives nearby. Around a quarter of pupils speak English as a second language and 27 per cent are eligible for free school meals – well above the national average. The thriving parents' association runs murder mystery evenings, quiz nights and other social events. OG: Ms Dynamite.

Entrance: Heavily over-subscribed, with a catchment area of half a mile or less. First preference to those with a statement of special educational needs, then siblings, then proximity.

Exit: About 65 per cent go on to the sixth form, part of La Swap consortium. Of these, two thirds go on to further or higher education, including many to art college and about seven a year to Oxbridge.

Money Matters: As cash-strapped as any other comprehensive. There's lottery cash, Excellence in Cities money, extra for teaching children with statements of special educational need, 'but it is never enough'.

Remarks: Creditable exam results from a very mixed intake, remarkable for its art and for the egalitarian effects of its anti-bulling and peer mentoring programme. 'It's incredibly informal,' said a student. 'The staff are good enough at their jobs to enable them to be friendly.' 'There's a real feeling that if you want to do something, you can,' said another.

ACS Cobham International School

Linked to ACS Cobham International School Junior School in the Junior section

Heywood, Portsmouth Road, Cobham, Surrey, KT11 1BL

Tel: 01932 867 251
Fax: 01932 869 789
E-mail: w.green@acs-england.co.uk
Website: www.acs-england.co.uk

- Pupils: 1,300 boys and girls; 110 board, rest day • Ages: 2 1/2 - 18 • Size of sixth form: 450 in the High School • Non-denom • Fees: Day: £4,900- £15,650. Boarding (grades 7-13): seven day £10,550, five day £7700 • Independent

Head: Since 1992, Tom Lehman (fifties), serious, thoughtful and articulate, and moves with the relaxed ease of a tall, rangy athlete (swimming and baseball). Went to Thiel College and Syracuse U (USA), and U of London, arrived at ACS in 1987, made head in 1992, and has no plans to leave. He does not mince words, answers questions with care and deliberation – in fact like the philosopher of his undergraduate training – and has a reputation for listening hard and following through. He runs a very busy school with a lot of balls in the air, but families see him as very much out and about on campus. He feels that a large school like Cobham offers a bigger pool for students to find more opportunities – for developing confidence in one's skills, for finding friends with common interests, for developing individually thereby contributing to the whole.

Academic Matters: American preparatory honors courses (towards American High School Diploma), with 14 Advanced Placement courses and the International Baccalaureate (IB Diploma) offered in the upper grades, maximum 20 in classes for all grades. Lower school emphasis on personal progress rather than grades, using carefully designed rubrics assessing progress (that can be readily translated into letter grades for transition to other schools). Very concerned that student gets a truly sound foundation and understands where he has been and where he needs to go, not compete against each other at this age. Strong fundamentals in math; even those arriving not properly prepared are strengthened by the process (in one example going from 40s to 90s in ERB math scores). Children work well together in teams, share ideas; are mixed well in terms of letting different ones lead, 'even forced into leadership.' Parents report that these are exceptionally empathetic teachers. There is a certain amount of traditional lecturing in the upper grades but the school encourages and looks for 'proficiency in the Socratic method,' teachers who are excited, engaged in inquiry-based, collaborative teaching, and are themselves learners. Frequent professional training in academics and all aspects of dealing with young people.

Very strong EAL assistance, both in specific EAL classes and mainstream classroom help. 15 per cent of students arrive speaking no English, by ninth and tenth grade may still receive assistance but, by high school, must be proficient to handle the workload. Special Ed assistance is good and getting better – new specially trained teachers in lower and upper grades are particularly good at helping kids deal with learning difficulties, and teachers deal with kids' disabilities and different learning styles. Exhaustive efforts to make educational experience work and to find (and keep) teachers who feel that education is a vocation and bigger than the sum of its parts. Students are placed according to proficiency in math and languages, mixed but challenged in other classes. Super language choices; courses in nine languages, classes arranged for other languages not offered or in native tongue. Very good exam results, especially considering there are so many EAL students: 98 per cent IB pass rate with 4 or above (out of possible 7); 37 per cent of SAT Verbal scores were 500-590 (including EAL students), 44 per cent of SAT Math were 600-690. Last year, 112 students took 207 AP exams, 148 made a 3 or above (out of possible 5).

Games, Options, The Arts: One of the strongest sports programmes of all the American schools, no doubt because of endless acres of playing fields (and 6 hole golf course, baseball diamond, tennis courts etc) but especially now because of the major school-wide 'healthy schools initiative.' New, very competent staff has been brought on to expand the PE offerings and see to the drop-dead terrific new sports centre. Few gyms, clubs, or schools in the world have such state-of-the-art aquatic facilities (computerised touch pads, movable pool bottom, water temp that can change at will depending on activities, UV-based cleaning all but eliminating heavy, eye-stinging, chlorinated atmosphere), or individual computer-card operated work-out equipment, plus suspended wood floors in the dance studio and gym, in a stunning light-drenched interior that looks like an ocean liner. All hands do sports in middle school, for skill and fun.

By high school, teams are selective (varsity teams compete in ISST competitions around Europe), but so many options (total of about 24 teams in various sports and ages per season) 'any student in this school who wants to do sports, can.' Even by the intensely academic senior year, elective classes are so appealing that most people, including non-athletes, stay in at least one. As everywhere else in the school, teachers come up with an optimum match that fits students' interests while it gives them something they need. Even in their dreams, staff can only come up with one thing more they might desire- maybe an outdoor skills component (to complement DofE programme) with an indoor climbing wall. Not unexpectedly, there are excellent facilities and classes for visual and performing arts, community service like Habitat for Humanity, international academic competitions, clubs, and a million field trips – cultural, historical, or service throughout London and the UK, Europe, Namibia, you name it.

Background and Atmosphere: Started in 1972 in attractive 1820s manor house built by Prince Leopold (later King of the Belgians) for his mistress. Finding herself too far from the bright lights of London, she promptly upped sticks and left, but ACS families who move here love it (poor Leopold would have appreciated today's 30 minute train trip to Waterloo). Apart from said love nest (now the bright and elegant home of the ACS kindergarten) and the charming pre-k village by the old walled garden, most of the upper school buildings are contemporary purpose-built and highly functional (of dark brick and rather in the stepped style of 1970s Florida golf condos), a bit dark in the halls but the rows of glass in classrooms and dorms help. Additional 'Early Childhood' building housing purpose-built classrooms and office space was completed in 2005. The school has the snappy feel of a first rate large public American high school, without the overwhelming numbers.

Pastoral Care and Discipline: In lower school, family buddies are matched with families of same aged children. Boarders are watched over by a sympathetic team of houseparents, the head of which feels the school nurtures teachers and staff as well as it does students. School rules are clearly stated, with a staged process of discipline depending on severity. A peer group buddy system for students, plus parent, teacher and student training for sensitivity to drugs, sexuality, bullying etc (using self-assessing interactive software, weekly group discussions, speakers) all keep awareness high to catch problems as they arise. School feels it's failed if someone must go; the process even for expulsion is compassionate – concerned with what is best for the child as well as the school.

Pupils and Parents: 51 per cent American, and 10 per cent from the UK plus students from 55 other countries. Standard louche appearance of non-dress-code-restrained teenagers, but alert and amiable with each other, attentive and focused in classes. Kids love the international diversity, say – 'someone closed-minded wouldn't like it.' Capable, involved parents help throughout the school; enormously successful international parents' committee integrates non-English speaking families, initiating and maintaining contact parent to parent in their own languages – quickly creating a high level of confidence and excellent network of communication. Good parent support seminars, welcoming picnics, transition meetings, and close contact throughout with administration. Families move here because of the attractive town and more space for children, yet easy commuting distance from London. Boarders are often children whose diplomatic or corporate parents don't have appropriate schooling in their current posting, or because kids want to finish here once they've started.

Entrance: Roughly 25 per cent turnover of student body from year to year but most of it occurs during summer – average stay is three years, due to vagaries of corporate moves. Selective entrance, looking for children 'willing to take on or grow into the challenge, given the space.' School tries very hard to see how they can address any child's needs, whether in achievement, language, or learning difficulties.

Exit: Colleges attended cut across spectrum of usual suspects, from Harvard to Stanford U, Yale, Princeton, with large handfuls going to good British, European and Asian Universities. If students stay in the country but leave after middle school, it is usually for a completely different and perhaps smaller school experience.

Money Matters: Strong financial stability thanks to the private corporate ACS owners; no endowment, fees fund the school and include tuition, loan of books, classroom materials, curriculum-related field trips. Quoted boarding fees do not include tuition, but do include autumn break holiday trip. Some financial assistance available.

Remarks: Their last New England Association of Schools and Colleges accreditation report commented: 'the visiting team senses the possibility of greatness at Cobham.' Outstanding suburban, bustling, something-for-everyone school, with high school IB and AP courses; the only one of the three ACS schools with boarding students as well as day.

ACS EGHAM INTERNATIONAL SCHOOL

Linked to ACS Egham International School Junior School in the Junior section

Woodlee, London Road, Egham, Surrey, TW20 0HS

Tel: 01784 430 611
Fax: 01784 430 626
E-mail: w.green@acs-england.co.uk
Website: www.acs-england.co.uk

• Pupils: 445 boys and girls, all day • Ages: 2.5 yrs-19yrs • Size of sixth form: 85 in High School • Non-denom • Fees: £2,360 (Pre-K) - £15,550 annual fee (grades 11-12) plus some hefty extras • Independent

Head: Since 1998, Moyra Hadley (fiftyish) – brisk, perceptive and knowledgeable, with a laugh that rumbles up from her toes. She was hired to initiate the IB programme in the newest American Community School. Born in Wales, with degrees from London University, California State U, and Boston U (USA). She has worked as a middle school principal or in system administration about everywhere in the world – USA, Indonesia, Zambia, Egypt, Germany, Sri Lanka. ACS tried to get her for several years before she decided to come back to Britain, and the sturdy seedling of ACS Egham is flourishing under the full and brilliant light of her attention.

Academic Matters: American college prep programme ending in an American High School Diploma but, most unusually, this is one of only 3 schools in the UK authorised for full IB programme from age 3 (scramblers) through primary, middle and high school levels – meaning much more IB Office oversight, biannual teacher training, comparison of work to others around world, and independent projects in fifth, tenth, eleventh and twelfth grades. In the very lively lower school, the six units of study are integrated across the curriculum; in middle school, five 'areas of interaction' (such as environment, or homo faber – man/woman the maker encouraging and understanding original work and its risks) are addressed through the usual academic subjects both in class and hands-on work. Wide use of rubrics throughout school so students, parents, and teachers all understand expectations and students can self-evaluate as they go.

Super IT backbone – more than adequate labs plus all high school students receive ipods (wireless, phoneless) upon entry to the school. Small classes of no more than 16 are mostly mixed in ability and learning style but with high expectations for achievement; more homogenous grouping in language and math (French taught from first through twelfth grade, Spanish from middle school on). EAL classes can be taken as a second language as needed through twelfth grade but, from the academically tough tenth grade on, students must be English fluent. Some special needs can be accommodated. Assessed on an individual basis, a child study team develops specialised strategies for the student that will work in and out of the classroom. SAT combined verbal and math average 1260. In 2004, Egham achieved a 100 per cent passrate on the IB Diploma.

Games, Options, The Arts: All students take music lessons in lower and middle schools, band practice divided between school and after-school time. Most students take private lessons after class, paid for by parents and organised by school. Inclusive sports policy in middle school, then breaks into more competitive varsity and JV, in nine high school sports. Extensive field trips offered related to curriculum at every age (London Museum of Science, CAS trip to Bangalore, India, language trips to France and Spain, Centre of Alternative Technology in Wales, history trip to Pompeii etc). Many after-school clubs at all levels. Particularly good design arts department, dealing with most forms of design from concept to implementation, and ranging from sets or costumes for school productions to furniture or musical instruments.

Background and Atmosphere: The campus is centred on a sprawling brick Victorian-Italianate manor house complete with tower, in lovely manicured grounds. Classrooms in the main house are bright, well proportioned and sunny. The rest of the classrooms, gym, labs and studios are tucked into sturdy, brick cottage-like outbuildings – surprisingly attractive considering they were built as a WWII soldiers' rehab centre – still connected by sloped paths, gardens and rolling lawns under large old trees that also provided excellent camouflage during the war for the secret testing of armoured vehicles (presumably before they moved in the veterans). Plans are underway to build or renovate various buildings and mews into sports centre, auditorium, and arts and design technology centre. Even for such a new school (started in 1994), there are already beloved patterns and traditions (eg a fifth grade archaeological dig, breathlessly anticipated by all in the lower school, fondly remembered by older students and certainly teachers.) There is a sense of real excitement at being in at the beginning of such an unusual, blossoming place.

Pastoral Care and Discipline: The school feels that children must be comfortable in their own skin before they can handle the rigorous curriculum. A good advisory programme deals with stress and time management, personal and health advice – 'at least one adult knows each child well.' Nurses and advisors have regular training; student council very involved in peer leadership and self-governing. Lower school students decide their own playground rules to avoid discipline problems. The international values of respect and responsibility are promoted often and well.

Pupils and Parents: 47 per cent Americans, 13 per cent British, 33 other nationalities. Pupils are absorbed and animated in their classes, polite yet enthusiastic in groups. They come from US schools, also private UK schools. Parents throw themselves into the fray, enjoy the involvement, are appreciated and very much part of implementing and setting policy. Like their children, many have relocated frequently, and are eager to ease the transition for others. School life anchors its families for however long they stay.

Entrance: Non-selective. Rather than looking for student qualities that fit the school, they look for ways the school can serve the student. If special services, classroom aids or other help is required that is not already provided by the excellent Special Ed or EAL teacher, parents need to pay for the extra assistance, and work that out in advance of acceptance. School is growing every year, has a total capacity of 626. The structure of ACS allows them to contract and expand according to need and class size at a given school. Applications and new students accepted year round (about 20 per cent turnover per year).

Exit: They leave for a very respectable range of colleges in the US, Canada, and the UK, including some to Oxford.

Money Matters: ACS Egham privately owned, fee-supported, no endowment but funding seems more than adequate to pay for ever-improving facilities and services. Limited financial aid. Huge door-to-door busing catchment area.

Remarks: Even with the high-octane academic IB programme from age 3 through high school, the rich warm environment of Egham should foster any child's growth and achievement. Class sizes are small and will remain so; as new students apply, new classes will simply be added. It will be fun to be along for the ride as Egham takes off.

ACS HILLINGDON INTERNATIONAL SCHOOL

Linked to ACS Hillingdon International School Junior School in the Junior section

108 Vine Lane, Hillingdon, Middlesex, UB10 0BE

Tel: 01895 259 771
Fax: 01895 818404
E-mail: w.green@acs-england.co.uk
Website: www.acs-england.co.uk

• Pupils: 500 boys and girls • Ages: 4-18 • Size of sixth form: 200 in High School • Non-denom • Fees: £7,250 - £15,000pa • Independent • Open days: October and February

Head of School: Since 2002, Mrs Ginger G Apple,(fifties), observant, gracious, composed and quickly absorbing the Hillingdon culture. She's worked her way through meetings with every single student three at a time and moved with sure but deliberative steps to make her own imprint on a school she thinks is already very good. She's taught or run American international schools from South America to South Africa, from Zambia to Scotland, and has degrees from Miami U (Oxford, Ohio) Trenton State College (NJ) and an EdD currently underway at Oxford Brookes U (UK) (in educational research).

Academic Matters: American college prep programme leading to the American High School Diploma, with Advanced Placement Courses (12) and/or International Baccalaureate (IB) and very good results (usually about half the graduating seniors are IB diploma candidates, with a 95 per cent pass rate – 100 per cent for the class of 2003). 2002/3, 41 students took 88 AP tests; 84 per cent passed with 3 or better. Avg SAT: 608 Math (all students), 553 Verbal (not including EAL students). School says its results 'place them among the top ten independent schools in the UK'. Spanish offered from fourth grade, French from sixth grade through twelfth, EAL available from kindergarten through tenth grade. Adequate and growing IT (portable pod of laptops available to classes as needed, plus three computer labs), with innovative training offered to teachers.

Small classes of no more than 20 in most grades. Some special needs assistance in lower grades (pull-out program approx 2 hours a week); special needs classes plus specific learning strategies for use in regular classrooms available in middle school.

Games, Options, The Arts: Middle and high school students may do intramural sports (PE compulsory through twelfth grade) or compete in three varsity and JV sports per year, girls' and boys' teams, with tournaments in UK and abroad. Student-run drama and musical productions with multiple departments contributing; major concerts for band and choirs, solo and ensemble performances held in the beautiful rococo Red Room. Great field trips in all grades to London, UK and abroad.

Background and Atmosphere: The heart of the school is the beautifully restored, white, C19th neo-classical Hillingdon Court, surrounded by eleven acres of formal garden and woodlands, and ten acres of playing fields nearby. By contrast, the substantial addition in which the lower school and most of the middle school are located looks dishearteningly like a corporate headquarters. But it's functional and well-maintained and the high school classes, library, music, and meetings take place in the marvellous, light-filled, baroque interior of the original house. New music centre plus digital recording studio, rehearsal rooms, practice studios and computer lab for music tech opened 2005. Students are sharp, interested and like their school. In fact, they actively like the activities both during and after school – writing workshop, sports, art. One, after assuring me that he wouldn't mind missing his bus and staying on at school the rest of the day, pointed out that even the less studious like to learn, because there 'are a lot of activities and not just desk work'. Teachers often go above and beyond, scheduling time to help students on Saturdays and over spring breaks.

Pastoral Care and Discipline: Students say 'a person who wants to slink into the shadows and disappear might not choose to come here but, once he came, we'd make it work'. They comment that peer helpers and teachers keep in touch with students and parents and are on the lookout for problems and stress how accepting this fluid, international student body is. International students stay an average of three years, so 'no real time to set up fiefdoms.' Problems are handled quickly; serious offences like drugs could trigger immediate suspension but coupled with counselling. Students are allowed to make mistakes and grow past them but protection of other students is key.

Pupils and Parents: About 46 per cent American, 12 per cent Japanese, 7 per cent British, 35 per cent from 51 other nationalities; heavy preponderance of international corporate families, therefore a 25 per cent turnover within the student body during the year; families move to the area just for this school as well as the English suburban village experience but some 32 buses take students door to door

as far as central London as well as in the catchment area. Strong PTA, particularly Transitional Assistance Network (TAN): over 60 volunteer parents, plus students, of every nationality, help in family transitions.

Entrance: Non-selective, looking for ways to serve most children who apply, who have good character, want to learn and can do the work.

Exit: Graduates go to range of American first and second tier large universities and small liberal arts colleges but even more go to good British, European and Canadian schools, with an additional smattering to Japanese universities, South Africa, and Australia. When younger students leave it's because of family transfers, usually going on to another international school or back to the US.

Money Matters: Fees include loan of textbooks, lab fees, classroom materials and day-long field trips (except theatre tickets); one-off debenture payment; some sports, daily bus, travel, tutoring expenses are extra, depending on needs and activities of the student. Also IB Mother Tongue languages with fewer than three students are paid for by the parent. Hillingdon is supported by its fees but owned by a private company, so no endowment as such. Some financial aid available.

Remarks: Large enough for lots of extra-curricular options but small enough for easy interaction amongst teachers and students; solid suburban American international school offering strong academics through AP classes and/or high school IB, for families who want to be out of the city but with an acceptable commute and a good school enabling ease of transition anywhere.

AIGLON COLLEGE

1885, Chesières-Villars, Switzerland

Tel: +41244 966 161
Fax: +41244 966 162
E-mail: info@aiglon.ch
Website: www.aiglon.ch

- Pupils: 350 boys and girls, almost all board • Ages: 13-18
- Size of sixth form: 130 • Ecumenical • Fees: SFr 45,800 - SFr 64,600 annually for boarding • Independent

Head: Since 2000, Rev Dr Jonathan Long DPhil MTh (University of South Africa) BA (Natal) MA (plus one or two others that he doesn't use) (forties), he came to Aiglon as chaplain in 1998. Educated at Monkton Combe, Bath, he first taught in South Africa and was previously chaplain and housemaster at The Dragon School, Oxford. While in Oxford, apart from adding to his degree portfolio and breaking athletic records, he was instrumental in helping independent schools develop sound approaches to PSE/PSHE and pastoral care. He is married to Sue, DipEd (primary education), BPhilEd (Hons) (Warwick) who teaches special needs. The Longs have two daughters. A manic triathlete, snowboarder and enthusiast, Dr Long was dead worried before he took up his post at Aiglon, having 'spent the last years looking after little ones, I've forgotten how to deal with the older version'. Obviously not a problem now, this is a supremely happy and self-confident headmaster.

The GSG has long been a fan of the gifted and inspirational Dr Long (or Revlong as he used to be). Dr Long took over as head of Aiglon following a period of some turmoil – the previous headmaster left in the context of an acrimonious divorce. At the same time, media interest in the school was especially high after it was announced that the Duke of York's children were coming to Aiglon. A suspected intruder in a girls' boarding house led to heightened media attention and a great deal of anxiety. 6 years later – no royalty but a very expensive new security system.

Already familiar with the running of the school, Dr Long has busied himself over the last five years with restoring confidence. A sensitive and sensible head, he regularly spends time with various student groups thrashing out the problems of the moment. Still a pastor at heart – albeit a slightly unconventional one – Dr Long and his two deputy heads (pastoral and academic) run an 'open-door policy' and are always on hand for advice. 'No problem at all about getting staff' – a recent ad for houseparents elicited almost 200 replies and a shortlist and their spouses were flown out to Aiglon so that both parties 'could take a look'. The days of photographs of Swiss mountains and interviews at the East India Club are long past.

Academic Matters: Follows a British curriculum, adopting the pick 'n' mix attitude to GCSE, IGCSE, AS and A2 levels. Setted according to ability in English, French and maths. A-level and GCSE results have risen steadily over the past 5 years (99 per cent pass at A-level and 87 per cent A*-C at GCSE in 2005). Most students have English as a second language and the tiny classes means creditable results at A level and a good university track record. The school is an accredited SATS centre (US qualification) and we were particularly impressed by the school's American university entrance programme. All students must study English and some maths in sixth form, though SATS qualify. A good, but not enormous, range of A level subjects on offer – the sciences, maths, humanities, languages – French,

Spanish and German – plus philosophy, psycology, media, business studies economics etc. Cyberspace link-up lessons where tutors in the UK can, via a pan-tilt-zoom camera, have instant access to pupils' work in Switzerland. Critical thinking popular.

Small classes, max 16, fabulous new teaching block and very recent modern languages centre with state-of-the-art computers and networked throughout (internet screened), history seminar room more like a boardroom than a classroom – cushy chairs, posh tables etc. 'But', says Dr Long, 'this is not a school for the straight academic who requires a lot of time to achieve results'. EFL and dyslexia help available, computers on hand to pull up pupil's assignments in special learning needs dept for extra assistance. Mark Readings two or three times a term are noted and go towards the final Transcript, which counts for university entrance in the States.

Games, Options, The Arts: Snazzy new art department with imaginative work and dramatic sculpture at entrance – bets were taken locally how long the thing would stay up – six years now and no sign of a wobble. Drama and music technology up to A2. Music department (along with computers and the like) in JCB building, four grand pianos, plus own recording studio. School puts out a local English radio station.

More team games than before (including rugby)but not a cricket school. Brand new Astroturf football facility on campus. Football popular, plus the minor sports; tennis strong, five courts, which adapt to basketball, scattered throughout the campus – well, it is on a mountainside. Skiing strong, but don't expect to spend all winter on planks, minimum four hours a week isn't bad though. Swimming in the local pool further up the village. PE compulsory, plus Exes (expeditions) which range from guided tours of the European capitals, to four-day ski-touring sleeping in huts, climbing Mont Blanc, community service and the like. Aiglon is part of the Round Square Association.

Background and Atmosphere: First founded in 1947 by John Corlette, who had previously taught at Gordonstoun, the school hiccuped along until 6th January 1949 when it opened with six pupils (including a Siamese princess), a headmaster, four teachers and two staff. Most of the pupils came to Villars for health reasons (think TB). The early years were beset with financial disasters, usually to do with currency fluctuations, but the school survived, went co-ed in 1969, and is the only British international school in Switzerland.

The school buildings – boarding houses/classroom blocks or a mixture of both – we are on a slope here so plenty of opportunity for multi-use, each with its own front door – are scattered around the bottom of Chesières (with one family still resolutely remaining in the middle of the campus). The boarding houses are single sex, with the opposite sex being allowed into the ground floor only. Major re-vamp nearly completed including brand new senior boys' boarding house. Dorms, usually in threes, but occasional singles, ski boots everywhere when we visited. Think a rash of slightly oversize chalets with lots of pine inside and out, juxtaposed with some fabulous modern architecture. No 'grounds' to speak of and no fenced-off areas.

Serious amount of fundraising for 55th anniversary and recently bought the local post office, no apparent current intention to sell stamps though, more likely that the '2,000 square meters of building land' will become part of an as-yet undesigned 'multi-purpose sports facility'. Serious house upgrading under way, school has leased le Cerf hotel as a sixth form girls' house. Ah the misery of life on a mountain.

Food much improved since out-sourced catering introduced; salad bars, and 'students are also served more of their preferred dishes and the different tastes and preferences between the boys' and girls' houses are taken into account'. Surprisingly strict dress code, no visible tattoos or piercing, no tongue studs, boys may not wear earrings but girls can have several. Fifteen minutes' meditation (much appreciated by pupils) scheduled daily before lessons.

Pastoral Care and Discipline: Houseparents, personal tutors, head and his two deputies all on hand to help. Enormous amount of support – with 57 different nationalities sometimes little problems can escalate out of all proportion. Fifty-seven nationalities also means grey areas in what is perceived as 'normal' behaviour in a British school. No smoking allowed on campus, or in any public place, but difficult to enforce a total ban when parents offer their children ciggies at home though help with quitting smoking available. Wine and beer from 17 OK with meals in the village. Regular random drugs testing – at least ten a week, from the third form upwards. Public displays of affection (PDA) discouraged, but the Italians are a warm and affectionate race, so forget the six-inch rule. 'Holding hands, or a friendly goodnight kiss after a school event are acceptable; heavy clinches, sitting on partner's lap, petting, couples being alone together in a closed room' are not. Strongly enforced PSE/PSHE programme. Series of punishments – laps, gating, suspension, expulsion.

Pupils and Parents: Truly international, half term only in the autumn term, long weekends in winter and summer, local students allowed out the odd weekend. Fifty-seven different nationalities, split in dorms as far as possible by language, max six from any one country. Mixture of princes, industrialists and the global A stream.

Entrance: Own series of admissions tests, interview with head and refs from present school for all. Satisfactory GCSE or equivalent for sixth form entrants.

Exit: Post-GCSE for sixth form elsewhere – A levels or IB. Otherwise to universities all over. Modest recent Oxbridge successes and tranches to Bristol, King's and University Colleges, London, LSE, Edinburgh, Durham (and quite a lot to the British 'new' universities – Oxford Brookes, Napier etc) as well as an impressive collection to America, Ivy League as well as Boston, Tufts, John Hopkins, NYU and Georgetown.

Remarks: Strong educationally, strong emotionally, tough physically. Aiglon, for all the glamour and the hype, is not an easy option. Neither for the shy and retiring nor the unstreetwise. Exciting, challenging, purposeful.

ALBYN SCHOOL

Linked to Albyn Lower School in the Junior section

17-23 Queen's Road, Aberdeen, AB15 4PB

Tel: 01224 322 408
Fax: 01224 209 173
E-mail: information@albynschool.co.uk
Website: www.albynschool.co.uk

• Pupils: 420 boys and girls in the whole school (but that includes toddlers doing a half day in the nursery); Junior school: 130 girls with (eventually) 150 boys; senior school: 200 girls • Ages: 3 months to 18 • Size of sixth form: 70 • Ecumenical • Fees: £2,633. NB termly fees vary with the length of the term
• Independent

Head: Since 2002, Dr John D Halliday BA PhD (fiftyish) who was educated at Abingdon School, did his BA in German and linguistics at Exeter and his PhD in Cambridge where his thesis was on Austrian literature. He just loves teaching and enjoys 'the developing relationship with children'. Married, with three children. Dishy, with a delicious sense of humour. His career path is a varied one, he started by teaching English In Passau uni, became a freelance translator for a couple of years before going to Merchiston as head of German, followed by head of langs and housemaster at Sedbergh thence to Rannoch, where he was head, which must have been a pretty dispiriting experience ('it was tough latterly but the school was inspirational'). Post Rannoch he taught langs at Dollar for a year.

Albyn had had a 'pretty rocky ride over the past five years', and was 'slightly wobbly' when Dr Halliday arrived but with 'an incredibly good core of loyal kids and parents' he has succeeded in turning the place around and attracting new blood. Ten year plan = boys. They start in the junior department (only) from August 2005 and two brave eight-year-olds were spending a day in the place when we visited. Clutching their tennis rackets they seemed undaunted by the monstrous regiment. Twenty-five boys have confirmed places, and 2005 saw 18 new girls arrive in P1 and P2. So numbers are up. New heads of geography, history, chemistry and PE appointed and school pretty much back on track, 'good common room, good supportive atmosphere'.

Academic Matters: No particular specialisms, broad range of subjects and results 'achieved with girls of varying ability', one or two fall below C. School follows Scottish system, with Intermediate II offered in art & design, sciences, business management, English and maths. Classical studies and Latin, not much take up of the latter above Standard Grade, accountancy and finance make a welcome addition to the usual suspects. Information systems to intermediate 2 only; business management (very popular and pleasing results) plus modern studies all offered up to Advanced Higher (school adds that all subjects can be taken at Advanced Higher). Higher biology produced an outstanding 11 candidates out of 16 examinees getting As, chemistry and physics both threw up six A candidates (out of nine and eleven candidates respectively). 100 per cent A-C in maths (with eight at A out of 19 takers); quite a number of takers and fair showing in English, more take up in German than French but better marks in the latter. Good music and creditable performance in art and design. Certain amount of almost individual teaching with only one pupil taking the subject; whilst one expects this with Latin (actually three) and Gaelic (learners), it is surprising to find only one candidate taking higher accountancy, and penny numbers doing business management, classical studies and history, but the results are impressive (if hardly cost effective). French and German throughout but Spanish only in the sixth form.

Max class size 23, with low teens for practical subjects (school sez 20, but in practice this is much smaller; most classes are 10/15). Comprehensive computer system, class taught as well as in suites, laptops abound, pupils can bring in their own. All pupils have their own email and can email homework and queries to staff. Impressive online support system in most subjects. European computer driving licence for all, key boarding taught early in the school; no interactive white boards (yet). Surprisingly only one learning support teacher, based in the primary department who covers the whole school, Dr Halliday talked of employing another SEN specialist who will probably be equally overworked as school caters for dyslexia, dyspraxia, mild Aspergers as well as having one pupil who is profoundly deaf (she came to the school with special microphone and class assistant funded by the LEA, who 'actually refused to give the girl any support at all once she came to us'). No EFL help available as such, but 'lots of support in the classroom', SEN teacher takes individual groups and double teaches a bit – she is very 'willing'. She would need to be. Scribing, readers and all the rest – extra time available for exams – this is no longer a blanket 20 per cent per pupil per exam, but different pupils may need different concessions in different subject. Case must be made for each. No extra charge for SEN help.

Games, Options, The Arts: Main games field at Milltimber five miles away, pupils are bused (and new games changers in pipeline to cope with the boys). Positive netball and hockey with regional representation, and masses of individual sports: national representation in athletics, swimming, rowing, riding, sailing and ten pin bowling. Stunning art dept, with a number of pupils going on to higher things in the art world. Very jolly with papier maché), acrylic and silk screen work. Hot on costume design and much use made of local museums. Strong art and architectural stream. Fantastic music, 'most girls play a musical instrument' and loads of participation in either choir or instrumental ensembles. Good representation in the National Youth Orchestra plus jazz, ceilidh bands and flute ensembles. Keen drama and dance (Dancercise important), the former still extra curricular. Couldn't do better. Enthusiastic YE, sweeties were the latest offering and highly competitive D of E with oodles of golds. Strong club culture, quizzes, chess, photography, gardening and Scottish country dancing. Keen on public speaking and debating.

Background and Atmosphere: School was founded in 1867 by Harriet Warrack who started teaching girls at home, advertising locally for pupils. Albyn Place (just down the road) became the school's home in 1881, hence the name, and Albyn School for Girls moved to Queen's Road in 1925 – all of which is pretty confusing as St Margaret's School for Girls is still based in Albyn Place. The son of one of the gardeners at Duff House, Alexander Mackie was an early moving light, writing books on English (he was university examiner) and made the school an Aberdeen institution, with emancipated Albyn girls on Aberdeen uni student council by 1907. The current school is based in four attached Victorian merchants' houses, with fantastic ceilings, two well-used libraries and the predictable garden expansion. An enchanting new-build houses the tinies (cots, high chairs and nappies). Dr H seems pretty non-plussed by this addition ('I never thought I would become a Pampers expert when I was at Cambridge') but it pulls in the punters. Tinies (as opposed to babies) are housed in the old stables, and there is a splendid new-build housing a dramatic science wing; equally impressive music dept above hall and gym in the west end of the school. New dedicated purpose-built primary on the stocks (to be opened in 2007); loos etc as well as classrooms will deplete the play area further. But it is not that cramped and there are dedicated enclosed nursery and pre-school play areas. School hopes to increase numbers to 650. The school has a strong family feel, which Dr Halliday is keen to keep, but logistically it is a complicated complex of corridors between the houses. Fire doors everywhere. Rather expensive looking prospectus tied up in a tartan ribbon which will have to have a new cover as it still boasts Albyn School for Girls.

Pastoral Care and Discipline: School divided into four clans, pupils can relate to heads of years and guidance staff when in difficulty. Sense of community – school aims to boost the confidence of the shyest child. Head has a policy of zero tolerance for drink 'n' drugs 'n' rock 'n' roll. So expect to be out for persistent bullying or drugs. Dr H has expelled elsewhere and would have no hesitation. Fags and booze on school premises = detention followed by exclusion followed by out. 'Bullying is usually changing friendship groups' seems about right, but actual bullying is regarded as a no-no.

Pupils and Parents: Mixture of professionals, lot of oil and gas, but farmers and marine engineers in the parent body. All hugely supportive and 'tightly knit' – as are the governors. Fair number of first time buyers, parents can drop off early and pick up late for pupils in the lower school but there is an extra charge. International bias, but lots of home grown ones too; nice strong middle class ethos with girlies neat in check dresses and a good line in frilly white socks which seems to be the craze of the moment. Check head bands too. Kilts mandatory for high days and holidays – even in the summer term – and they have to be proper kilts and not the kilted skirt variety – any tartan.

Entrance: Assessment for tinies up to senior school when formal exam (not many turned away, automatic advancement throughout the school, pupils can and do join at any time – throughout the year assuming space available; a very few years are full). Not many come post Standard Grades.

Exit: About five leave post Highers, the rest stay; most (95 per cent or so) will end by going to uni, often after a gap year, and almost all to Scottish unis. Aberdeen popular –

their business admin is particularly good, though surprisingly not that many opt for it. One recent candidate to Cambridge and the odd maverick to Sheffield, Belfast or film studies in Southern California and marine science at Miami.

Money Matters: Incredibly strict scale of rules for payment but (Aberdeen, remember) parents can get a 2 per cent discount if they pay the whole annual whack within a fortnight of the beginning of the autumn term. Discounts of 5 per cent for second child from pre-school nursery up, and fifty per cent rebate for third and subsequent children. School 'will do what it can to help parents in difficult times, as long as they are open and talk to us'.

Remarks: With numbers of potential pupils dropping along with the national birth rate this was a school in decline but new initiatives and a stab at lads have reversed this. Worth thinking about if you have tender flowers of either sex whom you would like to have educated together.

ALDENHAM SCHOOL

Linked to Aldenham Preparatory School in the Junior section

Elstree, Borehamwood, Hertfordshire, WD6 3AJ

Tel: 01923 858 122
Fax: 01923 854 410
E-mail: enquiries@aldenham.com
Website: www.aldenham.com

• Pupils: 451 boys, 33 girls (years 7 & 8 and sixth form only); 137 'proper' boarders (45 from overseas) + 30 flexi-boarders, rest either day or weekly boarders • Ages: 11-18 • Size of sixth form: 134 • C of E foundation with ecumenical overtones • Fees: Day: pre-prep £2,560; prep £2,831; junior £3,266; senior £4,741. Day boarders: junior £4,098; senior £5,662. Boarding: junior £4,892; senior £6,888 • Independent • Open days: June & October

Head: Since 2000, Mr Richard Harman MA PGCE (forties), educated at The King's School, Worcester, and read English at Cambridge. Tried his hand at the marketing side of publishing for a couple of years, then five years at Marlborough (with a sabbatical to do a PGCE) teaching English and drama, and twelve at Eastbourne College where he progressed from head of English via housemaster of girls' boarding to becoming part of the senior management team. Whilst at Marlborough, he met and married his wife, who currently teaches at South Hampstead High School. One daughter at Uppingham.

Urbane, charming, film star looks. Lots of staff changes – giving the place a shake-up – but off to head Uppingham in July 2006. New head is to be Mr James Fowler, currently deputy head of Highgate School.

Academic Matters: Not a fiercely academic place. Classes are small, 20 and lower, with four parallel forms, streamed across the board, and setted for English, maths, languages and science – three subjects taught separately but, below the top set, taken as dual award at GSCE. Six per class post-GCSE. Lots of modular exams. Classics back in the mainstream, plus a myriad of languages (native speakers). Best ever A level results 2004; excellent results in biology, business studies, chemistry, maths and further maths, as well as Japanese.

Excellent dyslexia provision with a head of learning support plus a dedicated peripatetic team – dyspraxia, 'mild Aspergers' and ADHD not a problem. One to one or just general support, computers important here – ie support staff can call up work in progress and give positive assistance. Indeed computers important all over, with network manager sitting in a little office below the art room (and next to the two computer suites) – all boarding houses have access to the school's network.

Games, Options, The Arts: A seriously sporty school. Intensely competitive, inter-house as well as inter-school matches in everything. Enormous sports hall with weights room attached, Aldenham Park with sailing lake, no swimming pool (it's on the ten year wish list), cricket popular, masses of footie fields, tennis courts all over. Fives court hosts trillions of matches, shooting range, hockey popular for both sexes, fencing, badminton, cross country, judo (and a dedicated judo hall which is also used for aerobics and dance). Climbing walls everywhere, both vertical and horizontal, look terrifying.

D of E, huge selection of clubs and rather grand expeditions all over the world. Excellent art results with some ambitious pieces of art on display within the art studios and around the school. Terrific pair of gates in a combination of MDF and pâpier maché depicting the whole sixth form – looked like the gates to hell. Impressive CDT complex adjacent to art rooms and computer suites, humming with activity, graphics room at the back, plus CAD-CAM. Our guide was justly proud of his fish tank coffee table, hell for hoovering, but an interesting conception, as were many others on show.

Imaginative conversion of the old chapel into music centre, with sympathetic recital hall and recording studio adjacent. Loads of practice rooms below – fairly pedestrian conversion here – very slabby, but computer linked to key-boards and networked round the school. Drama very popular in the somewhat utilitarian hall (new hall also on wish list). Good selection of plays and musicals in the past.

Background and Atmosphere: Stunning. Founded in 1597 by Richard Platt and endowed with 'three Pastures of Ground lying nighe the Churche of St Pancrasse in the County of Mid'x besides London.' Cometh the railway, cometh ornate Victorian gothic. Magnificent parquet floored dining hall, with benches and tables like an Oxbridge college. Impressive Robert Adam-style library, which is connected to a rather dreary careers library opened by Lord Denning. Guides hadn't a clue about the buildings, nor did they appear to have any interest or pride in the school's history or traditions, but knew all about the food (much improved recently). Chapel across the (quite busy) road; magical Burne Jones windows, and fairly hefty war memorial feel. School fell on hard times during the recession of the 1990s and caused waves when they saved their bacon by selling Stanley Spencer's altarpiece of the Crucifixion for around two million.

Games fields surrounded by gigantic red brick houses, three for boarders (the largest co-ed) and three for day. Single rooms post GCSE. Quantity of rather uninspired sixties/seventies buildings around – school went all out to celebrate its quartercentenary. New state-of-the-art classroom block housing English, media studies and modern languages opened in February 2005. Despite being an Anglican foundation, school pays more than just lip service to other faiths, and Muslims, Hindus and Jews all get time off for their own holy days (though they may have to do Saturday morning school).

Pastoral Care and Discipline: Very much based on the house system, loads of back-up. Those from abroad are taken on visits during exeats, to the Dusseldorf Fair, shopping in Calais etc. Tough on drugs, smoking and the like but head has only expelled one pupil, basically for going OTT. Good anti-bullying and PSE programme; 'the school is so small that we can smell trouble before it happens'.

Pupils and Parents: An interesting combination of boarding and day, with many of the day pupils coming from north London's very ethnically mixed community. Fair number from the Middle East and Asia, pupils happily chatting in Japanese in the art room. High proportion of first time buyers, often with two working parents who like to have their children home at weekends. Flexi-boarding popular. The pupils cover the entire spectrum, from those with a high IQ to those who need extra help across the board, but all are here because they flourish better in a small school environment away from the conveyor belt mentality. Pupils all wear uniforms, with sixth form of both sexes graduating to suits; praes (prefects) get to wear satiny grey ties. Manners immaculate.

Entrance: Tests in January for entry at 11, 13 and 16, plus interview and previous school's report. Waiting lists at 11 and 13. Pupils come either from local preps or primaries and the head is anxious not to be seen to poach, hence the double entry date.

Exit: Some leave after GCSEs, and places fill up with new blood, though a tiny trickle of pupils leave after AS levels. School takes enormous care in getting leavers into the right form of tertiary education, which the pupils will enjoy and last the course. Masses of new universities in the leavers' list, occasionally one to Oxbridge; some gap year. Business and IT type courses popular.

Money Matters: After the blip in the 1990s, the Brewers' Company gave the school its 120 acres, which is nice to have in your pocket when you go to the bank manager. Huge array of scholarships at 13 and 16, as well as bursarial help in financial need, plus Brewers' support as well.

Remarks: On the up. Good new head, fab surroundings; perfect for those needing an unpressurised school.

ALEXANDRA PARK SCHOOL

Bidwell Gardens, London, N11 2AZ

Tel: 02088 264 880
Fax: 02088 882 236
E-mail: admin@alexandrapark.haringey.sch.uk

• Pupils: 1,100 boys and girls, all day • Ages: 11-18 • Size of sixth form: 200 • Non-denom • State

Head: Since the school's opening in 1999, Ms Rosslyn Hudson, MA PGCE (fifties). Studied English at Edinburgh University, worked for VSO in Indonesia and the Bahamas, then started her teaching career at Latymer School in Edmonton. Was appointed head of English at Edmonton County School, then spent 10 years as deputy head at William Ellis School. Married with two children. Excellent leader and driving force behind the school's success. Was responsible more-or-less single handed for getting the school off the ground. 'It wouldn't have opened in 1999 if I hadn't been bloody-minded and determined.' Has put together a very strong senior management team and appointed many energetic young teachers (who tend to get short-listed for teaching awards). About half of the original staff is still at the school.

Academic Matters: Very mixed intake, with a large percentage coming in with lower than average attainment. However most do better than predicted: 'High expectations start at the top and permeate the whole school,' said Ofsted.

In the first GCSE results, with 51 per cent of students getting 5+ good grades, the traditional subjects of RE, English, history, geography, maths, science and modern languages showed up particularly well. More practical subjects with large amounts of course-work were less successful. 'We didn't have sufficiently robust systems in place, and we weren't strict enough. But that side has been addressed.' The school confidently predicts sharply improving results in future years. 'Our small really able cohort did brilliantly, with clutches of A*s and As.' Single sciences and classical civilisation are available as twilight classes. Everyone studies French or Spanish in year 7 and can take up the other language too in year 8.

The school has maths and science specialist status, and is using its position in the shadow of Alexandra Palace to follow a telecommunications theme, including topics on the health risks of mobile phones and the history of television. Staff are training in cognitive acceleration in science and maths. Some of the extra funds brought by specialist status are being used to split less able students into small science and maths groups.

Pupils with a practical bent can spend a day a week at the College of North East London studying construction crafts, hairdressing, beauty therapy or health & care. 'Our KS4 curriculum is phenomenally flexible. Whatever they want to study, we do our best to accommodate them.' The first sixth form cohort will take A levels in summer 2006; popular AS subjects include psychology, philosophy and critical thinking. Excellent SEN support, mostly in class. Three full-time SEN teachers, who all teach whole classes and are also form tutors. 'They are not shut away in little rooms doing one-on-one all the time. I have a vision for SEN. If you have sensible numbers of children you can do powerful work.' There are also some 20 teaching assistants, many highly-qualified. The school has been a honey-pot for parents of children with SEN statements. 'We have children here with very complex needs,' says SENCO Pauline Smith. 'Staff here are so receptive and willing to try different things to meet these needs. Everyone accepts that these children are part of the whole school community.'

Games, Options, The Arts: Large gym and spacious sports hall with a climbing wall, plus a tarmac sports area used for sports including netball, basketball and football, and a fitness suite. Plenty of inter-school matches, and sports and cultural clubs. High-quality art teaching; facilities include a dark room, kiln room and print room. Good drama; whole school musical every year. Music groups include a jazz orchestra, brass ensemble, cello quartet, boys' and girls' choirs and a rock group. Language trips to Spain and France, ski trips, football and netball trips to Europe, Duke of Edinburgh award scheme.

Background and Atmosphere: Opened in 1999 on a five-acre site between Muswell Hill Golf Course and Durnsford Park, which had been through several incarnations including Cecil Rhodes Secondary Modern and a sixth form centre for Fortismere School. Pleasant brick buildings with a rural outlook, including new science labs, performing arts rooms and sixth form centre. Friendly and welcoming but highly structured.

Pastoral Care and Discipline: The school includes its fair share of children with challenging behaviour, which is kept firmly in check. It has a structured behaviour management programme which includes rewards as well as sanctions, and does not tolerate unacceptable behaviour. The head is quite prepared to exclude those who try the patience of the school too far. 'We work very hard on behaviour management. I've got to protect the learning and safeguard the students that want to be here. I have to be ferocious about that.' Each form has the same tutor throughout the school, and staff get to know their pupils well. Teachers talk about feeling well supported: 'There's a real bond between staff to make the school a better place.'

Pupils and Parents: When the school first opened, middle-class parents were wary and its first intake included large numbers of children with special needs from a wide area. It has since become extremely popular and massively oversubscribed, with a genuinely comprehensive intake including children from the leafy west part of the borough and those from the grittier east. Mostly friendly, polite pupils who are enthusiastic and proud of their school, with a committed parent body.

Entrance: Those with statements get first preference, then siblings. The catchment area is in practice about three quarters of a mile, with most pupils coming from Rhodes, Bounds Green and Nightingale primary schools.

Exit: About two thirds have, so far, gone through to the sixth form, which is open-access, though some are encouraged to make a fresh start elsewhere. A few have moved on to FE colleges.

Money Matters: The maths and science specialist status has brought extra funds and school now employs a bursar, who is responsible for ferreting out other sources of finance and has an expert knowledge of what funds are available.

Remarks: Increasingly popular and oversubscribed comprehensive that caters well for pupils of all abilities, with dynamic and focussed head, and staff who are keen to find areas where all children can excel.

ALLEYN'S SCHOOL

Linked to Alleyn's Junior School in the Junior section

Townley Road, Dulwich, London, SE22 8SU

Tel: 02085 571 500
Fax: 02085 571 462
E-mail: registrar@alleyns.org.uk
Website: www.alleyns.org.uk

• Pupils: 570 boys, 588 girls; all day • Ages: 4 - 18 • Size of sixth form: 274 • C of E • Fees: senior £3,560 • Independent • Open days: Autumn

Head: Since 2002, Dr Colin Diggory BSc MA EdD CMath FIMA FRSA (fiftyish). Married to Sue, with three adult children. Previously teacher of maths at Manchester Grammar, St Paul's and head of maths at Merchant Taylors, Northwood, his first headship was at Latymer Upper where he stayed for 11 years. A physically impressive man, Dr Diggory moves and speaks with the alacrity and enthusiasm of a nimble and eager sixth former. Volubly articulate on all matters educational, both local and national, Dr Diggory knows his stuff and has done the homework. His doctoral thesis on leadership in independent schools is now complete, he has masses of experience and knowledge of management strategies, a special interest in the performing arts in schools, is a former A level examiner, a current HM school inspector and active on HMC committees.

If that gives the impression of a head forever away at conferences, the reverse is true. Parents speak of how he appears with his wife to cheer on school teams at weekends and, now in his fourth year at Alleyn's, he clearly knows what's what and has big development plans. Dr Diggory is a modest man but one who is generous with praise of others – staff, pupils and a very supportive board of governors. He is keen both to develop staff opportunities and improve delegation – 'leadership density' – yuk! He exudes a nervous energy and is clearly thrilled to take over this thriving school from his friend and predecessor, the much-loved Colin Niven. 'I've inherited a wonderful school and my priority is to protect and promote it.'

Academic Matters: 'We don't aspire to be a league-table killer,' says head but the results here need not hang their heads. 2005 GCSE students achieved 81 per cent per cent A*/A grades and 12 students got all A*s. At A level, 88 per cent got A/Bs, the average points per student being 339 which is better than AAB. Everyone takes the three separate sciences for the first five years and then can take them as individual GCSEs or as a dual award. Modern languages now being further developed to allow for enthusiasts to take three at GCSE if they so choose, as well as Latin. Greek still holding its own. This level of opportunity is rare.

Head has introduced politics and psychology (two of his own children did psychology degrees), which, together with business studies, photography, theatre studies and RS, get respectable numbers of takers at A level as well as the more trad subjects. English attracts large numbers and does well. History and geography also among the stars. Good IT suite and school recently upgraded resources here and the use of IT throughout curriculum – though not as a religion. SENs are quickly spotted and well-supported. 'We have a brilliant SENCO'. Those who need it get an individual education plan (IEP). 'Ideally everyone should have one,' says head -' that's the way education should go'. Buzz words here are 'choice' and opportunity' and parents speak appreciatively of the opportunities available in all areas of the curriculum. 'There's more to life than academics,' says head. But the academics are doing fine.

Games, Options, The Arts: Opportunities for everything. Games are big here but less sporty types are encouraged to do less competitive and intimidating things like fives, swimming, fitness, fencing, t'ai chi, trampolining. Very strong representation at county level in many sports though recent quirkiness in results – superb cricket and hockey and football now reviving after a noticeable glitch. Good pool – 'if they can't swim when they arrive here we make sure they can by the end of their first year', super huge sports hall, vast range of sports available and teams travel far for fixtures. School buildings spread around good fields; more fields plus an athletics track across the road. This is good provision in a grand suburb with a fair bit of local competition for large open spaces!

Opportunities in other areas – an excellent carousel programme for the first senior school years so that everyone has a shot at food tech – they design, cook and eat their own meals and love it, and CDT in metalwork, woodwork and ceramics etc. All taught in small groups. Results are weird, wonderful, clever and exciting. The art -taught in 5 studios – is astonishingly good – among the most impressively assured and proficient painting we have seen. Music thrives in converted brewery, loads of ensembles of all sizes and types. Recording studio, CDs, tours, concerts large and small, both on site and in grander venues like St John's Smith Square and the Queen Elizabeth Hall. An biennial concert with the 2 other foundation schools. Drama does remarkably well in the large and imposing, splendidly-beamed, school hall, a dingy old gym and various smaller spaces. An ambitious programme of development – planned for 2006 – is underway to provide a 300-seat theatre, sixth form centre and conference centre – will considerably enhance the school's facilities in all respects and do much to dispel any sense of being the poor relation in the trio of schools. The National Youth Theatre started here and school keen to exploit the link. 40+ clubs and activities, thriving D of E and CCF – the largest voluntary corps in the country, we're told. Community service is busy locally. Loads of trips to everywhere – educational and adventurous, and a good range of language exchanges. Posters advertising interesting speakers from outside make you want to book a seat.

Background and Atmosphere: In 1619 Edward Alleyn, actor and theatre manager who made most of his money from bear-baiting and who, at the age of 57, married the 19-year-old daughter of John Donne, founded his 'College of God's Gift' in Dulwich. This became Dulwich College (cf) but it had always had a lower school. In 1882, this lower school became a separate educational establishment – the present Alleyn's – continuing to share the College board of governors until recent times. The third school in the Dulwich estate is JAGS (cf) – the James Allen's Girls' School – which dates from the mid-19th century. Don't ask about the missing 'y'. The schools are a unique triumvirate, dominating independent education in this, mostly prosperous, part of South-East London and providing a rich – sometimes difficult – choice for local parents. Alleyn's is the co-ed one, the first independent school in London to go fully co-ed, and that is its particular distinction and selling point.

The main building, with its broad, unpretentious, 4-storey redbrick façade, on quiet Townley Road, faces chic Dulwich village to the south and the more modest terraced streets of East Dulwich to the north. Behind is the main site – around the fields – and the buildings are less impressive, plain and functional. The Derek Fenner library (named after pioneering past head) is terrific, well-run, well-stocked and here, almost uniquely, silent study seemed to mean just that. Sciences taught in a separate block and most subjects have their own teaching areas.

The atmosphere is relaxed, with the feeling of any well-run, mixed comprehensive except that it's, for the most part, in good nick, feels very orderly and well-resourced. Pupils are polite, friendly, articulate. Relations with staff seem open and cooperative. You get the feeling everyone is pleased to be here. Plain and sensible uniform. Good food – vegetarian option and salad bar – served efficiently in huge canteen with separate staff area. Sixth form have their own large common room with snacks available all day and their own servery at lunchtime so they can maintain their separate space. Feels like a university student bar. Hot breakfast available for everyone.

Parents speak warmly of the speed with which most pastoral problems are sorted out, especially in the lower school, of the good communications, excellent SEN support and happy children. The 'fantastic' music and brilliant sports are cited and the caring nature of the staff in general. Some feel that girls go there because of the boys, some feel that girls become cliquey in ways that don't happen in single sex schools but, for the most part, it's happy families all round.

Pastoral Care and Discipline: Junior school starts at 4 and school hopes for a nursery before too long. Lower school is for the 11-13-year-olds, middle school for the 13-16-year-olds and upper school is the sixth form. Lower school is comfortably separate from main school so that the youngsters have a haven but they are in the main building for about half their classes. Everyone has a tutor and, on entering middle school also joins a house. In year 9, heads of houses take over as tutors and establish close relationships with tutees. There are also academic tutors from year 10. Full-time school chaplain. School encourages pupils to be self-reliant and sort out their own problems but support is there if needed. Lower school staff highly praised for 'having it sussed'. Drugs policy clear but seldom needed – supply would mean 'out' and random testing used on rare occasions if felt necessary. Bullying is 'nipped in the bud' very quickly, we're told and most concur – though a few parental eyebrows raised at occasional less-well-handled instances. Head feels relaxed and orderly atmosphere is fed by the space and fields around the school site – less pressure from a harsh external world mean less within. A sense that, as head says, 'the community values everyone'.

Pupils and Parents: Strictly co-ed and any imbalance due to 11-year-old girls outperforming boys at 11+ is levelled when more boys than girls arrive at 13. Pupils come from a wide range of socio-economic and ethnic backgrounds, inner and outer London boroughs, nearish bits of Kent. Common denominators are brains and attitude and a relish of the all-round nature of what's on offer here. At 11, around 1/3 of new intake come from state primaries and much-admired head of lower school now spends a day a fortnight visiting these schools, telling them about the 30 scholarships and bursaries on offer (current total of 171 scholars and 71 on bursaries) to encourage more applicants. Notable former pupils include actors Julian Glover, Sam West, Jude Law and playwright Ray Cooney; writers CS Forester and VS Pritchett; surgical scientist Prof Ajay Kakkar and defence systems designer Prof RV Jones; industrialist Sir Ronald Leach and banker Sir Keith Whitson.

Entrance: Entry is now automatic from the junior school. Exams – taken by all in maths, English and reasoning. Interview given equal weight – not just the numerically top candidates are chosen. Priority to siblings and 'those with a prior connection'. Over-subscribed, of course. 125 places on offer at 11; in 2004, 600 applied. 10 places at 13. 20 places post-GCSE.

Exit: Lots of gap years. Otherwise to as wide a range of courses and destinations as anywhere – medicine at Leeds, London, Manchester; architecture at Edinburgh, Oxford Brookes, Nottingham; English at York, Homerton, Sussex; various kinds of engineering or IT courses everywhere. 2004 saw 19 to Oxbridge and the first ever leaver off to Harvard. Given the standard of art here, surprisingly few to art schools – but maybe that's where all the gappers end up.

Money Matters: Benefits both from the Dulwich estates (£1m) and Saddlers' Company (£1/4m) support – both of which fund generously. Scholarships at 11+, 13+ for which all candidates are automatically considered. More schols at 16+ - all worth up to 1/3 of fees. Means-tested bursaries at 11+ and 16+ worth up to 100 per cent of fees. Art, music and sports schols at different stages worth varying percentages. All worth serious investigation.

Remarks: Who would get on well here? – 'someone very self-reliant who has their own opinions, someone happy in a relaxed set-up, someone outgoing,' – so says head and parents concur. Perhaps the most academic, shyer girls will still head for JAGS. For boys the choice depends even more on individual personality. 'We're very holistic in our approach to education,' says Mr Diggory and this word, along with 'relaxed', 'opportunity' 'community' and 'valued' set the tone. Jot them down and now go and see the big brother down the road.

ALTRINCHAM GRAMMAR SCHOOL FOR BOYS

Marlborough Road, Bowdon, Altrincham, Cheshire, WA14 2RS

Tel: 0161 928 0858
Fax: 0161 929 5137
E-mail: agsbadmin@agsb.co.uk
Website: www.agsb.co.uk

• Pupils: 1,060 boys; all day • Ages: 11-18 • Size of sixth form: 260 • Non-denom • State

Head: Since 2003, Mr T J Gartside MA Edinburgh University (history). Early forties. Educated and taught at Hulme Grammar School for Boys and describes this post as 'coming home'. Lives nearby, three children at local state schools, 'I see myself settled for a good few years'. Taught history in a number of independent and state schools and came here from deputy head post of Westcliff High School for Boys, Essex. Boys describe him as 'well organised' and 'a good orator'. Parents feel he's reserved, but approachable, 'there's no spin, he speaks from the heart and he personally supports all events, often amongst the last clearing up'. Head says, 'leadership's about taking a strategic view and seeing the big picture but also being prepared to do the dirty jobs; then others follow, if only through guilt!' No showman but quietly ambitious for boys and school, 'this school should be giving parents a strong choice, an education and results that comfortably rival Manchester Grammar School.'

Academic Matters: Excellent. Consistently well over 50 per cent of A levels at A or B grade and half GCSEs A or A*, with maths and sciences particularly strong. Handful of boys receive high awards in national Maths Challenge, biology and physics Olympiads. Language College status coming into its own with fast track to GCSE for able linguists, options to study Russian, Chinese and Arabic with supporting trips to Russia, China, France, Germany and Spain, and after hours classes for community. Teachers take French and Spanish into some eight primary schools and offer accelerated group for new y7 boys. Historically compulsory CDT brought results down, it's now optional. Parents talk of one or two weak teachers but head believes exceptional results reflect recent full evaluation of 'teaching and learning for every teacher and setting of challenging but realistic targets.' Strong emphasis on extension work and national competitions for gifted and talented. SEN provision has grown but is still comparatively low-key, responding to needs arising and reflecting high ability intake. School copes with mild dyslexia in house. Physical access good since rebuild. Library revamped but still seems small for number of pupils. School defends minority subjects – Latin, geology, music and, hitherto, modern languages at A level – against economic concerns, with teachers willing to forego lunch hours if necessary.

Games, Options, The Arts: Exciting plans for new sports facilities following long awaited government grant in late 2005 for £3.5 million over three years. Astroturf, sports hall and land drainage to start in 2006 leaving days of 'soggy playing fields and smelly, down-at-heel gym' behind. 'It's very exciting to know we'll have top notch sports facilities which will benefit the whole community,' says head. Plans to introduce summer sport schools, non-mainstream sports (archery, martial arts), partnerships with local primary schools and sports clubs. Existing school teams already do well nevertheless, 2004 NW champions in hockey, tennis and badminton and national, regional and county players in several sports.

Parents and boys praise new injection of enthusiasm in music since staff changes, describing the standard as 'fabulous', and boys like the emphasis head has brought to live music and drama. Swing band is legendary. Head speaks of 'building a tradition of boys singing'; Manchester's Halle Choir recruits here. Barber Shop Quartet reached National Festival of Music finals. Lessons from peripatetic tutors available during school on no fewer than 12 instruments. Guitar building group. Spectacular two-storey art room with gallery bathed in light. Strong chess club fights inter-school competitions; U14 and U18 Greater Manchester Champions 2004. D of E. Global Challenge trips. TMFM web radio being set up by IT department to include soap drama, 'Marlborough Road'.

Background and Atmosphere: Founded in 1912 with just 57 pupils and three staff in 29 acres of well-to-do leafy SW Manchester suburb, the original redbrick school forms the heart of the buildings. Impressive building programme since becoming grant maintained in 1996, when school was given new coat of arms. Sixth form centre nearing completion, only a few 'huts' remain. Lifts newly installed for disabled students. Head attends and has strengthened links with nearby St Mary's Church, pictured in prospectus. Concerts and services now held there. About one third buildings new or newly refurbished; classrooms, IT suites, science and high tech language labs. School uses brand-new, airy Stamford Hall for dining with a smartcard system for reasonably priced meals. Boys still love occasional chip butties but school claims to have been ahead of the Jamie Oliver initiative; fizzy drinks have been banned on health grounds as agreed by boys and staff. Breakfast also available.

Boys and staff both friendly and welcoming, though corridor manners not always impeccable. Old corridors narrow so, despite one-way system, mayhem reigns between lessons. Relaxed but beavering atmosphere in classrooms – 'everyone wants to do well; it's expected you'll work hard – if you didn't want to work you wouldn't fit in here,' say boys. Healthy competition for commendations for accumulated effort marks and parents describe school as 'encouraging'.

Pastoral Care and Discipline: Head describes boys as, 'gentle folk who tend to respect boundaries; we do have naughty boys but generally they're accepting of authority'. Head's Saturday detention poses real threat. He's on site anyway to 'catch up' and support football and rugby. Sixth form prefects well-respected, first year forms have prefect mentors and boys say form tutors deal with problems quickly and well. Parents say school's really on the ball over bullying, pastoral care and any problems with drugs, which are few. Big emphasis on 'commendations' with prizes at the end of the year for individuals and form groups who win most. Boys welcome mix up of forms after first and second years, 'you make friends straight away and get to know everyone', and describe a 'good community spirit' throughout school. Head produces topical 'thought for the week' for assembly and follow-up in form discussion.

Pupils and Parents: Unpretentious, middle class. Two thirds of boys live near school in Altrincham, Hale and Bowdon. One sixth come from rural Cheshire and one sixth from less affluent parts of Trafford Borough. Twenty per cent of boys from ethnic minority groups, mainly professional families, but a third of them with English as a second language; Ofsted praised school for being 'racially harmonious and inclusive'. Fair smattering of children of Old Boys. Most celebrated OB is Ian Livingstone, creator of Tomb Raider, Lara Croft and Dungeons and Dragons and of companies, Games Workshop and Eidos. New IT suite bears his name after substantial donation. Cricketer Paul Allott and local Tory MP Graham Brady also OBs.

Entrance: Four applicants for every highly-prized place. Selective, using own exam with maths, verbal and non-verbal reasoning multiple-choice papers one Saturday in November. Place offered to every boy in the district who passes the exam, then to boys out of district with the highest marks. Member of the Northwest Consortium of Independent Schools which co-ordinates results publication and place acceptances. Not a level playing field; great demand for private tutors for state primary boys before entrance exam. Some parents prefer to pay for local prep schools to whip their boys into shape in time. Entrance depends on bare results, no reading between lines to discern who has been hothoused, but school's reputation is for bringing the best out of boys from a fair spread of ability.

Exit: A few out (to local colleges), a few in after GCSEs. Ninety per cent from sixth form to higher education, a good handful to Oxbridge, most to northern universities, Manchester, Leeds, Durham, Sheffield. Huge variety of courses.

Remarks: Top boys' state school in Manchester area with lots of extra opportunities in school that mixes tradition and state of the art. Welcoming, enthusiastic and not dauntingly large. Parents very satisfied with everything including new prospect of excellent sports facilities.

Altrincham Grammar School for Girls

Cavendish Road, Bowdon, Altrincham, Cheshire, WA14 2NL

Tel: 01619 280 827

Fax: 01619 417 400

E-mail: admin@aggs.trafford.sch.uk

Website: www.aggs.trafford.sch.uk

• Pupils: 1,163 girls, all day • Ages: 11-18 • Size of sixth form: 264 • Non-denom • State • Open days: September for entry into y7; January for entry into y12

Headmistress: Since 1999, Mrs Dana Ross Wawrzynski BSc MSc (Applied biochemistry) (mid forties – at a guess). Educated in Scotland, studied at Glasgow and Strathclyde Universities and taken south of the border by her husband's career; architect and university lecturer. Twin boys at MGS. A forthright Scot, friendly and approachable, she landed in teaching 'almost by accident' and found her true vocation. A rapid rise through the teaching ranks followed in a wide variety of schools from inner-city comprehensives to grammar schools, holding two deputy headships before this appointment. Refreshingly honest. 'Loves her job'. Her office is in the hub of the school and she likes to feel her door is always open. Passionate about the process of learning. Believes, 'we can all achieve our maximum if the barriers to learning are removed'. An ambitious head, studying for a Doctorate in Education in her spare time, she would like to put the school on the map; visualises expansion but strives to maintain a family atmosphere.

Academic Matters: Very strong academic results rivalling independent schools in the area. High expectations of the pupils by parents and staff alike. Head likes to minimise any disruption to the lessons and leave within term time is strongly discouraged. Traditional teaching with eager pupil participation. Average class size is 26, max 29. Streaming in maths and French from year 8. Girls take 9 GCSEs including 3 sciences or double award. 4 subjects are followed to AS level, 3 to A level ('better to get 3 good results than stretch to 4'), plus general studies. IT has been weak in the past but is improving with new equipment and staff. All pupils are encouraged to take the European Computer Driving Licence. In recent GCSEs, 60 per cent got five or more A* and A grades) and 75 per cent (excludes general studes) at A and B grade at A level. State of the art science labs are clearly not needed to produce excellent science results. Maths and music score well, though numbers taking the latter are small. A language college from 2002 – Italian, Russian, Mandarin, Japanese and Arabic on offer as well as the standard French, German and Spanish. School now has just four pupils who are listed as having SEN but continues to monitor and support a further eleven.

Games, Options, The Arts: Compulsory netball, hockey and gym in winter; tennis, rounders and athletics in summer, from years 7 to 9, plus dance from years 7 to 8. Years 10 to 11 are timetabled one general PE lesson per week plus the option of GCSE PE and/or dance. The school has achieved notable sporting successes in the past including the National Schools' U16 hockey champions in 2001, netball in 1998 and track and field athletics in 1995 and 1998. The teams feature regularly in the National Schools' finals in a number of sports. Girls represent Trafford, Greater Manchester, NW region and 5 girls have represented England in hockey, netball and athletics. Facilities include two full size all-weather hockey pitches and six netball courts, converting to tennis courts in summer.

Pupils praise the school for the breadth of opportunities on hand; 63 extra-curricular activities are on offer such as sport, music, dance, language and religious clubs. First and second orchestras, wind band, string groups and choirs provide a programme of concerts and lunchtime recitals, both public and in-house. Residential and non-residential trips abound, both at home and abroad, from field trips to ski trips, links with girls' schools in Beijing, Sydney, Tokyo, and work experience in Europe. A World Challenge expedition took ten sixth form girls to Brazil in summer 2001, 19 to Ecuador in 2003 and Puerto Rico is the destination for 2005. Drama is popular, taught by specialist teachers and backed up by regular theatre visits.

Background and Atmosphere: Founded in 1910, situated in the affluent suburb of Bowdon, the school buildings are on three separate sites, carved up by relatively busy roads. Grant maintained in 1997 and became a Foundation school in 1999. Head likes the girls to have a pleasant environment in which to learn and is keen to preserve the tradition of the school, enabling a sense of belonging to develop. Hence, original 'Sicilian Lion' wallpaper and lighting has been preserved in the lovely galleried main hall – sadly now too small for whole school assemblies. An ambitious building programme is in place, updating facilities. A new maths and English building with drama studio and a super new library were opened by Prince of Wales in April 2003. Redecoration is planned in the school and a relentless stream of successful grant applications funds continuing improvements.

The school is non-denominational but with a Christian ethos. Some parents comment that the school 'has more white Anglo-Saxon protestants than other Manchester schools' but pupils are from a variety of religious backgrounds, differences being respected but not highlighted. Navy uniform, with blazers reintroduced by the present head, producing a smarter finish. Designated skirt lengths according to height exist though rolling up the waistband allows the girls to be more fashion conscious. Mufti in sixth form.

Pastoral Care and Discipline: Head defies any head to say, honestly, drugs are not a problem. Staff are vigilant in looking for signs of drug use and will access appropriate help. Expulsion for any girl supplying drugs. Designated area for sixth form smokers, a handful of younger smokers are pursued by staff. Anorexia occasionally a problem as might be expected in a school of 1,200 girls; staff watch for excessive weight loss and access help. Cases of verbal bullying are effectively dealt with by close liaison with pupils and parents. A commendation system encourages self-esteem. Weekly certificates are given for achievements in all spheres and the recipients' names posted on the school board.

Pupils and Parents: Majority white middle class, happy to have their daughters close to home and mixing with other Altrincham girls but a broad spectrum overall, from the very deprived to professional families. A cohort of very affluent Cheshire 'new money' types occasionally ruffle feathers. Pupils are highly motivated, friendly and unassuming, praising the school for its friendliness and supportive, approachable teachers. Many without any broader aims or dreams go on to relatively local universities and never set the world alight. Some note rougher elements in the lower streams (not rough, 'boisterous', says head). The PTA is very active, raising funds and organising social events. Use is made of parental contacts; the principal of Somerville College, Oxford recently spoke to the school, arranged by a parental link. Good reports from parents. 'Why bus our daughters into Manchester?' Sons are bused in to MGS.

Entrance: Heavily oversubscribed. Apply directly to the school. A majority come from state schools – approximately 40 feeders. Complicated admissions system for entry into year 7, part academic part location. All applicants take the AGGS entrance examination involving papers in maths, verbal and non-verbal reasoning and a catchment area is defined by parish boundaries within Altrincham. Those who pass the AGGS entrance examination are prioritised as follows: first, girls living within the catchment area with sisters at the school; second, other girls from within the catchment area scored according to merit and proximity to the school. Any subsequent remaining places are then offered to daughters of staff, sisters living outside the catchment, sisters of former pupils and finally eligible candidates outside the area. Local parents often choose to send their children to independent primary schools in order to maximise their chances in the 11+ and many move house to be eligible for a place – the closer the better.

Admission into the sixth form requires six GCSEs at A-B grades plus satisfactory reports – this applies to internal and external candidates.

Exit: Vast majority to universities all over the place with Manchester, Liverpool, LSE, Birmingham, Warwick, York, Durham, Leeds and Nottingham being particularly popular. Twelve to Oxbridge in 2002, six in 2003. A wide variety of courses – nine into medicine, two into veterinary medicine, four into law.

Remarks: One of the top state schools in the country and, academically, rivals many independent schools in the area. Its approach may not be to everyone's taste (hence a fair number of girls still bus in to independent schools in Manchester, in preference), but it goes beyond the bounds of most state schools and is the automatic choice for many local parents and the answer to a prayer for bright local girls from less well-off backgrounds.

THE AMERICAN SCHOOL IN LONDON

1 Waverley Place, London, NW8 0NP

Tel: 020 7449 1200
Fax: 020 7449 1350
E-mail: admissions@asl.org
Website: www.asl.org

• Pupils: 1,312 girls and boys • Ages: K1 to Grade 12 • Size of sixth form: 463 in High School • Non-denom • Fees: £15,160 - £18,570 pa • Independent

Head: Since 1997, urbane, savvy, affable and highly competent, Princetonian Bill Mules AB MEd EdD (fifties) runs his school with great zest and very much in tandem with teachers, staff and the parent-based Board of Trustees. He came to London from the US to take this position, considers it to be the quintessential job in his career area and has signed on for three further years. He is available to parents whether in his office, chance meetings in the halls or the odd good-natured exchange through his open office windows.

Academic Matters: Parents and students alike assert that academics are the school's great strength and are given even greater impact through interdisciplinary studies. The lower school gives a well-rounded foundation in classes of 20 or fewer, fabulously enriched with a multitude of field trips around London. All children take Italian from K1 through fourth grade, as much for ease in this phonetic language as for the pathways early language opens in the brain. Middle school further prepares students for the high school American college prep program. The usual American broad-based high school mix of courses is taught by well-qualified popular teachers in classes that average 16 and includes 19 AP offerings.

Students are challenged to risk courses at their highest ability and it was said of one teacher, 'in a class with geniuses plus kids who aren't necessarily as interested or talented, he brings everyone up to the same level.' As in everything else at ASL, wide use is made of every possible venue in London, not to mention Europe, Africa, you name it. Five years of test results are published, with 86 per cent of 155 students scoring 3 or above (out of 5) on 368 AP exams last year and SATs averaging 628V and 630M. ASL is realistic and forthright about the limited number of students they can handle with mild specific learning difficulties and use testing as needed particularly in the lower school.

Games, Options, The Arts: With brand new space, the arts and particularly music are getting greater and more excited emphasis. Basic requirements plus interesting electives mean the impressive new studios for art, photography and woodworking are used by almost everyone at some point, as well as the enviable Annenberg Theatre for drama, concerts, evening lectures etc. Patient, well-liked music teachers lead students from the fifth through eighth grades, where everyone must play an instrument (and be in the choir along the way). That budding proficiency results in an enthusiastic take-up of seats in the junior and senior orchestras and jazz band. About eight practice rooms fill through the day with students working in class or in individual instrument groups even through lunch.

There's huge encouragement to take advantage of the cultural and historical offerings of London. To this end, because of a complicated but useful system of rotating class order, holidays, sports and numerous field trips can be flexibly accommodated with minimal disruption to any particular class. The imaginative after-school program keeps lower and middle schoolers constructively busy with everything from swimming to Latin, book club, cooking, volleyball, etc. The wildly popular annual three-day alternatives program, required of every high school student, offers a phenomenal choice of activities (included in fees) ranging from scuba diving in Spain, to study tours to Russia, to rock climbing in Alicante. There are two gyms, 42 high school teams with quite respectable stats and 21 acres of playing fields not far from school on the Jubilee line. ASL school buses transport students (to and from school as well as after-school activities) but even the athletes say the extra transportation time in a busy day means that 'the kid looking for a college athletic scholarship' is probably the only one who might not love this school.

Background and Atmosphere: Eager first graders in their classrooms are gently controlled by calm, pleasant teachers; buoyant middle schoolers work in duos or individually around school laptops in classes, ready at a moment's notice to explain their projects; high schoolers are at ease and friendly with each other in the halls, mildly scruffy (no dress code, just 'good judgement') but bright eyed, sharp witted and engaged. Teachers smile but don't miss a beat as visitors slip into the back. People come and go here and the inhabitants take it all in their stride. A massive and far-sighted five year renovation of the neo-brutalist 1960s building has added a third floor, another gym, scattered computer labs with 600 stations, wireless technology, state-of-the-art science labs and studios and, best of all, opened up the whole interior with new windows, colour and swaths of light.

A far cry from the first school, started in the fifties by another Princetonian for American diplomatic and military children, when football practice took place on the lawn of Winfield House and Truman came to speak at graduation. Current students are proud of the comparatively brief history, and know the details, including the years Elton John came to sing and Kathleen Turner graduated. Thanks to the open campus policy for high schoolers, students are everywhere, especially the library, where they use every corner, as a sort of beating heart of the school. They are also allowed to go off-campus during free times or 'opts,' which is unnerving for some parents, but it's one more way the school stresses and develops self-reliance. Above all, the amazing international diversity is cherished among parents and students alike. All realise that the nature of their transient community means, as a senior boy said, 'our time here is fleeting, the time you spend with your friends is valuable. You must make the most of it, and take nothing for granted.'

Pastoral Care and Discipline: It is the lucky child who finds himself transferred from yet another foreign assignment and plunked down at ASL. Because most students have been the new kid themselves and because 'it's so international, it opens up the whole student body to accepting differences.' 'Kids are incredibly accepting of the unusual,' students report. Sharp-eyed teachers are on the lookout for bullying, the lone ranger, the unusual slump – perhaps more than most because of extra potential for stress amidst so much coming and going. Concerns about students are noticed, monitored and quickly dealt with by teachers and advisors; easy, frequent communication amongst staff, parents and students is further facilitated by school email, conferences and the comfortable open-door policy throughout the school.

Zero tolerance and immediate expulsion for drugs, clear and firm prohibition on smoking. British laws complicate drinking restrictions off-campus but also ease student interest in abuse. Infractions are handled swiftly but always with an eye on the best interests of the errant child. Parents report that their concerns are met with serious attention, follow through and solutions. The middle school keeps adolescents hopping and on the move. Frequent interaction between parents, students and teachers keeps them talking and in the picture, encouraging 'kids to use this age to take risks, make mistakes, advocate for themselves, seek one-on-one meetings with teachers for help in anything.'

Pupils and Parents: American and international families looking for educational continuity, during short-term transfers from America or shifting assignments around the world (usually corporate or diplomatic), choose this very metropolitan school as much for its heart-of-the-ex-pat community role as for its scholastic excellence. Families don't just move across London to be nearby; in some cases, their preference for ASL has driven a career change in order to return here from America for their children's high school years. Economic and global shifts mean the student population changes as much as 20 per cent each year. But the school expects and plans for that and makes transition in and out of London and ASL a major part of its program for students and parents. Daylong parent orientations, neighbourhood coffees, evening lecture series, trips to local events and museums ... all create bonds and ready communication.

Entrance: The no-holds-barred, all-cards-on-the-table attitude of staff and materials mean that parents can judge the school pretty accurately. A recent survey showed that over 85 per cent felt their actual experience was even better than expected. This approach and consequent self-selection work is evident in the convivial buzz of a very disparate population as well as in the compelling, quantifiable results. The school looks for 'strong average to above' self-motivated students who can handle the rigorous academics; some EAL assistance is available in the lower and middle schools but the demands of the high school curriculum make absolute fluency imperative. Rolling admissions allow students to apply and receive a speedy response at any time in the school year. Almost by definition and certainly by long experience, the school is supremely capable in the task of integrating new students.

Exit: Most students only leave because of family transfers or because parents want something outside the realm of American day schooling, perhaps to 'go British.'

Graduates go on to most of the big and little Ivies, major state universities, and some British universities. An exhaustive five-year list is published in the back of the school handbook.

Money Matters: The only non-profit American school in England (gifts made by US citizens are tax-deductible), and a registered charity in the UK, ASL has very little endowment. Fees cover 95 per cent of what's needed, with the rest raised by annual giving. The well designed £22 million renovation has been completed, half was funded by parental and corporate donation, the remainder was conservatively budgeted from future tuition estimates. Fees include all books and materials, high school alternatives (mentioned above) and required curriculum-related field trips, although there are supplementary charges for some trips and theatre tickets.

Remarks: Probably one of the best of urban American day schools anywhere, whether US or international. An upbeat, nurturing sanctuary, yet fully engaged in the life of the great city around it. A boy was overheard saying to his mother as he left one afternoon, 'it looks like the other places I've been and it feels like the other places I've been but there's magic in there.'

AMPLEFORTH COLLEGE

Linked to Saint Martin's Ampleforth School in the Junior section

Ampleforth, York, North Yorkshire, YO62 4ER

Tel: 01439 766 000

Fax: 01439 788 330

E-mail: admissions@ampleforth.org.uk

Website: www.ampleforthcollege.york.sch.uk

• Pupils: 474 boys, 87 girls • Ages: 13-18 • Size of sixth form: 270 • RC - but not all are • Fees: Boarding £7,150. Day £3,815 • Independent

Headmaster: Since 2004, Fr Gabriel Everitt MA PhD. Fr Gabriel was educated at Dundee High School, studied history at Edinburgh and Balliol, Oxford (a doctorate in medieval history), prepared at Oxford for priesthood in the Anglican Church, at the same time gaining a first in theology. A curate in Hartlepool from 1987, he became RC in 1989 and joined the Ampleforth community in 1990. Started teaching in the school and was ordained in 1994. Successively head of christian theology (1997), housemaster of St Aidan's (1997-8) and then St Oswald's (1998). He was appointed third master in 2000.

Academic Matters: Top of the Catholic league but makes no bones about non-elitist intake – from A-stream scholars to fifth stream IQs of around 100 who get extra help with English and maths. NB Ninety per cent of this bottom stream achieve three A levels but 'the strong should be given something to strive for and the weak should not be over-burdened'. This is part of Ampleforth's mission statement and a quotation from the Rule of St Benedict. 'They never discard,' says a parent, 'the boys gain self-respect, the monks have an ability to home in on potential, to unlock talent to achieve.' Core curriculum plus compulsory Christian theology throughout (at which they do very well); most take three separate sciences at GCSE although the lower stream take the combined award. Liberal arts have traditionally had the edge here but science and maths continue to strengthen. Science has been helped by the

£4.2m investment in the new science centre, completed 2000. Christopher Belsom, head of maths, is also a member of the Advisory Committee for Maths Education(ACME). English is very strong and history and christian theology still very popular. Greek and politics and a wide range of modern langs among the options. Two thirds of the staff are lay (16 women), 20 are monks. All houses have a monk chaplain or housemaster.

NB pupils are allowed to have a go at an A level subject even if only from a pretty modest grade obtained at GCSE. Dyslexics taught 'for the most part' in the main stream but there is some additional specialist one-to-one teaching available. TEFL sets also in place.

Games, Options, The Arts: Powerful games school (games are compulsory); strong first XV. 'We have a depth of expertise,' confirmed previous head. Recently appointed John Liley ex-England and Leicester top points scorer, as director of rugby. Recent cricket tour to Barbados, cross-country, hockey (new Astroturf surface for this), netball (recent tour to Malta), lacrosse, athletics (own tracks), squash, golf (own 9-hole course), fly-fishing, renowned beagling. Phenomenal eighteen rugby fifteens, ten cricket elevens, eight tennis teams, 25-metre swimming pool, sports hall with plans for new £1.5m extension. Strong CDT and art (centre includes photography and electronics). Excellent drama (three recent Oscar winners!), main and studio theatres. CCF now voluntary. Duke of Edinburgh Awards (an OA heads the scheme now), scouts now taken over by Outdoor Activities Group, and clubs for everything from debating and gliding to bee-keeping. Music is particularly strong with the Schola Cantorum, the school choir, touring regularly – recent trip to Hungary. Annual pilgrimage to Lourdes for seniors. Own charity – run by students – raised funds to build school in Nepal and to sponsor eastern european students in school's sixth form. Also several other eye-openingly worthwhile international projects.

Background and Atmosphere: Founded in 1802. Fine setting in 3,000 acres of lovely Yorkshire valley, 'the half hour it takes to get boys here daily from York is as long as many London day school runs'. NB The fast train from London to York takes less than one hour 45 minutes. Beautiful Victorian Gothic main wing plus Giles Gilbert Scott's huge Abbey Church and school buildings (1930s) with late 1980s additions and much recent building, classrooms and boarding houses. 'The Benedictines have joined forces with Holiday Inn,' commented an architect, though the school points out indignantly 'there are other views!' Huge central hall – 'rather like a liner' – according to a pupil, and study hall with carrels (individual study desks). £20m

has been spent in recent years on improving facilities. Houses vary considerably in character with deliberate spread of ability throughout. From September 2005 three girls' houses run by married housemistresses and 7 boys' houses run by 4 monks and 3 married laymen – 'deeply thoughtful men, they've seen it all before'. En-suite bed-sits the norm in most houses. New double house for new 13-18 girls opened in April 2005. Parents can choose houses.

Though very much a country school and pretty remote, Ampleforth has links with the outside world via excellent and regular lecturers and far-away projects eg Chile and Eastern Europe on which previous head was 'mustard keen'. 'It's perfect for parents abroad.' No exeats except for one in the the winter term, otherwise half terms. Handy list of local hotels, restaurants and B&Bs is sent out to parents in the very comprehensive book – 'Confirmation of Entry – Your Questions Answered'. Not unknown for parents to rent a cottage in the area during their son's school years. The warmth of welcome is legendary – 'it's part of the Rule of St Benedict to welcome guests as Christ welcomed his guests'. Central feeding now in operation – at a cost of £2.4 million – but pupils are at least seated by house for lunch in sub-divided areas within the main dining hall. The monks of Ampleforth singing plainchant are now known to millions via Classic FM – a nice little earner. School recently part of a 'fly-on-the-wall' documentary – 'My Teacher's a Monk' – watched by 4m at Easter 2003.

Pastoral Care and Discipline: Pupils have a slight reputation for wildness (school prefers 'independence!'). Previous head's clampdown appears to have had effect – no shock horror headlines recently. Consciences worked on rather than harsh restrictions imposed. 'The philosophy is absolutely right,' says a parent, 'it is no good succeeding in life if you fail yourself'. The school's 'Handbook for Parents' spells out clearly what the policies are – tough, while bending over backwards not to hurt the offender's academic career. Fine for smoking, suspension for drinking spirits. 21 caught with drugs in February 2005. Bad language censored – 'they see tennis stars disputing, footballers spitting, we ask for standards to be different,' – hooray!

Pastoral care, say parents, is 'unique'. 'The monks are priests and friends, there is a loyalty from boys in return who come back to the Abbey to be married and to have their children christened.' All houses have resident housemasters/mistresses, visiting tutors and a monk chaplain or housemaster. No uniform but 'dress code' of jacket and black trousers with black or sports 'colours' ties for the boys and black trousers or skirts for the girls.

Pupils and Parents: Scions of top and middle Catholic

families from all over the place. Old Boys include Rupert Everitt, Hugo Young, Christopher Tugendhat, Lord Nolan, James Gilbey, Sir Anthony Bamford of JCB, Michael Ancram, Anthony Gormley (Angel of the North sculptor), Lawrence Dallaglio.

Entrance: Common entrance, with exceptions always allowed especially 'for reasons of faith or family,' or simply because boys have come up through the partner junior school, St Martin's Ampleforth. Entrants to sixth form are expected to have at least 6 GCSEs at C or above, preferably with Bs in their chosen AS subjects but pupils are taken in from outside the British system 'each case on its merits'. Need not be RC to get in – but you have to be prepared to be a full participant in the religious life of the school.

Exit: Ninety per cent to university, on average 10 per cent to Oxbridge. Popular subjects include history, classics, theology, music, medicine, estate and business management.

Money Matters: A generous 17 major and minor scholarships available, and others internally awarded. Seven music scholarships of varying value and Basil Hume all-rounder scholarships at 13.

Remarks: Unfailingly kind and understanding top Catholic boys' boarding school that has suffered, from time to time, as a result of its long-standing liberal tradition. Now getting more loyalty from the parents who form its traditional potential intake. Girls a success – very happy here – and happy, happy parents too. In confident mood.

ANGLO EUROPEAN SCHOOL

Willow Green, Ingatestone, Essex, CM4 0DJ

Tel: 01277 354 018
Fax: 01277 355 623
E-mail: reedb@aesessex.co.uk
Website: www.aesessex.co.uk

• Pupils: 1,300 boys and girls • Ages: 11 - 18 • Size of sixth form: 270 • Non-denom • State

Head: Since 1990, Mr Bob Reed BEd (fifties), previously deputy head of Cambridgeshire Village College. Was chair of the International Baccalaureate Schools in the UK organisation for ten years and is now on IB World Heads' Committee. Has also been an outdoor studies centre warden and an educational consultant with a major tour operator. Good, strong, visionary leader, passionate about his school.

Academic Matters: This is an international school, with about a third of pupils from families with strong overseas links. It was the first British state school to offer the International Baccalaureate and the first to become a language college. Everyone studies French and German from year 7, and can add Russian, Spanish or Japanese in year 9. Nearly everyone takes two languages other than English at GCSE, and continues to study a language in the sixth form. In the thriving Section Bilingue, geography and history are taught in French and German. Extensive study visits: nearly all year 7s visit Belgium for two weeks and there are two-week exchanges available for the other year groups. Year 10 pupils can spend eight weeks in Reims or Frankfurt.

Excellent GCSE results, with 78 per cent getting 5+ A* – C grades in 2005; as one would expect, languages show up well. A recent Ofsted report graded nearly three-quarters of lessons good or better and commented, 'the high proportion of consistently good and very good teaching is the main reason for the success of the students'. The only notable weakness it found was IT; staff changes have since been made.

The sixth form looks weak in league tables because it offers the IB, A levels and vocational A levels. Many students take a mixture. The IB, which does not show up on league tables, tends to attract the strongest students, and results are above the world average. Everyone studies a language but this can include vocational courses and even British Sign Language.

As a state comprehensive, the school gets its fair share of children with special needs. 'If they're appropriately placed in mainstream schooling then we will be happy to receive them,' says the head, though he feels that bureaucracy often takes precedence over finding the most suitable school for any particular child. The school has accommodated children with cerebral palsy and with sight and hearing impairments as well as the more usual learning difficulties. 'Two of our teachers use wheelchairs, so we have a very positive attitude towards pupils with disabilities.' The extensive overseas visits can be challenging for children with special needs, 'but we try to make reasonable adjustments. Some people think that if you've got special needs you can't learn languages – it's a load of rubbish. Plenty of our children with learning difficulties are bi- or tri-lingual.'

There are 77 languages spoken in the school, and although most of the international children come from well-educated families, some – including refugees from Afghanistan, fostered by a local Somali family – arrive speaking no English. They are well supported by learning support assistants and withdrawal groups. 'We will try to find someone who speaks the same language – for example, a Russian pupil could communicate with one from Afghanistan who also speaks Russian. We try to foster learning from each other.'

Games, Options, The Arts: All the usual sports, including badminton, trampoline and dance; there are three inter-house competitions every year, plenty of fixtures against other schools and lots of pupils play for local clubs. PE is an option at GCSE and A level. Good performing arts, with enthusiastic school musicals and talent shows and plenty of pupils learning musical instruments. Plenty of music, drama and sports clubs.

Everyone in the sixth form takes part in the IB creativity, action and service programme. This can include helping younger pupils who have special needs, organising a Christmas party for local elderly people and teaching sport in primary schools.

But the raison d'etre of the school is the international dimension. 'Europe and International Awareness is at the very heart of education,' says the school website. The school has 19 partner schools in Europe and further afield. Around 600 pupils travel abroad with the school each year. Older pupils represent other countries at a Model UN event with schools from all over Europe. Citizenship classes lead up to the European Citizenship award. Sixth formers take part in international conferences. There are art visits to Paris and Amsterdam, business studies visits to the Czech Republic, World Challenge expeditions to Peru and Namibia. The school is a corporate member of Amnesty International.

Background and Atmosphere: Opened in 1973 in this small Essex village on the site of a secondary modern which the LEA had been determined to close. A committee campaigned to keep a school in the village, and as Britain joined the Common Market, and employers such as Marconi brought international families into the area, there was pressure to set up a school with a European outlook. Anglo-European School opened with 180 pupils from the old secondary modern and another 180 new pupils in year 7. It was founded with the idea that children of different cultures should be able to work harmoniously together. 'We're about respecting other people's cultures and enabling them to respect ours. Most importantly, our children learn to become decent citizens.' Ofsted commented, 'pupils flourish in a setting where they are expected to be open to new ideas, different cultural traditions, varied ways of life and the possibilities of what they can do if they try. It encourages pupils of all backgrounds to take risks, explore unfamiliar cultures and ideas and learn to become independent.'

Pastoral Care and Discipline: Relaxed atmosphere with good relationships between staff and pupils. The influx of some 1,300 children into a small village every day can irk the mostly middle-class residents – more obviously, says the head, since the student profile has become less purely European and more international. Bullying tends to consist mostly of name-calling and bad behaviour of low level irritation from small groups. 'They usually stop after about year 9 and the occasional one or two who don't tend to become isolated.'

Pupils and Parents: Local, mostly middle-class children rub shoulders with children from virtually all parts of the world, including Kazakhstan and Mongolia. Children travel from the East End of London by train and from Essex coastal villages by bus. They tend to be mature and articulate, pleased to be at a school with such a broad outlook.

Entrance: The rather complicated bit. Sit down with a cup of coffee. Local children living in the parishes of Ingatestone, Mountnessing and Margaretting get priority, then siblings – but only of pupils who joined before the sixth form. All the other categories involve children 'who have been strongly and positively influenced by a different culture and language other than English'. Ten per cent of places are offered to those whose influence is as a consequence of 'one or more parent having visited a country other than the UK through their work or interests'. Then the rest of the places are offered to those in other categories, which include having lived abroad for some time and parents who promote language learning. Broadly, a holiday home in Spain or cousins in Australia won't count. As one would imagine, there is plenty of room for creative and wishful thinking here but the school seems to manage to sift wheat from chaff. 'We're trying to identify parents likely to support the ethos of the school.'

Entry to the sixth form is less complicated, with varying minimum requirements depending of courses but priority given to those who want to study the IB.

Exit: Around 75 per cent go through to the sixth form. Of those, most go on to higher education, with science, engineering and medicine amongst the most popular degree subjects. Other popular subjects include languages, politics, international relations and law.

Remarks: Exciting, successful state comprehensive with an international dimension and an unusual commitment to language learning, in an unlikely situation in a small Essex village. Just the place to broaden your family's outlook on life.

ARDINGLY COLLEGE

Linked to Ardingly Junior school in the Junior section

College Road, Ardingly, Haywards Heath, West Sussex, RH17 6SQ

Tel: 01444 893 000
Fax: 01444 893 001
E-mail: registrar@ardingly.com
Website: www.ardingly.com

- Pupils: 458 • Ages: 13-18 • Size of sixth form: 192 • C of E
- Fees: Day £5,120; boarding £6,840 • Independent • Open days: Some Saturdays in October, March and May

Headmaster: Since 1998 Mr John Franklin BA Dip Teaching M Ed Admin, fiftyish. An Australian with loads of teaching (English and geography) and boarding experience in both hemispheres including at Sedbergh and Marlborough. Previous job deputy, then acting, head St Peter's College, Adelaide. Mr Franklin inherited a benign but, perhaps, somewhat neglected institution with a brief to bring it up to date and beef up discipline. This he has clearly, rather spectacularly, done and all pay tribute to how much has been achieved. Friendly, communicative, with a sparkly wit lurking behind slight reserve, Mr Franklin talks of his regime as the iron fist in the glove. Certainly, he has made changes in standards of behaviour and discipline expected of pupils and, while some might chafe a bit, few would deny the benefits of the overall tightening up under his occasionally steely eye. Parents have welcomed the changes, colleagues admire what is being achieved. 'A lovely man and an excellent head,' was a fellow head's comment. Immensely and warmly proud of his pupils and their achievements, clearly hard-working and enthusiastic, a head to whose care most parents would confidently entrust their children.

Academic Matters: As part of head's drive to up the academic profile and aspirations, college adopted the International Baccalaureate in 2001 and this is having beneficial effects on both the quality of education offered and results. Head a great advocate -' it's a good, broad preparation for tertiary study....I like the overarching philosophy...it formalises all the things that a good independent education does anyway, emphasising creativity, academics and community service.' The first IB candidates achieved promisingly, getting an average of 34.5 points (45 is max) – comparing well with other schools. Five students scored the Oxbridge requirement 39 points or over. Now around 50/50 IB/A level students. Good choice of A level subjects – theatre studies, business studies (popular) along with more trad options. Good results especially in languages, art, physics and music; less good in business studies and DT but these often the choices of the less academic. Value added is good here. GCSE subjects include PE and drama plus all the usuals with 90 per cent achieving A-C grades and 36 per cent getting A*/A. Languages do well – so surprising how few take them in the sixth despite school's support – 'we might even encourage good linguists to take three languages in the sixth form', says head and certainly there are trips and links enough to fire enthusiasm.

ICT seen as a tool. Huge new PC suite September 2004. Every teaching room now networked and new access to school's library of 400+ CD Roms. Ceiling-mounted data projectors and more upgrading in progress. SEN well understood. 'We have a brilliant SENCO,' says head. 'If she says they will cope here, they will. She hasn't got it wrong yet.' All new entrants screened and individual support programmes drawn up for all who need one. Newest boys' boarding houses have lifts and, in general, school feels they could 'make it work' for the physically disabled on this large and undulating site. EAL available to few who need it.

Games, Options, The Arts: As far as you can see, pitches and sports fields stretch away into the Sussex landscape. School set in 275 acres, a third of which is let as fields. School has Astroturf pitch used for hockey or tennis, plus hard courts, plus use of reservoir for sailing and rowing five minutes walk from main buildings. More than 80 sports offered during the year and school especially successful in football, girls' hockey, cross country and shooting. Sports not compulsory here but everyone finds something they like. Sports hall built in 2000 but no weights/fitness rooms. Duke of Edinburgh Award scheme is popular here, as is CCF – a wide and challenging programme of activities. Music – now in attractive one-storey block at school entrance – very strong under charismatic director. A super choir – not, sadly, singing to herald our visit – was practising as we arrived – and bands, groups, ensembles, productions of all kinds flourish. Chapel choir sings in all the best places – St Paul's, Canterbury, St George's, Windsor. Individual lessons to top standards – some taught by London orchestral players and teachers include legendary bass guitarist and tuba maestro Herbie Flowers. Drama also good and adventurous, mostly in 'The Under', a super old three hundred seater theatre or in the smaller 'Friends' Barn'. Art is varied and lively – ceramics, sculpture, textiles among the try-outs.

Background and Atmosphere: A Woodard school ie founded in the mid nineteenth century by Canon Nathaniel Woodard and run on Christian principles, Ardingly moved to present impressive location in 1870. Main school in an imposing, three storey, H-shaped redbrick building high on the Sussex downs and with marvellous views over the landscape in all directions. Grandly solemn vaulted chapel used for weekly senior school services. In the winter, site can be cold and windswept but in the summer is a delight. Not a rich foundation and shackled by buildings' Grade II listings and doubtful privilege of being in an 'area of outstanding natural beauty;' school has major job to maintain and upgrade site and facilities but, under Mr Franklin, major changes have happened and more are planned. Good management, prudent changes, summer lets – all help to provide major investment now transforming school. Library to be greatly extended and upgraded by autumn 2004 and 3-year re-stocking plan in progress. Few spartan portakabins still around – one is to be a cybercafe we were told. While some stairwells, labs and corridors remain bleak, some depts, notably art, still awaiting relocating and updating and some boarding accommodation still to be raised to today's standards, Ardingly is on track and can now compete with the best in the area.

All but year 13 boarders now in village-like, small estate of 3 storey houses, moments from main building. Newest houses have ICT rooms, well-equipped games rooms, kitchens, 'brew rooms' and gardens with picnic tables. Year 9s are in 'pods' of 4 all with basins – one between two. Year 10s are in doubles and years 11-13 in singles. Beds look alarmingly narrow compared to some of the hefty types walking the campus. Attractive blue and white decor in house we visited. New day house made on top floor of one wing – from former boys' boarding rooms – comfortable, well furnished, spacious and with super views! Houseparents all living in house, many with families. All home-cooked, rather delicious food. Site is spacious, leafy, be-gardened, well maintained and feels relaxed.

Pastoral Care and Discipline: Pastoral care relies on tutorial system. Everyone has weekly meeting with tutor who is pupil's confidante, broker, spokesman and school's link with parents. Thereafter, hierarchy of support/discipline ending at the top. Long-term pupils appreciate Mr Franklin's tightening up. Foreign, principally German, boarders who enter for the sixth, strain at bedtimes and dress code but no major revolts after settling in period. Sixth form has dress code, lower forms have uniform – trouser option for girls. No recent drugs incidents but clear policy – automatic out for class A/B and possible police involvement, second chance over cannabis with testing/counselling/collaboration with parents regimen.

Pupils and Parents: Very much a Sussex school with a third of pupils living within 40 minutes drive, a further third – the English boarders – living within fifty miles and final third being overseas boarders. 'I could fill the school with Germans,' says head – the IB being, now, a prime attraction – but no more than 15 taken per year and those who come are, mostly, keen, highly appreciative of all on offer here and achieve impressively. Further few annually from everywhere else but no other large national contingents. Previously popular with Service families, numbers now in decline while diplomatic and other expat numbers increasing. Generally families are unpretentious, many making sacrifices to give their children 'the best'. Largest number from college's own prep. Former Ardines include racing driver Mike Hawthorn, Ian Hislop, composer Stephen Oliver, actors Terry-Thomas and Alan Howard.

Entrance: Selective via scholarship, CE or other exams depending on point of entry – English, maths, VR tested.

Exit: Around 20 leave after GCSE, mostly to local sixth form colleges. Rest stay and go on to everything from Oxbridge science to Nottingham Trent sport studies to employment to university abroad.

Money Matters: As part of necessary belt-tightening some scholarships funds have been reassigned however much still remains. Large number of academic, music, art, drama, sport and DT awards on offer at various stages - up to 50 per cent tuition remission. Special awards for clergy, Services, Sussex and Old Ardines' children. Worth scrutinising the literature.

Remarks: 'I would like to change the fact that we are the best kept secret in Southern England,' says head. Parents accosted on our way out were in no doubt. 'They praise the individual...they'll look at each child and work with them...they don't try to fit child into a mould...it's a very happy place.' We couldn't help noticing that, wherever we went, we were smiled at and that doesn't happen everywhere.

THE ARTS EDUCATIONAL SCHOOL (LONDON)

Cone Ripman House, 14 Bath Road, Chiswick, London, W4 1LY

Tel: 020 8987 6600

Fax: 02089 876 601

E-mail: head@artsed.co.uk

Website: www.artsed.co.uk

• Pupils: 140, about a third boys, all day • Ages: 11 – 18 • Size of sixth form: 35 • Non-denom • Fees: Main school £2,978, sixth form £2,665 • Independent • Open days: November

Headmaster: Since 2003, Mr Rob Luckham BSc PGCE MBIM, early fifties, a mathematician with an unusual career path for a head, having spent 15 years with the Ministry of Defence in various capacities. Even more unusual is that he, as a mathematician and scientist, should end up running this shrine to all things artistic. However, he began life as a teacher – science and electronics – and returned in 1995 as head of ICT/Year at Bourne Grammar. Thence onwards and upwards. He is a self-confessed amateur enthusiast for the performing arts but this, his first headship, is a brave one for someone from outside what is most often seen as a self-protective and precious milieu. He held off stiff competition to win the post and certainly looks different, neat and clipped in dark suit and smart tie, from just about everyone else in the place. Unlike most of his staff, he has, of course, never worked in the West End but, nevertheless, he feels he can 'talk meaningfully' with them without needing to be the specialist that they are. The school had been through a rough time before he came and needed a 'manager'. Quiet and assiduous, Mr Luckham is that and more.

Academic Matters: 'We are not a stage school,' asserts the head, keen to make the difference, and the pupils concur -'even when we're doing a show there is no excuse for not handing in work... the academic side is pushed as hard as the vocational'. This comes as a surprise to visitors who are surrounded by leotards and leggings, girls' hair scraped into buns, choruses and piano rehearsals booming out of each room. But the timetable – complex and on a two-week cycle – is firmly balanced and pupils not working on the vocational side are neat in trad turquoise (known here as 'lagoon') uniforms – which match the classroom doors and look quite demure!

Fewer subject options here than in 'normal' schools –

the curriculum simply doesn't allow for more. So, everyone takes human biology as the one and only science, along with 2 Englishes, maths, expressive arts, French and 3 options from a further 6 – art, dance, drama, geography, history, music. Results in 2004 were creditable and better than that in the Englishes, drama – all As – and art. The academic corridors look much as anywhere and good displays on historical topics make a reassuring change from the glitzy pics of past productions elsewhere else.

The sixth is separate and even existing pupils have to re-audition for admission. This means that most sixth formers come in at that stage. In 2004, only 8 of the 25 year 12 pupils had come up from lower school. 10 AS/A level subjects offered – all arts plus philosophy. Results in 2004 (all the candidates were girls) were nearly all Bs and Cs.

Games, Options, The Arts: Games don't exist here as everyone dances their socks off and football, etc are only played for fun in the lunchtimes. There is a gym/weights room for the sixth form. Some pupils obviously lament the lack of sport but everyone understands the reasons though the fear of injury is not so palpable as in the Tring Arts Ed. Yoga, 'combat fighting' and dancing like 'hip hop' use up surplus energies, if any.

Performing arts is what it's all about. Everyone belongs to either the Creative Arts (Drama) or the Dance stream and the two streams join for Choir and Musical Theatre lessons. Vocational courses include work in spoken voice, audition technique, text in performance, choreography, expressive arts, dance of all kinds and music. Music, criticised by the last inspection, is now impressive – loads of individual lessons, good resources and no-one now leaves unable to read music. Everyone performs all the time and it is most refreshing to go into a studio and see 13 year-olds, of both sexes, improvising without self-consciousness – no blushful hanging back here. Three major productions a year – aided by professional wardrobe and set-building staff. Though a professional attitude to performance is the main thing, pupils help on the backstage side and learn about the technical aspects of production, as well as film techniques. Production values are exacting and stand pupils in good stead when they move on. Unlike at stage schools, however, pupils are not encouraged to have agents and to take off long periods for professional work – school-life and work come first. The art rooms are a quiet relief and art is a popular GCSE here. Work is varied and clever and teaching makes stimulating use of past masters to prompt genuine creative responses in diverse media.

The school shares a building and facilities with the school of acting and the school of musical theatre. This means that as well as a theatre, music rooms and dance studios, a production manager, wardrobe mistress and carpenter are available to help with productions – 'they get a real professional experience of performance.' Part-time specialist dance and drama teachers hold master classes. Everyone has music twice a week – once as a whole class and once in streamed groups. There are four choirs, filled according to age group and ability, various instrumental groups including a jazz group, and many pupils have private music lessons too.

Art is popular throughout the school, with good GCSE results, lots of different media on offer and cross-curricular links such as making masks for a theatre performance. Plenty of trips to concerts and galleries. PE is more or less non-existent on a formal basis, though yoga and aerobics are available, and the boys often play impromptu lunchtime football games in the large studio.

Background and Atmosphere: It's a long, three-storey, plain redbrick building, unimpressively occupying about 100 yards of prime Bedford Park along the Bath Road in pricey West London and surrounded by leafy roads housing TV executives in semis which go for around £1m apiece. Inside it's a different world, via the entrance hall which is royal blue and crimson and lit with dinky mini stage lights. Plain corridors, plain rehearsal rooms – dozens of them which all look much the same to visitors apart from some being black and curtained and others bright and light – clearly have very different 'feels' to the students – eg 'that's where I do tap; I couldn't think of acting in there,' etc. A proscenium arch theatre, lots of storage space for costumes and sets, a good-sized, adaptable studio which mimics 'fringe' conditions – everything is geared to preparation for the outside reality.

Students look bright-eyed and busy – you cannot coast here and drown quickly if you try. There is little recreation space – the sixth form have space which acts as a common room but that's it and there is no outside. Little time for traditional teenage bickering here – 'it's very friendly and you have to work together', says sage 12-year-old student. A good canteen and good food, though sandwiches are not cheap. Most lower school pupils eat a hot meal at lunchtime – lots of pasta, always a vegetarian option and all prepared on site by unusually friendly staff. Good salad bar. Breakfast daily from 7.45 – a good idea considering that some pupils commute from as far as Kent or Reading. It's a long day, especially for dance students – 8.30am-5.30pm.

The building, in fact, houses two other schools – for post-18 students – the School of Acting and the School of Music Theatre, but some facilities are shared. School also borrows the local fringe theatre, The Tabard, and the excellent Questors Theatre in nearby Ealing, for performance space.

Pastoral Care and Discipline: A heady atmosphere on a major road between Chiswick and Hammersmith could make for some pretty spectacular lapses but the ambiance is energetic, purposeful and the emphasis is on self-discipline. Few, having got here, would want to jeopardize the places though some find it all a bit much and drop out, with relief, into something more conventional and less rigorous elsewhere. Carefully structured tutorial system. Students are remarkably focused and learn quickly that success isn't easily won. No problem with drugs, cigarettes or alcohol but all would be treated seriously – drugs by permanent exclusion. Cigarettes/alcohol – a first offence would mean a fixed term exclusion followed by meeting between headmaster, pupil and parents before pupil being allowed to return to school and any further offence = permanent exclusion.

Pupils and Parents: From a huge radius round London and very mixed in all ways – the common denominators are talent, a willingness to work, enthusiasm – and parents who can afford the fees. Some sixth formers from far afield are put up in local digs.

Entrance: By audition. Pieces prepared for audition depend on which course you are applying for eg – dance solos, drama monologues, sung or instrumental pieces. Then there is participation in unprepared workshops and classes. Tests are also given in core academic subjects. Don't come along seeing yourself as the next soap star or Billy Elliot. 'We're looking for team-workers.'

Exit: Not surprisingly, those who last the course and move into the sixth form, usually go on to acting courses in good colleges, to take drama and/or English at good universities or to gap years to think things out. School is very proud of those who beat off fierce competition from outside to win places in the two other on-site schools – 4 made it in 2005. Not too many embryonic accountants, lawyers and medics here.

Money Matters: One annual bursary given by the local authority.

Remarks: If you are sure that performing is your thing, if you have energy, drive, commitment and maturity, it's a great experience and you'll learn masses about what it takes to be a professional. But – if it doesn't work out, you can still go somewhere else for the sixth form and be an accountant after all.

The Arts Educational School (Tring)

Linked to Arts Educational School (Tring) Junior Department (The) in the Junior section

Tring Park, Tring, Hertfordshire, HP23 5LX

Tel: 01442 824 255
Fax: 01442 891 069
E-mail: info@aes-tring.com
Website: www.aes-tring.com

- Pupils: 273, mostly girls but 51 boys. Two thirds board, rest day
- Ages: 8-18 • Size of sixth form: 108 • Non-denom, but traditionally Christian • Fees: Day £3,965 - £6,200; boarding £5,460 - £7,710 • Independent • Open days: Contact school

Principal: Since 2002, Mr Stefan Anderson MA BMus ARCM ARCT ARCO, mid-forties. Previously director of music at King's Canterbury for 7 years and prior to that he was assistant director of music and organist at Wellington College. The first man to be principal of the AES. Now in his fourth breathtaking year at the AES, this likeable Canadian gives the impression of being permanently and happily swept off his feet by the sheer, ceaseless dynamism and creativity of the place, while, seemingly, having a pretty firm grip on its discipline and organisation. Having a teaching background in more trad and academic public schools probably helps in keeping feet on the ground here but he clearly relishes the diversity and populism of much of what goes on all over this place. A confident and confidence-inspiring head of a uniquely knock-out school.

Academic Matters: Unique also in its curriculum structure. Academic work takes up half of each day and 'vocational' work ie music, dance, drama and music theatre takes up the other half. Given that, and the fact that pupils are selected only for their abilities on the vocational side – not the academic – the academic results are more than creditable. A smaller number of subjects available here than elsewhere – 16 A level options and several of those are 'vocational' eg dance, theatre studies and performing arts and BTEC National Diploma in Performing Arts. Popular subjects are all the vocational ones plus art and design. Few other subjects get more than a handful of takers at A level. This makes for small classes and a range of decent results mostly in the A-C bracket.

Only one language can be taken at GCSE although private extra-curricular extra languages can be arranged. Eng lit, history and music among good recent performers at GCSE. New labs. SEN is big here – a quarter of pupils are dyslexic – something to do with people with aptitudes in drama and musical theatre having a tendency in this direction, apparently. But academic results often above expectations – 'if you've got a kid who's talented vocationally,' says principal, 'they get the confidence to do better academically.' One full-time SENCO and four trained assistants. 'Academic work is more fun here because we don't do so much of it', confided a shiny-eyed, recent refugee from a trad prep. Quite.

Games, Options, The Arts: Well, that's what this place is all about – minus the games. You simply wouldn't come here if sport matters much to you though impromptu football is played in the grounds by enthusiasts and off-site swimming is a regular activity. Dancers – and everyone dances – can't afford sports injuries and everyone expends huge energy and develops high-level fitness with the rigours of dance training. 'Dance' covers classical ballet, contemporary, tap, jazz, musical theatre, notation and choreography, dance medicine, dance journalism etc etc. Dance students take classes according to their level of ability not age – makes for unusual range of heights. Musical theatre students study acting, voice and speech, singing – and dance. Drama students do all the above plus more extensive theatre training in many technical areas. Musicians learn their own instruments, choral and individual singing, ensemble work and have groups and bands of all kinds. The chamber choir – we witnessed a rigorous bit of choir training – is voluntary but was 40+ strong and nobody yawning – and has been three time finalist and one recent winner of the Sainsbury's Choir of the Year competition. We were taken into various classes – the energy levels are dizzying – no shrinking or self-consciousness here – everyone gives their all. Everyone takes art to GCSE and a good range of media available. Super, purposeful art studios – not too tidy. Classes in film take in camera technique, story-boarding etc – all very practical and seriously undertaken.

Background and Atmosphere: The main building is as knock-out and as OTT as its denizens. Stunning, mostly red-brick facades, back and front and started in the C17th, this huge house has been tastefully added to, extended, embellished over the centuries, most notably by the Rothschild dynasty who owned it and lovingly improved it over many years. Few schools can boast an atrium, staircase, wallpapers and ceilings of this quality. The ballroom – used as a studio for performance classes – has C19th copies of Greek friezes and sculptures. One large dance studio – off the main, gloriously panelled, hall – has been cleverly glazed so that onlookers can watch the class. You want to pull up a chair and spend the day there.

Excellent, flexible, Markova theatre in constant use. Music and movement resounds from room after room. Only the quiet corridors where the academic lessons take place, the library – disturbingly tiny, whatever the reassurances about all departments having their own subject libraries elsewhere – and the conventional uniforms, strictly regulated eg no trainers, remind a visitor that this is a real school where coursework, prep and curriculum successfully co-exist with everything else. 'Below stairs' – mostly white-tiled and with narrower corridors – as much in use as the grander areas – for classes, dining, everything. 17 acres of super grounds in which the buildings sit comfortably and lots of huge mature trees make for a very pleasant, established feel. The upkeep must be a nightmare but a rolling programme of refurb and refurn keep it in good order and a 9-man team 'keeps on top of it'.

Girls vastly outnumber boys throughout – more than four to one. Boys only admitted since 1993 and principal allows that some parents, in the main fathers, have reservations about sending their sons to such a school. Boarding accommodation variable but much in splendid grand rooms and all is homely and cosy. Upper sixth girls live in Victorian houses down the road – much appreciated until you're ill and have to trek up to the san. Homely san with friendly staff and a welcoming extra sitting room for TLC. Good common rooms but this is not state of the art. We baulked at 7 fifteen year-olds sharing a room – though it was large and had wonderful views – but girls excitedly enthused about loving it and all being great friends. And this was no performance.

Local shopkeepers enthuse about the good behaviour of AES pupils. Enthusiasm abounds – in and out of the place. This was the first school visited by this gnarled old editor where the principal, the director of development and any numbers of bubbly pupils accompanied us throughout the entire, four hour experience – simply for the pleasure of showing it all off.

Pastoral Care and Discipline: You might think that with this amount of general artiness and hyper-activity, discipline would be a real problem here – but it isn't. A sense of self-discipline is palpable as you go around. Everyone seems to understand that, as the head says, 'they can't mess themselves up', without risking everything they work so hard for. So – only a few incidents of smoking and drinking and one exclusion for drugs since Mr Anderson's arrival. No random drug testing and school relies on its 'very clear policy' and the right to test if necessary.

The very long day means exhaustion by the evening and no boredom needing to be dispelled by illicit activities. Head acknowledges need for some 'down time' at the weekends so no pressure to join in various licit activities eg cinema, bowling, discos. Everyone is in a tutor group and pupils can choose their tutor – mostly getting their first choice. Excellent relationships between staff and students obvious everywhere – tangible affection and respect – these children want to please their teachers. Tremendous support for all the performing given by the academic staff – 'they turn up at every show', says head – and appreciated by students.

Sixth form wear own clothes and nothing flashy to be seen. Office-type suits for formal occasions. Good food, vegetarian option and salad bar and pleasant to spot large tubs of herbs and spices in the kitchen. Pupils grumble mildly about being only allowed one piece of fruit after each meal. Very careful monitoring of eating regularity and a sensible but strict attitude to eating disorders among staff and students. Ethos of discipline and work in evidence everywhere including in one studio plastered with homilies eg 'Dinner is served. Who's dinner? You or the audience?' and 'Fail, then figure out what to do on your way down'.

Pupils and Parents: From everywhere. Nineteen from overseas, otherwise from North Yorks to Cornwall. High proportion, especially, of course, day pupils, from Herts, Bucks and Beds. Equal diversity of backgrounds – many first time boarding families, some experienced public schoolers, some new to the whole thing, on full bursaries. Around a fifth from some kind of performing background. What unites them is the common purpose, the commitment and the energy. Eyes sparkle everywhere and everyone smiles. Ex-pupils include Jane Seymour, Stephanie Lawrence and Anna Carteret.

Entrance: By audition in your chosen specialism and, for under 16s, a 'very straightforward academic test'. Auditions have specific formats and requirements depending on course applied for.

Exit: A few stars straight into major companies eg Birmingham Royal Ballet. Some to university courses in anything from drama to physics. Many to drama or dance schools. Some gap years, some to employment.

Money Matters: 40 government funded music and dance school places plus 11 post-16 dance awards - all means-tested. 4 scholarships for 'outstanding all-round ability' - worth up to 33 per cent of all fees. Private music, music theory, SEN, word-processing and extra language help for non-English native speakers charged as extras.

Remarks: No sacrifice on the academic front if you send your budding Paige or Bussell or Flatley here – they'll get a pretty balanced regime but masses of what they love best. And, whether or not you end up with a West End star, you and they will get endless exhilaration and fun.

ASHBOURNE INDEPENDENT SCHOOL

17 Old Court Place, Kensington, London, W8 4PL

Tel: 0044 20 7937 3858
Fax: 0044 20 7937 2207
E-mail: admin@ashbournecollege.co.uk
Website: www.ashbournecollege.co.uk

• Pupils: 125 boys and girls in total (60/40 per cent split) of whom half are in the upper sixth (resits, condensed A levels or special uni foundation year), 60 in lower sixth (AS) • Ages: 16-19; plus 40 in the GCSE stream • Size of sixth form: 100 • None
• Fees: £4,500 per term for UK based students. International students applying directly from overseas £5,000 per term.
• Independent • Open days: At any time by appointment

Principal and Founder: Since 1981, Mr Michael (Mike) Hatchard-Kirby BApSc MSc (fifties) who was educated in Canada, where he did his first degree in engineering at Toronto University, followed by a Masters in maths at Birkbeck College, London. A deep-thinking, slow-speaking giant of a man, he founded the college in 1981 and is a member of CIFE (the Conference for Independent Further Education) and the British Council Education Counselling Service. Married, he has two grown up children and a toddler. Principal runs the college with the Director of Studies, Catherine Brahams, who graduated from the University of Durham with honours in English, Russian and Linguistics and also has an MA in Business and Administration. Much experience in education and in industry, mainly in the art world. The principal spends really quite a lot of time recruiting students around the world, and is very much a hands-on head. He is, one suspects, a bit of a stickler for discipline and will not tolerate any form of bad behaviour. Disobedience, bullying equals out.

The Principal actively recruits students from around the world but ensures that these are highly intelligent, motivated young people with a genuine interest in ultimately becoming university graduates in the United Kingdom. The Principal and the Director of Studies are keen to ensure that the overseas students fully integrate with the British students, hence their policy of allowing only English to be spoken on the premises (other than in language classes, obviously!).

Remarks: Tucked tidily in Old Court Place, behind Kensington Palace and next to Holmes Place Health Club, and describing itself as an independent sixth form college, the college has an additional building, that consists of an art studio, dark room, laboratory and language rooms, above the National Westminster bank opposite. Small, organised classes are ideally suited to the intimate environment with individual tuition and help across the board. Ashbourne runs a specific ESL programme for its international students in order to give them extra support. Six hours per subject (rather than the normal five), the extra period is a dedicated test period or is occasionally used for practical work.

The three year GCSE programme (Middle School) runs with max 10 students per class for the first two years and two parallel classes in the GCSE year. Ashbourne is now reluctant to accommodate students in the middle of term; however it is keen to recruit students at the beginning of any academic term, so offers real opportunities to those who need to find a place quickly. Students may, if necessary, arrive at any time and, with concentrated coaching, cope easily with the syllabus. GCSEs are regularly taken in one academic year, and one particularly bright child arrived at Easter and successfully did his GCSEs that summer term: no mean achievement. The GCSE stream has timetabled homework during school hours and can come in on Saturday mornings for extra help.

Vast number of GCSEs and A/As levels on offer – no combination too complicated, they pull in extra tutors to teach the more esoteric subjects like Russian, Arabic and accounting. 'Limitless timetable'. Results not displeasing: impressive selections of four (and five) A levels at A with only the occasional B; not quite up to the same standard as last year, but several straight A flushes (ie four A levels). Wow.

The A level stream has average class sizes of 5, rising to 10, including a marvellous media set up with a vast studio for art and design, and photography as well as a fully equipped multi-media room with video, sound-editing etc. Trails of successes getting students into the Architectural Association and the London Institute of Art. Students doing re-takes are encouraged to do an intensive extra A level in a year to improve their university prospects.

Dedicated medical school programme, designed in the main to help students get the necessary work experience, is backed with practice in interview technique and advice on uni application. The Medical School Programme has been enhanced by the college's strong mentoring links with Professor John Foreman who arranges interview practice with students in addition to giving an annual lecture about the changes in medicine. But advice and help with UCAS forms is the norm.

The International programme is basically a uni foundation course, geared to help overseas students find their feet more quickly when they do get to uni. Ashbourne offers 'many generous scholarships and bursaries each year to encourage those from both developing and developed countries to study in the UK', in particular at Nottingham university, where £750 is offered to students from the Republic of China, Vietnam and CIS.

Ashbourne is keen on organisation, and students are taught exam skills and structure. This place is about passing exams, and offers cramming in the Christmas and Easter hols for students in mainstream schools. Critical thinking and essay writing skills important. A certain amount of extra-curricular activity on offer. Ashbourne has recently set up a drama club and is expanding its teaching programme to include theatre studies as both a GCSE and A level option. One member of staff is an international chess player and successfully runs a lunchtime club for the non-sporty students. The five-a-side football team has won a plethora of trophies when in competition against its competitors in west London.

The college has successfully implemented a system of Personal Tutors to whom students report regarding their UCAS applications in particular. In addition to this, Ms Brahams runs the lower sixth diploma programme which enables the students to enjoy a demanding and challenging series of lectures which have included the principles of First Aid, critical thinking and essay technique and a talk about trial, arrest and drugs by Kensington Police.

Smoking is not permitted in college; however, is it tolerated outside. There is no uniform and the college prides itself on having an ethos not dissimilar to that found in universities.

Ashbourne finds accommodation for the international students 'some of it pretty basic but no worse than any London university digs'. Currently ranking fourth in the retake league, Ashbourne does well at what it does. Strong results, individual tuition, and really jolly civilised looking students with 20 per cent from abroad, 20 per cent foreign expats, and a diverse collection of others.

ASHFORD SCHOOL

Linked to Ashford Preparatory School in the Junior section

East Hill, Ashford, Kent, TN24 8PB

Tel: 01233 739 030
Fax: 01233 665 215
E-mail: registrar@ashfordschool.co.uk
Website: www.ashfordschool.co.uk

• Pupils: 338 girls; 95 board, the rest day. Going co-ed • Ages: 11-18. Will be 5-18 • Size of sixth form: 102 • Christian but all faiths welcome • Fees: Junior school: £1,588 - £2,808. Senior school £3,696 day; boarding £5,594 - £6,730 • Independent

Head: Since 2005, Mr Michael Buchanan (mid forties), previously the principal deputy head at Highgate School. Part of his brief there was to bring in co-education. Similar job to be done at at Ashford and head has ambitious plans to help the school and its status grow.

Academic Matters: Performing very well indeed with a non-selective entry. Many long serving, experienced staff along with several who, after completing their training at the school, felt attracted to stay. 90-96 per cent A to C grades at A level for the last 3 years, a notable achievement when you consider the challenge of Kent grammar schools – Ashford takes many whom the grammar schools have rejected. Science a strength – nine science labs, excellently staffed, many pupils taking the three sciences although physics is only the fifth most popular A level. Won the national ITN competition to send an experiment into space with the Endeavour Space Shuttle. English support (EFL) for many pupils – essential in a multi-racial environment. A fair number of dyslexics, included in usual classroom activity wherever possible. A private unit provides extra support but at extra cost.

Significant funding has been put into the IT, with an interactive whiteboard in every classroom being used adeptly by some staff, eg chemistry while boiling ice cubes the varying temperature was being plotted and displayed on the whiteboard. Mathematics is strong at all ability levels – good take-up at A level. Maths setted from the beginning of year 7 as are French, science and English – otherwise generally a mixed ability approach with 10-20 to a group. The timetable of 9 35-minute periods per day results in plenty of hot footing across the site from lesson to lesson and this may improve fitness levels but does not a 'punctual pupil make' – as was highlighted by recent inspection.

Games, Options, The Arts: Good usual variety of games including extra-curricular fencing, trampolining, judo and badminton. The pupils say the sport is getting better, probably aided by a new Astroturf and a good sports captain. Plenty of tennis courts and a small gymnasium but the school is not flush with facilities suitable for indoor games. Good-sized swimming pool. Plenty of clubs (up to 40 sometimes in one term). Young Enterprise Scheme, many pupils take the Duke of Edinburgh Award. Strong on community service – being on the outskirts of a town they have plenty of opportunity to help the disabled, charities etc.

Art work all round the school, amongst the best we have encountered – running out of superlatives at the level of design, craftsmanship of the textiles (that is approached from a fine art perspective), pottery and ceramics. Lots of students get As at A level and go on to study at St Martins, Falmouth etc. Pupils coming out of exams and clearly tired still seemed to be all heading for the art room! The sixth form goes to a chateau in France to learn and practise landscapes.

Music and drama, although perfectly adequate, pale in comparison. The pupils say that there could be a greater variety of instruments but 'what they do they do well': choir and strings. Drama department puts on one production a year; theatre studies is a popular option at A level. Good careers department, plenty of time allowed for one-on-ones with the upper sixth.

Background and Atmosphere: Founded in 1898 with the aim that the pupils should play an active role in the life of the town – still prevalent today. Christian ethos, although tolerant of all faiths, and became part of the United Church Schools Trust in 1999 (more financial backing). At the foot of the High Street, enclosed by high red brick walls with plenty of lawns and greenery stretching down the hill. The main senior school is ivy-clad and charming, with new additions built sympathetically with brick arches and rose-clad pergolas. Pathways lead to quiet benched areas for the students to meet or contemplate. The prep school moved over the summer to a spacious green site in Great Chart, a few miles outside Ashford. The pre-prep school now has expansive, bright accommodation next to the senior school.

A very international and friendly community with an emphasis on the integration of domestic and garden staff etc into the life of the school. Some internationals gripe at the food whereas some say that it is improving. 'Obviously a bigger budget these days,' says one – difficult though to achieve a menu to suit so many different cultures.

Pastoral Care and Discipline: Support from tutors, year tutors, house tutors, boarding staff, a chaplain and the deputy Mrs Williams 'the mother to us all,' say the pupils. Pastorally strong. Boarding houses recently refurbished and now with en-suite facilities and contemporary furniture. Caring but not a soft touch – zero tolerance drugs policy, though moderate drinking of alcohol at school functions is fine. No great degree of bullying although a pupil was recently withdrawn for such after due warnings. Inter-house competitions in music and drama involve younger working together with older. Boarders made to feel an integral part of the school though not allowed to return to boarding houses during the school day. Music, magic parties and a treasure hunt with clues in different languages get the pupils unself-consciously communicating in different tongues.

Pupils and Parents: A very international feel to the school with 21 different countries represented, significantly Hong Kong Chinese in the sixth form but 'we are very careful not to overdo any one culture, so that a healthy balance is achieved,' says the deputy head. The pupils seem a happy, friendly bunch, nothing toffy, and achievement and challenge is predominantly the cool culture. An impromptu quiz of the local boys' grammar school yielded a telling picture as to the girls' status – 'generally they have solid ethics'. Ashford is not leafy suburbia and many parents struggle with the fees but Ashford is expanding and there has been an influx of well-paid medics. The car park boasts a few posey cars but plenty that Jeremy Clarkson would place on his 'absolutely no fun' board.

Entrance: From independent schools, the junior school (automatic entry) and some state school pupils who were unsuccessful at the 11+. Generally non-selective. Tests and informal interviews – if the head believes they will thrive, they are accepted but if a child would struggle getting 5 A to Cs at GCSE he would recommend trying somewhere else. Quite an influx from abroad for the sixth form – lessons through the British Council to bring English up to scratch may be required before pupils are accepted.

Exit: Very few leave after GCSE; some to co-ed establishments (may return if they miss the support and commitment of the staff). Over 95 per cent go to universities.

Money Matters: Much healthier finances since joining the United Church Schools Trust five years ago – a healthy handful of scholarships on offer at age 11 and bursaries for the able child.

Remarks: In September 2005, Ashford School merged with Friars' Preparatory School, a co-ed prep with a good academic and pastoral reputation based in the outskirts of Ashford. The merged school operates in three sections – the pre-prep school (up to yr 2) on the Ashford School site, the preparatory school (yrs 3-6) on the Friars site, the senior school on the Ashford School site. The prep school is fully co-ed and boys arrive in the senior school in September 2006. We expect many of the school's virtues to survive the merger – but we will be unable to confirm that until well into 2006.

ASHVILLE COLLEGE

Linked to Ashville Junior School in the Junior section

Green Lane, Harrogate, North Yorkshire, HG2 9JP

Tel: 01423 566 358
Fax: 01423 505 142
E-mail: ashville@ashville.co.uk
Website: www.ashville.co.uk

• Pupils: 830 boys and girls, 145 board • Ages: 4-18 • Size of sixth form: 145 • Methodist • Fees: Senior school day £2,766 - £2,789; boarding £5,206 - £5,286. Junior school day £1,948 - £2,348; boarding £4,758 - £4,845. Pre prep £1,590
• Independent • Open days: October

Head: Since 2003 Mr Andrew Fleck MA BSc, early forties, educated at Marlborough College, did an MA in education at Sussex having read geology at Nottingham and studied for a PGCE at University College, North Wales. Previously deputy head of St Bede's School, Sussex, head of geography at Hurstpierpoint and teacher of geography at Ballakermeen High School. Married to Anne, with twin daughters, both at Ashville pre prep. Older pupils describe the head as confident, amiable and dynamic, younger ones as strict but nice. Loves watersports (especially sailing) and problem solving, spent four seasons canoeing in the Arctic. Believes balance and creativity are key, adds, 'sustainable success doesn't come from hammering the same nail all the time.'

Academic Matters: Good value added at GCSE, approximately 46 per cent of all passes are graded A/A* with 95 per cent graded C or above. Music GCSE is successfully replaced with AS and all pass. Art, Latin and RE traditionally strong, no let downs though slightly fewer pass German than other subjects. Approximately 50 per cent of A level passes are graded A or B, none fail altogether. Loiters round the lower regions of the independent schools' league tables but isn't highly selective in the first place. Taken as a whole, results wouldn't set the world on fire but most pupils exceed predicted potential and clearly those who are able do very well. In recent GCSE exams the school had 3 pupils in the top five nationally for German and Latin and were curriculum finalists of the National Maths Olympiad.

Average class size 18 with a maximum of 24. Shortish school day, 4pm finish and no Saturday school but option of after school care at extra cost. Six times Winners of the Institute of Directors Award for Business and Technology between 1995 and 2003 when (perhaps not surprisingly) the award was discontinued. All year 7 pupils (and year 3 in the Junior school) are screened for dyslexia using the Philips and Leonard Screening test with further testing and screening as necessary. No pupil has a statement of special educational need but the school identifies almost 100 pupils, mostly boys, as in need of special provision. Over half of these require extra English as English isn't their first language and approximately one third are dyslexic for whom specialist help is available at no extra cost. All access full curriculum, and are generally educated in the mainstream classroom by the class teacher with support as required. The norm is for pupils to be withdrawn for one period per week when assessments are carried out and help given on an individual basis. Individual Education Programmes (IEPs) are included in school reports. Those with dyslexia thrive thanks to the caring environment and carefully planned programmes of study; indeed in recent years only one child didn't get the benchmark 5 A-Cs at GCSE and most gain at least a B in English.

Games, Options, The Arts: Well-resourced music suite is home to a selection of choirs and bands. Talented musicians play in the National Children's and National Youth Orchestras but there are playing and performing opportunities for those just starting out too. Plenty of productions, latest offerings, Carmina Burana and Finzi's Imitations of Immorality well received. Sports facilities: two gyms, swimming pool, fabulous climbing wall, squash court, fitness room and ample pitches show importance of sport. All usual suspects on offer plus American influenced disc golf, something for everyone.

Background and Atmosphere: Founded in 1877 by the Methodist Church, the pleasant, uncontroversial site sprawls across an otherwise residential area. The school was evacuated to Windermere during the war as the premises were requisitioned for the war effort and used by Air Ministry. Run as a Christian school in the Methodist tradition. Plenty of well kept facilities, atmospheric Memorial Hall home to lectures, meetings and some concerts with larger gatherings filling the school hall.

Pastoral Care and Discipline: All year 7 are taken to the Lake District for a bonding weekend early in the autumn term, this receives rave reviews not only from the new pupils but also from sixth formers who work as liaison prefects. Those lucky enough to be assigned to Y7 go on the trip too.

Duke of Edinburgh Award Scheme available for pupils from year 10. Trip for older students to Malawi ties in with charity fund raising to support the Open Arms Orphanage which has close links with the school. School viewed as a day school with boarding. Four boarding houses are comfortably furnished with usual facilities: kitchens, common rooms, games areas and computers. A couple of largish dorms remain for younger boarders otherwise mainly one or two-man rooms. Biggest grumble is imbalance of pupil nationality – almost two thirds of boarders are Chinese with some resultant friction in an otherwise happy and relaxed environment. New head keen to redress the balance, possibly with enhancement of weekly boarding. Girls and boys encouraged to socialise, half-termly theme evening provides fun for all boarders. Plenty of activities on offer after school but all optional, pupils think everyone should do at least one or two to get the most out of boarding life. Fines if caught smoking with possibility of exclusion for repeated offences. Drugs: out for intending to or supplying, couple of expulsions in recent times.

Pupils and Parents: Hail from local professional and business families, quite a few first time buyers of independent education. A number of Americans from nearby Menwith Hill military base. For about ten per cent of pupils English is not a first language and overall approximately fourteen per cent come from a variety of minority ethnic backgrounds. Thriving Friends of Ashville run regular well-supported activities. Old boys: Ian Dodds (designer of the Moon Buggy), Commander Ian Grieve (head of anti-terrorism Scotland Yard).

Entrance: Interview, report from previous head and day of tests: academic and practical for year 7. Sixth form entry is via interview and satisfactory reference, minimum 5 grade Cs with grade Bs in subjects to be studied. Exams, interview and reference are norm for entry at other times. Majority of pupils come from own junior school and nearby preps: Belmont Grosvenor and Brackenfield in Harrogate, Westville in Ilkley and Richmond House and Moorlands in Leeds.

Exit: Just under a fifth leave at the end of year 6 and a third at the end of year 11. Majority of sixth formers go onto higher education, a couple to Oxbridge rest to a wide range of universities.

Money Matters: Means tested academic, music, art and drama scholarships available and worth between 10 and 50 per cent of fees. All scholarships are reviewed at the end of the stage of education ie y9 for y7 entry. Concessions available for the children of Methodist ministers and bursaries given to Service families.

Remarks: Plenty of happy pupils in a nurturing environment. High fliers tend to fly off to local competitors but those who stay thrive. Popular with locals and overseas Chinese alike. Worth a look if one school from nursery to university suits your child.

ATLANTIC COLLEGE

St Donat's Castle, Llantwit Major, Glamorgan, CF61 1WF

Tel: 01446 799 000
Fax: 01446 799013
E-mail: principal@uwcac.uwc.org
Website: www.atlanticcollege.org

• Pupils: 335 girls and boys from 76 countries • Ages: 16-19
• Size of sixth form: 335 • Non-denom • Fees: £8,450 per term (2 terms per annum) • Independent • Open days: October

Principal: Since 2000, Mr Malcolm McKenzie (fifty). South African-born, lectured at universities of Witwatersrand and Natal; left for political reasons. Studied at Oxford and Lancaster University as a Rhodes Scholar. Principal of Maru, a Pula international school in Botswana, from 1991 to 1999, then had a year's sabbatical in North America. Started Global Connections, a consortium of some 300 schools worldwide. Passionately interested in the plight of disabled people; has published extensively on academic and educational matters. Married to Judith, a ceramicist. They have a son and daughter.

Academic Matters: Students follow the International Baccalaureate Diploma (IB). This involves studying one subject from each of six groups, three at Standard Level and three at Higher Level, including two languages, science, maths, a social science and a visual or performing art. Students also study the theory of knowledge, write an extended essay and take part in community service activities. 'The IB's hallmarks are breadth, depth and coherence,' says the head. Generally 95 per cent pass the IB and, in 2004 four students out of only 50 in the world, gained 45 points, the maximum possible. 'It's wonderful for languages,' said a student. 'It's like total immersion.' Many students arrive speaking several languages and those whose English is not up to scratch are generally fluent by the end of the first term. The vaulted library stocks international newspapers and books in many languages. 'Whatever your interests, the teachers will really help you and there are the facilities to go the extra mile,' said a student.

Games, Options, The Arts: Community service activities form a major part of life at Atlantic College every afternoon. 'These occupy the place sport takes in a conventional independent school,' says the head, though there are soccer and basketball teams initiated by the students. 'We have a tradition of encouraging soccer, basketball and other sports like running and climbing where you challenge yourself, rather than competing with others. The community service activities encourage teamwork – the lifeboat crew, for example, must have total confidence in each other.' The college runs the local lifeboat and lifeguard emergency rescue cover for the area. Its social service unit and extra-mural centre work with disadvantaged people in the local community and further afield, including running outdoor activity, confidence-building, courses for children. Other students work on the college's organic farm, in a community education partnership with local schools or help run the public community arts centre on the campus.

Music is very strong. 'We are known for this among the United World Colleges (see Background) and students with a particular music interest tend to come here'. There are two full-time plus many peripatetic music teachers and a student commented on the massive selection of music scores in the library. The choir tours Europe every year. There is no standing orchestra but students form smaller groups. 'A fabulous jazz player in the first year got together with friends to put on a big band concert to raise funds for bursaries.' Drama is also strong with regular plays and festivals. Students get together with others from nearby parts of the world to put on performances – 'we take the mickey out of our own stereotypes,' said one.

In March and September the college shuts for ten days while students go off to work on their own projects. 'Some people went to Lebanon and worked in a Palestinian refugee camp,' said a student. 'It was very harrowing and they won't forget their experience. I worked in a school for children with learning difficulties and that was amazing.' The college operates a two-term system – first years arrive in September for a college year that breaks for about five weeks over Christmas then runs to late May. Second year students return at the beginning of August to spend four hours a day doing community service. 'It gives them the chance to establish themselves as a group and it's the most memorable month of their course,' says the head.

Background and Atmosphere: Atlantic College was founded in 1962, by Kurt Hahn and others and takes students from all round the world. It was the first of ten United World Colleges (UWC), in countries ranging from Swaziland to Singapore. The UWC is a global education movement which aims 'to foster international understanding, peace and justice'. Atlantic College's setting is stunning – the campus centres round the 12th century St Donat's castle, with terraced gardens stepping down to the sea. 'There's a power about the place. All the students feel it,' says the head. The grounds encompass the local parish church, and a ruined watchtower once used by smugglers (shades of Enid Blyton). The college owns and farms the surrounding 150 acres. A glass-fronted community arts centre, open to the general public, has fabulous views down to the bay. On the sea-front is the extra-mural centre, converted from cavalry barracks, and used for residential courses. Indoor and outdoor swimming pools. The tithe barn theatre shows films twice a week. Four students of different nationalities share each room in the seven co-educational residential houses. Informal atmosphere, with students and teachers on first name terms. 'We treat them more like university students than school children,' says the head. The Atlantic Appeal fundraising campaign will, over the next three years, rebuild the three oldest boarding houses, refurbish the castle and improve the IT facilities. An exciting part of this campaign has already been completed and this is the installation and commissioning of a wood burning, carbon neutral, heating plant. This is the first of its size and type in the UK.

Pastoral Care and Discipline: Students get plenty of freedom, with opportunities to visit the local pubs and towns. The head feels that alcohol is a bigger problem on the campus than drugs – 'my sense is that soft drugs are around on occasions but not a significant problem. Some of our students abuse alcohol and we are working on that. The problem is people who buy spirits and drink them fast.' Theft – perhaps inevitably in a community of people of a wide range of financial resources – is also an issue. 'The students feel very strongly about it. It is always a cancer in a boarding school.' The head would expel 'for theft, maybe for soft drugs, for regular anti-social behaviour, for dishonesty. We fall on the liberal end of the spectrum – we would try to correct unacceptable behaviour where possible.'

Pupils and Parents: Students come from some 76 countries, about a quarter from Britain. 'We expect them to be compassionate, interested in serving others, flexible, tolerant and curious,' says the head. They need to be able to adjust to the great cultural diversity and sufficiently self-disciplined to cope with the college's loose structure. The system of mixing nationalities within each bedroom seems genuinely to break down national barriers. 'Your dorm mates are like sisters,' said a student. 'If someone has a problem you have to take care of them.' An ex-student from Romania commented, however, that she would have welcomed more help with mundane matters like opening a bank account. One student said that global issues are swiftly given a real dimension, 'once I would have listened to the news then forgotten about it. But now news reports might be about the family of someone you know.' Because nearly all students have scholarships, there is a huge social as well as national mix. Most British students come from state schools. 'People think it's a posh, rich kids' school, but it's not,' said one. Ex-students include Jorma Ollila, CEO of Nokia, astronaut Julie Payette, MEP Eluned Morgan and Wang Guangya, the current Chinese Ambassador to the United Nations.

Entrance: National committees in 118 countries select students. Each has an allocation of places for overseas students. 'We don't know who's coming when they arrive in September from all over the world,' says the head. 'It's a big leap of faith for them and for us.' Academic ability is important – 'The IB is a rigorous programme, and if you're studying it in a new language, along with all sorts of other activities, you have to be jacked up to cope with it. But we are also looking for people who have demonstrated an interest in community service, an interest in international peace and justice, in environmental concerns, and have some kind of burning passion. We want them to be prepared to be ambassadors for their own countries'.

Eighty per cent of students come through the national committees, nearly all on full scholarships. British students apply to the UWC National Committee for Great Britain, filling in application forms which include a personal statement and a reference from their school. Seventy-five short-listed candidates spend a night at the college. They are interviewed by a panel of three, and play leadership and team-building games with past students, 'who are usually very astute judges of character.' Seventeen per cent are International Quota students, who have not lived in their country of citizenship for many years and so are not eligible to apply through the national committees. These, who can apply at different stages throughout the year, have a half-hour interview with the head and the director of studies.

About 45 Brits are accepted each year, the majority of these at Atlantic College but with the opportunity to attend all of the overseas colleges. The deadline for applications is during February in the year of entry.

Exit: 'We want students to go back home ready to make a difference.' About 95 per cent go to university, many to the world's top universities; others move straight to careers ranging from journalism to pottery.

Money Matters: The International Quota students pay full fees. Many British students were once supported by LEAs, but this is not longer the case, so most make some contribution, generally about half the fees. Nearly all the overseas students are on full scholarships. A good deal of the head's time is spent raising money to ensure that no-one is prevented from coming to the college for financial reasons.

Remarks: A small island of internationalism in a stupendous and improbable setting on a Welsh bay, with palm trees in the gardens and ever-changing light. The students seem uniformly passionate about the place, 'you're having such an amazing time you want everyone to know about it,' said one. Another commented on the abundance of opportunities to pursue one's interests. 'If you have a particular passion there's so much scope here for you. You come here thinking you have your ideals sorted out. You leave with more questions but a willingness to find out the answers.'

AYLESBURY GRAMMAR SCHOOL

Walton Road, Aylesbury, Buckinghamshire, HP21 7RP

Tel: 01296 484 545

Fax: 01296 426 502

E-mail: office@ags.bucks.sch.uk

Website: www.ags.bucks.sch.uk

• Pupils: 1,268 boys, all day • Ages: 11-18 • Size of sixth form: 345 • Non-denom • State • Open days: September for 11+. For 16+ mid November and late February

Headmaster: Since 1999, Mr Steve Harvey MA MSc (fifties). Previously deputy head of grammar in Lincolnshire. Cambridge educated, has spent entire teaching career in public or selective state schools, the majority of them single sex. Strong believer in single sex education. 'It avoids gender stereotyping,' he claims. 'Boys can choose the subjects they want to choose without any feeling that their particular choice doesn't have street cred.' Also believes the advantage of all-male classes is reflected in school's outstanding exam results. Trained as maths teacher, now teaches critical thinking. Earnest and enthusiastic, speaks in glowing terms of his boys and clearly wants the best for them – 'my aim is to make this school a centre of excellence in everything'. He seems to be going the right way about it.

Academic Matters: Granted Technology College status in 1997 with financial backing of well-heeled sponsor companies like British Aerospace and Research Machines. Historically strong in computer and techie areas but huge strides have been made in recent years to put arts on equal footing. History now the most popular A level choice and modern languages making major impact with student exchanges offered in French, German and Spanish, weekly video conferencing with German business and the introduction of Japanese to sixth formers from September 2001 and Italian in 2003. The most recent Ofsted report commented on the school's 'dynamic and charismatic' teaching – not just in languages but also sciences, DT, geography, history and music. We must agree – the Latin lesson we gate-crashed was decidedly more animated than we recall from our own hazy past. Good spread of subjects for GCSEs (though DT, general studies and three separate sciences a must for all) produced 100 per cent A*-C grades in 2000, a steady year-on-year climb from the 97 per cent 'low' two years before. Over 90 per cent of boys stay on to do A levels, achieving results that regularly put the school in the top 20 nationally. Some real high-flyers in the sixth form – a few get a whole fistful of A grades.

Top of the county A level league since 1995. But even so, head stresses, 'league tables are not important. What is important are the individual abilities of each pupil. If you get that right, the league tables will take care of themselves.' Excellent IT facilities networked throughout the school. Computer studies taught as stand-alone subject but also spills over into every aspect of school life, even Latin. When we visited, younger boys were engaged in on-screen science project while seniors were writing their own programs. Well-stocked library is much used and constantly updated with fresh material. Librarian told us, 'if a boy wants something that isn't here, we'll get it for him.'

Games, Options, The Arts: Not just a school for brains – brawn features strongly too. Very competitive, often extremely successful too on national playing field. One of 30 schools nationally to be awarded Sportsmark Gold status. County and national players in rugby, cricket and hockey, as well as cross-country where they've finished in top four over the last three years. Also regular winners of National Squash Tournament for schools and British Schools' Tennis Championship. Large, flat, well-tended playing fields are evidence of school's commitment to sport. Teams regularly tour as far afield as South Africa and Barbados. Less impressive gym (which has recently been refloored) but new sports hall now built. Swimming pool also updated last year and constantly in use. (Neighbouring schools and swimming clubs keep it busy.)

Extra-curricular activities seen as vital to well-rounded education as maths and English. They include art, chess, karate, Duke of Edinburgh Awards, war games, computer club (inevitably), robot wars (!) and model car racing. A thriving drama club was hoping to take up residence soon in an old barn on the school site (once they've found somewhere else to keep the lawnmower), but now a newly built drama studio is under construction. 'Grease' at the local theatre in summer. Public speaking a firm favourite. National finalists as well as producing 3 world champions.

Excellent art facilities in newish purpose-built block. Work on show (in process of being marked by examiner when we dropped in) was certainly high class. Music compulsory in years 7, 8 and 9, becoming increasingly popular option among older boys. School orchestra, jazz bands, string ensemble, barber shop, choral society and treble choir keep the musically minded fully occupied. School also has two CDs to its credit and boasts own recording studio. Head describes school music performances as 'very vibrant, very robust'. Firm believer in importance of non-academic extras. 'One of the reasons we are good in the exam room is because we have these extra-curricular activities.'

Background and Atmosphere: Founded in 1598, has been on present edge-of-town site since 1907. Original red-brick buildings set around lovely green college-style quad. Now dwarfed by later, less attractive additions (the dull exterior actually hides a surprisingly bright interior where much work is proudly displayed) and future plans include some demolition and reconstruction. Uniform, which includes black blazer with badge and striped school tie, a must for all – even sixth formers. General feeling in school of boys knuckling down and wanting to do well. One commented, 'we feel lucky to be here.' Boys positively bounce into lessons, no evidence of foot-dragging here. Class sizes no bigger than 30 with lots of interaction and input from pupils.

Pastoral Care and Discipline: Recently established peer support group helps deal with boys' concerns. Otherwise pastoral matters dealt with in-house. All boys put into one of six 'houses' on arrival and tutor put in charge of particular house group will look after set of boys throughout their schooling. Serious disciplinary misdemeanours dealt with swiftly by head. Tries to 'make the punishment fit the crime' but doesn't shirk expulsion (a number of boys have been given their marching orders since he took over) and drugs and violence are stamped on hard. Anti-bullying code pinned up on most notice boards. Boys and staff admit it happens but pupils taught how to handle it.

Pupils and Parents: Being a day school, most boys come from Aylesbury and environs though a few are prepared to travel further – from eg Milton Keynes. Mixture of backgrounds, though boys all have one thing in common and that's a drive to learn and achieve. 'We've got all sorts here,' said a prefect. 'Some from pretty poor families and others who're loaded. It's a good mix.'

Entrance: Very selective and hugely over-subscribed at a rate of 3:1. New intake of just 180 each year. Decided by examination and reports. Vast majority come from state schools, just 5 per cent from independent sector. Main admission at 11, but if places available can also join at 13, 14 and (rarely) 15 as well as small intake into sixth. Boys need seven A-C grades at GCSE to be accepted for A levels. Waiting lists.

Exit: Good representation at Oxbridge (ranked in top five state schools for successful entry in 2000), plus many other top-flight universities like Durham, Southampton, Birmingham and Bristol. Almost all (182 out of 189 leavers in July 2000) go on to some kind of further education. Favourite course last time round was computer science with geography, history and law not far behind. Section of school library devoted to higher education and careers.

Money Matters: Parents asked to contribute to cost of educational visits and activities where charging not applicable, or simply charged where it is. Fund-raising a full-time occupation for members of PTA.

Remarks: A large, fairly unattractive school that, notwithstanding, has a really good feel to it. Boys appear confident and content. And if they're lucky enough (and brainy enough) to get in, all the tools are there for them to soar to great heights.

BACKWELL SCHOOL

Station Road, Backwell, Bristol, BS48 3BX

Tel: 01275 463 371

Fax: 01275 463 077

E-mail: mailbox@backwellschool.net

Website: www.backwellschool.net

• Pupils: 1,650 boys and girls • Ages: 11-18 • Size of sixth form: 340 • Non-denom • State

Head: Since 2003, Mr Roger Mason BA BPhil (mid fifties), educated at Sussex and York Universities. Married with two children. Second headship. Committed to academic excellence and social inclusion. Recent successes in raising achievement and improving boys' performance. Keen to maintain Backwell's calm drive for individual success.

Academic Matters: Exam results above national average for GCSE (75 per cent of all entries awarded A*-C grades, with 25 per cent A or A* – but thin on the A*s) and A

level (55 per cent grades A or B). Girls do notably better than boys, as usual, and subjects show the traditional biases – English and art, girls' subjects, notably strong. Pupils' individual achievements recognised and valued in many fields beyond the academic. Not afraid of ability setting in subjects. Dual or single award sciences, French or German first language. Minimum of 8 GCSE subjects but usually 9. Options include Latin (10th subject), second modern language, drama, art, music, photography, child development and broad range of technology.

Wide choice of courses – AS, A level, GNVQ/AVCE, both commercial and general courses. Strong links with teacher-training programmes in Bristol, recruiting some of the most promising NQTs. Also very involved with developing professional support systems for young teachers. Range of extra-curricular activities includes annual Enrichment Week for all years 7-9, outdoor pursuits programme, Duke of Edinburgh Award Scheme, first aid, as well as subject-related field trips and visits. Does well in local debating and public speaking (winners of Bristol Gabbler of the Year 2001) against fierce competition from both state and independent schools. Strong links with the local community support eg work experience and two Young Enterprise companies.

Games, Options, The Arts: Facilities good with direct access to local sports and recreation centre, built on part of school site. Some parents feel sport under-powered, previous head robust in disputing this. Girls' soccer team (average age 13) are Bristol and Bath under 19 champions, boy reached finals of British schools tennis competition, one pupil plays cricket for England U15s, and many compete at local and county levels in a wide range of team and individual sports. Sport optional in sixth form. Music reputation strong, two orchestras (as well as string, wind and brass groups), senior and junior choirs give three concerts per year. Five pupils members of National Youth Orchestra in past 12 years. Plenty of opportunities for the ordinary mortal musician too. Drama ('fantastic') programme massive, a popular GCSE option and currently 60 A level theatre studies students. Regular productions in school theatre.

Background and Atmosphere: Situated on a spacious green site in a solidly middle-class rural area 8 miles south of Bristol, mixture of (mostly 1960s) buildings with a superb example of 1920s Art Deco (built, eventually, in 1954) at its core. Major efforts made (against a background of 10 per cent reduction in funding over the last 5 years) to create a pleasant and stimulating environment within the rather run-down buildings. School divided socially into Key Stage groupings and areas to allow manageable units. Pupils and staff cheerful and friendly. Uniform unpretentious and worn fairly tidily with some 'self-expression' tolerated. Girls mostly choose trousers rather than skirt. No sixth form uniform. 'Student culture' aims to develop independent learners. Atmosphere purposeful with the majority of pupils focused and well motivated. (' It is increasingly seen as 'cool' to achieve'.) Success ethic opens up possibilities for the not-so-enthusiastic and is reflected in results.

Pastoral Care and Discipline: Strong system. Lower school (years 7 and 8), houses (years 9-11) and sixth form all carefully structured so that pupils spend two years or longer with tutors who know them well. Code of discipline clearly spelt out in prospectus and sanctions applied (eg detention) after parents informed.

Pupils and Parents: Main intake from fairly prosperous out-of-town area, but there are pockets of deprivation within it. Some local parents perceive the school as rough and opt for Bristol independent schools, of which there is a wide choice. Those who do not have this option are joined by a good proportion of professional parents who choose the school for its reputation for delivery of a sound education, social spread and good results. Very lively parents' association, with social and educational activities and parents drawn in from the outset with an annual summer school (partly funded by National Lottery award) for parents and pupils, as well as the rest of the family. Good communication via newsletters as well as regular meetings. School policies (re eg drugs, homework) published in the prospectus. Pupil attendance well above national average. Pupils friendly and open, happy to talk to visitors. Caring ethic among pupils, with plenty of charitable activity and willingness of the older ones to help the younger. Lots of mixed-age co-operation in eg drama, house activities.

Entrance: Comprehensive intake, based on siblings, catchment area (mainly North Somerset villages) and distance. Parents outside area can request places and many, from both state and independent schools, do. About two applicants for every place. Applications to LEA in October of previous year.

Exit· Two thirds of year 11 pupils go into the sixth form and most go on to higher education, including Oxbridge. Most leavers remain in full time education with small proportion in employment and training.

Money Matters: Local authority funded, with constant belt-tightening constraints. Local management enables some creative balancing acts. Parents contribute to school fund to assist with societies and expeditions. Financial support available in cases of hardship in accordance with school's comprehensive ethos.

Remarks: A school where there is no cosiness, but

plenty of encouragement and support. Pupils learn early that independence and the confidence to take the occasional risk are expected and will increase their chances of success both now and later. A few move on. Not for the determinedly shrinking, but the vast majority flourish.

BADMINTON SCHOOL

Linked to Badminton Junior School in the Junior section

Westbury Road, Westbury-on-Trym, Bristol, BS9 3BA

Tel: 01179 055 271
Fax: 01179 628 963
E-mail: cbarker@badminton.bristol.sch.uk
Website: www.badminton.bristol.sch.uk

● Pupils: 300 girls, 170 board, 130 day ● Ages: 11-18; junior school 4-11 ● Size of sixth form: 100 ● Non-denom ● Fees: Senior school: £7,220 full boarding; £4,060 day. Juniors: £1,900 - £2,770 day ● Independent ● Open days: October and May - individual visits preferred

Headmistress: Since 1997, Jan Scarrow BA PGCE (late forties). Grammar school educated, married to an engineer. Deputy at Stonar prior to Badminton. Teaching career began at mixed state comprehensive in south Yorkshire. Now, a strong believer in single-sex education. Maintains pupil contact by teaching history to small blocks of the younger year groups.

Academic Matters: One of the top 10 performing schools in this country over the past five years for GCSE and A level results. Many taking maths and French GCSE early. No distinction in values between social and academic success. Setting for English, maths, science and languages without streaming; French is a must but Spanish or German are additional options. Outside specialist help available for girls with SpLD (eg dyslexia) requiring above the norm but plenty of individual support within school. Good UCAS and careers advice.

No grumbles about the additional stress of A levels – they work hard and play hard. Still plenty of time for school orchestras, choirs, D of E, community service and driving lessons. 'A busy life has always been part of their culture.' No dithering sixth formers wondering what to write for their personal statements for UCAS. Confidence oozes and they declare that they are well prepared for higher education.

Games, Options, The Arts: Competitive sport played widely and available as an AS option. Indoor heated pool, gym, tennis courts and new all weather surface. Younger girls try out all sorts of arts and crafts in the creative arts centre, many to GCSE and A2, along with textiles, jewellery making and photography. Drama is strong – seven productions a year with opportunities for front and back stage. Music continues to be traditionally strong, several taking AS in place of GCSE. 80 per cent of girls play an instrument and many two or three. Lots of orchestras, choirs, ensembles, jazz and rock groups.

Background and Atmosphere: Founded in 1858. Essentially a boarding school with day girls, where girls learnt to succeed in a man's world. Over the years in and out of fashion, currently on a high. Clustered elegant Victorian buildings mingle with purpose-built centres for science, art and music, as well as self-contained sixth form centre, impressive glass creative art centre and light airy library built by Sir Hugh Casson (ex-parent). Deceptively placed within 20 acres on the Bristol 'Downs', alongside the buzz of the city and the university with all that both have to offer with lectures, exhibitions and so on. Famous OGs include Iris Murdoch, Indian Prime Minister Indira Gandhi and Rosamund Pike, actress in the 2002 James Bond film.

Pastoral Care and Discipline: No chapel within the grounds but boarders can attend church on Sundays if they choose. Arranged activities for younger girls and trips encouraged. Sixth formers given extended freedom. Few rules in place as discipline not an issue. Successes celebrated but no individual rivalry and no dreaded prize giving. Balanced, healthy food cooked on site – the school won best school dinners in the UK last year – with own facilities for sixth formers after hours.

Pupils and Parents: Pupils from a wide geographical area. Normal termly reports and meetings. But independence encouraged and developed amongst pupils from very early on.

Entrance: At 11, 12, 13, 14 and 16 or otherwise if places become available. All-round ability preferred and those who excel in music, sport or drama but no prima donnas. English, maths and non-verbal reasoning assessed. Motivation and participation a must. High expectations which delivers high results.

Exit: Around 20 per cent each year to Oxford and Cambridge. Mostly into professions. Medicine, science research, engineering, finance and law favoured. Some to sport and the arts. Gap years becoming more popular. 100 per cent to to university.

Money Matters: As expensive as most of this calibre. Several academic, music, art and all- round scholarships offered, some up to 50 per cent.

Remarks: Definitely not breeding clones, room for indi-

viduality but an absolute common conviction in their ethos. Girls are articulate, develop a sense of confidence, self-belief and fairness, caring for each other. The secret of the school's success is in its size and a good deal of individual attention.

BALCARRAS SCHOOL

East End Road, Charlton Kings, Cheltenham, Gloucestershire, GL53 8QF

Tel: 01242 515 881

Fax: 01242 250 620

E-mail: admin@balcarras.gloucs.sch.uk

Website: www.balcarras.gloucs.sch.uk

• Pupils: 1280 boys and girls, all day • Ages: 11-18 • Size of sixth form: 280 • Non-denom • State • Open days: Last full week in September

Headteacher: Since 1996, Mr Chris Healy (early fifties) educated at Xaverian College, Manchester, Nottingham University where he read history and politics, Manchester University, where he completed his PGCE, and Leicester University for his MEd. Worked in six comprehensives before Balcarras, head of John Masefield in Ledbury and deputy head of Tewkesbury School. Married to Penelope, two daughters, both recently students at Balcarras and now at University in Bristol. Manages to combine forthright, dynamic leadership with laid-back, approachable personal style.

Academic Matters: Definitely a school on a roll. Value-added scores demonstrate extraordinary improvements between KS2 tests at 11 and all-important GCSEs. 76 per cent achieved 5 A*-C in GCSEs in 2002, 53 per cent A/B at A level. This in a town boasting one of the highest achieving selective schools in the country, Pate's Grammar, creaming off many would-be Balcarras high-flyers. Mixed ability entrants show across-the-board results, nearly all A*-E in core GCSE subjects of English, maths and science – all take double science award. Lots take art, results very good. Design and technology split into three, of which the food strand is the best performing. Very good language teaching under scrutiny by Ofsted for best practice tips. Long tradition of teaching Russian – apparently appeals to brighter kids for its 'crossword puzzle' make-up. Great enthusiasm for business studies, not entirely reflected in results. PE very popular.

Sixth form, in a separate building on site, only established seven years ago, but already results very strong. Of 18

A levels English, maths, history, chemistry, art and economics have all had particularly fine results, while psychology is almost scarily popular. GNVQ (AVCE) results exceptional – all 2001 health and social care entrants achieved distinction or merit. Boys and girls do equally well – comprehensive but flexible setting according to pure ability, not maturity. Great atmosphere in lessons – lots of smiley faces, fun projects and wide-open doors. Teachers young and keen – average age mid-thirties but many under 30 – and greatly praised by Ofsted. Around 20 statemented children and 140 special needs, many reliant on the solid extra help offered in all subjects. Numerous computer rooms and good access to around 500 terminals throughout the school.

Games, Options, The Arts: New facilities in every direction – teachers and pupils in awe of head's ability to secure funding for constant expansion. Extended music block, houses brand new keyboards, computers and lots of practice space and lots more pupils taking up partially subsidised individual lessons than used to be the case. There are orchestras and music groups and even a music tour to Tuscany in the summer. Large playing field for rugby, football and athletics, with hockey shifted onto brand new all-purpose Astroturf surface, complete with floodlights. School facilities, including large sports hall and new pavilion, act as sport centre for wider community. School expansion has freed existing rooms creating a drama studio and loads of light space for art. Oddly, there is no school magazine but the website, created and contributed to in-house, is accessible and chatty. Fine library run by professional librarians.

Background and Atmosphere: Balcarras School opened in 1986 on the site of Charlton Kings County Secondary School, itself reinvented in 1948 out of Charlton Kings Boys' School. Eighties reforms saw a shake-up in the local education system, notably scrapping single sex state schools and Balcarras became a true local comprehensive. The school was established on its present site in 1958, housing 450 pupils.

With its anonymous redbrick blocks and big, square windows, it looks every inch a product of its era, at least from the outside. New, matching blocks have been added virtually since the early days of Balcarras – first science, then geography, history and maths, then a new dining hall and the all-purpose sports hall. The sixth form centre opened in 1998, the modern languages block a year later. Only the lack of available flat space and the full stop created by Cotswold hills seem to put a lid on new construction. The beauty of its natural setting and sense of space do offset the perfunctory style of the building itself. Charlton Kings was a village, now engulfed by the outward spread of

Cheltenham, and retains a certain sense of separation – success of school credited with putting 10 per cent on nearby house prices. Tidy and well-kept inside, with sixth formers acting as reliable paid cleaners.

Pastoral Care and Discipline: Rather old-fashioned set-up for a modern comprehensive – 'kids see the value of tradition and having their status recognised'. Pupils organised into four houses and presided over by two sets of prefects, with school prefects having higher status and more responsibility than house prefects. No fixed number – anyone capable will be asked. House system basis of sound guidance and counselling system. House tutor a central source of help and guidance. House captains and vice-captains consulted periodically on school policy. Extensive action plan against drug-taking and dealing, including medical guidance, written code of conduct on bullying and guidance on behaviour – rarely needed, as such incidents are rare and children know to report problems early and talk them through with all involved. More usual problem is persuading parents that children should not stay home with minor ailments – head keen to drive good attendance ever upward.

Pupils and Parents: Confident, happy pupils, encouraged and able to work independently – faces buried in books or staring at screens all over school. Fairly good at sticking to uniform, which incorporates a school tie. Largely white, middle-class intake. Closest thing to a notable ex-pupil so far is Martin Devaney, footballer with Watford FC.

Entrance: Massively oversubscribed. No academic selection. School must be first choice, ie ruling out applications to Gloucester grammar schools. Proximity next factor, hence hike in local house prices – although outlying villages also have an overlap of catchment areas that includes Balcarras. Most come from half a dozen nearby primary schools. Siblings, being related to staff member or medical reasons may also help win a place. A couple of dozen formal appeals against rejection each year.

Exit: More than 70 per cent stay on for sixth form, with many of rest going to other schools and colleges. Majority of those go on to higher or further education in a huge range of subjects, from art foundation to business courses. Many attend local colleges, 'for reasons of cost, not ambition', says head. Bristol, Exeter and redbrick universities also popular. Five in 2005 to Oxbridge – school's reputation still to register with colleges. All pupils will have completed at least one week's work experience (in year 10) before they leave; most do another in year 12.

Remarks: Buzzing with ambition and plans, a school where every pupil is equipped with the confidence to try for what they want and the qualifications to achieve it.

BALFRON HIGH SCHOOL

Roman Road, Balfron, By Glasgow, G63 0PW

Tel: 01360 440 469
Fax: 01360 440 260
E-mail: balfronhs@stirling.gov.uk
Website: www.balfronhigh.org

• Pupils: 950 boys and girls, all day • Ages: 11-18 • Size of sixth form: 200 • Non-denom • State

Head: Since 2002, Mrs Val Corry BSc(Eng) ARSM PGCE (fifties) who was educated at Morpeth Girls' Grammar School, followed by Imperial College, London, where she read metallurgy and engineering and started her professional career as a researcher for British Steel. Into teaching via Moray House, she taught first at Grangemouth High and then ran a ceramics business before returning to teaching and leapfrogging up the academic ladder via Linlithgow Academy, Stirling High and Wallace High where she became assistant and then depute head. Very much the new girl, she has been involved with advising the government on staff development for the Advanced Highers programme and is in the midst of doing the SQH (Scottish Qualification for Headship) which encompasses leadership and key management skills, and is now working for her Masters – she is 120 points off, and is about to go back to uni to do her dissertation. She currently teaches one period of physics a week but hopes to increase this.

Academic Matters: Max class size 30. Fiercely academic, strong science school – and marvellous labs, but marvellous everything, see below – 24 students doing Advanced Higher biology, 'and huge numbers' coming through in the years below, biology lab has a greenhouse incorporated into its roof. Labs are an astonishing carpeted 90 metres square. Other sciences not far behind, good solid run of the mill academia, 'nothing esoteric' in the timetable, French and German on offer, Gaelic 'might be possible' as indeed is Russian. Flexible learning not a problem and sixth formers and local adults (evenings) can log on to do distance learning courses, psychology particularly popular. Computers abound, three pupils per machine, and emails for all. Mrs Corry is 'looking at' re-active white boards – trouble is they cost around £4,000, and you can buy an awful lot of books with £4,000. Humanities divided and pupils do either history or geography during their first year and the other in the year following. No problems with sup-

port for learning, the state can and will supply everything, one-to-one where needed, plus scribes etc; three full-time and two part-time staff plus a child ed psych on hand. This is an inclusive school, capable of dealing with physical handicaps (lifts all over the shop). Terrific library overlooking the atrium, with views out over the games pitches to The Campsies.

Games, Options, The Arts: School incorporates a fabulous leisure complex with pool, sports hall and weights much used by the local community and open from 7am to 10pm 365 days a year. Fantastic fitness then. Excellent swimming (25-metre pool), Astroturf, pitches and athletics track. Masses of games after school, Stirling Council (and the lottery) provide a sports co-ordinator; rugby good – and both national and international players in the school. Art is state of, with every possible medium catered for and finished products creeping on to the walls and a rather natty patio. Computer-linked CDT with every machine imaginable. First and third years do home economics – flash new kitchens with microwaves. Terrific theatre and drama, the theatre available to the community, and masses of music; with local involvement. Work experience for all at 14. Masses of trips and exchanges, for culture as well as skiing etc, Japanese exchange in November, school will underwrite those who can't afford it. Huge amount of charity work and much local involvement.

Background and Atmosphere: This is a split-new school, formally opened in May 2002 by Helen Liddle, Secretary of State for Scotland. Cathy Jamieson, MSP and Minister for Education and Young People, celebrated the partnership between Stirling Council and Jarvis by sticking the first leaf on the 'school tree of learning' which climbs up the corner of the atrium. How on earth later leaves will be added is anyone's guess – the tree is some thirty-odd feet high. The atrium adjoins the dining room, pupils bring their own or use swipe cards (which conceals the free school meals problem). This is a magnet school. State of the art in every dimension, each subject has a pod of rooms off the main core, terrific views, marvellous outside area – it does occasionally shine North of the Highland Line. Fortunately there is some scope for expansion, for, having built houses on the adjacent site where the old school stood (now demolished), the school roll is already dangerously near capacity. The school, built under a PFI/PPP will be run by Jarvis (of Railtrack fame) for the next 25 years, they provide the caterers and do all maintenance, the final design was a combination of staff and local community involvement. Slight big brother feel, all the rooms are networked for sound (as well as inter/intra netted) and at 9.55am and again at 10.05am, loudspeaker announcements about sin on the school bus and extra music lessons boomed over the speakers. Electronic notice board advertising weekend jobs at the local pub – £3.70 an hour. School became a community school proper in 2003 but the old boards still reassuringly in place. School uniform for all, trainers out, otherwise just polo shirts, sweatshirts etc; smart blue blazers with green trim loaned annually to sixth formers, who must have them cleaned before they are returned. Houses – Camsie, Endrick and Lomond – really only used for games.

Pastoral Care and Discipline: State system of guidance teachers, good PSHE and anti-bullying strategies in place. 'Balfriending' is a buddy system between first and sixth years which really works. Masses of contact, sixth pick up problems early; bullying incidents are logged, the victim supported and the bully sanctioned – and sanctions range from verbal warnings through 'the imposition of a written exercise' to temporary or even permanent exclusions and ed psychs etc.

Pupils and Parents: Mainly country folk, so friendly and welcoming children, few from ethnic minority backgrounds. Good middle class ethos prevails; a teacher at one of the local private schools (so discounted education) has sent his child here as the facilities are 'so much better'.

Entrance: From local primaries, 30 placing requests at the moment.

Exit: Few leave after Standard Grades, rather more post-Highers. Most to Scottish Unis and trad three or four to Oxbridge.

Remarks: Stunning school, happy staff, good work ethos, some of the best views in Scotland. Worth moving to the Trossachs for.

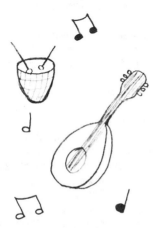

BANCROFT'S SCHOOL

Linked to Bancroft's Preparatory School in the Junior section

611-627 High Road, Woodford Green, Essex, IG8 0RF

Tel: 020 8505 4821
Fax: 020 8559 0032
E-mail: admissions@bancrofts.essex.sch.uk
Website: www.bancrofts.essex.sch.uk

- Pupils: 745 boys and girls (equal numbers) • Ages: 11-18
- Size of sixth form: 205 • C of E, but Jews and Muslims properly provided for • Fees: Prep £2,380; senior £3,140 • Independent
- Open days: June, September and October

Head Master: Since 1996, Dr Peter Scott (fifties). A graduate of St John's College, Oxford, he taught for 17 years at Charterhouse, where he was a housemaster, and was deputy head at the Royal Grammar School, Guildford. He has also been an inspector of schools and has written 8 text books on chemistry. A young-ish, energetic head with a frequently-deployed smile and a firm handshake, he states that he is 'committed to getting the best out of every individual in the school.' Bancroft's seems to attract, or perhaps create, very loyal headmasters; Dr Scott was only the sixth head to be appointed in the twentieth century.

Academic Matters: The record here is verging on the stupendous. 100 per cent 5 A*-C at GCSE; 50 per cent get at least 8 A grades which makes it the highest-achieving co-educational school in the country, in terms of GCSEs and A levels, and has been for the last 2 years. Pupils are repeatedly reminded of this fact and it's fair to say that a pretty academic atmosphere reigns. Latin is compulsory for the first 2 years and ancient Greek is an option. Some interesting AS levels on offer, including critical thinking and philosophy of religion. There is a teacher with responsibility for diagnosing and helping dyslexic pupils but if you had dyslexia in any but its mildest form, you simply wouldn't be at this school.

Games, Options, The Arts: A strong tradition of drama. Every year there's an inter-house drama competition, as well as a junior play, a middle school play and a senior play (serious stuff, eg Murder in the Cathedral, The Crucible). Rugby, hockey, cricket, netball and tennis are the principal sports; there are squash courts and a swimming pool. John Lever, ex-England bowler, is on the PE staff.

The school orchestra puts on a concert once a term. The school choir puts on a big annual concert at the

Drapers' Hall. Wide variety of clubs to join – the electronics club boasts 3 winners of the Young Electronic Designer Award. 10 gold and 22 silver D of E Awards last year. There's a Sea Scouts troop and CCF. Pupils produce an annual magazine, The Bancroftian. Also hot on trips and exchange visits. There are annual exchanges with France, Spain, Germany, Greece and even New Zealand.

Background and Atmosphere: Founded in 1737 by the Drapers' Company on behalf of Francis Bancroft as a school for poor boys. The original site was in Mile End; the school moved to leafier Woodford in 1889. The building is a red-brick Victorian pile with towers and crenellated walls, a large quadrangle with a war memorial in the middle, playing fields, a chapel and a wood-panelled library – same architect and design as Selwyn College, Cambridge. It's surrounded by Epping Forest on two sides and busy roads on the other two; large, expensive houses sit on the other side of the busy roads.

Pastoral Care and Discipline: The school is 'very keen on mutual respect', says the head. There is a written anti-bullying policy but in fact bullying isn't a problem here. There's a general atmosphere of good behaviour and politeness. All sixth form pupils are monitors, with responsibility for ensuring orderly lunch queues etc. They have the power to give detentions but this hasn't been done within living memory.

Pupils and Parents: There's quite an ethnic mix here. About 30 per cent of pupils are of Asian origin; there's also a strong Jewish contingent. Chapel is attended by most pupils but there is also a Jewish assembly and Muslim prayers. Pupils mainly drawn from affluent Essex suburbs rather than from east London. The boys wear dark grey suits and the girls wear Lindsay tartan kilts (or maroon skirts in summer). It's a crowded, bustling school – not quite enough space, really, but it's a good-natured sort of bustle. Kids are feisty but friendly. A parent remarks, 'there's a feeling of oneness about the school, from the prep school to the sixth form.' Alan Davies, the comedian and actor, is an Old Boy. So is David Pannick, Britain's youngest ever QC.

Entrance: Competitive entrance exam along the lines of the 11+. Of about 400 candidates, about 60 are selected (the rest of the annual intake is drawn from the prep school). The exam is on a Saturday but there is an alternative Wednesday sitting for Orthodox Jewish candidates.

Exit: Almost all pupils go on to university. 20 or so to Oxbridge.

Money Matters: Bancroft's has a strong link with the Drapers' Company, which offers a number of scholarships, usually for half or a third of the full fee. The school also awards six of its own Assisted Places each year. In total, about 170 pupils receive financial support.

Remarks: There's a certain amount of pressure to succeed academically but it wouldn't be fair to call it a hothouse. The school encourages plenty of interests besides academic ones. If your child is bright, they'll probably enjoy themselves here. If they're not, they probably won't get in.

BASIL PATERSON TUTORIAL COLLEGE

66 Queen Street, Edinburgh, Midlothian, EH2 4NA

Tel: 0131 225 3802
Fax: 0131 226 6701
E-mail: info@basilpaterson.co.uk
Website: www.basilpaterson.co.uk

- Pupils: 35 boys and girls. EFL College operates separately on same site • Ages: 16-19 (but currently some in their 20s)
- Size of sixth form: 20 • Non-denom • Fees: On application
- Independent

Principal: Since 2004, Mr Colin M Smith MA, previously Depute Principal St Margaret's School, Edinburgh. Educated at George Heriot's school followed by St Andrews University, where he read French and German. Having taught extensively in Scotland and been Depute Principal for 9 years, he is now in the process of changing Basil Paterson into a 'Scottish Sixth Form College' with a full-time programme as well as into a centre of flexible tuition (any subject, any level, any time). Twilight, evening and weekend tuition are now on offer. He leads the EFL College as well.

Academic Matters: Edinburgh's oldest and most famous tutorial college, BP was founded in 1929, and grafted onto Dugdale's Secretarial College (now defunct) which started in 1893. Currently owned by the Oxford Intensive School of English (OISE). Huge number of subjects on offer: Scottish Highers, Advanced Highers, Intermediates and Standard Grades plus all three of the English exam boards GCSE and AS/A levels. A team of part-time tutors to cover the various examination subjects (Edinburgh is rich in tutors). Max class size eight, plus many individual lessons where necessary. One well-equipped lab on site. Four lessons tuition per subject for Standard Grade/GCSE per week, five for Highers/AS Levels and six for Advanced Highers/ 'normal two year' A levels. An accredited exam centre for all four boards. Impressive success rate, 'but it does rather depend on the individual student'. Good careers advice, help with UCAS and clearing. The full-time course includes supervised study, general skills classes as well as the social programme.

Popular Easter revision courses in (almost) everything. In addition, flexible tuition is offered in any subject (twilight/evening and weekend). This is proving very popular with both parents and pupils. A suite of evening classes will soon be offered to the local community and beyond.

Background and Atmosphere: The college is now in superb new premises at 66 Queen Street, formerly home to one of Scotland's most prestigious solicitors' companies. It comprises two light airy Georgian buildings joined together with some original ceilings still visible and boasts state-of-the art computers, a student common room and student study centre, a wireless area for students to use their own laptops, 12 excellent classrooms and an outside cafe area. Classes can flow over into the EFL side during the busy Easter period. Outside café area. New computers with email for all. Good self-study area.

Pastoral Care and Discipline: Students on the whole live with families or in flats in and around Edinburgh, accommodation no problem for those from abroad or further afield. But students are expected to take a certain amount of responsibility for their own studies. The new social programme combines activities for both tutorial and EFL students. Each student and parent/guardian must sign a student support agreement.

Pupils and Parents: Currently 10 per cent from abroad plus first-time candidates, retakes and those hopeful of upping previous marks.

Entrance: An interview with the principal as well as a report from the previous school attended.

Remarks: Up and running and delivering the goods.

BEARSDEN ACADEMY

Morven Road, Bearsden, G61 3SU

Tel: 0141 942 2297
Fax: 0141 942 4681
E-mail: office@bearsdenacademy.e-dunbarton.sch.uk
Website: www.bearsdenacademy.org

• Pupils: 1,255 boys and girls (55/45), capped at 210 first-year intake (seven classes of 30); all day • Ages: 11-18 • Size of sixth form: 350 • Non-denom • State

Head: Since 2000, Mr P Michael (Mike) R Doig MA FRSA PGCE (mid fifties), who was educated at The High School of Glasgow (then in the state system), read mod langs at Glasgow University and did his teacher training at Aberdeen. Started his teaching career at Milngavie, followed by head of langs at Cumbernauld High School, was depute head at Kirkintilloch High and assistant head at Hermitage Academy in Helensburgh. Then head for 8+ years at Cumbernauld High. A state school baby then. He still teaches the 'occasional spot of PSE but it would be unfair to have a timetabled slot'.

Married, with two children who went through the school but who are now graduates and, as they say in Scotland, he stays locally. He arrived in the school after an unsettling period, the previous head having retired early through ill-health, and the one before that died in post. Bearsden was a school in a timewarp. However, now, head says, 'the school is in good heart again', with the staff 'united' after some pretty 'dramatic changes'. Head is 'largely autonomous' as far as choosing staff is concerned and is obviously running a successful school – the school that the Bearsden 'youngsters' ('nice neutral term') deserve. Although appearing almost horizontally calm and relaxed, head admits that life can occasionally be 'interesting'. An iron fist in a velvet glove perhaps?

Academic Matters: School takes Standard, Intermediate I, Intermediate 2, Highers and Advanced Highers. (Pupils may also be presented for both Intermediate 2 and 1 instead of the Standard; they have different weighting.) German and French but no Spanish, and three separate sciences; maths and English results had been disappointing (although head claimed 'they were the best in East Dumbarton') but now looking up – school says 'consistently strong'. New IT staff improving results are consistently strong. Youngsters (follow the drift) are setted in their second year for English, maths, French and sciences. Not a vast choice of subjects but totally adequate with the non-academic well represented. Most pupils take eight subjects at standard grade.

Pupils are allocated a guidance teacher during their last year at primary, who acts as tutor throughout their time in secondary. Smashing new library which also includes a careers office and much used sixth form study centre. Six fully equipped computing/business rooms – the library has a well-equipped computer room – fabulous dedicated space (more books needed). Work ethos is important here, ditto homework, and homework diary must be signed by parent or guardian but pupils can complain 'to their Guidance teacher if they feel that they are unable to cope with homework'.

Support for learning throughout, with learning support staff visiting the linked primary schools to ensure a smooth transition. Four support for learning assistants, who work with children both on an individual basis and in class, scribing if need be; no diagnosed ADHD, one or two 'high end' Asperger's – head 'is aware of their needs' – and they are integrated wherever possible. 'Can't cope with wheelchairs' (except in the new library) but no problem with a profoundly deaf child who gets peripatetic support. EAL on hand, over 22 different nationalities in the school, many of whom do not speak English at home.

Games, Options, The Arts: Stunning new games hall and, as a community school, this is much used by locals too. Good spread of games pitches; school does remarkably well at rugby, football, with hockey and athletics well-represented. Outstanding success in basketball, a former national basketball coach is head of the PE squad and the school was runner-up in the Scottish finals. No tennis courts or swimming pool but skiing, snowboarding are popular options, with regular trips abroad – the Alps as well as Aviemore. Superb home economics facility, with pupils learning how to wash and iron, as well as cook and operate electronic sewing machines.

Cultural trips to Paris and Florence and large successful art department, with fabric design as well as pure art. Music fantastic, choirs and orchestras of all description and a very sedate but popular rock band. Drama extra-curricular but a popular club – pantomime and Shakespeare in alternating years. Long standing Young Enterprise. Work experience in fourth year, with loads of private placements. Clubs highly popular, and the board game club specialises in esoteric conundrums which make the mind boggle. The web club is also well attended. Massive charity input from seniors in particular, with five-figure sums raised every year. World Challenge Expeditions to Thailand in 2003 and Mongolia in 2005.

Background and Atmosphere: Perched in the midst of leafy Bearsden and surrounded by seriously grand houses (whose denizens must love all the playing fields) the school was built in 1958 to a 1938 design, and has long outgrown its building. The site is littered with temporary structures and there are plans afoot to re-face and re-build (with a spot of selling of surplus land for little boxes to finance the new-build – derelict land we were assured – actually it looked really quite pretty). The alternative suggestion is a total new-build on the outskirts – we are looking at around eight million quids' worth of real estate. and well-maintained. Grounds tidy and well-maintained with staff parking in droves. Classrooms fairly old-fashioned but perfectly serviceable and in good heart; jolly canteen, though pupils often prefer 'to pop down to the cross for a carry-out'. Prefectorial duties include keeping a weather eye on behaviour around school premises. Pupils all neat and tidy in school uniform which is mandatory, with a very strict dress code – no advertising, track suit tops, denim, baseball caps or trainers outwith PE and particularly no football colours or any item of clothing which could potentially cause friction.

Pastoral Care and Discipline: Exemplary. School has a very positive attitude to bullying – 'Friends against Bullying', senior pupils volunteer to work with the first year group, visit them first thing each day and wear badges indicating that anyone who feels they are being bullied can come to them to discuss the problem. There are also 'supervised' lunch-time clubs that youngsters can come to, as well as study-buddies. Chaplaincy team of five – Church of Scotland, Baptist, all take a year each – Church of Rome refuses to allow Catholic priests to join this ecumenical team which is a bit odd considering one of the local primary schools (St Andrews) is Catholic and 85 per cent of their pupils come on. Room set aside during Ramadan for prayer.

Strong discipline code, range of punishments, from Behaviour Card which must be signed by all staff, with the ultimate sanction being exclusion. Pupils who persist in being disruptive or who are late are sent to the Behaviour Support Base for the rest of the lesson which they have disrupted and often for the next lesson in that subject; they also have detention at lunch-time. Head will exclude but has done so only temporarily so far; 'don't tolerate offences to staff'. 'No significant' drugs problem, 'hand on my heart, we've had nothing in the school as such' – they were patted on the back by drugs supremo Maxi Richards, who has an input in the senior PSHE programme.

Pupils and Parents: 5 per cent on free school meals; a good middle class bunch from Milngavie, Bearsden,

Canniesburn as well as Drumchapel, north west Glasgow. 'Somewhat' oversubscribed, school has a fair reputation and is handy for buses and trains. Priority to siblings, followed by East Dumbartonshire location (distance from front door to front door). Large number of ethnic backgrounds, over 100+ youngsters from non-English speaking families – most Asians and Chinese but Africans, middle eastern and east Europeans are well represented. Absolutely no problems with the mix, the school is a 'seriously harmonious group'. Good PTA with parents getting quite deeply involved with the school programme of speakers and interview skills as well as the trad charity role.

Entrance: Automatic from local primaries; then by formula. New arrivals can get immediate entry if space available.

Exit: 10 per cent leave post-Standard to do further education elsewhere or go into employment. Indeed one such came to the door to have his application signed by Mr Doig whilst we were with him – three weeks into the winter term and he'd decided he would be better off elsewhere. A few leave post-Highers with university entrance qualifications but most stay for sixth form, notably those going to uni down south. Majority of leavers go to central Scottish universities – no particular bias – industry, dentistry and medicine popular (12 medics in 2004). Regular two or three to Oxbridge annually. Some to study music, some to art school. Youngsters tend to go straight to uni, not a lot of gap year take up.

Money Matters: State, with help on hand to supplement low-income families to go on school trips. Two forms of financial help available to those who stay at school after the age of 16. Footwear and clothing grant for those whose family or guardian qualify as low-income; and the other, the Scottish Executive Education Maintenance Allowance Scheme (EMA), for any pupils living in the area and going to school in East Dunbartonshire.

Remarks: A positive school, firmly setting its sights on the 21st century, with an expert captain at the helm.

BEDALES SCHOOL

Linked to Dunhurst (Bedales Junior School) in the Junior section

Church Road, Steep, Petersfield, Hampshire, GU32 2DG

Tel: 01730 300 100
Fax: 01730 300 500
E-mail: admissions@bedales.org.uk
Website: www.bedales.org.uk

- Pupils: 446 boys and girls. 302 boarders, 144 day • Ages: 13-18 • Size of sixth form: 167 • Non-denom • Fees: Boarding £7,845; day £6,040 • Independent • Open days: Five each year

Head: Since 2001, Mr Keith Budge MA (forties). Educated at Rossall, read English at University College, Oxford and PGCE from Oxford. Rugby blue. Previously a housemaster at Marlborough and head 1995 to 2000 of Loretto. Married to Moony. Three children – one at Dunhurst, two at Marlborough.

A complex character. 'High calibre,' said a parent, 'But not a leader, not a visionary which is what Bedales requires.' We have previously called him a disciplinarian and some parents hold on to this view but others differ, saying 'he simply draws a line.' Whatever his gifts, they do not seem to lie in public relations and he can come across as cold/shy/arrogant, depending on one's point of view. Has weathered last year's troubles over the school's structure in the face of loudly voiced revolt from many parents (see below), and has brought to completion a stylish £7.5 million building project that would have been the undoing of many heads. Appears to have finally convinced sceptical parents that he is not set on turning Bedales into another Marlborough and that he is here for the duration. After five years as head, is finally becoming an accepted part of the furniture.

Academic Matters: Good results – notably better than other schools based on non-conventional principles. Students (they are not called pupils here) taught to organise themselves like university students. Average class size 15 with 22 max. Most subjects doing well. Maths, history and modern languages (how refreshing) particularly shine. Science well taught (chemistry classrooms must be best in the country) and head keen to point out that a fifth of Bedalians read science or engineering at university. Art, design and theatre see no more than average results. English, economics and art the most popular A level subjects. Plenty of spiritual discussion and theology and ethics are compulsory subject for all in year 13. Setting in maths and languages.

One sixth of the pupils is classified as having special educational needs of mild to moderate severity and are given help by three qualified special needs teachers – who also increasingly aid children without specific learning problems who need help improving their organisation and study skills. The whole is known as 'learning support' and is eulogised by those it supports and their families.

From September 2006 the school will offer a new curriculum. At the lower end of the school, there will be increased integration with the curriculum of (junior school) Dunhurst. In the GCSE years, Bedales students will take core GCSEs plus one or two others to a maximum of seven plus 'Bedales-accredited courses', which will include some that are parallel to GCSE courses, some which will replace GCSE as a preparation for A level, some which will combine aspects of several subjects and may underpin work in a variety of A levels, and some (such as courses in Outdoor Work) that are independent of any external assessment programme. The courses are intended to be ambitious, wide-ranging, creative and less restricting than the current GCSE straightjacket.

Games, Options, The Arts: Enlightened. All students must participate in games or 'outdoor work', the latter a godsend to youngsters who loathe lugging themselves around a rugby field. Three quarters opt for games. PE once a week for all (except the upper sixth). The school is almost comically sensitive about outsiders, like this guide, not taking Bedales' games seriously. It points out its sporting achievements, particularly in boys' and girls' tennis, hockey (four boys from Under 14 team represented East Hampshire, one-half of Under 17 Girls Hockey County squad from Bedales) and athletics. Bedales has poured money into its sports hall, indoor pool (renovated 2002) and floodlit Astroturf, and even rugby is starting to get a look-in. However, we still beg to suggest that it is a rare parent who chooses Bedales for its prowess at games. Quite the contrary, many choose it for the reverse. Still, we receive the odd moan from parents who want the school to do better at sport – lord knows why.

Outdoor work involves gardening, organic farming, tree-planting and livestock husbandry on school's farm. Also on offer are spinning and weaving (of farm's own wool, later used by textile department), blacksmithing, riding, baking bread in a wood-burning oven. We think the school would do better to crow about these phenomenal and unique opportunities rather than bang on about sport – perhaps Keith Budge agrees, as he told us that he would like to see more emphasis given to outdoor work. Quality art – though a few parents we spoke to called it elitist and say it is aimed at the talented few rather than the inept many. In students' first year they spend a half term experimenting with different artistic genres: painting and drawing, pottery, craft, textiles, technology. School runs own art gallery showing work of outsiders as well as students. Brilliant craft (DT) produces near-professional creations.

Amazingly high standards in music. 60 per cent of students learn at least one musical instrument, 20 per cent learn two or more, and many reach diploma level. Lots of concerts and opportunities to play in front of an audience, including a weekly performance for the poppets at nearby Dunannie pre-prep. Several school choirs encourage the masses and the most talented few. Music technology on its way in. Spectacular theatre, with Japanese-influenced architecture, used by outside companies and the public. Twice-a-week activities programme with options like 'tools for self-reliance', hydrotherapy (along with wide range of sports!). Lots of opportunity for creating your own thing.

Background and Atmosphere: Founded by visionary J H Badley in 1893 as an antidote to the education he received at Arnold's Rugby, with its emphasis on muscular Christianity, classics and rugby. Instead, the school would teach academic subjects alongside arts and crafts, rural skills, outdoor work and tolerance. Girls were admitted in 1898, partly to solve the horrendous bullying problem that had exploded in Badley's atmosphere of free choice.

Over the century since then Bedales has had to make periodic concessions to the mainstream – mostly for economic reasons – expanding in size and catering more for local children. Many mainstream schools have moved in the other direction, incorporating Bedales' 'alternative' approach, but the school remains distinctive and given the events of 2004-5 is likely, though not certain, to stay that way.

In September 2004, the board of governors announced plans to change Bedales' three school formula (pre-prep, prep and 13-18 senior school) to a two school system. In so doing, Dunhurst and Dunannie would have merged into a single 3-11 prep, and the entry age of Bedales would have come down to 11. It is no exaggeration that the storm of fury that this plan unleashed shook the school to its core setting parents against governors, parents against parents, governors against governors. 80 per cent of the Bedales' parents committee voted to keep the 3-tier system and the board of governors ultimately voted to back this by a majority of one, leading to the resignation of the board's chairman. For now, both sides have gone off to lick wounds. The governors have all but vanished under an invisibility cloak and are, parents say, conspicuously silent. 'There is a feeling of the craft being a little rudderless at present,' said a long-term parent 'which for the moment is no bad thing.' Meanwhile the dust has settled and the school has emerged surprisingly fit and well. It still offers parents a genuine alternative and, for all the disharmony, there are few parents who do not appreciate this.

That said, the school is not the school it was five years ago. Discipline has been greatly tightened, the trust that used to govern relationships with pupils has been replaced by eg the breathalyser, staff made much more 'accountable'. And perhaps that is inevitable. Many aspects of the old Bedales way of doing things are hard for conventional locals to accept – and their custom is increasingly important. Staff and students still call each other by their first names (reflecting the reality of the underlying relationship – hard for staff trained elsewhere and parents wanting respect from their children). Still no uniform – though the current Bedales fashion tends to muted colours, well cut and clean, this was not always so. The expression of opinions of all kinds continues, but also in a more muted way; mass student protest (eg over the abolition of 'Martin's Game') is dealt with politely – but without concessions – so the motivation for it fades; the B-Daily has lost its cutting edge – at least as far as opinions on school management are concerned, though it remains a startling read for conventional parents. Rules are increasingly enforced, under (by general standards) quite a fierce policy document.

Stunningly beautiful grounds, with arts and crafts style buildings making the whole look like some sort of Quaker or Pennsylvania Dutch utopian community. An aesthetic wonderland, with care and attention to detail in everything – a fertile setting for scholarship. Eyesore 'temporary' huts (have been up thirty years) now largely replaced by sumptuous new classroom/admin block (2005) within Bedales' arts and crafts tradition. Lovely grade I listed library is a war memorial with names of the dead listed along the walls. Food could be better.

Pastoral Care and Discipline: New head has discipline as a priority. 'It had got very lax,' said a student, referring to sex, drugs, illegal drinking, smoking, 'but now multi-busted people are expelled.' Students aware the school has a mostly-undeserved reputation for loose behaviour and are keen to rebut this. Two boarding houses with mixed-age dormitories, girls in Steephurst and boys in Boys' Flat. Noticeably fewer girly pictures on boys' dorm walls than in other schools. Final year students reside in a co-ed boarding house, with single-sex corridors. Sixth form bar open four times a week. Students expected to look after one another eg students caught accompanying a smoker will be given the same punishment as the smoker. Punishments include 'useful work' eg litter clearing and community service. Some parents have expressed concerns about cases of anorexia in this environment where being thin and beautiful is at a premium.

Pupils and Parents: Students a confident, verbal lot, concerned with one another's unique qualities and letting the individual bloom – order of priorities for them is work, then relationships. Not a lot of self-esteem problems among these kids. Extremely at ease talking to adults. If that's just not your child, be careful of plunging in here, but if you are the sort of parent who believes in reasoning with your child rather than barking out 'because I said so', then this could be the school for you. The students look little different from those at other no-uniform schools except for being a bit better-looking on the whole.

Parents with strong opinions and 'bloody impossible to govern,' according to one dad. For good or ill, Bedales parents 'mind terribly' what goes on here. It's not just the fees and natural concern for one's offspring. There is a depth of feeling here that has no parallel elsewhere. Making the decision to send one's child to Bedales is to take an exhilarating plunge – 'it's a way of life,' said a mum, 'and you have to continually defend yourself against those who question your decision to educate your children here – which increases your loyalty to the place.'

40 children of overseas Brits. 27 foreigners, ten with English as a second, but fluent, language (there is ESL tuition). Parents in media, arts, the British Council, Foreign Office, and professions. Famous OBs include successful musicians, artists and craftsmen (including the son and daughter of Princess Margaret), two ambassadors to Russia, business magnates, academics and actors, notably Daniel Day-Lewis and Minnie Driver.

Entrance: 88 students at 13, 60 per cent from Bedales' junior school, Dunhurst, the rest from preps mainly in London and the south east. 20 join at sixth form. At 13, candidates for entry spend two days at the school shortly before beginning of spring term preceding September entry. Applicants sit standard maths, English and reasoning tests, have a groovy time with art and games, and are 'observed' in their interactions with others. Will they fit in, deal with the freedoms of Bedales, show other talents? Used to be as much a chance for the school to sell itself as it is a way of vetting potential students, but now more of a real test (though league table ambitions are not yet overt). Overseas students may sit the tests abroad and UK applicants may be interviewed at other times of year, though the school discourages this. School is still full, despite last year's tumult. Indeed, Bedales is now taking a few extra day pupils, presumably to help fund its ambitious building programme.

Exit: Up to a quarter leaves after GCSE, often because they have been in the Bedales conglomerate since age 3 and need a change. Most go to sixth form colleges, almost none to other independent schools. Post-A level leavers mainly to degree courses; around 20 per cent to art foundation courses. Most popular destinations over past 5 years have been Leeds, Bristol, Oxford and Edinburgh (in that order). The net is wide beyond that but, in general, an impressively top-drawer list.

Money Matters: 13+ scholarships available for exceptional ability in almost anything, plus a separate category for music. At 16, scholarships are given for academics, art, design and music and, occasionally, science. From September 2006, a number of awards will be made to drama students at the end of their first year in the sixth form. NB All scholarships, with the exception of music, are means-tested. If you fail the means test, the maximum award is £750.

Remarks: Getting back on track and we look forward to seeing the new curriculum in action. Still good for 'individuals,' articulate nonconformists, and people who admire such qualities. But less distinctive than in the past. Said a parent who weathered Bedales' recent turbulent times, 'it wasn't perfect but if I had to go back and choose a school again, knowing everything I know now, I would choose Bedales all over again.'

BEDFORD HIGH SCHOOL

Bromham Road, Bedford, Bedfordshire, MK40 2BS

Tel: 01234 360 221
Fax: 01234 353 552
E-mail: officesec@bedfordhigh.co.uk
Website: www.bedfordhigh.co.uk

• Pupils: 865 day girls, 135 boarders • Ages: 7-18 • Size of sixth form: 200 • Christian ethos but respects other faiths • Fees: Junior school £6,285; Senior school £8,865. Boarding: Junior school £13,671; Senior school £16,251 • Independent • Open days: January and April

---

Head: Since 2000, Mrs G (Gina) Piotrowska, MA (forties). Married, no children. Educated at The Convent of the Holy Ghost in Bedford then University of Sussex before qualify-

ing as an English and drama teacher. Stayed in the Bedford area until 1991 when she became deputy head of The Barclay School in Stevenage. Appointed head of St Mary's School, Cambridge in 1998 before joining Bedford High School two years later. Taught in comprehensives in the maintained sector for 23 years and now firmly believes in the added value the private sector and single sex education offers, particularly for girls. Very approachable and friendly. Bowls of sweets (for parents and younger visitors) and cuddly toys sit on tables in her large, elegant office. Still 'gets a buzz every morning when the organ in the hall starts up ready for assembly.' Wants pupils to take risks and be challenged.

Academic Matters: Not as selective as you might imagine but very good results as far as one can judge without seeing value-added results. Setting in maths throughout the school and in English from year 9. Science groups are setted in the GCSE years. Class sizes 22 for seniors and 16 for juniors. Small groups for A level. 83 per cent A*- B at GCSE, biology and maths even stronger. Dual award and separate sciences. 30 subjects at A level as well as the International Baccalaureate in 15 subjects – introduced in 2002 and growing in popularity. 71 per cent A/B at A level; sciences, particularly biology and chemistry, popular and successful. Languages also popular with French, Spanish, Latin and German doing well. All 16 girls taking Chinese in 2003 gained an A or B.

Games, Options, The Arts: Has always had excellent sports facilities – representatives at district, county and national levels. Even better soon – the games field (about a mile from the school) is being redeveloped and a 22-acre facility for the school's main sports is being built further along with lacrosse and hockey pitches, tennis courts and a floodlit, all weather Astroturf. Back in the seventies girls used to walk in crocodile fashion to and from the games field; now a fleet of minibuses takes the strain. Rowing on the Ouse from year 9. Sixth formers may also sail and windsurf.

Fabulous music block with two recording studios and numerous practice rooms. More than half learn a musical instrument. Music technology offered at A level with 100 per cent getting A or B. Girls often join forces with boys from Bedford School, their brother school. D of E, and CCF from year 10 (joint with Bedford School) where they can learn to scuba dive and fly among other things. Thriving clubs, regular exchange visits and very popular supervised homework club after school each day.

Background and Atmosphere: Founded in 1882, one of two girls' single-sex schools run by the Bedford charity, the Harpur Trust, which benefits from the generous endowment of 16th century merchant Sir William Harpur and his wife, Dame Alice. Senior school in a rather imposing building which back in the seventies gave it a gloomy air, not helped by the dark, wooden floors – especially in the wood-panelled hall with its fantastic organ. It's amazing what a difference a bit of interior design will do – in the last few years floors have been stripped and walls painted and the place now feels light and airy and welcoming rather than foreboding. Old buildings mix with new. Very good computer facilities for both juniors and seniors. The junior school is on the same site but has its own playground, art room, library, assembly hall and science lab. (Varied) lunches in the adjacent former Holy Trinity church.

Four boarding houses split into age groups a short walk away. Comfortable and newly updated – cosy, friendly atmosphere now. Not a boarding school – a day school with boarding. Sixth form boarders get their own room, usually en-suite.

Pastoral Care and Discipline: Anti-bullying policy, although this doesn't seem an issue. Behaviour good. Mobile phones to be left with the form teacher. No expulsions during the current head's reign.

Back in the early seventies it was a serious place and a tough regime, particularly for boarders. Discipline was very strict. Hats and skirt length inspections took place regularly and any association with boys was discouraged. Time seems to have changed it for the better. Girls still work hard to achieve academic excellence but they can have fun too. Hats have gone and the current green and blue check skirt is worn below the knee. Sixth formers can either wear a black and white check skirt or trousers. As for boys – the High School recognises they 'can have a positive influence'.

Pupils and Parents: A large catchment area stretching from the Northamptonshire borders in the north to the depths of Hertfordshire in the south. Quite a large contingent from Milton Keynes. Parents have joined forces to organise a fleet of buses travelling from all corners of the county. Wide socio-economic mix with pupils from both prep and state schools.

Entrance: At 7, girls have an assessment day with tests in reading, writing and maths. Around 60 compete for 48 places. Juniors sit the entrance exam for the senior school alongside incomers; the vast majority transfer. When selecting, the head isn't just looking at academic interests, 'I want to see that sparkle too,' she says. New girls are linked to a 'first friend' via email. Minimum of seven GCSEs with a least a B grade needed for sixth form entry.

Exit: A handful leaves post GCSE to go elsewhere. Most go on to university or further education. Around eight to

Oxbridge. Medicine a popular choice. Old girls include Olympic pentathlete, Dr Stephanie Cook.

Money Matters: Academic scholarships in years 7, 9 and the sixth form. Bursaries for girls living in the local community.

Remarks: A happy school turning out feisty, confident girls ready to face the world.

BEDFORD SCHOOL

Linked to Bedford Preparatory School in the Junior section

De Parys Avenue, Bedford, Bedfordshire, MK40 2TU

Tel: 01234 362 200
Fax: 01234 362283
E-mail: registrar@bedfordschool.org.uk
Website: www.bedfordschool.org.uk

- Pupils: 1,112 boys (includes prep), senior school – 849 day, 263 boarding • Ages: 7-18 • Size of sixth form: 276 • C of E
- Fees: Day £8,151 - £12,600 pa; weekly boarding £12,861 - £19,161 pa; full boarding £13,491 - £19,812 • Independent
- Open days: Late November and early May

Head Master: Since 1990, Dr Philip Evans OBE MA FRSC (mid fifties). Fiendishly bright and highly entertaining, this is a man of ideas and an ethical approach, not only to his own, impressive, school but to education in general. Forward and outward looking, Dr Evans runs his, on first sight, conservative school, imaginatively and innovatively, drawing on a powerful combination of idealism, pragmatism and energy. A major player in HMC (chairs universities sub-committee, on academic policy committee etc), he is set to bring to his school the greater prominence it deserves. Clearly passionate about science and the teaching of science (he has a Cambridge first in natural sciences), his enthusiasms reach out to all areas of the curriculum and, to the capacities and the achievements of his pupils of whom he is touchingly proud. A hard-edged Welshman with a mission, whose determination to get the best for and out of his pupils, within a liberal and considerate community, permeates the ethos of the school. A good man to have on your side.

Academic Matters: Results are excellent. Almost 100 per cent get A-C at GCSE, almost 75 per cent get A/B at A level. Maths, sciences and French seem especially strong. Increasingly successful IB Diploma course offered since 2003 as an alternative to traditional A levels, 'provides diversification of opportunity, allowing for both the specialist and the talented student wanting to continue with a broad curriculum', says head. Good range of subjects available for the interested few: astronomy, Greek, German, Japanese, Spanish, Mandarin (school now twinned with one in Shandong province enabling joint projects, exchanges etc.)

On-site observatory and planetarium with astronomer in residence, 'allowing us to be undriven by assessment', justifiably enthuses head. Excellent IT facilities throughout school, including in boarding houses. Classics and English taught in two linked houses, with attractive 'schools' feel. Recently completed new facilities include 'state-of-the-art' library/resource centre (opened 2003) and £3m music school (opened 2005). Boys like 'Skills' syllabus – useful preparation for univ application. Academic Support Dept helps able boys with SEN and EAL (necessary as 150 boys from overseas – 25 different countries, making for excellent culturally diverse and homogenising mix). Good teacher/pupil ratio and impressive staying power of staff – over half have been in post for 10+ years.

On-site innovative and enterprising Bedford School Study Centre, a house for international students in which they spend 1-3 terms, mostly in intensive EFL, in preparation for entry to UK school to which they are best suited. Only 2 or 3 a year stay at Bedford but best advice given to help in choice. Integrated into whole school which includes prep, all under excellent leadership.

Games, Options, The Arts: Main sports rugby, hockey, rowing, cricket but 12 others played at team level. Rugby exceptionally strong, tours to S. Africa, Australia, New Zealand, junior internationals in 6 sports. Super fields integral to school site, good pool, sports hall, Astroturfs, rifle range. Also uses outside resources, eg athletics stadium. CCF is strong here, keenly supported by head who sees it as fostering leadership and believes it 'helps people to become rounded members of society, developing skills they didn't know they had.' Popular with boys, especially older ones, who see it as a chance to mix with girls from sister schools. Masses of varied activities on offer including Duke of Edinburgh Award, community service – visiting the local elderly or disadvantaged, as well as on-site theatre skills, pottery, journalism, house maintenance etc. Unusually rich choice which embraces CAS requirements for IB Diploma students. Annual ambitious music festival. Impressive and architecturally significant chapel used for concerts. Well-equipped theatre visited by outside companies. Pupils take productions to Edinburgh Festival. Imaginative DT.

Background and Atmosphere: An attractive site. Large fields, landscaped garden feel here and there and solid, unassuming school buildings. Calamitous fire in 1979 destroyed interior of main school building, now rebuilt, including large, light and unusual school hall. 450 years old in 2002, school enjoys its distinguished and significant history and relishes its promising future. Run by the Harpur Trust (along with Dame Alice Harpur and Bedford High Schools, both for girls) this charitable foundation still takes its status seriously and promotes outreach activities in the local community. Increased links with sister schools appreciated by pupils and enables sharing of some teaching and resources. Otherwise, resolutely but not aggressively single sex. Civilised atmosphere with touches of the antique, a 'Poem for the Day' in the library – Adlestrop on day of last visit. Pupils appreciate liberal and encouraging attitude of staff. 'Whatever type of student you are, you're given a chance to do your best,' said one. A chance most seem to take.

Pastoral Care and Discipline: 6 boarding houses on-site or nearby. The universally claimed 'family atmosphere' really is true of the converted, large Victorian houses with inviting sofas, well-equipped games rooms, computer facilities, decent bedrooms and a sensible regime, lovingly maintained by live-in housemaster and wife. Weekly boarding available (ie until after Saturday morning school). All boys in tutor groups, vertically grouped, all boarding houses twinned with day houses to encourage integration. Anti-bullying workshops. Inspection was enthusiastic about all aspects of pastoral care and boarding provision.

Pupils and Parents: Despite coming from more than 25 countries (including Estonia, Germany, Italy, Nigeria, Russia, Spain and many from the Far East) 90 per cent have English as 1st language and all mix happily irrespective of origins. School best-known in region and day places much sought after in locality. Boys seem relaxed and appreciative of school ethos. Not super-selective, induces loyalty in pupils, parents and OBs. Supportive parents increasingly involved. OBs include H H Munro (Saki), John Fowles, Paddy Ashdown.

Entrance: Most from on-site prep school but also from a range of local preps. School draws from five surrounding counties but 50 per cent of boarders from overseas. Prep school candidates take CE, state sector candidates tested in maths, English, science, French and VR. About 25 taken into sixth form. The IB has proved to be a successful attraction at this level.

Exit: Mostly to good universities, 'serious subjects' and a decent annual crop to Oxbridge. Head ensures best possible advice and guidance.

Money Matters: 18 page booklet details awards and requirements. Many and varied scholarships, bursaries and exhibitions. School generously endowed in specific arts subjects as well as general academic. Worth investigating for both boarding and day pupils.

Remarks: Key phrases in the head's vocabulary -'creative and innovative' and 'not anodyne' – very much characterise the approach along with 'not pretentious'. School much-respected by those in the know though not one of the big names, perhaps, says head, due to being in an 'unfashionable county'. Something, then, of a well-kept secret, likely, though, to be let out of its bag sooner rather than later as has so much to offer on all serious counts.

BEDGEBURY SCHOOL

Linked to Bedgebury Junior School in the Junior section

Goudhurst, Cranbrook, Kent, TN17 2SH

Tel: 01580 878 143
Fax: 01580 879 136
E-mail: registrar@bedgeburyschool.co.uk
Website: www.bedgeburyschool.co.uk

• Ages: 2 - 18 • Size of sixth form: 16 - 18 • Church of England Affiliated • Fees: £6,575 for boarding (full & weekly). £4,115 day • Independent • Open days: March and May

Head: Since 2000, Mrs Hilary Moriarty BA Hons, PGCFE, MA, diploma in educational leadership (late fifties, seems younger.) Married with four children – 3 grown up, one in sixth form at Worth. Educated Denbigh grammar school, read English. Previously deputy head of Red Maids' school in Bristol. An ISI Inspector. Has a regular monthly column in Home and Country, the national magazine of the WI and regularly contributes to the educational press. Straight talking, energetic and enthusiastic, wants the best for her students. Has a 'how can we do it better?' approach. Well-liked by the girls who say she has a good sense of humour, is approachable, friendly and understands their needs. Highly professional, runs a light ship, cares passionately about the school.

Academic Matters: Small non-selective, nurturing school. Wouldn't set the world alight academically but good value-added and provides some unusual options and creditable successes – past two years a Bedgebury girl has come within the top 5 in A level art & design. Most take nine GCSEs – 84 per cent graded C or above with 52 per cent graded A or B at A level. Average class size 12 reducing to 5 or 6 in sixth form. All usual curriculum subjects offered with additions of BTEC (Equestrian) – continually assessed, no written exams but equal to 3 A levels for University entrance;

A level equivalent NVQ3 fashion course communications studies; textiles. PE and drama GCSEs and PE and photography at A level are popular choices. The qualified and experienced learning support team cater for a range of mild to moderate special needs including ADD, ADHD, hearing and visual impairments, Aspergers and specific learning difficulties but a girl must be able to cope with demands of the mainstream curriculum. Approximately one third are on the learning support (LS) register – mostly for dyslexia; a high(ish) figure in part because school want to ensure potential is maximised so will offer support rather than risk leaving a girl to flounder. Norm is to withdraw for one or two lessons but support is geared to individual needs so eg child with dyscalculia may be withdrawn from all maths lessons and given individual tuition for a limited period. Senior girls tend to be supported with course work, lower school via specialised programmes. Limited, but valuable, in-class support exists but generally small classes, setting arrangements and differentiated work and prep reduce need for one to one assistance. LS register is used to monitor pupils with IEPs and where practical, staff, parents and pupils are involved with target-setting. Small successes celebrated. Gifted and talented belong to the NAGC and as well as the provisions of in-class extension materials, a range of activities is offered including competitions, spellathons, maths challenge and summer schools.

Games, Options, The Arts: Excellent and renowned equestrian facilities (BHS Registered) with stabling for 60 horses – third ride at least once a week benefiting from top class instruction provided in all major equestrian disciplines. Lots of other sports offered including lacrosse and swimming (outdoor heated pool). The very good facilities include a new sports hall with super abseil tower and climbing wall, fitness room and 22-acre lake for water sports and purpose built arts centre for ceramics, photography, art, design, jewellery and fashion. Drama not as good but refurbishment is on school's to-do list. All girls belong to one of four houses, lots of competitions in sport, drama, art, music, public speaking and photography. Plenty of clubs and activities, participation in Duke of Edinburgh Award scheme encouraged. A quarter of girls learn a musical instrument and regular concerts and recitals offer ample opportunities to perform. Day girls encouraged to join after school activities, choirs, orchestras and societies. Weekly boarders attend all school events so although there isn't any teaching on a Saturday, girls aren't always free to go home at the weekends.

Background and Atmosphere: The school was established in 1920 by the Church Education Corporation. The main building is a delightful nineteenth century version of a

French chateau, complete with spectacular rose gardens, terraces and a fountain, set in 200 acres (and oft requested as a film location).

Pastoral Care and Discipline: Dedicated team of supportive teachers, pastoral care a strength. Anorexia, drinking and smoking checked for but not a problem, indeed girls seemed rather surprised that we'd mentioned them at all. Boarding a popular option with many day girls choosing to board in senior years. Junior boarders sleep in small dormitories in the main school, progressing to shared or single rooms as they move up the school. Sixth formers housed in a purpose built block divided into 6 wings each with a common room, TV and kitchen – all have own study bedroom. Girls are expected to eat lunch and supper in the main school. No Saturday school but plenty happening at weekends including shopping trips to local towns, ice-skating, bowling etc. A few dances and socials are held with local boys' schools; girls would like more. Chapel twice a week and on Sundays, broadly Church of England but other faiths and denominations welcomed.

Pupils and Parents: Mostly professional, from a fairly wide geographical area – a number from London; school operates a weekly bus service to Waterloo. Approximately one quarter from a wide range of overseas destinations including: Spain, Germany, Croatia, Estonia, Ireland, Nigeria, Thailand, Japan, Hong Kong and Mainland China. Famous old girls include: Virginia Leng (Olympic Rider) and Trinny Woodall.

Entrance: Not overly difficult, girls are admitted at any time provided there's a place. Take school's own entrance papers and/or common entrance at 13. Many from own junior school otherwise from a wide range of prep schools. Entrance into sixth form relatively open, school attempts to tailor courses, academic cultural and vocational, to needs of students.

Exit: Twenty five per cent leave after GCSEs mostly to schools where there are boys – Stowe, Uppingham and Eastbourne popular. At 18 a few to the major universities eg Durham and Newcastle but majority go to new universities – art and fashion foundation courses popular.

Money Matters: Sixth form scholarships in BTEC National Diploma in business and finance (Equestrian Studies), art & design, fashion, drama, music and sports as well as academic and riding. Academic scholarships and music, art, drama and sport awards available for years 7 and 9 but not all offered annually.

Remarks: A homely school that aims to bring out the best in each girl – values the individual and regards vocational success as at least as important as academic achievement. A girl may arrive feeling she isn't much good at anything but will leave with a strong sense of self worth. Record number of hits on Friends Reunited supports view that girls make friends for life here. Parent commented, 'Bedgebury produces nice, level-headed girls with no airs and graces.'

BEECHEN CLIFF SCHOOL

Alexandra Park, Bath, BA2 4RE

Tel: 01225 480 466
Fax: 01225 314 025
E-mail: headmaster@beechencliff.bathnes.sch.uk
Website: www.beechen-cliff.bath.sch.uk

- Pupils: 1,040, mostly boys but 50 girls in the sixth form. All day
  - Ages: 11-18 • Size of sixth form: 238 • Non-denom.
  - Assemblies with Christian theme • State • Open days: September/October

Headmaster: Since 2005, Mr Andrew Davies, a history graduate, was head of humanities at Cirencester Deer Park School before moving to a deputy headship at Brislington School in Bristol. He became headteacher at Kings International College for Business and the Arts before taking up the post at Beechen Cliff.

Academic Matters: Beacon School status in 2000 and Technology School status in 1997. Third phase September 2003. At GCSE in 2005, 80 per cent achieved 5 or more A*-C GCSEs. Best in LEA in 2002 and 2005. 20 of the 62 staff have been here over a decade and are spoken of highly by pupils. TVEI-funded multi-media resource centre and an electronic weather station on the roof which is an official climatological station run by geography pupils. New state-of-the-art computer room with 30 work stations and electronic whiteboard (which local feeder schools also benefit from). Other electronic whiteboards in the school. English, science, maths, art, IT and history are strong.

Regular debating successes at Model UN, Cambridge Union, ESU and public speaking festivals. 80 per cent of pupils take Spanish, German or Italian as second foreign language from year 8, Latin offered in after-school lessons. Oxbridge candidates given additional tuition. Those with special needs can be taught in small groups or individually.

Games, Options, The Arts: 'More trips for theatre and art (New York, St Ives) than my private school', says new girl who recently sampled language trip to Catalonia where students worked in restaurants/bars in the evening and language school in the day. School's own cottage in Brecon Beacons is used throughout year. Masses of outward-bounding – mountain climbing in Morocco, Ghana in 2003. The only state school in the region to play Saturday fixtures (Pates Grammar, Monkton Combe, Millfield). County champs at rugby, football and cricket. Nationals for athletics, and Jason Gardener Gold Medal in the Athens Olympics. National and international stars in fencing – sabre, foil and epée! Rowing and golf among a host of other sports.

Over 100 play a musical instrument and bands toured Austria in 2000, Prague in 2001 and Veneto in 2003. Recorded first CD in 2002. 2005 tour to Tossa da Marra in Spain. Mid-Somerset festival winners 1998, 2000 and 2002. Master classes held by renowned musicians. Art is very strong – '14 out of 15 taking A level got As', says dedicated head of art. Photography A level all A grades too. Drama club, Amnesty International and Christian Union are strong.

Background and Atmosphere: Established in 1903 as City of Bath Boys' School and housed originally in the Guildhall, before moving up the hill in early 1930s to purpose-built premises which critics named 'the biscuit factory' – on the same hill as two old-money independent schools and Bath University. The school's constitution decreed that new-boy-on-the-block Beechen Cliff must never compete with King Edward's Boys' School. Despite this, it attracted high-calibre pupils – Arnold Ridley, playwright and actor was pupil and later schoolmaster; Roger Bannister, a 12 year old evacuee during the war, came 18th in a junior cross country! When Old Boy Dr Richard Roberts won the Nobel prize for medicine he donated a large slice of it to help to begin to refurbish the science centre. There are plans to sell a small, little-used piece of land to raise funds against much hue and cry – but not a penny is wasted here on vanity. School uniform has to be smart, even in sixth form (own smart clothes + jacket); no body piercings allowed.

Pastoral Care and Discipline: It's not unusual to find a senior teacher standing back to open a door for a boy with a pile of books. A sixth former who joined from an all-girls school says, 'I came here full of anxiety thinking it would be rough – like Grange Hill – but everyone has been so nice and a lot of my new friends have far more bonded family lives than anyone at my previous school'. Sixth formers give in-class support, coach junior teams and are attached to tutor groups. Strong discipline and a strict dress code is stipulated and adhered to.

Pupils and Parents: Largely white and English speaking from middle-class backgrounds.

Entrance: Apply in October for following September. No aptitude assessments or tests. Heavily oversubscribed;

criteria strictly geographic. At 16, 20 per cent added girls, from (Catholic) St Gregory's or other state schools, and a number from the private sector.

Exit: Over 60 per cent stay on to sixth form. Others to employment or further education. 70 places each year to Oxbridge, Durham, Cardiff, Sussex, London and local universities or art foundation. 30 gappers, who usually go to university following year. A few leavers to employment.

Remarks: Old fashioned values and high quality teaching. Fine results from all students; legendary sport and culture vultures.

BENENDEN SCHOOL

Cranbrook Road, Benenden, Cranbrook, Kent, TN17 4AA

Tel: 01580 240 592
Fax: 01580 240 280
E-mail: registry@benenden.kent.sch.uk
Website: www.benenden.net

• Pupils: 504 girls, all board • Ages: 11-18 • Size of sixth form: 160 • C of E • Fees: £7,850 • Independent • Open days: Three per term on Saturday mornings, contact the Admissions Secretary for dates

Head: Since 2000, Mrs Claire Oulton MA PGCE (early forties). Educated at Lady Eleanor Holles and Oxford, where she read history. PGCE at King's College, London. Taught history at Benenden from 1984 to 1988 before becoming head of history at Charterhouse, moving on to head of St Catherine's, Bramley for 6 years. Still teaches history at Benenden to year 8 girls. Married to Nick, a publisher – two young daughters (one has just started at Benenden; the other is at prep school). Very relaxed, calm and approachable lady (excellent feedback from parents). She makes a huge effort to know each girl personally – 'talks to them in the corridors' and organises tea parties with each 'layer' throughout the term. Believes in encouragement and praise as the best tools for helping each girl to achieve her own personal best. Has done a complete review of every aspect of the school since arriving and is making changes to several buildings; has had no need to make changes to the teaching staff. Took over from Mrs Gillian duCharme who was here from 1985.

Academic Matters: Consistently excellent GCSE and A level results. 95 per cent plus A*-B at GCSE and 90 per cent plus A-C grades at A level. These percentages have been rising each year. Maths equally as popular as English lang/lit at A level, with biology, economics, history and art subjects also taken up by many pupils. In 2002, three girls were placed in the top ten of highest scores at physics A level (Salters Horners Advanced Project) – two are Chinese. Nearly a fifth of all pupils live overseas, of whom 11 per cent are foreign passport holders from 26 different countries, mainly the far east; they don't all socialise well; some existing parents not keen to see any more far eastern pupils coming in.

Games, Options, The Arts: Strong on lacrosse – many girls being selected to play for county sides – and some have gone on to play for Junior England. Other local schools often request to play Benenden's B team against their own A team. Rounders, netball, hockey and tennis also popular (some 15 courts and plenty of coaching). Swimming pool (smart 25-metre indoor with a tiered stand at one end) – end of term games 'splash knockout' between houses much enjoyed by girls. Riding always oversubscribed and further arrangements are being looked into. Other sports/ activities offered include dance (ballet, modern and tap), fencing, judo/self-defence. Duke of Edinburgh also popular. Keen on drama – last performance of Cabaret was a huge success and previous plays have been performed at theatres in London. Lots of inter-house drama too. Fund-raising beginning for multi-million pound theatre. Impressive new library and study centre. Over 50 per cent of girls learn a musical instrument; choirs, wind band, full symphony orchestra – Benenden is the base for the Hemsted Forest Youth Orchestra. Flourishing music scholarships (four awarded in 2002). Computers in evidence all around the school including whiteboard technology in nearly every classroom.

Background and Atmosphere: Founded in 1923 by three mistresses from Wycombe Abbey. Huge, elegant and slightly gloomy Victorian mansion built by Gathorne Hardy, first Earl of Cranbrook, set in 244 acres. Approached by long driveway with 'lax' pitches on left. Some girls find this isolated position a bit tricky for shopping and boys! Discos with Tonbridge organised once a term (not enough, say girls). Other social events of various kinds organised with other schools. Six houses with dormies arranged in year groups ('layers') (first year, 7 beds to a room – considered too many by girls) – two of the houses have a housemaster (funnily enough in an all girls' school, very popular). Founders' centre (for sixth form) with four houses – girls allowed limited alcohol but many prefer to have the chocolate instead! The last bits of the institutional feel to the school, the old hospital-style corridor and dining room are being redeveloped into modern catering facility; this will then reflect the modernising of other buildings that has been carried out

recently throughout the school.

The snobby image from HRH Princess Anne days is still hanging on but the atmosphere is one of a relaxed, friendly, family feel. Despite the fact that it is a full boarding school, new head is keen for girls to go home when they wish (especially in their first year). Having said that, with the extensive weekend programme of outings and activities, most girls opt to stay in. No set limit to number of meals out at weekends with parents, families or friends.

Pastoral Care and Discipline: Many parents choose the school for its reputation as being very particular about its pastoral care. Aim is self-discipline and as a result the girls are well-behaved. Expectations for Benenden girls have always been high, which brings about tremendous self-motivation. Pink slips for good work or behaviour and blue slips for bad behaviour or poor/late work. The head sees any girl who receives three pink slips in a term and writes to parents; repeated blue slips lead to detention. Girls show a high regard for feelings of others and bullying seems almost non-existent. Those arriving in sixth form experience genuinely kind welcome. Strict policy on drugs – girls would expect to be expelled.

Pupils and Parents: Interesting and rich geographical and social mix – new money, overseas pupils and some upper crust. Parents seem down-to-earth, relaxed and low key – mostly Land Rovers and Volvos in the car park. Many live in surrounding counties of Kent, Surrey and Sussex; others from London and within 90 minutes' travelling distance; the rest from abroad. Active parents' association (each boarding house has a rep on this committee to provide feedback to the school) and parents' events committee, which along with organising events, assists with fund-raising. Most famous Old Girl HRH Princess Royal; also Charlotte Brew (the first lady to ride in the Grand National), Liz Forgan (ex head Channel 4 and currently chairman of Heritage Lottery Fund), Jane MacQuitty (wine writer), the Reverend Angela Berners-Wilson (one of the pioneer women priests) and – wait for it – Lady Moon (founder of worldwide Old Bags' Society for rejected wives – following the wonderful headline case in which she cut off the sleeves of her erring husband's suits and distributed his cellar of chateau-bottled clarets around the village).

Entrance: By CE and interview – from 60 different prep schools at 11, 12 and 13 (preview weekend for prospective pupils takes place prior to any exams). Some at sixth form – competitive exam for external sixth form entrants, plus at least 6 grade C GCSEs including As or Bs in A level subjects.

Exit: A good number do a gap year. Then on to degree courses. London very popular, also Bristol, Edinburgh and

Oxbridge (15 per cent).

Money Matters: By arrangement, annual fees can be spread over ten months. Sixth form (academic, music and art) and lower school (academic and music) scholarship exams are held at the school in January. Major (up to 50 per cent of fees) and minor awards. Generous bursaries are available for hard times. However, not a well-endowed school – half of all money for school development is raised by parents, seniors and friends of the school.

Remarks: A traditional girls' boarding school being brought into the 21st century by new, dynamic head. Emphasis very much on creating a caring community – parents report it's 'warm and welcoming'. Girls make life-long friends here. Expectations to achieve are high – and although there is a department catering for them – probably not the place to send a child with more than mild learning difficulties.

BERKHAMSTED COLLEGIATE SCHOOL

Linked to Berkhamsted Collegiate Preparatory school in the Junior section

Castle Street, Berkhamsted, Hertfordshire, HP4 2BB

Tel: 01442 358 002
Fax: 01442 358 003
E-mail: info@bcschool.org
Website: www.berkhamstedcollegiateschool.org.uk

• Pupils: 1,000 boys and girls. Mostly day, but around 55 full-time boarders. Single-sex teaching for girls and for boys from 11-16; co-ed teaching from 3-11 and from 16-18 • Ages: 11-18 • Size of sixth form: 280 • C of E • Fees: Day: prep £878 - £2,940; senior school £3,549 - £4,175. Boarding £5,992 - £6,618 • Independent • Open days: Early October

Principal: Since 1996, Dr Priscilla Chadwick MA PhD FRSA (mid-fifties). Previously Dean of Educational Development at South Bank University. Educated at Oxford High (briefly), later head girl Clarendon School in north Wales (now incorporated into Monkton Combe). Read theology at Girton College, Cambridge, then PGCE at Oxford. Jumped straight into teaching as head of RE. Similar role at next school before taking time off to travel around world. 'After seven years teaching I needed a break and I'm a great traveller,' head explains. Returned as head of RE at new Surrey comprehensive and spent next 10 years doing PhD in spare

time. Result was book, Schools of Reconciliation, published 1994. Second book published three years later, Shifting Alliances: Church and State in Education – a best seller in its field. First headship at big mixed comp – Bishop Ramsey School, Hillingdon.

Appointed BCS principal to oil wheels of 1996 merger, which saw Berkhamsted boys', girls' and prep schools, come together. 'I had a vision, an idea of how the school could be,' says head. 'The most important thing was that, for pupils, it should be absolutely seamless.' Nine years on, is delighted with result. Relies on strong team of deputies but this is not a hands-off, isolated head though she no longer teaches. Extremely proud woman (in best possible sense). Proud of school, proud of pupils but also proud of staff's achievement, own knowledge and interests which she takes pleasure in sharing. Sings in chamber choir when time allows.

Academic Matters: Lower selection cut-off than grammar rivals. Often (uncomfortably) seen as retreat for 'grammar school rejects', so there's much delight at taking them on at their own game. Results have steadily improved since merger (they were pretty good to begin with) and league table position ('I hate league tables – they're a total distortion,' states head) also in ascendancy. Large number of pupils allows for great choice of subjects – 27 in sixth form. Traditionally strong A levels in history, maths and physics, but no slouch in chemistry, biology and geography either; 75 per cent A/B grades.

Impressive too at GCSE with a full house of five A*-C grades. Sciences also feature strongly as does (no surprises here) RE. Other options include food technology, Chinese, classical civilisation, music, PE and theatre studies as well as the usual crop of arts and languages. Good academic foundation laid down at prep level where all classes totally mixed. Maximum class size 20, down to 18 for little ones. Most make grade to move into senior school (prep pupils not guaranteed a place in year 7) when boys and girls go separate ways until 16.

All GCSE subjects taught in single-sex classes on two sites separated by a brisk 10-minute walk across the town High Street divide. One senior staff member said, 'all the evidence shows boys and girls do far better at this age if they're taught separately.' Certainly the ones we spoke to had no argument with that. Sixth form brings them back together once subject choices have been made.

Class layout fairly informal throughout, loads of pupil participation and interaction encouraged. Walls everywhere smothered with artistic work, expedition photos, sporting activities and team lists – thankfully hardly a bare inch of paint to be found. Busy well-stocked libraries, all with computers linked to school network. Also ICT rooms and more computers in houses. Laptops allowed as learning aid (ie dyslexics). Extra support for dyslexics and dyspraxics with high IQ, plus specialist EFL. Study skills also offered. 'I was hopeless at history until I was shown a better way of learning it and then I got an A,' said one boy.

Games, Options, The Arts: Very sporty, very successful, particularly rugby for boys and lacrosse for girls – as a result of pupil power, they now try each other's sports too. Plenty to choose from – athletics, cricket, Eton fives, fencing, golf, shooting and squash to name but a few. New sports hall and pool completed in 2004, opened by the Duke of Edinburgh and named after OB, Sir Robin Knox-Johnston. Produced two trialists for 2002 Commonwealth Games – even before new facilities. Recent national fives champion, county cricket champions, also compete at national, regional and county level in other games. D of E, CCF and extra-curricular aplenty – certainly no excuse to get bored.

Art studios significantly better for boys than girls but hugely impressive work done by both. Lively well-used music rooms. Bagpipe lessons available. Choirs, orchestras, barbershop perform home and abroad. Spring interhouse music competition seen as highlight of the year. Rehearsals were well in swing when we visited. Fabulous tiered theatre (Centenary Hall) on girls' side of town used by whole school. Also smaller drama studio (boys' side) where all aspects of stage management, lighting as well as acting, taught on manageable scale. Two major productions a year, plus lots of little ones. Very popular choice for pupils. More opportunity for mixing in non-academic environment. Girls regularly give boys a pasting at Scrabble.

Background and Atmosphere: Three schools beating with a single heart since 1996 amalgamation. Boys-only Berkhamsted School (Castle Campus) had been around since 1541 when it joined forces with the 1888 Berkhamsted School for Girls (Kings Campus). Mixed prep came a year later. Each retains own largely autonomous head overseen by principal. Newly created collegiate school (BCS) a co-ed with a difference though, with single-sex teaching from 11-16. Parents, pupils and staff alike all agree – the system works! 'The pupils had absolutely no trouble adapting,' said one member of staff. 'But there was plenty of opposition from other quarters.' Very few left because of the changes however – now school is more popular than ever.

Buildings are mostly attractive, especially on Castle Campus which features the 'jewel in the Crown', a grade 1 listed Tudor hall (containing green baize door famous OB Graham Greene wrote of in early autobiography, A Sort Of Life), delightfully different 19th century chapel modelled on Venetian church, listed indoor swimming pool and more modern senior boys' houses surrounding the grass quad. A healthy helping of sixth form girls gives this impressive, if austere, dark redbrick backdrop a more relaxed feel. Similar picture on Kings Campus where sixth form boys a regular feature of this otherwise single-sex scene. Buildings here date from 1902 to 1990s, again set around a quad. School liberally scattered around this historic and very pretty town.

Lacks the stiff formality of many independents. Christian foundation school where religion still a vital part of daily life. According to head, the aim is 'to promote moral and spiritual values through the Christian ethos of the school, emphasising integrity, honesty, generosity, respect for other people and the environment and appreciation of other races, religions and ways of life'.

Pastoral Care and Discipline: House system completely overhauled in 1997 so now forms the backbone of all matters pastoral as well as competitive. Housemasters/mistresses (heads of houses) and tutors deal personally with problems in small 60-max size houses. Not just problems though, houses also the epicentre of social life. Bullying exists (though the pupils we spoke to seemed less aware of it) while one senior staff member claimed text bullying was the latest scourge. Bullying of any kind not tolerated. Culprits dealt with swiftly. 'We try to bring reconciliation and sometimes get both sets of parents involved.' Expulsion seen as last resort but not reluctant to take it.

Mobiles banned during school-time and use discouraged at lunch. Zero tolerance too of drugs and alcohol. Different approach to smoking – offenders fined £10 when first caught, £20 if caught again and so on. All money goes to leukaemia fund. Rewards given as well as punishments. Commendations awarded for outstanding effort in music, drama and academic work. Also one for community service. Good relationship between students and staff. Friendly, relaxed courtesy on both sides. Mutual respect. Boarding for the few in form of shared and single study bedrooms, not dorms. Plenty of beds for popular B&B arrangement.

Pupils and Parents: Refreshingly normal and not obviously products of a private school. Compulsory uniform, in cases informally worn. Special school ties – or pins – worn with pride, reflect commendations or team colours. Pupils switched-on and well-informed, either beavering away in class or making the most of their break. Give every appearance of wanting to do something rather than nothing. From broad sweep of backgrounds – as one girl put it, 'you've got kids here whose parents struggle to afford the fees and others who arrive by limo every morning.' Class divides don't seem to exist though. Another pupil added, 'what's important is that you enjoy doing what you're good at. That's where you find friends.'

Only around 45 per cent from in and around Berkhamsted. Remainder at least half hour's car/bus/train journey away. Small number of overseas students – less than 1 per cent – drawn mostly from Hong Kong by word of mouth. Lots of flexi-boarding. Eclectic mix of OBs and OGs who include author Graham Greene (his father Charles was headmaster), mariner Sir Robin Knox-Johnston, Lady Churchill, MP Michael Meacher, actors Emma Fielding and Stephen Campbell-Moore, antique dealer John Bly, musician Antony Hopkins and Sir Anthony Cleaver, ex-head of UKAEA.

Entrance: Over-subscribed. Entry to prep school by assessment, own entrance exam set for entry into senior school (same exam done by existing pupils in prep school as external candidates) and GCSE results all-important for sixth form places. Even though academic requirement is less than grammars, very much on the look out for potential. Head explains, 'we're looking for someone who enjoys learning, who has a reasonable level of academic excellence. We expect children to cope with a wide range of subjects.' Around half year 7 intake comes from own prep school, the rest from other preps or states. List of 50 feeder schools for 2004.

Exit: Not all who start at BCS finish the course. Few fallers in last year at prep, others 'weeded out' before A levels. 'Sometimes it's better for the pupil concerned to suggest another school might be more suitable,' said a senior teacher. On average 98 per cent of final year go on to higher education (many now opt for gap year first – out of 132 leavers in 2004, 53 were taking a break). Respectable number snapped up by Oxbridge. History, medicine and law traditional choices but media, film and art get their fair share too.

Money Matters: Solid financial foundations promise solid financial future. Limited number of scholarships, much sought after – 6 academic, 4 music, one art and one medical/army. Also bursaries in cases of need. Head can award exhibitions at her discretion.

Remarks: Suits 'youngsters who enjoy making the most of their opportunities – who want to have a go,' says head. We agree. Feels much like a college, especially the senior schools. Responsibility and respect are key, taught from the very earliest age 'until it comes naturally'.

BEVERLEY GRAMMAR SCHOOL

Queensgate, Beverley, East Riding of Yorkshire, HU17 8NF

Tel: 01482 881 531
Fax: 01482 881 564
E-mail: office@bgs.karoo.co.uk
Website: www.BGS.eril.net

• Pupils: 800 boys, all day • Ages: 11-18 • Size of sixth form: 350, joint with the girls' school • Non-denom • State

Head: Since 1998, Mr Gerald Broadbent LRAM (sixtyish). Studied at Royal Academy of Music and Westcott House Theological College, Cambridge, before becoming Church of England priest. Asked by vicar to become more involved with local youngsters, he took part-time job as a music teacher and loved it so much he gave up the priesthood! Went into full-time teaching because, 'I hugely enjoy working with young people'. Held various posts including head at Archbishop Thurstan School, Hull, before moving to Beverley. Genuinely loves his job and infects his school with fun.

Academic Matters: A solid performer. 75 per cent plus get five or more A*-C grades at GCSE – on a six-year upward trend. School graded A* at key stages 3 and 4, putting it in top 5 per cent of schools nationally. Students can also study for NVQ in engineering and GNVQ in IT. In the joint sixth form, almost half of all grades are either A or B. Sixth form blocks at both boys' grammar and nearby girls' high school so students divide their time between the two. 'I argue that it's a good half-way house between the school where they feel comfortable and what it will be like going to university where everything is new,' says head.

Games, Options, The Arts: Strong on music by state standards – about 120 have individual music lessons. Various choirs, orchestras, bands including a year 7 choir for all new intake. 'If any of the boys are reluctant, we take the view, "what do you mean you don't sing? Everybody sings!" And because it's the norm, they all do.' Drama has included an all-boy production of Macbeth. 'We had a boy as Lady Macbeth. It didn't cause a ripple.'

Also strong on sport ('you name it, we do it') and highlights include annual cross country race. 'The boys love it. I can't work it out, I used to hate it,' confesses head. And extra-curricular is, well, take your pick. 'If a boy wants a club to be started, we find a member of staff to start it.'

Background and Atmosphere: Founded in 700 AD, Beverley Grammar is England's oldest state secondary school. Cherishes its traditions but prides itself on moving with the times. On its present site since 1903 and now mix of the old (museum piece of a hall) and the new (£750,000 sixth form block). Though Grammar by name, it's a comprehensive by nature. There are no entrance tests, no fees, and it takes all-comers from its catchment area.

One of a handful of free-standing voluntary aided schools which means it can bid direct to the DfES for some of its finance. Downside is that the trustees have to find 10 per cent of the cost of major building projects. Recently granted specialist status in engineering bringing investment in technology, maths and science. All prizes at speech day awarded for effort – 'at least as important as achievement,' says head.

Pastoral Care and Discipline: Uses more carrot, less stick approach to learning. 'We believe in working hard, but having a lot of fun doing it so there's a lot of leg pulling goes on in the classrooms. And because we have a relaxed approach to learning, the boys learn because they want to, not because they're being threatened what will happen if they don't,' says head. 'We encourage everyone to show respect for everyone else and that's often about the little things – the way staff talk to pupils, the way teachers hold doors open for the kids as well as the kids for the teachers.'

Parents involved at earliest stage over any slips in discipline. School's own social worker may visit child's home to talk over problems. Only one permanent exclusion in three years and exemplary behaviour around school. Credible reward system of 'green slips' which lead to certificates and ultimate prize of special school tie. And mentoring system with a difference to keep learning on track – as well as teachers, mentors can also be volunteers from the community – industrialists, careers advisers, etc – to drum home the value of learning.

Pupils and Parents: Very supportive parents, encouraged to be involved with school from the off. Parents of new intake invited to sit with their child for half a day of lessons. One mum, fresh from a science lesson, described school as 'absolutely brilliant'. 'There's such an eagerness and keenness here. It's renewed in my son that excitement for learning.'

Entrance: Living in catchment area – Beverley and the surrounding villages of Tickton, Walkington and Bishop Burton – is pretty much a must.

Exit: About 70 per cent go on to sixth form and many more into some other form of further education. Ultimately, most go to university.

Remarks: A grown-up school, mature enough to nurture mutual respect and to know when to let its hair down. A school with a sense of humour. No wonder boys love it.

BEVERLEY HIGH SCHOOL

Norwood, East Riding of Yorkshire, Beverley, HU17 9EX

Tel: 01482 881 658
Fax: 01482 870 935
E-mail: admindept@beverleyhigh.net
Website: www.beverleyhigh.net

• Pupils: 860 girls all day • Ages: 11-18 • Size of sixth form: 350 in joint sixth form with Beverley Grammar • Non-denom • State

Head: Since 1989, Ms Ruth Vincent BA (fifties), read geography at Thames Polytechnic, MA education from Goldsmiths College, London University. Taught in London at Kidbrooke School SE3, George Green's School E14 and Sydenham SE26 before moving to Beverley in 1988. Married. A no-nonsense head, ambitious for her girls and her school.

Academic Matters: Breathtaking 85 per cent of pupils achieve 5 or more A*-C grades in GCSEs. 'We had one of those Kelly Holmes moments when we saw the results,' says head. 'You raise your arms in celebration and then can't quite believe it until you've been back to check.' Also good A level results at joint sixth form with Beverley Grammar (see their entry for details of sixth form).

One of only 18 schools in the country designated an Ambassador School by the National Academy for Gifted and Talented Youth. Children with particular skills, whether academic, arts, sporting, or even leadership, have their talents nurtured. Gifted A level science students from surrounding schools have joined them for lectures given by experts at top of their field. Key Stage 3 pupils get together for weekend study sessions at a local hotel to enable them to achieve at the highest levels in English and maths. Successful summer schools are held for bright students from within the school and also from feeder primary schools. Open University modules are offered to sixth form.

And for the less gifted and talented? 'If you do your best for the gifted and talented pupils, research shows that it benefits everybody in the school. By challenging all in the classroom, it moves everyone on,' says head. Subjects are taught in mixed ability groups apart from maths and languages at KS3 and science at KS4.

Games, Options, The Arts: Drama, dance, music and art promoted through the curriculum. Choirs, orchestras, annual carol service in nearby Minster and summer music concert in St Mary's Church. Sport very popular and soon to be enhanced by £1.5m sports hall to be shared with community. A new technology block and art block will follow. New developments are not a moment too soon. School, with its small hall, is desperately short of large meeting space.

Twenty-five clubs meet during the week, Judo to Japanese. Strong links and student exchanges with a school in Japan helped to win British Council's International School Award. Highlights of school year include more than 60 trips to places at home and abroad. Fund-raising for charities chosen by girls.

Background and Atmosphere: A tardis of a school with a small frontage on to a main road hiding extensive buildings and wooded grounds. Almost 100 years old but at the forefront of change. Became a Technology College in the first flush of schools adopting specialist status in 1998. A school where teachers give of their best. 'We have some wonderful teachers here who work hard to make learning fun and interesting,' says head. But much is expected of students, too. Classroom noticeboards show details of what pupils need to do to strive always for the next level of attainment. A girl expecting a B grade would never be in any doubt what she needed to do to lift herself to an A.

A real atmosphere of maturity and trust. School has three computer suites where girls can work unsupervised between lessons. Girls value the resources and look after them.

Pastoral Care and Discipline: Students closely monitored and pace of work is fast but hope is to encourage everyone from the most to the least able. Aim is that somewhere around the school, every child's name should be highlighted somewhere for some kind of achievement. Each form has a captain and deputy who keep their roles for a term so that everyone gets a chance at leadership. Merit system in lower school and good behaviour encouraged in upper school by a points system. Students can gain or lose points according to behaviour. Rewards on a sliding scale from a 'wear what you like' day to a trip to a theme park. But those who earn most points reap biggest rewards.

Pupils and Parents: Very supportive parents encouraged to share school's ambition for their girls. Pupils are drawn from local catchment area and come to take a real pride in their school.

Entrance: Substantially over-subscribed and draws pupils almost exclusively from catchment area – Beverley and the surrounding villages of Tickton, Walkington and Bishop Burton.

Exit: A hefty 97 per cent of year 11 stay in education, mainly in school's joint sixth form or the local colleges. Most of year 13 go on to university.

Remarks: A school that drives students forward but puts in extraordinary effort itself to give them every chance of standing on tiptoes and reaching out for the very best they could hope to achieve.

BIRKDALE SCHOOL

Linked to Birkdale School Preparatory School in the Junior section

Oakholme Road, Sheffield, South Yorkshire, S10 3DH

Tel: 0114 266 8409
Fax: 0114 267 1947
E-mail: admissions@birkdale.sheffield.sch.uk
Website: www.birkdaleschool.org.uk

- Pupils: 460 boys in the senior school; 132 boys and 49 girls in the sixth form. All day • Ages: 11-18 • Size of sixth form: 181
- Christian, but all faiths welcome • Fees: Seniors £2,577; juniors £2,128; pre-prep £1,799 • Independent • Open days: October/November

Head: Since 1998, Mr Robert J Court MA PGCE (fiftyish) who was educated at St Paul's, and read physics at Clare College, Cambridge. Previously twenty years as master, housemaster and in, 1994, second master at Westminster School. He lives on site with his wife, Andrea, who occasionally acts as receptionist at parents' evenings. He came to the school 'because of its strong Christian ethos'. God very important to the head and to the school.

Charming, incredibly prompt with a deliciously dry sense of humour, he has made a certain number of staff changes here, more difficult perhaps, than elsewhere, because of the high cost of housing (in local terms). Head has a house in the Peak District, and 'can be out walking' within thirty minutes of leaving the school. He has no intention of quitting but of raising academic standards, stabilising what he has.

Academic Matters: The sciences, maths, Eng lit and the humanities appear the most popular and successful A levels. Rather jolly ecology pool and masses of trips for geographers and historians. General studies for all at A level; not a lot of take up in either French or German (five in the former and two in the latter – twice as many pupils did Latin and performed considerably better) despite regular exchanges. However, recent GCSE results in the language dept were a great improvement, Spanish now on the curriculum and thriving. Greek on offer at lunchtime and can be taken to exam level. Dual award science at GCSE. Open-door policy in the common room, pupils can approach staff for help at any time. Dyslexia provision costs extra, mild dyslexics only, one pupil in the school is statemented. Huge library, many computer rooms, all linked, with email addresses for all; strong DT presence, subdivided into electronics, graphics and resistant materials.

Games, Options, The Arts: Rather jolly school mag with quizzes as well as the usual sporting achievements. Rugby important here, with trips to New Zealand and Fiji last year. Footie very popular and school has joined the independent schools' competition. Girls may do team or individual sport. 30-metre sports hall and designer gym with weights room. 125 year lease on a sports field some ten minutes drive away, complete with pavilion – new upgraded pavilion completed 2006.

Fabulous art complex run by husband and wife team, concentrating on perspective when we visited via a rather complicated machine of their own design 'which never fails'. Truly exciting work here. Regular As and A* at A level and GCSE respectively, masses of good 3D stuff and the walls of the art dept were positively papered in lively pics. Nice 3D guitar, and some Modigliani look-alikes. Well-equipped drama studio at Johnson House, with recording capabilities and an impressive wardrobe room. Theatre studies at A level. Much use made of the local countryside with trips to the Peak District, D of E. Whole school supports a school in Nepal, with annual visits both from members and friends of the school.

Background and Atmosphere: School founded at the turn of the twentieth century as a boys' private prep school, went up to 16 in 1988, then 18, and added girls in the sixth form only in 1996. Moved into current site in 1998, nice bit of Sheffield but hideously complicated campus, embracing Oakholme Road, Ashdell Road, Endcliffe Crescent and Fulwood Road. Masses of to-ing and fro-ing between the various Victorian/new-build houses on an incredibly steep site. Good octagonal concert hall, school hall bursting at the seams and it doubles as a dining room and badminton court, as well as stage – extension still planned.

Pupils are encouraged to get involved in a variety of lunchtime activities in the period when they are not eating. Pupil-inspired water fountains throughout the school. Separate sixth form block, the Grayson building, which also includes computers. Super Johnson House with listed (£20,000 to replace, said our guide) marble fireplaces, and RE dept on the top floor with a quote from Micah painted on the wall. 'What does the Lord require of you? To act justly and to love mercy and to walk humbly with your God'. Pupils not allowed to go down the main staircase (one-way system). Lockers line the broad passages throughout. As we said before, the atmosphere is lively, scruffy and fun with, it must be admitted, some of the dirtiest carpets we have come across – bits of chewing gum as well as scraps of paper and the odd pencil. Steps all over the place and no use for wheelchairs.

Pastoral Care and Discipline: Strong Christian ethos, pastoral care important here. And according to the school's policy statement, 'it is the policy of Birkdale School to promote a Christian lifestyle … any illegal use of controlled drugs by either staff or pupils will be treated as serious misconduct' – which is the first time we have seen staff mentioned in such context. Dealing in drugs equals out and no questions. If found using on the premises, the matter is 'taken very seriously' and previous conduct is taken into account. Pupil might be allowed to remain under a strict regime of testing. (Hasn't happened yet.) 'Drugs are contrary to all our teaching'. Smoking on site rare in school, would result in detention, increasing in severity if problem persists. Ditto booze. Occasional incidents of bullying are dealt with by (usually) confronting the perpetrator, 'might suspend', 'certainly involve parents'. Head of year groups, plus form tutors for all. Tutors first point of call if a pupil has problems but prefects equally used. Prefects spend a training weekend in the Peak District. School uniform throughout the school, blue, grey and white with dashing striped ties for the boys.

Pupils and Parents: Local lads and lasses, many first-time buyers, huge catchment area, parents operate local buses from as far away as Bawtry, Doncaster, the Peak District and North Derbyshire – over a thirty-mile radius. OBs Michael Palin, a couple of judges, a racing driver and an MP or two.

Entrance: Entrance test for all at 11, including those in the junior school, who don't come up 'if it is not the right school for them'. Perhaps a handful each year. CE at 13, but tiny intake then. Girls (and boys) join sixth form from many local schools, around 30 each year. Five passes at GGSE, with four Bs minimum, and at least B at GCSE in any subject to be studied at A level.

Exit: Excellent careers library and on-line for sixth form. Leeds the most popular university, plus ex-polys, which often offer more esoteric courses: De Montfort, Leeds Met etc. 9 per cent annually to Oxbridge. Business, medics, engineering, computing and law are popular degree subjects.

Money Matters: Not the rich school it appeared to be, having lost assisted places. Certain number of academic scholarships on offer – which can be topped up in case of need. Will carry a pupil to next stage if in real financial need.

Remarks: School has had a meteoric rise from a boys only prep school to a full blown senior school with girls in the sixth. No current thoughts about girls throughout, though anything is possible. Happily ensconced in Sheffield's education alley; strong and both academically and socially tough.

BISHOP LUFFA CHURCH OF ENGLAND SCHOOL, CHICHESTER

Bishop Luffa Close, Chichester, West Sussex, PO19 3LT

Tel: 01243 787 741
Fax: 01243 531 807
E-mail: webadmin@bishopluffa.org.uk
Website: www.bishopluffa.org.uk

• Pupils: 1,374, 50/50 boys and girls • Ages: 11-18 • Size of sixth form: 280 • C of E • State • Open days: October

Nick Taunt: Since 2000, Mr Nicholas Taunt MA PGCE NPQH (forties) educated at Exeter College, Oxford. Previously head of creative arts at Harwich School and then deputy head of Hedingham School. Married to a social worker, they have three children. Enormously positive about continuing and developing his school's excellent reputation. Mature, pleasant, a head who relates well to both parents and pupils; his interests are in literature, drama and music are reflected throughout the school.

Academic Matters: Impressive results for a non-selective school, GCSE 81 per cent A*-C in 2005, A level 99 per cent pass rate; 46 per cent A and B grades in 2005. Able pupils take up to 12 subjects at GCSE. Won the National Achievement Award for Excellence in 2001, 2002 and 2003. Pupils carry off a good share of competition prizes for arts, sports, debating and academics.

Well-resourced school, with capable staff and facilities to match; parents comment particularly on the school's innovative teaching of mathematics. A technology college, so ICT is used to facilitate all types of learning. A Leading Edge school too, and keen on professional development, staff training and thinking and learning skills. Strong English and drama, pupils produce their own poetry magazine and have had their poems published in the TES. Setting in some subjects. Motivated, caring and committed staff, hugely appreciated by parents, more than half have been at the school for 10 years.

SEN organised at both ends of the scale. Full-time learning support teachers, and extra training is provided for teachers to assist pupils with specific difficulties as the need arises. A programme of extension classes is run for the very able, which pupils from other schools attend. Individual needs really appear to be met and potential developed as opposed to just talked about as is sadly so often the case. Numbers with SEN tend to be below average but needs are wide ranging and include pupils with specific learning difficulties as well as some with physical or sensory needs.

Games, Options, The Arts: Sports have quality and breadth. Large playing fields, gym and indoor sports hall. Nine pupils in county or UK under-18 teams. Sailing judo and fencing. Good range of creative arts, modern/jazz dance, ballet, two choirs, orchestra, swing band; children compose their own music for productions. Much of the drama curriculum is linked with the English department – this happens far too rarely elsewhere – lots of productions, some produced at Chichester Theatre. One of few schools selected by the National Theatre for its International Connections programme. Actors and theatre directors amongst past pupils.

Background and Atmosphere: Founded in 1963, in a residential area on the edge of Chichester, by a group of parents who wanted a Christian based education for their children. They have been expanding and adding buildings ever since. Extensive new buildings opened in September 2004. A very busy place, with a warren of corridors, easy to get lost. Pupils appeared well behaved and hard working. School's philosophies are 'Nothing but the best' and 'Everyone matters'.

Pastoral Care and Discipline: House system, pupils are taught to support each other, feel valued and respect differences. Clear set of school rules and emphasis on Christian values. Parents and pupils feel a strong sense of community.

Pupils and Parents: From a diversity of backgrounds, as the school is non-selective. Mainly local and from surrounding villages, a few from as far as Arundel and Midhurst. Past pupils include Jonathan Thompson, Amanda Ursell, Paul Millar, Rupert Wingfield-Hayes and Zoe Rahmar.

Entrance: At 11 from 75 different Sussex primaries, both state and independent; Central School is a feeder. Majority of places go to practising Christians, then children living closest to the school. Unsurprisingly, always over subscribed.

Exit: A handful leaves at 16 to go to local colleges, most stay for A levels. 90 per cent go to university most years, 8 to Oxford and Cambridge in 2004; other popular choices are Imperial, Durham, York, Bristol and Cardiff.

Money Matters: Parents' group raise enough money to help less well-off children pay for school trips, foreign exchanges and in some cases instrumental tuition.

Remarks: A comprehensive that works. Interesting school to visit, offering wide range of opportunities to all its pupils whatever their ability, getting the results too at a personal level as well as academic. Parents comment, 'if all state schools were run and resourced as this one, British children could be really confident of competing and improving our world in the 21st century. I don't know any parent who does not feel blessed by attending such a wonderful school.'

BISHOP WORDSWORTH'S GRAMMAR SCHOOL

11 The Close, Salisbury, Wiltshire, SP1 2EB

Tel: 01722 333 851
Fax: 01722 325 899
E-mail: admin@bws.wilts.sch.uk
Website: www.bws.wilts.sch.uk

• Pupils: 810 boys, all day • Ages: 11-18 • Size of sixth form: 230 • C of E • State • Open days: Several afternoons in September; sixth form open afternoons in November and February

Head: Since 2002, Dr Stuart Smallwood BSc PhD NPQH (forties). Educated at Harvey Grammar School, Folkstone, then a glittering selection of academic qualifications: BSc (Hons) in geology from Leeds University, PhD from Cambridge and PGCE from Bristol. NPQH refers to the National Professional Qualification for Headship, in case you are wondering. First taught at Sir Thomas Rich's School in Gloucester before being appointed deputy head at Bishops in 1998. Wife Charlotte teaches English at Bishop's sister school, South Wilts. Three children at local schools. We met Dr Smallwood in his tracksuit and can verify that this is one superfit headmaster. Runs the school's cross country and broke off our interview to take the lads out for their run. Boys describe him as a 'strong disciplinarian'. Has introduced geology as an AS subject which he teaches jointly with the head of South Wilts, who also happens to be a geologist.

Academic Matters: Excels across the board at GCSE. Recently became a specialist language college which has brought innovation. Introduces French (compulsory for GCSE), Spanish and German all in year 7. Hoping to offer a non-European language soon and has launched an outreach programme for seven local primary schools. Head wants to buck the national trend of boys not learning languages ('this school swims against the tide!') and hopes languages will open doors for his boys to work overseas. A level results varied, with economics, chemistry and physics consistently outstanding. Art also excels, though few study it at A level. ICT, psychology (taught at South Wilts), biology and theatre studies have had less imposing showings. The boys we talked to singled out history for highest praise and English also got a keen thumbs up. Some joint teaching with South Wilts allows the sixth form to offer a wide(ish) range of A levels. Class size a constant aggravation but school works to keep this under control and boys looked attentive. Mixed ability teaching in year 7, with setting in maths and languages introduced the following year. IT provision improving and is especially good for languages. Special needs does not unduly trouble the school; two boys currently statemented, both for physical disabilities. Learning support coordinator looks after 'very small number with dyslexic tendencies' and your garden variety 'chaotic' boys. Virtually no ESL.

Games, Options, The Arts: You can play any game here, as long as it's rugby. OK, just kidding, but it is fair to say that Bishop's takes the game seriously. Not unusual for the school to turn out 10 rugger sides for its Saturday morning matches. Fixture card dominated by games against schools like (arch-rivals) Canford, Marlborough and Sherborne, though they will play against state schools in the area that can be counted on to give them a good game. Has done well in the Daily Mail Cup and at least one team is county champion most years. Several boys play for SW England or England development teams. Some boys grumbled that to be head boy or deputy you had to be in the first XV. Athletics and cross-country also strong – over 50 boys represent Bishop's at local cross-country fixtures. Football 'growing' with four sides recently in the county semi-finals. Hockey going well, and basketball, tennis and squash get a definite look in. Brilliant new sports hall (2004) inspires shock and awe. Clubs like judo, karate and trampolining on offer. Cricket undergoing a 'revival' say the boys, perhaps aided by sports centre's whizzy indoor nets. Playing fields a half mile jog away ('good exercise!' said one mum, loyally). Despite games emphasis, parents insisted that the slow and ungraceful can prosper here – 'there are plenty of nerdy boys who don't play sport'.

Huge range of well-chosen school trips – can't be cheap. Recent overseas extravaganzas have included art trips to New York and Barcelona, a language exchange to Peru, rugby tour to South Africa, skiing in France. Currently planning an Amazon expedition, and we don't mean the internet bookseller. Outstanding music department housed with maths across main road (take your life in your hands...) Narrow, winding, wooden staircase takes you through a fascinating warren of small rooms containing pianos, computers, instrument cases and other music paraphernalia – a world unto itself. Up to 100 boys sing in the choir which performs in the Cathedral and annually in France. Lots of concerts, both within school and outside, wind bands, string ensembles, jazz groups – over 150 boys learn instruments. Societies include the popular Christian Union, strong chess, drama, debating, a sixth form book club, D of E and an active community service programme. Lovely drama studio. Annual major play, plus smaller productions.

Background and Atmosphere: Founded in 1890 by Bishop John Wordsworth for the 'purposes of education in connection with the Church of England'. A compact site. Hemmed in on one side by one of Salisbury's most traffic-choked roads, Bishop's other three sides back on to the city's green and pleasant historical centre. Salisbury Cathedral towers above, both literally and figuratively, with the Bishop of Salisbury and one of his Canons amongst the school governors. School bumf warns, 'Please note that Bishop Wordsworth School is a Church of England Voluntary Aided School offering denominational teaching in Religious Education and Collective Worship.' A charming school chapel also serves as a war memorial for Bishop's boys and there is a monthly service in the cathedral. You don't have to be a believer, but confirmed atheists or rebels might cringe. Main building, 'Number 11', is old, quaint, dilapidated. But feverish building agenda in recent years has given the school a spectacular new 'E' classroom block – a lovely square of classrooms whose sliding glass doors all open onto a green courtyard; a brilliantly refurbished art block and IT suite; a luxurious sports hall. A shanty town of temporary huts remains – among them the most humble common room we have ever seen. School day finishes at 4pm but boys can stay for study or activities until 5pm.

Pastoral Care and Discipline: Boys speak solemnly of head's zero tolerance approach to vice, though reality is a bit less severe. In this cradle of middle-class civilisation, bad behaviour is not what it might be elsewhere. House system being strongly encouraged after many years of slumber – 'a bit Harry Potter' say the boys, while clearly enjoying the rivalry. Canteen serves standard school fare and about half the boys bring lunches; a few go home. 'Sixth form centre' a leaky shed. Boys commented wryly that it is soon to move into a larger shed. Many sixth formers use the small, but welcoming, library for work and quiet chat.

Pupils and Parents: Less of a colourful ethnic rainbow than a homogenous pail of milk. That said, we were much impressed with the boys we met here – easier to talk to and keener to meet your gaze than at a lot of boys' schools we could name. Many Services families. Boys arrive by bus, train and car, from as far away as Warminster, Andover, Ringwood, Southampton, Blandford, Shaftsbury. OBs: actor Ralph Fiennes and rugby international Richard Hill. William Golding wrote Lord of the Flies while teaching English here from 1945-62.

Entrance: Selected boys take tests in VR, maths and English in November before year of entry. Around one third of the 300+ plus candidates will be offered 120 places. Loads of appeals. Main feeders include local primaries St Marks C of E and Harnham C of E, and independent preps La Retraite Swan and Chafyn Grove. Some 25-30 new entrants come into sixth form, many from the local secondary modern Wyvern College; 6 A-C GCSEs required with minimum of a B in the subjects you wish to continue. Places allotted at other ages as available and always after examination.

Exit: With 15 boys off to Oxbridge in 2004 (an exceptional year) the school clearly has a handle on how to play the system. Engineering leads the charge, with medicine, sciences and history following. Good numbers to Bristol, Warwick, Bath, Cardiff and Exeter. A clutch to art foundation courses at the Bournemouth Institute. Heaps of gap years. Around 8 per cent leave after GCSEs, mainly to sixth form colleges.

Money Matters: The school depends heavily on parents coughing up annual voluntary contributions (which altogether come to £70-80,000) to keep class sizes down and to help fund extra-curricular activities.

Remarks: Heavy-weight state grammar blooming after extensive face-lift. Rugby, discipline, priceless historical setting – it is only the Nissen huts that remind us that this is a state school and education is available (almost) for free.

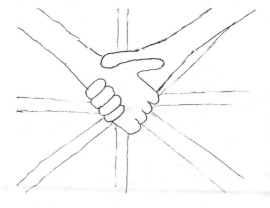

BISHOP'S STORTFORD COLLEGE

Linked to Bishop's Stortford College Junior School in the Junior section

10 Maze Green Road, Bishop's Stortford, Hertfordshire, CM23 2PJ

Tel: 01279 838 575
Fax: 01279 836 570
E-mail: admissions@bsc.biblio.net
Website: www.bishops-stortford-college.herts.sch.uk

• Pupils: 410 boys and girls; 130 full-time, flexi- and extended-day boarders • Ages: 13-18 • Size of sixth form: 180 • Non-denominational • Fees: Senior school, day £1,860 - 3,990; boarders £3,860-5,536 • Independent

Head: Since 1997, Mr John Trotman MA (late forties). Educated at Alleyne's Grammar School, Stevenage and Oxford, where he studied English. Was deputy head at the Leys, Cambridge for five years before taking headship. A pleasant man – easy to chat to and unintimidating. Enjoys writing poetry, drawing, travel and mountain walking in his spare time. Married to Alexandra, a garden designer and horticulturist. Two sons, one has recently left the school after taking A levels, the other is still there.

Academic Matters: Pupils are streamed and also setted for most subjects from entrance to the senior school. French for everyone, German for the top three sets. Latin is optional. All pupils take a minimum of nine subjects at GCSE and most (all but three or four) take ten. Excellent GCSE results, with the number of pupils receiving A* – C grades only ever a few per cent short of 100 over recent years. Twenty-one subjects on offer at A level, 60-ish per cent grades A/B, with a good proportion of A grades. Currently around 12 pupils in the senior school receiving help with dyslexia. Support is almost always one-to-one. Excellent computer facilities and laptop plug-in points around the school, including boarding houses. Average class size 16, with a maximum of 24. Average age of teachers is 42. Sixteen staff have been with the school for more than ten years.

Games, Options, The Arts: Very strong on sports, both for boys and girls. Plenty of recent successes, particularly in rugby and hockey (boys and girls). Across the whole school, 30 per cent of children play a musical instrument. Plenty of opportunities for both musical and dramatic performance. Wide choice of extra-curricular activities including D of E,

water polo, journalism and motorcycle maintenance. Involvement in the local community is strongly encouraged. Loads of trips to galleries, museums etc and abroad.

Background and Atmosphere: The school dates back to 1868 when it was set up as a non-conformist boarding school. The founders had ambitions to build 'the Rugby of East Anglia'. Plenty of land has been acquired over the years, some of it green belt and used for playing fields, resulting in an extensive campus. The school was originally on the outskirts of Bishop's Stortford and, despite recent new developments around the borders of the town, still has a rural feel. Old buildings are attractive and well-maintained; newer buildings fit in well with the original architecture. A new swimming pool in 2002. A lecture theatre, exhibition space and parents' meeting place are planned for the near future.

The school was boys-only until 1995 and some classes are still predominately male. This has not suited all of the girls although others are more than happy with the situation but will not be a problem in the future because classes coming through from the junior school have a good gender balance. The head is aiming for a 50/50 mix as soon as possible. Overall the school has a decidedly unstuffy atmosphere.

Pastoral Care and Discipline: All pupils go into either a day or boarding house and are under the care of a housemaster or housemistress. Each boarding house is run by a resident married housemaster or housemistress. Good family atmosphere in the boarding houses and happy boarders. There's a choice of termly boarding, weekly boarding, flexible boarding (mainly taken up by local pupils who may stay in the school one or two nights a week), or extended day boarding (pupils stay until after prep). Saturday school for everyone from 8.30am until 12.30pm. This is not popular with all parents, or indeed all pupils, but there are definitely no plans for change. Some moans from the pupils about the standard of the food but, judging by the evidence on the day of our visit, perhaps they just haven't had the opportunity to compare it to the meals in other schools. Few discipline problems. Two boys recently expelled for cannabis use. Both were under disciplinary warnings.

Pupils and Parents: The main intake comes from within daily travelling distance of the college and parents are middle class professionals – lawyers, doctors, high tech, the City. The majority of pupils are British but with an increasing number from Europe and the far east. A few overseas students are the offspring of British nationals.

Clearly an excellent training ground for any young person seeking a career in espionage. Sir Stephen Lander, current head of MI5, Sir Dick White, former head of MI5, and Peter Wright, author of Spycatcher, are all old boys. So is Lord Greenhill, former head of the Foreign Office. Entertainment is represented by BBC presenter Andy Peebles and sport by rugby player Ben Clarke. No famous old girls as yet.

Entrance: Pupils are selected through interviews, entrance tests and school references but parents who do not see their children as academic high-fliers should not be put off. 'We have a fairly wide ability range,' says the head. The majority enter at 13 from the junior school with around 10-12 entrants annually coming in from outside the school. Around eight pupils from outside join year ten every year in time for GCSEs.

Entrance to the sixth form is by interview and written tests; applicants are also expected to achieve at least three B grades and two C grades at GCSE, with A*-B in their A level subject choices. At the sixth form level, there is an external intake of approximately 15-20, some boarders, some day pupils moving on from local independent and state schools.

Exit: A handful leaves after GCSEs to study A levels elsewhere. With only a very few exceptions, sixth formers go on to university. Around five a year head for Oxbridge.

Money Matters: 'A considerable proportion of our income goes on scholarships,' says the head. 'If a child is talented but his or her parents can't afford us, we will do what we can to help.' Scholarship days, for both the main school and sixth form, are advertised in the local press or information is available from the school.

Remarks: The school faces stiff competition from excellent state schools in the Bishop's Stortford area but, since it started accepting girls, has found a definite niche as a strong co-ed independent offering a thorough, all-round education.

THE BISHOP'S STORTFORD HIGH SCHOOL

London Road, Bishop's Stortford, Hertfordshire, CM23 3LU

Tel: 01279 868 686
Fax: 01279 868 687
E-mail: office@tbshs.herts.sch.uk
Website: www.tbshs.herts.sch.uk

- Pupils: 1,175 boys aged 11-16, plus large mixed sixth form; all day • Ages: 11-18 • Size of sixth form: 270 boys and 115 girls)
- Non-denom, but strong Christian ethos • State • Open days: A Wednesday in early October

Headmaster: Since 1999, Mr Andrew Goulding BSc (mid-forties). Educated at De-Aston Grammar School, Market Rasen; BSc in mathematics at Hull, followed by PGCE at Cambridge. Has previously taught at John Bunyan Upper School, Codsall High and Haybridge High, and was then deputy headmaster at King Edward IV, Handsworth. One of his sons attends the school, the other left last year and is at Durham University reading physics. An approachable sort of man, boys find him 'friendly' and aren't intimidated by his presence.

Academic Matters: Academically very strong and pupils are expected to work hard. Setting by ability begins in year 8 and continues throughout the school. The vast majority of boys take nine or ten GCSEs, usually including English language and literature, maths and three science subjects, and achieve good grades. There are 29 subjects on offer at AS/A2 level and 3 AVCE courses in ICT, leisure and recreation and business education. Class sizes are around 30-32 in the early years, falling to 24-26 for GCSE and 13-19 for A level – not extraordinary. Staff turnover has been high but present staff are dynamic and generous with their time.

Games, Options, The Arts: Very strong sporting tradition, particularly in rugby, football and cricket, and boys are very much encouraged to take part, whatever their ability. When rugby trials for year 7s were held at 8.30am on a Saturday at the beginning of the autumn term, all but 4 of the 155 new pupils turned up. There are regular rugby football and cricket fixtures throughout the relevant seasons, many against schools from the independent sector, and results are impressive. Boys are expected to give priority to school fixtures.

Strong music with one in four pupils learning a musical instrument. The school's 'musician of the year' competition is open to students throughout the school and high standards of musicianship are always attained. Several drama productions every year. Other popular clubs include chess, public speaking, debating, Warhammer, subject-related clubs (maths, geography, science etc.) and D of E.

Background and Atmosphere: The architecture of its buildings is not one of the strong points of the school. Dating from the 1950s, utility was clearly the driving force behind the school's design. Additional accommodation has been provided in recent years – new English block (The Globe), new state of the art computing facility (Turing suite) and new music and drama block (Broadway) which incorporates a fully equipped recording studio. The sixth form centre (1989) is still too small for the 350+ students. The school's playing fields are extensive and excellent new sports grounds (35 acres)have recently been opened at a site 3 miles away.

The boys seem generally very happy – main complaints from a group of year 9s were 'it's a bit too strict', 'they should change the rule about briefcases' (sports bags or briefcases with logos or lettering are not allowed) and 'there aren't any girls in years 7 to 11'. No complaints about the lunches, which are unusually good.

Pastoral Care and Discipline: High standards of behaviour are expected from pupils. Some tutorial periods are used for pupils to evaluate their own performance at school, with the aim of helping them to recognise their own strengths and weaknesses. Disciplinary procedures are clearly laid out.

Pupils and Parents: In a prosperous part of town, and the parental mix reflects this. Many see the school as their first choice and opt for independent education only if their sons don't get in. There is a strong PTA that organises regular events and raises impressive amounts of cash. Uniform policy is strict. Sixth formers do not have to wear uniform as such but have firm guidelines as to what they may and may not wear.

Entrance: Demand for places at the school far exceeds supply. Although comprehensive, the school's strong academic reputation means that parents with less academically able sons or, at least, those with a realistic idea of their less academic sons' abilities, often prefer to send them elsewhere. The result is that average ability is high. Places are awarded firstly on the basis of compelling medical reasons, secondly by sibling link. Although there is no testing of academic ability, 10 per cent of places are allocated 'to pupils with a proven aptitude in music or sport'; there is great competition for these places, so a boy really does have to be outstanding in his field. The remaining places are allo-

cated according to where pupils live (the school has a traditional catchment area, defined by postcodes) and primary school attended. Obtain a copy of the criteria and study them very carefully.

The school currently offers 60 sixth form places to pupils who have not attended the lower school. For entry from outside, the requirement is at least 5 passes at GCSE (grade C or above) with a B in subjects chosen for AS/A2.

Exit: The vast majority of sixth formers go on to university, with roughly a 50/50 split between the old universities and the ex-polys. Half a dozen to Oxbridge each year.

Remarks: Academic school with ever-improving exam results. Any boy will fit in here as long as he is prepared to work hard and participate in the wider life of the school.

BLACKHEATH HIGH SCHOOL GDST

Linked to Blackheath High School (Junior School) in the Junior section

27 Vanbrugh Park, London, SE3 7AG

Tel: 020 8853 2929
Fax: 020 8853 3663
E-mail: info@bla.gdst.net
Website: www.blackheathhighschool.gdst.net

• Pupils: 300 girls, all day • Ages: 11 -18 • Size of sixth form: 60
• Non-denom • Fees: £3,063 • Independent • Open days: October and November

Head: Since 2000, Mrs Lisa Laws BA (geography at Liverpool) PGCE (fiftyish). Taught at two other South London schools before becoming deputy head, then head, at Bishop Challoner School, Bromley. A relaxed head, committed to her unusual GDST school's multi-ethnic, multi-cultural mix of pupils and their families , Mrs Laws believes in competition but not elitism and she likes to stress that there is no 'typical' pupil at her school. 'Girls here really can be individuals – we welcome diversity.' She believes the school is a good size for everyone to know each other – small enough to support the ethos of educating 'the whole person and for pupils to be valued as individuals but large enough to offer stimulating competition'. Endearingly restrained in lauding its many valuable curricular and extra-curricular features – perhaps taking them for granted? – Mrs Laws inherited an interesting school where much has been done and much more is to come ('imminent' says school, mysteriously). The 2002 Inspection found little to criticise and much to admire.

Academic Matters: The school sticks to the GDST ethos of rigour in its academic selection at 11. They won't take a child just to fill a place and would rather be down on numbers than lower standards – and, therewith, reputation – in this highly competitive location. Having got a place, though, a girl will do well here. 'Value-added is good here,' the head concedes. 56 per cent of grades at GCSE are A/A*, 98 per cent getting A-C. At A level, 77 per cent of grades are A/B. Class sizes are small, science, modern languages and ICT are well-served, teaching is uniformly good. Evidence for this is in the unusually wide range of heavyweight subjects taken at university by leavers. Probably not the place to send a girl with a serious SEN unless you are prepared for out-of-school lessons, though there is a SENCO on-site and individual support is offered.

Games, Options, The Arts: Games on super, poplar-lined fields, a mile (by bus) away, through well-appointed residential streets. Popular school football team coached by pros from Charlton Athletic FC. New pavilion and the only all-weather pitch in Blackheath. Good gym, new small fitness room. Sportsmark Gold awarded in 2004. Music room, the converted chapel of this former Church Army centre, has individuality and music is well-supported here – several choirs, two orchestras, a very popular jazz group and an enlightened policy of getting instrumental beginners into an orchestra from lesson one. A third learn an instrument. From September 2006, all year 7 pupils offered free tuition in a musical instrument – excellent, we like to hear this. Drama studio – everyone is involved in annual drama competition with many drama clubs and competitions. New performing arts block due in 2006. Newly expanded and refurbished DT facilities. First-rate art, ceramics, other 3D work, textiles and photography, also an A level option. Good extra-curricular activities, including DoE, an environmental garden and public speaking in which the school does well against classy opposition. Many trips, visits, including skiing and Russia. Good outside speaker programme.

Background and Atmosphere: Very much part of two contexts – the traditional GDST ethos of work hard/play hard and a thorough academic education for very competitive fees. Classic GDST Victorian core building – in this case, ex-Church Army HQ acquired in 1994 – with add-ons from various decades to meet updating requirements. Wood-panelled, plaster-worked ceilings in entrance hall and main rooms in the main building are welcoming and seem in keeping with school's history, while 1960s extensions work well and 1990s resource centre, well-stocked with ICT

equipment, networked and with intranet, with linking to pupils' homes underway, is up-to-the-minute and an attractively light and airy working area.

All this in up-market Blackheath, desirable Regency/Victorian South London suburb near palatial Greenwich and beside large common, surrounded by leafy streets full of impressive detached houses. Also near much less-privileged parts and girls drawn from all areas contribute to the stimulating social and ethnic mix here. Increasingly, gentrified North-of-the-River areas sending their girls here – the Greenwich Foot Tunnel assists access. The school's relatively small size seen by head as central to its special, collaborative atmosphere.

Pastoral Care and Discipline: Sensibly relies on personal relationships but has a formal policy to back it up. Discipline is good and self-policing. No drugs or related problems here. House system reintroduced by head along with deputy house captain from year 10 – an enlightened move. School council – girls are involved with whole school ethos here.

Pupils and Parents: Girls come from a wide range of social backgrounds and school competes with both heavyweight independents like James Alleyn's Girl's School and good local grammars. In addition to the white middle classes, Afro-Caribbean, Asian, Turkish-Cypriot and Chinese families send their girls here – 'a real reflection of London's population and a proper preparation for the world they will meet later,' says the head. Much increased parental involvement with the school, assisted by imaginative weekly newsletter, keeping families up to date.

Entrance: Many girls come from junior department but also from local primaries and preps. School part of South London Consortium. Assessment by test (maths, English and verbal reasoning) and interview.

Exit: Mostly to good universities to read serious subjects across range of arts, humanities, sciences. Recent trend to London. Impressive diversity and level of achievement. OGs include Baroness Jay, Helen Lederer, Mary Quant.

Money Matters: Unusually, for GDST school, well-off for scholarships and bursaries. Special new HSBC grant funds full fees + extras. Other schols - including for music and art - of varying values, some more for the honour than the honorarium. Additional sixth form scholarships competed for by internal and external candidates. Well-worth inquiring across the board.

Remarks: Not smart, not chic, not glitzy, but a school that holds its own in a competitive and complex area due to its no-frills, friendly and realistic approach, compromising neither on traditional values of sound education nor on up-to-the-minute innovation where needed. A really good blend of the city's diversity, the unselfconsciously academic and the far too seldom celebrated virtues of an all-girls' school with integral sixth form.

BLOXHAM SCHOOL

Bloxham, Near Banbury, Oxfordshire, OX15 4PE

Tel: 01295 720222
Fax: 01295 721 897
E-mail: registrar@bloxhamschool.com
Website: www.bloxhamschool.com

- Pupils: 260 boys, 145 girls (55 per cent board) • Ages: 11-18
- Size of sixth form: 140 • C of E • Fees: Senior school: boarders £7,235 - £7,380; day boarders £5,595 - £5,695. Lower school: weekly boarders £4,695 - £4,795; day £3,775 - £3,850
- Independent • Open days: March and September

Head: Since 2002, Mr Mark Allbrook (fifties) MA PGCE, who was educated at Tonbridge, and read classics at Trinity Hall; where he gained four cricket blues. Did his PGCE at Cambridge. Previously deputy head of Felsted. Helpful, articulate. Teaches classics six times a week, he reintroduced the subject on his arrival. He and his wife Mary, 'a computer wizard', have no children, are happy to be at Bloxham and much enjoy the local life. An enthusiast, the head has an open door policy, and our meeting was punctuated by knocks on the door from small people. Reckons 'he fell on his feet getting this job'. Has boosted the academic side of the school, appointing a new director of studies, which is having 'a knock-on effect'.

Academic Matters: Results good, given the intake, and last year saw one pupil getting four As at A level. School is aiming for serious academic improvement. Huge spread of languages (though less now than previously, as the number of exotic foreigners decreases – currently 10 per cent of pupils come from abroad: Germans, Russians, Hong Kong Chinese 'a good spread'. French, German, Italian, Spanish and Russian showed commendable results at A level last year, though the take-up in all cases was penny numbers, ditto the GCSE language results which included an A in Chinese. Stunning business studies department, fields more candidates at A level than any other subject, with varying results but a pleasing number of As. School plays the system (as do they all), certain amount of modules each term for A level candidates. All pupils now do the

new IBtech qualification which covers the whole spectrum of ICT skills. Laptops (free) for all from 14 at the start of their GCSE years, and much in use in the dyslexia department. School now 'fully wireless networked' and it works all over. No keyboarding taught as such, the head maintains that 'voice recognition' programs will make basic keyboarding skills redundant. And he is, himself, trying out ViaVoice.

Superb remedial facilities for dyslexia under Hugh Alexander (still) though school is anxious not to be known as a school for dyslexics and says it 'only accepts children with an IQ in the high 120s as members of the dyslexia course'. Maximum 20 in school at any one time. Serious dyslexia input, school has now gained CrestEd B status, with scribing and 'translating' for exams (ie a teacher who knows the pupil's work and writing will transcribe his or her answers into 'proper' English). Registered dyslexics gain 15 minutes per hour in official exams.

Games, Options, The Arts: Not the rugby powerhouse it used to be but lots of good variety. Two tennis/hockey Astroturfs, huge modern sports hall all just off campus, with two charming little cricket grounds a couple of hundred metres in the other direction (cricket professional recently appointed) and great indoor swimming pool, much used by locals, in the middle of the main school grounds. Sixth form club room now established above the cricket pavilion, complete with electronic score board. School good at individual sports, huge range of sports on offer from a highly acclaimed polo team via cross country, show jumping and dressage on the equine front to very serious clay shooting. Both girls and boys participate successfully at the National Championships on a regular basis. 'I challenge a keen sporting pupil not to be fulfilled at Bloxham,' says the proud head.

Music is on the up, recent senior school performance of West Side Story met with huge acclaim. Extension to music school planned, but currently still firmly based in the old converted gym. According to the young, Blox still more or less added to everything: guitar = fret-blox, jazz = swing-blox, you get the picture, latest additions = blox-idol and paper-blox. Art department open at weekends, much improved from our last visit, masses of quite successful uptake at GCSE and more at A than previously. Some exciting ceramics. Brilliant textiles. Drama in The Wesley, the old converted chapel popular and thriving. Young Enterprise, D of E etc. Workshops open at weekends too, staff put a lot of extra hours.

Background and Atmosphere: Founded in 1860 and given to the Woodard Foundation (group of schools originally founded by Canon Woodard to promote muscular

Christianity) in 1896. Handsome building of Hornton stone, quarried from below the foundations (very economical) with stunning chapel on first floor. Glorious re-shaping of dining room and kitchen area has released the basement to business studies (and an extra computer room). Extended light and airy dining room has good buffet and veggie options.

School proper is contained in playing-field-filled eighty acre campus with quite a lot of out-houses, pitches and buildings, a lot of walking ('max five minutes' said our guide – he must walk even faster than on our gallop round the grounds). Fabulous DT building on site, The Raymond Tec Centre; the top floor floats above the lower work stations joined with an alarming glass staircase. Lower school opened in May 2000 – this palace for 11-13 year olds is a magnificent transformation of the White Lion pub overlooking the main street and feels just like a ship with decking and portholes, though some of the passages seem a little narrow to accommodate two chattering creatures carrying books. Boys and girls allowed a certain amount of free visiting between houses, girls' houses much posher with girls graduating early from dorms to individual study bedrooms at fifth form while boys progress to shared studies – though many have their own at fifth form. Lots of repaints and re-organisation here, jolly colours abounds and the house captains have their own showers – even their personal jacuzzi. School uniform for all but sixth formers, who have a certain freedom in dress.

A tranche of day pupils and weekly boarding for years 7 and 8, and the odd flexi-boarding but a boarding school at heart. Days are long, from 8.30 am – 9 pm, but the week now ends on Friday for the lower school, and the rest can usually go home after games from 4pm on Saturday. Boarders 'are expected' to be in for the first weekend of term and the first after half term. Raft of school buses for day-boarders ferry them from 'convenient pick-up points'. The advent of boarding for tinies has pushed the numbers up and they recently moved into the former manor house, Park Close, really grand.

Pastoral Care and Discipline: Strong tutorial system via houses, children stay with same tutor throughout. Each house has five tutors who are often on hand during prep in the evening. God important here ('head prefers 'Christian ethos important') and indeed a goodly showing in RS at GCSE, but no A level provision apparently). Discipline 'not as big a problem here, we're a small school where you feel you might be letting someone down'. Urine testing on demand if drug use suspected, followed by probable rustication for a week and random testing thereafter. No pupil is automatically expelled, though they would be for repeated offences. Booze not a major problem, the villagers complain if they drop fag ends in the (very pretty) village, and the campus is too busy to find a quiet corner. Intra-house, boy/girl visiting in communal areas only, contact fairly controlled. 'But caught in flagrante equals out'.

Pupils and Parents: Lots of first time buyers. Parents with children in the state sector come to the school because they see it as 'an upmarket alternative to the state system' and parents from the independent sector come to the school because they want a smaller, more local school (as opposed to Stowe, St Edward's, Uppingham etc). Still suits the 'gentle and less able', but also numbers of very able who could have got in anywhere. Basically north Oxfordshire (not to be confused with North Oxford) farmers, businessmen, the services, considerable mix. 4x4s all over the car park when we visited. Pupils happy and confident, very polite and ready to help when you're lost. The teenage boys' rooms (relatively) wholesome.

Entrance: Large tranche from state primaries at 11, own test and assessment. At 13 from trad prep schools, Beachborough, Bilton Grange, Swanbourne, Winchester House, New College etc. CE pass mark of 50 per cent, but rest assured this is in no way an academic hothouse. Sixth form entrance by interview, report from previous school, and GCSE results.

Exit: Small leakage after GCSE. Majority go on to higher education. Great variety – from Russell Group to former polys and universities favouring practical hands-on courses, art foundation courses very popular plus, Southampton, Loughborough, Harper Adams (for ag/land management) Bristol (UWE). More or less the same as last time, possibly more reading business studies than before.

Money Matters: Parents in real need still get helped via the 'dreaded blue form means test'. Woodard Foundation can give help in an emergency for children of old Bloxhamists. Huge collection of scholarships for everything from music, sport (not at 11+), DT, art and academic, for all ages, take as many as you want, as often as you want, 11+, 13+ and 16+. Amazing.

Remarks: Interesting developments, and they continue. A thriving school with Christian values, academically more challenging than before. Very strong dyslexia course.

THE BLUE SCHOOL

Kennion Road, Wells, Somerset, BA5 2NR

Tel: 01749 678 799
Fax: 01749 836 215
E-mail: office@blue.somerset.sch.uk
Website: www.blue.somerset.sch.uk

• Pupils: 1,480 girls and boys; all day • Ages: 11-18 • Size of sixth form: 200 • C of E • State

Head: Since 1999, Mr Steve Jackson (forties); joined The Blue School as deputy head in 1989. Used to teach design and technology and PE; must have had some considerable impact on the high quality of these subjects within the school but is very reticent about claiming any direct responsibility. Married to a deputy head, so he can't leave the job at school, has three children, one already at the school. Insists on showing all new parents and visitors round the school himself. Proud of the success of the school and (notably) of individual pupils.

Academic Matters: A genuinely comprehensive school. Standards are high at GCSE and consistently good in the core subjects of English, maths and science. At A level there is a broad selection of subjects on offer. Was awarded science specialist school status in science and mathematics in 2003. Also outstanding work in design and technology and physical education. There has been a recent drive to increase the use of ICT within the classroom and to enhance the ICT provision and it shows. There are thirteen specialist computer suites, twenty-one rooms with full interactive whiteboards and a further 35 rooms fitted with modern audio visual presentation systems. The staff seem genuinely keen to embrace the new technology; they feel ahead of the game due to local company support. On arrival in year 7, boys and girls are taught together and in mixed ability groups, apart from in English and maths where they are setted. At GCSE almost all subjects are setted. Generally, there is little staff movement and a considerable proportion has been at the school for longer than 10 years. There is a strong belief that if a child is well-motivated then they can do very well here.

Games, Options, The Arts: Walking into the design and technology block feels like entering an art school department; fabulous work and ambitious projects. Regularly wins design awards eg Rover Midlander Open Design Award for Design and Technology, Arkwright

Scholarships etc and has established close working links with local businesses for funding specific projects and for work placements. Bench seating in the historic Palace Fields gardens in Wells was designed by A level pupils at the school. The presence of the sports development centre means that there is a huge choice of sports available in addition to the traditional – including caving and rock climbing – on site. The school encourages pupils to become involved in fund-raising activities and each year the school council will select three (one international, one national and one local) charities to support. These events are given a high profile within the school. Music is prominent with orchestra, wind band, jazz band, choir and guitar group – so plenty of opportunity to get involved. Drama is a strength with regular productions.

Background and Atmosphere: A big school in an impressively spacious 33 acres. Slightly elevated position means a fantastic view. Within the school there are three gyms, a school hall and three dining areas – exams have little impact on sports and drama activities. New £2m science block incorporating six laboratories and associated prep rooms and a large state-of-the-art ICT facility for use by own students and those from partner primary schools. The 'Blue' theme is carried throughout the décor – blue carpets, chairs, blinds, lino, walls. No glossy brochure; all publications are produced on site. Work is in hand to make the school more environmentally sustainable, with the lead coming from the school council. New dining facilities have won healthy eating awards; locally obtained fresh meat and vegetables are used and free chilled water is provided in each of the main buildings. Students also grow some of their own produce.

Pastoral Care and Discipline: The school is a 'telling school'. Pupils and parents are encouraged to speak up for themselves and on behalf of others. Although a church school, there are no signs of overt Christianity. There is an assembly every morning with hymn singing and reading from appropriate texts, however the format is guided by 'worthship' rather than worship. Achievement is valued, every opportunity is taken to publicise (bulletins, posters around the school and regular contributions to local press) and praise (Blue Roll of Honour in the school's newsletter). There is a daily, whole school, bulletin from which tutors can read out notices about the achievements of individual students or groups. The merit system is cumulative and results in tangible rewards in the form of gift vouchers, rather than certificates. There is a firm but realistic attitude towards all matters of discipline. Smoking within the building results in a 1 day exclusion as does swearing. The headteacher holds half termly Saturday morning detentions for students who need redirection.

Pupils and Parents: The school serves an area of generally advantaged, white, British, English-speaking households.

Entrance: Around 250 a year from local primary schools – mainly from within the city of Wells and surrounding villages. The school is oversubscribed and estate agents don't help this problem. It is worth getting a map of the catchment area from the school. Worth noting that free transport is only provided for those living within the catchment area and no further than three miles away from the school.

Exit: Over 50 per cent stay on to do A levels at sixth form and, of those, about 80 per cent move on to higher or further education.

Remarks: For such a large school there is an atmosphere of calm determination. The emphasis is on motivation and enthusiasm.

BLUNDELL'S SCHOOL

Linked to Saint Aubyn's School in the Junior section

Blundell's Road, Tiverton, Devon, EX16 4DN

Tel: 01884 252 543

Fax: 01884 243 232

E-mail: registrars@blundells.org

Website: www.blundells.org

• Pupils: 565; 335 boys, 230 girls (400 board/weekly board, rest day) • Ages: 11-18 • Size of sixth form: 170 • C of E • Fees: Junior: day £2,740 - £4,585. Senior: day £3,520 (locals) £4,400 (the rest) - £6,485 • Independent • Open days: Mid September

Head Master: Since 2004, Mr Ian Davenport BA (mid forties). Educated at Bloxham and Durham where he read politics. After five years in the city, Mr Davenport went to St George's Weybridge and thence to Radley where he was senior tutor, housemaster and head of dept (economics), also coaching rugby, fives and other school teams. Married with two young children.

Academic Matters: Strong results for a broadly comprehensive intake. Top of the tree recently are chemistry, geography and history, with mathematics and the other sciences not far behind. Class sizes between 6 and 22. 3 new modern technology suites completed in 2003. Full-time EFL specialist teacher, who is backed up by two part-timers. Requirements of some 60 special needs pupils are not over-

looked. 'Some' special provision for dyslexia. Education consultant used in advisory capacity.

Games, Options, The Arts: Some 16 annual school trips available. School planning for an indoor pool. Lively music department largely due to 'brilliant director of music' and possibly some intake from Exeter Cathedral prep. Choir tours central Europe each year. Art is equally impressive with enthusiastic teacher who, after 15 years, is quite at home in idyllic classroom with lush green outlook. Theatre taken seriously – West Side Story, Oklahoma-type productions, participation in Edinburgh Festival, hosting of English Shakespeare Company.

Lunchtime in huge canteen is a highlight – mouthwatering menu suits varying tastes; pupils extremely disciplined – queuing patiently, no pushing, shoving or shouting; returning trays to efficient conveyer-belt collection point. No parental concerns over diet. Good workshops (textiles, silver-smithing, cabinet making, engine repairs). Blundell's maintains traditional link with past through military service – all year 9 pupils join CCF for two compulsory terms. Ten Tors and D of E taken seriously. All mainstream sports offered, like hockey, football and cricket but rugby is particularly strong, alongside county-standard girls' hockey teams.

Background and Atmosphere: Set in 80 acres. Charming setting reminiscent of rural university campus; bisected by public road – a wakening reminder of outside world. Dignified collegiate main blocks, cloister and chapel; over the road the newer music block, huge dining hall, excellently designed Ondaatje Hall housing theatre plus photography, art, pottery – named after its Old Blundellian benefactor, self-effacing financier and explorer Christopher Ondaatje (brother of the Booker Prize winner). Do not be put off by the majestic-looking buildings though, as there's a friendly and supportive community atmosphere inside, where individuals count. Unpressurised environment, 'young adults' expected to make own decisions, consequently little sloppiness. Lots of banter among happy staff who tend to stay. Tiverton is 'proud to have it on the doorstep' although interaction with community is limited due to packed and varied schedules. Ginger brown tweedy jackets for 13 to 16 year olds, not every parent's cup of tea, sixth form boys and girls now wear navy blazers with 13-16 girls in red jackets and navy skirts.

Special burgundy and black striped jackets awarded to exceptional pupils as full colours – can be for sport, music, drama, academics or service to school. Founded in 1604 through the will of a local clothier Peter Blundell. Well served through long association with Amory family. Became fully co-ed in 1993. School mentioned in Lorna Doone by (Old Blundellian) R D Blackmore.

Pastoral Care and Discipline: Smokers caught on campus ordered to report to member of staff six times a day; boarders also put under curfew. Drunken pupils face temporary exclusion. No room for anyone bringing drugs into Blundell's; pupils also known to dabble off campus could face exclusion, although agreeing to random urine testing may save their bacon. Parents were comfortable with the 'fair' way a one-off incident was handled. Pioneering system of flexi-boarding allows pupils to stay as and when they wish and encourages them to come to board when they feel confident to do so; facilities are being adjusted to accommodate this.

Pupils and Parents: Farming intake has dropped from 20 to 2 per cent. Parents working in the professions (probably also looking at Kings Taunton); increasingly from the West Country, although some far-flung including Londoners with local connections. Fair number of Services children. 10 per cent are foreign nationals, especially German – Munich agency sends high-class pupils. Others from Eastern bloc, Japan, Canada. Strongly loyal and supportive Old Boys, include Christopher Ondaatje, Donald Stokes, Michael Mates MP, Anthony Smith. Pupils are pleasant, un-pushy, unspoilt – not afraid to hold opinions.

Entrance: Not a problem although some selection is being forced by oversubscription. CE at 11 and 13 from traditional prep schools (eg Mount House, St Peter's, St Michael's and King's Hall). Good sprinkling from local state schools. Internal and external candidates at sixth form need 5 C grades at GCSE.

Exit: Rising number to Oxbridge – 10 in 2001; 90-95 per cent to university. Mr Davenport considers that pupils who enter on a low entrance mark and leave with lowly A levels have achieved. Law and the Services are popular career paths; more recently graphic design. Not much migration towards London. The school has traditional links through Peter Blundell with Sidney Sussex, Cambridge and Balliol, Oxford.

Money Matters: Generous number of scholarships - academic and also for music, art, sport and drama, at different ages - well worth enquiring about. Approximately one-third of entrants hold awards of some sort, up to 50 per cent off basic fees. Foundation awards allow local boys and girls to attend as day pupils.

Remarks: Popular school if you can afford the fees. Don't be put off by any grandeur as it is only in the bricks and mortar. Everything else is really down-to-earth.

THE BOLITHO SCHOOL

Linked to Bolitho Junior School (The) in the Junior section

Polwithen Road, Penzance, Cornwall, TR18 4JR

Tel: 01736 363 271

Fax: 01736 330 960

E-mail: enquiries@bolitho.cornwall.sch.uk

Website: www.bolitho.cornwall.sch.uk

• Pupils: 300 boys and girls; 85 board, 215 day • Ages: infants 5-6, juniors 7-10, middle 11-13, senior 14-16, sixth form 17-18 • Size of sixth form: 35 • C of E • Fees: From £1,500 (infant day) to £5,300 (senior boarding) • Independent

Headmaster: Since 2004, Mr David Dobson BA BPhil MA (early fifties), previously head, for eight years, of Sir Christopher Hatton School, Wellingborough. Read modern history at Cambridge then did research into educational management at Middlesex University. Still teaches history, also interested in politics and drama. Married with two grown-up children. Relaxed and affable, busy expanding the school as well as 'fine tuning and polishing'.

Academic Matters: This is the place if you fancy your child learning fluent French. The previous head, who used to work at an international school in Switzerland, introduced the bi-lingual department, which starts in year 4 with eight lessons a week of intensive French, and continues with history and geography – and later RE – taught in French from year 5 to year 8. At that point lessons resume in English in preparation for GCSEs. Parents choose whether or not to opt for the bi-lingual department. Some pupils find it too taxing, but around half the year generally makes it through to year 8, taking French GCSE a year early and nearly always getting A* or A. Everyone learns French from Reception, and can take up German and Spanish in year 7. Chinese nationals – and there are several pupils from Hong Kong and China – can also take Chinese GCSE, and Latin is available as an extra. Pupils take KS2 and 3 SATs tests a year early, enabling them to start GCSE work in year 9.

This is a very small, mixed ability school, with fewer than 25 GCSE candidates a year so far, so results vary according to intake. Generally, however, between 80 and 100 per cent get 5+ A*-C grades. Most pupils take 10 GCSEs, including three sciences and IT; PE and Child Development are also options. Small class sizes – none are bigger than 15 and most are in single figures – enable pupils to get probably a couple of grades higher than they would have elsewhere, says the head. Pupils are grouped by ability for maths, English and science.

Sixth formers study the International Baccalaureate, which involves three subjects at higher and three at standard level, including humanities, maths, science and a language, plus an extended essay, theory of knowledge, and creative, sporting and community activities. It is particularly appropriate for an international school, as students can study their native language as well as English. All the lower sixth have work experience in Denmark, sponsored by a Danish company. Sixth formers are also working with those from eight other European countries on a three-year project funded by the British Council, producing books and a website for primary schools on life in the nine countries in 1900 and today.

The school has a learning support unit, including a dyslexia specialist, but is not equipped to deal with severe special needs. International students with little English can join the Intensive English section (at an extra £1,000 a term), studying the humanities and languages individually or in very small groups, and other subjects with the rest of the class.

Games, Options, The Arts: Music is a particular strength – around half the pupils learn an instrument. There are five rock groups, as well as an orchestra, choirs and other ensembles. Art is growing in popularity. Regular plays and musicals; the school has just purchased a redundant church which will be converted into a performing arts centre.

Team sports include rugby, football, basketball and rounders. Everyone has a weekly swimming lesson at the nearby public pool, and can also go sailing and surfing. The sixth form was, indeed, returning from the beach when we visited. The council is about to construct a public sports hall adjacent to the school. Plenty of camping and field trips; many take part in the Duke of Edinburgh Award Scheme and in the Ten Tors expeditions. A school tradition is a whole-school trip to the beach for three days in September, with activities such as writing about the sea, looking for wildlife in rock pools and sketching St Michael's Mount.

Background and Atmosphere: Founded in 1889 by the Woodard Corporation as the Church of England High School for Girls, the school moved to its present site – a former Bolitho family home with views to the sea – in 1918. It became the School of St Clare in 1928, and was renamed The Bolitho School in 1995 when it was re-launched as a registered charity by a group of parents who saved it from closure and turned it co-educational. A classic Cornish house with integral chapel surrounded by lawns, shrubbery,

trees and playing fields, with separate science labs, music centre, art rooms and boarding houses of varying constructions. Boarders live in comfortable bedrooms of two to four, with houseparents and gap year students to take care of them. September 2005 saw the opening of the new sixth form centre, Clarence House, a few minutes' walk away.

Pastoral Care and Discipline: In such a small school, disciplinary problems are rare. Students know that drug or alcohol abuse is liable to result in expulsion. The head comments that students from Europe are often used to a liberal, laid-back environment. 'We try to give them some independence – it's a bridge between school and university. But it's not run like an FE college – there's a clear code of conduct and they know what they can and can't do.'

Pupils and Parents: Local parents range from hoteliers to artists to estate agents. The school runs minibuses from Truro, Falmouth, Helston, St Ives and the Lizard. Many of the boarders are international students – the school takes up to three of each gender from any one country in each year group, mostly from Hong Kong and China, but increasing numbers of German students in the sixth form. OG: Rosamunde Pilcher, whose novel Coming Home depicts life at the school between the wars.

Entrance: More-or-less first come first served, assuming no great learning problems. Fifteen join in Reception, and one or two more each year throughout the junior school, mostly from local state schools or families moving into the area. Another intake into year 7, including several international children, who must produce a good report from their previous school; more come into the sixth form. Those coming into the sixth form without good English can take a foundation year before moving on to the full IB diploma.

Exit: Some who do not wish to take the IB move on after GCSEs to local FE colleges or other independent schools. Those leaving the sixth form take courses ranging from Disaster Management to Librarianship at a range of universities.

Money Matters: 10 per cent sibling and services bursaries; 50 per cent clergy bursary. New in 2005 were Elizabeth Bolitho scholarships of up to 75 per cent to attract local state school children into the sixth form.

Remarks: Small, friendly international school in a glorious situation on the Cornish coast, whose bi-lingual section enables pupils to become fluent in French by their teens. The most westerly independent school in the country, and the only school in Cornwall to offer the IB.

BOLTON SCHOOL BOYS' DIVISION

Linked to Bolton School Boys' Division Junior School in the Junior section

Chorley New Road, Bolton, Lancashire, BL1 4PA

Tel: 01204 840 201
Fax: 01204 849 477
E-mail: hm@boys.bolton.sch.uk
Website: www.boys.bolton.sch.uk

• Pupils: 891 boys • Ages: 11-18 • Size of sixth form: 224
• Non-denom • Fees: Junior: £1,854 + £105 for lunches; senior: £2,471 + £140 for lunches • Independent • Open days: October Saturday, plus conducted tours by appointment

Headmaster: Since 2003, Mr Mervyn E W Brooker BA (late forties). Educated at Jesus College, Cambridge (geography), taught at various schools, tried commerce with Proctor and Gamble, then deputy head of Highfields Comprehensive, Wolverhampton. Successful head of Camp Hill Boys from 1995, active on Birmingham educational scene. Exudes controlled energy (fast bowling blue at Cambridge, then minor counties; still plays), has a clear vision of what he wants for the school, admits he's impatient to achieve it. A confident, approachable, open door man. Took over from iconic Mr Alan Wright, here for 20 years. Married, with two daughters. Loyal Wolves supporter. Teaches 5 periods a week PSE.

Academic Matters: No streaming or setting except maths – not necessary as pupils are all bright. Science reigns supreme at both GCSE (separate sciences available for all) and A level. Over 30 per cent of year group takes chemistry, physics and biology at A level and gets excellent results. Maths also popular. French no longer a core subject, many do German and do it well. Russian an unusual speciality (regular visits to Russia). Lively classics (including Greek), shared in sixth with Girls' Division (qv), as are technology/design courses. English, history and geography good. All do general studies at AS or A2. High powered staff, many PhDs, etc., also committed to life outside the classroom. Class size up to GCSE averages 24.

Games, Options, The Arts: Surrounded by high quality games pitches; predominantly a soccer school – former national champions and six-a-side winners, coached by ex-Irish International. Rugby gaining in popularity and standard

– international representatives. Fine tennis. Also hockey, cross-country, golf. Games hall the size of four badminton courts, multigym and fitness training centre. Water polo popular – national champions at all age levels. Wide representation in National Teams. Regular timetabled residential trips for years 7 to 12 to Patterdale Hall, Ullswater; sailing, rockclimbing, expeditions, etc. Parents contribute towards food and travel. Not an extra activity but central to school's philosophy of developing independence and teamwork; an unusual operation. Over 60 foreign and residential trips; staff queue to go on them. Music and drama strong; arts centre and theatre shared with girls; also 25-metre swimming pool.

Background and Atmosphere: Founded in 1524, with links going back to 1515, the school was re-endowed and rebuilt in 1913 by the first Viscount Leverhulme, in equal partnership and on a shared 32-acre site with the girls' division. On direct grant list, then independent again in 1976. Imposing sandstone, Edwardian baronial structure, with spacious internal vistas, splendid hardwood doors and floors; a school to inspire pride in its pupils. Plenty of good modern additions too. 22 school buses from the city and local countryside serve both schools every day. Their position near Bolton's western edge means their catchment area could be even further extended.

Pastoral Care and Discipline: Efficient system of form tutors reporting to year head. Form tutors meet class twice a day and do major termly interviews with each boy. One official counsellor (head of business studies), plus several other staff specially trained in a small team led by impressive deputy head, Doug Wardle. 'No vast smoking problem.' Possession and/or trading of drugs within school could bring expulsion, especially if school's name is brought into disrepute. Mr Brooker 'will listen but will always take a firm line'.

Pupils and Parents: From far and wide, and a broad social range. Enormous parental pride and support. Fifteen per cent ethnic minorities. Boys are characteristically lively urban Lancastrian types, sharp, unaffected and forthright.

Entrance: Oversubscribed – 300 applicants for 120+ places. Exam in English, maths and VR. Four or five form entry, depending on standard of applicants. No automatic transfer from junior school (parents warned well in advance), and no automatic preference for siblings. Sixth form entry to balance exit (fluctuates around 10 each year); GCSE grade hurdle.

Exit: Nearly all to university, especially old established northern institutions such as Leeds, Manchester, Sheffield, Liverpool; 10 plus to Oxbridge.

Money Matters: Can and will help if need arises; Leverhulme Trust is generous to genuine hard luck cases (also supports Patterdale Hall visits). No straight academic awards, everything means-tested.

Remarks: Very strong all-round day school in urban grammar school tradition, impressive in science. Academic sharpness taken for granted; lively work ethos. Superb extra-curricular provision, especially Patterdale Hall experience. Successfully nurtured by revered previous head, now poised for take off – in Mr Brooker's words, 'ready to have their fires lit'. Could well rival Manchester GS (they probably think they do already).

BOLTON SCHOOL GIRLS' DIVISION

Linked to Bolton Junior School (Girls' Division) in the Junior section

Chorley New Road, Bolton, Lancashire, BL1 4PB

Tel: 01204 840 201
Fax: 01204 434 710
E-mail: info@girls.bolton.sch.uk
Website: www.girls.bolton.sch.uk

• Pupils: 1,229; 823 girls, all day in senior school; 206 in juniors; 200 mixed in nursery and infants, 0-7 • Ages: 0-18 • Size of sixth form: 217 • Non-denom • Fees: Seniors £2,471 (plus £140 for lunches); junior/infants £1,854 (plus £105 for lunches). • Independent • Open days: Mid October; sixth form in early November

Head: Since 2005, Mrs G Richards BA MEd (early fifties). Previously head of Belvedere GDST, Liverpool. Read history at the University of Wales, Bangor. After PGCE at Reading, taught in comprehensives in Shropshire and Chester, before moving to Rhyl High School as senior teacher responsible for staff appraisal. Gained an MEd specialising in Pastoral Care, Assessment, Special Needs and Appraisal. Went to Belvedere as deputy head in 1996, becoming headmistress a year later. Having taught in all boys', mixed and all girls' schools, she is a passionate advocate of the benefits of all girls' education, believing that boys and girls need different teaching styles for them to maximise their learning. Married with two grown up children, her interests include skiing, eventing, fishing, walking and cooking.

Academic Matters: Predominantly academic school, though not to the exclusion of all else. Head believes in 'working hard and playing hard'. Exam results place school consistently in top 1-2 per cent in country. Curriculum broad. Four-class intake in year 7. Class sizes quite big in years 7 and 8, around 30 in classes for most subjects, though this tapers down considerably as girls go up the school. Wide range of optional subjects in sixth form studies. Girls and boys join up for specialist courses. School well-equipped with computers. Average results over five years: over 74 per cent A*/A at GCSE, around 50 per cent A grade at A level, 77 per cent A-B.

Games, Options, The Arts: Something for everyone. Sport strong, athletics, lacrosse, netball, badminton, swimming (school has own pool, shared with Boys' Division). Notable for netball and lacrosse. Under 14 netball team were crowned National Champions 2003-2004. One pupil voted first ever BBC Young Sports' Personality of the Year. Lunch-time clubs across all areas of activity. Arts centre, drama productions. Music flourishing; many girls learning instruments in school. 300 instrument lessons given in school each week with others taking lessons outside. Beginners to grade 8+. More merits and distinctions than straight passes in associated board exams.

Background and Atmosphere: Founded in 1877 by local Bolton citizens; then in 1913 amalgamated with Bolton Grammar School (for boys) as joint foundation endowed by Viscount Leverhulme, and moved to present 32 acre site in 1928. Attractive Grade II listed building set in a wooded site one mile from centre of Bolton. Contact between Boys' (qv) and Girls' Divisions fairly frequent, including shared facilities and opportunity to mix socially at lunchtimes. Occasionally a subject may be taught jointly when this is the most logical option. Governing body rather dominated by the good and great in the business world but head claims this is a reflection of the north west more generally, and does not find it necessarily at odds with educational objectives.

Pastoral Care and Discipline: Yearly form tutors (two per form in years 7-9) meet with class daily and report to heads of school. Pupils say that 'teachers pick up on problems really quickly'. In addition, sixth form pupils offer confidential service to younger girls, with touching motto 'no problem too small'. In sixth form, girls describe teacher/pupil relationship as 'like friends'. Lower down the school, teachers take a stricter, more formal line. A very friendly and committed staff.

The absence of any signs of rioting in the long and hungry queue for lunch (hot food, including a vegetarian option, salads and sandwiches all get the thumbs up from their young consumers) suggests that discipline is firmly under control.

Pupils and Parents: Pupils an honest, down-to-earth bunch drawn from a wide range of primary and secondary schools and from many different social and cultural backgrounds, including a strong Asian presence. Unlike its obvious competitors, Bolton has no 'Cheshire' base, though more middle class parents with new-found wealth are moving into the area, and the profile of the parents changing accordingly. Old Girls include Angela Williams, Director UNRWA Affairs (Syrian Arab Republic), Ann Taylor MP, Harriet Steele MP, Monica Ali (nominated for Booker), the Baroness Morris of Bolton and Dame Janet Smith DBE.

Entrance: Own exam at 11, English, maths and Verbal Reasoning tests, and interview. Highly competitive, three applicants for every place. Almost half pupils from state schools, the rest from own junior department and handful of other prep schools. No automatic entry from junior school, though any problems will have been flagged up long in advance of date of transition to senior school. Entry at sixth form, preferably including A/A* grades in proposed sixth form subjects. Many pupils local, but school also attracts children from wider geographical area served by school buses – Wigan, Worsley, Preston, Rochdale and Oldham.

Exit: Almost all to university, studying a wide array of subjects from Anglo-Saxon to optometry, in universities old and new, north and south. Each year a significant number go on to Oxford and Cambridge.

Money Matters: Last cohort of Assisted Place students has now left. A number of 'foundation grants' maintain, as far as possible, the 'principal objectives of the first Lord Leverhulme - that no boy or girl of potential who qualified on academic grounds but whose family were able to offer limited support would be debarred from entry to the school'. Likewise several Ogden Trust bursaries may also be available. School can and will help in unexpected financial crisis.

Remarks: Big, action-packed school achieving high standards for hard-working girls. Its size (according to head, the biggest girls' independent school in the country) dictates need for slightly daunting degree of organisation. Systems certainly seem to be well in place, oiled and functioning. Despite this, room for healthy signs of eccentricity and non-conformity – school prefers 'individuality'. Girls very loyal to school, proud to be part of its success.

BOOTHAM SCHOOL

51 Bootham, York, North Yorkshire, YO30 7BU

Tel: 01904 623 261
Fax: 01904 652 106
E-mail: office@bootham.york.sch.uk
Website: www.bootham.york.sch.uk

- Pupils: 278 boys, 168 girls and 130 at Ebor, the Junior School
- Ages: 11-18 and 3-11 at Ebor, the Junior School • Size of sixth form: 140 • Quaker (but other faiths welcome) • Fees: Full and weekly boarders (y9 to y13) £5,700-£6,072; junior boarding (y7 and y8) £3,893; part weekly boarding (y9 to y13): £4,316 - £4,980; day pupils and day boarders £3,614 - £3,850; Ebor:£1,470-£1,800 • Independent • Open days: Saturdays in October, November, May

Head: Since 2004, Jonathan Taylor BA Hons Oxon, English, MEd, Sussex. Previously deputy head at Bedales School in Hampshire (described by his head there as 'my Mr Discipline'), he describes Bootham as his 'ideal headship'. Wife, Nicola. His interests include the arts, gardening and the outdoor life.

Academic Matters: Majority of pupils study for 11 GCSEs with a creditable 56 per cent graded A/A*. Particular strengths are DT, maths, music and art with no significant weaknesses. Usual range of subjects but no textiles, food technology or equivalent courses. 75 per cent of A levels are graded A/B with very few below D. Class sizes are between 10 and 20 for GCSE groups and 6 to 14 for A level. School tries to be as flexible as possible about A level combinations, pupils make guided choices then timetable is, as far as possible, designed around these. School houses a specialist science and geography centre, a music school, art and design studios and an IT centre. Computers are much more plentiful following the inspection report and a wireless network has been installed to facilitate the use of laptops. The super John Bright non-fiction library is well used and frequently updated. Teaching is lively and interactive, the expectation is that children will question, investigate and take responsibility for their learning. A wide range of special needs is catered for, including dyslexia, profound deafness and physical handicaps. The buildings have been partly modified for wheelchair provision but needs must be discussed prior to admission. School will do all it can to help – for example a biology lab was created on the ground floor to enable a pupil with a motor disability to be educated alongside her peers.

Games, Options, The Arts: All play sport including sixth form; tennis and football traditionally very popular. Facilities include a lovely new galleried sports hall – the result of an appeal, two squash courts, tennis courts, swimming pool (has had new roof and flooring but still requires further attention) and extensive playing fields. Competitiveness is not a dominant feature of the Quaker ethos, so teams will give as many players as possible the opportunity to compete, not just the most talented. This makes successes all the more commendable – both team (district basketball champions) and individual, where successes include a junior international fencer, Olympic games swimmer and Olympic cyclist, member of the England junior table-tennis team, county netball, hockey and cricket squad members and Leeds and York academy football players. Fantastic design work has received national critical acclaim and is mentioned in the design council guide as an exemplar for good practice. An impressive motorised go-kart designed and built by a sixth former was tested during the visit. We were offered a trial run but decided to leave that to the expertise of Jeremy Clarkson! Vibrant art department with results to match. Exciting expeditions to places as far flung as Peru, Bolivia, Iceland and Russia with regular exchanges in France and Germany. Over 60 per cent learn a musical instrument. Emphasis is on the individual enjoying music not pushing to achieve, yet several attain grade 8 and beyond as well as regular scholarships to the Guildhall and Royal Colleges. Pupils sing and play in national choirs and orchestras. Music technology rooms have digital recording facilities and variety of software to assist composition. All players afforded the opportunity to perform if they want to. School holds regular buffet concerts in the main hall, home to a permanent staging area with tiered seating and theatre lighting. Full-scale senior productions include a regular joint venture with the Mount School. Oh What A Lovely War, The Comedy of Errors and Guys and Dolls have taken centre stage in recent years. School has own well-used observatory and boasts the oldest school natural history society in the country. Hard to be bored here; plenty to do including regular activities and trips at the weekend for boarders.

Background and Atmosphere: The school was founded in 1823 based on liberal intellectual tolerant ideology. Originally a boys' school, it went co-ed in 1983. From the busy main road (minutes from York city centre) the only visible part of the school is a collection of fine Georgian terraces, so it is surprising to find such a deceptively spacious and tranquil campus to the rear. The school, originally the distinguished town house and grounds of the merchant, Sir Richard Johnstone, has been sympathetically extended over the years to provide mostly bright, modern, purpose-built facilities. Quaker meetings are held daily yet only a small percentage of the children and less than half the staff are Quakers. It is faith rather than a particular faith that is important. Head's joy is that the school is non-hierarchical (something that confused the inspectorate), staff are on first name terms and some pupils address certain staff by Christian names, no sirs or madams here.

Pastoral Care and Discipline: Street cred not important, just a warm and caring school with the intimate feel of a close-knit family. Pupils encouraged to question and to probe. Said one member of staff, 'the only thing you can be sure of is that you might be wrong.' Children are not judged, they are valued. No litany of rules exists; discipline is based on trust and mutual respect yet despite, or because of, high level of care, children are very self-sufficient. Pupils are encouraged to consider the impact of their actions not just on themselves but on others too. Effective punishment system operates whereby individuals are given columns of commonly misspelt words to write out, the number of columns depending on the offence. Columns are recorded collectively alongside credits for good work. Forms which achieve a positive number of credits are rewarded with a half-day off school to pursue an activity of their choice. The collectiveness of punishments and rewards works well and encourages pupils to think about the effects of their actions on the wider community. It also encourages the group to take responsibility for individuals and to help them. Alcohol not allowed on premises, drugs (3 expulsions in last couple of years) and bullying are no-nos, as are CCF and games involving violence, but war gaming based on model making and strategy is perceived as constructive and therefore permitted. Plenty of support, everyone from form teachers through to independent counsellors and the health centre, which may be used as a respite, on hand to help.

Good standard of boarding accommodation for both boys and girls. Houses are well decorated and rooms are generously proportioned; houses have a range of facilities but no computers although pupils are encouraged to bring laptops. Rowntree is the girls house, junior boys are housed in Penn, lower and upper senior boys in Fox with sixth form boys having the luxury of en-suite accommodation and single rooms in Evelyn. Children eat in the school dining hall, very good food, plenty of choice. All pupils belong to one of four houses independent of the boarding houses; these contain a mix of ages, sexes and boarding and day pupils.

Pupils and Parents: Regarded locally as the thinking parents' school, lots of children of dons, lecturers and those from the medical world as well as several first time buyers of independent education. Undoubtedly some well heeled parents but not the sort who flash their cash. Day pupils mainly from York and up to a 25-mile radius. 30 per cent of boys and 20 per cent of girls board. Boarders from UK and worldwide, all are English speaking or near fluent if foreign. Children are a happy, confident, savvy bunch accepted for who they are, individuality is appreciated and celebrated – no wonder they enjoy coming to school. Not a smart school, a sweat-shirt based uniform exists for the younger pupils with the older ones asked to dress in a clean, tidy and modest manner, so great variations on a theme! School supported by the Bootham School Association (BSA) and the Old Scholars' Association. The active BSA holds regular coffee mornings, barbecues, walks, lectures etc for parents and has even introduced Grandparents' day. Notable old boys: AJP Taylor, Brian Rix, Philip Noel Baker (Nobel Peace prize-winner and gold medal Olympic athlete), John Bright (parliamentarian), Stuart Rose (head of Marks & Spencer) and Silvanus Thompson (eminent physicist).

Entrance: Main feeder school is Ebor, the junior school to Bootham. Those entering at 11 and 13 sit school's own exam (and CE for those entering at 13). For sixth form (college) entry a minimum of six good passes at GCSE are required which must include maths and English. The head interviews applicants and a report is sought from the previous school. School is now at capacity so don't leave it too late to apply.

Exit: A few leave post-GCSE mainly to York sixth form college, either to follow vocational courses or to avoid Saturday school. Pupils encouraged to take a gap year prior to university and many do. Five or six per year to Oxbridge, rest mainly to wide-range of good universities. York, Newcastle and Leeds are popular choices.

Money Matters: Not a rich school, most income generated through fees and fund raising. Up to four scholarships for boarders of up to one half of fees. Major scholarships worth up to half fees and minor scholarships worth between twelve and twenty five per cent of fees. One art and one music scholarship worth up to half fees and some sixth form scholarships also available.

Remarks: Does well by all, especially the lost sheep and those considered different, but don't expect to find lots of meek souls. The end result is a bright, considerate, confident and articulate individual. Not many the school wouldn't suit after a time because Bootham is addictive – it gets under your skin – but rugby players, the very competitive and attention seekers may find it a tad too nice.

BOURNEMOUTH SCHOOL

East Way, Bournemouth, Dorset, BH8 9PY

Tel: 01202 512 609
Fax: 01202 516 095
E-mail: office@bmthsch.demon.co.uk
Website: www.bournemouth-school.bournemouth.sch.uk

• Pupils: 1,060 boys, all day • Ages: 11-18 • Size of sixth form: 310 • Non-denom • State • Open days: September; sixth form open day in early November

Head: Since 1996, John Granger BSc (mid fifties). Educated at Atlantic College where the stimulating international atmosphere gave him an appreciation of the value of education, 'there were pupils there whose parents had smuggled them out of their home country – knowing they might never see them again – to get them a British education. It had an impact.' (His ideals have been evident in his recent advocacy of a Moldovan boy taken in by the school a few years ago when he pitched up at Poole Port. After A levels, the young man took up a place at Bournemouth University. Mr Granger has been outspoken against government efforts to send the student back to his home country.) Read applied physics at Hull, then on to teaching at Plymstock and Torquay Boys' Grammar School. Married with children at university. Confesses little time for outside interests – 'you can't really do other things when you have a job like this. All my time goes to the school or to my family.' A top-of-the-range head whom we could imagine running any of the finest public schools in the country – one of the few state school heads who has been invited to become a member of the HMC, and not at all Clockwise either.

Academic Matters: Exam results are very good but not pushing out the inside of the envelope. Bright, hardworking boys will get top marks and go on to greatness, but there is a considerable 'tail'. Maths and sciences stellar, as one would expect from a selective boys' school (GCSE science dual award only). English, history, geography and RS also make strong showings. However, as a language specialist school since 2000, it is surprising that languages do not do better: in 2004 there was not a single A in French at A level and Spanish and German had no cause for celebration either. The head hopes that the buzz created by the school's specialist status may help these departments to pick up, and languages are certainly well-resourced. Many language exchanges, including a visit by a delegation of 15 Chinese teachers shortly before we arrived. All boys take two modern languages, plus Latin, through year 9. Afternoon classes in Mandarin, Italian, Portuguese, Chinese, Arabic and Japanese are open to Bournemouth pupils and to the community.

Sixth form subjects are coordinated with Bournemouth School for Girls (BSG), next door, and there is some joint teaching. There is also an invigorating rivalry between the two schools. Most boys take 11 GCSEs, dispatching their technology exams in year 10 (able linguists also sit French GCSE a year early). Large class sizes throughout. Learning needs section helps boys recognized to have special needs – and others. IT provision is good.

Games, Options, The Arts: Academic achievement definitely gets top billing here but, with over 1,000 competitive boys, it is no surprise that participation in sport is widespread and enthusiastic. A few parents felt it didn't quite get the attention it deserved. Sports centre, opened in 1999, provides a sports hall with two full-size basketball courts and eight badminton courts, eight outdoor tennis and netball courts and an all-weather training pitch for football and hockey. Annual sports day at King's Park. Outdoor pursuits on offer, including CCF, a long-established scout troop, and Ten Tors expedition.

Art and design technology very well-housed and we saw some super ceramic work. Music has an eccentric twist, with the head of music being a keen gamelan aficionado. We were told that the extensive assemblage of instruments occupying half a classroom was 'half a gamelan', so we gather it's not something you can practise at home. The magnificent instrument serves as the focus of some teaching and community outreach and there is a gamelan club. The annual 'band bash' with groups of hormonal boys vying to be chosen rock gods of the year is a highlight. Said one mum about the event, 'the boys enthusiastically support their friends no matter how hopeless and pitiful their music is'. Regular assembly performances by the big band, string orchestra or other ensembles, and we were enchanted by one boy's virtuoso piano playing. 'Ensemble', a wonderful series of guest lectures, helps on the enrichment front. Good debating society competes against BSG ('should polygamy be legalised?'). Chess popular among the tiddlies. Film-making club.

Background and Atmosphere: Founded in 1901 on the day that Queen Victoria died. Moved to present location after outbreak of WWII. Aimed at boys from Bournemouth and surrounds but has always taken pupils from a roughly 25 mile radius. Imposing brick building sets tone for the somewhat muscular, robust feel within the hallowed portals. Achievement is celebrated, not derided, academic success is unashamedly praised and boys who might coast elsewhere are motivated to do their best. The school harnesses the boys' natural competitiveness to steer them toward achievement – 'competition works!' says the head. Teachers at Bournemouth School commend the excellent support they receive from administrative staff – far better than at most schools. Games fields back onto BSG and boys and girls meet up at break time. Large well-resourced library closes at 4:30. Some parents would like to see better provision for study after school hours, until boys can be collected by working parents. Attractive sixth form block with sunken lecture theatre, also serves years 10 and 11. The canteen is small and space at lunch can be a scrum but pupils praise the new chef's cooking. We liked the new 'delibar' café.

Pastoral Care and Discipline: Flourishing and competitive house system. 'It helps you make friends,' said a pupil, 'especially with people in other years.' Tutor groups divided by house, though setting for maths and languages starts early. Pupils are assessed each term by each subject teacher and then discuss these results with their form tutor. Tutors keep an eye on pupils and most parents spoke very highly of the pastoral care (though a few had been disappointed). Discipline tight. Everyone knows the rules and knows they will be enforced – a real strength of this school. Unlike most heads who avert their eyes, mumble inaudibly and fumble with paperweights when we ask about exclusions, Mr Granger spoke of having 'an exclusion almost every term! A day or two at home won't do them any harm!' However, such measures are only ever used as a last resort or as a 'short, sharp shock' for very serious matters. Occasional drug incident – parents are brought in and the boy must attend counselling. Only two permanent exclusions in past nine years. The school bends over backward to root out any glimmer of bullying and pupils report that a strength of the school is 'how well everyone gets on'. Boys smartly turned out – definitely not the place for a lad who wants a pierced nose or dyed hair. In sixth form boys may wear any sort of business suit but, though a few express their creative soul in pinstripes or cream linen, the majority wear a dark suit almost indistinguishable from the school uniform. Annual ball with BSG.

Pupils and Parents: A broader academic range than might be expected and a reasonably inclusive social mix. As the head puts it delicately, 'we have very few on free school meals.' OBs: Daily Mail Editor Sir David English, BBC correspondent Mike Wooldridge, education guru Mike

Tomlinson, ITV news presenter Mark Austin, Blur guitarist Alex James and actor Christian Bale.

Entrance: Apply on LEA application form in October. No 'catchment area' – boys can come from anywhere. Competition for places is very intense but not hysterical – the school takes just over 35 per cent of the bright boys who take the entrance exam. Exam consists of NFER tests in maths, English and verbal reasoning (practice papers available at WH Smith) plus school's own test in creative writing. Offers sent out in March. Some 15-20 per cent of boys come here from independent preps but most from over 50 state junior schools. References for borderline candidates are taken up from their primary school unless parents ask that their son's school not be contacted. Ad hoc places may be available at ages 12-15, but don't reapply if you flubbed the test when you were 11 – you won't get in. 6 A-C GCSEs is minimum requirement for entry to sixth form, with at least Bs in subjects to be continued at A level.

Exit: 95 per cent to higher education 'everywhere'. Most popular subjects are sciences, maths, medicine and veterinary.

Remarks: Excellent, powerful, well-run grammar. Well-suited to focused, bright boys.

BOURNEMOUTH SCHOOL FOR GIRLS

Castle Gate Close, Castle Lane West, Bournemouth, Dorset, BH8 9UJ

Tel: 01202 526 289
Fax: 01202 548 923
E-mail: office@bsg.bournemouth.sch.uk
Website: www.bsg.bournemouth.sch.uk

• Pupils: 1,110 girls, all day • Ages: 11-18 • Size of sixth form: 290 • Non denom • State

Head: Since 2004, Mr Alistair Brien (early forties) – after being deputy head for five years. Educated at The Royal Grammar School, Guildford and read German and history at Exeter before PGCE at Birmingham. Previously housemaster of senior girls' boarding house at Keswick School, so no newcomer to shepherding teenage girls, then head of sixth form at the Arnewood School, New Milton. Gentle and insistent, rather than authoritarian; hopes he is thought of as 'approachable' and girls we spoke to agreed that he was. Keen on promoting school ethos and traditional values. Trying to tighten discipline, using carrot (stickers

and approbation) rather than stick, and we wish him well (see pastoral care). Spends free moments authoring German textbooks with former teacher wife, Sharon. Three children.

Academic Matters: Most parents describe school as 'good' and 'solid' rather than ground-breaking. But none we spoke to could fault the quality of the teaching. All girls do 10.5 GCSE subjects, including a compulsory full religious studies course. Results at all levels are excellent. Specialist status for humanities awarded 2005 – well-deserved, especially strong in history, politics, geography and sociology. Theatre arts and DT (esp textiles) also shine out. At sixth form collaboration with Bournemouth School (for boys) allows BSG to offer every pupil their first choice of A level subjects. Psychology far and away the most popular A level, dwarfing the numbers studying all other subjects. Class sizes average 27 in the first few years, shrinking to around 16 in a class by sixth form. Only around 40 special needs pupils, few of these with learning disabilities, but the school does well by them.

Games, Options, The Arts: Team sports not the centre of life here, but the school strives to offer something sporty for everyone. A few very talented pupils have achieved national success at sailing, dancing and archery. Art is impressive and mature. Food technology and textiles rooms lend the place a gently feminine touch. Music blossoming under new leadership, though exam results still have room for improvement. Recent co-production of Les Mis with Bournemouth School was a triumph. Traditional and gospel choirs on offer, plus variety of other ensembles and an orchestra. The new (2006) creative arts block, a cutting edge development, will give music and drama a new home and a helpful shot in the arm.

Background and Atmosphere: Scruffy younger sister of Bournemouth School up the hill (their playing fields meet and pupils from the two schools socialise at lunch break). Architecture an unremarkable sixties horror, now in varying shades of disrepair. Inside, the buildings hum with the bustle of busy girls. A lovely mural depicting the school in its pre-1961 location brightens up one prominent wall. Warm and inviting library includes good careers room. School originally designed to house 700 young ladies. Now heaving with over 1100. Says head 'We know we are a little bit shabby, but we're doing something about it.' The creative arts centre is certainly a great first step.

Pastoral Care and Discipline: Pupils repeatedly and enthusiastically praise the good relationships between girls and teachers. But there is a tension between management's desire to give these bright girls room to develop and the need to impose rules. Dress code was a constant irritant – new version from 2005 includes new jacket for younger ages but no jeans for the sixth. Canteen opens at 7:45 am for parents dropping girls off early. School day ends at 3:35pm but girls may stay at school to work until 5:30pm. Sixth formers can be mentors to younger girls, and prefects.

Pupils and Parents: Mainly from Bournemouth, but around a third come from outside the borough. Families travel from as far as Brockenhurst to the east and beyond Ringwood to the north (Parkstone Grammar, twenty minutes to the west, mops up bright girls in the Poole direction). A good mixture of school and parent-organised transport available. Racially homogenous (this is Dorset) but more socially mixed than might be expected. Tiny handful has English as a second language. School notes increasing numbers of split families – as everywhere. OG: Charlotte Moore, Commonwealth Games 800m finalist.

Entrance: Apply on LEA application form in October. No 'catchment area' – girls can come from anywhere. Around 430 hopefuls sit tests in English, maths and verbal reasoning on a Saturday in November, all vying for 162 year 7 places. Offers sent out in March. Past papers available to all, and virtually everyone who sits the test will have practised a bit – if you're too lazy to bother, then this isn't the school for you. A small chunk enters from independent sector, but most come from over 50 state junior schools. Prominent among the feeders are Bethany Junior, West Moor's Middle, St Thomas Garnet's Preparatory School and King's Park, Moordown St John's, St Mark's, Queen's Park, the Epiphany and Winton primaries. Admissions panel takes advice from primary school head teachers on borderline cases (for those schools where heads are willing to comment – those opposed to selective schooling can be unwilling to get involved). 25-30 pupils enter at year 12, mainly from local 11-16 schools like Glenmoor and Avonbourne: 6 A-C GCSEs the bottom line requirement for entry.

Exit: Vast majority to higher education – Exeter, Warwick, Southampton, Durham popular and a handful to Oxbridge. Just over 10 per cent to gap years, but this figure is growing.

Remarks: Good local grammar with high standards doing a great job serving the community. Lacks the powerful character of its brother school up the road, but many would say that is a good thing.

BOX HILL SCHOOL
Mickleham, Dorking, Surrey, RH5 6EA

Tel: 01372 373382
Fax: 01372 363942
E-mail: registrar@boxhillschool.org.uk
Website: www.boxhillschool.org.uk

• Pupils: 190 day pupils 160 boarders (rising to 400 by 2008) 63 per cent boy 37 per cent girls • Ages: 11-18 • Fees: Day £3,100 to £3,775; weekly boarding: £5,200 to £5,275; full boarding: £6,150- £6,225; International Study Centre: weekly boarding £5,990, full boarding £6,945 • Independent

Head: Since 2003 Mr Mark Eagers MA(Cantab) MA (Bath) PGCE (forties). Previously deputy head of Ardingly College, was a senior examiner for IB (history) and is an NCA coach (cricket). Married to Jane who teaches economics, business studies and ESL at the school. They have three children, oldest two at the school. Loves sport especially cricket, enjoys hacking round the golf-course and spending time with the family. Pupils say head goes by his name – Eager by name eager by nature. Personable, chatty, popular, his boundless enthusiasm and energy has lifted the spirit and atmosphere. Had a mandate to kick start the school in what is a highly competitive market.

Spent first year settling in and prioritising then started on the very many (and much needed) planned changes and upgrades. Not just facilities (more later) but a school council, greater communication with parents, captains' dinner, more sport etc. No room for complacency on the academic side, most staff swept along with him, a few voting with their feet, some retiring (staff profile older than in many schools). Staff say: 'he has vision, holds onto what's strong and good and that although changes are good, speed of changes have rattled a few cages, but he knows where school is going and where it needs to be.' Head gets universal thumbs up from pupils who say: 'school is more active, lively, he's younger, plays games with us, knows us all and has children the same age so he's in touch.' Teaches younger years and gets really involved in sport especially soccer matches (coaches the thirds) where he's often heard cheering on the lads and occasionally questioning the referee. Pupils love the fact he's revamping things and making everything more student friendly, younger ones agree adding: 'he's funny and nice; even if you're naughty he makes sure you understand what you've done.'

Academic Matters: Teaching styles vary but pupils say most staff work hard to make lessons interesting and accessible and use TVs, interactive whiteboards or OHPs to help. School introducing laptops for all from Y7 (included with fees). Smallish classes average 16. No Saturday school but prep on Saturdays for boarders. Positive value added with art, English language, French and History scores showing pupils gaining a grade higher than anticipated at GCSE. Lowest (though still positive) value added found in sciences and maths. Fashion very popular, A level theatre studies gaining in popularity, English, maths, history, science and art fine, modern languages come in for pupil criticism though German results are among the best at A level. Handful of U grades at A level but no particular subject – representative of policy of entering all who wish to.

Parents and pupils full of praise for SEN and learning support. Get one to one or small group support as necessary. One mildly dyslexic boy with poor organisational skills was thrilled to achieve 2 As in GCSE English, another told us, 'I was quite severely dyslexic when I came here but I'm not so bad now, teachers help you at every stage. You learn to get on with it. My teachers collaborate with the dyslexic teacher – it makes a difference.' Keen not to flood classes with learning difficulties as they don't have room for classroom support. Work on literacy and English plus strategies to help pupils in the classroom and with organisation, though older pupils may be given subject-specific help. Majority come out of activities on rotation but some drop a subject to fit learning support in. Department produce IEPs and meet, liaise and interact regularly with all teachers. Learning support staff say strength is the staff: all teachers are SEN aware and dedicated. Range of SENs catered for: physical difficulties (though not junior girl boarders), dyslexia, dyspraxia, mild aspergers, cerebral palsy, moderate hearing impairment, OCD and dyscalculia. Mild to moderate only. A quarter of pupils receive ESL tuition, 30 of whom attend the International Study Centre full time.

Games, Options, The Arts: All usual sports, good range of facilities: gym (doubles as main hall), small outdoor heated swimming pool, super climbing centre adjacent to a fantastic outdoor high ropes set-up, brand new assault/team-working course, a well-used, equipped and supervised multi-gym, dance studio with surround sound, etc etc.

Music and music technology is housed in an ugly brown portakabin. Plenty of opportunities to perform in concerts, productions, tours (Lake Garda for past 3 years), cabarets etc. Don't have to be grade 8 and gifted to join in, enthusiasm counts. Practical art, theatre, drama all popular. An hour and half compulsory activity slot is built into the daily timetable with diverse choice of activities ranging from candle making to ice skating. Plenty of outings – ys7-9 go on camping/out-door pursuits orientated expeditions twice a year; a big hit with pupils. Senior years do D of E (10 golds recently) and older children get opportunities to go overseas.

Background and Atmosphere: Founded as a co-ed school in 1959 by Roy McComish, a master at Gordonstoun. Still very much a Round Square school, following Kurt Hahn's principles of allowing children to discover themselves, furthering international cooperation, serving the community and participating in adventurous activities calling for initiative and responsibility. Main school in pleasant village of Mickleham, an important and integral part of the community. Pleasant red-brick building believed to have originally been a wedding present from DH Evans to his daughter. Mix of the old, modern buildings that blend well and incongruous ugly prefabs well past sell by date. Some refurbishment in progress.

Pastoral Care and Discipline: No plans to turn into an academic hothouse, believe education should be enjoyed not endured. Stress importance of finding something child is good at; success in one area enhances confidence, makes child feel better about self, leads to success in other areas. International centre attracts lots of overseas boarders – indeed it accounts for a high proportion of those who board in sixth-form, though some stay with guardians.

Boarding facilities vary considerably. Smart new house just built; other houses vary: mansions, cosy but comfortable; modern blocks in need of an upgrade and the externally hideous Ralph house (another brown pre-fab). Grim and impersonal living space in the junior girls' house – the girls loathe it. Another grumble is the cramped dinning hall (one of the worst we've seen but school says it's being revamped this summer). We sympathise with pupils who moan about the rush to get three sittings through lunch, not that we can imagine why they'd want to linger: for a school that prides itself on atmosphere the very blue dining room with its cafeteria system, plastic furniture, and poor acoustics is decidedly lacking; think gritty visions of transport cafés not romantic images of Hogwarts. Food ranges from healthy salad bar to stodgy puddings – not that anyone should go hungry, there's a school shop, vending machines stocked with sweets and a cyber café selling a range of snacks which provides a well-used communal area for juniors. Over 18s are allowed a couple of visits a week to the King William pub in the village (landlady checks ID) though we're told: 'anyone coming back hammered will get punished, but the cost of a pint in Surrey tends to limit quantity consumed anyway!' Sensible drinking allowed for older students at formal dinners. Clear guidelines are issued for those caught smoking, drinking or involved with drugs, random testing may be used.

The new tutor group system comes in for universal praise: pupils, parents and staff love it – only disadvantage is that tutor system is house based so you end up with single-sex tutor groups. Good and staged discipline system of coloured cards works well. Head introduced a student council which sixth formers praise but younger ones want improving – say they'd like to be asked for their opinions not just rely on a rep that doesn't always do the job properly.

Pupils and Parents: Lots of first time buyers of independent education. Majority from Surrey or Sussex, a quarter from overseas (24 nationalities). Pupils say it's more sporty, less academic than other schools they looked at and entry assessment procedure is more relaxed. 'I didn't want to be stuck in classroom and knew school really didn't approve of bullying and would do a lot to stop it.'

Children love the fact it's a small, close-knit community, where everyone knows each other. Need a 'have a go' attitude, good for the sporty. Couch potatoes and the vain may struggle as outward bound expeditions are compulsory A couple of girls told us how they hadn't fancied caving (water and the dark) but made to try and found they thoroughly enjoyed it. All agree expeditions are a highlight of the year, a great way to get to know people and make new friends. Pupils struggled to say what they hadn't enjoyed, other than exams. All agree school isn't known for its academic prowess, will never soar up the league tables but it does well with its intake and those capable of getting to Oxbridge do.

Entrance: Selection is by tests in maths and English and by interview, with previous school reports considered. Majority enter in year 7 or year 9 with selection days held in November and February prior to year of entry. Numbers are up and school is meeting challenges to find extra space. A truly comprehensive intake from those who achieve 5 grade A levels and take up Oxbridge places to those who struggle academically but may have talents in sports, the arts etc. Range of SENs catered for: physical difficulties (though not junior girl boarders), dyslexia, dyspraxia, mild Aspergers, cerebral palsy, moderate hearing impairment, OCD and dyscalculia. Withdraw from lessons up to four times a week for 40 minute sessions. A third receive learning support vast majority for dyslexia but it's not the place for those with severe difficulties who need classroom support though it's fine for mild to moderate who will benefit from intervention. A quarter of pupils receive ESL tuition, 30 of whom attend the International Study Centre full time.

Exit: Handful leave after GCSEs to local colleges. Majority of sixth form go to a range of universities selecting and recruiting, some to study degrees others HND. Odd one to Oxbridge otherwise range from Imperial to Thames Valley. Handful take a gap year, couple into employment.

Money Matters: Range of scholarships and bursaries offered, mainly means tested and worth up to 50 per cent of fees.

Remarks: We've been in far smarter schools with much better facilities but as a pupils told us, 'you don't need state of the art sports halls to play football, it's the package – the teachers, the atmosphere, the community, everyone is positive and school really helps to develop your talents.'

BRADFIELD COLLEGE

Bradfield, Reading, Berkshire, RG7 6AU

Tel: 0118 964 4510
Fax: 0118 964 4 511
E-mail: headmaster@bradfieldcollege.org.uk
Website: www.bradfieldcollege.org.uk

• Pupils: 630, including 120 girls in sixth form (540 boarders, about 80 day pupils) 40 girls each in years 9,10,11 • Ages: 13-18 • Size of sixth form: about 280-90 • C of E • Fees: Day £5,800, boarding £7,250 • Independent • Open days: Most Saturday mornings during term time. Call the Headmaster's PA to book - 0118 9644510

Head: Since 2003, Mr Peter Roberts, educated at Tiffin School and Merton College, Oxford (first class honours in history). Married to a former head of department of modern languages with three school-age daughters. Previously housemaster to Winchester College scholars – about as high-powered a job as they come. Committed to giving girls and boys 'the full Bradfield experience' throughout the five years – now co-ed throughout. Passionate about all-round education, his sports include football, cricket and hockey and his interests include watercolours, concerts and theatre. Strong belief in the importance of good manners, participation in all areas of school life and teamwork.

Academic Matters: 'Value added' is a significant feature here. 'Our pupils often surpass their predicted targets', says head. 2003 saw the best ever A level results at this school and GCSE also good. Several pupils gained all top grades in 2004 and one achieved the distinction of a place in the top five candidates nationwide – out of 400,00 entries – for GCSE English literature. Head pays tribute to good teaching across the board. Classes 15-20 max. Very lively and interactive. Pupils encouraged to join in rather than sit back 'and be taught'. New head bringing changes to the curriculum – year 9 curriculum reforms in place: cross-curricular teaching and the pursuit of learning for learning's sake. Introduction of a Bradfield Diploma (to give weight to Bradfield's extensive extra-curricular activities).

Games, Options, The Arts: Very sporty, loads of team games and much success. Bradfield is predominantly a football school – no rugby at all – but also plays hockey, cricket, tennis (notable for success here) and wealth of indoor sports. Well-kept playing fields, all-weather pitch and £3 million sports centre to die for. Huge heated indoor pool (underused by pupils, say PE staff, because of other commitments but often used by wider community), small well-equipped gym and vast hall. Built about seven years ago (opened by OB Lord Owen) to replace old chilly timber-framed gym which is still used for exams. Sporting extras include sailing, riding and golf on own course. Also Duke of Edinburgh and Combined Cadet Force.

Active music department with new music practice, teaching and ensemble rooms in a major extension (opened 2004), orchestras and choirs regularly tour and perform. Drama a 'big thing' for Bradfield. Known worldwide for performing Greek play every third year – in ancient Greek. Around 8,000 spectators packed last lavish production in school's own open-air amphitheatre (a roof was considered but thankfully rejected). Head says, 'it is regarded by pupils as the most important thing they've done at school.' Pupils agree it's the highlight of the school year. 'It's a lot of work but the sense of achievement is immense,' said one. Future ensured by summer 2006 production of 'Medea'. The cast, made up of boys and girls also taking public examinations, also does very well in academic studies. Very high standard on show. The excellent Bradfield Chronicle, the school magazine, – a must for prospective parents.

Background and Atmosphere: Very handy for M4 (Reading junction). Village itself in Domesday Book, completely dominated by school – in fact you'd be hard-pressed to find a building which isn't somehow connected. Founded 150 years ago by Thomas Stevens, rector and Lord of the Manor of Bradfield, set in over 200 acres (certainly not flat ones – hills are a particular feature). More buildings added in 19th and 20th centuries as school grew.

Boarding accommodation can't be faulted. Three purpose-built girls' houses quite superb on sunny hillside sites, all single or double rooms with en suite. Boys' houses head and shoulders above the usual dorm-style at rival schools. Maximum two per room, singles for older boys, many en

suite. Each house also has library with computers. Boys' uniform of dark grey trousers, navy jacket and house tie for juniors, suits for sixth-formers. Compulsory chapel once a week for seniors three times a week for juniors. September 2005 Faulkner's extension opened.

Real collegiate atmosphere. Slight feeling of isolation but public transport provides link to outside world. School bar Blundell's open most evenings except Sundays and Mondays. Beer, wine and cider available. Certain school traditions kept going (kitchens always known as 'Brewers', tuck shop 'Grubs', classroom corridor 'Bloods'). Generally open and friendly set-up. Parents can visit whenever they want and when fixed school events allow.

Pastoral Care and Discipline: School heavily underlines pastoral side – especially for younger boys and girls. First-year intake housed in Faulkners, lovely building specifically for new pupils. All eat and sleep under one roof (twin rooms), five TV rooms and games room. Big family atmosphere. Hailed as huge success in introducing younger boys and girls to boarding school life. Security obviously vital in all houses but independence encouraged – necessary, quite apart from anything else, due to spread out nature of school. Discipline not seen as a problem, more an issue underpinned by good pastoral care. 'We try to be steady and consistent without making people feel oppressed and under the cosh,' says head. Strict anti-bullying, anti-drugs, anti-sex rules (instant expulsion if caught breaking the last two and procedures followed for the first). In spirit of fair play, offenders given chance to jump before they're pushed. 'It means they don't have that black mark on their record for the rest of their lives.'

Pupils and Parents: Asked what was so great about Bradfield, one pupil answered, 'everyone here is so different – from different backgrounds. They're not a particular type.' Majority harvested from Thames Valley and increasingly London – a fixed 15 per cent (never higher) from overseas. Plenty of new money, less old than there used to be, fair number of 'ordinary folk'. No more than 10 per cent sons/daughters of OBs. Famous OBs include aforementioned Lord Owen, Nobel prize-winner Martin Ryle, cricketer and TV presenter Mark Nicholas, World at One's Nick Clarke, actress Claudia Harrison, Hants county cricketer Will Kendall and authors Louis de Bernieres and Richard Adams.

Entrance: By CE or scholarship, except overseas students. Sixth form girls' places heavily oversubscribed. Only 60 new girls accepted a year. Popular choice for A level theatre studies and girls escaping the hothouse approach of single-sex schools. Not such a problem for boys. Regularly take from M4 corridor preps like Elstree St Andrews and

Brockhurst. Entry to sixth form includes interview, IQ test and previous school report. Candidates may also have to submit written school work.

Exit: Virtually all to university. Traditional seats of higher educational learning still feature in likes of law economics maths and medicine (Oxford, Cambridge and Imperial College get their fair share) but 'less fashionable' colleges muscling in too (eg Bournemouth for computer graphics) where they're seen as specialists in certain courses.

Money Matters: Up to 10 academic, art and music awards in sixth form cover 10 to 50 per cent of fees over two years. Could be increased to 90 per cent in cases of need. Music scholarships include free tuition.

Remarks: A first division school in the process of losing its second division academic reputation. For setting, facilities, boarding comfort and 360 degree up-bringing it's hard to find better. Parents by all accounts couldn't be happier. 'Our son never looked back from the day he started,' said one. 'I'll admit, it wasn't our first choice but it was the best decision we ever made,' commented another. Visitors can see the evidence first hand – charming, confident, educated young people. How all this will change when the school goes fully co-ed remains to be seen.

BRADFORD GIRLS' GRAMMAR SCHOOL

Linked to Bradford Girls' Grammar School Preparatory School in the Junior section

Squire Lane, Bradford, West Yorkshire, BD9 6RB

Tel: 01274 545 395
Fax: 01274 482 595
E-mail: headsec@bggs.com
Website: www.bggs.com

- Pupils: 675; junior school 190; senior school 370; sixth form 115 • Ages: 2-18 • Size of sixth form: 115 • C of E • Fees: £2,643 • Independent • Open days: September, November and March

---

Head: Since 1987, Mrs Lynda Warrington MEd (early fifties), President of GSA in 2000. Read Physics at Leeds University, taught at comprehensive, QEGS Wakefield, then head of physics at BGGS. Married, no children. Very much in charge, clear-sighted, knows where school is going – 'I listen, then I decide,.' A touch daunting at first meeting, cautious of utterance (must go down well in Yorkshire), much

respected by girls, parents and staff – who are quick to emphasise warmth, too. Works through able senior management team (also approved by ISI) but aims to be accessible to prospective and current parents (currently sharpening up communication procedure here). Bradford Boys' Grammar School took sixth form girls in 1980s and went completely co-ed in 1999 but this challenge effectively neutralised during Mrs Warrington's reign.

Academic Matters: Consistently strong results at A level (A/B 87+ per cent), no failures. Surprisingly wide choice of subjects for year-group of 80 girls. Popular subjects – science, maths (excellent), English, IT, psychology. Good performance in extensive range of languages (French, German, Russian, Spanish, Latin, Greek), but small sets – no traditionally girlie choices here. Something of a blip in English language in last two years. GCSE predictably good (99 per cent pass, 65 per cent A*/A), IT particularly strong. Separate and dual award science on offer. Carousel of languages lower down school, including Japanese from year 9 (there is a link school in Japan plus visits). Plenty of DT. 220 networked computers support learning.

Senior library – with 'Mousy Thompson' furnishings – a pleasant place to work. Sixth form in Foster Beaver College (so designated 'to give older girls a sense of independence') hums along very efficiently. Academic achievement is clearly important but school also claims to satisfy needs of average child. Dyslexia etc catered for in-house; one teacher currently training with Dyslexia Institute. Staff predominantly from northern universities, as often in Yorkshire; extraordinarily committed. Five to ten per cent annual turnover; school regularly attracts young and energetic women teachers. Well established staff professional development/review scheme in place.

Games, Options, The Arts: Rich variety of things to do outside the classroom. Sport especially popular and successful – regular fixtures in 8 sports, frequent representation at county, regional and national level. Lots of drama – an all-girl affair – 'all the best parts are male, why give them away to boys?' Wide range of music from jazz and pop to classical, including home-grown folk band which has made a CD. 200 girls have instrumental and vocal lessons. Guides, D of E, and Young Enterprise.

Interesting and unusual scheme run by enthusiastic head of senior school encourages pupils to examine and account for all their time outside classroom; takes in, eg PSE, careers, health, grooming, exam preparation, moral dilemmas. In effect, a 5-year life-skills programme.

Background and Atmosphere: Founded 1875, but in fact deriving from the boys' school charter of 1662.

Dignified and occasionally handsome 1936 buildings in local Pennine sandstone, set in 17 acres of respectable Bradford suburb. Junior school in separate Victorian mansion with its own specialist rooms. Plenty of refurbished labs, attractive new glassed-in atrium (informal meeting and function area) plus 8 classrooms; brand new, neatly designed dining hall, open 8 am to 5 pm (for parents too). Sixth form centre has cheerful, well maintained common rooms. Not all A levels taught there – senior girls move about the rest of the school. Swimming pool, sports hall – used also by parents and Friends.

Very impressive calm, confident and purposeful atmosphere throughout school; these girls take life seriously but not solemnly. Single-sex community works very well – 'they need successful female role models', says Mrs Warrington. Not a big issue with pupils, apparently, who are simply busy getting on with life and work. Traditional, blue uniform (including trousers) worn throughout school – girls and parents seem content with it.

High quality publicity material (prospectus, statistics, termly newsletter) has real class.

Pastoral Care and Discipline: Disciplinary lines are clear, as one might expect; good behaviour encouraged by example, transgressions solved by staff listening and acting; not a big problem, it seems (see also life-skills programme above). Pastoral system form-based, supported by senior management team. Older girls have personal tutor for two years. Alcohol means suspension, drugs expulsion – last case about five years ago. Sixth form girls encouraged – and generally happy – to look after young ones.

Pupils and Parents: Pupils courteous and confident, with strong work ethic. Mainly middle class, from city and surrounding areas – buses from Ilkley, Leeds, Huddersfield, Halifax. Not as many Asians as at boys' school though a fair ethnic mix. First choice school for many ambitious West Yorks parents. Old Girls: Barbara (Lady) Castle, actresses Rebecca Sarker (Coronation Street) and Melanie Kilburn, Jill McGivering (BBC foreign correspondent), Isobel Hilton (journalist).

Entrance: At 11, from junior school, on results of 9+ exam and from local primary and prep schools on exam and interview. Competitive – roughly two applicants per place. School always full, though capacity can be stretched to accommodate unusually able year group.

Exit: A few leave at GCSE eg to maintained sixth form college, balanced by A level entry. Nearly all leavers go on to higher education, about five a year to Oxbridge.

Money Matters: BGGS Trust finances some bursaries at 11 according to parental means; average is half-fees. Six free music tuition (for two years) scholarships a year. Fees, in common with many northern schools, are well below national average.

Remarks: Very good traditional but forward-looking all-round city grammar school, with pronounced academic ethos; effectively led, with strong support from governing board (chairman has been in post for 15 years).

BRADFORD GRAMMAR SCHOOL

Linked to Bradford Grammar Junior School (Clock House) in the Junior section

Keighley Road, Bradford, West Yorkshire, BD9 4JP

Tel: 01274 553702
Fax: 01274 548 129
E-mail: hmsec@bradfordgrammar.com
Website: www.bradfordgrammar.com

- Pupils: 662 boys and 252 girls, plus 137 boys and 55 girls in the junior school (Clock House). All day • Ages: 11 - 18; junior school 6 -10 • Size of sixth form: 271 • Non-denom • Fees: Junior school £2,140; senior school £2,768 • Independent
- Open days: October and early January

Head: Since 1996, Mr Stephen Davidson DL BSc PGCE (fifties) educated at Tynemouth Grammar School and read metallurgical engineering at Manchester University. Previously head of the middle school at Manchester Grammar School. Married, with one young son now in the senior school. Described as popular in the recent inspection report.

Academic Matters: A powerful academic school, with strong traditions across the board – sciences especially so. GCSE results as you would expect, 98 per cent A*-C passes, 100 per cent in maths and English. A levels – an exciting collection with a 100 per cent pass rate at A to E. Now only a handful with lower grade passes. The school will stand by pupils even if they are not making the BGS grade. Business studies, economics, politics and psychology the most popular non-traditional choices. Small classics department which consistently gets As. School keen on AS, 'good for stretching'. Expectations high and pupils work hard.

Staff 'amazingly devoted and committed' – and teach sixth formers 'as if they are university students,' said a parent. Pupils are highly competitive, 'But not necessarily when we arrive here,' confided one – and thrive on it. The 1998 ISC inspection report notes though that 'evidence of independent learning is thin: pupils prefer to do what they are told.' Head says 'this is a grammar school', and points out that the ability to do what you are told is not evidence of lack of independence, but of independence under control. Low turnover of staff.

Games, Options, The Arts: Very strong successful rugby, netball and cross-country. Both the 1st XV and the u15 sides were beaten semi-finalists in the Daily Mail National Schools' Cup recently. Cricket good too (reached the last four in the national Lord's Taverners competition in 2004) and some outstanding results for tennis, table tennis and rowing. Keen drama. Three full-time teachers for design and technology (and the numbers choosing it as an exam option both at GCSE and A are still increasing). A new sixth form art studio has alleviated problems caused by previously cramped conditions for art with many taking it at exam level. Inspectors criticised lack of breadth at sixth form and below, and said that 'the development of spiritual values is not much in evidence'. Head disputes this strongly. Visiting speaker regularly as part of non-examined general studies. Half day each week is given over to sport, drama, music. Music lively.

Background and Atmosphere: School dates back to the 16th century. Formerly a free grammar, became direct grant, then private. Pleasant setting on the outer edge of Bradford, in 20 acres of grounds and all classrooms, games, etc, on the site – present sandstone buildings planned with 'incredible foresight'. Pleasing feel of space to corridors and quads between buildings. Subjects grouped together in classics 'row', geography ditto – rather like prison corridors, – (school demurs) – 'refurbished departmental suites', they explain. Large modern library and well-equipped IT rooms. Lots of new buildings opened in 2002 by Duke of Edinburgh including an indoor competition swimming pool, music school, auditorium, sixth form centre, junior school extension and superb multi-media modern language facility. New(ish) science block extraordinarily badly designed. Pupils and staff all purposeful and fully stretched. Faint sense of production line. There is a traditional morning assembly three days a week. Traditional the school is quite hierarchical. Co-education is well established.

Pastoral Care and Discipline: Lack of self-discipline is heavily frowned upon – and relatively rare. Northern hard-working ethos very much in place – and plenty of space to let off excess steam. Well-structured pastoral care system. Good peer support.

Pupils and Parents: Sons and daughters of local businessmen, professionals, 15 per cent Asians (usually bright and hard working – 'it suits us well here,' said one sixth form Asian girl). Old Boys include David Hockney, who comes back to the school and was president of the recent appeal – a source of inspiration, Denis Healey, Adrian Moorehouse. Pupils courteous and self-confident and neatly dressed. Lively Old Bradfordian Society now numbers in excess of 4,000 active members.

Entrance: 50 per cent from state schools, average IQ is 120; selective exam but any candidate showing any 'sparkle' in any part of the exam is interviewed with a view to selecting on potential rather than performance. Over half the entry at 11 comes in (also via exam) from Clock House (for 6-10 year olds), which has expanded in recent years and is going strong, tucked away at the side. Sixth form candidates need 20 GCSE points (4 for an A* to 1 for a C) plus interview – 18 points for internal candidates – a high hurdle.

Exit: 20 or so annually go to Oxbridge – it used to be between 40 and 50, but now 'the competition from other universities is greater'. The Bradfordian, the school's magazine, is full of interesting charts on, amongst other things, university choices and subject choices and the current swings in these. Durham, Newcastle, Bristol, Nottingham, Edinburgh, Liverpool, Newcastle, Manchester and Birmingham are all popular choices.

Money Matters: Fees kept purposely low - a bargain. NB 20 per cent of pupils were on Assisted Places and their abolition hit hard here, though school comments that these are being replaced by the school's own bursary scheme and 'we are determined to retain our all-round social ethos'. Ogden Trust, HSBC and several other corporate benefactors support the principle, along with Old Bradfordians.

Remarks: First-class, outward-looking grammar school having to face up to the challenges of co-education and the modern world.

BRAMDEAN SCHOOL

Linked to Bramdean Preparatory School, Kindergarten and Pre-Prep in the Junior section

Richmond Lodge, Homefield Road, Heavitree, Exeter, Devon, EX1 2QR

Tel: 01392 273 387
Fax: 01392 439 330
E-mail: info@bramdeanschool.co.uk
Website: www.bramdeanschool.co.uk

- Pupils: 50 boys and girls (10 weekly boarders girls only) • Ages: 13-18 • Size of sixth form: 12 • Inter-denom • Independent • Open days: October, December and May

Head: Since 1978, Miss Diane Stoneman who, after 10 years teaching at Bramdean, acquired the school and freehold from the retiring head. She was joined by Tony Connett, a family member, after 16 years in industry. Miss Stoneman was educated at Bishop Blackhall Grammar, Exeter, where she achieved eight O levels and three A levels in history, English literature and art. Appointed at Bramdean as an assistant teacher, Miss Stoneman successfully learnt from scratch under the guidance of experienced teachers. She is described as 'really approachable, brilliant' by parents whose children have passed through her hands.

Academic Matters: Continuing record of achievement from non-selective intake is attributed to the hard work, dedication and high quality of teaching staff. Among West Country's top – usually achieving 98-100 per cent of A*-C GCSE grades. 2003 GCSE results 100 per cent pass at grades A* – C, 72 per cent pass at grades A*A/B. Candidates sit an average of 11 academic subjects. All from a non-selective intake.

Maximum class size 19, average 14. Traditional teaching methods are used throughout the school including audio active language laboratory; well-equipped music and science labs. ICT suite has been completely refurbished with the inclusion of state-of-the-art equipment used by all children across the age groups. Video projectors and interactive whiteboards have also been installed in the science, ICT and humanities departments. 17 GCSE subjects are available including Latin and Spanish. 14 choices at AS/A2 level. Separate sciences taught from age 11. Main reference library and faculty libraries are well used. Teacher/pupil ratio 1:7 in main school; 1:11 in pre-school. No pupils with learning difficulties – apparently.

Games, Options, The Arts: Good facilities. Soundproof professional recording studio for media studies housed within impressive purpose-built chapel. Choir sings for Sky Television and BBC TV and radio. Large art department offers pottery, textiles, photography, fine art, sculpture, graphics and desk-top publishing. Brand new drama studio opened in October 2004. Other facilities include multigym, use of tennis courts, own games field, covered Uni-turf sports area, ballet and drama studios and field science equipment. Uses neighbouring university swimming pool. Numerous wins in cricket, football, rugby, especially since Keith Brown's appointment as games coach (former Middlesex vice-captain). Ten Tors, Duke of Edinburgh are popular. Weekly horse riding at local stables owned by sister of former Olympic champion who attended Bramdean. Archery and shooting well supported.

Background and Atmosphere: Founded in 1901, attractive frontage with gravel drive and flower beds; reminiscent of a Regency home. Became fully co-ed in 1995. Atmosphere described as 'distinctive' and likened to 'going into a time warp' by Ofsted inspector due to its emphasis on good behaviour and manners. It's a happy school where children are encouraged to realise their potential. Pupils can stay at Bramdean until 6pm and take tea in the dining room. 'It's an approachable school, you can walk in any time to talk to someone and feel comfortable'.

Pastoral Care and Discipline: Charming and charismatic resident housemaster; resident RGN matron. Homely boarding facilities at top of school; airy and light with nice views. Games room for boarders includes pool tables. Permanent exclusion for persistent bad behaviour. Sixth formers ask permission to leave premises; must return by 9pm. 'Any bullying is sorted on the day,' say parents.

Pupils and Parents: Cross section of parents from artisans to bank managers. Most live within 20-30 miles. About 10 foreign students, 8 from Hong Kong, 2 from Saudi Arabia. Former pupils include Sir Peter Stallard, governor and commander in chief of British Honduras, the secretary to Prime Minister of Nigeria and the governor of Isle of Man.

Entrance: Children admitted to kindergarten and pre-prep on understanding they remain in prep until aged 13. Must pass common entrance exam at 13 to stay at Bramdean. For sixth form entry, pupils need five GCSEs at grades A or B.

Exit: May lose one third to non-fee-paying sixth form colleges. All pupils go on to university (various) and choose varied career paths.

Money Matters: Competitive fees and many bursary awards and scholarships. Clergy children and siblings receive 10 per cent discount. Art, music and academic scholarships, sporting awards and bursaries. Voice trials available for any child wishing to join as choral scholar.

Remarks: An unusual non-school-like atmosphere with family values; respected for its firmness and fairness.

BRENTWOOD SCHOOL

Linked to Brentwood Preparatory and Pre-Preparatory School in the Junior section

Ingrave Road, Brentwood, Essex, CM15 8AS

Tel: 01277 243 243

Fax: 01277 243 299

E-mail: headmaster@brentwood.essex.sch.uk

Website: www.brentwoodschool.co.uk

• Pupils: 697 boys and 425 girls (includes 73 boarders) • Ages: 11-18 • Size of sixth form: 327; 200 boys and 127 girls • C of E • Fees: £3,647 day; £6,318 boarding • Independent • Open days: October

Headmaster: Since 2004, Mr Ian Davies, formerly head of St Dunstan's College, south London. A graduate of St John's, Oxford, Mr Davies, mid-forties, is a theologian, is married and enjoys skiing, golf, tennis and reading. He is an ISI inspector and helps select naval officers for training at Dartmouth for the Admiralty Interview Board.

Academic Matters: A good spread of subjects and school's size enables it to support strong modern languages dept and seven full-time classicists – one of the biggest such departments in the country. Good choice of A level subjects includes business studies, economics, classical civilisation, D&T product design, drama, ICT, Latin and Greek, PE, psychology and political studies in addition to the usuals. RS is a core subject at GCSE. Results are good. In 2005, 96 per cent GCSE passes A*-C. The sciences, Latin and RS especially strong. At A level, a steeper improvement in recent years and results especially impressive in sciences and minority subjects. SENs supported by two full-time SENCOs and 30-plus other staff all of whom have had training. Entrants tested on arrival and individual programmes devised where necessary. 'We want to minimise extraction from lessons … but we will take them out if necessary.' Children with SENs who inform the school prior to taking entrance tests will be given extra time. 'This is an important part of school life – it's our responsibility.' All subjects taught in their own buildings, floors or wings, many with bang-on modern facilities eg fantastic sports hall (used for major

school occasions and weekly whole school assembly), dance studios etc, super new science study centre. Impressive, purpose built Hardy Amies Design Centre, named after and opened by OB Sir Hardy Amies – the Queen's favourite couturier – houses DT, food tech, and ICT and is an inspiration to exceptional work. Elsewhere, in more antiquated areas, a few tired-looking classrooms and labs lag behind. Last head said, 'we're particularly good at getting the best out of those who are academically average … we operate fairly small groups … there is a tradition here of regularly monitoring progress, especially of those who are middle-of-the-road … we do it very thoroughly indeed.'

Games, Options, The Arts: Outstanding, above all in fencing. Current head of school is the U17 Sabre World Champion. At time of our visit, the 1st, 2nd and 3rd in the national U17s boys fencing squad and the Under 20 National Champion are pupils. In 2002 Commonwealth Games a sixth form girl achieved two gold medals. Coaches include two Commonwealth silver medallists. Superb facilities and school very proud and conscious of its prowess. Equally good at football – school holds best overall playing record in the Boodle and Dunthorne FA Cup in its 12 years. Other top sports include tennis, cross country, cricket and squash. An excellent pool, acres of pitches, fields and courts provide something for everyone. Games rooms for those who prefer not to get hot or muddy.

School has country's largest voluntary CCF corps. Also popular and still expanding community service unit does good things in the locality. Good spacious facilities for music and drama and a lively, ambitious programme for both. Galleried, adaptable music studio. Orchestra tours annually to Siena. Big Band much in demand for local events. Lots of instrumentalists and a whole, huge room devoted to the Sibelius computer programme. Good art studios in the Hardy Amies Design Centre with focussed themed work and, when we visited, lots of exuberant work going up for the annual art exhibition. Unique and glorious asset – an outdoor stage with grassed platform in a gorgeous walled and tree-lined garden.

Background and Atmosphere. An ancient foundation – school started life in 1557 and still has a building dating from not long after that – 'Old Big School' – in which relics are tenderly preserved. School clearly proud of its history and documents displayed on walls. John Donne signed its charter in 1622! Well-endowed and well-husbanded, school maintains its vast site, plus many buildings of varying architectural vintages and merits, with care and flair. Lots of domestic properties on the perimeter owned by school in which staff are housed – adding to the solid community feel of the place. Well-stocked and nurtured gardens fill spaces between blocks and pitches. Chapel built in 1867 is heart of pastoral life and is a bit of a gem. Also Memorial Hall – good wood-panelled building with splendid proscenium arch, organ, gallery and notable ceiling.

Unusual feature of daily life is that boys and girls are taught separately until the sixth form – popular with both sexes and parents and seems to resolve the perennial problem of single sex v co-ed in a sensible and equitable way. Also works academically, 'the gap between our boys' and girls' GCSE results is much smaller than the national one,' said head. Largely a day school, with a minority of indigenous boarders, life at weekends can seem a little limited for those who don't want to work all the time – though school stresses that all school facilities are available throughout weekends and explains that timetabled lessons, formerly on Saturdays, now take place during the week allowing more time for extra-curricular activities during the weekend with a hugely increased programme. Saturday school abandoned 2004. Uniform throughout – and stiffly enforced – though a relaxation of styles in the sixth. Girls are noticeably and distinctively smart in Amies designed mid-calf skirts and box jackets which seem not to have dated since arrival in 1995, though they are hot on warm days ('shirt sleeve order is applied on hot days' says the school). Brentwood is a prosperous area though, according to an insider,' the most boring town in England'. Fast trains into Liverpool Street and two minutes to the M25 help if you need to escape.

Pastoral Care and Discipline: Girls board in super late Victorian Mill Hill house. 2-4 share in first 3 years, 2 share in years 10-12 and most upper sixth have single rooms. These rooms are the largest we have seen in boarding houses – real nesting places and very unlike the cupboards and cubicles being built elsewhere. Boys in 1960s block on edge of pitch – with similar facilities – though less attractive ambiance. Both houses well-kept and well-maintained, comfortable and with a real family feel. Food, eaten in attractive and civilised dining hall with Head, staff and children all together, is good. We spotted chocolate sponge with chocolate custard for the first time since junior school days and – well, what would you have done? Discipline is tight. Pupils are tidy, the place is orderly and behaviour is unusually good. Praepostors – 'praes' – are prefects and do lots of jobs involving minor discipline etc. Have own room in sixth form centre and some privileges. Clear drugs policy. Works with parents, police and a testing régime after single offence but no mercy if you deal or 'persuade' a friend. Generally friendly relations between staff and students – a relaxed

and purposeful feel. Previous head felt by some to be too heavy on the discipline and much interest now in how the atmosphere changes under new regime.

Pupils and Parents: Vast majority from immediate locality. Proximity of Ford's UK HQ means plenty of high-paid execs send their children here but also builders, retailers and everyone else. Not much independent sector competition but lots from Chelmsford's highly selective – free – grammars, though no-one can compete with school's site and facilities. Boarders from all over the world. Many first time buyers but also loyal OBs who send their offspring. Pupils are friendly, courteous and unpretentious. Weekly boarding, and flexi is growing in popularity but little room for expansion at present. OBs include Robin Day, Douglas Adams, Peter Stothard, Griff Rhys-Jones, Noel Edmonds, Frank Lampard jnr, Nick Scheele – and Sir Hardy Amies.

Entrance: Significant number from own prep school but also from other good local preps and juniors. Assessment via school's own tests or CE – school looks for 55 per cent across the board but 'if they dip below and they're strong in the core subjects, I can take them on,' said last head. For the sixth, you need minimum of 6 Bs at GCSE with an A grade in subjects to be studied at A level.

Exit: Great range of destinations includes Reading, Loughborough, Birmingham, Kent, Essex, Royal Holloway and King's London. Seven to Oxbridge in 2005. Large numbers study economics/business studies; engineering also popular as are other science-based subjects – courses from robotics to criminology.

Money Matters: Fair range of academic scholarships and bursaries. Head believes in non-means-tested awards to attract academically top-flight students, 'though we do have an increasing number of means-tested bursaries'. Music, drama, sports and art scholarships.

Remarks: A good, orderly school offering a sound start in life. Especially worth considering if you like the separate teaching of girls and boys, if a small school is not a pre-requisite or if you aren't likely to make it past the stiff competition of the local grammars. So much going for it, it could hit the heights under promising new incumbent and well worth watching.

BRIGHTON AND HOVE HIGH SCHOOL

Linked to Brighton and Hove High Junior School in the Junior section

Montpelier Road, Brighton, East Sussex, BN1 3AT

Tel: 01273 734 112
Fax: 01273 737 120
E-mail: enquiries@bhhs.gdst.net
Website: www.gdst.net/bhhs

• Pupils: 420 girls, all day • Ages: 11-18 • Size of sixth form: 70
• Non-denom • Fees: £2,455 • Independent • Open days: Late September, October, late February and early May

Head: Since 2004, Mrs Ann Greatorex (rising 50), married no children. A linguist, with an MA in educational politics from Sussex University. Was head of City of Portsmouth boys' school and before that was deputy head at Bishop Luffa School Chichester. A wide range of experience and during her 4 years in Portsmouth she very quickly turned around a failing school. Took over from Miss Ros Woodbridge who had been in post for some considerable time and was loved by all, but new head is energetic, friendly and competent with a good sense of humour.

The school has a traditional and academic reputation and, whilst careful not to diminish this or make sweeping changes too soon, head has plenty of ideas up her sleeve. Believes in single sex education between 11-16 yrs but is considering the setting-up of Diamond schools (ie co-ed 3-11 and co-ed 16-18) the latter about to be launched in another Trust school in Cardiff. Wants to broaden the range of subjects, see the sixth form grow in size, and would like to cater for girls with a broader range of educational needs particularly the dyslexic and the very gifted.

Academic Matters: Academic results excellent, dedicated staff passionate about their subjects. Bright, stimulating, independently minded, confident girls – a description approved by parents, staff and the local general public. Pupils are very conscientious and pile the pressure on themselves but are encouraged to progress as individuals rather than through competitive peer rivalry. English very popular; particularly hot on poetry and awarded 1st place by the Keats House & the Poetry Society for the school Poetry Landmark of the Year. For book week 2005 they lured the Poet Laureate to work with the girls on war poetry. Also

involved with raising funds for the British Library for the specific conservation costs of editions of Pride and Prejudice and Robinson Crusoe. A published authoress is on staff; the book week runs as a cross-curricular activity involving history front page competitions, geography travel brochures and a dress up day – the new head dressed as Cruella de Vil calling the staff her 'puppies'. History is taught well – we popped into one lesson and witnessed a virtuoso performance in how to elicit facts and develop arguments with a captivated audience of year 11 girls. Some parents report that a watchful eye had to be kept on the volume of homework. Many girls leave for 6th form colleges because of the limited range of subjects available here; head is keen to eg extend languages beyond Europe and introduce Mandarin. Careers programme very impressive with close links with the local careers service and employers. Yr 9 girls receive individual careers guidance with consultants; all girls have free psychometric testing in yr 10 and prepare their own action plan. There is an intensive programme of visiting speakers and workshops. The Minerva network puts girls in touch with past pupils who are successful in the career in which they are showing an interest.

Games, Options, The Arts: Facilities much improved by the addition of modern new light sports hall with disabled access (lifts), two outdoor netball courts and an Astroturf court. Winners of the U12/U13 netball County Championship for the last three years, and recent Athletic Sports Champions. Plenty of clubs appear to be on offer, but the general consensus is that sport is not hugely high profile. Girls remark, 'if you are very keen on sport, you wouldn't choose this school or would have to follow up with activities outside the school' – disputed by school which considers that they fully support good athletes in their chosen sport.

Parents laud the singing. Policy of music for all, plenty of experimenting with instruments and sound. Drama well taught, housed in a brand new studio. The Art and Design block has a bright, industrious fizz about it. Excellent photography, sculptures, textiles/costumes.

Background and Atmosphere: The original building (the Temple) became part of the GDST schools in 1880. Still central to the site with pillars said to represent inverted cannons. The school has vastly changed in the past few years – the GDST has carried out extensive improvements, refurbishment and contemporary glass additions so that the past dowdiness has been transformed into a bright cluster of buildings. Food most acceptable – although many pupils bring packed lunches.

Pastoral Care and Discipline: Strong pastoral support system with form teachers and sixth form tutors and year heads – set up for easy communication and accessibility. Sixth forms and yr 10 offer a mentoring service for younger girls – this is made easy by the amount of inter-year, inter-house contact through drama, sport competitions and end of year entertainment. Imaginative PSHE – we have encountered this in other Trust schools – the special events and whole days given over to topical issues all help to raise awareness and assist pupils with self-expression on current affairs. Parents agree that the school exudes a disciplined, contained, respectful industrious environment that suits an ambitious, organised, self-motivated pupil. Some believe that within this there is still room for the individual eccentric, others feel that staff were fazed by combative girls. One past pupil told us 'they often celebrated feisty pupils – but distinctly rebels with a cause and not those without – there was plenty of room for spirited girls but not for those who did not value what the school offers'. Bullying not a problem – the school would take a serious stance and anti-bullying workshops are held.

Pupils and Parents: Principally Brighton with a good percentage coming from surrounding Pulborough, Eastbourne, Worthing, etc. A real social and ethnic mix and, due to competitive fees, a good economic mix. OGs Karen Pickering MBE – Olympic Swimming Gold Medallist, Heidi Cooper who won the 2004 Young Director of the year (IoD), Beth Cordingley from The Bill, several recent University Challenge competitors. One girl from the school won the Minerva Prize this year – national GDST award for all round excellence and jolly good egg!

Entrance: Not as heavily oversubscribed as in the recent past; girls come from a wide range of local maintained and independent schools and also the junior school. GDST entrance assessment for the main school, at junior level there are a range of tests, see children at play and interview them. Entry at sixth form requires 5 GCSEs at C grade or above with A or B in subjects to be taken at A level.

Exit: Some 20-30 leave at 16+ to enjoy co-ed at the local sixth form college, or because other institutions offer a wider range of subjects; some leave to go to co-ed private education. Those that stay are mainly destined for serious universities studying serious subjects, many into medicine, including medical science and veterinary medicine, sport science, natural sciences, earth systems science, geology, zoology, engineering, etc. 37 per cent have taken science degrees. A handful take a gap year.

Money Matters: A healthy bundle of bursaries. Academic scholarships up to 50 per cent of the fees.

Remarks: A successful and thriving school where girls grow focused and confident in their abilities. New head should bring in more flair and breadth.

BRIGHTON COLLEGE

Linked to Brighton College Junior School Pre-preparatory in the Junior section

Linked to Brighton College Prep School in the Junior section

Eastern Rd, Brighton, East Sussex, BN2 0AL

Tel: 01273 704 200
Fax: 01273 704 204
E-mail: registrar@brightoncollege.net
Website: www.brightoncollege.net

• Pupils: 720; 450 boys, 270 girls; 575 day, 145 board • Ages: 13-18 • Size of sixth form: 300 • Non-denom • Fees: Day £4,617; weekly boarding £6,286; full boarding £7,157 • Independent • Open days: One Saturday per term

Headmaster: From 2006, Mr Richard Cairns, previously Usher (sole deputy head) of Magdalen College School. Succeeds high profile Dr Anthony Seldon who has taken over at Wellington College.

Academic Matters: Performing very strongly, despite not being particularly selective. Over 77 per cent grades A/B at A level, over 67 per cent A/A* at GCSE ('I could push us radically up the league tables if I got rid of the bottom 10 per cent but I don't think that's the moral thing to do,' said Dr Seldon, the previous, very high profile, head). Twenty-nine subjects offered at A level. Class sizes are capped at 20 up to GCSE; after GCSE, the average class size is eight. No Saturday morning school. Good support for bright dyslexics and dyspraxics limited support for other SEN but will strive to work with any child in the school and to manage their needs. Occasionally advises parents to seek an alternative school.

School has a dyslexia centre with separate admission arrangements. Actively seeks out and welcomes the bright child with dyslexia. Entry based on recent EP report, assessment morning (observed in groups) and interviews by head and excellent head of centre, Mr David Ollosson. Severity of dyslexia isn't an issue, looking for potential. Says, 'if we feel a child will get there we will take them on that basis regardless of CE performance, even if they can barely read and write on entry.' Stresses, 'staff and peers recognise potential of dyslexics, we believe in their abilities, talents and needs, they often do better than their peers, we provide an environment in which they achieve.'

Approximately 160 children are taught in the centre (from all three schools). Work in groups, believes this is best way to offer full support, says group is very important, become fantastically supportive of one another, offer each other support even though it's not a discrete group within the year (included with peers in main school for all other subjects). One to one teaching offered only in sixth form but anyone can seek help outside of timetable if they have individual concerns.

Younger children are offered a mix of in class support and withdrawal. Senior pupils taught English in centre (max group size 9), offered maths support too if needed. Takes additional time from languages (though pupils can still study languages if desired). Concentrates on remediation with younger ones and study skills with older. Says taking complete control of English makes a huge difference, removes embarrassment and stress. Time to finish tasks not an issue – a good end product motivates students. Giving time results in outstanding imaginative works, brings on their English and increases confidence. Facilities include 'text help read & write' which was deemed fantastic by inspector on recent visit. (Programme reads back work punctuated as written and will read out spellings when spell checking.) Adds, 'take control of English as a whole process and help manage reading, writing and spelling together rather than in isolation. Can work up a particular area but for dyslexics, organisation and managing tasks simultaneously is difficult so we try to integrate skills from the start rather than concentrate on individual components.'

Games, Options, The Arts: Sport is enormously important here, with most pupils taking part in games two afternoons a week. Cricket, rugby, athletics, soccer and netball are popular, and pupils sail at a local reservoir. Wisden cricket school of the year in 2003. Girl cricketers reached the finals of the national girls' cricket competition at Lords at 2000, and one (while 15) played in an Ashes test. Clare Connor, captain of the England Women's Cricket team and former pupil, is Head of PR, teaches English and coaches girls' cricket. Heated swimming pool, two Astroturf hockey pitches.

Music thriving – the school has a choir, orchestra, concert band and various chamber groups – and parents rave about the school's drama productions. Excellent art department. Dance facilities much improved with the opening of a new performing arts centre. Lots of cultural trips and an impressive sixth form lecture programme – speakers range from diplomats to the chaplain of Wormwood Scrubs.

Community service is a vital part of school life – pupils help elderly people and disabled children, raise money for charity; some have even visited a Romanian orphanage. The college has formed strong links with disadvantaged state schools and Dr Seldon was involved in various (much-needed) initiatives to rejuvenate Brighton – 'I want our children to be aware they're in a privileged position. If we just turn out successful stockbrokers or lawyers without a social conscience, I think we've failed,' he said.

Background and Atmosphere: Imposing Victorian buildings designed by Sir George Gilbert Scott. In the winter, the buildings have a rather severe, Hound of the Baskervilles air; altogether more welcoming in summer. A short walk into central Brighton; sea views.

The school has had mixed fortunes since it was founded as a nursery for Christian gentlemen – bankrupt three times and almost closed twice. Dr Seldon was appointed head after its most recent financial crisis, in 1997. Enormous hoo-ha – 15 staff were made redundant – but he succeeded in turning the school around and there are now two-year waiting lists in some age groups. Lots of new teachers.

Massive (£4 million) recent building programme included putting in nine extra classrooms, building the performing arts centre, upgrading the sports hall, improving IT facilities, creation of the Rose Lecture theatre and upgrading the library. Pupils love the Café de Paris, a French-style café where they eat lunch once a week and meet to socialise. Despite the improvements, this is a town school and there is limited room for expansion. The new sports ground is a 15-minute walk away and some classrooms are rather cramped.

Pastoral Care and Discipline: Caring, motivated, youngish staff. 'They're very aware of what's going on and the kids trust them,' comments a parent. A 'family school,' with pupils encouraged to treat each other decently. The school's ethos is that discipline has to come from within – pupils who repeatedly step out of line will be told to leave. Liberal in many ways, but not on drugs (Brighton and Hove have a serious druggy culture, alas). Religion offered but not emphasised – indeed, the prep school chapel was recently turned into a library.

Pupils and Parents: The school's increasingly high profile means that more of its pupils commute from outside the Brighton area. Parents are an intriguing mix of old money and funky arty types – mothers waiting outside the school gates are just as likely to sport combat trousers and navel rings as Prada handbags. Serious commitment to co-education, as evidenced by the number of women in the senior management team. In 1997, 25 per cent of pupils were girls; that number has risen to almost 38 per cent. Pupils are generally cheerful, enthusiastic, friendly and polite and have an easy, relaxed relationship with teachers.

Entrance: At 13, by CE if they attend prep school; if not, after an assessment. Children who achieve 55 (used to be 50) per cent at CE are accepted, especially if they excel at music, sport or another activity. Entrance also at sixth form.

Exit: Almost all to university, with many taking a gap year. Wide range of subjects chosen. Old Brightonians include sculptor David Nash, racing driver Jonathan Palmer, writer Peter Mayle, explorer Sir Vivian Fuchs and actor Sir Michael Horden (who has a performance space named after him).

Money Matters: Fees reasonable. Some scholarships and bursaries available.

Remarks: Happy, modern, un-snobby, forward-looking school that has staged a remarkable comeback over the past few years – thanks mainly to its inspiring last head. Terrific for bright, energetic, robust pupils who like to keep busy; not ideal for the shy and retiring.

BRISTOL GRAMMAR SCHOOL

Linked to Bristol Grammar School Lower School in the Junior section

University Road, Bristol, BS8 1SR

Tel: 0117 973 6006
Fax: 0117 946 7485
E-mail: headmaster@bgs.bristol.sch.uk
Website: www.bristolgrammarschool.co.uk

• Pupils: Upper school: 1,015 boys and girls; all day • Ages: 11-18, juniors 7-10 • Size of sixth form: 320 • Non-denom • Fees: £2,705 • Independent • Open days: see website

---

Head: Since 1999, Dr David Mascord (fifties). Read chemistry at York, PhD in quantum mechanics at St John's College, Cambridge. Taught at range of schools, including grammar in Taunton, a sixth form college and Wellington before becoming assistant head at Aylesbury Grammar. Arrived at BGS in 1989 and was previously deputy head – and still seems surprised to have achieved headship in the first internal appointment in 140 years. Married with two sons in their twenties, both working in computing. Cheerful pragmatist who has always wanted to teach and still loves it – he continues to take year 7s for IT lessons.

Academic Matters: Highly selective, with very able children regularly achieving outstanding grades in wide range of subjects. Head, however, keen to stress that achievement is sought out at every level and in every area – 'it's too easy to underestimate children,' he says. Most subjects have 100 per cent A*-C pass rates each year at GCSE, with routinely impressive results in maths, English language and sciences (most taken singly). High grades, too, in languages, with all taking Latin in years 7 and 8 and French compulsory to GCSE. Russian and Latin particularly notable – two of the country's top five Latin scholars in 2002 came from BGS. Economics is often the Cinderella subject – long-standing apparent underperformance (which here means more Bs and Cs than As, so it's all relative). Design & technology and art results also excellent year after year. Comprehensive choice of 26 A and AS levels which includes sports studies, psychology and drama as well as more traditional fare. Fine results in maths, all sciences and English, although too many Ds and Es in business studies. Separate sixth form centre offers non-examined 'carousel courses', from ethical conundrums to cookery. Rigorous, lively teaching to astute pupils keen to join in – lots of hands up. Average class size 20 (and often far fewer, particularly in the final years). Special needs co-ordinator deals with the usual small complement of mild dyslexics.

Games, Options, The Arts: Strong no nonsense DT department. Boys play rugby, hockey, cricket; girls hockey and netball, tennis and athletics. PE is mixed. The school owns large acres of playing fields over the river at Failand (as do other Bristol schools) and pupils are bused out – it's part of Clifton school life. There is a sports hall on the site, much used (a large fencing class was in progress when we visited, both girls and boys). Inter-form competitions are held at lunch time ('we eat quickly', commented a pupil). Over 140 pupils are 'going through to gold' in the Duke of Edinburgh award scheme – an amazing number for a school without an outward-bound tradition. Trips to Mongolia, Borneo and Bolivia in recent years and the Summit Club for those committed to climbing British mountains. Public speaking is a popular option. Stunningly good library – county standard, and with a £15,000 a year budget, beautifully catalogued and laid out, and a joy to use – brilliant librarian.

Art school, in a house across the road from the main buildings, has lovely, calm atmosphere, with a sweet garden attached, although it concentrates on a relatively narrow range of options, including fine art and drawing. In the next-door house is music where lessons are streamed in the first senior year and where orchestras and various ensembles, including a jazz and a ceilidh band, are co-ordinated. Very encouraging of the whole theatre experience as a means of building confidence, whether budding actors or not – Dr Mascord was once a member of the National Youth Theatre. 'Stage crew' a strand of the activity programme, which once a week offers such courses as electronics and first aid to younger pupils, circus skills, yoga and Japanese to older ones. Performances take place either in the magnificent, vaulted Great Hall (which also doubles as the dining hall and, unusually, is on the first floor), which seats 1,000, or in the more intimate Mackay Theatre. Impressive library resources, with 40,000 books and a big budget. Well-produced school magazine, The Chronicle, and excellent, easy-to-use website.

Background and Atmosphere: Bristol Grammar School was founded in 1532 by the Thorne brothers, merchants made good. The school motto 'ex spinis uvas', from thorns to grapes, makes a play on their name. Became fully co-ed about 20 years ago. Bulk of the school buildings date from the 19th century, dark and gloomy Gothic, sited on the grounds of an 18th century mansion and grouped around the central Great Hall. Newer buildings tend to be obscured by the Victorian spires or, in the case of design technology, partially hidden underground. BGS is comprehensively shoe-horned into its corner space, tucked just out of sight of the city centre and next to the main university buildings. It feels very detached from bustling Bristol life, although the high metal fences and security gates act as reminders that this is an inner-city school (albeit in one of the nicest parts of town). School comes alive in break times, with noisy juniors careering around the play areas and teenagers furtively kissing behind handy gates. Lots of laughter. Also very caring and conscious of their good fortune, with lots of fund-raising efforts, such as Christmas boxes for Albanian orphanages and prefects selling themselves for charity (highly amused younger pupils demanded that they dance to earn money).

Pastoral Care and Discipline: Kind and gentle introduction to senior school, with newish Princess Anne building used as a designated base for the first two years, where pupils have their own classrooms and form teacher. Senior staff try to visit every potential feeder school 'so that they can see we don't have two heads,' says head. Each pupil assigned to one of six houses that, by 13, becomes a major source of support, with house-based tutor groups and the overall head of year. Sixth former tutors act as career as well as academic mentors (plus dedicated careers tutor, recently runner up in regional careers officer awards). In turn, peer mentoring, where sixth formers act as points of contact and support for younger pupils, is being introduced. 'School needs to be a place where you'll always find someone to talk to,' says head. Very open and clear policy on bullying and drugs, including alcohol and tobacco, stated in detail to parents. The social and personal development course also provides drug awareness sessions to all age groups.

Pupils and Parents: Resolutely middle class, while remaining genuinely welcoming of all comers. Most parents professional or leaders of local businesses, with a small number from the less salubrious parts of Bristol. Old Boys include cricketer Tom Graveney, Nobel chemistry prizewinner John Pople, actor Jeremy Northam and writer Robert Lacey.

Entrance: Entry exam at 11 (earlier, if 'mature') held in January for September – the exam is held in conjunction with several other Bristol private schools. A third of pupils come up from the grammar school's own junior school – on the same site, but separated by high wire fence – the rest from schools not just all over Bristol but as far flung as Weston-super-Mare. Typical feeds are Henleaze, Elmlea and Stoke Bishop primaries, Colston's Primary in Cotham, Westbury Park, Westbury C of E, plus Clifton, Red Maid's, Redlands, Clifton High etc. 20-25 pupils join at 13.

Exit: Almost all to university, 10-20 each year to Oxbridge. Manchester, Nottingham, Leeds and Cardiff perennially popular. Bristol generally not.

Money Matters: Seems to have survived the huge blow of losing assisted places – the school had up to 300 – with bursary scheme. Head says they have maintained the social mix of BGS (although there are only a third as many bursaries, including some from the Odgen Trust for full fees and others from a school endowment), so Bristol parents must be digging deeper in their pockets.

Remarks: City school where old-fashioned virtues of academic excellence, all-round endeavour and enthusiasm are nurtured and prized. Pupils happy and involved.

BRIT School for Performing Arts and Technology

60 The Crescent, Croydon, Surrey, CR0 2HN

Tel: 020 8665 5242
Fax: 020 8665 8676
E-mail: Admin@brit.croydon.sch.uk
Website: www.brit.croydon.sch.uk

• Pupils: 850, roughly two-thirds girls; all day • Ages: 14-19
• Size of sixth form: 600 • Non-denom • State

Principal: Since 2002, Mr Nick Williams (early fifties), previously head of Thomas Tallis comprehensive school in Blackheath. Teaches English. 'I love the excitement and enthusiasm of this school. We have to maintain the highest standards because we're a benchmark of excellence in performing arts.'

Academic Matters: The academic and the extra-curricular are closely entwined here. This is the only state-funded specialist performing arts college in Britain (possibly in Europe). It has a fully comprehensive ability intake with strong vocational interests and was previously not noted for its exam successes. However, in recent years, the school has put a major emphasis on raising achievement in National Curriculum subjects and the percentage of students getting 5 or more A*-C grades at GCSE increased from 25 in 2000 to 57 in 2001 to 95 in 2005 – well above the national average and roughly where the head expects it to stay. 'The school used to focus more on practical than academic subjects but we've resolved the curriculum issues that needed sorting. We now feel that the balance between the academic and the vocational is very good.' While some students are more inclined to put energy into performance than into essay writing, the last Ofsted report commented, 'many students are clearly making substantially more progress than might have been expected.' There is banding for core subjects and a special needs department supports all students as well as those with learning difficulties.

Everyone in years 10 and 11 does English, humanities, maths and science to GCSE. There is also a wide range of other National Curriculum subjects offered. Technology is delivered through BTEC First in either performing arts, media or visual arts and design. Many students also do dance, drama, music and media GCSEs. Sixth formers spe-

cialise in one of seven arts strands – theatre, visual arts & design, media, music, dance, musical theatre or technical theatre – and take AVCEs or BTEC national diplomas. 90-ish per cent get either distinction or merit. Many take one or two ASs and A levels alongside – mostly in performing arts subjects, media, art and design and English literature – and the A level A-C pass rate improved from 52 per cent in 2000 to 80 per cent in 2002. There is a year 14 course in arts management for students who are looking for further vocational qualifications and extended work experience. The school day is long, with sixth form lessons timetabled up to 6pm and plenty of rehearsals outside school hours. The school runs five eight-week terms a year, with a four-week holiday in the summer and two-week breaks during the rest of the year. 'This is very popular with our students because they have long stretches of intense work with a good break in between.' Most of the performance teachers are practitioners too: the head of music is also a commercial musical director and the production staff are all from theatre, film or TV backgrounds. 'This means that the students get not just teaching but an insight into how the industry works.' All the students get the opportunity for work experience, usually in their chosen specialism.

Games, Options, The Arts: Students have achieved A and AS levels in physical education, which is something of an achievement as the school's only on-site PE facilities are a room with multigym equipment, a gym plus a much used hard court area. Fitness is, however, a prerequisite for many of the courses. Many students travel to Crystal Palace national stadium and the local leisure centre for sport and there are after school basketball and netball clubs. But sport is a minor interest here, with most students throwing their enthusiasm into performance. They take responsibility for rehearsal schedules, back stage and front-of-house activities and take performances to primary schools. 'Students' commitment to preparing performances of all kinds is very impressive, involving many hours' work beyond the already long school day,' said Ofsted. 'These activities contribute very substantially to the development of both subject skills and their personal skills and qualities.' Students agree, 'no-one ever wants to go home.'

Background and Atmosphere: The school was opened in 1991, with great fanfare, as the only free, performing arts school in the country. It is funded not only by the government but also by the British Record Industry Trust, with funds raised from a number of sources including the annual BRIT awards. The extra cash, says the head, 'allows us to buy superb extra facilities but not extra staffing'. The school has a 350-seat theatre, a radio broadcasting suite, a

TV studio, a video-editing suite and music-recording studio with digital and analogue equipment (your children will explain the importance of this) and dance and drama studios. The main building is purpose-built in concrete, glass and steel, with a huge glass-fronted foyer, also used as a box office, and office-like pale grey décor. Next door is a red-brick building, comfortably shabby, reminiscent of a cosy old grammar school and used for National Curriculum subjects, theatre studies and musical theatre. There's plenty of high-class artwork about and a feeling of energy, with performances in rehearsal, dance practices in progress in studios and on the gallery which overlooks the foyer and media students with recording equipment preparing copy for Brit FM, the school radio station which runs for 10 days in the summer. 'Our approach is hands-on whenever possible,' says the principal.

Pastoral Care and Discipline: With the majority of students in the sixth-form, this is a half-way house between school and college with informal relationships between staff and students. Ofsted commented on the 'very positive attitude' of the students and their good behaviour in class. 'The level of focus and concentration achieved by students is very good and at times exceptional.' There's a general consensus that the school is largely free from bullying. 'Boys like the fact that it's not in any way macho,' says the head. 'They can escape the value systems elsewhere. You don't get loud boys (or girls) behaving in intimidating ways. We don't have to talk to them about behaviour, they get it right for themselves.' 'Everyone knows each other and helps each other,' said a student.

Pupils and Parents: Totally comprehensive in academic and social terms. The school suggests that students should live within an hour's travelling time but its authorised catchment area is more or less all of Greater London, plus some of Kent, Surrey and Sussex. Some sixth formers from further afield rent rooms in Croydon during term time. Students, many of whom were disaffected elsewhere, are mostly strongly motivated, full of enthusiasm to make the most of their opportunities. 'I always wanted to go in, however ill I was,' said an ex-student.

Entrance: 135 students admitted at 14, up to 350 at 16. Students must apply for a chosen specialism and those who meet the criteria are invited for a workshop or meeting with staff. 'We're looking for a commitment and interest in their chosen subjects, plus a good school report. We choose students with potential, not necessarily the highest performers.' Academic ability is not a prerequisite, commitment is. Those who appeal against a rejection are always given a second chance.

Exit: About two thirds of students go into entertainment, music and media industry employment and higher education courses. Ex-BRIT students include Katie Melua, Amy Winehouse, soul singer Lynden David Hall, Dane Bowers and Wayne Williams from R&B group, Another Level, singer/songwriter Imogen Heap and Quentin Clare, Music Director of the Sinfonia of The Hague. Others have become web designers, TV researchers, journalists and actors.

Remarks: Its unique status as the only free performing arts school in the country attracts dedicated students who, one feels, can't quite believe their luck at being able to concentrate on doing what they love most, with the help of top class teachers and facilities. 'Everyone loves it,' said a student. 'You can see it in their work. And the teachers enjoy it too.'

BROCKWOOD PARK SCHOOL

Bramdean, Alresford, Hampshire, SO24 0LQ

Tel: 01962 771 744
Fax: 01962 771 875
E-mail: enquiry@brockwood.org.uk
Website: www.brockwood.org.uk

• Pupils: 62 • Ages: 14 -19 • Size of sixth form: 20 • Non denominational, enquiry about all aspects of life is encouraged. • Fees: Phone for information • Independent • Open days: Phone for information on events

Head: School is run by two Directors:

Director of Administration: Since 1998, Mr Bill Taylor BA RSA TEFL (forties) who comes from New Zealand and read English literature at Waikato University in New Zealand. Bill originally came to the school as a mature student in 1983, spending five years here, including a spot of teaching, before going to university back in New Zealand. Returning to the school, he taught for four years, before joining the admin staff in 1994. He lives with his wife and daughter on campus, his wife previously taught here and both are keenly interested in Jiddu Krishnamurti, iconoclast, philosopher, educationalist and founder of Brockwood Park. A gentle soul, Bill does not proselytise but comes at you with clear-cut ideals, much charm and a quiet sense of humour. He originally 'came to Krishnamurti's teaching through Buddhism ... but Krishnamurti was in no way connected to Buddhism. Although his teaching has been likened to Buddhism, and Buddhists came to talk to him from time-to-time, he remains an independent spirit and very much the author of his own work.'

Toon Zweers, from Holland, first came to Brockwood in 1982 as a student, returning in 1996 to teach history and ESL. After finishing an MA in education with the Open University, he became the Director of Academics in September 2002.

Academic Matters: Not surprisingly, the school follows the ethos of Krishnamurti (whose name regularly cropped up in conversations with Bill). While attention is paid to matters academic, the school is equally concerned with the whole person. 'To explore what freedom and responsibility are in relationship with others and in modern society'. Self-reflection and caring for nature are as important here as pure academia.

While the school used to do GCSEs and opted for the international form (reflecting the international character of the pupil base) rather than the normal British exams, they now gear pupils for the AS/A Level exams. A foundation year precedes the AS/A Level exams if necessary and pupils are expected to take six ASs or some combination of AS and A level over two years. Core subjects include the humanities, languages – French, German and Spanish: taught by native speakers – English lang and lit, plus all the sciences. Classes are tiny, 1:7. EFL naturellement; and a whole raft of add-ons, which might not feature in a 'normal' school curriculum.

The majority of staff live in and adopt the Krishnamurti ethos. There are currently 30 adults on campus, plus a few specialists recruited from the outside world. The results themselves are 'too tiny to quantify' – there must be a certain number of examinees to qualify for inclusion in published A/AS level results. 'Structured' prep but students must be self-motivated. Some help available for special needs such as dyslexia.

Ofsted inspection May 2005, the results of which on the DfES website.

Games, Options, The Arts: Tennis court, few 'proper' team games as such, seven-a-side football for both sexes but no inter-school matches. Otherwise loads of individual sports, tennis, basketball, badminton, aerobics etc. Dark room, exciting drama. Arts brilliant, loads of music, and lots of contact with the Yehudi Menuhin School of Music – a cello concert from one of its prodigies when we visited. Fabulous art barn, designed by Keith Critchlow in the Arts and Crafts Cottage style: trad art the norm, plus loads of add-ons, it rather depends who has decided to come and work at the centre. Master classes are important here.

Background and Atmosphere: School founded by Krishnamurti in 1969 with a gift of £40,000, this was to be his retirement fund, instead he bought Brockwood Park and 40 acres. The school still has the same gentle feel he would have liked, the main building (a bit boring, but circa 1750 – after Robert Adam, and grade 2 listed) houses admin, classrooms and girls' dorms. A huge rambling and impressive library. Marvellous octagonal assembly hall. Quiet room with surprising linen fold panelling and William Adam fireplace (both apparently installed post-1930) with sag bags open for reflection.

Boys and male students live in purpose-built cloisters. Some staff live in cottages round the grounds, which boast 'one of the earliest outdoor swimming pools in the South of England'.

During the School winter break (January) there are optional trips to far flung places such as China, India, Brazil; during the course of the year there are language trips to Europe and camping trips in the UK. All at extra cost.

All decisions involve consultation with students and mentors. The day starts with ten minutes' silent time, followed by breakfast. There are no cleaning staff, staff and pupils alike work together to maintain the house and gardens. All food is vegetarian, with about 1/3 being sourced from the schools own garden, which is also home to their chickens. No coffee, the school has voted against such stimulants and has a tea bar with a range of herbal teas instead. No dress code (tidy casual – staff and students alike appear to affect the jeans and beanie culture), and everyone is on first name terms.

The Krishnamurti Centre, another marvellous Keith Critchlow creation, is shaped like a person seated in the lotus position and lies at the edge of the property; regular weekend retreats for jaded business folk and the like who are interested in studying Krishnamurti's work. £44 a night for full board. Occasional flurries of excitement locally about 'increased traffic', locals to whom we spoke said the school was 'a bunch of weirdos, but quite harmless really'. The car park was full of upmarket BMWs, Volvos etc.

Pastoral Care and Discipline: Not a school for drop outs, everyone here lives as one great family. All students have to sign an agreement – The Open Letter – which, amongst other things means that they must abstain from alcohol, tobacco, illegal drugs nor 'engage in sexual intercourse or inappropriate sexual activity'. Use of alcohol and illegal drugs is likely to lead to expulsion, other broken agreements are discussed openly with the whole school and the students are active in finding solutions to issues that arise. Students apparently spend hours ('time enough' says Bill) discussing what is 'inappropriate'.

Pupils and Parents: Students come from around the world to study at Brockwood Park School. Some come from families who are interested in Krishnamurti's teachings, although this is not a pre-requisite. More important is an inquiring and ethical outlook.

Entrance: Potential pupils (of all ages) spend a week's assessment at the school. If both sides are happy, then they are accepted. This is not the school for those who have failed elsewhere.

Exit: Around 80 per cent of Brockwood students go on to further education.

Money Matters: Fees are kept low to encourage international students from different socio-economic backgrounds. All staff are paid the minimum wage along with food and accommodation. Scholarships are available to students after their first year.

Remarks: A unique school.

BROMLEY HIGH SCHOOL (GDST)

Linked to Bromley High School (GDST) Junior Department in the Junior section

Blackbrook Lane, Bickley, Bromley, Kent, BR1 2TW

Tel: 020 8468 7981
Fax: 02082 951 062
E-mail: bhs@bro.gdst.net
Website: www.bromleyhigh.gdst.net

• Pupils: approx 900 girls, including 312 in junior school
• Ages: 4-18 • Size of sixth form: 115 • Christian, non denom
• Fees: £2,382 in the Junior Schools, £3,063 in the Senior
• Independent • Open days: First Saturday in October or by appointment

Head: Since 2001, Ms Lorna Duggleby BA MSc PGCE (early fifties). Read languages at York University. Married with two children, son at university, daughter studying A levels at a neighbouring school. Before taking the reins at Bromley, she was head of languages at Newstead Wood, deputy head of Wallington Girls High and head at Addington High. Focused, innovative, cheerful and a good communicator, she keeps in touch and updates everyone through her weekly newsletter.

Academic Matters: Strong across the board. 79 per cent A/B at A level, 95 per cent at GCSE. Languages and sciences particularly strong, a number of girls take the triple award extension course. Head has worked hard to make the curriculum really flexible so girls can have as much sub-ject choice as possible in all age groups and fit in some extra GCSEs like music and languages. Mrs Duggleby likes to get to know pupils by teaching Latin to all y7s. Modern classrooms, whiteboards now popping up everywhere, maths rooms have their own computers and latest software. Once a slightly weaker area, a small ICT revolution has been carried out over the last couple of years, report parents of both tuition and equipment. Superb refurbished library with opening hours that extend the school day.

Relationships between staff and pupils are friendly but respectful, many long serving teachers with a steady flow of new blood coming in. Support is available for SEN and EFL 'as it is required', study skills conferences for all in years 7, 10 and sixth form. Extensive range of lunchtime and after school clubs etc – strong emphasis on everyone reaching their full potential – practically and socially as well as academically. If Mrs D finds a rough edge, she'll sharpen it. Work experience in France and Germany is arranged for those studying languages.

Games, Options, The Arts: Again, strong all round, extremely successful mainstream sports teams, Kent champions for hockey, South East England champions for netball and gym and tennis team 3rd in national finals. Acres of space, athletics track, 8 netball courts, 3 hockey pitches including one Astroturf which is also used by Bromley Club, indoor swimming pool, the facilities are available to staff and families out of hours. Duke of Edinburgh Award Scheme, Neighbourhood Engineering, Young Enterprise schemes and World Challenge expeditions are popular with sixth formers.

Superior music department – though only 40 per cent participate; produces it own calendar of events and runs music trips all over the world. Tuition for voice and most instruments even the harp. Music and music technology an option at A'level. Three drama productions, a dance production and a drama festival each year; every pupil gets the chance to be involved. Several art studios and thoughtful displays all over the school, 80 per cent As at A level.

Background and Atmosphere: Founded in 1883 as part of the then Girls Public Day School Trust by a terrifying looking Miss Heppel whose photograph hangs in the past heads' gallery. Moved to the present fabulous 25 acre site complete with woodland and a lake in 1982. Not a speck of litter to be seen. Everywhere is buzzing with activity, lots of notice boards promoting forthcoming events or photographic displays of past ones. Uniform is a touch dreary, maroon and grey; no uniform for sixth formers, some think they could smarten up a little.

Pastoral Care and Discipline: Year 12 are taught peer counselling and all have access to a professional counsellor on a drop in basis or by appointment. Head and form tutors are always willing to discuss pastoral as well as academic matters with parents. Democratic discussion is encouraged through school committees, some of which junior pupils also attend. Elections are run for the selection of two head girls and four deputies. The school opens at 7.45am with a breakfast club and runs a homework club until 5.30pm.

Pupils and Parents: Girls are friendly, hard working and confident with a good sense of community. Predominantly from the surrounding areas but the catchment spreads from Tonbridge to Tooting. Mainly middle class plus a small social mix, good percentage of first time buyers. Parents are fiercely loyal to the school and see it as a leading light in Bromley. Well integrated PTA runs fundraising events, bus service and school bookshop. Old girls include Margaret Hodge, Professor Joan Walsh, Anthea Gaukroger (telecoms); Richmal Crompton once taught here.

Entrance: Almost all the junior school girls choose to go onto the senior school. At 11, all girls have an interview and sit exams in English, maths and a general paper which includes some non verbal reasoning. Girls applying for occasional places further up the school sit tests in English, maths, science and a foreign language. Sixth form entrance requirement is at least six GCSEs at A*-B.

Exit: Almost all to higher education. 6 – 10 to Oxbridge rest to top range of universities Bristol, Exeter, London, and Edinburgh. Needless to say many read maths and sciences; law and arts also popular. At 16+ the odd one leaves for a mixed sixth form.

Money Matters: All candidates sitting the 11+ entrance are automatically entered for academic scholarships. Music scholarships are also available. In the sixth form there are academic scholarships including one particularly aimed at science and maths, as well as special scholarships for music, art and drama and a sports scholarship courtesy of Bromley swimming club. Means tested Trust bursaries are also available.

Remarks: An efficient and business-like school for academic, sporting, artistic or musical girls.

BRUTON SCHOOL FOR GIRLS

Linked to Sunny Hill Preparatory School in the Junior section

Sunny Hill, Bruton, Somerset, BA10 0NT

Tel: 01749 814 400

Fax: 01749 812 537

E-mail: info@brutonschool.co.uk

Website: www.brutonschool.co.uk

- Pupils: 400 girls; 100 boarders • Ages: 3 -18 • Size of sixth form: 80 • Fees: Day £1,825 - £3,225; boarding £4,300- £5,830 • Independent • Open days: October, November, February. Sixth form information evening October

Principal: Since 1999, Mrs Barbara Bates BA MA MIMgt FRSA (early fifties); educated Accrington High School and London University. Taught at a London boys' comp and the awesome James Allen's Girls' School (JAGS) before arrival to herald centenary at Bruton. Intrepid and highly efficient, this new-style 'professional head' is married to Dr David Bates and has two German Shepherds: Horace and Hector. Will not rest on her laurels for a split second (the sort who might manage on three hours' sleep); injects a cosmopolitan flavour into a school consistently at the right end of league tables 'but you don't fatten a pig by constantly weighing it' she likes to say, sweeping cobwebs off this sleeping beauty. No time for teaching nowadays except to cover for absence. BB must be here to stay, a house is being specially built for her on site, so any member of her crew not prepared for the ride had best slip quietly into the nearby River Bru or come to heel.

Vice principal Pastoral Daphne Maclay MA, just plucked from Truro High is a jolly, cosy lady who will know the brigades of Emmas, Charlottes and Amys in a trice.

Academic Matters: Outstanding results with A level 60 per cent A/B grade means most stay on for sixth form, thus only 15 arrive – foreign or very cleverclogs. Bias towards maths and sciences but strong on history and languages too. Hot on public speaking. GKN Westland and Thomas-Marconi offer 'real' projects to sixth form physicists. Computers only just taking off with spanking new ITC room and bank of laptops to boot – 'when I arrived they mainly had Acorns,' says head, busily planting Oaks. Much change implemented in her short reign and we ain't seen nothin' yet as her 7-year plan thunders onward.

At GCSE A*s and As for 50 to 60 per cent. Latin and classical civilisation on offer. Counters inconsistent help from

Somerset Careers by involving OGs to lunch-time talks about their ad agency/law firm/industry. Rigorous teaching by (three-quarters) female staff. A token effort for mild dyslexia.

Games, Options, The Arts: Over half the school play musical instruments in two orchestras, a wind band, flute group. Several ensembles and three choirs (links with Bruton choral society) – ask for CD of choir recordings. Eye-catching art, well displayed, but no kiln. Enthusiastic and workmanlike drama dept. Nicely written school mag by pupils (hooray) reflects their busy busy life 'My week with the Beeb', 'What it takes to get to Vet school', reviews of gliding courses, French plays, Latin-speaking contests or George Melly discussing Dali.

Sports facilities inproved greatly by the addition of a new Astroturf (completed 2004) adding to the floodlit tennis courts, fitness suite (head's baby) and new dance studio. County players in hockey, netball, tennis and cross-country. Profuse activities from self defence to beauty therapy. Pru Leith's cookery course ensures gap/university students can always gain employment with a flash of a pan.

Background and Atmosphere: Sunny Hill School for girls was set up in 1900 by Henry Hobhouse and William Knight, head of Sexey's School in the same town. Forty acres of sweeping countryside surround an eclectic sprawl of buildings, some tired, some spacious. Many changes since new regime and much sprucing-up afoot. Bruton itself almost custom designed to provide not a drop of distraction. From her recently enlarged study (linen-clad sofas), Mrs Bates summons local gentry/cleverly chosen governors, visiting exotics or powerful OGs who magically donate a Steinway grand or turn inside out to please.

Pastoral Care and Discipline: Glowing well-scrubbed faces hide future Anne Robinsons. The Sunny Hill girl doesn't just think she is better than the girl next door, she knows it. Boarding comprises mostly Brits from beyond local area, Services, overseas contracts, ex-pats, some non-English speakers from Europe and the far east. Day pupils come from 30-mile radius by network of school coaches, mostly first-time buyers. Parents say they would prefer more rapport in interim rather than waiting for parents' day. However those who choose this mould (of Roedean or Cheltenham Ladies') are not wont to complain – except when fees recently doubled within short time. Staunch OG network provides loyal input with work shadowing etc: Ethel Knight (UK's first female vet), Louisa Grit (one of only two female RN commanding officers), Clarissa Farr (Chairman of Boarding Schools' Association).

Pupils and Parents: Enough older staff to retain a kindly environment, says mother of girl whooo glandular

fever was catered mistresses try to ke exam time. Pupils a mers allowed to pa banking, courtesy carte blanche to p

Entrance: Su joining at any age senior school is at ers with school's junior school. For the sixth form, places available after GCSE with B grades minimum. Limits intake of Hong Kong pupils to 5/6 per year.

Exit: Half a dozen to Oxbridge. All leavers to universities or art foundation.

Money Matters: Scholarships and exhibitions available at 11, 13 and sixth form. Scholarships awarded for academic merit, music, sport, art or drama. Exhibitions are means-tested bursaries available to talented students.

Remarks: Built for winners who work hard and play hard. Not a place for dyslexics or dreamers.

BRYANSTON SCHOOL

Bryanston, Blandford Forum, Dorset, DT11 0PX

Tel: 01258 452 411
Fax: 01258 484 661
E-mail: admissions@bryanston.co.uk
Website: www.bryanston.co.uk

• Pupils: 380 boys (330 board); 275 girls (255 board) • Ages: 13-18 • Size of sixth form: 260 • C of E • Fees: Boarding £7.669; day £6,135 • Independent • Open days: contact school

---

Head: Since 2005, Sarah Thomas (early forties)MA Oxon (Lit Hum) PGCE. Very good news. Brings experience from helping to run two of Britain's most successful and progressive co-ed public schools. Deputy head at Uppingham for 6 years and before that spent 13 years at Sevenoaks teaching classics and eventually heading the sixth form. Parents at Uppingham sang her praises. She is married with two school-aged daughters.

Academic Matters: Revolves around the school's following the Dalton Plan, a system of scheduling that allows pupils periods of non-lesson time each day to be used for assignments (prep) and extra-curricular obligations (eg music lessons). In past, this 'sixth form-style scheduling' presented a challenge to some dishevelled 13-year-olds

supervision. Prep assignments ...head, teaching pupils to organise ...on for university and adulthood. Junior ...assignments in subject rooms/libraries ...a teacher from that department. Older pupils ...k in their houses. Teachers see pupils in the sub-...ms and in class, plus individually in tutorials and ...to-one 'correction' periods. Lots of one-to-one teaching ...eans class sizes larger than at similar schools.

Exam results good given broad intake: good value-added scores. English and art usually the most popular A level subjects. School sensitive about artsy label – sciences stand up well, with some inspired teaching. Latin compulsory for all in first year. Ditto French, German, Spanish and technology. Setting in maths, sciences and languages. Not a cutting-edge IT school. Mac-based IT rather than PCs, reflects (dare we say it) arts leaning. For non-native speakers good English a must, although a handful receives ESL help. A fifth of pupils require special provision for learning disabilities.

Games, Options, The Arts: Much emphasis on rugby – surprising at this progressive school, and too much according to some parents. Football not a major sport. Girls have had success at netball and hockey, though parents say girls' sport lacks the consistent, enthusiastic direction that benefits the boys. Lots of choice a godsend for many. Fives, fencing and kayaking some of the more exotic choices. Rowing an important sport for both sexes. Two artificial pitches for hockey and tennis (one floodlit). Indoor pool but, sadly, school does not compete in this sport. Keen swimmers may join local Blandford swim club which trains at the school. Riding forms part of compulsory second year adventure training programme and several pupils study for road safety exams and the BHS Assistant Instructors certificate. Sailing at Poole Harbour.

Bryanston richly deserves its reputation as a fantastic art school. The department's teaching is second to none, the range of projects undertaken enormous, the results a joy to behold. Head of art full of enthusiasm and humour and not shy of the occasional tussle with pupils over which background music to play. Ceramics bask in massive, industrial kiln (it was on special offer). DT nearly as impressive. Extra-curricular drama is super, with no shortage of opportunities for pupils to act and direct. Lower sixth drama festival takes over the school for a weekend each year. Professional theatre – the 600-seat Coade Hall – hosts touring companies. Drama/theatre studies examined at A level only (not GCSE). Super audiovisual department provides studios for digital editing and recording. School's own

TV network provides information and shows videos. Music active with range of ensembles, five choirs and useful aural music exam prep sessions. Music building with own recording studio. Introductory orchestral music tuition is offered free to beginners in the first year. Annual trekking expedition to the Himalayas and many overseas sports trips and language exchanges. Adventure training, compulsory in year 10, includes camping, canoeing, caving, climbing etc. Lots of community service (known here as 'pioneering').

Background and Atmosphere: Very long drive from the front gates, through untamed woods, past riding centre and across 57 acres of playing fields to distant conglomeration of school buildings sets tone for this unusual school – 'uninstitutional' and 'unschooly' are how pupils describe it. Ostentatious Norman Shaw House for Viscount Portman is 'more like a town hall than a private house', to quote John Betjeman, but makes an aesthetically inspiring heart of the school (wood panelling and parquet flooring throughout). Set in 400 acres. Founded 1928, went fully co-ed in 1975. Religion back-pedalled but most Sundays pupils must attend either assembly or church. First-year pupils have compulsory weekly chapel in basement of main building. Pupils may go home at weekends from the end of classes on Saturday until bedtime on Sunday but management labouring to entice them to stay. School is investing £6 million in a new science block to emphasise science's importance in the school. Can't help wondering why not keep artsy reputation and current science block with charming indoor carp pond. Good food with stir-fry bar (pick your own ingredients), salad bar and famed omelette bar, all prepared by award-winning chefs (one was named chef of the year at a national competition involving 350 independent schools).

Pastoral Care and Discipline: School has reputation for giving pupils a loose rein but is little different from other co-ed, liberal schools. We continue to get reports of student misbehaviour – the full gamut – but parents whose children got into trouble as juniors appreciate how the school punished them but stuck by them, allowing them to emerge as responsible young adults. Upper sixth bar with two-drink limit (three on Saturdays). Boys and girls may visit each other's houses until 9.30pm. Security guards monitor woods etc. Those busted for drugs usually given second chance but must submit to continual testing. If they come up positive, they are out. Pupils found in bed together also liable to be expelled. Obsessive, almost excessive, pastoral care makes it close to impossible for misery/despair/going off rails to go undetected.

Boys enter one of two first-year houses (40 boys in each). The idea is to protect them from the rough and tumble, eradicate opportunities for bullying and allow new boys to make solid friendships. Thereafter they move into mixed age houses. Girls go straight into mixed-age houses. Dormitories very pleasant with lower sixth in double study bedrooms and upper sixth with rooms to themselves. Sky TV in every house. Not much rivalry among houses. Day pupils may stay overnight when they like.

Pupils and Parents: The beautiful people. Middle class arts and trendies' children, and media. One-third from Dorset and surrounds who will probably also have looked at Marlborough and Canford. Some 20 per cent from London. Rest mainly from South of England. Majority come from prep schools eg Port Regis (loads), Windlesham House, The Old Malthouse (Swanage), Highfield. 51 ex-pats; 17 foreign nationals from all over; 14 foreign nationals resident in the UK. These middle class pupils tend to see selves as non-conformist semi-rebels and Bryanston as a centre of cool. Most very fashion conscious (several articles about this in school magazine) and unlike other no-uniform schools where grunge rules, pupils here care how they look. Not many crooked teeth or weight problems. Girls not averse to make-up and 'Face Odyssey,' a beauty club, is popular. OBs Lucien Freud, Terence, Sebastian and Jasper Conran, John Eliot Gardiner, Quinlan Terry, Phil de Glanville, Frederick Sanger, Emilia Fox and Mark Elder.

Entrance: Do not need to organise years in advance: 18 months before September of entry will do nicely. At 13+, CE (50 per cent pass required) or school's own tests in English, maths and French, plus school report. Always strives to accommodate siblings, within reason. Entry to sixth form requires 40 points at GCSE.

Exit: 98 per cent to higher education, up to 70 per cent first taking a gap year. 8 per cent to art colleges. University destinations change enormously year on year but many to London, Leeds, Edinburgh, Durham, Bristol. 9 to Oxbridge in 2003 and several to study overseas.

Money Matters: Up to 27 scholarships: academic, music, art, ICT, DT, sport and all-rounder awards (all in February). For the last of these, leadership potential is an important criterion. Academic, music and sport scholarships available at sixth form. School is not wealthy, despite appearances. Bursaries available.

Remarks: Friendly, open, relaxed school where management has miraculously succeeded in making pupils feel they are treated like adults. Supportive relationships among pupils, and between pupils and staff, keep most everyone whistling while they work. Laid-back atmosphere belies some keen scholarship, but still not for everyone.

BRYMORE SCHOOL
Cannington, Bridgwater, Somerset, TA5 2NB

Tel: 01278 652 369
Fax: 01278 653 244
E-mail: office@brymore.somerset.sch.uk
Website: www.brymore.somerset.sch.uk

• Pupils: 150 boarders, 40 day; all boys • Ages: 13-17 • Inter-denom • Fees: Boarding £1,900 • State • Open days: Last Saturday in June - plus country fair

Head: Since 2003, Mr Malcolm Lloyd (early fifties), who was a boarder at Woodbridge, Suffolk before training as a PE teacher at College of St Mark and St John when it was still in Chelsea. Added PGCE in youth and community to his BEd degree and started career as PE teacher cum youth tutor at Tessbourne Community School, Barnstaple before moving to Harrow as youth officer. Spent 15 years as community education co-ordinator in Frome prior to appointment at Brymore. Whilst at Frome had organised joint skiing trips with Brymore so governors were aware that he would suit. Refreshingly honest and straightforward, he is respected by boys who catch his understated enthusiasm. Equally at home in front of a computer, on the rugby pitch or in the milking parlour. Lives on site during term time whilst partner Hilary still teaches in Frome and joins him at weekends. Had hoped to bring golfing handicap below 10 by age fifty. Loves sea and mountains. Enjoys painting and photography. Something of an entrepreneurial maverick who understands how boys tick and fits Brymore to a T.

Academic Matters: The curriculum is dominated by horticulture, agriculture and engineering which occupy a third of the time-table and most of a boy's spare time. Despite this, one third of pupils gain at least 5 GCSEs grade A-Cs - remarkable when a large proportion of 13 year olds arrive with a reading age less than chronological age. Recently introduced for year 12, and much applauded by Ofsted, a one-year BTEC Intermediate Diploma course in land-based skills and a one year NVQ level 2 course in engineering. Both involve 6+ weeks of work experience. Special needs dept kept busy with 24 statemented pupils and some 100 others with moderate learning difficulties/dyslexia.

Games, Options, The Arts: In keeping with the school's ethos, there is emphasis on team effort rather than individual winners. A rugby team for each year group have a healthy jostle with Millfield B teams. An impressive 19 athletes at county level (hammer, pole-vaulting, cross-country, road-running gets to Nationals), much made of D of E (bronze and silver). Enthusiastic golf, fishing, mountain biking, and badger watching. A resurgence of Young Farmers Club. Business incentive scheme linked with Barnardo's offers year 12 chance to be involved with a business venture while raising money for charity.

Background and Atmosphere: The Brymore school of Rural Technology was set up in 1952 for the sons of Somerset farmers in a stunning site of 60 acres between the sea and the Quantock Hills. A half-mile tree lined drive divides rape fields to the left, farm buildings to the right. The school and main boarding housed in a 17th cent mansion originally owned by a notorious Civil War figure, John Pym, Oliver Cromwell's right hand man. The original stable yard, complete with clock tower has been converted to metal and wood workshops, 2 blacksmiths' forges, and foundry to industrial standards. No wonder the ghost of John Pym still roams the ex-stable (noises of restless horse hooves on cobbles at night).

Motto 'Diligentia et Labore'. Classrooms in utilitarian blocks left behind by US Cavalry billeted during the war. In the impeccably kept one-acre walled garden dating from 1753 the school vegetables are tended and every boy can have his own allotment. The pupils are responsible for complete upkeep of entire estate – tree pruning, grass cutting, weeding, planting flower beds all lead to a NVQ. A self-financing farm is at the heart of this unique set-up, lambing a flock of 50 ewes, rearing free-range chickens, beef cattle and pigs (much of which ends up in delicious meals for pupils) and milking cows at 6 am on a crisp winter morning are essential parts of the learning. 'Backing a tractor through a gateway and getting 10 out of 10 in a spelling test are of equal value here,' says the head, who takes boys who have not thrived in mainstream schools. The knack of his resourceful staff is to turn boys who have seen themselves as failures into confident, responsible young men who all progress to further education or employment.

Golden jubilee 2002/3, supported by Prince of Wales, involved heli-pad purpose-built for his visit.

Pastoral Care and Discipline: No religious affinity. No written set of school rules. Instead, boys are instilled with common sense, given responsibility at an early age and taught by example. Ofsted was moved to wax lyrical – 'pupils respond like buds opening in the sunshine' and praised the personal development and behaviour of pupils. Serious offences dealt with by counselling, withdrawal of privileges, detention and ultimately exclusion. Years 11 and 12 become prefects to assist staff with operating rewards system. In farm and horticultural dept senior boys have real responsibility.

Pupils and Parents: Mostly white with one or two overseas. Mixed backgrounds: 40 per cent come from Somerset, rest mainly from Wilts, Devon, Dorset, Cornwall, South Wales but some from much further afield. All pupils wear blazers and ties for assembly each day, though black sweatshirt is the norm for daywear. OBs include Neil Parish the Euro MP; Mark Irish, English U21 rugby player; Julian Anderson, world windsurfing champion.

Entrance: Between 60 and 70 admitted at 13, selected on aptitude and commitment. Parents and boys interviewed after applying with questionnaire and short essay.

Exit: 71 per cent to horticultural/agricultural colleges such as Lackam, Sparsholt, Kingston Manward, Dutchy College, Cornwall or closer to home – Cannington College and Bridgewater. 13 per cent into employment. 10 per cent to apprenticeships/work based learning.

Money Matters: Boarding fees moderate. Some pupils funded by educational grants from their own LEAs. Up to 10 bursaries in each year, means tested, for one third of fees.

Remarks: State boarding school with a strong practical bias. Magnificently warm and empathetic staff know how to get the best from their boys. No-frills boarding with excellent teaching in practical domain. The only school of its kind in the country.

BURFORD SCHOOL

Cheltenham Road, Burford, Oxfordshire, OX18 4PL

Tel: 01993 823 303
Fax: 01993 823 101
E-mail: Headteacher.4040@burford.oxon.sch.uk
Website: www.burford.oxon.sch.uk

- Pupils: 1,150 boys and girls (90 board, the rest day)
- Ages: 11-18 • Size of sixth form: 200 • Inter-denom
- Fees: Boarding fee £2,000 • State

Head: Since 1995, Mr Patrick Sanders, mid-fifties. Read English at Hull, followed by PGCE at Bristol. Previously head of Cotswold School, Gloucestershire and prior to that deputy head of Wallingford School, Oxfordshire. Married with two children – daughter, ex-Burford sixth former, at Nottingham University, son still at Burford. Has brought stability to the school after departure of previous head. Rightly credited with putting a school relatively rich in resources back where it should be, focusing on rounded education and committed to inspiring self-esteem in all pupils.

Academic Matters: Rural comprehensive with rare boarding element, improving rapidly after period of decline, offering wide range of subjects to wide ability intake. Overall grades now above average – A*-C 2005 at 67 per cent – higher than county performance, reflecting combination of Oxbridge candidates and real strugglers. It is set apart by its boarding element, a fantastic resource for Services families, overseas students and local business people in particular. Wonderful community atmosphere – boarders lower the age profile of the entire town of Burford. Curriculum offers all the basics to a good standard, with solid results in English, maths and sciences, with drama, art and music popular at GCSE. Strong results in physical education and geography. A levels overall have disappointed in the past, but are now improving – criticised by Ofsted for 'inappropriate courses', school has now dropped the chief offenders. Also suffered from exam chaos of 2002 and forced to teach entire physics course with designated textbook unpublished. But no excuses – head took criticisms on board and has made necessary changes. Psychology newly introduced and wildly popular. All do French, Spanish and German taught alternately each year. Dozen who take exams in Chinese are from Hong Kong – not taught. Tight on discipline: no-nonsense teaching style and well-behaved classes, although a few teachers still favour grouped tables offering only side-of-head views of pupils. Learning support unit deals with wide range of special needs and underachievement – head rejects Ofsted criticism of poor lesson planning as 'just plain wrong'. Much new ICT equipment. School has become a technology college – good for status and dosh.

Games, Options, The Arts: Acres of wonderful green space and very committed sports staff – school awarded Sportsmark in recognition of efforts. Rugby and football both popular. Lots of competition with local state and independent schools. Plentiful tennis courts and huge sports hall, sitting like a vast yellow mushroom at the back of the site and the only building large enough to house the whole school, which it does annually on Charter Day. Dance of all descriptions and gymnastics a big hit with the girls – one girl represented Northern Ireland in the Commonwealth Games. Design and technology areas are well equipped and art space is welcoming and vibrant, utilising rooms that are nicely old-fashioned – high ceilings, lots of wood.

School proud of long-standing links with a Ugandan school, raising bucket-loads of money and creating fierce competition for annual exchange visits. Around 20 per cent

takes individual music lessons in range of instruments, from violin to electric guitar. Huge commitment to extra-curricular activities more akin to independent school, with thriving D of E, Young Enterprise and Formula Schools 2000, a forward-thinking scheme to encourage engineering via the creation of a racing car, to be raced at Silverstone. At least one musical and one play a year, with enthusiastic volunteers on and off stage. Nice new library, with its own excellent website, part-funded by legacy. Many trips to foreign climes. Annual Gifted and Talented Summer School offers practical challenges to 15 local children with particular skills.

Background and Atmosphere: Burford School was founded by charter in 1571 and maintains many of the old grammar school traditions, including house system, prefects and stringent uniform rules. Sole surviving state boarding school in Oxfordshire (of three). Old building in achingly pretty, tourist jammed Burford town centre now the boarding house, Lenthall House. Behind the honey-stone walls it's a bit of a Tardis, with modern facilities and warm, cosy rooms. Main school, on the main A40 out of town (just over an hour from west London on a good traffic day), dates from 1949, when the then Burford Grammar School was expanded to create Oxfordshire's first comprehensive school. Buildings are from a range of dates and run the gamut of styles, although they are refreshingly clean, tidy and warm. Odd patches of peeling paint and cracked glass a reflection of local education finance rather than a lack of pride in their environment – pupils and staff clearly have that in spades.

Pastoral Care and Discipline: Clearly defined rules, from Statement of Intent, detailing expectations of pupils and school, to home school agreements. Central tenet: 'Everyone will act with care and consideration to others at all times.' Head runs a tight, stable ship, with pupils comfortable and secure within a relatively strict list of dos and don'ts (although head retains right to judge any cases of drug-taking and bullying in its context). Excellent Student Record Book (SRB), with mini-version for sixth form, detailing and monitoring everything from homework to letters home, works well. Informal but respectful relationship between staff and pupils. School hot on self-esteem – one pupil bullied at primary school gushes with enthusiasm, saying, 'everyone here helped to build up my confidence and now I couldn't be any happier at school'. Committed, mature staff make ideal confidantes.

Pupils and Parents: Lots of buses bring pupils mainly from ten-mile radius, including the towns of Witney and Carterton (bordering RAF Brize Norton, base for many

Services parents) as well as outlying villages of west Oxfordshire and east Gloucestershire. Not much of any ethnic mix but quite a social range, with a council estate and various manor houses both on the doorstep. Alumni include Gilbert Jessop (cricketer) and Simon West (film director). Parents and former pupils in Burford School Association beaver away fund-raising and organise regular get-togethers.

Entrance: Places for all who want to come. Will 'move heaven and earth' if parents need to convert day place into boarding.

Exit: Almost all stay for sixth form and at least 70 per cent go to university or college, University of the West of England particularly popular. Usually one or two Oxbridge, although three times that number have been accepted in recent years.

Remarks: Happy, friendly school that offers far more than is evident on paper. Improving all the time, too.

BURGESS HILL SCHOOL FOR GIRLS

Linked to Burgess Hill School for Girls Junior School in the Junior section

Keymer Road, Burgess Hill, West Sussex, RH15 0EG

Tel: 01444 241 050
Fax: 01444 870 314
E-mail: headmistress@burgesshill-school.com
Website: www.burgesshill-school.com

- Pupils: 680 girls, boarding and day • Ages: 2 1/2 to 18 years
- Size of sixth form: 80 • Non-denom • Fees: Senior school: day £3,390; full board £5,885. Juniors school £1,620 - £2,835
- Independent • Open days: October, November, March and May

Head: From 2006, Mrs Ann Aughwane, previously deputy head at the school.

Academic Matters: Not for the work-shy. Very good results all round. At A level, the A/B percentage rose from 66 per cent in 1999 to 84 per cent in 2003 and has remained consistently above 80 per cent since. There is no stereotyping in terms of subject choices with large numbers attracted to psychology, maths, English lit, chemistry and biology amongst 24 subjects offered. GCSE results have improved to 63 per cent A*/A grades in 2004 and 2005 and school has 11th place in the national value-added tables. Girls talk of inspirational teachers. Quite a handful of male

staff although predominantly women. There are two very well equipped laboratories for each science discipline where the girls can unselfconsciously enjoy the sciences unencumbered by gender expectations. Science is split between 80 per cent doing the dual award and 20 per cent the individual sciences. Head of sciences denies that the dual is lightweight – 'many girls still go onto study medicine and sciences at university but it allows them more flexibility with other subject combinations.'

Uses MidYIS data for academic tracking, showing very high value-added. Only junior school participates in SATs at key stage 1 and 2. Streaming in maths and French begins in year 7 and for science in year 10. No unusual subjects on offer, some grumbles from the girls who would relish more – school says, 'a diverse and balanced sixth form programme' is on offer and cites '100 per cent success in placement to students' first choice university in 2005'. Parents happy, although they have to keep a vigilant eye on girls' stress levels as homework can be over-demanding (head is setting up a working party to review this). SENCO appointed to interpret psychological jargon and nip problems in the bud. Head very knowledgeable about how children learn to mask problems at an early age – will take some special needs if they can cope with the work but not a specialism.

Games, Options, The Arts: Sports facilities are not extensive, one well-manicured hockey/athletics field and one other rather inclined pitch. One floodlit and four other courts. Very good-sized gym and main hall for indoor sports – although dance hardly features. Good modern sports/ drama block. Efficient, popular staff and plenty of sporting success in hockey, netball with coaches employed for aerobics, squash and trampoline. The girls are bused to the nearby Triangle sports centre for the use of the pool and other facilities.

Exciting music and drama departments. A truly bustling music block, all practice rooms lively with orchestra, practising flute ensemble; 60 per cent learn one or more instruments, plenty of choirs. Uses the facilities of nearby Worth boys' school; annual get together for two drama productions and music festivals. Sixth form produces a performing arts festival each year, with fashion design and music. Good range of children's artwork colourfully prominent around the school and a quality display – good thoughtful compositions making one want to linger. CDT man keen for us to see impressive new machinery for welding. Both junior and senior school very up to date with IT equipment and girls use computers in all subjects. Smartboards in most classrooms, including the junior house. Well-stocked and modern library with full range of daily papers and flat computer desks with depressed computers (under smoked glass/ wood desks, no Margins here).

Ambitious building programme. Planning permission obtained for new sports hall and two practice areas, new netball and tennis courts.

Background and Atmosphere: School founded in 1906 as a PNEU (Parents National Education Union) school by Miss Beatrice Goodie, steadily grew and moved to present site in the 1930s. Now an independent charitable trust with 'an industrious, supportive bunch of governors,' says the head. Set in residential suburbia, a good mix of modern redbrick buildings and old turn of the (19th) century houses are linked by some elegant glass corridors. All buildings including the nursery, junior school, senior school (Webb House) and the sixth form (Cedar House) sprawl across a 14-acre site interspersed with large pockets of lawns, ancient trees, attractive paved quad, fenced pond – a colourful, happy atmosphere.

Takes care to accommodate special requirements eg prayer routines and festivals, religious diets, and even bathroom fittings. The three boarding houses, on the surrounds of the school fields, are comfortable and spacious with room to take more. Only the senior school boards; upper sixth have single rooms, year 9 three to a room. Excellent kitchens, new common room, sick bay, bathrooms adequate. Full programme of activities for boarders: ballet, fencing, drama workshops and theatre. Sunday is their day off, although they spend most of the day working. The majority of boarders are international.

Food more than worth a mention – anything but traditional stodge, a dining room and food any good restaurant would be proud of. Good hot food choices, excellent display of twelve different salad options, vegetarian option, halal meat for Muslims, and quality fruit. Queues too lengthy, grumbled some girls, but 'well worth the wait.'

Plans going ahead for an extension to the sixth form centre, new purpose built nursery and infants' school.

Pastoral Care and Discipline: Heads of the lower school, the upper school and head of sixth form strengthening the pastoral ethos of the school.

Pupils and Parents: Catchment wide and mixed – semi-rural and urban. Majority from professional/business backgrounds. Typically both parents work, often first timers to independent education. International contingent of Chinese (HK and China proper), Russian, Malaysian, Korean, Polish, Nigerian, make up most of the boarding populace. Teachers and pupils have ready beaming smiles – most charming and confident. Some pupils sweetly eidolined us

to hymn their teachers' praises. Notable Old Girls include Haydn Gwynne (actress), Caroline Atkins (cricketer) and Dr Francesca Happe (world authority on autism).

Entrance: Almost automatic from junior school so long as pupils can cope and are comfortable with the work ethos. External entry for years 7, 8 and 9 (the school will accept entrants at any year) – maths, English, verbal reasoning. Entering year 10 – sit a maths and English paper – plus formal interview. Head likes to interview in threes to see how pupils interact with each other, plus helps them to know familiar faces when starting school. Some minor dyslexics will be accepted – although no open policy on special needs.

Exit: A wide spread to universities, drama school etc. 95 to 100 per cent of pupils go to their first college of choice (100 per cent in 2005).

Money Matters: Numbers have always stayed steady, so there are no financial blips or disasters and the governors' current policy is to remain debt-free. Scholarships and bursaries are awarded for talented individuals and those whol will thrive in the school environment.

Remarks: Good results, steadily improved reputation, emerging as one of the most popular choices for girls' education in the area. Although lashing with rain during our visit, it was a sunny place to be.

CAEDMON SCHOOL

Airy Hill, Whitby, North Yorkshire, YO21 1QA

Tel: 01947 602 570
Fax: 01947 820 315
E-mail: admin@caedmon.n-yorks.sch.uk
Website: www.caedmon.n-yorks.sch.uk

• Pupils: 530 boys and girls • Ages: 11-14 • Non-denom • State

Head: Since 2001, Tony Hewitt BEd MA NPQH. Taught in four state secondary schools, most recently Blackfyne School, Consett, as deputy head. Still a principal examiner in history and sets GCSE paper for AQA examining board. Has written five GCSE history textbooks and teachers' guides. Married to Jenn, a special needs teacher. Two children. Enthusiastic, committed, with unstuffy sense of humour.

Academic Matters: With no GCSEs or A levels to steal the limelight, Key Stage 3 results are king. And, boy, does it show. Caedmon's results are in top 5 per cent nationally, rated an A* performance. Almost 90 per cent of pupils reach level 5 or above. Outstanding achievement regularly wins Caedmon the DfES's School Achievement Award – effectively a cash bonus for staff which Caedmon shares amongst everyone from teachers to dinner ladies. Placed in top twenty schools nationally in 2003 for value added. Across ability range, pupils judged to leave Caedmon a full academic year ahead of the progress they were expected to make on intake which means a flying start on GCSEs at their next school.

Caedmon also working on 'demystifying' exams by offering volunteers a chance to take information technology GCSE at 14. Impressive results from pupils – and even some teachers who were brave enough to sit the exam alongside them. School prides itself on doing well by less able pupils, including special needs. Intense monitoring means that any slip in standards is noticed and acted on.

OFSTED in 2005 reported 'no weaknesses' and head got an invite to St James' Palace 'as head of an outstanding school'.

Games, Options, The Arts: One of only three schools in North Yorkshire to win Sport England's Sportsmark Gold. Huge grounds including its own wood for cross-country. £500,000 new floodlit Astroturf, the first in the town, was completed 2004. New classrooms and changing facilities underway. Some pupils opt for junior sports leadership awards and pass on their skills in primary schools. Others return to coach Caedmon's athletes in their lunch hours after they leave. Wealth of after-school activities, including clog dancing.

Good music and drama, including two productions a year – though expect the unexpected. The sublime – performing a home-grown play on board the replica of Captain Cook's ship, Endeavour – was soon followed by the ridiculous – Caedmon's own Stars In Their Eyes with staff and parents doing their Freddie Mercury and Cher routines. Whitby's Captain Cook links mean that the school trip is as ambitious as they come. Caedmon gave up on its round-the-world tours after September 11th but still manages to bob over to Australia where civic receptions are part of the package.

Background and Atmosphere: Get up early, very early, to see what puts Caedmon in a class of its own. Its open school policy means that pupils are welcome from 7.45am onwards to use the library, computer rooms, do their homework or just socialise. The last pupils drift home around 6.00pm. And still the 1960s building, above Whitby harbour, is as tidy as your grandma's front room on Easter Sunday. So how do they do it? Largely, through a very structured system of rewards and merits and efficient prefects,

given a heady level of responsibility which includes running the school council and helping to suss out job candidates. Hard to believe they're still only 14.

And if you thought the days when house points meant anything in state comprehensives were long gone, Caedmon has found a way of making them doubly precious. The more points your house gets, the more balls it's awarded in the school's weekly lottery. And the prize? First place for your house in the school dinner queue. Priceless.

Pastoral Care and Discipline: Part of Caedmon's success is down to knowing its pupils well. And, while most would claim the same, Caedmon is small enough to mean it. Teachers pool knowledge of individual pupils at staff meetings. As much chance of disappearing in this school as of scooping a double rollover. Those who work hard are rewarded, those who don't are under the microscope. The head, who tours school several times a day, also does spot-checks on pupils' books. Bad behaviour means formal warnings and sometimes a phone call home to mum. And the ultimate deterrent? Saturday morning detention in full uniform. 'You see this forlorn figure in white shirt and tie trudging into school? They don't do it again,' says head.

Pupils and Parents: Very supportive parents who appreciate that Caedmon goes that extra mile. Accessibility to head verging on saintly. Gives parents his personal email address and mobile phone number. 'I know if they use that number, they're desperate to speak to me.' Blimey. And a newsletter goes home every Friday. That's more contact than most adults have with their mums.

Entrance: Mainly, but not exclusively, down to catchment area. About 20 per cent come from outside in one of those rare instances where parental choice means you can actually get into a very good school without having to move into the grounds.

Exit: Most go to Whitby Community College, the local 14 to 19 state school. Some come out of private sector for their three years at Caedmon.

Remarks: A peach of a school which combines respect and responsibility and still finds room for some classroom banter. You don't just send your child there, you wish you'd gone yourself.

CAISTOR GRAMMAR SCHOOL

Church Street, Caistor, Lincolnshire, LN7 6QJ

Tel: 01472 851 250
Fax: 01472 852 248
E-mail: administrator@caistor-grammar.lincs.sch.uk
Website: www.caistor-grammar.lincs.sch.uk

• Pupils: 275 boys, 310 girls. All day • Ages: 11-18 • Size of sixth form: 140 • Non-denom • Fees: None • State

Head: Since 1996, Roger Hale MA MA(Ed) (early forties), is a powerhouse. Educated Huddersfield New College and Cambridge (law and history), he is a modern headmaster with a top-flight MA in education management and administration, and his finger on the pulse of what's happening in the world of education. Was deputy head here for three years. Previous schools include Tewkesbury School (a Beacon School) and Haberdashers' Aske's, Elstree. Married with two young children. Subtle, capable and very switched-on. Much respected by staff and pupils alike for his commitment to the school. Glowing Ofsted report refers to his 'outstanding leadership'. Self-evidently proud to head the county's best grammar school and one of the country's top ten mixed state schools. Other half of the impressive double act is hugely popular and energetic deputy head, Eddie Cook (also Cambridge). 'I only realised how many hours Roger and Eddie put into their jobs when I became departmental head,' said one teacher.

Academic Matters: Consistently excellent results at GCSE and A level and still improving. Nearly 100 per cent get A*-C at GCSE and most of those are taking ten or eleven. The average point score for A level candidates over 30. Notably excellent results in English, biology, chemistry, French, German, maths. Smallish range of subjects on offer reflects size of school. Latin and/or classical civilisation is on the curriculum. All sixth formers do 3 A levels plus general studies, 'to broaden horizons' say students cheerfully. Good support is provided for those with learning difficulties. There is a mentor scheme for students in year 11 and a paired support scheme where sixth formers provide support for younger students as well as extra teaching.

Games, Options, The Arts: Sports pitches are a five-minute jog from the main school buildings. Despite being a self-avowedly academic school, sports are given plenty of time and a good range is available: football, hockey, rugby, netball, dance, gymnastics, volleyball, badminton, cricket,

tennis etc. 'Quite a few are playing for the county rugby team,' pupils relate proudly, and one for the England Under 19s. Cricket pretty good and athletics, including one county champion. Music quite strong (good results at GCSE) and all students are encouraged to play an instrument (tuition is subsidised by the school). One pupil is ranked no. 1 in Britain for Latin-American dancing. The art block is quite small but head of art is energetic, full of enthusiasm and imagination. Interesting work hangs on the walls.

Despite one or two grumbles to the contrary, there seems to be a mass of extra-curricular activity – house plays, exchange visits to France and Germany, public speaking teams (often successful up to national level), a Youth Parliament with its own Prime Minister's Question Time, mock trials, a school newspaper (highly commended in the TES competition), a creative writing magazine, helping with a lunch club for the elderly in Caistor, theatre trips to Stratford, ski trips, taking part in the Agricultural Challenge at the Lincolnshire Show, chess club, Young Enterprise Scheme, the Duke of Edinburgh Award and a host of designated days, eg Caring Professions Day, RE Day, World Issues Day etc etc. Gap year is now very popular and 'there's lots of advice to help you get the most out of it'. In September 2004 CGS gained Sports College Status.

Background and Atmosphere: Caistor Grammar lies along a narrow lane in the somewhat crumbling and faded Georgian magnificence of Caistor. Founded in 1631, the school is an attractively higgledy-piggledy collection of buildings, one of which dates from the original foundation. New blocks are being built at the moment which will provide much-needed extra space. 'If I could have one thing,' says Roger Hale, 'it would be more money for buildings and facilities.' Maximum benefit seems to be extracted from every inch. Some of the buildings are far from grand, and on the shabby side, but it does not seem to matter a jot.

Cheerful purposefulness and animation characterise the atmosphere. Teachers are strikingly popular with the pupils and much mention is made of friendliness and supportiveness. There is a considerable quiet pride in being at the school. 'Pupils feel they've been given a great opportunity,' says the head. 'They've seen the publicity and they're very conscious they're the next generation, carrying the baton, and they don't want to let the school down.'

All the sixth form are prefects and the head boy and girl with the senior prefect team are elected. There is a school council with representatives for each year 'to discuss issues – like food!' Lunch is in the school cafeteria – a fairly standard choice on offer – or pupils bring their own.

Pastoral Care and Discipline: Pastoral care is good. Staff know the children as individuals and they are valued as such – there are form tutors to keep an eye on things. Academic problems are quickly identified and appropriate action swiftly taken to provide support. The pupils are also supportive to each other – a weekly mentoring system operates whereby older students help younger ones with study problems. 'Bullying is very minor and really strictly dealt with,' say students. As for drugs, they say, 'there are none at school and very little out of school'.

Pupils and Parents: A fairly middle class school (parents are doctors, lawyers, businessmen, farmers) but far from exclusively so. Quite a lot from Grimsby but many also from villages. Pupils are well-mannered and open, very positive about the school, particularly those who have slotted into years post the 11+. 'It's so welcoming, it's fantastic!' Most notable Old Girl is Dawn French, 'but I'm sure there'll be many more quite soon,' says Roger Hale.

Entrance: Children are required to sit two verbal reasoning tests. If the applicant lives within 6.5 miles of the school, they will need 220 marks out of a maximum 280 (ie they will be in the top 25 per cent of ability range). Then they are guaranteed a place. For those out of catchment, it's a case of competing for whatever places are left over, typically about 40. There are 84 places in total per year and about 300 applicants. There are usually a few places each year subsequently. Applicants to the sixth form are particularly welcome.

Exit: All sixth formers leave for higher education. A good proportion go off to study science in some form or other. Out of 60 in the upper sixth in 2000, six to Oxbridge, seven to Imperial College, four to Nottingham, four to Birmingham. Medicine, law, maths, dentistry, computing etc.

Remarks: This is a school buzzing with motivation, energy and non-cocky self-confidence. They make more than most of what are admittedly not the most lavish facilities. Ideal for a self-propelled child who really enjoys learning. 'Ultimately we want to make ourselves unnecessary as teachers, and have the students doing it for themselves,' says Roger Hale. 'Everyone is moving in the same direction, wanting to do well, aiming for their best.'

THE CAMDEN SCHOOL FOR GIRLS

Sandall Road, London, NW5 2DB

Tel: 020 7485 3414
Fax: 02072 843 361
E-mail: csg@camdengirls.camden.sch.uk
Website: www.csfg.org.uk

• Pupils: 970; all day • Ages: 11-19 • Size of sixth form: 420 sixth form of whom 124 are boys • Non-denom • State

Head: Since 2000, Ms Anne Canning (forties), previously deputy head, and taught for many years at La Sainte Union convent school in Camden. Teaches maths to A level groups, 'which is an act of great self-indulgence'. Understated, thoughtful, a good listener. The previous much-loved head, Geoffrey Fallows, was a hard act to follow. 'But I think she is wonderful,' said a parent. 'She is gaining the respect and affection of everyone who knows how she operates. Self-importance has no meaning to her. She is a piece of real luck for the school.'

Academic Matters: A genuinely comprehensive school, taking equal numbers from each of four ability bands since 1999. For the first two years, nearly all the teaching is in mixed ability groups, with some setting for maths, science and foreign languages from year 8. 'The school puts great stress on inclusiveness – which puts high demands on the staff – because we don't like to label kids at an early age.' High quality staff is a priority and the teaching is strong more-or-less throughout the school. 'My daughter always bumbled along at primary school but Camden realised she could be doing better and now she's being stretched in every subject,' said a parent. 'They make great efforts to get the best out of every child.' 'Whatever your skills, you're made to feel wanted and valued,' said another.

2005 GCSE 75 per cent got 5+ A*-C grades – a very fine performance – included a rich mix of languages, from Chinese to Portuguese and Bengali. Classics is a Camden tradition – everyone studies it in year 8 and can choose Latin in year 9. Ancient Greek, studied before school, is another GCSE option. 'The school will bend over backwards to provide the curriculum your child wants to follow at whatever hour of the day,' said a parent. The large sixth form, offering 30 subjects, draws in a wide range of expertise that can be tapped further down the school. English literature is much the most popular A level, followed by history, art and maths. In 2005, 62 per cent of A level grades were A or B. ICT is a recent lower school addition – building work (at last!) has added three networked ICT rooms, as well as new science and technology rooms, extensive sixth form facilities and a new library with computers.

The school has a policy of entering everyone for exams they wish to take, regardless of their likelihood of success. With an intake of average ability and results at all stages well above average, it undoubtedly, in education-speak, adds plenty of value. Much of this is due to high expectations – 'the staff know the kids and their idiosyncrasies and how to get the best out of them.' Good SEN support, in and out of the classroom. The school employs three learning mentors, all ex-teachers, who help under-achieving girls to overcome their barriers to learning. Has its fair share of disaffected youngsters; the mixed-ability teaching policy means that they are not, on-the-whole, hived off into their own low ability sets but included and involved in mainstream activities. 'We always try to find something to engage them. Because there are always plenty of exciting things happening, most of the kids have a positive attitude to mainstream curriculum activities too. We're very good at identifying people's abilities and giving them opportunities.'

The school has beacon status for its Gifted and Talented programme, which focuses on enrichment rather than fast-track academics: professional artists, dancers, writers, musicians and storytellers come in to run workshops.

Games, Options, The Arts: Exciting things happening on the creative side most of the time, whether a Christmas talent show, the choir and orchestra performing the Brahms Requiem, or a high-profile writer running a workshop. The wonderful head of music, John Catlow, has now retired but there is great enthusiasm for his successor, Paul Newbury. The school has embarked on a formal relationship with the London Symphony Orchestra, whose musicians will give masterclasses to orchestra members and exam students and get involved in classroom music-making. The school choirs and orchestras perform ambitious repertoires and there's a whole school musical every year which includes singers, dancers and musicians. Theatre studies is an A level option, though at present there is no drama at KS4.

Art is very popular and very strong, with a high proportion of A grades at GCSE and A level. PE has greatly improved in recent years. Smallish gym, the main school hall, a dance studio and one netball/basketball court (usually monopolised at lunchbreak by sixth form boys playing football); otherwise pupils walk to Astroturf courts up the road in Islington. Games include football, rounders, athletics, cross-country and trampolining. Plenty of extra-curricular activities including lots of sports clubs, art, technology and modern languages. Lots of school trips.

Background and Atmosphere: Founded in 1871 by the indefatigable Frances Mary Buss, who also founded North London Collegiate (qv). Voluntary aided, which means it can, to an extent, set its own admissions procedure and have control over its own buildings. Its crammed site just off the busy Camden Road has a hotchpotch of redbrick and pebble-dashed concrete, with new labs, a huge new food technology room and a splendid new sixth form centre decorated in shades of lilac and rust-red. Phase 2 of the building works is now complete and houses English, D&T and music. The Music House is a brick-built semi with a wrought-iron balcony. The limited grounds do include some quiet green areas – which is an achievement given its urban location. Relaxed, informal atmosphere, 'but incredibly well-organised,' said a parent; no uniform. 'She was liberated by the atmosphere at Camden,' said a parent whose child came from a disciplined private junior school. 'It was like seeing a flower open up.'

Pastoral Care and Discipline: A supportive but tight regime comes down heavily and, on-the-whole successfully, on bad behaviour. A peer counselling scheme involves year 10 and 11 pupils who are trained to help younger pupils, mostly about friendship issues. In true Camden liberal tradition, there's a smoking area on site for sixth formers; younger pupils caught smoking will be temporarily excluded.

Pupils and Parents: A huge ability range, including a fair number from socially deprived backgrounds as well as plenty of middle-class girls, whose parents have often measured out the distance from the school gates before buying a house nearby (local estate agents should by rights donate a percentage of their proceeds to the school). Many use the selective independent schools as a back-up in case they don't get a place at Camden. Turns out confident, articulate, independent-minded girls. OGs include Emma Thompson, Arabella Weir, Deborah Moggach, Gillian Slovo. Strong informal OG network.

Entrance: Heavily oversubscribed; will now only consider the nearest 219 applicants, who must live within 1.4 miles of the school, under distance criterion. Applicants take the NFER cognitive ability tests in verbal and non-verbal reasoning and are divided into four ability groups, with equal numbers from each group being offered places. Sisters get first preference. Then there are five music places; in practice, those successful tend to be at least grade 5 or 6, though Camden sometimes goes for those with strong musicality but without formal grades. Those with social or medical needs come next. The rest of the places are given to girls living nearest the school gates (nearly always less than half a mile away, with different distances for each ability band, varying each year. Convenient for the school but a source of much anxiety for parents).

100-120 come into the sixth form (more than half of them boys, chosen from around 450 applicants, from private as well as state schools). At this stage, distance is not a factor and applicants are expected to have at least five Bs at GCSE for A level courses, less for vocational courses. 'We're looking at whether they're going to bring something to us, and get involved in all we have to offer.'

Exit: About three quarters go through to the sixth form; others choose more directly vocational courses elsewhere 'but they often stay involved with us'. About 90 per cent of sixth form leavers go on to higher education, often double figures to Oxbridge and many to art college.

Money Matters: Luckily, parents and friends are good at fund-raising. The £420,000 needed to fund the school's share of the recent building works was achieved by relentlessly pursuing charitable trusts, plus some staggeringly successful events – a promises auction organised by one set of parents raised £17,500. Otherwise, the school is as hard up as most, scraping together small amounts of money from various government initiatives.

Remarks: A successful, exciting comprehensive which has the middle-classes queuing up to get in. 'I had high expectations,' said a parent, 'and they've been fulfilled in every respect.'

CANFORD SCHOOL

Canford Magna, Wimborne, Dorset, BH21 3AD

Tel: 01202 847 207
Fax: 01202 881 723
E-mail: admissions@canford.com
Website: www.canford.com

• Pupils: 373 boys, 231 girls. (242 boys board, 131 day boys; 158 girls board, 73 day girls) • Ages: 13-18 • Size of sixth form: 254 • C of E • Fees: Day £5,525, boarders £7,360 • Independent • Open days: October and May

---

Head: Since 1992, Mr John Lever MA PGCE (fifties). Educated at Westminster, read geography at Trinity Cambridge – a rowing blue. Taught briefly at St Edward's School, followed by Winchester for sixteen years where he

was also a housemaster. Married to Alisoun with three teenage children, two now at uni. 'I enjoy my children, and I enjoy wild places ... and I enjoy silence'. Has highly strategically placed elegant study with gilt mouldings, perfect for bouncing out of and nobbling people as they tiptoe by, the door is often kept open and pupils know they can pop in and see him with problems.

Articulate and fun, with a good line in uplifting thoughts and bon mots. A five star head. Good to see him still in place. One of the few heads who make a point of seeing pupils when they have done well as well as when they have committed appalling acts of sinfulness and doshes out commendation cards with uplifting thoughts. This year's collection includes Goethe: As soon as you trust yourself, you will know how to live'; Woody Allen: 'Most of the time I don't have much fun'. Etc. Mr Lever is a robust advocate of boarding which he says 'develops unselfishness' and 'extends sense of community'. Believes that pupils having a 'positive attitude to their own talents and other people's values is absolutely critical'. Head keen to 'push children to dare' and to 'help more children to be braver and push to their own personal limits'.

Took issue with us when we said that the most important happening at Canford during his reign was the discovery and subsequent sale of the Assyrian bas relief. It was certainly a happy cash injection of something over six million quid but his greatest pride is in having turned the school into a 'proper co-ed', which it became in 1995 though it had had girls in the sixth form since the early 1970s.

Academic Matters: Greatly improved results across the board, with outstanding collections of As and A*s at GCSE level, ditto As at A in English, maths and the sciences. Creative writing important, and school takes part in national poetry competitions. Chemistry is still excellent with one pupil already having published an important scientific paper. Geography strong, also French and Latin, not much take up in German, Spanish or economics – the weakest of all subjects presented, though two new buzzy department heads should change all this.

For such a large school the spread of subjects at A level is not that impressive. But results are amazingly good given the wide ability range, owing partly to the head's knack of choosing dedicated staff, often coming in from other fields. Staff are often to be found whizzing round the school grounds on electric scooters which is another first (head sez 'only two, but aren't they fun?'). About two thirds of the staff live on site, and building in progress to convert the old stables into a dozen staff houses, Mr L calls his staff 'warm-blooded communicators'. Inspired head of IT (he runs a

Harley Davidson) was with Xerox and has the most imaginative new IT room where he teaches from a podium at the back with a white board at the front for the pupils to follow the lesson and he can see all the screens and watch for recalcitrant pupils playing games or going on-line. Chairs whiz round for closer explanations. Brilliant – we have already recommended other schools to follow suit.

Macs and PCs on stream, and computers throughout the school, course work and cross-curricular use. School currently operates an intranet via gigantic antenna, but 'is going wireless 'soon'. Enthusiastic and gifted science teachers and the results show. Lots of visits and lectures to inspire pupils, even for potentially tedious matters. Everyone does a language to GCSE and they don't fail, only three Cs last year in French – impressive. Setted for maths, all langs, max 23 per class, top movers streamed. Glorious library with impressive collection of books and twinkly chandeliers, not much fiction, and almost no books on view in the houses. Full time dyslexia help, one to one.

Games, Options, The Arts: Strong, as ever, on team games especially rugby, hockey and cricket for boys and hockey and netball for girls, with county players across a range of sports and recent good showing at Henley. Regular sculling on the River Stour which abuts the school grounds. Royal tennis court a feature but not much used as few other schools to play against; Astroturf pitches and hockey-field-sized games hall with all the ancillary activities like cricket nets etc, as well as dance practice rooms and proper weights room. Loads of specialist staff, pilates and yoga on offer. Good CCF, to die for assault course which only members of the CCF can use and a jolly good reason for joining.

Keen cabbage + ecology group alternative, otherwise community service – includes teaching science to local primary schools as well as getting involved in local charities. Canford partnership sponsors pupils on annual do-gooding trips to Kenya, India and South America which are then lyrically written up in the school mag, 150 sixth formers last year. Well-used swimming pool.

Music stunning, lots of little concertettes and the real thing, everyone can have a bash. Standard of music plumped up by music scholarships. Fantastic Layard theatre – state of the art – runs full schedule of visiting companies alongside student productions. The foyer was sound dead when we visited and filled with would-be thespians studying their parts scattered around with their shoes off (it seemed to be mandatory). School also uses theatre for Fame Academy type shows and Saturday evening films. Professional lighting and sound as you might imagine. Whole school appears to be carpeted in the same school-designed pattern with an oak tree and an open book. Art fun and thriving, with ceramics and rather good glass work, art students dive off to St Ives for master classes, enjoy visiting lecturers and regular artists in residence. Art department open at weekends. Sports facilities are open to (well-vetted) local residents.

Background and Atmosphere: Canford House, a magnificent Gothic Barry design, was built for the Guest family of GKN fame on a previous Norman building. Glorious 19th century interiors, splendid dining hall with deeply ornate dark wood panelling leading to a grand carved staircase. School was founded here in 1923, on three hundred acres of elegant, beautifully maintained, parkland now dotted with tennis courts, rugby pitches and various essential modern buildings. Enough parkland (and hideous bumps on the driveways) to make pupils feel that they are in deep country and not just a mile or so from the busy bustling town of Wimborne Minster. Historic arboretum with unusual specimens.

The house system important here, no more than sixty per house, with house chapel every week and regular monthly child-led house assemblies. Girls have cosy state-of-the-art new houses which feel exactly like motorway hotels with single and double bedrooms (they swap every term) and basins and sewing machines and kitchens as well as dedicated boy-socialising areas. All much expanded since our earlier visit and all pupils have proper work stations. Stunning new boys' house, Court House, is currently the sporty house, comes complete with a piano; younger boys have a jolly computer-filled common room, whilst older boys work in their rooms. Probably slicker than the girls' houses. The rest of the boys' houses are based in the main house. School House, over the main school building, has a state bedroom, wonderful old rooms and corridors and a positive symphony of creaks and squeaks from doors and floorboards. Three huge day houses (or Lodges) in the main building are mixed, with work stations and discreet lockers for clobber.

Heads of school have their own telephones and are supposed to be contactable 'at any time'. Splendid revamped assembly hall much in use for discos, and fabulous dining room with what the pupils tell us is excellent food, pasta and salad bar as well as burgers and chips. Absolutely stunning san, full of admonitions about booze. Tuck shop now rather bereft post Assyrian sale is full of reproductions, telly on tap everywhere. Regular themed weeks, and masses of visiting lecturers. Canford is one of the Allied Schools (for what that is worth, head says it doesn't impose much) with a Low Church foundation and 20 per cent of governors are appointed by the Martyr's Memorial. Now 'broad' C of E with chapel for all; two chaplains live 'with their families in the grounds' and are available 'to all members of the community at any time. Enchanting little Norman church in the grounds, much used by locals but not quite big enough for the whole school. Very security conscious, only two entrances in use.

Pastoral Care and Discipline: Some truly super matrons and 'good mature pastoral care', commented the head of a neighbouring prep school. Housemaster/mistress plus three tutors and matron in each house. Each sixth former has a tutorial either individual or by group with their tutor each week. Anti-drugs policy is 'to keep pupils busy' and teach them how to say no. Drugs testing on suspicion. Pupils may expect to be expelled if they indulge and indeed two had to leave the school last year. Booze more of a problem. Head has 'no hesitation in throwing child out for bullying if appropriate' – our guides told us that it really wasn't an issue, and that most was just first formers sorting out their pecking order. Head says they 'have remarkably few problems with drugs or alcohol, pupils have a lot to lose and cigarettes are no longer an issue'. Counsellor on hand. Prefects chosen for their moral qualities and good role model material rather than for flashy achievements.

Pupils and Parents: Most come from within one and a half hours' drive though numbers from London are increasing as the school's profile has risen. Small number of foreign nationals, plus about 30 or 40 service children. Foreign nationals all have to have some form of guardian, 'usually friends of friends'. Day pupils can come and go by school bus, occasional accommodation available if pupil has to stay late for any reason. Older pupils can bring their own cars. Lots of children of local professionals, Wimborne and Bournemouth. About five per cent first time buyers. A handful of Muslims. Set exeats, but no pressure to leave, pupils who don't go out can arrange informal 'sleepovers' in other houses. Comment from head – 'there are three weekends when they must go on exeat, about ten when we expect boarders to be in and, on the other 20 or so, they can choose'.

Entrance: First come first served basis, with waiting lists filling up earlier so try to get names down at least three years ahead. Those on waiting list invited for tests and activity day to see who will slot in best to the few remaining places. 55 per cent CE pass mark. Prep school commendation matters – fifteen regular feeders including Twyford, Highfield, Port Regis, Castle Court and Dumpton, over 40 different schools. Some from state system. About 30 come annually post GCSE.

Exit: 97 per cent to universities, about thirty of so try for Oxbridge and a regular dozen or so get there. School traditionally strong on engineers, professions. Southampton for scientists, but Bristol, Cardiff, Nottingham and Exeter all popular. Absolutely no policy of kicking pupils out for not doing well enough but if they are obviously 'not trying' then head might suggest that they would 'do better elsewhere'. Perhaps seven or eight a year. But if they really want to stay...

Money Matters: School made a lotta dosh selling the 3,000 year old Assyrian bas-relief which paid for the Layard Theatre (after the guy who brought the relief to Canford) plus a mass of vital repair work to the extensive fabric using good quality materials and architects, and set up a whole new scholarship fund. Scholarships at 13 for those with potential, 'likely leaders in their area of expertise, either academic, or cultural, or sporting.' Plus additional scholarships for sixth form entrants. Will keep a child in exam year if real financial need and work with parents but they must be up-front.

Remarks: This, still predominantly boarding, school is currently all singing and dancing – no change here then. Hard to fault, kind confident, enthusiastic, unpretentious and good all round. Quietly satisfied parents, not (yet) discovered by the fashionable set.

THE CARDINAL VAUGHAN MEMORIAL RC SCHOOL

89 Addison Road, London, W14 8BZ

Tel: 020 7603 8478
Fax: 020 7602 3124
E-mail: mail@cvms.co.uk
Website: www.cardinalvaughan.kensington-chelsea.sch.uk

- Pupils: 780 boys, plus 120 girls in sixth form; all day • Ages: 11-18 • Size of sixth form: 290 • RC • State

---

Head: Since 1997, Mr M A Gormally (Michael) BA FRSA ACP (forties) who was educated in Lancashire, read modern languages at London but teaches Latin 'to the first formers, 'it's my way of getting to know them'. He enjoys teaching Latin enormously, 'a secret garden'. He was previously deputy head and has been with the school for 25 years. He is a practising Catholic, as are three quarters of his staff, and religion is important here. Glorious sense of humour – we wanted to describe him as 'giggly' but he would prefer to be 'jocund'. Obviously enjoying the job, he exudes enthusiasm from every pore. Very much the traditionalist, he is affable and popular with pupils and parents alike. 'A rotund and orotund bon viveur,' said one witty member of staff – orotund = either of booming voice, or bombastic prose, neither of which seems appropriate. (Head spent much of our interview playing word games with the assistant headmaster who showed us round.) Thrilled with the 2002 Ofsted report, which is so good he could have written it himself. Goods, Excellents and Very Goods litter the pages, and the only adverse criticism was the size of the site (though interestingly the report describes the sixth form as containing 272 boys 'of whom 93 are young women').

Academic Matters: School has moved to teaching five one-hour periods a day, rather than the traditional 40 minutes; this has worked well, with pupils having to move round less and, according to staff, getting more done in the week. 'Less disruption'. Max 30 per class, with fewer for practical subjects and only 15 for art. Wow! First-formers are divided into four streams on entry and setted from the second year in maths and English but can move up and down. French for all but only the top two streams do Latin; Greek option 'sua sponte' for GCSE 'Latinists' (30 last year, plus 9 at A level) though this is not timetabled, and is not always available – depends on numbers. Alas, German has fallen by the wayside. All must take Eng lit and lang, maths, RE and DT. Pleasing number of As and A*s across the board, 2004 the best ever year for both GCSE and A level results. Christian theology important. Ablest pupils streamed into separate sciences for GCSE in the second year, with their weaker brethren taking dual award; strong science department, 'school ferociously keen on science' and a group in the second year came first in the Salters' science chemistry competition at Queen Mary's College, London. English, maths, history and economics the popular choices at A level. Small but vigorous classics department.

Design Technology (CAD/CAM and the like) in the new Pellegrini building is popular, with successes across the board at all levels. Not too much hands-on stuff in evidence. Computers abound, though not in every classroom. Super SEN plus support for learning, part of the Excellence in Cities for Gifted and Talented strand, which encourages the ablest. 20 pupils are statemented, with a further 70 on the school's own special educational needs register – they get support both within the class (mentor system by full qualified staff, as well as by older pupils) and on a one-to-one basis. 'This is a truly comprehensive school in every sense of the word'. Great emphasis put on homework. No major changes in staff, though there is a fair turnover in the younger members who find London living expensive and London weighting 'risible'.

Games, Options, The Arts: Extremely active sports – soccer popular but rugby catching up fast, and cricket gaining enthusiasts. Excellent playing fields next to the holy of holies at Twickenham. Pupils do one whole afternoon of sport a week and play other senior schools; large integrated gym. Pupils are bused to the river for rowing (strong), good fencing too. Swimming at the local Kensington Sports Centre. New art dept in the Pellegrini building, buzzing with terrific paintings and some fab 3D; impressive selection of AS stuff on show, being assessed when we visited.

Orchestra now of a 'quasi' professional standard – 'wonderful' – recently performed the whole of Beethoven's fifth and Dvorák's eighth. Impressive, plus a highly acclaimed big band jazz which has a regular monthly gig in the Bull's Head in Barnes, and travels abroad with great success. They sound pretty good too. Variety of ensembles plus 'the jewel in our crown' – the Schola Cantorum, which travels internationally, recently played in the Vatican, singing vespers in the basilica of St Peter's itself, when the choir was blessed by the Pope. This editor was given one of their recent CDs and jolly nice it sounds too – though not perhaps the high liturgy we were promised (there have to be some perks). Massive choral production at Easter and a range of other choirs. All these marvels come from a music suite in the basement, all singing and dancing, sure enough, but pretty grisly. New music suite due for completion 2005 to give this dept the accommodation it deserves. Drama is 'not taught as a discrete subject'; musicals rather than straight plays, put on by a combination of the English and music depts (fantastic much-praised head of music – a maestro). Guys and Dolls, West Side Story among recent productions. Regular French exchanges and trips all over the place both at home and abroad. Strong sense of community service fostered, pupils raise thousands for charity, with weekly charity collections in every form. Lots of voluntary work done in local primaries and with old people in the area.

Background and Atmosphere: The Victorian redbrick building which houses the senior three years was, apparently, originally built as a music hall, The Addison Hall, and we saw pupils doing their GCSEs in what could easily have been the auditorium. 1914 saw the building in use as a private school, it became a grammar school in 1944, and started taking girls in the sixth form in 1980. The Vaughan, as it is known, is a memorial to the third Archbishop of Westminster, Herbert Vaughan, and there is some rather jolly stained glass in the senior building, and a much neglected collection of mitres outside the tiny chapel – dedicated to self-reflection, the benediction is given here on

Friday afternoons at the end of school, every week. Voluntary, it is usually well attended.

The uninspired junior block across Addison Road (one way, humps, guarded crossing) dates from the sixties, functional and flat roofed, with a spanking new addition, the Pellegrini building, called after the previous head who was in the job for 21 years. Pretty boring collection of classrooms. All the classrooms have a crucifix in prime position. The mezzanine addition in the assembly/dining hall is a great improvement acoustically and certainly breaks up the barn. Not over-large library considering the number of pupils. Every nook and cranny crammed in the new building which houses the art room, DT and classrooms. It's jolly and bright, full of stainless steel – opened in 1988 by Cardinal Hume and the floor coverings are already showing bad signs of wear. When they decide to expand upwards, they had better stipulate a different contractor. Black and grey uniform, burgundy and grey for girls (school hot on this – 'no variation of uniform is permitted', nor are unconventional hair styles). Ties for sports teams. The Vaughan is possibly the tidiest school we have visited. Busy caring atmosphere, peaceful and friendly, where many other city schools are jungles.

Pastoral Care and Discipline: The Vaughan is a Catholic school and faith is important here. Junior pupils must attend Mass twice a week ('Mass is NOT optional'). The fifth and sixth forms have Mass once a month and the whole school attends the local Our Lady of Victories church on holy days of obligation. The Angelus is said each day at noon and the rosary recited at lunch between May and October (serious stuff this) and vocational education is part of the GCSE curriculum. Sex education is taught by a combined science and religious education clique – according, you understand, to the Catholic ethos. 40 of the sixth form are prefects with distinctive ties, the 'rest are pressed into service as and when necessary'. ' No real problems' with the perennial drugs 'n' booze 'n' fags, 'virtually zero-tolerance for illegal substances'. But discipline is 'under control'; school would like us to say that 'our discipline and pastoral care arrangements are excellent: see Ofsted report on this' – certainly more than under control, if younger pupils continue the habit of lining up in pairs at the end of break (leafy area, junior school) and filing inside, saluting our guide as they did so.

Pupils and Parents: No strategically placed primaries help here. Pupils come from all over the London area, from Tower Hamlets to Aylesbury, Hackney, Hampstead, south London and Bethnal Green, often travelling for an hour or so each way. Homework centre open until 4.45pm. 'School reflects the average inner London population', ditto the number of free school meals. Everyone from true working class to toffs. Huge amount of parental support with 'more than 300 turning up for the recent Ofsted parents' evening. Lots of moral support too. Head calls the parents 'exceptional, the secret of our success'. Almost 50 per cent from ethnic minorities from 50 different countries, with 22 per cent non-white according to Ofsted. Eng lang help on hand if needed.

Entrance: Primary criterion for admission – 'evidence of baptism or reception into the Roman Catholic Church'. As of 2004, new additional entrance tests – of how RC you are. Fiendlishly difficult and demanding questions and test has been failed by devoutly church-going and serious-minded RC candidates – much distress thereafter. Overall, the RC criteria for entrance now v v demanding and, some might think, pretty exclusive.

Massively oversubscribed – 300 for 120 places. 'All applicants are tested to ensure a balanced intake' – diagnostic rather than selective in maths and English – and designed to ensure that 'coaching is now useless'. The Vaughan does not aim to be an academic hothouse. Two As and four Bs or above for entry to the sixth form. Pupils come at 11 from a variety of primaries, and even some private prep schools, and at 16 from roughly the same spread, 40 girls and a handful of boys.

Exit: About 20 boys or so leave after GCSE, usually to take up some form of vocational education not available at The Vaughan. Otherwise a stunning ten to Oxbridge last year (six boys, four girls); Bristol popular, York and Warwick, as well as the London unis etc plus a selection to art schools. Some take a gap year, 'it is increasingly popular'.

Money Matters: Voluntary aided.

Remarks: A kind, religious state school with dedicated staff and a comprehensive intake which, by national state school standards, has consistently good exam results. 'More than good,' said the head indignantly. 'Our results are outstanding by any standards and bear comparison with those of many grammar and independent schools.'

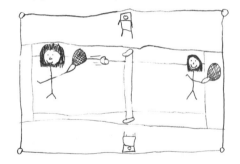

CASTERTON SCHOOL

Linked to Casterton Preparatory School in the Junior section

Kirkby Lonsdale, Via Carnforth, Lancashire, LA6 2SG

Tel: 01524 279 200
Fax: 01524 279 208
E-mail: admissions@castertonschool.co.uk
Website: www.castertonschool.co.uk

• Pupils: 260 girls (60 per cent board) • Ages: 11-18 • Size of sixth form: 90 • Christian foundation • Fees: Senior school: day £3,016 - £3,473, boarding £4,737 - £5,805. Prep: day £1,602 - £3,016 boarding £4,303 - £4,737 • Independent • Open days: October and February

Headmaster: Since 2005, Dr Peter Mclaughlin BA(Hons) PhD, who was previously principal of the British International School in Cairo.

Academic Matters: Consistently good at GCSE; only a tiny handful fails to make A*-C, and recently A* outstripped A; no obviously weak subjects. Languages good. A level results in 2005 84 per cent at A and B grades. This profile suggests excellence in teaching rather than exceptionally bright girls; certainly the school shows up remarkably well in national value-added tables. Everyone says the girls work very hard and expect to succeed. No culling of weak candidates either. Maximum class size 20. Can deal with 'mild dyslexia', but no EFL provision. Mixture of male and female staff, who like working here and tend to stay.

Games, Options, The Arts: Superb creative arts centre (1990), new performing arts complex planned. Art very strong, walls plastered with pupils' high quality work. Music and drama outstanding – 75 per cent have individual music tuition, choirs and ensembles perform demanding works all over the place (4 CDs produced). Same story for drama – sixth form play in public Kendal theatre, two girls recently joined National Youth Theatre. Lacrosse, hockey, netball, tennis (all-weather pitch 2002), indoor pool. Busy riding stables, where 60+ take lessons. Sailing and D of E take advantage of nearby National Parks.

Background and Atmosphere: The Brontë sisters' school, founded in 1823 as Clergy Daughters' School, hence attractively intimate scale of Georgian buildings, set on a hill overlooking handsome tiny village. The main building feels very much like a substantial residence which has grown rabbit warrens of classrooms at the back, the whole larger than it appears. Nice, secure old-fashioned feel; if senior girls sometimes sigh for something more exciting than the Saturday bus to Kendal it's perhaps inevitable in a boarding environment. The school aims to give pupils a relaxed but purposeful social life, with as much freedom as sensible parents would expect. School has a 'strong commitment to weekend activities including plenty of social events with boys' schools'. Nine boarding houses with own identity scattered round site; junior boarders (aged 8-12) housed separately. Sixth formers (also housed separately) have study bedrooms, and 18 year olds can go to the village pub. At the other end of the scale, younger pupils are allowed to be children.

Pastoral Care and Discipline: Thorough and professional pastoral system; priority is inspiring individual confidence. Discipline not a real problem, 'haven't sacked for many years'; will expel 'for the usual reasons'.

Pupils and Parents: A good split of local and international girls including expatriates and foreigners (Hong Kong Chinese, French, German and Spanish). 'Not a snobby school, lots of first-time buyers', said a parent. Feet on ground clientele.

Entrance: Not especially rigorous – which of course highlights results at the other end. Own exam (maths/English/VR) at 11, or Common Entrance. Most come via Casterton Prep School but places at other ages sometimes available. Small 16+ entry, with GCSE grade hurdle.

Exit: Around 95 per cent to higher education. Leakage post-GCSE was a small problem when Sedbergh up the road went co-educational, but has now virtually disappeared. Casterton regularly outperforms Sedbergh academically.

Money Matters: Bursaries and scholarships at 11 (less often 12 and 13); academic, art, music, all-round. Priority is support for hard luck cases (not a rich school – though it handles its money prudently).

Remarks: Small, friendly, unpretentious school, with excellent teaching; only girls' boarding school in the north west. Strong sense of identity – hard-working and busy, confident and poised girls.

CATERHAM SCHOOL

Linked to Caterham Preparatory School in the Junior section

Harestone Valley Road, Caterham, Surrey, CR3 6YA

Tel: 01883 343 028

Fax: 01883 347 795

E-mail: enquiries@caterhamschool.co.uk

Website: www.caterhamschool.co.uk

• Pupils: 746 boys and girls, roughly 3:2 • Ages: 11-18 • Size of sixth form: 241 • Christian • Fees: Prep £1,141 - £2,939; senior day £3,495 – £3,660; boarding £6,477 – £6,827 • Independent • Open days: September and November

Headmaster: Since 1995, Mr Rob Davey MA, Palmes Academiques (mid-fifties). Reminding this aged editor a mite of the young James Stewart, Mr Davey has a grave manner, a soft, engaging southern Irish voice, a tendency to talk at immense length when having begun his answer, 'I'll tell you exactly what it means...' and a smile which appears unexpectedly, betraying the fact that, despite his seriousness about his school, he finds it all tremendously exciting and fun. A modern linguist who has spent nine years driving this school to the considerable heights it has now attained, Mr Davey has a masterplan in mind which, in addition to yet more new-build on this large and leafy site, includes a much needed intention to up the profile of modern languages in his school which currently achieves very highly on the scientific and technical sides. Enthusiastic about 'independent learning' and cites many examples of what this means in practice. Previously deputy head of Wells Cathedral school, this gentle giant is a committed internationalist who was made an officer of the prestigious Palmes Academiques (an order set up by Napoleon Bonaparte for those who have made a notable contribution to culture and education) for his work on cultural exchanges. He is an elder in the United Reform Church, to which this school is affiliated, and is clear about the Christian nature and ethos of the school. 'We're not ashamed of being Christian and we're basically a very British school but we look at other viewpoints.' His school, its general approach and the substantial numbers of pupils from all over the world are testament to this open and truly internationalist attitude – a bit of a treasure in an, otherwise, very much Surrey-based community. Mr Davey was an Oxford Rugby Blue, is a member of the HMC Drugs Guidelines Working Group, is married and is clearly a popular and respected head.

Academic Matters: Caterham can now hold its head high in any company, especially in maths, the sciences and IT. 2004 results included 86 per cent A*-B grades at GCSE (a full 10 per cent improvement on 2000) and, at A level, 100 per cent A-C grades (in 1999 it was 78 per cent). Ninety per cent of leavers secured their first choice university place. Something is going right here. A good set of subject options (international students can take their own languages) includes business studies, economics, government and politics, textiles, psychology, photography and theatre studies, in addition to the usual staples. Modern languages, though encouraged by many foreign trips of all kinds, need beefing up to encourage more takers and this is now in hand. Excellent language lab will help. Greek survives here – hooray. Years 7 and 8 take a course in citizenship and all sixth formers take general studies. A good combination of the trad and the trendy but all in a sensible, purposeful manner. SENs are efficiently diagnosed and well-supported here though those with physical disabilities would find parts of this valley/hills site difficult to negotiate. Parents pay tribute to the caring and dedicated staff who 'really enthuse the pupils' but don't have unrealistic expectations of them.

Games, Options, The Arts: All onsite playing fields, pitches, all-weather surfaces abound. Superb sports hall, plus pool, giant fitness room with 25+ exotic-looking machines, plus plus plus opened in 1996 by Sebastian Coe and open to 'members' ie school families, former pupils etc. Superbly maintained Home Field for athletics etc. Boarding football enthusiasts are coached by a trainer from Crystal Palace FC and school achieves highly in sports which include swimming, rugby, hockey, lacrosse, netball, cricket and cross country. Riding too. CCF, Young Enterprise and D of E all popular.

Lots of drama though no designated studio; recent productions range from Bugsy Malone to The Comedy of Errors. Drama is an A level option. Workmanlike, well stocked workshops for DT and IT. Art is well catered for, though not in top-notch accommodation, and popular, especially with girls. Printmaking, graphic design, pottery and photography among many options. Nice interdisciplinary enterprises like a recent, beautifully produced, pamphlet of art and writings – a truly imaginative exercise done just for the pleasure of it and wonderfully encouraging for those whose work appears. Flourishing music with many in-school lessons on around 20 different instruments and every kind of band and ensemble – a range of small recitals to major choral concerts in the Humphreys Hall. Arcane and eclectic choice of other extra-curriculars includes Amnesty, bridge, chemistry,

Christian Union, debating, various language and minority sports and the splendid Melting Pot – a chance to exchange multi-cultural experience with over 20 countries represented. Visits here, there and everywhere – Bolivia, Botswana, mosques and temples, skiing and Spain.

Background and Atmosphere: In 1995 two schools merged. Boys' school, Caterham, founded in 1811, merged with nearby girls' school Eothen, founded in 1892. Both Christian foundations. Caterham had been set up to educate the sons of Congregationalist ministers – even thirty years ago around a third of pupils were Welsh and the relationship to the United Reform Church is still close. Christian background informs the ethos and is neither exclusive nor punitive. In fact, this is about as inclusive as a school can get.

School moved to its present, 100 acre site in 1884. One arrives at the school down a quiet lane out of Caterham centre with substantial, well spaced detached houses on one side and the school appears on rising ground to one's left. A three storey, immensely long, red-brick building, it is imposing though built in a plain and solid style – free from the excesses of later in that century. It faces banks of glorious, tree-festooned hills and its own sports grounds. Battalions of white mini-buses wait on hard standing. Further down is the prep and pre-prep, wonderfully secluded, be-treed and traffic-free. Later building has added necessary facilities and some views can seem a little cramped but, in general, there is a sense of space and light.

Inside the main building, there are redbrick and tile corridors which could be prison-like but aren't thanks to sensitive lighting and general decoration – even the somewhat violent yellow of the boys' boarding areas upstairs is well chosen. Boarding for girls and boys recently expensively upgraded. Years 7-9 in good sized rooms for 6, year 10 for 4, year 11 for 2 and year 13 students all have good rooms with en-suite loo and shower – better than most recently built undergraduate rooms. Good kitchens, lots of staff living in and school well-up on parents' need for flexi-boarding and very keen to help. New science block and dining hall now has planning permission. Uniform a sensible black/white/grey mix though 'smart business suits' for sixth form girls interpreted somewhat surprisingly by some.

Pastoral Care and Discipline: Commitment to excellent pastoral care evidenced by huge and touchingly accessible booklet, strong RSPE curriculum and general air of happy purposefulness everywhere. Clear but flexible structure. House system. Head believes links with parents work to mitigate problems and sees alcohol as a greater menace than drugs – no drugs exclusions for three years at time of visit. Around 70 per cent stay in over weekends – good programme. Many staff live onsite, either in purpose built houses or in boarding houses. Boarding staff seen as parents rather than staff.

Pupils and Parents: Most boarders from abroad and currently from 38 countries. Largest numbers from Hong Kong, China and eastern Europe. Day pupils from Surrey and a few from Kent or Sussex borders. Good bus services bring from all over. Large proportion of city and professional families, many first-timers – this is easy, prosperous, commuter country. Perennial problems of getting some hardworking foreign students to join extra-curricular activities and to mix generally being keenly tackled but remains an issue. Former pupils include Angus Deayton, Jon Finch, Michael Jecks and cricketers Alastair Brown, James Benning and David Sales.

Entrance: Getting harder for those outside school's own prep, especially as more folk grasp the fact that boys and girls from 3-18 get a pretty unbeatable start in life here. Usual tests at 11 and 13, via interview, and 6 good GCSEs expected at 16.

Exit: A spread of courses with economics most popular in 2003. Range of universities with Birmingham, Nottingham and Southampton most favoured. Three or four to Oxbridge.

Money Matters: Good number of scholarships awarded at 10, 11, 13 and 16. Extra science scholarships at sixth form. Also art and music awards. Bursaries available for children of clergy, OCs, Services and Foreign Service personnel. Special Caterham assisted places for the able but less well-off.

Remarks: Unaccountably neglected by the Guide before this edition, this is a top school. Parents pay tribute to the caring and dedicated staff who 'really enthuse the pupils' but don't have unrealistic expectations of them. Well-appointed in virtually every area and performing outstandingly in maths, science and IT, the school is set to build on the achievements of the last decade. Christian background informs the ethos only in good ways and is neither exclusive nor punitive. In fact, this is about as inclusive as a school can get. The site is leafy, spacious and comfortable. Hard to beat if a co-ed school in the Home Counties with a boarding option is your thing. It is exceptionally well-placed for commuters and those for whom Gatwick/Heathrow are significant – connections couldn't be better. 2004 inspection found no major weaknesses and commented on the 'humane values, the importance of the individual and the sense of community....the school....is very successful in preparing its pupils for their future beyond school'.

CENTRAL NEWCASTLE HIGH SCHOOL

Linked to Central Newcastle High School Junior Department in the Junior section

Eskdale Terrace, Newcastle upon Tyne, Tyne and Wear, NE2 4DS

Tel: 0191 281 1768
Fax: 0191 281 6192
E-mail: cnhs@cnw.gdst.net
Website: www.newcastlehigh.gdst.net

• Pupils: 620 girls, all day • Ages: 11-18 • Size of sixth form: 176 • Non-denom • Fees: Senior school £2,455; junior £1,779; nursery £1,470 • Independent • Open days: October/ November

Head: From 2006, Mrs Hilary French MA Oxon MEd PGCE NPQH (fiftyish). A historian with plenty of postgraduate study behind her along with four previous posts, culminating in four years as deputy head at Teesside prep and HS, followed by five years as head. Married to Durham University lecturer and has one daughter. Down-to-earth, warm and approachable (parents and girls alike at her last school said this). There she knew every girl by name and aimed to produce confident girls who would achieve their potential in all areas of life. Seems no reason why CNHS shouldn't be similarly blessed.

Academic Matters: Four class intake and all the way through, roughly 25 per form class, 28 max. Smaller groups for sets and options. Setted in January year 7 for maths and year 8 in English, speedy set for languages who then take the relevant GCSE early. Girls screened for learning difficulties if recommended, in-house assessments or the local Dyslexia Institute; peripatetic dyslexia support teachers – girls can be withdrawn from class or lessons before school. Limited provision for dyspraxia, ADD or ADHD. 'Quite a lot of recent retirements', and common room now a lot younger. Huge breadth of subjects, 'but not in any sense an academic hothouse'. Vast number of combinations available at A level, far and away the most academic girls' school for miles around, gets consistently super results. Philosophy for all. Strong classics; outstanding results in the sciences – labs recently upgraded. More than half take three separate sciences at GCSE. Purposeful library, computers all over. Well-run and popular exchanges to France, Germany and Spain and languages equally strong; digital language lab in a separate building. Senior school undergoing a £2.3m development to create new library and ICT suites, an art school, an additional lab, separate modern language and English centres as well as an extension to the sixth form facilities and conversion of the hall to a multi-use space. Due October 2006.

Games, Options, The Arts: Recent fabulous hockey and netball tour in Australia. Exceptionally strong tennis, national schools tennis champions at some age group seven times in recent years, and the LTA tennis 'School of the Year' not so long ago. Girls change in the gym and sports hall, jog to the nearby sports ground for actual play. Provision of sport for all, ethos is 'that everyone can have a go'. Awarded Sportsmark Gold in 2001 and recently extended until 2007 for its outstanding commitment to sport both within and without the curriculum. New development completed to link the music school to the super sports hall and creating an exciting new drama studio. 'Music is stunning, 'says the head. Subject has own building with keyboards, a charming wigwam-shaped recital hall and recording studios. Buzzy drama, biannual Greek play with the boys across the road. Art block above the dining room in a converted synagogue 'up the road', dining area itself and the hall outside filled with art and models. The whole of this building will become an art school as part of the school's redevelopment and will include ceramics and jewellery-making facilities. Imaginative art, all dimensions, photography etc and a lot of fabric work and girls run their own fashion shows. D of E very popular, one of the largest participating schools in the area.

Background and Atmosphere: Young and buzzy management team in place. School founded in 1895 and based in a selection of new builds and converted Victorian villas (some quite nice stained glass around but it's not a place you would come to for any aesthetic reason. Former synagogue with fabulous stained window gives stunning light for art department and the modern build is great. Really quite a lot of walking round Jesmond, school plumb opposite the elegant façade of the grammar school. A hundred yards from the metro station and brill for inner-city road connections. Large hall used for assemblies is being converted into a multi-use space to include dining at lunchtime.

Pastoral Care and Discipline: Strong caring team in action, good PSHE. Year heads, in charge of pastoral and monitoring progress, keep an eye on individual 'ups and downs' and safeguard the 'quality of life' of that year group, plus form teacher/tutor, plus qualified counsellor. Full new PSHE programme, anti-bullying policy: 'confronting if appropriate'. Much use of circle time, ie sitting down and arbitrating, getting together and 'support, support, support'.

'Girls must understand that there are firm boundaries' and if things get too bad, then out – either on a temporary or a permanent basis. No problems 'with smoking behind the bike shed'. Girls educated about the risk of drugs. Staff eternally vigilant for signs of drug abuse.

Pupils and Parents: No change, solid middle class from as far away as Alnwick, Co Durham; loads of professionals, ditto Asians. Rich mixture of regional accents. Articulate and friendly girls. School uniform now purple and grey in the senior school, still showing masses of leg and not quite flat shoes but then girls will always customise their clothes. Sixth form ditto, but in their own clothes.

Entrance: Very sought after, and relatively tough, with considerable competition at 11; do 'not lose any pupils between junior and senior school' – which presumably means that they all come on. If 10 leave post GCSE, then 10 more come in. School 'comfortably full', could take another 'one or two'.

Exit: No sign of many girls opting to go across the road for sixth form studies. Some leave post-GCSE, but places 'easily filled'. Medicine a popular career choice, also other sciences, regular stream to art colleges, normally 10 or so a year to Oxbridge. Other choices include Leeds, Nottingham, Edinburgh, Glasgow, St Andrews and Manchester.

Money Matters: Loss of Assisted Places was a blow, GDST funds as many bursaries and scholarships as possible. HSBC scholarship provides one 100 per cent grant (50/50 HSBC/GDST)for Year 7 entry for up to 7 years, for girls of outstanding merit. All bursaries and HSBC scholarships are means-tested annually.

Remarks: 'Powerful and deservedly popular academic girls' day school with a great deal to offer' – as we said in the last edition, now even more apt. The school is confident that the plans for the the grammar school opposite to take girls throughout will have little impact.

CHANNING SCHOOL

Linked to Fairseat in the Junior section

Highgate, London, N6 5HF

Tel: 020 8340 2328
Fax: 020 8341 5698
E-mail: info@channing.co.uk
Website: www.channing.co.uk

- Pupils: 360 girls, all day • Ages: 11-18 • Size of sixth form: 95
- Non-denom (Unitarian) • Fees: Junior £2,845; Senior £3,095
- Independent

Head: Since 2005, Mrs Barbara Elliott MA, previously acting head of St Albans High School for Girls. She studied modern languages at Cambridge, and has previously taught at mixed and all-boys schools. Married with four sons.

Academic Matters: Was traditionally the fallback for those who weren't suited to the pressure of the more high-powered north London schools. Now, increasingly, it is a first choice, delivering enviable results with 92 per cent A and A* grades in 2005. English, French, science and maths all seem particularly strong. A levels in 2005 included 67 per cent A grades and 28 per cent B grades. Theatre studies A level available since 2000. Classics and modern languages emphasised – all girls study French, Latin, German and Spanish in year 8; they can take up ancient Greek in year 9. Classical civilisation available at GCSE and A level.

A good selection of Apple Mac computers, plus a room full of laptops that can be booked by any class for internet use and cross-curricular activities. 'It's not a factory for A grade students, though they have some very bright girls,' said one parent. 'You can do very well there but they don't make the less able ones feel a failure.' Not as pushy academically as some other selective schools, for which many parents are grateful. 'They get them to a good level without pushing them too hard,' said a parent. But another commented that she felt her daughter could be given more encouragement to stretch herself – 'I feel that she is sometimes allowed to get away with the easy option.' Class size mostly 20 or fewer, particularly for exam classes.

Games, Options, The Arts: Not a particularly sporty school but does very well at athletics and gets good results in matches. 'We are remarkably strong for a school this size,' says the head. Tennis/netball courts and a rounders pitch also used by years 7 and 8 for football club, and playing fields nearby. Big sports hall. No swimming pool – 'we have nowhere to put it'; occasional use of nearby Highgate School pool.

'We are very proud of our creativity.' Strong art displayed up the stairs and in the airy top-floor art studios with panoramic views two ways across London. Major whole-school drama production each autumn term, eg Grease, Midsummer Night's Dream, Twelfth Night, and drama strong generally. About half the girls play an instrument and there are orchestras, choirs and wind and jazz bands – some in conjunction with Highgate School. 'It's standing room only for our big concerts.'

D of E, Young Enterprise, charity and community work too. Plenty of clubs, ranging from classics to gym. 'Almost every member of staff runs some extra- curricular activity'. Year 7 has a weekend camping in the mud 'to get to know each other'. Overseas trips include skiing; year 8 has a week in France; year 9 visits the WW1 battlefields; lower sixth trips vary from year to year but may include Amsterdam (for art), New York (for geography) and Pompeii (for classics and classical civilisation).

Background and Atmosphere: Founded by the Unitarians in 1885; encourages all faiths equally. Lovely quiet, seven-acre green site on Highgate Hill with a mixture of eighteenth century and 1980s buildings, of narrow corridors and spacious hallways. Possibly the only London senior school with a climbing frame and swings. Teacher-free sixth form centre – 'we trust them to look after it.' Large lecture theatre, three halls. Parents emphasise that it is a very happy school and pupils have a local reputation for politeness and courtesy.

Pastoral Care and Discipline: A cosy, sheltered school with a strong ethos of care and concern. 'In a school like this every staff member knows every girl.' Pupils found with drugs on the premises 'must expect to be suspended or excluded. But we judge each case on its merits.' Head says that as far as she knows any bullying is stopped instantly, 'if parents have told us about it and left us to deal with it. But much of the strength of our policy is due to the girls' willingness to look out for and help each other.'

Pupils and Parents: There is a family feel, with many ex-Channing mothers sending their daughters there. A large proportion of pupils are from the Highgate area, with less of a racial and religious mix than some other north London schools. Mostly professional families. Girls seem genuinely open and friendly. Old girls include Baroness Cox, Crown Princess Sarvath of Jordan and Peggy Vance.

Entrance: About a third from Fairseat, the junior school, the rest in more or less equal numbers from local state and private schools. Part of group two of the North London Consortium, which sets common maths and English exams at 11. Entrance into the sixth form is by interview; candidates usually take papers in three of their chosen subjects but this will depend on the individual.

Exit: A few leave after GCSEs, mostly to mixed sixth forms. About ten per cent a year to Oxbridge; the rest to redbrick universities, art or music college.

Money Matters: Some academic and music scholarships; a few bursaries for girls already in the school.

Remarks: Excellent small girls' school in a lovely green setting which gets enviable academic results without undue pressure. 'It's small, friendly, and happy,' said a parent.

CHARTERHOUSE

Admissions Office, Godalming, Surrey, GU7 2DX

Tel: 01483 291501
Fax: 01483 291 507
E-mail: admissions@charterhouse.org.uk
Website: www.charterhouse.org.uk

- Pupils: 635 boys; 104 girls in sixth form. Mostly boarders, a limited number of day boarders • Ages: 13-18 • Size of sixth form: 360 • C of E • Fees: Day boarding £6,601; full boarding £7,985 • Independent

---

Head: Since 1996, The Rev John Witheridge MA FRSA (fifties). Educated at St Albans School, University of Kent and Christ's College, Cambridge. Married with four children. Previously the Conduct of Eton. Universally respected; all agree that he has brought the school a long way. Believes that success lies in reform without change for change's sake and is keen not to lose the heritage and values of this flourishing school. Teaches English to all of the fourth form. Appears comfortable and at home in his cosily traditional study but, do not be misled, this is a man with a mission.

Academic Matters: All pupils take a minimum of 9 GCSEs, results consistently good across-the-board. In addition to the usual core subjects, all boys follow a non-examined course in RE. Twenty-four subjects are offered at AS and twenty-three at A level and every endeavour is made to satisfy individual choices. No particular strengths or weaknesses. Boys, and indeed girls, seem to feel that the outstanding results are due to good teaching rather than excessive pressure, and the understanding that only their best will be acceptable. Not unreasonable. Progress is closely monitored and regularly reported. Under School boys achieving high grades or putting in particularly good effort are praised and those with poor grades reprimanded, during the traditional system of 'calling over', where the form master presents his form to the Master of the Under School. Introduction of 'culture colours' means kudos is no longer limited to sporting heroes. Educational activities spread far beyond the classroom, eg geographical expedition to the Lake District, excursion through Thomas Hardy's Wessex, chamber music performance at St Martin-in-the-Fields, art trip to New York, classics trip to Greece, history trip to Germany, not to mention preparation for Duke of Edinburgh Scheme awards.

Games, Options, The Arts: Maintains a sporting reputation as competitive and difficult to beat. Focus is on soccer, hockey and cricket but the wide variety of sport (tennis, squash, rackets, basketball, shooting, karate, canoeing, fencing, water polo ...) means something for everyone. Busy schedule of fixtures in girls' hockey, lacrosse, netball, tennis and cricket. Plenty of inter-house activity and A-F school teams ensure that not only the superstars get to take part. Fabulous sports centre, administered by a separate company, which all pupils are required to join. Splendid facilities for budding musicians within the Old Music School and the Ralph Vaughan Williams (an Old Carthusian) Music Centre. Almost half of pupils learn a least one musical instrument, practice sessions timetabled. Active choral and chamber groups, orchestras and bands. Impressive art studio for the study of ceramics and textiles as well as fine arts. One of the best public school theatres in the country named after OC Ben Travers. Well supported CCF and an amazing number of societies. Fine main library, which has recently become even more glorious. IT is catching up, following recruitment of popular new head of department, and extravagant plans for a dedicated up-to-the-minute IT floor have been completed.

Background and Atmosphere: Stunning buildings and grounds exuding an atmosphere of history and tradition. School founded in 1611 by Thomas Sutton, originally in old buildings near Smithfield in London which had once housed a Carthusian monastery, hence Carthusians. The school, including a stone arch from the old building inscribed with the names of pupils, moved to the current site in 1872. Proud custodians of the largest war memorial in England, in the shape of the magnificent chapel, designed by Sir Giles Gilbert Scott, consecrated in 1927 to commemorate 700 Carthusians who died in the Great War. Eleven houses in all. The seven 'new' houses built in the 1970s have recently been completely refurbished and provide a comfortable and functional environment. Girls have their own boarding halls but during the day they belong to the main houses.

Pastoral Care and Discipline: Somewhat esoteric rule book, eg 'If you are put on "Satis" (daily report form) give your sheet to the "beak" (master) at the beginning of the "hash" (class)'. However, carefully thought out and clearly defined rules ensure that discipline is a co-operative process. Earlier drug and alcohol problems over-zealously reported in the press and antagonism between boys and locals, largely belong to the past. This is due to the fair but uncompromising policy of the new regime. Full boarding has been slightly adjusted to meet modern parental expectations. Boys may be allowed home on Saturdays but must return for Sunday service. The head insists this is a privilege not a right and will resist any pressure to become a weekly boarding school. Relationships within the school seem good. Older boys look out for the younger boys doing their best to help with problems such as homesickness and they all think this works, in practice as well as in theory. Master of the Under School overseeing the 13-16 year olds is reported to have his finger on the pulse. Parents stress the importance of choosing the right house, some perceived to be more popular and successful than others.

Pupils and Parents: Mostly from south London, Surrey, Sussex and Hampshire, a few from overseas, 7 per cent English not first language. Many children of middle class professionals – having money and being in business rated here. Traditional without being elitist. Confident, bright individuals, well mannered without over doing it. Long and distinguished list of Old Boys, Joseph Addison, John Wesley, William Thackeray, Lord Liverpool, Robert Baden Powell, Robert Graves to name but a few.

Entrance: Registration at least three years before entry. Guaranteed places offered two and a half years before entry based on satisfactory report from prep school but this must be backed up by CE performance. Results will need to be good across the board. Selective examination and interview for sixth form places for boys and girls, conducted in the November of the year prior to admission.

Exit: One a year might be asked to leave at the end of the first year if attainment and effort are not up to scratch, two or three ditto after GCSE mocks. If this happens to your son expect lots of warning, help with finding another school and a transfer of any unused fees to the new school.

About half do a gap year. Almost all go on to higher education, most to good universities in UK or Dublin, a few going to the USA or Europe. 50 Oxbridge places offered in the last 2 years. Carthusians were admitted to around 102 different courses; among the most popular were economics, politics, sciences, geography, languages, history and engineering. Mr Witheridge believes that their success is due, good A Level grades aside, to careful selection of the right course at the right university and conscientious support and guidance with applications.

Money Matters: Generous and diverse scholarships at 13 and 16, all of which can be supplemented by bursaries to cover up to full fees in cases of proven financial need. Six foundation scholarships worth half fees, music exhibitions cover the cost of music tuition. Continues to maintain its position as one of the most expensive schools in the country. As the head says, 'we have no excuse not to do everything well.'

Remarks: Most feel that, not least because of Mr Witheridge's achievement in developing a new and enthusiastic common room, the school is on an upward spiral. There is a new pride in the place.

CHEADLE HULME SCHOOL

Linked to Cheadle Hulme School Junior School in the Junior section

Claremont Road, Cheadle Hulme, Cheadle, Cheshire, SK8 6EF

Tel: 0161 488 3330
Fax: 01614 883 345
E-mail: Registrar@chschool.co.uk
Website: www.cheadlehulmeschool.co.uk

• Pupils: 1,352 boys and girls, all day • Ages: 4-18 • Size of sixth form: 270 • Non-denom • Fees: Juniors £1,968; seniors £2,490 • Independent • Open days: October, November, January, March

Head: Since 2001, Mr Paul Dixon (fifties). Read zoology at Oxford – teaching career entirely in the independent sector, includes a six-year stint as second master (deputy head) at Stockport Grammar and, since 1996, as headmaster at Reigate Grammar School, Surrey. Active sportsman, married to a PE specialist who has herself taught in independent schools. Three children.

Academic Matters: Cheadle Hulme has a strong record and consistently achieves impressive results. ISC inspection in January 2001 was favourable. The teaching methods are a mixture of traditional, all-class teaching and more informal approaches – not dogmatic – whatever is appropriate. A child who might shrivel up and under-achieve in a more pressurised academic environment could well blossom and achieve great things here.

Of the 103 full-time staff, many have been at the school for over 10 years. Ratio of staff to pupils is 1:12. Class size in years 7-11 averages 25/26; sixth form, average of 9/10, with a maximum of 16. Consistently good exam results; 98 per cent pass rate for 2005 at GCSE with 62 per cent at A* and A. A levels are modular. 2005 results best ever for the school with virtually 100 per cent A-C grades, and 74 per cent of all entries gained As and Bs.

Games, Options, The Arts: Games are compulsory and the school's sports reputation is high. Many pupils play for county as well as international teams. Year-round indoor swimming pool since 1911. School has good reputation for music – lots of groups, concerts; head of music aims to introduce children to wide range of music, not just classical. Facilities for fine arts, ceramics, textiles, new and fantastic – and now more take them at A level. Broad curriculum. Computer facilities and technical support excellent, under new partnership with computer firm Viglen. Science labs newly refurbished.

Background and Atmosphere: Site is large, spread out, and surrounded by greenery. Main school buildings are pure Victorian splendour. Established in 1855, as 'Manchester Warehousemen and Clerks' Orphan Schools', for 'orphans and necessitous children'. 150th anniversary in 2005/6. Compassionate and co-educational origins very much alive today; the word 'progressive' slips tentatively from the lips of a member of staff. Emphasis on child as individual, not just a cog in a system. Pupils comment on flexibility within school, staff prepared to accommodate different needs, eg optional drop-in sessions at lunch-time for children having difficulties in given subjects. The school feels it 'competes successfully with the most prestigious schools in the area as we aim to preserve our unique focus on the individual child'. Ratio of girls to boys roughly even. Enthusiasm and happiness evident, also creativity, pride in achievement. Lots of clubs and societies run by the children. No snobbery about industry, business – on the contrary, school proud of its links.

The school has its own sixth form centre, complete with café. Lunch-time is noisy, lively, possibly slightly overwhelming for quieter pupils but full of life for the more sociable. Pupils wear different coloured uniform (navy) from rest of school (green).

Pastoral Care and Discipline: Does not consider itself, or wish to be considered, an authoritarian school. Has detailed structure for pastoral care which 'reacts quickly' to any problems. Bullying identified and dealt with quickly – 'if we hear about it from a parent first, then we have failed'. For school council, pupils cast votes but staff have the final say.

Pupils have recently established their own peer support scheme.

Pupils and Parents: The school aims to further values common to all – pupils are from Christian, Jewish, Muslim and Sikh backgrounds and from secular homes. School takes parents' views into account – prides itself on listening to parents and finding 'enough common ground', even if not total agreement on all points.

Pupils come from all over the south Manchester/north Cheshire area, from as far afield as Delamere (near Chester) and Macclesfield. Many from Stockport, Didsbury, Hale/ Altrincham. Numerous school buses ferry children to and fro but a rather long school day for some – 'it's dark when I leave home and dark when I get back....but I'm still glad I've packed it all into the day.'

Entrance: Entry is by examination (including NVR test) and interview. Much trouble is taken to assess each child individually. Demand has increased in recent years – there are now six applicants for every place. 50 per cent of senior school intake comes from state primary schools.

Exit: Almost all to university, particularly northern universities, some to London, Oxbridge. Old Waconians (from 'Warehousemen and Clerks') include Katie Derham (TV journalist and presenter), Lucy Ward (political correspondent with The Guardian), Nicholas Robinson (BBC political editor), Susan Bullock (international opera singer), Chris Davies (MEP), Toby Sawyer (actor).

Money Matters: School offers some bursaries at 11 and at sixth form, based on academic merit and financial eligibility. Fees value for money.

Remarks: A vibrant, confident, action-packed atmosphere for children who intend to get stuck into life and make their way in the world.

CHELMSFORD COUNTY HIGH SCHOOL FOR GIRLS

Broomfield Road, Chelmsford, Essex, CM1 1RW

Tel: 01245 352 592
Fax: 01245 345 746
E-mail: office@cchs.essex.sch.uk
Website: www.cchs.co.uk

• Pupils: 850 girls; all day • Ages: 11-18 • Size of sixth form: 257 • Non-denom • State • Open days: September and October

Head: Since 1997, Mrs Monica Curtis BA (mid fifties). Educated at Bournemouth School for Girls and University of Manchester, where she studied English and history of art. Has held a wide and interesting range of teaching posts including a year at Cedars Special School in Gateshead, two years at Gateshead Technical College, head of lower school at Lancaster Girls' Grammar, then deputy head at Kesteven and Grantham Girls' School before coming to Chelmsford. Down to earth with a good sense of humour. Keen on skiing and travelling. Widowed with two grown-up sons.

Academic Matters: A highly academic school which achieves fantastic results. Very bright and self-motivated pupils don't feel the need to play down their abilities. 'I love the fact that it is not embarrassing to be clever – you have no reason to hide intelligence,' as one girl put it. Girls are divided into forms alphabetically when they arrive in year 7 and stay in these groups until the sixth form. There is no streaming in any subject. Everyone studies French and German in year 7, then Latin in year 8 (Italian, Spanish and Russian available for the lower sixth). The three sciences are studied separately. The school has had technology college status since 2000 and facilities for technology have been much improved over recent years by money from both government and industry. The electronics suite is particularly impressive. Traditional 'girls'' subjects have been dropped in favour of technology and there are no lessons in either textiles or home economics. Some of the girls expressed discontent at this because they liked the idea of taking home economics at GCSE. Alongside its technology college status, the school was granted music college status with English in 2004.

Both GCSE and A levels grades are regularly amongst the highest in the country. 'We have more or less eliminated failure at GCSE and also at A level. We don't expect them to fail if we are doing our job,' says the head. Drama has been introduced at GCSE. A design technology A level has recently been introduced in graphical products and is recruiting well. A levels in sciences and maths are very popular, as are English, economics and history. The average age of the teaching staff is late thirties and 22 members of staff have been with the school for more than 10 years.

Games, Options, The Arts: Sport is taken seriously, and the school holds the Sportsmark Gold award. Recent major achievements for the school include Schools National Junior Athletics Champions and National Schools Finals Gymnastics (under 13). A high number of girls learn a musical instrument and there are plenty of opportunities for performance. 'We've got orchestras coming out of our ears,' says the head. The excellent head of music was recruited from another Essex school. Competition is encouraged through the school's house system in everything from sports and music to karaoke!

Background and Atmosphere: The school was opened in 1906 in a traditional redbrick Edwardian building set back off the main Cambridge road and not far from the centre of Chelmsford. Pleasant quad area inhabited by a mother duck and her ducklings at the time of our visit. Extensive fields. Extra buildings have been added on over the years, most recently a new performing arts studio and the sixth form block. The school's swimming pool has recently been refurbished and an all-weather hockey pitch constructed. Sixth formers have their own house on the school grounds and a purpose-built common room.

Pastoral Care and Discipline: Form tutors are the first point of contact for both academic and pastoral welfare. Tutors report on each girl's progress to a student progress manager. Discipline isn't much of an issue. 'If there are any problems the teachers will pick up on them straight away. There is a healthy atmosphere here,' says one pupil. Strict policy on drugs: 'any girl who brings illegal drugs on to school premises will be liable to permanent exclusion.'

Pupils and Parents: Mainly the daughters of the white middle classes but a much higher ethnic minority presence than is found in Essex generally. Girls travel from all over Essex and beyond. Around 3 per cent have English as a second language but these girls have a high standard of English even if they don't speak it at home. Very few SEN pupils. Student dress consists of a grey suit, available with either trousers or a skirt, a navy striped blouse and navy sweater. No sixth form uniform but dress has to be 'presentable, practical and appropriate to the occasion'.

Entrance: Prospective pupils, both from Essex and outside the county, sit an 11+ exam made up of verbal reasoning (which accounts for 50 per cent of the total mark),

mathematics (25 per cent of the total mark) and English (25 per cent of the total mark). The top 120 are awarded a place at the school. The exam is hugely competitive – it's not unusual for over 600 applicants to take it in a year. There is an appeals procedure but appeals are rarely successful. The girls in any one year may come from as many as 70 different primary schools, so many arrive not knowing anyone else and every effort is made to help them handle the transition to a secondary school full of strangers.

Around 25-30 pupils are taken into the sixth form from other schools each year. Applicants need to meet the criteria for particular courses as well as an overall criterion based on their average points score at GCSE.

Exit: All but a very few go on to higher education, with a high percentage (85 per cent plus in recent years) achieving their first-choice place. Around 15 a year go to Oxbridge. Notable Old Girls include first woman under-secretary-general of the United Nations Dame Margaret Anstee and BBC foreign correspondent Emma Jane Kirby.

Remarks: Highly selective, powerful, bouncy girls' grammar school delivering top quality exam results.

CHELTENHAM COLLEGE

Linked to Cheltenham College Junior School in the Junior section

Bath Road, Cheltenham, Gloucestershire, GL53 7LD

Tel: 01242 513 540
Fax: 01242 265 630
E-mail: info@cheltcoll.gloucs.sch.uk
Website: www.cheltcoll.gloucs.sch.uk

• Pupils: 396 boys, 183 girls; two-thirds full boarders • Ages: 13-18 • Size of sixth form: 246 • C of E • Fees: Senior school: boarding £7,150; day £5,360. Junior: day £1,600 - £3,900; boarding £3,865 - £5,060 • Independent • Open days: Junior School - October. Senior School - October, April

---

Head: Since 2004, John Richardson (fifties) MA PGCE. Educated at Rossall School and Selwyn College, Cambridge, where he read engineering. Long-term teacher in top public schools, having taught maths at Cheltenham's Dean Close school, was a housemaster, acted as director of studies and run the RAF section of the CCF and the Christian Union, then on to Eton, teaching maths, taking up a house list and coaching the u16 rowing team. In 1992 he was appointed headmaster of Culford. Married to Ruth, he has three children at other local schools – 'it's hard on children to have the head as dad as well'.

Academic Matters: Distinct and deliberate upgrading of the importance of academic rigour. 'We are sharpening the focus,' says the head. In practice, this means higher selection targets – at least 50 per cent in all subjects at Common Entrance and 5 Bs at GCSEs (formerly 5 Cs) for admission to the sixth form. Strong, traditional timetable which has been tightened up to make sure that core subjects do not suffer through the proliferation of sports and their related fixtures, a key part of school life. Maths has long been a star subject here and continues to be so, with 50 per cent gaining A* and A at GCSE and more than 75 per cent As and Bs at A level. English, too, has been a strong performer, with the bulk scoring As and Bs at both GSCE and A level. Design and Technology is well established and popular, as are the sciences, with excellent results in physics and chemistry at A level. Art is very popular and results are good, with the endearingly messy art room testament to its popularity. Noticeably declining interest in languages – although reasonable passes at GSCE and top results at A levels for those choosing to continue – which the head aims to address.

Definite feeling that a new broom is sweeping through the school, although long-standing staff are very much part of the updating process, including the noted eccentrics of the science department. Good mix of younger and more mature staff reflecting both the need to look forward and retaining Cheltenham's sense of its own history. Information Technology is playing an ever-increasing part in all aspects of school life, with a college wide intranet, laptop-enabled teaching facilities throughout (all pupils are issued with a laptop on arrival at school), homework posted on the school's intranet, Powerpoint science projects, airports and internet connection. Apple Macs are everywhere and much more is planned, all maintained by a dedicated IT department. Classrooms are traditional with old-fashioned desks, with some in need of a lick of paint, although excellent work, including some outstanding art, is proudly presented all over the school. This, along with a huge plan to update and overhaul many of the older buildings, is in the pipeline.

Games, Options, The Arts: Sport is an important aspect of the character of the school and very popular at Cheltenham. The core games through the year for boys, played on Tuesday, Thursday and Saturday afternoons, are rugby, hockey and cricket, while the girls lead with hockey, netball and tennis. The girls also boast an unbeaten cricket team. But many other sports flourish, including rowing (the college has its own boat house), polo (Cheltenham are consistently National Schools' Champions), golf, shooting (clays and targets) squash, rackets and badminton. The games

department is supported by professionals in many team and individual sports. Monday, Wednesday and Friday are the big activities afternoons, with orchestras and ensembles, wind and jazz bands vying for popularity with a large number of clubs and societies, including a keen debating society, philosophy and astronomy. Arts groups include pottery, photography and dance. There is also a strong tradition of outdoors activities, with CCF and the Duke of Edinburgh Awards schemes. Facilities are extensive and relatively recent, with an excellent and well-used pool and a large sports hall. Pupils have resultant reassuringly healthy glow. There is a strong tradition of community service, with visits to local nursing homes and primary schools and two long-term humanitarian aid projects by staff and pupils to maintain and support Romanian orphanages, with reciprocal visits between the two groups, and the renovation of a school in Kenya. Drama very popular, with school and house plays, although the main school performance venue, known as Big Classical, has seen better days and urgently awaits its planned gutting and reinvention as part of the multi-million pound refit. Lots of music options and a fine choir (many ex-cathedral choristers and organ scholars) – and the gusto with which the daily hymns are sung in the chapel is legendary.

Background and Atmosphere: Traditional, and traditional-looking, Victorian public school, opened in 1841 to cater for the sons of gentlemen. Longstanding Services connections but balance has shifted so that, although boarding is still thriving, many pupils come from within a 50 mile radius of the school. An impressively Gothic array of buildings of Cotswold stone, set off by the expanse of the cricket pitch and its elegant pavilion, makes a statement to the visitor, although much of the interior, awaiting its refit, does not yet match it. The most notable exceptions are the grand 'new' chapel (completed 1896) and the only slightly less grand original chapel, now pressed into service as a well-used dining room after its position, light and acoustics proved to be all wrong. The library is also lovely, an oasis of calm and quiet (and kitted-out with wireless technology as well as newpapers, magazines and ranks of books) – and is due to be lovelier still after a planned overhaul. Pupils are chatty, polite and neat, particularly impressive given that the uniform brief seems fairly wide, with lots of different ties in evidence.

Pastoral Care and Discipline: House system is at the heart of the school, with girls' and boys' houses divided into boarding and day. Ports of call for support include housemaster or housemistress, tutors, chaplain, matron, teaching staff and an older mentor pupil, appointed to look after each new student on arrival, acting like 'an aunt or uncle'. Bedrooms are initially large and shared, graduating to single rooms in senior years. These are fresh and, by teenage standards, reasonably neat, with the older buildings having been newly upgraded to a high standard. Communal areas are thoughtfully kitted-out, with sofa-sized bean bags and snooker tables. Houses are spread along both sides of the road (the A40, busy elsewhere along its route but quiet here) and pupils are able to come and go from main school to house as they need to. The on-site medical centre has the added bonus of having Cheltenham Hospital, complete with A & E, directly opposite. Discipline is being quietly tightened – new head is making it clear that drug taking, bullying and general slackness will absolutely not be tolerated. Nor will any kind of sexual relationship – special friends is as far as it's allowed here. 'There's no uncertainty – if it's wrong, it's wrong. We aspire to high standards – there is no merit in mediocrity,' he says. 'We will not accept less than the very best.'

Pupils and Parents: The older boys seem to express themselves with outlandish amounts of hair styled in all directions, while the girls are stylish rather than overtly fashionable. All wear uniform from first year to last year. Well-integrated as a co-ed school, with girls first admitted to the sixth form in 1969 and from 13 in 1998. Ratio is around 60:40 boys to girls, nearing parity in the sixth form. It feels like a good, comfortable balance, producing confident, affable students. Popular with local families, who often find their children ask to board like their friends, even if they live just around the corner. Ex-pat quotient varies from year to year – strong links with Kenya. Lots of well-known Old Cheltonians: Scott of the Antarctic's companion Edward Wilson, General Sir Michael Rose, actor Nigel Davenport and his son, Pirates of the Caribbean actor Jack Davenport, and BBC war reporter Rageh Omaar.

Entrance: Most take Common Entrance – and will need good percentages in all parts to get in. About forty per cent are drawn from its own junior school, with others from a variety of preps. Those entering from the state sector will take an entrance exam and interview, as do those wishing to enter at 16, where there is stiff competition for places.

Exit: A handful leaves at 16, either to attend other schools or because pupils are not sufficiently committed to working to keep up – 'everyone who joins the school will be capable of achieving the required standards if they take responsibility and try their hardest,' says the head. Noticeably fewer have taken Oxbridge places in the last few years. Both Bristol Universities (the traditional and the former poly, BUWE), Oxford Brookes, Newcastle and UCL and

Kings' London are current favourites, with art and music colleges also popular. One in five takes a gap year.

Money Matters: Big range of scholarships, including art, sport, DT, music and all-round potential as well as academic, geared towards prep school entrants, although non-independent school pupils can be catered for.

Remarks: Strong all-round traditional public school, where league tables matter less than a complete educational experience – but matter more than they used to.

THE CHELTENHAM LADIES' COLLEGE

Bayshill Road, Cheltenham, Gloucestershire, GL50 3EP

Tel: 01242 520 691
Fax: 01242 227 882
E-mail: enquiries@cheltladiescollege.org
Website: www.cheltladiescollege.org

- Pupils: 850 girls (630 board, 220 day) • Ages: 11-18 • Size of sixth form: 285 • Christian but welcomes and respects all faiths • Fees: £4,863 day (£5,529 sixth form day); £7,243 boarder (£8,159 sixth form boarder) • Independent • Open days: 10 throughout year (Saturdays), also highly popular early May Bank Holiday

Principal: Since 1996, Mrs Vicky Tuck MA BA PGCE (fifty-ish). Came from City of London School for Girls where she was deputy head. Formerly at Bromley High. Married with two sons. Cool and collected. Former modern languages teacher. Keeps in touch with what is happening in the classroom by shadowing a girl twice a year for the day. Large school so pupil/head contact fairly limited (unusual in a girls' school) but housemistresses' job to ensure contact as frequent as possible.

Academic Matters: Continues to be seriously strong. In 2005 100 per cent pass rate at A level, 90 per cent at A/B. GCSE consistently impressive. Average 80 per cent A*/A at GCSE in 2004, with 97 per cent A*/A/B the following year; maths, English, chemistry, physics, economics, religious studies and geography being the most popular subjects. One or two do Greek. Spanish, German, Mandarin Chinese on offer, Japanese classes available. IT strong: all leave with an ICT qualification, masses of computers, internet and email for all using wireless technology and laptops. Contemporary art, design and technology block complete with artist and photographer in residence. The school prides itself on allowing almost 'any combination of subjects at every level'. Huge staff. Low turnover. Two well-equipped libraries both with full-time librarians. Can cope with 'mild dyslexia' (approximately 40 in college). Superb university advice/careers department, work shadowing in holidays.

Games, Options, The Arts: Excellent 'big' school facilities. Huge gym in main building, games hall, two fitness rooms, indoor tennis, competition-sized indoor swimming pool which generates great enthusiasm and spectacular results. Two all-weather pitches, one is floodlit, proving immensely popular. Teams for everything at various levels – a good number of girls play at county and national level. Increasingly popular alternatives to the traditional lacrosse, hockey and netball are fencing, rowing and judo. Off-site riding facilities – girls are allowed to bring ponies (popular among younger children especially), and polo is an option. Teams for everything at various levels – a good number of girls play at county and national level but some feeling that girls who aren't good at games just sit around.

Immensely strong music as always – over 800 music lessons weekly, all packed in round subject lessons, five choirs, three orchestras, dozens of chamber groups and lots of girls compose. Joint choral performance with other independent schools in Cheltenham. Drama and dance strong. Clubs for all ages and a plethora of productions including the annual Edinburgh Festival offering. Debating strengthening with societies dedicated to debating and public speaking. Debates, concerts and occasional drama with Cheltenham College (now co-ed, 'which doesn't help') half a mile away.

Active D of E programme. Two staff members dedicated to outdoor education programme – much growth here. Lack of things to do at weekends has long been, and for some continues to be, a parental moan. Adventure club invites girls to 'live life' by trying orienteering, canoeing, skiing, kayaking, scuba diving and the like. Something for the less adventurous (or active) too – like card making, needle skills, German cookery and magazine club. Strong on charity work – helping in primary schools, special needs, etc – 'Mrs Tuck's big thing,' said a pupil.

Background and Atmosphere: Founded in 1853, granted Royal Charter in 1935, main school revolves round huge purpose-built Victorian campus, with magnificent stained glass, marble corridor, Princess Hall, vast library, in the middle of Cheltenham. Boarders 'go home' to their house for lunch, tea and at night – table napkins, pianos, and sewing machines (but no longer pets), friendly homely atmosphere – it really works. Most houses are about 5-10 minutes walk away. Junior boarders live either in rooms converted into 'cubs' (cubicles), or in open-plan dormito-

ries. Sixth-formers have dedicated houses (one day, four boarding), boarders sleep and work in charming individual rooms, each with its own panic button but retain strong links with their junior house.

Housemistresses in junior houses are non-teaching (which works particularly well), whilst sixth form housemistresses also have academic responsibility. Sixth formers can 'have dinner in town' (taxi there and back) and invite their boyfriends back – 'the boys often become house friends'. Socialising with Radley, Shrewsbury etc including plenty of 'unofficial contact'.

Called 'greenflies' by townsfolk, the girls wear magnificent Loden coats in the winter. Uniform worn even by sixthformers. Food said to have improved. Few anorexics. Girls carry their books in 'sacks', send internal messages via 'slab' and have names for almost everything: Slodge (Sidney Lodge), St Mags (St Margaret's), the bunny run. No bells, just clocks. Very highly structured, very institutional, feels big (it is) and daunting to new girls.

Pastoral Care and Discipline: Head feels that this is good and lots of safety nets have been put in place. Bullying is 'taken very seriously'. Class teachers liaise with housemistresses for junior girls, sixth formers have tutors and all girls have a personal 'mentor'. Two day houses and a sixth form house are based at the newly refurbished Day Girl Centre, each with their own housemistresses. Confidential counselling service available to all girls run by professionally trained counsellors. 'No shame attached,' said a girl. Very comprehensive and tough drugs policy – nothing mealy-mouthed about it. Sixth formers commented that all prospective parents ask, when being shown round, if there is a drugs problem and wondered if any of them really thought that the girls would say 'Yes'! Reports of 13 year old collapsing drunk in games – she and seven others had polished off a litre bottle of vodka; two gated for three weeks, the others had to do a week's community service. Older girls encouraged to take responsibility in school affairs – prefects elected by staff and senior girls with each one given a portfolio of responsibilities.

Pupils and Parents: Ambitious parents of academic offspring – school has to manage the parents' expectations as much as the girls'. Broadish social mix, majority professional, not the 'posh' place the tabloid press think it is (accents are well-spoken but not smart). Lots of ex-pats. Around 20 per cent are international, mainly from Hong Kong and Singapore. Girls are good natured, bright and sensible, robust, astute and articulate. Perhaps a touch 'solid'. Girls' priorities are work, sport and shopping. Old girls: Rosie Boycott, Mary Archer, Cheryl Gillan, Rachel Lomax (first woman deputy governor of the Bank of England), Katharine Hamnett, Fiona Mactaggart MP, actress Kristen Scott Thomas, journalist Sue Lloyd-Roberts.

Entrance: Fairly stiff competition, at 11, 12, 13 – CE or own exam. Those from overseas need to have 'fluent and accurate English' before entering. Own competitive exam into the sixth form (lots join then and love it).

Exit: Of 150 leavers, 50 take a gap year, around 25 offered Oxbridge places. Others to traditional universities and art colleges. 'All girls are destined to have careers'.

Money Matters: Expensive but definitely provides value for money. 4.5 per cent of fee income available for bursaries at last count. Large number of scholarships (by girls' school standards) available.

Remarks: Famous and strong traditional girls' boarding school, with large numbers of day girls. Impressive results as always. Full and busy timetable. Described by Ofsted as an 'exceptional school' where emphasis on personal development – even for the timid girl- is encouraged.

THE CHERWELL SCHOOL

Marston Ferry Road, Oxford, Oxfordshire, OX2 7EE

Tel: 01865 558 719
Fax: 01865 311 165
E-mail: Headteacher.4116@cherwell.oxon.sch.uk
Website: www.cherwell.oxon.sch.uk

- Pupils: 1,055, boys and girls, all day • Ages: 11-18 • Size of sixth form: 370 • Non-denom • State

Head: Since 2003, Mrs K J Judson BA Med FRSA (forties), previously head of Maidstone Grammar School for Girls. Took over from Mr Martin Roberts, who was head from 1981.

Academic Matters: Arguably best state secondary in Oxford. Head hoped relatively slow rate of improvement at GCSE would be boosted when school became 11-18 in 2003. Cherwell has also applied for specialist science status. Wide and interesting range of subjects at GCSE, including sports studies, child development and information studies. Of the core subjects, above average results in English, strong scores in maths, and exceptional grades in French, history, art, drama, information technology (after a slow start and with the benefit of new IT facilities) and business studies. Most subjects well above national average. German second language on offer, with other languages subject to requirements and backgrounds of pupils. Girls

reap many more high grades at GCSE than boys, with a sizeable 20 per cent gap in most subjects between those achieving five A* to C grades. At A level they are much more on a par. Star subjects at A level are art, chemistry, French, geography (clearly popular with able sixth form girls) and maths and further maths, where the boys shine. Some A level courses offered at other sites (including Oxford College of Further Education), including law, graphics and psychology – small number of candidates, excellent grades. Very good AS results despite their hasty introduction – art the real success. Lots of distinctions in advanced GNVQs, offered in business and tourism.

Comprehensive SEN resources, with a full learning support programme and units for hearing-impaired and autistic pupils. 313 pupils currently on the SEN register, 53 IEPs, 25 or so picked up via school action plus. SENCO, who has an RSA diploma in dyslexia, plus administrator plus five teaching assistants, usually one to one, but popular small literacy group, withdrawn from class – normally a modern foreign language; all attend mainstream school. It may happen that SEN pupils are directed towards GNVQs or ASDN youth awards rather than GCSEs or A levels, but no harm in that. School is also home to hearing impairment centre for Oxfordshire with a number of outreach staff who work with families. Autistic centre.

Games, Options, The Arts: The setting is everything here. Adequate gym and good all-weather tennis courts and basketball area is supplemented by lots of green space for a big range of sports, including rugby and football, at which both boys and girls represent the county sides. Site also borders Ferry sports centre, which houses pools, larger sports hall and squash courts. Compact but well-resourced library. Drama very popular, with regular theatre visits to London and Stratford, an after-school club and excellent productions. Well-used, separate music block shows music of all kinds taken seriously and to a high standard – around a quarter take individual music lessons and a recent Young Musician of the Year was a Cherwell pianist. Regular concerts from school orchestras, wind band and choirs. Strong art – student sculptures grace the entrance and paintings line the stairwells. Sixth form art students study abroad for a week each year. More than 100 terminals on school computer network and internet use encouraged. Lively, interesting website includes the headteacher's regular and forthright newsletters. Linked to schools in France and Germany. Trips of all kinds in all subjects 'organised by staff at the drop of a hat'.

Background and Atmosphere: When it opened in 1963, The Cherwell School was a small secondary modern, for ages 11-16, surrounded by allotments and fields near Oxford's upmarket Summertown area. Two 1970s events shattered its peace: first, the building of the inner Oxford ring road; secondly, the shake-up of Oxford's schools. The Cherwell School became an ever-growing comprehensive upper school (ages 13-18), separated from its main feeder middle schools (9-13) by fast-flowing traffic. Its original box-shaped buildings were supplemented by a library and sixth form block and then, when the money ran out in the 1980s, rows of ugly temporary classrooms. When building restarted in 1991, a music and drama block and new permanent classrooms were finally added. The site was also land-scaped with help from the parents' association. It really shows, with a modern school that looks tidy and comfort-able in its leafy surroundings, if clearly bursting at its seams. Many more changes are afoot as the revamped 11-18 school swallows and extends Frideswide Middle School, across the main road, to house younger Cherwell pupils for the bulk of their lessons.

Pastoral Care and Discipline: Form tutors are first port of call for general matters – pupils retain the same form tutor for three years. School council, made up of elected representatives from years 9-11, discusses and formulates policy affecting the school community and arranges social and charity events. Sixth-formers lead working parties of younger pupils to deal with specific issues. Common sense, 'firm but fair' rules, formal detentions coupled with a positive approach results in, for the most part, decent behaviour and polite young people, though small number of pupils disrupt lessons on occasions. Temporary exclusions used sparingly, usually for bullying or fighting, and permanent exclusions very rare – a couple for violence and drug dealing in the last few years. But the lack of a uniform does leave some partic-ularly scruffy pupils looking as if they have been pulled from a skip.

Pupils and Parents: Pupils are generally all a school could wish for – bright, encouraged at home, used to aca-demic endeavour (this is Oxford, after all), imaginative and ambitious to realise their dreams. Parents are often aca-demics themselves or work in the mass of white-collar, high-brow and highly paid jobs on offer in Oxford. There are, however, pockets of poverty and disaffection in the heart of Oxford and Cherwell has its share of troubled and trouble-some children. Famous ex-pupils include Rachel Seiffert (novelist) and Yasmin le Bon (model).

Entrance: Only distance from school matters – unfor-tunately, this varies from year to year according to numbers applying. Oversubscribed by at least 50 for 220 places for last few years. Distraught parents falling just outside this year's boundary make up ever-increasing number appeal-ing – half a dozen usually succeed. Rise to 270 places per year from 2003 leads head to hope the problem will be solved. Most come from two nearest middle schools and the rest from within a small radius. A few arrive from pri-vate prep schools in Oxford.

Exit: Around 80-90 per cent go into sixth form, 60 per cent staying at Cherwell and the remainder usually joining Oxford's FE college. Almost all taking A levels will go on to higher education, while others take vocational qualifications and a small number start work. A few reach Oxbridge, with Cambridge favoured over the grand university round the corner.

Money Matters: Two successive years of financial cuts (1995-6 and 1996-7) in Oxfordshire mean that class sizes are larger, learning support has been cut and there are five fewer staff.

Remarks: A school whose star is very clearly rising, where a great deal is on offer for all abilities – and where one senses that the best is yet to come.

CHETHAMS SCHOOL OF MUSIC

Linked to Chethams School of Music Junior Department in the Junior section

Long Millgate, Manchester, Lancashire, M3 1SB

Tel: 0161 834 9644
Fax: 0161 839 3609
E-mail: lesleyhaslam@chethams.com
Website: www.chethams.com

- Pupils: 286, mostly boarding (60 day pupils) • Ages: 8-18
- Size of sixth form: 119 (56 boys, 63 girls) • Non-denom • Fees: Day £5,978, boarding £7,723. Choristers considerably less.
- Independent

Head: Since 1999, Mrs Claire J Moreland MA (mid forties). Read modern languages at Oxford. Previously housemistress and deputy head at Rugby School. Divorced, one son. Interests are music, literature, theatre, travel and walking. Plays classical guitar in private. Viewed by pupils as firm but fair and approachable; they comment that tighten-ing up in discipline since her arrival has been properly explained to them, not just dropped from on high. Her ambi-tions for the school are that it be 'even better known both locally and nationally' and properly understood as a 'centre of excellence', not of elitism. Developing outreach and part-nership programmes to make Chetham's resources, eg expertise and buildings, more widely available. Views not having come up through the music world as 'a bonus' enabling her to bring an independent and impartial perspective to the job. Has all-round support of staff and parents.

Academic Matters: About one third of timetabled time devoted to music. In view of this, and the fact that the school is academically non-selective, exam results are pretty good. Fewer GCSEs and A levels taken than in most schools (generally 7 GCSEs and 3 or 4 AS levels) to allow for exceptional music timetabling but the highly motivated attitude of pupils to their music seems to carry over into other subjects. Classes small – average size 15, maximum 22. Ratio of staff to pupils 7:1. Pupils keen to be perceived as highly successful across the board, not just as musicians. School careful to ensure that 'a decent Plan B' is in place, for those pupils who don't make it in a musical career or don't wish to pursue one. 39 pupils currently have some form of SEN, including dyslexia, dyspraxia and a few requiring ESL support. School uses the services of 3 SEN members of staff.

Musically, the school is highly thought of nationally and internationally. Head keen to emphasise that broad-based western classical tradition also complemented by other facets of musical education, including jazz and electronic music (a state-of-the-art music tech and recording suite available 2006) and use/impact of internet, as appropriate, 'to equip pupils for the 21st century'. Whiteley Hall (school concert hall) six years old. Numerous competition and other successes.

Games, Options, The Arts: Emphasis on personal fitness. Attention to physical well-being strongly encouraged. Gym open every evening and as much as possible at weekends – also walking trips and sailing activities. No compulsory team sports due to demands of timetabling music lessons, practice sessions, performances etc, though friendly matches, eg between staff and pupils, do take place. Prospective parents fearing that this might mean no competitive spirit in the school would be wrong; energy and adrenaline merely re-routed and very much in evidence in musical teamwork. Strong sense of pride in achievements of the school. Drama popular, including staff productions.

Background and Atmosphere: Site small, 15th-century listed buildings at its core, and located in the heart of Manchester city centre. Became school of music in 1969. Site a mixed blessing; on the one hand, absolutely beautiful, architecturally (something which the aesthetically finely tuned pupils appreciate) but on the other hand, its smallness and the security issues that any such city-centre location would pose, bring their own problems. These should not be over-emphasised, however. Bedrooms are not very big but not too many sharing. 3 or 4 to a room lower down the school, in sixth form 2 people per room. Girls in upper sixth not required to share. Bedroom tidiness evidently not a particularly high priority!

Atmosphere of school is tangibly charged with the excitement and enthusiasm of the pupils and has all the pros and cons of any tight-knit community. School has fairly close relationship with Manchester Cathedral (it educates the choristers) but has multi-ethnic and international intake and looks for common spiritual ground between people and religions rather than following any particular doctrine. The diversity of backgrounds of pupils is viewed as a plus. Pupils take advantage of good links with the musical community in Manchester, attend many concerts in the city.

Pastoral Care and Discipline: Various people to whom pupils can and do turn in difficulties. Relationship with instrument teacher generally very close. House parents, tutors, are available, also house assistants who are often a popular choice of confidant/e (not forgetting the laundry ladies, viewed by some as a bevy of 'mums'). Older pupils look after the younger members of the school and are touchingly fond of their 'little ones'.

Pupil handbook, setting out anti-bullying policy, general information and school rules, is a model document ('busking is strictly against the rules' – hard luck to the more entrepreneurially inclined pupils!). Due to extent of government funding, pupils not permitted to fall by the wayside – school has to justify, and be seen to justify, government support.

Pupils and Parents: Parents from many countries and all walks of life. Some are active in the musical world themselves, others have had no contact with world of music and are astonished to find themselves with a musical prodigy on their hands. Very occasionally a parent has musical ambitions for their child that the child does not share, leading to problems of motivation. Mostly the pupils are immensely motivated and committed, excited at the opportunity to learn at a specialist school. Pupils view 'modesty' and 'having your feet firmly on the ground' as essential prerequisites to happiness at the school. Mutually supportive atmosphere, in which pupils 'live or die' by remembering to read the noticeboards (there is a long corridor of them) and checking school's intranet several times a day – the more absent-minded pupils being suitably organised by the switched-on ones. Famous old boys/girls include Wayne Marshall, Peter Donohoe, Anna Markland, Max Beesley, David Hill.

Entrance: Most applicants hear of school, and are encouraged to apply, through their instrument/music teachers. The only criterion for entry is exceptional musical ability, which is assessed by two auditions. No academic criteria.

Exit: The majority (about two thirds) to music conservatoires and colleges, some to study music at university, others to read other subjects – a good proportion to Oxbridge, bearing out head's view that good musicians tend also to be very bright.

Money Matters: 98 per cent of pupils are at Chetham's with government support via DfES. Successful recent appeal to improve boys' boarding house by 2006.

Remarks: Very special pupils but not remotely 'precious'. Whereas a lot of schools like to pass themselves off as one big, happy family, Chetham's actually feels like one.

CHEW VALLEY SCHOOL

Chew Lane, Chew Magna, Bristol, BS40 8QB

Tel: 01275 332 272
Fax: 01275 333 625
E-mail: chewvalley_sec@bathnes.gov.uk
Website: www.chewvalleyschool.co.uk

• Pupils: 1,150 boys and girls, all day • Ages: 11-18 • Size of sixth form: 200 • Non-denom • State • Open days: September for y7 entry, November for sixth form. Tours by appointment any time

---

Head: Since 2003, Mark Mallett, LLB, MA and PGCE, University College, London. He taught in Borneo with VSO, London and Bristol before taking up deputy headship in Hexham, Northumberland. A passionate educationalist and classroom practitioner, he is a teaching head and enthusiastic promoter of extra-curricular activity in sport and the arts.

Academic Matters: Outstanding teaching in science, maths, English, technology and languages; small class sizes in the sixth form. 43 per cent A or B at A level; 75 per cent 5A*-C at GCSE. Highly effective Special Needs team (rated excellent by Ofsted) deals sensitively with 30 statemented pupils and varying degrees of specific learning difficulty through a modified curriculum. Also brilliant liaison with feeder primary schools on this score. Ofsted report (Jan 2005) confirmed it was a very good school with very good leadership and management, teaching, learning and value for money.

Games, Options, The Arts: Sportsmark, a lottery funded leisure centre and 35 acres of playing fields surrounding the landscaped grounds mean that sport has a high profile. County teams for rugby, badminton, squash, hockey, tennis. Two teams do Ten Tors challenge each year with 35- and 55-mile expeditions on Dartmoor. Sailing offered as sixth form option. Hockey and rugby teams toured Australia in summer 2003.

240 students learn an instrument and frequent concerts include a wide range of music and dance. Recent projects have included an artist in residence, Duncan Morrell, who worked with students on a large whale and dolphin mural. School diary is choc-a-bloc with debating visits, choirs at Bath Festival, drama performances including Twelfth Night at the Bristol Old Vic. Michael Eavis opened the new Music Centre in February 2005.

Background and Atmosphere: Most marvellous location in the midst of a beauty spot/green-belt between the affluent villages of Chew Magna and Chew Stoke, nestled behind the Chew Valley Lake. Unceremonious entrance hall gives you the feeling you had wandered past a back door of a Centre Parcs village. The photo-call of staff (beaming, bright, healthy smiles) could well be those at an up-market health hydro but these are highly skilled teachers and staff who inspire high achievement across the board.

Pastoral Care and Discipline: Much care taken over transplanting tender shoots at age 11. Parents' evenings are civilised, with private appointments – 'no scrums in the hall with everyone listening in,' remarks the head of careers. Sixth formers work with the year 7 students to help them settle into their new surroundings.

Pupils and Parents: So much in demand that 20 per cent of pupils live outside the catchment area. Pupils are a well-ordered bunch. Confident and happy. No signs of tension. They know exactly what they're here for and get on with it.

Old Boys and Girls become sporting stars (4 girls in England students' rugby team), successful musicians, fast-stream civil servants, careers in law, medicine or TV designers.

Entrance: Apply direct to the Director of Education, Bath & North East Somerset Council, Admissions & Transport Section, P O Box 25, Riverside, Keynsham, Bristol BS31 1DN by the 19th October prior to the year of entry. Outside entry into the sixth form needs 5 grades A*-C GCSEs but a key deciding factor is motivation and behaviour.

Exit: 60 per cent of GCSE students go on into the sixth form, 25 per cent to FE courses, 10 per cent into modern apprenticeship or employment – the rest move out of the area. 90 per cent of sixth formers go on to university (many after a gap year). Steady numbers to veterinary science, sports science, medicine and Oxbridge. In 2005, 2 students to Oxbridge and a further 2 to medical school.

Remarks: Hugely popular school in blissful rural setting.

CHIGWELL SCHOOL

Linked to Chigwell Junior School in the Junior section

High Road, Chigwell, Essex, IG7 6QF

Tel: 020 8501 5700
Fax: 020 8500 6232
E-mail: hm@chigwell-school.org
Website: www.chigwell-school.org

• Pupils: 710 (inc juniors); 300 girls, 410 boys; 35 boarders, rest day • Ages: 11-18 • Size of sixth form: 175; boys and girls nearly 50/50 • C of E but welcomes all • Fees: Juniors £2,290-2,894; seniors - day £3,523; weekly boarders £4,775-£5,069; full boarders £5,354 • Independent • Open days: October

Headmaster: Since 1996, Mr David Gibbs BA PGCE, a specialist in economics and politics (late fifties). Mr Gibbs came from Haileybury where he had been a housemaster, prior to which he taught at Charterhouse and, for ten years, at Sherborne where he was head of economics and i/c cricket. Gentle-mannered, quietly-spoken, spare, assiduous, this is a head whose ten years in post give no impression of sitting back. Our talk was of the ten year development plan – 'more of the same – we want to respond to whatever happens in the marketplace' – and it was warming to see the rapport he has with staff, parents and children. We arrived during The Macmillan World's Biggest Coffee Morning and the Gibbses – wife Philippa is very active in many areas of school life – were clearly comfortably at the heart of a relaxed and strong school community. Two boys, both at the school – and the Gibbses live on site – complete the family approach which is palpable throughout the place.

Academic Matters: ISI report of 2004 praised the academics particularly the teaching and attainment in the sixth form. 72 per cent A/B at A level. 2005, however, saw the best yet GCSE results. 61 per cent of grades achieved were A*/A and 100 per cent of students got A*-C in virtually all subjects. Highest performers of the most popular subjects were RE – astonishingly good, all the sciences and geography in which, out of 52 candidates, 41 got A*/A. History too consistently excellent. It's been a different story with modern and ancient langs – takers have been few after GCSE although the few who venture do well – German, Russian and Latin candidates all got A at A level. English results not really more than respectable at both levels. Head well aware of the problem and has recently appointed heads of both English and modern langs depts who should beef things up

a lot. If they can achieve as highly as the geographers we will see Chigwell soaring into the upper levels of the league tables everyone purports to despise. Economics is, not surprisingly, a popular and successful subject, – otherwise options pretty mainstream. ICT seen as a skill and not a religion – networked, home-school emailing links etc. Head impressively unobsessive about it all. SEN provision also criticised by ISI, now taken in hand by new head of learning support who will assess everyone and train staff to look out for problems. This is clearly not state-of-the-art provision yet but is clearly looking up.

Games, Options, The Arts: For a smallish school, Chigwell does remarkably well in sport. There is only a small outdoor, heated pool, a sports centre which is modest in comparison with the vast complexes elsewhere but the school has 75 acres of playing fields on site and they stretch invitingly over to Epping Forest. Also new £50,000 all-weather cricket nets site. They have national representation in a number of sports including the current captain of the national u16 soccer team and in 2005 were in the final of the ISFA u19s national 6-a-side soccer – defeating giants Millfield, Manchester Grammar et al on the way. 2 recent county cricket players and strong girls' hockey. Good range of indoor and outdoor exercise on offer including golf, squash, cardio-vascular room, volley ball and all the rest you'd expect.

Perhaps the pride of the school at the moment is the outstanding Chigwell School Drama Centre. On a site where all other buildings are a modest one or two storeys, this one means to be noticed. Opened in 2003, meticulously planned and designed by the arts team behind the Donmar and similar venues, the theatre is flexible, professional and a superb resource which must be among the finest anywhere. There are teaching rooms, studios, dressing rooms, workshops and an excellent foyer. The local primary school and outside drama classes borrow it – lucky them. Drama is strong as extra-curricular but it is, perhaps, surprising that, with this resource, so few take it for A level. Music also strong in purpose-built block and various bands and ensembles for the 50 per cent who learn instruments in school. Art and applied arts are excellent – judging by the witty and imaginative displays in many media we saw – clever photography and ceramics, super life-size cardboard figures, printing – inspired by ancient printing press in studio 'to show how it used to be,' lively, twisty, multi-coloured polypropylene lampshades and a carefully arranged installation of decorated paint-tins. Other extra-curricular stuff abounds – astronomy, D of E, 'Adventure Service Challenge', public speaking – frustrating if you want to try them all!

Background and Atmosphere: An interesting history still informing daily life here. A vast copy of a brass rubbing of the founder, the Rev Samuel Harsnett, greets a visitor to the main, original, school building – the real thing is in St Mary's Church next door – a Norman gem – and school has displays about its history from later times – all easy to imagine when the fine, first building is happily in daily use and is central to the life of the place. Harsnett started life here as the local vicar in the 1590s. He became Archbishop of York and Vice Chancellor of Cambridge University but lost his wife and only child and returned late in life to Chigwell, founding the school in 1629 in the solid but elegant brick building – now housing the head's office and admin rooms and having accrued various add-ons from other periods which blend in sympathetically. Over the centuries care has been taken with all newer buildings and, most unlike elsewhere, there is no building here one wishes away. Head believes school should have 'places to hide' perhaps in the tradition which saw its most famous alumnus, William Penn, having his 'first sense of God ...at Chigwell, being retired in a chamber alone', or so John Aubrey reports – the room in question being above the original schoolroom – now the library.

The 1920s chapel, built as a memorial to fallen alumni, like the rest of the school is emblematic of social history. The school had 250 pupils then. 77 boys died as soldiers in WW1. Of the 1st and 2nd cricket teams in 1913, half were dead by 1919. The chapel is a welcoming place and regular services are held there in this predominantly Christian school. Every pupil attends twice weekly. Current population has, of course, high proportions of non-Christians – around 33 per cent of pupils are Asian in origin, around 8 per cent are Jewish and there are handfuls of Hindus and others. School happily ecumenical – 'we look at what unites us not what divides us – we worship together but in the Christian tradition,' says head.

The school buildings are spread around what is, in effect, a garden – little planted plots and quadlets are everywhere – sunflowers lounge against a wall, trees look quite at home, hedges adorn and separate and the low-rise buildings nestle contentedly between flowerbeds. Music block centrally placed so that, says head, 'sounds waft across'. Two portacabin classrooms but even they look almost inviting here. Twenty-five per cent of, mostly younger, staff are housed on site – 'having the place lived in helps', thinks head and this is unusual but civilised in a predominantly day school. School's size contributes to family feel and, imaginatively, all new pupils of any age wear a navy tie so that, if they look lost, everyone knows to dash to their aid and take them back to where they should be. Parents pay tribute to caring staff and head's personal involvement, ' my far-from-academic son was struggling and instead of chucking him out', says one, ' the head took him on, really encouraged and motivated him, he got his A levels and is now happy at university'. Boys still outnumber girls in senior school but it's 50:50 in juniors so imbalance on its way out – and it's not really obvious anyway. About 50 per cent of staff now female.

Pastoral Care and Discipline: One of the most orderly – without feeling rigid – schools we know. House system. Pupils look smart – girls in attractive kilts – and civilized behaviour seems the norm. Two drugs instances in head's tenure – dealing meant out in one case. A few temporary exclusions for disciplinary matters but not common. Boarding is entirely for the sixth and largely for bright overseas students – mostly from central and Eastern Europe, with which director of boarding has forged strong ties – and mainland China. These pupils add greatly to diversity and all bring something extra – current Ukrainian sixth form girl in national ballroom dancing finals. Girls housed in two good houses nearby and boys in splendid, Georgian, Grange Court – three boys each to the well-furnished and equipped vast rooms and welcomed by equally vast Granger, the houseparents' highly congenial golden retriever. Food in dining room varied and excellent – masses of extremely tempting choice.

Pupils and Parents: Chigwell is prosperous, leafy and middle-class. School's neighbours are St Mary's Church and Ye Olde King's Head – super pub memorialized by Dickens as The Maypole in Barnaby Rudge. Estuary Essex this ain't. Locals are spoiled for choice – good independent alternatives in the shape of Bancroft's, Forest and the two City of Londons and excellent state grammars and comprehensives not far off. Lots of first time buyers – often second generation, Asian immigrant families – choose the school perhaps because of and contributing to the excellence in sciences and maths – also more trad independent education veterans. Sir Alan Sugar, whose house abuts the playing fields, sent his sons and now has his grandsons here – school assisted on the Apprentice series – but most parents come because of the small school, holistic and family values the school enshrines. A school for all-rounders above all. William Penn, Sir Arthur Grimble, Austin Bradford Hill, Edward Vulliamy, Sir Bernard Williams among lists of diverse worthies who make up distinguished alumni.

Entrance: At 7, 120 applicants for 40 places – sit exam, have interview, spend day in classroom and send feeder school report. At 11, 300 applicants for 30 places – exam and interview. Very few places at 13. At 16, 50 applicants for 20-30 places. 6+ Bs or better in GCSEs, As in chosen subjects, expected.

Exit: Good range of courses and colleges – economics looms large as does marketing. Quite a few practical courses eg property management, building surveying and business alongside theology, biology, medicine and philosophy but, unsurprisingly, few on the lang/lit sides at present. They go to universities old and new largely in the south – few further north than Nottingham. A creditable ten per cent annually to Oxbridge.

Money Matters: Up to ten Archbishop Harsnett schols at 11 for academic merit. More schols at 7, 13 and 16. All-rounder schols at 11,13 and 16 plus a drama schol at 16. Also exhibitions – like mini-schols and worth less financially. Means-tested bursaries – if family's combined gross income is under £30,000 pa may be worth applying.

Remarks: A lovely start in life for your happy all-rounder. Would probably make a happy all-rounder of just about anyone.

CHRIST COLLEGE, BRECON

Brecon, Powys, LD3 8AF

Tel: 01874 615 440
Fax: 01874 615 475
E-mail: enquiries@christcollegebrecon.com
Website: www.christcollegebrecon.com

- Pupils: 190 boys, 130 girls. 260 board • Ages: 11-18 • Size of sixth form: 130 • Christian • Fees: Day £3,490 - £3,975; boarding £4,650 - £5,940 • Independent

---

Head: Since 1996, Mr Philip Jones MA (fifties), educated at Midsomer Norton Grammar School and read geography at Fitzwilliam College, Cambridge. Taught at Downside and for twenty-four years at Sherborne where he was senior master, housemaster, head of department and a legendary rugby coach. Came relatively late to headmastering but has shown in his time at Brecon that he has a natural talent for the job. Has transformed Brecon into perhaps the leading co-educational boarding school in Wales.

Married to Jane and has two grown up children. When not involved in school (which is not often) he can think of nothing more wonderful than to fish the Tywi, which meanders right past the college. Exudes integrity and is a delightfully unpretentious and honest man who is very clear what he wishes Christ College to become. Steeped in his Welsh heritage (his father was a miner and later the first principal

of Midsomer (Mining and later Technical) College) whilst at the same time with a wide and extensive experience of the independent school system. His long service as a very effective and popular housemaster at Sherborne has led him to focus particularly on the quality of pastoral care. Brecon has a particularly strong and vibrant house structure. At least as impressive is the fact that he knows and greets every pupil he meets on his main excursions around the campus. A man who believes in the old-fashioned principle that the first obligation of a head is to walk the job. Understands that happy and fulfilled pupils are those who are stretched in a wide variety of academic disciplines and activities.

Academic Matters: Wide ability range – results are extraordinarily good. 90 plus per cent A* to C at GCSE, 75 per cent A-C at A level. In the sciences, A level pass rates were over 90 per cent. Design and technology is another great strength.

The range of subjects offered in such a small institution amazes one. Enormous choice offered for GCSE and even more at A level. Sixth form teaching groups are often very small with individual progress being very closely monitored – a particular strength. Not a school that has compromised its scholastic ideals in the pursuit of transitory success in league tables. The vast majority of sixth form pupils are undertaking real and demanding subjects even if this depresses the school's league table showing. Strong learning support provided (unusually) as part of the basic fee. The 12 per cent foreign student contingent is offered considerable assistance with English; again as part of the basic fee.

Games, Options, The Arts: Brecon is a boarding school. This means that, even nominally, day pupils will spend at least ten hours a day in school and sometimes as much as fourteen. The school is a hive of activities with the glorious Brecon Beacons being well used as a resource for adventure training and CCF activities. Christ College is perhaps most famous for its prowess on the rugby field. The annual match (perhaps better described as a battle!) between Brecon and Llandovery is a highlight of the Welsh school rugby scene. Yet it is clear that all sports are taken very seriously. Now the College is co-educational this is particularly true of hockey and netball. If proof were needed of the sporting focus of the College the twenty-odd pupils who have represented their country in ten different sports surely speaks volumes.

Art one of the particular strengths and some extraordinary work in photography. The way the pupils' success in this area is acknowledged and even celebrated shows that Brecon has totally shrugged off the bone-headed rugby image it once had. Also shown in the fine dramatic tradition the school has recently developed. Major dramatic productions take place in most terms and are designed to involve as many of the pupils as possible. 'Sweet Charity' and 'Oh What a Lovely War' are recent examples that do precisely this as well as exploiting and developing Brecon's strong choral tradition. Despite this tradition, only 33 per cent of pupils learn a music instrument.

Background and Atmosphere: Founded in 1541 by Henry VIII, together with Eton one of the two independent school royal foundations. Nestles on the edge of the sleepy Welsh market town of Brecon – the views are truly spectacular and whole assemblage is reminiscent of an idealised Dylan Thomas film set. The school campus is nicely compact with boarding houses, chapel, games fields and classrooms all jumbled together in a rather eclectic mixture of architectural styles. In truth one would not celebrate the majority of the post-war developments, yet on the whole the campus is of a human scale that enhances the very modest and unpretentious atmosphere of the institution. The key to Brecon's success is the friendliness and warmth that pervades the relationships here. The head's determination to be accessible to all is a key factor. His office right in the centre of the campus ensures that pupils and staff can simply pop in if need be. Bullying is hardly evident here.

Quite deliberately the head celebrates the old-fashioned values. The College has something of the feel of a 1950s grammar school. Everything and everybody is neat and tidy and a great emphasis is put on respect and courtesy.

Pastoral Care and Discipline: Very strong house system. Head focused on the need to deliver top quality pastoral care. A huge amount of money spent in recent years in upgrading the boarding accommodation. The two girls' boarding houses are now very attractive with charismatic and effective housemothers. Whilst the school expects high standards of behaviour from its pupils (and usually achieves them) discipline is enforced with a light touch. The emphasis is on the quality of personal relationships that seem to be especially good. Escapes some of the more extreme drugs and drink difficulties that plague schools closer to the fleshpots of the south east.

Pupils and Parents: Most of the pupils hail from within 50 miles, pretty evenly divided between those from Wales and from the English marches. There are small numbers from a total of 19 different countries as well as significant and unusually not declining numbers of military and ex-pat families. Not a smart school and has never attempted to be so. Significant numbers come from an agricultural back-

ground, although this is very much in the decline. The growth in the number of refugees fleeing London to the good life in Powys suggests that the English proportion will grow.

Entrance: About 60 per cent of the intake at 11, for two years in the delightfully prep school atmosphere of the Junior House, mostly from relatively local Powys and Herefordshire primary schools. A significant and growing intake from prep schools at 13 plus: St John's on the Hill, Llandaff, St Richard's Bredonbury, Abberley Hall, Moor Park and Moffats. Entrance is by a simple mathematics, English and verbal reasoning test and not usually Common Entrance. The growing popularity of the school has made it more selective than it was but it remains relatively relaxed in its selection criteria.

Exit: 97 per cent go on to university, between two and four a year to Oxbridge. A larger than expected number go on to read science degrees, a reflection of the College's particular strength here.

Money Matters: Extraordinarily good value. Lots of very generous scholarships and bursaries for the able and deserving. A rare and very attractive feature is that despite a competitive fee level there are no compulsory extras.

Remarks: No one is going to choose Brecon as an elitist icon, but it's a school that is very much on the up and achieves much more than one would expect given its size and location. Offers at least as much as many more prestigious and expensive alternatives; becoming seriously popular.

CHRIST'S HOSPITAL

Horsham, West Sussex, RH13 0YP

Tel: 01403 211 293
Fax: 01403 211 580
E-mail: enquiries@christs-hospital.org.uk
Website: www.christs-hospital.org.uk

- Pupils: 492 boys, 348 girls (all board) • Ages: 11-18 • Size of sixth form: 254 • C of E • Independent • Open days: March and October; November for the sixth form

Head: Since 1996, Dr Peter Southern MA PhD (early fifties), educated at Dragon School, Magdalen College School and Merton College, Oxford plus PhD from Edinburgh (medieval history). Previously head of Bancroft's School, Woodford Green, prior to that head of history at Westminster. Married, two children, plays tennis, golf and sails. A congenial, relaxed man who intends to stay until retirement. He works very much in conjunction with his two respected deputies. Now established in the school and a very present figurehead about the place 'with an amazing memory for names' say the parents and also very au fait with the children and what they are heading for.

Departing in July 2007.

Academic Matters: A strong academic tradition offering a rich diet of subjects. Consistently producing good results, and rightly so, given the tight selection procedure and their regard for academic spark and energy. GCSE core results look very strong, with art and music jumping out at you, while science, modern languages, history follow closely. Science lecturers were keen to forego lunch and discuss the sixth form science and electronic projects on display. A few pupils take up the classics option but a full languages department offers French and German. Spanish short course is offered at sixth form. The A level results are very good all round; in art, all 14 students scored straight As. Unusual subjects include archaeology, theatre studies and music technology. All A2 students are given laptop computers. Academic Buttons are prestigiously awarded to sixth formers as the highest distinction for outstanding performance in more than one subject.

Games, Options, The Arts: Superlatives abound when describing all areas of Christ's Hospital's arts. There is a new attic extension to the art school with wide-arched windows and parents wax lyrical about the variety and standards of art on offer – 'a creative bulls-eye'. The department has excellent young and vibrant staff plus artists in residence who are fully engaged in their work, share their expertise and ideas – hence record achievements at A level. Design, fine art and history of art are all offered at A Level. The school has a very strong musical tradition. The department buzzes and pupils have recently played at the Purcell Room, American Embassy, made TV appearances, led the Lord Mayor's procession, the Pasadena Rose Parade, California (first UK school band invited). Super theatre, modelled on the Globe, and drama is compulsory for the first two years. Productions are staged at Chichester Theatre, Edinburgh Fringe Festival and taken to the local community and primary schools.

Christ's Hospital is proud of its sporting achievements and boasts a commercial and lush leisure centre. The school also refreshingly fields B and C teams, as well as representing most sports on a highly competitive circuit. Plenty of activities are on offer, 40 at the last count. Community service is a high priority with cadetship or community service compulsory in some year groups and links with Romanian orphanages.

Background and Atmosphere: A charter was signed by King Edward VI in 1553 laying the foundations for London's poor and homeless to be educated. Ten days later he died but left a legacy that has given 'the best education money can't buy' (school advertising slogan) to thousands of children. It moved from London in 1902 to the present site (1,200 acres, 200 of which are occupied by the school) and was joined by the girls from Hertford in 1985. The site is a vast, spread-eagled miniature city reflecting different eras surrounded by acres of countryside. The main quadrangle is impressive, reminiscent in part of a cross between Hampton Court and a monastic academy surrounded with redbrick attractive cloisters, elaborate collegiate chapel, large oak-panelled dining hall into which the whole school formally marches into lunch to the accompaniment of the school band. Boarding houses and teaching blocks line the avenues, with the skyline of high domes, clock towers and minarets lifting the spirits. The peripheral buildings still resemble barracks but the school is undergoing a major refurbishment to all its boarding houses, including two new upper sixth form residences.

The school wants to get away from the austere Florence Nightingale boarding house image and they are succeeding. The sixth form Grecian houses are excellent, modern but sympathetic in style, 'it's the future of boarding'. Hilton Hotels – eat your heart out! A more relaxed style discourages barrack-like behaviour and house-by-house is being refurbished. 'If children are boarding here, they deserve to have equal boarding and teaching facilities. We are creating the right atmosphere for their social space', says the head.

Uniform is unchanged, boys wear long blue coats, black breeches and rich saffron coloured socks, girls wear similar. Initial impression is a surreal drama with blue-coated children wafting in and out of cloisters; some idly riding side-saddle on bikes to lessons, Harry Potter flying by with trailing cassock would not look out of place here.

Pastoral Care and Discipline: No rulebook but codes of conduct are written in the back of pupil's termly calendar, lest they forget. They are not molly coddled. 'The initial stages are tough', remarked a parent, 'they have to be very self disciplined and street-wise to survive'. The houseparents and tutors live on site and are very supportive and there is plenty of TLC for the more fragile pupils. The system of mixing older children with younger ones really works and 'they develop a good mix of freedom and responsibility and cope with whatever life throws at them'. Houseparents are vigilant concerning drugs, drink etc. The pupils have clear expectations and rarely receive a second warning.

Pupils and Parents: One parent remarked 'it can be a cross between Grange Hill and Dickens', which is a good indication of the diversity of the pupils. Mostly from London down to the south coast but pupils are drawn countrywide and there is a small connection developing with Russia and Romania. 'Would like to see the catchment area expand,' say staff. Parents range from farm hands, service officers, teachers, and freelance media. 3 per cent of parents pay full fees and 20 per cent are totally supported by the school. 70 per cent earn less than the national average. It is a very multi-racial community with a high volume of single parents. Lots of distinguished Old Blues, including Barnes Wallis (RAF benefactor connection), William Glock, Bernard Levin, John Snow, Coleridge, Leigh Hunt, John Edmonds, Mark Thomas, Charles Hazlewood, Sir Colin Davis, Roger Allam.

A lively, bright-eyed and bushy tailed group of children enjoying quite an educational extravagance. 'Refreshingly non-elitist', say the parents but there is still an embedded prejudice from outsiders. 'Here come the poor children', is occasionally heard at arrival for matches but both pupils and parents feel the NOCD brigade (not our class, darling) are missing the point and missing out. Children do not cloister among their own classes but blend, integrate and develop an ability and confidence to communicate, support and appreciate everybody. Pupils/parents talk of close, strong friendships that last for life.

Entrance: Anything but typical, and renowned for its rigmarole, but slowly implementing more user-friendly mechanisms for entry. The process is protracted and may seem complex due to the Foundation's rules that enable entry under geographical locations or family background. The Counting House (foundation office) oversees the procedure ensuring the ancient mission of education for all is adhered to. One is reminded of St Peter's big question – 'What should [did] you do that we should let you in?' For which lucky children do those big gates swing open? Take a long breath ....

Precedence is given to those children whose parents cannot afford a fee-paying education but whose child has a definite need for boarding education, and this is the raison d'être of the school. Places are given mainly by presentation, special category or competition. The admissions department will advise on which method of entry applies upon receipt of application form. Each child is given a score based on need, and that is looked at in conjunction with the results of the exam set by the school. Other skills are considered, eg sporting prowess, art portfolio, musical ability etc. Some entry categories are associated with the RAF, Guys Hospital and the Church. Individual governors or corporate bodies can present a child, and corporate or trusts' benefactor's presentees proudly display the badge bearing their benefactor's name. The remaining places are offered to competitive candidates, usually in order of merit but always with a close eye on the most needy children where flexibility may be applied: these places are more hotly contested. All parents are means-tested each year.

Having your finances (or lack of) laid bare can be a daunting and, for some, a humiliating process but it would be prudent to leave pride on the shelf, ignore the taboos that surround handouts and think of it as an alternative form of scholarship, ie the end (a fab education) justifies the protracted means. Get an up-to-date list of the governors to see who can help. Presently there is a 4:1 ratio of applicants to entries. Every year 35-40 sixth form places are granted to pupils from other schools; done by interview where both academic ability and need are assessed. 'They bring strength and variety to the upper end of the school'.

Exit: Most to universities and widespread – Cambridge, Imperial, University College, Bath, Bristol, Exeter – studying French and politics, archaeology/classics, physics/astrophysics, civil engineering, biology, English and German, psychology, chemistry and law.

Money Matters: The envy of school bursars across the land. 'A real pot of gold, but prudently accounted and wisely spent,' says the head. Everyone is means-tested and a sliding scale of contributions is payable depending on your net income (deductions for insurance, mortgage protection, dependencies). Nil fees for an assessed income below £7,500 pa to full fees for an assessed income above £57,000 pa. Music fees also relate to income. 'If I had less money, it would have been the choice for us,'says a would-be parent.

Remarks: Not an orthodox public school but successfully encompasses the comprehensive ideal. A continuing success story. RIP King Edward VI.

CHURSTON FERRERS GRAMMAR SCHOOL

Greenway Road, Churston Ferrers, Brixham, Devon, TQ5 0LN

Tel: 01803 842 289

Fax: 01803 846 007

E-mail: secretary@churston.torbay.sch.uk

• Pupils: 900 boys and girls; all day • Ages: 11-18 • Size of sixth form: 277 • Non-denom • State • Open days: July and September

---

Head: Since 1997, Mr Stephen Kings BA MEd (fifties). History graduate from University of Wales. Various teaching posts, including 14 years at an inner city Bristol comprehensive, prior to senior positions at Withywood School, Bristol and Torquay Boys' Grammar School. Married, with three children. Dedicated – 'I don't have time for anything else except my children'. 'Approachable,' say pupils.

Academic Matters: 99 per cent five A*-C grades at GCSE; approximately 60 per cent at A*/A. Good 'value added' education – pupils leave with better results than parents often anticipate – a reflection of good teaching methods. Not something Mr Kings is complacent about – believes teaching quality can constantly improve. Individual academic needs are taken seriously, 'they re-jigged the timetable to accommodate geography and history for my daughter at GCSE; they really care and do what's best for the individual', commented a parent. Maximum GCSE and A level class size 25; good subject choice at A level. Four computer rooms and five-year rolling programme to ensure all classrooms have computers.

Games, Options, The Arts: Some pupils choose Churston for its sports – excellent facilities, number one sporting strength is basketball, winning two national championships thanks to the two England coaches on its staff. Football, netball, hockey and athletics also produce county and some national players. Parental moans over lower standard of tennis.

School drama productions are renowned and always a sell-out. Eye-catching artwork – recent acquisition of a dedicated computer suite in the art room has made research far more efficient and enabled students to produce highly professional results. Orchestra and choir dependent on talent and enthusiasm. Serious about environmental issues.

Dedicated Combined Cadet Force classroom for year 9 upwards, managed by armed forces sergeant. Organised trips through CCF include exchanges with Germany, France and Poland. D of E and Ten Tors only available through CCF.

Background and Atmosphere: Community-orientated grammar with tight catchment area. At the southern end of Torbay, amid beautiful countryside. Extensive and attractive grounds. Surrounding tranquillity interspersed with idyllic 'Railway Children' style steam train, running alongside school – originally a popular mode of transport to the school. Pupils nowadays, however, arrive by bus and gum up the traffic. Extensively developed since opening in 1957 – lots of new classrooms. Strong links with local community; raises money for the Leonard Cheshire Foundation, Children in Need and others.

Pastoral Care and Discipline: Relaxing and harmonious atmosphere. Ask parents why they choose Churston and they'll reply 'pastoral care'; ranked as high priority and 'much better than neighbouring grammars or comprehensives.' 'The school really listens to you.' Pastoral team leaders, with experienced team of tutorial staff, provide guidance and support tailored to needs of each student. Additional support provided by trained adult and senior student listeners so any problems 'dealt with promptly and effectively'. Smoking and drugs policies adhered to; message hammered home via expulsion of pupil caught peddling drugs. Minor bullying problems resolved by bringing together those involved. Parents, teachers and staff alike view atmosphere as 'friendly but purposeful'; relationships as 'easy going and relaxed'.

Pupils and Parents: Pupils from 25 primaries including Brixham, Dartmouth and Paignton. 'It's very friendly here,' say pupils. 'I preferred it to other schools, the moment I stepped through the door'. Year 5 primary pupils are introduced to Churston via a one-day tutorial in a range of subjects.

Entrance: From 2003, Churston's own entry system (based on English, mathematics and verbal reasoning) will be in place – hoped to be an improvement on the LEA's. Priority always given to pupils who place Churston first. Between 30 and 35 students from Brixham and Dartmouth Community Colleges join sixth form.

Exit: Some 95 per cent to university with especially

strong links with Exeter, Plymouth, Cardiff, Bristol, University of West of England and Bath. Falmouth Art College also popular. Two or three into armed forces. Ninety per cent continue into sixth form, others migrate to nearby community colleges and South Devon FE college.

Remarks: Caring and close-knit feel, like a relaxed comprehensive. Strong pastoral system, effective academic teaching; 'ordinary' children achieve top grades.

CIRENCESTER DEER PARK SCHOOL

Stroud Road, Cirencester, Gloucestershire, GL7 1XB

Tel: 01285 653 447

Fax: 01285 640 669

E-mail: enquiries@deerparkschool.net

Website: www.deerparkschool.net

- Pupils: 1,112, boys and girls, all day • Ages: 11–16
- Non-denom • State • Open days: Late September

Head: Since 2003, Mrs Chiquita Henson BA(Hons) NPQH (forties). Read English at Sheffield University followed by PGCE at Bristol; subsequent professional training in leadership and headship. Educated at a comprehensive school herself, Chiquita Henson has been at Deer Park since 1989, becoming head of English when the school still had a sixth form and then deputy head from 1994 to 2003. Knows the patch inside out and has been at forefront of school's recent development as a 'Leading Edge' and 'Training' school. Outwardly reserved but combines steely professionalism with a passion to drive Deer Park forwards. Makes full use of ex-accountant director of support to do the number crunching she finds a chore. 'Incredibly hardworking,' said one parent; 'children find her a bit scary,' said another. A modern, no nonsense head who is good at getting recognition and money for the school. Partner, Tim is a science teacher with children at primary school in Stroud where they live. Still teaches some English. Predecessor was 'a hard act to follow' but general parental agreement that she is good news.

Academic Matters: Have made application to add second specialism to become a college for arts and technology. A truly comprehensive school with results fluctuating from year to year; incredible 80 per cent 5 GCSEs at grades A*-C achieved in 2003 partly attributable to a significant GNVQ factor. Has averaged 70 per cent plus over past four years; consistently impressive KS3 levels and improving

results in value-added tables with boys and girls doing equally well. Over 20 per cent gain 5 or more A* and A grades at GCSE. Curriculum structure is divided into modules across a 50 (hour long) lesson fortnight, run by faculties and overseen by mentors – brings the nearest thing to a personal timetable by GCSE level. Interesting links with industry. Mix of traditional and newer courses at GCSE where the 'normal' subject load for pupils is being reduced from 11.5 to 10.5 subjects, giving more time for non-examinable PE (4 hours per fortnight) and global citizenship. Dual award science so quite a challenge for those who go to academic science sixth forms. Can take science as a single subject – plus rural science or child development or a choice from citizenship/RE/ICT. 'Fabulous maths teaching,' said a parent; we saw a class tackling probability with plenty of intelligent participation. Innovative maths and drama scheme for year 7 pupils. 'Faculty in Focus' puts pupils and staff from a given area into the spotlight for a short period – visits to 'Starlab' and 'Maths Magic' have resulted. Parents like homework which they described as 'challenging without being too difficult.'

Well-sited learning support unit adjacent to art area. SENCO carries out audit in year 7; 16 statemented pupils; about 20 per cent of pupils receive help in some form: extraction, spelling and literacy groups; alternative curriculum pathway with support from teaching assistants based in different faculties; value-added results highlight successes, with one pupil in 2005 achieving 5 GCSEs at grades A*-C from a baseline VRQ of 70. Enrichment activities for gifted and able have included designing a refectory in collaboration with Plymouth University.

Games, Options, The Arts: Vibrant young head of expressive arts having tremendous impact. Orchestra, choir and jazz band with music tours abroad. Major drama production every two years with plenty of shorter works in between. We saw a drama class which was totally absorbed and never noticed us watching. NCFE award in music technology rarely found in 11-16 sector. Good sports hall plus larger Astroturf for football, hockey and lacrosse (!) plus smaller one for netball. Plenty of teams and extra curricular sports activity. Art is well taught (parents amazed at what their offspring have achieved); adequate accommodation with some impressive pieces on display. Standstill days give each year group a chance to do something outside the curriculum and the annual enrichment week approaches citizenship from a different angle eg 'European Awareness' for year 8 and 'Personal Challenge' for year 9. Hosts South Cotswold Science Fair – a fun event to bring science into everyday experience.

Background and Atmosphere: Celebrates fortieth anniversary as a comprehensive school in 2006. Origins stretch back to middle ages but 1960s legacy evident in featureless external appearance. School shares attractively wooded site on western edge of town with Cirencester College next door and the Royal Agricultural College opposite. Youngish staff with the average age below 40 but over one third have taught here over ten years. Specialist technology status translates into computers everywhere plus digital projectors and interactive whiteboards in every classroom; Powell's Learning Centre a hive of activity and remains open after school. Some aesthetically pleasing internal features such as the drama studio, atrium social area and art exhibition corridor. We liked the simple polo shirt uniform and the positive buzz in lessons and corridors.

Pastoral Care and Discipline: Strong pupil services team divides years into half-year groups with learning coordinators for each supported by tutors and mentors. We felt that pupils here have a positive attitude to work and an understanding of a good range of global issues. Pastoral database is bought by other schools. Emphasis on restorative justice. Good attendance levels point to policies working.

Pupils and Parents: Mainly middle class catchment but with some from surprisingly deprived areas in Cirencester. Friendly, polite bunch who get stuck into the challenging work environment. Year 11 pupils seem more mature for age than in average 11-18 school. Some pupils involved in unusual exchanges with Inuit children from Canadian Arctic and with a day school in New Delhi. Most of school's governors are parents. Friends of Deer Park is active in supporting school events and raising funds. Website allows parents access and publishes weekly newsletter.

Entrance: Over-subscribed – comprehensive intake with geography and siblings most important criteria. Majority from Cirencester primaries and outlying villages but quite a few come from Stroud direction where it is seen as an attractive alternative to secondary moderns for some.

Exit: About 90 per cent go into further education with majority going to Cirencester College next door. Significant number go further afield to sixth forms such as Pate's in Cheltenham where Deer Park pupils have done extremely well.

Remarks: 'Can do' philosophy rubs off on everyone – 'everything is an opportunity,' said one teacher. Plenty of human endeavour and creativity behind the high tech world on offer here which 'doesn't take over.' Quite a place, with pupils liking the modern approach and responding well across the board.

CITY OF LONDON FREEMEN'S SCHOOL

Linked to City of London Freemen's Junior School in the Junior section

Ashtead Park, Ashtead, Surrey, KT21 1ET

Tel: 01372 277 933
Fax: 01372 276 165
E-mail: headmaster@clfs.surrey.sch.uk
Website: www.clfs.surrey.sch.uk

- Pupils: 825 pupils; 430 boys, 395 girls; 40 boarders • Ages: 13-18 • Size of sixth form: 190 • Inter-denom • Fees: Day £3,834; boarding £6,098 • Independent • Open days: October, November, January, March and April

Headmaster: Since 1987, Mr David Haywood MA (late fifties). He has a background in geography and prior to this appointment he was deputy head in a school in Wiltshire. Married with a grown up sons, 'he is just like a friendly giant' said one pupil. A very likeable 'gent' with lots (and lots) of chat about his school and its pupils. 'He is CLF School,' said one parent. Although not in day to day contact with many students (has a hands on management team) he has a strong and visible presence in the school and still enjoys the formality of being called 'headmaster' by pupils, staff and parents alike. Mr H sees his key role as appointing the right staff and selecting the pupils.

Academic Matters: Goes from strength to strength – excellent results and now up there on a national level as well as being a leading local player. 80-ish per cent A/B grades at A level. Sciences, IT and maths are all strong. Numerous science labs in purpose built centre – very impressive – and science teaching particularly praised by several parents. Good IT facilities – all students have e mail and internet access, and there are projectors, TV and videos in classrooms. The Haywood Centre, which opened in 2000, is the 'hub' of the school and houses an excellent library – open after school for homework and private study – a multi media centre and most of the classrooms.

About 40 students with a range of needs receive help from two part time SEN teaching staff. School is happy to discuss whether it can provide the right support for those who need it. Quite encouraging, but it would need careful consideration as to whether a SEN pupil would be happy here, as there is a definite academic pace to maintain.

Those who receive extra tuition do so at extra cost to parents.

Games, Options, The Arts: Not a school for couch potatoes – sport is actively encouraged and is compulsory for all. Teaching is of a high standard and facilities are excellent. PE is offered at A level and results are good. Boys play rugby and cricket and for the girls it's hockey and tennis. Swimming all year in the recently refurbished indoor pool; lots of praise for the swimming tuition from pupils and parents. Sports hall complex and extensive grounds provide everything from floodlit Astroturf pitches to squash courts. Some surprising mutterings from parents that the range of sports on offer is quite 'narrow'. Huge level of commitment needed from school's sporty souls- lots of matches on Saturdays as well as after school. A v competitive bunch, they like to win; many are in regional and national teams.

Art & design building has an impressive range of facilities. Students' work exhibited throughout the school. Drama teaching is very strong, several pupils are members of the National Youth Theatre and in 2005 five students formed a production company and secured a two week run for a new play at the Edinburgh Fringe. Music plays an important role in the school – teaching is good. Heaps of choirs, orchestras and ensembles providing opportunities for all abilities. After school activities include all the usual and many, many, more; so many in fact that a booklet containing all the details is published each term. DofE is well supported as is Young Enterprise for those in year 10.

Background and Atmosphere: Founded in Brixton as a school for the orphans of Freemen of the city of London in 1854, and paid for by the Corporation of London. Moved to its current site in Ashtead Park in 1926 and began admitting fee paying pupils. Maintains strong links with Corporation of London, who own and financially manage things, and the school still educates orphaned children of Freemen. Corporation has funded the £15m improvements over the last few years. Set in 57 acres of stunning parkland on the edge of Ashtead Village, the school is housed in a number of buildings ranging from the beautiful18th Century 'main house' to the recently completed 'state of the art' Haywood Centre.

A superb setting (difficult not to be completely overawed by the location) reminiscent of a stately home, with beautifully kept grounds and immaculately maintained buildings. Somewhat taken for granted by the pupils who see it every day, but much admired by staff and parents. 'Who could fail to learn in such a delightful setting,' said one parent. Sixth form centre newly refurbished, much to the pupils' delight and long overdue they said, and a mezza-

nine floor has been added to create more study space. Located in the old stables, there is lots of comfy seating, new workstations for private study and a smart new kitchen – complete with dishwasher but no TV!

'The food is quite good,' said pupils and staff alike. Several choices, a popular salad bar and more traditional school fare. Has improved recently, but lots still take a packed lunch. Quite hot on uniform and pupils do look very smart. More relaxed for sixth formers who wear a different uniform to the rest of the school (navy/charcoal/black jacket and trousers/skirt/suit with shirt) – 'more of a dress code,' said one, 'but still quite strictly enforced.'

Boarding numbers are relatively low though boarding houses v homely. Rooms are attractive with lots of space and wonderful views of the grounds. Pupils are allowed to personalise their space within reason. Lots of activities for boarders during the week and at weekends and many spend time with friends they have made who live locally. Annual trip to the Lord Mayor's Show for all boarders followed by a meal – usually in Chinatown and organised by the students.

Pastoral Care and Discipline: Strong house system. Sixth formers act as mentors to the younger ones through their first years at the school. Discipline is fair and 'if you adhere to the code of conduct you won't go far wrong' says Mr H. Pupils say the school is very tough on bullying and as a result there are few instances. Zero tolerance drugs policy -and staff have dealt with occasional breaches swiftly – they don't pretend it doesn't happen.

Pupils and Parents: Predominately from the affluent surrounding Surrey towns: Ashtead, Epsom, Cobham, Leatherhead and Bookham, but also increasingly from South West London. There is school transport from most of these areas and also a minibus to and from Ashtead Station for those who travel by train – popular with parents who can then avoid the school run. Parents are from a wide variety of backgrounds, many are professional – lawyers, bankers, doctors, etc. Loads of siblings in both junior and senior schools – a very good sign – they find it easy to fit in and it enhances the family atmosphere. Increasing numbers of overseas students who also make up the majority of the boarders. Mr H makes an annual trip to a schools exhibition in Hong Kong to recruit and has developed good connections in the Far East. Several boarders have also come from Russia in recent years. The most notable old boy is Joe Strummer of rock band The Clash – a fact that probably impresses more parents than pupils!

Entrance: Selective, and standards are high. Majority enter from junior school at 13 – they know the drill and do not have to sit an exam. For the rest – mainly from local preps including Downsend, Danes Hill, Cranmore, Feltonfleet and Parkside – screening tests are completed at 11 and the school sets its own entrance exam in English, maths, science and languages at 13. Interview with the head is given equal importance, as is the report from previous school. 'It took a lot of effort and was v stressful but worth it in the end,' confessed one delighted parent on gaining a place for their child. Mr H confirms standards have increased in line with the national drive for improvements in education – this equates to a fair degree of pressure on students throughout their time at CLFS. At sixth form there is an intake of about 20 – students mainly from overseas and a few from local state schools such as Nonsuch.

Exit: Only a handful leave after GCSE, usually to attend local sixth form colleges. Of those who stay, about 95 per cent go on to universities such as Nottingham, Southampton, Leeds, Exeter and the London colleges with half a dozen each year to Oxbridge.

Money Matters: The Corporation is very generous and (despite the tangle of red tape) they fund a variety of scholarships both for new and current pupils (including sixth formers) which can be worth up to half of the fees. Academic, music and other awards for exceptional candidates in art, drama and sport.

Remarks: A traditional academic (and sporty) school in a stunning setting with impressive facilities but not at all elitist – in fact quite the opposite. Not for the faint hearted (there are high standards to achieve), but while the school is home to a goodly number of academic high fliers, it offers everyone their moment to shine.

CITY OF LONDON SCHOOL

Queen Victoria Street, London, EC4V 3AL

Tel: 020 7489 0291
Fax: 020 7329 6887
E-mail: headmaster@clsb.org.uk
Website: www.clsb.org.uk

• Pupils: around 870 boys; all day • Ages: 10-18 • Size of sixth form: Approx 260 • Non-denom • Fees: £3,615 • Independent • Open days: Several - please contact Admissions Secretary for details. 020 7489 0291

Headmaster: Since 1999, Mr David Levin BEcon MA FRSA (fifties). Went to school in South Africa, read economics at the University of Natal, then a research degree at Sussex. Previous post was as head of The Royal Grammar School, High Wycombe, and before that he was second master at Cheltenham College but he started his career as a solicitor. South African in origin, with a strong interest in development economics. Keen sportsman, particularly rugby and swimming – he has swum the Channel. Tall, with charm, very able, accessible, a brilliant manager. His wife Jenny is a management consultant.

Governors are made up of representatives of the Corporation of London (not noted for being long-sighted or easy to work with) which owns the school; as such, the headmaster is termed a 'Chief Officer' and, as such, must meet with other 'Chief Officers': of parks for example. Has succeeded in co-opting governors from outside the City.

Academic Matters: Grammar school ethos, some setting, limited specialisation below sixth form level. Pupils take 4 AS exams, followed by 3 or 4 A2s. Results remain steady and pleasing and continue to improve – now largely A grades. Mathematics continues as the most popular A level subject, followed by history, 'brilliantly taught', say boys, chemistry, biology, politics, French and economics. Pupils regularly distinguish themselves in mathematics Olympiad. Remarkable English master, Jonathan Keates – distinguished author of biographies on Stendhal and Purcell. Staff closely monitor academic performance to find ways of picking up problems early. Big emphasis on modern languages, with work shadowing schemes in Germany and France and an exchange with families from the Northeastern University of Shenyang, Republic of China.

Games, Options, The Arts: For a central London school, this is a sporty place, with numerous teams. It fields up to 20 football teams and recently reached the finals of the Inner London Cup. Traditionally strong on basketball and has won the London Independent Schools Basketball league at several age groups. Successful in water-polo too (superb pool on site), also badminton. Keen sailing. Lots of staff involved in games, with 17 acres of playing fields at the school's disposal some thirty minutes bus ride away. Real tennis sadly no longer played at Queen's but Eton fives can be had at Westminster. Sports facilities on site are splendid and well used. CCF bristling with participants.

Extremely good music department; art and design technology reveal pockets of fine work. Enthusiastic drama. Good on trips, 127 organised in 2004-5, very lively political debates, big programme of clubs/activities at lunch break and some after school. Boys run societies (heaps of these) and get speakers galore – a prime site for getting the great and the good and also the famous. Square Mile Club (head's baby) with four or five other City schools (state and private), fruitfully netting more speakers and exchanging ideas.

Background and Atmosphere: Started in 1837 on medieval foundation (1442); in 1986 moved to purpose-built high-tech U-shaped building with river frontage, just east of Blackfriars Bridge, and bang opposite the Tate Modern, right beside the Millennium footbridge. Terraces for the boys, one enclosed so a football can be kicked around, constant hum of boats from the river. Stunning view of St Paul's – altogether, an exciting setting. Good library, attractive small theatre and drama studio, large hall for assemblies, slightly airless locker-lined corridors, large classrooms where you can hear the proverbial pin drop. Work hard, play hard atmosphere. Sixth form common room reeks of toast and Nescafe with pool table and a poker game in progress at time of our visit.

Pastoral Care and Discipline: Well-developed tutor and year head system, with all boys reporting to their tutor first thing each morning and afternoon. Links with parents increasingly fostered (parents mainly pleased) Good clear guidelines on drugs, bullying etc. Misdemeanours are 'discussed by reason'.

Pupils and Parents: Recent survey breaks down the pupils as about 35 per cent WASP, 22 per cent Jewish, 20 per cent Asian, 10 per cent Greek and Cypriot – probably one of the broadest social and ethnic mixes in any school. Over half come from north London; some East Enders and a few from south London (good trains). Handy for City yuppie parents and increasingly for US/Europeans working there. Gritty, an edge of sophistication, quite a few mobile telephones busy at break (allowed), boys not afraid to voice their opinions, not afraid of life, by and large bushy-tailed with a sense of curiosity and they know how the world works. Old Boys include H H Asquith, Mike Brearley, Kingsley Amis, Julian Barnes, Denis Norden, Anthony Julius (Princess Di's lawyer).

Entrance: Entry at 10, 11, 13 and 16, with the school's own exam set at three different standards according to age group: 10 and 11 – maths, English and reasoning; 13 – maths, English, French, 3 sciences. Past papers from the admissions office. Interview lasts 20 minutes. 10-year-old entry includes 5/6 choristers (all day boys) who sing at Temple Church and Chapel Royal, St James' Palace; c.75 come in at 11, at least 65 per cent from state schools; 40 places at 13 (well over 100 trying for places) from 25+ prep schools. Sixth form takes in 12 or 13 boys – and typically about 12 leave, invariably for co-educational schools.

Exit: All to university or medical school, including nearly 20 per cent to Oxbridge, then high-powered hard working careers.

Money Matters: Financially in the thrall of the Corporation of London, not short of lolly, but Byzantine system of organising it prevails. New fund provides 14 full fee bursaries at 11 and 5 at sixth form for able boys from poor backgrounds. Academic Corporation scholarships at all ages, some for music, and there are several Livery Company scholarships. There are 71 full fee scholars in the school. Choristers are bursaried pupils; some bursaries available for hard-pressed parents of fifth and sixth formers.

Remarks: Busy cosmopolitan urban London boys' school with an international outlook, slightly on the soulless side but delivering the goods and with high morale.

CITY OF LONDON SCHOOL FOR GIRLS

Linked to City of London School for Girls (preparatory department) in the Junior section

St Giles Terrace, Barbican, London, EC2Y 8BB

Tel: 020 7847 5500
Fax: 020 7638 3212
E-mail: info@clsg.org.uk
Website: www.clsg.org.uk

• Pupils: around 670 girls, all day • Ages: 7-18 • Size of sixth form: 149 • Non-denom • Fees: £3,528. Lunch extra in the senior school • Independent • Open days: In autumn and summer terms

Head: Since 1995, Dr Yvonne Burne BA PhD FRSA (who requests us to omit her age), educated at Redland High School in Bristol, read modern languages at Westfield College; taught at Harrow County School for Girls, moved to Washington – and elsewhere – with her diplomat husband and worked in educational publishing. Daughter just left university, son just gone there. Head of St Helen's Northwood before coming here. A low profile lady, terrifically efficient. Busy fostering the American 'can do' attitude in City girls and emphasises her interest in 'expanding opportunities' for girls. NB The Corporation of London appoints the governing body, which is a mixed blessing.

Academic Matters: Continues to get good results – over 95 per cent achieved A* and A at GCSE, over 97 per cent per cent A and B grades at A level in 2005. Three classes of 26 per year, then numbers drop to far smaller groups in GCSE years; four divisions for maths and French from the age of twelve. Some staff changes in recent years, with several youngsters - 'it's great,' said a sixth former, 'you feel they're on our wave-length.' The school day has recently been extended, lessons elongated. Increased emphasis on modern languages, with French for everyone from the start, and Spanish or German as a second language; Latin GCSE optional. Ancient Greek also offered at GCSE. Strong science teaching, with double award GCSE. Biggest A level take-up is for history; English, biology, maths, art are other popular and successful subjects. Politics and theatre studies now appear on the A level menu. Work and progress carefully monitored at all stages, including sixth form. Very strong work ethic.

Games, Options, The Arts: Lovely art, up in the sky-lit attic, producing a huge variety of objects of good quality, achieving rows of A* grades at GCSE and As at A level. Brilliantly equipped design technology department making rapid progress under its new young head of department, producing exciting work. Impressive music – a keen subject, as you would expect with peripatetic teachers from the neighbouring Guildhall School of Music and Drama, and the same is true for drama. Ambitious productions of their own by various ages/groups, new drama studio and lots of interest. 'And we do more drama with the boys' school now,' say girls happily, 'they ask us to be in their plays.' Surprisingly sporty, and, even more surprisingly, it's all done here in the concrete jungle, even athletics. Excellent swimming pool, large gym/indoor sports hall, next door to the compact well-equipped fitness room. Netball and tennis do well (two outdoor courts). Five-a-side teams for football. One small games pitch, the only grass for miles around. Girls are also taken to use the Honourable Artillery Company playing fields a few minutes' walk away.

Young Enterprise and Duke of Edinburgh both very active, also fund-raising for the third world, and environmental issues are a hot subject. Careers advice strongly emphasised. Increasing numbers of girl-led initiatives these days – grunts of parental approval – among them setting up an Asian society, also a law society, with prominent figures lured in as guest speakers. A group of girls from the senior school do a two-week swap with pupils at Chapin School, New York.

Background and Atmosphere: Concrete purpose-built 1960s block in the centre of the Barbican, with a few ancient historical monuments peeking through and a skyline of towering glass and steel city blocks. Khaki coloured water (the lake) and well-planted tubs occasionally relieve the eye in this relentlessly urban environment. Bustling and purposeful atmosphere. The school was founded in 1894 on Victoria Embankment by coal merchant William Ward, with the express intention that girls receive a 'broad and liberal education with the emphasis on scholarship'. Entrance foyer with its waiting area feels more like a hospital than a school. Functional in layout and design, with five floors plus design technology and sport beyond the main block, making an L shape around the small lake. 'It lacks charm,' is often the first impression of parents more used to traditional old-fashioned establishments ('awful' said one). That said, the place buzzes with enthusiasm and energy; girls are cheerfully noisy between classes, noticeboards all bulge with information and are keenly read. New library developed 2005 (one silent, one to talk/teach in), lots of computers, often found out on the broad corridors, 'so you learn to work with quite a racket going on around you,' commented one pupil. All computers are networked and internet is much used. Sixth form common room next to the lake is quite a haven. A climbing wall has been built, a new addition to the sports department. Interesting history of the school recently published (James & James).

Pastoral Care and Discipline: Democratic ethos, with all sixth formers acting as prefects, active school council and suggestions book. Recently set up 'initiative course' for all sixth formers has proved popular. Discipline has not been a problem here. No sense of spiritual values – 'the emphasis is laid on community values rather than religious doctrine,' says the school.

Pupils and Parents: Lots of Jewish girls and large numbers of Asians. Top choice for Islington and lots from NW areas; numbers from Essex who commute to Liverpool Street. A really broad ethnic and social mix, children of ship brokers and shop-keepers, heavy on professions. Happy, confident and talkative girls, 'quite prepared to be outspoken,' said one parent, 'and they are encouraged to take the initiative.' Butch uniform of black trousers and red sweatshirt, the skirt option is less fashionable. Sixth formers are uniform-free.

Entrance: Sharply competitive, with around 400 girls sitting the exam (English and maths), which boils down to interviews for 200 for the final selection of 57, plus around 45 from the school's own prep. NB interview counts for a great deal, with beady staff seeking the X factor. Girls come from a huge number of state and fee-paying schools. Some new arrivals at sixth form, to take up additional places on offer and to fill vacancies (girls exit to Westminster, boarding school or sixth form college – some then change their minds and return to City).

Exit: The most popular exits in 2005 were Cambridge, Nottingham, Edinburgh, Oxford and UCL. The most popular subject choices were history, English, classics and modern languages.

Money Matters: The school is part of the Corporation of the City of London (which is financially generous) and has established connections with the livery halls. Varying numbers of academic scholarships for girls at 11, totalling five full-fees, and now spread at the head's discretion. Also academic bursaries.

Remarks: Academic and hard-working day school that currently produces good results and unspoilt articulate girls but remaining low profile. Sought after, but not among the chattering classes.

CLAYESMORE SCHOOL

Linked to Clayesmore Preparatory School in the Junior section

Iwerne Minster, Blandford Forum, Dorset, DT11 8LL

Tel: 01747 812122
Fax: 01747 813187
E-mail: hmsec@clayesmore.com
Website: www.clayesmore.com

• Pupils: 234 boys, 136 girls; 220 board, the rest day • Ages: 13-18 (but Clayesmore Prep School offers 2-13 on the same site) • Size of sixth form: 111 • C of E • Fees: Boarding £6,915; day £5,060 • Independent • Open days: Late September/early October, May. Prep school holds its own Open Days and very popular boarding taster weekends

Headmaster: Since 2000, Martin Cooke BEd (Hons) FCollP (forties), an ex-St Paul's chorister and organ scholar who was educated at Monkton Combe and did his BEd in music at Sussex. Describes his hobbies as music in general, playing the organ and information technology. A human dynamo, he originally came to the school in 1994 as head of Clayesmore Prep, a job which he has now resumed and he whizzes between the two (closely interlinked) sites like a dervish. We met and lunched with him (and his pretty wife Eleanor who plays an active part in both schools) in the senior school and found him again in the prep when we hijacked his office for a chin-wag. He was previously head of music at Bembridge school and, whilst he no longer teaches, he plays the organ for chapel on occasion and 'interferes' (his word) with the musical output 'occasionally'. He reckons that running a music dept is excellent training for a headship as 'you do a lot of handling people, dealing with the whole 'congo' (as in congregational choir practice).

Vast number of new appointments since his arrival in the senior school – though junior school too during his reign there eg new deputy, assistant head, director of studies, heads of maths, English, drama and major building programme. (Four staff houses in the village, most commute from Shaftesbury, Blandford et al). Enthusiastic IT pundit, one of his two children is currently 'gapping' and 'earning a fortune' writing websites in the Cooke spare room; his daughter is still in the school.

Trenchantly hands-on, keeps himself well-informed on all pupil issues including bullying. Has focused lots of attention on making the sixth form an exciting environment and spruced up the school's image. Clayesmore is now a member of HMC and Mr Cooke had just come back from his first conference when we met. 'We are now a small school of 400 rather than of 300,' but there is no intention of changing the central ethos of a small, caring school dedicated to bringing out the potential in each individual child. Wish list includes new prep school building and classrooms, improved boarding facilities plus new upper sixth house and an extension to the chapel.

Academic Matters: Year groups of 90, five sets in most subjects except maths for which there may be six. Pupils are setted in French, science and maths. French, Spanish and German are all available to A level, with a goodly number getting As and Bs at A level, splendid number of As in business studies, 30 candidates and 29 passes; history, English, maths, French and art all in the ribbons. Good sprinkling of A*s across the board at GCSE – double science particularly impressive, followed by French, German and English, plus art and PE. ICT provision is very strong. First year in senior school tends to be a 'stabilising year' for children to get up to speed. Tiny class sizes equals more attention from committed staff. Tutors responsible for a small group of pupils and monitor assessments every three weeks. Autumn half-term report for new students. Fantastic new extensive builds all over the shop including the award-winning Jubilee Building housing an entire new science department, two large computer suites and the new learning support centre with small lecture hall. Plus the Spinney Centre, which opened in 2004 with new classrooms for geography, history, business studies and careers, all bristling with the latest computer technology. Impressive.

This is a school on a roll. All the dys-strata catered for and a certain amount of Aspergers, autism and ADHD, new build fine for physical handicaps, rest a bit dodgy. Outstanding learning support for children with moderate to medium learning difficulties from a full and part-time staff of 12 (all fully qualified) in the superb new learning support centre (LSC) atop the new Jubilee building 'and anyone can get there' though, sadly, the senior school SENCO was on a school trip in Rhodes during our visit. All children are assessed, edpsyched if needed, extra help in maths, English and science (but not mod langs). More than 35 per cent of all pupils have some form of support, and a 'tiny number' have serious needs. Progressively more group lessons, max eight in a group, particularly in study skills. 'Need children to laugh and feel successful'. Pupils generally come out of language classes and extra sessions can be timetabled if necessary, plus evenings, but can pop in whenever, early morning sessions, exam and course work, 'try anything'.

'The Dore' exercise programme 'quite beneficial'. Good communication between LSC staff and subject teachers means that each pupil will have the individual attention they need, detailed pupil profiles for each. Help for the most able too. CReSTeD category B – CreSTeD listing essential for 'forces stock' who will be deprived of 'unlimited help indefinitely' if the school is not part of the system. Strong EFL too, with up to six hours a week, either individual or in pairs. Extra charge for both, from £21.50 for individual lessons to £5.43 for lessons shared by up to five.

Games, Options, The Arts: All pupils do sport three times a week. You name it, they play it: swimming, rugby, squash, badminton, hockey, football, netball, athletics, cross-country, rounders, sailing and tennis. Lots of matches and some notable successes against bigger schools. A good sprinkling of county players. School is 'potty on orienteering', and regularly in the ribbons. Locals use the 'leisure complex' on site with pool, gym, squash courts and modern fitness suite, including weights (from 16 and under supervision), and a mirrored salle, but pupils say 'the public are not that much of a hassle'. Presumably a planning requirement. Sports science strong. CCF for pupils in years 10 and 11, and enthusiastic D of E participants – tranches of golds et al (New Chaplain keen on D of E too). Sailing at Ringwood popular. Thriving music school in purpose-built building run by enthusiastic head of music. Vibrant, terrific impromptu piano recital during our visit ('actually my main instrument is the flute'), terrific head of music in a class room filled with primitive instruments collected from all over the world. And some of them sound amazing. Sophisticated electronic key boards too, recording studio and good participation in national choirs and yoof orchestras. Composition master class in Salisbury, loads of internal concerts, plus mass of travel, pupils can play almost anything, plus woodwind ensemble, brass group, flute choir and string ensemble. Trails of visiting artistes – including Evelyn Glennie – who only goes barefoot on stage.

Strong thespian tradition, with a terrific head of drama, whom we met in the (tiny) black theatre, but he is keen that actors should give several performances and not just be a one off. Tremendously strong, with masses of tripettes: Bristol, the Old Vic, London. Pupil technicians (approximately 60 in the school at the moment) as important as actors themselves; fantastic costume dept, with sewing machines and London type input. 'Reading plays' gives access to more pupils, who need not learn the part, but can perform, on stage, in costume, with script in hand. 'Theatre Studies A level and drama work closely together'. Mystery plays for all, including the prep, at Christmas. Outstanding art department housed in lovely old primary school past the pub in the village – pottery, photography, textiles, drawing, painting and ceramics, really bustling and fun, sixth formers have a dedicated wall. Pupils take their lives in their hands when they cross the sometimes A350.

Trips to galleries in London and Paris. Huge range of extra activities four afternoons a week and all staff are expected to run at least one. Pupils can do anything from fencing and yoga to textiles and pottery. There is even a wine tasting club (sixth form only) though, post November 2005, the school bar can only function if it serves food as well as booze, and the wine tasting may well get blairised or nanny-stated too.

Background and Atmosphere: Idyllic setting; large country house set in sixty two acres of well-maintained grounds with lake, in the pretty village of Iwerne Minster in rural Dorset, 5 miles north of Blandford Forum, which boasts a post office and butchers (and an awfully large collection of those blue/grey morris minors), plus a school shop which sells skool uniform as well as other essentials for school life. NB sixth form uniform is not provided by skool shop. Some slightly surprising room divisions in the main house, but fireplaces to die for (and glorious computer room on ground floor still showing signs of the most recent roof leak). Well-used social centre, lots of inter-house competitions, sixth form bar twice a week (but see above). Superb grub with salads and vegetarian option. Good cross-cultural influences; staff helped the small group of Chinese pupils cook a celebration meal for Chinese New Year and school meals are occasionally themed around different international celebrations.

Pastoral Care and Discipline: Head keeps a well-practised eye: 'no overt and terrible sin', 'occasional smoking bush' – dissing (as in dismissed which was a new word to the head) about once a year, the odd fag equals letter home and it can get more severe; 'jolly cross' about 'smoking in the building'. A tiered system of punishments ranging from academic 'satis' for prep missed/inappropriate clothing etc to gating and suspension for more serious behaviour problems. Tight eye kept on discipline by the deputy head. Pupils air complaints and suggestions at pupil forum with the head, who is well on top of the situation and not as relaxed as you might think. Has a 'very bad memory' for sin, which means that the next time a pupil sins 'he is down upon him like a ton of bricks' but otherwise the offence is delete. 'Fantastic collection of house parents' currently, five boarding houses (three boys' and two girls' houses) – all on site except one boys' house in the village. Trad smell of toast, pupils graduate from dorms to study bedrooms. Houses run by married staff often with small children and dogs, with full support staff of matrons and house tutors (choose own in sixth form), 'a good school for the expatriate child who might otherwise have been lost with parents far away'. Campus living in a small school is a double edged sword, on the one hand there is this big family feel with lots of people to turn to, and on the other there can be pervasive claustrophobia and great efforts are made to have buzzy weekends for boarders, including discos, talent contests and popular sixth form parties, houses take turns to organise. Shopping buses are organised to local towns such as Blandford, Shaftesbury and Sherborne (none of which will set the world alight). The new Southampton shopping mall streaks ahead of the rest, staff go too. Duty staff organise excursions to local places of interest such as Bath (ditto) after Sunday Chapel, which is compulsory twice a year. C of E school chaplain much involved in the whole school. Children of any denomination are welcome.

Pupils and Parents: Number of day children, local buses: Salisbury, Poole, Bournemouth, Dorchester and the A30; can't flexi-board, but can stay over if late night activities, weekly boarding ok (casual boarding – for parents' or pupils' convenience £20, post school function £20). Senior pupils can bring their own cars. 'Always 150 boarders at weekends'. Progressively more London refugees (this is getting to be the norm) Home Counties and a good sprinkling of ex-pat children (Services, diplomatic etc) plus a small number of foreign students, Dubai, Barbados, the Channel Islands. Fair number of first time buyers. No great green wellie influence. Two-night exeats have recently been introduced twice a term.

Entrance: Waiting list of 20 currently. By Common Entrance at 13 (50ish per cent) and interview with the head who looks for potential, and the all-roundedness of prospective boys and girls. Just under half come through from the prep with the rest from a variety of local (and some further afield) prep schools: Forres Sandle Manor, Hordle Walhampton, Highfield, Durlston Court, Port Regis, Dumpton, Sherborne Prep and Castle Court plus local maintained schools. Rash of academic, music and art scholarships, several species of all-rounder awards are made each year. Sixth form entrants need five A/C passes at GCSE. Popular, but space will become a problem as the larger number further down the school progress up – next project is expanded sixth form. Currently year group expands from 90 to 110 (number of Germans plus overseas as well as Brits).

Exit: Some unis, certain number of Oxbridge candidates, some Services, some vocational courses. School turns out vets, medics, all the usual suspects plus strong art, drama and music stream.

Money Matters: Oodles of scholarships: sixth form up to eight, ranging from 75 per cent down, with min four reserved for those not presently in the school, plus for local candidates (means-tested) plus internal, plus music (string players preferred). Trillions too (though not quite so many) of scholarships, exhibitions and bursarial help for academics, music and art for entry into senior school, plus continuity awards from 11 to A level via the prep school (bursarial help available here too) and more closed awards at 13 – means-tested again. Plus closed School Service bursaries for serving members of the armed forces, and a further bursary occasionally for children of past and present members of the Devonshire and Dorset Regiment. Impressive collection.

Remarks: A well-structured school, ideal for a child needing a supportive environment, with a bubbling far-sighted head in charge. Not a snooty school, perfect for the child who needs extra care.

CLIFTON COLLEGE

Linked to Clifton College Preparatory School (The Pre) in the Junior section

32 College Road, Clifton, Bristol, BS8 3JH

Tel: 0117 3157 000
Fax: 0117 3157 101
E-mail: admissions@clifton-college.avon.sch.uk
Website: www.cliftoncollegeuk.com

- Pupils: 660 boys and girls (60 per cent board) • Ages: 13-18
- Size of sixth form: 280 • C of E but pupils come from many different faith backgrounds • Fees: Boarding £7,305; day £4,835
- Independent • Open days: Termly

Head Master: Since 2005, Mr Mark Moore MA (mid forties). Educated at Wolverhampton Grammar School and Downing College Cambridge, where he read English. Taught at Marlborough followed by seven years at Eton, then eleven years as head of English, and latterly director of University Entrance as well, at Radley. Captained Cambridge and a National Champion at Eton Fives; also enjoys squash and soccer (anything with a round ball really). Married to Jo with four children (two boys, two girls). 'Very enthusiastic and energetic, clearly with a love of ideas and learning, and good at celebrating the work and achievements of pupils. A fine sportsman too,' says a (possibly partisan) source.

Academic Matters: In a pilot of 200 schools, Clifton College came out top of the value-added table – on average, a two grade advantage at GCSE. Wide choice of subjects, with non-examined courses and balancing of arts and sciences designed to reap long-term rewards rather than short-term gains. Flexible timetable means that all options and subjects, however diverse, are possible. Excellent range of GSCE options, with strong performance in maths, Eng lit and history. French and Spanish grades consistently high. Sciences mostly examined separately – (they have a lot to live up to – Clifton has produced two Nobel prize-winners in science).

At A level a diverse and comprehensive selection, with lots of As in maths and science. Excellence also in both fine art and history of art. Huge range of languages which may include Polish, Japanese, Hebrew and Mandarin (growing rapidly, currently 80 in the Pre and Upper School). Many As in German. Previous head supported broadening principle of AS levels; results are admirable across the board with a big increase in A grades at A-level in 2004 and 2005. Pupils take four AS courses with a fifth, non-examined, course to broaden horizons. Small classes, lots of individual attention. Learning Support (eg for mild dyslexia) reflected by performance of former strugglers turned Oxbridge candidates.

Games, Options, The Arts: Sport is compulsory throughout the school but the choice is broad and the facilities outstanding, with rackets and fives courts as well as squash and tennis, a sports hall with indoor cricket nets, indoor swimming pool, huge gym full of state-of-the-art equipment and a miniature shooting range. And that's just one side of the Clifton Suspension Bridge – on the other side are new international-standard Astroturf hockey pitches, a new covered pitch allowing year-round tennis and netball, 24 tennis courts, a Real Tennis court, a new fitness centre and pavilion. Oarsmen and oarswomen row on the River Avon. A school used to winning at sport, particularly at cricket and rugby, with England players galore. Girls' games very successful at County and National levels.

Music and drama also a vital part of school life, with its music school stuffed with Steinway grands and rehearsal and practice space, yet embracing modern technology in the shape of synthesisers, a computerised composition suite and a new DJ course. Thriving choirs and all kinds of ensembles, from the full orchestra to a swing band, give regular concerts. Named after old Cliftonian Sir Michael, the Redgrave Theatre hosts up to 40 productions each year. The art department, with two main studios, caters for potters and photographers (with a well-equipped darkroom) as well as fine artists. Wonderful ICT suites, including the library's newly refurbished (to the tune of £1 million) centre of learning, seamlessly integrated into lofty Gothic spaces at the heart of the school.

Long and strong Services connection reflected by 250 in CCF, with girls as enthusiastic as boys. D of E also very popular. School has own property in Wales as base for orienteering or walking weekends. Amazing trips – Ecuador and Himalayas for mountain lovers, Australia and Canada for CCF. Everyone involved in some form of community service.

Background and Atmosphere: Justly famous for the beauty of its campus, overlooking the lovely Close, Clifton College was founded in 1862 by Bristol merchants. It expanded by building or buying the correspondingly tall, Gothic townhouses that surround the main buildings. Backs onto Bristol Zoo in thriving Bristol's jaw-droppingly expensive Clifton. Fully co-ed since 1987. Main entrance through Memorial Arch marks the hundreds of Old Cliftonians, privates and generals among them, who have died in wars – a very poignant daily reminder of which pupils are touchingly conscious. Recently refurbished Percival Library is the jewel in the crown. Houses (literally, in this case) for day and boarding pupils – East Town or West Town, for example, for day, Worcester and School House for boarding. Day houses are well-used for studying, chatting and slumping in breaks. Boarding houses have had major face-lifts – introducing a clever fusion of tradional and modern designs. New houses (one for girls to reflect increased per cent in the school) opened in September 2004. Strong Jewish presence remains, though no longer with their own house and now fully integrated into the life of the school. Nicely laid out dining hall, more popular since advent of new chef with more extensive repertoire than the last, complemented by Grubber, a tuck-cum-uniform shop with an offshoot of little tables. Bustling, busy and cosy feel to the school.

Pastoral Care and Discipline: Comprehensive, compassionate support, with a family feel, via the house system, particularly for the many pupils thousands of miles from home. Forays to the pub or into town usually foiled by houseparents or the Marshal, a former serviceman based on the edge of the site and in charge of security, discipline and general reining in of excess. Clifton's lovely chapel, with its stained-glass window depicting a cricket match, also gives a spiritual focal point. The whole school meets here four days a week, and three or four Sundays a term, with each house choosing a theme for the week and expanding it – recent topics have ranged from immortality to WWF wrestling.

Pupils and Parents: Parents mostly professionals – lots of solicitors and accountants – and many in the Services. Boarders make the most of the flexi-, weekly- and full-boarding options, with a significant number from a wide

range of countries abroad. Many day pupils within walking distance, although a few travel from as far as Weston-super-Mare. Famous Old Cliftonians run the gamut – legendary schoolboy cricketer A E J Collins, Victorian poet Sir Henry Newbolt, Sir Michael Redgrave, Earl Haig and John Cleese.

Entrance: Cut-off is 50 per cent at CE and signs of potential. Also internal tests and interviews. Around 70 per cent from own prep (entry to Upper School not a given). Few leave at 16 and popular sixth form is massively oversubscribed.

Exit: Almost all to universities of their first choice and 10 plus to Oxbridge. Many also go on to captain sporting sides and some to Olympic glory.

Money Matters: Variety of scholarships and bursaries. Maximum 25 per cent on merit but supplementary means-tested bursaries up to 100 per cent possible.

Remarks: Traditional school with a modern outlook, offering much to pupils with a range of talents. Lovely to look at, too.

CLIFTON HIGH SCHOOL

Linked to Clifton High Lower school in the Junior section

College Road, Clifton, Bristol, BS8 3JD

Tel: 0117 973 0201
Fax: 0117 923 8962
E-mail: enquiries@cliftonhigh.bristol.sch.uk
Website: www.cliftonhigh.bristol.sch.uk

- Pupils: 690; 325 juniors inc 135 boys; 365 in senior school; 2 family boarders, rest day • Ages: 11-18 • Size of sixth form: 82
- C of E • Fees: Lower school from £1,935; upper school £2,660
- Independent • Open days: Several in October/ November

Headmistress: Since 1998, Mrs Colette Culligan BA MEd PGCE (mid-fifties). An English teacher who taught in the state sector in Liverpool and Swindon and who then spent some years in the USA. She came back to teach at St Mary's Calne, becoming head of English and then deputy head. Bright-eyed and smiley, efficient, sensible, open and good company, Mrs Culligan took over a school in some disarray and gently nurtured it back to being the confident and happy place it now is. 'A peace-maker rather than a trail-blazer,' we were told but some trails are being discreetly blazed here and she's not finished yet. A head to whom most parents would gratefully entrust their daughter and clearly many are eager to do so.

Academic Matters: Traditionally not the starriest in Bristol's glittery academic firmament but that is changing. Grades across the board are at least respectable, frequently impressive and, in one conspicuous subject area, outstanding. Classics – Latin and Greek, under uniquely good leadership – is the diva here. Lots of takers and superb results. We have never read an inspection report so busy falling over itself with superlatives. Otherwise a good spread of subjects and school takes pains not to restrict options. Modern langs are well supported, German thrives and Italian is available in the sixth form. English, maths, business studies and geography seem strong and have most takers at A level. Science labs completely refurbished in 1999. IT recently much expanded and developed. Everyone takes a short GCSE IT course; new, flat-screened PCs for everyone. Psychology now offered as an A level, as are DT, classical civilisation and IT – though none, as yet, with many takers.

A small percentage has SEN here and head speaks of 'the dyslexia friendly classroom'. On-site SENCO but pupils not screened on entry at 11 although some picked up later and some attend nearby Dyslexia Centre in school hours – their timetables adapted to fit in. Head stresses that more than mild cases might struggle as school cannot provide one-to-one support. Impressive careers room – well-used. Overall, parents are happy – 'they're on the ball, academically', said one and the results bear her out.

Games, Options, The Arts: Sport is good here. 'This is not a school where it's not cool for girls to enjoy sports!' On-site facilities limited to an old-style gym – no massive sports hall – and an exceptional pool with viewing gallery. However, excellent facilities a bus ride away at Coombe Dingle provide playing fields, athletics track and numerous pitches, all-weather and grass, indoor and outdoor courts. Results are good and girls represent the county in all school sports plus some at national level in hockey, rounders, swimming and tennis – remarkable. In 2004, some school teams, notably U14 netball and hockey, unbeaten all season. Sports on offer include squash, scuba diving, fitness, wall climbing and football. Sports optional in the sixth form but these latter activities popular and how wise not to make them compulsory!

Music, in a dull 1960s building shared with home economics but under energetic leadership, is good; lots of individual instrumental lessons, many ensembles, chamber and full-scale, bands and groups of all kinds. Much involvement with major ensembles outside school such as the National Children's Choir, National Youth Orchestra and, of course, with the Bristol Schools' Symphonia. Bristol schools' music is famously good and all the major schools work closely –

and not too competitively – together. CHS loses out in the music schols states – having less, financially, to offer than its richer neighbours – with the not distressing result that performers not quite up to Young Musician of the Year standard might get more of a look-in here than elsewhere.

Art and design is good. Everyone in years 7 and 8 on a rotation scheme trying out food technology/design technology textiles/resistant materials and making a choice in year 9. Inviting, bright studios, lots of lively, colourful work in many media – painting, textiles, ceramics. Textiles in good, spacious room, popular and imaginative. Good art history library. Sixth form has 'enrichment' programme -includes car mechanics, cookery on a budget, well-woman issues – all practical, sensible and seems to fit with the general ethos. Lots of opportunities for all kinds of trips – linguistic and others. Lots of clubs, D of E etc.

Background and Atmosphere: In the heart of beautiful, chic Clifton – an enviable location and one that certainly helps in recruitment of pupils. Main building is grand Italianate villa, splendidly tiled and porticoed, built as a private house and maintaining some stunning rooms and many wonderful ceilings under which everything goes on as if they weren't there! Apart from its elegant 'waiting room' there is little here that is smart and much that could do with a face lift but this is not a 'posh' nor rich school nor one that will impress with its resources, glitz or glamour. It's quiet, off a quiet residential road in ultra-respectable Clifton. The buildings are, mostly, unremarkable, mainly in the honey-coloured brick common to the area. Good, old-fashioned, galleried school hall used for everything – productions, concerts, assemblies, events and 'wet PE'. Goodish library but, although not small, has a crampy feeling – sofas on the way, we're told.

Separate 'schools' all, more-or-less on one site. Nursery, prep and junior dept are co-ed. At 11, boys depart for one of the many local schools eager to take them. The nursery, with 35 children, is in a separate large Victorian house. It has limited outdoor space but some safe surfacing and good play equipment and apparatus. Large classrooms, lots of varied play activities and much parental involvement make for a super, secure-feeling start to school life. The prep, for the 4-7-year-olds has, again, unusually spacious rooms – light and airy and the atmosphere all over was of contentedly absorbed and productive activity – sometimes aided by sixth formers. Junior school is also housed in a separate Victorian building. Its hall with flexible seating is used by whole school for different events but this was one of the most malodorous school spaces we have encountered. Classrooms are, again, large, orderly and quiet with imaginative displays. Head has long-term plans to unite nursery and reception.

Head sees sixth form very much as a stepping stone between school and university and girls allowed unusual privileges and given important responsibilities – but 'we do it with a light hand'. So very few leave after GCSEs and then mostly to take subjects not offered here. Some come in from outside at this point. Sixth form centre on top of main building includes attractive, small teaching rooms, rooms for quiet study with PCs and big, colourful, mercifully messy common room with kitchen facilities. Super views over Clifton, including the big local competition, lift the heart. School food looks good and varied with daily vegetarian option and vast range of salads – we counted 22 choices – but middle school girls were unenthusiastic. Civilised dining room with separate staff area. Main school uniform is attractive – a smokey blue called, we're told, 'heather' for the pullovers and tartan skirts. Sixth form in own clothes – an eclectic mix from plain, floor-length black to the miniest of tartan skirts but school 'insists on smart jacket'. Lovely touches here and there such as beds of snowdrops (we visited in January) – all planted in fives by girls, parents, staff and governors to commemorate the millennium.

Pastoral Care and Discipline: Somewhat startling to go round school and be assailed by large posters saying (in cerise): 'Never settle for less than your best' or 'Be Your Best, Be Kind'. Old-style, on-site boarding is now gone though some 'family boarders' are accommodated in local families, most with traditional connections with the school. School ethos 'broadly based on Christian principles' works a tutorial system supported by a full time nurse, a counsellor and heads of house and year also monitor progress and happiness. Parents pay tribute – 'what I love is that there's a wonderful family atmosphere. The teachers always know everyone's siblings and take a personal interest.' Another said, 'there's a very clear anti-bullying policy but when we had a problem it all worked out informally. The pastoral system is great.' Certainly there is a relaxed and happily collaborative atmosphere and all pupils we spoke to would n't want to move to any of the rich diversity of competition though some have gripes and would like 'more contact with boys' schools' and repair work (especially on leaky loos, some middle schoolers grumbled, though school says such repairs are dealt with immediately) attended to with more urgency. But, on essentials, a general agreement – 'it's a lovely school,' said one middle-teenager. 'The best things are my teachers and my friends,' said another. 'It's very special,' agrees head.' Mutual respect, trust and liking between girls and staff.'

Pupils and Parents: A real mix. 'My parents are real people' says head, ie they do real jobs and live in real local communities. Not, for the most part, the most well-heeled in this prosperous part of the world and some will struggle over fees. A few on 100 per cent full school assisted places, 'maintained as a point of ethos', asserts head with energy. Nice girls (and nice little boys!) happy to make a contribution to this and the wider community come here and do well. 'We're good at being all-round and we're good for all-rounders', says head.

Old Girls include Jo Durie, Sarah Keays, Mary Renault, Stephanie Cole, Elizabeth Filkin and Bernice McCabe (current head of North London Collegiate).

Entrance: No test for tinies – 'classroom observation and assessment'. Exams and head's report at 11. Approx 45 per cent coming at 11 from outside. 80-90 per cent stay on after GCSEs.

Exit: Lots locally to the University of the West of England to study, mostly, the arts/humanities and to Bristol and other good universities. Others just about everywhere and to study everything from American studies to zoology. Oxbridge a bit disappointing, perhaps – only 4 offers out of 12 applications in 2004/5 – an increasingly common experience, of course. Two leavers in 2003 to Oxford to read medicine. In 2004, one to Oxford and three to Cambridge.

Money Matters: 10 per cent sibling discount. Range of academic schols at year 7. Offers made to selected candidates following entrance examination. Schols also available to girls entering in years 9 and 12. Music scholarships, covering cost of tuition in either one or two instruments, assessed by audition. Few assisted places for girls who satisfy the academic requirements but whose families are not able to meet full fees. Means-tested. Bursaries where needed to help families through short periods of financial difficulty.

Remarks: Not an 'ooh-ah!' school where facilities and privileged surroundings blind one to the quality of experience actually underlying the glamour. A relaxed, civilised, secure and happy place where your outgoing, bright daughter will bloom and flourish. Much has been done under present head but much still to do and she is eager to do it – without rushing. A 'single unified learning centre' is on her wish list as is...'Ah', she says, 'I've got all kinds of ideas......'

COBHAM HALL

Cobham, Gravesend, Kent, DA12 3BL

Tel: 01474 823 371
Fax: 01474 825 906
E-mail: enquiries@cobhamhall.com
Website: www.cobhamhall.com

• Pupils: 200 girls of whom about 55 per cent board • Ages: 11-18 • Size of sixth form: 65 • Multi-faith • Fees: £3,800 to £4,900; boarding £5,800 to £7,100 • Independent • Open days: May and November

Head: Since 2003, Mrs Helen Davy (forties). Read modern history at Oxford followed by postgraduate study at King's College, London. Then worked as a radiographer at the Royal Free Hospital for four years before beginning teaching. Has taught history, history of art and politics at Roedean and The Towers Convent School. Before coming to Cobham she was head of the faculty of cultural studies and acting senior mistress at Roedean. During a career break she ran a small fine wine business and still retains an interest. A warm and enthusiastic person who seems to be very much in touch with the outside world. Married but has no children; her husband works in the City and spends much of his time travelling abroad. He is a biodiversity enthusiast.

Academic Matters: 68 per cent A/B at A level. GCSE 90 per cent A*-C. 3D design, fine art, photography and maths have the best results at A level but increasingly strong in modern foreign languages and sciences; a breadth of courses including critical thinking, theatre studies, IT and business studies. All do Latin for three years and can take it to GCSE. Head says that her aim is to teach children to see the value in themselves and to release it. Encouraged to 'think outside the box or even take the lid off'.

Cobham Hall accepts students with a broad range of abilities and is a truly international school, with 40 per cent coming from abroad. Pupils come from 25 different countries with a growing proportion coming from mainland Europe but there's no dominance from any one country. Strong and impressive EAL presence: about 20 per cent of pupils have EAL requirements. Lessons are timetabled alongside the general curriculum, and students are given extra English tuition either individually or in small groups as well as attending mainstream lessons.

The Susan Hampshire Centre for girls with specific learning difficulties was founded in 1990 and can cater for a fair spectrum of learning problems, providing one to one, multisensory support in most subjects. About 15 per cent of pupils have some form of learning assistance under the aegis of the very experienced Mrs Christine Ostler (who has written several books on teaching dyslexics). The Centre is recognised by CreSTeD as a Dyslexia Unit. Pupils need to be of at least good average ability – they are expected to attend mainstream lessons. Specialist help available for dyscalculia. Well equipped computer suites – all wireless networked.

Games, Options, The Arts: Games are compulsory for everyone throughout the school. Stunning games and fitness centre for aerobics, dance, self defence, etc – locals use it in the evenings and summer schools in the holidays. Good success both with team games and individual sports – netball and volleyball rather than lacrosse and hockey. Rowing on the river Medway is a popular option. A Cobham girl won a bronze medal in British Junior Modern Pentathlon team.

Varied and impressive art, with kiln, mixed media, photography. The fusion of cultures makes for some wonderful artwork. Drama a popular subject and theatre studies is offered as an A level. LAMDA exams on offer too. Tenison Smith Studio Theatre recently opened with state of the art sound and lighting. Drama and music of some sort are compulsory for the first three years and music technology and music are both offered at A level. Fifteen peripatetic teachers, masses of small choirs and bands. Some go to Trinity School of Music or the Guildhall for extra tuition. 2 girls got distinction at grade 8 violin in 2005. Extracurricular activities for everything from craft to cooking and including riding, gardening and golf – ice skating lessons can be arranged at Gillingham. Duke of Edinburgh also popular.

Background and Atmosphere: Founded in 1962. A member of the Round Square, an organisation of schools (eg Gordonstoun) throughout the world committed to education through service, conservation, adventure and international understanding, and run along the lines of Kurt Hahn's philosophy though the outdoor life perhaps not as prominent as in some other schools in the group. Member schools arrange exchange visits for pupils and teachers, and undertake aid projects in places such as India, Kenya, Venezuela and Eastern Europe. Pupils encouraged to see themselves as genuinely international citizens. Cultural Festival a highlight of spring term. Different nationalities cook their local dishes for a feast which is followed by an entertainment or storytelling – Cobham Hall ethos of students from all over the world working together learning from each other and enjoying the experience.

The elegant Tudor hall, previously the home of the Earls of Darnley, is surrounded by 150 acres of parkland designed by Humphrey Repton with a deer park and golf course. The hall itself is pure magic with magnificent marble fireplaces and a fantastic coach on the first floor. Assemblies are held in the Gilt Hall, a masterpiece of high relief plasterwork covered in gold and superb marble fireplace. English Heritage help with the upkeep of the fabric of the building and the house is open to the public during the holidays .The BBC have recently filmed Dickens' Bleak House here. Worship is available locally for almost all faiths – C of E in the village, Catholic and Sikh in Gravesend, and there's a synagogue nearby too; the chef can provide food early and late during Ramadan.

Modern class rooms are strategically placed away from the main building. Boarders progress from the main building to sixth form houses with their own kitchens – due for refurbishment. Lots of privileges for sixth formers, who wear their own clothes and run the dungeon café in the basement as a commercial venture.

Pastoral Care and Discipline: School run on democratic lines with each girl expected to take responsibility for themselves. The election of the new guardian (head girl) is run like a general election with a manifesto and pupils and staff vote by secret ballot. Guardian and three deputies and four heads of house elected in March and serve for three terms. They meet with the headmistress once a week, and see their role very much as a pastoral one. Links with other head girls to compare leadership styles. Lots of work in keeping open atmosphere and making girls self-assertive. New girls supported by 'big sister' scheme. Genuine sense of family.

Pupils and Parents: Lots of first time buyers, many of whom scrimp and save to send their children here. The main UK catchment area is north Kent, London and the Thames Gateway. Strong overseas contingent. Famous Old Girls include journalist Mary Anne Sieghart, photographer Amelia Troubridge and newsreader Mishal Husain.

Entrance: Not overly difficult. At 11+, 13+ and post GCSE but pupils can usually be accommodated at any time with a letter from the current school and possibly a test. School's newcomers' entrance test day in early January: English, maths and a general paper plus two areas of assessment out of music, drama, art and sport. Plus confidential report from present head teacher plus interview. Scholarships usually awarded as a result of performance in the school's entrance exam. Dyslexic candidates also sit the entrance tests although their results are viewed in the light of the educational psychologist's findings.

Exit: Wide diversity of universities all over the world – lots to art school, some to top universities, one or two to Oxbridge. Several to London University to read medicine. Lots seem to end up in media and the arts.

Money Matters: Cobham Hall Scholarships for the academic, awards for special talents and abilities. Four major sixth form scholarships worth up to 50 per cent of fees plus several subject scholarships. Plus bursarial help, usually only for those with acute temporary financial problems and often only to the next public exam.

Remarks: A gentle school which somehow manages to meet the educational needs of a polyglot community of pupils, provide excellent help for those with specific learning needs, and release potential at all levels of ability. Stunning house and grounds bring creativity to the whole.

COKETHORPE SCHOOL

Witney, Oxon, Oxfordshire, OX29 7PU

Tel: 01993 703 921

Fax: 01993 773 499

E-mail: admin@cokethorpe.org

Website: www.cokethorpe.org.uk

• Pupils: 605 boys and girls. All day • Ages: 5-18 • Size of sixth form: 80 • Joint C of E and RC foundation • Fees: £2,440 - £3,940 • Independent • Open days: First Saturday in October, Early Lent term, May

Headmaster: Since 2002 Mr Damian Ettinger BA MA PGCE, late thirties. Educated St Joseph's College (Beulah Hill), Universities of Manchester and Surrey. Previously head of theology and housemaster, Prior Park College, Bath, 1989-96; head of St Oliver's and head of theology, Downside 1996-2002. Mr Ettinger is married and has 4 sons and 1 daughter. Brisk, relaxed, confident, this is a young man in a hurry. He has inherited a school which he believes was seriously underperforming and in which underachievement was almost part of the culture and has set himself in double-quick time to change entirely its character, aims and reputation.

Certainly he's right in that the place has masses going for it in terms of location and site and he has initiated extensive staff changes. His Roman Catholic faith underpins his ethical approach to this job – 'I want to introduce a prayer life into the school' – but this is no preaching softie – 'I want teachers to get angry with the children. How can anyone give 6 out of 10 and say, "Well done?"'. This is a tough, modernizing head who wants his own high standards reflected in all areas of this, traditionally rather relaxed, school and means, in particular, to move away from the name it had established for being 'a special needs school'. A roller-coaster of a man going, perhaps, too fast for some but he looks pretty unstoppable from where we're standing.

Academic Matters: Results are moving steeply upward – remarkably quickly. Hard to gauge, owing to the widely varying numbers in each year, but in 2002 7 out of 40 A level entries got A/B grades and 17 got D/E/Us; in 2004, 63 out of 101 entries got A/B/C and 38 got D/E/U. Hardly extraordinary, but this school had a high proportion of children with learning difficulties and this represents a considerable improvement and, no doubt, for many, a huge achievement. GCSE grades show a comparable shift. Also notable is that more good candidates are now staying on here post-GCSE and school keen to build on this.

Excellent head of sixth form has introduced range of new A level subjects – psychology, politics, media studies and law; new performing arts space should also help in retention as must centrally located 'bistro' – for sixth and staff – a good idea. £80,000 spent on upgrading ICT and school has startling new block housing two large IT rooms – well-used, if not only for work. We wondered whether some supervision might help here.

Head has beefed up modern langs – all do French, and Spanish is on offer from year 8 (as, now, is Latin). German from year 10. School has a link with school in Lyon and there are some trips abroad – more, perhaps, needed to boost this vital area. At GCSE, geography and business studies are popular. Most take double science but triple also available – taken by decent number. Head has also introduced discrete subject setting – you are setted separately for each core subject not, as before, put in the same set for everything irrespective of your varying aptitudes. He has also moved to a two-week timetable of one-hour lessons – more flexible and better for consistent work.

More controversial is the resolute shift away from learning support. More rigorous assessment at entry and the refusal any longer to take children with more than mild specific learning difficulties – head sees the school as being less able than the nearby special schools to give such children appropriate help – means a decided change in the culture and aspirations of the entire school community. Not that the head doesn't want to help children with SEN but he is convinced that these children, as much as any, need higher aims and need to be helped to achieve far more highly than before – 'when a child is shown excellence in one area it raises his or her expectations across the board ... when they've done something brilliant they need to know it'. As it

is, most of children with SEN have some degree of dyslexia or dyspraxia. Some of the older children look mildly shell-shocked – possibly also because of the far stricter discipline than they were used to – but they haven't pulled out and that must be telling.

Games, Options, The Arts: School has 150 acres of parkland and a vast sports hall. Clay pigeon shooting is a passion here – available four times weekly and very popular. Lots of pitches and Astroturf arriving March 2006. Everyone takes part in inter-house cross-country. Head has reintroduced house system, importantly for competitive sports, and believes in excellence – 'we're elitist about our sports'. Rugby, netball and football played. Also on offer are golf, fencing, riding, canoeing, aerobics and judo inter alia. New young head of music set to revitalise dept – at present, fewer than a quarter learn individually and, apart from two class teaching rooms, dept's current housing isn't inviting. Good DT studio but art, too, needs a bit of a boost – nothing specially striking on display here, though graphics, textiles and photography on offer – but head has plans! Old huge maintenance hut now converted to make new performing arts space seating 200+ – a good new asset. Various clubs – chess, sketching, cookery, design, film, BMX biking and very popular 'gadgets and gizmos' – should be something for everyone here. However, a school with this amount of space can offer more and it's hard to imagine that, under the new regime, our next visit here won't be struggling with the range of options.

Background and Atmosphere: A very attractive, solid-looking (though long-standing member of staff called it 'jerry-built') Queen Anne house – 'the Mansion' – greets the visitor. It's set in acres of flattish but undeniably rural parkland with grazing sheep and even has its own Norman church – St Mary the Virgin – a hundred yards or so from the house – used for services and assemblies. Estate has a worthy history and links with the literati of the eighteenth century – Pope, Swift and Gay were visitors here. The mansion now houses the junior school and administration and the entrance hall and some of the rooms are quite splendid. The mansion fronts three courtyards around which, partly in converted farm buildings, teaching takes place, mostly in subject blocks. Some new buildings have been added to complete the quadrangular arrangements – all sensitive and in the appropriate Cotswold stone except for the prosaic and incongruous canteen which is something of an eyesore in this, otherwise immensely attractive, site. Lovely features like a centrally placed little round building – formerly a dove-cote – now the school shop and a rather grand arch to one side of the estate.

Site is well-maintained and orderly – very visible maintenance team hard at it. Atmosphere is hard to judge. School still feels something like the boarding school it was until 2003 but also something like a fee-paying, mixed comprehensive which, essentially, it is. Head is moving towards a far more trad public school ethos – new crests on blazers are emblematic in many ways as are reintroduction of real life versions of school emblem – the peacock.

Pastoral Care and Discipline: Again, the Ettinger Effect creating palpable ripples on the discipline front – 'I want pupils to stand up when I come into the room and feel proud of their uniform ... I can't stand children eating and walking ... I can't stand mobile phones'. Has long had local reputation for good pastoral care. Teacher:pupil ratio is unusually high – most classes between 5-15 pupils and never more than 18. Joint RC and C of E foundation underpins ethos. School lunches look appetising and have improved – 'we've tried really hard to give them proper food,' says cook.

Pupils and Parents: From wide catchment area and school runs in 400+ children using 16 buses with many pick-up points – a real plus for working parents. Children come from as far as Oxford, Swindon, Wantage, from Witney and all villages round about. Some complain of the long school day and it is tough if you have an hour's journey each way on top of a school day that ends at 5.00pm. Wide range of families – old school to first-timers – a sizeable proportion. Copies of Homes and Antiques and Cotswold Life on reception room table. Pupils do not look particularly smart – unkempt hair is clearly height of cool here – hard to imagine the reforming Ettinger eye won't be trained on this soon. Parents increasingly involved – head sees this as essential – and school community set to grow in this area. Overall, head wants a 20:60:20 school ie good 'middle order batsmen' with a starry top and a slower bottom and aims 'to get the best out of every child'.

Entrance: Getting tougher and no longer automatic from the school's own junior dept. Maths, English and VR assessed along with applicant's social and sporting skills so other aptitudes taken into account – 'if he's a fantastic fly-half I'd be interested even if he's not academically strong – the question is, what can he offer the school?' says head. Hitherto, 'we've obviously gone with what's come through the door' but that's changed now and increased competition for places seems to justify the change. Between 2-4 applicants now for each place depending on the school stage. At year 5, parents of junior school pupils unlikely to make it into the senior school are helped to look elsewhere – 'we have to learn to say "no" to parents'. Juniors enter mostly from local nurseries including school's own linked nursery, Westfield House, and primary schools. Seniors from outside come at 11 via Chandlings, The Manor, Ferndale, Our Lady's Convent Junior, St Andrew's Wantage, or, at age 13, from Josca's, The Dragon, New College School, Christ Church Cathedral School and St Hugh's. Criteria for sixth form entry also upped – must have 5+ GCSEs at A*-C including maths, English and a science plus good grades in your A level subjects.

Exit: Some to redbricks eg Manchester, Bristol; most to newer universities eg Nottingham Trent, Oxford Brookes though this trend will probably be reversed. Courses taken cover the range though 2004 saw a lot of embryonic psychologists.

Money Matters: Lots of schols/bursaries of all kinds – academic, art, music, sports, drama, classics, modern langs, and (nice!) all-rounder - now all means-tested. Minor schols for two years from 11. All gauged on exam performance and interview with head. Sixth form schol candidates take two subject papers, a general paper, a reasoning paper and have interviews. Value of schols from 5 - 50 per cent of fees depending on parental means.

Remarks: Ettinger-speak: 'we have to get away from too much patting on the head of children who could have done much better... we haven't got time, we've got to get on with it. I love this job... I'm free at the moment, I've got nothing to do... I'll practise my golf swing.' Interesting to see if he can stay on the ride without too many people – including himself – falling off.

COLCHESTER COUNTY HIGH SCHOOL FOR GIRLS

Norman Way, Colchester, Essex, CO3 3US

Tel: 01206 576 973

Fax: 01206 769 302

E-mail: office@colchestergirls.essex.sch.uk

Website: www.colchestergirls.essex.sch.uk

• Pupils: 763 girls, all day • Ages: 11-18 • Size of sixth form: 230 • Non-denom • State

Headteacher: Since 1998, Mrs Elizabeth Ward BA (fifties). Educated at St Mary's Abbey, Mill Hill and Orange Hill Grammar School, Edgware. BA in English from the Open University. Previously taught at schools in Hertfordshire, Essex and Suffolk, all large mixed comprehensives. Senior teacher at Copleston High School, Suffolk and then 12 years as Deputy at Colchester County High before being promoted to head. Enjoys the country life, particularly walking her springer spaniels. Married to Alan, an academic lawyer. No children.

Academic Matters: Very high standards, and the head and staff are confident that what they do works. 'We looked on Ofsted as a fun thing to do,' says the Head. Excellent GCSE and A level results. All of the girls take 10 GCSEs and the expectation is that all but a very few will achieve A*-C grades in all 10, with many achieving a high number of A* and As. Selection means that the pupils are all very bright, 'an amazingly buzzy atmosphere – the girls really spark each other off,' says the head. Pupils are taught in form groups right through until the end of year 10. No streaming, although there are two groups for maths – accelerated and normal. French from year 7 and a little Latin. German from year eight. Separate sciences. A high percentage of the girls take science A levels and go on to study science subjects at university and, with this in mind, the school has successfully gained science specialist school status. 18 teachers have been at the school for more than ten years and the average age of teachers is 45.

Games, Options, The Arts: Some major sporting successes. Girls' District Champions in athletics for 14 consecutive years but, rather annoyingly, are disqualified from being overall champions because they have no boys. Apart from traditional girls' sports, rugby, golf, football and cricket are offered according to demand. Plenty of opportunities for music, theatre etc. Numerous musical groups. Regular music exchanges with Giessen in Germany. Good choice of clubs, particularly at lunchtimes, including veterinary science, medicine, law. A large number participate in D of E with many achieving gold.

Background and Atmosphere: Set back off a quiet road about a mile to the west of central Colchester. The school was established at the turn of the century and has been at its present site since 1957. The main buildings from that time are typical of the era and have little to recommend them aesthetically but are light and pleasant enough inside. Extra space has been created over the years by 'demountables'. Now totalling 12, these eyesores were never meant to be a long-term solution but some have been there since 1958. The head is keen to get rid of them but they are likely to be around for some time yet. Fairly extensive recent building work has produced some large and airy rooms that are a very welcome addition to the facilities but more building work is needed. 'Our next project will be to improve buildings for music and sport. We don't have good facilities for these subjects, although we certainly have the talent,' says the head. Sixth formers now have a large common room and a private study area.

Pastoral Care and Discipline: Form tutors are responsible for pastoral care. Very few problems with discipline. Detentions were introduced in 2002 but are not used very often. 'The staff needed a sanction for girls who don't hand in their work,' says the Head. No exclusions in the past 15 years.

Pupils and Parents: The main intake comes from south Suffolk and central and north Essex. Girls come from 65 different primary schools. Variety of backgrounds but generally white and middle class. A few girls have English as a second language but clearly use English to a high enough standard to pass the entrance exams. Several statemented pupils over the years with hearing or sight impairments. Parents are very supportive and raised £430,000 towards new buildings in two years. Old Girl, gardener and writer, Beth Chatto OBE is president of the building fund and hosts an annual musical event in her gardens.

Entrance: Highly selective. All prospective pupils sit an 11+ exam made up of verbal reasoning (which accounts for 50 per cent of the total mark), mathematics (25 per cent of the total mark) and English (25 per cent of the total mark). The top 108 are awarded a place at the school. It's not unusual for over 500 to try for a place. The main test date is in late November but provision is made for those who are ill and late entrants. Entrance to the sixth form is open to those with at least 6 GCSEs at grade C and above. Sixth formers come from far and wide and a few stay in digs in Colchester.

Exit: 99 per cent go on to university, with around 20 going to Oxbridge each year. Many go on to careers in law, medicine and academia.

Remarks: A very successful school that turns out highly qualified and confident pupils.

COLCHESTER ROYAL GRAMMAR SCHOOL

Lexden Road, Colchester, Essex, CO3 3ND

Tel: 01206 509 100
Fax: 01206 509 101
E-mail: admin@crgs.co.uk
Website: www.crgs.co.uk

• Pupils: 750 boys and girls (girls in sixth form only), all day, apart from 30 sixth form boarders (boys only) • Ages: 11-18 • Size of sixth form: 250 • Christian • State

Head: Since 2000, Mr Ken Jenkinson (mid forties). Educated at Danum Grammar School, Doncaster. BA in French and German from University of Leeds and MA in French from University of Sheffield. Started his teaching career in a Doncaster comprehensive then moved on to Blundell's where he was head of modern languages. Five years as deputy head at Colchester Royal Grammar before becoming head. Enjoys sport (football, rugby and cricket), travel and spending time with his family. Authoritative but pleasant and friendly manner with pupils. Married to Jackie, a librarian currently working as a school secretary. Two teenage daughters.

Academic Matters: Extremely high academic standards. No setting in years 7 or 8. French and maths set from year 9. 'But this is only a question of pace,' says the head. 'Set four pupils will still be expected to achieve A* at GCSE.' French and Latin in year 7, choice of German or Greek in year 8. One of the very few state schools that offers Greek, the Greek government funds a teacher. For a state school, an above average number go on to study classics at university. Fantastic results at GCSE and A level, regularly among the top five state schools in the country for A level results. In some league tables, top state school for A level results in 2002 and 2003. Occasional SEN pupil with physical disabilities; any EAL pupil will have had a high enough standard of English to pass the selection tests.

Games, Options, The Arts: Cricket and rugby particularly strong. Regular fixtures against state and independent schools. Hockey and netball for the sixth form girls. Many other sports available as extra-curricular activities including athletics, sailing and weight-training. Also plenty of non-sporting activities. Great music department with loads of opportunities for any pupil with any musical ambitions.

Background and Atmosphere: The school is directly descended from a Colchester town school that existed in 1206 and was granted royal charters by Henry VIII in 1539 and Elizabeth I in 1584. Set in an affluent residential area of Colchester, the main buildings date back to the late 19th century. Latest additions, which include a new history and classics block, a new art block and renovated music and drama facilities, fit well with the attractive old school buildings. Lovely, well-tended gardens of a standard unusual in a state school and featuring quiet and private sitting areas for pupils. Extensive playing fields five minutes' walk from the main school and a heated outdoor swimming pool. Two boarding houses with a mixture of single and double bedrooms; family-style facilities, with five resident staff members for the 30 boarders. The uniform includes a vivid purple blazer not very popular with the boys – school begs to differ! – no uniform for sixth formers but smart dress is required.

Pastoral Care and Discipline: Generally very high standard of conduct and not many discipline problems. Punishments include loss of privileges and lunch-time and after-school detentions. There have been few expulsions in the head's time at the school. Zero tolerance of drugs – possession leads to expulsion.

Pupils and Parents: Years 7-11 mainly from Colchester and surrounding area but pupils travel up to an hour each way each day. Sixth formers come from further afield. The boarding house caters mainly for those who would have too far to travel to school each day and pupils from abroad; the school is very popular in Hong Kong and a member of staff visits the country each year to interview potential sixth formers. Very active parents' association raising funds for the school. Old Boys include Telegraph columnist Giles Smith, economic commentator Tim Congdon, costume designer and double Oscar winner Jim Acheson, founder of Freeserve, John Pluthero and BBC education correspondent Mike Baker.

Entrance: Highly competitive 11+ exam – 50 per cent verbal reasoning, 25 per cent English and 25 per cent maths. 'Places will be awarded in rank order to the top 96 boys in the order of merit who have named Colchester Royal Grammar School as a preference.' The exam is set by the Consortium of Selective Schools in Essex, of which the school is one of 12 members, and is held in November at the school. Candidates do not have to live in Essex. Four places available for entry to the school in year 9, but the competition is stiff. Report, plus tests in maths, English, science and a modern language. Minimum of 3 A and 2 B grade GCSEs for entry into sixth form for internal and external candidates. The 40 or so external entrants (half of them girls) also require a school report and must satisfy the school's academic requirements. Candidates for sixth form boarding places must meet the academic requirements. Overseas boarders must be British or EU passport holders.

Exit: Virtually all pupils go on to higher education. 20-25 to Oxbridge each year.

Remarks: One of the country's top selective boys' state schools, rivals many independents. Any academically able and hardworking boy (and sixth form girl) should thrive here.

COLFE'S SCHOOL

Linked to Colfe's Preparatory School in the Junior section

Horn Park Lane, Lee, London, SE12 8AW

Tel: 020 8852 2283
Fax: 020 8297 1216
E-mail: head@colfes.com
Website: www.colfes.com

• Pupils: 510 boys and 200 girls, all day • Ages: 11-18 • Size of sixth form: 180 • C of E • Independent

Head: Since 2005, Mr Richard Russell (forties) read classics at Jesus College Cambridge. Previously deputy warden at Forest School and, before that, director of studies at Sevenoaks.

Academic Matters: Strong academic record, but it's also strong in sport, music and drama. Don't want to simply produce eggheads; it's a school that turns out rounded people. The pupils do get a lot of homework, the school expects results, but at Colfe's they're told the most important lesson of all is how to learn, so they are equipped to cope with university. The school is great at putting pupils forward for exams – it's more interested in encouraging them than worrying about them pulling the results down.

Results pretty consistent. 2002 was a record year with 66 per cent grades A or B at A level and, at GCSE, 93 per cent, with 37 per cent A*/A grades. 2003 grades rather lower at A level but better at GCSE. Performing well, particularly as they draw on a cross section of academic ability and there are many highly selective schools nearby. Class sizes are small. Nearly a third of the staff have been there for over 10 years, although staff are mainly youngish, around 40 years old. Plenty of children have special learning needs

including dyslexia and dyspraxia. Help for this is mainly confined to mild cases, with only one or two having more serious problems.

Games, Options, The Arts: Sport is an important part of the curriculum: rugby training twice per week at eleven for almost all (soccer is also played). Other schools may have a better sporting record but, again, the all inclusive ethos pervades; for example, if you're taken as a reserve to a match you still get a chance to play, unlike some schools. Typically inter-house competitions and inter-school competitions abound, as do sports tours abroad. Sporting personalities, John Gallagher, rugby and Grahame Clinton, cricket, among the committed sports staff. 30 acre site with a modern sports complex and an Astroturf pitch planned in the foreseeable future. Girls' sport was lagging behind – it hadn't really been thought about as the school moved to co-education, but it's now developing in netball, hockey and rounders.

Visual and performing arts centre opened in spring 2003 with facilities for practice and recitals, art and a dark room for photography. Walls adorned with very impressive works – looked like an art gallery in town. Soloists perform, group performances, ballroom dancing – all sorts of activities. 400 pupils in the senior school learn a musical instrument up to post-grade 8.

Various expeditions. Extra-curricular very important – each pupil must attend two (of forty) clubs during the week, either during lunch or after school, ranging from pet care to cookery. Most attend five. You can change clubs each term and they reflect the all round ethos of the school – a club is still learning but it's fun.

Background and Atmosphere: Dates back to 1652; the Leathersellers' Livery Company supports the school, which went independent in 1977. The frontage is an unprepossessing 1960s ILEA building – don't be put off, it's better behind. Tucked away, but there is a real feeling of space once in the grounds, which is quite something when it is so close to London. Generally in good order, bits such as the science block and staff room due for an upgrade. The pre-prep and prep schools are situated in self-contained buildings at the far end of the site, although the younger ones visit the main school for regular assemblies and lunch.

A welcoming school, with a genuinely all-inclusive feel – the sports centre is used by the local community. Broadminded and encouraging, would appeal to parents who believe, 'a happy child is an achieving child' – not a hot house. A sufficiently small sixth form for the head of sixth to know every pupil. They have not found undue discrimination from universities like Bristol – possibly because

Colfe's is a lesser-known independent school.

Pastoral Care and Discipline: 'Firm but fair' is an expression that rolls off the tongue of pupils – they've obviously heard it often. They know bullying, stealing and drugs would not be tolerated (and parents know of no bullying), the school's strategy is tough and well documented but it seems to be accepted that there's a class clown in each year who will be in trouble all the time. Mentors from sixth form help year 7 settle in, not surprisingly, the girls seem more conscientious over this.

Pupils and Parents: Parents are very happy with the school – 'I rave about it to everybody, both my boys love it'. Parents range from ladies with manicured nails to those who've just raced back from a quick trip to Sainsburys after work – though some of the pushier ones push off to Eltham and Dulwich College after pre-prep. Lots of professional parents but not an old boys' network. 18 per cent from ethnic minority families, which reflects the immediate local community, but all pupils speak English. Lots of two-parents-working families, so school opens at 7am for breakfast, the library is supervised until 5pm, and the prep school runs an after school club till 6pm (you don't have to commit to a whole term). Network of school coaches.

Children level-headed and pleasantly not over-indulged. Wearing of home clothes on comic relief day does not turn into a fashion competition, as in some schools. Old Colfeians society is active and maintains the heritage.

Entrance: School is oversubscribed at 11. Colfe's promotes itself as taking a cross section of pupil abilities (well, it is at least noticeably less selective than some of its neighbours), so the interview (of child and parent) is crucial. Not unknown for the child to pass the interview but the parents to fail – eg not committed enough. Said to be harder for boys to get in than girls – better local provision for girls means less competition for places.

11+ entry by exam in January, reference from present school and interview. Examination consists of maths, English and Verbal Reasoning. Half the pupils come from own prep school, though it's not a foregone conclusion that you'll get into the senior school from there: one or two fail each year, but parents are warned well in advance.

Entry to sixth form by interview, reference and conditional offers on GCSE results.

Exit: Most to good universities, with around 4 to Oxbridge.

Money Matters: Fees are competitive for a London day school. The Leathersellers' Company helps over 100 children in the school through bursaries (and to a lesser extent scholarships) if the household income is below £30,000. The school also has its own bursary funds.

Remarks: Pleasant, family atmosphere. Takes a broad mix of children yet it still performs well. Not the place for social climbers or swots.

COLLINGHAM

23 Collingham Gardens, London, SW5 0HL

Tel: 020 7244 7414
Fax: 020 7370 7312
E-mail: london@collingham.co.uk
Website: www.collingham.co.uk

- Pupils: 250 in total: 50 in GCSE dept, 200 over two years in senior dept; roughly 50/50 boys and girls • Ages: 14-19
- Independent

Head: Still under the thriving leadership of Gerald Hattee who has been in the position since 1989. Educated at St. Peter's, York and read history at Keble. Teaches history and politics. Very amiable man who clearly has a good rapport with the students, whose welfare is paramount.

James Allder, BA, is in charge of the GCSE department in Queen's Gate Place. A keen skier and snowboarder.

Academic Matters: Offers an impressive range of subjects and in any combination. Popular subjects are English, history, maths and business studies. Photography at AS increasingly popular and some take it on to A2 where it works well with media studies. Sciences are strong with a number of students going on to read medicine. 75 per cent ABCs at A2. Music is taught to A2 but there are no rehearsal rooms.

Students can join a course half way through and the college will pick up the threads, preparing the student for examination. Class sizes are on average five at AS and A2 with a maximum of nine at GCSE. It's a long day starting at 9.30am and finishing at 6pm with lessons taught in two-hour slots, with a short break in the middle. Students can expect six hours tuition per subject a week at A2, with individual lessons if deemed necessary. For November and January re-takes, this goes up to eight hours.

The college runs Easter revision courses for A, AS and GCSEs, fitting in a staggering amount of tuition, enabling a keen student to thoroughly revise three AS/A2s or six GCSEs. Not surprisingly, these are very popular.

Games, Options, The Arts: The college makes use of its location in central London, with gallery and theatre visits. Weekly football match in Wandsworth – voluntary but very popular. Students can keep fit using the facilities at Imperial College where there is a pool, gym, squash and tennis. Sport is compulsory in the GCSE department. Chess is about to take hold of the college and there is also a thriving debating group.

Background and Atmosphere: Founded 30 years ago. Housed in a seven storey building in a leafy residential square, it's in good condition. Space is obviously a limitation but the house has been cunningly divided up, making 27 classrooms, with three well-equipped laboratory, art and dark rooms. You couldn't expect the facilities to be state of the art but they are surprisingly good and combined with teaching excellence, it all adds up to the provision of a sound education. The library, with a bank of computers, overlooks the square, providing a tranquil place to study and is always monitored by a tutor. The coffee room in the basement allows students to meet and sandwiches are made to order. For a tutorial college, there is a strong sense of community that seems to go beyond the boundaries of the classroom. There is an air of inspiration about the place.

Pastoral Care and Discipline: The college prides itself in its pastoral care and is clearly good at it, cleverly bridging the gap between the care that you would expect to find at school and the degree of freedom that the students enjoy here. The support of staff is subtle but highly effective. The overriding mood at Collingham is decidedly upbeat on both the student and staff fronts. The head's door is always open and he is happy to talk. He is keen that students develop and succeed in their own interests outside school hours.

Registers are taken at the beginning of each class and should a student fail to show, this is followed up immediately. Students have personal tutors for their two years, who are adept at picking up on problems and praising the triumphs.

There are no boundaries within the building and so tutors and students are free to go wherever they like. This garners openness. The smokers can usually be found on the pavement opposite the school at break and are not fussed when a member of staff pops out for a word. Mr Hattee prefers to have them in sight rather than round the corner.

Pupils and Parents: You might expect a London tutorial to be full of misfits. This is certainly not the case at Collingham. Many of the students come from the larger public schools: for one reason or another it hasn't worked out. They may have found the set up just too large or the rules too confining. The friendly environment that Collingham provides is often the catalyst needed to fire the imagination and the will to succeed.

It is often the first time that the students themselves have been in part responsible for making a decision in their future education. This means that they are unlikely to fight the system and consequently put more effort into their work.

Students are largely local, travelling in by public transport. Generally there is parental support, with a parent or guardian at the end of a telephone, should the need arise.

Entrance: Students are interviewed and need five GCSE passes to get a place. The student also has to assure the Head that he really wants to come here.

Exit: Students are taken through the UCAS process with a number of presentations and are given guidance with personal statements. The majority go on to the major universities and art schools. A number to Oxbridge.

Remarks: Collingham appeals to children who haven't quite fitted into the public school system. The level of support given to students is exceptional and this is reflected in a growth of confidence and the desire to succeed.

COLYTON GRAMMAR SCHOOL

Whitwell Lane, Colyford, Colyton, Devon, EX24 6HN

Tel: 01297 552 327

Fax: 01297 553 853

E-mail: admin@colytongrammar.devon.sch.uk

Website: www.colytongrammar.devon.sch.uk

• Pupils: 745 boys and girls • Ages: 11-18 • Size of sixth form: 180 • Non-denom • State

---

Head: Since 1990, Barry Sindall BA Med (fifties). Graduated at Exeter University in history and theology. Previously deputy head at Torquay Boys' Grammar School for three years, director of studies for 11 years at Colyton, head of humanities at a comprehensive in the Bahamas with 2,000 students, history and RE teacher at secondary in Ashford, Kent. Mr Sindall describes his association with Colyton as a 'love affair', ecstatic at being able to return as its head teacher to complete his career. Down to earth demeanour, non-critical, relaxed and approachable but with firm expectations of students' behaviour. Parents view his focused and organised direction as paramount in the school holding its academic position.

The head's pride in Colyton extends outside the classroom to the tidy courtyards and splendid roses. He 'values classroom contact' – teaches RE up to year 11 and general studies to sixth form. Married to Maggie, a Colyton science teacher. Two children, one educated at Colyton.

Academic Matters: Excellent, steadily maintaining its

position as one of the strongest academic state schools in the country. Head teacher's happy and relaxed personality seems to have rubbed off on students, allowing academic study to flow. GCSE class size of 29, A level 18. All students take a minimum of 10 GCSEs, 4 or 5 of the available 22 A levels, as well as key-skills in ICT, communication and numeracy. Useful exchange links fostered with France and Germany extend to European work experience to encourage linguists. All students have access to Advanced Extension qualifications.

Ofsted inspectors report 'total absence of any area of subject weaknesses'. In 2004 Ofsted reported, 'this outstanding school continues to accelerate away from similar schools'. All students excel here – even the less confident – and in all subjects. Girls commonly pursue engineering projects at A level. In 2003 one student gained award for the country's highest marks in A level physics and another in A level English; in 2004 individual students from the school were amongst the highest achievers in GCSE biology, chemistry, RE,and ICT and in 2005 this included Mathematics and French; in GCSE technology individual Colyton Grammar students were ranked 1st, 2nd and 3rd in the UK. Other wins include involvement in National Mathematics Challenge, British Biology Olympiad, Physics Olympiad and Chemistry Top of the Bench (national finalists). In 2003 and in 2005 one student represented Britain in the International Physics Olympiad. The school is an Ambassador School of The National Academy for Gifted and Talented Youth.

Games, Options, The Arts: Good sporting facilities here now, with dedicated playing fields, new (2003) sports hall, floodlit all-weather Astroturf hockey and tennis area, netball courts. Acquisition of a neighbouring field has doubled the area available for sport since 2000, allowing more scope for future athletes, and cricket and soccer fixtures. Strong competitive traditions, with keeping fit as a complement to study taken seriously. Students gain county honours across the board.

Choir is popular and enjoys a national reputation, performing at the Barbican, Westminster Abbey, Dublin Cathedral, St Mark's, Venice, St Nicholas, Prague, Edinburgh Festival. Well-established orchestra, woodwind, folk, jazz band: uplifting lunch-time concerts as well as seasonal ones. Visits from performers of international standing. Cherishes involvement with local community – often entertaining local groups and supporting charity with performances of music, singing and dancing.

Expressiveness plays major role in art lessons, with flamboyant teacher successfully encouraging personality to shine through different media in open-plan classrooms. Perhaps not for the shy types who want to sit quietly in a corner.

Strong links with primary school – year 11 students provide drama workshops and sixth formers help with science master classes. Young Enterprise, National Magistrates' Court Competition (finalists three years in succession and were winners in 2004) and National Bar Mock Trial Competition finalists 2002 and 2003 and National and International champions in 2005 extremely popular for the industrious team and law graduate types. Regularly enters at least two teams in Ten Tors and Exmoor Challenge. D of E popular too.

Background and Atmosphere: Founded 1546, amongst the oldest state schools in the country. Moved to town of Colyford when school outgrew premises in Colyton. Attractive low-level redbrick school with views of the sea from playing fields. Happy atmosphere which comes from the top, with teachers made to feel integral part of team. Proud students speak highly of the school with an air of unpretentious confidence.

Pastoral Care and Discipline: Students working with, rather than for, teachers help prevent emergence of disruptive behaviour. Excellent attitudes and behaviour, much praised by parents.

Special needs children, including profoundly deaf, partially blind, dyslexic, well supported by students and teachers, their academic progress closely monitored with supportive action plans where necessary. Parents say the school can find students' weaknesses and bring them up to par with other subjects, or transform them into strengths, by the time they leave.

Ample opportunity for responsibilities for sixth form students – organising assembly, extra-curricular activities, teaching in primary schools. Zero tolerance policy against smoking, alcohol, drugs and bullying seems to be working, with one exclusion in ten years.

Pupils and Parents: As students are drawn from 30 mile radius from more than 60 primary schools, there is no sense of competition with other schools. About 50 per cent of students live in Axe Valley. Social background is varied.

Highly thought of, especially for all rounders. Former students include Sir Rex Richards, President of the Royal Society of Chemists and former Vice Chancellor of Oxford University; Ben Way, a Young Entrepreneur of the Year who, despite being dyslexic, made his first million in his first year of work.

Entrance: 11+ exam using NFER mark scheme; a score equivalent to the top 25 per cent of the ability range nationally qualifies a candidate for consideration. If more qualify than the 120 available places allow for, preference is given to: firstly, those with siblings at Colyton, secondly, those who live closest. Entrance to sixth form requires 50 GCSE points achieved in over eight subjects.

Exit: 90 per cent go on to sixth form; leavers post GCSE either enter further education college or are relocating to other areas of the country. At least 95 per cent of the sixth form enter university, with 10-15 per cent gaining Oxbridge places. A wide range of degree courses but more than average head for science, medicine and engineering.

Remarks: Academically outstanding grammar school instils self-belief and a can-do attitude. Not for the faint-hearted.

CONCORD COLLEGE

Acton Burnell Hall, Shrewsbury, Shropshire, SY5 7PF

Tel: 01694 731 631
Fax: 01694 731 389
E-mail: theprincipal@concordcollegeuk.com
Website: www.concordcollegeuk.com

• Pupils: 175 boys, 160 girls; 300 board • Ages: 13-18 • Size of sixth form: 250 • Inter-denom • Fees: £6,312 • Independent

Principal: Since 2005, Mr Neil Hawkins MA (forties), presently director of studies at The Leys School Cambridge. Has a difficult act to follow (see below), but already involved himself in the life of the college and intends to build on Tony Morris' success. His wife Vanessa will continue the tradition of principal's wife looking after the girls' welfare. Took over from Tony Morris, who in his thirty-year reign has overseen the most remarkable development of Concord from a lesser-known international college to perhaps one of the most respected and successful in the entire country. His enchanting enthusiasm, can-do philosophy, high expectations and close involvement with the day-to-day life of the pupils were an important component in the relaxed, yet focused, atmosphere that pervades the college.

Academic Matters: In recent years Concord's A level league table position has rocketed to the very top: currently number one in Shropshire and is sixteenth in the Times top schools league. Remarkably Concord has now left very prestigious local public schools such as Shrewsbury, and Malvern in its wake. This is despite the fact that most of its students speak English as a second language and selection criteria are very broad indeed. The reasons for this success are many, but first amongst them is the atmosphere of focussed endeavour that pervades the institution. In some

sense it is refreshing that there is little attempt here to lay claim to a liberal educational agenda. The public school tradition of chapel and games field simply does not exist here and student status is a consequence of academic effort and success. This celebration of avowedly meritocratic values underlies everything the college stands for. In 2004 one A level student secured eight A grades at A levels and she together with other successful scholars have their photographs and achievements prominently displayed and celebrated. Academic work is the first priority and every other aspect of college life takes second fiddle to this. To emphasise this point all students sit internal examinations every Saturday morning. This, according to the principal, ensures a very close monitoring of progress and gets students used to the experience of examination nerves.

80 per cent of all A level teaching is science based – no attempt to massage league table position by offering soft subject options. Science-teaching facilities, already extraordinarily good, have just become even better with the building of yet four more laboratories. Up to 25 per cent of all students go on to read medicine at British universities. The balance of the curriculum in the sixth form is somewhat skewed by the emphasis on science. Neither history nor geography are offered as A level subjects (though history is now offered at AS level), and those opting to pursue a non-scientific track are likely to find themselves studying economics, law or business studies, all of which are extremely strong.

In 1995 the College expanded from its strictly sixth form identity to develop a lower school of pupils aged 13 to 16. It is still early days, and the lower school is only 70 strong. Moreover, it is significantly local and day and in atmosphere and ethos is quite different from the core sixth form. GCSE results have been very satisfactory with 83 per cent of pupils achieving A- C grades, but in truth these result do not yet compare with the exceptional achievement of the A level scholars.

Games, Options, The Arts: The college offers a wide range of games and activities. There is remarkable freedom of choice to the student. The college policy is to offer what the student wants rather than demanding that the student accepts what the college can provide. Currently no one wishes to play rugby so despite an excellent pitch it is not played. On the other hand there is demand for kick boxing, so facilities and coaching are provided.

Some lovely art facilities are to be found in a separate house in the local village. Art is popular, not only for its own sake but also because quite a few students aspire to architecture as a future career. Despite some wonderful music facilities only 70 pupils take individual tuition: a consequence of the primacy of academic matters. It would be wrong though to suggest that Concord is merely a glorified crammer, and it is clear that it possesses a lively and creative cultural life. The musical standards are high and informal concerts are a very regular feature of college life. There is a brand-new theatre/concert hall which must rate as one of the most opulent anywhere and especially in so small an institution. Drama too is a regular feature of life here, but like music the emphasis is on informality and personal choice.

This consumer led approach to games and other activities is one of the great strengths of Concord. Students really feel that their views and concerns are central to college policy. They seem to feel that their wishes are taken serious by the college management. However, the essentially voluntary nature of these activities means that it is difficult for the college to compete effectively with local rivals and is one reason for its relatively low profile within the local community.

Background and Atmosphere: The campus is centred on Acton Burnell Hall which was once the family home of the Smythes who were a leading Catholic gentry family. The building has a fascinating history, and during the Napoleonic wars housed what later became the Benedictine schools of Ampleforth and Downside. The building is maintained to an extraordinarily high standard and the feel is one of a particularly prestigious country house hotel. Furniture and decoration are all of the highest quality and does much to enhance the civilised feel of the college. The library is especially attractive, housed as it is in the Strawberry Hill early 19th century Gothic chapel. The many new buildings (approximately one a year over the last twenty years or so) are sympathetically styled to fit in to this quintessentially English landscape. The position of the college in the stunningly beautiful Shropshire countryside hard by the market town of Shrewsbury and close to Birmingham makes it a popular venue for summer schools, which are offered every year to students from overseas, but not yet from the UK.

The college recruits its students from all over the globe. Around 85 per cent are overseas pupils and of these the largest component are from South-East Asia. However, there are growing numbers from Eastern Europe. The college is very careful to avoid developing national cliques and it is quite clear that the various national and religious groups mix freely with a real sense of mutual respect and tolerance.

The college is keen to stress its lack of any religious affiliations. However, great efforts are made to accommodate various religious faiths with transport provided to church and mosque if required.

Pastoral Care and Discipline: Concord has avoided the English educational obsession of uniform and traditional ethos and rules. The atmosphere is very relaxed with students free to wear more or less what they want. However, this is not a free and easy institution. The students are expected to be polite and considerate of others. The impression one has is that they are. This is very much the product of old fashioned high profile staff involvement. Teaching staff are all expected to be fully involved in all aspects of pastoral care with particular responsibility given to the eight house parents. The principal considers evidence of such a committed attitude to be an essential component of staff selection. Rules only exist when they are deemed essential and this seems to avoid the often mindless rule bashing one sees often in some English schools. Essentially the students are trusted, but if that trust is abused the consequences can be dire. Smoking and drinking are not tolerated and can quickly lead to expulsion; any drug taking will ensure the immediate departure of the offending student.

One unique feature of the college is that overseas pupils can and do stay during the Christmas and Easter holidays as well as half-term holidays at no extra cost. Sometimes as many as 250 are to be found resident during these times. This is a remarkable service and does much to enhance the college's popularity with overseas parents.

Pupils and Parents: Generations of the same family have often attended the college. Pupils tend to hale from the richer and more socially mobile groups of South-East Asia, Africa and Eastern Europe. However, the opening of the Lower School has made Concord attractive to some local families. Local prep school heads are taking the college increasingly seriously.

Entrance: An informal online test of mathematical and English ability is the only real requirement. Beware – you only get one chance!

Exit: 15 this year to Oxbridge, 30 plus going on to do medicine. The vast majority go on to British universities although a growing minority now aspire to American, Australian, and European higher education.

Money Matters: The fees are very competitive, this is especially so when one considers that pupils may stay during the whole academic year. The college is very generous in providing bursaries and scholarships setting aside as large a proportion of its fees as many grander and richer public schools.

Remarks: Concord offers a fascinating and creative alternative option to overseas pupils aspiring to a British education. Combines strong pastoral care, fabulous facilities and an extraordinarily focus on academic achievement and the sciences. Not yet clear how the new principal will change things (if at all).

CRAIGHOLME SCHOOL

Linked to Craigholme Lower Junior School and Nursery in the Junior section

72 St Andrews Drive, Pollokshields, Glasgow, G41 4HS

Tel: 0141 427 0375
Fax: 0141 427 6396
E-mail: jkerrigan@craigholme.co.uk
Website: www.craigholme.co.uk

• Pupils: 520 girls, all day • Ages: 3-18 • Size of sixth form: 90 in fifth and sixth forms • Non-denom but Church of Scotland roots
• Fees: £1,960 - £2,500 • Independent

Principal: Mrs Gillian C K Stobo MSc BSc DipEd (fifties), previously deputy rector at The High School of Glasgow: 'I am the rags to riches of the education world,' she said, adding that her original ambition had been to become depute head. Educated at the Girls' High School of Glasgow, she did chemistry at Glasgow followed by Dip Ed at Jordanhill and taught 'for a bit' before taking almost ten years out to have a family (one is now a doctor and the other a lawyer). Did the odd bit of supply teaching et al before joining the High School of Glasgow as a part time chemistry teacher in 1993, becoming head of science before depute director. She also completed an MSc on a part time basis: her thesis is on learning support for able pupils and she is currently working on her doctorate. What a role model.

Quite seriously into the jargon (well, she is a chemist at heart), the principal is good at initial-speak and runs the school with an SMT or senior management team of two deputy principals. No staff changes to date, but she was involved in selecting the two teachers who were replaced last year, including the head of chemistry, which must have been fun.

Academic Matters: Trenchantly academic, small classes usually 12-18, with one primary of 21 pupils. All start French at four, with a German taster at 10 and Spanish at 13/14, and all three taught to Advanced Highers. Science from the top of junior school and into labs at 10, human biology on offer. Large number into the world of bio-medical and sports science. Maths and English setted at 11, maths regularly taken a year early, occasional standard grades. Classics a thing of the past. Curriculum adjustments in the pipeline: archaeology et al. Computers from three up, age-specific resource centres and all singing and dancing in the library. Key-boarding for all, and pc passports mandatory. Interactive white boards and smart boards, and a purpose-ful air of concentration throughout the school.

Girls screened for dyslexia if staff concerned, no ed psychs on site, but fully trained learning support team, offer-ing one to one, monitoring, extraction, team-teaching and study skills, which should cover most problems. Not keen on the autistic spectrum. 'We are open about what we offer, nothing is automatic, and nothing in extremis.'

Games, Options, The Arts: Teams for everything, trips all over the globe, in almost every discipline: geography to China and India, history to the Somme and hockey to Eindhoven. School mag full of happy smiling victorious faces. Mega-million sports complex in Pollock Park (home of the Burrell collection), school has a 99 year lease from Glasgow City. Hot on athletics. 'Our presence is felt.' Presumably bored athletes can while away their time at the Burrell itself, much used by the art complex: imaginative stuff, including some fairly way out jewellery. Textiles. Choirs and bands for all, clarsach currently popular and head was keen to emphasis that the school produces a cross-curric-ular play, this year Macladdin, written by the staff with music composed by the staff. Such enterprise appears to be unusual in the west of Scotland. YE, D of E, much as you would expect.

Background and Atmosphere: Basically a collection of rather grand Victorian villas tacked together with some imaginative glass add-ons. Wouldn't be allowed in Edinburgh, but generous Glasgow planners have been kind. Not a lot of the original bits left, but good sized classrooms (hence availability to add the odd girl at the off time) and the occasional vestige of Victorian decoration – brilliant piece of adaptation, girls will need a map when they start in the senior school. Nursery and junior school more or less on site, but different buildings. Houses bustling with assorted check-clad girls, red pinnies for littlies, graduat-ing to skirts for older girls. Totally unpretentious pupils, none of the (presumably unconscious and automatic) preening we are accustomed to seeing elsewhere.

Pastoral Care and Discipline: School keen on health, healthy eating and proud of their new in house 'smart café', which is organised by a former mum. Girls sit in year groups, and school is 'small enough' so that everyone knows all the children, lunch is a 'pay as go' experience, with chicken curry and lentil dahl tops. 'Everyone who can eats the school food'. Free tasters, buffet salad bar, veggie option and water at every desk -'we are keen on water'- and smoothies but no fizzy drinks; the head keeps a stash of real coffee for visitors. Positive anti-bullying strategy in place: 'we take it seriously'. Vertical house system, strong right down the school, siblings in the same house; activities, year groups and tutorials on Thursdays. Staff allocated to houses too. No reported miscreants to date.

Pupils and Parents: A few from ethnic minorities. Solidly middle class, massive catchment area which includes not only Pollokshaws, Pollokshields but also north of the Clyde, Bearsden down to Kilmarnock and Ayrshire. Victorian burgers would be pleased to see what their homes have become. Buses. Loads of professionals, good number of first time buyers. Number from ethnic minorities. Parents can drop their daughters at 8 am; final collection time is 5.45 pm which might be tight for some. After school costs extra.

Entrance: Full, though spaces may become available at odd moments; and as this is 'a Victorian house it is often possible to squeeze an extra desk in'. Plots afoot to expand nursery. Otherwise regular entry at five, with girls joining (often from the state sector) at 11, or post Standard Grades for their Highers.

Exit: Most stay the course, apart from the odd logistical departure. A few girls leave at 11, 12 or 13 to trad girls' boarding schools (perhaps one or two every five years) though some will go elsewhere either post standard grades or, as happened recently, post Highers in order to qualify for Oxbridge from the maintained sector. Craigholme is a school which breeds loyalty, over 90 per cent to university (some after gap years) and trails of happy mini-biogs in the school mag: school obviously encourages lawyers, mathematicians (or accountants) and medics.

Money Matters: School in good heart, will carry child whose parents have fallen on hard times as long as parents are up front about it. Not a rich school, 'no large bursary fund', but still a modicum of means-tested bursaries on offer at 11/12, and some fiercely sought after (discretionary) academic scholarships available at any time.

Remarks: Useful school. The infrastructure is there, and impressive staff with it.

CRANBROOK SCHOOL

Waterloo Road, Cranbrook, Kent, TN17 3JD

Tel: 01580 711 800
Fax: 01580 711 828
E-mail: registrar@cranbrook.kent.sch.uk
Website: www.cranbrookschool.co.uk

• Pupils: 392 boys, 359 girls. 242 board • Ages: 13-18 • Size of sixth form: 302 • Non-denom • Fees: Boarding £2,675; £2,880 for sixth form • State

Head: Since 1998, Mrs A S Daly (early fifties), married with two children one of whom was at Cranbrook. Was head at Tunbridge Wells Grammar School but moved to avoid being at same school for 18 years. Previous head retired. Feisty, brisk, smart, energetic, down to earth, state educated, wants pupils to do well and they do do exceedingly well. Teaches English and RE wherever and whenever she is needed. Well up on the history of the school, past heads, beneficiaries etc. Believes in the importance of moral teaching.

Academic Matters: Strict adherence to National Curriculum with tremendous number of extras. Saturday school abolished so sports feature heavily on Saturdays. Languages offered are Latin, French, German and Spanish – very public school, good science labs, very well-equipped large kitchens for pupils to learn food and nutrition. All the classrooms are a bit small but aesthetics are not top priority. Almost every facility here a child could need. Overseas students including Chinese are given the opportunity to take GCSE and A level in their native language but any teaching needed for this is outside the curriculum. Independence massively encouraged, which leads to pupils seeming very mature. Staff are relaxed and down to earth, focused on getting the best out of each pupil. At A level, maths, the sciences, English (decreasingly) and history (increasingly) popular; 71 per cent A or B. 99 per cent A*-C grades at GCSE. A fine performance.

Games, Options, The Arts: A wide range of bands, musical instruments taught, and a new music centre is being built. Every sport is played and they beat local public schools at cricket and rugby regularly, much to the horror of 'smarter' schools. Climbing wall, gym – this school has facilities that most state schools don't. Huge theatre with countless productions including the Cranbrook panto in the holidays.

Background and Atmosphere: The energy of the school hits you as soon as you walk in. Has the look and feel of public school, yet on closer inspection feels far too unsnobby to be one. Newly completed building projects include a performing arts centre (with recording studio), sixth form centre, administration block, medical centre and an observatory to house the fantastic telescope donated to the school. The school has been awarded Science Status and Training School status.

NB the unusual (for state schools) entry at 13 means that most children will have attended a private school prior to attending Cranbrook, so it feels less rough than perhaps a large, non-selective state school would. Absolutely no arrogance here and, if pupils board, it is often because the parents both work or live abroad. Incredibly funky assemblies – pop music and overhead screens displayed a controversial debate with sixth formers talking to the lower school, on this instance on the corruptiveness of the WTO. Make-your-mind-up assemblies rather than your average hymn and a prayer and, at the end – after a piece of music performed by pupils – 'right then, off back to lessons'. Incisive, thought-provoking and not traditional at all.

Pastoral Care and Discipline: Has a chaplain, but 'in house' care groups are the way ahead at this establishment, ie student listeners, school council and the senior house members look after the younger pupils.

Pupils and Parents: The pupils seem relaxed and laid back despite the fact that they must be working extremely hard to get such amazing results. They were all chatty, busy and smiling, thoroughly engrossed in whatever they were doing. There is a uniform up to sixth form and then they have 'dressing up' days when they don suits – none of the sixth formers looked really scruffy. All pupils are well spoken, polite and extremely motivated – they talked about how they could achieve more and get more ticks in their boxes before applying for their various universities. Parents are middle class and unstuffy and most mums work. Very few families on benefits and very few very rich either. One parent commented that she wanted her daughter to come here so that she could have a normal education and life.

Entrance: Competitive. Own closed exam (ie no past practice papers available) and a reference is required from current school – most pupils who take or would have taken Common Entrance achieve over 75 per cent. Over-subscribed by 100 per cent. Day pupils MUST live within 6.2 miles from the boundary of their property to the school gates on normal roads – ie no cutting across forests in four wheel drive vehicles to attend as has been tried in the past – and houses reputedly cost £20,000 more if within the 'Cranbrook catchment area'. Can live further afield if a boarder but the pupil still has to pass the entrance exam – this is not a 'back door' to the school. Boarders only pay boarding fees ie tuition is free to all.

Unusual (for state schools) starting age of 13. The main feeder schools are Angley (35 per cent), the local 11 to 18 comprehensive school which has a special stream to try and get pupils in to Cranbrook, and Dulwich Preparatory School, Cranbrook (30 per cent); otherwise most from Kent/E Sussex prep schools.

Exit: 98 per cent go on to university or higher education. There is an outstanding UCAS support system, with staff closely monitoring every pupil. The few pupils who leave after GCSE all take A levels elsewhere.

Remarks: Feels like a public school without the old guard staff. Not for the faint-hearted, sensitive child or for parents with social aspirations but there is not much that this school cannot offer a child that it suits. A dynamic, unfussy, unpretentious school.

CRANLEIGH SCHOOL

Linked to Cranleigh Preparatory School in the Junior section

Horseshoe Lane, Cranleigh, Surrey, GU6 8QQ

Tel: 01483 273 666
Fax: 01483 267 398
E-mail: enquiry@cranleigh.org
Website: www.cranleigh.org

• Pupils: 401 boys, 205 girls; about 70 per cent board • Ages: 13-18 • Size of sixth form: 245 • C of E • Fees: Boarding £7,450, day £6,035 • Independent • Open days: Usually end of September

Headmaster: Since 1997, Mr Guy de W Waller, MA MSc PGCE FRSA (fifties), educated at Hurstpierpoint, and read chemistry at Worcester College and educational psychology at Wolfson College. Cricket and hockey blue. Former headmaster of Lord Wandsworth College. He has obvious enthusiasm, energy and self-confidence. Clearly doesn't feel he has to impress anybody – PR machine was definitely switched off the day we looked round – also a tendency to be rather glib and flippant (he doesn't have much time for this guide!). Describes himself as a 'frustrated housemaster – definitely not a career headmaster.' Feels that co-ed schools 'reflect the world we live in.' Has no doubts that school is doing it right – right balance of boys and girls, right approach to education. Describes the school fondly as 'this crazy place with heart.' Still teaches chemistry and philosophy – believes being in the classroom 'focuses you'. Likes to be kept informed and involved with pupils and he says 'the key is to have a good team in place.' Cuts something of a controversial figure amongst parents – variously described as 'charming, dynamic, running a tight ship' as well as 'distant, arrogant, autocratic, doesn't listen to parents' and all range of comments in between. Some parents feel that he is rather resting on his laurels (head hotly denies this – he has recently researched and completed a major development plan for the school), the school really being the only serious contender for senior co-ed in this part of Surrey, and thus a virtual monopoly. For others, he can do no wrong.

Academic Matters: Although academia is not wholly what Cranleigh is about, academic results have improved greatly of late, not least because of the introduction of girls throughout the school. At GCSE 60 per cent A/A* with particular success in drama and classical civilisation. At A/AS level, individual strengths vary from year to year but drama, economics, business studies, English, history and the sciences are usually up there with good grades. At A level between 75-80 per cent A/B grades. Head says that pupils 'don't have to be superstars,' but one parent commented that the academic side is definitely hotting up and 'B and C students may struggle.' School employs a SENCO who screens all entrants, support offered for those who need it – one-to-one sessions which cost extra.

Games, Options, The Arts: 'Sport is a very important part of just about every Cranleighan's life,' says head. The sheer range of sports available is staggering – there really is something for everyone. Sports facilities are extremely impressive – 100 of the 200 acres of the school land are given over to playing fields. Facilities include the Trevor Abbott sports centre (opened in Jan 2002), an all weather pitch for hockey in winter which converts to 12 tennis courts in summer (all packed with Wimbledon wannabees when we visited), indoor and outdoor swimming pools, cricket and rugby pitches stretching away as far as the eye can see, championship standard squash courts, six Eton fives courts, nine hole golf course, stables with own horses (pupils can bring their own horse(s) if desired), and so on. Key sports include rugby, cricket, hockey, lacrosse, netball, tennis and athletics. Football has nowhere near the same emphasis as rugby – might put off a soccer-mad boy. There are opportunities for all levels of talent – parents with non-sporty but enthusiastic children say that they really enjoy what they do. But certainly don't bother applying if your child absolutely loathes sport.

Art generally praised but one informed parental critic 'wasn't that impressed'. Drama is particularly strong with fantastic theatre facilities (very professional tiered auditorium) and lots of chance to perform throughout the year in a variety of different shows. Musically, the opportunities are vast, with choirs, orchestras, individual instrument tuition, concerts throughout the year. Interestingly though, music has not been hugely popular at either GCSE or A level.

Head does not feel that the description 'after-school activities' is apt for Cranleigh – 'it's not an expression that fits with our ethos as here after-school activities equal going to sleep. You have to be careful not to say 'going to bed' in a co-ed school.' Quite! However, call it what you will, other than sport, the options are wide ranging and children have loads of opportunities to fill their day – 'too many' says head.

Background and Atmosphere: Founded in 1865 for farmers' sons, is going through something of a renaissance and is currently wildly fashionable – 'the school has become very popular since Guy Waller became head,' was how one prospective parent put it. Another described how it was her daughter's 'dream come true' to get in. Set in stunning grounds totalling some 200 acres, the school certainly fulfils every expectation of an English boarding school. Beautiful, impressive façade – breathtaking architecture which continues inside to the chapel, library, quad.

Six houses: 4 boys, 2 girls. Boarding houses seem well designed – the newer ones are obviously more swish with bright and airy feel, dorms (generally sleep four) on the whole seem like the typical teenage bedroom – posters on wall, clothes strewn everywhere, but a homely atmosphere. Dining hall atmospheric, pupils help themselves from a choice of food – 'rather like motorway services,' says head. Boarding is actively encouraged – majority do board – not out of necessity but desire to engage in all the school has to offer. If you are looking for a school where the kids are home at 4.00pm lounging around and chatting to parents, forget it – this is not the school for you. Absolutely key at Cranleigh are the sporting/extracurricular opportunities and a long school day – whether you are boarding or not. A parent of a day pupil commented 'she loves the social whirl and doesn't want to come straight home.'

Pupils are encouraged to eat, sleep, and breathe Cranleigh. They are busy from dawn till dusk – school day is from 7.30am until potentially 9.00pm at night. 'If they really want to go home after that, they can,' says head. Everyone is expected to participate in the school fully and the head is very pro boarding and quite disparaging of what he calls 'five day' schools. Do expect resistance if your boarding child wishes to change to being a day pupil. Parents have been told it's disruptive to boarders, and affects the school's cash flow.

Everyone has Saturday school virtually every Saturday, and over a third of boarders stay at the weekend – although one boarding pupil said 'we all go home at the weekend' so it depends what a particular peer group does. A number of parents we talked to felt that there should be more weekend exeats. 'My children aren't usually home till 6.30pm on a Saturday, which makes going away for the weekend or seeing friends very difficult' said one parent of day pupils. Boarders need to be back by 7.0pm on a Sunday, so an even shorter weekend for them.

Pastoral Care and Discipline: Christian values underpin school society. Huge crackdown in recent years on sloppy discipline – drugs definitely not tolerated in any way; two boys expelled recently for drugs possession, although 'those expulsions surprised nobody,' says a not-particularly-shocked parent. Personal possession of alcohol and smoking are also big no-nos leading to a variety of sanctions including gating and detentions. Persistent offenders will be suspended. Sex education, not surprisingly, is quite high up the agenda here and romantic attachments between pupils are definitely discouraged. 'Inappropriate' sexual behaviour will lead to suspension or expulsion.

Head says that whole feel of school is 'more like a university' and that pupils will need self-reliance. Pupils' daily pastoral care is managed within each of the six houses and weekly meeting between head and tutors allows specific problems to be discussed. Bullying is tackled via the tutorial/house system where pupils can talk in confidence. Individual housemasters and housemistresses have their own views on mobile phones, going out etc – it's the luck of the draw – 'nonsense!' says the head, 'the only variation is whether the house actually collects phones overnight/during prep.' Surprisingly, considering tough line on transgression, school is not a pageant of well turned out pupils – lots of customised uniform in evidence, stiletto heels, short skirts, and funky hairstyles. Sixth formers wear suits – but for some girls the word suit is no way synonymous with smart and Mr W is trying to tidy them up. All this trendy dishevelment and urban cool seems a bit incongruous in such glorious surroundings.'

Pupils and Parents: Interestingly, for a predominantly boarding school, parents tend to be from quite a small, local radius (certainly no more than 30 miles is the norm) – and it's not unusual for parents to actually live in Cranleigh. Parents are 'a mix of backgrounds' says head – although as the school is hardly cheap presumably most are well-heeled

(though Mr W keen to stress that a significant number have bursarial assistance). One parent said that school is 'like a movie set – full of beautiful people' and certainly pupils are particularly cool souls who come across as mature, self-possessed individuals.

Entrance: The entrance list is opened in May, 2 1/2 years before September entry. Candidates and parents interviewed for interests/values/aspirations – conditional offers based on these and prep school reports, pending CE results. School very oversubscribed so they can afford to be choosy about who gets in. Head is looking for pupils who 'enjoy being at school and have the capability to be interested in a wide range of things.' For entrance to the sixth form (about 15-20 come in at this stage), the expectations are fairly modest: three Bs and three Cs at GCSE. Candidates will also be interviewed and reports sought from previous head. Sixth formers in general would be expected to board.

Exit: 15 or 20 a year leave at 16 for 'places offering more diverse AS/A2 courses than us', but the vast majority stay and go on to a wide range of universities – most popular recently include Nottingham, Exeter, Bristol, Leeds, Oxford Brookes with 8 or 9 a year to Oxbridge.

Money Matters: Fees are by no means cheap, but most parents seem to feel that 'you get what you pay for' with the huge amount on offer. There are scholarships available – academic, music, art and the Eric Abbott for candidates of 'strong academic ability and at least one other area of excellence' - up to a maximum of 25 per cent of fees for the top awards. Other than that you'll need to remortgage.

Remarks: Hugely popular school with loads on offer, improving academia and mega street cred. Ideal for the sporty, energetic, sociable, and independent child.

CROYDON HIGH SCHOOL

Linked to Croydon High Junior School in the Junior section

Old Farleigh Road, Selsdon, South Croydon, Surrey, CR2 8YB

Tel: 020 8651 5020
Fax: 020 8657 5413
E-mail: info2@cry.gdst.net
Website: www.gdst.net/croydonhigh

• Pupils: 520 girls, all day • Ages: 11-18 • Size of sixth form: 80
• Non-denom • Fees: £2,383 - £3,063 • Independent • Open
days: October

Head: Since 1998, Ms Lorna Ogilvie BSc MSc PGCE (fifties). Educated Mary Erskine School Edinburgh. A geographer, started her career at Inverness High before heading south to the Royal Russell. Head of St Margaret's Aberdeen for 10 years before taking the reins at Croydon. Down-to-earth, forward thinking and approachable, say both parents and pupils. A keen sportswoman in earlier days, says her interest and knowledge of music has been kindled by Croydon's highly successful music department. Aims to produce independent, confident girls who achieve their potential in all areas of life.

Academic Matters: GCSE results excellent, more than 65 per cent A/A*, after that mainly B's. Strong all round with good reputation for sciences, languages and English. Some lovely new light science and language labs, with the latest in resources. 80-ish per cent A and B grades at A level; strong maths, chemistry – even physics. Library and ICT centre are open until 5 pm run by enthusiastic staff – the new librarian will find you anything, say girls. Well-stocked library includes audio books and DVDs, inspiring place to work, desks looking out onto beautiful grounds. Reasonable mixture of long serving and new younger staff. Experienced SENCO runs special needs provision which includes screening and running non lesson time study skills groups.

Games, Options, The Arts: Something for everyone. Energetic sporting calendar, fielding teams for hockey, netball, tennis, cross country, rounders and gymnastics. School has won the netball national finals 14 times in the last three decades and is successful in many other national events. Large sports centre which doubles as a private club, houses gym, sports hall, dance studios and pool, where the highly successful swimming teams train. Recreational sports include badminton, self-defence, table tennis, aerobics and salsa. Thriving D of E Award scheme, also regular field trips

as well as adventure holidays, music tours and skiing. Sixth formers are encouraged to be involved in the supervisory roles around the school and run clubs. Sixth form activities programme offers over 10 non exam options. Very accessible Careers Centre which maintains links with outside agencies.

'Music to die for' say parents, instrumental tuition available on almost any instrument including tuba and harpsichord. Wonderful choirs, orchestras and bands in-house; Fairfield Hall concerts are always a sell out, musicians involved at local and national levels. The school holds its own annual chamber music competition judged by an external adjudicator. Music and drama departments work together to produce spectacular musicals each year. Great art department with an open door policy, professional artist runs life drawing classes, very popular extra with sixth formers. Pottery studio and dark room recently opened.

Background and Atmosphere: Founded in 1874, moved to its present purpose-built site in 1966. Buildings rather utilitarian from the outside, excellent well proportioned rooms inside. Classrooms well maintained, cheerful; high-quality up to date facilities. Superb sporting and recreational space – a few well-loved school pets enjoy the grounds too. Friendly comfortable atmosphere – many links encouraged between older and younger girls.

Pastoral Care and Discipline: Head likes to keep rules to a minimum; most are common sense or based on health and safety requirements. Deputy and school nurse look after counselling, recently set up 'Friendly Faces' a scheme where year 11 and sixth formers are trained to counsel and befriend younger pupils.

Pupils and Parents: Pupils come from over a hundred feeder independent and state primaries. The majority comes from a 5 mile radius around the school but the catchment stretches from south London to rural Surrey. Mostly professional, reasonable racial mix – over a dozen nationalities in the school. The school recently welcomed a group of Chinese students from the Shenzhen Province who have joined the sixth form. Old Girls: Jacqueline du Pré, Helen Chadwick, Elizabeth Laird, Jean Uro, Jane Warr, Marilyn Cutts, Rabbi Helen Freeman, the list goes on.

Entrance: At 11, annual entrance test in January, also informal interview with the head or deputy. All those offered places attend a special induction day during the summer term before entry. At 16, interview, report from the previous school and seven GCSEs grade C or above.

Exit: 8-10 a year to Oxbridge, otherwise anywhere from London to Edinburgh. Dual degrees becoming particularly popular: engineering or law with modern languages. Handful leave at 16 to other schools or sixth form colleges.

Money Matters: Standard GDST scholarships and bursaries are available. Music scholarship for year 7 entrant and Jacqueline du Pré scholarship for year 12. Considered very good value for money by parents.

Remarks: Consistently good results for arts and academics. Suits lively, motivated girls; probably not for the dreamers.

CULFORD SCHOOL

Culford, Bury St Edmunds, Suffolk, IP28 6TX

Tel: 01284 728 615

Fax: 01284 729 146

E-mail: admissions@culford.co.uk

Website: www.culford.co.uk

- Pupils: 335 girls and boys (140 board) in senior school • Ages: 13-18 in senior school; 2-8 in pre-prep, 9-13 in prep • Size of sixth form: 170 • Methodist foundation • Independent • Open days: Beginning of October and November but prospective parents are welcome to book a visit at any time

---

Headmaster: Since 2004, Mr Julian Johnson-Munday (early forties), educated Norwich School, Leicester (Eng lit) and Durham (MBA). Previously housemaster at Cranleigh and deputy head at Mill Hill. Married with one son. Highly approachable, unstuffy and energetic, he refers to himself as a 'shameless hustler' when it comes to furthering the interests of the school. He feels the school has languished in anonymity in the past, even in the area, and is busy giving it a higher profile. He is very keen to invest in the boarding side (he aims at half and half day and boarding), and has already done a lot to improve the provision of weekend activities. School should be 'challenging, enriching and fun'.

Academic Matters: Results are very sound indeed, considering the wide ability range, with 92 per cent achieving 5+ A-C grades at GCSE and 72 per cent A-C at A level. The 2002 inspection was concerned that provision was not as good as it could be at the top and bottom of the spectrum. Now, an excellent SEN teacher liaises with subject staff to support pupils with difficulties (individual help is an extra), and scholarship pupils (and anyone else who wants to) attend an extra-curricular course of challenging lectures, organised by a newly appointed head of scholars.

Since the new head's arrival, many classrooms are very high-tech – there are computers, laptops and interactive whiteboards everywhere – and IT is thoroughly integrated into lessons. The classics are alive and well, with extra-curricular Greek attracting good numbers. French is largely compulsory at GCSE, with German and Spanish as the other modern languages. Science is very strong and has its own state of the art centre. Roughly a half do separate sciences at GCSE.

Choice of subjects at GCSE and A level is, at least for the moment, fairly strictly mainline academic. Until September 2006, when psychology will be on offer at A level, the only '-ology' is biology.

Classes are small (average 16, maximum 24 across the school, average 10 in 6th form). The school day is quite packed, with a very short 40 minute lunch hour break, to accommodate 8 periods (4 on Saturday), plus every day after school activities. Day pupils don't leave until 5.30pm. There is a well-established system of rewards for good work (which add up to bronze, silver and gold medals), and closely monitored sanctions for unsatisfactory work.

Games, Options, The Arts: Provision for sport is nothing short of spectacular – a 25m indoor pool, squash courts, fitness suite, huge sports hall, floodlit Astroturf and games pitches as far as the eye can see. Competition within the school and with other schools very much encouraged. The new head has introduced CCF and clay pigeon shooting to add to an already impressive list of outdoor activities. He hopes in the future to improve facilities for music and drama, although these departments do well even as thing are, and there is already a very good dance studio. There is a wide range of choirs, bands and orchestras, plenty of concerts and two major dramatic productions annually. Art is clearly imaginatively taught in pleasant, lively studios, but it would be nice to see more of the pupils' efforts around the place.

Background and Atmosphere: The main building is a fine late 18th century mansion (with much older bits), originally belonging to the Cornwallis who lost the American war of independence, and it is gloriously set in 480 acres of beautiful well-kept parkland, with a fine grade 1 listed bridge and a garden designed by Humphrey Repton. The interior of the main building, with the exception of the large and rather gloomy assembly hall, is ravishing. The head's study was Lady Cadogan's boudoir, the very fine library served as Queen Alexandra's dining room, and giggling new pupils may be taken to see the loo where Edward 7th once sat enthroned. Dotted about are various pleasant purpose built subject blocks (some the result of handsome bequests), and boarding houses. The latter are currently undergoing a major overhaul. Comfort in the one already finished is definitely 5 star. Everywhere is amazingly tidy, well equipped and well cared for. Uniform is worn throughout the school, with girls in long pleated skirts looking rather quaint and elegant. Pupils and parents alike rate the school highly and one has the feeling of a quietly self-confident, happy establishment.

Pastoral Care and Discipline: A thoroughly efficient hierarchy, responsible for care and discipline, operates, in which everyone seems to know where they are and who to turn to. Discipline problems are very rare – it helps, of course, that the school is well away even from the very minor fleshpots of Bury St. Edmunds. The ethos of the school is decidedly Christian, with two religious assemblies a week, but not overtly denominational. The parish church in the grounds is used by the school.

Pupils and Parents: 25 per cent of pupils are Services children, 11 per cent from overseas (lots of German girls and boys doing a year or two at the school, quite a few Hong Kong and mainland Chinese). Otherwise pupils are very much East Anglian, coming from within a radius of 50 miles, and from middle class professional and business backgrounds. A sizeable number of families have attended the school for generations. Old Culfordians are generous in their support eg William Miller, who funded the building of the splendid science block.

Entrance: Not highly selective, entry is by exam and interview at 13, and 6 A-C passes are required for the sixth form. Pupils come from local prep schools (including Culford prep) and from state schools.

Exit: Most go on to further education, with a good smattering making it to Oxford and Cambridge.

Money Matters: Various academic, sport and arts scholarships (up to 50 per cent of fees) and exhibitions (up to 25 per cent), renewable annually. Up to 4 boarding scholarships, various bursaries and Services allowances.

Remarks: A well rounded, thoroughly reliable school, in a wonderful setting, which deserves to be better known.

D'OVERBROECK'S COLLEGE

The Swan Building, 111 Banbury Road, Oxford, Oxfordshire, OX2 6JX

Tel: 01865 310 000
Fax: 01865 552 296
E-mail: mail@doverbroecks.com
Website: www.doverbroecks.com

- Pupils: 210 boys and girls in the sixth form, of whom approx 45 per cent board. About 80 in Leckford • Ages: 16-19; Leckford Place 11-16 • Size of sixth form: 210 • Non-denom • Fees: Years 9-11 £3,370; sixth form £4,850. Boarding £6,050 - £7,265 • Independent • Open days: February, May and October

Principal: Since 1996, Mr Sami Cohen BSc (forties). Educated in the Middle East followed by A levels in London, Mr Cohen read chemistry and French at Leeds. He first joined d'Overbroeck's in 1979, became director of studies, left, went to Paris, came back, et voila … . Teaches languages, though not currently, French, Italian; sympa, thoughtful, quiet sense of humour, knows absolutely everything about everyone,thoroughly competent. Married, with three young children.

Head of Leckford Place School: Since 2005, Mr Mark Olejnik (late forties); has a first in history and ancient history. Joined d'Overbroeck's from Bury Lawn School in Milton Keynes, where he was deputy head.

Academic Matters: d'Overbroeck's Sixth Form – huge numbers of subjects on offer (40 at present); serious labs, good library, tiny classes – max ten. 'Rigorously academic', excellent teaching (north Oxford of course), terrific staff specialising in A levels need one say more? Third-year-sixth picks up any retakes from other schools or extra A levels for a career change. Almost any combination possible, three or four A levels the norm. Good university advice and UCAS pick up

Leckford Place School – for many years d'Overbroeck's had some students joining at 13 – something of an 'alternative' environment. In 2005 they established Leckford Place School 11 to 16 year olds on a separate site. Target intake per year group of 40-45, max class size is 15. Entry at 11+ and 13+. d'Overbroeck's says 'focus still very much on the individual, small class approach, a school where the individual child is at the centre of everything the school does'. We have yet to visit – or indeed hear much from parents.

Games, Options, The Arts: Sixth Form: serious art room, with sculpture, pottery, ceramics, fashion design, print making et al. Good music, games provision improving all the time from previous rather ad hoc basis (now two afternoons a week) – voluntary in the sixth form. Theatre studies dept have an arrangement with a company in Oxford for hands-on experience. Strong debating. Good IT and music technology. Special medic and vet and Oxbridge courses. The facilities are there, it is rather up to the pupil to enjoy.

Leckford Place School: 'PE and sport play important part in the life of the school'.

Background and Atmosphere: Sixth Form: two main sites near to each other and close to city centre. All pupils expected to find their own lunch but food available to buy in the student common room/cafe. University environment, informal, relaxed, friendly but focused. No uniform.

Leckford Place School: we shall see.

Easter revision courses (GCSE, AS and A levels). Jazz holiday courses for ages 10-16.

Pastoral Care and Discipline: Sixth Form: 40 per cent of all sixth formers board, either in the college-owned student accommodation – super bedrooms, ghastly carpet – or with host families organised by and well known to the college. The rest are day. No boarding facilities for juniors. All students have personal tutors. Attendance and work rate very closely monitored. Regular feedback to parents.

Pupils and Parents: Sixth Form: Those who want or need an alternative to more trad schools.

Leckford aiming to see parents 'as partners: open door policy.'

Entrance: At 11+ and 13+: own exam, references and interview.

Sixth form entry: references, interview and minimum of 5 GCSE passes.

Exit: Universities all over. Tops (in order) for 2004 were Bristol, Imperial, Oxford Brookes, University College, Edinburgh, Manchester, Oxford, Royal Holloway, St Andrews, Warwick.

Money Matters: Academic scholarships, science scholarships and art scholarships available. New performing art scholarship.

Remarks: Probably the most exciting school for secondary education in Oxford, and a very strong candidate for the best independent sixth form college in the UK.

The new Leckford Place junior school is, to us, an unknown.

DAME ALICE HARPUR SCHOOL

Linked to Dame Alice Harpur Junior School in the Junior section

Cardington Road, Bedford, Bedfordshire, MK42 0BX

Tel: 01234 340 871
Fax: 01234 344 125
E-mail: enquiries@dahs.co.uk
Website: www.dahs.co.uk

- Pupils: 910 girls, all day • Ages: 7-18 • Size of sixth form: 176
- Fees: Senior £2,898; Junior £2,075 • Independent
- Open days: October and May

Head: Since 2000, Mrs Jill Berry BA (forties). Married to a further education science inspector. No children. Studied English at Manchester then completed an MEd at Liverpool. First job teaching English at Range High School, Formby. Has taught in both the maintained and independent sectors at comprehensive, selective, boys', girls' and co-ed schools. Before moving to Dame Alice, was deputy head at Nottingham High School for Girls GDST. Very down to earth and approachable. Her door is 'always open to staff and pupils.' Teaches year 7 every year and so knows all the current year 7 to 11 girls by name. Knows most of the other pupils by sight and attends as many events as possible; can be seen regularly on the touchline cheering on the girls. Her aim is for each girl to fulfil her potential, whatever her talents, and hopes they develop into friendly and confident, but not arrogant, girls.

Academic Matters: Not too highly selective but excellent results nonetheless. 99 per cent A*-C grades at GCSE; particularly fine results in maths and double science, despite separate sciences for the stars. Around 80 per cent A/B at A level, with chemistry and English notably strong and popular. Setting in maths from year 6; girls in year 7 choose two out of three languages (French, German and Spanish) and add Latin. GCSE Greek can be taken in twilight sessions. Every girl takes nine GCSEs and is expected to achieve at least eight passes to go into the sixth form with at least a B grade in the chosen A level subject. Traditional subjects offered at A level, also Spanish and English language and, now, psychology. In the sixth form there's a range of examined and non-examined supplementary courses, including fitness training, preparation for driving, self-defence and study skills. Class sizes in years 7 and 8 can be 24 or 25 but this reduces in subjects where there is setting and girls are taught in groups of, at most, 24 in science and in half form groups for all practical activities. Class sizes further reduce as GCSEs approach.

Games, Options, The Arts: Excellent facilities on site include a floodlit, all-weather area which provides one full hockey pitch, two seven-a-side hockey pitches, 12 tennis courts and six netball courts. There is also a gym, excellent indoor pool, fitness suite and versatile sports hall which stages indoor hockey events. Hockey is the main sport but, because of the school's closeness to the Great Ouse, rowing has grown in popularity over the last decade and girls have enjoyed increasing success in local and national events: some internationals.

Excellent music and drama, with 400 individual music lessons and 45 speech and drama lessons taking place each week. The girls often join forces with pupils from other schools to put on productions – from small informal gatherings to major concerts where the other three Harpur Trust Schools (Bedford High School, Bedford Modern and Bedford School) combine to fill the Birmingham Symphony Hall. Girls can also join the CCF along with boys from Bedford School where they can learn to scuba dive and fly, among other things. Thriving clubs including debating and a popular Saturday Youth Theatre group.

Background and Atmosphere: The school was opened in 1882 to receive 58 girls who were among the earliest in the country to enjoy an education previously reserved for boys. One of four schools of the Bedford Charity, the Harpur Trust, which benefit equally from the generous endowment of Sir William Harpur (a Bedford merchant who became Lord Mayor of London in 1566) and his wife Dame Alice. The school moved to its present site, a short walk from the town centre and by the banks of the Great Ouse, in 1938. Makes education available to as many girls as possible through the Harpur Bursary scheme. Modern buildings surrounded by attractive gardens and playing fields. Two listed Georgian houses provide a sixth form centre and music facilities. A purpose-built drama studio and separate drama room have been sympathetically added. The most recent building project has enhanced the art and textiles facilities and a new sixth form common room is planned for September 2006.

Pastoral Care and Discipline: Discipline does not seem an issue. No 'rule book'. Girls know what is expected of them.

Pupils and Parents: A wide mix from a large catchment area attracting pupils from many corners of Bedfordshire. Some parents make considerable sacrifices to send their girls here. A mix from state primaries and prep schools. Some girls come by train; others make use of the coach service which has been set up jointly by local coach companies and parents.

Entrance: At 11,12 and 13 girls have a group interview then take a test in English, maths and verbal reasoning. 47 took the 11+ entrance test in 2005 and 40 girls were awarded places. The head insists on writing to each girl individually to say whether they have been successful or to explain why they have not met the required standard. 'I believes it's important to explain why I don't feel a girl will benefit from a Dame Alice education rather than just telling them they haven't got in.' There is no waiting list but parents can contact the school at any time to see if places become available.

Exit: A dozen girls leave post-GCSE, for financial reasons or to pursue courses not available here. Most go on to university or further education. A handful to Oxbridge. Old Girls include Jean Muir, designer, and Gail Emms, Olympic silver medallist in badminton 2004.

Money Matters: No scholarships. The head and governors feel strongly that a Dame Alice education should be available to as many girls as possible and are able to offer a number of bursaries through the Harpur Bursary scheme.

Remarks: A large school in numbers but with a small school feel. Girls seem happy and confident and enjoy school life, take pride in their appearance and, although trousers have been introduced as an option from year 7 upwards, the majority wear the smart navy skirt. Girls come with a broad range of ability but end up producing excellent exam results.

DAME ALICE OWEN'S SCHOOL

Dugdale Hill Lane, Potters Bar, Hertfordshire, EN6 2DU

Tel: 01707 643 441
Fax: 01707 645 011
E-mail: admin.damealiceowen@thegrid.org.uk
Website: www.damealiceowens.school-portal.co.uk

• Pupils: 1,400 boys and girls • Ages: 11-18 • Size of sixth form: 430 • Non-denom • State

Head: Since 2005, Dr Alan Davison (late forties). Two previous headships. Married with four children.

Academic Matters: An all-ability comprehensive but definitely not 'bog standard.' Results and facilities are a match for some independent schools in the area, which is why the school is so popular. Some 96 per cent of pupils achieve five GCSEs at grade A* to C. Good A level results too. At 11 pupils are placed in an upper, middle or lower band for their first three years. Class sizes are around 30, reducing to 20 at GCSE. Some subject setting is introduced from year 7. Science is taught on an integrated basis for two years then separately in year 9.

The school was awarded Language College status in 1996, and offers Spanish, Italian, Chinese, Portugese and Japanese as well as French and German. For budding classicists there is now Latin – hooray! At 11, pupils take French, Spanish or German then, in year 8, they all study an extra language. The vast majority of pupils stay on for A levels. Some leave to pursue GNVQs elsewhere as only ASs and A2s offered here.

Games, Options, The Arts: Sports facilities are impressive for a state school. There is a large sports hall, floodlit, all-weather Astroturf pitch and games field. Boys enjoy soccer, rugby, hockey, cricket, athletics, cross-country, gym, badminton and basketball. Girls play football, netball, hockey, badminton, cross-country, athletics, tennis, rounders and crickets. County and national representatives.

Music is also strong – some 400 learn a musical instrument. There are two full orchestras. The symphony orchestra has come second in the National Festival of Music for Youth at the Royal Festival Hall twice. There are also five chamber groups, three bands and four choirs. Music tours abroad to France and Austria. Drama is also popular with regular productions. New performance arts centre and concert hall which has been well supported by former pupil, Gary Kemp of Spandau Ballet.

Background and Atmosphere: Alice Wilkes, thrice widowed by a brewer, a mercer and lastly by Judge Thomas Owen, established a school for 30 boys from Islington in 1613. She entrusted the running of the school to the Worshipful Company of Brewers who, for the past three and three-quarter centuries, have supported and encouraged the school. A girls' school was added in 1886 and in the late sixties a search was made for a new location. The new school opened on its present site – 35 acres on the southern borders of Potters Bar in Hertfordshire – in 1973. Today, all year 7s receive one crown each at a ceremony at Brewers Hall in the City of London.

The school entrance is welcoming and pupils' work is well displayed around the school. Buildings are modern and purpose-built. In 1989 the trustees provided the Edinburgh Centre to house computer suites, labs and a high-tech library. Arts facilities are a little cramped. Smart school uniform – red V-neck jumper and dogtooth check kilt for girls. Black jacket and dark grey trousers for boys.

Pastoral Care and Discipline: Innovative way of dealing with bullying and other issues. A sixth form group called Talk 33 provides a sensible ear for anyone in the lower school.

Pupils and Parents: A wide mix from a large catchment area attracting pupils from the northern reaches of Hertfordshire through parts of Essex and down to north London. This does mean some pupils travel quite long distances by bus and train which, as one pupil said, 'can affect friendships.'

Entrance: Unusual admission rules. Well oversubscribed. Some 1,400 children compete for 200 places. Siblings take priority, then 65 places awarded on academic ability. Tests in English, maths and verbal reasoning. Ten places for musical aptitude. Then places offered to applicants from specific parts of Hertfordshire, Barnet and Enfield, plus 20 places to children living in or at school in Islington.

Exit: About 10 per cent leave post-GCSE to pursue courses elsewhere – to start A level courses pupils must have five GCSEs at grade C and above. Vast majority go on to higher education after A levels. Twenty-two pupils won Oxbridge places in 2005.

Remarks: A school that shines out in the state sector. Self-motivated pupils genuinely enjoy themselves. 'What you put in is what you get out,' said one. It's a friendly school where pupils are keen to get on and committed teachers are proud of their academic record. Notable former pupils include the Kemp brothers, Dame Beryl Grey and Joss Ackland.

DAME ALLAN'S BOYS' SCHOOL

Linked to Dame Allan's Girls' School in the Senior section

Linked to Linden School in the Junior section

Linked to Dame Allan's Schools Junior Department in the Junior section

Fowberry Crescent, Fenham, Newcastle upon Tyne, Tyne and Wear, NE4 9YJ

Tel: 0191 275 0608
Fax: 0191 2751502
E-mail: l.stephenson@dameallans.co.uk
Website: www.dameallans.co.uk

• Pupils: 900, all day. Seniors: 300 boys, 280 girls; juniors 55 boys, 40 girls. Plus Linden Prep (a separate entity) • Ages: Seniors 11-18, juniors 8-11, Linden Prep 3-11 • Size of sixth form: 220 • Christian foundation • Fees: Linden £1,370; Junior £1,899; Senior £2,413 • Independent

Principal: Since 2004, Dr John Hind (mid forties), read history at Cambridge, previously deputy head of Kingston Grammar and before that at Durham School.

Academic Matters: Given it's not the usual first choice for Newcastle's academically ambitious, results are consistently respectable: A level A/B grades above 60 per cent. Good haul of As, no obvious weak points. Much more academic confidence evident since previous head's arrival. Popular subjects: English, French and German (flourishing exchanges), geography, economics, psychology, science. Girls tend to do better than boys at A level. GCSE very solid, again with good results in geography and languages; A*+A hover around 60 per cent. Pupils need 5 A*-C GCSEs to do AS/A2, including B/A/A* in chosen subjects. MIDYIS and ALIS value-added markers used; too early to draw firm conclusions. Average class sizes, 10 in years 7-9, 20 in years 10-11. All must take one language to GCSE; 60 per cent do separate sciences.

Dame Allan's big selling point to parents and pupils is its mix of co-education and single sex: boys and girls taught together 8-11, separately 11-16, together again in sixth form, ie kept apart during difficult adolescence. It works, they all say. Support from Dyslexia Institute one day a week; school has its own SEN co-ordinator. All pupils screened on arrival. Staff turnover about 10 per cent; good balance between stayers and movers.

Games, Options, The Arts: Lots of sport for both girls and boys – eight pupils have played at national level in recent years. Participation stressed. Grand sports hall, plenty of room for games on site; nearby swimming pool, all-weather area, extra pitches hired as and when. Many team tours to far-flung places (S Africa, Barbados, Canada). Wide range of minor sports, actively followed.

Nature of site limits extensive activity in music and drama, but both well supported – music particularly lively. National reputation for dance (girls and boys learn together). Excellent careers department.

School takes its Christian foundation seriously: many links with local charities and churches (two services each year in cathedral, Dean is ex-officio governor). Links in schools in eg Kenya, India, Bolivia, Borneo. Vigorous outdoor activities programme: D of E, regular overseas expeditions (Uganda, Mongolia, Bolivia, Ecuador).

Background and Atmosphere: Founded 1705 by Dame Eleanor Allan, widow of wealthy merchant, to educate 40 poor boys and 20 poor girls from three city-centre parishes (trades for the boys, sewing for the girls). Moved 1935 to Fenham; this rather dreary suburb now encircles open 13-acre site. Long range of fairly unprepossessing buildings; flagpole outside midpoint used to mark frontier between boys and girls – and their heads – up to 1988. Schools now coexist easily, working identical curriculums. Much useful interdependence, though separate 11-16 identities preserved. Most staff teach in both schools.

Facilities being modernised in thorough continuous programme, especially art, ICT and labs (£3.5m in last 8 years). New building planned, including sixth form centre, dance/drama studios; all-weather pitch under way. Computer provision being extended.

Inescapably hugger-mugger conditions of life have been turned to remarkable advantage by staff and students. Boys' and girls' behaviour ('exemplary', according to recent ISI inspection) seems to be largely self-regulated, responsible and tolerant. Cheerfully chaotic sixth form common room scheduled for upgrade.

Everyone matters, eg sick pupil recently visited in hospital by dinner lady. Students' official handbook/diary a model of its kind. As well as eg How to study/What to do if/Where the labs are, there are three pages on spelling and punctuation. Hooray.

Pastoral Care and Discipline: All staff involved in traditional pastoral care system; high expectations come from the top. Staff/pupil relationships clearly defined but easy: 'Do as I do' is the rule. Boys and girls appreciate being taken seriously, are expected to look after each other – interesting

'Link' scheme, whereby 24 trained sixth formers act as strictly confidential listeners via drop-in sessions for other students. Good discipline really does seem to issue from shared objectives, while avoiding caring/sharing daftness – which would hardly catch on in Geordieland anyway. Suspension for antisocial behaviour (three cases in last three years), usually after 'totting-up' process. Drugs = sacking (no recent cases).

Pupils and Parents: Numbers holding up despite end of Assisted Places scheme. Pupils come from as far as Durham and Berwick, or walk round the corner to school; much pride in keeping up service to local community. Wide social mix of parents, many Asians (non-Christian faiths easily accommodated). 'No snootiness about the place,' said last head. Former pupils include Peter (Lord) Pilkington (a Fenham scholarship boy), Anne Gibbs, Ian La Frenais, Sir David Lumsden.

Entrance: Via own entrance exam and interview at 11 and 13 (strong entry at this stage from prep schools). 50 per cent of entry from junior department (which has its own entrance exam) plus 3-11 prep school. About 20 leave each year after GCSE to FE/sixth form colleges; 8-10 enter.

Exit: Almost all to higher/further education; a handful to Oxbridge, many to Durham. Popular courses: medicine, English, law, engineering, modern languages.

Money Matters: 'Good value', said previous head, and indeed it is; Newcastle fees among lowest in country. Some academic scholarships (up to half fees) on entry, six bursaries every year (up to 100 per cent). Some academic scholarships in junior department.

Remarks: A no-frills, thriving school, retaining the best of city grammar school ethos; strong social sense. Happy amalgam of twin schools; pupils (and staff?) benefit in terms of common sense and maturity. Not an academic powerhouse, but will bring out the best in above-average as well as average girl or boy who reacts positively to family atmosphere.

DAME ALLAN'S GIRLS' SCHOOL

Linked to Linden School in the Junior section

Linked to Dame Allan's Boys' School in the Senior section

Linked to Dame Allan's Schools Junior Department in the Junior section

Fowberry Crescent, Fenham, Newcastle upon Tyne, Tyne and Wear, NE4 9YJ

Tel: 0191 275 0708
Fax: 01912 751 502
E-mail: enquiries@dameallans.co.uk
Website: www.dameallans.co.uk

• Independent

Remarks: For Good Schools Guide entry see Dame Allan's Boys' School.

DAUNTSEY'S SCHOOL

West Lavington, Devizes, Wiltshire, SN10 4HE

Tel: 01380 814 500
Fax: 01380 814 501
E-mail: information@dauntseys.wilts.sch.uk
Website: www.dauntseys.wilts.sch.uk

• Pupils: 748; 52:48boys to girls; approx 40 per cent board
• Ages: 11-18 • Size of sixth form: 240 • Inter-denom • Fees: Day £3,980; boarding £6,720 • Independent • Open days: Early May and mid-October, boarding evenings late September and in March

Head: Since 1997, Mr Stewart Roberts (fiftyish), educated at Birkenhead School and St Peter's, Oxford, where he read physics. Previously housemaster at Shrewsbury School, he was the founding head of Chand Bagh School, Lahore, Pakistan. Briefly second master before being offered headship. Married to musician Anna, with two children, both now at Dauntsey's. Jovial, forward-thinking and caring.

Academic Matters: Imaginative expansion of academic curriculum and after-school programme in tandem has paid dividends in results at GCSE and A level. Excellent results in core subjects English language, maths and French at GCSE. Languages score well, although solid string of A* and A grades in Chinese a credit to the regular number of

Hong Kong based students. Dual and single sciences offered – strong results all round. In 2005 79 per cent of A level results were at grades A or B; at GCSE 67 per cent were A* or A.

Excellent art centre, housed in a former primary school building in the school grounds. Wide choice of 23 A levels, including biology, music and music technology, classical civilisation, physical education and theatre studies. Best results in the more standard subjects – maths, further maths, English Literature and languages real strengths.

Fabulous new library, with banks of computer booths – there are 300+ all told throughout the school. Teaching conducted in an atmosphere of easy-going discipline, with plenty of positive encouragement and clear explanation. Dauntsey's has been co-ed since 1972 so long enough for there to be little sign of friction or competition between the sexes – results show very little difference between boys and girls. Special needs support for dyslexics and non-native English speakers – there are a small number of these each year.

Games, Options, The Arts: Head is a passionate believer in rounded education that nurtures fulfilled, happy pupils. To this end the extra-long lunch hour and hours after classes are filled with clubs and activities, from bee-keeping and aerobics to model railways, kites and, for sixth formers, wine-tasting. It certainly seems to stop the boarders, rather marooned in a quiet Wiltshire backwater with only a Costcutters mini-market to pass for excitement, from becoming bored. Sport compulsory throughout the school, with a very wide choice of activities, even for non-games players.

Facilities are outstanding, with 120 acres of floodlit Astroturf and grass courts and pitches, a state-of-the-art gym, large heated indoor pool and options including horse-riding, canoeing and sub-aqua. Popularity of all sports – and the restaurant quality of the school canteen – clear from the rude health of the pupils. Ultimate in sporting options is ocean-sailing on the Jolie Brise, the school's own boat, a gaff cutter that won the Millennium Tall Ships race and three Fastnets. On site is a croquet lawn; at the Manor, the junior boarding house a mile away, is a nine-hole golf course and trout stream. Regular foreign tours – during 2005 there was both a netball tour to Malta and a rugby tour to Hong Kong and New Zealand.

Very outdoors orientated, with a big deal made of canoeing and trekking and the outward-bound course, called Moonrakers, compulsory for all year 9 pupils. Art centre open for individual work and venue for termly exhibitions – visits by students to galleries includes regular over-seas trips. Drama is very popular, taught in the first two years, for GCSE and in the sixth form and offered more informally via acting clubs and talks from visiting experts. Productions every term, either at the 700-seater Memorial Hall or the more intimate studio, with lighting and sound and room for 45. In 2003 the School performed Les Miserables to wide acclaim at The Prince of Wales Theatre, Leicester Square. Most pupils have individual music lessons. Two concerts a week is average, from rock to concertos, and the school is awash with choirs. Not a school to skimp, it also has its own recording studio.

Background and Atmosphere: Dauntsey's was founded in West Lavington in 1542 on the deathbed largesse of Sir William Dauntsey, master of the Worshipful Company of Mercers. Originally sited beside the village church, the large current school building opened in 1895. School remains closely linked to Mercers' Company. Absolutely drips money, evident from the moment you sweep up the drive, past the immaculate lawns to the pristine building, complete with entrance hall that could grace a five-star hotel. Similarly, The Manor, taken over as the junior boarding house in the 1930s from an impoverished landowner, boasts vast rooms around a stunning central staircase, overlooking floodlit tennis courts in one direction and views across the Vale of Pewsey in the other. Can feel a bit bleak on wintry days, not all traces of its pre-monied past yet extinguished. Dauntsey's is an immediately impressive school, not just because of the obvious affluence on display, but also the care and dedication given to providing the best in opportunities. Ask the head what he takes most pride in and he says, without hesitation, 'the boys and girls here'. Has a tangible family atmosphere, commented on by all visitors. New senior girls' boarding house opened 2005. Sludgy beige uniform now replaced with chirpy petrel blue, much more in line with the cheery feel of the place.

Pastoral Care and Discipline: Support broadly organised along house lines – day pupils and boarders are in separate houses. Big network of ready listeners – tutor, housemaster or housemistress, school counsellor, chaplain, school doctors and sanatorium staff, even former staff, depending on the problem. Student listening service, made up of specially trained pupils, have their photographs up for all to see, but can be contacted anonymously, via e-mail or scribbled note, as necessary. Rules seem a bit trendy liberal – 'a breach of common sense is a breach of the rules'. Apparently harder on smokers than on bullies, who broadly remain unpunished under non-confrontational approach, in return for a full confession and a promise not to do it again. Yet it appears to work, as bullying is rare and the nearest most pupils come to rebellion is colouring their hair (strictly forbidden here). Christian foundation but embraces other faiths – upper room with a nice view of the lawn set aside for quiet reflection by allcomers.

Pupils and Parents: Very confident pupils, smart in both senses and cosmopolitan, with good balance of largely Wiltshire and home-counties children and those with parents overseas. School took part in BBC programme Trading Places, with Dauntsey's pupils experiencing life at a Newcastle comprehensive and vice versa, and came out as level headed and adaptable. Mr Roberts subsequently tried to fund Newcastle pupils who had cried at leaving Dauntsey's, but good intentions foundered on the distance involved. Famous old Dauntseians include Thomas the Tank Engine creator Reverend Awdry, anthropologist Desmond Morris, TV theme writer Simon May and Sydney Olympic rowing silver medallists Miriam and Guin Batten.

Entrance: At eleven, 80 places are up for grabs by examination. Further 30 offered at age 13 via common entrance exam, and 25 join in sixth form on basis of school reports and predicted GCSE grades – 6 B grades the minimum, even for existing pupils. Extremely sibling friendly – half the school has a relation there.

Exit: Almost all go to university of their choice, mainly traditional ones, including at least half a dozen Oxbridge applicants. Art foundation and vocational courses are also popular.

Money Matters: Not cheap, but lots of scholarships and awards available at 11, 13 and 16 for outstanding scholars, artists, musicians, sportsmen (and women) and all-rounders. Clearly would try everything not to sacrifice talented potential pupils for lack of cash. Sad to lose assisted places, but will strive to make them up with help from the Mercers' Company and Old Dauntseians. Sizeable discounts for boarding siblings.

Remarks: Kind, sensible but also innately clever children in a nurturing environment.

DAVIES LAING AND DICK COLLEGE

100 Marylebone Lane, London, W1U 2QB

Tel: 020 7935 8411
Fax: 020 7935 0755
E-mail: dld@dld.org
Website: www.dld.org

- Pupils: 400 boys and girls, all day • Ages: 14-19 • Size of sixth form: 350 • Non-denom • Fees: £4,920 • Independent

Principal: Since 1996, Ms Elizabeth Rickards MA PGCE (fifties). Read history at St Andrews University. Spent ten years at Duff Miller College, including five years as Vice Principal. Joined DLD in 1993, and was appointed principal three years later. Has also worked at the Young Vic, and is passionate about the importance of creativity in education. Outstanding leader. 'She's very sharp, very quick, really on the ball,' said a parent. 'The kids know that they can't get away with anything.' 'She's fantastically persuasive,' said another, 'but most of what she said has been borne out by our experience.' Known to staff and students as 'Topsy': 'which shows our affection as well as our respect,' said one. Married.

Academic Matters: A small minority of pupils are there to do one- or two-year GCSE courses, the rest one- or two- year A level courses. There are also retake courses of varying length. Maximum class size: 10. Commendable results from a mixed-ability intake. Most GCSE students take eight subjects, from a limited list that includes the basics plus French, Spanish, business studies, ICT, art and drama. Latin, Greek and German are available via individual tuition. Generally over 80 per cent get 5+ A*-C grades.

A level students get a choice of 40 subjects, including Chinese, photography, film studies and law, in more-or-less any combination. Art, business studies and psychology are consistently popular, alongside English and maths; just over half of all grades are generally A or B.

Some students are disaffected when they arrive. 'But it is unusual for them to be anti-education after a few weeks. It's important to fit the right course to the right student. Because of the small class sizes they get lots of individual feedback and huge amounts of encouragement, and most start making progress very quickly.'

The college can cope with special needs such as dyslexia and dyspraxia, though not ADHD, generally picking up several previously undiagnosed cases each year. Most need group support with study and essay-writing skills; individual help is also available at extra cost. 'Our SEN students get more or less the same level of results as the others – due to getting the subjects right, and to plenty of support.'

No quarter is given academically: 'We will not accept scrappy work. We believe in raising standards and in making students believe they can move up to the next level.' Many staff are from Oxbridge, and come from non-teaching backgrounds: the theatre, the City, the BBC. 'They work unbelievably hard,' said an insider. 'They put in a lot of effort for the students.'

Games, Options, The Arts: A surprisingly arty college: A level art is one of the most popular and successful subjects, and several students are refugees from high-powered academic institutions where the creative side is less valued. The main aim of most students is to pass their exams, and extracurricular activities are not high on the agenda except for those in plays and sports teams. A level students, in particular, often work long days. However, all GCSE students play sport at local centres on Friday afternoons, including football, basketball, tennis, netball and aerobics, and there are sports clubs and matches after school. The DLD youth theatre puts on two performances a year; the house band – organised by the drummer of Van der Graaf Generator, who is also the music technology teacher – plays well-attended gigs; there are film, debating and art clubs.

Year 10 and 12 students take part in Activities Week at the end of June, which could involve putting together a newspaper or a CD, making a film, playing plenty of sport or going on an art trip to Italy.

Background and Atmosphere: Now one of a group owned by Alpha Plus, the college was founded in 1931 to provide tutoring for Oxbridge and Colonial Service entrance exams. After the second world war it began to specialise in A and O level teaching. In 2004 it moved from Notting Hill to light, airy, refurbished premises in Marylebone, with an 80-seater theatre, recording studio, three art studios, science labs and photography studio.

Informal atmosphere, closer to a college than a school, with staff and students on a first name basis. 'They're unfussy about clothes, and about students in clinches on the stairs,' said an insider. 'But academically they're pretty tough. Students don't get away with things.'

Pastoral Care and Discipline: Strong pastoral system. 'Many students have had a shifting lifestyle, and it's a real haven for them,' said an insider. 'There is a lot of respect, because students know we care about them.' An attendance officer checks that students are present at each lesson and contacts parents of absconders. Each student has a weekly meeting with their personal tutor, to talk about progress and future plans. Tough sanctions for misusing drink and drugs; those under suspicion are sent for drugs tests, to general parental approval. 'There are a few troubled and troublesome students,' said a parent, 'but most buckle down eventually.'

'Occasionally there are students we don't manage to turn round,' says the head. 'Then I'll often suggest to parents a gap year in the middle of the sixth form, preferably working in Waitrose. It concentrates their minds on the consequences of failing to work, and the difference in maturity when they come back is often amazing.'

Sanctions include detentions and supervised study, and there is a system of verbal and written warnings based on employment law. Bullying is taken very seriously. A few students are excluded, mostly for consistently failing to turn up, some for drug offences. 'They don't care about superficial things, but on work, drink, drugs and bullying they clamp down very quickly.'

Pupils and Parents: Most students have come from private schools. Some have had enough of boarding; some have been ill; some have found their previous school too rigid or too stressful. Others come from peripatetic diplomatic families. Some lack confidence, and need to learn good working habits. Most thrive in the informal but structured atmosphere.

Entrance: Those going into the sixth form need a minimum of 5 grade Cs at GCSE; if they haven't passed maths or English they will need to retake these. Everyone is interviewed, and previous schools are asked for references. The college will not consider students who have been disruptive elsewhere.

Exit: A few GCSE students move on elsewhere – perhaps to state sixth form colleges – but most go through to the sixth form. Those aiming at Oxbridge are given an intensive course including lectures, seminars, mock interviews and individual tuition; around half a dozen a year generally get places. Extra help also for potential vets, doctors and dentists. Arts foundation courses are popular; other students move on to a huge range of courses varying from mechanical engineering at Edinburgh to sports and exercise science at Brighton.

Money Matters: Several scholarships available, usually of 20 – 50 per cent of fees, plus bursaries.

Remarks: Good at stimulating the very bright as well as re-motivating the disaffected. Informal atmosphere with strong staff/student relationships underlies a structured regimen where everyone is kept up to scratch.

DEAN CLOSE SCHOOL

Linked to Dean Close Preparatory School in the Junior section

Shelburne Road, Cheltenham, Gloucestershire, GL51 6HE

Tel: 01242 258 000
Fax: 01242 258 003
E-mail: office@deanclose.org.uk
Website: www.deanclose.org.uk

• Pupils: 468 boys and girls: 118 day boys, 92 day girls plus 137 boys and 121 girls boarding • Ages: 13-18 • Size of sixth form: 190 • C of E (Anglican Foundation) although all denominations welcome • Fees: Day £4,640; boarding £6,585 • Independent • Open days: September, November, March and May

Head: Since 1998, the Revd Tim Hastie-Smith MA CertTheol (fortyish), who was educated at Cranleigh, followed by Magdalene. He took orders at Wycliffe Hall, Oxford. One of our favourite heads, dashing (lilac shirt, purple-patterned tie, orange and turquoise socks when we visited), personable and fun; he is relishing the challenge and enjoying it hugely. Taught briefly at Felsted between Oxford and Cambridge: St Nicholas Scholar, with three years curacy at St Ebbe's before going to Stowe in 1991 where he was chaplain (and a very popular one too), admissions tutor and head of theology. Married to 'the beautiful Joanne', with three children, the elder two are in the school, plus a 'brilliant new baby'. Hastie-Smith (nicknames Tastie-Hastie, Tastie Bits haven't changed) arrived to find the school in less affluent circumstances than he had been led to believe, and spent the first couple of years performing financial miracles. With two new boarding houses under his belt, a new pre-prep and a £2.5 million refurbishment of one of the boys' boarding houses underway (autumn 2003), he is now set to go for it. New sports hall scheduled for 2004. Lots of new staff employed, certain amount of 'dead wood' replaced, plus some dynamic new appointments: almost every housemaster/mistress and many new heads of departments. All bar one of the senior posts have changed. This is a school in flux. 'Shaking the school out of its time warp', says the head. New director of studies, new management structure (previous head insisted on signing all the cheques himself), loads of delegation. 'Each department should be autonomous.'

Head has spent time introducing pupils to the real world: regular and interesting programme of external speakers – ranging from Jonathan Aitken via Lord Marshall (of BA) to John Julius Norwich and Jilly Cooper. Plus serious entertaining in his own (rather grand) home, when he has up to 70 (mostly local) guests for a visiting speaker and supper, which 'raises the school profile'. Tries to get away from the previous slightly introverted evangelical image and invites both staff and pupils to face important challenges. Enthusiastic on promoting confidence (as do they all) and 'develop as people, YOU matter, you have a unique roll to play; you are significant, you have the ability to do something'.

Keen to raise the academic standard (and has already done so) and is 'flirting with the idea of IB'. Though whether he finds time to read all the books in his study is open to question: this editor will be first in line when he does a rummage sale (and he says he has many more at home).

Academic Matters: 'On the cusp, academically', increasingly more selective, though the average ability of students can vary from year to year. Class size 20, five streams in each year; all pupils must do RE at GCSE, and take it a year early, most also take the three sciences and English early too. Super labs, combining practical areas with 'proper' lecture auditorium. Huge variety of GCSEs: French, German, Spanish. Latin, Russian and Chinese successes.

We originally said that 'pupils are equipped with laptops on arrival, and can connect into the infrared networking facility throughout (only occasional glitches) which should connect them both to printers and to the internet'. This is apparently no longer true and, while they are essential for some lessons, only 90 per cent now have them, others lease them from the school. Head says 'IT is not an educational panacea, but it is a basic piece of kit which all must be competent and confident at using'. Pupils do super power point presentations. Excellent dyslexia provision, with a dedicated unit, including dyslexia-sensitive software, programme targeted for each child as necessary; as is EFL; pupils are assessed on arrival, and they are encouraged to take the relevant exams to enable them to enter British or American universities.

Games, Options, The Arts: Little change here: primarily a hockey school with national representation still at all levels, Decanians regularly feature at county and regional levels as well, and regularly reach National finals, their under 14 boys' team won in 2001 and, in 2002, the under 14 girls' team won. Rugby, cricket, tennis, sailing etc all on offer, 25-metre swimming pool not yet up to speed, and sports hall due for a revamp shortly (£1.5 million campaign). Water polo strong. Huge number of clubs, 120+ 'activities' on offer currently, everything from astronomy via clay pigeon shooting, to theatre maintenance and woodwork. The kit car building option means real cars, though perhaps not popular for driving lessons. Polo, yoga and Tai Bo are new entrants into the list. Plus octa hockey 'in which a small piece of wood around eight inches long is used to push a lead puck around on the bottom of the pool'; masks, fins and protective gloves are the only equipment required. Heptathlon as well as pentathlon. D of E as you might expect, CCF from the age of 13, though sixth formers have dropped it for community service: working with asylum seekers and wheelchair basketball popular, as well as teaching in a special needs school. Head is chairman of ISC Community Service Group.

Thriving Young Enterprise. And a host of spectacular trips all over. Currently seven scholars on various expeditions organised by the British Schools Exploration Society 'to undertake expeditions to harsh environments and to carry out adventure-related scientific fieldwork'.

Superlatives fail to describe the brilliant new music wing, attached by overhead bridge to professional theatre, much used by locals. Music vibrant, with a strong choral tradition and various orchestras. Music and drama very strong and timetabled with spectacular productions. Outdoor Tuckwell theatre in the grounds, CDT with CAD, and home economics for both sexes.

Background and Atmosphere: The school was founded in 1886 in memory of Dean Francis Close, Rector of Cheltenham for 30 years, before becoming Dean of Carlisle. 'Voluntary' Christian Union and Bible study still feature in each house; Christian ethics important. School worships together three times a week in the slightly austere chapel (porch with interesting stained glass). Head has replaced the compulsory weekly Sundays service for all (including day pupils) with evensong on Fridays, though all must still attend chapel on two fixed Sundays a term.

Set in 80 acres of manicured grounds, shared with prep school, who also share sports, some drama and music facilities. Original buildings much altered, with fantastic library like an upturned boat with beech galleries and refurbished parquet flooring. Spectacular lofty dining room, with 'God's Word a Guiding Light' inscribed below the rafters. Café-style feeding, vegetarian option. Modern cloisters with unusual sculptures contrast with older classrooms – many now revamped; and boarding houses, now almost all state of the art. Larger dorms have been divided into smaller cabins. Boarding encouraged and flexi-boarding on offer, strong family feel. Single rooms for (almost) all at the top of the school. Brilliant new girls' house.

New uniform 'on the stocks'; suits and trouser suits for older girls, and head was amazed to be approached by female staff on his arrival to be asked whether it was OK for them to wear trouser suits. Wow.

Pastoral Care and Discipline: House system, with houseparents and ancillary tutors. Dedicated houses for day children. Strong anti-bullying policy. Head expelled 'masses' his first year, but now discipline is 'firmly under control'. Out for OTT, but 'hardly anyone lately' – the odd one or two. Automatic expulsion for drugs and sex; warnings, followed by 'junkers' (hard labour/estate work) for booze, fines for fags.

Pupils and Parents: As we predicted, under the new regime, the profile has been gradually creeping up: the green wellie brigade is advancing. Fair number of ex-pats, military parents on the up (20 per cent) – they tend to choose the school and then buy a house in the area. Around 15 per cent of locals board, lots of self-employed people 'the mercantile gang', quite a number of proper foreigners – who must attend chapel.

Entrance: To prep school by own entrance exam (English, maths, verbal reasoning). To senior school by Common Entrance, special arrangements for children from state primaries. More or less automatic from own prep school but school has now a vast number of feeder prep schools on its books and head is governor of an amazing six of them: Aldro, Orwell Park, St Anselm's et al. 30 pupils joined at sixth form level last year: VR plus six GCSEs 4 Bs, and 2 Cs, plus 'special exams' in potential A level subjects.

Exit: Almost 50 per cent took a gap year last year (a sign of changing profile – parents can afford it – right); fair number of re-applications, and 'applying this year', no particular bias, three baby doctors, five art foundationers. No particular bias either in university choice (re-applying and applying this year are undoubtedly the favourites in the leavers' list) and only one to Oxbridge (head says they usually apply after A level results). One or two train for holy orders, but business and economics are important.

Money Matters: School now back on a firm financial footing, squillions of scholarships: academic, art, music, sports, and bursarial help where needed – automatic for clergy children, and popular with the Services. Tough on non-payers, but lenient in family crisis or emergency.

Remarks: Non-stuffy new head is performing miracles, and kicking the school out of its time warp; less dauntingly evangelical than before, though Christian ethos still prevails, but, we suspect, the c is getting smaller. No challenge from Cheltenham College going co-ed.

DEVONPORT HIGH SCHOOL FOR BOYS

Paradise Road, Stoke, Plymouth, Devon, PL1 5QP

Tel: 01752 208 787
Fax: 01752 208 788
E-mail: headmaster@dhsb.org
Website: www.dhsb.org

• Pupils: 1,150 boys • Ages: 11-18 • Size of sixth form: 240
• Non-denom • State • Open days: Early July and mid September

Headmaster: Since 1993, Dr Nic Pettit (early fifties). Graduated in biochemistry at University of Herts, PGCE at Bristol, PhD in microbiology, University of Kent. Research scientist for five years. Offered biology teaching post at Simon Langton Boys Grammar, Canterbury. Loved it so much changed career to teaching. Head of biology at Dane Court Grammar, Broadstairs; deputy head of Royal Latin School. Firm disciplinarian who believes research background enabled him to work fast and hard but also taught him when to stop. A country lad at heart who enjoys family life. Likes to share a joke. More familiar with boys who share his passions for academic excellence, the great outdoors and orienteering. Married to Pam, Bristol University classicist, now part-time school librarian. One son, David, educated at DHSB (now at Cambridge reading engineering) and younger daughter, Ruth, educated at Devonport High School for Girls (DHSG)(also now at Cambridge, reading classics).

Academic Matters: Excellent results. Average class size 29, reducing in number for practical subjects such as science and technology and for GCSE. Setting from year 9 provides small sets for pupils who need more help. Latin compulsory in years 7 and 8 and an option in year 9. Year 9 mini option system allows additional drama, music, Latin or physical education. In year 10 all boys study ten GCSEs, RE and PE. Four/five AS subjects in year 12 and three/four A levels in year 13 is common, sometimes five or six. 26 A level subjects at DHSB; consortium arrangement with four local schools (DHSG, Notre Dame, St Boniface and Eggbuckland) increases number to 30+ and gives boys opportunity to work alongside girls. 'The teachers are brilliant, they don't push but guide pupils to bring them up to speed,' comment parents. As the new engineering curriculum is developed, partnerships with Plymouth and Loughborough University enhance course provision.

Games, Options, The Arts: Regular county, regional and often national sporting achievements in rugby, football, athletics, basketball, cross-country running, cricket, fencing, judo and water polo. No swimming pool, so civic facilities are used. Hockey off campus. Picturesque Mount Edgcumbe Country Park and Dartmoor used for cross-country and orienteering. Art is on the up with newly appointed head of department working in newly refurbished art rooms. Music in new department base from autumn 2003. Lots of before and after school clubs – scrabble, poetry, French conversation, robot wars/robotics, rock climbing, running. Community drama productions and musicals co-presented with DHSG. D of E and Ten Tors popular. School boasts French centre in Brittany where up to 400 pupils, including year 7, enjoy week's break for £168, practising French, orienteering, canoeing and riding.

Background and Atmosphere: DHSB founded in 1896 by head teacher Alonzo Rider to give able boys opportunities that they otherwise might not have – still true today. Moved to present splendid Grade II* listed building in 1945 alongside Tamar Technical High School. DHSB took over whole site in 1991. The interior is now being extensively refurbished, the school benefiting from engineering sponsorship and LEA capital grants, although DHSB still prioritises spending on teachers. Smart and tidy, talented-looking students. The youngest seem inquisitive and polite, while the older 'young-gentlemen' seem quietly confident, a trait Dr Pettit approves of.

Pastoral Care and Discipline: Since Dr Pettit's arrival, pastoral care team has more than doubled to ten. 'Dr Pettit's very approachable, always there at the end of the telephone,' say parents. 'My child suffered mild name-calling because he wore glasses but as soon as I contacted the school the problem stopped with no lasting side effects.'

Behaviour on-site seems remarkably good, minus the odd scribble on toilet cubicles. It's perhaps less presentable outside school, eg food fights on the buses. Three caught with cannabis in eight years, resulting in fixed term exclusion and police involvement. Dr Pettit is a realist, 'I don't like mistakes but can tolerate one in some circumstances.' Rules state hair must be of 'natural colour and conventional style' although short-cropped dreadlocks have crept in; more lax sixth form style allows ponytails. No jewellery includes earrings.

Pupils and Parents: Mixed bag. Pupils from extremely impoverished backgrounds have achieved success at Oxbridge via DHSB. Pupils from 160 feeder schools desperately want to come here, dragging their non-committal parents along on open day. DHSB takes up to 12 per cent of

Plymouth's boys.

Pupils travel from within 750 sq-mile catchment area, even from Truro, Exeter, Okehampton. Parents established contract with local bus company for eight double-deckers to bring children in from neighbouring Plymouth districts to city's three grammar schools. Many old boys in positions of influence, including Sir Austin Pearce, chairman of British Aerospace, many Navy admirals and professors, MP Anne Widdecombe's dad.

Entrance: Written English paper (comprehension and composition), two multiple choice papers on mathematics and verbal reasoning. PTFA organised practice exam held beforehand, then the real exam on two successive Saturdays. If 174 places oversubscribed (happens often) candidates are admitted in the order of their score, with siblings (of those at DHSB, DHSG and Plymouth High School for Girls) having priority in the event of a tie for 174th place (rare). Results are age-standardised. Transfer to DHSB is possible at 12, 13, 14 and 16.

Exit: 80 per cent proceed to sixth form, remainder begin GNVQs, modern apprenticeships, local employment. 90 per cent of sixth form to higher education. Popular university choices include Plymouth (increasingly), Durham, Cardiff, Bristol, Nottingham and Imperial London, not forgetting Oxbridge. Various careers – medicine, dentistry, sports management. Many engineers, mathematicians and scientists a testament to the school's generous sponsorship from the consortium led by the Engineers Employers Federation and BAE Systems.

Remarks: Provider of broad and demanding education. Well-driven and focused head.

DEVONPORT HIGH SCHOOL FOR GIRLS

Lyndhurst Road, Peverell, Plymouth, Devon, PL2 3DL

Tel: 01752 705 024
Fax: 01752 791 873
E-mail: dhsg@dhsg.devonportgirls.plymouth.sch.uk
Website: www.devonportgirls.plymouth.sch.uk

- Pupils: 825 girls • Ages: 11-18 • Size of sixth form: 220
- Non-denom • State • Open days: September. January for the sixth form

Head: Since 2000, Mrs Maureen Smith BA PGCE (fifties). Deputy head of Devonport since 1986. Classics graduate of Bedford College, taught Latin and Greek at girls' grammar in The Wirral, relocated to Plymouth when husband, a biochemist, began lecturing at Plymouth University. Spent seven years teaching Latin at former girls' grammar, then took a seven year gap to raise her two sons (one now an engineer in USA, other history graduate of Leicester University.) Returned as head of classics at Newton Abbot comprehensive. Enthusiastic about role. Will remain teaching some Latin to years 8 to 11. She enjoys being in the classroom and places great importance on integrating well with pupils. Avid reader, keen gardener.

Academic Matters: High standards. 100 per cent of all GCSEs A* to C, 68 per cent A/B at A level. Choice of 20 A level subjects – further choices available at DHSB, Notre Dame and St Boniface and Eggbuckland Community College – part of a new consortium, 'The Link Partnership' – , including politics, psychology, sports studies and media studies – allows more timetable flexibility. English, the sciences and maths are particularly popular A level choices and students often sit additional Institute of Biology British Olympiad exam. French, Italian, Latin, Spanish and German available at GCSE and A level. Budding engineers invented collapsible mobile platform to lift equipment on and off ships, which has been adopted by the Royal Navy. Weaker achievers or students with SEN receive ample support.

Games, Options, The Arts: Thriving basketball squad. Dance taught in main school hall. Girls' sporting talents have reached the England stage in hockey, netball, basketball, swimming and athletics and improved sporting facilities are likely to boost success all the more. Music is considered a strength by parents with more than one third of girls playing an instrument and achieving grade 7 or 8 by year 10.

Flourishing orchestra and choir have good reputation within Plymouth and perform a carol concert in the city church each year. Several pupils perform at county level. Drama group often teams up with St Boniface College for Boys and Devonport High School for Boys; annual whole school drama production. Some pupils and staff support an active Christian Union which produces several assemblies for the school. Duke of Edinburgh available elsewhere through local YWCA; windsurfing and sailing offered through school.

Background and Atmosphere: Founded in 1911, moved to its present purpose-built site in 1937. The red-brick building is off a busy road opposite parkland. No great views and access by car is somewhat puzzling. Originally built for three forms of entry but since expanded to four – still waiting to dispose of ten temporary classrooms. First phase of building programme completed September 2005. Low turnover of staff – teachers almost seem relieved to be here, 'pupils listen and like to learn'. Sixth form has own centre with kitchen and study. Every girl has free access to internet and own email. Amazingly the system is not abused.

Pastoral Care and Discipline: Good level of care and support; discipline is a 'quiet word in their ear'. School nurse and youth counsellor from Youth Enquiry Service each run weekly drop-in sessions. School council instead of prefect system – each form elects a member. Girls have been sent home for minor incidents but no exclusions in Mrs Smith's 15-year history; letter sent home to parents if caught smoking. Sixth formers expected to dress as if they were at work; body piercing items must stay home. Everyone in school is 'expected' to contribute to school's chosen annual charity.

Pupils and Parents: Attracts girls from some 50 feeder schools in Plymouth, west Devon and south east Cornwall. Good attendance record and extremely positive attitudes. Many professional parents from doctors and nurses to lawyers and scientists.

Entrance: Plymouth exam in verbal reasoning taken on four successive Saturdays – one practice and three real. Best two scores added. Pupils who have named the school as their first choice are admitted in the order of their exam score until the maximum intake of 120 is reached. Sixth form entry is open to students who have achieved at least five GCSEs at grades A*-C with B grades in subjects (or equivalent) they wish to pursue at AS and A2 level.

Exit: Some 85 to 90 per cent migrate into sixth form, others move away or choose vocational courses. Few go into modern apprenticeships. Most continue to further education, although taking a gap year seems popular. About four Oxbridge candidates annually although not necessarily considered to be the best destination by the girls. Cardiff, Exeter, Bristol, Southampton and London universities are favourites.

Remarks: Currently preferred choice for parents wanting single sex selective education for girls. Students seem well prepared not just for academic success but for life after school.

DOLLAR ACADEMY

Linked to Dollar Academy Prep and Junior School in the Junior section

Dollar, Clackmannanshire, FK14 7DU

Tel: 01259 742 511
Fax: 01259 742 867
E-mail: rector@dollaracademy.org.uk
Website: www.dollaracademy.org.uk

• Pupils: around 1,240 boys and girls, 50:50; 100 board, rest day
• Ages: 5-18 • Size of sixth form: 275 • non-denom • Fees: Boarding: £5,214 - £5,850; day: £1,932 - £2,568 • Independent
• Open days: 'Every day is an Open Day - come and see Dollar at work.'

Rector: Since 1994, Mr John Robertson MA DipEd (fifties); deputy rector from 1987, he was previously assistant head at Stewart's Melville. Educated at Jordanhill College School (then the teachers' demo school in Glasgow) he read English at Glasgow. He still teaches occasionally but has no timetabled class, operating on a 'partner another teacher' basis. An enthusiast, though not 'a one man band', he 'runs the school with as good a senior gang as you can get anywhere'. We arrived during a cross country run; Mr Robertson was nowhere to be found. 'Mr Robertson is with the runners'. 'Running?' 'No, Mr Robertson is just interested – in everything – and he always watches – everything.' (In fact he turned up an hour after the allotted time and our meeting ran on so long that we ended up examining the re-constructed science labs in mad dashes along unlit corridors from light switch to light switch – there must have been an easier way!) Here is a man in charge, confident and happy in his work, with 'no intention of going elsewhere'. Proud that he has improved the 'quality of the bedrock' of the staff at Dollar, 'we used to have almost 90 per cent of the staff living in and around Dollar, now it is less than 30 per cent and they come in every morning fresh and full of new ideas'. Good common room mix, energetic young plus committed older staff, with some appointments from overseas. We met an effervescent drama teacher from the States during our visit – he had problems coming to terms with calling it 'the Scottish play' as opposed to.... NB prospectus still too big to fit into an A4 folder but it's on the website now and it's a splendid website.

Academic Matters: 'Science in Dollar is sexy,' says the rector and the results certainly show an impressive collection of As. Dollar is the Scottish school centre for biotechnology and with funding from the Wellcome Foundation, who underwrite 'half a member of staff' annually. English and langs not too bad either, German and French more popular than Spanish or classical studies (heroes for zeros). All three langs on offer from junior school. Good take up in Japanese (regular rugby tours and exchange visits to Japan), plus Russian, Italian, as well as philosophy, car mechanics and other jolly options. Pupils choose the subjects they want to study and classes are worked round them, rather than the trad system of block choice. Broad streaming for English (with EFL if needed), tight setting maths, and mixed ability in most subjects. A compressed science option on offer for 15, 16 year old high flyers aiming for medical school, two classes in each year group. Equally popular compressed business option which combines economics, business management, finance and accountancy - ' a powerful statement,' says the rector and a popular one at that. There is a distinct emphasis on the academic rather than the vocational.

Classes of 18-26 in junior school and 5-22 in senior school. Efficient support for learning in place, with rector getting progress reports. One to one, small groups and support learning in class all on offer. School has a positive approach to those with ADHD. Pupils can drop in to the dyslexia centre at any time. Serious homework, carefully spelt out in a smart little green book full of info for parents which interestingly persists in referring to the school as the Academy, whilst the rector himself calls the place Dollar. 'Whatever else, we expect that all pupils in the Academy should have enough work to occupy their evenings and any child who indicates otherwise misunderstands.' Not quite all singing and dancing new computer system, still one or two teething problems, but touch typing for all as well as the Scottish word-processing Higher course for all, thus cutting out the need for short courses in keyboarding at university. Specialist ICT course to Higher grade.

Games, Options, The Arts: No sport is compulsory. That being said, Dollar boasts a first XV rugby team which still has not been beaten in a home game this century (work it out – it fooled this editor). Regular tours to Europe and further afield, went to Canada in 2003 as 'the holder of the Scottish Schools' Cup'; as Scottish Cup winners again in 2004 and 'Rugby World' Team of the Year; and, would you believe, Dollar won again in 2005, a magnificent hattrick. Dollar represented Scotland in the World Schools tournament in Japan. Shooting 'phenomenal' (Dollar was half of the UK U18 team). The shooters won the Ashburton at Bisley in 2005, for the first time ever. Hockey pretty strong, current holders of independent boarding schools' cup. Individual pupils regularly get through to county level in major and minor sports; golf, skiing and badminton particularly successful, as well as the more esoteric activities such as shotput, curling and triathlon. Large collection of games fields, sixty-three acres of school grounds, as well as much used hall and swimming pool.

Strong volunteer CCF, good following, not just because of the trips to Canada; excellent pipe band, all of whom wear the McNabb tartan. The pipe band has been champions for the last six years. Fab art, now in the splendid new Maguire Building, we saw a jolly fifth form exhibition in the sugar pink painted library when we visited ('don't call it sugar pink call it regency coral'). Strong drama club and masses of productions; the head of drama specialises in doing sound commentaries for the blind on films. Clubs for everything, oodles of choirs, orchestras, jazz bands, a raft of choice. Munro bashing (Munros = mountains over 3000 feet), fabric technology and D of E, work experience at home and abroad, plus ballroom dancing on Fridays. Participants earn Latin American and rock 'n' roll – medals (bronze, silver, gold or Scottish Awards) which they wear proudly on their blazers thereafter; Scottish country dancing too – but no medals. Seventy-six options in total, with excellent facilities – powerful charities committee. Our spies in the district comment enviously that bird-watching of the non-feathered kind has grown in popularity recently, with last year's harvest garnering a dozen or so in one field.

Background and Atmosphere: Captain John McNabb, a former herd boy who rose to become a ship's captain, and, latterly a ship husband – literally looking after ships in port – died in 1802, leaving half his fortune, £55,000, to found a school to educate children of 'the parish wheir I was born'. Rumours abound whether the monies came from slavery or piracy but they were certainly augmented by bribes from ship owners eager to be first past the post and the Rev Andrew Mylne opened Dollar Academy in the elegant Playfair building in 1818. McNabb's ashes are entombed in the wall above the main 'Bronze Doors'; this is the only school in the land where pupils pass under the founder every day. By 1830, the grounds at Dollar had become an Oeconomical and Botanical garden, boasting some of the rarest trees in the country – certainly the most northerly tulip tree, as well as a Corsican pine. The interior of Playfair's original building was gutted by fire in 1961 and a certain amount of re-arrangement dates from then, with a zinging concert hall (the Gibson Building) and much improved science block. Current wish list which has just received planning approval, is for an 'ambitious new building to house PE, art and drama' – to be built out of 'funds'. The grounds are open to the public daily and war seems to have broken out between the great unwashed and pupils to see who can cover most tarmac with chewing gum.... It costs over £3,000 per year to remove (petrol, if you're interested).

Formerly a direct grant school, Dollar became independent in 1974 – a day school with an international boarding element. Easily accessible from most of Scotland and just a short hop from the Forth Road Bridge and Edinburgh Airport. The boarding houses are small, no more than 25 in each; McNabb house has had recent half million pound face lift and many of those who do board have rellies round the corner. Wet weather a feature of the place and masses of matches are rained (or snowed) off – it even rained on the bicentenary celebration in 2002 – 'but it couldn't have mattered less,' said the rector, 'all the FPs wanted to do was talk.' NB the school uniform includes beanies (first time ever for us on a clothes' list) and macs with fleecy linings.

Pastoral Care and Discipline: Rector boasts that, 'few schools in the country handle child protection better than here' and refuses to allow the word 'bully' to be used at all. He will always ask for clarification, 'are we are dealing with mugging, name-calling or what?' Automatic out for drugs. Lousy work equals detentions post school or early morning – dead unpopular with parents, plus out if, in the opinion of the rector, 'the pupil is not deriving benefit from being at the school or indicates by his/her conduct that he/she does not accept the rules of the Academy'. Pupils not perceived by rector as being particularly streetwise – 'pupils have a reasonable amount of self-knowledge but on the whole they are not young people obsessively interested in the major interests of the day; it is no bad thing for them to remain children for a little longer'. Victorian values, with clear rules, many of the petty restrictions have been done away with, and the kilt may be worn by chaps at almost any time, though most prefer to be 'breeched' except for dances or reels.

Pupils and Parents: The vast majority comes from within a 30 mile radius – impressive number of buses, plus an ever-dwindling number of Services' children and a contingent from the Scottish diaspora worldwide. Dollar itself has the reputation of having the 'highest percentage of graduates of any town in the country'. School has a long tradition of looking after the children of tea-planters, missionaries and engineers – still. 'Travelling' scholarships for Dollar's seniors to study abroad – pour encourager le gap, peut-être? Rector agrees with his predecessor that pupils are perhaps 'too conservative' though whether, as we said previously, 'that pupils might have difficulty discussing the concept of rebellion', is still the case, is open to slightly more debate. 'But,' says the rector firmly, 'this is not a parochial school, neither is it full of Sloanes'. Exceptionally strong and active FP network, including Sir Frank Swettenham the first Governor of Malaysia, Sir James Dewar the inventor of the vacuum flask and the sculptor George Paulin. The governing body is mostly FPs, which ensures that the place has freedom to develop.

Entrance: At 5, 10 or 11. The latter two by examination which is very selective. Well oversubscribed for entry at V and VI forms, each case individually considered; good GCSE or Standard grades required plus good refs and an ability to put something into the school. No open days as such – 'school is open every day', says the rector.

Exit: 90/95 per cent to some sort of degree courses. NB one pupil recently left Dollar to go to Gillespie's post first year sixth with an adequate supply of Highers (ie enough for university entrance – nb: this is still OK on ordinary Highers, Advanced Highers are not yet required) and then applied to Oxbridge as from a state school. Nine Oxbridge offers in 2004. Otherwise most students head for the Scottish unis eg Edinburgh, Glasgow, Aberdeen with barely a quarter going south or abroad. Not much take-up for gap years though the rector pushes it like mad, brochures all over the shop. 'Sometimes an entire group will head off but it is rare,' he sighs.

Money Matters: Collection of academic bursaries at 11, 15 and 16 plus ESU and boarding bursaries (means-tested, with tuition not covered). Very reasonable, governors tough on non-payers.

Remarks: Very sound; this large, solid, co-ed school provides education in the best old Scottish 'get on with it' manner, facing the twenty-first century with the traditions and values of an earlier age, mercifully free of most of the excesses of the sixties. 'Robust teaching and meritocracy' are important here. March 2005 brought an outstanding Inspectors' report which can be accessed on the Dollar website. Dollar is up there with the best of the merchant schools, though 'possibly not quite so trendy'.

DOUGLAS ACADEMY

Mains Estate, Milngavie, G62 7HL

Tel: 01419 562 281
Fax: 01419 561 533
E-mail: office@douglas.e-dunbarton.sch.uk

• Pupils: 1,060 boys and girls • Ages: 11-18 • Size of sixth form: Fifth form: 155; sixth form 130 • Non-denom • State

Head: Since 1989, Mr Gordon Wilson BSc PGCE (fifties) who came to the school as depute in 1983, rising to acting head, and, with the coming of the School Board, had to announce his own appointment as head. He formally took over in December 1989. Educated at the then Bellahouston Grammar School, he read chemistry at Glasgow University and did his PGCE at Jordanhill. Married, with three grown-up children, two of whom came to the school on 'placing request', he lives 'three and a half minutes' away. He 'misses classroom teaching, but enjoys running the school and manages to fit in hockey on Saturdays', relaxed and proud of his pupils' achievements; no problems in getting staff. Keen that pupils do not necessarily make career decisions at 11 or 12, but take a spectrum of subjects across the board. Care and welfare are equally as important as exam results.

Academic Matters: School is on the up academically, with last year's results brill. Three sciences on offer, many take two, outstanding results in the Chemistry Olympiad, ditto Biology Olympiad; junior success in Junior Maths Challenge, and Junior Maths Olympiad. Successes in Physics Challenge and Physics Olympiads. Get the message? French and Italian (replaced German), 'nothing to do with the music school'); Spanish option at sixth form, had more pupils with five Highers than any other state school in Scotland a couple of years ago. 'Fair amount of autonomy' in employing staff', 'but if there are teachers free within the authority, then we have to take them'; otherwise school advertises and can make their own appointments. Regular success across the board at Standard Grades, music specialists take both Standard and Higher music without fuss and, 'effortless'. Specialists take 'specially tailored courses', but see below. Most pupils get a clutch of eight subjects at Standard Grade, some may leave after Highers, and some stay on for the Advanced Higher – school responds to 'the needs of the pupil' and there is a certain amount of mix and match with Intermediate grades.

Staff visit local primaries and meet new pupils the term before they hit big school. Children are setted for maths in October of their first term, and in the second year for everything else. Programme in place for teachers to be trained in how to make use of ICT in the classroom, which software to use and how to make power point presentations. Exceptional computing department, school got best results in Advanced Highers in Scotland, and won the STAR trophy (well 'equal top marks'). Computers all over the shop – a certain amount of room revamping to form study areas. School also acquired a couple of dedicated computers via the Tesco voucher scheme – parents had to buy £270,000 worth of shopping to fund them! Two rooms for CDT, plus computer studies, business studies, as well as a computer suite in the library – well stocked, which also contains the careers department. Excellent support for learning, with a strong team which offers both guidance and support in class. When we visit a school we always ask for detailed exam results over the last three years, regretably not available here – an unacceptable attitude to parents, we feel. School responds,'exam results outstanding. Published annually in School Handbook, updated in December'. Douglas Academy, apparently uniquely in Scotland, was hit by a national, targeted strike by Unison, 'owing to the high profile of the school' and the teaching staff ran the school with no janitorial, office or technician staff for over three months. Now that's dedication.

Games, Options, The Arts: The school does outstandingly well – head says 'embarrassingly well' – at rugby, hockey and athletics. 'Strong competitive edge'. This is not a school for layabouts, this is a doing school. 'Lots of land', internal cross-country course, pool – much used by the community, who also do evening and keep-fit classes here. Mass of charity involvement. Spectacular art, and marvellous art complex at the top of the building, with three dimensional as well as pottery etc. Home economics classrooms reduced from an astonishing five to two, but well used. Regular charity fashion shows. Mass of extra-curricular activities ranging from fitness training to paired reading and debating. French exchanges.

School became a Centre of Excellence for Music in 1979 and boasts a first orchestra of 'almost professional standard' plus 'an outstanding chamber orchestra, senior wind band, second orchestra – very full (60+) which often has first year pupils playing, as well as non-music specialists. 'On a par with St Mary's Music School in Edinburgh. Adjectives tend to fail when dealing with Centres of Excellence but take it as read that any superlative would be inadequate. Pupils follow the normal curriculum, but 20 per cent of their time is spent on music. Music specialists come from all over Scotland, Ullapool to Newton Stewart, and their chosen instrument can be in any discipline from fiddle to piano. (There are no quotas for entry, 'around about eight or ten annually', and 'might all play the flute'.) Places at the school are free and open to all (help given with transport), with pupils from further away boarding at Dalrymple House, opposite the Botanic Gardens in Glasgow's west end (they share with pupils from the Centre of Excellence for Dance at nearby Knightswood). Two homework tutors. Music lessons carry a nominal charge for non-music specialists (22 per cent), and local concerts are always a sell-out, particularly the annual Christmas concert at St Paul's in Milngavie. Not as many boy choristers but very good girls' choir and serious senior choir, the junior one is merely 'good'but, by any other school's standards, it would be outstanding. Most of the music staff have top jobs in Scotland's orchestras and choirs.

Background and Atmosphere: Fairly boring square sixties building round a grass quadrangle with a mass of interesting add-ons. Magical views of the Campsies to the North. Millennium project involved re-landscaping the campus and revamping most of the fixtures and furnishings. Health and Safety complain that there is too much glass, but it is clean, light and airy. School dress equals white shirt/blouse, school ties, trousers or skirts and NO trainers. School monitors occasionally do a dress-code blitz. Music specialists wear blazers, as do the debating team, who won the 2002 European Parliament UK final in York and travelled to Turin to represent the UK.

Pastoral Care and Discipline: Team of ministers from local churches welcome involvement with the school. 'Drugs not an issue' in the school and good (state) guidance system in place, plus link tutors who have informal relationships with the pupils offering both emotional and social support. Recent HMI Inspection was enthusiastic about the fact that 'almost all enjoyed coming to school and were treated as family'. Clearly defined rules about bullying and loads of staff back-up. 'Good extended team'.

Pupils and Parents: No 'significant number' from ethnic minorities and no problems with religious festivals – 'praying (as in five times a day) never an issue'. Parents 'feel welcome', and good fund-raising and pastoral parents association in place. Homework diary and home study invitations plus the Home Study Pack 'really bumps up exam performance' and gives parents detailed info as to what is going on at school; and the results have improved spectacularly over the last six years.

Entrance: Four associated primary schools; one of which is tiny and rural. Pupils from (the Catholic) St Joseph's

may come here, and almost all do, or they may prefer to be bused the 30 minutes or so there and back to the local secondary Catholic school in Kirkintilloch. Excellent child-orientated joining handbook.

Exit: Some leave after Standard Grades, ditto after Highers, most stay on for Advanced Highers. Good percentage to uni, 75 per cent of leavers go to higher education with five or six Highers, local unis popular with a regular trickle to Oxbridge. Some to art school, most music specialists to some form of further music.

Money Matters: Funds available for trips, those on 'free meals' not expected to pay, though the take-up here is less than anticipated and with swipe cards, this is not an issue.

Remarks: Stunning state school for musicians but worth moving house for if you are not in the catchment area. Exam results impressive and getting even more so.

DOWNE HOUSE SCHOOL

Cold Ash, Thatcham, Berkshire, RG18 9JJ

Tel: 01635 200 286
Fax: 01635 202 026
E-mail: correspondence@downehouse.net
Website: www.downehouse.net

● Pupils: 560 girls; 550 board, 10 day ● Ages: 11-18 ● Size of sixth form: 166 ● C of E ● Independent ● Open days: By appointment

---

Head: Since 1997, Mrs Emma McKendrick BA (fortyish). Nickname 'Kenny' (reference to South Park intended, but not for any obvious reason). Educated at Bedford High and Liverpool University where she read German and Dutch 'just to be difficult.' Previous post was head of the Royal School Bath (1994-97), and head designate of the Royal School Bath/Bath High when the two schools amalgamated in 1998 (having been previously head and deputy head of sixth form at the Royal). This didn't work out, however, and so here she is – and good, super, confident, though also shy and friendly. Comments that school is 'very much about preparing girls for the next stage and not an end.' Has argued in the education debate why single-sex schools give the best answer. Husband is in banking. Altogether good news – steady stream of parental plaudits.

Academic Matters: Splendid and inspiring science block and good solid results at GCSE (single sciences); sciences amongst the most popular subjects at A level; physics the least so. A good collection of modern languages on offer including Italian, and Chinese at A level, with options for all 13 year olds of Spanish, German and Italian as well as Latin and Greek. Property, previously Ecole Hampshire (in the Dordogne) has been bought; 12-year-olds go out for an entire term (in batches of 25), and LOVE it. 'Magic for the French, of course,' says a mother. Projects, art, music, etc, also benefit from the French experience. English literature the most popular humanities subject at A level – very good results. Becoming a bit of a hot-house say some parents (and a prep school head).

Class subject rooms rationalised, cutting down on endless movement hither and thither. Good IT. Technology introduced nearly ten years ago 'we're starting gently', and is popular. Can cope with mild dyslexia and dyspraxia – two qualified members of staff co-ordinate all forms of learning support, also one peripatetic. EFL undertaken by a member of the English department (qualified). General studies taken by all, which improved league table performance no end (though not included in league tables any more except, perhaps, government ones). Results good by any standard, however.

Games, Options, The Arts: Round-the-year tennis coaching (oodles of courts), strong on lacrosse, also very strong swimmers – splendid pool. Netball introduced five years ago as a serious competitive sport and hockey in 2004 from 13 plus to give all girls the maximum chance to play in a team. New sports hall. Music everywhere (90 per cent of girls play an instrument), practice rooms in nuns' former cells; particularly good choir and chamber orchestra. New performing arts centre opened in September 2004. Cookery and needlework for everyone; Leith's cookery course in the sixth form. Art (includes textiles, screen printing and ceramics) good but not very good (examples of work used by examination board as best practice in their latest publication for teachers). Enthusiastic drama, 'and', said one girl, 'quite a lot of it.' Good Young Enterprise, Duke of Edinburgh.

Background and Atmosphere: Whitewashed building in Hispano-Surrey style, disjointed and scattered (lots of to-and-fro, with the library well down the hill), set in 110 acres. Lots of new building over the past few years. Definitely a house-orientated school. First two years lead a cosy life apart, under strict management, but 'attached' for the purpose of drama, sports etc to one of five mixed-age houses which they move into in their third year. In the sixth form, the girls move into the newish sixth form block: four boarding houses (lower and upper mingled, large single rooms for upper, doubles for lower), huge common/telly viewing rooms and own dining room. Cafeteria system intro-

duced – 'we know our manners have gone downhill' – good food.

Chapel is too small for the whole school but much used, with some complaints of 'too much.' Highly structured set-up but subtly so, with uninstitutional buildings and atmosphere (which comes as a disappointment to potential parents who imagine it might be a really traditional girls' public school). Weekend programme with considerably increased options (Saturdays and Sundays), 'but some girls still choose to mooch around,' and Oxford and Windsor are within easy reach. Strong work ethic, pleasantly non-institutional atmosphere.

Pastoral Care and Discipline: Smoking a persistent irritant, 'no matter how disagreeable the evidence against it,' sighs the head. Surrounding woods thick with head-high nettles appear to keep the boys at bay. Girls very much on trust. Ages mix freely, plenty of staff to turn to. Occasional drugs incident. Some pupils report peer group pressure to be thin.

Pupils and Parents: Upper class parents with cohesive backgrounds and values, some (25-ish) Services children. Geographically fairly widespread (Scotland, Cornwall and of course London and Thames Valley). Delightful and open girls, a good advertisement for their school, who comment on themselves, 'we're very untrendy – lessons finish at 6.00, and no one bothers to change into mufti afterwards' – though there's a strong weekend/holiday social life and an 'It' girl would be at ease here too. Old Girls include Baroness Ewart-Biggs, Dame Rosemary Murray, Geraldine James, Clare Balding.

Entrance: By exam at 11 (the bulk), also 12, quite a lot at 13 and some at sixth form. Competitive, but not fearsomely so. Minimum of seven GCSEs at A or B grade for entry to sixth form, plus, for those coming from outside, entrance exam and interview.

Exit: Some leave post-GCSE, and some come in. Almost all to university (Durham, Edinburgh and other green wellie choices), ten or so to Oxbridge (extra coaching for Oxford and Cambridge), increasing numbers take a gap year.

Money Matters: Major and minor scholarships at 11 and 12. 13 also at sixth form; open music and art scholarships.

Remarks: Has enjoyed a long innings as the most popular and fashionable girls' boarding school in the country. The previous head's abrupt departure plus small exodus of staff rocked the boat in the mid 1990s but the new regime has succeeded in re-establishing confidence – a pretty good school, all in all.

DOWNSIDE SCHOOL

Linked to Downside St Oliver's in the Junior section

Stratton-on-the-Fosse, Radstock, Somerset, BA3 4RJ

Tel: 01761 235 100
Fax: 01761 235 105
E-mail: admin@downside.co.uk
Website: www.downside.co.uk

- Pupils: 367 boys, 260 board. Girls since 2005 • Ages: 9-18
- Size of sixth form: 94 • RC and Christian • Fees: St Oliver's (Junior school) boarding £5,186; day £3,408. Senior school boarding £6,530; day £3,408 • Independent • Open days: October, November and March (call Registrar on 01761-235103)

Head: Since 2003, Dom Leo Maidlow Davis MA BD STL (fifties), who was educated at Downside, spent three years reading archaeology and anthropology at Cambridge and returned to his alma mater in 1975, teaching classics here for 20 years. He enjoyed teaching classics and enjoys being a monk: 'people talk to monks as they can't talk to others', 'monks are part of the furniture'. Latterly housemaster of Smythe House then novice master in the monastery. 'It is a great privilege to be headmaster' but it does sometimes make it difficult 'to get some daily meditation and to find time for reflective reading'. An intellectual, he has that precise way of talking that belies an underlying sense of humour and a constant twinkle in his eye. A delight to be with. Parents say he is 'unprepossessing at first but has abilities and a vision for the school; he's a good listener and good at delegating'. As we said in our previous guide, 'a thoroughly nice man, witty, intellectual, a typical Benedictine'.

Father Leo, who has three headmasters watching him from the monastery, has changed quite a number of staff since his appointment; some were retired, and some were 'moved on'. The age of the common room is much reduced, and while it is not essential for all staff (men and women) to be practising Catholics, Father Leo admits 'that it is preferable'. 'A consultative kind of head' he runs the school with a board of governors, the monastic community and headmaster's council plus the staff. He is currently fronting an enormous change in Downside. 'School needs to grow to 400' and girls arrived in September, moving into the currently pretty sad looking Caverel House which is about to be transformed. Conversion work, if not in the pipeline as we write, will be soon and the boys are terribly jealous of what they think the girls are going to have. The school had a slight flirtation with girls at the end of the 1970s which was not a success and they are pleased that already some 25 girls have signed up.

Academic Matters: Whilst in principle all do RS at GCSE, it is not mandatory, 'the odd Chinese boy not getting anywhere much with RS might be allowed to give it up'. Wide spread of results reflecting wide range of abilities. Over half the A level grades are A or B. English and theology departments swinging, as is science, following new appointments here. English, maths, history, RS and science are all setted and pupils are graded every three weeks. Full written reports sent home at the end of term and shorter report every half term. Tutors for all, and weekly meetings to keep 'em on the straight and narrow. Huge amount of dosh recently spent on new IT suite, trad teaching methods 'still around'. School on line, and nanny-netted. Some (3) teaching monks. An excellent and highly thought-of special needs department which can 'help pupils manage mainstream curriculum'. ADHD and mild Aspergers 'not a problem' but 'serious cases need serious treatment'; school manages well with tiny classes and masses of individual attention. Extra cost if need be for special needs.

Games, Options, The Arts: Currently unbeaten rugby squad, school keen on soccer, hockey, cricket, golf, orienteering, fencing. Girls play hockey, netball and tennis. Splendid sports hall, squash courts, Astroturf and swimming pool, for some reason much loved by the younger pupils and not so much by those further up the school. Flourishing CCF, Ten Tors, regular summer camps in Cyprus and popular pilgrimage to Lourdes where boys remain on duty throughout the night. Superb art, dotted round the school, good showing in A levels, ceramics, 3D, school makes its own sets for drama.

Choral music integrated into the school – it is now cool to play, the school has signed up with Virgin records, jumping on the Gregorian chant bandwagon. Slaughterhouse Seven jazz band, popular and constantly on tour, raising money for charity, often abroad. Half the boys learn an instrument and all try one out free for the first term. Theatre productions recently widened to include as many as possible and they need no longer emulate the Elizabethans and can have real girls playing Viola.

Background and Atmosphere: Benedictine Monastery transferred to rural Somerset from Flanders (via Shropshire) in 1814. Rather austere, imposing, 19th century granite buildings house the monastery, its guest wing and the school in close proximity. A goodly mix of not quite matching architectural styles greets the visitor, but the windows line up and the overall effect is grandly elegant (the grotty utilitarian stuff is tucked away out of instant view, thank goodness). Virtually the whole school is under one roof surrounded by lovely grounds and the monastery farm. Magnificent Abbey, monks worship there four times a day. Fantastic choir. World renowned monastery library (which we, being female, couldn't see) houses 150,000 books some of which aren't in the British Library.

During the 1980s the school boasted eight houses including some new-builds (hence the grotty jobs), and six hundred boys; the governors in their wisdom actively pruned the numbers of boys and now there are but five houses, one of them the girls' manor. The junior house, St Oliver's is separate from the main campus, and only shares facilities where necessary. All first year boys in the senior school occupy the same house, allowing boys to make friendships across the year before joining their main grown up house, which they choose 'by negotiation'. Delightful wide passages, imposing corridors and ecclesiastic architecture everywhere; you can almost feel the calm.

Terrific library, apparently about to be re-located, has a vintage encyclopaedia chained to the lectern by the door. Charming intimate 'old' chapel, which the monks used before the Abbey was built. Popular chaplaincy centre, where pupils can pop in for a coffee or a chat, usually staffed by a monk who will act as counsellor, but pupils can and do use it on their own. Slight pressure on chaps to think about joining up, monastery hosts taster weekends, and our guide said he was seriously thinking of 'giving it a go'. Spiritual matters pervade the atmosphere everywhere, with team photos alternating with religious pictures along the corridors – all pretty jazzy and not in the least oppressive. Every classroom has a crucifix. School motto 'Apud bonos iura pietas': 'For good men, loyalty is the lawgiver'. Pre-(first) world war uniform of black jackets and pinstripes; prefects wear grey waistcoats with jazzy hankies in their breast pocket (our guide said he habitually wore an orange one but spent our visit clad only in his waistcoat). Girls in burgundy tops and grey/black kilts. Food good, but not a huge range, hot buffet (curry) and salad bar. Most seemed to leave their stewed fruit and custard. Teaching staff, including the (teaching) monks, and pupils all sat together in a homogenous mix. All very chatty.

Pastoral Care and Discipline: Lots of rules, starting with The Downside Rule: the priority of a Gregorian is duty to others. Currently over 80 per cent are practising Catholics. Father Leo is keen 'not to go to expulsion too quickly', but out for dealing, drugs testing on suspicion, stealing currently on the wane; bullying 'means children need to get noticed'.

'Chaplaincy centre a great help' plus usual selection of matrons and tutors. This is a caring school. Punishment for mundane offences is either 'gating' or detention; gating means boys have to report in to members of staff or prefects at certain times during the day. Spiritual development is taken seriously and there is a religious assembly every morning and evening in house as well as an all-school assembly weekly, plus weekly house service and religious meditation groups two or three times a week. When Great Bede is rung twice a day, all stop for prayer even in the middle of a lesson or a cricket match. Pupils bused into Bath at the weekend, standard exeats, can go home for the afternoon on Saturdays and Sundays. Good family feel. Sex education is always a knotty one with monks, but Father Leo is keen that pupils should 'be prepared to relate in a happy and mature way with the opposite sex'.

Pupils and Parents: 40 per cent or thereabouts children of old boys, in some cases several generations have come to Downside. Fair number of overseas pupils, from grand Catholic Europe (Austria and Germany well represented and Father Leo about to trawl in Vienna) to South America and Hong Kong. Foreigners either arrange their own, or have school-appointed local guardians. Social spread from aristocratic downwards and from very wealthy to those who have very little. Notable Old Boys include Sir Rocco Forte, the late Auberon Waugh, David Mlinaric, Richard Holmes (biographer), Lords Hunt and Rawlinson and Father Timothy Radcliffe (first English world head of the Dominican order).

Entrance: By assessment at 9 and 11 for St Oliver's, by exams in English and maths; CE or scholarship at 13. References, school reports and recent exam results for foreigners, good English is essential. Regular feeders include Moor Park, All Hallows, Farleigh and Winterfold House, plus some further away.

Exit: Almost all to some form of tertiary education including regular flow to Oxbridge, eight last year. Gap year popular.

Money Matters: According to Father Leo, 'monks live a hand-to-mouth existence' but bursarial funds usually found 'somewhere' to help in extremis. Load of scholarships, but most for not much.

Remarks: Traditional monastic education for boys and girls aged 9-18, smashing children, smashing teaching and an environment second to none. Big and basic Catholic education.

DR CHALLONER'S GRAMMAR SCHOOL

Chesham Road, Amersham, Buckinghamshire, HP6 5HA

Tel: 01494 787 500
Fax: 01494 721 862
E-mail: admin@challoners.com
Website: www.challoners.com

• Pupils: 1,275 boys; all day • Ages: 11-18 • Size of sixth form: 365 • Non-denom • State

Head: Since 2001, Dr Mark Fenton MA MSc PhD (late thirties – making him probably the youngest secondary school head when appointed). Previously deputy head of Sir Joseph Williamson's Mathematical School (known locally as The Math School) in Rochester for four years. Read history at Peterhouse, Cambridge before landing first teaching post at a Chelmsford comprehensive, then senior teacher at King Edward VI Grammar, also Chelmsford. Did MSc and doctorate in 'spare time'.

Passionate supporter of state education. 'I have never been tempted to go into the private sector.' Can understand arguments for and against single sex schools; no plans to introduce girls to DCGS but close links with all-girl sister school, Dr Challoner's High, nearby. Bright-eyed, bags of energy. Acutely aware of boys' academic and extra-curricular needs and strengths. Sees education as more than good grades and certificates. Aim is to 'prepare students for life beyond school'. 'You have to keep moving,' he says. 'Look at ways of doing things better all the time. We have high expectations of our boys and they don't disappoint. It's amazing.'

Academic Matters: Consistently high marks and impressive exam results in all areas. At GCSE all get 5+ A*-C grades, 90 per cent-ish A*, A or B. Similar picture for A levels where pass rate over last five years an almost unwavering 97/98 per cent with over 70 per cent As and Bs. Maths especially strong (a fact reflected in further education choices), boys head and shoulders above similar selective schools. Top two sets take GCSE a year early and easily most popular A level subject. Science good, the focus of attention now that the school is a science college.

Multitude of improvement projects underway to make good 'years of government underfunding', according to head, who has overseen the improvement of many of the buildings 'to match the quality of the work which goes on

inside them'. Boys seem sufficiently focused not to be distracted by such on-site disruption. Class sizes a cramped 30+ (fewer in sixth form)' but even in snuggest settings (eg geography lessons) behaviour witnessed was impeccable. Teaching both inventive and inspirational. Computers aplenty, four dedicated and networked IT rooms in constant use.

Strong links with industry, careers conventions and industrial days a regular feature (all part of the 'life beyond school' philosophy). Language labs for French, German and now Spanish – foreign-speaking from day one – with exchange visits arranged for boys. Learning support available. 'We work hard with the boys who find life a bit of a struggle,' says head. 'Once boys are here, we want to do out best for them.'

Games, Options, The Arts: Equally outstanding reputation for matters non-academic. Standard of art on show throughout school (including fabulous 3D face on exterior school wall) more than impressive with an energy of tuition to match.

Hugely successful on sporting field with boys representing county and country in almost all sports. A new floodlit all-weather pitch has recently been completed, along with a new cricket square, pavilion and improved drainage for the playing fields. Particular hot-shots at tennis (national and county level) with six outdoor hard courts. U12 and U14 cricket teams won county cups in 2005 and both U12 and 1st XI soccer teams were also county champions. Rugby is a fast emerging sport, while swimmers won the national championships, beating Millfield. The sports hall, opened in 2000 and funded entirely by donations, provides lovely facilities now for basketball, badminton, gymnastics and cricket nets.

Music good too with determination to appreciate as well as participate. Relatively few (about 160) learn an instrument at school but many more have lessons outside. Most orchestral instruments taught, no tuition for piano and drums. Two orchestras and range of groups including wind band, jazz band and string ensemble. Classrooms equipped with electronic keyboards, synthesisers and music computer system. All boys encouraged to have a go. Also class singing lessons and three choirs. Main school choir undertakes major choral work annually and has performed at the Royal Albert Hall. Drama productions run in conjunction with sister High School.

Great debaters – winners of the Oxford Union debating competition and one boy was recently in the victorious England team in the world public speaking championships. Strong work experience tie-ups with businesses in France and Germany but ground-breaking link with Fasiledes School in Gondar, Ethiopia (first British school to do this). Much time spent in foreign climes – for cultural, sporting or other reasons – Sweden, Venice and the Himalayas. More extra-curricular than we have room for here – everything from Amnesty International to stage lighting, from chess to weight training.

Background and Atmosphere: Steeped in history having been founded in 1624, transferred to present site in 1903. From 30 boys, school expanded and turned co-ed. In 1962 the girls broke away to form Dr Challoner's High. Now has a large number of boys on a fairly confined site, hence the crowded classrooms. Parking/pupil drop-offs a problem because of its residential location.

Mixture of buildings. Best parts are the newish brick-built cloistered quads (which photograph particularly well for the prospectus) containing various classrooms, libraries and sixth form common room. Nasty 1950s blocks still serve a purpose and have been recently refurbished but boys certainly not spoilt by their surroundings.

Movement between lessons quick and orderly. Keen sense of learning here – boys attentive in class and behaved well around the school site. Not a place for time-wasters, we suspect. Uniform compulsory up to sixth, then smart work-wear. Easy relationship between boys and staff – courteous yet friendly and relaxed. Head has good rapport with pupils – aims to know all names within three years.

Pastoral Care and Discipline: Pride themselves on providing a 'caring community'. Care begins with form tutor responsible for individual day-to-day well-being, supported by heads of year who also handle PSE matters. Two teachers undertake counselling role, there's a qualified nurse as matron and ultimately the headmaster. Meetings are held weekly to discuss current issues. Bullying, theft, drinking and drug taking are not tolerated at any level. 'I am absolutely determined to keep this school a drugs-free zone. Pupils need to know where they stand.'

Firm anti-bullying policy, plus bully box for named or anonymous complaints. Boys urged to stand up for each other as well as themselves. 'If you see bullying going on and do nothing about it, then you are allowing it to happen,' says head. 'I encourage boys to take a very positive sense of their own responsibility.' System of commendations and rewards. Large team of prefects and head boys play part in daily running of school – help with junior classes and organise school events.

Pupils and Parents: Pretty well-to-do on the whole with brains and bucks going hand in hand. Massively affluent area which can make fund-raising easier, though one parent complained the appeals never stopped. 'Unfair,' cries head. Claims they ask parents for less than other schools. The downside is that staff are hard to find and keep due to high property prices. Famous OBs include James Bond actor Roger Moore.

Entrance: Mixed intake, in terms of feeder schools rather than ability. Claims not to be 'super selective' – takes roughly the top third of ability range. Boys come from independent preps as well as local primaries and is heavily over-subscribed by around 4:1. Entry at 11 (for 180 boys) is determined solely by the LEA on the basis of verbal reasoning tests. The school sets its own tests for entry between the ages of 14 and 16. Entry to lower sixth (for around 25 students) requires 46 points (A*= 8 points, and so on). Again, more than twice as many apply as get in.

Exit: No surprises that Oxbridge features heavily here (17 places in 2005), as do similar top-flight universities like Southampton, Birmingham and Bristol. Eclectic range of courses from perennial favourites like engineering and computer science to music, medicine and a whole clutch of 'ologies'. Tiny number of boys lost post-GCSE to co-ed sixth forms or employment.

Money Matters: State funded, so been feeling the pinch for a while now. Hard working 'Friends' society (school PTA) constantly in fundraising mode. Parental support buys minibuses, equipped a new language lab and provided books and equipment. Well in excess of £20,000 raised each year.

Remarks: A busy, bustling, beehive of a school which turns out high achievers. As such it's much in demand and struggles to cope with its catchment area let alone the high level of interest from further afield.

DR CHALLONER'S HIGH SCHOOL

Cokes Lane, Little Chalfont, Buckinghamshire, HP7 9QB

Tel: 01494 763 296

Fax: 01494 766 023

E-mail: office@dchs.bucks.sch.uk

Website: www.dchs.bucks.sch.uk

- Pupils: 1,060 girls, all day • Ages: 11-18 • Size of sixth form: 280 • Non-denom • State

Head: From 2003, Mrs Hilary Winter BSc (fiftyish). Educated at Chelmsford County High, studied for BSc in Geography at St Mary's College, Durham, before PGCE at Bath. Teaching posts include head of resources at Filton High, also head of lower school at Cotswold School in Glos. Arrived at DCHS from Ribston Hall HS in Gloucester where she was deputy head from 1998 to 2002. Married with two grown-up children, varied interests – from cooking to gardening, good wine and friendships (invariably together!), theatre to music and reading. Succeeded Mrs Sue Lawson BA, head since 1993.

Departing Easter 2006.

Academic Matters: Max class size 30, unstreamed except in maths, a strong department. In fact, tough to find any weak areas. Early language diversification with French, Spanish, or German and Latin on offer at KS4 and KS5; girls can choose two languages for GCSE. Dual or single sciences available, large take-up in all three sciences at A level. 50 per cent (70+ girls in Y12) of KS5 cohort do chemistry and biology and 25+ per cent do physics. Computers throughout and growing use of other technology such as IAWB and data projectors – their use being led by maths and languages; keyboarding teaching in lower school. Super library still 'about to be enlarged'. Support lessons for those experiencing learning difficulties.

Games, Options, The Arts: Superb arts and technology faculty. Good art, which festoons the building – large numbers taking it at GCSE and good number at A level; results in both excellent. Masses of drama, mostly via English department, and lots of competitions. Music strong – over 250 learn instruments in school in addition to examination and class music – largest uptake of peripatetic teaching in the county; string, wind, brass ensembles, hugely adaptable. Choirs and good links with Dr Challoner's Grammar School (qv) for orchestras, societies, drama etc.

Arts Week and Annual Art Show in the summer term, with masterclasses, and artists and dancer in residence. Sport extremely popular, regional, county, national and international level across athletics, hockey, netball, fencing, basketball, cricket, football, rugby and swimming (but no pool). Strong on extra-curricular sports clubs with fully developed Sports Leadership programme in sixth form. Work experience, D of E, and many clubs for everything. Strong charity involvement – especially with link school in Mvumi in Tanzania.

Background and Atmosphere: Founded in 1624 by Dr Robert Challoner, becoming co-ed in 1906, the girls hived off to Little Chalfont in 1962, concentrating, in the words of the then headmistress, 'not on looking backwards, but upon a forward vision'. Splendid suburban site, with mature trees and acres of playing fields, the school is a combination of ghastly (head says 'dated'), flat-roofed 1960s and marvellous curving brick-built recent extensions, encompassing an outdoor amphitheatre. Large and versatile sports hall completed in 2002. Very close to Metropolitan tube line station. Lots of foreign visits.

Pastoral Care and Discipline: Girls have the same form tutor from the time they arrive until sixth form level. Girl-orientated school council and students' sports council, and parents involved in pastoral curriculum – 'an awareness-raising programme.' PSHE in place, little bullying, will exclude for involvement with drugs on site and/or dealing; mutual support with all schools in area. Helpful daily assembly.

Pupils and Parents: From SE Buckinghamshire and Chiltern district; sixth formers may enter from further afield; predominantly middle class, with fair share of ethnic-minority backgrounds. Parents very supportive financially, underwrote original computer lab. Parents can visit the school at any time, with head's 'clinic' once a month for queries.

Entrance: Selective. 150 pupils each year at 11; administered by LEA. School has no say in intake (it's done by Buckinghamshire selection procedure), though preference given to siblings and girls within the catchment (grammar schools in Bucks take approx top 30 per cent of ability range). Sixth form entrants apply direct to school, need minimum five GCSEs at C or above and a minimum of B in the subjects they want to do at A level.

Exit: Few leave after GCSE, usually to do different A levels elsewhere, otherwise 95 per cent to university. 8-12 annually to Oxbridge.

Money Matters: State funded. Parents' Association involved in fund-raising events.

Remarks: Strong and worthy academic traditional girls' state grammar school with dynamic head who 'is seeking to combine the best of these traditions with a proactive approach to the rigours of twenty-first century life'. Perceived as an excellent solution for impoverished middle class.

DRIFFIELD SCHOOL

Manorfield Road, East Riding of Yorkshire, Driffield, YO25 5HR

Tel: 01377 253 631
Fax: 01377 256 922
E-mail: office@driffieldschool.eril.net
Website: www.driffieldschool.net

• Pupils: Almost 2,000 boys and girls • Ages: 11-18 • Size of sixth form: 300 • Non-denom • State

Head: Since 2004, Mr Martin Green BEd MA (late forties). BEd from University of Leeds, MA Educational Leadership, University of Hull. Started career as chemistry teacher in Hull area, later deputy head of Winifred Holtby School, Hull, and head of Withernsea High School and Technology College. Married to a teacher wife with two daughters at university.

Academic Matters: Exam results on oxygen-sapping uphill gradient as children benefiting from changes in recent years reach exam age. In 2003, 55 per cent of pupils achieved at least five GCSEs at A*-C; 67 per cent in 2005. A level results currently among the best in the East Riding. How do they do it? By tracking every single child in every subject all the time. Teachers log progress of pupils every four weeks on an electronic registration system. Computer flags up any student who fails to make hoped-for progress and hapless pupil is brought up to speed in whatever way the school decrees, be it extra homework or late study. Child is attached to a mentor – a teacher designated to get them instantly back on track. Parents love it, school loves it, even students accept it's for their greater good. Apparently. And it's not all bad news for pupils. The mentor can negotiate deadline extensions, etc for a student genuinely snowed under.

Debbie Dalton fronts the SEN dept, now called Student Services (ie inclusive); can cope with (almost) any learning difficulty from moderate to severe – the entire dys-strata, ADHD, plus severely (rather than profoundly) deaf – the school operates a soundfield system. 200 children on the register with IEPs for all including 49 with statements. One to one, one to two, small groups, anything from one hour to two/three hours a week, alpha smart (computers) – in and out of school, and all networked. 18 teaching assistants, all

highly trained, most remedial help is provided in class, but occasional 1:1, max one and a half hours a week, but 'can buy in more'. Very accommodating, 'can adapt to different needs'; special co-ordinator for their able, gifted and talented programme too.

Games, Options, The Arts: International recognition for performing arts. Winners many times of international Rock Challenge competition for dance, drama and music. Represented UK in Australia in 2003. Strong on sport, particularly cricket, rugby, hockey. Thriving Duke of Edinburgh scheme. Range of activities outside lessons excellent. Extracurricular activities given priority because of rural catchment area where, for many children, school is core element of their social life.

Background and Atmosphere: A whopper of a school, among the biggest in the country, set in a vast 40-acre site and with considerably more people than most of the students' home villages in the Yorkshire Wolds. Feels less like a school, more like a campus, not least in sixth form which boasts own internet café. School only 40 years old but has just spent millions on new design and technology and ICT blocks with specialist performing arts building imminent. Shares use of council swimming pool and sports centre.

Biggest asset? Its own residential studies centre in the North York Moors National Park for everything from geography field trips to intensive study seminars. Pupils encouraged to use school with its 600-plus internet-linked computers out of hours. Doors open at 7am and library is open until at least 7pm, sometimes later. Children can go home for a meal, then catch special late bus back to school for more study or activities before school bus takes them home again.

Pastoral Care and Discipline: Potential for swamping enormous as intake largely from relatively small rural primaries. Problems prevented by putting students into six houses and having registration forms comprising six students from each year group. New pupils instantly taken under wing of old hands. One of many ways school encourages responsibility. Sixteen-year-old student governor says views of pupils are taken seriously. 'They really listen to us.'

Discipline tight. School prides itself on standing absolutely no nonsense. Will not tolerate pupils disturbing lessons and disrupting education of the majority.

Pupils and Parents: Parents from wide range of backgrounds but many have caught school's ambitious bug and work hard to support it. Pupils' progress reports to parents three times a year and full report annually. Newsletters to many parents sent out via email so no chance to 'lose' that letter about extra homework. Parents' briefing evenings about, for instance, study leave.

Entrance: Seriously over-full and only takes pupils from 130 square mile catchment area.

Exit: Most stay on to sixth form and then to universities including Oxbridge.

Remarks: A beacon state school combining innovation and risk-taking to fire up the ambitions of a whole community. Outstanding.

DULWICH COLLEGE

Linked to DUCKS (Dulwich College Kindergarten and Infants School) in the Junior section

Linked to Dulwich College Junior School in the Junior section

Dulwich Common, London, SE21 7LD

Tel: 020 8693 3601
Fax: 020 8693 6319
E-mail: info@dulwich.org.uk
Website: www.dulwich.org.uk

- Pupils: 1,450 boys. 128 boarders • Ages: 7-18; junior school 7-11; lower school 11-13; middle school 13-16; upper school 16-18 • Size of sixth form: 390 • C of E
- Fees: Day (tuition fee): junior, middle, lower and upper schools £3,775; full boarders: tuition fee plus £3,830, weekly boarders: Tuition fee plus £3,530. DUCKS fees vary according to age
- Independent • Open days: Many throughout the year

Master: Since 1997, Graham Able MA Hons (natural sciences) MA Hons (research into boarding education), late fifties. Known as the Master, Mr Able is probably the highest profile head around and not just because he was recently Chairman of HMC and therefore seen as rent-a-quote on matters educational by the journalistica. His strong views, 'I'm always prepared to tell people what I think', controversial pronouncements on matters such as divorcing parents and their 'selfish and self-indulgent attitudes', immense empire building at Dulwich and abroad have earned him the respect of many, the envy of some and the dislike of others.

Awareness of all that doesn't entirely prepare one for the man himself who is not so self-evidently the international business man some describe. However, the development of the Dulwich brand abroad in its burgeoning number of schools, has led the Master and the governors to appoint a deputy Master who can give attention to the franchise schools in China and oversee the commercial aspects of the College. The Master is clearly on top of the latest research in every aspect of his field – can quote research studies with impressive ease. Past pupils from his teaching days at Sutton Valence, Barnard Castle and Hampton pay tribute to his teaching skills and humanity – qualities harder, perhaps, to discern now as he oversees Dulwich College unlimited. However, he maintains that 'our prime job here is to educate boys. Everything else we do is to provide the means to do it or to enhance their education.' His ultimate aim is to provide 'needs-blind' places, ie boys with the requisite ability will get a place at the College regardless of their finances. 'It may take us fifty years to get there but I'm sure we will.' If something of a traditional headmaster's personal touch and knowledge of his pupils is lost in that aim, it is surely a laudable one – though the approach may not be for everyone. Mr Able is clear that there is no loss, 'it would not be right to have too much of my time divorced from my prime job of being academic and pastoral mentor of Dulwich College – you have to get the right balance.' The balance is achieved, at least in part, with a carefully structured senior management team. In its scope and global reach this is a school like no other – one has to admire how it's done.

Academic Matters: The breadth of academic opportunity here is pretty breath-taking and in this, as in other respects, one has the sense that this is a small campus university rather than a school. Subjects are studied in their own buildings, blocks, wings or on separate floors and cover as wide as range as you'd find anywhere. 2005 results (in 27 subjects) include nearly 80 per cent A/Bs at A level with impressive showings in art, English, maths and further maths, religious studies, physics and Italian. At GCSE in 2005, 95 per cent achieved A*-B grades. French taken early allowing for Italian in two terms and a bit with impressive results. IT seen as a skill not a subject and school has pioneered – with collaborators – a multi-level BTec course, now marketed to other takers. 'We were frustrated with what was available ... now every boy goes through all the basic skills very thoroughly and then produces work from their own subjects ... assessed individually and tested online.' Computer science is also a separate A level. 1:11 teacher:pupil ratio – about as good as it gets. SEN catered for by 3 full time staff offering 'flexible help' dependent on need. 'What we don't do is take boys out of classes after year 7.' Help is given in breaks or library periods. Overall, given the mixed intake, the College does exceptionally well by its boys and, understandably, the head has robust contempt for league tables.

Games, Options, The Arts: They play everything you'd imagine and a few you wouldn't. Water polo and fencing are among the exotica. Sixty acres of fields, 2 full sized Astroturf pitches, a synthetic athletics track, numerous other pitches, courts and practice areas, swimming pool, vast sports hall and weight training room, Thames boathouse and a field centre in the Brecon Beacons keep everyone fit and provide, surely, something for all. Many games eg rugby and football played to highest international levels. CCF and Duke of Edinburgh Awards scheme offer further opportunities as do the 60+ clubs and societies comprised by the College union – everything from Christian Union to the Urban Culture society via the Think society and the Goons Appreciation society. Drama is strong and the College publishes a leaflet detailing productions on a professional scale. Super studio theatre. Music 'powerful' and prodigious, housed in good new block and masses of individual lessons to highest levels. Every kind of band and ensemble and events on a daily basis. Art also good and varied. Ceramics, block and intaglio printmaking, animation, graphic design and drawing and painting among available options. Community service programme and some boys help out at DUCKS – good for both.

Background and Atmosphere: Founded in 1619 by Edward Alleyn, an actor whose flamboyant entrepreneurial approach still informs his legacy today. His foundation, called 'Alleyn's College of God's Gift', was in two parts, one charitable and the other educational, on one site, and sharing a chapel. Twelve poor scholars, aged between six and eighteen, were to be educated by resident Fellows. Present Head likes to feel that these principles are still part of school's ethos and, in fact, 30 per cent of current pupils receive some sort of help with fees. Moved to its existing site in mid nineteenth century and the main buildings are grand, confident Victorian redbrick, embellished with stucco worthies in cream niches. Architect, Charles Barry jnr, the son of the great designer of the Houses of Parliament and it shows. Main building has treasures such as the masters' library and the great hall, the Wodehouse (PG – an Old Boy) library where his own study is recreated and wonderful archives – as grand and imposing as you'd expect. In one library we enjoyed a lively game of chess with many onlookers commenting and giving loud advice. Later buildings less happy 1960s and 1970s additions but all contribute to the campus feel familiar from the universities of the great industrial towns. Large fields and pitches surround the buildings, with a stand of mature chestnut trees. Everywhere, though, are cars and traffic – this is not a quiet concentration of academe but a big, busy place with teachers bustling by on mobile phones, three motorised groundsmen on one field, and car parks around and in the centre of the teaching blocks.

Lunch is eaten in one of the recently refurbished dining halls and food is excellent. 'The commercial branch of the College does a lot of catering – it's fashionable to get married here....our executive chef is high quality,' says deputy head. All part of Dulwich College Enterprises (office building on site.) Staff and boys eat in the same rooms. There is nothing formal here – again, more of a tertiary college feel. To a passing observer, this looks like good working relationships if not the warmth and cordiality noticeable elsewhere. Staff and pupils carry swipe cards which let them into buildings and which act as debit cards for meals etc. Around 40 female staff, including heads of DUCKS and junior schools and heads of some years.

Pastoral Care and Discipline: 'The importance of the pastoral role of form tutors for these age groups cannot be overstated,' so says recent College job description and for most boys, their tutor is first resort in times of need. Recent inspection praised all aspects of College's pastoral policy, noting that 'the great majority of tutors are effective and understanding'. Sound approach to bullying which occurs, as it always will, but infrequently and is rapidly dealt with. If you are found with drugs you're out but the College will accept expellees from elsewhere and give them a second chance. Boarding accommodation is up to the standards of elsewhere with all sixth formers now having their own room with en suite 'facilities'. Medical centre with 24 hour staff at heart of College site. House system involves everyone, even those shy internationals or workaholics. Weekly, flexi and occasional boarding available.

Pupils and Parents: Mostly from local areas though some from quite a distance. Buses – another part of onsite commercial operations – combining with 3 other schools, shift nearly a thousand children daily. Intake visibly and cheeringly reflects south London environs and is multiethnic – around 35 per cent are non-white Caucasians. Every socio-economic band represented here – thus intake about as mixed as anywhere. Most of the 128 boarders (out of 1,450) are from around 12 countries, many in the far east. Parents involved in many ways and the College fosters close cooperation with home. Boys are not generally smart – shirts out, ties loosely knotted, shambling gait, longish hair – not a number one in sight – but faces look engaged and purposeful. OBs PG Wodehouse, Lord George of St Tudy, Trevor Bailey, Peter Lilley, Roger Knight, Sir John Willis. Also Shackleton, whose Antarctic expedition boat is dramatically on display in the entrance hall.

Entrance: Kindergarten and DUCKS start as non-selective and co-educational but boys sit entrance test to the junior school at 7. 3-4 boys per year will have been pre-advised to look elsewhere in case of not making the grade. Sizeable intakes at Years 3,7 and 9 and for the sixth. Intake at 11 largely from the state system. Testing via written and oral assessment in English and maths, reading and spelling, non-verbal reasoning at 7, via written papers in English and maths, verbal reasoning at 11. At 13, via own entrance examination.

At 16 via 6+ GCSEs with 6 A*/A grades minimum, which should include English lang, mathematics and A level subjects. Boys at the College must achieve 14 points (A*=4)to be admitted to the sixth form – and half a dozen or so a year fall at this hurdle. The College says 'Any boy admitted to Dulwich should do much better than this, and (barring exceptional circumstances which should be discussed with the school immediately results are published) will do so if they work hard enough. There are assessments, parents' evenings and full written and predicted GCSE grades are published after the mock GCSE examinations in year 11 providing a final warning of a boy's likely GCSE outcome in June. The College 'stands ready to help find another school – we have always been successful in this given enough time – should the need arise.' It is not clear to us, from this or from conversations with parents, that boys on track for non-selection have their predicament brought to their parents' attention sharply enough or early enough.

Though this system is common in London, and convenient for the school, we think that the very best schools regard themselves as having made a commitment to their pupils, and will strain every sinew (not always successfully) to see them through. It saddens us greatly to see Dulwich slipping.

Exit: Around 25 boys leave after GCSEs. The rest go everywhere to study everything. Head is convinced that, despite press hysteria, there is no discrimination for or against schools like his and people go where they should. 2005 leavers included large number to London colleges and Oxbridge.

Money Matters: At 11 and thereafter, scholarships worth 10-30 per cent of tuition fees. Also music and choral, art and sports scholarships of varying values. School is among the best provided for in the country. Well worth investigating.

Remarks: A multi-national operation although the average boy on the ground is probably unaware of just how significant that side of College life is to him and his future. There are five schools more or less on one large site,

making a huge and layered community. It feels impersonal – we couldn't resist an eyebrow raise at the 'Commissariat', being the school shop. However, it undoubtedly works and homogenises a disparate clientele into a successful, stimulating educational and social mix. 'We want to open as many doors as possible for our boys.' says head.

DURHAM HIGH SCHOOL FOR GIRLS

Linked to Durham High School For Girls Junior School in the Junior section

Farewell Hall, Durham, County Durham, DH1 3TB

Tel: 0191 384 3226
Fax: 0191 386 7381
E-mail: headmistress@dhsfg.org.uk
Website: www.dhsfg.org.uk

- Pupils: 600 girls, all day • Ages: 3-18 • Size of sixth form: 100
- C of E, accepts all faiths and none • Fees: Seniors £2,550; Infants/Juniors £1,770 - £1,900 • Independent

Head: Since 1998, Mrs A Templeman MA DipT (fifties), previously deputy at Haberdashers' Aske's, Elstree. Married with three children; calm, reflective, gentle style; teaches classics. Educated at Watford Grammar School for Girls and at St Hugh's Oxford (Lit Hum). Reader in the Church of England. Wants girls who are 'excited about life and learning', encourages hard work and dedication alongside a social conscience.

Academic Matters: 98 per cent five or more good GCSEs, 94 per cent grades A to C at A level. Stronger than average take-up in maths and science; geography and religious studies also strong. French, German and Latin taught from 11, though not the widest range of languages for keen linguists; a safe but not expansive range of A level options includes politics and sociology. Average class sizes, a number of age groups surprisingly not yet at capacity. Some girls with mild to moderate dyslexia, the occasional one with other special needs; teaching assistance offered at extra charge.

Games, Options, The Arts: Sports not overly obvious around the place (in contrast to Durham School), though a good range of the usual options – hockey, netball and tennis being favourites; represented at county level in hockey, national level in tennis and skiing. World Challenge expeditions to Rajasthan and Madagascar; Duke of Edinburgh awards also popular; community service and charity work encouraged. Music workshops, outdoor activity trips and overseas visits invite the wider world in and encourage the girls out; music, art and drama popular with larger productions held in Durham's Gala Theatre, the girls not afraid to tackle the occasional all-male play with an all-female cast.

Background and Atmosphere: Founded in 1894 by the Church of England, now accepts all faiths and none. Relatively new site with mostly modern buildings and programme of refurb throughout. Attractive open location in good residential area, convenient for city centre. Juniors in attractive new buildings, including delightful Rainbow nursery ('the promise of a good beginning'); all very proud of new senior library and dedicated librarian forging links with a school in New York to share ideas and opinions across the Atlantic. Upgraded ICT and science labs. A translation of the school motto causes some consternation – 'The fear of the Lord is the beginning of wisdom' which, for avoidance of misunderstanding, rarely surfaces these days. Yet there are reminders everywhere that this is a church school, the affirmation of faith and 'spiritual growth' is mentioned throughout. The recent appointment of a lay chaplain proved a great success, inspiring girls with her desire to learn salsa dancing as well as her teaching. Staff are 'wonderful and slightly wacky'; average age 44; a number of 'characters' generating real fondness between staff and pupils.

Pastoral Care and Discipline: House system (though the girls had some difficulty remembering what they were). Form tutor for each class. Staff and girls vote for head girls and deputy. Buddy system; nurturing approach to discipline.

Pupils and Parents: Very diverse social spread, significant number from educational action zones in East Durham, others from business and professional families. 10 pupils on free places; 20 per cent of senior house on bursaries. Intake chiefly from County Durham and Sunderland; fairly narrow cultural spread, reflective of the local community. Supportive Old Girls' association. Girls are bright, vivacious and enthusiastic with that refreshing naivety that they can take on the world and win. Free (but not too free) thinking, challenging but not groundbreaking, girls are glad to be here and feel 'safe'. No uniform for sixth form and unusually relaxed dress code, rare to see girls in denim in this type of school, girls admit they relax and 'stop thinking about what to wear for school after the first couple of weeks or so', apparently an advantage of a 'boy-free zone'.

Entrance: Assessed 'by observation' for nursery and reception, appropriate testing in subsequent years for junior house. English and maths tests at 11 based on Key Stage 2

SATs with references from junior heads and interview, style of testing reflects intake from local feeder state primary schools. For entry at 16 5 GCSE passes A* to C, references and interview with head. Generous number of scholarships and bursaries 'to attract bright, enthusiastic and gifted pupils who can make a real impact on the life of the school'.

Exit: Some leave post-GCSE for the boys of Durham School or local state schools, most stay for sixth form then go on to trad, predominantly northern, universities, plus a good number of Oxbridge candidates. Notable old girls include Wendy Craig (actress), Joanna Burton (opera), Wendy Gibson (BBC journalist), Sarah Blair (sister of PM).

Remarks: A refreshing change, a school that doesn't oversell itself. A combination of all that is new in education with core traditional values.

EALING INDEPENDENT COLLEGE

83 New Broadway, Ealing, London, W5 5AL

Tel: 020 8579 6668
Fax: 020 8567 8688
E-mail: ealingcollege@btconnect.com
Website: www.ealingindependentcollege.com

- Non-denom • Fees: variable according to courses
- Independent • Open days: contact college

Principal: Since 2001, Dr Ian Moores BSc PhD, a chemist with impeccable independent education credentials, in his late forties but looking a decade younger and definitely 'cool'. Previously taught at Wellington College, then head of chemistry and science at Bedales and latterly head of science and IT at Cheadle Hulme. Something of a polymath – a sportsman and musician – his main commitment is to 'the individual' and the, currently, small scale nature of his college allows for all-comers to be given close individual attention. 'I'm an innovator,' he says, 'very flexible and adaptable.' He is certainly easy to talk to and very open about the challenges of the job – those he has already confronted and others to come. He's relaxed but focussed, with an intensity and quiet purposefulness which makes this college an interesting prospect for the future.

Academic Matters: Its raison d'etre. No-one would come here for the ambiance or the architecture but it is a place in which work is palpably central. There is not much else to do anyway and the importance of consistent work – often neglected in comparable establishments – is stressed here. Results are quite hard to evaluate – partly because, for example, the GCSE cohort consists of early and late takers, resits and of candidates of varying ages. 2004 saw 22 candidates sit papers in 9 subjects – all 3 sciences – individually or as a double option, maths, ICT, business studies, French and English lang and lit. 85 per cent achieved A*-C grades, with 24 per cent getting A*/A. At A level, in 2004, 24 students achieved a range of grades with 85 per cent getting A-C grades, the total pass rate being 100 per cent.

Not a great range of subjects offered – college disagrees – but they will get in tuition for minority subjects and 2004 saw papers taken in law, Japanese and accounting. Permanent part-time staff in accounting and law. Business studies very popular supported by Dr Moores' new back-up programme of visits to companies, talks from outside speakers, work experience and IT. This in tandem with new medical sciences programme to support aspirational medics with visits to hospitals, speakers etc. Music now a GCSE option, as are geography, history and Spanish. PSHE compulsory at GCSE level. Economics, psychology and sociology among available A level options. No qualified SEN support though an English teacher is available for extra help. This is not the place if you have SpLD but EFL help is available though 'we won't take a child whose English is very poor'.

The strength of the place is in the tiny classes, the teaching – 'crucial' says principal – and in the close monitoring of all students. GCSE students work in a supervised study room when they don't have classes. Every lesson/study period begins with registration and parents are telephoned in cases of no-show. A level students have supervised study programmes worked out with their personal tutors. Everyone has an individual learning plan and parents get written feedback every 5-6 weeks. One-to-one tuition also on offer as an extra and, unusually for a college of this size and type, a large proportion of the staff is full-time. League tables – inasmuch as they are an indication of anything – suggest that, at A level, the college performs as well as the smarter, up-town competition and better than some.

Games, Options, The Arts: Nothing on-site. Sport is compulsory for GCSE students and they are bused to a local sports centre. A 'circus' of games is offered around the year: football, badminton, tennis, handball, rock climbing and swimming. No formal games programme in the sixth form but football team meets weekly, voluntarily. Music newly available and college will arrange private lessons if required. No art, music ensembles, drama – no space and, as yet, no demand though locality abounds with classes, clubs and courses of all kinds for those who want out-of-school arts.

Background and Atmosphere: College began life as Ealing Tutorial College in 1992 in even smaller premises. Moved in 2001 to present 3 storey building – ex-social security offices – just off the Broadway in the centre of Ealing. The building itself is entirely undistinguished – a glass and steel cube with a bumpy tarmac carpark – all in need of renovation. The rooms are smallish but the right size for the small group teaching they accommodate. Good IT suite, two neat labs for chemistry and physics but no library and principal keen to develop that area, though Ealing Central Library – an excellent resource – is minutes away. College has good computer facilities with links between home and staff.

Low ceilings, strip lighting, carpeting awaiting replacing when we visited – it isn't cosy. Much could be done to refresh the inside with displays/posters on the walls and it cannot be that this would be at odds with the austere purposefulness of the ambiance. Ealing Broadway is a lively shopping area with plenty of cafes and bars and students get their lunches from these – or bring their own – eaten in the sizeable common room which has vending machines for coffee and chocolate bars. Common room out-of-bounds during lesson times. Bus and tube connections are excellent and students come from quite a wide area – Hammersmith to Uxbridge, Harrow to Richmond.

Pastoral Care and Discipline: Everyone is in a tutor group – 10-12 students to a tutor and the tutors are responsible for academic and pastoral matters. Close supervision picks up problems and links with home are crucial to progress and welfare. Principal holds a compulsory weekly assembly followed by meetings with tutors – an unusual and healthy feature for a college of this kind. A cheery atmosphere prevails and there is a sense that individuals who were unhappy or uncomfortable elsewhere could find a niche here. 'We're good at individuals who need to be pinned down more,' says principal – 'they're not lost in the crowd here. We get several who have been bullied. That doesn't happen here.' Lateness, late appearance of work and erratic attendance are now minor problems due to reporting system, letters home and sanctions. 'We put them on probation if necessary', says principal. For the majority, the approach works well and results are showing it.

Pupils and Parents: A few come as young as 13 and they do, indeed, get a privileged education – taught alone or in tiny groups. Great for tuition and they get used to coexisting with older students but – otherwise socially and in terms of extra-curricular opportunities – this must be an outside option for most at this age. The largest cohort in this small college – only 90 students with a capacity of 130 – is at A level and these overwhelmingly are there to study the sciences – though this may broaden according to demand. 65 per cent of students are Asian, 20 per cent is white; the rest a mixture reflecting local population. Some from overseas and local accommodation is found in hostels or with host families. Special link with school in Singapore. Common denominator is a willingness to pay for top tuition to achieve results.

Entrance: On exam results, reports from schools and interview. Principal likes to give those who have failed elsewhere or been expelled – once, no more – a second chance. Place could be a lifesaver for those who have seen the light.

Exit: Some stars – 4 leavers in 2004 off to read maths, medicine or dentistry at top universities. Sizeable number to Brunel and other more local universities – engineering, sciences and business subjects, obviously, dominate. Some with no places after results, often due unrealistic parental aspirations which push offspring into applying for unrealistic courses. The majority does end up in colleges of higher education.

Money Matters: Fees according to subjects taken and number of lessons. 8 subjects at GCSE works out at £8,150 pa. 3 A2s works out at £9,100 pa. More lessons are given for retakes and one-year courses and these are proportionally more expensive. Few scholarships available up to 50 per cent of fees.

Remarks: College keen not to be seen as second option or refuge for those who have failed elsewhere but this may well be a mistake. There is a real need in unglitzy west London for a haven for those with support – financial and moral – from home who need a second chance or for real individuals, oddballs or bullees who will find a haven here and be taught expertly, monitored closely and given every chance to succeed. Not the place for those for whom the extra-curricular side is what schooldays are all about. There are some who will opt out wherever they go and whatever support they are given but this college offers an unusual opportunity for those with the wit and maturity to seize it.

EASTBOURNE COLLEGE

Headmaster's House, Old Wish Road, Eastbourne, East Sussex, BN21 4JX

Tel: 01323 452 323
Fax: 01323 452 354
E-mail: admissions@eastbourne-college.co.uk
Website: www.eastbourne-college.co.uk

- Pupils: 609, 382 boys and 227 girls; 50 per cent boarders
- Ages: 13-18 • Size of sixth form: 258 • C of E • Fees: Day £4,565, boarding £6,895 • Independent • Open days: May and October

Head: Since 2005, Mr Simon Davies (early forties). From Bedford School, vice master. Previously at Abingdon, head of biology, senior housemaster. Married with children.

Academic Matters: All achieve 5 or more A*-C grades at GCSE, 68 per cent at A or A*. 65+ per cent A/B at A level. Science is very strong, new science centre, new DT centre, school intranet is a major component in the academic life of the school and the use of laptops is positively encouraged. Cavendish Learning Resources Centre 'the most up to date library on the south coast'. Maths well taught with consistently excellent results.

Games, Options, The Arts: Very sporty school. Rugby and cricket are de rigeur; rugby pitch (College Field) dominates the front of the school; training and coaching sessions are offered by the school to neighbouring clubs and schools. Girls play hockey and compete in athletics competitions to national level. CCF mandatory in year 10 with a large (voluntary) following thereafter. DT department led by a strong, dynamic teacher (Wayne Trinder) who positively oozes enthusiasm – has already produced 20 Arkwright scholars and 5 Young Craftsman of the Year. Over 50 per cent take DT at GCSE. Frederick Soddy, Nobel Prize winner for physics is an OE, and The Casson Art School is named after Sir Hugh Casson RA, another OE. A full activities programme, running from 7.00am on Monday to 10.00pm on Sunday, offers such diverse subjects as fishing, textiles, D of E, chamber choir, horse riding and electronics. Plenty to do if College Field fails to thrill.

Background and Atmosphere: The school was founded in 1867 by the seventh Duke of Devonshire (the current Duke is President of the Eastbourne College Council) together with other prominent Eastbourne residents, initially as a boys' school. It is tucked away behind the seafront, close to the railway station (one and a half hours from Victoria) and right in the heart of the town. Nearby is Devonshire Park, home to the Eastbourne Ladies' Tennis Tournament which precedes Wimbledon each year. The atmosphere in school is busy and energetic. Not the place for a delicate blossom. Although day pupils are admitted, it is run as a full-boarding school rather than a school with boarders. Day pupils have their own house and can stay over if necessary. No weekly boarding.

Pastoral Care and Discipline: About 80 per cent of the staff live on the site so help is always on hand. It is not unknown for pupils to email their teachers when stuck on their prep. 'Chapel is central point of college' with two chaplains to provide pastoral support to all irrespective of their beliefs – large chapel choir sings almost every Sunday morning. Pupils are encouraged to serve others through S@S (Service at School) which involves helping in primary schools, running clubs for old people, links with local schools. Discipline is good.

Pupils and Parents: Niche market for local families who prefer the boarding option. The majority of parents live within commuting distance. There is a flourishing Eastbourne College Parents and Friends Society which organises social functions and strengthens links between the school and parents. Parents and OEs are encouraged to maintain contact with the school – a careers fair is organised annually by the Old Eastbournian Association.

Entrance: At age 13 in year 9 or at 16 in year 12 (lower sixth). Prospective pupils are invited to join in school life for 24 hours. Candidates sit CE or the school's own entrance exam. Academic, music, art and all -rounder scholarships are available. Most pupils come from surrounding prep schools. Overseas students are admitted provided their English is proficient.

Exit: 95 per cent go on to higher education. About a third follow the current trend of taking a gap year. Some to Oxbridge, others to art college or drama schools.

Money Matters: Apart from the scholarships at 13 there are further sixth form scholarships worth up to 50 per cent of the fees. Music scholars receive free music tuition. There is also the Scoresby science scholarship awarded to a student who wishes to take 3 science A levels. The school also has its own assisted places scheme for 10 day pupils entering at sixth form and subject to the usual academic criteria.

Remarks: A demanding, energetic, busy school under the strong leadership of current head. A well-kept local secret – boarding numbers have hardly altered over the last eight years – very much a part of the community.

EDGBASTON HIGH SCHOOL FOR GIRLS

Linked to Edgbaston High School for Girls Preparatory Dept in the Junior section

Westbourne Road, Edgbaston, Birmingham, West Midlands, B15 3TS

Tel: 0121 454 5831
Fax: 0121 454 2363
E-mail: admissions@edgbastonhigh.bham.sch.uk
Website: www.edgbastonhigh.bham.sch.uk

• Pupils: 480 girls, all day • Ages: 11-18 • Size of sixth form: 120 • Underlying Christian ethos and respect for all traditions • Fees: £2,925 • Independent

Head: Since 1998, Miss Elizabeth Mullenger (fifties); educated Bolton School, universities of Wales, Bristol and Birmingham. Very wide experience: started her career in a Brighton Grammar School, went on to be head of English and head of year in what she describes as a quite demanding comprehensive, then to Birmingham where she was head of English at King Edward VI for Girls at Camp Hill, head for ten years at St James and the Abbey in Malvern, and finally at Edgbaston since 1998. A genuinely different head, with a sense of vision and a no nonsense view of what is really important in schools. Bubbly, charming and full of joie de vivre, but no pushover. She was a remarkably successful head of St James and the Abbey, managing to buck the boarding trend in smaller girls' schools. That experience has left an indelible mark on her. She believes that girls respond to a holistic experience of school where there is a genuine balance between the academic and creative and is determined to offer within the day environment the best that she saw within boarding schools. This means that she makes a real effort to know as many girls as she can and is incredibly accessible to pupils, staff and parents. A bundle of energy and enthusiasm, always thinking of new ideas and ways to do things better. Demands similar enthusiasm from her staff and pupils. This is someone with a real passion for education in the sense of the drawing out of the best in her pupils. Loves drama and even runs her own Youth Theatre on Friday evenings. Entirely hands-on, a very charismatic lady who is clearly doing great things for Edgbaston.

Retiring July 2006.

Academic Matters: Superb results by any standard except in comparison with the super-scholastic King Edward V1. 60 per cent As at GCSE and over 85 per cent A/B at A level. Considering that the academic cream tends to (but does not always) go to King Edward VI down the road this is testimony to the very high standard of teaching that goes on here across the board. Business studies, science, geography and modern languages seem to be especially strong at A level. The head's philosophy of getting the very best out of the girls by confidence-building is having the effect of improving already commendable results. Academically on the up.

Games, Options, The Arts: Wide range of sports from cricket to dance. Rather unusually for a city centre school there is lots of space in their four acre site. Fine (if not outstanding) facilities including an indoor swimming pool. Edgbaston is by tradition a very sporty school, untypical in this respect of most inner city independents. The head is trying to expand the options available – no easy task with many children obliged to return home on the school buses. Extensive range of clubs at lunchtime: fencing, German, dance band, science and art amongst many. Impressive music, nearly a quarter of the entire senior school took part in a recent concert extravaganza. Choir regularly tours Italy. Dance and drama are other areas of special distinction, aided by the head's passion for the stage. New multi-purpose hall adds to the possibilities.

Background and Atmosphere: Founded in 1875 by the burgesses of Birmingham to provide an equivalent education to that already available for their sons. A tradition of no-nonsense, non-conformist, unpretentious belief in the value of education in its own right has served it well in the increasingly multi-cultural world of modern Birmingham. The school fully reflects the cultural and racial mix of the city, says the head and she says it with real pride. There is an underlying Christian ethos and the head is a practising Christian, yet the emphasis on respect for all traditions means that this is a school at ease with itself.

The buildings form an attractive complex, with senior school, prep school and pre-prep cheek by jowl. The core building, dating from the beginning of the sixties, has been sympathetically added to over the years. Lots of refurbishment internally with the most attractive common room areas for the sixth form (the school does not use this term: years 12 and 13 are the local coinage). Classrooms are bright and airy and particularly well-equipped especially as far as IT is concerned. Perhaps the most impressive area of the school is the library, well stocked with an enthusiastic switched-on librarian – just the place for private study. A more relaxed, less pressured place than King Edward's.

Pastoral Care and Discipline: Responsibility for pastoral care falls onto the year heads. The head is particularly exercised by the need for a joined-up system where girls are genuinely cared for as far as is possible within a day environment. Knowing the girls and treating them as individuals are the central values of the school and, as you would expect, the system works extremely well. There is a strictly enforced uniform up to year 11; the sixth form are allowed to wear casual clothes – quite liberally interpreted. Muslim girls are allowed to wear a headscarf in the school colours. Discipline does not appear to be a problem with well-motivated, confident, engaged pupils.

Pupils and Parents: The pupils are drawn almost entirely from within the city boundaries with many living in the immediate area of the attractive district of Edgbaston. Buses to more distant suburbs. Parents from a wide cultural mix are predominantly from commercial and professional backgrounds. Notable Old Girls include Estelle Daniel, Jenni Mills and Molly Dineen. Can also claim two eminent Old Boys (they used to take boys up to 7) Sir Adrian and Sir Dominic Cadbury – Sir Adrian used to sit on their council and Sir Dominic currently does.

Entrance: Many pupils enter from the prep school, which in atmosphere and ethos is modelled on the senior school. More than half the intake comes from outside, mostly from local primaries at 11. Unusually amongst Birmingham girls' schools, Edgbaston is very relaxed about taking girls at 13 from local preparatory schools, if places are available. Standards of entry are rising. 'Not the pushover it used to be,' says a local parent.

Exit: Loses many of its junior school pupils at 11 to more prestigious alternatives – a trend that is slowly being reversed by the present head but which speaks well for the quality of the junior school. Vast majority in the senior school stays onto to sixth form, virtually 100 per cent exit to university, few to newer universities and fewer still on Mickey Mouse courses. Half a dozen to Oxbridge, including the first female organ scholar at Gonville & Caius Cambridge. Lots go on to do medicine.

Money Matters: Remarkable value for money - everything thrown in except for meals. A limited number of scholarships at 11 and 16 which can be combined with bursaries in case of special need.

Remarks: A rising star in the Birmingham independent school world where average and bright girls can do extremely well. In The Daily Telegraph 2004 league table, was the highest performing school in the West Midlands at A level.

THE EDINBURGH ACADEMY

Linked to Edinburgh Academy Junior School (The) in the
Junior section

42 Henderson Row, Edinburgh, EH3 5BL

Tel: 0131 556 4603
Fax: 0131 556 9535
E-mail: amu@edinburghacademy.org.uk
Website: www.edinburghacademy.org.uk

• Pupils: 450 boys, 30 girls (all in sixth form), all day except for 25 boarders • Ages: 11-18 • Size of sixth form: 140 • Non-denom • Fees: Senior school £2,750, Geits (top of Junior school – but based in senior school) £2,150 Junior school £1,950 - £1,440; nursery £1,350 full time, £626 - £1,565 (2+) • Independent

Rector: Since 1995, Mr John V Light MA (fifties) who refers to himself as 'Lighty'. Educated at Sedbergh, he read modern langs at Clare followed by a diploma in business admin, and came to The Academy (as it is known to aficionados) via a spell in industry, plus teaching in Glenalmond, Uppingham, Haileybury and Sedbergh where he was housemaster. Married, with four grown-up children, his wife still runs in marathons – wow! Keen on sport and singing but, whilst he still sings, he no longer referees, but is 'still doing most things, including hill-walking, tennis, golf, sailing. I ain't dead yet'.

An iron fist in a velvet glove but, having said that, boys approach his room with problems through the day. Lighty has strong policies and believes in producing individuals who are 'competitive and realise that while their best is as good as anybody's, their second best will get them nowhere'. Keen on grades 'but they are not an end in themselves; qualifications will get you a job, but personality will get you customers'. 'Good values and the ability to work important'. And we are looking for thinkers who get to university and think, rather than get to uni and struggle'. The head is master of the bon mot. A lateral thinker, with a keen sense of humour, 'tell me if I am talking claptrap'. Not at all keen on policy statements – 'you're stuck with them'. A lovely man, wish there were more like him.

Academic Matters: Hybrid public exam structure (still), with GCSEs for all across the board, followed by either Highers or AS, and then A levels (A2); any child showing interest in a Scottish uni is encouraged to take Higher English more or less by default. Sciences are 'still utterly wonderful', and a good showing in all the public exams last

year, particularly geography (except for some reason at AS level), maths results impressive, and ditto biology (new head of biology and two more appointees in the maths department have obviously paid off). Business management or studies, government and politics and philosophy – often regarded as the softer option – did not appear to attract many As, but a goodly showing nonetheless, with only the occasional slippage. Sport and PE popular. Greek and Latin poking their heads briefly if successfully above the parapet. Oodles of As. French, German and Spanish. Good collection of subjects at higher level, though some parents find it 'Frustrating because specialist subjects not available' (as in Chinese, Russian, law and psychology). Not too many of the poncier modern subjects around; and whilst school could teach the more esoteric langs, it is hardly 'viable for the 'Russianist' on the staff to teach seven lessons a week for two pupils.

Staffing levels good, 'steady turnover', lots of both internal and external appointees. Expect a broad academic range of pupils in mixed-ability classes, with the exception of maths, which is setted from age ten, ie the top year of the junior school, which is based in the senior school building. Remember always that most of the junior school come on, and there is no way of sussing out their IQ at five. Max class size 24. Some streaming, but basically three parallel classes. Good learning support throughout with the 'absolutely wonderful' Mrs Marsh, both one-to-one and withdrawn from class. Results commendable given the mixed intake, but, says the rector, 'we are only as good as the next year's results'. He is keen on playing your strengths – 'some are spectacular, you never know who will be the success at the end of the day'. Parental comment about, 'mixed academic results, the top quartile is extremely high, the others satisfactory' – can be interpreted as Edinburgh-banker-speak for doing fine. The tradition of 'dux', the brightest boy or girl in the school (Magnus Magnusson was dux in his day) has been enlarged to include a clever group of scholars – the Dux Club.

Games, Options, The Arts: The school tradition for providing a mini squad for the Scottish Rugby side continues and this year is no exception, with usual rash of caps, would-be caps, and waiters in the wings. Main games field down beside the junior school with its fantastic (community) sports hall shared with lucky local residents. No pool, but specialist weights and gym. School sold five (disused – and needed money spent on them) tennis courts during the past year (little boxes built on them) which caused a press furore. Cash already earmarked (and no begging letter in the offing, promises Mrs Bashford, the head of the junior school) for a major £4 million upgrade at junior school plus new science block at the senior school and some fairly hefty tinkering. Pavilion badly burnt couple of years back, thought to be arson.

Outstanding art department, with notable achievements in every discipline, brilliant ceramics; life class in the evenings a popular option. Music outstanding, all singing and dancing. Superlatives from our informants reach awesome proportions. Tales of sight-reading Missa Brevis in record time, and a complicated series of concerts, both open to parents and to other divisions (or houses); any pupil learning an instrument can play in concerts 'even if it is only three notes and child has been learning the trombone for three weeks'. Loads of productions with St George's; polished public speaking. Strong choral tradition, plus every other discipline – CDs you name it – 'but we don't use the choir for PR,' says the rector. This is obviously not flash in the pan school-only stuff, as two FPs shot to stardom in the most recent James Bond film. Concerts outstandingly professional, Chamber Choir broadcast on Radio Four. CCF hugely popular, piping particularly strong, with successes in both quartet and trios. Keen D of E; and good charity input – Academy Action does a massive amount of fund raising and even the Rector has been known to take part in a charity sleep-out (not for a bit, he sez).

Background and Atmosphere: School was founded in 1824 by Lord Cockburn and Sir Walter Scott amongst others. Built in trad Edinburgh inspired granite (Greek mode), the Greek motto on the main portico reads 'Education is the mother of both wisdom and virtue'. Buildings in main school a mixed bunch, some obviously designer-inspired additions including a fabulous oval assembly hall, plus a mass or add-ons as well as classrooms and labs around huge tarmac courtyard. Stunning new music department. Look for generous Edinburgher-sponsored libraries etc; successful FPs remember their font of learning with pride. Boarders live some 15 (very brisk) minutes' walk from the main school, near the Botanical Gardens and Inverleith Park (the green lung of Edinburgh North) and all meals are taken in the superb parquet floored dining room at Arboretum opposite. Not much change in boarding numbers, weekly boarding and flexi boarding (B&B) on offer, good take up. School owns a field centre in Angus. Boys wear tweedy jackets in winter, blazers in summer; sixth form girls look neat in navy blue blazers.

Pastoral Care and Discipline: Pupils divided into four houses, pastoral care via heads of year plus form takers (class teachers); good PSHE. Head ephor (prefect) is a key link with rector and school. Rector 'not complacent that

drugs are confined to an area south of Princes Street', or 'stop at the railings'... 'Incidents do occur'. No automatic exclusion unless dealing is involved. 'If at all possible we give the pupils a second chance'; parents are involved etc, 'pupil may forfeit the right to remain in the school (for a varying length of time). Last year was a difficult one but the school faced a much publicised teenage crisis as fairly and as openly as it could against much press comment'. City temptations are close, whizzy new houseparents in place in boarding house. One or two teeny reports of bullying still around, but are really just aggravated teasing, and no more than any nit-picker might expect.

Pupils and Parents: All sorts, with a large traditional tranche of the Edinbourgeoisie. St George's School for Girls is their sister school. Not many from abroad. Rector and head of junior school keen on playing down trad middle class image of the school – hence extended and very popular nursery hours. On the whole, pupils are pleasantly self-confident and polite; occasional lout but not more than teenage adolescence. Robert Louis Stevenson and Archbishop Tait of Canterbury are FPs as are partners of many of Edinburgh's institutions today.

Entrance: Traditionally patronised by the great and the good of Edinburgh (the Edinbourgeoisie), and does well by them plus an increasing number of first time buyers (around 40 per cent).

Exit: 'Around 90 per cent' to various universities, roughly two thirds Scottish, the rest elsewhere. Steady trickle (7/8 regularly) to Oxbridge, with quantities currently trying their hand as we write. As ever, sciences, engineering and art feature strongly. Enlightened careers department (rector again: 'vv good'). Quantities of embryo lawyers, doctors and merchant bankers; plus, it has to be said, a fair tranche of pupils going off to uni to read engineering, physics, technology, English, modern languages, sports studies, history, international relations. 'What they do thereafter may be different – but they are not cloned down the three routes which you mention' says the head. 'Some into the professions, but progressively more into art, drama, interior design and admin'.

Money Matters: School still continues to protest that it is not well-funded, and recent tennis court capitalisation will take care of the next building boom. (NB remember Mrs Bashford's words - 'no begging letters'.) Tranches of scholarships for musicians and academics, school may support pupils in financial difficulties, but parents must be upfront about the problem. 'No endowments per se, all scholarship and other bursaries come out of fee income'. Familial discounts for third child (and more) at either Ed Academy or St George's.

Remarks: Trad and distinguished academic day school which is absolutely back on form again, with a much broader pupil base, capable of producing a clutch of really well-rounded creatures in the nicest and widest possible way. Last word from Lighty – 'a school for those who still want something that is reliable, with good values and respect for other people but with the stamina and ability to work'.

EDINBURGH RUDOLF STEINER SCHOOL

Linked to Edinburgh Rudolf Steiner Lower School in the Junior section

60 Spylaw Road, Edinburgh, EH10 5BR

Tel: 01313 373 410
Fax: 01315 386 066
E-mail: bursar@steinerweb.org.uk
Website: www.SteinerWeb.org.uk

• Pupils: 305 boys and girls; of whom 55 board • Ages: 11-18
• Non-denom • Fees: £1,777 - £1,898 • Independent

Chairman of the College of Teachers: No head as such, school run as an egalitarian society, and requests for interviews with 'the head' over a two-year period were politely refused. For the first time in this editor's seventeen years with the guide, we turned up at a future parents' open day. This we found slow, irritating, 'no-one was available to answer questions' and ill-managed – a crocodile of grown-ups criss-crossed the crowded campus in the rain, with no apparent direction, often visiting the same building several times. At one point we were almost knocked over as an enthusiastic male teacher (whose class we had already visited) pushed past us to force open the door, whilst urging four of his pupils 'to get a move on'. School denies that this is parents' usual experience – pointing out that staff are 'always on hand to answer questions', going into classrooms while lessons are in progress is most unusual (true – and a great plus), and that it does not always rain in Edinburgh.

Teachers are trained over 'at least a two-year training seminar' – one evening a week, plus Saturdays from 8.45am to 4pm. Courses include 'an introduction to Rudolf Steiner and Anthroposophy, study of the book 'Esoteric Science', Goethean Science and artistic practice' (and this is in the first year) plus 'Parsifal: biographical questions with reference to the Grail legend, Eurythmy, Creative speech,

painting drawing etc etc etc'. During the third year all must do teaching practice. 'Each school determines its own teachers' pay scale. Some schools have a definite scale, other schools pay according to teachers' needs and circumstances. Teachers working in a Steiner Waldorf school share responsibility and authority for the daily running of the school and the educational programme. Collaborative leadership is practised in the management of schools and particular tasks and areas of work, such as finance, administration and building development are carried by individuals or groups within the College of Teachers, together with administrative staff and a school Council'.

Academic Matters: 'The education at the Edinburgh Rudolf Steiner School strives to engage and nourish each child's innate curiosity and love of learning. It offers a balance of academic, artistic and practical activities, so that the child is thoroughly prepared for all life experiences'. Books appear not to be a priority here. We saw few (if any) during our tour, and no reference was made to either a library, or computers (though we gather that there are 'one of two for older children'). Children are taught to read and write from the age of six, reading first from what they themselves have written. They make their own workbooks for each subject.

The 'main lesson' is a two-hour period on 'reading, writing, maths, history, geography, the sciences, house-building, farming, mythology, botany and astronomy,' taught over a three to four week period. The rest of the day is 'timetabled to provide a real balance between academic, artistic and practical activities'. Pupils keep a 'tidy' book for their main lesson work.

French and German from the age of six, and those who join the school later may have to take extra lessons (and pay extra) to catch up. Sciences taught in such antiquated labs as to defy belief. 'By teaching science, art and religion in this integrated way, we hope to implant in our young people a holistic view of life, so that they may regard the world with understanding and serve it with respect'. Loads of exchanges with other Rudolf Steiner schools all over the globe.

GCSE English, maths, German and French taken aged 16, followed by humanities, the sciences and art at 17, and either Highers or AS levels at 18. Although there is no academic selection, results are good: 70 per cent plus A*-C at GCSE, ditto passes at Standard Grade and Highers. No homework until the age of 9+.

Games, Options, The Arts: Small basketball court, but no other apparently organised games. Hall used for gym, theatre etc. Options and the arts integrated into the syllabus and the art which was dotted around was not that fantastic for the year group – though art AS exam results consistently very good.

Music and drama integrated into the syllabus, and we were pleased to see one of the early years included a child with Williams' syndrome, performing amongst her peers (she needs a scribe for normal academic activities). Cooking lessons for fifth year, though all actually bring packed lunch and break, and eat in their classrooms.

Background and Atmosphere: Three trad Edinburgh Victorian villas, set betwixt George Watson's extensive campus and various parts of Napier University – this is conversion land in Edinburgh. Tiny conglomeration of town gardens, in appalling condition when we visited – but then it had been the wettest January since forever. But the routes between the three houses were ill-conceived and complex (the puddles round one particular tree made it impossible for anyone to arrive at any lesson in that building dry shod). New build gym, and new build and rather glammy area for tinies.

Pastoral Care and Discipline: Enormously caring. Lots of TLC. Loads of 'understanding'.

Pupils and Parents: Apart from Steiner aficionados, most are middle class locals who are fed up with, or whose children do not get along with, other local schools. Plus some 'out-boarders', pupils from further afield, who stay with local families, plus some exchange students from other Rudolf Steiner schools elsewhere, as well as those from non-Steiner schools. This is a hands-on school, and parents are expected to contribute, during the term, as well as 'helping with redecorating etc' during the work week at the end of the summer term.

When we queried the dress code – as in 'do you have one?' – we were assured that yes, there was one. However, some older students were wearing oversized flares, earrings or studs, and hats – either baseball caps (worn any way), sunhats (it was January) or beanies (which we take to be the trad woollie bunnet without the pom pom). Dress code, apparently means not wearing trainers – this however, has been abandoned, as being impractical.

Entrance: Turn up, as we did, on the first Friday of the month – but book in beforehand, state what age group you are interested in, and follow the crowd. Younger would-be pupils are placed in a class of their age group, to see how they – and presumably the class – react. If parents are interested they are offered an interview, and if they are not quite certain about the school, they are offered a preliminary interview. Children are accepted at all times, throughout the year.

If a child does not follow the Steiner system from nursery, then the most likely time for them to arrive is 'around 12' when they have either discovered problems with their current school, or need to have their self confidence boosted.

Exit: 95 per cent of pupils leaving at the upper end of the School go on to 'some sort of higher education'. Oxbridge 'not out of the frame'.

Money Matters: Bursaries are available for those in financial need. There is currently a campaig aimed at the Scottish parliament to secure state funding to ensure that those wishing this type of education are not discriminated against for financial reasons. No luck yet with persuading the Scottish Executive to emulate its European peers.

Remarks: Super school for the refuseniks, the alternative parent, or the child who fares badly at a trad school. Could be brill for your dyslexic et al child.

ELMHURST, THE SCHOOL FOR DANCE

Linked to Elmhurst School for Dance

249 Bristol Road, Birmingham, B5 7UH

Tel: 0121 472 6655
Fax: 0121 472 6654
E-mail: enquiries@elmhurstdance.co.uk
Website: www.elmhurstdance.co.uk

• Pupils: 215 total – 155 girls, 60 boys – majority boarding
• Ages: 11-19 • Size of sixth form: 90 • Non-denom • Fees: Boarding £5,500 - £5,700; day £4,300 - £4,550 • Independent
• Open days: Around the ends of September, January and April

Principal: Since 1995, Mr John McNamara BA MPhil (fifties). Read drama and theatre arts at Birmingham, then English studies at Nottingham. Previously director of drama at Marlborough, having earlier taught drama and theatre studies at Liverpool, Manchester and Reading universities. Served as chief examiner for drama A level course. Married with three grown-up children, all pursuing non-theatrical careers. Former actress wife, Julie, head of pastoral care and boarding. McNamara is a patriarchal principal who shows real affection for his small Elmhurst family. Talks about pupils' achievements with swollen chest and fatherly pride. Also monumentally impressed by their commitment. 'They all want to be here. They feel privileged to be here. They are fulfilling their aspirations.' Appears to be well-liked and respected by staff and pupils alike. 'We have only the very best here,' he says. 'This is not a place for the faint-hearted.' When time allows, he likes Elizabethan and contemporary theatre, historical fiction and travel, and is a fan of Manchester United.

Academic Matters: First and foremost a ballet school but academic studies do still matter. Regularly found midway down the schools' top 500 league table, also winner of three Good Schools Guide awards in 2004 (for dance and performing arts, inevitably). But still quite good results for a school with no academic selection and a timetable spotlighting vocational training. In GCSEs, latest figures show 80 per cent passes A*-C, with 25 per cent of all grades A* or A. Usual curriculum subjects as you'd expect but with science only as a double award and French the only language choice. As principal explained:, 'French is the language of the school – it's the language of ballet.' Most students take five core GCSEs, another two from a list of options plus dance and drama. English taught as additional language to sizeable number of overseas students. Some learning support for mild to moderate dyslexics. Subject choices at A level very restricted due to nature of Elmhurst's three-year sixth form which is heavily vocational. All graduate with qualified dance teacher status (the national diploma in professional dance is degree-level), plus a couple of A levels in, say, art, music, French, English literature or office skills. No science. Principal insists the curriculum is 'broad and balanced'. 'We are not in the business of just producing happy hoofers,' he says. As the prospectus points out, 'in the event of a career cut short by injury or a change of aspiration, they (non-vocational qualifications) constitute a reliable insurance policy'. Lots of non-ballet careers followed by former pupils would seem to support this. State-of-the-art ICT room, also interactive whiteboards in bright airy classrooms, well-stocked library as well as plenty of books in departments and boarding houses. Class size 30 max, with English and maths streaming in GCSE years. Six-day week starts at 8.20am, finishing at 9pm after prep, but there are five meal or snack breaks during that time.

Games, Options, The Arts: Exclusively classical ballet since move to Birmingham. Tap, contemporary and jazz only taught as appendages to ballet rather than disciplines in their own right. Superb dance studios with slightly sprung floors rarely out of use. Surrounded by both external and internal windows so young dancers can get used to being on show. Top notch dance teachers (ex professional dancers) from around the world under artistic director Mary Goodhew, all the crème de la crème. 'They have reached the top in their profession,' says McNamara. 'They're the best.' Each class also has own piano accompanist. As the official feeder school now for Birmingham Royal Ballet, students often invited to perform with the company and take up apprenticeships. 'It's the kind of experience dance students would normally only be able to dream about,' says principal. BRB director David Bintley CBE also school's artistic advisor. Fabulous 250-seat theatre at hub of school which is hired out for summer school conferences. Great evidence of artistic ability on show, with students' own work adorning the walls. Sports necessarily limited. No team sports like rugby or hockey but students put through Sthenos body conditioning (exercise) programme and allowed to use neighbouring school's swimming pool. Can also kick a football around school grounds (unfortunately the cause of a recent ankle injury, explained the principal). Music, not surprisingly, extremely popular. There are around 200 individual music lessons (both instrumental and vocal) a week as well as class music for all for the first three years, then music as GCSE, AS or A2 option.

Background and Atmosphere: Relocated to Edgbaston area of Birmingham in summer 2004 from its former home in Camberley, Surrey, the culmination of five years' planning and building. 'We believe it's the first purpose-built ballet school in Europe for this age range,' says principal. School originally set up in 1922 by Helen Mortimer as the Mortimer School of Dancing, re-named Elmhurst Ballet School in 1947. Uncertain future in Surrey forced total rethink and its now purpose-built edge of city campus is the glorious result and 2005 winner of Birmingham Civic Society's 'new building' prize. McNamara is first to admit that, despite present day delight, the move was traumatic. Only 11 staff could relocate (including principal and wife), mostly on the academic and pastoral side. 'At least that meant there was a sense of continuity for students and their parents,' he said. Vocational (dance) faculty built up from scratch. Move had total support of parents, pupils and governors though. Two other bits of Camberley relocated – an old painting of the former Elmhurst, still waiting to find wall space, and a bronze 'Girl with otter' standing outside a boarding block. School designed so dance studios and classrooms form ring around theatre while medical centre and boarding houses do same around small outdoor amphitheatre. Four nurses and two physiotherapists on the payroll so help always on hand. Treatment room always busy as the least twinge is quickly repaired. Never a dull day on site. Constantly buzzing with visitors (Friends of Elmhurst were sitting in on dance classes the day of our visit and you could hardly move without bumping into a governor or two) but students plough on regardless. The overall impression was of complete contentment – the smiles never stopped coming. And even though the aroma emanating from the school 'Bistro' smelt like school dinners, the food looked very different. Choices ranged from salads to curries to jacket potatoes and pupils sat at tables with plates piled high. 'We have our own catering team so we have total control over diet and nutrition,' said the principal. 'We take eating disorders very seriously and our menus are regularly reviewed by a leading dietician.' Each boarding house has live-in house parent, common room and kitchen. Younger pupils live next to the medical centre, sharing double rooms, while year 11 students and some first year sixth have spacious single study bedrooms with en suite shower-rooms. There are also two off-campus houses five bus stops away for other sixth formers (both with resident members of staff). Students in their final year can choose to live in rented flats and houses. 'It gives them the independence they need at that age.'

Pastoral Care and Discipline: Pastoral care primarily the responsibility of tutors and house parents. But McNamara says it's a responsibility taken on by everyone where older pupils also help and support younger ones. Bullying quickly stamped on through mediation rather than sanctions. Both sides (including parents) brought together to sort it out. Would have zero tolerance of drugs if they became an issue but principal stresses, 'there are no drugs.' In such event, the course pursued would be 'negotiated withdrawal'. Discipline generally not an issue either. The discipline students show in the dance studios spills over into their daily lives. (Certainly true if the state of classrooms and study bedrooms is anything to go by). Head of pastoral care Julie McNamara tells us, 'the difference is that all our students want to be here. They know how lucky they are to have a place here and they're happy.'

Pupils and Parents: Numbers up significantly since move to Midlands – especially among the boys. Principal puts it down to the 'Billy Elliot effect'. Both boys and girls are bright, cheerful and totally focused. 'They have an emotional maturity you don't normally find in youngsters of that age,' he says. Come from far and wide. Now 13 nationalities represented. Full range of backgrounds dictated by sliding scale of fees support. But McNamara says, 'the children blend together seamlessly because they have one thing in common – the common concern with excellence.' OBs and OGs (known as old Elms) include actresses Helen Baxendale, Hayley Mills, Juliet Mills, Jenny Agutter and Joanna David, singer Sarah Brightman, and ballet dancers Dame Merle Park, Diana Fox and Isobel McMeekan.

Entrance: By audition only. No academic test. Selection made on 'perceived potential' and 'commitment' rather than technical brilliance. 'That can be taught, but this isn't a place for recreational dancers.' Auditions held between October and March (fee non-refundable). At least 12 applications for each place, so youngsters really need to be something special. Big sixth form in-take to replace those weeded out.

Exit: Around 50 per cent lost before sixth form to dance careers or other vocational schools more suited to them. Regular assessments throughout school career will have identified weaker members who will be directed elsewhere. Ruthless maybe but principal explains, 'we're all about producing classical ballet dancers. It's a very demanding art form and there's no point in giving youngsters false hope.' Of those who stay the course, several each year secure contracts with international ballet companies before leaving and head says 90 per cent are in professional employment within six months of leaving.

Money Matters: One of eight specialist schools that get government support through music and dance aided places scheme. School receives funding for 85 aided places across lower school and sixth formers helped through National Dance and Drama awards. Means-tested support given to most gifted and eligible 11-year-olds, with funding continuing until end of year 11 if youngsters get through artistic appraisal in year 9. When visited in 2005, school had 145 students on state scholarships. Fees not extortionate compared with similar specialist schools. Few extras include text books, exam and audition costs, and any medical expenses not covered by compulsory BUPA membership.

Remarks: A very special place for very special students. It was easy to forget at times that Elmhurst was, in fact, a school as pupils looked happier than they had any right to be! Certainly not a school that would suit all though but then that's the whole idea. Only the best need apply – it's as simple as that. 'We are going to be the Ivy League in classical ballet training,' vows McNamara. 'We aspire to being one of the best classical ballet schools in the world.'

ELTHAM COLLEGE

Linked to Eltham College Junior School in the Junior section

Grove Park Road, Mottingham, London, SE9 4QF

Tel: 020 8857 1455

Fax: 020 8857 1913

E-mail: mail@eltham-college.org.uk

Website: www.eltham-college.org.uk

- Pupils: 745 boys plus 65 girls in the sixth form. All day • Ages: 11-18 • Size of sixth form: 215 • Christian Free Church • Fees: £3,434 • Independent • Open days: Late September, mid November for 11+ entry; early November for sixth form entry

Head: Since 2000, Mr Paul Henderson BA FRSA (early fifties). Educated at The Leys Cambridge and Nottingham. Taught at Norwich School for 15 years (head of classics, director of studies, i/c cricket), then second master at St Albans until he came here. Not someone that students naturally talk to, but 'teaches every pupil in the school and attempts to get to know each of them well.' A cricket lover and singer, keeps a bat lolling in his study, so perhaps the sports field or the concert hall are where he opens up. Wife and two grown-up children.

Appointed with a mission to raise the profile of the school, redevelop the junior school and enhance music. Sees his most important job as choosing staff and pupils; 20 staff have been appointed to the community since 2000 and all pupils are interviewed. Parents find him approachable despite his previous informal title 'Prince of Darkness' at St Albans – a strict disciplinarian.

Academic Matters: Good results overall. Head tells pupils 'you can do better'. Grades have improved c 20 per cent since 2000 with new initiatives; closer monitoring of pupils' academic results (now 5 sets of grades per academic year), biannual staff appraisals with a focus on how a head of department appraises staff. The governors have allocated a healthy budget for in-service training and professional development. Eltham is part of the South London Teacher Training Scheme; encourages links between private and maintained sectors with team work. The usual wide curriculum for years 7 – 11, Latin and French are now compulsory for those in year 7 for 2 years. The head teaches Latin to year 7. All year 7 are screened for SEN and special needs are taken seriously. One SEN teacher. Pupils view SEN help as an aid to attaining the required rising grades. English, history, maths and the sciences the most popular A

levels. Teachers good at their subject but required for extra curricular activity too. Boys look academic smart in blue blazers; girls are in dark power suits.

Games, Options, The Arts: Strong rugby tradition with successful annual entry into Daily Mail Cup. Head introduced hockey despite pressures from OEs and there was a hockey tour to Greece in 2003. Hockey now the norm for all but only the best play external matches. Long history of cricket with Eltham as a Centre of Excellence in Kent. Frequent cricket tours to the Caribbean. Annual match Gentlemen of Mottingham v Eltham for the W G Grace trophy – it is rumoured he lived in the village. The Eric Liddell Sports Centre keeps sport going in inclement weather. Plans are in place for a partnership with the local community for a flood-lit Astro surface. Non sporty types welcomed for their arts.

Eltham values the making of music for teamwork. New music school opened 2005 – a refurbishment of the boarding house that closed summer 2004. Free lessons for a term to introduce an instrument – watch this space for music lift off. Art is large and big – positive displays in the main entrance hall and a sculpture walk along the path from the senior to the junior school. Many sculptures donated by Dr Gerald Moore OE. Clubs are very popular especially chess and D of E for years 11, 12 and 13.

Background and Atmosphere: A school with a sense of purpose – Get the best As possible, go on to uni, aim high in life. Has its origins in Walthamstow in 1842 and then Blackheath as a school for the sons of missionaries. It moved to its current site in 1912 when the Royal Naval School sold up. Warm reception for visiting parents – good telephone warmth too. The 36 acres of level playing fields surrounding an elegant 18th century mansion are a green and pleasant oasis in busy South-East London. The tranquil setting belies the compressed bustle of an academic day school (8.30am – 4pm) – well run, lots of management consultancy feel. Refurbished junior school has a separate entrance from the senior school; each school has an individual identity under the same brand name. Christian principles to the fore but all faiths are embraced.

Pastoral Care and Discipline: Strong anti bullying and drugs policy. Parents sign a contract which outlines the conditions under which a pupil is accepted at Eltham. Innovation of pastoral evenings for years 10 and 12 pupils together with parents to discuss diverse issues organised by the pastoral deputy head. Too early to assess real benefits but parents value involvement, pupils less enthusiastic. Parents and pupils, especially girls, regard school nurse as a high profile pastoral team member. Strong tutor system with a head of girls to monitor the 60 girls in the sixth form. Still a hint of a male dominated ethos but no plans for Eltham to go fully co-ed.

Pupils and Parents: Good mix socially and culturally. Most parents work in and around the City; very keen for a good education but not an elite education. Most are entrepreneurial professionals. Five mile radius catchment area including Blackheath, Bexley, Bromley, Croydon, Hayes, Orpington and Sidcup. Notable OEs include Eric Liddell (gold medal Olympian and missionary), Fenner Brockway (Pacificist), Mervin Peake (Novelist), John Willis (BBC) and Barnaby Lennon (Harrow head).

Entrance: 75 places at 11 – English, maths, verbal reasoning. 50 per cent come from the junior school and c 5 from state schools, places at 13+ reserved for Bickley Park style prep schools. Girls and boys coming in for the sixth form – must have 6 B GCSE grades, not that hard for an average pupil. This applies to boys in the school too, so there's a 'small natural wastage' post GCSE.

Exit: Recent average of 10 places to Oxbridge otherwise to Durham, Nottingham, Bath and London – particularly medicine, law and social sciences. About 40 per cent of leavers go gapping.

Money Matters: Up to 20 academic awards available to sparky 11 year olds and 20 sixth form scholarships including art and drama. Music and sports scholarships too. Current development fund raising scheme is helping to meet Eltham's aim for 25 per cent of students to have financial support. Attempts to keep students to the next academic stage if financial clouds appear - a dialogue with the bursar is crucial.

Remarks: A beacon of quality in South-East London. Traditional day school with a boarding school feel – Saturday matches. Popular in the local area and with the surrounding gated properties.

EMANUEL SCHOOL

Battersea Rise, London, SW11 1HS

Tel: 02088 704 171
Fax: 02088 771 424
E-mail: enquiries@emanuel.org.uk
Website: www.emanuel.org.uk/

- Pupils: 480 boys, 220 girls, all day • Ages: 10-18 • Size of sixth form: 138 • Christian Foundation • Fees: £3,658
- Independent • Open days: One each autumn and tours each Wednesday throughout year; ring in advance to book a place

Headmaster: Since 2004, Mark Hanley-Browne MA (early forties). Nat Sci BA at Oxford, PGCE at Cambridge. 22 years in teaching including time at Charterhouse, Sevenoaks and was the pastoral deputy at Highgate School before moving here. Keen to discuss strategies and challenges with others in the United Westminster Schools group such as Joe Davies at Sutton Valence. Dedicated and ambitious, with a clear vision for Emanuel, building on good work of previous heads. Married to Rachael, a management consultant, lives within walking distance across Wandsworth Common, so is a recognisable local presence for children and adults. Excited about recent improvements to school and very proud of the pupils and growing reputation of the school.

Academic Matters: The careers of old boys (Sir Tim Berners-Lee, creator of the World Wide Web, Peter Goddard CBE, director of Institute for Advanced Study at Princeton University) illustrate that in Emanuel's academic heyday it turned out intellectual heavyweights. At present it is at the bottom end of the best 200 schools in the country, with members of the current lower sixth having 50 per cent grade As and A*s in their GCSEs. Pulling up the academic socks of a school always takes a while – 7 years to be precise, the time that a pupil spends working his/her way through to the sixth form. The head recognises that Emanuel's current academic reputation is its Achilles heel, but comments, 'annual league tables are always a snapshot of the academic achievements of a school's intake 7 years previously.' He is confident that his latest group of year 7s are first division with many choosing Emanuel over competitor schools.

Newly refurbished science labs are impressive and well-used, a mini lecture theatre faces an interactive whiteboard, the use of which clearly benefits the pupils (rather than it just being shown off to prospective parents). Dedicated ICT rooms including one in the wonderful, and separate, sixth form building (paid for by a princely old boy). CDT takes place in a well-equipped workshop. The SENCO also has devoted space at back of school, above Hill form (year six). She visits every form for one day per year to introduce herself and the resources, after that 'you can go in yourself and ask for help – people do, especially with revision.' Dyslexic pupils and those with statements receive scheduled help.

Good range of languages – French, German, Spanish and Latin from year 7. £1.5m renovation of the main building on its way in 2006 which will result in smarter corridors, a new library and two new ICT suites – walls will be knocked through and leather sofas spread around the new space.

Games, Options, The Arts: Shining sports hall with climbing wall, ergometers on which you can race other people on the internet, fencing equipment, PE classroom, excellent rowing available at Barnes, 14 acres of sports grounds at Blagdons and 12 acres at Mitcham as well as swimming pool and fives courts on site. The pitches are verdant – the work of two dedicated groundsmen – and pupils have won awards at county, regional, national and international levels, throughout the huge range of sports on offer. Also a healthy emphasis on general fitness with gym machines available in free periods if supervised.

Fantastic music department run by a dedicated couple, he provides inspiration while she keeps the feet on the ground. Kids play in the National Youth Orchestra, sing in the National Youth Choir and go on tours to Malta, Italy and the US. Drama is popular, especially the sixth form review, always a golden opportunity for mickey taking and cross dressing. Visual art leaps out of the rabbit warreny art department and is everywhere in the school – shelves, walls, ceilings. The standard is very high and showcased once a year in a school exhibition.

Background and Atmosphere: Many pupils say that Emanuel's atmosphere is why they chose to attend. It is a friendly and welcoming one, with 85 per cent white European, 10 per cent Asian and 5 per cent Afro-Caribbean pupils reflecting the mix of residential Clapham now. The Dacre legacy (the school was originally richly endowed in 1594) stretches to support not only these 12 acres of green land in centre of London, but a boarding school in Kent (Sutton Valence) and a state comprehensive (Westminster City School). Links with WCS include teacher exchanges and practical advice on ICT use with mixed ability groups.

The school grounds are very secure, the main building is an ex-Crimean War Orphanage, sandwiched between two train lines, with pupils approaching across Wandsworth Common or from Clapham Junction BR station. Emanuel pupils mix well across years, with prefects' visits to the con-

tained Hill form and sibling relationships encouraging this. The new dining room and choice of food provides a good focal point as well, pub tables outside make mealtimes in the summer look idyllic.

The school council has two representatives from each year and has a £2,000 budget. They have had a positive influence on the school uniform – 'the horrible yellow shirts that were cut to fit lumberjacks' are being removed from the girls' clothing list and replaced with tailored blue blouses. The general pupil consensus is that things have got much better since the new head came in, especially in the lower years. Kids are not afraid to disagree with each other at all – or the teachers, but this confidence does not seem to bleed into insolence.

Pastoral Care and Discipline: Each pupil has a tutor (20 in a tutor group) and a head of year, as well as belonging to one of 8 junior and senior houses. This ensures designated individual attention in addition to that stemming from friendships with peers and subject teachers. The chaplain is the school counsellor and has a sixth form team to help him but pupils say most problems are picked up and dealt with by friends. Demonstrations of care for each other and the world outside ranges from community service to boys having their legs waxed during charity week! Prefects and heads of school enforce discipline – conduct cards are carried by all to record school and homework timetables, commendations and signatures (5 signatures and you are sent to the year head to go on daily report). Academic and behavioural detentions for misdemeanours take place after school and on Saturday morning respectively. Exit for cumulative misbehaviour and possession of drugs in school – as a day school, any drug use is likely to go on outside grounds...

Pupils and Parents: Reflect the mix of modern south London, parents in media, arts, law, and finance. Reports and grades sent home every half term and meetings held where appropriate. Full written report once a year, twice in first year. Emanuel Parents' Association focuses on organising social and educational events rather than fund raising.

Entrance: 1,500 people at a recent Open Day so 'easy to sell'. Recently 330 applicants for 90 places at y7. Interviews for 60 per cent of applicants and the interview really matters here. Aiming to continue raising academic standards but not at the expense of the arts and sport.

January exam at 10: up to 20 places available. At 11: up to 90 places. At 13: up to 20 places. At sixth form level, interview and own tests, so they can offer unconditional places (usually in December). The aim here is to take the worry away from pupils and parents as they open their post at results time in August: 'when we offer places at sixth form level, those places are guaranteed. The "hurdle" (8 A*-C GCSEs including maths, English and Bs in the subjects to be studied) is merely a guideline – we have the courage of our convictions!'

Exit: Nearly all to university, most to first choice, about a third take a gap year. Four to five Oxbridge offers per year.

Money Matters: Academic, music, art, sport and drama scholarships on offer – at present 17 in youngest year, 20 scholars in the lower sixth.

Remarks: A diverse and caring school which is improving academically although the best aspects are still music and art (86-88 per cent As and Bs at A level). Looks outward as well as in for inspiration and education with plentiful trips within London and abroad for classics, sport, languages and music.

EPSOM COLLEGE

College Road, Epsom, Surrey, KT17 4JQ

Tel: 01372 821 234
Fax: 01372 821 237
E-mail: admissions@epsomcollege.org.uk
Website: www.epsomcollege.org.uk

• Pupils: 720; 498 boys of whom 263 board, including 151 weekly boarders. 222 girls: 127 board, including 81 weekly boarders • Ages: 13-18 • Size of sixth form: 318, including 114 girls • C of E • Fees: Day £5,266; day boarding £5,607; weekly boarding £7,159; full boarding £7,463 • Independent • Open days: May and September/October

---

Head: Since 2000, Mr Stephen R Borthwick (early fifties), previously head of Aldenham. Educated at a Surrey grammar school, then physics at the University of Wales, Bangor. Previously head of physics at Marlborough and then deputy head at Bishop's Stortford. Enjoys golf, walking, portrait photography and music. Personable and business-like. Married to Glynis, a modern linguist (they met at university), who teaches English as an Alternative Language at the school. Parents' main point of contact seems to be with house masters/mistresses rather than the head.

Academic Matters: Not a premier league academic powerhouse but very strong overall performance. At GCSE consistently good A/A* performance in languages (French, German, Spanish), art, maths, geography, history and the separate sciences. Overall GCSE pass rate of 100 per cent grades A-C. A level results also impressive with 80 per cent achieving A or B.

In the lower school there is a broad curriculum. Choice between German and Spanish. Generally, pupils take 10 GCSEs; the most able at maths can sit a year earlier. Sixth formers take 4 A/S levels, some continuing with 4 subjects for A2s but most taking 3. Recent introductions proving popular for A/S level include classical civilisation, theology, philosophy, business studies, politics and government and theatre studies. The newly introduced critical thinking has also proved a popular choice for candidates. One parent with a son keen on serious computer programming settled on Epsom after a long and frustrating search.

Each subject has its own teaching block, except for economics, business studies, history and geography which are housed in the new Mackinder building. Each block has a dedicated library, seminar room and departmental office. Impressive modern main library converted from the old gym in 1996, with link to the careers department. Qualified librarian always on duty and it also functions as a community area, with broad selection of daily newspapers and current cinema guides.

Average class size 18 in the lower school; 10 in sixth form. Pupils with SEN admitted provided that they can cope with academic mainstream (full-time teacher and assistant solely for this), but extra charge. Support for dyslexic pupils is 'impressive', according to one satisfied parent. Saturday morning lessons for all with games or activities in the afternoon, after which weekly boarders can depart until Sunday evening.

Games, Options, The Arts: Sport compulsory for all – more than 25 sports available. PE is offered at A level and the sports centre has a dedicated form room for this. The centre also houses two large sports halls (one with cricket nets), a fencing salle with two pistes, a multigym, climbing wall and everything else you would expect. School very, very good at target rifle shooting, with a 25m indoor range – popular with both boys and girls and the master in charge of shooting (an historian) has been adjutant to the British cadet rifle team. Epsom has been Public Schools' Champions 9 times during the last 14 years.

Better spectator provision for the swimming pool almost complete at time of writing. Hockey very popular with both sexes (master in charge was member of British Olympic team); rugby is main boys' field sport (winners of The Daily Mail U15 Rugby Cup). Soccer also on offer, although budding David Beckhams should note that soccer is not often played competitively below sixth form. Good squash courts, some with spectator galleries, and golf available on the neighbouring private Epsom Downs course.

School surrounded by extensive playing fields. Splendid

CCF assault course (used by the Army as well) and which has featured in ITV's 'The Bill'. CCF compulsory for first two years – it's not popular with everyone – thereafter optional. Duke of Edinburgh Award scheme also operated at all 3 of its levels. School exceptionally strong on art (see famous OB artists), with most pupils having their own studio space for their work – no tedious packing away after each lesson. One parent said, 'my son was especially talented at pottery and he was given the greatest encouragement.' Music also very good (over 350 lessons per week) and sensibly scheduled so that no pupil misses an academic lesson – other schools take note! Modern music block has own recording studio. Vocal groups very popular with both sexes, including the Downs Singers (secular as well as holy music) and the chapel choir. Old squash courts destined to become a centre for performing arts, relieving the somewhat small school hall (also being developed) from housing these activities as well as exams and assemblies.

Background and Atmosphere: School founded in 1855 along with The Royal Medical Foundation for the sons of doctors and occupies 80 acres on Epsom Downs – an oasis in the heart of the built-up Surrey commuter belt. All accommodation, facilities and sports are within the grounds or adjacent (except for sailing in the summer at Ripley). Used to have small, idiosyncratic museum housing, probably unique, collection of medical instruments and items of biological interest – still on view and of great interest to some parents and, we hope, to the fortunate pupils.

Buildings of mellow red brick, including the chapel and the modern structures blend in well, creating a collegiate atmosphere – although some would argue the site is not over-endowed with character and atmosphere. A recently developed 'social centre' very popular with both sexes and all age groups – open at specified times during day and 'good for hanging out,' says one sixth former. Boarding houses cosy, each with small library, music and IT rooms. Meals are compulsory for all (peace of mind for mothers with potentially anorexic daughters). Girl boarders share no more than 4 to a room, with a single room in the upper sixth. Boys boarding share between 4 and 6 in first year, then between 2 from second year, with own room in upper sixth.

School now fully co-ed and has benefited enormously from this, says head, becoming a 'more civilised and congenial community.' Numbers expanding, mainly to cope with demand from girls, which has necessitated an additional house, increasing houses from 11 to 12. Around 30 day boarders (20 boys, 11 girls), who stay at school to do their prep.

Large numbers of brothers and sisters in the school which, head says, brings a better sense of partnership with the families. Courteous, middle class pupils, with noticeably easy relations between boys and girls. All wear uniform, with wider choice available to sixth formers including trousers for girls. Generally smart but some girls a bit dishevelled and with surprisingly short skirts.

Pastoral Care and Discipline: We have had a few reports of bullying in the past (head accepts that this may have been the case) but it is now definitely history. Recent parental survey on key issues resulted in 97 per cent voting that pastoral care was either satisfactory or very satisfactory. There is a published anti-bullying policy and the issue is addressed in PSE lessons and in-house talks. House support for pupils is strong with a house tutor for each year group in each house, providing supervision for academic and pastoral matters as well as house matters. More than 50 per cent of the staff have been here over 10 years, indicating a stable and contented bunch. School counsellor available. Zero-tolerance on drugs with head finding it 'difficult to envisage any circumstances in which a pupil found in possession or dealing could remain.' Recent social services report on boarding very positive.

Chapel compulsory on Wednesdays and on Saturday, together with a weekly congregational hymn practice, alternative arrangements eg supervised study for non-C of E students. Chapel on Sunday morning is voluntary, followed by optional sports and visits eg to Tate Modern. One pupil says, 'very few boarders want a seventh day of being organised, they want flexibility.' Boarders allowed into Epsom but control exercised depending on age, numbers and time.

Pupils and Parents: Predominantly from Surrey and fringes, even among the boarders. Pupils come from a wide range of local prep schools but no formal links with any particular one. Ample daily school transport laid on from west London and several Surrey towns, with minibuses between school and local rail stations – means many parents can avoid the dreaded school run.

Parents mainly professionals and company directors, with 14 per cent ex-pats and non-UK. ' The school is not a pretentious one,' says one mother. Has a long tradition of overseas students and the sixth form entry especially reflects this, with pupils continuing to come from the same schools in SE Asia and Hong Kong, many of them the children of former pupils.

Well-known Old Epsomians include artists John Piper and Graham Sutherland and, for no obvious reason, a strong line in TV reporters, including Jeremy Vine, Nicholas Witchell, Mark Mardell and Jonathan Maitland (also the author of 'How to Make Your Million From the Internet' and, subsequently, the same with 'And What to Do If You Don't' added to the title), together with lots of medical luminaries and some politicians.

Entrance: Via CE at 13 (pass mark for entrance 55 – 60 per cent). An 11+ exam can be sat before CE based on tests in English, maths, IQ and an interview – useful for borderline candidates. Non CE takers can sit special tests at 13. At sixth form, there is an intake of about 50 – including 30 girls. Sixth form entry is subject to entrance exams, interviews and actual performance achieved at GCSE.

Exit: Vast majority to university (most popular are Southampton, Edinburgh, Nottingham and Cambridge or gap year). Subject-wise, of 155 about 10-15 go on to study medicine and 10-20 engineering or economics, with business, English, law and geography next in popularity. School has reputation for producing more medics than any other and used to be the number one choice for doctors' sons – intake broader now.

Money Matters: The usual awards for art, music and sport, together with academic, all-rounder but also design technology and theatre studies awards and all available at both 13 and 16. Closed scholarships for children of doctors who have fallen on hard times. More than 40 awards made each year - their value is up to 20 - 25 per cent of full fees but can be topped up by bursaries.

Remarks: Solid co-educational school with healthy proportion of boarders both weekly and full-time. Good academic achievement, very good on-site facilities and increasingly popular with girls who generally integrate well.

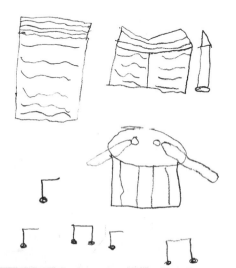

ERMYSTED'S GRAMMAR SCHOOL

Gargrave Road, Skipton, North Yorkshire, BD23 1PL

Tel: 01756 792 186
Fax: 01756 793 714
E-mail: admin@ermysteds.n-yorks.sch.uk
Website: www.ermysteds.n-yorks.sch.uk

- Pupils: 673 boys • Ages: 11-18 • Size of sixth form: 174
- None • State

Head: Since 1998, Mr T L Ashworth BSc MSc (fifties), previously deputy head at Reading School and head of mathematics at Ripon Grammar. Warm, enthusiastic and approachable; married with two daughters; originally from Birkenhead. A mathematician, he teaches sixth form four periods a week. Appears very laid-back but the success of the school and an appetite for further progress suggest otherwise. Justifiably proud of the school's achievements, both academic and sporting, but not complacent. His overriding view is that the boys and, indeed, the staff, should come to school and enjoy themselves and their success will follow on naturally from that.

Academic Matters: Academically selective, boys are competitive and hardworking. The Sunday Times Parent Power supplement described Ermysted's as the most consistent school (in terms of examination performances) in the north of England. In August 2004, at A level, depending upon which national paper one reads, Ermysted's was placed 12th or 13th nationally, second in the ranking for all-boy schools. In new-style value-added league tables the school outperformed all other schools in North Yorkshire. Average class sizes vary from 28/29 in years 7-9 to approximately 22 in years 10-11. Sixth form groups range from around 12 (though sometimes smaller) to maximum of 17. French and German taught from year 7; Latin in years 8 and 9. Science strong throughout the school and provision of II facilities much improved of late, a direct consequence of criticism of facilities provision in the 2000 inspection. Economics at A level thriving. 20 courses offered to sixth form, further opportunities coming from closer cooperation with the nearby girls' grammar school, expanding into new territory with joint lectures, theatre visits, drama and curriculum opportunities in years 12 and 13.

Games, Options, The Arts: Rugby, cricket, cross country and athletics – the strongest being cross country where the school is represented at both county and national levels. The school also boasts international honours at orienteering – viewed by school as a perfect fit for this trad grammar school in that it requires a 'fit body and an agile mind'. Badminton, golf and football also options for older pupils – although essentially a rugby-playing school where rugby skills are practised on the pitch and football skills 'honed in the school yard'. An attractive sports hall (1992) is useful area for team games and school functions with added climbing wall, also table tennis and snooker on the upper floor. Swimming at the nearby local authority pool.

Music and drama productions lend life to the academic curriculum; varied and interesting school visits valued by parents, notably geography trips to Iceland, for which the boys believe they are extremely well-prepared by 'freezing games lessons endured on windswept playing fields'.

Background and Atmosphere: Founded circa 1492, originally the school for the sons of dour Dalesmen, local townsfolk and professionals from industrial Yorkshire ('escaping for the clean air of Skipton'.) The school's uncomplicated motto 'Suivez La Raison' or 'Follow the Right Path' (alternatively translated as 'You can't go wrong here' or 'Follow the Grape') is echoed in the blunt, hard Yorkshire gritstone buildings and style. Well-supported Old Boys' Association shows an active interest in the continued success of the school and the continuation of its selective status.

Generally well-kept and with a sympathetic mix of old and new buildings. Old prefabricated canteen due for replacement (£1.7 million grant received – completion date August 2006), as is the library; sixth form common room to be relocated and given an overdue face-lift. Additional teaching block, opened September 2003, offers more classrooms, an additional IT suite and impressive design technology areas.

Hard core of long-established, experienced teachers, with some newer, younger staff; the addition of a small number of women teachers has 'mellowed the staff common room'.

Pastoral Care and Discipline: A great deal of time given to careful induction into year 7, with staff visiting boys in their primary schools prior to joining, followed by visits to the school for new boys and parents and 'taster' lessons. Pastoral care wrapped around the house structure and a newly introduced merit system working well, particularly with the younger boys. Boys appear focused and purposeful, are aware of what is expected and generally conform to expectations.

Pupils and Parents: Pupils come from a wide-range of backgrounds, many travelling from outlying rural villages and the industrial areas of West Yorkshire and Lancashire; a number, with a good eye for a Yorkshire bargain, emigrating from the more affluent areas such as Ilkley. The diverse population, both in cultural and socio-economic terms, is undoubtedly a strength. Has many of the features of its independent counterparts (Speech Day, Founders' Day), parents value the high quality of education and the traditional approach without the added fee-paying burden that would make it inaccessible for much of its existing population. Small core of active parents fundraise significant amounts of money for the school each year. Old Boys include Ian Mcleod (politician) and Simon Beaufoy (scriptwriter 'The Full Monty').

Entrance: For entry at 11, LEA oversees testing procedure at this age – verbal and non-verbal reasoning tests. Priority given to boys living in catchment area and those with a brother at the school; Common Application Form requiring preferences before outcome of tests known (this will change for September 2007 entry) has caused difficulty for some parents – not fully subscribed in September 2005. The school actively discourages coaching for entry but little doubt that it happens anyway as parents and feeder schools are aware that this is a highly selective school and the pressure for places is great. Entry to years 8 to 11 if places available. Tests in mathematics, English, science and a modern foreign language (French or German). Entry to sixth form needs 6 GCSEs at grade C+ including at least B in AS subjects (grade A in mathematics required).

Exit: Not surprisingly, most stay on to sixth form; of these by far the majority go on to good universities (most popular for 2005 entry were Newcastle, Oxford and Cambridge – 8 to Oxford, 6 to Cambridge in 2005); small number into industry and the Services.

Remarks: A gritty no-nonsense school, not groundbreaking but unashamedly competitive and academic, with a caring edge.

ETON COLLEGE

Eton, Windsor, Berkshire, SL4 6DW

Tel: 01753 671 249
Fax: 01753 671 248
E-mail: admissions@etoncollege.org.uk
Website: www.etoncollege.com

• Pupils: 1,298 boys (all boarding) • Ages: 13-18 • Size of sixth form: 520 • C of E (other faiths 'excused' chapel, but many attend anyway) • Fees: £7,896 • Independent • Open days: Tours and briefings on 60 afternoons a year

Headmaster: Since 2002, Mr Anthony (Tony) Little ARM MA PGCE (forties) who was educated at Eton, read English at Corpus Christi (where he was a choral exhibitioner) and did his PGCE at Homerton. Previously head of Oakham, having taught English at Tonbridge and Brentwood, and was head of Chigwell ('a steep learning curve') before Oakham. Keen on music, the theatre, film and rowing (nostalgically the latter). A lovely man; he speaks immaculate English, in paragraphs, with 'whoms'.

Some radical moves – the head man (as all Eton heads are known) has instituted a parent/teacher evening in E and F block, before long leave in the first half (Eton speak: read before half term in the first term); this is a dramatic turnaround and no longer will parents be able to complain that they 'don't know what the darlings are up to'.

Certain amount of jealousy from other headmasters – 'he hasn't even been head of a first division school and now he is head of the heap' – but he appears comfortable in his (holey) shoes and is good at working the public and the parents, 'super directed, makes a terrific impression'. 'Keen on raising the public perception of the school.' 'Not a stuffed shirt and always open to new ideas.'

This is a head who reckons that, 'there must be a regular appraisal of teachers and housemasters'. Health and Safety are also much involved, and there has been a proactive appointment. The head's wife, Jenny, is very involved in school activities ('too involved' said one beak (ie teacher); 'not at all hands-off' said the head man; she regularly acts as school guide. And no, she has not done her colours test. The Littles have a grown up daughter.

The lower man (as the previous deputy head was known) is now a two-man position, with 'computer freak', the erstwhile head of maths, The Rev. John Puddifoot ('jumped up director of studies,' said one colleague) run-

ning the curriculum side, with Dr Bob Stevenson looking after the trad pastoral role of lower master.

Academic Matters: First class all round, though not necessarily first class in all the league tables. Outstandingly good teaching, Eton can pick and choose (and cash has quite a lot to do with it – heads of departments elsewhere join the also-rans for extra pay). Prospective staff have a series of interviews, spending time in the department, taking a class (head man is 'keen that everyone should be in a class with boys') and culminating with lunch (knives and forks test). Boys setted by ability from the first year and all take some (it varies) GCSEs early, plus a full complement the following year. No thought at all of abandoning GCSEs, though a certain amount of miff about AS levels. Plenty of va et vient among sets, boys are constantly changing beaks and peer groups.

Tutors allotted for junior boys, who may then request their specialist tutor post-GCSE. Highly structured, lots of sticks and carrots. Monthly order cards and show-ups – the former now apparently delivered by email. Certain amount of irritation from older beaks about 'having to fill in the class register by computer'. Fab langs, one of the most successful departments in the country in terms of results – packs in talk and chalk. Japanese is an option (NB if Eton offers a subject it really happens – unlike many other schools which often have an element of window dressing). Proper language exchanges throughout the school (like two weeks in Japan, a whole term in Germany – usually on an exchange basis). Indeed exchanges in every discipline – France, Spain, Russia ... Plus Casa Guidi in Florence.

Vast choice of A levels, results outstanding; maths a popular subject, with ancillary economics; geography and history strong. English results are phenomenal. Twice yearly internal exams ('trials' – the top boys' results are read out). Boys are treated much as university students and need considerable stamina and self discipline to cope with the work load, no quarter is given for those who fall by the wayside. (School comments that 'this is utterly untrue, and every effort is made by housemasters, tutors and teachers to help boys through difficult periods').

School reports sent to parents have a curious formula: beaks report to tutors, who in turn report to housemasters, who in turn write to parents, enclosing relevant reports as well as their personal assessment of the situation.

School took us to task for saying that 'this is absolutely not the school for a dyslexic' and though school has good links with the Dyslexia Association, and has had for many years, pupils and beaks alike say that 'it is not really the best place for pupils who are seriously challenged'. 'Too much working on your own,' said one former (mildly dyslexic) Etonian of our acquaintance. But that having been said, there is a strong learning support system in place and the school takes in 'a significant number of dyslexic and indeed dyspraxic boys corresponding to the proportion in the general population ... and does so consciously at the point of selection where their potential is recognised, and it then provides them with extensive support'. Dyslexia unit in place, with one to one, and group therapy on tap, school can also cope with boys with Aspergers and ADHD, on the 'mild to moderate' spectrum in all cases.

Most of Little's previous headships have leant in the direction of co-education and/or the IB. When we asked him about the possibilities of such radical change his reaction was to say that, 'I first learnt that we were going down the IB route on the radio when I was filling the car with petrol in Norfolk'. He doesn't reckon it is 'good for enthusiasts, nor for scientists', but is 'much better for girls'. 'The best part of the IB is the extended essay or Theory of Knowledge – complete with footnotes – but now that all lower sixth do divinity' (which he teaches) 'this acts as an embryonic ToK, and we find nuggets of outstanding excellence, exposing as many boys as possible.' On the question of girls: we got an enigmatic 'who knows?' (the boys wondered about their uniform).

Games, Options, The Arts: Excellent all round – every conceivable extra-curricular activity is on offer to amazing standards in some cases. IT now in the vanguard, with the local expert maintaining that he had rarely come across such infrastructure. (Head man complains about 'the tyranny of the email culture'). Each room in every house now with infra-red and net connections; all boys have mobiles and discount-available laptops. Brill music, generally acknowledged to be one of the best departments in the country; and attracts the brightest and best in music scholarships. Regular and very polished concerts; wonderful chapel choir.

Superb and inspirational art department, oodles of dosh spent here in the last few years – marvellous open aspect over playing fields to the northwest. Remarkable and challenging work; masses of prizes and skols here too. The art department that all other schools envy. Drama important. Skule plays as well as house plays; both housemaster and boy-inspired, plus more trad stuff.

Main games are soccer, rugby, fives, hockey, cricket – very good; plus Eton's own Wall Game and the Field Game; good fencing, swimming (squad recently trained to swim the Channel), water polo, sailing etc, also judo, polo, beagling. Over forty teams in action most Saturdays but,

though still successful, the school does not appear to be winning the way it once did. And sport is no longer worshipped the way it once was. Housemasters not pushing hard enough say some. Head encourages boys to continue with sports through exam terms – brownie points for this.

Huge number of outings, visits and field trips etc, and good provision for amusing pupils post-exams. CCF very popular – pace Harry Windsor, and full time officer seconded. Excellent and popular post-school camp offers fantastic range of experiences – helicoptering, parachuting, speedboat driving licence (popular this and essential for hiring boats in the hols). Vast number of clubs and societies, with top notch speakers, often run by boys themselves, and almost all of which boast a variety of club sox – by which Etonians can be easily identified – they usually wear a non-matching pair (warning here, the school bill may well be augmented by several hundred quid's worth of extra 'essential' club kit – sox and scarves only).

Background and Atmosphere: Founded in 1440 by Henry VI (sister college of King's College, Cambridge, which was founded a year later), and 70 King's Scholars still live in the original buildings (most elegant dining hall and really ancient classroom still with original benches and graffiti). Buildings of mellow old red brick, grounds run down to the Thames. Magnificent chapel built by Henry VI and a second chapel for Lower Boys; war memorials all over the shop, deep nostalgia. School has appointed an Imam, RC chaplain on staff too.

Twenty-four boarding houses, including separate one for King's Scholars; single study bedsits for all, from day one. Huge variety in spec, housemasters employ different strategies as to which boy chooses first. Décor differs – one mother described one as 'like a working brothel'; another has carpet up the walls. Boarding houses scattered down the High Street and beyond; houses are known not by name but by the initials of the housemaster in charge – housemasters in the job for 13 years, so of course the name of the house changes... irritating for Eton buffs who like to pretend they know the place. Boys no longer wear bum freezers but tail coats for all, with stiff (paper) collars except for office bearers, who wear proper wing collars and white ties. Brilliant for posture, as boys stuff pockets in their tails with all sorts of essential school kit, pulling even the most round-shouldered creature straight. (Must be the cheapest school uniform out, with good second-hand trade both boy-inspired and via the school tailors in the High Street). Head describes the uniform as 'anally retentive'. Fancy waistcoats worn by members of the self-electing Eton Society, most memorable one was entirely made of condoms. However pupils no longer wear tails across the bridge to Windsor, or even now (much) in the High Street, and much changing and half-changing throughout the day.

Atmosphere very much alive, not easy, and every day is structured and active. Everyone – boys, beaks (often flying round Eton on their bikes – in white tie, with their black gowns flying and trousers tucked into their socks). All beaks must wear gowns and these come into their own during their three line whip coffee break – Chambers – when one beak will attract the attention of another by tugging at his gown... this can become addictive, with long lines of tugging beaks forming. 'Like a line of elephants,' says the head man.

Eton has its own trad but ever evolving school language: halves (terms) long leave (half term) etc, currently the buzz is to add 'age': as in 'pubage', 'birdage', 'tabage' (tobacco), lebage (as in plebs) etc. In general the school is a solipsistic attitude to life. Excellent school mags (The Chronicle, The Junior Chronicle) which are sold on high days and holidays for commission (usually by younger boys). An unwritten law discourages boys from speaking to the press, which may be the reason why beaks often hear the latest gossip via their houses and not from their peers – this can lead to not so funny situations, when a quick email to all housemasters concerned could calm the matter down. All boys now allowed mobile phones, though talking on them outwith the house is frowned upon, if not action is usually taken.

New poet in residence: the normally yellow PVC clad (in night clubs) Patience Agbabi. Chosen by the head for her 'raw vitality' and she has lines from her poems tattooed on her body. Keen on lesbianism and sado-masochism – or so says the Evening Standard.

Pastoral Care and Discipline: Broad-minded and liberal in principle, though quite capable of firing a pupil at a moment's notice for drugs offences, often to the consternation of parents. Drugs and booze and fags a perennial problem. If there is a suspicion that a pupil may be dabbling with drugs, then a 'more flexible' view is taken, to 'motivate' the pupil. Parents are informed and boy is subjected to lectures and random drugs testing. The idea, according to the head man is to 'turn around the drug culture'; this is not necessarily how it is perceived by housemasters and dames who may be involved. 'Not so much boozing' now, but 'smoking is still fairly prevalent'. Expect dismissal for repeat performances. Drunken boys are usually sobered up in house – with much love and care from housemaster and dame – other boys equally supportive. The alternative is an overnight stay in the local (extremely expensive) private hospital with stomach pumps et al. Immediate rustication thereafter, and not a

lot of sympathy either. The most normal punishment is 'to go on the bill' – this involves a quick trip to the head man with a preposter (aka sixth former) within and without the head man's office. The former acts as watchman, and the latter as marshal. The only time a preposter is not used is in the case of bullying when the head man deals with suspected culprits on his own.

The most popular form of punishment – and here the range is from missing chapel to going AWOL – is early rising. Some pupils are never 'off the bill' and some are never on it. School takes exception to our comments that 'boys are allowed out on any Sunday', and indeed true that younger boys have to have some sort of permission in place, usually given by email or fax, and on a fairly laissez-faire basis. But the King's Road in London heaves with Etonians of all shapes and sizes on any given Sunday, with boys in C having one extra weekend off in each half, B blockers two such indulgences. For those left at school though, there are masses of extra-curricular activities, choral, dramatic, what have you. The art and music schools are open, as well as the swimming pool, plus organised cross country runs (strong house competition here) rowing, cricket, football, whatever. This is a school well provided with opportunities as well as the staff to run them, and house noticeboards bulge with info on rehearsals, debates, groups, matches (both inter-house, and friendlies), clubs and activities.

Pupils and Parents: Still the trad school it always was, with numbers of Old Etonian families in the ascendant again. The Fourth of June (aka school speech day) is still as buzzy as ever, with minibuses decanting lovelies from local girls' schools to join the baying throng of picnickers but (fortunately for the school), the mass of royal watchers have gone, and the hype has subsided. A huge mix of families, from scholarship boys in the remote Welsh valleys via a percentage of first time buyers to foreign princelings and the deeply grand.

Numerous notable Old Etonians: Hubert Parry, 19 Prime Ministers, Captain Oates, the poets Gray and Shelley, Keynes, Fielding. Surprisingly few real stars among the living; politicians (William Waldegrave, Nicholas Soames, Douglas Hurd, Boris Johnson) a clutch of journalists (Charles Moore, Nicholas Coleridge, Craig Brown) also Martin Taylor, Humphrey Lyttleton, Nicholas Charles Tyrwhitt Wheeler, Matthew Pinsent and Michael Chance; plus gaol birds: Jonathan Aitken and Darius Guppy amongst others. Successful old boys tend not to describe themselves as Old Etonians; preferring to describe themselves as 'having been at school'; as in 'there is no truth in the rumour that Jeffrey Archer was at school'.

Entrance: 700 candidates for 256 places; currently from 91 different prep schools. 'A record' says the tutor for admissions. New (as in not the trad put down at birth and forget about it regime) entry procedures appear to be working well. The head man has taken the new exam himself – 'I did pass, but did rather better in the oral part'. Boys do a combination of an interview and a multiple choice computer driven exercise and results are marked by five independent assessors who then spend two days discussing their findings. Prep school reports are important, and family background is taken into account when reaching the 'global mark'. It is important that a boy 'will thrive in a boarding environment', and be able to cope 'working under his own steam'.

Successful candidates then make their choice from a possible four or six houses – as each housemaster has a potential 13 year tenure, then the odds on actually getting the particular housemaster you opt for is higher than if you chose him when little Johnnie is two or three months old. So that's a bonus. Housemasters find the extra strain of these late interviews a bit of a bind, and sometimes reflect nostalgically on the days of the general list. School has taken to visiting prep schools, we think for the first time ever, to reassure them that Eton is still the place for their darlings. Prep schools to whom we have spoken report that yes, after the first year's blip, when school seemed to 'be choosing clever creatures without much oomph', procedure does seem to be working well, and the chaps who get in would mostly have been the chaps who got in under the old procedure. They did, however, express concern that Eton should be 'pleased with the results' when boys chosen by the new procedure have not yet gone right through the school.

Entries for King's Scholarships (14 per annum) accepted until the beginning of May for exam in May at 12/13+ (these scholarships may be up to 100 per cent, with school paying for uniform, and occasionally travelling expenses). Scholars still chosen by the examiners sitting as an electoral college, looking for imagination and enterprise as much as competence – hopeless Latin forgiven if maths superb, or vice versa. Past papers freely available from the school.

Up to four continuation scholarships (aka junior scholarships) for younger boys from state schools at 10, at which point Eton pays for three years' prep school education in trad Eton 'feeds' for successful candidates. Four scholarships for state school pupils at sixth form – for the whole two years; plus regular one year (usually lower sixth) scholarship for bright boys globally.

Exit: Average of 70+ boys to Oxbridge, though not all who might be Oxbridge material apply. 'Anyway, who would we meet there?' is a regular comment from potential Oxbridge scholars. Successful in organ scholarships to Oxbridge. Most go on to university, to Bristol, Exeter and Edinburgh in droves, plus over 70 different institutions in the UK, 10-15 annually abroad. The army is popular in some quarters (pace Prince Harry), and one or two fall through every net. Tranches of gap year. Thereafter the City, estate agencies, auction houses, journalism, family estates, politics.

Money Matters: Pots and pots of money and assets; it is said that Eton is funded not by fees but by rental income; popular sideline from films (The Madness of King George etc). Eton can afford to, and does, have everything of the best, and pays its staff very well indeed. Good value. Large number of bursaries etc for parents on hard times plus eight music scholarships year, plus countless exhibitions. The posh thing is to win a King's Scholarship and turn it down in favour of someone who needs it financially. The original KS then has the (less important than ever) kudos of E marked against his name in the school house list, ditto for regularly coming tops in trials. Regular subsidised summer schools - rowing a popular option for prep school wannabes. Masses of public activity; the rowing lake is used nationally for training international rowers, and the new athletics hall and track are much in demand by locals. Eton is one of the few schools confident in its charitable status and, if it goes, they assume that parents will be able to pay the VAT on fees which is what the government is after.

Remarks: Still the number one boys' public school. The teaching and facilities are second to none. School was cross about our saying that it was 'a hard place to be for a boy who is neither one of the lads nor a gifted sportsman'; a quick survey of recent starry leavers thought, 'it must have been ghastly' for those whom they regarded as nonentities or nerds; the nonentities disagreed, saying 'that they had great fun', and 'wouldn't have been anywhere else for the world'.

EXETER SCHOOL

Linked to Exeter Junior School in the Junior section

Victoria Park Road, Exeter, Devon, EX2 4NS

Tel: 01392 258 712
Fax: 01392 498 144
E-mail: admissions@exeterschool.org.uk
Website: www.exeterschool.org.uk

- Pupils: 485 boys, 181 girls • Ages: 11-18 • Size of sixth form: 202 • Non-denom • Fees: Senior £2,660; junior £2,385.
- Independent • Open days: July and October; January for the sixth form. Taster days in November for all entry ages

Head: Since 2003, Mr Robert Griffin (early forties). First in modern languages (French and Spanish) at Oxford University. Taught overseas in Peru before being head of modern languages at Haileybury. Came to Exeter from The Royal Grammar School, Guildford where he was second master for five years. Teaches English, French and Spanish. Married with two children, one at Exeter Junior School and the other at the senior school. Is overseeing much development and building work at the school, including a new library, enhanced departmental facilities, a fitness suite and dance studio.

Academic Matters: Excellent record – 'results speak for themselves', 'no complaints', say parents. 86 per cent A-B grades at A level in 2005. Fortieth nationally at GCSE. A and A* grades 54 per cent. Top sets in maths and French up to 24 pupils to allow bottom sets to be 10-14. Average GCSE class size is 16-18, other year classes average 20. AS maximum class size, 16; A2 averages 10. Broad subject choice – 18 GCSEs including Spanish available in lower sixth; 25 A level subjects, with strong uptake of all major academic subjects. High numbers in economics and politics. Four AS choices with critical thinking and key skills is usual in lower sixth; 30 per cent study four A2s in upper sixth. Some learning support available, especially in years 7-9.

Games, Options, The Arts: On national stage for shooting, squash and hockey. Plenty of fixtures organised in various other sports – rugby, cricket, netball, golf, soccer, shooting, cross-country, athletics and swimming. Appealing cricket ground and club house, plenty of fixtures but not top of the league. Annual trips abroad include exchanges to Rennes, Hildesheim, USA. Trips with British Schools' Exploration Society and Adventurous Training Expeditions popular. CCF, D of E and Ten Tors well supported. Music is exceptionally strong, many and varied ensembles, reaching the National Music Youth Finals at the Festival Hall and schools prom at the Royal Albert Hall. Regular recitals in Exeter Cathedral. Artistic talent abounds, stunning results in all media.

Background and Atmosphere: Founded in 1633 originally for sons of freemen of Exeter. Reverted to independent status in 1976, stopped boarding in 2000. Sixth form has been mixed for 20 years, went fully co-ed in 1997, partly due to the end of the Assisted Places scheme. Female integration evidently pleasing to both sexes, and most parents – transition 'as smooth as one could expect'. Separate and mixed common rooms available. Co-ed now firmly established with head boy and head girl and prefects taking a more prominent role in running the daily life of the school. School not as lavishly endowed as one might think and décor is typically dated but much refurbishment has taken place between 2003-5. New library and study centre to open in September 2006. Third large computer room opened in summer 2004. A dance studio is part of the refurbished and extended sports centre opened summer 2005.

On 25-acre site with views of countryside and backdrop of Haldon Hills, less than a mile from city centre. Original buildings designed by famous Victorian architect William Butterfield – designer of Keble College, Oxford. Sixth Form dress code not uniform. Active and social parents' association – 'great at making parents feel included in the school'.

Pastoral Care and Discipline: Senior staff and heads of house nip minor indiscretions in the bud. Pupils failing to produce homework more than once might expect detention. Saturday detention for cigarette smokers. 'Extremely caring staff,' say parents. Teachers usually stay for years.

Pupils and Parents: Pupils, staff and parents seem to get on very well. Happy pupils, seem glad to be here, especially appreciative of extra-curricular activities. Past pupils include High Court judge Sir Charles Collingwood; politicians David Bellotti and Tony Speller, Nick Barnes of Radio 1; General Sir Anthony Farrar-Hockley, historian and TV expert on military issues; commanders, generals, actors and a former Bishop of Hull. Middle class parents – doctors and lawyers, farmers and leisure industry professionals – 44 per cent live within five miles of school, the rest up to 30 miles away.

Entrance: Entrance to junior school is by informal assessment and school report. Examination and school report for candidates at 11, 12 and 13. Pupils come from 60-70 different schools including 6 per cent from other counties.

Exit: 9 Oxbridge in 2004. Most junior school pupils progress to senior school. A trickle is lost to other independents or Colyton and Torquay grammars; 90 per cent of Exeter pupils stay on for sixth form.

Money Matters: Maintenance of numbers in recent years has enabled a range of academic and music awards at 11-13 and also a sixth form art award. Governors' awards may be offered to applicants, whose parents are unable to afford the full school fees, who show academic potential and a talent perceived to be of benefit to the school. Special awards from generous local benefactors. Support from Ogden Trust for one sixth form entrant.

Remarks: Unexpectedly unpretentious and relaxed. Produces high-achievers.

FARMOR'S SCHOOL

The Park, Fairford, Gloucestershire, GL7 4JQ

Tel: 01285 712 302
Fax: 01285 713 504
E-mail: farmors@farmors.gloucs.sch.uk
Website: www.farmors.gloucs.sch.uk

- Pupils: 1,105 boys and girls, all day • Ages: 11-18 • Size of sixth form: 170 • None • State

Head: Since 2000, Mrs Anne Stokes MEd (forties). Taught English in a comprehensive in Somerset before moving to Gloucestershire and taking up posts in a secondary modern, Linden Secondary School, then at the Catholic St Peter's High School in Gloucester. Joined the teaching staff at Farmor's in 1988, becoming deputy head before taking over the headship. Approachable, friendly and organized.

Academic Matters: Very much a school for and serving its local community, with a broad ability intake, although has in recent years taken bus loads of children from over the border in Wiltshire, including a sizeable number from Swindon opting against lower performing local schools. Always has been a school where high flyers shine, with many A grades; overall results have risen since Mrs Stokes took the reins. Excellent results in business studies, particularly at A level: became a specialist school in Business and Enterprise in 2004. Farmor's real star subject is English, both language and literature and at GCSE and A level, with results awash with As every year. And this with no setting for English, although maths, sciences and languages are streamed. French GSCE results very good, although few take it through to A level. Sports studies is popular with

strong results, psychology and music technology popular too. Consistently solid science results, with the most able taking triple science. Five A*-Cs at GCSE needed for sixth form, with Bs preferred for A level choices, although some leeway allowed. Vocational choices are limited, but Farmor's either supports students through courses elsewhere, such as Swindon College, or suggests alternative colleges. Engineering is newly introduced, aimed at the most able. Large network of PCs throughout the school, well used by students. Good mix of much-loved long-serving staff and fresh enthusiastic new ones.

Games, Options, The Arts: Lots of space for sport, but no large all-weather surfaces. Sports Centre on site but school limited by its public usage. Despite that, pupils excel in the main competitive sports of rugby, football, hockey, netball, basketball, tennis, cricket and athletics, with many representatives in county teams and regular wins in district and county sports. Nice bright spaces for art and for design & technology. A quarter of students take individual music lessons; singing a current favourite. Numerous orchestras, groups, ensembles and a choir; regular concerts, musicals and dramatic productions. Lots of foreign trips, mostly sports and language related. Interest in healthy eating initiated by staff and pupils in the form of their Ecobytz meal-options project, and now continued by the school kitchen. Lots of quiet space for reading and research.

Background and Atmosphere: Modern school with long history in a largely rural area. Farmor's School was founded in 1738 with money left by Elizabeth Farmor and Mary Barker to educate 50 boys in Fairford. Girls were admitted in 1815 and the school became fully co-educational in 1922. It was originally in the centre of town, in a building that is now the community centre, but in 1961 it moved to its present site in 18 acres of parkland a short walk away, becoming an 11-18 comprehensive in 1966. Although showing its age in places, the site is very well kept, with older buildings having had a recent facelift, and the new business and science rooms large and airy.

Pastoral Care and Discipline: Clear, open rules pinned up in every classroom regarding bullying, insolence and disobedience; well adhered to – permanent exclusion, the ultimate sanction, not seen now for several years. An air of studious calm. No detectable signs now of once reputed friction between locals and the Swindon intake.

Pupils and Parents: Intake from Fairford and villages around make it a broadly, though by no means entirely, middle class intake. Parents very supportive of school events and fundraising. Widely regarded as a decent bunch of kids (the local driving instructor says they are the nicest learner drivers in the area). Neat, polite, enthusiastic and eager to learn. Reasonably well turned out – uniform until sixth form and then 'decent' attire, which translates as jeans and plain tops in the main. Eminent former pupils include vulcanologist Dr Philip Gravestock.

Entrance: Oversubscribed (despite doubling in size in the last ten years) at both 11 and 16. School takes siblings, feeder school pupils, locals, Swindon applicants, independent school pupils and, if room, a few from further afield.

Exit: Two thirds stay on at Farmor's for the sixth form – some go to nearby Cirencester to college, although some come the other way. Almost all A level students continue their studies. Favourite destinations including Royal Holloway, Nottingham, Bristol, Cardiff, Swansea and Manchester. One a year to Oxbridge.

Remarks: A happy, forward-looking school with excellent academic results where everyone can fulfil their potential.

FELSTED SCHOOL

Linked to Felsted Preparatory School in the Junior section

Felsted, Great Dunmow, Essex, CM6 3LL

Tel: 01371 822 600
Fax: 01371 822 607
E-mail: info@felsted.org
Website: www.felsted.org

- Pupils: 450 boys and girls (around 40 per cent girls, 150 day and 290 boarders) • Ages: 13-18 • Size of sixth form: 200 • C of E • Fees: Boarders £6,847; day £5,124. (Prep day £1,179 - £2,945) • Independent • Open days: October and May

---

Head: Since 1993, Mr Stephen Roberts MA (mid forties). Educated at Mill Hill and University College, Oxford. Degree in physics. Formerly head of department and housemaster at Oundle. Spent an unfulfilling year as a credit analyst before switching to teaching. Friendly, chatty and approachable. Enjoys golf and reading when he has time. Married to Joanna, an occupational psychologist. Two teenage sons.

Academic Matters: Setting according to ability in core subjects from the beginning of year 9. French is a core subject, with a choice of Spanish or German as a second language; Latin to A level, Greek to GCSE. IT is integrated into all subjects, not taught separately. The International Baccalaureate is to be offered from September 2006 in addition to A levels; lower sixth pupils all attend a selection

of four five-week courses to 'broaden their intellectual horizons and to complement their mainstream studies'. Exam results are impressive at GCSE, with around 95 per cent achieving C or above. A level results are good, particularly considering that the GCSE grade requirements for sixth formers are lower than those of many competing schools, and are improving year by year. Currently about 50 on the SEN register, the majority of them dyslexic. About 30 have extra time in exams. 'We provide extra support for those children who need it but the school isn't right for the severely dyslexic,' says the head. Full-time EAL support. Children with EAL take extra English instead of French in year 9. After that, language study is dependent on progress.

Games, Options, The Arts: Rugby, hockey, cricket and tennis for the boys; hockey, netball, tennis and rounders for the girls. Winners of Twenty/20 Cricket Schools Championship for 2 years running. Boys' and girls' hockey is strong. Plenty of other sports on offer as extra-curricular activities, including soccer, golf, squash and shooting. D of E and Combined Cadet Force. Many pupils involved in community service. Around 50 music scholars and many more taking music lessons. Regular overseas music tours and a recent tour of the USA with a theatre production. A 30-strong social committee ensures that there is no shortage of entertainment for boarders, particularly at the weekends.

Background and Atmosphere: Set in the rural Essex village of Felsted. Founded in 1564 by Richard, Lord Riche, Lord Chancellor of England, a villain who developed a social conscience after playing a part in the decapitation of Thomas More. A building dating from this time is still in use for music but the main building dates from 1860. Some grade I and II listed buildings. New additions, the latest being an extra boarding house for girls, are architecturally pleasing and fit well with the existing buildings. Extensive and well-kept grounds and an extremely pleasant environment. Girls came to the sixth form in 1971 but not to the rest of the school until 1993. Numbers grew fairly rapidly and Felsted feels like a proper co-ed school now.

Pastoral Care and Discipline: Strong house system with plenty of inter-house competitions. Parents choose their children's houses several years in advance. Eight boarding houses – five for boys and three for girls – with small dormitories and single rooms for everyone in their last year, if not before. Home-from-home atmosphere in the boarding houses, with house staff performing tasks beyond the call of duty – ie picking boarders' clothes up off the floor and putting them away. Many of the day pupils board several days a week, often because they want to take full advantage of the extra-curricular activities but 'a child won't feel second- rate as a day pupil,' says the head. Home boarding option (school day starts at 8.30am and ends at 9pm) also available. Pupils attend chapel three mornings a weeks, plus boarders attend on two out of three Sundays. Three grades of detention, with the most serious – and most effective deterrent – being the Saturday night detention.

Pupils and Parents: Pupils come from Essex (daily buses run from a number of Essex towns), Suffolk, Cambridgeshire, north London and Hertfordshire. A fair number from abroad, with around 50 speaking English as an additional language. The sixth form is particularly popular with Germans. Notable old pupils include theatre director Max Stafford-Clark, England cricketers Derek Pringle, John Stephenson and Nick Knight and architect Prof Sir Colin Wilson.

Entrance: CE for pupils from schools that prepare for the exam. The pass rate is 50 per cent, although around four or five pupils are taken on each year who don't quite make it. 'It would be absurd to put up a solid black line,' says the head. 'And usually those who don't make 50 per cent go on to achieve good A levels.' Entrance from schools that do not prepare for CE is by interview, VRQ test and confidential reference. Lots come in from Felsted Prep School – of a prep year group of 60, 50-55 will move on to the senior school. Holmwood House in Colchester also provides a significant number of pupils. Entrance to the sixth form is with five GCSEs at grade C or above.

Exit: All but a few go on to university. Five plus to Oxbridge per year.

Money Matters: An unspecified percentage of fee income goes towards bursaries and a variety of academic, music and art scholarships worth up to 50 per cent of the fees at 13 and 16. Scholarships also at 11 and some means-tested awards. Had around 80 assisted places (at last count). School does not have heavy endowments.

Remarks: Plenty to attract parents to this school whether they are looking for a day or boarding place for their offspring.

FERNHILL SCHOOL

Fernbrae Avenue, Burnside, Rutherglen, Glasgow, G73 4SG

Tel: 0141 634 2674

Fax: 0141 631 4343

E-mail: info@fernhillschool.co.uk

Website: www.fernhillschool.co.uk

• Pupils: 165 girls, all day • Ages: 11-18 • RC (but all faiths welcome) • Fees: Primary £1,650 - £1,905; secondary £2,019 • Independent

Head: Since 2005, Mrs Anne Crammond DA (Design – as in product) PGCE (forties) who is teaching in tandem with the outgoing head and assumes 'sole responsibility' in August. The first external appointment in the school's history. Previously depute head at St Ninian's in Giffnock, she has popped in and out of the state sector and head office – Trinity High School in Renfrew, seconded to Renfrew divisional LEA as staff tutor in art and design and Holy Cross High School in Hamilton. She first came to Fernhill as a pupil in primary 'absolutely lovely', then went to Notre Dame and followed by Glasgow School of Art and Jordan Hill College of Education. Her first few years were spent in industry before marriage, motherhood and education beckoned (her son is now off to Glasgow University and psychology).

Immaculate, bubbly and bouncy, our trip round the playground was a pied piper of an experience, with tinies demanding to tell Mrs Crammond that she knew their auntie, big cousin or sister, or that she had been 'at school with Mummy'. Obviously a popular choice, Mrs Crammond is as relaxed as 'one can be' at this time, but admits to 'having a ball', 'it's just gorgeous to be back'. Currently co-head Mrs Louisa McLay, who leaves after 30 years at the helm; Mrs Crammond 'has a record of managing change' (her words), she looks forward to 'further develop the school's unique qualities, expand numbers where possible but not to the detriment of a healthy school delivering education'. We 'need to harness and take the school forward and build, as in Bob'. Fortunately, the chairman of the governors is a rare beast with whom she can discuss future plans. No mention of her at all on the (rather basic and impersonal) school website.

Academic Matters: 'Does vv well' says Mrs Crammond (well she would); trenchant spread of results, including three As at Advanced Higher, but generally more

Bs than As at Highers (geography the notable exception in 2004) and no great spread of subjects. Tiny classes with max 24 and down to 11/12 for specialist subjects. French, German and Latin, classical civilisation, lots of cross-curricular activity. An academic school, 'a wonderful spirit of team work' pervades and pupils 'work well together'. 'Curriculum support second to none', five Highers the norm, but no music, drama (extra-curricular) or home economics. Huge investment in IT over the past five years, key boarding for all, flat screens, local area network, and forty stand alones as well. Computing offered as an exam subject up to advanced higher level. Staff all dual qualified and can book computer suites for lessons. No interactive whiteboards yet, but LCD projectors around the place. Humanities well taught, and good SEN provision.

Games, Options, The Arts: Huge range of sports on offer, rugby for primaries of both sexes, plus all the usual girl affiliated activities; netball, volley ball, hockey, house matches as well as interschools. Good athletics, with mums involved in annual sports days, keen swimming at Castlemilk swimming pool nearby (which is absolutely stunning) and successful cross-country team. Saturday sports for teams. Clubs post school and during lunch, for everything. Chess popular. Singing and debating important, with masses of woodwind and violins, the occasional trumpeter and pianist; no orchestra as such, but lots of playing and groups, house competitions; music is fun here. Regular trips to the Royal Concert Hall in Glasgow. No drama – as yet 'basically this is an academic school', stunning art department including fabric and fashion design, 'band box smart into the bargain'; pupils design the fabric and follow all the way through to the finished item. Impressive.

Background and Atmosphere: Perched on the edge of a golf course and bounded by council houses on one side, this Victorian family home, which overlooks the city of Glasgow on one side and the Cathkin Braes on the other, is set in nine very nook and crannyish acres, with locked gates and security at all times. The school was founded in 1972 as a primary school, and pushed the leaving age up: demand and supply. Classrooms were added when necessary, and though the quad itself is quite splendidly uniform, the road up to the main building is lined with the most extraordinary architectural mish-mash. One might almost be tempted to say that a new brown field site might be a bon idée. School run on Christian ethos, and pupils deliciously polite, tons of praise for all, and cups awards and prizes for (almost) everything. Immaculate. Strap shoes, caps for boys (caps!) and round felt hats for girls, even with their summer dresses and long white socks. Strong links formed between senior girls and tinies, with buddies at break time. Packed lunches for all, no vending machines, pupils appear to eat lunch all over the place in little unsupervised gangs for older girls.

Pastoral Care and Discipline: No bullying – school founded on respect for other people, and 'treat them properly', though head would 'certainly take steps to see that no-one was unhappy'. Strong PSE and MRE programmes, four houses and tutor system in place. This is a Catholic Christian foundation, the school has its own priest and all practising pupils are prepared for their first confirmation within the school. The school mag has enchanting pics of boys proud in their kilts and girls in their mini bridals. Primary school staff must be practising Catholics, but it is not essential for teachers in the senior school; non-Catholics may be excused services. The school caters for all: Hindu, Moslem etc. there is no religious or sectarian bigotry. The Asian pupils 'celebrate their feast days' and the school 'acknowledges other faiths with understanding and respect'. Drugs, smoking and alcohol awareness days.

Pupils and Parents: From all over, some travel quite a long distance. North Lanarkshire, Ayrshire, buses. An oasis of middle class respectability. Can leave pupils from 8.30 am, which is handy for commuting parents.

Entrance: Own mini test and interview for littles, otherwise entrance exam for all.

Exit: Some logistical, boys leave either for the independent sector (sometimes at eight) or go into the state system. Few girls leave post Standard grades 'to further studies elsewhere', but not many fill the resulting places. Gap years for some post Standard, most go to uni, usually somewhere in Glasgow. Vast cross section of degree courses; last year also saw a collection going into the service industries: hairdressing, beauty therapy and the like.

Money Matters: Will carry a child if parents up front about financial difficulties if public exams looming, but not a rich school.

Remarks: Could be just the answer for the gentle child who needs a small loving and caring environment with the benefit of a strong religious backbone.

FETTES COLLEGE

Linked to Fettes College Preparatory School in the Junior section

Carrington Road, Edinburgh, EH4 1QX

Tel: 01313 116 744

Fax: 01313 116 714

E-mail: enquiries@fettes.com

Website: www.fettes.com

• Pupils: 280 boys, 190 girls; 195 boys and 120 girls board, the rest day • Ages: 13-18 • Size of sixth form: 180 • Non-denom • Fees: Prep: £3,270 day, £5,120 boarding. Senior: £4,953 day, £7,070 boarding • Independent • Open days: October, senior and prep; February, prep only

Headmaster: Since 1998, Mr Michael C B Spens MA (fifties) educated at Marlborough and Selwyn College where he read natural sciences. Came to Fettes after five years as head of Caldicott, having previously spent 20 years at Radley where he was housemaster and taught geology, after a short spell in business. The transition between junior and senior schools is always an interesting one but Mr Spens has weathered his double change with charm and élan – one might say nonchalance but that would be harsh, and misleading – quarter is not easily found here; there is a tightly wound spring beneath the cultivated appearance of charm and relaxation. Expect zero tolerance on the drugs front. 'The students don't want it around,' and the Fettesian druggy alcy image no longer makes headlines in the Scottish press. Fettes is challenging allcomers as Scotland's school of choice, surprisingly, even on the day front, 'and we're more expensive than the others,' says the head – but then we are talking Edinburgh (think mink and nae knickers). Married to Debbie, they have three young children (all at Fettes) and a much loved labrador ('Kiwi, because she's all black'). Charismatic, vibrant, fun. Fettes and Mr Spens are zinging. He is currently forefront of the campaign to keep Scottish independent schools' charitable status and all over the Sunday papers.

Academic Matters: Almost all heads of departments have changed during the past seven years, 'new young staff', 'very good', 'strong', 'Edinburgh is a strong draw'; and, having played the Scottish versus the English system along with all the other big players, Fettes is adding the IB to its exam choice from 2006. Pupils will be able to choose whether they want to specialise – in which case they will be encouraged to do A levels, or decide whether the broader

IB syllabus, with its extended theory of knowledge will suit them better. Highers will still be on offer over one year 'to broaden' those on A level courses. This is a brave decision, but Mr Spens appears to think that it is possible to mix the three disciplines. Pupils will be offered positive advice and encouragement on which route to take, 'but parents' wishes at the end of the day are followed'. Three sciences on offer throughout, plus trad French, German and Spanish, as well as Russian, Mandarin Chinese and Japanese (available for beginners as well as for native speakers); and all these can be taken as a one year higher, from scratch if need be. No particular bias, physics, chemistry, history and geography outstanding at GCSE level, Maths and English almost equally strong, results in all disciplines equally impressive at A level (88 per cent A+B grades). Art results outstanding throughout the school (3 out of the top 5 A level candidates nationally for the second year in succession). Tranche of outstanding French GCSEs taken early. Strong tradition of classics; government and politics and history of art available at A level. Broad range of subjects available but not the biggest take up at A level in langs, classics or further maths.

Foreign pupils with minimal English are no longer accepted willy-nilly unless they happen to be particularly bright, or have siblings in the school. EFL is on hand, but pupils who don't have 'a pretty good working knowledge of English' are encouraged to do an English lang course before they arrive (Edinburgh School of English is popular). Good staff:pupil ratio. 'Computers zooming ahead'. School wirelessly networked throughout, with all senior school students having their own laptop, school can provide at 1500 quid a pop including software and insurance, or pupils can opt for their own. A very high proportion of leavers (95+ per cent) go on to university; on average 12 Oxbridge places each year.

Fettes is creaming off the academic elite of Edinburgh, be they boarder or day.

Games, Options, The Arts: Wide range of opportunity for games. 'Rugby is strong, though no longer a religion' (73 blues to date). Needle matches with Glenalmond and Merchiston on the rugby field and Strathallan in hockey. Lacrosse impressive, girls play hockey and netball as well – sixth form not forced to play team games at all – swimming or aerobics are also available. Big new sports centre and swimming pool providing a wide range of other sports, old pool (a delicious antediluvian gem) is used for sub-aqua, canoeing and the like.

Music 'a huge strength' with loads of bands and orchestras and three choirs and a string quartet etc etc, two popular concerts in spring and autumn plus carol service (strangely not for charity – that is left to the sportsfolk who run mini marathons et al). Les Mis the most recent production with over 100 pupils involved. Keen drama with imaginative productions, pupils often perform at the Edinburgh Festival (and win awards). New art centre in pipeline (still) and 'very inspirational head of art' (another one if you follow) recently appointed. Pipe band popular. CCF, community service, D of E etc. Masses of trips, everywhere, for everything.

Background and Atmosphere: Vast Grimms' fairytale of a building, turreted and with acres of wood panelling and shiny black floors (are they granite or stone flag underneath the tarry surface?) purpose-built in 1870 by Bryce. Part of the main building still has the original steam driven heating which starts up twice a day with alarming groans and wheezes – ripe for the engineering museum methinks.

Various Victorian edifices scattered about the school's wonderful 90 acre grounds plonk in the middle of Edinburgh. 'School uses Edinburgh much more now,' says the head, Spectacular development after school sold 'redundant' acres to build Fettes Village, a collection of neat little boxes which splits the games field and provide the cash for much needed expansion. The collection of new and converted buildings that house the new prep department are much bigger than they look from the outside, an example of space well used, and about to be extended. The school is also about to build itself a new house to accommodate the expanded sixth form which is due to increase by 25 per cent: both events to coincide in 2007. The new build, which will include a sixth form centre but not a bar (illegal in Scotland – but of course they can leave the grounds and go out for their two units of alcohol) will house 125 upper sixth pupils in two identical wings (surely this should be 126 or 124?) each with their own individual room and will provide a transition between the disciplines of school and uni with pupils being able to cook their own meals if they want to. Planners have accepted a fifteen year development plan (well done those architects – difficult with conservation and all that) and whilst funding is in place for the new sixth form house, some serious fund raising looms for the future.

The school has gradually metamorphosed from famous trad boys' school to genuinely co-ed. Girls have been head of school twice in recent years and the flavour has changed from home-grown Scots to more exotic, with an influx from the Far East.

Pastoral Care and Discipline: Despite colourful stories in the Edinburgh press in past years – drugs, booze, sex etc, grossly overstated says the head – there is a clear framework of discipline that is well understood by all. This is a school with a zero tolerance policy on drugs. Edinburgh is the drugs capital of the north and running a school in the middle of it is no joke. Under-age drinking is an acknowledged problem. Three tier system on the discipline side: housemaster/deputy head/head = rustication/formal warning and suspension or expulsion. Ditto smoking. Very clear house visiting rules – no overt demonstrations of affection; bonking equals out. And yes, they do lose the occasional pupil for all these misdemeanours ditto bullying. Strong anti-bullying ethos. Prefects very responsible: imaginative bullying (anti-bullying?) code involves culprits writing down what they must or must not do and signing it. Expulsion is always an option.

Pupils and Parents: School topped up with many non-Brits in the bad old days, now the mix is veering more towards the British norm but still collections of exotic foreigners – Russians, Chinese, Japanese, Americans, Ukrainians but fewer Bulgarians than previously. School not keen on European pupils who 'only want to come for lower sixth, leaving a hole in upper sixth'. Increasing numbers of locals and Scots from all over. 'Pupils from 34 different countries, East European connection sadly dropping off.' Very strong old Fettesian stream, plus loads of first time buyers, intellectuals etc etc. Good vibrant mix. Old Fettesians include John de Chastelaine, Ian McLeod, James Bond, Tilda Swinton, Lord Woolf and Tony Blair – remembered fondly for 'his acting ability'.

Entrance: CE or school's own exam for those not coming from UK preps. 'Hurdle' exam from own prep; approx 25 students a year join the sixth form after GCSE elsewhere, currently much sought after as pupils pile in from other, mainly Scottish, schools.

Exit: University or further education the norm with 12 Oxbridge places last year, and about one third taking a gap year; favoured universities are – as ever – Newcastle, St Andrews, Durham, London, Bristol, Leeds, Warwick, Nottingham, Edinburgh, Glasgow and Aberdeen.

Money Matters: Well endowed with academic scholarships which can be supplemented with bursaries when the chips are down – if necessary up to 100 per cent - 'the level of these awards depend upon parents' financial means and can cover up to the full value of the fees'. Special (Todd) bursaries for Old Fettesians, 12.5 per cent discount for Services (not so many of these around).

Remarks: Undoubtedly the strongest school in Edinburgh – possibly riding too high? – to quote one governor, 'it is better to have a challenge, otherwise we become complacent'. Head adds, 'no danger of becoming complacent, the most dangerous thing in a school is to stand still'. Exciting cosmopolitan mix in an exciting city.

FILEY SCHOOL

Muston Road, Filey, North Yorkshire, YO14 0HG

Tel: 01723 512 354
Fax: 01723 512 165
E-mail: admin@filey.n-yorks.sch.uk
Website: www.filey.n-yorks.sch.uk

• Pupils: 780 boys and girls • Ages: 11-16 • Non-denom • State

Head: Since 2003, Mrs Lorraine Gill BA (Hull) (late forties). Twenty-five years a teacher, latterly as deputy head at Kelvin Hall School, Hull. Married, used to foster children. Extremely focused, mightily determined. Previously specialised in boosting under-performing schools. 'Here, I want to take a good school and turn it into an outstanding school. I'm going to complete my career here so it has to be right. It's my mission.' So, no pressure there, then.

Academic Matters: Awesome improvement in exam results. 2002 saw school's best ever GCSE results with 66.4 per cent of students achieving five or more A*-C grades, a 27 per cent increase over three years. Winner of Government's School Achievement Awards bonus scheme for three consecutive years, and dubbed 'Ofsted-on-Sea' by one national paper. Not bad for a true comprehensive – the only one serving the Filey area – with often a below-average ability intake despite excellent feeder schools. Special educational needs numbers often 20 per cent plus, partly because children with disrupted schooling move in and out of resort; does well by special needs students and just as well by the gifted. Gifted and Talented Co-ordinator nurtures students with special skills – academic, musical, sporting, whatever.

Under-achievement is spotted and dealt with, whichever side of the fence it falls. 'We have a rigorous programme of performance management,' says head. 'Myself and my deputies observe all our teachers, and samples of books and homework planners are seen on a regular basis.' Teachers are keen to start videoing their own lessons to see how they can improve. They are committed to becoming excellent. 'We touch and change people's lives and to me that's a sacred trust. I can't do with teachers who come in to this profession for bad reasons. They have to be on a mission. The students have to come first.' Now you know why she got the job.

Games, Options, The Arts: Good sporting achievement but thank the staff, not the facilities. It's not just that

the school lacks a sports centre, it's the town. Head and community now working together on bid for sports centre funding. School also has the only community swimming pool, 30 years old and still open to the public. New music suite but as yet no adequate drama space. Usual hobby clubs. Accessible community education with facilities open 50 weeks of the year.

Background and Atmosphere: Built in the sixties, school's growing reputation and thriving population have seen numbers virtually double in 14 years. One minute you're in a science lab straight out of your childhood with roller blackboards and woodwork by Noah, the next you're in a state-of-the art IT suite. Schizophrenic, or what? The solution? Specialist technology college status, hopefully by October 2004, bringing a much-needed £1m investment. 'That doesn't mean technology at the expense of the rest of the curriculum,' assures Mrs Gill. 'We want to use the best of technology to enhance, say, drama and music. We want a 21st century school.'

Meanwhile, head stamps her mark on the school in ways all those little ways teenagers love. The word 'pupil' is out, 'student' is in – and that's how they're treated. Youngsters who once sat on the floor in assemblies now sit on chairs, the canteen – though still hopelessly too small – has been given the Ikea look, toilets are graffiti-free and Mrs Gill checks personally that the new soap dispensers are always full. She's fanatical about litter – and she's no time for teenage slouches. 'Come on, tuck your shirts in,' she says with a hint of good humour to some 16-year-old boys in the library. And they do. They don't even seem to mind. This is a school buzzing with good pupil/teacher rapport. No wonder they learn.

Pastoral Care and Discipline: School rules mercifully brief and standards of behaviour high. Isolated study, possibly with head, as ultimate deterrent for bad behaviour. Parents informed if pupils misbehave. 'Disturbances in lessons cannot go unchallenged,' Mrs Gill says. Well, hurrah to that.

We spring a visit on one class where the pupils are heads down working when we go in, polite when I address them, complimentary about the school. 'Some of our most challenging pupils are in that class,' Mrs Gill says later. You could have fooled us.

Pupils and Parents: Parents, desperate to secure children's future in an area hard-hit by fishing and farming decline, treasure school as a focal point in community. Good school/home links. 'Nothing is too much trouble,' says one parent. Head sets aside regular sessions when her door is open to any pupil for any reason. 'Well, they are my kids.'

Entrance: Same old story. Unless you live in catchment area, appealing for a place in this chock-full school is your only hope.

Exit: Two thirds go to sixth form or further education colleges in nearby Scarborough, most ultimately to university. Modern apprenticeships take much of the remainder.

Remarks: If it's gloss you're looking for, this is neither the school nor the town for you. What you see is what you get – good behaviour, good teaching, good results.

FOREST SCHOOL

Linked to Forest Preparatory School in the Junior section

College Place, Snaresbrook, London, E17 3PY

Tel: 020 8520 1744
Fax: 020 8520 3656
E-mail: warden@forest.org.uk
Website: www.forest.org.uk

• Pupils: 1,200 (includes 220 in prep) boys and girls • Ages: 11-18 • Size of sixth form: 250 • C of E foundation with a sizeable proportion of pupils from other faith groups • Fees: Prep £2,258 - £2,761; senior £3,572 • Independent • Open days: Main Open Day in September each year followed by a number of information mornings

---

Warden: Since 1992, Mr Andrew Boggis MA (fiftyish), of New College Oxford and King's College Cambridge. Formerly Master-in-College and housemaster to the King's Scholars at Eton. Three children all of whom are at Forest School – the middle child has something called an honorary scholarship. Chairman of HMC in 2006.

Academic Matters: Exam results are good – 75 per cent A/B grades at A level, 65 per cent A*/A grades at GCSE. Pupils are taught in single-sex forms up to GCSE, with setting from the second form onwards in some subjects, particularly English, maths and science. Languages offered are French, Spanish, German and Latin. Co-ed in the sixth form. Class sizes around 20 maximum for GCSE subjects and 15 maximum for A levels. 25 A2/AS subjects including drama, further maths, philosophy, textiles, music technology plus all the usual suspects. One report that the school is not so hot on dyslexia – unconfirmed so enquire carefully.

Games, Options, The Arts: Forest is big on games. Good sports facilities – several games pitches, a sports hall, tennis courts, a heated swimming pool. Strong football tradition – Forest is the only school ever to have played in the FA cup, and Quinton Fortune, South African international

and Man United star, is an Old Boy. Hockey and netball are the main winter sports for girls. Cricket the summer game – strong Essex CCC link. Ditto athletics. Minority sports include golf, fencing and tae kwon do. New sports complex with two swimming pools, cricket gallery, gymnasium et al due for September 2006.

Big CDT/art/drama block opened in 2001. New performing arts extension opened in 2004. Drama is one of the main co-ed activities. Inter-house drama competitions – there are 8 houses in the boys' school and 6 in the girls' – regular productions with musicals and plays such as Me and My Girl, The Rivals and plenty of Shakespeare. The school has four orchestras, four bands, ten choirs and numerous ensembles; 42 visiting music teachers and a pianist in residence. Other extra-curricular activities include CCF, D of E, Young Enterprise and various trips and exchanges – around 30 a year.

Background and Atmosphere: As its name suggests, the school nestles on the edge of Epping Forest. The school address – Snaresbrook, London E17 – is a revealing contradiction. The E17 bit (Walthamstow) is geographically accurate, while the Snaresbrook bit – an affluent suburb about a mile away – is more socially accurate. The school was built in 1834 and the oldest building (the boys' school) rather resembles a large country mansion. Set around it are the more modern preparatory school and girls' school, the sports fields and of course lots and lots of trees.

Pastoral Care and Discipline: Looked after by the head of the boys' school, Marcus Cliff Hodges, the head of the girls' school, Mrs Penny Goodman, and the head of the preparatory school, Mr Ian McIntyre. Sixth form boys are made monitors and sixth form girls are made prefects. The school has an anti-bullying policy, not that bullying is a problem. A friendly school but the discipline is pretty strict and hones the pupils' competitive instincts.

Pupils and Parents: Pupils tend to be drawn from the more affluent Essex side than from the equally proximate east London side, as you'd expect, but with increasing numbers from Hackney, Islington and Docklands. Around 25 per cent Asian pupils, reflecting the demographics of the area. Long list of interesting Old Foresters includes sportsmen such as Nasser Hussain, James Foster and Quinton Fortune; Peter Greenaway; actors Adam Woodyatt (Ian Beale in Eastenders), Sharat Sardana (Goodness Gracious Me) and many others; murderers Eric Brown, Gerald Lamarque and Omar Sheikh; numerous businessmen; Old Girls include Natalie Ceeney of the British Museum and Jackie Smiles, first woman Chinook pilot etc etc. A school that is proud of its progeny.

Entrance: By exam and assessment at 11 and 16.

Exit: Almost all to university, ten-twelve a year to Oxbridge.

Money Matters: Clearly, the school isn't short of a bob or two - they've recently built a new 3-storey art, drama and CDT block (2001), a performing arts and sixth form extension (2004), and are currently building a sports complex. The equivalent of 9 full scholarships and 3 full bursaries are offered each year (split between multiple candidates) - for a bursary you need some extra-curricular ability, eg in sport or drama. Three sixth form half-scholarships, 1 full sixth form bursary, and four music scholarships, which (says one parent) are the easiest to get, if your child can play an instrument at grade 5 level or above. Fee reductions for children of clergy. School involved with the Ogden Trust and other sponsorship initiatives for bright sixth formers.

Remarks: A London school that feels as if it's in the country. Top tip — it's open for breakfast from 7.15am (£1.25 for a cooked breakfast), which is very useful for parents who have to get to work early.

FORTISMERE SCHOOL

South Wing, Tetherdown, Muswell Hill, London, N10 1NE

Tel: 02083 654 400
Fax: 02084 447 822
E-mail: anixon@fortismere.haringey.sch.uk
Website: www.fortismere.haringey.sch.uk

• Pupils: 1,651 boys and girls; all day • Ages: 11-19 • Size of sixth form: 441 • Non-denom • State

Head: Since 2005, Mr David Jones has been acting head while consultants seek a new head 'for up to £100k'.

Academic Matters: This is a comprehensive, but has more than its fair share of bright children (it is, after all, at the top of middle class, liberal, intellectual Muswell Hill). It also has a number at the lower end of the academic spectrum but relatively few middle-of-the-roaders. Not overtly pushy, it does well by its intake, with a respectable 80 per cent or so of pupils getting five A-Cs at GCSE. Art, English, mathematics, science and history are particularly strong and popular at GCSE and A level; Spanish is improving; ditto IT, due largely to a reorganisation and re-staffing of both departments, plus a considerable investment in the learning resources centre so everyone has easy access to computers. There are 50 interactive whiteboards in the school.

French, German and Spanish are all taught to A level; each pupil is allocated to a language group in year 7. ('Of course nearly everyone wants to learn French, so people do tend to feel disgruntled if they're given German or Spanish,' commented a parent. 'And they deliberately don't let you learn a language if you've already got experience of it.') Two thirds now take up a second language in year 9; an accelerated learning programme is available only to particularly able linguists. 27 A level options, including business studies, drama, economics, media studies, philosophy, performing arts, physical education, psychology and photography, plus some GNVQs.

Although this is a technology college (and has smart labs and DT rooms to show for the extra funds), there is no particular technological emphasis. 'It is my pride and joy that they all get a fully rounded education up to GCSE.' But the school does run a Neighbourhood Engineers scheme, which sees older pupils working on projects with companies like Arup. 'We've made engineering really fashionable – it's no longer seen as a blue collar activity. It now has the cachet it has in countries like Germany and Switzerland.' Pupils have also worked with Interbrand, whose founder is now on the governing body, and whose aim is to put the design world in touch with the education world.

Money from the government's Excellence in Cities programme – 'the best bit of government policy there is – it recognises the extra challenges of inner cities and gives them extra money to cope' – funds two learning mentors, who mostly do outreach work with families and counsel children on a one-to-one basis. Part of the project is to encourage youngsters from non-academic backgrounds to stay on to the sixth form and go to university. The money also funds curriculum extension work and extra-curricular activities as part of the government's Gifted and Talented programme. These are available to everyone, though high-achievers are particularly encouraged to take part. 'Extras can benefit everyone. You need to make sure you're not selling anyone short.'

This is an inclusive school and the teaching is as mixed ability as it can manage, though maths is setted from year 8 and modern languages from year 9. 'Our intake is skewed towards the top end and these bright, motivated pupils help to pull up the tail end – they encourage the less motivated to do their best. You have to take each child as you find them, get to know them inside out, set appropriate targets and go for it in a big way.' Some parents are less than totally convinced about mixed ability teaching – 'my son has expressed frustration about the influence of disruptive pupils in a couple of science subjects. But he did two science papers early and got As in both of them, so the teaching is obviously good.'

Effective special needs department – 'we've cornered the north London market in dyslexia'. On site, and part of the rebuilding programme, is the secondary department of the Blanche Nevile School for deaf and hearing-impaired children. These pupils are integrated into the main school for anything from 5 to 95 per cent of the time.

Games, Options, The Arts: Enviably for a London school, Fortismere has a 20-acre site which includes three football pitches, cricket pitch and outdoor swimming pool, as well as a sports hall and gym, a dance studio and seven tennis courts. Football, tennis and athletics particularly strong. It runs endless clubs and teams, down to C teams, 'so even if you're not that good you can still join in,' said a pupil approvingly. There's a full Saturday mornings sports programme. Fortismere was awarded the Sports Mark in 2003. Art, as mentioned before, is extremely strong, with excellent results. 'It's stunning,' said a parent. 'The children take it very seriously and work very hard.' Drama, dance and music are all taken seriously; there are three choirs, a string quartet, steel band, jazz band and orchestra. 'The jazz is wonderful,' said a parent. Music students have visited Prague and Beijing. On the head's wish list is a new performing arts building.

Background and Atmosphere: Bracing hill-top site amidst leafy Muswell Hill Edwardiana. An amalgamation of a grammar school and a secondary modern in 1967, the school mirrors the history of secondary education in Haringey. It has two wings, joined by a quarter-mile pathway round the playing fields – 'in the depths of winter, in the midst of a hailstorm, it's like being out in the North Sea,' says the head. A rebuilding programme completed 2003/4 funded by the government's private finance initiative scheme. This is providing a library/learning resource centre, four new labs, food technology rooms, the all-weather pitches and new tennis courts. No uniform, relaxed atmosphere.

Pastoral Care and Discipline: Each class keeps its form tutor and head of year for five years (staff turnover permitting), – 'it is nice to have the continuity in such a big school,' said a parent. Bullying is mostly dealt with well, with disruptive behaviour kept in check. Good home-school communication, and accessible teachers. A parent commented, 'there's very little for the children to rebel against – with no uniform, and very basic rules. And it works, partly because the parents of the majority are very proactive at home.'

Pupils and Parents: 'It's a good reflection of what I'd describe as a balanced society,' said a parent. 'It's very multi-cultural, very multi-ethnic, with a good solid base.' Plenty of middle class professional and creative types from the surrounding leafy streets (many of whom moved there with Fortismere in mind), plus a good number from less affluent parts. 'One big advantage of the school is that I know all my son's friends, because they nearly all live nearby. They can walk to school and to each other's houses, which is brilliant for their independence. And they're all very nice kids.'

Entrance: After special needs and siblings, preference goes to those living nearest as the crow flies. In practice, the catchment area is about a mile. Although technology colleges are allowed to select 10 per cent, Fortismere does not do so – 'my governors would never select by aptitude. We believe very strongly in inclusiveness.' All year 11 students get the opportunity to move up to the sixth form and are joined by about 50 new students, from independent as well as state schools. Those wanting to do A levels need a minimum of 5 A*-C grades at GCSE.

Exit: About 80 per cent go on to higher education, mostly the traditional universities, including three or four a year to Oxbridge.

Money Matters: Technology college status has brought extra funds for improvements, as has refurbishment under the council's private finance initiative scheme. This is a comfortable area with a high proportion of professional families, many of whom are enthusiastic fund-raisers.

Remarks: One of the successful genuine comprehensives that put a premium on the prices of nearby houses. Excellent facilities, an inclusive ethos and highly creditable exam results. 'My kids might have been pushed slightly harder at a selective school,' said a parent. 'But here they get an excellent balance and recognise the broader range of society. It's a lovely school.'

FRAMLINGHAM COLLEGE

Linked to Framlingham College Junior School in the Junior section

Framlingham, Woodbridge, Suffolk, IP13 9EY

Tel: 01728 723 789
Fax: 01728 724 546
E-mail: admissions@framcollege.co.uk
Website: www.framlingham.suffolk.sch.uk

- Pupils: 274 boys, 153 girls; 304 board, 123 day • Ages: 13 - 18 • Size of sixth form: 186 • C of E - Inter-denom • Fees: Day: £1,740 - £3,026 Brandeston Hall and £3,967 Framlingham College per term. Boarding: £4,866 (BH) and £6,172 (FC)
- Independent • Open days: Late Jan, May and early October

Head: Since 1994, Mrs Gwen Randall BA, early fifties, husband retired, budding barrister daughter. Read French at Bristol University, was head of modern languages and drama at St Mary's, Calne, then deputy head of Dauntsey's, before setting about, with enormous energy and considerable publicity, transforming and modernising the college. A very lively person, completely open about the downs as well as the ups, much in love with the school and excited about future plans. Describes herself as 'one of the pithier backbenchers at HMC.'

Academic Matters: A well performing school at both GCSE and A level, not amongst the highest fliers, but nowadays more top than bottom heavy. Prides itself on catering well for the whole ability range. Provision for ESL and learning support is excellent, with a separate suite of rooms and a lovely atmosphere. Facilities in general, for such a large, rambling place, are very sensibly thought out, business-like and well equipped. This is very much due to Mrs Randall's excellent eye for maximisation of space, of which the superb split-level library is a prime example. Class sizes are small, with rooms deliberately designed to hold no more than 22. Maths very strong through to A level; Design and Technology department is stunning and produces quite exceptional work.

Games, Options, The Arts: Sport clearly of major importance (there is a fine new indoor pool) and highly successful but the head makes a point of musical and academic achievement featuring strongly in inter-house competition. Drama is immensely popular -quite a few pupils go on to RADA and the like – with frequent first-rate performances. Lots of concerts too and exciting plans afoot for the updating of the theatre. Endless interesting leisure

activities. Radio enthusiasts have their own room bursting with equipment.

Background and Atmosphere: College founded in 1864 with rather austere Victorian main building. Beautiful setting, perched on a hillside with a gorgeous view across the valley to Framlingham castle. Everything beautifully kept, including 50 acres of playing fields. A woman's hand at the helm has helped to give a greater sense of light and cohesion to what was a bit of a hotch-potch. Boarding facilities are pleasant enough and have certainly come a long way since the best boast of a (very) early prospectus that, 'each boy has a separate bed.' The school is enviably tidy and well-organised. Relaxed politeness the order of the day for relationships between staff and pupils and the atmosphere is tangibly unpressured but businesslike. Some very nice touches, like the airy central meeting hall, where pupils can gather and chat, currently being extended into a charming outside piazza.

Pastoral Care and Discipline: A major change has been the abolition of day houses and the absorption of day pupils into boarding houses, where they have desks and can sleep over in boarders' rooms; clearly a good move, as now the tutor system looks after day pupils and boarders with complete even-handedness. Prefects are carefully trained (the top ones do a week's residential leadership course) and given plenty of responsibility. Open discussion of problems such as bullying is encouraged and prevalent. Occasional cannabis experimenters are given a second chance but not one has ever re-offended. Discipline in general is good – a calm atmosphere prevails.

Pupils and Parents: Pupils are drawn largely from middle class East Anglian families, although there is a largish contingent of students from abroad including numbers of German students who come for one year in the sixth form and frequently stay for two. Most integrate seamlessly into the school. The college is highly thought of locally. No problems recruiting on any front.

Entrance: Most applicants and Brandeston Hall pupils accepted but only if the head considers they will cope. Big influx into the sixth form (dependent on GCSE results), where virtually all subject combinations are accepted.

Exit: Most to university, with a fair smattering of Oxbridge.

Money Matters: Head says she likes to balance the books and give value for money and has worked small miracles on the site. One coup in 1999, when she changed the 'scruffy' uniform, now remarkably tidy (including the sixth form who all, boys and girls, wear suits), was to give every pupil a free set! Good number of scholarships of all sorts, reductions for siblings.

Remarks: Very pleasant, well-ordered school which bears the stamp of a lively, charismatic head. When she came she saw 'pockets of excellence in a sea of despair.' No sign of despair now.

FRANCIS HOLLAND SCHOOL (NW1)

Clarence Gate, Ivor Place, London, NW1 6XR

Tel: 02077 230 176
Fax: 02077 061 522
E-mail: admin@fhs-nw1.org.uk
Website: www.francisholland.org/nw1/showpage.asp

- Pupils: 400 girls, all day • Ages: 11-18 • Size of sixth form: 90
- C of E • Fees: £3,625 • Independent • Open days: Please contact school office for details

Headmistress: Since 2004, Mrs Vivienne Durham, MA. Read English at Oxford, previously taught at various London independent girls' schools, including Haberdashers' Aske's and Godolphin and Latymer. Former deputy head of South Hampstead High School.

Academic Matters: Very strong academic results in all subjects at A level and GCSE. In August 2005, 93 per cent of all A level results were grades A-C : almost half were grade A. More than 71 per cent of GCSEs A or A* in 2005. Particularly strong results in French, history, Latin and Greek. The most recent inspection report found progress in science particularly good in the sixth form.

Some setting – in French and maths from year 7 and Latin from year 9, with science GCSE groups for those who find the subject tough. Choice of Italian, Spanish, German or Classical Greek from year 9. GCSE PE is offered. A level possibilities include psychology, government and politics, history of art and theatre studies. The sixth form curriculum includes current affairs, ethics and general studies as well as a rich weekly lecture programme. Eminent recent speakers include Kenneth Clark, Diane Abbot, Simon Sebag Montefiore, Joely Richardson, Kazuo Ishiguro. The senior mistress is the learning support co-ordinator and monitors those with mild dyslexia, as well as giving one-to-one guidance on study skills. 'The slightly broader range of ability gives a slightly less competitive edge to life.'

Games, Options, The Arts: Sports include yoga and water polo (in the subterranean swimming pool with floating floor) as well as hockey, netball, rounders and tennis in Regents Park, just over the A41. Large, state of the art basement gym, refurbished in 2005. Not a hugely competitive school but 'the sports teachers are very keen,' said a parent. It does well at netball and provides members of the London schools U16 girls' water polo team. All sixth formers have a wide choice of sports activities, such as tennis, swimming, aerobics, yoga. In Easter 2005, there was a sports tour to South Africa; choir tour to St Petersburg in October 2005. Great enthusiasm for music, with choral standards particularly high; large numbers of girls take singing lessons. The school was invited to sing at the re-opening of the Royal Opera House. Joint choral productions with Harrow School, with sporting and social links also under development – 'it's only 20 minutes away down the Metropolitan line.' Music groups include the Pink Ladies jazz group.

Art is also strong, with A level results consistently good and GCSE results 'improving'. Big, light art room with Mary Poppins-esque views of London roofs and chimney-pots. Plenty of drama, including clubs, competitions and ambitious school plays eg Amadeus. The yearly form play competition gives everyone the chance to take part. A wide variety of extra-curricular activities, ranging from vaulting to pottery; debating is particularly popular. Has links with Jack Taylor School for children with severe physical and learning difficulties, which uses the swimming pool and joins in on picnics, sponsored walks and other social events. 'We get a huge amount out of this relationship,' says the head. 'It draws great qualities out of the girls, often those you'd least expect.' Destinations of trips abroad have included India, New York, Costa Rica, Iceland and Russia.

Background and Atmosphere: A wedge-shaped red-brick building tucked away near the top of Baker Street, a hedge or two away from Regents Park. Founded as a church school by Canon Francis Holland in 1878. In May 2005, the school acquired the adjacent building in Ivor Place, a four storey former pub – will provide a number of new large classrooms.

Aqua corridors stretch away at unlikely angles due to the building's shape, adorned with noticeboards crammed with photos of clubs, activities and lessons. Some stairs are painted red and some classrooms lilac or pink. Friendly and welcoming – parents often comment that the atmosphere sold them on the school. Like most inner-city schools, cramped for space. The seven-sided panelled central hall has a traditional atmosphere; large concerts take place in St Cyprian's church next door. Upstairs, there is a roof terrace for sixth formers, between the glass-roofed cloisters and the central dome. Basement loos, 'probably the best in London', are based on a design from Ally McBeal. Small tarmac outside area where barbecues are occasionally served – the food is reportedly excellent. 'You need to get the fundamentals right,' says the headmistress, 'and that means the loos and the food.' She adds, 'I love this building. There's a huge warmth about it.'

Pastoral Care and Discipline: Very strong on pastoral care – 'they really do mean it,' said a parent. 'They're good with individual girls and on whole class issues.' The head is very keen on developing girls' self-esteem. 'I want girls to get a feeling of security and warmth here but also of opportunity and challenge.' Freedom to go out at lunchtime increases gradually with seniority, 'but if work isn't getting done we can draw in the net.' No drug problems to speak of – 'ours are mostly pretty caring parents who know what their daughters get up to,' says the head optimistically. She hopes, 'it is still true there aren't any stupid rules.'

Pupils and Parents: A good cosmopolitan mix. Plenty of media parents, plus others looking for an informal, warm and friendly, environment in which the pressure is not intense and their daughters can thrive as individuals. Famous OGs: Joan Collins, Jackie Collins, Amanda Donohue and Saskia Wickham (actress).

Entrance: One of Group 1 of the North London Consortium of girls' schools that use common maths and English exams. Everyone is interviewed. 'They may be fantastic at something we don't test and we like to find out about their hobbies and interests.'

Exit: To a spread of major universities, to do wide range of courses. A few leave after GCSE, mostly to co-ed sixth forms.

Money Matters: One music scholarship at 11. Means-tested bursaries also available at 11. FHS pupils in year 11 can apply for the sixth form academic scholarships and a music scholarship.

Remarks: Consistently popular inner-London girls' day school with praise for its friendliness and community feel. Recent exam results 'show that academically we do mean business – and the girls can do lots of other things too.' 'It's a nice, positive place that takes all its girls very seriously,' said a satisfied parent.

FRANCIS HOLLAND SCHOOL (SW1)

Linked to Francis Holland Junior School (SW1) in the Junior section

39 Graham Terrace, London, SW1W 8JF

Tel: 02077 302 971
Fax: 02078 234 066
E-mail: education@fhs-sw1.org.uk
Website: www.fhs-sw1.org.uk

• Pupils: 290 girls, all day • Ages: 11-18 • Size of sixth form: 50, rising to 65 in 2003 • C of E • Fees: £3,120 - £3,735
• Independent • Open days: Several

Headmistress: Since 1997, Miss Stephanie Pattenden BSc PGCE (fifties). Educated at St Anne's Sanderstead (now defunct), Durham (maths) and King's College London (PGCE). Formerly deputy head at South Hampstead High. Energetic, efficient, enterprising. Keen on bell ringing and hill walking. Teaches maths to year 7 while managing a multi-million-pound expansion completed in 2004. Deeply respected by the girls, whom she knows by name. 'We are a caring community.'

Academic Matters: 70-ish per cent A/B at A level. Traditional teaching approach 'not for the unmotivated.' Staff devoted to providing pupils with wide range of experiences and successes. Many teachers on staff over 10 years but not fossilised – plenty of young too. Sympathetic to mild special educational needs but no specialist provision; currently one physically disabled pupil; staff track individual pupils where help may be needed and parents are kept informed.

Games, Options, The Arts: Well-patronised DofE, bronze or silver level. Good library. Lots of visits to galleries, etc. Good careers advice.

Background and Atmosphere: Fortress-like but impressively spacious, light-filled school on residential road behind Sloane Square. Large courtyard playground separates senior from junior school. Late 20th century blends well with 1881 portion (including hall with stained-glass windows). Affiliation with St Mary's Church; no special emphasis on religion.

Pastoral Care and Discipline: School divided into four 'houses'. Senior girls help juniors with reading and where requested.

Pupils and Parents: Self-aware girls who sparkle. Daughters of diplomats, bankers and captains of industry as well as TV presenters. International flavour, 'hard pressed to find a child with four grandparents born in the UK.' Pretty uniform, grey skirt with blue and white check blouse. 'What you want your daughter to look like.' Kings Road style own clothes for sixth formers. Growing American presence as evidenced by barbecues and other 'nice' fundraising activities.

Entrance: Stiffer than before due to increased demand (8 applicants for each place). No sibling preference. Majority comes on from own junior school – some go from there to St Paul's and some to boarding. Part of the North London Consortium Group 1. Written exam in English and maths, plus interview and attendance at two lessons for assessment.

Exit: Almost all to university; 10 per cent to Oxbridge. Emphasis on matching pupil to the right course with a wide range of destinations. Courses from law, medicine and maths, to journalism, psychology and history of art. Languages include Chinese, Russian and Italian.

Money Matters: 3 full fees bursaries and some scholarships, also help for clergy daughters.

Remarks: Growing in stature as the expansion works through. Feels safe; works well for children who might flounder in a larger, more demanding, establishment.

FRENSHAM HEIGHTS SCHOOL

Linked to Frensham Heights Lower School in the Junior section

Rowledge, Farnham, Surrey, GU10 4EA

Tel: 01252 792561
Fax: 01252 794 335
E-mail: headmaster@frensham-heights.org.uk
Website: www.frensham-heights.org.uk

- Pupils: 480, roughly 50/50 boys and girls; Boarding from 11 (37 per cent board, 62 per cent in sixth form) • Ages: 11-18, juniors 3-11 • Size of sixth form: 90 • Non-denom • Fees: First school: £1,480 - £2,220. Lower school: £2,220 - £3,920; boarding £6,040. Upper school: day: £4,130; boarding £6,250
- Independent • Open days: Five each year - see website

Headmaster: Since 2004, Mr Andrew Fisher BA MA (forties), educated at Geelong Grammar in Australia (where his father was headmaster) followed by the University of New South Wales (history and Eng lit) and a masters in education management at Sheffield. Comes from Wrekin College in Shropshire, where he rose through the ranks to become deputy head. Married to Catherine, with two young children who are not in the school: 'as the son of a head, grandson of a head and nephew of a head I realise that they must have a bit of a life outside school'. Teaches 14-year-olds, 'loves teaching', 'children only get one chance', 'school should be the best experience they ever have', 'students should get the chance to make mistakes'.

Recently appointed deputy head academic whose job it is to 'ensure that all pupils fulfil their potential – not with the eye to any league table but with an eye to them not wasting their own time, other pupils' time or their parents' money.' 'Several got quite a bump when Andrew did as he said he would and did not allow them up into the next year as they had not worked hard enough. It has had a remarkably salutary effect'. Head is, nonetheless, delighted to be fronting this seriously artistic school, but keen on rugby and cricket too, so watch out for a slight change in emphasis.

Personable and fun, some pupils are still slightly wary of Andrew (this is a first name school): those who have regular contact were reassuring: 'he's OK' (highest form of praise). 'You can hear him whistling in the morning', but not apparently later in the day. Suspects that he is probably a people's person rather than a builder.

Predecessor, Peter de Voil, went to head The English College in Prague.

Academic Matters: Average class size 17. Not the best collection of A levels we have ever seen, but that's not really what this school is about. Fair number of As in German, French and Chinese, but Eng lang and lit scoring more Bs and Cs in GCSE, and ditto at A level recently. Science and maths strongest, history OK. Two of: drama, dance, music, art, ceramics, DT required at GCSE, the first by far the most popular. Vast range of different and busy A levels: photography, PE new additions. Setting in maths and science but not other subjects to avoid labelling perennial slow-streamers. 100 plus pupils receive support for mild specific learning difficulties, and virtually all get extra tuition. Parents interested in personal development, not league tables. No classics. No RE after age 14 (pupils thought they might like it). Some good, unconventional teaching, using drama etc to get the message across.

Lower school classrooms are dotted along the ground floor of the converted and much expanded stables, IT in the hay loft (power point presentations the norm), ditto (but not the same hay loft) busy multi-media library, well-used with audio books, videos and appealing paperbacks and classical music buzzing gently in the background. Ceramics everywhere. Library is open till 6.30 pm, points for lap tops, teaching sessions on how to run a library and use a catalogue, along with quizzes and games for 13+ make this one of the more imaginative libraries we have visited.

Games, Options, The Arts: Head keen on sport, rugby now in place, and first XI have just beaten Charterhouse 'and are walking about 50 foot tall'. Sport is 'improving'. Enormously. 'Both in the quality of the schools against whom they play (for instance boys' matches v Eton, Winchester and Charterhouse) and in the results they are achieving – several sides are unbeaten'. Games compulsory twice a week, whole class play the same games up to sixth form, when they can choose. All the usual games are played but probably not yet the place to send a prep school rugby champion. Plenty of minority sports – basketball strong, also fitness training. One or two already involved in colt County cricket, all-weather nets in the offing. (Apparently the original cricket ground was laid down by the Charringtons in 1900 so that Daddy could play and Mummy could entertain the Prince of Wales).

The most terrifying high frame ('it looks even higher from the top,' said Andrew) which combines every conceivable superman movement plus some that even stunt men would be amazed at. Woods filled with serious and popular climbing frames: Jacob's ladder impressive. School was the first to be licensed as a centre for outdoor education, and 'the ropes course is partly about personal challenge, but it is actually far more about respecting and supporting others, and taking responsibility for one's own actions, which is why it is a timetabled lesson'. Forges strong staff/pupil links and is much used in summer by business workshops. Forget convention: this is the most imaginative playground we have ever seen. Trad gym looks Neanderthal by comparison. Certain amount of D of E, but not the religion you find in many schools. Expeditions important, huge range, staff 'give up weeks of holiday time to take pupils to The Red Sea and the Sahara'. Trekking, camping, mountain climbing, survival skills, first aid. Lots of weekend trips away for boarders which day pupils can join, most sound rather scary.

Intimidatingly good performing arts, the building itself has won oodles of awards, with several pupils in current TV programmes and films. Award-winning dance in stunning dance studio: shiny black floor, wall of mirrors and no shoes allowed. New slightly surprising music centre (fires are in fashion at Frensham: this time it was a squirrel which apparently ate the wires; horrifying photographs of the detritus left by the blaze). Music centre has a glass roof in the main auditorium which means that it is almost useless sound-wise when it rains, and like an oven when the sun shines. Fortunately the house itself boasts a glorious ballroom which can be co-opted for concerts. Music strong, with loads of opportunities to play and sing, including an annual concert tour abroad. 22 peripatetic music staff, some of them international performers, two orchestras, three choirs, string quartets, masses of concerts and a soirée in June – for some reason they also teach the bagpipes. More ceramics dotted all round the place, with children's art on every wall, everywhere, the main hall, the passages. 'We like having our work on show, it is very encouraging,' said our 11 year old guide. Not quite big enough art department (extension probably on next wish list), but some superb results. Glorious pupil-designed panther in foyer of the Performing Arts Centre.

Background and Atmosphere: Founded in 1925, this was a school ahead of its time: co-ed school capable of taking children virtually from cradle to university with no uniforms, no bullying, no competition, no house points, no prize-givings. Creative learning, creative thinking important, plus the arts. Think Bloomsbury in the country. Teachers and students all on first-name basis. No uniform, vague dress code, 'we do insist on more formal dress when the occasion demands' but no overt fashion dictates.

Magnificent Edwardian pile, built by a brewery magnate, set in beautiful 150 acre grounds with stupendous views – over fifty miles on a clear day, Frensham ponds just over the hill. Massive outside use of Performing Arts Centre, which was set ablaze by an electrician's halogen light just days before it was due to open. Fair amount of new build lately, and lots of titivating going on. No Saturday school, day pupils may leave at 4.10 on weekdays. Boys' houses across the road, girls live in the main building in not very satisfactory conditions: dorms are perfectly OK, with decent study bedrooms for older girls, but if they want to invited boys into their common room they must 'find a member of staff and ask them to come and sit in the common room too'. The new sixth form centre (due 2006) and consequent re-jigging of accommodation should deal with this problem.

Pastoral Care and Discipline: Very nurturing pupil/teacher relationships with teachers widely available out of school hours. 'If you get a bad mark it's easy to discuss it with your teacher,' said a pupil. 'Mentors counsel younger students: 'nice and easy to talk to'. Strict about getting prep in, discipline is taken seriously. Smoking used to be allowed here, no longer; bar twice a week, school gets cross if boozing overdone. Drugs the same perennial problem: though Andrew will always give everyone a second chance, even to taking on pupils dissed by other schools. Though immediate expulsion if caught indulging on school premises. Pupils with a drug history coming from other schools must agree to a contract, and will be subject to regular – periodic – drugs testing. Three pupils out last term. No chapel or assembly, but morning talks on Wednesdays, varying from the 'enlightened to the mundane'. Annual parent teachers meeting, which doesn't seem quite enough, plus parents' committee 'which meets each term to discuss matters of common interest'. (Fly on the wall stuff that).

Pupils and Parents: Pupils come from state and independent schools in Surrey, East Hampshire, West Sussex and the A3/M3 corridor into South West London. About 7 per cent ex-pat and no more than 10 per cent from overseas. Unusual international dimension, echoing the founders' international conscience, with the head keen on bringing overseas kids into a 'parochial part of Surrey'. Large numbers of those whom we met lived 'within two minutes' of the school, and neighbouring villages are rapidly becoming school annexes. Sir Claus – now Lord – Moser is an Old Boy (he came as a refugee from Nazi Germany). Many from the arts, publishing, film, entertainment, design etc. Also academics, professionals and IT people.

Entrance: Mainly at 3+, 11+, 13+ or 16+. Assessment, interview and school report at age 10 (or below). Entrance exam required for the older children. Considerably 'oversubscribed for our January entrance exam'; 'there will therefore be those who are not offered places. BUT, and it is a big but, the selection will never be just about academics

(the reason we have our own entrance exam: the reason we offer all pupils the chance to show us skills/interests they have irrespective of whether these skills are of themselves scholarship standard'. Need six Cs or better at GCSE for sixth form entry. Hate to turn anyone away, 'the worst thing you can say to anyone is – you failed'. Some children come here from schools where they were not happy.

Exit: Some to music conservatories, drama schools and art colleges in the UK and abroad. Most to a wide range of universities, studying everything from marine biology and coastal ecology to Arabic with politics, dance and fashion. The odd one or two to Oxbridge. Some Gap.

Money Matters: Some help for academia, music and other creative and performing arts. Bursarial help reserved for 'funding those pupils of excellence whose parents would not otherwise be able to afford a Frensham Heights' education'. Busy-bee development officer, helping the school to make a bob or two letting out facilities like the outdoor education centre to visiting schools, the Prince's Trust. Also does a brisk trade in weddings. Competitive music festival and summer schools also pull in the loot.

Remarks: Friendly and inspiring school, achieving its aim of providing good alternative education with lots of freedom but no hint of chaos.

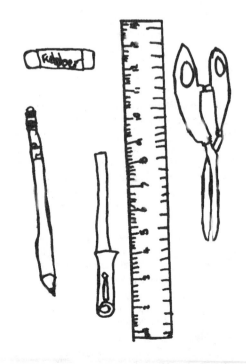

FRIENDS' SCHOOL

Linked to Friends' Junior School in the Junior section

Mount Pleasant Road, Saffron Walden, Essex, CB11 3EB

Tel: 01799 525 351
Fax: 01799 523 808
E-mail: admin@friends.org.uk
Website: www.friends.org.uk

• Pupils: 220 boys and girls; 50 boarders • Ages: 11-18 • Size of sixth form: 40 • Quaker ethos • Fees: Day £2,050-£3,590; boarding £5,790 • Independent • Open days: Termly

Head: Since 2001, Mr Andy Waters BEd MA (forties); went to local grammar and then London University, was house tutor of St Christopher's, Letchworth and deputy head at Oswestry in Shropshire. A human dynamo; meticulous, ambitious, verbal, going hammer and tongs on marketing the assets with new prospectus to mark 300th year. Climbs mountains and does Triathlon for kicks (ex-tutor of Outward Bound Wales) so serious re-construction of the place is merely his warm-up exercise. Still time to teach history, play guitar and mandolin in a ceilidh band. Says he has a complete intolerance of bullying. Bends over backward to be Robin Hood with deserving cases who can't afford fees – 'my door is always open though my desk is seldom clear.' Wife Hazel works in Cambridge, with son at junior school and daughter in senior school. Sixth formers like his tenacity but still undecided on suitable nickname.

Academic Matters: For a school whose policy is to select as wide a range of pupils as will benefit from its curriculum, it does wonders: 83+ per cent 5 or more GCSE A-C grades, half of them gaining 8 or more. Does not worship at altar of league tables – no policy of withdrawing borderline candidates in order to improve GCSE statistics. In year 11 pupils achieved on average 2.6 more A*-C grades than expected from standardised tests in year 9 – due to quality of teaching. French and German taught to all in years 7 and 8.

Member of National Association of Gifted Children – the more able as well as Special Needs catered for. 3 dedicated full-time specialists and 6 assistants assist dyslexics, mild Asperger's syndrome, impaired hearing and some statemented pupils.

Cosy sixth form (most tutor groups only 6) attracts those who can't face 'factory farm' sixth form colleges nearby. Bias towards science, maths, exotic languages, history of art and art. Recent additions to A level subjects are film studies, theatre and media studies. 25 per cent A or B grades at A level, about 8 per cent fail – around the national average. Adequate IT facilities but don't hold your breath. Well-meaning careers advice needs more business-like approach from the real world.

Games, Options, The Arts: Despite acres of playing fields, hard tennis courts, a 25 yard indoor pool (one of first in the country) and a sports hall for indoor hockey, badminton, basketball, football and cricket, no county teams as yet. Much enthusiasm though and 90 per cent of girls represent school in hockey teams; 80 per cent of boys in football teams. D of E given full rein. Mr Waters will no doubt improve the motivation to compete.

Young Enterprise Scheme gains an extra qualification. 185 instrumental lessons in purpose-built music school ranges to post grade 8. Zestful drama puts on flamboyant musicals with casts of all ages. LAMDA exams.

Established ESOL takes Chinese, Japanese, Russian students and integrates them into all classes. The Octopus Art Gallery (in fabulous space of disused water tower) provides ample exhibition space for local artists as well as pupils and very vibrant artist in residence.

Background and Atmosphere: Founded in 1702 this well-travelled school began its life in Clerkenwell attached to a workhouse, lifted off to Croydon and, when typhoid threatened, came to its present site 20 minutes away from Cambridge in an imposing gothic Victorian building (land donated by two Friends).

Stunning artwork by ex-students and various artists in residence displayed in the old wood-panelled dining room and all round the school. Otherwise not a penny wasted on vanity. Has the atmosphere of an unpretentious grammar combined with a small country school with tight community ties. With its cosily old-fashioned feel it's a place where individuality is cherished, catered for and celebrated. Head is pumping new blood into the school with heads of departments, so give it a year or two under his energetic reign and this friendly teddy-bear could metamorphose into a savvy 21st century fox.

Pastoral Care and Discipline: Where the Quaker element comes up trumps. School-phobics or those bullied elsewhere come and thrive here. Day scholars encouraged to stay on after school hours to join in activities/prep/tea. Boarders live in comfy, large and airy rooms with cheery resident staff. Quartet of senior scholars are the head boy/girl and deputies.

Pupils and Parents: Only a sprinkle of teachers and pupils from Quaker background these days, though the governing body is still essentially Quaker. Day pupils come from a 30 mile radius, boarders from London, Herts, Suffolk, Essex, Cambridge – teachers, doctors, entrepreneurs and 'estuary up-market East-Enders', commented local taxi driver.

Uniform is due for overhaul. Sixth formers in own clothes. No trendies, alcohol banned, campus is strictly a no smoking zone. Old Scholars: BBC 'Blue Planet' producer Martha Holmes, rock star Tom Robinson, former Speaker of the House of Commons, Lord Newton of Braintree and quite a few of the Rowntree clan.

Entrance: Easy for those who fit the type of pupil the school looks for. Interview and assessment at 11. 40 per cent arrive from junior school. Most outside entries to sixth form are currently via EFL.

Exit: 3-4 to Oxbridge. 70 per cent to universities like Bristol, University College London, Lancaster. 30 per cent leave post-16 for sixth form colleges in London and Cambridge which offer a broader range of subjects.

Money Matters: Despite 70 assisted places lost, school continues to grow strongly (by over a third in three years in senior school). Two scholarships for academic excellence in years 7 and 9 (means tested); bursaries in art, music, sport in years 7 and 9 and for new entrants in year 9. Sixth form: head's discretion to award (max) £2,000 to those who contribute substantially to school life. Quaker bursaries for Quaker families.

Remarks: Head is contracted till retirement so major improvements are expected. Thus very good value until fees catch up with 21st century. Ideal for an unusual child or one who would shrink in the high pressured hot-houses.

GATEWAYS SCHOOL

Linked to Gateways Preparatory School in the Junior section

Harewood, Leeds, West Yorkshire, LS17 9LE

Tel: 0113 288 6345
Fax: 0113 288 6148
E-mail: gateways@gatewayschool.co.uk
Website: www.gatewayschool.co.uk

• Pupils: 535 girls, 25 boys aged 3-7 • Ages: 3-18 • Size of sixth form: 60 • C of E foundation, but 'all faiths or none' accepted • Fees: £1,089 - £2,655 • Independent

Head: Since 1997, Mrs Denise Davidson BA MEd (fifties). Read history at Manchester, and has done just about everything since then, including living in a Little Gidding community with her family, teaching history to Borstal boys and car maintenance to motor mechanics, starting a school on Tuvalu (where her husband was attorney general), running a smallholding, being appointed as the first housemistress at Oundle, and picking up an MEd in educational management at Cambridge. Five grown-up children. This all adds up to a range of experience and knowledge of the world unusual at the top of any school. It's said the more conservative elements on the staff were somewhat startled by her arrival. Warm, attractive and welcoming personality; a good listener, much respected by pupils and parents, also clear-sighted about where she wants the school to go and how to guide it there – which includes extensive professional development for her staff (two senior teachers were recently awarded MAs from Leeds, in education and music). Her immediate ambition is to construct a winter garden between the school's attractive main buildings.

Academic Matters: Results getting better all the time (value-added index too), as numbers grow and teaching becomes more focused; former 'rejects' now getting Ds and Es at A2 level, while more As are coming from the brightest – 'identified and pushed' by staff. Girls at opposite ends of the ability range seem to coexist contentedly. English outstanding at both levels, art and IT show very well. 2004 GCSE was a bumper year in numbers and achievement, with strong languages (including Greek and Latin) and dual award science. Interestingly, some girls were entered ahead of or behind their chronological group, thus 'highlighting our policy of treating each pupil as an individual'. Average class size 17, and student:staff ratio 8.7 to 1. Serious SEN provision: currently two statemented pupils (1 to 1 attention), while another 17 get extra support.

Games, Options, The Arts: Games flourish under recently-appointed male director of sports. The usual netball, hockey and swimming, plus some football, and an emphasis on general health; fitness suite just opened, with an Astroturf area in the pipeline. Wittily titled games news sheet – 'Sporta', school mag is 'Porta', OK you Latinists? – helps to raise profile. Enthusiastic involvement in drama (some with boys of nearby Leeds GS), art and music (director is an expert on music and liturgy). D of E and World Challenge cater for the adventurous.

Background and Atmosphere: Founded in 1941, the school occupies the handsome former dower house of the nearby Harewood estate, midway between Leeds and Harrogate. Plenty of additions since then, much of it good to look at and work in, especially recent science/languages building, sports hall, and performing arts centre. An attractive site, if a touch bleak in winter – but these are (mostly) Yorkshire lasses who can cope with a bit of wind and rain. Mrs Davidson is a strong advocate of single-sex education, for all the familiar reasons but with a gritty extra dimension – self-esteem in adolescence depends to an extent on experience in risk-taking, public speaking and conflict handling. Much is made of providing opportunities for these – and preparing girls for a changing world where teamwork and communication skills count for more than old hierarchies – in the school's admirably terse and guff-free prospectus. Fine if it all works in practice; the intention is certainly there. Equally, you find evidence of thought for others, something a good small school can do very well – from 'wraparound care' for the 3 to 11s (ie before and after school provision, charged as an extra) to involvement in the locality (ask about the Gateways Link). A senior girl observed how satisfactory it was that younger pupils weren't altogether separated on the site, and that prefects could keep a motherly eye on the little ones as they played. Neat, trad uniform: cherry red blazers and black skirts, with sixth formers in acceptable own clothes. Altogether, an impression of quiet, unpushy confidence, and girls ready to converse unaffectedly but respectfully with adults.

Pastoral Care and Discipline: As you might expect, a well-conceived pastoral system in which every teacher is involved, and just about everyone knows everyone else. Very little problem with the common school sins, though Mrs Davidson did suspend two girls for smoking – on safety grounds, since they were standing next to some gas bottles.

Pupils and Parents: This used to be a faintly posh establishment for girls perceived to be nice but dim and who couldn't make it to boarding school or the grammar schools of Leeds and Bradford. No more – Gateways increasingly figures on the local prep school circuit for parents who choose what it offers in preference to other places. Local primary schools are also taking an interest. Girls come from Leeds' more comfortable suburbs and the affluent arc of villages from its NW to NE; also Harrogate, and further afield from Skipton and York. Parents are typically doctors, lawyers and financiers, also transient foreigners (Danes, Australians, French) drawn to Leeds' booming economy. Plenty of large shiny cars and smart mums in the car park at picking-up time. Prominent OG: Henrietta Hill, human rights barrister.

Entrance: Applicants for nursery places spend some time in the school on a 'carousel' of activities; 4-11s assessed. 11+ tested in English, maths and VR, also art, ICT and PE. Selection 'not on academic criteria alone'. Transfer from prep to main school is automatic; parents warned in good time if this is unrealistic. Relocation at any age considered if the school has room; post-16 candidates need a minimum of six GCSEs at A*-C. All 11+ girls have a 30-minute slot with Mrs Davidson, then asked to say what they thought of the process (and each other).

Exit: Vast majority to northern universities and colleges; subjects range from molecular biology to equine science.

Money Matters: Some scholarships at present, but system being revised to offer only bursaries; reductions for siblings.

Remarks: An impressive small school on the way up, with strong visionary leadership and a real concern for the all-round development of the individual, but by no means comfy and girly. Increasingly making its mark, and respected by big-hitter neighbouring schools. It may suffer temporarily from the forthcoming amalgamation of Leeds Boys and Girls, but it has the confidence to continue carving out its own niche. Definitely worth a trip into the Yorkshire countryside.

GEORGE ABBOT SCHOOL

Woodruff Avenue, Guildford, Surrey, GU1 1XX

Tel: 01483 888 000
Fax: 01483 888 001
E-mail: ga@webmail.digitalbrain.com
Website: www.ga.digitalbrain.com

• Pupils: 1,939 boys and girls • Ages: 11-19 • Size of sixth form: 400 • Non-denom • State • Open days: Tours each week

Head: Since 1999, Mr Daniel C Moloney ('Danny') BEd MA FRSA (early fifties). Previously head of Feltham Community College and, before that, deputy head at George Abbot and Carshalton High School for Boys. Very experienced head, well in control. Wife, Sandra, is a primary school teacher; two teenage children.

Academic Matters: George Abbot School is a Leading Edge School, working in partnership with local secondary schools in four key areas. Awarded specialist status for the visual arts in September 2000, providing an extra £1 million over 4 years. Head points out that the school has so many strong suits, it could have applied for specialist status in any number of fields, 'we could have become a language college but opting for arts had the least effect on our curriculum structure.' Accredited as a teacher training school by Investors In People. Academically, there is lots of setting, allowing the able to push ahead and the slower to take a gentler road. Fantastic after-school and lunchtime masterclasses for the brainy eg one on forensic science investigating how blood splatters onto different surfaces from different heights and at different angles. Generally good GCSE and A level results. 35 A level options, including a few rare specimens eg geology, textiles and graphics. Year 11 students achieved 75 per cent pass rate at A*-C in their 2005 GCSE examinations, 81 per cent in 2004; 99 per cent of students got A-E (a record 2 per cent increase) in their A level examinations in 2005 and 99 per cent in 2004.

Games, Options, The Arts: Art is displayed everywhere and the talent is breathtaking. All pupils benefit from the buzz emanating from the art rooms and the enthusiasm of the art teachers. Textiles is especially strong, led by wonderful women described appreciatively by the deputy head as 'completely bonkers.' Every youngster has a go at textiles as part of art and it is a very popular option at exam level. Artist in residence is designing a sculpture garden. Music now very good with pupils last year going on the school's first ever overseas music tour (swing band to Italy). Drama a big GCSE subject (100 a year).

The school has a good sporting record, thanks partly to the huge number of pupils. Football predominates for the boys (not much rugby). The fantastic Surrey County Cricket centre was built on site in 1997 with a lottery grant. The county team uses it for winter nets and other practices, but George Abbot has run of the centre during school hours. Surprisingly, the school seems to make nothing of this glamorous link to British sporting heroes but renting out the upstairs conference rooms provides a nice little earner. Swimming off-site. Many sixth form pupils work for a sports leadership award by supervising local primary school pupils' PE lessons at George Abbot. Very good boys' and girls' gymnastics, trampolining and dance. Offered GCSE and A level dance from September 2002.

Background and Atmosphere: Separate boys and girls schools amalgamated in 1976 to become one enormous, muscular, semi-urban comprehensive. Set in leafy Guildford residential streets (nearness to the school said to have inflated house prices in the vicinity). Slightly daunting real-world atmosphere offset by school's successful efforts to treat each year group in an age-appropriate way. Main canteen open for early drop-offs and breakfast from 7.45am. Resounding agreement from pupils and parents on school's least pleasing feature: the food!

Pastoral Care and Discipline: Excellent precautions abound to protect tender eleven year-olds from shock when joining the heaving George Abbot metropolis. Induction in July helps them (through treasure hunts etc) to suss out the school's maze of buildings and corridors. Every single year group has its own playground which helps to protect younger children from unwanted botheration. Year 7s have their own tuck shop, toilets and specially allocated members of staff and there is a full-time youth worker. Best of all, year 7s are based in the new Wilson Building, far and away the loveliest structure on site.

Pupils and Parents: Pupils are homogenous, white, middle-income or above, fashion-conscious, streetwise, conformist; high-heeled, bare-legged girls teeter about alongside snazzy boys sporting carefully gelled-up fringes. No uniform in sixth form. 20 EAL students (out of 1,900 pupils)- a melting pot this isn't. Old boys/girls: England spinner Ashley Giles and the artist who created the sculpture for the Sydney Olympics, Dominique Sutton.

Entrance: Entry not a problem if you live in the catchment area (which shifts slightly annually). Can be difficult if you are just over the line. Siblings always admitted. Main feeders: Boxgrove, Burpham, Holy Trinity and Bushy Hill.

Selective sixth form admits around 25 pupils from outside, mainly from private schools (5 A-C GCSEs minimum – stiffer requirements for some subjects).

Exit: One third leaves after year 11, mostly to further education elsewhere. After sixth form, 85 per cent go to university (some after gap years), many to study fashion, sports science, media arts and such. Vast numbers to art foundation courses at Surrey Institute or Kingston. A dollop to Oxbridge (5 in 2005).

Money Matters: Has brilliantly tapped into every special programme/funding source/DfES initiative going.

Remarks: Heavyweight comprehensive in affluent area, successfully providing challenge to its most able pupils and aid to those who are struggling.

GEORGE HERIOT'S SCHOOL

Linked to George Heriot's Junior School in the Junior section

Lauriston Place, Edinburgh, EH3 9EQ

Tel: 01312 297 263
Fax: 01312 296 363
E-mail: admissions@george-heriots.com
Website: www.george-heriots.com

• Pupils: 900 boys and girls • Ages: 11-18 • Size of sixth form: 145 fifth form, 110 sixth form • Non-denom • Fees: Senior school: £2,348; Juniors £1,557 - £1,909 • Independent

---

Head: Since 1998, Mr Alistair Hector MA (fiftyish), who was educated at Edinburgh Academy, read modern languages at St Andrews and came to Heriot's from Warwick School, where he was deputy head. Before that he taught at King Edward's School. Started his career at Merchiston, after a spell in Germany teaching EFL. Married, one of his children currently attends the school. Pleased to be back in Scotland and quite liked taking over mid-way through the session – 'you don't have to worry about the timetable and you've got a couple of terms to settle in'. He is head of the whole school. No longer has a timetabled class to teach but pops in and does the 'odd bit of supply teaching for PSHE'; rather misses the daily contact – 'pupils are the core of what the school does'.

Academic Matters: Not easy to extract detailed examination results (by subject by grade) – so keep asking. Solid results at all levels. Max class size 26, 'but usually much less'. Classes streamed early, setted for maths at 9; also for English from 11. Steeped in 'Euro-awareness' a sort of Euro-starter course at 8; with either French, German or Spanish at 10. A second lang can be taken at 13. Strong sciences across the board but actually no particular bias. Eight Standard Grades the norm; Latin available to Standard and classical civilisation to Higher level is surprisingly popular. Finely-tuned support for learning but limited in the amount of help they can give, will not take children with a formal statement of needs except in 'exceptional circumstances' but any child with a suspected problem is seen by the Support for Learning department, which then swings into action. Both withdrawn and team teaching on hand, either individual or in small groups. School will bear the cost of extra lessons and may, in certain circs, cover the cost of an outside ed psych; they have their own who is free. Can cope with ADD/ADHD up to a certain degree, Ritalin is not an issue – 'we would consult with parents to see how their children might be best served'. EFL lessons are charged for. Computers all over the shop, loads of new suites.

Games, Options, The Arts: This is a games school. Outstanding rugby and cricket and girls' hockey very powerful; games played down at Goldenacre, along with all the other Edinburgh schools mafia; FPs use the pitches too. Pupils bused across Edinburgh, cross-country running and rowing are favourite alternative sports – the school has a boat house on the canal. Badminton and extra-curricular football are all in the frame, plus fencing and very good swimming, there is a small training pool on the (very cramped) site, but basically they use the baths at Warrender. Drama now timetabled and taken at both Standard and Higher levels. New head of music recently appointed which has done wonders for this department – choirs as well as a variety of chamber and other orchestras. Art streaking ahead, and photography on offer but not to exam level. Sixth year does voluntary service, working in the nursery, helping with lower primary pupils and outside placements eg the outpatients at the Ashley Ainslie.

Background and Atmosphere: George Heriot, jeweller to King James the VI (and I), who had started business life in a booth by St Giles, left the princely sum of £23,625 'for the building of a hospital' (ie a charity school) on a 'site at the foot of Gray's Close', for boys whose fathers had died. Fabulous ogee curved-roofed towers, the place was first inhabited by Cromwell in 1650 and, whilst principally designed by William Wallace, the magical inner-city school can boast almost every important 17th century Scottish architect – finishing with the court favourite, Robert Mylne. The school claims to be the longest-inhabited school in Scotland. Magnificent Pugin chapel revamped by James Gillespie Graham in 1837; pupils still sit on backless benches. A rather snazzy library in the lower half of a hall has been disastrously (school rejects this epithet – not surprisingly) split in two to provide a concert hall above. While all schools are perennially short on space, this is the most blatant piece of architectural sacrilege we have ever come across.

Founders day celebrated with 'buskins' (garlands) round the founder's statue on June Day. The foundation was feudal superior of great tracts of Edinburgh, and has close links with Donaldson's hospital for the deaf (the school's after-school club is held there daily). The hospital became a school in 1886, changed its name and the 180 foundationers were joined by paying pupils but the 180 registration marks are still visible in the quadrangle. Boarding was phased out in 1902 and girls admitted in 1979; the school became 'fully independent' in 1985. FPs are known as Herioters. School has fantastic views of Edinburgh Castle but the site is cramped; they had hoped to be able to buy part of the about-to-be-defunct Edinburgh Royal Infirmary but were thwarted by developers who propose transforming the place into upmarket flats and office blocks. The former, says the head, 'will be handy for more pupils' but they currently need space more than bums on seats. One or two possibilities in the pipeline – a certain amount of in-filling, plus some internal revamping (the head's office smelled of paint during our visit). The school has leased space from Edinburgh College of Art and the wish list includes plans to improve the old gym, expand the music department and create a sixth form centre for starters. Uniform for all, different ties for prefects and sixth. Trips all over the shop in every discipline.

Pastoral Care and Discipline: Code of conduct equals schools rules which parents and pupils have to sign, based on 'personal safety, safety for others and respect for others, property and the environment'. Ladder of sanctions. Good PSHE team who are proactive in reducing tension, both sides must face up to an issue. Persistent misbehaviour and not responding = out; detentions and discussions with parents more normal. Occasional suspensions, no real problems with drugs, booze and fags but head is on the ball – 'can honestly say that there have been no expulsions because of drugs in my time here'. Concern if school work suffers, no random drugs tests. Church of Scotland chaplain; school uses Grey Friars Kirk (of Bobby fame) for services.

Pupils and Parents: Sturdy middle class lot, Edinburgh-average ethic. Thriving parents' association.

Entrance: Test (English, maths, VRQ) at primary and senior level, including from own junior school; predicted grades for pupils joining post-Standard Grades.

Exit: Regularly four or five to Oxbridge; school runs induction weekends down to Oxbridge along with St Mary's Music School to familiarise pupils with the collegiate system, otherwise mostly to Scottish unis, some leave after Standard Grades either to employment or further education elsewhere.

Money Matters: School felt the loss of Assisted Places keenly but is pretty well back up to speed. Foundation still provides 100 per cent bursary for 'children of primary or secondary school age, who are resident in Edinburgh or the Lothians, whose father has died and whose mother might not otherwise afford the cost of private education'. Raft of other bursaries and scholarships, will keep children in place during financial crisis – but rather depends on child for how long.

Remarks: Thunderingly good inner-city school in a spectacular position, doing what it does do well.

GEORGE WATSON'S COLLEGE

Linked to George Watson's Primary School in the Junior section

Colinton Road, Edinburgh, EH10 5EG

Tel: 0131 446 6000
Fax: 0131 446 6090
E-mail: admissions@gwc.org.uk
Website: www.gwc.org.uk

• Pupils: 1,100 (boy:girl ratio 55:45 • Ages: 12-18 • Size of sixth form: 426 • Non-denom • Fees: Junior £1,681 - 2,026; senior: £2,606 • Independent • Open days: October

Principal: Since 2001, Mr Gareth Edwards MA (forties). Born in Wales and has a 'keen affinity with the Celts.' Educated at Tudor Grange Grammar, Solihull; read classics at Exeter, Oxford. Taught at King Edward VIth Edgbaston, before becoming head of department at Bolton Boys, followed by vice principal of Newcastle-under-Lyme School. He was previously rector at Morrison's Academy in Crieff. Married, with one daughter.

A slow speaking, deep thinking head, he has all the Welsh charm and a quiet charisma. He is also very giggly, though he was considerably offended by this comment saying that 'a reputable publication such as ours would not pass such personal comments'. Little does he know.

Academic Matters: One of Scotland's most successful schools; follows the Scottish system; excellent results. One of a few schools to teach study skills throughout the school. Careers advice starts from 15 upwards beginning with Morrisby testing so that pupils can make informed choices when deciding on 5 or 6 subjects from the choice of 26. Extension modules and additional subjects available for the last year. Foreign language teaching is strong, with great emphasis put on speaking skills. Numerous native speakers within the department and opportunities for exchanges. Superb networked ICT department used for backing up the curriculum.

Dr Weedon, a practitioner at the forefront of dyslexia research and development, is still strongly at the helm of their special needs team. In this buzzing department all manner of support is made available for pupils, and parents speak highly of special needs provision. Dr Weedon seems to have adopted the school credo of 'developing independence of thought'. Lots of children referred for help but most feel confident enough to refer themselves. Frequent 'inset' and personal development training for all staff throughout the school.

Games, Options, The Arts: Renowned for their successes on the rugby field and strong rowing but now most definitely on the map for their success in winning the juvenile World Pipe and Drum Championships. A wealth of music and sports to choose from as well as the chance to appear in spectacular dramatic productions. But with clubs and societies galore, at the last count close to 80, including 20 sports clubs, 4 orchestras, 3 bands, musical ensembles and several choirs, they are spoilt for choice. Many school trips too, at home and abroad. The third year 10-day excursion backpacking with their peers and teachers, features high in most students' memories. Amazing art (students sit English board for this).

Background and Atmosphere: Founded by a legacy left by George Watson, the merchant and financier, in 1741. Some 250 years on, the school still adopts his original principles in offering a good academic and moral education, making room for children from less privileged backgrounds along with the more fortunate. Moved to current site in 1932, now a listed building. Splendid and impressively approached on a long sweeping driveway.

Pastoral Care and Discipline: Ethos of respect for others. Excellent system in place to control such a large school, with a year head following pupils all the way through the school. First year pupils keep the same form teacher for the first two years; the next two years follow suit and get to choose a tutor. Sixth formers are actively involved throughout the school. Strong anti-bullying policy, parents immediately informed and consulted if child is involved. Overall, parents report being impressed with the help given in difficult situations. Detentions plentiful but expulsion rare.

Regular training for specialist guidance staff who help with listening and advising.

Pupils and Parents: Bright pupils, stretched in every direction. Claim never to be bored. Mainly children of professionals. Very much a local school but some travelling quite a distance. OBs and OGs include Sir David Steel (The Right Hon Lord Steel of Aikwood KBE DL, presiding officer of the Scottish parliament), Sir Malcolm Rifkind, former foreign secretary, Chris Hoy, Olympic and Commonwealth medal cyclist, Gavin and Scott Hastings, former Scottish rugby internationals, Sheena McDonald and Martha Kearney, broadcasters and journalists.

Entrance: At 12 and upwards where vacancies arise by selection taking maths, English and VR papers along with interview.

Exit: 90 per cent plus stay on after Highers for further studies. 90 per cent plus go on to higher education. 66 per cent to Scottish universities.

Money Matters: A range of up to 11 academic and 2 music scholarships each year. Also sports bursaries, Enablement Fund and part of Ogden Trust Science Scholarship Scheme. Numerous short-term or long-term bursaries for those in need with assistance for more than 100 pupils. In 1997 the school's own foundation was established to maintain the original Watson purpose and replace the loss of Assisted Places. It also funded the new music school extension and a lift for disabled students.

Remarks: A fine traditional reputation. Well-organised structured school. Despite the size, communication with parents and pupils is very strong. Every pupil treated as an individual.

GIGGLESWICK SCHOOL

Linked to Catteral Hall in the Junior section

Giggleswick, Settle, North Yorkshire, BD24 0DE

Tel: 01729 893 000
Fax: 01729 893 150
E-mail: enquiries@giggleswick.org.uk
Website: www.giggleswick.org.uk

• Pupils: 325 boys and girls (215 board, 110 day) • Ages: 13-18 (associated junior schools, Catteral Hall 7-13 and Mill House pre-prep 3-8) • Size of sixth form: 140 • C of E • Fees: Senior school: boarding £6,990; day £4,700. Catteral Hall, years 7 & 8 boarding £4,910; day £3,835. Catteral Hall years 3-6 boarding £4,140; day £3,400. Mill House pre-prep £1,700 • Independent • Open days: October - nursery - year 9; February - sixth form

Head: Since 2001, Mr Geoffrey Boult BA (mid forties). Read geography at Durham University. Previously a housemaster at St Edward's, Oxford. Married to Katie, four daughters, two at Giggleswick. A friendly, good-humoured, youthful figure, well liked and respected by pupils, teaches civics and religious studies. Fast developing a love of life in the north; appreciates the straightforwardness of northerners who 'tell it like it is.' A committed Christian and keen sportsman, once a county hockey player now enjoys coaching games and indulging his passion for golf. Staff now used to the new boss, lots of positive feedback, emphasis on academic target setting caused a stir but now accept head wants to balance the academic, blending it with the breadth of opportunity that Giggleswick offers.

Academic Matters: Hard working pupils confident but not arrogant, good solid staff, blend of age and experience. School selective, but not greatly so, good value added. Separate and combined sciences offered, 94 per cent A* to C pass rate at GCSE (100 per cent in single sciences) and new generation of enthusiastic science teachers. Sets for English, French, maths, science with top set French taking GCSE a year early then studying Russian. A good selection of A level courses offered though these 'have been rationalised to ensure viable teaching groups'. Those wanting to pursue vocational courses are directed elsewhere at 16. Most subjects sport a few Ds and Es but none fail altogether, art a particular strength. No massaging of results here, if you study for a subject you sit the exam. 'Failure not necessarily a bad thing,' says the head, 'sometimes it can provide a much needed wake-up call.'

Full time special educational needs co-ordinator and successful buddy system where older children with experience of a learning difficulty mentor younger ones. EFL provided (two to four lessons a week), one-to-one, in study periods but anyone arriving from abroad must have a basic level of English. Class sizes 22 maximum, 4-12 for A level. Lots of computers, including some in each boarding house; every pupil has email and a computer link in their study bedroom.

Games, Options, The Arts: Keen drama started by Russell Harty, several OGs and some pupils active in the profession, but luvvies and their tantrums not tolerated. Art and design taken seriously – impressively ambitious design work in particular. Strong links with half a dozen large companies and all pupils take IT qualifications. Public speaking encouraged.

Sport keen, traditionally cross-country and rugby, international level coaching over the past few years has led to success in hockey, cricket and athletics. Seven hard and four grass courts, together with the opportunity to train in Portugal, ensure continued popularity of tennis. A third of pupils learn an instrument (some play professionally), glorious chapel choir and lots of bands regularly tour home and abroad. Splendid sixth form centre with bar, alcohol allowed at weekends but consumption strictly monitored. Oozing with outward-bound opportunities including Duke of Edinburgh Award Scheme and CCF (compulsory in y10) but plenty of other activities: car maintenance, conservation projects and all the usual opportunities. Exchanges with schools in France and Spain, tours, eg of drama and jazz, to the US, sports to Barbados, Australia and Hong Kong and historians to the WW1 battlefields. Sports' trips charged as extras but those identified as curriculum trips included in the fees.

Background and Atmosphere: Set in the western margins of the magnificent Yorkshire dales beneath an imposing limestone escarpment, 60 minutes' drive north of Manchester. Giggleswick was founded in 1512, moved to present site in 1869. Attractive buildings overlook Giggleswick village beneath the fabulously restored chapel complete with landmark copper dome well worth the walk up the steep hill (bring your crampons). Large development plan continues but wonderful new library with IT suite and internet café now complete (a popular venue for nightly prep). Other recent additions include floodlit all-weather pitch and dining hall (cafeteria system, separate sittings, lots of choice, quality middling rather than Michelin.) Work on the new science centre is underway and once finished a new sports hall will be built on the site of the old. Girls' quarters in better decorative order than boys' where a lick of paint and the odd new carpet wouldn't go amiss. Pupils welcome to decorate their own study bedrooms, most do but some communal areas impersonal. A full boarding school, exeats only one weekend in three. Happy relaxed but purposeful atmosphere: James Herriot meets Wainwright.

Pastoral Care and Discipline: Six houses (four boys, two girls) mix of boarding and day. Senior house staff tutor year 9 and 10 with pupils choosing their tutors in year 11. Pastoral care is supported by the medical centre, school doctor, professional counsellors and chaplain. Expulsions are rare, a couple a year. Sniffer dogs brought in termly for drugs checks and compulsory drugs testing is used on known and suspected offenders. Anyone caught supplying faces immediate expulsion. Boys and girls are allowed to visit each other's houses but permission must be sought to move away from public areas. Behaviour between sexes 'should not cause embarrassment to anyone.' Staff vigilant for anorexia and similar, system in place to check on pupils suspected of skipping meals including height/weight monitoring and meal attendance cards. Chapel an integral and important part of the school but faith more important than denomination.

Pupils and Parents: 75 per cent board, the rest are local children from a large catchment area, more boys (65 per cent) than girls, mid-range academically. School fully co-ed since 1983. Fifteen per cent foreign, 15 per cent expats and Services and popular with all these. Suits those who are team players, keen on the out doors and enjoy the varieties of life. Not for city types, loners or those who mind getting wet! Parents in business and the professions. OGs: James Agate, Richard Whitely, William Gaunt, Sarah Fox. OG society well established on the internet.

Entrance: Not a great problem. At 3 (pre-prep, Mill House); at 7 (junior department, Catteral Hall) via own test and reports; at 13 CE or Giggleswick entrance exam for those from state schools and Catteral Hall together with interview and previous school's report. Entrance into sixth form is by a minimum of five GCSEs at A*-C grade with AS level subjects at B grade. Around 25 new sixth form entrants per year. Catteral Hall Prep school, the main feeder for Giggleswick, is situated in the same grounds and has moved away from following what it describes as the rigidity of common entrance to the breadth of National Curriculum. Year 7 and year 8 pupils at Catteral Hall use the senior school facilities for some lessons easing the transition from junior to senior school and allowing for specialist teaching.

Exit: Five plus to Oxbridge, others principally to a wide spread of universities or art foundation courses. 20 per cent do a gap year.

Money Matters: 30ish scholarships a year, including general distinction, art, music, and locals, ranging in value from 10 per cent for an exhibition to 50 per cent for a top scholarship award, bursaries including Services available. School in good shape financially owing to large gifts from OG Norman Sharpe and more recently Graham Watson (late governor).

Remarks: Friendly, character building co-ed boarding school serving the locals and the English community abroad. Extremely strong links with business reflected in curriculum and attitudes through the school. Doing a good job for a broad intake in this relatively isolated area. A useful school for the less academic pupil, those who don't know what to do next or the multi-talented who want to pursue a diverse range of interests.

THE GLASGOW ACADEMY

Linked to Atholl School in the Junior section

Linked to Glasgow Academy Preparatory School (The) in the Junior section

Colebrooke Street, Glasgow, G12 8HE

Tel: 0141 334 8558
Fax: 0141 337 3473
E-mail: enquiries@tga.org.uk
Website: www.theglasgowacademy.org.uk

• Pupils: 307 boys, 267 girls; all day (plus prep schools, see below) • Ages: 11-18, prep schools see below • Size of sixth form: 200 • Non-denom • Fees: £865 - £2,560 • Independent • Open days: November

---

Rector: Since 2005, Peter Brodie MA PGCE (forties) who was educated at Abingdon and did his Masters in English at St Johns, followed by a PGCE at Oxford and a (later) Masters in education management (part time) at Canterbury Christchurch University College ('a good intellectual training exercise'). Unmarried and a self-confessed thespian, chalk is in the blood, his father was headmaster and his mother taught PE. He started his teaching career in a 'split-site comprehensive school'. Comes to Glasgow Academy from King's, Canterbury, where he was press officer, having risen via the ranks of head of English, housemaster, and more recently 'held public relations responsibilities and was Arts Festival Manager. Has also 'produced numerous plays and organised a wide range of activities and events, from debating to Duke of Edinburgh

Award training. 'He is passionate about encouraging children to make the most of the opportunities good schools can provide and believes strongly that a culture of high expectations combined with good pastoral care helps children grow in confidence and achievement'. Has contributed to various training courses for new heads and is part of the Longmans editorial clique.

Academic Matters: School follows Scottish system, all singing and dancing, with fabulous computer labs, science labs and lots of ancillary add-ons (as you might expect with the amount of dosh they must have accumulated from selling the grounds of Westbourne for up-market housing). Max class size 24, 20 and down for practical subjects. Sciences – biology, chemistry, computing studies, geography, maths and physics outstanding at Standard Grade, and both Highers, and Advanced Highers, as is English; slight blip in the humanities and languages, though Latin on offer – with a commendable take-up – throughout, two out of two at grade 1 in Advanced Highers last year. A stirring achievement. Grade 1s are on a roll, with ever improving performance figures in Standard and Advanced Higher levels and only a slight glitch overall in the Higher results for 2001.

Remedial help on hand for the lesser and the brighter child, laptops in evidence, and extra help in exams. No problems with children with ADHD, support for learning much in evidence. Fabulous new computer suites all over.

Games, Options, The Arts: Serious rugby school (more than 80 FPs have won their Scotland caps). Three playing field areas with Astroturf, some hundreds of metres apart from each other at Anniesland (the home of all Glasgow school playing fields) plus an all weather pitch on site in the middle of the campus. Hockey, cricket, footie, a proper athletics track as well as tennis. Games are important here. Zillions of inter-house competitions as well as inter-school matches. And masses of inter-house activities at lunch time.

CCF became non-compulsory the day we visited (May 2002) and community service is now an acceptable alternative, D of E, and trillions of golds, etc. Trips almost everywhere, in every dimension, art as well as skiing. The rector feels that there is a real need to get the Glasgow young out of their cosy environment and see the big bad world outside – super visit to Japan last year. Music is good and strong, with choirs for all, as well as orchestra, string, wind band and various ensembles, lunchtime concerts a popular feature in the 'little concert hall'. Drama is outstanding, the Cargill Hall was set up for The Miser by Molière when we visited.

Spectacular art, and stunning art room at the top of the recently converted terrace house in Colebrooke Terrace. Strong follow-through to art schools all over. Very popular design technology, with a huge number of girls participating, though as our guide pointed out, this may have something to do with the dishy member of staff in charge!

Background and Atmosphere: School was founded in 1845 and re-constituted as a memorial to the 327 staff and pupils who fell in the First World War, post the First World War (as, incidentally, was Kelvinside Academy, their nearest rivals). The school merged with the girls' school, Westbourne School for Girls, in 1991 and still occupies a fabulous site on the banks of the river Kelvin, with the Glasgow underground system but a hundred yards away. Hub of the school is The Well, or library, where children can come and study in their free periods, computer linked, it hummed during our visit.

When we last visited the school, they had one or two houses in the lovely Victorian Colebrooke Terrace under their auspices; they now own most of the terrace, which is shut of from the general public with fancy iron gates – though there are one or two houses still in private ownership. However, behind the Victorian façade, a great transmogrification has occurred and the school boasts art rooms, computer suites and is home to the prep school.

Children are not allowed out at lunch time (minor scraps with local – state – schools). There is an excellent dining hall, adjacent to the Cargill Hall, buffet/cafeteria style meals, with vending machines. Transport is easy-peasy. The Cargill Hall and its ancillary dining area are let out for functions – when we visited, the Georgian glass of one of the doors to the dining hall had been punched out during a let. All pupils wear uniform and there is an excellent sixth form chill-out area on two floors in an area which used to be the old 'writing room'.

Pastoral Care and Discipline: All pupils join one of four houses and much of the extra-curricular activity is organised through these. Good PSE and anti-bullying procedure in progress. The occasional theft, 'yes, we're into sin' said the rector, but no recent problems. Only one recent expulsion for drugs related offence and that was a pupil whom the head had taken in 'out of kindness'. Smokers are usually excluded for a week.

Pupils and Parents: The usual Glasgow mafia; excellent links with the West and M8 conurbations, good PTA, basically sound middle class, plus ancillary huge scholarships for the less financially able. Loads of FPs' children, plus first time buyers.

Entrance: More or less automatic from junior schools, otherwise school's own test. Some incomers at sixth form level, usual requirement of Grade 1 at Standard for courses to be studied at Higher level.

Exit: Trickle post Higher – ie at S5, otherwise most stay till S6, usually adding to Highers rather than Advanced Highers. 90 per cent plus to unis, most to Scottish unis, with a steady stream south of the border, three or four regularly to Oxbridge. Engineering a popular subject.

Money Matters: Post Assisted Places, the school has worked hard to set a very comprehensive scholarship scheme in place. They hope to be able to offer 100 per cent of all fees and uniform. The trouble is getting the words in place not to offend government guidelines. Priority looks like being given to all-rounders rather than nerds.

Remarks: A good solid school, with a good solid head. Should not be over-looked under any circumstances.

GLENALMOND COLLEGE

Glenalmond, PH1 3RY

Tel: 01738 842 056
Fax: 01738 842 063
E-mail: registrar@glenalmondcollege.co.uk
Website: www.glenalmondcollege.co.uk

• Pupils: 385 pupils (235 boys, 150 girls; all board except for 59 day pupils) • Ages: 12-18 • Size of sixth form: 182
• Episcopalian • Fees: Day: £3,635 - £4,840. Boarding: £5,325 - £7,100 • Independent

Warden: Since 2003, Mr Gordon Woods MA (Oxon) PGCE (forties) who was educated at Durham where he was head boy, and previously taught at Shrewsbury, where he rose through the ranks to become head of geography and finally second master. He also ran a couple of houses. Keen on rowing, he stroked the winning Oxford lightweight crew in 1976 and 1977. He and his wife, Emma, are much enjoying their Perthshire appointment, couple of partridges hanging in the porch, that sort of thing. Two teenagers, one in the school, and one still at Shrewsbury.

A human geographer, he is 'passionate about geography and the part that the subject can play on the way the other half lives'. 'You must always look outwards.' Currently teaching upper sixth Highers geography – to learn about the pupils as well as the Scottish system. Has retained the practice of breakfast for new pupils that he inherited from his predecessor who was here from 1992 and directed a considerable recovery of the school's fortunes. He and his wife also have lunches for the lower sixth. Articulate and enthusiastic, 'he is a good thing', the pupils reckon, apart from the occasional (and more than that) mutterings about being a little 'petty- minded'. Mr Woods says of his aims, 'Glenalmond needs to be outward-looking and not just outward bound, to retain a strong sense of its own past but to be modern in its approach to pupils and parents. Seeing boys and girls through the teenage years has to be a three way partnership – pupils, parents and the school'. A credo that was seriously put to the test two summers back, when miscreants included the son of one of the governors.

Academic Matters: 71 per cent A & B grades at A level. Some good staff at all levels, but still one or two who reckon that teaching at Glenalmond is 'a way of life'. Pupils complain about 'inadequate teaching aids', and head admits that 'teaching methods are under review'. Several recent retirements and seven new and enthusiastic staff appointed, including a new deputy head (Academic), a new head of geography from UCL and a new head of girls' games. The new chaplain, previously a choral scholar, keen on rugby and cross country running, is a real plus.New(ish) science and maths block, awkwardly placed on the slope to the north of the main complex and connected at various levels – the trad build-it-by-numbers confection we see so often, with tubular rails and bog standard three level classrooms (well difficult to be imaginative with the sciences but given some of the glorious architecture around ...). Some excellent science results, but school still leans towards the arts. Fibre optics in place, two networks throughout school, apple and PCs, computers in most classrooms and houses, intranetted, nanny internet all over, and broadband. Software used to detect fraud with pupils down-loading course work from elsewhere (does it work we wonder?).Setting in the third year, core subjects still setted individually, four sets. Exotic new additions to the A level syllabus: music technology, RS, PE at GCSE level; history of art, apparently, with internet input, which most other schools find difficult if their internet is properly nannied. Ditto politics AS (language in the House of Lords can be truly blue). Good GCSE results with quantities of As and A*s across the board.School follows mixed bag of A levels and Highers. Always a difficult row to hoe. About ten per cent take Highers over two years: maths, English, geography popular plus economics and theatre studies. Loads of class related trips. Dyslexia support now represented at meetings of heads of departments (goodness gracious) and salaried professional in charge of learning support 'loads of one to one lessons'. All screened on entry, and certified with Ed Psych report for extra time in exams. Most of the male chauvinists are now a thing of the past, though girls still complain of one beak.

Games, Options, The Arts: This is still a school which majors in outward bound activities and uses its fantastic site to good advantage – all sorts of activities (and active is the word) – conservation projects, Munro Club, terrific CCF (remember Coll has strong army links), full-bore shooting as well as clays, indoor and outdoor .22 range, Scottish Islands Peaks Race, skiing (own artificial ski slope now out of commission thanks to Health and Safety regs) regular trips to freezing Glenshee – school boasts a number of past and current members of Scottish ski teams), curling a surprising newcomer, own nine hole golf course at Cairnies, sailing. Two gold D of E assessors on the staff, and hugely popular, with trips to Norway and the ruggeder parts of the USA.

Rugby is a religion, but good, rather than sweeping all before it. Boys' hockey coming up fast, girls' hockey and lacrosse strong, the appointment of hockey international as head of girls' games has done wonders. Enough girls now to muster full strength sports teams who keep tennis/netball teams flying the Glenalmond flag. Sports are a key part of life here, and daily participation is compulsory, but the constitutionally disinclined can get by with a spot of umpiring. NB sports regularly interrupted with vile weather. Rich in all-weather spectacularly floodlit pitches and more in the pipeline. Fishing (on the River Almond), sports hall, indoor heated pool. Two Pipe bands – which is hot shot on the charity front.

Design and technology now holding its own. First XV matches timetabled to ensure that players can participate in music and art – which they do with enthusiasm. Head keen that we would be as keen on the new art dept head as he is. He also did not like us calling her 'a jolly dolly', insisting that 'there is an intensity and passion about her art that goes well beyond the jolly dolly image'. We stand corrected. Head of art very keen on fabric and design and appeared proudest of the hat collection pupils had fabricated during the previous session. Hat making seems the strangest choice for what is a pretty butch school, but the art room is filled with zany pics of girls modelling their own creations, with one or two chaps as well. Fifth form CCF (both sexes) now an option, regular camps throughout the term very popular (our girlie guide was not absolutely convinced how much

she loved the expeditions, but it is so much fun to look back on). Sixth form can grannie bash or work in special schools instead.

Background and Atmosphere: Known to the pupils as Coll. Founded in 1847 by Prime Minister Gladstone, this is Scotland's oldest, most elegant, school. Spectacular self-contained quadrangle of cloisters, centred round the chapel and set in its own mini 300 acre estate, beautifully tended parkland and surrounded by some of the smartest grouse shooting in Scotland. Several modern additions stuck round the back, including Basil Spence music block. Also the aforementioned science and maths block.

This is a proper boys' boarding school which admitted girls at sixth form in 1990 and went 'all the way' in 1995; admissions now running 50/50. School currently sports five boys' boarding houses and two girls' and, whilst a third girls' house is on the wish list, a new boys' house will be open in 2007 in order to totally revamp the somewhat jealous boys and to convert some of the current boys housing into staff flats (all staff must live on site, part of their contract). Boys and girls mix socially during the day and after prep in school and not in each other's houses, although moves are afoot for each house to have a co-ed common room for limited access. All houses will also have one dedicated common room. Sixth form bar on Saturdays.

Rather set apart from the world and protective – you can't just wander round at will. 'Shopping bus' to Perth twice a week. Fixed exeats on either side of half term, 'parents have free and welcome access to their children at any time and can take them out on Saturdays and Sundays (after chapel). New trenchant school prospectus, which actually acknowledges that parents and guardians can read the spoken word rather than resembling a Scottish Tourist Board guide to Perthshire, is full of muscular pics of kids in action. Boy and girl now joint heads of Coll for the first time ever.

Pastoral Care and Discipline: Following a fairly hectic last few weeks at Glenalmond two summers back, head has been accused of regarding high jinks as serious. Certainly the affair saw some rather boring removals. Head has counteracted with a massively impressive tightly worded code of behaviour which covers everything from cycling without a helmet to public displays of affection between pupils as well as a massive drugs etc document. 'Smoking is a major social gateway to the smoking of illegal drugs, the College may regard persistent tobacco smoking as a reason for asking parents and pupils to agree to future drug testing'. These documents are unique in our experience and we are slightly concerned that sometimes alleged offences may be judged in black and white.

Basically, random drugs testing on suspicion, out if positive; fags equals house gating, Warden's gating and letters home, followed by suspension. Smoking in a building equals suspension even for the first time. Boozing to excess in permitted zones equals Warden's gating, followed by bans and possible suspension, no spirits allowed in the recognized pubs and watering holes. No bringing booze back to school under any circs. Stories of booze trenches, which we have heard ad infinitum over the years from staff and boys alike (well known to staff cos they borrow it and replace like with like), dismissed by the warden as 'nothing other than an unsubstantiated allegation'. No reported bullying, senior mistress both neutral and approachable. Anorexia said to be less of a problem, couple of girls under watchful eye, but nothing serious. 'Not completely clean' admits the head. Local keepers still complain about empties and other detritus on the neighbouring grouse moor.

Pupils and Parents: Scotland's school for toffs. 'Jolly nice parents'. Traditionally Scottish upper middle and middle class, army, Highland families. About twenty per cent locals and ten per cent foreigners from all over, plus three to four per cent ex-pats. School has previously trawled abroad and this year seven Chinese pupils arrived from Shanghai via an agency. All real foreigners must have guardians, either via parents or contacts or school will fix them up with guardianship agencies 'with whom we have worked successfully in the past'. Large number of first time buyers. FPs (known as OGs) a generous bunch and include Sandy Gall, Robbie Coltrane, Miles Kington, Allan Massie, David Sole and Andrew MacDonald (Train Spotting fame), Charlie (Lord) Falconer, erstwhile flatmate of Tony Blair – who was of course at arch-rival school, Fettes.

Entrance: Own entrance exam at 12, most at 13+ via CE, oodles from Ardvreck, Craigclowan, Lathallan (who are about to take pupils up to age 16) St Mary's Melrose and Belhaven, with a clutch from Cargilfield, state primaries or overseas. Some at sixth form; twenty this year, with a number from Germany, six passes at standard grade or GCSE or entrance test and previous school's recommendation. Entrance not a difficult hurdle at the moment.

Exit: 96 per cent + to university of some form of higher education. Half a dozen to Oxbridge.

Money Matters: Discounts for siblings of 25 per cent, a whopping 50 per cent for fourth child. 10 per cent for children whose parents are in the Armed Forces, and Fil Cler Bursaries for offspring of the Clergy. Otherwise a clutch of bursaries (means-tested) plus help if circumstances change. Music, art and academic scholarships too.

Remarks: School popular and highly thought of, saved by the 'belles' after a period of falling numbers, more girl friendly than previously, but still really a boys' school at heart. Not for retiring flowers, rebels or non-joiners in. We gave the school the soubriquet 'the Eton of the North' in our first edition; despite its best endeavours, we still don't think it's fully back on form.

THE GODOLPHIN AND LATYMER SCHOOL

Iffley Road, Hammersmith, London, W6 0PG

Tel: 020 8741 1936
Fax: 020 8746 3352
E-mail: registrar@godolphinandlatymer.com
Website: www.godolphinandlatymer.com

• Pupils: around 700 girls; all day • Ages: 11-18 • Size of sixth form: 200 • Non-denom • Fees: £3,922 • Independent • Open days: Check with school

Headmistress: Since 1986, Miss Margaret Rudland BSc (late fifties), educated at Sweyne School in Essex and Bedford College, London. Her first job, in 1967, was maths teacher at Godolphin and Latymer. She left to do VSO in Nigeria and has since taught at St Paul's Girls and been deputy head of Norwich High. Friendly and approachable, she is held in high esteem by parents, girls, staff and other heads. 'People choose us,' she says, 'because we can offer a good balance between the academic and the extra-curricular and because of the interest the staff take in all the girls.'

Academic Matters: Examination results are impressive – 95 per cent of A level results at A or B. English lit, maths and biology are particularly popular, with chemistry close behind. A level choices include philosophy, government and politics, Greek classical civilisation. In 2004/05 99 per cent of GCSE results were A*, A and B. The school will offer Mandarin from September 2006. Particularly strong on individual attention, with informal help for the few with special needs from the staff member in charge of study support. Streaming for French and maths from year 8. Unusually, girls in the first three years study technology (food and design) including a cookery lesson every other week, and a masterchef competition in the summer. 'The quality of the food is amazing,' says the head. Class sizes start at about 26 in the first three years, reduce to fewer than 20 in the GCSE years and to fewer than 12 in the sixth form. The school introduced the International Bacalaureate Diploma in September 2005 and girls have a choice between the Advanced level or IB route.

Games, Options, The Arts: Plenty of extra-curricular activities, starting at 6.30am some days with rowing squad on the river and ending at 8pm on the floodlit Astroturf games field. Drama is a great strength – year 7s, in their first term, perform a pantomime for local elderly people written and produced by the lower sixth, and the school is famed for its large-scale plays which often feature cast lists in the hundreds including actors from all year groups. There is a drama studio but no theatre. However, the school makes use of local theatres – including the Lyric Hammersmith and the Cottesloe – and has taken productions to the Edinburgh Fringe.

An Astroturf hockey pitch, recently floodlit, plus netball courts, which convert to tennis in the summer, means most sporting activities can take place on site. 'We don't want to waste time busing them around.' Hockey is the main sport, though netball has recently been reintroduced, and football and basketball are other winter options. They play tennis and rounders in the summer. Music is also strong. There is a joint orchestra with Latymer Upper School and various choirs, ensembles and bands including a jazz band. 'My daughter is very happy there musically,' said the mother of a talented musician. 'You can get involved even if you have no musical talent whatsoever,' said another pupil, approvingly.

There is a ski trip to USA and the school sends a team to the girls' schools' ski championships in Flaine. There are two polo teams and extra-curricular sports such as fencing, cricket, football and triathlon. Sixth formers do work experience in Versailles and Berlin with Latymer Upper School students; there are joint French and German language exchanges; plenty of overseas trips to locations ranging from the Sinai desert to New York and Moscow.

Background and Atmosphere: Built as a boarding school for boys in 1861, became an independent day school for girls in 1905, and evolved through different state-aided statuses before turning independent again in 1977 rather than becoming a comprehensive school or being closed down altogether. The original buildings are yellow brick Victorian, with some distinctly church-like windows and a formal panelled assembly hall. Recent yellow brick additions blend in fairly harmoniously and have provided new science labs and art studios, a pottery room, computer studies rooms and language labs. 'I like the way different buildings have different feels,' said a pupil. The ecology garden is used in biology lessons, there's a quad with pond (plus dolphin statue) and a courtyard where girls can eat lunch in warm weather. The spacious top floor sixth form centre resembles an airport lounge with roof terrace and tuck shop. 'We feel privileged to come up our own staircase to our own room,' said a sixth former. The school is valued for its friendly and supportive atmosphere. Although some of the local brightest are creamed off by St Paul's Girls, others choose Godolphin for its less pressured approach to life. 'There's lots of positive teacher input,' said a parent. 'They're very approachable if I have any problems.'

Pastoral Care and Discipline: The girls have produced their own anti-bullying strategy. Sixth formers visit each form on a weekly basis, 'so younger girls can take advice from older girls.' The head says that girls know drugs are not allowed in school; she would look at instances on a case-by-case basis and has not excluded anyone permanently so far.

Pupils and Parents: Mostly from within a five-mile radius – Westminster to Hounslow and Harrow to Wimbledon. The school has tried to persist in the grammar school ethos of educating bright children regardless of income. Inevitably, the abolition of Assisted Places – which used to make up around a quarter of the intake – has narrowed the social mix but the school tries hard to raise money for bursaries. About a fifth of applicants come from state primaries.

Entrance: A member of group 2 of the North London Consortium of girls' schools that set common maths and English exams. Generally 450-500 applicants for 104 places. Everyone has two interviews – 'it gives them a chance to see us and for us to see them.' Ten or twelve come into the sixth form to replace those who have moved to co-ed or boarding schools. They have a test and interview on subjects they want to do in the sixth form. 'I want them to fit in with the current cohort and to sit and talk about the subjects they want to do. I'm keen that they shouldn't make mistakes.'

Exit: Nearly all to the old-established universities, including a dozen or so to Oxbridge and a few to art schools.

Money Matters: The school has appointed a development director to raise funds, particularly for bursaries. 'I'm adamant that no-one should leave the school because their parents have fallen on hard times,' says the head. One music scholarship at 11 and music and art scholarships in the sixth form.

Remarks: Very strong academic school with a friendly atmosphere, an outstanding head and a broad range of extra-curricular activities. 'I always try to persuade people to come here because I've had such a wonderful time,' said a sixth former.

THE GODOLPHIN SCHOOL

Linked to Godolphin Preparatory School in the Junior section

Milford Hill, Salisbury, Wiltshire, SP1 2RA

Tel: 01722 430 500

Fax: 01722 430 501

E-mail: admissions@godolphin.wilts.sch.uk

Website: www.godolphin.org

- Pupils: 411 girls; half board, half day • Ages: 11-18 • Size of sixth form: 116 • Christian foundation • Fees: Day £4,295 boarding £6,600 • Independent • Open days: October, November, January, March

Head: Since 1996, Miss Jill Horsburgh MA (late forties). Educated at Ipswich High School GDST; studied history at Oxford and education at Leicester; did post graduate work at Sheffield and Surrey. Taught history at Downe House followed by Benenden – head of history, then housemistress and deputy head. Has wide-ranging interests from riding and walking her dogs to literature and music. Keen to maintain present ethos of the school while improving facilities. Next major development planned for 2006 is the opening of a new boarding house in January and a sixth form centre incorporating study, boarding, careers and leisure facilities in September. Very popular, described as a busy little sparrow – she is tiny, and buzzes about.

Academic Matters: Impressive GCSE (58 per cent A*/A – 88 per cent A/B) and A level results (81 per cent A/B). Average class size of 14 dropping to far smaller groups at A level. Wide range of subjects offered in the sixth form including activities (eg photography, creative textiles, debating and salsa dancing) alongside traditional A level subjects. French, German and Spanish are part of the curriculum but Japanese, Chinese, Russian and Italian can be studied as optional 'activities'. Head perceives strengths to include mathematics, modern languages, music, geography, sciences, English and art, although girls do well in a broad range of subjects.

A high-achieving school but emphasises that they try not to put too much pressure on the girls and sums it up with a quote from a parent praising the school for its 'success without stress'. One of the girls puts it a different way – 'work is not something we get stressed about here as we're all pretty good'. Not a lot of extra support for those with learning difficulties (between half an hour and an hour a week from qualified SEN teachers). However, girls who are

falling behind are picked up quite quickly and given extra support after school on an informal basis by staff. Probably not the place to aim for if your child is used to getting more support than this and, indeed, they would probably not get through the selection process. Some leave after GCSE, including a few who want a less demanding academic sixth form programme.

Games, Options, The Arts: Wonderful art work on show everywhere and girls anxious to point out some striking pieces: an oil painting (destined for a church), a sheep made of barbed wire and some lovely black and white photographs. Art department is open at weekends and pupils make full use of it. Photography, ceramics and metal work on offer. DT department humming with activity with girls making silver jewellery – last year's products included a windsurfer 'designed for Dad' and fibreglass canoes. The school is well known for its music; at least 85 per cent of students learn an instrument to grade 6 or higher. Lots of concerts and some unusual music workshops eg Indonesian music, drumming and jazz. Music lessons are timetabled outside lessons in the sixth form and where possible in GCSE years, otherwise lessons are missed on a rotating basis (some complaints from parents here). Practising is timetabled. Biannual music tours.

Sports compulsory throughout school, with a wide range of options from the fifth year. Lacrosse, hockey, netball and tennis are the main sports, with year round swimming and options range from badminton and basketball to touch rugby and indoor cricket. Indoor swimming pool opened 2001. Sports tours in recent years to Barbados, Australia, Malawi and Zambia. CCF contingent formed in 2000 (a first in a girls' school so lots of publicity). Plenty of field trips locally and also overseas; also a biannual adventure expedition, last year to Namibia and Botswana. Sixth formers have preference for these, otherwise on a first-come basis to middle school students. Splendid theatre, the Blackledge, used for several drama productions a year which aim to involve all those interested as well as numerous concerts, debates and talks by visiting speakers. Girls full of enthusiasm for the annual inter-house drama competitions in which everyone is involved.

Masses of after-school activities to choose from; younger girls do 3 a week, optional, but still very popular, for older students in the sixth. They are also on offer at weekends. Activities range from 'glass slumping' to martial arts and special exam revision classes.

Background and Atmosphere: Cluster of buildings situated in a 16-acre campus at the top of a hill, 10 minutes walk from the centre of Salisbury. Has the advantage of being self-contained but still feels very much part of the city. Girls like the fact they can pop down to town easily though on a carefully restricted basis. Has close links with the cathedral. Head's study in the centre of the old Victorian main building as is the central school hall with classrooms, complete with iron fire-grates, leading off it. Other classrooms, art, science and music and boarding houses are only a couple of minutes walk away. The atmosphere is positively humming with bright, bubbly girls slightly incongruously dressed in blue 'pinnies' (girls say 'pinnies' are much loved). Sixth form have no uniform. New developments – sixth form centre, incorporating study, careers and leisure facilities and a new boarding house.

Pastoral Care and Discipline: Parents comment on the friendly atmosphere. A small school where everyone knows each other and there are good relations between the girls and with the staff. The aim is to quickly pick up on any bullying and deal with it effectively. Girls claim the friendly relations between all age groups is in part due to the system of mixed-age dorms (11-14) where the older girls can help with any homesickness problems. Prospective parents are less keen on the idea of their 11 year-olds being in with older girls, though current parents appreciate the advantages. Single and 2 bed studies for GCSE year and above. There are 4 boarding houses usually with married house parents; lots of teddy bears, posters and bright scatter cushions in evidence. One of the rare schools where there is still eating in houses and staff tend to spot problems quickly as they eat with the girls.

All ages allowed into Salisbury starting with an hour a week for the first years, in groups of 5, and gradually extending through the school. Sixth formers may go down freely after afternoon school; they may also spend one or two evenings in town, on a Saturday. All dependent on work schedules being up to date. Girls can invite friends (who must meet the housemistress) at weekends and they have parties, socials and debates with local boys' schools. Weekends are packed with activities after Saturday prep (no Saturday lessons) and many 'Sarums' (day girls) come back to join in. One local parent comments that it's difficult to extract his daughter for a weekend, as she wants to stay in school.

Pupils and Parents: A very popular school locally. Girls come from a wide region around. A handful of foreigners (8 per cent) and some ex-pat kids (mostly Services). Parents generally solidly middle class. Flexi-boarding policy where boarders must spend 5 full weekends a year in school but may otherwise spend weekend time in or out of school as they and their parents choose. 'Sarums' may spend the odd

weekday night in school if they are staying late for activities. Boarding is very popular in the sixth form and there is a press on places with some coming in from outside. Old Girls include lots of writers, Amanda Brookfield, Minette Walters, Jilly Cooper, Dorothy Sayers, Elizabeth Lemarchand and Josephine Bell. Girls emerge totally non-streetwise (school says 'confident and prepared for the modern world'), which is either just what local parents tell us they want (if we are right), or not, if the school is right.

Entrance: Registered pupils invited for a preview day and night in the autumn before CE including tests. 'As much for them as us,' comments head. Everyone has to take CE. Girls come in from many different private and state schools including Godolphin prep. Head says, 'we are looking for girls who can cope with the curriculum and are able to enjoy the opportunities available and be part of the community'.

Exit: Nearly all to higher education, mostly to universities to do anything from medicine to Japanese. Others go to art schools, music conservatoires and, sometimes, drama school. About half take a gap year.

Money Matters: Scholarships for 11 and 13 and sixth form, up to 50 per cent of boarding fees for outstanding merit and promise in academic work, sport, drama, music or art. Also six Foundation Scholarships (worth 70 per cent) for girls from divided families and with financial need.

Remarks: A very good, all-round girls' school, strong academically and in the arts. Positively buzzes with confident, gregarious girls. A good place for girls seeking a supportive environment without being in a 'pressure cooker'. Perhaps not the place for a timid type or one not prepared to work hard but the bright, enthusiastic girl will do well here. One parent comments,' a nice family atmosphere – full of tradition but ideas and outlook are modern and kids are kept very busy'.

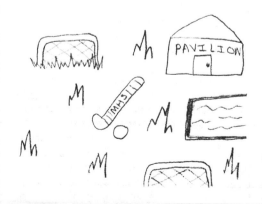

GORDON'S SCHOOL

West End, Woking, Surrey, GU24 9PT

Tel: 01276 858 084

Fax: 01276 855 335

E-mail: registrar@gordons.surrey.sch.uk

Website: www.gordons.surrey.sch.uk

- Pupils: 643 boys and girls (57 per cent boys); approx one third boards • Ages: 11-18 • Size of sixth form: 117 • Inter-denom • Fees: £3,013 full boarding; £2,729 weekly boarding • State

Head: Since 1995, Denis Mulkerrin MA (fifties) CBE. Educated at Guernsey Grammar School, then read history at Hull and Kings College. Looks, speaks and behaves as though he walked straight out of the military – we can picture him running an RAF boot camp – but he is actually a lifelong teacher and Gordon's is his third headship. He was head of two comprehensive schools in Brighton before coming here. Married, his wife helps with school functions. One daughter, a BBC producer. His main interest outside of school is weight-lifting – has competed for Britain and is secretary of the British Schools Weightlifting Association (so that explains the school's newly installed multigym). Gruff but friendly and intensely proud of the school which he transformed from an unknown school limping along at 3,011th in the government league tables in 1994 to the 14th highest-achieving non-selective school in Britain – ('it's all a matter of expectations,' he says). Keen on discipline and tradition. Would fit in nicely as the head of any major public school.

Academic Matters: Admirable, traditional teaching methods that we thought had been exorcised from the state system decades ago. Big on setting and sceptical of mixed ability learning. Relatively small classes. Homework diaries are one of the head's favourite educational tools and they are strictly kept, taken home to parents and always brought to class.

The school can list a wealth of statistics confirming its greatness: the best GCSE results of any state school in Surrey for the last six years, the second most improved school in Britain (1999) – 90 per cent of students get five or more pass grades at GCSE. There are graphs up all over the school, charting the school's dramatic uphill climb in GCSE scores, prompting some pupils to worry about what might be expected from them in years to come! No independent school could take exams more seriously and the children

are well-prepared with practice papers, after-school 'clinics' etc. Art & design, English literature, physical education and drama show particularly strong GCSE results. In 1998 Gordon's created a small sixth form of 19 students in conjunction with Heathside School, a comprehensive eight miles away in Weybridge. Although this sixth form technically comes under Heathside, all students are taught at Gordon's by Gordon's staff. The sixth form has now grown to 116 students, all doing A levels. Over half the grades in 2005 were either A or B, and 83 per cent were A to C. All of these students went to university.

Games, Options, The Arts: Sport is outstandingly strong – especially rugby – and of the several dozen pupils we spoke to, each and every one singled out sport as his or her favourite thing about the school. Huge range of after-school extra-curricular activities in the hour immediately after lessons, known as Period Six. Music is another strength: 205 pupils take singing or instrumental lessons (including the bagpipes) and music is a popular GCSE option.

Two elaborate dramatic productions each year, performed in the gym on what looked like a few upturned orange crates (euphemistically referred to as a 'stage'). Pipe and drum band, as well as orchestra, choir and concert band. Gordon's has a remarkable tradition of parades; marching practice happens every Friday. On eight Sundays a year the children, bedecked in tartan trousers and military jackets (the original uniform worn by the orphan boys in 1886), march to the music of bagpipes and drums before an audience of over 1,000 parents. The high point of the year is the annual London parade to commemorate the death of Gordon. The pupils march down Whitehall past the Cenotaph, ending up at the bronze statue of the General on the Embankment. All Gordon's pupils have the opportunity to take part in this traditional pageant at least twice during their time at the school.

Background and Atmosphere: Founded in 1885, by the Gordon Foundation (which still runs the school), at the express wish of Queen Victoria who wanted a memorial to her favourite general (killed that year in Khartoum). The foundation decided the best memorial would be a boys' home ('they could have built a huge statue instead' notes the head). Since then, the reigning monarch has always been its patron.

Beautiful, original buildings with sympathetically designed newer ones, including two new sixth form houses. The school is slightly squeezed into a quad around a large tarmac playground. Ample playing fields. Lovely, St Edward the Confessor Chapel built in 1894 at the request of Queen

Victoria ('you wouldn't find a chapel like this in many state schools, would you?' rightly boasted the head). Recently renovated small gym built in 1886 (possesses dubious distinction of being one of the four oldest gyms in England). Fine swimming pool, well-used by boarders. The school day is long (until 8pm) – ecstasy to any dual career couple struggling to get home on the train from London. Day pupils may leave at 3.30pm but almost none do as they would miss activities, supper and – the mums' favourite – supervised prep. Non-academic Saturday morning school (10am to noon) with sports, clubs, music etc.

Smart uniform, a green blazer with grey trousers or skirt (we haven't seen schoolgirls wearing skirts so long since 1957). No uniform for sixth form. Loads of computers. Boarding houses are pleasantly scruffy, with homey common rooms and a definite 'no frills' air. The youngest boarders are packed five or more to a room but gain a bit of privacy through strategic placing of study/bunks. By 13, numbers are down to about three in a room and this continues to decrease until sixth form where it is only two, or even one, per room. All the dormitories are wondrously tidy and feel friendly and welcoming.

Pastoral Care and Discipline: Well-liked houseparents in each boarding house. Bullying kept at bay through lots of discussions and zero tolerance. Apparently few troublemakers – no exclusions for several years. Lessons are conducted rather formally but pupils speak of an easy relationship with teachers, especially during supervised prep when there is often time for one-to-one attention. The entire set-up exudes a somewhat martial air, in keeping with its origins (General Sir Anthony Pigott is chairman of the Gordon Foundation).

Pupils and Parents: Children unusually polite and apparently keen to get on and do well. About ten per cent from overseas – a mixture of ex-pats, Services families and a sprinkling of foreign nationals (Hong Kong, Canada and South Africa). Parents of all types, a few who would otherwise have paid the full whack for an independent school if they had not got their children in (a few children come to Gordon's from the private sector). Some Services/diplomatic families who genuinely need the full boarding facility.

Entrance: Academically unselective intake but horrificly oversubscribed with five applicants to every place. Siblings are given first whack, then, for day pupils, places allotted exclusively by proximity (there is a white spot painted in front of the main school gate and all distances are measured from this). Full boarding and weekly boarding (and some day) places are parcelled out according to need (so you had better have a convincing one). We noticed a striking number of pupils who had moved to Gordon's (some from independent schools) in the middle of their education (ie not at 11 or 16). Entry at sixth form is selective. Applicants must have five A*-C grades at GCSE and no less than a B in the subjects to be taken at A/AS level. Some Gordon's pupils are turned down.

Exit: 100 per cent of upper sixth students in 2005 gained university places. One student gained a place at Oxford.

Money Matters: Bursaries are available.

Remarks: No-frills boarding and splendid academics for the privileged few who can wangle a place. Consider moving round the corner if you are interested in a day place.

GORDONSTOUN SCHOOL

Linked to Aberlour House the Junior School at Gordonstoun in the Junior section

Elgin, Moray, IV30 5RF

Tel: 01343 837837
Fax: 01343 837 808
E-mail: admissions@gordonstoun.org.uk
Website: www.gordonstoun.org.uk

- Pupils: 429 boarders, 30 day; boys and girls 60/40
- Ages: 13-18 • Size of sixth form: 274 • Inter-denom
- Fees: Junior school - £2,723 day; £4,881 boarding. Senior school £4,901 day; £7,263 boarding • Independent
- Open days: November, March, May - junior school. April - senior school

Head: Since 1990, Mr Mark Pyper BA (fifties). Educated at Winchester, dropped out of Oxford and finished his degree externally at London. Father, grandfather and great grandfather were all prep headmasters and Mr Pyper started his teaching career in the prep school world. Came to Gordonstoun from Sevenoaks, where he was deputy head. 'Rather like it here,' 'suits me'. His wife likes it too, 'she jogs, plays the guitar'. In a world where headmasters are progressively a scruffy bunch, he is unique (in our experience) in wearing a natty tweed suit come summer come winter. Study (drawing room more like) of lairdly splendour full of Mr Pyper's ancestors in stately frames. 'Likes to give the impression of being laid-back', but would like the world to know that he 'is quite switched on and can be quite tough as well'. HRH The Princess Royal is no longer a governor but is now Warden ('she wanted to keep in touch') and fronts the fundraising campaign 'and is very supportive'.

Academic Matters: Academia is not what Gordonstoun is about. 'Pupils are here for the whole broad experience'. 'The balance is important'. Huge range of ability from children 'at the lower end of the academic scale for whom two Ds at A level is a real achievement' to the really bright who get to Oxbridge. Exam results are occasionally pretty uninspiring, with their sprinkling of Ds, Es, Ns and Us; perhaps no better or worse than one would expect, though we have heard complaints of low quality teaching. Staff are often selected for their alternative skills. Maths consistently good, with French, Spanish and German throughout, the latter remarkably successful (but then school has a large number of German students). Classes setted for maths and English from 13. Excellent new networked computer set-up on stream, not wireless, buildings have over-thick walls. New International Citizenship course in place, not PSE or RS but examining real problems against a global background. Good remedial support, all pupils are now screened on arrival. Will scribe for exams. EAL (English as an additional language) available at all levels.

Games, Options, The Arts: Community service is important at Gordonstoun and many chose the school for just this reason. All children must take part and do service training in year 11 before opting for the fire brigade (the most popular), mountain rescue (MR), off-shore and in-shore rescue, ski patrol, visitng the elderly etc. Lots of exchanges with other Round Square schools – Canada, Germany, Australia etc. Joint international expeditions to India, Sinai, Thailand, Kenya, Honduras to work on conservation/ecological 'projects' (expensive), popular and full of teenage japes. School has its own yacht and timetabled sailing weeks (when the weather can be 'pretty wild' according to the skippers), as well as expeds – outward bound expeditions. Tall ships race now a regular feature. Mainstream games on course but long distances to other schools for matches cause problems. Good sports facilities and trips all over – Europe, Australasia, points west. Drama very popular, new 200-seater theatre opened in 2005. Magnificent art, lots of disciplines, graphic design impressive. Particularly strong DT with pupils learning not only to make lights but to cost them effectively.

Background and Atmosphere: Founded in 1934 by the German educationalist Kurt Hahn, founder of Salem School in Baden-Württemberg and believer in educating and developing all aspects of children not just the academic. Grounds and setting lovely, half a mile from the Moray Firth with cliffs and beaches nearby, and not as cold as one might think. The Gulf Stream is useful. Gordonstoun House is a former residence of Gordon-Cumming of card-cheating fame. Beautiful circular stable block (hence the Round Square tag) houses the library and boys' house. Cunning music rooms round exotic chapel (shaped like an open book – magnificent but repairs to the pews are incredibly botched). New library conversion in round square, sixth form study area in attic area – lots of nooks and crannies – very busy. Houses spread all over, some quite a hike from the main school. Minimal exeats, distances are huge, but pupils often do not want to go home. Prospectus lists nearby hotels, B&Bs (with prices) and ways of getting to school (a good four hours from Edinburgh but less than that flying from London). Non-stop social life which swings right through the holidays – caveat for Southerners. Excellent prospectus information booklet.

Pastoral Care and Discipline: The Betts parents (father and step-mother of Leah who died after taking one ecstasy pill) give harrowing anti-drugs lectures. Occasional problems with smoking and boozing 'not totally whiter than white'. Head tough on perpetual offenders – particularly bullies and 'children have eventually had to leave the school as a result'. Commendably clear rules. Girls and boys can visit each other's houses with a certain amount of freedom. Each pupil has an academic tutor; house parents and assistant house parents in each house. Shopping bus to Elgin on Tuesday but only the upper sixth can visit on Saturdays and can 'have meals out in the evening'. Elgin can be pretty rough.

Pupils and Parents: A third English, a third Scottish and a third from the rest of the world, the Pacific Rim popular. Can be cliquey, some deeply rich, some less so, with locals benefiting from serious scholarships. Quite a number of first time buyers. FPs include royals, William Boyd, Eddie Shah, the composer of The Flower of Scotland – Roy Williamson, Martin Shea, Alan Shiach, Lara Croft.

Entrance: School is bulging. Pupils come up through the school from Aberlour House, Ardvreck in Perthshire and Pembroke House, the Kenyan prep school in Gil Gil near Nakuru. Pupils usually come up automatically from the junior school, Aberlour House (get there by 11). Assessment for those joining at year 10 (about ten each year) and influx to sixth form. Pupils are assessed both academically and for personality. Odd places sometimes available for pupils 'at any level of the school for short periods – although not normally less than one term'.

Exit: Some leave after GCSE 'because they believe they might get higher grades elsewhere', some to crammers, otherwise standard 80/90 per cent to universities all over. Newcastle, Leeds, Bristol and Edinburgh currently popular. Occasional Oxbridge entrants.

Money Matters: Set fee; parents can 'opt above'. Scholarships and bursaries awarded after means-testing. Hardship fund. Vast sums accumulated via flourishing summer school for foreigners. Despite offering scholarships with a pro-active hardship fund, school has launched a £4 million appeal for revamping the 1960s sports hall, plus extra scholarship fund. Gordonstoun has also picked up the tab when Aberlour School was closed earlier this year (it was losing money); the buildings were sold and the funds realised more or less paid for the stunning new build, Aberlour House, in the grounds.

Remarks: Children and parents appear happy. Fashionable co-ed outward-boundish boarding school with vast range of pupil backgrounds. Increasingly popular, particularly with the new younger boarding house in action.

THE GRANGE SCHOOL

Linked to The Grange Junior School in the Junior section

Bradburns Lane, Hartford, Northwich, Cheshire, CW8 1LU

Tel: 01606 74007
Fax: 01606 784 581
E-mail: office@grange.org.uk
Website: www.grange.org.uk

• Pupils: 493 boys and girls, all day • Ages: 11-18 • Size of sixth form: 190 • Christian • Fees: £1,645 - £2,195 • Independent • Open days: First Saturday in November

---

Head: Since 2005, Mr Christopher Jeffery BA Hons (History) York (early forties). Mr Jeffery (who shares Shakespeare's birthday) previously taught History at Bristol Grammar School then at The Perse School for boys, where he became deputy head (in charge of pupils). He is married with three school age children. He follows Mrs Jenny Stephen who, along with her husband, Martin, heads south for a high-profile post – he to St Paul's boys (qv), she to South Hampstead HS(qv).

Academic Matters: In view of the ordinarily selective intake (top 25 per cent ability range) results are impressive. Over 80 per cent A-B at A level (94 per cent A-C), maths and science popular. GCSE 96 per cent get A*-B. Pupil/ staff ratio is 11.2: 1. Classes never bigger than 26 in years 7, 8, 9 (average 24.4), tailing off to max of 12 in years 12, 13 (average 9.5). Pupils enthusiastic about commitment and dedication of staff, who are accessible and available outside lessons. School days action-packed. Sense of healthy competition to reinforce, rather than undermine, self-confidence. As head put it, 'children can gain success by competing'. Not much time for standing and staring. Head adamant that co-education does not mean girls lose out.

Games, Options, The Arts: Sport high up the agenda, particularly team games and rowing (school has its own boat-house on River Weaver). Science facilities superb. Lots of extra-curricular activities. Drama, the role-play and performing it encourages, are viewed as life-skills central to the school's work of preparing pupils for their futures in the outside world. Drama and music facilties are brand new as a result of £3.6 million project providing a 300 seat theatre and superb associated music and drama teaching block. Just over half of pupils learn an instrument. Art facilities still very ordinary, which only goes to prove that it is people, not equipment, that matter – art teaching inspirational, including background classical music to help pupils give their imaginations free rein in their collage-making.

Background and Atmosphere: Founded in 1933 as prep and kindergarten school. Senior school opened in 1978. Pupils feel pride in their own achievements and a sense of being valued. Successes are given prominence – all those shining trophies! – and perhaps success, as an end in itself, occasionally overshadows the importance of pupils' individuality. Head is unusual and exemplary in emphasising need for risk-taking as part of learning process. School positions itself to compete with local maintained sector, also with independent schools in Manchester, Chester and Stockport.

Pastoral Care and Discipline: Discipline unobtrusive but part of the fabric of the school. Pastoral care offered by teachers, to whom pupils genuinely feel they can turn, also trained counsellor who works with children – and, where necessary, their parents – to sort out any difficulties. Peer support scheme, co-ordinated by school counsellor, works well. Special area set aside for younger pupils to seek out older ones at lunchtime. Children seem to feel very much part of a community, not isolated if they hit a problem.

Pupils and Parents: Pupils are drawn from local population and are an honest, hard-working bunch. Largely come from within a 20 mile radius and tend to be white, middle class; only a few belonging to ethnic minorities. Parents are business people, professionals, and farmers. Great parental pride in the school, an almost proprietorial interest in it. School encourages parental involvement, including AGM for parents and open financial accountability.

Entrance: 4 form entry in senior school. Main intake at 11, when 63 per cent of places go to pupils from junior school, hence tough competition for the remainder. Entrance tests in English, maths and verbal reasoning.

Exit: Almost all to university, including a few to Oxbridge. Business studies, management, law, medicine, economics and engineering currently popular degree subjects.

Money Matters: Compared with other independent schools in the area, fees are very competitive, although school not able to offer much financial assistance to children from less privileged homes, due to development programme eating up income.

Remarks: Just beyond reach of the cosmopolitan sophisticates of Manchester, the school reflects back its local community – proud of itself, caring for its own, determined to prove itself every bit as good as longer-established schools in the area.

GRAVENEY SCHOOL

Welham Road, Tooting, London, SW17 9BU

Tel: 0208 682 7000
Fax: 0208 682 7075
E-mail: info@graveney.wandsworth.sch.uk
Website: www.graveney.org

- Pupils: 1,913 boys and girls • Ages: 11-18
- Size of sixth form: 621 • Non-denom • State

Head: Since 1989, Mr Graham Stapleton MA (fifties). Read history at Cambridge, and has spent almost his entire career in Graveney and its predecessor schools. Very busy, dedicated and disciplined. Married. Two children.

Academic Matters: Described by Ofsted as 'outstanding'. No other south west London state school is so oversubscribed or has better GCSE results. In 1995, 55 per cent of students obtained at least 5 A*-C grades at GCSE; this increased to 68 per cent in 2000, 73 per cent in 2001, 77 per cent in 2002, 84 per cent in 2003 and 81 per cent in 2005. A level results are good for south London (average point score is 274). In 1995 Graveney became an Information and Communication Technologies College.

Students are banded in most subjects. Average class size is 28 pupils for KS3 and 22 for KS4. The school day is longer than usual – 8.30am to around 4pm (depending on the day of the week); more homework than average too – between 45 and 90 minutes (years 7 and 8), 60 and 120 minutes (year 9) and 150 to 270 minutes (year 10 and 11).

Games, Options, The Arts: Strong musical, drama, sport and poetry traditions. Four choirs, an orchestra, many bands and a number of sophisticated music workstations. Creative writing promoted through the student magazines.

On the sporting side it has a sports hall, two other large gyms and seven open courts. Graveney has links with the London Cricket Project, Belgrave Harriers Athletic Club and Tooting Bec Football Club. Aerobics, basketball, hockey, volleyball, badminton, tennis, soft-ball, netball, table tennis and cross-country are also practised.

Background and Atmosphere: Graveney was founded in 1986, as an amalgamation of two selective and two community schools, the oldest one being the Battersea Grammar School set up in 1669. It has remained a mixed, partially selective and comprehensive school in a middle class (school says 'very diverse') area. Around half of its students live nearby but many of the pupils who have entered through the fiercely competitive exams have to travel from other London boroughs.

No other good-quality state school in London is so large or has so big a sixth form. Graveney has double the average number of students, so don't expect the head teacher to know all of the pupils and parents. On the other hand, Graveney has a broad range of facilities, a wide variety of courses (29 A level courses, 33 at KS4 including six languages – French, German, Spanish, Italian, Urdu and Latin) and some notable specialised teachers (some of them are authors of many books). Graveney has two campuses either side of the quiet Welham Road; one a Georgian building, the other dating from around the first world war – rather cramped. Good public transport – bus, train and tube – but a half-mile walk from the stations to the school. There is a good atmosphere amongst students and between them and their teachers.

Pastoral Care and Discipline: The head of year and form tutor move up the school with the pupil. Younger students have their own separate buildings. Strong discipline.

Pupils and Parents: A very cosmopolitan school with 45 per cent of pupils from ethnic minorities. Students behave well. There is an active PTA, and special IT courses for parents.

Entrance: The yearly intake is 250, of whom 63 are chosen by selection. Around half of the intake are siblings, who have priority, and about 80 are children who live no more than 500 metres from the school's main door. The 63 chosen by selection take the standard Wandsworth NFER exam, but Graveney only takes into account two of the three parts (verbal and non-verbal reasoning). In 2005 there were about 2,500 applicants for the 63 selective places – only one out of twenty five achieved the more than 97 per cent needed for entrance – more competitive than any other London grammar or public school.

Exit: About 15 per cent leave after GCSE – mostly to

vocational courses elsewhere. More than 95 per cent of sixth form students go on to university. In 2005, 10 students gained places at Oxbridge.

Remarks: Very good in academic and non-academic matters. Lacks the familiar atmosphere of a smaller school but seriously believes in its motto: 'Committed to excellence'.

GREENHEAD COLLEGE

Greenhead Road, Huddersfield, West Yorkshire, HD1 4ES

Tel: 01484 422 032
Fax: 01484 518 025
E-mail: college@greenhead.ac.uk
Website: www.greenhead.ac.uk

• Pupils: 1,750 boys and girls; all in the sixth form
• Ages: 16-18 • Non-denom • State

Principal: Since 2002, Mr Martin Rostron BA PGCE (early fifties) who was educated at Chadderton Grammar School in Oldham and read English at Liverpool. He came to Greenhead in 1991 and was previously vice principal. He has always taught in the maintained sector and has taught all ages from 11-18 but, more recently, at Priestley Sixth Form College in Warrington. He has had a son and daughter at Greenhead; third child (son) hopes to come. Much enjoying his time here, 'life has got to be fun', 'people here work extraordinarily hard', and 'the staff are quite phenomenal'; good intra-staff support, little turnover of staff. Took over from the seriously wonderful Kevin Conway, the foundation of Greenhead's excellence.

Academic Matters: College is one of three in Huddersfield and they have a concordat whereby all will provide the basic AS and A level subjects but each will specialise in a different sphere. Hence Greenhead offers a business studies at AVCE level (much more difficult than NVQ) as well as A and AS levels in law, government and politics, IT, maths ad infinitum and the humanities and sciences. Psychology and RS currently top of the pops and sociology. An astonishing 199 students took psychology last year, with 40 per cent getting A. French, German, Spanish and Italian on offer but no classics or esoteric languages – one might have expected Urdu, given the ethnic mix but that is studied elsewhere. Computers all over the place. Fantastic suite of brand new labs.

Good take-up for RSA qualifications. Average class size 18 for A levels, and 19 at AS. Most students opt for four AS and three or more As; College will 'tolerate' re-takes but

only if space available in that particular course and candidates 'have a realistic chance of improving their grades' – perhaps half a dozen a year. They will also 'investigate the possibility' of grafting on extra subjects if 'there is sufficient demand' and if there is sufficient space. A level general studies for 'almost all'. No real break between some lessons – the distances can be quite far. College operates an 'open door' policy, staff cluster in subject rooms during their free time and any pupil can walk in to any subject room and ask for help. Magic. We met a larger than normal cross-section of teachers during our visit. Library designated a 'place of silent study', well, quiet rather than silent, but ferociously well-equipped. Supplemented in 2004 by the 'Reading Room', a new large area for 'sociable' study.

Kevin Conway developed the College's own value-added system, now widely followed – picks up students who are falling behind or who deserve particular praise very early and, most particularly and without rancour, helps bring teachers who are performing below par up to scratch.

Games, Options, The Arts: PE and music popular; enormous art rooms in £2 million new building, shared with law and business. Stunning, with inspired work in progress. No large sports hall of their own but has 'use of' one five minutes' walk across the park; major playing fields (cheap to hire, use all the facilities going, and dance studios.) 92 took PE last year, one third grade As. Strongest rugby side in the county, cups all over the place, squash, basketball good; national representative in hockey – popular, and football 'expanding' – four competitive teams. Music 'absolutely stunning at the moment', orchestra, plus jazz, string quartets – positively 'humming'. Impressive music dept with full recording gear, music computers and PCs. Vibrant drama, often with play rehearsals at 7.30am as well as pm and at weekends. Serious enrichment programme, students are offered an amazing 70 different courses, everything from Freudian psychology, to crime in society or yoga. D of E, Young Enterprise, any key skills you want plus hints on how to handle Oxbridge. Every student MUST attend one course but if you don't fancy any of them, then you can start your own. Probably the best work placement programme anywhere.

Background and Atmosphere: Plumb in the middle of Huddersfield and a stone's throw from the centre of town with train and bus stations, Greenhead, set in what is now an enormous car park, bustles with purposeful students. Huge complex with masses of add-ons, very handsome hall, big wide corridors with lockers on either side, and remarkably tidy. College has 'no problems with disabled'; 'we move the teaching room to the ground floor to accommodate wheelchairs' but possessed of four new lifts; most areas are now fully accessible. They have blind students and, of course, support for learning is a given. Prospective students are advised to contact the college's learning support coordinator for advice prior to admission so any specialist support or facilities can be put in place (strive to meet all reasonable requests). Good support and back up once in the system. This is, after all, state-funded. Student Union, self-elected prefects, social areas are the hall and canteen; smokers exiled to cancer ward = outdoor area beside canteen, with huge chimney, presumably from the boiler, presiding over all.

Pastoral Care and Discipline: Excellent pastoral system, with tutors taking a personal interest in each student, and all students having a day off each term to discuss their grades with their teachers and being given a rocket if they are not up to scratch. PSHE for all. College will exclude for violent or abusive behaviour, smoking 'not tolerated' but see above (they all light up as they leave the campus anyway). Students with real problems can make an appointment to see a counsellor. No racial tension, though ethnic groups tend to stick together – 'most stick with their school peer groups'. Regular 'whole block' assemblies – unusual in most sixth form colleges.

Pupils and Parents: What you would expect, mainly solid middle class, not a lot of 'twocers' (taking without owner consent). Strong work ethos. Huge catchment area, about two thirds of the students come from partner schools.

Entrance: Apply well before mid-Feb of the year you want to go to, College nearly 40 per cent oversubscribed, fed by 12 local partner schools in the same catchment area, and around 55 other schools nearby on a placement basis. Places allocated on the basis of interview, plus results of mock GCSEs, and school reports. 8 per cent from the independent sector.

Exit: About 90 per cent go directly to higher education, including 30 or so to Oxbridge; very strong medical bias – at one point the college was responsible for 1 per cent of the new medical intake in the country. Musicians may choose the Northern College of Music or the Conservatoire but, equally, may decide to go to uni first and then study music full time. 5 per cent gap (and then presumably to higher ed) and rest to work.

Money Matters: Students qualify for state hand-out (EMA), to keep them in sixth form education.

Remarks: As we said before, an outstanding sixth form college, with an ordinary load of students in an ordinary town doing extraordinarily well. The brightest do succeed here and all can expect to do markedly better than in the average state (or independent) school. Terrific.

GRESHAM'S SCHOOL

Linked to Gresham's Preparatory School in the Junior section

Cromer Road, Holt, Norfolk, NR25 6EA

Tel: 01263 714500
Fax: 01263 712 028
E-mail: bmccombie@greshams.com
Website: www.greshams.com

- Pupils: 450 boys and girls (two thirds board, one third day)
- Ages: 13-18 • Size of sixth form: 194 • C of E • Fees: Senior school: boarding £6,890; day £5,340. Prep school: boarding: £5,025; day £3,855. Pre-prep: from £1,905-£2,115
- Independent • Open days: First May Bank Holiday Saturday, plus taster days in September, October and November

Head: Since 2002, Mr Antony Clark MA HDE (forties), educated at St Andrew's College, South Africa, followed by Rhodes University; read history (and played cricket) at Downing, Cambridge and started his teaching career at Westerford High School in Cape Town.

After a brief spell in the 'investment business' he was appointed head of St Joseph's Marist College in Cape Town, which is RC and 'non-racial, ahead of Independence'. Challenging stuff. He expanded the school roll by almost 50 per cent during his time there, before becoming head of St Andrew's College in Grahamstown.

Married to (Dr) Brigitte, who lectures in law at the University of East Anglia; three children in the school. Very much a hands-on head, pupils say 'he is everywhere', turns up at (almost) all matches, has a good recall of their names (all were impressed – apparently his wife tests him in the kitchen). According to a previous head boy, 'he appears to be shaking up the whole school with a new regime'. Teaches history – though probably not enough to satisfy the teacher in him. A 'listening head', he is gradually 'making changes to the pattern of education here'. Asked for a wish list, he replied he 'would like to make the school as happy a place as possible' (first time we have had a metaphysical here), 'build an all-embracing sports pavilion' (the school sports ground hosts a mass of ex-Gresham's matches on the Astroturf, so it could also be a permanent fund-raiser) and 'build a resources centre to house the library etc, etc'). And, yes, when pushed, the sports pavilion beat the resource centre on priority.

Academic Matters: 50 per cent pass rate at Common Entrance is probably the reason for the really quite large number of Ds and Es at A level, though the bright do really well, with a starring number of pupils in the top five per cent in English literature at GCSE, and 25 pupils (out of fifty) getting A in maths at A level (English and French good too). Classics currently popular, Greek is an option. Huge variety of languages: French, German, Japanese, Russian (good take-up here from the German contingent) and Spanish, and proper brand new lang labs.

No class larger than 21, mostly much much smaller. Pupils are setted from 13 in English and a variety of disciplines thereafter. Utilitarian collection of classrooms, the width of corridors depends on the age of the building. Business studies and the sciences all good, pupils usually do two sciences at GCSE. And one bright chap not only got an A in physics last year, but was also published in the States. CLT (chemistry lecture theatre) in newish science block, with the tiniest staircase imaginable up to the chemistry library. Powerpoint presentation under way during our visit in the biology lab but not a sign of an interactive white board anywhere. Masses of flat-screened computers and, in every department, good use of laptops, school internetted and nannied.

Excellent booklet on sixth form choices. Pupils coming into the school from outside, ie not from the prep school, are screened for suspected problem areas during the year before they arrive: spelling, comprehension, writing and reading and dyscalculia. They may also have an IQ test and an ed psych's report. They may then be given extra help in the lamentably tiny SEN department, which strives manfully to cope with both accelerated learning and dyslexia et al. The visitor creeps past three pupils, each on different programmes, to reach the head of department's over-cluttered hq; three other pupils are tucked away in corners, working away with individual teachers, who may also be teaching EFL. The department boasts three full time learning support teachers and one dedicated EFL in about the same area as half of one normal class room. Money needs spending here – we are surprised that games facilities should be given priority. Pupils are usually withdrawn from study periods, but support teaching in class is also on offer, and any pupil in the system is offered 'supervised' study time. The school 'can cope' with very mild Aspergers, ADD but not ADHD, and offers scribes, readers, and voice-activated computers, all for £200 extra per pupil per term.

Games, Options, The Arts: Strong games, particularly hockey – fantastic say the pupils – national championships, county players all over the place. Probably over-used Astroturfs, masses of pitches, keen external coaches and a sports physio on hand at important matches. Cricket spec-

tacular and head regards himself as assistant coach. Rugby on the up. Much used swimming pool (and open to all comers) with three mornings a week for early swimmers ex school, BASC course an option. (Indeed masses of options). Weights room, gym, rowing machines regularly used by both boys and girls. Regular prizewinners at Bisley, CCF (army and RAF) popular and D of E, imaginative car building also part of CCF, grannie bashing for non-joiners-in.

Aerobics and dance at GCSE, but no proper dance studio, school needs larger, properly mirrored premises. Auden theatre much used by locals and tremendously varied selection of performances, free to school. Mass of dressing rooms, and sophisticated professional lighting and sound systems for those interested in theatre studies who don't want to strut the boards, enthusiastic set designers happily painting when we visited. Spectacular music with vast range of instruments on offer and good collection of orchestra, band and choral activities. Loads of tours in all disciplines.

Strong art, with good showing at A level, but sadly only flat art and photography, the latter particularly impressive. Our pupil advisors were at odds as to whether the art was fab or not – one who had come here on an art scholarship was particularly dismissive. 'Better in my last place,' she said. Life class open to outsiders and the art rooms were filled with naked fat ladies from every conceivable angle. Regular artists in residence but no history of art. Some of the pics around the school are fantabulous; the photography master recently held an almost sell-out (when we visited) exhibition in the foyer of the art block. Pupils' work is displayed there too. Pupils wondered about textiles, with painted fabrics and the like; though there is a tapestry and embroidery option 'it isn't the same'.

Background and Atmosphere: Founded by Sir John Gresham, Lord Mayor of London and 'a wealthy Midlands landowner' in 1555, 'the school was placed in the control of the Worshipful Company of Fishmongers', with which it still has close links. Somewhat haphazard development of a 170 acre site (including 90 acres of woodlands) demonstrates a variety of architectural styles around 'the parade ground'. Lutyens-style classroom blocks mingle with The Big School, a vast Edwardian hall with polished wood floors. Greek theatre in the woods, optimistically used for prize giving, 'but it almost always rains and we have to run for cover'. Charming chapel. Curious combination of Norfolk knapped flint, and 'temporary' twenties thatched huts ('scruff shacks') which are now listed buildings. Fair amount of walking involved, school straddles (the now by-passed but still fairly busy) main road: bridge for all but upper sixth mandatory.

Friendly, happy and relaxed atmosphere between pupils and staff, 'they don't put us under any pressure' said a pupil (why not?). Masses of lectures, concerts and debates, lively internal social life within the school. More or less ad hoc clothes for upper sixth, lots of jolly jerseys and 'no more than one ring per finger,' said our informant – she was sporting at least three on each. Fetching line in female make-up too, no need for this lot to learn about life skills. No bleached hair (house gating). Sixth form divided by those who do, and those who don't, qualify for BOP (bar on premises). Much used tuck shop, Dave's Diner, offers solace to the rest. Both open five nights a week: post-prep hot spots.

Houses important here, with a host of inter house competitions, 'hysterical house music competition' where all indulge in a spot of cross-dressing. Houses undergoing a senior revamp: Farfield now decorated in what the boys call vomit green, but jolly and with real flowers in strategic places. Ditto the jolly girls' houses. Huge light dining hall (CFB – central feeding block or 'trough'), all pupils eat in houses with staff strategically placed, standard buffet fare, with vegetarian option. All eat at the headmaster's table once a year – empty during our visit, he was wandering around with a rather sad ham sandwich and some salad. Milk and water machines all over the shop, we didn't see a fizzy drink dispenser anywhere. Pupils are allowed into Holt (not a den of iniquity) three times a week, and would love to have a cooking option.

Pastoral Care and Discipline: Good pastoral back-up with tutor, house parents, school counsellor and popular school chaplain. Escalating scale of punishments for fags: smoking 'within school buildings will normally involve a movement of two points up the scale' (which could mean permanent exclusion). 'Pupils found in the company of smokers can expect to be punished at 50 per cent severity. (Brill: more schools should copy). Over-18s are allowed to visit The Feathers with permission, otherwise there is an equally comprehensive scale of punishment for boozers, head 'reserves the right to impose the punishments in whatever order seems to him appropriate', which could equal expulsion for a first offence. Zero tolerance for drugs. Sixth formers have sessions on stress, strong anti-bullying policy. Laziness and non-participation frowned upon, particularly by pupils. This is a joining-in school. Sixth formers baby new pupils for their first couple of days.

Pupils and Parents: Delightful, open and friendly, not over-sophisticated boys and girls. Interesting mix of boarders, both weekly and full and day pupils where the day pupils often live further away than the weekly boarders. Some flexi-boarding. By and large farmers, solicitors,

accountants, etc., about nine per cent real foreigners (Hong Kong Chinese, Russians, Bulgarians and Germans the main players) plus a handful of ex-pats, some of whom live in Holland (oil: good links via Norwich airport to Amsterdam). Most come from East Anglia, Lincolnshire etc, plus refugees from London. Old boys include Sir Stephen Spender, W H Auden, Benjamin Britten, Ben Nicholson, Sir Christopher Cockerell (inventor of the hovercraft) James Dyson, Lord Reith, Prof Alan Hodgkin.

Entrance: CE, pass 50 per cent plus interview, keen on siblings, though will not take siblings if not up to standard. Either up from own pre-school, or from Taverham Hall, Beeston, Town Close (Norwich) or many many others, plus the maintained sector. Some arrive at 16.

Exit: Annual trickle to Oxbridge. Otherwise all over the place with the (regular) odd one to Harper Adams, UMIST, London Guildhall plus the perennial Durham, Newcastle, Leeds etc. About 90 per cent go on to higher education with a percentage taking a gap year, practical subjects like engineering, business, economics and accounting feature strongly.

Money Matters: 450th anniversary appeal launched to give increased bursarial help as well as a spot of building; Fishmongers give generous scholarships. Restricted scholarships to those who have lived in Norfolk for five years, pupils from African prep schools and candidates from the maintained sector. Otherwise 12 academic scholarships or bursaries (up to 100 per cent 'upon demonstration of financial need'), plus art, drama, music, sports and all-rounders awards, plus sixth form scholarships either for those doing fantastically well in GCSE within the school (who are not already getting a scholarship) or for those coming in at sixth form – academic, art, music etc. Annual award of £1,500 for mathematical genius. Plus a bursary of £750 for pupils who 'undertake voluntary work through Students Partnership Worldwide'. Though staff told us that 'school will hold pupils whose parents fall upon hard times until the next public exam,' head is not quite so sure.

Remarks: All singing, all dancing, unsophisticated public school catering for a not so niche market under the positive direction of a powerful head. As we said before, well worth driving to the top of Norfolk for.

THE GREY COAT HOSPITAL

Greycoat Place, Westminster, London, SW1P 2DY

Tel: 02079 691 998
Fax: 02078 282 697
E-mail: info@gch.org.uk
Website: www.thegreycoathospital.org.uk

- Pupils: 1,000 day girls; a few boys in the sixth form • Ages: 11-18 • Size of sixth form: 240 girls and 40 boys • C of E • State
- Open days: September/October, sixth form in December

Head: Since 1999, Mrs Rachel Allard BA (fifties). Married with two grown-up children. Previously deputy head of St Saviour's and St Olave's and advisory English teacher for Hackney. Tall, eloquent lady with a special interest in African and Asian literature. Consciously raising the academic profile. Strong management team and governors.

Academic Matters: Sound and very thorough, some high-powered teaching with GCSE and A level results improving annually apart from one blip, very few failures in any subject. Beacon status for good practice shows in the results and in happy motivated pupils through the ability range. Evening Standard Award for academic excellence is proudly displayed in the head's office. School recently became a specialist language college: hard-working, dynamic language department offering wide range of choices, girls do particularly well in French. Girls found to have an aptitude for languages may be studying three by year 8, one of which will be Chinese. Exciting exchange programmes are run with other schools all over the world; presently they are developing good partnerships with Japan and China.

Pupils are encouraged by incentives such as 'mathematician of the month'. Debates are welcome. Single and dual award sciences on offer, girls now benefit from lovely new modern science labs at St Michael's. The staff who are mainly women have a good rapport with the girls and are a 'committed bunch', claim parents. Small number of boys in the sixth form. 'We come for the friendly atmosphere and better facilities,' say boys. Active careers department and careers roadshows. Head has arranged a link with Westminster School so pupils can study there, free of charge, some subjects not available at Grey Coat. (This year, A level Latin & history of art.) SEN overseen by a head of special needs; there's a programme for gifted pupils.

Games, Options, The Arts: Amazingly successful sports considering the limited facilities, run by a really dedicated head of sports. Makes the best of a small on-site space; girls are bused to Battersea Park and swim at Queen Mother's sports centre. National champions of cricket and have produced national football and cricket players. Under 15s rowing team shares facilities with Westminster independent schools. Hoard of trophies for almost everything.

Strong music and drama, four large choirs that have performed at the Albert Hall, wind band and strings group. Subsidised tuition on any instrument. Theatre studies A level and drama GCSE are becoming very popular, several plays produced annually. Successful competitors in the Mock Magistrates and Bar competitions. Huge list of lunch-time and after school clubs to choose from, including Korean — set up by an enthusiastic sixth-former; D of E awards and community service.

Background and Atmosphere: Founded by concerned parishioners to reduce crime and get urchins off the streets in the days when the parish of Westminster was considered a den of iniquity, the school has a colourful history. In 1701 the governors bought an old workhouse and set up a school to provide education board and lodgings and care (hence hospital in the name) for 40 boys and 40 girls. Benefactors' portraits still hang in the Great Hall. There was a murder in 1773 and a rebellion against the dreadful conditions in the school in 1801. In 1874 The Grey Coat Hospital became a day school for girls, led for some years by one of the great pioneers of education, Elsie Day. The lower school continues today on the same site (St Andrew's). A new building for the upper school, St Michael's, is a short walk away. Both premises have gyms and libraries. A small school feeling prevails due to the separate sites, with a sense of busyness, staff and pupils going places.

Pastoral Care and Discipline: Long tradition of caring and solid Christian values with good home-school contact. Form tutors, heads of year, girls are expected to be responsible for themselves and care for others. Good community feel with plenty of opportunities for spiritual and moral development, seniors run their own Christian Union. Older girls have the opportunity to take on serious responsibilities and serve the school. 'Everyone feels really involved here and if something goes wrong there is always someone to listen,' say pupils. Sensible set of school rules aiming to produce good citizens. Many past pupils return for the annual school celebration service in Westminster Abbey. Strict uniform code.

Pupils and Parents: Big inner-city mix, very few locals, pupils come from all over as catchment is anyone living in the dioceses of London and Southwark. Popular choice for the children of education professionals. Streetwise, polite and orderly (mostly), sensible hard-working girls, plus a few boys in sixth form.

Entrance: At 11, 15 selective places by exam for girls showing an aptitude for languages, then standard LEA criteria: 25 per cent top band, 50 per cent middle band, 25 per cent lower band, with priority given to practising C of E and other Christian families. 27 open places. Sibling policy.

Exit: At 16, one third leaves to follow vocational courses or A levels elsewhere, mostly because the school does not offer the A level courses they want; handful to work. At 18, most to university: London, Durham, Bristol; 3-4 to Oxbridge.

Money Matters: The Parents' Guild raises money for the school and charity, keeping up the long tradition of serving the community. Small foundation which provides instrumental tuition.

Remarks: The pioneering spirit lives on as does the tradition of care; many girls benefit from time spent here.

THE GRYPHON SCHOOL

Bristol Road, Sherborne, Dorset, DT9 4EQ

Tel: 01935 813 122
Fax: 01935 816 992
E-mail: john.jordan@gryphon.dorset.sch.uk
Website: www.gryphon.dorset.sch.uk

• Pupils: 1,327 boys and girls • Ages: 11-18 • Size of sixth form: 307 • C of E • State

Head: Since 1992, Mr Chris Shepperd BA (fifties), educated Queen's College, Oxford, and Warwick University. Was head of maths at Hinchingbrooke School, Huntingdon under the renowned Peter Downes before arriving for baptism of fire: amalgamation of three schools into one. When not writing mathematical tomes, he sings and is learning to fly. Has been known to take assembly seated in a gryphon-crested wooden throne which may give lead to his nickname – God. Says the Gryphon is rising from the ashes – 'we have finally brought together a divided community'.

Academic Matters: 50 per cent of A level results are A or B, with 315 UCAS point score average for students (equivalent to better than 3 Bs). Strong on business and economics, arts, ICT, history, languages. Sixth form has breadth and variety, 27 subjects – ancient history, Latin at GCSE, law, history, philosophy & ethics, further mathemat-

ics, theatre studies, sports studies and economics with a range of vocational advanced subjects. At GCSE, 70 per cent of students gain 5 A* to C, 58 per cent gaining 5 A* to C with maths and English included. New learning resource centre with internet and a regularly updated set of books – open three afternoons per week after school for additional study. Maths and science setted from year 7, modern languages from year 8. Five IT suites and 350 computers with all departments networked. Gifted and talented programme includes provision within the curriculum and outside of timetable with whole day activities, residential stays and summer schools. SEN and dyslexia centre outstanding, draws pupils over the borders from Dorchester, Gillingham, Shaftesbury, Blandford; serves a total of 230 (23 dyslexic, 53 statemented) with help for mild Aspergers too. Says an LEA official, 'the Gryphon School has created an ethos over the past ten years which is based upon inclusive practice. All teaching and support staff are actively engaged in designing, creating and delivering a curriculum appropriate to meeting the needs of all pupils. The school has developed highly effective tracking and monitoring systems and analyses data in a very systematic way to inform future planning and pupil progress. This ensures that the additional resources provided for pupils with SEN have very positive outcomes.' Says the school, 'we provide for special needs right up to A level. A student with Aspergers who had been rejected by mainstream schools in his area and basically written off came here and we got him through 6 GCSE levels. Our dyslexia base is full simply because of the excellent provision. We never take more than 4 in each year group. We offer special needs right up to A level so children with severe learning difficulties are not excluded from acquiring good A levels.' Realistic careers advice begins as motivation for work-related curriculum in year 10; a new programme provides one or two day vocational training for students in agriculture, mechanics, health and child care, catering, electical and plumbing and hair dressing.

Games, Options, The Arts: Thirty per cent plays an instrument in one of two school bands or four ensembles. Tuition for any instrument possible. Three choirs with umpteen lunchtime musical groups get frequent showcases and three main concerts. Recording studio and main music rooms have composing software on 15 computers. Artsmark silver awarded 2001 in recognition of results in drama, music, art, design, media and literature. Art exhibitions raise local critical acclaim for arts, crafts and photography. Recent theatrical productions range from Lorca to Les Miserables to West Side Story with a cast of fifty and an orchestra of thirty.

Leisure centre on site provides fitness suite, squash courts, outdoor pool, dance studio. Attempts to gain Sportsmark to match attained Artsmark seen as ambitious by some who feel school ought to focus on sciences. Rugby and football teams play private schools and links with Sherborne rugby club; athletes get to county level but team sports further down the school don't often get the attention or the manpower to keep them going. Healthy menu of foreign exchange trips/theatre and dance shows and art trips everywhere.

Background and Atmosphere: The result of an amalgamation of three schools in 1992 is a bustling, well-marketed, consumer-orientated institution with snappy newsletters and an eye-popping social calendar. For a purpose-bred school it lacks some essentials (lockers for pupils) but youngsters are cheerful as they hover round large quadrangles and foyers. Pretty it ain't but locals are won over with the new and well maintained buildings. Hot on parent-rapport and student voice but PTA has fizzled out.

Pastoral Care and Discipline: Bursting with political correctness it bends over backwards for children from difficult homes, employs a counsellor to see pupil referrals of any age; provides access so the disabled can reach every part of this vast building; puts emphasis on charity activities.

Pupil guidance centre for youngsters with problems integrating, eg school phobics, can have specialist attention from senior staff in much smaller groups here, and move back into classrooms as confidence grows. Parents moan that well-behaved plodders don't stand as good a chance here as kids 'with problems'. Care taken over tender shoots before re-planting at 11; teachers visit the eight rural primaries to familiarise youngsters with the big move and each is allowed two friends to have in their tutor group. Tutors remain for 5 years.

Pupils and Parents: Many teachers from independent Sherborne schools – and state schools – choose Gryphon for their own children. Education is the largest employer in Dorset, thus a huge proportion of teachers' children. Nearby Yeovilton airbase instils a drop or two of Malaysian, Dutch or Spanish blood (pilots on 3-year stints) into an otherwise white community 'wo also have top lawyers, dentists, doctors and they want a proper university!' says head. Uniform strictly adhered to, sixth form wears mufti. Ex-Sherborne, first-team rugby player who chose Gryphon for his sixth form, says he likes it because 'it's relaxed and liberated'.

Entrance: Non-selective. At least 220 enter at 11 from 80 square mile catchment, 25 or so from local independent schools. For sixth form 5 A-Cs but will make exceptions for students with special needs.

Exit: Post-16, 30+ per cent or so leave for further education at agricultural college, vet training school, engineering apprenticeships, Yeovil College and art foundation courses. 'All but 1 or 2 per cent of our pupils have a positive outcome. Just because they don't get an A level it does not mean they are on the scrap heap. Of the 30+ per cent not staying on for our A level, about 28 per cent go into work-based learning or colleges of further education (Strode College, Weymouth Tech etc). The best way forward for them might be to be a motor mechanic and I'm sure you will be very pleased to see them the next time your car breaks down.' Parents of children who have left at 16 confirm that Gryphon did well for them while they were there. Post-A level, four or so to Oxbridge, 91 per cent to first choice or second of universities.

Remarks: A modern school. No longer reserves its academic emphasis for A levels, with very good GCSE results as well. Parents say it does well for a non-selective school in a rural area; good SEN teaching too.

GUILDFORD HIGH SCHOOL

Linked to Guildford High School Junior School in the Junior section

London Road, Guildford, Surrey, GU1 1SJ

Tel: 01483 561 440
Fax: 01483 306 516
E-mail: alex.kearney@church-schools.com
Website: www.guildfordhigh.surrey.sch.uk

• Pupils: 600 girls (plus 300 girls in junior school) • Ages: 11-18, junior school 4-11 • Size of sixth form: 155 • Christian • Fees: £1,979 - £2,698 • Independent • Open days: Several per term, please see website

---

Head: Since 2002, Mrs Fiona Boulton BSc MA (fortyish). Had been deputy head for 6 years so the school is not striking out on a risky new course. Previously taught at Stowe and Marlborough. Practical, down to earth, well-liked, very easy to talk to. Not yet the grand dame of girls' education that predecessor, Mrs Singer, was.... but watch this space.

Academic Matters: Regularly 99-100 per cent A-C grades at GCSE – 89 per cent A*/A grades in 2005. A level results mostly As, some Bs, scattered Cs and negligible numbers of grades below that. Superb maths, brilliantly taught – we were impressed to find that no calculators are allowed until after year 7. Sciences also strong (biology and maths are the most popular A level subjects). Unusual languages programme – Spanish introduced in year 1 (age 5), German in year 3 and French in year 5. In year 7, girls study two languages of their choice. Italian available at AS level. All girls do Latin in years 7 to 9 and Latin and Greek are available at GCSE and AS level. Head discourages girls from doing more than 9 GCSEs (although some do) because the girls 'need time to talk to their parents'. Wonderfully sensible. No early GCSEs. Setting only for languages and maths in year 7, English and science at GCSE. In the junior school, girls are streamed for spelling and maths. NB Don't coach your child too much to help her get a place. If she isn't genuinely bright enough, she will sink like a stone.

Games, Options, The Arts: Sports fields (four acres) a few minutes' walk from the school, opening onto Stoke Park. Girls may only walk there in pairs. Very strong lacrosse teams (regularly Surrey champions in many year groups, National Champions in 2005) but also successful in netball, athletics, rounders, tennis and gymnastics. Additional sports offered at the indoor Spectrum Leisure Centre. Some parents say that, as at most competitive schools, the chosen few tend to show up on the lists for every team. Curently the school is building sports hall + fitness suite + 6 lane 25-metre pool development – planned for Michaelmas term 2006.

Strong musical tradition with a high percentage of pupils receiving individual tuition (550 music lessons every week) and a number of choirs, orchestras and ensembles. Class music lessons for junior school pupils and during first three years in the senior school. Music technology also part of the curriculum. No dross among the music staff which includes a Suzuki violin teacher (traditional violin tuition also offered). Annual dramatic productions for most year groups. The 11-year-olds perform in an annual school pantomime, written and produced by sixth formers and girls in year 11 and sixth form can take part in the senior school play. Many joint productions with RGS. Lots of clubs including very active debating. School trips, many and exotic (Cuba, Mongolia, Russia, Peru, Tibet). 80 per cent of girls take part in D of E. Despite all the above, many girls race around in the afternoons attending extra activities out of school.

Background and Atmosphere: Founded 1888 by consortium of 'worthy locals.' Member of the United Church Schools Trust, a group of eight schools which share a common governing council but otherwise appear to have nothing whatsoever in common. Main school building Victorian but overshadowed by proliferation of attractive modern additions. All has been thought out and no corner is allowed to skive. Awash with interactive whiteboards, computers and creative uses of space. 11 new science labs,

ingenious underground sports hall (1999) and dining room (1995) (both superb), help make the cramped site, wedged in along a main road, unexpectedly pleasant. Even the 'old' bits ain't bad. Lovely hall for daily school assemblies. Nice library, full of girls, absolutely silent. Bright art room, recently expanded. Main computer rooms brilliantly designed so that one teacher can see all the screens at once ('to make sure they're not all on hotmail').

The refurbished (2003) sixth form centre is well-planned with private study areas, classrooms and rather bleak, university-style common room. For these older girls, classes are sometimes large but the school will also run a course for just one girl. No uniform in sixth form – uniform trousers now available for the rest. Surrey University library much used (sixth formers all have cards). Ample careers guidance with specialist careers adviser on tap and well-equipped resource room. General studies taken with Tormead and the Royal Grammar. This and the many joint drama productions (Les Mis hoped for in 2006) provide opportunities to mix with boys.

School day finishes at 4pm in the senior school (earlier in the junior department) so all prep done at home. Lack of space grimly felt in the junior school play areas – 4 year olds are corralled in a narrow strip of tarmac overlooked by the sixth form centre. The rest of the junior school plays in a square that must be on the brink of breaking government space per child regulations. None of this seems to bother the bubbly, smiling girls happily racing around the yard. Inside, the junior school hums with efficiency and enterprise. Marvellous time line showing 2,000 years of history runs up the staircase (painted by a teacher). Girls all sit facing the white board and teachers address the pipsqueaks as 'ladies' eg 'Do sit down, ladies'. Class sizes of 16, 18, 20 up to age 7, 24/25 thereafter.

Pastoral Care and Discipline: As at most schools, sixth formers play a big role in this, helping the younger pupils. Drug offences would be dealt with individually and the head reminds parents that 'it might be your own daughter.' No exclusions in recent times. One or two minor suspensions for OTT behaviour. Sixth form pupils may sign out to walk to town but younger girls may not leave the school (they can sometimes be found in High Street shops, nonetheless). With many girls commuting to school by train, parents have expressed concerns over the girls' behaviour on the journey – 'that's where they get their education about life,' says one parent, 'on the train with the RGS boys.' Indeed, London Road station, opposite the school, has become a centre of social life, even for girls who do not travel by rail.

Pupils and Parents: Generally, middle to upper middle class, two-income families who want the best education for their daughters. Guildford High has carved out a position for itself at the pinnacle of hard-edged academic success, regularly winning very narrow edge in the A level league tables over Tormead and St Catherine's, Bramley, the two other local girls' academic powerhouses. 'Some parents are dreadfully pushy,' says one mother, 'not socially, but academically'. Perhaps to counteract this tendency, all upper sixth girls receive a prize at prize-giving. The catchment area tends to be around Guildford and anywhere with good access to the A3 or rail.

Entrance: At 4 girls are seen on two separate occasions to make sure they are bright as berries. Reading ability is not assessed. 2-3 applicants for each available place. At 7 there are tests in English comprehension, creative writing and maths, oral language and reading. At 11 the school gives its own maths and English exams, plus interview. A small intake of around 15 girls at sixth form – candidates need a minimum of 8 GCSE passes with grades A or A* in the subjects they plan to follow at A level.

Exit: Virtually all to university. 15 per cent to Oxbridge, then Durham, London, Warwick popular. A few dribble out after year 11 to attend sixth form elsewhere (eg Godalming Sixth Form College).

Money Matters: Fees must be paid by direct debit, either termly or monthly. Price very reasonable but everything other than tuition and books is excluded. Reductions for siblings. Academic scholarships available at 7, 11 and 16. Music scholarships at 11 and 16. Offers own assisted places, and bursaries based on financial need are available to scholarship winners and to all sixth form candidates. Two United Church School Trust Assisted Places available annually. Clergy bursaries also available.

Remarks: This is a class act from start to finish, with little or no room for improvement. It's more streetwise and hard-edged than you would expect from a clever girls' school in the stockbroker belt. But it is a marvellously challenging environment for your clever, confident daughter offering her the type of education that makes you want to go back to school. Not for anyone who suffers from claustrophobia.

GUMLEY HOUSE RC CONVENT SCHOOL, FCJ

St John's Road, Isleworth, Middlesex, TW7 6XF

Tel: 02085 688 692

Fax: 02087 582 674

E-mail: general@gumley.hounslow.sch.uk

Website: www.gumley.hounslow.sch.uk

• Pupils: 1,180 girls; all day • Ages: 11-18 • Size of sixth form: 250 • RC • State • Open days: Early July, late September and early October

Headteacher: Since 1988, Sister Brenda (Miss B Wallace BA PhD) (mid fifties). Previously taught French and Italian and loved it. Now a non-teaching head – felt she was not giving enough time to lesson preparation and this was unfair to girls. Read modern languages at Liverpool and a PhD in Italian poetry at London. Diminutive and approachable, whereas her study is large, airy and reassuringly cluttered; 'you'll just have to take us as you find us,' she declared in a soft Lancashire accent. An outstandingly successful inspection by Ofsted in 2001 showed that they liked what they found very much indeed.

Academic Matters: For a non-selective state school very good results. Compares extremely favourably with local and national averages. Comes top in local league tables. 80-ish per cent gain 5 or more GCSE grades A*-C. A and A/S levels well ahead of local and national averages. On vexed subject of A/S levels, head feels weaker pupils benefit from leaving school with some qualification but regrets loss of free study periods 'so essential for independent learning'.

Very committed to special needs provision. Two fully qualified teachers and fourteen learning support assistants. SENs catered for include physical difficulties, learning difficulties, ASD, dyslexia, Downs Syndrome. To make sure that they miss nobody, policy is to screen for literacy at the start of year 7 and to organise support as appropriate eg literacy tuition, in-class support, reading clubs or monitoring as appropriate. Preferred method of support is in the classroom. Where possible, try to avoid withdrawing girls from subject lessons. Classroom support now widely accepted by staff and students alike. No stigma associated with classroom support, in fact the girls often ask for it. Wheelchair access throughout the school seen as part of ethos – 'we encourage concern for the disabled, the marginalised and the needy'. Sixth formers involved in helping younger pupils.

Games, Options, The Arts: Netball, hockey and athletics all very strong. School regularly wins all local tournaments. Eight tennis courts, a new all-weather surface hockey/football pitch set in spacious 10 acres. New dance and fitness studio (very popular), new drama studio. Thriving orchestra and plethora of private instrument lessons on offer.

Background and Atmosphere: Founded in 1841 as a school and convent by the Faithful Companions of Jesus. The Queen Anne house surrounded by lovely grounds creates a peaceful oasis in west London. Strong support from parents, 'we couldn't run it without them'. Superbly equipped library in former chapel (just the place for inspired contemplation), sensational octagonal assembly hall for whole school events. Despite rigorous religious requirements at entry level the atmosphere is cheerful and tolerant with no hint of religious oppression.

Pastoral Care and Discipline: Prides itself on discipline. Truancy very rare. Emphasis on strong school/home links. Distinctive uniform worn with pride. Strong emphasis on religious, spiritual and moral formation of pupils. Very supportive staff.

Pupils and Parents: The catchment area covers a wide area of west London from Southall to Twickenham so a broad mix of intake. Most parents make a voluntary contribution to the school's development fund each month.

Entrance: Non-selective academically at age 11. However (and here's the rub), girls and their parents must be practising Roman Catholics (written proof required from parish priest) and that means attending Mass every Sunday. Other entrance criteria are distance from school and first choice on application form. School is heavily oversubscribed; head has no plans for further expansion – 'we'd rather like to keep our grounds as they are'.

Exit: 60 per cent and rising each year go on to higher education. The remainder either take a gap year (increasingly popular) or go directly into employment.

Money Matters: Voluntary aided so run by head and board of governors. Funded through the local council but parents' contributions (voluntary) keep it running as a Catholic school, provide extra facilities and offset maintenance costs.

Remarks: For a budding Mr Bennet who is also a fully paid-up member of the Catholic Church now would be a good time to visit an estate agent in Isleworth. This is an excellent school in lovely surroundings, which will give all your daughters a good education. Well worth a visit.

HABERDASHERS' ASKE'S BOYS' SCHOOL

Linked to Haberdashers' Aske's Prep School in the Junior section

Butterfly Lane, Elstree, Borehamwood, Hertfordshire, WD6 3AF

Tel: 020 8266 1700
Fax: 020 8266 1800
E-mail: office@habsboys.org.uk
Website: www.habsboys.org.uk

• Pupils: 1,100 boys (plus prep school, with 210 boys); all day
• Ages: 11-18, prep school 7-11 • Size of sixth form: 300
• C of E • Fees: £3,200 • Independent • Open days: October

Head: Since 2002, Mr Peter B Hamilton MA (mid-forties). Youngest head here since school moved to current Elstree site in 1961. Educated at King Edward VI Grammar School, Southampton and read modern languages at Christ Church, Oxford. Taught French and German at Radley College, later became head of modern languages and Wren's housemaster at Westminster School. Returned to alma mater as head before landing Haberdashers' post at Easter, replacing Jeremy Goulding who moved to be head at Shrewsbury in 2001. Was also governor of three Hampshire primaries. French wife Sylvie, two daughters. Big outdoorsy type – into canoeing, mountain walking, riding, and sailing. Also likes a bit of karate, classical music and comparative literature when time allows.

Academic Matters: All pupils bright as beavers. Classes of around 20/25 at the youngest age, then 10/12 for A level. Remedial help on hand for mild dyslexia. Three separate sciences at GCSE (dual award not an option). The school is very computer literate and has £350k worth of PCs at last count – over 250 networked machines where each boy has his own space and can use it in his spare time. Increasing use of IT across the curriculum. CD-ROM machines in the library. Low turnover of staff, 'terrifically keen teaching', report many parents. Hugely successful in a wide range of national Brains Trust-type competitions. Consistently outstanding exam results, both at GCSE and A level, particularly in maths. Strong sciences and popular humanities and French, though possibly not the most exciting place for arts people who, nevertheless, do well.

Games, Options, The Arts: Strong on the games field – rugby and hockey both good (regular tours abroad), also some budding athletes and swimming. Badminton very strong. Cross-country. Water polo still very successful. Good games pitches, two Astroturf pitches, sports hall. Magnificent pottery and art department – 11 taking art at A level in 2004. Lively drama – usually in conjunction with the Haberdashers' Girls', next door. See The Skylark magazine for an 'insight into a wealth of extra-curricular activities'. Masses of clubs and activities, thriving community service, CCF currently popular.

Background and Atmosphere: Founded in 1690 in Hoxton by the Worshipful Company of Haberdashers, who continue to play a powerful role in the governing body. Moved to the present site in 1961. Much of the original sixties flat-roofed classrooms now being replaced by purpose-built facilities which cluster awkwardly round Lord Aldenham's pretty redbrick former home now housing the admin offices and accommodation upstairs for young teachers. Charming grounds with rustic bridge leading towards the girls' school. Purposeful, grammar schooly atmosphere pervades as does dreary uniform.

Pastoral Care and Discipline: Tight on disciplinary matters, a school where prefect power counts for something. Staff beady-eyed ('relaxed', says school) over to-ing and fro-ing with the girls next door. Staff also watchful of bad language.

Pupils and Parents: Polyglot. Parents mainly professionals; school busily fosters links with 'the home'. School appeals to first-time buyers. Pupils come from an ever-increasing large catchment area – boys and girls are bused in together (parking permits for the lucky few). Old Boys include Sir Leon Brittan, Sir Nicholas Serota, Dennis Marks (English National Opera), Michael Green (Carlton TV), David Baddiel, Sacha Baron Cohen (aka Ali G), racing driver Damon Hill and the wonderful Brian Sewell.

Entrance: Tough, currently oversubscribed and highly selective. Exam and interview at 11, one third comes from Haberdashers' own prep school; about 25 at 13. Some at sixth form. Top GCSE grades expected.

Exit: Very small post-GCSE leakage (mainly to sixth form colleges) – pupils expect and are expected to last the course. To university – with rare exceptions. Anything between 35 and 45 to Oxbridge annually.

Money Matters: Had 230 Assisted Places now replaced by own bursary funds. Some small scholarships, plus 20-25 bursaries for those in financial need.

Remarks: Thorough and rock solid academic day school for boys but not for social climbers. Delivers the goods and expects a great deal from its pupils.

HABERDASHERS' ASKE'S SCHOOL FOR GIRLS

Linked to Haberdashers' Aske's School for Girls, Junior School in the Junior section

Aldenham Road, Elstree, Borehamwood, Hertfordshire, WD6 3BT

Tel: 020 8266 2300
Fax: 020 8266 2303
E-mail: bcohen@habsgirls.org.uk
Website: www.habsgirls.org.uk

- Pupils: 1,135 girls (including 300 in junior school), all day
- Ages: 11-18 • Size of sixth form: 250 • C of E
- Fees: £2,508 - £2,990 • Independent
- Open days: October & July; Open mornings: November

Head: Since 2005, Mrs Elizabeth Radice MA PGCE (forties), former head of Channing and formerly director of studies at the Royal Grammar School, Newcastle-upon-Tyne. Educated at Wycombe Abbey and Somerville, read English. Married to writer and lecturer at the School of Oriental and African Studies, two student daughters. Feels that, 'important as the academic side is, real education is about a whole lot of other things too. It's about learning to get on with others and making yourself vulnerable by having a go at things.' 'She seems like a typical headmistress,' said one parent at Channing, 'but she can be very caring about the individual girls.' 'Formidable,' said another.

Academic Matters: Enviably consistent results keep Habs way up the league rankings. Performance to be expected bearing in mind highly selective status. But head at pains to point out, 'we don't always pick the cleverest. We want people who have the Can Do mentality.' Sciences (taught separately) and maths hot options for both GCSE and A levels. Overall 95 per cent A*/A grades, well up with the best. No failures at A level. In 2005, 97 per cent A/Ds at A level. 33 girls gained places at Oxford and Cambridge in 2005. Large, well-lit classrooms set around quad with girls' work well displayed. Corridors also lined with fine artwork, picture galleries, activity lists and more.

Languages hugely important here. New block opened September 2003 – new home for language labs, 240-seat lecture theatre and more classrooms. French taught from day one, two modern languages the norm at GCSE. Girls are not allowed to speak English to language teachers, even outside classroom. Opportunity to learn Japanese as part of sixth form general studies; Japanese part of the curriculum in junior school. 250 IT stations in the main school and 50 in the junior school. Every classroom has at least one computer, some have tablet PCs and many have digital projectors; both juniors and seniors have ICT suites. Internet plus intranet (each department has own page). More computers in library and sixth form study room. Used to support every subject (in chemistry, for example, it's a safe way of simulating a dangerous chemical experiment). Digital camera, video/data projectors, scanners all for student use – IT seen as crucial to today's education. Girls can also access network securely from home if off school for a while. Video conferencing possible for those on long-term sickness absence. 110 teaching staff, 37 non-teaching. Years split into four classes according to where girls live. Streaming for some subjects, like maths. Class sizes anything from 18 to 28. 'Individual Needs Co-ordinator' now providing learning support and guidance across senior and junior school.

Games, Options, The Arts: 'Is there nothing these girls can't do?' asked one visitor. Looking at their achievements in art, music and on the sporting field, the answer would seem to be obvious. Much weight thrown behind lacrosse (no hockey played at Habs') and teams littered with national and county players. Regularly victorious over other famous lackey-playing schools. Large sports hall, opened in 1982 by the late Princess Margaret, for badminton and basketball (the favourite indoor sports, according to girls), also fencing. Floodlit tennis courts alongside, lovely new gym (doubles as exam room) that has own section for junior school, older covered pool – next on head's list of projects. 'We try to do something every four years, but we're well ahead of ourselves,' she says. Purpose-built music and art building opened in 1995 a real treasure. Class music compulsory (girls have to sing the register), at least 75 per cent learn a major musical instrument, many more than one. Three orchestras (including chamber), three bands, six ensembles and six choirs. Head says, 'it is part of the creative side of the school that they have always loved making music.' Terrifically high standard of art pieces. 'Even if you're not in the least artistic, you can surprise yourself,' said a girl. DT starts at upper end of junior school. No cookery, no needlework. Lots of sculpting, carpentry and computer design. Numerous after-class activities. Chess particularly popular, as are community and charity work. Drama productions involve everyone without exception – and often include boys from neighbouring Habs' school. Great debaters.

Background and Atmosphere: History dates back to 1689 when Robert Aske (Master of the Worshipful Company of Haberdashers) left £20,000 to found school and almshouses in East London. Moved to present location next to Haberdashers' Aske's Boys' School in 1974. Modern, self-contained and set in almost 55 acres of countryside. Closely linked with 'brother' school. Separated by pair of black gates, formerly known as the 'Passion Gates'. Absolutely no plans to join forces totally and become co-ed. 'Wouldn't dream of it,' says head. Boys and girls allowed to mix at breaks and lunchtimes, as well as taking part in limited number of joint clubs. Also mingle on vast bus network – 84 routes in all – bringing pupils into both schools from north London, Hertfordshire and Middlesex (from Welwyn Garden City in north to St John's Wood in south). 'It's not unusual to spot a boy peering through the gates trying to catch a glimpse of his beloved,' said head. Plain red-brick classroom blocks not exactly bursting with character but newer additions have greater appeal. Also display of pupils' work and out-of-school adventures give rooms and long bleak corridors an enormous lift. Huge stained glass window of school's patron saint, St Catherine, a true jewel in this functional crown. An atmosphere of endeavour, achievement, also enjoyment. No long faces spied – there's a real buzz here. Assemblies daily and very important. Compulsory for all, whatever religion. Breakaway gatherings once a week for girls of Jewish, Hindu and Jain faiths.

Pastoral Care and Discipline: Responsibility and care for others instilled in even the youngest. Active leadership and teamwork training. (We saw one year 6 girl acting as peacemaker in a minor playtime dispute in junior school. Handled confidently, maturely and compassionately.) 'It's peer support not peer pressure.' Pastoral system runs down through form tutor to sixth-formers (allocated to all lower classes in 'big sister' role), and form prefects. More serious matters dealt with by heads of junior, middle, and upper schools and sixth form. Overall school head has final say. No drugs, no drink, no smoking. 'Girls know they have too much to lose if they break the rules,' says head who has never yet had to expel anyone. Full PSHE programme. Discipline not a problem, she says. 'We're terribly lucky. The girls want to be here, they are good to each other and the parents are very supportive.' School council a strong force – much listened to. Brought about end to heart dissection in A level biology and pushed for RS at A level. 'They put a good case,' says head. 'This is a school that thrives on change.'

Pupils and Parents: A really nice bunch of girls from mainly professional backgrounds. Families don't stay in the background though. Very involved in fund-raising activities to pay for 'luxury' items. (School fete expects to raise £15,000 alone.) Parents also encouraged to get actively involved in daughters' education. Says head, 'I feel passionately about partnership with parents.' Large ethnic mix. No extra English tuition needed – nor is it offered. Famous OGs? 'We don't do fame, we do salt of the earth,' she says, being rather coy. TV presenter Vanessa Feltz was there, among other notables.

Entrance: At 4 and 5 by assessment, then own papers at 11. Oversubscribed by a long chalk. At least 5:1. Looking for something special, not just intellect. Examines English, maths and verbal reasoning. Reduced number of prospective pupils called back for interview. Parents also seen alone by head but 'not part of the selective procedure. It's important the parent feels they can trust the person they're handing their daughter over to for the next seven years'. Head adds, 'it means in the end you get the whole family.' Five A-C GCSEs lowest requirement for entry to sixth, preferably As in chosen A level subjects.

Exit: No-one lost after GCSEs to schools with co-ed sixth form, we are told. A handful only to boarding schools, sixth form colleges or because of finances. 'We never throw people out,' says head. Though the odd girl might agree she'd do better elsewhere. Leavers destined for university (almost without exception), some after gap year. In 2004, 43 girls gained places at Oxford or Cambridge. Medicine very popular – lawyers, engineers and linguists aplenty too.

Money Matters: Fees cover tuition. Extras include lunch, music, exams and coach travel. Academic and music scholarships up to 50 per cent tuition fees (plus free music lessons with latter). No awards for junior school entry but governors' bursaries available at year 7 entry. Haberdashers' Company provides for special 'emergency' fund each year.

Remarks: Dubbed 'the friendly school' and if current crop of happy, smiling faces is anything to go by, it lives up to it. Room here for the shy as well as out-going. But 'got to be reasonably robust in intellectual terms,' adds head. Lots of jollies, lots of fun alongside an unquestionably heavy workload. A first-rate girls' school where enjoyment is seen as most effective learning tool.

HABERDASHERS' MONMOUTH SCHOOL FOR GIRLS

Linked to Haberdashers' Agincourt School in the Junior section

Linked to Gilbert Inglefield House in the Junior section

Hereford Road, Monmouth, Monmouthshire, NP25 5XT

Tel: 01600 711 100

Fax: 01600 711 233

E-mail: admissions@hmsg.co.uk

Website: www.habs-monmouth.org

- Pupils: 695 girls; 110 board (full and weekly), the rest day
- Ages: 11-18 • Size of sixth form: 120 • Christian foundation, non-denom • Fees: Day: £2,310 in the prep; £2,766 in the main school, £2,940 in the sixth form. Boarding £2,316 extra
- Independent • Open days: October

Head: Since 1997, Dr Brenda Despontin BA MA PhD MBA (forties). Educated at Lewis Girls' Grammar, in the Welsh valleys, and Cardiff University, where she completed her BA in psychology, an MA on Thomas Hardy and a PhD in children's literature. Intended to become an educational psychologist and took PGCE, at Bath University with this in mind, but found a love for teaching instead. Taught at British school in Brussels (where she met her husband, also a teacher), then moved to take up 'very interesting' post as residential supervisor in home for disturbed teenage girls. After seven years each at a comprehensive and an independent school, she set up new girls' division at King's School, Macclesfield. Principal for five years before coming to Habs' Monmouth – 'it felt like coming home,' she says. One son, house tutor at Old Swinford Hospital. Manages difficult job of being dynamic leader and friendly, approachable face. Totally committed to continued learning and opportunities for all staff, whether cleaners or teachers (and recently completed her MBA from Hull University by distance learning). President of GSA 2005. Regional award for leadership in a secondary school from The Teaching Awards Trust.

Academic Matters: Across-the-board excellence, as expected from a highly selective school. Wide-ranging choice of subjects, particularly at A level, which has a timetable of more than 30 A and AS options organised with military precision in conjunction with Monmouth School (the boys' school on the other side of town). Boys arrive for psychology, business, Italian, German and classical civilisation, with girls going off for Russian, history of art and computing. Particularly strong results in art, biology, maths, French and German. Italian (a relative newcomer) yet to fully find its feet at A level. These girls regularly produce the expected strong performance that takes them where they want to go. Similarly near perfect (99 per cent plus) A*/A/B grades at GCSE, 80 per cent A/B grades at A level. One girl, in 2004, in top 5 for country in statistics. Eleven candidates placed in the top 5 marks in the country in 5 different subjects 7 in French, out of 163,000 candidates! Previously weakish chemistry now doing fine. Outstanding results in IT, Latin (taken from 12), Spanish (just increased to two sets to take account of its popularity), maths, English, music and art (taken in year 10). Sciences taught both doubly and singly in wonderful, state-of-the-art labs with separate lecture facilities, with creditable results all round. Welsh taught in sixth form as an after-school option by teacher from Monmouth Comprehensive (so far of limited appeal, particularly to the sizeable English contingent). Good number of male staff, occasionally the subject of gentle ribbing by the girls.

Games, Options, The Arts: Head has been careful to maintain the huge and diverse extra-curricular programme in the face of exam demands (and achieving it so far). Drama is particularly popular and is given the space for all to take part and enjoy it, in a fine studio with professional standard lighting, in addition to the main hall – the venue for many memorable productions. Dance of all kinds, including ballet, enthusiastically embraced by many girls. Keen on the outdoors without being overtly jolly hockey sticks (it's lacrosse here anyway, with Habs' teams regularly trouncing those from all over the west), with large and scenic playing fields, and a new flood-lit, all-weather pitch. A huge, well-equipped sports hall and a lovely, well-used pool with spectacular views across the Wye Valley. Big commitment to D of E, Young Enterprise and all kinds of community service around the town. Annual expeditions, to such places as Ecuador and the K2 base camp, made possible by fundraising by the participants. Lots of space for textiles, which has a strong following. Lovely art department, with beautiful examples of work on the walls. Annual inter-house Eisteddfod showcases all sorts of talents, from music to cookery. Large music space, kitted out with a range of equipment including keyboards, with recording studio next door – a cacophony of sound during our visit. School choirs compete internationally and many girls take individual music lessons. Superb careers department, praised by staff and girls alike, with a well-stocked room big enough to take entire classes for careers sessions.

Background and Atmosphere: Haberdashers'

Monmouth School for Girls was founded in 1892, a late complement to the boys' Monmouth School, whose foundation dates from 1614. It was funded by the original bequest of William Jones, a member of the Haberdashers' Company and local man made good. The guild and the Jones Foundation still provide excellent support of all kinds for both schools, which remain closely tied through siblings, the academic programme and social events, including the May Ball. Imposing turn-of-the-century buildings, supplemented by a liberal sprinkling of '60s cubes, perch on a hill on the edge of Monmouth, with lovely views of rolling valleys and the pretty town centre. New classroom block planned for 2006. Some departments are across the road, linked by a pedestrian flyover, where school owns most of buildings ('the hospital isn't ours but we've got our eye on it,' says head). Twiston Davies boarding house, tucked unobtrusively behind main school building, has some of the nicest boarding facilities imaginable – lovely, cosy, colourful rooms, some with en-suite bathrooms and plenty of cool, chilling-out space. 'It's just like an IKEA catalogue,' sighs one envious day girl. Separate junior boarding house. Flexi-boarding and range of evening activities has reinvigorated boarding here, once in decline but now stable. Uniform compulsory throughout, although slightly more grown up for sixth-formers. Lots of badges on jackets to show who and what girls are. Top quality food on offer in the comfortable, panelled dining room – girls look reassuringly well-nourished.

Pastoral Care and Discipline: Happiness is paramount and pastoral support comes in many forms. Peer mentoring, with trained sixth formers offering an ear to younger pupils, works well. Girls are always encouraged to speak out early to head off any bigger problems, and will turn to friends, head of year, head of house (there are four), tutors or school chaplain, depending on the nature of the problem. As a result, bullying is barely an issue. School reserves right to search lockers, involve police or drugs test if illicit substance abuse is suspected (although head points out that she has never had to deal with such an incident). Recent inspection praised the 'spirituality' of school, particularly for its warmth and caring attitude. Comprehensive PSE programme also offered from years 7 to 11. Pupils seem genuinely and effortlessly supportive of each other.

Pupils and Parents: Mainly professional parents, farmers and business people. Enormous catchment – from Ledbury in the north, the Forest of Dean to the east and across south Wales to the west and south, including a non-stop bus from Cardiff. Boarders relatively local (from Wales and England, including children of London commuters). A few from overseas.

Entrance: Most arrive via 11+ entrance exam, some from junior school, others from local primaries and preps. School also takes candidates at 13 via CE. Lots of demand at sixth form level. School aims to spot potential as well as taking out-and-out high-flyers through interviews and previous heads' reports.

Exit: Girls equipped to achieved their objectives, with around 10 per cent a year to Oxbridge and many others to top universities all over the country, with Birmingham, Exeter, LSE and Durham particular favourites. Lots of doctors and dentists – Cardiff University apparently a home from home for Habs' Monmouth scientists. Others go to art college or into the Services.

Money Matters: Well-supported school able to be generous, with music and academic scholarships of up to 50 per cent available at 11 and 16 and a hardship fund for those in genuine need. Not feeling the loss of Assisted Places as acutely as most, not least because fees kept at reasonable level.

Remarks: Friendly, happy school where achieving potential in every sphere, including social, is genuinely as important as getting the grades.

HAILEYBURY

Hertford, Hertfordshire, SG13 7NU

Tel: 01992 463353
Fax: 01992 470 663
E-mail: registrar@haileybury.com
Website: www.haileybury.com

- Pupils: 718 (including 434 boarders); 422 boys, 296 girls.
- Ages: 11-18 • Size of sixth form: 273 • Christian foundation
- Fees: Day £3,320 to £4,993; boarding £4,219 to £6,650.
- Independent

Master: Since 1996, Mr Stuart Westley MA (fifties). Educated at Lancaster Royal Grammar School and read law at Corpus Christi College, Oxford. Cricket blue and has played as a professional cricketer for Gloucestershire. Previously principal of King William's College, Isle of Man, and before that deputy head at Bristol Cathedral School. Also taught at Framlingham College, Suffolk. Married with one daughter who boards at Haileybury. Believes the three main strengths of the school are its 'academic programme, the quality and quantity of its extra-curricular programme and its excellent pastoral provision.' Keen to stress that Haileybury is predominantly a boarding school – while day

pupils are made welcome it is on the understanding that they will board at some time in the future. An enthusiast of the International Baccalaureate, which Haileybury introduced in 1999 – growing in popularity with 116 participants in 2005-2006.

Academic Matters: Not hugely selective but becoming more so at every point of entry. Good and improving results. 2005 results include 59 per cent of GCSE grades A* or A and 72 per cent of A levels A or B. Average IB points score 35 out of 45. Popular subjects are history, psychology and maths. Sports studies, theatre studies and general studies are available at A level along with Russian, Italian and Chinese. Separate sciences and dual award (very good results) offered at GCSE. Small classes – 15 pupils. Setting in year 7 in maths and English and in year 9 for maths, English and science. All pupils study French and Latin from year 7 with German or Spanish an option in year 9. No GNVQs offered. Entry to sixth form requires a minimum of four GCSEs at grade B or above, including four at grade B or above. All pupils are screened for special needs when they join; there is one full-time special needs teacher and three other members of staff who provide extra, individual help part time. A small number of pupils get extra help with English as a foreign language.

Games, Options, The Arts: Outstanding sports facilities on 50 acres of playing fields including the impressive Terrace pitch, a multi-million pound indoor sports centre, floodlit all-weather pitch, indoor pool and squash, rackets and tennis courts. All usual sports on offer with sailing an additional option. A huge range of extracurricular activities also available. Boys and girls can learn to fly through the CCF. Music is growing in strength since the arrival of a new director – some 300 pupils learn a musical instrument. Strong drama with performances ranging from Shakespeare to Alan Ayckbourn OH.

Background and Atmosphere: Haileybury opened as an independent school in 1862 occupying the buildings formerly used as The East India College, which between 1809 and 1859 was the training ground for generations of boys destined to govern India. In 1942 Haileybury College and The Imperial Services College at Windsor amalgamated on to the Haileybury site. The buildings surround a central quadrangle, in neo-classical style by William Wilkins whose later works included the National Gallery, Downing College Cambridge and much of London University. Old buildings have been refurbished and new ones added in a sympathetic style and at vast expense, the last project was two stunning new girls' boarding houses which offer hotel-style comfort to the 120 or so lucky girls who are housed there.

Long gone are the days of large, Spartan dormitories. Today's boarders sleep in cabin beds with more individual space. Sixth-formers get their own study bedrooms complete with wash basins, desk and wardrobe. They can also bring their own fridge. All pupils eat together in the impressive domed dining hall sitting at grand oak tables on benches. Cafeteria-style with traditional meat and veg dishes on offer alongside salads, pasta and jacket potatoes. The Russell Dore lower school (named after OH who left a £3m windfall) is bright and welcoming for the first years. The tuck shop is popular and busy.

Boarding houses are homely and welcoming and try to create a family atmosphere. Some teachers keep their own pets on site which helps pupils feel more at home. But remember, this is a boarding school – in the senior school on Saturdays there are morning lessons then sports fixtures; even during the week, day pupils stay at school until 6.30pm but are encouraged to stay for supper and evening prep. Not much point going home really. So if you are set on a day school it's probably not the best choice.

Pastoral Care and Discipline: Strong house system. Pupils choose their own house. Housemaster and housemistress are the first points of contact for parents and pupils and are supported by a team of tutors. Good Tickets reward improvement. Six or more Good Tickets equal a book token. Pupils' progress is constantly monitored with three weekly reports. ('It keeps us on our toes,' says one teacher); over the academic year The Master writes at least one report on each pupil. School has clear policies on bullying, illegal drugs, alcohol and smoking. Not as hardline a stance on drugs as some other schools but those caught supplying illegal drugs are expelled. Several recent cases involving cannabis.

Pupils and Parents: Range from middle class professionals and those running their own businesses to the 'seriously rich.' About one-tenth have a parent who went to Haileybury. Most of the British pupils live within 50 miles of the school; some 18 per cent currently have overseas addresses. Pupils from a large number of feeder schools, mainly prep schools, although some come from state primaries; they seem polite and confident. Notable Old Boys include Clement Attlee, Sir Stirling Moss, Sir Alan Ayckbourn, Sir Clive Martin (former Lord Mayor of the City of London), John McCarthy and Dom Joly.

Entrance: A total of 48 join the lower school at 11 out of 95 sitting tests in English, maths and verbal reasoning. A total of 70 are admitted at 13. Some places for sixth-formers from other schools provided they fulfil the GCSE criteria and pass the school's own entrance exam.

Exit: Majority goes on to further education to a wide range of universities. About ten to Oxbridge each year.

Money Matters: At 11 academic and music (at least grade 4) scholarships (worth up to 50 per cent of the fees) and an 'all-rounder' award (worth up to 20 per cent) available. Similar scholarships available at 13 with additional art, music and design technology awards, art scholarship and design technology scholarship. Academic and music and art scholarship also offered for sixth form entrants. Bursaries also available for the needy. Haileybury offers a 10 per cent discount for a second child and 20 per cent for a third. Books and stationery not included in fees.

Remarks: Parents like what they see – you can't fail to be impressed by the stunning facilities. A happy, relaxed atmosphere with an international flavour.

HALL SCHOOL WIMBLEDON (THE)

Linked to Hall School Wimbledon Junior School (The) in the Junior section

17 The Downs, Wimbledon, London, SW20 8HF

Tel: 020 8879 9200
Fax: 020 8946 0864
E-mail: enquiries@hallschoolwimbledon.co.uk
Website: www.hallschoolwimbledon.co.uk

- Pupils: 155 boys, 80 girls • Ages: 11-16 • Non-denom
- Fees: £2,957 • Independent • Open days: Open days twice termly, parents must apply to attend

Head: Since 1999, Mr Timothy Hobbs MA (forties), educated at Eastbourne College and St Andrews where he read mediaeval and modern history. Abandoned accountancy training in favour of a teaching post at Hill House International Junior School, which he left six years later (encouraged by parents) to set up in 1990 his own school – the original Hall Junior School (qv). (In 1999 his brother Jonathan joined as principal of the junior school). Unmarried – other than to the school where he spends seven days a week in any of his five offices which range from a gorgeous cream sitting-room complete with three-legged black cat, to a more functional workspace in a converted garage where the children can drop in as they pass by. Erudite, energetic, entrepreneurial, passionate about the school and a stickler for old-fashioned good manners. He has the demeanour of a favourite uncle. Entertainingly opinionated, he writes the most readable newsletters we've seen – wonderfully indiscreet and quite philosophical at times. He prides himself on his prescience – currently has a date in a sealed envelope in his safe, predicting abolition of the Euro. More pertinently, he served his first home-cooked organic school dinner when Jamie Oliver was still a school boy, and wrote The Hall's code on bullying eight years before it became law for all schools to have one. He has recently closed down the school's ICT suite and predicts that computers will no longer be used in classrooms in the UK by 2015. He (and his school) have a certain local reputation for being quirky – but underpinning some of the less conventional practices, he espouses traditional, old-fashioned values. 'It can only come out as the usual collection of clichés, but I absolutely cherish the individual and want to foster their spirit,' he says. 'He puts the needs of the children above all,' agrees one mother. 'And truly celebrates their individuality.' TJH is The Hall School Wimbledon – parents should consider all the pluses and minuses such a close association with the brand can bring. You wouldn't want him falling under a bus the day after your child starts the school or any time during their time there.

Academic Matters: If you love league tables and prize academia above all else, look away now. As a mixed ability school with a largely non-selective entry, exam results are not the be all and end all here. Ethos is that learning must be a pleasure, not a burden. The prospectus says that 'thought is the most important activity taking place at our school.' That said, the school works to the Common Entrance and GCSE syllabuses, while 'noting the spirit and content' of the National Curriculum, all combined in its own 'Works Programme'. Pre-GCSE, the core subjects are English, French, maths and science, alongside the usual history, geography, religious studies art, music and the less common 'gardening'. No SATs. At GCSE, the timetable will be written around that year's cohort and always include German and PE - 'PE is our most popular choice,' says TJH – additionally a broad choice of languages, textiles, and rural science among others. Generally academic matters are not considered more important than any other matters at this school. (That's not to say that the children don't work hard – they do.) But TJH stresses equal emphasis across the school day: 'Maths is as important as lunch, which is as important as poetry and football.' He is anti-league tables – would be more interested in something which gave a better idea of value-added. 'Getting a 'refuser' to take exams is a success' he says. 'A year 10 boy who joined us with not much more than his 2 times table and went on to get a B in his GCSE a year later – those are success stories.' For the record, in 2005 84 per cent gained five GCSE passes at A*-C.

Class sizes average 20. English and maths classes (for which the pupils are set) usually have a second teacher with them. Language classes (also set) have about 15 pupils. At GCSE class sizes are anything from 1 to 20, averaging 10. The school no longer offers ICT as a GCSE option and use of computers in other lessons is selective: 'IT skills are taught to avail real curriculum needs rather than as a general subject – we don't teach how to use a hammer, we teach the skills to make a box,' says TJH in typical TJH fashion. Books are preferred. 'I simply felt that the ICT GCSE syllabus did not deliver,' he adds. However, the school aims to have all the children touch-typing by the end of year 9. GCSE year groups additionally study the ASDAN programme promoting 'key life skills.'

School has its own unique and rather elaborate homework system called 'Flints'. Based on a 'little and often' philosophy, the pupils get bite-size exercises in four or five different subjects every night, and are then tested at school on Friday morning in what is called 'a flint wall'. These results are fed back to parents each week. One mother said she felt the children aiming for Common Entrance were pushed harder than the rest. No weekend homework (the envy of other private school pupils?) except for GCSE coursework in years 10 and 11, though the students invariably have a project on the go.

Special needs are met within the classroom with as little one to one as possible. Three learning support teachers are on the staff (parents contribute towards the cost of special needs provision). School currently caters for mild dyslexia and for two amputees from the Iraq war who both have one to one help in all classes for writing and translation. The specialist autistic unit based at the junior school (qv) can take secondary age pupils. Around 15 pupils have EAL needs – met by an EAL teacher and classroom support as necessary.

Games, Options, The Arts: Sport is an integral part of school life. Every day begins with the major wake-up call of 30 minutes circuit training from 8.30am – and this goes on all through the year, rain or shine. Similarly a hurricane would have to pass through before outside playtime was dropped, and some parents grumble about slightly damp children trooping back for lessons – school's attitude is that a drop of rain never hurt anybody. Sport is timetabled every day – a good range with the emphasis on racquets and netball (pupils recently returned from a netball tour of New Zealand). There are no elite teams – places are rotated to allow everyone to have a go. Some parents of sports 'stars' would prefer set teams and can resent the wobbly beginnings of newcomers – but the school will not leave someone on a bench all term.

A very active school – makes the most of any opportunity to get out of the classroom for anything from a 45-minute investigation of the school's ponds, to a three-week field trip incorporating literature, history, philosophy and geography. The field-trip programme is enormous and led by TJH, includes expeditions such as walking the 105 mile South Downs Way, climbing in the Brecon Beacons in Wales and camping in Pevensey. 'This is a huge plus point,' says one mother. 'TJH really gets to know the children on these trips and follows up when they are back in school.' Downside according to another is that it makes him hard to track down: 'parents are not his priority- though he's very good when you get him.' The head replies that 'any parent that wants to see me does so – parents can always see a senior tutor who will contact me and may act on my behalf.' Additionally, all the children are taught to climb (head likes the analogy with achievement in life). Musical abilities are strongly encouraged – no orchestra but there is a choir and a regular pantomime and musical production each year ('always a treat' says one parent). Art facilities have recently expanded to fill the space vacated by ICT suite. No after school clubs (school day runs from 8.30 to 5pm) but there are break time clubs in design technology, art and music. There are also inter-house sports competitions in morning break (which is 45 minutes long).

Background and Atmosphere: TJH founded the school in 1990 and began teaching in a church hall in Wimbledon Village with nine pupils, intending to steer them through to Common Entrance. He was teaching, cooking, keeping animals – and it's probably from these early beginnings that the 'wacky' reputation gathered hold. Things took off very quickly as word spread and new pupils joined. The senior school (formerly Hazlehurst's school premises) was purchased in 1998 – an extended Victorian residential property 10 minutes from Wimbledon station. Grounds not huge, but beautiful and well-used. There is a gazebo, a grassy area, five ponds, some landscaping and other interesting nooks and crannies. Some classrooms on the small side – functional rather than fantastic. Walls a bit bare when we visited but it was the beginning of term. Impressive central staircase hung with professional artwork belonging to the head. Lunchtime is a pleasant social occasion. The children get wholesome organic food (no packed lunches allowed, nor any vending machines) and they set and clear tables themselves. A child having a bad day may be distracted by an invitation to come and help prepare the food – all done on site. Lunchtime functions as an 'assembly' – there is no other whole school gathering. 'It's a wholesome school rather than a faith school,' says TJH. Children look ready for action in outward-bound style uniform of polo shirts, sweat shirts and chinos. They are proud of their school. All encouraged to do lots for charity. Overall a happy, stimulating environment, with a relaxed atmosphere.

Pastoral Care and Discipline: A tolerant regime with as little regulation as possible. No punishments as such and certainly no detentions or being kept in at break time ('What message does that give? That fresh air and exercise are not important,' says TJH). Zero tolerance of bullying – which has a wide-ranging definition including ignoring somebody. This is about the only 'crime' for which there is a punishment. Serial offender would be deemed to have 'spoilt his/her community' (his class) and would be moved to another year group while things were sorted out, otherwise suspension and expulsion follow. 'Some of the children who join us have been bullied elsewhere and we simply will not tolerate it here,' says TJH. Children are encouraged to report any incident, to sit with somebody different in each lesson (no saving places for friends) and indeed not to have a 'best friend' to the exclusion of others.

Every child is given a cake to celebrate their birthday – whole school sings and there's enough to share with their class. Until recently TJH made each cake himself ('great chance to really focus on that child and think about their needs in the coming year,' he says.) Has had less time for this lately but would like to reinstate. 'Tutors always very supportive. It is like a family', said one parent. Average age of teaching staff is 35. Around 20 per cent have been with the school at least 10 years, others put in more fleeting appearances – a hefty contingent are recruited from Australia and New Zealand (their can-do attitude appeals to the school).

Pupils and Parents: A cosmopolitan school including lots of nationalities and social groups. Ideal for parents looking for an international school type atmosphere: 'our children slotted in quickly and happily,' says one well-travelled parent. 'Children with a need will have it catered for here,' says another mother. 'Consequently it attracts children with a 'story' or history of some kind.' TJH worries that people will equate quirky/eccentric with mediocre achievement – 'we have many very bright children and a few 'gifted,' he says. Pupils are not obviously different, and the youngsters who showed us round were pleasingly confident. School is boy heavy – 60/40. Very mixed parent population but notable minorities of actors/playwrights and producers; others from the music world, and football and tennis players. No PTA or sports day (by design) so parents don't get to know each other so easily – particularly if they have not had children in the junior school.

Entrance: By assessment at 11+. All applicants take papers in English and maths, are observed undertaking arts and sports activities and are interviewed. Parents must supply a report from the previous school and disclose any ed psych reports. TJH says purpose of interview is to ensure compatibility with existing children and ensure that all who join 'may benefit from our teaching,' and he aims to make it a good experience for the child even if no place is offered at the end. Special consideration is given to children with particular merit in a non-academic field. Around two thirds of the places go to pupils from the junior school. These children also take the 11+ exams, but are guaranteed a place. Lots of word of mouth recommendations. 60 per cent of pupils live within three miles of school.

Exit: Bit of an exodus at 13 – 'it is about 15 per cent, sometimes fewer' – when the Common Entrance bunch leave. No particular trend, but pupils go to King's Wimbledon, St Paul's, Epsom College and Latymer among others. Off in all directions at 16+, Epsom College a popular sixth form choice. To the question 'Any notable old boys/girls?' comes the reply 'They are all notable!'

Remarks: An unusual place – conventional parents may balk at some of the thinking here – but it's different rather than completely alternative. Mixes the off the wall with the traditional and could be perfect for children who are the 'square pegs' in more traditional establishments.

HALLIFORD SCHOOL

Russell Road, Shepperton, Middlesex, TW17 9HX

Tel: 01932 223 593
Fax: 01932 229 781
E-mail: registrar@hallifordschool.com
Website: www.hallifordschool.co.uk

- Pupils: 370 boys, all day • Ages: 11-18 • Size of sixth form: 45
- Non-denom • Fees: £2,900 • Independent • Open days: March, May, October, November

Head: Since 2002, Philip Cottam MA (fifties) previously a senior master at Stowe, a housemaster at Sedbergh, and an officer in the army. He has two grown-up children from his first marriage, and a 13 year-old stepson from his 2003 re-marriage – 'I'm sorry I left it so long,' he laughs. Bristling with energy and enthusiasm, his interests include history (which he still teaches 'as an indulgence') the theatre, concerts and wine tasting. Also a keen skier and climber ('though I do less of that now!'). Describes his approach as 'traditional – with a soft- centre' – which also serves as a good description of him personally. His especially popular and long-serving predecessor was a hard act to follow but he seems to have pulled it off. The boys like him, long-serving staff are still in post ('he has a very strong team' stresses one mother) and parents describe him as 'super' and 'very approachable'. He is more of a disciplinarian than the previous head and has brought in plenty of new ideas, while apparently retaining the best of the old. 'He has tightened things up all round,' says one delighted mother. Very hands-on, he makes a point of attending most of the school's weekend home matches.

Academic Matters: Deserves a pat on the back for genuine willingness to take in the less academic and late developers. Not an academic hothouse – which is part of its appeal for parents – but that's not to say it doesn't get very reasonable results from the mixed ability intake. Almost all get five or more A*-C grades at GCSE. Latin compulsory until year nine and mentioned as a highlight by several parents – a fair few boys go on to GCSE (75 per cent A-C passes) and even A level. 40 percent-ish A/B at A level. The sixth form is currently run as a consortium with nearby St David's, an independent girls' school, although plans are afoot to cut these ties so there will be no joint teaching by 2007. Mr C will then be able to implement his vision for the school, including making the sixth form fully co-ed instead of just 'the few girls we have at present' and to offer critical thinking AS in year 11, to be completed in the lower sixth.

The first two years in the school are taught in three sets with 22 boys in each. After this, boys are put into four sets for all academic subjects. Staff are generally very willing in lunch hours and after school to help those prepared to put in some extra effort. Good value-added – head cites example of a boy in the lower sixth whose predicted attainment in year seven was two GCSEs. He went on to pass nine, and studied for three A levels. ICT is one of the few weaknesses, and although steps have been taken to address this, still some parental concern – something to watch. A few pupils have EAL, but there is a dedicated teacher. No provision for SEN; boys with mild dyslexia and/or mild dyspraxia 'are dealt with by virtue of small class groups', says the school.

Games, Options, The Arts: Certainly a sporty school with bags of opportunity for those so inclined. But don't be put off if you have a not-so-keen son. It's not rammed down their throats (much of the action is outside the timetable) but several mothers of non-sporty sons said their boys really enjoyed the four timetabled periods of sports per week. Main sports are rugby, football and cricket. Rowing is also popular (old boy Steve Trapmore of the Sydney Gold Olympic eight is a shining example to today's eager crews) and golf is on offer to the older boys. A new building, 2005, includes a sports hall- the size of four badminton courts with a climbing wall, all topped off with a viewing gallery.

State of the art theatre, masses of drama and is also used for extra-curricular lectures (which are plentiful and popular), as a cinema and as an assembly hall, and is home to the house unison competition and the debating society meetings – both Cottam initiatives from Stowe. Art is a strength, music too – drums and guitar popular with teenage boys of course (too much electric guitar head grumbles good-naturedly). Evidence of a rich after-school life, including a wide selection of clubs, which are all free. Some born out of adversity (when building works restricted playground space). The cinema club proved so popular it has been retained for rainy days – though it can take several days to see a whole film – said one pupil good-naturedly.

Background and Atmosphere: Established 1921. On six acres beside the Thames. Georgian house, behind which, separated by a courtyard, are modern buildings housing light and airy classrooms. Hard surfaced play area is bijou – one mother moans that boys are not encouraged to get out in the fresh air at lunchtime. Mr C disagrees and says boys are actively encouraged to be outside, but building works caused temporary problems. Sports pitches are plentiful and well used. The school is small (for a secondary school), very friendly and nurturing – 'a real boy's school' – enthuses one parent. Good manners seem second nature to the boys – doors routinely held open for others, teachers greeted with respect – and they in their turn know all the boys by name. A healthy sprinkling of female teachers (called ma'am by the boys). 'The staff have a great rapport with the boys,' says one parent. 'They are approachable and not at all stuffy and really seem to get the balance right so that things are not regimented, more relaxed but respectful.' Several parents mentioned that their son's confidence had been really boosted after just a few months at the school.

Most pupils must have the 'school dinner' – 'they learn to eat what is put in front of them – no bad thing,' says one mother, describing the food as 'slightly better than typical.' Another said the food was 'rather heavy on carbs' – but this is probably necessary for all the rugby players and rowers around. Staff eat it too – with the boys. Uniform is not ruinously expensive – M&S trousers and shirts are allowed – but standards are strictly applied. No silly business with ties or untucked shirts is tolerated, and there are also fairly strict rules about hair – no gel and must be kept above collar-length. All this results in smart boys.

Pastoral Care and Discipline: Great efforts to help the boys feel at home from the start, with a honed programme of induction including taster days and a sports day during the term before entry, Q&As sheet – aimed at the boys rather than their parents – answering common concerns, generally plenty of opportunities to make contact with soon-to-be classmates. Healthy house system in operation, which provides the foundations of a discreet, but highly effective, discipline system based on merits and censures. Anti-bullying policy seems equally effective – head claims zero-tolerance. The mother of a (briefly) bullied son has nothing but praise for the way things were quickly and successfully handled. Head is keen to stress the importance of distinguishing between a bad dose of adolescence and genuine bad behaviour. Four boys have been asked to leave in recent years for incidents involving stealing, drugs and rudeness – this sort of behaviour is very much the exception.

Pupils and Parents: Not snobbish or full of rich kids. A largely local intake from Middlesex, Surrey and SW London using good transport links and a school bus service. Fairly equal numbers arrive from state primaries and private preps.

Entrance: Mostly at age 11, armed with a suitable reference from their previous school, applicants must pass an entrance exam and an interview. 'It's getting harder to get in,' says head. In 2004, there were 140 applications for 66 places. Word among parents is that the school will look kindly on applications from siblings (even overlooking a bad test result). 'I definitely believe the interview counts more than the test,' says one parent. Some pupils join at 13+, based either on Common Entrance or a separate Halliford exam. For entry to the sixth form, it's a minimum of five GCSE (A-C) and an interview with the head. School does take boys at odd times – always worth a try.

Exit: Currently approximately 60 per cent of boys move on to the sixth form (school is aiming to increase to 70 per cent). Most leavers at 16 go to sixth form colleges – there is a glut of them in the surrounding areas – some to do courses the school does not offer and for others Mr C says 'there is a feeling the grass is greener on the other side with more freedom etc, but we do keep the majority of the most academic.' From the sixth form, it's university in the main, including a 'steady trickle' each year to Oxbridge (two in 2004).

Money Matters: 'It's one of the cheapest,' admits one honest mother amid her list of reasons for choosing the school. A limited number of academic scholarships (50 per cent of fees) at 11, also art, music and sports scholarships. Sixth form bursary system rewards students for GCSE results.

Remarks: Does well by all; although clearly not first choice for those after a hothouse academic environment, the bright boys who get here are well looked after. Going from strength to strength.

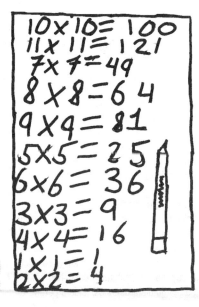

HAMPSTEAD SCHOOL

Westbere Road, Hampstead, London, NW2 3RT

Tel: 020 7794 8133
Fax: 020 7435 8260
E-mail: enquiries@hampsteadschool.org.uk
Website: www.hampsteadschool.org.uk

- Pupils: 1,300 pupils; 55 per cent boys and 45 per cent girls
- Ages: 11-19 • Size of sixth form: 270 • Non-denom • State
- Open days: September and October

Head: Since 2000, Mr Andy Knowles (forties). Was deputy head here for 10 years and head of the technology department before that. Has also taught technology in Greenwich and EFL in Greece. He is a widower with two primary aged children. Full of energy and enthusiasm. He is 'utterly wedded to the job and cares passionately about the school,' said a parent, 'but he is also very good at looking at the bigger picture'. Very concerned about the children and can understand their problems. Respected by both staff and children.

Academic Matters: Hampstead got a special mention from the Chief Inspector of Schools in 2001 for its outstanding inspection report, which gave it a grade A for its 1999 GCSE results in relation to similar schools. Its results have now risen and 55 per cent of its students now get five A*-Cs at GCSE. It now takes more disabled pupils, including two with cerebral palsy, and 14 each year with statements of special education need. Nearly half the pupils are bilingual, speaking a total of 48 languages, and there is an enormous ability range. 'We have what we call a mixed economy,' says the head, 'and that is one of our real strengths.' Nearly all the lower school teaching is mixed ability, with some setting from year 10 in maths, science and languages. Heads of departments who want to change the system must have good reasons. Setting in maths, science and languages for GCSE is more or less inevitable because of the syllabus differences between the foundation and higher level papers. 'But when we tried setting in DT it made no difference to high-achieving students, while the low attainers did slightly worse. We stress to staff during interviews that mixed-ability teaching takes far more teacher input and preparation – but most of our teachers like Hampstead because of our philosophy.'

Plenty of young, able, enthusiastic teaching staff, many of whom are studying for further qualifications and many of whom move on to be heads of department elsewhere. 'The teachers are so creative,' said a parent. 'They can achieve the most amazing things – like getting the least academic kids to appreciate Romeo and Juliet.' There is extension work available for bright children as part of the curriculum, 'though a lot depends on the child,' said a parent. 'If they're happy to coast along, they're mostly left to get on with it' and some take maths and a humanity GCSE early. The school gets government funds for its Gifted and Talented programme, which provides workshops and master-classes, though these activities rather go against the school's ethos of providing equal opportunities for everyone and are not emphasised. 'And, of course, some parents are very bitter that their children aren't ever chosen,' said a parent. Some complaints that the lack of homework in the first three years does not prepare children for the rigours of GCSE preparation.

Very effective SEN support on and off the site, with help for disruptive pupils which includes a behaviour modification programme. 'We're very successful with students who couldn't cope elsewhere.' The school stresses that while it is not specialist in any key areas of SEN, it is always willing to acquire the necessary skills in order to support its students. All those with a reasonable attendance record who complete the course work – and this does not apply to a significant minority – are entered for exams. 'We give them a chance right up to the last minute. Some of our students achieve enormously by getting a D.'

There is a open recruitment policy into the sixth form, with one-year vocational courses available to the less academic. A level options include electronics, sociology, media studies and government and politics alongside more conventional subjects. There are intermediate GNVQs in leisure and tourism, health and social care, art and design, business and performing arts; the latter three can also be studied to advanced VCE level. The extra funds brought by technology college status have provided excellent ICT resources which are used across the curriculum.

Games, Options, The Arts: No playing fields on site and pupils are bused to Hendon to play games. However, the school does its best and there's a good range of sports clubs and fixtures. There are three gyms on site, including one used mainly for dance, a swimming pool in the basement of the DT building and two tarmac courts called the Front Cage and Back Cage. Students can also go skiing, camping and orienteering.

Perhaps surprisingly for a technology college, there's lots of emphasis on the creative arts, to a very high standard. Art, music and drama are consistently strong at GCSE.

The school has links with the National Theatre and, with local theatres and drama schools, puts on ambitious musical productions and co-ordinates the National Playwright Commissioning Group which commissions plays for schools from well-known writers. Pupils are very enthusiastic about drama productions they have been involved in and several students have had their plays performed in various London theatres.

Very high calibre art department with an excellent head – over 90 per cent of art A levels have been grade A for some years. There's plenty of diverse artwork on display including textiles and 3D art, and visits to galleries in London, Barcelona, Paris and Venice. Some of the many choirs, orchestras and smaller music groups – which include steel bands, salsa band and boys' a capella choir – do regular tours abroad. The school won a national award for curriculum extension in 2000. There's a full-time youth worker based at the school, which also employs a community manager to run adult ICT courses. 'We hope to be seen as a focal point for community activities.' The school's Children of the Storm charity supports refugee pupils, of whom there are over 100.

Recently became the first comprehensive to win the cup for Best Delegation to the Model United Nations international debating competition, beating the likes of Eton and other top public schools.

Background and Atmosphere: Situated on the Brent and Camden borders, surrounded by a mixture of local authority housing and genteel West Hampstead suburbia. The school buildings are a mixture of red-brick Edwardiana and 1960s pebble-dash concrete, with paved areas somewhat reminiscent of an underground car park, and a pond full of lilies and yellow irises. A mixture of shabby and refurbished, with plenty of computers, extensive modifications to accommodate a severely disabled pupil, and a new library with state-of-the-art multimedia facilities. An excellent new sixth form facility has just been added which was badly needed; also on the head's wish-list is a sports hall. Relaxed atmosphere; while it has its fair share of difficult pupils, many others are intensely loyal, enthusiastic about the drama, the science projects, the support they have had from teachers. 'It's a very caring school,' said a parent.

Pastoral Care and Discipline: This is a very inclusive school, taking on and coping with children who would struggle elsewhere. 'We can do this because our population is so diverse. We don't have that negative critical mass that can sink other schools.' The discipline is quite strict – 'I can honestly say that my children's education has not been disrupted by the disturbed kids,' said a parent. Excellent pastoral care system. Bullying 'is a fact of life in all schools and you need to be vigilant. We encourage parents to look out for signs. Aggressors are dealt with very severely but most bullies have also been bullied in their lives and we provide anger management and behaviour modification courses.' Parents confirm that any bullying is dealt with very quickly – 'and the head of year rang me when she thought my son might be being bullied – when in fact he wasn't.' There's formal and informal peer support; permanent exclusions 'are very rare but likely to be for extreme acts of aggression.' The school has the usual policies on drugs, with exclusion for dealing and an extensive drug education programme. 'It's about making sure children have the right information and having clear, explicit boundaries.'

Pupils and Parents: Immensely diverse, from Hampstead and West Hampstead intelligentsia to those from nearby local authority housing estates. A great ethnic mix, a high proportion of refugee children, children with disabilities and children with learning difficulties. OG: author Zadie Smith.

Entrance: Those with special educational needs get first preference – the school takes 14 with statements each year – then siblings, then pupils living closest, which, in practice, means less than a mile. Anyone already in the school may go on to the sixth form and about 70 per cent do. Most of the rest go on to FE colleges. Around 15-20 students, mostly from abroad, join the sixth form each year. 'We have an open recruitment policy into the sixth form, because we run vocational courses that can give people an extra year to develop.' Students aiming at A levels need six grade Cs at GCSE, with Bs in the subjects they intend to continue. Advanced vocational courses need four grade Cs; the one-year intermediate vocational course has lower requirements. 'We don't like to turn anyone away.'

Exit: About half go to university, including two or three a year to Oxbridge. Many students get into higher education via the vocational route at Hampstead. School feels that this is a particular strength of its sixth form. Others go to further education colleges, training and employment.

Remarks: Successful, inclusive inner-city comprehensive which has its fair share of disaffected as well as high-flying pupils but also has enthusiastic and creative teachers and 'fantastic' performing and visual arts. A parent commented, 'they do their utmost to give everyone the opportunities and make them all feel valued.'

HAMPTON COURT HOUSE BUDDING SENIOR SCHOOL

Linked to Hampton Court House in the Junior section

The Green, Hampton Court Road, East Molesey, Surrey, KT8 9BS

Tel: 020 8943 0889
Fax: 020 8977 5357
E-mail: office@hamptoncourthouse.co.uk
Website: www.hamptoncourthouse.co.uk

• Pupils: boys and girls, some weekly boarding • Ages: 13-14, but rising to 18 • Independent

Remarks: See main (ie junior) school.

HAMPTON SCHOOL

Hanworth Road, Hampton, Middlesex, TW12 3HD

Tel: 020 8979 5526
Fax: 020 8941 7368
E-mail: registrar@hamptonschool.org.uk
Website: www.hamptonschool.org.uk

• Pupils: 1,110 boys; all day • Ages: 11-18 • Size of sixth form: 330 • Inter-denom • Fees: £3,530 • Independent • Open days: Open morning late September. Visitors' afternoons throughout the year

Head: Since 1997, Mr Barry Martin MA MBA FIMgt FRSA (fiftyish). Educated, and later assistant master, at Kingston Grammar School. Bags of experience in independent schools; formerly director of studies at Mill Hill and principal of Liverpool College. Career in economics for Bank of England before teaching. Maintains interest in world of business; author of business studies textbooks and chief examiner A level business studies. Slightly difficult to read, with a bluff manner, but innovative, humanitarian and admired by the boys – a capable hand on the rudder. Married to Fiona, with teenage son (at the school) and daughter at university.

Academic Matters: Fairly exigent academically, increasing pressure on places is pushing up pass mark for 11+ entry test which is, locally, already considered demanding. Head expresses concern that this is the case, with equal pride in the pupils' intellectual prowess. Levels of homework average-high, tempered by emphasis on extra-curricular involvements. 'We have set our face against being a hothouse pure and simple, the main thing is that boys are busy and happy.'

Results are of high standard; typically 99 per cent pass at GCSE A-C (70 per cent grades A*/A) but, unlike some other schools, no one asked to leave as a result of GCSE results alone. For incumbents and newcomers alike, minimum of GCSE A grade in given subject is preferred for A, A/S level options. 99 per cent pass at A level (70 per cent grades A-B). Languages are strong and well represented in A level choices which, otherwise, show science/maths bias. Year 7 boys choose between French, German and Spanish for modern language slot in timetable, Latin is compulsory until year 8. Maximum class size is 25, lower school tends not to exceed 22. Approximately 70 dyslexic/dyspraxic pupils, offered specialist individual support at extra charge.

Games, Options, The Arts: Sport is of a very high quality. Each boy is allowed to choose the sport he wants to play with no compulsion to play a particular game. Visiting physiotherapist. Leading UK rowing school (by medals and representations) – rowing has been established here for over 50 years – also rugby – spawns several professional players. Football likewise. The sports hall is large enough and has a multigym built in. Four well-equipped IT suites. Modern extension houses English, technology and art with art gallery-cum-corridor adjacent to large light studios with plenty of easels and equipment and reserved space for sixth formers. Recently installed, state-of-the-art, design suite – row upon row of inviting, funky Apple Macs. Design technology workshops are spacious and stuffed with tools and heavy machinery. Wonderful library with open access even in school holidays, large, cheerful, well-stocked, enormous selection of newspapers and periodicals – great libraries are rare and it is good to see a boys' school leading the way. Another comparative rarity is its cellular language laboratory.

Opportunities for performance in national-level debating, drama company that travels to Edinburgh Fringe and takes Shakespeare (back!) to Hampton Court. Plenty of music – choir, orchestra and several pop/rock/jazz and chamber music groups. Individual instrument lessons are school-subsidised and boys routinely win scholarships to music colleges. Most clubs and much sport take place during long lunch breaks. Meals are fitted around extra-curricular activities, but so sufficient is the service (school is well-known on the culinary front) that school lunches are taken up by 80 per cent of pupils, despite being completely optional. Exciting field trips to far-flung destinations plus school travel awards and some worthy links with Africa.

Background and Atmosphere: Spacious suburban location, low on traffic. Central building dates from 1939 and, if not glorious, is at least attractive. Unlisted and, therefore, unimpeded, sympathetic extensions have been added over the years. It all hangs together very well; roomy classrooms, new buildings that link smoothly with the old, added floors and corridors that are distinctly unwarren-like and maintenance which is tip-top. Outdoor space in the form of quads and lawns allow for plenty of steam-letting at breaktimes. On-site playing fields (27 acres) are, by London standards, downright magnificent. The new sixth form centre feels quite separate, offering status and privacy to the older boys.

Formerly a state grammar school (went independent in 1975) and about half the pupils come from state primary schools, majority from state-educated parents. This said, in atmosphere, school makes a good fist of resembling a traditional public school of long-standing – blazers and flannels, jacketed and tied sixth formers, Old Hamptonians' Association, flourishing cadet corps, burgeoning rowing, shooting and field sports societies; all very 'Tom Brown's Schooldays'.

Not surprisingly, given the head's background, there's a sharp business-minded approach to the running of the school. Member of staff dedicated to PR and fund-raising from alumni and other corporate sponsors. Semi-funded fabulous performing arts centre is the project in progress. Super-slick lunch-time programme of speakers (high-profile Old Boys, left/right politicians and others) keeps boys enthralled and ensures oodles of local press coverage. Upper school divides into two competing entrepreneurial businesses with laurels going annually to the most profitable enterprise. Valentine's Day roses selling well on day of visit! Omni-supportive careers department, responsible for comprehensive handbook, UCAS pamphlet, annual careers convention, high-profile work placement programme and 'mock' interviews. Much emphasis on achievement post-Hampton (after all they may need you to dig deep towards another extension one day!). Ex-pupils' university successes are published back to back with current year's A level results. Illustrious Old Boys include lions of industry, lawyers, politicians and the like.

Pastoral Care and Discipline: Youngish staff with plenty of female role models – one of the deputy heads, head of modern languages, head of maths and head of art – are all women. Proximity to The Lady Eleanor Holles (adjacent premises, some shared facilities, drama and music, same bus service) ensures all-round healthy access to the opposite sex. Informal support pyramid whereby newcomers are paired with a mentor in the upper school. Boys and parents are encouraged to approach form tutors and heads of year with any concerns and pupils rate the 'very friendly nurse' as a good back-up. Ready access to counsellors. Plenty of commendations and merit marks and all-round opportunities to shake the head's hand. On the other side of the coin, detentions, work clinics and suspensions for serious infractions of school rules. Stringent illegal substance policy – expulsion is a serious threat.

Pupils and Parents: Wide west London and Surrey catchment area, bolstered by extensive school bus network. Good mix of boys – not at all pushy and precocious – and an unpretentious parental set 'You can tip up there in your anorak.' All faiths represented and celebrated according to the head.

Entrance: 120 join at 11 (85 per cent from state primaries) and 60 or so at 13 (65 per cent required score in Common Entrance). Majority of 13+ candidates are pre-selected, sitting school's test at 11, success in which reserves a place. Advance place examination available for 10 year olds, sufficient precocious intellectual ability sees exemption from the scramble for places at 11. Failures at this test are encouraged to re-sit for unprejudiced reconsideration at 11. To join at sixth form, there is an absolute requirement of 6 GCSEs at A or A*.

Exit: Almost all to university, up to 25 to Oxbridge. Oxford, Cambridge and Leeds the three most popular universities in terms of numbers – impressive.

Money Matters: Academic, all-rounder, art, music and choral scholarships are available to candidates demonstrating exceptional promise. A limited number of means-tested bursaries may be offered by the head.

Remarks: High-achieving, well-respected, unpretentious, modern meets traditional independent boys' school. Reasonably large (but not expanding) numbers accommodate a refreshingly wide range of personalities/interests. Possibly not for trembly snowdrops or non-joiners, however. Should your 10 year old son need convincing of the school's merits, note that Hampton once fielded a team in the BBC's 'Robot Wars'!

HARRIS ACADEMY

Perth Road, Dundee, DD2 1NL

Tel: 01382 435 700
Fax: 01382 435 701
E-mail: harris@dundeecity.gov.uk
Website: www.harris-academy.com

• Pupils: 1250 boys and girls, all day • Ages: 11-18 • Size of sixth form: 290 • Non-denom • State

Rector: Since 1997, Mr John Thewliss (the name comes from the North of England) BSc PGCE (fifties) who was educated at Broadhurst High in Motherwell, read geography at Glasgow University and did his PGCE at Hamilton College. Previously depute head at Dalziel High in Motherwell and before that depute head at Wallace High. V experienced, a chap who knows the area, married, with two children, his daughter is up and flying and his son is about to take up residence at Dundee University (and as the halls of residence are opposite Harris Academy, he is dreading the bags of washing). Charming, articulate and fun, 'love this job, I cannot believe how lucky I am to have it. 'Everyone thinks I am nuts'. It's not so easy to get good staff, fairly high turnover, and this problem is reflected in the 2004 HMI report 'Overall, the quality of learning and teaching was variable'.

Academic Matters: Well above average: no particular bias, but with around fifty per cent of all pupils leaving after standard grades (most go to Dundee College) it is a little difficult to give an accurate picture. Masses of computers etc, all heavily used with waiting systems in place if need be. Impressive library with yet more machines, class teaching on computers as well as IT. Pupils do keyboarding and basic ICT skills and use the skills in presentations: power point, sound, film-making, animated flow charts and present to the rest of the class. Max class size (legal limit) 33, but down to 20 for practical subjects. First couple of years all study Eng, maths, science, hist, geog, mod studies, home economics (magic), technology (great etc etc) plus one mod lang: French, German or Spanish. Latin on hand, but no Greek. Streaming after first year when a fast track for English, maths and mod langs comes into force. Teaching disciplines are a combination of individual, small group, whole class teaching and discussion. Strong learning support (but see below).

School attracts a number of ethnic minorities whose parents are billeted to the local uni, hospital or area, 14 currently in the school. Russian, Bengali, Urdu and Cantonese the most frequently spoken at home – native speakers can take these at standard grade. EAL is taught by the special educational needs team, and the HMI thought they were a bit stretched. Pupil support staff co-teach where necessary in class, but 'such support may result in a revised elaborated or alternative curriculum and include individual or small group tuition'. Supported study includes homework clubs, and a teacher is in waiting early on Tuesday mornings or Thursday evenings to help pupils with problems. Good encouragement too, for the more gifted. Terrific use of external facilities.

Eight standard grades for all as far as possible. Langs, humanities and modern studies above average and good showing in the Scottish and UK Maths Challenges; ditto the Dundee Enterprising Maths competition. Wish list includes re-vamped labs on the top floor. Good diversity, inspiring programme of lectures from outside speakers. Serious advice for all pupils on which road to take. Good choice post Standard with the option of intermediates 1 and 2 as well as Highers and Advanced Highers in a raft of subjects, plus tourism and hospitality at standard grades. Regular assessments and good parental feedback.

Autism: School is an important cog in the education of children in the autistic spectrum and, since 2000, takes ten pupils (never less) by request and allocation from the west of Dundee and the city itself (Morgan Academy takes those who live East of Dundee). These pupils are scattered across the age range, and school only accepts the next pupil when space becomes available. 'Lovely laddies' (mainly boys, but that's the nature of autism) all have individual educational programmes which are regularly monitored and amended. Some are totally supported individually and educated in the base (only one currently); others attend mainstream lessons, but may be entirely supported in class, or allowed to attend certain classes for a short period – eg physics: in mainstream for six weeks, and then back to the unit. Most take standard grade maths and all have speech and oral communication. School OK for physical handicaps – 'only one lift, but there are ways of moving round the school'. The base is popular with 'normal kids' who choose to join those in the autistic spectrum at lunchtime – a reverse integration. Many of these pupils will go on to Elmwood College in Fife, where the school has close links.

Games, Options, The Arts: Games fields half a mile away, gyms (still labelled boys and girls) on site – but used by all, ditto swimming pool. Large sports complex off-site.

PE timetabled, and impressive line-up of games (extracurricular) but including the v popular rugby, hockey, football for boys and girls, athletics, basketball (enthusiastic coach) water polo etc. Art, as you might imagine, deeply computer-linked: ceramics, painting, ICT, no CAD as such but the facility to use computer based design. Computer suite in art room, home economics, metalwork area, all computer based and hands on. Other schools please note. Mass of instrumentalists, music strong and popular with ceilidhs and rock concerts (including FPs) – huge charitable input, 'everything and anything'. Choirs, bands, orchestras. Popular theatre club, though not available as an exam subject despite pupils' requests. Outstanding debating, thrashing all comers; vibrant YE and truly popular D of E, with a whacking list of Gold, Silver and Bronze successes. Not the longest list of clubs we have ever seen, but thoroughly active, mass of trips abroad: humanities with proper exchanges popular.

Background and Atmosphere: Founded in 1885 and 'the oldest public school in Dundee', moved to the handsome granite building in 1930, school then added on a hotchpotch of flat-roofed excrescences in the '60s. Thirties class rooms elegant and airy with corridors wide enough for children and their bags to pass: '60s nasties – apart from the inevitable flat roof drip – boast beastly narrow passages, scarred by teenage book bags. Stunning views to the south, with really quite a lot of playground. Tiny dining hall in basement, next to library, students wait their turn in a surprisingly orderly queue at the 'red line'. Work experience at 14; some – less academic – pupils can study vocational subjects; Access courses in communication and maths or apprentice-shops locally.

Free school meals (but the cafeteria is cashless). Help with school uniform (skool provides the basics ex-stock) and trips. Grants available. If pupils stay for fifth year the odds are they will stay on to sixth: five Highers the norm; school qualifies for £40 educational maintenance allowance for those staying on after 16, which is a carrot.

Pastoral Care and Discipline: Sixth formers buddy first formers- 'very protective and good anti-bullying strategy'. Strong PSE reinforced by RME. Pupils are divided into four houses, and the pupil support strategy is handled by house representatives, each house having two guidance and two support-for-learning teachers. Defined sanction system: if pupils disobey one of five clearly defined rules then they 'may be excluded for up to three days' for continuous disobedience and head will meet with the parents. He 'is not prepared for disruptive children or anti-social behaviour' to permeate the school and would much rather produce 'decent sensible sensitive citizens' who are a lot 'more use than an anti-social chemist'. To this end (and this is a first for us) he has installed a splendid reward system: (Pavlov eat your heart out). Each pupil (who has the school code drilled into them during their first week 'so they can't say they don't know what is expected of them') is given a personal plan which must be stamped at the end of each lesson. Pupils earning 250 marks are awarded a certificate, can skip an afternoon's school and see a film of their choice – and get a Mars Bar. 500 stamps qualify for a silver certificate and a free ticket for Megabowl, gold equals a trip to Alton Towers and a certain amount of parent in-put and platinum a three day trip to London. Platinum winners have to have their cards stamped after almost every lesson to qualify. Head just loves these trips. Links with top year of feeder primaries, guidance staff and teacher visit regularly (HMI reckoned the school 'could try harder') and first year pupils all decamp with their teachers to Falkland Youth Centre for bonding and team-building stuff.

Pupils and Parents: A mixed bunch, some here briefly, a caring bunch of kids, charming and well-mannered. (The lure of London perhaps?) Good parental support and school booklet encourages this. Farmers, business people as well as the uni and hospitals.

Entrance: Always full. Pupils come from five main feeders with a couple of dozen placement requests annually. Certain amount of logistical movement. Standard rules about addresses and siblings.

Exit: Either post Standard Grade, or (usually) post sixth form. Some 70 odd per cent to unis, mostly to Scotland but the occasional trickle to Oxbridge. Inspired careers advice.

Remarks: Inspirational. An outstanding head, pity he can't inspire the building with as much enthusiasm as the children.

THE HARRODIAN SCHOOL

Linked to Harrodian Preparatory and Pre-preparatory schools in the Junior section

Lonsdale Road, London, SW13 9QN

Tel: 020 8748 6117
Fax: 020 8563 7327
E-mail: admin@harrodian.com
Website: www.harrodian.com

• Pupils: 812 • Ages: 4-18 • Size of sixth form: 70: 35/35 boys/girls • non-denom • Fees: Pre-prep £2,944; prep £3,306; senior school £3,786; sixth £4,146 • Independent • Open days: Regular small group tours. Phone for appointment. 11+ open afternoon, October

Headmaster (Mr Hooke); Principal (Mr Thomson): Since 1999, Mr James Hooke BSc Hons PGCE, a geographer, mid-forties. Mr Hooke was director of studies and deputy head for four years prior to taking over as head so he has been at the heart of the building of this remarkable school from the start. Quietly spoken and serious, Mr Hooke produces a first impression of an eager sixth former but this quickly gives way to a sense of a man intensely proud of the school he has helped to form and of a very focussed, though understated, professionalism and pleasure in the achievement.

Before the Harrodian, Mr Hooke spent three years at St John's School in Buenos Aires and it is perhaps this experience which informs the internationalism he sees as so important and which is reflected in the very mixed backgrounds of his pupils. Mr Hooke is the headmaster, deals with the curriculum and the day-to-day running of this fast-developing school. He is a head who clearly knows his children. The school also has its principal, Mr Peter Thomson. Mr Thomson was headmaster in the early years until his 'retirement' in 1999 but, if he is in any sense retired, it is far from obvious in his intimate involvement with all aspects of school life and his clear delight in what the school has become in so short a time. If Mr Hooke is the head in all the usual senses, Mr Thomson is the benign eminence grise, dealing, perhaps, with the more public face of the school among various other responsibilities he is clearly happy to shoulder. A former head of history and surmaster at St Paul's Boys, yards up the road, this is a highly experienced, more 'old-school', type of master who seems to have taught, during a long career, everyone one meets on the tour, and many of their parents too. An enthusiast, Mr Thomson pays fulsome tribute to the founders of the school in all aspects of their vision and approach.

Academic Matters: 2004 saw the pioneer sixth formers leave for higher education with much success at A level. As the school has grown, it has become academically more selective. Concurrently, fewer parents have seen it just as a prep and taken their children out at Common Entrance. Nonetheless those who do are winning places at good schools elsewhere.

Results are now making the dramatic improvements we predicted some years ago. 2005 GCSE results included 97 per cent with A*-C, and 49 per cent with A*/A grades and eight pupils scored all A*/As. Impressive stuff. Pupil numbers at this level have more than doubled in the last four years and results show steady improvement. Modern languages are essential to the school's being, and all learn French to a more-or-less bi-lingual level, taught wholly by native speakers. Other popular languages include Italian and Spanish; Russian and German are also taught. Japanese, Chinese etc are available by arrangement. It is a rare pleasure to find a school where a command of modern languages is seen as central to civilised life.

The curriculum is a mainstream one with all traditional subjects on offer. Classical Civilisation has been introduced 2004 at GCSE; Latin and Greek survive. Media studies and business studies also popular options. ICT in two good rooms, everyone has a lesson a week and is encouraged to use it in other academic areas. GCSE and A/S options. Senior school and sixth form centre fully networked for laptops etc and science facilities recently updated with new whiteboards. School not rushing into this area. An appealing suite of four rooms nicely tucked away at the top of the main building houses strong SEN dept – mostly for one-to-one. 'Support staff work closely with mainstream staff,' says principal, and explains that, with so much sport on offer, school can afford to withdraw pupils from a lesson or so for SEN or, with the less academic children, from Latin. 'We like to think we can cope with mild dyslexia or dyspraxia but we have to be confident they can survive on the academic curriculum,' says head.

Overall, good and promising better academically. Head has aim of upping the overall performance and, increasingly, with the pick of the local clientele, he won't have a problem.

Games, Options, The Arts: You'd be forgiven for imagining that the builders of the old Harrodian Country Club knew that one day it would become a school. Or for being pretty impressed with the vision that has transformed an old squash court into a good modern dance studio, the ballroom – art deco skylight and all – into the school hall and theatre, the kitchen into a library and so on. This school has no sports hall or designated gym – maybe a drawback for some – but it has, half a mile from Hammersmith, 25 acres of pitches, courts, play areas and gardens. Sport is seen as central to the school day. 'We have a very good sports dept', stresses head. 'I'm very proud of what they've achieved. Everyone does sport daily and even the youngest are taught by highly qualified staff – not just a granny in a track suit', says head. All the usual sports on offer as well as lots of dance. Small but heated outdoor pool in super courtyard setting. Art in various art rooms – not over-spacious and pleasantly cluttered with variety of lively work. GCSE class were thoughtfully painting and varnishing bottles when we visited and some textile and fashion work, somewhat haphazardly on display. Good, careful drawing done lower in the school. Music school opened in 2003 provides flexible small recital/theatre studio with fixed raked seating and other facilities including teaching/practice rooms. New 'high energy' head of music set to build on recent 'huge progress'. All usual instruments taught to increasingly high levels. Bands allowed to record CDs on site and make their own photographed cover – very popular, of course. Battle of the Bands competition judged by celeb from music world. Performing of various kinds going on contentedly in pairs or small groups everywhere we went. Extra-curricular options include board games, dance, film, music ensembles and umpteen bands, computer club and 'animation' – many of which happen after school.

Background and Atmosphere: Unusual to say the least. Not a very 1990s idea – buy an old country club on the banks of the urban Thames and turn it into a co-ed school with a bias to modern languages and civilised values. Preserve the faux-neo-classical architectural style, add to it seamlessly with first class new-build and imaginative, charming features eg a pool in a cloister with ambulatory, and embellish it tastefully with any number of inessential but elegant and stylish jeux d'esprit – little fountains and stone vases, olive trees, balustrades, loggias and parterres, York stone courtyards and reception areas, real carpet, real gardens, real three course lunches, yet manage not to be precious or to spoil the pleasant and unpretentious children lucky enough to start life here. Space is used to create large halls and atria, a feeling of space everywhere except in some of the smaller teaching rooms/studios/labs which would be cramped with more than one or two more children. This place began life in the 1920s as the resort of staff from Harrods – clearly Mr H wanted his employees to have a taste of the grand style. After a tri-partite bidding match in 1993, a couple with vision, Sir Alford and Lady Houstoun-Boswall, he the eighth baronet and she an American multi-lingual teacher, headmistress and restorer of historical buildings, bought the site (beating St Paul's Boys and the Lycée to it) and proceeded to create a dream – a co-ed school run according to civilised values in a civilised environment to produce relaxed, happy children. School has expanded up and down – now taking from 4 to 18 though it began with ambitions to be no more than a prep. Existing prep and pre-prep part of the whole school in all respects – all share facilities though designated areas for younger pupils all purpose-built, thoughtful and charming. Mini 3-piece suites abound in social areas – velvety sofas and clubland chairs. Thus the school is the newest of its kind in London and unique in many of its qualities. A visitor chances her luck – there are no signs directing you to reception – or anywhere else. There are no bells or buzzers, children are smart but uniform is not a religion – there is a dress code. Few restrictions, 'children are civilised, cultured, accepting and disciplined without huge numbers of rules', says head. 'If the school had a motto, it would be 'Support The Individual', he thinks and parental noises convey that it does exactly that. Head and parents agree about the strong pastoral support, the 'fantastic' success in integrating new children – whatever their educational background, the general happiness. Staff seem to love working here – 'it's such a joy,' said a prep school teacher, in passing. It's certainly about as civilised an environment as one could find – perhaps not wholly surprising in leafy Barnes – the river on one side and large, detached houses on the other side of the school site – but there are older, less congenial schools taking from similar clientele not a million miles away so something is different here. It's not trendy liberal either – conventional and traditional in many things including the teaching style and the curriculum.

Pastoral Care and Discipline: A carefully structured system which works. High teacher pupil ratio which helps create the excellent relationships the school fosters. Parents are lavish in their praise,'...it's very much for the individual...so positive about each child...seems to find the best in everyone...such good support throughout the exam period...'. Few discipline problems, though, says head, 'children who push too far at the boundaries wouldn't fit in.' Zero tolerance for drugs and no safe haven here for those who have been expelled elsewhere. 'I have expelled children for drugs and wouldn't hesitate to do so again. We try to deal with such matters with PSHE and advice and try never to get into that situation.'

Pupils and Parents: Very middle class, professional, mostly very local though with very international – mostly European – origins. The cosmopolitan west London area not yet really reflected in the ethnic mix of the intake but this presumably only a matter of time and word getting out.

Entrance: Now has huge waiting lists for pre-prep. Non-selective. Strong sibling policy. Competitive at 8+ and 11+ and for occasionals. 'I will interview lots,' says head, 'and try to find children who are happy and have something to offer. I don't just take the top twenty off the list.' Takes few more at CE. Entry to the sixth now requires 6 A/s at GCSE and As in A level subjects.

Exit: A decreasing few at CE to trad day and boarding schools eg St Paul's Boys, King's Wimbledon, Marlborough, Eton, Bryanston, Haileybury and a bunch to Stowe. A few at 16 to tutorial colleges. Thereafter – it seems likely – to range of further education – good universities and art colleges.

Money Matters: Fees pretty average for location and what is on offer. No scholarships or bursaries.

Remarks: When it opened, school developed a local reputation for being for 'the thick rich' but this has been rapidly dispelled. An unusual, gentle and happy place, with a liberal but purposeful atmosphere, harmonious relationships, an exciting present in which everyone takes pride and a promising future in which everyone takes an interest. Set to gain from local Latymer Upper's becoming co-ed – more clever boys looking for a good school – and from the secret now being out that something rare and special is happening up river.

HARROGATE LADIES' COLLEGE

Linked to Highfield Prep School in the Junior section

Clarence Drive, Harrogate, North Yorkshire, HG1 2QG

Tel: 01423 504 543

Fax: 01423 568 893

E-mail: enquire@hlc.org.uk

Website: www.hlc.org.uk

• Pupils: 350 girls; 190 board, 160 day • Ages: 10-18 • Size of sixth form: 120 • C of E • Fees: Senior boarding £5,900; day £3,500 • Independent • Open days: May bank holiday Monday

Headmistress: Since 1996, Dr Margaret Joan Hustler BSc PhD (fifties), biochemist. Previously head of St Michael's, a missionary foundation in Surrey, prior to that deputy head at Atherley School, also taught at Lady Eleanor Holles. Well liked by students and staff, accessible approachable and interested. Described as a good egg and excellent leader. Aims to develop confident girls, equipped and able to cope with the challenges they'll face in life. Born and bred in Harrogate married to David Wraight, the school's estate manager. Has eight children, 5 girls and 3 boys aged between 10 and 21, two currently at HLC.

Academic Matters: Improving, results are regularly in top five nationally. 97 per cent A* to C pass rate at GCSE. Strength is with sciences but modern languages are fine – normally only the odd D at GCSE otherwise all A* to C passes. Only a handful (3 or 4 per language) opt for modern languages at A level but achieve very good results. Girls seem to enjoy the subjects and get on well with teaching staff and language assistants. Teaching is very good – friendly good-humoured staff. Art & design, history, and design & technology particularly strong too. Overseas students encouraged to sit exams in their native language and despite lack of additional tuition results are extremely good. EAL students take IELTS rather than GCSE English. 77 per of A levels graded A or B. Computer facilities excellent, touch typing and office skills taught to all. AVCE business course equivalent to two full A levels and accepted for university entrance offered as an alternative to traditional route. Young Enterprise a regular and successful feature. Good and stimulating facilities, displays everywhere – a striking balance of pupil work and thought provoking material. Energetic, competent and caring staff, lessons an inspiring blend of instruction, innovation and investigation. Good provision for a range of special needs and specific learning difficulties including dyslexia and deafness. Class size averages 18 in lower school. Reports always discussed with head or tutor prior to being sent home.

Games, Options, The Arts: Sport, the life-blood of the school, is keenly pursued by all. Lacrosse ('Lackie') is king (at expense of other sports?) Girls are frequently the northern champions and a good many achieve representative honours. Super much-used sports facilities include plenty of tennis and badminton courts, multi-gym, 25-metre pool and an enormous indoor general-purpose court. The extra-curricular menu embraces sub-aqua, riding, golf, windsurfing and ski trips as well as keen D of E and masses of charity and community work. School also boasts a flourishing ham radio station (callsign GX0HCA), historic triumph was a hook-up with the Mir space station and the International Space Station.

Dedicated music house accommodates ensembles galore. Majority of girls learning an instrument or two and the choir regularly features on BBC Radio, at cathedral services across the land and on tours, eastern Europe being a favoured destination. AS and A level theatre studies on offer with plays and productions acted out in the suitably equipped drama studio. Curriculum supported by regular trips to concerts, theatre and cinema. Many girls take LAMDA lessons (honours and distinctions the norm). Careers education taken seriously, two weeks work experience for all followed by presentation and dinner.

Background and Atmosphere: School founded in 1893 on a nearby site and was one of the Allied Schools. Within walking distance of the busy town centre, in the heart of Harrogate's leafy prime real estate, originally part of the Duchy of Lancaster. The pleasant Victorian mock-Tudor buildings with sympathetic additions blend gently with the locality. C of E (own chapel, resounding hymns et al) in small doses for all without exception. Super sixth form centre in main school complete with common rooms, study centre, kitchens, AV room etc. The six well-presented boarding houses each have generously sized attractive study bedrooms, a common room centred round the TV, kitchen and games room.

Up to four share a room in lower school but most sixth formers have their own room. Friendly comfortable feel, not snobbish or overtly feminine. Girls are encouraged to mix across the ages with a buddy system operating for new pupils. Upper sixth housed in Tower – a half way house between school and university where pupils prepare and eat breakfast and a couple of evening meals in house and have greater freedom than lower down the school (team building exercises at start of upper sixth aid the bonding process). Flexi and weekly boarding as well as day and full boarding, weekends brimming with trips and activities. Food improving but often stodgy and unimaginative, however chocolate machines and toast galore in houses compensate. Residential staff and girls dine together in main house, self-service at lunch, grace and formal sit-down at other times.

Pastoral Care and Discipline: Manners strictly monitored. At 16+ girls are allowed out one night a week. Occasional links with other schools but not into creating artificial exposure to boys. Drugs and similar problems uncommon and treated with firmness, head retains discretion, expulsions rare. Health centre, specialist counsellor, teaching female chaplain, tutors and staff all on hand to help if things go wrong.

Pupils and Parents: Mostly from Harrogate and the environs. Number of boarders from overseas, including Hong Kong, USA, China, Thailand, Spain, Germany. Buddhists, Jews and Muslims in the school. Parents predominantly from the professions, farming and self-employment – popular with the Services. Turns out informed, assured, polite and articulate girls, cooperative rather than competitive. Strong OG network, including Anne McIntosh MP, Jenny Savill (author), Juliet Bremner and Henrietta Butler.

Entrance: Own entrance test (maths, English, verbal reasoning) taken on assessment day together with reports from previous school. Main entry points are 11, 13 and 16 but school flexible. Highfield Prep is the linked feeder school. Minimum seven GCSEs at grade C or above required for entry to sixth form.

Exit: Trickle to Oxbridge, otherwise to a widespread selection of universities including Durham, Imperial and Leeds. Lack of boys cited as main reason for handful of pupils leaving at 16.

Money Matters: Academic scholarships of up to 50 per cent of fees and a couple of music scholarships at 11 or 12 with two or three at sixth form and discounts for siblings and Services.

Remarks: A lovely school providing a happy, caring environment and offering a myriad of opportunities. Suits wide range – bright sporty girl, the spirited, independent free thinker and those who need TLC or nurturing to realise their potential. Weak academics and couch potatoes should look elsewhere.

HARROW SCHOOL

1 High Street, Harrow on the Hill, Middlesex, HA1 3HT

Tel: 020 8872 8007
Fax: 0208 8872 8012
E-mail: hm@harrowschool.org.uk
Website: www.harrowschool.org.uk

- Pupils: 800 boys (all board) • Ages: 13-18 • Size of sixth form: 350 • C of E (but 135 RCs) • Fees: £7,875 per term
- Independent • Open days: One Saturday every month

Head Master: Since 1999, Mr Barnaby Lenon BA PGCE (fiftyish) who was educated at Eltham College in London during its direct grant days, read geography at Keble, Oxford and did his PGCE at St John's in Cambridge – a double Oxbridge graduate then. Previously taught at Sherborne, followed by thirteen years at Eton, Highgate where he was deputy head, and head of Trinity School, Croydon. 'A meteoric rise,' said another, presumably jealous, head. Still super, still a mover and a shaker – he has appointed 8 new housemasters out of 11 and 11 new heads of departments – an overall change of twenty five per cent since his arrival. Not bad for starters. He is also charming with a puckish sense of humour and gives his answers with measured reasoning.

He has taken a view on all aspects of the school and is asking everyone, 'can things be done better?' hoping for the answer, 'yes', 'so that we can move on'. His ambition is to make sure that 'everybody makes Harrow their first-choice school'. A first-class school with full boarding (and no little trips to London on Sundays) so that the school can run a full timetable on Sundays, orchestra practice, play rehearsals and the like. Sixth form pupils can earn extra Sundays out, otherwise it's exeats only. Keen on yomping through the desert, he is married with two young daughters.

Academic Matters: Takes a fairly wide spectrum of able boys, 'with the top fifty getting three or four A grades at A level and the bottom fifty getting ABB on average'. Sixty per cent pass mark at CE – up from 55. All must take at least ten subjects at GCSE, including one science subject, which makes for better all-rounders, of course. Sparky young common room. Like policemen, they all seemed to this editor to be about sixteen. As one beak once put it, they 'all look like KGB agents: thick necks, mid-twenties and three piece suits.' Usually eight or nine sets per subject, with more pupils in the higher sets than the lower ones, max class size fourteen for A level subjects and myriad of subjects and combinations available.

Head proud of Harrow's climb up the league table list but prouder still of their showing in the Durham University value added table. Popularity stakes still rate maths, English, geography, chemistry, history, economics and physics, with languages coming up fast. Generally ten to twenty pupils get A grades in five subjects, thirty get As in four. GCSE results equally fine. Not bad for a school which goes for all-rounders rather than nerds. Vast array of languages on offer, ranging from the predictable French, Spanish or German to the esoteric Chinese, Japanese, Russian, Portuguese and Italian – native speakers abound. Classicists abound too, with classical civilisation as well as conventional Latin and Greek. Regular trips all over for all language students – both the quick and the dead.

Excellent dyslexia provision, with small dedicated staff and help given to those whose native language is not English to gain fluency.

Games, Options, The Arts: Awesomely successful rugby teams; 16 out of the 18 teams that played Eton last year won their matches and two national players in their midst, playing for England and Wales. Traditionally and actually very strong on all main games including Harrow football and keen with a great many house competitions and special ties for everything. 'Competitive to the eyeballs,' said one visiting parent. One of the last two Lord's cricket schools and this year produced the captain of the England under 15 cricket side. Smart indoor sports complex with magnificent 'ducker' (pool). Huge, brand new tennis and athletics complex. 'Too much emphasis on sport,' said one disenchanted youth – plus ça change.

Popular CCF and pipe band. School got six out of the fifty army scholarships on offer last year. Successful Royal Marine section, with regular success in the Pringle Challenge and a tough trip to Borneo last year. D of E, plus community work. The spectacular Ryan Theatre – school claims one of the best seen in any school, though seats a little too short even for this editor – has given drama a boost. Jolly professional productions with girls from North London Collegiate and Heathfield. The Speech Room (Burgess in a restrained mode) is annually transformed into a Globe Theatre replica for the Shakespeare production. 'As a non-sports player in a sporty school the theatre got me through the five long years'.

Music now outstanding with the choir giving performances in the Vatican, St Paul's and Westminster Abbey as well as regularly in school and, joy of joys, 'we now no longer give concerts with no audiences'. Amongst winners of National Chamber Music for Schools Competition for last four years – a sign of real strength.

Sculpture has moved out of the Art Schools down near the squash courts, vibrant and different. AS pupils' work was being displayed when we visited, some very exciting, some pretty peculiar and some downright daft – (veggies rotting on a frame) – but all imaginative and interestingly carried out. Ditto art itself. Some of the art was spectacular and some of the canvases just ridiculously large, one offering, stuck in place with drawing pins, covered the entire wall of the art room. Good to see such variety. The design technology centre – The Churchill Schools – possibly the most impressive we have come across, is light and airy with teaching rooms flanking the enormous machine room. CAD/CAM, robots, technogames and graphics as you might expect and of course everything singing and dancing here: the newest of Harrow's buildings. An enormous number of extras in other areas, this is a rich school, including a farm with longhorn cattle.

Background and Atmosphere: Founded in 1527 under a Royal Charter from Good Queen Bess, to a local landowner, John Lyon, on a site of some three hundred acres on the hill. John Lyon's endowment originally included a requirement to 'maintain the road between London and Harrow'. All this has now changed, although funds from the bequest helped start the nearby John Lyon School, and the endowment is now used to support other charities.

The school straddles the High Street with collegiate buildings on either side and crossings are now manned by guardians in yellow jackets at break time and the road is criss-crossed by effective calming measures. The oldest buildings date from 17th century, worlds away from the nearby Betjemanesque, and a mellow, mainly red-brick oasis of tranquillity in a sea of suburbia. Impressive Gilbert Scott chapel, used by 'all Christians', the RCs hold their own service there and, indeed, have their own priest. The Vaughan Library (also Gilbert Scott, as, we suspect, is the rather handsome pillar box outside with a splendid topknot) has been recently revamped, now providing a much-used, three and a half floored, boy-inspiring learning area. Integrated careers library and mini-teaching areas. Much used, boaters were scattered all round the place when we visited, with chequered bands for those in the cricket XI. Balconies reach the highest level and the older reading booths have been swept away. IT on every level, both intra- and internet. Good collection of antiquities in the museum and fine watercolours – mostly 19th century. The quality of modern buildings is outstanding and should be seen by other schools for non-carbuncular possibilities. The older teaching blocks have been mostly redesigned to give spacious and light classrooms.

Magnificent uniform with 'bluers' (blue jackets), braid, straw boaters, tail coats on Sundays, with monitors wearing bow ties – not to mention top hats and sticks – an inspiration for Coco Chanel who had an Old Harrovian lover. Pecking order keenly felt by boys – the boarding houses themselves have an ancient order – and it is the houses themselves that matter rather than the housemaster – though all this, says the head, is changing – slowly. Very male atmosphere often remarked upon by visiting mothers – traditional with a very keen entrepreneurial streak. Exeats every three weeks, though more can be earned by sixth formers for good work, otherwise Sundays particularly are filled with choir practice, rehearsals, outings and inter-house games.

Houses now totally refurbished, most share double rooms for the first two years, followed by study bedrooms; no dormitories.

Pastoral Care and Discipline: Excellent pastoral care: an outside survey is carried out by an external agency each December to check on undetected problems. Each boy is quizzed. If a problem is found then, 'immediate action is taken'. Head felt recent problems to have been, 'perceived bullying by small boys of other small boys'. Weekly health education in every house. Masses of back-up here, house masters and their wives, house tutors, and matrons. Pupils can be sacked (though rarely) for being 'off the Hill' without permission, dishonesty or (irredeemable) sloth – 'about three or four a year'. Outstanding 'Way of Life' course still continues, with discussion groups including girls from three local schools who reflect on – amongst other things – 'their experience of the environment, society, ourselves and God' – under the guidance of specially trained counsellors. School also has a consultant psychiatrist on call.

Pupils and Parents: One of the rare schools that can truthfully claim to be truly international. Long traditions of exotic foreigners, including maharajas and royalty, Lots from Scotland and Ireland, loads of fiercely loyal Old Harrovian families; visiting rabbi and own RC chaplain. Strong links with trade, old landed and aristocratic families as well as first time buyers. Polite, with a trace of arrogance, is the norm. Long and distinguished list of old boys including seven prime ministers, Churchill, Baldwin et al; plus Byron, Peel, Trollope, Palmerston, Galsworthy, Terrence Rattigan, King Hussein of Jordan, the Nizam of Hyderabad, the Duke of Westminster, Evelyn de Rothschild, the Fox brothers, Julian Metcalfe (who founded Pret à Manger) Bill Deedes,

Lord (Robin) Butler, Lord Guthrie, Sir Peter de la Billière, Alain de Botton, Richard Curtis and James Blunt.

Entrance: Names down by age of ten ideally, no longer for a particular house – this changed in 2001; sixty per cent pass mark at CE, and lists well over-subscribed. Pre-selection test (verbal reasoning) twenty-three months before entry. Some places reserved for late developers and late applicants.

Exit: Gap years are popular, twenty-five or so annually to Oxbridge, otherwise Bristol, Edinburgh, Newcastle, plus Durham, Oxford Brookes, Exeter plus a tranche to the American unis. No particular bias though the humanities have given place to science, arts and social sciences.

Money Matters: Forty scholarships per year. 'Everyone thinks we're well endowed, but we're not well endowed,' emphasises the head. We would say, all is relative. The school does indeed appear to be rich (and has lots of very rich Old Boys) and definitely comfortable with a sense of quality - extremely well kept, freshly painted and no ugly rubbish bins or lurking crisp bags. School had a huge unbreakable fund rolling up for the upkeep of the road between Harrow and London - a task now undertaken by others - the income now goes to local charities.

Remarks: An outstandingly good, all-round school, with a healthy waiting list. Has upped the entrance requirements, sad to see. Does well, does the boys well, couldn't do better.

HEADINGTON SCHOOL

Linked to Headington Preparatory School in the Junior section

Headington Road, Oxford, Oxfordshire, OX3 7TD

Tel: 01865 759 100
Fax: 01865 759 113
E-mail: admissions@headington.org
Website: www.headington.org

- Pupils: 695 girls; day, weekly and full boarders • Ages: 11-18
- Size of sixth form: 225 • C of E • Fees: Day £3,230; weekly boarding £5,920; full boarding £6,150. Prep school £1,575 - £2,360 • Independent • Open days: October

Head: Since 2003, Mrs Anne Coutts BSc MEd (late forties). Educated at King's High School, Warwick and Apsley Grammar, followed by Warwick University, where she read microbiology and virology. Research posts at Oxford Institute of Virology and Nuffield Institute, then taught at Trent College and Edgbaston C of E College. Vastly experienced. Headington is her third headship – previously head at Sutton High School and before that Eothen School in Caterham.

Married to C of E clergyman and has two grown-up daughters. Outgoing, warm and super-efficient. Very much a hands-on head, she lives in a house in the grounds, lunches alongside girls in the school dining room and teaches chemistry to the youngest pupils. 'It's fun and enables me to get to know the girls really well,' she says. Thrives on the variety of being a head, from financial planning – 'parents want value for money and I do too' – through to academic matters. 'I'm a round peg in a round hole here,' she says. Staunch believer in the merits of single-sex schools. 'Girls develop differently, learn differently and need encouraging in different ways to boys.' Very proud that there's no such thing as a Headington stereotype. 'It would worry me if people said they could spot a Headington girl at 60 paces. That's not what education is about. It's about drawing on what is within, building on skills and talents. I was thrilled when a sixth former said "you don't want us all to be the same, do you?" I emphatically do not.'

Academic Matters: Impressive performance at all levels. School prides itself on offering 'a first class and rigorous academic education and a breadth of choices and opportunities.' 70-ish per cent A/A* grades at GCSE – science (usually taken as dual award), history, geography, music and art particularly strong. V good AS level results and

excellent A levels – no fails and 83 per cent A and B grades. Maths, physics, chemistry, history, geography and English literature all star performers. In 2005, all art A level candidates achieved A grades – wow! Wide choice of subjects for sixth form. Girls took A2s in 29 different subjects in 2004 – choices included psychology, home economics (food and textiles), theatre studies, law and environmental science.

Setting by ability for maths and French from first year and for English from second. Girls take Latin from first year and embark on second modern language (Spanish or German) in second year. School supportive of individual choice – particularly good for girls who want to combine humanities and sciences. Around 40 pupils have English as second language – lessons given one to one or in small groups. When it comes to SEN provision, school 'considers it important to track and monitor pupils of all abilities, including the gifted and talented.' In 2005, 67 girls needed support (mainly for mild dyslexia/dyspraxia) or extra challenge. Individual SEN support lessons cost £30 per hour.

Well-provided library. Book group for 11 to 14-year-olds, with Anthony Horowitz, Diana Wynne Jones and Garth Nix among favourite authors. ICT networked throughout school and interactive whiteboards galore. Friendly, ultra-committed, highly-qualified teaching staff – average age is 46 and a quarter have been at school for more than 10 years. Member of English department recently voted best teacher in Oxfordshire. Maximum class size is 24 but average of 17 to a class up to GCSE and 8 in sixth form.

Games, Options, The Arts: Fantastic facilities across the board, from sports hall kitted out with multi-gym to stunning 25-metre indoor pool. Rowing, as you might expect at an Oxford school, is first-class – three pupils in junior GB rowing squad at time of our visit. Games – hockey, netball, athletics, swimming, gym, dance, rounders, tennis, basketball, badminton – are compulsory for all, though sixth form can choose pursuits like golf, squash, riding or martial arts. Lots of optional sports too, including trampolining, fencing and judo.

Music very popular, with 420 instrumental lessons timetabled every week. Excellent world-touring chamber choir has released two CDs and recently won its class at Oxford Music Festival for seventh year running. Loads of other orchestras, bands, gospel choir and even a harp sextet. Split-level art complex opened in 1998 has four light, airy studios, full of exciting work (traditional through to Brit Art) and stays open till seven or eight at night. Drama takes place in Headington's brand-new £2m theatre – used for school productions, lectures and concerts as well as shows by professional companies. Girls trod the boards of the

National Theatre in 2004 and own touring company, Venue2Venue, took production to Canada and another to Edinburgh Fringe in summer 2005. CCF introduced in 2001 – a big hit – and World Challenge goes down a storm too – girls were about to leave for Botswana and Zambia when we visited – school reports that all returned safe and sound! Pupils can also get involved in D of E and Young Enterprise.

Background and Atmosphere: School founded in 1915 to enable girls 'to fulfil a professional career and be financially independent.' Moved to present 26-acre site just a mile from city centre in 1929. Main building spacious and south-facing, with impressive redbrick façade – 'it feels like a proper school should,' says one girl. Loads of new additions, including music wing, library and state-of-the art dining room. Beautifully-kept playing fields, gardens and woodland. School is a Church of England foundation, with lay chaplain, morning assembly and confirmation classes, but welcomes students from different faiths. Day girls and boarders and staff vote for head girl and prefects every spring term.

Girls (and their parents) can choose the set-up that works for them – whether it's as a day pupil or full/weekly/flexi/occasional boarder. Four boarding houses – girls divided according to age and each house has own unique character. Davenport, a rambling Victorian pile for the younger boarders (including a few Headington Prep girls), is cosy and welcoming, with bedrooms in the eaves, games room decorated by the girls, pretty garden and a loo called Everest on account of the high step up to it! Newly-built Napier is second to none, with three colour co-ordinated corridors, each based around own kitchen where girls can watch telly, use toasters, microwaves, washing machines etc. Very popular with girls, who share in twos or fours. Feels just like home, with abundance of jolly Cath Kidston duvet covers, pop posters on walls and stray shoes on the floor. Envious parents say they'd move in like a shot given half a chance! Celia Marsh, the sixth form house, offers more freedom in preparation for university. New head of boarding (ex-Downe House) is a big fan of full boarding but reckons weekly and flexi boarding work 'brilliantly' too. 'It's so good for parents with busy working lives to be able to drop their daughters off on Monday morning and collect them again on Friday afternoon,' she says. 'It means the time they spend with their daughters is quality time; no time lost battling through traffic jams and no nagging about getting the prep done.' Lots laid on for full boarders at weekends – Tate Modern, backstage tour of the BBC, strawberry picking and much-prized trip to see Billy Elliott.

Girls look smart and well-turned out in uniform of check skirts and pale blue blouses. Sixth form wear own clothes (jeans allowed but no crop tops or flip-flops.)

Pastoral Care and Discipline: Pastoral care is second to none. Up to GCSE, each form has two tutors – the 'front line,' who see girls daily and don't miss a trick. Rest of team made up of heads of year, three heads of pastoral care (for sixth form, middle and lower school), a trained counsellor who visits school on regular basis, chaplain and head (who operates open door policy, enabling girls to talk to her in confidence if they wish.) Communication with parents good. Regular reports, newsletters and parent-teacher meetings. Befriender scheme helps new girls settle in, with sixth formers taking them under their wing. Very clear rules. Everything laid out in writing in excellent handbook – from zero tolerance on drugs, alcohol and smoking to anti-bullying policy. Mobile phones 'must not be seen or heard' in school, although separate rules apply in boarding houses.

Pupils and Parents: Thirty nationalities represented, including two annual Brunei scholars – high-achieving Muslim girls heading for medicine. Day girls travel in by car, bus and train from 30-mile radius while boarders come from all over. Many opt for weekly boarding – particularly popular as girls get older. Some Londoners hop on handy Oxford Tube bus line from Victoria, Notting Hill etc at crack of dawn on Mondays and get off right outside school gates. Pupils bright, confident and brimming with enthusiasm – but not at all toffee-nosed. Old girls include Baroness Young, Julia Somerville, Lady Longford, Baroness Mallalieu, Comic Relief founder Jane Tewson and Christina Onassis.

Entrance: School isn't 'aggressively selective' but gets around 140 applicants for 90 or so places at 11. Head looks for girls with originality, sensitivity to others, enthusiasm and lots of potential – not impressed by 'over-coached children.' Headington Preparatory supplies around half, with rest coming from prep schools like The Manor, Chandlings Manor, Rupert House, Ashfold, Dragon, Godstowe etc and local primaries. Entry at 11 and 13 by Common Entrance and at 12 and 14 by internal exam. Incoming sixth-formers (around 25-30 a year) take papers in proposed A level subjects and need at least six GCSEs at grades A-D. Reports from previous schools and all candidates interviewed by head or senior staff.

Exit: A few leave after GCSE for sixth form colleges or co-ed schools but vast majority stay on. Popular universities for sixth form leavers include Cambridge, Bristol, Edinburgh, UCL, Durham and Nottingham. Ten or so to Oxbridge. Law, medicine and sciences always figure highly but art foundation and other arts courses well-represented too.

Money Matters: Offers very wide variety of scholarships (academic, music, art, drama, sport) and bursaries. Celia Marsh awards – funded by £1.2 million bequest from much-loved senior mistress who taught at school between 1934 and 1963 – for those of 'outstanding academic ability or potential' who might not be able to come to Headington otherwise.

Remarks: A delightful school, nurtures and entertains its pupils while at the same time achieving excellent academic results. Fun and stimulating to be at.

HEATHFIELD SCHOOL

London Road, Ascot, Berkshire, SL5 8BQ

Tel: 01344 898 342

Fax: 01344 890 689

E-mail: registrar@heathfieldschool.net

Website: www.heathfieldschool.net

- Pupils: 210 girls; all full boarders • Ages: 11-18 • Size of sixth form: 65. NB this can fluctuate • C of E • Fees: £7,630
- Independent

Head: Since 2003, Mrs Frances King BA MA MBA (forties), who was previously deputy head of St Mary's Ascot and arrived here after a couple of years of turbulence. Mrs King was educated at Ashford School, Kent, did a gap year in Israel where her parents were on secondment (and where she improved her Hebrew), and read theology at Oxford, followed by a (much later) part time degree in philosophy and religious ethics plus an MBA in international leadership (ie headship) in the independent sector. Quite. She comes to Heathfield via Lady Eleanor Holles, Francis Holland, Guildford County School plus Tormead School in Guildford (head of department of religious studies at all of them).

Personable, chatty and fun, her key ambition 'is to turn out girls who think about their lives'; 'don't judge each day by the harvest you reap but by the seeds that you plant'. Having spent her first year consolidating 'and not really tinkering that much', Mrs King is now 'putting the academic front under the spotlight' and has made several new appointments. The girls would dispute her claim about not tinkering; she has introduced cafeteria style posh nosh, with a massive buffet and oodles of salads – 'the food is much better' say pupils. Mrs King, who teaches the first year theology, has appointed a 'breezy' chaplain, and is married to a clergyman who is currently studying to become a psychodynamic counsellor (double quite). Two children: a daughter in the state sector and a son bound for Shiplake.

Academic Matters: Strong English, history, languages. 80 per cent A/B at A level, and a third get 3 A grades.

School is wireless; staff take computers into class and will respond to an e-mail regarding almost any subject almost by return. Senior girls do their work on computer and often e-mail course work to tutors. Pleasing number of male staff. Keyboarding for all. Senior girls' study bedrooms with internet access. All internet nannied (which usually means no real history of art). Moves afoot to revitalise teaching methods and introduce 'more up to date learning methods'. Senior library needs a face lift.

Dyslexia help on hand, though not more than one to one for one hour a week which may not be enough support for some – 'girls move at a bit of a pace'. EFL on tap. EFL and dyslexia coaching cost extra.

Games, Options, The Arts: Games popular, but not a religion; good lacrosse currently on a winning streak, and tennis and athletics. Stunning millennium swimming pool with loads of competitions and water polo, aqua aerobics, rowing practice (!), scuba diving and PADI certificates. To die-for sports centre, with weights room, dance studio (ballet, ballroom dancing and perfect for tap dancing) and nautilus type gym. Wow. Pristine squash courts, bursar lamented that they were sadly under-used by all except the staff, and presumably locals, who can besport themselves at certain times. Good take-up of D of E, particularly at the younger level.

'Divine, scatty' head of music; music very strong, most learn at least one instrument, singing by far the most popular: recent choir trip to St Petersburg. Class music taught in small groups in engagingly chaotic music room stacked with all kinds of instruments in every nook and the drum kit looks as though it is trying to escape out of the window. LAMDA drama awards a regular feature, though drama a bit of a poor relation, and head has new music and drama complex complete with theatre and recording studio as number one on her wish list. Art exciting and varied with a recent hat exhibition at Sotheby's in London. Textiles popular, but no sewing machines. Odd bits of sculpture all over the shop and good showing in both art and history of art at A level, ditto photography, ceramics to GCSE.

Trillions of clubs, expanded, now run mainly by staff, rather than over-worked house-parents: options include kayaking and the Leith cookery course (wish list again, new kitchen, current teaching kitchen can only hold eight). Polo popular, either on own ponies or hirelings – about £50 a chukka.

Background and Atmosphere: Handy for London and Heathrow and six miles from Windsor (Eton) (the bus stops at the door), the about to be revamped Ascot racecourse is ten minute's walk away and a further five to the station. Heathfield is discreetly tucked away on the London road with an impossible turn off by the traffic lights, and boasts nothing other than a tiny easily missable sign board to announce its presence.

One of the last small all-boarding school for girls (Benenden is their only rival). Founded in 1899 by Eleanor Beatrice Wyatt who moved the girls out of her London school in Queens Gate to this charming now much extended stucco-fronted villa of Georgian proportions (low windows, incredibly restrained panelling and stripped wooden floors or decent velour carpet). Good feeling of space. Jolly if utterly impracticable conversion for the 21st century, the whole place reeks of Dornford Yates and elegant country house parties of a bygone age. We met a charming selection of girls in a very OTT 'drawing room'. And our coffee with the head was brought in by TWO uniformed maids with frilly white pinnies and mob caps.

Fairly pristine on the whole. School set in 35 acres of highly manicured grounds dotted with tennis courts, lax pitches, and sixth form house, charming late Victorian chapel resplendent with girl-crafted tapestry kneelers (chapel three mornings and one evening a week) and a glorious Gertrude Jekyll-like abandoned fencing hall.

Most of the sleeping accommodation is in the main block, with the youngest three year groups in dormitories (supervised by members of the lower sixth); single study bedrooms thereafter. The lower sixth provide prefects so that the upper sixth can concentrate 'on enjoying their last year at school'. Ostensibly the upper sixth have their own house, an overlong L shape partly two storey affair, with long narrow passages (excellent for ten pin bowling) and fairly underused, not quite big enough common rooms (not many books but a goodly supply of periodicals).

Upper sixth wear their own clothes, otherwise they swing around the place in an assortment of jeans, no dangly earrings, but a spot of nail varnish and a mass of bracelets appeared to be OK. They also wash their own clothes, and cook all meals except weekday lunches in the sixth form centre, 'to promote independence before going to university' – but as two housemothers take orders and produce the food the poor darlings have absolutely no sense of budgeting. Lesser mortals live neat in blue skirts and jerseys with green ties and a plethora of badges (aka 'bows and bearings' awarded for manners, deportment, kindness etc) worn vertically up their jerseys, mufti post school during the week and at weekends. The rhodie walk round the perimeter is still much loved by the girls.

A certain amount of garden and interior design would not go amiss. Whilst tradition for tradition's sake is all very well, the school does need a new build, the promised new class room block for 2003/4 has not materialised and was not even mentioned during our visit. Mrs King has done a good calming job, now all she needs are much better facilities and bums on seats. Numbers currently buoyant-ish – essential if the school is to remain all-boarding.

Pastoral Care and Discipline: The upper sixth may visit the pub across the road once during the week and on Saturday evenings, though this privilege is withdrawn if they drink too much. The upper sixth also have free access to Ascot after school and Windsor on both Saturday and Sunday until 9 pm and can (and do) have regular dinner parties in their house kitchens. Boys not a problem, though they must be formally introduced to a member of staff and are not allowed 'upstairs' (though this has been known). Regular joint socials, Caledonian society activities, playing croquet, whatever. Streams of visitors for lectures in the evening: Wellington, Radley and chaps from Harrow as well as Eton are regular visitors. Joint Eton/Heathfield trip to China at discussion stage.

School runs on the trad fixed exeat system plus half term. No Saturday school, but masses of scheduled trips for all ages. Chapel on Sunday. Good supply of house parents. No recent reports of wickedness, smokers the worst offenders. Head says suspended for boozing and out for drugs. No recent reports either of expulsions and we were assured 'that there was no bullying' by the girls, who were charming, chatty and quite prepared to hold their own. PSE timetabled, and lifestyle skills too. School is keen on instilling confidence.

Pupils and Parents: Loads of trad families, plus an increasing number of first time buyers plus loads from abroad 'some rich, and some even more rich'. Large selection both from London and country (usually all girls) prep schools, as well as from all over the UK plus smattering from overseas, about 8 per cent in the services or ex-pat community and about the same amount of real foreigners – US, Portugal, Russia, Hong Kong, Singapore etc, who must have a good command of English. Not many ethnic minorities.

Entrance: 11+, or girls who have done their common entrance and then decided they don't want to go to a co-ed school at 13+. School aims to have year sizes of 35/40, of whom 25 might arrive at 11+ rising to 35 at 13+ (head did admit that might be a trifle optimistic in the current climate). Entrance exam day consists of workshops in various subjects, PE or drama class, oral English and an interview with the head followed by Common Entrance. Sixth form entry is currently quite tight, girls queue to fill the available places. Expect to sit an exam in two subjects you want to do at A level; 7 GCSEs the norm for sixth form entry.

Exit: Most to university all over. Edinburgh, Durham, Bristol, Newcastle perennially popular, ditto Northumbria, humanities and general subjects the norm. Many take a gap year and few leave post GCSE, the draw of the upper sixth centre is too great.

Money Matters: Bursaries on line to replace scholarships; will keep children till the next obvious stage if parents have financial difficulties. NB: this is a very expensive school. Revenue much increased by popular summer school for boarders and day alike.

Remarks: Jolly nice girls' school, offering a good range of subjects and turning out charming pupils. Perfect for the girl who needs stability and cherishing.

HEATHSIDE SCHOOL

Brooklands Lane, Weybridge, Surrey, KT13 8UZ

Tel: 01932 846 162
Fax: 01932 828 142
E-mail: mail@heathside.surrey.sch.uk
Website: www.heathside.surrey.sch.uk

• Pupils: 1,400 pupils; girls and boys • Ages: 11-18 • Size of sixth form: 195 • Non-denom - but affiliated to the diocese of Guildford • State • Open days: Mid October

---

Principal: Since 1989, Dr G A Willoughby EdD MSc BSc PGCE. Educated at Tiffin School in Kingston, Dr Willoughby was appointed deputy head in 1986 and head in 1989. Energetic and hands-on, he believes strongly in the merits of lifelong learning and, to prove it, has completed his doctorate in education at Surrey University. Appears to lead by example and 'walk the talk' – both his daughters have attended Heathside from the age of 11 to 18. Parents describe him as friendly and approachable – 'a head who lives, eats and breathes the school.'

Academic Matters: Heathside has grown dramatically in size and stature since 1988 when it had only 487 pupils. Its grant-maintained status was changed in 1999 and it is now well established as a Foundation Community Technology College (in affiliation with the diocese of Guildford). Heathside gets good academic results and their GCSE and A level results put them up with the top performing comprehensive schools nationwide. Although it is a Technology College, Heathside offers a broad and balanced academic curriculum. For the first three years, all students follow a general foundation course (including French and German or Spanish) with a fair amount of extra ICT work being included in all subject areas. Students work in mixed ability groups and are also setted for others – system seems fairly flexible. However, by year 9, setting is more extensive. There is a wide choice of subjects on offer for GCSE including a new GNVQ qualification in ICT and the sixth form offers AS and A levels. Class sizes are larger than many fee-paying schools but, at an average of 29, perfectly acceptable (drops to 10-15 in sixth form).

Design and Technology and IT are particular strengths of the school but not, one feels, to the detriment of other areas (wonderful art in evidence). Lots of homework set but head feels it isn't a problem as most students come with homework culture ingrained. Can provide EFL support if required (majority of students are British) and has a special needs facility within the learning resource centre. School works closely within the community and has links with many outside agencies for additional help if required. Well-equipped new ICT centre has recently been completed and is at the heart of all student-directed learning at Heathside.

Sixth form been in place for 9 years but is growing every year. Separate sixth form centre where most lessons and relaxation take place. Fairly bland common room with pool table and kitchenette provides students with the autonomy they feel they need. No uniform requirements, only an understanding that dress be 'acceptable'. Careers area located in this centre is open all day for student use. Strong links also being formed with the traditional universities (particularly Oxbridge) to widen the options available to the students. A number of additional opportunities also exists for sixth formers, such as acting as senior councillors on school council, working with industry mentors (meet on a regular basis with a mentor from a local business) or directing and managing large drama productions, producing the annual year book, the school's termly newspaper and mentoring younger students.

Games, Options, The Arts: Many students at Heathside have chosen the school because of its strong sporting profile and the school has been awarded its second Sportsmark. Heathside has a sports hall, gym, tennis courts and hard play area. All students are encouraged to participate but selection for teams is tough; recently the trampoline team came third in Great Britain; an ex-Heathside tennis player beat the no 1 U14 player in the world; the under 15 squash squad came second in the Schools' National championships and there are a number of other players in various sports who represent the district and the county.

Drama and music play an important role in the life of the school with plenty of activities. There is a large concert band (70 players), jazz group, choir, and a number of ensembles (flute, string, brass, clarinet, guitar). Students regularly perform at venues within the community and the choir has appeared at the Albert Hall and Docklands Arena. Over three hundred students have individual music lessons on a weekly basis. The concert band undertakes a bi-annual tour in Europe. The head is a percussionist and likens his role to that of a 'lift-man in a bungalow.'

The 'school production' is an annual event and the drama department's major activity but other drama activities take place through the weekly drama club. Other extra-curricular activities include Duke of Edinburgh Award Scheme, Young Enterprise, Book club, science club, art club and many other societies and clubs.

Background and Atmosphere: The school is tucked away down a side street in Weybridge, Surrey. Surrounded by trees and looking onto playing fields, there could be an air of green, leafy tranquillity but for the buildings, some of which look prefabricated (flat-pack council design) and in need of a lick or two of paint. So the first impression – of a scruffy exterior and unkempt grassy areas – is a pity in view of the reality being a good school with great teachers who genuinely want the best for their students. And, very often, they get it.

The canteens have been refurbished. New contractors now provide healthy options; fresh fruit salad, salads, panini and stir fry vegetables as well as trad meals. No fizzy drinks sold on site. Many students bring their own packed lunches but now more uptake of the food in the canteens.

Pastoral Care and Discipline: Good pastoral care system with an advanced mentoring scheme whereby all new students in year 7 are linked with trained student mentors from the upper school. They are responsible for these students throughout their first year in school. Tutors and year managers form the additional rungs of support through close monitoring of students and constant feedback with parents. 'You cannot afford to be complacent about any student,' says head, 'everyone has a special talent or strength and the school must find out what it is.'

Strong culture of discipline within the school and it works very closely with parents and the community to ensure that all areas are being upheld. Zero tolerance towards substance abuse. Close co-operation with Surrey Police and involvement with Youth Against Crime Scheme. Head has worked as a magistrate and feels he has good insights into adolescent behaviour. Strict blazer policy and they try to enforce dress code. School does not stop at the gates and the school takes complaints from members of the public very seriously. Every complaint is followed up. Firm anti-bullying guidelines.

Pupils and Parents: The students are reflective of the Weybridge, Walton, Hersham area and a good international mix. Most social classes and faiths are represented and there are up to 21 feeder schools with St James School, Cleves School and Sayes Court being the main contributors. The school is popular and oversubscribed. Students a bit scruffy, however more girls have recently taken up the option of wearing black trousers and a friendly, happy-looking bunch on the whole.

Entrance: At 11. The closing date for applications is in October of the year before a pupil is due to attend. Siblings at the school and proximity of home to the school can affect admission. The school will also consider applicants who live outside the catchment area who show exceptional musical, sporting, IT or design & technology skill and who are successful in the challenges in these skills.

Exit: About 50 per cent of students leave after GCSEs, for the likes of Strodes College (Egham), Esher College and Brooklands College; a few seek employment. Many traditional university choices. In 2005 84 per cent of students gained their university or college place of choice.

Remarks: A thoroughly all-round school that will prepare your child well for the demands of the 21st century. It may be a bit shabby, lacking the grandeur and facilities of its privately funded counterparts but it is unpretentious, gets on with the job and is a community school in the real sense of the word.

THE HENRIETTA BARNETT SCHOOL

Central Square, Hampstead Garden Suburb, London, NW11 7BN

Tel: 020 8458 8999
Fax: 02084 558 900
E-mail: hbs_school@btconnect.com
Website: www.hbschool.org.uk

• Pupils: 720 girls; all day • Ages: 11-18 • Size of sixth form: 260 • Non-denom • State

Head: From April 2006, Mr Oliver Blond, an English and drama specialist, who has taught in a variety of schools in London and Essex. Married with two children. Interim head is Mrs Mandy Watts, deputy head.

Academic Matters: Invariably excellent exam results, rivalling any of the north London selective independent schools, particularly at GCSE. Very few grades below B, 83 per cent A* or A in 2005. At A level, 87 per cent of results were grade A or B, with biology, chemistry and maths all very popular and very strong out of a range of 18 mostly mainstream subjects. 'The sixth form is enormously academic but not particularly broad,' said a parent. Class size 31 at Key Stage 3, some GCSE groups smaller. Streaming for maths from year 8. Support within the English department for the small number of dyslexics – 'but they have mostly sorted out strategies themselves before they get here.'

Everyone does French, German and Latin at Key Stage 3; classical Greek is an AS/A2 option. Everyone takes IT GCSE in year 10; it is an option at AS level in the sixth form. The school also has two rolling IT classrooms so anyone can sign up to use computers when they need them. The science department is at present a couple of labs short but the school has part funding and planning permission for new ones. Many top-class teachers, who tend to move on to be heads of department elsewhere. 'My daughters like the friendly working environment,' said a parent. 'They find most of the teachers open and willing to discuss things they disagree with.'

The last head said of league tables, 'it's nice for us to come out on top, but with our calibre of students we should do so. It's more pleasing to see that our value-added is good too'.

Games, Options, The Arts: 'Most parents send their children here for our academic standards but we're becoming more holistic – doing more PE and performing arts,' said

last head. Apart from a smallish gym and three tennis courts – plus the use of others in Central Square opposite – the school is lacking in sports facilities. However, girls visit Copthall School sports centre for swimming, athletics and field sports, and teams do well. 'Barnet's hockey team is basically our girls,' said last head. 'We have poor facilities but, due to the PE Department, we do very well with very little.' 'If you're good at games there's plenty of scope,' said a parent, 'but there's not so much for the ones who aren't.' After-school activities are restricted because the Hampstead Garden Suburb Institute still has the right to use many of the facilities after 5pm.

The school owns a field centre in Dorset, once a village school; everyone in years 7-9 visits for a week a year for activities ranging from orienteering to field trips. However, parents complain of a lack of trips abroad (by comparison with independent schools). The annual drama competition is popular – each class in years 8-11 organises its own play ('to a very high standard,' said a parent) – and the much-praised director of music has introduced a musical production involving girls from throughout the school. 'I'm really impressed that my daughter recently spent three days at the British Museum learning from a Japanese musical theatre teacher,' said a parent. There are concerts involving the orchestra, choir and ensembles, including the annual Bernard Hooton Music Festival, which includes one day of pop and one day of classical music. 'The music is wonderful,' said a parent. 'They play really exciting things that reflect the ethnicity of the school.'

'Because the school suffers from a lack of facilities, it creates an atmosphere of having to sort things out for yourself,' said a parent. 'The girls aren't spoon-fed – they're encouraged to get on and make things happen.'

Background and Atmosphere: Founded in 1911 by the formidable Henrietta Barnett, who fought for educational opportunities for girls equal to those of boys. A long-running dispute with the Hampstead Garden Suburb Institute is now resolved and the elegant Lutyens building is in the early stages of redecoration – 'but it's rather like painting the Forth bridge,' commented the last head – with plenty of areas still comfortably shabby. Lovely quiet suburban situation amidst cherry trees, greenery and upmarket Garden Suburb houses. The magnificent Main Hall and foyer area have been restored to something like their former glory. 'There is a real sense of community in the school,' said a parent. 'People don't mind putting themselves forward because they know they will be supported.'

Pastoral Care and Discipline: Informal mentoring system. 'We try to make everyone feel safe here. Then they can fulfil their potential.' Sixth formers are trained to teach sex education to year 9 – 'the girls are more likely to feel able to ask them questions they'll either assume we don't know the answers to or are too embarrassed to ask us.' Parents report that there seems to be no problems with bullying or prejudice. 'The girls feel they have a voice in the school,' said a parent. 'If they say that something's not right they'll be listened to.'

Pupils and Parents: A wide social and ethnic mix from a huge area. More-or-less everyone is very pleased to be there and extremely motivated, 'and parents have to be committed too,' said a mother. Parents and pupils cite the huge variety of pupils as one of the school's great strengths. 'There are girls who came over as refugees and have really pulled themselves up by their bootstraps to be there,' said a parent. 'It can be a great launching pad for some girls.' 'I love the mix of people here,' said a sixth former. 'Everyone is so friendly and welcoming.'

Entrance: One of the most competitive in the country, with around 1,000 applicants for 93 places. The first round is verbal and non-verbal reasoning exams, with the top 300 called back for maths and English papers. These are designed to measure innate intelligence and creativity rather than cramming; the maths paper gives examples in which logic is used to solve further problems, and the English paper may include some comprehension and some creative writing. There is no interview, and reports from primary school heads are only considered in special circumstances eg family bereavement or special educational needs. The word in north London is that this is a harder school to get into than any of the selective independents. Around 25-30 join the sixth form, each with a minimum of 6 grade As at GCSE.

Exit: Quite a few leave after GCSE for buzzier, often co-ed sixth forms with a wider A level range. Virtually all sixth formers go on to university, mostly the old-established ones, including about 10 a year to Oxbridge. Large numbers study medicine or other sciences.

Money Matters: The Parents' Association is a highly successful fund-raiser, contributing around £55,000 a year to the school and a development office has been set up to raise further funds (parents are asked, but not obliged, to donate £60 a term, and around a third do so). A 'Ball for the Hall' paid for the recent refurbishment of the magnificent Lutyens hall. But apart from this, the school is as short of money as any other voluntary aided state school.

Remarks: One of the top academic state schools in the country, with fiercely competitive entry and highly committed pupils. 'The facilities are not brilliant, and I'd like my

daughters to have had more sport, extra-curricular activities and school trips,' said a parent. 'But the teaching and the open, friendly atmosphere make it all worthwhile.'

THE HERTFORDSHIRE AND ESSEX HIGH SCHOOL

Warwick Road, Bishop's Stortford, Hertfordshire, CM23 5NJ

Tel: 01279 654 127

Fax: 01279 508 810

E-mail: admin.hertsandessex@thegrid.org.uk

Website: www.hertsandessex.herts.sch.uk

• Pupils: 1,015, mostly girls; some boys in the sixth form • Ages: 11-18 • Size of sixth form: 205 • Non-denom • State • Open days: End of September or beginning of October

Head: Since 2005, Ms Alison Garner BA (forties). Married, no children. Has spent all of her career in the state sector, for the past 9 years in single-sex girls schools.

Academic Matters: An all-ability comprehensive and very good too. Results at GCSE are exemplary with 90-ish per cent five A* to C grades – in the top five per cent of state schools in England. History notably strong. The school has Science College status. Because of the churn post-GCSE, the sixth form are a rather different cohort; results at both A level and GNVQ (business education and ICT) are above the national average but by no means startling. Sciences a popular choice for girls at A level. At 11, pupils are taught in mixed ability classes of around 32 pupils in each; setting in maths in year 7 and languages from year 8. French in year 7, then German, Latin or Spanish added in year 8. One written report a year, with tracking grades 2 – 3 times a year, plus annual parents' evenings and regular home-school contact.

Games, Options, The Arts: Sport is strong with individual representatives at all levels. The main sports pitches, five-minutes' walk away, include four hockey pitches and a 400-metre grass athletics track. On site there are tennis courts, rounders pitches, netball and basketball courts and a football pitch a 25-metre indoor swimming pool, a gym and a dance studio. School competes at district, county and regional levels. Clubs in trampolining, gymnastics, judo, dance, basketball and lifesaving – RLSS Lifesaving Awards at bronze, merit and distinction levels.

Some 10 per cent of girls learn one or more musical instruments – so not a great feature here – but there are flourishing choirs, an orchestra, wind band, swing band and several instrumental groups. A wide variety of extra-curricular clubs, many at lunch-time.

Background and Atmosphere: Opened in 1908 as The Bishop's Stortford Secondary School for Girls; fees were £3 a term and girls were trained for teaching careers. Stopped charging fees in 1944 when it was granted self-governing status and committed to remaining an all-ability school. Grammar-schooly buildings with adequate later additions – not much room to build more. The girls are proud of the uniform because it is associated with Herts and Essex High School even though it – long brown kilt-type skirt, matching blazer and fawn jumper – might just make you think this an old-fashioned school, stuck in the dark ages. Far from it. Plans to re-locate school to a new site with state-of-the-art buildings in Bishop's Stortford, possibly by 2010, planning permission allowing.

Pastoral Care and Discipline: The first point of contact is a pupil's form tutor although there is a 'buddy' system where pupils can talk to a particular sixth former about any worries or concerns. Pupils are encouraged always to act with honesty, equality and fairness and the head expects the girls to show respect and consideration to each other. Links with a school in Uganda. Strong policy on bullying.

Pupils and Parents: Large catchment area. Although the town is affluent there are pockets of deprivation, so there is a range of pupils from diverse backgrounds.

Entrance: About 300 apply for a total of 160 places at 11. Priority is given to those who can offer a compelling medical and/or social reason for admission, followed by siblings. Daughters of someone who works at the school come next. A total of 10 per cent of places (16) is allocated to girls with a proven aptitude in music or sport. Any further places go to children on the basis of distance in relation to primary school attended.

Exit: Up to 35 per cent leave after GCSE to pursue courses elsewhere. Minimum entry at sixth form is five C grades at GCSE. Vast majority goes on to higher education after A levels. Pupils are encouraged to sit Oxbridge if they wish; a handful succeed each year.

Remarks: Traditional values but prepares pupils well for the modern world. Girls are encouraged to do well academically and they seem to do so, whatever their ability.

HIGH SCHOOL OF DUNDEE

Linked to High School of Dundee Junior School in the Junior section

Euclid Crescent, Dundee, DD1 1HU

Tel: 01382 202 921
Fax: 01382 229 822
E-mail: admissions@highschoolofdundee.co.uk
Website: www.highschoolofdundee.co.uk

• Pupils: 730 (roughly 50/50 boys/girls) • Ages: 11-18 • Size of sixth form: 230 • Non-denom • Fees: £1,740 rising to £2,475 • Independent • Open days: Early November

Rector: Since 1997, Mr Michael Duncan (Mike) MA Dip Ed BPhil (fifties) who was previously deputy head of Robert Gordon's in Aberdeen whence he arrived in the late seventies as head of English before becoming assistant and then deputy. Read English at St Andrews, did his teacher training at Dundee College of Education (with a Diploma from Dundee University) he then 'taught for a bit' before winning a research scholarship at St Andrews where he spent a happy two years studying popular fiction in 19th Century Scottish periodicals.

Articulate and very much in control of his school, he is quietly proud of his achievements. Certain amount of structural re-jigging: offices, proper reception area, that sort of thing. The junior school has been pulled together: and a new teaching block has been created for English, plus a sixth form common room and separate study area. Computers all over the place and masses of dosh spent here, but head is keen for them to be working computers and not just dust-gatherers. Fair number of new heads of departments, and exam results reflect this in the main. Rector has introduced strong links with Dundee University where some members of S6 can follow uni modules which, if successfully completed, will allow them to start in the second year here (if that is their uni of choice). This pilot has now been copied by a number of state schools – a super initiative.

The rector believes it is vital for pupils to be 'happy in the school' and keen to encourage more independent learning so that pupils do 'not just parrot out facts': ('Abandon spoon feeding'); and would like to be able to offer a broader syllabus to accommodate the small minority of pupils who needs a more vocational programme. The school is academically selective, but there is a broad church of ability (siblings et al) and the rector is concerned that one or two may slip through the net. He has also just appointed a member of staff to pick up the minority of pupils who don't even join in activities. Charming, affable and well in control, Mr Duncan, who is not married, has a nice sense of the ridiculous, and is – quite definitely – prudent.

Academic Matters: School follows the Scottish system: Standard Grades mixed with Intermediate I and II, plus Highers and Advanced Highers. A good collection of subjects offered, including quite a few esoteric ones: technical studies, computing studies plus health and food technology, hospitality, information and modern studies as well as drama, business management and graphic communications. PE at Higher level only. Philosophy and moral ethics a new addition, home economics popular, with cooking courses for sixth formers to prepare them for uni. Tranches of success in chemistry, physics, biology and history. Top chemistry and top history marks in last year's Highers (wow); good links with Burn House at Edzell where historians go for weekends of outside speakers. 14 labs revamped so far and science strong over all. Impressive. Recent English results disappointing, new head of dept in place, so these should improve; head of English busy building relations with the English department at Dundee uni, creative writing popular last year. Mathematics not all that it could be: too many failures and D grades around. Pretty poor take-up in languages, even though all must take two, starting French at Primary 6. French and Spanish the leading contenders, with German a poor third – but new head of dept on stream, so watch this space. Latin scholars in penny numbers (no official Greek, but 'can be organised'. Classics trip to Italy last year.

Max class size 28ish (though usually 'in the teens or low twenties') and 20 for practical matters. No bias in subjects chosen by gender. Efficient looking computer rooms, locked at lunch time, but used for classroom teaching as well as for IT, 300 desk tops, the internet link comes via adjacent Abertay University. Old computers are tweaked by pupils and sold via YE for charity and rows of computers wail for attention in the design department, their red guts hanging out like a butcher's shop. Computer links with art, graphic art and design et al. No lap tops yet 'not ruled out for a year and a day'. Library in the undercroft below elegant school hall, used for year assemblies (the whole school gathers in the nearby Caird Hall), has been re-furbished; computers and good tables to work at as well as a plethora (but not a huge plethora) of books, but the school mag says that borrowing has gone up by 50 per cent. Free photocopying for skool stuff. Learning support throughout the school, two dedicated staff about to be joined by another.

Support starts in the junior school (exercises for all to help dyspraxic students), keen on early intervention, some ADHD but 'not much below', mild aspergers and dyslexia OK, some help for the very gifted, head keen to avoid the bored child syndrome. Extra English on hand where necessary.

Games, Options, The Arts: Sports field a mile away with brand new three million quid Mayfield Sports Centre under construction as we write, pupils bussed. Strong on rugby, regularly at the finals of the Scottish cup, number of district and Scottish players. Girls' hockey strong, boys play too, cricket, athletics, tennis, swimming at Dundee uni, netball popular and athletics 'very powerful'. New outdoor instructor has taken over D of E which is thriving. Strong CCF and pipe band. Impressive music, with lots of charity concerts, ensemble groups: 500 pupils do instrumental music, a huge range: symphony orchestras, choirs, regular trips to Europe and masses of participation in local competitions. Separate drama department, plus media studies both curricular and extra curricular. 'Art is stronger on design' says the rector, 'than on painting'; and a jolly art suite stretches across one wing of the building: jewellery expert has recently joined the art staff, and the extra-curricular jewellery club is incredibly popular. Fearsome debating with school regularly thrashing all others and often in the ribbons in the Oxford, Cambridge, Durham etc. uni/schools debating competitions.

Background and Atmosphere: Claims to be the oldest school in Britain: tracing links back to the thirteenth century 'when the Abbot of Lindores was instructed to build a grammar school in the burgh of Dundee'. Good adaptation of old building plumb in the centre of Dundee and surrounded by secure patrolled playground and janitors all over the place (though they did let me park there for a couple of hours). CCTV cameras everywhere. The junior school, based in the 1880s former girls' school (the Margaret Harris Building) is adjacent. School has acquired all the buildings down Bell Street and the school is rapidly expanding along. School uniform for all (boys may wear highland dress as an alternative – though we didn't see any), with girls wearing rather jolly Dundee High check, pinafores for juniors, skirts for the rest – another of the Rector's changes. Those sixth formers who are following classes at the university are allowed to change into mufti on site. Goonies for posh for all staff, the head wears his for assembly. Thrift shop once a month. School has good strong links with the Dundee worthies: directors elected by the Chamber of Commerce, the Guildry and Nine Trades of Dundee, as well as ex-officio the Lord Dean of Guild and the Parish Minister of Dundee and whilst nominally following the Presbyterian ethic, this is truly a broad church.

Pastoral Care and Discipline: Not many problems with drugs or booze or rock and roll, brief incident three years ago equalled pupils out. Tough and stringent anti-bullying policy, pupil welfare committee meets regularly, with regular reviews and impressive PSE. Two dedicated members of staff deal with 'child protection' – this is a first for us. List of possible misdemeanours includes hacking (another first), gambling or bringing laser pens or camera phones into school. Mobiles OK but mustn't be used during school hours or taken into exams. Sanctions range from a 'mild reprimand' via punishments, detention, letters home, suspension and very very occasionally expulsion – though children under threat of expulsion these days are more likely to be withdrawn by their parents first. Sixth formers befriend juniors both buddying and helping with reading or learning support. Four houses run throughout the school each house providing guidance as well as academic support and individual tutors for all.

Pupils and Parents: Fair number of first time buyers, ditto ethnic minorities, traditionally a mixture of – predominantly – farmers and professionals. A number of incomers from the universities and the life science department (particularly) of nearby Ninewells Hospital. 50 per cent come from outside Dundee, with buses from St Andrews, Perth, Forfar, Blairgowrie, Alyth and Arbroath: one or two pupils from Kirkaldy, school is close to railway station. Drivers can bring their own transport with the usual strictures about driving other pupils in place. Famous former pupils include Sir Lewis Robertson, Lord Cullen (Lord President), Lord Ross (Former Lord Justice Clerk) Andrew Marr of the beeb, the novelist AL Kennedy and former Scottish rugby captain Andy Nicoll.

Entrance: Pupils can and do arrive throughout the school year if space available. Two thirds come up from the junior school, the rest from other primaries. Waiting lists currently at P4, P5 and P7. 'School readiness' test for tinies; entrants for P2 up take standardised tests in maths and English for the junior school, and all pupils take the senior school entrance exam – no automatic transfer. Not many come post Standard Grades.

Exit: Logistic throughout the school, otherwise few post Standard (six or so), some post S5 and Highers, with uni entrance, or stay on for Advanced Highers. 93 per cent of those who do stay on go to uni, with a regular trickle of 4/6 to Oxbridge.

Money Matters: School not that rich, and loads of cash recently poured into the infrastructure. Number of bursaries (only); school will move heaven and earth to help families who have come financially unstuck, but hard on non-payers who won't co-operate. Selection of continuation scholarships available for FPs going on to university, some of which are dedicated to The High School and some of which are directed to inhabitants of Dundee. Trusts can often be persuaded to help an individual but might not be prepared to help the school itself. Foundation set up four years ago, and rafts of FPs are under pressure to give little and often 'which when combined might pay for one pupil for one year'.

Remarks: This is a thunderingly good school in the best of the Scottish tradition with all the right vibes and modern teaching aids in place, though some of the results need tweaking a bit. And, with the projected demand from the junior end, the Rector might abandon prudence.

THE HIGH SCHOOL OF GLASGOW

Linked to High School of Glasgow Junior in the Junior section

637 Crow Road, Glasgow, G13 1PL

Tel: 01419 549 628
Fax: 01414 355 708
E-mail: rector@hsog.co.uk
Website: www.glasgowhigh.com

• Pupils: 675 boys and girls in the senior school; all day • Ages: 10-18 • Size of sixth form: 195 • Non-denom • Fees: Secondary £2,274 - £2,616; primary £1,596 - 2,247; nursery £849 • Independent • Open days: October/November

---

Rector: Since 2004, Mr Colin D R Mair MA Cert Ed (fifties), who was previously depute rector here. Educated at Kelvinside Academy, read Latin and French at Glasgow, did his Cert Ed at Jordanhill, first came to the school in 1976. Charming, affable and well-versed in the ways of the school, he reluctantly relinquished his teaching role (classics) at the end of last session, but 'would be keen to cover whenever the chance arises'. He would also be keen 'to help out on either the cricket ground or rugby pitch' and hopes that being rector won't 'make him too remote' from the school itself (not a chance says this editor who has met him on earlier visits to the school).

Academic Matters: Scottish system exclusively. A thunderingly good school on all fronts. 79 per cent 1, 98 per cent 1-2 for 714 subjects at Standard Grade; 64 per cent A, 88 per cent A/B for 481 subjects at Highers; and 49 per cent A, 79 per cent A/B for 182 subjects at Advanced Higher level in 2003. This statement was taken from the school reports. Previous years' exams have shown strong results across the board, with perhaps less take up in home economics, though art & design and modern studies still in the frame. A pleasing 13 out of 13 got grade 1 in Latin. English and maths particularly strong, but impressive results across the board in all disciplines. Classical Greek on offer as well as Latin. Latin for all first two years, French and German throughout, Spanish offered as a crash course in the sixth year. Business management popular. Almost as many girls as boys doing Highers physics. Greenhouse attached to biology lab, school offers human biology as well as the 'normal' option, and pupils can take this as a crash subject in their final year at school – useful for those entering the medical profession (Glasgow uni is popular for medics). One of the best sixth form handbooks we have ever come across, complete with university entrance requirement and advice. Other schools would do well to copy. Huge variety of subjects and options, keyboarding skills on offer, home economics and sewing for all – fluffy toys and natty embroidered lined denim bags being sewn in the lunch hour. Max class size 26, with 20 for practical subjects. Excellent and organised learning support throughout, with masses of liaison from junior school, and good follow-on in all disciplines. Dyslexic pupils from junior school teamed up with senior pupils for the first three years, to encourage and help them with any organisational difficulties and with homework etc. Impressive library, computers everywhere; dedicated for the fifth and sixth form only, during their study time, but all pupils can and do use them during their lunch break. New IT suite opened August 2003.

Games, Options, The Arts: School surrounded by 23 acres of games fields and car parks; masses of district, county, country players (Alison Sheppard FP, Olympic swimmer) lots of reps on West of Scotland teams in almost every discipline. Huge range of activities, including sailing, skiing (trips to Canada popular) as well as D of E. Granny bashing popular (Rector, and probably Social Services, do not like this description, this editor's 86 year old mother, who has been subjected to the latter, thinks it totally accurate!) and good strong links with local group of autistic children. Lots of charity projects, often house-based. Masses of popular clubs, lunchtime and post school.

Impressive debating skills, silver mementoes of previous glory all over the shop: the Observer Mace, The Cambridge Union, the Oxford Union and ESU. Massive and exciting drama and music. The former in super new purpose built studio – always interesting to have the theatre on the first floor, but much use of sponsoring, the Fraser of Allander lecture room and such like. Regular spectacular productions. 'Really exciting music department', which won three chamber music awards the week before our visit. Smart new music practice rooms with mirrored walls. Choirs and orchestras abound, trips abroad, travelling for competitions and the like. Faure Requiem in Paisley Abbey highly acclaimed.

Sparky art department with a gallery, but not much take up at higher levels – work is a serious matter in the west. Rector challenges this, saying there is 'an encouraging take-up at Higher levels with pupils regularly going on to art colleges'.

Background and Atmosphere: Founded as The Grammar School of Glasgow in 1124, the school was closely associated with Glasgow Cathedral but despite (because of?) its high academic standing, was closed by Glasgow Corporation in 1976. An appeal launched by the High School Former Pupils Club funded the new purpose-built senior school on the sports ground at Anniesland Cross, already owned by the FPs and the new school opened the day after the old school closed. A triumph. The High School merged with the former PNEU Dame school, Drewsteignton in Bearsden, three miles away, now the junior school.

The flat roofed purpose built building at Anniesland has expanded considerably; with new additions sprouting all over the place, though fortunately without any obvious loss of playing fields. Square split level assembly hall, artificial flood lit pitch, new Stand Complex. Sixth form area houses coffee shop and loud music as well as dedicated computers and work areas. The additions are humming and no longer buttercup yellow. School uniform for all, with girls in tartan skirts. The old house system remains, with each house having its own particular area in the school.

Pastoral Care and Discipline: Highly defined house system with colours but not names carrying on from junior school, siblings follow siblings into the same house. 'Transitus' (10 year olds) pupils are lovingly tended with lots of back up from junior school, particularly with learning support. The Rector has enormous parental support and says that he 'is not complacent, but no problems' – still – no recent drugs cases, though a couple have been asked to leave for going OTT, but certainly would expel if drugs were brought into the school. Suspensions for 'major offences'. Otherwise punishments range through sanctions, lunchtime detentions, clearing up litter (black bags) – how about scraping the gum off the tarmac? – school detention after school on Fridays.

Excellent blue booklet on Promoting Positive Relationships. Good PSE step guide, practised from the junior school.

Pupils and Parents: Ambitious, strong work ethos, almost half come from the affluent Bearsden/Milngavie complex and the remainder from different parts of Glasgow and outlying towns and villages. Bus system, some pupils from Ayrshire, the Trossachs (aka the edges of Argyll). Popular amongst the middle classes. Pupils can and do drive to school, large pupil car park. The geographic jump from the centre of Glasgow to the West End has changed the bias of the school, which now has fewer Asian or Jewish pupils (no synagogue in the West End), though there are a significant number from the South Side. Still large element of first time buyers plus one or two recently arrived Europeans – Russians and the like. Previous pupils include Bonar Law, Sir John Moore of Corunna, Campbell Bannerman, Lord Macfarlane of Bearsden.

Entrance: 10 and 11. Automatic from junior school (qv), otherwise three times oversubscribed. 50/60 applicants for every 22 places at Transitus, and a third as many again for first year. Odd vacancies in most years, own entrance exam, small number after Standard Grades, 'not many, not really looking for customers'. Fifth year candidates should have grade 1 passes in virtually all their Standard grade exams, or As at GCSE if they have come from England.

Exit: 98 per cent to degree courses all over, with a fairly high percentage to Scottish universities, a regular ten or so to Oxbridge and about 15 per cent going elsewhere. Only about seven taking a gap year this year (out of 94), but numbers rising. Work experience popular and exciting new project, the 'pioneering Mentoring scheme' shadowing senior managers and sponsored by the Scottish Education Business Partnership, currently in tandem with the local police officers – this is management training at its best. No particular bias in career – medics, engineers, accountants, IT course, lawyers, possibly less enthusiasm for the humanities.

Money Matters: School sympathetic to genuine problems, three or four academic scholarships each year and about 40 bursaries awarded on a financial need basis (and Rector is pleased when he can find pupils in financial need of a suitably high calibre). Bursary fund being built up to replace the old assisted places.

Remarks: School on a roll, going from strength to strength. A remarkable success story – and, as we said before, a High School truly worthy of its name.

HIGHGATE SCHOOL

Linked to Highgate Junior School in the Junior section

Linked to Highgate Pre-Preparatory School in the Junior section

North Road, London, N6 4AY

Tel: 020 8340 1524
Fax: 02083 407 674
E-mail: admissions@highgateschool.org.uk
Website: www.highgateschool.org.uk

• Pupils: 600 boys in senior school; girls in the sixth form and up to year 4, joining year 7 from 2006, gradually becoming fully co-educational; all day • Ages: 3 - 18 • Size of sixth form: 270 • C of E • Fees: £1,777 nursery (half day); £3,565 pre-prep; £3,820 junior; £4,195 senior (includes lunches) • Independent • Open days: Call school office

Head Master: Since 1989, Mr Richard Kennedy MA (fifties). Educated at Charterhouse and read maths and philosophy at New College, Oxford; taught at Shrewsbury and Westminster and was deputy head at Bishop's Stortford. Represented GB at athletics, musician; married to a high-powered civil engineer with an OBE. Two sons, one at Highgate. Governor of The Hall.

Retiring July 2006. Mr Adam Pettitt currently deputy head of Norwich School will be next in line.

Academic Matters: With the current teacher famine, the school's ability to offer staff accommodation in desirable Highgate Village gives it a huge edge. 'We've appointed some fantastic able young staff in the past few years.' Not an academic pressure cooker but does well all round with its broad intake. Runs extra classes in maths, economics, physics and modern languages for high achievers. Partnership schemes with local primary supported by the Sutton Trust. 77 per cent plus A*/A at GCSE, and over 84 per cent of A levels were A or B in 2005. One classical Greek A level candidate was in the top 5 in the country; a GCSE student got full marks in French in 2005. Economics, maths and the sciences are the strongest subjects but a major new centre for art, design and technology was opened this year and may change that emphasis. The head of physics is particularly interested in space and astronomy and boys can control a telescope in LA via computers. One chemistry teacher 'is an expert on alchemy and the boys love being taught by him.' 'My son is not the most academic child but that doesn't matter,' said a parent. 'He is encouraged every step of the way.' Flexible setting for most subjects. Full time learning support staff who can encompass lack of motivation as well as learning difficulties.

Games, Options, The Arts: Games very strong, with excellent facilities, including extensive playing fields and splendid sports centre, plus the Caen Wood Hall newly opened for dance. Opportunities range from soccer and cricket to Eton fives (the school teams are often national champions), fencing, golf, dance, sailing and climbing. Plenty of school and league matches, often including more than half a year group. Music also strong, and characterised by 'a lot of enthusiastic middle-ranking instrumentalists, alongside some exceptional soloists', says the head, though the number of pupils learning instruments is 'not as high as I would like'. There is an annual choral concert in conjunction with Channing School, usually in Southwark Cathedral. As well as the usual orchestras, there is a mixed chamber choir, a swing band, a dance band and a barbershop quartet. The house music competition is strongly contested.

The art is of a high standard, fine results at GCSE and A level. 'We're thrilled with the art our son is producing,' said a parent. New art centre with good facilities.

Optional activities include CCF, community service, the Duke of Edinburgh Award scheme and the unusual Urban Survival, as well as around 25 clubs that range from meteorology to car restoring. Plenty of trips abroad including classics trip to Greece and Italy, skiing in France and diving in the Red Sea.

Background and Atmosphere: The school was founded by Sir Roger Cholmeley in 1565 – 'and I love the fact that my son plays games on fields boys have used for centuries,' said a mother – at the top of Highgate Hill, by the tollgate north of London. The senior school is at the heart of old Highgate, with playing fields, sports centre and the junior and pre-prep schools a few hundred metres away. The site is a difficult one to manage and the school worked hard on preparing for its first co-ed intake, a decision which is proving very popular in the area. 'We're trying to keep ten years ahead,' says the head.

The school is a Christian foundation – albeit a multicultural one, holding different services for different religions – with a chapel attached, and the vaulted central hall has church-like features. The earliest buildings date from the mid-19th century, but the feel of the school is much older. Building styles range from the panelled assembly room, through the library in an ex-non-conformist chapel, to 1960s Dyne House, mostly used for the arts, with a brick terrace giving views across London. Various quadrangles with flower beds where boys and girls gather during break times.

Pastoral Care and Discipline: 'It's a very kind school,' said a parent, 'as long as you abide by the rules. It's not the place if your child wants to buck the system.' 'We haven't had a whisper of bullying,' said another. The school house system, viewed by the head as 'one of our great strengths', is arranged by geography, which means that students get to know others in different years living nearby. 'It's nice to meet others you know when you are out shopping,' said a sixth former. Housemasters visit students' homes before they join the school.

Some of the biggest changes have been on the pastoral front, says the head. 'We had a big internal review and threw out the old rewards and punishments system.' Now, as recognition of positive achievement, gold, silver and bronze alphas are awarded to around half the pupils each prize giving. 'We are very reflective as a school about these things. We have such confidence in the overall pastoral structure that we know the school can help pupils in turmoil keep their lives together.' The school chaplain is highly respected. 'You can talk to him about anything,' said a sixth former. There is a successful peer counselling service involving a team of lower sixth formers. Drugs are viewed as an educational rather than a disciplinary issue, though 'students are clear that the possession and use of drugs in school is treated seriously'.

Pupils and Parents: Traditionally viewed as having WASPish tendencies, the school is surprisingly multi-cultural. Plenty of local pupils as well as ones travelling in from all points north and south. OBs include Sir John Tavener, Barry Norman, Sir Clive Sinclair, Gerard Manley Hopkins and Anthony Crosland, John Box, John Rutter, Jan Latham-Koenig, Douglas Lowe, Sir Martin Gilbert, Geoffrey Palmer, Dan Damon, Sir John Betjeman and Charles Clarke.

Entrance: At 3, 32 boys and girls join the pre-prep. Another 34 or so 7-year-olds come into year 3. At 11, 30 boys and girls join the junior school (see below), almost all from state primaries. Forty-five more come into the senior school at 13, joining the 80 or so who have come up from the junior school with a virtually guaranteed place. Highgate's approach used to be more about finding 'nice boys who would fit in' but increasing demand has led to much more rigorous academic assessment. A few leave after GCSEs to go to boarding school or go to sixth form college, but the arrival of girls is making sixth form entry very competitive.

Exit: Most to good universities; one in six this year to Oxbridge.

Money Matters: Scholarships and bursaries at 11 have replaced most of the assisted places. There are also scholarships and bursaries at 13 and 16. The school does not, says the head, have many budgetary constraints.

Remarks: A London day school bang in the middle of old Highgate but with a suburban acreage of sports fields, which does well by its increasingly academic intake. Has confounded its traditional, hearty, masculine reputation by its bold decision to become fully co-educational. Will be watched with interest.

HILL HOUSE ST MARY'S

Linked to Hill House Saint Mary's School

65 Bawtry Road, Doncaster, South Yorkshire, DN4 7AD

Tel: 01302 535 926
Fax: 01302 534 675
E-mail: info@hillhousestmarys.co.uk
Website: www.hillhousestmarys.co.uk

- Pupils: 225 boys and 235 girls • Ages: 3-16 • Non-denom
- Fees: £1,850 - £2,643 • Independent

Head: Mr Jack Cusworth BA CertEd (fifties), who has been head of Hill House since 2000 and joined the school in 1973, teaching maths and PE, and 'gradually worked my way up'; sole deputy head and principal from 1990. Educated at a grammar school in Doncaster, followed by Sheffield College of Education and the Open University, his wife is head of the sixth form at Danum school – the local centre of excellence for 16-19 year-olds ('very, very good,' he says, 'but then I am a bit biased'). As nice a chap as you could hope to meet, open, friendly, frank; the children think he's brill. The governors of Hill House effectively bought out the proprietors of St Mary's and the whole is now run as a charitable trust.

Entrance: From reception upwards, put name down on the list. Mini-testette if joining later. Progressively more pupils staying on to combined senior school, with others joining from the state sector. Pupils come from within a fifteen-mile radius of Doncaster.

Exit: A few leave at 11 or 13 and go to trad public schools with fair number of scholarships – Repton, Worksop and the like. Older pupils at 16 mostly go to further education, with a fair number to trad sixth forms and local techs.

Remarks: The combination of these two independent schools in Doncaster happened over the summer hols 2002. St Mary's previously had pupils till 16, as well as in the prep; Hill House, a much stronger and bigger prep, had an enviable reputation locally. GCSE results include a goodly collection of A*s and As across the board and a very commendable pass rate all over. However, when we arrived, the chaos in the office was such that they appeared to have 'thrown everything away', well, couldn't find it anyway. Pupils can take GCSEs early, otherwise, French, Spanish, business studies, ICT, geography, history, art, CDT, home economics, Eng lang and lit, music and maths. Brightest pupils studying at AS and A2 levels. Very good recent ISI inspection report.

Going upwards in age: nursery perfect, lovely collection of Victorian houses with secure play areas (masses of white fences – infuriating for drivers). Excellent pre-prep and prep mostly housed in converted convent, brimful of up to 11 year olds when we visited, each wearing their own school uniform and each with their class teacher in charge. Special needs catered for, both withdrawn from class, small groups as well as one-to-one, the school adopts a multi-sensory approach, dyspraxia, Asperger's, 'will cope if we can'. One of the current pupils, an epileptic, has full-time learning support (parents pay). Dedicated labs, wizard libraries, masses of computers and IT, vast hall with stage which doubles as gym, bags of child-inspired art on all the walls.

Art dept full of sumptuous art, pottery, papier mâché and textiles and masses of art scholarships further up. Altogether humming. Thriving music dept with staff travelling between the two buildings. Impressive dining room, tinies are served, otherwise canteen style, staff preside at the ends of the tables. Halal meals on offer and special kitchen. Late supervision till 6pm, plus activities and juice and bikkies for the prep and nursery. Both convent and the extensions overlook Town Field, much used for games by school and town, and absolutely charming. Indeed the whole Rutland Street complex is absolutely charming, with only one smallish property for sale which would complete the corner (and as the school is planning to sell this inner-city site and move further out, this would be a logical – and financially rewarding – step).

At 11, all youngsters move to the more spacious Bawtry Road site, out past the racecourse; regular shuttle between the two sites. Sadly the detached Victorian villa, with its stables and various purpose-built outhouses in a fairly substantial garden (netball pitch, loads of play area) came with a limited lease, now extended to five. The main house is in good heart and the numerous outbuildings have been appropriately refurbished to a high standard to accommodate an additional rather smart science laboratory, new music area and larger home economics room. Certain amount of other internal tinkering with space, smashing art dept atop the stables, good CDT, enviable oak room, used for assemblies and mini-productions. Dining cafeteria-style with stools, halal food, always salads, fruit and cheese and bikkies. Much use made of local facilities sports-wise. PSHE important – 'occasional problems always possible' but good pastoral systems in place. Each division of the school has its own head, plus tutors (pastoral). The academic and the pastoral operate side by side.

Exciting developments. Watch this space.

HILLS ROAD SIXTH FORM COLLEGE

Hills Road, Cambridge, Cambridgeshire, CB2 2PE

Tel: 01223 247 251
Fax: 01223 416 979
E-mail: aclarke@hillsroad.ac.uk
Website: www.hillsroad.ac.uk

• Pupils: 1,750 girls and boys • Ages: 16-19 • Non-denom
• State • Open days: Evenings in November

Principal: Since 2002, Dr Rob Wilkinson BA PhD (fifties) to whom we spoke but did not meet. Vast experience of sixth form education and as a college inspector. Came here after eight years as principal of Wyggeston and Queen Elizabeth I College in Leicester. Before that he was vice principal at Hills Road (1989-1994), head of history at John Leggott College, Scunthorpe, and taught at Scarborough Sixth Form College.

Academic Matters: Most years tops the league tables as highest achieving sixth form college. The great majority of its students – 85 per cent – come from maintained schools in Cambridge, south Cambridgeshire and surrounding areas. The remaining 15 per cent come from private schools, some of which haemorrhage 16 year olds each year to Hills Road. Latest inspection report (2001) awarded Hills Road 11 grade ones – 'outstanding' – for every subject inspected and for the college's leadership and management – a unique achievement nationally. The college has a distinctive, palpable academic buzz; it may have a top class sports centre and be renowned for music but many students choose this college first and foremost for its academic reputation. No snobbishness about A level offerings – the more the merrier, including accounting, archaeology, electronics, film studies, Italian, media studies, music technology, dance, sociology, performance studies (not to be confused with theatre studies – also on offer) to name a

few. Despite these more glamorous options, maths remains the most popular A level subject – double many other departments. All students do four subjects in their second year – which can include either A level general studies or AS level critical thinking.

One of the most technologically impressive colleges in the UK. Awash with computers, more than 650, all networked and internet capable, they are wedged into every spare open space, not just IT rooms (head of IT was brought in from Unilever). Two language labs (many private schools have none), video cameras to loan, media studies studio with 3 editing suites, darkroom, 2 satellite systems for receiving foreign language programmes and meteorological information. £5m building programme has provided a new science building, new teaching accommodation for psychology and computing, student guidance centre, student cafe, more music facilities, and new landscaping around the campus.

Excellent study skills centre copes with everything from time management, handwriting and essay writing to ESL, dyslexia and Asperger's syndrome. Centre is available to all students and helps over 20 per cent of the student body and this percentage is growing each year. Laptops used by a few students with special needs. Average class size is 19 with 22 max; lunch-time surgeries in all subjects give students an opportunity for more individual attention.

Games, Options, The Arts: Students must attend at least one 'enrichment' session once a week in a discipline outside their studies. Massive range of options available, including most sports. Fields teams in major sports and many unusual ones and those not already going can be rustled up if interest demands. Girls' swimming team, set up by 4 students, won the English Schools' Swimming Association's Senior Girls' Freestyle and Medley Relay titles against the likes of Millfield School (2001) – some achievement as the college does not have a pool. Recent national players in cricket, hockey, rowing, rugby and tennis. College's sports and tennis centre includes superb cricket hall, opened in 1997 by Sir Colin Cowdrey, indoor and outdoor tennis courts run in conjunction with the Lawn Tennis Association, sports hall and squash court. Ten acres of sports fields a 5-minute walk away.

Drama, theatre administration and stage management flourish in college's Robinson Theatre, built 30 years ago through the donation of a multi-millionaire Old Boy, but looking as fresh as if it were completed yesterday. High standards in music with incredible range of ensembles and fab facilities, including top class recording studio and new music technology suite. Artists in residence and spacious areas for creating art masterpieces. Lots of clubs, including language groups (for non-linguists), life skills, art, fitness, D of E. 60 students involved in Young Enterprise. Overseas visits and exchanges with 17 destinations in Europe, the USA and Africa, including work placements in Germany for language students, a brilliant idea.

Background and Atmosphere: Has been described in the press as a half-way house to university but could more accurately be called a seven-eighths-way house. After coping here, university is a doddle. Opened in 1903 as a selective boys' grammar (nearby private school, the Perse, complained to the government and tried to get it closed down). In 1974 relaunched as a co-ed sixth form college. In the early 1980s there were 600 students, no adult education (4,500 adults now attend evening and weekend classes) and the college site consisted of the original building plus decrepit temporary huts. Foundation building now swallowed up by tasteful, bright, well-designed blocks. Social area in basement a bit of a squash for all these students but almost everything else rivals some universities for excellence of facilities. Big, bustling, friendly; looking out over the central quad as 1,750 sixth form students move from lesson to lesson, the scene resembles a mammoth beehive, or a film on fast forward with everyone moving at double time. New students may feel anxious at first as they have to become used to academic challenges, a diversity of social and economic backgrounds, co-education, and independent work and study. There is nevertheless strong support and guidance for students from day one. 'Although we treat them as young adults, we don't really expect them to be adults', the principal said. Thanks to felicitous Cambridge location, state school cred and excellent reputation, the college enjoys a stream of celebrated speakers, eg Professor Stephen Hawking, John Major, Lord Dearing, Zandra Rhodes and Sir Martin Rees, the Astronomer Royal.

Pastoral Care and Discipline: Hills Road requires teenagers to have a measure of self-discipline, subtly reinforced by the pastoral system. Students have been consulted on most college rules, are expected to behave like adults, and generally rise to meet expectations. There is no smoking behind the bike sheds because the college provides an area for those who choose – despite the principal's advice! – to smoke. Students can freely come and go from campus – as long as they are there for lessons. As well as working hard, students are quick to point out the fun they have: freshers' disco, two annual balls and ... all this freedom. The tutor is the pastoral care mainstay and students see their tutors regularly in tutor groups of around 20 students. There are also regular individual sessions and careers guidance. Previously some gripes about this system but a review of student guidance has been completed and a specialist tutor team, based in a brand new large student guidance centre, became operational in September 2005. Drugs and drink not problems here, although – as everywhere – opportunities exist.

Pupils and Parents: Students do not choose to come here unless they want to work (there are lots of good local alternatives) so are mostly motivated and mature. Some commute well over an hour each way to be here, bus stop opposite and Cambridge rail station five minutes away. Popular with parents of independent school pupils who move their children to Hills Road from local independents like the Perse and the Leys and even from famous London public schools trusting their kids will have a better chance of getting into Oxbridge from a state school than from an independent. Parents are involved, committed, ambitious for their youngsters. Former students include prominent government officials and Anil Gupta, director of the TV programme, Goodness Gracious Me.

Entrance: All prospective students from the local 'Collegiate Board' area are interviewed – a phenomenal feat given the numbers. For A level courses, students need GCSE grade Bs or better in the subjects they will be pursuing or related subjects. Priority is given to students living within the Collegiate Board area and most students come up from one of the area's 11-16 community or village colleges. Up to 80 places offered to pupils outside the area, mostly within a 30-mile radius of the college, but a few from other parts of England. Each year 200 applicants are turned down, some because they do not meet academic requirements.

Exit: Around 95 per cent to degree courses, over 70 a year to Oxford and Cambridge. 35 per cent take gap years and the college is unusually proactive in helping students arrange these, even providing limited funding. A few students don't stay the course but retention rates are well above sixth form college norms. The college has occasionally asked unmotivated students not to continue.

Money Matters: Previous head was a genius at magicking pots of funding out of thin air. With luck, this happy pattern should continue and the signs are that it will, with over £50,000 already raised from donors and the £5m building project having just been completed.

Remarks: Big, powerful, ambitious, top of the range sixth form college for confident and motivated young adults. Challenging atmosphere but most students positively thrive here.

HOCKERILL ANGLO-EUROPEAN COLLEGE

Dunmow Road, Bishop's Stortford, Hertfordshire, CM23 5HX

Tel: 01279 658 451
Fax: 01279 755 918
E-mail: admin.hockerill@thegrid.org.uk
Website: www.hockerill.herts.sch.uk

• Pupils: 710 boys and girls; 225 boarders • Ages: 11-19 • Size of sixth form: 140 • Non-denom • Fees: Boarding fees £2,206 - £2,850 • State • Open days: October

Principal: Since 1996, Dr Robert B Guthrie BSc PhD MBA (early fifties), educated at Sale Grammar School and Leeds and Durham Universities. First degree in physics, PhD in ceramics and MBA in business administration. Previously head of the International School in Rome. Taught in the independent sector for almost all of his career until coming to Hockerill. A keen sportsman in his youth, he played rugby for England Schools and Great Britain Universities. Married to Christine, who is in charge of the junior boarding at the College. Two adult children.

Academic Matters: A language specialist school that is recognised (and therefore awarded additional funding) as both a language college and training school by the DfES. Pupils are setted from year 7 and those with an aptitude for languages are not only fast-tracked in a modern European language (either French or German) but also learn history and geography in their chosen language in years 9, 10 and 11 up to GCSE. These pupils also take their foreign language GCSE one or two years early and nearly all achieve an A*. Across all subjects, GCSE grades are now well above the national average and improving. Hockerill's GCSE results last year were in the top 50 comprehensives in the country and it was listed as the country's 3rd most improved school. The 2003 Ofsted report described Hockerill as an exceptional college, which gives very good value for money.

The school had no sixth form until 1998. There is no provision for A levels and all pupils study for the International Baccalaureate Diploma. In 2005, 97 per cent were successful, with half gaining a bilingual Diploma and displaying equal competence in two languages. Lessons are held on approx two out of every three Saturday mornings but school holidays are longer than those of state day schools (an extra three weeks in the summer, for example).

Games, Options, The Arts: Floodlit Astroturf pitch; plenty of sporting fixtures including soccer, rugby, hockey, netball, basketball, tennis and athletics, against both state and independent schools.

Wide range of extra-curricular activities, including D of E, CCF (both army and RAF), community service and golf, to keep the boarders occupied, but day pupils are strongly encouraged to join in. Numerous exchange trips and foreign visits; year 10 pupils are offered two weeks of work experience in France, where the college has a rural base.

Background and Atmosphere: Set well back from the road and close to Bishop's Stortford town centre. Dates back to 1852, originally an Anglican teacher training college, and only set on its present course since 1994. Traditional Victorian buildings with the addition of standard modern blocks, overall appearance and atmosphere of the 20-acre site is very pleasant. A new uniform from 2005 – blue blazers, pinstripe trousers and striped tie for boys, blue jackets, distinctive blouses and pinstripe trousers or skirts for girls. Sixth formers wear plain dark suits. Uniform rules strict.

Pastoral Care and Discipline: 'Our approach to behaviour and discipline is generally old-fashioned,' says the principal. Pastoral care for boarders is highly rated, although pupils think that they are treated rather strictly. Good behaviour by the boarders rewarded with a system of privileges.

Pupils and Parents: Boarders from around the world and seem to mix well. On the day we visited a history class studying the causes of the second world war included a group of Germans. 'We have plenty of lively and stimulating discussions,' said the very enthusiastic history teacher. Hockerill has found favour with the local middle classes over recent years, so day pupils are increasingly from relatively affluent backgrounds.

Entrance: It's getting more difficult to get a place here every year – 8 applicants for every day and every boarding place in 2003. Top priority goes to applicants with a brother or sister on the roll at the time of admission. Next in line are applicants with a compelling medical and/or social reason for admission. Then 10 per cent of places are awarded to the applicants who attain the highest scores in the college's language aptitude test. After that places are awarded to applicants who can demonstrate that they may need to take advantage of the college's boarding facilities at some point in the future. All other places are allocated according to the primary school the applicant has attended. Out of 107 year 7 places, 32 are allocated to boarders. Boarding places are heavily oversubscribed. Entrance is by interview. 'We look for evidence of a positive commitment,' says the principal.

Entrance to the sixth form is dependent on GCSE (or equivalent) results and interview.

Exit: All of 2005's sixth form went on to higher education. A high proportion studies law or medicine.

Remarks: In little more than five years Hockerill has changed from a relatively unknown school with places to spare to a very highly regarded and massively oversubscribed academic institution. Even for those who don't regard language as a priority, this school has plenty to offer. Latest Ofsted inspection October 2003.

THE HOLY CROSS SCHOOL

25 Sandal Road, New Malden, Surrey, KT3 5AR

Tel: 02083 954 225
Fax: 02083 954 234
E-mail: hxs@rbksch.org
Website: www.holycross.kingston.sch.uk

• Pupils: 875 day girls • Ages: 11-18 • Size of sixth form: 140
• RC • State • Open days: October

Head: Since 2001, Mr Tom Gibson MEd NPQH BSc DipEd,(forties). Educated Wimbledon College, read physical education and sports science at Loughborough University. Previously taught at St Joseph's, Beulah Hill, Glyn ADT and St Gregory's, Kenton. Married to a fellow teacher, four young children. Well experienced in different areas of education, a pleasant, unassuming gentleman who looks set to brighten all horizons.

Academic Matters: A mostly long-serving, committed staff of all age groups delivers an 'innovative curriculum' (OFSTED 2004) to a high standard. Class sizes are around 30. A level results getting better while GCSE results have improved to 80 per cent A*-C. Awarded Specialist Science College status from September 2003 which enables the school to develop its provision in science, maths and ICT over four years. Independent working habits are encouraged and study skills taught although touch-typing is now only taught within the GNVQ ICT. Two large bustling ICT suites, reasonable-looking library. Staff and students are developing a video conferencing project with NASA. The sixth form is in partnership with a local boys' school, Richard Challoner, enabling them to offer a wider choice of subjects – much appreciated by pupils and parents. SEN and EFL are catered for by specialist teachers throughout the school.

Games, Options, The Arts: Two garret-style studios provide an inspiring setting for art and DT. A hard-working music teacher is making new waves with the orchestra, individual instrumental tuition on most instruments can be arranged. Strong choir, tours at home and abroad. Sport is an area the head is looking at developing over the next few years. A new sports hall and dance studio will be complete by September 2007. The school has been selected to train year ten as Wimbledon ball girls. Creative drama department is growing, many do GCSE. Duke of Edinburgh Award Scheme along with a selection of after-school clubs.

Background and Atmosphere: The Sisters of the Holy Cross founded the school in 1931. It became grant maintained in 1993 and in 1999 became a voluntary aided school within the diocese of Southwark. The original buildings have been much added to, updating and redecoration is currently underway. A £5.2 million building programme is underway and will provide excellent new facilities. Caring and moral values help deliver a smooth, organised atmosphere. Whilst Roman Catholicism predominates, all other faiths are welcomed. Pupils are encouraged to be involved in the community through voluntary work.

Pastoral Care and Discipline: Sensible set of school rules, girls are expected to be mature and aware of others' needs; all have form tutors. Strict uniform code, girls ticked off if not properly dressed. Sixth form pupils are expected to be self-disciplined and present themselves well.

Pupils and Parents: Good ethnic mix; 65 per cent are Catholics. 'We are from all walks of life here, professionals to refugees, most are somewhere in the middle.' The common interest is a well-balanced and Christian education. Serious PTA.

Entrance: Pupils come at 11 from a wide catchment area as the school has twenty grammar stream places, the remaining 130 places go firstly to Catholics living in Kingston and surrounding boroughs. At 16, at least 5 GCSEs and an interview.

Exit: Currently 80 per cent of students return into the federated sixth form, with 15 per cent moving to local colleges and a small number to the world of work.

Remarks: With a young and dedicated head, a school for parents to watch develop. March 2004 OFSTED stated that Holy Cross is a 'good and rapidly improving school... behaviour and relationships are very good...and students achieve well as a result of good teaching and learning'.

HOWARD OF EFFINGHAM SCHOOL

Lower Road, Effingham, Leatherhead, Surrey, KT24 5JR

Tel: 01372 453 694
Fax: 01372 456 952
E-mail: Howard@the-howard.demon.co.uk
Website: www.howard-of-effingham.surrey.sch.uk

• Pupils: 1,575 pupils; girls and boys • Ages: 11-18 • Size of sixth form: 350 • Non-denom • State

Head: Since 1999, Mrs Rhona Barnfield MA BSc (fifties). Initial impressions are of a strong, positive personality with a very clear vision of what is best for the school. 'She comes over as very committed and probably quite determined,' says a parent. Mrs Barnfield declined to be interviewed.

Academic Matters: 'The Howard' – as it is known locally – enjoys an excellent reputation and many families move into the catchment area to enable their children to attend. It is a mixed comprehensive school that achieves very good results. 70 per cent plus get 5 A*-C grades at GCSE; average point score at A level in 2004 was 317. The school has larger classes, lesser facilities and fewer resources than most of its Surrey fee-paying counterparts. Yet the Howard's results are as good, if not on occasions better, than some of its private competitors, particularly when you consider the school's mixed intake. Modern languages, art and design and technology are particularly strong with great examples seen all over the school. Latin, too, is offered as an additional subject option from year 9. There are light and airy new science labs (sponsored by Brown & Root). The Howard is among the first 24 schools in the country to become a Science College. With support from businessman Peter Harrison, they have built a brand new lab and ICT suite; older labs have been refurbished. A new cyber cafe was opened last January and there are new courses in applied sciences at KS4 and A level, plus science-based events for the wide community. In the core subjects, maximum class sizes likely to be 30, but numbers do get smaller higher up the school. Very few foreign students so no current EFL requirements. Some special needs support and sixth form students also get involved, giving up one free period a week to help students. It works out to about 2 hours per fortnight and sixth formers seem to enjoy the challenge. Also a reading scheme that helps year 7 students

achieve required levels (operated on a voluntary level by sixth formers). There is a large sixth form resulting in a wide range of options. Vocational A levels on offer and praise for the sixth form teaching – 'the teachers are very helpful and friendly, we get a lot of support, yet a lot of opportunity to work on our own,' said one (ex-private school) sixth former, whose only fear was of turning into a couch potato in the state system. 'I'm not particularly sporty, there should be proper timetabled PE lessons, but at least now we have voluntary sports lessons.' Adequate sixth form block has relaxation area and study classrooms.

Games, Options, The Arts: For a comprehensive school, there is a lot of sport on offer. Facilities could be larger for the number of pupils but the school uses additional fields from a nearby sports club as well as the facilities of the Effingham Community Sports Centre. Hockey, netball, football, cricket and rugby are major sports with tennis, badminton, athletics, basketball, rounders, cross-country, squash, volleyball, softball, orienteering, dance and gymnastics also available.

Drama and music play an important role in the life of the school with regular musical activities each week. There are numerous choirs, a jazz band, orchestra and ensembles. The orchestra provides the music for many of the drama productions and both orchestra and choir have performed at the Albert Hall. The drama productions are popular, with the sixth form being very involved in the lighting, sound and staging. Any other extra-curricular activities take place before school, at lunch-time and after school. The Duke of Edinburgh Award Scheme is available from year 10 onwards and enjoys popular support.

Background and Atmosphere: Named after the second Lord Howard of Effingham (admiral who commanded the fleet which defeated Spanish Armada in 1588), the school was built in 1940. Although it has been extensively enlarged and expanded since then, the school feels as if it is bursting at the seams. There are so many pupils that the school operates a one-way system during lesson changes to avoid congestion in the narrow pale green corridors. Yes, it needs a coat of paint in places and it would be nice if there were green lawns where there is black tarmac, but instead of window dressing, the school seems to be spending its funds on great teachers and educational resources. 'The staff seem extremely committed and very hands-on,' says one impressed parent. Food is adequate, say pupils – hot and cold options, plus snacks. Many pupils bring their own packed lunches.

Pastoral Care and Discipline: School is conscious of the need for strong pastoral care in such a large community.

House system in place to encourage co-operation, community spirit and competition. Older pupils are encouraged to be role models for younger ones. All new pupils are invited for an induction day in July before they join. School has a code of conduct which pupils are expected to adhere to. 'If there are any difficulties, the staff are in there pronto,' says a parent.

The size of the school is undoubtedly an issue – but it bothers some more than others. One pupil did say that if she could change one thing at the school it would be the 'class sizes', because 'you sometimes feel as if you could disappear.' A parent shared this view and said, when discussing her child with a teacher, she was not sure whether the teacher really knew who she was talking about. However, another parent had the opposite view and felt, despite the school's size, the staff had a good insight into her daughter. Lots of consultation with parents re any changes.

Common complaint from outsiders is the scruffiness of the pupils – the usual parade of micro skirts skimming their backsides, school socks disappearing into clompy shoes, and shirts and ties for both boys and girls worn at ever more rakish angles – although head and staff are trying very hard to encourage pupils to take more pride in their appearance. Not a particularly authoritarian school but encourages children to behave responsibly with respect and consideration. Policy on drugs and smoking is firm according to pupils, as is anti-bullying.

Sixth form is relatively autonomous. There are fewer pupils in each class and, as the students feel closer to and more relaxed with their teachers, they really seem to enjoy themselves – 'my daughter found her feet very quickly, and there was no prejudice whatsoever that she had come from a private school. She is very happy,' said one impressed mum. Sixth formers don't wear uniform but have to conform to a standard of acceptable dress, which was certainly adhered to when we visited. Biggest gripe of the older students seems to be that there is not enough parking for their cars!

Pupils and Parents: Main catchment areas are very middle class – Horsley, Effingham, Bookham and Fetcham, although a few pupils come from the equally upmarket Cobham and Oxshott areas. Most pupils are bused in, as parking facilities are limited; parents are discouraged from dropping their children off. The school is popular and usually oversubscribed. Pupils seem well-mannered and happy in the environs of the school. A smattering of real scruffs and others the school would not be proud of, including the odd smoker or two, are spotted on their way to or from school –

a fact of life unfortunately common to many schools and something they can do little about.

Entrance: At 11. The closing date for applications is usually around mid-November of the year before a pupil is due to attend (for example, Nov 2006 for entry Sept 2007). Siblings at the school and proximity of home to the school seem to be the main factors affecting admission. Places are then offered during the spring term and, if unsuccessful, one can apply to be put on a waiting list. There is also an appeals procedure.

Impressive A level results mean that the school is popular with outsiders, including ex-private school pupils, for sixth form studies.

Exit: Approximately 65 per cent stay on into the sixth form; the students who leave the school tend to enrol at a local college to pursue more vocational courses, and small number take up employment or join training schemes. Sixth form leavers to many traditional university choices, about 20 per cent via a gap year, a good few straight into employment. A good half dozen to Oxbridge each year.

Remarks: A very large, but very successful, state school that offers a good alternative to the ubiquitous Surrey private schools. It doesn't have the manicured grounds and gracious old buildings of the private environment but it does boast many pupils whose parents are teachers in both the private and state sectors.

Good academic results mean that the school is an option for cash-strapped parents of private school pupils at age 11. However, 11 year old timid girls and shy, awkward boys – particularly those from cloistered private schools – may feel overawed by the sheer sink-or-swim size of the place. At A level, the school comes into its own and can hold its head up high with the private schools academically and with the big plus of an atmosphere and social mix more in tune with university life.

HOWELL'S SCHOOL, LLANDAFF

Linked to Howell's School Junior School, Llandaff in the Junior section

Cardiff Road, Llandaff, Cardiff, South Glamorgan, CF5 2YD

Tel: 02920 562 019
Fax: 02920 578 879
E-mail: headsec@how.gdst.net
Website: www.howells.cardiff.sch.uk

- Pupils: 535 girls, all day – but boys in the sixth form from 2005
- Ages: 11-18 • Size of sixth form: 180, including 25 boys
- Non-denom • Fees: Junior £1,293 to £1,565. Senior £2,159
- Independent

Principal: Since 1991, Mrs Jane Fitz (forties) was born and educated in Tasmania, then London University (chemistry). Has always taught in GSDT schools, rising through the ranks in London. Husband is a professor at Cardiff University; teenage daughter presently at the school. Diligent, professional, able and committed. Chaired the Welsh Independent Schools Council, now a council member of Cardiff University. Described as 'fascinating' and 'a visionary with the ability to see the whole picture and work through the minutiae of detail to see things through to completion'. Such tenacity has not always endeared her to staff but, when applied to the welfare and aspiration of pupils, has proved very successful. Bubbly and delightful deputy principal, Mrs Sally Davis.

Academic Matters: Academically very strong indeed – a selective entry and a busy, vibrant management team ensures there's no room for slack. 87 per cent A/Bs at A level in 2005 and 64 per cent with A/A* at GCSE. Parents make contented noises at the quality of teachers and general standards. Science does very well – eight labs with a collection of enthusiastic staff – and many girls later taking up medicine. We sat in for part of a biology lesson with very attentive pupils who eagerly informed us that we had missed the 'best and gory bits'. Only dual award at GCSE, to leave room for ICT, DT, drama within the school's limit of 8 or 9 GCSEs. Keen that all students take at least one creative subject – which they do. Maths sure-footed – 'my less mathematically able daughter felt safe and confident due to the dedication of the teachers'.

The breadth of curriculum is not extensive, but is improving: no social sciences, but government & politics, psychology, critical thinking, theatre studies, drama, business studies and IT recently introduced. The head is keen to point out that many go on to study social sciences at university and choices are pragmatic and made with each pupil's university requirements in mind, and the school will jump through hoops to accommodate an individual's passion. There's a pupil doing Arabic, another Italian, another (as a result of some girls winning a national science competition, visiting Cape Kennedy and Houston, returning to form an astronomy club) astronomy. The school celebrates its Welshness and pupils learn about and play their part in Welsh culture – plenty of exhibitors in the Eisteddfod with one pupil winning the Learners' Recitation. Raises the profile of the languages generally in the school. The emphasis on Welsh language and the uniqueness of Welsh culture is strongly supported by parents but does elbow some other subjects out of the curriculum. Wales as famous for exporting teachers as it is for coal – Welsh lilts can be heard in staffrooms across the land and many of the best have come back here. A congenial, jovial and committed bunch. Tenish mild/moderate dyslexic pupils annually – satellite unit gives individual tuition at extra cost. Talented children with specific gifts are also catered for. Clear ethos of the school is that the girls can achieve academically and be productive in society. The sixth form is housed opposite the main school in two large Victorian redbrick houses with gardens that stretch to the Llandaff fields. An exciting time is ahead for Howells as – uniquely within the GDST – they have become co-ed at sixth form with capacity increased from 120 to 200 (they argue that single sex education works well from 11 to 16 but co-ed is equal or better from 16 to 18).

Games, Options, The Arts: Some fine art and textiles on display. A couple of quality drama productions a year, drama perceived as very important in the curriculum. Sport includes badminton, horse riding, fencing, a dry ski team (currently Welsh champions) apart from the usual netball, hockey, swimming and gymnastics, where national successes are numerous. Lacrosse has been a long tradition at the school although fixtures are limited due to the lengthy trip to rivals Malvern and Haberdashers Monmouth. Dance is popular – but not taken to GCSE level. 50 per cent pupils play an instrument, significant numbers at county level (some at national) – parents really laud this department. Light, fresh, octagonal, concert hall and plenty of practice rooms – soon to be extended. We saw pupils being talked through Dawn (by Benjamin Britten) by one of the celebrated music staff who broke into extravagant, enraptured gestures much to the amusement of the girls – very infectious enthusiasm. All types of bands, five choirs, three large orchestras and many chamber groups. Duke of Edinburgh increasingly popular – we met a large troop setting off for their gold award. Impressive involvement in community and charity work – working with a local special school, Envision, Fair Trade etc; the canteen stocks only fair trade approved goods. Also links with a school in their sister country, Lesotho; staff have already visited for a week and now the pupils are raising money for a new science laboratory and library. Excellent careers programme – conventions, visiting speakers etc.

Background and Atmosphere: In 1537, Thomas Howell left a substantial sum to the Drapers Company for orphans and from this charitable bequest the school was founded in 1860. Joined the GDST in 1980. A short walk from the centre of Cardiff off a busy main road. On entering the school, all feeling of congestion disappears – the site is much larger than is visible from the road. A grey stone chateau-style building of turrets and spires with extensions bolted on over the years. Grand old cast iron staircase, wood panelling, stain-glassed windows, original fresco in the Grand Hall, etc. Much fustiness dispensed with over the past 10 years – no more straw boaters, even the pink and white striped shirt is soon to change. Good food. An atmosphere of 'hwyl' ie spirit and heartiness, respect but not deference.

Pastoral Care and Discipline: Head is not fazed by feisty pupils – 'I often find they become great contributors to society' and the deputy says their motto is 'don't let small things become big things' and 'work hard with parents to nip problems in the bud'. Very effective pastoral systems. Drugs, alcohol not big issues, but out if caught.

Pupils and Parents: Catchment area from Cardiff to Newport, Bridgend and the Valleys means a diverse group of pupils – a lot of bursaries so the selection is academic and not exclusively social. 15 per cent ethnic minority and 60 per cent from state and own linked junior schools, the rest well-heeled parents from eg the medical and legal professions. A shared desire to achieve – the parents are as ambitious as the pupils. Parents very involved with life of school. OGs include the first woman QC in Wales, Jane Crowley; the first women chair in Egyptology, Professor Rosalie David; and Charlotte Church.

Entrance: Usual GDST entrance criteria at nursery and junior school of observing at play and interview. Yrs 3-6 sit papers in maths, English, non-verbal reasoning. Entrance papers mainly taken at year 7 in maths/English. Scholars are chosen from results and interview. Mainly automatic entry from junior to senior unless a pupil is struggling with the level of work.

Exit: Only a handful escape university. Some to art foundation, a double handful go to Oxbridge, others mainly to top brass universities with the highest numbers reading medicine, dentistry, pharmacy, veterinary sciences, engineering and law. Plenty do business studies, IT or performing arts.

Money Matters: Healthy. Apart from the support of the Minerva Trust common to all GDST schools, there is the added benefit of the Thomas Howell Trust managed by the prosperous Drapers Company. About 20 per cent of the senior school are on some kind of bursary – with a small pot available to those falling on hard times.

Remarks: A school where academic excellence, the arts and Welsh culture are celebrated.

HUISH EPISCOPI SCHOOL

Wincanton Road, Langport, Somerset, TA10 9SS

Tel: 01458 250 501
Fax: 01458 250 262
E-mail: office@huishepiscopi.somerset.sch.uk
Website: www.huishepiscopi.somerset.sch.uk

• Pupils: 615 boys, 595 girls. All day • Ages: 11-16
• Non-denom • State

Head: Since 1996, Mr Graham Roff BEd MEd AdDipEdMngt (early fifties). Educated in Stockport then Madeley College before reading geography and education at Keele and adding further qualifications along the way. Has moved around the country and was deputy head at Cheadle Hulme High School for six years before coming to Huish Episcopi. Lives locally and wife Pam teaches infants in Ilminster; both their sons have gone through the school. Takes a keen interest in sport particularly basketball which he used to play. Enjoys hill walking and foreign travel but says he has little time for these. Slightly reserved but shrewd with a pragmatic approach to educational issues. Likes to engage with parents and staff; chats to pupils informally in corridors and says that they are 'comfortable' about seeking his help when needed. Proud of what has already been achieved and would love to see school develop a sixth form.

Academic Matters: Head believes in setting children from the outset. School operates two distinct 'populations' (or bands) in each year group. Two 'top ability' groups identified within each band for English and a number of other subjects but 'tight' setting in maths and science. Choice of second foreign language from year 7 (for all except those with 'extreme' special needs) allows pupils to see whether to continue with one or two languages from year 9. GCSE results have improved consistently over recent years, in top 25 per cent nationally in value-added tables. Noticeable effort being put into making teaching livelier and more flexible. Strong emphasis on ICT with more than 250 computers in the school; specialist science status has provided funding for additional laboratories. Majority take dual award science but similar numbers of gifted and weaker scientists take triple science or GNVQ (due to end in 2006) courses respectively.

Attractive languages area with particularly impressive GCSE results in French. History, English and art also good but in all these subjects it's mostly girls who get the best grades; boys fare better in geography. A large number of pupils are entered for statistics in year 10 (a policy questioned by some parents) and many take short GCSE courses in RE and citizenship. Some pupils follow an optional extra subject after school. Large laboratories accommodate up to 32 pupils in top sets allowing lower ability groups of 16-19. Less flexibility in other core subjects. Links with Bridgwater College have led to highly popular and useful courses in practical skills such as engineering and vehicle maintenance with a few in year 11 getting extended work placements.

All year 7 children are screened on entry using computer based (Cats) testing despite close liaison providing plenty of information beforehand from feeder primary schools. SENCO works with staff to support pupils with SpLD and other special needs largely within normal timetable and the 13 learning support assistants work alongside mainstream teachers. Small numbers of statemented children. Few with Aspergers traits get help with socialisation and use of free time in school.

Games, Options, The Arts: Longstanding reputation especially in boys' football, girls' hockey and cross-country with huge numbers involved. Regularly comes out as county champion in football, cricket and hockey; also individual representation at district and county level. Has produced national champions in athletics and high national placings in cross country. PE is a popular GCSE option and pupils have benefit of purpose-built leisure centre on site which is shared with the community and includes fitness centre, dance studio and superb squash courts; floodlit multi-use outside courts, heated 25 metre open air pool and extensive playing fields.

Music and drama join forces for many productions with good results considering lack of sixth form. Dance is popular but not a GCSE option yet. Lower school hall doubles up as a drama studio. Well-resourced music area where pupils get hands-on experience in lessons. 120 learning music instruments plus choirs and ensembles with regular concerts. Art is well displayed despite the limitations of the buildings; innovative and enthusiastic department which gets good number of students into specialist art and design courses at local colleges.

Background and Atmosphere: Motto: Conemur (Let us strive) which head feels is as appropriate now as ever. The unassuming, single storey, redbrick buildings at the front of the school date from 1939 with seven subsequent additions behind them. From outside and on entering it still feels like a small, rural school. Enjoys its village location and for many years was a 'lovely secondary modern' able to go comprehensive slowly and steadily. No nine day wonder, it has built up a reputation locally as a school which 'gets the best out of children' who go there.

School opens up inside like a tardis but despite its multiplicity of specialist accommodation the original appeal of the place has not been lost. The assembly hall which doubles up as a dining (snacking is probably nearer the truth) area can only accommodate a year group at a time. We witnessed an unusual year 10 assembly which used overhead projection of a Liverpool FC footballer as a positive rôle model and succeeded in carrying pupils along in a way which had relevance for them. Five lessons per day of one hour duration – four before lunch break (which doesn't start until 1.20pm) – a pattern which brings good trade for mid-morning snacks (breakfast for some). Old style classrooms can be viewed from corridors which are now too narrow during lesson changeovers (fortunately not too frequent). Many groups seen knuckling down to real academic work.

Pièce de résistance is the vanguard pupils' loo – all gleaming hardware and surfing murals – which has provoked local media interest. CCTV 'not infringing pupils' privacy' has stopped vandalism. Languages and science suites particularly impressive with results to match the facilities provided. Study Centre is perhaps the greatest success of all offering multi-media facilities including well stocked library. A real oasis of civilisation where pupils are allowed to bring food into a hugely popular weekly storytime. Workshops with visiting authors for both the gifted and those with low literacy levels.

Pastoral Care and Discipline: Pastoral care in hands of experienced senior staff and year heads who make themselves accessible to parents. Year 7 head is especially active around feeder primary schools to make sure children look forward to joining senior school. Attendance is carefully monitored with dedicated staff member to ensure first day notification of absence. Small but adequate learning support area in the heart of the school and separate student guidance and learning centre introduced recently to tackle the educational and social needs of the disruptive and disaffected few.

Pupils and Parents: From within and outside a 200 square mile catchment area. Slightly undersubscribed at present which is good news for those parents willing to ferry their offspring. Martock parents have clubbed together to run their own coach. Informal parental car sharing gets pupils back home if they stay for sports, rehearsals etc.

Parental views are sought and involvement is maintained through regular newsletters; turn-out at parents' evenings is usually about 90 per cent. We heard no parental gripes about discipline or teaching standards but some criticism of homework policy as being both too little and too much. School tries to strike the right balance but may have to work harder with parents on this one. Parents' strong support for sixth form was revealed in a recent survey. At present students move on to any of five tertiary colleges located in the main towns of Somerset, all some miles away.

A certain amount of scruffiness but staff chip away at keeping pupils' appearance up to the mark. Children we met definitely enjoy the school, thought the teachers were good – 'no evil teachers' said one of them – and were keen to show us the best bits. Interesting array of former pupils include fashion designer Alice Temperley, winner of the Walpole Award for British Excellence as well as Sarah Ball, creator of 'Bob the Builder.'

Entrance: Children come from about thirty villages across mid-Somerset including 17 per cent from outside the catchment area.

Exit: Vast majority proceed to tertiary colleges in Somerset.

Remarks: Friendly, close-knit and not daunting for the younger ones. Not many 11-16 comprehensive schools do as well as this.

Hurst Lodge School

Bagshot Road, Ascot, Berkshire, SL5 9JU

Tel: 01344 622 154
Fax: 01344 627 049
E-mail: admissions@hurstlodgesch.co.uk
Website: www.hurstlodge.freeserve.co.uk

• Pupils: 220 girls, 18 boys (aged 3-7 only); 28 boarding (weekly and flexi), 192 day • Ages: 3-18 • Size of sixth form: 14 • Non-denom • Fees: Senior day £3500, Junior day £2,920, boarding £5,750 • Independent • Open days: Autumn

Principal: Since 1999, Miss Victoria Smit (early forties), a Hurst Lodge old girl. Unusually for a head, she doesn't have a teaching background. Spent early part of career in industry and reckons it helps to have worked 'in the real world.' Took over from her mother, Mrs Anthea Smit, who bought the school in 1978 to save it from closure. A dynamic, hands-on, open-minded head with great sense of humour, Miss Smit is a 'chronic dyslexic' who tells pupils she's never let it stop her doing anything. 'If a child ever says, "I can't do that – I'm dyslexic," I tell them that I am too,' she says matter-of-factly. Works very closely with deputy principal and experienced teacher, Siobhan O'Connor – they form impressive senior management team. Miss Smit knows all pupils by name and encourages girls to pop into her study to chat about successes and/or disappointments. Spends spare time studying for OU degree, learning Chinese and going to theatre.

Academic Matters: Definitely not an academic hothouse but school gets very solid results. In 2005, 88 per cent of GCSE grades A*-C and 29 per cent A*/A. Tiny number of A level candidates but all A-C grades last time round. School firmly believes in tailoring approach to girls' needs and abilities – a few take French, maths and RE GCSEs a year early but pupils who aren't ready may well wait an extra year. 'It plays havoc with the league tables but we don't just push people through,' says principal. Long-serving and loyal staff who know pupils well. Small classes – rarely more than 16 to a class. Girls setted for English, maths and science.

About 70 pupils – a third of the school – have specific learning difficulties, including dyslexia, dyspraxia, Aspergers Syndrome, ADD, ADHD and mild deafness. Lots of individual help available, with SEN pupils offered one-to-one classes (up to five sessions a week) in cosy dyslexia and educational support dept. Mrs Judith Parker runs the department with trained staff of six dyslexia and SpLD teachers, who follow multi-sensory approach. Speech therapist comes in twice a week and occupational therapist available too.

Games, Options, The Arts: Sport definitely on the up. Small numbers used to mean that netball, hockey, rounders teams etc regularly got thrashed but this is no longer the case – several teams were undefeated in 2005. School excels at swimming (open-air pool in walled garden) and also holds annual biathlon and cross-country championship for local schools. Currently boasts national synchronised swimming and polo champions among pupils. Performing arts form a key part of school – past pupils have gone on to work at the RSC and the National. All pupils have timetabled dance classes every week up till year 10 and ballet, tap, modern dance, jazz and musical theatre offered as extras too. Three performing arts studios for ballet shows, drama productions, concerts etc. Girls' creativity encouraged as much as possible. This must be one of the only schools in the country to allow two and a half tons of sand to be deposited in its performing arts studio for a drama production. 'Some schools are far too anxious about what people will think,' says deputy principal. 'And the kindergarten loved getting what was left over afterwards!' Around 85 per cent of girls take music lessons, with singing far and away the most popular choice. School has junior and senior choir as well as ensemble groups and a mini recording studio where girls can compose own music. Art and photography very popular at GCSE and A2 and loads of extra activities on offer, from flower arranging and cookery to football and judo.

Background and Atmosphere: Founded as ballet school in London in 1942 by Doris Stainer, sister of Oscar-winning actor Leslie Howard (Gone with the Wind...) – 'a very formidable woman with a cane,' recalls present head, who was one of her pupils. School later moved next door to Agatha Christie in Sunningdale and then to leafy 22-acre site on outskirts of Ascot in 1997. Main school building a rambling Victorian country house. Poignant rolls of honour from First and Second World Wars take pride of place in tiny chapel, now used for choir rehearsals. With 220 girls currently on roll, school is bigger than it's ever been and fizzes with activity from dawn till dusk. Small number of boarders live at far end of house – traditional dorms for younger girls, with older ones getting singles or doubles.

Strong family atmosphere abounds. Despite its posh reputation the school isn't in the least bit snooty. Smart frocks and a marquee for prizegiving are 'as posh as we get,' says principal, who hands out gongs for all sorts – from the kindergarten child with smiliest face to the Spirit of Hurst Lodge award, given to the pupil who embodies 'all the things we think are important, like enthusiasm, politeness and hard work.' Girls tolerate old-fashioned brown uniform with good humour. 'People are always complaining about it but it's very comfy,' says one girl. Sixth form wear suits, though they look more like trendy art students than city-slickers.

Pastoral Care and Discipline: Emphasis placed on good manners, respect for others and integrity. Clear list of school rules – girls getting fresh air at break-times and making sure they eat properly at lunch – but discipline not a problem here. Principal says can count on fingers of one hand the number of times she's ever had to raise her voice! Very helpful welcome book for new girls lists everything they need to know, from what to call the teachers to the stationery they need in their pencil cases. Head girl and prefect system, as well as three competitive houses – one named after Miss Stainer and the others after ballet legends Margot Fonteyn and Ninette De Valois. Weekly school council gives girls chance to have their say. Recent innovations include water fountain and more comfy (and back-friendly) school bags. Girls also run buddy system to look after new pupils and offer friendly ear to anyone who needs it. Head prides herself on regular contact with parents and produces weekly newsletter to update them on forthcoming events. Each form has parent rep who attends a termly school management meeting.

Pupils and Parents: Day pupils from up to 50 miles away, boarders from as far away as Hong Kong (eight EFL students). Friendly, personable girls who are very proud of their school and stand up when teachers or visitors enter the room. Notable old girls include Duchess of York, actresses Juliet Stevenson and Claudie Blakeley and TV presenter Emma Forbes.

Entrance: Entrance exam at 11. Girls entering at other stages spend day at school and have interview with principal. Most girls starting year 7 come from Hurst Lodge's own junior school, others from local primaries and preps. School looks at educational psychologists' reports but always keeps an open mind. 'Reports sometimes bear no relation to the child we see,' says principal. Girls entering sixth form must have a C or more in chosen A level subjects and 'a commitment to work hard.'

Exit: Junior school has handful of boys, who leave at seven for preps like Woodcote House, Hall Grove and Papplewick. A big exodus of girls after GSCEs, mainly to sixth form colleges – 'they want to see boys,' says principal with note of exasperation in her voice. Not the place for girls wanting to do A level chemistry and physics but reasonable choice otherwise. Sixth form leavers head in loads of different directions, to university (LSE, Exeter etc), art college and performing arts careers.

Money Matters: Academic, dance, drama, music and art scholarships on offer, as well as the school's annual Racov award – three terms of basic fees given in memory of eminent neuroscientist Achi Racov.

Remarks: Mainstream school that caters for all. Great for raising self-esteem and getting the best out of pupils in nurturing, friendly, purposeful environment. Splendid performing arts and more academic than sometimes given credit for. Particularly good at helping pupils who have the ability to succeed academically but may need individual help.

HURSTPIERPOINT COLLEGE

Linked to Hurstpierpoint College Preparatory School in the Junior section

College Lane, Hurstpierpoint, Hassocks, West Sussex, BN6 9JS

Tel: 01273 833 636
Fax: 01273 835 257
E-mail: info@hppc.co.uk
Website: www.hppc.co.uk

- Pupils: 276 boys, 145 girls; 287 board: full, weekly or flexi
- Ages: 13-18 • Size of sixth form: 166 • C of E • Fees: Preprep: up to £1,890. Prep: day £3,420; full boarding £4,600. Senior: day £5,035; full boarding £6,595 • Independent • Open days: 4 per year - 2 in autumn, 1 early spring, 1 late spring

Head: Since 2005, Mr Tim Manly BA (Oxford in Lit Hum) MSc from the LSE. After a career in commerce lasting six years, he took his PGCE at Cambridge and became a classics teacher at Sevenoaks in Kent becoming HoD in 1997. He was also a housemaster before moving to Oakham School as deputy head. Mr Manly is married with 4 young children, 2 sons and 2 daughters.

He succeeded Mr Stephen Meek who left to be principal of Geelong Grammar in Australia.

Academic Matters: Takes a wide spectrum of boys and girls and gets the best out of them; academic work clearly taken seriously, with good GCSE and A level results (nearly 70 per cent A/B in 2005). Geography and business studies the most popular. School uses a value-added system for eg target setting in the GCSE year. The staff are generally well liked and there are plenty of them with a ratio of pupils to full-time teaching staff of 8:1. Strong careers programme.

All pupils are screened on entrance for special needs. As there is only one special needs teacher and no pupil can have more than one session a week with her, the school is unable to admit pupils needing more full-time help than this. The kids have a very full and long day but seem to get used to the regime quickly.

Games, Options, The Arts: Sport is high on the agenda here, played 3 afternoons a week, with an enormous variety for pupils to choose from – including, in addition to the obvious – squash, weights, badminton, basketball, aerobics, outdoor pursuits (such as kayaking, sailing and shooting), cross-country, rounders, athletics and volleyball. The school also has an Astroturf hockey pitch and a climbing wall. Wednesday afternoons devoted to an extremely popular and well-run CCF or conservation and community service. Travels include sixth form geography field trip to Morocco, CCF expedition to Wales, rugby tour to Australia, New Zealand and Fiji. The Duke of Edinburgh scheme is very popular, currently involving 70 students. Music, dance & drama are also popular – new dance & drama studios and a 250-seat rather old-fashioned theatre staging termly productions.

Background and Atmosphere: Founded in 1849 by Nathaniel Woodard as part of his vision of schools pledged to provide a Christian education and give accessible education to all classes. Still the ethos of the school today, with pupils coming from a wide variety of backgrounds – not unusual to see Porsches and old bangers parked next to each other. Children may be confirmed if they wish but religion is more an ethos of the school than something enforced.

Built in 1853 of traditional Sussex knapped flint to the design of Richard Carpenter, now greatly extended, in 140 acres within sight of the south downs. All upper sixth girls and boys (including day pupils) have their own rooms in their own house, which is slightly away from the rest of the school and has a bar and other social facilities. Neat uniform up to lower sixth form; in the upper sixth, students can wear their own clothes as long as they are smart (blazers and ties for boys, suits for girls).

Introduced girls in 1995, and now has the feel of a true co-ed school. Warm and friendly with courteous, enthusiastic pupils. Communication between school and home extremely good; pupils' 'effort marks' are accessible by parents through a website link, as are the termly reports.

Pastoral Care and Discipline: Countless rules and regulations but the pupils appear to live happily within their boundaries, creating a relaxed atmosphere. The school chaplain runs a Guardian Scheme, taken very seriously by the pupils themselves, which involves two volunteers per year group (who have appropriate training) and helps to catch issues early and ensures that there is a regular system of communication between pupils and staff.

Entrance: At 13 by Common Entrance and by the school's own entrance exam at 16.

Exit: Most go on to a variety of universities, with a few taking a gap year.

Remarks: A good all-round school, where almost any child could thrive.

HURTWOOD HOUSE SCHOOL

Holmbury St Mary, Dorking, Surrey, RH5 6NU

Tel: 01483 279 000
Fax: 01483 267 586
E-mail: info@hurtwood.net
Website: www.hurtwoodhouse.com

• Pupils: 300, half boys half girls; almost all boarding • Ages: 15-18 • Non-denom • Fees: £8,200 • Independent

---

Head and Founder: Since 1969, Mr K R B (Richard) Jackson MA (sixties) who was educated at Cranleigh (just down the valley) and read history at Corpus Cambridge. He started his working life in marketing, followed by a spell at the now defunct Heatherdown prep school and founded Hurtwood, the first co-ed sixth form college in the UK, with his wife, Linda. The school is his 'baby', he owns most of the buildings (one of the five boarding houses is rented from the National Trust) and is paid rent on these but the school operates as a charitable trust but without the trustees – ie a not-for-profit company.

We previously described Mr Jackson as avuncular and easy to communicate with – he would prefer the term 'grand seigneurial' – no matter, his jolly exterior (with beard and paunch) does hide a sharp business brain. And he is an entertaining and inspiring mentor. Our meeting took place in the central hall of the elegant former shooting lodge of Hurtwood, invaders being repelled by a red rope on which hung the notice 'keep out, meeting in progress'.

Mr Jackson's aims are two fold – to make sure that students feel they are 'in the most exciting place imaginable' and that their parents feel they are in the 'safest place'. No cars, no pubs for miles (and very hilly both ways) and no distractions.

Academic Matters: This is a sixth form college, offering the odd GCSE, all boards, retakes, or a one year GCSE foundation course – aimed at the sma... eigners (EFL on offer). The range of ASs ... the trad subjects plus accountancy, eco... studies, law, sociology and philosophy. Tin... range of foreign languages, outstanding scie... and brill new chemistry lab. Maths strong, and modules throughout. Humanities popular but by far the largest contingent is taking courses in theatre, media studies, music technology and art. Results impressive, high numbers of As, way above average, some Bs, very few failures. School is proud to have finished in the top 50 in the 2005 Daily Mail A level league table, an outstanding achievement with such a mixed intake. Super library, with nooks and crannies, rather like a prep school library; computers throughout. Each pupil must devote six periods a week to 'non-academic' subjects, ie something in which they will not be taking an exam, though these non-academic subjects do include music, theatre, aromatherapy and creative writing. Some dyslexic help available.

Games, Options, The Arts: Busy art department – 95 students currently studying art at AS/A2 with five full time tutors. Department completely revamped under Russell Gray. Course now includes sculpture, 3D, print-making, computer-generated design, fine art, constructed textiles and photography. 100 per cent grade As at A-level in 2005.

More than a third of the school currently studying theatre studies and this is undoubtedly the most professional media set-up we have ever seen. Anywhere. Squillions of pounds and a wealth of experience on the teaching side. This is professional stuff. The media/theatre complex is huge; think masses of green rooms, mixing studios, dance studios, recording studios, video studios. Think students avidly rehearsing – some in costume, some in corners, think half a million quid's worth of kit, with students plugged into mickey mouse earphones avidly mixing and then recording CD-ROMs. By A2 level, students are up to a truly employable standard. Impressive, superlatives fail, the vast theatre has roll up chairs, the lighting equipment is brill and the sound fantastic.

Organised games on offer every day but not aggressively pursued – rugby sevens, hockey, football, netball and tennis on site, golf, swimming down the road. School was South East England area netball champions when we visited.

Background and Atmosphere: School is perched on a chilly site of outstanding beauty between Dorking and Guildford, with fabulous views to the south coast. Whilst it sounds temptingly close to London, Guildford is a senior step away and there are no shops/pubs for miles. Students in five elegant mega-villas and one castle, with a fleet of 22 mini-buses to ferry them to and fro. Classes are held in mainly purpose-built blocks round Hurtwood itself and, below the eye-line, it is all very elegant and surprisingly buzzy. All the facilities you would expect to find at a major public school, though the dining room is quite small 'and we eat in drifts', says Mr Jackson. Halal meat on tap for Muslims – not that there are many of them.

Pastoral Care and Discipline: Houseparents, house tutors plus personal tutors overload the tutorial system and pick up the merest hint of hiccup. No uniform is worn and staff are called by their first names. Not a lot of sin; zero tolerance for drugs, boozing out of the question and Mr Jackson has built 'a bike shed' for committed smokers. One or two 'requests to leave' but it is 'not a serious problem'.

Pupils and Parents: The fed-ups, and the 'I need a change' fraternity, and the performing arts enthusiasts. Basically Sloane, though some first time buyers and currently a quarter from abroad. Many come from single sex boarding schools and relish the prospect of added fun and games; though the sexes are aggressively separated by houses, which prevents too much naughtiness.

Entrance: Non-selective but the place is very popular so apply early to be safe.

Exit: To trad universities in the main, tranches, as you might expect, to the performing arts. Continuing help with UCAS forms and university choices.

Money Matters: Fees are in line with major public schools.

Remarks: Exciting, could be just what you want for the child fed-up with school or who needs the extra pick-up of very small classes and high academic standards.

HUTCHESONS' GRAMMAR SCHOOL

Linked to Hutchesons' Junior School in the Junior section

21 Beaton Road, Glasgow, G41 4NW

Tel: 01414 232 933
Fax: 01414 240 251
E-mail: rector@hutchesons.org
Website: www.hutchesons.org

- Pupils: 1,055 boys and 985 girls • Ages: 11-18 • Size of sixth form: 400 • Ecumenical • Fees: £1,615 rising to £2,289 • Independent • Open days: Late October / early November

Rector: Since 2005, Dr Ken Greig MA PhD who worked for some time in the world of practical geology with BP and was previously headmaster of Pangbourne. Educated at George Heriots where he was dux. 1st at Oxford, then went on to complete a PhD in geology at the University of Edinburgh before taking a post with British Petroleum as an Exploration Geologist. After travelling extensively with BP, in 1987 Dr Greig turned his talents to teaching, becoming a mathematics teacher at Christ's Hospital School in Sussex. He then became head of maths at Dollar. Succeeds Mr John Knowles who retired to go into the ministry; a great loss to Scottish education.

Academic Matters: Very strong results (60 per cent plus grade A at Highers) and strong work ethos – the day often lasts from 7am to 7pm. Five Highers the norm, 15/20 per cent get six, with early morning classes and twilight classes (from 3.30 to 5 pm) to top up to seven: in 2004 only 4 pupils in the whole of Scotland tackled 7 Highers – all were from Hutchie and all achieved 7 A passes.

This is very senior stuff. Mixture of SYS and A levels, though watch this space as the new Higher Stills are absorbed into the curriculum. Masses of languages, all the normal ones, plus Swedish and Russian, language labs, satellite TV. Vast classics department and Latin compulsory till third year. New double-decker library stacked with as many videos (Shakespeare on film) as books and computers everywhere intranetted, internetted. Biology currently top of the pops, but children encouraged to take as wide a spread as possible. And they do. No particular bias, beyond the traditional Scottish 'feel' for engineering, but as many pupils now opt for careers in arts or media as follow the engineering, medicine, accountant route. EFL on offer for non-

English speaking foreigners – we are after all, on the edge of silicon glen.

Games, Options, The Arts: Small Astroturf, plus Clydesdale ground adjacent to the school but mostly pupils are bused to Auldhouse for the main games pitch. No swimming pool on site (problems with old coal minings underneath) but huge sports hall with fitness centre and gym. All the usual games, rugby (almost a religion like so many schools in Scotland), hockey (one teacher in the UK olympic team) etc, plus rowing and '25 sporting options'. School currently holds gold medal for taikido. Quite.

Good and busy drama, new theatre and church now on line; lots of external competitions, winners of recent Scottish drama and music festival and off south for the finals. Three big shows each year. Surprisingly, no pipe band (though a few pipers) or CCF; granny bashing and masses of charity work popular. Masses of music, several orchestras. Art fantastic, with kiln and fabric design options and thankfully, for an academic (and the strongest academic) school, home economics is a popular option. And in sixth form, pupils can do advanced driving, archaeology, first aid, Italian plus a raft of other options. Lots of trips abroad and pupil exchanges. D of E.

Background and Atmosphere: Both Hutcheson's hospital and school were founded in Ingham Street in 1641 by the brothers, Thomas and George Hutcheson. In 1841 the school moved to the 'quietness of the situation, good air, roomy and open site' of Crown Street in Glasgow's Gorbals, moving to leafy Pollockshields in 1960, five minutes' from the M8 and easily accessible from both sides of the river. Good local buses, plus a fantastic train service. The school amalgamated with the girls' school in 1976 (with the junior school moving into the girls' school) and went independent in 1985, and the current board of governors is full of the great and the good of Glasgow: the Merchants House, Hutchesons' Hospital, the Trades House plus the Church of Scotland Presbytery.

Newly enlarged dining area, and local Congregational church converted into a music and ICT centre – the congregation still able to use the church. Think large, flat roof, wide open corridors, huge blocks of classrooms – think Hutchie. Super chunks of new-build on what is basically a sixties flat roof horror, masses of photographs, good pupil-inspired art. Subjects are grouped either horizontally or vertically, and there is a certain amount of moaning about more labs being needed NOW – they only have fifteen.

School runs on swipe cards, the original cashless economy, where pupils top up their cards at the beginning of term (or when needed) and use them to buy lunch (very good, lots of veggies and salads), brekky, or whatever (but no fizzy drinks) from the vending machines. Swipe cards also act as passes in the library.

Pastoral Care and Discipline: School divided into four houses for games, competitions and the like. Seniors 'buddy' littles when they join senior school. Strong emphasis on PSE, with fatigues or detention in place for minor wickedness (eg 'dogging off'), though individual teachers may set their own punishments; the ultimate deterrent is expulsion. Tutors for all over a two-year period.

Pupils and Parents: A mixed bag. 'Social, ethnic and economic A-Z'. Cosmopolitan collection of parents, about a third bus their children daily – over 20 miles – from Paisley, Renfrewshire, Lanarkshire, north of the river. Pupils from as far afield as Ayr and Drymen – made possible by improved road links and school bus services. Tranche of Australians, Koreans; pupils either stay with relatives or have surrogate mothers. Long tradition of having a significant (10 per cent) number of Jews – separate assemblies for them; Muslims may go to the mosque at lunch-time on Friday, have separate lessons for gym and no problem with scarves. Number of FPs' children. FPs include John Brown of the shipyard, plus John Buchan, Russell Hillhouse, Carol Smillie, James Maxton, Richard Emanuel, Lord McColl, Ken Bruce, Lord Irvine, Olivia Giles.

Entrance: Either from local prep or state. 100 a year more or less automatic up from the junior school, plus a 100 extra (and all pupils then get mixed up), otherwise by written test 'with interview for a number of candidates', pupils are actively encouraged to join the school at sixth form 'to top up Highers'. Admission usually in August but, if space available, can join at any term and two pupils were being assessed (for the junior school) when we visited in October.

Exit: 95+ per cent to universities: 15/18 a year regularly to Oxbridge, and many leave with firsts; an impressive list of firsts (and double firsts) from all graduates. More gap years taken than previously, lots do work experience and then travel, most to Scottish universities, but a fair trickle down south.

Money Matters: School previously had 250 Assisted Places, their phasing out is a real problem. Currently discounts for siblings, some scholarships for sixth formers and more funds being sought. All scholarships are means-tested.

Remarks: Awesome. Fiercely academic but children achieve their impressive grades from a fairly unselective background. This is old-fashioned teaching, with enormous breadth, at its very best. As the rector says, 'it's cool to succeed here'.

HYMERS COLLEGE

Linked to Hymers College Junior School in the Junior section

Hymers Avenue, Hull, HU3 1LW

Tel: 01482 343 555

Fax: 01482 472 854

E-mail: enquiries@hymers.hull.sch.uk

Website: www.hymerscollege.co.uk

• Pupils: 980 boys and girls • Ages: 8-19 • Size of sixth form: 200 • Non-denom • Fees: £1,965 - £2,235 • Independent

Head: Since 1990, Mr J C Morris MA (fifties), previously deputy head and head of history at Hymers. Read history at Oxford, married with adult offspring. Thoughtful, courteous and sincere, more of a Major than a Thatcher or Blair in leadership style – 'we appoint decent people and leave them to get on with it and make a success of it'. Exudes quiet control without looking over teachers' shoulders; former cricket and rugby master, he is a team player, relaxed and open about sharing responsibilities with large management team.

Retiring in July 2006.

Academic Matters: Average class sizes 27 in lower school to 12 post-16. Academically selective on intake, 'though not as selective as most grammar schools'; standards and expectations are high and exam results very commendable. This school has a high credibility rating in the academic stakes, little, if anything, to match it locally. Traditional teaching styles prevail; classrooms are formal with a nod to modern technology, desks in straight rows very much the order of the day, even in the all-new junior school. Science is popular – widespread aspirations (both pupils and parents) towards medicine. French, German, Spanish and Latin on offer, though linguists in the school would appreciate even more choice. Several pupils in top ten nationally in A levels in recent years. No specialist SEN staff, parents advised to seek professional (external) help; about thirty dyslexic pupils in school.

Games, Options, The Arts: Where talent is recognised, be it sport, music or the arts generally, then pupils are expected to demonstrate commitment and be prepared to give extra time and effort after school and on Saturdays – opting out isn't an option. Games compulsory – rugby and cricket for boys, hockey and netball for girls, tennis (notably successful) and athletics for both; boys and girls well represented in national competitions. Successful and nationally

recognised music department, eight pupils in National Youth Choir. Army Cadet Force (voluntary and after school) popular with some, though my pupil guide seemed a little unsure, 'they go in those sheds over there and do whatever they do...'

Background and Atmosphere: Opened in 1893 as a school for boys, its founder, The Reverend John Hymers, Cambridge Fellow and Rector of Brandesburton, leaving money in his will for a school, 'for the training of intelligence in whatever social rank of life it may be found among the vast and varied population of the town and port of Hull'.

'It's hard to get excited about Hull,' as its most famous adopted son, Philip Larkin, wrote, 'I wish I could think of just one nice thing to tell you about Hull... oh yes, it's very nice and flat for cycling.' Harsh perhaps, but it does capture something of the character of a town that reaches few heights, physical or otherwise. But despite such unpromising geography, Hymers is to be commended for scaling the heights of academe. A curious mix of tatty classrooms, a fine old assembly hall and attractive new buildings – labs, theatre, sports hall, sixth form centre, junior school and swimming pool – clearly there has been extensive recent investment in new facilities, perhaps at the cost of refurbishing the older ones. Attractive site, well-maintained playing fields, all-weather pitches and even a lake for those keen ornithologists on balmy summer post-exam days. Hard core of long-established experienced teachers, average age forty-five, majority ten+ years at the school. The boy/girl ratio is 60/40 but women under-represented on the staff generally, particularly on the senior management team.

Pastoral Care and Discipline: Apparently the children are expected to 'jolly well behave themselves'. Good, that's that sorted then. Pupils can expect to be expelled for serious misdemeanours, such as bringing drugs into school but there have been no expulsions for ten years. Head rarely gets involved with disciplinary matters, this is picked up through the robust pastoral care system where pupils feel 'genuinely supported' but understand the rules and know they will be pulled up quickly, probably by 'a furious but fair' deputy head, if they get it wrong. Good pupil/staff and pupil/pupil relationships, all fairly relaxed for much of the time.

Pupils and Parents: Large catchment area – Hull, East Yorkshire, North Lincs, buses in all directions. The school reflects the lack of ethnic diversity in the area. Wider social spread than most independents, due mainly to generous bursaries and lower than average fees, remaining true to its founder's intentions. About fifteen fee remission places per year, mostly full fees. Parents mostly first-time buyers, ranging from professionals (preponderance of medics) to owners of local takeaways. Pupils bright, cheerful and enthusiastic and most apologetic when our car was hit by a football for the third time; uniform, like some classrooms, scruffy around the edges.

Entrance: For entry at 11+ competitive entrance exams in maths, English and verbal reasoning, plus interview. Four-form entry, 108 places in all, about 30 for external pupils, remainder transferring from own junior school. For sixth form, five GCSE grade B or above passes, usually about 12 enter at 16.

Exit: 90 per cent stay post-GCSE, favoured universities mainly in the north/midlands – Leeds, Newcastle, Durham, Nottingham, also a good number annually (around ten) to Oxbridge.

Remarks: Hull is a conventional, unpretentious place and the school mirrors this. 'Perform and conform' could be the school motto, though isn't, but that's the message coming over loud and clear. Do this and the school will support and deliver quality traditional learning at its best.

IBSTOCK PLACE SCHOOL

Linked to Ibstock Place School, Junior and Kindergarten in the Junior section

Clarence Lane, Roehampton, London, SW15 5PY

Tel: 020 8876 9991
Fax: 020 8878 4897
E-mail: registrar@ibstockplaceschool.co.uk
Website: www.ibstockplaceschool.co.uk

• Pupils: 761; 399 boys and 362 girls; all day • Ages: 3-11 primary school, 11-18 senior school and sixth form • Size of sixth form: Sixth form opened in September 2005 • Inter-denom • Fees: £2,989 up to year 2; £3,040 up to year 6; £3,870 from year 7 • Independent • Open days: Throughout the year

---

Head: Since 2000, Mrs Anna Sylvester-Johnson BA PGCE – 'Mrs SJ' to the pupils – (fifties). Previously head of English at the Green School for girls in Chiswick for 9 years and before that was at the Lycée Français. Theareafter, head of The Arts Educational School, London. Has lived in the area for 25 years. When she took on the post she said she was going to make changes and so she has. A very feminine and professional person who has gone quietly about her business and transformed this rather plodding school into a sleek, vibrant operation without losing any of her senior management team in the process.

Academic Matters: Bearing in mind that there is a non-selective entry to the school at age 3, although there is selection at 11, GCSE results are extremely creditable. Committed staff, many of long service, offer stimulating teaching and generate enthusiasm for their subjects. Study is backed up by visits and trips, 'not glitzy', making full use of London's wealth of institutions. Not a school that would attract devotees of league tables but most subjects are strong with 100 per cent obtaining grades A*-C. French starts in year 2; German, Spanish, Italian, Latin and Greek taught too. Pupils are setted in science, maths and French. Has invested hugely in DT and ICT – 'we need female engineers'.

Support for minor learning difficulties where child can still access the broad curriculum and there are three qualified support staff part time but no special needs support beyond that. Where a child is having difficulties, parents are fully informed. 'There are no shocks in this school,' says Mrs Parsons, the registrar, formerly of St Paul's Girls. 'There's always an awareness of whether a child can go into the senior school as all problems are actioned.' The school opened a sixth form in September 2005.

Games, Options, The Arts: 'A sport-rich school' with excellent facilities and everything on site. No busing out, just a stroll across the bridge to the football and rugby pitches and the all-weather pitch with lines marked out for several different options. Having its own indoor (very warm) pool means they frequently play host to other schools for swimming galas. Matches take place after school with teas served in the rather grand sports pavilion (it was the coach house to the main house originally), and are enthusiastically supported by loyal parents. Parents' Association is very strong with an ebullient and enthusiastic, completely non-political chair who runs a social programme throughout the year – concerts, bingo suppers, fireworks. 'Helps the children realise that staff and parents are also social beings'.

Large outdoor education programme and sports tour culminating in year 11's expeditions to a variety of places, eg Canada, Kenya, Thailand, China, where pupils contribute to charitable causes. 'It's pro bono by the school. Makes them aware of their privileged position. No point having high achievers if they are not sensitive to those who are less privileged.' Closer to home the pupils are involved with a local state MLD (moderate learning difficulties) school, putting on dance shows. Music is very strong here. Practice rooms throb to the sound of guitar or drum during breaks, music groups in each year with a strings initiative, choirs, concerts, quartets, recorder groups, singing, percussion, jazz, flute, oboes, bassoons, to name but a few. After-school clubs until

6pm offer debating, film, kick-boxing, model-making, drama, a range of non-team sports and outdoor pursuits.

Background and Atmosphere: The school was founded in 1894 on the principles established by Friedrich Froebel and started life in a small house in West Kensington with only 4 pupils. After being evacuated during the war, the school re-opened in a former private residence designed by GK Chesterton just outside Richmond Park. The surprisingly spacious grounds (6 acres) have three buildings housing the nursery, the junior and the senior school respectively. Campus atmosphere with wooded areas one side and more formal gardens on the other. On the downside is the distance from any local tube and the proximity to the notorious Roehampton Estate – not so says school, 'now that 50 per cent is university and large population of Somali families' – and reminds us of good buses and trains. However, parents who are anxious for their offspring not to spend too long in a car could always drop them off at Richmond Gate and make them walk across the park every day – they might even enjoy it.

The nursery (3-7) is housed separately at the bottom of the hill with its own playground, pupils then progress to the junior school (7-11) and finally arrive at the main house at the top of the hill (11-18). Each move is accompanied by a little ceremony to mark the occasion. On entering the senior school a team-building day is held on the first Saturday which really promotes a sense of challenge and excitement.

Pastoral Care and Discipline: One of the school's strengths. Progress reports issued to the seniors every 6 weeks on effort and achievement and structures in place which stop little nagging problems slipping through the net. One parent commented, 'the staff are like the thought police' – problems are dealt with before they are even recognised as such. Standards are very much led from the top. Notices in classrooms are polite and always use the magic words and you won't get away with bad table manners at lunchtime. No notable discipline problems.

Pupils and Parents: Friendly, mature, self-confident, likeable pupils who look you in the eye and are responsive. Neat appearance. Uniform is adhered to and is reasonably attractive for both boys and girls. A conscious effort is made to keep numbers of both equal so that it is truly co-ed. Even though most parents live locally – Barnes, Richmond, Fulham, Chelsea, Chiswick, Putney, East Sheen – lack of tubes is a problem so they could easily be dismissed (unfairly) as those 4 x 4 or MPC types responsible for all the traffic chaos at Roehampton Gate morning and evening. Earliest pupils from pre-war days include Iris Murdoch. Mrs SJ would not be drawn on identities of present Ibstonians – rumours abound but her lips are sealed.

Entrance: At 3, 11 and 16. Names down at birth, long waiting lists. One class of 24 is admitted to the nursery at age 3 and one into reception at age 4. Siblings are given priority but there's no testing of any sort at this age and, provided there are no educational problems, all entrants will proceed into the junior schools. At 11, however, all applicants are interviewed and tested in maths, English and reasoning and then (250 of them for 35 places in 2005) take part in classroom activities. Included in the process is having lunch with the staff: best to make sure they know one end of a soup spoon from the other. Pupils come from. inter alia, Holy Cross, Kingston, Ravenscourt Park, Tower House, King's House, Prospect House, Orchard House, Cameron House, Sheen Mount, East Sheen Primary, St Osmund's. Occasional places available at 7, 13 and at 16.

Exit: Most pupils go on to school's own senior dept but some to boarding schools or to St Paul's or Godolphin and Latymer.

Money Matters: Music scholarships and exhibitions are offered from age 11 and various scholarships from 16. Auditions and interviews are held in January for 11+ and November for 16+.

Remarks: An ambitious, forward-looking school where 'happiness underpins everything' and progressive – turning out well-rounded young adults. Was previously most regarded for its still excellent junior department but senior school now seriously over-subscribed. Recent inspectors had no recommendations to make and, under current head, school growing considerably in local status.

BY ROSIE HAMILTON

ILFORD COUNTY HIGH SCHOOL

Fremantle Road, Barkingside, Ilford, Essex, IG6 2JB

Tel: 020 8551 6496
Fax: 020 8503 9960
E-mail: enquiries@ichs.org.uk
Website: www.ichs.org.uk

- Pupils: 845 boys, all day • Ages: 11-18 • Size of sixth form: 245 • Non-denom • State • Open days: September

Head: Since 1993, Stuart Devereux BA BEd (mid fifties). Down-to-earth, genial northerner who studied PE at Leeds Carnegie with the aim of becoming 'the best PE teacher in the world'. Quickly rose through the ranks at The Coopers' Company and Coborn School, Upminster, before taking an Open University degree in IT. Became deputy head at Ilford in 1990. Married to a special needs teacher with two daughters. Still teaches IT to the sixth form. Keen rugby player, who participates actively in the school's rugby club.

Academic Matters: A strong, academic, highly selective grammar school which in 2004 became a specialist science college.

The admission test is by verbal and non-verbal reasoning alone, so the school tests all new boys to ensure other skills are up to scratch. Loads of extra help given to those who need reading support, with professionally trained older boys mentoring younger ones, 'you'll find pockets of sixth formers all over the schools reading with year 7s.'

All do 10 GCSEs (98 per cent A*-C): English lang and lit, maths, chemistry, physics, biology, a modern foreign language (French, German, Spanish) – plus two options. Set in maths and science for two years before GCSE years and class sizes kept down to 20 in English, maths and science. Technology (electronics, graphic design and resistant materials) part of the curriculum; electronics clearly a strength.

All year 12s take 4 academic AS, plus an AS in critical thinking. 'It's more useful than general studies for those thinking of medicine or law'. 23 A level options, most take three. 'Our boys are nothing if not pragmatists,' says the head. 'Their view is, "what does my career or university ask? I'll do that to the best of my ability".' Clearly a successful strategy since the average point score is 330-360. Very strong history, mathematics, business studies, biology and geography.

Homework from 5-7 hours a week in year 7, up to 20 hours a week at A level. 'Though not all the parents agree, there's enough homework,' says the head. 'Boys need time to watch television.'

All pupils given twice yearly assessments of progress and an annual full school report known as a record of progress. Also one-on-one pupil interviews once a year to discuss progress. Reports sent out at times when most useful to parent and child – in year 7, before parents' evening; in year 12 before mock GCSEs, otherwise at the end of year.

Games, Options, The Arts: Until recently the school lacked a decent gym, and PE was not its forte, but a state-of-the-art sports hall will be completed summer 2006. Main sports, football, cricket and swimming, with two football pitches, a swimming pool, tennis courts and cricket nets. Strong sporting tradition outside the curriculum and boys are fanatical about cricket ('Winter, summer, rain or snow,' says the head.) Last year's sixth form included the England Under-19 captain.

Music teaching singled out for effusive praise in recent Ofsted. Jazz a strength, and, as well as the usual medley of rock bands, the school also caters to its ethnic audience with a sitar teacher and traditional Sri Lankan instruments on offer. Concerts and plays are multi-cultural, with a recent triumphant Asian West Side Story.

Probably not the place for aspiring fine artists. Two pleasant art rooms with some strong work and an enthusiastic teacher, but these are boys devoted to practical ends and few do art at A level. Drama, too, not a major component of the curriculum – taught only as an academic subject in Year 7 – and housed in a less than enticing Portakabin, but a lot of fun clearly had at the annual talent competition.

Three well equipped, air-conditioned computer rooms, plus inter-active white boards in many classrooms. Two trolleys of laptops also accessible to every department. 10 labs, including one period piece from 1935 and another recently refurbished. Beautiful – if small – library, with energetic librarian who organises popular author visits.

Wide range of educational trips – World War 1 battlefields for history, the UN for economics. The head helps out to give teachers time off. Definitely not, however, all work and no play – end-of-year activities week includes outings to Alton Towers and paint-balling. Popular after-school clubs – often organised by the boys – include table tennis, maths, Warhammer, sailing, Sudoku and rugby. Sixth formers also recently won The Schools 'Question Time' Challenge.

Background and Atmosphere: School moved to its current site in 1929 and the main core of the building is still two gracious floors of deco-influenced brick built round internal courtyard gardens. Elsewhere the fabric is somewhat patchy.

The long-serving head very much sets the tone. More a father figure than a tyrant, he's clearly liked by staff and boys. Strong family feel, relaxed but respectful: ties must be tied, shirts tucked in, but the odd sweet wrapper is tolerated. Older boys in particular given a fair bit of autonomy. Most of year 12 made prefects from midway through the year. Plus three head prefects and three senior prefects, selected from 12 by formal interview.

Very little communal non-academic space. No playground, for example, and only the most Spartan sixth-form common room. As a result sixth formers allowed to attend according to their timetable, except for Wednesday assemblies.

The canteen, a walk away from the main building, has recently been re-equipped by caterers Scolarest, who now provide healthy options. 'We try and teach them the difference and offer them the choice, but most still end up with chips and pizza.'

Pastoral Care and Discipline: All religions welcomed and celebrated. Weekly whole-school and year-group assemblies, given by boys and topped and tailed by staff. Separate assemblies on Tuesday and Thursday for Sikhs, Hindus (who have the largest hall), Muslims, Christian and Jews. Also plans to introduce a Humanist assembly.

Behaviour admirable – courtesy and consideration in evidence without prompting. The schools very much operates an open-doors policy, so occasional instances of theft have been known. Discipline firm but reasonable. 'My policy is to allow boys to make one big mistake,' says the head. Fixed-term exclusions can, very occasionally, be followed with permanent exclusion. Truancy virtually unheard of.

Pupils and Parents: Supportive parents with high expectations. Primarily from Redbridge, Barking and Walthamstow. Extremely ethnically diverse with a high percentage of pupils whose main language may be English, but who speak something else at home. About 30 per cent WASP, then largely Asian (Indian, Pakistani, Bangladeshi), British born and first generation. Few free school meals.

Entrance: At 11, by age-adjusted verbal and non-verbal reasoning tests set by the local education authority, Redbridge. Top 120 given places. Level of ability very high and the school is over-subscribed by about 10 to 1. 50 feeder primaries and independent prep schools. Gaps occasionally appear higher up the school. About 30 new boys admitted to sixth from with a requirement of 7 A*-C, with A*-B in A level subjects.

Exit: A handful at 16, to co-ed sixth forms or schools with a different choice of A levels and facilities. Thereafter, the majority to Russell Group universities to read practical, career-oriented subjects, law, medicine (15 last year), dentistry, business, economics and mathematics. A consistent handful to Oxbridge. Old boys include Lord Shepherd, former chairman of Grand Met, England footballer Trevor Brooking, West Ham manager John Lyall, and conductor Bramwell Tovey, musical director of the Vancouver Symphony.

Remarks: A friendly, orderly school, which takes able, focused boys to exam and career success without undue pressure and with a considerable sense of enjoyment.

IMMANUEL COLLEGE

87-91 Elstree Road, Bushey, Hertfordshire, WD23 4EB

Tel: 020 8950 0604
Fax: 020 8950 8687
E-mail: enquiries@immanuel.herts.sch.uk
Website: www.immanuel.herts.sch.uk

- Pupils: 273 boys, 287 girls • Ages: 11-18 • Size of sixth form: 126 • Jewish • Fees: £10,398 pa • Independent

Head: Since 2000, Philip Skelker MA (late fifties). Previously headmaster of King David School in Liverpool and Carmel College and a beak (master) at Eton. A very impressive and hugely experienced man. Fatherly without being paternalistic, a motivator, amusing, energetic, knows every child. Mr Skelker has two of his six children at the school, one as a teacher. His commitment to enlarge the school and elevate its academic standing as a whole are paralleled by his enthusiasm for and personal interest in the development of each individual student.

That Immanuel College's reputation has grown immensely over the past year is due in no small measure to his regime, with parents hoping that their children will want to model themselves on a head who himself embodies the school's motto, 'Torah im Derekh Erez', the study of Torah together with secular education. Amongst a devoted and enthusiastic staff he is primus inter pares and makes a point of teaching English to all age groups. 'Although my son really has no great love for the subject, he absolutely loved Mr Skelker's English lessons and was inspired by them,' says a mother.

Academic Matters: Solid teaching in very small classes (girls and boys separated except for ICT and art in the upper years and all subjects in the sixth form) with an impressive teacher/student ratio especially in the sixth form. 'The separation works well, making girls feel more confident in their academic studies and boys more confident about expressing their feelings,' says the head.

Throughout the syllabus there is a very strong emphasis on linking secular subjects with Jewish history, tradition, literature and ethos. 'There is no reason why, for example, matters of kashruth (dietary laws) cannot be linked with the issue of, say, zoology,' says a Jewish Studies teacher, reciting chapter and verse. The modern language department is surprisingly imaginative and solid, with these subjects, again, being linked with Jewish studies. Students speak fondly of their teachers and feel they can always approach them with any questions and do so at all times in the corridors.

While some parents welcome the relaxed atmosphere, in which students of all levels are taught together and streaming is reserved for only a few subjects and only in some age groups, others would like to 'see more drive'. The aim, however, is to boost the confidence of students and nurture their potential, says Skelker who, in the same vein has expanded the A level curriculum to include subjects like psychology and theatre studies. The result seems to be a very happy student body, one that enjoys learning for its own sake rather than simply for the marks. The results are impressive by any comparison, almost all pupils achieving grades A*-C at GCSE. About 20 per cent of pupils score A or A* grades in eight or more subjects. At A level, all but a few achieve A-C.

Support teachers on hand for students with learning difficulties but this area seems to be kept rather 'low key' – students get a very large amount of individual attention in all subjects at all times.

Jewish studies takes up almost one third (taking morning prayers into account) of the school day. The enthusiasm and dynamic teaching of this department's head is reflected by students' immense interest, knowledge and love for the subject. The Jewish studies staff clearly take both their subject and their students very seriously. While being completely versed in Jewish texts, teachers are capable of broadening class discussions to include consideration of other religions and of dealing with sophisticated political issues without being exclusive or unduly partisan. 'Since there is no need to do outreach for our children,' says a teacher, 'we can focus on the actual study of text and issues.' All pupils take Jewish Studies to AS level, very many continue to A level, thus being superbly prepared for Yeshiva (further study of the Jewish holy books) and seminary stud-

ies. Indeed study at Yeshiva or seminary is very much the preferred gap year option for Immanuel graduates, though this may also reflect a certain hesitation to venture beyond the tried and true.

Games, Options, The Arts: Thanks to the very large and beautifully equipped grounds, sporting activities could be featuring high on the curriculum but these take third place after the intensive Jewish studies and secular curricula. Late coach service encourages take up of sports after school. The music department is in the process of being built up – a tempting scheme through which students are being offered free instrumental tuition and free use of instruments. 'I was absolutely amazed by the level, creativity, and brilliant results achieved in the arts department and the GCSE projects are worthy of exhibition,' said a parent – we can only agree. School trips aimed at enhancing students' understanding and appreciation of Jewish history start in year 7 with a week's visit to York, a trip to Strasbourg and Israel in the middle years and, finally, in sixth form, a trip to Eastern Europe.

Background and Atmosphere: With its very rural setting, late Victorian main building, surrounded by a medley of nondescript modern buildings and bungalows and long school days, Immanuel College has the atmosphere of a boarding school. A warm community, with wafts of homemade cooking as you walk across the campus.

Pastoral Care and Discipline: While disciplinary rules are in place, these do not seem to be imposed on students but simply reinforce family values. On the whole, students support, promote and talk kindly and respectfully to one another.

Pupils and Parents: Most students hail from solidly middle class, warm and quite protective homes. This makes for quite a homogeneous student body, with children socialising comfortably during and after school. This is 'exactly what we were looking for when my child left a very protective primary school environment and was not really able to cope with a more anonymous large scale inner-city operation,' says a father. The dress and language of the students as well as the cars of the parents are 'rather swish', comments a staff member.

There is definitely a feeling of well-behaved, quite docile and 'fortunate' children, perhaps at the expense of not being exposed to a more diverse or cosmopolitan way of life. You will not see these students roaming around aimlessly in the coffee shops of north London. A leaning towards the conservative/modern orthodox way of life does not preclude pupils/parents from all backgrounds and of all degrees of religiousness being welcomed and respected.

Entrance: Students come from varied academic and Jewish backgrounds but have to be committed to want to pursue both these areas with equal zest, says Mr Skelker. About 40 per cent of the students come from non-Jewish primary schools. Very few students join the college at sixth form level, since the head feels quite strongly that students should continue their sixth form studies in the school in which they started their secondary education.

Exit: Historically, a flood left after GCSE. Under the new head and owing to improvements in the sixth form, this has slowed to a trickle. After A levels most students continue to university, after having taken a year off to study at a yeshiva or Seminary.

Money Matters: Several scholarships are awarded annually and bursaries are offered in cases of proven need. Sixth form scholarships may be awarded for outstanding results at GCSE level.

Remarks: While Immanuel College would not feature in a list of scholastically vigorous secondary schools, it certainly would rate among the most caring. A place where no one will 'slip through the net'.

IMPINGTON VILLAGE COLLEGE

New Road, Impington, Cambridge, Cambridgeshire, CB4 9LX

Tel: 01223 200 400
Fax: 01223 200 419
E-mail: office@impington.cambs.sch.uk
Website: www.impington.cambs.sch.uk

• Pupils: 1,370 boys and girls, all day but provision made for far-travelled pupils to be put up locally • Ages: 11-19 • Size of sixth form: 280 • Non-denom • State

Warden: Since 1997, Jacqueline E Kearns MA FRSA (early fifties). Earned a BA Hons degree in German from Liverpool and MA in German Literature from the Freie Universität, Berlin. First teaching jobs were at inner London schools. Then headed a large comprehensive in Kent and two international schools in Germany before taking the reins here. Totally dedicated and inspirational, she is a popular head and an ideal spiritual guide for the multi-layered Impington enterprise. Speaks in a calming and reflective manner and is warm, humorous and genuine (as far as we know, the only head to have addressed an unfamiliar Good Schools Guide editor phoning to arrange an interview as 'my lovely'). Interests include theatre, concerts and dance. Husband, a former teacher, stays busy at home doing up

their 16th century house. Two children – both attend Impington Village College.

Academic Matters: A unique school with a split personality. For ages 11-16, it is a happy, successful comprehensive, with unusually strong arts provision and a healthy international conscience. The sixth form is something else – a bona fide international college, offering both the International Baccalaureate (since 1991) and A levels, and taking pupils from 33 nationalities. Running throughout the school is its excellent languages programme (it is one of the government's specialist schools for languages). All pupils learn French in year 7, then German is added, and in years 10 and 11, Spanish and Japanese and, in the sixth form, Russian becomes available. The school won a European Language Award (2001) for its non-traditional approach in introducing French to local primary schools. Lots of extra challenges available for the most able (eg studying Latin and Greek and sitting some GCSEs early).

Pupils praise the school for its excellent teachers and rewards for achievement. Said one, 'you don't get laughed at for wanting to work hard.' As for exam results, what other schools summarise in half a page here extends through 23 pages of statistics, tables and graphs. We think they are telling us that 70 per cent of pupils normally gain 5 A*-C GCSEs, a solid result given the mixed intake. And the IB/A level scores must be good – in 2001, Impington Village College ranked first among all British comprehensives in the Financial Times' league table of sixth form examination results. This put it above Cambridge's famously good Hills Road Sixth Form College and many independent schools in the area.

Currently 75 per cent of students follow the International Baccalaureate diploma programme – a huge increase in the last two years; 24 per cent take AS/A2 levels and 1 per cent follow the IDEAL course for students with special needs. Of the A level cohort approximately 30 per cent will be taking the full arts provision, and be members of 'The Performance School'.

Games, Options, The Arts: Pupils encouraged to try everything, with spectacular results. Usual range of sports in the lower school, though even in games, Impington's emphasis on individuality, creativity and social justice can be felt. Pupils speak solemnly of the school's scrupulously fair methods of team selection, and where but Impington would we have found a group of cool 12-year-old footballers chatting enthusiastically about how much they enjoy their dance class? Games not mandatory in sixth form and enthusiasm for team sports, abundant among the younger kids, tends to fizzle out.

Deservedly one of the first schools to achieve the government's Artsmark Gold in September 2001 (a composer, a fine artist and a professional dancer in residence). Performing arts are a particular strength and sixth form candidates without academic qualifications may apply directly to Impington's School of Performance via audition. The college stages a dance performance every term, and there is an annual showcase at a venue in Cambridge. Ballet classes available before school. Music department provides masses of opportunities and good teaching (excellent, says Ofsted), popular and successful at GCSE. Lots of clubs, including active Amnesty International group and SFPAN (sixth formers political awareness network!). IB requirement of 150 hours of community service fits in nicely. Many international exchanges and assorted trips overseas. Enthusiastic and popular D of E. Active student council and pupils say they feel 'listened to.'

Background and Atmosphere: Founded in 1939 as part of Cambridgeshire Education Secretary Henry Morris' village college movement – an attempt to provide rural England with educational and social centres serving all ages. Main building designed by the founder of the Bauhaus, Walter Gropius. True to its roots, the college offers adult evening classes, runs a workplace nursery, provides a base for local youth clubs and maintains a sports centre open 364 days a year from 6am to 10pm. Much emphasis is put on international politics, the environment, human rights and other global issues (the student council has been debating whether to introduce Fair Trade vending machines). Pupils' views are respected and children of all ages are encouraged to speak out and share their beliefs. Some elegant facilities (indoor pool, beautiful library with separate sixth form area, cutting-edge language teaching lab, good science labs, dance and drama studios, editing suite). This equipment, along with the international buzz of the place, amusingly at odds with overall down-at-heel condition of the mostly-standard-government-issue-drab site. Head hopes to build a new sixth from centre, and new building for 600 students, replacing temporary huts, opened in 2005. Would also benefit from a larger canteen and a bigger cleaning budget. Sixth form feels separate from the rest of the school but has a beautiful 'learning centre'. No sixth form uniform.

Pastoral Care and Discipline: Behaviour we witnessed was impressive, including an assembly of several hundred 15-year-olds who sat in rapt silence through a twenty minute exposition by a teacher. Behaviour policy speaks in 1970s psycho-babble (much discussion of 'spiritual development', 'unique human beings' and 'the self' – with miscreants requiring an 'inclusion manager behaviour support plan' – yuk) but it is all meant well, and the overall caring and friendly atmosphere is the first thing to hit any visitor. With all the talk of inclusion and social conscience, the college's zero tolerance drugs policy comes as a (pleasant) shock. Any pupils found to be taking illegal substances (including alcohol) or who are under the influence of illegal substances on site or during the school day will be excluded permanently. Only a hip state comprehensive could get away with such a firm stance at a time when most independent schools speak more of counselling and second chances. 'The children love the policy,' says the head, 'because it is clear. Cambridge is a druggy town and the rule makes it much easier for them to say no.' International pupils and youngsters from outside Cambridgeshire are housed (carefully) with local host families.

Pupils and Parents: Parents of 11-16 year olds range from Cambridge academics to severely underprivileged. 25 per cent of children are on the special educational needs register (including a small group of children with severe disabilities – wheelchairs possible here). In the international sixth form one third of the pupils come up from Impington and a further third from other schools in the area and throughout the UK (a few from independent schools). The rest hail from 33 countries all over the world, although the majority come from Europe. Sixth formers we met (of several nationalities) were mature, non-competitive and self-motivated. 'We're not spoon-fed', said one boy who came here from an independent school.

Entrance: Oversubscribed, but appeals often succeed, boosting class sizes above the target level of 28 pupils (12 in the sixth form). Intake at 11 mainly from neighbourhood primaries. At sixth form, from a wide area in Cambridgeshire and adjoining counties, plus abroad. The sixth form offers four distinct courses. The selective IB course is aimed at highly motivated students earning mostly B grades or above at GCSE. Somewhat less academic children may be steered towards A levels, though they will still normally need 5 C-or-better GCSEs. The School of Performance accepts pupils with virtually no academic qualifications and, although these pupils will take one or two A/AS levels, it is essentially vocational training for young people planning a career in dance, theatre or music. There is also a special course providing one-to-one tuition to youngsters with severe learning disabilities.

Exit: Leavers at 16 (about two thirds of the school) go to local colleges (Hills Road, Long Road etc) for A levels and GNVQ. Those who leave at 18 go on to a dazzlingly wide array of destinations. Examples from last year's list of leavers: London School of Contemporary Dance (BA programme), Academy of Arts in Rome (to study sculpture), Trust House Forte (hotel management training), Cambridge University (Anglo-Saxon, Norse and Celtic Studies), national service in Germany, medical studies at the University of Padua (Italy), employment in Uzbekistan. 87 per cent to university. Many gap years, deferred entries.

Money Matters: Pupils from outside the EU (very few) must pay roughly £4,700 annually for tuition. Free for everyone else. Pupils residing with host families pay for room and board.

Remarks: The state school system's best kept secret. A genuinely international sixth form college, on the outskirts of one of the most appealing towns in England, offering the IB and A levels, free of charge to all EU residents. And a brilliant head to boot.

INTERNATIONAL COLLEGE, SHERBORNE SCHOOL

Newell Grange, Sherborne, Dorset, DT9 4EZ

Tel: 01935 814 743
Fax: 01935 816 863
E-mail: reception@sherborne-ic.net
Website: www.sherborne-ic.net

• Pupils: 130; 57 per cent boys. All board • Ages: 11-16 • Non-denom • Fees: £8,270 per term • Independent

---

Principal: Since 1997, Dr Christopher Greenfield MA MEd EdD (fifties). Previously head of Sidcot (Quaker) School, Somerset for 11 years and worked for the Quakers in the Middle East for four years. The ideal man for the job, he describes his work as 'doing my small part for increasing global peace and understanding.' An active politician, Dr Greenfield has stood as a Liberal Democrat candidate 4 times. Sees the aim of International College as not just to instruct pupils in English and other academic subjects but to teach them how to cope successfully in a British boarding school.

Entrance: No exams. A place is yours if you have a reasonable school report. Pupils' academic abilities and knowledge of the English language vary widely. Students entering the one-year intensive GCSE programme need to have at least Lower Intermediate Level English (Equivalent to IELTS score of 4+).

Exit: Here, the college really comes up with the goods. Its 'future schooling advisor' is devoted to slotting pupils into good schools when they leave International College. Many go to Sherborne (9 last year) but also to a wide range of other schools. Few disappointments so long as you're not counting on Eton or Winchester. However 2005 saw one alumnus offered a place at the former and two into the latter!

Remarks: Set up in 1977 by Robert Macnaghten, then head of Sherborne School, who found himself turning down bright overseas applicants because their knowledge of English was inadequate. The International Study Centre, as it was then called, aimed to help pupils improve their English while studying a British-style curriculum. The college keeps a low profile in the UK, but is promoted by 250 agents overseas. Located on a small, pleasant site, just above Sherborne School (five-minute walk), it is a miniaturised version of a British boarding school. There are 25 dedicated small classrooms (classes average 6 pupils), a small library, computer room, 8 science labs, playing fields and basketball court. Pupils use some Sherborne School facilities eg tennis and squash courts and the indoor swimming pool. Lovely canteen with piles of fresh fruit and wonderful, varied menus (much pupil input). Excellent teachers all trained in EFL as well as their subject of instruction. Strong feeling of industry and purpose – parents are not coughing up this kind of money for their children to have a holiday.

Pupils stay for at least one year, often preparing for Common Entrance or GCSEs. The college offers a 'normal' two-year GCSE course and also a more demanding 'express' course – essentially a one-year crammer for older children some of whom may have covered much of the material already and just need to nail down some exams and spruce up their English. Last year, 84 per cent of the pupils on the express course earned 5 A-C grades as did 70 per cent of those on the two-year course – an amazing achievement considering the linguistic hurdles.

Unsurprisingly, the subjects studied lean heavily towards maths and sciences where language ability is less crucial. Fine arts also superb. School is expanding its admission of younger pupils. Also runs a popular summer course attracting students from 31 countries, 40 per cent of whom are preparing to take up places at UK schools in September.

Friendly atmosphere. Wide range of nationalities represented but majority of pupils come from the far east (Hong Kong, China, Korea, Taiwan, Thailand and, less so, Japan). In their free time, these youngsters tend to stick together and, despite staff's best efforts, speak their own language. Older boys board on site in single or double rooms. Girls live a three-minute car journey away in Westcott House, a converted Georgian residence (they are bused to and from school, as are the junior boys who live nearby). 'Graduate resident assistants,' fresh from university, help look after the boarding houses and seem to have an easy-going relationship with the pupils. Pupils age 13 and over are allowed to wander freely in town (must sign out and wear school uniform) and can be found hovering in newsagents and over the sushi display in Sainsburys. An education in itself and lovely Sherborne is an ideal town in which to wander.

A good option for families that can afford it. But don't expect the college to turn your disaffected son into a scholar. Schools that have accepted International College pupils tell us that they find their levels of English and general academic ability do vary widely. OBs: King Mswati III of Swaziland and the heir to the Kingdom of Qatar.

INTERNATIONAL SCHOOL OF ABERDEEN

Linked to International School of Aberdeen, Preschool and Elementary in the Junior section

296 North Deeside Road, Milltimber, Aberdeen, AB13 0AB

Tel: 01224 732 267
Fax: 01224 735 648
E-mail: admin@isa.aberdeen.sch.uk
Website: www.isa.aberdeen.sch.uk

• Pupils: High school; (15-18) 85 middle school; (12-14); 165 elementary (5-11); 30 in pre-school (3-4). Variable ratio boy/girl • Ages: 3-18 • Fees: Underwritten by the oil companies 'who meet the tuition fees for their employees'. Some non-oil pupils: £500 registration; £2,000 capital fee; £ 4,375 to £ 4,900 • Independent

Head: Since 2002, Dr Daniel Hovde PhD (aka Dan) (forties) who came to the granite city from the jungles of Sumatra where he was head of another International Services contract school, in this case contracted to Chevron. Before that he taught in the Canadian Academy in Japan, which was founded as a missionary school in 1913 and was home to some 35 different nationalities. Dr Hovde, who is married to Karol, a counsellor with the school (they adopted their daughter in China whilst in the far east), was educated in Seattle, studying history, social studies and majoring in education from Washington State University followed by a masters in education and a doctorate in educational leadership – 'it seemed to take forever'. He taught in between his lengthy education and was pleased to come to

Aberdeen as it was 'the right size and make-up for himself and his wife and good for the daughter' They could 'all work in the same place'. Delightful, outgoing and friendly, he runs the school with a pair of principals and positively bounced this editor round the school.

Academic Matters: School nominally follows the IB, but they also cover High School Diplomas. Those pupils who only do the IB diploma average 33 credits (24 is pass). Pupils get advanced credit for having taken the IB, but it is by no means suitable or even needed by all. Some standard grades taken 'for curiosity benchmark'. Fair mish-mash. Massive amount of to-ing and fro-ing, 32 different languages spoken, most pupils come for two or three years, some only for one, and 'odd much beyond five'. Pupils go on the roll of honour (spelled, of course, 'honor') society if they have done well in the realms of academe, leadership and service. All very American and fairly in your face.

60 per cent of all staff are British 'local' hire, with husbands in oil – or 'just living here' and 40 per cent have a mixture of backgrounds, from English-speaking countries in the main, though native speakers employed for Spanish and French (the two langs offered for IB). School appears to run as a commune with 'no heads of departments', and two counsellors – whilst senior pupils seek advice from staff, younger pupils are ambivalent about whether they go to a teacher or an older pupil for help. EAL where necessary, and a dedicated teacher. Roughly 25/30 pupils in each year group, 12/15 per class. Choices accelerated, and learning support available – two dedicated members of staff, school is brutally honest, if pupils need more than one hour's support per day, then they will have to go elsewhere – ie local mainstream. Dedicated computer labs, and flat-screened computers in the class rooms, home economics also in a classroom ('there is a cooker and a sink in the corner' – sorry chaps, we missed it). Head of computing negotiating with oil companies for outdated computers expects to pick up thirty or forty of them which he will use for special projects, whizzing them round the school on a trolley. All wireless.

Games, Options, The Arts: Stunning sports hall about to be superseded by an even grander sports hall, trad games football and golf (which they also play internationally and in the Scottish league) plus basketball and volley ball. Teams visit London, Spain as well as running their own internal league. Cabinets of shining silver. No orchestras, but number of instruments taught, ditto choirs – pupils make music outside school. Rather clever computer programme which goes red when you hit the wrong note. Deeply popular. Current sports centre also houses drama etc productions, and will be home to the music and drama department by next year, music dept currently housed in the rather charming Victorian manor house, but stage is tiny: 50 max in the audience. History of lavish drama. School has a high charity presence, sleepovers for the homeless, shoebox appeal and the eight-year-olds visit local 'rest' homes and read and perform to them. American boy scouts but no D of E.

Background and Atmosphere: School founded in 1972 by Mr McCormick, and bought by the oil companies in 1980. The oil companies own the buildings (and undertake all the improvements – wish lists et al) leasing them to the school for a peppercorn. The school is run by a charitable trust with the members of the board being appointed in proportion to the number of employees' children in the school at one particular moment. A local solicitor sees fair play. School owns six, fairly cramped, acres on the north of the Dee, with an almost-impossible-to-see sign tucked away up the drive at a rotten angle – perhaps it might be more visible were one to drive on right? (Prospectus details 9.5 acres of land, school secretariat appears to plump for five, including an acre bought last year. Looks more like nine or so.) Huge spaces, huge magically filled classrooms, wide passages. Gosh. Pupil-pics abound so not that soulless.

Pupils eat by year group in the dining room, choice of healthy option, main meal, veggie meal = pretty pathetic – mini waffles and spaghetti hoops! Come in Jamie Oliver – or panini and pud. Menu for whole week, and really pretty expensive. Not quite the overflowing library one might expect, but humming with more computers and boasting a book hospital. All pupils have lockers, decorated in rather uninspired wrapping paper on their birthdays. Lots of singing of happy birthday at lunch. Much talk of how super Scotland is, and a certain amount of Celtic indulgence. Trips all over the shop. Tinies have dedicated play area outside with squidgy tar. (NB: peanut butter is not allowed in pre-school...)

Pastoral Care and Discipline: Head anxious to dispel the myth of spoilt little rich boy, keen PSE and strong RME. Guidance by clans or houses. Staff are trained in different cultures and dealing with people in a different fashion – how things are done at home. 'Kids are kids', 'knock on wood – no overt bullying, but quite a lot of teasing'. No bullying because of habits, more 'teasing because of personality traits' (his words not ours). Drug presentation evening, and head has 'oh ya, on occasion' disciplined and suspended (never expelled) miscreants for a day or two – details of all suspendable offences in handbooks complete with list of drug test cut-off levels. Head keen on independent study and motivation and no gum may be chewed in class.

Pupils and Parents: No school uniform but of course everyone conforms. Most students arrive via school bus. Good contact via monthly letter.

Entrance: Whenever.

Exit: Universities in America and Britain the most popular.

Money Matters: Fees paid by oil companies, otherwise one or two non-oil American ex-pats, scholarships in pipeline so that school more reflects the cost of a 'normal' British school, most about 25 per cent, but 100 per cent is on the cards.

Remarks: Smashing school – an eye-opener and totally logical, of course, to follow an international programme but, with such an influx of non-native teachers, it might be possible for a family to be billeted in Scotland for a year or so and experience no native culture at all. Thank you for sharing.

INTERNATIONAL SCHOOL OF LONDON

Linked to International School of London Junior School in the Junior section

139 Gunnersbury Avenue, London, W3 8LG

Tel: 020 8992 5823
Fax: 020 8993 7012
E-mail: mail@ISLondon.com
Website: www.ISLondon.com

• Pupils: 140 seniors, 120 juniors • Ages: 3-18 • Size of sixth form: 40 • Non-denom • Fees: £3,416 - £4,583 • Independent • Open days: Early October

---

Director: Since 2005, Mr Amin Makarem who taught at the school for four years before taking up the directorship.

Academic Matters: School has followed the IB programme since 1976 and has been accredited to the European Council of International Schools since 1983. Implemented the Primary Years Programme and the Middle Years Programme (now authorised) in 2002. Recent recruitments 'have been made with that in mind' but 'we have been training and jetting new staff and teachers all over the world'. GCSEs are no longer on offer. The IB Diploma is successfully up and running, with 100 per cent of all candidates getting the diploma in 2004.

A student's mother tongue is 'usually available' – notably Japanese, Italian, Arabic, Spanish and French.

Students can also take almost any language in their IB syllabus; hence Norwegian and one or two other non-mainstream tutors are shared with other schools. A cost is incurred if there are fewer than five studying the particular language that you want. EFL and EAL automatically on hand but not as expensive as one might think, as 'a one time only additional charge of £750 payable for pupils enrolled in the intensive course at the secondary level'. The summer course is particularly popular with families who have just arrived in Britain.

Limited help for dyslexics, dedicated special needs co-ordinator; school not keen on taking pupils who arrive with a known problem – but they will deal with any problems that arise during a child's progress through school. Combination of Dyslexia Institute (nearby) plus specialist help both internally and externally. No ADD/ADHD enthusiasm (for want of a better word!) although again pupils in situ will not be asked to leave – school not keen on Ritalin but will 'give support'. Tiny classes at all levels, max class size 20 and down, streamed in English and foreign languages in middle school. Very keen on homework, with homework diaries which parents are required to keep an eye on – 'they are an effective means of communication between teachers and parents'. Up to fifteen hours homework a week by sixth form. Computers all over the shop but no laptops.

Games, Options, The Arts: PE is part of the curriculum; no cricket in school but pupils are encouraged to become part of their local community and join clubs for sports. Football, volleyball, tennis and athletics all played at Gunnersbury Park (almost) adjacent to the school; the primaries swim at Brentford leisure centre, five minutes' walk away. Loads of lunchtime activities; sport as well as hobbies. Music timetabled to 15, oodles of individual lessons, choirs, bands in almost every discipline. Drama also timetabled and an annual production involves both disciplines. Masses of trips – the usual tours round the highlights of London, plus educational visits, both at home and abroad, with a special bonding session for the oldest of the primary children when they spend a long weekend at an adventure centre. Weekly visits for older children. The creativity, active and service part of the IB syllabus includes mega-community work at the Age Concern Centre in Acton; pupils have to do home helping at weekends as well. They also get involved with Model United Nations and UNESCO and help the littles with reading, 'riting and 'rithmetic.

Background and Atmosphere: School was founded in Camden in 1972 and moved to the current converted (very boring in appearance) RC purpose-built school ten years ago, plum next to the Catholic Church. School sited on the North Circular road so cars and lorries speed past the entrance with impunity and noise. Playground in front of school dedicated to child-inspired games, hopscotch, basketball and some strange game that involves angled lines across the forecourt as well as goalposts. Children bused – door to door – and rather strict rules about bus behaviour. Ditto sports clothes, otherwise no uniform. Tremendous school back-up for new parents, who 'will be contacted by a member (who speaks the same language) of the parent-teacher association who will assist them in ensuring that the move to London is as smooth as possible'; and introduced to pretty tortured English too. Weekly assembly for all.

Pastoral Care and Discipline: Rules, absolute commandments and playground rules, as well as bullying (policy document – presumably anti-bullying policy document) disciplinary procedures, school detention, off-campus behaviour and drugs, alcohol and tobacco are all covered in great detail in the handbook. The ISL rules are merely common sense and courteousness and sanctions range from confiscating beanies worn in class or phones ringing, to litter collection, detention, exclusion, suspension and expulsion. Zero tolerance of drugs, suspension considered and automatically out for dealing. Very strict censure in place for pupils discovered taking drugs off campus, counselling and warnings about the seriousness of a repeat performance in place – but no need of these sanctions to date. This is ruthless discipline but it works. Fags banned between Acton Town and Kew Bridge. Strong PS(H)E programme, with external specialists.

Pupils and Parents: Only about 25 non-foreigners; the rest a combination of multi-national, international, diplomatic, middle class families. Large number of Japanese, Italians at the moment but it changes according to the economic climate. School works hard to instil community spirit.

Entrance: From all over, previous school records and interview, ability to speak English is not a priority. Pupils come and may well be accepted throughout the year, though school not keen on anyone arriving between Easter and the end of the summer term.

Exit: Most to unis, some stay on for British unis after their parents have returned to their motherland; some take SATs here (recognised centre) and go for the American option, some go home with their parents. Otherwise strong science bias, with students taking accountancy, business studies, business admin and heading for medical schools.

Money Matters: Will keep a child in extremis – companies usually pay the school fees, but if there is a job change, this may well go out of the window 'we don't want any one to leave because of money'.

Remarks: The most cosmopolitan collection of pupils we have ever seen, could be anywhere in the world, and they really do become a sort of homogeneous mass, no obvious problems with global spats overflowing into the classroom. Works well, the entire IB programme should bring more academic uniformity.

IPSWICH HIGH SCHOOL

Linked to Ipswich High School Junior Department in the Junior section

Woolverstone, Ipswich, Suffolk, IP9 1AZ

Tel: 01473 780 201
Fax: 01473 780 985
E-mail: admissions@ihs.gdst.net
Website: www.ipswichhigh.gdst.net

- Pupils: 465 girls • Ages: 11-18 • Size of sixth form: 105
- Non-denom • Fees: £2,455 senior; £1,470 - £1,779 junior.
- Independent • Open days: In autumn and summer terms

Head: Since 1993, Miss Valerie MacCuish BA (mid-fifties). Educated at Lady Edridge Girls' Grammar and Westfield, London University. Modern linguist. Formerly deputy head at Surbiton High then head, Tunbridge Wells Girls' Grammar. A twinkly, approachable head, with a shrewd and pragmatic approach to her rather special school and its girls.

Retiring July 2006.

Academic Matters: An academic school in 'happy competition' with excellent (free) local grammars and with town centre Ipswich School which now takes girls throughout. Value-added good, girls performing above their innate abilities across the board. An unusual bias for a girls' school towards the sciences and maths at sixth form level; surprising, as the head is a modern linguist and the many who do take languages, art and English do well. Head attributes shift to sciences at year 12 partly, at least, to science/engineering bent of girls' families. Recent major investment in upgrading labs, maths and geography rooms, in particular, with new interactive white board system – girls very enthusiastic. Progress in English at sixth form level singled out for praise in most recent inspection. Impressive individual achievements in sciences and maths, pupils regularly winning awards in Olympiads and other competitive events.

Games, Options, The Arts: Tennis especially strong, county champions at several levels. Athletics also good, along with hockey, netball, riding, skiing and sailing. School has held Public Schools Fencing Cup for 11 consecutive years. Sports trips around the world. Good sports hall and brand new pool. Hockey played on fields in front of architecturally decorous and elegant main building – a wondrously incongruous sight for a visitor. Astroturf for hockey and tennis: in the winter this can be a windswept, wet and chilly place. Many clubs and activities include chess, foreign films, philosophy and young reporters. Also Duke of Edinburgh, Young Enterprise and Engineering Education Scheme. Music is lively – 40 per cent learn an instrument – but less popular than drama at GCSE . Annual concert at Maltings, Snape. Speech & drama also taken by 25 per cent of school. Excellent theatre. Ballet very strong with good individual achievements. Super purpose-built theatre. Art results good and school tries to allow pupils to work in whatever media they feel drawn to. CDT popular, especially metalwork, and taken by everyone to year 9. ICT provision much improved and up-to-date.

Background and Atmosphere: Founded in 1878, only six years after the GDST began, Ipswich has twice had to move to larger premises, most recently to present fabulous site in 1992. School's central building is splendid Georgian Woolverstone Hall, grade 1 listed, which one approaches up a long straight drive with grazing sheep on both sides. School set in 80 acres of parkland on banks of the Orwell, and many rooms look over fields, woods and down to the very picturesque river, marinas, distant low hills etc – a unique view, especially for a GDST school which, so often, are in crowded urban settings. Hall's rooms have glorious ceilings, views and other features – a privilege to be educated in such surroundings – in particular, in the round Elliston Room, used for meetings. A previous school on the site built some of the existing blocks and the Trust has added some excellent new ones. Library now has higher profile in school with enthusiastic full-time librarian and a slowly growing stock in pleasant surroundings – under another wonderful ceiling. School adapted well to building though one-way system employed on some staircases and, possibly, needed elsewhere notably in teaching block where most of curriculum is taught and which, though attractive as a building, has cramped corridors and other public spaces.

All-girls atmosphere, appreciated by its pupils and which the head sees as providing them with opportunities to 'learn how to speak up and not defer to the boys', especially in maths and the sciences. 'Love it or loathe it' cerise uniform.

Pastoral Care and Discipline: Tutorial system at the heart of effective pastoral care. Mentoring system for year 7s in which they are befriended by a senior girl. Discipline unobtrusive and relaxed. Few serious problems and a theoretical 'zero tolerance' over drugs offences – which present head has yet to invoke. Smokers and other serious transgressors made to 'do socially desirable things' like litter picking and school has litter duties anyway which keep place immaculate. Girls pay tribute to staff who 'always have time for you' and whose 'door is always open.' Good friendly relations between staff and pupils and place has civilised, harmonious atmosphere. Girls have less independence than city school pupils – there's nowhere much to go in breaks except, within bounds, the fields and woods. Sixth allowed to the river, through the woods and past the pet graves made by past owners of the Hall.

Pupils and Parents: Mostly local girls, bussed in from surrounding areas – Colchester, Felixstowe, Harwich, Hitcham, Stowmarket, Sudbury, Woodbridge and Ipswich itself. 60+ pick-up points for coaches. The journey – lengthy for some – is seen as part of the school's social life (and probably saves hours of mobile phone time). Families very mixed – strong professional contingent – lawyers, teachers, doctors. Some from large local BT research station, some small business families, many farmers. Some parents could buy the school outright while many struggle on two incomes to find the fees.

Entrance: Mostly from school's own junior dept but also 35 or so taken from other state or independent juniors at 11. Entrance via tests in English, maths and school report.

Exit: Most to good universities, a high proportion to Durham, Sheffield, Nottingham, Birmingham, Leicester. Wide range of disciplines studied with an interestingly high number taking medical and veterinary subjects. A few annually to Oxbridge. No starry OGs but good proportion successful in many professions including broadcasting, law, accountancy, business, engineering and medical.

Money Matters: A few Trust scholarships at 11 and 16 up to half fees but most for less. No means-testing, awarded on academic merit alone. Music scholarships at 11 - awarded by audition - for up to a quarter fees. Means-tested bursaries at 11 and 16 awarded on need and academic merit up to full fees. Short-term assistance also available if needed.

Remarks: A stunning location – almost like an august girls' boarding school in position, with all the advantages of accommodation and space as well as the advantages of a day-school way of life and timetable. All in all, highly desirable so long as you're the sort who can make bus deadlines and not the sort who needs the fix of shops and busy streets round about.

IPSWICH SCHOOL

Linked to Ipswich Preparatory School in the Junior section

Henley Road, Ipswich, Suffolk, IP1 3SG

Tel: 01473 408 300
Fax: 01473 400058
E-mail: registrar@ipswich.suffolk.sch.uk
Website: www.ipswich.suffolk.sch.uk

- Pupils: 735; 510 boys, 225 girls; 38 boarders. Plus 303 in prep
- Ages: 11-18 • Size of sixth form: 200 • C of E • Fees: Seniors: full boarding £4,555 - £5,258; weekly boarding £4,343 - £4,950; day £2,729 to £3,019. Juniors £1,953 - £2,221
- Independent • Open days: September for 11 & 13; November for the sixth form

Head: Since 1993, Mr Ian Galbraith MA (mid fifties). Educated Dulwich College, Cambridge (a double first in geography). Previously head of geography at Kingston Grammar, then head of Upper School at Dulwich. Married (wife, Kathryn, teaches history and general studies in school), with two children. A genial, effervescent head who says he's 'very, very committed to pastoral care' and means it. Mr Galbraith's study alone is worth a visit – the extraordinary ancient 'Old Town Library', a unique collection of 1,000+ volumes, mostly from the 15th and 16th centuries, in mint condition and a miraculous asset for any school (though it actually belongs to Suffolk). Mr Galbraith's enthusiasm for this trust is matched by his enthusiasm for, knowledge about and pleasure in his school, the changes he has overseen, his future plans and the achievements and general character of his students.

Academic Matters: School's results have improved significantly in recent years – partly due to the advent of girls throughout. Head does not pretend to stratospheric league table showings but school now gets very respectable results – most pupils getting A*/A or B for all GCSEs. A levels also respectable with a good showing in history and economics. Also good for the few who take Latin and art. SEN well-supported – includes learning support for children without specific problems to bolster confidence etc. Pupils do better here than their abilities would suggest.

Games, Options, The Arts: Main sports are rugby, hockey and cricket and, for the girls, netball, hockey, tennis, rounders but many others on offer. Boys' hockey especially strong, teams regularly in national finals. First XI cricket on beautiful pitch in centre of school, lovingly maintained and everyone else kept off for most of the year! Beautifully refurbished pavilion with squash and fives courts. 35 acres of sports fields ten minutes' walk away. 1992 sports hall, indoor nets, cricket gallery on professional standard surface. School is centre for Suffolk County Cricket coaching. 1999 excellent design technology centre with good multimedia workshops. Exceptional theatre for 200-400 depending on use of flexible seating. Drama very strong though, admirably, not part of the curriculum ie no public exams, thus freeing subject to everyone. CCF, community service, conservation among huge and inviting range of options. Also costume design, golf, journalism, photography, silversmithing & jewellery, textiles and windsurfing. Very good music.

Background and Atmosphere: An ancient foundation – possibly 14th century – royal connections date back, at least, to Tudor times and present 'Visitor' is HM Queen. School moved to present Victorian buildings in 1852. Main building a wonderful mock-Jacobean extravaganza, now among many newer blocks all on a well-maintained, well-planted site surrounded by leafy middle-class Ipswich residential roads in this conservation area. School became fully independent after World War Two. Newer blocks have excellent imaginative touches eg coffee bar in sixth form building, where they also have computer suite, study room and changing rooms. Also clever 'loggia' for Middle School relaxation with picnic tables, coffee machine, TV and ponds – though in a heated space. Wonderfully anachronistically-housed ICT centre with beamed roof and parquet floor. Super chapel. Stunning library – inside and out – a rarely inviting working space, airy, spacious yet intimate. Special feature the John Piper round stained-glass windows depicting seasons. This feature echoed throughout school site where stained glass pops up here and there – much done by previous school chaplain or pupils under his tuition. Gives school real individuality. Much light, airy space with wood much used, throughout school. Altogether a very pleasant place to be in, a sense of loving care and imaginative development pervades the whole site.

Pastoral Care and Discipline: House-based and year-group-based tutorial system plus other staff with specific pastoral brief. Chaplain also seen as important in pastoral care. Head's commitment reflected everywhere and he is sure that many parents choose school over substantial competition because of reputation for 'value-added' – in pastoral matters as well as academic. Discipline good and occasional serious transgressors dealt with on an individual basis – 'we wave a big stick'.

Pupils and Parents: A real mixture – rural and urban, Essex and Suffolk, from preps and primaries. 'We are delightfully mixed', says Head. In fact pupils come from the whole of Suffolk and north and east Essex, many farming families but also many whose parents commute to Liverpool Street. Good complex coach service helps to ferry in and out. 20+ overseas nationals, mostly from Hong Kong, live with increasing number of weekly boarders – more local pupils – in 'Westwood' – super house, minutes away, in which years 11-13 have individual study bedrooms and years below in threes and fours.

Girls now in all years though still a minority. Girl pupils in the main seem unaffected and grateful to be here and although achievement of the ultimate aim of being co-educationally equal may be some way off, the feeling of imbalance seems likely to ease over time. Children are relaxed, collaborative and quietly purposeful.

Entrance: 40 per cent from Ipswich Prep, transfer virtually automatic. Large number from other local prep and various state primaries. Via school's exam, interview and current head's report. Takes pupils who do well enough in entrance tests but won't take below the set standard. The natural choice for the less than super-brilliant as the school, head feels, will get the best out of them in a way that top grammars may not. Results would suggest that he's right.

Exit: Wide range of courses across the spread of disciplines, academic and vocational. Wide range, too, of destinations, from a few at London/Oxbridge to rather more to the newer universities. Old Boys include Cardinal Wolsey, Rider Haggard, Sir Edward Poynter PRA, Nobel Laureate Sir Charles Sherrington and physicist, Sir Charles Frank. Also Edward Ardizzone and composer David Sawer.

Money Matters: Maximum scholarships are Queen's scholarships, equivalent to half tuition fees. A number of smaller awards are made each year. Academic, music and art scholarships for entry at ages 11 and 13 plus new sports scholarship at 13. Academic, music and all-rounder scholarships for entry at age 16. A limited number of Ipswich School Assisted Places at ages 11, 13 and 16 are available to help able children whose families could not otherwise afford the fees - these are means-tested.

Remarks: Super school, a warm and aesthetically educational environment. Severe competition from Essex grammars and from Ipswich High School for Girls but offering unbeatable attractions in many areas – one being its position just to the north of the town centre.

James Allen's Girls' School (JAGS)

Linked to James Allen's Preparatory School (JAPS) in the Junior section

East Dulwich Grove, London, SE22 8TE

Tel: 02086 931 181
Fax: 02086 937 842
E-mail: juliee@jags.org.uk
Website: www.jags.org.uk

• Pupils: 748, all day • Ages: 11-18 • Size of sixth form: 181
• C of E Foundation but all are welcome • Fees: £3,275 - JAGS: £2,766 - JAPS, plus lunch • Independent • Open days: September, October and November

Headmistress: Since 1994, Mrs Marion Gibbs BA MLitt (fiftyish). Read classics at Bristol, where she also did her PGCE and part-time research. Previous post was as an HMI inspector – still inspects for ISI. Before that she taught in both private and state schools, including Burgess Hill, and at Haberdashers' Aske's School for Girls, Elstree. Very keen classicist, has been an examiner in the subject, and is the author of books and articles (under the name Baldock). Highly efficient, business-like, fast talking, direct and lively. Teaches up to nine lessons per week – Greek mythology to year 7; Latin to year 9, citizenship to years 10 & 11; classical civilisation to year 13 at A2. A hands-on head who knows all her girls – quite a feat in a school this size. 'Interested' in IB, but leaving it alone for the time being – all staff debated the issue in 2001/2 and decided it would not suit all JAGS girls.

Academic Matters: Perennially very strong and consistent. Maths and English the biggest takers at A level, followed by biology, chemistry and history. GCSE results also impressive – 6 girls in top 5 in the country for their subjects this year. Good teaching in modern languages including writing poetry, with provision for those in the fast track and school/family exchanges for children learning Italian, Spanish and French; German and Russian also on offer. Hard work ethos firmly in place. Noticeboards bursting with information, courses, articles, and girls reading them. Some outstanding staff, reasonable turnover, 20 per cent men. Head keen on professional development, very proud when staff get promotion and a better job elsewhere.

Games, Options, The Arts: Very strong in the arts – Silver Artsmark awarded May 2003. Outstandingly good art – demanding teaching with high expectations. Music is also outstanding, under new, young director of music, Leigh O'Hara. Drama intensely keen, in small but inspiring theatre, modelled on the Cottesloe. Good careers department and DT another strong department. Traditional games compulsory for the first three years and a wide range of sports played in all years, with masses of games and matches at all times. Awarded Gold Sportsmark, a rare achievement, in 2003. Good playing fields and sense of space. PE an option at GCSE (unusual in an academic school). Impressive debating – they win competitions. JAGS girls always do well in the Youth Parliament, a seriously politically minded streak runs through the school. Broad outlook and general studies encouraged, good use made of the wonderful Dulwich Picture Gallery, occasional studies with Dulwich College at sixth form level. Huge new swimming pool, linked to the new sports hall. Partnership with state schools keenly fostered; JAGS girls help in local primary schools which also use JAGS pool – head dead keen on community work – impressive community service programme involves girls locally and abroad.

Background and Atmosphere: Founded in 1741 (claims to be the oldest independent girls' school in London, though Dulwich was not London in those days) in 'two hired rooms at the Bricklayer's Arms' – a nice symbolic beginning. One of the three schools of the Foundation of Alleyn's College of God's Gift to Dulwich, named after James Allen, warden in 1712 of Dulwich College and described as 'Six Feet high, skilful as a Skaiter; a Jumper; Athletic and Humane' – not a bad role model. School became girls only in 1842 and moved to present 22 acre site in leafy Dulwich in 1886 following Act of Parliament passed to reorganise the Foundation. Large rather dour purpose-built building plus lots of additions, including new very fine library. Huge development programme ('we're borrowing money from ourselves') well under way, to include a new dining room (in place of old swimming pool). Famous Botany Gardens planted by Lillian Clarke (pioneer ecologist at the beginning of the 20th century). As we have said before, the whole place bounces with energy and pride.

Pastoral Care and Discipline: School council to discuss problems/complaints – girls are very articulate at these sessions. Head girl and deputies elected by girls and they are 'pretty powerful' according to one. Detention the usual punishment for misdemeanours (parents warned in advance). All staff act as shepherds.

Pupils and Parents: Mostly from south of the river, as far away as Bromley. Also increasing numbers from north of the river – girls from the city and Islington (London Bridge to East Dulwich train takes twelve minutes), school bus from Victoria. Unusually rich social and ethnic mix. Old Girls include Anita Brookner, Lisa St Aubin de Terain, Mary Francis, Dharshini David.

Entrance: At 11 by exam and interview – all 400 children trying for places are interviewed – mental liveliness an essential ingredient. About one quarter from their own excellent junior school (see separate entry), though all must pass the exam – January, for places in September. Nearly 50 per cent from the state sector, altogether from nearly 100 'feeder' schools. Constantly oversubscribed and hot competition to get in. NB overshot on applications for 2000 entry and had to add on an extra form (five forms, each of 26 girls), 'but never again'. Sixth form entry: six A or B grades at GCSE, with a minimum C in English language and maths (for girls already in the school, as well as those coming in from outside). Variable numbers come in at 16.

Exit: 95+ per cent to higher education, with at least 12-15 to Oxbridge, and sometimes around 25 offers. Wide variety of top universities, often reading tough subjects. Medicine popular, also history. Foundation art courses popular, also a gap year. Usually around ten girls leave post GCSE. Old Girls offer careers talk, good work experience/ work shadowing.

Money Matters: Almost 40 per cent of pupils on financial assistance of some sort. A well-resourced school, with an annual grant from the Dulwich Estate, all of which goes towards scholarships, including bursary elements (where necessary). Generous with the help they give. Up to 20 scholarships per year currently offered at 11, including one for music and one for art – major scholarships of £1,000 pa, minor ones of £500 (all can be means-tested up to 90 per cent and 80 per cent respectively); some at sixth form too. Fifteen James Allen's Assisted Places (means-tested up to full fees) each year and ambitions to increase this; one or two offered at sixth form.

Remarks: Strong, strong, strong on all fronts; works and plays hard.

JAMES GILLESPIE'S HIGH SCHOOL

Lauderdale Street, Edinburgh, EH9 1DD

Tel: 0131 447 1900

Fax: 0131 452 8601

E-mail: headteacher@jamesgillespies.edin.sch.uk

Website: www.jamesgillespies.edin.sch.uk

- Pupils: 595 boys, 540 girls • Ages: 11-18 • Size of sixth form: 310 • Non-denom • State

Head: Since 2005, Alex Wallace, previously assistant head teacher and depute head teacher over the past 12 years.

Academic Matters: Class size 30 (20/25 for practical subjects), setted early for maths in the September of their first year, second year setted for English. Three separate sciences for all from the third year onwards. No classics, but French, German and Urdu, a tiny number also learn Gaelic (there is a feeder school where pupils do all subjects in Gaelic). All languages are taught up to Higher level. School does complicated mix of Standard, Higher, Advanced Highers and A levels for physics, art (in order to form a portfolio) and geography. An interesting diversification for a state school. Good support for learning, dyslexia, dyspraxia, and help with exams, both withdrawn from class and team teaching in class. ADHD is OK, 'most reasonably well-behaved'. 250 of the pupils come from 40 different countries 'the most diverse population in Scotland', EFL available (free) for all who need it. CDT is 50/50 craft and design and all computer-based – 350 computers in the school. Recent BECTa award for best website.

Games, Options, The Arts: PE and swimming on site; huge games hall plus Astroturf, much used by local community. Football, rugby, hockey pitches about 1.5 miles away at Kirkbrae, pupils are bused. Games are basically extra-curricular, girls' football and netball are popular. Short lunchbreak, 45 mins, so no lunch clubs, kids either go home or to the local carry-outs, rather jolly dining room. Massive music uptake, with carol service in the Usher Hall last year, this year they are off to The McEwan Hall, over 350 regularly on the stage. Senior orchestra, junior orchestra, lessons free, but music dept needs drastic revamping. Ditto labs, DT, libraries and PE area. Strong, spectacular art, photography, 'the lot', impressive fabric design. Huge dance area, media popular with lights and editing studios, three drama studios. Wizard home economics dept – better than most homes we know. Trips all over the place, in many disciplines, skiing, Paris for art, historians to the trenches, geographers to do glacial research in Norway.

Background and Atmosphere: Founded in 1803 as a result of a legacy from James Gillespie, 'a wealthy Edinburgh manufacturer of snuff and tobacco', who was born in Roslin. The school started with 65 students and one master and led a peripatetic existence. At one point it was the prep school for the Merchant Company's secondary schools. By 1908 the school had a roll of over a thousand, including girls, and offered secondary education under the aegis of The Edinburgh School Board, moving to Bruntsfield House, just off The Meadows, in 1966 and going fully co-ed in 1978. The earliest building on this site dates from 1300, and the current schloss was built in 1605, with later additions and improvements. (Sir George Warrender, whose family was to be awarded the title Bruntsfield, bought the house from the original owners and was intrigued to find that if you hung a sheet from every window you could access from the inside, there were still sheetless windows outside. A secret room was discovered, with blood-stained floor, ashes in the grate and a skeleton under the wainscot. The Green Lady haunts the top storeys to this day.)

The head has a grand office in the main building, with a spectacular ceiling, and an impressive fireplace, almost exactly replicated by the music room not quite next door. Now surrounded by predominantly sixties-type classroom blocks, relieved by swards of green and mature trees with a singular clock in the middle of the campus which, despite thousands spend on renovation, will never work properly as the hands were found to be too long. It remains as a memorial to the follies of the architects of the day, though interestingly, Colin MacWilliam has nothing but praise for the design. The campus is hidden amongst decent Victorian tenements, and more grass and trees than you would expect. Woefully short of space, there was a certain frisson when the local electricity board sold an adjoining substation without first offering it to the school, who desperately need room to expand. No uniform 'at the moment'.

Pastoral Care and Discipline: Follows the state guidelines, good PSHE, good anti-bullying strategy in place, 'we get the youngsters to talk it through....we bring them together and get the bully to accept their behaviour is wrong'. 'No current problems' with fags (though pupils light up as they leave the school gates), booze or drugs, but head will exclude on either a temporary or permanent basis if necessary. Last head only ever made two drugs-related temporary exclusions, but it would be permanent if there were any hint of dealing. Also out permanently for a violent attack, though merely temporary exclusion for 'physical violence'. Homework books which must be signed by parent or guardian.

Pupils and Parents: Free intake, so diverse. Large number of professional families, Marchmont is a popular area for the university, plus 'a significant group of working class, with relatively poor backgrounds'. Huge ethnic mix, with some girls wearing the chador – they may well do PE and swim wearing full leggings and long-sleeved T-shirts (though parents can ask to withdraw their daughters from these lessons, few do). Lifts being installed next year for wheelchair-bound pupil, minor physical handicaps OK. Strong parent/teacher involvement.

Entrance: First year capped at 200 but catchment area usually only offers 140, the extra 60 places are by request (and some come from as far as Musselburgh). Last year there were 150 such placement requests; school is obliged to take children on a first come first served basis.

Exit: Number leaves after Standard Grades, either to further education or work; good proportion to unis, mainly Scots, studying medicine, science, art college, followed by social subject and music in that order. Annual trickle to Oxbridge.

Remarks: Much at stake here as new head succeeds very successful predecessor.

JFS School

The Mall, Kenton, Harrow, HA3 9TE

Tel: 020 8206 3100
Fax: 020 8206 3101
E-mail: admin@jfs.brent.sch.uk
Website: www.jfs.brent.sch.uk

• Pupils: 900 girls; 980 boys • Ages: 11-18 • Size of sixth form: 500 • Jewish • State

Head: Since 1993, after twenty years of working herself up the ranks, Dame Ruth Robins DBE BA TTHD (early fifties); hails from South Africa. Her life is committed to the school, where she is often the first one in and the last one out. Although slight in appearance she is almost military in presence. Her message on Open Days on discipline and hard work is repeated throughout the years and conveys to students and parents alike a feeling of 'I mean business'. When speaking of her pupils one gets a Jean Brodie impression, which is substantiated by her students. She continues to teach French, as she always has and her reputation as an inspired teacher is known to all students. Although Dame Ruth does not hover over students or over her staff, her presence behind the scenes is felt throughout the school. 'I don't know how she does it but she knows every single student even if they have not been to her office,' marvels one student. It takes in fact a long route indeed until a student actually ends up at Dame Ruth for any disciplinary reason and whatever steps ultimately taken are without question with the student's welfare in mind.

Her teaching staff respects her and tries to live up to her high standards and expectations. They seem to do so most successfully.

Academic Matters: JFS has now thoroughly left behind its reputation as a school for the less bright and is now one of the top comprehensive schools in the country, showing up well in value-added tables. 88 per cent got 5+ A* – C grades at GCSE in 2005; 75 per cent of A level grades were A or B. Strong GNVQ courses – all this is impressive for a genuine mixed-ability intake. Maths, sciences, history and geography are strong depts but students less enthusiastic about the modern langs depts especially French. At GCSE students may choose any 2 of French, Hebrew and Spanish. A particular strength of the school's policy is to set students in each subject early on, with students being constantly evaluated and new targets set. No

student, however, is ever 'labelled' and can easily move down or make their way up. Some excellent teachers take on lower sets.

At awards ceremonies, effort and achievement are rewarded on an equal footing. It is thus 'heart warming to see a student with learning difficulties pick up the academic prize of his year or a child with a handicap receive the certificate for PE,' says a parent. A lot of other 'incentive prizes' encourage students to participate in the community life of JFS – and the wider community – with rewards going to students who, for example, help with fund-raising – a high item on the JFS agenda – or with visiting the elderly or contributing to the religious life of the school.

Across years 7-13, a range of programmes is offered for the gifted and talented, as well as for students in need of one-to-one mentoring. Much thought has clearly been given to special needs at JFS, dyslexia, for example, already becoming almost a 'cachet' – with dyslexic students proudly walking with their laptops through the corridors. Their academic achievements seem to prove that, with the right support, results can be very satisfactory. SEN services range from 1:1 tuition to in-class support.

In addition to the standard KS3 and KS4 curriculum is Jewish education (including Jewish studies, Israel studies and modern Hebrew). Jewish education has a strong moral basis and takes into account the concerns of, and dilemmas encountered in, today's world. PSE is part of the Jewish education curriculum. Diploma in Childcare and Education (DCE level 3) is also offered.

Games, Options, The Arts: There is little opportunity for formal sport, with the curriculum being occupied by secular and religious studies. However sports are offered and include dance, gymnastics, trampolining, badminton, volleyball, football, netball, hockey, rounders, cricket and athletics.

There are quite enjoyable drama performances; music (choir, barbershop quartets, instrumental performances etc) is quite outstanding, above all due to the enthusiasm and camaraderie inspired by the department's staff. Every performance is received by fellow pupils like an Oscar performance and self-confidence soars. Unlike her predecessor, Dame Ruth likes music and can be spotted at every school concert (albeit in the wings). Teachers, who themselves are excited about a particular type of instrument or style of music, have readily joined in.

The (selective) year 9 Israel residential scheme, which is a 3-month stay on a Kibbutz in Israel, offers students a unique experience to study and live in Israel whilst keeping pace with the academic progress of their counterparts back at home '... the best thing that has ever happened in my life', enthuses a student. Visits to galleries, museums, theatres etc are 'an integral part of school life', says school – to the surprise of some. Music master classes, a week-long reading festival, a three-week long music festival, poetry and debating competitions, an architecture project, the science Olympiad, D of E and Young Enterprise.

Lots of trips abroad.

Background and Atmosphere: While the origins of JFS go back to 1732 and to the East End, the school moved to Camden after the second World War and, in 2002, to a superb new purpose-built campus in Kenton with 15 science labs, an ecological garden, 5 technology labs, a 450-seat theatre, a television/media studio, a music suite with recording studio and keyboard laboratory, a large learning resources centre, an ICT suite, an open-air amphitheatre, 2 large sports halls, a dance studio, a multi-gym and acres of playing fields. The school has its own beautiful synagogue.

Pastoral Care and Discipline: Religious staff, professional counsellors and individual tutors are on hand at all times and deal with personal problems swiftly and with sensitivity. On entry, each class is allocated to a tutor who accompanies the students until graduation. This is a very effective system that helps students and parents communicate and sort out personal or academic problems. 'It's an overwhelmingly big school but you would never know it, once your child has settled down,' comments a father. However, information about the school can be hard to extract.

Students come from a very wide range of backgrounds (ten per cent on free dinners), displaying different abilities and talents all of which become recognised and appreciated at JFS very early on. On the reverse side, there is zero tolerance for bullying, roughness and discourteous behaviour. 'There are clear guidelines on the school's ethos on entry. Anybody displaying contravention of this does not get a second warning', says the head. 'School has very high standards of discipline and believes in "old-fashioned values".'

Pupils and Parents: JFS students are extremely happy and enthusiastic and mix in such a way that transcends economic and social barriers. They are friendly and respectful to visitors and care about one another. Those more able need little encouragement to help those with difficulties, the school's paired reading scheme being a case in point. For the most part, students are very proud of their school and of who they are; they carry themselves with confidence. JFS is a very large school but students quickly find their feet. Senior students ease the integration of the new arrivals and

make them feel welcome. It is not, say parents, the comprehensive nightmare so many parents fear exposing their protected children to; indeed, the vast majority of students are bright, cheerful and Jewishly committed with 70 per cent coming from Jewish primary schools.

Entrance: The school seeks to have a fully comprehensive intake. Prospective applicants sit tests which are used to divide them into four ability bands. Interviews (which take place after acceptance) are used to allow teachers to gain a wider insight into the interests of each child. Priority is given to looked after children, siblings, those at a Jewish primary school continuously since the start of year 3, siblings of former students and then distance from the school, proportionate to the numbers from each borough. Oversubscription criteria are listed in the full policy, available from the school. The sixth form has 500 places. Approximately 25 per cent join from other schools, many from the private sector.

Parents should not be surprised at being asked to produce their marriage certificate (United Synagogue or equivalent) on application, nor at being asked at the interview about the stability of their marriage.

Exit: Almost all students go on to university; well over half go to Russell Group institutions. Six to Oxbridge in 2005.

Remarks: A big school, but with a warm and caring family atmosphere; students reach their full potential. Aims to guide students 'towards a fulfilling career and towards becoming tolerant and responsible citizens and committed members of the Jewish community'.

THE JOHN LYON SCHOOL

Middle Road, Harrow, Middlesex, HA2 0HN

Tel: 020 8872 8400
Fax: 020 8872 8455
E-mail: admissions@johnlyon.org
Website: www.johnlyon.org

• Pupils: 557 boys, all day • Ages: 11-18 • Size of sixth form: 150 • Non–denominational Christian foundation, welcoming pupils of all religions • Fees: £3,395 • Independent • Open days: October

Head: Since 2005, Mr Kevin Riley, BA (UCW, Aberystwyth) MEd (Bristol) (late forties), former head of Bristol Cathedral School. Three sons, the youngest at neighbouring Harrow (because they play rugby). Teaches English, drama and games. A jovial, energetic, outgoing soul, he's clearly made a good impression on boys and parents. Took over from Dr Christopher Ray who departed for Manchester Grammar School, after a two-year headship, in September 2004.

Academic Matters: Strong academic record, but this is no exam factory. The school's priorities lie in providing 'the foundation for a happy and successful life' and John Lyon, unlike some North London schools, puts the child rather than the exam results first. 'The summit of our ambition is not 4 As at A level,' says the head. 'We're looking to university and beyond.' (And, indeed, the school magazine publishes old boys' degree results). Nonetheless, in 2005 over three quarters of all papers sat at both A and AS level were awarded A or B grades and 95 per cent of the boys received A*-B at GCSE in at least five subjects.

Four modern languages – French, German, Italian and Spanish. Latin now being phased out. All study French to GCSE, with some taking the exam a year early, but few pursue languages to A level – and then with unspectacular results. Sciences taught as double award. Setting by ability from year 8 in maths; sciences banded into upper and lower groups in years 10 and 11. Maximum class size 25 in the lower school, 2-10 at A level. Work monitored with a school-wide system of grades for attainment and effort, submitted to parents six times a year and available to teachers for remedial action on the intranet. Teaching resources OK. Some good labs, but ICT fairly lacklustre, and the library, though well-stocked and spacious, is a bit like the Marie Celeste.

A level choice not restricted, but pupils are 'guided to realistic decisions'. Mathematics a particular strength with over three quarters gaining A* or A at GCSE, and 70 per cent A or B for A. Economics also strong, and drama taken very seriously, with a dazzling head of department, who's steered both GCSE and A level students to straight As in 2004 – a shame that so few took it on to A level.

Games, Options, The Arts: For an independent school, facilities are not outstanding, though there's an attractive pool, a well-used fitness studio, a modern sports hall, an indoor archery range, a climbing wall, an athletics track, three decent art rooms (including a sixth form studio), plus studios for photography and print making. Playing fields a walk away. Main sports football and cricket. Boys regularly represent the county or region (or, in one case, Arsenal). Loads of extra-curricular sports from riding to basketball, golf to water polo. A wide range of options, including jewellery and robotics. Duke of Edinburgh, Young Enterprise and Outward Bound for sixth formers.

Strong music which aims to include as many as possible in some sort of ensemble, band or orchestra. (Boys can try out a musical instrument for one term for free) Artist and musician in residence, and music technology taught – very successfully – to A level. Drama extremely popular. A major musical and straight play annually with nearby girls' schools, plus numerous smaller productions.

Background and Atmosphere: Founded in 1572 as part of the Harrow School Foundation to provide an education for the sons of local tradesmen, it became an independent school in 1876. Links with Harrow remain – including a shared founder's day concert and an archery competition – but John Lyon sits rather in the shadow of the great public school and, if you thought about it much, you could easily feel yourself the poor relation here. Clearly boys don't. A few listed Victorian buildings, but otherwise a motley collection of uninspired 20th century and pre-fab architecture, not particularly aesthetic inside or out. 'A tad utilitarian' is the new headmaster's comment, something he hopes to rectify. There are, however, attractive pockets – The Mall, a focal atrium is light and airy with well displayed artwork.

Quite a small school in terms of numbers, so plenty of space for everyone. Sixth formers enjoy their own, much-appreciated, common room. Dark blazer, white shirt and tie for younger boys, dark business suits in the sixth. A friendly and relaxed atmosphere, from the efficient and helpful school secretary to the smiley porter. Food well sub-Oliver. 'I believe it's got better,' said one boy, 'but I bring my own lunch.'

Pastoral Care and Discipline: Both parents and pupils feel pastoral care is one of the school's key strengths, with teacher-pupil relations noticeably relaxed. 'My son chose to come here because he thought the teachers were so friendly,' says one contented father of a sixth former. 'And he's not been disappointed.'

School divided into four age-based sections and four houses (named after former heads of Harrow). House system provides strong support and encouragement, and form tutors, who see pupils regularly and know them well, are the mainstay of pastoral care. Boys given a lot of responsibility for themselves and others. Concern for others clearly not just lip service – alongside a profile of the departing head in the school magazine, full-page coverage was also given to the porter and a school chef. Excellent links with parents, with a comprehensive handbook and regular newsletter.

A non-denominational Christian foundation, welcoming pupils of all religions. Bi-weekly spiritual assemblies taken by representatives from different faiths, and SPACE (Social, Personal and Citizenship Education) Lesson, held weekly in Years 7 to 11 – covering drugs and alcohol, bullying, etc – to help pupils develop their own moral code. Twenty-three temporary and two permanent exclusions in 2003-4. 'This is a high figure but indicates a determination not to tolerate certain types of anti-social behaviour rather than a draconian regime,' says a recent Independent Schools Inspectorate report. Pupils generally courteous, co-operative and friendly.

Pupils and Parents: Majority from Harrow and the surrounding areas, such as Ruislip, Ickenham, Kenton, Wembley, Pinner and Northwood. Some from further afield. Varied ethnic mix. Professional and business parents very supportive – 'sometimes too supportive,' jokes the head – and are generally very happy with the education their children receive.

Entrance: At 11, via the school's own entrance exam in English comprehension, essay, maths and verbal reasoning. All candidates interviewed before the exam - 'if you interview afterwards, boys get nervous.' Half from state primaries: 'We're looking for potential not well-coached mediocrity.' Oversubscribed by roughly 3 to 1 – though many applicants will also be sitting for nearby top maintained selective schools, as well as Haberdashers' Aske's, UCS and Merchant Taylors' Northwood, with whom they share a commonly agreed acceptance date. Late-entry exam held for those who've failed to find a happy berth elsewhere. At 13 via tests in mathematics, science, English and French, with options for two further papers (no Common Entrance requirement). At 16, new entrants need 6 B grade GCSEs.

Exit: A few leave for sixth form colleges, 'but we want the Full Monty,' says the head. The majority to Russell Group universities, with some unusual options including, in recent years, music technology and transport management. About 10 per cent to Oxbridge.

Money Matters: Competitive entrance scholarships (up to 25 per cent of the fees) for academic achievement, art & design, music and drama at 11, 13, and 16. Also sports scholarships - including cricket and chess - but significant potential considered in any relevant area. Some means-tested bursaries.

Remarks: A low-frills independent school producing very good results and confident, independent boys who show a genuine concern for others and a mature understanding of the world outside.

JORDANHILL SCHOOL

Linked to Jordanhill School Primary in the Junior section

45 Chamberlain Road, Glasgow, G13 1SP

Tel: 0141 576 2500
Fax: 0141 950 2587
E-mail: info@jordanhill.glasgow.sch.uk
Website: www.jordanhill.glasgow.sch.uk

• Pupils: 575 boys and girls, all day • Ages: 11-18 • Size of sixth form: 180 • Non-denom • State

Rector: Since 1997, Dr Paul Thomson BSc PhD Dip Ed (forties), educated at Dollar Academy and took combined honours in maths and physics at Glasgow University where he also did his PhD, and then did his teacher training at Jordanhill College next door. Started his teaching career at Boclair in Bearsden followed by Chryston High School where he was principal teacher of physics, then assistant head at the Vale of Leven and depute head at Hermitage Academy: a speedy career path. Dr Thomson, whose wife is depute head of St Margaret's High School in Airdrie, has two children; he is also exceedingly keen on cooking. That apart, he has a fearsome intellect and spouted facts and figures faster than most heads we have met, adding all the while 'that it is available on the web page' which then turned out to be off line for a spot of tinkering.

Jordanhill is the only direct grant-aided non-special school in Scotland, runs its own budget and indeed so does each department. A block grant comes from the Scottish Executive Education Department to whom the school is answerable. Dr Thomson regards himself quite rightly as a

CEO, working 'with the staff' and running the place with a budget of £4,500 per child per annum. One of the youngest heads – state or independent – in Scotland he says he has no intention of moving though he obviously misses teaching, and his entire demeanour changed during our tour round the school; whenever we found a child to be talked to – about anything – gone was the efficiency question-answering model and in its place appeared an interested smiley friend. (He also does all the 'early' UCAS references). But youngsters apart, we suspect he does not tolerate fools with ease. (He thinks he has 'mellowed a little' recently). The school is due for a spot of new build to accommodate the reduced class sizes in primaries 1 and 2 and to replace some 'hutted' class rooms well past their sell-by date. Unlike many heads, Dr Thomson regards this as a pupil-necessity and therefore worth spending time and thought on rather than an end in itself for the glorification of Jordanhill and his own cleverness in getting the necessary funding.

Academic Matters: The school is inclusive, but is still the most successful state school (albeit grant-aided) in Scotland. Four classes of 25 (rather than the trad legal limit of 33) with practical classes of 15 (max 20). Some setting in maths and French. French from primary, German taster at 13, and enormous success with credits all over the shop at intermediate II; Spanish is only open to those who do OK in French and only in S5 and S6. Head doesn't seem to think that Latin happens anymore, but the current website happily talks of minimus and classical civilisation clubs (the latter cunningly disguised as lives and cultures of the Romans), and there is much discussion of classical availability at higher still level. The school plies both standard and inter-mediate II (and results have become sharper in the last eight years); biology and art and design results strong at both standard and higher grade. English, French and maths results are impressive as is French, physics and chemistry. Masses of external activity in the science department with pupils doing project work with the university of Lyons, taking part in the Royal Society of Chemistry quiz and challenges run by Paisley uni.

Outstanding music results with seventeen candidates getting A. The recent HMI report praises the economics results (eight at A, five at B at higher level). Higher psychology in conjunction with Anniesland College and a good partnership developing. Terrific art. Excellent use of computers: everywhere, in the art rooms as well as the class rooms, three hundred of them, interactive white boards all over the place too. Smart new media studies room which doubles for English having interesting star-shaped six seater tables and two overhead projectors with an interactive white board,

pupils won a prize with their first film. One of the best equipped schools we have visited. Ever. Clusters of lap tops motor round classrooms.

Homework clubs and some homework on line. Ditto supported study. Several groups of pupils doing research projects have direct links with staff. Power point demos by all, from P7; P6 are observers and rector then discusses the P7 presentation with them (face lit up like a beacon when he described this). Loads of interaction. Evening support classes for exam years, labs are open at lunch time and post school. Good modern library, more computers and even more in the careers department. Special needs well catered for, 'if they can cope then we will take them, unless their needs are such that the school cannot accommodate them', some pupils have a record of needs. Two dedicated staff who work across both primary and secondary schools, plus a host of classroom assistants and auxiliaries, scribing where necessary. Lifts and ramps all over the shop. With one or two exceptions, the staffroom looks incredibly young and vibrant.

Games, Options, The Arts: Fantastic games and oodles of caps: capped pupils wear green ties, though we didn't spot any. Rugby, hockey, football (and school was second in the Glasgow league – a stupendous achievement), volleyball, basket ball and athletics. Two gyms and a recently acquired sports hall nearby courtesy of Hutchies who bought the former Laurel Park complex. Stunning if cramped art complex, and excellent art on display all over the place: the staff room and on various corridors. None of it too big, but impressive. Kiln and new silk screen machine in place. Sculpture and good CDT. Drama strong, though not the biggest studio we have seen. Inspiring music, with specialist staff from P6 up. 'The best music department in the country' says Dr Thomson, 300 plus pupils play an instrument, 26 different ensembles, serious orchestras. All swinging, and particularly keen on composing.

Clubs for everything, chess particularly popular and a current pupil is in the international squad. Hot on debating, and citizenship. Home economics a serious contender now, but rather more post standard grades when students also study international cuisine (head's face lit up again). Ambitious outdoor education programme with pupils spending afternoons or weeks away depending on year group: Raasay, Castle Toward, senior pupils have a bi-annual trip to the developing world, part project part tourism (forty in Thailand when we visited). World Challenge in Peru a couple of years ago. Oodles of trips abroad: Euroscola at the European Parliament in Strasbourg, Paris, Spain et al. Massive charity involvement, both fund-raising and community work in the locality. Jolly pupil produced school mag, clearly laid out with brilliant editing: nice one, easy to read, with none of the trendy undershadowing that doting grannies find so irritating (not to mention GSG editors).

Background and Atmosphere: School founded in 1920 as a demo school for Jordanhill College of Education and became direct grant aided in 1987. Handsome classical grade B listed building – plus some temporary accommodation which is about to be replaced on the other side of the (rather sad) games pitch. Rector has stunning panelled offices (think Eltham Palace); super huge classrooms with wide pupil-proof corridors. School surrounded by (some) games pitches but a high fence now divides them from the university. Strong links with local Jordanhill Parish church. Strong links too with Glasgow state schools, joint improvement meetings for staff and pupils whilst the latter have a joint pre-vocational programme plus Your Turn project involving pupils across the city. Pupils from other schools can come to Jordanhill to pick up the odd higher or advanced higher not catered for in their own schools.

Jordanhill pupils are neat in brown uniforms – except for the primary when we visited who were in mufti as were their staff – the head of primary particularly dashing in a black T-shirt. Efficient and fairly unforgiving uniform guidelines in the prospectus supplement. Sixth year have a dedicated common room and two separate ones for boys and girls in S5, the new build will give them better social areas. JOSS operate an after-school club for tinies in the nearby church hall.

Pastoral Care and Discipline: Four houses, the heads of houses are guidance staff with a combined office and interview rooms. Pupils have tutors who are responsible for PSE and the school policy is to clamp down hard on any form of bullying. Neither Dr Thomson nor his predecessor have ever permanently excluded; and there is a clearly defined code of sanctions, including letters home, litter duty (brill) and detention. Regular links between sixth form and littles, combined reading, and the BFG club. Minister from Jordanhill Parish church takes assemblies, but this is an ecumenical school, with all religions' festivals observed, rector is keener that pupils learn 'to conduct themselves properly in church' and understand other faiths (by eg visiting local synagogues, mosques and temples) than pay lip service to any particular religion.

Pupils and Parents: Jordanhill serves a predominantly owner-occupier area; professionals, who form an enthusiastic parent teachers association, with parent volunteers in primary dept and loads of fund raising. Seven per cent ethnic minority.

Entrance: Inclusive, by address, over-subscribed, waiting lists. Siblings get priority. Some places (never advertised) available post standard grades. First come, first served.

Exit: Some 75 per cent to university. Trickle to Oxbridge, certain number to unis down south, Imperial for engineering, Liverpool, Manchester, the odd musician to the Royal Academy of Music, and tranches to art school, with or without a foundation course. But most stay in the West of Scotland. Dentistry, medicine and vet school all popular.

Remarks: Outstanding, with an inspirational if slightly left of centre rector. Better resourced than many schools in the independent sector: and it's free. A beacon. Glasgow independent sector eat your heart out.

THE JUDD SCHOOL

Brook Street, Tonbridge, Kent, TN9 2PN

Tel: 01732 770 880
Fax: 01732 771 661
E-mail: headmaster@judd.kent.sch.uk
Website: www.judd.kent.sch.uk

• Pupils: 915 • Ages: 11-18 • Size of sixth form: 290 (includes 55 girls) • non denominational • State • Open days: First Wednesday in October

Headmaster: Since 2004, Mr Robert Masters. Educated at The Harvey Grammar School, Folkestone, Reading University (BSc mathematics) and Bristol University (PGCE). Previously taught at Gravesend Grammar School for Boys and Torquay Boys' Grammar. Married with three children. Believes strongly in 'the old traditions of grammar schools' ie academic strength, leadership, social concern, wide programme of extra-curricular activities.

Academic Matters: A high achieving school – the combination of creaming off the top 15-20 per cent at 11 and excellent teaching staff. Ofsted undertook a short inspection in 2001 (the short one is only done when the school is deemed to be doing well) and categorised school as 'outstanding'. Pupils/parents laud both English and the outstanding music department.

Maths popular and strong – the top maths set can take GCSE from year 9 and go on to study statistics or pure maths or give more time to other studies and the maths staff generally need to be pretty sharp to keep on top of the crucifying questions being fired at them. 10 science labs, 3 very modern, the rest museum pieces. Good IT and effective IT-based parents/pupils/staff communications. Sixth form economics/politics/business studies described as 'exceptionally good with A1 teachers', and the sixth form generally is highly valued because the school tailors the curriculum to each individual based on a lengthy personal interview – attracts many pupils from surrounding schools. Not a huge variety of subjects on offer, eg lacks psychology, sociology, media studies but, as the headmaster commented, 'these are not subjects accepted by some universities and thus resources are better utilised elsewhere'.

Maths is the only subject which is streamed (from year 8) but otherwise the head is keen to keep 4 equal groups with a range of ability in each. These are regrouped in year 9 – often for social reasons. Every boy is given a full dyslexic test on entry (the 11+ in Kent is pretty writing-free). 'This highlighted a weakness in my son who was immediately given extra tuition,' says one parent. Parents affirm that, 'this is as much a school for the plodder as the boffin'. Homework surprisingly undemanding and the culture full of encouragement; the boys become organised very quickly.

Games, Options, The Arts: Very, very strong games, do exceptionally well at all levels on a competitive circuit. Loads of rugby and cricket teams, basketball reached final Kent Cup – virtually no soccer. Cross-country team are second nationally. Outdoor swimming pool, good swimming and tennis teams.

Music built into the very fabric of the school, described as inspirationally good with many excellent musicians, some first class, yet all abilities catered for. Director is Mr Richard Walsaw who oversees an impressive roll call of orchestras (professional and training), choirs, wind and swing bands, chamber music and countless rock groups. 'One of the perks from a stressful profession is to have the spirits uplifted when attending concerts performed by the pupils,' says the head. The school has been designated as a Specialist Music College – one of very few in the country. Vast expansion into music technology planned. Colourful art department. Drama good, timetabled once a week and one main production plus year 12 charity review annually, plus plenty of mini productions. The usual excursions and adventures on offer including Borneo jungle complete with leeches. CCF (Army and RAF) occupies a shack on the periphery of the playing fields – very well attended. Vast Duke of Edinburgh's Award participation.

Background and Atmosphere: A traditional, outwardly attractive, late Victorian red-brick building. Playground space now being swallowed up with new handsome red-brick/Cotswold stone buildings and annexes. The rear of the school sports 3 pitches but also uses pitches approx 5 minutes away. The corridors and classrooms of the main school building are still undistinguished and Dickensian, however a traditional, snug feel to the place – sixth form common room has been given a major makeover including a servery.

Pastoral Care and Discipline: A happy relaxed atmosphere, although a traditional grammar school – nothing staid or finger-waggingly strict. The care of pupils high on the agenda for the head – 'you can be any sort of person here (eg quirky, dyspraxic) but still feel accepted, valued and thrive'. Very experienced staff who are used to dealing with individuals. Pupils with any concerns have access to a mentoring system supported by the staff and sixth form.

Pupils and Parents: Pupils are unpretentious, alert, unstifled and look you confidently in the eye. A complete mix from high-flying parents to those who qualify for financial help with outings etc (all done discreetly). Famous past pupils include Admiral Sir Terry Lewin – Chief of the Defence Staff, Neville Duke – WW2 test pilot, Royal portrait painter Bernard Hailstone and Cecil Powell – Nobel prize winner (physics).

Entrance: Selection at 11 with an exam set by Kent CC. Always over-subscribed, the top 120 are chosen in order of merit. Distance from the school is a very minor factor.

Parents and staff alike speak of misapprehensions and the 'fear factor' of the school's academic reputation and some refrain from applying but head of lower school feels the 'overall standard is more within reach than people assume'. Care is taken to put pupils in with friends, as there are 60+ feeder schools. There are waiting lists still for years 8 & 9. The sixth form admits 150 students – inc 25 girls from surrounding schools; external applicants likely to need 5 GCSE As.

Exit: Almost 100 per cent to university.

Money Matters: In the 19th century the sensible burghers of Tonbridge, finding the fees for Tonbridge School beyond their reach, requested that the Skinners' Company provide affordable academic schooling for their offspring. The Company obliged, opening The Judd in 1888. Doubtless the inhabitants of Tonbridge continue to be relieved that their children can enjoy state-funded academic education. They, and Old Juddians, show their gratitude by contributing most generously to the much-needed building funds required as a voluntary aided school.

Remarks: Not uncommon for parents to hop county borders to ensure they are in the catchment area of a first class education. Very normal, honest, able pupils amongst similar staff, bristling with confidence and intelligence.

KELLY COLLEGE

Parkwood Road, Tavistock, Devon, PL19 0HZ

Tel: 01822 813 100
Fax: 01822 612 050
E-mail: admissions@kellycollege.com
Website: www.kellycollege.com

• Pupils: 370. Boys 215; girls 155. 50:50 day/boarding • Ages: 11-18 • Anglican foundation but all faiths and denominations welcome • Independent

Head: Since 2001, Mr Mark Steed MA (early forties). Theology, religious studies and teacher training graduate of Cambridge; MA from Nottingham. Worked at Radley for three years as assistant don, then at Oundle for ten years, both as head of RS and housemaster. Married with three children, one of whom is educated and boards at Kelly. Teaches ICT and plays rugby fives; gets on well with pupils. Has a refreshing and infectious outlook on life, full of enthusiasm and energy. A charming and amiable fellow who gives anyone with a talent a chance. Talks to pupils as if they are important and is shown courtesy and respect in return. Likes to share a laugh with the children.

Academic Matters: Has climbed the academic ladder in recent years from 37 per cent A and B grades at A level to 61 per cent. Has much to offer talented pupils. 'Positive' teaching, to enhance self-esteem and belief in abilities. Class sizes less than 20. Economics, business, geography, history and biology are popular A level choices. Most pupils learn French; Spanish and German are options. Parents and pupils speak highly of the staff. Average class size is 10 at A level, 20 at GCSE.

Learning support coordinator will ensure any SEN pupils receive tuition outside of usual lessons. Can take pupils with ADHD, if it's under control, dyslexia and dyspraxia but not Aspergers.

Games, Options, The Arts: Outstanding swimming reputation, squad coached by former Olympian. Devon County Championships see many Kelly swimmers taking gold and qualifying for National Championships and Commonwealth Games. Kelly successes however are now increasingly broader than swimming alone – under 20s Great Britain fencing champion went to Commonwealth Games; English Schools Champion in 1500m; European Cross Country Champion. Promising GB Triathlon champion has just packed in three GCSEs to concentrate on his talent.

Kelly has produced more than 20 Olympians since 1980, has two World champion Para-Olympians and 14 national champions. Rugby-passionate pupils boast Kelly has the best rugby pitches (five) in Devon & Cornwall, a bonus for its county-standard players. Annual six-month rugby exchange link with Australia for third form players. 'Many people think of Kelly as very sporty but my son isn't he just has access to everything and has a go', said a parent. New permanent artist in residence has raised the standard of art among inspired pupils. On-site CCF (compulsory) benefits from a dedicated training and rifle range; opportunity to construct vehicles in purpose-built garage; join Ten Tors; do D of E; gain the PADI open-water diving qualification; compete in the 125-mile Devizes to Westminster canoe race; go sailing, rock-climbing or orienteering. CCF instructor is a former Royal Marine who is also Kelly's Health and Safety officer. A Dartmoor farmhouse is used for expedition training. Think of a club or society and it is probably possible to join it at Kelly and excel. Every lower sixth pupil has public speaking 'to help prepare them for the real world'. Performing arts expected to be more 'up and coming' with opening of new theatre.

Background and Atmosphere: Founded in 1877 as a school for the sons of naval officers. The land was donated by the Duke of Bedford and the money was provided by a bequest from Founded in 1877 as a school for the sons of naval officers. The land was donated by the Duke of Bedford and the money was provided by a bequest from Admiral Benedictus Marwood Kelly. Attractive grounds; no shortage of scenery. Ample space for students. Kelly first admitted girls to lower sixth in 1970 and became fully co-ed in 1991. Lots of good new building. Wireless networking allows pupils to use their laptops anywhere.

The six-day week starts at 8.30am with house meetings, chapel and registration; activities from art to surfing from 3pm to 5pm. 'Boarders at some other schools are left with nothing to do at the weekend, but at Kelly they have lessons on Saturday morning, music or games in the afternoon and on Sunday there's a range of activities they can choose from. They even have a 'chill-out' night on Saturday and watch a film. It works very well.' Long weeks compensated for with longer holidays.

Pastoral Care and Discipline: Teachers talk to pupils on the same level, encourage them to speak up and let them share their ideas so everyone feels valued. Good at instilling confidence, respect for self and others. 'Self-esteem is the key. Kelly pupils can look in the mirror and feel proud that they are a top netball player or grade five violinist,' said Mr Steed. Flexi-boarding arrangement allow day pupils to stay overnight at a minute's notice. Day pupils can stay until 9.10pm.

Pupils and Parents: Confident but unpretentious pupils, seem comfortable and on a level footing in each others company. Not afraid of chatting with the staff, who dine in the same canteen. Still retains much of its appeal to naval families, but some 85 per cent live within three post-codes. Parents come from all walks of life, from medics at nearby Derriford Hospital, solicitors and businessmen to single mums, builders and farmers. Parents relocating to England have chosen Kelly for their children's education before finding a home or place of work and still have no regrets. Foreign nationals at its lowest ever at nine per cent – 20 from the Far East, 13 from Europe. Old Kelleians include author Gerald Seymour, Olympic medallist swimmer and broadcaster Sharron Davies and Olympic gold medal hockey goal keeper Veryan Pappin.

Entrance: 'Selective on non-academic grounds, we are a broad church,' says Mr Steed. The entrance procedure includes tests in literacy and numeracy; an assessment of the potential for extra-curricular contribution, and an interview with the headmaster who looks for 'a certain type of answer rather than a right or wrong one'. If the head feels the pupil has potential then he will give him a chance.

Exit: Average two Oxbridge places. Popular universities are London, Bristol, Nottingham, Manchester, Bath and Southampton. Many Kelleians become lawyers, engineers, doctors, join the armed forces or work in media and sport.

Money Matters: Will take one financially stricken pupil a year under his wing and give him a bursary. Boarders can receive a maximum bursary of 40 per cent. Naval and Services families, the police and siblings get 10 per cent discount.

Remarks: Delightful ethos and charismatic head teacher.

KELVINSIDE ACADEMY

Linked to Kelvinside Academy Junior School in the Junior section

33 Kirklee Road, Glasgow, G12 0SW

Tel: 01413 573 376

Fax: 01413 575 401

E-mail: rector@kelvinsideacademy.org.uk

Website: www.kelvinsideacademy.org.uk

• Pupils: 600 pupils, including 100+ girls throughout ('it's still a new pioneering spirit'); 30 in nursery • Ages: 3-18 • Size of sixth form: 97 • Inter-denom • Fees: nursery £700-£1,748; primary £1,500-£2320; secondary £2,320-2460 • Independent • Open days: November x 2

Rector: Since 1998, Mr John Broadfoot BA MEd (fifties), who arrived at the school 'along with the girls'. Educated at Merchiston, he then read English at Leeds and 'is delighted to be teaching English to the fifth year Highers set'. Comes to Kelvinside after ten years at Strathallan, having briefly dabbled in the state system – 'very boring, no drama', and spent a short time teaching in the West Indies. Married with three children, two of whom are in the school. Keen for the children 'to have achieved not only their academic potential, but also to have realised their talents in other areas and to leave the school full of self-confidence'. Interested and interesting.

Academic Matters: Mr Broadfoot is only too aware of the pitfalls of converting to co-education. His solution is to 'radically shake up the system' and divide the school into four faculties each with its own management structure – which should get round the problems of 'dyed in the wool' department heads and make the school more girl-friendly. The faculties are science, maths and computing; social studies, including geography, history and RE; the expressive arts, including music, art etc; and a language faculty, embracing French, German, Spanish and Latin (and can 'pull on experts' to teach Russian and more esoteric languages); Italian on stream for the top end. 'The shake-up is much bigger than originally anticipated and has had a much speedier impact'.

Follows the Scottish system, with the odd A level in sixth form, as well as Sixth Form Studies and the new Advanced Highers, which can be combined with SQA modules. School traditionally strong on maths and sciences, 'science within the class' but strong across the board; with the advent of girls, the arts may get a better image. Max class size 20, parallel classes, upper school setted for English, maths, and modern languages. Good work-shadowing arrangements. Strong learning support with trained teachers in each faculty.

Games, Options, The Arts: Lots of music – masses of tinies carrying instruments bigger than themselves were struggling off to junior orchestra when we visited; a lovely sight. Drama timetabled and impressive. Masses of extras. Liberal studies includes a wide range of classes – eg philosophy, psychology, cooking.

Rugby and cricket powerful, girls play hockey. PE is mixed and can be taken by staff of either sex (to the distaste of some parents). Curling and Olympic wrestling on offer. Two serious gyms, school uses Glasgow University games fields ten minutes' walk away. CCF compulsory for all for one year, thereafter voluntary. D of E, and camping at Rannoch (costed into fees).

Background and Atmosphere: Kelvinside school is technically The Kelvinside Academy War Memorial Trust, in a purpose built-building in Kelvinside. The school has expanded down to nursery level, with parents dropping off early and collecting late (late waiting till 5.30pm). Certain amount of spreading across the road – the two houses here are destined to become a sixth form house – and plans are afoot to roof over part of the frankly disorganised area at the back of the school proper to form a social area. Super new computer complex which includes a multimedia lab 'that anyone can use', and a small lab for the website, with conference and digital enhancing facilities. Rather a fine double-decker library. Stunning new Gilchrist theatre recently opened in Kennedy Mall (Nigel Kennedy was major donor, natch).

This traditional Glasgow boys' school held out against the tide of girls until 1998 but two years later one has no feeling that this is a boys' school with girls tacked on.

Pastoral Care and Discipline: House system, strong PSE. 'A certain amount of smoking' – 'we flush the smokers out'. Only one recent drugs incident; will use random testing if suspected evidence of involvement; counselling on hand, but miscreants are probably out anyway. School boasts 'a strong partnership with parents'. Holiday club to help with baby sitting problems.

Pupils and Parents: Middle class, professional, a significant number of first-time buyers, lots of travelling. From Gairlochead, the Trossachs, to Dunlop in Ayrshire. Bus from Newton Mearns/Southside.

Entrance: Through the nursery, or wherever; traditionally at 5, 11, 12 or sixth form level. Not academically selective; by interview and assessment.

Exit: Over 80 per cent to universities – usually Scotland; Glasgow and Strathclyde Business School popular – 'we're a parochial lot' – but trickle elsewhere and the very occasional Oxbridge candidate. Lots of engineers.

Money Matters: Usual discounts for siblings, good collection of scholarships and 'bursarial fund' being put in place. Will help 'wherever possible' if financial difficulties occur.

Remarks: Strong traditional school subject to big changes; watch this space. The girls look as though they have always been there.

KESWICK SCHOOL

Vicarage Hill, Keswick, Cumbria, CA12 5QB

Tel: 017687 72605
Fax: 017687 74813
E-mail: admin@keswick.cumbria.sch.uk
Website: www.keswick.cumbria.sch.uk

- Pupils: 1,075; 543 boys, 532 girls; all day except 45 boarders
- Ages: 11-18 • Size of sixth form: 240 • Non-denom • Fees: £1,930 boarding • State

Head: Since 1996, Mr Mike Chapman MA (mid-fifties). Cambridge natural scientist, taught biology at City of London School, then from 1980 at Sexey's School, Somerset, where he ran boarding and sixth form, became deputy and briefly head. Fast-talking, buzzy non-northerner, up-front leader, has made quite an impact in Cumbria. Full of ideas, ambitious for the school, with its growing reputation for good practice; loves it here, and so he should, with the finest study window view in England. Believes in 'sheepdogging'; claims chivvying pupils to observe minor rules helps to set right conditions for getting big things right.

Academic Matters: Results at GCSE and A level remarkable across the board in view of non-selective comprehensive entry. GCSE A*-C passes around 80 per cent, English regularly does well and science too (unusually – separate sciences taught by specialists to almost all pupils – school has been awarded science specialist status). Setting in most subjects from year 8. A level taken by about three quarters of original year group; vocational courses laid on for year 12 leavers, including popular ACVE business studies. A + B passes at A level around 50 per cent. Science again popular, maths surprisingly less so. General studies taken by all, now improving after a couple of indifferent years. Few take modern languages but they do well. Art regularly gets many As and Bs. Some provision in small department for SEN; other local schools specialise more in this area.

Teaching styles lean towards the traditional. Facilities are excellent (see below). Staff tend to stay in Keswick (who wouldn't?); about half have been there more than 10 years, average age is 40+. Will this be a small problem in 8 years' time? Pupils appreciate staff commitment and teaching quality. School has Leading Edge status and Ofsted Outstanding School Award.

Games, Options, The Arts: All the usual team games, with regular successes at county level; extensive playing fields, dry ski slope, lottery-funded sports hall shared with local community. Particular emphasis on outdoor education (strong staff team, Lake District on doorstep). Music thrives; much instrumental and singing tuition, very successful choir. Serious efforts made to overcome geographical isolation through visits abroad and eg to theatres.

Background and Atmosphere: Re-founded in 1898, briefly grant maintained, now voluntary-aided again, this is one of that rare and under-vaunted breed, a state boarding school. A lot of civic pride about, strong sense of identity. Moved in 1996 to one half of original split site, on town outskirts. New buildings are airy and good to work in, blend with refurbished older ones, all surrounded by stunning vistas of lakeland fells. Up-to-date ICT network throughout means internet access from anywhere, video conferencing etc; all can email. Circulation areas generally tidy and litter-free. Striking bottle-green and maroon uniform; only sixth form are allowed into nearby tripper/tourist town.

Pupils are cheerful, busy and positive. Not much sign of small-town doziness (pupils don't see rural setting as a disadvantage), though inevitably life moves in a more uncomplicated way than in a big city. Boarders (boys and girls together, in purpose-built house) add variety and breadth to the school atmosphere – a particular enthusiasm of Mr Chapman's. Originally intended to accommodate children from remote settlements, the boarding list is now made up of UK and EU passport holders from all over the world, including Scots escapers; applicants are carefully weeded on academic and personality grounds, ie they have to fit in.

Pastoral Care and Discipline: Efficient and unfussy pastoral system, plus the now common formal home/school contract. 'Conduct and discipline' is an important area. Keswick attracts the usual holiday town bad behaviour but drugs and alcohol are not a real problem. Governors may permanently exclude persistent offenders.

Pupils and Parents: Most of the school's catchment area beyond Keswick is occupied by sheep, hence it draws substantial numbers from the decaying industrial belt of west Cumbria. Aspirational parents eg from Sellafield run a large fleet of buses from as far away as Egremont. This broadens the social intake and parental support helps to push up attainment. Some have moved into Keswick, which has allegedly inflated house prices.

Entrance: No entry tests, though headmaster may ask for recent report from current school (feeders are overwhelmingly state primary). Preference given to siblings, prospective boarders. Out-of-catchment applicants considered on strict basis of distance from school. Small intake into year 12.

Exit: About 15 per cent leave after GCSE and a further 15-20 after year 12. 90 per cent of year 13 leavers go on to university, mainly in the north; a handful each year to Oxbridge.

Remarks: In some ways, more like a traditional country independent school (but without the pretentiousness) than a rural comp. Headmaster – 'not "headteacher", please' – happy with this aspect, as with his unashamed advocacy of middle class values but he and the staff are proud of the school's history of service to its all-ability, wide social range.

KILGRASTON SCHOOL

Linked to Kilgraston Junior School in the Junior section

Bridge of Earn, Perthshire, PH2 9BQ

Tel: 01738 812 257
Fax: 01738 813 410
E-mail: registrar@kilgraston.pkc.sch.uk
Website: www.kilgraston.com

• Pupils: 235 girls; 98 board, the rest day • Ages: 13-18 • Size of sixth form: 50 • RC but inter-denom as well • Fees: Junior school from £2,020 day to £4,950 for boarding; Senior school from £3,500 day to £5,930 boarding • Independent • Open days: May and October

Principal: Since 2004, Mr Michael Farmer BA PGCE (forties), who was educated in the state system in Leicestershire, did economics at Portsmouth and then became a yacht skipper. He did his PGCE at Bristol and comes from Headington School in Oxford, where he was deputy head and head of sixth form (having moved there from Godolphin with the erstwhile headmistress Mrs Hilary Fender). A Roman Catholic. Mr Farmer heads a school very different to that to which he first applied. Kilgraston absorbed the 8-13 section of the much loved girls-only prep school, Butterstone (which was going broke) at the end of the summer term 2003. The girls from Butterstone have now almost all gone (most went down south) and the junior school is no longer Butterstone Grange at Kilgraston, but Kilgraston Preparatory school.

An open door head, he is looking forward to 'teaching economics next year' but currently still admits to 'wearing big L plates'. His wife Mary Ann 'is deeply supportive' and runs the sixth form creative cuisine course. They have a son at Strathallan and a daughter in the school – 'who never comes home, she really loves the place'.

Academic Matters: Not the sleepy place it used to be, placed in top 3 at Higher in 2005. School runs primarily on the Scottish system, with Standard grades followed by Highers to university in lower sixth, and A levels. Certain amount of fast track standard grades in French and English. Science on the up, with new head of physics, excellent science labs. English lit not strong. 'Bright and encouraging results from lesser sparks,' claimed the previous head. Pupils can 'top up' Standard grades in sixth form, and often take French, maths and Latin a year early. Tiny classes, 8/20, with tiny maths classes to bring the less academic up

to status. No change here. Piloting Scotvec clusters, four modules equals one cluster. Only one or two do secretarial studies/keyboarding skills. Business studies popular. Computers everywhere plus two dedicated computer rooms. Really good IT and lap tops for everyone on the way (still). E-mail for all. Mass of personal lap tops. Library a mess, needs a new broom, drastic re-organisation and a whole lot of new books. Good remedial unit (CReSTeD B status – Wow), with specialist teachers for dyslexia and dyspraxia – one to one teaching and EFL on offer. Language labs popular. Masses of exchanges, French, German and Spanish (both pupils and staff) via Sacred Heart network.

Games, Options, The Arts: Magnificent sports hall faced in sandstone, with niches echoing those in the stable building (well converted into junior school with attached nursery); Historic Scotland at its best. Nine Astroturfs with floodlighting (good grief). Wide choice of other sports. Climbing wall. Indoor swimming pool on the wish list. Strong drama, and inspired art - 'going from strength to strength'; the art department overlooks the Rotunda and currently boasts an enormous computer-linked loom. Tremendous ceramics and regular masterclasses. D of E, debating, leadership courses. Music centre in the attics, with keyboards and individual study rooms; guitars and stringed instruments everywhere, sound recording studio on wish list too. Writers' group. Cooking and brilliant needlework, the girls make their own ball gowns for the annual ball with Merchiston. Couple of school ponies and several more due to arrive shortly, but school is not yet totally into the equestrian scene: pathetic pic of uncollected, out of control pony and rider in current prospectus (stirrups too short, back not straight, air below the seat, pony's neck not bent, ears back etc). The page is entitled 'Balance, poise and composure in all things'! New director of weekend activities recently appointed, and all sorts of options in the pipeline, whitewater rafting, canyoning, sailing.

Background and Atmosphere: Founded in 1920, and one of 200 networked schools and colleges of the Society of the Sacred Heart. Moved to the handsome red Adamesque sandstone house in 1930, masses of extensions including spectacular Barat wing, light and airy with huge wide passages. We previously said that 'religion was very much in evidence, with saints on tap,' this is no longer the case. Mr Farmer has removed many of the saints from the Central Hall, as it was felt that this would be an excellent place 'to show off some off some of our superb artwork'. And indeed pupils' work does look smashing but school looks a bit bleak. A Lawrence Bowen-Jones makeover is desperately needed. Sixth form common room needs an influx of books.

Bedsits from third year, tinies dorms now divided into attractive cabins for each. Huge development following the Butterstone debacle, and masses of revamping going on in the dorms area. School stops at 4.10 on Fridays for day and weekly boarders, but masses of alternative activities for those who stay back – though usual moans about 'not having enough to do', these should now be under arrest with the new appointment. Computers, games hall/courts, art, music and sewing rooms open throughout the weekend. Boyfriends can and do visit at weekends. God still important here, most attend assembly and mass on Sundays. Feast Days still special. Local priest holds regular confession.

Pastoral Care and Discipline: Sacred Heart ethos prevails, staff enormously caring, and staff 'will go the extra mile'. Pastoral conferences every week, independent counsellor on tap. Disciplinary Committee, gatings, suspensions, fatigues round school for smoking. Drinkers are suspended and a not so recent problem was 'nipped in the bud'. Will test areas, not girls, if drugs suspected. The girls here are not the dozy lot they used to be. Counsellor on hand, and bullying handled by BFG (Big Friendly Group). Charming little handbook for new pupils full of helpful advice.

Pupils and Parents: Day children from Fife and Perthshire, though bus no longer collects children from the school's front door – the main gate was damaged too often. Boarders from all over Scotland, and Old Girls' children. Toffs' daughters, including non-Catholics, and Muslims. Academically pushy parents may move their children elsewhere but the school breeds loyalty among those who value 'other things'. Currently 21 from overseas ('the internet is handy,' says the head).

Entrance: Not that difficult. All sit the school's own exam in February in tandem with scholarship exam. Junior school entrants also do CE. Otherwise 11+ from primary schools, and 12+ from prep schools. Pupils can come whenever, half term if space available. Sixth form entry – 'good Standard grades/GCSEs to follow A level course, pupils come 'from overseas', or from local state schools. Pupils steered to 'appropriate' levels of study. Has been known to 'pick up' the odd casualty' from Glenalmond – 'they (the pupils) weren't tough enough'.

Exit: Toffs still abandon at 11+ or 13+ to go elsewhere. 80/90 per cent annually to universities. Occasional departure for sixth form in boys' schools; some leave after Highers, though not currently.

Money Matters: OK financially, the nuns have left rich pickings. Up to ten academic, art and music scholarships. Also riding, tennis and sporting scholarships. Almost one

third receive assistance of some sort. School is 'good at finding Trust funding' for those who have fallen on hard times.

Remarks: The only all-girls boarding school left in Scotland and popular. Small, gentle, not overtly Catholic, with terrific facilities. Useful prep facilities; Scots parents see it as a viable alternative to St Leonards (recently gone not very successfully co-ed).

KING ALFRED SCHOOL

Linked to King Alfred Lower School in the Junior section

Manor Wood, 149 North End Road, Golders Green, London, NW11 7HY

Tel: 020 8457 5200
Fax: 020 8457 5249
E-mail: pressoffice@kingalfred.barnet.sch.uk
Website: www.kingalfred.barnet.sch.uk

• Pupils: 600 all day, roughly 50:50 boys:girls • Ages: 4-18
• Size of sixth form: 75 • Non-denom • Fees: £3,000 - £3,780 + optional lunch • Independent • Open days: July

Head: Since 2003, Ms Dawn Moore BSc MA PGCE (early forties). A biologist with a further degree in education management, Ms Moore began her teaching career at King Alfred in 1986 and has been there ever since. Her own children now attend the school. All that suggests a profound commitment and that's exactly what one senses on first meeting this unassuming, unpretentious, unheadmistressy but intensely impressive and likeable head. Ms Moore is informal, open about and very proud of the school she admits she has grown up in. She is also clearly proud of the terrific vote of confidence from the school community that her appointment must have been. A year before her elevation, an ISI inspection produced a report on the school which included many trenchant criticisms of its academic side – something Ms Moore is clearly still upset and angry about. She is herself a trained and experienced inspector of schools and, while acknowledging that some of the criticism was justified and conceding that 'we have taken on much of what they said', feels that the inspection team wholly failed to engage with the nature of the school. Our overall impression of the quality of the education and the values inculcated here would suggest that she is right.

Academic Matters: No exams taken here until year 10. So, no SATs, no end-of-years and somehow the children manage to learn and to do themselves credit in GCSEs and A levels without having wasted weeks each year in satisfying assessment criteria and league tables. The vast majority of the pupils arrive aged 4 so the intake is virtually non-selective. In 2005, 97 per cent got A*-C grades at GCSE and 98 per cent got 5 or more subjects. At A level in 2005, 56 per cent of subjects taken achieved A grades and practically all the rest got B or C. All 11 photography candidates got A and the dept wins awards annually for the quality of the work. English is another strong subject and there are no weak ones. 'All my teachers are good,' said one cool young sixth former, 'and I like them all too.'

The range of subjects available at A level is pretty fair for so small a school – 20 of them with the recent addition of media studies and business studies. Most people get the combination they choose. GCSE choice is limited though Ms Moore has plans to extend possibilities here: whereas only French and Spanish are curriculum modern languages at present, extra-curricular lessons in other languages are possible and she is currently looking at introducing other languages earlier in the school to boost the later uptake. There is a Russian club and Latin is about to reappear! Everyone takes double award science. Lots of computers in special IT rooms – hardware and software recently updated and supplemented with noticeable results.

However, the ISI report found much to criticise in the standard of academic work, largely on presentation but also on attainment in basic subjects. This is hard to assess on a flying visit but, if the spelling in the school's magazine, the otherwise delightful and beautifully produced 'Alfredian', is anything to go by, they might have had a point. Perhaps the lack of emphasis on basic skills – compared to unashamedly 'academic' schools – is the price you pay for all the stimulation and real childhood that is part of the ethos here. SEN is well-supported and school has to protest against being seen as 'a school for special needs' because it does so well by such children. Five statemented children at time of visit seem seamlessly integrated. Lower school buildings are single storey and could accommodate wheelchairs. Middle and Upper School have a two storey building without a lift: 'a disability access plan is in place'.

Games, Options, The Arts: Sited around one large field – very muddy in wet weather but used for lessons in summer. It all looks charmingly like a village around a village green and the field is supplemented by four on-site Astroturf tennis courts, a sports hall and mini-bus to off-site facilities elsewhere. Everyone does PE and options include squash, aerobics and yoga along with all the ones you would expect. Everyone goes on a camp once a year when socialising and self-sufficiency are part of the unwritten syllabus. Arts are

universally strong. Drama thrives and the school is well provided for with a theatre and a small 'black box' of a studio. Many parents are in the profession and come in to give masterclasses which would be coveted by top drama schools. Theatre, now with extra EU funding, is on an international scale with collaborative writing and production projects with schools from many countries. Music, too, is popular and strong and has more takers at GCSE than many far larger schools. Orchestras, bands and ensembles of all kinds thrive.

However, it is in CDT, DT, ceramics, photography and art generally that this place is on the wing. Underpinned by inspirational leadership and a pervasive philosophy of sustainable technology in design, the pupils produce work that is both professional and principled. They have built three boats, and laid the foundations for a kindergarten/community centre for the village Gaus in Africa. In the school's own forge they designed and made the school gates – metalwork birds and hearts. Everything is used – from coppiced wood from the plantation opposite to 'smart' materials, but all from a 'green' and socially aware point of view. The head of CDT is also the head of PSHE and 'citizenship' and clearly sees them as indivisible. All lower school classrooms have ovens for baking. Every flowerbed sports home-made ceramic pots and dishes; ponds and water-features everywhere are evidence of the creativity and fun to be found here. A vast treehouse dominates one side of the field. A cheery ceramic King Alfred reading a book sits on a wall near the school gates and makes you smile.

Background and Atmosphere: Unique in background and atmosphere. The school was started in 1898 by parents who rejected the authoritarian methods of Victorian education with the objective of arousing 'interest and the spirit of enquiry, to cultivate working power and the faculties of observation and imitation as well as the memory; and especially to encourage self-reliance hand-in-hand with the sympathetic faculties.' Always labeled 'progressive', its principles embody the best that is meant by the term – 'child-centred education, aiming to draw out the best in the individual....principles of mutual respect, of relationships based on trust rather than authority and punishment'. The result today is rather like the atmosphere in a huge extended family. Everyone is on first name terms, everyone wears home clothes and the working of the whole place relies on willing cooperation and everyone taking responsibility for the whole. Pupils here tend not to hold the door open for you, people interrupt, leave bags in heaps and litter abounds – though we have seen worse elsewhere – and gum-chewing seems not to be challenged even in lessons.

Everyone eats together – deliciously – but groups of children chat noisily and insouciantly around the staff in a way that would be unthinkable elsewhere. It might all be hard to take if you come from a trad prep or public school background. However, the pluses are impressive and, as in a family, learning to live together pays off.

Included in the family are various pets including a duck called Duck who has a central domain in a clumpy pond. The family idea is enhanced by the school's myriad international links – the global family being seen as just as important – and pupils travel to, and are visited by, schools and delegates from all over the world in, possibly, a uniquely diverse and rich way. All this is part of the school's knock-out 'international enrichment' programme. Trips to, projects in and visits from16 countries including Namibia, Lithuania, Sweden, China, Egypt and Cuba. Rare, mind-expanding opportunities here. Following the tsunami the school is working with a non-government organisation and is running a pre-school in Tamil controlled Sri Lanka.

The whole school – lower (in glass-fronted, single storey blocks giving a very open feel), middle and upper are all housed around the field and everyone shares communal space. Only the infant children are off the main site – over the road in the newly acquired Ivy Wood, formerly Anna Pavlova's home. The glorious house overlooking the garden is let but the nursery is in newly refurbished and redesigned buildings inherited from previous tenants and is a delicious haven for tinies with pond, caravan and garden and some of the most stimulating classrooms we've seen. Nothing here is smart, the buildings are a mix and a jumble but the staff turnover is low, class sizes are small – the overall teacher:pupil ratio 1:8 – remarkable – and the sense of a noisily collaborative and productive community based on respect and consideration is irresistible. Also, everything is fiercely recycled here. The sixth form has recently expanded and pupils realize that, compared to other schools, provision for them, in terms of a sixth form centre and resources, is unimpressive. But few are tempted away.

Pastoral Care and Discipline: Pastoral care is in the essence of the place and is palpable. It's hard to imagine anyone getting or feeling lost here. The obverse of the not-holding-doors here is that pupils and teachers greet each other in a genuinely friendly way and affection and pride in each other is obvious. Few incidents in recent years requiring serious disciplinary action and head looks bemused at the thought of having to come down hard on anyone. 'We're very supportive if a child is getting into trouble,' and she talks of how pupils will confide in a teacher if they fear a friend might be in trouble. 'We try to be proactive and head off trouble.' Clearly, the clientele know what they are doing when they send a child here – 'parents here know what they want and what they don't want for their child.'

Pupils and Parents: Very diverse from north and north-west London, reflecting the local population in that some are very well able to pay the fees while many struggle doggedly to do so. Arts and theatrical families abound but doctors, lawyers also. Perhaps fewer first-timers for independent education and less representative of the ethnic diversity of the local population than the many 'academic' schools nearby. Parents are devoted to the school and, effectively, own it. Many are former pupils. All are articulate and will quickly react if anything is not up to their expectations. Very few complaints, though.

Entrance: At 4, 11 and 16. At 4 children are assessed on how they get on with each other during activities on a relaxed visit as well as on basic motor skills. At 11 they come for a two-day visit and, again, social skills and the attitude to learning is more important than brilliance. Hugely over-subscribed. At 4 there are between 100-200 applicants for 40 places.

Exit: Pupils leave for a range of good courses, mostly in the arts and humanities.

Money Matters: No schols. Lunches charged on top of fees but are so good few pupils now opt to bring their own.

Remarks: It's not for you if academic rigour and starry results are what you're shelling out for. If you believe that learning and childhood are not incompatible, that discipline comes from within and from belonging to a cohesive community and that ethics and values come before exams and virtuosity then go and look. It's a big surprise, just off the road from Golders Green to Hampstead, but a pretty convincing one.

KING EDWARD VI HIGH SCHOOL FOR GIRLS

Edgbaston Park Road, Birmingham, West Midlands, B15 2UB

Tel: 0121 472 1834
Fax: 01214 713 808
E-mail: admissions@kehs.co.uk
Website: www.kehs.org.uk

• Pupils: 545 girls; all day • Ages: 11-18 • Size of sixth form: 160 • Non-denom • Fees: £2,553 • Independent • Open days: January and July

Head: Since 1996, Miss Sarah H Evans BA MA (forties); educated at King James' Grammar School, Knaresborough and Sussex, Leicester and Leeds universities. Previously head of the Friends' School, Saffron Walden, and before that taught at Leeds Girls' High School, also Fulneck Girls' School. A lovely, chirpy, calm Quaker, passionately committed to the children and their education. Wants to give her pupils 'wings to fly somewhere unexpected'. Focused on community – working with other schools, Birmingham University etc – and on breadth – building characters for life. Much liked and appreciated by pupils. Took over from Miss Ena Evans ('Old Miss Evans').

Academic Matters: Outstanding academically for decades and undoubtedly one of the country's top academic schools, with outstanding teaching and an ethos of hard work (lunch is soon done). Excellent across the board. No weak subjects. Biology, chemistry, maths and English are currently the most popular subjects – Latin not far behind. Brilliant teaching all round – staff of long standing but excellent, lovers of teaching who have decided not to move on to administration. GCSEs – nothing fancy on offer, but what it does comes out with astounding results. Girls are achievers with high expectations who 'learn to want to excel'. Lots of individual attention given to the girls, help is available from all and any staff at all times.

Wide academic syllabus. Classes of 'mixed ability' (on a very narrow range, however), maximum class size 26. One third of pupils takes A level sciences (and must follow a non-A level English course), one third takes arts (and must follow a non-A level maths course) and one third mixed. General studies taken as fifth A level – and girls get mostly As in this too. Russian, Italian, German and Spanish on offer. Classics department flourishing and innovative. School moved to IGCSE maths in 2005 – 'much more fun and challenging'.

Nine science labs, two computer rooms (free access during day); equipment recently upgraded. Classrooms double as subject rooms, with old-fashioned desks in some, but filled with pupils' work on display. Some classes taken with King Edward's School (qv). 'Outsiders sometimes think teaching here must be a soft option', commented one member of staff, 'because all the girls are bright – but the fact is that a little doesn't go a long way: they lap it up and want more'. Girls are adept arguers and class discussion and debate is encouraged from the earliest forms.

Games, Options, The Arts: Formidable hockey teams and lots of county representation, netball good, also tennis and athletics. Fencing, basketball, good, strong dance group, ballroom dancing, aerobics. Girls picked for county squads in several sports, 'They get madly keen'. Sports hall, two artificial hockey pitches. Swimming outstanding, own pool, boys have their own next door. Girls in sixth form must take some type of exercise but team games not mandatory.

1983 Centenary Art and Design block filled with textiles and tie-dyeing; as well as trad painting and superb ceramics. Girls combine A level art with science and arts subjects. Many concerts, plays and dance productions – most shared with the boys from over the drive; school symphony orchestra outstanding but lots of performance opportunities for all levels. Food technology (cooking) and video technology (filming) on offer. Careers advice and work experience all on offer. Masses of fund-raising and community service. Drama/theatre studies shared, popular, challenging and, by now, deservedly famous under 'very professional...inspirational' (according to latest Ofsted) and extraordinary teacher. Productions big and small throughout the year to top standards. Music also outstanding – combined again. Girls bring out school newspaper, High Profile.

Background and Atmosphere: Part of the King Edward Foundation group of schools (all bursarial work carried out jointly), founded in 1883, and followed King Edward's School to present site in 1940. Share same architect and campus is a pleasing blend of red brick plus usual later additions (not always totally in keeping); feeling of space and calm inside. Girls leave their stuff in piles all over the place in the certainty that it is safe anywhere. Direct Grant school until 1976. 'KEHS' girls wear uniform to sixth form, when free rein is given to fashion.

Pastoral Care and Discipline: Marked discipline. Staff hold a short weekly meeting to discuss concerns, but have 'been very lucky'. Girls follow a pastoral care and personal decision-making programme, and can discuss problems with any member of staff, but normally with form tutor, year co-ordinator, deputy or head. No prefect system, no head girl, no houses. No school drugs offence policy – 'any cases would be dealt with on an individual basis'. Good parental contact. In principle, parents can contact senior staff, head or her deputy 'certainly within the hour' if it is clearly an urgent matter (other schools please note). There are clear rules on smoking – a 'letter home works wonders'.

Pupils and Parents: Seriously bright children of professional families, middle to lower middle class. Shares transport system with boys at King Edward's, girls come from as far away as Lichfield, Bromsgrove, Wolverhampton, Solihull. 'There's not a school in this league for miles, and precious few anywhere,' say parents. Approx 35 per cent ethnic minorities as you might expect – no problems here. Ecumenical outlook.

Entrance: School's own very selective test 'designed to test the children not their teachers' (nice one). School spends two weeks searching the completed tests 'for potential not raw marks'. About half come from state primaries. Tough entry post-GCSE (and girls are 'warmly welcomed' at this stage) – school's own exam in relevant subjects, plus interview and previous school's report. By their statutes girls have to be resident in the area of the West Midlands with their parent(s).

Exit: Very few after GCSE (having the boys next door removes the urge to fly off to a co-ed), and nb does not chuck girls out for doing badly at GCSE, but stands by its commitment to them; 10-20 to Oxbridge and the rest to the top range of universities – Bristol, Leeds, Nottingham, London etc – almost always to their first choice. After university to the professions, arts, media, industry, business; school records 'noticeably more and more high achievers – no glass ceiling'.

Money Matters: Had a very large number of Assisted Places and their loss is felt, though some have been replaced by an 'equivalent governors' means-related' scheme - up to 14 places a year. Academic scholarships up to the value of two full-fees at 11 (not more than 50 per cent per pupil). Now has some Ogden Trust bursaries for 'above-average children from a state school of limited or no parental means'. Parents' Association does the odd bit of fund-raising (though mostly used for social activities), second-hand uniform shop in summer term.

Remarks: One of the country's top academic girls' city day schools, turning out a long line of academic high-flyers, and an example to the grammar school tradition of how this can be combined with breadth and civilisation.

KING EDWARD VI SCHOOL

Kellett Road, Southampton, Hampshire, SO15 7UQ

Tel: 023 8070 4561

Fax: 023 8070 5937

E-mail: enquiries@kes.hants.sch.uk

Website: www.kes.hants.sch.uk

• Pupils: 625 boys, 345 girls, all day • Ages: 11-18 • Size of sixth form: 225 • Non-denom, with C of E ancestry • Fees: £2,962 • Independent • Open days: Mid November

Head: Since 2002, Mr Julian Thould MA – Pembroke College, Oxford. He's an historian and, thereby, arguably leavens the atmosphere of this notably scientifical school. Worked in industry before beginning teaching at Westminster School, and arrives at King Edward's via Cranleigh and King's Worcester. A man whose brains can be read in his eyes and demeanour – alert, astute, assiduous. Decidedly likeable. An educationist and a humanitarian, capable of radical action, probably always with his feet on the ground. He's removed the school from the league tables (would be well above the snow line if it were still there) and is determined that, in addition to superb exam results – 'parents take those as read' – the school will turn out pupils with 'well-tuned minds'. He wants his school to be 'happy and safe', busy in and out of the classroom. His big things are outward bound, charitable work, sport, new technology and creative arts. Has developed strong links with local state schools, especially in the teaching of science, and you can see he'd like his school to be accessible to children from deprived backgrounds. There's still a strong whiff of direct grant about this place, a very agreeable aroma of old-fashioned grammar, and Mr Thould asserts 'We are only doing here what a state school should do'. He's proud that over 200 children receive financial support. The school is making a big bow wave under his headship and he's getting rave reviews. Parents like him, say he's a good communicator. Pupils 'love him – he's always having new ideas, he lets them in on the plans and asks them what they think.' Well up, too, to having an apple shot off his head at a medieval banquet. Very much a family man, three children at the school.

Academic Matters: 'We are the leading school in the area, and known to be,' says the head without vanity or vainglory. Exam results speak for themselves – superb in all respects. For all the pupils' penchant for sciences, the arts are just as well done, history and English in particular. Last year's GCSE English results, you should know, were the best in the country. Why are the sciences so popular? Partly because there are a lot of medical parents, partly because this is what the school is known for – to which we may add, perhaps, the reflections of a sixth former: 'I did history AS. Writing those essays took forever. I can do my chemistry homework in half the time.' They're all-rounders. The range is broad – three modern languages at A level, theatre studies, philosophy. In 2002 the school inspectors worried that there was too much focus on exam teaching. By now, the head's breadth-making policy has dissolved that criticism. There's the sort of work ethic here that you would expect wherever a thousand or so very bright people are gathered together, and, yes, they know they are expected to butter the parsnips. In the classes we saw the atmosphere was purposeful, civilised and, in the sixth form, urbane. We shan't quickly forget a GCSE design technology class where boys and girls were designing board games. Independent thinking and high intellect were generating seriously clever projects. An attractive school to good teachers, you can't help but reflect.

There has been a fair amount of decamping, post-GCSE, to sixth form colleges in recent years. The flow is being stemmed both by a more young adult-friendly regime plus uniform to match, and also by a growing perception that, when you see how the émigrés get on, staying here offers the stronger certainty of best grades. Parents praise uni selection and preparation which, for Oxbridge interviews, leaves the syllabus far, far behind. Lots of recent refurb in the science zone part funded by the Abraham Trust. No shortage of space anywhere, everything bright and kempt. Marvellous concourse, a great meeting area with highly readable notice boards. Mild SENs addressed, literacy and numeracy support from Senco, but you've got to be able to keep up – SEN has been a blind spot for years.

Games, Options, The Arts: Sport a serious matter for the sportiest, and it's well resourced – acres of playing fields, sports hall, Astro. Compulsory for all, sixth formers do min 1 afternoon. Unsporty types do merrymaking lollopy things. Very inclusive. Top coaching. 'We probably win more than we lose.' Website has multimap links for all competitor schools. Sailing especially strong – Olympic gold medallist Iain Percy was here. Also Keith Wiseman (past chairman of the Football Association), John and Simon Francis (county cricketers), Dudley Kemp (England rugby cap and past president of the RFU) and Rob Moore (hockey Olympian). Parents like the Saturday fixtures: they keep 'em out of town.

Lots of good art going on, especially the drop-in session at lunchtime when you do just as you please, radical as you like. Purpose-built in-the-round theatre doing good stuff. Plays well supported by fellow pupils. Lively music, Henry Mancini to Henry Purcell, lots of public performance, often with a charitable fundraising focus. Christmas carols in Romsey Abbey. Fifty-plus clubs, many of them formidably intellectual. Sure, there's cooking and wargaming, but there's also chess, of course, and Conversationalists (they debate someone's essay), and classicists, and creative writing (popular, we note, with all academic persuasions). Raising money for good causes is a big thing, thinking up events – £21,000 raised last year. Summer camp for deprived children, links with an orphanage in Romania. D of E is big, too – 27 Gold Awards 2005 – the school has a bothy on Dartmoor awaiting planning permissions. Young Enterprise does very well. They're a busy lot and egged on to be so. The school is, say parents, very good at picking out wallflowers and discreetly nudging them into things. Last Easter hols 50 per cent of the teaching staff took groups away on residential trips.

Background and Atmosphere: Founded by William Capon in 1553 to elevate the customary impoverished wretches. Though non-denom now, the school maintains its historic relationship with St Mary's church. Has been at its present site since 1938, the period feel of the buildings imparting, you can't help thinking, their bit to the ethos.

Pastoral Care and Discipline: Notably relaxed, adult relationships between pupils and teachers, a collaborativeness about them that's very good to see. There's no better insight into this than the superb school magazine, entirely produced by sixth formers. They even have to get print quotes and oversee every aspect of production – a truly adult expectation. The writing is sprightly, irreverent, funny, intelligent, unmediated by teachers and a huge tribute to the confidence of the school. Read it and you will know the place. There's an annual review, too, another excellent window. Rules try not to be petty, uniform is worn mostly as intended, attitude met with intelligent, unpatronising debate, though the school is impatient of recalcitrance. No earrings for boys, no nose studs for anyone. You pass the beadle-like deputy head's office on your way in, and he picks up on the slightest. Lots of drugs education. Is this a worry? Say parents, 'not an issue'. Food has been Jamie Olivered, now a source of pride. Boys and girls observably natural in each other's company. Tutorial system works. One mum reported a teasing thing at breakfast and was phoned back before she got to work. Sorted.

Pupils and Parents: Unstuffy, unsnobby. That's how parents want it and that's how they intend to keep it. They want a traditional, co-ed grammar school and they inhabit a 25-mile radius. No local competitor. Around a third come from Winchester. School has its own buses but, a trad, certainly a green touch, this, around a hundred flood in by bike or on foot. So does the head, and so do quite a few teachers. The school is rooted in its community and, hard though it is to get in, it doesn't do exclusivity nor does it breathe rarefied air. Typical of its values, it has never borrowed a penny to build anything. Ethnic mix evident, testimony to its meritocratic nature. Buzzing PTA, KESSoc – secondhand uniforms, social events.

Entrance: Hard, of course: around two up for every place (reputation depletes aspirants). Entry exam: maths, English and reasoning plus interview plus previous school's report. Around half from state primaries, then from around 25 local independents, with big lumps from Stroud and Sherborne House. For sixth formers (own brochure) you'll need 6 GCSEs at Grade B including English and maths.

Exit: Almost all to Russell Group universities – the cream. Around 10 per cent to Oxbridge. Recent OEs range from Hugh Whitemore (playwright and dramatist) and Michel Vickers (pop group Manfred Man) to Michael Langrish (Bishop of Exeter), Ian Bruce (President of the RNIB) and Sir Edward Abraham FRS (Oxford academic – groundbreaking work on penicillin and synthetic antibiotics). Also His Honour Judge David McCarraher, Sir Michael Bichard and Her Majesty's Ambassador Richard Kinchen MVO.

Money Matters: Bursaries, means tested, 100 per cent remission for the most deserving. Scholarships, academic and music, up to 20 per cent of the fee. Entry at 11, 13 and sixth form.

Remarks: We arrived through the tight-squeeze entry at the back of the school in the middle of break, air thick with balls, shoals of flushed boys, gaggles of chatty girls. Not much enchantment to the eye here. Yet from the moment the bell dissipated them first impressions fell away to reveal not only top-notch teaching but also great charm. This is a downright and a decent place, an independent school socially comfortable in its surroundings.

KING EDWARD'S SCHOOL (BATH)

Linked to King Edward's Junior School (Bath) in the Junior section

North Road, Bath, BA2 6HU

Tel: 01225 464 313
Fax: 01225 481 363
E-mail: headmaster@kesbath.biblio.net
Website: www.kesbath.com

• Pupils: 663 (177 girls, 486 boys), all day • Ages: 11-18 • Size of sixth form: 207 (63 girls, 144 boys) • Non-denom • Fees: Pre-prep: £2,175; junior: £2,318. Senior £2,936 - £2,970 • Independent • Open days: Late September

Head: Since 2004, Mr Crispin Rowe (late forties). Went to Bryanston then read history at Newcastle which he taught first at Watford Boys' Grammar then at RGS Newcastle, where he was head of lower school before joining KES in 1992 as second master. Passed over by the governors when Peter Winter left to become head of Latymer Upper in 2002, but stepped in immediately as acting head when newcomer Caroline Thompson departed abruptly in May 2004. She had upset some parents but pleased others by beginning to tackle areas of the school that needed upgrading. The new head looks set to carry on with the improvements. He has a thorough understanding of the school and a business-like approach. News of his appointment brought a 'roar of approval' in the staff room. He wants 'to uphold the academic tradition of KES whilst ensuring that the school is rounded and not narrowly academic.' Considers himself fortunate to be unexpectedly in charge and is obviously enjoying discovering what heads get up to. Married to Jill with three grown-up children. Knows his staff and pupils inside out. Takes a real interest in music and sport – plays the clarinet and still runs half-marathons.

Academic Matters: For a school which the head describes as 'not desperately selective' results are impressive and especially so since the loss of 130 assisted places. KES currently tops the academic results tables in Bath with consistently high percentages of A/B grades at A level and of A*/A grades at GCSE. Results reflect school's academic bias especially in English and maths where large numbers of candidates get top grades, likewise history and geography.

Latin, modern languages and physics lead off the success story across smaller departments. Biology has had the longest 'tail' at A level in recent years but does very well by stronger candidates aiming at medicine etc. AS entries are not necessarily just a preamble to A2 with subjects like art, electronics and psychology attracting punters in the way the exam originally intended.

GCSEs are underpinned by strong results in English and maths with non-scientists and non-linguists probably accounting for most of the lower grades in dual award science and French respectively. ICT has not seized candidates' imaginations judging by recent results. Religious studies is available as a GCSE option but is also compulsory through to the end of year 11. When we visited, pupils were studying Buddhism which has been adopted as part of the GCSE curriculum by popular demand. Parents feel that teachers deliver their subjects well. Class sizes are around twenty in the lower school, 25 or less in the middle school but much smaller in many GCSE option groups and below 15 in the sixth form. Limited special needs programme.

Games, Options, The Arts: Rugby is still top dog in what is a notoriously fanatical rugby playing city. Impressive fixture list and tours to places as far away as Kiwi and South Africa. Cricket and hockey are both strong for boys as are netball and tennis for girls but with hockey doing better as girl numbers steadily increase. Good sports facilities on site are complemented by extensive playing fields a mile or so down the A36 at Bathampton and for swimming and athletics at neighbouring Bath University. A school swimming pool is high on the parents' wish list. Strong tradition in minor sports includes pole vaulting and, more recently, fencing. Parents like the choices available for the non team players. Current KES pupils have reached world level competition in sailing and canoeing.

Despite music having been something of a Cinderella subject at KES, musicians have got into top national youth orchestras and now with improved facilities, including for music technology, music has raised its profile. Great drama for all ages in the school with loads of variety and challenging productions for the many who get involved both within the curriculum and in their own time. Conversion of a former gymnasium into a theatre has been a success. Visually explosive art department is looking to expand digitally plus more exhibition space to show how good it is across a range of media.

Scholarly head of English inaugurated highly successful and intellectually stimulating Café Philo for sixth formers and local cognoscenti. It meets regularly in a Bath hotel and forms part of the Bath Festival of Literature. The cerebral influence permeates many of the school's clubs and activities: chess, bridge, national cipher challenge, Egyptological society, young investigators and others. Plenty of fund-raising including a one-girl effort in a school assembly on national water day and the school also has an amnesty branch. Activity weeks held annually to break the academic mould and there are other expeditions and visits through the year. Over 100 pupils are involved in the CCF, and D of E is also flourishing. Young Enterprise, work experience scheme and industry day all help to foster local links with industry and commerce.

Background and Atmosphere: Founded in 1552 by Edward VI, the school moved from the centre of Bath in 1961 to its present site still within walking distance of the city; spreading out from an elegant, Georgian house on the hillside via clusters of mainly utilitarian buildings dominated by a large sports hall and adjacent Astroturf. Overlooks much of Bath's less attractive housing as well as prehistoric Soulbury Hill which is now scarred by dual carriage access to M4. Apart from Nethersole mansion built in 1830 there is little of architectural merit here but thanks to the naturally contoured grounds the buildings are not displeasing to the eye and subject areas are adequately accommodated. The science laboratories have been largely refurbished and two new ones added. There is also an impressive manufacturing suite equipped with CAD/CAM facilities largely funded by an outside trust.

Nothing much provided in the way of social facilities for younger pupils but this might explain why they are keen to do activities such as street dancing. At lunch-time some pupils queue for sandwiches dispensed in bags (apparently they asked for this) from a now redundant hot meals' servery. Staff and hungrier pupils feed in the dated and dual purpose Willett hall where there is little incentive to linger over lunch. Here and in some other ways KES still feels more like a former boys' grammar school than a fully co-educational independent school, but less so in the sixth form where the ratio of girls to boys is higher. Average age of staff is 43, good proportion of female staff. Most stay for about eight years and many younger ones got promotion elsewhere. Teachers work flat out – 'the pace is unrelenting' said one resilient head of department. When we visited, the staff room certainly looked more like an ops room than an oasis of tranquillity.

A free thinkers' school rather than a religious foundation though Bath Abbey is visited twice each year for collective worship; small group of committed Christians however who meet regularly under name of Ichthus. The careers department is well resourced and effective, especially in terms of preparing year 12 pupils for their UCAS applications. The library has plenty of periodicals, foreign language newspapers and reference books. Despite the provision of laptops there is still a need to increase the use of computer-based learning resources here and modern teaching technology in several areas of the school. A notable exception is the cutting edge language laboratory which allows pupils to work at their own pace. Co-educational CCF meets on Wednesday afternoons and has its own indoor range and parade ground. There is also a burgeoning community service programme.

Pastoral Care and Discipline: Parents and pupils find it a friendly school which takes a genuine interest. There is no house system. Gowned prefects give an anachronistic impression but they play more of a caring role these days and share leadership responsibilities in one way or another with half the sixth form. When we visited, the prefect selection procedure was nearing completion, involving spirited discussion and friendly banter between out-going prefects and head. PSHE programme runs through the school. Rather surprising that the designated school chaplain is not on the staff and neither is there a school counsellor.

Pupils and Parents: Pupils appear to be articulate and keen to learn – no 'creep' culture here! Pupils are proud of the school's tradition and academic achievements. They are tidy but unpretentious, articulate but not condescending. Growing number of informal links such as a staff and parent choir.

Entrance: By interview and written tests (verbal reasoning, numeracy, literacy and short essay) at 11 and also for those seeking places in years 8 -10. Still seeks to select top quarter of ability range with a significant proportion in top 5 per cent. At sixth form, entrance is based on an interview (held in the preceding November), school report and a points score of 48+ from GCSE (with A* worth 8 points and grade C worth 5).

Exit: Almost all to higher education with between ten to fifteen per cent to Oxbridge. Good numbers to UCL, Nottingham, Exeter, Cardiff, Leeds, Manchester, Durham and Birmingham. A small but regular number of pupils go on to have Services careers; art foundation and drama courses also popular.

Money Matters: Doing best to build up a bursary fund with 9-10 entrance bursaries (always income related).

Remarks: Efficiency without frills. Parents feel that it succeeds in educating the whole person and represents good value for money. KES will attract those escaping from the 11+ merry-go-round in London.

KING EDWARD'S SCHOOL (BIRMINGHAM)

Edgbaston Park Road, Birmingham, West Midlands, B15 2UA

Tel: 0121 472 1672
Fax: 01214 154 327
E-mail: office@kes.bham.sch.uk
Website: www.kes.bham.sch.uk

• Pupils: 840 boys; all day • Ages: 11-18 • Size of sixth form: 250 • C of E/multi-faith • Fees: £2,583 • Independent • Open days: Early July, October, November

Chief Master: From 2006, Mr John Claughton, MA Hons (an Oxford classicist) (fiftyish). Educated at King Edward's, he was previously housemaster at Eton and then headmaster at Solihull School 2001-2005. Married with three young sons. Loves cricket, having gained his blue at Oxford and subsequently played County cricket for Warwickshire. He now serves on the Warwickshire CC Committee.

Succeeds popular, successful and charismatic Mr Roger Dancey who retired in December 2005.

Academic Matters: School gets outstanding results by means of first-rate teaching, a well-organised curriculum and an emphasis on educating the whole person, not merely turning out impressive exam statistics. Roughly 12:1 boys to full-time teachers, no class bigger than 26, sixth form 16. Results among the best in the country, especially so in maths, chemistry and geography. Maths A level in 2005, 42 out of 57 candidates got As, out of 59 chemistry candidates 55 got As or Bs; all 25 boys who took history got either A or B. Maths and geography seem especially strong among so many strengths. French compulsory to GCSE, other languages having to be taken as options.

Almost all passes at GCSE, the overwhelming number of grades in all subjects being A*s or As. Head emphasises the importance of special needs support, 'a bit of a crusade', and its place in enabling all candidates to achieve their potential. The recent full inspection which regarded the school as 'outstanding' in all but a very few respects, did point out the need to upgrade the library. This currently enthusiastically in hand. Middle school curriculum also re-evaluated with a view to making it more flexible in the light of report.

Games, Options, The Arts: Main sports rugby, hockey, basketball, cricket, athletics. Boys can also take archery, badminton, cross-country, Eton fives, fencing, golf, orienteering, sailing, squash, swimming, table tennis, tennis and water polo. Boys participate in many regional teams in various sports, also in U15 and U16 national sides in rugby, water polo, cricket. Extensive playing fields, extraordinary in a school one mile from centre of city. Also huge new Astroturf pitch shared with King Edward's VI High School for Girls (qv) which shares the school's huge campus and many activities, facilities and some staff. Extra-curricular options include conservation and environmental studies, leadership, CCF. Arts are famously good. Drama to professional standards under inspirational, unequalled teaching and production values. Music similarly outstanding – school justifiably proud of both. Art also impressive.

Background and Atmosphere: School founded in 1552 by King Edward VI, now flagship of King Edward Foundation group of seven Birmingham schools, including King Edward VI Camp Hill, an excellent grammar and school's main academic local rival. The chief master is head of the Foundation though each school is autonomous. School moved to a famous Charles Barry building in 1838 but in true Birmingham spirit of renewal and regeneration, this was demolished and the school moved to its current impressive 32-acre site in 1936.

Buildings are 1930s red brick and solid-looking, and manage to be both elegant and functional, though the length of the corridors might daunt newcomers! Newer buildings have been sensitively incorporated, including latest addition, an imaginative 'tea pavilion' for the entertainment of parents during matches and so on, known, up to now, as 'Dancey's Diner'. Now to be...? Much recent refurbishment especially flooring and lighting, greatly improves ambience.

The adjacent King Edward VI girls' school, founded 1883, is a real boon to the school, especially in matters dramatic, musical, social. Good friendly working relations between the two schools, assisted by some shared staff. Most pervasive feeling in school is a genuine warmth and unaffected enthusiasm among both staff and pupils and a sense of privilege – of the best kind – and good fortune in being there. The school has a sense of being geared to the realities of working life. A cooked breakfast is served every day and school uniform buying arrangements are geared to a working parent's schedule.

Pastoral Care and Discipline: School publishes an impressive-looking Pastoral Handbook with a carefully constructed Code of Conduct and Policies on sex education, PSE, drugs, bullying etc as well as advice on whom to speak to in the event of 'matters of pastoral concern'. System, however, is not restrictive and boys are encouraged to talk to person who is right for them, rather than to specific tutor or master. School has trained student counsellor. Also very approachable masters, including deputy head. Prefect system. Head would assess individual infringements of rules individually but hypothetical serious issues, eg drug selling, would mean instant expulsion.

Pupils and Parents: Intake reflects greatly diverse local ethnic and social mix. Between 35 – 40 per cent of boys from ethnic minorities, only 35 per cent from the city of Birmingham, many commute from as far as Coventry, Wolverhampton, Lichfield and consider it 'worth it'. 45 per cent from primary schools and 55 per cent from prep schools. Uniform throughout the school but sixth formers don't seem to mind. Liberal attitude to self-expression in hair etc and on 'own clothes' days. A place at this school clearly regarded as a prize by parents and pupils alike.

Entrance: Highly competitive (400 candidates for 125 places) at 11+. Entrance tests in English, maths, verbal reasoning, interview, report from current head. Five or so places available at 13+. Sixth form entry dependent on entrance examination in proposed AS subjects, Headteacher's report and interview. Academic scholarships decided on performance in entrance tests. Music scholarships (up to one-half fees) also offered.

Exit: Vast majority take up places at good universities (24 out of last year's 121 leavers went to Oxbridge, 26 to London colleges, 10 to Birmingham, 9 to Nottingham, 9 to Leeds and so on.) Unsurprisingly for a school which is so strong in maths and science, maths and medicine accounted for 30 leavers; natural sciences, computer sciences, engineering, economics made up a further 22. The traditional bias towards science has changed over recent years; leavers are now fairly evenly divided between science and the humanities. Old Edwardians include Tolkien, Enoch Powell, Nobel medical Laureate Sir John Vane, Kenneth Tynan, Bill Oddie.

Money Matters: School - and pupils - hugely fortunate to have Foundation able to compensate to great extent for loss of Assisted Places. Up to 14 places a year still funded out of school resources including 2 HSBC scholarships. Means-tested remission of up to full fees. Additional help in subsidising educationally useful school trips for those who need it. Altogether generous help for the genuinely worthy. Fees compare very favourably to comparable schools elsewhere.

Remarks: On all counts this is a very impressive school combining academic excellence, a real commitment to wider values of education, genuine exuberance and enthusiasm and turning out unpretentious, independent-minded, well-behaved and confident young men. Worth moving for.

KING'S BRUTON

Linked to Hazlegrove School in the Junior section

Plox, Bruton, Somerset, BA10 0ED

Tel: 01749 814 200/ Registrar 01749
Fax: 01749 813 426
E-mail: office@kingsbruton.com
Website: www.kingsbruton.com

- Pupils: 235 boys, 85 girls; 220 board, 100 day • Ages: 13-18
- Size of sixth form: 130 • Christian • Fees: Boarding £6,700; day £4,910 • Independent • Open days: October

Head: Since 2004, Mr Nigel Lashbrook (forties). Chemist. Read it at Oxford – where he played in the university 2nd cricket XI and captained his college rugby side – then taught it at Manchester Grammar where he also coached top rugby and cricket teams. Moved to Tonbridge in 1992, was a boarding housemaster then deputy head. They reckon he's 'totally different' from predecessor Richard Smyth and, for that reason, an 'inspired choice'. Not that there was anything wrong with the excellent Mr Smyth (now at St Peter's, York), he just defied imitation. He was also pretty defiant of contradiction, while with Mr Lashbrook 'you don't feel as if you've gone 15 rounds after you've raised a problem'. He's softly-softly, carefully consensual, rigidly insistent. He's approachable, affable, humorous, with that restless intelligence and ambition you want to see in a head. He's also clearly loving the job. Parents now say they feel confident that, under him, the school is 'really going to go places'. The change of style has led to no change in ethos – 'old fashioned but with a modern outlook' in the words of a parent – but he wants, particularly, to up the academic standard and raise the profile of drama. In both causes he has made firm first strides. He's also kicked out the caterers and improved the food immeasurably, thereby eliminating a long running gripe. He worries that the school is a 'well-kept secret' – this despite years of earnest marketing and some very good building – and he wonders why. Answer: because the school has always been unexceptionable. Sorry. And yet, and yet, the very qualities that have made it so may, in today's boarding market, make it exceptional. We rather think so.

Academic Matters: Good standard fare served up just as you would expect. No eccentricities and no vocational A level equivalents – a shame, perhaps. Some outstanding facilities – top science centre, IT and technology labs with computer-aided design and metal forges. Admirable IT, fully intranetted campus-wide. Classes really are remarkably small – max 20 to GCSE, max 14 in the sixth form. Expectations are rising, underpinned by statistical pupil monitoring. The head interviews every boy and girl at A level revision time, mulls over what they're up to, puts them on the spot. Smart move. 2005 has yielded a best-ever crop of exam results at all levels and the new school year was launched with Henry V-style oratory, but this is not the sort of place where youth grows pale and spectre thin and dies, good heavens no. There's pressure but, observes a sixth form girl fresh from a single sex school, it's not relentless neither does it nag – it's there, yes, but not so you're acutely aware of it. Parents feel the school does a good job by the brightest (always an Oxbridge handful) and the not so bright. Very bright director of studies. The social atmosphere is remarkably free of academic snobbery. Established special needs department – 1 full time, 2 part time – caters for 35 dyslexics and dyspraxics, and is reckoned to do well by them, most fall within the dyslexia stream, literacy and study skills important. One pupil currently has a statement of needs. Some help with study skills, especially the sixth form, one-to-one throughout with pupils withdrawn from ancillary rather than core subjects, 'we nurse them through literacy and study skills plus organization and curricular support'. School not good for wheelchairs, but would 'never turn anyone away'; can and have coped with mild Aspergers, profoundly deaf (hearing aid and voice magnifier for teacher rather then specialist mentor). All the normal aids, scribing, readers (expensive in public lessons = extra invigilators) the odd 'Irlen lens' but not a proven treatment', extra cost for lessons about £25.

Games, Options, The Arts: Terrific sport – a heritage feature. Stirring feats of valour weekly. There's a Spartan quality about the boys' rugby team (the haircuts, of which more anon, add to the impression), as this small school confronts overweening opponents and habitually overcomes them. Coaching excellent all round. Girls not yet quite so mighty but getting there. Parents, lots of them, pound touchlines intently and with camaraderie, while visiting parents comment on the warm welcome. You don't have to be sporty to be happy here, but it must help. Old boy Haydn Thomas is now Gloucester scrum half, Joe Mbu plays for Wasps. Long, strong cross-country tradition: the Tickner brothers were here. Rugby compulsory in first year only. Superb fitness suite approached by way of an art gallery – good art. Drama in its brilliant little in-the-round theatre is going from strength to strength as the head, having just appointed a full time manager, has added dance to the menu and is looking to involve the community. They already do the Edinburgh Fringe. This is a notably team-spirited school. Music is strong, ambitious director, ensembles of all sorts, a military band and, jewel in the crown, a very good swing band – ask for the cd. 40 per cent learn an instrument. Strong choral tradition and collaboration with the community to make the very biggest noises. Growing trend to do things with other schools in this school-filled town, including the Steiner school. Activities convention on first day of each term to advertise the array on offer. It's the usual long list but, observed a pupil, 'they all actually happen'. Now, that's rare! A thoughtful touch for parents coming to watch their progeny play away matches – a booklet with detailed maps and directions to 25 other schools in the vicinity.

Background and Atmosphere: When the Bishop of London founded King's in 1519 he intended to turn out 'perfyt latyn men' in a school where prayers were said only in Latin. They've gone vernacular now but the golden stone emanates ancientness of an agreeable, lost-world sort of quality. At times, as you walk about the campus, you feel as if you are in a Cambridge college. The town lies in a part of Somerset where the busy world is hushed, making it increasingly attractive to metro-exiles, downsizers, good-lifers, artsy folk, but it's neither ragged-arse bohemian nor is it Cotswold-twee. It's intelligent. The railway station at nearby Castle Cary is the last frontier of the commuter. There are five schools in this wee town and they rub along in a contentedly unfederated way. Coed since 1997. Good prospectus, gorgeous long-lens photos which, unusually, depict the boys and girls much as they appear in real life. Very good website. Splendid school mag which offers lots of insights.

Pastoral Care and Discipline: Boarding is apparently so well done here that we were inspired by incredulity to investigatively expose its underside for, as we know, to visit many a boarding school on a wet Saturday night in November is to spectate adolescents falling into hedges. We found no shred of evidence. As one mum put it, 'other schools turn a blind eye to drink. Not Bruton.' 75 per cent of the students board (no weekly, no flexi), and they do so in safety. Expect to see 65 per cent of them on any weekend. Why the good order? 'It's the measure of control we exert,' says the head. 'And the boys and girls like this place, they don't want to rock the boat.' Parents concur – 'there's a healthy respect for the line – this is a tight-knot community. They look after each other.' There's also a breathalyser to focus minds and, clever touch this, a chill-out period in houses every Saturday from 7 o'clock till 8 which tames the fever in the blood. Vigilance is the key, not the sanctions.

Pastoral care here has got so much better. Parents talk of some splendid housemasters coming through – 'my son responds to emails almost by return'.

Relationships with the community are necessarily good and, because town-gown standoffs sometimes inevitably happen, the school part-pays the salary of the local bobby. Boarders can go home for 4 weekends a term – you choose. Not all take them all up. Why not? 'Because they are happy in the company of their friends,' reflects the head to whom, in his first year, this seems to have been a happy revelation. It is certainly evident in the tenor of relationships as you walk around and is corroborated by the social care inspectors' report, which uncovered one of the lowest bullying rates in the country. They're an unusually well-turned-out lot, boys' hair collar length mostly, giving them a preppie look, especially the sixth formers in their business suits. Oh, they're all terribly nice, some would say terribly conventional. No sign of attitudinous rebs and rads. Character is indulged and enjoyed, says the head, 'unless it undermines safety.' Day boys and girls join boarding houses and feel hardly different at all.

Pupils and Parents: Those who want trad values. Increasingly popular with sophisticated incomers, ever popular with local families who reckon the big school nearby lah-di-dah. Not a school of choice by any means for the M4 corridor brat pack. All the small pool attractions and, yes, good at nurturing those who need it, but by no means exclusively so. Around 20 expats, 30 Europeans and 35 from China and Japan.

Entrance: The intake is truly comprehensive, so the hurdle is the waiting list. Main feeder schools are Hazlegrove (own prep), Chafyn Grove, Salisbury Cathedral, Port Regis, with a smattering from any of the many prep schools hereabouts. The academic range is wide because parents and children choose the school for its own sake, not for its place in the academic pecking order.

Exit: Almost all to higher education – all manner of courses everywhere. For a school that not many people have heard of, it's produced lots of former pupils that people have: R D Blackmore (Lorna Doone), explorer William Dampier, Air Marshal Sir Peter Squire, The Sunday Telegraph's Mandrake, Adam Helliker, historian and author of 'Fortress Malta', James Holland, and comedian Marcus Brigstocke.

Money Matters: Masses of generous scholarships and awards including sixth form, academic and music.

Remarks: A thoroughly well turned-out school in every respect and – we think it high time someone blew their cover – a pre-eminently eligible candidate for parents looking for boarding.

KING'S COLLEGE (TAUNTON)

Linked to King's Hall in the Junior section

South Road, Taunton, Somerset, TA1 3LA

Tel: 01823 328 200
Fax: 01823 328 202
E-mail: admissions@kings-taunton.co.uk
Website: www.kings-taunton.co.uk

- Pupils: 148 girls, 267 boys; 184 boys board, 94 girls board – the rest day • Ages: 13-18 • Size of sixth form: 170 • C of E
- Fees: Day £4,550; boarding £6,660 • Independent

Head: Since 2002, Mr Christopher Ramsey MA; educated Brighton College and Corpus Christi, Cambridge, and was head of modern languages at Wellington College. He is married to Lynne, with three small children. He is a football coach, an amateur painter and keen director of plays.

Academic Matters: Some excellent results in design technology – the GCSE work produced in design is jaw-droppingly magnificent. Links with successful Old Boys and Girls are useful – biologist Patrick Morris from the BBC's Natural History unit is a frequent visitor. Senior biology teacher Roger Poland's work with Mediterranean marine turtles led to EuroTurtle, a conservation project which has gained many awards and was selected by the American Science Teachers' association for inclusion in the national teaching programme. Links with Exeter University at the cutting edge of contemporary physics. Separate sciences for most at GCSE and very fine results too. 60 or so per cent A/B grades at A level, with history, the sciences, maths, DT, business studies and art all popular; DT again consistently good. Not a school that withdraws candidates from borderline A level subjects to massage the statistics.

Games, Options, The Arts: Designated a centre of excellence by English Cricket Board under cricket guru Dennis Breakwell. Sometimes takes the scalps off Millfield, Clifton College and closer to home for hockey, rugby, fencing (national champ) and netball, athletics, badminton, cross-country (several county champs). Goes big time on CCF (two Lord Lieutenant's cadets), Duke of Edinburgh and fund-raising. New theatre and drama studio for wonderful home-grown musicals involving entire school. A jazz CD par excellence and others featuring choir and various ensembles are sent to prospective parents.

Background and Atmosphere: Founded in 1880 to mark anniversary of King Alfred's death 1,000 years before. Set in 100 acres of grounds on the Exeter end of town, King's is a member of the Woodard Corporation developed by Christian educational pioneer Nathaniel Woodard. Pupils who are not christened are welcomed provided they will be present at ordinary religious instruction and services. Gothic-looking dining hall straight out of Harry Potter, recently refurbished with modern cafeteria providing meals to appeal to 21st century customers. Looks after its employees too – the floor above the spacious staff room is a club-style bar with luxurious sofas.

Pastoral Care and Discipline: Sees itself as looking after ordinary boys and girls and doing well to hold up the weaker brethren. Seven houses mix both day pupils and boarders. Pupils allowed to choose décor of attractively furnished common rooms. Sixth formers have their own social centre. Leadership and adventure score high (pioneering BTEC in leadership) so maybe not the place for those who can't keep up.

Pupils and Parents: A fair slice from the Services, others are business, ex-pats, farming, county; middle class and mostly white. OBs are Geoffrey Rippon, cricketer Roger Twose, rugby internationals Tom Voyce and Matthew Robinson, historian John Keegan, singer Alexandra Edenborough and children's broadcaster Dominic Wood. Says mother of future pupil, 'we went back to look at Kings 3 times before deciding. It's got a very good feel'.

Entrance: Selection through Common Entrance or VRQ at 13 when 85 enter from large geographical area. Several from Port Regis, Exeter/Salisbury Cathedral schools, St Michael's Jersey, plus 35 per cent from Kings Hall, their own prep down the road.

Exit: 98 per cent to universities. 5 or 6 each year to Oxbridge.

Money Matters: Academic awards of a third fees at 13. Several music scholarships, plus art, drama, DT awards. At sixth form there's a sports bursary; music and academic scholarship exams held in November each year.

Remarks: Civilised with strong Christian ethos. New young head is bound to have some changes up his arty, clever sleeves.

KING'S COLLEGE SCHOOL (WIMBLEDON)

Linked to King's College Junior School (Wimbledon) in the Junior section

Southside, Wimbledon Common, London, SW19 4TT

Tel: 020 8255 5352
Fax: 020 8255 5357
E-mail: admissions@kcs.org.uk
Website: www.kcs.org.uk

- Pupils: 755 boys; all day • Ages: 13-18 • Size of sixth form: 290 • C of E (but other faiths welcome) • Fees: Senior £4,350; junior £3,285 - £3,695 • Independent • Open days: Late September

Head Master: Since 1997, Mr Tony Evans MA MPhil (fifties). Educated at De la Salle School, London, followed by the French Lycée in Kensington, then Paris University and St Peter's, Oxford, where he read modern languages, and University College, London. His mother was Jersey French and he married a French wife (widowed) and has two children. Previously head of Portsmouth Grammar, which he ran with great flair and espièglerie for 15 years, helping pioneer, among other things, language courses in France in the hols. Also taught at Eastbourne College, Winchester and Dulwich. Keen (energetic!) committee man, including Admiralty Interview Board 1984-1997, and Chairman of HMC in 1996, where he made a very thoughtful inaugural speech on the problems of children today and the need not to sweep them under the carpet.

A governor of Sevenoaks, Winchester and of St George's, Montreux. Recreations (and we quote) 'soccer, France, theatre, avoiding dinner parties' (the latter is a pity as he would make an erudite and interesting dining companion). Forward-thinking 'European' in his attitude. A fan of the International Baccalaureate, has introduced it here.

Academic Matters: Strong, strong, strong. School committed to enriching the boys' academic diet, encouraging study of subjects 'because they are intrinsically interesting subjects to study rather than because they're going to lead to X'. Head wants boys to think creatively as he says there is a 'touch of autism in over- stimulated and structured children'. Setting from the first year. Sciences taught separately towards dual award examination. Ten GCSEs the norm (some early) but several take as many as 13. English

is an outstanding department, also maths and classics, 'but every department is good', commented a parent. Many distinguished members of staff – some of whom stay several decades. Has offered the IB alongside A levels since 2001 and intends to move to it exclusively. In 2003, IB results good across the board with history and biology popular and the most successful. In 2004 the mean points score reached a remarkable 39.1, the highest in UK. At A level, popular subjects were maths, all three sciences and English and 92.3 per cent A/B grades in all subjects was achieved. Average UCAS points 392 – pretty unbeatable. At GCSE 100 per cent got A*-C in five or more subjects and results show a good spread across curriculum. New large library and IT centre opened in 2003.

Games, Options, The Arts: Lots of everything – 'boys aren't just eggheads', said a pupil. Get a copy of the school mag – very glossy, black and white bar the fat section on art – and you will get the gist of the breadth of activities. Rugby, hockey fields etc, on site (plus 15 more acres at Motspur Park), cross-country on Wimbledon common, good rowing from the school's boathouse on the Tideway at Putney. Notably good tennis – national winners 2004. Renaissance of extra-curricular activities since Saturday school was abolished (though up to a third of the boys come in for sports or rehearsals on Saturdays). Ceramics must be among the best in any school. Music also very vigorous and so is drama with what one mother calls 'surprisingly sophisticated productions', including 5-star performances at Edinburgh Festival. Societies busy at lunchtime and after school, and the great and good drawn in to talk on all manner of topics – recently, for instance, Lord Saatchi, Lord (Robin) Butler, Bob Ayling, Anne Widdecombe and Lord Cranborne.

Background and Atmosphere: Situated on the edge of Wimbledon Common. Curious hotchpotch of buildings, including fine collegiate hall, elegant 18th-century house and sundry modern additions with plenty of elbow room, pleasant grounds, junior school (qv) on site. Sixth form block with good tidy common room. Originally founded in 1829 in the Strand, as the junior department of King's College, University of London. See the recent history published by James & James which, among other things, recounts the ghastly death by bullying of a boy in the 1880s. Back to the present – a sombre and busy seat of learning with bustle and purpose. Lively place with boys involved with all sorts of activities as well as excelling at exams.

Pastoral Care and Discipline: Well disciplined school. Well organised looking boys. Third Master in charge of pastoral care holds open forums with parents, big emphasis on responsibility. No long hair; manners are OK but not polished. Prefects now sent off on leadership training courses (like many others), and regard themselves as junior managers. Copes with the occasional odd-ball. Excellent Learning Enrichment department, serving the very gifted and less able alike.

Pupils and Parents: Middle class, professional parents, 'the parents and pupils are mostly life's natural hard workers', joked one of them. Largely from central and south west London, Kingston and Surrey, lots of ethnic minorities (mainly Asian). Sixth form allowed to drive to school. 'Boys not born with a silver spoon,' commented another, 'but often well aware that they are the intellectual elite.' Old Boys include vast numbers of university dons, Dante Gabriel Rossetti, Walter Sickert, Roy Plomley.

Entrance: Two thirds from school's own wonderful prep (qv), the rest from a wide variety of schools, pre-tested at 11. CE pass mark is 65 per cent, 'but boys need spare capacity as well'. Head says they are not a hothouse and that they take boys who have something other to offer than academic excellence.

Exit: Virtually all to university (conservative in their choices), heaps to Oxbridge. Engineering, the law, the city and medicine continue to be likely careers.

Money Matters: Up to 15 entrance scholarships at 13 and several at 16 of varying values from 10 per cent to a maximum of 30 per cent fees. Three awards for boys showing 'outstanding promise as scientists, classicists or modern linguists'.

Remarks: A hot-shot boys' academic day school in south west London, with less of the high-pressured atmosphere than some London establishments, helped in this by being situated in a desirable suburb of London (ie lots of space).

THE KING'S SCHOOL
CANTERBURY

25 The Precincts, Canterbury, Kent, CT1 2ES

Tel: 01227 595 501

Fax: 01227 595 595

E-mail: headmaster@kings-school.co.uk

Website: www.kings-school.co.uk

- Pupils: 798 pupils. 434 boys, 364 girls (610 board, 188 day)
- Ages: 13-18 • Size of sixth form: 351 • C of E • Fees: Boarding £7,760 day £5,760 • Independent • Open days: 6th form: October and May . 13+: June

Head: Since 1996, Canon Keith Wilkinson BA MA FRSA (early fifties), previously head of Berkhamsted, senior chaplain at Malvern and Eton. Married, twin grown-up daughters, one of whom attended the school. Mrs Wilkinson, also a teacher, is part of the SEN team. Parents have great admiration for him, his hard work and calm manner; a thoughtful speaker; his interests include music and drama.

Academic Matters: Highly successful, producing excellent results. A high proportion of As and Bs at A level, and 100 per cent A*-C at GCSE. Academic work is taken very seriously, with some setting and streaming; bright children can take some GCSE subjects early. English is presently the most popular A level, well backed up by exciting drama department and extensive library. The library is housed in its own building and opens to pupils 85 hours a week, twice as long as most schools. Somerset Maugham and Sir Hugh Walpole both left their personal libraries to King's. 'There is nothing our librarian can not help you to find out, I was amazed,' says young pupil. The school's great strength is intellectual growth, constantly encouraging children to find out more and aim high. Good languages dept staffed by mainly by native speakers, nine options including Japanese and Russian. Sciences are really alive here, imaginative teaching in single and combined, head of science recently came in the top three in a Tomorrow's World competition. Science Research Initiative involves pupils in research work.

ICT is now up to the mark having been fully updated recently, all are encouraged to learn to touch-type. All studies linked to the net. Once dominated by older men, staff is a good mixture of male and females from varying age groups. 'Teaching is very sound and motivating, lots of cerebral types around,' say parents, everyone has an academic tutor to monitor their progress. EFL and SEN support is available though only minor difficulties can be coped with, those who need to may use a laptop.

Games, Options, The Arts: Thriving sports department – sport held in high regard by pupils; trophies all over the school. Acres of playing fields and modern sports centre incorporating pool, indoor courts, climbing wall, café and gym which is open to pupils at any time. Needless to say, they have produced international players in various sports, particularly strong fencing, excellent rowing (boys and girls) many professional coaches. Long tradition of excellent drama and music. Professor of Royal Academy conducts an orchestra; high-quality concerts and theatre are brought together in the famous and popular summer 'King's Week.' Countless clubs and activities including silversmithing and archaeology, staff always keen to add new options. Many do D of E awards. Art department runs in a sympathetically converted twelfth century priory, different artist in residence each year. 'We do arrive home for the holidays exhausted – there is always so much going on,' say pupils.

Background and Atmosphere: Has to be one of the most inspiring settings – in the shadow of Canterbury Cathedral, pretty gardens, well-kept, mostly listed, buildings, whose conservation can cause the head problems when updating. Beautiful wood-panelled dining room; food is reported by pupils to be fantastic. Busy, get up and go campus with smiling faces buzzing everywhere in smart pinstripe uniform, gowns for scholars and monitors. Rich variety of architectural styles for different boarding houses; recital room is a former synagogue (this last a monument to Egyptomania). Beautiful at every turn (pretty gardens, flint walls), and, said a housemistress with glee, 'when parents see the place they are instantly won over'. Atmosphere of ancient customs and traditions in fact totally at odds with the truth, which is that a small school on the site was turned by Canon Shirley (head of King's from 1935-62 and one of the great pioneering entrepreneurial heads) almost overnight into a place with smart uniform, quaint customs, in a marketing exercise of which any captain of industry would be proud.

Pastoral Care and Discipline: Girls now 46 per cent of pupils and wear smart uniform, pinstripes and jacket, and white shirts with wing collars – like little barristers, and pupils so taken with it apparently some go on wearing it when they leave school. 'Now very sound,' say parents, pastoral as well as academic tutors for all. 'A much gentler place than in my day,' says Old Boy, though some reports of heavy-handed housemasters. However, recent big influx of new, young housemasters and mistresses. Big effort has been made to address everyone's needs and happiness, several pupil/staff committees to ensure all have their say. Boarding houses are clean and friendly with areas where pupils can make their own snacks and relax. Pupils are articulate, alert and very enthusiastic about their school. Member of the Eton Group, a network of schools that pools ideas for successful running of independent schools.

Pupils and Parents: Good mix socially and culturally, popular with locals, London and county sets, ex-pats and foreigners: USA, Indians, Far East, Germans particularly in sixth form. 'Travel is nothing, when you see the opportunities there are here, if your child has the stamina,' say parents. Scholarship pupils are encouraged from all backgrounds and nationalities. OBs and Gs: David Gower, Michael Morpurgo, Michael Foale, Jacquetta Wheeler, Patrick Leigh Fermor, Harry Chistophers, Lord (Charles) Powell, Jonathan Powell and 2005 world champion rower Frances Houghton – to name a few.

Entrance: At 13, by Common Entrance, or special exams for those not prepared for CE; looking for around 60 per cent, and for children who will make the most of their time here. At 16, 30-40 places by entrance exam plus at least seven B grades at GCSE.

Exit: Almost all to a wide range of universities, a couple of dozen to Oxbridge each year, popular choices include biological sciences, English, languages and medicine.

Money Matters: Head and governors are developing a long-term endowment plan. Up to 50 scholarships and bursaries a year: academic, music, sport and art.

Remarks: You need to be creative, academically able and hard-working, as everything moves fast here. Lessons every Saturday morning including on exeat weekends! Stretches its pupils beyond the usual bounds of the curriculum. Glorious setting.

THE KING'S SCHOOL (CHESTER)

Linked to King's Junior School (Chester) in the Junior section

Wrexham Road, Chester, Cheshire, CH4 7QL

Tel: 01244 689 500

Fax: 01244 689 501

E-mail: info@kingschester.co.uk

Website: www.kingschester.co.uk

• Pupils: 855 boys and girls • Ages: 7-18 • Size of sixth form: 141 boys and 42 girls • C of E, cathedral foundation • Fees: Junior £2,010; senior £2,625. Plus lunch • Independent • Open days: Second or third Saturday in November

Headmaster: Since 2000, Mr Tim Turvey BSc FIBiol FLS (fifties). Read botany and zoology at University College, Cardiff. Came from The Hulme Grammar School, Oldham, where he spent the 1990s as deputy head and head from 1995 – 'Oldham's huge mix of urban, ethnic minority backgrounds was a big contrast with Chester.' Principal examiner for Nuffield A level biology from 1981 until 2001 and editor and author of various Nuffield biology textbooks. Commutes from Didsbury in Manchester where he lives with his wife (a principal manager at AQA). Keen churchgoer, BBC radio 'Pause for Thought' contributor and takes seriously the school's cathedral foundation and faith implications – 'we, as a community, are founded in faith'. Describes the main changes he has made in five years as being, 'initiating major improvements in and additions to the facilities of the school for the benefit of the pupils and the introduction of full co-education.' Pupils describe him as modern, with a driven approach. Mr Turvey is very enthusiastic about the recent admission of girls, 'we believe that educating bright girls and boys alongside each other is the best preparation for university and careers'. Some parents had mixed feelings though most embraced the changes enthusiastically.

Academic Matters: Strongly and unashamedly academic with consistently outstanding GCSE results – 91 per cent A or B grades, around 70 per cent As, very few Cs and only a handful below that. Outstanding at A level too with 30 students gaining 3,4 or even 5 A grades; a few Ds, Es and Us which school puts down to not pressurising pupils to choose subjects in which they are bound to excel and not insisting that pupils who have only mediocre prospects

should leave. Active SEN provision with SENCO giving extra support before school. Parents describe school as 'not too pushy.' Head explains that an A at GCSE might indicate an A, B or C at A level and says that where A level grades are not what they should be it reflects the difficulties students face making the transition to A level study. Most pupils choose to take general studies AS level. Most popular, and most successful, subjects are maths and sciences. Pupils do well in Maths Challenge and some reach dizzy heights in the maths and physics Olympiads.

Games, Options, The Arts: Very strong rowing tradition (since 1877) with boathouse on the River Dee in city centre though recent coaching style doesn't appeal to all boys. Teams compete with universities and at Henley regatta etc and one of the recent Olympic eight was a pupil here. Boys proud of football, first XI players have hero status and match reports dominate school newsletter but rugby is also on the up. Heated indoor pool on site, acres of flat playing fields, an outstanding new all-weather pitch for hockey and soccer, six full and four half tennis courts and an annual fitness test for students, D of E, Combined Cadet Force, outdoor pursuits trips for first years and trips abroad aplenty – Italy for classics students, WW2 sites for history, geographers go all over Europe, language-related trips and skiing to Europe and North America.

Enthusiastic drama performances, four or five productions a year, enhanced by presence of sixth form girls. Pupils say art has taken huge leap for the better with new teacher and recent results show significant upward trend. Plenty of music activity, private instrument tuition and opportunities for involvement in cathedral worship. Parents like new brochure with forthcoming arts programme.

Background and Atmosphere: Founded by King Henry VIII in 1541, the school moved out of its city centre cathedral site in 1960. Plenty of air and space around the campus just inside Chester ring road where large car parks and bus bays (school bus services are organised by parents and shared by Queen's girls) lead to dignified central buildings and less elegant later additions. New art and design technology studios opened in summer 2004 and a new music school in spring 2005. The 'head's house' used to be exactly that but is now agreeable space for sixth form economics though, from the outside, is dated. But sixth formers say it has a nice atmosphere and love being set apart – 'we get priority at lunch too.' The sixth form block has common and private study rooms and a careers reference room. The common room has a newly introduced cafeteria service with seating to match – a foretaste of student life. Relaxed atmosphere with head of sixth in his room with door open and corridor full of chatting students during private study period. Super new 'Wickson' library named after previous head, over 10,000 books, 60 journals and daily papers. 'The librarians are helpful but they're strict about noise,' say pupils. Hooray! Circle of twenty computers for accessing info adjoins extensive IT suites. And at the heart of it all a beautifully planted quad with dramatic statues – 'that garden's only for the teachers,' pupils shrug.

Pastoral Care and Discipline: Head says that, despite prevailing youth culture in Chester, the school is drug free, 'although you never know what tomorrow will bring.' Pupils seem genuinely aghast at the question of having anything to do with drugs. Head says he believes alcohol is far more of a danger for today's youngsters, 'in a culture where smoking is very uncool they can still be naïve about drinking.' The school does appear genuinely friendly – parents think that new pupils joining any year are welcomed and present pupils say there's a great social life amongst students, which is encouraged by staff, who sit among the children in dining hall.

Removes in first year have prefect mentors to look up to, otherwise pupils say form tutors sort out problems and parents praise the accessibility of teachers, many of whom make personal numbers and voice mail available. An onsite school nurse is appreciated by parents, pupils and head. Head has strengthened links with cathedral, moving from what he calls a superficial spirituality to one which, 'in an unobtrusive way makes faith lived and talked about.' He has introduced two Christian Unions, weekly staff prayer meetings, a Christian parents' group and a significant input from boys in the cathedral on the first Sunday of each term. Pupils have noticed a change of emphasis in assemblies but say, 'he doesn't ram it down our throats.'

Pupils and Parents: The school reflects its catchment area and is predominantly white and middle class, with a few very wealthy Cheshire families represented. Pupils come from miles around, from far along the North Wales coast to areas south of Manchester. Pupils are self-assured, polite, friendly and unpretentious. Smart uniform with dark green, navy and gold striped blazer and sixth form attire only slightly relaxed. Since going co-ed in 2003, years 7, 8 and 9 have thirty per cent girls; 'very encouraging', says head, 'the girls are loving it and they're contributing hugely'. Still some joint ventures with Queen's, notably CCF.

Entrance: By examination at 11. Academic entrance scholarships reintroduced in September 2005 for pupils entering at 11. Every place has 1.6 applicants – 'we take from the top 25 per cent of ability,' say staff. Most seniors carry on into sixth form needing at least 7 GCSEs at a minimum of grade B and an A in prospective A level subjects, so a few are encouraged to go elsewhere for sixth form.

Exit: Most leavers go on to traditional universities to study a wide variety of subjects including film studies, aerospace engineering, equine and human sports and dairy herd management as well as the more traditional PPE, law, medicine and engineering. Thirteen to Oxbridge in 2005, lots to Nottingham, Manchester, Leeds and London. Notable OBs include comedy actor Hugh Lloyd and former M&S finance director Keith Oates, but, 'alas,' says head, 'no serious benefactors proffering huge endowments!'

Money Matters: Some bursaries available, after means-testing, for pupils of high academic ability.

Remarks: Friendly and unpretentious with great results and lots of opportunities. Head is revamping the infrastructure at the same time as encouraging deeper thinking on matters spiritual, in keeping with the school's cathedral foundation.

KING'S SCHOOL ELY

Linked to King's School Ely, Junior School in the Junior section

Barton Road, Ely, Cambridgeshire, CB7 4DB

Tel: 01353 660 702
Fax: 01353 667 485
E-mail: admissions@kings-ely.cambs.sch.uk
Website: www.kings-ely.cambs.sch.uk

• Pupils: 410: 155 day boys, 125 day girls; 70 boy boarders, 60 girls boarders • Ages: 13-18 • Size of sixth form: 130 • C of E • Fees: Day: pre-prep £2,100; years 3 & 4 £2,965; years 5-8 £3,235; years 9-13 £4,470. Boarding: year 4 £4,725; years 5-8 £4,990; years 9-13 £6,470 • Independent • Open days: Whole school open morning September; but tours/visits available all year

Head: Since 2004, Mrs Sue Freestone GRSM MEd LRAM ARCM (late forties), formerly head of Sibford – a Quaker school – and Mrs Freestone is a Quaker. Married, with a grown-up son and daughter, she was educated at Clifton High School in Bristol before training at the Royal Academy of Music and was appointed head of Sibford in 1997 having taught 'all over'- Bryanston, Canford, Claviesmore, Colston's Girls' School in Bristol and was previously director of music at North Foreland Lodge. A success at Sibford – bubbly and fun, with a great sense of humour.

Academic Matters: Does not churn out only academics, offers huge support to all its pupils, treats each as an individual. Maths is the most popular subject at A level with mostly As and Bs. Other successful subjects include biology, business studies, RE, physics, English. Art & design becoming very popular with excellent results helped by a highly qualified and enthusiastic teacher who takes students on lots of trips – The V & A, Tate Britain, Tate Modern, Barcelona etc as well as local visits. Photography new option. Strong SEN department with a full-time teacher and assistant. King's International Study Centre provides a 'bridge' for international students to acquire the language and study skills they need to gain access to education at Britain's top boarding schools. 45 or so students a year, about 90 per cent A*-C pass rate at GCSE – some doing the course in only one year. Wide spread of nationalities. The Study Centre has its own classrooms and boarding houses but shares dining and sports facilities with the main school, and its students get the opportunity to play representative sport for the school. Some nice success stories eg a Hungarian boy who took a year's GCSE course at the Study Centre went on to be a scholar at the main school, head of his boarding house, a school prefect, member of the 1st XV rugby team and is now reading law at Cambridge.

Games, Options, The Arts: Wonderful art department and CDT section with textiles being particularly popular. Photography new in 2005. School has own computerised sewing machines and there is a great deal of experimenting going on and encouraged. Students' artwork all over the school, extremely high quality. Take a close look at the clock on the mantelpiece in the waiting room.

Music very much central to the school's ethos with over 50 per cent learning at least one instrument, many reaching grades 7 and 8. Orchestra, bands, choirs and instrumental ensembles. Performances in Ely and Peterborough cathedrals, locally and abroad. Superb facilities with a large theatre for concerts, many practice rooms, a percussion studio and specialist IT suite for composing or rearranging music. Music technology introduced in 2005.

Sport flourishes and is compulsory in years 9 and 10. Girls' hockey is extremely popular as is rowing, football, basketball and netball with cricket, tennis, rounders and athletics in the summer. Rugby has been reintroduced as a major boys' team sport. Many county players, one won five gold medals in the English Schools' Athletics Championships and represented England at the Athens Olympics in 2004.

D of E and the school's own Ely Scheme, which replaces CCF, are very popular. Ely Scheme compulsory in year 9, one afternoon a week and two weekend camps during the year. The Scheme 'promotes initiative, self-reliance, teamwork, communication and a sense of responsibility.' Annual overseas expeditions ranging from the French Alps to the Himalayas. Activities include canoeing, kayaking and climbing (not the easiest thing to do in east East Anglia.)

Background and Atmosphere: Exceptionally friendly – staff and students, just like one big happy family. In the middle of spectacular Ely city with the cathedral always in sight, the school can trace its origins back more than a thousand years. Still in use by the school are many of the original medieval and monastic buildings including the monk's barn (a tithe barn) used as a magnificent dining hall – excellent food, breakfast being particularly popular. The ancient library building, which is reached via a spiral stone staircase, has been beautifully modernised.

The sixth form centre, originally a terraced cottage, a comfortable place. Own garden for BBQs in the summer. Chapel is compulsory twice a week, optional on Sundays.

Pastoral Care and Discipline: Very caring school, allows the children to develop naturally and encourages children to think for themselves. A Christian school, pupils from all denominations (or none) are welcome but are expected to join in fully with all school spiritual activities. Discipline is self-regulating as much as possible. If any student is caught with drugs, discussion takes place prior to exclusion; if necessary, random tests instituted – this usually sorts out most problems. Similarly with bullying – discussions between the parties will always take place first to try and solve any misunderstandings.

Pupils and Parents: Students from a variety of backgrounds, traditionally farming, clerical and the Services but increasingly business, entrepreneurial and professional families too. Locals plus Cambridge, Newmarket and Huntingdon, also Norfolk, Suffolk, Hertfordshire and Essex. 60 from abroad of whom about 12 from the Far East, 20 or so from Europe and the others ex-pats or Services. Notable Old Scholars include Lord Browne of Madingley (group chief executive of BP Amoco), Alan Yentob (BBC), Ms Jo Marks (national finalist in the Entrepreneur of the Year awards having launched her own multimillion mobile phone group with one handset).

Entrance: Own exam at 11, also Common Entrance for entry into year 9 (75 per cent from King's own junior school). Sixth form entry based on GCSE results (minimum 2 grade Bs plus 3 grade Cs). Not too difficult to get in, overall picture of student taken into consideration.

Exit: Very few leave after GCSE, usually to go to the very good sixth form colleges in Cambridge. Music very high on the agenda post A level, with many going on to study at the Royal College of Music, others to a wide variety of universities including a good number to Oxbridge.

Money Matters: Some scholarships available for achievement and potential at academic work; also music, art, design & technology, drama and sports and award holders whose families are unable to meet the remaining fees may apply for bursary support. Choristerships carry a 50 per cent bursary in junior school as long as the boy remains in the choir and a 33 per cent bursary in senior school. Girls in a senior school girls' choir (starting in September 2006) will receive a 33 per cent bursary on the boarding fee. Discounts for clergy and Services.

Remarks: Everyone is given the chance to flourish – lots of support at all levels. A very happy and productive school.

THE KING'S SCHOOL (MACCLESFIELD)

Cumberland Street, Macclesfield, Cheshire, SK10 1DA

Tel: 01625 260 000
Fax: 01625 260 022
E-mail: mail@kingsmac.co.uk
Website: www.kingsmac.co.uk

• Pupils: 500 boys, 370 girls; all day • Ages: 11-18 • Size of sixth form: 270 • C of E • Fees: Infants £1,665; juniors £1,925; seniors £2,440 • Independent • Open days: Autumn and spring term plus weekly tours all year round

Head: Since 2000, Dr Stephen Coyne BSc PhD MEd (chemistry/polymer science) (fiftyish). Grammar school educated before studying at Liverpool and Manchester universities. Taught at Merchant Taylors', Crosby and The Manchester Grammar School, becoming head of science at Arnold School, Blackpool and deputy head at Whitgift School, Croydon. Married to a teacher with no children and is very happy here; softly spoken, quietly confident with clear ideas and ambitions for the school. Quite understated but appears to provide good leadership for the King's foundation. Makes his presence felt at both sites, regularly making the mile journey between the two.

King's has had the reputation of being a sports school and, whilst anxious not to diminish this, the new head visualises improved academic results, putting King's on a level with other academic schools in the area. Indeed, it is already on a par with some. Since his appointment he has tightened up on 'housekeeping' issues eg uniform, presentation of the school and monitoring of standards ('many more assessments of academic performance,' comments one pupil). He enjoys teaching chemistry to the sixth form – 'the only way to keep in touch at ground level'. A believer in breadth of education, not academic pressure cookery.

Academic Matters: Now a leading school in Cheshire. Maximum class size is 26 with average sizes around 20. 50-ish per cent A*/A grades at GCSE, 70 plus per cent A/B grades at A level. A wide range of subjects on offer, including psychology, classical civilisation and geology. A Gifted and Talented register offers opportunities for exceptional pupils and learning support is available for pupils with dyslexia (for which there is a fee).

Games, Options, The Arts: Excellent facilities include 40 acres of playing fields, all-weather pitches, gym and squash court. The girls' division has a sports hall and Macclesfield leisure centre provides a swimming pool. High pupil participation in all sports, with teams of all abilities playing on Saturday mornings. Hundreds of sporting fixtures occur throughout the year and many King's pupils achieve county and national success; regular tours abroad to places such as Kenya, Singapore and Australia. Outward bound activities are particularly well catered for, including a compulsory programme of activities in years 7 to 9, making use of the centre at Hathersage in the Peak District – rock climbing, pot holing, sailing, mountaineering, orienteering – the list goes on.

Music is important at King's. Timetabled lessons in years 7 and 8 provide a broad exposure to the subject and include hands-on learning in the keyboard lab. 30 peripatetic teachers provide individual lessons. There is a full programme of recitals by the choirs [(they were the BBC choir of the year in 2003)], barbershop, and chamber groups as well as orchestras, wind bands, percussion and string groups; the more talented musicians, boys and girls, combine to form The Foundation Choir, Orchestra and Big Band. Results at GCSE and A level are excellent. Art and design are well catered for with dedicated art rooms at both sites and an impressive technology rooms at both sites. Pupils enjoy residential weekends, workshops and hold biannual art exhibitions.

Background and Atmosphere: Founded in 1502. Originally a grammar school, its status has evolved over the years and it became an independent fee-paying school in 1946. C of E foundation but an ecumenical ethos. The King's School Foundation is organised in four divisions, the boys and co-ed sixth form divisions at the Cumberland Street site that the school has occupied since 1855, whilst the girls and co-ed junior divisions occupy the site formerly known as Macclesfield High School for Girls. Boys and girls are therefore taught separately, with very little mixing, between the ages of 11 and 16, the school promoting the advantages of single sex and co-ed education at the different stages of development.

Boys and the sixth form occupy an impressive site with lawns sweeping up to the imposing main building. The girls and junior site is less grand but is situated on the edge of the Peak District with glorious views over open countryside; it has a bit of a poor relation feel compared with the dynamic boys' division ('simply not true,' says the head). However pupils here extol the virtues of their division and the head points out that the girls represent much of the academic success of King's. Houses at both sites encourage achievement, academic or otherwise.

Pastoral Care and Discipline: Head likes to deal with anti-social behaviour before it reaches the point of bullying. The few cases that occur are dealt with quickly and in close liaison with parents. A peer support network enables younger pupils to turn to a known older pupil with problems they may be unwilling to take to a member of staff. Drug offences would invite expulsion but head comments he would look 'at circumstances of each individual case'. Warnings and detentions for other troublesome behaviour. School councils (pupil run) operate at many levels. The sixth form council has its own boardroom and seems to have real clout.

Pupils and Parents: Majority professional, some farming families and a sizeable minority of blue-collar workers. Traditionally rather WASPish but now popular with families relocating to the area so has an international element. Good parent support. Head 'rarely buttonholed at events with concerns or complaints'. Pupils are relaxed, chatty and warm. They clearly enjoy school. The head girl was outstanding – very confident, articulate, with oodles of charisma, clearly going places. The rest are a sociable bunch with their feet on the ground, polite and fiercely loyal to their school. They defy any pupil not to find a niche here.

Entrance: The school draws from a large geographical area within Cheshire, Derbyshire and Staffordshire. Non-selective entrance into the infants. Assessment for entry into juniors plus report from feeder school. Entrance is not automatic from own infants. At senior level, entrance is by examination, report and interview; again there is no automatic right of transfer though vast majority does. At sixth form, 2 As and 4 Bs or equivalent are required by internal candidates, higher for externals. The majority at senior level come from the junior school, the local state schools and local prep schools.

Exit: A small number leaves post GCSE to go to sixth form colleges. The vast majority of sixth form leavers go on to higher education – a mix of universities, including the new universities and art foundation colleges. Around 10 each year go to Oxbridge (support and preparation for candidates). Pupils praise the careers advice.

Money Matters: Bursaries (means-tested) for bright children with limited resources are available. Some minor scholarships. To mark the quincentenary year, a fund to provide for sixth form bursaries, has been launched and 7 students are going through on this scheme.

Remarks: A relaxed, friendly school offering oodles of opportunities for its pupils. Academic results are improving and, under the new head, look set to continue to do so. Head comments that pupils who may not have achieved in a pressured environment do well here because they enjoy school, find that they can excel in an area, and hence their overall performance improves.

KING'S SCHOOL, ROCHESTER

Linked to King's Preparatory School in the Junior section

Satis House, Boley Hill, Rochester, Kent, ME1 1TE

Tel: 01634 888 555
Fax: 01634 888 505
E-mail: walker@kings-school-rochester.co.uk
Website: www.kings-school-rochester.co.uk

- Pupils: 310. Boys outnumber girls 2:1 throughout the school.
- Ages: 13-18 • Size of sixth form: 123 • C of E • Fees: Day: pre-prep/prep £2,375 - £3,460; senior £4,470 plus lunch. Boarding: prep £5,335, senior £7,520 • Independent • Open days: Second Saturday in October

Headmaster: Since 1986, Dr Ian Walker (fiftyish), hyperactive and charming Australian polymath whose PhD on Plato and string of degrees are complemented by his multilingualism, artistic and sporting enthusiasms and complete involvement with every aspect of his extraordinary school. Wife, super, ex-teacher and now a practising solicitor, warmly and closely involved with the school. Two children, both at university.

Head's passionate dedication to the school, its staff and pupils informed by powerful personal morality and exuberance which makes the highest demands – of no-one more, it seems, than of himself. Loopy sense of humour as evidenced by his published collection of 'Howlers', available from the school.

Academic Matters: Extraordinary, because this is a school with a truly comprehensive intake. Takes at 4 years old pupils it keeps, with no academic weeding, throughout. Gets results comparable with the academically selective competition with an intake 70 per cent of whom would not make it into grammar school. 60 per cent A*/A/B at GCSE, 53 per cent A/B at A level. Special features: German taken from pre-prep level so pupils leave school bilingual, cross-over between the three schools on site so that younger children are taught by senior school teachers and vice versa, unusual emphasis and level of achievement in divinity, reflecting head's commitment, no rigid 3 science GCSE insistence though all 3 sciences on offer, flexible curriculum allowing for Russian, Irish and other languages to be studied and, across the board, very impressive results, getting the best from all pupils. Excellent individual support for children with special needs of all kinds. School not afraid to take on children that other schools would shy away from – and then get the best out of them.

Games, Options, The Arts: High standards in all sports especially rowing, fencing, rugby, hockey. Excellent outdoor facilities, less extensive hard surface areas. Wide range of options including wine tasting, bridge, home economics, CCF. Drama excellent despite lack of proper drama studio or special facilities. Music good and enthusiastically supported and includes various ensembles, classical, jazz and pop. School supplies choristers for cathedral choir. Outstanding art under inspirational teaching.

Background and Atmosphere: School inseparable from cathedral and chapter, to which the school buildings are integral. Ancient foundation, dating from 604, re-established in 1541 by Henry VIII, many classes take place in buildings of astonishing elegance and beauty. Sixth form centre in The College, 17th century gem in which new sixth form common rooms are panelled, painted, superbly furnished and immaculately kept, self-policed in this disciplined, though relaxed, atmosphere. School blends ancient with state-of the-art, having fully networked computer centres, direct satellite linked systems and a pioneering European Initiative. First rate new buildings include Chadlington House, stunning new pre-prep. Some older buildings in need of refurbishment and school well-aware of its responsibility to maintain its inheritance. Seven new buildings or major refurbishments in current head's fourteen year regime.

Pastoral Care and Discipline: Pastoral care via tutor system though pupils also encouraged to go to anyone in case of need and many feel comfortable going direct to the head. Clearly a well-run and happy school. Discipline and considerate conduct is emphasised and high standards of dress and behaviour are expected and achieved. Very warm, open and spontaneously polite pupils.

Pupils and Parents: Most pupils live within 10 miles of the school, Rochester, Chatham, Gillingham, Gravesend, Maidstone, Tonbridge, Sevenoaks. Ethnic and cultural mix comfortable with the unashamedly Christian ethic and atmosphere. Parents are warmly supportive and appreciative, especially of the school's clear commitment to the pastoral welfare of each pupil as well as to his or her academic achievement. Only 48 boarders (with room for more) – many happily from abroad – in delightful, family atmosphere, separate girls and boys boarding houses.

Entrance: Over-subscribed at all stages. Common Entrance or special entrance test for maintained sector candidates. Sixth form entry conditional on 5 GCSEs at A*-C, preferably B or higher in chosen A level subjects and especially if maths or sciences are to be studied. Most children start at 4 and stay until 18.

Exit: Virtually all to university to study the full range of academic and vocational subjects. A decent number to Oxbridge and more to the University of London colleges. Old Roffensians include the brothers John and Peter Selwyn Gummer (now Lord Chadlington) the late actors David King and Dinsdale Landen, and many Services and industry chiefs.

Money Matters: Scholarships include cathedral choristerships for boys of 40 per cent tuition fees + a reduction on music tuition fees, King's Exhibitions (from 11), up to 5 awarded annually, of 50 per cent of tuition fees; King's scholarships (at 13+), up to 5 awarded annually, of 50 per cent of tuition fees and 5 Minor King's scholarships of 25 per cent tuition fees. At least 5 of these for pupils from the maintained sector. Also one art, five music, an organ, and a sports scholarship on comparable bases. Governors' exhibitions, means-tested awards for able children from less well-off homes. Reductions for clergy, service personnel and siblings after the second child. Bursaries in case of sudden need.

Remarks: 'In theory we shouldn't survive,' says the head of his 'best performing comprehensive intake school in the country'. 100 applicants for 8 places at 11+ despite the formidable competition from 26 local grammar schools. Deserves to be far more widely known and appreciated.

THE KING'S SCHOOL (WORCESTER)

Linked to King's Saint Alban's Junior School in the Junior section

Linked to King's Hawford School in the Junior section

5 College Green, Worcester, Worcestershire, WR1 2LL

Tel: 01905 721 700
Fax: 01905 721 710
E-mail: info@ksw.org.uk
Website: www.ksw.org.uk

• Pupils: 506 boys, 376 girls; all day • Ages: 11-18 • Size of sixth form: 229 • C of E • Fees: £3,022 (seniors); £1,575 - £2,785 (juniors) • Independent • Open days: Early October and January; November for sixth form

Head: Since 1998, Mr Timothy H Keyes MA (fifty). Educated at Christ's Hospital, read classics at Wadham College, Oxford, then PGCE at Exeter. First headship. Came from Royal Grammar School, Guildford, where he was second master having previously held classical teaching posts at the Perse, Whitgift and Tiffin. A committed and active Christian. Says, 'I think that's important because the school is run on Christian principles.' But keen to stress all faiths 'welcomed and valued'. Sings with Worcester Festival Choral Society, also a keen campanologist. Inherited school in transition – lengthy transformation from traditional boys' boarding (with girls in sixth) to fully co-ed day was only just reaching completion. Outgoing, friendly and infectiously enthusiastic, he's a man on a mission. Knows all pupils by name, knows what's going on. 'I'm interested in every one of them,' he says. 'I hope they know that.' The friendly face of authority but not a soft touch. Rule break at your peril! Wife Mary Anne teaches maths and science to juniors (King's St Alban's) and takes Christian Union club. Two sons – one at King's, the other at university. Pet lurcher, Tess, rounds off family unit.

Academic Matters: Usually to be found in league tables' top 150. Selective though flexible intake with generous approach to lower entry exam marks if child excels in other areas. Much emphasis placed on 'unlocking potential' and pupils 'doing the best they possibly can'. Class size maximum 24 with setting introduced pre-GCSE in maths and English. May be more setting in future but not much as head believes it can be 'demoralising'. Overall performance good. GCSEs 97 per cent A*-C grades at last count, a small but steady rise over the years. A levels a couple of points short of 100 per cent passes (ICT letting the side down a bit). Maths and sciences (which can be done separately or as dual award) consistently good at both GCSE and A levels. Modern languages equally impressive – 100 per cent A*-C in French and German, Spanish coming up fast, now beating German in popularity but not in results yet. Geography shines in sixth, English lang and lit good to average. Interesting observation by head. 'The shelf life of GCSEs and A levels is very short,' he says, their main use being to secure university places. 'It's our responsibility to produce people who can work in teams, manage themselves, take responsibility, who can lead and who are well-balanced.'

Great choice of subjects includes drama, music, theatre studies and textiles. Classrooms bright, freshly painted and well organised with mixture of eyes-front and huddle teaching according to year group. Changeover from boarding to day school freed up loads more rooms giving lessons new lease of life and increasing year sizes. Science labs in typical 1960s block but labs themselves in process of updating, so far with great effect. Oddest, most inaccessible library you're likely to find. Housed in slightly spooky medieval gatehouse (like something out of Hogwarts) up wooden spiral staircase. That's all going to change in 2006 with a new £2m library which will be central to academic life and fully integrated with a very active careers department. Already well-stocked but move will make it more e-friendly putting bytes on more equal footing with books. Elsewhere computers much in evidence. Dedicated IT rooms as well as classroom provision. Specialist help for mild learning difficulties only.

Games, Options, The Arts: Awarded Sportsmark Gold in new millennium. Sport an important part of school life – but not an obsession, says head – with fine facilities like sports hall, fitness suite and 25-metre pool, also used by outside bodies. Games played once a week. Very competitive and successful – in particular the girls' rowing eights (national champions), an undefeated rugby XV, strong cricket and netball. Dance a popular activity among both boys and girls, apparently. Outstanding art – and lots of it. Might have been the unsung hero a few years ago but deservedly celebrated from the rooftops now. More A grades than any other at A level – in the 2005 Edexcel A level exams, 5 of the top 10 students in the country were from King's. Art school in separate building secreted behind red brick wall, but visitors discover a paint-splattered Aladdin's cave inside. Extremely high-quality work. Pupils and energetic staff ably assisted and inspired by artist in residence. Work shown off well in dining room, around school and in specially designed and lit gallery. A new art department is expected to open in 2007.

Much music, as you might expect at a choir school. 15 boy choristers boost ranks of cathedral choir (until voices break so most come from junior school). Over 100 musicians, three school orchestras (two pupils recently in National Youth Orchestra), two school choirs and a jazz band. Two school organs for pupils' use. Oxbridge organ and choral scholarships not unheard of. Flourishing drama department. Newish 310-seater theatre in frequent use for plays, concerts and big screen presentations. Plenty of opportunities for travel, home and abroad. School's own outdoor pursuits centre in the Black Mountains hugely popular; art and language students, historians and geographers also venture far and wide. National finalists in Young Enterprise Scheme. Very involved in local community (sixth formers help young readers at local primaries) and further afield (young Nepalese student sponsored through university). Extra-curricular can mean anything from chess club to climbing the Himalayas. The school day might not be long (8.30am to 3.50pm) but it's certainly packed. The school remains open and busy until 5.30pm each day.

Background and Atmosphere: Superb green setting under the watchful gaze of Worcester cathedral, founded in 1541 by Henry VIII after the suppression of the priory. Described by head as 'an oasis of calm' at heart of busy modern city. Oldest part is 14th century former monks' refectory now serving as vast and imposing assembly hall. Despite school's great age, no school motto (dismissed as fatuous by head). Closest it comes to one is Greek inscription (translated for us by classicist head) on heavy oak assembly table: 'I learn the things that can be taught; the things that can be discovered I seek, and the things that can be prayed for from the gods I pray for.' (Well, that just about covers all eventualities.) School could be said to be completely co-ed from July 1998 when first girls to arrive at 11 left after As. Now make up 43 per cent of pupil population. Despite hundreds of years of history and tradition, it feels refreshingly unpretentious and certainly doesn't tolerate self-indulgent navel-gazing. From early age, pupils encouraged to look beyond school gates, to try new things and help those less fortunate. Keen communicators internally and externally. Slightly stodgy and worthy annual school mag The Vigornian records the year's high points, regularly supplemented by a more upbeat 4-page bulletin, various newsletters, tabloid newspaper, The King's Herald (free) and countless activity leaflets. Much has changed since going all day (eg giving new arrivals in year 7 their

own building) with more changes (eg music school moved into refurbished house in 2003, leaving room for improved centralised library). King's underpinned by two junior schools – one right next door (King's St Alban's) shares senior school facilities; the other more recently acquired (King's Hawford) lies to north of city in country setting. Have own individual heads but Mr Keyes is supreme head.

Pastoral Care and Discipline: Pastoral care still run along boarding school lines. Based on old house system. Newcomers at 11 put into groups of 20-22 for first two years to make friendships and settling in easier. For remaining five years pupils assigned to one of eight houses (around 75 per house) with five tutors per house responsible for pastoral issues (staff paid extra to take on this role). Sixth formers volunteer to act as 'mentors' for youngest pupils. An active school council and pupils also have voice through elected monitors. Also sit on food and uniform committees. Pretty hot on rules. Suspension for smoking and drinking (even in Worcester city centre). Drugs more complicated. Automatic expulsion for dealing, final warning for using. 'We are very tough when we have to be,' admits head. Best summed up as firm yet fair. Parents always contacted and consulted, particularly in rare cases of bullying. Daily matters of appearance, behaviour, punctuality and so on dealt with through system of coloured papers issued by staff which collectively give overview of pupils' activities.

Pupils and Parents: A fairly mixed bag. Reputation for old money but far more professionals and new money these days plus a number of strugglers. Enormously supportive. Annual fete or charity walk regularly raises tens of thousands. Prepared to travel some distance too since King's went day (Stratford, Birmingham and Evesham, to name but a few). Pupils appeared smart, interested but above all confident – from the youngest up. Well-mannered, not afraid to speak up, enthusiastic. 'We are not seen as having a mould,' says head. 'We turn out interestingly different characters.' OVs (Old Vigornians – they take their title from the Roman name for Worcester) include TV presenter Chris Tarrant and comedian Rik Mayall.

Entrance: Selective entry exam at 11 (qualifying for those coming up from the two junior schools, competitive for external candidates). 132 new places at 11. Own entry exam at 13 for 20 places. School looking for 40-50 per cent minimum pass but consider all-round performance and potential. About 20 places fall free each year in sixth – at least five Bs and two Cs needed at GCSE. Entry to junior schools also selective. Chorister voice trials held throughout the year. A good voice is not enough in itself to win school place.

Exit: At least 95 per cent to higher education with a few heading for Oxford and Cambridge. Medical studies perennially popular, as are art, drama and mechanical engineering. Very few losses post-GCSEs. No weeding-out policy to improve overall A level results.

Money Matters: Good crop of scholarships (worth up to a third tuition fees) up for grabs in the junior schools and at 11, 13 and 16. Include academic and music. Boy choristers awarded 50 per cent scholarships by cathedral to cover their time in the choir. Head says, 'the school will do its very best to make sure no chorister has to leave after that scholarship ends.' Limited bursaries available. Big appeal under way to make more funds available. Small discount for third and fourth siblings.

Remarks: Big enough to offer much, small enough to keep it personal. Individual choice and achievement count for a lot here with boys and girls given the right mix of guidance and freedom to discover their own strengths. There's a real feeling of relaxed respect among students and staff with co-operation seen as the key to reaching goals. 'It's quite simply a lovely school,' says one parent. Very well thought of locally (even by those who haven't got kids here) and much sought after. Book early.

KINGSTON GRAMMAR SCHOOL

70-72 London Road, Kingston Upon Thames, Surrey, KT2 6PY

Tel: 020 8546 5875
Fax: 020 8547 1499
E-mail: head@kingston-grammar.surrey.sch.uk
Website: www.kingston-grammar.surrey.sch.uk

• Pupils: 415 boys, 290 girls; all day • Ages: 10-18 • Size of sixth form: 95 boys, 75 girls • Non-denom • Fees: £3,595; £3,501 for prep form • Independent • Open days: September, October and November - or just ask

Headmaster: Since 1991, Mr Duncan Baxter MA (fifties). Read English at Oxford. Previously deputy head at Wycliffe College, Stonehouse. Married to a former teacher (his wife gets involved with school life and fund raising), they have two grown-up sons. Music is his great passion (he was a choral scholar at Oxford) and he goes to lots of concerts and opera, loves Italy where he holidays, and enjoys cricket, serious walking and writing. Polished and urbane, he knows how to work a room and makes the most of a number of celebrity connections to improve the school's profile and coffers. Not afraid to ruffle feathers for the greater good ('unbending,' says one parent) he is clear about his aims for the school and proud of his entrepreneurial streak. As the prime mover behind the school's 2005 £12.5 million redevelopment, he admits to feeling 'quite emotional' when the work was completed and opened by HM the Queen. 'It's been like a re-foundation of the school,' he says. He keeps in touch with school life by walking around the place and 'bumping into' pupils he'd like a word with. In the spirit of self-inspection within the school, he frequently visits lessons and runs departmental reviews. Parents impressed that they see him at all the school's events and say he is an impressive public speaker – clever and well prepared. Approachable – but scary when he needs to be. 'As a headmaster he's a great businessman,' said one mum. Respected rather than adored.

Academic Matters: Selective intake and good teaching equals impressive academic results across the board. In 2005, five KGS pupils were among the top five nationally in GCSE English, French and Spanish. 80+ per cent A/B at A level – 2 geography students were in the national top 10. Maths, history, geography, and biology attract most takers at A level – and an A/B at GCSE is required for entry to the A level course. 'The leap is too large otherwise,' says Mr B. 'but we do not cull those who don't make the grades. There would only ever be one or two pupils we would have a conversation with about this – and then not every year.' Over and above the usual A level offerings are politics and sports studies, with psychology and theatre studies recently introduced. Excellent ratios of pupils to staff in A level classes: one modern languages student said she regularly got 40 minutes one to one conversational practice with a native speaker teacher or assistant. Class sizes generally are not small – between 22 and 25. Not a crammer – academic standards are high but it's not a slog. Homework felt to be reasonable and well regulated.

Lessons we saw were full of action and pace – children were fully engaged in what they were doing. Some of the younger ones looked set to pop with excitement as they eagerly raised their hands to answer questions. Older pupils more restrained but no less involved. Extension classes for the gifted and talented; school is quick to spot and nurture talents in all areas – downside is that Miss Average and Master Plodder may not feel so special. Learning support staff on hand as necessary – currently 19 pupils have extra lessons. School says it can cater for dyslexia and dyspraxia – though one parent with some experience said the school's 'not interested' in any special needs: 'It's looking for the crème de la crème – and certainly doesn't want any 'xics' of any kind!' Others agree it's a place which loves its high-fliers – the scholars and sports internationals. Over 50 pupils speak English as a second language – but none has special help in school. Parents praise 'thorough' parent consultation interviews, lots of grade cards and 'extremely revealing' reports. High praise also for teaching staff across the board – generally considered an impressive bunch. Lots of male staff. Solid, long serving team.

Games, Options, The Arts: So much going on here, it could make you feel quite dizzy. Head is v keen that students fit in as much extra-curricular stuff as possible. 'If you manage your time well, you can fit in an awful lot,' he says. 'Pupils must get tired of hearing me say that if you want something done, ask a busy person. Generally our most successful academics have always been active elsewhere around the school too.' In practice you can't impose it, but tutors 'strongly encourage' at least one extracurricular activity.

A sporty school – especially successful nationally and internationally in rowing (Olympic gold medallist James Cracknell is an old boy) and hockey. Smart boathouse on the nearby Thames and fantastic pitches and other facilities at its 22 acre sports grounds off site (15 minute bus ride) in Thames Ditton; main sports are netball, soccer, cricket and tennis. Although everyone is encouraged to 'have a go', regular team places are hard won. Music strong and plentiful – about one third of pupils learn an instrument and there are more than 25 musical events each year: 'second to none' say parents. Music, drama and art departments are major beneficiaries of the school's new Performing Arts Centre – includes a recording studio, a 250-seat theatre and new art, design and technology facilities.

Extra-curricular activities (lunchtime and after school) are endless, 'and they are certainly not frightened of taking the children out and about,' says one mother. 'There are tons of trips – locally and abroad.' Stamina at a premium – mother of a committed hockey player says he would often not get home till 10pm and then start his homework. 'He loved the place though, so he didn't seem to mind,' she says. Another mum praises the way the school interests and entertains the children outside lesson time. 'My daughter is so involved with different things that she has no time or inclination to go and hang around the shopping centre,' she says with relief.

Background and Atmosphere: The school can trace its history back to the late middle ages and was endowed by Queen Elizabeth 1 in 1561. Was a boys' public school for many years, direct grant from 1926 until the late 1970s, when it became fully independent and began to take in girls.

Now truly co-ed, with no whiff of 'boys' school with girls.' Ultra-urban location beside the busy four-lane A308 into Kingston, close to good bus and rail links. Head cites accessibility as an asset – weigh that against the traffic and bustle of a busy town. Opposite Tiffin Boys (state grammar school qv), what barely passes as friendly rivalry is intense. Victorian frontage (offering the best aspect) belies the actual size of the much-extended school behind it – other parts having been added in the 1920s '50s and '90s. Expansion was restricted geographically rather than financially until the school acquired land next door and built the mega impressive glass-fronted, high tech new building that increases the school's size by a third. Despite extra space, pupil numbers will not rise above 780 – Mr B cites the school's medium size as one of its defining features and would be loathe to lose its 'intimate feel – a bit like a boarding school but without the sleeping.'

KGS is a traditional place, but not stuffy, and it has a modern edge. Definitely a happy atmosphere – camaraderie abounds. Spacious and well kept – classrooms and corridors lined with good displays. Lovely sixth form facilities include common room, study room and cafeteria. Outdoors less lovely – but pupils are encouraged to get out into the playgrounds for fresh air. Only sixth form allowed offsite at lunchtime. School lunch compulsory for prep and first years (Y7) after that packed lunches are allowed. Pupils are cheerful, and appear confident as they move around in a polite and courteous way. All wear conventional smart uniform and hair must be 'natural'. Sixth formers wear business suits. Things loosen up a bit for sixth formers – but essentially they remain in a 'school environment'.

Pastoral Care and Discipline: Pastoral care generally considered 'good': form tutors deal with day-to-day issues. Good relationships between junior and senior pupils. Very strong house system with lots of inter-house competitions. 'It's quite tribal in a healthy way,' says Mr B. Much responsibility given to these older pupils who run the houses and organise school productions for the lower years, as well as being generally available in a well-run mentoring system. School operates a policy of 'firm reasonableness': read this as 'no-nonsense'. Standards and boundaries are clearly laid out and largely adhered to. Absolutely no smoking (anyone brave enough to try will be fined £25 for Cancer Research). Hierarchical system of prefects under the headship of the school captain and deputies – and it is taken seriously. Bullying dealt with 'pretty severely' – while acknowledging it can happen anywhere, head believes that the co-ed feel of the place tends to defuse the intensity.

Pupils and Parents: Most are reasonably local – 50 per cent live within 2 1/2 miles, others commute from south west London and Surrey: a fair mix of social and cultural backgrounds. Parents mainly professional (business, finance, arts/media) and apparently a friendly lot – more involved with each other and the school than is usual at secondary level. 'I've made really good friends here,' says one mother. 'The staff are very good at introducing us to each other and the many events are good social occasions.'

Entrance: Local reputation as 'hard to get in'. School's own written exams in maths, English and reasoning. Those likely to be offered a place plus borderline cases will be invited for interview ('We try to look at them in the round – borderline interviews are often the most interesting', says Mr B. 'We're looking for copeability and potential'). Entry at 10+ (25 taken for one prep form); majority join at 11+ (four-form intake). Common Entrance at 13+. V bright intake from around 20 local schools and no preference for siblings. Increasing popularity: more than 3,000 attended one open evening. Entrants to sixth form will be told at interview what GCSEs they need – generally A/A* .

Exit: At 16 a chunk – approx 20 per cent – leave, usually for a sixth form college. Mr B says many move for financial reasons, others to find a subject not offered at KGS or because they like the sound of a 'college environment.' At 18+ pretty much all to university – lots of redbricks plus half a dozen to Oxbridge.

Money Matters: Scholarships for academic work, music, sport and art. Means-tested bursaries (worth 25 per cent of fees). Otherwise be prepared to cough up regularly on top of fees – all the sport and foreign travel does not come cheap. 'I would always recommend the school - but it was a costly experience,' said a parent who put two children through.

Remarks: An academic school with a modern edge and determined head. A great school for do-ers who get involved over and above academic studies. A 'swim or sink' place.

THE LADY ELEANOR HOLLES SCHOOL

Linked to Lady Eleanor Holles School, Junior Department (The) in the Junior section

Hanworth Road, Hampton, Middlesex, TW12 3HF

Tel: 020 8979 1601
Fax: 020 8941 8291
E-mail: office@lehs.org.uk
Website: www.lehs.org.uk

- Pupils: 880 girls; all day • Ages: 7-18 • Size of sixth form: 190
- C of E • Fees: Senior £3,401; junior £2,565 • Independent
- Open days: Contact the Registrar

Head: Since 2004, Mrs Gillian Low MA Oxon PGCE Cantab (mid forties) formerly head of Francis Holland NW1. Educated at North London Collegiate School, read English at Oxford, taught at various comprehensive schools, former deputy head of Godolphin and Latymer School. Approachable, down-to-earth. 'She's very warm and caring,' said a FH parent. Another commented that she will deal immediately with any concerns. Three children, all at independent schools.

Academic Matters: Undoubtedly, one of the top academic schools in the country. As one parent says, 'given the high level of intake, exam results ought to be good and they are.' Typical pass rate of 100 per cent A*-C at GCSE, with over 90 per cent of these at A*/A grades. Separate sciences more popular than the double award. Latin is popular. General studies compulsory for A level and average points per candidate including this subject is around 34; excluding this subject it is 26. About 70 per cent of grades are A at A level, with English literature, mathematics, biology and psychology being the most popular subjects. Not many do art and few do music but those who do obtain top grades. A parent says that great efforts are made to accommodate unusual combinations of subjects. In spite of terrific results (and probably because the school is an academic front runner), last head had no truck whatsoever with league tables. Clearly there is some exceptional teaching but one parent said that 'pupils do complain that some of the older teachers bore them rigid.' Not a school for slackers. A parent sums up academic life – 'pupils and staff have high expectations of their academic achievements and though it is not cool to be seen to work hard, a great deal of hard work goes on. Most pupils take this in their stride but it must be hard for the ones at the bottom of the class.'

Games, Options, The Arts: Great rowing school – the Millennium Boat House (opened by Sir Steve Redgrave) was a joint project with neighbouring Hampton School, enabling 80 boats to be stored; balcony with far-reaching views over the Thames at Sunbury, 'it would be the envy of any professional rowing club,' says one appreciative parent. For winter, there is lacrosse (lacrosse teacher plays for England, and three girls have recently played in the England squad) and netball (netball teacher played for England in Commonwealth Games 2002) and in the summer, athletics, tennis and rounders. Usual complaint from parents that sports are played to win and 'once the teams are picked, there is not much chance for the rest to represent the school.' Swimming in on-site heated pool. Fencing optional. Splendid new sports hall and trampolining especially popular. No compulsory PE in sixth form but options broaden to include other activities such as Real Tennis at Hampton Court, aerobics, jazz dancing and use of the climbing wall at Hampton School. Recent sports tours have been to the US and Australia.

Dedicated art block enjoys great natural light and shows high quality work. 'Art is done to a very high standard with some fabulous artwork up on the walls,' confirms an impressed parent. Good music – 350 girls have individual music tuition, a considerable number attaining grade 8, with wide variety of choice available. Instruments can be safely left at school. Lots of ensembles, orchestras and choirs. 'The pupil has to be keen,' says a parent, 'no one tells you to go to the practices.' Annual choral and orchestral concert with the boys at Hampton School. Speech and drama is optional extra and annual drama festival of plays by sixth formers (with participation from throughout the school) held with Hampton. Lots of clubs from Scrabble to Amnesty International. Young Enterprise groups in sixth form and CCF.

Background and Atmosphere: School dates from 1711, when it was established in the Cripplegate Ward of the City of London. Moved to Hackney in 1878 and then to its present site in 1936. It has to be said that the main building is not an aesthetic gem by any stretch of imagination, unless one has a special passion for the functional 1930s early Gaumont style, but art historians may appreciate the touches of art deco here and there. Set in the heart of suburbia in largely terra incognita for public transport – shares large school bus network with Hampton School, which means that those keen on after school activities may have a tricky and time-consuming journey home. 'Advantage is that at the end of the day the girls go home, so you don't see any

sign of bored teenagers hanging around the school gates,' says a parent. Not that these girls would fall into the bored teenagers category – they are too busy working and doing after school activities.

Has a huge (for outer London standards) thirty acre site, which includes gardens, playing fields and many, mostly modern, additions to the original building. Of particular note is the splendid sixth form centre, which has its own library and where sixth form lessons are taken in most subjects, using small seminar rooms. Both upper and lower sixth have their own well-equipped and comfortable common rooms. The school's 'Statement of Purpose' reflects one of the earliest documents relating to the school. It aims (among other things) 'to produce young women of grace and integrity,' 'which', sighed the previous head, characteristically, 'can occasionally require nothing short of a miracle.' Very much a grammar school feel to the place, although it has never been a state school. The uniform is distinctly understated, being mostly grey, with flashes of cherry red; many skirts considerably above the knee and lots of chunky shoes in sight. In fact, the pupils are surprisingly a bit on the scruffy side – in some ways rather endearing – a change from all those prissy, not above the knee, hair tied back, bags must be black, girls' private schools. No uniform for sixth form – required to dress 'suitably'. Sixth formers can also bring their cars into school and park in their dedicated car park. Security is tight, all girls have swipe cards to gain access to site and buildings. Many parents appreciate the easy relationship with Hampton boys' school next door, 'it's a great leveller. If any LEH girls show signs of getting up themselves (as teenagers quaintly put it), the Hampton boys soon bring them down to earth,' says one parent.

Pastoral Care and Discipline: One mother says, 'I find the staff very considerate and open, with genuine kindness.' Another says: 'Staff are very highly motivated and get the best out of the girls and many of them are great characters.' The girls stay in the same form groups throughout the school until they enter the lower sixth, with four forms of around 24 girls each with a form tutor and deputy, although the tutors tend to change every other year. 14 tutor groups in the sixth form. The girls are bright and confident and a parent says that any trouble is soon nipped in the bud. The school encourages independence and self reliance from day 1 -'could be a bit daunting for new pupils who are having trouble adjusting to life in a big new secondary school,' says one parent. School counsellor available. Sixth formers can leave premises at lunchtime (some have driving lessons then) and invite Hampton boys into their common rooms (arrangement is reciprocal).

Pupils and Parents: Intake is mainly suburban, middle class from professional and middle management families; many first time buyers. Increasing numbers from the London postal districts but otherwise from Guildford, Esher, Richmond, Twickenham, Walton, Windsor and Weybridge. 'Definitely not a snobby school,' says a parent, 'you do not get the impression that parents are likely to show off their money – there aren't really any opportunities to do so.' Famous OGs include actresses Charlotte Attenborough and Saskia Reeves.

Entrance: By interview and examination at 11 in maths, English and a general paper. Over-subscribed and some girls do get dropped at interview stage. Intake is 100, around a third of whom enter from the junior school, via exam, but transfer not automatic. The rest tend to come from a wide selection of private preps including Newland House, Twickenham; Rowan, Claygate; Old Vicarage, Richmond; Bute House, Hammersmith and Queens Junior School, Kew; about 20 per cent from state primaries. £50 application fee and £500 reservation fee (refundable on completion of studies). At 16, entrance is by comprehension and analysis, maths and modern language(s) if appropriate, required standard at GCSE and satisfactory school report. About 8 or 10 places at sixth form level available to replace those who leave (see Exit). Registration should be by 1 November for entry to sixth form in following autumn term.

Exit: Virtually everyone to university – Oxford, Cambridge, Bristol and Leeds recently the favourites. Those who leave after GCSE tend to go to co-ed independent schools such as Westminster, Marlborough, Wellington or Charterhouse, or to sixth form colleges.

Money Matters: A few entrance bursaries are available for 11, based on the results of the entrance exam. A small number of scholarships for excellence in music or academic subjects. Some sixth form scholarships of up to 25 per cent of fees for the two year course - these are awarded on basis of performance in entrance exam.

Remarks: Top-notch academic, highly sought-after, girls' day school, run adeptly by a redoubtable head. Forget private tutoring for borderline candidates, academic expectations are high and it would not be a lot of fun struggling at the bottom of the lowest sets – choose somewhere else. Probably best suited to the outgoing, self-reliant type; the wilting wallflower and those in need of the gentle touch might find it hard to find their feet (and survive) unless they already have a talent to offer, for example, in music or sport. As one mother says, 'it's a "go for it" school for a "go for it" child.'

LADY LUMLEY'S SCHOOL

Swainsea Lane, Pickering, North Yorkshire, YO18 8NG

Tel: 01751 472 846

Fax: 01751 477 259

E-mail: admin@ladylumleys.freeserve.co.uk

Website: www.ladylumleys.org

• Pupils: 997 boys and girls • Ages: 11-19 • Size of sixth form: 225 • Non-denom • State

Head: Since 2003, John Tomsett (fortyish). Former deputy head at Huntington School in York; before that, director of sixth form at Hove Park School in Sussex. Wife also teaches. Two young sons. Warm, approachable; main aim, 'to inspire everyone in our school community with a love of learning and, by doing so, maximise their life chances.'

Academic Matters: Good GCSE and A level performances. No prima donna departments here – school claims its strength is quality of teaching across the whole curriculum especially at Key Stage 4, and Ofsted largely backs that up. Strongest performances consistently in the basics – English, maths and science. Able linguists given the option of taking GCSE French a year early, with German to follow in year two. Early results impressive.

School also does well by less academic pupils – 15 and 16 year-olds can take a double GCSE in engineering, studying partly off-site with engineering firms. Others opt for GCSE health and social care, drawing on links with GPs and hospitals – would-be paramedics, chiropodists etc please note. Vocational path can continue into sixth form with packages including modern apprenticeships. Students encouraged to pick and mix, customising education to boost chances of achieving career goals. Strong, award-winning careers education and guidance, and work experience programmes.

Games, Options, The Arts: Very strong sports department. Extensive sports facilities in glorious rural setting. New fitness suite and floodlit all-weather pitch used by pupils and local sports clubs with benefits to both. Sports hall, gym, learner pool, good athletics facilities, all helping to encourage all-round sporting achievements. Drama taught in every year group and those with a musical interest can join the orchestras and choirs. All the usual extra-curricular clubs and societies too but pupils have to risk indigestion to join. One downside of a sprawling catchment area is that buses whisk pupils away at the final bell. Makes for busy lunchtimes with sports practices, science clubs, revision workshops and even dreaded detentions all competing with the butties.

Background and Atmosphere: Set on the edge of the market town of Pickering, Lady Lumley's is a mix of every architectural style over five decades. Built in the fifties, the older buildings are offset by a new £1m+ administration block, sixth form and community learning centre which should soon also incorporate a conference centre for use by school and community. Besides, who couldn't live with a bit of dodgy fifties architecture when the view is of sweeping school grounds framed by countryside with even the puff of an old steam railway in the distance? Good disabled access, including lifts.

Biggest surprise? Classroom doors are left open during lessons and all you can hear in the corridors is the teacher's voice. And the orderly cloakrooms are full of children's coats and bags. In how many comprehensives would pupils leave their bags unattended on a peg? Even the morning rush into school is orderly. No school-run congestion because of the buses and an uncanny absence of the teenage sillies.

Pastoral Care and Discipline: A no-nonsense school which sets high standards and expects pupils to meet them. 'It irons out problems before they escalate,' said one parent, which seems, to use a third metaphor, to hit the nail on the head. Unacceptable behaviour is dealt with quickly and efficiently. Students are given 'cool off' time which can include that most excruciating of all punishments – writing a letter of apology.

School policy to keep children busy, in and out of lessons, and 'treat them like human beings', giving them the courtesy of decent catering, clean toilets and graffiti-free walls. Strong on caring and community, and rolls up its sleeves to practise what it preaches. School still collects food to make into harvest festival parcels and gets pupils to deliver them to nominated neighbours over many miles. One of a dying breed, we suspect.

Pastoral care boosted considerably by Lady Lumley's Education Foundation, named after its founder, an Elizabethan landowner. Her bequests to the school mean that it can still spend upwards of £20,000 a year on pupil support, from subsidising trips to encouraging pupils' projects. A very nice carrot indeed.

Pupils and Parents: A true comprehensive drawing from an area of affluent professionals and farming communities. Lots of the Range Rover set but also its fair share of children from disadvantaged homes. Good rapport with parents who receive a report in every term of every year. Pupils' progress tightly monitored with regular tutorials. No hiding

place here. Parents talk of a happy school and are pleased with children's achievements.

Entrance: Living in the catchment area is the only way to be sure of a place. A whopping 22 per cent of pupils come from further afield after winning appeals, but if your heart's set on Lady Lumley's you might have to move house to get in. People do.

Exit: Almost 60 per cent of pupils stay on into the sixth form, expected to increase as vocational courses expand. Around 85 per cent of sixth formers go to university.

Remarks: A solid school which feels part of the community it serves. Letter just received from newly qualified graduate thanks school for giving out-of-class tuition to him and others who needed that extra push. 'It has made all the difference to my future. You made me feel I was somebody and I could achieve my goals,' he writes. Says it all.

LADY MARGARET SCHOOL

Parson's Green, London, SW6 4UN

Tel: 020 7736 7138
Fax: 020 7384 2553
E-mail: admin@ladymargaret.lbhf.sch.uk
Website: www.ladymargaret.lbhf.sch.uk

• Pupils: 586 girls; all day • Ages: 11-18 • Size of sixth form: 130 • C of E • State • Open days: First fortnight in October

Headmistress: Since 1984, Mrs Joan Olivier BA (sixties). Came from Camden Girls as deputy in 1973. State educated, read history at London and did her postgraduate work at Cambridge. Splendidly vocal lady, totally open-door policy, wedded to the school. 'I love it here, I say: why should I want to move?' – to possible poachers. Cheerful, positive, liberal with praise, also firm in rebuke where necessary. Husband worked in the city, own son at university. Insists on bright colours on the walls, flowers in the hall etc. 'People think it's rather odd, but I tell them that if you give children a bright environment, they'll be proud of it and won't wreck the place.'

Retiring in July 2006.

Academic Matters: Rigorous teaching and expectations. Traditional approach. Several staff with both private and state school experience who are exceptionally committed. Homework from one hour per night from the start. Class sizes variable. French and Spanish options. Offers music at both GCSE and A level – music is a great strength of the school. Does excellently at GCSEs and at A level – top in the nation's comprehensives for A* and A grades in 2004 – 97 per cent A*-C, 74 per cent As and Bs at A level and 6 Oxbridge places. Good and well-used library. Brand new ICT facilities.

Games, Options, The Arts: Imaginative drama. Sixth form put on their own ambitious productions. Loads of outings and trips, sleep-overs in the school, special leavers breakfast. Netball/tennis courts on site, energetic sport matches programme. Good art (good uptake at A level); signs of embryonic fashion designers in evidence.

Background and Atmosphere: School has its origins in Whitelands College School, founded in 1842, threatened with closure in 1917 and rescued by Miss Enid Moberly Bell and other staff to become Lady Margaret in 1917. Elegant Georgian bow-windowed mansion with the Green in front and gardens behind, plus modern gym, hall, etc. Super design and technology building (for which the school energetically raised vast sums). Moral values and caring aspect breed deep loyalty and a distinctly happy atmosphere, much commented on by parents and staff. Feels like a private school and very much run along those lines. Even girls who might be disaffected elsewhere are warm in their praise.

Pastoral Care and Discipline: High marks for discipline. 'This is a Church school,' says the head firmly. Truancy is negligible. Uniform standards upheld. No drug related incidents.

Pupils and Parents: A big mix, including a handful of very keenly involved parents. Some brilliant fund raisers. Some refugees from the private sector, more middle-class professionals than many state schools. Girls are polite, articulate and fiercely supportive of each other.

Entrance: Incredibly difficult and no flexibility – parents wring their hands and ask what must they do to get children in. Accepts 50 Anglican girls (letters from vicars needed) and 40 others: from eight boroughs – including Ealing, Barnes, Wandsworth. No preference to siblings. 600 children tested in December (maths, English) to ensure a mixed ability intake.' Five GCSEs at B or above usually required for entry at sixth form level (some departments require A or A*).

Exit: Some always leave post-GCSE, but the majority stay on for A level, and are joined by pupils from other schools. Almost all go on to university.

Money Matters: State-funded. Parents regularly raise money for the school. Head keen on boosting coffers by letting school for Weight Watchers, weddings etc.

Remarks: Super successful state girls' school, with a well-deserved reputation for being a nice, caring place under an exceptional head.

LANCASTER GIRLS' GRAMMAR SCHOOL

Regent Street, Lancaster, Lancashire, LA1 1SF

Tel: 01524 320 10

Fax: 01524 846 220

E-mail: lggs@kencomp.net

Website: www.lancastergirlsgrammar.lancs.sch.uk

• Pupils: 890 girls, all day • Ages: 11-18 • Size of sixth form: 325 • Non-denom • State

Head: Since 1987, Mrs Pam Barber BA (fifties); read modern languages at NW Poly, taught in Bradford girls' comprehensive, then deputy at two Halifax schools. Easily in charge after 19 years, a strong hands-on presence around the place and all staff call her Pam. Forthright, what you see is what you get; keeps open door for pupils and staff. Plenty of style but no side. Lives outside Lancaster, keeps horses and donkeys (used to show jump), drives smart Mercedes two-seater. Loves travel, goes on many school trips abroad, eg to Peru.

Academic Matters: Very sound, regularly in top five per cent of national state school results. First para in distinctly unglossy prospectus says '[the school] provides a centre of learning dedicated to encouraging quality and excellence...where hard work and commitment are a part of everyday life'. Strong languages (French, German, Spanish), no classics. Dual award science at GCSE seems no brake on popularity of science and engineering at university (many girls do these). A level A+B averages over 70 per cent (bumper year in 2004); maths and history consistently good; very few Ds and Es generally. Media studies and psychology popular (latter taken by weaker girls?). Marked technology emphasis (specialist status since 1995); sponsorship and collaborative projects with BAe Systems, enviable technology and IT teaching provision.

High computer count, interactive whiteboards everywhere. DfES Leading Edge school since 2003. Able staff (one third men), most appointed by Mrs Barber; age profile creeping upwards – they don't want to leave and you can see why.

Games, Options, The Arts: Sports fields 5-10 minutes away from school. Astroturf pitch and Mrs Barber would like a sports hall – but where to put it? Sport is important, and keenly played, especially hockey and running (representative successes). Much variety beyond these, including rugby, fencing and swimming in the local boys' school pool. Music strong and multi-form, many joint ventures with boys' school; also drama and public speaking. Lots of overseas visits and exchanges; a current EU Comenius project, shared with European schools, is centred on CERN in Switzerland. Links with schools all over, eg Madagascar and India. Serious community involvement in Lancaster.

Background and Atmosphere: Founded nearly 100 years ago on central site, surrounded by private houses. Despite ingenious use of limited space, and a thoroughgoing 1990s rebuilding programme, the overall impression is inevitably cramped. But there is a clear sense of purpose and busyness as the cheerfully confident girls go about their day. Chatter in the stylish art deco dining hall is deafening. It's not easy to get into this school and pupils are obviously proud to be there. Atmosphere is relaxed but not lax; staff expect old-fashioned standards of behaviour, and trust and respect between them and pupils is evident. School was GM, now has Foundation status, which allows a degree of control over its destiny, including (vitally) academic selection. This comfortable relationship with the LEA may or may not continue.

Pastoral Care and Discipline: Usual form tutor system, backed up by year heads, works well. 'There are hardly any rules,' says head, 'they know what standards are expected.' She thinks it is 13 years since she expelled anyone. Lancaster isn't the outback, but it's hardly Leeds or Bradford either, and the school can count on solid parental support plus a good dollop of pupil common sense.

Pupils and Parents: For the most part, straightforward girls who are keen to get on and to do their bit for society. Wide range of parental backgrounds, not surprising in middle-size county town. Selection and history confer prestige, northern good sense prevails, hence a strong sense of identity and unity of purpose.

Entrance: Heavily oversubscribed at 11+ (3 to 1). Admission (November exam) is 'according to ability and aptitude', ie you have to be pretty bright to stand a chance; by test, primary school record and headteacher's report. First chance goes to inhabitants of Lancaster and surrounding parishes (list available from school), then residual places to families living outside these. Sisters of existing pupils looked on favourably. Up to one third of post-GCSE year group has entered from other schools – minimum qualification five or more GCSEs at C or better.

Exit: A very few leave after GCSE; nearly all go on to higher education, 6-10 annually to Oxbridge.

Remarks: Confident, sought after and successful state grammar school, taking the pick of local catchment area and doing well by them. Led by experienced and visionary head.

LANCASTER ROYAL GRAMMAR SCHOOL

East Road, Lancaster, Lancashire, LA1 3EF

Tel: 01524 580 600
Fax: 01524 847 947
E-mail: genoffice@lrgs.org.uk
Website: www.lrgs.org.uk

• Pupils: 1,000 boys, including 170 boarders • Ages: 11-18
• Size of sixth form: 300 • Christian foundation • Fees: £2,100 boarding fee • State • Open days: A Saturday in September and otherwise by appointment

Head: Since 2001, Mr Andrew Jarman MA (mid-forties). Read maths at Oxford, taught at Aylesbury Grammar , Portsmouth Grammar, Haberdashers', Cheltenham College (Director of Studies). Followed Mr Peter Mawby, revered head for 18 years. Wife Kerstin runs an INSET consultancy. They have twins (13), one of them at the school, and an 11-year-old. Energetic, bags of unaffected charm, voluble, strides around the place with evident pride and pleasure – 'I always like to have a building site somewhere'. Sees himself leading by example, while keeping his fingers on all the buttons. Aided by capable and experienced senior management team, most appointed by him. Good cricketer and golfer, lists 'family' among his interests.

Academic Matters: Superb tradition – regularly near top of table for state grammars, strong value-added results. Aiming high taken for granted, as is the graft to support it. Very much the traditional grammar school ethos, challenging boys to 'fulfil their potential in a competitive environment'. Narrow ability range, so no setting (except maths) up to GCSE; class size averages 28. Maths outstanding, stronger classics than in most independents. All do technology up to GCSE; school has had Technology College status since 1995. Sciences separately taught up to dual award and all three are popular sixth form options. Modern languages not quite up to exalted standards of the rest recently, but climbing. A few special needs pupils (eg Asperger's) looked after in house. The especially gifted (also classed as 'special needs') are stretched by enhancement schemes and wide-ranging extra-curricular provision.

Games, Options, The Arts: Strong rugby and cricket, taken seriously – they beat most independents, go on frequent foreign tours. An impressive list of other sports, including rowing on the Lune, and plenty of outdoor pursuits in nearby Lake District. Much encouragement to join in; couch potatoes don't seem to figure. Music popular, regular drama productions (often with sister school in Lancaster). Very good art and design results.

Background and Atmosphere: An ancient foundation, 'in existence by 1235' and endowed in 1472. Now has voluntary aided status. Buildings extend on both sides of hilly East Road; mixture of Victorian houses and purpose-built blocks, leading to impressive recent additions (science and business/design centres, junior boarding house). Boys scuttle purposefully between classrooms which range from slightly tired looking to smartly refurbished. Though the school in most ways resembles its independent competitors, it differs in that there isn't much money to do the things that the private sector usually takes for granted. It doesn't matter, of course, since the school concentrates on the important transaction of the classroom but it does mean the place can look a touch untidy at the edges. Older parents will be reminded of the grammar school of their youth; 'no-nonsense, no-frills', says one successful and grateful old boy. Prospectus has more print and fewer pictures than home counties counterparts; southern incomers may find this quaint, Lancastrians probably don't worry about it.

Boarding gives the school an edge and identity. Mr Jarman, a grammar school boy who spent formative years at Cheltenham, is a great enthusiast, keeps closely in touch with boarding staff. Younger boys have splendid new house (2001); middle school pupils sleep in large rooms under the eaves punctuated by stable-like partitions. These are due for replacement, which will probably please parents and annoy their conservative sons. Seniors have pretty comfortable single studies. Weekly boarding is popular. A new senior boarding house is planned for 2007/08.

Pastoral Care and Discipline: Thoroughgoing systems for boarding and day work well; pastoral staff heavily committed to pupils' welfare and relations between boys and teachers admired by parents and inspectors. High personal standards expected. Not much evidence of real wickedness; Mr Jarman suspends for possession – and would expel for dealing – and the boys know it.

Pupils and Parents: Local day boys given preference; after them about 60 places go to those further afield; brothers and family connections considered. Boarders come from all over but must be a UK subject or have an EU passport and a UK guardian. Boys and parents very proud of school and its regional standing (juniors love wearing blazer and tie, says Mr Jarman). Parents are easily persuaded to contribute regularly to the development programme – not a burden, given free day education and bargain boarding fees.

Old boys include Prof T Hugh Pennington, microbiologist; Kevin Roberts, CEO Worldwide Saatchi & Saatchi; James Crosby, CE HBOS plc; Jason Queally, Olympic and Commonwealth cycling champion; Brigadier Alex Birtwistle (foot and mouth star); Tom Sutcliffe (journalist) and Sir Richard Owen (dinosaur man).

Entrance: By oversubscribed competitive exam at 11 (English/maths/VR). Boarders have separate test but all 'must be of an aptitude and ability suited to an academic curriculum'. Regular increasing intake at 16, popular for boarders.

Exit: A few leave after GCSE; vast majority to good universities, mainly in the midlands and north. 10-15 annually to Oxbridge.

Remarks: Buoyant selective grammar school with big reputation in the region, has managed to retain marked degree of independence within maintained system. Unashamedly academic but takes all-round education seriously and delivers it.

LANCING COLLEGE

Linked to Mowden School

Lancing, West Sussex, BN15 0RW

Tel: 01273 452 213
Fax: 01273 464 720
E-mail: admissions@lancing.dialnet.com
Website: www.lancingcollege.org.uk

• Pupils: 471: 340 boys, 205 board; 131 girls, 85 board • Ages: 13-18 • Size of sixth form: 211 (68 girls) • C of E • Fees: Boarding £6,550, day £4,555 • Independent • Open days: September, October, May. November for Mowden. Visits welcome throughout year

---

Head Master: Interregnum. Mr Peter Tinniswood (head since 1998)was due to retire in July 2006, but has gone earlier on health grounds.

Academic Matters: Not an academic hothouse but nevertheless, very respectable results with around 30 per cent of grades being A* and over 97 per cent A to C grades at GCSE. More than 40 per cent of A level grades are As.

In the lower school, children are placed in sets for some subjects according to ability and performance in entrance exam. Separate science subjects, subsequently either dual or single award sciences available. Good range of languages. Pupils choose between Latin or classical civilisation, together with French, then choice of one from German, classical Greek and Spanish. Divinity compulsory and includes personal, health and social education, together with comparative religion. Very impressive DT provision. Great new library building with good, up-to-date stock.

Pupils take between eight and twelve GCSEs. 'Clinics' held twice a week by subject tutor for pupils to catch up or seek clarification. Unusual subjects available at GCSE include Italian, Greek and occasionally astronomy. No home economics at GCSE available as yet. Lower sixth students are expected to select 4 AS levels, most reducing to 3 A2s in the upper sixth. In the lower school, average class size 11, with maximum of 23; for AS/A level 9 and 15 respectively. About one third of staff is female.

Games, Options, The Arts: Very strong on music with a choir that periodically tours Europe. Annual concert by candlelight with the chapel full to capacity – a sight to behold. Christmas carols often broadcast on TV and pupils able to use wonderful chapel organ. At any one time about 150 pupils learning at least one instrument.

Very sporty school with extensive playing fields. However, die-hard rugby fanatics beware – rugby is played at Lancing and the school has London and South-East rugby squad members, but ' football and hockey are the major team sports for boys.' School has football players in the Public Schools squad and pupils have recently won the Sussex Youth Cricketer of the Year competition in their appropriate age groups. Sporty souls also take part in national events in various disciplines including swimming, riding and ball sports. Refreshing to see a girls' football team with inter-school matches. Recent sports tours to Hong Kong and Holland and USA. School has traditional links with Kamazu Academy in Malawi and there are trips there every other year.

Debates held once a week in old library – great success at local competition level. Two former head girls have been President of the Oxford Union in recent years. Excellent drama provision with more than 12 productions annually both in the indoor (seats 200) and open-air theatre. Musicals performed every other year. Sailing on River Adur, clay pigeon shooting and conservation projects also on offer. Head says, 'the emphasis at Lancing is on breadth of experience,' – the hugely popular school farm underlines this. Areas of the farm which are not cultivated support livestock raised by pupils (great enthusiasm at lambing time) and life down on the farm encourages steady trickle of pupils who go on to become vets.

Background and Atmosphere: Enviable location high on the Sussex Downs overlooking the sea in 550 acres, which commands superb views of the River Adur estuary and surrounding area of outstanding natural beauty. Can be very windswept in winter but glorious on sunny day. Some lovely flint-knapped buildings and quadrangles. Huge chapel (largest school chapel in the world and open to the public) of the upturned-pig school of architecture – you either love it or hate it – with stunning interior that should lift up the heart of the most hardened atheist. School founded by Revd Nathaniel Woodard in 1848 – his tomb is in the chapel. The Woodard Corporation is now the largest group of independent schools in England and Wales with Lancing as its senior school.

Girls' accommodation in modern houses, very homely. Boys' accommodation not so good but quality increases as boys get older. Some boarders share their room with a day pupil, who uses the room as a base. No weekly boarding as such (ie no reduction in full fees) but pupils able to go home for weekend from Saturday lunch-time onwards if they wish.

Fully co-ed since 2000, the sixth form has been co-ed for 30 years. Girls now comprise about 30 per cent and they fit in well – the school does not feel macho and laddish, a common teething problem when boys' schools initially venture into co-education. Numbers healthier than in recent years. Since 2002 Mowden School, a prep school in Hove, has been the junior school for the College.

Pastoral Care and Discipline: According to one mother, 'the high standard of pastoral care is one of the school's main attributes'. House system very strong but does not mean that pupils are isolated in their own houses; much inter-house activity and friendship. Integration of day pupils with boarders encouraged by sharing rooms during the day. Pupils choose their own tutor after the first year (to give them time to make up their minds). Inevitably, some tutors more in demand than others but, thankfully, the popular ones take on all-comers. Counselling available from school counsellor if required and peer-support group run by pupils with help from staff. School rules clearly defined in The Pupil's Charter, given to all new pupils. Compulsory attendance at chapel but faiths other than C of E welcomed. Bullying and drugs dealt with severely and generally not a problem. Pupils neatly decked out, although the uniform regs are not that strict; girls will need a Lancing cloak in the winter. Noticeably relaxed and warm atmosphere.

Pupils and Parents: Mainly from south east, with about 15 per cent from overseas – Europe, Hong Kong, mainland China and eastern Europe. A 'significant minority' of ex-pats. New school transport services from Horsham, Brighton, Hove and Lewes has widened the day catchment area. Parents mainly local business people, professional, financiers and academics, with some commuters but, as one parent says, 'well away from the pushy, yuppie London types.' Pupils from many prep schools in the area and, now, Mowden School. OBs: playwrights David Hare, Christopher Hampton and Giles Cooper, lyricist Sir Tim Rice, novelists Tom Sharpe and Evelyn Waugh (headmaster at pains to point out that Waugh's 'Decline and Fall' is not based on Lancing), Shakespeare scholar and writer John Dover Wilson, singer Peter Pears, Archbishop Trevor Huddleston and TV 'yoof' presenter Jamie Theakston. 'Not a snobby school,' says one parent.

Entrance: By CE. Pass mark 50 per cent. Pupils from state sector separately assessed. For entry into the sixth form, outsiders need a satisfactory reference from present school, good GCSE results and they undergo interviews, a verbal reasoning test and have to produce an essay on their interests and aspirations.

Exit: Oxbridge popular as well as Nottingham and other redbrick universities. A couple every year to art or agricultural college.

Money Matters: Small number of smallish continuation scholarships available to age 11s whose parents intend to send them to Lancing at 13. Around 23 awards annually up to 50 per cent of annual fees - includes two for families of clergymen and one for a naval family. Limited number of bursaries for children whose parents are serving members of the Services. All awards can be augmented up to a maximum of two thirds of the full fees, depending on family circumstances. Special awards for music and art. About four awards available annually for sixth form entrance, again these can be augmented.

Remarks: Not one of the premier league public schools if you are looking solely for academic results (which is not to say that clever pupils don't do well) but more than compensated for by first class pastoral care, community spirit and family atmosphere – almost tangible. Well worth a look if these qualities are high on your list.

LANGLEY PARK SCHOOL FOR BOYS

Hawksbrook Lane, South Eden Park Road, Beckenham, Kent, BR3 3BP

Tel: 020 8650 9253
Fax: 020 8650 5823
E-mail: office@lpbs.org.uk
Website: www.lpbs.org.uk

• Pupils: 1,425 boys; 75 girls in the sixth form; all day • Ages: 11-18 • Size of sixth form: 445 boys and girls • Non-denom • State • Open days: October

Head: Since 2000, Robert Northcott MA (forties); his third headship, previously at St Katherine's Bristol. Married, two teenage children. Strong leader, boundless energy and enthusiasm, a great communicator with an entrepreneurial streak. Popular with parents, pupils and colleagues. The school, having had its up and downs, has been put firmly back on the map by Mr Northcott and his staff.

Academic Matters: Takes a wide range of abilities; all are tested on entry and tracked thereafter; setting in maths, English and science. GCSE and A level results moving upwards; popular subjects are maths, ICT and media studies. Teaching is sound with pupils pushed to go further and understand that homework is essential for success. Everyone is expected to work to the best of their abilities and are praised for their efforts. Numerous ICT suites, school has now been designated as a specialist in maths and computing and links with other schools to offer masterclasses. Dual and single sciences – some labs refurbished, others when they can afford it, says head. Regular 'living history' trips to battlefields and other sites; boys are encouraged to research events thoroughly. Thriving sixth form, co-ed since 2001 and still expanding, has own club house which is also open to neighbouring girls' school. Enthusiastic, smiling teachers, men and women mainly under forty-five; pupils get on well with them and are given lots of encouragement. Good SEN provision, pupils well integrated into school life. Programme for more able pupils who seem to do as well as they would in a grammar school.

Games, Options, The Arts: Very strong sports; links with professional sportsmen have proved an excellent influence. Various sporting tours, under 13 cricket county champions, well-used on-site facilities that could do with updating when they have the money. Staff are keen on getting out and about – all go to camp at school's own field-centre in Derbyshire; annual mountain climbing trips; sixth form recently went to the top of Kilimanjaro. Corridors are lined with pupils' murals, art and poetry. A recent residency was held by an African dance group; all the boys learn to dance here! Broad exposure to drama and music, numerous choirs, bands and orchestra, links with the Royal Academy. Interesting range of lunchtime and after-school clubs includes African drumming, air training corps and drama.

Background and Atmosphere: Previously Beckenham and Penge Grammar, became comprehensive in 1976. Large green site next door to Langley Girls' School, a not very attractive main school building with various modern additions some of which have (briefly) seen better days. Well-balanced with a quite exceptionally friendly and welcoming atmosphere, Mr Northcott's enthusiasm getting through to staff and pupils. Boys calm, well-behaved and clearly involved in their school.

Pastoral Care and Discipline: Boys, who are referred to as gentlemen, are expected to be courteous, co-operative and use their common sense. Everyone is given lots of encouragement to join in and communicate well. Sixth form is given responsibilities such as running the library, lunch hall and helping younger pupils. Smart uniform, suits for sixth formers.

Pupils and Parents: All very local Beckenham and West Wickham types, small ethnic mix. Mostly hard-working parents who expect the same of their children. OBs Henry Mee, Bill Wyman, Derek Underwood, Sir Douglas Henley.

Entrance: At 11, no entrance exam. Priority to siblings of those in the school, then closest proximity. Waiting list is kept for those not lucky enough to get a place first time round. 16+ girls and boys: 5 A*-C grades at GCSE.

Exit: At 16, a quarter go to local colleges for A level and vocational work. At 18 most go to college or university, 2 or 3 to Oxbridge, a handful to work.

Remarks: A most impressive comprehensive.

LATHALLAN BUDDING SENIOR SCHOOL

Linked to Lathallan School in the Junior section

Brotherton Castle, By Johnshaven, Montrose, DD10 0HN

Tel: 01561 362 220
Fax: 01561 361 695
E-mail: office@lathallan.com
Website: www.lathallan.com

• Pupils: boys and girls, some board • Ages: 13-14, rising to 18
• Independent

Remarks: See main (ie junior) school.

THE LATYMER SCHOOL

Haselbury Road, London, N9 9TN

Tel: 020 8807 4037
Fax: 020 8887 8111
E-mail: office@latymer.co.uk
Website: www.latymer.co.uk

• Pupils: 1,417 girls and boys (in equal numbers); all day • Ages: 11-18 • Size of sixth form: 502 • Non-denom • State

Head: Since 2005, Mr Mark Garbett MA MEd NPQH. He was previously head of Stretford Grammar School in Trafford, Manchester and served in independent schools prior to that. Mr Garbett is keen that pupils should take part in a wide range of activities and gain self-confidence akin to that of many independent school pupils.

Academic Matters: The super academic results you would expect from a high-powered co-ed grammar school with devoted staff. 'Latymer pupils are ... more than three years ahead of most pupils when admitted to the school,' said the latest Ofsted report. 'GCSE results are very high overall and well above those for similar schools. 'Over 80 per cent A and A* grades at GCSE, over 80 per cent A/B grades at A level. Awarded DfES School Achievement Award in 2000 for improvement in GCSE results. Particularly strong on maths and sciences but universally good – the best department in 2002 was media studies!! Russian, sociology, theatre studies and PE are among the 23 A level subjects on offer. Classes of 30, banding for maths from year 8 and languages from year 9. Came top of the Sunday Times value-added survey in 2002, measuring progress between key stage 3 and GCSEs.

Special needs co-ordinator and a teacher co-ordinating provision for gifted children. Excellence in Cities money used to fund a mentoring programme for under-achieving, able children. 'Exams and brilliance are two different things. Some very able children find it difficult to put things down on paper.' 'It's a bit of a sink-or-swim school,' said a parent (last head disagreed). 'Some children find it a bit over-whelmingly big and overwhelmingly competitive. But I've never felt the school was pushing my children too hard – they give them the opportunities and let them get on with it.'

Games, Options, The Arts: Twelve acres of playing fields and two gyms. A new sports/dining complex is being built and will open in early 2006. Fields plenty of teams – 'there will be a hundred youngsters playing football and rugby on a Saturday morning'. Music is outstanding, with three orchestras, a concert band, choirs and some 600 children learning instruments. 'The head of music tries to provide opportunities for the most talented youngsters we have at any time,' said last head and a parent commented, 'you couldn't get better music anywhere.' Drama is also very strong and a new performing arts centre was opened in 2000, with facilities for music, drama and media studies. The school puts on a large-scale musical most years involving actors and musicians. Plenty of art on display around the school and good results at GCSE and A level.

Outdoor pursuits weeks for years 7 and 9 at the school's own field centre in North Wales, plus plenty of trips abroad eg Barbados. Senior musicians tour Europe each summer. 'We have able children – we don't have to force-feed them,' says the head. 'We have as wide a range of extra-curricular activities as many independent schools.' The school invests highly in staff, who have less teaching time than most. 'This means they are willing to take on extra activities and are less likely to take sick leave.'

Background and Atmosphere: The school was first established in the 17th century with an endowment from merchant, Edward Latymer. It moved to its present site in 1910 and has been expanding ever since. Red brick buildings on a quiet site off the A10 just beyond the North Circular. Well resourced, with refurbished science and technology rooms and a new sports hall and dining hall. Now also specialist ICT rooms and learning resource centre. Large hall that can house the whole school for assemblies, concerts and plays. New sixth form common room. Very active association of parents and friends. 'It's got a nice atmosphere – casual but purposeful,' said a parent.

Pastoral Care and Discipline: Peer counselling system as part of anti-bullying policy. There is a strong, committed team of nine year heads. Visiting school counsellor.

Pupils and Parents: The sort of social mix one would expect from a catchment area that spreads from Islington to Walthamstow – pupils must live within a one hour public transport ride from the school. Parents generally very supportive and pleased that their children have got a place at Latymer. A mother commented, 'some parents compare it unfavourably with independent schools, and of course the classes are bigger, but the teaching is just as good.'

Entrance: Around 1,800 applicants for 180 places. The first round is a non-verbal reasoning test – 'supposed to measure innate ability'. 'It's to give an opportunity to children who haven't been to a good primary school,' said previous head. The second round is maths, verbal reasoning and literacy tests. Points also given for extra-curricular interests. The school can give up to 20 places to talented musicians (which, in practice, means around grade 5 distinction), 'but generally we only choose two or three because most get in anyway on academic grounds.' A minimum of six A grades at GCSE is needed to enter the sixth form, with between 50 and 80 students coming in from other schools. 'We select youngsters who wouldn't otherwise have peers working at that level. It is a marvellous thing to give them the opportunity to study at a school where working hard is seen as "cool"'.

Exit: Nearly all to university, about 20 a year to Oxbridge.

Money Matters: The Latymer Foundation, as well as funding the Snowdonia Field Centre, funds selected capital projects and helps those who cannot afford uniform or school trips. The financial side is looked after by the Bursar, who is on the senior management team.

Remarks: Hugely successful and sought-after outer-London co-ed grammar school. 'There is no doubt in my mind that Latymer is an excellent school,' said a parent. 'Dedicated, hard-working head and staff, loads of extra-curricular activities, very strong music. My three children – very different personalities – have all been extremely happy there socially.' New head will make changes in this flagship – well worth keeping a weather eye on rate of knots.

LATYMER UPPER SCHOOL

Linked to Latymer Prep School in the Junior section

237 King Street, Hammersmith, London, W6 9LR

Tel: 020 8741 1851
Fax: 02087 485 212
E-mail: registrar@latymer-upper.org
Website: www.latymer-upper.org

• Pupils: 1,052, still mostly boys (girls in sixth form) but co-ed started in 2004 from year 7. All day • Ages: 11-18 • Size of sixth form: 355 including 90 girls • Non-denom • Fees: Prep £3,625; upper school £3,995 • Independent • Open days: September and November

Head: Since 2002, Mr Peter J Winter MA (Oxon) (early fifties), formerly head of King Edward's School (Bath), educated at Trinity School, Croydon and Wadham College, Oxford, where he read French and German. Taught at Latymer Upper and Magdalen College School (Oxford) before going to Sevenoaks School, where he was head of modern languages, then ran the International Centre, the sixth form boarding house for boys with his Ghanaian-born wife Adwoa. Two children. A keen all-round sportsman and Francophile, he is a strong advocate of co-education and is happily over-seeing Latymer's transition. 'I have never been more fulfilled in my work.' 'He clearly has his hands on the reins,' said a parent, 'and he seems to have the support of a good staff team. I value his recognition of all the pupils – including those who don't win the prizes.'

Academic Matters: Results have improved year on year for the past 6 years – 77 per cent A*/As at GCSE in 2005, 56 per cent A grades and 87 per cent AB at A level. English and maths followed closely by history and RE, and then sciences, as most popular A levels, from a total of 35, including business studies, government and politics and photography. Ten new staff appointments in 2005; the head has done some weeding out and now says confidently, 'we don't have any weak staff any more.'

Around 100 pupils have specific learning difficulties and there is now a learning support teacher who backs up classroom teachers with diagnoses, advice and support. 'We screen every child on entrance and we are conscious that it is an area of real need. Parents are very grateful that it is now being recognised.' Good careers advice and imaginative work experience scheme in Paris, Berlin and Stockholm.

Games, Options, The Arts: Rowing is a particular strength, giving an opportunity for boys and girls who are not talented at ball sports to represent the school. Plenty of opportunities too for more conventionally sporty types, including cross-country, badminton, netball as well as football (girls as well as boys) and rugby. The sports ground at Wood Lane, a 20 minute bus ride away, has been completely refurbished at a cost of £4.2 million, with a new pavilion and changing rooms, grass and Astroturf pitches. This came into use in Sept 2004. 'We want to give the girls the same quality and range of sport as the boys.' Large sports hall with swimming pool and fitness suite on site. Strong musical tradition; joint orchestra with Godolphin and Latymer and exchanges with The Johanneum in Hamburg, plus bands and choirs. Saturday music school for local children.

The creative and performing arts centre, opened in 1998, includes a central atrium café – beloved of the sixth form – with impressive exhibitions lining the stairs leading to large, light art, ceramics and photography studios. Well-equipped theatre with galleried seating; drama is another strength – timetabled throughout the school.

Each summer, all the pupils who are not doing public exams go off for an activities week – which might include caving on Dartmoor, rafting in the Alps, surfing in Newquay or visiting the Futuroscope in France. Other school trips include language exchanges, classics tour to Sicily, geography field trip to Switzerland and art trip to New York. Lots of pupils get silver and gold Duke of Edinburgh Awards. Plenty of extra-curricular activities eg bridge, karate, French drama, debating.

Background and Atmosphere: Founded in 1624, the school moved to its present site in 1895. It was once a direct grant grammar school and still has a somewhat hybrid feel: jammed and very urban from the front entrance, straight off a busy Hammersmith road, but with a vaulted great hall lined with Oxbridge scholarship boards, and a boathouse emerging onto the banks of the Thames at the back. An elevated section of the A4 was actually built through the playground after WW2. But an underpass emerges by a tarmac sports pitch which leads to a lawned garden, swimming pool, sports hall, boathouse and the elegant town house with river views occupied by the prep school.

An 'Italianate piazza' with plants, seats and tables has been created in the centre of the site, giving a spacious and airy feel and room for outdoor recreation away from ball games. The cars have been exiled – hooray!

Pastoral Care and Discipline: Historically, not a place for shy, sensitive souls – quite a few stories of bullying. The present head has expelled several aggressors and beefed up the pastoral side. 'We do not tolerate bullying.' He has improved the pastoral side of the school and a tiered system of tutors, year heads and division heads ensures that children do not fall through the net either socially or academically. 'We've sent out some strong signals. I now have a first class pastoral team and we are serious about our pupils' welfare.' The new regime, plus increasing numbers of girls, should create an atmosphere where tender flowers can flourish.

Pupils and Parents: This is an urban inner-city school that still has a grammar school feel, and parents value the social mix that comes from taking in plenty of state school children at 11. Its clientele is mostly local – middle class professional families, including plenty of media and acting folk, many races and creeds. Turns out 'hard-working, solidly unpretentious chaps'. OBs include Sir James Spicer, George Walden, Mel Smith, Hugh Grant, Alan Rickman and lots of MPs.

Entrance: Going co-ed has naturally upped the ante on the entrance front. About 40 boys and girls come up from the prep. The rest are chosen at 11 and 13 from a variety of state and private schools – at 11, 50-60 per cent come from state primaries. 2004 was the first mixed gender entry and the acceptance rate has been very high with 40 per cent girls in years 7 and 8. The 13+ entry will be scaled down in future. Around 50 places in the sixth form mostly go to girls.

Exit: To a wide variety of universities, including 15-20 a year to Oxbridge, to do a wide variety of courses ranging from sports science to theoretical physics. University of London is particularly popular.

Money Matters: A rich enough school, which offers a range of scholarships, bursaries and awards including academic, music, sports, art and drama. The new development director's task is to raise sufficient funds for many more bursaries, 'so that academic ability is the only entry criteria' (sic).

Remarks: Popular with local parents who know their sons and daughters will emerge with creditable results. Image softening under new head, likely to soften further. Aims to set new standards for co-education in west London.

LAVANT HOUSE

Linked to Lavant House Junior in the Junior section

West Lavant, Chichester, West Sussex, PO18 9AB

Tel: 01243 527 211
Fax: 01243 530 490
E-mail: office@lavanthouse.org.uk
Website: www.lavanthouse.org.uk

• Pupils: 145 girls; 20 board, 125 day • Ages: 3-18 • Size of sixth form: 15 • C of E • Fees: Day: junior £1,670-£2,800; senior £3,365. Boarding: junior £4,445; senior £5,330 • Independent • Open days: October

Headmistress: Since 2001, Mrs Marian Scott MA (natural sciences) (fifties), took over from Mrs Watkins. Educated at Talbot Heath, Bournemouth and Newnham College, Cambridge, was the deputy head here for 5 years. Two grown-up children; interests include sailing and gardening.

Academic Matters: Traditional, small, girls' school catering for a broad range of abilities. Small classes with a nurturing environment with an emphasis on the individual. Strong science department for small school, a team from the second form recently won first place in Salters Festival of Chemistry, and physics, chemistry and biology are all running at A Level. Girls are also keen on entering national maths challenges. English and drama popular at GCSE. Four languages on offer, others can be arranged when there is the demand. Almost all A*-C at GCSE; at A level 100 per cent. Girls follow a fairly full and varied curriculum but one or two subjects missing at GCSE, like food technology, which seems a shame in such a practical school; IT results are improving. Staff are mostly local and long staying, mainly female, well qualified and teach able pupils to the highest levels.

All staff have SEN awareness training and are sympathetic to children with difficulties. SpLD teachers are available for both group and individual help. EFL teaching is available for the few foreign pupils attending, school is happy to take pupils for a term/year who want to learn English and experience life and living in the UK.

Games, Options, The Arts: Plenty of sports especially athletics, netball a main game, all facilities are close to the school and accessible at any time. Three new tennis/netball courts including the highest specification surface for netball; outdoor heated pool. Teams frequently placed in top three in area championships for netball. Lavant House

Stables are on site offering individual or group lessons, a showjumping course and dressage arena. Set in wonderful countryside for hacking, these facilities are also open to the public. Very active Duke of Edinburgh awards, most do bronze some go onto silver and gold. All do First Aid certificate. Good music and drama, new drama studio; there are regular house drama competitions. Many chamber concerts which children from the junior school can join in, emphasis on musical productions, girls made their own CD of carol service. Light art studios with girls' work well displayed, textiles, ceramics, mixed media very popular GCSE and A level.

Background and Atmosphere: The school was founded in 1952 by Dora Green primarily for her own children, two of whom serve on the current governing body of the trust. The main building is 18th century brick and flint, with spacious rooms and well-tended gardens. The verandah has recently been restored providing an idyllic place for pupils to have tea and chat after school. You could be forgiven for thinking you were a guest in a large country house; everyone looks so comfortable in his or her surroundings.

Pastoral Care and Discipline: Staff are always on hand to help with any problems large or small; the school nurse has a counselling roll. Pupils comment, 'I like it here because everyone is your friend, even the older girls.' Boarding houses are homely, sixth form can cook their own meals and gain some independence and may bring their own cars. Sensible set of school rules and house point/order mark system. High standard of behaviour is expected. Flexi-boarding can be arranged to meet individual requirements. Excellent boarding inspection report in January 2004.

Pupils and Parents: Reasonable social mix, many run local businesses, mainly local from a radius of 25 miles. Girls are friendly, well-presented and supportive of each other.

Entrance: At 3 on a first come first served basis. Most stay on for the senior school or enter by an 11+ exam and assessment day.

Exit: 50 per cent stay on for the sixth form, leavers go to local colleges or to sixth form at boys' public schools. At 18 they disappear to the four winds mostly to university or art colleges. Recent university entrance includes medicine at Imperial College, history at Hull and at Exeter, English and Latin at Bristol.

Money Matters: 1 or 2 academic scholarships each year at 11, 13 and 16; girls are selected by exam and an assessment day.

Remarks: Possibly not a school for really high-flyers but a useful option for a less confident child to be nurtured and excel. Would also suit the pony-mad well.

LEEDS GIRLS' HIGH SCHOOL

Linked to Ford House in the Junior section

Headingley Lane, Leeds, West Yorkshire, LS6 1BN

Tel: 0113 274 4000
Fax: 0113 2 752 217
E-mail: enquiries@lghs.org
Website: www.lghs.org

• Pupils: 606 girls; all day • Ages: 11-18 • Size of sixth form: 160 • Non-denom • Fees: Senior £ 2,602; Ford House (7-11) £1,896; Rose Court (3-7) £1,741 • Independent • Open days: Mid October, early November

Head: Since 1997, Mrs Sue Fishburn BSc (fifties). Educated at Dursley Grammar School and Birmingham University. Previous post deputy head, Stafford Grammar. Has taught in private and maintained schools. Two grown-up children. Very involved at all levels of school in hands-on way; energetic, approachable, good sense of humour, listens to girls and parents. Wide interests, eg folk music, sailing. Wants to produce 'happy, confident, well-motivated girls' and to provide opportunities for developing wider as well as academic skills. Will retire when the merger with Leeds Grammar is completed in July 2007.

Academic Matters: Very strong. 74 per cent A*/A at GCSE and steady growth to 84 per cent A/B (75 per cent As) at A level in 2003, with only small numbers below C. Very good range including psychology, British politics and government, home economics. All take general studies. Maths setted in year 8 and modern languages at GCSE. Thriving classics department. Highly experienced, dedicated and enthusiastic staff; very good relationships with girls. Classes of around 25. Good IT provision – qualifications taken in years 8 and 9 and sixth form. Very strong careers education: assertiveness training, management skills courses, links with local and national industries.

Games, Options, The Arts: Outstanding art displayed all over the school – mainly mixed-media drawing and painting but a sculptor has been in residence for a week to teach girls about working in wood; silversmithing available as an extra. Strong home economics department. Purpose-built drama studio; joint drama productions with Leeds Grammar School for Boys. Exceptionally strong, very varied music, eg folk, jazz, classical (two organs in school); music links with boys' grammar and local comprehensive. Recent tours to eastern Europe and Australia. 60 per cent learn instrument at school in separate music block. Very lively magazine mainly edited by girls – ambitious and satirical writing; plenty of humour.

Successful mainstream sports teams; sports hall with indoor pool and multigym; lots of courts but no Astro on site. Wide range of extra-curricular activities, Duke of Edinburgh Award Scheme, very successful in debating, Young Enterprise and various other national competitions. Funds raised for Malawi causes (a trip there every two years) and reading work done at local primary school.

Background and Atmosphere: Founded in 1876 by Yorkshire Ladies Council for Education with close links with Leeds Grammar – with whom it is to merge in July 2007. 1920s building with 1970s and 1990s additions. Traditional hall with organ and wooden panelling but some dreary corridors and parts with just artificial light. Variable quality of classroom decoration. Attractive sixth form common rooms. Well-resourced, networked library. Minority religions catered for, eg Muslim prayer room. Hard-working, lively, creative atmosphere with a strong sense of community. Scope for humour and individuality; singing in the corridors. Girls encouraged to use initiative and express views, eg in school council.

Pastoral Care and Discipline: Comprehensive set of school policies form basis of a well-established system for handling problems. Discipline based on co-operation and acknowledgement of individual needs. Exclusion rare – for serious offences, eg theft, supplying drugs. Motivating rewards policy. Head of lower school takes endless pains with girls' upsets. Year 7s have year 11 buddy who they meet in summer before entry.

Pupils and Parents: Socially mixed with several academics/teachers, medics and other professions. 15 per cent Jewish and 10 per cent Asian girls. Mostly from Leeds but some travel for up to an hour. Large number of school buses, flexible about routes. Articulate, friendly girls enthusiastic about school and caring towards others. OGs include Dame Pauline Neville Jones, political director of the Foreign Office, Nicolette Jones and journalist Jill Parkin.

Entrance: Girls from junior school assessed by last two years' work; external candidates sit maths, English and verbal reasoning tests, plus interview, at 11. Older entrants sit maths, English and French/German paper; entry to sixth form – 7 GCSEs at A-C with A/A* in AS subjects. Entrance to pre-prep based on informal assessment of school readiness. Caters for top 25 per cent of ability range.

Exit: 15 leave after GCSE mainly for sixth form colleges or state sixth forms. Almost all go to university, almost always their first choice. A dozen to Oxbridge; large number

to very good universities, often to study science or medicine; business/management/accounting quite popular. Adventurous gap year projects. Produces several barristers and consultants.

Money Matters: 4 scholarships per year - one sixth reduction in fees plus means-tested bursaries up to 100 per cent (these include 2 Ogden bursaries reserved for state school pupils entering at sixth form level to study a science curriculum); Also one or two music scholarships. New means-tested bursaries for 6th form students.

Remarks: Very successful all-round school for girls, especially suited to high-flyers with wide interests. Merging with Leeds Grammar in July 2007 – not clear yet what the detailed implications of this are.

LEEDS GRAMMAR SCHOOL

Alwoodley Gates, Harrogate Road, Leeds, West Yorkshire, LS17 8GS

Tel: 0113 229 1552
Fax: 0113 228 5111
E-mail: info@lgs.leeds.sch.uk
Website: www.leedsgrammar.com

- Pupils: 1,380 boys • Ages: 4-18 • Size of sixth form: 247
- Non denominational • Fees: Junior school £1,683 - £2,280; senior school £2,796 • Independent • Open days: October, November, January and June; sixth form January. See school website for dates

Headmaster: Since 1999, Dr Mark Bailey (early forties), read history at Durham and Cambridge. Previously Fellow in History at Caius, Cambridge, then at Corpus Christi (including some bursarial duties). Author of four books on medieval England, played rugby on the wing for England between 1984 and 1990. Wife works as freelance Human Resources consultant; young son and daughter. Unusual (no school experience) but highly successful appointment. A committed meritocrat, 'hugely ambitious for school' he says, wedded to importance of a firm academic basis for all-round education. Very visible round the place (teaches year 7 history, shadows pupils, visits lessons). Consensual leadership style – including listening seriously to pupils' views – insists on staff taking responsibility – 'HM's job is to articulate the way forward and trust others to get on with it'. Strong yet affable personality, say approving parents; he clearly relishes the challenge of his career change of direction, in a brand new school (see below).

Will be head of the merged school when the combination with Leeds Girls' High School goes ahead in July 2007.

Academic Matters: Well up the league tables; results compare favourably with similar selective grammar schools – negligible failures at A level, average 70 per cent at A/B grades, similar record at GCSE. Not a hot-house, however; any boy who passes the entrance procedure should cope, with impressive staff help. There is a real sense of academic purpose about the place and all subjects share in enviable results. Pupils noted in 1999 ISI report as 'smart, engaged and eager to learn'.

Maximum class size to GCSE is 25, with many sets at about 20; subjects almost entirely setted from Year 9. Teaching mainly traditional but supported by up-to-date IT and library facilities, encouraging self-directed learning. Dual award science for all; brightest sets get beyond GCSE before year-end. All do RS to GCSE as an integral element in PSE. French, German, Latin and Greek offered. Up to 5 ASs per student in sixth form, boys 'encouraged' to do the lot (about 60 per cent do). Modern science block with 17 specialist labs; dedicated suites for all subjects. All boys screened for dyslexia on entry; some help given thereafter.

Staff commitment is enormous – half of them have 20+ years of experience and about a quarter have been at LGS since the 1970s. The challenge involved in a move to a completely new school seems to have invigorated those who might otherwise be fading in late career. Also a sufficient number of keen young things. One fifth women staff. Head insists on teachers 'living values they profess to teach'.

Games, Options, The Arts: Extensive windswept playing fields, with room to expand, sports hall and squash courts, swimming pool. Sport is important – strong reputation in rugby (frequent representation at county level and beyond) and cricket (this being Yorkshire, the 1st XI tend to moonlight in the tough world of league cricket). Soccer recently introduced. Many other team and individual games on offer. A lot of drama goes on – there is a studio theatre – and music has always been vigorous in this very musical city; choirs and orchestras all over the place. Plenty of opportunity beyond the curriculum for creative activities stemming from art and DT and the usual spread of clubs and societies.

Visits to the outdoor centre in splendidly wild Teesdale form part of every pupil's curriculum. Also on offer are the voluntary CCF, Scouts and the D of E Scheme.

Background and Atmosphere: In 1552 Sir William Sheafield left £14.13s. 4d. to found a school, 'for all such young scholars, youthes and children as shall come to be taught, instructed and informed'. New premises were found in 1624 and then, in 1857, increasing numbers prompted a further move to a site a mile from the city centre, with confident ecclesiastical buildings – now part of Leeds University – designed by EM Barry (brother to the then headmaster and a member of the famous architectural family). In 1997, renewed pressure of numbers and curriculum brought the courageous decision under Dr Bailey's predecessor to build a completely new school on the northern edge of Leeds. The result is a very handsome set of buildings, 'a blend of function and quality', designed by an architect who did imaginative work at the previous site. Vital historical bits from the old school are incorporated, thanks to the efforts of its extraordinary teenage historian. Few if any major schools start with an advantage like this (visitors are wafted by lift from reception to the elegant administrative area and invited to admire the campanile, piazza and porte-cochere). Purpose-building does not come cheap but expanded numbers and stringent financial control now mean that the school's future looks secure.

Clearly everyone got a shot in the arm from having to reinvent themselves on a fresh site; now settled down into a determined atmosphere which is also civilised, to a degree unusual in a large city boys' school (though of course generous and well-lit circulation space helps). The students seem genuinely proud of the place and look after it (though the sixth form centre is beginning to look a touch tatty). Rare inadequacies like art provision are being remedied. Confidence buzzes in the air and so it should.

Pastoral Care and Discipline: Traditionally form-based, with horizontal divisions into two-year sections; also all-through houses, mainly for sporting and other competitions. Chaplain offers counselling to boys of all religions. General discipline firm but understanding; key figure here is long-serving and universally admired deputy head.

Pupils and Parents: From Leeds and a wide arc to the north; significant proportions of boys of minority ethnic backgrounds reflecting the area's cultural diversity. Many professional families, especially doctors. A booming region but the school doesn't serve only the rich. bursary fund on its way to a second million pounds. Parents generally supportive and probably grateful – this is the best boys' school in the area. Old boys include Barry Cryer, Tony Harrison, Gerald Kaufman MP and Colin Montgomerie (who has given a sports-weighted bursary) and Ricky Wilson (Kaiser Chiefs).

Entrance: Mostly from local primary schools, who are pretty keen (but state secondary provision in Leeds is hardly an attraction), some from prep schools. Selection by in-house assessment from junior school, exam + interview +

report at 10 to 13, interview + 5 Bs at GCSE for sixth form. Places occur at other ages from time to time. More than two applicants per place overall.

Exit: Nearly all go (predictably) to higher education: 15+ a year to Oxbridge, otherwise overwhelmingly to Ivy League northern universities (21 to Newcastle in 2001), many to medical school, also history and English. Gap years popular.

Money Matters: Up to three scholarships at 11, plus a rising number of bursaries at 11 and 16 (ongoing fundraising to increase these) to encourage bright boys from low income families.

Remarks: Excellent all-round school under strong and clear-sighted leadership, greatly enjoying its new life at Alwoodley Gates. No reason why both quiet and pushy should not prosper here, provided they are determined to join in and get the work done. There's still an element of West Riding grittiness about but the school increasingly looks more cultured and sophisticated than its competitors.

Merging with Leeds Girls' High School in July 2007 – not clear yet what the detailed implications of this are.

LEIGHTON PARK SCHOOL

Shinfield Road, Reading, Berkshire, RG2 7ED

Tel: 0118 987 9600
Fax: 01189 879 625
E-mail: admissions@leightonpark.reading.sch.uk
Website: www.leightonpark.reading.sch.uk

- Pupils: 450 girls and boys; 163 board • Ages: 11-18 • Size of sixth form: 120 • Quaker (all faiths welcomed) • Fees: Senior: boarding £6,950; weekly boarding £6,196; day £4,618. Junior: boarding £5,906; weekly boarding £5,267; day £3,926
- Independent • Open days: September as well as a monthly open morning and also individual meetings with head are available

Head: Since 1996, Mr John Dunston MA AIL (fifties), a Churchill fellow educated at Cambridge and York universities with a degree in modern languages. The only Jewish headmaster chosen for two Quaker schools (previous headship was Sibford). Wife teaches at a local prep, two children, son is a pupil. A likeable man and diplomat manqué who accompanied the school choir on USA trip (sings baritone).

Academic Matters: For 7 consecutive years, students achieved 97 per cent or more passes at A level (99 per cent in 2005). 66 per cent A/B grades at A level in 2005. Almost half the A level students take maths, and about a third physics or chemistry. Unlike the discrepancy seen in national figures, boys here perform as well as girls. Sciences taught separately as three subjects. GCSEs; 95 per cent achieved five or more A*-C, with 35 per cent at A*/A. Pupils averaged 9 passes each. Religious studies, called 'beliefs and values', includes the philosophy of Quakerism. Individual learning centre (mainly for dyslexia) with highly skilled staff. New multi-media languages centre opened September 2005.

Games, Options, The Arts: An impressive list of county athletes, runners, hockey, netball and rugby players. A rugby and hockey South Africa tour made time for bush excursions and ocean safaris. Individual success at ice dance, swimming, world-class sailing. Wide choice of hobbies include ceramics, electronics, good causes, Duke of Edinburgh, photography, textiles, plus wide choice of sports and musical groups. Young Enterprise is an ambitious throng.

Choir and orchestra tour Europe regularly. A successful US tour to Philadelphia performed Fire & the Hammer – a musical written by the school's music director. 100 pupils learn a musical instrument, some to grade 8, a few to diploma. Timetabled lessons. Practice before school/lunch hour/evenings. Jazz band in finals of Music for Youth at South Bank. New music technology studio. Masses of cultural exchanges – recently with a lycée in Nantes; Barcelona, Hamburg, Athens and joint ventures with other Quaker schools. Adventure training trips recently include Ecuador (sixth form), skiing in Canada and Pembrokeshire (year 8). A level art trip to European capitals.

Background and Atmosphere: A welcome oasis of greenery, calm and gracious buildings amidst the hustle and bustle of Reading's maze of tarmac, cheek by jowl with the University of Reading in 60 acre parkland. Though not as ancient as most other Quaker schools, LP began as a public school in 1890 (though there are links with Grove House Tottenham which dates earlier) with the specific intention of educating scholars for Oxbridge. Girls were added in 1975. Boarding houses, some smart as a whistle, some a tad dowdy, but Fryer House where 11-13-year- olds live is a lively, warm environment with lots of space for recreation/prep/outdoor activities housed in a wonderful self-contained building – a 3 minute walk from main campus – recreational café area and skateboards/roller blades appropriately in evidence. New Dining room 'Oakview' opened October 2004, offering wide choice of high quality meals for the whole school community (breakfast, lunch and tea) plus sixth form cafe. Library to die for in the oldest building with 9 separate rooms, themed artful displays prepared by a librarian who lives to make people want to go in there and read.

Pastoral Care and Discipline: Dedicated older staff inject a great deal of warmth and behind-the-scenes support. Lots of effort, so not much division between day pupils and the rest. 'Day boarders' stay for evening meal and supervised prep if required; breakfast also available if needed. All pupils participate in residential week of team building/adventure training. Anyone bringing drugs onto premises permanently excluded. Alcohol is banned.

Pupils and Parents: All major faiths represented here. 20 per cent from overseas and a sprinkle of ex-pats but mainly from Berkshire, Oxfordshire, north Hampshire and Bucks. Only 10 per cent staff and pupils Quaker. All seem confident and vital. Dress code for senior school, uniform for Years 7 and 8. No Saturday lessons so many of the boarders are weekly, hence exodus on Friday nights though much to do for those remaining. Old Leightonians: Sir David Lean, Sir Richard Rodney Bennett, Jim Broadbent, Michael Foot, Lord Caradon, Lord Frederick Seebohm (who reformed social services) and a fair clutch of MPs, Rowntrees, Cadburys, Clarks, Reckitts, Morlands and Frys.

Entrance: Tests autumn and spring for year 7-10 (though alternate dates can be set if needed); entrance tests include maths, English, non-verbal reasoning. Pupils chosen on previous report, interview and reference from current head. At sixth form about 35 enter from outside with at least 5 A-Cs with A*-B grades in chosen subjects.

Exit: Most go to universities (often getting firsts). Few leave at 16 for sixth form colleges.

Money Matters: Several major and minor awards. Means-tested bursaries. Friends' schools' bursaries given to those with Quaker parents. David Lean Foundation awards one annual scholarship for 100 per cent of day fees, for academic excellence.

Remarks: The feel of a busy London day school on a mini-university campus. Strong moral code and self-esteem.

THE LEVENTHORPE SCHOOL

Cambridge Road, Sawbridgeworth, Hertfordshire, CM21 9BY

Tel: 01279 836 633
Fax: 01279 600 339
E-mail: admin.leventhorpe@thegrid.org.uk
Website: www.leventhorpe.herts.sch.uk

• Pupils: 1,150; boys and girls; all day • Ages: 11-18 • Size of sixth form: 300 • Non-denom • State • Open days: October; 6th form open evening in March

Head: Since 1995, Mr Peter Janke BA BSc (mid fifties), studied philosophy at Birkbeck College, London and chemistry at University of Nottingham. Head of chemistry at several schools before becoming deputy head at Cheltenham Bournside School and sixth form centre, the post he held before moving on to Leventhorpe. Married to Marian, a resting maths teacher. A keen sportsman, he's run three marathons in the past and hopes to do one more in the future. Sailing is also a passion.

Academic Matters: Head is a strong believer in setting according to ability and children are setted for most subjects from entry to the school in year 7. Initial set groupings are based on children's National Curriculum records (forwarded by primary school) and further tests but regular assessments ensure that there is plenty of opportunity for transfer between sets. Separate sciences at GCSE (physics, chemistry, biology) for the most able pupils. GCSE results, though not spectacular, are well above the national average and improving each year. At A level, pass rate is 100 per cent in almost all subjects and the proportion of A and B grades is about 48 per cent; business studies the most popular subject by far, with fine results. The sixth form has expanded rapidly over recent years. 28 subjects are currently on offer at A level, plus a couple of applied GCEs.

Average class size at key stage 3 is 26, at key stage 4, 22 and in the sixth form, 12. Plenty of committed staff – 21 teaching and 7 non-teaching staff members have been with the school for more than ten years.

Games, Options, The Arts: The school's swimming pool is used for activities both inside and outside school hours. Participation in sport is encouraged through regular sports fixtures in a wide range of sports and there are currently a number of county players. The school holds the national Sportsmark award. A good choice of extra-curricular activities includes D of E. The weekly sailing club attracts pupils of all ages. Other activities include the Costa Rica World Challenge and year 7 camp. Music and drama are both strong, with regular concerts and productions involving large numbers of pupils. The annual exhibition of GCSE and A level art work attracts increasing numbers of the public, as well as parents and friends. Countries visited regularly on school trips include France, Germany, Spain, Switzerland and Kenya.

Background and Atmosphere: Set back from a main road, a series of unattractive, mainly single-storey, flat-roofed buildings make up the school. Inside some of the buildings are scruffy and in need of redecoration work (not a priority with the LEA), although staff have done what they can to brighten up the walls with plenty of artwork and displays. Playing fields are extensive. Plans are afoot to sell off a piece of unused land to fund a new sports centre and to improve library facilities. Uniform policy is strict, previous disgruntlement among the girls that they are not allowed to wear trousers has to some extent abated with the introduction of a rather smart black/red tartan kilt. Sixth formers do not wear uniform but there are guidelines as to what is suitable dress – basically office attire.

Pastoral Care and Discipline: Pupils belong to one of four houses and their progress is overseen by the house head as they move up through the school. House heads work with a team of form tutors, each of whom looks after a tutor group for two or three years. Sixth formers remain members of their house but are under the care and guidance of the head of sixth form. Competition between houses, both sporting and academic, is encouraged. The house system also gives older children the chance to develop leadership and organisational skills. Discipline policy is clearly defined and high standards of behaviour are expected and, on the whole, achieved. Parents are told before they apply to the school that they are expected to support school disciplinary procedures. Pupils report a strong and successful anti-bullying policy and staff members are generally regarded as caring and approachable.

Pupils and Parents: As the majority of pupils come from the pleasant and prosperous town of Sawbridgeworth, children tend to be mainly from middle class backgrounds. A small number of pupils come from ethnic minorities, reflecting the make-up of the local population. A very active PTA runs numerous fund-raising events throughout the year.

Entrance: Oversubscribed. Children with a brother or sister currently at the school take priority. Next in line are children of staff and then those attending one of 8 named feeder primary schools. 10 per cent of places are allocated to children with a proven aptitude in music. Remaining places (not usually many) are allocated to children living closest to the school. The school's application form is only available from the head in person. He believes that this system provides a good opportunity to meet the parents and explain the disciplined and hard-working ethos of the school. 'The support of the parents is absolutely crucial,' he says. 'If they don't like the package the school has to offer and are not prepared to give us total support, they shouldn't apply.'

Entrance to the sixth form is offered to those with five grade A-C GCSE passes, including three at grade B, plus specific requirements according to course studied.

Exit: Most year 11 pupils go on to the sixth form. About 90 per cent go on to university, with a handful a year going to Oxbridge.

Remarks: The school has a very good reputation locally. Some parents find the head's approach a little heavy-handed but nevertheless regard him as a strong and successful leader. Any child of any ability should fit in well, provided he or she is prepared to go along with the school's ethos.

THE LEYS SCHOOL

Linked to Saint Faith's School in the Junior section

Trumpington Road, Cambridge, Cambridgeshire, CB2 2AD

Tel: 01223 508 900
Fax: 01223 505 303
E-mail: office@theleys.net
Website: www.theleys.net

• Pupils: 545; 330 boys, 215 girls (390 boarders, 155 day) • Ages: 11-18, plus associated prep St Faith's 4-13 • Size of sixth form: 200 • Methodist/inter-denom • Fees: Boarding £6,990; home boarding £5,255; day £4,475; years 7-8 boarding £5,035, years 7-8 day £3,190 • Independent • Open days: October, November, March and May

Head: Since 2004, Mr Mark Slater MA (early fifties), previously head of St Lawrence College (Ramsgate).

Academic Matters: Traditionally middling, though exam results have been improving. Head says that he is concentrating on 'the two ends': Oxbridge candidates and pupils who are struggling. A level results strong in religious studies, German, Spanish, geography, physics and maths. Setting in every subject. Garden-variety learning disabilities well supported in a low-tech way (but do own up to known problems in advance – the school's literature is a bit threatening on this point).

Games, Options, The Arts: Games are popular, diverse and more inclusive than at many schools (ie they often lose). Lots of flexibility and minor sports flourish. 'Some in the common room would prefer that everyone did the same games,' moaned the head. Games compulsory two afternoons a week but offered on an additional afternoon and after school. 'If you're no good, the teachers help you get better,' said one lad – surely the highest praise. The Leys participates in the Cambridge University Leagues for some sports and gifted athletes can be assured of top-level competition (though girls say that 'boys' sports are taken more seriously'). Swimming and rowing strong and the LTA funds a tennis scholarship. Brilliant sports facilities, first class sports hall (shared with local sports clubs), floodlit Astroturf hockey pitch (converts to twelve tennis courts in summer), rowing from own boatyard on the Cam.

The bright and modernistic 'Rugg Centre' houses design technology, art, photography and ceramics. Music department 'much improved' and now offers a large orchestra, string groups, excellent choir, parents' singing group etc. 27 per cent of pupils learn a musical instrument. Drama a notable strength (all schools say this, but here it is really true). Drama scholarships are available and LAMDA exams are given, with the majority of pupils achieving distinction or honours. The school produces some marvellous theatre and talented Leysians sometimes perform in local professional productions. The annual sixth form festival provides a week of cultural and media events in the school and around Cambridge, including theatre and film outings, art workshops, musical events and lectures. Masses of school trips 'and not too expensive,' said one grateful parent.

Background and Atmosphere: Opened in central Cambridge 1875 with 16 Methodist boys. Attractive red-brick Gothic buildings with many additions, densely packed in alongside playing field and other sporting facilities. With additional games fields nearby, the school has an ample 50 acres. Went co-ed in 1994 and maintains a roughly 60:40 boy/girl split. Pupils now have a choice of being boarders (the majority), home boarders (at school for all but breakfast and sleep) or day pupils (home by 6pm). Still a relatively small school with an unusually friendly atmosphere and a strong sense of community. NB: Home boarding carries the distinct advantage of being able to return home after Cambridge rush hour, but is only available from age 13. Girls' boarding rooms nicer than boys' (as usual).

Pastoral Care and Discipline: Pupils say pastoral care is the school's biggest strength, citing dedicated tutors, a supportive house system and the school's small(ish) size. Twice a week chapel gathers up the multitudes. The school maintains an admirable balance between tradition and discipline on the one hand, and progressiveness and brotherhood on the other. 'Traditional but not formal,' according to a teacher. Easy-going rapport between teachers and pupils. One expulsion a year. Bullying well handled with a 'no-blame' approach (co-education also helps) and pupils say there is virtually none. Prefects very supportive of children in the younger years (known to the older pupils as 'the little ones').

Pupils and Parents: Hefty international component (and plentiful ESL support available, especially in sixth form). 17 per cent from overseas, plus ten per cent from British expat families and 5 per cent from foreign families living in the UK. Pupils from over 21 countries, but mainly Malaysia, Hong Kong, Russia, Germany, Nigeria, Taiwan and the USA. The school is proud of these overseas links, which have been strong for many decades. The occasional whiff of East Asian noodles through a boarding house kitchen window, everyone seems to blend right in. Local pupils mostly from St Faith's – the Cambridge prep owned by The Leys – St John's College School and King's College School. Known locally as the 'rounded' education option in Cambridge (with obvious reference to the highly academic and single-sex Perse schools up the road). In truth, many parents of super-brains take a deep breath and cross their fingers when the time comes to accept a place at the Leys. But many do, and the school seems to do jolly well by its most academically-able pupils. Old Boys: Martin Bell, Sir Alastair Burnett, Nobel Scientist Henry H Dale, mathematician Andrew Wiles and writers J G Ballard, Malcolm Lowry and James Hilton (who wrote Goodbye Mr Chips).

Entrance: At 11, 13 and 16. Very broad ability range: Common Entrance of 50 will do. However, has moved away from Common Entrance, preferring its own entrance exam administered in February, but uses CE marks for setting. At 16, pupils need GCSE Bs in subjects to be studied at A level and at least 5-6 passes (overseas applicants may sit alternative tests in place of GCSEs). The school produces a brilliant information booklet with, among other things, the details of dozens and dozens of Leys parents who are willing to be contacted (grilled mercilessly) about the school. West and Fen said to be the sporty houses, while North A reputedly more academic.

Exit: 95 per cent go on to university. London far and away most popular choice, then an even spread across the field.

Money Matters: Two 11+ scholarships (30 per cent of fees) usually to great brains, but other talents considered. Up to 14 awards at 13, notably for design & technology and drama, as well as academics, music, sport, art and all-rounder. Some special awards restricted to St Faith's pupils and to sons/daughters of Methodists and Old Leysians. Scholarship exams in February, for 11+ and 13+, and in November for sixth form.

Remarks: Popular, friendly, well-rounded school taking children from the very top to (close to) the bottom of the ability range – and doing very well by one and all.

LINCOLN MINSTER SCHOOL

Linked to Lincoln Minster Preparatory School in the Junior section

Upper Lindum Street, Lindum Terrace, Lincoln, Lincolnshire, LN2 5RW

Tel: 01522 551 300

Fax: 01522 551 310

E-mail: enquiries.lincoln@church-schools.com

Website: www.lincolnminsterschool.co.uk

• Independent

Principal: Since 1999, Mr Clive Rickart BA PGCE. Head of the prep school for three years prior. Read history at Manchester, was a boarding housemaster at Stamford School and then head of Junior School at Oswestry before arriving at Lincoln. Married with 3 children who have been through the system. Quiet, direct, not at all flashy. Competent – highly regarded by his staff. Not one to spend a lot of time mixing with the pupils. A man of vision, who is doing great things for the school both here and in Hull, where the United Church Schools Trust is merging two schools. Believes that the focus should be on the individual, allowing them to achieve their best and to build on their leadership skills.

Academic Matters: A perfect environment for learning – pupils noticeably responding to it: keen, feel the world is their oyster. Interactive white boards in each classroom – and well used by teachers. Pupils who miss a lesson are able to print off material or access it on the school's network. Science, IT and art facilities are fabulous, some with far reaching views across the Trent plain. Given that the school is mixed ability, the results are well spread but the head believes that there is usually improvement in each individual's performance. Over half A/B grade at A level. At GCSE, a very respectable 82 per cent A* to C.

Subjects are spread well across the board, with geography, sociology and art & design notably popular.

Languages on offer are French, German and Spanish. Staff are seriously dedicated and thrilled by the new premises and the challenges that lie ahead.

Games, Options, The Arts: Music plays a very large part in the school's curriculum with its close relationship to the Cathedral. The director of music's role is divided between the Cathedral and school, the school providing 40 choristers, so the standards are incredibly high with a number of orchestras, bands, and groups making for a busy concert programme. The school runs a GCSE Express Music course for year 9 pupils which allows them to complete the full course two years early.

Drama thriving and taught to A level. All year groups encouraged to take part.

Less emphasis on sport – facilities are a walk away – but the school is proud that their netball team is the fourth best in the country. Will go to great lengths to look after an individual talent, eg a swimmer who is showing great potential at an international level: to fit in with absences for training, the pupil is able to keep up with schoolwork over the internet.

Background and Atmosphere: In the shadows of the Cathedral: magnificent setting. An uplifting and immensely successful new build (there are old bits there, but the feel is modern). Food exceptionally good and the atmosphere in the dining hall one of enjoyment. An adult environment – pupils want to get on and do well.

Pastoral Care and Discipline: A strong sense of Christian values. Issues spotted early and dealt with immediately. Tutors are always on hand to help pupils and answer parents' concerns. Prefects too are approachable, even by the younger members of the school.

Pupils and Parents: There is no denying that this is a county school attracting children from Lincolnshire's further reaches, with buses ferrying them in, as well as a number of forces children. Boarding is popular with four houses in close proximity to the school. The boarding side looks a bit tired when compared to the modernity of the new facilities at the school. The houses are cosy, spotlessly clean and run by kind and sympathetic staff.

Enthusiastic kids, tidy, look you in the eye and chat easily. No foot-draggers here.

Parents stuck with the school through its redevelopment, and their children are now reaping the benefits tenfold.

Entrance: A number of children come from the Minster's prep school. Others attend a personal assessment day in January, which largely indicates the breadth of ability.

Exit: Durham, Newcastle, Leeds, Reading, Nottingham.

A few to Oxbridge. The Virtual Careers Library is a tremendous resource for leavers, which can be accessed from computers outside the school.

Money Matters: Well endowed. Scholarships (academic, art, music and sport), plus bursaries (up to full fees) from the United Church Schools Trust.

Remarks: State of the art facilities. Turns out well rounded and thoughtful children, with the desire to succeed.

LOMOND SCHOOL

Linked to Lomond School Junior Department in the Junior section

10 Stafford Street, Helensburgh, G84 9JX

Tel: 01436 672 476
Fax: 01436 678 320
E-mail: admin@lomond-school.demon.co.uk
Website: www.lomond-school.org

• Pupils: 560 boys and girls; all day except for 70 boarders
• Ages: 11-18 • Size of sixth form: 50 • Non-denom • Fees: Nursery £700; junior £1,230 senior £2,515 Rebate of 50 per cent for third sibling, on tuition fees only. Plus termly levy of £35 for capital purposes. Boarding fees add £2,705, or £2,650 for weekly boarders, or £38 b&b • Independent • Open days: Early November

---

Headmaster: Since 1986, Mr Angus Macdonald MA DipEd (mid fifties), educated at Portsmouth Grammar and an exhibitioner at Cambridge where he read geography; his previous post was as depute rector at George Watson's and before that he taught at Alloa and Edinburgh Academies. Married, two grown-up daughters.

This is the most hands-on head we have come across; he keeps records of every pupil's potential (CAT) and each youngster is under constant surveillance to make sure that they achieve their predicted potential. Whilst one child might find Bs and Cs an effort, others will be chided for not turning in regular As, and not just chided, extra work, a certain amount of hauling over the coals as well as regular two-hour detentions (like every night until their work improves). Children are given their targets and, if they get five commendations, a certificate; if not, then it is form reports; if no improvement after five weeks they go on depute's report and finally head's report. The final sanction for a non-working child is expulsion. Head knows each child personally and he knows them well. He monitors the seating plan in each lesson – boys share with girls, chattier ones with those who never put their hands up, and has a range of highly thought out classroom skills. He also plays a pupil for the day (last time he shadowed a fifteen year old girl). Wow, never have we found any head quite so intimately involved with their pupils' achievements. This is tough stuff. No obvious problems in getting staff, Helensburgh is a lovely (if expensive) place, what with the sailing and the Clyde and all, and no recent turnover.

Academic Matters: Well, with a headmaster who keeps pupils quite so up to the mark, what else would you expect? – tranches of As across the board though biology not so hot. Setted in English, French and maths at the age of 12, French taught from 8, German from 11. Huge range of subjects on offer, including such esoteric activities as graphic communication and English & communication, as well as French, German and Spanish and French, German and Spanish writing. Gaelic on offer but not much take up. Three sciences. Latin GCSE and psychology AS taught by video conference link and distance learning. School takes Standard Grades, Intermediate 2s, Highers, Advanced Highers and A levels – notably in the sciences, maths, statistics etc and the humanities. 90 per cent do Higher maths and can then move on to A level. Max class size 20. Sixth form were working – supervised (which is unheard of at that age) in the library when we visited. Homework very important, children keep a diary and expect to do at least two and a half hours each night in their Standard Grade year. The school has strong links with a private school in China and pupils follow GCSE and A levels in Chinese. Computers everywhere, networked and all have access to the internet; keyboarding skills for all, electronic interactive whiteboard presentations for all by all. Tutors for all. Good support for learning, with scribes and readers (but no provision for those with ADD or of ADHD), both withdrawn and team teaching on offer. English as a second language on hand.

Games, Options, The Arts: Huge playing field just along the (tree-lined) road. Rugby and hockey the two main winter games, with tennis, cricket and athletics in the summer and oodles of add-ons. Swimming in the local pool, option of squash, riding and badminton. Inter-house matches popular. Mass of lunch time clubs, D of E popular and, of course, sailing, The Scottish Islands Peaks Race, Lomond Challenge (a beastly tough triathlon). This is not a school for sissies.

Traditional Scottish music important here, well-subsidised (by the Glencoe Foundation in the States for one – that must please the headmaster, him being a Macdonald and all), and clarsach players, fiddlers, pipers and singers are in regular demand. Music, based in the old stables, is important here – one wall entirely covered with guitars, not just for decoration judging by the enthusiasm the guitar teacher generated. Recording facilities in place but tape only. Big bands and chamber orchestras, over 20 instruments on curriculum with some 150 individual lessons. Spectacular graphics department, where the teacher in charge was architect of the new school building and magical art department with old school desks press-ganged into use. Huge variety of disciplines, from photography with spit-new kit, magical screen printing, jewellery making as well as the more prosaic (which it wasn't) sculpture, painting and etching. Tremendous enthusiasm here and enchanting flower costume complete with design and basque and wings on show which was made for last summer's play. Strong drama.

Background and Atmosphere: Based on the northern edge of the posh, sleepy, seaside town of Helensburgh, school was originally housed in a series of Victorian villas. Present school is an amalgam of Larchfield founded in 1845 and the girls' school St Brides, which was founded in 1895. The schools combined in 1977 and, in February 1997, the St Brides' building suffered a massive fire, which gave them the chance to do a stunning re-build, partly financed by insurance and part by the sale of the Larchfield building. The resulting school is a curious combination of old and new, with three floors replacing the original two, and subject rooms being grouped in series. Most impressive, massive amount of glass, super new dining hall, good gym, and terrific entrance hall with glorious views out over the Clyde. Burnbrae, the boarding house, is currently being rebuilt to house both boys and girls, with a cunning fingerprint device to keep the two sexes apart (gives bundling a totally new meaning). New boarding houses on the way. All pupils wear uniform – kilts – neat and tidy with ties and a thoroughly purposeful air. Fairly uninformative prospectus, full of quotes from pupils and parents who, one suspects, are no longer part of the school, and remarkably short on fact.

Pastoral Care and Discipline: Strong anti-bullying procedure in place – the 'no blame' circle appears to be the most effective. Confidential suggestion boxes throughout the school are really part of the anti-bullying programme. Good PSD programme. CCTV cameras throughout the school. Children not 'given a lot of rope'; taking a puff of the odd joint equals letters to parents and discussion, dealing equals straight out. Smoking is apparently 'not happening just now', but smoking in uniform is 'not on'. The school tries to educate 'through' booze, but expulsion would, in any case, be the last resort.

Pupils and Parents: An upmarket lot; good middle class, from the surrounding area (they organise the buses) some from as far away as Glasgow, picked up quite a few with the recent closure of Keil School in Dumbarton. Number of Services families, Faslane next door, and some from further 'round the bay' send their children here. (The local state school thought to be too state.) Seven or eight mainland Chinese usually come for most of their secondary schooling, plus connection with Germany, whence the occasional pupil comes for a year or a term. Not much take-up with Scots going to Germany in exchange. Bonar Law was educated at Larchfield, as well as John Logie Baird – his school report, displayed in the dining room, apart from showing that he was fourteenth out of fourteen in maths, expresses the hope that he will eventually 'go on and do something with his life'.

Entrance: Either up via nursery or from local state primaries.

Exit: Usual dribble away after Standard Grades and could fill up the resulting places several times over, trickle leaves after Highers; some, again those going south to uni, tend to stay and do their A levels or Advanced Highers. Most will end up at university, usual trickle of two or three annually to Oxbridge. Gap year popular, particularly the Chinese option, where girls and boys have their fares paid, receive two thirds the normal salary and go and teach in China for a year, complete with lessons in Chinese.

Money Matters: Not a rich school. Will support pupils in financial difficulties, variety of scholarships and bursaries available at the age of 10 and 11 and post-Standard Grades. Good scholarships for those studying trad Scottish music.

Remarks: This is a jolly, busy school, perfect for those who want to keep their children at home and don't want the hassle of going daily to Glasgow, with one of the most outstanding heads we have come across. Steadily growing influx of Chinese pupils – from both mainland and Hong Kong.

THE LONDON ORATORY SCHOOL

Linked to London Oratory School Junior House (The) in the Junior section

Seagrave Road, London, SW6 1RX

Tel: 020 7385 0102
Fax: 020 7381 7676
E-mail: admin@los.ac
Website: www.london-oratory.org

• Pupils: 1,385; all boys except for 80 girls in the sixth form; all day • Ages: 7-18 • Size of sixth form: 350 • RC • State • Open days: Junior House - September and November

Headmaster: Since 1977, Mr John Charles McIntosh MA OBE FRSA (mid fifties). Educated Ebury School, Shoreditch College, Sussex University. Determined, dedicated, a builder and creator. Married to the school. Retiring July 2006.

Academic Matters: Takes a broad spread of ability. Classes are streamed on entry, with some setting in later years. Teaching styles are mostly formal; hard work is expected, whatever your level of ability. A steady performer in the academic league tables for some years. A strong profile of GCSE results – a good number of A*s, not too many Ds and Es, few laggards; the brightest take 5 GCSEs a year early and go on to take English AS, maths AS and Spanish GCSE from scratch, as extras in the fifth form. Consistent results at A level. Lots of computers, much used.

Games, Options, The Arts: Music immensely strong and popular (the good old hymns are sung here). Art OK but we saw comparatively little display of it – though school now tells us there's lots. Purpose built arts centre which also houses music department and fully equipped theatre. Sport is compulsory, and played with enthusiasm (but limited facilities); the CCF (Army and Air Force) is well supported. Every pupil will have had strong experience of IT and of public speaking by the time they leave – would that we could say this of more schools.

Background and Atmosphere: A very Catholic, very disciplined, hard-working all-ability school in pleasant modern buildings. The school's foundation derives from Saint Philip Neri (1515-95), a humorous and innovative preacher whose unorthodox views and behaviour (he was said to have shaved off half his beard for fun) would get him into considerable hot water here. Catholicism permeates everything, much more so than in many fee-paying Catholic schools. The discipline is exceptionally firm, again more so than most private schools – the pupils daren't even visit the local McDonald's, let alone smoke within a mile of the school.

Pastoral Care and Discipline: It's clearly fun to teach here and the teachers go out of their way to be helpful and friendly to pupils (but are called 'Sir' at all times). Pastoral problems are quickly passed on to one of the six housemasters. Operates the 3H rule – hair, homework and hard work. Pupils a happy and communicative lot nonetheless. Parents sign a written promise to monitor homework, ensure punctuality and control absence. Uniform for all at all ages, strongly-enforced policies on hairstyles etc.

Pupils and Parents: Committed Catholics from all walks of life from all over London.

Entrance: Apply a year in advance. You must be practising Roman Catholic and prepared to accept the firm discipline, school regulations and parental commitment – none of which are to be sneezed at. All applicants are interviewed – what counts is attitude: yours and your child's. Other factors taken into account include whether you have made the school your first choice and family connections with the school. Girls (and some boys) come in at sixth form from Catholic schools all over London; five grade As, and Bs or better in the subjects to be studied, required; attitude to work and responsibility are additionally important at this age; those already in the school sometimes find that their sixth form place is made conditional on this. For entrance to the junior house you need an IQ of over 100 and a strong aptitude for music; juniors have a right of entry to the senior school at 11 and are expected to use it. Don't worry about where you live – pupils (such as young Blairs) get in from miles away.

Exit: Rapid and certain if you (or your child) kick consistently against the unbending pricks of the school's policies ('not quite the case,' says the school). A few leave at 16 for a change of air but you should expect a strongly indignant reaction from the school if you are caught looking around while trying to keep your sixth form place open – you will have made a commitment to stay until 18 when applying. Of those who stay on for A levels, virtually all go to university, with ten or so per year to Oxbridge.

Remarks: Unique, strong, hard-working Catholic state school. Those the school suits, it suits well.

LORD WILLIAMS'S SCHOOL

Oxford Road, Thame, Oxfordshire, OX9 2AQ

Tel: 01844 210 510

Fax: 01844 261 382

E-mail: Headteacher.4580@lordwilliams.oxon.sch.uk

Website: www.lordwilliams.oxon.sch.uk

- Pupils: 2,190 boys and girls; all day • Ages: 11-18 • Size of sixth form: 450 • Non-denom • State

Head: Acting head since Sept 2005, Mr David Wybron MA (forties). Previously head of lower school, and deputy head of Lord Williams's overall, he joined school in 1991 as head of humanities faculty. History graduate from Swansea University who taught in Cambridgeshire and Great Missenden, Bucks, before settling in Thame. Still teaches GCSE history to one class a week. A softly-spoken Welshman whose drive and determination should not be under-estimated. 'I am passionate about this place,' he assures us. Has already drawn up two to three year plan of improvements with better GCSE results a top priority. Wife a secondary school teacher, one child at school in Aylesbury, the other at university. Took over from Michael Spencer, head since 2000.

Academic Matters: Still one of top state schools in Oxfordshire. A level results seen as major success in 2005 with 99 per cent pass rate, 74 per cent A-C grades. GCSE results might seem less impressive; 64 per cent gained five or more A*-C grades with 94 per cent exam passes overall – but still far exceeding national and county averages. OK, but could be better, says head. Focus now very much on improving those grades though and broadening choices, including vocational subjects. Head says, 'I'm looking at the core agenda for all students and looking to see how we can be sure our students get the right package and develop the right skills.' As children of all abilities entered for exams, results are pretty sound and school commended by Ofsted for adding value, 'well above the national average'. Girls beat the boys in most subjects (as per national trend) but boys come out on top in core areas of English, maths and science. Huge curriculum choice at every level. Special needs very well catered for. Resource unit for 20 children with autism on site, also plenty of classroom and extra help for others with dyslexia and other learning problems. Well-stocked libraries in both lower and upper schools, regularly updated. ICT taught as subject in its own right to all from

year 7, also as learning support for later studies. 10 purpose-built computer networked suites boast latest technology and are in constant demand. Loads of classroom assistants as well as subject specialists mean large classes of 30-odd are kept under control.

Games, Options, The Arts: Sports college status, also awarded an Artsmark Gold award for its creative arts provision. Both areas of school impressive, highly productive and successful. But head keen to point out, 'we are not just a sports school, we haven't slanted things so that it's just about sport.' Happy with the health, leadership, fitness and community agendas. Shared use of Thame sports centre (right next door to school), acres of playing fields and plans for all-weather pitch. Regularly produce county (sometimes national) players and winning teams. NVQ football course launched in 2005 for sixth formers. Art studios well used and well resourced. Excellent examples of work on head's study walls. Good displays at lower school. Good music uptake. Individual lessons as well as compulsory class music for all early on. Traditional orchestras now complemented by assortment of bands. Drama, dance and theatre studies all popular time-table and exam options. Impressive results too.

Background and Atmosphere: A true comprehensive. Known affectionately as Lord Bill's, it's a big school – much bigger than average secondary with 2,000+ pupils – but split over two sites about two miles apart. School founded by Lord Williams of Thame in 1575. Current set-up dates from 1971 when Lord Williams's Grammar and Wenman Secondary merged. Both sites on leafy edge of market town, well spread out, and despite high numbers on school register, there's room to breathe. Buildings mixed in age and mostly functional, parts much in need of TLC, but well laid out and absolutely buzzing. 'It's an ideas place. There's a sparkiness here about teaching and learning.' Students allowed voice in decision making process. 'Sometimes people are afraid of the student voice,' says head. 'But we harness it.' Recently played major role in choosing new caterers. (Plumped for healthy option rather than one offering fatty fry-ups and burgers.) Canteen style lunches, good selection of fresh salads, some vending machines still with the usual contents. School sites very open and security has recently been stepped up. CCTV installed at cost of £38,000 at lower school, all staff and visitors to upper school must wear ID and anyone not wearing a badge will be challenged by staff and students alike. Maintains close ties with local primaries through well-established system of networking. Much effort made to ease the transition to 'big' school through team-building activities.

Pastoral Care and Discipline: Small tutor groups, communications and family workers, plus close links with parents all provide solid student support. Nurture groups set up for students who are particularly vulnerable. Children shown how to deal with own problems too, as well as being encouraged to seek help. Few serious misdemeanours but guilty parties swiftly dealt with. Sliding scale of exclusion periods for offenders. No instant dismissal for drugs, but police will automatically be involved. Head readily admits bullying exists, but is not tolerated. All unacceptable behaviour dealt with initially in the same way – with a range of sanctions used – detentions, internal isolations and fixed term external exclusions.

Pupils and Parents: Confident, sometimes outspoken, but articulate and secure. Hard workers will achieve and the less academically able are being increasingly catered for. Students seen on our visit appeared focused and involved in their lessons. Their relationship with staff seemed generally relaxed and informal. A socially mixed catchment area obviously results in a wide social mix at school. Some from professional backgrounds, plenty of rural and an increasing number who qualify for free school meals. Parents range from the supportive to the demanding, rather than the apathetic.

Entrance: From Oxfordshire state primaries in Thame and surrounding villages like Chinnor and Tetsworth, but also a number of Buckinghamshire schools (like Brill and Long Crendon) due to school's proximity to county border. Over-subscribed by about two to one. Head describes Lord Williams's as 'truly inclusive'.

Exit: Up to 70 per cent stay on to sixth form, most of those leaving after year 11 go onto college courses or into employment. Majority go to university or college after A levels, annually two or three to Oxbridge. No single area of expertise evident – courses and jobs right across the board.

Money Matters: Extra funding given through sports college status has been well spent and clever bit of land sale (a small triangle of unused playing field) is paying for the new all-weather pitch.

Remarks: A perennially popular school which maintains a good local reputation through its ability to do well by its students. Seen by some as a safety net for Bucks grammar school failures but hard-grafters won't be disappointed. In many respects worthy of first choice status, certainly not second best.

LORETTO SCHOOL

Linked to Loretto Junior School aka The Nippers in the Junior section

Musselburgh, East Lothian, EH21 7RE

Tel: 01316 534 444
Fax: 01316 534 445
E-mail: admissions@loretto.com
Website: www.loretto.com

- Pupils: 141 boys, 129 girls, of whom 182 board • Ages: 13-18 • Size of sixth form: 113 • Non-denom • Fees: Senior school: £7,010 boarding; £4,633 day. Junior school: £4,955 - £5,286 boarding; £1,748 - £3,507 day • Independent • Open days: One each term; see school website

Head: Since 2001, Mr Michael Mavor CVO MA (fifties), who was educated at Loretto (head boy and head of almost everything else), he is umbilically attached to the place), read English at St John's (trails of scholarships). Previously head of Rugby, he worked in the States before his appointment as head of Gordonstoun at 31. Married to Elizabeth, with a son at Oxford and a grown-up daughter. Mr Mavor, who is renowned for his PR skills, was chairman of the HMC in 1997; and previously a governor here. He came to Loretto like a knight in shining armour.

No more building pro tem: masses of tidying-up and rather efficient house-keeping: new paint jobs, some new staff, and a 'change of ethos' in the school. 'It is now cool to work'. Loretto prides itself on being 'a family school'; the headmaster talks to the whole school, on his own, two or three times a week (known as doubles). This is unique in our experience. Having come from Rugby, with its massive secretarial, bursarial, you name it back-up, Mr Mavor initially found it 'interesting' to run a smaller school with a much smaller organisation. (We previously quoted his actual words – 'quite tough going' – he prefers the word 'challenge'.) Mrs Mavor much in evidence and regularly joins the staff, and indeed the whole of the school, for lunch. Both are enjoying the Edinburgh social scene.

Academic Matters: Monthly tutorial assessments, which are 'minuted and followed through' with pupils and parents. School now exclusively follows the English system. GCSEs for all, plus AS and A2s. Normally pupils take four AS, followed by three A2 levels though, increasingly, top end pupils go for 5 AS and four A2. Yet another AS can be added in the upper sixth. Maths, biology, physics and business studies the most popular subjects, each attracting up to a third of the year group. Traditionally strong on science and engineering, A level physics course now has encouraging numbers of girls. Three sciences standard at GCSE, though thankfully one can be dropped for art or music. AS results have pleasing numbers of As across the board and 100 per cent pass at A level in 2003. In 2004 10 out of 60 candidates achieved straight As at A level. GCSEs now better too – 50 per cent A*s or As. French, history, geography strong at GCSE, Spanish increasing in popularity. Russian and Mandarin Chinese new additions at all levels.

Pupils are setted in English, maths and languages, according to ability – from fourth form, most subjects setted. The girls apparently set the academic standard and boys try to match them. The staff whom we met were all bright, bubbly and enthusiastic. Mrs Shepherd, the 'sums lady', is also deputy head and was particularly impressive. Lunchtime viewing in the dining room showed a remarkable lack of young blood, though this has now changed with the appointment of twelve new 'young' staff in last two years.

ESL and support learning available throughout, though both at extra cost. Networked computers everywhere, even in study-bedrooms if requested (you need 'your own card') Masses of visiting lecturers, interview practice for all.

Games, Options, The Arts: Singing as ever good and keen, the whole school sings in the war-memorial chapel choir – soprano, alto, tenor, bass, also performers at the Schools Proms at the Royal Albert Hall. A burgeoning orchestra, most of the third (ie 13 year olds) study one or more instruments, and, as always an acclaimed pipe band which still travels globally. Drama on the up, theatre studies now available at AS and A2 levels, as is PE. Art scholars take life classes as well as screen printing and textiles.

Loretto used to be famed for its prowess on the rugby field and is beginning to recover its reputation under a new director of sport. Cricket XI and hockey teams put on a creditable performance. The girls' athletics and lacrosse do well (rows of lax sticks were waiting to be cut down to size for younger players when we visited). Impressive all-weather court now surrounded by a security fence – as much to keep out the local ungodly ('what happened to the 'honest toun?') as to pre-empt the Right to Roam Act. Skiing once more a serious activity, the school won the army championships in 2001. CCF, Young Enterprise and D of E etc.

The Golf Academy which opened in September 2002 is flourishing (school has a long tradition of senior golfing FPs), and golf is professionally coached throughout the school to all pupils using top class practice facilities on campus

including a nine-hole Huxley all weather putting green. Rounds are played at the local Craigielaw Golf Club and the Musselburgh Old Course. Older pupils can have their lessons re-jigged to accommodate coaching. Recent accolades include three Golf Scholarships to leading American Universities, two qualifiers to the Daily Telegraph Golf Championship finals and wins in many of the county championships. Last year seven of the top squad played for their countries (Scotland, Ireland and Italy). Talent spotting days and Easter and summer residential Golf camps are run to encourage new golfers to apply.

Background and Atmosphere: Founded in 1827, and bought by Hely Hutchison Almond in 1862 (a distinguished scholar of unconventional convictions – Scotland's answer to Dr Arnold), the school went fully co-ed in 1995. The traditional East Lothian ochre-coloured buildings straddle the main road. Swimming pool off-campus, and early morning (6.30am) swimming popular. Various outbuildings, including The Nippers, across the River Esk. Holm House (with lift for disabled access) and Balcarres, the two girls' houses, are adjacent to the (small) sports centre. Girls of both houses are mixed up for the first year (and indeed the two houses are joined at both levels) and then move on to study bedrooms. Senior common rooms for sixth form with a certain amount of male access, but the 'social communication' of the sexes has not really been thought out. Linkfield, the sixth form bar, open at weekends, is not really the answer, though barbecues are popular at the girls' houses and attended by all. This will all change in September 2006 as a major development and refurbishment programme is underway to accommodate the structural changes that will be introduced into the school then. All six houses will be completely refurbished by 2007.

The corridor to the dining room is lined with photographs of Lorettonians of the past – pupils delight in pointing out photographs of the head in shorts (but remember it is not so long ago that all Lorettonians wore shorts, daily). The famous haunted Pinkie House, with its important painted ceiling in the gallery under the roof, is home to the youngest pupils – though we understand the ghost is not much in evidence. The first three years of boys share mixed dorms, with SBUs (study bed units) which must be tough on those taking GCSE – though there are other study areas available in the houses.

Kilts on Sundays. Some remnants of the trad uniform remain. Red jackets the norm for all. The sixth form must wear them for public occasions (our guides showed us round the school in red and instantly changed into navy blue for the rest of the day), but the rest of the school was in red and still no ties for daily dress. Rather dreary long skirts for girls and an absolute ban on any form of platform heels – no more 'tottering on the asphalt'.

The CRC (Communication and Resource Centre), untouched at our last visit, now shows slight signs of wear, computers out of their stations, and the smirr of cleaning materials on the black plastic which covers the keyboard has gone polaroid which must make working there difficult. But libraries full of books, learning support and EFL and new head of ICT has 'ambitious plans....'.

Plexi-glass now covers all but the memorial window in the chapel. Full boarding, weekly boarding and flexi-boarding on offer as well as day pupils. Buses from all over – mainly East Lothian, and more in the pipeline. School operates a six morning, three afternoon schedule, and day pupils can and do go home during the week at 4.30pm if they have no further activities (otherwise it is 6.30/8.30pm). Sixth form boarders can get permission to go into Edinburgh on any night of the week 'providing that their work is in order'. They can go to a film, to the theatre, to concerts (rock or otherwise), and the upper sixth can go to the races in Musselburgh. The young told this editor that they take taxis, though apparently buses are gaining in popularity. Younger boarders take the school bus of a weekend to Kinaird Park, which houses a multiplex cinema as well as a collection of utterly desirable shops – a great improvement on Musselburgh. This is a chilly corner of East Lothian and the east wind whistling across the race course from the North Sea is an almost permanent feature (headmaster is not so sure!).

Pastoral Care and Discipline: Small school, so great family feel, and this is much emphasised by the head. Zero tolerance for drugs no longer the norm: head operates the same system he used at Rugby – automatically out for being caught actively using any drug or for dealing, 'but the alternative policy which can be adopted if the facts are not clear, involves the whole truth from everybody, and no disciplinary consequences if drugs have been involved. 'Instead parents are told, counselling may follow, and the pupils concerned go on random urine testing for the remainder of their school career. A positive test would then mean expulsion' School is tough on persistent bullying ('we spend hours on it, please don't use the word tough'). Recognised ladder for punishments, no longer entirely in the houseparent's domain: breathalyser, gatings, rustications and out for booze; gatings and letters home for fags.

Pupils and Parents: Usual Scottish collection, not a lot of foreigners here; large number of OL's sons, daughters and grandchildren, some of whom join for the sixth form only. Fair number of first time buyers. Not really a Sloane/Charlotte Ranger school. OLs include the current headmaster, plus a gang of MPs, Lord Lamont, Lord (Hector) Laing, Andrew Marr, Alastair Darling, and the current chairman of the governors Ronald G Graham CBE.

Entrance: Own entrance exam or CE from Scottish and northern prep schools; pupils come up from The Nippers en masse. Special exam and interview for those from the state sector, or from overseas. Five GCSEs at C and above for entry into sixth form – about 10/15 annually. Scholarships are available at 12+ for those from state primary schools.

Exit: 98 per cent or so to tertiary education with a regular four to six to Oxbridge – 85 per cent getting into their first choice of university.

Money Matters: Masses of scholarships for all-rounders, musicians, drama, art, sport, golf, plus scholarships for those from the state sector, and for those coming up from The Nippers etc etc, also sixth-form scholarships and post-school bursaries awarded to those 'who have deserved well of Loretto'. 19 scholarships awarded in 2005, excluding golf scholars.

Remarks: We have previously described Loretto as a 'Famous Scottish public school, now co-ed, for gentle middling souls in need of nurturing'; all this is true. With Michael Mavor at the helm the school itself is getting the nurturing it needs to return it to the forefront. Extra day pupils are being actively sought, extra buses in the pipe line and a lot of tightening up, both academically and socially. Loretto is back in the frame.

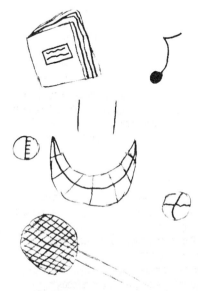

LOUGHBOROUGH GRAMMAR SCHOOL

Linked to Fairfield Preparatory School in the Junior section

Linked to Loughborough High School in the Senior section

Burton Walks, Loughborough, Leicestershire, LE11 2DU

Tel: 01509 233 233
Fax: 01509 218 436
E-mail: registrar@loughgs.leics.sch.uk
Website: www.loughgs.leics.sch.uk

• Pupils: 1,010 boys; 50 boarders, the rest day • Ages: 10-18
• Christian - non denominational • Fees: Day £2,715 boarding: full £4,824, weekly £4,260 - all per term • Independent • Open days: October

Headmaster: Since 1998, Mr Paul Fisher MA (late forties). Taught at Prior Park College in Bath and Marlborough College. Teaches classics and RE to years 7 and 11, a good way to get to know the pupils and maintain the relationship throughout the school. A very likeable person who clearly has huge support from his staff, pupils and their parents. Plenty of humour which is reflected in the extremely happy atmosphere of the school. Married to Helen who teaches Spanish and French here; two boys, both at university.

Academic Matters: Not an academic sausage machine and all boys given full opportunity to shine in any way they choose. Having said that, A level results are very good indeed with 65 per cent (out of 62 entries) getting an A in maths and all but one pupil gaining an A in further maths (and his result was not to be sniffed at). Other popular subjects are biology, chemistry and physics, English and French. Maths and a modern foreign language are compulsory subjects to GCSE level and Latin to the end of year 8. The first three years are used to emphasise the fun in learning and boys go confidently into their GCSE years. Average class size 19, maximum 26. Average age of the staff – early to mid forties with about 50 per cent having 10 or more years' service.

Superb new language lab with state-of-the-art facilities proving very popular and encouraging. Computers evident all around the school and much used. Although selective on academic grounds, every pupil is screened and, if necessary, assessed for SEN. The school is highly supportive with about 60 boys currently receiving extra help – individual targets, very confidence-boosting.

Games, Options, The Arts: Sport in good variety and much enjoyed, and is compulsory in some form twice a week with matches on Saturday afternoons. Rugby remains very popular as do hockey, basketball, swimming (own heated indoor pool) and cross-country, with cricket, athletics and tennis in the summer. Popular extra-curricular activities include D of E, CCF, music and drama. Magic club run by sixth former who is a member of The Magic Circle. Also a hugely popular lunchtime and weekend bridge club which boasts national and international players, and a karting club where the boys build their own go-karts and then race, with much success at national level.

New drama studio allows for some marvellous productions, once a term in conjunction with the girls' high school, and as an integral part of the school. Approximately 60 per cent of pupils play at least one musical instrument; very enthusiastic musical department with two big bands, one of which was selected for the National Festival of Music for Youth at Queen Elizabeth Hall in London, who perform bi-annually abroad in eg Prague, Italy, Austria and Spain, often on sea-front bandstands as well as concert halls. Popular choir which tours both at home and abroad, two string orchestras and a woodwind and brass ensemble.

Background and Atmosphere: Founded in 1495, Loughborough Grammar School is now part of the Loughborough Endowed Schools and shares the same extensive campus as Loughborough High School for Girls and Fairfield School, the co-educational junior school. Although independent of each other, the three schools share a common board of governors and the links joining the three are very tangible. There is joint sixth form teaching but this is not a co-educational senior school.

All boys from all backgrounds are fully integrated and made to feel welcome and part of the community. Although generally Christian, with 20 per cent of pupils from other religious denominations, all faiths are celebrated and included in the curriculum. Lovely mixture of old and new buildings surrounding an attractive cherry tree-lined grassed quadrangle; boys behave better because of the way the place looks and feels. There is, for instance, a distinct lack of litter and general dumping of school bags and blazers.

Pastoral Care and Discipline: Small tutor groups, with a great deal of support at all levels, staff always have time to talk and help where necessary, said one pupil, a view echoed by others and parents. Boys are made to feel that they contribute in some way. Anyone who is prepared to join in and have a go, in whatever capacity, will fit into this school. In a sixth form with a broad ability range, those boys who come out with lower grades at A level are made to feel that they have really achieved something and are encouraged to apply to university.

Pupils tell us that bullying is really not a problem. If it does occur it is dealt with quickly at the root. Boys seem to be able to separate what is acceptable at home and at school. The two small boarding houses offer a homely atmosphere with comfortable dorms and sitting rooms both within easy reach of the campus, so sports facilities can be used outside school hours. Staff always willing to find the time to talk to parents.

Pupils and Parents: Some middle class, others not; about 25 per cent from ethnic minority backgrounds as well as approximately a dozen boys from mainland China and Hong Kong and a few from other parts of the world. Buses from all over Leicester, Derbyshire and Nottinghamshire, as well as the immediate local area. Old scholars include Patrick McGoohan (actor, 'The Prisoner'), Colin Dexter (author of the Inspector Morse books), Peter Preston (editor of The Guardian), Marcus Rose (England Rugby International), Bruce Woolley (Pop singer/composer, 'Video Killed The Radio Star'), the late Johnnie Johnson and Felix Buxton of Basemant Jaxx.

Entrance: By own examination, at 10, 11 and 13, or CE at 13, with about 40 boys coming in at 11 from Fairfield School. Sixth form entry based on GCSE grades – overseas pupils may sit an entrance exam in the subjects to be studied in the sixth form.

Exit: About 10 per cent leave after GCSE, usually to go to a sixth form college or other school that offers a specific course that Loughborough Grammar does not. University places are varied, from Oxbridge (15-20 each year) reading law, theology or maths to other universities reading medicine, dentistry, engineering or computer sciences etc. Generally a good range of subjects being read at a good variety of universities.

Money Matters: Financially secure and not pressured into taking students who would not fit into the school. A number of scholarships and exhibitions at 10, 11 and 13, awarded on academic merit, regardless of parents' means. Some music awards each spring for boys entering the following September. School assisted places are available upon request.

Remarks: Any boy willing to have a go and join in would be welcome here. A very happy, productive school, excellent facilities and support from staff and pupils. Very well respected in the area and beyond, the current head is continuing to attract a wide range of boys who really contribute to the success of the school.

LOUGHBOROUGH HIGH SCHOOL

Linked to Fairfield Preparatory School in the Junior section

Linked to Loughborough Grammar School in the Senior section

Burton Walks, Loughborough, Leicestershire, LE11 2DU

Tel: 01509 212 348
Fax: 01509 215 720
E-mail: admin@loughhs.leics.sch.uk
Website: www.loughhs.leics.sch.uk

• Pupils: 580 girls, all day • Ages: 11-18 • Size of sixth form: 161 • Non-denom • Fees: £2,493 • Independent • Open days: October

Headmistress: Since 2002, Bridget O'Connor MA (mid forties). Read literae humaniores at St Hugh's College, Oxford. Taught classics at Francis Holland and became head of classics and year head at Old Palace School, Croydon. Moved to Haberdashers' Aske's School for Girls as head of classics and head of sixth form, then deputy head, before moving here. Married with one daughter. Very keen to make improvements, particularly extending the IT and music departments. A very fair head, with a good sense of humour, liked by her staff and pupils.

Academic Matters: Very academic school with excellent results. Impressive GCSE results, particularly in double science, English literature and maths, leading on to equally impressive A level results – 89 per cent plus A/B. Huge support from teachers who, according to a number of pupils, 'really care how well you do and therefore put themselves out for us.' The most popular subjects at A level are biology, chemistry and maths closely followed by history. Classics in year 7 (taught by the head), Latin compulsory in years 8 and 9, those who continue this through to GCSE level generally get A* or A. German or Spanish as additional modern foreign language in year 9. Three computer suites with 15 to a room – not enough, but gradually being improved.

Does not cater for statemented children but pupils with diagnosed specific learning difficulties are put on the school's own Individual Education Plan. Excellent library, with computerised fingerprinting instead of library card, very popular – 'I kept losing my library card before this was introduced,' said one girl. Lots of computers in the library and a separate resource room with internet access. Appears to be very well used.

Games, Options, The Arts: Traditional sports – hockey, netball and cross-country in the winter, tennis, athletics and rounders in the summer. Great use made of the recently introduced Astroturf. Some excellent achievements in all sports at county level; one national success at U14 tennis.

Music increasingly popular with about 85 per cent learning at least one instrument; some very talented musicians amongst the pupils with one student being a member of the National Youth Orchestra, some girls play in the County Symphonic Wind Band and many pupils in the Leicestershire Schools' Orchestras at various levels. Some joint ventures with the boys' Grammar School.

Excellent art department with some really superb work displayed throughout the school; a great variety of media and small group taking art at A level. Lively drama department with a good mix of productions from traditional plays to musicals, often in conjunction with the Grammar School. Popular lunchtime drama clubs.

Plenty of extra-curricular activities, including a very popular mind games club at lunchtime in conjunction with the Grammar School, chess, Chinese chess, bridge, Scrabble and Go as well as other games that many people may not have heard of. On the day of our visit, pupils were playing a Japanese game called Pini.

Background and Atmosphere: Loughborough High School was founded in 1850 and is one of the oldest girls' grammar schools in the country. Academic work and excellence are central to the philosophy of the school, though personal and social development receive much attention. Pupils commented that the school offers such tremendous support and friendship that it is just like one big happy family. Popular school council chaired by the head girl and her two deputies discusses canteen changes, the introduction of Spanish, a change in the school uniform. Staff sit on the periphery, listening and allowing the pupils the chance to debate.

Pastoral Care and Discipline: Staff and pupils are really attentive to each other's needs and each girl treated as important. Staff always available and willing to chat, go out of their way to iron out problems.

Pupils and Parents: From a 40 mile radius covering Leicestershire, Derbyshire and Nottinghamshire. Huge variety of backgrounds including Asian and European; a recent survey showed 21 languages spoken by families and extended families. Only two pupils from overseas (China) who seem to fit in very well. Parents and pupils very enthusiastic about the school; the happy atmosphere really shines thorough as you are shown round.

Entrance: Exams at 11, 13 and at 14 when a foreign language is tested, usually French but an alternative if French has not been studied. Entry at 16 has a mixture of tests and interviews. Approximately 40 per cent come up from Fairfield Preparatory School (part of the Loughborough Endowed Schools), others from prep and primary schools (and state secondaries at 12,13 and 14).

Exit: A few girls take a gap year but most go on to university, about half a dozen to Oxbridge the rest to universities around the UK reading a diverse range of subjects. Many choose the sciences, others subjects as such as anthropology, economics, a variety of languages, architecture, law, medicine and classical civilisation. Not many leaving after GCSE, only those wanting either to board, to go onto a sixth form college or, more usually, to study a subject not offered at Loughborough.

Money Matters: Three scholarships and three exhibitions at 11 and one of each at 13. Some music scholarships and exhibitions are offered annually, details of these are sent to applicants who are offered a place following the academic exams. School assisted places and bursaries are awarded on each individual's merits.

Remarks: An excellent and very friendly school for the academic girl who has lots of energy and commitment together with a love of learning, and who can keep up with the rigorous pace.

LYCÉE FRANÇAIS CHARLES DE GAULLE

Linked to Lycée Français Charles de Gaulle Primary in the Junior section

Linked to Ecole André Malraux in the Junior section

Linked to Ecole Charles de Gaulle - Wix in the Junior section

Linked to Lyceé Français Charles de Gaulle (British Section)

35 Cromwell Road, London, SW7 2DG

Tel: 020 7584 6322
Fax: 020 7823 7684
E-mail: proviseur@lyceefrancais.org.uk
Website: www.lyceefrancais.org.uk

• Pupils: 3,500 (including primary and nursery school); all day (but see below) • Ages: 3-18 • Size of sixth form: 400 (100 in the English section; 300 in the French) • No religious affiliation • Fees: French section - subsidised by the French Government - primary £970 secondary £1,191 - 2,031, British section £1,868 • Independent

Proviseur: Since 2001, M André Becherand (fifties). Married with two children, with degrees from universities of Nancy, Lyons, Toronto. Taught English at various schools in France before becoming lecturer (French studies) at Loughborough University; had a spell as consultant for General Motors in Indiana, followed by four headships, latterly in Alsace. Manages to teach one period per week (French studies) to the GCSE class.

A four/five year post. Feeling his way, M Becherand inherited the school in excellent shape and appears even more dynamic than his predecessor.

Head of English Stream: Mrs R E Nichol.

Academic Matters: Formidable, and results considered extraordinary by French standards. Academic success has made it difficult to make changes. 30 per class. First lesson is at 8.40am, and lessons all last 55 minutes. Lots of learning by rote, and it is important to reproduce what the teacher has taught. For the Bac, students choose literary, economic or science 'stream' at the age of 16 – and the most brilliant pupils go for the sciences.

Children can move to the British section – for GCSEs and A levels – from the age of 14, following staff/parent meetings, consideration of end of term reports and thorough discussion. Pupils entering the British Section are (according to the Lycée) 'usually those who, although bilingual, are more at ease in English.' A member of staff told us they were often the strugglers – 'and it's a joy to see them flower.' The British Section allows these pupils to prepare British examinations while maintaining their contact with French language and culture. (French GCSE and A level compulsory for all pupils in this Section.) Currently there are 225 children in the British Section of the school. Entente very cordiale – British and French systems now collaborate far more than they used to.

Philosophy for all in their penultimate year. At the start of the academic ladder, true to the French tradition, children repeat a year if their work is not up to scratch – a threat that is regularly carried out – and fear of this humiliation makes children work hard. The head commented that lots of children get extra tuition, which he declared to be 'quite unnecessary'.

Especial strength of the French system is training the young to become good at analysing and expressing themselves. Extra work on Saturdays in school for slackers. Not much time for the individual. NB All teachers are appointed directly by the French government (through the ministry for education and foreign affairs), though the head's own assessment, made via application papers (no formal meeting) weighs heavily. Immensely dedicated teachers. Famously heavy homework loads. No school on Wednesday afternoons at primaire (traditionally this is for home-based catechism classes) but a recent development (to cries of delight) are the Wednesday afternoon clubs and activities for littles with older siblings in the school, and nowadays open to all the children in the primaire.

Games, Options, The Arts: The shortcoming of the place, by and large. Head of sports does his absolute best – busing pupils to Raynes Park: basketball and volleyball both keenly played. Playground bursts with activity and noise but parents will need to allow their sons and daughters to let off physical steam at weekends.

Background and Atmosphere: Busy and noisy in the main huge block in Cromwell Road, stretching back to Harrington Road. Huge quad and playground, admin offices mainly on the Cromwell Road side. School's history is linked with the Institut Français (the increasingly dynamic centre for French culture in London), and this lycée first opened in 1915 near Victoria Station with 120 pupils (mainly Belgian and French refugees, though Belgians seem to be given short shrift these days). Present building inaugurated in 1958. Teaching blocks consist of lengthy corridors and rather soulless classrooms. Though French is the main language you hear plenty of English, Spanish, Italian, German,

Russian and Arabic – but the whole place feels French, down to the chicly dressed secretaries and above all attitudes – be warned! The whole quartier is frenchified, with boutiques, boucheries, patisseries, book shops etc. Surprisingly strong school spirit (nb a very un-French trait).

The atmosphere is very, well, French. Institutional even. Et cool. Tinies may be flattened. Do not be put off when they answer the telephone in French, however: if you speak loud enough they will give in in the end and speak English. NB sartorial note: the Lycée has an Old School Tie – the only Lycée in the world to have one. Not a lot of people know this. Food: you would expect, would you not, at least a Michelin star in this home from home for the French in London, and indeed the menus are little poems of delight: couscous mouton (the chef's speciality, explained the member of staff who very kindly showed us round), boeuf bourguignon, jardinières des légumes frais etc etc. However, we have to relate that the reality is somewhat different: about three-quarters of pupils were eating frites. However, marvellous patisseries have sprouted up all round the area, to cater for those who could kill for a baguette.

Pastoral Care and Discipline: Surveillants (kind of monitors, often young students themselves) patrol the building, supervise meals, keep a watchful eye on the classes in the five minutes between lessons etc – leaving the teachers free to teach. The French system decrees that matters spiritual and pastoral are mainly the province of the parents and the church, however the school's attitude is not exactly laissez faire – but there is a rough element, though pupils mainly courteous and easy. Nasty drugs incident in 2002 swiftly dealt with by the head who immediately brought in the police.

Pupils and Parents: Wonderful broad mix – fifty different nationalities. The majority of children come from the French-speaking world, plus mixed marriages, embassy children from all parts of the globe. Parents from all walks of life, dress-makers, civil servants, dukes, bankers, actors, ex-pats. Huge effort in last few years to involve parents far more in their children's education. 'Parents need to support their children,' said a mother, feelingly.

Entrance: Complicated. Registration, preferably before Easter, for the following September, interview and test. Starting from scratch (ie at 4 years old) children do not need to speak French. However, entry at almost any other stage and certainly from the age of 8 upwards (if, that is, there is a place going) necessitates absolutely fluent French, and also requires the applicant to have successfully completed the previous year's National Curriculum, and be deemed capable of/ready to move on. The school is at pains to point

out that this can be done outside school time – but in practice it means that most children join from following the French system elsewhere. Secondaire starts at sixième (ie when children are 11 years old). Staff good at informing parents about junior nursery schools elsewhere in London. Make sure you have a strong French connection (house in Normandy or a French granny) before you apply. Well worth considering for sixth form A levels if you want change with a French flavour.

Exit: French and English universities: Imperial College very popular, also USA, Columbia, Princeton, Yale and Canada (McGill) – international business studies, European law with languages for instance. Fair numbers opt out aged 11 or 13 and switch to English schools (but the Lycée does not prepare them for CE).

Money Matters: 13 scholarships selected by the French department of education. Fees a snip - subsidised by the French government.

Remarks: First-class academic education in the real French style – but don't even begin to consider the place if you mind about extra-curricular. Robust and confident children best suited here.

LYMM HIGH VOLUNTARY CONTROLLED SCHOOL

Oughtrington Lane, Lymm, Cheshire, WA13 0RB

Tel: 01925 755 458
Fax: 01925 758 439
E-mail: sch_lymm@warrington.gov.uk
Website: www.lymmhigh.co.uk

• Pupils: 1,960 boys and girls, all day • Ages: 11-19 • Size of sixth form: 430 • Non-denom • Fees: Free • State • Open days: 6th form open evening November

Head Teacher: Since 1998, Roger A Lounds (fifties). Married with two grown children. Down to earth, enthusiastic, deemed 'very approachable' by parents. Dismisses his letters BA MSc MA DMS (Ed) DipCEdG CertEd as not making any difference to Roger Lounds the person. Passionately believes in non-selective co-education 'because society is mixed; if you can create a school that mirrors society, youngsters find it easier to cope as they grow up.' Came from challenging headships at Brumby Comprehensive in Scunthorpe and Vermuyden School, Goole.

Academic Matters: Lymm High School ranks in top 30 non-selective state schools for results. 93 per cent plus 5+ A*-Cs at GCSE. Specialist language college since 1996 – five language assistants, in separate block of eight classrooms with state of the art technology, offering German, Spanish, French, Russian, Italian, Japanese and Mandarin – 80 language on-line learning packages available. Staff from LHS teach and support language learning in partner primary schools; this is regarded as exemplar practice by CILT. Languages being worked into vocational corners of the curriculum – take-up improving from a low base. Many students take intermediate and advanced vocational GNVQs/BTEC each year, most passing at the higher level. Hospitality and catering course, with the opportunity for study/work experience in France, and sports vocational course with work experience in Spain. New courses in art/design, fashion, health science, travel and tourism, construction, design and performing arts.

Setting in two ability 'populations' is standard throughout school in most subjects and parents like the way pupils readily move up and down sets depending on performance. Good provision for dyslexia and dyspraxia in designated block; currently 200 special needs pupils. School works closely with parents of SEN children from years 5 and 6 before transition to secondary school. Huge developments in SEN provision over past six years from single SENCO to learning development team of 25 staff working to evaluate and improve support. Extra literary sessions at 8.15am before school, lunchtime typing/homework club popular for those who need extra help and those escaping hurly burly of playground. Wheelchair-friendly sixth form, lift and automated doors. Timetabling for ground floor access if necessary lower down school. Advanced skills teacher identifies and encourages gifted and talented pupils through 'gifted scholarship programme' for over 200 pupils in all subjects including sport, using mentoring, advanced public exams, university work in addition to A levels, summer schools, outside lecturers and trainers and the National Academy for Gifted and Talented Youth in Warwick. Parents describe this area of school as 'really on the ball' and versatile with the possibility of a child having, for example, extra help for dyslexia while on the honours programme for art or sport.

LHS has links with schools in South Africa and is supporting developments at Quashana High School in a black township near East London. This school is also supported by one of Lymm's partners, Glen High in Pretoria.

Developments in teaching and learning styles are changing 'a dependency culture where pupils come to rely on teachers instead of taking responsibility for their own learning. The best teachers in any school put learning first and regard teaching as just a way to access learning.'

Games, Options, The Arts: Sport is a key strength; 'best thing about the school,' say many pupils. Head believes, 'to be the best you have to bring in the best' so employs teachers who are county coaches for hockey, has appointed an England U16 squad coach for soccer and there are strong club-school links for rugby. Vastly improved fixture lists against some of the best independent schools in the north west. Rash of county players in hockey, netball, rugby, cricket, football, tennis, athletics, cross-country – including two female county players – and under 18 male and female water polo nationals. Pupils frequently selected for England U18 Rugby Union. Rowing established at junior and senior levels. Won the gold medal at U15 in the National Schools Championship and two silver medals in the National Championships. The 22 metre pool, gym and sport hall double as local community leisure centre. Full size all-weather pitch, and recent land purchases mean the sports fields stretch out in several directions with additional pitches. Lymm HS now leads a School Sports Development partnership involving 50 schools in Warrington and Cheshire. Chosen to be the location for the All England Netball Association North West 'Centre of Excellence' and home for the professional side 'Northern Thunder'.

Half a dozen dinghies are over-wintering in one of the quads – the school has 14 GPs, Mirrors, Lasers and Toppers and sails every weekend from April to October at local Budworth Reservoir and Tatton Mere. Summer sailing courses held at Roscolyn on Anglesey where the school has an outdoor residential centre in 38 acres – Ty'n-y-Felin is a 1600s farmhouse with new dormitory wing where all first years bond in form groups and which is busy all summer with camps. Long list of clubs and societies, several bands (one has cut CD), mainly meeting in lunch hour. D of E, Young Enterprise, Whole School Enterprise Challenge. Lots of trips to exotic locations and international sports tours(Australia 2004, South Africa 2007).

Music now a strong element of the school. All students in year 7 have musical tuition in strings and brass free of charge. Voice and oboe are also free. Music is also taught by LHS staff in partner primary schools.

Background and Atmosphere: Lymm High School, Lymm Grammar until 20+ years ago, serves a wide area of rural England. Set on a hillside with far reaching views over the Cheshire plain, all the outlooks are green. Easy access to the motorway network makes Lymm an ultra-leafy suburb – recently acclaimed the most expensive place to live in the North West with average house price over £200,000. Not quite as neat as a private school, nevertheless well-presented, with work, projects, trips and very impressive ceramics on display everywhere. Prefects on entrance doors at breaks and lunch – a nice touch and welcoming. Staff and pupils friendly and communicative. A busy place with leisure and language centres and on-site uniform shop open almost every day.

Grey and navy blue uniform described as 'comfortable' by pupils who accept ties, even in sixth form. Logoed sportswear also compulsory. School has own caterers though the dining hall looks small, 'lunchtime is not dignified,' admitted head,'we need to get a lot of children through in a short time'. School has a healthy eating policy with chips ('they're good,' say pupils) only available on one day each week. Day starts early at 8.20am.

Notable past pupils include Ruth Lea, head of the Institute of Directors and business commentator; Maurice Flanagan CBE, group managing director of Emirate Airlines; Catherine Bruton, author; Neil Fairbrother, cricketer; Richard Eggington, rower.

Pastoral Care and Discipline: Parental concerns that size of school is daunting for first years – addressed by established Five Halls system, so each child belongs to smaller unit. Two forms from each year in each of five halls – Arley, Dunham, Moreton, Tatton and Walton, each with own tie. 'It gives me more chance to say "well done" to more children,' says head. The Halls are the backbone of the school and afford many more students the chance to succeed.

Active mentoring and pupil peer scheme through the Hall system – pastoral care seems to fall to form tutors in Hall teams. No-nonsense approach to discipline; head doesn't hesitate to temporarily exclude for serious misdemeanours and permanently exclude for assault and drugs but describes school as 'pretty clean' for its size. 'You can count the scallywags on one hand; they're great kids but we demand and expect high standards.'

Pupils and Parents: White, rural Cheshire, quintessentially middle class. Ethnic minority faces and faiths almost non-existent. Christian with a small 'c' – no church connections. Parents say they're 'bowled over' by the school and describe it as 'the cream of secondary schools for miles'.

Entrance: Non-selective. Place virtually certain for children from one of nine feeder partnership primaries. Heavily oversubscribed locally so entrance difficult from out of area – for 11+ rejects from neighbouring Trafford for example, but some with grammar school places choose Lymm High School in preference.

Exit: A good handful to Oxbridge. About 90 per cent go on to higher education, most to university.

Remarks: A forward looking, happening place; full of life and more opportunities than you would expect even from a large secondary school. Good results with a lot of fun to be had along the way.

MAGDALEN COLLEGE SCHOOL

Linked to Magdalen College Junior School in the Junior section

Cowley Place, Oxford, Oxfordshire, OX4 1DZ

Tel: 01865 242 191
Fax: 01865 240 379
E-mail: admissions@mcsoxford.org
Website: www.mcsoxford.org

- Pupils: 675 boys, all day (including 100 in junior school)
- Ages: 7-18 • Size of sixth form: 162 • C of E • Fees: £2,672 years 3/4; £3,294 years 5-13. Plus lunch • Independent
- Open days: Late September and early January

Master: Since 1998, Mr Andrew Halls MA – a double first in English from Gonville and Caius (mid-forties). Previously deputy head of Trinity Croydon and head of English at Bristol Grammar School. Inherited a school stuck in a time warp but you now get the feeling it's really going places once more. Young, dynamic, driven and determined to regain MCS's academic crown. 2003 saw 3rd best boys' A-level results and 2nd best boys' GCSE results in UK according to one national table, so head clearly true to his word. Has made pretty radical changes since his arrival – abolished Saturday morning lessons, lowered age of junior school intake, introduced staff reviews and study skills for all boys. Good listener. Not scared of upsetting people if convinced he's right or has silent majority support. 60 per cent of staff new since his arrival (mostly through natural wastage). Finally feel they're singing from the same hymn sheet (more modern than ancient). French wife Veronique teaches French, two young daughters are at Oxford schools. Firm advocate of single-sex education. 'I believe boys do better in this kind of environment,' he says, 'and that's all I ask of them – that they do their best.' Numbers have risen from 520 to 675 since head's reign began. Applications in that time have almost trebled.

Academic Matters: MCS boys continue to break records – 96 per cent A/B passes at A level in summer 2005, 93 per cent in 2004, 52 out of 73 candidates with 3 or more A grades, 20 Oxbridge entrants. At GCSE, 98 per cent gained A*, A and B grades. Eight boys secured awards for gaining one of the top five marks in the country at GCSE (out of tens of thousands of candidates). Biology, maths and English very strong and the most popular choices in sixth form. Other sciences also hot – all three sciences compulsory at GCSE. Much investment in improving facilities – each science now has three or four labs, all refurbished and refitted. New ICT centre opened in 2002 complete with 50 new PCs, laptops, whiteboards and ergonomically designed desks and chairs. About to build a spacious new library alongside the ICT department, thus creating a vast new information and study centre at the heart of the school. French a must for all to GCSE, German and Spanish additional options. Spanish shooting up the popularity polls in recent times. History rather on the small side but new head of department beginning to expand the subject. Geography a front-runner with non-scientists – loads of great trips, we're told. Class sizes anything from 16 to 24, depending on age, in large, well-lit rooms – junior classrooms in particular papered with boys' work. Good proportion of female staff (around 14) and plenty of new blood.

Improvements to junior school since intake age dropped from 9 to 7. Lots of new painting and bright colours – much more a school in its own right. All children encouraged to play full vocal part in lessons; long gone are the days of sit up, shut up and listen. Five-day school week (Saturday mornings ditched by head despite some staff protests). Head says, 'we were the last day school in Britain with Saturday school. There were some fears that sport would suffer but I'm delighted to say that hasn't been the case.' No class streaming until 11, then only in French, Latin and maths.

Games, Options, The Arts: Greater success in sport since major investment in £2 million sports centre and all-weather courts. MCS determined to excel in all things. Football up to 11, then rugby, cricket, hockey, tennis, and indoor sports various. Centre also has squash court and state-of-the-art gym. School teams taken very seriously, says head. 'Boys are told that if they've been selected to play for a team it takes precedence over everything.' Particular emphasis on getting as many boys as possible involved in school teams – 'an inclusive rather than exclusive approach,' says head. Previous successes included a three-season unbroken record in cricket and a top three ranking for tennis. Commitment to sports clear as scholarships now available. Eleven acres of playing fields on doorstep – school claims 'the most beautiful sports fields in England', but there is stiff competition for this accolade! Another 13 acres three miles away as well as use of Christ Church grounds adjacent to the school site.

Art, once the poor relation, now enjoying better fortunes. Large, bright studios stretch across top floor of one building (junior school has its own) and impressive work on display throughout school. 'When I arrived work was only shown in the studio and that's something I wanted to change straight away,' says head. 'Much of it was far too good to hide away.' Arts scholarships introduced by Head. Very strong musically, choir still sings from top of Magdalen Tower at dawn on May morning (worth getting up early for though the bulk of the crowd down below normally has yet to get to bed) and supplies choristers to the college from which it takes its name and a number of governors. School's 16 choristers sing regularly in college chapel and have made several recordings eg sound track for Shadowlands. Quality orchestras, also jazz bands, wind bands and the like (annual senior school concert in Sheldonian Theatre involves over 160 boy musicians.) A number of boys are also members of the Junior Royal Academy of Music. Plenty of extras. Friday lectures by visiting speakers. Recent visitors have included Soviet spy Oleg Gordievsky, historian David Starkey, George Galloway MP – quite a mix! Always get a good turn out, debates with all-girls Oxford High and Headington, active CCF (again twinned with local girls' schools) and community service (boys have to do one or the other) and highly competitive chess club including five England internationals – the Under 9s were crowned English Champions in 2003, defeating 148 other schools.

Background and Atmosphere: An extraordinary mix of old and new and awkward in-between. Founded in 1480 by William of Waynflete (MCS leavers invited to join Old Waynfletes organisation) to prepare boys for Magdalen College. Former masters include Cardinal Wolsey, former pupils St Thomas More. Oldest part, School House, home to enlarged junior school, head plus family and admin. Opposite is array of newer buildings, some horribly dated but functional, others late 20th century and much better laid out, furnished and aesthetically pleasing. Pretty near the middle of Oxford but calm setting none the less. Pleasantly green surroundings, spanning the Cherwell. Not the hothouse you might expect, bearing in mind their (now reclaimed) academic reputation. Boys look cheerfully relaxed and some refreshingly scruffy – untucked shirts, crooked ties, that kind of thing (not the norm, head insists. 'Local feeling is that MCS boys are a good deal tidier than of yore,' he tells us.) But very polite and respectful too. From juniors to seniors, a feeling of friendliness, a school of good mates. Relaxed approach to uniform adds to that. All boys must wear the school tie, juniors have a school jumper, otherwise general rule is sober shirt, formal jacket and trousers. Regular morning assembly important part of school day. Dual purpose school hall – boys face one way for prayers, the other for plays. RC pupils also get their own weekly prayers.

Pastoral Care and Discipline: House system run geographically to help parents (so son's friends are hopefully close at hand) and competitively. Tutors, matron, chaplain and boys themselves all play a part in pastoral welfare. 'Special bond between juniors and seniors the key to a happy school,' says head. 'There's something precious about the Magdalen atmosphere – an interdependence. There's a certain naturalness in relations between the boys, there's a sense of looking after each other.' Head alert to bullying, but no evidence of it, a fact commented on in most recent inspection (2001). A pretty laid-back, 'few rules' school but very purposeful and well-ordered nonetheless. Expulsion for drug use on premises, theft and systematic bullying. No expulsions in head's time but has parted company with seven to eight boys by mutual consent.

Pupils and Parents: Great mix of background, dons' sons making something of a comeback, not a big magnet for the mega-rich. As a day school, catchment area fairly tight but private buses service further-flung regions of county. Particularly welcoming to new intake – lots of social evenings for new parents. Professionals well represented but many 'making sacrifices'. Parents' association active and productive. OBs down the centuries too numerous to mention but include Ivor Novello (an MCS chorister), William Tyndale (who translated the New Testament and was killed for doing so on the orders of his fellow OB St Thomas More), film director Sam Mendes, Blur portraitist Julian Opie, 2002 Nobel prize winner Tim Hunt, Sir Basil Blackwell, and sports commentators John Parsons, Jim Rosenthal and Nigel Starmer-Smith ... to name but a few.

Entrance: At 7, 9 and 11 by tests and assessment, 13 by CE, scholarship exam or by school's own 13+ exam for state school applicants and, into sixth form, at least six to eight GCSE passes at B or above with As in A level choices. Same applies to existing MCS boys. School spoilt for choice. Head says, 'for the first time last year, I really did feel I was saying no to boys who would have done well here'. Boys not expected to flunk at 11, 13 and sixth form stages if selection process further down school has worked well. Should be a case of once there, stay there. Main intake at 11 from primary schools – mainly local state schools. Feeders at 13 include The Dragon, New College and Christ Church schools. Pre-assessment service available if unsure whether son is MCS material.

Exit: Over a quarter of 2005 upper sixth secured places at Oxford and Cambridge. Over last ten years, Cambridge

and Oxford far and away the most popular destinations. Nottingham, Southampton, Warwick, Bristol, Manchester, Durham and Sheffield well up the rankings. Good spread of destinations and courses, from physics with astrophysics to journalism.

Money Matters: Seen as good value for money. Best value for money boys' school in London and the south east according to Sunday Times survey in 2003. Fee remissions total £250,000 a year, excluding the sport and art scholarships, and choristers' 66 per cent remission. Hard-up cases need only ask. 'No boy has had to leave because his parents have fallen on hard times.' Help is always at hand.

Remarks: Not what you might expect a boys' public school to look like or feel like. A comfortable mix of brains, brawn and artistic flair but demanding and challenging too. On a roll.

MALVERN COLLEGE

Linked to Malvern College Preparatory School and Pre-Prep in the Junior section

College Road, Malvern, Worcestershire, WR14 3DF

Tel: 01684 581 500
Fax: 01684 581 615
E-mail: enquiry@malcol.org
Website: www.malcol.org

• Pupils: 355 boys and 213 girls; 449 board, 119 day. Plus own prep and pre-prep schools – 188 boys and girls • Ages: 13-18, prep and pre-prep 2-13 • Size of sixth form: 294 • C of E but ecumenical • Independent • Open days: Early in the Autumn term and May day

Head: Since 1997, Mr Hugh Carson MA PGCE (late fifties), educated Tonbridge (head boy), joined the army and discovered, whilst at Sandhurst, that he loved teaching. Came to Malvern via the Royal Tank Regiment followed by London and Reading, where he read history, history of economics and politics – which he still teaches. Came to Malvern via Epsom College, where he became housemaster, and Denstone College – a Woodard school – where he was headmaster.

Urbane and charming but serious minded too, with an underlying sense of purpose and a certain reserve; pupils hold him in high regard. He has definitely made his mark on the school. His wife, Penny, is a JP and 'freelance historian'. Both great dog lovers, his black and white spaniel is never far from his heels.

Retiring July 2006. New head is to be Mr David Dowdles, currently headmaster of Warminster School.

Academic Matters: Number of recent staff changes in heads of departments and further down the school. Malvern is one of the highest profile schools to teach the IB – with great success: about 50 per cent of sixth form pupils take this option – though, having said that, the A level results are also very good. This is not an overtly academic school but achieves good results, with a fair number of As and Bs at GCSE and A level and AS level. Placed 19th in the Times league tables of top 800 schools. Max class size 23, streamed and setted, no obvious star subject, though both maths and English strong. Economics strong in sixth form. Separate or dual award science (science labs look pretty tatty) plus impressive success in modern languages – do not be deceived; there are a number of native speakers in the school. EFL on offer to top up wobbly English for non-native speakers but good basic English essential before joining the school – and many foreigners go to the prep school at 11 before transferring to the senior school. Loads of trips abroad, German exchanges and French work experience.

Apart from the IB, the school has also pioneered the Nuffield Science course, and the Diploma of Achievement, a skills-based course that includes life skills as well as learning, healthy eating and fitness for life. The key skills qualification counts as bonus in the UCAS total. Networked Apple Macs in banks throughout the school, as well as the library, the IT dept and the houses.

Excellent dyslexia pick-up under Mrs Jackie Thomas, who runs a unit for pupils with learning difficulties at South Lodge with four part-time assistants; no facilities to deal with serious problems but lots of good advice and help. Mrs Thomas can pull up pupil's work in progress to iron out hiccups.

Games, Options, The Arts: Main games football and rugby, lots of tours abroad – but boys complain they keep being beaten by schools who do two terms of rugby rather than a mixture of football and hockey. Rackets, fives, large games hall, refurbished swimming pool in divine Victorian exterior. Adventure training at cottage in Brecon Beacons, all go there for a week. Serious popular and successful clay pigeon shooting team. Masses of music in converted Victorian monastery with monks' cells as practice rooms; former Catholic church is now a concert hall with sixth form centre in the crypt. Charming little theatre in former gym. All weather playing surface recently laid down.

Fabulous new IT block – all the normal disciplines (though dust extractor pipes have thick layer of sawdust on the inner surface which Health & Safety has required to be addressed) plus home economics and textiles – for both sexes. IT block cunningly linked to existing art department, huge exciting variety of work on show and proper (ie grown-up post-school-age) art foundation course started in September 2001 under the charismatic head of art, Mr Tim Newsholme, which leads to a BTEC diploma. Strong CCF, but also extensive community service and D of E.

Background and Atmosphere: Collection of impressive Victoriana perched on sloping site beneath the Malvern Hills (imagine immaculate terracing dotted with playing fields and Betjemanesque limestone piles). Main railway line traverses the grounds. Founded in 1865, the school grew rapidly and there are now ten houses scattered throughout the brightly lit grounds – no house apparently more desirable than any other. The separate chapel built in 1899 replaces the earlier one, which has now become an imaginative double deck library. In 1992 (falling numbers, Lloyds etc) the school amalgamated with nearby Ellerslie Girls' School and Hillstone prep school – which moved into the original Ellerslie site (just up the road).

Unusually, Malvern still has in-house feeding, with around fifty pupils in each. This is both a noisy and a cosy experience – and the houseparents feel much more hands-on. Younger pupils sleep in dorms with separate studies, and graduate to study bedrooms (some said to be too small for modern Health & Safety standards, but they looked perfectly OK to us). Day pupils are either in boarding houses and stay till around 9pm or in day houses where they chose to do prep in school or at home – all day pupils can do B&B whenever parents require it. School operates on a three-week cycle, with every third weekend out from Friday lunch, masses of activities on Sundays and head is particularly proud that he usually has 'at least 400 pupils' on site during the weekend. Trousers and jackets or blazers till sixth form when boys wear 'their own suits'; dark jackets and serviceable dark striped skirts for girls who move into rather natty trouser suits at sixth form.

Pastoral Care and Discipline: Good house and tutor system; pupils allocated tutor in lower school and choose personal tutor post-GCSE. Headmaster brooks no nonsense on sin: out for drugs, out for sex, drinking is only allowed for sixth form but smoking not allowed. Persistent offenders will be required to leave the school – so there you have it. Hard, too, on petty crime.

Pupils and Parents: Middle class, professional (princes to paupers) but not a posh school. 15 per cent discount for Services families, a fair number of foreigners – 'about 20 per cent climb on an aeroplane at the end of term,' says the head, that includes ex-pats. Fair number of Germans, often for the sixth form for IB only. Not an overly sophisticated school.

Entrance: Registration and CE or separate test for state school entrants. 20 per cent from own prep school, lots from other preps (only a trickle now from Beaudesert); CE essential for these but waived for state school entrants. Sixth form entry six GCSEs at A to C for AS/A2 subjects, about seventy join the sixth form each year, mainly for IB.

Exit: 97 per cent to university – up to twenty to Oxbridge (nineteen last year) some to the States, some to Europe (the IB again), plus art college, the Services etc.

Money Matters: Demise of Assisted Places hit hard but numbers rising again and school now has own funds in place and can offer both bursarial help and scholarships. Will pick up any financial shortfall 'up to the next public exam', but parents must be upfront with the problem. Huge appeal both for bursary dosh and funds for new language labs – head proud of the fact that the school 'has no overdraft'.

Remarks: Trad co-ed rural public school with a surprising number of aces up its sleeve.

MALVERN GIRLS' COLLEGE

15 Avenue Road, Malvern, Worcestershire, WR14 3BA

Tel: 01684 892 288
Fax: 01684 566 204
E-mail: registrar@mgc.worcs.sch.uk
Website: www.mgc.worcs.sch.uk

- Pupils: 310 girls; 260 board, 50 day • Ages: 10-18 • Size of sixth form: 130 • C of E • Fees: From £3,300 day (£4,800 new sixth form day); from £6,100 weekly boarders (£8,160 new sixth form full boarders) • Independent • Open days: October, November, February, May and June

---

Head: Since 1997, Mrs Philippa (Pippa) Leggate BA MEd PGCE (fifties), educated at Royal School, Bath, read history at York, returned to Bath for Masters. Impressive pedigree. First taught history in state system, moved to Middle East and was founding head of new international school in Oman. Last post – head of Overseas School in Colombo, Sri Lanka, from 1993-97. Very clued up, smart in mind and appearance, enjoys support of staff, pupils and parents. Passionate believer in single-sex education. 'Girls benefit from working alongside other girls because you can appeal to their particular interests'. High achiever ideally placed to

nurture future generations of female high achievers. Intelligent, articulate (but chooses words carefully), efficient, means business. In many respects, more like chief executive than headmistress.

Academic Matters: Consistently high exam results. 2005 saw 100 per cent passes at A level with 82 per cent A/Bs. Broad range of hot subjects include Chinese (large overseas intake could have something to do with this), drama, further maths and RS. Huge focus on sciences (over a third opt for science-related subjects at university) now housed in award-winning three-storey science block (built on head's private garden). Girls scored high at GCSE in maths and sciences but history, modern languages and English lit are right up there too. A*-A grades 78 per cent, almost all A-Cs. Good, solid teaching. Not as traditional as once was – now more challenging, but not so way-out as to risk damaging fine academic reputation. More to education than 'what takes place in the classroom', says head. MGC is 'springboard into adult life'. Great choice of subjects at AS level include drama, Greek and philosophy. Extra help available for dyslexics.

Games, Options, The Arts: Art department is one to benefit from space freed by sciences' departure to new block. Now has bags of room with three large light studios. A level arts students have own work area, can drop in whenever they like. Big lab too for cookery classes, still popular with 21st century MGC girls. 'Well, they get to cook their own food and eat it, don't they? It's always preferable to school food,' we were told. Music a key ingredient in MGC life – 75 per cent study at least one instrument. Two orchestras, three choirs (girls audition for chamber choir), and energetic new music head bursting with ideas. Sees chamber music as best way of bringing music to the masses. Successful in schools' chamber music competition in consecutive years. 'Music here is very, very strong. These girls are bright conscientious kids', he states with pride. Instrument tuition an extra charge, of course, except for girls with music scholarships or exhibitions and those doing music A level. Computers all over the place, internet access, girls free to surf in spare time.

Loads of action on the sports field, big in hockey and lacrosse but also keen on less mainstream girls' sports, also rowing, scuba diving, tennis, swimming, netball but no cricket. Large sports dome for badminton, squash and aerobics, much-used all-weather pitches and surely one of the few listed indoor swimming pools. Lovely arched beams and changing cubicles (dating from previous life as Victorian hotel) but not much to inspire potential medal-winners. Much emphasis on community service work: locals can use pool and old folk helped with shopping etc. Head says, 'we see ourselves as a community but also a community within a community. We take our role in Malvern very seriously.' Success in Young Enterprise scheme, big following for D of E awards, many extra activities from needlepoint to white-water rafting.

Background and Atmosphere: Set against breathtaking backdrop of the Malvern Hills. Formerly the Imperial Hotel, large redbrick imposing building with later additions, right by railway station (it was built to serve the hotel). School life revolves around the houses. Five houses organised in age groups, so girl who goes right through the school will start in the lower middle school house, move up to one of two middle houses and end in one of two sixth form houses. Comfortable accommodation ranges from multi-bed dorms to study bedrooms, plenty of opportunity for privacy as well as mixing in common rooms, girls encouraged to bring home comforts, laptops/mobile phones welcomed (mobiles banned from classrooms though). Weekend activities timetabled. Include riding, bowling, games coaching and the cinema. Pretty unexciting school uniform (no ties) compulsory until sixth form when 'suitable' home clothes can be worn. Very security conscious – all external doors have coded locks. C of E school where religion high on agenda but other denominations well catered for. Long-standing link with Muslim school in Gambia. Daily assembly with regular church/chapel for all. Glorious well-stocked library (21,000 volumes, multimedia computers, CD-ROM etc) with one end devoted to careers information. Girls' work shown off in school corridors, notice boards display scale and range of non-curricular activity. Busy, fast-moving school which won't tolerate less than 100 per cent effort. One teacher said, 'this isn't a school for the shy retiring violet. Girls here tend to be rather outgoing.' MGC not an island – plenty of link-ups through sport, drama, debates and discos with other schools (independent and state) in Malvern and further afield. Maintains contact with Malvern College since going fully co-ed. No bad feeling/competition. 'What we offer in a girls only school is something quite different.'

Pastoral Care and Discipline: Provided through housemistresses/parents and form tutors, as well as sixth formers. Successful 'peer mentoring' system in operation whereby younger pupils encouraged to talk problems through with an older girl. Few school rules but strong code of conduct. Girls taught to take responsibility for their actions, also made to see how actions affect others. Impressive PHSE skills course in middle school and learning for life programme in sixth form. 'We teach self worth and respect without arrogance,' says head. Discipline may be dealt with by head, housemistress or sixth form council (pupil/staff mix) depending on seriousness. Expulsion ('exclusion') for drugs 'at the head's discretion', smoking only allowed off school premises by over 16s, and alcohol can extend to wine with a meal for over 18s but no booze or cigarettes ever in study bedrooms. Girls allowed to walk into town (middle school pupils must go in groups), behaviour 'which brings school into disrepute' reported to council for possible disciplinary action. No evident problem with bullying. Pupils anonymously complete bullying questionnaire every year giving their views/experiences. Any problems dealt with swiftly.

Pupils and Parents: A large contingent from abroad (girls from more than 20 countries), make up about a third of school. Lots from far east in particular who seem to excel in sciences but less so in sports. Cross section socially, academically and geographically. Some local, majority from midlands and London. Increasingly dominated by professionals, like lawyers, rather than 'the fabulously rich', some farming stock still but less since hard times and the rest first-timers. Naturally attracts brains and much artistic talent in evidence. The late Dame Elizabeth Lane, first woman High Court judge, is old girl. Also novelist Barbara Cartland and Vogue editor Liz Tilberis. Not to mention, adds the head, numerous 'doctors, vets, lawyers, architects, scientists and good mothers'.

Entrance: At 11, 12, 13 and sixth form. Common entrance and own entrance papers and scholarship exams. For sixth form, GCSE results must include Bs in chosen A level subjects.

Exit: Around 99 per cent to degree courses, up to 12 to Oxbridge. Careers taken very seriously. Top of the popularity charts are medicine, the City, Foreign Office, law and engineering.

Money Matters: Scholarships for academic, music, art and PE at middle school, and academic, expressive arts including music, art and drama, plus PE at sixth form level. Special scholarships for daughters and granddaughters of Old Girls, some bursaries and some assisted places. Discount of 5 per cent for younger sisters while both at MGC.

Remarks: Much good work and modern thinking going on inside the old-world façade. Very sure of its single sex status, giving parents a choice as well as a first class education for their daughters. Girls come across as confident and content, those in their last year now impatient to get out there and get going. Girls taught how to stand on own two feet (but not without help, insists school – ie through comprehensive network of support systems).

THE MANCHESTER GRAMMAR SCHOOL

Old Hall Lane, Rusholme, Manchester, Lancashire, M13 0XT

Tel: 0161 224 7201
Fax: 01612 572 446
E-mail: general@mgs.org
Website: www.mgs.org

• Pupils: 1,440 boys; all day • Ages: 11-18 • Size of sixth form: 400 • C of E links, but basically non-denom • Fees: £2,413 plus lunch • Independent • Open days: Early October

High Master: Since 2004, Dr Christopher Ray, educated at Rochdale Grammar School and University College London, followed by postgraduate study at Churchill College Cambridge and Balliol College Oxford. Taught at Marlborough, Framlingham, director of studies at King's College School Wimbledon. From 2001, headmaster of The John Lyon School, Harrow, who were rather surprised to see him go. Married. Has also worked at The Bank of England and for Oxford University Press, and has taught in universities (Oxford, Singapore and Oregon, USA.)

Academic Matters: Outstanding academic power house, one of the best in the country. Predictably brilliant results – 85 per cent A*/A at GCSE 87 per cent A/B at A level. Quite apart from exam and league table success, school has striking academic ethos. Love of learning comes out of the boys' pores. High academic standards are valued for their own sake. Staff a mixture of old and enthusiastic and young and enthusiastic. Inevitably, the odd dud. Most are very committed, dedicated to the true aims of their profession. People want to teach at MGS and are trusted to get on with the job. Handing initiative and responsibility over is a feature of the school; a 14-year-old said, 'they help, but really it's up to us'. Increasing number of women appointees but not for political correctness, simply 'the best person for the job'.

Class sizes now reduced at lower end of school to maximum 25/26, thinning down to 22/23 in middle school, 10/12 at A level. Most take (and pass) 9-11 subjects at GCSE. Own lower school general science course to even out differences in pre-11 teaching, then all take separate sciences at GCSE. Latin optional after two years. Greek, Spanish, Russian, German, Italian. Boys 'banded' for maths, thereafter classes defined by subject grouping. RE compulsory up to 5th year. Learning support team quietly picks up

fallers by the wayside, dyslexics, et al in fourth and fifth years. Membership of this 'at risk' group more a cachet than a stigma, claims head of middle school.

The academic successes of the past – long list of high-flyers in every conceivable field – does not seem to over-whelm boys; they feel cherished for what they can bring to the school, not required to live up to an impossibly high standard. The wealth of talent is mirrored by the resources for the inquiring mind. Both libraries are fantastic. The range of periodicals covering arts, physical and social sciences, current events, sport etc, tells its own tale – academic excellence fed by the intellectual ferment in the outside world. Excellent careers room and bookshop. Major new development in DT.

New pattern of post-16 curriculum is four ASs plus four A2s but very wide-ranging general studies in sixth form has been retained, with philosophy course compulsory in lower sixth; school no longer feels it can dictate a particular faith to its pupils, but believes that 'any young person leaving school at 18 without either a moral code or a structured pattern of thought relating to morality and ethics is both at risk and has not been educated'.

Homework expected to take from one hour a night (first form) to 16 self-directed hours per week in sixth. Five As at GCSE means automatic passage to sixth. If this looks unlikely, boys and parents given plenty of warning.

Games, Options, The Arts: The range of non-academic and extra-curricular activities is mind-boggling (pity about cookery – future spouses and partners may lament this omission?). Huge amount of energy invested in what goes on outside the classroom, both for its own sake and also, equally importantly, to encourage and engender self-esteem; especially popular, all-muck-in-together camps and treks and compulsory first/second year drama. Non-academic achievement valued highly. Regular visits to Edinburgh Festival. Unique full-length play-writing award, the Robert Bolt Memorial Prize, open to any pupil and judged by Royal Exchange Theatre (£500 for winner). Fantastic new sports hall, named after old boy Mike Atherton. New tennis courts (from anonymous donor). No great pressure to play games but school still licks most of the opposition; recently became first northern school to win Rosslyn Park Sevens. Music much prized. Regular visits to school by BBC Philharmonic; James MacMillan composer-in-residence in 2000; Biennial concert at St John's Smith Square.

Outstanding facilities for ceramics and fine arts and an approach by which art history, theory and practice dovetail naturally. Staffing in these two subjects greatly increased in recent years. Absence of tension between arty and sporty fraternities; each perfectly confident of their own worth.

Background and Atmosphere: Founded in 1515 by Hugh Oldham, Bishop of Exeter, a year before he founded Corpus Christi College, Oxford with which MGS has links, to educate able boys regardless of their parents' means, to go on to university and the professions, and open what the founder called the 'yate of knowledge'. Moved to present purpose-built 28-acre site in 1931, though facilities enormously extended since then. Now the biggest private senior school in the country. The founding ideals hold steady, fuelled by high master's and staff's convictions. School determined to continue to offer education to boys from less privileged backgrounds. Prides itself on being 'colour blind', ie not differentiating on grounds of race. Atmosphere very positive, vibrant, full of life, supportive, ambitious in the sense of purposeful – school sets, and rises to, challenges.

Cheerful, polite boys. Most of all, a pervading, almost tangible, love of learning, and sense of happiness, pride in achievements of all kinds.

Dining room noisy but efficient. 'Butty Bar' for older boys enamoured of fast food. Sixth formers wear school tie and tailored jackets, otherwise blue blazers. On first arriving at MGS, boys – many from small, local schools – generally feel overwhelmed by its size, despite pastoral measures to prevent this. But once they find their feet (and their classrooms), they seem never to look back.

Pastoral Care and Discipline: The caring ethos of the school, hardly touched on in its prospectus, is nonetheless real and alive. In such a big school, good pastoral care is a priority. There is a striking general standard of decency towards, and respect for, each other, unobtrusively underpinned by discipline. School goes to great lengths to catch problems early and to make available lots of different routes for boys having difficulties. Various schemes – friend (for new boys), peer support system, form tutor (key role) are backed up by less formal network, such as school nurses, who are trained in counselling. Non-teaching staff contribute to pastoral care. One teacher described as 'fairly flabbergasting' the rapport between staff and pupils. Occasionally, problems or injustices slip through the net, inevitably.

Carefully worked out and rigorously implemented drugs policy – possession means suspension, usually followed by readmission, on condition the boy concerned submits to random tests thereafter. Discipline not hampered by pointless pettiness, and occasionally rules more honoured in the breach than in the observance, eg no running in the corridors unless it's to get to the front of the lunch queue, in which case stampedes are perfectly in order; it's all visitors can do not to join in, just for the fun of it. High Master has last word on choice of captain (head boy).

Pupils and Parents: Wide range of backgrounds, social, religious, racial. One pupil commented that anyone would enjoy the school, provided they were willing to 'get involved'. And loners? Yes, so long as they 'get involved ... as loners'. Very wide catchment area. School delays start until 9:05am but even so it's a long day for some boys – dropped off early, picked up late, or facing long bus journeys both ways. Communication with parents is good on the whole – tutors encouraged to phone parents if they feel there is a problem. Otherwise contact fairly minimal, restricted to parents' evenings and reports. Parents' Society arranges events and network, including optional scheme to pair up 'old' parents with new, to aid settling-in process.

Dozens and dozens of distinguished Old Boys, including rows of FRSs, not least Sir Michael Atiyah. Also Mike Atherton, Michael Wood, the Crawley brothers, actors Ben Kingsley and Robert Powell, Robert Bolt, Steven Pimlott, and National Theatre head Nicolas Hytner, writer Alan Garner; John Ogdon, LSE boss Sir Howard Davies, Thomas de Quincey, plus several members of the Sieff family and Simon Marks. One we came across this year was Steve Robinson who runs a language school on the south western frontiers of Brazil – 'I owe an awful lot indeed to MGS. Apart from an excellent array of curricular and extra-curricular activities, the highly competitive environment exacts the very best from you and makes you into an active person who goes out there and does things. I have fond memories of my time there and I wouldn't be out here in central Brazil, running a language school if it hadn't helped broaden my horizons and expectations in life. My background in classics has been fundamental in helping me redesign the teaching of English to Brazilians and I hope to be able to publish my ideas in the near future. I think it will always be with a certain sense of pride that I recollect my time there and recognise the value of the balanced education I received.'

Entrance. Not easy. Main entry is at 11, where 550/600 boys vie for 200/210 places. Entrance by exam only. No interview (is there a risk of a bright lad missing out because of an off-day in the exam room?). 50 per cent of intake from state primaries. School draws from around 80 preps/primaries.

Exit: All but a few to degree courses, mostly trad tough subjects at older universities. Law, medicine, languages, natural sciences, history/politics popular, also accountancy. 60 or so to Oxbridge.

Money Matters: High master has clear priorities: 'money goes on bursaries and teachers'- salaries first, buildings second'. There was a large number of Assisted Places and their phasing out has threatened the very purpose and ethos on which the school was founded. However, massive amount of energy, determination and goodwill has been channelled into Foundation Bursary Appeal (Patron is The Prince of Wales, signalling his strong support for provision of free places at school for deprived, inner-city children). More than £10 million raised since 1998. Rigorous procedures mean that money goes to deserving cases only. School trips are often to exotic locations and can prove expensive. According to the school, dedicated fund-raising and funding for needy pupils prevent such trips from being divisive. Parents in the middle income bands might wish for a few cheaper options.

Remarks: Impressive, five star academic day school, well deserving its reputation for excellence. Its enlightened founding principles, and the vigour with which the school still carries them forward, make it exemplary among independent schools. Such is the level of intellectual challenge, as well as non-academic and extra-curricular activities, some boys must have little, if any, time or energy left over for that trifling detail, the outside world. Manchester parents with no boys, eat your hearts out.

MANCHESTER HIGH SCHOOL FOR GIRLS

Linked to Manchester High Preparatory Department in the Junior section

Grangethorpe Road, Manchester, Lancashire, M14 6HS

Tel: 0161 224 0447

Fax: 0161 224 6192

E-mail: administration@mhsg.manchester.sch.uk

Website: www.manchesterhigh.co.uk

• Pupils: 940 girls, all day • Ages: 11 - 18; preparatory department 4 - 11 • Size of sixth form: 200 • Secular • Fees: £1,718 - £2,412 • Independent • Open days: October/November

Headmistress: Since 1998, Mrs Christine Lee-Jones MA MIMgt FRSA (fifties). Previously principal of Eccles Sixth Form College (seven years) and before that vice-principal of Leyton Sixth Form College, in London. Studied education. Married with a daughter. Interests include travel, theatre, tennis and reading. Refreshingly non-judgmental style and not heavy-handed as a manager.

Academic Matters: Placed in the Daily Telegraph's premier league of independent schools in 2002- 2005 for A Levels and a school which always performs well. Results at A level and GCSE are excellent; 86 per cent of GCSE grades A*/A, and 91 per cent grades A/B at A level. Popular subjects are biology, chemistry, mathematics, psychology and philosophy. Average class size in years 7-9 is 25; years 10-11 is 16 and in sixth form, 12, although much smaller for some subjects, eg sixteenth century history. Average age of staff 42. A few pupils are dyslexic. Facilities very good. New language labs. Language teaching impressive. French begins in year 7, Spanish and German as well in year 8. Much use made of local theatres, museums and galleries to support curriculum.

Games, Options, The Arts: Arts, music and sports facilities impressive. Evidence everywhere of pride in these activities. One girl commented that if she needed materials for art, which the school didn't have, they went out and got them for her. Wonderful swimming pool. Sports hall with climbing wall, dance studio and fitness suite in the offing. All girls have music lessons in school; additionally, 300 girls take individual instrumental/singing lessons, including children in prep department. Individual speech and drama lessons also very popular. School accommodates exceptional pupils wishing to realise their talents in outside activities – eg if necessary, letting them miss occasional school days to pursue their ambitions at a national and international level.

Background and Atmosphere: School set up in 1874 by group of Manchester citizens convinced of the value of educating girls and wishing 'to provide for Manchester's daughters what has been provided without stint for Manchester's sons'. Current head emphasises that school celebrates diversity. Handbook for parents and pupils contains slightly mind-boggling details of rules and regulations but school has had positive feedback from parents. Overwhelming impression on arriving at school is of great friendliness – girls and teachers. Caretaker, whose daughter is at the school, describes it emphatically as 'tops'. Striking atmosphere of happiness. When asked what sort of girl wouldn't fit into school, one pupil replied, 'someone who mucked around and spoilt it for the rest of us'. A fitting, and telling, response, consistent with overall feel of positive, happy general outlook. Despite fairly heavy homework and full school day, girls seem relaxed and unpressurised – but with sense of purpose. This reflects head's opinion that 'competition is a part of life' but that it is also important to keep a balanced perspective.

Pastoral Care and Discipline: Form tutors are first point of contact if pupils have a problem; also Big Sister scheme, whereby younger girls can turn to trained sixth formers for help. Volunteer student mentors available to give academic advice. School nurse, heads of year and a learning support co-ordinator provide a strong support system. Discipline not heavy-handed. Role of discipline is as general backdrop rather than motivating principle; it does not feel like a 'carrot and stick' school. Rather, assumption is that pupils will want to learn and will enjoy the process, within a secure, orderly but not unnecessarily strict, environment. Residential trips at the start of year 7 and year 12 help students settle into the school and create a co-operative, friendly and supportive community.

Pupils and Parents: Parents seen as very important as contact with them enables school to understand pupils in more rounded context. Annual handbook of information for parents. Parental opinion is consulted by means of regular detailed questionnaires. Parents and pupils constitute a great mix. School highly thought of in local mixed religious and cultural communities. Bursary scheme means that girls from wide range of backgrounds are represented. Girls can stay at school until 6pm but extra-curricular activities after the end of the school day avoided as much as possible because most girls use buses to get home. Old girls include,

famously, a clutch of Pankhursts, assorted businesswomen such as Clara Freeman OBE, Marks and Spencer's first female executive director; leading lawyers such as Ann Alexander who acts for the families in the Shipman case; and, doing her bit for the cult of TV celebrity, Judy Finnigan, of 'Richard and Judy' fame.

Entrance: Selection is by examinations in maths, English and verbal reasoning and by interview. Four applicants for every place. Pupils come from very wide geographical area across Greater Manchester and beyond. Fifty per cent of year 7 intake is from state primary schools. Approx. 200+ feeder schools.

Exit: All girls go on to further education, some taking a gap year before starting courses. Sizeable numbers read medicine and law, also dentistry. Some girls to art foundation courses. Northern universities popular, a number also to London and a respectable handful (approx 13 per cent each year, according to school) to Oxbridge.

Money Matters: School has appointed a director of development. A variety of means-tested bursaries are available from the Sylvia Pankhurst Bursary Fund.

Remarks: Friendly, happy school. Fantastic staff. Humane values. Brilliant for bright, hard-working all-rounders.

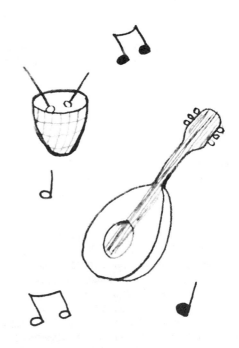

MANDER PORTMAN WOODWARD

90–92 Queen's Gate, London, SW7 5AB

Tel: 020 7835 1355
Fax: 020 7259 2705
E-mail: james.burnett@mpw.co.uk
Website: www.mpw.co.uk

• Pupils: 400 boys and girls • Ages: 15–19 • Non-denom
• Independent

Principal: Since 1998, Mr Steven Boyes BA MSc PGCE (thirties), who read geography at Lancaster followed by a PGCE at Durham (where he also did research into employment law). An expert on education matters, Mr Boyes came straight to MPW. 'We are not a crammer but the second largest independent sixth form college in the country, after Eton'.

Academic Matters: 'We live or die by our results'. Courses on everything, for everyone. Easter revision courses, two-year A level, one-year intensive A level, AS, GCSE plus re-takes and a specialist science department for the medical stream which includes hands-on courses at Ealing Hospital in London and Heartlands Hospital in Birmingham. Notable success rate, eight to Oxbridge last year, and trails to trad universities countrywide. Specialist preparation for students wishing to go on to study art and design.

Excellent and detailed course information – should be the yardstick for all schools, never mind sixth form colleges. Can pick up second year A levels from all over (lower sixth form transfer). Huge range of options, plus extra-curricular activities if course requires it – visits to museums and the like. Small classes. Lots of exam practice and help with UCAS forms. Computer suites. Some dyslexia provision and lots of help with everything (surgeries). Tough on homework and supervised study periods if necessary, 'for slackers'; good libraries and reading rooms for in-house work. Max class size eight. Hours 9am to 6pm. Popular internet library.

Games, Options, The Arts: Some sporting activity, plus art, music, drama, Duke of Edinburgh, voluntary work, college newspaper etc and quite a strong football team which plays in the school leagues, plus debating society.

Background and Atmosphere: Founded in 1973 and ever expanding. Good conversion of a site in Queen's Gate, easy working ambience, mass of labs, language labs etc etc.

Pastoral Care and Discipline: Principal, the vice principals, the directors of studies as well as personal tutors for all. Immediately out for drugs, bullying and persistent absenteeism. Local boozers warned about lunchtime drinking and told to check on age of customers – principal will call the police if necessary – no smoking on the premises. This place is tough. Principal will call pupil's parents (wherever they are in the world) to ask why child has not turned up for class and, during our visit, we came across one being given a real dressing down for absenteeism. Help with finding accommodation but, 'it's up to the pupils really'.

Pupils and Parents: In the main, 'public school movers', no to druggies, some ex-state school ('parents take out second mortgage'), plus 'limited number of foreigners' (EFL on offer if needed but tested in English before entry). Fairly scruffy lot.

Entrance: All prospective students attend an interview, and GCSE students sit English and mathematics tests.

Money Matters: Some scholarships and bursaries available. Scholarship examinations in February. Contact principal for details.

Remarks: Huge, efficient, well-run, does exactly what it says it does. The sheer scale of the operation might well daunt a tender flower or school refuser but, that said, the personal touch is impressive for such a large organisation. Has branches in Birmingham and Cambridge.

Manor House School

Manor House Lane, Little Bookham, Leatherhead, Surrey, KT23 4EN

Tel: 01372 458 538
Fax: 01372 450 514
E-mail: admin@manorhouse.surrey.sch.uk
Website: www.manorhouse.surrey.sch.uk

• Pupils: 370 girls, all day • Ages: 11-16 • Christian non-denom • Fees: Prep/junior £1,805 - £2,725; senior £3,395. • Independent • Open days: Late October, late March and late May

Head: Since 2000, Mrs Alison Morris BSc (fifties). Joined school in 1982 and has worked her way up the school ranks from maths teacher to deputy head and then head – she describes herself as 'a real Manor House girl.' Has two grown-up children, was educated at Sutton High and read maths and economics at University of Kent. Very smartly dressed, very business-like, yet a very friendly, approachable head who truly loves the school. One parent commented that 'she does her job well with the girls.' She knows them all by name – no mean feat for a head. Another parent summed her up by saying that 'she is very in tune with what people are trying to achieve with their girls in a realistic way.' Her warmth when dealing with parental problems – divorce etc – is much praised. Happily admits that 16 is the right age for the girls to move on 'as they need a couple of years to get in touch with the real world before university life or whatever they choose to do.'

Academic Matters: Caters for girls of all abilities from the very bright souls who do not want the pressure of the big name academic schools, to those for whom academia is not the be-all and end-all of school life. Excellent GCSE results from such a mixed bunch, with the academic girls scooping up not just bucketfuls of As and A*s, but also academic scholarships from schools such as Cheltenham Ladies, Cranleigh, and City of London Freemen's. For those wishing to pursue other avenues, there is encouragement and support and a wide range of vocational GCSEs including PE, home economics, art, music, drama and child care. Popular optional GCSE subjects include geography (very impressive GCSE geography results), drama, and religious studies. The girls are set for maths, science and French, but not for English. The school prides itself on the introduction of Spanish – alongside French and German – a good variety of languages for such a small school. Latin is also on offer to most.

15 of the current teachers have been with the school for more than 10 years and many are liked and respected by the girls. They are complemented by the fresh blood of younger teachers (a few more would not go amiss). Seeing the teachers is easy, according to a mother of two girls in the school. 'You can happily walk in and will always be welcomed.' Another said, 'they are much more approachable than in other schools.' Classrooms are large and bright as are the corridors – displaying art work by the girls.

All girls are screened for SEN and, according to the head, never turned down solely on those grounds. Currently 15 are receiving extra help. There are 3 part-time qualified SEN teachers and a full-time study skills support teacher for senior girls. 'Terribly supportive, fabulous' is a widely felt attitude by parents for the SEN provision. The girls are also encouraged to use computers to help them with their work if need be. Computers are gently being introduced throughout the school – with two computer rooms and a fully networked system – the school is getting there, slowly but surely, and plans are afoot for the introduction of interactive whiteboards in all the classrooms.

Games, Options, The Arts: Sports facilities on site. School praised by parents for putting out not just A teams, but regular B and the occasional C team – problem being a lack of opposition with many other schools not interested in anything other than fielding one team of top players. Games' teaching is generally very strong (though sometimes appears stretched, particularly in the busy summer months) and the school regularly gathers in sports scholarships when the sporty souls leave at 16. Music, art and drama are impressive. In line with the school ethos, everyone has an opportunity to take part, even if it is only in the back row of the chorus. Lots of music ensembles including choirs, orchestras, brass and string groups – but the teaching of individual musical instruments by outside peripatetic teachers leaves room for improvement. Average choice of after school clubs including jazz dancing and tap as well as ballet, fitness, skiing and calligraphy. D of E also popular.

Background and Atmosphere: Founded in 1920, but moved to its present site in 1937. The main building is a beautiful Queen Anne house surrounded by 17 acres of land. Allocated play areas keep the little ones happy, while idyllic grounds with flower beds and benches are at the older ones' disposal. Two small libraries – however, it does not seem to faze the girls. 'We always find what we're looking for,' was a 14 year-old's comment. School offers an 'early-birds' free of charge facility from 8am and an after-school chargeable (and not cheap) late club till 6pm. Car parking and pick ups (as with most schools) seem on the difficult side but 'we manage like clockwork,' said a satisfied parent. Administration/communications with parents is not the school's strongest point. School food also leaves something to be desired – although it is said by the girls to be improving. Cosiness a strong point – a tangibly friendly atmosphere, a pleasure to visit.

Pastoral Care and Discipline: 'To Love is To Live' is the motto of the school – a motto which seems to fit well. The size of the school means all the girls know each other. Senior girls actively help out in the junior school and spend time with the younger girls. The girls seem to feel confident approaching teachers and the head with any worries or concerns.

A peaceful community. Drugs, bullying, smoking and drinking not evident to parents. The head commented, 'you always get the odd teenage girl who thinks she knows much more than you do; in those cases, you have to set boundaries as well as win their trust'. Rewards, sanctions and rules are clearly defined within the school as well as in the girls' homework diaries! There is plenty of discipline. Girls happy and calm – break-time not as chaotic as it can be.

Pupils and Parents: A mix of parents; the children of city executives to those who come in from the state sector on well-earned scholarships, although it is fair to say most are not short of money. Many parents choose Manor House to avoid the competitiveness of the 'Surrey Schools mafia' and the academic powerhouses. Girls are friendly, polite, smartly dressed – with hair (supposed to be and mostly) its natural colour, no outrageous skirt lengths nor the ubiquitous shirts hanging out. School is very successful charity fund raiser – both the girls and the parents. Bus service available to pick up from surrounding areas (but only in the mornings) and free shuttle bus to Effingham station. Old Girls include Susan Howatch (author), Elinor Goodman (political editor Channel 4), Sarah de Carvalho (founder of the charity, Happy Children) and Rose Gray (co-owner of The River Café).

Entrance: Many enter via the junior school, but spaces are available at 11 – entrance exams in English, maths, verbal reasoning plus small group interviews. Exams not a huge hurdle, but the school is becoming more popular (about 60 girls compete for 38 places). Scholarships and bursaries available. There are often occasional places at odd times, so worth a try at most ages: girls would spend the day with peer group and take tests in maths and English.

Exit: All girls leave at 16 – leavers go everywhere from the highly academic schools to art college or drama school.

List varies from year to year but usually includes: Howard of Effingham, St John's Leatherhead, Godalming College, Cranleigh, Reed's Cobham, Charterhouse and City of London Freemen's.

Money Matters: Girls from the state system can compete for The Mason Scholarship - up to 50 per cent of the fees. Other academic scholarships plus art, drama, music and sports awards.

Remarks: A small, friendly school which offers a traditional and caring environment for girls of all academic abilities. Not for the rebel or rule breaker – she would stick out like a sore thumb.

MARLBOROUGH COLLEGE

Marlborough, Wiltshire, SN8 1PA

Tel: 01672 892 400
Fax: 01672 892 307
E-mail: admissions@marlboroughcollege.org
Website: www.marlboroughcollege.org

- Pupils: 550 boys, 315 girls. A very few day, rest board
- Ages: 13-18 • Size of sixth form: 373 • C of E • Fees: Boarding £7,720; day £5,490 • Independent • Open days: One in the autumn, one in the summer

Master: Since 2004, Mr N A Sampson MA (forties), who was educated 'in the state system' in Kent, read English at Selwyn College, Cambridge, fast-tracked into the civil service and diversified into education. After ten years at Wells Cathedral, where he was housemaster, he became head of Sutton Valence, thence to Geelong Grammar (which had a hefty drug problem at the time) where he was 'brutal, dramatic and unpleasant but let someone else build on that' (his words) and really loved it and 'wouldn't have come back for anywhere else'. Plaudits all over the place, as we write, as Marlborough has just won a landmark case involving a teenager whose father objected to the school's decision that the pupil would not be welcome in its sixth form and took the school to court. The resulting highly publicized, costly and stressful, court battle (the parent eventually withdrew) has done wonders for the morale of many heads who have felt under attack from parents who assume their teenage tearaways will be transformed into angels as they pass through their public school gates; heads throughout the independent sector are heaving sighs of relief. The word from Marlborough staff is that 'The master was very supportive', 'solid' which might also be a physical description of this former rugby player who keeps a stylish, black-covered set of golf clubs in the corner of his study – 'I'm just a beginner,' he confesses.

The school itself is in excellent heart, no more than the usual whiff of drugs and waiting lists as long as your arm. Great strides in the IT provision at the school, though the master despairs of IT provision in Britain. 'We were much further ahead in the outback'. And he is keen to shake the place out of its academic complacency and encourage some 'educational independence'. Having introduced the IB at Geelong, he is thinking (no decisions yet) of offering the dual system at Marlborough, has committees reviewing the lower school syllabus, and wants to introduce an early assessment (like Eton at 11) to cut the interminable waiting lists, review the entrance procedure and perhaps encourage, a more 'cosmopolitan dash' – moving away from what is basically a solid middle class institution to something more intellectually challenging and 'enliven the academic structure and leave our cocoon behind'. 'Education should be exciting and enriching.' He would like to introduce 'resident experts: scientists, song-writers and poets'. 'This is a chance to grow, we don't want to expand, [rather] encourage independence of mind'. Recently appointed two new heads of departments: English and modern langs, and six changes of housemaster. Married, with twin daughters at Pinewood prep school nearby. It is good to find an inspired Trojan at the helm.

Academic Matters: 'Not an academic hothouse'. Max class size 20, fining down to 16 for GCSE. All pupils must have a bash at everything during their 'shell' or first year, before deciding which subjects they will take at GCSE. Absurdly young common room – probably the policeman syndrome – many of whom looked as though they ought to be sitting the other side of the desk. English the most popular A level, with a respectable clutch of As, followed by business, English and history, also the sciences, now all in the ribbons at GCSE. Maths not bad either, at either level, though it was sad to see some Ds, Es and Us. Good trenchant collections of As in 2004, though only around 50 per cent of those taking each exam got A. Science mainly taught in fabulous 1920s building with shuttered concrete and Crittall windows magically light and airy; the adjacent biology department is stuffed with dead Victorian offerings (including a great bustard menacingly next door to the live chipmunks). A camera is permanently trained on a clutch of eggs in a nest on The Mound – eat your heart out Seabird Centre in North Berwick – and when the eggs are hatched, a repeat video is shown a regular intervals, 'useful for impressing parents on open days,' said our guide. Business

studies, which was pioneered here, has now been deposed in popularity by religious studies. One or two esoteric languages – regular Arabic regularly in the ribbons; Russian, Spanish, French and German the norm, Italian an option. Greek as well as classical civilisation. Rather a fine Egyptian mummy (out of Rome, from Alexandria) was recently discovered in a store cupboard (!) by some pupils and now graces the foyer of the languages and classics dept. Pretty hands-on stuff. Astronomy on offer at GCSE.

Current thinking seems to be that pupils take three A levels over two years and a different AS level each year. Modules as far as poss. 'Not very far down the road of learning support,' with two full-time and one part-time staff who cope with the dys-strata, ADHD but not full blown Aspergers, 'support where needed' though NOT a full remedial department, and support for the brightest too. Extra help either in the afternoons or during sixth form study periods: old fashioned study skills are in great demand. Computers everywhere, laptops for those who need 'em but mostly kept in rooms or study areas. EFL on hand but 'not a huge demand'. Each department has its own library so that pupils can have instant access to books, which they use regularly, as well as having computer links with the main library.

Games, Options, The Arts: Every child must take one creative subject at GCSE and art results good – and a good number taking A level too. Stunning new glass-filled art department opened just before our visit, incorporating much of the old art department, gallery, spiral staircase, but with loads of light and moveable walls, dedicated department areas, seminar rooms H of A library, photography (with sexy revolving door) digital stuff, plaster, clay, etching press to be joined by another, terrific exhibition space, artist in residence. Inspired, though no textiles at the moment. The head of art, slightly like a child with a new toy, currently moving bookcases and display cases around 'to see how they look there'. Stunning newish music dept with curved corridor (think acoustic wizardry) and incredible recording room with baffled walls. Orchestras, bands, choirs, inspired music with the famous brass band, the 'brasser' still going strong. Magical theatre dept with huge hall(3) which adapt with adjustable seating to lectures, open spaces, in the round, whatever; theatre studies well down from a high of 23 in 1997, though this seems to be changing since the opening of the exciting new performing arts centre: only 11 AS candidates in 2004.

Traditionally strong on mainstream games, the girls are now holding their own in the hockey world; rugby results, too, have been jolly good of late. The pitches are 'plateaued' out of the wildly sloping site, with infill dug out of the new swimming pool being used to level off yet another pitch. The new swimming pool, 25 metres long, has an adjustable floor – either sloping or deep for diving and is in addition to the one in the leisure centre that the school shares with the town, an arrangement that has never really worked, but it did wonders for the planning process (and the school itself now doesn't use the place). Trad games hall, weights room and the rest. Dozens of societies, good recent success on the polo field, alas the beagle pack has been blairised. D of E popular. Huge number of weekend activities – everything from trad games to ceramics.

Background and Atmosphere: Founded in 1843 for the 'sons of clergy of the Church of England', imposing red-brick quadrangle, with elegant Queen Anne building at the head of the court, contrasting with Memorial Hall built after World War I, and earthwork known as The Mound. Raft of new departments and buildings, neat little interconnected modern boxes. The classroom doors have a cunning dia-mond-shaped window so that staff and pupils can be observed from outside. Stunning IT building has an impres-sive mirrored wall. Two floors of it. Some really super archi-tecture, elegant gardens with duelling lawn, indoor and outdoor theatres.

Main Calne-Marlborough road runs through the school, lots of pelican crossings. Has its own shorthand: Shell = 13/14 year olds, followed by remove, then hundreds; plus sixth form. Houses are divided into those 'In' campus and those dotted round the town = 'Out' houses. Housemasters and mistresses are contracted for up to fifteen years, juniors tend to choose their house, those arriving later usually are allocated according to whim. The ones with their own dining facilities are generally reckoned the best. Girls' quarters cosy and comfortable, though sixth form girls share senior houses with boys – well separated.

Boys wear tweed jackets and grey flannels, very trad, shirts sticking out etc etc, suits for sixth form; sixth form girls wear incredibly elegant (truly) black bias-cut full-length skirts, with a jacket – the current choice is black – ear rings OK (giant hoops more like). Littler girls wear longish kilted skirts with a number of pupils defying the Wiltshire wind and wandering around with only the top buckle done up (or the second one moved up) and exposing a fair expanse of tight. Pupils graduate from dorms, to sharing, to bedsits, as the study bedrooms are known. Arriving sixth form girls often share for the first year, 'to bond'. Mobile phones only in rooms. Carefully controlled booze ('not a free flow') at week-ends only, in the posh (slightly soulless, café-style tables with only a sprinkling of sofas) social – The Marlburian; sixth form only, other houses have various nooks and pupil-

painted crannies for more intimate socials. Interestingly, unlike some co-eds, we saw little fraternisation between the sexes and single-sex groups of all ages drifted past in ani-mated twos or threes. Marlborough was the first trad boys' school to take girls but do not send your daughter straight into the sixth form here unless she is a toughish egg on all fronts: mature, outgoing, streetwise. Sixth form entrants of our acquaintance say that it can sometimes be a bit of a rocky ride to start with but 'the boys are fine'.

Pastoral Care and Discipline: In-house tutors to help housemasters, Dames (as at Eton); good pastoral back-up on all fronts, prefects pretty beady. Random drugs testing and immediately out for dealing. One recent miscreant experienced a 'negotiated withdrawal', pupils who do drugs get 'a second chance, with counselling, testing and suspen-sions; and 'run a book for minor transgressions' where they can work off their sins via community services. If students notch up 'four live major sins then they have to go'. Transgressions include 'breaking the boarding code', booz-ing, fags, out at night.

Pupils and Parents: Middle and upper middle class – accountants, lawyers, bankers, more army (strong on gen-erals), less clergy than before, tiny handful of real foreigners, selection of expats from all over. Clutch of prep school heads' children (discounts). More first time buyers than before and fewer OBs children (distant OBs now choosing schools local to them, says the school). School runs buses to all over the south coast of Britain – Oxford, Newbury, Tonbridge – wherever there is sufficient demand – at start and end of every exeat and half term. OBs include William Morris, Anthony Blunt, John Betjeman, Nicholas Goodison, Wilfrid Hyde White, James Robertson Justice, Lord Hunt (of Everest fame) Francis Chichester, Louis MacNeice, Siegfried Sassoon, Bruce Chatwyn.

Entrance: 'Waiting lists at 13: CE, average 60 per cent with 'not less than' 55 per cent in English, maths, French, science is the 'benchmark'. Over 200 feeder prep schools. Sixth form entrants must have five GCSEs at B (not a high hurdle) with applications for sixth form girls overflowing. But see above and proposed new assessment test which will be based as much on character as on academic ability.

Exit: In 2004, over 80 per cent of A level candidates got to their first choice university, strong Oxbridge presence, 24 last year. Wide spread of universities, plus gap years etc. Careers office help with problems around exam result time. Still trad tranche to Services, usually army.

Money Matters: An appeal and increased pupil num-bers have funded the recent rash of building – a case of putting your money where your mouth is perhaps. A moveable percentage of fee income goes to children of clergymen (who used to number 20 per cent of all pupils but now not as many as previously) plus large numbers of scholarships for academics as well as music, sport and art. Bursarial help for parents facing financial hardship, school will try and get pupils to the next 'break point'. School runs a popular summer school. Currently has uncommitted dosh in the bursary fund. Collection of academic, music, sporting, and OBs' scholarships plus sixth form academic and music plus means-tested Anniversary Bursaries for all (see above).

Remarks: Top choice for girls at sixth form, jolly good all round, girls no longer feel in a minority. Famous, designer label, co-ed boarding school still riding high, but watch this space – head would truly like to cast off the designer label and make this one seriously exciting school, both on the academic and the social fronts.

THE MARY ERSKINE SCHOOL

Linked to Mary Erskine and Stewart's Melville Junior School in the Junior section

Linked to Stewart's Melville College in the Senior section

Ravelston, Edinburgh, EH4 3NT

Tel: 0131 347 5700
Fax: 0131 347 5799
E-mail: principal@esmgc.com
Website: www.esms.edin.sch.uk

• Independent

Remarks: See Stewart's Melville College.

THE MAYNARD SCHOOL

Linked to Maynard Junior Department (The) in the Junior section

Denmark Road, Exeter, Devon, EX1 1SJ

Tel: 01392 273 417
Fax: 01392 355 999
E-mail: office@maynard.co.uk
Website: www.maynard.co.uk

• Pupils: 508 pupils, a quarter of whom are in the junior school. All day pupils • Ages: 7-18 • Size of sixth form: 105
• Non-denom • Fees: Junior £2,156; senior £2,698 per term
• Independent • Open days: October, December, June; sixth form February

Head: Since 2000, Dr Daphne West BA PhD LTCL (late forties). Predecessor was tough act to follow but Dr West's abounding enthusiasm, professionalism and efficiency have made their mark – 'she's small but powerful,' say teachers. Educated Durham University (1st in Russian and French). Leningrad-based, researched Russian poet who died during Stalin's purges. Various teaching posts – Middlesbrough comp, Millfield prep, Sherborne School for Girls. In 1987 became community education tutor for Somerset LEA. Returned to Sherborne as head of languages. In 1997 went to Sevenoaks Independent (co-ed) as international development officer and French/Russian teacher, then head of languages. 'I feel I'm in the right place,' she says. If her door blind is up, pupils can pop in to see her. Runs middle school choir on Thursdays, teaches French and Russian. Married with no children, enjoys walking.

Academic Matters: Shining results. Consistently over 50 per cent grade A at A level, 75 per cent A*/A at GCSE. Biology, chemistry, history and English popular. Modern languages now much stronger – excellent GCSE and A level. 24 subjects to choose from at AS level. Some teachers boast more than 20 years with the Maynard. Special Education Needs co ordinator in place, geared mainly towards dyslexia.

Games, Options, The Arts: Fine art facilities and equipment, low pupil numbers, a breadth of courses and good results. Music strong – some go on to scholarships for specialist music education in colleges and universities. Pianos in every music room, the main hall and the gym. Three orchestras, three choirs, plus a Chamber Choir and Chamber Orchestra, jazz and wind bands, oboe and flute groups, various ensembles. Mostly in-house drama productions and concerts. Girls take LAMDA exams in speech and participate in the Exeter Competitive Festival each spring.

Three on-site netball and tennis courts and a large sports hall, pupils walk to external swimming pool, while two minibuses take pupils to Exeter University Astroturf for hockey. National reputation for netball, basketball and hockey. Plenty of annual French, German and Spanish exchanges and welcome introduction of Russian ones organised by Dr West. Work experience abroad is popular as is foreign travel in gap year to eg Belize, India, Vietnam and South Africa, all arranged through recognised student volunteer organisations. Young Enterprise scheme is outstandingly successful.

Background and Atmosphere: Founded 1658; moved to present 'island' site near Exeter City centre 1882. Attractive mosaic floor tiles and marble staircase creates sense of grandeur in main senior block – clean and well maintained. A £500,000 project for the redevelopment and extension of sixth form block was completed in January 2004. 'Happy and caring community spirit,' comment parents, with evident peer support. Parents are impressed by the life force of the school and its confident pupils.

Junior department housed in its own building, within the senior school site. Above National Curriculum levels in all areas, especially English and science. Various junior groups run by older pupils – drama, dance, art. Pupils seem mature, supportive of one another, polite and well-behaved.

Pastoral Care and Discipline: Misdemeanours treated cautiously, second chances. Persistent bullies will be suspended; counselling provided. Sixth formers are forbidden to smoke off-site until out of sight of school boundaries; problems are rare however and non-existent for alcohol or drugs. One head girl and three deputy heads elected by peers and teachers. Peer Support Group, run by trained sixth formers, well-used especially by younger pupils. Initial contact is made via a confidential note being placed into a secure box; teachers believe it works well for pupils who don't wish to share their 'problem' with an adult. Variety of lunchtime clubs run by sixth formers for younger pupils. Parents say, 'the teaching staff use fantastic methods of encouragement and motivation'; 'my daughters have gone from strength to strength'.

Pupils and Parents: One third from city, remainder as much as 50 miles away from Plymouth, also Taunton, Barnstaple, South Hams. Most parents are professionals – businesspeople, doctors, solicitors, accountants. Handful of foreign students. Old Girls include Professor Dame Margaret Turner-Warwick – first woman president of British Medical

Council; Claire Morall, author, shortlisted for Man Booker Prize 2003.

Entrance: Admission at 7 to 15 is by examination or assessment and interview, and by proven examination success and interview at sixth form. Feeder schools include Maria Montessori, Exeter Cathedral Prep, St Peter's, Lymphstone, Hylton, The New School and Elm Grove.

Exit: 99 per cent of the sixth form to higher education. High proportion read medicine or science. A few year 11s head off to other sixth forms in locality (financial pressures as much as anything else, and fewer than used to) – this outflow made good by new arrivals.

Money Matters: Governor-assisted bursaries pay up to 45 per cent of fees for those without financial backing. Newly-established Joan Bradley Memorial Fund available to help girls of conspicuous potential. Music scholarships - up to 50 per cent. Sixth form scholarships for music, art, science and sport. Sibling discount available.

Remarks: A 'smashing school', providing ample opportunities for pupils, achieving excellent results. Likely to improve further under the direction of enthusiastic head.

MAYVILLE HIGH SCHOOL

Linked to Mayville High School Junior Department in the Junior section

35-37 St Simon's Road, Southsea, Hampshire, PO5 2PE

Tel: 023 9273 4847
Fax: 023 9229 3649
E-mail: mayvillehighschool@talk21.com
Website: www.mayvillehighschool.com

• Pupils: 440; 205 boys, 235 girls, all day, of which nursery, 6 months-4: 42 girls and 37 boys; pre-prep, 4-7: 42 girls and 36 boys; junior school, 7-11: 58 boys, 55 girls; senior school, 11-16: 80 boys, 97 girls • Ages: 6 months to 16 • C of E, all creeds welcome • Fees: Pre-prep £900; junior £1,675; senior £2,170 • Independent • Open days: Tours daily, taster days by appointment

Head: Since 1994, Mrs Linda Owens, BEd. Has overseen what in recent years has been rapid evolution from genteel girls' school to mainstream co-ed (100 per cent when boys enter year 11 in 2006) catering for a number of particular needs locally. She and her fellow strategists have read market forces incredibly intelligently, their acumen abetted by their strong sense of what education should be about, namely, putting children in touch with the best ways of making the most of themselves. An indefatigably hard worker and a disciplinarian in a kindly old-fashioned sense – the pupils shoot to their feet and full-throatedly incant 'Good mor-orning Mrs Ow-wens' when she enters a classroom – you also see the littlest girls rushing up to hug her. Catchphrase 'everyone here is a star in some way', her words meaning what they say – this is what the school is predicated on. Teaches drama and oversees the school's monster musicals. Loves what performance does to a child's sense of itself.

Academic Matters: The spectrum is broad. They do particularly well by dyslexics and those who need the emotional nurturing of a small, caring school. It's all about focus on individual needs, of course, and it's this that's made them locally famous – 'Others say they do it, we have to do it.' Class teaching is trad, structured, careful with – we saw it happen – the clever being stretched while the rest work at their own level, and no sense of anyone looking down – or up. These children rate each other according to personal attributes, not marks, and that's instilled by the teachers. Parents say 'they lay down the building blocks of learning one by one and don't move on until everything is consolidated, no matter how much reiteration is necessary. It's very systematic.' It's also segregated. Boys, they reckon, develop differently from girls so they teach them maths, science and English separately, the boys for shorter periods according to male attention span, and bring them together for modern languages, history, geography, art, drama and sport. This is increasingly popular with members of ethnic minorities, the separate sex education in particular. One father praised the way his daughter can wear the hijab with pride, attend festivals and is encouraged to tell the other pupils at assemblies all about her faith – 'They accommodate individuality at no cost to the community.'

A number of children here are victims of the coercive, target obsessed National Curriculum – they fell behind, gave up on themselves and became the prey of all manner of emotional fallout. Refugees from other independents here, too. Mayville turns them around by, first, 'understanding the problem,' say parents, then making them feel secure, reacquainting them with success and giving them 'an amazing sense of belonging'. Discipline is strict in terms of expectations, never heavy-handed. Teachers here understand learning styles; they're up to date, not a bit faddish, and unusually well qualified. Relationships are warm, often giggly. Say parents, 'they know them and they like them'. But it's 'not cushy'. The school believes that 'hitting barriers gives them the strength to overcome and learn. It sets them up for life. Our job is to keep them going though this period.'

The dyslexia unit is justly lauded by inspectors (CReSTeD DU) who know what's what, and by parents who see the difference. Highly qualified teachers do all the right polysyllabic things – multi-sensory, kinaesthetic – and they do it expertly, but this isn't the half of it. Remediation has to be much more than a mechanical process because every dyslexic is different. Kindness matters most, and it is the emotional intelligence of those who work here that generates their best work. It's all about how children feel about themselves, and one thing they certainly don't feel is sorry. This is a victim-free zone. Lots of 1-1 – 'expensive but worth it'. In addition to GCSEs, some pupils are entered for dyslexic-friendly BTecs. Some parents say they'd like to see more vocational subjects – and wish the school wouldn't worry so much about b league tables. Well, it wouldn't if they didn't.

Mayville is not a school for the marginalised. There are conventionally bright children here, too, they benefit in all the ways the rest do, they resist the urge to go off to Portsmouth Grammar at 11 and they pick up fine GCSE results. The school is currently developing a programme to stretch them even further.

Games, Options, The Arts: Sport four times a week squeezed in after lunch, fixtures with schools of similar size and they play in local leagues. Drama is big because 'it's a whole life skill'. Public speaking big, too, and they win Rotary Youth Speaks comps. Art good. Music doesn't stretch to orchestras but they do super choirs, a jazz group and rock bands. All learn recorder, then a brass instrument and violin for a term each. Fab after school clubs and supervised prep: they are open, would you believe it, from 8 till 6, 50 weeks a year.

Pastoral Care and Discipline: Strict uniform code – smart blazer – and strict behaviour code underscore the sense of security the school instils. Justly famed for its standards of care. One mum says 'I wish I could be a fly on the wall to find out exactly how they do it.' Teachers 'very approachable. Any problems, they pick up the phone or write a note.' Expectations of parents are rigorous: 'They let you know early, and they expect your backing.' Children notably pleasing in their manners and demeanour and shiningly proud of their school.

Pupils and Parents: Local. Some move to be near the school, some make quite long daily journeys. Down to earth, unsnobby. Active PTA.

Entrance: No academic hurdle. Interview. They recruit for balance, so where SENs are concerned they do turn away 'the one too many'. Dyslexia's the big thing, but they also consider dyspraxia, ADHD and mild ASD. No emotional and behavioural disorders – 'There's only so much we can do'.

Exit: Havant College v popular. Local sixth form colleges and independent sixth forms.

Money Matters: Fees decidedly competitive, and after-school care a real bargain. Academic and creative arts scholarships worth 50 per cent of fees. Some means-tested bursaries up to 80 per cent.

Remarks: Very much its own place. Very inclusive. Operating out of four town houses a stone's throw apart, they cheerfully concede 'we don't look good' yet modifications are apt and they nurture development plans. The point is this: the school's a raging little success story.

McLaren High School

Mollands Road, Callander, FK17 8JH

Tel: 01877 330 156
Fax: 01877 331 601
E-mail: McLarenhs@stirling.gov.uk
Website: www.mclarenhigh.com

• Pupils: 693 boys and girls • Ages: 11-18 • Size of sixth form: 132 in the fifth, 63 in the sixth • Non-denom • State

Rector: Since 2005, Peter Martin MA (Hons). Mr Martin was appointed Rector, having been acting head for eighteen months and depute head for 6 years prior to that. A geographer who knows the school and the catchment area well. Strong commitment to quality improvement. Keen on using outdoor education as a vehicle for delivering other educational objectives – leads annual ski course to the Alps.

Academic Matters: Follows Scottish system only. All mainstream subjects, including wonderful classics teacher (still) – Latin popular at senior school level. Good results all over. Careful setting, max class size 30, with no more than 20 for practical subjects. Pupils work in flexible ability groups, 'they move up and down as necessary' (eg in maths). Lots of 'individual timetables' and varying amounts of work experience where necessary (nb large farming community). Science strong, also humanities – history and geography good. Pupils are encouraged 'to aim for the best', 'take as many (exams) as you can'. There is a strong emphasis on support, both academic and pastoral, for everyone, the gifted as well as pupils with additional needs. Good prefect system, strong links with local primaries. The head of each year group is tutor to that year group throughout. IT is good and the physics web site is second to none, with pupils logging on to do their homework. They can ask for and get help online.

Games, Options, The Arts: Given the time restrictions, the school manages to pack in a lot. Lots of clubs and activities in the lunch hour, very keen and good music (pipe band = junior section of Callander and District pipe band). Loads of choirs, jazz, swing, guitar ensembles plus violin groups (ie fiddle, they do well at the Mod). In-school music festival with outside adjudicators – over a hundred pupils took part last year. Masses of trips, skiing popular with regular sorties to France and Austria. The school has reinstated the role of dux ludorum; ie the head of games, a title which dates back to 1904, disappeared in the sixties, and is now awarded (by medal) to the top boy and girl in the games field. School uses the on-site McLaren Leisure centre during the day for gym and the like.

Background and Atmosphere: Donald McLaren, a banker from the Strathearn area, originally endowed the Free Church School in Callander in 1849 with a view to providing a 'salary of sufficient amount to induce men of superior talents and acquirements to become and continue to be teachers in the said school'. McLaren High was established in 1892. After Donald McLaren's death in 1894, 'his daughter Mary McLaren ensured that the McLaren Educational Trust endowments were used for the benefit of the children throughout West Perthshire, including Balquhidder, without distinction of income or class' and the school handbook is still supported by the clan McLaren.

Stunning site on the edge of the river just south of Callander in the Trossachs. Sixties buildings received civic trust award though, after recent £600,000 arson attack, causing enormous damage to both the swimming pool area and the music school, a major rebuild/refurbishment through PPP is in the offing.

Masses of student involvement, student forum includes the top team – ie the head boy and girl, plus deputies. Pupil representatives are involved on local civic panels, the Stirling Council Student forum and Community Councils. Active pupil council of all ages meets regularly to discuss specific problems. First year pupils have a 'buddying system' (the McMentor system) to ease their arrival into the senior school. Community service volunteers. Very strong PTA. This is true community spirit at its best. All pupils wear uniform (parents who don't support the uniform code must give their reasons in writing). Prefects wear rather smart gold edged blazers.

Pastoral Care and Discipline: The brisk no nonsense approach we described earlier has not changed (school says it has). Time-keeping is emphasised, good community policing. Very high profile prefects. Letters to parents and 'withdrawal of privileges' eg the culprits cannot go to the

PTA-organised monthly school disco – a vital mainstay in the rural social calendar. Good back-up procedure in place.

'ORCA' values important here (Order, Respect, Care, Achievement). School divides its loyalties between the local Presbyterian Church of Scotland, the Roman Catholic church and the Episcopalian Church in Scotland, with services from all three denominations. Plus an outreach week, when 'trendy Christian groups' organise drama, lunchtime concerts and discos.

Pupils and Parents: All sorts, from a 400 square mile catchment area – tourism, farming, home-workers, Stirling University.

Entrance: By registration; automatic, places for all.

Exit: 40 per cent go to higher education – Glasgow, Edinburgh, Aberdeen Universities all popular – large numbers to further education locally and some straight into farming, whatever.

Money Matters: Tiny foundation (land only now – not a lot of income); well supported by local businesses, which can and will provide extra funds for outings and the like.

Remarks: Sound, much admired school on the edge of the Highlands with lively friendly pupils (as before); the work ethic is on the up.

MERCHANT TAYLORS' SCHOOL

Sandy Lodge, Northwood, Middlesex, HA6 2HT

Tel: 01923 820 644
Fax: 01923 835 110
E-mail: info@mtsn.org.uk
Website: www.mtsn.org.uk

• Pupils: 815 boys, all day • Ages: 11-18 • Size of sixth form: 250 • Multi-faith • Fees: £11,260 pa • Independent • Open days: May and September

Head Master: Mr Stephen Wright MA (forties) took over in 2004 from the long-serving and widely respected Jon Gabbitas. Educated at King's School, Macclesfield, and Queen's College, Cambridge. Former deputy head at The Judd School, followed by six years as head of Borden Grammar School, north Kent. Married to Penny, a nurse, they have three children, one son at Merchant Taylors'. Very keen on sport – volleyball half blue at Cambridge – and continues to teach history and general studies. Enthusiastic gardener and opera buff.

Academic Matters: As is the case with many heads of schools near the top of the league tables, the head says he's not a great fan and then details just how good the exam results are. In this case, exceptional. Nearly 90 per cent A or B at A level, 86 per cent A and A* at GCSE. Used to demand 6 Bs for sixth form entry now at least 3 As required in the mix. 'They're looking to match schools like St Paul's,' said one parent.

Teaching a major strength of the school – with added value in every subject. Predominantly male staff oversee classes of 20 up to GCSE, 10 at AS and A level. All boys take 9 or 10 GCSEs – about 50 per cent do maths and/or French a year early. Four academic subjects at AS; most take 3 As. Everyone also takes AS general studies in years 12 and 13.

Wide range of subjects on offer throughout – over 20 in the sixth form. Science taught as three subjects – more able sit all three at GCSE, less do the double award. Chemistry one of most popular A levels (along with mathematics and economics). Very strong modern languages department in superbly equipped, purpose-built centre. Two thirds take two modern languages to GCSE, 50 per cent at least one at AS. All boys study French in years 7 & 8 (though this is under consideration) and begin German, Italian, Spanish or Ancient Greek in year 9. French, German, Spanish offered at AS and A, plus Italian, Japanese and Mandarin as part of the general studies programme. Latin now being phased out. English offered as three different A Levels (Eng lang, Eng lit, and Eng lang & lit).Extensive written reports three times a year, identifying strengths and weaknesses. Grades and comments sent to parents each half term, plus a full parents' evening once a year with teachers, tutors and headmaster. Study skills built into the curriculum. Once a year each boy writes his own report in considerable detail and discusses it privately with his tutor. Bright, modern library – 'a jewel' waxes the Independent Schools Inspectorate – with over 18,000 books, periodicals, tapes and CDs.

Games, Options, The Arts: Games taken seriously in this outstandingly well-equipped school. Fabulous on-site pitches, large sports hall, cricket nets, heated indoor pool, floodlit all-weather hockey pitch, lake for sailing and wind-surfing, grass and hard tennis courts, squash and fives court, fencing salle, huge, level, playing field for athletics, etc. School teams in rugby, hockey, cricket – as many as four a year – and PE includes basketball, athletics, swimming and tennis. Soccer, badminton, croquet, cross country, golf and shooting too.

Art a growing strength with a dynamic head of department – 'great man' say parents and boys – determined to add to the growing trickle leaving for top art schools. Light, spacious and well equipped four-year-old art block with well-used display space. Gallery trips and lectures, exhibitions in school and beyond, residential courses include a week painting at St Ives. Excellent design and technology department. Self contained music school arranged around an octagonal 150-seat recital hall seating. Annual concert at the Merchant Taylor's Hall in the City, plus a medley of orchestras, band and choirs. Active drama department with numerous large and small scale productions. Strong link with 'sister school' St Helen's Northwood, a mile away, for drama, music and other activities.

Impressive range of extra-curricular options. Over 50 clubs – everything from Scrabble to Outward Bound – including a Young Enterprise Business Company to form rival businesses and a school bank run by senior boys as a branch of Barclay's. Large cadet force – army, navy and air force – with purpose-built HG, assault course and shooting range.

Background and Atmosphere: Founded in the City of London in 1561 by the Worshipful Company of Merchant Taylors and Linen Armourers, it was then the largest school in the country. In 1933 moved to current impressive green-belt site, which remains one of the outstanding features of the school. Core of buildings still date from that period, with a dominant Deco angularity complemented by municipally neat grounds. Playing fields surround the school in an impressive sea of green. Funding clearly not an issue with recent additions including a new library and information centre, new computer centre, new politics and economics centre and a new entrance hall and sixth form. No lack of direction here – administration and management evidently clear and precise. Despite its high academic standing, the non-academic side is given equal weight, and the school sees its objective as equipping boys for the world beyond their schools days – 'a broad and balanced education that prepares pupils for life,' says the head. Old boys include Sir Edmund Spenser, Clive of India, Titus Oates, the artist Samuel Palmer and the founding editor of The Times; and, more recently, Lord Coggan, Archbishop of Canterbury and the sculptor Lynn Chadwick (whose work graces one of the many manicured lawns).

Pastoral Care and Discipline: Eight day houses and a very strong tutor system for individual guidance. Each boy is allocated a tutor on his arrival, whom he sees once a week throughout his time at the school and who monitors his progress – academic, sporting and extra curricular – and reports regularly to parents.

Two school assemblies a week, plus one house assembly. Religious leaders from different faiths invited to address the whole school. Christian services held in the chapel. Plus a Muslim prayer room, a Jewish society, a Christian discussion group and an Asian Cultural Society. All faiths work happily together with tolerance and consideration. Probably not, however, a school for the very observant Jew, since a significant number of activities take place on Friday evenings and weekends.

School rules kept as simple as possible. Boys encouraged to show kindness, common sense and respect in their day-to-day behaviour – and good manners here are clearly not restricted to high days and holy days with evident courtesy displayed in boys' dealings with each other. Boys take considerable responsibility at registration, lunch times and assembly, and also run the Duke of Edinburgh's Award, the Asian Culture Club and house-based teams and activities.

Series of lessons and courses on health and diet, sexual behaviour and risks of alcohol and substance abuse. Qualified school counsellor, with whom boys may book appointments and talk in confidence.

Pupils and Parents: Pupils reflect the affluent, suburban, middle-class area in which the school sits – Asian, Jewish, and commuter-belt Wasps. 'Children of the Thatcher Revolution,' remarked one parent, 'with a competitive spirit to match.' Primarily local intake and points along the Metropolitan Line – Moor Park Station within walking distance. Coaches from Beaconsfield, Ealing, Harrow, Mill Hill, Radlett, Stanmore.

Entrance: 11+ entrance (about 50 per cent from the state sector) by January exam in English, maths and verbal reasoning. Boys who do well are asked to return for interview. 13+ entry – need to be registered a year in advance, with interviews in autumn preceding entry. School's own exam in all CE subjects with the scholarship exam running at the same time. Scholarship candidates invited back for further interviews. A small number of sixth form places by examination in March. Candidates must register by January 31st and will be tested in the subjects they wish to study, followed by interviews.

Exit: About 15 to Oxbridge in last two years, and another 10 to medical schools, as well as a broad range of academic subjects at Russell League universities. University and careers advice clearly a strength. Each sixth former is assigned to a senior head of department who acts as his university adviser. Careers guidance from year seven, with a careers test and a careers conference offered later. Work experience – some of which can be done abroad – is highly developed, including a companies links scheme which helps boys find work in major companies in varying sector of business and industry.

Money Matters: No separate scholarship exam but roughly a quarter receive some financial help. At least five scholarships at 11 (maximum 30 per cent of fees), 11 scholarships at 13 (up to 30 per cent of fees), one sixth form scholarship (15 per cent of fees) and one exhibition. Four internal scholarships and exhibitions in the upper and lower sixth for up to 5 per cent of fees. Music scholarships at 11, 13, 16 include one for 25 per cent of fees, one for 15, and two exhibitions of up to 10 per cent, as well as free instrumental or singing tuition. Three Assisted Places up to 100 per cent of the fees.

Remarks: A tightly-run, high-achieving academic school in beautiful surroundings preparing well-rounded and courteous boys for good universities and good jobs. New head yet to make his mark.

MERCHISTON CASTLE SCHOOL

Linked to Pringle, Merchiston's Junior School in the Junior section

294 Colinton Road, Edinburgh, EH13 0PU

Tel: 0131 312 2200
Fax: 0131 441 6060
E-mail: Admissions@merchiston.co.uk
Website: www.merchiston.co.uk

• Pupils: 430 boys (70 per cent board, 30 per cent day) • Ages: 8-18 • Size of sixth form: 145 • Non-denom • Fees: Day: £3,175-4,950; boarding £4,660 - £6,925 • Independent • Open days: Information mornings (ie a morning in the life of the school): March, May, October

Headmaster: Since 1998, Mr Andrew Hunter BA PGCE (forties), educated at Aldenham and Manchester University where he read combined studies: English, theology and biblical studies. Came to Merchiston after eight years at Bradfield, where he ended as housemaster of Army House and, before that, eight years at Worksop, housemaster of Pelham House. Trails of glory on games fields, ex-county hockey, squash and tennis player. Head admits to 'ditching his MBA' which he promised us he would complete when we first met him seven years ago. Occasionally teaches A level classes and presentation skills. An ex-pat, he was brought up on a Kenyan coffee farm, and started school at Kenton College, Nairobi. Married to the glamorous Barbara who teaches art and design. The Hunters have three children, one son at Merchiston, one son at a special school and a daughter at St George's. Keen on the arts, theatre, wine tasting etc. He goes from strength to strength – spot of tinkering with the syllabus, mass trawling all over the UK, Europe, and the world on behalf of school, plus a dabble into building. The next great project is the sixth form house opening in September 2007, and a six million quid fund raisor is on the starting blocks (some cash already in hand following the sale of strategically placed geriatric staff houses, which will, of course have to be replaced as well). Excellent Hunter-inspired forty-five page Information Booklet that is undoubtedly the best guide to any school we have ever seen, plus a really comprehensive leaflet on exam results including a rather complicated value-added section – other schools please note.

Academic Matters: School continues to ply the mainly English system, though some may move from AS to Highers over two years. All boys must do two separate sciences at GCSE, and goodly whack go on to study science at A level. Maths, Eng and science results OK, better than the humanities, which, in many cases had a lesser take-up. The labs have all been refurbished – interesting design, repeated throughout the school, a mixture of trad tables and octagonal plinths, but not an interactive white board in sight. White boards at Merchiston, non-reactive and well used (torn in some places) seemed curiously old-fashioned: staff seemed pleased enough with their overhead projectors. Not that much use of computers as teaching tools either (though all must take their European Driving Licence), some pupils have their own laptops and there is a good IT suite plus more computers in the magical double-decker Spawforth library, but prep is not necessarily done on line. Good showing in out-of-school activities, physics challenge, chemistry Olympiads and the like.

School now offers full junior school facilities, and littlies can start at eight. Good take-up but not that many boarders, tiny classes, max 12, but in reality smaller than this. Snazzy new Pringle Centre provides a teaching block for eight – ten year olds, we were treated to a treatise on tropical fish by the youngest year group, and whilst there were computers in every classroom, there was no dedicated IT area for the youngest. No dedicated dyslexia unit either, but a learning support available and all pupils screened on entry. Pupils must score 100 in IQ assessments in order to follow main curriculum and do the standard 8/9 GCSEs. Certain amount of learning support included within the fees, but extra charge if extra help needed, both for this and for EFL, but see below.

School has CReSTeD B status, though Mrs Carol Watson, head of support for learning, was fairly noncommittal about the fact. No pupil taken who can't 'access mainstream education'. She heads a team of roughly four part-timers, though one of these is a four-days-a-week part timer and she 'often comes in on her day off Friday' (and is basically in charge of the junior house). All pupils are assessed on entry on a whole year group basis for their reading riting and rithmetic, though some boys arrive already diagnosed. Support is specially geared for each pupil, all have individually tailored profiles. Timetabled support varies from year to year, with small groups for foreign languages and Latin, as much to get boys up to speed as for actual diagnosable problems. In-class support too, plus 'concentrated units' for spelling, reading and individual subjects. Maths on the whole catered for by the maths department, whilst the SEN specialists can and do provide support lower down the school, complex problems need more info

and background than she feels the SEN dept can give. Lower school miss few lessons, with help available after or before class and in the evenings (boarding school), though pupils may miss Latin, French (some don't do it all) and Spanish or design technology and thereby do one GCSE less. Support for the gifted too. Mrs Watson (who is attached to a boarding house) appears to be a one man 24 hour referral unit, boys can and do come at all times. All the dys-stream catered for, plus two or three currently with 'mild Aspergers' diagnosed in-school; ADHD not a problem, physical handicap not 'a real problem': classes are re-located if access complicated; profoundly deaf boy recently went through the school with a (free) monitor paid for by West Lothian authority. Wow. Can and will scribe in exams and pupils get extra time both in school and public exams. Really quite a large number of boys 'in the system': 'looks like a lot between 80 and a 100'. Laptops not provided by the school, but masses in the special needs dept, all on the school network, and parents often buy their own. Extracurricular (ie not timetabled) classes cost extra.

Games, Options, The Arts: Rugby popular, cricket, athletics, curling back in favour, skiing, sailing etc, ditto all macho field games, well-used sports hall, and very well used swimming pool, weights room replaced by fitness centre. Golf encouraged. Wide variety of activities and successes in many areas. Popular CCF, grannie bashing and work in special schools a viable alternative, rifle range built in to school wall. Masses of trips all over the place in every discipline. Fantastic pipe band, sounding good during our visit, with some of the smallest pipers looking like embryo masons lugging their oblong bagpipe cases with grave determination. Strong choral tradition, including close harmony group, and huge number of orchestras and bands. Super art department, with terrific paintings both in the department and displayed all over the school, apparently not much take-up post school, only one to St Martins last year. Surprising, this is a strong department. History of art only within the A level curriculum, no ceramics; new printing press in the offing. DT uses Cad Cam, and good juxtaposition with computer suite and music hall – open till late.

Background and Atmosphere: Founded in 1833 by scientist Charles Chalmers, school moved from Merchiston Castle (now owned by Napier University) to the rather gaunt purpose-built Colinton House in 1930 (ruins of Colinton Castle in grounds). Set in 100 acres of park-like playing fields, with stunning views to the North. Pringle House, for junior boarders (aged eight to 12 or 13) recently much extended and a bit rabbit warreny, enclosed in its own private (secret) garden, own houseparents. Boys can climb the tree as far as the white mark, and generally allowed to be their own age without being pressurised 'to join the grown ups'. Book inspired day room, plus obligatory telly and rather complicated game of Diplomacy up on the wall. School in good heart, well used, nothing flash here but no signs of real distress either – some minor blemishes in the chipboard desks and cabin-beds. Huge amount of cash recently spent on revamping loos and individual showers.

Boys work in their dorm areas and day boys have desks in the same area. Wicked posters. First year sixth formers are billeted to each house for the year to act as monitors and have pretty snazzy kitchens to make their tasks less onerous. Cooking the flavour of the month, both in Pringle and, certainly, in Chalmers West: stunning pupil inspired kitchens. Pringle boys are running a self-financing cook-in. Older boys are encouraged to deviate from pizza and Pepsi. 'Steaks would be good,' said our guide and housemaster. Sick bay with visiting sports physiotherapists, own ultrasound machine and a delightful bubblegum pink isolation room (which would put any self-respecting boy off thoughts of malingering). Dining hall surprisingly small, with new servery and buffet service. Food good, soup, meat and veg, acres of white bread and rice pud when we visited, impressive salad bar for a boys' school too. Boys praise the new arrangement – 'the food is still good at the end of term' – when the budget is low.

First floor Memorial Hall doubles as a chapel (service inter-denominational) and dance hall and boasts Cameron tartan cushions on removable pews, and an impressive tartan stair carpet up to the entrance. Girls are regularly corralled in from (primarily) St George's but also Kilgraston and St Margaret's for reel parties, with lots of practice before the real thing. Merchiston boys are regularly voted the best dancing partners in Scotland. Visiting girls 'not a problem' – they come and go at weekends and can join the boys in the sixth form bar. Various departments already plotting what they will do with the about-to-become redundant areas which will be freed up when the sixth form centre finally materialises; we heard three possible uses within the same number of hours. Vast number of trips and options for boarders, day pupils can join if space available.

Pastoral Care and Discipline: Good rapport between pupils and staff. The horizontal house system is said to have made bullying practically 'non-existent', and 'anyway physical bullying has been superseded by text bullying from mobile phones' (banned until senior school). Head will and has asked pupils to leave. Believes in tough love, though a couple of prefects to whom we spoke obviously hadn't heard the phrase before. Mr Hunter is keen on parent/pupil/

school partnership; will take in boys who have been dissed elsewhere: both boy and parent will sign a contract and the boy will be subject to very stringent and regular drugs testing routine. NB urine testing now regarded as useless ('any fool can purchase antidotes from the internet,' said the head) pupils are tested by hair (think Napoleon). Expect to be drugs tested if either caught or suspected of dealing, or dabbling, followed by (but nothing in black and white) temporary, or permanent exclusion. Ordinary misdemeanours (alcohol, smoking etc) are treated on their own demerits. No longer cool to smoke. Discipline seminars. Jolly school policies booklet, re-printed every year, of which head is justifiably proud, lists all the dos and don'ts of the place. Purchase of fags or booze on or off the campus and dealings with betting shops are no-go areas. Betting is a new one to the GSG but perhaps other schools aren't as clear-cut in their expectations.

Pupils and Parents: 'A down-to-earth school, rooted in values' (says the head). The only all-boys boarding school in Scotland. Strong middle class ethos, good values, no change here. Record number of pupils in the school. 14 per cent from abroad, of whom about five per cent are ex-pats. Real foreigners come from all over, Japan, Hong Kong and Mainland China as well as the States, plus a number from Europe usually for the sixth form. Germany popular at present. No quick short stay fix, pupils must stay the full year. Head keen not to lose the boarding ethos, and littlies at Pringle are encouraged to flexi-board. Day officially ends at 4.10 pm, but pupils can stay till after tea (and presumably supper) if they want to. Must be the cheapest baby sitting service in the country. Senior boys can flexi-board too, often without charge if they are about official business – 'debates, plays and the like' – but £25 a night if for 'parental convenience'. Housemasters spend their 'ill-gotten' gains on boy treats: microwaves, new cookers. Boys open, friendly and well-mannered.

Entrance: At 8 and 10, also 11, 12 and 13, and 16 always via exams; 55 per cent pass mark at CE, boys come from prep schools all over Scotland and the north of England. Entry to sixth form automatic from inside school, others need a satisfactory report from previous school.

Exit: Refer again to the useful little booklet for details of the favoured unis – almost 80 per cent to England (Durham, Bristol, London etc), eight per cent to Oxbridge), rest stay in Scotland (Edinburgh, Glasgow, Aberdeen). Science, engineering, economics, management/business and languages/ classics/English the favoured subjects. Pupils go on to be fully paid up members of the Edinburgh mafia – law lords etc.

Money Matters: Myriads of scholarships and bursaries for almost everything but the school is working towards means-tested awards. Sibling discounts with Kilgraston, Casterton and Queen Margaret's York.

Remarks: No change. Still the top boys' school in Scotland, which extraordinary position has been achieved by defection to co-education by the rest – and it is on the way up anyway. Quite. Charismatic head, boys are encouraged to 'try their hardest, make the most of their talents and look after each other'. 'No thoughts of going co-ed,' say head, staff and boys – the latter positively shuddered at the idea.

MICHAEL HALL SCHOOL

Linked to Michael Hall Lower School in the Junior section

Kidbrooke Park, Forest Row, East Sussex, RH18 5JA

Tel: 01342 822 275
Fax: 01342 826 593
E-mail: info@michaelhall.co.uk
Website: www.michaelhall.co.uk

- Pupils: 600 boys and girls; all day, bar 20 who board with local families • Ages: 0-19 • Size of sixth form: 60 • Non-denom: Steiner Waldorf Schools Fellowship • Fees: Annual Early Years £3,735, Annual Lower School £5,310 - £6,090, Annual Upper School £7,890 • Independent • Open days: Two a term

---

Chairperson of the College of Teachers: There is no head teacher. Steiner schools are self-governing communities and a 'college of teachers' administers and manages pedagogical issues without a traditional hierarchy supported by the Council of Management (trustees).

Academic Matters: An interNational Curriculum which enables children whose parents' professions take them abroad to slot into a new school with minimum difficulty. The Steiner Waldorf curriculum includes cultural studies, sciences, arts, humanities, music, drama, languages – German and French both taught from 6, Spanish, Dutch and Italian are additional options. No use of calculators or computers until 12 and 14 respectively. No exams until mock GCSEs. At 14 the National Curriculum is introduced and pupils take GCSEs at 16. Results above the national average last year: 93 per cent achieved 5 A-Cs at GCSE, 100 per cent passed at A level.

Three-month EFL course for 15-18 year olds three times a year brings 30 pupils to experience intensive courses in English with a Waldorf flavour.

Games, Options, The Arts: Practical projects feature in their curriculum on grand scale. New environment studies building designed and constructed by several groups of age 14 pupils over two years. Sports at Michael Hall are largely non-competitive. 'One of the things that creates bullies is a competitive environment. We don't like to use competition as a motivational tool.' Volleyball and basketball in regional and county championships; also fencing, gymnastics, orienteering, athletics, softball, cricket, canoeing, sailing on offer.

Music, art and movement are treated as powerful tools for learning in areas like science, maths and languages. Every child learns recorder at 7. At 9, a second instrument is encouraged and, thereafter, often a third. Chamber ensembles, choirs, orchestras galore provide concerts throughout the year either in ballroom or open air theatre. From age 10 upwards each class has its own class orchestra.

Background and Atmosphere: In 1919 the Austrian philosopher and scientist, Rudolf Steiner, began a school in Stuttgart for children of the workers at the Waldorf-Astoria cigarette factory, using a curriculum based on nurturing emotional and cognitive intelligence. Today 890 schools in over 60 countries now use this holistic approach, making it the fastest growing independent education system in the world. Their curriculum is unique and, in the lower school, all teaching is done 'through the teacher and not via text books'. Michael Hall, founded in 1925, is the longest established of the 4 English Steiner schools to offer the National Curriculum and mainstream exams. Based in an 18th century mansion (with later additions and a spectacular Early Years edifice resembling an upside down mushroom) in 50-hectare parkland originally laid out by Humphry Repton on the edge of Ashdown Forest. It has links with two biodynamic farms, Tablehurst and Plaw Hatch, which play a vital role within its curriculum. 'Home boarding' of distant pupils arranged with families of local pupils.

Pastoral Care and Discipline: Pupils benefit from continuity and commitment of their teachers. The 'looping' system means a teacher remains with the same class from age 6 to 14 and this long-term relationship enables the teacher to evaluate the pupils' development. The ethos effects a strong partnership between parent and teacher, who work together in best interest of pupil. Teachers will pay home visits to discuss a child's progress. Teaching ratio is 10:1. From 14-19 the students get support from a 'class guardian' and a self-chosen tutor. Most teachers are from the state sector and Steiner-Waldorf trained; 25 of them have been here more than a decade.

Pupils and Parents: Michael Hall strives hard to reflect a multicultural community but in middle-class white Sussex that's quite some task. Few Asians about. One black student. 80 per cent of students live within a 30-mile radius. 10 per cent come from overseas. But parents will move house to be within reach of a Steiner school they regard highly, downsize, travel miles or go into debt to finance it. They are expected to play a big role in school community and some own shares in Forest Row co-operative. WOW (Waldorf One World) raises funds with monthly craft market.

Difficult to find parents with a bad word to say. We visited on the day pupils of all ages were in costume and make-up to celebrate carnival; the festive air made pupils behave as though it was the last day of term. One 9 year old had experienced problems with a London Steiner and come here for a 6 week 'trial' – of mum and dad's ability to shuttle back and forth from London – to spend half a week at Forest Row. Despite everything, his mum beams, 'it's worth even that. At last he is happy and that is what we both wanted.' No uniform. No prefects or head boy/girl. No competitive houses. Past pupils: Oliver Tobias, Sean Yates (international cyclist), Bella Freud, Esther Freud, Marty Boysens (mountaineer), Prof John Pearce (author and professor of child psychiatry at Nottingham University), Stuart Koth (osteopathy centre for children).

Entrance: Non-selective in academic sense. Some previous experience of French or German and music an advantage. Class teacher will interview potential parents/ pupils. Most enter through own Early Years Kindergarten before 7. Brighton Steiner and Steiner School of south west London are main feeders at age 14. Sixth form entry: interview.

Exit: 60 per cent of sixth form leavers go on to degree courses. Each year a handful leaves at 10 for local secondary schools. Roehampton University admits Steiner pupils on their year 12 diploma and GCSEs. Universities in Norway take Steiner pupils without external qualification (Holland, Sweden, Switzerland, Austria and Germany have state funding for Steiner schools).

Money Matters: No scholarships. Means-tested bursaries. There is a fund to see through any family in difficulties for a year.

Remarks: A child orientated and compassionate school which turns out well-rounded, focused young.

MILL HILL COUNTY HIGH SCHOOL

Worcester Crescent, Mill Hill, London, NW7 4LL

Tel: 0844 477 2424
Fax: 02089 596 514
E-mail: wynneh@mhchs.org.uk
Website: www.mhchs.org.uk

- Pupils: 1,656; roughly 55 per cent boys and 45 per cent girls, all day • Ages: 11-19 • Size of sixth form: 420 • Non-denom • State

Head: Since 2004, Geoffrey Thompson MA (Cantab) MBA (Ed) MIMgt. Mr Thompson came from headship of the Duchess's Community High School in Alnick. Degree subject was music. He previously taught in Bromley and was a deputy head in Norfolk. He is a performing musician, mountaineer, married with three children.

Academic Matters: Heavily oversubscribed, with high expectations and achievements. Selects 10 per cent on 'technological aptitude'. In 2005, 89 per cent of GCSE pupils got five or more A* – C grades. At A level, English, maths and the sciences are all popular. 68 per cent of A level grades were A or B in 2005, with 24 students getting at least 3 grades As. Strong, as one would expect, at science and maths, but very good results also for RS and English literature GCSE. Vocational options are ICT and leisure and tourism GNVQ. Other popular options are law, psychology and sociology and vocational courses including media studies and ICT. Pupils are grouped by ability for most academic subjects right from the start. Express groups of students can take one or two GCSEs in year 10, then do a one-year course in law or geography, or an AS in critical thinking.

The Inclusive Learning Team works with students with a wide range of special educational needs – mostly within mainstream lessons. Two blind students have recently joined the school. 'My son, who has dyslexia, has had plenty of support,' said a parent. 'They're helping him to achieve to his capabilities.'

Games, Options, The Arts: Perhaps surprisingly for a technology college, performing arts are important here – 10 per cent of places are given to talented musicians and 5 per cent to dancers. Everyone does combined dance and drama lessons for the first three years and can take either or both as GCSE and A level courses. 'The drama department is wonderful,' said a student. 'I love it to pieces.' There's a drama festival every autumn, often including plays written by the head of drama, and a school musical production in the spring, involving actors, dancers and musicians. 'The quality is amazing,' said a parent. There are 32 music and choral groups and six dance clubs. Art used to be the poor relation, but has improved considerably over recent years.

The school overlooks playing fields and netball courts and has a gym and sports hall. There's plenty of sport going on in PE lessons, clubs, house and school teams, alongside other activities such as Duke of Edinburgh, field trips, ski trips, language exchanges and summer camps. 'There's so much to get involved in,' said a pupil, though a parent commented that it takes organisation – 'getting a place in clubs and on trips can be competitive, so you have to be on top of what the activities are and be first in line to sign up.'

Background and Atmosphere: Its 21-acre site on the edge of the green belt should be spacious but the school is so popular that the site is almost too small for pupil numbers. It is also, incidentally, a tricky place to get to, with no tube station for miles, though buses do stop around a quarter of a mile away, and the LEA is planning to extend the existing public bus routes. The technology college status has brought extra funds for major refurbishment and building projects over the last decade, including new science and art rooms, a business and ICT centre and a media studies centre. Another round of building work has provided English, music, dance/drama rooms and a new library. This is a large school and by no means cosy, but it doesn't seem that children get lost in the crowds. 'They expect a lot but they will also put their arms around the children,' said a parent. 'Whenever we've had problems they've always solved them.'

Pastoral Care and Discipline: The school prospectus states that it is 'highly traditional in its approach to student behaviour and attitudes'. 'Their discipline is very tough and their expectations are high too,' said a parent. Sixth formers provide peer mentoring and also help with literacy in year 7. A pupil commented that her brother, who has learning difficulties, has received lots of help with friendship problems. There's a system of merit awards for service to the school and for academic achievement. Zero tolerance of selling drugs on the premises.

Pupils and Parents: The presence of the school puts a premium on house prices in the surrounding estates, with plenty of parents measuring the distance to the front gate before they buy. With a large proportion of the places going to technology and performing arts buffs and to siblings, the catchment area stretches as far as Borehamwood. So there's a good mix, ethnic and otherwise, of locals from leafy Mill Hill and families from further afield. OBs: Angus Fraser, Middlesex cricketer, and Robert Elms, journalist and broadcaster.

Entrance: Highly competitive, with over 1,300 applicants for 240 places. Looked-after children, then siblings, get first preference (siblings usually take around half the places); then the 24 with the highest scores in technological aptitude tests. There are also 24 music places, awarded after aural tests, and generally to those at around grade 4 or above, and 12 dance places. Children of staff are offered places next, and at least 10 places to those who live closest, which in practice means rather less than a mile away. Around 70 per cent go through to the sixth form; places are offered to all those who 'have previously displayed a positive attitude to study and a determination to succeed'. Entry requirements at this stage for outsiders are five Bs, including As in the subjects chosen for A level, or five Cs for vocational courses, and there are around five outside applicants for every place.

Exit: Nearly all sixth form leavers go on to university, and 7 got Oxbridge places in 2005. Law, business studies and medicine are all popular courses.

Money Matters: Not short of funds, through its technology college status and other initiatives. Plenty raised by parents.

Remarks: Successful, tightly-run state school with high standards and rigorous teaching. Strong at performing arts and sport as well as technology. 'It's a fantastic school,' said a parent. 'They expect a lot of the children and they give them the support to achieve it.'

MILL HILL SCHOOL FOUNDATION

Linked to Grimsdell Mill Hill Pre Preparatory School in the Junior section

Linked to Belmont School in the Junior section

The Ridgeway, Mill Hill, London, NW7 1QS

Tel: 0208 959 1221
Fax: 0208 906 2614
E-mail: registrations@millhill.org.uk
Website: www.millhill.org.uk

• Pupils: 480 boys, 150 girls; 460 day, 170 board (about half of the boarders are from abroad) • Ages: 13-18 • Size of sixth form: 240 • Non-denom • Fees: Day £4,402; boarding £6,905 • Independent

Head: Since 1996, Mr William Winfield MA (fifties), educated at William Ellis School, Clare College Cambridge (where he read French, German and Norwegian) and the Royal Academy of Music. Has been at the school since 1970, joining as assistant master of languages. Set up the much admired Section Bilingue (which sadly expired with the advent of GCSEs) and initiated a programme of exchanges and links with European countries. 'It is a remarkable programme,' said a recent Independent Schools Council (ISC) inspection report. 'He absolutely enshrines the humanistic ethos of the school,' said a parent. 'And he has a very clear vision of where he wants the school to go.' His wife, Margaret, is a professional musician with the Apollo Consort. Head of governors: Dame Angela Rumbold.

Academic Matters: Despite its strong overseas links – around 50 per cent of the pupils go to Europe each year and many Europeans visit the school – the school's academic strengths are in business studies rather than languages per se. 'Overseas students come here to learn English as a business language and our students tend to learn languages for vocational reasons'. Many go abroad for work experience. 'We're not an international school but we are looking outwards. We expect our students to travel and they do.' The school has a relatively broad ability range, including foreign students who may arrive with little English, but it achieves 60 per cent A and B grades at A level, and 45 per cent A* and A at GCSE. Overseas students may go into a transition class for a year to concentrate on getting their English up to scratch. One recent ex-transition pupil won the top scholarship in medicine at the University of Toronto.

Business studies, economics, maths and physics are consistently popular A level subjects. The breadth of languages at GCSE and A level – including Chinese, modern Greek and Russian – suggests the range of mother tongues of overseas students, as does the tendency of students to achieve top grades in these subjects. Latin is taught to A level, classical civilisation only at AS and A level. Setting for most academic subjects throughout the school. The school tests for dyslexia and will bring in outside help where necessary. 'Our philosophy is to play to people's strengths,' says the head. Outside the core subjects, pupils get a wide choice of options and timetables are made up round their choices. Gifted musicians, for example, can get in several hours practice a day if necessary. 'There is an excellent academic education available there,' said a parent. 'The top 25 per cent will get results as good as in any school in north London.'

Games, Options, The Arts: Saturday school – plus weekdays up to 5pm – opens up plenty of time for extracurricular activities and art, music and sports scholarships attract those with particular gifts. 'They think of the cultural, sporting, moral and ethical life as well as the academic,' said a parent. 'We used to have the reputation of being a hearty, sporty school,' says the deputy head. 'Now, and this is mostly due to the girls, it's as cool to be good at drama, music or art as to be captain of the first XV.' Having said that, the school has 120 acres of grounds, and sport is a serious business, with rugby and hockey tours of South Africa and Canada and netball players visiting Barbados. The school provides many county players. Major sports are rugby, hockey and cricket for boys and hockey, netball and tennis for girls. Minor sports include fives, fencing, shooting and golf.

High standards of art, with many media on display and a high proportion of A grades at A level and GCSE. The school visits European and New York galleries as well as London ones. The small numbers who take music at GCSE or A level do well, and there is plenty of music around, with choirs visiting New York and Denmark and performing at the Wigmore Hall. The head of music composes pop and classical music, and had a composition premiered at the Proms in 2000. Drama is popular at GCSE and AS level, and plenty of plays are performed in the school theatre, including the House Drama Festival. Two recent productions at the Edinburgh Fringe have sold out, one dubbed 'must see' by the Daily Mail.

Strong Combined Cadet Force, with an induction for all year 9 pupils. Conscientious objectors can do private study instead. The house system, with ten day and boarding houses, provides plenty of opportunities for taking part in inter-house competitions. All the houses have their own common and study rooms and act as social centres for their members. The school has links with two local schools – one for children with learning difficulties – and centres in India, Nicaragua and Ethiopia.

Background and Atmosphere: Mill Hill was founded in 1807 by a group of non-conformist Christian ministers and city merchants, who placed their school outside London because of the 'dangers, both physical and moral, awaiting youth while passing through the streets of a large, crowded and corrupt city'. The buildings form a time-line. The original neo-classical building with huge pillared entrance, housing a dining room with sweeping views across parkland and playing fields, gives way to Edwardiana, a neo-Jacobean chapel and a prefabricated Scandinavian addition to the music department. Boarding houses, some single-sex and some co-ed, are scattered round the grounds, with a refurbishment programme in process. Huge amounts have been spent on redevelopment over the past few years. Grotty squash courts have been converted into the magnificent Piper library. The panelled Murray Scriptorium, where Sir James Murray wrote the Oxford English Dictionary whilst teaching English and geography at the school, has been converted slightly incongruously into an ICT suite. Newly-refurbished classroom block and multi-sports complex with new indoor swimming pool.

The atmosphere is informal and multi-cultural. 'The school wants to treat them as responsible people,' said a parent. 'They really encourage self-reliance. And because there's such a wide range of activities, everyone has the chance to shine in his chosen field.'

Pastoral Care and Discipline: Pastoral care 'is widely recognised as one of the major strengths of the school,' said the ISC report. Housemasters and mistresses, tutors and the chaplain are all involved. 'The chapel is a spiritual centre of the school, without being strictly Christian,' says the head. There is an anti-bullying council staffed by pupils and teachers – 'we aim to make bullying culturally unacceptable.' Pupils dealing in drugs are liable to expulsion; those using them are put on a supportive regime with regular urine testing. 'It's easier for under-age pupils in north London to buy drugs than a bottle of vodka – and cheaper. We like to give people a second chance.'

Pupils and Parents: Girls make up about 25 per cent, a percentage that is gradually increasing ('though the girls have about 50 per cent of the influence,' says the head). A cosmopolitan ethnic and cultural mix typical of north London, with overseas students added in for good measure. Plenty of parents run their own businesses and many are first-time buyers of private education. Few of the boarders, says the head, also considered country boarding schools. 'They want the buzz of London and its population mix.' OBs and OGs include Richard Dimbleby, Francis Crick, Denis Thatcher, Simon Jenkins, Norman Hartnell, Timothy Mo, Katherine Whitehorn and Keith Murray.

Entrance: Fifty per cent comes from the junior school, Belmont, which takes in a new class at 11. No guarantee of going through to the senior school, though very few don't make it. At 13, all applicants are interviewed. 'We're looking for people who want to be part of a community, rather than just going to school.' Plus points for achievements in art, music or sport.

Exit: About 95 per cent to a wide range of universities and art colleges.

Money Matters: A selection of scholarships and bursaries. Academic, drama, art and music awards at 11. At 13, bursaries for those on a low income, plus academic, sport, music and art awards. Music scholarships and bursaries at 16.

Remarks: 'The whole structure is based on boarding lines,' says the head, who comments that, when parents of 11-year-olds first look round, they see Saturday school as a disadvantage. By the time their children are 13, they'd much rather they were wholesomely engaged at school than roaming north London at weekends. A genuinely multi-ethnic and multi-cultural school with a strong European dimension. Its parkland setting encompasses enviable – and improving – facilities, and a huge range of extra-curricular activities. 'The academic opportunities are there,' said a parent, 'but they are just as interested in turning out good, well-rounded citizens.'

MILLAIS SCHOOL

Depot Road, Horsham, West Sussex, RH13 5HR

Tel: 01403 254 932
Fax: 01403 211 729
E-mail: admin@millais.w-sussex.sch.uk
Website: www.millais.w-sussex.sch.uk

• Pupils: 1,500 girls, all day • Ages: 11-16 • Non-denom • State

Head: Since 1997, Mr Leon Nettley BEd MA. Educated at Fosters Grammar School, Sherborne, and Exeter University, where he read maths. Taught maths for 15 years before coming to Millais as deputy head in 1990. Wife, Fiona, is a reception teacher and they have two girls, both educated at Millais. Loves sport – 'all sport.' Committed to a 'personal vision' of how international links can be used to 'create a vibrant learning community'. Good at promoting ties with local businesses that provide sponsorship and work experience placements. Tall and well in control, with an understanding and easy manner, Mr Nettley is described by parents and pupils as 'supportive'.

Academic Matters: Among the first comprehensives to be given specialist status as a language college (1996) and language teaching is a great strength. All girls learn French and another language through to year 9 (usually German, Spanish, Japanese or Italian; Latin is available). 75 per cent continue two languages through GCSE. Not surprisingly, the pupils do well in language exams and results also very good in sciences and statistics. Virtually all girls do 10 GCSEs with over one third grades A or A*. Percentage of pupils achieving five or more A-C GCSEs hovers around 84 per cent, a good showing for a school with no selection. Wonderful, dedicated teachers provide twice-a-week after-school tutorial sessions – popular when pupils have been ill (also with year 11 students before exams). Every academic subject setted from year 8 (sometimes earlier). Pupils who are struggling receive extra literacy sessions, access to a special homework club and small-group teaching. All children sit exams in every course they are following, regardless of ability. The school has earned lots of official recognition and pats on the back (charter mark, investor in people etc). Glowing Ofsted report with praise for the school so effusive it almost makes one cringe.

Games, Options, The Arts: Two hours of games compulsory each week. Lots of sporting triumphs, with team sports – especially hockey – strong. No swimming. Good DT, offering projects with a feminine touch like using computer-aided design to produce garments on a knitting machine. Drama GCSE very popular. Exceptional art, praised highly by parents. Music good but a bit delicate. Just over 10 per cent of girls have tuition on a musical instrument; orchestra now properly financed and organised. Good musicians said to be (perhaps overly) pushed. Lots of thriving clubs, including the popular engineering club in which girls build and race a car. Many D of E bronze and silver awards. Plenty of overseas trips and exchanges ('can get a bit expensive,' said a parent).

Background and Atmosphere: Physically nondescript school in a nondescript section of a nondescript town. Clearly the school is not squandering resources on paint. However, long-term Millais parents are impressed by improvements that have been made to the facilities over recent years: sports hall, library, drama studio and computer facilities excellent. A bright new science block opened September 2001, with nine classrooms. Lovely atmosphere of respect amongst pupils, and between pupils and staff. Outside, there is an all-weather hockey pitch, grass playing field and four tennis courts (more in summer). An inconspicuous day nursery is plonked in one corner of the school property (a helpful local resource, although bosomy ladies shouting, 'Sally, I already told you not to wee on the grass' may not enhance the savoir-faire of this centre of language excellence). Good canteen, becoming very popular since the school introduced brand names and a salad bar. Be prepared for the short school day, with lessons ending at 3pm (clubs etc run for an hour afterwards).

The language department – the school's pride and joy – is housed in a scruffy but well-equipped block. The emphasis on languages and international affairs is ingeniously woven through the school, enriching all subjects. From the newsletter, Millais International (with stories of foreign visits and discussions of third world debt) to the mock European parliament elections (the winner received a prize trip to Brussels), the girls see they are part of a big, exciting world. There are multilingual signs for everything in the school – brilliant fun and they give the place the buzz of an international airport. Pupils visit British Airways at Heathrow and spend a day practising languages while pretending to be cabin crew (in BA uniform!). Through the 'Comenius Project,' Millais girls work with pupils in the Netherlands, Portugal, Poland, Italy, Germany and the UK to create a common curriculum for some topics. The school had to drop its innovative and successful 'business studies in Spanish' course (temporarily, we hope) owing to (inane) government requirements and lack of examination support.

Pastoral Care and Discipline: The school made headlines in January 2002 during the trial of its IT teacher who was accused of murdering his wife, a Millais maths teacher, after discovering she was having an affair with a colleague – another teacher at the school. Worse, when the alleged murder took place in March 2001, pupils were still recovering from the car crash death of their deputy head who had been a teacher at Millais for 28 years. Most parents commend the school's handling of these tragedies. The head spoke directly to the girls, counselling was provided and parents and pupils closed ranks against unwanted press and public attention, helping the story to die down.

The episode was a shock to the generally quiet, well-ordered school (even some parents roll their eyes at a few of the school rules). The girls say Millais is famous for its uniform (hideous) and dress code (draconian). However, the cream blouse and bottle-green sweatshirt seem to inspire 'we're all in this together' loyalty and, to us, the girls do not look much squarer than their peers at other schools. Fixed-period exclusions are meted out to troublemakers: possibly not the place for a rebel, regardless of academic ability. No permanent exclusions in the past seven years. Students and teachers elect fifty prefects. From them, a 'senior team' of six girls is elected. The team attends weekly coffee and biscuit sessions with the head where school news is discussed and student grievances can be raised. Very active elected student council to which, say the girls, the school really listens.

Pupils and Parents: Lots of girls whose parents could and would pay for private education if Millais were not around. A few girls travel quite a way to come to the school, but most are local Horsham girls. Extremely homogeneous: 97 per cent white and mostly middle(ish) class. No pupils from abroad (two girls came last year from Germany, but only for a term). Parents involved and supportive – don't want the standards to drop.

Entrance: Comprehensive, so no selection. Apply through the West Sussex LEA. The school is oversubscribed, but not hugely, so it is worth having a go even if you do not live in the immediate area.

Exit: 95 per cent to further education. Vast majority to the local College of Richard Collyer in Horsham (known as 'Collyers Sixth Form College').

Remarks: Very good state school for local parents and hard-working girls.

MILLFIELD SCHOOL

Linked to Millfield Preparatory School in the Junior section

Butleigh Road, Street, Somerset, BA16 0YD

Tel: 01458 442 291
Fax: 01458 447 276
E-mail: admissions@millfieldschool.com
Website: www.millfieldschool.com

• Pupils: 1,260 boys and girls (about 75 per cent board, the rest day) • Ages: 13-18 • Size of sixth form: 573 • Inter-denominational • Fees: Available on application • Independent • Open days: May and October

Head: Since 1998, Mr Peter Johnson MA CertEd (fifties). Educated at Bec (as in Tooting) Grammar (at the same time as Tory hopeful, David Davis) read geography at Oxford on army scholarship, rugby and judo blue. Retired and distinguished captain in Parachute Brigade – remains ultra-smart with tell-tale gleaming shoes; he has a deliciously confidential manner and his eyes positively sparkle when discussing successful or future projects. Fifteen years at Radley followed by seven years as head of Wrekin. Absolutely fits the Millfield bill – passionate about sport, opportunities and winkling out talent in equal measure. Has direct personal experience of inspiring confidence and providing support, as he and wife Chrissie have two sons, one a keen sportsman, one in a wheelchair (spina bifida), both high achievers making dad proud by following him into teaching. In firm control of the whole vast Millfield operation, rather like a compassionate MD, backed up by a welter of committed senior staff. New heads of physics, chemistry, drama, maths, music – 'a superb chap who enjoys rugby and now there are more boys in the choir' – plus new head of languages and history. (School can house 38 staff, the rest must rent or buy roundabout). Good young 'feisty' common room. Says 'you need a passion' to do well at Millfield.

Academic Matters: You name it, they do it, or very nearly. Huge range at GCSE, from dance to design by way of classical Greek and, of course, physical education. More than 40 A levels as well as AVCE courses in leisure & recreation and BTEC in art & design. Languages, a movable feast depending on the origins of the intake, more popular here than in many schools, with French particularly strong, although with 50 nationalities represented it is not surprising. Academic Society for the brightest and the best. Staff constantly irritated by some parents' perception that Millfield's truly comprehensive, all-ability intake makes it a school solely for the nice but dim. Individual results attest that brilliance is enhanced as much as struggle is aided, and overall grades' and points' tallies have steadily increased over the last six years. School results highlight 100 top scores rather than dwell on the huge spread of results that reflect the ability range. Well-stocked library but still not open very late and only on the occasional Sunday. Head points out that Millfield's long-established and much admired language development unit supports children with IQs of 140, whose abilities are not always mirrored by their performance, as well as dyslexics, dyspraxics and the odd statemented child with severe difficulties. Mild Aspergers, autism, ADHD – some come with statements of needs and ed psychs' reports, others are identified during their school career. 'Jolly nearly' wheelchair friendly (and of course head is ultra-aware of this problem), 'but can certainly cope, enough classrooms on the ground floor'; one child at the school is deaf, hearing aid rather than monitor. Currently some 400 children get some support, for those with lesser difficulties this may be only once a week when they are taught in groups, but there is an entire English class in each year (of a greater or smaller size, ca depend) who are taught English in the SEN dept which is on the top of the academic floor, with proper classrooms as well as individual teaching units. Strong emphasis on spelling as well as on personal attention, each challenged pupil has an individual pupil profile which is constantly updated, unit is open before school, during break and at lunchtime with a drop-in centre (well used during our visit) plus some mainstream guidance for those in the main school. No shame in visiting the unit. Sixth formers meet with the unit at the start of the year, can do preps here (some concentrate better in an organised environment). Five full-time staff and two part-timers, all qualified teachers and either dyslexia qualified or with loads of experience. Strategies and help for the bright bored too, 'one to one', must commit to come. Some non-English speakers receive EAL teaching from specialist staffing in the Millfield English Language School (MELS), either graduating to core subjects or preparing for university interviews. Millfield may seem dauntingly large, yet classes are pocket-sized (maximum 15, usually much smaller) and the pupil:staff ratio a long-standing constant 1:7.5. Boys do just as well as girls, bucking the national trend. Staff usually stay for the long haul.

Games, Options, The Arts: 'Outstanding' barely covers the range, quality and availability of the fantastic sporting facilities for which Millfield is justly famous, 25/30

pupils compete internationally each year. Olympic-sized swimming pool, freshly upgraded sports halls, equestrian centre with indoor and outdoor arenas with fabulous accommodation for the pupils' own horses, recently increased in size: there is a waiting list for horses, polo very popular and played at Millfield Prep (£295 per term plus livery of £115 per week per pony). Pupils can take their BHSAI, as well as competing against the outside world. Purpose-built fencing salle, nine-hole golf course with indoor tuition centre (and golf clubs everywhere), indoor tennis centre (plus lots of all-weather courts), plus running track, water-based astro hockey pitches (you scoosh it with water at half time and it remains super smooth) and acres of playing fields. To further aid the quest for physical excellence, there is a well-staffed physiotherapy department and weights rooms. Predictably, Millfield teams trounce all comers as a matter of course – two pupils competed in the Commonwealth Games and one pre-teen swimmer narrowly missed the qualifying time. As head says, 'I could cover my walls just with pictures of famous Millfield sports men and women' (the admissions stairway is covered anyway, with winners from all walks of life). Two PE lessons a week the norm, including dance or orienteering for the less overtly muscled. Trips to everywhere in most disciplines.

Fantastic fine arts centre teaches everything from photography to painting, with regular artists in residence, but closed on Sundays so budding painters will have to do it elsewhere. Regular exhibitions – fab new space – from visiting artists, to staff and pupils. Outsiders invited in. Impressive new home economics dept under Leith's aegis popular with all, and massively increased design technology department positively humming (BTech as well as GCSEs on offer). New concert hall and music school under construction during our visit (Peter's Palace) should increase musical awareness in the school although huge numbers have individual music lessons and there are tripettes all over the place. The string quartet and piano trio were among the finalists at the Nat Chamber Music Competition held at St John's, Smith Square recently. Interest in academic music tends to tail off at A level. Drama well-supported, with pupils having the 500-seat Meyer Theatre at their disposal, as well as a professional-standard TV and recording studio.

Background and Atmosphere: Always a pleasure to come here – the immaculate campus is dotted with sculpture, some by artists in residence (and pupils watch them grow) and some specially commissioned, courtesy of the Millfield Sculpture Commission. Founded in 1935 by Jack Meyer with seven Indian pupils, of whom six were princes, and swiftly adopted the Robin Hood principle – squeezing money from the exceedingly rich to subsidise the needy, talented poor. From day one, in a large, rented Somerset house, he set about promoting individual ability, in whatever sphere. Millfield feels less like a school than an old-style university campus, with buildings in all directions in a mishmash of styles, rubbing shoulders in a relaxed, appealing way rather than clashing. The new on-site boarding houses are particularly impressive, smashing kitchens with Sky and huge common rooms, almost all upper and lower sixth have individual cabins. The old boarding houses, mainly ageing manors around Street and Glastonbury, have almost all been sold off, three only remain, pupils are bused in and out. Six hundred acres of ground and school is still adding to its portfolio. Millfield is proud of having been built up from nothing and owing nothing. Used to paying its way – school hosts range of Easter revision courses and summer English language courses as well as conferences. A large dining hall, notable for its finer than average fare, sits at the heart of the campus and is given a universal thumbs up by pupils, even the vegetarians. One wall consists entirely of Olympic contenders as well as others decorated with heads of school and more ordinary mortals. Fantastic glass fronted sixth form bar, which serves real food (as indeed all school bars will have to do post November 1st). And incredible new glass cricket pavilion, the glass walls etched in cricket balls (this silly editor thought they were coffee beans until put right). Clubs for almost everything, chess highly popular.

Pastoral Care and Discipline: Seems to have eased off the throttle of 'one strike and you're out' methods of old, no doubt helped by now having a larger number of boarding pupils on campus and in clear sight. Head judges any case of bullying, drug-taking or drinking on its individual merits, although on-site drug dealing would inevitably earn a one-way ticket home, 'one sniff' and off with his head, 'unless there is a good reason why not'. Posh parents; no reason to keep the blighters. Random drug testing for individual pupils by agreement with the parents. Head acknowledges bullying cases, particularly at boarding school, can be complex – needs of the victim a priority, though. All pupils are in houses. Houseparents are usually the first port of call with problems – caring, family-orientated people making boarders feel at home (the cleaning staff important too, and we trotted off with the tutor for admissions to take in a farewell party to a lady what did for 32 years, thereby meeting a rash of houseparents, the head's wife and a raft of the cleaning squad). School keeps going throughout the term with activities for those who live abroad (though guardians etc pick up during half term and exeats). Long-standing, and successful, 'no

private assignations' rule – couples would need houseparents' permission to meet. School counsellor available, as is school doctor or chaplain. Definite sense of separation from more worldly atmosphere of nearby Glastonbury – a relief. Chaplaincy centre a haven for exam-stressed pupils, plus other counsellors in the place, dedicated prayer room for Muslims. Strong community service locally.

Pupils and Parents: Sensible, mature pupils from a wide range of backgrounds, from the dyslexic sent by a local authority in north Wales to a Middle Eastern prince wallowing in cash. Girls notably smart and stylish after revision of uniform to prescribe tailored suits but tidiness very important here for boys too (though shirt tails still a problem), ties for every achievement, and the head girl has rather a natty gold brooch, senior prefects the same but in silver. Expected to work hard and play hard – not for those who duck out of being part of a team. Day pupils mostly local, boarders from anywhere and everywhere, with around 16 per cent from overseas. Increasing numbers (24 per cent) from London and the Home Counties, 'we seem to have been discovered by the trad parents and not just the first time buyers'. The list of alumni, famous and notorious, is endless, with Duncan Goodhew, John Sargeant, Tony Blackburn, James Hewitt, Ben Holliaoke and Sophie Dahl just the tip of a very eclectic iceberg.

Entrance: Interview and previous head's report the usual route in, with CE used to determine set for core subjects. Millfield has anything up to 80 feeder schools but by far the largest day number come from its own prep school (see separate entry). Many more arrive than leave in the sixth form.

Exit: Most go to universities here and all over the world (America a big favourite), eight last year to Oxbridge, quite a number to sports courses at uni, Bristol is popular, also accounts, business management and law.

Money Matters: A large number of scholarships at all levels for all-rounders, sportsmen, academics, musicians and artists, dedicated scholarships for those coming in at sixth form. All are individually assessed (vestiges of the Robin Hood principle linger), nearly 50 per cent get some form of bursary, with higher special bursaries and for local hardship cases. Reassuringly expensive for the affluent – in top ten for big-budget full fees. School setting up a foundation to be able to offer more help to more.

Remarks: Impressive, good-looking school with a genuinely all-inclusive urge to seek and find the best in everyone. Strong in every area and a great confidence builder, particularly for those who have struggled elsewhere. Not for those content to hide in a corner.

MILTON ABBEY SCHOOL

Blandford Forum, Dorset, DT11 0BZ

Tel: 01258 880 484
Fax: 01258 881 194 or 01258 881 250
E-mail: info@miltonabbey.co.uk
Website: www.miltonabbey.co.uk

• Pupils: 220 boys (21 day boys, the rest board); 9 girls in the sixth form • Ages: 13-18 • Size of sixth form: 90 • C of E • Fees: £7,490 boarding; £5,620 day • Independent • Open days: November, February, May

Headmaster: Since 1995, Mr W J (Jonathon) Hughes-D'Aeth (pronounced Daith) BA (fifty), educated at Haileybury and Liverpool, where he read geography which he still teaches throughout the school – doesn't teach as much as he would like, enjoys it a lot – 'good fun, but other bits fun as well'. Twelve year contract now abandoned ('indefinitely'), he is really enjoying 'being here in a 'little school' – not really a proper school, so enjoying real education'. No thoughts of moving anywhere. Bubbling, he has grown (perhaps a trifle literally) with the job and, when he showed us out to our car (parked somewhat perilously in front of the rugby pitches), he was instantly surrounded by chaps in diverse garb clamouring for attention. We kept an eye out of the rear window and, no, he didn't actually kick a rugby ball – but he might well have done. Obviously very popular. Previously a housemaster at Rugby, he still helps out with the CCF. Married, with four children spread all over the place – The Old Malthouse, Hanford, Haileybury and Charterhouse.

Charming, gassy, enthusiastic, keen that Milton Abbey should not be known as a special dyslexic school – 'boys are loved and treated as individuals'; the basic idea is to boost their self-confidence. Talks in metaphors (and not very good puns), 'Jaguar engines with lawn mower gearboxes'. Aims to boost self-confidence – 'how to deal with imperfections, that's what education is all about'. If a boy wants to bring back his gun dog for training, fine; the pigs, fine (Fatima and Felicity are being fattened up for summer barbles – when we last visited it was Babe who was bacon, and Bertie and Basil for barbecuing); a couple of Suffolk rams, fine; though no more than two and a half dogs (currently two beagles ex Marlborough). Captains of ferrets, captains of pigs, captains of sheep et al, if it makes a chap happy, then why not? 'If it's legal, honest, decent and doesn't scare the horses' he will

try anything. 'A happy boy is a confident boy, and they are much more ready to learn'. The head believes in 'preparing chaps for life', reckons that they don't grow up 'until they are 26', loads of energy, and 'don't worry too much'. Enormously flexible, he says of pupils here that he immediately 'perceived them to be gentle men' (as in gentle/caring). But he still can't get the hang of having girlies too and still refers to his pupils as men.

Academic Matters: Huge range of ability, IQs between 80 and 156; very frustrated bright boys and the rest. A key school for helping boys with learning difficulties, dyslexics are integrated with the rest (lots of remedial help where needed and instant tutorials on anything at any time). School is anxious not to be known as a 'specialist school' and all pupils must be able to access mainstream education. That having been said, thirty per cent of the pupils come with an educational psychologist's report, a summary of which stays in the staff room and tutors and staff have instant access. Three dedicated SEN teachers plus three classroom assistants and more to come, 'dual teaching is the way forward'. Some pupils withdrawn, a core group – usually from French – five lessons a week, either one-to-one or in small groups but it varies according to need. Extra time in exams, scribing, amanuensis, laptops – 'exams really exciting time' with invigilators for every pupil with an amanuensis or a scribe – each in separate rooms. School now CRESTeD (ie indefinite learning support paid for by Services et al). No DORE or trendy exercise gismos, 'scaffolding rather than tricks'. GCSEs taken ad nauseam, no shame in failure here. 'We learn through failure,' says the head. AS levels often taken over two years and, though the A level results are perhaps not as convincing as they might be, many get A*s in their practicals, which subsequently lead to job offers after school. Spanish a popular option, and of course German speakers do German. A D or E at A level is often way beyond anything that might have been predicted. Modules as far as possible in everything. Smallish classes, max 20, 16 the norm. 'No problem' in getting staff, 'though sometimes the choice is restricted', much emphasis on staff training. Academic tutors do study skills and monitor progress; teaching staff set aside two periods each week for official tutorials or help with problems. IT popular and computers everywhere, most boys have them for private study, and laptops both in class and exam. Business studies linked to economics dept, 'excellent take-up in BTechs: countryside management popular (and two boys recently organized the delivery of 140 pheasants with 40 boys up at crack of dawn to welcome them to their release pen, the game farm was so impressed that they delivered 40 partridge for free the following day and boys organized a shoot the Saturday before our visit with nearby fathers bringing guns in on the day (no they did not shoot 180 birds). BTechs also in sports and exercise management and hospitality management, with the school currently offering a popular chalet cooking course in Shaftesbury and looking to organize its own cooking course in the kitchens which are about to undergo a serious facelift, ditto the food (wood-burning ovens, making own bread and cutting down on the Es – which 'lengthens the attention span'). BTechs = two A levels and are a 'fantastic good qualification'.

Games, Options, The Arts: Compulsory activities on Tuesday and Thursday afternoons, huge choice: art, very active theatre, boat maintenance, clay-pigeon shooting (popular), fencing, model making etc. Art and design revamped with the addition of good, practising (commercial-eyed) artists and 'excellent' photography. Natural history still strong with moth traps shining through the summer months. Boys do regular head counts of birds. Ferrets (captain of etc). CDT (under theatre) popular, as well as CCF. School has strong links with Royal Armoured Corps at Bovington as well as the Royal Navy and masses of D of E (oodles of golds). Indoor heated swimming pool popular, games hall has sexy under floor heating – a bonus in winter; new Astroturf. Peter Allis inspired golf course (his son was here) and very enthusiastic sailing (lots of prizes) plus success in off-shore yacht masters certificates and days skipper courses. County participants in athletics.

Background and Atmosphere: Friendly, caring, prefects are called pilots and a 'big brother' atmosphere is encouraged, particularly where new and vulnerable pupils are concerned. Weirdos are not picked on and almost all recent Old Boys report that they 'loved it' at the school, though – as ever – the occasional chap slips through the net. Approving noises from prep school heads.

Magical listed grade 1 building, with fabulous plasterwork (begun by Sir William Chambers and taken over by James Wyatt), set in fold of valleys and Dorset hills. Abbot's Hall and King's Room breathtaking. School does weddings 'in the holidays', used for the occasional film and telly set; the Sallie Army have a couple of summer schools a year. Rather jolly prospectus with masses of brightly coloured inserts. School owns the fabric and grounds, diocese of Salisbury owns the Abbey – which is gorgeous – a peculiar arrangement, the diocese bought it when the place was up for sale in the thirties, to prevent it falling into 'the hands of a faith-healing group'. Locals occasionally worship here too and school uses it daily. Each year group takes chapel and even the most dyslexic read a lesson or say a prayer. School

founded in mid 1950s. Modern blocks cleverly hidden, stable block converted into light classrooms plus art, music etc. Stunning theatre, with efficient CDT below (very cunning), all classrooms/sports hall/theatre quite close to hand. Houses, now with carpets, being revamped (£46,000 last year, £60,000 this), all in main building, each with its own territory.

All housemasters (one of whom is a woman, Jane Emerson) are married, family atmosphere pervades – boys know each other well, graduating from dormitory/common rooms (ie with working spaces round the beds – and much less cramped than previously) to single study bedrooms, still untidy and refreshingly scruffy. Lots of new paint everywhere, some surprisingly bright (and some currently looking a trifle worn), head aiming to bring the school 'somewhere towards the 20th century', and is going for 'the faded country house look', 'buildings and the whole environment are so important'. School not as bulging as when we first visited and could hold one or two more, but no wish to grow.

Boys are kept busy in this isolated school. Lovat trousers and jerseys, suits on Sundays, ditto for girls, who are expected to be joined by another dozen or so September 2006. Certain amount of to-ing and fro-ing still with local girls' schools – St Mary's, Godolphin, St Anthony's, and stunning new basement sixth form centre ('the best night club in Dorset'). Two fixed exeats, plus half term, but enormously flexible. Saturdays off for hunting (still), polo 'they would lose the same time if they had to go to an away match' (but no horses in school – stables converted you see, good links with local riding school). NB this is the only school where reception has Hurlingham and Country Life to read and a glossy on sporting achievements rather than recent skool mags and prospectuses.

Pastoral Care and Discipline: Housemasters, who are normally also academic tutors, plus assistant house tutors. School is small enough to pick up any worrying vibes via the bush telegraph and head usually knows within hours if drugs have been brought back. 'Boys don't like drugs because it forms cliques which are unpopular in a small school'. Rehabilitation and random drugs testing on suspicion (and boys apparently like to be able to say, when offered drugs during the exeats, 'no thanks, I am tested at school' – even if they aren't). Not automatically out for drugs but out for dealing or going OTT. Booze a permanent problem, with parents tending to slip a chap the odd six pack in the hopes that a beer here or there will keep them off drugs, and the introduction of girls will compound the problem, ditto the recent government diktat that schools can only have a bar if food is served, hence the introduction of school feasts – a massive Saturday night blow-out followed by gassing to staff 'over a beer or two'. 'Constructive restrictions' for smoking in building, plus rustication – 'if we made smoking compulsory, and Latin illegal then all the boys would sneak off to the woods to read Virgil and throw the fags in the fire'.

Pupils and Parents: Gents, plus a handful of first-time buyers, more so than previously, and from further away. A handful of real foreigners, slightly more ex-pats, and an increasing number of Services children. Pupils are courteous, relaxed and friendly and 'really miss it when they leave'. 'Boys here have three great loves in their lives – their Ma, their Pa and the head'. Geographically widespread. Monthly rendezvous for old boys at the Duke of Wellington pub, Eaton Terrace. Presumably girls will turn up there too.

Entrance: Via CE, very flexible though, 'it's not really the school for children who need the bright lights and the Kings Road'. (Staff too, have to come for a twenty-four hour interview rather than a short sharp committee quizzing.) Boys come from all over, over 100 feeders, including all the top preps, plus state system. Girls currently from Cranleigh, Westonbirt, St Mary's Shaftesbury and the maintained sector. Entry post-GCSE if they have the right qualifications – currently five Cs or even Ds at GCSE is 'good enough'. 'But we have to be very frank and honest and say if a child is not up to it'.

Exit: Around 90 per cent to some form of further education, with 50 per cent to degree courses. (The chap who went to Peterhouse, Cambridge, at 14, graduated in 2001.) An 'increasing number positively choose not to go to uni' preferring instead to get a positive life experience: two years before the mast, a year in an African game park, coaching sport in a shanty town in India' and then hitting the jobs market. But still Cirencester, Newcastle, Bristol WE, Bournemouth, Oxford Brookes, Manchester Metropolitan all popular, as are colleges of higher education like Cheltenham and Gloucester. Boys given career briefing from the moment they arrive, and tend to opt for careers where 'they have to sell themselves' – very entrepreneurial. Practical subjects such as business studies, the record industry, and hotel and catering are popular. Some leakage (to sixth form colleges everywhere) this year post-GCSE, 'chaps tend to get restless' said our guide.

Money Matters: Some scholarships including academic, music, art, drama, sailing. Will carry pupils through exam year in cases of hardship.

Remarks: Boys' boarding school which resolutely continues to give good experienced professional help to those with learning difficulties, now with an increasing number of girls in the sixth form (a third of whom have learning difficulties). A great confidence-building place which runs on kindness and encouragement. Don't take our word for it, read Dr Rae's Letters to Parents (Harper Collins). 'What is more, the self-confidence gained by the school's pupils is not the shallow "effortless superiority" of the traditional public schoolboy but the self-belief that comes from fighting back and proving the pessimists wrong.'

MOIRA HOUSE GIRLS SCHOOL

Linked to Moira House Junior School in the Junior section

Upper Carlisle Road, Eastbourne, East Sussex, BN20 7TE

Tel: 01323 644 144
Fax: 01323 649 720
E-mail: info@moirahouse.co.uk
Website: www.moirahouse.co.uk

• Pupils: 420 girls day and boarding • Ages: 3 -18 • Size of sixth form: 80 • C of E • Fees: Day £1,660-3,850; weekly boarding £4,725-5,900; full boarding £5,175-6,625 • Independent • Open days: Any day

Principal: Since 1997, Mrs Ann Harris (fifties). Initially joined the junior school in 1973 to promote music after specialising in music and religious studies at Newton Park College of Higher Education in Bath and gaining her ARCM. Completed a part-time BEd at the University of Brighton in 1987. Became head of juniors in 1982, headmistress in 1986 and finally principal with responsibility for both junior and senior schools in 1997. Elegant, calm, dignified, totally committed careers person. Has time for everyone. Knows every girl's name. Travels extensively (visited Thailand, Vietnam and Jordan in 2001 and 2005, Japan in 2004/5 Ukraine in 2005) to promote the school. Says, 'travel is important to understand people's cultural background'. Believes 'education should be about getting out and about – girls need to be introduced to the world'. Mrs Harris is chairman of the East Sussex Centre of the Incorporated Society of Musicians – she is rightly proud of the school's international reputation for musical excellence though modest about her own musical proficiency.

Academic Matters: Very strong English and science departments. Could be a reflection on the 'demanding, strong characters' who teach there? 25-30 per cent of girls enter a career in science. Old Girls are encouraged to return and talk about their career choice to pupils. Actress Prunella Scales maintains close contact, described the school at the

130th anniversary in 2005 as a 'safe haven'. Has had a full-time careers advisor at the school for the past 28 years. In 2005, 90 per cent pass rate for grades A*-C at GCSE. At A level, 98 per cent grades A-C. Sixth form is 65 per cent boarding – 'it gives them independence' – and this is encouraged. The school has a history of cultural mix since opening 130 years ago – 40 per cent of the boarders in the sixth form are from overseas giving it a buoyant, international flavour. Intensive language courses are offered by the EFL department to help integrate foreign language speakers into the life of the school.

Games, Options, The Arts: Very strong musically with an international reputation for excellence. Drama and debating are both keenly studied. The effervescent Mrs Ritzema inspires the girls with her enthusiasm for both subjects. Trips to the theatre and performances by Moira House girls abound and they participate in the Cambridge Union Debating Competition and have an annual Youth Parliament Competition which is fiercely contested. Girls also programme and present on the radio for an annual community youth project in the area. In 2005, girls took a performing arts tour to Thailand and Australia. All sport is popular, especially now that girls can play indoor hockey, tennis, football in a spanking new sports hall. MoHo girls are selected each year as ball girls for the International Ladies Tennis Tournament in Eastbourne. Was the first girls' school to play cricket. A two-hour break at lunchtime allows plenty of time for activities, games, sports or even maths surgeries for those in need.

Background and Atmosphere: Founded in 1875 and established on its present site in 1887 by Mr and Mrs Charles Ingham, pioneers of female education. It consists mainly of three large old houses on a hilly site just outside the surprisingly busy and colourful centre of Eastbourne. Lots of bracing sea air. Very traditional feel to the place. Principal is vocal advocate of single-sex education for girls – very involved in GSA locally and SHMIS nationally. Head girls and prefects are quaintly known as knights and standard bearers. Boarding popular, with weekend boarding also on offer. Full programmes of activities available at weekends – day girls are welcome to join in. The school minibus fleet is a familiar sight around Eastbourne picking up and dropping off. MoHo choirs and orchestras in demand locally and further afield with performances at Canterbury Cathedral and Bath Abbey and also tours of America and Australia. Girls very involved with local community helping out in rest homes; visiting/shopping for pensioners.

Pastoral Care and Discipline: Boarders have a continuity of pastoral care from their housemistress and housemother which extends across all aspects of a girl's life. Day girls have their own house which provides them with a social centre while they are in school and house tutors for their pastoral needs. Close links with parents are integral to the school's ethos. Grades for academic achievements, effort and attitude are given monthly in all subjects. Girls are encouraged to discuss their reports with the principal at the end of each term, 'an invaluable system'. Discipline is good and run along family lines.

Pupils and Parents: Good cultural mix particularly in the sixth form. Attracts girls from local area and all over the world. Has a reputation as a small, friendly school ideal for nurturing blushing violets. Parents and Old Girls very involved. Prunella Scales and Susannah Corbett (actor Harry's daughter) are OGs, as were author Rumer Godden and explorer Virginia Fiennes.

Entrance: Mostly from the junior school. Non-selective – 'would only refuse a girl who would really struggle in the senior school'. Also from overseas due to enthusiastic promotion of the school by the principal and by word-of-mouth recommendation.

Exit: Majority to universities in UK, a few to USA, Hong Kong, Japan. Strong bias towards science subjects; engineering popular; business, finance and accounting gaining prominence. Increasing number takes gap year.

Money Matters: Several exhibitions and academic scholarships available annually. Strong PTA known as Moira House Association. Voluntary subscription from each family per term. Supports the school through fund-raising and social activities and was instrumental in helping raise funds for the new Junior School playground.

Remarks: Friendly, family-orientated school with a good academic record. Given the immediate example of other girls' achievements day to day throughout the school, even the most retiring female would come out of her shell – very non-threatening and supportive. 'Moira House Girls are confident and articulate and go on to a wide variety of careers' – The Independent.

MONMOUTH SCHOOL

Linked to Haberdashers' Agincourt School in the Junior section

Linked to Grange (The) in the Junior section

Almshouse Street, Monmouth, Monmouthshire, NP25 3XP

Tel: 01600 713 143

Fax: 01600 772 701

E-mail: enquiries@monmouthschool.org

Website: www.habs-monmouth.org

- Pupils: 580 boys; mostly day, 145 board • Ages: 11-18
- Size of sixth form: 180 • Anglican • Fees: Day: senior £2,989;
prep £2,065. Boarding: senior £4,983 • Independent
- Open days: Early October and mid-January

Head: Since 2005, Dr Steven Connors (late forties) previously deputy head of Christ's Hospital, an English specialist. Succeeded Dr Tim Haynes who now heads Tonbridge. Dr Connors is married with two sons, aged 15 and 18. He started his teaching career at Denstone College, going on to become head of English and drama at Queen's College, Taunton, and then head of English at Sevenoaks. He was also head of boarding and housemaster of the sixth form International Centre. He was appointed deputy head of Christ's Hospital, in 2000. Keen rugby player and coach, also cricket and athletics. Other hobbies and activities include theatre, music and hill walking.

Academic Matters: Does extremely well with a fairly comprehensive intake and very strong in the area. Reportedly much improved in recent years, and the stats bear this out with a solid all-round performance – 71 per cent A/B at A level – which has been consistently maintained over the last five years. Intensity now about academic feel of place – modern languages, maths, sciences and history are all strong areas. Over 30 options at A level made possible by timetable co-ordinated with the girls' school and lots of shared classes. Has taken AS in its stride – 'helps to keep you focused'. Impressive GCSE results and Ds now a rarity. Sound IT, with lots of new machines. Small classes, though can rise to 24 at the lower end of the school.

Games, Options, The Arts: Sets enormous store by games and has a considerable reputation on the rugby field. To be expected perhaps when you are coached by John Bevan (referred to as The Legend – played for Wales and British Lions, and previously ran Welsh rugby). Compulsory for the first three years – helps with integration. Athletic

achievement is underpinned by the much coveted choccy blazer, with its rather Wodehousian flavour, – a brown coat, with gold piping and buttons, awarded for all manner of sporting endeavour and worn with unconcealed pride. Head says he is moving the emphasis to acknowledge more cerebral areas of achievement, though not without resistance, from the artists, actors and musicians as much as from the hunks of the XV. Strong rowing tradition. Soccer, cricket, swimming, tennis, cross-country, hockey, golf, sailing, climbing all flourish. Vibrant music department, with all manner of ensembles, groups, chorales in atmospheric music school. Superb drama studio, and new 500 seat theatre. Lively debating in sixth form. Art block refurbished and the results are fantastic. Efficient and popular CCF.

Background and Atmosphere: Founded in 1614 by William Jones, a member of the Haberdashers' Company of London (a connection from which the school benefits hugely still) beside the Wye in what was then the outskirts of Monmouth, now a very attractive, thriving and bustling country town. Pleasant 70 acre site, based round original impressive sandstone buildings, but much added to and imaginatively adapted to meet modern needs. Essentially a town school and space is at rather a premium but relieved by one or two grassy areas. Wonderful library, now more fully used. Bisected by the busy A40, but pupils live quite happily with the traffic, and a pedestrian underpass minimises the hazards. Very splendid sports centre (sports hall, 25-metre indoor pool, fitness suite), boat house, Astroturf and playing fields over the road.

Predominantly a day school now and most boys disappear in a fleet of buses at 4pm but it does its best to retain the flavour and ethos of a boarding school, with a full 6 day week and lots going on at weekends. 150 boarders (flexi-boarding increasingly popular) in three boarding houses within campus, which offer good, if rather institutional, accommodation. Complemented by its own attractive and well-run prep, The Grange, which is just up the street. Well-established link with Haberdashers' Monmouth Girls' School provides shared academic, social, dramatic and artistic opportunities.

Pastoral Care and Discipline: All the academic and pastoral back-up that one might expect, with housemasters and tutors in the front line. Lots of capable and enthusiastic young staff who say it's a wonderful place to work but enough veterans too to give the right balance. Relations with boys are relaxed but respectful. The usual controls on drinking and drugs but reportedly not a big problem. Boys allowed freedom of Monmouth but expected to behave responsibly.

Pupils and Parents: 'Old money, new money, no money,' says the head. The last is a reference to the keenly-priced fees and the high degree of financial assistance available to those who could not otherwise afford to come. The result is a more diverse community – which gives the school its tone. Parents anyone and everyone therefore. Many run small businesses in the area especially in IT but the school pulls day pupils in from as far away as Chepstow, Cardiff, Bristol, Gloucester and Hereford. Teachers, doctors, accountants, solicitors, farmers, Services, shopkeepers. Small foreign and ex-pat presence. Boys are straight-forward and confident, polite and open, have 'bearing without arrogance', and clearly expected to stand on their own feet and make the most of what they are offered. David Broome, Lord Moynihan, Victor Spinetti, Major Dick Hern, the Very Reverend Christopher Herbert, Bishop of St Albans, and Steve James (Glamorgan and England) all spent their formative years here.

Entrance: Large majority in at 11, from its own prep, The Grange, and primaries – sit school's own entrance exam. Significant number from a loyal handful of feeder preps sit CE at 13. Some in at 16 (5 GCSE passes A*-B, plus test and interview). Broad academic entry, but 'they have to be able to cope'. Some 25 with mild learning difficulties get some support.

Exit: Small number after GCSE. Ten or so a year now to Oxbridge, and all but a handful to wide spread of universities – Exeter, Cardiff, London, Birmingham, Bristol and Durham among the more popular.

Money Matters: A huge selling point and amazingly good value for what you get. Support of Haberdashers, and its substantial endowments, makes possible generous scholarships (some for music and games) and bursaries, and its own assisted places scheme, which gives a high level of means-tested help where it would otherwise be impossible. Application should be made to the bursar's secretary.

Remarks: A once-traditional boarding public school that has metamorphosed into a day school with boarders, without losing the traditional. Very strong in the area. Well-run, solid, high-achieving. Not perhaps for the very tender flower but produces robust all-rounders who are going to get stuck in.

MORE HOUSE SCHOOL (LONDON)

22-24 Pont Street, Chelsea, London, SW1X 0AA

Tel: 02072 352 855

Fax: 02072 596 782

E-mail: office@morehouse.org.uk

Website: www.morehouse.org.uk

• Pupils: around 230 girls, all day • Ages: 11-18 • Size of sixth form: 55 • RC, but others welcome • Fees: £3,525 • Independent • Open days: October

Headmistress: Since 1999, Mrs Lesley Falconer BSc. Studied microbiology at London, then combined research with teaching at a sixth form college. Teaches some biology and science. Off to head St Teresa's in Dorking in July 2006.

Academic Matters: OK. Science, maths, history and languages are consistent hot spots at GCSE; English and geography less so. 100 per cent pass at A level, with around 60 per cent A/B grades. The aim is to teach the girls to work with others and do well for themselves, hence there is little notice taken of who does best in the class but much pleasure gained from the maths and public speaking teams beating other schools. A few head off for boy-rich pastures at A level, so some of the remaining students find themselves receiving tuition in small groups. Class sizes now range from four to twelve.

Games, Options, The Arts: Games are restricted by the location and an un-gamesy past but are being taken more seriously. Wins now recorded in running and gym – there is a large entry for the London mini marathon and a refurbished gym. Arts OK, with one or two each year winning places at art colleges such as St Martin's. Many alumnae are artists or art historians. Music, most notably the choir, very good. Drama and photography groups, D of E.

Background and Atmosphere: Pont Street Dutch architectural rabbit-warren in prime location (two minutes to Harrods) but the rooms are well proportioned and the whole effect quite comfortable. Founded by RC parents in 1953, the school retains a strong RC ethos which, nonetheless, doesn't hit you in the face as you go round – 'all faiths are welcomed,' says the school. Food all cooked on the premises and smells good; no packed lunches allowed, though some of the senior girls run a flourishing trade in break snacks, undercutting the caterer's prices. The girls most hoped-for development – 'build a boys' school next door.'

Pastoral Care and Discipline: Solid, supportive, small-scale, cosy set-up with lots of personal attention from caring staff 'who bother about us, take us out for coffee' approves a sixth former. Partly for this reason and partly because of the lack of bike sheds to smoke behind, the problems of the world seem to be left behind at the door. Strong PHSE programme.

Pupils and Parents: Bi- and tri-linguals among the pupils who, though mostly London residents, are notably diverse in their national origins. RC status steady at around half, a draw for diplomats etc. Quite a sheltered environment, produces nice unspoilt girls. Not a Sloane school and proud of it. After a long history of anything-goes for clothes (which left some parents bothered about the Fast Set) the dark blue corduroy and gingham uniform came as something of a relief.

Entrance: From prep and primary schools across London – from Wimbledon to Hampstead but particularly from nearby Hill House and surrounding area.

Exit: A few to co-ed schools at 16. After A level to wide spread of courses at a spread of good universities and the odd Oxbridge.

Money Matters: The mid-range fees include items which most others would charge as extras. Academic, music, sixth form scholarships and bursaries for established pupils in financial need.

Remarks: Small, inner London, girls' day school at smart address. All the girls we talked to said that they themselves had made the choice to come here and potential pupils have reported they 'much preferred' More House to other private schools in the vicinity. Felt by some to be somewhat limited, it does well by those it suits.

MORETON HALL SCHOOL

Linked to Moreton First in the Junior section

Weston Rhyn, Oswestry, Shropshire, SY11 3EW

Tel: 01691 773 671
Fax: 01691 778 552
E-mail: admin@moretonhall.com
Website: www.moretonhall.org

• Pupils: 320 girls; 60 day, the rest board • Ages: 4-18 • Size of sixth form: 102 • C of E • Fees: Moreton First: £1,900 - £2,600. Senior: boarding £6,690 - £7,035; day £1,900 - £5,350.
• Independent • Open days: November, May

Principal: Since 1992, Jonathan Forster BA PGCE (mid forties). Formerly housemaster in charge of girls and head of English at Strathallan. Educated at nearby Shrewsbury School and Leeds. Steered the school out of deeply troubled waters in early nineties into the sunlit uplands it now enjoys and says that he remains excited by new challenges there (new sixth form 'en suite' boarding house, brand new all weather surface and much else planned), though another career move must at some time be a possibility. Strong-minded, clear-sighted pragmatist but also chatty, with a strong sense of fun and people relate to him easily. He takes all new parents round personally and remains at the heart of the school. Married to Paula, who oversees the superbly resourced working library and teaches English. Two daughters, one at uni (Edinburgh), both attended MH. Supported by strong management team and staunchly Moretonian governing body.

Academic Matters: Now punching substantially above its weight academically, given its broad intake (35 girls getting special help) and competing successfully with much bigger academic fish – down to excellent, and sometimes inspirational, teaching in nearly all areas (staff reported as 'deeply, deeply committed'), a hugely supportive system, and a feeling among the girls that opportunities are something to be seized. A*-B now the norm at GCSE with 22 options (inc Welsh and Polish). A levels scarcely less good with English, maths, French, geography, biology and business studies strong performers. More run of the mill art and history results but wonderful art evident on the walls of splendid art studio. All underpinned by superb IT department, which is effectively used to enhance school work. Internet connections everywhere. Good dyslexia and dyscalcula support, and EFL where necessary.

Games, Options, The Arts: Sporty tradition. Lacrosse is the flagship sport and MH more than holds its own on competitive circuit but performs capably in all areas. D of E keenly pursued. Outstanding drama at all levels. Impeccable music, with lots of groups, ensembles, choirs, some with Shrewsbury. Very successful public speaking. Excellent careers dept – 'such a help'. Moreton Enterprises, the sixth form business enterprise group, is a truly ground-breaking affair. Past initiatives have seen girls running their own railway station, bank, mail order, commercial recording studio and their own radio station. Whatever next! Superb school mag.

Background and Atmosphere: Founded in 1913 by Mrs Lloyd-Williams ('Aunt Lil') of Oswestry for her own daughters and local friends. An unhomogeneous, but by no means unappealing (only the severely 1960s science block looks seriously dated) mixture of building styles, centred on the original 17th century Moreton Hall. The buildings are dotted round an attractive leafy campus, which incorporates both formal gardens, and beautifully kempt parkland, where there are fine games fields and a 9-hole golf course. Running full at 320, and pressure on boarding places. The relaxed and unstuffy style sits easily with expectations of mature and responsible behaviour and the result is friendly, self-possessed and cheerful girls, who well understand the connection between giving and gaining.

Pastoral Care and Discipline: A very strong area. Each girl is supported by a web of houseparents, tutors and mentors, to whom they relate in a typically relaxed and easy manner. 'Everyone looks after you.' Head says that its people are its best resource and there is a strong sense of the 'Moreton Community'. Small classes and constant monitoring means that no-one gets overlooked. Firm views on teasing. Drugs simply not tolerated. Excellent focused weekend programme for boarders (up to sixth form.)

Pupils and Parents: Drawn largely from within a 50-mile radius of the school and a wide mix – from Manchester and Cheshire double-income business people to doctors, solicitors and academic types and the odd big farmer from the remoter parts of north Wales. Sees itself as the girls' boarding school for the area. Girls are truly a delight – open and outgoing – 'have confidence, approachability and don't take themselves too seriously' – they say. They argue strongly the merits of single-sex education (there is close proximity without consciousness of image or the need to seem cool), but the school shrewdly allows them a good degree of social freedom, sensibly regulated to avoid unhelpful pressures. Many have brothers at Shrewsbury, with which school is twinned and shares much in ethos and style, not to mention abundant dramatic and social opportunity.

Entrance: At 4 into Moreton First, at 11 from primary school, and at 13 from a number of feeder prep schools. Up to 10 a year at sixth form level. Not competitive, but test, interview and report. 'They need to be able to cope.' Parents always welcome. Taster visits very popular.

Exit: Increasingly Ivy League (4 to Oxbridge this year) but all to one uni or another.

Money Matters: Small number of scholarships and bursaries.

Remarks: The best sort of smaller girls' boarding school, offering super teaching and a marvellous range of other opportunities and going great guns.

MORRISON'S ACADEMY

Linked to Morrison's Academy Junior School in the Junior section

Ferntower Road, Crieff, Perthshire, PH7 3AN

Tel: 01764 653 885
Fax: 01764 655 411
E-mail: principal@morrisonsacademy.org
Website: www.morrisonsacademy.org

- Pupils: 171 boys, 146 girls, 28 boarders including weekly
- Ages: 3-18 • Size of sixth form: 98 • Inter-demon • Fees: Day £850 - £2,573; full boarding £5,956 - £6,274; weekly boarding £4,586 - £4,904 • Independent • Open days: October and February

Rector and Principal: From 2004, Mr Simon Pengelley BA PGCE (forties) who was educated at Repton, read history at Bristol and did his PGCE in London. Started his teaching career at Abingdon before moving to Strathallan where he was head of history and comes from Rossall; he spent twelve years there, ending as director of studies and deputy head. He and his wife Louise love Scotland and have 'loads of friends in the area'. So that's all right then. Has two sons, one at uni and one still at Rossall. He joins the school after an interregnum, fronted by the depute, who has returned to the common room 'and is enormously supportive'. Outgoing, enthusiastic and bubbly. When we asked about the last head but one's plan to return the ceiling of the Memorial Hall to its original height, we both rushed off to have a look; it is back to its former Victorian glory, with stained glass shining in the Perth sunshine and portraits of those who died in the First World War strategically placed round the balcony.

Academic Matters: School follows Scottish curriculum: good take up for Advanced Highers. The traditional bias towards science is slightly fading in favour of arts-based courses. Masses of computers on site and many staff have to taken their European Computer Driving Licence as have the pupils (the head of the computer department often builds his own). 17 Highers, with photography for media a recent addition at sixth form only, plus Intermediate 2 more or less across the board. Sciences perform consistently well, also maths; English Highers impressive last year, also accountancy. Goodish art and design, not really much language take up, humanities OK. Ditto geography and history. No obvious terminal cases; human biology popular at Higher level and results indicate that it is obviously either better taught or more interesting to the candidates. Can cope with special needs and programmes much used: dyslexia, dyspraxia and mild Aspergers not a problem.

Games, Options, The Arts: Masses of pitches at Dallerie, a ten-minute walk from the main buildings, and school plays all the standard games. Good rugby. Strong pipe band and very popular – with Chinese students forming a part (plus locals of course) but it does make interesting photographs. Band plays at Murrayfield rugby internationals as part of massed bands. CCF on curriculum, D of E strong, almost all get bronze, lots of silver and gold. Enthusiastic art dept in inspired converted attics but still no CAD. Music and drama strong with a stunning girls' chamber choir which plays regularly to local acclaim. 45 extra-curricular activities in total.

Background and Atmosphere: Built in 1859, this Scottish baronial-styled building with its crow stepped gables was described at the time: 'Its healthful locality and commanding view of extensive and beautifully romantic scenery cannot be surpassed, if at all equalled, by any such public building in Scotland.' The gift of Thomas Mor(r)ison, who lived in the neighbouring village of Muthill and made his fortune as a master builder in Edinburgh. He instructed his trustees to erect an institution carrying his name 'to promote the interests of mankind, having a particular regard to the education of youth and the diffusion of useful knowledge'.

Always independent, at one stage the school did have grant-aided pupils but this finished in the late 1970s. Boarding numbers declined in the 1990s but have stabilised at two houses. Some of the current boarders are Scots but many come from overseas, and add an exotic flavour to what is a fairly pedestrian environment – almost all religious festivals are celebrated. Fabulous buildings revamped following the sale of underused outlying houses. The swimming pool, the nomenclature BATHS carved in (whitewashed) stone above the entrance, is still in daily use. The original school building is fantastic with large open corridors and a terrific hall which doubles for daily assemblies and socials. A somewhat convoluted reconstruction of the former girls' school has made a jolly music room, with excellent practice rooms carved from the earlier loo block. Recording studios on the wish list. A magnificent newer build for maths and jolly attic transformation into a vast art complex.

Pastoral Care and Discipline: Excellent pastoral care and guardianship for boarders and the same applies across the school. Head quite tough on sin (early days yet) though pupils on the whole 'quite docile': 'tobacco could get you suspended and Chinese pupils do like smoking' and often arrive addicted. No booting out for fags, regular boozing could ultimately result in expulsion and use of drugs means that 'you should expect to be expelled'. Not really a streetwise school.

Pupils and Parents: Day pupils from all over the middle belt, Falkirk, Stirling, Dunblane, Comrie, Perth, Auchterarder are bused to school. (No trains since Beeching). Masses of boarders from abroad – agencies and regularly dominie-type visits, head expects 'to show his face in the Far East shortly' and is keen to target the highland professionals, 'estate factors, solicitors, accountants and their like.'

Entrance: Children can and do arrive at any time, during the term and at the start of any term – particularly for boarding from abroad, if space available. The school operates an open presentation policy – 'we don't prevent pupils from taking exams in order to improve our statistics.' Interview and testing for nursery and junior school and more or less automatic entrance into senior school from the junior school. Some join the senior school at 11 from the state sector or from local prep schools such as Ardvrec or Craigclowan. Interview and examination. Sixth form entrants are assessed on their potential, taking into account their grades at Standard level or GCSE.

Exit: Three or four off to (usually) Scottish independent schools at either 11 or 13. Otherwise a dribble occasionally to Oxbridge, one to Cambridge last year, though four to London, Imperial and Kings. Regular mini stream usually to engineering or allied science at Imperial London, or Manchester, Newcastle, Leeds. Most stay in Scotland with law, computing, business and sciences prevailing, though sports science and sports medicine in the ribbons. Plus ca change

Money Matters: Discounts for siblings, one or two means tested bursaries, scholarships for the final year.

Remarks: A good proud school which does well by its pupils.

THE MOUNT SCHOOL

Linked to Tregelles in the Junior section

Dalton Terrace, York, North Yorkshire, YO24 4DD

Tel: 01904 667 500
Fax: 01904 667 524
E-mail: registrar@mount.n-yorks.sch.uk
Website: www.mount.n-yorks.sch.uk

• Pupils: 251 girls; 66 full, 185 day • Ages: 11-18 • Size of sixth form: 64 • Quaker • Fees: Weekly full boarding years 7-13 £5,535; weekly day boarding years 7-13 £3,565 • Independent • Open days: January, May and October

Head: Since 2001, Mrs Diana Gant, BD PGCE (mid fifties). Read theology at King's College London; previously deputy headmistress at Norwich High. Prior to that was head of RE at King's Worcester and head of careers at Tonbridge Grammar. Married to Brian, an Anglican priest; two grown-up daughters. Very pleasant, modest, approachable – 'open door' office. Not a Quaker but determined to preserve Quaker ethos.

Academic Matters: Strong AS/A level results – about 80 per cent A/B with only a few below C. At A-level the overall pass rate in 2004 was 100 per cent. General studies taken by all. 60 per cent or more A*/A at GCSE. French and maths setted in years 7/8. IT provision developing, including one very state-of-the-art computer suite; qualifications taken in middle school and sixth form. York used for local history work; archaeology as an extra in sixth form; links with university. Does well with all abilities including EAL – support available; also specialist dyslexia teaching. Girls enjoy lessons and have good relationships with friendly, cheerful and enthusiastic staff. Very good careers education with work experience.

Games, Options, The Arts: Beautifully kept grounds with numerous tennis courts, indoor pool, sports hall allowing eg indoor cricket, football; also fitness suite. Successful at traditional team games as well as fencing and orienteering. Very strong and varied musical life, from classical to rock; all abilities participate in Christmas concert; regular concerts with other Quaker schools. About one third learn instruments at school; regular speech and drama successes. Drama co-productions with Bootham (older brother Quaker school, now co-ed). Over 50 after school activities, eg jewellery making, photography. Impressive art, especially 3D work. Creative writing competition successes. Duke of Edinburgh popular; strong tradition of community involvement.

Background and Atmosphere: Origins go back to 18th century; present building has a very fine 1857 façade with modern additions, set in 16 acres of gardens and green fields close to the centre of York. Calm, friendly, happy, purposeful atmosphere. Girls work hard because they want to do well for themselves and the school, but are not competitive or driven. Though only a small percentage of staff and girls are Quakers, the ethos is central, manifest in respect for everyone in the community, a high degree of tolerance of differences, caring for others, and democratic practices like the school council, which discusses internal affairs. Morning Meetings include a period of silent reflection. Widespread involvement is regarded highly, not just achievement.

Pastoral Care and Discipline: Considered very important; girls feel they receive a lot of individual attention. Four sixth form girls to a tutor group. Non-confrontational approach to discipline; exclusion only for persistent offences or major breach of rules (eg alcohol abuse). Plenty of contact with parents – school website; weekly newsletter. Year 7 girls go on initial two-day residential for team-building exercises and trips to gel as a group.

Pupils and Parents: Not just those with Quaker connection (it's the only all-girls Quaker school in England), but large number of local parents, often without an independent school background; not a county-set school. Wide range of religions or none. Several boarders from Hong Kong and others from a variety of other countries, plus overseas Brits. Girls wear white shirt, tartan skirt and blue jumper; no uniform for sixth form. Famous Old Girls include Dame Judi Dench, Margaret Drabble, Antonia Byatt, Mary Ure, Kate Bellingham.

Entrance: Assessments for years 7-10 entry in English, maths and verbal reasoning plus interview with head, who looks for 'spark – interesting girls with wide interests'. School report also important. Average and above average abilities catered for. Six GCSEs A-C and interview for sixth form.

Exit: About 8 leave post-GCSE, most for local sixth form college. Otherwise to a variety of universities, old and new, several to Oxbridge; a wide range of subjects studied. Some students choose to take a gap year prior to University entrance.

Money Matters: Scholarships are available across specific subjects ranging from 20 - 40 per cent. Bursaries available, separate bursary fund for Quaker children.

Remarks: Well-established Quaker girls' school – multi-faith and with an international student body. Lively, creative, warm atmosphere in a framework of orderly calm.

NEWLANDS MANOR SCHOOL

Sutton Place, Seaford, East Sussex, BN25 3PL

Tel: 01323 890 309
Fax: 01323 898 420
E-mail: newlands1@msn.com
Website: www.newlands-school.com

• Pupils: Total 420; ages 8-13 220 pupils; ages 13-18 200 pupils • Ages: 8 to 18 • Non Denominational • Fees: Senior school - day fees £3,625 , boarding £5,950 • Independent

Head: Since 1998 Mr Oliver Price, BEd (Loughborough University). Oversaw the amalgamation of the three schools (pre-prep, prep and senior), now Newlands School. Big adjustments were necessary, difficult times experienced but now transformed into a more settled and positive school. Known as Buster, he's a charming, approachable, cuddly 'teddy bear' type described by parents as an honest, caring, no frills type. Married to Patricia Snowdon (in charge of the hugely successful Theatre Arts programme), they have two children in the school, one in prep and a daughter in the sixth form. Says school has developed a niche market and a national reputation for offering a broad spectrum of pupils with varying needs – a specialised and fulfilling education, whilst in the context of a mainstream school. His vision for the school is to maximise the potential of each individual, to drive on strengths and build on weaknesses, to produce decent rounded human beings so that he sees a school of smiling children.

Academic Matters: Operates as a mainstream school with small classes, where the individual is valued more than league table position. For the record, the results at GCSE and A level are slightly above the national average. In 2004, 56 per cent were graded A*/C improving in 2005 to 73 per cent. Almost all pass 'A' level with 30 per cent A or B grades in 2005. However results alone don't give a true picture of the achievements of the school and pupils. 'There are some staggeringly bright pupils,' says the head but many results reflect the excellent teaching within the SEN department. Some children arrive after 'failing' at other schools with well

below appropriate reading age yet achieve nine GCSEs and get A levels with A grades. Maths, dance, physics, art, Spanish, business studies and English literature all popular, with law and psychology newer additions to 'A' levels. Setted from year 5 in English, maths, science and modern languages; will look at ability not obstacles. For example, one very intellectually competent pupil with data recording problems was placed in the top set. Whole school screened in reading and spelling at the beginning of Autumn term with writing speed cannily assessed (changing from a blue pen to a red pen after twenty minutes). Special exam requirements extra time, use of scribe or a transcriber, utilised as required. One dyslexic boy, whose computer skills were poor, whose writing deteriorated when under pressure, was allowed a transcriber and achieved A* in English literature and language. Of the present three Oxbridge candidates, two are dyslexics. Most parents are happy with the prep school but within the mainstream Manor School there have been murmurs of discontent. The recent inspection report revealed some unsatisfactory teaching, lack of in-service teacher training, uninviting library and inadequate boys' boarding. However, the head assures us that all the above are being addressed, particularly with the purchase of the new building.

A third of the school receives extra learning support through the Gannon Centre (warrants a separate prospectus due to its profile and specialisation). Established by a retired headmaster, Tom Gannon, who taught English and noticed that many pupils could easily accommodate facts and be discerning with them but found recording difficult. Predominantly for dyslexics but also with experience of dyspraxia, mild Aspergers and mild attention difficulties, the centre specialises in literacy and numeracy needs, often using a multi sensory approach: 'feel it, touch it, see it'. Originally for pupils of average to above average ability, the core still fit that profile though all abilities are catered for; will take any child they think they can help. Children are withdrawn for one-to-one tuition from a mutually agreed lesson (charged as extra). 'Withdrawing them into groups almost always does not work – they do not like to admit in front of their peers that they do not understand something.' Withdrawal begins as early as pre-prep, with complete continuity through the school if required. School not suitable for those needing to be withdrawn for more than five lessons a week. Often the SEN staff stay with one pupil through their entire school life, encouraging independent learning and developing firm relationships that are the springboards for remarkable successes from previously deemed hopeless cases. Staff are all specialists, familiar with accurate diagnosis of a child's need. No SALT or physiotherapist but pull in specialists if needed. Communication and, feedback to the Gannon Centre, plus liaison between prep and senior school is well-established.This, together with the appreciation of different learning styles by all teachers, contributes to centre's success. Parents and pupils say there is absolutely no stigma attached to a child being withdrawn to the Gannon Centre. Everywhere there is a relaxed friendly atmosphere with a supportive network; self-esteem problems vanish shortly after arrival. Many happy faces in evidence. One child decided on Newlands because 'the sun always comes out when I come here'. Many parents felt the confidence and self-assurance their children developed was a direct result of the non-pressurised, supportive environment. School also has a new International Study Centre offering TEFL courses in large light new classrooms.

Games, Options, The Arts: Approximately one third of the school involves itself in dance, jazz, drama and singing. Indeed the school attracts dancers of the highest calibre and currently one boy is Samba in the Lion King at the Lyceum Theatre. There is excellent specialist teaching on offer with examinations at many levels and great facilities. Three large dance studios and a good proportion of SEN pupils involved. 'The art is also highly thought of' one pupil remarked, 'it's absolutely my most favourite place to be in the whole school. Staff are open to many creative outlets, animation, photography, etc. – pupils feel inspired. The music department is small with few ensembles- but plenty of individual practice rooms. Sport has a solid reputation with good facilities including a sizable swimming pool and sports hall. The emphasis is on fun and variety. Certain activities would be encouraged for those finding competitive team games difficult, eg gym, orienteering, riding, golf. Coastal location means plenty of sailing on offer. New head of sport, changed the curriculum to ensure that years 4-5 have more co-ordinated activities, attention to flexibilities, etc.

Background and Atmosphere: Set in 21 acres, a stone's throw from the sea, the pleasant Edwardian redbrick building proves an attractive setting but some areas weary and in need of a makeover. There's nothing very glitzy, no wall to wall carpeting but there's a happy buzz amongst the children and varied and delicious food. A good proportion of boarders are Asian or African, while many are from Services families. A multi racial group that mixes well.

Pastoral Care and Discipline: Children know they will be listened to and are valued, have good rapport with staff so little in the way of behavioural problems. Support flexes so children with attention difficulties will be given time out to help them refocus if necessary. Staff so au fait with pupils that problems are spotted quickly and nipped in the bud. The level of pastoral care is deemed a strength by parents and inspectors. A new school has been bought nearby that is large, light and will house the boys boarding and later some of the girls. Recent inspection critical of existing boys boarding facilities and associated activities; certainly the accommodation is now good but check out what is on offer at weekends etc. – other than the usual trip to the local town.

Entrance: School is not selective. SEN pupils often come to the school with educational psychologists' reports but all are tested so literacy and numeracy needs are detected. 'If we feel they have potential, we will take them but we never set a hurdle too high, too soon'.

Exit: Some to Further Education Colleges, art school or performing arts courses. Many to universities particularly helpful with SEN needs, eg Newcastle, St Mary's Exeter, Southampton or Wolverhampton.

Money Matters: Small bursary available if a child would clearly benefit but lacks the extra funds. Slight reduction for Services children.

Remarks: The prospectus picture of a girl in her white and red chorister robe running to kick a football is a fitting image of this school, reflecting an underlying spirit, learning to express itself. A mainstream school that boosts the confidence of pupils. An inclusive school for all abilities, with emphasis is on the well-rounded individual.

NEWPORT FREE GRAMMAR SCHOOL

Bury Water Lane, Newport, Saffron Walden, Essex, CB11 3TR

Tel: 01799 540 237
Fax: 01799 542 189
E-mail: admin@nfgs.essex.sch.uk
Website: www.nfgs.essex.sch.uk

• Pupils: 1,013 boys and girls • Ages: 11-18 • Size of sixth form: 196 • Non-denom • State • Open days: 2ndSaturday in October

Head: Since 1991, Mr Richard Priestley BA (early fifties). Educated at Southend High School for Boys and University College, London, where he studied classics. Previously taught at Peter Symonds College and Lord Williams's School. Came to Newport Free Grammar School in 1984 as deputy head. Is both the first deputy head and the first non-Cambridge graduate to be appointed head. His strong interest in foreign travel and his commitment to encouraging international communication between young people is reflected in the extensive and unusual opportunities for foreign visits offered to pupils at the school. Married to Wendy, a teacher. Their now grown-up two sons and a daughter all attended Newport Free.

Academic Matters: Not an academically selective school (see below). GCSE results in most subjects are well above the national average. Boys do significantly better in their exams compared to those in many similar schools, a fact that has been noticed by the DfES. The headmaster puts this down to the fact that the school was formerly a boys' grammar school and has maintained a strong tradition. He also believes that high-quality teaching combined with a commitment to monitoring and goal-setting helps to keep the boys on track. Latin is strong; the head teaches the subject at A level. Modern languages also strong. Pupils are setted in French after Christmas in year 7, from year 8 in maths and from year 9 in science. All other subjects are taught in mixed ability groups to GCSE. Pupils with special educational needs are supported by teaching assistants in mainstream classes. Twenty-two members of staff have been with the school for more than 10 years.

Games, Options, The Arts: Plenty of opportunities for sport with regular fixtures in hockey, netball, rugby and football, cricket and rounders. Both boys' and girls' sport is strong, especially hockey – school feels that parental criticism of lack of support for girls now in the past. The school

has an all-weather, floodlit hockey pitch and clubhouse and a new sports hall. There is a purpose-built arts centre with a drama studio and music suite that has recently been extended to cope with large numbers taking instrumental and voice lessons. Two school plays and a musical are staged each year. Twenty-four different music groups rehearse every week of the year. Participation in extra-curricular activities is strongly encouraged. There are plenty of activities to choose from, including D of E. Foreign trips include visits to Holland, France, Germany, Italy, Spain and South Africa. Sixth formers have the chance to spend three weeks in India and may also attend a Model United Nations General Assembly at the Palais de Nations in Geneva. Newport is one of only two state schools in the country to be invited to this event. The school is a founder member of Euro School Net 2000, a network of 15 schools and 3 teacher training universities across Europe, which provides educational opportunities for staff and pupils. The school is also worldwide co-ordinator of IDEAS, an International Day of Environmental Action and Service. 'Our aim is to get the children out into the world and bring the world into the school,' says the head.

Background and Atmosphere: 'The ffree Grammer Schole of Newport' was founded by a wealthy benefactress in 1588 in memory of her only son. Education was free to the children of Newport, hence the inclusion of the word in the name. Foundress day is still celebrated. The school has been at its present 35-acre site since 1878 and the original building is now listed. Cloistered garden outside the reception area. New accommodation has been added over the years as the school has expanded. The school is strong on tradition and still maintains links with Gonville and Caius College, Cambridge – a connection that has existed since the school was founded. Uniform for years 7-11 is inoffensive. Sixth formers are expected to dress 'as if for work in a professional capacity, such as a bank or office'.

Pastoral Care and Discipline: The school is divided into six houses and pupils are put into a house tutor group of 27 from when they start at the school. Relatively few discipline problems and pupil behaviour is generally very good. There is a brief code of conduct which pupils are expected to follow. Sanctions for pupils who fail to follow the code are clearly laid out.

Pupils and Parents: The school serves a relatively affluent, white middle class area and the pupil population tends to reflect this. There are strong family links within the school and generations of extended families have passed through its doors. Best known former pupils are TV chef Jamie Oliver, pig farmer Jimmy Doherty and Irish international footballer, Matt Holland. The parents' association is very active, as is the 1,000 strong alumni association.

Entrance: Heavily oversubscribed. There were 550 applications in 2005 for 162 places. Boys and girls residing in the parish of Newport are given top priority. Next are those who live in 13 named parishes for whom Newport Free is their nearest secondary school, followed by siblings of those attending the school. The final criterion based on a map produced by the school defining nine areas. A number of places are allocated to children from each area based on a ratio of the number of applications. In practice, children come from a wide area – from as far as Cambridge to the north, Epping to the south, Royston to the west and Braintree to the east. Each applicant is offered a taster day at the school – they come in and spend the day with a year 7 class.

Most pupils go on to the sixth form but there are also places for pupils who have not previously attended the school. Anyone who has five grade Cs at GCSE is welcome to study for A levels – a less-selective entrance policy than many other schools. 'Our policy may mean that we appear further down the league tables but the parents fully support us in giving students the opportunity,' says the head.

Exit: Most sixth formers go on to university, with between one and five a year gaining places at Oxbridge.

Remarks: A school with a sound academic reputation. Stronger on history and tradition than most state schools but with an up-to-date approach to education.

NEWSTEAD WOOD SCHOOL FOR GIRLS

Avebury Road, Orpington, Kent, BR6 9SA

Tel: 01689 853 626
Fax: 01689 853 315
E-mail: office@newsteadwood.bromley.sch.uk
Website: www.newsteadwood.bromley.sch.uk

• Pupils: 960 day girls • Ages: 11-18 • Size of sixth form: 296
• Non-denom • State • Open days: September

Head: Since 2001, Mrs Elizabeth Allen BA MA FRSA (fifties), married with two grown-up daughters. Previously head of Altwood School, Maidenhead, which she turned round very positively during her time there. Her degree subjects are English and RE. A neat and sympathetic person, her serenity disguises a character full of insight on many different levels, a scholarly and talented leader of women. Newstead's success markets itself, so Mrs Allen can concentrate on academic fulfilment and developing talents.

Academic Matters: Very strong, one of the top performing schools in the country, consistently high A level and GCSE results, 95 per cent A* or A – not that surprising considering the intake. Broad curriculum delivered by committed, stable, predominantly female staff. Big drive to encourage girls to be responsible and work independently right from the start. All departments of equally high calibre, master classes for the gifted, rigorous monitoring assessment, results of which are reported to parents. Girls feel supported and difficulties are dealt with swiftly. Twenty-three choices at GCSE, sciences taught as three separate subjects or as dual award, all take DT a year early, most go on to take four A levels. Setting only in mathematics, everyone does Latin for two years, recently refurbished language department enhanced by interesting trips and exchanges. Science and mathematics based, but staff insist that equal importance is given to the arts and humanities. Since September 2004, Newstead Wood is a specialist engineering school, focusing on problem-solving, thinking skills and creativity across the curriculum.

Four ICT suites, state-of-the-art engineering suite, well-stocked – about to be refurbished. Annual enrichment weeks are run, though some feel they could be more dynamic. Separate sixth form centre, boys from neighbouring schools come in for specialist courses and debates. Superior careers advice, the utmost importance is given to ensuring pupils are aware of the options open to them and making the right choices. Girls are introduced to university life through conferences and courses at Oxford and the school has good links with industry. SEN a positive approach with parents and pupils aware of teaching needs. Thinking and study skills taught, laptops can be used. EAL specialist teaching can be arranged if required.

Games, Options, The Arts: Ample sports grounds, the challenge is to think of what's not on offer here rather than to report what is. Access to sport is excellent and the school has been awarded a Sportsmark for the second time. Swimming and tennis are particularly good, indoor courts opened in 2003, with athletics up and coming. A year 7 pupil recently won the London mini marathon. Needless to say the girls win many local and national competitions. Healthy Schools Award achieved as well.

Artsmark for expressive arts and often has an artist in residence – musicians, poets or artists. Clean bright art and design studios, RIBA awards for pupils' architectural design. Dance and drama very active, with new initiatives starting all the time. Debating and conferencing groups abundant, they are part of a United Nations programme, also mock trial training, competing successfully at a national level. Music is supported by Bromley Young Musicians Trust amongst others, three orchestras and two choirs tour with the Trust. One third of the pupils play an instrument, tuition can be arranged on any instrument if not in house, new composing software is on its way. Imaginative music and drama productions. Good choice of clubs and enrichment programmes including film club and 'arguers anonymous'; the school tries to satisfy any unmet demand.

Background and Atmosphere: On the edge of a residential area overlooking the Kent Downs. Thoughtfully planned, there is plenty of space and greenery. Everywhere hums with activity and excellence, 'No goal is unachievable'. There is fun to be had but this is a seriously hard-working environment with a reputation, along with Tiffin Girls', for supplying the NHS with a large percentage of its female staff.

Pastoral Care and Discipline: Guidance good all round, girls are far too busy to cause much trouble but, of course, there is always the odd one. Rules have been tightened by the new head, home/school contract, clear guidelines; parents must return a slip confirming receipt of communications. Harmonious relationships and respect for everyone's opinion are strengths, all have a personal tutor. Sixth formers run the school council and are house captains.

Pupils and Parents: Reasonably mixed though more middle class than not, rural and city families as catchment stretches from Deptford to Sevenoaks. Most of the pupils would not have the opportunities they have here if it were fee-paying – 'most of us realise how fortunate we are compared to others', pupils say. Comfortable community feel with confident pupils, though some feel they lack etiquette and manners and presentation could be improved. Girls who are keen to gain new experiences, many are the first generation of females in their families to go to university. Academic tutoring ensures one-to-one recognition for achievements and target setting for all students. Parents receive two interim assessments as well as a report annually. School encourages parental participation; parents help with open days, careers talks and can get involved in policy making. Alumnae: Christine Hancock, Barbara Harriss-White, Emma Johnson, Susan Tebby.

Entrance: Furiously competitive, 700 apply for 130 places, non-verbal and verbal reasoning test, highest achievers awarded places. At 16 interview and reference from previous school plus at least six GCSEs grades A-C. All girls must live in the 9-mile catchment area – map provided by the school.

Exit: Nearly all to university, up to 15 a year to Oxbridge, lots to medicine and law.

Remarks: School for motivated, mature, academically able girls with committed parents, not for the faint-hearted.

NONSUCH HIGH SCHOOL FOR GIRLS

Ewell Road, Cheam, Sutton, Surrey, SM3 8AB

Tel: 020 8394 1308
Fax: 020 8393 2307
E-mail: admissions@nonsuch.sutton.sch.uk
Website: www.nonsuchhigh.co.uk

• Pupils: 1,220 girls, all day • Ages: 11-18 • Size of sixth form: 350 • Non-denom • State • Open days: September (yr 7) and November (sixth form)

Head: Since 1995, Mrs Genefer Espejo BA (mid-fifties). Previously head at a girls' comprehensive in Reading. English, despite her exotic sounding name (courtesy of her Colombian husband). Theatre, art, travelling and shopping among her interests, also a keen supporter of Southampton football club! Looks younger than her years and comes across as a woman entirely at ease with herself and her school – very pleasant manner. 'She definitely has a presence and you are in no doubt about who runs this place,' said a parent – though, as in most large state schools, the vast majority of parents have little or no face-to-face contact with her.

Academic Matters: Impressive, as you would expect from one of the top selective schools in the country. Science facilities are good – but results not so sparkling. Nice to see astronomy available as a GCSE option (school has its own observatory). At A level, English, psychology, sciences, geography and maths are among the favourite options. 'It's almost as if they don't want to be labelled as a girls' school, they are always emphasising the more traditionally masculine subjects,' said one parent. Lots of homework but parents say it is 'manageable'. 'My daughter works very hard and is definitely stretched here. In year 8 she was looking at GCSE papers,' says a mother. Definitely not a school for slackers. 'We actually chose this school because we thought it would be less pressured than Tiffin Girls but we were wrong – it is quite pushy,' says another mother. Little call for special needs support here, but SENCO assists those dyslexic pupils who are able to pass the entry test and some physical disabilities are catered for. Approximately 20 EAL students but no beginners.

Games, Options, The Arts: Sports facilities are excellent and well used, thanks in large part to an innovative deal with a David Lloyd sports club. Nonsuch was the first state school to go into such a partnership – the school leases land to the club and in return can use its facilities – including exclusive use of the swimming pool in the mornings and the tennis courts in the afternoon. Additionally as part of the deal, David Lloyd provided the school with a dedicated sports hall, a floodlit all-weather hockey pitch and a new music centre. All the usual main sports on offer and pupils compete at national and county level in several including netball, football and hockey. Tennis is popular and the school provides the ball girls for the Stella Artois tournament at Queens.

Very good reputation for music (old girls include 'cool' singer Katie Melua and harpist Lucy Wakeford) with many choirs, orchestras, and ensembles. Some 350 girls take extra-curricular music lessons and aim for grade 8 by the time they leave. Budding dancers and actresses might struggle to express themselves – some parents feel these subjects are the poor relations. 'They have spent all the money on maths and science facilities – the drama department is a temporary hut and was like that for the entire seven years I was there,' says one former pupil. (Head says work on a new drama studio will begin soon and that uptake and results for drama at both GCSE and A level are high despite the 'very modest physical means'). Clubs and societies from cheerleading to philosophy. CCF and DofE.

Background and Atmosphere: Lovely setting on the edge of the 22 acre Nonsuch Park. Plenty of outdoor space, mix of buildings – admin and some classrooms are in the charmless original building, which has been extended in different directions with newer, fresher facilities and a few separate blocks. Workman-like rather than flashy. There was an untidy pile of clutter in the lobby when we visited at short notice. This is a school so confident of its strengths that it doesn't have to try too hard to impress. Girls are lively – even noisy. Strong house system.

Pastoral Care and Discipline: Usual system of tutors and heads of year in place, and working well. Issues dealt with rapidly – nothing festers. Discipline is strict. No major discipline problems – 'I tolerate absolutely no nonsense and treat everyone exactly the same,' says the head. Parents feel their daughters clearly know and understand the boundaries. No tolerance of smoking anywhere while in school uniform – including travel time – prefects patrol the huge school site.

Pupils and Parents: A refreshingly multicultural bunch (30 languages). Pupils proud to be here, and generally smart – school uniform kilts are difficult to shorten. Parents are mainly professional, ambitious for their daughters, and supportive of the school. Communications with parents are good – lots of up-to-date information on the website, 75 per cent of parents opts to receive and send all communication by email.

Entrance: Hugely oversubscribed – in 2004 there were 830 applications (from some 50 primary schools) for 180 places. Applicants must list Nonsuch as a preferred school on the foundation grammar school application form to sit the test – two parts (maths and verbal reasoning), no interview. Places are allocated to those who pass, according to the usual criteria of siblings and proximity – families move into the area to be as near to the school doorstep as possible. However the top 50 highest scores get a place regardless of where they live. In practice the school maintains a local intake, with 95 per cent of the pupils living within 5 km of the school. 10-20 external students join the school in the sixth form.

Exit: Over 80 per cent of the girls stay on for the sixth form – of the rest some join colleges (probably in search of a mixed environment) and a few go to the private sector. At 18 most go on to university – 10 or so to Oxbridge, lots to the redbricks and a handful each year to leading medical and dental schools.

Remarks: A super school for the disciplined and hard-working, not for the rebel, slacker or drama/dance diva.

NORTH BERWICK HIGH SCHOOL

Grange Road, North Berwick, East Lothian, EH39 4QS

Tel: 01620 894 661
Fax: 01620 895 495
E-mail: northberwick.hs@eastlothian.gov.uk
Website: www.northberwick.e-lothian.sch.uk

• Pupils: 925 boys and girls, all day • Ages: 11-18 • Size of sixth form: 240 • Non-denom • State

Head: Since 1999 (previous head, George Smuga, having been seconded to East Lothian Education Department), Mr Colin Sutherland BSc (forties), who comes from the West (as they say in Scotland). He started his teaching career at Garnock Academy, Kilbirnie in Ayrshire, before spending 11 years at Castlehead School in Paisley. Previously depute at Port Glasgow High School, before that assistant head at Greenock. Educated at Paisley Grammar, 'when it was still selective'. He read maths and geology at Glasgow University plus PGCE and 'masses of courses'. He would love to teach more but still does 'the odd bit, supply teach-

ing mainly' but no set classes as such. Mr Sutherland runs the school with three depute heads, who are responsible for the school's three houses, plus a whole host of add-ons. There is also a recently-appointed school business manager.

A charming man, thoughtful and very aware of children's needs, he has a lovely sense of humour and 'just loves it here'. An enthusiastic cyclist and walker, he has not yet taken up the North Berwick vice of golf though is otherwise much involved in the community (he lives at nearby Port Seton, safely out of the catchment area).

Academic Matters: School follows Scottish system. Standard Grades followed by Highers and Advanced Highers the following year. The school picks up children from five associated primaries, the huge (over 700) Law Primary, which is adjacent and shares many of the school facilities including the fabulous local sports centre, and the much smaller local primaries of Aberlady, Athelstaneford, Dirleton and Gullane. Pupils in primary 7 visit the school before their actual arrival here and follow part of the big school timetable. There are however six parallel classes at S1 and S2, with pupils being setted for maths in S1 and S2; French is also setted in S2. Thereafter, the school runs six parallel classes, taking into account option choice, when specialist subject teaching kicks in – 'deliberately made broad to ensure that pupils' needs and interests are met within the national framework'. 'Max class size 25 (head says 'could be up to 30, but the school strives to ensure that classes contain no more than 25/26'). 18/20 for practical matters.

School consistently turns in better results than any other in East Lothian and recently ranked 37th overall in Scotland for Standard Grades and 17th for Highers. In Standard Grades biology, chemistry, English, French, geography, history and, to a lesser degree, physics, were outstanding. French writing and German less so, maths had a bad year. Pupils can take Spanish up to Intermediate level in S5/6 – usually the latter.

At Intermediate 2 (which many schools are using instead of Standard Grades) chemistry, English and maths are very strong and this trend continues at Higher level, with excellent showings across the board in English and the sciences, as well as geography, history and modern studies. Pupils take an amalgam of exams, often topping up with another batch of Highers rather than opting for Advanced Highers. Little problem with getting staff – well it's North Berwick isn't it? Head is autonomous in being able to choose his own staff ('scheme of delegation').

Good remedial back-up, children with Records of Needs not a problem, nor are those with ADHD. Double teaching in class. Laptop computers where required, plus extra time in exams and for those with learning needs, 'which cannot be tackled in the classroom'. There are 'workshops on basic processes, individual educational programmes and individual tutorials'. Reading Recovery programme, as well as educational psychologists, outreach teachers et al. Support for learning for the most able as well as for those with learning difficulties. This school has a number of profoundly deaf pupils, for whom there is an excellent programme. Blind and partially sighted pupils and wheel chairs all easily absorbed. Laudable.

In session 2003-2004, an integrated Pupil Support Faculty was established, including a Pupil Support Base in which the most vulnerable pupils have a 'sanctuary.' This was extended further in Session 2004-2005 with the addition of a Base for pupils with Additional Support Needs.

Outstanding report from HM Inspectorate of Education in January 2002.

Games, Options, The Arts: The school has an enviable collection of games pitches with the local sports centre and swimming pool next door – they have priority over local users. New Astroturf. Two gyms in school, plus dance studio plus mirrors of course. Strong rugby and school recently toured Canada with great success, they all wore the kilt and the piper came too. Two current sixth formers in national squad. Plus basketball, hockey (huge fixture list for girls), badminton, netball club, sailing, swimming and local authority development officers on hand for coaching. D of E popular – head would like us to add 'VERY', with half a dozen pupils every year going to Holyrood for their Gold Award'. Trillions of clubs for everything.

Music outstanding, though no pipe band of their own, pupils (of both sexes) play with the town band. Bands, orchestras and choirs in every discipline: wind, jazz, brass, piano. Senior and junior choirs, the school sings carols outside the church for charity at Christmas, and plays at The Lodge. The school provided the brass band for the opening of the local Sea Bird Centre. Musicians have been known to come back to school and join in the school orchestra – often with no warning at all. Scottish country dancing popular, as are the regular ceilidhs, much to the amazement of the bunch of Kosovan refugees who were billeted in the town recently – 'they loved it'- (and came with extra resources).

Recording studio, huge assembly hall used for school drama, very good, and by the locals – for partying as well as plays. Deaf loop in operation. Keyboards, guitars, large number of practice rooms. Whizzy art department, absolutely fabulous, with excellent ceramics and tranches of young going on to art schools all over the country. Amazing cut glass. Fabulous screen printing (though the sewing-up was less impressive). Art work all over the school. Huge art library and dark room. CAD and computer links to art department, impressive DT, though mainly in wood. Home economics but not much take up. Impressive computer suites (one hundred new computers in 2004) set out like an office and due to be expanded shortly; computers and tellies in every class room.

School is twinned, as is the town, with Kerteminde in Denmark; children do exchanges and four-weekly study visits are a regular feature. This is a growth activity.

Background and Atmosphere: The school was founded in 1893 with thirteen pupils. Originally North Berwick boasted two schools: the Parish School (which started in 1661) and the Burgh School; these amalgamated in 1868 and joined forces with the High School in 1931. The current buildings date back to 1940 and very impressive they are too. The temporary classrooms which had provided schooling for the extra post-war pupils were replaced during the 1990s and a further extension under the PPP initiative began in April 2003. This was scheduled to be complete by March 2005, and, at time of writing (autumn 2005) is at last nearly so. However, as reported in the Daily Express (so it must be true) the contractors went bust, having removed (and presumably chucked out) the specialist cabinets needed to store A1 paper and all the rest. Staff had to hunt for substitute desks at local (upmarket) scrap merchant and pupils came back to find not only a leaky roof but also fifties-style desks some of which were more suited to kindergarten than a senior school. Balfour Beatty are now in control but red faces and ruined art work abound. Or so we hear.

Light and airy, the school must have some of the best views in Britain, with the Law to the south and views over the North Berwick coastline and the Bass Rock to the north. The school has strong links with the recently opened Sea Bird Centre, which is used for regular study, as well as providing summer and weekend jobs for impoverished pupils. A grade one bonus.

This is a community school at its best. Loads of town participation, a squad recently cleaned up the East Beach, and local countryside a haven for hands-on teaching. Masses of inter-school/town involvement, and the Community Council has recently 'donated a prize for community service which is awarded annually'. Huge library, divided into little seminar areas, as well as crannies for private study. The tidiest school we have ever visited, only two bags in evidence, the rest neatly tucked into lockers. Having patted the back, one has to say that there was quite a lot of detritus and candy bar wrappers lying around, despite the enormous (labelled) litter bins everywhere.

School operates with a three house system, a focus for pastoral care as well as discipline and games. Sibling led. Each of the three depute and heads fronts one of them. And house boards vie for imaginative notices.

Children wear their school uniform with pride; move currently afoot to introduce fleece jackets, all wear white shirts, with black and red ties and sweat shirts. Pupils not encouraged to leave the school at lunch time but no dining rooms as such, cafeteria-style food available, and can bring packed lunch or eat in the sports centre. Head boy or girl chosen via ballot of staff and sixth form – 'not a beauty contest', said the head, the top four are then interviewed before selection. A pretty onerous task, they have to do the Burns night supper at the local Marine Hotel, which brushes up their public speaking skills. Two prize givings – the head boy and girl are principal speakers at the prize giving for S1/2/3 at the trad time in June, and then return for the senior prize giving in mid September which is followed by soft drinks, wine for the adults and nibbles in the library. Very popular.

The school closes at lunch time on Fridays for 'staff training' which may not be over-convenient for working parents. School bus for all outlying districts. Masses of trips, for everything, all over.

Pastoral Care and Discipline: Good PSE programme in place; strong anti-bullying programme in place 'secrecy is the worst enemy'. No obvious problems with booze, fags or drugs in school, but North Berwick itself had some recent horrendous publicity with children being found paralytic on the beaches during the weekend and underage drinking is certainly a problem locally. The local community health boys take this seriously and are very 'proactive'. School is much involved in this and 'ever vigilant in educating youth'. Slight glitch last autumn when pupils were 'temporarily excluded from school for smoking cannabis at lunch-time'. Regular smoking patrol.

School uses three chaplains, two Church of Scotland and one Episcopalian, who tackle moral issues. 'An honest school', no history of theft, and most classrooms are left unlocked.

Pupils and Parents: Mostly a middle class bunch but a diverse intake, everyone from baby bankers to impoverished shepherds. Incredibly supportive, usually over 95 per cent turn up for parents' evenings, and a very strong PTA. Good at fund-raising. Minuscule number of ethnic minorities. Parent-led school board, parents, staff and a couple of members of the local community.

Entrance: Automatic from local primaries and if children of school age move into the area. At any time.

Exit: Two departure dates a year, one at Christmas, the other at the conventional end of school year. Around 80 per cent stay on for sixth year; some leave to go into 'further education', some work, 50 per cent to university, quite a mix: 'medics, law, business admin, economics, English, maths, education etc. Primarily to Scottish universities but a regular and quite impressive trickle to Oxbridge annually.

Money Matters: No child disadvantaged, good back-up from the local LEA, as well as parent-inspired foundation.

Remarks: A stunning and successful local school. Couldn't do better anywhere.

NORTH BRIDGE HOUSE SENIOR SCHOOL

Linked to North Bridge House Nursery School

Linked to North Bridge House Junior School in the Junior section

1 Gloucester Avenue, London, NW1 7AB

Tel: 020 7267 6266
Fax: 020 7284 2508
E-mail: seniorschool@northbridgehouseschools.co.uk

- Pupils: 900 boys and girls, all day • Ages: 2-16
- Non-denom • Fees: £3,125 • Independent

Heads: North Bridge is divided into five departments on three sites (two in Hampstead and one round the corner from Regent's Park, with mini-buses running between them).

Head of senior school since 2003 is Alexandra Ayre, formerly deputy head and head of English.

Head of upper prep school since 2005 is Brodie Bibby, previously deputy head at Westminster School.

Head of the lower prep school is the highly-regarded Ms Battye.

Head of the junior and nursery schools is Mrs Allsop. 'She's wonderful,' said a parent.

Entrance: Most lower school pupils come into the nursery at 2, 3 or 4, generally on a first come first served basis though NB treat the school tour as an interview in disguise.

Senior school pupils nearly all join at 11, mostly from state primaries. They visit the school for a day and go through a routine of lessons which includes assessments in maths and English. 'We're careful not to call them entrance exams,' says the head. 'We're looking for potential, so even if they have weaknesses we'll take them if we think they'll be able to get at least five A-C grades at GCSE.'

About 80 per cent of candidates are offered places. A few – probably around half a dozen a year – come up from the lower school.

Exit: Nearly all the preparatory school pupils leave either at 11 (girls) or 13 (boys) to go to major London day schools eg South Hampstead, North London Collegiate, Westminster, St Paul's, UCS and Highgate. Senior school pupils leave at 16 to go to eg Davies Laing & Dick, Camden School for Girls, Mill Hill School, Westminster, La Swap sixth form consortium, Woodhouse College.

Remarks: This is really two separate schools: the preparatory school – including the junior school and the lower and upper prep schools, which prepare pupils very successfully for senior independent schools at 11 and 13; and the senior school, which takes mostly state school pupils at 11 and achieves creditable GCSE results. (NB some of the parents of boys joining the senior school at 11 were not aware that the prep school boys working for the Common Entrance are in a completely separate school, following a different syllabus. The senior school does not prepare children for 13+ exams.) Boys thought unlikely to succeed at common entrance may be advised to move to the senior school rather than the upper prep but the decision is ultimately made by the parents.

Around 96 per cent of senior school pupils get at least five A*-C grades at GCSE – about 30 per cent tend to be A* or A – in a range of subjects that includes media studies, photography and drama.

French from the nursery upwards, plus Latin in the upper prep only. Setting for maths in the lower and upper prep schools; final year upper prep boys are divided into classes depending on whether they are competing for either a scholarship or for a place at St Paul's or Westminster, or for schools like UCS, City and Highgate. The senior school moves at a gentler pace. It sets for maths from year 7, English and French from year 8 and science from year 9 but since there are only two sets, each contains a wide ability range. Traditional, rigorous teaching with plenty of assessment.

The school has no intention of becoming more selective; it occupies a useful niche outside the relentless pressure of most of the north London private senior school system. 'Nicely laid-back,' said a senior school parent; this is less true of the lower and upper prep schools which have the pressure of 11+ and CE.

Can cope with mildish dyslexia, offering up to four 40-minute sessions a week in small groups. This help has just been extended to the junior school.

Around 3:1 boy:girl ratio at senior level. More-or-less 50:50 in the junior school, but the upper prep, from 10-13, is virtually boys only (girls spend another year in the lower school then take the 11+). The half-dozen or so boys and girls who are staying on to the senior school form a tiny year 6 class together.

Housed in what used to be a convent – including a chapel – with pillars and gilt ceiling, now used as the school hall – the school suffers acutely from lack of space. There's no library nor language labs but the art department, though compact, produces consistently good results – 'minor miracles,' said the previous head, 'given the space available.' No grounds but the school is a five-minute walk from Regent's Park, which it uses at breaktimes as well as for sport.

The boys play football, rugby and cricket, the girls netball, rounders and hockey. Not the sportiest of schools but great things are expected of the new head of PE, 'and because it's a small, mixed school your child can get more opportunities to shine,' said a parent. Drama has tended to lapse in recent years but the new drama teacher is hoping to return to the tradition of producing big musicals and drama is now a GCSE option. Music, too, suffers from lack of space – there are no specialist practice rooms – but there is plenty going on, with brass and string groups and choirs (though no orchestra) performing in summer and Christmas concerts. This is not a slick school – parents report disorganised concerts, a Christmas drama production repeated at Easter and floundering swimmers being entered for a gala – but some find the bohemian aspects endearing. Chess, outstanding in the lower school, has not yet fed through to the senior school but the head is activating a club. Other clubs include fencing, drama and photography.

The school's situation just up the road from Camden Town, which is quite possibly the drugs capital of the UK, means that the head is scrupulous about the subject. 'We watch this very carefully and even bringing cannabis into school could be an expulsion issue.' Bullying 'exists but we jump on it quite quickly.'

An eclectic mix of pupils from all sorts of backgrounds. 'It's very nice socially,' said a parent. 'It's a happy school and parents tend to be far less pushy than lots of private school parents. The school has always been very accommodating whenever I've had a problem.' 'It's very buzzy, very jolly, very friendly,' said another parent. 'My boys have been so happy there.'

View as two separate schools: the lower school will do what it takes to prepare your child for senior school entrance exams; the senior school provides a useful refuge for those opting out of the high-pressure choices – and they'll probably get decent GCSEs anyway. Bought by Asquith Court Schools, then sold on to Cognita, www.cognitaschools.co.uk, Chris Woodhead's company. Not clear yet if this will lead to any notable changes.

NORTH CESTRIAN GRAMMAR SCHOOL

Dunham Road, Altrincham, Cheshire, WA14 4AJ

Tel: 0161 928 1856
Fax: 01619 298 657
E-mail: office@ncgs.co.uk
Website: www.ncgs.co.uk

• Pupils: 290 boys • Ages: 11 – 18 • Size of sixth form: 65 in sixth form; co-ed since 2005 • Non-denominational • Fees: £2,090 • Independent

Head: Since 1996 David Vanstone MA history, Cambridge, then PCGE and Sabbatical Union Post from Goldsmiths' College, London. Youthful early fifties. Came from six years as deputy head at Stafford Grammar. Chair of ISA, ISI Inspector. Passionate about what small schools can offer pupils in developing individual potential, speaking of 'the ethos behind the mission'. Jocular with pupils but commands friendly respect. Boys like him but say, 'he does like making speeches and the sound of his own voice'. Parents appreciate his pastoral care – 'once your son is under his wing he's really one of his boys, he looks after them like his own sons'.

Academic Matters: Founded in 1951 as a grammar school for boys who hadn't passed the 11+ and who might therefore be disadvantaged. 'People see us as a non-academic school,' says head, 'but many who have passed the 11+ actively chose our small, personal environment where they're known individually and looked after.' Justly proud of reputation for 'value-added', nurturing unfulfilled potential and enabling dyslexic boys to thrive. Two classes of 25, streamed from y8. 14 GCSEs and 14 A level courses on offer. 73 per cent GCSEs A – C. Most boys exceed expectations, delighting parents and themselves, and many go on to university. All encouraged to develop in extra-curricular ways too. 25 per cent SEN, mostly dyslexia. Parents describe extra dyslexia tuition as, 'very available, timetabled, sympathetic, open-minded, an extra cost but marvellous'. Some boys have restricted curriculum to succeed in 6 GCSEs rather than struggling in 9, 'so they learn they can cope, to boost their confidence and self-esteem.' Boys seem willing to give up breaks to finish work. Trafford Connexions careers service and parents praise school's

help in decision-making during upper years. Sixth form classes average 7 pupils.

Games, Options, The Arts: Large sports hall and gym and four tennis courts on site. 20-acre playing fields rented from National Trust with modern pavilion and changing rooms, five minutes walk through leafy suburbs, downhill there, uphill back, 'miserable in the rain after two hours football,' say boys. Very strong tradition of DofE, accounting for over half local borough's gold and silver awards. The only local school with in-house training to gold. 'Though we're a small school we try and provide everything you'd find in a bigger school,' says head. Strong emphasis on outdoor pursuits during weekends, evenings and holidays including rock climbing, snow boarding, golf, white water rafting. Well-equipped music and art rooms, private tuition on seven instruments, impressive ceramics on display round school. Recent trips include skiing in New England and theatre workshops in New York, plus less expensive outward bound nearer home.

Background and Atmosphere: Stately home aura with portico entrance, pink front door to grand carpeted entrance hall with wallpaper. Large front room of 1850s mansion was home to original 1951 intake of 39 boys, now head's study. Brand new hall seats all by former stable block housing technology. Former hall now home to library with work stations. Outdoor area at break seems cramped. Unstuffy, bustling but relaxed atmosphere prevails. 'The best thing about the school is the co-operation and understanding between boys and staff,' says head, 'they get the best out of each other.' Parents say there's a lot of fun here; teachers join drama productions, one even flick-flacks across the stage. Lunches pre-paid, compulsory. Head firmly believes, 'boys need to be fed' and while there are healthy options, defends provision of stodge, 'better than them being hungry all afternoon and I abhor Ruth Kelly's abominable attacks on vending machines. This school is full of thin boys and we educate them to make choices.' Inevitably most choose stodge but do seem to stay thin.

Pastoral Care and Discipline: On very busy A56 but boys keep to footbridge and nearby pelican crossing. Otherwise very secure with gated grounds sandwiched between Loreto prep and girls' senior schools. Caretaker and wife live on site. Classes and hall routinely locked when not in use. Boys stand for staff and the word 'sir' is on the tip of every tongue, though pupil-staff relationships friendly. Head says, 'I know every boy, not just their names but their family and whether they need me to shout at them or not'. Four houses, Grenfell, Hillary, Livingstone and Scott. Strong pastoral care, going to great lengths through year heads and form tutors, older prefects mentor lower forms. Parental contact is good, termly reports and homework diary has scope for communicating home. Parents describe school as 'very approachable' with lots of awards for effort as well as achievement but say that the influx of boys who're not thriving elsewhere before GCSE courses begin can be disrupting for existing settled boys and class groups.' Head says, 'we rarely fail a pupil and, if we do, they generally end up outside mainstream education'.

Pupils and Parents: Largely white middle class. 10 per cent Jewish, 10 per cent Muslim with strong link to local faith communities. Two thirds from nearby, others travel out from Manchester or in from far flung parts of Cheshire. Diverse but harmonious community embracing those needing extra tuition or nurturing as well as the eccentric and recalcitrant. Co-ed sixth form since September 2005 when five girls joined as response to parental requests. 'They'll flood in once word spreads,' says head. No plans to include girls from 11. Notable OBs include ice skater Nicky Slater, floating weatherman Fred Talbot, Kevin Godley – 10cc rock star, and James Goulding – Chief Executive of Deutsche Asset Management Europe, Just Pidcock – Olympic hockey medallist, Kevin Godley – 10cc rock star, Gary Davies – Radio One DJ.

Entrance: Relatively un-daunting exam looking for GCSE A-C potential, so not all pass. Papers in English, maths and reasoning in autumn term. Entry to co-ed sixth form based on anticipated GCSEs and interview with head. Some exchange of pupils at sixth form, some boys leaving for a bigger school for better transition to university, others coming here for more individual attention.

Exit: Many to university, some to high flying courses.

Money Matters: Means-tested bursaries available, 'we would like to issue more,' says head who also offers some academic scholarships based on entrance exam merit.

Remarks: Justly deserved reputation for realising potential, especially in boys who, for whatever reason, have not passed 11+ and for dyslexics who can pass entrance exam. Many local boys sit exam as safety net, some 11+ passers also choose NGCS for its size and ethos of individual attention. Parents say, 'it's a brilliant school for the right boy, I can't speak highly enough of it for our son.'

NORTH LONDON COLLEGIATE SCHOOL

Linked to North London Collegiate School Junior School in the Junior section

Canons Drive, Edgware, Middlesex, HA8 7RJ

Tel: 020 8952 0912
Fax: 020 8951 1391
E-mail: office@nlcs.org.uk
Website: www.nlcs.org.uk

• Pupils: 790 girls; all day • Ages: 11-18 • Size of sixth form: 225 • Christian foundation, but all faiths welcomed • Fees: £2,832 - £3,339 • Independent • Open days: Two in the autumn term. See website for information

Head: Since 1997, Mrs Bernice McCabe BA MA FRSA (forties). Educated at Clifton High School and Bristol University (English followed by a PGCE). Was previously deputy head of The Heathland School in Hounslow, then head of Chelmsford County High. Smart, glamorous, dynamic. Gets to know all the girls by teaching English to everyone in year 7 and is keen to emphasise her philosophy of providing 'floors, not ceilings'. 'Our focus is to encourage girls to be confident and believe in their own abilities and we have a pastoral system to support this.' 'She's very forward-looking,' said an insider. 'She's not content to let the school rest on its laurels. But she delegates well, she takes advice when necessary, and she doesn't shy away from dealing with issues.' 'I've always found her very supportive and insightful,' said a parent.

Academic Matters: Stunning results consistent with the academic profile. In 2005, 97 per cent of A levels were A and B grades, with 74 girls getting all straight A grades. The GCSE results in 2005 were equally outstanding, with 95 per cent of grades at A* /A. This is hard to beat. A level options now include philosophy, theatre studies and Italian. No streaming except for maths from year 9 and broad bands for GCSE science; the very few girls with special educational needs get extra support eg laptops where necessary.

The school offers the International Baccalaureate alongside A levels in sixth form. 'The IB programme really matches our academic aspirations – it ensures girls continue to study a broad range of subjects and gets them to think for themselves. The extended essay and theory of knowledge parts of the programme are in tune with our thinking and so is the creativity, action and service element – we will ensure that these will all be part of the curriculum whichever pathway girls choose.' As part of a crusade to get girls to think beyond the syllabus, the school organises symposia that involve sixth formers pairing up with boys from schools including Winchester College and Whitgift School. Communicating largely by email, the students prepare and deliver a paper on a theme such as theory, space time or humanist thinking. Philosophy, ethics and critical thinking are part of the sixth form general studies programme, and there is a weekly choice of lectures at senior societies.

'We had 38 Oxbridge offers in 2004-5 – the numbers are improving each year. We believe it is a result of the intellectual stimulation we provide, with plenty of lectures and discussions outside the syllabus. But I'm very opposed to identifying "Oxbridge hopefuls". We don't encourage competition – they're well-motivated enough.' The school does not award academic prizes nor give class positions and parents agree that it does not intend to put pressure on the girls. 'The girls put intense pressure on themselves and everyone is scared of being the one who lets the class down by getting a grade C,' said a mother.

Games, Options, The Arts: Excellent facilities include a sports centre with large hall, multi-gym and swimming pool, all-weather netball/tennis courts and lacrosse/athletics pitches. Plenty of sport in the lower forms (though instrumental lessons can take preference), plus extra-curricular clubs every day, including badminton and cross-country running. Teams do well in local tournaments and quite a few girls play for county sides. Dance is increasingly popular – year 7s enthuse about their dance display in which everyone plays a part.

Large, light art centre overlooking the lake; the small numbers taking art A level more or less all get A grades. 'Very beautiful, very controlled art,' commented a parent. Smallish but effective DT department.

A performing arts centre is under construction. It comprises a 350-seat auditorium, orchestra pit, 12 rehearsal rooms and exhibition space and will open in winter 2006/7. At present, the school hall hosts three major performances a year, 'but this can limit its other uses for weeks at a time.' There's a drama studio with lighting equipment; drama GCSE and theatre studies A level are options. Year 7 devises and performs a pantomime and school productions have been favourably reviewed at the Edinburgh Fringe Festival.

Three orchestras, choirs and various instrumental groups including a popular jazz band ('more and more girls are getting into playing the drums,' said a pupil). The school nearly always wins the Founder's Trophy at the National Chamber Music Competition. Some extremely talented musicians eg junior school girls playing at grade 8 level, but the middle school orchestra is inclusive, and anyone can join. ('My daughter complains that she has to play stuff that's too easy but I like the ethos).

Everyone is encouraged to take on responsibilities, from year 7s showing visitors around to sixth formers running clubs or becoming form assistants. Plenty of school trips eg netball tour to Barbados, classics trip to Italy, skiing in Alpe D'Huez, year 9 adventure week in the Peak District, lots of language exchanges.

There's a strong emphasis on community service which is further enhanced with the introduction of the IB – girls work in local hospitals and on conservation schemes, while events such as the Mencap Funday, the Fantasy Fashion Show and the Party Near the Park talent contest raise funds for charity. 'Everyone finds something they like to do,' said a pupil. 'And it's such a supportive environment you don't mind having a go at things.'

Background and Atmosphere: Glorious setting on the outskirts of suburbia, with 30 acres of playing fields, terraces, lawns shaded by cedars, lime tree avenue, rose garden, duck pond. The gracious Old House was built in 1760 and was once owned by the Duke of Chandos; the modern additions blend in fairly well. Girls roam freely in the grounds, play a rowdy game of Budge outside the head's window, chatter and giggle in the corridors. 'We expect them to concentrate in lessons, so outside class they need to be able to let off steam,' says the deputy head.

Founded in Camden by Frances Mary Buss in 1850 (she also founded Camden School for Girls), the school moved out to Edgware in 1939. It has formed links with local comprehensive schools; middle school girls share academic, creative and sporting activities with pupils from the Sacred Heart High School in Harrow; year 10 girls have debated the topic of war with pupils from The Heathland School in Hounslow; the sixth form links up with boys' schools for symposia. But it is a very self-contained community, with an almost boarding school feel, far removed from the grittiness of London life. Despite its size, it is very close-knit – 'you get to know people throughout the school,' say pupils. Parents comment that a bit more contact with boys' schools wouldn't go amiss, but sixth formers are less keen. 'Doing the symposium made me very pleased I was at an all-girls school. The boys just assumed they were right.' 'If we did plays with boys they'd get all the best parts.' Occasional parental complaints of school inflexibility over rules and regulations.

Pastoral Care and Discipline: Praise for the pastoral care system, beefed up in recent years and designed to pick up problems early. 'If a girl's work isn't going well it's often because she's fallen out with friends or has pressure at home. We have a strong tutorial system which ensures that no-one slips through the net.' 'The pastoral care teams are really on the ball and pick up on events before they get out of proportion,' agreed a parent. Girls entering year 7 are allotted a 'buddy' from the year above to look after them for the first few weeks, and sixth formers are trained as peer counsellors. Behaviour, said a recent Independent Schools Inspectorate report, is 'exemplary', though parents comment that free spirits are not well tolerated by some of the staff.

Pupils and Parents: Around a third Jewish and a third other ethnic minorities, mostly Asian. Not overtly rich – the minority with oodles of dosh are counterbalanced by large numbers of girls on generous bursaries. The catchment area extends from Northwood to Islington, along the school bus routes which encompass Radlett, Hampstead, Highgate, Kentish Town, St John's Wood and Queens Park – a large proportion of the north London intelligentsia. But the diligent, hard-working girls from solid professional families in the surrounding suburbs form the core of the school's intake. Old Girls include Stevie Smith, Marie Stopes, Helen Gardner, Judith Weir, Esther Rantzen, Eleanor Bron, Barbara Amiel, not to mention Susie (Fat is a feminist issue) Orbach, who was expelled.

Entrance: Around 40 girls come up from the junior school. Another 65 are chosen by the highly competitive English and maths paper set in common by the North London Girls' Schools' Consortium. Five of so leave after GCSEs (no-one is thrown out for academic reasons), and about 25 come into the sixth form, having sat a testing one-hour paper for each AS level subject.

Exit: All to university: a third or more to Oxbridge, others to medical schools and the old-established universities.

Money Matters: Pays out £250,000 plus in scholarships and bursaries, including music scholarships (grade 6 or 7 probably needed). Has set up a bursaries fund to pay for even more.

Remarks: Academically stunning outer London school in a glorious setting, which is demonstrating its refusal to rest on its laurels by introducing the IB. Ideal for girls confident of their academic ability with a appetite for all the other opportunities too.

NORWICH HIGH SCHOOL FOR GIRLS

Eaton Grove, 95 Newmarket Road, Norwich, Norfolk, NR2 2HU

Tel: 01603 453 265
Fax: 01603 259 891
E-mail: admissions@nor.gdst.net
Website: www.gdst.net/norwich

• Pupils: 650 girls, all day • Ages: 11-18 • Size of sixth form: 160 • Non-denom • Fees: Junior £1,779, senior £2455; plus lunch • Independent • Open days: October

Head: Since 1985, Mrs Valerie Bidwell BA PGCE FRSA (fifties). Read French and German at Newcastle. Taught in two Suffolk schools as they went co-ed before coming here. Tall, enthusiastic, hugely entertaining but a force to be reckoned with. 'She knows everything about all the students, even the ones who left 15 years ago,' say girls, 'she's a good teacher, she'll speak in any language, even Latin and Greek.'

Believes in parental choice but likes girls having freedom from gender stereotyping, 'many are deeply into electronics and the physics syllabus, and no workman will ever fool a girl from this school; she'll know just what the job entails.' Homely head's study with piles of ongoing projects. However, parental criticisms include a sense of some areas of school life being better supported by the head than others – music?

Academic Matters: 'It's cool to work here,' say girls, 'everyone wants to do well.' And they do, with almost all GCSE results A* to C, most of them A* to B, and a third of girls gaining eight or more A and A* grades. At A level two-thirds of results are A or B. Outstanding ICT results – all girls take GCSE two years early in year 9, over half, 75 per cent in 2002, achieve A or A*. 'They need these skills for their GCSE coursework, why wait?' says head. Four main IT suites and computers with specialised software in departments. European Computer Driving Licence at sixth form.

'The teaching is interactive and vigorous,' says head, 'anybody learns best by doing. The really bright cookies do Greek; very good for the academic mind.' Designated learning support teacher. Impressive creations from the DT department where a large mirror hangs beneath a notice that says, 'Here's a picture of the sort of student who'll do really well at GCSE or A Level Design Tech at Norwich High School.' DT lunch club regularly has 'Sorry, Full' on the door.

'We move mountains to give the girls their choices at GCSE and A level,' says head, and some courses have run with just one or two students. Settled staff with two-thirds over 40, many in place for at least a dozen years.

Games, Options, The Arts: Tennis courts and pitches flank the buildings. Good lacrosse but teams travel miles for suitable competition. Hockey has been re-introduced. Superb 25-metre pool, swimming taught to lifesaving levels. Some 40 girls involved in rowing, 'supported by brilliant parents. We enjoy the buzz of competing but the Wensum isn't quite the Thames – we're always glad not to come last,' says head. Community Sports Leader award. Good D of E, Young Enterprise.

Strong and inspirational music includes performances in the glorious Norwich Cathedral. Some projects with the Norwich School (boys). Large new performing arts studio. Good careers department in lofty garret, includes personality testing. Visiting speakers to inspire older girls.

Background and Atmosphere: Founded in 1875 (the first GDST outside London). Main building is Eaton Grove, an attractive Regency house. 'The heating is either on or off,' say girls, 'but we love the old parts of the building.' Particularly gracious bay window in studious Jameson library. Navy and green tartan uniform, pinafores for juniors, kilts 'which blow up in the wind' for lower seniors and straight skirts 'which you can't walk in' for upper seniors. All seem quite happy with charmingly old fashioned lengths. Sixth form dress supposed to be appropriate for a managerial job, seems relaxed. Casual, vibrant sixth form common room where microwave is a hit and profits from football table go to charity.

Pastoral Care and Discipline: House system called companies. Care through staff and mentoring across the years. Girls feel well cared for. Sixth formers help in junior school. Head girl and deputies elected by peers and staff, attend GDST head girls' conference. 'There are lots of moral guidelines, Christian-based assemblies and a good Christian union,' say girls. Sanctions include day suspension for misdemeanours such as theft, 'they soon get the message,' says head. And catch up time during Friday lunch break. Breakfast club from 7.45am, teas until 5pm and Bishy Barney Bees juniors after-school care until 6pm.

Pupils and Parents: Hard working girls from middle class homes. Very few from ethnic minorities, but four times more than Norfolk demographics. Many parents connected with nearby University of East Anglia, lots of second and third generation girls. Attracts girls from wide area but most within 15-mile radius. Buses, and mini bus service from station. Notable OGs include authors Pat Barr, Anne Weale,

Stella Tillyard, Raffaella Barker and Jane Hissey, soprano Jane Manning, dress designer Ann Tyrell, scientist Dr Jenny Moyle and composer Diana Burrell.

Entrance: At 11 by exam, one and a half applicants per place. Some at sixth form, needing six A-C grades at GCSE and As or Bs in A level subjects.

Exit: From sixth form most to university. Enormous spread of locations and courses. Some join boys for local co-ed sixth forms or go elsewhere to be closer to home.

Money Matters: Annually approx 15 means-tested bursaries and a few academic or music scholarships at head's discretion. Hasn't fully replaced 200 former Assisted Places.

Remarks: Happy and enthusiastic school where girls can achieve highly. Charming, unspoilt girls, without airs and graces.

NOTRE DAME SENIOR SCHOOL

Linked to Notre Dame Preparatory School in the Junior section

Burwood House, Convent Lane, Cobham, Surrey, KT11 1HA

Tel: 01932 869 990

Fax: 01932 589 481

E-mail: headmistress@notredame.co.uk

Website: www.notredame.co.uk

- Pupils: 375 girls, all day • Ages: 11-18 • Size of sixth form: 50
- RC • Fees: £3,180 • Independent • Open days: June, October, November, March

Head: Since 2003, Mrs Bridget Williams MA (forties). Previous headship at St Mary's Convent, Worcester. Moved back to Surrey for family reasons. Married with son and daughter (at Notre Dame). A softly spoken, honest and open lady who is smart, efficient and friendly. Her faith and the spiritual ethos of the school are important to her. She quickly gets to know pupils and their parents and still teaches quite a lot because she 'enjoys exchange and interchange with young people.' Has worked hard to increase academic standards.

Academic Matters: A wide range of abilities catered for and lots of emphasis on getting the best from each girl. Mrs W keen to emphasise that 'the school has the highest value-added in Surrey'. There's not a huge amount of academic pressure, but academic standards gradually rising – Mrs W describes them as 'already very high,' helped by new initiatives such as extra tuition and Easter revision classes. 50 plus per cent A/B pass rate at A level: there are bright sparks at the school – girls in the top 5 in the country for A level English literature and history. Sixth form is relatively small and A level options can be limited due to the size – however, big plans for growth.

School deserves a pat on the back for bucking the trend for sciences in girls' schools. Although the facilities, especially for physics, are ancient in the extreme – Mrs W prefers to describe them as 'needing up-dating and there are plans for a new building' – an increasing number of girls choose to study science to A level and results are improving. Mrs W says 'The school is at the forefront of science teaching – we teach and train the teachers of other schools in the area.' There are already biotechnology workshops and head sees science as a big growth area for the school and will back this up with future investment.

Everyone does theology and all take GCSE in religious studies. French, German and Spanish from year 7 (Latin available) Italian as an optional extra at lower sixth. Exchange trips with sister schools overseas reinforce language provision. Good design & technology (food and textiles) with large, well resourced rooms. Average class size 17, although they can get quite large and some reach 23 – a bit too large some would say. However classes split into tutorial groups and set by end of year 7 in English, maths, languages, sciences, history and geography. SEN provision is limited. Entrance tests used to reveal learning difficulties. Mild dyslexia and dyspraxia catered for. Two part-time specialist teachers, but a very small number of girls receive extra help.

Games, Options, The Arts: Everyone involved in Sport for All – swimming, tennis, athletics, rounders, netball, fitness, dance, cross country – all compulsory. Netball v strong with tours to Tobago and Grenada. Full-sized heated indoor swimming pool, which is looking a bit worn at the edges – Mrs W says 'refurbishment is scheduled'. Super sports hall. Parents comment that sporting facilities need more investment – they are putting their hands in their pockets to fund raise for a new health and fitness suite. Better use could be made of outdoor space – there are three tennis courts, running track and area for playing lacrosse, but no Astro turf pitch or hockey pitch although there's plenty of room for them.

Art is exceptionally strong and is held as a model of good practice by examining boards (OCR and EdExcel both use photos of pupils' work as examples in their booklets). The pupils' beautiful artwork decorates the school walls and is updated yearly. Currently two art rooms, but facilities could be improved. New kiln and dark room planned. Drama is well resourced -one large production each year and pro-

ductions taken to Edinburgh Fringe Festival.

Investment in music is evident, including music technology equipment and loads of different instruments. Everyone gets the opportunity to learn a musical instrument from a vast range taught by peripatetic teachers. Successful string orchestra and choir – but be prepared for religious element to singing groups – it may put some girls off. Few after school clubs. Mrs W says 'Parents choose to pay for their daughters to use a coach to travel to and from school – thus after school clubs are limited.'

Background and Atmosphere: First and foremost a Catholic community with a strong family value: parents agree that the head is 'bringing faith and spiritualism to the forefront again.' The school was opened on its present site in Cobham in 1937 and is part of a worldwide educational order, The Company of Mary Our Lady. The core of the school is the rather beautiful Burwood House where four elderly nuns remain in the convent and from which the junior school is run. However, a maze of large modern blocks attached to the house has overshadowed it. Stunning library which is resourced to a very high standard and employs two librarians. A mezzanine floor houses the new sixth form study area that any university would be proud of. Real wow factor here. Classrooms are tidy, well maintained and spacious. Girls move about the school in a polite, quiet and orderly fashion, and the atmosphere is calm.

The prep school and senior school are inextricably linked (prep school girls regularly use senior facilities and vice versa) – girls move easily between the two schools through a large adjoining corridor. Communal chapel sits between the two. Security around the school is tight. Not near any public transport, seven coach routes laid on from the surrounding areas- for very local families these can be pricey. Alternative is the school run – cars nose to tail down a v narrow road to the school. Children of working parents can use the breakfast club open at 8am. Study centre stays open until 5.45 for late leavers.

Pastoral Care and Discipline: Strong pastoral care and a routine of regular contact, including personal, social and health education forms part of every day. School chaplain lives on site and is available for chats. Supportive mentoring system. A nice touch is the blue post boxes discreetly scattered about the school where girls can post slips asking mentors for help of any kind. Parents say new girls settle in well – (particularly important for the 30 or so who are not from the prep school) helped by 'big sister' scheme where each lower sixth girl is given responsibility for four year 7 girls. This scheme also operates if your daughter joins later up the school.

Pupils and Parents: Although strongly Roman Catholic (with attendance at mass and assemblies compulsory), the school does not discourage pupils from other denominations. In fact, no more than 50 per cent of the pupils are RC. The girls are beautifully turned out and uniform guidelines are strict. Hair tied back and no jewellery except a cross if wanted. Any holes in tights are fixed at reception.

Many families dual income professional in and around Cobham, Walton, Weybridge and Esher areas. Majority are British, but strong multicultural feel which parents regard as a plus (constant turnover of ex-pats from around the world) and some celebs (Chelsea football training grounds are just down the road). School has a long history of charitable involvement in the community and all girls are encouraged to take part.

Entrance: Entrance exam at 11: English, maths, verbal or non-verbal reasoning (non-verbal for girls with learning difficulties). Past papers not available. Of the 72 places available, approx 40 are filled from own prep school. General feeling among the prep school parents is that new head 'wants to make the senior school stand out academically' with no longer the guarantee that prep school girls automatically have a place in the senior. Competition for the remaining places comes from up to 20 different schools including Danesfield Manor, The Ursuline Prep, The Study Wimbledon and Holy Cross Prep Kingston. Spaces become available in all years – quite a transient parent population– so always worth a try. Entrants into sixth form need a minimum of five or six subjects at C grade or above (B grades for the subjects to be taken at AS level).

Exit: After GCSEs, a hefty number of leavers (Mrs W does not accept the word 'hefty') – between 30 and 50 per cent – move to pastures new to experience co-ed sixth forms or to increase their A level options. Big financial input into sixth form resources may encourage more to stay. Post A level most opt for higher education: universities include Oxford Brookes, Surrey and Leeds.

Money Matters: A number of short-term bursaries which are based on personal hardship. Limited number of scholarships into year 7 and the sixth form, these vary and can be up to 50 per cent of the fees. Also some special awards into the sixth form linked to a particular talent or expertise such as music, drama or sport.

Remarks: A solid, all round, school with an orderly, nurturing atmosphere and a head who is pushing to drive up academic standards (not least to boost the numbers in the sixth form).

NOTTING HILL AND EALING HIGH SCHOOL

Linked to Notting Hill and Ealing High School Junior School in the Junior section

2 Cleveland Road, London, W13 8AX

Tel: 020 8799 8400
Fax: 02088 106 891
E-mail: m.cleary@nhehs.gdst.net
Website: www.nhehs.gdst.net

• Pupils: 560 girls, all day • Ages: 11-18 • Size of sixth form: 140 • Non-denom • Fees: Junior school £2383 per term, senior school £3063 per term • Independent

Head: Since 1991, Mrs S M Whitfield (late fifties). Read natural sciences at Cambridge. Previously taught biology at St Paul's Girls' School. Married with five children. 'She's very eloquent and hearing her talk fills you with confidence,' said a parent.

Academic Matters: Around 85 per cent A* and A grades at GCSE and nearly 90 per cent A/B grades at A level from a range of subjects that now includes psychology and economics. Year 12s also choose a general studies option, which could range from jewellery-making to Greek. Class sizes 28 – 29 in year 7, though about half the subjects are taught in smaller groups. Maths is setted by ability from year 8. Many excellent teachers, with a new, younger influx as long-standing teachers leave.

The school can deal with mild dyslexia and dyspraxia. 'We look for it, and when we find it we try to make sure we give the best help we can.' Parents praise the school for its breadth of education, with plenty extra-curricular opportunities, but are uneasy about variations in teaching standards – the head feels that they are no greater than in most other schools. Some mention infelicitous responses to complaints when problems arise. 'I don't feel that my complaints are taken seriously,' said one parent, reflecting a fairly widespread feeling. The head comments that every school has issues, and she feels that they are addressed wherever possible.

Games, Options, The Arts: Plenty of trips abroad, with artists going to New York, geographers to Iceland and Spanish students to Madrid and Barcelona. There are also museum visits, maths challenge competitions, Duke of Edinburgh expeditions, sports fixtures and drama performances. Sports facilities on-site include a gym, netball/tennis courts and a new indoor swimming pool; sixth formers are trained and employed as professional lifeguards. Hockey, rounders and athletics at a sports ground a mile away. Around half of the girls play a musical instrument, and there are orchestras, choirs and ensemble groups. There is a successful Amnesty International group; girls have raised funds for a school in Tanzania and an arts centre in Uganda.

Background and Atmosphere: The West Wing, completed in 2003, provides new art rooms, including a sixth form studio, a recital hall with recording studio and splendid acoustics, several other music rooms, and new English classrooms. 'We now have three large spaces: the main hall, the gym and the recital hall.' There are four new computer rooms, including a PC-based language room with specialist software. The GDST is installing broadband in all its schools.

One parent said: 'It does offer a wide education in the broadest sense. It's been a lovely environment for my daughter to grow and flourish as an individual.'

Pastoral Care and Discipline: Generally happy and motivated with few discipline problems. 'I've always been very keen on pastoral care. With five children of my own, it matters to me how they are seen as individuals. The academic and the pastoral go hand in hand. There are some boundaries a school has to impose, and we make these clear. How can young people operate within them unless they know what they are?'

Pupils and Parents: Broad social and cultural mix of mostly local families, including many of Eastern European and Asian extraction. Girls emerge articulate and confident, full of west London sophistication, but without the trendy, street-wise demeanour characteristic of pupils of other local establishments. OGs include Angela Rumbold, writer and TV presenter Bettany Hughes and Blue Peter's Konnie Huq.

Entrance: Competitive consortium examination in maths and English plus interview. About half come up from the junior school. Sixth form applicants sit entrance exams in their potential A level subjects plus a general paper; they're expected to get at least 7 B grades, with As in their A level subjects. Most go through to the sixth form.

Exit: Varying, but increasing, numbers move on after GCSE to eg Latymer Upper or Richmond College – a trend not uncommon in girls' schools. Courses range from civil and architectural engineering at Bath to molecular and cellular biochemistry at Oxford; art foundation courses are also popular.

Remarks: Popular and over-subscribed GDST day school, valued for its high academic standards without undue pressure.

NOTTINGHAM HIGH SCHOOL

Linked to Nottingham High Junior School in the Junior section

Waverley Mount, Nottingham, Nottinghamshire, NG7 4ED

Tel: 0115 978 6056
Fax: 0115 924 9716
E-mail: info@notthigh.rmplc.co.uk
Website: www.nottinghamhigh.co.uk

• Pupils: 847 boys, all day • Ages: 11-18 • Size of sixth form: 212 • Fees: Senior: £2,798. Junior: £2,271 • Independent • Open days: Mid November

Head: Since 1995, Mr Chris Parker CBE BA FRSA (fifties), educated at Windsor Grammar School read geography at Bristol University and studied for his PGCE at St Catharine's College, Cambridge. Previously head of Batley Grammar School. Married to Maggie who donated the Margaret Parker cup for individual verse speaking and takes a cookery club for y8 boys; two grown up sons. Speaks with genuine pride about his boys, knows most individually and they're comfortable with him. Says, 'boys refuel you – when you're tired, you pick up energy from them and qualities – they give so generously.' Some boys say head is out of school a lot (head agrees – chairs lots of committees and works on various projects – including assisted places and independent/state school partnerships). They add that discipline is tight and they know what won't be tolerated – but think head runs school very well and say staff he's brought in have upped the ante.

Retiring at Easter 2007.

Academic Matters: This is not a swot-house, boys don't need to be force-fed facts and figures; they are capable of independent thought and enquiry, encouraged to challenge accepted doctrine and discover the joys of serious thought and intellectual discussion. Boys say 'school has a reputation of taxing, challenging work but you find you can do it and teachers will help if you have difficulties'. All pass – 70 per cent of GCSE entries graded A/A* and commendable 80-ish per cent of A levels graded A/B. Enter lots of academic competitions – maths challenge, maths Olympiad (highest scorers), Engineer for Britain (winner most innovative award), physics and biology Olympiads (gold medal winners), to name but a few. Super well-kept facilities (save the odd bag strewn on the floor), school has many generous benefactors and it shows. Wireless networked throughout, interactive technology, super library with own laptops, DVDs, periodicals, new arts centre, well equipped labs, DT centre etc.

Class size varies from 16 to 26 reducing to fewer than 10 in the sixth form. Lots of fizzy teaching – use technology and skills to make lessons come alive: practical demonstrations and the concrete even extend to A level mechanics – believe it's important to appreciate practical applications. Older pupils expected to research, plan, and take model lessons – it enhances understanding, makes them think. Pupils clearly appreciate dedication of staff who willingly give up free time to help boys both academically and with extra-curricular activities (45 staff assist with games alone.)

Head, a keen champion of special needs, brought in enthusiastic and very capable head of learning support who has done much rapidly to transform attitudes – lots of inset and training on learning styles, kinaesthetic learning etc. Not only have old-school staff embraced provision but children are gaining confidence to self-refer. School identifies 70 children as being in need of additional help or support, majority are dyslexics but there are a handful of dyspraxics and smattering of Aspergers, ADD, ADHD. Head fighting off those staff keen to offer extra help and support. No additional charge for those requiring 1 to 1 though outside help such as occupational therapy will incur a fee. They stress that the main thing is pupils requiring additional support are able to achieve. Say to pupils, 'this is you, this is your profile, you can give up, or go for it.' They go for it – SEN input reaping rewards.

Games, Options, The Arts: School motto: Together Everyone Achieves More (TEAM) summarises the spirit of the school. All are encouraged to do far more than pursue academic interests and virtually all do. Games and music are the mainstay but not the only offerings. Chess plays a large part in school life and the school boasts national champions and international representation across several age groups. Very good facilities – large sports hall, climbing wall, full size swimming pool and excellent multi-gym puts many leisure centres to shame – there's even a TV to take your mind off going the extra mile. The school's first-rate sports pitches are located a short bus-ride away and are used for school matches as well as area and national trials and training; astro-turf and additional tennis courts on the wish list. Sport is an important part of the boys' education – don't gloat over victories, happy to accept defeat. Rugby (couple of international players) and swimming particularly successful (lots of cups) but sports such as orienteering (national champions) get a look-in too. Trying to encourage and develop sport for all, especially for those where enthusiasm exceeds talent or who have difficulties such as dys-

praxia. Music is active, alive and practical, numbers opting for GCSE shooting up, lots of bands (big band medal winners in Boosey and Hawkes competition), choirs, performing opportunities and now latest computer equipment adding a new dimension to music technology. Trips and tours aplenty.

Background and Atmosphere: Founded in 1513 by Dame Agnes Mellers (with help of Sir Thomas Lovell) after the death of her husband, Richard, partly in his memory but also as an act of atonement for his several wrongdoings against the people of Nottingham with the foundation deed sealed by King Henry VIII in the November. Moved to its present pleasant site in 1868. A long programme of building and development results in today's facilities. Immediate area not the most salubrious – a police raid was taking place opposite the school on the day of our visit and ladies of the night are known to pound the nearby streets (school say police efforts reducing the problem) but, apart from odd incident of graffiti, school appears to escape the downfall of its near neighbours.

Pastoral Care and Discipline: Plenty of graduated awards for good work, helping out etc. Celebrate, enjoy and respect success at any level – not just rugger buggers – mutual respect, family feel. Head or deputy sees those with 10 or more distinctions. All belong to a form and a tutor group. Forms have a horizontal structure but crux is the carefully thought-out vertically operated tutor-system – tutor even phones parents to invite them to the introductory parents' evening – get to know families as well as boys. No detentions for y7 but one boy reported that 'detention runs from y8 to y11' which we thought a bit excessive! Tutor often the one batting for a boy when chips are down. Students encouraged to seek help, support or advice from any of the school nurse, tutor, form teacher, head of year, form prefect, school counsellor or other person they trust – school medical service open daily. Compulsory testing for suspected drug misuse. Bullying of all kinds dealt with promptly, boys encouraged to report all, however trivial, and certainly the many children we spoke to agreed bullying wasn't a problem, saying they felt the tutor system, where they got to know boys from all years, really helped.

Sixth formers are expected to act as role models for those younger than themselves. Usual opportunities for leadership, and for personal and social development offered through CCF, Duke of Edinburgh, young enterprise, business leadership scheme or as prefects. In addition, the organisation of house teams and events relies solely on the initiative of sixth formers and this is serious stuff – everything from four part choirs to producing, directing and coordinating up to 50 youngsters at a time in the uniquely inventive and dramatic verse-speaking competitions. Dire threats issued to those who might think about skiving a rehearsal or two. Plenty of joint activities with Nottingham Girls' High School: politics society, arts society, drama club and explorer scout unit as well as a couple of balls and an annual major dramatic production.

Pupils and Parents: A genuinely mixed bag – offspring of millionaires to those in care. From a wide geographical area: Nottingham, Bakewell, Loughborough, Leicestershire. 50 per cent from own junior school, 15 per cent from other independent schools, rest from state primaries. Twenty per cent identify their ethnic mix as other than white but fewer than 4 per cent have English as an additional language. Boys smartly dressed in blazers distinguished by house ties, suits in the sixth form (tufty tie for those who gain a minimum 10 grade A GCSEs), say they feel privileged to have a first-rate education and fantastic opportunities. These are genuinely grounded, rounded individuals with bags of personality and myriads of interests, not a swot in sight – we doubt arrogance, even a mild dose, would be tolerated by anyone. Many have a string of successes to their bow – grade 8 instrumentalists, national representation in the sporting, academic, and musical world but they don't let on – they present as great lads, able to hold their own in conversation and debate but with a wicked sense of humour and lovely ability to poke fun at themselves – what more could you ask? A sample of famous old Nottinghamians include Edward Balls, Jesse Boot, Kenneth Clarke, Geoff Hoon, Robert MacFarlane (author) and Andrew Turner (Olympic hurdler).

Entrance: Majority at 11 a few at 16. Occasional places available at other ages. Tests for all in English, maths and verbal reasoning, plus short interview for non-junior boys. Details about the exam are sent out in January prior to September entry. Advise all to visit school on open day in November. Entry to sixth form is by interview and achievement at GCSE, sixth form open evening held early October. Don't admit boys they feel wouldn't be happy.

Exit: Small number (between 5 and 10) leave after GCSEs. Large numbers to Oxbridge, 11 to Cambridge alone in 2004, most of rest to wide range of Russell group of universities studying for traditional gold standard degrees. Birmingham, Leeds, Manchester, Newcastle popular.

Money Matters: Generous means-tested bursaries (up to 100 per cent of fees) available at head's discretion. Believes any boy who is able should be given all the assistance necessary to attend the school. Ogden bursaries and HSBC provide 50 per cent which school must match plus

additional help (if needed) via a one-off grant to offset start-up costs such as school uniform. School financially secure enough that no boy will be turned away because of a lack of funds.

Remarks: A very good school, hard to fault. Media studies types should look elsewhere though media types would do very well. Only for the seriously bright with personality and plethora of pursuits and passions.

NOTTINGHAM HIGH SCHOOL FOR GIRLS GDST

Linked to Nottingham High School for Girls Junior School GDST in the Junior section

9 Arboretum Street, Nottingham, Nottinghamshire, NG1 4JB

Tel: 0115 941 7663
Fax: 0115 924 0757
E-mail: enquiries@not.gdst.net
Website: www.gdst.net/nottinghamgirlshigh

- Pupils: 820 in senior school of whom 220 are in sixth form
- Ages: 11-18 • Size of sixth form: 220 • Non-denominational
- Fees: Senior £2,455; Junior £1,779 • Independent • Open days: November

Head: From 2006, Mrs Sue Gorham BA MA (early fifties), head at Burgess Hill (qv) since 2001 and previously deputy head at Dame Alice Harpur School. Educated at Manchester University (BA in French) and the Open University (MA in education management). Has three children at university and is married to a senior lecturer at the Open University. Took over Burgess Hill when it was successfully coasting along, applying a more dynamic approach and tightening up on discipline – but, as the new girl, had been watching from the wings before making major changes. Comments on her reign at BH include: 'very approachable' (according to staff and the girls); welcomes calls from parents – 'immediate feedback helps to defuse any problems or resentments'; would like to think that her pupils get as much pleasure from an E grade as an A grade (providing that this reflects their potential); feels that one of her strengths is spotting potential during selection interviews.

Academic Matters: Sits comfortably in the higher echelons of the league tables. 75 per cent plus A/B at A level; all study and pass 9 GCSEs with 80-ish per cent of entries graded A* or A. Average class size 25, relatively stable staff though sufficient turnover to ensure steady injection of new blood. Results clearly play an important part. Parents feel there's an over-insistence on everyone doing well all the time – easy to feel like a failure if you get an A not an A*. It makes those who are a little bit unsure feel less confident but, parents add, 'it's better to have high expectations and odd upset than not have pressure at all.' School says, 'we do let up eg after exams and at the ends of term when we do pantomimes and other silly things ... much of the pressure comes from the parents.' Most say they are well-taught and staff work hard to make their subject enjoyable – 'I'm starting to try again.' Sixth formers comment that, 'school makes you fulfil your potential even if you don't want to.' Some younger ones feel there's too much instruction in lessons; older girls say they're encouraged to question and to challenge as they progress through the school.

Many facilities – comfortable rather than state of the art – and include a well-stocked library with several computers for student use, separate careers library, modern lecture theatre, large drama studio, recently refurbished music house and well equipped medical centre. Sixth form has own facilities, no wireless network or interactive whiteboards, but school is fully networked. All usual subjects available, modern languages choice of: Spanish, German, Russian and French, Latin and Greek. Wide selection of A level subjects including psychology, economics and sociology; all take general studies.

Homework a source of angst – parents say girls get too much – but accept that it's a selective and competitive environment so a necessary evil. Pupils add homework causes friction at home especially at weekends – eats into family activity time. After-school club until 5.30 for those who want it.

35 children currently feature on the learning support register, majority have dyslexia or dyspraxia but also caters for profoundly deaf and mild visual impairments. Any specialist individual tuition incurs an extra charge.

Games, Options, The Arts: Wide range of activities – dance, chess, debating, drama/theatre studies, Duke of Edinburgh, life saving/first aid, orchestra/band, outdoor pursuits, practical engineering, skiing, young enterprise allows girls to have fun. Range of sports facilities includes newish sports hall with viewing gallery, gym, fitness centre, large all-weather pitch, and sports field a bus ride away. No swimming pool so use one at the nearby boys' school. Lots of sports, netball and tennis (currently U16 national netball champions, national finalists and loads of county players), plus national representation in hockey, netball and badminton, large range of other sports on offer. Bands, choirs, concerts and plays provide performing opportunities –

including joint ventures with the boys' school. Expeditions and strong house system hosting numerous competitions such as debating, general knowledge.

Background and Atmosphere: Founded in 1875, situated just north of the City of Nottingham. Originally housed in a group of Victorian mansions, the school, an incongruous mix of old and new buildings, has expanded and sprawls across both sides of a fairly quiet road, each part impersonally referred to as A block B block etc. This is a big school in a grotty part of town (improving says school) where nearby sign announces the number of kerb crawlers arrested the previous month. Parents comment compact grounds leave something to be desired, facilities frayed and corridors tired but new administrator is overseeing rolling programme of refurbishment, which has now started in earnest.

Pastoral Care and Discipline: Pastoral care is good – school expects girls to fire on all cylinders all of the time and provides help and support to ensure they do. Staff very encouraging when working hard but some parents feel pressure shouldn't always be on full pelt – good to let go occasionally. Head will write to parents and look for different strategies to assist any girl thought to be falling by the wayside. Discipline matters dealt with swiftly, aim to get a girl back on track – rely heavily on peer group pressure to make a girl want to do well. Drug related issues taken and dealt with very seriously. Girls involved in writing of anti-bullying policy – bullying box emptied by school nurses. New girls seamlessly integrated. Younger pupils comment many teachers are strict and scary but no such feeling in sixth form.

The new dining hall provides snacks and meals throughout the day with breakfast available for pupils and parents. Packed lunches permitted and special dietary requirements catered for. Wide selection of the healthy and the not so but we think Jamie Oliver would mostly approve. Several vending machines around school sell chocolate and fizzy drinks – school jury out on whether they should stay or go.

Pupils and Parents: Parents socially a mixed bag, majority lives within a 20 mile radius of the school. Caters for all types of personalities from make-up brigade at one end to country girls at the other; school lets girls be themselves so a few wonderful eccentrics among the flock but shy overwhelmed. Active parent/teacher association supports the school. Head reports good relations with nearby boys' school. Famous OGs Stella Rimmington, Julie Myerson, Helen Cresswell.

Entrance: At 11 by interview and a written test (including maths and English) designed to identify potential and understanding. Occasional places available at other times in other years. At 16 entry is by interview, report from current school plus a minimum of 8 GCSEs (average grade B), usually with grades A or B in subjects to be studied.

Part of the GDST which aims to provide an all round education for girls of intellectual promise, at an affordable cost.

Exit: About 10 per cent leave after GCSE some to go to sixth form college, some to co-ed a number choosing the state sector. Several take a gap year prior to university.

Money Matters: A number of scholarships worth up to 50 per cent of fees are awarded at 11 and 16. Scholarships are awarded solely on the basis of academic merit not means- tested. Additionally, the GDST Minerva Fund provides bursaries on the basis of financial need though academic merit is taken into account. Good value for money.

Remarks: Takes academic work very seriously but plenty going on outside the classroom too. Parents sigh with relief when girls are offered a place, saying, 'it's a very nice school if you can cope with the pressure.' We have high hopes for the new head.

OAKHAM SCHOOL

Chapel Close, Oakham, Rutland, LE15 6DT

Tel: 01572 758758
Fax: 01572 758595
E-mail: admissions@oakham.rutland.sch.uk
Website: www.oakham.rutland.sch.uk

- Pupils: 545 boys, 530 girls; 50 per cent board, 50 per cent day
- Ages: 10-18 • Size of sixth form: 350 • C of E • Fees: Jerwoods - day £3,880; day boarding £4,970; boarding £6,110. Upper/middle school - day £4,270; day boarding £ £5,740; boarding £7,140 • Independent • Open days: See website

---

Headmaster: Since 2002, Dr Joseph Spence BA PhD (mid forties. A powerhouse with immense charm. From 1992-2002, Dr Spence was Master in College at Eton ie had charge of the scholars – one of the top academic jobs in independent education. A history and politics graduate, Dr Spence is a polymath who also writes and directs plays, plays sport 'quite well', is knowledgeable about and interested in just about everything and is an acknowledged specialist (several books) on Anglo-Irish history and culture. Thus the ideal head of a school in which, traditionally, 'the total curriculum' was the by-word. He has quickly got to

grips with the school and, while revelling in the excellence of the sporting, musical and other activities he inherited, emphasises 'the primacy of the classroom' and now sees work 'at the heart of the total curriculum'. While at Eton he had to work to get the scholars involved with extra-curricular life, here it has been something of the other way round. However, it's working and they seem to like it! 'Delighted' and 'honest' are frequently used words in the vocabulary of this energetic, direct, highly capable and warmly welcoming head. Pupils who spot him in the Oakham streets wave affectionately. 'You must meet Oakhamians', he enthuses. 'They're having fun and I'm having more fun than all of them.' Married to a lawyer, with a son and daughter at Oakham.

Academic Matters: One of the lowest pupil:teacher ratio we have encountered at just over 7:1 though obviously this varies, depending on year and subject. Average A level class size is 10. It's been all change since 2001 when the IB became an option in the sixth. After a dip in take-up, interest is picking up and the head, wholly committed to it on academic principles, sees A level candidates becoming, eventually, a minority. Good choice of A level and IB subjects with a general spread of take-up. GCSE subjects include very popular art and design, D&T and drama. Not a league table driven school, nonetheless, results have leaped since head's advent to 74 per cent A/B at A level in 2005. Especially good: art, English, French, further maths, history, physics, RS and several minority subjects. IB results in 2005 100 per cent – average worldwide rate is 80 per cent. GCSEs 98 per cent pass rate. History imaginatively presented – wonderfully realistic WW1 trench in head of dept's room plus very lively work on display. Sane policy on ICT – 'it must serve us not master us'. Internet points in every room but school does not provide the lap tops. Good computerised language labs. SEN supported by 'two brilliant teachers' and school moving away from withdrawing to more in-class support. Physical disabilities copeable with onsite but some buildings separated by roads.

Games, Options, The Arts: Interesting to discover what you couldn't do here. 'Sport here is massive' asserted pupil. In addition to the standard sports, a further 30 are offered – cycling, rowing, sailing, shooting, sub aqua, fencing among them. Superb onsite pitches used by county cricket teams – 'it's better than Lords', claimed modestly proud student – 2 Astroturfs, 25 meter pool, fitness centre and 1972 sports hall with weights room and squash courts. Achievements include victory for 1st XV rugby team in Daily Mail U18 national schools rugby cup in 2002 and 2003. 8 England schoolboy rugby internationals since 2000. Past pupils represent country in women's cricket and hockey. Duke of Edinburgh Awards scheme very big here: first school to achieve 1000 D of E golds (in 2001). CCF also strong and we witnessed inspection of massed troops by imposing RSM on our visit.

Music almost as strong. Former head of music J L Dussek 1922-83 commemorated on a plaque – presumably a descendant of Jan Ladislav Dussek? 40 per cent learn instruments, events large and small include concerts at St John's Smith Square, Southwell, Ely. Music tour to South Africa in 2003 leading to links with township schools with whom school shares charitable projects. Orchestras, bands of all kinds. 3 CDs recorded by 2004. Excellent Queen Elizabeth Theatre – like a small professional theatre complete with foyer and bar and displays of ambitious, professional-looking productions. House plays and other shows abound and everyone enthusiastically involved. Both music and drama productions feature at the Edinburgh fringe. Art and design impressive, especially textiles and jewellery to art college standards – highly imaginative and creative work – very popular. Younger pupils encouraged to work alongside older students. Few boy takers at higher levels thus far. Witty work in ceramics and pottery. Superb D & T work – covetable steel and wooden hammocks on display. You want to roll up your sleeves and get in there.

Background and Atmosphere: Founded in 1584, there are still a few reminders of the school's long history in its location in the centre of this prosperous market county town, snug in the truly rolling Rutland hills. The oldest, main parts of the school have the feel of a small Cambridge college – quiet quads, old stone buildings round lawns and immaculate flower beds – civilised, donnish, conducive to study and thought. New status accorded to scholars enshrined in College House – special sanctuary with quiet study areas for those applying to Oxbridge and other high level university courses – at the heart of this carefully laid-out campus. Much is owed to pioneering head, John Buchanan, whose tenure from 1958-77 oversaw move to full independence and coeducation as well as landscaped garden feel of the whole site. Present head relishes day/boarding mix and the centrality of school to town, 'we're not a capsule-like school in Oakham town that has nothing to do with it'. No weekly boarding offered here, 'this is a full boarding school for its 550 boarders,' says head and day pupils often appear to join in activities on Sundays. Day boarding, ie two or more stays during the week, a popular option. Atmosphere is civilised, collaborative, appreciative. Boarding is seen as a desirable privilege, 'I wish I'd been a boarder all the way through,' sighed one wistful sixth form recruit.

Subjects taught in, mostly, attractive 2-4 storey, purpose-built blocks, continuing the quadrangular theme, giving feel of small-scale 1960s university campus – but better designed than most. School shop where, according to a cheery sixth former, 'you can buy everything and stick it on the bill. Mum always ends up paying for her birthday card'. Superb Smallbone library – up to public library standards – spacious, well-stocked, computerised – a rare resource. Campus studded with entertaining metal sculptures (watch out for the crocodile!) by visiting Kenyan sculptor. Most boarding houses abut playing fields – peaceful and, again, reminiscent of collegiate Cambridge. All are attractive, well-maintained – large vases of flowers in entrance halls. Trips of all kinds, everywhere and excellent programme of visiting speakers, artists etc. Plans include Jerwood Sphere project – a hoped-for concert hall to serve school plus East Midlands to professional standards together with new teaching accommodation. Also wonderfully enlightened bi-partite 20:20 project – a woodland scheme to inculcate entrepreneurism, teamwork and leadership – as well as an African solar power project to provide for a whole village. Mind-broadening stuff.

Pastoral Care and Discipline: Pupils express confidence in carefully structured pastoral system – not just a written policy but one which actually does what it is designed to do. A few drugs-related incidents since Dr Spence's arrival but he relies on a policy of testing pupils if worrying reports reach him and collaboration with home. 'I'm a comfortable convert to the right to give someone a second chance – so long as they understand the policy.... I feel we've got a pretty clean campus.' A rather more honest and realistic approach than many. Super boarding houses and, unusually, all house staff also on teaching staff. Programme of room refurbishment continues and new accommodation is being built for 7th form girls and style moving from youth hostel functionality to home-like comfort. All year 13s to have own study bedroom. Lots of common rooms and meeting areas. Huge choice of excellent food in civilised dining rooms – allergy warnings on walls.

Pupils and Parents: Boys and girls, day and boarding equally mixed. Boarders mostly from 1-3 hours drive though a few from Fife to Hampshire. 85 foreign nationals from 30+ countries – numbers of Germans – direct train to Stansted helps here. 70 expat children. Day and boarding pupils from 50+ preps and juniors but largest number from Jerwoods – onsite junior school. Recent OOs include media personalities Julia Carling and Charlotte Uhlenbroek; theatre folk Katie Mitchell, Greg Hicks and Matthew MacFadyen, and international sports stars Lewis Moody, Lucy Pearson and Crista Cullen. First OO fellow of All Souls, Philip Woolfe, elected in 2003.

Entrance: Exams at 11+ (maths, English and VR), 13+ or CE (55 per cent expected though rare exceptions made for those who 'have something to offer even if they don't quite make it'. Siblings looked upon kindly. Commitment matters as does sufficient ability, 'I'm interested in people who are going to be with us from 11 or 13 until 18. I don't want to be a culler at 16,' asserts head. At 16+, minimum of 7 good GCSEs (4 As and 3 Bs) .

Exit: All but a few to higher education and a vast range of places and courses. 2005 saw 13 Oxbridge offers and large numbers to Leeds, Newcastle, Nottingham, Durham and handfuls to Bristol, Loughborough, UCL. Business management, history, economics popular but everything else from African studies to sports science.

Money Matters: Remarkably (reasonably, says school) well-endowed. Generous spread of scholarships, exhibitions, bursaries at 11, 13 and 16 for general ability and specific talents, including sports, drama, A & D, D & T, music and chess. A new bursaries policy seeks to offer funding where most needed.

Remarks: A privileged – but unpretentious and non-spoiling start in life for the lucky. All-rounders who also like work will get the best out of it but most will love every minute here. The place somehow summed up in the fact that a new rugby coach has started a Chaucer-reading prize.

OBAN HIGH SCHOOL

Soroba Road, Oban, Argyll, PA34 4JB

Tel: 01631564231/2/3
Fax: 01631 565 916
E-mail: enquiries@obanhigh.argyll-bute.sch.uk
Website: www.obanhigh.argyll-bute.sch.uk

- Pupils: 1,124 boys and girls (capacity 1,300); 75 boarders
- Ages: 11-18 • Size of sixth form: 101 • Non-denom • State

Rector: Since 1998, Mrs Linda Kirkwood BSc (early fifties), formerly head of Dalbeattie High. Strong, dynamic leadership, firm but friendly approach. Head has worked hard to create a pupil-centred environment, operates an open-door policy. Changes introduced are generally viewed positively, though some staff reportedly feeling the pressure.

Academic Matters: Full range of subjects offered at Standard Grade, Highers and Higher Still, including Gaelic. Results significantly above average for Scottish State Schools in most subjects. Good emphasis on the academic. Effective learning support operates for those with records of needs or specific learning difficulties. ICT is taught in five well-equipped rooms but other departments have good access to the school's many computer facilities. Class sizes generally smaller than in most state schools, average 23 for academic and 20 for practical subjects.

Games, Options, The Arts: Large games hall, well-equipped dance/fitness studio, two gyms, wide range of sports available including sailing, climbing and curling. Football and badminton popular with boys and girls, one pupil is a regular in the Scottish National Badminton team. Plenty of extra-curricular activities on offer, difficulties because of long distances and buses are generally overcome. Older students are encouraged to participate in Duke of Edinburgh Award Scheme. All S1 and S2 pupils learn keyboards, selection of bands and choirs for those who show interest in music.

Background and Atmosphere: The recently completed renovation and rebuilding programme provides a bright, spacious and stimulating learning environment. Lots of informative well-presented displays throughout the school including an imaginative art gallery exhibiting student's creations. Wealth of reminders that this is Scotland's first Eco School, recycling bins everywhere, newly developed, pleasant, peaceful eco garden area for all to enjoy. A healthy eating policy operates and children are encouraged to remain in school at lunchtime. Uniform is largely adhered to with individual styling by some. Pupils say they feel cared for and valued. Functional boarding hostel provides for those residing a long distance from school.

Pastoral Care and Discipline: Comprehensive range of support: each year group has a year head and every child is allocated a guidance teacher with key workers and mentors assigned to those in need. Prefects work with younger pupils. School boasts an attendance officer, health worker and social worker. Good discipline prevails with effective sanctions for those who don't conform. All staff trained in assertive discipline. Successful Truancy Watch scheme operates in conjunction with the local community. Lots of certificates and awards, including trip to Strathclyde Park for winners of 'annual class of the year.'

Pupils and Parents: Majority Scottish, many travelling long distances from North Argyll and the Islands. Famous Old Boys/Girls: Iain Crichton-Smith (writer), Kirsteen Campbell (BBC political correspondent) and Maureen Scanlon (MSP), Shona and Mairi Crawford (British Ladies Ski team) and Lorne MacIntyre (author and journalist).

Entrance: Takes anyone residing within the catchment area and receives and accepts a few placing requests. Twenty-three feeder primary schools.

Exit: Most (90 per cent) remain at school until 17 or 18. Of those taking Highers vast majority continues to higher education, mostly Scottish universities.

Remarks: A good, caring state school.

OLD PALACE SCHOOL OF JOHN WHITGIFT

Linked to Old Palace School of John Whitgift Junior Department in the Junior section

Old Palace Road, Croydon, Surrey, CR0 1AX

Tel: 020 8688 2027
Fax: 02086 805 877
E-mail: info@oldpalace.croydon.sch.uk
Website: www.oldpalace.croydon.sch.uk

• Pupils: 840 day girls • Ages: 4-18 • Size of sixth form: 140
• C of E • Fees: Senior school £2,698 • Independent • Open days: October; sixth form open day in February

Head: Since 2005, Ms Judy Harris (forties). Formerly deputy head at the Abbey School in Reading, where she taught French and PE. Grew up in Purley and went to Croydon High School for Girls.

Academic Matters: Stellar. Around 85 per cent of girls earn As or Bs at A level and this is steady, year after year. School leaflet lists girls who in 2005 earned at least three As at A level with an A at AS – six pages of names. Chemistry the most popular A level subject, politics notably good. However, most other subjects also excel, particularly languages. Latin for all in years 7, 8 and 9. French compulsory through year 9 when girls may switch to German, Spanish, Italian or classical Greek. Routinely wins awards in national essay competition run by Italian embassy. Girls may study for Russian GCSE in the sixth form. Head hopes to expand Japanese tuition and introduce Mandarin Chinese. Handful of girls sit GCSEs in their mother tongue (Gujarati, Bengali, Turkish, Japanese etc). Reasonably broad choice of GCSEs with almost no grades below a C (some years virtually nothing below a B). All girls take A level general studies paper. Brilliant Key Stage 1 and 2 test results in the prep. IT provision getting better and better. Setting for French and maths. Special needs co-ordinator helps small number of girls. EAL teaching available. School owned and administered by Whitgift Foundation which also runs the Croydon boys' schools, Whitgift and Trinity. Class sizes: 26 in the senior school, 24 in the prep, 20 in the pre-prep (max).

Games, Options, The Arts: Emphasis on physical activity for health and fitness rather than blasting the competition on the hockey pitch (lists table tennis among its main games). But these are competitive girls and sport is surprisingly strong. No playing fields, but girls are bused to Trinity School for hockey. Swimming excels in school's heated indoor pool. Netball successful, dance and aerobics popular. Fencing and self-defence recently introduced. In the prep school, girls play netball, swim and take part in athletics. Short tennis introduced when girls are ten(!)

Very hot on speech and drama lessons – virtually all girls in the prep take these and huge numbers earn LAMDA awards. NB Drama examined at GCSE but not A level. Seniors team up with Whitgift and Trinity boys for some dramatic and musical productions, recently 'Taming of the Shrew' and 'Carmina Burana'. School has staged a number of operas and operatic musicals, including 'The Magic Flute' and' The Beggars Opera'. Impressive steel band. All girls learn recorder in year 2 and in year 3 they are offered a year's instrumental tuition free of charge. Chess very strong in the prep and becoming more so in the senior school (head considering offering a chess scholarship). Good range of prep school clubs, including cookery and photography, some taking girls on a rota so everyone gets a go. Art proficient and beautifully presented through the school. Rich mix of extra-curricular offerings to stimulate the brain eg Young Enterprise, debating, English reading group with Trinity School, careers evenings. Huge take-up for D of E (almost 100 per cent to at least bronze).

Background and Atmosphere: Rose-decked oasis in the middle of a grotty (school says 'historic') part of Croydon. English Heritage site in conservation area with parts going back a thousand years to when in 1070 King William granted the Manor of Croydon to Archbishop Lanfranc. Medieval Banqueting Hall, a 15th century wonder, used for assemblies and prep school PE. Library housed in the Guard Room where the young James I of Scotland was held prisoner. A very tight ship where everything has been painstakingly crafted to make the most of inner-city campus. School has undergone enormous redevelopment and expansion, while keeping numbers steady, resulting in a much more pleasant environment for all. Beautiful new preparatory school has transformed school life for the youngest girls and given them a great sense of pride. New indoor pool, new theatre on its way. Working on buying eyesore house across the road. School acquired Shah building, previously a Pickford's depository, in 2001 and it now houses the sixth form centre, a gym and a sorely needed new dining room. New classrooms have allowed school to flatten remaining temporary huts to be replaced by gardens. A well-equipped modern langages laboratory was opened in September 2003. Girls are supervised at school from 7.30am (godsend to working parents) with the school day starting at 8.20am

and ending at 3.45pm (3.15pm in pre-prep). Girls may stay at school until 5.30pm, senior girls working in the library (free of charge) and prep school girls in an after-school programme (there is a fee). Girls and parents appreciate teachers' availability for early morning chats.

Pastoral Care and Discipline: Discipline tight, manners immaculate. Drugs and drinking not an issue in this intense day school environment. Sixth formers wear no uniform, may go out at lunchtime and are allowed to finish early one afternoon each week. Every girl in year 6 spends a term as a prefect of the prep. Almost all girls in the prep are driven to school through the rush hour. Older girls may come by tram (it stops a stone's throw from the school at the end of Old Palace Road though one has feeling of life taken in hand as one negotiates colourful scenes along the way) or train to East and West Croydon stations five minutes away. The school offers self-defence classes and sells personal alarms but parents say the walk is not a problem – teachers are on the prowl and these are savvy girls who can look out for themselves. Sixth formers who have walked from the station every morning since age 11 say they can report nothing worse than the occasional teasing about their (fawn and green) uniform. Assembly four times a week with hymn and a prayer. Classes use lovely small school chapel on a rota. One service each term in grand parish church just over the school's back wall. Old Palace steers careful line among its many faiths and parents are impressed by the school's general spiritual values and sensitivity.

Pupils and Parents: No doubt the most spectacularly ethnically diverse independent school to appear in the top echelons of the exam league tables. In London it has no parallel. Ability is everything – money, family, address count for nothing. Girls from inner-city estates learn side by side with offspring of professional high-flyers. Parents committed and involved – it starts with coaching their girls through the entrance exam to the prep school and continues right through until the university place is in the bag.

Entrance: Over-subscribed but not massively so. Entrance tests are tough but not impossible. Tests for entry at 4 and 11 given in early January (11+ tests only in English, maths and verbal reasoning, to ease entry from state sector). 13+ candidates tested in February. Virtually all girls in the prep go on to the senior school. Entrance at sixth form requires 7 subject passes at A*-B grades, with at least A grades in the subjects to be studied at A level.

Exit: Overwhelming majority go on to university in London. Numbers to Oxbridge vary widely each year. Eleven in a good year (one sixth of leavers), four in more typical years. Medicine, dentistry and optometry popular. Very few gap years taken – these are motivated girls whose families expect them to crack on. A few leave after GCSEs to attend sixth form colleges (eg Reigate) – some because they can't take the pace, others because they have been at the school from age 4.

Money Matters: The three schools overseen by the Whitgift Foundation benefit from an enlightened sliding fee structure by which parents pay for what they can afford. Some girls attending Old Palace will pay as little as £45 in fees for the entire year, while others pay full fees (in themselves a bargain). The majority falls somewhere in between. In addition to these bursaries, merit-based scholarships are available for academics and music. Money matters openly discussed. School provides fantastic list specifying every extra penny pupils may need to shell out during their sixth form years (eg to attend Mathematics in Action Study Day or for theatre visits – not all pupils will be expected to pay for these extras).

Remarks: A unique and inspirational school. Genuine ethnic, religious and economic diversity in a happy, historically rich atmosphere of scholarship and fun. Well-endowed. A gem.

THE ORATORY SCHOOL

Woodcote, Reading, Berkshire, RG8 0PJ

Tel: 01491 683 500
Fax: 01491 680 020
E-mail: enquiries@oratory.co.uk
Website: www.oratory.co.uk

• Pupils: 400 boys – 220 board, 180 day • Ages: 11-18 • Size of sixth form: 125 • RC Foundation • Fees: Junior: day £3,990, boarding £5,380. Senior: day £4,930, boarding £6,835.
• Independent • Open days: Saturday mornings in May and October for the 11+ and 13+ entry

Master: Since 2000, Mr Clive Dytor MC MA (forties). Born and bred in Wales. Read oriental studies at Trinity, Cambridge (played rugby and rowed). Joined Royal Marines, served in Belfast and Falklands (where he earned that MC). In 1986 read theology at Oxford, followed by church work and teaching post at Tonbridge. Converted to RC. Housemaster at St Edward's, Oxford, before Oratory appointment. Inherited a listing ship – much bailing-out ensued. No longer paddling furiously – school now returned to state of buoyancy. First crop of 'new regime' A level results have jumped up the league tables. 'We've passed

the 400 mark. The fact that we are full, the fact that we are attracting a good quality of boy, speaks for itself.' Ambitious and determined. Has put the 1990s doldrums behind him. 'Our pastoral side is excellent,' he says. 'Is it too much to want our academic side to match?' Straight-backed and strict, head keeps a close eye on all comings and goings. Jumps hard on slackers but quick to reward effort and achievement. 'A busy boy is a happy boy,' is head's unofficial motto. Great talker, good listener too. Wife, Sarah, a professional violinist, son 15 and daughter 9 (at Oratory senior and prep schools), dog Basil – first XV mascot.

Academic Matters: There was room for improvement and head knows it, though recent signs promise well. 65 per cent As & Bs, 88 per cent A-C. School less selective than many and results reflect that, though many now showing steady improvement and closer inspection reveals some outstanding performances in specific areas. Art streets ahead of the rest with 24 A*-A grades out of 32 (the rest B and C) with solid back-up provided by maths and sciences. Hopes rest squarely on more choosy intake (already begun), greater discipline and committed teaching (huge staff changes since head's arrival). Strong leaning towards languages (ancient and modern) with Chinese, French, German, Italian, Japanese, Russian, Spanish and Latin all on offer (Greek has gone) Portuguese and Ukrainian too at times. RI now on curriculum for all. Art and maths also clear winners at A level. Too many D grades and below (geography now better) used to drag down overall performance level but this seems to have been consigned to the previous regime. On the plus side, school prides itself on its flexibility. Heaven and earth moved to cater for almost any combination of subjects. Small class sizes, 20 and fewer, throughout school. Traditional eyes-front teaching methods (not many huddles or horseshoes here) but plenty of scope for one-to-one. Key subjects streamed so boys can work at their own pace. Individual achievement seen as all important. Fortnightly effort and achievement reports produced on all boys so staff and parents alike can monitor progress electronically. Saturday lessons still seem popular (boys resigned to it). Library under-used but now librarian now in situ with task of beefing it up. Computers in classrooms as well as in new open-access IT centre and boarding house study areas. Terminal points in study bedrooms. Boys can hire laptops from school. Specialist tuition for Oxbridge hopefuls, also study skills and extra help for dyslexics and dyspraxics.

Games, Options, The Arts: Great sporting tradition head is passionate to promote. 'Sport is vital,' he says. 'It's important for boys in particular to exercise – it keeps them healthy and keeps them busy.' Primary winter sports rugby and football, cricket and rowing in the summer, with not inconsiderable success. Struggles a bit against larger schools but hold their own well against fair competition. Strongest school in local area at rugby and shooting (superb record at Bisley). Enthusiastic, rather than medal-winning, rowers (regulars at Henley) with own boathouse nearby. Also own sailing fleet. Fantastic facilities for these and secondary sports. Prince Edward a familiar face here. Well-maintained multi-purpose hall for indoor games complete with real tennis court – one of only 28 in country. Winners of national schools' real tennis championships – in fact strong racket tradition overall – real and lawn tennis, badminton, squash. 12 courts, six grass (set in exquisite original walled garden) and six hard. Nine-hole golf course recently professionally redesigned. Big favourite with parents, we are told. Terraced football/rugby grounds very high quality. No hockey here so no all-weather pitch. Boys report, 'no-one's forced into sport but everyone's encouraged to take part.' Major games days Wednesdays and Saturday afternoons for both boarders and day boys.

Music and drama much improved. Orchestra, choir and many ensembles (many fine individual musicians). Oversubscribed CCF with boys queuing up to get in. Persuasive debaters too, so brains as well as brawn. Impressive artwork throughout school confirms head's claim that art outstanding. Regularly updated to celebrate new talent.

Background and Atmosphere: Founded in 1859 by Cardinal John Henry Newman as school for sons of well-off Catholics. Moved to present Georgian manor location in 1942 with just 30 boys. Sympathetic conversion of original building with more recent (slightly less sympathetic) additions but first impressions still make impact. Set on a hill, surrounded by 400 acres of playing fields, greenery and woodlands, the school commands breathtaking views across both Berkshire and Oxfordshire. Back lane allows boys limited shopping in Woodcote village. Otherwise, school quite isolated and self-contained. Strengthens community side of life though as does large number of boarders. Bulk of staff also live on site or in school-owned accommodation in village. 2003 saw £5 million building programme to clear away second rate boarding accommodation.

School finished the 20th century at very low ebb after decade of dwindling numbers, poor results and low morale. Previously fine reputation suffered badly. New head has done more than put sticking plaster on old wound. Boarding houses have been refurbished and new ones built as well as two new teaching departments; an overhaul of all classroom facilities has also taken place. Cosmetic changes to help modern extensions blend in with old. Pupil numbers back in the ascendant pushing past 400 for first time since 1996. 'Won't take more than 450,' stresses head. Real air of excitement about school's future. 'It's changed so much over the last couple of years,' say boys. 'It had got really slack. But now you know just where you stand, what's expected of you and everyone gets on so much better now.' Head well on course to create a 'can do' ethos in place of 'can't be bothered'. This has now translated into performance in the exam hall and on the sports field.

Pastoral Care and Discipline: Though established as Catholic school, now only 50 per cent of boys are RC. Rest anything from Anglican to Hindu. Daily prayers in houses and weekly assembly a must for all. Sunday morning Mass a must for boarders (regardless of faith) and option for day boys. Vast modern chapel for main school, juniors in St Philip House attend exquisite little chapel converted from old tithe barn. Spirituality (rather than religion) an increasingly important part of school life. 'This isn't a heavy duty Catholic school,' says head. 'What I'm offering isn't THAT rigorous but I am trying to make it MORE rigorous.' Boarding also increasingly important. Juniors (11-13) in separate house (over a third board) while older boys split into four houses. Day boys have study areas with boarders. No dorms but open-plan sleeping arrangements for youngest – 'new boys settle in more quickly that way,' said one boy – and shared or single study bedrooms for rest. Functional more than homely but clean, freshly decorated and boys clearly proud of having own space. Married housemasters and tutors live in. Housemothers being introduced to keep female eye on things.

Older boys, particularly prefects, encouraged to watch out for younger ones. Bullying dealt with swiftly. 'I don't think there's a lot of bullying,' head says. Boys caught smoking will be warned, fined then suspended. Zero tolerance of drugs at present. We say 'at present' as head considering showing yellow card on first offence in place of instant exclusion. Has expelled nine boys for drug use or possession so far plus three more for other matters. All were allowed back to take exams. 'We have to try to establish a culture where taking drugs is not the done thing...determined to work with parents to establish boundaries.' Prefects given important, supervisory roles in younger boys' prep periods.

Pupils and Parents: A thoroughly nice bunch of boys. Head says, 'traditionally the Oratory boy was considered to be a gentleman. I would like to think the Oratory boy today is a courteous boy. It's said we produce nice people.' All the evidence would support that. Boys encountered or questioned were confident, respectful and polite with 'Sirs' aplenty. Not scared of speaking their minds though. 'I think there's a pretty healthy culture if boys express themselves,' says head. Smart in appearance. Uniform for all below sixth form, grey tweed jackets and grey trousers. Pupils used to come from rich Catholic stock, far more mixed these days. Basically middle class, professional types. Some posh, some titles, some Services. 12 per cent overseas including regular intake from Catholic schools and families in the far east. No parent/staff association, though support at sport events good. Famous OBs include Hilaire Belloc. Gerard Manley Hopkins taught here.

Entrance: Can afford to be more choosy – and certainly plans to be. Most come from own prep school nearby (co-ed till 13) or on-site junior house, a few from good primaries. Entry test. CE at 13 requiring 50 per cent pass (though more flexibility granted to siblings and Old Boys' sons plus others who make out a good case). Also head's report from last school and interview. Five Cs at GCSE generally needed to get into sixth form.

Exit: All depart for university after As (some opt for gap. Substantial non-academic post-GCSE leakage to sixth form colleges largely in search of alternative, less academic subjects. Lots of science-based subjects, also art and engineering. 'We don't produce a certain type but we do seem to turn out a lot of leaders'.

Money Matters: Scholarships and exhibitions up to half fees available. Academic, music, art, sport and good all-rounders. Fees middle of the range. Extra charges for books, cultural and sports trips, laundry and haircuts. Generous bursaries.

Remarks: A school which still has Newman's motto – Cor ad Cor Loquitor (Heart Speaking to Heart) – running through it like a stick of rock. Some may have lost heart a bit in the 1990s but the new regime has done all it can to consign that to history. A caring, sharing environment where relationships are central and effort on the sporting field and stage stand shoulder to shoulder with exam success. Emphasis very much on the rounded individual, preparing boys for challenges later in life. Still a bit to do here, not least in the classroom, but it's a school with a lot of heart and a lot to offer.

OUNDLE SCHOOL

Linked to Laxton Junior School in the Junior section

Great Hall, New Street, Oundle, Peterborough, Northamptonshire, PE8 4GH

Tel: 01832 277 125
Fax: 01832 277128
E-mail: admissions@oundle.co.uk
Website: www.oundleschool.org.uk

- Pupils: 630 boys, 435 girls; 835 board, 230 day • Ages: 11-18
- Size of sixth form: 405 • C of E • Fees: Day £3,424 - £3,995; boarding £5,268 - £6,897 • Independent

Head: Since 2005, Mr Charles (Charlie) Bush MA (early fifties), formerly head of Eastbourne College and before that at Marlborough for 11 years as head of maths; also ran a boarding house. Married with children, very charismatic, youthful looking, dry sense of humour. Rattles off facts and figures with alarming alacrity. Is a fervent advocate of co-education. A commanding personality whom some might find intimidating.

Academic Matters: Superb DT facilities through to A level, fairly good uptake at GCSE. Lots of languages in very modern language block, mostly A or A* results. French the most popular followed by Spanish and German. Latin and Greek well subscribed at GCSE and increasingly popular at A level: science is strong across the board among boys and girls, though all are outrun by history (very fine teaching). Overall results continue to be consistently good. The head comments, 'this is a school for children with stamina, mental and social'. The pupils work really hard but are very enthusiastic about the teaching staff, who are always available to support students in any way they can.

Games, Options, The Arts: Pioneered DT and the idea of learning through doing at the turn of the century – the subject is still very much part of the fabric of the school and pupils all come out with a proper and very useful grounding, way above the standard of most schools. School has magnificent DT workshops for designing and constructing individual projects. The atmosphere is more like industry than school, with casting, lasers, wind tunnels, micro-electronics and many computers. The school will try to accommodate and help build any idea that pupils may have so long as it is safe and legal. Huge new science and technology department in the pipeline, the first phase of which should be completed by about 2005.

Superb multisports complex completed in 2001 with large swimming pool (canoes and scuba diving equipment), climbing wall, indoor football and cricket pitches, six squash courts and a fitness room. Outdoor athletics track, rugby pitches, tennis courts, rifle range and hockey pitches – used also by the town and local schools. Two full size Astroturf pitches for hockey.

Music a high priority, compulsory for the first year. Exceptional symphony, chamber and junior string orchestras and a very strong choral tradition. Numerous instrumental ensembles perform regularly in competitions and consorts, both inside and outside the school, at home and abroad, St John's, Smith Square, Peterborough Cathedral, Barbados, Spain and Italy to name but a few. Stahl Theatre in converted church in Oundle High Street puts on both professional and pupil productions, good and popular and gives pupils a feel for the real thing as they take up the acting, producing, lighting, scenery production etc.

The art and sculpture department has recently extended its space, the work being carried out is of an outstanding standard, The Yarrow Gallery regularly displays pupils' work although not much of it on show around the school outside the department. The lovely stained-glass windows in the chapel which was part of the school's millennium project, designed and made by Mark Angus are based on ideas submitted by the pupils. Long-running community scheme in association with MENCAP. CCF, D of E and adventure training together with exchange programme with schools in China and Europe all on offer. D of E and CCF much enjoyed, with as many girls choosing these options as the boys. The community scheme very popular too, students feel they are well integrated within the town.

Background and Atmosphere: Pupils highly motivated in all aspects of school life. 'Exhausting but fun' said one. Boarding houses scattered throughout the pretty medieval town with pupils scurrying to and fro like university students. Furthest boarding house a good 10 minutes walk from central quad. All pupils go back to their boarding houses (or Laxton for day pupils) for all meals, so boys and girls are segregated at these times and are only allowed in the opposite sex boarding houses at very restricted times, with boys only allowed in one specified room in girls' houses. Happy comments from parents, 'the boarding is fabulous, she is in with such a good bunch of girls and can't wait to go back after the holidays,' or praising the emphasis on self-reliance. Compulsory chapel on a Sunday and on two other slots in the week.

Wonderful avenue of trees, games fields etc. Massively built boarding houses, all of which have recently been refurbished to a very high standard, but homely atmosphere. 20,000 volume library, open late in the evenings and on Saturdays and offering a book ordering service. Computers in the library for students' use together with a good selection of DVDs and CD-ROMs.

Pastoral Care and Discipline: Pastoral care very much on the house tutorial system and each pupil has his/her time at school with clear cut boundaries. Instant exclusion for drugs and sex. No public display of physical affection is permitted but upper sixth formers allowed into one public house in Oundle (next door to headmaster's house). Exeats few and far between but pupils are allowed out for good reasons (for example, to go on the Liberty and Livelihood March in London as long as they were collected by, accompanied by and returned by, their parents). Good staff/parent contact. Students choose (if they want to) a boarding house which they will stay in for the whole of their time at Oundle so all year groups get to know each other and mix well. Bullying, on the odd occasion it occurs, is dealt with by the housemaster or mistress which seems to sort out most problems (often misunderstandings).

Pupils and Parents: 12 per cent of pupils are children of old Oundelians; the family network is strong here. 7 per cent from overseas, half continental Europeans or British ex-pats, others from Hong Kong, China. Old boys – Arthur Marshall, Peter Scott (ornithologist), Cecil Lewis (the aviator), A Alvarez, Anthony Holden (Royal biographer), Richard Dawkins, Professor Sir Alan Budd, Charles Crichton (film director), Bruce Dickinson (lead singer of 'Iron Maiden'). Lively bunch of students, highly ambitious and obviously enjoy the social aspect that the school offers as well as the academic.

Entrance: Common Entrance, scholarship or own exam for entrance at 13. A tough (school protests at this – 'we require at least 55 per cent in maths, English, French and science at CE') exam and pupils should be well prepared before sitting it. Six GCSE passes at B or above for sixth form entry, even within the school. Local feeder schools are well used to starting the preparation early.

Exit: Large percentage to Oxbridge, 31 offers in 2002, with across-the-board subjects, others to Edinburgh, Bristol, Durham. About sixty per cent now take a gap year. Very few leave after GCSE. Of the small number of leavers after GCSE, some have just had enough of boarding school, others would like a sixth form that prepares them for university by offering a more relaxed atmosphere, no uniform, less formal over all.

Money Matters: Scholarships and bursaries policy has been recently reviewed to place a greater emphasis on needs-based assessment. Scholarships are awarded at 11, 13 and 16 in a variety of subjects - academic (15), music(10), drama, technology(2), art(1) and general(8). Old Oundelian bursaries for their sons and daughters, depending on circumstances.

Remarks: Very strong traditional public school where pupils need stamina and energy to thrive. A huge amount going on; happy, confident, outgoing pupils.

OXFORD HIGH SCHOOL GDST

Linked to Greycotes and The Squirrel, Oxford High Junior Department in the Junior section

Belbroughton Road, Oxford, Oxfordshire, OX2 6XA

Tel: 01865 559 888
Fax: 01865 552 343
E-mail: oxfordhigh@oxf.gdst.net
Website: www.gdst.net/oxfordhigh

• Pupils: 586 girls, all day • Ages: 11-18 • Size of sixth form: 164 • Non-denom • Fees: £735 (nursery), £1,779 (junior), £2,455 (senior) • Independent • Open days: October

---

Head: Since 1997, Miss Felicity Lusk BMus DipEd DipTeaching CertMusEd (mid forties). Previously deputy head of Hasmonean High School, London. Unusually for a head, a musician – by training, an organist – with wide interests and experience in education. A governor of Guildhall School of Music and Drama. Stylish, relaxed and warm, this head lights up when talking about the excitement and fun of her job, her school and of what being a pupil there should be about. Staff pay tribute to her leadership and the regeneration of the school under her regime. Similarly, she sees the job of running this outstanding school as a necessarily and happily collective one. Clearly, an inspiring head to work under, whether as teacher or pupil.

Academic Matters: Popular A levels are maths, English, history, biology and chemistry. School gives good support to modern languages and a good range is available. Results at both GCSE and A levels are uniformly and consistently excellent, virtually 100 per cent A*/A or B at GCSE and 93 per cent A or B grade at A level. Everyone takes GCSEs in maths, English lang and lit, dual award science and a modern language. School continues to win awards in biology, chemistry and physics olympiads and prizes in national maths and classics competitions. Good

sixth form extra-syllabus options include ethics. School equipped with state-of-the-art computer facilities including intranet and satellite links. Current massive investment from Girls' Day School Trust, to which this school belongs, has meant improvements across the board in refurbishment and updating facilities and, in addition, school has had a generous grant from Wolfson Foundation to further develop science and technology. All pupils screened on entry to determine particular needs and given extra help accordingly. Special needs co-ordinators who support dyslexic or other educationally needy children, and the most able have the opportunity to spend weeks away on enrichment courses in a variety of subjects. Pupils confirm that the approach is to educate each as an individual – with corresponding results, both educationally and in terms of confidence. Hard to beat.

Games, Options, The Arts: Music is outstanding. 300 individual instrumental and vocal lessons weekly. All juniors and virtually all seniors learn an instrument, many learn two. 18 instruments available, 16 in-school ensembles, including four orchestras, five choirs and African Drumming. Art is breathtaking, especially textiles to professional standards and stunning ceramics. Inspirational teaching at work here and textiles is a popular and successful subject at GCSE and A level. Well-equipped and inviting art and design school makes one want to get one's hands dirty! School represented in various national sporting teams and up to 30 sporting activities on offer at different stages of school life. Good on-site playing fields and a new swimming pool. Young Enterprise, CCF, Duke of Edinburgh Awards among many other options. Drama flourishes and is innovative and lively.

Background and Atmosphere: The school moved to present modern site in north Oxford in 1960s and has successfully integrated two new sites for the junior department at The Squirrel (ages 3-6)and at Greycotes (ages 6-11)- both former independent schools housed in Victorian houses minutes away from main site and both now benefiting from updating and additional wings. The Squirrel has air-conditioned classrooms – a real plus. The junior department is to maintain its co-educational tradition: boys leave at 7 for good, local junior/prep schools. Head of the junior department, Mrs Judy Scotcher, is very enthusiastic about the 'wonderful team' she has. Pupils have love/hate feelings for senior school plate glass buildings but great efforts have been made with gardens, plants and landscaping to humanise site and it is welcoming and attractive to visitors. Schools bears its impressive one hundred and thirty year history lightly (Baroness Warnock head mistress 1966-72) but pupils are rightly aware of the importance of school in relatively brief history of women's education.

Pastoral Care and Discipline: Unusually high profile and authority of school council which influences decisions in many areas of school life. Breeds a healthy sense of co-operation and shared responsibility. Strong tutorial system and good, mutually respectful and friendly staff/pupil relations probably a greater strength. School nurse/counsellor with 18 years in post is warm and approachable. House system reviving. Purposeful, happy and relaxed atmosphere in civilised environment.

Pupils and Parents: Intake from 30-mile radius of Oxford, a third from dons' families. Obviously over-subscribed so places prized. Girls intelligent, articulate and intellectually curious as you would expect but also appreciative of stimulation and opportunities presented by school. Parents very supportive in all areas of school life. Old Girls include Dame Josephine Barnes, Elizabeth Jennings, Dame Maggie Smith, actress Miriam Margoyles, conductor Sian Edwards, cook Sophie Grigson, Chess Grand Master Harriet Hunt.

Entrance: At nursery and reception, where assessment is oral and practical, and then various possible entry points in junior school where maths, English, reading and spelling are assessed. At 11 there are tests in maths, English and reasoning and candidates are invited to bring a sample of work or item of interest to stimulate discussion at interview (this is my brother's front tooth which I knocked out yesterday ...). Entry possible throughout the senior school. At 16 by interview and minimum of 5 B grades at GCSE, including maths, English and one science, and As in 'A' level subjects. Many pupils begin at junior department and stay until 18. Pupils moving up from the junior department at 11 transfer automatically but, 'if there is concern, school does give advice and support to parents of girls less likely to benefit from an academic curriculum so that they have time to look elsewhere, in the wider interests of their daughter'.

Exit: Boys, at 7, mostly to nearby New College School and Magdalen College School. Virtually all at 18 to impressive range of good university courses, a high proportion to Oxbridge.

Money Matters: Fee includes additional sum for compulsory school lunch until end of year 11. Academic and music scholarships available at 11 and 16. Art and Sports scholarships available at 16. Academic scholarships are for up to half tuition fee, not means-tested. Bursaries in case of need - short or long term - also available up to full fees, means-tested.

Remarks: If you live in or around Oxford and want a

day school for a bright girl – or boy up to 7 – who will make much of opportunities, a place here must be top of your wish list. She or he will find an exuberant, stimulating environment, exemplary, enthusiastic teaching and a whole school driven by a shared vision. This is the GDST at its best. An unbeatable start in life for able pupils who will be inspired to put in as much as they will get out of it. Recently opened indoor swimming pool, Mary Warnock School of Music and English Department at senior school.

PARKSTONE GRAMMAR SCHOOL

Sopers Lane, Poole, Dorset, BH17 7EP

Tel: 01202 605 605
Fax: 01202 605 606
E-mail: enquiries@parkstone.poole.sch.uk
Website: www.parkstone.poole.sch.uk

• Pupils: 1,050 girls, all day • Ages: 12-18 • Size of sixth form: 335 • Non-denom • State • Open days: Early October, but parents welcome at other times

Head: Since 2001, Mrs Anne Shinwell MA (early fifties). Read history and politics at Glasgow. First teaching job was at John Kelly Girls' School in London where she rose to be assistant director of the sixth form and head of careers and economics. Went on to spend eight years striding the hallowed halls of Tiffin Girls', one of the most revered and oversubscribed girls' state schools in the land – most of her time there as deputy head. Leaving no stone unturned, she became head of Queen Elizabeth's Girl's School, Barnet, an academically successful comprehensive. In short, this lady knows a thing or two about educating clever girls. Exudes authority, confidence, and joie de vivre. Married to a solicitor who has two children.

Academic Matters: Luminous SATs results. GCSEs and A levels almost uniformly excellent. Parkstone was given science specialist status in 2002 and the subject is popular, successful and well-resourced. The school has loosened up its compulsory GCSE requirements – pupils can take separate sciences (more fun to teach, say teachers) or dual award. Girls learn French and German in years 8 and 9. Since September 2004, modern foreign languages has become part of the GCSE options choice with the vast majority of girls still continuing with at least one MFL. At GCSE pupils may add Spanish or Italian and be examined in three languages – or none at all. No GCSEs taken early. Computing and graphics A levels and geology AS courses around the corner at Poole Grammar (the boys come to Parkstone for economics, food technology and politics). Psychology all the rage and media studies has become very popular since its introduction in 2004.

Tries to give girls every opportunity. There are 'Da Vinci' enrichment classes for year 10 pupils with Poole Grammar in subjects like photography, philosophy and Japanese. Overseas trips take girls to unusual destinations eg Russia and Iceland. A year 11 homework club helps to keep motivation high. Class sizes large throughout. Very little call for special needs support here (3 girls officially), although the school is coping well with a pupil who is a wheelchair user, and hopes to improve further in this regard.

Games, Options, The Arts: Sport good, and heartily played – up to a point. All girls do games or training of some kind through to the end of year 13, and girls' rugby, cricket and football are popular (Parkstone hosted Dorset's first tournament for girls' rugby). Netball strong; hockey less so. Girls who came here from the independent sector comment wryly how they were suddenly promoted from the D hockey team at their prep, to prime position on the school team at Parkstone. School is raising funds in hopes of building a new sports centre. Playing fields are ample, with loads of tennis courts. At sixth form, girls can go off-site to local sports clubs etc. Music well-housed and said to be very good, with some talented girls. A big drama production every second year in conjunction with Poole Grammar. Theatre studies A level. High quality art and textiles. Unusually good range of extra-curricular activities – some in the sixth form combined with Poole Grammar. Ms Shinwell eager to increase links between the two schools.

Background and Atmosphere: Founded 100 years ago in nearby Parkstone, hence the name. Moved to 20 acre site, next to the sewage works, in 1961: the smell takes some getting used to – 'only very occasionally', says head. The main building not a thing of beauty but serves, and several new buildings, especially the sixth form/music block, are downright pleasant. Classrooms bulge with brainy girls who are proud of their school and know they are privileged to be here. Despite their dedicated (and very attractive) common room, sixth form girls say that the school is a bit short of space for their study and computer use. Impressive new lecture theatre. Little canteen opens at 8am for early birds and serves as a social area/study throughout the day. Cheap, very good food.

Pastoral Care and Discipline: Girls stay with same tutor group for first four years. Mentoring and big sister schemes help new girls fit in. Uniform quite attractive, though our heart goes out to girls who can't wear yellow. Trousers a

recent new option. Sixth form pupils allowed to wear what they like and seem relaxed with it. Some parents dismayed that the school has permitted nose rings and exposed tummies, but this is not a school that wages war over minutiae. A very few girls have received fixed-term exclusions for 'friendship group problems' – headspeak for bitchiness.

Pupils and Parents: Rich and some poor, but few from ethnic minorities (reflecting Poole's residents) and virtually nil who do not speak fluent English. Parkstone Grammar has a reasonable social cachet and families that can well afford to pay for education can be found earnestly coaxing their daughters to swot for the entrance exam. Head laments that there are still areas in Poole where families say 'we don't send girls to the Grammar'. 65 per cent come from Poole, the rest from up to an hour away. Around 40 per cent of girls come to school by bus – local bus company, city bus or via private arrangements made by parents. Sixth form girls distinctly mature and focused.

Entrance: Poole's current three tier system (junior, middle and senior schools) makes the entry age of 12 out of sync with many schools (the borough is currently reviewing this system and Parkstone could move to a year 7 start). Around 330 girls sit entrance test in late November vying for 168 places each year. Girls who pass and attend a school in Poole automatically receive places. Out of area girls are allotted places in exam rank order – distance away from school only counts if two applicants receive the same score on the exam. Further places can be awarded via the Independent Admissions Appeals Panel: 35 extra in 2004! Appeals on the rise, esp if parents can give a good reason why only Parkstone will meet their daughter's needs. Girls come from all over but usual suspects include Broadstone Middle School, Baden Powell and St Peter's School, Canford Heath Middle School, Oakdale Middle School and independent preps like Castle Court in Corfe Mullen. Can take up to 50 girls at sixth form – the school requires a bare minimum of five GCSEs at A-C, with at least a B in subjects to be studies at A level.

Exit: 10-15 leave after year 11, often to schools nearer home (some competition from good comprehensive sixth forms like Thomas Hardy's and Brockenhurst). Occasionally girls 'return' to the independent sector. At 18, 'practically all' go on to university – loads locally to Southampton, Bournemouth, and Portsmouth. Also Exeter, Bath, Reading, Kings' College London. A few to Oxbridge.

Remarks: Very together, very confident, very forceful place. We don't know how they manage it but even fragile or disorganised girls seem to blossom here.

PARLIAMENT HILL SCHOOL

Highgate Road, London, NW5 1RL

Tel: 020 7485 7077

Fax: 020 7485 9524

E-mail: headteacher@parliamenthill.camden.sch.uk

Website: www.parliamenthill.camden.sch.uk

• Pupils: 900 girls, all day • Ages: 11-19 • Size of sixth form: 550 in joint sixth form with William Ellis, part of La Swap consortium of 1,250 sixth form students in four schools • Non-denom • State

Head: Since 2005, Ms Susan Higgins MA MA(Ed) (fifties), previously head of Brentford School for Girls. Read English at New Hall, Cambridge.

Academic Matters: Wide ability range. It was a designated Beacon School and is now a Leading Edge School (the only one in north London) – which means that it gets extra money from the government to share its innovations and expertise with others. It is also a Technology College – 'I thought it was important to choose the subjects where girls don't traditionally excel. They can see that all subjects are equally worthwhile.' This has resulted in a good supply of computers, used across the curriculum, and electronic whiteboards in almost every classroom – 'the teachers love them'. Particularly good teaching in design and technology.

Around half the pupils get at least five A* – C grades at GCSE – 57 per cent in 2005, the best ever result. Graphic products, product design are popular subjects, as are business studies and drama. Year 7 pupils learn French or Spanish and can take up the other language in year 10; Italian and Bengali are extra-curricular options. Everyone does short courses in RE and IT and takes the GCSEs at the end of year 10. Mixed ability teaching throughout, except for science, which is setted in year 11, languages, setted from year 10, and maths, setted from year 9. 'My girls say that some of the mixed ability classes aren't very challenging,' said a parent, and the latest Ofsted report comments that more able children are not always stretched in the first three years. But the head feels that setting can be too rigid and 'one of the best ways of learning is explaining to someone else'. Key stage 3 SATs results for 2004 were 15 per cent higher than the previous year, and well above targets.

The maths department – which has, to great cheers, ditched the SMILE (secondary maths individualised learning experience) system in favour of whole-class teaching and small-group work – is one of only six in the country designated Leading Edge. This means it is considered particularly innovative, though the GCSE results are not yet amongst the school's strongest.

In the forefront of developing vocational GCSEs, including a successful Life Skills and Skills for Working Life course, aimed particularly at disaffected pupils who are not suited to a more academic route. Quite a few of the teachers are inspiring, report parents and pupils, and Ofsted rates 77 per cent of lessons as good, very good or excellent – a very high percentage.

The successful La Swap sixth form consortium of 1,250 students includes Parliament Hill, William Ellis, La Sainte Union and Acland Burghley schools, with students able to study one or two subjects at other schools. This system can mean large subject groups with a wide range of abilities but it gives large choice of subjects eg film studies, law, psychology and photography at A level, leisure and tourism and art and design at GNVQ, and business and performing arts for AVCE. 'We try to respond to students' needs and will put on an extra class if there are enough students.' Results are hard to quantify, as La Swap sixth formers study different subjects at different schools, but nearly 45 per cent of the A level grades were A or B in 2003, and results are always around the national average.

Games, Options, The Arts: Plenty of sport. The school borders Hampstead Heath and has two tennis/netball courts, a small playing field, a gym and a dance studio. Thriving football and basketball teams. A youth club at the school, open to all Camden secondary students, runs dance, drama, computing and trampolining sessions after school two days a week. Drama is a popular GCSE and A level option and there are plenty of productions throughout the year.

Art studios a riotous mix of painting and sculptures. Courses include photography and textiles; art A level is popular and produces a good crop of A grades. School choir and orchestra, run jointly with William Ellis School, recently visited Barcelona and Tuscany, and there are bands, groups and ensembles too. 'Very enthusiastic music staff,' say pupils. Increasing numbers take GCSE and A level music, and GCSE grades are always A*-C.

Background and Atmosphere: Lovely setting on the edge of Hampstead Heath, with plenty of outdoor space including a sculpture park and a maths garden. Refurbished science labs and new IT rooms, plus an information resources centre. Under construction are state-of-the-art music, dance and drama studios, and a new technology building, landscaped to blend in. Relaxed, informal, harmonious atmosphere. 'We work hard on positive social relationships,' says the head.

Pastoral Care and Discipline: Attendance and punctuality have been a problem and support staff are employed to monitor this. One of the school's 'Leading Edge' roles is looking at ways of motivating disaffected youngsters eg life skills courses. There is always a member of staff on duty to cope with disruptive pupils and a 'traffic light' system of graded sanctions. Some students not suited to academics are found placements outside eg Arsenal football ground, arts centre, sports centre, while still connected to the school. The head says – and pupils agree – that drugs are not a problem. Nor does there seem to be much bullying. 'The girls like to think of themselves as being quite moral and like to deal with issues themselves,' said a parent. 'But when my daughter was bullied, the school reacted very well.'

Pupils and Parents: Wide social mix, from the million pound houses nearby and from the council estates of Gospel Oak. Pupils, of some 70 nationalities, come from over 60 primary schools. They include refugee children and those from well-known political and legal families. OG: Ms Dynamite.

Entrance: Controlled by the LEA. Siblings and those with particular needs get preference, then girls who live closest – in practice, within about a mile and a half. About 600 students apply for 200 places in the joint sixth form. Those coming in from outside are asked for at least five grades C at GCSE with Bs in their A level choice subjects.

Exit: About three quarters go through to La Swap. Of these, some three-quarters go on to further or higher education, to a huge range of old and new universities, including five or more a year to Oxbridge. Courses range from medicine to media technology.

Remarks: Increasingly popular and successful comprehensive in beautiful setting, which is pioneering ways of keeping disaffected pupils on track. Particularly harmonious atmosphere – 'Most people just get on well together,' say pupils.

PARMITER'S SCHOOL

High Elms Lane, Garston, Watford, Hertfordshire, WD25 0UU

Tel: 01923 671 424
Fax: 01923 894 195
E-mail: admin.parmiters@thegrid.org.uk
Website: www.parmiters.herts.sch.uk

• Pupils: 1,250 boys and girls, all day • Ages: 11-18 • Size of sixth form: 310 • None • State • Open days: Early October

Head: Since 1993, Mr B (Brian) Coulshed BA (geography) PGCE (University of Manchester) (early fifties). Started his career in 1972 at Longdean School, Hemel Hempstead where he progressed to head of year. Left in 1979 to become head of geography and head of year at Hemel Hempstead School and in 1986 was appointed deputy head at Goffs School in Cheshunt. Joined Parmiter's as head seven years later. Wife Gill is head of department at a nearby secondary school. Two sons, 21 and 19. Approachable and likeable head who is proud of what he and the school have achieved in all areas. Still teaches geography to the younger pupils. Enthusiastic about the school's future, always available to parents, and insists on wearing a gown to meet them or any students. Doesn't see this as pompous but rather, 'it emphasises the traditional feel of the school.' Says the school never closes and for him the job 'is a way of life.'

Academic Matters: Banded by ability in all subjects from year 7. Setting in maths, sciences and languages from year 8. Class sizes very good for a state school – around 25 and going down as GCSEs approach. 93 per cent got five or more A*-C grades in 2004, 46 per cent of grades at A*/A, with maths and English being particularly strong. A levels well above the national average too; 311 UCAS points on average per student in 2004. English and maths were the most popular choices. Latin has been squeezed out of the timetable, much to the head's disappointment. No language laboratories, although a new modern foreign languages block is being built in 2005. Separate sciences as well as the dual award. Holiday courses in maths and twilight lessons every week in physics, biology and chemistry. AVCEs in business, travel and tourism and IT.

Games, Options, The Arts: Proud of its sporting tradition and success, awarded a Sportsmark Gold for its facilities (extensive playing fields, floodlit tennis and netball courts and an impressive new sports centre – new floodlit

Astroturf and another new sports pavilion opened in 2004 plus floodlit synthetic pitch for football and hockey) and extra-curricular activities. The main sports for boys are football, basketball, rugby, cricket, tennis and athletics. Girls choose from netball, hockey, football, athletics, tennis, dance and rounders. Reaches national level in many sports. Very good reputation for music with some 250 pupils learning an instrument in school; two symphonic wind bands, four choirs, an orchestra, a big band and a recorder group as well as smaller woodwind, brass and string chamber music groups. European concert tours aarranged biennially.

A host of extra-curricular clubs including dance, drama, trampolining, debating, robot, chess and technology. D of E strongly supported, the public speaking team has been national champions and thriving house system. Regular foreign exchanges and visits to France, Germany and Spain, and sixth form exchanges with Eton and Sherborne Girls'. Owns its own field centre in Wales.

Background and Atmosphere: Founded in 1681 in Bethnal Green, Parmiter's moved to its present 60 acre rural site in 1977. As well as public funding from the government, the school receives additional financial support from Parmiter's Foundation which owns the school and its site. From the outside the school is modern, seventies style and purpose-built but on the inside it has a traditional feel. Portraits of former head teachers look down on you as you enter the welcoming reception area, honours boards give you the feeling you are in a school where achievement is highly valued and recognised. But traditional doesn't mean stuffy. 'It's a traditional school which is progressive and forward looking,' says the head. It's very much a family school. Siblings, regardless of academic ability, take priority in the admissions process. 'We believe every child has a talent and we celebrate it.'

Pastoral Care and Discipline: Minimal set of rules. Pupils are expected to be punctual, tidy, hard working and courteous. Pupils are publicly rewarded for good effort and excellent work. All children undergo diagnostic testing on joining the school to identify strengths and weaknesses and those with special needs. In twelve years only 13 pupils have been expelled.

Pupils and Parents: Vast majority come from Hertfordshire post codes although some travel from as far away as the Wembley/Harrow/Stanmore areas in north London. Most come from state primary schools, a few from prep schools. Pupils are well behaved and polite and feel they are given every opportunity to reach their full potential. Former pupils include Tommy Walsh from TV's Ground Force, Keith Medlycott, manager of Surrey CC and Alper Mehmet, current British Ambassador to Iceland.

Entrance: Partially selective and rather complex criteria for places at 11 plus. Current siblings take priority followed by those for whom there are compelling medical grounds and then 10 per cent allocated to those living closest to the school. 35 per cent of places are then awarded on academic ability (test in maths and verbal reasoning) and up to 10 per cent on the basis of music aptitude (test and audition); remaining places are allocated to the children of staff. Entry into sixth form is based generally on B grades upwards at GCSE.

Exit: Around 20 per cent leave post-GCSE to go to further education colleges and occasionally to other schools. More than 95 per cent of sixth formers progress to higher education with around 16 per cent taking a gap year. Five or so a year to Oxbridge.

Remarks: Private-school-standard facilities in a state school. Excellent results at Key Stage 3, GCSE and A level and excellent value-added. Parmiter's was named in the Chief Inspector of Schools' Annual Report of 2003 as an 'outstandingly successful school'. As a result the headmaster received the personal congratulations of HRH The Prince of Wales at Highgrove.

Parrs Wood High School

Wilmslow Road, East Didsbury, Manchester, M20 5PG

Tel: 0161 445 8786
Fax: 0161 445 5974
E-mail: pwtc@parrswood.manchester.sch.uk
Website: www.parrswood.manchester.sch.uk

• Pupils: 2,000 boys and girls; all day • Ages: 11-18 • Size of sixth form: 400 • None • State • Open days: Late October/early November

Head: Since 2005, partnership heads Ms Rachel Jones and Mr David Ashley, both in their forties. Ms Jones was deputy head and fixed term sole head here. She came from English teaching background with extensive experience in large, multi-cultural comprehensives in London and Manchester, and still teaches occasionally. Mr Ashley was head of Hathershaw Technology College in Oldham, where he was praised in the national press for 'driving the ICT agenda in education'. He has a design and technology teaching background.

Academic Matters: One of the first UK schools in 2004 with dual specialist status, for technology and the performing arts. Ofsted in 2001 said, 'compared with schools in the same free school meals category, results are well above average, placing them amongst the top five per cent in the country.' Of note is the school's attitude to ICT with over 1,000 computers on site, trolleys of laptops for use in lessons and a staff of five technicians. Each pupil has own electronic filing cabinet. Students can borrow a PC if they do not have one at home – access through the school's system with its many safeguards. 'We're attacking the social disadvantage,' said previous head. 100 per cent of year 9 students take ICT GNVQ (equal to 2 GCSEs at grade A-C), with extra ICT training available during lunchbreak and after school.

The school has programmes for the gifted and talented, with extra sessions after school, as well as a learning support department of 17 staff working with 198 children of designated special needs. At GCSE, 60 per cent achieves five A-C grades. Wide GCSE curriculum including PE & dance, sociology, drama, business studies and Urdu. 32 A level subjects offered here and, in 2004, 100 per cent pass rate in 90 of subjects taken. The school sets targets for each pupil from day one and offers early starts and Saturday morning sessions to those not achieving their potential. There are 118 full-time teaching staff, with a young profile

(40 in post for less than 5 years, only 28 for 15 years or more.) Additional staff (admin, technicians and other assistants) number 120. Some subjects are streamed, some taught in mixed ability groups. Department of Education Leading Edge School working with local secondary schools to support raising standards. Future Vision award for innovation in ICT and North West regional Focus school for the Specialist Schools and Academies Trust's ICT register offering consultancy and support for other secondary schools across the region, UK and abroad.

Games, Options, The Arts: The extensive school playing fields, with airy views of trees and sky despite proximity to Manchester, can be subject to flooding from the Mersey in heavy rain, but the school also boasts an Astroturf area which survives occasional submersion, as well as indoor sports halls and a fully kitted gym. There are teams for every sport imaginable and a commendable list of high placements in local and regional competitions. Community Sports Leaders Award has run for many years.

Pupils and parents say the best thing about the school is the wide range of extra-curricular activities, 'there are so many things on after school it's hard to decide what to do'. D of E, drama, music and dance productions, student governors' body, public speaking (recent area finalists in Rotary competition) and clubs for chess, maths, design technology, science, art and music, oh...and homework club nightly. Over 10 per cent of students take advantage of the wide range of instrumental lessons on offer for £15 a term or just £40 a year, including steel pans, balalaika and Indian music. 'There are loads of different bands, choirs and orchestras,' say pupils, 'and at lunch-time you can hear them practising.' Seventy per cent of the instruments are loaned from the Manchester Music Service but demand for lessons does exceed availability. Standards are high; a string quartet reached recent finals in the Music for Youth festival.

Background and Atmosphere: Today's Parrs Wood Technical College, occupied since April 2000, bears no resemblance to the former crumbling Parrs Wood High School thanks to swapping valuable school land for new premises. The new buildings are tucked away behind the huge entertainment complex that made them possible. A multiscreen cinema, bowling, health club and pizza joints now shield the school from the A34, one of Manchester's main arteries, running south from the city. The result is a quiet, leafy, ultra-modern campus where state-of-the-art, low maintenance buildings in honey-coloured brick with red painted upper floors and waveform rooflines are softened by one elegant refurbished building which houses the music department. The new buildings are within a steel frame so internal walls can easily be altered if future teaching needs dictate. The downside of the deal is the loss of land; one of the very few criticisms on recent reports is the lack of space to expand the sixth form and for pupils to play in wet weather. Aristotle's maxim, 'we are what we repeatedly do. Excellence, then, is not an act but a habit,' is inscribed large above the entrance to the school from the main foyer where a reception office and security desk give the feel of a large new office block.

Acres of blue carpet lead to wide corridors, flanked with hundreds of lockers painted in the same jade green as the school uniform; no piles of bags and coats here. Each subject has its own coloured corridor and professionally made poster-sized sign that includes montage pictures of the students involved in relevant activities, 'look, here's me,' they delight to point out. 'We do every sort of charity fund-raising,' said head. Jade polo and sweatshirts, black in year 11, over black trousers (for girls too) or skirts are the order of the day. The atmosphere isn't refined but there's no rough air or graffiti. New dance studios; hearing impaired unit integrated into the school.

Pastoral Care and Discipline: Parents say some children are unnerved by the enormity of the school but there is a pass to a safe room with board games, reading and peer counsellors. Students belong to and wear the badge of one of four houses, Griffin, Orion, Pegasus and Phoenix, which compete for points in quizzes, sports, charity fund-raising and attendance and which 'develops a sense of belonging, togetherness, unity and community.' The school states its ethos as 'celebration and reward' and uses a system of slips for behaviour; bronze, silver and gold for good conduct and effort. Blue slips for bad behaviour counteract the good slips and students speak enthusiastically about prizes they can earn, 'you can swap slips straight away for cinema tickets or you can save them for a really good prize at the end of the year, you can even earn a CD player, and the house with the most points gets to go on a brilliant trip, like Alton Towers.' Parents say, 'the school's really encouraging, always drawing out the best and making children feel good about themselves.'

No permanent exclusions for many years. 'We work really hard to achieve that,' said last head, who also maintained tough line on drugs, and parents report that any minor bullying incidents are handled well. Presumably a tradition to be continued under new regime. Granted a Healthy School Award in 2002 for all areas of the personal education programmes.

Pupils and Parents: Thirty-five per cent pupils non-white and thirty per cent entitled to free school meals reflecting the diversity of catchment area which includes seriously disadvantaged areas and prosperous suburbs favoured by Manchester's academic and media communities. Parrs Wood has the widest and most balanced distribution of ability of any school in Manchester.

Entrance: LEA driven, hugely oversubscribed with over 600 applications for three hundred places each year, and waiting lists for every year, even the final ones.

Exit: More than 80 per cent carries on to post-16 education. After A levels 75 per cent goes on to degree courses, and some 10 per cent to other further education courses. A handful to Oxbridge yearly.

Remarks: Parents feel, 'it's fantastic, I can't praise them highly enough.' True comprehensive education at its very best for those lucky enough to secure a place.

PATE'S GRAMMAR SCHOOL

Princess Elizabeth Way, Cheltenham, Gloucestershire, GL51 0HG

Tel: 01242 523 169

Fax: 01242 232 775

E-mail: office@pates.gloucs.sch.uk

Website: www.pates.gloucs.sch.uk

• Pupils: 950 pupils, equally mixed. All day • Ages: 11-18 • Size of sixth form: 360 • Non-denom • State

---

Head Master: Since 1999, Mr Richard Kemp MA (early fifties). Educated at Westminster School and Christ Church, Oxford, where he read geography. Worked in marketing and advertising before embarking on teaching career. Following a short spell at Eton, he taught at two state schools before returning to Oxford to complete a further degree in education. After acting as senior education advisor in Buckinghamshire, he returned to teaching in 1992 as senior deputy and then acting head of Aylesbury Grammar School. Married to Denise and with two grown-up children, he lists travel, gardening and military history among his interests. Warm and friendly, exudes quiet control.

Retiring July 2006.

Academic Matters: Extremely impressive, with 100 per cent A*-C in almost every subject at GCSE. Separate sciences are also very strong. At A level there is a 100 per cent pass rate in every subject except general studies, which is taken by all. Maths, physics, chemistry and languages fare best but no subject is anything other than strong. A specialist language college since 2001, offering French, German, Spanish, Italian, Latin and Mandarin;

student exchanges with China and Europe. Some funding given for French teaching in six local primary schools. Pate's is also a Beacon School and has a unique project to provide curriculum enrichment to children from local primaries. Separate DT block but no vocational subjects are offered at examination level.

Class sizes average 30 in years 7-9, dropping to 25 in years 10-11 and 10 to a maximum 18 in the sixth form. Youthful looking staff, average age of 45, more than half having been at the school for ten years or more. There are 30 pupils on the SEN register, with specialist assistants typically dealing with the dyslexic maths genius but able to cater for other, mild, special needs. Pupils help to set their own personal academic targets on 'progress cards', monitored by teaching staff.

Games, Options, The Arts: Variety of sporting and cultural extra-curricular activities on offer, often organised on an inter-house basis by senior pupils, and a big programme of school matches on a Saturday. Adventurous spirit evident in the large outdoor pursuits centre on site and the school has recently installed an Astroturf pitch and a climbing wall. More than 250 pupils are CCF members and the D of E Award scheme is popular too. Inter-school matches can be international affairs – the hockey tours to Barbados and South Africa and rugby tours to Australia and South Africa for example – and destinations for expeditions include Peru, the Himalayas and Thailand.

Most learn an instrument, with the various orchestras and bands giving well-reviewed concerts in Cheltenham venues. A new arts building centre, for visual arts and music, opened in 2002 to complement the existing performing arts centre, with a library development to follow.

Background and Atmosphere: Although housed in bright new buildings, opened in 1996, what hits the first-time visitor is Pate's location, smack in the middle of Cheltenham's grottiest council estate. As one parent put it, 'it can feel a bit like running the gauntlet to get here'. At odds with both the largely genteel and affluent town and the polite, self-possessed pupils who come here. Few Pate's pupils are from local state primaries, despite the best efforts of a head who doesn't want the school to be 'just a middle-class enclave'. Parents more bothered than the pupils by faint air of menace outside the gates, with sixth formers, who all wear uniform, happy to pop out to the chip shop at lunchtime.

Founded in 1574 by local bigwig Richard Pate, the school was a free grammar school for boys for more than 400 years. In 1904, a grammar school for girls was opened alongside it, with the two schools amalgamated in 1986. Problems for pupils shuttling between the two old buildings,

mainly involving minor thefts and intimidation, almost entirely solved when the purpose-built new single building opened. Now an oasis of calm, with visiting schools marvelling at the total absence of graffiti, even in the toilets. Beautiful artwork, from all years, covers the walls and building is amazingly clean and tidy. Very laid back, with no sign of tension from pupils. They know they must be bright to be here, accept it and just get on with it.

Pastoral Care and Discipline: Remarkable scheme where sixth formers train and act as counsellors to other pupils seems to work well. Form teachers also act as personal tutors. Personal targets mean that pressure is most often self-imposed. No compromise stance on drugs. Bullying very rare, but addressed with suspension and a dire warning. Behaviour is rarely an issue – pupils are universally well-mannered, mature and conscientious.

Pupils and Parents: Bulk are from in and around Cheltenham but some travel from all over Gloucestershire and even Worcestershire, from more than 100 feeder schools. Head suggests a limit of 45 minutes' safe travelling time and puts parents in touch with others nearby to organise their own transport. Buses only offered to those in Cheltenham. Parents tend towards middle class professional but school keen to take all comers and some do make it from the less affluent areas. As ethnically mixed as Cheltenham, ie not very. Famous former pupils include Gustav Holst, the Rolling Stone Brian Jones and a clutch of minor sporting figures.

Entrance: Absolutely rigid. With 750 applications for 120 places, selection based on school's own VRQ-based entrance test. A line is drawn under the 120 top scorers and they are offered places. No special pleading or circumstances taken into account. The rest can remain on a waiting list for the handful of places that come up each year. The 50 extra sixth form places are offered on the basis of interviews, after a bucketload of As and Bs have been predicted at GSCE and a favourable report received from the pupil's present school.

Exit: Virtually no leavers after GSCE. In most years 100 per cent go to university, with occasionally a few opting for employment. At least 15 Oxbridge a year and rising fast, with 20 offers in last two years.

Money Matters: State funded. Strong parents' association organises a range of money-making schemes, complementing the head's sharp eye for both government and charitable funding.

Remarks: Outstanding school combining old fashioned values with a modern outlook in a very modern setting. A place where the very bright will thrive.

THE PERSE SCHOOL

Linked to Pelican Pre-Preparatory School (The) in the Junior section

Linked to Perse Preparatory School (The) in the Junior section

Hills Road, Cambridge, Cambridgeshire, CB2 2QF

Tel: 01223 403 800

Fax: 01223 403 810

E-mail: office@perse.co.uk

Website: www.perse.co.uk

- Pupils: 600 boys; around 50 girls in the sixth form. All day.
- Ages: 11-18 plus junior schools • Size of sixth form: 210 •
Non-denom • Fees: £3,465 • Independent • Open days: contact school: usually late Sept/early Oct

Head: Since 1994, Mr Nigel Richardson MA PGCE (mid fifties). Educated at Highgate and Trinity Hall, Cambridge. Eighteen years in Uppingham and thence to first headship at The Dragon. Deputy head at King's, Macclesfield. Married with two boys. A softly-spoken, reforming head, who combines a quiet but intense enthusiasm with a sane and humane realism and dependability. A historian who maintains an active interest in his subject while also developing and giving tremendous support to other disciplines. Staff pay tribute to the changes to the school's atmosphere and ethos under his sound regime, citing especially the improved structure of the senior management team and the benefits to the pastoral care system which have followed.

Academic Matters: Results good across the board, most candidates getting As or Bs at A levels and A*/A at GCSE. Japanese and Russian, sports science and philosophy are among sixth form options. An unashamedly 'seriously maths and science school' and results are especially good in these areas. English, history and geography numbers and results also holding up well. School teaches a technology syllabus that is unusually weighted to engineering and practical skills – its previous emphasis on and reputation for egg-headed intellectualism is now outdated. New technology building in 2003, aided by grant from the Wolfson Foundation. All labs recently refitted to highest standard. Arabic option introduced for high-flying GCSE linguists 2005. Plans for classroom expansion and new resources centre/library as the school moves towards full co-education from September 2010.

The Perse is the academic boys' school in Cambridge – where, needless to say, brainpower is not thin on the ground; it aims high academically and has the pupils and staff to achieve the highest standards. SEN provision much improved in recent years. All boys screened on entry, on-site SEN teacher plus liaison with Ed Psychs. 50 pupils with some kind of SEN support.

Games, Options, The Arts: Surprisingly for a day school, The Perse manages to keep two/three afternoons a week for games and other extracurricular activities throughout the school. This is, in the main, a very popular policy and pupils relish the opportunities to develop sporting, musical or dramatic skills along with the various other options on offer – among them CCF, a, perhaps surprisingly, popular choice for many girls. Scout and Explorer scout troops. Excellent sports hall block includes two squash courts and a large and well-appointed fitness suite which – an enlightened and appreciated policy – the sixth are allowed to use in free unsupervised time.

Art is rich and colourful, evidence of inspirational teaching, and includes ceramics and printing. Local artists exhibit in The Pelican Gallery within the teaching space. Good lecture theatre doubles as drama studio seating 180 – big expansion in drama productions in recent years. New music building – an extension to existing block – provides new teaching/practice rooms, space for larger ensembles and exciting new rehearsal hall to accommodate full-scale symphony orchestra with chorus; doubles as concert hall, available to local community. About half learn at least one instrument and musical activities of all types flourish here – baroque string ensembles, jazz, brass, wind and chamber groups, choirs and music technology. The school's musical excellence now seen by parents as a principal reason to apply and attracting correspondingly good budding musicians. Good careers room and resources in sixth form centre which also has well-used common room area recently expanded to provide a separate work area for growing number of sixth formers.

Background and Atmosphere: The school's history – nearly 400 years of it – is chequered and includes embezzlement in the 18th century, an assault on the head in the 19th and an incendiary bomb hitting it in 1941. Since 1960 it has occupied award-winning, purpose-built accommodation on a 28-acre site. Buildings are low – few higher than two storeys as is customary in this part of the world – but although not imposing they are inviting and well-integrated into the site. Hall doubles up as dining room necessitating daily quick setting out and packing away of tables. Meals taken by staff and pupils together perhaps explaining the unusually orderly atmosphere. Girls have their own small but charming building by playing fields, housing changing rooms and a small lobby for getting away from overwhelming male presence. Astroturf pitch, very attractive, tree-lined playing fields, good feeling of space. Big shake-up after 1998 Inspection led to streamlining of management. Now a sense of a new common vision and sense of purpose. While being efficient and well-organised, school has room for eccentricities and individuals.

Pastoral Care and Discipline: Three deputy heads in newly streamlined management structure, including one with specific responsibility for pastoral matters. All pay tribute to new system and head clearly sees pastoral care as central to his regime. No house system but various vertically grouped activities compensate and pupils mix comfortably across the year groups and sexes. 'Code of conduct' – highly reasonable rights and responsibilities. New more pastoral role for prefects who are – a novel approach – required to apply for the job. Head well aware of need to support self-esteem of the less obviously able in this academic school and encourages strong relationships between boys who 'need to feel liked' and staff. Strong drugs policy seldom needed.

Pupils and Parents: Fees prohibit mass takeover by bright children of poorly paid Cambridge academics though many still manage it. School ceased taking boarders in 1993, two years before girls arrived in the sixth form. Girls vastly outnumbered at present but most blossom here with opportunities and resources few girls' schools can offer. Pupils are relaxed, unpretentious and natural indicating that, altogether, this school gives them a very good start in life.

Many come for science but also relish new sporting/artistic possibilities. Lots of local competition for pupils at sixth form level (not least from the state sixth form colleges) and about 20 per cent of fifth-formers do leave – more than compensated for by those who come in from outside. Majority live close by though many come from as far as Ely, Saffron Walden, Newmarket, Royston and elsewhere. Annually, a very few from abroad, under special guardianship scheme, seen as bringing new and refreshing dimension to school life. Distinguished list of Old Boys includes Sir Peter Hall, Rev Dr John Polkinghorne, David Tang, Dave Gilmour, Pete Atkin, Sir Mark Potter and the late lamented Mel Calman.

Entrance: At 11, about 40 from Perse preps but also 30 from other local juniors and preps. About 25 more at 13+. Commendably, school won't take pupils at 11+ from other Cambridge preps which don't expect pupils to leave until 13. Competitive entrance at 11+ and 13+ via own exam and interview. Very good GCSE grades required for entrance at 16+. School stresses that competition for

places at 11+ – at about 2:1 – is tough but not that tough!

Exit: Many to Oxbridge and top medical schools with a good spread of other universities. Engineering, medical and natural sciences preferred subjects, engineering single largest degree subject.

Money Matters: Scholarships 10 per cent at most. Means-tested bursary schemes look more promising, especially for science-biased candidates.

Remarks: School much expanded in recent years and now set to expand again as it takes girls at 11 and 13 from September 2010. An academic school which has, in recent years, put much effort – and cash – into raising the standard and profile of the other areas of excellence it offers. Justifiably, but not forbiddingly, sought after, this school will get the best out of its boys and do the best by them. All but the shyest girls will thrive here too.

PERSE SCHOOL FOR GIRLS

Union Road, Cambridge, Cambridgeshire, CB2 1HF

Tel: 01223 454 700
Fax: 01223 467 420
E-mail: office@admin.perse.cambs.sch.uk
Website: www.perse.cambs.sch.uk

• Pupils: junior school 170, senior school 520 • Ages: juniors 7-11; seniors 11-18 • Size of sixth form: 115 • Non-denom • Fees: £2,810 - £3,300 • Independent • Open days: One morning in October and one evening in November (sixth form)

Headmistress: Since 2001, Miss Patricia Kelleher MA (early forties), read history at LMH Oxford, did a further MA at Sussex, taught at Haberdashers, then Brighton and Hove GDST, was deputy head at Brentwood School before joining the Perse Girls. A warm, engaging and not at all headmistressy person. The marked absence of grandeur about her and her office make a visit a totally undaunting experience. Staff and girls are clearly at ease with her. She feels she has helped to create a school for the 21st century with an international flavour, where girls are not pressed into a narrowly academic mould or screwed down to their desks, but are outward-looking and having fun.

Academic Matters: Results are outstanding, with nearly 90 per cent A*/A at GCSE (girls take 10 – 11 subjects), and nearly 90 per cent A/B grades at A level. All subjects do extremely well but languages are a particular strength (the GCSE score rises to 100 per cent A*/A for those taking languages early in y10), with eight on offer, including Latin, ancient Greek and Japanese. The curriculum is very broad at all levels and a low pupil/teacher ratio ensures that classes with only one or two pupils survive at GCSE and A level. There is streaming for maths and French from the word go, and in science from y10. Maximum class size is 22 up to GCSE and 14 at A/AS level. ICT provision is good but does not dominate the scene; the overall impression is one of lively teaching and responsive pupils unaffected by the fact that quite a few classrooms are still in need of modernisation. The library is in a bit of a time warp and little used but, until funds allow this to be rectified, departments have their own libraries and parents certainly don't see it as a problem. Most labs, on the other hand, are sparkling with modernity. Pupils' work is in evidence everywhere, including a shower of favourite literary quotations spilling over banisters for all to read.

Being a selective school, there are few girls with any learning problems, and any mild dyslexia is quickly identified and referred, staff are advised, but there is no SEN or EFL provision in the school. Sixth form has a bright and airy centre across the road from the main school, with its own IT facilities and study areas.

Games, Options, The Arts: Governors have recently poured £1m into the games field, ten minutes' walk from the school, and it is now a splendid facility with a state of the art pavilion and outside bodies forming a queue to use it. The school has been thought of as 'ungamesy' in the past but a dynamic new head of department has put an end to all that and teams in all sports are a match for anyone. The help of top class professional coaches is frequently enlisted and girls not only represent the county and England, but are also Cambridge champions in various sports. Last year netball teams went on a memorable tour to South Africa.

Eye-catching and very imaginative work is produced by the art department, particularly in ceramics and textiles, and enthusiasms are fired by visiting professionals such as sculptors and printmakers. The school is part of the prestigious Comenius scheme, which shares projects with schools in Hungary, Finland and Portugal. These are built into an exciting programme of creative arts and technology which is part of the y9 curriculum, and has modules in everything from architecture to robotics, through masks and make-up and musical composition.

The music department has an excellent separate home with a performance area and numerous instrumental lesson rooms, where more than 20 instruments are taught. There are several choirs and vocal ensembles, orchestras, bands and chamber groups, performing frequently, sometimes in the University concert hall. David Willcocks recently came

and conducted a performance of parts of the Fauré Requiem to celebrate the school's 25th anniversary. Music tours are organised as far afield as Australia.

The school prides itself on the international flavour of many of its activities; in 2004 it gained a sought after 'international school' award from the British Council. The list of foreign visits (as far afield as Japan) is endless.

There is a vast range of extra-curricular activities taking place before and after school and in the lunch break. What the 2002 inspection saw as a rather congested timetable is in fact a minor miracle of logistics, offering at least 25 opportunities for broadening horizons. One of them, The Gambia club, raises money for projects there and sends out a group of L6 girls to help every year. Drama is hugely popular, and plays often have an international flavour. About every other year the sixth formers studying Greek produce a classical Greek play, with choruses in Greek, and the rest translated by themselves.

Background and Atmosphere: Founded in 1881 as a sister school to the much older Perse Boys. The head stresses, however, that the two schools are very different, and the Perse Girls is not at all the traditional public school that the boys' school is. It feels, indeed, more like a sort of updated grammar school. Situated near the centre of Cambridge it is in the fortunate position of having some excellent facilities and lecturers on the doorstep, which are made good use of. It also has its own nature reserve near the Cam, used by both the junior and the senior pupils, where keen moth-watching members of the public are also made welcome. Entering the school, one feels a bit like Alice in Wonderland. An insignificant door gives access to a large and slightly labyrinthine complex of buildings dating from the late 19th century to the present. Some of it looks a bit run down, but there is a sort of homely cheerfulness about the place. A new dining room and assembly hall, to replace the cramped and battered existing ones and to be ready early in 2007, will make a huge difference. But there is no sign that the odd creaky floorboard and old-fashioned classroom in any way detracts from the business-like and go-ahead atmosphere.

Pastoral Care and Discipline: Year heads and form tutors forms the backbone of the pastoral system, and this has recently been complemented by the appointment of a second deputy head responsible for pastoral care, and of a school nurse, who provides another listening ear. Relations between staff and girls are so relaxed that girls feel they can talk to a number of people, including the head! There are six 'houses', and although form loyalties are the strongest, house competitions (sport, drama and a very popular talent contest), are keenly fought. Sixth formers play a key role in the organisation of these and help with form charity events, as well as being prefects. They choose their own tutor groups, so as to be with their own particular friendship group. There are three full assemblies per week, and all forms get a chance to be involved. Girls are committed, well-behaved, enthusiastic, and not more than usually messy.

Pupils and Parents: Pupils are almost all local, fairly solidly middle-class, with a smattering of dons' daughters. Parents are very keen on the school, and supportive of it. Quite a few highly distinguished old girls eg the author Philippa Pearce, archeologist Jacquetta Hawkes, broadcaster Bridget Kendall and Olympic gold medallist Stephanie Cook.

Entrance: Exam and interview at eleven, some from local prep and primary schools, the largest number from Perse Junior School, from which entry is more or less automatic. A few join in y9, a few more in the sixth form. Girls are expected to have gained an A at GCSE in subjects they wish to study at AS/A level.

Exit: Some leakage at the end of y11, mainly to Hills Road SFC, though some join the co-ed sixth form at Perse Boys. They are to become co-ed throughout in the near future, and it is not known what effect this will have on Perse Girls. About a quarter or more girls gain places post A level at Oxbridge, with a definite preference for Oxford. Others go mainly to top universities. The number opting for engineering courses is a good indicator that there is no sign of a glass ceiling here.

Money Matters: Governors' scholarships at KS3 and also 6th form scholarships, plus means tested bursaries. Every year the school is awarded several Nuffield bursaries for science and there is currently an Arkwright scholar in y13.

Remarks: A top notch selective school which manages to deliver a first rate education at the same time as offering a truly outstanding cultural and creative extra-curricular experience.

PETER SYMONDS COLLEGE

Owens Road, Winchester, Hampshire, SO22 6RX

Tel: 01962 852 764
Fax: 01962 849 372
E-mail: psc@psc.ac.uk
Website: www.psc.ac.uk

• Pupils: 2,500 boys and girls; most day, 100 board • Ages: 16-18 • Non-denom but with strong links to C of E • Fees: Boarding (average) £7,000 • State • Open days: Three open evenings in November and one in February

Principal: Since 1993, Mr Neil Hopkins BSc MEd (early fifties), read maths at University of East Anglia. Taught maths in a comprehensive, then Eccles Sixth Form College. Previously acting principal at Rutland Sixth Form College. Married (wife lectures in further education) with three children, all of who have been through Peter Symonds. His role is essentially general manager – five faculty heads are more in touch with the pupils themselves and he 'only knows the very good and very bad by name'. Approachable and dynamic, he is very results-orientated and has overseen a period of great expansion and building at the College. Peter Symonds is now the biggest A level centre in the country.

Academic Matters: Academically well up amongst the top 10 (out of 100) sixth form colleges. Overall A level pass rate approaching 99 per cent with over half of A levels graded A or B. AS results are equally impressive for a non-selective school. Principal keen to point out that results can be compared directly with Winchester College's when you select only the top performing 500 pupils. 'Value-added' scores were not available but are used to encourage pupils and teachers alike. Wonderful, wide selection of courses on offer – pupils can choose from 35 A level subjects. Lots of non-traditional subjects available such as performing arts (dance, theatre and music 'outstanding' course according to the Inspectors' report), film studies and sport and PE as well as classical civilisation (but no Greek or Latin) and economics (now largely overtaken by business studies in most schools but very popular here). Some courses are 'victims of their own success' and pupils have reported that they could not study their first choices. Candidates now have to audition for performing arts and pupils cannot opt for 2 art subjects together (such as art and photography).

Numbers are huge – there are 21 sets for biology for example. No streaming though. Some unevenness in teaching is addressed by close results' monitoring and regular classroom observation. All pupils report that they have excellent and inspiring teachers, though some are reportedly less than stellar. Computers are much in evidence throughout the college and banks of them are available and used in the library.

Around 12 students a year are selected for the Hampshire Specialist Music Course on which they study 2 instruments to a post Grade 8 standard as well as studying for music plus 2 or 3 further A levels.

Less academic students (about 100 of the total) can pursue vocational courses – foundation and intermediate level GNVQs and/or VCEs (vocational A levels) in such subjects as health & social care or business & finance – 'much more useful than re-sitting GCSEs and struggling with A levels'. Just 4 GCSEs are on offer, for retakes. Academically, the pupils are watched very closely and attendance is monitored electronically by lesson. Each pupil has a tutor (who is not necessarily teaching him or her) and regular tutorial sessions to monitor progress and prepare for university entrance. Falling attendance and not handing in assignments triggers action and a letter to parents. Predicted grade summaries are sent home 3 times a year but parents are only encouraged to parent-teacher meetings if there is a problem. Pupils report that there is all the help they need if they ask for it – but they have to ask for it. This is not an environment for those who need spoon-feeding and pushing along. Strong learning support system in place – those with learning difficulties are actively sought out and helped in the specialist department. Some 15 per cent of pupils benefit from some form of help including essay planning and self-organisation. Corridor to learning support centre lined with pictures of successful and famous dyslexics. Similarly, those aiming for Oxbridge or competitive courses such as medicine, vet science, physiotherapy have additional guidance and interview practice. Ofsted report of 2005 rated Peter Symonds College as 'outstanding'.

Games, Options, The Arts: Pupils must choose a minimum of one activity from a long list (50+) ranging from Amnesty International to windsurfing. Progress is monitored by personal tutors and used in reference writing for university entrance. A fifth of the courses are accredited, such as the Community Sports Leader Award and the Duke of Edinburgh award. Sports are very competitive because of the large size of the school – those who were used to being in a team cannot automatically expect to be selected to play for the College. Fund raising and local community work is greatly encouraged. Drama is strong because of the performing arts course. The college orchestra, jazz band and choir all perform to a high standard.

Background and Atmosphere: Peter Symonds originally founded Christes Hospitall (no relation to Horsham school) in the sixteenth century to look after aged brethren, assist two divinity students and educate 4 poor boys. Sale of land during the expansion of the railways at the end of the nineteenth century allowed a boys' grammar school to be built on the current site, becoming a sixth form college in the early seventies. College buildings located on top of a grassy hill overlooking the suburbs of Winchester and train station. Town centre and lure of coffee bars and shopping just a mile away. Original late Victorian building now completely converted into enormous and comprehensive learning and resources centre (library plus) and is surrounded by marvellous, dedicated buildings purpose-built in the last ten years. Everything being used to full capacity.

Pupils socialise in giant departure lounge style common room and outside in pubs and coffee houses. Large canteen provides cheap and plentiful food. No uniform (but all pupils tidy and purposeful, with backpacks and mobile phones). Teachers are called by their first names. Friendly, casual atmosphere. This is really a half way house between school and university.

Boarding is provided in 2 houses, both mixed single en-suite rooms to sharing with 3 others. Quiet study time for 2 hours each evening and curfew at 10.30. 'Very happy atmosphere' report boarders.

Pastoral Care and Discipline: Discipline minimal. Although there is a zero tolerance policy on drugs and alcohol on site, there are 2 designated (outside) smoking areas. Principal has expelled occasional miscreant for possession of cannabis. 'Litter is our biggest headache'. This sudden freedom can go to their heads but surprisingly few (3 per cent) drop out. No prefect system but elected student union handles social and philanthropic matters and is the student voice on college committees. Personal tutor system greatly appreciated by students to help them with progress and direction. Full time counsellor available for personal matters. Very little parking for students.

Pupils and Parents: Intake is 40 per cent from the 3 main Winchester state schools plus Perins Community School in Alresford, 15 per cent from independent day and boarding schools and the rest from far and wide – Reading, Salisbury and Isle of Wight included. Principal says you can't tell what sort of school the students came from after the first few weeks and students confirm this. Student social profile directly reflects Winchester skew towards ambitious middle classes – one teacher remarked that there is 'nothing as formidable as a Winchester mother protecting her young'.

Entrance: Deadline for application – mid-March for starting in September. Non-selective – requirement for A level courses is a minimal 5 grade Cs at GSCE level, which should include maths and English. Some courses are over-subscribed and an unofficial geographical selection exists for these – priority is given to the Winchester state schools. Less academically able children are encouraged to pursue vocational courses. For the Hampshire Specialist Music Course candidates have to audition on 2 instruments, one of which should be at grade 7/8 standard. For boarding, priority is given to Falkland Islanders, Services children and those on the Specialist Music Course. Apply early for the few remaining places.

Exit: 85 per cent to universities of all descriptions, with a steady 45 to 50 to Oxbridge.

Money Matters: Students must pay for their own books, meals and transport. Hardship funds are available for those who need them, at the school's discretion.

Remarks: A huge, friendly, highly successful sixth form college which falls neatly between school and university in approach. The self-motivated can take advantage of the myriad of A level courses and resources on offer.

PIMLICO SCHOOL

Lupus Street, London, SW1V 3AT

Tel: 02078 280 881
Fax: 02079 310 549
E-mail: enquiries@pimlicoschool.org.uk
Website: www.pimlicoschool.org.uk

• Pupils: 1,350 boys and girls; all day • Ages: 11-18 • Size of sixth form: 180 • Non-denom • State • Open days: In the autumn term

Head: Since 1995, Mr Philip Barnard (late forties). Educated in Singapore, Darlington and UMIST. Joined Pimlico in 1973 to teach maths and has risen through the ranks. Active and engaging, fully involved in the everyday life of the school, but refuses to meet the Guide, so we do not have his views on the school's progress. Married with a teenage son, at state school in Wandsworth.

Entrance: All London state school admissions are now co-ordinated. If you want to apply for Pimlico, list it on your own borough's application form, along with every other London state school that you are applying for, in order of preference. Priority to looked-after children, then those with a medical or social reason for choosing Pimlico, then siblings, then children at Westminster primary schools. Remaining places go to those living nearest which, in practice, means about a mile and a half.

Pimlico also runs a special music course, taking 24 talented musicians a year from about 150 applicants – apply direct to the school. In theory Westminster primary school pupils get preference but, in practice, most special musicians come from outside Westminster.

Exit: About half go on to the sixth form, others moving on to local sixth form colleges. About 80 per cent of sixth formers go on to a range of old and new universities, to study courses ranging from Arabic to nursing. Two or three a year to Oxbridge.

Remarks: Over-subscribed, inner London comprehensive which had a few uncertain years of in-fighting (presided over by then chair of governors and parent, Jack Straw) over whether or not the school should be rebuilt via the government's favoured Private Finance Initiative, with developers using part of the grounds for luxury flats. The award-winning 1960s building is like a cross between a car ferry and a giant greenhouse, tending, as one would imagine, to freeze its inhabitants in winter and boil them in summer. Rebuilding now seems to be off the cards. There has been £1 million refurbishment over the past year or two eg science labs, but the future of the, now somewhat dilapidated, building is still undecided. However, the middle classes, who were deterred by the in-fighting, are now returning.

Performing arts particularly strong; the school is now a Specialist School for Visual and Performing Arts. Music instrument tuition is free – though there can be long waiting lists for eg guitar lessons – and there are extremely impressive concerts. The special music course gives the school a strong musical base and large numbers take music GCSE – some in year 9 – though relatively few continue to A level. Excellent drama, with large and lavish whole school productions of eg West Side Story, Little Shop of Horrors. Theatre and media studies popular at A level and BTEC. Good art, including GNVQ Art and Design, with much use made of London's galleries and museums. Good PE, including dance, despite a lack of outdoor space. The school has four tarmac football pitches, two gyms and a swimming pool.

Science and maths are weaker: the school suffers from the general inner-city difficulty in recruiting and keeping experienced staff. Most teaching groups are mixed ability, and Ofsted commented that work is often not matched to the abilities of the least and most able pupils. The school has started master classes for gifted and talented children, in lunch hours and after school. Staff are encouraged to provide extension work. The school uses the SMILE maths system, with students working at their own pace. Few girls take maths, physics or chemistry A level. Languages come out well. Some 40 per cent of pupils speak English as an additional language and are used to studying languages at home. Many are encouraged to take a GCSE in their first language. Good history and geography too.

In 2005, 45 per cent of pupils got five or more A* – C grades at GCSE. Ofsted commented, 'achievement would improve further if students took a less relaxed attitude towards attendance and punctuality. Most students behave well but a small yet significant minority does not.' Parents express concern about behaviour management and lack of homework. The head comments that social inclusion means including badly behaved students. 'I am of the opinion that everyone has a saving grace, so we try to work with them.' The school has three learning mentors who help with target setting and monitoring and a learning support unit where those who are struggling with the work can get small group tuition. 'You promote assertive discipline by promoting work. We're trying to accentuate the positive.' There is good EAL and SEN support, inside and outside lessons. Some year 10 and 11 students go to college one day a week to study eg motor vehicle maintenance, photography or electronics. A gate has just been installed inside the entrance hall and pupils have to sign in or out before passing through – an initiative to improve attendance and punctuality. A huge social and ethnic mix, including about 10 per cent refugees and asylum seekers, children from grim inner-London estates and some from the progressive middle classes. Students tend to be opinionated – 'some of the boys talk too much and write too little,' says the head – and socially conscious. Good racial harmony, 'you have to work at it.'

Corridor walls are vibrant with photos of performances, paintings of eminent authors, illustrations of DNA – and some graffiti (mostly, says the head, by visitors coming to after-school or weekend events). The school, too, is a vibrant place, which works hard to deal with disruptive elements while holding on to its progressive values. 'We're on an upward curve,' says the head.

PLYMOUTH COLLEGE

Linked to Saint Dunstan's Abbey, The Plymouth College Junior School in the Junior section

Ford Park, Plymouth, Devon, PL4 6RN

Tel: 01752 203 300
Fax: 01752 203 246
E-mail: mail@plymouthcollege.com
Website: www.plymouthcollege.com

• Pupils: 280 girls, 360 boys. 105 boarders, the rest day • Ages: 11-18 • Size of sixth form: 210 • C of E • Fees: Pre-prep: £1,779, Years 1-2: £1,867, Years 3-6 £2,000 • Independent • Open days: September

Head: Since 1990, Alan Morsley BSc ARCS CMath FIMA FRSA (sixties). Maths graduate from Imperial College, London. Began career as maths teacher at Essex comprehensive. Also worked as house master and head of maths before becoming the head of a Yorkshire independent. Married with three grown-up children. Has a passion for the history of art. Also enjoys music and cricket. Concentrates on the management demands of the schools.

Academic Matters: Strong academically. At 95 per cent, the A* to C pass rate at GCSE is the school's best ever, with A*/A grades up around 45 per cent. 60 per cent A/B at A level. Very strong economics, physics and engineering students, winning top competitions. Upper sixth students provided two of the four teams in the 2005 national final of the business CIMA Management Challenge Competition – school were runners-up in 2004. Strong sciences and business studies generally. French compulsory from year 7. Students can choose Latin, German or Classical Civilisations in year 8. Pushes strong linguists towards Latin – also useful for medics, lawyers and English experts. Small classes: two to seven pupils is common at AS & A level; the average is about 15 lower down the school.Hot learning support system with some 80 students including some very bright who have a mild specific educational need including three Aspergers. Will take Dyslexics with reasonable IQ (this is a school for those who are capable of achieving a minimum of eight GCSEs) but not so geared up for ADHDs or those with general learning problems. Any stragglers will be advised to drop a subject and will receive extra help to concentrate on the main ones. 'It really helps your child be the best they can be.'

Games, Options, The Arts: Ample on-site sporting facilities. Excellent sporting reputation. Outstanding rugby teams with Devon Cup champions in each year group. Shares on-site swimming pool with Plymouth Leander club that sees pupils swim for Great Britain. Girls' team beat other independent schools in 2005 to become HMC Schools Champions for the third year running. County successes in netball, hockey, athletics, cricket and tennis. Plenty of practice, specialist teaching and performance rooms for music including a recording studio and performance hall with professional audio and lighting equipment. Discussion groups of a director, producer, editor, DJ announcer and publicity officer develop varied performing skills. Drama is not as strong here, although it is 'up and coming'. Separate art house houses fantastic artwork with extremely broad styles. Visiting lecturers from poets to sportsmen.

Background and Atmosphere: Acquired girl's preparatory school in 1995 and the nearby St Dunstan's Independent in 2004. 'It works very well with the Prep being on a separate site. I don't think four and 18-year-olds should be on the same site,' said the head. Founded in 1877, the site is a vast maze of large buildings with a myriad of corridors and doors creating an extremely quiet school. Must be somewhat daunting for newcomers. The students seem to have masses of space – a table or even a row each although the head is determined to reduce the number of pupils to 600. Not an elite or tough city school. Adopts a more gentle, seemingly laid back air, perhaps quietly confident. However, in class the students are extremely attentive and studious – a dream for any committed teacher.

Pastoral Care and Discipline: No behaviour problems in evidence here. 'Very helpful' resident married housemaster and housemistress and a member of the sixth form team support boarders on a one-to-one basis or in small groups. Boys are accommodated in three houses on one side of the housemaster's home, with girls in the three houses on the other side. Lots to do for weekenders, from surfing to skating.

Pupils and Parents: Overall well-presented and polite individuals. Sixth form senior prefects adorned with graduate-style gowns when accompanying visitors or on special days. Varied social and professional backgrounds. Many from the local area whose parents work at Plymouth's Derriford Hospital. Some 10 per cent foreign nationals, including 50 from Hong Kong resulting from the St Dunstan's merger; some German, South Korean and African.

Entrance: Only mildly selective, so enormous range of ability on entry, following satisfactory performance in entrance exam. Typically lower ability than neighbouring grammars on entry but GCSE and A level results compete. Six passes including maths and English are required at GCSE, including a minimum of three B grades, to enter the sixth form. Some 70 per cent enter from Prep. Intake likely to be reduced, particularly fewer foreign nationals.

Exit: Half head for traditional universities but many are increasingly staying local. Aspiring doctors, surgeons etc look to the new Peninsular Medical Training School in Plymouth, others to Plymouth University for subjects like maritime studies.

Money Matters: Some scholarships, the odd bursary.

Remarks: A huge school with ample space, excellent teaching and many opportunities to excel.

PLYMSTOCK SCHOOL

Church Road, Plymstock, Plymouth, Devon, PL9 9AZ

Tel: 01752 402 679
Fax: 01752 484 018
E-mail: info@plymstockschool.org.uk
Website: www.plymstockschool.org.uk

• Pupils: 1575 boys and girls, all day • Ages: 11-18 • Size of sixth form: 260 • State

Head: Since 2002, Dr Sean Sweeney (PhD MA BMus MIMgt (late forties). Honours graduate from University of Wales. Previous managerial posts included vice principal of Stoke Dameral Community College, Plymouth, and headteacher of Ridgeway School, Plympton. A studious looking man, passionate about sport and music. As a musician, he has recorded for radio and television and has made a CD of choral and keyboard music. At Plymstock, he has taught music and general studies and played piano for school productions. Dr Sweeney has high expectations of himself and others. He likes to keep his fingers on the educational pulse – part of editorial board for international teacher development journal, external examiner, chairperson of South West Educational Leadership. His energy and enthusiasm finds him in the thick of it – active in the classroom and local community, holding officer posts on the Community Council, Civic Society, Academic Council and Plym Adult Education Governors. Parents believe his enthusiasm rubs off on his pupils. Lives in Tavistock with his wife and three children.

Academic Matters: Top (75 per cent A* to C) at GCSE for Devon. 25 A level courses, besides good GNVQ, NVQ, RSA opportunities via a training consortium. Lots of awards.

Games, Options, The Arts: Excellent reputation for county, national and international sporting achievements – hence has Specialist Sports College status. Students clinched 2003 Junior World Championship title in Mirror Dinghy class. Enviably large, outdoor floodlit sporting area with flat grass track and netball/tennis courts. Parents believe separating boys' and girls' groups for PE works. The less academic will not fade here and budding acting professionals still have a chance with drama and performing arts A level. Growing percentage of students do PE, dance and sport studies. The art adorning the corridors shouts high quality. Parents impressed with varied range of musical and dramatic performances from Shakespeare to Rock and Roll. Work experience in Germany popular for A level German students – a big confidence booster.

Background and Atmosphere: Attractive school with garden courtyards. Teachers and parents work well together. Quiet and hard-working atmosphere of which it is proud. Recent investment of £5m has replaced temporary classrooms with well-facilitated dance and drama, modern languages, mathematics, pottery and sport areas. Science, technology and humanities refurbished. Plymstock keeps up with leading edge ICT development – electronic whiteboards in every department, digital music recording.

Pastoral Care and Discipline: Parents don't seem to be the worrying type as Plymstock has a reputation for finding and supporting everyone's talent. Enhanced Specialist Provision coordinator for communication difficulties and intensive numeracy and literacy programme for SEN in years 7 and 8. Good extension studies for gifted/talented students through faster moving classes, earlier entry into subjects, supportive services include reading and homework club. Bullying or behavioural problems are dealt with quickly. It's 'cool to be clever at Plymstock' so ridiculing swats is out. 'Unreserved support' for any necessary punishment is expected from parents. Wheelchair friendly.

Pupils and Parents: Mixed social backgrounds, although Plymstock is more affluent than many parts of Plymouth. Parents are 'proud' to send their children to Plymstock: 'It really encourages individuals to celebrate their talents'. Students believe they achieve because the teaching is good. Olympic swimmer and gold medalist Sharon Davies came here before winning a scholarship to Kelly College.

Entrance: Pupils from eight feeder schools: Oreston, Elburton, Hooe, Dunstone, Pomphlett, Goosewell, Downham, Wembury – belonging to The Plymstock (Plymouth) Area Academic Council. This family of schools communicates well. One per cent choose Plymouth grammar schools instead.

Exit: Approximately 65 per cent of year 11 students progress to Plymstock's sixth form, others head for the local College of Further Education, the College of Art and Design, employment based training and other schools. Plymstock regularly sends students to top universities, including Oxford and Cambridge.

Remarks: Highly successful and good all-round comprehensive in a pleasant suburb of Plymouth.

POLAM HALL SCHOOL

Linked to Polam Hall Junior School in the Junior section

Grange Road, Darlington, County Durham, DL1 5PA

Tel: 01325 463 383
Fax: 01325 383 539
E-mail: information@polamhall.com
Website: www.polamhall.com

- Pupils: 440 girls and the odd boy; 60 board • Ages: 3-18 • Size of sixth form: 50 (including boys) • Quaker origins • Fees: £2,690 (day); £5,235 (boarding). Juniors £1,320 - £1,955
- Independent

Head: Since 2004, Miss M Green BA PGCE (early fifties), previously head of English at Withington Girls' School, Manchester. Extremely cheery and welcoming, Bolton Wanderers supporter with one of the warmest handshakes ever encountered; studied English and French at Lancaster, exudes a love of literature. Although still somewhat the 'new girl', hugely enthusiastic and genuinely sincere in her affection for the school and pupils of all ages and stages.

Academic Matters: Moderately selective on intake, pupils expected to work hard and results impressive with non-high flyers achieving beyond expectations in all areas; maths very strong, bucking the trend with the largest A level group; French, German, Spanish and Chinese all available, pupil-run Russian club; art, music and drama vibrant and popular; science labs in need of (and due for) refurb; ICT much in evidence; comprehensive range of A level subjects for size of school. Very buzzy nursery and junior departments, colourful and enthusiastic displays abound.

Games, Options, The Arts: Hockey, lacrosse, netball, cross country, tennis, athletics all popular, little for boys as yet; attractive playing fields, courts and sports hall on school premises; school represented on England netball training squad; national golfer and fencer. Major sports tours to Canada, Australia. Purpose built theatre; termly music concerts; intimate 'coffee' concerts held in the conservatory to showcase developing talent. Mini bridge club – pre-drive schemes for sixth formers. Duke of Edinburgh Awards operating with sustained success at all levels. Extended view of the world encouraged with inspirational speakers, annual overseas visits, World Challenge to Malawi.

Background and Atmosphere: Founded in 1848 by Quakers with the descendants of founding families still represented on governing body. Tight, cohesive site including main school, junior school and boarding houses with a number of newer additions to original school house. Residential on three sides, attractive open parkland adjoining school grounds to one side lends a feeling of open space. Boarding facilities homely but tired, plans afoot to extend and improve.

Hard core of long-established, experienced teachers, fairly stable but with an appropriate injection of new blood, average age 37; mutually supportive, spirit of goodwill 'working together for the good of the whole' encouraged by collaborative leadership style.

Pastoral Care and Discipline: Regular assemblies ('Reading') reflecting Quaker foundations; awareness of the wider world and strong spirit of generosity. Successful and enthusiastic fundraising. Before and after school care, homework clubs and activity club during school holidays. Few formal rules; high standards of courtesy and behaviour expected based on respect for self and others. Strong anti-bullying policy; serious misconduct extremely rare.

Pupils and Parents: A broad cross-section of abilities, backgrounds and cultures here in a community that welcomes diversity. A changing profile with a large influx of overseas pupils mainly into upper school – including proud International Boarder of the Year finalists. Shocked local press recently by adding a handful of day boys into sixth form, mainly from nearby Hurworth House – so few, however, you'd be forgiven for missing them altogether.

Pupils are friendly, remarkably modest about their achievements and down-to-earth, reflecting the honest, unpretentious character of this northern school. School council produces manifestos and submits thought-provoking proposals, with even four-year-olds effectively negotiating the right to wear watches to school. Parents a mixture of urban and rural, first-time buyers and second and third generation Polamites. Strong Parents' Association organising free events for parent body. Parents' Focus Group presents views/perspectives to head.

Entrance: For entry at 11, diagnostic tests in English, mathematics and verbal reasoning, interview with head. Scholarships, means-tested bursaries and music awards available. At 16, examinations in three subjects, two of pupils' own choosing, plus a general paper, interview with head.

Exit: Varying numbers depart post-GCSE, most remain but small proportion move to local sixth form college or co-ed boarding schools. Northern universities favoured by pupils; small number of Oxbridge candidates. Notable old girls Nadine Bell, NASA scientist; Ruth Gemmell, actress.

Remarks: Ignore, if you can, the rather drab and uninspiring visitors' waiting room reminiscent of a tired B & B, and the tour improves remarkably from here on. Suddenly we remember we are in a school, with impressive work adorning the walls and cheery girls to meet and greet. Enthusiasm abounds, busy pupils at work and play with the well-organised, self-reliant manner that girls, with support and encouragement, do so well.

POOLE GRAMMAR SCHOOL

Gravel Hill, Poole, Dorset, BH17 9JU

Tel: 01202 692 132
Fax: 01202 606 500
E-mail: office@poolegrammar.com
Website: www.poolegrammar.com

• Pupils: 940 boys, all day • Ages: 12-18 • Size of sixth form: 300 • Non-denom • State • Open days: September

Head: Since 2004, Mr Ian Carter BSc PGCE NPQH (forties), member of the Institute of Biology, chartered biologist. Educated at Worthing Sixth Form College, then read zoology at Durham and earned PGCE from Pembroke College, Cambridge. Blue chip teaching career includes stints at University College School in London, Cranbrook Grammar School, Monkton Combe and Woodbridge School in Suffolk. Came to Poole from The Perse in Cambridge where he was deputy head. Wife, Suzy, works in modern languages at arch-rival Bournemouth Grammar, where their son is a pupil. Daughter at nearby comprehensive. Informally arranged hair conceals a stickler for detail. Keen that the school should focus on serving the local population, rather than drawing in the brightest berries on the bush from anywhere. Keen sportsman, played cricket and hockey in university and still surrenders to the call of leather on willow in the springtime. Sings in the local choral society. Lifelong interest in Borneo and spent time in Sarawak 'studying headhunters' in his twenties.

Academic Matters: A mathematics and computing specialist school and, not surprisingly, maths is the most popular A level subject here. Sciences also big – separate sciences for virtually all at GCSE now – with some stellar individual performances (but too many Ds and Es overall). Surprisingly, the subjects where the results really shine out lately are the more verbal ones – English, history, French, politics – and also art (though very few candidates for this last).

Enthusiastic and innovative IT. All pupils are entered for short course IT GCSE at end of year 9 and computing is a popular A level. The school has Cisco Academy status and students can earn the CCNA networking qualification in sixth form. Modern languages a bit limited (only French and German) but plans afoot to add Spanish. Currently no setting in languages but head appreciates the mind boggling boredom some French whizzes experience when they arrive here and may introduce it (some setting in maths at present). Media studies robust – not the vacuous piece of fluff it can be at some schools. Joint sixth form teaching in some subjects with Parkstone Grammar School (girls). Very good careers programme and all pupils do two weeks work experience in year 11. All take A level general studies, with mixed results, and a few do an AS in critical thinking. Class sizes under control, especially in sixth form.

As grammar schools go, Poole Grammar has made thoughtful provision for learning support via a part time specialist teacher and 7 learning support assistants. 'We're not afraid of special needs,' says the head, 'we want to celebrate differences.' A teacher at the school agreed, saying, 'we are working harder now to look after boys who are not achieving.' Currently two boys in wheelchairs.

Games, Options, The Arts: Considered a sporty school. Some activity compulsory all the way to the end of sixth form and a significant minority of boys are involved in teams. Football the most popular sport but rugby, cricket and athletics are probably more successful. Teams from Poole Grammar have recently been U13, U14 and U15 county cricket champions and South West Schools Athletics champions. Tennis played in the summer on new courts. Two old-fashioned gyms, one with diminutive climbing wall. Fencing available as an after school activity. Sailing (at Hamworthy) plus swimming and squash off the premises. After school participation in games and activities constrained by the bus schedule but much happens at lunch time. Music department enthusiastic and accomplished. Unconventional ex-actor has added a certain je ne sais quoi

to the drama department. Big theatrical production alternate years with smaller studio play in between. Some boys also take part in Parkstone Grammar's big musicals. Art a little less central here, with a slightly fringe following. Large, multi-faceted DT area, with a different room for each aspect of the subject, including food tech. Keen Young Enterprise.

Background and Atmosphere: A 'late' grammar school, founded in central Poole in 1904. Strangely, the school admitted boys and girls until 1937, when it became boys only. Moved in 1966 to Gravel Hill, a nondescript wooded artery into Poole famed for its speed traps. Large grounds, well cared for with, 'the best cricket square in Poole!' enthused the head. Much recent building, though the contractors seem to have mastered the retro sixties look, as the whole place looks of a piece. Library, with small sixth form study areas, used for an hour or so after school and at lunch. Science labs being upgraded – some now spiffy and we saw an unfathomable range of ultra-high-tech equipment. Boys expected to work hard and they do. Over 150 academic and non-academic prizes given annually. Although this is a place of work for nearly 1,000 manly adolescents, it feels surprisingly civilised and less macho than Bournemouth Grammar, only fifteen minutes away – not sure why.

Pastoral Care and Discipline: Heads of year take responsibility for all boys in the year. Head of year 8 makes sure the little lambs settle. Their year 9 tutor will then stay with their boys for the next 3 years. Uniform requirement relaxes over the years – from blazer and tie for years 8 and 9, to jumper and tie for years 10 and 11, to ties only in sixth form. Out (either temporarily or permanent) for bringing drugs on site – the policy was recently put to the test. Bullying will land you in school's exclusion room for a day. Parents praise the discipline here and the rapt and concentrating faces we saw in lessons certainly bore this out. School holds some social events with Parkstone Grammar.

Pupils and Parents: We dug long and hard but did not find parents who found fault with any major aspect of the school (the demon headmaster?). Families from range of social backgrounds, mainly united by good work ethic. Not a rich tapestry of ethnic diversity but this is Poole. Ability range broader than you would expect, perhaps owing to proximity of similar grammar in Bournemouth, plus very good local comprehensives, plus entrance policy that favours local pupils above potentially brighter but more distant applicants (see below).

Entrance: Complex and intensely controversial. In 2005, Poole Grammar was forced to change its entrance criteria that had until then discriminated against pupils living outside the borough. Aiming to keep Poole Grammar a local school, it changed the admissions policy to now favour pupils attending schools in Poole. This subtle change brought a wail of outrage from Poole residents whose children attend school on the wrong side of the borough line. The local independent preps, most of who are just outside the borough and turn a tidy sum by preparing pupils for the grammar, were among the loudest complainants. Meanwhile, Poole Grammar will continue to take some pupils attending schools outside the borough (there are not enough Poole boys to fill it). Entries by late October; test (in maths, English and reasoning) in late November for 162 places at 12+. Loads of appeals – 34 last year of which 10 were successful. Main feeders: Broadstone, Oakdale, and Canford Heath Middle Schools and Castle Court Prep. NB: Borough currently consulting over whether to move entry age to 11+: decision due by 2009. Sixth form entry much less competitive – surprising that more people haven't caught on: 6 A-C GCSEs required with at least a B in any subjects to be continued to A level.

Exit: One or two boys scram after year 8, often in search of small class sizes and hand-holding at a local independent school. 10 or 20 leave after GCSE to vocational courses or sixth form college. Later, to universities mainly in the southwest – Southampton, Bristol, Bath, Bournemouth (for media programmes) – also to Durham; few to London. Half a dozen or more to Oxbridge, mostly Ox. Staff includes seven Old Boys.

Remarks: A solid, commendable treasure serving the people of Poole.

PORTLAND PLACE SCHOOL

56-58 Portland Place, London, W1B 1NJ

Tel: 02073 078 700
Fax: 02074 362 676
E-mail: admin@portland-place.co.uk
Website: www.portland-place.co.uk

- Pupils: 323 (242 boys, 81 girls); all day • Ages: Ages: 11 - 18
- Size of sixth form: Size of sixth form: 59 (43 boys and 16 girls)
- Non denom. Independent • Fees: £3,650 • Independent
- Open days: Wednesday mornings - please contact the school

Headmaster: Since 1996, when school opened, Mr Richard Walker BSc (Hons) Chartered Chemist, PGCE, FRSA (early fifties). Educated at Hinckley Grammar School, Loughborough University and Goldsmith's College. Was head of chemistry at St Paul's Girls, then principal of Abbey College (also owned by Alpha Plus group, formerly DLD Group, which owns Portland Place and several other London schools and colleges). Married with two young daughters. Engaging, enthusiastic, very popular with parents. 'He is absolutely charming,' said one. 'He is easy to talk to and understanding – he sold me on the school.'

Academic Matters: Very unusually for a London independent school, Portland Place is deliberately aimed at a broad ability range. This means results do not compare well with the more selective schools except in value-added terms. 82 per cent of pupils got five or more A* – C grades at GCSE in 2005. The choice of subjects is limited partly by the small size of year groups – in 2005 there were 56 students in year 11 – and by the need to spend more time on English and maths than the very selective schools do. There is no RE or classics; DT is available in year 10, though the head is luke-warm on the subject. 'There isn't much demand for it and they do plenty of 3D work in art.' Everyone learns French and Spanish in years 7, 8 and 9, choosing one in year 10 to continue to GCSE. Other GCSE options include history, geography, music, business studies, ICT, art, drama and PE.

About 10 per cent of pupils have special needs – mostly dyslexia. These get specialist outside help once a week during a sports lesson, paid for directly by parents. 'We treat it as like a trombone lesson.' Some parents suggest that the school should have its own special needs department. 'But I make it very clear during open days that we are not a special needs school. I tell parents that their child will have to be able to work in a classroom with 19 other children.'

A level results tend to be poorer than GCSE results because many of the more academic pupils move on at 16, and their replacements are mostly from overseas, many on the borderline of qualifying to do A levels. The head sees it as his job to persuade the best students to stay on and is broadening the range of sixth form options. There are usually fewer than 30 A level candidates, so all sixth form classes are small, and the proportion of A and B grades fluctuates between about a quarter and a half. Business studies, economics and politics are all popular A level options.

Children are divided by ability into three groups for all subjects; these groups vary in size, averaging about 20 pupils, and the higher groups are usually the largest. Interactive teaching; lessons tend to be lively and informal. 'My son came from a very formal school and found this hard to cope with at first,' said a parent. 'But now he really enjoys it.' Others comment that their children find the lessons fun and interesting – if occasionally boisterous – and the teachers enthusiastic and encouraging. Occasional complaints of work not being marked nor misspellings corrected.

Games, Options, The Arts: Because the school has no outdoor space for letting off steam at lunchtime (which for this reason lasts only half an hour), everyone in years 7 – 9 has a double sports lesson every day. All the sports staff are national athletes; two recently competed in the World Bobsleigh Championships and one is British shot putt champion. Two have been selected for the 2006 Commonwealth Games. PE lessons take place in Regents Park, at Parliament Hill athletics track, or the University of Westminster gym. Plenty of after-school sports clubs, and the sports teams compete regularly. 'My daughter never did much sport at her junior school,' said a parent, 'but now she's very keen and plays in the teams.'

Everyone studies music in the first three years, though few continue to GCSE or A level. But plenty learn instruments; most visiting teachers are post-grads nipping in from the Royal Academy of Music just round the corner. The orchestral ensemble has a professional conductor. There are music concerts every term with solo and ensemble playing. 'My daughter is very musical and it's nice to have a platform for that,' said a parent.

A wide variety of artwork covers much of the communal space as well as the light, top floor art room. It is a popular and quite successful GCSE option; photography is available at A level. The school has only a small hall, but senior and junior drama productions take place in various London theatres, in the school's drama studio and in the RIBA head-

quarters just up the road. Sixth formers direct lower form plays and groups perform in assembly.

The school is ideally situated for outings to central London theatres and museums. Groups also visit France, New York and Barcelona, and years 7-9 spend the last two weeks of the summer term doing activities like climbing and sailing.

Background and Atmosphere: The head was in charge of a London sixth form college in the mid 1990s when he realised there was a desperate need for a co-ed broad ability school in central London. His employers, the DLD group (now the Alpha Plus group), agreed to buy two adjacent gracious grade II listed James Adam town houses in Portland Place and the school opened with 90 pupils in 1996. In 2002 it bought Harford House, a rather less beautiful ex-office building round the corner in Great Portland Street, where art, drama and science are based. In 2004 the school bought a fourth building, also in Great Portland Street, for the sixth form centre. The central London location means easy commuting for students and staff, some of the latter young New Zealanders. 'New Zealand is producing the most amazing quality of teachers.'

Lack of space is pupils' main complaint – the only common areas are the small-ish L-shaped hall (which accommodates some assemblies, packed lunches and concerts) and the examination hall in the sixth form centre. There is no outdoor space.

Pastoral Care and Discipline: The atmosphere and uniform are informal and, though the head takes drug and alcohol abuse very seriously, some parents complain of too much tolerance of scruffiness and bad language (head disagrees). All emphasise that their children are very happy here – 'students are very kind to one another.'

Pupils and Parents: A huge mixture, ethnically and socially. Many families see it as a haven from the more selective and demanding London independents, happily accommodating children who could not cope elsewhere.

Entrance: Most come in at 11. The school sets tests in maths and English and offers places to everyone of average ability and above. Pupils joining in year 8 are mostly, says the head, rather bright children who have found their state secondaries insufficiently challenging. There is another influx into year 9 of pupils from prep schools who have generally failed to get a place at their chosen public school. Those coming into the sixth form are usually expected to have at least five A* – C grades at GCSE, with Bs in their chosen A level subjects.

Exit: Some leave at 13 to go to more selective schools. 'This hurts, because the good teaching here has helped them to reach the level they need to move.' About a third usually leaves after GCSEs, again for the selective independents. Some three quarters of sixth formers go on to higher education, with London colleges being particularly popular; the rest go abroad, take gap years or retake A levels, or go straight to work.

Money Matters: One 50 per cent academic scholarship per year; bursaries may be available to see existing parents through hard times. 'We like to look after the ones we've got.'

Remarks: Increasingly popular central London co-ed school that does a good job of educating children of all abilities from average upwards, including many with special needs. Lively, fun teaching. Some parents find it too informal, others are grateful for a school that accommodates children that have not fitted in elsewhere. 'I wanted my daughter to have a gentle education where she could feel confident and find her strengths,' said a parent. 'She has been happy here from day one.'

THE PORTSMOUTH GRAMMAR SCHOOL

Linked to Portsmouth Grammar Junior School (The) in the Junior section

High Street, Old Portsmouth, Portsmouth, Hampshire, PO1 2LN

Tel: 023 9236 0036
Fax: 023 9236 3256
E-mail: admissions@pgs.org.uk
Website: www.pgs.org.uk

• Pupils: 989, two thirds boys. All day • Ages: 11-18 • Size of sixth form: 240 • Christian non-denom • Fees: Senior school £2,847; junior school £1,826 - £2,024 • Independent • Open days: Late September. Open afternoons, November, January, March

Head: Since 1997, Dr Tim Hands BA AKC (theological diploma) DPhil (forties). Read English at King's London, then on to St Catherine's Oxford, followed by Oriel where he ended up as lecturer. Housemaster at King's Canterbury and second master at Whitgift School before coming here. From a long line of teachers, including both parents and an ancestor who was schoolmaster on HMS Victory. Likes rugby, cricket, music and writes books, articles etc. Married, two children. An ideas man, who has carried through many ambitious and imaginative plans for the

school. Stickler for detail. Parents think he's great and credit him with softening PGS's slightly masculine, military reputation. Keen to celebrate Portsmouth's naval and literary history (Dickens was born here) and to enthuse his pupils with the special qualities of the city. Appointed to key role in 2005 as joint Chair of the HMC/GSA University Sub Committee.

Academic Matters: Very good A level results with large numbers sitting maths and sciences (school came top in 2002 UK Biology Olympiad), but also English. In last ten years 50 pupils have been awarded Examination Board Prizes for coming in the top five nationally. In 2005, a record 10 GCSE board prizes included five in AQA GCSE English Literature and 3 in AQA GCSE French. A levels also surprisingly strong in theatre studies, music, art, philosophy/religious studies, electronics – all of these attracting smallish numbers and doing those pupils proud. Unusual AS/A2 arrangement. Sixth form pupils commit at the start of year 12 to three A levels, plus either one or two ASs or another A level. Pupils in some subjects can do an AS over two years, if teacher and pupil prefer. School proud of this arrangement because of its flexibility and because it leaves more time for general studies (Radley was profiled in the national press as the only school with the courage to take ASs at the end of the sixth form – not entirely so!). GCSEs impressive across the board. Languages introduced in year 2, age 6, when junior school pupils experience a little French, Spanish, German, Italian and Latin (in rotation). Two modern languages plus Latin compulsory in years 7 and 8. Mostly mixed ability teaching, but setting in maths, languages and science. Average class size 21 in years 7-11; down to 8 (and often fewer) in the sixth form.

Games, Options, The Arts: Strong sport, with eight current internationals and several county cups. Pupils have competed in 5 national finals in the last two years in rounders, netball, athletics and hockey. The usual games are played one afternoon a week (twice a week in year 7) and rugby dominates (only a little football and no lacrosse in the senior school). Games optional after year 9. School owns 17 acres of playing fields at Hilsea, a couple of miles away, where a new all-weather hockey pitch was opened in 2005. Younger pupils travel there by school coach but, from year 9, pupils make their own way on public transport. Sea rowing and sailing on the doorstep. Lower school has covered swimming pool; upper school uses nearby city pool. Sports centre (1989) with three squash courts, sports hall, fitness suite and aerobics/dance studio, shared by members of school sports club. Inter-house competitions, from which team members are excluded, give less talented sportsmen chances to shine. CCF popular in this centre of naval activity (over 200 pupils). D of E also successful and several teams enter the Ten Tors expedition on Dartmoor each year.

Performing arts a great strength. School drama energetic and popular, with lots of performances and good record on LAMDA exams including a major musical production every year in one of the city theatres. PGS helps to organise the Portsmouth Festivities, a city-wide cultural festival involving music, theatre, talks, walks and more. Parents rave about the music taught in its own building with loads of practice rooms, new recording studio and lovely rotunda for concerts. All year 3s receive a term's free violin tuition. Strong singing tradition – choir has toured Czech Republic and travelled to Salzburg in 2005. Partnership with the prestigious London Mozart Players. Popular swing band. Some successful art but the department does not produce the same buzz as drama or music. Brilliant, meaty, pupil-produced school mag, with loads of good writing. Masses of overseas trips and exchanges. Masses of clubs and societies. Masses going on in general.

Background and Atmosphere: Founded 1732, went independent in 1976 and fully co-ed in 1995 though senior school still feels like a boys' grammar. Faint lingering scent of regimented past in the air, mostly owing to the stern, brick, listed architecture and shortage of greenery. Recently acquired former naval building, Cambridge House, next to the school's Cambridge Barracks. Substantial landscaping began 2003. Major re-development in 2005 has produced a new dining and theatre complex, a new library and state-of-the-art science laboratories. Much less pressurised environment than some of its rivals. PGS publishes thoughtful occasional series of monographs on topics to do with the school and Portsmouth's history.

Pastoral Care and Discipline: Four houses, each divided into mixed-age tutor groups, meet three times a week. Tutor stays with same group for two or three years and is the pastoral care lynchpin. Tutors speak by telephone to all their new tutees' parents within their first three weeks at the school (head sees the transcript of the call). A complementary system of heads of year, including head of sixth form, introduced in 2005. Buddying system for year 7 and 8 pupils to guard against bullying. Fairly rigorous discipline, with precise dress code (no multiple ear pierces) and 'no public displays of affection'. Pupils have to get the head's permission before accepting a weekend job. Pupils don't appear to follow all this to the letter but adhere to general principles. Sixth formers may go home for lunch or leave for the day at 12:50pm if they have no afternoon lessons, but no others allowed off campus. Active sixth form council. Expulsions/suspensions from time to time for drugs and OTT behaviour.

Pupils and Parents: Large proportion of pupils come to the senior school from state sector. Some travel from as far as Southampton, Winchester and Isle of Wight (and beyond). Six parent-organised coaches bring in the hordes and others take public transport. Pupils not polished but generally diligent and polite. Parents work for IBM, the Navy, professions; some humble backgrounds. One of school's monographs tells the stories of three former pupils who won the VC.

Entrance: January entrance tests for 11+ (125 places, but half these are filled by junior school children) in maths (no calculators), English and verbal reasoning, plus interview. For prep school pupils, CE usually replaces school's own test at 11 and 13. Families frequently transfer in and out of Portsmouth, so places open up in most years at odd times. Always worth inquiring. Entry to sixth form requires 7 GCSE passes at C or above, with 'high results' in subjects to be studied at A level. School's own pupils who fall short may be encouraged to look elsewhere.

Exit: Almost all to universities far and wide, a majority studying sciences. In 2005 over 90 per cent of pupils gained a place at their first choice university. 10 per cent to Oxbridge. 15-20 pupils leave after GCSEs, some for a wider curriculum, others because their GCSEs are not up to scratch.

Money Matters: Music and drama lessons a bargain. Range of academic scholarships at range of ages. Peter Ogden scholarships for state school pupils at 11 (pupils asked to bring 'their favourite thing' to the interview; article in The Times described some of the objects brought, including an artificial rib, once lodged within the candidate's own chest). Ogden, Rank and other bursaries also available at 16. Music scholarships at 13 and 16. Sixth form art, drama, science and sports scholarships.

Remarks: Traditional grammar, enthusiastically getting on with educating a wide range of pupils, including some of Portsmouth's best and brightest. At first glance it appears it may have expanded beyond manageable limits but seems to be juggling it all quite nicely. Markedly less macho than in former days – and girls very happy here – and now, it assures us, increasingly in touch with its feminine self.

PORTSMOUTH HIGH SCHOOL

Linked to Dovercourt - Portsmouth High Junior School in the Junior section

25 Kent Road, Southsea, Hampshire, PO5 3EQ

Tel: 023 9282 6714
Fax: 023 9281 4814
E-mail: headsec@por.gdst.net
Website: www.gdst.net/portsmouthhigh

- Pupils: 615 girls, all day • Ages: 3-18 • Size of sixth form: 95
- Non-denom • Fees: Seniors £2,455; juniors £1,779; nursery £1,470 • Independent • Open days: Open Day in October. Regular 'Drop-in' Mornings throughout the year and taster days

Head: Since 1999, Miss Peg Hulse BA (mid fifties). Taught English and drama for thirteen years at Newcastle-under-Lyme School, then deputy head at Northampton High. A solid and serious individual, soft-spoken but steely. Popular with girls and parents. Dedicated to the school which absorbs most of her time and talents. A Quaker.

Academic Matters: The straightforward, colour prospectus sets the tone for this school which is one of substance rather than gloss. Consistently very good results year in, year out. Outstanding sciences. Science block situated off-site, a short walk down a bustling shopping street, blocks of flats on all sides. Top-notch new sixth form laboratory (interactive whiteboard etc – 2000). Good maths. Emphasis on languages – French or Spanish compulsory up to GCSE and German or Latin compulsory in years 8 and 9. New AS/A2 subjects inc theatre studies (2002), psychology and design technology (both 2003). No EFL. A few girls with mild dyslexia. Has to compete head on with the enormous co-ed metropolis of Portsmouth Grammar School (over a thousand pupils) – the two schools stand cheek by jowl in recent A level league tables.

Games, Options, The Arts: Surprising amount of sport played on a shoestring. Talented sportswomen have every opportunity but some parents feel the school could do more to encourage everybody else. Up to 50 per cent of girls are involved in extra-curricular sport at some point during their time at the school (a low figure), 30 per cent regularly. Good at water sports – no pool (at present) but use Navy facilities – and netball. No games fields so school pays to use stretches of Southsea Common on the waterfront for hockey, rounders, tennis etc. University facilities used for hockey and athletics. Enthusiastic girls' football. New sports centre with

a new director of sport to go with it – September 2005. Gym has a sprung floor – good for dance, aerobics and gymnastics. The art building generates much good work. DT becoming very popular – new classrooms opened 2005.

Sprightly new drama studio (2002). Challenging performances that 'raise eyebrows' but more wholesome fare for the younger girls. Fantastic LAMDA exam results. Music wing has welcoming practice rooms and department boasts many accomplished players though some parents reckon this owes more to the encouragement and private tuition provided by parents than to the school's efforts. The school provides musicians with ample opportunities to progress and gain experience in public performance (including overseas music tours). Young Enterprise active.

Background and Atmosphere: Founded 1882. Historically not a thing of beauty. Inside, it feels like a London school – wedged in and multilayered, with lots of staircases and unusual passages. Extensive building programme has had a phenomenal effect, however, lightening and brightening the site. Parts are now quite lovely. Good IT facilities. Small, new (2000), mainly girl-run library (librarian supervises) – very pleasant and heavily used. Careers department lodges in a cubicle in the corner. The school has a warm family feel with the teachers knowing all the girls – even those they don't teach. Approach is very down-to-earth and unfussy. Short school day: 8.30am – 3.40pm. Suits those girls who travel long distances to be here. A fleet of coaches and minibuses brings girls from distant spots like Chichester and Southampton and girls come by train from as far away as Petersfield. Girls in sixth form mature and confident – look adults straight in the eye. Treated like adults and most live up to expectations. No uniform for sixth form – dress cheerfully scruffy (fashionable, says school). Sixth formers may come and go freely from site and enjoy many other privileges. Head girl elected by peers. Groovy sixth form centre (2000) wins most astonishing mess award which testifies to the sixth form's genuine autonomy. Relationships (balls etc) with co-ed St John's and Portsmouth Grammar.

Pastoral Care and Discipline: Works well in this relatively informal and egalitarian school environment. Year 7 girls are allocated a year 11 mentor. Each form has one or two sixth formers attached as helpers. Girls register twice a day with their form tutor. School day too short for issues of drugs and drinking to raise many problems.

Pupils and Parents: Girls generally mature and hard-working. Parents mostly on the middle side of middle class, educated, professionals and some Services families. Many humble backgrounds in on bursaries etc.

Entrance: Three form entry at 11. Girls also welcome at sixth form and most ages in between. At 11 girls sit maths and English papers based on the National Curriculum, meant to be user-friendly for girls from the state sector. Looking for average ability or better. Entry at sixth form requires seven GCSEs at grade C or better, with Bs in future A level subjects. At the junior school, 4-7 year olds attend an individual assessment session, plus a group assessment the following week. Older juniors attend school for a morning during which they are tested in English story writing, reading, spelling, comprehension and maths.

Exit: 30 per cent of girls leave after GCSE, with majority going to local sixth form colleges. Girls and parents who stayed are glad they did. They appreciate the high school's small size, its high standards and the close, nurturing relationships between teachers and students. Leavers tend to go on to universities in the south west: Bath, Exeter, Southampton, Portsmouth. A clutch to London. Two or three each year to Oxbridge. Gap years less common than at most schools.

Money Matters: A bargain. Always does well in charts evaluating value for money. Still awards huge numbers of scholarships and bursaries for such a small school (one-quarter of girls are recipients), though fewer than in the days of assisted places.

Remarks: A super no-frills choice for almost any girl. Small enough to be intimate, big enough to sparkle. Prestigious local reputation.

PRIOR PARK COLLEGE

Ralph Allen Drive, Combe Down, Bath, BA2 5AH

Tel: 01225 831 000
Fax: 01225 835 753
E-mail: admissions@priorpark.co.uk
Website: www.priorpark.co.uk

• Pupils: 300 boys, 248 girls (74 boys board, 226 day boys; 43 girls board; 205 day girls) boarding year 9 upwards • Ages: 11-18 • Size of sixth form: 170 • RC • Fees: Boarding £6,356. Day: 13+ £3,525; 11+ £3,164 • Independent • Open days: October and March

Head: Since 1996, Dr Giles Mercer MA DPhil (mid fifties). Went to Austin Friars School, Carlisle then read history at Churchill, Cambridge, then on to St John's, Oxford. Started career as head of history at Charterhouse before brief spell as assistant principal, MoD. Subsequently director of studies at Sherborne, then 11 years as headmaster of Stonyhurst before coming to Prior Park. Married to Caroline with one son. Likes travel, art and music. A committed Catholic with a realistically broad approach. Compassionate, articulate and approachable. Keen to emphasise positive praise whenever possible and to foster a family atmosphere in the school. Seen as an involved, effective head by parents and pupils. Cares deeply about kindness between pupils and in leading his staff from the front. Believes in maintaining a boarding ethos and structure despite vast majority of day pupils at PPC. Parents amazed at how 'he really knows pupils as individuals.'

Academic Matters: Results impressive given the broad band of ability. English and history are strongly-led departments with outstanding results at both A level and GCSE. Music, design & technology and theatre studies are impressive whilst maths results are also good with more candidates. Fewer pupils opt for physics, chemistry or modern languages at A level but there is plenty to lure them elsewhere such as music technology, sport studies and theology which all do well by their followers. Most pupils take ten subjects at GCSE with particularly good results in sciences where pupils generally have a choice between separate or dual award entry. Almost all pupils take two foreign languages in year 9 and at least one to GCSE. There is setting in all subjects by year 9 apart from English except in small subjects where there is only one set. Class sizes do not exceed 23 and are generally much smaller in GCSE sets and beyond. An excellent and oversubscribed Language Development Programme (LDP) accepts four pupils into year 7 each year and addresses mild dyslexia and dyspraxia (Asperger's syndrome also accommodated). EFL available.

Games, Options, The Arts: Fields strong teams in all ages in the major sports (rugby, hockey, netball, tennis, cricket and rounders) with good use made of its indoor heated swimming pool, gymnasium and fitness centre. Games timetabled and do not squeeze out other activities. The nearby 'Monument' playing fields were acquired from the National Trust in a swap for the landscaped grounds to which the school still has access and the Astroturf is adjacent to the school buildings. Use is made of superb athletics facilities at Bath University. Hilly surroundings well-suited to x-country including an idiosyncratic annual school relay event which engenders great excitement. Army and navy sections of the CCF, D of E with expeditions in the south-west and to Europe. Facilities, coaching and choice, particularly in the upper years, ensure that sports people are more than satisfied, with some playing at county level. The less athletic can find enjoyment and recognition too.

Exceptional diversity and quality in music, drama and dance with a majority of pupils involved in one or more activities. Julian Slade Theatre hosts wide range of musical and dramatic productions; well-equipped and brilliantly managed music department oversees five choirs, orchestra, chamber strings, quartets, piano trios, jazz band, wind band and rock bands. Magnificent new classical organ was installed in the college chapel in 1996 and the chapel choir has toured extensively in Europe. Pupils have won places at all the major music colleges and several pupils are currently members of leading national youth orchestras. Boys as well as girls take dance within theatre studies and high octane performances are much appreciated. Performing arts generate a tremendous buzz. Despite a reputedly strong art department there could be more evidence of visual arts around the school.

Background and Atmosphere: Founded in 1830 and run by the Christian Brothers until 1981, Prior Park is now the largest independent, co-educational, Catholic day and boarding school in the UK. Only 20 per cent of all pupils are boarders, but the proportion increases to about one third from year 9. And with 40 per cent practising Catholics, PPC does not feel like yet another largely day school with token boarders or nominal religious affiliation. It is also unmistakably co-educational with fairly even numbers of boys and girls throughout. The magnificent Georgian architecture with a view from the 'mansion' over the grounds (much of which are now National Trust property including the famous

Palladian Bridge) and Bath stretching out beyond is unsurpassed. The mansion has been painstakingly renovated and completely refurbished since the 1991 fire destroyed much of the interior. The College Chapel accommodates the whole school for weekly assemblies and mass, held roughly once each half term, plus particular feast days. Boarders have to attend mass on Sunday mornings and theology is compulsory throughout. The well established PSE programme also reflects Catholic thinking and the resident school chaplain plays a central role.

ICT has a new centre and is networked throughout including in the well-resourced and study-friendly library. Day pupils have a nominal workspace in their rather crowded house accommodation where daily prep is supervised between 4.45 and 5.45pm. Junior pupils are split into small vertical groups which counters the risk of year eights dominating. Roche and Allen are relatively civilised boarding houses for boys on the upper floors of the mansion whilst girls are accommodated in enviable surroundings in St Mary's house which occupies the nearby 'Priory'. Some day pupils opt to be in boarding houses because they prefer the ethos and flexi-boarding is popular. Most of the residential staff are Catholic as opposed to 40 per cent as a whole.

Pastoral Care and Discipline: The reward system is central to the head's philosophy and breeds a positive approach to work and behaviour. There is little evidence of a punishment culture. Pupils are generally well turned-out without being ostentatious. The deputy head is respected for being 'firm but fair' and remarkably there have been no expulsions in recent years. There is a strong counter-bullying policy. There is a good mix of 'old guard' and new staff with an average age in the common room around forty-one. All sixth formers are expected to involve themselves in running the school. Food gets a thumbs up, esp the baked spuds.

Pupils and Parents: Most come from within an hour's drive. Six daily mini-bus and coach routes transport day pupils from a 30 mile+ radius including a 7:15am start from junction 16 on the M4 which makes one wonder why those pupils don't board? Boarders generally come from further afield including a fairly traditional mix from overseas. Relatively few foreign nationals most of whom are Catholics from the Far East. Former pupils and current parents are very supportive with a range of fund-raising and social events and pages on the school website. Famous old boys include Cardinal Cormac Murphy-O'Connor, archbishop of Westminster, the impresario Sir Cameron Mackintosh, international rugby player Damian Cronin and television presenter Hugh Scully.

Entrance: Registration at least eighteen months before entrance is recommended. January entrance tests for either two or three form entry at 11+ with entrants coming from local 3-11 or 7-11 preps and about 20 per cent from state primaries. Lists close at least a year in advance for LDP applicants. About 40 pupils join at 13 with about half of them from the junior school at Cricklade, Wiltshire. November interviews for entrants into lower sixth who need a satisfactory reference and a minimum of 6 A*-C grades at GCSE with higher grades in chosen AS subjects.

Exit: Almost all to universities with Cardiff and Liverpool the most popular choices in recent years. Nine per cent to Oxbridge. Many take a gap year. A few leave after year 11.

Money Matters: Not a school for the super-rich – no five star frills. Range of scholarships and bursaries with good academic scholars typically gaining 30 per cent off fees. Services bursaries. Currently around 150 award holders. Some continuity scholarships from junior school. Generous discounts for siblings. Bus services charged monthly and quite pricey. Music tuition fees excellent value for money.

Remarks: A school which has transformed itself over the past twenty years and where most pupils will feel happy and busy. A strong Christian rather than heavily Catholic feel to the place. 'Non Catholics are made to feel welcome and involved,' said a recent leaver. Talents can blossom here without fear of censure from peers. The only school in Bath to run along boarding school lines, even for day pupils.

PRIOR'S FIELD SCHOOL

Priorsfield Road, Godalming, Surrey, GU7 2RH

Tel: 01483 810 551
Fax: 01483 810 180
E-mail: registrar@priorsfield.surrey.sch.uk
Website: www.priorsfield.surrey.sch.uk

• Pupils: 325 girls; 130 boarders (full and weekly), rest day
• Ages: 11-18 • Size of sixth form: 63 • Anglican • Fees: Day £3,695, boarding £5,950 • Independent • Open days: February, May and September - Boarding taster weekends in May and September

Head: Since 1999, Mrs Jenny Dwyer BEd (early forties). Educated at Bradford Girls Grammar and then Homerton College, Cambridge. First job at Benenden (teaching/ housemistress), then went on to Queen Anne's School, Caversham, where she was deputy head responsible for pastoral care. Young and dynamic, Mrs Dwyer has a warm and charming manner. Married to a 'very supportive man', they live on site and have two school-age sons who attend Milton Abbey and Charterhouse. She is interested in maths and hockey and maintains that pastoral care is her particular passion – a sentiment that is borne out by her pupils who describe her as 'approachable' and a great listener.

Off to head Sherborne Girls in July 2006. The new head is to be Mrs Julie Roseblade, currently deputy head of St Helen's School, Northwood.

Academic Matters: Mixed ability school achieving good results both at GCSE (86 per cent at A*-B grade) and A level (80-ish per cent at A-C grades). The girls are offered a wide variety of subjects given that it is such a small school. French and Spanish are taken from the first year and at least one of these has to be taken at GCSE. The school will try to organise less mainstream subjects such as Russian even if there is only one pupil.

Strong art and design department with some really imaginative pieces adorning the school. Textiles and food technology are also popular but so too are the sciences, geography and maths. PE is, surprisingly for a small school, offered at GCSE as well as at AS level and the superb new sports hall and dynamic staff ensure that it remains a popular choice.

Pupils are setted for maths, English, French and science from 11 but these sets are fluid and pupils can move up or down. Head believes that education is about far more than results on a certificate and thus there are a lot of practical courses on offer during the first few years. This is to ensure that all girls get some sort of grounding in life skills and perhaps help the less academic girls to find a niche for themselves.

The average class size is sixteen, going right down to one or two in the sixth form. School offers full-time support for pupils with SEN (mild dyslexia etc) and has virtually full-time EFL tutors for foreign students (8 per cent).

Games, Options, The Arts: Superb new sports hall built to celebrate the school's centenary. Locker rooms, for once designed with teenage girls in mind, are clean and airy with excellent showers and built-in hairdryers. Everyone is required to take part in sport at Prior's Field right through to the sixth form. The main sports are hockey, netball (county league players), tennis and athletics. Cross-country, gymnastics and swimming are popular activities, as are trampoline, basketball, badminton, fencing and archery clubs. Horse riding is an area in which the school excels, winning the national schools' championship recently. Enthusiastic, friendly sports staff, over the moon with their marvellous new facilities.

Over half of the girls receive individual instrument tuition. There are three choirs, orchestras, chamber, wind, string and jazz groups and the music department has its own facilities with practice rooms and a recital room. The school regularly gives concerts and performs at the Woking and Godalming music festivals. An interest in music is encouraged from when the girls first start school. Strong drama department with regular productions and A level options. Main hall now transformed into drama/arts centre. All the usual school clubs on offer as well as a few unusual ones such as lace-making. Girls are encouraged to take part in as much as possible. Some interesting options are Thai or Italian cookery courses, offered by parents.

Background and Atmosphere: The school was founded in 1902 by Julia Huxley, the granddaughter of Thomas Arnold of Rugby and the mother of Julian and Aldous Huxley. Members of the Huxley family still serve on the governing body. The main school building was designed by Charles Voysey (Arts and Crafts Movement) and the gardens by Gertrude Jekyll. Much has been added over the years but, thankfully, the modern buildings have been designed with more than a nod to Mr Voysey. The school has a genteel, albeit slightly shabby, air from the outside – a bit like an old manor house for distressed gentlefolk – but the whole effect is rather charming. School has good website that gives a feel of what the school is all about.

Unlike in many schools, boarding is growing in popularity here and there are taster boarding weekends to tempt the waverers. All the boarding facilities have undergone major refurbishment – it was needed. Pupils are allowed to bring their own bedroom furniture (space and room-mates permitting) and all tend to decorate them with scarves, posters and other girlie flotsam.

The common rooms are great with televisions, sofas, stereos and pool tables. Prep is supervised and television viewing is monitored, as is choice of videos. Day girls can sometimes board overnight or for short periods if parents are going away – they are also welcome to join in any weekend activities with boarders.

The sixth form house is separate from the rest of the boarding establishment. 20 en-suite bedrooms have been added together with additional kitchen and staff flat. Comfortable and laid-back, it is designed to have a university campus type feel to it with a great common room (complete with squishy sofas, stereos and television), kitchen and study rooms for the day girls. The majority of bedrooms have been refurbished and the girls can and do decorate them and they are private. New study rooms for all day girls.

Pastoral Care and Discipline: A nurturing environment is probably Prior's Field's greatest strength. Pressure down and achievement up underpin all that the head does for her school and she feels that it helps each girl find her level. 'If you take on a girl,' she says, 'you have an utmost responsibility to get the best out of them.' She describes the school as quietly disciplined with the rules being sufficiently reasonable to maintain equilibrium. 'There is a culture of being respectful to one another.' Strong house system in place as well as head girl and prefects. Head of year and form tutor each have a prefect linked to them and, because of small class sizes, problems are spotted and sorted out very quickly.

Anti-bullying policy and clear rules on smoking, drugs and alcohol. Not cast in stone though and each case will be dealt with on individual merits. School is anorexia-aware with an eye kept on those who seem to skip meals. Catering facilities transformed 2005. New processes and procedures in production together with a renovated kitchen and dining room. A varied selection of hot meat dishes and vegetarian as well as large salad bar and desserts on offer. All eat together and the bread, cakes and biscuits, which are made on site, are extremely popular and were very good, we thought. School has an Anglican leaning but is non-denominational. Everyone attends assemblies and representatives of various faiths are invited to lead assemblies.

Pupils and Parents: Wide cross section of pupils from all social environments. Most of the day pupils are dropped off by parents (not really on any bus route) and come from the local areas. School bus service from Haslemere, Milford and Godalming Station in mornings. Weekend bus service to London. 44 schools are feeders with the largest number coming from St Hillary's in Godalming. About one third comes from the state sector.

Entrance: Entrance is not a huge hurdle but it is becoming tougher to get in because of the growing popularity of the school. Entrance procedure kicks off in November prior to entrance with a preview day. Own exam taken in January – maths, English and science. The school is full, so early registration is recommended and becoming more crucial. There are also a number of sixth form imports.

Exit: Most go on to sixth form, although there are some who want to experience different things and exit to other schools or to sixth form colleges – usually ones where there are boys. The majority of sixth formers go on to tertiary education, which ranges from architecture to law to music or media studies. Institutions are varied and can be anything from the traditional universities to art colleges.

Money Matters: The school offers two academic scholarships and some drama, music and art scholarships. There is also a number of fourth year and sixth form scholarships, which can be up to 50 per cent of the fees.

Remarks: Someone once said that Prior's Field was 'the school for turning out politicians' wives.' It was meant to be an insult but was laughed at by the head who said that, if it meant her girls were confident, articulate and intelligent members of society who would know what to do in any situation, she had done her job. A well-rounded education is the hallmark of Prior's Field and it is well worth a look if you feel your daughter would wilt under academic pressure or if she needs a safe nurturing environment to spread her wings. Not the school for your headstrong or unconventional girl.

PURCELL SCHOOL

Linked to Purcell School Junior Department in the Junior section

Aldenham Road, Bushey, Hertfordshire, WD23 2TS

Tel: 01923 331 107
Fax: 01923 331 166
E-mail: info@purcell-school.org
Website: www.purcell-school.org

- Pupils: 172 boys and girls. Two thirds board • Ages: 9-18
- Non-denom • Fees: Day £6,788 day; £8,682 boarding
- Independent • Open days: September

Head: Since 1999, John Tolputt BA (fifties), read English at St John's, Cambridge, and Cert Ed at Bristol. Was head of English and drama at Bromsgrove and Cranleigh before moving to Rendcomb College, Glos, in 1987 where he remained as headmaster for 12 years. Non-musician but oozes appreciation. 'I'm musical in an audience sense,' he says. Is clearly his highly-gifted pupils' greatest fan and applauds their commitment. Knows the school is different. 'Music is at the centre and other things have to work in from the edges,' head explains. But keen to stress that Purcell pupils are 'amazingly normal children. They do all the things normal children do'. True up to a point. No longer plays teaching role though retains interest in drama productions. An earnest but unassuming head who quietly gets on with running the show while his young prodigies take centre stage. Comes from a musical family – wife Patta is musician and teacher (elsewhere), son Ed was choral scholar now actor and daughter Anna acts and sings.

Academic Matters: Despite being a specialist school, the ideal of a good, broad education is taken seriously here. Education is unquestionably 'good' (as evidenced by both the standard of the music and the surprisingly respectable A level results), but 'broad' is an exaggeration. No GCSE or A level computing courses (although music technology is an option). If your child is into science, physics and chemistry are on offer at A level but biology only at the next door school. There is no GCSE or A level economics, politics, classics, religious studies or business studies. Nonetheless, there are far more academic options than at most specialist schools and certainly ample for pupils who will be devoting so much of their time to music. Most pupils take three, sometimes four, A levels. Sixth formers earn heaps of As in A level music (which helps to explain the overall good exam results). Everyone sits the GCSE music exam one year early. Children seem earnestly attentive in their somewhat informal lessons and general level of academic achievement is laudable.

When it comes to managing time, there's an understanding that music comes first and academic lessons second. 'Such a relief,' said one pupil who had suffered under the opposite premise at his old school. Most pupils have three hours one-to-one tuition each week and study a wide repertoire, including contemporary classical music and jazz. In addition, there are lessons in theory, singing, music composition and music technology. Loads of performances, rehearsals and practice. A parent described it as a 'tough regime' but very few find it too much and leave. Excellent, enthusiastic, young-adult 'practice co-ordinators' provide both a big brother/sister pastoral role and a 'policing element,' making sure that the younger children clock in their time in the practice rooms. Good EFL provision for overseas pupils, some of whom come with almost no English. A Special Needs Coordinator monitors the few children with learning disabilities. Teachers 'do their best' to offer support.

Games, Options, The Arts: Not the place to send a child who is passionate about sport. Well-rounded these children may be, but most have neither the time, the interest nor – frankly – the ability to rustle up a serious game of rugger. Good sports field and we're told that there's a basketball team. Sports like weight training, table tennis and basketball are popular. There's a good gym. Teamwork skills are, of course, honed through playing in the orchestra and smaller ensembles. One or two dramatic productions each year. Art is a popular A level and GCSE subject and the work on display was encouraging. Lots of community outreach projects (to earn all that government funding) and the school has been effective in bringing musical performance to children in Bushey schools.

Background and Atmosphere: Founded in 1962 (called the Central Tutorial School for Young Musicians with fees £50 a term) as the UK's first specialist music school. From small beginnings, pupil numbers have grown steadily. Now boldly states, 'it is our mission to produce the world class musicians of tomorrow.' Has been at its current austerely impressive red-brick location on the edge of the Hertfordshire countryside for seven years. Outgrew its old home in Harrow so raised £2 million to buy former Royal Caledonian School, established for orphans of Scottish soldiers. Officially opened by patron Prince Charles in 1998. Since then, science labs and art school have been added on, and parts of original building partitioned to form practice rooms, small dorms and sixth form studies. Future plans for purpose-built music teaching and rehearsing facilities. Private funds already promised to cover one-third of costs, launching public fund-raising soon with hope to start building next year. Daunting dorms have now been cleverly converted into cosy study bedrooms and all sixth formers live in single studies. Younger pupils are cared for in 'family-style' junior house.

Generally relaxed atmosphere, helped by fact that pupils don't wear school uniform on daily basis (only for concerts). Have inevitably developed own 'uniform' of bootleg jeans and trainers. Informality offset by the deeper intensity and dedication of pupils themselves. Surprisingly non-competitive but supportive. A real feeling of pulling together and appreciation of fellow musicians. Little evidence of pupils' other work in classrooms and corridors. But live music heard everywhere – from a jazz classic being played by students in the canteen to a phenomenal classical performance in the head's study by a 15 year old Chinese girl on a piano once played by Liszt. Feels much more like a college than a school. Kids seem very happy and together.

Pastoral Care and Discipline: Houseparents and house tutors responsible for general pupil well-being. But fifth and sixth formers willingly take on big brother/sister role for younger children. As do practice supervisors. One such said, 'we're here to help the youngest members of our community practise but often we act as a liaison between pupil and teacher and we quite often get involved in pastoral care.' Pupil behaviour in general not a cause for concern, says head. No suspensions or exclusions necessary since his arrival. Anyone found with drugs would be given a second chance, if willing to accept ongoing blood testing. Cigarette smoking not allowed.

Pupils and Parents: Pupils come from wide range of backgrounds but up to 50 per cent are children of musicians (this figure is much higher among the youngest in the school – the vast majority of the children under 12 have musician parents). Some children of very well-known people and a few are stars themselves (a parent commented that the school has, in the past, put too much of a spotlight on its 'stars' to the neglect of the more 'normal' musicians, but the head seems to have this problem in hand). Many pupils arrive from state schools where music provision was poor and they were teased for being music nerds. Parents have worked out that it's cheaper to send their child to the Purcell School, with a full government scholarship and all music lessons included, than to a mainstream private school where their child would win a music scholarship of, at best, half the fees. Truly international, 40 per cent of pupils from abroad – Korea, Japan, China, Taiwan, Russian and France. Most pupils coming to Purcell move from having been a famous musician in their school to being just one of many. 'Makes you realise you're not so great,' said a pupil. Staff at the school repeatedly emphasise that, music talent aside, 'these are just normal kids'. We are not so sure. Even the rowdy seem to possess a focus and maturity, advanced for their years. Pupils at Purcell given lots of freedom and need to possess self-discipline.

Entrance: Officially by audition, interview and a report from current school, but almost everything rides on the audition. Most children play second (and third ...) instrument (but there are exceptions). Auditions take place every Thursday. Younger candidates usually take an informal preliminary audition to spare the feelings of those deemed not up to scratch – if they are good enough they will be invited to return for main audition. Largest intake is at 16 but children can join as young as nine. Standard for acceptance is high, high, high.

Exit: Seventy per cent move on to one of four music colleges: the Royal College of Music, the Royal Academy of Music, the Guildhall School of Music and Drama and the Royal Northern College of Music (in that order). A number of leavers choose to study music at mainstream universities, with some each year to Oxbridge music departments. A few read other subjects at university.

Money Matters: Painfully high fees which few, if any, parents actually pay in full. School comes under the government's music and dance assisted places scheme. Parents means-tested before getting grant of up to 100 per cent. Scheme currently covers around 80 per cent of pupils – remaining 20 per cent mostly overseas students getting corporate or individual sponsorship from home countries. Head says, 'I don't think we have any full fee payers.' Help also available from school's scholarship and bursary fund and some LEAs might also chip in.

Remarks: Undoubtedly and unashamedly a musical hothouse which has already produced a wealth of great musicians and is now helping more reach greatness. A top heavy sixth, with relatively few lower down, due to large intake after GCSEs. Can't help feeling the little ones run risk of being socially isolated with so few friends their own age. But head stresses how most feel more comfortable in school with like-minded youngsters rather than feeling the odd ones out at their old schools. Despite obvious emphasis on music, children certainly not let down academically. But do not be tempted to push your child into it unless this sort of education is something he or she wants very, very much.

PUTNEY HIGH SCHOOL

Linked to Lytton House in the Junior section

35 Putney Hill, London, SW15 6BH

Tel: 020 8788 4886
Fax: 020 8789 8068
E-mail: putneyhigh@put.gdst.net
Website: www.gdst.net/putneyhigh

- Pupils: 565 girls, all day • Ages: 11-18 • Size of sixth form: 140 • Non-denom • Fees: Junior £2,383; senior £3,063 • Independent • Open days: Late October or early November

Headmistress: Since 2002, Dr Denise Lodge (fifties), formerly headmistress of Sydenham High. Married with two grown up children. Can come across as remote and unapproachable. However she is obviously good with staff and efficient at organising the academic side of school life. The younger girls seem disappointed that she doesn't have much to do with them 'apart from at boring assembly'. Very proud of the girls' academic results. She says she and her staff are good at challenging bright girls but accept girls with promise, at year 7 entry, 'to bring them on'. Loves the gardens with the well-established fruit trees that surround the lawns. This is where the girls go to relax in break times and hold sales of cakes as a part of the school's commitment to charity work.

Academic Matters: High academic expectations with results to prove it/to match. 90+ per cent A*/A at GCSE, 85 per cent A/B at A level. English, biology and maths the most popular subjects. The mildly dyslexic and dyspraxic are monitored and supported. Extensive ICT labs with more computers in classrooms plus use of interactive white boards for teaching. Maths Direct, a brilliant innovation, where a sixth former takes any girl needing extra help in maths for a one-to-one lesson.

Games, Options, The Arts: Gym particularly strong, with teachers who are very keen to actually explain how to do everything so no one is left on the side. Two of them represented England at lacrosse so are a great example to the girls. Lacrosse/tennis, gym/netball/dance and rounders/athletics take place in rotation. Unusual system of paying a deposit and fee for borrowing kit – it does work, fewer girls forget. Only years 3 – 7 go swimming; school says 'the girls are less interested in swimming as they get older' – which would make them a pretty unusual bunch. We prefer the explanation that we heard when we went round: that staff consider that girls become too aware of their bodies, and by the same token they don't expect them to wear leotards for gym. Athletics is hard if you are not sporty and it's difficult to get in any sports club if you're not in one of the teams. The same people tend to get into all the teams, girls say. School prefers 'teams are very competitive' and points out that they have increased the number of sports groups for those not in teams. Rowing popular.

The music department is very encouraging and really helps the girls with composing, spending time showing them exactly how to do it step by step. Puts on informal concerts that the girls love. Music in the senior school becomes very serious; if you learn an instrument you have to be in the orchestra just as those having singing lessons have to be in the choir. 'Requires commitment' is the phrase the school prefers.

Drama sounds really fun. Drama production for years 7/8 includes everyone who wants to participate, giving huge encouragement even to those who are not budding actresses. The sixth form run the drama clubs which, of course, are hugely popular, relaxed and great fun because no teachers are involved. Art department has the right blend, a real interest in the girls doing well; lots of help and advice given with a great sense of humour but firm when necessary. DT and textiles well taught.

Plenty of outside trips to support subjects studied, making good use of educational and cultural opportunities in London with parents encouraged to do the same. Three residential trips a year: French language, Birmingham to study canals and industry (visit to Cadbury's factory being a highlight, say girls) and activity centre in Dordogne.

Background and Atmosphere: Laughter and chat can be heard around the building and outside on the lawns. Girls describe school as cosy, homely and colourful with lots of work, art and information up on the walls. Uniform purple and grey (a seriously un-flattering combination). Some of the girls wish it didn't stand out so much when travelling on public transport. All the girls seem to make their own way to school. 'It wouldn't be cool to be brought by mummy'.

Despite busy London traffic close by, amazingly quiet inside the grounds. Well looked-after buildings. One of the few schools that has decent food (huge good choice of food at lunchtime), 'even delicious baguettes'.

Pastoral Care and Discipline: Form tutors generally have an unusually good rapport with the girls and take a real interest in each. They seem quick to deal with problems both personal and work related. Discipline tight, for instance time extensions are not generally given for late homework.

School tries to be democratic with good representation throughout the school. 'Great to feel we are listened to and that the teachers are interested in us as people'.

Pupils and Parents: Pupils' backgrounds reflect the locality from which they come, says headmistress, roughly a four mile radius. Past GDST schoolgirls send their own children – a huge network that the school makes full use of, continuing long after graduation into the working environment. Mix of religions (prayer room for all religions to use) plus other nationalities. The girls seem to appreciate the mix - 'it's more interesting, more like real life'. Arts, media and politics feature amongst alumnae eg Elizabeth Symons, Virginia Bottomley, Sophie Raworth, Melanie Phillips, Pippa Greenwood, Sophie Kinsella and Sophie Daneman.

Entrance: Assessment at 4 for 44 places. Exam and interview at 11 for 84 places but most of the juniors stay on. Some from local prep schools with up to 40 per cent from state primaries. Sixth form entrants normally have A grades in the subjects they want to study at AS, with a minimum of 6 GCSEs A*-B.

Exit: Some leave of their own accord, at 11+ or post GCSE. 'A few', says the school; 'about a quarter' say we – to quite a spread of schools, notably co-ed boarding. Majority of sixth form to university, with about 25 per cent opting to take a gap year. 10 per cent to Oxbridge.

Money Matters: Scholarships at 11+ and 16+ for outstanding academic and musical ability. Financial assistance with fees available for those who need it.

Remarks: Impressive head. Teachers employed for their interest in pupils, not just academic/teaching qualifications. Positive, friendly but hardworking atmosphere with good balance of sport, art, music, etc. Girls seem fulfilled, confident and happy – well prepared for outside world.

QUEEN ANNE'S SCHOOL

6 Henley Road, Caversham, Reading, Berkshire, RG4 6DX

Tel: 0118 918 7300
Fax: 01189 187 310
E-mail: ssec@queenannes.reading.sch.uk
Website: www.qas.org.uk

• Pupils: 330 girls. 170 board (full and flexible), rest day • Ages: 11-18 • Size of sixth form: 90 • C of E • Fees: Boarding £7,064; day £4,778 • Independent • Open days: September

Head: Since 1993, Mrs Deborah Forbes MA (fifties), educated at Bath High School, read English at Somerville, Oxford. Previously taught English for 10 years (later head of English) at Cheltenham Ladies College. Responsible (not single-handedly, she would insist) for complete overhaul of Queen Anne's School (QAS), putting it back on pedestal and reinstating it as a first choice school for girls. New school buildings up, school confidence up, outside interest up. 'We've been very busy,' head understates. Not all change though. 'We have retained the same ethos – it's still a small school where everyone knows everyone else. It's a friendly school, essentially a happy school.' Firmly behind single sex education. No unwanted distractions or pressures. Married to poet with two grown-up children. Comes across as determined, unfussy achiever – the embodiment of school motto: Quietness and Strength. Retiring July 2006.

Academic Matters: Consistently good results over past few years, particularly noticeable in sciences. GCSEs overall hover around 85 per cent A*-B grades, with around half A*/As. Strong passes in maths, separate sciences and double awards do much to hold up the percentage. Some good linguists too. Spanish increasingly popular with occasional Turkish, Russian, Japanese and Chinese popping up as and when. 'If someone wants to do a particular language or subject which isn't catered for, the school will do all it can to help,' one girl explained. A levels show quite heavy science bias too. Maths and separate sciences top for A grades. Head adds, 'the most important thing for the girls, and indeed for me, is not whether they are A grade students, but whether they have achieved their own personal goals.' Impressive octagonal two-tier library well-stocked and constantly updated with hardbacks, softbacks and software. Two dedicated IT rooms fully equipped with latest technology. Intranet and guarded access to internet for girls'

own security. Small classes for all – standard size 16-18. Many classrooms situated off rat-run of narrow corridors (hence school rule stating girls must walk in single file) which, despite fresh coat of magnolia, feel dingy and claustrophobic especially when filled with lots of girls sporting bulging rucksacks. Large lecture hall (once the library before the new one was built). Next major project is a £3m new science block, which will open in September 2006. Only mild dyslexics catered for – no specialist teacher. Careers room full of pamphlets on university courses, careers, gap years and so on. Housemistress doubles as careers adviser (helped by sixth former) and is in constant demand. Saturday morning school compulsory (variety of activities according to age) with games in afternoon. Lots of new faces on teaching side since head's arrival – very few men (9 full-time out of 40).

Games, Options, The Arts: Focus of huge investment in recent years. Superb sports centre (as you'd expect) opened in 2000 by Princess Royal. Multi-functional hall plus squash courts and fitness suite (latter can be used at any time by sixth formers, only under staff supervision by younger girls). Great reputation on lacrosse field. Constant stream of Old Girls feed national teams (three in the under 21s, another in under 19s, five represented England in World Cup). Tennis traditionally strong too with good range of hard courts. Netball very popular and gaining in strength and, since opening of sports hall, basketball. No hockey. Indoor 25-metre pool with underwater lighting and music (presumably to meet sudden demand from synchronised swimmers, though none have come forward to date).

Skilled and enthusiastic art department. Bulk of work seen was excellent, but you have to seek it out. Aforementioned narrow corridors don't allow for displays so pupils' work mostly confined to 'showpiece' reception hall and dining room. The old science lab is to be transformed into gallery. Great passion at QAS for music and drama. Based in purpose-built performing arts centre, incorporating fabulous 250-seater theatre plus music practice rooms. Productions and concerts a vital part of school life. Three orchestras, two choirs. Both theatre studies (drama) and music offered at GCSE and A levels. Full programme of out-of-hours and weekend activities range from gym club, dry skiing and go-karting to jewellery design, photography and public speaking. D of E, Young Enterprise, Team Challenge etc. As one girl put it – 'there isn't time to do everything you want to do.'

Background and Atmosphere: Dates back to 1698 when the Grey Coat Hospital was founded for children of Westminster. (Bear with me – there is a connection.) In

1706 Queen Anne granted it a charter and, somewhat later, the governors decided to use part of the endowment to found a country boarding school. QAS was born in Caversham in 1894. The school still has Queen Anne's favourite flower, a deep red rose, as its emblem. Girls' traditional capes (now only used triannually for special service at Westminster Abbey – pretty well last remaining link with the old days) are also red, while their more up-to-date replacement, the fleece, is navy. Set in charming red-brick assortment of original and modern buildings up hill from the Thames in 35 acres. Girls sorted into houses on arrival – two for boarders, two for day girls and two for sixth form. Small dorms (largest sleep five), plenty of privacy, large common rooms (known as the Sit), accommodation recently extended and refurbished. Sixth-formers given more independence and can go to local shops or into nearby Reading at specified times. Male guests allowed in house Sit and Café 6 – the striking purple and green sixth form snack bar/café/games room created out of old school gym. 'We trust the girls,' says head. 'They don't give us cause not to.' Despite modern developments, QAS retains strong girls' school feel in many respects. Home economics and ballroom dancing sit comfortably alongside chemistry and further maths. While girls more likely to be found poring over their 'personal statements' for college applications than sewing machines, the sewing machines still get plenty of use (as the brilliantly beaded and coloured cushions scattered around registrar's office amply demonstrated). Plenty of mingling with the opposite sex – school socials with likes of Wellington, Radley, Shiplake and Oratory (also Harrow and Eton, adds head). No involvement on music/drama side though. Point worth noting here – among the academic, musical and sporting prizes handed out on speech day is one for happiness awarded to 'someone who relishes and embraces life, who greets it joyously and is not afraid of opportunities, or of sharing.' Doesn't that say more than a prospectus ever could?

Pastoral Care and Discipline: Daily assembly in lovely school chapel – not just daily notices but hymns and prayers too. Christian ethos is key. Individual behaviour obviously important but doesn't give rise for concern. If problem arises, girls know how to deal with it. 'We have arguments and fall out for a bit but it soon blows over,' says one girl. All given diary (student organiser) each year which gives school rules and sanctions, plus anti-bullying policy. Drug offences warrant immediate expulsion. Smoking banned (sliding scale of punishments for offenders). Alcohol supplied for girls of age at some school events, otherwise no drinking allowed. Pastoral care handled mostly in house through chain of command, but form tutors might also get involved. One girl explained, 'you can turn to anyone if you have a problem – there will always be someone who can help.'

Pupils and Parents: Girls well turned out, whether in uniform or not. Only sixth formers allowed to wear home clothes for lessons but must look businesslike (and not trousers for lower sixth). Uniform, compulsory for everyone else, comprises red and white striped shirt with navy skirt and jumper sporting red band on cuff. Strong backs are clearly a must as heavy book-filled rucksacks are carried from class to class. Mixed family backgrounds, we were assured (though one parent does arrive by helicopter). Broadly middle class, professional and well-heeled from the Home Counties and silicon valley. Average 10 per cent overseas (China, Hong Kong, Korea, Nigeria and Russia mainly) and same again ex-pats. Fewer Services. Famous OGs include actress Jenny Seagrove.

Entrance: Usual CE and interview at 11, 12 and 13 (though some girls arrive mid way through the school year and are welcomed, one girl told us) with generous pass rate. 'We are academically selective but not ferociously so,' says head. Will accept less than 50 per cent on CE but girl should be able to offer other qualities. Hopefuls invited to fun day, then assessment day, before sitting CE. Main feeder schools Rupert House, in Henley, and Oratory Prep. But increasing interest from loads of others including the odd state primary. Head says, 'I think the school suits all rounders who are keen to get involved and it suits those who enjoy being in a smaller school where they know everybody.' Entry to sixth form conditional on entrance exam and at least five GCSE grade Cs.

Exit: Handful lost to good sixth form colleges, art colleges or mixed independents after GCSEs. Several opting for gap year after A levels, returning to higher education later. Most go to university. Top of the pops are Exeter, Durham, Nottingham, Southampton and Birmingham, and a few to Oxbridge. Scientists aplenty, others include likes of art foundation, fashion and film studies.

Money Matters: Well-funded, though extra equipment paid for through efforts of able and willing parents' association (like a digital camera and camcorder for PE department and piano for music department). Several scholarships, including foundation scholarships, on offer to candidates under 15 years for academic work, art, music or sport. Top award valued at full tuition (two thirds total boarding fees). Also sixth form scholarships up to value of half tuition fees. Help on hand in cases of hardship.

Remarks: A feel-good school which keeps its eye on the future without losing sight of the past, aiming to produce, 'flexible, confident, well-balanced girls'. There's a real sense of community and appreciation here where girls openly support each other's efforts and achievements. As one explained, 'we're made to realise what we have and not to waste it. Our days are full and long; we pack so much into them and get so much out of them and it's worth every second.'

QUEEN ELIZABETH GRAMMAR SCHOOL (PENRITH)

Ullswater Road, Penrith, Cumbria, CA11 7EG

Tel: 01768 864621

Fax: 01768 890 923

E-mail: reception@queenelizabethgrammar.cumbria.sch.uk

Website: www.queenelizabethgrammar.cumbria.sch.uk

- Pupils: 804: 365 boys and 439 girls; all day • Ages: 11-18
- Size of sixth form: 202 • Non-denom • State

Head: Since 2004, Mr Christopher Kirkup BA PGCE NPQH (mid forties). Read history at Queen Mary College University of London, taught at Torpoint School, Cornwall, Bourne Grammar School Lincolnshire, deputy head at Devonport High School for Girls, Plymouth.

Academic Matters: Results at GCSE and AS/A2 are very good and, in view of the school's wide ability range at entry ('wider than all other 163 UK grammar schools'), they are remarkable.

Expectations are high, and targets consistently challenge pupils; they seem happy to accept this. There is a real sense of academic purpose about the place. Average class size up to GCSE is 28, without noticeably damaging effects on achievement (independent schools take note). Broad banding and setting in maths and science at KS3, minimum 9 subjects per student at GCSE. About 81 per cent go on the sixth form. Usual prescription is 3 x AS plus general studies in year 12. 2005 A level results – 56 per cent at A/B. Extra lessons for Oxbridge. SEN catered for in-house.

Teaching is broadly traditional without being rigid. Well qualified and very experienced staff, and they tend to stay (Penrith quality of life is very attractive.) There is a well-developed programme which helps feeder primary schools in the teaching of science, design & technology, ICT, art and PE.

Games, Options, The Arts: Good range of team games for boys and girls; rugby (boys) and cross-country (both) are strong. They breed them hardy up here. Playing fields on site, and now vast new sports hall that extends games

options. Instrumental music and drama (students in National Youth Orchestra and Theatre) reach a high standard; all year 8 have a 'residential experience' in the Buttermere valley in the Lake District. Otherwise the usual run of clubs and societies, trips abroad and theatre visits – the school is a long way from most urban centres, and knows it has to work at this. Much fund-raising by students.

Background and Atmosphere: Founded by Royal Charter in 1564, moved to present site in 1915, changed from 13-18 comprehensive to 11-18 selective grammar in 1993; grant-maintained since 1992, and now a foundation school, which means that governors have control over finance and buildings.

The site includes two rugby pitches, two for hockey and one for football as well as three netball and three tennis courts. Plenty of grassy areas and some fabulous trees. Some rooms in the main building are a little cramped but the school works hard at its upkeep and has just completed an office, staff room and new reception extension (2004)in keeping with the original architecture.

Since 1995 a continuous building programme has provided fine IT, technology and science facilities, classrooms for the English Department and an impressive sports hall. What sells the place is the pupils' demeanour – cheerful, confident, purposeful and courteous; they are happy to be here and show it. Sixth form centre in a recently re-furbished former primary school across road from main site; students treated as if at college (no uniform, but 'smart and appropriate' formal dress, visits to nearby MacDonald's in school time allowed), and live up to responsibility. Years 7 to 11 have traditional uniform, blazers shirts and ties for both boys and girls in year 7.

Pastoral Care and Discipline: Pastoral unit is form-based up to year 11, then tutor groups. Parents seem happy with school's attitude; minor incidents are quickly and effectively dealt with. Big city wickedness (drugs, alcohol etc) not really an issue, says head. There are advantages in small rural town life; it may lack urban buzz, but there is a lot to be said for old-fashioned virtues and a strong common interest between school and home.

Pupils and Parents: Enormous catchment area of 400 square miles; half pupils live in Penrith, half in country. 28 buses a day bring them in. Whole range of wealth and status. Parents very supportive; still a strong desire for self-improvement, especially in rural areas.

Entrance: Almost entirely from primary schools, by entrance test sat in December. 120 places on offer annually. Five GCSEs at A*-C qualification for sixth form entry.

Exit: Well over 90 per cent to higher education, a few to college diploma courses. Several to Oxbridge every year (three in 2005), otherwise predominantly northern universities. Gap years popular. About a dozen a year leave or transfer schools after GCSE.

Remarks: The only grammar school in Cumbria and proud of its favoured status but the school works hard at self-awareness and outward vision. Remarkably successful at sustaining academic ethos on a broad ability intake. Pleasant location, happy and business-like students. World-weary parents moving from the south east will appreciate its refreshingly uncomplicated air – if their children can get in, that is.

QUEEN ELIZABETH GRAMMAR SCHOOL (WAKEFIELD)

Linked to Queen Elizabeth Grammar Junior School (Wakefield) in the Junior section

154 Northgate, Wakefield, West Yorkshire, WF1 3QX

Tel: 01924 373 943
Fax: 01924 231 603
E-mail: admissions@qegsss.org.uk
Website: www.wgsf.org.uk

• Pupils: 720 boys • Ages: 11-18 • Size of sixth form: 170
• Inter-denom • Fees: £2,632 • Independent • Open days: Early October

Head: Since 2001, Mr Michael Gibbons BA AKC PGCE (forties), educated at the City of Leicester Grammar and read a double whammy history and theology at Kings, London before becoming an accountant in the City for a couple of years. Then back to do a PGCE and variously taught at Ardingly before becoming housemaster at Rugby, thereafter second master at Whitgift. An incredibly fast talker, ideas and enthusiasm come pouring out. Delightful turn of phrase – 'Gentlemen, can we please be gentlemen,' seemed to do the trick quite nicely. (The miscreants concerned shut up with alacrity.) Teaches some RS. Slightly anxious about HMI inspection, imminent at time of writing (can't see why). Married, with a son in the school and a daughter in the senior school. 'Really like it here, it is easy to be biased but I am enjoying it'. Made a 'positive choice' to come here and very much wants to 'lift the school and genuinely serve this community, with a really great school in south-west Yorkshire, doing all the things that (senior) schools should do'. Wants to strengthen the academic and

help children from all backgrounds to realise their potential and aim for excellence. Numbers rising again after the Assisted Places blip.

Academic Matters: New appointment of assistant head (pastoral). 'Reasonably healthy turnover, and good mix of youth and experience in the common room'. School now operates a ten-day revolving timetable, with six fifty-minute lessons a day. Strong across the board with commendable results and, whilst still bursting with mathematicians, biology popular. English and humanities are equally good. French and German on offer to all, plus Spanish, business French and Latin. Business studies and some languages studied with the Girls' High across the road, and there is much to-ing and fro-ing across the cobbled lane. Exam results for GCSE in 2004 were good – 29 per cent A*; 69 per cent A*/A and 93 per cent B. Five parallel classes each year, max at bottom of the school 22/23 per class. Work clinics for all at lunch-time. No setting (though given the desired academic thrust, this may not be too far away?)

Computers throughout, and 'loads' of interactive white boards. Good remedial help on hand for mild dyslexia and the like, can 'cope' with mild Asperger's. Children are automatically screened and additional help can be organised, usually at lunch-time, laptops allowed. Fantastic double-decker library, with false floor through which the brill Victorian roof is clearly visible, the new build will return the library to an archive area and, though they would dearly love to remove the false floor, it looks as if it could be quite expensive. New build, due late 2005, includes a 240 seat theatre, learning resources centre, library, sixth form centre and English department.

Games, Options, The Arts: Art continues to blossom, both curricular and extra-curricular, still a good and popular A level subject, plus all the add-ons – terrific art department in the top of the school with masses of light. Screen printing, photography, etchings. Outstanding music, the brass section wins prizes, over 300 individual players, swing band (played in front of the Queen during her Jubilee) and junior swing bands (hired out for local weddings and things, the dosh earned funds trips abroad). Concerts often held in Wakefield Cathedral, where the junior boys provide choristers, joined by girls from the High School (BBC said second only to St Paul's). Music is often a joint activity as, indeed, is drama – Kiss Me Kate and The Mikado recent productions. School has 'use of' over 27 acres of playing fields, the senior boys play 'up the road' (which is also used by the nearby Police Academy as a helicopter landing pad – great excitement). Pavilion opened in 2000 as well as the new sports hall with special 'resilient' flooring, which is used by local rugby team and came on stream in 1999, state-of-the-art facility, and hired out to locals. Training pool for junior school only, seniors use the pool in town. This is a games school, oodles of Internationalist old boys in the field of rugby – including Mike Tindall, and masses of trips to South Africa, South America, Australia and hockey to Canada, cricket team to the West Indies. Plus cultural tours. Bridge and chess clubs well attended and 300 regularly take D of E.

Background and Atmosphere: QEGS (pronounced kwegs) for short. School founded by Royal Charter in 1591 and moved to present site in 1854. From 1944-76 it was a direct grant school and reverted to fee-paying in 1976. Marvellous Victorian Gothic façade hides a multitude of extensions and make-overs, some very imaginative and some less so. Junior school also on site, and they play games on the grass in front of the school.

Pastoral Care and Discipline: All boys carry record book at all times (homework diary) which incorporates the school rules and can be inspected by staff at any time and must be signed by parents at preordained levels. If a boy misbehaves in public, the line is to remove the record book which is then sent back to school, and the owner will be reprimanded. Ladder of sanctions, Friday afternoon staff detention for minor sin, Saturday morning (real bore, no school otherwise apart from games) detentions for more serious matters and an essay, 'set according to pupil's requirements'. Good bullying policy. Keen to educate, school holds strong beliefs and expectations. Advanced pastoral system in place, tutor first point of inquiry, followed by referral to head of year. 'No problems this year' with drugs, but automatic expulsion. Smoking equals detention, three detentions equals suspension. Suspensions and exclusions for bullying, vandalism and aggressive behaviour. Tough, but it works. NB school will also 'kick out' under-performing pupils.

Pupils and Parents: Wonderfully close to the motorways and bus and rail stations; a timetable comes with the prospectus; wide catchment area. QEGS is the 'only' acceptable alternative to the state system for miles around and progressively getting more middle class as the middle classes prefer to keep their little darlings at home. Good strong work ethic. Parents and pupils must make a 'positive choice' to come here. Fair assortment from ethnic minorities. Good breeding ground for bishops, Lincoln and York; plus John Scott, director of music at St Paul's and a tranche of internationalists.

Entrance: Not automatic from junior school, transfer is based on academic record and satisfactory results – 'may toss out if not up to it' – but less than 5 per cent each year

(two or three). Those from the junior school make up 60 per cent of the first year intake, the rest coming either at 11 or 13 – most come at 11. Pre-test CE, plus interview, and then on basic CE results. Oversubscribed, last year 110 applicants applied for 47 places (the answer of course is to start at the junior school). Pupils come from local preps – though most of these now seem to go up to 16; plus state primaries. Baseline qualifications for entry at sixth form are 6 GCSEs (but most come with 7 or 8) with at least two As in subjects to be taken at AS/A level. Essentially school is looking for an 'aggressively' academic pupil, though whole lifestyle will be looked at, no 'bias to sport, music or drama'. Boys can and do move into the school at other times, subject to academic OK and space available, 'penny numbers' says the head.

Exit: Some post-GCSE occasional dropouts, one or two to art foundation courses, ditto to employment, a handful to Oxbridge, the odd one to re-takes or improved offers but the majority to degree courses all over Britain – Sheffield, Durham, Newcastle, Leeds and London the favoured destinations. Medicine and law popular.

Money Matters: Was hit hard by the end of Assisted Places. Part of the Ogden Trust (which supports 32 former state high or grammar schools with bursaries for 'talented children through independent secondary education regardless of parental ability to pay'). Bursaries of up to 100 per cent plus travel, uniform and school trips. Children must be in the state sector, high scoring at key stage 2, with parental income of less than £30,000 per annum. State 'education maintenance allowance', available nationally to keep pupils in sixth form, school will top up if necessary. Sprinkling of other scholarships and bursaries (which are awarded post exam and reviewed annually each year, so - no work = no sub) plus music and sixth form schols. Bursaries for choristers in junior school, paid 50/50 by school and Cathedral, but only whilst boy is in the choir. Ogden Trust sixth form science scholarships available (worth up to 100 per cent of fees) each year for a student wishing to study maths/science at A level.

Remarks: No change. The best boys' city day school in this area. Serious, unpretentious former grammar school. Results up, intake up, and very tough. Could one need more?

Queen Elizabeth's Girls' School

High Street, Barnet, Hertfordshire, EN5 5RR

Tel: 020 8449 2984

Fax: 02084 412 322

E-mail: office.queenelizabethsgirls.barnet@lgfl.net

• Pupils: 1,100 girls, all day • Ages: 11 – 18 • Size of sixth form: 220 • Non-denom • State

Head: Since 2001, Mrs Kate Webster BA PGCE MA (Education Management), forties. Studied geography at Sheffield University and taught at Furze Platt School in Maidenhead and Herschel Grammar School in Slough, before joining Henrietta Barnett as deputy head. No children; likes walking, music, theatre and art. Amiable, competent and straight-forward; excellent manager. Teaches where needed – geography, RE and PHSE.

Academic Matters: Some at the top end are creamed off by Barnet's selective and semi-selective schools, but this is a comprehensive with a full ability range, achieving commendable results because of good teaching and high expectations from the start. Around 70 per cent of girls get 5+ A*-C grades at GCSE, with some 30 per cent A* and A grades. RS, media studies, psychology and sociology are all popular and successful A level choices alongside English and biology. The 20 subjects available include vocational courses in ICT and business studies.

The school's media arts specialism means a focus on English, drama, art and media studies. 'It's about teaching and learning styles which use IT and the media as much as possible. But this does not deflect us from a broad and balanced curriculum and we don't allow overspecialisation.' There is, indeed, a good selection of computers around the building; 'though you are always running to catch up with IT – it's a priority to keep updating our provision.'

Setting for maths from year 7, talented linguists are hived off to take up a second language in year 8, but all other subjects are taught in mixed ability groups. 'We tried setting for science, but the results didn't improve.' Ofsted comments that most teaching caters well for the whole range of abilities. Maths has, historically, been one of the weaker subjects. 'But we've made lots of progress at KS3 and we hope to see that feeding through to GCSE results.'

Good SEN support, mostly within the classroom. The school's split-level site is unsuitable for children with phys-

ical disabilities but around 10 per cent of pupils have special educational needs, mostly dyslexia and dyspraxia. The Gifted and Talented Co-ordinator identifies very able girls, who are encouraged to take on extension research projects; a year 11 group recently visited the Guardian Newsroom. 'But we don't want to be exclusive, and others can join in too.' Masterclasses in eg music and history. Good careers advice; has Investors in Careers status, recently renewed.

Games, Options, The Arts: As befits its media arts specialism, drama GCSE is very popular, involving regular show-cases to parents. A new drama studio is planned and part of the present large canteen will become a media studies studio and editing suite. Music is also strong, though relatively few take it to GCSE or A level, where it is available through Barnet Music Centre. There are senior and junior orchestras, a jazz band and various ensembles depending on the strengths and numbers of musicians. Links with the ENO, Wigmore Hall and various orchestras. Several art studios, and plenty of innovative art on display. Good sports facilities; there's a newly refurbished swimming pool, sports hall, gym and several tennis/netball courts; girls compete in county football and cross country tournaments. Girls doing PE GCSE often organise dance and games tournaments for local primary schools. Trips abroad include skiing in the Alps, trekking in the Atlas Mountains, language exchanges, art trips to New York and history trips to the battlefields of France.

Background and Atmosphere: Opened in 1888 as a grammar school; has been comprehensive since the 1970s. Hilly site on the edge of London's green belt. Buildings range from Victorian to 1960s. Looks rather tatty round the edges and could do with a major influx of cash for refurbishment. The loos, however, were revamped at a cost of £150,000 at the request of the school council when the head first joined. 'We've done what we can in terms of improving the environment but we have no space to rebuild.' Relaxed atmosphere with confident, articulate girls, used to speaking up in public.

Pastoral Care and Discipline: The school is renowned for making new girls feel at home quickly. The dedicated head of year 7 'puts lots of time and effort going to feeder schools and getting information on the girls who will be joining us.' There are high expectations of good behaviour, and discipline does not appear to be problematical; only two permanent exclusions in the last four years. Clear policies on drugs and bullying. 'Obviously girls are exposed to drugs outside, but inside it is not an issue. Our PHSE programme is very good and we put a lot of effort into equipping girls to make informed decisions on all aspects of life. The form tutor or head of year is the first port of call if a girl is troubled but they are not phased about coming to find me if they feel strongly about something.'

Pupils and Parents: This is not a purely middle-class school; it has a higher than average percentage of girls on free school meals. But neither is it a gritty inner-London comprehensive. Plenty of nice, confident Barnet girls. OGs: Elaine Paige, actress and singer, and Stephanie Beacham, actress.

Entrance: Generally around three applicants for every place. First in line are girls with a statement of social or medical needs specifying the school; then siblings; then those living closest – which in practice tends to mean within about two miles. Girls entering the sixth form – and about 18 do so each year – are asked to have five grade Cs or above at GCSE, though many A level courses specify a B grade in the A level subject.

Exit: Nearly half leave after GCSEs, with some high achievers moving on to selective sixth forms, some to co-ed sixth form colleges, others to FE colleges to pursue vocational courses. Some return when the grass elsewhere proves to be less green than it had appeared. About 80 per cent of sixth form leavers go on to higher education, to do courses ranging from medicine to audio-visual production at old and new universities, including one or two a year to Oxbridge.

Money Matters: Not a rich school. Low down in the queue for government cash for refurbishment but does its best with available funds. Loyal parent body works hard at raising money.

Remarks: A successful comprehensive with high expectations that caters well for all abilities, and produces self-assured girls used to discussion and debate.

QUEEN ELIZABETH'S GRAMMAR SCHOOL

Linked to Queen Elizabeth's Grammar Junior School in the Junior section

West Park Road, Blackburn, Lancashire, BB2 6DF

Tel: 01254 686 300
Fax: 01254 692 314
E-mail: headmaster@qegs.blackburn.sch.uk
Website: www.qegs.blackburn.sch.uk

• Pupils: 665 boys, 100 girls, all day • Ages: 11-18 plus junior school (see below) • Size of sixth form: 115 • Inter-denom on C of E Foundation • Fees: £1,449 - £2,567 • Independent • Open days: October. Additional junior/early years open day in January

Headmaster: Since 1995, Dr David Hempsall MA PhD (late fifties). Read History at Sidney Sussex, Cambridge, followed by PGCE at Cambridge and PhD at University of Kent. Spent 12 years teaching at Rugby (was head of history and director of Oxbridge admissions during time there). Then head of Scarborough College. Enthusiastic, pragmatic and hugely experienced, with great sense of humour and reputation for being firm but fair. Says he wants pupils to be stretched '105 per cent' while they are at QEGS (pronounced 'Quegs'). Firmly in favour of co-education – school went fully co-ed in 2001. Still teaches several times a week and says, 'it's the best job in the world – I've never had a day when I haven't wanted to come to work'. Widower, with two grown-up children. Due to retire in 2007.

Academic Matters: Head says 'realising potential is our aim'. Science particularly strong, with maths and chemistry most popular subjects in school. A QEGS sixth-former recently represented the UK in the four-member International Biology Olympiad in Latvia. Exam results good. 59 per cent A/B grades at A level in 2005; 16 pupils got at least 3 grade As. At GCSE, 100 per cent got 5+ A*-Cs in 2005, with 10 pupils getting all A* or A grades. Class sizes of around 20-25 in main school and 8-10 for A levels. Pupils take nine GCSEs, including English, maths, a modern foreign language (French or German) and a combination of sciences (dual award or separate sciences on offer). Latin and Greek available too. School has adopted six-day revolving timetable with eight 35-minute lessons a day – system looks puzzling to outsiders but pupils insist you soon get the hang of it. Loads of computers (four networked IT suites) and state-of-the-art science and language labs. No remedial help but less able taught in smaller sets. Staff very impressive bunch – average age 43 and nearly half have been at school for more than 10 years. More than a third of staff are women.

Games, Options, The Arts: Dazzling games reputation. QEGS awarded Sportsmark Gold award for third time in 2005, 'with distinction'. Historically a soccer school, it won the Independent Schools FA Cup in 1996, 2001 and 2004 – the first school to win the cup more than once. Close links with Blackburn Rovers – old boy James Beattie played for them before signing for Southampton. Rugby, cricket, swimming, athletics, golf and cross-country all good too. House system enables pupils of all abilities to play competitive sport. Trickier for girls because of smaller numbers but sports department organises combined year teams. Splendid six-lane swimming pool with electronic timing system – used in out-of-school hours by appreciative locals.

Around a third of pupils play musical instruments. Drama is popular too. All pupils get opportunities to sing, speak, act or perform in front of an audience, whether it's singing in a choir or taking part in the annual school play – Barnum was a recent choice, wisely staged minus the high wire. Exchange trips galore, Young Enterprise, Duke of Edinburgh Award Scheme etc, plus lunch-time and after-school clubs.

Background and Atmosphere: School founded in 1509 by the second Earl of Derby, granted Royal Charter by Queen Elizabeth I in 1567. Moved to present site in leafy Blackburn suburb in 1884. Went direct grant in 1944 and returned to private sector in 1976. Traditionally admitted girls in the sixth form but took the plunge and opened doors to girls of all ages in 2001. Girls now in every year of main school. Staff reckon girls are integrating well and confident numbers will gradually build though it may take a while. New Early Years department, catering for ages 4-6, opened in 2002 and extended to include nursery for ages 3+ in September 2005. Original school building, with stunning stained-glass windows, known as 'Big School' and used as school dining hall. Portraits of previous heads, school silver, team photographs and press cuttings proudly on show.

Campus comprises five acres (not counting playing fields) and numerous buildings. Bit of a hotchpotch, some purpose-built, some converted houses, and on a sloping site so lots of steps. Games fields and sports hall 20 minutes away at Lammack – pupils travel there by minibus. Grounds and buildings immaculate – not a scrap of litter or graffiti in sight. Light airy library with 17,000 books and panoramic views across Blackburn and surrounding countryside on top floor of Queen's Wing. Pupils can use it for private study at break and lunch-time. Sixth form housed in purpose-built Singleton House. Has own café, common room (complete with table football, pool table, comfy chairs and Atomic Kitten blaring out of the stereo system), careers suite and private study room. Pupils wear uniform – distinctive royal blue blazers for under-16s, black blazers for sixth form. Idea of scrapping uniform for sixth form mooted a couple of years ago but pupils themselves opted to keep it.

Pastoral Care and Discipline: Head says school has lost its 'rough and tough' reputation over the last 10 years – 'we are a much more caring society, more family orientated and able to poke fun at ourselves a little more these days'. Staff rightly proud of pastoral care at QEGS. Problems great and small relayed via form tutors and heads of year to deputy head (pastoral) and head. Chaplain, school nurse and head of complementary studies often involved too. Punishments range from pink referral slip sent to form tutor and detentions through to temporary or permanent exclusion. School rules succinctly outlined in 13-point code. Hot policy on bullying, verbal abuse, smoking, alcohol and drugs.

Pupils and Parents: School open to 'anyone with ability'. Pupils bright, industrious and confident without appearing complacent or alarmingly sophisticated. Very mixed backgrounds – parents range from wealthy Ribble Valley families to those who make huge financial sacrifices to send their sons and daughters here. Around one-fifth Asian. Massive catchment area. One third come from Blackburn with Darwen, but rest from 20-mile radius, including Preston, Colne, Burnley, Bolton and Clitheroe. School bus service covers 12 routes. Former pupils are an eclectic bunch, including the late Russell Harty, scientist Sir Ernest Marsden, businessman Sir Kenneth Durham, designer Wayne Hemingway, film director Michael Winterbottom, professional golfer Nick Dougherty and Krishnan Guru-Murthy, the Channel 4 news presenter/reporter.

Entrance: At 11, school test in English, maths and verbal reasoning, plus school report and interview with the head, who says he looks for 'character, spark, sparkle'. Boys and girls come from huge array of state primaries and local preps, including Clevelands, Highfield Priory, Sunny Bank and Park Hill Convent. Virtually all QEGS juniors move up to main school. Sixth form entrants need minimum of five Bs at GCSE.

Exit: Handful leave after GCSE, mostly for local FE colleges offering subjects like law and media studies (head rolls his eyes at this subject) that are not available at QEGS. 95 per cent of sixth form go on to university – normally at least five to Oxbridge each year. Medicine far and away the most popular subject to read and Manchester – 25 miles down the road – currently the favourite university, though Newcastle and Nottingham gaining popularity.

Money Matters: Head says, 'we live off our fees and use our money wisely'. School previously had large number of assisted places (about a third of the intake) – their loss affected pupil numbers for a while. One scholarship (one-third remission of fees) offered to best new main school entrant each year, plus one Ogden Trust science scholarship for a sixth form entrant from a state school. There are also over 20 main school and sixth form bursaries (up to one-third of fees).

Remarks: Very impressive school under strong leadership. Has made huge changes in recent years and will take a while for girls' numbers to build but a stimulating place with friendly, articulate pupils.

QUEEN ELIZABETH'S HOSPITAL

Berkeley Place, Clifton, Bristol, BS8 1JX

Tel: 0117 930 3040
Fax: 0117 929 3106
E-mail: headmaster@qehbristol.co.uk
Website: www.qehbristol.co.uk

• Pupils: 570 boys (30 board) • Ages: 11-18 • Size of sixth form: 151 boys • Non-denom • Fees: £2,664 day; £4,909 full boarding; £4,465 weekly boarding • Independent • Open days: Usually a Saturday in mid-November

---

Head: Since 2000, Mr Stephen Holliday MA (early forties), read history at Jesus College, Cambridge. Formerly deputy head of Queen Elizabeth's Grammar School, Blackburn. Wife a teacher, 2 young sons. Teaches PHSE to all of year 7, also year 9 history. Welcoming and approachable, spoken of with warmth by colleagues (some long-established) and respected by parents. Maintains the personal management approach of his predecessors, believing in 'evolution rather than revolution', based on the valued traditions of the school (founded in 1590). Quietly innovative and building on the school's strong reputation. 2005 sees the launch of a multi-million pound development programme.

Academic Matters: Exam results well above national average for GCSE (70 per cent A or A*) and A level (85 per cent A/B). Emphasis on quality rather than quantity with minimum of nine GCSE subjects – 'our boys are stretched but not stressed', says head. Pupils' individual achievements recognised and valued in many fields beyond the academic. Curriculum balance carefully maintained, options include Latin, drama, art, ceramics, Greek and Spanish for GCSE. All do three sciences until end of year 9 and after that choose triple or dual award science. A level choices include politics, theatre studies, electronics, business studies, psychology and sports studies. Video conferencing enables some partnership teaching with local schools (eg classics). Very wide range of extra-curricular activities and clubs, from art club to wind band via ornithology and Scrabble. Additional boarders-only activities include 'Sunday Sunshine Tours'. Impressive programme of visits abroad has included a world rugby tour and a choir tour to the United States. Hugely successful in local and national debating and public-speaking competitions, frequent finalists and winners of the national European Youth Parliament competition. Strong traditional links with the local community enhance work experience programme. Increasingly strong following in Outward Bound and D of E. Several flourishing Young Enterprise teams. School very highly regarded locally for many contributions to choral (boarders' choir sings regularly in the Lord Mayor's Chapel), musical and theatrical events. On-site theatre 'most vibrant in the West'.

Games, Options, The Arts: On-site games facilities good given city-centre location, squash courts, gym and weight-training room, large recreation yard. Extensive playing fields 10 minutes' away at Failand (boys bused there) with pavilion facilities. Other off-site activities include hiking, climbing, sailing and swimming. Many pupils compete at local, county and national levels in a wide range of team and individual sports, the list is long and their achievements celebrated. Music a strength. Orchestral and choral concerts as well as house competitions in which participation is encouraged at every level: organ, comb and paper, rattling a tin of beans. Drama offered as a GCSE option as well as A level theatre studies. Regular ambitious productions involving large numbers and other schools.

Background and Atmosphere: Extraordinary main building, initially intimidating, reveals inside the very best of over 400 years of grammar school tradition. School has clearly moved with the times (the 'dungeons' now house electronics and ICT). Purposeful, but not over-aggressive, atmosphere in which individuals count.

Pastoral Care and Discipline: Strong system with good tutoring by staff who know boys well, student counsellor also available. New boys feel well cared for and boys generally are relaxed with staff. Senior boys volunteer to train as peer counsellors, and give effective and valued support. Parents impressed. On a site well suited to mountain goats (and training rugby players) with steep stairways and narrow corridors, consideration and self-discipline are the normal order. Civilised behaviour is expected and the boys are treated as young adults. Sanctions, when imposed, are seen as fair. School rules are few and straightforward.

Pupils and Parents: 'We are academically selective but not socially exclusive'. Pupils from all areas of Bristol and beyond, local primary schools and independent prep schools. The historic charitable foundation supports pupils from many different social backgrounds, and there is a perceptible family feel. Inspectors commented on the strong contribution of boarding to the life and character of the school. Day boys can stay to do prep with the boarders. Close involvement of parents is encouraged and Friends association very active. Good communication maintained via termly newsletters. Attendance well above national average. Pupils friendly, open and polite. Firm guidelines issued about appearance (uniform, no long hair, no jewellery) and great pride in traditional bluecoat uniform worn by boarders and the choir – but only on special occasions! Pupils and staff complimentary about meals, taken in the shadow of the organ in a rather baronial hall.

Entrance: Selective intake, via joint entrance exam with Bristol Grammar School and Bristol Cathedral School for entry at 11 (exceptionally 10) and 13, taken in January. Entry to sixth form typically 6 B grades at GCSE and headteacher's reference. Two applicants for every day-boy place, fewer for boarders. Weekly, flexi- and occasional boarding offered and steady trickle of day-boy converts.

Exit: Nearly all year 11 pupils go into the sixth form and most go on to higher education. Significant number to Oxbridge. Some interesting gap year student projects (eg teaching English in a Tibetan monastery). Thriving and very supportive Old Boys' society.

Money Matters: Large endowment income enables school to offer assisted places to about 20 per cent of pupils. Academic (six) and music (four) scholarships awarded based on achievement in entrance procedures at 11+ and 13+. Ogden Sixth Form Scholarships.

Remarks: The only single-sex boys' independent school in the Bristol area. With a wealth of history behind it, QEH remains true to its long-established values, but is nonetheless thoroughly up-to-date in all that it does, offering a relevant curriculum in modern facilities. A school not noted for blowing its own trumpet but battalions of pleased parents testify to its well-deserved reputation for excellence.

QUEEN ELIZABETH'S SCHOOL, BARNET

Queen's Road, Barnet, Hertfordshire, EN5 4DQ

Tel: 020 8441 4646
Fax: 02084 407 500
E-mail: office.queenelizabethsboys.barnet@lgfl.net
Website: www.qebarnet.co.uk

- Pupils: 1,150 boys • Ages: 11-18 • Size of sixth form: 260
- Non-denom • State

Headmaster: Since 1999, Dr John Marincowitz BA PhD FRSA (fifties). Joined the school as a history teacher in 1985 and taught part-time while completing his PhD. Previously taught in South Africa for seven years. Son attended Queen Elizabeth's and daughter went to North London Collegiate. Teaches some history. Quietly spoken but very approachable and has a clear vision for the school. 'We are not an exam factory. We want to develop boys to be rounded individuals who will go on to make a serious contribution to society.' Believes the school has outgrown GCSEs and doesn't feel they prepare pupils for A level. Hopes to see an alternative that is accepted by universities in the near future.

Academic Matters: Outstanding results, competes with the top private schools in the area. Boasts a 100 per cent pass rate at GCSE (grades A*-C) with 80-ish per cent getting A*s or As. 90 plus per cent A/B at A level. Class sizes stand at around 30, getting smaller as GCSEs approach. Setting in all subjects from year 7. No Latin, but Russian offered at A level. Single sciences available. School is very strong in science and maths with more than 50 per cent of boys opting for these at A level. AVCEs (formerly GNVQs) offered in IT only.

Games, Options, The Arts: Sport is important. Boys represent the school at district, county, national and international levels in a range of sports including rugby, swimming, athletics and cross-country and cricket. Water polo also very successful – new indoor pool opens in August 2006 and multipurpose hall is scheduled soon after.

Music attracts large numbers to a range of ensembles, orchestras, bands and an established choir. Almost half the pupils play a musical instrument. A new music block and art extension thanks to parental fund-raising.

Clubs and societies are strong and flourishing at lunch times, after school and at weekends; fencing to chess, debating to CCF. Nine boys sporting internationals in the past year, plus members of the science or modern language British Olympiad teams, the National Youth Choir of Great Britain, English Schools Orchestra and National Children's Wind Orchestra. Twice National and European winners of the Young Enterprise award scheme.

Background and Atmosphere: Founded in 1573 by Queen Elizabeth I as a grammar school for the education of boys in manners and learning, it moved down the road from its Tudor building to its present 30-acre site verging on green belt Hertfordshire in leafy High Barnet in 1930. It briefly turned comprehensive from 1971 but opted out of council control in 1989 and became fully selective in 1995. Very traditional atmosphere, although the siren sounded between lessons brings you up to the present day.

A mixture of original 1930s architecture, attractive new buildings and some ordinary sixties and seventies, flat-roofed buildings that are gradually being refurbished, thanks to parental fund-raising and external contributions. Majority of parents contribute from £50 a month towards their child's education. Over the last ten years, parents, local businesses and Old Boys have enabled the school to invest £3.5 million in improvements. A new sixth form and private study centre with computing facilities has been opened and changing rooms, showers and toilets which were criticised in the 1999 Ofsted report have all been extended and refurbished. All boys now have access to a locker.

Pastoral Care and Discipline: Homework diaries in years 7 and 8 teach boys how to organise their work. This seems to be taken very seriously. Parents are required to sign the diary weekly. The first point of contact is the house tutor who monitors a boy's progress and provides a link with the family. Efforts and successes are rewarded with house points and commendations from year heads, the headmaster and chairman of governors, culminating in senior and junior awards days. The head says there are few discipline problems; he would expel a boy for violent behaviour or being in possession of drugs but has not had to yet. No lengthy rule book but quite strict on appearance – no shaved heads for instance!

Pupils and Parents: A real ethnic and socio-economic mix with about half the boys coming from ethnic minority backgrounds. No immediate catchment area. Some pupils come from central London. Some applicants apply from as far north as Bedfordshire. A private coach service funded by parents brings about a third of the pupils from surrounding areas. About one fifth of entrants have been educated at a prep school. There's a thriving Friends of Queen Elizabeth's organisation. Notable old boys include Sir Tim Bell and Richard Aylard.

Entrance: Very selective. Some 1,200 boys sit for 180 places. No practice papers available – the school 'doesn't want to encourage the coaching industry'. The school is reluctant to say much about the tests other than they are made as accessible as possible. Up to 160 places are allocated on academic ability and up to 20 on musical aptitude (at least grade 3 standard). Entrance exams take place in December; the minimum pass mark is 70. Those achieving this (about 600) are invited to return to take a second test in January; the first 160 get places. No priority for siblings unless there is a tied score.

The school takes no outside applicants into the 6th form.

Exit: About 25 per cent leave after GCSE, 'some go elsewhere to pursue courses that we do not offer; some take up places at independent school sixth forms; some take up scholarships at independent schools; some want a mixed sixth form environment and some are offered places on courses elsewhere which are not offered to them here.' says the school. Has long had a reputation for hoofing out underperformers, but head says 'every one of our boys who expresses a desire to stay on in our sixth form is offered a place in the sixth form' – so take him at his word. He says, 'pupils are continually assessed during years 10 and 11 and places on A level courses are offered on the basis of internal assessments. Parents are kept informed throughout of their son's progress in relation to A level expectations and the final subject recommendations are made in February of year 11'.

All sixth form leavers go on to university, the overwhelming majority to Russell Group and redbricks and a good bunch to Oxbridge.

Remarks: Some boys turn down scholarships at excellent private schools to come here and it's not difficult to understand why. But it is very selective and only the brightest will be admitted.

QUEEN ETHELBURGA'S COLLEGE

Linked to Chapter House Preparatory School in the Junior section

Thorpe Underwood Hall, Ouseburn, York, North Yorkshire,
YO26 9SS

Tel: 0870 742 3300

Fax: 08707 423 310

E-mail: admin@queenethelburgas.edu

Website: www.queenethelburgas.edu

• Pupils: 277 girls, 162 boys; 330 boarders, 109 day; plus prep school 'Chapter House': 57 girls, 50 boys, of whom 40 board; plus Queen's Kindergarten of 30 tinies (open all year) • Ages: main school 11-20, prep 2-11, kindergarten 3 months to 2 years • Size of sixth form: 140 • Inter-denom • Independent

Head: Since 2001, Mr Peter Dass JP BA MA (early fifties). Started life as an engineer with General Motors. Then full-time CertEd at the University of Wales, then BA in maths and MA in educational management (specialising in the use of value-added systems in schools – a very good sign) while he worked his way up the ladder – maths teacher, head of maths (Herne Bay, Bedgebury), deputy head and head of senior school (Bedgebury) from whence here. Married to Mary, a teacher; two grown-up children. Flies. Hopes to carry on growing the senior school. Keen on value-added measurement of pupils' (and one hopes teachers') progress – a good sign. Substantial growth throughout the school since his advent.

Academic Matters: On the steadily up – good results in the last 3 years up from average of three C Grades to three A grades per pupil in 2005 – The Times placed the school in the top 50 of all independent schools for A Level results in 2005. Some do very well with at least one fifth getting 4 or 5 straight A grades. Not an academic power-house but a pleasing absence of lower grades. French from 6 and German from 10 (which means that pupils arriving at the senior school form a different class for these subjects). Spanish for all at 14, dual science, very popular – and fab modern labs with spectacular views, plus the usual trad subjects. Science and maths a strength with many A grades. Plus an unusual spread of alternative A levels embracing psychology, photography, performing arts, as well as business and fashion and design A levels. Dyslexia help available and free in the junior school, EFL free throughout the school. Not a school that can be judged by the league tables – ask to see the value-added data.

Games, Options, The Arts: Horses are an important part of QE. The Royal Court Equestrian Centre (which cost three million quid) has an impressive indoor riding school, outdoor manège and masses of pony paddocks plus three serious cross country courses. Pupils may (and do) bring their own animals, all living in a vast American-style centre capable of holding 80. Pupils get up to muck out at 7.30am, and generally do their own horses but full livery is available at £1,600 per term, indulgent fathers please note. £895 a term to use a QE horse (the school has seven) but there is a variety of options available if you are prepared to share your own. BHSAI on offer in the sixth form and riding is timetabled. Their own Polo team for 2005. Cor. Plus 10 acres of floodlit all-weather courts for hockey, soccer, rugby, high jump, volleyball etc.

CCF popular and clubs for IT, archery, fencing, golf. Magical fitness rooms (one in each house plus sauna and suntanning beds). Music on the up, masses of keyboards and regular musical either performed in York or in house. The lecture theatre converts into seating for the stage in the sports hall (if you follow), all very cunning. Small swimming pool (the Martins' original one) now roofed over in slightly strange juxtaposition with the refectory. Art and psychology good and strong. Enthusiastic home economics and Leith's food and wine course for sixth formers (no more than two sets of eight per year group) with the smashing new kitchen used for grown-up classes in the holidays. D of E with masses of gold participants. Very popular new internet café. Fantastic new refectory and leisure complex.

Background and Atmosphere: Founded in 1912, QE was the intellectual doyenne of the Northern Circuit, rivalled only by St Leonard's in Scotland. However, falling numbers and threatened closure precipitated the move to Thorpe Underwood, conveniently situated 15 minutes from York and Harrogate and ten minutes' drive from the A1. Surrounded by 100 acres of beautifully manicured grounds, Thorpe Underwood dates back to the Domesday Book where it is described as Chirchie, Usebrana and Useburn, before becoming part of the monastery of Fountains Abbey in 1292 (the stew pond used by the monks to supply food for the passing travellers has been meticulously restored). The hall itself was rebuilt in 1902 in best Edwardian Tudor style and the extensions have been sympathetically carried out with leaded paned windows to match the original, though some of the blue wallpapered classrooms are a bit surprising (not to mentioned the rather grand Sanderson curtains).

Previously home to the Martin family, the front hall is filled with stuffed tigers and hung with odd guns, halberds and the trappings of posh country house living. Impressive new-build dormitory blocks – dorms would be a misnomer for these elegant little bedrooms, the majority now with private bathrooms, all with tellies (on a timer) and telephones with voice mail. The school has recently built substantial extra boarding accommodation to cope with the increase in boy boarders. Boys' and girls' accommodation is separate. Charming little chapel due to be expanded this year and a Muslim prayer room.

Leased for a peppercorn from a charitable foundation (originally the brain child of Brian Martin) QE has benefited from twenty million quid's worth of investment. Good, if not lavishly stocked, libraries, banks of computers, teletext business info displayed in series of fours around the school, free availability to the internet including 6th form boarding houses, though not intranetted. Regular formal dinner parties with silver service and speaker for sixth form 'to give them practice in the real world'. Immaculate parking facilities, just like the army.

Now over 40 per cent boys, with boarding numbers up 25 per cent this year alone. Mr Dass would like to see the school with two parallel classes throughout and six hundred on the roll. Given the dramatic increase both in pupils and boarders over the past eight years, this may not be so far off the mark.

Pastoral Care and Discipline: Tutorial system which changes yearly, no more than a dozen tutees to each. Pupils are not streetwise and the house system, though a bit wobbly, seems to pick up any real problems. Bullies are confronted head on and the bully box where notes, either signed or not, can be deposited for scrutiny by the head or his deputy, is rarely used.

Regular socials, the sixth formers have a bar twice a week (non-alcoholic since new laws) and lots of inter-school beanos like karaoke and the like. The sixth form also has a smoking room where pupils may smoke 'with parental permission' – another first for the GSG.

Twice a week the head hosts a discreetly separated lunch table where pupils can let their hair down; if the matter raised is contentious then the pupil concerned is 'invited to see me in my office later'. Charming 'leavers' letter' inviting any former pupil (until they 'leave university, or their 21st birthday, whichever is the later') to contact the college or Mr Martin – reverse charge – at any time – if they have got into a scrape and need help or (free) legal advice. (Another GSG first.)

Pupils and Parents: Fiercely middle class, pupils come to board from all over – Scotland, Wales as well as East Anglia and locally on daily basis; horses come too. Expect a mass of regional accents, some 16 per cent 'real

foreigners' from abroad – Chinese, Germans, Russians, Scandinavians et al, most of whom come via the internet, with quite a lot just coming for the sixth form. Eight buses collect day pupils from all over Yorkshire (not cheap), though not all locals feel comfortable with the glitz.

Entrance: Either via Chapter House but generally Level 4 at Key Stage 2 SATs – As and Bs at GCSE for potential A level candidates at sixth form. External candidates tend to come from the local state schools or out of the area. Pupils accepted at any time during the school year 'if places available'.

Exit: Most, who want to go to university, go to the university of their choice – these tend to be Edinburgh, Durham, Liverpool, London and Nottingham, with usually 4 or 5 a year to Oxbridge.

Money Matters: Well underpinned financially but quite expensive. Masses of scholarships, rebate if you move to QE from another independent school; 20 per cent discount for Services, diplomats and professional bodies. Sports, art and music scholarships plus a discount for the first year for boys entering the senior school and many many more – including a Karen Dixon scholarship for equestrians. 'You can also pay by Barclaycard or Amex' but it costs extra to spread the payment over several months. Lots of awards and scholarships which include free 'Blue' livery and free BHSAI tuition.

Remarks: This is a mind-boggling transmogrification from a moribund institution to something more like an American campus. Gentle and not aggressively academic or street wise, this is a nurturing school, which in view of the amount of cash thrown at it, is as good as it looks. Boarders are on the up and boys are gradually creeping their way up the school.

QUEEN MARGARET'S SCHOOL

Escrick Park, York, North Yorkshire, YO19 6EU

Tel: 01904 728 261
Fax: 01904 728 150
E-mail: enquiries@queenmargaretsschool.co.uk
Website: www.queenmargaretsschool.co.uk

• Pupils: 362 girls, all board except for 26 • Ages: 11-18
• Size of sixth form: 119 • C of E • Fees: Day £3,945;
Boarding £6,225 • Independent • Open days: No open days
but individual tours and a meeting with the headmaster can
be arranged for parents

Headmaster: Since 1993, Dr Geoffrey Chapman MA (late fifties), educated at St Bartholomew's Grammar School, Newbury; read classics at Trinity College, Oxford. Teaches some Greek and Latin (to one or two). Previously head of classics at Christ's Hospital, Horsham, and before that was professor of classics at University of Natal. Known for serious research on Aristophanes, keen on golf. Wife (a popular lady) teaches drama; two grown-up children. Keen on breadth and choice. 'No one can excel at everything, but everybody can excel at something.' A listener, of considerable and common sense, and the quiet authority of a man who has been twelve years in the job and seen the school improve steadily.

Academic Matters: Although entry is not particularly selective, academic success matters, but without too much of a hothouse atmosphere. Fine GCSE results: 62 per cent plus A*/A, the rest B or C. At A level, French, chemistry, art, history, biology and history of art popular, but no weaknesses. Overall performance very good: 80 per cent plus at A/B. Special needs department (one full, one part time), and two teachers for EFL.

Games, Options, The Arts: Lots of healthy outdoor life, games keenly played: 9-hole golf course, lacrosse (long journeys for fixtures), hockey (newish Astroturf), squash, tennis, etc. Riding popular (private riding school on campus); some girls bring ponies, school keeps 15. Good art, but not an 'arty' school. Home economics for all. Strong choral music, and lots of drama. Catholics go to York for Mass.

Background and Atmosphere: Founded in Scarborough in 1901, moved to this fine Palladian house (by John Carr), with later 'rustic timber' purpose-built classrooms in 1949. Lovely setting in 60 plus acres of parkland (more leased from nearby estate). Victorian additions, clever conversions; recent building includes centenary theatre and chapel (shortlisted for RIBA award), swimming pool. Superb library: panelling, wood everywhere, open fire, huge windows looking out on to lawns. Circular dining hall (once an indoor lunging school), with somewhat noisy acoustics. Food much improved in recent years, say parents. The school was once part of the Woodard Foundation, and was taken over by parents in a 1986 drama. Now not at all what it was (a stuffy finishing school for well-heeled farmers' daughters). Still feels more traditional and structured than its Yorkshire competitors but manages to be relaxed and civilised at the same time.

Welcoming, homey boarding house for 11-year-olds. Girls live in year-groups all the way through (though keeping the same tutor for two years); 'prevents them from growing up too fast', observed one pleased parent, though other views are possible. Sixth form have independent rooms in attractively converted cottages on site. New building planned for fifth form boarders, which will release more room for the three years below. Girls are kept 'pretty busy' all the time. Uniform is tartan and charcoal; own clothes worn after tea – don't provide anything that you wouldn't want boil-washed.

Pastoral Care and Discipline: The pace of life in this attractive rural idyll (and you don't get more rural than N. Yorks) is inevitably slow and there is a noticeable air of protectiveness towards the girls. 'There are no silly rules,' say parents and girls but it is by no means light on rules. 'We are pretty old fashioned about smoking and drinking' – though senior girls do have their own club which serves limited quantities of alcohol. Sixth formers can go into York during free time on Wednesdays and Saturdays; they are usually careful not to abuse this freedom.

Pupils and Parents: Friendly, unaffected pupils, less touched perhaps by the world than some of their contemporaries (many parents will not complain about this). Parents mainly upper and middle class: landowners, farmers, professionals, a small Hong Kong contingent, many from Scotland ('it's the first real boarding school you hit driving south'), Cumbria, the East Coast, and of course Yorkshire. OGs include Winifred Holtby (author), Ann Jellicoe (playwright), Eleanor Hamilton QC.

Entrance: Own exam at 11, 12 and 13. Heavily oversubscribed at 13. A few into sixth form (minimum 8 GCSEs, with at least three Bs and two Cs including English language, maths, a modern language and a science).

Exit: Virtually all go on to universities (predominantly northern). Three or four a year to Oxbridge. A few leave for co-ed sixth forms, eg Rugby.

Money Matters: Scholarships at 11, 12, 13 and sixth form; music scholarships, art scholarship. Some bursaries.

Remarks: Ex-posh girls' boarding school now moving into the top rank, academically and socially. Not for aspiring urban sophisticates. It earns many approving noises from parents, and quite right too – a confident and successful school, where the individual girl matters.

QUEEN MARY'S SCHOOL

Linked to Queen Mary's Prep School in the Junior section

Baldersby Park, Topcliffe, Thirsk, North Yorkshire, YO7 3BZ

Tel: 01845 575 000
Fax: 01845 575 001
E-mail: admin@queenmarys.org
Website: www.queenmarys.org

• Pupils: 215 girls; 55 boarders, mostly weekly, a dozen or so stay at weekends, plus flexi-boarding • Ages: 3-16 • C of E (Woodard school) • Fees: Reception £1,620. Pre-prep £1,950. Senior prep day from £2,990; boarding from £4,380. Senior school day £3,630; boarding £5,040 • Independent • Open days: October and April

---

Headmaster: Since 2003, Mr Robert McKenzie Johnston MA (Cantab) (fifties), known as Mr MJ (as in emjay). Previously joint head with his wife Kate at Hanford, he was educated at Rugby, read economics at Cambridge, and taught at Shrivenham. No PGCE, grandfather's rights. In a former life he was Lt Col in the Queen's Royal Lancers, though he no longer uses the title and can't believe how lucky he is to be at Queen Mary's. The MJs live in the house, and his wife Kate, an occupational therapist, is now an assistant in the nursery: 'such fun, a perpetual three year old birthday party'.

Ebullient, sensitive and very on the ball, the MJs arrived at the school after a period of great turmoil; the previous heads (who did wonders re-decorating the inside of the main house)had left after a fraught proposed amalgamation with Cundall Manor, and the school had been under the guiding hand of previous much-loved heads, long since retired, Peter and Felicity Belward, for a couple of terms. Mr MJ arrived to 'a school full of tension, worry, with no development plan', 'full of lovely dedicated staff', some of whom had been in situ since the school's previous incarnation in Duncombe Park. Certain number of staff changes; the head of English, who left to teach A levels, has been replaced, and there is a new whizzy head of art. Mr MJ teaches maths

to the C stream (who all therefore passed maths GCSE last year – a first for the school). The MJs' daughters come and go, living in the school when they are at home. With so few full-time boarders, the MJs treat the weekending girls as an extended family, with 'jolly trips all over the place'. As they work every weekend they take Wednesdays off and go hunting locally. Not a PC head then! Twiggy is a much loved lurcher, often amongst the children.

Academic Matters: No A level stream. This is a very mixed ability school and all take English, maths and the sciences, most (nearly all) French as well; French starts early. French email exchange with school set up by previous French assistante. 'It is good because you can practise your grammar. It makes it a lot easier in exams!' seems to be the general opinion of the pupils. Excellent showing across the board at GCSE, with a pleasing number of As and A*s. Classics on offer at 11, but not that much take-up further up the school until recently, new classics-teaching chaplain has turned the tide and a couple of girls are now learning Greek as well. German results consistently good and the humanities well represented.

Streaming and setting, tiny classes. New timetable. Good and sensitive dyslexia help, with great celebration when the most dyslexic pupil in the school got her five Cs last year. Buzzy library with sagbags. Classrooms in the main building and converted outhouses, plus stunning new build for tinies. Science department boasts a greenhouse and freshwater pond for hands-on experience. A goodly supply of computers throughout, plus dedicated IT rooms, many of the girls also have their own laptops; internet OK, but girls not allowed to used hotmail (chatrooms). Senior girls do coursework online. Tinies have computers too, and good basic three Rs in the lower school. Thirty-five staff on hand plus 12 part-timers. School never closes and girls can be found wandering around in the Easter holidays having been 'doing extra workshops' with the staff, who never seem to take holidays either.

Games, Options, The Arts: Long time head of music can't quite understand why the school does not 'revolve round music' and the place hums with junior and senior choirs and natty concerts and concertettes open to the general public as well as for inmates; impressive for a school of this size. Chapel choristers wear much coveted green sweat shirts and give regular performances both home and away. Stunning art in the attics under new head including creative textiles and ceramics, sewing machines in the DT room. Home grown art all over the place. Drama good and popular, everything about this school spells fun. Cooking timetabled, the smell of frying onions pervading the steps to the art room (instant hunger pangs and we had just had lunch).

Trad sports, with lacrosse, athletics and tennis teams all doing well. Superb equestrian facilities, children can and do bring their own ponies and ride daily (Mr MJ has started the children riding before breakfast in the summer months), outdoor manege of Olympian size, as well as rides across the local landowner's fields, Mr MJ in constant negotiation with his neighbours to increase riders' scope, cross country course on site. Tadcaster polo club is nearby and looks like becoming the next horsy activity. Terrific little swimming pool (though the surrounding wood panelling needs help – new estate manager should help with maintenance) and tiny adjacent fenced in area for littlies. Climbing frames. Superb selection of expeditions for all, plus D of E. Canoeing on the adjacent River Swale popular in the junior school.

Background and Atmosphere: Baldersby Park is a grand Palladian mansion (Colen Campbell 1721, Jacob-ethanised following a fire in 1902) and was converted into residential flats in a previous existence so the girls have a rash of good sized dorms with private bathrooms. Posh. Splendid library in the former ballroom presided over by a rather dreary portrait of Nell Gwynn (why?). Glorious main hall used for daily service, with the girls sitting on the carpet, Mr MJ sitting in front of the stairs, the choir ranged behind him in serried ranks. School uniform evolves over the years with girls graduating from beige jerseys to green jerseys and royal hunting Stewart tartan kilts, slight pressure currently to change the uniform but neither the MJs nor the girls can see the point.

Staff and pupils bring their pets to school and girls are happy with the relaxed atmosphere – like an extended family – all ages mix – with a mass of sisterly teasing. Prefects lock up at night, though they may come and get Mr MJ if it is dark and they have to check the stables. Charming new-smelling chapel, resident chaplain, Mr MJ is keen that religion should be 'part of the school routine' but not rammed down the throat. The early assumption of seniority (at 16 rather than 18) gives girls confidence and maturity. All pupils have to play some part in keeping the school neat, clean and tidy. Really helpful and supportive gang of governors.

Pastoral Care and Discipline: Like home. No petty rules, and others which are bendable but there is an underlying sense of organisation. 'Suspension,' says Mr MJ, 'is a sign of failure on the part of the school and not the pupil'. Parents' requests granted when reasonable. Not a sophisticated place, no obvious sin.

Pupils and Parents: Local as opposed to county school, combination of first time buyers, local farmers, landowners and professionals and has long since shed the image of the school that looks after the daughters of local nobs. Relaxed 7.30 drop off time for working parents. Quite a lot of army families, Catterick is just up the road, some of whom pop their daughters in the school 'whilst they are based in Yorkshire' and are so pleased with the place that they leave their darlings there when they are posted elsewhere. Quite a lot of flexi-boarding, with some full time boarders living closer than some of the day girls, ditto the flexi-boarders. ('Girls come to escape.') If girls regularly stay three nights a week they get their own permanent space rather than living in truckle beds, no charge for extra meals, only for bed. Boarding mainly from 11, and day girls often opt to stay at least on a weekly basis. Parents and pupils can use school facilities in the holidays. No real overseas presence, one or two ex-pats. Parents run a website and are delighted to answer any queries.

Entrance: At any time, middle of term if needed. At all ages. Testette but only those with special needs beyond the school's capability are liable to be turned away.

Exit: At all ages. Some take common entrance at 11, some at 12 and some at 13. Girls have previously mainly gone to Queen Margaret's Eskrick, with one or two to Tudor Hall, Heathfield or co-eds, Uppingham, Millfield, Rugby. None appear to be leaving at this stage in 2006. Senior girls go on to do A levels at Ampleforth, St Aidan's, Ripon Grammar, Oundle, Queen Margaret's Eskrick, Uppingham etc. etc. Good collection of scholarships, music predominates, plus academic and sports.

Money Matters: Not a rich school and not endowed but scholarships for academics, music, art and sport plus bursaries for clergy daughters, sisters and Services discount.

Remarks: Useful, popular, small, girls' – predominantly weekly – boarding school without a sixth form. A home from home and a good education too. Needs one or two more bums on seats but, under the inspired guidance of (we think) one of the best headmasters around, this shouldn't prove too much of a problem.

QUEEN'S COLLEGE

Linked to Queen's College Junior School in the Junior section

Trull Road, Taunton, Somerset, TA1 4QS

Tel: 01823 272 559
Fax: 01823 338 430
E-mail: contact@queenscollege.org.uk
Website: www.queenscollege.org.uk

- Pupils: 710 boys and girls (160 boarders, 550 day) • Ages: 11-18 • Size of sixth form: 125 (50 boarders, 75 day) • Methodist foundation • Fees: Junior day £1,377 - £3,342 boarding £2,629 - £4,929. Senior: £3,792 day; £5,724 boarding
- Independent • Open days: A whole college open day in October and 2 further days for junior school

Head: Since 2001, Mr Christopher J Alcock BSc FRSG (mid forties). Geography and anthropology graduate of Durham University, 1981. After PGCE, taught geography at Stamford School where he was boarding housemaster and rugby coach. Became deputy head of King Edward's School, Witley, in 1997. Relaxed, self-assured and pragmatic nature seems to be rubbing off on pupils. He takes an 'omni-present' approach – tries to watch every match, debate, concert performance, play, sporting fixture. Married with two sons at the school, one in senior and one in junior.

Academic Matters: 'Everyone has the chance to fulfil their potential here', said the head girl. Good raw GCSE and A level results – even better on value-added. Passionate about accelerated and individual learning – evidently working. Broadly follows National Curriculum. Huge investment in high-speed IT network linking 150 computers, mainly grouped in one of three dedicated suites including for science but many positioned in individual classrooms. It makes parents, pupils and staff proud – 'enviably this improves resourcing to enhance pupils' work'. Interactive whiteboards are also seen as an asset. Excellent teaching quality in modern languages, resulting in good marks, compensates for the bare and uninspiring classrooms, with little to show for resources.

Multi-sensory approach used to teach dyslexics, often on a one-to-one basis, although methods and techniques are adapted to suit the individual; good exam performance as a result. Supportive of SEN children generally; pupils withdrawn from classes rather than taught in class. Allowed the space to be what they are: dyspraxics thrive in individual sports like diving; ADHD pupils are allowed to 'fiddle qui-

etly' with Blu-tac under the table. Pupils can (and do) come up to the SEN department at any time for support, advice and TLC. Informs/enlightens all colleagues about SEN difficulties through special booklet and guidance notes and through INSET. Liaises with tutors and house parents to make sure SEN children are happy and well cared for. Each pupil gets an individually designed programme to suit his/her unique needs. Expect as much from their SEN pupils as they do from the rest. Currently has former SEN pupils studying medicine, dentistry, marine biology, chemistry etc.

Games, Options, The Arts: Leadership, teamwork, confidence and self-esteem encouraged through broad, cross-curricular programme of music, drama, art, sport, Duke of Edinburgh's Award and outdoor pursuits. 'You don't need to worry if your child isn't sporty as they'll soon find a sport to suit,' comments a parent. 30 acres of enviably flat playing fields, quaint benches and trees line the sides. Impressive, high-tech gym for sixth formers and staff.

A suitably noisy art room allows students to express their ideas and creativity freely. D of E is popular among pupils and staff alike – in year 10 every pupil is expected to be involved at bronze level, for older groups it is optional. Community service and charitable work comes about both under the formal D o E umbrella and via various activities specific to the school. Staff willingly give up their time to run activities as diverse as rock-climbing and computer training. 'There's something to suit every whim,' said a parent.

Background and Atmosphere: Relaxed, peaceful and friendly atmosphere. Somehow has a hint of mainstream openness about it. Sixth formers looking like they're allowed to be teenagers – chilling in the corridor, a cool kiss or hug here and there, chatting and milling in the students room. However, on entering the well-resourced, well-used media-friendly library, students knuckle-down to work. School motto 'non scholae sed vitae discimus' ie 'We learn not for school but for life' – is followed today as it was when the school was founded in 1843. Elegant 19th century buildings combined with state-of-the-art science labs. Average class size: 17. Committed and happy teaching staff of high calibre, some who have written internationally recognised textbooks on their subjects.

Pastoral Care and Discipline: 'The pastoral care is fabulous,' say parents. 'Never heard of any bullying'. 'If you treat others the way you wish to be treated yourself then you can't go far wrong,' says head. Parents feel the house system is 'broad and challenging' but 'friendly and family-orientated'. It was the 'family feel-good factor that struck me when I visited Queens.'

Pupils and Parents: From various social backgrounds.

50 per cent of borders are Services children, the rest from all over the country and beyond.

Entrance: Broad intake. Pupils at 11, 12 or 13 sit school's own entry papers in English, maths and verbal reasoning or Common Entrance. Sixth form entry is dependent on good GCSE results and, for newcomers, a sound school report.

Exit: 65 per cent leave with all As and/or Bs. Most secure places with the Russell group of universities. Medicine, veterinary science, law and arts are popular. Dyslexics to a notably wide range of subjects: art, biology, chemistry, dentistry, electronic engineering, environmental sciences, geography, history, international business, medicine, PPE (politics, philosophy and economics) and law.

Money Matters: Awards up to eight academic scholarships a year, worth up to 50 per cent of fees. A music scholarship was won by girl in Kuala Lumpur after she auditioned via video link. Up to three boarding scholarships for seniors. Sibling discounts. A couple of boarding bursaries care for juniors whose parents fall on hard times.

Remarks: An interestingly confident school with effective teaching strategies.

QUEEN'S COLLEGE LONDON

Linked to Queen's College Prep School in the Junior section

43-49 Harley Street, London, W1G 8BT

Tel: 020 7291 7000
Fax: 020 7291 7090
E-mail: queens@qcl.org.uk
Website: www.qcl.org.uk

• Pupils: 380 girls, all day • Ages: 11-18 • Size of sixth form: 90
• C of E • Fees: Senior school £3,800 • Independent • Open days: September, October, November, February for senior school. Junior school by appointment

---

Principal: Since 1999, Miss Margaret Connell MA (fifties). Read physics at Oxford. Previously head at More House for eight years and before that deputy head at Bromley High. Also spent ten years in the maths department at North London Collegiate. A strong and popular head, she clearly knows and cares about each girl and interviews every child personally before taking them on board. Interests include music, theatre and travel.

Academic Matters: Small classes – 20 pre GCSE, 12-15 in the sixth form – ensure all girls get plenty of attention. Most take 9 or 10 GCSE, 4 AS, three As. Languages a

strength, with six modern languages on offer. Everyone studies French for at least three years, with a chance to try Italian, German, Spanish and Russian. Also strong classics department, with Greek from year 8. (Girls regularly enter Latin and Greek reading competitions.) Setting in maths and French. Three sciences taught separately from year 9, taken as double award. All girls take English and Eng lit, mathematics, a science and a modern language to GCSE, 'after that the choice is up to them'.

Parents with struggling daughters find the teaching exemplary. 'If one approach doesn't work, they try another,' says one enthusiastic mother. 'Girls want to work hard because they make it fun.' It has been said that high flyers are not quite so well served, but in 2005 65 per cent of those taking GCSE received A* or A, 6 out of 35 sitting A levels proceeded happily to Oxbridge.

27 subjects offered at A level, with much timetabling gymnastics. Particularly good results in French, chemistry, art and geography. Girls allowed a free choice of subjects, though guided on potential downside. 'We never ask a girl to discontinue a subject to improve our ranking in the league tables,' says the head. Some provision for special needs, with a screening in year 7 followed by help from a part-time specialist.

Games, Options, The Arts: Not really a school for the very sporty. A well-equipped gym, but only a miniscule Astroturfed playground. Traditional games (with inter-school matches) take place a 15-minute walk away in Regent's Park. Swimming at nearby Seymour Baths and Westminster University. Emphasis more on keep fit than 'go-fight-win' with a wide range of exercise on offer – gymnastics (excellent record in competitions), dance, fencing, yoga, self-defence, Pilates and kick boxing. No time-tabled PE in the sixth form (hurrah, say the girls!).

State-of-the-art glass-sided computer room ('the goldfish bowl'), provides the latest flat-screen computer technology, where girls can do internet research. (Staff and girls all have their own email address.) A large (and beautiful) wood-panelled assembly hall for morning assemblies, lectures, concerts and major dramatic and musical productions.

Art – extremely popular both at GCSE and A level (textiles also an option) – has its own airy roof-top quarters, with a suitably Bohemian feel. Many girls proceed to top art colleges, and even those intending to pursue an academic career often choose art foundation at one of the London colleges first. ('They use it as an alternative gap year to focus the mind,' says the head.) Design technology not on offer.

Well-equipped music department – with computers and a multi-track recording studio – in basement, 'because we've found the thick walls are great for sound insulation.' Singing lessons extremely popular, as well as a wide range of instruments. Both music and music technology offered at A level. Other musical activities include a choir, wind band, jazz choir and singing club. Parents, too, encouraged to have a go with a scratch Messiah.

Senior library definitely one of the glories of the school. 17,000 volumes (including Spanish, French, German and Russian in the original) spread over three distinguished Listed rooms with an Oxbridge feel. Careers advice taken seriously, with a well-equipped and central careers room and a careers specialist on tap three days a week. Year 9 girls take part in the Take Your Daughters to Work programme and careers lessons form part of the GCSE curriculum. Popular basement canteen paid for with a swipe card so parents know what their daughters are eating. Girls not obliged to have school lunches, but most do.

Active charitable involvement and also participation in schemes like Young Enterprise, where a recent successful venture included the creation of pink 'hoodies' fringed in diamante. 'You'd have thought we had a uniform; they sold out in one day.'

Background and Atmosphere: Founded in 1848 by one of the great Victorian reformers, Frederick Denison Maurice, Professor of English Literature and History at King's College, London, Queen's was a pioneer in the higher education of women and the first to provide academic qualifications. Maurice encouraged girls to take responsibility for their own actions and this remains a central premise of the College today. The atmosphere is controlled laissez-faire, the approach to dress non-didactic and this is definitely not a school where you'll get lines for lateness. Sixth formers, in particular, given increased freedom (swipe cards record arrival and departure times throughout the school).

A generally non-competitive atmosphere – 'We're not aiming for a certain level of results, we want each girl to get the best results for her,' says the head – leads to an unusually happy environment. 'Girls pop in after two years at university with fond memories of the school. They're often surprised to find this is not always the case everywhere.'

Still on its original site, the College is housed in four elegant 18th-century town houses, which provide a higgledy-piggledy arrangement that's been cleverly adapted for modern needs.

Early students included Frances Mary Buss, founder of North London Collegiate and Camden School for Girls, and Sophia Jex-Blake, the first English-educated woman doctor. More recent old girls include Anna Wintour, editor of American Vogue, actresses Emma Freud and Jennifer Ehle,

and Asma al Assad, the glamorous wife of the President of Syria.

Pastoral Care and Discipline: A liberal school in every respect, but one with an underlying Christian tradition. Broadly Christian prayers held four days a week in the Hall. Jewish prayers held separately twice a week and Muslims have a quiet area set aside for worship during Ramadan. Strong pastoral care. Parents' evening at least once a year, reports twice. In between, parents can contact staff by telephone or email – 'Most of our parents are working and that's often the most efficient means of communication' – or arrange a meeting.

Few rules and few exclusions – mainly over abuse of emails. 'If anybody is unpleasant to another girl they're banned from the system and suspended from school.' Drugs not an issue. Head girl ('Senior Student') and prefects voted for by girls and staff.

Pupils and Parents: Accessible from everywhere in London, but girls mainly from the north and west. Its central London position gives it a cosmopolitan and sophisticated feel. Parents from a wide variety of backgrounds and professions but a strong showing of media. About 25 per cent ethnic minorities.

Entrance: At 11 by exam (part of Group 1 of the North London Independent Girls' Schools Consortium.) Not unduly selective by London standards, but the majority fall into top quarter of the ability range. The head interviews all candidates before the exam – 'afterwards they're much more nervous' – and allows parents their say. Recently launched prep school the biggest feeder, 'perhaps because it's easier to assess suitability', but 'definitely not a junior school.' Twenty-five per cent from state primaries. Some places available higher up the school. Sixth form entrance by interview, school reference and six grade C GCSEs. (Scholarship exam held in December).

Exit: Some leakage after GCSE to co-ed state (Camden School for Girls very popular) and independent schools. The vast majority go onto good universities. Many stay in London, including a strong sprinkling to top art colleges. 'Elsewhere they tend to look for universities with a London feel, not a campus in the middle of nowhere.'

Money Matters: Small number of art and music scholarships at 11, and several scholarships awarded by competitive examination for A level. Bursaries also available for those 'whose circumstances change'. More than 10 per cent receive some sort of funding.

Remarks: Not a school for those who want their girls in neat uniforms and ranking order. Creates confident, articulate, street-smart young women whose career choice is more likely to be in the arts and media than the civil service or banking.

QUEEN'S GATE SCHOOL

Linked to Queen's Gate Junior School in the Junior section

133 Queen's Gate, Kensington, London, SW7 5LE

Tel: 02075 893 587

Fax: 02075 847 691

E-mail: registrar@queensgate.org.uk

Website: www.queensgate.org.uk

• Pupils: 270 girls; all day • Ages: 11-18 • Size of sixth form: 45 • Non-denom • Fees: Junior £2,900 - £3,050 Senior: £3,625 • Independent • Open days: October

Principal: Since 2006, Mrs Rosalynd Kamaryc, previously head (for ten years) of Wykeham House School in Fareham. Took over on the retirement of Mrs Angela Holyoak, the most elegant head we have interviewed and a terrific head all round.

Academic Matters: Small classes, max 20, vaguely streamed, half-termly tests, girls move up and down. Pupil:staff ratio of 7:1 which is impressive – 'good staff fairly thin on the ground' – not, you understand at Queen's Gate, where 'contracts for new staff are half a term's notice on either side during the first half term, thereafter a term's notice.' Following an earlier 'incident', all short-listed staff 'are required to teach while observed by the head of department and the principal or the head'.

Stunning male head of science (fair number of teaching chaps in evidence) who teaches chemistry, is justifiably proud of his pupils' 100 per cent As success at A level. Dedicated labs in the basement and three separate sciences taught from 11. However, sciences still the pretty poor relation, with tranches taking classical civilisation, history of art, art, theatre studies and Eng lit. Lots of desktop publishing and study skills masquerade as English. History popular, and at uni level. Languages stronger at GCSE level than at A. French, German, Italian and Spanish offered, all taught by native speakers with masses of hands-on and trips abroad. Latin for all for the first two years, and a certain take-up at GCSE. Maths (regular Monday maths clinic) and geography making a good showing. An interesting collection of specialisms: sociology, graphic communication/products and information studies. Mrs H disputes our comment that, 'this is not a place you would choose for a straight up and down academic', pointing to a string of recent successes –

As across the board and honours degrees thereafter (engineering and maths would you believe), but this is a school for girls of mixed ability and they do jolly well.

Tellies, videos and computers in most classrooms, serious computer suites (cool new machines), all learn word processing, and do touch-typing in the junior school. Dyslexia provision, dyscalculia, dysphasia, you name it, two individual lessons a week. EFL as required. Not keen on behavioural problems – 'though', said Mrs Holyoak, 'there is usually a reason for it and school can often work through it.'

Games, Options, The Arts: Good sized gym, marked out for fencing in the mews of the middle house, and an impressive string of wins on the games field. Girls are bused to Battersea for tennis, rounders, hockey and basketball, and to the Kensington Sports Centre to swim and use their sports hall. Fantastic roof conversion for art suite, with fabric design, screen printing, CAD-CAM and a clever new vinyl cutting machine, lots of real hands-on stuff. Good strong work on show, much of it research based. Use made of local museums, art galleries and theatres.

Drama vibrant – the latest production was As You Like It, performed at Imperial College, the girls do everything – play every part and design the sets. Regular end of term house plays in impressive new hall (converted across two of the houses, much fund-raising, runs into the internet library). Most take the LAMDA exams in acting and the speaking of verse and prose. Terrific music, chamber orchestra, individual lessons and popular singing; girls join the W11 choir and take part in West End musicals, much visiting the West End for opera and musicals too. Clubs for almost everything at lunchtime, girls must go to two a week, the range is huge, everything from debating, yoga, jewellery making and cookery (microwave). Hot on charity, with regular fund-raising events, and particularly keen on cancer research – sponsored readathons, spellathons.

Background and Atmosphere: Founded in 1891, the school is based in three large Victorian mansions in South Ken. The head points out that 'we've more space than you might imagine' but former broom cupboards in erstwhile mansions of this size provide useful dark rooms/tutorial rooms and offices. Immaculate, the place has recently been rewired to allow for computer/internet access throughout. The school spreads into the mews behind and all but one of the rooms have at least two fire exits – some of them about five feet high. New pupils should probably be issued with a map, compass and bits of chalk for orienteering practice in their first few weeks.

Two libraries, not snazzy enough says the last inspection report, well-used careers library. Lots of the old features still remain, imposing marble fireplaces, ornate cornices and fire doors make curious companions. Sixth form common rooms dotted all over, ditto fifth form – much talk of tidying them up for our visit. They were – very. Walls filled with photographs, children's work and noticeboards, and a sense of calm prevails, girls remarkably well behaved, stand up when the principal enters, but sadly, they no longer curtsey or wear white gloves (haven't for years). No official uniform: T-shirts, skirts and jerseys, no facial or body piercing. Food excellent, vegetarian option, older girls may bring packed lunches which they eat in their classrooms, otherwise the whole school eats in two sessions in either the white or the black (definitely the grander) dining room. Coffee bar in the basement.

Pastoral Care and Discipline: Two of the sixth form girls are attached to each of the younger forms as 'sisters' – 'often easier to confide in than a member of staff, after all,' said our informant, 'they leave'. Mrs Holyoak is passionate about discipline, 'won't tolerate drugs', but equally won't deliver 'blanket' punishments, each case is treated individually, and wouldn't comment on 'any disciplinary subjects in school'. Not many rules. Three roll calls daily, in the morning, after lunch and before they go home, 'we are in loco parentis'. Tutor system for all (they meet twice a term). Good PSHE system in place, outside counsellor, health advisor, vigilant for anorexia.

Pupils and Parents: We would stick with our previous comment, 'pretty upper class' – 'wide range of parent' says the principal; fair enough; from a range of ethnic backgrounds, though principally of Sloane extraction. A good number of foreigners, encouraged by the principal as long as their English is up to it, 'this is London and we're a cosmopolitan city' – useful network for later gap and other travel too. Girls are fiercely loyal, delightfully mannered and very pretty. OGs: Redgraves, Sieffs, Guinnesses, Amanda de Souza, Jane Martineau, Nigella Lawson, Lucinda Lambton, Camilla Parker Bowles and Tracey Boyd, Aurelia Cecil and Suzanna Constantine. The new head of MI5, Eliza Manningham Buller, used to be on the staff.

Entrance: From Junior school – three quarters of junior girls come on to the senior school – and a huge variety of other schools, confirm entry for the January exams the November before you want to come. Above all priority given to sisters and OGs' children. New arrivals throughout the year, but preferably in September, though pupils who have left and have then been unhappy at their new school often re-join again mid-term. School holds three open days a year for potential parents and it is not unusual to have 800 parents attend. Girls take London day schools' exam for entry

at 11, assessment and test for entry at other times. For sixth form entry 5 A*-C grades with at least A in subjects to be studied at A level and B in AS subjects. Usually over-subscribed, but, because of the volatile nature of London, places do occur all over.

Exit: Tiny dribble to Oxbridge, strong medical faction at the moment, most take a gap year, otherwise to unis all over, Durham popular, some to art school. Small leakage after GCSE to other London day schools, co-ed boarding, or local sixth form colleges, either because they want a change, or a larger variety of A levels.

Money Matters: Two internal scholarships for sixth form entry.

Remarks: Plus ça change. Charming popular school, with a mixed intake, which does jolly well by its girls. Touch of the Miss Jean Brodies.

THE QUEEN'S SCHOOL

Linked to Queen's Lower School (The) in the Junior section

City Walls Road, Chester, Cheshire, CH1 2NN

Tel: 01244 312 078
Fax: 01244 321 507
E-mail: secretary@queens.cheshire.sch.uk
Website: www.queens.cheshire.sch.uk

• Pupils: 600 girls; all day • Ages: 4-19 • Size of sixth form: 110
• Non-denom • Fees: Senior school £2,645 lower school £1,755
• Independent • Open days: October and November

Head: Since 2001, Mrs C M Buckley MA (early fifties). Read French and German at Oxford. Won two language prizes for French but started career teaching English to German speakers in Bavaria. Still teaches one class German. Came here via Manchester High School, Cheadle Hulme and King's, Macclesfield. Slim, stylish and ultra smart. Admired by girls as, 'very intelligent, a modern thinker, strict but an encourager, celebrating achievements including those out of school,' her catchphrase to them being, 'go on, you can do it.' Writes glossy termly newsletter stuffed with praise for girls and other members of the school community. Redesigned the entrance to the school with new ground floor reception and admin areas, curriculum developments and electronic reporting.

Academic Matters: Traditionally an academic school with hard work ethic prevailing. Girls' definition of a Queen's girl: 'academic, but not just academic, she'll have other talents including sport and music'. 70 per cent GCSE results are A or A* and at A level 40 per cent As, 70 per cent A or B. A number of girls achieve top five national marks at GCSE and A level each year, and over half the girls gain eight or nine GCSE A* grades. Sciences popular but good results across the board. Latin, and classical civilisation as options. Good breadth and training for the world outside. Sixth form general studies is expanding to include AS critical thinking and life skills such as cooking on a budget, ethics and fitness (outside speakers for this). Good careers and university advice, also work experience schemes. 'Totally dedicated staff,' say head and girls, giving up lunch, after school and free times to help.

Games, Options, The Arts: Very sporty. Head expected the academic strengths but describes herself as surprised by how good the sport is. Star in the firmament is Beth Tweddle, European and Commonwealth medal-winning gymnast. One all-weather pitch on wedge-shaped playing fields across the road beneath the city walls. Strong lacrosse, some county, North West and England players. Ruth Evans, ex pupil, plays lacrosse for England and hockey for Wales. Good tennis (Cheshire champions), basketball club, inter-school rounders teams, indoor cricket and football during lessons and extra-curricular activities. Extra sport coaches hired. Running club navigates the two miles of city walls at lunch times, some run for Cheshire. Rowing, self-defence and dance on offer.

YE and D of E have slots in timetable. Traditional links with King's include RAF and Army cadets, joint drama and music productions and discos. Varied foreign trips such as wilderness experience in Kenya after fund-raising for fare, and skiing supported by parents (second British girls team). Charity fund-raising, Barnardos and Amnesty International feature. Lots of clubs, Christian Union, community voluntary work. Several music groups, two choirs, annual music festival celebrates instruments and singing and includes competition and concert. Good art in airy top floor room. Home economics rather than food tech for the practical life skills it offers.

Background and Atmosphere: Founded by Dean of Chester in 1878. Some cathedral links remain, chamber choir takes evensong sometimes. 'We're Christian with a small c,' says head, though assemblies include Bible readings, prayer and a thought for the day. Site was originally Chester's house of correction, the cells long since filled in and tarmac'd for a playground, where staff parking competes with pupil space. Limited city centre site on Chester's tourist trail and city walls; a mix of Georgian, Victorian and modern buildings all on top of Roman remains. Conservationists and archaeologists precede builders on any new project.

Grounds overshadowed by Moathouse Hotel across inner ring road, but charming, leafy, walled gardens offer oasis for girls. 'Nightmare parking,' say parents but sixth formers enjoy popping out for coffee. MacLean House has separate common rooms for years 12 and 13 each with microwave and kitchenette. New head introduced suits for sixth form; attractive uniforms in lower years of navy and white with deep fuchsia wool jumpers, 'itchy,' girls, 'tend to shrink,' parents, 'sweatshirts would fade so,' says head. Superb school magazine, 'Have Mynde', first produced in 1887 for the sake of the 'noble industry of thought'.

Pastoral Care and Discipline: Girls describe teachers and year heads as really caring. Peer support scheme, four houses, head girl and two deputies elected jointly by students and staff. Elected form captains and council members. Merits for younger pupils, 'recognising and rewarding effort as well as achievement, we don't want anyone to feel a failure.' Head likes to bring in strong women role models for annual prize giving.

Pupils and Parents: Solidly middle class, well-spoken, unspoilt girls. From wide catchment area including far along north Wales coast, travelling by train and then bus. Other buses shared with King's, some long journeys. Very few ethnic minorities reflecting Chester's population. 'The challenge is pronouncing the Welsh names correctly,' says head. Notable OGs include Vivienne Faull, Dean of Leicester Cathedral, Ann Clwyd MP and Anne Minors, architect. Building bridges with OGs, especially younger ones, is priority for head.

Entrance: By exam, interview and primary school report, 'we're looking for a spark,' in late January. Number of applicants up by 25 per cent to 2.5 for every place as a result of increased marketing – helpful as new competition when King's started accepting girls in 2003. 'Parents have to find the right school for their daughter and in this school girls can really be themselves. They don't have to pretend to be anything but bright,' says head, 'it's boys who benefit from co-ed.'

Exit: Some leave for local college sixth forms. Otherwise all to universities with a wide range of location and course. Lots opt for medicine and more than a handful to Oxford or Cambridge each year.

Money Matters: Some means-tested bursaries and a variety of scholarships including a long-standing annual £30 university scholarship 'tenable at a college of Oxford or Cambridge Universities.' Two travel bursaries annually for older girls.

Remarks: Really good, full, encouraging education on

cramped (school says 'limited') site with lots of extra interests. As one girl said, 'I absolutely love my school, it's such fun and there's excellence in everything.'

QUEENSWOOD SCHOOL

Shepherd's Way, Brookmans Park, Hatfield, Hertfordshire, AL9 6NS

Tel: 01707 602 500

Fax: 01707 602 597

E-mail: registry@queenswood.herts.sch.uk

Website: www.queenswood.org

- Pupils: 411 girls: 214 boarders, 197 day boarders
- Ages: 11-18 • Size of sixth form: 113 • Christian/Non-denom
- Fees: Day boarders £5,020 - £5,480. Full boarders £6,665 - £7,265 • Independent • Open days: Lots

Principal: Since 1996, Ms Clarissa Farr BA MA PGCE (forties), read English at Exeter, followed by a Masters in modern literature and previously taught in a sixth form college, a comprehensive school, a grammar school and abroad before coming to Queenswood as deputy head (academic) in 1992. Married to the sports news correspondent of The Times; two children. She teaches English and theatre studies. Fun and outgoing, Ms Farr's hobby is running marathons; she was wearing a chic trouser suit when we visited and is much approved of by her pupils. Aims not to produce a 'typical girl' but to turn out 'charming, confident and kind' pupils who will be efficient and have a sense of values without being 'shrinking violets'. She passionately believes in producing 'whole girls', whose range is broader than pure academe.

Off to head St Paul's Girls in September 2006.

Academic Matters: Exam results on the way up – 93 per cent A/B at A level. Girls often do two modern languages at GCSE and continue with at least one in sixth form. Hooray! Options in Italian, Russian, Japanese and Spanish Culture; girls encouraged to continue studies in their own native languages. No child is refused 'a go' at a GCSE. Setted in maths, French, English and science, no class larger than 24. Theatre studies and drama strong. Girls follow a general studies course of their choice alongside their A levels. Laptops for all from year 8. Internet on tap all over and computers in classrooms. Younger pupils work at carrells, with plug below each for laptop (NB iPods, mobile phones etc not allowed in study areas!). Refurbished, state of the art library with CD-ROMs, SKY and internet access. Careers advice and learning support throughout.

Games, Options, The Arts: Sports are 'high on the agenda'. School is a national LTA clay court centre and hosts the annual National Schools Championships. The Lawn Tennis Association suggests it for would-be tennis stars. With 27 courts in all – 12 clay, 13 all-weather and 2 indoors. 'You can play tennis at any level,' and at almost any time. There is a community-based letting programme. Masses of inter-school competitions. Astroturf hockey pitch, indoor swimming pool completed October 2004, weights room, aerobics room and huge sports hall. This is a school for budding internationalists. Keen on music, with impressive music centre and re-vamped organ in the chapel where there are regular lunch-time recitals, as well as lots of community use. Strong choral and masses of orchestras, loads of inter-house competitions. Good drama with workshops; new theatre December 2005. Fabulous art and spectacular ceramics. Textiles important. Regular art history trips to Europe. Model United Nations, Young Enterprise, debating society, plus charity works. School awarded bronze level 'eco-school' status, September 2005. The place hums.

Background and Atmosphere: Only just out of suburbia. Founded in Clapham Park in 1894, school moved to purpose-built neo-Tudor building in 1925 with masses of later additions. Spectacular Audrey Butler Centre (aka the ABC) houses lecture theatre, language labs and masses of classrooms; science labs opposite functional and uninspired. 120 acres of sports fields and woodland two miles out from the M25, a 'short hour' out of London. Houses divided by year for youngest (Trew), with some resident lower sixth on hand to help. Upper sixth have own houses, with single or double study bedrooms. Rest of school lives in mixed age houses, with each house having a common room where other houses can visit. Sixth form common room known as the Pizza Hut, tellies everywhere, but viewing restricted. Boarding breaks and sleepovers on hand for 'day boarders', who are, anyway, at the school from early till very late. Fixed 'activity' and 'home weekends', otherwise boarders can spend Friday and Saturday night at home, as long as they are back in time for evening chapel on Sunday. Daily chapel; sixth formers line the cloister 'to make sure socks are pulled up', school wear purple and grey but mufti in sixth (the school prefers the term 'smart own clothes' and indeed they were).

Pastoral Care and Discipline: Each house of 40-90 girls is run by teaching housemistresses with assistants and a team of academic tutors. Each tutor has around ten tutees and sixth formers choose their own tutor. Deputy principal (pastoral) in charge of boarding. Parents informed, plus fines (out of pocket money) and community service for smokers and boozers – fines and time spent on community service increase for second offence; immediate suspension for smoking indoors or third offence. Girls taking drugs 'lose their right to be a member of the school'.

Pupils and Parents: Lots of first time buyers, with both partners working, masses from London, very strong parent supported Queenswood Fellowship much involved with social activities throughout the year. 10 per cent from abroad, with some ex-pats. Not a snob school, 'no social overtones' – 'this is a school for real people,' said a visiting educationalist.

Entrance: Registration advised three years before entry date, either by CE at 11 and 13 or by own entrance exam. Strong sixth form intake, candidates must get six GCSEs at B or over, with As in the subjects they want to study at A level.

Exit: Most to university, a couple to Oxbridge. Many do gap years, organised by the school. Few now leave post GCSE to do A levels elsewhere.

Money Matters: Academic scholarships throughout, two at sixth form. Music (including organ scholarship), tennis and sport scholarships. All scholarships renewed annually while the holders are at Queenswood provided they prove themselves worthy. Occasional bursaries. School will pick up any financial disasters as long as parents are upfront about the problem.

Remarks: Refreshing, zappy, highly-structured girls' boarding school, extremely handy for busy London parents. An all-round education, where sport and the community are as important as academic results. Parents current and prospective will be crossing their fingers over the succession to a very healthy regime.

RADLEY COLLEGE

Radley, Abingdon, Oxfordshire, OX14 2HR

Tel: 01235 543 000
Fax: 01235 543 106
E-mail: Radley@goodschoolsguide.co.uk
Website: www.radley.org.uk

• Pupils: 625 boys; all board • Ages: 13-18 • Size of sixth form: 250 • C of E • Fees: £7,580 per term • Independent

Warden: Since 2000, Mr Angus McPhail MA (forties), educated at Abingdon School and read PPE at University College, Oxford. Previously head of Strathallan School in Perthshire and started life as a banker before switching to teaching ('far more satisfying'). He taught first at Glenalmond, followed by Sedbergh, where he was housemaster, and still teaches 'a little' economics at Radley (half an A level set).

Charming and fun, interesting and interested (in everything) he is pleased to be back in the Abingdon area; a delightful man with ease of manner, many talents and interests. A keen cricketer, all-round sportsman, very musical, sings, plays the violin and guitar. Wife and three children; fond of children – 'you can't be a good teacher unless you like children – and I've met lots of people in the profession who don't like them'. Has fourth form boys 15/16 at a time for cocoa on a regular basis – 'very relaxed and fun'. Took over from the redoubtable Mr Richard Morgan (aka the king maker) a top class head with a genius for gathering a good common room around him.

Academic Matters: Results excellent given intake (see Entrance); 88 per cent A/B at A level, 80 per cent A*/A at GCSE. Maths – in all its disciplines – outstanding, also physics, English and history; economics popular. French, German, Spanish on offer with an Italian option. School operates on an eight-day timetable; the half days are always on the same day but otherwise classes move around 'so that sometimes you can do a whole week without your worst subject' said our guide. EFL and dyslexia tuition (on a fairly pedestrian basis we said, to which the warden replied 'very unfair, it is a great strength of the school') if required. Laptops not a problem; stunning new library in converted medieval barn; masses of computers, all intra/inter-linked; e-mail for all. Magical circular Queen's Court (aka the doughnut) houses six departments, plus new arts building, which includes modern languages, English, drama (including theatre workshop) and RS. All very state of the art.

'Fantastic standard of teaching' says the warden, 'remarkably balanced in what we do, good overall consistency'. All staff at Radley are assessed and observed regularly. Parental suggestion 'that teaching staff are going for achievements and not willing to allow A level students enough choice' negated by the insistence on breadth under the AS/A2 system. Policy of taking ASs and A2s together at the end of the second year – most unusual – felt by warden to be a great success.

Games, Options, The Arts: All boys expected to take part in community service during the hols, projects include helping the elderly or disabled, conservation projects; seniors run a camp in Romania or build a house in India (very popular). Drama strong and important, with a new theatre in the offing, though complaints have been heard about lack of public speaking – 'pupils have not enough self-confidence to open their mouths, put their shoulders back and spout,' said a dissatisfied parent (warden 'truly amazed by this' – speaking, debating, reciting all strong, he says). Masses of 'high class' speakers, boys have a reputation of asking 'proper' questions and don't need to be tipped the wink or have plants in the audience. Music strong – huge choice of instruments, fab music school.

Very keen games school, rugby important (20 teams play each weekend) – and needle matches with Wellington; also rowing, cups everywhere – 'awesome at the moment' says a recent sixth former – now at Oxford (and a rather peculiar boat – for want of a better word – suspended in the library!). Hockey in spring term for 'dry-bobs' and masses of cricket, tennis etc, in summer. Own beagle pack. Wizard swimming pool with probably the best diving facilities in private sector in the country. School in general has a slight aura of a country club at times with tip-top facilities all round including two Astroturfs, plus 'tartan' athletics track. Non team-games players have been heard to comment that there are 'not enough games for them' though school (and our guide) say there are lots of minority sports.

Stunning art with levitated figures hanging everywhere. The Sewell Centre (aka the art department) continues to produce amazing work. A level results good, albeit with a limited take-up; GCSE competent. CCF compulsory at 14 until proficiency test is taken. D of E, 'masses of societies'.

Background and Atmosphere: Stunning. Green and pleasant site – Turner was moved to paint it in his youth, lots of mellow red brick (1720) and Victorian Gothic, overlooks the school's golf course, lake, games field and pavilion; 800 acres of prime Oxfordshire, totally self-contained and away from the rest of the world. School founded in

1847 by the Revs William Sewell (don at Exeter College) and Robert Congleton Singleton on Oxford college model – with cloisters, quads, and dons (masters) and has its own slang – presumably based on 19th century undergraduate speak? Certain amount of house fagging, newspapers and the like – but not, you understand, personal fagging – 'not a problem' said our guide, 'you know it won't last forever and it will be your turn next'. JCR = bar in basement.

Brilliant tuck shop where pupils have their own 'jam account' – bacon butties at all hours. Jolly red theme to school and uniform, though pupils allowed to wear any sensible dark jacket and shirt – status marked by type of tie. The school still feels slightly inward-looking and its strength and current status is a source of amazement to some other schools – not to mention some ORs, though the memories of that infamous telly programme are now a blip in the past, it didn't do the school any harm at all, indeed inquiries increased in the weeks following. John Murray has published a history of Radley College by OB Christopher Hibbert – worth a browse, though not cheap.

Houses = socials, no particular bias, housemasters and tutors for all, yearly then specialists. Boys graduate via dorms (horsebox configuration) with prefects on tap to single rooms with basins; kitchens everywhere. Eight socials plus one 'overflow' sixth form house which provides for the academic or those who 'would prefer a change of scenery'.

Pastoral Care and Discipline: Complicated hierarchy of 'stigs' (new boys: gits spelt backwards) each with a nanny for the first year or so (not usually used after the first six weeks). Pups = prefects. Staff lean on 'pups' who have intricate privileges in exchange for their responsibilities. Compulsory evensong four nights a week (chapel fabulous) and dons go too, 95 per cent of staff live on campus in school accommodation – brilliant for packing in talent. Warden admits to there being a 'trawl round Oxford colleges to see who is available'. Staff, young and old, have an annual MOT, one-to-one meetings with head at which they can air grievances/produce ideas and the like.

Complicated system of leave-outs, floating weekends (pupils' choice) plus fixed half term, Michaelmas and Advent weekend. School tough on discipline, little quarter here. Couple of recent suspensions – for malicious (very malicious apparently) phone calls and for 'being rude to matron'. Anti-smoking feeling at top end of school pervades and senior boys will still report juniors; booze a perennial problem and JCR (bar) popular. 'Not a sniff of drugs' (so true says a recent leaver), strong drugs education and good PSE.

Pupils and Parents: As you might expect with the intake, good homogenised middle class lot. Very British (stiff upper lip), few foreign pupils here (they tend to turn up too late), but may make the grade via scholarship or Warden's List (see below). ORs include Andrew Motion, Sir (now Lord) Richard Wilson of Dinton (former Cabinet Secretary), Lord Scarman, Ted Dexter, former world rackets champion James Male and England cricketer, Andrew Strauss. An eclectic bunch.

Entrance: Still largely on a first come first served principle which explains why the lists are consistently full for years ahead. Name down as soon as poss but the registration is usually closed by the time the little blighter is 5 or 6. Entry by Warden's List (usually ten or twelve a year) is by prep school recommendation ONLY. Note the weedy little pictureless prospectus – status symbol.

Exit: On to the usual universities, 40-50 regularly apply for Oxbridge, with a bias towards the former. Typical former pupil says he was 'brilliantly prepared for university life in all its entirety' – he is now studying law at St Cats, playing rugby for the university, and enjoying a serious social life. Traditionally Radley produces headmasters, barristers, Servicemen, one or two art dealers and some jolly good all rounders.

Money Matters: Silk bursary (named for a previous warden); school quite rich, though fund-raising on the cards for new build. Music, art, and academic scholarships plus further scholarships and bursaries (Foundation awards) plus Thompson scholarships for all-rounders. Bursarial help for the needy. 'Paintings bequeathed by the Vestey family have now been sold and a collection of work by contemporary artists has been started' - and some of them look pretty strange in the 18th century Manor House.

Remarks: Plus ça change, plus c'est la meme chose – outstanding public school which has had a long innings as one of the most popular public boarding schools in the country. 'A friendly school', now very much first division; Old Boys report that there is still a slight pressure to conform. Continuing contented reports from parents – though the odd dissatisfied one.

THE RED MAIDS' SCHOOL

Westbury Road, Westbury-on-Trym, Bristol, BS9 3AW

Tel: 0117 962 2641
Fax: 0117 962 1687
E-mail: admin@redmaids.bristol.sch.uk
Website: www.redmaids.bristol.sch.uk

• Pupils: 490 • Ages: 11-18, junior school 7-11 • Size of sixth form: 81 • Non-denom • Independent

Head: Since 2001, Mrs Isabel Tobias BA (forties); took an English degree at New Hall, Cambridge, and worked in book publishing before training to be a teacher in 1988. Taught at Henrietta Barnett, London and was head of English at Bath High during a long and complex amalgamation with The Royal; then deputy head after the deed was done. Married to a doctor with 3 children, she understands the challenge in taking on a school eager to be re-packaged for the new century. She believes every pupil is talented and valuable. This underpins a school ethos where every student is encouraged to discover and develop her own abilities and strive for success.

The bright-eyed girls are thrilled to bits to have a young head who 'allows them to come and talk to her'.

Entrance: At 7, 11 and 16, selected by joint entrance exam and informal interview in January. Broad ranging intake from local primaries, prep schools and Red Maids' Junior School. Places available in other year groups.

Exit: 6 per cent to Oxbridge, 100 per cent to higher education.

Money Matters: Scholarships: 4 academic and 2 music per year group; Up to 6 sixth form scholarships awarded annually; Discretionary 13+ entrance; discretionary additional head's awards for year 7 entrance; school assisted places available up to 50 per cent of fees; sibling discounts.

Remarks: Founded as 'Red Maids' Hospital' in 1634, enjoys unique position in Bristol City's heritage with annual procession and Cathedral Service on Founder's Day. Longer established than Badminton, Redland or Clifton High School, Red Maids had an authoritarian reputation when Mrs Tobias took over four years ago. Trad rigorous teaching in the chalk and talk vein churned out formidable grades (60 per cent A-A* at GCSE) and future Cherie Blairs, 'fiercely competitive at matches with other schools,' say opponents. After much discussion boarding phased out over 2 years, ending July

2004 – this accounts for big drop in pupil numbers since our last report.

Science and English are strong and languages include Russian and Latin. Music is taken seriously with 50 per cent of girls having private instrumental lessons timetabled, so bands, orchestras, jazz group, a samba band and choirs performing all over the place. Lovely music block and recording studio and vibrant stage productions from Guys and Dolls to Oh, What a Lovely War! with brother school, QEH – and yet no tapes or CDs.

Things are on the move at last with this head – a school to keep a hopeful eye on. Head talks of her school's 'strong work ethic coupled with sense of fun and emphasis on involving everyone, meaning high academic standards and broad range of interests among students and staff.'

REDLAND HIGH SCHOOL

Linked to Redland High Junior School in the Junior section

Redland Court, Redland Court Road, Redland, Bristol, BS6 7EF

Tel: 0117 924 5796
Fax: 0117 924 1127
E-mail: admissions@redland.bristol.sch.uk
Website: www.redland.bristol.sch.uk

• Pupils: 500 girls, all day • Ages: 11-18 • Size of sixth form: 130 • Non-denom • Fees: Junior £1,625-£1,915; senior £2,715 • Independent • Open days: October

Head: Since 2002, Dr Ruth Weeks (early fifties). Went to girls' grammar in Sutton Coldfield then read biochemistry at Birmingham before post-doctoral research; married to brewing executive Michael and lives in Wye Valley where she has helped raise funds for a village community shop; daughters Heather and Lucie pursuing medicine after leaving Haberdashers' Monmouth where Ruth Weeks taught for 19 years, ending up pastoral deputy. Delightful, empathetic personality. Necessitated quantum leap of faith for some staff after serving revered and 'old school' predecessor; made immediate hit with girls by modernising uniform; described as 'first rate chemistry teacher' by one senior girl; 'she's tuned in to our wavelength' said another; described as a 'wonderful head' by parents; well honed brain.

Departing in July 2006.

Academic Matters: 30 or so A level subjects on offer. Impressive recent track record of 75 per cent+ A/B grades at A2. Psychology a strong newcomer at A level but good showings too in English, maths and geography; not much of a 'tail' in any subject. High volume successes in biology and chemistry feed medicine and allied subjects. Popular DT department covers food, textiles and construction (using CAD/CAM technology) in plastic and wood.

Little feeling of academic hothouse despite results. Top set take separate sciences with physics coming out best though girls subsequently shy away from it; majority take GCSE dual award. Latin and Greek survive well at GCSE, small numbers continue beyond. Lively teaching in modern languages reaps glut of top grades in French and German with Spanish still building up its following; department craves specialist area – link with La Baule has led to British Council funded performances of 'Le Petit Prince' on either side of channel. RE is unusually strong and offers short GCSE course as well as A level: popular trips to experience religions and other cultures in far flung corners of globe.

Individual programme for dyslexic pupils co-ordinated by SENCO who is also junior school deputy head.

Games, Options, The Arts: Music the dominant extracurricular activity and overall strength of school; two thirds of girls play an instrument; frequent low key lunch and tea time concerts plus bigger events for choirs and orchestra. Drama very popular; performances highly rated by audiences; public speaking, debating and model UN encouraged. Half year 12 get involved in young enterprise scheme which lets loose hitherto untapped entrepreneurial skills.

Legacy of poor playing and practice facilities for games now ended by acquisition of Golden Hill site; nearby Redland Racquet Club used as well as school courts. Few girls reach county standard; majority probably not desperately sporty though hockey, netball and cricket have been successful. Dance popular outside timetable with biannual show; likewise fashion with highlight for girls on catwalk at end of year.

Wonderfully creative vibe strikes visitor from top to bottom of separate art building with a wide spiral staircase providing vantage point from which to relish offbeat feel. Shame that profusion of artistic talent cannot be splashed more around school. Good range of lunchtime and after school activities on offer; D of E scheme from year 10 with expeditions; house system centre of high volume charity giving. PSHE to year 11 termed 'education for life' becomes enrichment programme in sixth including discussions with school doctor and life skills such as car maintenance and self defence.

Background and Atmosphere: Founded in 1882, school moved to 18th century Redland Court in 1885 where it still dominates one of Bristol's classier areas. Motto: 'So

Hateth She Derknesse' engraved in wood over doorway from assembly hall reminds girls of characteristics of daisy (school emblem). Current girls struck as unlikely to shrink from limelight anyway.

Limited outside breathing space includes pond area, vestige of formal Dutch garden plus newly created 'peace' garden; good hard tennis courts below main mansion for more energetic. Development here suffers double whammy of cramped city site and trying to overcome 'listed building' restrictions. We overshot entrance to only parking area and wondered how everyone coped on parents' evenings. Teaching areas housed in mix of architectural styles; refurbished laboratories show what can be done.

We really liked content and layout of library with quiet area for swots open until 5.00pm. 48-station ICT suite opens for business at 8.00am so girls can always clear their inboxes before lessons. Well-resourced careers suite shows how seriously RHS takes preparing girls to hold their own in world of work. Mary Crook Sixth Form Centre across road from main site, where teaching and social areas sit cheek by jowl in altogether comfortable and civilised surroundings.

Pastoral Care and Discipline: Rapport generally excellent and builds up through school. Lacking in social areas for younger girls who were observed huddled in classrooms during breaks. Popular, healthy school lunches on an 'eat as much as you like' basis.

Pupils and Parents: Girls see absence of boys as 'definite plus' for their short-term academic achievement but don't doubt that they'll cope at university and beyond. A few still slope off after year 11 but looks like head will counter with some mixed sixth form teaching. Bustling, purposeful atmosphere with no danger of remoteness in this multicultural and commercial city.

Noticeable growth in girls' confidence towards upper end; very little posturing or bitchiness; loads of co-operation and positive innovation. Senior girls have open and relaxed approach to adults. Famous old girls include Dame Elizabeth Hoodless, chairman of CSV, and Geraldine Peacock, charity commissioner.

Entrance: Exam at 11 with about one third coming from junior school (qv). Remainder mainly from Bristol state primaries.

Exit: Virtually all to higher education with about 10 per cent to Oxbridge. Wide choice of courses at leading universities.

Money Matters: Scholarships at 11, 13 and 16 include academic, art, sport and music. Bursaries for a few needy cases.

Remarks: Few frills and short on wow factor in terms of facilities it nevertheless has impressive record of sustained academic success. Girls work hard, support one another and take full advantage of what's on offer outside classroom. Looks set for a good spell under current head.

REIGATE GRAMMAR SCHOOL

Reigate Road, Reigate, Surrey, RH2 0QS

Tel: 01737 222 231
Fax: 01737 224 201
E-mail: info@reigategrammar.org
Website: www.reigategrammar.org

- Pupils: 535 boys, 325 girls; all day • Ages: 11-18
- Size of sixth form: 205 • Non-denom • Fees: £3,303
- Independent • Open days: Main open day in October, open afternoons every month during term time

Head: Since 2001, Mr David Thomas MA (forties), educated at Magdalen College School, Oxford where he was a chorister and later an organ scholar at Queens College Oxford. Followed a musical teaching career and was previously deputy head at Trinity, Croydon. Married to Andrea, an historian, who also teaches part time at the school, they live in a beautiful house adjacent to the school. 'One of the main attractions of the job,' he jokes. Very business-like but friendly and easy to talk to, he enthuses about his school, 'I'm a big fan of co-ed and I love the atmosphere of this place'. Mr Thomas is very visible around the school and the children respect that – 'he comes to loads of sports matches,' said a pupil. 'A top man,' said one parent. 'The kids really like him and he's turned the place around,' said another.

Academic Matters: Strong. 75 per cent A/B grades at A level, GCSE results equally good with 60 per cent A*/A grades. Head believes the school is about more than just academic work. Generally good standards of teaching and super IT facilities with networked classrooms and interactive whiteboards. The aim is for all pupils to leave with IT qualification from the Microsoft Academy – very useful in the real world. Mr Thomas is a big fan of IT and it shows throughout the school – electronic registration is very efficient and the staff even have their own IT trainer. Well-stocked library stays open after school for homework and private study.

About 40 students with a range of needs receive help from two part time SEN teaching staff. School is happy to discuss whether it can provide the right support for those who need it. But it would take careful consideration as to whether a SEN pupil would be happy here, as there is quite an academic pace. Those who receive extra tuition do so at extra cost to parents.

Games, Options, The Arts: Sports teaching is exceptional. Stunning 32 acre sports complex at Hartswood (about two miles from the school), complete with astro pitches, cricket field, athletics track, golf course and pavilion. All pupils are bused there to spend at least one afternoon a week taking part in a variety of sports. Netball, hockey and rounders for the girls, rugby, cricket, hockey for the boys. School is renowned for its prowess on the rugby pitch and proudly claims to field up to 18 teams on match days. Most matches are played on Saturdays, the school is mega competitive and always up there at inter school sporting competitions – the high numbers who take part are expected to show a huge level of commitment. Surprisingly little complaint from the less sporty souls, as swimming, tennis and visits to the local leisure centre for badminton and squash are also on offer. Heated outdoor pool on the site only used in the summer.

Music, art and drama receive a lot of praise from parents. Art building has an impressive range of facilities, students' work is frequently exhibited within the school and often achieves some of the best exam results. Music teaching is excellent; good facilities, opportunities for all to join in. The head continues to teach some A level music classes. 'It's my haven in the week,' he says 'and it's a good reminder of the staff workload.' Super drama department led by 'an inspirational teacher' according to parents, puts on several productions each year. Lots of individual drama successes including two students who have won places at the National Youth Theatre. Numerous after school activities including all the usual; CCF is well supported as is DofE.

Background and Atmosphere: Founded as a boys' school in 1675 and became a grammar school in the nineteenth century. Girls in the sixth form from 1976 when it became independent and fully co-ed from 1993. Located minutes from Reigate town centre, school is housed in 'hotch potch' of buildings – some very old and in need of replacement but many newer and very attractive. Outside space is at a premium. Quite a walk from class to class and to different buildings. Our pupil tour guides were none too keen on the footpath by the cemetery in the winter! 'The food is good,' say pupils and staff alike. Lots of choice. All meals served in a light airy building: 'the best place in the whole school,' said one pupil. Bit of a crackdown on uniform recently but generally not overly strict – 'life's about more than uniform,' says the head. On the whole pupils look

smart – a few need reminding to tuck their shirts in and Mr Thomas does so quite regularly. More relaxed for sixth formers but still within guidelines – quite unusual but popular especially with parents.

Pastoral Care and Discipline: Head only gets involved in really serious issues and readily involves parents. Sixth formers apply each year to become mentors to the younger ones through their first years at the school. 'My mentor's lovely,' said one pupil 'she even bought me a Christmas present!' 'It's a very good idea,' commented one parent, 'although I'm not sure they get involved in serious problems – it seems to be more about going bowling and having fun.' New pupils are invited to an admissions evening in June when they are formally welcomed to the school by Mr Thomas in full cap & gown. 'Parents love it,' commented staff, and 'it's an excellent photo opportunity,' said one proud father. Comprehensive parents' handbook of school life and each term parents are invited to a parents' forum to discuss issues such as bulimia, exam stress, drugs etc. Pupils discuss the issues during the day and parents are invited in the evening. Parents find these very informative and useful – but several comment that they would like more time to discuss their child's progress on an individual basis. Discipline fairly relaxed, pupils are given space to 'get it right' and are encouraged to feel they can talk to teachers about any problems they have. Clear alcohol, drinking and smoking policy – the head and staff have dealt with occasional breaches swiftly. Very little evidence of bullying – in fact quite the opposite – but staff don't pretend it doesn't happen.

Pupils and Parents: A very unpretentious place – parents say it is just like the state grammar schools they used to attend. Pupils are a likeable bunch – confident but not full of themselves and very honest. Pupils mainly from the affluent Reigate and Redhill area and the surrounding Surrey towns. Parents from a wide variety of backgrounds: professionals, former pupils, but also plenty of first time buyers. Mega cool rating for its former pupils with many notable Old Reigatians: Norman Cook (aka DJ Fat Boy Slim) and BAFTA winning writer and comedian David Walliams are the most famous as far as pupils are concerned. Many old pupils return to the school to talk about their careers and experiences – a recent visit from David Walliams and his 'Little Britain' co star Matt Lucas was very popular with pupils and staff alike!

Entrance: Selective but not excessively so, although two applicants for every place in 2005. Majority enter at 11+, small number at 13. The school sets its own entrance exam in verbal reasoning (from 2006 this will be computerised with sample questions on the school's website), English and maths. Interview is given equal importance as is the report from previous school. The school places emphasis on academic achievement but wants to give more children an opportunity to apply, so a new test has been designed in consultation with several local state primary schools who gave it the thumbs up. Approximately 50 per cent of the pupils come from state schools, particularly Reigate Priory Junior. The rest from local preps including St Mary's Prep, which is now amalgamated with Reigate, although admission is by no means automatic. Other regular feeders include Mickelfield, The Hawthorns and New Lodge School.

Exit: About 15 per cent leave after GCSE, usually to attend the large local sixth form college. Of those who stay, around 98 per cent go on to traditional universities eg Durham, Edinburgh, York and Exeter; 5-10 students each year to Oxbridge.

Money Matters: Scholarships have a fixed value of £1,000 pa, but parents can apply for a means tested additional fee reduction up to 90 per cent. In addition, the school operates its own Assisted Places Scheme for gifted children whose parents cannot afford the fees; again this is means-tested.

Remarks: A good all round school with a strong head. Not at all posh.

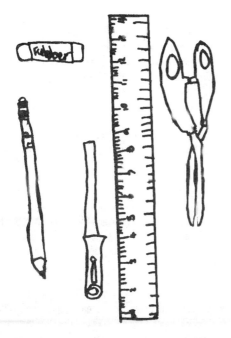

RENDCOMB COLLEGE

Linked to Rendcomb College Junior School in the Junior section

Rendcomb, Cirencester, Gloucestershire, GL7 7HA

Tel: 01285 831 213
Fax: 01285 831 331
E-mail: info@rendcomb.gloucs.sch.uk
Website: www.rendcombcollege.co.uk

• Pupils: 270; ratio 50:50 boys to girls; 50:50 boarders to day pupils • Ages: 11-18 • Size of sixth form: 70 • C of E • Fees: Nursery £1500; Junior £1,510 - £2,345; Senior: day £3,535 - £4,860; boarding £4,730 - £6,255 • Independent • Open days: Late September, February and early May

Headmaster: Since 1999, Mr Gerry Holden (mid forties), educated 'in Scotland' and St Andrew's University, where he read medieval and modern history. Previously deputy head of Frensham Heights school after heading history departments at Millfield and Forest School. Former examiner and qualified soccer referee. Takes particular pride in being a teaching head, taking English and history classes. Married to Liese, who works both locally and in school, helping out particularly with riding – keeping her own horse at school. Son Alex at Rendcomb. Highly organised, with a penchant for business terminology, he has made many changes at Rendcomb and clearly enjoyed it. Advocate of the personal touch – great sender of handwritten postcards.

Academic Matters: Rendcomb's main motto is 'educating the whole person' and, as a small school, it isn't aimed solely at academic high flyers. But strong, if not spectacular, results in recent years – 58 per cent A*/B at GCSE, with 40 per cent grades A or B at A level – lots of Bs. Concentration mainly on traditional core subjects. Languages a real strength, although availability of Spanish, Russian, Chinese and Italian ebbs and flows according to background and inclination of potential students. Lots of As in art at GSCE and A level. A third of each year group takes double science instead of single GCSEs. Food and nutrition GCSE being phased out in favour of drama, to complement theatre studies A level. Business studies A level very popular, particularly with boys, although exam performance has been patchy.

Sailed through start of AS levels by restricting choices to four in first year, down to three at A level and timetabling more teaching time than needed for each subject. Every three weeks pupils assessed for effort and achievement. Head's watchword, 'rigour', evident in all aspects of school life, from making pupils stick rigidly to the dress code to the Spiral Study Skills programme – classes on planning, organisation and working effectively. Emphasis on self-discipline rather than heavy-handed control – it was criticised by inspectors for this in the past – brings relaxed classes full of eager contributors. Two EFL teachers support regular batch of overseas students, including five annual Japanese students. Some light special needs support but no current pupils statemented. End of the school day is 'blurred', making it easy for day pupils to slide into prep alongside the boarders.

Games, Options, The Arts: School is a six-day a week – long days too – commitment for pupils and parents, off-putting for some potential parents. Only a few years ago day pupils faced seven days at school. Realistically it's the only way to fit in 50 or so, mainly sporting, extra activities on offer – most take three or four but two is the minimum. Sport is a big deal, enthusiastically supported by staff and pupils alike, although boys' rugby and boys' and girls' hockey teams tend to struggle against bigger schools with greater strength in depth. Facilities are excellent, with grass pitches and Astroturf, squash and badminton courts, a heated outdoor swimming pool and a large sports hall. Individuals regularly make it to the county teams. On-site there are traditional country pursuits of clay pigeon shooting, at which the school excels, fishing and golf, while the nearby Cotswold Water Park hosts windsurfing and fishing.

Indoors, art is very popular and run by an extremely enthusiastic head of department. Most play a part in annual fashion shows, almost all at least embark on individual music lessons and the choir is highly rated. There are regular in-house productions performed in the school's theatre, once the orangery of the Victorian main house. All seniors have their own studies with a bed – making flexi-boarding very common for day pupils cramming as much into a day as humanly possible.

Background and Atmosphere: Rendcomb College was founded in 1920 when a member of the local fags-to-landowning Wills family bought a vast Italianate pile sold off after the first World War. Noel Wills was inspired by the notion that 'the only aristocracy is the aristocracy of brains and character', offering poor local boys the benefits of a typical upper class boarding education but without the snobbery he had encountered. Until relatively recently, the county chipped in to fund places. Now continued support from founder's family enables Rendcomb to try to follow broadly its original philosophy.

Stunning grounds, eulogised by Alexander Pope in 1721, with the house looking out over rolling greenery and woodland in all directions. The Victorian main house is supplemented by a stable block and a couple of bland recent constructions. Reorganisation of site has given sixth formers their own block, a perfunctory 1970s addition, but suitably separate from main school. The shared rooms of younger boarders have refreshing air of light and space, while seniors' rooms are bright but compact and practical. All the boarders' rooms are notably clean, fresh smelling and tidy – signs of Mr Holden's rigour coupled with diligent cleaning staff. The grounds spill into the village of Rendcomb – the village store doubles as the school tuck shop – and the chaplain is shared by school and village. Feels very secluded, although nearest town Cirencester is only a bus ride away.

Pastoral Care and Discipline: All staff, from the head to the maintenance team – who run sports activities as well as keeping the grounds beautiful – are immersed in school life and help out. Real sense of caring abounds. Relatively new chaplain – dual role as school and church pastor notoriously hard to fill. Two school nurses most often source of initial advice, although house parents also on hand for support, as well as part-time counsellor. Achievement, whether good results or a small kindness, rewarded more by word than by deed – praise in assembly or commendation from the head. Rules spell out that you can't bring a gun or explosives to school – penknives are allowed but chewing gum expressly forbidden. Drugs users face immediate expulsion, while alcohol offences mean suspension. Smoking is forbidden but treated more as a problem than a crime. A taste of independent living is provided via the new sixth form flat – a single sex group of pupils lives in a flat on site for a week, manages a budget, cooks meals and invites a member of staff and partner for dinner at the end. Pre-university students love it.

Pupils and Parents: Children are smiley, polite and quiet – very low noise levels for a school. Traditionally a haven for farmers' sons and Services' children, now there are many 'first-time buyers', often with one parent from independent school, the other from state school. Many travel in on the newly completed bypass between Swindon, where many schools are poor, and Gloucester. Most pupils, whether day or boarding, come from within an hour's travelling time. Jockey Richard Dunwoody is Rendcomb's most famous old boy.

Entrance: Mainly at age 3 to the nursery, at 4 and 11, by examination, at 13 by Common Entrance (or special exam) and 16. But would consider each application on individual basis. Not solely concerned with exam aptitude but also ability to try hard and function as part of a team. Effort not grades the acid test.

Exit: Most go where they want to, a few to work but 90 per cent to higher education. Loughborough is a particularly favourite, otherwise slight southern bias. Subjects are often business related. Generally one a year to Oxbridge.

Money Matters: Good value, particularly boarding. Almost everything included in price. Individual music tuition extra but ensemble lessons free. But EFL teaching and learning support is charged to parents. Generous academic, choral, music and art scholarships on offer, supported by Wills family and Dulverton Trust, plus Noel Wills full scholarship to one local state primary pupil.

Remarks: Beautiful site a gentle home from home for all pupils, following its aim to bring out the best in its charges. But you have to be wholehearted about school life to get the most out of it.

REPTON SCHOOL

Linked to Foremarke Hall in the Junior section

Repton, Derby, Derbyshire, DE65 6FH

Tel: 01283 559 220
Fax: 01283 559 223
E-mail: headmaster@repton.org.uk
Website: www.repton.org.uk

• Pupils: 595 total – 345 boys, 250 girls; 457 board, 138 day. Plus prep school 'Foremarke Hall' • Ages: 13-18 • Size of sixth form: 241 • C of E (other faiths welcome) • Fees: Boarders £7,060 day £5,240 • Independent • Open days: September

Head: Since 2003, Robert Holroyd MA (mid-forties). Educated at Birkenhead and Christ Church, Oxford. First in modern languages. Still takes French and Spanish at Repton twice a week as 'floating' teacher, stepping in where timetabled tutors allow. Previously head of department and housemaster at Radley College. Wife Penny also a teacher but now fully involved in life of school community. 'We function very much as a team,' he says. Devoted to Repton and all it stands for. Delights in having raised its profile since his appointment. 'I inherited a terrific ship and we have tried to maintain the core values of the school,' he says. 'But you won't catch us standing still.' Fervent believer in co-education. Good cricketer at Oxford, still enjoys choral music and drama. Big plans for the future. Has two daughters at Repton and its prep.

Academic Matters: Strives to extract the best from its broad intake – and frequently succeeds. Sound but unexceptional past exam results well and truly put in the shade by more recent year-on-year improvements. Latest available figures (2005) show 98 per cent overall pass rate at GCSE, 67 per cent of them A* and A. In fact every pupil got at least five A*-C grades with eight among the top marks nationwide. Top A level grades also up 4 per cent. Of the overall pass rate of virtually 100 per cent, just under a half were As, with nine students gaining four or more top grades. Lots of As taken a year early too. Most subjects set according to ability. Traditional teaching methods with all teachers living on site or in village – key to the success, says head, of the all-round boarding experience.

Good blend of ancient (library in Old Priory building) and modern (all pupils have free internet access and own email address). School's first ever full-time librarian actually in process of dragging library into 21st century after school inspectors twice highlighted it as weakness. 'I was surprised at the state the library was in when I got here,' head told school magazine, the Reptonian. Cataloguing and re-stocking now well underway, also refurnishing and carpeting planned 'to make it a more welcoming place where students will want to spend some time to read or study'. Plans include installing ICT and DVD technology in adjoining room to bring old and new learning tools together. Should be ready 2007. Computers currently located in other areas and pupils encouraged to bring own laptops for use in boarding house studies. Wide choice of subjects on offer with business studies, PE, theatre studies and IT more recent additions.

Appointment of new academic 'tsar' has seen more outside involvement in school curriculum with top business names invited to lecture students. Has also introduced electronic reporting on pupils' progress. Parents get usual end of term reports as well as mid-term updates on effort and achievement. Learning support for dyslexics. Two hours plus extra tuition a week can be given in most serious cases, though might be at the expense of French classes. Information and strategies passed to subject teachers to ensure support continues in class. Good teaching environment, new classrooms with state-of-the-art interactive whiteboards under construction, staffed by dedicated team. Students report tutors will 'go the extra mile'. Head can't speak highly enough of them! Those we saw appeared to have boundless enthusiasm and energy to spare. Prep 7-9pm each evening for both boarders and day pupils – only youngest supervised, rest work independently in house studies.

Games, Options, The Arts: Sport now in league of its own. At time of visit school celebrating huge national success. Girls' 1st XI hockey champions (U-18s) and boys victors in U-18s tennis. Repton has long been outstanding tennis school, recommended to parents by the LTA. Played all year round on outside and indoor courts. Now equally strong in hockey, much thanks to vast sports hall and similarly vast Astroturf pitches. Cricket is no slouch either with county and test cricketers regularly produced. And whereas most independent boys' schools still favour rugby as the major winter sport, Repton remains among the handful to stay faithful to football – again with considerable success. (Girls also play football here, sadly with less success to date.) Large indoor pool (also used by locals). Popular extras include D of E, while CCF is compulsory for all for some time. Three half days (Tuesdays, Thursdays and Saturdays) leave time for matches and non-curricular activities. Drama thriving at all age levels. Great competition between houses. Two theatres; a small hall and a more traditional school hall waiting for a facelift. Music also flourishing, with regular choral performances and trips abroad, orchestra and variety of bands from string ensembles to rock. Best bands even get chance to record. Immensely impressive art studios. Work on show was of extremely high standard and shown prominently all round school as well as at some local businesses. (Money made from hiring out pieces goes into pot to fund foreign trips for art students.) From fine art to sculpture to wall hangings – so big, bold and brilliant. Also plenty of scope for budding photographers and architects. Old squash courts due soon for transformation into new textiles school. Where will it all end?

Background and Atmosphere: Found on the banks of the River Trent, it's absorbed into village of Repton rather than dominating it. Boarding houses can be found up leafy lanes, art department tucked down a side street, sports centre and games fields alongside another. Pavements regularly populated by throngs of well turned-out boys and girls making their way from one part of school to another. With a busy B road running through the middle, Repton was never going to be a sleepy idyll, but the school lends a certain vitality. Founded under the will of Sir John Port who died in 1557, school is fast approaching its 450th anniversary. A Bloody Mary Foundation, with a long and interesting history dating back to the medieval monastery, the peaceful heart of which still exists (minus the cloisters). Chapel a key part of weekly routine with evensong and Sunday services. Head says, 'all faiths come along to chapel and they love it. If someone from another faith wants to be excused they can be but no-one has asked me yet.' School once boys only, fully co-ed since

1991. Boy/girl ratio roughly 60/40. Correspondingly there are six boys' boarding houses to four girls'. House system still very strong – all pupils return to houses for both lunch and tea. All food cooked in-house and given big thumbs up by regular diners. Small two- to four-bed dorms, sixth formers have own study bedrooms. All-age mixing in communal areas but separate common rooms for juniors and seniors 'just to give us our own space'. Emphasis on homely with mistress/master in charge seen as 'house parent'. As one girl told us, 'it's so nice to be able to take a break from whatever's been happening during the day and be with the family in your house. It's very special.'

Pastoral Care and Discipline: House system again all important. All new arrivals (whatever age) given a 'buddy' (existing Reptonian) to show them the ropes. Pupils encouraged to turn to more senior students, house parents or matron with problems. Plenty of 'motherly' input in both boys' and girls' houses. Miscreants dealt with severely though. Zero tolerance of drugs, demonstrated recently with five expulsions. 'My first and hopefully my last,' says head. Smoking and drinking both yellow card offences. Bullying (yes, there is obviously some but we are never complacent, insists head) is handled more sensitively with all parties getting involved. Parents encouraged to get involved in school activities at every level and contact with staff can be as often or infrequent as they want. Three exeats by arrangement. Some local pupils allowed to nip home on Sundays – after chapel. Good relationship between teachers and students seems based on mutual respect.

Pupils and Parents: Overall a very down-to-earth bunch. Pretentions go un-nurtured. Hard work is rewarded and with 97 per cent getting the 5+ C grades at GCSE needed to gain entry to the sixth form, is, more often than not, delivered. Uniform is compulsory – black suits and ties for the boys, grey plaid skirt and blazer for girls who can accessorise with their own choice of one-colour V-neck jumper 'for that bit of individuality'. Pupils are polite, easy-going, confident. Past OBs and OGs include author Roald Dahl, columnist and TV presenter Jeremy Clarkson and Lady Carole Blackshaw, Lady Mayoress of London. No one particular type of parent here. Some good northern hard-graft, others from the Cheshire corridor and a good smattering of professionals as well as plenty from overseas.

Entrance: Largely from own prep (sited nearby and co-ed since early 1970s). Rest from growing array of other prep schools. Head says recent good exam results making Repton first choice further afield. Common entrance pass mark required around 50 per cent but can be flexible. Takes those with special needs who can cope with the curriculum. Majority are dyslexic but can cater for others, including dyspraxics and those with severe hearing impairment. Considers needs on individual merit. As well as five Cs at GCSE, potential sixth formers also need at least Bs in chosen A level subjects. But again, rule not written in tablets of stone and other strengths will be considered.

Exit: On average, 11 students to Oxbridge, bulk of rest to northern universities, but business, drama and art all have their followers at various destinations.

Money Matters: Scholarships a-plenty. Worth up to 50 per cent of fees. Offered as academic awards, also art, drama, music and sport. Also exhibitions of around 10 per cent of fees. Open to pupils at 11, 13 and sixth form. We are assured that school's five year development plan (including new classrooms, new science centre, reworking of library, large theatre and music school and new textile school) will not mean big hike in school fees.

Remarks: No bargain but value for money. So much on offer, such an all-round experience. Repton is impossible to pigeon hole. Why would anyone want to send their child here? 'We have a strong emphasis on the whole person,' says the head. 'It's standards without snobbery. They come out of Repton proud of their schooldays but able to look out beyond the school.' A feel-good school filled with real youngsters happy to be themselves.

THE RIDINGS HIGH SCHOOL

High Street, Winterbourne, Bristol, South Gloucestershire, BS36 1JL

Tel: 01454 252 000
Fax: 01454 250 404
E-mail: office@ridingshigh.org
Website: www.ridingshigh.org

• Pupils: 1,865 boys and girls • Ages: 11-18 • Size of sixth form: 355 • Non-denom • State • Open days: Early October

Dr Gibson: Since 1995, Dr R S Gibson (fifty), string of qualifications from the universities of Liverpool and Oxford. Friendly and welcoming with evident enthusiasm and a smooth-running organisation around him. Teaches history and politics, pupils think it a privilege to be taught by him. Highly regarded by parents and colleagues. Wife a teacher, son working and daughter at local school near family home.

Academic Matters: Exam results significantly above national average for GCSE, 81 per cent gain five or more passes at grades A*-C. A level, AS level and GNVQ results excellent. Dual or single award sciences, very strong ICT delivered across the curriculum. Technology college status has major impact on funding of additional resources not only for ICT-related activity but also throughout the curriculum. School awarded International School status in August 2005. Cisco Regional Academy provides training both in the school and for the whole of the south west region. Minimum of 8 GCSE subjects but usually 9. Options include second modern language (French or German only as the first), drama, art, music, photography, and broad range of technology (includes graphics, systems control). Wide choice of AS and A level courses, also GNVQ/AVCE, commercial and general courses. Strong links with teacher training programmes in both Bath and Bristol – as a popular school with both newly trained and experienced teachers, there are no recruiting problems. Individual achievements recognised and valued in many fields beyond the academic. Curriculum balance carefully maintained, not afraid of ability setting or banding in subjects, extensive tutor programme in social and moral education, citizenship. The school is aiming to introduce the International Baccalaureate in September 2006 to complement existing post-16 provision.

Games, Options, The Arts: Sports facilities being updated. Within the context of the present rather limited space for sport, the achievements are quite remarkable –

many individuals compete at local and county levels in a wide variety of sports, some internationals too. U12 rugby team national champions. Sport is optional in sixth form. In November 2004, the school launched its new all weather pitch – phase one of The Ridings Sports Village development. Arts centre is an exceptional resource, providing the school and the local community with huge range of opportunities for exhibitions, dramatic and musical activities, workshops led by professional artists, writers, and musicians. Music lively – orchestra, choir, wind and string groups and 3 rock groups. Four concerts each year, two orchestras (as well as string, wind and brass groups), senior and junior choirs. Drama programme massive, a popular GCSE and A level option.

Range of extra-curricular activities strongly linked to community education, and includes popular summer schools, outdoor pursuits, Easter revision courses and opportunities on Saturdays and evenings to do GCSE ICT award (80 per cent pupil take-up) and Key Stage 3 subjects. D of E as well as subject-related field trips and visits. Does very well in local debating and public speaking: winners of Oxford Union debating competition in 2000 and runners up in Bristol Schools' European Youth Parliament competition in 2001, both against fierce competition from state and independent schools. Three Young Enterprise companies supported by local business.

Background and Atmosphere: Situated in a solidly middle-class suburb of Bristol, though actually in Gloucestershire, the school sits at the heart of an essentially village-like community and the two are closely connected. The first impression is of well cared-for buildings and a general orderliness. Major efforts made (against a background of 10 per cent reduction in funding over the last 5 years) to create a pleasant and stimulating environment. School divided socially into Key Stage groupings and areas to allow manageable units. Pupils open and articulate, staff cheerful and stable. Uniform straightforward, worn tidily, and pupils like its simplicity. Girls mostly choose trousers rather than skirt. No sixth form uniform. 'Student culture' encourages independent learners and the school's motto, 'maximising potential through partnership', is deeply rooted in its daily operation. Culture of pride in their school's reputation. Pupils complimentary about teaching standards and also acknowledge their own responsibility. Involved in their personal Record of Achievement. They are focused and well motivated and it shows in their results.

Pastoral Care and Discipline: Strong system. Tutors remain with their groups from years 7-11 supported by a head and a deputy head of year. Small tutor groups in the sixth form. Pupils identify tutor support and guidance as a strength. The school is at the cutting edge of and invests heavily in diagnostic testing and performance management, with close monitoring of pupil performance data to ensure that each maximises their potential, the first school in the area to adopt this practice. Behaviour policy clearly spelt out and school/parent/pupil contracts in place. Clear sanctions (eg detention) for miscreants, after parents have been informed but little need to apply them for anything serious. Crime and punishment do not appear to loom large on the horizons of pupils.

Pupils and Parents: Main intake from fairly prosperous out-of town area but there are pockets of deprivation within it. Parents generally regard themselves as fortunate if their children are offered a place and express confidence in the school. The sixth form attracts pupils from nearby independent schools. Very lively and supportive parents' association, with social and educational activities and parents drawn in from the outset with an annual summer school (partly funded from Technology College monies) and opportunities to participate in the varied adult and community education programme (eg RYA shore-based course). Good communication via newsletters as well as regular meetings. School policies (re eg drugs, homework) published in the prospectus. Pupil attendance well above national average. Caring ethic among pupils, with plenty of charitable activity and willingness of the older ones to help the younger (some pupils help with reading development schemes in local primary schools). Lots of mixed-age co-operation in drama, debating.

Entrance: Comprehensive intake, based on siblings, catchment area (mainly local primary schools in surrounding villages plus adjacent Emersons Green area of Bristol) and distance. Parents outside area can request places and many, from both state and independent schools, do. About two applicants for every place. Applications to South Gloucestershire Education Service in October of previous year.

Exit: 70 per cent of year 11 pupils go into the sixth form and the majority of those into higher education, including Oxbridge. Most leavers remain in full time education with small proportion in employment and training.

Money Matters: Local authority funded with constant belt-tightening constraints and often frustrating lack of speed. Local management enables some creative entrepreneurial balancing acts and initiatives as well as links with the business world generate additional funding to enable greater opportunities. Parents contribute to school fund to assist with societies and expeditions.

Remarks: A school where confidence, but not complacency, is in the air; constantly challenges its own performance as well as that of its pupils.

RIPON GRAMMAR SCHOOL

Clotherholme Road, Ripon, North Yorkshire, HG4 2DG

Tel: 01765 602 647

Fax: 01765 606 388

E-mail: enquiries@ripon-grammar.n-yorks.sch.uk

Website: www.ripongrammar.co.uk

• Pupils: 817 boys and girls, day and boarding • Ages: aged 11-18 • Size of sixth form: 213 • Non-denominational • Fees: Boarding £1,955 - £2,715 • State • Open days: Early September for year 7 entrants. January for sixth form

---

Head: Since 2004, Mr Martin Pearman (pronounced Pierman), mid forties. Educated at Bournemouth School, read chemistry at Oxford. Previously taught at Woodhouse Grove where he was deputy head. Started teaching at Bristol Grammar. Married to Fiona, has 3 sons, one at Ripon Grammar (had to go to appeal to secure a place), one at Woodhouse Grove and youngest at a local primary. Staff positive about their new head and the way he's got involved, teaching sixth form, spending time in boarding houses and of course running the school. Friendly but focussed, biding his time before introducing changes: 'if it's not broken, don't mend it'. He has already attracted significant funding to improve facilities, and plans for a new classroom block and lab refurbishment have already been secured. Wants to make a good school better and has appealed for funds to Old Riponians during the 450th anniversary.

Academic Matters: Exam results are good and supported by very good value-added at KS3 (fifth in the country in 2004). Teaching mainly traditional rather than innovative. Virtually all gain 5+ A* to C at GCSE with 58 per cent graded A/A*. Excluding general studies, approximately 65 per cent of A levels passes are graded A or B. At AS over 70 per cent of the grades are at A or B. Chemistry is historically very popular (75 in the lower sixth) throughout the school and results are impressive, outstripping other sciences, which merit a 'could do better'. French provides very good value-added, economics and business studies perennial favourites with sixth form. Further maths is thriving. The school is bidding for Specialist Status in Engineering reflecting outstanding success in the sciences at GCSE, where the vast majority of students follow separate sciences. New courses are planned in GCSE statistics, systems and control, astronomy as well as engineering. Sixth form subjects are academic in orientation though sociology, government and politics, theatre studies and psychology are available and those wishing to study law or sports studies can pop across to the local college. Staff turnover is low though not as static as it used to be.

Games, Options, The Arts: Variety of extra-curricular activities provides something for everyone. Lots of enthusiastic musicians; Big Band performs frequently in Ripon Cathedral, tours Europe and even entertained the Queen. Two samba bands make for an interesting distraction. Vocalists are encouraged to join one of the two choirs. Sport is compulsory, rugby and cricket mainstay for boys and hockey for girls. School counts among its members county and country representatives in sports such as rugby, hockey and karate and boasts the British Junior Orienteering Champion though readily admits much of this is due to pupil involvement in external activities. The well-used pool is a valued resource but generally facilities at the school need updating, although significant change is now underway. No dedicated playground, assembly hall doubles as the dining room and, despite overwhelming popularity of sport, there isn't a sports hall, but the new drama space is well used. There are some saving graces – well resourced and used library, new sixth form art studio and vibrant displays that disguise the tired corridors.

Background and Atmosphere: The school originally housed in Ripon Cathedral was granted a royal charter in 1555. It moved to the present, green and pleasant 23-acre site in 1874. The original Victorian buildings have been added to over the years not always sympathetically. Rapid growth of school has led to an assortment of incongruous Portakabins. Planned new classrooms will allow the phasing out of these classrooms. A recent conversion has added 6 new teaching rooms.

Pastoral Care and Discipline: The idea that bright kids don't need pastoral care was laid to rest some years ago with children now benefiting from a caring and genuinely supportive system. Pupils look after each other, sixth formers train as listeners and teams of form tutors ably support heads of school. Genuinely good relationships between staff and students throughout the school; friendly, compassionate house-staff create a relaxed, easy-going boarding environment though you could be forgiven for thinking the boarding houses, Johnson for the girls and School House for the boys, belong to different schools. The girls' house is in a good state of repair, reasonably furnished and homely. The boys' house is clean and very tidy but dorms lack atmosphere. William Hague was a boarder here and, although much may have changed since then, we suspect the fading furnishings haven't. Girls have an in-house prep room with networked computers; boys must use the library and have no sizeable common room yet girls have two. Both have in-house dining and a home-from-home feel. Some evenings there is an organised activity otherwise pupils are free to go into town, watch TV or use common room facilities. Only a handful stays at weekends but an activities programme includes visits to local attractions.

Pupils and Parents: Boarders tend to be from the Services or Yorkshire Dales, day pupils from the locality. EAL and SEN don't really feature, had one statemented child but he got on so well he lost his statement. A friendly, grounded bunch of rounded individuals proud and privileged to be at the school. Notable Old Boys: Bruce Oldfield (fashion designer), Peter Squires England Rugby and Yorkshire cricket, David Curry (MP).

Entrance: Mainly from local primaries but smattering from schools throughout North Yorkshire and from local preps including Ripon Cathedral Choir School, Belmont Grosvenor and Cundall Manor. Heavily oversubscribed at 11 but places are available in sixth form, although competition increasing. Pupils selected at 11 by verbal reasoning (VR) and non-verbal reasoning (NVR) tests administered by the LEA. Takes 116 pupils (top 28 per cent of cohort). At other times entry is via tests in maths, science and French plus VR and NVR. Minimum six grade Cs at GCSE for entry to sixth form.

Exit: Approximately one fifth leaves at the end of the year 11, often in search of broader A level choice. Vast majority of sixth formers go on to university, mostly northern ones, with 20 per cent taking a gap year first.

Money Matters: Yorkshire's only state boarding school, free for day pupils, boarders charged on a sliding scale.

Remarks: Well worth forking out for the tuition needed to get 10-year-old Johnny up to scratch on his VR and NVR and ensure his 120+ IQ is brought to the fore! A good school for genuinely bright young things but tread carefully if your crammed, coached or cajoled child only scrapes the grade.

ROBERT GORDON'S COLLEGE

Linked to Robert Gordon's College Junior School in the Junior section

Schoolhill, Aberdeen, AB10 1FE

Tel: 01224 646 346
Fax: 01224 630 301
E-mail: h.ouston@rgc.aberdeen.sch.uk
Website: www.rgc.aberdeen.sch.uk

• Pupils: 1,450 boys and girls (60/40 split), also nursery 40 boys and girls. All day • Ages: 5-18, nursery 3-5 • Size of sixth form: 146 post-Highers • Inter-denom • Fees: Nursery: from £2,400 (half day) - £4,800 (whole day) primary £4,840 - £6,600 (annually, but fees not divided into equal termly chunks) (2 per cent discount if you pay the lot in September which is surely a typical Aberdonian economy!) • Independent • Open days: November and May

Head of College: Since 2004, Mr Hugh Ouston MA (Oxon) DipEd (fifties). Educated at Glenalmond, he read history at Christ Church (aka The House), Oxford and DipEd from Aberdeen. Previously deputy head of George Watsons, head of history at Beeslack High School in Penicuik (under the 'headmastering genius' of Sir Richard Staite), and assistant head at Dunbar Grammar. An SQH boy. He runs the school with a deputy head of College plus three deputy heads (not quite the same thing) plus Mrs Mollie Mennie MBA DipEd who is head of the junior school and a deputy head of junior school. 'Would love to teach' but 'impossible', 'not fair to the children'; however he (and some of his senior staff) make a point of watching every member of staff take an entire lesson, 'a good insurance policy'. A wandering head, 'though I am liable to get to the end of the corridor and then be called back.' Made 28 new appointments last year – 'for the three best possible reasons, retirement, maternity and promotion', 'quite a well balanced common room, some of them are as old as me'. 'I inherited (from Brian Lockhart) a tightly-run school, superb' and has spent a very happy first year enjoying the tremendous academic achievements of his pupils, 'boasting like mad', 'tops in everything', 'absolutely nothing to do with me but I get all the credit'. Says 'greatest strengths of the school are its co-educational and cosmopolitan community, the work ethic of its pupils and the fact that a quarter of senior school pupils are on bursaries.' Own four children at Robert Gordon's, two in primary and two in secondary.

Wife 'terribly happy here'; she comes from Aberdeen and her mother lives close by. Relaxed, confident and outgoing. Mr Ouston is very much in control, an iron fist in the velvet glove perhaps but riding on a serious high.

Academic Matters: Unashamedly academic, claims to have got the top results overall in Scotland in 2005. 'Top passes per pupil, top passes per candidate; essentially very strong'. Follows the Scottish system, traditionally very strong on maths and sciences, 'science strong, exceptionally large number of excellent results and pretty good on languages,' says the head, which more or less echoes the majority of parental careers (oil, business). (And last year provided the winner of the SQA Chemistry Prize for the top marks in Scotland – and a hundred quid). Five Highers the norm after fifth year (lower sixth) and masses of add-ons in sixth form: philosophy, psychology, entrepreneurship (in conjunction with Robert Gordon's University which shares the campus) plus pre-med courses, Scots law course, university skills and Japanese. An educational triumvirate with Aberdeen University and Robert Gordon's.

ICT strong and internet connection sourced through the university (ie = free), computers throughout, from nursery up, with banks of PCs on hand for sixth form in their free time. Email for all. Computer-based projectors in every room, plus a quorum of interactive white boards (they must be used). Eight parallel classes throughout, max 22, two classes of mixed ability in each of the four houses, French for all, Latin for all, Greek for the bright (up to higher). Mandarin Chinese for the ambitious (seven currently). Setted at 12 for English and maths, but otherwise 'continuous assessment'. German a popular option with Italian and Spanish – the latter to advanced higher level in 2007. Spectacular biology room groaning under the weight of various heads and skulls of horned beasties. The SEN dept now 'straddles' junior and senior school and is linked into guidance. Actual hands-on assistance plus dual teaching in class, mainly from specialists. School doesn't really do dyslexia per se, though any pupil who hits 'either a temporary or a permanent barrier' will be given as 'much help as is necessary' to overcome that blip 'Learning and teaching and support for learning definitely comes into that'.

Games, Options, The Arts: Art school at the top of one of the many wings; variety of disciplines, and particularly keen on photography, graphic communication now on stream. Drama now timetabled and a Highers subject, good and thriving. Magnificent 45-acre sports ground at Countesswells with artificial pitches for tennis/hockey et al; the amazing water-based hockey pitch (gets hosed down at half-time to keep it super smooth) is used by the international squad. The ground at Countesswells is also used during the hols both for junior sports camps and international hockey practice. Historically, school fields strong rugby, hockey and cricket teams, and rugby strong, plus hockey, golf. Internationalists in all disciplines as well as trips abroad for fun as well as for rugby (Italy, South Africa) hockey (Ireland) skiing (USA). Well-used swimming pool (water polo, canoeing) on site. Two gyms.

Music department recently refurbished, and strong. Masses of instruments on offer, and the recent, not quite a hundred strong, trip to Czechoslovakia was a tour de force. Enormous (brass) oompah band of over 200, plus pipe band, part of the CCF (army and RAF sections only). Hugely popular D of E, 'biggest in Scotland' says the head, and contracted out, with oodles of basic, plus silver and gold galore. Impressive pupil-led Piranha weekly news letter. Zillions of clubs and societies.

Background and Atmosphere: 'Robert Gordon was born in Aberdeen in 1668, he spent most of his life as a merchant in the Baltic ports, building a significant fortune in the process. He always had the idea of building a Hospital for maintenance, aliment, entertainment and education of young boys and, when he died in 1731, that was his legacy'. Magnificent William Adam quadrangle in the centre of Aberdeen, The school currently occupies the northern side, with masses of modern add-ons behind a fabulous front. The Governors' Room still visibly W Adam. Originally occupied by Hanoverian troops under the Duke of Cumberland on their way to Culloden; the first 14 boys did not take up residence until 1750 and The Hospital changed its name to Robert Gordon's College in 1881, went co-ed in 1989, and added a nursery unit in 1993 (popular after-school club for nursery and junior pupils until 5.30 each day, where they can either play or do supervised homework). Thus endeth chronology. To date.

The school currently shares the quad with Robert Gordon's University to whom it sold the lion's share in 1909, but the uni is off to amalgamate its entire campus down by the riverside at Strathdon and RG governors have agreed buy back the rest of the quad for £10.4 million (out of 'housekeeping'; no special fund needed). The school gets possession of the Blackfriars building and the engineering workshop in June 2007, and the final tranche falls in (technology building and total control of the quad) between 2012 and 2015 when the school will be able to spread back into its wings, demolish the excessively nasty 'temporary' buildings which were going up in the playground during our last visit, and equip itself for the 21st century. Current thoughts are that all the specialist teaching in the junior school will move into the wings, science, French, drama, art – and art will become a curricular subject; junior class numbers will fall from a current max of 23/26 to 20 pupils per class and an extra class in each year group. And there will be more floor space for nearly all the senior school. The engineering workshop will be converted into an expressive arts building incorporating a theatre, and the final phase of the technology building will be absorbed by the science department (though of course it will be out of date by then). This is exciting stuff; few inner city schools get such an opportunity, though some of the plans are so grandiose that they may not all fit into the current footprint, and the school has no thought of expanding its actual role.

Sixth formers who help with school meals are spared paying for lunch, though from 14 onwards they can (and most do) go into the town for food. New caterers on board – The (upmarket) Olive Garden – and 'food fantastic' said the head (whose girth we shall examine with interest at our next meeting). Girls wear rather jolly Dress Gordon kilted skirts. The whole school processes behind the pipe band down the streets of Aberdeen to St Nicholas Church on Founder's Day.

Pastoral Care and Discipline: House system recently reinforced, with class captains at all levels plus sixth form assistants at 11 to help those newly arrived in the senior school feel more at home. Guidance system in operation = tutors, as well as good PSE. Fairly sin-free school, pupils allowed out for lunch and 'no bad reports'. No smoking on the premises (campus too small), one expelled for drugs during head's reign. Strong anti bullying programme – would be suspended for booze, and it's a bit obvious out of school, ditto smoking.

Pupils and Parents: This is THE school in Aberdeen. Lots of university parents (easy to drop off), oodles of professional and oil-related ditto, plus farmers etc. Day starts early at 8.30 and children often come from as far away as Montrose ie 35/40 miles away. Parking at drop off and collection times hideous. Vast and increasing number of first time buyers consistent with the vagaries of the oil industry, and strong global ethnic mix. Good PT newsletter and parental involvement. Parents love the school so much that often, having spent years in the oily wilderness, they buy a proper house, and at the next placement maw and the wains stay behind, leaving paw to travel the world alone.

Entrance: Interview for nursery and five year olds entering junior school; test for those over nine and exam for senior school. Fewer leave post Highers than arrive: usual strictures for entry plus test. Four/five post-Standard and eight/ten post-Highers for sixth. Pupils either come up from primary school, or from local state schools, hugely oversub-

scribed – particularly in the junior school, but Aberdeen has a fluid population and it is worth applying at any time – school can cope with a short period of 'overlap' if they know a family is about to be re-located. Rather jolly in-house instruction manual for S1s (ie first year senior school).

Exit: Coming and going with relocation, otherwise (95 per cent) to universities all over, the odd gap year, 'few don't go to university'. Still fairly conservative in choice, almost a third of last year's leavers elected to go to either RGU or Aberdeen uni, followed by Edinburgh and Glasgow; trickle – penny numbers – down south, and an astounding ten to Oxbridge last year. Medics, lawyers and would-be scientists top the wish-list, all got into their first choice uni, 'but then we have no delusions,' said the head.

Money Matters: Huge number of endowments - Robert Gordon's expectation that 'those who came to the Hospital and did well in later life would plough back some of their gains'. In 1816 'a generous bequest by Alexander Simpson of Collyhill made it possible to extend the accommodation' and Gordonians and FPs have continued to do so ever since. 250 children (22 per cent) on some form of bursary, with 100 per cent help available to those in real need with bright kids. Plus The Aberdeen Educational Endowment which takes up slack left by the demolition of the Assisted Places scheme. And guess what, there will be an appeal to help convert the newly re-acquired bits of quad.

Remarks: Very strong co-ed day school with a far-sighted new head relishing the unique challenge of masterminding the transition into such a happy acquisition. If you want to keep the little darlings at home, and you live near enough, you couldn't do better. Not a school for social climbers and probably rather intimidating for gentle souls.

ROEDEAN SCHOOL

Roedean Way, Brighton, East Sussex, BN2 5RQ

Tel: 01273 603 181

Fax: 01273 676 722

E-mail: admissions@roedean.co.uk

Website: www.roedean.co.uk

• Pupils: 387 girls, all board except for 53 • Ages: 11-18 • Size of sixth form: 218 • C of E, but all faiths are welcome • Fees: Day £4,130; boarding £7,400. Plus extra fee for those who join as international sixth formers • Independent • Open days: October and May. School recommends personal visits by appointment

Head: Since 2003, Mrs Carolyn Shaw BA (English) London, PGCE Liverpool (mid fifties). Late of St Mary's, Calne where she was head for 7 years, prior to which she taught English at Cheltenham Ladies' and other schools including one in Bermuda. Lots of experience in the GSA and on various high level education committees and busily involved in the promotion of girls' education in general, this is a very active and pro-active head with a clear vision of what she wants her school to be. A seemingly inspired appointment, Mrs Shaw has the energy, dedication and leadership qualities needed to re-create this, formerly celebrated, school, as a powerhouse in the world of girls' education today. And she's nice too. Likes quoting local taxi drivers who she sees as useful sources of vox pop on the (excellent) local reputation of her charges. If the public perception of Roedean has not kept pace with its character today, Mrs Shaw is the person to change all that and, while loving the school's multi-national make-up, is already doing much to show local families that Roedean could be their local school. 'She's made it brighter, sharper, fresher,' said a parent. Above all, she's an enthusiast, enthusing wildly about the enthusiasm of her girls and her staff. It's infectious.

Academic Matters: A rare 26 A level subjects on offer – rare, that is, for a school as small as this. Subjects include German and Latin which the school is determined to support despite few current takers. Maths taken a by a huge proportion – 50 out of 81 candidates – 39 of whom got grade A in 2005. Other popular subjects include chemistry (26 takers), biology (21) and economics (22). Large proportion of As in all sciences and maths and no question that these subjects predominate in general – partly, though not entirely, through the influence of the substantial far eastern cohort. 80 per cent got A/B at A level in 2005. At GCSE, 60 per cent of the candidates obtained an A or an A*. German less popular than Spanish but resolutely supported by school and results in all languages would suggest that some girls might be missing a trick by not taking them further. EAL taken by many although a good level of English is a pre-requisite for all candidates for places here – around 100 have one-to-one language/learning support which includes good support for a wide range of mild SENs. Group lessons to prepare for the IELTS exam. School's location and sloping site make wheelchair access virtually impossible though a range of other physical disabilities eg mild visual or hearing impairments catered for. Good careers room and good library with first-rate full time staff.

Games, Options, The Arts: Around 30 sports available here including riding at Ditchling riding school where own ponies can be stabled and very active polo club, popular with girls from all types of backgrounds. Multi-purpose sports hall and additional fitness suite for older girls, inviting indoor pool and plenty of outdoor space – fields rolling seawards and robust attitude to go with it – 'we don't stop because it's raining a bit,' we were told. Girls return from matches envying the Astroturfs on offer elsewhere and school currently managing doughtily without, though head says, 'in due course there will probably be one' and they do borrow a couple at nearby sports centre. Everyone takes dance for the first two years and many thereafter. Successes in many sports including, most recently, U16 netball. Lovely new adventure playground for younger girls (money raised by parents) and a great attraction to visiting prospective pupils. Arts flourish though in rooms of varying sizes and much work in many media delights the eye – super textiles, ceramics and very lively DT – all witness to clever and inspirational teaching – as are excellent results. Music is strong in good size class teaching room and many smaller spaces. Music tech 'there if you want to' but, as yet, not many do. Concerts in the wonderfully atmospheric Edwardo-Romanesque chapel or the hall or theatre – an exceptional asset with wholly flexible staging, allowing for theatre-in-the-round or an orchestra pit and seating 320. House plays, one senior and two junior productions a year. All looks professional, well-supported and enjoyed with no hint of flashiness. D of E, Young Enterprise and masses of highly enjoyable and very effective charity work. In late 2004, a 'bath race' – carrying a housemistress in a bath all the way from the school into the centre of Brighton – raised £1,200 for Water Aid.

Background and Atmosphere: You drive away from Brighton heading east, the huge marina clinking below between you and the open sea and there, in front, bolted to the hillside and above the cliffs, you see a vast, grey, pebble-dash, twin turreted and red-roofed pile and, if you don't know, wonder what on earth it could be. This is Roedean of unique and, now outmoded, reputation – with as stern an aspect as could have been wished by any Victorian school-marm – facing the sea and seemingly outfacing any pre-sumptuous invader. But, the sign says 'Welcome' and welcomed you feel in this relaxed, orderly, spacious and warm – in all senses – school and any notion of being in an uninviting spot rapidly recedes.

Having begun at the end of the 19th century as a school with 10 pupils and two mistresses, 10 minutes walk away in Lewes Crescent, the school rapidly expanded and the present building, designed in 1898 by the former Wembley stadium architect – hence the trademark twin tur-rets – bears witness to the confidence, solidity and dura-bility its redoubtable founders felt about girls' education. The building has a medieval baronial feel with huge high windows, vast tiled fireplaces and many pretty massive rooms. One feels the place could take twice the number of pupils and be far from crowded. Corridors and many other areas being cheerily redecorated when we visited – a bright primrose yellow giving a fresh, warm feel and school eagerly anticipating the arrival of smart new blue carpets. Clearly it's a nightmare to keep up and the battering of the elements visible not just outside, as patches of bubbly damp on many walls, but the place is warm, attractively and not skimpily furnished and it feels like home. A few atmospheric rather Gothic corridors and staircases and a lovely cloister area on the way to the chapel – for quiet and repose. Girls in 'French navy' uniforms seem relaxed and friendly and keen to give of their best.

Pastoral Care and Discipline: 'I don't see discipline as a problem,' says head. No drugs or similarly serious inci-dents in her time but 'there would be no alternative to exclu-sion' if anyone is caught with an illegal substance. Head sees 'respect for others as what we value here – respect of girls for girls, for different nationalities and cultures. The youngest pupil, the newest cleaner and I all merit respect from everyone – we are all equally worthy.' Integration of overseas pupils far more successful here than in many comparable schools – far less struggle in getting everyone to join in after the first few weeks. Head uncompromising about her community – 'to talk loudly in a language others can't understand is rude and can be hurtful. Everyone agrees with this and, by and large, they all speak English.'

Strong pastoral system and all staff on the alert for a long face or other signs of unhappiness or disturbance. All girls have open and wholly confidential (except in cases of actual danger) access to a counsellor. Active peer-listening scheme. Pride taken in caring for each other and family atmosphere. 'My daughter finds it a very nurturing environ-ment,' said one parent, 'and she's very happy there'. All female teachers are called 'Madam' and head maintains it is said 'with real affection, not prissiness' – certainly borne out by what we saw. Boarding accommodation undergoing rolling programme and best upper school rooms now quite large and with en-suite bathrooms. Younger girls share in rooms of 4 (one of 6) but all have space and all rooms are quite cosy. Some newer rooms have blu-tac embargos which seems a little sad. All sixth formers in Keswick House in single rooms with proper sized beds, good kitchen and common room. Nice touches like hot choc and coffee on tap all day. Food, in general, excellent complete with dietary warnings/info where necessary and special needs catered for. Special help given on occasions like Ramadan fasting. New wing with excellent conference room used for outside speakers, careers talks, house meeting etc. Sixth form girls do their own laundry – good practice! Other houses linked by 'bunnyruns' so you don't have to go outside from one to the other. Good support for overseas boarders includes escorted service to/from Victoria and taxis to airports. Some belongings can stay at school over hols. Excellent onsite shop sells everything including uniform. Everyone has email and access to the internet. Help for day pupils includes a bus which takes girls away from school late into the evening, after the extra-curricular activities no-one wants to miss.

Pupils and Parents: From 30+ countries and every continent. Lots of Chinese, but also Thai, Russian, Korean and Europeans of all sorts. Also more than half indigenous or ex-pat Brits, most from the south of England and school busy recruiting in this area. Clientele not the stiff upper class and diplomatic types of yesteryear but everyone and it's hard to imagine a girl who would not feel welcome here. Lots of famous ORs include Baroness Chalker, Verity Lambert, Sally Oppenheimer, Tanya Streeter, Honeysuckle Weeks, Rebecca Hall, Philipa Tattersall.

Entrance: No main feeder schools. Entry at 11, 12 or 13 is via Common Entrance, scholarship or the school's own entrance exam. All entrants are required to visit the school for interview and may spend a couple of days at the school prior to joining. Candidates should be registered as early as possible in the academic year prior to their entry in school to ensure the availability of a place.

Exit: Very few leave before 16 and then, a few, for co-ed. Some – as elsewhere – return, gratefully, after a few weeks outside. 2004 leavers went in large numbers to the

LSE and to Imperial College, also to UCL, Bristol, Nottingham and Durham universities and to a long list of others. Courses in everything from cosmetic science to veterinary medicine, German to law.

Money Matters: Lots of scholarships - academic, music, sport, art or performing art - competed for at 11, 12 and 13 by exam and audition -worth up to 40 per cent fees. Sixth form schols also by exam in A level subjects and a general paper.

Remarks: Early in 2005, the new triumvirate – head/bursar/chair of governors – undertook a major overhaul of staffing and resources. The hard look at management and structure was long overdue and resulted in a more efficient system better suited to the school's needs now though some staff were lost on the way. Pupil numbers are at least holding up and in some years – notably the sixth form – over subscribed, as one would hope for a school with such a healthy spirit and so much to offer. The tough approach, though sensible, will have scared a few but the head is relaxed – 'confidence is strengthening', she says. We would be surprised if the school doesn't spur on more strongly from now on.

Head asserts, ' we're a cracking good school and I need to get parents in to see – they're overwhelmed when they come.' Previous emphasis on filling top end means you may have missed the boat there but spaces still available at the lower end and well worth getting your 11 or 13-year-old in before the word gets out.

ROSSALL SCHOOL

Linked to Rossall Junior School in the Junior section

Broadway, Fleetwood, Lancashire, FY7 8JW

Tel: 01253 774 201
Fax: 01253 774 282
E-mail: enquiries@rossallcorporation.co.uk
Website: www.rossallschool.org.uk

• Pupils: 407: 250 boarding, 250 day; about 40:60 girls:boys. Plus 78 in the International Study Centre • Ages: 11-18 • Size of sixth form: 200 • C of E • Fees: £2,455 - £6,860 (Senior); boarding £3,005 - £7,565 (IB); ISC £5,307 (below 13) - £7,570 (above 13) • Independent • Open days: October, January and April

Headmaster of Rossall Schools: Since 2001, Mr Tim Wilbur BA PGCE (mid forties). Read history at Kent. Taught at Millfield until 1998 (housemaster), then deputy head of Sutton Valence until he came here. A serious hockey player. Married, with three children all at Rossall and all playing hockey. A modest, approachable man and a good listener. Walks about the school a lot, talks to pupils, takes school teams.

Academic Matters: Hard work insisted upon. Acceptable results overall at GCSE (86 per cent A* – C, excellent science and maths) and A level given unselective nature of intake. School by no means complacent and always looking to improve. IB taken seriously and enthusiastically by staff and pupils; one third of year do it, excellent 100 per cent per cent pass in 2005.

International Study Centre (ISC) in existence for ten years; for overseas students, mainly from Hong Kong and SE Asia, but rising numbers from Germany and Eastern Europe (parents disenchanted with domestic system and looking for secure pastoral care). Intensive English language courses lead to International GCSE or a transfer to main school (about 25 a year). As much academic integration as the organisation can cope with (eg science staff teach in both areas), and more hoped for. ISC numbers have doubled in recent years.

Special needs support taken seriously, though difficult cases have to go elsewhere. Senior SENCO doubles as housemistress and has one fully trained teacher who oversees English and maths classes during first two years in senior school. Good links too with the junior school. Currently 45 pupils turn up at the ILU (individual learning unit) twice a week for an hour long session, either one to one or one to three. Chiefly of the dys-strata, plus occasional mild Aspergers, ADHD or semantic pragmatic disorder (can't say a sentence the right way round). Some deaf, but not profoundly so, no mentors in living memory, the occasional statemented child. Campus not brill for wheelchairs – though they have had them. £300 per term extra for two weekly sessions: cheap. Clone the SENCO.

Games, Options, The Arts: The usual games, and famous for Rossall ('Ross') hockey, played on the beach, tides permitting, and very popular; invented in 1860s, with esoteric rules. CDT and art strong. Good music – choirs and orchestras, and professional subscription concerts, in the Sir Thomas Beecham (Old Boy) Music Schools. Performing arts building planned. Keen CCF (all three arms) includes girls; leads to BTec in year 11. School has its own outward bound award; Lake District and Yorkshire Dales used.

Background and Atmosphere: Founded in 1844 on the windswept north Fylde coast, an easy tram ride from Blackpool. Confident looking and mellow redbrick buildings open up into Oxford-type quad with a handsome chapel to one side. Healthy sea air, pretty brisk in winter, with views of the Lake District. A full programme of refurbishment of the boarding houses commenced summer 2004. Day pupils have their own houses, with studies, common rooms and changing rooms, where they can stay until 8.30 pm. Sixth form centre and bar popular with boarders and day pupils. Religious observance not obtrusive; thrice-weekly compulsory chapel 'a chance for quietness and reflection', says head. Hymn practice for all.

The ISC obviously looms pretty large – a quarter of the school, exceeded in size only by Sherborne international school. Students mix socially, eg in sports teams. Some are clearly well off, judging by the Mini-Coopers in the car park. Their parents have presumably opted for the benefits of the English system (and access to higher education), plus the security of life in west Lancashire. A full programme of events, activities and field trips runs each weekend.

Pastoral Care and Discipline: Strong anti-bullying ethos and not a druggy school. Blackpool a temptation, but head says whole-school vigilance pays off. Foreign pupils 'often set our boys and girls very fine examples'.

Pupils and Parents: Now mainly a local school, with (apart from ISC) a somewhat parochial feel. Parents are farmers and business people. A growing number of Services children. Over 50 per cent first time buyers. Chirpy, courteous students, happy to be at Rossall. (Very) Old Boys include Leslie Charteris (creator of 'The Saint'), Patrick Campbell, David Brown of Aston Martin fame, Paul Herbert and Sir Thomas Beecham.

Entrance: Entry 'flexible', and generally not a problem. All pupils assessed for dyslexia on entrance.

Exit: 95 per cent go to a wide range of universities, mainly in the north; some to Oxbridge. Gap years are popular.

Money Matters: Half a dozen or so half fee academic awards, plus one full academic and one full all-rounder scholarship.

Remarks: Very successful international study centre. Trad British day/boarding side seems to be finding the competion tough, to judge by the numbers.

ROYAL GRAMMAR SCHOOL (GUILDFORD)

Linked to Lanesborough School in the Junior section

High Street, Guildford, Surrey, GU1 3BB

Tel: 01483 880 600
Fax: 01483 306 127
E-mail: tmsyoung@rgs-guildford.co.uk
Website: www.rgs-guildford.co.uk

• Pupils: 890 boys; all day • Ages: 11-18 • Size of sixth form: 240 • Non-denom • Fees: First & second forms (incl.lunch): £3,305; third - sixth forms: £3,154; lunch : £151 • Independent • Open days: First Saturday morning in October

Headmaster: Since 1992, Mr Tim Young MA (early fifties). Educated at the Dragon, Eton and Cambridge, where he read history. Previously a housemaster at Eton; has taught in California and New Zealand. Popular and easygoing. Father was headmaster of nearby Charterhouse. Wife a consultant radiologist. Two sons, both at Aldro prep nearby. Retiring in December 2006.

Academic Matters: Outstanding teaching plus selective intake equals superb results. Boys come in expecting to work hard and most do. Reputedly and actually strong at maths and sciences. Maths is the most popular option at A and A/S level and nearly 50 boys take the maths GCSE a year early. Economics comes second, with physics, chemistry and biology close behind. Still, boys praise the English teaching and A level results from the minority who opt for the subject are super. French compulsory to GCSE plus choice of German, Greek or Spanish at age 13. Each year a dozen boys take the Japanese and Chinese GCSEs which are examined off-site. Sixth formers join up with two local girls' schools (Tormead and Guildford High) for weekly general studies programme. All homework done at home. No streaming but setting in French and maths from years 10-11. No ESL provision. Handful of dyslexics.

Games, Options, The Arts: Perceived as less sporty than bevy of heavyweight public schools that surround it but RGS more than holds its own. Outstanding rifle shooting and athletics and wide range of minor sports. Rugby, hockey and cricket each get their own term and the school turns out 27 rugby teams, 15 hockey teams, 12 cricket teams (not a huge number considering they are spread over seven year groups). Very little soccer. The 15-minute drive to the school's luxuriant games fields south of Guildford is not the boys' favourite interlude – the travel eats into the once-a-week two-hour games session. But newly completed £6 million indoor sports centre and all-weather pitch has improved the school's games facilities dramatically.

High standard of music with huge array of opportunities including sax quartet, guitar ensembles, big band and a jazz group. Top musicians or singers can join the high-powered Guildford Sinfonia or the Guildford Chorale, along with the cream of other local schools. Good drama – offered as an A/S option but not at GCSE or A level. Small but useful drama studio. New auditorium opened in January 2005. Annual musical production also incorporates girls from Tormead and Guildford High. Space for art lessons is limited, particularly at sixth form, but the output is impressive. Big on brainbox activities eg chess, the Schools National Quiz Competition (finalists for several years), and radio communication (with MIR and Space Shuttle astronauts!). During 'period 8' every Monday afternoon, boys are obliged to participate in CCF, scouts or D of E. The school day ends at 4pm, and although a few boys stay on for team practices and clubs, most extra-curriculars take place at lunch to allow transport connections to be made.

Background and Atmosphere: Ancient and historic, dating from first decade of the 16th century. Mouldering 1552 charter from King Edward VI kept behind glass in head's study and the school's official title is still King Edward VI's Grammar School. Tall white 400 year old building on one side of busy Guildford High Street oozes charm. Shame about the huge main teaching block on the other side which is strictly 1960s Awful. Was run as a state school for 30 years after the war but went independent again in 1977. Class sizes reasonable: 21 22 up to age 14, then 16-17 during GCSEs and an average of 10 in sixth form. Space at a premium wherever you go. Cramped library with spacious study area tucked above. Cramped lunchroom (excellent food) with boys queuing down the hall. Breakfast service for early risers. All classrooms should have interactive whiteboard by September 2006.

Pastoral Care and Discipline: A continual challenge as the school stands smack in the centre of Guildford town centre (sandwiched between Argos and McDonald's) but the school manages it well. Boys maintain that this urban location is the school's greatest strength, teaching them how to manage – and excel – in the real world. Head agrees, 'it's real life. The boys see guys selling The Big Issue as they walk to school from the station.' Shops out of bounds until age 14 and even then access is a privilege, not a right, and boys learn quickly to be responsible to safeguard that right. Littlest boys are well looked after and boys joining the school at 13 are put in lessons as a group so they can all be new together. Each boy's tutor checks him in twice a day. Sixth formers all have a chance to be prefects. Much more freedom in sixth form when boys may go off campus when they choose but must still wear uniform. Social life abounds in the High Street and on the trains and buses where there is no shortage of contact with young ladies from the local girls' schools.

Pupils and Parents: Clever, mature, hard-working boys. Parents committed to education and high standards. Many were educated by state grammar schools and overwhelming majority have university degrees. About 15 per cent of mothers are teachers. Large numbers join from own prep, Lanesborough. Other main feeders: Cranmore, Danes Hill, Hoe Bridge, Yateley Manor and state schools South Farnham, Busbridge, Holy Trinity and Waverley Abbey. Many boys travel from as far as south west London, Portsmouth and Reading as the school is close to main Guildford train and bus stations. OBs: Terry Jones of Monty Python and cricketer Bob Willis.

Entrance: Selective but not impossible (three applicants for every two places). 75-100 boys enter at 11, after attending entrance exam in January before the September of proposed entry. Tested in English, maths and verbal reasoning, plus short interview. Weight also given to report from current school. Further interviews in English and maths for borderline cases. 50-75 boys enter at 13 after having spent a day at the school for pre-CE assessments at either 11 or 12. On the basis of this they will get an offer conditional on satisfactory performance on CE or scholarship papers. 12+ exam covers a little bit of French conversation, science and IT in addition to English, maths and VR. Small number join at sixth form – GCSE As required in all subjects that will be continued to AS. This school is a bargain and many thankful parents, who could never afford more expensive schools, can scrape together one set of fees for RGS. The 'Charter Award' funds several free places for deserving, needy state school pupils. NB If you fail to get a place at 11, don't be afraid to have another go at 13.

Exit: Around 20 a year to Oxbridge and big clutches to Bristol, Exeter, Nottingham and Durham. Large numbers reading medicine, economics, engineering, physics, chemistry. A few trickle out after GCSEs to local sixth form colleges.

Remarks: Thriving top notch grammar school, which happily whips in the brightest 10 per cent from its juicy catchment area and, on the whole, does them proud.

ROYAL GRAMMAR SCHOOL (NEWCASTLE)

Linked to Royal Grammar School Junior School (Newcastle) in the Junior section

Eskdale Terrace, Newcastle upon Tyne, Tyne and Wear, NE2 4DX

Tel: 0191 281 5711

Fax: 0191 212 0392

E-mail: a.bird@rgs.newcastle.sch.uk

Website: www.rgs.newcastle.sch.uk

- Pupils: 1,075 boys plus 65 girls in the sixth form. All day.
- Ages: 11-18, juniors 8-10 • Size of sixth form: 340
- Non-denominational • Fees: Senior school £6,849 pa; Junior school £5,739 • Independent • Open days: A Saturday in mid-November

Head: Since 1994, Mr James Miller MA (fifties), educated at Douai, read classical mods followed by PPE at Merton College, Oxford. Previously head of Framlingham and before that a housemaster at Winchester. Very busy when we met, as he was chairing the HMC/GSA study-links web portal, sitting on the HMC academic policy committee and whizzing up to London on an almost daily basis trying to iron out the glitches with the A and AS level results (he promises that he is not normally 'an absentee landlord'). He was also much in evidence on Radio 4, stoutly defending the A level corner versus the IB, and, nb, recommends the Bell Media web portal or study-links as amazing guides to web sites for A level students to use. His wife, Ruth, teaches special needs locally; they have two sons, who were in the school.

An economist, infectiously outgoing and enthusiastic, he is continually surprised at 'how much is going on that I don't know about' and recently discovered a drama group doing 'an independent production' of the Scottish play, and regularly finds groups rehearsing at 7.30 in the morning. Says 'the school is humming, far more going on than you would believe possible'. Fair amount of staff change over the past eight years, almost half the heads of departments have been replaced, common room now buzzing with top class teachers of all ages. Head is 'loving the place', has no intention of moving, and was most indignant that we should dare to suggest in our last edition that the school might have a 'complacent attitude' – 'we're normally accused of moving too fast'.

Academic Matters: Impressive. Outstanding results in 2005. All take three sciences at GCSE, ten GCSEs the norm, seven core and three options – which range from the classics (Latin, Greek and classical civilisation) to design technology, economics and the humanities. Not much take-up on the classics side (though a fair showing at AS and A level), but enormous enthusiasm for economics and history and a pleasing collection of A* and As across the board. Recent introduction of girls at sixth form level has allowed the introduction of a wider choice of A levels; psychology the latest addition. The sciences particularly strong at A level, and have been given a boost with fabulous science and technology block, with state-of-the-art labs running off broad corridors filled with home grown art. Regular success and prizes nationally.

School is keen on local partnerships and runs practical courses on Saturdays as well as after the summer term, with local comprehensives, genetics and DNA analysis and the like (The Newcastle Science Enrichment Programme). Computers everywhere, four dedicated suites, plus more in the library, the science resource room and in the sixth form centre – 250 machines, easy access and open at lunch time, and before and after school. Email for all, ICT is 'not currently offered as an examinable subject' but the European Driving Licence is about to come on stream. Computer-based lang lab, but French and German only, with exchanges. Max class size 24. Support for learning in place, 'the new Special Educational Needs and Disability Act (SENDA) means that we have got to consider applicants with any disability, and consider fairly and reasonably whether we can do a good job for them and whether we can make reasonable adjustments to cater for them'.

Games, Options, The Arts: Rugby unbelievably strong, beating all contenders, with regular trips abroad. Vast array of sport on offer, the usual chestnuts – cricket, athletics and gymnastics, plus hockey, basketball etc. Football for sixth form, by special request, plus swimming, tennis and squash. Enviable new sports hall, with, surprisingly, no mirrors in the weights training room – how else do pupils know when they are performing properly? Own rugby pitch on site, and outfields rented nearby, much use made of local facilities. Huge variety of clubs, chess meets three times a week and bridge is popular. Outstanding debating, and regular prize winners. Technology club equally successful. CCF for both boys and girls (and a certain amount of naughtiness), 'granny bashing' as well as involvement with the local community – the Inner-City Partnership, where pupils work with deprived children on a one-to-one basis. Strong charity commitment. D of E flourishing.

Music flourishing, though only a trickle take it at GCSE level. Masses of orchestras, bands and ensembles. Regular concerts (though recent moans are that they could be better attended) and trips abroad; the choir recently sang mass in St Mark's basilica. Drama important here, and a new four million quid performing arts complex on the wish list. Five or six plays annually, plus French plays and a biannual Greek production with girls from Central Newcastle High School opposite. Theatre studies and film studies now added to the A level syllabus. Masses of take up in art in all disciplines (screen printing, 3D and expressive) both at GCSE and A level, more trips abroad, and pupils' work is exhibited in local galleries. Trips to battlefields for historians, to Greece and Italy for classicists, as well as World Challenge.

Background and Atmosphere: Foundation dates back over 450 years, current buildings much revamped with stylish glazed arches linking the main buildings and making the whole place look more put together and elegant. Redbrick 1906 Queen Anne style frontage conceals a mass of add-ons round the impressively large, five acre sports grounds (remember this is a city centre school) and new build planned. School surrounded by inner ring road motorways and a hundred metres from Jesmond metro station. Well-used old hall, apparently endlessly filled with pupils waiting for something else to happen. It is a busy place. Lecture theatre with magical stained-glass windows. Sixth form centre flourishing. Libraries recently upgraded, and a certain amount of re-jigging in the classroom area. New performing arts centre to be completed in Sept 2006. Junior school extension completed Sept 2005.

Boys move from blue blazers to purposeful black in senior school, with suits or jackets in the sixth form; girls admitted in 2001, max 22 in any one year, and wear neat dark suits. Younger pupils a fairly scruffy lot – 'regular battles on dress,' says the head. 'School was a hard place, austerity was the name of the game, now much more civilised.' Junior school a couple of hundred yards away at Lambton Road, pupils come over for computer studies, science and games.

Pastoral Care and Discipline: Pupils are allocated a personal tutor who stays with them throughout, weekly meetings. Vigorous anti-bullying policy, PSHE for all. 'Tackled bullying head on,' loads of help from prefects, on the whole it appeared to be 'careless insensitivity' rather than malicious bullying. Girls a civilising influence. Out for violence, the usual suspects, and drugs. Smoking not tolerated, and no particular problems with drinking or smoking off-site. Crack now appearing in certain parts of the north east and head and staff are constantly vigilant.

Pupils and Parents: First choice for clever boys from every corner (inner and outer) of Newcastle and Sunderland, Durham and County Durham, and also from far-flung rural corners eg Berwick, Wooler, Alnwick. Broad social mix, a fairly scruffy bunch who don't always observe the school's dress code. Popular with local bigwigs in industry, the professions, academics from the universities, the Asian community. Closer relations with parents now actively fostered – some like it, some don't. Pupils in the main hard-working, keen to succeed and 'don't feel life owes them a living,' observed a master with memories of working in a famous public school further south. Old boys include England winger David Rees, Lord Taylor, Brian Redhead, composer and saxophonist John Harle.

Entrance: Tough and competitive via the school's own entrance exam at 11, hardly any now come at 13. 50 plus from the junior school, as long as their work is up to scratch. 24 girls and around 11 boys come post-GCSE, min six GCSEs at A/B plus report from school. Whole school moving towards full co-ed in 2006. Co-ed entry available in years 3, 4, 7, 9 and sixth form for Sept 2006. Girls come from an amazing 46 different schools, the majority from Central Newcastle High across the road, but otherwise from a good cross section of state and independent.

Exit: Recent average of 22 a year to Oxbridge; otherwise to Newcastle, Leeds, Edinburgh, Manchester, Nottingham and London, science, particularly medicine and social sciences popular, not a lot of change here. 21 students to medical schools around the country in 2004. Small coterie to art and/or music colleges, though the latter are often more likely to read music at uni and then go on to conservatoires. Two recent professional footballers. Six left at the end of last session post-GCSE, either for financial reasons, 'or because the RGS sixth form was inappropriate for them'. Gap year gaining in popularity.

Money Matters: Was hit hard by the loss of Assisted Places. Four bursaries now under the aegis of the Ogden Trust for 'above average children from a state primary school or limited, or no parental means', school splits damage 50/50. Mega bursarial appeal now in place, school hopes to raise three million quid. School keen not to be seen as socially elitist, some bursaries available – up to 100 per cent if need be.

Remarks: Powerful traditional grammar school, with high morale under dynamic head and an obvious choice for ambitious locals.

ROYAL GRAMMAR SCHOOL (WORCESTER)

Linked to RGS The Grange in the Junior section

Upper Tything, Worcester, Worcestershire, WR1 1HP

Tel: 01905 613 391
Fax: 01905 726 892
E-mail: office@rgsw.org.uk
Website: www.rgsw.org.uk

• Pupils: 1,067, still mainly boys but going steadily co-ed • Ages: 11-18 in senior school; 2-11 at RGS The Grange • Size of sixth form: 220 • Non-denom • Fees: £2,644 senior school; £1,410-2,352 junior school • Independent • Open days: Senior October/Jan; prep October/Jan; Pre-prep Oct/Jan; 6th form Nov

Head: Since 2005, Mr Andrew Rattue MA PGCE (forties). Educated at Bishop Wordsworth's Grammar School and Brasenose College, Oxford, where he read English. Taught English at Mill Hill School and The Haberdashers' Aske's School, Elstree, before becoming head of English at Highgate School in the early 1990s and then second master at RGS Guildford. Also taught in Thailand and the USA, where he was a Fulbright Exchange teacher at Greenhill School, an independent co-educational school in Dallas, Texas in 1990-91. Married to Jacky, four children. Interest include all sports, American culture, France and the French, the Victorians, hill walking and cooking.

Academic Matters: In a challenging environment. Worcester and its environs are well provided with independent schools (King's, Alice Ottley, Malvern and Bromsgrove) and there are some good state grammar schools as close as Stratford. The ending of assisted places in 1997 cost the school 35 pupils in each year (one of the highest proportions of any school in the country), which forced it to look closely at its potential market and the sort of school it wished to be. The Grammar School is now committed to co-education, not as selective as it was, and has excellent provision for dyslexic pupils (although there is not a great number of them). There is already a minority of girls in the sixth form and the intake has been entirely mixed since

September 2003 which will make the school genuinely co-educational by 2007.

Given the loss of pupils on assisted places (who were generally the more able part of the intake) the continued impressive academic showing is remarkable – far stronger showing in the league tables than any of the local rivals. No obvious curriculum weaknesses most subject areas, having a 100 per cent pass rate at GCSE and, at A level, A and B grades have not dipped below 60 per cent. The school has a particular reputation for its science and mathematics teaching, which will doubtless be strengthened by recent improvements in laboratory facilities.

Games, Options, The Arts: Traditionally very strong in the boys' team games – rugby, soccer and especially cricket. In recent years has much extended its range and will do so again with the influx of girls. Delightful complex of city-centre pitches within easy access of the school; generally adequate sports facilities. Rowing is increasingly successful with the junior quad sculls crew national champions two years in succession; six pupils selected for national rowing teams in 2002. Cricket remains the pre-eminent sport and it is perhaps significant that the two most famous old boys, Imran Khan and Tim Curtis, both made their name as cricketers. The head is very supportive of games – 'he is at every match,' comment parents, 'we don't know how he finds the time'.

Art and drama are playing a greater and more significant part in the curriculum. New art house opened Sept 2004. Engineering seems to be an especially strong element of design and the school has some wonderful examples of winning go-karts built by the pupils. There is a choir; orchestra and music generally taken seriously – but with the proximity of a choir school the Grammar School does well to compete in this area. Wide range of activities on offer both at lunch time and in the evening up to 5.30 pm; 'an incredibly committed staff,' commented a parent. CCF seems to be especially popular. However, after school activities are limited by the fact that 250 children have to catch buses rather promptly at the end of the day. Full fixture programme on Saturdays (there is no Saturday school).

Background and Atmosphere: Proud to point out that it is certainly the oldest scholastic institution in Worcester – its foundation in 1291 (and descent from an episcopal school dating from 685) makes it rather older than the vast majority of leading public schools – notably Eton and Winchester. Non-denominational, which marks it out from the avowedly Anglican King's and Malvern. Occupies a site in Upper Tything, perhaps not the most attractive part of Worcester, yet its campus is particularly charming with largely Georgian and Victorian buildings clustered around attractive and well maintained gardens and lawns. Many of the buildings including Perrins Hall were designed by an Old Boy, Alfred Hill Parker, and were funded by Charles William Dyson Perrins, Worcestershire Sauce owner. It even has the ruins of the old medieval convent chapel to add a further air of antiquity to the landscape. The only unattractive building is the dining hall, built by the LEA in the days when the school was a voluntary aided grammar – it became independent in 1983.

The school has suffered from being seen as the second choice to King's. In part this is because of the obvious cathedral links and consequent status of its rival. Until the abolition of grammar school selection, King's got the first tranche of pupils and the Royal Grammar School got the second. However, for the last decade or so the Royal Grammar School has been the stronger institution academically. Rather unfairly, this is often not adequately recognised. Has the ethos of an old fashioned grammar school, with none of the pretentiousness so often associated with the minor public school.

Pastoral Care and Discipline: The school's ethos is firmly reflected in its pastoral system and discipline structure. It retains a traditional prefect system which gives real authority to senior pupils, closely monitored by a year tutor system – a structure very clearly set out in easy to understand guidelines. The head takes bullying very seriously and much emphasis is placed on good manners, as was obvious when walking round the school. The boys (and the growing number of girls) were delightfully relaxed, charming and very welcoming. The impression was of young people who were genuinely proud of their school and had an easy relationship with each other and the staff.

Pupils and Parents: Some local parents would tend to choose the slightly grander (more expensive) King's, Bromsgrove or Malvern. The better informed ones choose RGS where most of the children are from middle class commercial and professional families; lots of first-time buyers. Wide catchment, with buses going as far afield as Tewkesbury, Evesham, Droitwich and Tenbury Wells. Good train links to Malvern, Kidderminster and Bromsgrove.

Entrance: Many from the school's own preparatory school RGS The Grange; many, too, from local primary schools by test at 11. Some come at 11 from local prep schools and a few at 13 by Common Entrance (head quite happy to see more of them coming in at this age). Selective, but not excessively so. Highly regarded by local heads, both prep and primary, seen as very good value for money.

It has become attractive for girls to enter the sixth form from, especially, Alice Ottley – the source of some bad feeling between traditionally neighbouring schools which will be made worse by the decision to go entirely co-educational. Negotiations to combine the two schools seem to have failed – Alice Ottley seems likely be the loser here!

Exit: Head is aware of the growing threat from sixth form colleges, especially attractive to some of his financially challenged parents. Virtually all sixth form leavers attend university. Most of them to pretty sound establishments, not too many to the University of Nether Wapping. A solid core of around eight a year make it to Oxbridge.

Money Matters: There are a few bursaries and scholarships and it is clear that the head is keen to help able children from poorer backgrounds. However, very limited funds for this.

Remarks: Unpretentious and on the way up. Offers great value for money and will become a larger player in the local independent scene.

THE ROYAL GRAMMAR SCHOOL, HIGH WYCOMBE

Amersham Road, High Wycombe, Buckinghamshire, HP13 6QT

Tel: 01494 524 955
Fax: 01494 551 410
E-mail: admin@rgshw.com
Website: www.rgshw.com

• Pupils: 1,275 day boys plus 70 boarders • Ages: 11-18 • Size of sixth form: 400 • Inter-denom • Fees: For boarding only: £3,104 weekly, £3,500 full • State • Open days: September and November

Headmaster: Since 1999, Mr Tim Dingle BSc MBA (forties), educated at King's Cambridge as a chorister and then The Perse School, going on to read biology at the University of East Anglia. He taught at Mill Hill, where he went on to become deputy headmaster. He has a MBA in educational management and recently won a Churchill Fellowship which he used to look at Australian education. He enjoys an amazing array of interests and hobbies with a passion for rugby. Parents and boys alike find him easily approachable and comment on how he makes time for chat.

Off to head St George's College in Argentina in July 2006.

Academic Matters: Average of 11 GCSE passes per pupil. Students prepare for four AS levels and continue with four A levels. Results are well above grammar school and national averages, with boys achieving on average 28 UCAS points. Results for modern foreign languages are amongst the highest nationally. It is one of the largest sixth forms in the country with a choice of 25 subjects including an impressive list of languages: French, German, Spanish, Italian, Japanese, Swedish, Bahasa Malay and Mandarin to name but a few.

Games, Options, The Arts: Rugby, cricket, hockey, athletics, rowing, basketball and fencing are the main sports with opportunities in many other sports. The head is an English rugby schools' selector. An outstanding music department ensures something for all and when girls are required for stage productions they are 'borrowed' from the excellent nearby high schools. Superb range of opportunities for trips home and abroad and activities from CCF, community service, D of E as well as Young Enterprise and World Challenge. A myriad of clubs too from go-karting, to the 'Jeremy Paxman' society. Work shadowing and opportunities to do work experience at home and abroad.

Background and Atmosphere: Founded in the 12th century and received its Royal Charter in 1562. Red brick Queen Anne style building with various additions in similar style built around a quadrangle. Newly built boarding facilities offer en-suite rooms with telephone and communal facilities including IT. Other recent additions include a refurbished music centre, science block and admin offices as well as new language facilities. An overall impression of being orderly and purposeful.

Pastoral Care and Discipline: The school expects high standards and boys adhere to them – parents kept well in touch with any slips. 'Old-fashioned courtesy and manners are the norm', says school. The boys are proud to be part of the school. Boarders have plenty of extra activities and full care from matron, houseparents and tutors.

Pupils and Parents: An abundance of professional parents. School unwilling to be seen as exclusive and is proud to be the local grammar school. There are boys of every shape and size from all types of background. They seem to find a niche to meet their needs in terms of interests and friends. Matches and other functions strongly supported by parents. OBs include Professors Roger Scruton, Michael Zander and Denis Stevens; Henry Sandon of the Antiques Road show; Richard Hickox, conductor of the LSO; England cricketer Philip Newport and England rugby players Matthew Dawson and Nick Beal, GB hockey captain and Olympian Jonathan Wyatt, professional golfer Luke Donald, Olympic gold medal gymnast Ross Brewer, rock star Howard Jones, BBC news commentator Fergus Walsh, Lord McIntosh of Haringey, MP Paul Stinchcombe and Ian Fraser VC.

Entrance: Selection subject to Bucks criteria and VR score in 11-plus exam. In recent years only first-choice applications within catchment area have been successful. School's own selection procedure adopted if places become available further up the school as well as for the 10 boarding places for each year. Worth considering if outside catchment area but definitely not convertible to day places. Independent school candidates attracted to the small number of places available at sixth form, and EU students with good English are considered for full boarding then.

Exit: 100 per cent into higher education, with about 25 each year to Oxbridge. Remainder to other established universities.

Money Matters: Some company sponsorships, but parents lead strong fund-raising initiative, seeking commitments for the coming seven years.

Remarks: Overtly a boys' school excelling in boys' activities. As good as top public schools but no frills. Not many schools of this calibre offering so much for free. A school to move house for. High position in league tables with excellence in the classroom, on the sports field and in drama and the arts. Proud to be recognised as 'the local grammar school'.

THE ROYAL HIGH SCHOOL (EDINBURGH)

East Barnton Avenue, Edinburgh, EH4 6JP

Tel: 01313 362 261
Fax: 01313 128 592
E-mail: admin@royalhigh.edin.sch.uk
Website: www.royalhigh.edin.sch.uk

- Pupils: 1,160; 585 boys and 575 girls, all day • Ages: 11-18
- Size of sixth form: 139 • Non-denom • State

Rector: Since 1998, Mr George M R Smuga MA DipEd (fifties) who was previously head of North Berwick High School, with a brief interregnum when he was seconded to East Lothian Education Department where he was manager of quality assurance. Educated at Kirkcaldy High School, he read politics and modern history at Edinburgh University, followed by Moray House. He had thought of a career in journalism; wrote text books, but enjoyed teaching. After Portobello High, where he built up his department as principal teacher of modern studies, he became Assistant Head Teacher, before moving to Beeslack School in Penicuik, where he was depute rector. A man of parts then. Thoughtful, concerned and sensitive. He has two grown-up children.

Enjoys the school, enjoys the challenge and has become an expert on building control and such-like since his arrival here.

Academic Matters: Max class size 30, going down to 20 for practical subjects and much less in higher years. Certain number of new staff appointed. Maths, English and modern languages set in S1/S2, other subjects set in S3 where necessary. Strong on social subjects; modern studies popular. In 2003 sixth year student awarded the Beazley Prize from the Royal Historical Society for performance in Advanced Higher History exam. Good showing in the National Enterprising Maths competition and maths results outstanding. English impressive, CDT very strong; fair showing in the field of science; excellent human biology as well as biology department. The Nuffield Science Bursary was awarded in 2001 to one of the pupils 'to carry out an investigation into flamingo behaviour at Edinburgh zoo'. Languages trail slightly. History popular with oversubscribed library lunch-time club (library lunch time clubs generally oversubscribed anyway). Clubs for almost everything, often curriculum related: maths, chess etc.

Computers everywhere, six suites, plus 'computers in a box' – a mobile trolley armed with 20 laptops which motors round each class room in turn. Good support for learning; one-to-one, plus support teaching, as well as curricular support for the staff; advice on how to differentiate work sheets and the like. Sixth form help with 'paired reading for younger members. Prefects also 'befriend' younger pupils – either for specific subjects or just general back-up. Number of statemented pupils ('record of needs' as it is known in Scotland). Recognised fast track for primary pupils, who may combine studies in both places. French and German, plus optional Spanish, with Urdu on the side. Masses of trips abroad in every discipline. Year tutor stays with that class for their time at school. Classrooms and facilities used by adults and locals out of hours – this is a community school in all but name.

Games, Options, The Arts: House system (nations) in place, but mainly for games. Mass of rugby/football pitches; the school does well on the games front with masses of individual and team activities; athletics, badminton, cross-country, fencing and curling. Rugby and football for both boys and girls; plus basketball. Ski trip to the States in 2003. As ever, problems with those who think it cool not to play the game (any game). Swimming pool much used and FPs (who have a rather posh sports pavilion on campus) use all the sporting facilities (car parking a bit tight).

Music strong. Long-established pairing arrangement with Munich and Italy where school orchestras perform in each other's home towns in alternate years; outstandingly popular concert, choral and orchestra, which used to be in the Usher Hall. Jazz, woodwind, but no pipe band. Mass of choices. The Keith Thompson 'KT', singers are much in demand and contribute a sizeable amount to the Sir Malcolm Sargent Fund for Children at Christmas each year. Drama on the up, strong links with the Edinburgh Festival fringe. Art soldiering on in the current circumstances – life in a portacabin is not necessarily conducive to productivity.

Background and Atmosphere: Unique history: dates from 1128, the school 'provided education for 60 boys'; the site most people associate with the school is on Calton Hill, a site much loved by the telly news cameras. (Think overnight vigils, think home rule for Scotland). Girls admitted in 1974. Established on the current site in 1968, the school buildings have been recently completely refurbished under a PFI scheme completed August 2003 with half the school refurbished and the other half in new build. One constant however, is the memorial door, out of which each graduating student steps, to be greeted on the other side by the president of the former pupils club. The huge marble door is a memorial to those who died in the first world war and the west-facing stained-glass windows to FPs who fell in the second. 'Significant prize-giving'. Highly vaunted end of school leavers dance, often held in Edinburgh City Chambers, strong charity commitment.

Uniform worn by all, with a variety of sports and club ties. 'Bonding' week during the first year, when the whole class plus class teachers take off during November/December.

Pastoral Care and Discipline: Regular assemblies, good, strong PSE programme, school has to follow City of Edinburgh 'guidelines', so difficult to exclude, but will do so in the case of drugs, bullying, physical or otherwise, and abuse. Strong prefectorial presence. Very few 'refusers'. 'Civilised guidance strategies in place,' says the head. Regular school assemblies.

Pupils and Parents: Strong PTA and School Board organisation, basically 'affluent middle class, but a very wide intake – with a whole range of social and ethnic backgrounds', the catchment area covers Davidsons Mains, Clermiston, Blackhall and Cramond. The school is capped at a 200 pupil intake and there is always a waiting list.

Entrance: Automatic but see above. Some join the school from other state schools post standard grades, otherwise, 'penny numbers' arrive on a re-location basis.

Exit: In 2002, 91 per cent of all pupils stayed for fifth year (ie Highers) and 75 per cent stayed for sixth year. Trickle to Oxbridge, masses to the Scottish universities or tertiary education. FPs include Sir Walter Scott, Alexander Graham Bell, Lord Cockburn, Ronnie Corbett, Sarah Boyack (MSP) and the principal of St Andrew's University.

Money Matters: Current building has been revamped under the aegis of the PPP. Regular PTA fund-raising including discos and jumble sales, tranche of endowments (including Mary, Queen of Scots) provide tiny scholarships for pupils who have done well of the school; not a lot, 'just a nice wee extra'.

Remarks: This is a high school in the old fashioned sense – strong discipline and work code, good results, masses of extra-curricular activities – which also doubles as a local centre with adult learning classes and much use of the sports facilities. You can't get much better for nowt.

ROYAL HIGH SCHOOL, BATH GDST

Linked to Royal High School, Bath, Junior School GDST in the Junior section

Lansdown Road, Bath, BA1 5SZ

Tel: 01225 313 877
Fax: 01225 420 338
E-mail: d.sheppard@bat.gdst.net
Website: www.gdst.net/royalhighbath

- Pupils: 600 girls (approx 500 day, 100 boarding) • Ages: 11-18
- Size of sixth form: 150 • Non-denom • Fees: Seniors: boarding £4,814, day £2,455. Juniors: £1,779 • Independent
- Open days: Usually a Saturday in early November and a Thursday in late April

---

Head: Since 2000, Mr James Graham-Brown (fifties), previously head of Truro High School (also all girls), educated at Sevenoaks, University of Kent, University of Bristol. Popular with staff and parents. Totally committed to single-sex education (as is the head of the junior department), he is the first man to head a GDST school. In his fifties, but seems much younger, fit (ex-professional cricketer), dapper even. Carefully spoken but with conviction, having strong opinions on education and educating girls, and sure to make his mark on the school. Teaches English to all year groups, including junior school, and PE to sixth form. Passionate about literature and theatre. Married with two teenage daughters.

Academic Matters: There was some worry about academic achievement when the two schools (Bath Royal and the High School) merged in 1998. However, both GCSE and A level results have remained consistently good (overall pass rates of over 95 per cent) across the board. With the merger of the two schools, there has been a number of staff changes and new appointments, with the result that the number of male teachers has increased – generally felt to be a good thing in a single-sex school. Sciences are strong and popular at A level, with biology in particular having consistently good results. Resources for science are impressive, with separate facilities for sixth form, and flexibility at GCSE with both double science and separate subjects. Excellent language teaching reflected in the results, and a good choice too – French, German, Spanish, Greek, Latin, Italian, Chinese. Languages not just reflecting overseas pupils – the school has a long-standing exchange programme with China and its own member of staff teaching Mandarin. Good provision for special needs, in particular dyslexia and EFL. Senior SENCO Mrs Teasdale who is also head of food technology has 60 girls on her special needs register. This is not the school for a seriously challenged girl. The Royal Bath is 'a highly academic school' and the girls 'pretty much cope extremely well'. One-to-one or small groups, £12 an hour, no lessons missed, either before, after school or during lunch.

Games, Options, The Arts: Girls are encouraged to be themselves and 'aim for excellence' in whatever field appeals. Drama is very strong, and the Memorial Hall is well kitted out for performances, of which there seems to be a continuous programme. Everyone does PE, lots of outdoor sports. Well-equipped sports hall with dance studio. Sporting achievements reflect the diversity on offer – diving, showjumping, rowing. About a third of pupils take individual music lessons, there are choirs, orchestras and a swing band. 'We don't shout about the music but it is of very high quality'. Although art is valued within the school and there are interesting, and often large, pieces of work displayed, it is only compulsory up to year 9; not many go on to art school. Technology gets more timetable time and includes information technology, design technology, and food technology (very popular). There is a programme of activities on Saturdays, and outings on Sundays, which are open to all.

Background and Atmosphere: Impressive but somehow austere Gothic architecture in the main school, not welcoming but doesn't seem to bother the girls. Huge overwhelming internal spaces and corridors seem to suppress rather than magnify noise, and the school feels cool and calm. Plenty of space, and the many common rooms encourage mixing and 'the opening up of friendships'. Lovely boarding facilities, on two sites according to age, girls sharing rooms of generous size between two or three. Sleepover facility and provision for friends to stay for tea, or to do homework, is an added bonus for working parents. Boarding is popular and usually over-subscribed. No house system for boarders – prefer vertical pastoral structure for boarders 'to promote a sense of one community', all very friendly. Four day houses, with fine names – Austen, Du Pre, Wollstonecraft and Brontb – for the whole school for competition purposes. No boys, and really very little contact with boys – 'the problem is a lack of single-sex boys' schools in the area'. Links with Beechen Cliff for drama and involvement with Kingswood for Model United Nations, also joint debating with King Edward's School. But some parents (and many girls) are disappointed that there is not more opportunity for mixing.

Pastoral Care and Discipline: Manners and courtesies are taught and expected, with a very strong emphasis on self-discipline and self-sufficiency. Smart dress code, the uniform with tweedy skirt, often worn quite short, perpetuates the 'Angela Brazil' image that the school has, in reality, moved away from. Sixth formers wear suits. Jewellery and pierced ears are discouraged and therefore decidedly low-key or absent.

Pupils and Parents: In the main, girls come from professional families where both parents work, living in the city of Bath or surrounding villages; could do with its own school bus – and parents are beginning to lobby on this front. Wide social mix; girls are confident, polite, sure of themselves and instilled with 'can do' ethos. Small numbers from overseas, the school has a policy of only two from any one country in each year group in order to encourage integration and English language learning.

Entrance: As selective as possible, by school's own exam at 11, with just under 50 per cent coming up through junior department. It is also possible to enter at years 8, 9,10 subject to passing exams in English and maths, but there are no formal dates for these. Entry to sixth form is dependent on a minimum of six GCSEs with top grades for subjects to be taken at A level.

Exit: Some leave after GCSE to join co-educational schools, majority go on to sixth form and then higher education with the overwhelming majority getting places at their first choice university.

Money Matters: The GDST has its own means-tested bursary scheme, maximum value is the full day fee. There are also a number of Trust Entrance Scholarships awarded on merit for a few year 7 entrants, these offer reduced fees

(up to 50 per cent) for duration of school career. Services discount.

Remarks: A good, solid, GDST school. Not too flashy, emphasis on providing good value, all-round education with an emphasis on the academic side but no hothousing. Parents feel that the school offers good value for money – 'you might get a bit more elsewhere, but you'd be asked to pay for it'.

RUDOLF STEINER SCHOOL

Linked to Rudolf Steiner Junior School in the Junior section

Hood Manor, Dartington, Totnes, Devon, TQ9 6AB

Tel: 01803 762 528
Fax: 01803 762 528
E-mail: enquiries@steiner-south-devon.org
Website: www.steiner-south-devon.org

• Pupils: 285; 140 boys, 145 girls • Ages: 3-16 • Christian foundation • Fees: £810-£1,150 • Independent

Head: None. Non-hierarchal system; a 'college of teachers'. 'It has its ups and downs,' say parents; the principle is that sharing leadership lends itself to more diplomatic, well-rounded and better thought-out policies despite lengthier deliberation. Point of contact for parents is education manager and parent facilitator Gillian Mills, late thirties. She joined the school in 2002, following a career in local government and off-shore banking/trust fund administration. Has two children at the school; interests include gardening, walking, sailing and furthering her knowledge of Steiner Waldorf education.

Academic Matters: GCSEs not rated highly (only entered for four GCSE exams) with results in them around the national average. The Steiner curriculum focuses on the 'evolution of consciousness' eg progressing from fairy tales to farming, moving on to local, European and world-wide geography. Lots of cross-curricular links. In the upper school, ages 14-16, specialist teachers bring foreign languages, music, sports and crafts into the classroom. School trips are described as 'inspirational', 'social', 'fun' by pupils and parents. They are integrated into the curriculum theme and organised for every year including a trip to Germany to study history of art and work on a surveying project involving camping on-site. Teaching quality/commitment is high. Only one class per year and only one teacher per class, therefore teachers are like second parents – first point of call if problems arise.

Games, Options, The Arts: Pictures decorate the walls created with natural plant pigment using a 'wet on wet' Steiner technique. Everyone plays a musical instrument. Piano, violin, cello, flute, clarinet, guitar, saxophone, trumpet, trombone, horn, accordion and recorder lessons. Some parents like the way music and the arts are 'given as much preference as academic subjects'. No competitive sports (although basketball is played internally). Football forbidden except for class 9 and 10 students between 12.45 and 1.30pm on the Turnip Field on Wednesdays. Parents believe this prevents it monopolising all other sports. Football enthusiasts can join out-of-school clubs. Instead, pupils enjoy rock climbing, canoeing, swimming and Bothma gymnastics – reminiscent of Tai Chi. Duke of Edinburgh often available.

Background and Atmosphere: The South Devon Rudolf Steiner School was initially founded by parents as a small kindergarten in 1979 before settling at Hood Manor where it continues to expand. Outline planning permission to extend the upper school to cater for 16-18-year-olds has been granted, alongside a new tract of kindergarten buildings and a sports hall that would greatly improve the facilities. Appeal under way. Younger pupils confidently approach teachers. Youngsters' imagination and creativity abound, in the classroom and out. Teachers have transformed part of the attractive wooded grounds into a play area with rope-bridge and tree house. A neatly-wrapped parcel of leaves and berries will be presented to you on ordering from the children's pretend playground café. Wheat (ground and used for bread baked and eaten by the pupils) flowers, fruit and vegetables are harvested from the pupils' biodynamic garden and sold at the mid-week sale. The wild strawberries are a tasty treat for those who find them first. Parental involvement is central to school's life and well being – mums and dads expected to clean/decorate classroom, make curtains, maintain grounds, help with class events such as camping trips, plays or transport. A grind for some parents, but they accept it's all part of the contract.

Pastoral Care and Discipline: Not an extended hippy community as some may perceive. Equally they don't put pupils into blazers and 'address people as "sir" to create discipline'. Strict on rules. Immediate suspension if pupils found smoking at school, expulsion for third offence. Possession of drugs or alcohol can lead to immediate expulsion. No sign of graffiti. No mention of bullying or aggressiveness. Parents refer to 'strong positive relationships' between peer groups. Some parents/pupils like the continuity that they have with one teacher throughout lower and upper school (additional specialist teachers introduced in upper school). Parents say 'It's the care and consideration

that teachers give to individual pupils that stands out'. Emphasis on developing the physical, emotional and spiritual side in unison.

Pupils and Parents: 'Wholesome-looking' children. Real clarity of expression on faces perhaps due to rich educational experiences. One parent said, 'I think the pupils are encouraged to ask questions to discover what there is to be discovered!' Taught to help one another. Socially delightful. 10 per cent from abroad but with English residency. Estate agents aware parents move to Dartington to be near school. Very few working class families. Lots of 'cultural creatives', former company owners, bank managers, lawyers, who have moved to Devon for its beauty and tranquillity. Many special needs. Caters well for dyslexics but serious cases may leave to benefit from LEA-funded specialist support.

Entrance: Entrance to Upper School (Class 8) is not automatic. Meetings with parents to assess 'commitment'.

Exit: At age 11 average of three pupils leave for Exeter or Kevics College, Totnes. Some to Atlantic College at 16, or Cornwall – a centre of excellence for English and dramatic art. Students mostly move on to local colleges at 16, and seem to do well there.

Money Matters: Lots of bursary places available, applicants judged on individual merit. Christmas market at nearby Totnes Civic Centre is a big fund-raiser and hugely supported by parents.

Remarks: Child-focused with a caring and homely environment.

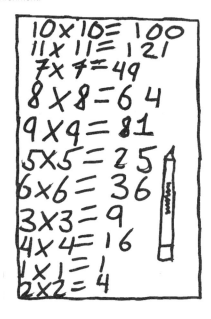

RUGBY SCHOOL

Lawrence Sheriff Street, Rugby, Warwickshire, CV22 5EH

Tel: 01788 556 216

Fax: 01788 556 277

E-mail: registry@rugbyschool.net

Website: www.rugbyschool.net

- Pupils: 805 in total: 370 boys boarding, 75 day; 295 girls boarding 65 day • Ages: 11-18 (day pupils only at 11 and 12)
- Size of sixth form: 341 • C of E • Fees: Day £6,900-13,800 pa; boarding £21,750 pa • Independent

Head: Since 2001, Mr Patrick Derham BA PGCE (forties), who started life on the naval training ship Arethusa, a 19th century wooden frigate, now in cold storage. Training on the Arethusa was abandoned quite suddenly, and he found himself at Pangbourne, from whence he read history at Pembroke College, Cambridge. His early teaching career was at Radley, where he became housemaster, before joining Solihull School as headmaster in 1996. He still teaches an A level set, 'vital to do it', and 'nice to teach an exam group'. He also delights in the fact that he is sitting in Thomas Arnold's study, complete with a contemporary portrait. He is potty about the Victorian period, so it is even more apt that boys (and now girls) still come and go through the staircase in the corner, through which boys could slide without having to run the gauntlet of the school secretary – as they did in the days of Tom Brown's Schooldays (and indeed as this editor did, on the way to her car). Said staircase recently starred in TV programme with Stephen Fry impersonating Thomas Arnold.

'This is not a highly selective single-sex boarding school but a broad church where everyone is encouraged to achieve their full potential.' Has had two of his own children in the school (one remains), which has worked well, 'a tribute to the school'. Not a lot of tinkering with the staff and he is first to acknowledge the change in ethos engineered by previous head Michael Mavor, who transformed a backward and bullying school into its superb present. Head conscious of modern realities – 'you're walking a political tightrope. It's important for the school to remain true to its traditions and values but we can't rest on our laurels and we have to move forward.'

Academic Matters: Has come shooting up the FT league tables, with a very strong showing in mathematics, physics, chemistry and economics at A level (and these of course may yet be improved). Recent English results phenomenal, also politics, art, classic and photography but not too many geographers, despite the extraordinary geog room. Business studies and economics popular, as is biology, interestingly computing is an A level rather than the European Driving Licence. All pupils now have their own laptops or computers and a stiff little plea is enclosed with the school bumf requesting that pupils have school issue, which makes servicing them that much easier. Many classrooms now have Prometheus whiteboards.

Wide range of languages on offer: French, German, Spanish, Russian plus Japanese, Chinese, Arabic and Italian – all getting As, might well be native speakers. Trip to St Petersburg for Russian speakers last Easter. Other trips include Paris, Vienna, Ecuador. New state of the art lang labs, with computers and software in every language. Japanese and Italian are also offered as non-examinable options. Three separate sciences at GCSE for all but the bottom set; all are streamed and setted in every subject. Class sizes max 24 and down. Labs undergoing serious rearrangement, certain amount of new build, with an interesting window in the biology lab, angled to get more sunlight; the complex must be hideous to work in. However, phase 6 of new build now complete. Transformation in the common room, much younger staff and quite a high proportion of women. Dyslexia provision on tap, OK dyspraxia ('tremendous team, getting better and better') and EFL programme in situ. Enrichment programme for academic scholars. Loads of extra-curricular clubs.

Games, Options, The Arts: 'Huge investment' recently in sports facilities but school still boasts the only listed gym in the world and it is still in use (looks like a church). Town uses their Astroturfs, tennis courts and cricket wickets as well as pool – on the main campus. Rugby, cricket, tennis, hockey and athletics all stunning. Polo on the ascendancy. PE A level quite popular. Swimming pool available to all from 7am, early bird swimming.

Art flourishing and spectacular and photography dept much improved – 'outstanding' says school. Professional stuff this, locals use the studio, and 16 pupils took the subject at A level last year. GCSE drama and theatre studies offered at A level and an utterly stunning all singing and dancing Macready theatre. Oodles of productions, including a Latin play – 'magic'. Modern langs 'culture evening', recent productions include West Side Story, The Crucible, Snow White. Fantastic media studio with all the gear for pupils to practise making tapes, videos and cut their own CDs. Magical music, with masses of orchestras, bands and huge concert hall and, vibrant throughout the year, music at A level. Orchestras, choirs, ensembles – everything you would expect from a school of this size and importance. Keen voluntary CCF, loads of community service and other charity input.

Background and Atmosphere: Founded in 1567 but metamorphosed as a Victorian 'railway' school in the 19th century. Home of the famous Dr Arnold of Tom Brown's Schooldays. Head anxious to dispel the Tom Brown image. 'It has gone', he says. Imposing buildings, very much in the middle of the town, heavy traffic on one side of the campus. The glorious Victorian library has had a face lift, which, for some reason, has included covering the old stone staircase in blue nylon carpet. Why? Feels rather like north Oxford, with school houses scattered all over the place. Sixth form centre, a house in its own right, has a bar and those over 18 and house prefects allowed out into Rugby on Sat nights. Three-weekly weekends off, school buzzes at weekends – buzzes all the time really, everyone seems to be involved in half a dozen things at once.

School went fully co-ed in 1993. Now has seven houses for girls and eight for boys, which will bring the number of boarding houses to an astonishing fifteen by 2005, and increasing the boy/girl ratio to 55/45. All pupils eat in their own houses, one of the last large public schools to do this, head 'wouldn't dream of changing this' (hurrah!) – despite the fact it costs a bomb to get all the kitchens up to scratch. 'Social' eating in each others' houses by invitation. Girls' houses very civilised, particularly the sixth form one, Stanley (the food is reasonable here too). Boys' houses have been less ritzy, but a huge amount of dosh has been put into upgrading them. Refurbishing programme rather like the Forth Bridge in place. Two day houses.

Girls' uniform elegant long skirts, now redesigned so that it is possible to run in them, they swan round the place looking elegant with tweed jackets. Wish list includes new mod langs area, senior common room, and to finish the science development programme – which seemed pretty far through when we visited. School has its own language: co = roll call; levee = school prefects.

Pastoral Care and Discipline: Well, first of all forget the fagging of Tom Brown's Schooldays. Very strong pastoral care and PSHE in place and each pupil is issued with a book of Guidelines for Life at Rugby School, which details everything, from bedtime to fast food carry-outs (delivery before 9.00pm and never on Friday or Saturday). Stringent anti-bullying policy, stealing is unacceptable, final warnings and being sent home are the normal sanctions. Strict guidelines about where the sixth formers can eat and drink and how much, in place. No fags at any time. Crescent Centre =

bar. Boozing in school hours has a variety of sanctions, four sins and you're out. Counselling for smokers. Using drugs does not necessarily equal out, though out if dealing, otherwise random testing may be required (and if positive, out).

Pupils and Parents: The girls' ('and boys', prompts school) coeducational school of choice. So girls from all over and not many first-time buyers here. Otherwise from the Midlands, sprinkling from overseas, Scotland regard it as 'just down the road', the north of England and London. Wide social range but school is not 'snobby' and not impressed by social credentials. 12 per cent are sons or daughters of ORs, who usually regard the place with nostalgia. ORs Rupert Brooke (who has a girls' house named after him), Bishop Hugh Montefiore, Ian (Lord) Laing, Robert Hardy, A N Wilson and Anthony Horowitz as well as Tom King, Salman Rushdie, Lewis Carroll, Harry Flashman and Tom Brown.

Entrance: Oversubscribed, interview with school the lent term of the year before entrance – ie four terms before CE. Takes from a huge range of prep schools. Front runner is The Dragon but recent years have had a stunning 80 feeder schools. Approximately 10 per cent from overseas, either ethnic or ex-pats. Sixth form entry equals a day-long programme of exams and interviews and six GCSEs including Bs in A level subjects – very competitive. School comments that an IQ below 110 would be struggling. Choice of house may be deferred until nearer the time of entry and, in any case, head tries to avoid clique houses.

Exit: Careers dept 'extraordinarily good'; all go on to further education (the Services are an option), with a stunning 15 per cent of leavers going to Oxbridge last year. Edinburgh and London popular, also the perennial chestnuts, Newcastle and Bristol. Not a lot going into art or music schools.

Money Matters: Huge numbers of scholarships and bursaries, and major schols for those living within ten miles of the school. Over 20 per cent on some sort of a bursary. The original foundation was for 'local boys' to be educated. Will keep any child to the next level in times of hardship. School owns property in London, including Great Ormond Street. Newly launched Arnold Foundation offers up to 100 per cent scholarships to boarders otherwise unable to afford fees. Scholarships now up to only 10 per cent but augmentable up to 100 per cent in case of need.

Remarks: Famous public school going from strength to strength. Has undergone huge changes in the last few years and is now one of the most popular, and deservedly so, number one choice among all the co-ed boarding schools. The co-ed school of choice at sixth form level and many are turned away. Friendly, hard-working and fun.

RYDE SCHOOL WITH UPPER CHINE

Linked to Ryde School with Upper Chine, Junior School in the Junior section

Queen's Road, Ryde, Isle of Wight, PO33 3BE

Tel: 01983 562 229
Fax: 01983 564 714
E-mail: headmaster@rydeschool.org.uk
Website: www.rydeschool.org.uk

- Pupils: 490 boys and girls, 50 board (mostly weekly), rest day
- Ages: 11-18 • Size of sixth form: 100 • C of E • Fees: Senior school £2,730 • Independent

Head: Since 1997, Dr Nicholas England MA DPhil, previously at Wellington College for some 19 years. A physicist, he still teaches, using his own textbook, 'Physics Matters'. 'We are very impressed with him,' said a parent. 'He's always approachable, always available,' said another. 'Since he's been there the pastoral side has taken off and he's well liked and respected by the pupils.' Both his children moved to Ryde School when he became head. 'It was wonderful to see them enjoying it and exceeding my expectations.' Many of the other staff have children at the school. Two extremely capable deputies.

Academic Matters: A non-selective school. 'Our profile is about half-way between a typical state comprehensive and a selective independent.' Some very high-flyers – 'and it is as good as any mainland public school at the top end,' said a parent of one – and about 15 per cent receiving learning support (mainly dyslexics but a couple of children with Asperger's), plus the whole spectrum of ability in between. About 90 per cent get five A*-C grades at GCSE. The more practical subjects are very successful – art, drama, IT, music and PE show up well at GCSE, while biology and physics look weaker, though they are popular A level choices. Twenty-four A level subjects, including environmental science, government and political studies, psychology and theatre studies. 'And the school is very flexible about A level choices,' said a parent. 'If you let them know your options in time they will do their best to accommodate them.' Around half the A level grades are A or B. Chemistry results particularly good, with 90 per cent A and B grades over the last few years; languages also come up well, though with much smaller numbers. Many do general studies.

Class size is around 15 or 16, divided into four streams for most subjects. Two ICT rooms, plus a trolley with 20 laptops; a number of classrooms have Powerpoint and interactive white boards. In 1997, Ryde took over Bembridge School, which specialised in learning support. As a result, that department is particularly strong, housed in its own unit with pictures of famous dyslexics (eg Einstein) on the wall alongside photos of its own pupils and their achievements. But the head emphasises that while he wants the school to cater for any Island children with special needs – though not behavioural problems – who want an independent school education, he does not intend to expand the department. 'We have a good balance of children and I do not want to upset that.' High calibre, committed staff. 'Hard work is rewarded and respected,' said a parent. 'The children are motivated and set their sights high.'

Games, Options, The Arts: Excellent music, with four choirs, an orchestra and a jazz combo (and good exam results, with virtually all candidates getting A and B grades at GCSE). 'The standard is higher than I would have thought possible,' said a parent. Music tours abroad every year to eg Barcelona and Verona. The annual school musical, performed in Ryde Theatre to an audience of paying public as well as parents, 'is reckoned to be the best amateur dramatics on the island,' says the head; parents agree. The art department produces excellent work in limited space; the new head of art is particularly keen on 3D work and is planning a sculpture exhibition in the grounds of a nearby monastery. 'My daughter finds him inspirational,' said a parent. DT also popular and imaginative, with pupils working in any medium from stained glass to concrete. The new 3D milling machine linked to a computer enables pupils to feed their computer-aided design straight into the machine. 'Our practical subjects are particularly good,' says the head.

A variety of sports are played on the school's 17 acres of playing fields (including a rifle range), tennis courts and a sports hall on site, plus an Astroturf hockey pitch a mile away. Teams play Island state schools ('though they often can't get a team together,' said a parent) and mainland independent schools; the girls' hockey and netball teams are particularly successful. Swimming at the public pool down the road – 'it's far cheaper and easier to use someone else's pool'. The school has four houses, mostly for sporting and other competitions. 'The younger ones are very competitive over the Citizenship cup.' CCF is available in year 10 for one afternoon a week, with air force or navy options. 'My children loved it for the sailing,' said a parent. 'They didn't take the parading terribly seriously but there were lots of opportunities to go on exciting camps for amazingly low prices.' Reports of these camps fill several pages of the school magazine. One pupil at 16 became the youngest person to sail across the Atlantic. 'His parents asked if it would disrupt his GCSEs. I said of course it will but it will look very good on his CV.' D of E popular. 'It's one of the things Mrs Till-Dowling (a new deputy head) is involved in,' said a parent. 'She's absolute fireworks.' Notwithstanding the barrier of the Solent, which can limit off-Island school trips, the whole school recently had an outing to London, with visits to plays and art galleries, the Planetarium and the Science Museum.

Background and Atmosphere: Founded in 1921 and moved to its present site in 1928; in 1995 it merged with Upper Chine girls' boarding school, and in 1997 took over Bembridge School, which specialised in learning support and had a large number of overseas pupils. It is now more-or-less the only independent school on the Island, and its fortunes tend to depend on the reputations of Island state schools. Ordered but relaxed atmosphere. Pleasant situation at the top end of Ryde, a 10 minute walk from the esplanade where hovercrafts and Seacats dock; at least one family commutes from Portsmouth every day. Buildings range from the Georgian admin and sixth form block to the light, galleried library block which was built in 2000. The science block was refurbished in 1997; the head has hopes for a cantilevered gallery addition to the 200-seater school theatre. The junior school has been newly expanded. The boarding houses are six miles away at Bembridge, overlooking 100 acres of playing fields and woodland.

Pastoral Care and Discipline: 'I was impressed that the head wanted to show us round at break-time,' said a parent. 'That's when a lot of heads want to keep you clear. But the children were very courteous.' Discipline firm but low key. 'We don't have institutionalised bullying; we do have personality differences. We use a no-blame policy and we tend to be successful by sorting it out without making it a huge deal. Calling in the parents is usually enough.' 'PHSE is superbly taught,' said a parent. 'It addresses real issues.' Two expulsions in the past five years, one for supplying drugs. 'If a head hasn't expelled for that they don't know what's going on in the school.'

Pupils and Parents: About half of the boarders are from Portsmouth naval families; a few full boarders from overseas. The day pupils, from a wide cross-section of families, come from all round the Island (and one or two from the mainland). 'Island children tend to be very pleasant,' says the head.

Entrance: Non-selective but all are interviewed by the head, do some maths and English and an IQ test. 'We want

to ensure that they're of a standard to fit into the school. The tests are to look for discrepancies between their IQ and their maths and English standards. We hope everyone will get five A*-C GCSEs, and unless they're going to get close to that they won't feel comfortable here.' Three or four a year turned away, mostly for misbehaviour. Most go through to the sixth form. 'We accept people into the sixth form whom we believe will cope with A levels. Normally, we would recommend a starting baseline of three B and three C grades at GCSE.' The school has open days but prospective parents can make an appointment to look round at any time.

Exit: About 90 per cent to university, mostly redbrick; three or four a year to Oxbridge.

Money Matters: Some means-tested assisted places, plus a few external scholarships worth 10 per cent of fees, which can be added to an assisted place. Because the Island has a middle school system, the senior school's main intakes are into years 5, 7, 9 and 12, and its awards are available at all these times.

Remarks: A mixed, non-selective school that aims to cater for any Island child that wants an independent education, plus a few mainland boarders. Particularly strong on practical subjects. 'My daughter has been very well taught and has developed a real love for nearly all of her subjects,' said a satisfied parent.

RYEDALE SCHOOL

Gale Lane, Nawton, York, North Yorkshire, YO62 7SL

Tel: 01439 771 665
Fax: 01439 770 697
E-mail: admin@ryedale.n-yorks.sch.uk
Website: www.ryedale.n-yorks.sch.uk

• Pupils: 572 boys and girls • Ages: 11-16 • No religious affiliation • State

Head: Since 1993, Geoff Jenkinson BEd (Nottingham) MA (Open University) (fifties). Married, two children, wife also teaches. Previous posts include deputy headship at Worle School, Weston-super-Mare. Big believer in rolling up sleeves and getting the job done. 'In all the other schools I've worked in, there's been a limit to what you can achieve. Here the size of the school and the support of the community means that you can make changes and very quickly see results because people pull together.' Example – cost of new music suite, paid for through fund-raising, was halved when school decided to manage the building project itself. Well, if you want a job doing …

Academic Matters: Broadly average intake, well above average results. Pledge to parents that 60 to 70 per cent of pupils will gain at least five A* to C GCSEs each year. Good results with special needs and no-one leaves without at least one GCSE. School achievement award for excellent results.

The secret? Hard work. Lessons rattle along at a cracking pace and students are fired up for learning. Good thing, too, because this is no school for shirkers. Regular diligence reports grade pupils not on what they're achieving, but how hard they're trying. A-grade pupils can be in firing line if more effort would mean A*s. Across the board slacking leads to monitoring by the school – and a chat with mum. 'No parent wants to hear in an end-of-year report that their child hasn't been working hard. If there's a problem, they want to know about it at the time – and they want us to sort it out,' says head.

Games, Options, The Arts: Ryedale's undoubted speciality. No such thing as a lunch break in this hell-for-leather school. No-one goes off-site at lunchtime – not least because there's nowhere to go – so Ryedale crams its lunch hours with all manner of extras, from sport to composing, creative writing to cribbage. All voluntary, but volunteering is this school's forte. In one morning alone, 87 children out of

a year group of 116 spotted a notice for the Duke of Edinburgh awards and signed up for more info. These kids are up for anything – canoeing, fund-raising, handing out sticky buns at a pensioners' party. Mother Theresa would have loved this school.

Success breeds success. 'What we have noticed is that those who get involved in the most activities also achieve the most academically,' says head. 'There's a fine balance between getting the best out of children in exams and squeezing them so hard that they have no chance to do all the other things that children need to do as part of growing up.' Already holds Sport England sportsmark and has excellent community links. Future plans include becoming specialist performing arts college, hopefully bringing new studio theatre and no doubt a whole new raft of projects for these eager beavers to volunteer for.

Background and Atmosphere: Fifty-year-old school in the middle of nowhere. Draws pupils from nearby Helmsley, Kirkbymoorside and a vast chunk of the glorious North York Moors. This isn't just school for many of the pupils, it's their entire social life. Some have an hour-long journey so be prepared to join the chauffeur rota if your child and his pals like after-school sport. Head has pupils up on stage for a pat on the back for any achievement. 'I never want a pupil here to have that feeling that if you do something special you have to be ashamed of it. It is not uncool to achieve in this school.' We arrive unannounced in an English lesson where children are writing poetry. A 13-year-old is asked to read his work aloud. It's good, very good. His peers spontaneously applaud. We feel like we're in Narnia.

Pastoral Care and Discipline: Step out of line in this school if you dare. Sliding scale of punishments keeps children on the straight and narrow. Lots of support on discipline for teachers. 'If there's a problem, we want to know early so we can nip it in the bud,' says head. 'Pupils resent nothing more than a teacher who doesn't make them work.' Students like feeling of security, 'you don't ever feel excluded or picked on here,' says 15-year-old pupil. 'You feel safe.'

Entrance: Once seen as the poor relation because of its lack of sixth form, now rapidly growing and over-subscribed. Move into highly desirable catchment area or gamble on appeal.

Exit: More than 70 per cent go into further education all around the county and many ultimately to university.

Remarks: A school that believes there's more to life than GCSEs and still comes up with the goods in exams. Pupils leave with secondary school qualifications and primary school enthusiasm.

SACRED HEART HIGH SCHOOL

212 Hammersmith Road (Entrance Bute Gardens),
Hammersmith, London, W6 7DG

Tel: 020 8748 7600
Fax: 020 8748 0382
E-mail: ybrennan@sacredh.lbhf.sch.uk
Website: www.sacredh.lbhf.sch.uk

• Pupils: 780 girls, all day • Ages: 11-16 • RC • State

Head: Since 1992, Dr Christine Carpenter BA PhD FRSA (fifties). A hard-working head, known for having a keen interest in her girls and all their activities. 'Definitely a safe pair of hands and a no-nonsense head,' remarked one parent. A leader.

Academic Matters: A well-respected and committed team of teachers, majority are Catholic. Now a beacon school, helping other schools in the borough with good practice and to develop the skills of newly qualified teachers. GCSE results well above the national average – 60 plus per cent A*/A. Covers the National Curriculum plus – a wider range of subjects and activities is offered compared to some of its neighbouring schools. Good choices and results for modern languages; English and history departments are especially strong. Most classes are mixed ability though there is some streaming for English and maths. Modern science and technology wing (some parents would like to see more action in this department).

There is support for girls with learning difficulties and an effort is made to ensure that all pupils can access the curriculum. An enthusiastic attitude to studying prevails, everyone is expected to do their best. The girls are polite and well-motivated.

Games, Options, The Arts: A better than average sports programme, with tennis and netball as firm favourites though, as with many inner-city state schools, the sports facilities are not very extensive. Annual activity weeks, D of E. Some talented artists; not much music; drama and dance more popular.

Background and Atmosphere: The convent is built on an historic site with a long Catholic tradition; four different orders of nuns have taught girls here for the past 330 years. A grammar school until 1976 when it became comprehensive.

Pastoral Care and Discipline: A strong Catholic ethos. Many parents feel the school's size, which is smaller than average for a London state senior, is of particular benefit in promoting a friendly and supportive atmosphere. Girls all have year tutors. Links within the local community are given particular attention, girls are encouraged to want to live purposeful lives, think about and include others. Discipline is strict and a very high standard of behaviour is expected at all times.

Pupils and Parents: An inner-city multicultural mix, most live in Fulham, Hammersmith or neighbouring boroughs. The majority are very committed to the school and serious about education. OGs Pauline Collins and Patricia Hayes.

Entrance: At 11 years all applicants have an interview and take a non-verbal reasoning test, results are divided into three bands. Places then allocated 25 per cent top band, 50 per cent middle band, 25 per cent lower band to ensure a comprehensive intake. When any band is oversubscribed additional criteria come into play: first in the queue are practising Catholics whose first choice of school it is, then siblings, girls with a medical or social need and those who have attended a Catholic primary school. Parents need to complete an application form and return it with the child's baptism certificate and a reference from their parish priest. The test takes place in the autumn term and place offers are made in January.

Exit: At 16 most go on to take A levels at local sixth form colleges or other Catholic schools, a popular choice being St Charles sixth form college. A few go to the private sector.

Remarks: Traditional school aiming to promote the education of women and academic success. Doing a fairly good job with pupils of all abilities.

SAFFRON WALDEN COUNTY HIGH SCHOOL

Audley End Road, Saffron Walden, Essex, CB11 4UH

Tel: 01799 513 030
Fax: 01799 513 031
E-mail: info@saffronwalden.essex.sch.uk
Website: www.saffronwalden.essex.sch.uk

• Pupils: 2,000 boys and girls, all day • Ages: 11-18 • Size of sixth form: 500 • Non-denom • State • Open days: End September, plus tours in the week following

Head: Since 2004, Mr John Hartley MA (late forties). Born Leeds, educated Oundle and St Catharine's College, Cambridge. Has taught (physics) since then, most recently as head of Notley High School, Braintree. Enjoys fell walking, photography, social and local history.

Academic Matters: Children are setted for maths and languages (all children initially study French and German) by the end of year 7 and broad-banded in English and science from year 9. Otherwise they are taught in mixed ability groups right up to GCSE. Results well above the national average. Children with special needs well integrated in the school. Sixth formers have the option of doing work experience in Germany, France and Romania.

Sixth formers follow one of three routes, route one being for the most academically able pupils and requiring a minimum of five GCSEs in grades A*-B. Route two is for those with five GCSEs at grades A*-C. Route three is open to pupils with five GCSEs at grade D or above. Course options are determined by route.

Games, Options, The Arts: A strong emphasis on traditional team games, such as hockey, netball, rugby and cricket, with between 50 and 60 sports teams playing regularly, depending on the time of year. Artsmark Gold and Sportsmark Gold. Plenty of musical opportunities – 700 children learn an instrument and there are numerous choirs, orchestras, bands and ensembles. Many staff help lead the well established D of E programme, which is enormously popular, and there are plenty of other extra-curricular activities.

Background and Atmosphere: Set on the edge of the very pleasant town of Saffron Walden and surrounded by rolling countryside. Grounds are unusually extensive – there's even enough space for grass tennis courts (there are plenty of hard courts as well). Typically unimaginative 1950s architecture, although recent additions, particularly the new music block, have been thoughtfully designed. Very well-equipped sports centre. The school continues to invest heavily in its premises. 2005 saw the opening of a new multi-purpose hall, classroom block and library extension.

Pupils are generally happy with the school with few gripes apart from the usual – they have too much work and the uniform policy is too strict.

Pastoral Care and Discipline: The emphasis is on establishing relationships between staff and pupils. In years 7-11 each year group is headed by a senior tutor (head of year), who moves up the school with his or her year group and oversees academic and pastoral care. Each form also has a form tutor who remains with that form from years 7-11. Relatively few formal rules but pupils are expected to exercise self-discipline. Few exclusions, rarely more than one a year.

The only worry expressed by some parents is that the school is so big that it can be difficult for children to settle in, especially as many of them are moving on from very small primary schools; most children settle in well.

Pupils and Parents: Catchment area is predominately middle-class. A small number of pupils come from ethnic minorities, reflecting the make-up of the local population.

Entrance: Heavily oversubscribed. Siblings first, then residents of twelve listed parishes. There are a further six criteria but the vast majority of places are offered on the first two. 'To be sure of getting a place here, you do need to live in the catchment area,' says head.

The majority of pupils go on to the sixth form but there are around 40 places for newcomers. It's not uncommon for pupils from London to board with friends and relations in the area so that they can attend the sixth form.

Exit: Most go on to university, seven or eight going to Oxbridge.

Remarks: Highly regarded locally. A co-educational comprehensive with high academic standards and well-behaved children.

St Aidan's Church of England High School

Oatlands Drive, Harrogate, North Yorkshire, HG2 8JR

Tel: 01423 885 814

Fax: 01423 884 327

E-mail: admin@st-aidans.n-yorks.sch.uk

Website: www.st-aidans.n-yorks.sch.uk

- Pupils: 1,217 boys and girls; plus 604 in the joint sixth form
- Ages: 11-18 • Size of sixth form: Associated sixth form: 904 (604 from St Aidan's, 300 from nearby St John Fisher RC High School) • C of E but welcomes children from all Christian traditions; allocates 5 places per year for children from other faiths 'where the circumstances are clearly exceptional' • State

Head: Since 1989, Mr D Richards MA BD FRSA (mid fifties). Previously deputy head at Bishop Stopford C of E School, Kettering. Educated at Queen Elizabeth Grammar School, Wakefield. Read modern languages at Manchester University. Spent early part of career teaching in south Yorkshire state schools, before embarking on a degree in theology at King's, London. A teaching head with a highly visible profile around the school, often pops into lessons. A true Yorkshire man with a lovely Michael Parkinson lilt and shared passion for cricket. Has a genuinely Christian outlook on life and treats everyone with respect and kindness. Believes his early days teaching in south Yorkshire help him keep his feet firmly on the ground. He is well aware of the privileges afforded to the school and its pupils. Very highly thought of by all within and beyond the school, loyal and supportive staff, plenty of goodwill. Aims to produce pupils who are happy, tolerant, compassionate and rounded individuals. Member of QCA Advisory Committee to Tomlinson 14-19 group.

Academic Matters: Excellent value-added. Year on year, improvement in results at all levels. In 2005, 95 per cent gained 5 A*-Cs at GCSE with over 46 per cent A*/A considerably above the previous year. This is a proper comprehensive school, entering all children for exams, including those with special needs who are integrated into the main school (very good provision here). Head said one of his proudest moments was a pupil with Down's Syndrome receiving rapturous applause at the presentation evening for gaining two GCSEs. Setting in some subjects from year 7 increasing to all academic subjects by year 10. Excellent range of A level courses; 99 per cent pass rate (52 per cent

graded A/B), asssociated sixth form entered 414 A2 students – by far the largest school entry at that level. School gained specialist status in science in March 2003. Most subjects have fine accommodation adorned with first class displays of pupils' work and relevant information. The technology rooms are modern, bright and brimming with up-to-date equipment but growth of school means some lessons have to be carried out in inappropriate areas. Computers and modern technology throughout including a new £1 million data-handling suite opened in September 2004. Students regularly compete successfully in YORTEK and Young Engineers For Britain Competitions. Sixth formers have own study centres and facilities with a magnificent new library extension due to open in the spring of 2006.

Lively, innovative teaching, a variety of methods and styles, excellent use of modern technology. Pupils encouraged to think for themselves, to question and to investigate. Most classes 30 but lower ability and some options taught in smaller classes.

Games, Options, The Arts: One sports hall and one purpose-built fitness centre, well-maintained grounds. Lots of sport – strength in cricket, football and netball with many teams competing at national level. Superb new synthetic grass surface added in September 2004. Vibrant art department, with splendid displays, consistently secures excellent results at GCSE. Very good drama – one major and many minor productions performed each year, also touring theatre group puts on plays and workshops in the wider community. Eleven ensembles play under the guidance of the music department ably directed by Mark Pallant. Concert band in National Schools Prom in Royal Albert Hall in 2001; chamber choir achieved same accolade in 2003. Swing band also won National Festival event in 2004 and so become 3rd St Aidan's ensemble in 4 years to play in Schools' Prom at Royal Albert Hall, an unrivalled achievement. Own recording studio. Good range of outdoor pursuits, several older students achieve D of E gold.

Background and Atmosphere: Founded in 1969 in the renowned spa town of Harrogate close to the famous Stray. Originally a secondary modern school, it has grown steadily to accommodate ever-increasing numbers. Latest additions include a new dining room, modern languages and maths block and beautiful Constance Green Chapel Hall (named after a Harrogate philanthropist and benefactor), renowned for its acoustics and regularly used by the wider community. Award-winning careers library staffed by full-time careers officer.

You have to come from a committed Christian background to get here but there's no feeling of religion being rammed down your throat – just a genuinely caring Christian ethos where everyone is valued. The assembly we attended had prayers and story but otherwise just messages and information. A resounding hymn would have been nice but, we are told, new from September 2004 is Christian rock band, Aidan's Flame, which has revolutionised assembly music. Uniform doesn't have a blazer. Vast majority of girls now wear trousers.

Not easy to find a real downside to the school – and this editor tried awfully hard – stopped the fat boy (but he wasn't being bullied – at least not until we arrived …), went into classes (spent longer than intended as they were interactive, dynamic, fun …), got two of the more streetwise boys (of my choosing) to show me round – kept saying how good the football was and how they weren't very good at maths but the maths teacher was great and made lessons fun and interesting! (They then tried to hijack me and take me to meet the chap!) Spoke to locals, parents (of academic, average and SEN children), staff – and still had nothing untoward to report.

Pastoral Care and Discipline: Pastoral system swings into action as soon as pupils are allocated a place. Lots of meetings and visits for parents and pupils prior to arrival, trips and weekends away help year 7 bond as a group and settle into their surroundings. Staff very much put the children first and treat them as individuals. All children in years 7 to 10 must remain in school at lunch-time. School employs its own award-winning chef and excellent health-conscious food has attracted national attention (featured in Times and on BBC). Large proportion take part in extra-curricular activities organised by staff with some parental involvement.

Harrogate is prime drug territory – an affluent area situated close to Leeds and Bradford. School very aware – knows what goes on – effective policy of support – police involved where necessary (not usually minor first offence ie possession – though any intent to deal would involve immediate police contact). Strictly a no smoking school (staff and pupils). Any child excluded (figures are very low) can expect to receive help and support funded by the school in addition to that from the authority. Emphasis is very much on rewarding good behaviour and parental contact is usually instantaneous following any indiscretion by child – pupils very much aware of this.

Pupils and Parents: In a very middle class area – so social mix is not comprehensive – though there is the odd council house even in Harrogate. There are no pretensions here – Yorkshire folk are far too canny – and can spot a bargain – St Aidan's is certainly that – a state school that matches many independents. If you can't get in here then it's probably Ashville College, Harrogate Ladies, Leeds Grammar etc (ie parents will fork out if they have to). Parents are extremely supportive of the school (no wonder, after the efforts to secure a place). Plenty of fund-raising (though more goes to charities than to school). School raised a huge £33,000 for worthy causes in 2004-2005. Pupils are polite, articulate and considerate, demonstrating respect both for others and their environment.

Entrance: At 11. 66 per cent from town area, 34 per cent from wider area (diocese of Ripon). School very oversubscribed, lots of calls from people asking if purchasing a house in the catchment area will guarantee a place (absolutely not). Admission procedure is clearly laid down and locals know what needs to be done to get children in – 'start praying at conception, often and publicly', said one parent – and in reality it's much worse than that.

See website for full details but, in summary: approximately 150 places go to pupils living within the Harrogate catchment area and a further 76 to those outside. If more than 226 applications are received (and they always are), points are allocated as follows: where the family's main residence is within the geographical boundaries of the Archdeaconry of Richmond (9 points); frequency of attendance of the child at services, including Sunday school or Youth Fellowship in any branch of a Christian Church affiliated to Churches Together in England (weekly, fortnightly, monthly, occasionally and for how long this has been the case) (0-9 points); frequency of attendance of the parent(s) ditto (0-9 points); an older sibling in the school at the time of application (9 points); a parent or guardian working in the school (9 points); the child attends organisations working for the Church, or for the community or supports the Church in other ways, eg choristers, servers and readers (0-9 points); the voluntary service given by the child's parent or guardian to their church or to the community eg PCC membership; working for charitable organisations (0-9 points). Places allocated by the total number of points scored. Heaven's gates slammed firmly shut in the face of unbelievers; strong bias towards the middle classes in some of these criteria.

Exit: 96 per cent remain in full-time education at 16. Sixth formers – 86 per cent to higher education predominantly to northern universities, steady flow to Oxbridge, 9 per cent into employment, 5 per cent gap year.

Remarks: A top-flight state school, does well by its children regardless of ability or disposition. Only for Christians and a very few others.

St Albans Girls' School

Sandridgebury Lane, St Albans, Hertfordshire, AL3 6DB

Tel: 01727 853 134

Fax: 01727 831 157

E-mail: admin.stags@thegrid.org.uk

Website: www.stags.herts.sch.uk

• Pupils: 1,100 girls; all day; Boys in the VIth form come to us from consortium schools • Ages: 11-18 • Size of sixth form: 240 • Non-denom • State • Open days: A Thursday evening in early October

Headteacher: Since 2004, Mrs C Murrell BA,MEd, NPQH (fiftyish) married to John, also a teacher. Educated at West Park Girls Grammar Technical School Sunderland, Coundon Court School for girls in Coventry then University of Sussex school of education and later Nottingham University. Taught physical education and drama at Garth Hill Comprehensive in Bracknell, Tewkesbury High School and the Chase High School in Worcester where she was head of department and head of year. For ten years was teacher, SENCO and housemother with her husband who was senior housemaster to 80 boys at the King's School Peterborough. In 1994 became deputy headteacher at The Gleed Girls' School in Spalding and in 1998 became headteacher. Says of STAGS, 'it has a strong examination record but school is more than just lessons ... what sets us apart is how we care for the particular needs of individual girls, the strength of our links with parents, the expectations we have of every girl and the way we encourage her to be conscious of the needs of others'.

Academic Matters: Consistently very good academic results which is why it is a popular school. 88 per cent get 5 A*-C grades at GCSE (no separate sciences). At A level popular subjects are psychology, maths and media studies. Class sizes are good for a state school – 27 max. Setting in maths from Christmas in year 7 using MIDYIS scores and internal testing. All girls take French and most study a second language – Spanish or German. Language setting introduced from year 8. In years 7 to 9 there are extra English lessons as an alternative to a second language for girls with basic skills difficulties. Setting in science from year 9 and English from year 8.

Games, Options, The Arts: Strong in sport, music and drama. There are nine tennis courts, three hockey pitches, a cricket square, athletics track, outdoor pool and gym. Teams are very successful at district, county and national level. Pupils can choose from 20 extra-curricular music groups; two drama studios provide ample opportunity for those interested in taking part in performances or helping behind the scenes. Dance groups practise on a regular basis and take part in local productions with some girls taking part in national productions.

Background and Atmosphere: Founded in 1920, STAGS now occupies a large, modern site towards the north of the city. Some buildings are a bit dreary and in need of a lick of paint, however facilities have recently improved considerably because of specialist school status.

Pastoral Care and Discipline: Pastoral care is co-ordinated through year heads and prefects. All girls are placed in one of 7 houses. Each named after an important woman such as Jane Austen, Mary Seacole etc. Simple list of rules. Pupils are encouraged to take pride in their school. House points and commendations reward good work and behaviour. Learning support is available throughout the school.

Pupils and Parents: Mainly from St Albans and surrounding towns. Some affluent families who opt for STAGS rather than the private sector.

Entrance: At 11 from a wide range of primary schools in the area and 'in accordance with the county's admissions criteria.' Administration of admissions is carried out by Hertfordshire County Council and not by school and these 'criteria' are baffling to those who attempt to navigate their way through to a place. Parents complain of weird anomalies in terms of where accepted/refused pupils live and placements taking no account of whether or not applicants actually wanted a single sex school. Some mistake here surely.

Exit: Vast majority (over 80 per cent) goes on to higher education. Some Oxbridge entrants every year.

Money Matters: Has an excellent PTA known as Friends of STAGS which raises considerable amounts of money.

Remarks: While the exam results continue to be strong, STAGS will always be popular with those parents wanting a single-sex education in an all-ability school.

St Albans High School for Girls

Linked to Wheathampstead House in the Junior section

Townsend Avenue, St Albans, Hertfordshire, AL1 3SJ

Tel: 01727 853 800
Fax: 01727 792 516
E-mail: admissions@stalbans-high.herts.sch.uk
Website: www.sahs.org.uk

- Pupils: 950 girls, all day • Ages: 4-18 • Size of sixth form: 170
- Christian • Fees: £2,955 • Independent • Open days: October and November

Headmistress: Since 2005, Ms J C Pain, MA, MA, MBA. Mrs Pain was previously headteacher of the Henrietta Barnett School in London. Prior to this, she was deputy headmistress of Northwood College, London.

Academic Matters: At 11, girls are put into four parallel forms. Average class sizes 24, reducing to 20 at GCSE and 15 at A level. Four sets for maths. French, German, Latin and Spanish offered. Regular exchanges and visits abroad. Excellent results – 100 per cent A*-C at GCSE (nearly 70 per cent got A* or A grades). At A level 84 per cent A/B; art particularly strong – facilities are very good (two studios) with each A level pupil having their own dedicated workspace.

Special needs taken seriously. No statemented children but some pupils with dyslexia and dyspraxia. All girls are screened to ensure appropriate support is provided if necessary.

Games, Options, The Arts: Strong sporting tradition; sports fields are a ten-minute walk away. Girls play lacrosse, netball and tennis as well as doing gymnastics, modern dance and athletics; lots of other sports. Indoor pool and leisure complex under construction adjoining current sports hall for completion September 2006. Music and drama popular with half learning a musical instrument. Four orchestras, three bands, five chamber ensembles, four choirs and a choral society. Drama and theatre studies a popular GCSE and A level choice. Thriving clubs in gym, drama, choir, orchestra, sports acrobatics, fencing and tennis.

Background and Atmosphere: Founded in 1889, about half a mile from the centre of St Albans, referred to as The High School by locals to distinguish it from St Albans Girls' School. A strong, traditional, city school turning out successful, polite and confident girls who come from near, and as far as Bedfordshire and north London, courtesy of some 12 coach services. Entrance area gives the school a rather stuffy air but, walking about, the girls seem happy and lessons have a fun element. Separate primary school located in Wheathampstead, has its own gym/hall, music and computer rooms, library and science lab. The main school has seven bright science labs, two computer rooms housing both Apple Macs and PCs (all pupils have internet access), a technology centre, two fully-equipped food technology rooms and a well-stocked library with videos and computer facilities. Has close links with the diocese of St Albans through the Bishop who visits and the Dean who is a member of the Council of Governors.

Pastoral Care and Discipline: Minimal set of rules. Girls are expected to behave with common sense and consideration for others. Pastoral policy under the umbrella of a 'statement of care and consideration.' Uniform of navy blue blazer with a thin yellow stripe and airforce blue skirt. Sixth formers can wear own clothes (no shorts or crop tops), have their own common room with kitchen facilities and are allowed into the city centre. Head girl and four deputies are chosen by teachers and pupils after each has submitted a manifesto and spoken at 'hustings'.

Pupils and Parents: A wide mix from both state and independent schools. Pupils polite and confident. Old Girls include Dame Anna Neagle and Isobel Lang.

Entrance: Very oversubscribed. By assessment and interview, at 4,5 and 7 into the primary school and at 11 and 16 for the senior school. Vast majority of girls progress from the primary school to the senior school 'provided they have reached the expected standard'. The head talks to individual parents if she has concerns about the transition and may advise them in advance to look elsewhere.

Exit: A handful leaves post-GCSE to go to other schools or a local sixth form college. Otherwise, most do A levels then leave for first degrees at a wide selection of universities across the country – 6 to Oxbridge in 2005.

Money Matters: Academic scholarships available at 11 and post GCSE, music scholarships and a number of bursaries for those less fortunate. Special terms available for daughters of the clergy.

Remarks: An organised, well-run, academic school, which aims to teach girls to respect and value one another. It sets high standards and achieves them.

ST ALBANS SCHOOL

Abbey Gateway, St Albans, Hertfordshire, AL3 4HB

Tel: 01727 855 521
Fax: 01727 843 447
E-mail: hm@st-albans.herts.sch.uk
Website: www.st-albans.herts.sch.uk

• Pupils: 780, all boys except for 38 girls in the sixth form • Ages: 11-19 • Size of sixth form: 240 (38 girls) • Multi-faith
• Independent • Open days: Several throughout the year. Contact school

Headmaster: Since 1993, Mr Andrew Grant MA PGCE FRSA, early fifties, a Cambridge English graduate. Active on HMC committees, Mr Grant is the perfect example of what a difference can be made to a school by a professional head with a sustained long-term commitment. He has overseen an impressive revival in his school and shows no signs of flagging. Relaxed, energetic, chatty and with appropriate toughness when required, he is good company and visibly 'hands-on'. Mr Grant communicates a buzz which permeates the place as a whole. 'I feel very personally identified with this place', he says, enjoys life 'outside the magic circle of the M25' and says of St Albans, 'it's a great place to be.' Mind you, he also modestly describes it as, 'a small cathedral city on the outskirts of our school playing fields' – but with justification! (see below). His own two boys have been pupils – one as head boy by popular choice and this, too, says a lot for the popularity and democracy of his regime. A good, solid head running a solidly strong school, now getting some of the acclaim it deserves.

Academic Matters: Everyone does GCSEs in core subjects plus 3 options chosen from a pretty standard range. In 2004, 100 per cent of pupils got A*-C in at least 5 subjects and most of those got A*-B. Top performers were art, maths, music, RS, science and the minority languages but results in all the other major subjects not far behind. History, geography, drama and business studies the most popular options. A levels, in a total of 20 subjects offered, similarly strong. Big numbers in maths and strong showings in all sciences, economics and English. Results good across the board and in The Independent's 2004 list of the country's top 50 schools, based on A level results.

As is so often the case in boys' schools (which this is, until a small number of girls move into the sixth) languages are less popular. However, a lapse in take-up in 2004 isn't typical and the school is keen to support langs, both ancient and modern. So numbers in all modern langs are again up throughout the school and Latin and Greek are picking up too. Staff changes are enlivening interest in German, so sadly threatened elsewhere. French, German and Latin are on an equal footing in year 7; pupils choose any 2 to continue into year 8. Ancient history popular and results at A/S level were the best nationwide in 2004. Big recent investments in IT – school now well-equipped with PC suites here and there and inter-active whiteboards – used effectively and enthusiastically by those staff who like them and eschewed by others who don't – a sensible policy.

Unobtrusive but efficient SEN provision with those who 'appear to need it' informally assessed by SENCO; edpsychs pulled in if necessary, pupils are assessed termly. 25 currently get some form of help (none with a statement of needs), usually one to one, rarely withdrawn from lessons and if they are, then they are rotated on a six weekly cycle so that no boy misses too much of the same subject. Extra help at lunch time, post school popular. OK on dyslexia and dyspraxia, plus the occasional ADHD and those who find exams threatening. This is old fashioned proper back up, good for confidence and building self esteem: no tricks, just patient ground work. Costs £25 per child per hour, 'works well for the school, works well for me' says the SENCO who works four full days a week and is chocabloc. School not really good for wheelchairs.

Games, Options, The Arts: In 2003, after a nine-year planning battle and two public enquiries, school finally opened 'Woollams' – 'the best school playing fields in the country'. School sold a 12-acre plot plus planning permission inside the purlieus of the city of St Albans and bought a 400-acre farm two miles down the road with the proceeds. Letting the rest, they then proceeded to level 75 acres to make 19 winter pitches for football and rugby, an all-weather hockey pitch, 7 cricket squares and 2 blocks of tennis/netball courts. Two elegant and impressive pavilions, one 'boyproof' and the other belonging to the energetic Old Albanians.

A 15-minute bus ride from the school but well worth it and pupils become gooey-eyed when they talk about it – as does the long-serving head groundsman and who can blame him? Twenty sporting activities are on offer here including all the major games but you can also try sailing, squash, badminton, aerobics, golf, cross country athletics and table tennis. Regular tours worldwide.

The facilities are matched by the achievements. National and international honours, including, recently, 3 athletics internationals, an U16 England rugby cap, a Cambridge blue in hockey, two in cricket. 'Too numerous to mention' are school's representatives in county teams in many sports. In the 2005 English Schools AA national cross country championships, half the county senior team came from St Albans. You get the picture. Younger, less sporty pupils feel that 'there's not so much to do for us' on the extracurricular side but this apparently picks up as you move through the school in the shape of more, less physically demanding, clubs etc.

In case you think it's all sports, drama is strong and benefits from recently acquired house across the road from main school into which have been built teaching spaces and a good studio with top-class technics – a real boost for the subject. There is a large, well-equipped school hall which acts as a theatre for major productions as well as – how nice – a small outdoor theatre. School publishes 'The Albanian' – one of the most intelligent school mags we have seen. John Mole has been resident poet here for yonks – again a sensible and novel idea. Music is also strong – though music tech isn't big here – and lots of ensembles flourish. Annually, a huge tour taking many groups of all sizes goes to eg Barcelona, Paris – New York on the agenda in 2005. Annually also an oratorio concert, jointly with St Albans High, takes place in the cathedral. The school choir, which sings at school services twice weekly in the cathedral, is 60 plus strong and professional in approach and sound. We were treated to a Scarlatti motet – a privileged start to a morning for the whole school as well as for those who sing. School does not provide the choir for the cathedral – that is made up of boys and men (there is a girls' choir too) from all over the area but 5 pupils here are also in the cathedral choir – a double and challenging commitment but those we met who make it were articulately proud of the their involvement.

DT in first-rate new robotic suite, CDT is impressive and creative. D of E is popular and begins with the silver award. CCF also strong. School owns Pen Arthur, a 'rugged' farmhouse in rural Wales and everyone goes there for a variety of activities and field work – a rare and well used resource.

Background and Atmosphere: School founded in 948 making it one of the country's oldest. It is next to the cathedral and has inherited many of the foundation's buildings and some extraordinary rooms and nooks. It is not, however, the cathedral school and relations with the great building and its foundation are, says head, 'cordial, loose and ideal, with all the advantages of being thought a cathedral school and none of the disadvantages'. We know what you mean. We visited lessons in the old dungeon building

and the library (well-stocked) is housed in a super ancient hall with gothic windows and yard-thick walls. Busts and memorials to the school's venerable history abound and sit comfortably with all the accoutrements of a thoroughly modern educational environment. Other buildings nestle amid beautifully kept gardens and school is reached by many via a walk over the cathedral green. A privileged setting. Strong involvement with the local community including excellent work on local conservation projects and links with local maintained schools.

Boarding went in the 1950s, the direct grant in the 1970s – 80 per cent had been on free places – and girls arrived in the sixth in 1991. Of the 40 or so new pupils into the sixth, most are girls but this still means that, proportionately, their numbers are small. The attitude of the school to them is healthy and we did not detect any of the cattle market mentality observable elsewhere. The girls, many from STAGS the local state girls' school, clearly love it and, despite – or because of? – their small numbers, thrive. A third of the staff are women. Perhaps this, together with the few girls and the sensible, unmacho attitude of the staff, makes for the relaxed, cheery and comradely atmosphere we observed throughout.

Pastoral Care and Discipline: Carefully structured tutorial system, prefects and a, now full-time, school nurse make for effective pastoral care. 'Anyone who brings drugs on site is too stupid to be here so they have to go,' says head, refreshingly. Random testing used 'on good grounds' and in coordination with home. Head has expelled for drugs and would again but no incidents for two years. School feels orderly but not oppressively so. A sense of self-discipline prevails. Food 'very good', enthuse pupils.

Pupils and Parents: Many come in on good network of school buses. 70+ per cent from local Herts area and about half of those from St Albans itself. The rest, including a good number of Jewish pupils, from north London, mostly from Enfield. Parents mostly professional/business/commercial and a large proportion new to independent education. A smaller number from other ethnic minorities or families where the first lang is not English. Very strong Old Albanians many of whom send their sons here and, later, their daughters. Many siblings so a strong family/community feel. Notable former pupils go back to the year dot but recent ones include Sir Tim Rice, archaeologist Lord Renfrew, film producer Mike Newell, General Sir Richard Lawson and Prof Stephen Hawking – himself.

Entrance: At 11 years old, 260 apply for 72 places. Tests in English, maths and VR and interviews all on the same day. Average IQ of 128 of those who make it. At 13,

90 applicants for up to 48 places. Tests as above plus 3 interviews and entry dependent on CE results. Around 50 applicants for 20+ places at 16 – predictions of A*-C at GCSE with As in A level subjects. Increasingly school the first choice and can afford to be choosy.

Exit: A very impressive list of subjects and destinations. All good solid stuff eg large numbers in 2003 to read maths at Warwick et al, equally large numbers in 2004 to read philosophy, economics or history at places such as Bath, Leicester, London. A sprinkling of Oxbridges in a spread of disciplines – all testament to a broad and serious education.

Money Matters: Variable numbers of schols worth 10-50 per cent of fees awarded on the basis of performance in the entrance tests at 11 and by separate exam at 13 and 16. Also means-tested bursaries up to 100 per cent of fees. Special bursaries for instrumental tuition from 11 and art.

Remarks: Justifiably in the Indie's top fifty on more grounds than the merely academic, unjustifiably omitted from this Guide until now, this is a correction we are happy to make. If the glitzy north London heavy-weights or the big boys in the shires are not your thing, quietly relocate to a spot on the St Albans bus route – and then gloat over your friends.

St Aloysius' College

Linked to Saint Aloysius' College Junior School in the Junior section

45 Hill Street, Garnethill, Glasgow, G3 6RJ

Tel: 01413 323 190
Fax: 01413 530 426
E-mail: mail@staloysius.org
Website: www.staloysius.org

• Pupils: 945 boys and girls in senior school, all day; roughly 50/50 boys/girls • Ages: 11-18 • Size of sixth form: S5 and S6: 250 • RC • Fees: £2,140 - £2,313 • Independent

Head: Since 2004, Mr John Stoer BA PGCE (forties) who was educated at Dowie School, read theology at Bristol and originally went down the accountancy road, but rapidly changed to teaching, taking his PGCE at London University. A committed Catholic, he is the first lay head at St Aloysius and has always taught in the Catholic sector; starting at St Thomas More School in Chelsea, followed by being head of RE at St Philip Howard School off the East India Dock Road, thence Gunnersbury Catholic School in London where he

was director of sixth form, followed by deputy head of The Campion School in Hornchurch. He comes to St Aloysius after ten years St Joseph's College in Staffordshire where he was also the first lay head. ('Steadily moving north'). A thoughtful man, entertaining and interesting, with a puckish sense of humour, Mr Stoer applied for St Aloysius because of its links with the Jesuit tradition which he first encountered at The Campion School (though it was, by then, out of Jesuit control). A theologian and a born teacher, he couldn't resist giving this editor a quick history lesson on Jesuit education via his (heavily marked in turquoise) copy of Ratio Studiorum, the Jesuit handbook, first published in 1586.

Mr Stoer arrived with a wealth of experience, a confidence to change and a subtle way of persuasion. The school, which had previously eschewed standard grades is now opting for the stronger Intermediate II (in the Scottish system) with music and religious studies taken as GCSEs (the latter is the only exam board with a Roman Catholic syllabus). Highers and advanced highers in S5 and S6. 'Real change doesn't happen quickly, you need to change hearts and minds'. No mass staff evacuations which might be expected to follow such radical surgery: just two or three who were of an age to retire. Mr Stoer and his wife, who have two children in the school, live in the West End of Glasgow.

Academic Matters: Year sizes of 156, S1 = mixed ability, but expect some setting further up the school into classes of around 22; pupils can move up and down. School moved to five one-hour lessons daily from September 2005, with ten minutes added on to the working day – five in the morning and five at the end. Curriculum in a state of flux currently, no standard grades at all, with pupils expected to aim for five highers in S5 and at least two advanced highers in S6. Recent results show that twice as many pupils took higher Latin than Italian, with French and Spanish the only other languages on offer. French, Spanish and the sciences the strongest kids on the block. English and maths perhaps a tad sad; we might expect more than 57 per cent getting A in these subjects and, frankly, nine failures in maths is too many, ditto seven in Geography. Music produced an astounding 10 out of 11 getting As at Higher grade. IT computing et al less than brilliant performers but new computing block should produce miracles 'ere long. Some of the classes are tiny – six in Latin five in drama; Spanish and media studies at A level, the latter outstandingly popular in S6. No recent take-up in Greek.

The school has heads of faculties rather than departments and it could be that some radical pruning may become necessary before too long. Impressive new computer suites used for straight IT and class learning with open access (staff not so keen on this as new Clavius building is vast and needs quite a lot of patrolling and there is no staff room in Clavius, though admittedly that was part of the original design). Dramatic chemistry labs with interesting clusters of really quite high tables round six dedicated work areas with gas and water access. Well-used library. School keen (very keen) on homework for all ages and has a dedicated learning website which children can access from home or wherever and carries lesson notes and homework assignments, homework club for all plus after school club for extra help – no stigma about popping in at any time. Huge strides in the SEN department, Mr Stoer was having a planning meeting with the head of SEN during our visit (and so of course we asked to stay). Number of pilot schemes afoot: laptops (and growing), mentoring (which is proving highly successful with four mentors now on staff) scribing, reading (team readers practise); this is a school aware of SEN disabilities and which is taking serious steps to facilitate learning. Aspergers, ADHD, dyslexia, dyspraxia, ok for the visually impaired ('we work with guidance from the eye hospital' – which includes using coloured lenses and overlays. NB apart from the dedicated Old Rectory, this is the first time this editor has come across coloured lenses being treated with anything other than lip service). Learning support either for the individual or small groups of pupils. The two new-builds have lifts, with Braille on the lift buttons, but the slope is such in the primary school that it would be impossible without hefty carriers to get a wheelchair into the classroom currently used for music.

Games, Options, The Arts: For an inner city school there is a surprising amount of playground space (this includes car parking for important visitors – like this editor – otherwise it is hideous round here), and young were fooling around on the all-weather surface in a serious Glasgow rain at break time during our visit. Games are important in the Jesuit culture – 'sport helps pupils learn to accept both success and failure graciously' – and team games for all (at least once a week). The dedicated playing fields are down the M8 towards Stepps (our guides hadn't a clue where – they just 'slept on the bus'). Old-fashioned gym on site and impressive looking weights room. Quite good representation in rugby and regular winners of the Scottish Schools' Cup plus local and national caps in rugby, hockey and athletics. Annual rugby tour to Ireland and the occasional trip abroad. More for skiing than for rugby. Girls' games important too. Full time co-ordinator of outdoor education and D of E just appointed, so expect masses more expos – kayaking, climbing, sailing, all good hearty stuff. The whole senior school decamps for a week's brisk outdoor education between S1 and S4, and post the public exams there are more jaunts and tripettes: walking the West Highland way, film making, trips to London and the like.

Glorious, light, sunny art department in the top of the elegantly stained-glass Mount building, nice line in flat painting, one or two jolly sculptures and some terrific fabric design plus a wizard Roman helmet made out of ring pulls from cans (our guide had been photographed in it and made sure we had seen quite how cunningly it had been made).

Music important with a vast range of instruments on offer and compulsory weekly lessons up to S2. Vibrant school orchestra, terrific and popular choir. This is a school where music really matters. Strong drama throughout the school, we were kicked out of a junior rehearsal with alacrity. Enthusiastic inter-house music as well as sport. Keen debaters; mass of clubs, chess, debating and film making popular, ditto D of E, and YE. Regular school links with other schools 'especially Jesuit ones' for exchanges and the like give pupils a 'broader outlook on life'.

Background and Atmosphere: School founded in 1859 to educate the Catholic community in the west of Scotland and is run still very much on the Jesuit principles that God is in all things, that human excellence and service to others and the 'fullest possible development of all the God-given talents of each individual' is paramount. St Aloysius College St A (St Aloysius Gonzaga 1568-91) was the patron of young people and the school is part of a network of over two thousand Jesuit seats of learning 'educating over two million students in sixty five countries', and one of the principle missions of Jesuit teaching is education. The school is based on not quite the apex of Hill Street, opposite the convent and next to the splendid Victoria Baroque Jesuit church, which the school uses for whole school mass and regular assemblies (about three times a week) – very much in the centre of Glasgow, just off the M8; brilliant for public transport and well-nigh impossible for car-bound visiting editors to find. The Hanson and Mount buildings are redbrick, serious Victoriana and have well withstood the test of time, however the two newer buildings, one housing the junior school, and the Clavius building which is home to the IT and scientific world, are already showing their age. The junior school is lovely, full of jolly hanging pics and tiny chairs in groups of six. It is fully self-contained but adjacent (and too many steps). The Clavius building, however glam it is, causes problems: the staff think it is too big to patrol, the pupils think it is 'pretty weird' to have form mass in the atrium surrounded by blocks of lockers, and the bright blue paint on the doors and cupboards is

already   chipping   off
it has been repainted once); passages and stairs are horren-
dously narrow. Both new-builds are prize winners with
Clavius top of the pops but neither look particularly clever
next to the Rennie MacIntosh Glasgow School of Art, which
is apparently just what the planners wanted.

Charming tiny little chapel in the main building, voluntary mass for all at 8.30 every morning – well-attended by
parents pupils and staff and 'over by the time school starts'.
Crowded during lent and the run up to exams. Crucifixes in
every class room, two Jesuits still on staff.

Pastoral Care and Discipline: New chaplain
appointed. Jesuit principles pervade: formation in all things
important including theology, philosophy, a commitment to
ecumenism, and the resistance of atheism, materialism and
consumerism, with an emphasis on 'service to others even
as a lawyer or a doctor' (think UCAS forms). In the real world
this means strong anti-bullying dogma in place and sin and
wickedness treated with the contempt they deserve. Expect
to be dismissed for trading in drugs at school, otherwise
subjected to the expected scale of punishments – 'we would
gradually raise the ante, but make sure that support programmes were in place to try and solve all problems in a
positive way'. Sex education officially taught via RE 'and
lousy', says a parent. Junior school operates discipline Stars
and Stripes cards. Strong house system (based on the
Jesuit saints: Campion, Loyola, Ogilvie and Xavier). Heads of
houses double as guidance teachers and are responsible
for 'the academic, pastoral, co-curricular and disciplinary'
side of school life. Siblings in the same house as far as poss.

Pupils and Parents: Predominantly middle-class core,
almost exclusively RC, which, in the west of Scotland, historically means predominantly Scots, Irish and Italians, plus a
tiny ethnic minority. Strongly supportive of the school, pupils
come (in the main) from the wealth of suburbs that surround
the city. Tranches of FPs who seem to accept that the school
is progressively changing to lay staff. Fair number of first
time buyers. 'Wide diversity'.

Entrance: School claims 'to admit pupils in the top half
of the general population. 75 per cent of our pupils come
from the top quarter of the population' – we are talking academically here. Priority given to practising Catholics and
those who 'share the aims and values of Jesuit education'.
More or less automatic from the junior school. Active sibling
policy. Assessment, tests but previous school reports, school
reference (and preferably one from the parish priest) are all
taken into account. If pupils transfer from another independent school, St Aloysius checks that there are no outstanding
fees as well as getting a reference.

Exit: Fair number leave post Highers with uni entry in
the bag – a bare 70 per cent stay on. (Mr Stoer was surprised by this, but it is the nature of the Scottish uni entrance
system and high time it was changed.) Some 95 plus per
cent go on to tertiary education, the school provides a regular (tiny) trickle to the priesthood (some 15/20 pupils are
serving in the local diocese) slightly larger trickle to
Oxbridge. Deep reluctance to strike out from familiar territory, fair number seem to end up at Glasgow and
Strathclyde unis, but they are getting 'progressively more
adventurous'.

Money Matters: The school receives no state funding
– not even apparently for class room assistants for those
with a record of needs which is odd. The original Jesuit concept was that their role was to educate free and the school
has a certain amount of funding available. Parents are
asked whether they need bursarial help at the time of application, almost automatic for families on income support,
plus family discounts, but no named or dedicated bursaries.
School does what it can to help. Will also try and help out if
family hits financial crisis but with the usual strictures, parents must be up-front about the extent of their problems.

Remarks: A traditional and unusual school which has
served the local community well – dedicated to providing
'improvement in living and learning to the greater glory of
God and for the common good' (St Ignatius Loyola 1491-
1556). St Aloysius has adapted well to the twenty-first century; it will be interesting to watch the developments in the
exam department. So much better to get some exam prac-

tice at 16 rather than go straight to highers as previously.

St Antony's Leweston School

Sherborne, Dorset, DT9 6EN

Tel: 01963 210 691
Fax: 01963 210 786
E-mail: admissions@leweston.dorset.sch.uk
Website: www.leweston.co.uk

• Pupils: 264 girls; 98 full boarders (flexi-boarding available and popular) • Ages: 11-18; plus co-ed pre-prep and prep on site for ages 2.5-11 • Size of sixth form: 76 • RC - but the majority are other denominations • Fees: Day £4,090 Boarding £6,290
• Independent • Open days: October and May

Head: Since 1999, Mr Henry MacDonald, MA, Oxon (fifties). Head of classics from 1981, then deputy head. Went part-time in 1995 so that he could spend more time on creative writing. When head's position came up he was persuaded to go for it, to the pupils' delight – 'he was one of our favourite teachers'. Kind, understanding and family-orientated – his two daughters attended Leweston. A believer in emotional literacy which he thinks indispensible for effective teaching and learning – 'many young people growing up at the moment lack affection and find it difficult to build relationships with adults'. Italian wife, Luisella, a translator and teacher of Italian, is involved on the pastoral side. 'Omnicompetent,' says her husband, she does a weekly prayer group with boarders plus evening lessons in Italian GCSE and AS level. Off to resume, inter alia, his literary career in July 2006.

Academic Matters: Impressive GCSE results every year, with geography, music and the sciences outstanding. A level pass rate consistently above 95 per cent. Value-added very high. Language results good, bolstered by native speakers. All year 10s spend eight days in an 18th century French manor house near Caen studying their normal curriculum plus French language and culture. Latin, IT and music compulsory in year 7. Enthusiastic and devoted teachers – beloved by the girls and their parents. Good support for EFL and dyslexia. Supervised prep for one hour during the first two years, two hours thereafter. Small classes – one girl commented that her biggest class had 11 pupils, her smallest 4.

Games, Options, The Arts: Excellent and active music department – two thirds of girls play an instrument, half play two. Top musicians join Sherborne School and Sherborne

School for Girls in a stunning joint orchestra. Drama GCSE introduced 2001; newly refurbished school theatre includes a redesigned stage. Good theatrical productions, some involving other local schools. Sports popular and successful. During 2004 the school produced 6 County Champions and 15 County representatives in netball, hockey and cross-country. Current Great Britain Catholic schools cross-country champions.

Background and Atmosphere: A caring, relaxed school founded by the Sisters of Christian Instruction in 1891 (31 per cent of pupils RC). 40 acres on a lovely, secluded site, a 3 mile drive south of Sherborne through apple orchards and country air tinged with the scent of manure. No one chooses this school for architectural coherence – it is an astounding jumble of discordant styles. But once the shock has worn off, it is possible to appreciate the floodlit all-weather pitch, elegant new library (both 2001), lovely DT, art, jewellery and ceramics rooms, science labs, sports hall, outdoor pool, superb health centre and music block – all spread out among the greenery. The grounds offer a warren of wild paths through splendid nature. An ethereal calm pervades with, sometimes, a feeling of a few girls knocking around a huge site. Since September 2003, sixth formers are no longer required to wear school uniform, which for the younger girls consists of an open necked shirt and kilt. Highlight of day – afternoon tea but lunch is fast catching up with the extensive and varied menu – homemade bread a speciality. Building starts soon on an impressive new kitchen and dining facility.

Pastoral Care and Discipline: The girls are well cared for, feminine, well-mannered – changes to the sixth form over the past year have handed more responsibility over to the girls for school administration and discipline. Girls may go into Sherborne town in the afternoons (minibus takes them on Thursdays, taxis available other days). Upper sixth may visit the Sherborne School bar. Dormitories very tidy and pleasant – six to a room to start with, gradually working up to singles by sixth form. Well-organised, wholesome weekend activities available to day girls as well as boarders. RC boys from Sherborne School come to Leweston for weekly mass and the two schools mix for dramatic productions, social activities etc. The social programme is constantly being enhanced to provide further opportunities for girls to meet with pupils from other schools. Recent total refurbishment of sixth form boarding provision including the introduction of a kitchen and laundry and internet provision in every study bedroom.

Pupils and Parents: Mostly local girls, farmers' daughters, service families, professional couples, doctors etc. Some from co-ed prep located on site. 15 per cent from overseas. Old girls: actress Kristin Scott Thomas, novelist and radical anti-feminist Erin Pizzey, Serena De La Hey, artist and creator of the West Country's Wicker Man.

Entrance: Entrance is via Common Entrance, school examination or scholarship examinations. Scholarships offered for art, drama, music, PE, science and academic excellence. The school accepts pupils with a cross-section of abilities. Good individual needs support.

Exit: Majority to university – London, Bristol, Birmingham, Cardiff, Durham, 11 girls to Oxbridge in the past five years. Some to Art foundation courses; Gap years are popular.

Money Matters: Good value for money.

Remarks: Caring school, quietly bringing out the best in its pupils.

ST BEDE'S COLLEGE

Linked to Saint Bede's College Prep School in the Junior section

Alexandra Park, Manchester, Lancashire, M16 8HX

Tel: 0161 226 3323

Fax: 0161 226 3813

E-mail: head@stbedescollege.co.uk

Website: www.stbedescollege.co.uk

- Pupils: 422 girls and 498 boys; all day • Ages: 11-18 (plus own prep 4-11) • Size of sixth form: 288 • RC • Fees: Day: prep £1,412; senior £2,260. Additional boarding fees: £1,572
- Independent • Open days: Mid September to early November

Head: Since 1983, Mr John Byrne BA MEd (History) (fifties). Educated at Priory Grammar School for Boys, Shrewsbury, studied at London and Birmingham universities and returned to Shropshire to teach at Church Stretton School. A post at Blessed Robert Johnston Catholic College, Telford, followed, then deputy head at St Augustine's Catholic High School, Redditch. Married with 5 children aged 11-18 years, all of whom attend St Bede's. A firm and committed leader, quietly spoken, unswerving in his Catholic faith; he believes that 'without inner confidence we are nothing' and aims to 'inculcate the teachings of the Catholic church over the pupils' school careers, giving them a firm foundation on which to build and to embrace fully in later life'. Sees St Bede's as an academic education rooted in the teachings of the Lord Jesus Christ producing 'a generation of well-educated, articulate, theologically literate and compassionate young people who will ensure that the Christian case does not go by default'.

Academic Matters: Strong academic results; pupils are expected to work hard. Class size 28 maximum with an average of 25, smaller in the sixth form. Setting in maths and statistics to stretch the more able. At GCSE 68 per cent A* and A grades – one pupil scooped 10 A* grades. At A level 67 per cent A to B grades. The broad range of subjects includes the classics, Chinese, Polish, politics and business studies; religious education is compulsory throughout the school though in the sixth form the approach is less formal and pupils enjoy discussion groups. A healthy age and gender mix of staff.

DT (the proud recipient of many awards) and art have excellent facilities and display impressive creations. Some science labs are dated, nevertheless producing robust results, but the multimedia language lab is impressive and fully computerised. IT facilities good, computers abound, linked to the school's intranet. Impressive Maher library with approachable and knowledgeable librarian. Open after school and during the holidays in the run up to exams.

Games, Options, The Arts: Games compulsory throughout the school. Football achieves notable success, being in the final of the Boodle and Dunthorne Independent Schools' Football Association Cup and Greater Manchester county champions. Netball is strong with U13s and U15s county champions. National runners up at U16. Head determined not to focus on the two best sports, as this would limit opportunity for others; hence rugby, hockey, cricket, athletics and tennis are also offered. New floodlit all-weather surface opened in 2003 for netball and hockey.

Plenty of extra-curricular activities from chess to robotics. Sports and studies are enhanced by foreign tours, field trips, pilgrimage to Lourdes etc. Less than expected uptake

of individual music tuition possibly due to costs involved for many. Nonetheless there's an orchestra, a string orchestra, a concert band and three choirs.

Background and Atmosphere: Founded in 1875 by Cardinal Vaughan, the school moved to its present site in 1877, taking over the buildings of the Manchester Aquarium, and has since expanded onto an adjoining site separated by a quiet road. Originally a boys' Catholic grammar school, it became direct grant but reverted to independence in 1976. Girls were admitted from 1984. Traditionally, the school served the local inner city area but now draws pupils from a 25 mile radius encompassing a wide social spectrum. The Christian spirit is omnipresent but not, according to pupils, repressive; there's an atmosphere of mutual respect and warmth with excellent pupil-teacher interaction.

Pastoral Care and Discipline: Pupils comment on the excellent provision of pastoral care. All pupils have a member of staff to whom they can turn and peer support is available, though this is not formalised. Clear moral framework; pupil behaviour is good with very little bullying, theft etc.

Pupils and Parents: Majority white British or Irish with a number of 1st and 2nd generation African children who have settled in Manchester. 4 per cent non-Catholic Christians 'unhappy with secular schools'. The social mix is broad, in line with the school's ethos. Pupils are courteous to each other and staff, polite and hard working. Uniform is worn throughout the school, with 'office wear' in the sixth form.

Entrance: Selection is by examination and interview. The interview is of particular importance for those children from inner city state schools who have not been 'prepped' for the entrance exam. Sixth form admission requires 7 GCSEs.

Exit: On average 14 per year to Oxbridge. Other top redbrick universities are the most popular for the remainder, to follow a broad spectrum of courses.

Money Matters: Two half-fees music scholarships. Applications for financial assistance are otherwise means-tested, one third of pupils receiving financial assistance from St Bede's Educational Trust.

Remarks: An excellent choice for committed Catholics seeking an academic education within a Christian environment. 'I cannot recommend St Bede's more highly,' comments one such parent. A fantastic opportunity for bright young Catholics from underprivileged homes.

St Bede's School

Linked to Saint Bede's School-Eastbourne in the Junior section

The Dicker, Upper Dicker, Hailsham, East Sussex, BN27 3QH

Tel: 01323 843 252
Fax: 01323 442 628
E-mail: school.office@stbedesschool.org
Website: www.stbedesschool.org

- Pupils: 485 boys, 315 girls. About half board • Ages: 12-19
- Size of sixth form: 295 • Inter-denomination • Fees: Day £4,055; boarding £6,595 • Independent • Open days: May, September

Head: Since 2002, Mr Stephen Cole (fiftyish) formerly head of St Paul's Collegiate in Hamilton, New Zealand. Took over from Mr Roger Perrin, who was here from the beginning (1978). Energetic and passionate about sport, remains loyal to the original philosophy of not selecting on academic grounds.

Academic Matters: Non-selective at entry but produces a good proportion of A/B grades at A level. A teacher/pupil ratio of 1 to 7 allows for lots of individual support – and the academically able have the Curriculum Enhancement Programme to keep them on the fast track. Students are not expected to take subjects where they have no natural aptitude, except English and maths. One pupil, who was floundering at a nearby, more pressurised, school and recently joined St Bede's and is now thriving (there are numerous such cases) said, 'here I am allowed to make mistakes – the pressure is off'. Another exceptionally able boy was not performing at a traditional school. Offered full academic scholarships at two top league schools, he chose St Bede's as the only school that would be flexible enough to accommodate his request to fast track some subjects so he could concentrate on a range of further subjects. Teachers take the view that for some pupils an E grade is a marvellous achievement. English, modern languages and art & media studies are particularly strong.

Games, Options, The Arts: Absolutely extraordinary choice – it's difficult to imagine anyone being bored here. All students take part in a club activities programme that runs every afternoon. Students must do one energetic activity each week but can get away with, for example, table tennis. At the moment, there are more than 140 activities on offer, with a daily choice of over 40. Clubs for everything, from car restoration to art appreciation. Facilities for the arts

include a graphics design room, art studios and a photographic area and dark room. Music is a strength of the school, with nearly half the school involved in the musical programme. Numerous concerts, workshops and choirs performing every term at different levels. Parents are very welcome to attend. 'Everyone is allowed to do their own thing and is accepted for what they are but this is not an easy option and the students work hard.' Drama is doing very well and there is a new drama studio under construction which will open in January 2006. Lots of productions, musicals etc with a thriving weekly club for drama scholars. Own riding stables with a recently enlarged menage and excellent local riding. National success in tennis and swimming.

Background and Atmosphere: Leafy bit of East Sussex – many have long school runs or journeys on the school minibuses. Newly built extensions visible everywhere and on the 'to do list'. School runs the village shop and post office and helps look after the village church. An English School with a strong cosmopolitan element, staff and pupils are drawn from all the continents of the world. A happy, buzzy and diverse bunch – diversity breeds a tolerance and understanding that is perhaps the school's greatest strength.

Pastoral Care and Discipline: Parents much appreciate St Bede's' tolerant atmosphere and its caring pupil/teacher relationships. No major discipline problems reported – 'if people feel the school supports them, they're more likely to be kind to each other,' says the head. Students are told that the worst thing they can do is to make others unhappy. Strict drugs policy and anyone caught using or possessing drugs is out, and those suspected of drug use are tested. Choice of a multi-religious school meeting or an organised church service.

Pupils and Parents: About 20 per cent from overseas – 30 different countries. Most British pupils are from schools in Sussex, Surrey and Kent, with most day pupils coming from prep schools and community colleges in Sussex.

Entrance: Non-selective. Most children enter at 13 after an interview with the head, following references from the student's current school or through Common Entrance, scholarship or entrance test, although some enter in the sixth form. It is unusual for any pupil who has been interviewed and received a satisfactory report from his or her present school to be refused admission. Considerably oversubscribed, so pupils are admitted on a first come, first served basis.

Exit: Most go to university in this country, with a good number to Oxbridge. Many return to overseas universities. A sizeable number follow relatively unconventional careers, especially in art and design, theatre and dance.

Money Matters: Healthy – plenty of new builds and expansions demonstrates this. Numerous scholarships and bursaries for academic work, art, music, sport, dance and drama.

Remarks: Not a typical public school – not for tidy, traditional or tweedy types. Good for self-disciplined children who want the freedom to pursue their own interests.

ST BEES SCHOOL

St Bees, Cumbria, CA27 0DS

Tel: 01946 828 000
Fax: 01946 823 657
E-mail: mailbox@st-bees-school.co.uk
Website: www.st-bees-school.org

- Pupils: 190 boys, 120 girls. 125 board (40 weekly), the rest day
- Ages: 11-18 • Size of sixth form: 117 • C of E • Fees: Day £3,107 - £4,013; weekly boarding £3,985 - £5,713; full boarding £4,856 - £6,696 • Independent • Open days: October and May Day bank holiday

---

Head: Since 2000, Mr Philip Capes, previously deputy head of Warminster School; engineering degree from Exeter, married to a primary school teacher, three children, one of whom attends St Bees. Safe, experienced pair of hands; an approachable head, clear about school's future. Many new staff since he arrived; planned retirement scheme for some long-servers.

Academic Matters: Broad range, from special learning unit to top scores at A level. Not a hothouse and doesn't claim to be. Much satisfaction over Ds and Es turned into Cs and above. 'Everyone is stretched,' says one satisfied parent, whose two sons' indifferent junior school achievements were turned into 3 As at A level – attributed to confidence instilled by being treated as an individual. Usual small school constraints on A level choices, but Latin, Greek and further maths available. GCSE – over 40 per cent at A and A*. IT, French and Spanish taught in innovative Management Centre (see below). Year 10 do some OU foundation courses. Very committed staff, who insist on hard work and high standards.

Games, Options, The Arts: Games fields everywhere in stunning 150-acre site. Rugby strong (tough fixture list), girls' sport also good. Large sports hall, squash and fives courts. Much PE teaching mixed. 60-acre 9-hole golf course on headland, shared with locals. Proximity to unspoiled part of Lake District has led to development of distinctive and successful tradition of outdoor activities. CCF for all aged 13-15. Artwork in evidence everywhere, drama lively, music very good; refurbished music school opened 2000 – many instrumental groups, choir sings in chapel and village priory, tours abroad with chamber orchestra every other year.

Background and Atmosphere: Founded as a grammar school in 1583; original schoolroom now a dining hall with past pupils' names carved on wall panels. Handsome Victorian additions in local sandstone spread over fine site 'between the sea and the sheep', and well integrated with St Bees village, where pupils wander freely. Girls admitted since 1976, so a proper co-educational school. Girls' houses in attractive terrace on the far side of useful local railway (footbridge), senior boys in two houses, one in the same building as the head. All new staff do boarding house duties. International Centre offers specialist EFL plus general courses for one year for up to 18 overseas students aged 11-16 – doubtless a useful boost to numbers. Many now from mainland China. Some join St Bees after basic course, some return home. All international pupils integrated into existing boarding houses.

Management Centre, opened in 1992, is an unusual and successful joint venture – used commercially as a conference centre in the week, by the school in evenings and at weekends.

phisticated – neatly dressed in formal uniform, frank and unaffected in manner. Many bright boys and girls attracted to St Bees, says head, because of greater chance of representing school in multifarious activities.

Parents very supportive (some allow their names to be used in prospectus for potential parents to telephone – what a good idea); Cumbrian farmers and professionals, local industrialists (Sellafield – still – a huge employer). Very efficient marketing department; its boss goes on frequent recruiting trips abroad.

Entrance: Not very competitive – though International Centre students have to show realistic level of competence. Two-form entry, mainly from state schools, topped up at 13 and 16. Possibility of extension downwards into prep and nursery departments.

Exit: Nearly all to higher education (very little fall-out after GCSE); a sprinkling to Oxbridge, mainly to a wide range of old and new universities. 2004 leavers' list shows good cover of engineering, law, medicine; straight arts underrepresented.

Money Matters: Bursaries for children of clergy, Services and former pupils, and a few for deserving cases. Up to 50 per cent academic and music scholarships; art and sports awards post-16.

Remarks: Good local school, strong reputation, not averse to change; palpable atmosphere of security in beautiful surroundings. Endless care taken over individuals.

ST BENEDICT'S SCHOOL

Linked to Saint Benedict's Junior School

54 Eaton Rise, Ealing, London, W5 2ES

Tel: 020 8862 2000/2002
Fax: 020 8862 2007
E-mail: headmaster@stbenedicts.org.uk
Website: www.stbenedictsealing.org.uk

- Pupils: 600 boys, all day (20 girls in the sixth form) • Ages: 11-19 • Size of sixth form: 175 • Roman Catholic • Fees: £2,910
- Independent • Open days: October and by arrangement

Headmaster: Since 2002, Mr C J Cleugh (pronounced Clough) BSc MSc, educated St Mary's, Crosby and Hull University where he read Chemistry. Mr Cleugh began teaching at St Kevin's Kirby and then returned to his own old school, St Mary's, where he remained for 17 years, becoming head of sixth form and deputy head. Headmaster of St Anselm's College, Birkenhead for 9 years. Married, with four adult children. Mr Cleugh succeeds the charismatic Dr Anthony Dachs who put the school back on the rails. Mr Cleugh is less of an obvious charmer, has his own style of leadership and vision for his school.

You know where you are with this head – easy to talk to, open, straightforward – you feel he would always be honest with you and your child. Not afraid to risk unpopularity – for the good of the community – and is a man of quiet but total conviction. Knows, and knows about, all his pupils, and has a sensitive understanding of their concerns. Mr Cleugh is charged with – and is keen on – upping the Roman Catholic life of the school. This has various knock-ons. Faith is, literally, more visible now – texts on walls, mottos and quotes from St Benedict everywhere, and more charity work is now part of everyone's school life. Some non-Catholic parents find the new emphasis irksome but a price worth paying for all the pluses; most children either welcome it or take it in their stride. Numbers of non-Catholics have not fallen under the new regime, despite the desired wish of the new head to increase the Catholic percentage – while stressing equally the inclusiveness of his approach.

Academic Matters: A school which, though not highly selective academically, regularly puts in a more than respectable showing. The ethos of the school means that a starry place in league tables is not what they're about. 'What I want is every child to fulfil his or her full potential,' declares the headmaster, and is quite happy if that means 2 Ds at A level for a particular child – so long as that child has worked and fulfilled said potential. However, Mr Cleugh wants to up the general academic performance and hopes, among other things, to attract bright RC boys who currently go to the more traditionally academic local schools, St Paul's and Latymer Upper. A good range of GCSE subjects on offer with everyone taking RS. RS curriculum largely RC in content and other faiths learned about in PSHE instead. Modern languages just about holding up as is Latin, and school still manages to field candidates in Latin and Greek at A level – hooray. Other A levels offered include sports science, classical civilisation, drama and music. Average class size 20-24 in years 7-11, 11-16 in the sixth.

Well-equipped ICT rooms – the subject is well-taught and IT skills used increasingly in other areas. Newly refurbished labs – clinical, white, orderly, purposeful. Interactive whiteboards everywhere – well used. F/t librarian assisted by 'decans' (prefects) in recently refurbished tiny library, equipped with slimline computers and state-of-the-art facilities. No-one obviously looking at any books when we visited, though. Adjoining the new library is Reading Room – a supervised, sixth form study area – like public library with huge oak tables – in which silent and serious work – with books! – takes place. Dyslexic and dyspraxic pupils – about 35 currently, catered for by SENCO/learning support teacher and her assistant – but some parental concern that problems are not picked up or properly addressed still persist.

Games, Options, The Arts: Rugby is the main sport here so not the place for a boy who can't see beyond Beckhamworld, although there are plans for changes in 2006/7 (see below). Recently won the U15 Daily Mail Cup at Twickenham. School uses 14 acres of playing fields in Perivale about a mile away and plays hard, winning and losing about equally. Less than world-class pupils appreciate school's attitude to sports – 'everyone's given a chance', said one in heartfelt tones, having experienced the 'if you're not in the first team you're nobody' syndrome elsewhere. Cricket main summer sport, and school has good number of county representatives. The school is heavily represented in rugby county squads (also currently two U18 England rugby team in sixth form). Sixth form girls frequent the local gym, play netball and football among other choices. Basketball, rowing, tennis also offered and plans for more diversification in 2006 with the appointment of a new director of sport covering years 7-18. On-site sports hall, decorative outdoor climbing wall. School plans multi-gym and fitness centre as part of development scheme.

Music and drama both keenly supported and well-taught. About 60 per cent learn an instrument in school, more outside and much enthusiastically supported musical activity. Music festival in the abbey which is focus of regular performing and choral singing. Photographic evidence of lively drama productions up on walls and the sixth form guide on our visit to the school, having starred in a recent production, was stared at by lesser denizens as if he were a TV celeb. Good big drama studio plus new lanterns, good new music rooms and facilities, lively work witnessed in both. Good theatre and attractive one-storey modern art/DT block with evidence of intensely imaginative, disciplined, creative work on show. Before and after- school study supervision in the library on offer. Over 65 clubs now – meeting earlier complaints of not enough on the extra-curricular side – from karate, chess, debating, history society, drama, CCF, D of E, Saint Vincent de Paul charity fundraising to current affairs; these take place before school at lunchtime and after school.

Background and Atmosphere: A Roman Catholic school, and this is evident in every aspect of the atmosphere and environment of the school, its publications, its ethos. Doubly unique in that it is the only Benedictine day school in Great Britain and the only RC independent senior boys' school in London, it was founded in 1902 by the monks of Downside Abbey. The monastery of Ealing became an independent community in 1947 and an abbey in 1955. Leafy, residential, prosperous setting: something of a surprise to round a corner and find Ealing Abbey – a large and imposing church with a power and grace to disarm the most unbelieving unbeliever. The school abuts the abbey and the juniors look onto it – something of a privilege in a London suburb! The buildings are a mix of un-gloomy Victorian redbrick and various twentieth century extensions, additions and blocks – some of which are wearing better than others. The whole site is functional rather than welcoming and cries out for some planting and gardening. Internally, much has been done in the last two years – frankly, it was necessary! – to update and maintain the school. Sixth form area completely refurbished with pool room, all science labs, library and reading room, plus classrooms regularly repainted.

However, more importantly, the Benedictine ethos of respect for each other genuinely informs life here and the school has an unquestioned local reputation for quite exceptional pastoral care. Parents pay tribute to the trouble taken over the smallest worry, and pupils feel supported and secure. 'It's been fantastic,' says one mum, 'it's given him the self-esteem he never had at primary school. It gives him clear boundaries and a real structure -he knows what he has to do to get recognised. He feels a valued person.' Monks are always available for individual counselling and support and many are much loved permanent fixtures. Small chapel in the middle of the classroom area in which a Mass is said for anyone who wants to go. Whole school assembly in large, draughty, atrium-like hall, unaccountably not in huger, more congenial and attractive Orchard hall used for dining and productions. Sixth form area includes sizeable common rooms with sofas and vending machine. Pool and snooker tables and TV in rooms unlocked during breaks. Mr Cleugh said to be tightening up on uniform, but boys seemed pretty relaxed about it while not being scruffy.

Pastoral Care and Discipline: 'First and foremost I'm a parent – I know children can get it wrong sometimes,' is Mr Cleugh's immediate humane response when asked about discipline. Drugs, booze, fags no real problem and only two exclusions for repeated theft since head's arrival – 'I don't like doing it but sometimes you have to put the betterment of the whole before the individual'. Clearly, though, this school would not give up on any individual in a hurry. School prefects – known here (though they weren't quite sure why) as 'decans' (apparently the term derives from a word for 'dean' in the Benedictine Rule which is the core of spiritual life here) – assist staff in running things and have some (enough?) privileges in reward. Good system of merits and badges provides incentives and rewards.

Pupils and Parents: 60/40 RCs/non RCs and head hopes, eventually, to up the RC contingent by 10 per cent while seeing 'the academic performance as crucial' and hoping always to attract pupils from other denominations who 'are prepared to embrace our Benedictine ethos'. Multiplicity of ethnic and religious backgrounds in this very multi-racial area. Ealing is home to the second largest Polish community outside Poland (after Chicago) – reflected in school. 50 per cent come from on-site junior school and most of the rest from local state primaries. Some at 11 and 13 from Durston House, Orley Farm and other local preps. Most live within 5 mile radius but some come from much further afield. Mix of professional backgrounds as you'd expect from its situation. Many pupils have sisters at nearby Notting Hill and Ealing HS GDST and some of the sixth form girls are escapees from there. OBs include Chris Patten CH, Peter Ackroyd, Declan Donnellan.

Entrance: Most come at 11. 80 places. All do entrance exams in maths, English and verbal reasoning. Most interviewed and only the academically least able RCs and no siblings are turned away. About 16-20 places at 13, entrance via school's exam and CE. Sixth form requirements a minimum of 6 GCSEs at C or above and Bs in A level subjects.

Exit: Virtually all to good universities and to an impressive range of courses – no stereotypes here. Half a dozen or so to Oxbridge (seven in 2005 and 11 applying for 2006).

Money Matters: Limited number of academic scholarships at 11 and 13 and at sixth form - up to 50 per cent fees and can be augmented by bursaries. Also a number of means-tested bursaries.

Remarks: Exactly the school for your brightish but quietish lad who would sink in a larger, or tougher, environment. Not a smart school – nor would strive to be – but an honest, straightforward, hard-working place with a gentle and loving approach.

ST CATHERINE'S SCHOOL

Linked to Saint Catherine's Preparatory School in the Junior section

Station Road, Bramley, Guildford, Surrey, GU5 0DF

Tel: 01483 893 363
Fax: 01483 899 608
E-mail: schooloffice@stcatherines.info
Website: www.stcatherines.info

- Pupils: 535 girls; 135 boarders, rest day • Ages: 11-18 • Size of sixth form: 140 • C of E • Fees: Day: senior school £3,710; prep school £1,830 - £3,010. Boarders £6,105 • Independent • Open days: Senior: November, February, May

---

Head: Since 2000, Mrs Alice Phillips MA (forties), followed a traditional teaching career and was previously deputy head at nearby Tormead. Married with a young daughter, very smart and businesslike, a proud Yorkshire woman – 'I know what is right for my school'. A hands-on teacher, she gets huge enjoyment from teaching and not just being office bound – 'if I can't teach, I can't do my job properly and anyway it helps me know what's going on.' A dynamic head ('with lots of stories about her wonderful girls,' said a parent), but parents and pupils find her very approachable. 'A true professional, who really cares about her school and her pupils,' sums up the opinion of many.

Academic Matters: Very impressive – a tip top local and national player in the academic league. In 2005, 92 per cent grades A/B at A level – many girls with 3 or more grade As. At GCSE, results equally praiseworthy with 40 per cent achieving A* and 98 per cent A*-B grades. In recent years, more than one student has achieved the highest national GCSE mark in a subject. High standards of teaching throughout. Sciences and languages very popular – numerous science and language labs in the school – and full marks to the increasing number of girls studying Latin and Greek. IT facilities are state of the art and would put many companies to shame. Each pupil has her own email address and PC access and increasing amounts of homework can be submitted online – 'very handy' commented one pupil. The sixth form is now wireless networked. Well stocked library – with library stock on the web.

The head is very keen to fine tune independent study. All girls in the first year of the school have lessons in 'Grey Matters' taught by Mrs P, covering learning methods, emotional intelligence etc. Bit trendy, think some, but probably useful in higher education. All this could translate into academic pressure, but most parents agree that the girls are stretched rather than pressured. Some parental grumbling that the focus at the school is always on academic achievement, but as entrance standards are high and girls are very bright, only a few struggle and those who do are supported and encouraged. All girls are tested for SEN on entry particularly for literacy. There is a 'very good' SEN co-ordinator who covers both the junior and senior school. About 5 per cent of the girls have extra help at extra cost. Provision is made for dyslexia, but a girl must have the IQ to support the required level of learning says Mrs P. Not a first choice school for girls who cannot easily keep up with the rigorous academic regime.

Games, Options, The Arts: PE teaching is very strong – netball, lacrosse, swimming, rounders, athletics and gymnastics are all compulsory in games lessons until year 10. Several girls have played lacrosse and netball nationally and an U19 England netball captain was a St Caths girl. The school is very competitive and always up there at inter school sporting competitions – those who take part are expected to show a lot of commitment – pupils often practise netball and lacrosse before school – even in January! Some parental disquiet that there is little opportunity for sport outside PE lessons if you are not part of the 'sporty set'. Mrs P disagrees.

Art building has a stunning range of facilities. Students' work is frequently exhibited both within the school and outside – one piece displayed at Guildford Cathedral received a bid of several hundred pounds. Musical children thrive at the school – teaching is excellent and practice rooms are housed in a purpose built block. There are a number of choirs, orchestras and ensembles providing opportunities for all to join in – not just the talented ones. One parent commented how proud her daughter was of her musical ability – it was not 'cool' at her previous school. Lots of music tuition available – girls are taken out of lessons (not all parents approve but they never do in any school) on a rotational basis so they do not miss the same subject each week. Enthusiastic drama department puts on several productions each year. Older girls take on the main roles but there is usually a part for every one who wants one – a group of students took a play they wrote, directed and performed, to the Edinburgh Fringe. Numerous after-school activities – 'there is a club for everything here,' said one pupil – some parents worry there is just too much and it is difficult to choose.

Background and Atmosphere: Located in a beautiful Surrey village only 10 mins from Guildford, school is housed in attractive buildings – mix of old and new – within extensive grounds. Lots of space and a very rural feel. Generally tidy though some parts are beginning to look a little tired. School chapel nothing special on the outside but beautiful tranquil interior. Used regularly for services and assemblies and for girls to just sit and reflect.

Sixth form centre is well planned and cosy with quiet study areas for day girls. Sixth form boarding popular – it is good practice for university, commented one pupil. Two share a typical teenage bedroom. 'We get lots of privileges,' and there is plenty to do. Pilates classes in the evenings. Weekend activities include trips to rugby matches and West End shows (weekly boarders can go along too). Occasional social events with boys' schools at weekends. Younger boarders' houses comfortable but certainly not plush, up to six to a room. Most boarders go home at weekends. Flexiboarding for those parents who have to work away for periods – space permitting. Girls can also have supper at school when competing in sport or music activities in the evenings – very useful. 'The food is fantastic,' commented girls and staff alike, and all meals are served in a light airy building more reminiscent of a restaurant than a school dining hall. Lots of choice, healthy options, popular salad bar and more traditional school fare. Very lively atmosphere but pupils are well behaved. Uniform enforced fairly strictly.

Pastoral Care and Discipline: House system. Lots of inter-house activities and a fun day for new girls at the beginning of each year to get to know new house members. The house system is more light hearted than competitive, thought one parent – girls may think differently as there are lots of inter house events such as drama and even 'Pop Idol' competitions.

Communication between home and school is frequent. Discipline fairly strict – although Mrs P prefers to describe it as 'firm'. System of rewards and sanctions operates linked to the 'Traditions of St Catherine's' – basically the school rules. Clear alcohol, drinking and smoking policy – breaches are rare according to staff. The girls take an obvious pride in the school. Very little evidence of bullying – nothing more than usual school banter said parents. As a C of E school, everyone attends chapel once a week. Services are led by a local chaplain who is 'really good' – a refreshing remark – acute boredom is the more usual comment from pupils in other schools.

Pupils and Parents: Thought by many outsiders to be 'very posh', St Cat's is upmarket but not intimidatingly so. Pupils mainly from the surrounding affluent Surrey towns Guildford, Farnham, Godalming, Esher, Oxshott and increasingly from the homes of the chattering classes in south west London – the school has become very fashionable in recent years. There is also an international flavour particularly among the boarders. Parents are largely professional – lawyers, bankers, doctors, diplomats etc. Obviously intelligent and necessarily wealthy, there are a number of first time buyers. Parents who chose St Cat's say they are looking for an alternative to the sophisticated, 'city centre' atmosphere and freedom of the other nearby academic schools of Tormead or Guildford High. Notable old girls include actress Juliet Stevenson and poet Ursula Fanthorpe. Many old girls return to the school to talk about their careers and experiences – much appreciated apparently by the pupils.

Entrance: At 11+ by exam in verbal reasoning, English, maths and science (and the report from the previous school is also very important). School places emphasis on academic achievement and 'they are looking for the brightest girls,' said one parent. A useful tip – several parents checked how well their daughters had done in the entrance exam before accepting a place – they were worried whether an average girl, who just passed the exam, would be able to keep pace in the future. About 45 per cent come from own prep school, although admission is by no means automatic, with a growing list of other regular feeders which include St Hilary's Godalming, Rowan, Halstead, Amesbury and Waverley Abbey. Prospective pupils can have a taster day. Increasing number of requests to enter at sixth form – boarding is very popular. Seen as a good opportunity to 'enrich the mix,' entrance requirements are an IQ test, general studies paper, interview and a minimum of 6 GCSEs Grade C or above – though in reality applicants have much higher scores.

Exit: 10 -15 per cent leave after GCSE mainly to mixed sixth form colleges locally (the temptation of more freedom and boys no doubt). Of those who stay, most go on to traditional universities Durham, Bristol, York and a handful to Oxbridge.

Money Matters: Four academic and one music scholarship offered at 11. In the sixth form, there are also ten internal academic scholarships, one sport, one music, one art and three external academic scholarships. Amounts range from one sixth to one third of the fees.

Remarks: An increasingly fashionable, upmarket school with superb academia and facilities. Ideally suited for the clever and the outgoing.

ST CHRISTOPHER SCHOOL

Linked to Saint Christopher School Junior School in the Junior section

Barrington Road, Letchworth, Hertfordshire, SG6 3JZ

Tel: 01462 679 301
Fax: 01462 481 578
E-mail: admissions@stchris.co.uk
Website: www.stchris.co.uk

• Pupils: 370 boys and girls, including 67 boarders • Ages: 11 - 19 • Size of sixth form: 95 • Non-denom • Fees: Junior school £2,415 - £3,000; senior school £3,855 - £6,775 • Independent

Head: Since 2004, Mr Donald Wilkinson MA MLitt (early fifties). Educated at the Royal Grammar School, Lancaster and Keble College, Oxford, where he got a history first. Previously at Manchester Grammar, Oakham and Newcastle-under-Lyme, then appointed head of Cheadle Hume in 1990. His second headship was Jerudong International School in Brunei. Married with four children; interests include sport and running ('depressingly slowly'). He feels that the traditional St Chris virtues of informality and tolerance need a strong academic underpinning. 'It has always considered itself set apart from the rest of the world but must recognise that there are important functions that the world expects it to fulfil. Good results and idealism are not mutually exclusive.'

Academic Matters: St Chris prides itself on taking children of wide-ranging abilities from 'average' upwards. Its results are very commendable, with over 98 per cent of pupils getting 5+ A* – C grades at GCSE in 2005, with 34 per cent A*/A grades. More than half of A levels were graded A or B. Art and psychology are two of the most popular A level subjects, from a list that includes photography, business studies and government and politics. Classes are small, averaging 18, with many A level classes in single figures. Pupils get a wide choice at GCSE, as only five subjects – two English, double science and maths – are compulsory. Other options include three modern languages, PE and IT. 'A broad education is vital to an individual's development but it is also vital that they are stimulated academically. I am very keen for the academic side to be as strong as it can be.'

Excellent support for individual needs from a specialist, highly-trained team. The school copes well with dyslexia and dyspraxia. A 'second to none' in-house counselling service is available. A handful of pupils have Aspergers. 'But we are certainly not a specialist unit,' says the head of Individual Needs. 'Other schools can cope better.' Some have one-to-one tuition (at extra cost), others are helped by a learning support assistant. Mainstream staff are given information and training on different needs. 'We have a strong individual needs department and we hope to make it stronger,' says the head. 'The true aim of learning support is to help with difficulties with a view to the child eventually managing on their own.'

Games, Options, The Arts: Not, traditionally, a school that excels at team sports. It is known rather for its magnificent climbing wall, its skateboard park and the outdoor pursuits club, which goes off for weekends surfing, climbing, potholing, white-water rafting. However, competitive sports are increasingly important; netballers are off to Spain and basketball is particularly popular. Standards in team sports like soccer and rugby are improving. 'Because we are so small, everyone has got a better chance of being part of a team.' Extensive playing fields, sports hall, new indoor swimming pool and the Letchworth Tennis Club is handily situated next door. At the end of the summer term the school decamps to a range of destinations from the Cotswolds to Saas Fee. Art, including pottery, ceramics and photography, is strong at all levels, with plenty of spectacular work on display. DT is also important, with much emphasis on craftsmanship.

Plenty of performance opportunities, from major school musicals to orchestral concerts to recycled fashion shows. Great praise for the drama – 'the teacher took care to get to know all the children before he cast the play' – and the after-school music club. 'It's all about sharing and enjoying the experience of playing in a group.'

Lower sixth formers have the opportunity to spend time in Rajastan and/or Kosovo, visiting schools and development projects with which the school has had considerable involvement over the years.

Background and Atmosphere: Set up in 1915 under Theosophist principles, which include a wide age and ability range and co-education. Excellent, vegetarian meals; many Quaker influences, with pauses for silent reflection in meetings and assemblies. Self-government is central to the

school ethos, and the head is in the process of reviewing the workings of the school council, which meets every two weeks. 'We need to find ways of ensuring that the council has an effective part to play. It should involve pupils in how the school operates, including what goes on in lessons. As a teacher, I like to ask pupils occasionally what works and what doesn't work.'

The 35-acre site accommodates a harmonious blend of old and new buildings, including the award-winning junior school extension, with its glazed roof and low energy use, and the new senior school IT and English building, built of wood and glass with a grass roof. The school has a very active environment committee and has won the Eco-Schools green flag award for energy monitoring.

Pastoral Care and Discipline: Liberal, caring, nurturing ethos, with no uniform and staff and pupils on first name terms. 'There's an air of tolerance here,' said a parent. 'They don't stamp on you for being eccentric.' Some parents are concerned that the greater emphasis on academic achievement may come at the expense of the liberal ethos. 'It is very important to look after children as individuals,' says the head, 'but not by allowing them to do as they please. We work for the child's best interests, but do not allow them to fulfil themselves at the expense of their work or behaviour.'

Drugs and alcohol are 'occasional problems that are dealt with as appropriate'. No prefects: sixth formers are elected to take charge of aspects of school life such as games, the environment and social events. The boarding system has been reviewed and will continue on largely weekly boarding lines.

Pupils and Parents: A liberal lot, who have found an alternative to more hot-house, authoritarian establishments, and tend to be fiercely protective of the school ethos. The school runs a daily bus service from north London; most other pupils live nearby or along the rail route which runs from Kings Cross to Cambridge. After school, a steady stream of pupils make their way the mile or so to the station.

Entrance: Most junior school pupils move on automatically, 'unless we feel in the light of experience that the child wouldn't benefit from the senior school. We try to keep parents fully aware and school and family will make the decision together.' Outsiders come in for half a day, take part in assessments which include cognitive ability tests and extended writing, and have an interview. Parents can chat with senior staff at the same time. 'We take children whom we think will do well. We try to assess their underlying ability and to build up a rounded view.' Students coming into the sixth form need at least five grade Bs at GCSE.

Exit: A few leave after GCSEs for sixth form colleges,

schools closer to home or those with greater vocational opportunities. Nearly all sixth form leavers go on to higher education – including two or three a year to Oxbridge – to do courses that range from Astrophysics at Exeter to, wonderfully, Surf Science and Technology at Plymouth.

Money Matters: A few bursaries are available for families who fall into financial difficulty, but not a hugely endowed school.

Remarks: Liberal, creative school with strong spiritual underpinning and environmental values. The new head is set on greater academic rigour; parents are happy with this while still wishing to preserve the liberal outlook.

St Clare's, Oxford

139 Banbury Road, Oxford, OX2 7AL

Tel: 01865 552 031
Fax: 01865 513 359
E-mail: admissions@stclares.ac.uk
Website: www.stclares.ac.uk

• Pupils: 360, mixed • Ages: 15+ - 20, plus adults on senior courses • Size of sixth form: 199 • No affiliation • Fees: Full boarding £24,080 pa; weekly boarding £ 22,415 pa, non residential £14,840 pa • Independent • Open days: October and March; arranged visits to sit in on classes welcomed

Principal: Since 2005, Ms Paula Holloway (early fifties), who took a BSc in Geography at London University. From 1991 – 2000 she was deputy and then head of Latifa School for Girls in Dubai, and from 2000 – 2004 head of Ashford School in Kent. She is married to Stephen, a management consultant. Former head (Since 1998), Mr Boyd Roberts, has departed for pastures new and unspecified.

Academic Matters: St Clare's is a complex beast; the main thrust of the programmes is threefold. Around 200 students study for the International Baccalaureate Diploma (27-year history of teaching this – longest in England, with centuries of experience on the staff – and an impressive pass rate, particularly given that 'students are not selected as certs') with a pre-IB course (30 students, up to one year) for those whose English or academic standard is not high enough. The University Foundation Course is primarily geared to overseas or indeed home-grown students whose English or qualifications may not be up to entry requirements. With adult, ie 18+, English language, they number 80 students on a separate site, with separate boarding. The liberal arts programme offers around 45 students (mostly

from US universities) a taster of the intellectual way of life in Britain, as well as serious academics, and can count for credits at American universities. Help with dyslexia throughout. An IB Institute offers short summer courses for students and officially approved workshops for practising IB teachers.

Well-equipped classrooms – more like boardrooms than any we have seen elsewhere, good labs, art rooms and study areas. Banks of computers. Fabulous resources centre and library. Staff (20 nationalities) are inspired and not all part of the north Oxford mafia, quite a number relocated from abroad, which contributes to the international outlook of St Clare's.

Games, Options, The Arts: CAS (Creativity, Action and Service) is an essential part of the IB course and all students must spend at least one afternoon a week doing something. St Clare's has use of local playing fields and sports centres; basketball is very popular and the range of activities on offer is huge. Choose from aerobics, tennis, dance, yoga, environmental action, soccer, Model UN, photography, Young Enterprise ... and the notice board when we visited also offered lessons in DJ-ing and trips everywhere. Good strong art, which can also be taken along with drama, as part of the CAS option. Debating popular and masses of lectures and International Days open to all IB students across the country – gender and human rights, science and ethics. Service includes projects with homeless people in Oxford, Oxfam, and conservaion work. St Clare's supports a rural primary school in Tanzania with awareness raising, fund raising and individual projects.

Background and Atmosphere: Main buildings are stunning conversions of Edwardian Oxford houses; the recently converted library building has the back knocked out to accommodate a lift and fabulous classrooms in pale ash. Impressive. Accommodation available for all, some quite close along the Banbury Road with twenty supervised halls of residence, and some further out – a manor house in Kidlington has been converted into mini-flats for older students on senior courses. Weekly and full residential, although day students welcomed and attached to a house.

Gorgeous dining room with conservatory (the gardens are not bad either) and inspired café, The Sugar House, which was filled to capacity with students at break time – coffee, buns, pizza – that kind of thing with loud music and a terrific atmosphere and very, very popular. Students have a card topped up to a certain amount of cash daily and they choose where they want to eat and how to spend their allowance – usually buying bottled water to use up their allowance at the end of the day.

A recent initiative is an attempt to promote global citizenship throughout the college. The IB academic programme has been tweaked to reflect this – houses deal with conflict resolution; recycling prominent; inter-cultural understanding promoted. Principal a leading voice on such matters within the IB.

Pastoral Care and Discipline: Excellent. Each student has a personal tutor; the halls of residence – single sex – have wardens and are closely supervised. Strong PSE programme; last principal reckoned that 'education is a balance of making mistakes and learning from them', but asked about one a year to leave, plus some 'assisted departures'. Relatively few rules, firmly implemented; students respond by staying within them – for the most part. Fierce on absenteeism, drugs not necessarily out, but counselled, as with over-toping; dealing automatically out, help with stopping smoking – clinics and the like, but otherwise very restricted smoking area – out in the open in a dingy corner. Overt displays of sexual nature discouraged, more relaxed rules for the adult students. Reflection room but no organised religion.

Pupils and Parents: Over forty different nationalities, so huge variety. Slightly more girls than boys as we write.

Entrance: By application, on school record, reference and interview (where possible – essential for UK applicants). Non-English speakers may have to take a written test.

Exit: Over seventy UCAS referrals annually, St Clare's is an SAT centre for American universities. Regularly sends five to Oxbridge, lots to London, Warwick and other premier/first league universities. Also some to US universities. Full-time higher education adviser, plus US university adviser.

Money Matters: Scholarships and bursaries (up to full fees) available (mandatory interview at St Clare's). First round before Christmas, second round (for larger awards) in February.

Remarks: Truly international, buzzy, fun, gets the right results, couldn't do better for Henry and Caroline if you want to go the IB road.

ST COLUMBA'S SCHOOL

Linked to Saint Columba's Junior School in the Junior section

Duchal Road, Kilmacolm, PA13 4AU

Tel: 01505 872 238
Fax: 01505 873 995
E-mail: secretary@st-columbas.org
Website: www.st-columbas.org

• Pupils: 360 boys and girls, all day • Ages: 11-18 • Size of sixth form: 120 • Non-denom • Fees: From nursery £654 - senior VI £2,490 • Independent • Open days: November

Rector: Since 2002, Mr David Girdwood BSc PGCE MEd SQH (forties). (SQH = Scottish qualification for heads – the latest wheeze from the Scottish education boys, which will be mandatory in the state sector from 2005, but makes Mr Girdwood a fairly rarefied beast amongst independent heads.) He first taught at Lornshill Academy; was educated at Alva Academy followed by St Andrew's University, Jordanhill, Stirling and Edinburgh universities and comes to St Columba's from Stewarts Melville where he 'taught chemistry for fifteen years'. 'I went to Stewarts as head of chemistry, rising to become head of science and head of upper school and part of the management team', as well as doing his day release in headmastering. A man o' pairts then.

Married to a solicitor wife who works in Edinburgh, he has two children in the school, which he first visited as part of an HMI team and was 'enchanted that pupils gathered for assembly should be so numerous that transitus sat on the stage in front of the rector'. Not so the boss of the HMI team and, as we reported previously, the transitus 11-12 year old class is now banished – apart from forays to the art and music block – to the (admittedly all singing and dancing) junior dept. Early days yet in Mr Girdwood's Renfrewshire experience, but he bemoans 'the lack of policies' and is setting up committees 'to develop anti-bullying policy, ditto health and safety, child protection' et al, as well as encouraging staff appraisal weekends (cor!), combined with 'an explosion of staff going on courses' as well as studying for their SQH. (Look for a rash of new heads ex-St Columba's soon) Keen to involve both management and governors in decision making as well as staff, Mr G has produced a raft of questionnaires and analysis documents. This is definitely new broom stuff, yet the man himself comes over as caring, gentle with only the faintest hint of a rod of iron, and full of really quite sensible ideas. Plans afoot to dramatically improve the facilities at the senior school, the head has schemes for major development, increased facilities (much needed – particularly in the IT, art and science departments) – and is busily eyeing up adjoining property, ditto the disused railway 'across the way').

Parents pleased with the way things are going.

Academic Matters: No change. Highly structured learning with masses of parental encouragement, French very popular, 'Spanish booming' with ten pupils currently following the normal Higher course this year, and ten others doing a 'crash course' of Higher Spanish in one year. Three languages possible at Higher level, 'but not simultaneously' – head of lang dept writes text books. German 'holding its own remarkably well' – some native speakers. Latin for all, Greek 'on demand' but not much take-up recently. Named by Sunday Times as Scottish Independent School of the Year 2004. Results for 2005 'the best ever' and St Columba's came top of the Scottish league. Mod langs and the sciences particularly strong, though revamped labs on the urgent list.

Support for learning to be increased, with dedicated staff in both the senior and junior schools; help on hand for dyslexics and for those who find some subjects particularly difficult. 'Can cope' with ADHD and Ritalin. No problem with pupils with disabilities (but no lifts in the classroom block) though parents of any child needing a dedicated teacher would have to underwrite the cost of that teacher. Class size 20, three classes per year, and pupils setted at 12 (transitus) for English, French, and maths. Exciting new library above former gym; old library now a business study centre. Pupils can work in the library in their free time (with fabulous views to the south to distract them).

Games, Options, The Arts: Good and enthusiastic rugby team, school won Scottish rugby plate in 2001, not bad for a school with only 180 chaps. Regular rugby and hockey tours to Canada. New Astroturf and rugby pitches near senior school though most games are still played on local park near the junior school where there is a vast games hall and weights room. Loos and showers in new primary building are next to the sports hall and the boys' showers have the controls outside, which could cause hours of entertainment. School now plays tennis at the Kilmacolm tennis club adjoining Shallot (as the junior school is known, previously the girls' boarding house, and set in six manicured acres). D of E hugely popular.

Stunning new art and music centre in the Cargill Centre (the old Cargen house adjoining Gryffe Road has been demolished, which means the school now occupies the whole site. The Princess Royal opened the centre in June 2000 – the self-contained ground floor houses the technology department. Music and pipe band popular, for girls as well as boys, as is choir – lots of travel. Art a little prosaic but fabric (design) stunning in interpretation. Home economics for all, but no pottery, photography, or sculpture evident – head promises 'this will be seen to'. Regular exchanges with Canada and Australia on an individual basis but no longer with Europe; recent links with St Petersburg and a one-way Russian exchange! Public speaking all over.

Regular revision classes, weekends, evenings, and classes for all locals, from seven to seventy-year olds, everything from computers, to languages, to bridge. Very popular and good for the community, classes run from September to May.

Background and Atmosphere: Originally part of the Girls' School Company, the school was founded in 1897 and went co-ed (in the face of falling numbers) in 1978 (the junior department) and 1981 (the senior department). The junior department is a long half mile from the senior school. As a result of the fantastic new build and the subsequent shuffling round of classes, transitus, the youngest class in the senior school, is based down here. Fair amount of walking as juniors visit senior school for music, art, IT, HE (home economics) and the sciences, but Shallot is otherwise self-contained. Seniors visit for PE and games. Fair amount of tinkering with senior school fabric under the previous (impressive) incarnation but whilst the original red-brick building is still 'just' recognisable, it seems to have a lot of space dedicated to cloakrooms and passages; the dining hall doubles as assembly, with fold up stool/tables that stack in a cupboard. Imaginative architectural over-view badly needed here despite, or possibly to complement, the recent of new-build. The senior school campus is pretty cramped, with some spare, rather dreary, tarmac, most of which is car park!

Pastoral Care and Discipline: Four houses (sibling and FP tradition) and inter-house everything. Zero tolerance; drugs/theft means out. 'No significant problems with bullying,' said the rector.

Pupils and Parents: 'Very much a Renfrewshire school, with about 80 per cent from within a five mile radius, but regular bus comes from north Ayrshire, and a small nucleus from Dunoon 'across the watter'. Pupils catch the 7.30am boat and join up with the Greenock/Port Glasgow bus. Kilmacolm, a popular sprawling suburban village, once served by the railway, is booming: first time buyers, a tiny wide ethnic base as well as the traditional Kilmacomics (sic). FPs Lord (Ian) Lang, and Eleanor Laing MP. Don't get it wrong, this is not a toffs' school by any means, just good and sensible; pupils 'are not terribly street-wise'.

Entrance: Automatic from junior school to senior school, otherwise own test and interview. Waiting lists all over (except primary five at the moment) and fifteen vying for the dozen places available at other ages. Otherwise places only available as pupils leave.

Exit: Small trickle (very small trickle) leave to go to trad prep schools at 8 or public schools at 13, plus occasionally after they have got university entrance qualifications – ie first year sixth transfer (latest wheeze is to opt for the local state school and apply to Oxbridge – or Bristol – from there). Otherwise 90+ per cent to university, usually in Scotland, 2/3 to Oxbridge on occasion (two currently to Cambridge, 2003) one or two to art college.

Money Matters: Odd bursary available (currently under assessment), means-tested. 'No fall-off' post assisted places scheme. The school can be hit hard when one of the local companies goes down (and suffered badly on the demise of the local sugar company.)

Fees remarkably reasonable, but all parents must cough up £350 for a debenture when their child is accepted; this is returned at the end of the child's time at school (without interest or increase in value). There is a fifty per cent penalty if a place is accepted and not taken up, and a levy of £50 is charged per pupil per term for the Development Fund. Discount of 75 per cent for the third child, 50 per cent for any subsequent children, but the Development Fund levy remains the same. Bursar has been replaced by a business manager (and it shows).

Remarks: Huge waiting lists, academically outstanding, very middle class, stolid, perhaps not terribly imaginative. Victorian values, terribly popular, and may be the reason that houses in boring old Kilmacolm (and this editor once lived there) change hands at a premium, and, to quote a local landowner, 'they actually move into the village because of the school'.

ST DAVID'S COLLEGE, LLANDUDNO

Llandudno, Conwy, LL30 1RD

Tel: 01492 875 974
Fax: 01492 870 383
E-mail: headmaster@stdavidscollege.co.uk
Website: www.stdavidscollege.co.uk

• Pupils: 265, 200 boys, 65 girls (170 board) • Ages: 11-18
• Size of sixth form: 60 • Non-denom • Fees: Boarding £5,260 - £5,465; day £3,420 - £3,553. Dyslexic pupils boarding £5,914 - £6,177; day £4,032 - £4,199 • Independent

Head: Since 1991 Mr William Seymour MA (mid fifties). Educated at Aldenham (head boy) and read natural sciences at Christ's College, Cambridge. Arrived almost by chance at St David's in 1969, liked it, and stayed on, becoming director of studies, housemaster and then head. His wife, Shirley, is a huge support on the pastoral side. One of his two children attended St David's and his daughter has returned as wife to one of the living-in housemasters. A thoughtful, sympathetic man, wise to the ways of the young, and, he says, 'still much stimulated by the environment'. Committed to providing opportunities for young people for whom success, for one reason or another, has proved elusive. Nearing the end of his span – retiring July 2006, but he has established a strong team.

Academic Matters: St David's cannot be judged in any conventional academic sense. It makes no bones about being a school for dyslexics and is rightly proud of both its sense of purpose and achievement in this field. Two thirds of the school have specific learning difficulties and receive special help. In any straight league table comparison it would languish at the lower end but, in what the children achieve against their own capacity for learning and academic success, it would tell a very different tale. Even so, there is a good range of A level options (16 including philosophy, sports science and performing arts) and a respectable showing of As and Bs. In this, and the solid 98 per cent pass rate at all grades, can be found some astonishing personal success stories.

The school has pioneered a multisensory teaching policy for dyslexic pupils, evolving a whole school approach, with much cross-referencing between mainstream and individual lessons. There is an outstanding level of specialist help, given individually or in small groups, in the superbly equipped Cadogan Centre. Surprisingly though, no central library worthy of the name and year group libraries seemed only adequate. Very strong on business studies and powerful performers in the Young Enterprise field. IT provision is excellent, as one would expect in a school like this, and it is used both intensively and extensively. CAD is a speciality, and City and Guilds qualifications are on offer. DT much enhanced by the brand-new centre opened in October 2002. Pupil/teacher ratio 6 to 1.

Games, Options, The Arts: The school aims to 'develop the whole person, promoting self-belief and confidence and meeting the needs and aspirations of each pupil'. So, the emphasis is very much on challenge, teamwork and developing physical and mental robustness and a huge range of activities is on offer. Regard is paid to conventional team games and all children take part and with fair success, but it is up in the hills of Snowdonia, the Alps, the Arctic Circle or Kilimanjaro that St David's comes into its own. There is a powerful team of outdoor activity instructors and the school is full of enthusiastic scuba-divers, kayakers, climbers, trekkers, ocean sailors, kite-buggy riders, 4x4 offroaders, skiers, fell-runners, mountain bikers etc both losing themselves and finding themselves in their own particular activity. Some even go on to represent Wales. D of E an important element. Art is very strong, and half the children learn a musical instrument. Photography is another popular speciality. Drama provision being developed with new investment in theatre equipment.

Background and Atmosphere: Founded in 1965 by John Mayor, who saw dyslexic children in the public school system sinking without trace. He acquired a fine late medieval mansion with 30 odd acres on the edge of the Snowdonia National Park in the outskirts of Llandudno in a wonderful situation and St David's was born. The heart of the school is its dark oak-panelled reception rooms, hung with fine portraits of long-departed Mostyns, but it has spread into every conceivable outbuilding and, while some of the further additions have not exactly added to the aesthetic appeal, they are very fully and inventively used (hobbies rooms, multigym, squash court). It has a delightful unselfconsciousness and no-one, staff or children, seemed aware of tarmac walk areas that looked as if they have been the subject of a not unsuccessful carpet bomb attack, or its dingy corridors. There is however a programme of improvement, with appealing new boarding blocks for both girls and boys already up and running, in which it might be hoped that a general spruce-up one day be included. The effect, though, is friendly and all-embracing, with a good bustle about it, and a warm family atmosphere, and a feeling of care for each other. Very positive Christian ethos.

Pastoral Care and Discipline: The great benefit of a small school, says the head, is that it is difficult to get forgotten. Each pupil is supported by a veritable web of housemasters, tutors and team leaders and no area of life is overlooked. The staff profile leans towards youth, enthusiasm and energy, though there are enough grizzled veterans of the chalkface to give a good balance. Hot on bullying and drugs, though neither is a serious problem.

Pupils and Parents: The pupils are not particularly polished or sophisticated but they are confident, articulate and friendly and enormously proud of their school and what it has helped them to achieve. Dyslexia is no respecter of social or geographical barriers and the children come from every possible walk of life and every part of the country and abroad. At least 30 are statemented by different local authorities and, for others, the fees are a struggle, while at the other end of the scale, the Earl Cadogan was so delighted with what St David's did for his son that he became a school governor and the family showed their appreciation by supporting at least three major building projects which bear the family name. Quite a strong local element too, who choose the school for its good all-round education.

Entrance: Largely at 11. No formal test. Interview and school reports. At the discretion of head, who will take them if he feels children can benefit from what the school has to offer, and the school is sufficiently able to cope with such difficulties as they have. Fills school on a first come, first served basis. Some vacancies at 16.

Exit: Some to vocational courses at 16. Mainly to university, where the large majority will study the more technical subjects.

Money Matters: Excellent value, given marvellous staff/pupil ratio. Non-dyslexics pay on a slightly lower scale.

Remarks: Has no academic pretensions and would not wish to be thought of as smart. Its greatest resource is its people. What they do for children with educational difficulties and, in particular dyslexia, is just marvellous. They are given not just a high level of educational support but the wherewithal, through a huge range of sporting and creative activities, to achieve success and self-esteem and the confidence to take life's difficulties in their stride.

St Dominic's Sixth Form College

Mount Park Avenue, Harrow-on-the-Hill, Middlesex, HA1 3HX

Tel: 0208 422 8084

Fax: 0208 422 3759

E-mail: stdoms@stdoms.ac.uk

Website: www.stdoms.ac.uk

• Pupils: 805; just over half are girls • Ages: 16-19 • RC but other faiths accepted • State • Open days: Contact college

Principal: Since 2004, Mr Patrick Harty BSc PGCE MA(Ed) NPQH, early forties, a scientist and engineer, open, relaxed and positive. Previously taught at 3 schools, then a first deputy headship at Parmiter's School in Watford, a second at Nicholas Breakspear RC School followed by his first headship at Marlborough School – both in St Albans. Mr Harty spent between two and four years in all his previous posts but is clearly in no hurry to move from St Dominic's about which he is infectiously enthusiastic and has plans! Faith is the common denominator here – 'our faith base is just as important as our academic performance', he stresses, and these two factors come up again and again. 'The fundamental mission for the college is to provide education for the Roman Catholics of Harrow – in a multi-faith community ... one of the reasons for our success is that we provide an academic atmosphere.' The job has its challenges and its frustrations but the rewards are palpable too and Mr Harty has the energy and the humour to take it all on. He is impressively and vigorously supported by his vice principal, Mr Mark Nicholls – they were colleagues in St Albans – and clearly enjoy working as a mutually supportive team.

Academic Matters: Teaching is good here. Staff are efficient and pupils warmly praise their dedication and care. Expert help is given to prospective pupils about their subject choices and to existing pupils about their future courses and destinations. A very good range of courses and subjects offered – A levels include art history, business studies, classical civilisation, further maths, human biology, four modern languages, PE and Latin – in addition to all the ones you'd expect. Results are impressive. More than 82 per cent A – C pass rate in 2005. 55 students got three or more A grades, with 18 getting four and two getting five. Biggest cohorts by far in biology, chemistry and psychology – results impressive in all three. Large numbers also taking the other sciences, maths, Eng lit and business studies and average

75-85 per cent A-C in most. AVCEs taken in business studies, ICT and travel and tourism with, again, respectable results or better. GNVQs taken in business – results more mixed but some stars. Few takers for modern languages but results pretty good and outstanding in Italian – all langs taught by native speakers.

SEN is good here and individuals' physical as well as educational needs can be met. Almost everywhere is accessible by wheelchair. Everyone is assessed on enrolment and individual learning programmes are constructed where necessary. A 'Skills for Life' manager, ie a SENCO with add-ons, organises support in class or one-to-one. Little EAL required. Average class size of 16 with max 22.

Games, Options, The Arts: Very little on site – simply there is no space. School borrows facilities from Harrow School down the road but for A level PE only. Games not compulsory but football and a few other sports are options in the Wednesday 'activities' slot. One tarmac playground on which football is played. New block to be opened in September 2006 will free more space for art and DT rooms and facilities – much needed. Art and design and DT taken by small but significant numbers with creditable results. Music is currently taught at a partner school but will move back on site from September 2005 and into the new block the following year. One small trapezoid drama studio – theatre studies taken by 19 students in 2004 with mixed bag of results but this is not a such a high profile subject here. Space is at such a high premium that the school's few larger rooms cannot be spared for large productions.

Work experience, trips, lectures, opera visits, talks, the Duke of Edinburgh Award scheme, conferences – there is plenty going on, though some students feel that more could be done and that peers elsewhere are offered more on the extra-curricular side. Space, again, is a factor. However, the Comenius project sponsored a trip to Malta, a politics group went to Florida, history of art to Rome and the college has good links with schools in Italy. You wouldn't come here on account of the extra-curricular but there are more opportunities here than immediately meet the eye.

Background and Atmosphere: It's like a mini mini university campus – with the stress on mini. A cluster of buildings of different ages and styles sits on a leafy bit of Harrow-on-the-Hill, surrounded by some of the priciest bits of residential north-west London. Private schools are all around – John Lyon, Orley Farm and, of course, the local Big Brother. It's quiet, attractive, enhanced by the super chapel – a 1920s bit of retro Arts and Crafts – but none of the buildings are unappealing and the site has been developed with sensitivity, since giving up being a convent school in 1979. The new 4 storey block is taking up outdoor space the college can ill afford to lose but needs must when you are oversubscribed 3 to 1 and teaching and IT rooms are essentials. It took 7 years to get planning permission so no-one should expect the college's enviable reputation to lead to a rush of new-build to meet demand.

We visited on a sunny spring day so students were gathering everywhere, especially on the few grassy patches. On wintry days there are few places to go and the canteen, in which lunchtime sittings are, of necessity, staggered, is small and unappealing. The food is criticised – 'too expensive and horrible', we were told and certainly there was a preponderance of pasta and pies. Sales, however, are very high so it can't be all bad. There is a salad bar but a two-slice white bread sandwich was £1.20, a jacket potato with tuna mayo £1.50. There is no common room – nor plans for one – and this lack of social space is the students' main complaint. However, there are plans to extend the social space of the canteen and provide an outdoor sheltered area. Off-site there is nowhere much to go either so everything is conducive to work – and these are, in the main, highly motivated students. The atmosphere is harmonious and cooperative and discipline – mostly in the firm-but-fair hands of Mr Nicholls – is enforced, much as you'd expect at any well-run school. There may not be anywhere much to go in non-lesson time but he will make sure you go there. One such resort is the excellent, well-stocked and workful library, another is the ICT room and, by September 2006, the new building will greatly increase workspace. Considering the number of people packed in here it was surprisingly orderly and tidy – we have seen far more mess in far more august and spacious establishments.

Everyone in this very ethnically mixed college looked happily integrated and 'there is no racism here' though we did hear regrets from a few that the ethnic groups didn't mix as much as in students' previous schools. The principal was mystified at this and, certainly, the visual evidence didn't support it. Staff and students seemed on good – first name, in fact – terms and there is a feeling of mutual respect.

Pastoral Care and Discipline: The faith base of the college is crucial and homogenising although no more than 50 per cent of students are Roman Catholic. What counts is faith: 'I will expect the young person to talk about their faith at interview,' says the principal. There is a chaplain and a weekly, voluntary, mass. Everyone has two lessons weekly of Religious and Moral Education. The staff monitors attendance very carefully and there is an electronic registration system at each lesson that picks up unauthorised absence very quickly but absenteeism isn't a problem here. Students realise how prized places are and don't want to jeopardise theirs. Tutors monitor all aspects of a student's life and progress. Many staff stay for 10 plus years – stability counts. Student council and a peer listening system. Progress grades are issued half-termly. Zero tolerance of violence and drugs.

Pupils and Parents: There are 7 boys to 9 girls because more girls meet the academic entrance requirements. Of the 50 per cent who are non RC, 25 per cent are Hindu, 16 per cent Muslim and the rest a mix of everything else. Most live locally in Harrow but they come from more than 50 schools in 5 other boroughs as well as from Berks and Bucks. A commitment to religious faith is the common denominator as well as, increasingly among the non-Catholics, academic ability.

Entrance: The vast majority come from the Salvatorian College and Sacred Heart on unconditional offers. The rest must meet various criteria based on verifiable religious commitment and academic predictions. Criteria vary depending on courses applied for but, for example, for a full A level course in 4 subjects 7 GCSE passes are required + at least Bs in the A level subjects. All are interviewed.

Exit: Local ie the various London University colleges and Brunel predominate here but there's a good crop of other redbricks etc notably Manchester, Southampton, Leicester and so on. Lots of law, business and medical courses but there are fine arts students and teaching students – they go everywhere to do everything. It's a very impressive list and notably lacking silly courses at exploitative institutions. Students from here clearly mean to have proper careers.

Money Matters: Free if you're under 19. Excellent and enlightened system of bursaries for students and staff to fund specific projects and trips.

Remarks: Measured against its peers on academic achievement, St Doms outscores virtually all the local competition. If the serious work/faith combination does it for you and outweighs the space and facilities other places offer, get onto your priest/imam/rabbi pronto and get those grades.

St Dunstan's College

Linked to St Dunstan's College Junior School in the Junior section

Stanstead Road, Catford, London, SE6 4TY

Tel: 020 8516 7200
Fax: 020 8516 7300
E-mail: jdavies@sdmail.org.uk
Website: www.stdunstans.org.uk

• Pupils: 480 boys and 340 girls, all day • Ages: 11-18 • Size of sixth form: 150 • Anglican foundation • Independent

Head: Since 2005, Ms Jane Davies BSc. She joined the College in 2000 as deputy head having been head of maths at Trinity School in Croydon.

Academic Matters: At A level 66 per cent of grades A or B, at GCSE 44 per cent A or A*. Class sizes small, 20 max in prep, pre-prep and lower senior school, smaller thereafter. Youngish staff, average 35 years, one third female. Pupils are setted for maths in years 7-9 and in all subjects for GCSE. Lessons are well structured, homework is taken seriously and there is a feeling of serious intent and work to be done around the busy and sometimes crowded school corridors. Staff training taken seriously. Achieving well especially given the competition from selective schools on its doorstep, which take the highest flyers. Very few children have special educational needs.

Games, Options, The Arts: Sport is important, although if you're not a rugger bugger you'll still fit in and get along OK. Less sporty pupils head for the popular after-school clubs – pets to chess. National U13 fives champions and school judo champions. Enthusiastic games staff include specialists such as Neil Taylor, a former county and England cricket player. One third of the school learns a musical instrument and there is plenty of activity, with two school orchestras, concerts at Southwark cathedral, six choirs, and regular overseas visits. Drama strong, with 15 in-house productions each year, an electronic workshop for learning the art of theatre production. Corridors are adorned with pupils' art – run of the mill stuff. Duke of Edinburgh Award Scheme: second nationwide for number of awards; CCF strong.

Background and Atmosphere: Originally built as a boys' school in 1888, went co-educational over ten years ago. The old building, fondly described by some as Hogwartesque, is dark and imposing, though there's some

OK new build. Busy inner-city site next to a road junction is not enviable, nor is tangling with the South Circular a joyful way to spend your mornings, nor is the immediate area notably salubrious. Parents and the coaches drive inside the gates to drop the children off.

Pastoral Care and Discipline: Pastoral care is excellent, 'cannot be faulted' according to parents, a real strength of the school with a lot of effort and manpower invested in it. 'St Dunstan's picked up instantly on a special educational need for my child, which had not been noticed in two other independent prep schools. They were extremely supportive and my child was not singled out in any way.' There are heads of year, heads of section, a prefect system and mentor if needed.

Discipline is firm and the school take a harder line than the rest of society on misdemeanours. Straight out for drugs. Bullying not tolerated – it (but one hopes not the bully) is stamped on as soon as it appears.

Pupils and Parents: Parents are professional but in no way snooty – would consider Alleyn's to be stuffy, Dulwich College to be overwhelming; school suits a more laid-back, happy-go-lucky child. 30 per cent of pupils are from ethnic minorities, which reflects the immediate neighbourhood; all pupils speak English. Children come from all over south east London; coaches daily from Blackheath, New Cross, Clapham, Streatham, Farnborough and Bromley. After-school club until 5pm.

Entrance: With improving results it's become easier to recruit staff and the school is becoming more academically selective. Oversubscribed – half from the prep school and most of the rest from other independents. Exam preparation available on Saturday mornings in the autumn term.

Exit: Most pupils go to their first choice of university, one third of those are to the top tier universities to read medicine and other academic subjects. A couple to Oxbridge.

Money Matters: Competitively priced for a London day school. Around 10 pupils per year get some help with fees - to be eligible household income must be under £25,000.

Remarks: Busy, bustling feel. A useful option

St Edward's Oxford

Woodstock Road, Oxford, Oxfordshire, OX2 7NN

Tel: 01865 319 200

Fax: 01865 319 202

E-mail: registrar@stedwards.oxon.sch.uk

Website: www.stedwards.oxon.sch.uk

- Pupils: 660; 430 boys, 230 girls. 480 board, 180 day
- Ages: 13-18 • Size of sixth form: 255 • C of E
- Fees: £7,208 boarding; £5,694 day • Independent
- Open days: Contact school

Warden: Since 2004, Mr Andrew Trotman MA PGCE, a Balliol English graduate, fiftyish. Married with two school-age children. Previously a teacher at Radley, Abingdon and the Edinburgh Academy where he was deputy rector, Mr Trotman's first headship was, from 1995, at St Peter's, York where he was much and warmly respected. At St Edward's he incorporates into his timetable half a term's teaching of each class in year 9 – good to see. Soft-spoken, relaxed and friendly, Mr Trotman has inherited a super school in superb nick so the challenge is to build on existing success and keep ahead of the not especially fierce competition. The school is a bit of a treasure – an essential bit of the North Oxford landscape, physically and spiritually – with a high-achieving, demanding and largely prosperous clientele. Mr Trotman's quiet assurance and civilised approach seems likely to strengthen St Edward's established reputation as one of the best co-ed boarding schools we have.

Academic Matters: School famously accepts children with 50 per cent at Common Entrance – 'we are broad but not mediocre,' affirms the warden. Maintaining this breadth of ability is at the heart of the school's ethos. 'I want them all to be challenged,' says the Warden, 'no child deserves second best.' The most able clearly achieve as highly here as anywhere and in 2005, 14 per cent of the year 13 students were offered Oxbridge places. At GCSE in 2004, A*-C grades were achieved in 96 per cent of subject entries by boys and in 97 per cent by girls – remarkable congruity. Of the majority subjects, good results in history and geography and, of the minor options, statistics, Greek, art and design and music did especially well. 2004 A level results – good showings in all languages – old and new; also in further maths, physics and, again, art. English is popular as are history, maths and – you guessed it, art. Everyone does political literacy – we approve.

A quarter of the school has some kind of, usually, minor learning difficulty eg mild dyslexia or organisational/study skills problems and gets well-supported by the Learning Support dept – two and a half teachers. This is probably not the place for more serious SpLDs. A few each year need some kind of EAL help – as does a sizeable proportion of the domestic staff – and all are supported by the EFL dept – most enlightened. The EAL help usually means withdrawal from a foreign language class – fair enough. Two scholars' groups have a special programme of events laid on for them but all are welcome to take part. This group tends to make up the Oxbridge hopefuls later on. The timetable is, unusually, constructed on an eight-day cycle – you get used to it.

Games, Options, The Arts: The glory of St Edward's. Pupils pay tribute to the 'co-curricular' – 'you can never do it all', said one. A clever subway under the Woodstock Road leads to the stunning fields – 90 acres of them – and all kinds of pitches, courses and courts abound as far as you can see. The Esporta Sports Centre at the heart of the site is vast, open to the public and clearly very popular but also, of course, a central asset to the school. It has everything you have ever seen in a sports centre – only bigger and more of them. For example: 4 indoor tennis courts on wonderful velvety carpet-like flooring, the most enormous gym in the world with endless banks of machines of every kind, indoor and outdoor pools, studios for all kinds of dance and other activities, beauty centres and a vast sports hall. Teddies' pupils have open access to it all along with time-tabled classes – a very special privilege for the sporty and non-sporty as there are alternatives for everyone. Results are correspondingly strong – school is first XI county hockey champion and has pupils in various national sides at all levels including twelve in the U16s rugby; they row, they win at netball and have individual stars in several sports. Silver and gold Duke of Edinburgh Awards come in barrowfuls; CCF is very strong.

Likewise art and music. We were treated to some of the biggest studios and most impressive results in many media, notably ceramics, we have enjoyed anywhere. Art and design are clearly big here – in range, inventiveness and in results. There is a gallery which displays work by both pupils and inspiring visiting professionals. A huge design workshop with woodworking and metalworking machines, as well as a 'hot metal room', CADCAMs, and jewelry-making facilities – terrific equipment turning out witty and clever things eg a brilliant Hollywood-style dog-bed, coffee tables, water sculptures, natural lighting projects and a bike-powered salt spreader. If you like making things, you'll make your dreams here. No textiles on the syllabus, though there are sewing facilities.

Music strong too despite uninspiring building which houses it – loads of individual lessons and more ensembles of all kinds than there was room on the noticeboard to advertise – large numbers seemingly signed up to everything. Parents and staff join in large scale events. Terrific programme of musical events including recitals, full scale choral works, trips, tours and visiting high calibre professionals – music is high profile and arguably richer here than in many more prominent schools.

Background and Atmosphere: North Oxford = large and solid, well-proportioned, Victorian redbrick houses in broad, comfortable and peaceful leafy streets. Combine that with the college quad idea and you have the essence of Teddy's – a super quad, spacious with central lawn and flower bed, well-spaced, attractive buildings around the perimeter and others, mostly boarding houses, behind them. Other boarding houses abut the playing fields – and all within a short walk of Oxford's heart and a moment from the local Summertown shops. Quiet, civilised values pervade the atmosphere – exemplified in the Warden's practice of lunching twice weekly in the beautiful wood-panelled dining room, with different year/tutor/house groups and once weekly with guests selected by the head boy and girl eg a winning side or cast of play or even the Reformed Naughty Pupils' Club.

About two thirds of pupils are boys, about three quarters board – proportions that seem to work and are unlikely to change much pro tem. Atmosphere is a relaxed amalgam of the traditional and the bang-up-to-date. The chapel is a sober, plain but attractive building in which lines of plaques touchingly commemorate OSEs fallen in the Matabele wars, the Boer war and, of course, WWI and II. ICT used sanely as a means rather than an end – prep is given with helpful attachments eg videos, extension work, notices sent out electronically and not posted on boards which no-one checks; PCs are everywhere including 10 in each house and every block has a large computer room. There is a vast school hall used for all major events but a new performing arts centre with a 300-seat theatre, also to be shared with the local community, is due to open in 2006.

Boarding accommodation is good. Rooms are relatively large and are shared by boarders and day pupils – it seems to work. Innovations include clever siting of desk, cupboard and basin downstairs and a mezzanine reached by ladder to the bed above in single study/bedrooms. Corridors are carpeted and well-kept with pictures – this feels more like a plain but good hotel than a boarding school.

Pastoral Care and Discipline: A relaxed but controlled attitude prevails. The Summertown shops are accessible to everyone, in small groups for the younger pupils, and Oxford itself is there for the taking on some Sundays or Saturday evenings for the upper sixth – also in the evening for the older pupils. There are, of course, temptations and Mr Trotman uses the word 'firm' repeatedly when conveying the school's attitude to misdemeanours. 'We've worked hard at tightening control,' he asserts but there have been no major problems in his first two years though 'youth and alcohol is always a battle.' An uncompromising attitude to drugs – it's out for possession or use. Minor recent rumblings about bullying not as quickly dealt with as we would like.

Students feel supported and praise the democratic house and year councils – 'if you have a comment or a complaint they do listen' – and they cite examples of good changes after pupils have made a case. Clear tutorial system supported by prefects. No weekly/flexi/occasional boarding – you're here for the whole ride. You'll be happy if you join in.

Pupils and Parents: From a vast number of schools – 53 preps in 2005 and, especially girls, from local and less local primaries too. Most but not all from within the Berks/Bucks/Oxon/London areas. Small handfuls from the world but no specially large groups from anywhere. School has strong links with Thailand but few Thai pupils. Parents a considerable mix – the urban, the rural, the academic – as you'd expect. OSEs of note include Guy Gibson and Douglas Bader, Nicholas Budgen, Laurence Olivier, George Fenton and John Berger, Katie Knapman, Jon Snowe, Kenneth Grahame, Bishops Paul Burrough and David Bartlett, numerous sportsmen, MDs and academics.

Entrance: Apply early and in consultation with your child's prep. There is no vast pressure nor oversubscription but it works in a civilised way through the Warden's relationship with the child's existing school and the aim is to take children who are right for the school – and for whom the school is right. Warden hates to turn down a child but will if he feels that it simply won't work. CE is the main means of entry but doubtful candidates and non-CE candidates, eg girls at schools which stop at 11, will take school's own assessment tests in the May prior to entry. Such girls, of course, need to find a school for the next two years before entry. Occasional places thereafter.

Exit: No bias here – they go everywhere to do everything from politics at Aberdeen to physiotherapy in Wales. The range suggests a sane and liberal approach. A good Oxbridge contingent each year.

Money Matters: Boarding and day schols/bursaries for academic/sports/arts all available but anything above 10 per cent is now means-tested.

Remarks: An urbane school with a country feel but with all the advantages of a splendid city and London within easy reach. Best for your all-rounder boy or girl and for those who want to socialise and take part in everything. A less grand place than its obvious competitors and less pressurising than some, but offering every kind of opportunity in a highly privileged and civilised setting.

SAINT FELIX SCHOOLS

Linked to Saint Felix Schools, Preparatory School in the Junior section

Halesworth Road, Reydon, Southwold, Suffolk, IP18 6SD

Tel: 01502 722 175
Fax: 01502 722 641
E-mail: schooladmin@stfelix.suffolk.sch.uk
Website: www.stfelix.co.uk

• Pupils: 148 girls and boys in the senior school, 140 girls and boys in prep/pre-prep, 54 in nursery, 51 boarders • Ages: 1-18 • Size of sixth form: 37 • Non-denom • Fees: Prep/pre prep £1,200 - £2,200. Senior: day £2650 - £3850; boarding (weekly and day from year 6) £4,200 - £5.850 • Independent • Open days: Saturdays in May and October

---

Head: Since 2004, Mr David Ward (early forties), is overall head of the merged schools. Taught at Kimbolton School, then was deputy head at Cokethorpe. Married, two young children, both in the prep department. Is fulfilling a life-long ambition to be a headmaster. Very approachable, with lots of boyish charm and a shrewd business sense. Keen to raise profile and numbers and hopes to attract more weekly boarders with second homes in the region, and has already successfully launched a 'sponsor-a-window' scheme to repair and restore 1,000 windows. Enthusiastic sportsman (loves rugby). Some teachers claim they have been led out of jail as they feel more in charge of their own areas. A committed Christian.

Academic Matters: Results largely reflect wide intake but small, even sometimes tiny, groups and very committed teaching staff mean that individuals do their very best and high achievers achieve highly. The new head quickly spotted areas of weakness and didn't hang back. Maths support has been introduced, for example, for those with difficulties, in addition to already good provision for English (both as first and second language). Maths particularly good at A level. A modern language (choice of three) is compulsory at GCSE, and school is keen to keep Latin as an option,

although it is only taught as an extra-curricular activity to begin with. Classrooms in senior school are a bit of a nondescript hotch-potch, but adequate, and the main library, which hasn't changed since the year dot, is about to be re-equipped for the 21st century. As of recently, there is no Saturday school but lessons finish at 5pm every day except Friday (4pm).

Games, Options, The Arts: Impressive art department obtains amazingly bold results from seemingly quiet and well-behaved children. Photography is outstanding, with exceptional results at A level. Very vibrant and creative music department – a high proportion of pupils learn an instrument. Great emphasis on sport (and on winning!), with excellent facilities including a super swimming pool, fitness suite and equestrian centre, all also used by local community and parents. A GB swimming coach is now in charge of swimming and she intends to train an Olympic champion! Good programme of non-overlapping evening and weekend activities.

Background and Atmosphere: Beautiful if windswept 82 acre site, with fine red brick purpose-built buildings dating from 1897, with more modern additions. A well ordered, friendly atmosphere manages to prevail despite a certain echoing emptiness about the place. Numbers still stand at not much more than half what they should ideally be. Particularly under the new head, the school is very involved in the local community through sporting activities, local radio, music and the church. Head promotes strong Christian and traditional ethos.

School came close to extinction, with governors losing heart, but parents rallied and it's now again on the up.

Pastoral Care and Discipline: No discipline problems. With small numbers, pupils are well cared for as individuals. There is a 'buddy' system for new pupils, and one for new parents too. Foreign students spend exeat weekends with school families whenever possible.

Pupils and Parents: Largely from north Suffolk, south Norfolk and the A12 corridor, but a significant number of overseas students (from Ethiopia, Nigeria, Russia, Holland and China), particularly in the 6th form. Parents much involved and highly supportive. The school will be fully co-ed by 2007.

Entrance: Via exam and interview at 11 (most-comers accepted). 5 GSCEs and interview for sixth form.

Exit: To a wide variety of courses, with a very good smattering of top universities.

Money Matters: Academic scholarships (up to 50 per cent of fees), academic and music exhibitions (up to 25 per cent) for entrants 11-16. Academic, music, sport, art and drama scholarships and exhibitions for sixth form entrants. Also bursaries for needy pupils.

Remarks: The new head really looks as if he might succeed where others have not entirely done so in expanding a thoroughly worthwhile school, where the whole person is well catered for (very well gastronomically), but which has struggled to survive in the past. The atmosphere of optimism is palpable.

St George's College, Weybridge

Weybridge Road, Addlestone, Surrey, KT15 2QS

Tel: 01932 839 300
Fax: 01932 839 301
E-mail: contact@st-georges-college.co.uk
Website: www.st-georges-college.co.uk

• Pupils: 320 girls, 520 boys, all day • Ages: 11-18 • Size of sixth form: 205 • RC but others welcome • Fees: 1st and 2nd years £3,275, then £3,770 • Independent • Open days: September and March

Head: Since 1994, Mr Joseph Peake (fifties) educated at Oxford (degree in chemistry), previously director of curriculum at Millfield and taught at Manchester Grammar School. Married, a chief examiner in A level chemistry, and chairman of SHMIS (Society of Headmasters and Headmistresses of Independent Schools). A strong leader: sits erect and upright, knows what he is doing is right and knows exactly what he expects from his staff and pupils. Very confident and hugely ambitious for the school (particularly to make it more academically selective), 'I want us to be the best in the country, an exemplary Christian role model for a 21st century co-ed school.' Parents generally speak well of him: 'he is doing a great job – we don't see enough of him because he is so busy.' Some niggles about him being 'self-assured' and 'somewhat intimidating.' When asked to describe himself, he is 'still enjoying life to the full.'

Academic Matters: Solid. Caters for most abilities with noticeably improving exam results (62 per cent A*/A GCSE), but not a real academic powerhouse (although one feels Mr P would like it be). Academia has (rightly or wrongly) always been perceived as secondary to the stunning sporting/extracurricular side of the school, but the academic souls do get some very good results and Mr P is obviously on a mission for the school to rise up the academic league tables. Pupils are setted in maths and French from year 1. Latin is also

taught in year 1, but can then be substituted for a technology based subject. ICT taught in the first 2 years, but is optional thereafter – an issue with some parents – slightly compensated by the introduction of ECDL (European Computer Driving Licence – a certificate to verify computer skills and competence) though this is still at its early teething stages. Max class size 22, bright, quite large class rooms – some in need of modernisation. Library well equipped but ICT could be improved. Academic support is provided for those with mild dyslexia and dyspraxia – one dedicated teacher. However, check thoroughly before applying whether the school would be right for a SEN pupil. Mr P says: 'We do not face issues with academic support since our entrance exams are so highly selective. About 25 students (3 per cent) receive extra help and they have been able to pass the entrance exams.'

Games, Options, The Arts: Much praised in all areas. A sporty soul's delight particularly for tennis, hockey and rowing. Tennis facilities are mega impressive – jaw droppingly extensive courts the envy of any school. Rowing is also high profile. Huge grounds, lots of pitches, the school oozes sport (though v surprising that no swimming pool). National and regional sports cups and awards ad infintum, and justifiably proud of its sporting achievements. Not the ideal school for idle couch potatoes or those only able to bumble around on the sidelines, but the glowing example of others might gee them up. Music is another strength (much praised music department), recent head boy snapped up an organ scholarship to Cambridge in 2004. Drama rooms are in need of improvement, but new development and expansion is in hand and despite the facilities, drama productions are 'amazing' according to a happy parent. Art department: excellent facilities and about 40 per cent take GCSE art. Extra curricular: a vast range of activities from the usual to the more unusual African drumming, public speaking, video club and scrabble.

Background and Atmosphere: School was originally opened by the congregation of Josephites in Croydon in 1869. Moved to its present breathtaking 100 acre site in 1884 and continued to be primarily a boarding school for RC boys until 1992 when it became a day school. Has become fully co-ed (though still boy heavy) and increased in size dramatically within the last 10 years. Multi-million development is on the cards: including replacing some of the 'shabby' classrooms, new centre for art and drama and a water-based astro turf pitch. Mr P's aspirations come to the fore again with his aim 'to have top-class facilities, the best in the country.' School day starts at 8:45 and ends at 4:00, but pupils can be dropped off from 8:00 and clubs tend to go on till quite late – useful for working parents. RC ethos is paramount (although 51 per cent of pupils are not Catholic). Mr P is the first to admit that families from other faiths might feel fazed by the RC influence of the school. He does, however, encourage an atmosphere where the pupils learn tolerance. 'A very real environment. I could not be happier with the school,' commented a mother.

Pastoral Care and Discipline: It is a large school on a very large site and 'not for the faint hearted!' says one parent. However, much parental praise for pastoral care and nurturing atmosphere: 'although my child's tutor is not the greatest, I am quite enamoured by the teachers' carousel system – having the same tutor till you leave.' Strict rules when it comes to discipline. Detentions seem to be handed out on a regular basis. The head has no problem admitting that he expelled 4 children from the sixth form. Has no tolerance for drugs and drinking. Smoking seems to be less of a problem – perhaps these sporty teenagers are more aware of health risks. Bullying has raised its head, but has always been swiftly stamped out.

Pupils and Parents: Almost all Christian, white and middle class. Quite a few American and Irish. Pupils smart yet stress-free – some imaginative hair styles and slightly relaxed ties, but not messy by any means. School says parents include those who 'work in the City and high achievers.' OBs and OGs include Lisa Tarbuck and Sir Clive Sinclair.

Entrance: Entrance exam at 11, many come via their own junior school and from other feeder schools including Bishopsgate, Cranmore, Feltonfleet, Hall Grove and Hoebridge. Also CE on offer at 13. Entrants at 16 must achieve 6 Grade Bs at GCSE – about 12-15 a year come in at this stage.

Exit: Around 10 per cent leave at 16, usually to various sixth form colleges. Those who stay on go to a variety of universities, including Leeds, Warwick, Oxford Brookes and Loughborough, with four or five a year to Oxbridge.

Money Matters: Academic, music, art and all rounder (which includes sport and drama) scholarships for entry at 11, 13 and 16 ranging from 10 to 50 per cent. Lunch and a number of clubs are not included in the fees, neither are academic support lessons; a direct debit system is available though!

Remarks: An all round school with a very strong RC ethos (though 50 per cent non-RC pupils). Head on a mission to raise the profile of the school, academically and otherwise.

ST GEORGE'S SCHOOL (ASCOT)

Wells Lane, Ascot, Berkshire, SL5 7DZ

Tel: 01344 629 900
Fax: 01344 629 901
E-mail: office@stgeorges-ascot.org.uk
Website: www.stgeorges-ascot.org.uk

- Pupils: 290 girls; 140 board, 150 day • Ages: 11-18 • Size of sixth form: 83 • C of E • Fees: Day £4,600; boarding £7,200
- Independent • Open days: Any Tuesday or Friday by appointment

Head: Since 2005 Mrs Caroline Jordan MA PGCE (early forties). Mrs Jordan succeeded the highly respected and much-loved Mrs Joanna Grant-Peterkin. Educated at St Helen's and St Katharine's, she then went onto St Edmund Hall, Oxford to read Earth Sciences. After a period of running her own business, she then took her PGCE at Manchester University before taking her first teaching job at Wycombe Abbey. Ten years later she left there for St George's, having taught both physics and chemistry. She gained boarding experience as a housemistress and latterly joined senior management as head of sixth form and deputy senior housemistress. Married with one son.

Academic Matters: A level results excellent, 88 per cent A/B, and 2004 GCSE results were commendably good with trails of As and A* and no failures. Average take-home was AAB in 2005. All girls take science at GCSE, double for most, but single for some weaker brethren, rather than three separate sciences. Maths 'surprisingly good,' said the last head, 'and popular' – but not as popular as English, biology, history of art and theatre studies. 24 subjects offered at A level.

Foreign nationals can and do take their own languages to exam level, which has a dramatic effect on results! French on particularly fine form, with German and Spanish on offer, Russian, Japanese and Chinese also taken. No apparent Greek take-up, nor business studies and the like. Lots of IT. Inter/intra-netted computers everywhere and available at all times (though an ominous notice on the door announces 'that if more evidence of food is found in the computer room then it will be locked at the weekend'). Personal laptops can be connected to the system. Keyboarding skills are important here and girls get CLAIT and RSA qualifications. E-mail and voicemail for all.

EFL and good dyslexia/dyspraxia cover plus study skills for all, from the Helen Arkell Centre which operates from 'a new facility' ie a portacabin in the grounds.

Games, Options, The Arts: Art, textile and design strong as ever. Super fashion, make your own pattern/ball gown, and rather natty corsets on show in the entrance to the art block. Fabulous music, joined-up concerts with Eton (popular), lots of own CDs, masses of instruments – and lessons can be arranged for any instrument. Drama and public speaking popular with regular awards for the former, LAMDA exams. Photography popular, own dark room.

30-acre campus, new multi-purpose building opened in 2002. Very versatile: the hall can be used as a lecture theatre, auditorium, dance floor and for exams. Funds from the sale of Queen's Hill paid for the stunning sports hall, with enviable dance and weight training area (indoor swimming pool is next on the agenda). Games important here, especially lacrosse and tennis.

Background and Atmosphere: Founded in 1877 as a boys' prep school and converted to girls at the turn of the century. This is rhodie-land. Mega rebuild following sale of Queen's Hill, with purpose-built dorms, and interlocking classrooms – incredibly narrow claustrophobic staircases and passages everywhere – single file only. Guides said careers advice and university suggestions tiptop.

There is a certain amount of B&B (currently £25 per night) and flexi-boarding on offer. Day boarders often move to becoming real boarders further up the school. Boarders move from dorms of six to dorms of one or two (always called dorms even if it's only one). Common rooms, pay phones (mobiles OK but only in dorms) and kitchens for each year group. Sixth formers can take driving lessons and entertain boys in the common room (dinner parties still popular) and go out one night a week. Increased privileges come with age, no uniform in sixth – though our guides were wearing very smart black suits (skirt or trousers a choix), plus trips to Windsor (Eton next door) etc. Cookery club popular and sixth formers often cook their own supper. No timetabled lessons on Saturdays, but all girls start with an hour's prep, juniors then do games, riding, drama lessons and, with the exception of four closed weekends a term, can go out from lunch time on Saturday till Sunday evening. Complaints that there was 'not enough to do' at weekends were refuted by our guides who said there was masses to do, lots of activities organised by the girl-led school council. 'Changing rooms' a popular activity, when girls redecorate and paint their common rooms – which are then opened to great fanfare.

Pastoral Care and Discipline: Good pastoral care via house and prefectorial system; day girls are assigned to boarding houses where they have work stations – surprisingly cocooned off from each other with gloomy grey screens. Shadows for first year pupils, form deputies and year tutors for all, girls choose a personal tutor at sixth form, plus a director of studies. School operates school code, enforced on the seven deadly sins – 'girls are in big trouble' if they get involved with drugs, sex (boys in bedrooms), booze, fags, bullying, going out without permission, or theft. 'Straight out' for drugs; fags = chores, fine and gating; booze ditto and contract, strong bullying policy and 'quick follow-up'.

Pupils and Parents: From the south, rather than London but masses from further afield, around eight or nine per cent foreigners. 'No visible impact' yet from the Yorks' decision to send their daughter here. Some first time buyers.

Entrance: 'Lots of different schools', basically the toffs' prep schools: Cowarth Park, Upton House, Windsor, Maltman's, Garden House, Lady Eden's, Thomas's etc plus local primary schools. CE at 11 and 13, pass mark 50/55 per cent plus previous head's report. Plus interview. Sixth form entry, standard six GCSEs at C and above for all. B or above recommended for A level subjects; A essential for maths and science at A level plus talk to heads of departments for external pupils.

Exit: A few do leave after GCSE, going to Wellington, Stowe, Bradfield or sixth form colleges, otherwise 98 per cent to tertiary education. Small tranche to Oxbridge.

Money Matters: Academic and music scholarships on offer at 11 or 16; art & textiles, drama and sport scholarships at 16, which can be further means-tested, plus bursarial help (means tested annually) for those already in the school.

Remarks: School increasingly popular locally (ie day boarders), good for the less academic, with impressive results. Still a bit Sloane.

St George's School (Edinburgh)

Linked to Saint George's Junior School in the Junior section

Garscube Terrace, Edinburgh, EH12 6BG

Tel: 0131 311 8000

Fax: 0131 311 8120

E-mail: head@st-georges.edin.sch.uk

Website: www.st-georges.edin.sch.uk

- Pupils: 995 girls; 945 day, 50 board. Nursery 72 including 8 boys • Ages: 2-18 • Size of sixth form: 165 • Non-denom
- Fees: £1,830 - £2,120 in primary; £2,335 £2,925 senior school. Boarding £2,875 extra • Independent • Open days: October and visits are welcomed throughout the year

Head: Since 1994, Dr Judith McClure CBE, MA, DPhil, FRSA, FSA,(fifties). A Scot educated at Newlands Grammar School, Middlesbrough (was briefly a nun – at 18), studied law, then read history at Oxford where she got a first and lectured at Liverpool and Oxford. She came to St George's after a stint at St Helen and St Katherine, followed by an assistant headship at Kingswood and was previously head of the now merged Royal School, Bath. Married to 'portable' historian husband, Dr Roger Collins, who specialises in medieval Spain. No children.

Fast talking, super, enthusiastic head – she leapt up and down during our interview getting us yet more policy statements and exam results – larger than life and incredibly elegant – a long black dress, with shocking pink jacket and matching pashmina when we visited. 'She loves it here, loves Scotland, loves Edinburgh' and loves running St George's; she is also much involved both with the Scottish education policy makers and with the local universities. 'So much is happening, so fast, such fun.' Pretty OTT, and not necessarily every parent's cup of tea – think Miss Jean Brodie, think Edinburgh. A great exponent of single sex schools, she runs the best in Scotland and puts pupils, parents and staff in that order. 'No problems getting staff' and those who are there change jobs every so often which eliminates the boredom factor, though whether Dr McClure is reaching that particular plateau is open to debate. A five-star head, St George's is lucky to have her.

Academic Matters: School no longer narrowly academic, the courses are much broader, with girls taking units of Intermediate I and II, as well as following the English or the Scottish system as appropriate. A choice might therefore be Standard Grades, followed by a unit or two of Intermediate in lower sixth (Intermediate studies incorporate a much wider range of options than the regular exams) as well as Highers, followed by further Highers or Advanced Highers. Again extra Intermediates can be added in the upper sixth (geddit?). Equally, girls can opt for the English system after Standard Grades and switch between Highers and Advanced Highers, and ASs and A2s. It is very much horses for courses and a timetabling challenge. Oodles of As and Credit 1s in both disciplines, and 'lots of flexibility' in course selection. School employs VLE – Virtual Learning Environment – to allow students to access course work, collect work or refer to notes provided by staff online.

Pupils help with scientific research with the universities, share seminars with staff and undergraduates and take part in an impressive outreach programme which encompasses both the academic and the appreciation of the wider world. No particular bias – English, maths, languages, the sciences and the humanities all outstanding. The new, very popular, Chinese centre has girls studying Mandarin – results only now coming through – but otherwise French, German, Spanish and Russian (school is twinned with Pushkin's town, as well as schools in Moscow and St Petersburg). Good general studies and careers advice.

School is split into three distinct departments – junior, which encompasses the nursery, lower (where Dr McClure has her office) and upper. Good learning support throughout, four specialist teachers in all. Small ESOL department to help with non-nationals. NB league tables are meaningless in this school, given that two systems are followed.

Games, Options, The Arts: Fabulous Centenary sports hall with imaginative viewing area over hall and squash courts; much used lacrosse pitches (recently upgraded) plus a floodlit all-weather pitch, all trad games played with a vengeance. Magical Robertson music centre houses untold numbers of choirs, ensembles, three orchestras, over 600 musicians. Vibrant art department, with fantastic sea sculptures (sadly the lobster didn't sing), conventional art – and some pretty rum portraits, we hope they don't really look like that – as well as pottery, textiles et al. Drama and theatre good. D of E popular, as is CCF with Merchiston (well, it would be, wouldn't it?); sixth formers join forces with brother school Edinburgh Academy and Merchiston Castle School for sport, art, music etc. Zillions of after school clubs that offer everything from keyboarding to extra IT.

Background and Atmosphere: Founded in 1888, St George's is Edinburgh's foremost school for girls and sister to Edinburgh Academy – shared holidays, sibling discounts, that sort of thing. Purpose-built 1912 complex, much altered and expanded, is still home to the school. Long corridors with classrooms but also fab recent add-ons. Lower school now in converted earlier boarding house; primary school much expanded and previously dreary classrooms totally refurbished late 2005. Stunning new dining hall (exit bridge known as Bridget) with entertainment area below has released valuable space for extra libraries and study areas. Parents can (and do) use the new dining centre as a coffee shop. Recently opened a sixth form reading room. Totally refurbished library.

Pupils have a purposeful air, mufti in sixth form. Boarders occupy a couple of converted Edwardian mansions with a purpose-built bungalow for sixth formers, singles and twins, all very jolly, lots of extra activities.

Pastoral Care and Discipline: Head has made no real expulsions, though several miscreants have been given very heavy hints that they 'move elsewhere' (two in seven years). 'No need to break out, this is a liberal environment.' The boarding housemistress tells tales of boys trying to sneak in and gaspers handing her their lighters and their Lucky Strikes when they have been rumbled – but that's only a few occasions in eleven years and none recent. 'No sniff of drugs'. Good PSE, positive behaviour policy which incorporates the best of human rights legislation.

Pupils and Parents: Boarders from the Highlands and Islands and from the borders; some from 'abroad', links and exchanges with Germantown Friends School in Philadelphia. Otherwise, good straight Scots parents, some with Charlotte Ranger background, incomers and some first time buyers. Unashamedly elitist, lots of parent/pupil forums – on every subject under the sun; The Friends of St George's for social events.

Entrance: Selective and seriously so. Via nursery and elsewhere at four and a half. Otherwise, exam, school report and interview. Entry to sixth form is more or less automatic for home-grown pupils; external pupils need five A/1-C/3 passes at GCSE/Standard grade.

Exit: Usual (but rare) trickle down south at 8 and 13, a few leave after GCSE/Standard grade to go co-ed, otherwise gap, degrees, and higher education of all sorts – Scottish law popular, as are the sciences and medicine. Around 50 per cent opt for Scottish universities, Aberdeen, St Andrew's plus Edinburgh and Glasgow.

Money Matters: Bursary scheme now replaces assisted places; 'mustn't let the really bright down'. Sibling discounts which walk hand in hand with brothers at Edinburgh Academy.

Remarks: The top girls' school in Scotland, particularly in the academic field; much more liberal than previously and offering a broad sweep of academia – the main building still looks archaic but this is not a school to judge by its exterior.

ST GEORGE'S SCHOOL (HARPENDEN)

Sun Lane, Harpenden, Hertfordshire, AL5 4TD

Tel: 01582 765 477
Fax: 01582 469 830
E-mail: admin@stgeorges.herts.sch.uk
Website: www.stgeorges.herts.sch.uk

• Pupils: 990 boys and girls (including 120 boarders) • Ages: 11-18 • Size of sixth form: 250 • Non-denom Christian • Fees: Boarding £2,350 • State • Open days: October - boarder parents receive tour and interview on payment of registration fee

Headmaster: Since 1988, Mr Norman F Hoare OBE MA FRSA (fifties). Historian. Married to teacher and has two sons who attended St George's. 'I couldn't have considered anywhere else; there was no better way to show confidence in what I believe this school can do.' Is determined to provide chances for all in a school based on Christian principles. Founder member and chairman of STABIS (State Boarding) for three years and was appointed chairman of the Boarding Schools Association between 1999 and 2000. Is a Governor of Welbeck College (Army's sixth form college) but avoids too many commitments outside school. 'I miss the place dreadfully – the privilege of daily Chapel and being with young people and first-rate teachers'.

Academic Matters: Very good academic results for a comprehensive. In 2005, 95 per cent of pupils gained five or more GCSEs at grades A* to C. At A level, all departments score highly, especially art, English and history. 55 per cent A/B grades in 2005. Maths is very popular with the great majority of candidates gaining A and B grades. Year 7 is taught in mixed ability groups but setting begins after the first three months. French taught from year 7 with German and Latin being offered later. Some departments set A grades for entry. In 2001 the school was awarded specialist status for maths, science, technology and ICT. The school holds Artsmark GOLD and Sportsmark Awards and received the DfES School Achievement Award for three consecutive years.

Games, Options, The Arts: Strong in music, art, drama and sport. There are four choirs and two orchestras. A level theatre studies and music technology are popular choices. Competes well on the sports field too, with rugby being the main sport for boys (county and national players) and lacrosse for girls. St George's is the only maintained school in Southern England to play lacrosse so all fixtures are against independent girls' schools. The school is proud that former pupils now teach lacrosse at some leading private girls' schools. The school also offers cricket and netball, rounders, basketball, tennis and athletics. Representatives at regional and national level. Recent rugby tours to South Africa and lacrosse to the USA.

A range of extra-curricular clubs is offered; D of E popular. World Challenge Expeditions to Madagascar, Argentina and Mongolia. The school also owns a sailing boat, the Verulamia, based on the Solent.

Background and Atmosphere: Founded in 1907 by the Rev Cecil Grant, St George's was one of the first, fully co-educational independent boarding schools in England. In 1967 it became voluntary-aided. The school is a non-denominational Christian foundation with, according to tradition, its own Anglican Chaplain. Sunday chapel attendance three times a term is compulsory for every pupil and is a condition of entry. Family attendance is a big feature, as is belief in the house system and competition. Original buildings are Victorian Gothic style (1880s) but have been adapted and added to, especially over the last ten years. State-of-the-art technology centre, new drama studio and four computer suites around the campus.

Pastoral Care and Discipline: School is divided into four houses, each with a head of house, an assistant and a

team of tutors. Tutor groups are organised into lower, middle and upper school groups so a child will stay within one house and have only three tutors in seven years. School attaches importance to courtesy, integrity, manners and good discipline.

Pupils and Parents: Majority of day pupils come from Harpenden and surrounding areas, some boarders from overseas. Many well-to-do families choose the school because of its Christian ethos. There's a high demand for places so many move to Harpenden and attend church regularly (a major criterion for admission) to get a better chance of a place. OBs include Kenneth Horne, Patrick Heron, Michael Oakeshott, Sir Maurice Drake, Andrew Hunter MP and Rex Warner.

Entrance: For the 130 day places each year, there is a complicated system of priorities. Preference is given to siblings of present and past pupils, staff children, and children of former pupils (2 years minimum) who live (at the time that they apply) in Harpenden and other named civil parishes. Remaining places are then divided into three sections: 70 per cent to those living in the civil parishes of Harpenden and Harpenden Rural, 20 per cent to those from four other civil parishes, 10 per cent to those further away. Within those sections places are allocated to children living with parent(s) who have attended a recognised church with their children at least once a month over the past two years (certificate from priest/minister required). Recognised churches are members of The Council of Churches of Britain and Ireland or are in association with Churches Together in England or the Evangelical Alliance – ask the school if you are uncertain which churches qualify. Unfilled places in these sections are then used to cater for excess demand in other sections. There are further criteria (eg medical need) but rarely any places left for them to apply for.

Application lists close early November the year before entry, but late applicants are given places on the waiting list according to their ranking on the above criteria so a few slip in.

Boarders are interviewed and a full report from their current school is required. Flexible boarding was introduced in 1990. St George's is now one of the country's leading state boarding schools and early applications (six to twelve months ahead) are necessary.

Exit: Majority goes on to undergraduate courses with a few entering employment directly.

Remarks: A successful and popular school, which is hard to get in to. Your best chance is to move to Harpenden and start attending church regularly.

ST GREGORY'S CATHOLIC COLLEGE

Combe Hay Lane, Odd Down, Bath, BA2 8PA

Tel: 01225 832 873
Fax: 01225 835 848
E-mail: stgregorys_sec@bathnes.gov.uk
Website: www.st-gregorys.bathnes.sch.uk

- Pupils: 811 girls and boys, all day • Ages: 11-16 • Catholic
- State • Open days: First Thursday in October to see the school in action; last Thursday evening in September

Head: Since 2004, Raymond Friel MA(Hons) NPQH (early forties). First class degree in English from Glasgow University in 1987; PGCE from University of Wales, Aberystwyth. As head of English introduced A level English to new sixth form at St Augustine's, Trowbridge after 'good start' to career at St Charles Sixth Form College, London. Two and a half years as head of St Joseph's, Salisbury which he took from 'challenging circumstances' to receiving a 'good' Ofsted rating. Then 'too good to miss' opportunity arose at St Gregory's. Thoughtful and caring head who follows long-serving predecessor. Good listener and fits St Gregory's academic and Catholic profile. 'Has handled changes with sensitivity,' say parents. Married to Janet Anne, an artist and teacher, with three sons at local Catholic primary school. Interests include sport, literature and performing arts. Former co-editor of Southfields literary review and a regular contributor to London Review of Books.

Academic Matters: Outstanding results in core subjects, especially English (with GCSE results in both language and literature more than 20 per cent above national average). Religion compulsory to GCSE. A modern foreign language compulsory for nearly all; we were particularly impressed by quality of teaching and range of languages offered. Most other subjects also strong and drama, music and dance more than justify the college's specialist performing arts status. Children streamed academically and setted in maths from the beginning of their second term in year 7. At key stage 4, pupils follow courses in one of three 'pathways' stretching the most able, providing qualifications alongside appropriate experience for small vocational group and giving 'mainstream' pupils a sensible compromise in terms of breadth and workload. No sense of 'second class' or disaffected pupils. Class sizes vary according to subject and ability.

All year 7 children are screened on entry. 6 statemented children and 29 with IEPs. Early morning reading programme and a lunch club for vulnerable pupils. Close liaison with range of outside agencies. SENCO works with staff to support pupils with SpLD and other special needs largely within normal timetable; learning support assistants work alongside mainstream teachers. High ranking (recently ninth in the country) for value-added at key stage 4 attributed in part to success of support programmes. Head of RE also runs small behaviour and attendance unit with experienced support assistant.

Games, Options, The Arts: Active sports department organises range of after school fixtures across the major games. Pupils spoilt for choice when it comes to performing arts. 220 pupils receiving instrumental tuition in school and another 100 outside. Annual tour for musicians of all kinds and many play in county bands. Parents 'really grateful' for trips abroad organised by staff. New music technology offers twilight tuition to AS level for those who can manage extra workload, likewise after-school dance and language options. Strong drama with school productions involving dance and music too. New, purpose-built dance/drama studio opened in 2003 in addition to main stage in school hall. When we visited, one of two professional dancers in residence was inspiring a creative class of uninhibited year 7 pupils. Annual Artsweek in July has performances every day and draws up to 500 key stage 3 pupils; stunning choice of workshops with local artists and performers volunteering their time. Artists, writers and poets, theatre visits and cross-cultural exchanges add to the heady creative mix here. Children prove resourceful in getting themselves home and many stay after school.

Background and Atmosphere: Motto: In Christo floremus (In Christ we flourish) expresses the Christian core of the school. Every day begins with corporate worship plus extra masses through year and voluntary mass in school's small chapel which also provides a sanctuary where some pupils have left touching prayer dedications in an open book. Each year group can experience a retreat and there are all kinds of good works for charity. Non-Catholics 'don't feel left out' confirm parents.

School located on attractive 12-acre site on 'socially mixed' southern edge of Bath; extensive playing fields, new Astroturf for hockey and soccer plus hard tennis courts and gym. Good facilities for graphics, design & technology. Modern 12 classroom block for mathematics, geography and modern languages in spacious, purpose-built accommodation. Well-resourced and airy library; interactive whiteboards, overhead projection and plenty of computers around without being techno crazy. Pleasant bistro area for year 11 lunches with healthy food options and smart card payment system. School day begins at 8.55am and ends at 3.35pm with many getting back to far-flung homes by bus ahead of those crossing congested Bath. Strong PTFA runs fund-raising events through year.

Pastoral Care and Discipline: Deputy head (former LEA adviser and Ofsted inspector) pioneered 'peer counselling' here; truancy almost unknown with attendance monitored closely. 'Name and praise' assembly and rewards system plus clear sanctions where necessary. House system under review.

Pupils and Parents: 88 per cent Catholic; very active PTFA. Parents receive six progress reports plus full written report at end of year. Homework set by all and journals for parents to see and sign. Quite a few refugees from private sector and many staff have children here. Strong sense of community; pupils appear relaxed, confident and tolerant of each other. Those who showed us around were articulate and sensitive. Moral values and full of good works for disabled, homeless etc. Smart, green uniform has replaced dreary brown predecessor still worn by older year groups. College Senate has representatives from across years and has influenced uniform and catering changes including introduction of popular breakfast club.

Entrance: Oversubscribed. Prides itself on transition arrangements into year 7; children come from 200 square mile catchment area and complicated preference system for Catholics operates. Pupils mainly from six linked primary schools (St Benedict's, Midsomer Norton; St John's, Bath; SS Joseph and Teresa, Wells; St Mary's, Bath, St Mary's, Chippenham and St Patrick's, Corsham) plus siblings. Apply through Bath & North East Somerset LEA for admission into year 7, but apply direct to school if moving into the area.

Exit: Around 65 per cent to St Brendan's and other sixth forms; 25 per cent to further education; 10 per cent to training and employment. A few to Oxbridge via St Brendan's or other colleges.

Remarks: Much sought-after and dynamic 11-16 Catholic comprehensive which combines creativity with academic success.

St Helen's School

Eastbury Road, Northwood, Middlesex, HA6 3AS

Tel: 01923 843 210
Fax: 01923 843 211
E-mail: Office@StHelensNorthwood.co.uk
Website: www.sthelensnorthwood.co.uk

- Pupils: 1,140 including junior school; all girls; 30 board • Ages: 3-18 • Size of sixth form: 185 • C of E but all faiths welcome
- Fees: Nursery £2,115; Little St Helen's £2,332; Junior school £2,529; Senior school - day £3,230, weekly boarding £5,774, full boarding £5,986 • Independent • Open days: June and October

Head: Since 2000, Mrs Mary Morris BA PGCE (fiftyish). A geographer who taught at Dr Challoner's High before coming to the school in 1998 as deputy head. An internal appointment then and, unlike many such, received with popular acclaim which no-one has since regretted. One of the most engaging heads we have encountered – voluble, smiley, relaxed and frank. It's a bit like talking to your best friend except that Mrs Morris is, clearly, a wholly professional head. So many girls' schools still seem to be run on the 'we're-ever-so-nice-really' principle without the forward-looking, cutting edge taken for granted in the boys' equivalents. Not so here.

Mrs Morris is an inspirational head who is also huge fun. She knows her girls, her staff, her stuff, her school and her market and underpins the lot with a profound belief in spiritual and moral values. Conducted an 'audit' of the spiritual content of the academic curriculum – 'we need to be moral in lessons – there should be social, spiritual, moral and cultural elements in every single lesson.' Unashamedly partisan about single sex education for girls, she parried a question from a potential (male) parent who asked why he should send his daughters to a girls' school rather than to a co-ed, 'this is not a girls' school – it's a school and, unfortunately, we don't have room for any boys'. Clearly still thrilled about her appointment, she says, 'this is an incredibly moral job. Above everything else, we are role models.'

Academic Matters: School moved to the International Baccalaureate in 2004 and, taught in parallel with A levels, it is now taken by around 25 per cent of sixth formers and growing. Excellent range of subjects available in the sixth including two history syllabuses, English lit and lang and economics. The overwhelmingly popular subjects at this level – A or IB – are the sciences and maths – 98 takers of chemistry, 99 of biology and 110 of maths to only 16 of English lit, 23 of art, 38 of French and 5 of Latin. Results outstanding – 2005 saw St Helen's jump into the top 25 of The Daily Telegraph's independent schools' list on the strength of its A levels and The Evening Standard placed it as 36th in the south east for its performance at GCSE . Practically all A level grades are A/B and very few GCSEs lower than B. Teaching strong across the board but pupils drool over sciences – 'the department is absolutely amazing', said one.

Main curriculum includes art history, psychology, business studies, lots of languages – school's support for and involvement in langs, especially given the scientific bent of so many pupils, is a joy. Head says, 'I don't want people who can speak French – I want linguists'. Hooray! So, Japanese, Mandarin Chinese, Italian, Russian – along with Latin for all and Greek as an option – available alongside the more predictable lingos. Lots of trips and exchanges abroad.

Head is 'passionate' about IT and there can be few girls' schools – and not many boys' schools – which are as far ahead and well-provided for as St Helen's. 100 Mb per second broadband recently installed – 'it's very fast' – it's wireless now throughout the senior school and everyone can access everything from everywhere. School has a partnership with Toshiba and is now the UK Centre of Excellence in Mobile Education ie there are stacks of laptops for girls and staff to be used wirelessly everywhere; two rooms using the Virtuoso multi-media system which facilitates, for example, language learning, enabling the teacher to talk individually to each pupil and each pupil to talk whatever lang it is, individually without disturbing – or waiting for – anyone else – extraordinary! And it's not that IT is an end in itself – 'it's teaching them to use that enormous resource as well as we teach them how to use their books and their teachers and everything else,' reassures head.

Everyone is screened at 7 and 11 for potential educational difficulties. 'We then discuss with parents how we can make it better.' One qualified SEN teacher with lots of help. School can and does support autistic spectrum difficulties, mild dyslexia and dyspraxia, mild speech difficulties and children with hearing impairments. EAL also taught and some children have extra help with maths. One-to-one is given to all those with SENs and school has a positive and helpful attitude to these girls. 127 children currently identified as Gifted and Talented and supported with 'differentiated work schemes and activities'.

Games, Options, The Arts: The huge surprise for anyone visiting St Helen's and who, perhaps, has only seen it behind its sedate hedges and modest perimeter walls, is the unbelievable amount of space it has. Acres of playing fields, courts and pitches extend in all directions and you begin to realise that most of this end of Northwood is St Helen's! Vast new sports complex in development and superb, seemingly endless pool, in stunning new building, already in enthusiastic use. Lacrosse, netball, tennis, athletics, badminton and rounders all popular and many other games and activities available including pilates, aerobics, fencing and trampolining. Lots of success – representation in lacrosse, swimming, cross country and netball county teams and much success for school teams in all these sports plus athletics and rounders at impressive levels.

The school's extensive landscape accommodates numerous blocks and houses, often purpose-built. One such is the Leader building, named after school's outstanding, and aptly named, head of recent years, June Leader – the great builder of the school, both in physical terms – numerous new blocks rose up in her 16-year tenure – as well as in terms of the quality of education and values promulgated here under her uniquely humane regime. This block houses art, DT and drama – all spacious, well-equipped , bright and inviting and matched by the excellence of what is achieved here. We saw much classy wooden furniture – clever designs, beautifully crafted and finished; imaginative ceramics, good painting and drawing – life drawing taken very seriously here. Art is varied, witty and serious. Very good drama studio but main productions happen in good old-fashioned huge school hall – good light and sound systems recently installed. Lots of plays – some in the Founder's Arts Festival. Lots of collaboration with Merchant Taylors' boys up the road – the annual musical now a tradition and very professional.

Music less glamorously housed in one of the older and grimmer buildings still remaining – but it's cosy inside and has a large and inviting recital room. Orchestras, choirs, bands. The jazz band has made a CD, the huge choir tours abroad but possibly fair to say that music is not school's strongest suit. Dance is popular and strong. Loads of extra-curricular opportunities – masses of charity work especially PHAB very much part of school's ethos. Collaboration with Merchant Taylors also in CCF. Dof E and Young Enterprise also popular. Visits from Profs, writers and theatre companies. Successes in debating, maths and physics Olympiads, technology competitions. Lots of trips – Ypres, Kew, Rome, House of Commons, Paris, British Museum, galleries – you find it on a map, they've been there.

Background and Atmosphere: The site is everything. Unbeatable in its generous, green space, its trees and gardens. The buildings have sprouted all round the site and none of it feels crowded, although the main senior school blocks are, for the most part, picturesquely, at the main entrance end of things. Most subjects taught in own blocks or in main, extended, building. One of the joys here is looking through the windows of whichever building you're in – stunning views over the school from every one. St Helen's was founded at the end of the nineteenth century with a vision and ambition for its first pupils which has informed its ethos ever since. It does not aim at league table stardom – that seems to be a happy spin-off.

The junior school (see below) is an integral part of the whole. Situated centrally, it is natural for girls here to stay the course – now from 3 to 18 – and continue to feel that it's all in the family. Equally natural here, despite one of the most diverse ethnic and cultural mixes anywhere, is the happy co-existence of girls from all over the world. In particular, the boarders – mostly from abroad – are seamlessly integrated and clearly value the specialness and family-feeling that the single boarding house and their small numbers provide. The house – Gwyer – is attractive, comfortable mock-Tudor – well-furnished, well-kept. A good kitchen, common and games rooms. Bedrooms are spacious – doubles for the younger girls and singles for all the upper sixth. Posters of Colin Firth not, we understand, obligatory but clearly a popular option. Girls currently from Kenya, China, Hong Kong, the US and Germany. Weekly, flexi and occasional boarding offered.

More significantly, around 33 per cent of the school's population is Asian – (mostly Hindu) – and a further 25 per cent is Jewish – these stats reflecting, of course, the local population. There can be few stronger arguments for heterogeneous school populations than to see the unqualified friendships between these groups. A sixth former we quizzed looked baffled by our questions – 'from when I was four I've been friends with people from every kind of background – they're just your friends.'

Staff tend to stay – 44 with 10 or more years in school – but lots of young teachers and NQTs as well – average age 38. Staff/student relationships palpably cordial. 'A lot of our teachers are role models,' said one sixth former. 'They are so kind and helpful and it doesn't just stop in the classroom. They will keep helping you achieve what you want to achieve.' A younger pupil agreed, 'and', she added, 'you just have to be friendly here because everyone is. The teachers are so sweet – they really look after you – there's always someone to talk to and problems are sorted out really quickly.'

School has several special places. The chapel is one –

now used as a quiet place during Ramadan as much as for services and Christian prayer – a beautiful, tenderly cared-for room with a particular atmosphere which should be cherished. The school library is also special though not as quiet as, perhaps, it might have been. Another asset is Longworthe – a day boarding house in which pupils with busy parents can spend a long day – breakfast and supper included and quiet places for prep and recreation. Younger members of staff live above – this adds to the lived-in feeling of the place. When we visited on a leafy October day, a vast bonfire – mostly old desks, tables and prunings – was being assembled in the centre of the parkland. You could anticipate the fun of bonfire night just looking at it.

Pastoral Care and Discipline: Civilised behaviour the norm here. No rule book but a 'Code of Conduct' and a Behaviour Policy which are called upon if – rarely – anyone needs reminding. Clear sanctions policy. System of warning and detention cards. Walkmen/mobiles illegal in schooltime. No drugs incidents in Mrs Morris's time – or in living memory. The occasional foolish smoker is dealt with individually but, in the head's words, 'sanely. It's never public, it's not about humiliation – ever'. Food looked appetising and reasonably varied though we were perturbed to see successive nine-year-olds carrying off plates of pasta and chips with never a word said. Otherwise, pastoral care very good. You're allowed to slip here. Head says, 'they have to be able to fall down and you have to pick them up again because it's safe in school'. Quite.

Pupils and Parents: Couldn't be more ethnically and culturally diverse. The families of junior school pupils alone come from 40+ countries. Northwood is prosperous, with lots of large detached houses – no shortage of dosh in most cases. Parental occupations just as mixed – as you'd expect. Girls come from wide area – good coach service covers Beaconsfield, Elstree, Barnet, Amersham, Ealing and points between. Old Girls' network huge and devoted. St Helen's inspires a, perhaps unique, loyalty. Alumnae include Patricia Hodge, a great supporter, Vanessa Lawrence (director general Ordnance Survey), Lady Lowry, Luisa Baldini and Penny Marshall, Maria Djurkovic.

Entrance: School part of North London Consortium which shares tests at 11. First point of entry is at 3 into Little St Helen's (see below). At 11, exams in English, maths and VR; around 300 apply for 50 places – not too terrifying as lots apply elsewhere but school is increasingly candidates' first choice. At sixth form, around 40 apply for about 15 places. You need 7+ GCSEs at B+. Few leave along the way – around 10 leave at 11 for state system, boarding or (few) other local independents. Very few leave after GCSEs.

Exit: Everyone to higher education. Everything from medicine to maths, fashion to finance. Everywhere from the LSE to Leeds, St Andrews to Sussex. Half dozen+ to Oxbridge annually.

Money Matters: Range of scholarships and means-tested bursaries. Bursaries awarded annually and are either awarded to girls whose parents could not otherwise meet fees or to girls whose families are experiencing temporary difficulties.

Remarks: So what is this extraordinarily unsung haven – unaccountably neglected by us till now? A poor man's Habs? A refuge for NLCS refuseniks? We don't think so! Get in at 3 if you can and crow over your neighbours for the next fifteen years.

St James Independent School for Senior Boys

Pope's Villa, 19 Cross Deep, Twickenham, Middlesex, TW1 4QG

Tel: 020 8892 2002
Fax: 020 8892 4442
E-mail: admissions@stjamesboys.co.uk
Website: www.stjamesschools.co.uk

- Pupils: 300 boys, all day except for 30 weekly boarders • Ages: 10-18 • Size of sixth form: 65 - rising to 80 • Inter-denom (but see below) • Fees: £2,915, plus £1,200 for weekly boarding • Independent • Open days: Late October, early November

---

Head: Since 2004 Mr David Boddy (early fifties). The school reports that he: 'has known the St James family of schools and their approach to education since their formation 29 years ago. Mr Boddy is a founder Trustee of the Education Renaissance Trust, a charity which works to promote and support schools across the world which are seeking to deliver an education enriched by philosophical principles similar to those at the heart of the St James Schools. He has been responsible for the organisation's teacher training programme since its formation in 1990. In that time the Trust has worked with over 500 head-teachers and teachers in the UK on the application of spiritual, moral, social and cultural values into daily classroom activity. He is also the Chairman of the Lucca Leadership Trust, a charity which runs leadership training and development courses for young people aged 16-28. Mr Boddy has been the course Principal working with a staff of young men and women, many of whom are former St James' pupils, in the delivery of the week-long courses held annually close to the ancient Tuscan city of Lucca. In order to take up the Headship at St James, Mr Boddy is retiring from his active business life. He has been the Senior Partner in the management and training consultancy firm, Farsight Leadership, and has pioneered a number of innovations in leadership development for some of the country's major manufacturing and commercial enterprises. His work was recognized by the Department for Education and Skills in 2001 when the consultancy's work with Unilever plc was a finalist in the prestigious National Training Awards.

'A New Zealander by birth, Mr Boddy trained as a journalist and broadcaster and came to England in 1973. He commenced the study of practical philosophy shortly after his arrival at the School of Economic Science, and over recent years has been lecturing in Philosophy and Meditation in the United Kingdom and affiliate schools around the world. He and his wife, Marian, have three sons, all of whom attended St James schools as pupils throughout their entire schooling, and who went on to achieve significant academic success at Oxford, Durham and Bristol universities. Before moving into business consultancy, Mr Boddy spent several years as Director of Press and Public Relations for the British Conservative Party, serving the Rt Hon Margaret Thatcher MP as a political press secretary in her 1979 and 1983 general election campaigns. Following that he established Market Access International Ltd, a public affairs consultancy, which grew into one of Europe's leading political consulting companies.'

We reserve judgement till our next visit early in 2006. The history of heads brought in from outside the world of teaching is not encouraging, and the choice of someone steeped in the School of Economic Science rather than someone steeped in schoolmastering presumably reflects the underlying priorities of the school's governors. Numbers up – an encouraging sign.

Academic Matters: Broad intake reflected in exam results – typically, a handful of really clever boys per class, one or two strugglers at the bottom end and all shades in between. Teaching is traditional, English a particularly strength – see the school magazine for its creative writing and poetry both important. Mathematics does well. Sanskrit for all pupils (those coming in from the junior school have a head start), also Greek, Latin and French. The less able drop some of the classical languages and do classical civilisation instead. Philosophy taught at all levels. 24 maximum per class. Laptops not computers – there are some, of course, but no IT suite. Good help for mild learning difficulties – particular emphasis on helping teach boys to get organised.

Games, Options, The Arts: Notably good drama, the school produces budding thespians. Good on games, three full afternoons each week (mainly nearby at Teddington). Rugby and cricket the main games – there are teams at all levels, and there is a laudable choice of minor sports (fencing, squash, rowing etc) especially considering the school's size and surprisingly large numbers of (part time) games staff. Good strong music (some with the girls school), emphasis on singing. D of E, keen cadets under ex SAS officer ('a real tiger'), and popular mountaineering club with trips to the Alps every two years. Also a wilderness trek in Africa on offer – shades of Laurens van der Post.

Head considers games and physical activities for boys 'absolutely vital – just as important as spiritual and academic development'. Challenge and learning to face and overcome difficulties part and parcel of these adventure projects. Work experience week well thought out and varied. Good debating – as you might expect in a school where speaking and discussing issues and ideas are important.

Background and Atmosphere: On the site of Pope's villa, red brick neo-Tudor on busy road one side – and stunning river frontage behind, looking over to trees and parkland the other, a peaceful haven. Terrace and grassy playing area. Pope's Grotto remains (American visitors come to look), and the school is all set to restore this with the help of English Heritage. School moved here (from Eccleston Square in 1996), previously a Catholic convent (St Catherine's) which moved directly over the road. Continues to expand – they arrived with 175 boys, and will go up to 300. Linked to the School of Economic Science – www.schooleconomicscience.org. Meditation (voluntary – but most choose to do it) starts each day, and each lesson begins and ends with a minute of stillness ('well, ten seconds, sometimes!' said a teacher): interestingly, this feature is extremely popular with young teachers who come to work here as part of their training. After school homework period is an option. Very good vegetarian food.

Pastoral Care and Discipline: Good shepherds abound, and fairly old fashioned/traditional in its outlook: mucking about in class means a boy is sent out for part of the lesson. Poor work has to be repeated after school hours. Saturday morning detention if necessary. One of the last schools to give up corporal punishment, and recent complaints of what some see as rigid rules, harsh punishments and unsympathetic teachers.

Pupils and Parents: Largely middle of the road, middle class. Mainly well motivated boys, mature and enthusiastic. 'They like adults and get on with the staff', according to a father. Strong parental involvement. Good at getting pupils to concentrate.

Entrance: Straight up from their junior school at Olympia, or at 11+ via entrance exam – lots from local state schools – and at 13 via CE. Not very fussy about the academic level – what matters is that parents and boys like the school ethos.

Exit: Vast variety – from Oxbridge to minor unis or drama college. Gap year popular – particularly to teach at one of the affiliated schools (New York, Dublin, Sydney, Melbourne, Auckland, Johannesburg, Leeds, Trinidad).

Money Matters: Bursaries available.

Remarks: Interesting and unusual small school with a strong ethos (emphasising the spiritual, intellectual and physical aspects of education), and producing self-confident young men who are keen to do something useful in life. New head without much educational provenance coming in against a background of some recent parental disquiet.

St James Independent School for Senior Girls

Earsby Street, London, W14 8SH

Tel: 020 7348 1777

Fax: 020 7348 1717

E-mail: schoolsec@stjamessengirls.org.uk

Website: www.stjamesschools.co.uk

• Pupils: 246 girls • Ages: 10-18 • Size of sixth form: 42 • Non denom • Fees: Senior school £2,915 years 6 - 8; £3,045 years 9 - 13 • Independent • Open days: October and November

Headmistress: Since 1995, Mrs Laura Hyde CertEd (fiftyish) attractive, calm, a firm upholder of traditional values – occasionally branded 'old fashioned' by racier sixth formers straining at the leash. Mainly grammar school educated. Taught at a church primary school, then at St James' Junior Girls and subsequently became PA to Leon MacLaren, founder of the School of Economic Science. Later took time off to bring up her family, before coming back to teaching. Teaches philosophy (about which she is passionate) once a week to every form and twice a week to sixth formers with whom, besides exploring Plato, she plunges into issues at the heart of society. She explains the school's daily practice of meditation (not obligatory) to parents as a way of focusing, being quiet and still – 'most parents welcome this in the noisy, busy world of today.'

Academic Matters: Extremely creditable results, especially bearing in mind the comprehensive intake, and this is one of those rare schools where girls probably do gain the best results of which they are capable. Ds and below are few and far between. Small sixth form means lots of individual attention. High standard of teaching, very thorough, with high expectations. Unusual feature – Sanskrit is taught – and is burning a small trail in school circles. However, such is the complexity of this most ancient language, that only those who have begun learning Sanskrit in the junior school can take it up in the senior school – where it has a keen following. Latin for everyone and Greek under splendidly bright head of classics, Mrs Sarah Labram, a young St James's OG. French for all and Spanish starting from September 2006. All girls take 9 or 10 GCSEs. Full programme for sixth formers of non-examinable subjects despite the demands of AS levels. Excellent study support department – deals with everything from learning difficulties to accelerated learning. IT suite – and laptops available for lessons as well.

Games, Options, The Arts: Fabulous music, with glorious and ambitious singing, not just for the choir – the whole school sings twice a week before lessons start – Mozart's Magic Flute and Requiem both performed in full plus Handel, Pergolesi's Stabat Mater, Purcell, Tallis, Gabrieli under the amazingly energetic Mrs Loulla Gorman. Very good drama, imaginative and educative and fun. Good on games, played at Chiswick, lacrosse especially. Plenty of outdoor pursuits – the school runs its own adventure training club, the St James Challengers (abseiling, canoeing, climbing etc). D of E. Impressive lectures shared with boys' school. Short 'Art of Hospitality' (cooking plus) a week's residential course for 14 year olds and twice-termly lessons for all in the school. Dance lessons for Years 7 – 13. Full programme of extra-curricular activities for all ages.

Background and Atmosphere: Fairly new and still growing – settled in grand new premises in Olympia in 2001, along with both junior schools (qv). Formerly an adult education centre, on a one-acre site with sizeable playground and pleasant large arcaded courtyard entrance, pale lemon paint and flowers throughout. All four schools founded in 1975 (originally in Queen's Gate). An unusual feature – each lesson starts with a couple of minutes silence, for children to 'collect themselves'. Girls kept at full stretch and kept busy most of the time, 'an unhappy teenager is one who isn't doing enough – keep them busy', is part of the head's philosophy. Teachers all madly professional, more women than men, respect for the spiritual world a prerequisite. Very good advice on careers, or, to use the school's terminology, 'vocational guidance'. The emphasis is on giving, not getting, 'preparing our talents for the needs of the community and not to get the most out of it for me.' A few projects jointly undertaken with the boys' school. School day starts at 7.55am with meditation. Happy friendly and purposeful atmosphere – high spirited but calm too. Very good food – fresh and healthy (own cooks).

Pastoral Care and Discipline: Girls are taken care of, emphasis on responsibility, and discipline is not a problem. Care and attention key words here, also consideration for others – typical of the school. Lunch dishes are put on each table and girls serve their neighbour, not themselves. Parents of 14 and 15 year olds corralled to discuss all the going issues – parties, alcohol, drugs etc. Poor work repeated after hours.

Pupils and Parents: Mutually supportive and agreeably confident. Close communication encouraged. Actress Emily Watson is an Old Girl.

Entrance: Via own entrance exam at 10 and 11. Two form entry at 11 consisting of a mixture from St James's Junior School and from other schools. Broad intake and places only offered to pupils who the school reckons to be willing and able to make good use of what is on offer.

Exit: University for most, one or two to Oxbridge, one or two to art college.

Money Matters: Some bursaries available.

Remarks: A small and unusual school you might well consider if the more conventional, larger establishments don't seem to fit your way of thinking or your way of life. Striking a brave posture upholding spiritual values in the modern world – and absolutely not weird – focusing on the whole person. Not for slackers.

St John Fisher Catholic High School

Hookstone Drive, Harrogate, North Yorkshire, HG2 8PT

Tel: 01423 887 254
Fax: 01423 881 056
E-mail: office@sjfchs.org.uk
Website: www.st-johnfisher.n-yorks.sch.uk

- Pupils: 660 boys, 660 girls • Ages: 11-18 • Size of sixth form: 310 (+ 490 from St Aidan's) • Roman Catholic • State

Head: Since 2001, Mr Paul C Jackson MA Cantab (forties). Previously head of St Mary's Catholic School, Bishop Stortford, a Londoner and committed Catholic, he first taught at St Bonaventure's School where he'd been a pupil. Also taught at The Campion School, Hornchurch and All Saints Catholic School, Dagenham. Took over from Terry Keelan who head credits with revitalising the school and raising its profile. Head is working hard to raise Catholic awareness, stressing faith. Loves the buzz of the school, lots of camaraderie between staff, cynics marginalized. Head well-liked by all, energetic, ebullient, approachable but focused. Good on PR although he does admit to upsetting the diocese a little on arrival (it's their school after all!) Says he's learnt to do what's important not what's urgent, so priority is people.

Academic Matters: It's fine to be clever here and commendable results suggest many are. 83 per cent achieved 5 or more A* to C passes at GCSE, none fail altogether. English, geography, history and sports studies are particular strengths but German and DT (Resistant Materials) have had comparatively disappointing results in recent years. Maths very strong at KS3, English a little weaker but improving and differentials disappear by GCSE.

Good system of learning support operates and curriculum tries to accommodate differing abilities. KS4 pupils can opt for a GNVQ in IT or the performing arts in place of some GCSEs. The sixth form is shared with nearby St Aidan's C of E school and operates as an ecumenical and educational venture. Pupils are on the roll of one of the two schools but will move between them according to subject options. Students love this arrangement and it's hard to find any evidence of rivalry between the two closely located schools. A level results are creditable, 56 per cent are graded A or B, again sciences are particular successful and only general studies with an 85 per cent overall pass rate doesn't come

up to scratch. In addition, GNVQ courses in business, health, ICT and science AVCE record a 98 per cent pass rate. Cross-curricular links well established in many areas. Careers department good.

Games, Options, The Arts: Granted specialist arts status to promote creative development of pupils with particular support for art, sport and performance in dance, music and drama. Purpose-built Keelan centre (named after previous reforming head) houses a large music room, suitable for an orchestra, music ICT suite, digital recording studio, individual practice rooms, an art gallery, a series of sixth form art studios as well as a computer graphics room. Plenty of computers around and school is fully networked. Main productions (Godspell in 2004) are staged in the hall but there is a 120-seater auditorium and dance studio for minor works. Have artists in residence, hold regular workshops with visiting professionals and pupils recently participated in a RADA-led Shakespeare workshop. Regular successes recorded at the Harrogate Speech and Drama Festival. Successful Bridge club, winners of the Harrogate Schools' cup and placed second and third in the Nationals.

Lots of fund-raising throughout the year; recent venture involved pupils making hand-crafted rosary beads in technology which were sold to raise money for charity; a fund-raising maths challenge, annual participation in CAFOD and Red Nose day. School has 4 netball courts, 3 soccer pitches, 4 floodlit tennis courts, a mini hockey pitch, artificial cricket strip, gym and sports hall. Sports on offer include athletics, cross-country, soccer – popular with both sexes, girls are county champions, and boys U19 are North Yorkshire champions and reached the last 8 of the English National Schools Competition, netball (some county players), orienteering (area winners), cricket and tennis. School received special award from the Table Tennis Association in recognition of its achievements and many year 11 pupils gain junior sports leadership award. Annual skiing trips, USA in 2004, ample opportunity for theatre, opera and concert visits.

Background and Atmosphere: Set in 22 acres of parkland on the south side of Harrogate. The original 1900s building was a girls' private convent school and the cells where nuns slept are now offices and art studios. Much added-to over the years – mostly sympathetic additions but who commissioned those dangerously narrow corridors? The adjoining Chapel is used by the public for Sunday services though school has sole use throughout the week. School was the first in North Yorkshire to be granted Arts College status, a community-inspired effort undertaken with the financial backing of over 400 sponsors. Catholic ethos pervades yet no sense of, 'I'm not a Catholic...get me out of here.' All faiths welcomed, tolerated and accepted. Despite stiff local competition, children say they don't feel under undue academic pressure – staff do, not just from school but parents, league tables and professional pride.

Pastoral Care and Discipline: This is not a Hail Mary school but pastoral care remains true to Catholic traditions and aims to reinforce positive behaviour and attitudes. Form teachers and heads of year look after most pupils but pastoral head handles the more time-consuming cases. School genuinely supportive and views care as a working partnership between home, church and school. Follows Catholic teaching but divorce, abortion etc tackled head on – no dodging the issues or debate. A day of recollection retreat is held for years 7, 8 and 9, trip to Lourdes for year 10, and years 11 and 12 have opportunities to participate in residential retreats – organised by exuberant head of RE and newly appointed school lay chaplain. All pupils up to year 11 must stay in school at lunchtime – good choice of edible and generally healthy food. Children are allowed to use form rooms or to attend clubs and are encouraged to start up new ones if their interests aren't served. Every pupil is issued with a super planner, containing tons of useful information for recording homework and achievements – what's more pupils really do use it properly, give or take the odd doodling eg 'Hi, I'm in maths and I'm bored....' (Strange because most pupils spoke very highly of maths and even expounded its benefits.) Sticker system used for misdemeanours – can be red-carded for more serious offences. Only one expulsion for drugs in last couple of years.

Pupils and Parents: Predominately white, middle-class, Catholic professionals from Harrogate and the environs, smattering from rural villages. Children bused in from wide area of North Yorkshire and north Leeds but the chance of a place for those outside the catchment area is now as rare as a personal audience with the Pope. Pupils are a charismatic bunch, polite, well-mannered but chirpy and not afraid to question.

Entrance: Over-subscribed. Acquire a Catholic Baptism Certificate then purchase a house in the catchment area – (yes of course you'll pay extra for the privilege but it is a nice leafy middle-class area, clean streets, Neighbourhood Watch...). Otherwise not really much hope – even siblings who already attend Catholic schools (but aren't baptised Catholics) are finding appeal is a necessity. Officially it goes like this: all applicants are required to declare their positive support for the mission, aims and Catholic ethos of the school. Over-subscription criteria are applied as follows: looked-after children from Catholic families have priority, followed by baptised Catholic children

who are resident in the parishes serving the school and attending the Catholic primary schools serving those parishes. These are: Deanery of Harrogate – all parishes, St Joseph, Bishop Thornton; St Edward, Clifford; St Robert, St Joseph and St Aelred, Harrogate; St Mary Knaresborough; St Wilfrid, Ripon; St Joseph, Wetherby and Our Lady Immaculate, Pately Bridge. Deanery of Selby: St Joseph the Worker, Sherburn-in-Elmet only (served by Barkston Ash Catholic Primary School). Baptised Catholic Children who are not resident in the parishes but who attend the above listed primary schools will then be given priority followed by baptised Catholic children who are resident in the above named parishes. Fifth on the list are other baptised Catholic children who have brothers and sisters currently attending St John Fisher followed by other baptised Catholic children then other children who have brothers and sisters currently attending the school. The criteria go on to include other children attending one of the Catholic primary schools listed who can provide evidence of religious practice both of the child and parents/guardians, children attending a Catholic primary school not listed and finally children of other Christian denominations or of other faiths whose parents are in sympathy with the aims and ethos of the school and can provide evidence of religious practice. Catechumens and members of an Eastern Christian Church are given priority after baptised Catholics in each of the above categories.

Exit: At 16, ninety-seven per cent to further education (80 per cent transfer to the associated sixth form) rest to employment. Of those who stay on to the sixth form, 86 per cent enter higher education, 9 or 10 to Oxbridge, rest to wide range of recruiting and selecting universities, 9 per cent embark on courses at FE colleges, remainder to employment.

Remarks: A good state school that's still very much on the up – worth moving into the catchment area for. Produces articulate, well-rounded and endearing Catholics, a credit to the partnership between all involved.

St John's School

Epsom Road, Leatherhead, Surrey, KT22 8SP

Tel: 01372 373 000

Fax: 01372 386 606

E-mail: secretary@stjohns.surrey.sch.uk

Website: www.stjohnsleatherhead.co.uk

- Pupils: 417 boys plus 60 girls in sixth form • Ages: 13-18
- Size of sixth form: 200 • C of E but other denominations
accepted • Fees: Day £5,050; boarding £6,950 • Independent
- Open days: October and June

Head: Since 2004, Mr Nicholas J R Haddock MBE MA FRGS. He was educated at St Edward's School and St Edmund Hall, Oxford, where he read geography and played hockey for the University. After leaving Oxford, he was commissioned as an officer in the Royal Green Jackets, where he attained the rank of major. Married with four children. In 1998, he was awarded the MBE for work involved in planning military operations worldwide and was selected for promotion to Lieutenant Colonel but left to pursue a career in teaching.

Academic Matters: Not an academic hothouse; more of an all-round ethos catering for a broader intake of pupils. Examination results have risen sharply over the years – the percentage of GCSE top grades (A* to B) is 84 per cent. Four AS levels taken in lower sixth and usually three A2s after that. At A level, the percentage of A and B grades now stands at 76 per cent and at A2 it is 65 per cent.

The most able academic high-flyers in the area in the past have tended to gravitate towards more prominent day schools such as King's College School, Wimbledon and the Royal Grammar School, Guildford. Equally, St John's competes for potential boarders with Epsom College, Charterhouse, Winchester, Eton, Tonbridge and Lancing. One prospective parent summed up the school as, 'a good all-round school suitable for those not academic enough to get into King's,' however the head responds that a significant percentage of his pupils would be able to meet King's academic rigour! He does accept that it remains a major challenge for St John's to become the first choice senior school for the most academically able. To this end, the school has introduced 'The Scholars' Initiative' which is designed to stretch and challenge these sought-after able pupils from day one onwards. The aim is to widen the general cultural perspective of members of a selected group by addressing matters of current affairs and political, scientific and cultural issues. Others can ask to join the group.

Up to GCSE average class size is 17, the 80 pupils in each year being divided into sets, the more able in larger sets and the less able in smaller. Average size of sixth form class is 10. Youngish (39) average age of staff. Provision for dyslexics is 'super', according to one parent, 'a great confidence booster.'

Games, Options, The Arts: About one third of pupils learn an instrument, several of them are at grade 8 standard. Tuition largely scheduled so as not to clash with academic lessons. Orchestra, wind band, two jazz bands, chapel choir, madrigal and choral societies, string quartets and more. In 2001, its 150th year, school put on a concert at St John's, Smith Square, Westminster, in presence of its patron, HRH the Duchess of Gloucester. First school allowed to perform Shakespeare in public at Globe Theatre, Southwark, in same year. New three million pound performing arts centre was officially opened in May 2003 with an auditorium, a music school and a Sixth Form Social Centre. Good opportunities for sport – including conventional pitches and large Astroturf pitch for hockey, football, rugby and tennis. Girls play netball and hockey. PE available at both GCSE and A level.

One mother praised the summer post-GCSE programme in particular, 'the boys had trips to France, driving theory lessons and such-like, when all my friends' children at other schools were being chucked out after the exams – a bit galling when their parents had paid for the whole term and after the children had had study leave at home as well!' Another mother with a daughter due to start at the school was a fan of lessons on Saturday morning, 'great for keeping 16-year-old girls from hanging around Guildford on Saturday mornings.'

Background and Atmosphere: Founded in 1851 in St John's Wood to educate the sons of Anglican clergy; moved to existing site in 1872. Set in the middle of a residential area in prosperous commuter town of Leatherhead. Red-brick buildings and quad, with modern chapel, which is light and airy with tiered seating, unlike a lot of older ones.

Girls (in sixth form only) from 1989 – ' brilliant integration,' says head but no plans to go fully co-ed. Girls' boarding house converted and extended from Victorian house situated just across the road from main school site. Bit of a rabbit warren but cosy and the girls like it and draw up their own rotas for minor domestic chores – not just left to domestic staff – mothers will probably approve. Two or three lower sixth girl boarders share rooms with own room in upper sixth. Another girls' house for boarders and day girls opened in September 2004. All boys' houses have day boys and three take boarders as well. Boarders initially share rather cramped dormitories for up to six, which by no stretch of the imagination could be called luxurious. 'Boarding facilities not up to much,' said a prospective parent who was put off the school by the sleeping arrangements. However, many a boy (if not their parents) may welcome the camaraderie of dorm life and, as usual, accommodation improves with age of pupil – sharing between two to five in fifth form, between two in lower sixth; own room in upper sixth.

School very proud of its computer facilities and aims to be one of the most computer literate schools in the country. Sixth form boarders have school computer provided in their houses, all linked to the school network. Splendidly equipped modern language lab. Library converted from former chapel and has good stock of 12,000 books, together with suitable videos and CDs for loan, daily broadsheet papers and periodicals, including foreign language journals. CCF compulsory for first 18 months but 50 per cent of school tend to stay on after that. Duke of Edinburgh Awards also popular with 100 or so members and 13 gold awards in 2002/03. Great inter-house rivalry.

Many day pupils make their way by train – five minutes walk from station and public bus routes from Epsom and Guildford pass the door. School minibus service from Woking under consideration.

Pastoral Care and Discipline: Head points to school's 'caring Christian ethos.' A fourth former agreed, saying that he 'likes the way that everyone looks out for each other right from the start.' Assemblies held daily in Chapel with themes being introduced by the head, chaplain, staff and pupils. Once a month pupils attend a compulsory act of worship on Sundays. No specific provision for those of faiths other than C of E.

Tutors meet all their pupils in small groups for ten minutes at start of every day and for 30 minutes on Friday. Each year group in each house has its own tutor, with two tutors per year group for the girls. Pupils have different tutor every year as they progress through the school – means lack of continuity – but advantage is that tutor becomes very experienced with the foibles of that particular age group. Tutor meets parents of pupils within four weeks of start of academic year. Sixth formers are involved in a range of voluntary service activities including work with disabled adults and football coaching with autistic children.

Pupils neat and tidy in their navy blue blazers; sixth formers also have a uniform regime – a suit of their choice – and prospectus refreshingly says that some of the girls' uniform can be purchased from M & S. Smoking dealt with by graded system of punishment and fine. Drugs cases dealt with on an individual basis and the rules apply to offences either on or off school premises. Student Council with representatives appointed for each house and for each year group – the elected Chair liaises with head. Parents agree that pastoral provision is good.

Pupils and Parents: Unspoilt youngsters, mostly from middle class families and without a trace of arrogance in sight. Boys come from large selection of local Surrey preps and girls mainly from local independent schools. Virtually all live within 20 miles, even boarders. About 50 per cent first-time buyers, with very few ex-pats and around 30 from overseas. Now 14 Foundationers (children of Anglican clergy, see Money Matters), probably because clergy prefer these days to educate their children in their local communities. Notable OJs include architect Lord (Richard) Rogers, archaeologist Sir Leonard Woolley, novelist Sir Anthony Hope (wrote 'The Prisoner of Zenda'), Bishop Leonard Wilson (a former Bishop of Birmingham) and Sir Paul Bryan (a Cabinet minister in Harold MacMillan's government).

Entrance: Boys enter at 13 via CE (pass mark 55 per cent) or Common Scholarship exams. The few coming from the state sector sit an internal test. Both girls and boys can enter at 16 via school's entry interview and their GCSE results, which should include at least 6 passes at A-C with a minimum of 4 Bs, and with B for their chosen AS level subjects.

Exit: Very few leave after GCSE, those who do invariably go to sixth form colleges. Vast majority to university – favoured ones include Oxbridge, Durham, Southampton, West of England, Bristol, Birmingham, Loughborough, Exeter and Kings College, London. About 30 per cent choose a science-based subject, the same percentage plump for humanities, then around 25 per cent a business-orientated course, the rest opting for art.

Money Matters: 170 pupils receiving some sort of fee assistance at present. Awards at 13 for academic, all-rounder/sports, music and art scholarships, ranging in value from 25 to 50 per cent of fees. Similar awards at 16. Fees for children of Anglican clergy (Foundationers) are based on total family income. School is able to offer up to 67 per cent remission of fees for Foundationers. In some cases, fee remission could be higher.

Remarks: Solid, all-round, school with good pastoral care and well sought after but lacking the glitz of its more illustrious competitors. However, a big plus – the super pupils, un-snooty and unaffected while still displaying confidence.

ST LAURENCE SCHOOL

Ashley Road, Bradford-on-Avon, Wiltshire, BA15 1DZ

Tel: 01225 309 500

Fax: 01225 309 572

E-mail: admin@st-laurence.wilts.sch.uk

Website: www.st-laurence.wilts.sch.uk

• Pupils: 1,140 boys and girls • Ages: 11-18 • Size of sixth form: 210 • C of E • State

Headteacher: Since 2004, James Colquhoun LLB PGCE (fifties); educated at Kelly College, Devon. Read law at Bristol before 'a few years in the wilderness.' PGCE at Bath then first teaching post in Swindon followed by promotion to deputy headship in Market Harborough and headships in Bishop's Stortford and Kettering. Married to former special needs teacher with grown-up family. Appointed to restore St Laurence's fortunes after predecessor's sudden departure; follows two year spell in noteworthy DfES 'Fresh Start' headship in Newcastle-upon-Tyne. Track record of raising academic standards, a hands-on manager with clout and business acumen. Energetic and determined to see school back amongst top state schools. Generally liked by parents and respected by pupils; keeps banging out mantra of 3 core values: commitment, creativity and community. Has dispensed with bursar, privatised support services and restructured staff. Some parents unhappy about shorter teaching day but, overall, reforms have been well received with improved results at Key Stages 3 and 4.

Academic Matters: Academic strengths across the board with science and modern languages strong. Provision for exceptionally able. A Levels 98 per cent pass rate, 59 per cent A-B. At GCSE, average of 67 per cent achieved 5 or more A* – C in 2005; almost all get five A*-Gs. Setting progressively from year 8. 'Oxbridge awareness programme' in sixth form.

Games, Options, The Arts: Grass athletics track; playing fields provide enough space for cricket, tennis, hockey, rugby and football. Some athletes at county and national level. Riding once a week for SEN students. A hits-you-between-the-eyes art department where dynamic and dedicated team nurtures each pupil to locate the ceramicist, sculptor, textural artist, colourist or draughtsmen they didn't know they were. Unusual projects such as Burning of the Dragon (30 x 40 foot wooden sculpture which 'came alive' when pyrotechnically injected) seen on Channel 4 news,

was aided by local industries/parents. A talented young sculptor gained a very rare 100 per cent at art A level same year. Strong on drama, dance and music – close links with Theatre Royal in Bath. One in five take an instrument. Two choirs – linked to a school in Japan, several string groups, two jazz bands and an orchestra. Foreign exchanges to Sully (France) and Norden (Germany), and sixth form trips to Paris, Israel, Berlin, Prague and participated in Model United Nations. Supervised private study an option. Each year timetable is collapsed for a week of special projects/outward bound/challenge programmes for all years. Drama and dance trips aplenty. Late bus operates following 3.00 – 5.00 programme for after-school sports and activities.

Background and Atmosphere: The prosperous Italianate town of Bradford-on-Avon spawned rich merchants in the wool trade. In 1860, a freethinking philanthropist, Lord Fitzmaurice, set up a technical school with the radical aim of educating young people for the 19th century. In 2002, archaeologists unearthed a vast Roman Villa on the playing field and uncovered a rare mosaic in almost perfect condition. Half-hour documentary on BBC2 Time Flyers October 2003. Fitzmaurice Grammar merged in 1980 with 250 year old Trinity Secondary Modern on a site above the picturesque town. The marriage was St Laurence, blessed with enough land to offer a slice for the Wiltshire Music Centre to be built 4 years ago by £2.8 million lottery and local sponsorship. Although independent, the 300-seat auditorium, recording studio, music technology suite and nine workshop spaces are used for pupils as well as 2,000 visitors a week for concerts/jazz and voice workshops/dance/lectures/filming. The Schubert Ensemble, The Orchestra of the Age of Enlightenment, Howard Skempton, Jason Rebello, Pee Wee Ellis hold workshops for the school. This fairy godmother has done much to glamorise the image of St Laurence's shabby barrack-like shell. Enthusiasm from staff is infectious. Rock star Midge Ure recently visited – 'I wish I'd been to a school like this!' Recently opened restaurant serves healthy options and gives the kind of lift to the place that the head is keen to see generally.

Pastoral Care and Discipline: No rebels given reins here. Hitherto discipline achieved through reward and sanction system. Hot on parent-staff rapport. Inter-personal skills highly valued – sixth formers taking part in mentor scheme get certificate of recognition as part of record of achievement. School counsellor and nurse on staff. Clear policy on dealing with drugs – rather than expulsion that sends the problem further down the road, parents are involved and they work in close co-operation with police and other agencies. Tries to lure students into dining room with imaginative sandwiches. Also – excellent idea – breakfast from 8 to 8.45am. Why, oh why, cry pupils, do only year 7s and sixth formers get lockers, forcing the rest to troll around with books, PE kits, props for drama and kitchen sink from class to class? Or is this set to change now under new regime?

Pupils and Parents: Large contingent from affluent villages of Freshford, Westwood, Winsley, Limply Stoke. Most from middle class catchment area. Professors/teachers/county hall bods/self-employed media/musicians/actors/architects. 'All our teachers send their children here which is a good sign,' says old-timer. Students willingly swap from private schools like Sherborne to endure the mundane uniform of navy sweatshirt with logo, navy trousers/skirt. Body piercing or dyed hair is out. For sixth form, nets are cast wider than catchment, and casual dress allowed. Parent who dumped a 100 per cent Assisted Place from a private school in Bath to send girl here instead, says 'every child in private education needs to come to a place like this to get ready for the real world'.

Recent stars of small screen: Charlotte Long, Emma Pierson, Michael Rouse, singer Mike Edwards, Joe England (Royal Shakespeare Company).

Entrance: 180 places at year 7 are over-subscribed but anyone in catchment area automatically gets in. Head is wise to all tricks to gain entitlement such as renting a house in the area for a year. (The school's cachet has driven up house prices by 10 per cent.) Induction days for sixth form in June and September.

Exit: 90 per cent to higher education. Mostly Aberystwyth, Cardiff, Nottingham, Sussex, Leicester, London. 2 to Oxbridge. Small tranche to art/photography colleges.

Remarks: Stimulating environment, which can take just about anybody and get magnificent results. Good relationships between teacher and parent; teamwork and creativity to the fore with new head capable of putting St Laurence back where it was in terms of local reputation.

St Leonards School & Sixth Form College

Linked to Saint Leonards - New Park in the Junior section

South Street, St Andrews, Fife, KY16 9QU

Tel: 01334 472 126
Fax: 01334 476 152
E-mail: info@stleonards-fife.org
Website: www.stleonards-fife.org

• Pupils: 390; 67 girls board, 149 day; 41 boys board, 133 boys day; Some flexi-boarding available • Ages: 16-18 sixth form college; 12-16 senior school, 3-12 junior school including nursery • Size of sixth form: 97 • Non-denom • Fees: Senior School and College boarding: £6,754; day: £2,757 Junior school: day £1,999-£22,41; nursery: £1,595 • Independent • Open days: October and May but visit any time

Headmaster: Since 2003, Mr Robert Tims MA PGCE (fifties); comes with Heidi, whom he married not so long ago (she has a grown-up son). Seen very much as a joint appointment. The Tims were (briefly – Malvern was in a state of flux) houseparents at Malvern and Mr Tims, who joined Malvern in 1978, rose to become head of chemistry and was head hunted while he was senior master. Much involved in setting up the IB at Malvern, he helped mastermind the introduction of co-ed and was a popular soccer referee, cricket umpire and PPL.

Educated at Eton where he was a chorister, from thence via a choral bursary to Jesus, Cambridge, where he read natural sciences combined with a PGCE over four years. Started teaching at Abcross School in Hornchurch, where he learnt the rudiments of showmanship teaching – 'brilliant head of department'. Such skills will no doubt stand him in good stead as he tries to instil confidence back into this somewhat battered, once-great school in windy St Andrews. A smashing, thoughtful couple, comfortable with each other (loads of teasing) and their new challenge, they have already met many of the local prep heads, and a mass of potential parents – quite a lot from abroad. Golf at St Andrews is a great draw – the latest recruit has a handicap of three (and the one before, eight). Heidi has over twenty years' worldwide experience teaching, also teaches EFL and has recently become involved in working with pupils in the Aspergers/autistic spectrum.

Academic Matters: Mixed reports. School now follows the English syllabus. Classes are setted but not streamed and the norm is to take four AS levels, followed by three subjects at A level. Both dual and separate sciences offered at GCSE. A levels on the up, with a pleasing number of As in biology, chemistry, English, French, Spanish and German; Latin and some Greek at A2. 'Classics amazing', so the take-up here could be in for a growth spurt. Italian is an 'activity'; Russian speakers take A levels, and all native speakers take their own lang at GCSE, occasional slight problems getting specialist tutors for A level and lit. Psychology A level not currently on offer. Will offer the IB from 2006.

'Much use made of St Andrew's University' but not quite as much used as it should be, say pupils, though sixth form pupils have total access to the university library, 'where they do serious academic work'. The principal of the university is one of the governors of St Leonards and there is much to-ing and fro-ing of staff. This is a two way game – pupils have been known to take part in university psycho-type research. Head keen to foster stronger links, but it is early days yet in his tenure. Good dyslexia programme, usually one to one. EFL in place and Mrs Tims was off to teach it as we left. Good IT but more in the wings.

Games, Options, The Arts: Girls' sports still strong, with usual mass of international lax players. Boys' sport strong. Loads of individual sports: judo, trampoline, skiing, badminton, swimming (university uses pool for water polo – and remember who played water polo at the university?), football (seven a side only). Great new all weather pitch, slight problems with Historic Scotland, who own the fabric of the walls and are reluctant to allow floodlights (this is an ongoing hassle). Sports hall probably on the wish list, though school has quite a lot of spare cash after some judicial sell-offs, but talk of lottery funding and community type use. Strong art department, often studied outside normal lessons – huge range of alternative media, reception hall decorated with magical red felt balls made in art dept by the girls plus one rather wonderful origami flower made by one of the chaps. DT centre on cards. Music strong in fabulous Bob Steedman (husband of three heads ago) designed centre. Drama on the up; school does AVCE (which used to be GNVQ) in drama and has an option to perform twice a year in the newly revamped Byre theatre in St Andrews (and this is popular with both school and public). All pupils are taught self-defence, plus D of E and all sorts of options.

Background and Atmosphere: Founded in 1877, now a conglomerate, calling itself St Leonards School and St Leonards sixth form college, St Leonards junior and middle schools. Perhaps some PR might not come amiss with the nomenclature. 'Mother' school of Wycombe Abbey; purpose-built and slightly awesome with many additions, though fewer than there were. This is a chilly corner of Fife, on the sea, bracing air, track suits popular for games. Golf, riding and the beach all great draws, as well as trips up town and forays to the surrounding countryside. Mega library and selection of maryana in Queen Mary's House (less used now since the opening of the sixth form college).

School recently shed 'a number of redundant buildings' and land outwith the wall. Much redistribution of territory, with the girls' sixth form houses now housing the boys' sixth form and the lower sixth now in former classrooms. The boys' house above the nursery, in the old St Kat's building, now aptly renamed Hepburn House, after 16th Century Bish Hepburn, whose motto 'ad vitam' was adopted by St Leonards all those years ago. NB pupils do their own laundry, and sixth form wear own clothes; previous head changed school uniform (again) apparently 'even the boys don't mind wearing' the specially designed St Leonards' kilt. (With such a vast range of proper tartans it seems odd to design a school tartan – where else could the poor dears wear it?)

Day pupils may board on occasion, either if parents are away, or after a particularly late rehearsal. Buses on hand for day pupils and juniors may be dropped off early and collected late. Popular nursery department, boys often 'just' stay on.

Pastoral Care and Discipline: School rules feature punctuality, security and civilised behaviour; the student handbook has a rash of rules, most of which are sheer common sense. L-drivers may not drive college friends and the like. But members of the sixth form college have a mass of privileges – can visit local pubs (some are out of bounds), smoke off-campus and are generally expected to behave like grown-ups. No smoking on campus, no under-age drinking and absolute zero tolerance of drugs (a draft of the newly written drugs policy has gone to parents for approval). Out for pushing, 'forfeit right to remain in school' for using – depends on individual and other factors and for how long, and pupils may be allowed back under fairly arduous conditions – random testing and the like. Testing on suspicion of drugs use, suspension for continued failure to observe the booze rules. Police are called for theft. No chaplain currently, each girls' house takes it in turn to attend the three local Presbyterian churches; others follow their own faiths. Regular visiting preachers.

Pupils and Parents: Still strong Scots contingent, around 66 per cent from Scotland, plus 6 per cent ex-pats, some 24 per cent foreign nationals, which rises to 56 per cent in the sixth form, and 4 per cent from south of the border (who probably ought to be classed as foreign nationals in the current climate!) Growing influx from abroad for the sixth form college – this is encouraged as the internationalism of the college is seen as one of its strengths. A particular interest in golf – golf scholarships proving a popular draw, pupils can and do play the Old Course. St Leonards has a strong Old Girls' network and many at the school are offspring or grand offspring of Seniors. Famous Seniors include Betty Harvey Anderson, Dame Kathleen Ollerenshaw, the previous President of St Leonards, Gillian Glover of the Scotsman (who didn't last the course), Stella Tennant (ditto) Baroness Byford (current President) and Angie Hunter.

Entrance: Accept CE, usually own entrance exam or scholarship exam. Six GCSEs or equivalent for sixth form with As and Bs in subjects to studied at higher level in the IB.

Exit: Usual dribble away post GCSE, otherwise around 90 per cent to universities, with Newcastle, Bristol, Exeter, Durham, Nottingham and Edinburgh the most popular (particularly the latter). A regular 8-10 per cent to Oxbridge. Most do a gap year, armed with addresses of welcoming Seniors throughout the world (a boon for worried parents).

Money Matters: Serious – though only of nominal monetary value – collection of scholarships, ranging from academic through music, drama and sport – golf scholarships very popular (as you might imagine).

Remarks: Famous traditional academic girls' boarding school which has been hit hard by Scottish chaps' schools going co-ed. School went fully co-ed in 2000 – after a brief spot of top and tailing, the trickle is not yet a flood, but they come. Boys who started in the nursery are going through the junior school.

Previous head reckoned St Leonards to be 'Fife's best kept secret'; certainly it is one of the more under-used schools we have come across. Not a lot of change here, though whether Seniors will approve of having a man at the helm, or of selling off the family silver is debatable. However, the facilities are second to none, the sixth form college is superb, more like a university foundation course than many we have seen. More aggressive marketing may be the answer and, just possibly, the governors may have got it right this time.

St Leonards-Mayfield School

The Old Palace, Mayfield, East Sussex, TN20 6PH

Tel: 01435 874 600
Fax: 01435 872 627
E-mail: enquiry@stlm.e-sussex.sch.uk
Website: www.stlm.e-sussex.sch.uk

- Pupils: 400 girls; around 190 board • Ages: 11-18 • Size of sixth form: 120 • RC (but non-RCs welcome) • Fees: Day £4,220 (plus £38 per night flexi-boarding); boarding £6,480.
- Independent • Open days: At least one per term. See website for dates

Head: Since 2000, Mrs Julia Dalton BA PCGE (fifties), educated at Bedales School and University of York (read English). Started teaching career at Wakefield Girls' High. Took 10 year career break to have her daughter and two sons. Husband is director of education planning for Hertford LEA. Resumed teaching career when children reached school age and taught at various schools in Hertfordshire, rising to deputy head at St George's School, Harpenden, before coming here. Succeeded the very popular and long-running (twenty years) Sister Jean Sinclair.

Academic Matters: GCSE results very good – more than 50 per cent A/A* in the last two years, after that mostly Bs. A level – more than 70 per cent A/B. Maths/science subjects as popular as arts – teachers well-liked by girls. Maths classrooms have their own computers with latest software. Average class size at GCSE 14, dropping to 8 for A level. Strong on languages; 4 modern languages on offer as well as Latin and Greek. EFL well catered for. Girls are encouraged to try the many different subjects on offer before making a choice for GCSE – all 13-year-olds are doing a minimum of 16 subjects and most do 18. At A level, teachers try to build time-tables around individual preference.

Games, Options, The Arts: Absolutely amazing ceramics department, fantastic pieces displayed all around the school. Art department very inspiring too (female life drawing once a week). Girls use artwork to 'express themselves' with some thought-provoking work at A level (all students achieved grade As in 2001). Music active – 5 choirs, orchestra, wind and string bands; involved in the Mayfield Festival under Sir David Willcocks. Keen on drama – inspiring teacher – but concert hall needs updating for large productions. Sport facilities within easy reach of main block. Strong generally, excellent results in tennis, hockey and volleyball. Girls can keep own ponies at nearby farm; outdoor/small indoor school available and cross-country course; many competitions. Successful debating society, City & Guilds professional cookery course and inter-house Masterchef competition. Main library disappointing – updating promised.

Background and Atmosphere: Founded in 1846 by Cornelia Connelly as a religious congregation for the education of Catholic girls. Buildings set in wonderful grounds of The Old Palace of The Archbishops of Canterbury. Stunning medieval chapel where performances of 'The Live Crib', prepared by the school prefects every Christmas (real baby, real donkey), are always crowded. All classrooms and facilities on one site; exceptional new science block opened in 2000; five boarding houses, split by age; girls in years 11, 12 and 13 have study bedrooms and can share or opt for single rooms. Approx half of pupils board – some weekly (no school on Saturday). New state of the art boarding house opened September 2005. Years 7 and 8 have their own classrooms separate from other teaching rooms to facilitate the transition from a small prep or primary school to a larger senior school. Three dining rooms for lunch; excellent food (catering manager very popular); girls comment that 'food is too tempting not to eat'. Sixth form don't wear uniform. Very impressive school magazine, 'The Cornelian'. Friendly, caring feel to the school.

Pastoral Care and Discipline: Strong spiritual ethos running through school – 'teachings of Christ provide our moral cornerstones', says Mrs Dalton; this helps the girls to understand and learn the difference between right and wrong. Any bullying is dealt with immediately.

Pupils and Parents: Mainly from south east and London. Around 75 non-Brits – 40 from Hong Kong, the rest Mexico, Asia, Spain and other European countries. Girls are polite, well-behaved, relaxed and open; good relationships with teachers, who treat them as individuals. Parents past and present involved in many social and fund-raising activities. Very strong Old Girls' association – friendships last a lifetime.

Entrance: Main intake at 11, then 13 and sixth form entry. By CE at 13 plus interview and previous school reports. Own entrance tests for any girl not able to offer CE. Equal opportunities at 11 and 13 for Catholics and non-Catholics.

Exit: Wide spread of universities; many to London – Imperial College/Kings/Queen Mary – University. 8 to Oxbridge in 2004.

Money Matters: Scholarships - offered to years 7 and 9 (divided on discretionary basis) for all round academic, music, sport and art. No one award worth more than 50 per cent discount. No bursaries, except to pupils already in the school whose parents face financial crisis.

Remarks: Head forward thinking, very positive and has great vision for this caring and impressive school; she plans to stay until retirement. Pupil numbers rising since 2000.

ST MARGARET'S SCHOOL (EDINBURGH)

Linked to Saint Margaret's Junior School (Edinburgh) in the Junior section

East Suffolk Road, Edinburgh, EH16 5PJ

Tel: 01316 681 986
Fax: 0131 667 9814
E-mail: contact@st-margarets.edin.sch.uk
Website: www.st-margarets.edin.sch.uk

- Pupils: 300 pupils; 15 board, 285 day • Ages: 11-18 years
- Size of sixth form: 100 • Non-denom • Fees: £2,185 - £2,677
- Independent

Principal: Since 2001, Mrs Eileen Davis (fifties), educated at Queen Mary Lytham, read geography at Hull, 'no ideas really what I was going to do', who had been the most efficient deputy head at St George's School for Girls in Edinburgh. Married, no children. She previously taught at Dollar Academy and before that taught at Bolton girls and the state sector. Super, fun, relishes the challenge, 'the conundrum'.

Academic Matters: Strong results – 60+ per cent grade 1 at Standard, almost 70 per cent A/B grades at Highers. ESL and excellent learning support on hand throughout, also support for gifted pupils. Adapts the upper levels of Scottish 5-14 curriculum to start National Qualifications courses early – in Senior 1 or 2. Standard Grade and Intermediate presentations are made in S3 so that Highers or Intermediate 2 Levels can be 2 year courses in up to 6 subjects as well as modules in wider variety of subjects. Pupils take short courses or work experience or voluntary service.

Games, Options, The Arts: Girls are bused to Edinburgh University's Peffermill sports grounds. The gym is above the music studios (still) in a converted church. Music good, with a thriving choir, plus plainsong, masses of orchestral, jazz, strings, etc. Home economics, and 'survival skills in cookery', also strong ceramics, photography, jewellery.

Background and Atmosphere: Known as the saints, or all saints; this rich conglomerate is now a serious player in the Edinburgh property circus. The former Oratava hotel, which until recently has been the school's boarding and computing sixth form centre, is currently on the market. As well as its adjoining villa, and huge car park, all adjacent to The Cameron Toll shopping centre and utterly desirable in flat conversion terms. A sign outside Suffolk Hall Hotel further up the road, proclaims it to be acquired for St Margaret's school, plus the building behind. This property tinkering should do wonders for the school finances, and will concentrate the school buildings in a tighter area (albeit with the main road through the middle) but whether, with boarders currently down to sixteen, it makes any sense at all to offer boarding facilities is open to debate.

Quite a number from the ethnic minorities, with orthodox Moslems traipsing along the pavement between classes in chic headscarves and mini-kilts. This is not really for the aspiring middle classes or the yuppies. Useful, though for parental drop-off when heading into the city from the South, and with the possibility of a huge capital gain on the property front, should be able to offer fairly substantial scholarships to attract brighter pupils when the buildings are completed and funds realised from the sell-off.

Pastoral Care and Discipline: No complacency here, but 'seeing the principal is usually enough'. Anti-bullying is given high priority by all staff: four guidance staff, plus form teachers on hand to advise.

Pupils and Parents: School subsidises daily buses from North Berwick, Lauder and the Gyle. A thorough mixture, with gentrified children departing for their country estates on the one hand, and solid Edinbourgeoisie, plus children whose parents work at the local supermarket on the other. Head keen on 'diversity of backgrounds'.

Entrance: Throughout the school, any term. Whenever, very flexible, but primarily at 11, 12 and 13. Boys up to 8 only – links into Merchiston. Interview with principal, short assessment, day visit and references.

Exit: Greatest tranche to tertiary education, mixture of UK universities, but more to Scottish universities.

Money Matters: Scholarships worth up to 30 per cent of tuition fees for entry to the Senior School (S1) - academic, art, drama, sport or musical achievements as well as assessments. The assessments (papers in English and maths, an aptitude test, an interview with the principal, specialist interviews where relevant and a good current school report) are held in January.

Remarks: Worthy, still an educational dinosaur; not perceived as either a smart or an intellectual establishment by Edinburgh citizens, there is a touch of the Miss Jean Brodies about the place.

St Margaret's School (Exeter)

Linked to Saint Margaret's Junior School (Exeter) in the Junior section

147 Magdalen Road, Exeter, Devon, EX2 4TS

Tel: 01392 491 699
Fax: 01392 251 402
E-mail: mail@stmargarets-school.co.uk
Website: www.stmargarets-school.co.uk

- Pupils: 360 girls: juniors 70; seniors 290. All day • Ages: 7-18
- Size of sixth form: 85 • C of E • Fees: Junior school £2,128, senior school £2,570 • Independent • Open days: Autumn and summer

Head: Since 2004, Miss Rowan Edbrooke (mid-forties). Started her teaching career at Queen Elizabeth's Girls School, Barnet. Progressed to senior teacher and head of department at South Hampstead High School then moved to Haberdashers' Aske's School for Girls as head of sixth form; promoted to deputy head. Has promoted students' interest in sport since her arrival; teaches PE to all years, so gets to know the children quickly and remains in contact with them. Enjoys theatre, music, literature and outdoor pursuits. A charismatic lady, believes in the encouragement of leadership, independence and initiative. Values extra-curricular activities for the development of a good all-rounder. Her enthusiasm and energy has rubbed off on the school, say pupils.

Academic Matters: Excellent A level and GCSE results; 75 per cent A/B at A level. Two girls received 100 per cent for Religious Studies GCSE placing them in top ten nationally. Broad curriculum. Compulsory French taught from year 7; Spanish and German taught 50:50 so preferred second modern language can be taken in year 8. Separate sciences from year 7 with good facilities and teaching, regularly producing medical students. Average class size of 15. Years 8 and 9 take ICT CLAIT exams. Lots of homework but workload and progress are closely monitored during exam years to ensure students cope.

Two learning support assistants work three days a

week under guidance of SEN coordinator. Separate SEN room for children to have one-to-one support. Caters for dyslexics, dyspraxics and a range of other needs and disabilities. School willing to adapt to cater for individual needs.

Games, Options, The Arts: Nationally recognised reputation for music. Chapel choir often triumphant at finals of National Festival of Music for Youth, recently receiving top accolade: 'Outstanding Performance Award' for the 4th year in succession. Performances include involvement in the School Proms at the Royal Albert Hall. Two jolly music teachers oversee three orchestras, five choirs; jazz bands, a chamber orchestra and chamber choir, plus a variety of other ensembles. Aspiring fashion designers, photographers etc produce outstanding art work. Drama is also extremely popular. Good co-ordination between music, art and drama departments. 'The standard of music, art and drama is amazing,' say parents.

Plenty of D of E gold award participants: 33 off to teach at Indian orphanage. Combined Cadet Force and Ten Tors also popular. Well-established exchange programme with many girls choosing to spend some time in France, Germany, Spain. Head keen to foster leadership and sense of adventure in girls.

Despite lack of sporting facilities, girls still reach county standard in sports particularly swimming, running and tennis. On-site tennis courts and good-sized gym caters for other sports like gymnastics, aerobics and dance. Since appointment of head, enthusiasm for netball and rowing is increasing. 'This not a school for top athletes,' say parents, '...although it makes the best of what's available'.

Background and Atmosphere: Ribbon of Georgian houses along an urban street. School founded 1902 'for the

daughters of gentlemen'. Seven headmistresses later it's 'still producing young adults with qualities you would wish for in your own daughter', say parents. The girls and staff present very caring attitudes. 'They are thoughtful, helpful, well-integrated kids,' say parents. 'They look after the younger ones'. Noticeably welcoming and friendly atmosphere. You get the feeling there is no bullying taking place. 'It's a marvellous school'. Strong home economics department has resulted in health-conscious students and staff forming the School Nutrition Action Group to educate their peers. The old chocolate and fizzy drinks-filled vending machines are now redundant and have been replaced by a new Green Machine with healthy and Fair Trade alternatives.

Pastoral Care and Discipline: The emphasis here really is pastoral care and preparing pupils to be independent in the future. Parents choose school for its strong focus on the individual. Mentoring support system and excellent career guidance help students to stay focused. Small, light chapel provides pleasant, quiet retreat to contemplate. Separate place of worship for different faiths.

Pupils and Parents: Happy and confident girls; supportive of one another. Parents living up to 25 miles away choose this school. Mostly middle class professionals – farmers, clergy, GPs, doctors, policemen. OGs include broadcaster Mary Nightingale, Royal Ballet musician Emma Granger, Archers' actress Hedli Niklaus.

Entrance: Entrance examinations consist of, at 11, maths, English & VR; 13+: same tests plus a language paper. No past papers given. 'For good all-rounders who have a sparkle in their eye and aspire to be the best they can be,' says head. Not just for top academics. Parents can choose between independents like Maynard (girls), Exeter School (co-ed) and Blundells. Main feeders 20 state primary schools and preps: St Peter's, Lympstone, St John's, Sidmouth, Exeter Cathedral etc. Would like to attract more external entrants to sixth form – traditionally three annually.

Exit: A couple of pupils leave to start senior school at Colyton/Torquay grammars or Central Middle School. Five per cent of year 11 leaves for Exeter College. Sixth form students all to university or further education. Regular Oxbridge entrants.

Money Matters: Academic scholarships of up to 50 per cent, plus music. Council awards for means-tested parents earning below £27,000.

Remarks: Girls with moral values, high standards of work and behaviour. If your child is academically bright but also loves music, dance, art or drama, definitely one to consider.

St Margaret's School for Girls

Linked to Saint Margaret's School for Girls Junior Department in the Junior section

17 Albyn Place, Aberdeen, AB10 1RU

Tel: 01224 584 466
Fax: 01224 585 600
E-mail: info@st-margaret.aberdeen.sch.uk
Website: www.st-margaret.aberdeen.sch.uk

- Pupils: 385 girls, all day • Ages: 3-18 • Size of sixth form: 65
- Non-denom • Fees: Juniors from £1,381 to £2,189; Seniors £2,409 • Independent

Head: Since 2001, Mrs Lynn McKay BA PGCE ACCEG (fifties), who has a stunning list of schools behind her: previously head of Parsons Mead at Ashtead in Surrey, and before that deputy head of sixth form of Guildford High. Educated in Wales, she went to Ardwyn Grammar School in Aberystwyth, followed by Swansea uni where she read French (which she still teaches). Keen on Spanish, youth work and the 'extra-curricular side of school life'. She also sings and is a member of the local church choir.

Don't get the wrong impression: Mrs McKay is a modern re-invention, zinging, swinging, and totally on the top of everything. She took over a school which had 'been through a difficult year': the school is on course again. Mrs McKay's incredibly elegant office overlooks the playground and she is much entertained by the fact that when pupils want to plan something 'really wicked' they sometimes squat on the stairs immediately below her window, not realising that she can hear everything they say.

Academic Matters: Academically strong across the board, though not really such a formidable selection of subjects: Business management and information studies (one candidate only) stand out among all the usual suspects. Italian and philosophy in the pipeline, and ethics has been introduced as a non-exam subject next year. French and German, plus Latin on the langs side – all can be taken to Advanced Higher level, but hardly any classicists – though all get top grades. Tranches of excellent results in maths, English, mod langs and sciences. Head keen that girls should have the advantage of 'learning independently' and enjoy their lessons. Three new ICT suites, all intranetted, travelling trolley of lap tops motors round the school.

Strong support for learning throughout the school with help for the most gifted as well as the underperformer, dyslexia, dyspraxia, ADHD and mild Aspergers all catered for, both individual and group teaching, plus support in class if needed. Each department keeps detailed notes of problems that might be 'just around the corner'. Impressive paired reading initiative where girls in senior school 'trained in specific reading techniques' work with younger pupils in their free time – apart from fostering community spirit, senior readers also get brownie points through 'certification from the Institute of Management'. The learning support team also provides EAL (Tefal trained helpers in the nursery): Aberdeen is, after all, the oil capital of the North and has a huge through-put of non-English speakers.

Games, Options, The Arts: Stunning netball team who were Scottish champs last year. School keen on promoting team games, but loads of individual activities too: swimming important, athletics, tennis, rounders etc. Mrs McKay keen for school to have an 'ungirly' image, so food technology only up to second year (though it reappears again as preparation for living in sixth). Dramatic fabric design in art, girls make bags with their products, sewing club post school. Art and soldering 'fantastic', and juniors had art on display at Crathes castle last year. Art, music and PE can all be taken to Advanced Higher level, good music and PE results, art the least impressive, drama seems to have fallen by the wayside as an exam subject, can it really be relegated to a couple of club slots a week? Music vibrant, school uses the Kodaly method and boasts a collection of orchestras, string, chamber, jazz plus outstanding 'travelling' choir with regular trips to the States, Europe and St Paul's Cathedral. Impressive collection of FPs in the national youth orchestra. St Margaret's schools worldwide band together for choir tours, heads' chit-chat. 'Gives the school a global dimension'. Collection of clubs, but not a vast collection and some of them might be seen to be part of the school curriculum: tennis, French, dance but also debating and chess. Strong D of E proponents, regular golds. YE (finalists in 2005) and masses of charity input, strong international pupil base and good global awareness. Comprehensive careers department with every girl spending a day at BP.

Background and Atmosphere: Founded in 1846, St Margaret's is the only all girls school in the North of Scotland. Based in a hotch potch conversion of Victorian Merchant's houses (and Albyn Place and the adjacent Queens Road in Aberdeen are home to some six or seven various schools – not all of them clearly labelled, this editor happily tried to go to the (state) school next door.) The deep gardens at the back have been neatly filled in with massive new builds, and recently refurbished art studio, resources centre and dining area. Charming well equipped library. Pupils chose lunch from a menu provided by a local restaurant, and are served by volunteer parents in a jolly nice but pretty cramped bistro style room in the basement adjacent to the recently revamped and very posh loos. Girls eat by class, own sandwiches OK. School is wheel chair friendly, lifts. Early drop off from 8 am, with special provision in the nursery for tots to stay up till 5.30pm, though it costs extra if after school's official closing time. Holiday activities club run during the Easter, summer and October holidays. Nursery staff – and the nursery is called daffodil, wear charming yellow tops and green track suit bottoms. Good second-hand shop (well this is Aberdeen).

Pastoral Care and Discipline: Strong moral back ground, with joint PSE and RME syllabus. Some 15 Moslems in the school, headscarves and longer skirts OK, and pupils made to feel inclusive with Ramadan respected and a special prayer room set aside. Ecumenical assemblies. All join in the Easter service and Christmas concert and the whole school troops off to the Cathedral for St Margaret's day when the smallest have to be restrained from trying to find St Margaret's shield on the roof and falling over in the process. Girls have form teachers, with a dedicated head of guidance for each year, and can go 'to anyone if in difficulties'. Strong anti-bullying programme. Detention now apparently against human rights (not a lot of other schools seem to know this) and recalcitrant pupils get 'an extra learning opportunity to brush up their skills'. Sometimes this takes place after school ...

Pupils and Parents: Large number of first time buyers, large number of non-Brits, strong parent association. And very strong FP links, we met several coming back to help during their gap year, or just to say how they were getting on. Charming. Polite and well-mannered. Tessa Jowell was an old girl. Girls come from all the surrounding areas, as well as the city itself.

Entrance: Test for all, mini test for tinies where they play in groups and are surreptitiously assessed by experts. Siblings not usually turned away.

Exit: Regular trickle to Oxbridge, one last year, but most to Scottish universities studying an astonishing variety of subjects.

Money Matters: Couple of academic and music scholarships, means-tested from September 2005. Will keep a child to next public exam if parents have problems but with the usual caveat about parents being upfront and realistic.

Remarks: Jolly nice old fashioned school with proper values and the best of modern teaching methods. Some of the fabric is a bit sad ('although recent inspectors said it was very good') and the well-used lawn in the tiny play area is a disgrace (thanks to the recently laid new gas pipe). But if single sex education is what you want, St Margaret's is a school which does its girls exceeding well.

ST MARY REDCLIFFE AND
TEMPLE SCHOOL

Somerset Square, Redcliffe, Bristol, BS1 6RT

Tel: 0117 377 2100
Fax: 0117 377 2101
E-mail: enquiries@smrt.bristol.sch.uk
Website: www.redcliffe-school.co.uk

• Pupils: 1,420 boys and girls • Ages: 11-18 • Size of sixth form: 415 expanding to 450 from 2006 • C of E • State

---

Head: Since 2005, Mrs Elizabeth Gilpin, formerly head of St Augustine's RC/CofE Upper School in Oxford.

Academic Matters: Exam results well above national average for GCSE (norm 10 per pupil) and in line with it at A level. Pupils' individual achievements recognised and valued. Curriculum balance carefully maintained, and complemented throughout by a wide-ranging enrichment programme. Currently engaged on a 5-year 'values education' project with Bristol University, to develop pupils' sense of social responsibility through the curriculum. Will fund pupils to attend some courses at local colleges if not able to provide them. Special needs resourcing 'adequate but not generous'. History, maths and RE teaching particularly strong; art department linked with local community creative projects; many other departments involved with visits, exchanges and links abroad (Tanzania and China in 2000). Specialised status in humanities applied for.

Games, Options, The Arts: On-site facilities for games surprisingly good given city-centre location, with courts, an all-weather pitch ('the arena') and indoor pool. Further sports facilities out of town. Many pupils compete at local, county and national levels in a wide range of team sports (rugby, soccer, hockey, netball, basketball and others) and individual activities such as athletics, judo and aerobics. The list is long. Music vibrant and encouraged. Orchestral and choral concerts held in adjacent and outstandingly beautiful church of St Mary Redcliffe, a superb historic setting, very inspiring, which also serves as school 'chapel'. Drama offered as a GCSE option, and regular ambitious productions involving large numbers of pupils.

Background and Atmosphere: In the typically 1960s purpose-built and now very over-crowded buildings, space is a problem, particularly in the communal areas such as the dining room and the corridors. However, the school functions in a civilised and orderly manner. (What better way to pass the time, while waiting patiently in a long lunch queue, than to stop one's head teacher and tell her a joke?), and some aspirations are already becoming bricks and mortar – new science and English buildings. Parents are kept up to date about all aspects of the school's life via the monthly newsletter.

The close relationship with parents and their underpinning of the school's Christian ethos create positive attitudes to the development of each pupil's potential. Thanks to DfES funding, the new 16+ centre housing 450 students has now opened and is in its second year of operation.

Pastoral Care and Discipline: Impressive system of mixed-age tutor groups reflects the powerful ethos of the extended Christian family. Warmly appreciated – 'a strength' – by parents and former pupils. Valued by staff despite its demanding workload. Enables older students to know and mentor younger ones. Year 7 spend a year in separate house to establish their own year-group relationships before moving into the senior houses; These provide the cornerstones of very good discipline, based on exceptionally effective tutoring. Quick response to any anti-social behaviour, offender withdrawn from class and supervised by (senior) duty teacher. Problems, academic or other, generally detected at an early stage. Parents involved and feel confident about it.

Pupils and Parents: Pupils come from all areas of Bristol and beyond as this is the only C of E VA school in the diocese. The educational provision is explicitly Christian with daily worship, much of it pupil-led, a distinctive feature at its core. The broad social and cultural mix is absorbed comfortably and the close involvement of parents is encouraged, including in worship. Attendance well above national average. Pupils friendly and open . Firm guidelines issued about uniform, and recent reminders to staff, parents and pupils. Girls comment that the grey sweatshirts are 'itchy' but like the option of trousers or skirts. Boys must wear ties for most of the year and always tie and blazer when travelling outside. Tucking in of shirts appears to be a good-natured battleground. Pupils as cheerful as they ever are about school meals, lunchtime visit of ice-cream van on site very popular.

Entrance: Comprehensive intake, admissions policy based on family church attendance history and other priorities (siblings, residence). Some pupils of other faiths admitted. More than 2 applicants for every place. Applications for year 7 close in October of the previous year. Sixth form admission based on academic performance at GCSE and 'agreement to 'respect the faith of others'. Applications close in January of each year.

Exit: Nearly all year 11 pupils go into the sixth form. 75 per cent go on to universities or other higher education institutions – a few to Oxbridge. Some gap year students go abroad on scholarships and as community service volunteers.

Money Matters: No charges. Generous enabling fund supports those from disadvantaged background for school visits etc.

Remarks: 'If only we had qualified...' the cri de coeur of many parents in the area. This is a school born of faith and led with conviction. Its atmosphere is purposeful but also welcoming and considerate. Parents and staff did not need Ofsted (Feb 2004) to tell them that the school offers 'a very good education' and that 'pupils attain high standards'. Not over-focused on league tables, but undoubtedly able to hold its own academically.

St Mary's Catholic School

Windhill, Bishop's Stortford, Hertfordshire, CM23 2NQ

Tel: 01279 654 901
Fax: 01279 653 889
E-mail: info@stmarys.net
Website: www.stmarys.net

• Pupils: 899 boys and girls, all day • Ages: 11-18 • Size of sixth form: 173 • RC • State • Open days: Early October

Head: Since 2001, Mr Anthony Sharpe BA MMus NPQH (late thirties). Took over from Mr Paul Jackson who had a good reputation. Has ambitious plans for the school, 'I'm not here to just oversee everything staying as it is,' he says. Educated at Cardinal Langley High School in Greater Manchester and University of Liverpool, where he studied music and divinity. Taught music and RE in Liverpool before taking up post of deputy head at Loreto RC Girls School in St Albans. Music is a passion – his liturgical compositions have been published and broadcast. Married with three young children.

Academic Matters: Pupils are taught in mixed ability groups in year 7, apart from setting in maths. In years 8 and 9 they are setted for further subjects. IT teaching has been integrated into other subjects but the head is keen to prioritise it and it is now taught as a separate subject. GCSE results are good – 70 per cent achieved five grade Cs or above in 2001 – and A level results tend to be some of the best in the area. There doesn't appear to be any major gender gap in the results. All sixth formers study a general studies programme that includes both religious education and sport. Pupils with learning difficulties are well supported and there are currently ten pupils with SEN statements. Twenty of the 50-odd teachers have been at the school for ten years or more. Average age of teaching staff is 43.

Games, Options, The Arts: Plenty of trips to theatres, exhibitions and places of interest and opportunities for travel abroad. Wide-ranging extra-curricular activities include D of E. High numbers of pupils participate in extra-curricular sports, particularly boys. Regular music and drama performances involving large numbers of pupils. Specialist Arts status, awarded in September 2003, will build further on the reputation of the school in this area. Pupils are encouraged to help in the community through the Saint Vincent-de-Paul Society.

Background and Atmosphere: Established by an order of nuns in 1896 as a girls' convent but co-ed since 1976. Situated near the centre of Bishop's Stortford on a large and pleasant site. Near to bus routes but about a 15-minute walk from the rail station. A mixture of old and new buildings. Some of the older ones are a bit scruffy and there is a big current building programme and plans for refurbishment. Recently built sixth form centre with plenty of space for both study and relaxation. Current sports facilities are adequate but plans for a first class new sports centre. Unobjectionable uniform for years 7-11; no uniform for sixth formers although they are expected to dress smartly.

Pastoral Care and Discipline: Very strong Catholic ethos. There are regular lunch-time Masses and residential retreats. Pupils report a very supportive atmosphere and find it easy to confide in teaching staff who they believe will deal swiftly and effectively with any problems, whether they are related to school – including bullying – or at home. Discipline is firm, but fair. 'We have a reputation for being strict but overall this is a happy school. We have no major discipline problems and pupils are very aware that if they cross the line, there will be sanctions,' says the head. One pupil has been excluded in the past two years. Ofsted rated leadership and management as very good and noted the very good relationships between staff and pupils, saying that staff are excellent role models.

Pupils and Parents: Predominantly Catholic families. In the past, non-Catholic pupils have fitted in well but increasing pressure for places from Catholics has meant that fewer non-Catholics have been admitted to the school over recent years. St Mary's serves the Lea Valley Deanery, which stretches from Bishop's Stortford to Hoddesdon, Cheshunt and Waltham Cross and many pupils travel significant distances across Hertfordshire and Essex. Unlike some local schools, St Mary's does not practise backdoor selection so has, the head stresses, a truly comprehensive intake. The area served is fairly affluent so pupils tend to have relatively few social problems. Very enthusiastic support and fundraising from parents through the PTA.

Entrance: Has recently expanded to five form entry. Heavily oversubscribed. First priority goes to Catholic children with a brother or sister in the school. Next in line are Catholic applicants with no sibling connection. Places are awarded according to where applicants live, with 40 per cent going to children in Bishop's Stortford and Sawbridgeworth, 40 per cent going to children in other parts of the Lea Valley Deanery and 20 per cent to those living in another five surrounding Essex parishes. Next come any other Catholic applicants who don't fit the above criteria. Criterion four offers places to those with a non-Catholic sibling in the school. Effectively, apart from rare cases, the only non-Catholics who will now be gaining a place are those who have an older sibling already at the school. Contact the school for full admissions information.

Entrance to sixth form is dependent on GCSE grades but 'some students come to us without the necessary grades if we think they can cope,' says the head. 'Equally, if students are not able to sustain the level, we ensure that they leave that course and take up alternative provision.'

Exit: A few pupils leave after GCSEs to move to other sixth forms in the area, a few go straight to work. The vast majority of those leaving the sixth form go on to further education. One or two a year head for Oxbridge but the head hopes to see this figure increase with the introduction of a new year 12 extension studies programme.

Remarks: You can more or less forget about applying to this school at the moment unless your child has been baptised in a Catholic church, although places may possibly be available again to non-Catholics following expansion to five form entry. For Catholic parents who are keen to have their children educated in their faith in a happy and academically successful environment, St Mary's should be ideal.

St Mary's Music School

Linked to Saint Mary's Music School in the Junior section

Coates Hall, 25 Grosvenor Crescent, Edinburgh, EH12 5EL

Tel: 0131 538 7766

Fax: 0131 467 7289

E-mail: info@st-marys-music-school.co.uk

Website: www.st-marys-music-school.co.uk

• Pupils: 70 in total; 22 are choristers; 15 boys, 7 girls • Ages: 9-19 • Size of sixth form: 15 • Non-denom • Fees: individually assessed • Independent • Open days: October

Head: Since 1996, Mrs Jennifer Rimer BMus LRAM DipEd (fifties), previously head of academic music, career guidance and guidance in the school and, before that, was principal teacher of music at St David's High School in Dalkeith. Educated at Buckhaven High School, she read music at Edinburgh University. Married, with three children; she and her husband live in Edinburgh and all have a high involvement in music. She was bubbling with glee when we visited – Scottish Gas had just delivered two pairs of angel wings (jolly realistic, with wands) which two selected pupils (one girl and one boy) were to wear (and be filmed in) for the Ministry of the Environment Energy campaign. Not often we find ourselves in such exalted company.

The school has close links with the four specialist music schools south of the border; musical excellence is a priority but academic results are also consistently excellent and the school is regularly at the top of the Scottish schools' league tables.

Academic Matters: School follows normal Scottish National Qualification exam syllabus, Standard Grades followed by Highers and Advanced Highers. A pleasing number of A passes in all disciplines (music tops though). Small classes as one might imagine, and no problem with staff, grades are pleasingly high with over 85 per cent credit passes at Standard Grade and similar successes at Highers. A level music also on offer. 'Support for learning' available and languages include French, German, Gaelic, Italian and Latin.

Games, Options, The Arts: School has an all-purpose games court on site and also uses the sporting facilities a couple of roads and a teeny hike away – (school says 'nearby') – at Donaldson's College. Swimming club popular, busy art classes, debating, plus regular workshops, masterclasses, rehearsals and concerts. Dedicated staff in every

discipline – this is a centre of excellence and if a pupil's music specialism is not normally covered, then a specialist will be pulled in. Music libraries and practice rooms all over. Rooms full of clarsachs and harps; pupils practising in the quaintest corners. Pupils are occasionally joined by musicians from other local schools.

Saturday morning music classes are non-selective, where senior pupils act as class assistants, along with professional staff. Huge variety of choice, from the very basic to quite complicated string ensembles, chamber concerts et al. 'Classes are non-selective and waiting lists are in operation'. Over 200 local children attend.

Background and Atmosphere: Encouraged by Sir Yehudi Menuhin, the school was founded in 1973 in the grounds of St Mary's (Episcopal) Cathedral, and moved to the present site, previously a theological college, in 1995. Delightful if slightly scatty building, the chapel, with all the ecclesiastical trappings, is used for school assemblies, concerts and rehearsals and staircases seem to run in every direction. Some classes held in the 'principal's house' or the 'fives court' in school grounds. Tiny number of boarders who mostly share rooms and can go out with '16 year olds at night and with two or three of our own age during the day' said our charming junior guide. Flexi-boarding if space permits. Weekly assemblies include 'praise time'. School uniform for choristers, junior pupils, otherwise tidy dress and the most elegant and put-together collection of teenagers we have ever come across.

Pastoral Care and Discipline: Tiny numbers, not a lot of sin. 'No drugs – as far as I know' says the head; no obvious smokers. Good guidance system from year staff and the career staff. All of the sixth form have some sort of responsibility, either head of school, or deputy head of school or head of library; but all are prefects in one way or another and contribute to the running of the school.

Pupils and Parents: Primarily from Scotland and the north of England, with a trickle from overseas; these are all dedicated pupils, from every corner of society. The school has an equal opportunities policy but the physically handicapped might find the building a challenge.

Entrance: By vocal audition involving the master of music at the cathedral for choristers: aged 9-13 (though a boy may leave earlier if his voice breaks early). Thereafter all pupils are chosen by instrumental audition, involving the head teacher and the director of music, plus two or three specialists, who change according to instrument. Each child is assessed differently; a successful musical audition is followed by a two-day assessment. Two audition sessions each year, which are always full. The head keeps a waiting list.

Exit: Choristers leave at 13, though some may re-apply for an instrumental place. Almost all pupils go on to tertiary education, be it the conservatoires or music departments in universities. This is a focused school with excellent career guidance for musicians. Good history of music scholarships.

Money Matters: School is basically fee-paying, but with 'aided places' ie parents pay according to means, supported by the Scottish Executive under the St Mary's Music School Aided Places scheme. Government funding (up to 100 per cent) available and Cathedral bursaries.

Remarks: For a musical child, there could be no better start in Scotland or thereabouts; outstanding musically and educationally and, possibly, financially.

ST MARY'S SCHOOL ASCOT

St Mary's Road, South Ascot, Ascot, Berkshire, SL5 9JF

Tel: 01344 623 721

Fax: 01344 873 281

E-mail: admissions@st-marys-ascot.co.uk

Website: www.st-marys-ascot.co.uk

- Pupils: 356 girls; 340 board, 16 day • Ages: 11-18 • Size of sixth form: 103 • RC • Fees: Day £5,128, boarding £7,349 • Independent

---

Headmistress: Since 1999, Mrs Mary Breen BSc MSc (early forties), who was educated at St Mary's Convent, Bishop's Stortford, followed by Exeter University where she read physics, and Manchester where she read philosophy of science and 'rather fell into teaching' when she married James, who taught English at Wellington. As a housemaster's wife she was encouraged to teach physics and progressed, via the Abbey School in Reading, to Eton where, with a two-month intermission when she taught physics on a temporary basis at St Mary's, she became head of dept. The first lay head of St Mary's, she was head-hunted by the chairman of the governors, whose daughter she had briefly taught during her two terms – and, it must be said, much to the chagrin of Etonians who felt that 'it was a terrible waste for her to be going to a girls' school'.

Pretty, bubbly and fun, she is much enjoying her headship. Pupils say she's image conscious, and trad parents find her 'a bit populist but very professional and popular with first time buyers' – this could of course be due to the downturn in the number of girls born to trad families – 'we no longer have families with four or five daughters who have come to us for generations', said a member of staff (10 to 15 per cent are daughters of Old Girls). Still teaches some physics.

The transition to a lay head appears to have been seamless. The school ceased to be a convent in 1988 and Mrs Breen says she has had, 'a great deal of support from the governors and the CJ trustees', 'no interference at all' and considers herself, 'incredibly lucky to have the nuns'. Head lives on site with her husband who was, apparently, only too thrilled to abandon his housemastership. Thirteen male teachers currently.

Academic Matters: Stunning, given the size of the school. Trails of As and A*s throughout, 100 per cent A*-C in GCSEs, with commendable A level results as well. Languages very strong (French, Italian, German and Spanish) and impressive language lab with dedicated computers. Good classics take-up at A level, theology strong. Sciences growing in popularity. Parents say that, 'the staff have a way of making children work'. Computers everywhere, with masses of plugs for laptops in the library – very impressive – and a wireless computer system throughout, intranetted, internetted and email addresses for all.

Full-time teacher for those with mild dyslexia/dyspraxia, one lesson per week, but all staff have some evening duties, so there is a gang of teachers willing and able to help the less able. EFL if asked for. Each pupil has a tutor, which changes biennially until sixth form, when they may choose. Classes streamed for academic subjects and mixed for things like RI and PSE.

Games, Options, The Arts: Outstanding art, the tradition of only getting As and A* in GCSEs and A levels continues; the fabric design and ceramics are to a truly professional standard. Drama good and popular (and the only oversubscribed after-hours club) and available at A level, though little take-up. Tennis the top game, and keen coach is at the nets morning, noon and night; swimming popular, with 'free swimming at weekends' as well – staff use the fab pool at lunch time and it is let out during the summer months. Parents report girls' complaints 'that there is not enough sport, we want to have more exercise to keep fit and trim', though head disputes this, claiming trails of glory on the hockey field and, when we visited, girls were attacking an aerobics lesson with enthusiasm. New purpose-built £4 million sports complex.

Music to die for, most girls learn at least one instrument, with public concerts in London a feature – again parents mutter 'that games are often side-lined for music/drama/choir (the current thing) practice' – head disagrees.

Background and Atmosphere: Commuter-belt rhododendron country – 55 acres of immaculate grounds, the former nuns' burial ground neatly tucked away beside the car park. Purpose-built in 1885 under the auspices of the Institute of the Blessed Virgin Mary (IBVM), founded in the 17th century by Mary Ward, one of the great English educationalists. The charming chapel holds 350 and is the mainstay of the school, used both for mass and morning assembly – notices given out and all that; and for some extraordinary reason there was a sponge in the font when we visited. Much extended and expanded, the head's husband described the red-brick neo-Gothic building as 'Legoland' – apt, but misleading. The imaginative Mary Ward Courtyard for the upper sixth should be copied by all schools – and whereas the girls must eat lunch in the stunning recently decorated school refectory (good food, masses of salads and yoghurts, huge choice), they make their own breakfast and supper.

An excellent halfway house twixt school and the real world. Younger pupils live in bedrooms – not dorms, masses of storage, lots of posters with good cheerful colour schemes and curtains everywhere (and everywhere round the school, with jolly tie-backs). The school is at the end of a private road, with security cameras everywhere and panic buttons in the downstairs bedrooms of the Mary Ward Courtyard. No uniform in sixth form, the girls can also do their own laundry.

Pastoral Care and Discipline: Good PSE programme in operation, and school not known 'for bullying' according to pupils who talk of a 'close knit community across the ages'. Head had a hideous induction when she expelled six girls for possession of cannabis (though not on school grounds) in February 2000; and subsequently had massive number of letters of support from over 90 parents, including letters from most of those whom she had expelled (and subsequently found places for elsewhere). Tough on smoking (£20 fine for the second offence plus letter home, thereafter suspension), and equally tough on booze (not so much a problem) but as house mothers see children into bed, the chance of smoking or boozing not being picked up is remote. Masses of organised weekend activity, arranged by the houses on a rota basis and by the girls on a 'must go to London' basis – head seemed surprised by the latter. Masses of larks with Eton boys.

Pupils and Parents: Top trad Catholics. Conventional. Plus, recently, a number of first time buyers. 'A mixed bunch,' says the head (often with brothers at Eton). Seven per cent non-Brits, a few smart foreigners, diplomats' daughters, OGs' daughters etc. OGs include Caroline of Monaco, the Spanish Infantas, Sarah Hogg, Marina Warner, Antonia Pinter, Poppy Frazer and Fran Hickman.

Entrance: From over 250 different prep schools: school's own exam at 11 for 40 places, and at 13 for 15 places each year. Traditionally lists close 12 months before estimated time of entry but worth asking whenever, though school normally full. Strong preference given to practising Catholics – only a dozen heretics in the place. Sixth form applications entail interview, predicted GCSE results and essay paper.

Exit: As ever, '100 per cent' to university. 10 to Oxbridge, otherwise to the 'fashionable' universities: Newcastle, Edinburgh, Bristol etc. Dribble leave – usually to go to boys' schools – after GCSE.

Money Matters: School will and can pick up some slack if parents fall into difficulties, otherwise two scholarships for tuition fees only at 11 and 13, plus a 10 per cent Mary Ward scholarship for girls at 11 as well as annual music, art, science and sixth form scholarships. This is not a rich school.

Remarks: A charming school where girls learn self confidence and come out with high academic qualifications – 'a very happy school' say girls, who claim to be a lot less sinful than they are painted in the press.

St Mary's School (Calne)

Curzon Street, Calne, Wiltshire, SN11 0DF

Tel: 01249 857 200
Fax: 01249 857 207
E-mail: admissions@stmaryscalne.org
Website: www.stmaryscalne.org

- Pupils: 275 girls; over three quarters board • Ages: 11-18
- Size of sixth form: 90 • C of E • Fees: Day £5,180; boarding £7,580 • Independent • Open days: None; phone for an appointment to visit

Head: Since 2003, Dr Helen Wright MA MA EdD PGCE FRSA (thirties). Educated at James Gillespie's High School, Edinburgh and Lincoln College Oxford where she read Modern Languages (French and German). In December 2004 she earned a Doctorate in Education with a thesis entitled 'Understanding Moral Leadership in Schools'. Taught languages at Reed's School, was head of German at Bishop's Stortford College, then head of German and girls' games and deputy housemistress at St Edward's Oxford. Came to St Mary's from Heathfield School where she was head for two years having arrived as deputy head (was catapulted into acting headship after one term). Is firm that girls do better in a single sex school. A small human fireball, intense, lots of energy, always on the go. Dr Wright wants everything at St Mary's 'to be first class so girls can leave here and do anything.' Recoiled at the description of St Mary's as 'elite' preferring 'cutting edge'. High aspirations for the school which seem to be paying off. Husband, Brian, an IT consultant works from home. Their tiny son can be glimpsed in his pushchair perambulating around the school grounds, a living symbol that a demanding working life and motherhood can (almost) coexist.

Academic Matters: Still prides itself as being the most academic of the small, rural girls' boarding schools and works hard to preserve this. Keen peer pressure to work – and they do. Over half of last year's upper sixth got straight As at A level (2005). GCSE results remarkable as well, with nine and a half GCSE subjects the aim. Girls here lean heavily to English, history and geography (consistently superb results for all three) – less towards maths and sciences though some exceptions. Latin compulsory up to 14 and a few stick with it through to A level, one girl even grinding through Greek A level most years. New A levels include PE, politics and ICT (only one or two girls for each so far). Sixth form lecture programme – from politicians to teenage current affairs – very well received. Three fab but very different libraries to accommodate changing demands as girls move up the school. Not the ideal place for dyslexics etc.

Games, Options, The Arts: Super attitude to sport. Keen on games 'but we don't usually win', say the girls with (too much) modesty. Head wants everyone in a team in the first three years -'if they don't do it now, then, when they leave school, it's too late.' The big five here are lacrosse – new lax coach from the States – netball, hockey, tennis and athletics. Fencing and riding (through local stables) two of the more unusual sports/activities on offer. New indoor pool with fitness suite upstairs. Very well-subscribed D of E with lots of girls going for gold. Drama excels in purpose-built theatre. One grand annual school production which can involve a large proportion of the girls in one way or another (especially when it's a musical). Sir Tim Rice visited St Mary's (his daughter a useful former pupil) while the school was working on its recent production of Chess. 80 girls are doing LAMDA exams, there are several small plays each year, and groups from St Mary's have taken part in the Edinburgh Fringe. School developing links with RADA and working on a plan whereby girls would skip the drama GCSE ('discredited' says head) and go straight to AS with girls spending their final year on a theatre studies foundation course. Lovely music building produces high quality performances, especially the chamber choir which tours, often abroad. Fourth form music competition a fun event 'even if you're no good' said a girl. Music exam results for singing are outstanding, less so for instrumental music (eg only one exam attempt on violin last year – grade 4, pass). Art and history of art A level get brill results.

Background and Atmosphere: Not a school you would choose for its sumptuous grounds. Functional, practical, purpose-built building, founded 1873 by Canon Duncan (Vicar of St Mary's Church, Calne) in 25 acres of central Calne, an unglamorous little Wiltshire market town once best known as home of now defunct Harris' sausage factory. Mostly white, light and airy throughout. Uplifting, though a few classrooms impersonally bare. Each year group has its own house; pupils move each year while remaining throughout in multi-age 'companies', accumulating 'red points' for good deeds. Inter-company competitions in eg drama, music and sport, and each company has annual black-tie dinner. Pet corner exists (one ailing guinea pig) though not much in fashion.

Pastoral Care and Discipline: Quietly supportive tutorial system, staff keep a careful watch – 'we are well aware of social pressures'. Fine and letter home for smoking, and suspensions (occasional) for alcohol and straight out for drugs. Dorms serviceable; nothing truly depressing and all girls from age 15 up have their own study bedroom – even the day girls. Girls all seem to appreciate the school's small, intimate feel – 'everyone knows everyone'. Nice touch – making individual named cake for each of a very large class of pupils being confirmed. Fantastic food, big on soups and salad. Closer to a Michelin star restaurant than to school grub as we know it, with teriyaki salmon a favourite. School has been praised by Social Services for its 'self-harm policy', keeping an eye out for anorexia and bulimia. No make up and only one ear stud per ear allowed. Quite strict on mobile phone use, though some wiseacres try to outwit system by bringing two. Girls involved in running the daily services in attractive modern concrete and metal chapel. No sixth form uniform, but girls very elegantly turned out.

Pupils and Parents: Largely establishment intelligentsia, in strongly C of E ethos. 'They are demanding but in a very positive way,' says the head. Many girls from Wiltshire, Hampshire and Gloucestershire (within hour and a half drive) plus London. 8 per cent overseas pupils – must have fluent English when they arrive. Dedicated travel office a testament to the complex web of journeys that bring the girls here. Bright-eyed, unhearty upper-crust girls whose parents tend to know each other. Sophisticated, feminine and clever. And considering the no make-up rule, an awfully striking set of young women.

Entrance: At 11, 12 or 13 – a little bit intricate. First visit (an absolute requirement), then register, then a conditional place will be offered. In the summer term of year before entry, girls are asked to attend a Taster Day, not to be confused with Entrance Day which they will attend in October. For the latter day of activities and assessment, girls are asked to bring along examples of recent work and references etc will have been sought from their current school. St Mary's will then give a 'firm indication' of whether the school will suit, subject to CE or entrance test performance. Many pupils from the cream of London preps. Also from own prep, St Margaret's, plus Farleigh, Danes Hill and St Francis Pewsey. Siblings encouraged. Sixth form entry more straight-forward and based on good GCSEs – very few places at this age.

Exit: Hardly anyone leaves post-GCSE; a very strong sixth form. Post A level, the majority goes on to first-rate universities (Bristol, Edinburgh, Durham etc). A dollop to Oxbridge in a typical year and the school is good at preparing girls who are attempting this route. Vast numbers currently going on to read art history, history and geography. Gap year is popular.

Money Matters: Selection of academic, music and all-rounder scholarships at 11 and 13. At sixth form, three academic, one art, one drama and one music scholarship. Scholarships can be as much as 40 per cent of fees but all are means tested and only the first 15 per cent is automatic – parents are invited to apply for the remainder of the award. A foundation scholarship may be offered to a highly gifted child whose financial circumstances would otherwise prevent her from attending the school (could cover the full fee amount). School has no endowments so this is no mean feat.

Remarks: Has nailed down mini-niche as the small, rural, academic girls' boarding school. Long seen as a good place for well-bred brains to mix with their own kind but there is more depth here than first meets the eye.

St Mary's School (Cambridge)

Bateman Street, Cambridge, Cambridgeshire, CB2 1LY

Tel: 01223 353 253
Fax: 01223 357 451
E-mail: enquiries@stmaryscambridge.co.uk
Website: www.stmaryscambridge.co.uk

• Pupils: 490 girls, 50 boarders including full time, weekly and flexi, rest day • Ages: 11-18 • Size of sixth form: 90 • RC but all faiths welcome • Fees: Day £2,990; weekly boarding £5,290; full boarding £5,990 • Independent • Open days: October and May

Head: Since 2001, Mrs Jayne Triffitt MA PGCE (forties), educated at Truro High School, read chemistry at St Hilda's, Oxford, where she also did her PGCE. Having benefited from a direct grant scholarship when she was at school, followed by a full grant at Oxford, Mrs Triffitt 'always wanted to put something back into education'; bright, pragmatic, with a twinkle in her eye and a memory like a computer, she has all the easy charm of someone who is not accustomed to not getting her own way. Married to the head of history at The Leys (but she got her job first), they have two young children, a son at King's College School and a daughter at St Catherine's, the main feeder school for St Mary's.

Came to the school after a period of some turmoil – five heads (two acting) in six years. A practising Catholic (and a convert) she was previously head of sixth form at one of the sister schools, St Mary's Ascot; before that, she taught for 17 years in the state system, ending with a ten year stint at La Sainte Union girls' comprehensive school where she was head of science. Mrs Triffitt arrived in Cambridge to find a much more rudderless ship than she had anticipated, 'it was incredibly challenging...the school had really good academic standards, the teachers were excellent, the pastoral care was good' but the school was falling in numbers. It wasn't 'selling itself', it was also losing money. Not surprising really, the external walls were decorated with graffiti and some parts of the inside hadn't been 'touched for thirty years'. Now, decorated in uplifting tones of cheerful yellow, cream, jonquil – except for one very nasty (inherited) bubble gum pink passage – with clean white woodwork everywhere; the school looks fresh and inviting.

With fewer than thirty boarders when she arrived, Mrs Triffitt has invested heavily in a whizzy marketing director, assistant and registrar and does a fair amount of trawling herself. A smart young bursar with an IT background (what do former army officers do now, we wonder?) and an academic housemistress in the boarding house are among the latest appointments. Plus new assistant head from an international school in Brazil. Over 60 staff, with a regular 10/15 per cent turnover. No problem appointing high calibre staff (head keen to make the right appointments and will re-advertise rather than taking a 'might-do') but cost of housing in Cambridge is high for those with families.

Academic Matters: Huge recent investment in IT, with over 250 computers around the school; dedicated computer in sixth form IT centre for girls to edit video footage – multi-split screen and high tech mikes. Recent ISI inspection high-lighted lack of teacher-skills in this direction – one suspects the young may be rather more with it than their mentors. Breezy attractive library, but possibly not enough novels or newspapers in evidence throughout the school. Efficient labs, bright and sunny on the whole, and school has a history of doing well in the biology and chemistry Olympiads; strong A level results too in the sciences, ditto GCSE. Individual or dual award.

Stunning results across the board. Actually results overall pretty outstanding, especially when you consider this is a 'fairly' unselective school. Italian about to be phased out, 'just French, German and Spanish'. Latin on hand, and the odd girl does Greek. Theology for all to GCSE, we sat in on a lesson, brilliant. Classical civilisation, drama, textiles, art and design all make a good showing. Statistics quite popular, also art and design plus psychology or RE at A level. Range of subjects at A level includes theatre studies, textiles, critical thinking, economics and business studies. Max class size 22, but most are way below, certain amount of streaming throughout, but not in science, girls can and do move up and down. Regular collection of time-tabled drop-in surgeries for girls with problems – in any subject – and much used.

The school also runs an International Study Centre. This offers a year's concentrated course in English for girls going to secondary school in the UK (and some will end up at St Mary's, but by no means all) as well as EFL, and lang labs for their own students and summer courses. Ages from 11-17. The site (which is plumb opposite the main school buildings) also accommodates an overspill from St Catherine's, the main feeder school to St Mary's. Girls from abroad at the international study centre are either found accommodation with host families nearby, or, if space available, in the main school itself.

All pupils assessed on entry for reading, spelling and maths, unit 'logs and monitors' problems at the beginning and may pick up one or two during their time at school. Dr Goddard head of SEN, plus two full team co-ordinators and specialists, plus peripatetics for one-to-one, and double teaching in class. Edpsych consulted if required. Only 'about ten' see specialists, some help available outside school, and some help with study skills, plus individual departments help out on an 'informal basis'. Norm is one lesson a week, though 'up to three' is possible. School reckons it is 'dyslexia friendly' but not Crested 'and not likely to move into that area' though there is a 'dedicated teaching space with full rescources'. Individual classes in lunch time and post school. One girl in school diagnosed ADHD with one or two further suspicions. Will not let any pupil needing help 'slip through the net'. Good EFL provision too.

Games, Options, The Arts: An inner city school, games pitches some distance away, pupils are bused, various hirings from The Leys, swimming pool and the like, one or two courts on site, and really quite an adequate play area. Own (smallish first floor!) gym. School plays matches on Wednesdays, and does 'jolly well' in hockey, netball with one or two county players and good match successes. Currently under 16 county netball champions. Tennis and gymnastics impressive, taster rugby sessions available in the sixth form. Regular tours abroad, hockey in Holland popular. Popular too are water sports holidays in France. Outstanding D of E, the best we have ever (and we mean ever) come across – 38 participating in gold in sixth form. Mega mega WOW factor. For any school this would be impressive, for an inner city girls' school, this is incredible. Incredible performance too in Young Enterprise, where school regularly tops all others in the district. Can't do better than that.

Music was the weak link, new staff and getting stronger by the term. Serious investment. Bigger variety of instruments on offer, and take up encouraging, with 'lots more' extra-curricular. Three choirs (and trips abroad) two orchestras, jazz band etc. Drama 'fine', with dedicated drama room, and a couple of main school productions a year. School piloting a new Arts Council sponsored Arts Award scheme for young people which includes journalism, dance, digital film work, music and drama. Art rooms a trifle cramped but good work nonetheless, entertaining ceramics. Textiles allied to art, with huge bright classroom filled with sewing machines (brill), adaptable tailor's dummies leer out from the most unlikely corners all over the school.

The sixth form society runs their own esoteric activity programme from kayaking to wine-tasting. Varied programme of visiting speakers and debates. School hot on charity, raised £14,000 last year, and do an annual and popular Lourdes pilgrimage (the Catholic nobs' unofficial marriage market).

Background and Atmosphere: Former convent, moved out of nun-control in 1989, built round one side of the Botanic Gardens. Stunning sixth form centre in a separate building where girls, who wear their own clothes, have dedicated study areas and classrooms. Main school has a diverse collection of '60s, '70s and '90s add-ons to a primarily early Victorian structure. Architecture at its worst in almost every case. Dorms cosy, well-used, with teddies and boy inspired posters, single rooms for those post GCSE and some for those in their GCSE year, but a map would come in handy for visiting GSG editors and suchlike. Rising popularity has meant that you have to be quite quick off the mark to book boarding before the school has filled all available beds with an influx from abroad (not more than 11 per cent in total, though it may feel more). Dedicated flexi-boarding space available. Local boarders are enthusiastic and rate the place highly – 'hilarious in the evening...quite a lot of freedom and regular trips to Cambridge'. Junior common room full of dress-up clothes, painting kits as well as games and the inevitable telly and DVDs – the former two are a first for us. Excellent. Dining room (stools folding into tables set-up) part of brilliant halls (A+B) arrangement, noisy, busy, with good buffet, hot, veggie and cold and the food, according to our informant is 'super, all hand-made'. So there you are. Constant anorexia watch but no current concerns.

Pastoral Care and Discipline: Strong Catholic ethos. Very strong form tutor team backed up by 'six experienced heads of year'; girls get 'loads of individual attention from subject teachers' and their 'progress is noted on a personal basis'. Every girl knows that someone is watching out for her and is encouraged 'to share her problems with any member of staff with whom she is comfortable'. Happy self-confident girls. Recent report picked up a certain laxness in sixth form registration and sixth formers now have to register twice a day. Smoking, boozing, drugging – expect suspensions at the very least, head has permanently excluded two girls.

Pupils and Parents: Broad day pupil base, some very local, some commute by car, but over 100 come by train (station five minutes away). School vies with The Perse and The Leys locally. Mixture of first time buyers, dons' children, medics and lawyers plus a few (Catholic) toffs and the like from East Anglia. Good selection of weekend activities.

Entrance: Quite a number at 11, usually the entire output from St Catherine's next door, plus those who are coming at the state sector break, more at 12 and 13 plus a small influx post GCSE. Own exam throughout but not 'necessarily an easy ride'.

Exit: Fair number of locals leave after GCSE to Hills Road (qv) and a few others may go to co-ed boarding schools or merely elsewhere. That having been said, the sixth form centre appeared full of utterly happy and poised young ladies busily getting on with life. Most to unis, with impressive numbers to Oxbridge and equally impressive course selection.

Money Matters: School now financially OK. A Mary Ward school, with two Mary Ward bursaries (up to 95 per cent) at 11, one at 13 and at sixth form; these are reviewed annually; as well as academic scholarships, and music scholarships. Will 'try and help' with pupils whose families fall upon hard times, usually to the next public exam. Always worth a try.

Remarks: School on a roll. Not the sleepy neglected place it used to be.

St Mary's School (Shaftesbury)

Linked to Saint Mary's Junior School (Shaftesbury) in the Junior section

Donhead St. Mary, Shaftesbury, Dorset, SP7 9LP

Tel: 01747 852 416
Fax: 01747 851 557
E-mail: registrar@st-marys-shaftesbury.co.uk
Website: www.st-marys-shaftesbury.co.uk

• Pupils: 320 girls; 205 board, rest day • Ages: 9-18 • Size of sixth form: 75 • RC • Fees: Junior boarders £6,065, day £4,140. Senior boarders £6,390, day £4,350 • Independent

Head: Since 2003, Mrs Margaret McSwiggan MA (early fifties), who was educated at St Rita's in Brisbane and started her career teaching home economics in the state sector. She becomes the second lay head at St Mary's and was previously first lay head at Notre Dame School in Cobham, and before that at King Edward's Witley. Asked why she came to St Mary's, she simply says 'I missed boarding'. Got her MA in educational management from University of Surrey (whilst at Cobham). Married, with a daughter (at St Mary's). Loves skiing and walking and spends any spare time in Alps.

Believes strongly in encouraging each girl to achieve her potential, not only academically, but also through playing a part in the life of the school. Since her arrival she has 'got rid of those awful velvet curtains', revamped the staffroom, and spent an awful lot of money on the sporting side. (Parents and pupils agree that this was money well spent – though one father grumbled that he had thought they were getting an art department and not a wretched indoor swimming pool – fear not, the art school cometh next – complete with planning permission). Her husband is big in IT. Head is also keen on IT and has revamped the IT, wireless in the boarding houses and points all over the main school. Pupils are encouraged to bring their own laptops. ECDL for all. Keen that pupils should 'achieve their potential' through IT and not in spite of it. New heads of staff include director of sport plus heads of ICT services, RE, geography and history (the latter's predecessor is now housemistress) and Mrs McS is appointing 'high calibre academics as house mistresses', and is thrilled to have a chaplain under retirement age. 'All jolly fun' said the head, who is enjoying her time at the helm here. IB in tandem currently under investigation.

Academic Matters: Results are excellent for mixed intake. Almost half the girls do A level English; RS, French and art/history of art popular too; maths and the sciences have 'smaller numbers' – ie minimal take-up. Separate sciences for all at GCSE and rather whizzy science labs with just the whiff of Dr Strangelove about them, GCSE results impressive, and an astrophysician in the making (so why so few at A level). New head of geog in place and numbers of girls taking AS and A levels on the up. Impressive classics master. One or two esoteric languages: exams usually taken by native speakers, otherwise Spanish, German and French. Trained staff stretch the most able ('through our gifted and talented programme'). 'Girls being pushed more and harder these days'. Good calibre of staff and increasing numbers of them. 'We won't give in over little things' – homework must not be late, poor work is not accepted. All screened on entry, five part time and one full time co-ordinator in the SEN department; good links with preps (and pre-preps come to that), and can cope with mild dyslexia etc; no ADHD or Aspergers. SEN lessons usually take the place of a language. Good provision for physical disability – has accommodated muscular dystrophy and cerebral palsy.

Games, Options, The Arts: Strong on netball, tennis and hockey, Astroturf, new pool, oodles of dosh lately spent on the sports side, polo popular, but new art department not too far down the wings, planning permission and expect it in a couple of years. Old art rooms burgeoning, and with textiles (sewing machines natch – after all Mrs Mc S started her teaching career in home economics). Stunning music dept, with practice rooms and concert hall. Jazz, rock, orchestras, choirs, trips abroad. Envy making. Keen drama, LAMDA. Strong on extra-curricular activities – self-defence, modern dance, masses of clubs for just about everything and stunning cooking facilities. Duke of Edinburgh Award taken to Gold level. Retreats, pilgrimage to Lourdes (that well-known smart European marriage bureau) etc.

Background and Atmosphere: Sister school to St Mary's Ascot (the choicest of the three) and St Mary's Cambridge (the most street-wise), founded by IBVM (now CJ) in 1945. Charming converted late Victorian house with hotch potch of architectural miss matches: class rooms scattered all over the shop with a shabby wooden shack (sponge bags in the windows) home for the smallest – 'due for demolition shortly – in next stage of development – linked with art school project'. Fifty-five (ominously previous reports said sixty two) acres of rolling grounds, wonderful views and – for the boarders – rather a sense of 'being out in the sticks'. Shaftesbury three miles away does not swing; and trips to Bath and Salisbury at weekends will hardly set the world alight.

All must spend two compulsory weekends in school each term. Girls allowed cars in the sixth form, offsets the isolation a bit. Weekend activities considerably boosted in the last two years. Recent building includes new junior school, infirmary and library. Strong community happy-family feel. Boarders graduate from larger bedrooms (never dorms) to individual bedrooms (think nun's cells – head says 'individual bedrooms are actually quite spacious compared with other schools ' – yeah?) all with concealed 'sinks'. Refectory and fantastic new pastry chef 'so close to the hearts of so many'; long flowing kilts for all, curious when worn with short white (head sez 'beige' but we actually saw quite a number of white) socks, and full length for the sixth form.

Pastoral Care and Discipline: Shock horror: Mrs McSwiggan suspected drugs had been brought back to the school and called the police who arrived with every dog they could lay their hands on (search and rescue as well as drugs) and searched the school, having corralled the sixth form. Nothing found. Pupils duly impressed and neighbouring heads enchanted at the idea. 'but St Mary's...'. Fierce anti-smoking policy – fine and letter; suspended; expelled.

All newcomers (even the head) have a mentor for the first term, and welcome cards (decorating the altar during our visit) abound. Pastoral care improved and improving with increased numbers of staff per house; pupils meet with their tutor each morning. Spiritual life important, two thirds pupils Catholic, two thirds board; school chaplain takes mass in Spanish once a week. Quite a number of C of E girls, Anglican priest comes once a week and 'occasionally' celebrates eucharist in the chapel.

Pupils and Parents: Wide variety, including some from overseas (but not more than 10 per cent non-nationals) – 22 currently: Mexico, Spain, Germany, Hong Kong. Unspoilt, jolly nice, articulate, uninhibited girls – and relatively unsophisticated. One or two refugees from the hurly burly of London. Day girls go home at 6 pm. Parents largely enthusiastic about their choice, though recent personnel changes seem to have led to an increase in first time buyers. Parents wanting to use the school as a conventional prep school are scuppered as there is no provision or preparation for CE (head says 'This is not relevant because we are not a prep school, we just have two small junior classes'.

Entrance: At nine, 11, 13 and into sixth form. Tranches of scholarships in all disciplines, music, art and sport as well as academic with the option of bursarial top-up. Numbers currently steady, minimal testing for those who come into the junior school to go up to senior school.

Exit: Tiniest trickle to trad girls or co-ed senior schools, stronger trickle post GCSE to sixth form elsewhere. Of those who remain almost all to university, occasional Oxbridge candidate (head sez: 'special Oxbridge preparation classes. Each year we have at least two or three Oxbridge offers often 'post A level, so they do not appear in our statistics', loads to various art courses: foundation or history of art plus medics and chemical engineers, astrophysics.

Money Matters: Not a rich school but does its housekeeping well. Bursar an acknowledged genius.

Remarks: Jolly nice girls' Catholic boarding school, from the same stable as St Mary's Ascot, but with less social cachet, unpretentious and good at bringing out the best. Parents and pupils pleased with the increase of sport, but there are equally those who would prefer slightly sharper academic facilities. School has come a long way from the days when locals used to ride to school and leave their mounts in the stables during the day.

St Mary's School, Wantage

24-28 Newbury Street, Wantage, Oxfordshire, OX12 8BZ

Tel: 01235 773 800
Fax: 01235 760 467
E-mail: admissions@stmarys.oxon.sch.uk
Website: www.stmarys.oxon.sch.uk

• Pupils: 200 girls, 90+ per cent boarding • Ages: 11-19 • Size of sixth form: 75 • High Anglican • Fees: Boarding £7,330; day £4,900 • Independent

Head: Since 1994, Mrs Susan Sowden BSc PGCE (forties), educated at Clarendon House Grammar School in Kent and read geography at King's College, London. Previously deputy head at Headington School, where she had two daughters; also has one son. Divorced and recently remarried. Also has a theological qualification, AKC, and an advanced diploma in educational management. Super lady, extremely popular with staff, pupils and parents, energetic and jolly with it. Operates totally open-door policy. 'She knows us all!' say girls appreciatively. Teaches geography.

Academic Matters: Head is determined to maintain present first-come, first-served policy which does not require demanding academic selectiveness at entry. However, recent results and her successful regime mean that there is a growing pressure on places. Excellent teacher/pupil ratio 1:6. Art is superb and much the most popular A level subject. Many go on to higher education in this and related subjects. Otherwise a good spread through all subjects and with very small A level classes. 25 A level subjects on offer. Enlightened policy of RS (compulsory) GCSE taken in year 10, followed by a year 11 course in ethics and philosophy. GCSEs at least respectable across the board; 43 per cent A*/A grades in 2005. Excellent support for EFL, EAL and SEN. 'Value added' is especially good here, girls achieving results in GCSEs and A levels beyond expectations. School is first to have complete wireless laptop computer system, virtually doing away with need for designated IT rooms – a liberating innovation especially on a site spread over several buildings. Library provision improved under new librarian over last two years.

Games, Options, The Arts: Sport, especially 'lax', is good here, remarkably so for so small a school. Huge sports hall and good sixth form gym. A horsy school – large-scale regular riding, as befits its geography and its tradition. Girls appreciate school's policy of trying to help everyone find things they are good at – will find teachers of obscure instruments if there is a demand etc. Super new music block linked to newer drama block creating many opportunities as well as increasing links with locality as residents invited for events. Art is extraordinary in the variety available – ceramics (wonderful), painting, drawing, textiles (professional), printing, pottery (done by everyone in first three years), metalwork, photography, sculpture, stone-carving, casting etc etc – and in the execution. Justifiably, the school is full of the stuff. A splendid cookery room used for years 7-10, a 'survival cookery' course, as well as a Leith Cert of Food and Wine course and other sixth form options. Resident artist, musician, dramatist and sports person an enlightened extra.

Background and Atmosphere: Gradually and naturally shedding its previous image as being for thick, rich horsy types, but not its well-earned reputation for exuberance and self-reliance. It is an immensely civilised place, set in a jumble of attractive Victorian red-brick and later buildings on a corner of the pleasant Oxfordshire town of Wantage – the town centre being only minutes walk away. Girls stress school's friendliness and there is an almost palpable gentleness in the air. A High Anglican Foundation and still centred on the splendid Anglo-Catholic chapel in the Gothic heart of the main building, the school's ethos is now a relaxed Christian one where all faiths are welcome and religion is not forced on anyone though 'chapel' is compulsory. Community service is strong, there are close ties with local old people's homes and school supports children in Africa via pen-letters as well as cash. Long-term refurbishment plans in progress, having begun with labs and needed in other areas, though 90 per cent board and boarding regarded as superb. Girls clearly happy with it and food is also excellent. Totally new school buildings on an expanded single site on the other side of the town centre due to open in late 2007.

Pastoral Care and Discipline: 'We give them responsibility for themselves and teach them how to use it', says head. 'We aren't wishy-washy.' There is a policy of 'restorative justice' actively practised in matters great and small. Few disciplinary problems and girls given much freedom to visit town, have weekends away etc. Sixth form has pool table, Sky TV and bar in JCR . 'Day boarders', ie day girls who spend some nights at school, fully integrated and welcomed. No official weekly boarding. Many staff live on site and school has good relaxed atmosphere. Good sixth form block.

Pupils and Parents: From range of local, London and national preps. Up to 15 per cent from up to 20 other nationalities make for a stimulating mix. Natural constituency 'Countryside Alliance' but increasingly business families send daughters here – a broader spectrum in all respects. Interesting bunch of OGs include ten per cent of the baronesses in the House of Lords (there by merit not inheritance, a truly extraordinary record), Dame Ruth Railton, Mrs Ian Duncan Smith, polar explorer Victoria Riches, Lady Helen Windsor and the first Who Wants to be a Millionairess, Judith Keppel. Old Girls (SMOGS) and current parents very supportive of school.

Entrance: Via school's own assessment procedure and Common Entrance at 11 plus interviews and current head's report. Few places at 12 and several more at 13. Overseas candidates assessed via current school's report and piece of written English. School does not admit to years 10 or 12 without fluent English.

Exit: To a good range of university and college courses. Excellent art results naturally produce good crop of entries to art schools.

Money Matters: Scholarships at 11 and 13. Various sixth form scholarships - academic, musical and one for an all-round contribution. All well-endowed and worth investigating. Bursaries available particularly for daughters of clergy, St Mary's OGs and from Services families.

Remarks: School site and buildings in process of being totally replaced by a new build but ethos will remain the same – a rare mix of work, fun and caring for each other and the wider community. A lovely school, especially so if the arts are your thing and you want a happy atmosphere in a small school nestled in the Oxfordshire countryside.

THE ST MARYLEBONE C OF E SCHOOL

64 Marylebone High Street, London, W1U 5BA

Tel: 02079 354 704
Fax: 02079 354 005
E-mail: stmaryleboneschool@yahoo.co.uk
Website: www.stmaryleboneschool.com

• Pupils: 821 • Ages: 11-18 • Size of sixth form: 179, including around 50 boys • C of E • State

Head: Since 1993, Mrs Elizabeth Phillips (fifties), previously at Feltham School in Hounslow. Spent 16 years abroad in places ranging from Hong Kong to Zambia; ran a language school in Rome. Neat, smart, married, with one daughter and two sons who were all educated privately but she is passionately committed to the state sector, 'I want to fight for those who have no-one else to fight for them'. A historian, and 'a brilliant, inspiring teacher,' said a parent. 'She is very focused and has turned the school around,' said another.

Academic Matters: Hailed in 2000 as the most improved school in England – over the previous four years the proportion of girls achieving five good grades at GCSE shot up from 39 per cent to 89 per cent – it's now 94 per cent. Most subjects achieving 90 per cent+ A*-C grades. A level options have expanded dramatically and now include media studies, ICT, politics, RE, psychology and economics. Key Stage 3 SATs results are well above average. It is a genuinely comprehensive school, taking 25 per cent from the top ability band, 50 per cent from the middle and 25 per cent from the bottom band. 'The results are staggering considering the intake,' says the head. She puts the results down to setting pupils in all academic subjects from year 7, and to excellent teaching – 'inadequate teaching is not accepted'. 'In a good percentage of lessons learning was outstanding,' said the last Ofsted report, which talked of 'an environment for teaching and learning based on mutual respect and high expectations of all'.

The school invests highly in teachers to get a staff:student ratio of around 1:17. Although tutor groups are 33, each has two form tutors. The four tutor groups in each year divide into five ability groups and the lower sets are particularly small. 'We are here to see that all the children achieve. It is really important not to let some pupils become an underclass.' 'The teachers are very good at spotting need

and doing something about it,' said a parent, 'and they get astounding results from girls who don't speak English at home.' There is an effective special needs department and a language and learning department to help those with difficulties. There is a gifted and talented programme that builds extra opportunity for able pupils with mentoring from a GT co-ordinator. In years 9 and 10 there are special programmes in history, English, maths and science for gifted and talented children, plus after-school enrichment classes. All take ICT and RS GCSEs in year 10. All the staff are specialists (it is the only state school in Westminster with a full complement of qualified mathematicians and scientists). Many girls do vocational subjects, 'it is a real preparation for the world of work and the universities are very happy to have students from the AVCE courses'.

The school runs a homework club, 'many of our girls have nowhere quiet to work. But the most deprived have to get home to look after the younger kids.' The sixth form is a haven for some boys (with their own football team, dance group and rock band) 'who had a terrible time at macho boys' schools. And accepting these boys in a girls' school has a beneficial effect on their results.'

Games, Options, The Arts: St Marylebone is a specialist Performing Arts College, 'though we're not a Fame school – the arts are for enrichment' – which awards 12 places a year to talented music, dance and drama students. All year 7 pupils get free music lessons, the head would like to expand this but lacks money and space, and all key stage three students have three hours a week of music, dance, drama and expressive art as well. There are two orchestras – one of which recently played concerts in Venice and Barcelona – plus salsa bands, string quartets, percussion and African drumming bands. There are major concerts three times a year, plus plays and pageants. 'I like that fact that the events involve everyone but the standards are very high,' said a parent. The school has extensive music technology equipment.

Spectacular artwork is displayed all around the school including a wide range of textiles, 'this is where you see the effects of the multi-ethnic nature of the school, and we display a whole class's work, not just the best.' The school has its own printing press that can print copies of artwork. Sport suffers from lack of space but this is being rectified (see atmosphere section). 'The girls are very competitive,' says the head. A parent comments, 'there's always something going on, like weights or dancing or keep-fit. The sports teachers are brilliant'. The school uses the sports pitches in Regents Park, All Souls gym for dance and the Seymour Baths for swimming and hopes to get access to the old

Pineapple Dance Studios.

The central London location enables many cultural outings and trips in the UK and abroad include outward bound, skiing and exchanges with French and German schools. Much of this, though not skiing, is subsidised for the needy by charitable funds. 'I want to give my pupils all the music, the theatre, the trips abroad that private school children take for granted,' says the head. A group of 22 sixth formers, 'many of them inner-city pupils from high-rise estates', are off to Zambia on a World Challenge trip in 2007, building on successful trips to Vietnam and India in the past.

Background and Atmosphere: Wonderfully situated in an oasis of quiet off a paved courtyard at the top of Marylebone High Street with the Conran shop almost opposite and Regents Park across the road, albeit the six-lane Marylebone Road. Desperately tight for space. 'I've expanded into every space I can possibly think of,' says the head. The video editing room was once a coal-hole and a music practice room was once the cleaners' cupboard.

The school has recently shoe-horned three classrooms into one high-ceilinged Victorian room and many of the upper classrooms have marvellously shaped windows and ceilings. The rooms are mostly light and airy, in a colour scheme of green and white to match the school uniform. The staff room is painted tasteful blues and purples, redecorated through business sponsorship – 'I'd never have spent the money on it myself', says the head. 'We use everything we can for the children.' Newly refurbished science labs, plus new professional recording studio and two dance and drama studios. Assemblies are held in the wonderful Regency church next door. A major building programme has been approved by the DfES to create a large subterranean sports hall and a purpose-built performing arts centre with dance and drama studios, music teaching rooms, music practice rooms and art studios. This will be completed by October 2006.

Pastoral Care and Discipline: There is a peer mentoring system to help children who are having trouble settling in, making friends or coping with homework. 'The children will say there's no bullying,' says the head. 'Year 10 counsellors are there if they need someone to talk to. All the drama we do gives them confidence to speak out. They learn the ability to stand up and talk in front of the school.'

Drugs have not been a problem, 'we're really harsh about that and we do lots of preventative work. We're vigilant and strict. I expect there is smoking, especially amongst the sixth-formers, but they don't do it in the toilets or on the school premises.' In general, the school has a no-exclusion policy, 'we never write a child off.' The school has a quiet and orderly feel, with silent concentration in most of the lessons. 'Pupils' behaviour both in lessons and around the school is exemplary,' said Ofsted. 'We're nit-pickingly strict – people need to know the rules. The staff can teach here, because they're not spending their time keeping order,' says the head, who feels, 'you can't take the spiritual dimension out of all this. It's not fashionable to talk about faith but I think the nation is yearning for spiritual belief.' 'There is a strong caring and achieving philosophy,' said a parent. Another said, 'it's not over-pressurised – they just help them as much as they can.'

Pupils and Parents: Mixed socially and culturally, including many races and religions. 'We have working class children, immigrants, refugees – someone needs to bother about them,' says the head. Very popular with middle class parents, some of whom undergo miraculous religious conversions a year or two before applying. Very active PTA does successful fundraising for the new building project.

Entrance: Hugely oversubscribed, with 1,027 applicants for 120 places in 2005. Apart from 12 performing arts places, religious faith is a prerequisite. Within the academic banding, about 55 per cent of places are reserved for C of E, while the others go to girls of any other faith – including Muslims, Jews, Buddhists and Zoroastrians. Girls from two linked Westminster primary schools get preference along with all Westminster Church primaries; coming from any other church primary school helps, with distance as a tie-break.

Exit: The school has a wide catchment area and because local boroughs don't pay for transport after 16, some girls leave then to go to local schools. Some high-flyers get scholarships to private schools, 'though value-added data shows that they would do better here – the boys who come in do particularly well,' says the head. All go on to higher education (about one a year to Oxbridge – parents tend to be wary of it from a social point of view) or to blue-chip training companies, apart from a few Muslim girls destined for early marriage.

Money Matters: As well as being a specialist performing arts college, St Marylebone is a beacon school and receives Excellence in Cities money for supporting gifted and talented students. All this brings in extra cash. However, one parent commented how sad it was that bidding for extra money from various sources takes up a lot of the head's time and she agrees, 'fund-raising is my nightmare – it's what I do. It's cost me five years of my life.' The result, however, is a school that is well-staffed and well-equipped, if not to lavish private school standards.

Remarks: Hugely successful and popular small girls' comprehensive in wonderful West End setting. Caring and dedicated staff, determined that girls of all abilities should succeed. A parent whose two older children went through the private sector commented, 'it's simply a brilliant school'.

ST MICHAEL'S CATHOLIC GRAMMAR SCHOOL

Nether Street, North Finchley, London, N12 7NJ

Tel: 020 8446 2256

Fax: 0208 343 9598

E-mail: office.stmichaels.barnet@lgfl.net

Website: www.st-michaels.barnet.sch.uk

• Pupils: 742 girls, all day • Ages: 11 - 18 • Size of sixth form: 265 • Catholic • State

Head: Since 1995, Miss Ursula Morrissey BA PGCE (fifties), educated at Queen Mary College and Institute of Education, London University. She has been at St Michael's for her entire career, joining in 1971 to teach history and rising through the ranks to become deputy and then head. Charming, approachable, excellent leader. 'She's immensely committed and that shows in the school's ethos,' said a parent. 'She's very human, very caring,' said another. 'She really listens to you.'

Academic Matters: St Michael's is less ferociously selective than other north London grammar schools because all applicants must be practising Catholics. However, its results put it not just in the top 5 per cent of schools but in the top 5 per cent of grammar schools. In 2005, 77 per cent of GCSE grades were A* or A. Most girls do 11 GCSEs, including RS, DT and one or two foreign languages; everyone learns French in year 7 and has a taster of Spanish, Italian and German. Latin lessons start in year 8. This can result in a crammed timetable – 'we work at a bit of a gallop. The girls are bright and keen and that compensates for having less time for each subject.' Maths is setted from year 8; everything else is mixed ability. There is no SEN department but heads of key stages are responsible for the few girls with sight or hearing problems or dyslexia.

The sixth form collaborates with Finchley Catholic High School, a non-selective boys' school ('and there are plenty of grammar schools that would be sniffy about linking up with a comprehensive,' commented a parent). It is not a joint sixth form but students from each can study one or two subjects at the other school, which helps to avoid timetable clashes. St Michael's offers 31 A level subjects, including theology, economics, government and politics, and PE. Excluding general studies, 71 per cent of results were A or B in 2005. Classics is a popular A level choice, as are psychology, maths and biology. Relatively few take foreign languages. OFSTED describes the sixth form as 'first class.' Many sixth formers go to Europe for two to four weeks' work experience. It is compulsory for linguists but non-linguists can work in Sweden.

Games, Options, The Arts: On-site are netball/tennis courts, a grassy area and an ageing gym (a sports hall is on the head's wish-list); girls swim the Finchley lido in year 8 and visit the Sobell sports centre in year 9 for climbing, trampolining and basketball. Although facilities are lacking, 'we are usually vying to be borough champions in netball and athletics'. Football and hockey are popular extra-curricular activities and dance GCSE is a new option. There are Outward Bound and skiing trips, plus field trips and language exchanges. Year 12 is a 'year of service', with girls organising clubs and events and running committees. Sixth formers also help with reading in local primary schools. A very enthusiastic sixth form arts and cultural committee organises dance and music performances.

Background and Atmosphere: Founded in 1908 by the Congregation of the Sisters of the Poor Child Jesus as a prep school for boys and girls, it became a girls' grammar in 1958. Sandstone lower school building, once inhabited by the nuns, including a chapel with bright stained glass windows, also used for assemblies and dance classes. Nineteenth century sixth form centre, plus new sixth form study centre; the rest is mostly 1950s buildings, mostly refurbished. State-of-the-art technology block produces very strong DT GCSE results. The top floor science labs have views to Mill Hill; modern maths rooms; plenty of computers. Traditional, ordered atmosphere; very welcoming. 'The head has an absolute care and love for the school and this permeates the atmosphere of the whole place,' said a parent.

Pastoral Care and Discipline: Year 7s are each allocated a year 13 'Guardian Angel' to help them settle in. A parent commented, 'everyone knows each other and the sixth formers look out for the younger ones inside and outside school'. The school's strong spiritual underpinning shows in its pastoral care. 'We have parameters but we work first and foremost on forgiveness.' 'When my daughter had emotional problems, they were so supportive,' said a parent. 'And they dealt very fairly with it when she had a clash of personalities with a teacher.'

No drugs problems to speak of. 'Because we're a traditional school we probably over-react on the small things. This sends out a message that certain things are unthinkable – the girls probably think we'd have apoplexy if they took drugs.'

Pupils and Parents: A big mix of Catholic families from a large area of north London. Pupils tend to be keen and motivated and parents relieved they have found such a high quality education in such a sane school. The sixth form offers a broader experience of life by taking in non-Catholics and linking up with Finchley Boys' High. OGs: Jill Paton Walsh, Jessica Martin (actress), Vanessa Gearson – prospective parliamentary candidate for Cheltenham.

Entrance: Only girls from practising Catholic families (letter needed from priest) may take the entrance exam, which consists of English, maths, verbal and non-verbal reasoning. The four sections are given equal weighting and girls ranked in order of merit. The school no longer interviews. Generally around 300 girls after 96 places.

Students after sixth form places – about 50 join year 12 – do not have to be practising Catholics but do have to attend services and play a part in the spiritual life of the school. They also need at least a grade B in the subjects most closely related to those they want to study to A level.

Exit: A few leave after GCSEs, to pursue vocational courses or join co-educational establishments. The school has a target of 10 per cent of leavers applying to Oxbridge and about half of those – general six or seven – are generally given offers. Other students go on to a wide range of mostly old-established universities, to read anything from Italian and Management Studies to Forensic Science.

Money Matters: The Government pays only 90 per cent of refurbishment costs, so the school is constantly fund-raising. Parents' committee runs international evenings, summer barbeques etc.

Remarks: Small girls' grammar school which gets impressive results as well as being universally popular with pupils and parents. 'My daughter has blossomed and grown in confidence there,' said a parent. 'It's a very human, very caring place.

ST OLAVE'S AND ST SAVIOUR'S GRAMMAR SCHOOL

Goddington Lane, Orpington, Kent, BR6 9SH

Tel: 01689 820 101
Fax: 01689 897 943
E-mail: office@saintolaves.net
Website: www.saintolaves.net

• Pupils: 836 boys, plus 76 girls in the sixth form, all day • Ages: 11-18 • Size of sixth form: 324 • C of E • State • Open days: First Saturday in October

Headmaster: Since 1994, Mr Anthony Jarvis BEd MA FRSA (fifties), educated City of Oxford Grammar, previously head at Sir Thomas Rich's, Gloucs, deputy head at St George's, Rome. Very involved in education generally, member HMC, Fellow Woodard Trust, Governor Hurstpierpoint College, Member of Army Scholarship Board. Married with two grown-up children. Mr Jarvis teaches English to year 7 and general studies to the lower sixth form, ensuring that he knows all pupils personally as well as academically. Keenly supports school sports. Authoritative without being intimidating, a busy man.

Academic Matters: One of London's leading grammar schools, hugely sought after – 'a traditional education for the academically able'. All pupils are assessed on entry and their progress tracked to ensure they reach their potential. Streaming for Latin, French and Maths from year 9. Outstanding facilities and spacious classrooms in all departments. Construction will be completed by September 2006 of new music, performing arts and sixth form blocks. A new computing suite came into use in September 2005 following designation as a mathematics and specialist school.

Good blend of high quality staff, newer and longer-serving, and a well developed pastoral structure – definitely a place where teaching posts are probably as sought after as pupil places. Often gets better GCSE and A level results than its fee-paying neighbours. Some choices that are not often available in other state schools, eg Greek, Latin, Japanese, Mandarin, Italian, Dutch, Modern Greek and Gujerati. School also does particularly well in academic competitions for maths, sciences and languages. Super library and IT suite both full of activity. Lots of extra-curricular activities and clubs from debating to community work – 'boys are constantly encouraged to try out new things'. A handful of SEN pupils who are well supported by the

SENCO, with individual assistants for statemented pupils. No EFL support.

Games, Options, The Arts: Again outstanding choices, tuition and facilities, many competitions and awards won. On site, well-used playing fields. Rugby team provides players for Kent. The only state school to play Eton Fives at national level, a few bemoan the lack of football. Indoor swimming pool, new sports pavilion. Very strong music, informal and formal concerts are part of school life, hall has orchestra pit, tuition on any instrument is available. Several successful choirs and orchestras, chamber, barbershop, jazz, brass, symphonic, wind – you name it, they do it. Not uncommon for pupils to get choral and organ scholarships to Oxbridge. The school provides choristers for the Queen's Chapel of Savoy, four choristerships each year are offered to 10 and 11 year olds. Interesting displays of art work, again of a particularly high standard. School occasionally has an 'artist in residence', the most recent being a worker in stained glass. Some parents would like to see DT developed more but you can't have everything. In 2004, five students won Arkwright Design Scholarships.

Background and Atmosphere: 16th century foundation. St Olave's and St Saviour's amalgamated in 1899 and moved to a site in Southwark. The school moved to Orpington in 1968 for more space and its own playing fields. A not unattractive set of modern buildings based on quadrangles surrounded by pleasant gardens and playing fields. The school's original foundation stone plaque was found by workmen while widening the road at London Bridge in the 1890s, now in situ in Kent. Determined high focus atmosphere, pupils calm and fully involved, friendly whilst respectful. Good staff/pupil relationships.

Pastoral Care and Discipline: Thought by parents to be excellent; a 'do as you would be done by approach'. The deputy head 'pastoral' works with year heads and form tutors who stay with the pupils through each key stage. Older students arrange outings and house games competitions for younger ones to encourage social skills and responsibility. All aspects of pupil well-being are attended to, even the food is thought to be better than in other schools in the area!

Pupils and Parents: From all walks of life socially and culturally. Has always had an enormous catchment area but is particularly keen to receive applications from its original boroughs of Southwark and Lambeth.

Entrance: At 11 by competitive exams in November. 700-800 boys apply for 112 places, which are awarded to the highest achieving. For sixth form, competitive exams plus at least 6 Bs at GCSE. Well over 200 boys and girls apply for 40 external places.

Exit: Handful leaves at 16, 97 per cent stay at the school for sixth form, all go on to higher education. Good few to Oxbridge every year, other popular choices include Bristol, Durham, Edinburgh and Warwick in addition to London colleges. Good numbers take engineering, law and medicine.

Money Matters: Basic state funding together with its own fairly well-endowed foundation, which provides most of the funds for new buildings and additional teaching staff. School employs a professional development director while active PTA also raises funds for different projects. Sixth form runs a charity week and raises an impressive amount for various charities. OBs: John Harvard, Squadron Leader Andy Green, Baron Hill of Luton, Roy Marsden, Sir John Smith.

Remarks: Going from strength to strength, an excellent and well deserved reputation as an inspiring place.

St Paul's Girls' School

Brook Green, London, W6 7BS

Tel: 020 7603 2288
Fax: 020 7602 9932
E-mail: admissions@spgs.org
Website: www.spgs.org

• Pupils: 684 girls, all day • Ages: 11-18 • Size of sixth form: (known as seventh and eighth forms): 200 • Anglican foundation • Fees: £3,948 • Independent • Open days: Autumn

High Mistress: Since 1998, Miss Elizabeth Diggory (fifties), read history at London. Was head of Manchester High for four years and, prior to that, head of St Alban's High for 11 years. Articulate, purposeful and forthright. Her aim for the school is, 'that it should continue to reflect excellence in all ways.' She has no intention of letting the school rest on its laurels – 'addressing change is part of a dynamic institution.'

Retiring in July 2006. Successor will be Ms Clarissa Farr BA MA PGCE (forties) head of Queenswood since 1996. Read English at Exeter, followed by a Masters in modern literature and previously taught in a sixth form college, a comprehensive school, a grammar school and abroad before coming to Queenswood as deputy head (academic) in 1992. Married to the sports news correspondent of The Times; two small children. Teaches English and theatre studies. Fun and outgoing, Ms Farr's hobby is running marathons – much approved of by her pupils. Aims at

Queenswood to produce 'whole girls', whose range is broader than pure academe. Feels like a good choice – should prove an interesting head.

Academic Matters: A recent Independent Schools' Council (ISC) report commented that St Paul's' standards are well above even the expectations for such highly able pupils. With over 96 per cent of GCSEs graded A or A*, and 88 per cent of A levels grade A, the school has few – if any – academic equals. The atmosphere is fiercely intellectual. 'There is such a strong ethos to succeed that the teachers don't need to put pressure on the girls,' said a parent, 'the girls put it on themselves.' 'The standard of teaching is amazing,' said another parent. 'The teachers exude intelligence and enthusiasm.' Considerable pace and variety of work. Particular praise for the history teaching and for the high status of foreign languages – everyone takes one language GCSE a year early and could then, in theory, take two more. Setting only for maths. Not a school for the academically challenged, 'but we can give a lot of individual attention to those who are struggling,' says the high mistress. 'We hope to sort them out before it becomes a huge problem.'

There is help for the few with dyslexia or English as a second language. Students between the seventh and eighth forms may complete the Senior Scholarship, a piece of independent research in any field which might range from a musical composition through a stem cell investigation to an essay on the history of asylum. 'It's one of the two things I'd defend with my back to the wall,' says the high mistress. (The other is the Colet Play, which is chosen and organised entirely by the seventh form.) The Friday lecture sees eminent speakers from a huge variety of backgrounds talk to seventh- and eighth-formers.

Games, Options, The Arts: Very strong in more or less every field. 'We try to give them an interest that will last a lifetime.' Gustav Holst was once director of music here and wrote many pieces for SPGS. The school offers its own, more challenging, GCSE music course, 'because GCSE music is not a sufficient preparation for music A level.' Over 60 per cent of pupils take music lessons, many learning several instruments. There are two orchestras plus choirs, madrigal groups and chamber ensembles, as well as a strong commitment to jazz. Art GCSE is also a school-directed course – in the first year pupils work through a series of introductory modules in different media including oil painting, ceramics, photography and 3-D design, plus critical and historical studies. They then go on to complete coursework projects in their chosen media. 'We can introduce more breadth and structure the course to suit the stu-

dents,' says the head of art and design.

The purpose-built Celia Johnson Theatre hosts two or three drama productions a term and a studio theatre opened in 2002. The five or six productions each term have ranged from a junior form production of Bugsy Malone to the aforementioned Colet Play, which enables seventh formers to plan everything from the budget to the stage setting and lighting.

Excellent sports facilities, including a playing field, swimming pool, tennis courts and the new sports centre, with a multigym, dance studio and sports hall. Championship-winning lacrosse teams; pupils regularly gain places in county and area squads. Sports lessons do, however, tail off higher up the school. A great variety of extra-curricular activities, with over 60 clubs ranging from photography to debating to volleyball. Travel opportunities include a yearly ski trip to the USA, exchange visits to schools around the world from Sydney to Prague and Washington, cultural trips to Europe including a musicians' tour (to Venice in 2002, Barcelona 2005), lacrosse matches in Baltimore and World Challenge Expeditions – to Madagascar in 2001, Ecuador in 2003 and Borneo in 2005.

Background and Atmosphere: In the 16th century, John Colet founded a school 'for the children of all nations and countries'. The Mercers' Company, guardians of the Colet estate, used some of the endowment to set up SPGS in leafy Brook Green in 1904. The mellow red-brick building, with marble-floored corridors and a panelled and galleried great hall, has enviable facilities and a spacious and peaceful feel. 'The place has a calm confidence, and the girls pick

up on that,' said a parent. No uniform – jeans and sweat-shirts are almost universal.

Pastoral Care and Discipline: Each new girl is allocated a 'big sister' (in the seventh form) and a 'middle sister' (two years older than herself) to help ease her way into the school. No prefect system – the head girl and her team of five help out at school events rather than ruling the roost. Drugs 'have not been a problem in my time,' says the high mistress. 'We make the girls very aware of what we feel about drugs from the point of view of their health.' She would expel for out-and-out defiance – 'there are situations where a school and pupil have reached the end of what they can do for one another. But I would hope to smooth her passage elsewhere.' A parent commented that the relationship between staff and pupils is more akin to that of a university than of a school. 'There is a real camaraderie.'

Pupils and Parents: A cosmopolitan mix of professionals and business people. 'Some of the parents can be pretty daunting,' said a mother. 'So can the girls,' said another, who commented, 'the ones who have a great time there are socially very relaxed and confident, as well as very high achieving.' The impressive list of Old Girls includes Rosalind Franklin, Celia Johnson, Harriet Harman and Shirley Conran.

Entrance: The schools sets its own maths and English entrance tests, plus an extra comprehension paper to throw in a surprise, 'they're tailor-made for us and demand a little bit more than normal tests. The really bright child will probably find something to keep her thinking.' Successful candidates are likely to be eager to voice their questions and ideas and 'to be excited by work, by school and by learning.' A number come from Bute House, the rest from preps all over west London, with between 10 and 20 per cent from state primaries. Around 20 places a year available for A level students, with a two-day entrance procedure – 'we like to have girls coming in from outside with new experiences'.

Exit: Virtually all to university. Between 30 and 40 per cent to Oxbridge and up to 10 to major universities in the States.

Money Matters: Increasing number of means-tested awards at 11 and 16. Junior and senior academic and music scholarships (2 music at 11+ worth half the school tuition fees), and senior art scholarships (mostly honorary).

Remarks: Confident in its role as the top academic girls' day school, much praised for its positive ethos. 'The music, the sport – everything is fantastic,' said a parent, 'as long as you have the self-confidence to cope with it.' 'My daughter has had the most amazing opportunities there,' said another.

ST PAUL'S SCHOOL

Linked to Colet Court in the Junior section

Lonsdale Road, Barnes, London, SW13 9JT

Tel: 020 8748 9162

Fax: 020 8746 5353

E-mail: hmsec@stpaulsschool.org.uk

Website: www.stpaulsschool.org.uk

- Pupils: 855 boys, majority day; one boarding house (around 40)
- Ages: 13-18 • Size of sixth form: 340 • C of E • Fees: Senior school: £4,680 + £2,855 boarding; Colet Court: £3,640
- Independent

High Master: Since 2004 Dr Martin Stephen BA PhD (early fifties), formerly High Master at Manchester Grammar School. Educated at Uppingham and Leeds University, followed by PhD at Sheffield. Read English and history for first degree. Taught at Uppingham, housemaster at Haileybury, deputy head at Sedbergh. Head of The Perse, Cambridge from 1987 -1994, MGS from 1994 – 2004. Married (wife Jenny is headmistress of South Hampstead High School, coming from The Grange, Northwich) with three sons.

Likes drawing and painting as well as writing – has published 15 books on English literature and naval history. Combines love of intellectual matters with impressive leadership skills. Astute, massively energetic, volubly passionate about the school. Great sense of humour and team player. Clear leadership, management team given a lot of responsibility; sees himself as first among equals.

Follows the estimable, Mr Stephen Baldock who gave most of his life to the school and who can be credited with its humanisation during his twelve year tenure.

Academic Matters: As ever, superb in all subjects, with an especial sparkle about the maths results. Most recent Inspection praised all areas with only minor qualifications about a lack of timetabled 'spiritual' guidance (which head fools is inherent in many extra-curricular aspects of school's rich life, visiting speakers etc) and about size of some classes in labs. Overall, teaching, as one would expect, has flying colours with few exceptions. Head positive towards A/S exams, backed up by pupils. Enlightened general studies options for year 12. Five resident language assistant native speakers, French, German, Spanish, Italian; everyone sits French GCSE at end of year 10. Enthusiastic classics, English and history taught to highest levels. School fabulously equipped in all areas scientific, technological, electronic. New streamlined floor dedicated to geography, science and electronics, including data-logging lab and IT control lab. SEN supported here but probably not the place for more than mild cases. Library tastefully revamped in soothing wood invites quiet study. Staff tend to stay long term. School invites those interested to inspect its website – www.stpaulsschool.org.uk – where all results are displayed.

Games, Options, The Arts: Again, superb. School has impeccably-kept playing fields, large swimming pool, offers 30 sports including rackets, taught by pro., housed in new court – funded by single benefaction – which hosted World Championship. Notable successes in fives, basketball. Music in world class, new Wathen Hall (linked by bridge to main building to remain integral to school). Practice rooms designed for specific instruments and an exhilarating concert hall seating 316, in demand by professional groups for rehearsal, recording and performance. Musical pupils (half learn at least one instrument) have a rare privilege in this new resource. Drama well-provided for in versatile theatre and smaller equally flexible studio space – both well-used and producing impressive work. Pupils attest to the range of extra-curricular activities available and school makes the most of its central London location and accessibility of celebrated locals.

Background and Atmosphere: Too much has been made of the 'hideous' 1968 buildings. School now on its fifth site since foundation by much-commemorated Dean John Colet in 1509. School foundation run by the trustees of the Worshipful Company of Mercers. Some Old Paulines still lament move from Waterhouse building in West Kensington but few can regret acquisition of this superb, 45-acre site between Thames and chic Barnes residential streets – extraordinarily peaceful for such a location – well-kept and humanised with rose beds and trees in all available spaces. Increasingly, relics from former buildings coming out of store and integrated on site. Newer buildings and improvements sensitively use existing motifs. Boys' sculptures and canvases also break up starker areas and the place is mellowing nicely. Head balances idealism with practicality and realism – hence CCTV in new locker room to guard against petty pilfering (not a major problem), also huge new common room for final year pupils as well as splendid, commemorative millennium sundial. Development office, staff of four, works on links with outside. 30-40 boys board with some spare capacity for temporary pressing need. Dormitories – four to a room for younger boys – graduating to individual study bedrooms – small, functional but not spartan. Common room with snooker and table tennis, TV room. Boarding, though used by minority, seen as central to school tradition.

Pastoral Care and Discipline: Tutorial system works well and has much improved overall pastoral and academic supervision. Tutors visit pupils' homes and 'look out for' tutees, as one boy put it. Boys are consulted in curricular decision-making which affects them and this, as well as vastly increased parental involvement in various aspects of school life, contributes to more integrated care of pupils. Tough but realistic drugs and smoking policy relies on co-operation with parents and balances what is best for the individual with the needs of the school community. Dress code exists in theory but is imposed with difficulty in practice, however boys are relatively kempt compared with many. School feels orderly but not constrained.

Pupils and Parents: Boys come from all over London. Many faiths represented. School community is cosmopolitan, strong US, Asian and European contingent. Parents mostly professional middle classes, ambitious, with solid work ethic. This is the school parents aspire to for their bright, motivated sons. Boys are independent-minded, articulate, the most mature aware of their privileged position. School fosters a competitiveness to which boys contribute – fine if you can take it and make it work for you. 'To succeed here you need to be smart, competitive and be able to do things under your own steam', says one – a challenge or a concession? Judging from a sample of final year Paulines, most boys appreciate the challenge and rise to it. Celebrated Old Paulines, an embarrassment of riches, include Milton, Halley, Marlborough, Chesterton, E H Shephard, Compton Mackenzie, Edward Thomas, Field Marshal Montgomery, Paul Nash, Isaiah Berlin, Sir Alexander Graham, Eric Newby, Lords Janner, Baker, McColl and Renwick, Sir David Rowland, Sir Jonathan Miller, Oliver Sacks and the playwrighting Schaffer twins, Peter and Anthony.

Entrance: 45 per cent come from Colet Court, the rest from assorted prep schools. Registration for the senior school, accompanied by non-returnable fee, should be at least five years in advance of entry (at 13+). All 13+ candidates from external prep schools are interviewed two years before entry once a reference from head of prep school has been received. CE taken at prep school, 65 per cent in every subject required. Scholarship exam taken at St Paul's. A few boys join school at sixth form level – minimum 8 good GCSEs expected with As in proposed A level subjects.

Exit: Vast majority to good universities, reading heavyweight subjects. A quarter to Oxbridge and, a dramatic new phenomenon, about ten a year to US Universities, including Harvard and Princeton. Old Paulines feature prominently in most professions needing brains and enterprise.

Money Matters: Means-tested bursaries where needed. Scholarships awarded by exam taken in May by candidates under 14. Compulsory papers in all CE subjects + optional Greek. About 30 Foundation scholarships awarded each year. Up to 12 of these (John Colet awards) give 25 per cent fee reduction and the remainder are worth £60 per annum. Means-testing can increase this to up to full tuition fee. Overall number of scholars in the school fixed by John Colet to match the number of fishes caught in the Miraculous Draught. Music scholarships competed for by candidates with at least Grade VI on main instrument. Further scholarships - academic, music and art - available in later years. Some remission for families who send three or more children to the school.

Remarks: Remains one of the two top London boys' schools and the one to remain single sex throughout.

St Peter's School

Linked to Saint Olave's School (pronounced Olive's) in the Junior section

Clifton, York, North Yorkshire, YO30 6AB

Tel: 01904 527 300
Fax: 01904 527 302
E-mail: enquiries@st-peters.york.sch.uk
Website: www.st-peters.york.sch.uk

- Pupils: 318 boys, 202 girls • Ages: 13-18 (pre prep and junior school 3-13) • Size of sixth form: 200 • C of E (but other faiths welcome) • Fees: St Olaves: Day £2,163 - £2,809. Boarders £4,323 - £4,931 • Independent • Open days: September, October and May

---

Head Master: Since 2004, Mr Richard Smyth MA, previously, from 1993, head of King's Bruton. Read history and law at Emmanuel College, Cambridge, taught at Christ's Hospital, housemaster at Wellington College, is a child-friendly head who really does know all his pupils by name. Teaches history, coaches cricket. Unashamedly Christian. Married to Nicole (Swiss) with a teenage son and two daughters.

Academic Matters: Strong work ethos. Teaching and learning is of utmost importance This is a school for those who expect to achieve at least a fistful of GCSE grade As (approximately 75 per cent of GCSEs are graded A/A*) though weaker brethren struggle through and often exceed expectations. Ideal child is one who is not only prepared to give things a go but also has a genuine interest in learning. School recog-

nises more needs to be done for the lower streams and is experimenting with smaller classes in some subjects, the gifted simply study for more exams. Handful with mild dyslexia, limited support, must be bright and able to cope. Emphasis is very much on the academic with sport, for the talented, a close second. Theatre studies GCSE and AS level. Both staff and pupils comment that less pressure would have all-round benefits without affecting exam success. Last head acknowledged the school tries to be good at everything and this can result in undue pressure and resources being spread too thinly. Class size averages 20 in the middle school and 12 in the sixth form. Six pupils at the school received letters from the exam board for scoring within the top five marks in the country and the art department appears in the Guinness Book of Records for a remarkable 100 per cent A*/A grade pass rate achieved four years running. The odd D or E grade creeps in but all pupils pass at least six GCSEs at grades A* to C with approximately 95 per cent achieving ten passes. Commendable 75 per cent of all A level entries graded A or B with half those entered gaining straight As. Additionally all pupils study for the CLAIT course in IT.

Games, Options, The Arts: Sport is compulsory for all. Facilities include two sports centres, gymnasium, indoor swimming pool, extensive playing fields, boathouse and tennis and squash courts. Rugby popular and strong, winners of the U15 Daily Mail Cup held annually at Twickenham. Rowing crews regularly pick up honours and awards, gold and silver medallists at the National Schools' Regatta. Hockey, rowing and netball are the most popular girls' sports but tennis, athletics, fencing, squash, swimming and all usual suspects on offer for all.

Professional coaches are employed in most sports but pupils complain that only first team players are properly coached, catered and cared for and that once a squad is chosen it's difficult to break in, though school does offer a range of teams and there are frequent house competitions. Competitiveness a prominent feature of the school and success universally applauded at weekly assembly. Trips and tours include expeditions to Ecuador, rugby tours to Canada and Australia, history treks to WW1 battlefields and musical excursions to Europe.

Majority learn a musical instrument or two. Practice sessions aren't timetabled so have to be slotted in but each boarding house has a practice room with piano. Several choirs and ensembles including Barber Shop and Barbie Shop quartets meet regularly. Recent performances include The Messiah (performed at York University) and Guys & Dolls. Some pupils involved with community service projects and all participate in charity fund raising.

Background and Atmosphere: The school was founded in 627 AD by Paulinus, first Archbishop of York, and is one of Europe's oldest schools. In 1844 it was established on its present attractive site in Clifton and is within walking distance of York Minster and the city centre. The recent acquisition of the defunct Queen Anne's Grammar school has allowed reorganisation and expansion of the campus. Additions include four bright new biology labs together with a sixth form microbiology lab, an IT lab and, most notably, a superb art department with facilities to rival the best. Classrooms are a mix of ancient and modern but generally well cared for and many with interesting and informative displays. Three computer rooms are complemented by clusters of computers throughout the houses and school, all pupils have access to email. Strong Christian ethos, pupils meet thrice weekly for collective act of worship in school chapel with assemblies at other times.

Pastoral Care and Discipline: Pupils are members of one of the five day or four boarding houses. Boarding houses are well equipped with a selection of common rooms and games rooms, a kitchen and generously sized study bedrooms. Strong house loyalty, pupils and staff share a healthy mutual respect and relations are good. Houses are headed by husband and wife teams and supported by resident and non-resident assistants. A pupil mentoring system is being piloted in a couple of houses and, while this is a caring school, it isn't as touchy-feely as some – the tender, sensitive child who requires constant TLC and support should look elsewhere. New intake start the term with a world challenge day, a fun programme of problem solving, team building and bonding activities designed to ease the transition to senior school. School rules lay down clear boundaries and sensible guidelines on boy/girl relationships, smoking and alcohol. Four expulsions for drugs within living memory underline the school's zero tolerance policy. An anti-bullying policy is in operation and any minor incidents are quickly nipped in the bud. When problems arise advice, help and support may be sought from tutors, house staff, health centre staff or the school chaplain. Additionally the school has an appointed Child Protection Officer and an independent listener. The long school day at St Peter's and academic and sporting demands can leave some with little spare time. Pupils are allowed to visit town twice a week (more in sixth form) and for younger ones a timetable of supervised events is on offer, answering earlier complaints of not enough to do.

The dining hall and menu have undergone a most necessary recent major overhaul and we are told the menu is now varied, balanced and of a good quality.

Pupils and Parents: Day pupils mainly from north Yorkshire, the Leeds conurbation, York, and surrounding villages. Majority of boarders live within an hour's drive but others from wide area in the UK. Parents in business and the professions, a popular choice for Services families, small minority from overseas, mostly Hong Kong. Sixty three per cent boys, twenty eight per cent board, rest day. Pupils bright, articulate, friendly and biddable, confident not arrogant, an endearing bunch who cope well with the pressures of expectation. Old boys include Guy Fawkes, Alcuin (8th century scholar), Greg Wise, John Barry and Clare Wise (director of the British Film Commission).

Entrance: Automatic entry from Clifton pre-prep to St Olave's (own prep school) and from St Olave's to St Peter's. Otherwise by CE and school's own entrance test at any age including 16. Assessment and filtering takes place in prep and pre-prep to weed out those who won't cope with the demands of St Peter's. Generally entry to St Olave's requires a child to have a reading age at least a year ahead of chronological age. Will take pupils who pass exam at any time provided a place is available. Other main feeder schools: Terrington Hall, Minster School and Cundall Manor.

Exit: Approximately six per cent of pupils leave at the end of year eleven to go on to sixth form colleges. Ninety per cent of those leaving after Y13 go directly to university, vast majority selecting Leeds, Bristol, Newcastle, Durham and UCL. Nine or ten to Oxbridge, seven per cent take a gap year, remainder enter paid employment.

Money Matters: Not a rich school but the recently created St Peter's School Foundation aims to create a culture of long term giving and support for major capital expenditure and fund raising. Foundation Awards based on need are available allowing a wider group access to St Peter's. Up to 5 academic means-tested scholarships worth £900 per year at 13 and twelve at sixth form are available regardless of previous school. Additionally there are foundation scholarships for sixth formers in science, business or economics and design technology worth up to £1,000 pa plus a modern languages scholarship of up to 100 per cent of fees.

Remarks: The middle of the road child who scrapes through the entrance exam could rapidly lose confidence and feel overwhelmed by multi-talented peers. Not for the delicate, indecisive or those with low self esteem but the quirky eccentric or confident academic, especially those who are sporty or have a musical bent, will blossom in this high pressure environment.

St Swithun's School

Linked to Saint Swithun's Junior School in the Junior section

Alresford Road, Winchester, Hampshire, SO21 1HA

Tel: 01962 835 700
Fax: 01962 835 779
E-mail: office@stswithuns.com
Website: www.stswithuns.com

• Pupils: 479 girls; 221 board, 258 day • Ages: 11-18 • Size of sixth form: 121 • C of E • Fees: Senior: day £3,950; boarding £6,510. Junior: nursery £1,000; reception - y2 £1,985; years 3-6 £2,550 • Independent • Open days: For sixth form in September

Head: Since 1995, Dr Helen Harvey BSc PhD (fifties). Did her PhD in cancer research at the Royal Marsden in Surrey. Previously head of Upper Chine School on the Isle of Wight, has two children. Keen on sailing and on music. Held in high regard by parents. 'She is superb,' said one. 'She's dealt instantly with any small problems I've had and rang back later to check that things were all right.' The girls like and respect her. The school 'visitor' is the Bishop of Winchester, council members include the head of Winchester College, the Dean of Winchester and the Mayor of Winchester.

Academic Matters: For a not particularly selective school, it consistently comes up with impressive exam results. GCSEs in particular tend to be awash with A* and A grades, with scarcely anything below B. 'You're pushed to get good results but you're not pushed too far,' said a pupil. 'There's plenty of time for other activities.' Chemistry and languages are particularly strong. French and German are compulsory for at least two years; Spanish and Russian are sixth form options. The sciences are all popular A level choices; everyone does general studies A level. 'The girls are not all top-of-the-heap academics,' says the head, 'but they all want to do well. They are aiming at A£.' Setting in maths and modern languages. All take nine GCSEs and no-one takes any early. 'There's a big difference between qualifications and education – and we don't let them tot up one at the expense of the other.' The only compulsory GCSE subjects are two English and maths – plus a foreign language and a science.

Beyond that girls get a free – 'but very guided' – choice, from a list that includes Greek, classical civilisation and food technology. IT has a relatively low profile, 'we don't have much IT-driven teaching.' The school is not, however, lacking in computers, with a recently-refitted IT room. The learning support department is staffed full time, giving one-to-one help to some 50 or so girls who may have dyslexia or dyspraxia or just need help with planning their work.

Games, Options, The Arts: With after-school activities until 6pm four days a week, 'you're nicely tired by the end of the day,' said a pupil. Plenty of lacrosse fields, tennis and netball courts, impressive swimming pool and a sports hall; the school fields quite a few national and county players in lacrosse, netball and judo. Other possibilities include fencing, volleyball and landsailing. 'My daughter, who is not particularly sporty, has been encouraged to get out and do a lot,' said a parent.

Music is high profile, with a range of orchestras, choirs, bands and ensembles, playing, said a parent, 'to an extremely high standard.' The senior choir sings at least two services each term in Winchester Cathedral. The new performing arts centre, which was completed in September 2003, has provided a superb new facility for drama in the school. Few art results below grade A at GCSE or A level. DT is popular as a GCSE and A Level subject and as an after-school club; girls pop in to make presents for relatives (they have designed a production line to make fridge magnets) or get involved in projects such as designing and building a fleet of racing cars – and racing them very successfully at Goodwood – and creating a robot for the Schools Robot Wars competition. 'We made a hovercraft,' said a pupil, 'and we go to Weston-super- Mare to drive it on the sands.' Everyone does food technology for the first three years and there are after-school clubs 'where you can just come in and cook'. Increasing numbers of trips abroad, including sports tours to Australia and the USA, a classics trip to Greece and choir visits to Prague and Barcelona.

Background and Atmosphere: Founded as Winchester High School in 1884 by Anna Bramston, daughter of the Dean of Winchester, who remained as school secretary for over 40 years. It changed its name to St Swithun's in 1927 and moved to the present 45 acre site in 1931. The vast, red brick, Queen Anne style building with polished wood and large windows looks out over the playing fields. Spacious, excellent facilities, with a feeling of plenty of funds for upkeep and expansion. Separate day and boarding houses, except for the upper sixth. Since the completion of a new boarding house in September 2002, all houses are now on campus. The younger ones share rooms while the older ones have their own individual cubicles, where homework is often done curled up on the bed. More or less all the boarders are weekly ones and a large proportion come from within an hour's radius – 'we're a very local school,' says the head.

Because there are only around 40 full boarders, activities at weekends tend to be sporadic. 'We don't have the regimented structure of a full boarding school, so the boarders may spend weekends doing the sort of things they would do at home, like going to Tescos to buy food for supper.' Because they have separate common rooms, day girls and boarders tend to make friends with their own kind, at least initially. 'Later on, I don't think you can spot the join,' says the head. One ex-student complained of having felt molly-coddled, with very little freedom to roam, even at 16. Occasional links with Winchester College eg the odd mixed play, society and jazz group, but 'we are not joined at the hip. We don't feel we need to organise the girls' social lives'.

Pastoral Care and Discipline: 'It's a nice relaxed, informal atmosphere,' commented a parent. While the housemistress is the important pastoral link, girls and parents are encouraged to talk to any member of staff with whom they feel comfortable – 'we see it as a collective responsibility.' Senior girls are responsible for helping junior ones in their own houses, 'though we don't use senior girls in a hierarchical sense.' A pupil confirms that there is a good back-up system involving the housemistress, sixth form and form tutor. 'And you can go and have a good old chat to the sister in the san if you want to.' Alcohol is seen as more of a problem than drugs (despite Winchester being the drugs capital of Wessex). It is allowed only at a few senior bashes; otherwise, 'if they are caught drinking in school I will send them home.' The head comments that their most effective anti-drugs talk was about which countries won't give you a visa if you have a drugs conviction.

Pupils and Parents: Middle class, middle-of-the-road, Wessex girls with mostly professional parents. 'Our girls are not natural rebels or rule breakers.' Any of these will tend to leave after GCSEs for more free-spirited establishments.

Entrance: Entry at 11 and 13. Everyone must pass common entrance and produce a decent report from their previous head but are accepted in order of registration. 'They're above average intelligence but not all greatly above. We like to think that if a girl meets our criteria we will be able to take her.' A few join the sixth form, generally with A grades in their chosen A level subjects.

Exit: About a quarter leave after GCSEs, bound for the local sixth form college or for other co-ed sixth forms. Almost all the others go on to university, mostly the old-established ones, including a good number to Oxbridge.

Money Matters: About one in five pupils has a bursary, an academic scholarship or a music award. These are available at 11 and 13. Academic scholarships range from 10-50 per cent of school fees. Music scholarships pay up to 30 per cent of school fees; awards give free music lessons. The £500 registration deposit is not returned if your daughter is offered a place but goes elsewhere.

Remarks: A well-funded, well-equipped day/weekly boarding school with consistently excellent results, producing confident, articulate girls who are unlikely to rebel against the system. The good local state schools compete effectively in some respects – though not in academic selection, funding or social cachet.

St Teresa's School

Effingham Hill, Dorking, Surrey, RH5 6ST

Tel: 01372 452 037

Fax: 01372 450 311

E-mail: info@stteresas.surrey.sch.uk

Website: www.stteresas.surrey.sch.uk

- Pupils: 330 girls, including 87 boarders • Ages: 11-18 • Size of sixth form: 75 • Roman Catholic but all faiths welcome • Fees: Prep/junior £930 - £2,750; Senior £3,450 - £3,700. Additional £2,125 - £2,585 for boarding • Independent • Open days: October, March and May

Head: Since 1997, Mrs Mary Prescott, BA PGCE (fifties), formerly head of languages at the school and before that had a spell in the state sector. Also has experience out of academia – working in the city – and is a confident, business-minded head, immaculately dressed and eloquently spoken. She clearly has a passion for teaching and draws on her own experiences – 'I want to help the girls be the best they can be. I want for them what I wanted for my children.' Describes herself as optimistic, lively and interested in people. Stresses that she likes the girls to believe that, 'if you think you can, you might, but if you think you can't you certainly won't.' Parents see her as 'very approachable', 'friendly' and 'very caring'. The girls say she is 'firm but fair'.

Retiring in July 2006. Her replacement will be Mrs Lesley Falconer BSc, currently head of More House in London. Studied microbiology at London, then combined research with teaching at a sixth form college. Teaches some biology and science.

Academic Matters: The school is selective but not hugely so and caters for girls of all academic abilities. Good results from such a cross section: in 2005, 64 per cent of girls got A/B grades at A level (100 per cent A-E), with 60 per cent A*/A at GCSE (98 per cent A*-C. Languages are strong, perhaps not surprisingly with Mrs P being a languages specialist. French, Latin, German, Spanish, Italian on offer and Japanese as an extra. Unanimous thumbs up from parents for the language teaching 'a huge asset to the school.' Girls are setted in maths, French, science and humanities. Computers and interactive facilities used in the classroom in all subjects. Classrooms are large and colourful and a new library offers a very wide range of books and resources. Teaching staff are mainly in their forties, with 7 who have been there for more than 10 years. One SEN teacher on site full time and the girls are regularly assessed – parents have to pay extra for SEN support. 'It might be an idea to have more than one dedicated SEN teacher,' said one parent.

Games, Options, The Arts: Sports facilities aplenty! A new swimming pool and all weather hockey pitch, hard tennis courts and a multi-purpose sports hall means that the girls are spoilt for choice. Strong in netball and hockey says a mother. Musically, at least 50 per cent play an extra instrument and the school choir beavers away preparing for a main concert every term. There are 22 opportunities in the year for girls to perform musically and professional musicians are invited to perform to the music society. A new performing arts theatre hall opened in September 2005. It is fully equipped with a 750 seat theatre, sound recording studio, two large interconnecting drama studios, dressing rooms and two music teaching rooms as well as 5 music practice suites. 'Much needed,' according to a satisfied mum. Photography, art and textiles are impressive 'The girls produce work of professional standard,' commented one enthusiastic mother and the artwork we saw was of gallery standards. Textiles, photography and jewellery making classes are popular -taught in a relaxed atmosphere with the radio playing in the background – you feel as if you are walking into a gallery or a workshop rather than a classroom. 'I can't even sew a button, my daughter can make dresses!' says a parent. School is constantly buzzing – 'there's always something going on' with lots of clubs; even the astronomy and lifesaving clubs are popular.

Background and Atmosphere: St Teresa's was founded in 1928 by the Religious of Christian Instruction on what was originally part of a manor site recorded in the Domesday Book. The present house, dating from 1799, is the centre of the senior school (there are still nuns living there) set in 45 acres of parkland – the small buildings where the classrooms are located and the gravelled walkways give the feeling of a small, self-contained town.

Boarding girls comment that it is like 'a home away from home.' (Girls have the option to full board, weekly board or simply stay one night a week – useful for the odd nights when parents are short of baby-sitters). Full boarders are taken out to nearby Kingston or Guildford on the weekend and are generally kept occupied. They certainly seem to enjoy their time. Boarding girls are very down to earth – older girls do a great job taking care of the younger ones. Boarding facilities are very clean, spacious, but simple. A nice touch for those who board occasionally (eg once a week) – they get the same beds and do not have to play musical beds changing every time. Non boarders say that 'sometimes we wish we were boarding' – day girls can be left till 6 or 7 in the evening. The school has a pleasing atmosphere and environment. As one parent says 'It has a feeling of old-style establishments. Might even need a bit of a boost, but everyone is very approachable and friendly.' 'Focused and happy' is the general feeling amongst parents.

Pastoral Care and Discipline: As one ex-pupil with a daughter at the school said, good pastoral care is one of the main reasons for choosing the school. Strong RC ethos based on 'the unique value of the individual,' but girls from all faiths are embraced. Mrs P wants her girls 'to know that they are not better than others – they are, however, gifted – everyone is.' Teaching staff are respected and liked. Discipline well-managed, structured, strict but fair. Drugs have not surfaced at the school, there have been smoking and bullying issues, but they were swiftly eliminated. Parents are kept in close contact generally, and are encouraged to approach staff with any concerns.

Pupils and Parents: A noteworthy number of pupils are daughters or even grand-daughters of ex-pupils: 'I went there, my mother went there, my daughter is there and hopefully, one day, her daughter will too.' Also popular with the Far Eastern community, and 14 per cent of the girls is from overseas. Pupils are smart, skirt lengths are decent, one or two unnatural blondes in the school but not enough to call the highlight brigade! Some experiment with fashionable hair styles and makeup in the sixth form but nothing too worrying. Local parents are a mixed bunch – professional mums and dads as well as first time buyers. The school seems sheltered from the growing 'Surrey Mums' syndrome: the atmosphere at sports days and school events is still quite relaxed with no obvious competition between the mothers.

Entrance: Many enter via the junior school after sitting the entrance examination in year 6, but a large number also come from other schools including Hoe Bridge, Halstead, Danes Hill, Downsend, Feltonfleet and Rowan and from local state primaries. Tested in maths and English – not too oner-ous. A handful of girls join at 16 for the sixth form. Special exam for entry from overseas.

Exit: About 35 per cent – quite a chunk – leave at 16 to sample co-ed independent schools, to sixth form or spe-cialist colleges. Others finish their A levels and head for a variety of universities which include Bristol, LSE, York, Birmingham, Leeds, Warwick, Bath, Durham and occasion-ally one or two to Oxbridge. In 2005 five girls were offered unconditional places to Central St Martin's College of Art, London.

Money Matters: Academic, music, sport, drama and art scholarships are available and can amount to 50 per cent of the fees. Good to see that tuition fees include lunch and before and after school care facilities.

Remarks: An ordered, friendly, all round school with strong religious ethos and good pastoral care.

THE SCHOOL OF ST HELEN AND ST KATHARINE

Linked to School of St Helen and St Katharine Junior School (The) in the Junior section

Faringdon Road, Abingdon, Oxfordshire, OX14 1BE

Tel: 01235 520 173
Fax: 01235 532 934
E-mail: info@shsk.org.uk
Website: www.shsk.org.uk

• Pupils: 633 girls, all day • Ages: 9-18 • Size of sixth form: 177
• Anglican foundation • Fees: £2,837 • Independent • Open days: Late September or early October

---

Head: Since 1993, Mrs Cynthia Hall (fifties) educated at North London Collegiate School and St Anne's College, Oxford, where she read English. Previous post as head of English, St Paul's Girls' School. President of GSA 2004; current vice president and co-chair of the HMC/GSA University sub-committee, closely involved in the develop-ment of government policy for university access. Married to Tony Hall, chief executive of the Royal Opera House. Daughter attended the school, her son attends Abingdon. She is dynamic, sparky and charismatic – knows what needs doing and makes sure it's done well.

Academic Matters: Excellent GCSE and A level results. Only a tiny handful achieve less than a B at GCSE across all 20 subjects. Sciences offered as separate or as

double award. Choice of languages, very much encouraged here, includes Latin and Greek, as well as Italian, Spanish, German and French. State-of-the-art language facilities. IT, once somewhat of a weak point, now taught to all girls to GCSE and used as a tool in lessons across the board. Eclectic mix of 25 A levels includes economics, psychology, classical civilisation and art history, with choices pretty evenly divided between arts and sciences. Some subjects jointly taught with Abingdon. Varied teaching styles actively encouraged with traditional emphasis on essay structure, spelling and grammar combined with the use of modern technology to make learning an enjoyable experience. Authors are invited to the school to talk about their books and reading for fun is very much encouraged.

Small classes are the norm, with an average of 20 in years 7-11 and 10 in A level classes. Year 5 and year 6 classes, of 16 and 24 girls respectively, have separate form-room base within school grounds, with the older year treated as part of main school. A special needs co-ordinator is responsible for the five per cent of pupils with dyslexia or disability problems – none are statemented. Pupils encour-aged to think independently and take responsibility for organising their own work.

Games, Options, The Arts: Music is central to school life and a new performing arts centre now provides first class accommodation. Harp, saxophone, trombone, double bass and singing amongst the huge range of instruments that find their way into various school orchestras, bands and choirs. Organ scholarships are available at senior level. Fierce competition to get into school musicals, with older pupils taking past productions, with boys from Abingdon School, to acclaim at the Edinburgh festival. New studio theatre.

Sports facilities generally good, with a large all-weather surface for tennis and netball and a new sports centre opened this year, providing gym, fitness suite and changing facilities. Many pupils compete at county level at lacrosse, netball, tennis and cross-country running, some representa-tion at regional and national levels, despite constraints of a small site hemmed in by a major road on one side and a newish estate on the other. The school pool, however, is small, elderly and outdoor, surrounded by high wire fencing to deter vandals. Sailing is increasingly popular with a number of girls selected for national development squads. Hockey recently introduced.

Debating is very strong, with girls winning the regional final of the Observer Mace competition and featuring strongly on the national circuit. Big success is the Young Enterprise scheme, with its business schemes and pupil-run companies enthusiastically supported even by younger years and picking up prizes across Oxfordshire. Over three hundred girls involved in Duke of Edinburgh Award Scheme.

Background and Atmosphere: St Helen's was founded in 1903 to provide a 'liberal and advanced' Christian education for young ladies in Abingdon. Taught by Anglican nuns, the girls joined forces with the pupils of St Katharine's, Wantage in 1938. The school still occupies the same neat, if slightly draughty, redbrick buildings and beautifully kept gardens on the edge of town. 2000 saw the addition of a separate, modern sixth form building and the huge, hi-tech Jean Duffield building housing English and modern languages blends in surprisingly well for a modern extension. The performing arts centre, opened in 2004, provides music department accommodation, art display space, a dance studio and a very high quality studio theatre with rehearsal space and costume storage etc. Enormous donation made by the son of a late teacher and governor of the school has brought 21st century comfort to St Helen's, along with IT facilities that had been noticeably lacking. The same benefactor is funding further improvements, including a new library. State-of-the art touch pad security system (door codes to each block) installed throughout, according to head, in line with parents' wishes, but looks slightly paranoid to the outsider.

Pastoral Care and Discipline: Christian values underpin everything. School exudes an air of intellectual spirituality and there is a strong sense of community spirit. Questions and personal views on morals actively encouraged. Form tutor responsible for day to day welfare, with full time school chaplain, nurse. Doctor and counsellor available as needed. Girls in the upper sixth take positions of responsibility in form, charity or sport – younger girls encouraged to do the same. All efforts made to make occasional perpetrators of bullying or drug taking take personal responsibility – home-school agreements a favourite tool. May look softly-softly but head not afraid to remove those who don't play ball.

Pupils and Parents: Polite but rather shy younger girls blossom into confident, courteous, well-dressed seniors. Not particularly socially mixed – overwhelmingly nice, middle-class girls with professional parents from Oxfordshire and Berkshire. A comprehensive bus service covers most of the catchment area. Alumnae, generally worthy rather than starry, include Belinda Bucknell QC, former Arts Council executive Mary Allen, author and journalist Alice Thompson and Sue Wyatt, executive director of the Rambert Dance Company.

Entrance: Entry is at age 9, 10, 11, 13 and 16. Large numbers apply for approximately 60 places at 11 from both local state and private feeders. Entrance based on exam, headteachers' reports and interviews conducted with prospective pupils before exams. Around a dozen with good GCSEs and a positive report join the sixth form to replace leavers. Head prides herself on never denying access to the sixth form to existing pupils, even those with relatively poor GCSEs, regarding exclusion for academic reasons as an unfair way of bumping up A level results.

Exit: Almost all go on to further education, with a school record 19 Oxbridge places in 2004. Bristol, Leeds and Birmingham universities are favourite destinations – there's a distinct southern bias – with English, medicine and sciences all popular.

Money Matters: Fees reasonable but every extra is paid for, whether it is modern dancing, squash or any musical instrument. Small number of academic and musical scholarships - inc new ones at 13 - and bursaries for those with financial need. Long-term fund raising is underway to expand bursary and scholarship programme.

Remarks: Bright, neat buildings house bright, neat girls who are given a rigorous intellectual workout in a caring, harmonious school. Getting hothouse results without the hothouse atmosphere.

SEAFORD COLLEGE

Lavington Park, Petworth, West Sussex, GU28 0NB

Tel: 01798 867 392
Fax: 01798 867 606
E-mail: seaford@clara.co.uk
Website: www.seaford.org

• Pupils: 439; 120 boarders (85 boys, 35 girls), 319 day (216 boys, 103 girls) • Ages: 10-18 • Size of sixth form: 99 • C of E • Fees: Day £4,180, juniors £3,350. Boarding £6,370, juniors £4,920 • Independent • Open days: Two a term

Head: Since 1997, Mr Toby Mullins BA (economics) MBA (forties), came from a retail background, previously deputy head of Churcher's, Petersfield. A committed head, working hard to build up the school's reputation, also an inspector for ISI/HMC. Voluble, tells you like it is, emphasises regularly at school speech days that 'this Seaford is no longer the dumping ground for staff and pupils that it used to be', but some pupils with troubled histories still. Parents also regularly reminded not to moan alone but to call him on his direct line if they have any problems at all – 'we're all big boys now, let's get to the heart of the problem'. Pupils reckon they can

go to him at any time, not frightened of him. Married with 2 young children, both at the school, wife active in the school.

Academic Matters: Traditional, catering for a wide range of pupil. Results improving steadily, the sixth form growing each year, pupils achieving well according to their abilities. 90 per cent plus 5 A* to C grades at GCSE, a fair share of As for English. Humanities and history are strong departments with brilliant staff who are popular with the pupils; lots of living history and travel included. IT is all high tech, the whole school campus has a wireless network – broadband access to the internet from anywhere.

Children's progress is monitored carefully and study skills are taught. Learning support team regularly update themselves on new ways of assisting pupils – about one third of children have a SpLD such as dyslexia or dyscalculia (but not dyspraxia) – such pupils need to provide an educational psychologist's report, otherwise will be assessed on entry. Those who need to can work on a laptop. EFL support available but the school only has a handful of overseas pupils. Staff are predominately young and long-staying. Parents comment 'staff are approachable and work very hard here to get results with all pupils whatever their difficulties, which is no mean feat'.

Games, Options, The Arts: Sports play a very important role in school life, vast playing fields and courts of every description, all pupils participate in sporting activities every afternoon. International water based hockey pitch (makes balls go faster and players get wet as balls splosh down), only 2 schools in the country have this facility; all UK teams use the pitch for practising on, so excellent links with professional sportsmen. Regular winners of the West Sussex Cups for hockey and rugby for the under 14s. Lake for fly fishing, golf course, Multigym and clay pigeon shooting. Indoor swimming pool is next on the new building plan. Golf course not up to par.

High-profile music, no more free instrumental tuition for new pupils, but there are various orchestras and jazz band. Renowned choir in high demand to perform both here and abroad – they have made numerous CDs and are given air-time on Classic FM. Drama is equally strong, every term offers good quality dramatic and musical events with theatre studies being popular at GCSE and A level. Pupils also do LAMDA awards. The art and CDT department are well resourced – 5 full-time members of staff, pupils produce some excellent results. The school invites professional artists to visit and four different art A level courses are on offer.

Background and Atmosphere: Founded in 1884 and moved to Lavington Park (not surprisingly, known as Lavy

Park) in 1946, pretty Georgian house set in wonderful grounds with great views of the South Downs in all directions; charming Sussex flint stone cottages for staff, ghastly collection of add-ons for teaching – changes afoot. Planning has been granted for a brand new maths and science block, scheduled for completion in January 2005. Walking round the campus feels like being in a small village, peaceful with sound of children cheering at matches in the distance. Some children find the size of grounds a little overwhelming at first – 'you definitely need an umbrella as departments are miles from each other', commented one younger pupil. Girls live in main house, boys in a cluster well past their sell-by date though redeemed by fab common rooms, sag bags, DVD, telly – Playstation 2; 'better than at home' we were told. Dorms for younger boys, sixth form have study bedrooms. Brand new boys' boarding house should be ready by September 2005.

Pastoral Care and Discipline: Tutor system, pupils say they feel well supported and there is always a housemaster/housemistress available for them to talk to. Chapel in the grounds. School has a good standard of behaviour and good manners, and consideration for others is expected. Sin – very much three strikes and you're out. Bullying – letters home, warning of suspension next time around. Out for serial wickedness. Drugs usually equals out.

Pupils and Parents: Mainly professional middle class families, on the whole affluent rather than grand, but some polo-set girls (Cowdray just up the road). Overseas pupils predominately in the sixth form. Old Boys include the De Haan brothers.

Entrance: From a variety of local preps and state primaries within a 30-mile radius; popular with Haslemere and Chichester parents. Small number of 10-year-olds, mostly at 11 or 13 by Common Entrance or school's own exam and a report from their current school.

Exit: 70 per cent stay on to do A level courses, 90 per cent then go onto university or art school, many to Central St Martin's. Leavers at 16 tend to go to local colleges for A level.

Money Matters: Annual scholarships worth £500 for art, design & technology, music both choral and instrumental, sports and academic, and sixth form.

Remarks: Definitely a good choice of school for a sporty child – facilities and training some of the best on the market; the same can be said of the art departments. Parents comment, 'its ethos lies in confidence building and developing people; whatever their strengths, staff at Seaford will help them be realised'. Kids seem happy, results speak for themselves, good for dyslexia etc.

SEDBERGH SCHOOL

Linked to Sedbergh Junior School in the Junior section

Malim Lodge, Sedbergh, Cumbria, LA10 5HG

Tel: 015396 20535

Fax: 015396 21301

E-mail: hm@sedberghschool.org

Website: www.sedberghschool.org

- Pupils: 324 boys, 118 girls; 431 boarders • Ages: 13-18 • Size of sixth form: 172 • C of E • Fees: Senior: boarding £6900; day £5140. Junior/prep: day from £2,720; weekly boarding £3,990; boarding £4,635. Pre-prep £1,820. Reception £1,590.
- Independent • Open days: Senior School - September. Junior School - September, March & June

Head: Since 1995, Mr Christopher Hirst MA (mid fifties), educated at Merchant Taylors' and Cambridge. Previously head of Kelly College before that senior housemaster at Radley. Historian and Cambridge cricketer. A member of the full HMC Committee and currently Chairman of HMC (NE) Division. Good and energetic, a genuine and committed enthusiast for full boarding and co-ed education. He is married to Sara who is senior mistress; they have three daughters, two at Sedbergh one at nearby Casterton.

Academic Matters: GCSE averages 95 per cent A-C passes, 35 per cent A/A* not bad for a school with a comprehensive intake and a policy of entering all pupils for exams, very good value added. 99 per cent pass rate at A Level. Some learning support is offered for those in need, principally children with dyslexia. Average class size is 15 with a ceiling of 25. Pupils have good relationships with the helpful, caring and dedicated staff. Some classrooms showing signs of age and several areas would benefit from greater display of pupils' work. Modern technology is now weaving its way throughout the school, boarding houses and many curriculum areas – not before time. Departmental libraries are well stocked. Main library, housed in a super conversion of Georgian building on the site of Lupton's original school, is rather frayed not only round the edges but also on the shelves.

Games, Options, The Arts: Renowned for its sporting prowess (34 sporting activities on offer) with many pupils winning representative honours, especially in rugby and shooting. Good, very keen cricket school, sports hall, 25-metre indoor pool. Also famous for its Wilson Run – a 10-mile fell race open to ages 16+. All pupils participate in CCF in year 9 but involvement is optional after that, though many continue. Magnificent music school, lots of ensembles; the CCF band recently toured Austria, lots of good drama with productions each summer at the Edinburgh fringe. Regular trips and tours abroad. Many clubs and societies available including D of E award scheme. A Sedbergh group climbed Everest and reached the highest point ever by any school team.

Background and Atmosphere: Founded in 1525 by Roger Lupton, a provost of Eton. School lies in the centre of a small, picturesque town surrounded by magnificent fells, in the heart of the splendid (if often wet and cold) Yorkshire Dales National Park but only a short drive from the M6. Departments housed in several separate buildings which gives rise to a mature, campus feel appreciated by pupils. Each pupil is assigned to a house where they live and eat (excellent food, lots of choice, special diets catered for). New entrants quickly develop keen house loyalty and rightly see the system as pivotal to the success of the school. New girls' boarding houses are bright, modern and well furnished. All the boys' boarding houses have been refurbished over the last three summers except for one house to be completed by September 2006.

With the arrival of girls in 2001 and reverting to a 13 to 18 school in 2002, the school is now better placed to serve its population. Younger children are catered for at the newly established prep and pre-prep school developed on the old Bentham Grammar School site, 30 minutes drive away but managed by the senior school head. At the start of the fourth year of the co-ed intake the 118 girls form a significant, vibrant and impressive part of the school. Smart and business-like in appearance (super navy uniform with tartan skirt) the Sedbergh females are a force to be reckoned with, very much keeping the boys and staff on their toes. Look out for improving results in the coming years and famous Old Girls in the not too distant future.

Make sure to check out the Sedberghian, the school magazine, for well reported information on every facet of the place and the students who populate it.

Pastoral Care and Discipline: Effective house system with strong, popular and caring housemasters and mistresses heading up dedicated teams. Well thought-out punishment system. Bar available at weekends to sixth formers, school encourages a sensible attitude to alcohol. Over-familiar relationships between boys and girls actively discouraged.

Pupils and Parents: Mostly northern professionals but some from Scotland and increasingly from the south. Traditionally a school for landowners, industrialists and farmers' sons (Wordsworth was a parent) but now an eclectic mix including Services, expats and a few foreigners. Pupils are confident, sparky and generally though not universally sporty. A straightforward bunch admirably demonstrating many typical northern values. Not afraid to get their hands dirty, they might call a spade a spade but willingness to help others, loyalty and compassion are values universally to the fore. This is a very happy school, lots of laughter in and out of lessons. Still not a place for the timid or loner but anyone else, especially those who appreciate the fantastic surroundings and teamwork, will love it here. Old boys include Simon Beaufoy (Full Monty), Will Carling, Will Greenwood, Lord Bingham (Lord Chief Justice), James Wilby, Sir Jock Slater (First Sea Lord) Sir Christopher Bland (Chairman BT), Robert Napier (Chief Exec WWF and Chairman of Governors.)

Entrance: For most, Common Entrance is the normal route, others applying in years 9-11 sit exams in English and maths. A current school report is required. Sixth form requires a minimum 5 GCSEs at C or above. Main feeder is Sedbergh Junior School but significant proportion come from prep schools across the north of England and beyond.

Exit: Mostly to university, many choose to stay in the north. Steady trickle to Oxbridge (traditionally strong links with Cambridge). A Sedbergian won one of the coveted Morehead Scholarships to the University of North Carolina. Several opt for a gap year having secured their university place. Handful embark on vocational courses or careers at 18, trickle leave at 16.

Money Matters: Several scholarships: academic, all-round, sport, drama, DT, music and art: awards vary but may be up to half-fees. Couple of index-linked major scholarships. Exhibitions and bursaries also available. In 2004/5 41 awards made, averaging 26 per cent of fees.

Remarks: Sedbergh has faced up to the demands of the 21st century but managed to retain traditional values and ethos – increasing numbers esp for boarding indicate parents very much approve. It rightly retains its reputation as a formidable force on the sports field but away from there provides a happy and caring environment for all its pupils regardless of ability or sports prowess.

SEVENOAKS SCHOOL

High Street, Sevenoaks, Kent, TN13 1HU

Tel: 01732 455 133
Fax: 01732 456 143
E-mail: regist@sevenoaksschool.org
Website: www.sevenoaksschool.org

- Pupils: 490 boys, 490 girls; 160 boys and 170 girls board
- Ages: 11-18 • Size of sixth form: 433 • Non-denom • Fees: £4,471 - £5,078 (direct entry to sixth); boarding £7,203 - £7,810 (direct entry to sixth) • Independent • Open days: May and September

Head: Since 2002, Mrs Katy Ricks MA (early forties) first female Head. Fast-track career at good schools: King Edward's Birmingham, Latymer Upper, St Paul's Girls, latterly deputy at Highgate. First in English from Balliol. Husband, David, teaches Byzantine and Modern Greek at King's, London. Energetic, stylish and bright woman, exudes confidence from her cool, minimalist office (stripped floor, Eames chairs), clearly very proud of her school and staff. Keeps open door for students despite school's size – 'it's people that matter, not policies'. Well-informed about what's going on, has big plans for school's future (see below). Enjoys teaching International Baccalaureate (IB) Higher Level English literature.

Academic Matters: Prospectus says, 'not all learning is fun but young people learn better if they are genuinely involved and can see the relevance...to their own lives'. Hooray! – it needed saying. From 2005/06, A level phased out; all will take IB, which Sevenoaks has been offering as an option since 1970s, the first big-hitter public school to do so. This, with its international sixth form, set the school apart as a trend-setting and outward-looking institution. IB requires students to study three higher and three standard level subjects, covering the areas of English, another language, experimental sciences, the arts, maths, and humanities; plus a theory of knowledge paper and an extended essay of 4,000 words. They must also complete a programme of at least fifty hours each on activities classed under creativity, action and service, over two years. Results are issued in July, an advantage for university choice. Sevenoaks is on an impressive academic roll: GCSE results superb (over 90 per cent at A* and A in 2005) and IB/A level performance puts it near the top of the heap on every newspaper's list. Languages strong and varied, reflecting cosmopolitan sixth form, but by no means the only centre of excellence. Mrs Ricks claims a strong learning ethos in the school's upper part and students seem to agree – 'you're not expected to be a swot, it's just that everyone gets on with it'. Able and internationally-minded staff help to drive things along.

Games, Options, The Arts: Games pretty good all round, plenty of enthusiasm: usual county representation at several sports, with sailing, shooting and tennis strong nationally. Not in the same rugby and cricket leagues as prominent south east boys' schools but probably untroubled by that. Shiny new sports centre now open, including 25-metre pool. Music outstanding: multiple concerts, recitals and masterclasses throughout year, including St John's Smith Square. Regular finalists in national chamber music competition; 700+ instrumental lessons a week. Thriving drama department (own theatre), regular tours abroad and annual play in a foreign language. Studio for budding TV reporters. National pioneers of voluntary service in 1960s and boys and girls still encouraged to be community-minded. Students run projects in orphanage and hospitals in Romania and Moldova each summer, as well as go on numerous language exchanges to partner schools in Europe. Modern UN vigorous and popular. Flourishing D of E programme; voluntary CCF popular, includes many girls.

Background and Atmosphere: Traditional but relaxed and informal. School founded in 1432 by William Sennocke, mayor of London and friend of Henry V, as a thank-you for his share in the victory at Agincourt. Campus of varied buildings within walking distance of Sevenoaks town centre straggles agreeably over 100-acre site and opens up on to gracious grounds of Knole House (new chairman of governors is a Sackville West). Seven boarding houses, including cosy junior house and two for international students, though school is predominantly day. Big influx from abroad (started in 1962) swells roll for last two years but both sides appear to shake down happily enough together. Big development ambitions, with all users involved in 10 to 20-year planning exercise – more boarding provision, centres for performing arts and science/technology, more space for students, also enlarged bursary fund.

Pastoral Care and Discipline: No reports of recent problems. Discipline not especially strict, much along lines of other mixed boarding schools. Pupils rarely booted out (one to three a year); school reserves right to test pupils for drug abuse. Alcohol now less of an issue since recent change in law (as everywhere else). Senior boarders allowed into town, but not pubs – centre of Sevenoaks predictably 'lively' at weekends – and locals praise their behaviour.

School counsellor works alongside house staff. Strong house system.

Pupils and Parents: Largely local until you get to the sixth form, favoured by professional, media and diplomat parents. Many bi-lingual families. Large numbers of foreigners post-sixteen, from over 40 countries. Old Boys and Girls: Professors Simon Donaldson and Oliver Taplin; Lord Prout, Jeremy Harris, Chris Tavare, Paul Downton, Jonathan Bate, Emma Johnson, Lucy Cousins.

Entrance: At 11 via own exam in January. At 13 via CE, scholarship or school's own exam; candidates must first attend a screening day in October before entry. Standards are tough and parental anxiety can be high – but Mrs Ricks insists the school's not super-selective. Post-sixteen incomers need seven passes at mainly A* or A. Fluent English a must for overseas students.

Exit: To wide variety of universities, mainly Russell Group; 90 per cent get first choice university. Many to top US institutions (Yale, Berkeley, MIT etc); 30-plus a year to Oxbridge. Lots of gap years, as you would expect.

Money Matters: About fifty scholarships a year at 11, 13 and 16, including music, art, sport and all-rounder. Some bursaries available.

Remarks: Trail-blazing co-ed day and boarding school, proof that IB works; now riding high academically. Learning ethic fostered by both staff and pupils – it's OK to do well. Confident and assured students but with little trace of public school arrogance. Strong tradition of altruism. Much sought after, enjoys its success. Unique sixth form.

SEXEY'S SCHOOL

Cole Road, Bruton, Somerset, BA10 0DF

Tel: 01749 813 393
Fax: 01749 812 870
E-mail: Admissions@sexeys.somerset.sch.uk
Website: www.sexeys.somerset.sch.uk

• Pupils: 500 boys and girls; majority board years 7-11 • Ages: 11-18 • Size of sixth form: 200 • C of E • State

Head: Since 1996, Mr Steve Burgoyne BA PGCE DMS (fifties). Coaches cricket. 'Children should be happy at school and really enjoy it,' says this John Majoresque head. Parents say, 'quiet, intelligent, stands no nonsense'. Wife Carole is a special needs teacher, an unsung presence but staunchly supportive, coaches badminton and helps with learning support. Two graduate children (daughter attended sixth form here). Head of sixth form Dr N E Hooper was Science Teacher of the Year in 2000 – charismatic.

Academic Matters: Consistently high in the GCSE league tables with just over 90 per cent gaining 5 or more A*-Cs, fine results for a non-selective school. 2004 not a stellar year for A levels, especially sciences where there was not a single A in chemistry or physics (biology had no cause for celebration either). Average teaching group size in years 7 to 9 is 20, in years 10 and 11 it is 18.

From year 8 there is setting in maths, languages and sciences. No classics. Adventurous foreign cultural exchanges. School applied for humanities specialist status at the end of 2005 – head hopes to funnel some of the funding into improving ICT. All departments are networked, email for pupils. New computerised library reserves a mezzanine for sixth-formers' self-supported study. Learning support well staffed; mentor system for every student who needs it. 35 students have Individual Learning Plans.

Games, Options, The Arts: One in 6 play an instrument. Girls play prominent part in the school band but now music room is boosting participation of boys. Drama tackles everything from the challenging Jean Anouilh 'Antigone' to A level students putting on Macbeth for benefit of year 9s studying the play. Talented but chaotic art department; effective art and DT trips. Well-used gym provides cricket nets, bowling machine and 4 badminton courts. Rugby and football teams play top private schools, and there are links with Dorset Rugby Club and Bruton Cricket Club. Athletes gain top places at county level. Parents complain that not

enough advantage is taken of Mill on the Brue Adventure Centre next door and 'D of E tends to fizzle out for lack of enthusiasm'. However, flourishing ATC under enthusiastic leadership.

Rich variety of foreign trips (was one of first English schools to have an exchange to Russia), regular exchanges to Lahnau, Germany for years 9-13. Recent mind-and-soul enlightening trip to Zambia and repeat trip planned. Visit the website if you want it from the horse's mouth.

Background and Atmosphere: Founded in 1891 after a local, Hugh Sexey, who rose to become auditor to Elizabeth I, established Sexey's Hospital which still provides care for 30 elderly people. Trustees later founded a school for apprentices and, under guidance of The Honourable Henry Hobhouse who drafted 1902 education act, the current premises were built. Sexey's has metamorphosed through boys' grammar, voluntary controlled, grant maintained to voluntary aided; went co-ed in early 80s; took its first 30 day pupils into year 7 in 2003. Day pupils now moving up through the years, radically expanding the school roll.

Buildings are a mishmash of styles and houses often pressed for space but the countryside that bounds up on three sides makes up for its dishabille. Fast shaking off its old-fashioned image with new science labs, drama studio, smart library/ ICT room. Alas giving way to sloppy dressing for sixth form, seen as retrograde step by long-serving staff. Sixth form boarding oversubscribed. New sixth form centre opened late 2005.

Pastoral Care and Discipline: Prefect system now streamlined – a dozen appointed after applying in writing with CVs and being interviewed as if for real jobs (with debriefing for those not chosen). Punishments ensure fair discipline, however immediate expulsion for drugs or sex. Crisis Care Anti-Bullying Code. The Christian ethos important to school life but remains low key. Almost every aspect of this place pleases the 2001 Ofsted team and particular praise is heaped on the moral fibre of pupils.

Not a lot arranged at weekends, complain those with homes abroad. Weekly boarders leave Friday afternoon (a respite from the nosh), back by 8.30am Monday. Four houses have usual house-staff as well as much heralded sun-tanned surfers in the guise of gappies (cross between an older sibling and pastoral assistant). Sexey's own reciprocal gap scheme started 20 years ago, so post-sixth form students from Bathhurst in New South Wales have a taste of England and vice versa. Younger children shed tears when favourite gappies depart. A family atmosphere prevails.

Pupils and Parents: A school for real people. Most are first-time buyers and many have siblings here. One third are Services, 10 per cent ex-pats, 7 per cent Brits from Nigeria and Hong Kong. Rest are farmers and wide spectrum of local folk including some who can afford Marlborough or Winchester but prefer this for lack of snobbism, happy atmosphere and non-pushy way they attain results. Girls minimise their maroon check kilts, girls and boys wear black blazer and tie. Parents annoyed at plague of 'borrowing' – 'I gave up sewing name tapes in the end.' Nearly all staff stand in for houseparents' days off so get to know pupils out of classroom. Enthusiastic parent governors who really muck in. OBs as un-flash as the Sexey's image – professors at universities, botanists, Douglas Macmillan (founded Macmillan Nurses), ambassador Peter January and Ned Sherrin. City kids won't go a heap on it.

Entrance: Now takes up to 30 very local day pupils into year 7, alongside 50 boarders. For boarding places at 11 and 13 entrance based on interview and suitability for boarding, two terms prior to arrival. Can only accept EC citizens or those with British passport since tuition is free. Large intake at sixth form, the less able weeded out to make way for incomers who virtually all go on to university: 5 A-Cs required with Bs for main subjects. Boarding not compulsory for sixth form.

Exit: 95 per cent to university degrees especially business studies, engineering, architecture, media, biomedical; some to employment; many gap years.

Money Matters: One of the best boarding bargains anywhere. No bursaries or hardship funds. One or two pupils kept by social services, 6 aided by charities. Bursar waves an iron rod.

Remarks: 'Pupils who've been bullied elsewhere have come here and thrived,' says head. Parents and staff alike are loyal to this little known gem in the sleepy Saxon town of Bruton, and word of mouth is how most people hear of it. 'The atmosphere is worth everything,' say satisfied parents. Keeping this character, while expanding rapidly, is the school's new challenge.

SHEFFIELD HIGH SCHOOL

Linked to Sheffield High School Junior Department in the Junior section

10 Rutland Park, Sheffield, South Yorkshire, S10 2PE

Tel: 0114 266 0324
Fax: 0114 267 8520
E-mail: enquiries@she.gdst.net
Website: www.sheffieldhighschool.org.uk

• Pupils: 963 girls; all day • Ages: 4-18 • Size of sixth form: 173 • Non-denom • Fees: Junior £ 1,674; senior £2,310. Lunches extra • Independent • Open days: October - Infant, and Junior; November - Senior

Head: Since 2004, Mrs Valerie Dunsford, BA Hons (forties). Mrs Dunsford read French and did her PGCE at Manchester. She taught at Ryland Valley HS in Halifax, Benfield in Newcastle and then was head of modern languages, head of sixth form and deputy head at Durham HS.

Academic Matters: Strong A level results – steady growth to 81 per cent A/B with only small numbers below C; almost all get into their first choice universities. Fourth consecutive year at 100 per cent pass rate. A good range of subjects including sports studies, Russian, psychology, gov-

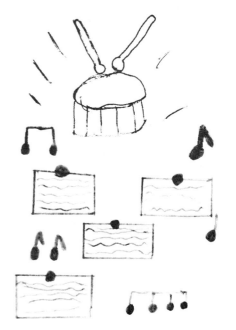

ernment and politics, with some very small sets; all take general studies AS. Strong GCSE results – 99 per cent average pass rate over last four years, 67 per cent A/A* with only a small proportion below B. Four modern languages offered, a particular interest in Russian culture – Love Russia, a charity for Russian orphans, well supported. Only sets for maths. Experienced, hard-working, enthusiastic staff who use very up-to-date teaching methods, are generous with their time and enjoy good relationships with girls. Classes of up to 28 (there are only two private all-girls schools in Sheffield and only one with progression from 4-18). ESL teaching available. Very good IT provision and use in teaching, particularly in modern languages and music; qualifications are taken at GCSE and in the sixth form. Library well-stocked and pleasant – despite its origin as a gym. Strong careers education – has links with local industry and commerce and organises work experience in Europe.

Games, Options, The Arts: Very successful mainstream sports teams, trampolining, badminton, cross-country, skiing and orienteering as well. A new sports hall with a dance studio; all-weather courts, a new Astroturf hockey pitch, but no swimming pool. Music strong, including a swing band that has performed at EuroDisney; converted stables with recording and drama studios. Yamaha C5 grand piano inaugurated with a recital and masterclass by Benjamin Frith.

Wide range of extra-curricular activities with local, national or international successes in Young Enterprise, public speaking, chemistry, technology, maths and creative writing competitions; Duke of Edinburgh Award Scheme very popular. Several do LAMDA exams. Trips to Mongolia and Argentina (World Challenge), Ecuador, Ski trips to Europe and Americas, Russia plus residential visits to France and Germany. Sports tours to Australia and South Africa, New Zealand in summer of 2005. Excellent art, eg ceramic work, fabrics; new extension to art suite imminent. Trips have been organised to France and New York and there is an artist in residence annually.

Background and Atmosphere: Founded in 1878 as part of the Girls' Day School Trust. A city school, with the focus on moral/spiritual development rather than religion, it occupies a cramped (school says 'tight') site in a surprisingly leafy residential area but uses the available space effectively. Architecturally very mixed, including a church that housed the original gym, a graceless but now refurbished 1960s science block with an extension from 2005, a converted old lodge with an elegant ex-billiards' room, and a separate sixth form in a Victorian house. The class-

rooms are well-resourced; the decoration has been upgraded with interactive whiteboard facilities, and a number are attractive. Relatively new dining hall with a popular breakfast club.

Pastoral Care and Discipline: Clearly a virtue of the school. There is a strong pastoral support system with a sensible code of conduct written by staff and the Student Council and a successful merit system. Sixth form tutor groups are formed by combining self-selecting friendship groups. Exclusion is for repeated unacceptable behaviour eg drugs, smoking, theft, intransigence – the whole picture is taken into account. There is a thoughtful year 7 induction and they have all their lessons in classrooms off one corridor for the first year.

Pupils and Parents: From Sheffield, south Yorkshire, north Nottinghamshire and north Derbyshire. Most come from professional and business families but there is a social mix because of the large number of Trust bursaries. Well-motivated, confident girls who feel happy and secure and speak appreciatively of their teachers.

Entrance: Tests in English and maths plus an interview at 11; 40 per cent from state schools. Entry to sixth form: girls need 7 GCSEs at A-C with A/B in AS subjects. Scholarships available in subject areas. Entry to the junior school is through observation during a child-friendly day – they are looking for bright, lively girls who are ready for school. All proceed from the junior school as less able girls are counselled out by end of year 4. It caters for average to above-average ability, 'sparky girls who want to learn and are interested in their own development'.

Exit: 12-18 leave after GCSE, for local state schools, other independent day schools (eg co-educational ones) and sixth form colleges. Almost all go on to a range of universities, most to very good ones; about 10 per cent to Oxbridge. Many do a range of science/medically related courses; business courses are also popular.

Money Matters: 20 per cent have Trust bursaries which can go up to full fees; anyone who passes the entrance exam can apply. 2 full fees HSBC/Trust scholarships including uniform. Scholarships based on academic ability give a 10 per cent reduction; also available at sixth form entry (usually 7) plus a sixth form music scholarship awarded through a music exam.

Remarks: A successful all-round city school, especially suited to academic, musical and sporting high flyers. Excellent value added, staff especially proud of lower ability girls who achieve outstanding grades at A level. Must be prepared to work for it, though.

SHERBORNE SCHOOL

Abbey Road, Sherborne, Dorset, DT9 3AP

Tel: 01935 812 249
Fax: 01935 810 426
E-mail: enquiries@sherborne.org
Website: www.sherborne.org

• Pupils: 570 boys; all but 40 board • Ages: 13 -19 • Size of sixth form: 230 • C of E • Fees: Day £5,995; boarding £7,595 • Independent • Open days: Mid September and early October

Headmaster: Since 2000, Mr Simon Eliot MA (late forties). Educated at Radley, read history at Queens', Cambridge. Taught at Winchester from 1976 where he was a well-respected housemaster for 12 years. Wife, Olivia, read English and history of art at Cambridge and was a history of art examiner. Two children. Quiet, thoughtful, unimposing – not a stereotypical headmaster. Interests include drama, music and sport. Keen to 'jazz up' the school's academic reputation and 'emphasise academic achievement as the most important thing we do here.'

Academic Matters: Strong and steady A level showing every year, usually squatting at the bottom of the top 100 British schools in the league tables. Languages setted from the start, other subjects in both arts and sciences streamed. Two modern languages plus Latin compulsory during first year. Greek available at GCSE and A level. Nearly all boys take separate sciences to GCSE and high numbers continue with sciences to A level. Generous music scholarships and excellent range of orchestras, choirs, bands etc. ESL help available. SEN support where necessary. A number of sixth form courses are offered jointly with Sherborne School for Girls (currently German, Italian, Russian, Spanish, history of art, philosophy, law, electronics, drama and theatre studies and PE.

Games, Options, The Arts: Traditionally seen as sporty but head is gently trying to tone this down, 'we don't want to go back to the days of worshipping rugby'. Parents praise the games, saying boys who were sidelined at their preps are given a chance here. Recent termly newsletters feature fives, shooting, golf, tennis, squash, basketball, riding, cross-country, swimming, hockey, skiing and the Ten Tors hike. Boys may opt for soccer after the first year. 50 acres of playing fields, new all-weather pitch, 20 tennis courts, fives courts and sports centre comprising indoor pool, squash courts, fitness centre and sports hall. No rowing. Exotic sporting expeditions – recent cricket tours to Barbados, Grenada, Sri Lanka and hockey team to West Indies!

Musicians also seeing the world – joint symphony orchestra (with Sherborne School for Girls and nearby girls' school, St Antony's-Leweston) recently toured France and the Czech Republic, the choir sang in Rome in 2000 and St Mark's Basilica in Venice in 2001, Portugal in 2003 and Tuscany in 2005; the nationally famous swing band plays to packed houses around Britain and abroad and the jazz band lately toured Cuba. A dozen dramatic productions each year, often in co-operation with Sherborne Girls' or Leweston, staged in the Big School Room or the professional Powell Theatre.

Art continues to thrive in elegant new home, gutted and refurbished science labs. The design and technology Department has also recently been completely refurbished. Loads of activities – golf, sailing, canoeing, rock climbing, excellent boy-run debating club, sub-aqua, D of E, Combined Cadet Force. Weekly extra-curricular activity session (ACE), undertaken with the girls' school – compulsory for 13 year olds but optional thereafter. Officially described as 'cultural, practical and fun,' it is the sort of wholesome jollity (car maintenance, orienteering, badminton) that looks a good idea to adults but is, sadly, abhorrent to some teenagers, though school disputes this. Lower sixth pupils may apply for travel grants to fund overseas visits relevant to their studies (24 pupils benefited last year).

Background and Atmosphere: Glorious mellow-yellow stone wonder, set in charming, safe country town, in shadow of ancient abbey. Founded by Edward VI as grammar school in 1550, though origins go back to 8th century and subsequent arrival of the Benedictines in 998, who were removed by Henry VIII. One of the few schools that has managed to keep its new additions aesthetically pleasing, decade after decade – the new Pilkington science block is particularly well-designed. Splendid library, now completely computerised, with hammer-beam roof. Loveliness of setting and collegiate atmosphere brings in nice little income from visiting film companies. Many parents choose the school for its town setting, preferring a quiet, rural town to isolation in the sticks. School also trades heavily on its proximity to Sherborne School for Girls and Leweston Girls' – 'all the advantages of single-sex education combined with the best aspects of co-education,' reads the prospectus, a point reiterated by every teacher, pupil, parent and dinner lady.

Excellent train service to Waterloo (2 hours). Good food, with lots of choices, dished up in one large recently refurbished central dining hall. Superb uniform for lower forms:

dark blue shirt with non-school-looking navy jumper (suit and tie dragged out a few times a term). Jacket and tie for sixth form. Worship takes place in school chapel, with regular services at glorious Sherborne Abbey (which shares a wall with the school). 40 RC boys bused up to Leweston School for Mass.

Pastoral Care and Discipline: New boys carefully integrated, first by spending a day at Sherborne during their penultimate year at prep, then spending a night or two in their future house the following year. All new boys start one day before the rest of the school and each has a mentor from a higher year for the first few weeks. Eight boarding houses, each with some 70 boys who are well looked after. All boarding houses in very good nick, done up recently. Biggish dorms to start, but individual study bedrooms from fifth form (age 15) upwards. Each house assigned at least six members of staff as tutors. Girls always around the place in a low-key way, though still feels very much a boys' school. Boys and girls may visit one another's houses, during certain hours, so long as they have housemaster's or housemistress's permission. Sixth formers from Sherborne Girls' and Leweston frequent the boys' sixth form bar. A few misdemeanours in recent years resulted in suspensions. Some 'minor bullying' reported and some less than 'minor'. Most, but not all, parents are satisfied that it is quickly dealt with.

Pupils and Parents: Pupil numbers back up. Uncomplicated, earnest boys lacking some of the more unpleasant social and financial snobbery of similar schools, summed up by one boy's description – 'we're not really a laptop school ...'. Boffins and loners can do well here – school makes space for them and will even let them off games – you need a good brain, though. Appeals to parents in professions and Services. Boys come in ones and twos from 50 or 60 preps in the south of England. 8 per cent foreign pupils, some coming across from Sherborne International College (qv), 5 per cent overseas Brits. Old Boys: Cecil Day-Lewis, Nigel Dempster, Alan Turing (Enigma code breaker), Jon Pertwee (Dr Who), David (now Lord) Sheppard, Sir Christopher Chataway, John Le Carré, Sir David Spedding (former head of MI6), A N Whitehead, Jeremy Irons, John Le Mesurier (Sergeant Wilson in Dad's Army) – and lots more, from all walks of life.

Entrance: 110 boys enter at 13 via CE, scholarship exam or school's own papers as appropriate. About 15 join at sixth form; 5 A-Cs required at GCSE, with at least 4 Bs. Sherborne boys have been asked to leave when they've not made the grade. Currently booking 5 years ahead, full three years ahead. An unusually informative prospectus, worth a read.

Exit: Highest numbers to London (mainly UCL), Birmingham and Bristol. Oxbridge entrances down a bit over past couple of years but still around 10 per cent. School says decline is result of fewer pupils choosing to submit Oxbridge applications. Excellent, switched-on careers advisor. Up to 50 per cent of boys opting for gap years.

Money Matters: Sherborne Foundation, set up in 1998 as a 'permanent fund-raising vehicle', seems to be doing the trick. Old Boys coughing up large donations including through assemblages of overseas Old Boys, eg American Friends of Sherborne. Generous scholarship provision, including up to 3 half-fees-worth of scholarships for music, and awards for outstanding ability outside the classroom, including art and sport.

Remarks: Strong, traditional public school in delightful setting, working hand in hand with neighbouring girls' school. Hard to resist once you've had a look. Excels at producing down-to earth, well-rounded boys.

SHERBORNE SCHOOL FOR GIRLS

Bradford Road, Sherborne, Dorset, DT9 3QN

Tel: 01935 818287
Fax: 01935 389445
E-mail: enquiry@sherborne.com
Website: www.sherborne.com

• Pupils: 365 girls; the great majority board • Ages: 11-18 • Size of sixth form: 140 • C of E • Fees: Day £5,270; boarding £7,195 • Independent • Open days: Spring and autumn

---

Headmistress: Since 1999, Mrs Geraldine Kerton Johnson (fifties). Read chemistry and botany at the University of Natal Pietermaritzburg (South Africa), then taught chemistry, physical science and biology in state and private schools in SA, ending up as principal of Epworth High School, Pietermaritzburg, before joining Sherborne. Married to an Anglican priest and has 4 grown-up children, two living in England. Comes across as gentle, maternal and deeply Christian, but with a steely inner core. 'Has her finger on the pulse and really understands young people,' said a parent. Banned the 'new girls' test' (a sort of initiation), improved relations between younger and older girls and 'boosted morale.' Professes to be possibly the only head teacher in England to like the AS exams – 'it helps girls come into their second sixth form year better prepared and with more confidence.'

Retiring July 2006. New head will be Mrs Jenny Dwyer BEd (early forties), currently head of Prior's Field. Educated at Bradford Girls Grammar and then Homerton College, Cambridge. First job at Benenden (teaching/housemistress), then went on to Queen Anne's School, Caversham, where she was deputy head responsible for pastoral care. Young and dynamic, Mrs Dwyer has a warm and charming manner. Married to a 'very supportive man', they have two school age sons. Interested in maths and hockey and maintains that pastoral care is her particular passion – a sentiment that is borne out by her pupils at Prior's Field who describe her as 'approachable' and a great listener.

Academic Matters: GCSEs brilliant every year – it is hard to fault a single department. At A level, modern languages (which include Japanese, Chinese, Russian and Italian) are particularly strong (overseas pupils do not hurt the pass rate). Maths comes through with flying colours year after year. Music is astonishing – in 2001, every girl who sat an A level, AS or GCSE music exam received an A (and all the GCSEs were A*!). Art and design produces high flyers, art history less so. In the popularity stakes the prizes go to RS (with excellent results), English (so-so results), history of art and the sciences (physics as ever the poor relation, but much better results than of old.)

Much setting and streaming from 13. Roughly 10 per cent of pupils have ESL lessons and 12 per cent have mild SEN. Teaching staff not what you would describe as 'spring chickens.' A level block system has become more flexible but can still irritate.

Games, Options, The Arts: Stunning art, brilliantly taught in inspiring – if slightly cramped – art and design centre. Head of art is an A level examiner. Each A level candidate has her own fenced-off studio space in the large general art room. Some keen artists appear to virtually live here. Weekend workshops offered on juicy topics eg book-binding, stained glass and paper making. State-of-the-art computer-aided design and manufacture suite opened March 2003. Successful music, with lots of concerts, competitions and trips. The excellent music director shows understanding of the time and dedication that good music requires. 55 per cent of girls take individual music lessons (including singing). Practice sessions time-tabled for girls in four youngest years. The school takes part in the Sherborne Schools' Symphony Orchestra which skims off the cream of musicians from Sherborne Girls, Sherborne Boys and nearby St Antony's-Leweston to produce two stunning joint orchestras. Some girls complain about the music building's slightly depressing breezeblock design, with extra music classrooms scattered far and wide through the school.

Famously sporty, with games 'more than every day!' according to one exuberant 11-year old. Mostly excellent facilities – a proper sports hall, fitness centre, squash courts, Astroturf hockey pitch, plenty of grass pitches and 27 tennis courts. Girls very proud of school's fantastic lacrosse record – 12 Sherborne girls currently on the Dorset/Wilts County lacrosse teams (NB Sherborne Girls is reputedly the only school in Dorset to play lacrosse). Hockey also fearsome. Scattered complaints from girls about the outdoor swimming pool. Many extra activities available but not a great uptake (beyond those that are obligatory). The school is working to encourage involvement, but parents speak of girls sometimes feeling intimidated into non-participation by 'cool' older girls who look down on extra-curricular activities.

Background and Atmosphere: Founded in 1899 – large architecturally undistinguished conglomeration on a 40-acre site on the edge of the town, looking out over open country. The school trades heavily on the perceived benefits of close co-operation with the boys' school nearby – 'the best of both worlds.' Parents, pupils and teachers are all very enthusiastic about the concept. Much to-ing and fro-ing between the schools, with sixth form pupils able to attend courses at each other's schools if the subject is not on offer at their own. The two schools also combine for some activities, two orchestras, GCSE drama and A level theatre studies (not to mention social events) and many girls have brothers at the boys' school. Boys may visit the girls' houses at the weekends and the older girls can visit the boys' houses. Upper sixth girls are allowed into the sixth form bar at Sherborne Boys. Girls have quite a bit of freedom to go out of school and a quiet backwater like Sherborne is a wonderful place for them to gain a little independence. Girls do not wear school uniform on their visits to town. There is currently a push to expand numbers of day girls. Day girls all have a bed at school; they may go home at 6pm though some stay until 8pm.

Pastoral Care and Discipline: Lovely, feminine, homely boarding houses all recently done up or in the process. House loyalty very strong and houses play a big part in girls' experience of the school. All 11 and 12 year olds start off in West house sharing dorms sleeping 3 or 4 or sleeping in cubicles (curtained or walled-off compartments in a dormitory). Thereafter, girls disperse into eight mixed-age houses, though some will stay on in West as their 'proper' house. Meals eaten family-style in each house. Seating plans change frequently to avoid cliques forming. Prefects sit at the head of table, with teachers and other adult staff often joining in. Many cosy touches eg girls get to choose the menu on their birthdays. Sporty house – Wingfield. Most popular – Aylmar. In the upper sixth, girls move into the hotel-like Mulliner, with its more grown-up feel (self-service cafeteria and individual study bedrooms). Exclusion for drugs offenders. One exclusion in past couple of years (a girl caught smoking for a third time).

Pupils and Parents: Mostly homogenised, friendly, gamesy English lasses. Many Services families, diplomats, Londoners with south west connections. Also 11 per cent of girls from Hong Kong and 8 per cent from elsewhere abroad (including British ex-pats). Several pupils referred to tension created by what they perceive as large numbers of pupils from the far east some of whom do not integrate into the school and 'stand in the stairways speaking at the top of their lungs to one another in their own language.' Other comments – 'we feel outnumbered' and 'they are so good at maths.' One or two girls expressed concern that too many foreigners would be a turn-off for British parents. Parents, however, are unfazed and like the idea of their daughters making friends with girls from all over the world. School says, 'girls are encouraged to mix and to learn about other cultures.' Old girls – Emma Kirkby, Maria Aitken, Dame Diana Reader-Harris and the first woman to make the board of M & S – Clara Freeman.

Entrance: Scholarship exams, common entrance papers and placing papers. One small form enters at 11, a few girls join at 12 but the majority (three forms) enters at 13. Mainly from Hanford, Port Regis, Hazlegrove, Knighton, Broomwood Hall, Mount House, Sherborne Preparatory, Kings Hall and Cottesmore. About 20 join for sixth form – at least 5 grade B or above GCSEs required.

Exit: Practically all go on to university (usually a good number to Oxbridge), the fashionable choices – Edinburgh, Manchester, St Andrews, Nottingham, Durham, Bristol – all popular.

Money Matters: Fees steep but scholarship provision generous for a girls' school. Range of academic, art and music awards pay up to half of fees, plus bursaries based on need. One all-round award each year worth one quaarter fees. At any givon timo, nearly 100 girls are receiving some sort of award or bursary.

Remarks: A traditional, girls' school sitting next door to a famous boys' school in a charming and safe small town. Dynamic head giving the school the firm push it needs.

SHIPLAKE COLLEGE

Shiplake Court, Shiplake, Henley-on-Thames, Oxfordshire, RG9 4BW

Tel: 0118 940 2455
Fax: 0118 9405 204
E-mail: registrar@shiplake.org.uk
Website: www.shiplake.org.uk

• Pupils: 306 pupils, mostly boys (16 girls in sixth form). 220 boarders • Ages: 13-18 • Size of sixth form: 105 • C of E • Fees: Day £4,445 Boarding £6,590 • Independent • Open days: Normally October with sixth form taster day in January. See college website for more details

Head: Since 2004, Mr Gregg Davies. Fresh from Fettes College, Edinburgh, where he was briefly deputy head before stepping up to lead a complete transformation of Fettes prep school. Joined Fettes in 1989 as schoolmaster and games coach. Has been described to us as 'charismatic and deeply caring' and known for his 'energy, enthusiasm, total commitment and easy charm'. Top class international rugby referee and fine singer.

Academic Matters: Good value-added results. Unfussed by league table ratings – allows pupils to sit exams when they are ready, early or late. One of the first schools to accommodate pupils with specific learning difficulties, 24 mild dyslexics admitted to learning support department each year, pupils drop French to allow for specific tuition. Shiplake seems to have recognised that they had coasted along on their old reputation. Response has included appointment of head of pupil development, 16 subject teachers trained in specific learning difficulties to complement the head of learning support, three new part-time specialist teachers and additional support offered off time-table. Despite all this, reports still reach us of pupils falling through the net and not getting the learning support that parents expect them to receive.

Good overall pupil/teacher ratio – 45 full-time to 306 pupils at last count. Healthy turnover of staff after five to ten years on average. Accommodation provided for about half eases crippling cost of living in Henley area (and helps hang onto them for longer). Classrooms in newer buildings light, airy and well furnished. Good language facilities – French said to be a particular favourite, German replaced by Spanish. Maths and sciences relatively weak (in numbers, not teaching, insists head). An upper sixth boy taking chemistry, physics and biology is a rarity. A boy explained, 'Shiplake is more creative'. Currently a choice of 16 subjects at A level, theatre studies new this year. Girls slowly increasing in numbers, boarding girls from September 2006. State-of-the-art accommodation in new £2 million upper sixth house and broadening range of activities are helping.

Games, Options, The Arts: Well-earned reputation for fine sports – boys put much emphasis on it, U19 Rugby County Cup winners last season. Real strength lies in rowing (see below). Frequent race winners at National Schools Regatta at Nottingham and boys winning gold medals for GB team. Sixth form girls successful competitors in their own right. Extra-curricular rowing club for less competitive aquatic activities. Mixed fortunes at rugby (understandably struggle against much bigger schools but regularly thrash those of similar size. Large, rarely empty sports hall (squash, badminton etc), 25 metre outdoor pool very much for leisure rather than competitive use. Hockey, tennis and cricket all good – derive particular pleasure in taking on rivals Pangbourne. Foreign tours – eg rowing in Switzerland, cricket in Barbados. Plenty of travel opportunities too through CCF (no longer compulsory but still 100 strong), D of E and educational trips to likes of Kenya, Strasbourg and Brecon Beacons. Astronomy, cookery, film club and debating are all broadening the options. Pupils have to choose something extra to do. Head says, 'I don't mind if boys get bored at weekends – I just won't have them getting bored alone, so boarders staying at weekends should have lots to do.'

Art traditionally strong and current artists certainly upholding that. Fabulous work on show around the school and immensely popular A level choice. Music more for fun than a serious career option for most. 'We have a terrifically good jazz band and we hold some great rock concerts,' says head. Part of 19th century water tower sound-proofed for music practice (namely drums, keyboards and electric guitar). Drama productions in own theatre, also an open air show (often riverside) in summer. Good links with local girls' schools. Regular dances with Queen Anne's (Caversham), lots of parties with Wycombe Abbey and 'we flirt with schools in the Ascot area. They like us because our boys are well behaved,' adds head.

Background and Atmosphere: By public school standards, still relatively new. Founded in 1959 by first head, Alec Everett, as school for 120 boys. Opened up sixth form to girls forty years later in response to demand from families for female siblings to attend same school as brothers. Managed to achieve that 'without too many difficulties', girls

boarding from 2006. Head insists mixed sixth form works – boys readily agree. Main building is elegant red-brick mansion which has converted well to school use. Wood panelled Great Hall doubles as dining room and assembly hall (also occasional overspill concert hall), four-bed dorms and study bedrooms above, some with balconies. Breathtaking views over tennis courts and glorious grounds to river. Despite long school days (prep till 9) and wealth of activities, a sense of calm pervades. More recent class blocks and boarding houses blend almost seamlessly with old, also barn and stables converted to theatre, careers room and more classrooms. Large site but all within easy reach. Separate upper sixth centre (College House) providing university-type accommodation. New bursar and new catering manageress investing in dramatic food improvements.

Pastoral Care and Discipline: Very supportive, they all look after each other. Head gives example, 'when a known weak reader is reading in chapel, you could hear a pin drop.' Chaplain delightful, 'genuinely Christian', matrons good at handling teenage problems and will help finding lost socks and laundry (always a problem with children who are dyslexic). Shiplake famed for its caring approach to education and this extends to all school life. Anyone found upsetting equilibrium is given marching orders. Particularly important in small school. 'Very concerned' about bullying and deals with it 'as well as anyone, providing support for all parties involved'. Boys excluded in past for this and drugs offences (sinful Henley nearby). 'I'm certainly not loath to expel,' says head, and parents would vouch for that; does not seem to be as helpful as other schools in finding a new school for the sinner. Allowed back for exams but only on daily basis (no boarding). No drink problem (licensed bar on premises).

Chapel at least once a week for assembly, also on Sunday for those still in school, central to Shiplake. House system organised according to pupils' day or boarding status – ie there's one day house, one weekly, one full boarding and two hybrid.

Pupils and Parents: More middle class professional types than there used to be. Still favoured in Surrey and SW postcode area of London, 'we get more recommendations from SW dinners than anywhere else', head jokes. Around 10 per cent overseas (Russia, Europe, Thailand, Hong Kong and Korea) and some Services. Also strong ex-pat support. Boys appear comfortable and content. Exude confidence, not arrogance. Very polite, relaxed in appearance and keen to help. 'Chaps who leave us will have a confidence about them and a set of values from being constantly talked to about how one should conduct oneself in society,' says head. Some say that boys can lack a sense of destiny and ambition. Famous OBs, Olympic (gold medal) rower Ben Hunt-Davis, Nick Jones founder of Soho House/Babington House.

Entrance: Around 40 feeder schools, no favourites. At 13, interview with head, prep school report and CE (in order of priority). Looking for character, boys who will make the most of Shiplake, rather than outstanding academic excellence. Around 10 taken annually from state schools. Must sit school's own papers in English, maths and IQ. Early assessment for learning problems (contact school around 18 months before entry). External entry at sixth form dependent on interview; at least five C grades preferred. 'We expect people to work and turn people down if I feel they wouldn't benefit or contribute to Shiplake.' Few arrivals at sixth form – reportedly quite hard for some newcomers to fit in.

Exit: Oxford Brookes and Bristol UWE perennial favourites; also Bristol, Exeter, Leeds and Reading. Business studies and art foundation courses both popular choices in recent years as are sport and leisure. Vast bulk of leavers do degrees, diplomas, HNDs etc. Clutch of gap students.

Money Matters: Lack of charge for extras (like rowing and books) make fees pretty reasonable. Scholarships up to third of fees in music, art and sport.

Remarks: Small (fundamentally single sex) school with close-knit family approach. Boys here may not be destined for Oxbridge but charm, good manners and respect for others as well as themselves will get them far. Fills niche as demand for this kind of supportive education steps up in line with increasing academic pressure on pupils in league-chasing establishments. Parents equally supportive and fiercely defensive of Shiplake. 'The school's really brought the best out in our son,' said one. 'It's never let him down.'

SHREWSBURY HIGH SCHOOL

Linked to Shrewsbury High School Junior Department in the Junior section

32 Town Walls, Shrewsbury, Shropshire, SY1 1TN

Tel: 01743 362 872
Fax: 01743 364 942
E-mail: enquiries@shr.gdst.net
Website: www.gdst.net/shrewsburyhigh

• Pupils: 490 girls, all day • Ages: 11-18 • Size of sixth form: 112 • Non-denom • Fees: Junior £1,779, senior £2,455
• Independent • Open days: October and November

Headmistress: Since 2000, Mrs Marilyn L R Cass BA MA (in education management) (forties). Educated at Royal School, Bath. 6 years in WRAC – recruitment, PR, intelligence officer. Travelled all over world with husband, a former naval officer, who now works for charity. Two sons, twenties. Did her degree at Exeter, after children arrived and went into teaching. Previously deputy head at Redland High, Bristol. After four years in post says she could be good for another 11! Unstuffy, articulate, energetic, enthusiastic, no-nonsense and an excellent communicator. Prefers to enthuse and motivate rather than drive but strong expectation of hard work and good behaviour. Expects to know her girls well – teaches geography, PSHE and current affairs at different levels. She and her husband

To Love is to Live

MHS

take the annual ski trip to the Alps – both are keen skiers and are qualified instructors. Girls said that she has 'sharpened up and modernised the school, with a new uniform, a wider curriculum which included psychology.' It is now more formal and structured but also more flexible and broadening.

Academic Matters: Robust academic, top level but with three form entry now planned throughout, it aims for a broad intake, with lots of middle-of-the-road girls. Takes great pride in its impressive academic results – well up from 1999 and four out of five now expected to gain A*/A (GCSE) or A/B (A level) – and the number of girls placed at popular universities but is genuinely concerned too for the underperformers, who are supported sympathetically. There is a small number of dyslexic children – 30 with individual educational plans – who are helped to cope with normal classroom life and the school will 'see them through'.

The academic routine is lively and stimulating and the result is interested, excited children all striving to fulfil their potential. Girls report 'unpressurised but as academic as you might want it.' 'Challenging at the top end but does well with the less able.' 'Lots of after school help from the teachers.' 'Doesn't worry about league tables.' 'Brilliant teaching atmosphere.' So, who wouldn't fit in? 'Someone who wasn't enthusiastic about learning.' Only French and German and Spanish available in languages. Superb IT facilities and music and art and particularly drama (super drama studio) are clearly strengths. On the value-added side, the ALIS Assessment suggests that it is up a full grade from GCSE to A level. Class sizes can rise to 26 but the average is 20. A level forms average 12.

Games, Options, The Arts: Space for games is limited (two hockey pitches for the whole school, though others nearby). While it could not really be described as a 'gamesy' school, more sport is planned for the sixth form and they do have up to 30 county players in a variety of sports. Also holds its own with the best at tennis. Superb sports complex, the Kingsland Centre, opened in 2005. Uses fine facilities at Shrewsbury School – Astroturf, rowing, swimming pool.

Background and Atmosphere: A GDST school, it was opened in 1885 in much older premises along the old town walls, with grounds running down to the river Severn. The buildings are a pleasing mixture of old and new, largely concentrated within one site, but with a splendid new sixth form centre and music school on other parts of the campus. The head has a strong vision for the school and the Cass effect is visible nearly everywhere. It is losing its hitherto rather institutional feel, with brand-new labs and lots of cheerful paint, though the old-fashioned library and some of the classrooms and displays await attention. Two new classrooms have been incorporated in a new sports complex, the Kingsland Centre, which has just been opened. It is joined by the Kingsland Bridge to nearby Shrewsbury School across which there is much to-ing and fro-ing. There can also be found its own popular junior school, with all its own facilities (entry at 4, 7 and 9). Staff, of whom most have been there ten years plus with no sign of staleness, include one or two thirty-somethings to take the culture of the school forward. All like working there. Clearly a good working environment with inspiring and enthusiastic management.

Pastoral Care and Discipline: Not only do all girls have form tutors but in the GCSE years they are individually mentored by other teaching staff. In addition, there are pupil mentors, drawn from the sixth form, who are attached to every form group. Strong House system. Head stresses importance of communication with parents and talking through problems which are handled firmly but sympathetically. Head says, 'children need to expect anything in life and cope – to persist and not give up – they need a culture of achievement.'

Pupils and Parents: Girls confident, out-going, assured, friendly, cheerful, with a strong sense of community and greatly supportive of each other. There is a wide social mix, with children drawn from the 'county set', professional classes, business and farming and from new industries in Telford. It is a very popular option for staff at nearby Shrewsbury School and the headmaster's two daughters attend. Girls come from wide radius – Ludlow, Telford, Bridgnorth, Wolverhampton.

Entrance: Its popularity locally ensures a good stream of able girls and it can afford to be selective, though projected increases in numbers give a chance for the not-so-academic. It is largely fed from its own junior school (a certain amount of filtering here). The rest of the intake come from prep schools and some thirty odd state schools.

Exit: Some leave at 16 – to sixth form college and to co-ed and girls' boarding schools. All go on to some form of higher education at 18 and the large majority ends up at university, with at least half a dozen going to Oxbridge.

Money Matters: Fees - extremely modest and wonderful value and, unlike most except other GSDT schools, include almost everything (exam fees, personal insurance, external careers advice etc.) Bursaries available.

Remarks: Strong academic girls' school but with plenty of time and space for the ordinary mortal as long as she is enthusiastic about learning. New head doing great things.

SHREWSBURY SCHOOL

The Schools, Shrewsbury, Shropshire, SY3 7BA

Tel: 01743 280 552
Fax: 01743 351 009
E-mail: enquiry@shrewsbury.org.uk
Website: www.shrewsbury.org.uk

• Pupils: 695 boys; 565 boarding, 130 day • Ages: 13-18 • Size
of sixth form: 285 • C of E • Fees: Boarding £7,180; day £5,045
• Independent • Open days: None

Head: Since 2001, Mr Jeremy Goulding MA (early fifties).
Previously head of Haberdashers' Aske's (from 1996), and
before that Prior Park, Bath. Went to school in
Nottinghamshire, then Magdalen College, Oxford, where
he started to read classics, then switched to philosophy
and theology. Keen sportsman and accomplished cellist.
Taught at Abingdon and Shrewsbury. Married to Isobel, also
a philosophy and theology graduate; four children. Very
able and experienced, calm and reassuring, with a twinkle
in the eye. Inclusive management style – he heads a very
strong staff team – but not afraid of decisions. Delighted to
be back at Shrewsbury. Took over from charismatic Mr Ted
Maidment, who did the school a lot of good.

Academic Matters: Very sound across the board,
does very well for average as well as scholarly. English and
maths remain popular at A level; all three sciences and
geography healthy. School team recently represented UK
in recent successful International Young Physicists
Tournament. Many other successes in physics and maths
Olympiads. Art spectacular, backed up by trips to everywhere including Italy and USA (with history department);
classics and second and third languages well supported,
also RS and business studies. Wonderful Jacobean library.
AS pattern is four subjects, turning into three at A2. Boys
can cope with this in the boarding school day; staff are
becoming more familiar with the new exam. They give off an
air of confidence about this kind of thing and certainly aren't
bullied by the currently faddish assessment culture.

Learning support available for mild dyslexia, dyspraxia
et al; ok for the mild wild (ADHD, Aspergers). If pupils arrive
at school with an edpsych's report then they get free remedial help for the first term, thereafter it costs. Keen on boosting morale, and helping youngsters to 'work through'
dyslexia (it happens). 15/20 per cent of school has some
form of help, one-to-one and regular drop-in clinics. No big

deal. Moderate ok for handicapped, new house wheelchair
friendly, but still stairs. 'The odd disabled child not a problem,' can cope with visually and hearing impaired, with
assistants if necessary. SENCO plus six fully trained staff
plus one dedicated EFL teacher.

Games, Options, The Arts: Famous for rowing (marvellous facilities on the Severn, representation at national
level), and strong on cricket and most games. Soccer is
main winter game; cross-country club – 'The Hunt' – claims
to be oldest in the world. Just about any sport can be played
somewhere on the 100-acre plus site. Music very vigorous,
now housed in state-of-the-art new Maidment Building;
professional string quartet in residence. Drama strong –
home-grown musicals transfer every other year to the
Edinburgh Fringe. Lots of theatre trips – Birmingham (1
hour) and Manchester (11/2 hours) theatres within day-trip
reach. Wonderful Jacobean library. Many visiting speakers;
despite idyllic setting, the school does not feel isolated.
There are two management conferences a year, and each
year one young graduate from Harvard and one from
Bordeaux University come on a teaching fellowship. The
annual Salopian Review, written by pupils, is a mature and
stimulating production. Well-known for outward-boundish
activities – camping, fell walking, leadership, based on
school's farmhouse near Betws-y-Coed; and serious
community work centred on Shrewsbury House youth club
in Liverpool.

Background and Atmosphere: Founded in 1552 and,
at one time, reckoned to be the biggest school in England;
revived at the end of the 18th century, moved in 1882 to
present position, across river from town. Beautiful, spacious
campus, vistas everywhere, boys seen scudding about all
over the place. Grounds superbly kept. Classrooms
upgraded recently, now starting on boarding houses again
(emphasis on quiet space for individual learning). Day boys
have their own houses with studies. Houses in general very
strong, excite tremendous loyalty. All staff engaged in personal tutoring one way and another, very committed; 'a 24
hours-a-day community,' says Mr Goulding, where mutual
responsibility is clearly understood. 'They learn how to tolerate adults,' remarked one teacher. Staff and pupils do
appear to treat each other in an enviably grown-up way.

All meals are now cafeteria-style, doubtless to the
regret of some, but the food is good and the noise level
acceptable. Sunday chapel plus sectional assemblies.
Several school buildings available for outside use, concerts,
lectures, summer activities; headmaster is keen not to be
seen as 'the posh school on the hill'; in fact relations with
local schools are generally good. Some drama and music

with Moreton Hall, Shrewsbury Girls' High and Shrewsbury Sixth Form College.

New outpost in Thailand, Shrewsbury International School, on the Chao Phraya riverfront in Bangkok, opened September 2003 with a roll of 670, ages 3-18; cost £29 million. Follows 'same curriculum as its English original' with masses of exchanges of staff and pupils. Two reps from Shrewsbury sit on Thai school board. Headmaster Stephen Holroyd – former deputy head at Shrewsbury.

Pastoral Care and Discipline: Excellent house system picks up most personal problems, backed up by sanatorium and counselling service if needed. Boys choose their own tutors for the last two years. Good relations with parents. Headmaster takes firm line on drugs – expulsion in clear-cut cases and it doesn't matter whether the offence took place in or out of school. Little if any bad behaviour reported in town.

Pupils and Parents: Remarkably poised and civil young men as a rule; a recently appointed master was asked (genuinely) if he was enjoying his new job. Perhaps not as edgily sophisticated as in some urban schools, but none the worse for that. Parents come from a vast catchment area – many from West Midlands and Marches, also Yorks, Lancs, London, East Anglia and Scotland. Lots of sons of Old Salopians – loyalty a strong point. Pretty Middle England, really. Interesting list of former pupils includes Sir Philip Sidney, Sir Martin Rees (Astronomer Royal), Charles Darwin, Michael Heseltine, Richard Ingrams, Willie Rushton, Paul Foot, John Peel (ask to see the 1552-2002 'scrapbook').

Entrance: By CE, but the lists are pretty full, and early registration is recommended (before age 10). Many boys from top prep schools for miles around, especially Abberley and Prestfelde, also Malsis, Bramcote, Lichfield Cathedral School, Locker's Park, Aysgarth, Yarlet, Moor Park, Packwood Haugh and Kingsland Grange and increasingly from the home counties. Sixth form entry via school's entrance exam plus specified GCSE grades. No open days, all done six days a week by interviews with characterful registrar (ex-English master).

Exit: Almost all to university, a good number to Oxbridge.

Money Matters: Seventeen academic, four music scholarships at age 13, two at sixth form. Fourteen boys supported by Shrewsbury Foundation, and 200 on bursary support from the school.

Remarks: Remains one of the strongest boarding schools in the country, about which we hear virtually nothing but good; 'a school wholly at ease with itself,' says one experienced observer. Has a good blend of tradition and forward-looking attitudes, conscious of the temptation to complacency and works hard to avoid it. Leavers are confident and mature. A connoisseur's choice, and well worth slogging up/down the motorway to get to it. NB Girls from September 2007, new boarding house, sixth form only, both boarding and day; no more than a hundred, though that could be a few years hence.

SIBFORD SCHOOL

Linked to Orchard Close in the Junior section

Sibford Ferris, Banbury, Oxfordshire, OX15 5QL

Tel: 01295 781 200
Fax: 01295 781 204
E-mail: info@sibford.oxon.sch.uk
Website: www.sibford.oxon.sch.uk

• Pupils: 391 boys and girls; 75 board, the rest day • Ages: 4-18
• Size of sixth form: 67 • Quaker • Fees: Day £1,879 - £2,986; weekly boarding £4,033 - £5,403; full boarding £5,688 - £5,802
• Independent • Open days: Twice a term

Head: Since 2004, Mr Michael Goodwin (late forties), married with four children, and fluent in Spanish, who came from Sheringham High School and sixth form centre in Norfolk where he was head for five years. Says he felt drawn to Sibford as soon as he saw job advertised. Has big plans for school, starting with asking parents about school's strengths, their perceptions of it, changes that could be made. 'I felt the school was very special and the interview process comfirmed that for me. There is a wonderful atmosphere and ethos to the place.'

Academic Matters: Sibford is a 'gentle nurturing school' and follows the National Curriculum – with enhancements – 'more suited to our pupils' needs and talents'. There is a strong and well-known SEN department, though not more than a third of the children need remedial help, 'though sometimes, because we are good at catching dyslexia, we recognise it when it wasn't previously diagnosed and the numbers go up a bit'. However, A, AS, levels, GCSEs, GNVQs and Certificates of Achievement are regarded as equally important. The 30 per cent in the remedial stream include those with dyslexia, dyspraxia, the odd Asperger's, as well as fragile children plus refusers and those who have been bullied elsewhere – 'we are so thrilled when they break the rules'. A maximum of five pupils in each year are admitted to the learning support department and the tiny well-stocked specialist rooms only have six-sided tables. Pupils follow the mainstream curriculum, being withdrawn on a regular basis from French.

Laptops important and pupils encouraged to have one, but computers throughout, though in banks rather than dotted around – 'the staff said it was a distraction'. Internet/intranet/networked. School is trialing voice recognition software. The academic side is on the up, though university results won't set the world alight, 'it is more important to raise their self-esteem'. Having said that, this is a school where the children do hold their heads up high, look you in the eye and say hello. The normal GCSE syllabus includes English lang, possibly English lit or media studies, maths and double science plus a whole raft of options including business studies, DT, IT, music, art, textiles, drama et al. School keen to 'identify talents' and encourage self-esteem, 'GCSE results day absolute magic. Pupils who might previously have thought themselves worthless, can then judge themselves on the same basis as others.' Results surprisingly good 'by their own lights'. 'Any child who does the course can take the exam – if they want to and personally feel up to it'. Sibford is not really a high-flying school. Countryside and environment, for which the school is famous, can be taken in conjunction with single science. Numerous A level courses on offer at sixth form and can be mixed and matched with vocational qualifications. Large English as an Additional Language department, particularly well subscribed at sixth form level; pupils take EAL exams and work in tiny classes of eight.

Games, Options, The Arts: All the normal trad games are played in regular matches against other schools plus (very special this) dyspraxic children practising balancing on their tummies on fat skate boards and zooming around the gym like turtles, with dyspraxia specialists on hand, for fine motor control. Large sports hall, squash courts, proper playing fields and recently-opened swimming pool.

The arts are 'confidence building, and underpin the Quaker ethos – all have a right to be seen and be heard'. Drama, art and music are of first importance and during our trip round we found no fewer than five different groups rehearsing some form of theatrical entertainment. Art is taught in conjunction with textiles, design and technology (wood cutting is good for measurements), and music is everywhere. The aim is for children to find self-expression and give them 'wings with which to fly'.

Background and Atmosphere: School originally founded in 1842 and the charming motley collection of Cotswold stone buildings 'on the hill' were put up in the thirties. The school itself is fairly pedestrian – passages with add-ons, some spanking new boarding houses (boarding numbers down and extra houses have already been sold), staff houses look like impoverished farm workers' dwellings, contrast with Orchard Close and super duper new art and music blocks – very state of the art. Fabulous 98-acre grounds.

Masses of flowers and plants everywhere – as you might expect – and it appeared as though the Triffids were on the march, as tractor after tractor came trundling down with ever more impressive collections of greenery.

Pastoral Care and Discipline: Very strong Quaker ethos, but having said that, head locked her door when we left to go on our tour. Self-discipline and treating others with respect emphasised – 'you only abuse once', which means great freedom but, if bullying does occur, authority 'comes down like a ton of bricks'. 'Two strikes and suspension, three strikes and you're out'. Fatigues (not Quaker PC) for smoking, one warning for drugs and booze then suspension; immediate out for trading or providing. Head has only had to expel twice in three years – this is not a very streetwise place. Tutors, but every child has someone in whom they can confide.

Pupils and Parents: A mixed bunch, from those who come daily and use the school like any other, to those – often quite grand – whose children come for the special needs department. A small tranche from overseas, both for the English language department and for the special needs facility.

Entrance: Fairly relaxed at Orchard Close, though children needing help have an educational psychologist's report and an IQ test. Pupils are generally accepted if the school has the necessary staffing and provision in place to deal with specific problems and they will do their own assessment if necessary.

Exit: 'Pupils usually go to the courses they want to.' Strong emphasis on performing arts and art foundations courses, music, business and language courses or straight into employment. Majority of Orchard Close pupils go through to the senior school but some still opt for Cokethorpe, Bloxham or other local schools.

Money Matters: LEAs' contribution appreciated, otherwise not a rich school but host of scholarships at all ages, including special Orchard Close and dyslexia scholarships.

Remarks: This is a school highly thought of by parents with children needing special help either because of learning difficulties or because they find 'ordinary schools' daunting and over their heads. Friendly, fun and could be just the ticket.

SIDCOT SCHOOL

Linked to Sidcot Junior School (The Hall) in the Junior section

Oakridge Lane, Winscombe, BS25 1PD

Tel: 01934 843 102
Fax: 01934 844 181
E-mail: admissions@sidcot.org.uk
Website: www.sidcot.org.uk

- Pupils: 350 boys and girls; 146 boarders • Ages: 11-18 • Size of sixth form: 118 • Quaker • Fees: Day £1,250 - £3,330; weekly boarding £5,350; full boarding £4,850 - £7,200
- Independent • Open days: First Friday in October and first Bank Holiday in May. Scholarship and test day last Saturday in January

Head: Since 2001, Mr John Walmsley BSc PGCE (fifties), educated Leeds and Lancaster universities, is a veteran traveller who taught at Mexico City International School before becoming head of IT at Simon Langton Girls' School Canterbury and deputy head at Sidcot in 1998. Married to Barbara, a stonemason and teacher, has James 14, Dominic 12, William 7 and Cissy 4. An engaging man with razor-sharp perception, was chosen against high calibre candidates while holding post of acting head. Seems like the one-school-head sort; teaches Octopush, scuba dives, enjoys cooking, cinema, music. Although not a Quaker, his father was one and he is currently an Attender (one who attends Quaker meetings). 'I want our students to engage with the world, to forge links across international boundaries and religious divides,' he says.

Academic Matters: A rare breed of school; excellent exam results within a holistic education. Ratio of staff to pupils is 1:15 and drops to 1:7 in sixth form. 65 per cent A/B grades at A level but some students take exams a year early and so don't show. In the last five years five students have been amongst the top five in the country for maths and music. 25 A level subjects. Bucks the national trends with boys doing as well as girls at GCSE – says it's because they don't have peer group pressure problems.

Highly successful English as a Foreign Language centre recently integrated into school campus, teaches intensive English language/business English/ IT to up to 25 students at GCSE while maths, science, games and arts subjects are taught within shared classes amongst rest of school. Latin taught from 12 onwards.

This isn't a special needs school but they don't shy away from pupils with SEN. Dyslexics well catered for with provision monitored by CreSTeD. Lots of successes too: recent head boy and head girl got straight A grade A levels, one had dyslexia other didn't, yet the one with dyslexia had been written off by a previous school as someone who'd never achieve academically. Say it's not unusual for dyslexics to get top grades though not all do. Recognise for some, lower grade passes represent great achievement and massive success.

Games, Options, The Arts: Perfect place for a child and horse who will not be parted. Own stables on site. Though all students are encouraged to participate in wide variety of sports, compulsion does not fit with Quaker ethos. Competitive teams for rugby, football, cricket, hockey, basketball, rounders, netball, athletics on 20 acres of playing field, three short tennis courts and lush heated swimming pool. Recently Kate Reed was middle distance England runner. Vibrant table-tennis tournaments, Octopush, canoeing, fencing, riding, dry-slope skiing, golf, competitive squash, skateboard ramp and 60 activity clubs offer everything from chess, Judo, photography. Hot on public speaking, Environmental Action Group and United Nations Club.

Music school built in 1957 has lunchtime concerts for parents and locals to air the two choirs, a jazz group and the school band 'Crumpet'. One in three play instruments and 20 per cent of students learn instruments to diploma. Several go on to music colleges. Around 3 a year to Royal Academy. Innovative textiles department

Background and Atmosphere: It is unusual to find a school of this calibre of which so little is known. Facilities are good and current population scant because of last head being Bob-the-Builder variety, extending buildings rather than numbers. Library and luxurious sports centre donated by OB from the Cullis family. State of the art canteen. Impeccably kept gardens amid 150 acres of Cheddar countryside, buildings purpose built over 3 centuries provide spacious labs/classrooms. Five un-ritzy houses on campus. Resident staff are often couples with own children so family atmosphere prevails. Does well from its inheritance – 'we sold a field for £2 million last year,' comments head.

Founded in 1699 when Quakers in the west of England set up schools to educate their children in liberal, intellectual, tolerant ideology. Equality of sexes and critical enquiry valued from year dot. Though only 15 per cent of school are now Quakers, ditto staff, emphasis on nurturing the individual and exploring potential are key to their ethos. Morning meeting based on silent worship begins each day though pupils can and do address the meetings. Strong community feel with lots happening at weekends. No Saturday school. Quaker schools celebrate and respect differences so the 10 per cent with SEN issues have high self-esteem, know they can achieve, are valued and have many fine examples of others with similar difficulties leading the way.

'Sidcot pioneered the teaching of sciences by allowing students to partake in lab experiments,' says a chirpy physics head. Visual impact of the place not lost on pupils. Art students designed a circular stained glass window for dome of new library; younger ones worked with interior designer for an eye-popping common room in indigo/saffron yellow. 'It's a very pleasant place to work; people come and stay,' say staff, 11 of whom have stayed more than a decade.

Pastoral Care and Discipline: 'College of Teachers' confers on important decisions. Teachers live by example so that 'nothing should humiliate any pupil or their religious belief'. This is obvious in relationships between pupils and staff. 20 upper sixth prefects called 'office holders' organise social events and seniors involved in running their own houses. Current head boy from Saudi, previous head boys from Russia and Thailand. Bad behaviour dealt with by Quaker gentleness rather than by stamping on it.

No alcohol served on premises though Quaker ethos does not forbid it. Not druggy. Much care taken over transition from junior, and new pupils given pupil mentor to break them in gently. Guardians arranged for foreign pupils. School choir includes staff and parents too. Barbecue parties each Friday evening at the swimming pool.

Head and staff switched on to the needs of all individuals. Recognise a child with a prestigious talent may not be straight down the line, won't fit in neatly or think as majority do but will make own way with help, support and guidance. Recognise some aspects of SpLDs are an advantage; help a child think outside the box, won't write children off, use role models where they can including parents. Say parents who chose it for 3 very different types of offspring – 'it is unusual to find a school which takes itself seriously academically to be this kind and caring, particularly amongst the Bristol 'hothouse' schools'.

Pupils and Parents: Not a flash school despite some well-heeled customers. Popular with media/arts folk. 25 nationalities making up 20 per cent of the pupils. A school bus and flexi boarding attracts 75 per cent locals from Glastonbury, Yeovil, Frome, Bristol. Pupils in uniform of blue and white striped shirts and grey skirts/trousers seem happy and confident. Old Scholars: Sir George Trevelyan, Robert Shackleton, George Palmer (Huntley & Palmer) historian Edmund Ashby, Justin Webb and some of younger Dimbleby clan, Zoe Wanamaker, Tim Bevan, Deborah Warner (RSC director), one of the Baroness Millers.Each

Easter old scholars gather for a week's pow-wow when pupils put on concerts/theatricals/art exhibitions. The snappy and professional newsletter, Sidcot Matters, that keeps track of recent OS successes and school news, can put to shame many a school magazine.

Entrance: Automatic entry from junior school. Entrance test at 9 and 13 can be taken at applicant's present school. Common Entrance as possible alternative to school's own entrance exam in February. A taster day and night can be arranged. Entrance to sixth form needs 6 GCSEs though the school reserves the right to be flexible. Students of EAL can enter any time of year. A genuinely mixed ability school, handful of students has a range of needs: exceptionally bright, gifted and talented, dyslexia, dyspraxia, dyscalculia, Aspergers, ADD, ADHD and physical difficulties (improved wheelchair access on cards). Looks at every single child, takes those who'll benefit from school and give a bit back, though severe SEN cases may be better placed in specialist schools; only has room for occasional child requiring a learning support assistant.

Exit: Geared up to finding right course at right institution, however talented a student. Recently helped a very bright dyslexic student who wanted to study medicine find a course with a practical bias (a great comfort to those of us who'd rather be opened up by a surgeon with a steady hand and good eye than one who's a whiz at spelling!) 70 per cent to select universities: LSE, Imperial, Exeter, Manchester, Leeds etc. 4 per cent to Royal Academy of Music and music colleges. 20 per cent to art foundation/art colleges, a couple to Oxbridge.

Money Matters: Eight academic scholarships at years 6 and 8 worth up to 25 per cent of fees. Exceptional candidates may get awards younger. At sixth form 10 major scholarships for pupils inside or outside the school planning on 3 A levels. Music and arts scholarships at any age for outstanding youngsters on basis of portfolio/sculpture. Six other Quaker schools in UK contribute to a fund, which distributes up to 80 per cent bursaries to Quaker families.

Remarks: An international boarding environment in a safe and secure community where every teacher can know the name of each pupil. Ideal for a bright child who might shrivel up in a pressured environment or one who needs creativity unlocking.

SIR WILLIAM BORLASE'S GRAMMAR SCHOOL

West Street, Marlow, Buckinghamshire, SL7 2BR

Tel: 01628 816 500
Fax: 01628 816 501
E-mail: enquiries@swbgs.com
Website: www.swbgs.com

• Pupils: 1,000 boys and girls; all day • Ages: 11-18
• Size of sixth form: 135 • Inter-denom • State

Head: Since 1997, Dr Peter Holding MA BA MA(Ed) (early forties), educated in the United States. Previously taught at Rugby and then went into state comprehensive system before taking over this co-educational grammar school. Married, with no children. Considered innocuous and extremely approachable and liked by the children – Ofsted described him as 'very effective'.

Academic Matters: Entry is selective and pupils must be self-motivated. A wide range of subjects taught to GCSE including a choice of three languages and there are strong links with foreign schools. 45 points required at GCSE and A or B grades for chosen AS subjects to secure entry to sixth form. Requests for fresh subjects are welcomed but all students are expected to take critical thinking as a fifth AS. Most pupils then drop to three or four A2s plus general studies at AS.

Games, Options, The Arts: All students are encouraged to take at least one sport from the wide selection on offer but both hockey and rowing are played to national and international standard. Excellent art department with practice in different mediums and the option for foreign studies in this area at sixth form level. The music and drama departments are equally strong, again with chances for trips home and abroad. Prospects for using talents with orchestral ensembles, jazz, rock, gospel choir, drama and choreography. Pupil-driven performances with frequent major and minor concerts and productions all year round. Nevertheless tickets for plays and musicals need to be secured early to avoid disappointment. Creativity is encouraged and children can be found just leaping on to the platform dying to perform. D of E, Young Enterprise and World Challenge.

Background and Atmosphere: Founded as a boys' school in 1624 by Sir William Borlase in memory of his son. Even now as a co-educational grammar school its long-term future is safeguarded by a Board of Trustees. Buildings still on original site, very public schoolish, without the fees but with courtyards, cloisters and private chapel. New additions have been sympathetically added to this listed brick and flint building to provide excellent facilities overall. Special little picnic areas with tables, chairs and umbrellas for shared lunches. Children gathered together chattering with ease. Currently planning major new development to provide design centre, performing arts facilities and sixth form centre.

Pastoral Care and Discipline: A happy caring community with good discipline policies and pupil counsellor system. Bullying is not tolerated.

Pupils and Parents: Children do not feel compelled to conform to fashion modes. Instead, individuality is respected and creativity admired. Strong PTA.

Entrance: At 11 by county exam with only top 25+ per cent admitted from local catchment area – the school is now one of the most over-subscribed grammar schools in the county. A further limited number of places become available for sixth form for suitably qualifying candidates.

Exit: A good number each year to Oxbridge and other established universities. The Times in 2003 rated the school 16th nationally of state schools getting pupils into Oxbridge.

Money Matters: Very lively, active and supportive parent association enabling the school to purchase resources that they would otherwise have to go without. Where possible all parents are expected to make small annual contribution towards the general school fund, and there is also a strong voluntary covenant scheme in place. The Old Boys too have established a trust for long-term projects.

Remarks: Maybe not an academic hothouse, but achieving results at the top end of county grammar school tables and turning out confident, responsible individuals. Parents choosing not to put money into education but rather into property to secure catchment area points will be making an excellent decision providing their child can make the grade at 11. Past and present generations are proud to be able to say they went to Borlase.

SIR WILLIAM PERKINS'S SCHOOL

Guildford Road, Chertsey, Surrey, KT16 9BN

Tel: 01932 574 900
Fax: 01932 574 901
E-mail: reg@swps.org.uk
Website: www.swps.org.uk

- Pupils: 555 girls, all day • Ages: 11-18
- Size of sixth form: 125 • Non-denom • Fees: £3,111
- Independent • Open days: October and July

Head: Since 1994, Miss Susan Ross BSc (fifties), read physics at Manchester. Previously deputy head and head of science at Godolphin & Latymer. Very approachable head. Although she's been with the school for a while, she moves with the times and understands the changing needs of her girls. Her plans for the school are well thought out and parents say 'she's spending money appropriately'. An efficient manager without losing the personal touch – she remains strongly involved with pupils and staff. Parents say she doesn't allow things to get out of control but takes 'prompt and fair action – she's good on discipline.' A much praised head.

Academic Matters: Academic standards are consistently good, though the school does not aim to be an academic hothouse. Miss R says 'We have very many bright girls but there's room for not just the academic child but the sporty and musical one too.' She wants her girls to find the academic work challenging and expects them to do well but she is adamant that their desire to succeed must come from within. The school won't pile on the pressure – they find that the girls push themselves. 86 per cent A/B grades at A level; popular subjects include English, sciences, maths, languages and history. Maths is particularly strong throughout the school, results are very impressive (a refreshing change for a girls' school). Critical Thinking is now a regular part of sixth form studies. Class sizes can be fairly large – average 21, but can get up to 24. Facilities good, notably the language and science labs, and the design and technology facilities are out of this world – another unexpected delight in a girls' school. The ground floor houses loads of machine tools for wood, metal and acrylic work and the first floor has a laser cutter, drawing tables and computers dedicated to CAD/CAM work. Parents comment that the 3-dimensional work the girls produce is 'fantastic.' Home Economics room

on the other hand is due for modernisation, with old fashioned ovens and formica units, but very usable and spacious. There are two air conditioned IT suites – modern and airy and all pupils have their own email accounts.

SEN provision limited, mild dyslexia catered for. Specialist SEN teachers on hand or outside help after school by private arrangement.

Games, Options, The Arts: There's a great selection of sports on offer, from rowing to orienteering, football, volleyball, fencing etc etc. Clubs after school and at lunch time. 'Girls have a go, and enjoy most things and get included in matches, even if they're not very good,' say parents.

Drama very prominent; the performance hall has been impressively refurbished to include electrically operated retractable seating and smoke machines (much to the delight of the drama students). There's also a large dedicated drama room. The performing arts centre has performance rooms with good acoustics, a private drama room and seven music practice rooms, all with pianos. Music very strong, loads of after school music groups (swing band popular). Artwork is bold, bright and creative and very much reflects the girls' own characters. There are two lovely big, bright and airy art rooms, a kiln and print making facilities with a resident print making artist. Head of art encourages the use of lots of different types of media and graphic art is done in the IT suite.

Background and Atmosphere: Founded in 1725 by Sir William Perkins, a wealthy Chertsey merchant. Originally started with 25 boys but a decade later extended education to 25 girls. Moved to present site in 1819. 12 acres of gardens and playing fields. Original 1905 red-brick building has been imaginatively extended to form a figure of eight shape of interlocking buildings with two pleasant courtyards which are a tranquil oasis among the red brick.

Lots of energy and enthusiasm about the place. Miss R says, 'we try to ensure that girls achieve academically but not in an environment that makes them think that only academia is valued.' Very friendly school with good teacher/pupil relationships – 'the teachers are always willing to help; they're concerned, friendly and very welcoming.'

Pastoral Care and Discipline: Head places a strong emphasis on pastoral care with rigorous policies, which parents like. No problem is ignored and staff deal with issues quickly and sympathetically. Fully accessible to physically disabled pupils, to the extent that there are stair lifts on all short flights of stairs where a lift is not available.

Discipline is good and rules are adhered to for things that really matter. Girls comment that you could get a detention if uniform rules are not adhered to, but there's still the odd ladder in tights, scruffy shoes and skirts rolled up. No summer dress – the girls successfully lobbied through the school council. They're now trying for permission to introduce trousers and the only sticking point seems to be the choice of fabric – a brave move in a private school, reflects the head's modern outlook and openness to change.

Pupils and Parents: Large school bus network. Girls are lively, fairly boisterous individuals, who are down-to-earth, friendly and enthusiastic. They like to 'get involved'. Really strong Duke of Edinburgh Award Scheme – usually 50 per cent of the sixth form do gold award and the scheme has its own training room and office. Parents are a cross section – as one commented 'there's a good mix of cars in the car-park. Its not all Porsches and Mercedeses. Some parents are obviously making sacrifices.'

Entrance: Forty per cent come from surrounding state schools, the rest from a wide range of independents. Lots of care is taken over the selection process. (A pat on the back for the school as it will accept girls who are out of year). Parents need to register their interest in the October before the pupil is admitted. Entrance exam is based on Key Stage 2. Maths and English are tested, backed up by report from current school. Girls do need to be academically inclined – it is not for the non-motivated. Entrance for sixth form is at least five GCSEs at grade B or above including English language and maths – and interview.

Exit: A few want the experience of mixed schooling after GCSEs but most stay on to sixth form. Majority then leaves for top of the range universities where maths, science and languages are popular choices. About 5 per cent to Oxbridge.

Money Matters: Fees 'good value for money.' Some short-term bursaries to deal with personal hardship and a Foundation Bursary for one child each year from a state school in the Runnymede area who would otherwise be unable to come here. Some scholarships - academic and musical.

Remarks: A friendly school with a strong, forward thinking head and very good academic standards – ideal for unstuffy girls who enjoy healthy competition and getting stuck into what is on offer.

Skipton Girls' High School

Gargrave Road, Skipton, North Yorkshire, BD23 1QL

Tel: 01756 707 600
Fax: 01756 701 068
E-mail: sghs@sghs.org.uk
Website: sghs.org.uk

• Pupils: 729 girls, all day • Ages: 11-18 • Size of sixth form: 216 • Non-denom • State

Headteacher: Since 2002, Mrs J Renou BA PGCE ATD NPQH (forties), previously vice principal at Landau Forte College, Derby and head of sixth form and design at Djanogly City Technology College, Nottingham. Highly professional and business-like yet warm, welcoming and unassuming; two daughters. Originally from North Yorkshire coast. Design Technology background, clearly focussed on taking the school forward as befits its new spin – 'Engineering the Future'. Encourages girls in the belief that they 'can do anything', readily challenging gender stereotyping. Led the school to specialist status in engineering in 2003 (first all-girls' school to achieve this) to some surprise from staff but support from governors. Proud of the girls, wants them to 'know how to behave in any given situation'.

Academic Matters: Academically selective on intake; girls competitive and hardworking, GCSE and A level results highly impressive. Regular position in top 50 best state schools. Top 25 per cent for value-added (this, given the selectivity, is a crucial measure). Average class sizes vary – 28 in lower school to 18 post-16. All academic subjects strong – no surprises in science/DT focus (girls buzzing with knowledge and interest whilst making complex lighting circuits); home economics still surviving here and art vibrant. French and German taught as standard, Japanese and Russian available as extra-curricular. Post-16 collaboration with nearby boys' school has widened A level options in minority subjects. Some provision for special needs. ICT currently being upgraded, computer suites, a scattering of laptops and interactive whiteboards. Homework club recently introduced and proving popular, mainly for research tasks as internet access can be a problem for those living in the outer reaches of the dales.

Games, Options, The Arts: Not the school for your highly sporty girl, team games and competitive sport limited mainly due to lack of facilities (no sports fields or sports hall on site). Several tennis courts, small gym; aerobics and dance popular. Duke of Edinburgh Awards also popular with North Yorks National Park on doorstep. Music is strong, majority of girls play an instrument; drama popular (in the 'Judi Dench Drama Studio' opened in 1996 by the good dame herself) and increasingly so since scheduling joint activities with the boys' school down the road. Centre of excellence for dance; lectures, workshops and professional performances. Overseas visits popular and encouraged.

Background and Atmosphere: Founded in 1886 as a girls' boarding school. Tight, cohesive campus, space limited; mix of buildings works well and is tidy, attractive and welcoming. Original Victorian and Edwardian houses; sixth form centre housed in recently refurbished large Edwardian house complete with 'bistro' courtesy of IKEA and a rabbit warren of small but useful cubby holes for private study. Extensions include hall, gym, labs and classrooms; current embargo on further building. Parking and access restricted and therefore troublesome, hairy at 4pm.

Hard core of long-established experienced teachers, average age 42, even a few Old Girls of the school who can tell a tale or two about the changes they have seen but remain loyal to the cause. Teachers here have to be of 'high calibre and secure in the knowledge of their own subject' otherwise they are in danger of being severely tested and possibly tormented by these confident, articulate girls – expectations both of self and others are high. Austere portraits of previous headmistresses are a bit of a surprise in modern surroundings but remind the school community that, despite recent innovation, long-standing traditions and history of success are to be maintained.

Rolls Royce plc is a key sponsor of the specialist status but this is not a Rolls Royce school. The academic engine is undoubtedly first class but it lacks the flamboyance and frills. More of a Volvo.

Pastoral Care and Discipline: Communication between home and school quick and efficient thanks to web-based communications package. Parents/staff given access to each other for discussions on progress and homework and extension tasks posted on site for students. Code of conduct and drugs policy rigorously enforced; small amount of bullying especially amongst younger girls with 'wicked tongues' taken seriously and dealt with. Unusual and reassuring lack of lockers – coats, belongings left in cloakrooms, stealing very rare. Active student council requested 'healthier' lunches and the removal of the soft drinks machine in favour of water.

Pupils and Parents: Full range of social and cultural spread on intake. Shy and confident girls do equally well.

Girls are delightfully enthusiastic and eloquent with a genuine social conscience – charities, anti-Iraq war demo ('allowed but with strict parameters' ie school grounds only). Pupils fully supported engineering status spurred on after hearing from the charity WaterAid how engineering had changed the lives of African women. The best thing about the place? A spontaneous and unanimous 'the teachers... because they listen to us'. And the worst? They struggled to come up with one but, when pressed, 'the pressure'. From whom? 'Ourselves – it's the way we all work here but we thrive on it'. These are the offspring of liberal quirky 1960s roots – only the hairstyles and clothes have changed – parents are very vocal, demanding, yet supportive and 'know what they want'; a real mix of middle class professionals, university staff and sheep farmers – free-thinking people who encourage their daughters to challenge, investigate, accomplish something, with open minds and hearts and are quick to leap on the school should it attempt to over-restrain. Local house prices soaring as parents move to secure a place in catchment area.

Entrance: For entry at 11, LEA testing procedure – verbal and non-verbal reasoning tests. Coaching for selection discouraged as less able will struggle here. Priority given to girls living in catchment area, greater competition for those out of catchment.

'How bright does a girl have to be to get in?' is apparently a question that no one ever dares to ask (or answer): it would be easier to obtain classified information from the Menwith Hill spy base up the road than to get an answer to this question. We would say (though the school might not) that girls should have a high pass at 11+, with the ability to attain 9 or 10 GCSEs at A or A* and 3 or 4 top grade A levels. Anything else would be a real disappointment to all concerned.

Exit: 99 per cent stay post-GCSE. Favoured universities – Newcastle, Leeds, Edinburgh, half a dozen to Oxbridge. Notable Old Girls Elizabeth Harwood, opera, Ruzwana Bashir, Chair of Oxford Union 2004.

Remarks: The press loved this school's move to engineering status because the 'blend of girls with engineering' was seen as 'sexy' – forcing a wry smile in this unpretentious market town sandwiched rather quietly between industrial West Yorkshire and the dales. Won't turn heads but it's as sound as it comes, will get your daughter safely from A to B (or rather from B to A*).

SLOUGH GRAMMAR SCHOOL

Lascelles Road, Slough, Berkshire, SL3 7PR

Tel: 01753 522 892
Fax: 01753 538 618
E-mail: office@sloughgrammar.berks.sch.uk
Website: www.sloughgrammar.berks.sch.uk

• Pupils: 1110; mixed, all day • Size of sixth form: 360 equally boys/girls • Non-denom • State • Open days: November

Head: Since 1988, Mrs Margaret Lenton BA FRSA (fifties), a historian. Previously Mrs Lenton worked in a bank and in a solicitor's office after which she became a teacher and taught in Derbyshire, Haringey and Southend, latterly as deputy head at Westcliff High School for Girls. In her long tenure as head, Mrs Lenton has appointed most of the current staff and has transformed the place into one of the best mixed grammars in the country. The Ofsted annual report for 2003/4 included SGS in its highly prestigious list of most successful schools. Mrs Lenton is highly experienced, thoughtful, quietly assertive and a firm believer in order and being tough when appropriate. 'Once you have order you can do anything,' she claims and the quiet and purposeful air of her school bears her out. She stickles over uniform – 'button!' she says as she spots an undone collar and the hole is quickly buttoned up. An eyebrow scarcely needs to be raised over a coat illegally worn inside school – it is off almost before she notices. She is regarded with respect but not fear. 'I take risks,' she says and can cite examples of sticking her neck out for her pupils or her school and getting results. This seems to be appreciated and understood by pupils and parents alike.

Not afraid to buck trends and question established tenets, Mrs Lenton learns from experience and then turns that learning into highly effective teaching practice. Boys and girls, for example, are taught separately in some subjects for the first three years – and achieve more as a result. 'We have driven up the performance of girls doing physics ... boys prefer fact to fiction – we choose girl-friendly and boy-friendly books eg Treasure Island and Jane Eyre.' They have separate drama lessons – 'young men will not perform in front of girls.' The 2004 Ofsted inspection report, one of the most lyrical we have read, noted that there is 'very little difference between pupils of different ethnicity or sex' in terms of their achievement and praises the 'inspirational leadership' of the head. 'The danger is,' she says, 'of

being in a comfort zone. I hope I'm not.' She could be – many would be – but this one clearly isn't. 'My aim in life is to create genuine, independent learners and we're not there yet.'

Academic Matters: In addition to a full National Curriculum programme, school offers a vast range of other options and opportunities. Food technology is popular – 'everyone learns how to make a samosa', as are textiles and languages – modern and ancient – both Latin and Greek are taught here. 15+ other languages also available as extra-curricular options though, perhaps surprisingly, the majority of pupils in the school – those whose families originate from the Asian sub-continent – mainly choose to study the languages and the music of their culture outside school. The sixth form offers both A levels and, since 2003, the International Baccalaureate. 'It's a really good course, it helps you to think creatively and it offers opportunities to those who don't want to specialise', asserts head. School also offers AVCEs in travel and tourism and in business studies – useful qualifications and results are a spread across the grades. School works to a fortnightly time-table facilitating a more-or-less free choice from the huge range of options.

Results in core subjects show a spread, mostly across the A/C grades, with a good sprinkling of A*s, notably in English lit and maths. Very few grades below B in the sciences. In the optional subjects, RS is very popular and the results are exemplary. Food and nutrition also does well – for both sexes. 15 A levels are offered and results seem pretty evenly spread, some subjects being vastly more popular, eg biology, chemistry and psychology, than others. Languages and RS have tiny groups at this level. First IB results expected in 2005 and eagerly awaited. This side of academic life here – as elsewhere – is sure to grow.

Overall, results are more than respectable and indicate a serious and successful approach to learning and preparation for professional life. The plan is that, by 2006, every child will have his or her own Individual Learning Plan – ie a programme and plan of work tailored to their own abilities and aptitudes. This is a dream elsewhere – here it is close to being realised. SEN not a big deal here – few with SpLD – and a SENCO and teaching assistants give, mostly, in-class help. Physical disability catered for though there is no lift but visually and hearing-impaired students are supported as are wheelchair users and few autistic spectrum pupils. Extra support and masterclasses for those identified as gifted and talented.

Smallish library with helpful f/t librarian who works closely with the academic departments. Limited but well-chosen books and extensive fiction section – again well-chosen and well-used, as is the library as a whole. Library also houses UCAS handbooks though there is a good careers library and staff elsewhere. IT is impressive – 'the equivalent of 13 computer rooms' – and the school is 'wireless' so that anyone can access anything anywhere. A system of wall-mounted screens in the corridors keeps everyone in touch with school information. A spanking new website up and running in March 2005 enables pupils and parents to access masses of information from home.

Games, Options, The Arts: Wednesday afternoon is spent on diverse 'activities' such as 'Out and About in historical Slough', digital photography, music composition, bell ringing, health and beauty, first aid, football refereeing, cycle proficiency and sports and languages galore – this is serious 'enrichment'. The 17 sports on offer include all the usuals plus badminton, 'new age kurling', and cricket at which the school is more-or-less unbeaten. School has a good, large, on-site field, several courts for tennis and netball and buses pupils to the Thames Valley Athletics Centre in Eton. Buses also go to the nearby municipal pool, the Montem Sports Centre.

Instrumental music is not huge here but there is a choir and an orchestra and five rock bands. 'They can learn jazz or rock but they have to learn it properly – the rules of composition and so on', says head. Drama also is not high profile but major productions happen in large school hall. Art is strong and painting, drawing, sculpture, cartoon animation, ceramics and textiles all produce lively and attractive results. Super aboriginal work on 'self-identity' on display when we visited. Good woodwork and DT. Artists and writers come and give masterclasses. Provision for all these subjects was described as 'good' in the recent Ofsted. In all these areas, though, as with staff and office accommodation, school suffers from a lack of space. The abilities and enthusiasm are there – more space and facilities could make a huge difference. Projects with local companies eg GSK, provide training and experience in problem solving and the world of work. Young Enterprise students were taking orders for Valentine's Day roses when we visited. They'd been up at Nine Elms at 4.00am to get them!

Lots of trips all over the place – in and out of the country – many linguistic but also scientific and geographic as well as cross-cultural. School has links with another in China and one in Norway. School participates in the British Council's Comenius project to encourage such links.

Background and Atmosphere: The main, two-storey, long building is a classic 1930s design, brick, unbeautiful but practical. Pupils do not admire it nor its add-ons but it is well-maintained and kept in good order. In a quiet, prosperous residential road, lined with well-spaced detached houses – hardly the Slough of unfair repute. Two minutes from the M25 intersection with the M4 and just off the A4 but it feels safe, suburban and very respectable.

We saw far less litter inside the school and roundabout and fewer heaps of back-packs than in most comparable schools. Orderliness is the theme and it is palpable in every class you pass and in the disciplined and purposeful movement of pupils around the place. Some, inevitably, find the regime too rigid but most appreciate it and feel what it does for them. We met two prospective sixth formers hoping to be offered places partly because 'there's no racist fighting here' – unlike at their existing schools.

School institutions are democratic and important. Houses – Herschel, Hampden, Brunel etc, count in the school structure and cultural life as does the exemplary school council which, as in another place, has committees for such concerns as health and safety, learning and teaching, bullying, the school environment and so on. These committees research questions of importance to the school community, report back and their findings and recommendations are implemented. This is impressive democracy and is also part of the school's citizenship programme.

Sixth form centre in converted squash court. Lunch here would not delight health campaigners – a high proportion of pizzas, pies, sandwiches and crisps and a very small salad bar. The least impressive thing we saw on our visit.

One of school's major successes is in the happy co-existence of students from such diverse backgrounds. Head is clear – 'we celebrate the cultural diversity of the school, which is huge, but these are British children'. Many children are bi-lingual and you hear odd snatches of other languages as you move around but head says her parents want the children 'to absorb other languages'. She is keen to unite them in a common British heritage and 2005 sees everyone making trips to Portsmouth to learn about Nelson in the bi-centenary of his death at Trafalgar. 'I said they could have their money back if they didn't enjoy it and no-one's asked for it yet.' School has British Council's International School Award status and is now also accredited as an Initial Teacher Training provider – high level stuff.

A high-flying institution with an atmosphere of high standards and aspirations. School elects 'honorary fellows' – people with no direct connection but who help in different capacities eg in careers advice or support. Ex-head of Eton – across the river – Sir Eric Anderson, came to give the prizes and, when you wait in the school's entrance foyer, a large screen shows the occasion, with staff in gowns all sitting on the platform. Screen apart, this could be a scene from fifty years ago.

Pastoral Care and Discipline: Pupils rise when a teacher enters the room. Lessons are orderly, disciplined, quiet. Pupils move along the corridors in a civilised manner and treat each other and staff with respect and courtesy. Everyone wears uniform. Zero tolerance of drug-taking and stealing but only two exclusions in recent years – for drugs. For stealing – 'I will call the police,' says head but 'we're a pretty honest community'.

Pupils and Parents: Pupils come from Slough but some from Ealing, Chiswick, Twickenham and Harrow and some from as far away as Paddington and Reading. Considerable ethnic mix but the majority is of Indian and Pakistani origin and the rest mostly white Brits. Once you're there it becomes an irrelevance. Most people's first language is English, Punjabi a not-close second. Sikhs, Muslims and Christians in more-or-less equal numbers. Very supportive parents. 90+ per cent turn up to parents' evenings and many support school in diverse ways eg work experience. Former pupils include novelist Susan Cooper, Lord William Bradshaw, transport expert, ophthalmologist Prof Anthony Moore, Olympic swimmer Philip Hubble, Andrew Watts, opera singer.

Entrance: Via Slough 11+ NFER exam. Highly competitive – it's about 5 children trying for each place at 11 and about 3 for each sixth form place. School can afford to be highly selective – 'we're educating people who are going to be the bedrock of the community,' says head, citing the numbers of lawyers and doctors produced during her time there. The 2004 intake came from 67 primaries. For entry into year 12 students will need 5+ GCSEs at C+ for vocational subjects and 6+ good GCSEs at, at least, B in their A level subjects.

Exit: Most to study scientific or business courses. London, Brunel, City, Westminster or other local universities. Some to everywhere from Stirling to Southampton to read everything from languages to aerospace engineering, from history to drama. A few to Oxbridge.

Remarks: Impressive at all levels. Head's aim is 'to be better than we are'.

SOUTH HAMPSTEAD HIGH SCHOOL

Linked to South Hampstead High School Junior Department in the Junior section

3 Maresfield Gardens, London, NW3 5SS

Tel: 020 7435 2899
Fax: 02074 318 022
E-mail: senior@shhs.gdst.net
Website: www.gdst.net/shhs

- Pupils: 635 girls, all day • Ages: 4-18 • Size of sixth form: 166
- Non-denom • Fees: £3,063 • Independent • Open days: September and October

Headmistress: Since 2005, Mrs Jenny Stephen BSc (early fifties), previously head of The Grange in Cheshire. She is married to the high master of St Paul's School and has three adult sons. In her previous post we recorded of her that she is 'highly organised, efficient, purposeful, sees her role as taking the school forward in terms of new buildings and ever greater achievements, and carrying on its tradition of striving for excellence. Commands respect of staff (has introduced successful staff reporting structure) and pupils. Eagle-eyed, in the most charming way possible, and determined. Qualities of leadership shine out of her – could easily be mistaken for a high-calibre government minister. Quotes the Chinese proverb, 'educate the man for the day' to illustrate some of the choices made by the school and its pupils.' Has already discarded the unpopular grading system whereby a set proportion of girls were placed in each of levels 1 – 4 regardless of actual marks, amidst parental cheers.

Academic Matters: As befits one of the most high-profile girls' schools in north London, the majority of the teachers are of the Jean Brodie type – without the picnics. Some are able to instil enthusiasm and interest, even in those students who may lack a natural proclivity for a particular subject. 'The teachers themselves love their subjects and it is infectious. They liberally give of their time during breaks and after school hours,' says a student. Extensive and very impressive project work particularly in the higher years allows students to study themes in art or literature in great depth, giving them a scope for discussion and debate which compares favourably with university level. Students tend to exude enthusiasm for the humanities, while still insisting that all the sciences 'are brilliantly taught', above all, physics. The new science block 'has further encouraged us to take up sciences for A levels,' says a sixth former.

Overall, parents feel that while the first year is quite tough and students are certainly not being mollycoddled – 'my daughter could have done with some more individual care' – as time goes on, and students themselves become more aware of their strengths and weaknesses, increased individual attention is given, with students feeling freer to approach teachers of their own accord. Students and teachers monitor and discuss progress and the agreed targets together. 'As I was preparing for my exams, I felt that both the teaching and the advice given were tailored to my needs,' says a sixth former. However, a parent commented that she does not feel that the school necessarily instils a love of learning.

In terms of results, the school lives up to its reputation. The highest grades are being achieved consistently across all the subjects by a very high percentage of students, both at GCSE level and at A level. Students are not only bright and high-achieving but genuinely motivated, with any student being able to feel prima inter pares.

Games, Options, The Arts: In theory a wide range of clubs and societies – more than 40 – though some eg dance are by audition only and there is some feeling that younger girls could get more encouragement to join in. Girls appreciate being able to make their own choices and prove their independence. Despite the recent acquisition of four acres of sports fields, sport is not a priority for those not in teams. A few sports clubs are open to all but most are for those in squads, and curricular sport tails off higher up the school with year 10 having only one double lesson a week. Sixth form sport now compulsory – options include yoga and rock climbing in association with UCS. Very high quality music, with various choirs and music ensembles enjoyed for performing abroad, sharing each other's company and getting to know how to present themselves in public. Opportunities are increasing, but concentrated on those at the highest level. The more shy and withdrawn girls may well find it harder to establish themselves at first, particularly when surrounded by a large number of very accomplished and self-assured students. 'At the beginning it was tough,' says a recent leaver, 'but gradually competition gave way to friendship'. Overall, friendship figures extremely high on the SHHS agenda, transcending cultural, religious and social boundaries. Links with the boys' University College School up the road are firm 'and fun' says a student, covering projects in music and drama. The head is keen to expand on those. An extremely impressive tradition of self-initiated projects to raise funds for the less fortunate. School trips abroad include language exchanges, a ski trip for year nine and art trips to Italy, but field trips and outings to local museums, galleries and theatres are low on the agenda.

Background and Atmosphere: The main building is Victorian redbrick, complemented by several more modern buildings on a compact north London site, tucked conveniently behind Swiss Cottage.

Pastoral Care and Discipline: A qualified school counsellor is available to the girls on a self-referral basis. Some parents feel that the more everyday concerns are being given short shrift, that they 'are being thrown back into the parents' laps'; the head, however, remarks that the counsellor is simply 'a listening ear'. Students seem to be able to enjoy each other's company and still get on with their studies.

Pupils and Parents: The SHHS girls – who cover a refreshing range of religions and ethnic backgrounds – are bright, well-bred students eager to do well academically and socially. There is a tangible sense of decorum, refined speech, an air of sophistication and good breeding exuded by the students, coupled with a relaxed sense of informality. Walking from one building to another you bump into cheerful groups of girls gathering around walls and niches who are equally happy poring over homework as discussing the latest fashion; girls who, though bright and high-achieving, generally have their feet firmly on the ground, though there have been several cases of girls getting carried away with self-imposed pressure to (over)achieve. OGs include Rabbi Julia Neuberger, Helena Bonham-Carter, Antonia Forest, Fay Weldon, Joanna McGregor.

Entrance: Highly selective. Searching entry tests and interviews. Oversubscribed. Increasingly via the school's own (enlarged) junior school. Many from state schools. Ten or so places at sixth form – to fill leavers' places and new places available to clever girls (entrance exams in proposed A level subjects, plus you need three As at GCSE in your A level subjects).

Exit: Practically all to university – destinations swing considerably from year to year; medicine popular; Some to Oxbridge, one or two to art foundation courses. 40 per cent take a gap year.

Money Matters: One or two scholarships of half fees for girls who top entrance exams, plus bursaries. One (or two) sixth form scholarships (available internally and externally).

Remarks: Friendly, no-nonsense, no-frills, academic day school.

SOUTH WILTS GRAMMAR SCHOOL FOR GIRLS

Stratford Road, Salisbury, Wiltshire, SP1 3JJ

Tel: 01722 323 326
Fax: 01722 320 703
E-mail: head@swgs.wilts.sch.uk
Website: www.swgs.wilts.sch.uk

• Pupils: 920 girls, all day • Ages: 11-18 • Size of sixth form: 310 • Non-denom • State • Open days: September

Head: Since 2003, Mrs Frances Stratton BSc (fifties). Read geology at UCW Aberystwyth, before embarking on teaching at Luton Sixth Form College where she spent 24 years. Moved for five years to Corfe Hills School near Poole before coming to South Wilts. One grown son now working as a project manager. A veteran builder, she has overseen big construction projects in every job she has had, sometimes drawing up the plans herself (speaks of the new mathematics hub here as 'my third maths block'). Has no plans to tinker with the curriculum – 'it's too good as it is'. Together with the head of boys' grammar Bishop Wordworth's – also a geologist – Mrs Stratton has introduced geology as an AS subject. Parents of girls in the lower years of the school describe her as 'fair' and are delighted to be here. Parents of older girls, who admired Mrs Stratton's predecessor, not yet convinced.

Academic Matters: School covered in glory, as you would expect given the selective intake. School points out that its value-added scores are excellent and that its exam results are on a par with far more selective grammars. Academic pressure can be intense, with 12 GCSEs not unheard of for girls in the top sets (head says 11 tops). Don't coach your academically average daughter to get through the 11+ or she is likely to wither here. GCSE results so good it is impossible to fault any major department. No language compulsory at GCSE and only French and German on offer at that level. Separate sciences an option since school became a specialist maths and computing college in 2003. At A level the range of subjects (and abilities) broadens out and some subjects eg Spanish are offered jointly with Salisbury's boys' grammar school, Bishop Wordsworth's, a 20 minute walk away (the schools have synchronised schedules to allow sixth form pupils to get to and fro). English lit the most popular subject for many years, recently overtaken by biology and psychology. Softer subjects fare better than at most schools. Communication studies has been popular and the results ain't bad, especially at AS level for which it received a Good Schools Guide A level award. Economics (offered at Bishop's), which often attracts the intellectually challenged like wasps to a honey pot, managed As for all of its six entrants in 2004. Class sizes look big and feel big, with up to 32 girls per class in years 7-9, and up to 22 in sixth form. SEN barely figures here, though the school is taking steps to improve wheelchair access.

Games, Options, The Arts: Well tried, as the coaches would say, though parents who have been involved with the school for a long time say the quality of extra-curricular activities has suffered as the school has devoted more resources to technology. PE said to be a 'happy department', especially for the younger girls; sport is less vigorous as girls move up the school. Good range offered, including tag rugby, football, gymnastics, yoga/relaxation, hockey. Girls say netball and tennis are strong. Also cricket – school won a national six-a-side indoor cricket competition at Lord's. Some county and even national representation, especially at athletics and lately at specialist sports like canoeing and orienteering. Generous games fields, plus all-weather athletics track used out of hours by community.

Music famously good. Head of music was one of Classic FM's five national finalists for 2005 Music Teacher of the Year and promotes inclusivity ('music for all') rather than elitism (focussing on the most talented). Choral music especially hot, with 120 girls singing in the senior choir. Usual range of orchestras and bands, plus guitar ensemble and recorder groups. Music A level results outstanding and quite a few girls go on to music college or to study music at university. New music block needed and is the next building project looming in the diary. Art thrives. New 'theatre' (more of a studio, really, with seating for 70) is a well-used resource. However, at the time of our visit, there had not been a major school theatrical production in over two years. Much of year 7-9 drama, as well as music and other activities, run by sixth form pupils (pros and con...) Quite a lot of uptake for D of E at all levels, and has won awards for Young Enterprise. Scores of lunchtime clubs (bring a packed lunch to save time) but after school the place tends to empty out.

Background and Atmosphere: Opened in 1927 with 207 girls. Imposing brick main building with constantly improving additions, all in a jumbled heap at one end of the school's large property. Girls beadle along the maze-like paths between buildings – ('it took us ten minutes to get from one lesson to another when we were new!'). Building programme has done wonders and the new sixth form block is a tour de force, its computers gleaming and its 'study centre' awash with comfy sofas. Super new maths block. Science labs a mixture of new and old, improbably interspersed among language classrooms. Good technology – the place is certainly not short of computers. Girls spoke with enthusiasm of their DT projects and we admired the glistening food tech kitchens. Much recent staff turnover (mainly retirement, says head).

Pastoral Care and Discipline: Girls say they feel 'trusted' and relish the freedom they are given. Younger girls in years 7 and 8 seem to be kept out of main school fray (our young guide did not know where the sixth form centre was). School currently winning battle on skirt length.

Pupils and Parents: Not a hotbed of ethnic diversity. Girls come by bus and train from over 50 primary schools – some from up to 40 miles away – plus from a few local preps. Unlike the boys' grammar, which stands alone as the premier boys' school in the area, South Wilts has plenty of local competition from the independent sector, especially from the Godolphin School which narrowly pips it in the A level league tables most years. The sorts of parents you will find at the two schools are almost indistinguishable, a few will have one girl at each.

Entrance: Some 370 girls sit the 11+ and around 110 are offered places (the top 29 per cent of the ability range to be exact). 15 to 20 additional girls are awarded places through South Wilts' review process (eg girls who performed below par on the exam, but whose primary schools can vouch for their indisputable academic ability). A small handful enters at years 8, 9 and 10. Up to 60 girls join at sixth form, mainly from local 11-16 schools; entry requires 6 A-C grades, with a B usually required in subjects to be studied at A level.

Exit: 15 per cent leave after GCSEs, mainly to sixth form college, often because they are tired of commuting a vast distance to school (60 per cent travel more than 5 km to get to South Wilts, many much more). Top university destinations, by far, are Cardiff and Exeter, followed by Southampton, Surrey, Bristol. Usually a good lump to Oxbridge. Surprisingly high numbers into sciences, technology, medicine, engineering etc. Also many to read modern languages.

Remarks: A superb, free education for clever, self-motivated girls. Lacks the imposing atmosphere of Salisbury's boys' grammar, but most parents consider that a plus.

SOUTHBANK INTERNATIONAL SCHOOL (W1)

Linked to Southbank International School (NW3) in the Junior section

Linked to Southbank International School (W11) in the Junior section

63-65 Portland Place, London, W1B 1QR

Tel: 020 7243 3803
Fax: 020 7727 3290
E-mail: admissions@southbank.org
Website: www.southbank.org

• Pupils: 265. 50/50 boys/girls; all day • Ages: 11-18 • Size of sixth form: 80 • Fees: £4,200 - £5,900; plus 'capital development fee' • Independent • Open days: Information sessions in March and November

Head: Since 2001, Mr Nigel Hughes BSc MEd (fifties), who has been with the school (with various sabbaticals in the States and elsewhere) since its foundation by the previous head Mr Milton Toubkin in 1978. Educated at King's, Rochester, and read psychology and cybernetics at Reading University. After VSO in Trinidad, where he taught science and maths, he spent a period in the wilderness with BP and the Tavistock foundation studying behavioural and human relationships, before coming back to teaching. On the steering committee of the UK IB schools and colleges association. Married, three children.

Academic Matters: Southbank follows the IB system, and is run on 'international lines'. Divided into primary (3-11), middle (11-13) and high school (14-18). Small classes; some primary classes as small as ten, dictated by classroom size, but good for early learning. All primary children follow the IBPYP Inquiry method, 'what do I want to know?' etc, they also learn the violin or cello – the Suzuki method. Through the middle years, students follow the IBPYP programme, leading to an IB Diploma for the academic in high school or IB certificates for the less able (though often the school will suggest they go elsewhere to take NVQs or similar). The IB exam results average 32 points over 15 years, 33 points 2004.

Setting occurs in mathematics and languages as well as English as a second language. French/Spanish (German in Primary) the norm, but extra tuition in many other languages possible for an extra fee – Arabic, Danish, Dutch,

Finnish, German, Hebrew, Italian, Japanese, Mandarin, Norwegian, Persian, Portuguese, Russian, Swedish.

IB diploma is now accepted at all universities and the certificate is sufficient for entrance to most of the American colleges at foundation level. Pupils from Hampstead and Kensington may transfer to the high school in Westminster; some joint activities take place between campuses and staff often get together for inservices. Some help with special needs.

IT is important at Southbank, and pupils are encouraged to use the internet for research. School is open from 8.30am, masses of uptake for after-school clubs and societies. Very good university placement advice. No religion as such, though comparative studies regarding 'world religions' are dealt with in humanities.

'No problems' in getting staff, the school recruits internationally, though there are problems for young staff in joining the London housing ladder – 'you really need two incomes to cope'.

Games, Options, The Arts: Art popular and compulsory in the IB syllabus till 15, loads of drama and music. Masses of trips to museums, good use made of local libraries, strong tradition of using 'London as a classroom'. Model United Nations popular and masses of IT. PE and swimming in the Kensington Sports Centre and pupils bused to games pitches. In the high school, soccer, volleyball and basketball are the main team sports. All students joining in middle school or high school participate in a five-day adventure trip as a team-building exercise. Pupils bused – even to the closest venues.

Lots of extra-curricular activities and community service. The whole school gets involved in various projects and recently held a water day – investigating the use globally and locally of water, including sports, and testing the purity of the Thames.

Background and Atmosphere: Originally founded 25 years ago on the South Bank, the school was the first all-IB school in the UK, now located on 3 campuses.

Kensington (3-11 year olds) is housed in 2 Victorian villas. A playground has been created in rear garden and an assembly room, library and other classrooms in an adjoining building. The original houses are now a rabbit warren, subdivided by passages and narrow staircases, the ornamental cornices divided by partitions peppered with photographs and student work. The huge drama/assembly room is part of a building previously used by a car rental company and the rather impressive library was their showroom. Other classrooms have been hived out of the car parking area above. Art room, decent-sized classrooms are interspersed with

tiny rooms for individual tuition. Canteen facility at Westminster or children bring packed lunch. Some children play in Ladbroke Square gardens opposite; the bigger ones are bused to Kensington Gardens at lunch time. No disabled access in Kensington.

The Hampstead building is a purpose-build behind an Edwardian façade (the local planners refused development consent and insisted that the building be retained for educational use). Standing in its own grounds, the campus is big enough for PE etc.

Since 2003, there is a third campus at Portland Place, Westminster in a grade II* listed Regency building and serves as the senior school (11-19 year olds). This has been completely refurbished, with new laboratories and new equipment throughout, canteen. Although no outside space, children are bused to local sports centres (Regents Park is just up the road).

Pastoral Care and Discipline: Good PSE programme in place, no bullying, occasional expulsion – always expelled for dealing in drugs – but the occasional user will be counselled and advised. No history of children coming back at lunchtime 'drunk or stoned'. Counsellors on all campuses.

No uniforms other than for PE, no 'overtly offensive' messages on T-shirts and no hair spec. The pupils whom we saw looked perfectly normal.

Pupils and Parents: More than fifty different nationalities, oodles of ambassadorial kids or those whose parents work for international firms. The largest number from the States, followed by the UK, plus dribs and drabs from elsewhere. Mainly affluent, mainly upwardly mobile parents, who instil in their offspring the same parameters. Most come from within two or three miles of each campus but some come from farther afield and there are buses that collect (with preference given to younger pupils) from all parts of London.

Entrance: Waiting lists for most classes. Admission is on previous school reports/recommendations plus interviews where possible. This is a highly mobile school; average length of stay 5 years, lots of 'short notice departures' and consequent aggro over the requisite one term's notice (usually paid by the company who pay the parent – negotiable), so the waiting list may disappear overnight. Shifting the sixth form to Westminster has allowed an expanded early years' programme in Kensington. Don't give up at any stage.

Exit: Trickle to Oxbridge, otherwise a selection of universities; a lot to the States, plus globally; though more to UK unis than previously – 'pupils tend to stay in Britain'.

Money Matters: Bursarial help on hand for those

whose life styles have dropped dramatically, and a brand new scholarship - the Milton Toubkin Foundation.

Remarks: Brill for the international family, good for those who would like to be, and all those extra languages ...

STAMFORD HIGH SCHOOL

Linked to Stamford Junior School in the Junior section

Linked to Stamford School in the Senior section

St Martin's, Stamford, Lincolnshire, PE9 2LL

Tel: 01780 484 200

Fax: 01780 484 201

E-mail: info@ses.lincs.sch.uk

Website: www.ses.lincs.sch.uk

• Pupils: 612 girls; 55 board, rest day • Ages: 11-18 • Size of sixth form: 180 • Non-denom • Fees: Day £3,004; boarding £5,700 • Independent • Open days: October

Head: Since 2003, Mrs Dyl Powell BEd NPQH, educated at The King's Norton Girls School and Warwick University where she studied physical education and mathematics. She was among the first cohort of applicants to complete the National Professional Qualification for Headteachers in 1999. Previously taught at The King's School in Peterborough where she became deputy head in 1994. Throughout her career Mrs Powell has been involved in a large number of activities, including sport, where she is an international level umpire in hockey and outdoor education. Her enthusiasm for this has already led her into taking up a role within the Schools' Combined Cadet Force.

Academic Matters: Has always been a popular local school but recently the school has lifted its performance. The school has own entrance exam where the final grading is linked to chronological age. Excellent overall improvement in GCSE results over the last four years; art, DT and drama still being the most popular subjects, and excellent results in English, French, geography, maths and science (dual awards). A levels are taught in mixed groups with Stamford School. The 2005 A level results were the best yet with a spread of popular subjects from chemistry, biology and psychology to English, art, history and French. Academic standards are high but there is a caring attitude to students from everyone involved in the school and sixth formers are encouraged to integrate with the younger ones, particularly evident in entertaining fund-raising events.

Of the 56 full-time staff, 30 have been with the school

for more than 10 years with the ratio of staff to pupils being 10:1. Average class sizes are 24 with a small number of pupils with SEN. Only 8 pupils from overseas, though there are more ex-pats' children.

Games, Options, The Arts: Sport is compulsory with netball and hockey very popular in the winter, and tennis and competitively successful athletics in the summer. Very enthusiastic girls' football team and a large sports hall. There is a new artificial hockey pitch on site. D of E popular (trips to Peru, Kenya etc; students are encouraged to raise as much of the cost as possible eg by working in the school shop), CCF (with the boys' school – plenty of enthusiasts, surprise surprise). Popular drama and dance. Charity fundraising much encouraged including staff sports day with wheelbarrow races, slow bicycle race etc. Good numbers for music, with all the usual bands. Concerts in Peterborough Cathedral and the choral society sang in Washington. Plenty of school trips and exchanges – Europe mostly.

Pupils' pictures and pottery all over the school – pop art to still life. Painting, life drawing, pottery, sculpture and DT are all available on site but, for larger DT projects, students can use the facilities at Stamford School. Computer facilities and technical support excellent; large computer room plus electronic white boards; computers dotted around the school.

Background and Atmosphere: On the edge of the spectacular town – setting for many films and TV series, including latest Pride and Prejudice. Part of The Stamford Endowed Schools group which can trace its history back to the 16th century. The girls' school was founded in 1877 and, together with the boys' school and the junior school, is under the direction of a single governing body. The three schools work closely together with mixed teaching in the sixth form. Spacious, with numerous pockets of garden between buildings, one garden for each year group to use but everybody has access to all of them. Both pupils and staff very outgoing and enthusiastic, lots of fun and humour – take a look at the school magazine. Staff put on a spoof Harry Potter production recently and the lower sixth enter tain the whole school annually – sadly not open to the general public!

Boarding houses have a homely feel, bedrooms decorated with posters and other personal effects (with some obvious restrictions). Comfortable common rooms with a good selection of books for use during prep (encyclopaedias etc). Well-equipped kitchen, popular with the students, visits to cinema, ice rinks and other local places at weekends.

Pastoral Care and Discipline: School rules are few and self-regulation is encouraged, with all girls expected to conform to agreed standards of behaviour, punctuality and academic discipline. Should bullying or substance misuse be a problem then this is discussed between the parties. The staff dealing with such matters like to come to a satisfactory conclusion through discussion with the parents and students involved rather than taking automatic draconian measures.

Pupils and Parents: Students come from local schools over a wide area, own junior school, local prep schools and state local primary schools. Buses from Peterborough, Oakham, Uppingham, local villages etc. A few from abroad, notably RAF and Foreign Office Brits, Hong Kong, Germany, Spain and France. Pupils from many different social and economic backgrounds all seem to mix well. Pupils treated very much as individuals and, although it's an academic environment, all who pass the entrance exam fit happily into the school's way of life. Well-balanced and all-round individuals. Notable Old Girls include Lucy Cohu (actress), Sarah Cawood (TV presenter), Kirsty Stewart (RAF, first girl to fly Tornado), Joanna Parfitt (author), and Suzanna Ivens (won the 1988 Dressmaker of the Year Award).

Entrance: Selective, with own entrance exams at 11 and 13, broadly following Key Stages 2 and 3 in National Curriculum. Good GCSE standards needed to go into the sixth form, otherwise students would find it hard to cope.

Exit: Most students go on to university, with just a few deferring for a year. Oxbridge candidates increasing, subjects range from biomedical sciences, philosophy, medicine, engineering and forensic science to English, art, law and languages.

Money Matters: Not a well-endowed school but generous state scholarships available and allocated to 25 students at 11 who have been resident in the Lincolnshire LEA area for the last three years. Other scholarships and prizes from year 7 upwards.

Remarks: Lively boarding and day school, ideal for independently minded children who are self-motivated enough to cope with the good academic standards.

STAMFORD SCHOOL

Linked to Stamford Junior School in the Junior section

Linked to Stamford High School in the Senior section

St Paul's Street, Stamford, Lincolnshire, PE9 2BQ

Tel: 01780 750 300
Fax: 01780 750 336
E-mail: info@ses.lincs.sch.uk
Website: www.ses.lincs.sch.uk

• Pupils: 662 boys, 75 board • Ages: 11-18 • Size of sixth form: 200 • C of E • Fees: Day £3,004; boarding £5,700 • Independent

Head: Since 2005, Mr Stuart Burns MA Hons Cantab, a linguist, mid-thirties. A rugby 'blue'. Previously at Kingston Grammar School, Dulwich College and was senior master and head of boarding at Brighton College. Married to Claire with two children, both at Stamford Endowed Schools. Teaches French and games daily, mostly lower and middle school.

Academic Matters: A sound (the school's choice of word) academic school but the boys are extremely motivated and enjoy their time at Stamford. Maths continues to be the most popular subject at both GCSE and A level and results are consistently As and Bs with 90+ per cent A-C at A level. Other popular subjects with good results are chemistry, English and religious studies. Superb DT facilities, with every machine available for whatever project pupils want to carry out. Very computer-orientated, particularly in the DT department, much appreciated by the pupils. Average class size 22 until sixth form when drops to 14 – 16. Only a small number with SEN. These children are given extra help where needed and encouraged to build on their own strengths.

Games, Options, The Arts: Sport is compulsory and encouraged in the school and hugely popular with excellent sporting achievements, notably two shooting internationals and one chess international. Rugby and hockey are at the top of the popularity stakes after shooting and inter-school matches are held every Saturday afternoon with excellent results both locally and at county level. Cricket, athletics and tennis predominate in the summer but there's golf, badminton, squash and swimming too. Excellent and well-equipped sports hall offering opportunities for indoor games and wonderful Astroturf pitches for hockey in the winter and tennis in the summer.

Long-established connection with the armed forces.

CCF and D of E (run jointly with the girls from Stamford High School) extremely popular, so much so that many boys are keen to join the armed services having had a taster through the CCF. Serving officers regularly visit the school to provide training, and local RAF stations offer flying experience – several flying scholarships each year. Regular expeditions abroad, recently to Peru, New Zealand, Ecuador and Kenya as well as exchanges with schools in Russia and Europe.

A third learns at least one musical instrument and there are plenty of opportunities to join the various orchestras, ensembles, jazz bands etc. Some boys have junior exhibitions at the London conservatoires. The choral society is extremely popular with performances in Peterborough Cathedral and choir trips to Venice, Norway, Spain and Washington DC. Music is encouraged throughout the junior and senior schools with lunch time practices and recitals popular.

Background and Atmosphere: In the spectacular town of Stamford, which has been the setting for many television programmes and films. Founded in 1532, forms part of The Stamford Endowed Schools group with the girls' Stamford High School and Stamford Junior School (mixed). The three work closely together with joint teaching in the sixth form. Voluntary attendance for all the Stamford Endowed Schools at 'Saturday School'- no uniform and a less formal atmosphere. Sports, a variety of languages, drama, art and much more. Not only does the majority of pupils choose to attend, so do some of their parents! Recently refurbished boarding houses, comfortable accommodation.

Pastoral Care and Discipline: All boys are expected to conform to agreed code of conduct – stresses community, contribution, responsibility and respect – agreed to and signed by pupils and parents and reviewed every year.

Pupils and Parents: Best suited to boys with an all-round love of sports and those who are willing to have a go at anything on offer. A well balanced lot, from local schools over a wide area as well as own junior school, local prep schools and local state primary schools. Wide catchment area with buses from Oakham, Uppingham, Peterborough and local villages. 25 per cent overseas Brits, traditionally from the MoD but also foreign office and ex-pat workers. Not a huge number from overseas, but a good variety from Europe, Hong Kong and Poland etc – they mix well and often go on to a UK university. Notable old scholars, Sir Michael Tippett, Sir Malcolm Sargent, Simon Hodgkinson (England rugby full back), Mark Dauban (Olympic hockey gold medallist), Revd Philip Goodrich (formally Bishop of Worcester), General Sir Mike Jackson (Chief of the General Staff) and Colin Dexter (Morse books).

Entrance: Selective entry but not highly so. Own entrance exams at 11 and Common Entrance at 13. Many coming up from own junior school, can go right the way through from nursery to A levels.

Exit: A few to Oxbridge, to read such subjects as mathematics, bio-chemistry and history. Elsewhere American business studies, theology , sports science as well as maths, medicine, history and modern languages.

Money Matters: Not a wealthy school but state scholarships available and allocated to 25 students at 11 who have been resident in the Lincolnshire LEA for the last 3 years. Other scholarships and prizes from year 7 upwards.

Remarks: Generally a traditional boys' school, which has altered significantly, following the introduction of mixed sixth form teaching. Not too academic but the performance of the 25 LEA scholars places the school in the top 50 of maintained schools in the country.

STEWART'S MELVILLE COLLEGE

Linked to Mary Erskine and Stewart's Melville Junior School in the Junior section

Linked to Mary Erskine School (The) in the Senior section

Queensferry Road, Edinburgh, EH4 3EZ

Tel: 0131 311 1000
Fax: 0131 311 1099
E-mail: principal@esmgc.com
Website: www.esms.edin.sch.uk

• Pupils: (SMC) 715 boys (almost all day) (MES) 705 girls (almost all day) • Ages: 11-18 • Size of sixth form: Joint: 220 boys and girls • Non-denom • Fees: Day £2,643; boarding £5,015.
• Independent • Open days: Late September

Principal: Since 2000, Mr David Gray BA PGCE (forties), who was educated at Fettes, read English and modern Greek at Bristol, where he did his PGCE. Taught English in a Bristol comprehensive before moving to Greece to run a language school, after which he became head of English at Leeds Grammar. Mr Gray comes to this vast conglomerate from Pocklington School in east Yorkshire, where he was head for eight years. Brought up in Inverness, he is proud of his Scottish roots and is 'keen to give something back to Scotland, having been away for almost a quarter of a century' – (his father is the wonderful, long-standing, former Conservative MP, now Lord Gray of Contin). Married, he has twin daughters and a younger son. He and his wife live on campus and she is actively 'attempting to make the place like a large family', including entertaining members of staff for dinner (an activity which has not apparently met with universal acclaim). Mr Gray himself spends part of the week in each school. We visited him at his base in Mary Erskine, where there is a strict policy of no coke vending machines; this editor was amused therefore, to see an empty crumpled coke can on the principal's desk when we arrived.

Very much a hands-on head, the principal reckons to keep sane by swimming and jogging at 7am each morning, and is a familiar sight as he cycles between the two campuses. He also 'works the room' quite beautifully, 'we all think we know him well and that he knows our children almost as well as we do,' said one father (a gift no doubt inherited from his politician father?). Keen on promoting self-confidence in his pupils, he sees himself as an 'educator'; 'no man is an island'; interdependence is important here. Mr Gray also admitted that, in a better world, he would prefer 'his pupils not to party during term time' – some hope – and maintains that 'only eleven children have been expelled for drugs offences in Scotland during the past academic year' – it is, apparently all a 'press hype'. (Head says 'we have a Personal and Social Education policy which is important in encouraging well-informed young people to make wise judgements'.)

Pupils slightly dismissive about the new regime, 'he has tightened up on our shoes and our clothes but not a lot else'. All staff wear the school badge – post Dunblane – and yet again, this editor was charmingly challenged by a pupil.

Mr Gray runs the twin senior schools with two deputy heads, and the head of the co-ed junior school, Bryan Lewis, who is also vice-principal. Mrs Lesley Douglas took over as deputy head of The Mary Erskine School in August 2002; she was previously assistant rector at The High School of Glasgow and her predecessor, Mrs Norma Rolls, moves to front up the massive new five-year ICT development programme as co-ordinator and director.

Academic Matters: Boys and girls educated together at junior school, separately from age 12-17, then combine again for the last year at school. 'Not a highly selective school', however described by an educationalist as a 'grade one academic machine'. Classes of up to 25 (20 for practical classes) setted, groups subdivided to extend the most able. School has embraced the new Advanced Higher in depth – greater analysis, independent study, projects and dissertation and recent results show a pleasing number of As and Bs across the board in both schools. 'The Mary Erskine results are outstanding' said the principal, 'particu-larly on the languages front'. French, German and Spanish on offer to Higher Grade but Spanish is not available at Advanced Higher. Latin and Greek on offer, if demand high enough.

From August 2002, Standard Grades phased out in favour of Intermediate 2 (which is based primarily on unit assessments, as are Highers) except in the modern languages and maths departments. Stirring stuff this. Very good links (still) with the Merchant Company who do masses of business breakfasts and links with professional firms around Edinburgh. New IT multiplex in the pipeline, to be fronted up by Mrs Rolls. Biology dept strong links with the horticultural dept of the world famous Edinburgh Botanic Gardens. Impressive careers structure across both schools and excellent library facilities. Pupils can sign in for private study and technology is taken at GCSE level rather than following the Scottish norm.

Schools combine for sixth form, most extras, and pastoral structure – ie you might find one girl doing science at Stewart's Melville and seven boys doing RE at Mary Erskine's. With such a large sixth form, the variety of course permutations is almost limitless, though, as our informant muttered, 'the amount of free time you can wangle by saying you are taking the bus up the road is equally limitless'. Outstanding back-up for those with learning difficulties, school has its own educational psychologist; 'some on Ritalin'; 'will never abandon anyone'.

Games, Options, The Arts: Girls still better at shooting than boys and both sexes join the voluntary CCF (trillions of girls, over 400 members in all) – and at a recent camp in Scotland, produced more candidates than the rest of the schools put together. Super new floodlit Astroturf. Twenty-seven rugby teams; swimming pool (at Stewart's Melville) with dramatic sixth form slump-out room adjacent, new gym (at MES), cricket pavilion (MES again). FPs and current pupils share sporting facilities at MES; mutterings about needing more – but one of the play areas at SMC is about to be developed into a new performing arts centre. Extra games pitches at Inverleith. Needle matches in almost all disciplines; with FPs representing both county and country across the board. Stunning swimming pool adjacent to dining room complex with sixth form centre above for better viewing the SMC pitches.

Incredibly strong drama (regular performances at the Edinburgh Festival and throughout the year – Sir Cameron Mackintosh much in evidence). 600 pupils were involved in Noye's Fludde – (super video) and, more recently, 80 pupils from the junior school took part in Joseph and the ATD at the Edinburgh Festival theatre. Masses of orchestras in every discipline. Pupils can learn to fly, ski (Hillend and the real thing: the Alps, Canada); brilliant debating team (regularly the Scottish Debating Champions, European Youth Parliament finalists) and SMC has represented Great Britain abroad all over the shop. Masses of clubs, for all, lunch time and post school. Popular. Good home economics. Arts spectacular. Dramatic art room atop MES (with adjoining pottery and greenhouse), and art displayed all over.

Background and Atmosphere: Stewart's Melville campus is based round the magnificent David Rhind-designed Daniel Stewart's Hospital which opened in 1885 and merged with Melville College in 1972. Fabulous Victorian Gothic with a cluster of moderately successful modern additions, surrounded by ever-decreasing games pitches and car parks. Huge and impressive school hall. The old chapel is now a library complete with organ and stained-glass windows. Stewart's Melville is also home to the senior department of the junior school – see separate entry.

Mary Erskine was founded in 1694 (originally the Merchant Maiden Hospital) moved to Ravelston House in 1966, changing its name to The Mary Erskine School, and amalgamated with the boys' school in 1978. (Girls wear charming Mary Erskine tartan skirts, with matching Alice bands.) MES clusters in decidedly 1960s architecture – with, now, quite a lot of more modern extensions, round the charming (1791) Ravelston House: swimming pool, tennis courts, games pitches, Astroturf etc. The last much used by FPs. The nursery department and the youngest classes of the junior school are also based here – see separate entry.

Two boarding houses, Dean Park House and Erskine House, furnished like large family houses and based on the edge of the Stewart's Melville campus. Tremendous family feel, boarders are encouraged to invite friends home, caring house parents. No more than 50 boarding places. Lockers for all woefully inadequate in both schools, and piles of bags everywhere. The tarmac outside both schools is hideously covered in blobs of discarded chewing gum, particularly in front of the sixth form centre at Stewart's Melville. School disputes this.

Regular buses from East and West Lothian and Fife service both schools, which operate as one, under the auspices of Erskine Stewart's Melville Governing Council. Each school, however, is fiercely proud of its individual heritage.

Pastoral Care and Discipline: Both schools have a tutorial system for the first year, followed by house system in Upper Schools which is common to both. Good links with parents. Brief is that 'all children have a right to be happy here'. Excellent anti-bullying policy, keen on 'children not slipping through the net'. Sophisticated PSE programme right up the school, including study skills. Buddy system for those coming up from junior schools. Automatic expulsion for those bringing in illicit substances – 'those on the periphery of the same incident will not necessarily be excluded but can come back in as long as they agree to random testing'. This is a policy that the principal has applied in the past, and no-one has yet tested positive. Though 'each case is judged on its merits'. Fags 'unacceptable and pupils suspended'. Booze 'not an issue in school'.

Pupils and Parents: Edinburgh hotch-potch of New Town and suburbs, with many first-time buyers and lots up from England. Siblings and FPs' children. Less elitist and perhaps less dusty than some Edinburgh schools. Children living far out can spend the night when doing evening activities. Pupils 'relaxed and happy, friendly and responsible' to quote school inspector. Parent teacher group ('the red socks brigade') slightly better organised into a Friends of the School group, fund-raising, ceilidhs, 'good cash cow'.

Entrance: At 11,12, 13 or sixth form – otherwise 'by default'. Automatic from junior school. Entrance assessments held in January but can be arranged at any time. Waiting lists for some stages but just go on trying. Entrance to upper school is by interview, plus school report plus GCSEs/Standard grades (five credit passes for fifth form entry.) Numbers up, 'the number sitting our entrance exam has increased by 100 per cent in three years,' says the deputy head of Stewart's Melville. Whilst Mary Erskine's is 'buoyant, absolutely full'.

Exit: Some leakage after Standard Grades, 12 left after Highers last year, most sixth year (95 per cent) go on to university (few gap years, though growing in popularity), most opt for Scottish unis (30 per cent go south). SATS (the requirement for American Colleges) not a problem. Art college, music/drama are popular alternatives.

Money Matters: Scholarships/bursaries available, some linked to the Merchant Company, others sibling directed. 'No child will be left wanting in a (financial) crisis'.

Remarks: An outstanding school, happily focused.

STOCKPORT GRAMMAR SCHOOL

Linked to Stockport Grammar School Junior School in the Junior section

Buxton Road, Stockport, Cheshire, SK2 7AF

Tel: 0161 456 9000
Fax: 0161 419 2407
E-mail: sgs@stockportgrammar.co.uk
Website: www.stockportgrammar.co.uk

- Pupils: 1,030, all day, equal numbers of boys and girls • Ages: 11 - 18 • Size of sixth form: 290 • Secular • Fees: £1,635
- Independent • Open days: A mid October weekday evening and a Saturday morning in late November

Head: Since 2005 Mr Andrew Chicken BA (early forties), head of Colfes (qv) since 2001. He read history at London, trained as a teacher at Oxford, followed by a career in both state and independent schools, notably Cheadle Hulme and before that Manchester Grammar. Married to a teacher, no children. A straight-talking northerner who faces problems head on, he would be the first to make a joke of his name. Parents warm to him. Places a strong emphasis on academic matters. At Colfes he was difficult to track down as he was either on PGL camp, coaching cricket or teaching students – but parents put up with the inconvenience for the sake of the involvement. Knows students, from first year upwards. Prepared to go the extra mile – sees parents at weekend if there's something that needs sorting out.

Academic Matters: Particularly in past five years, results have been excellent, with well over half of candidates gaining A* and A grades at GCSE and never less than 90 per cent gaining B grades or above. Likewise, impressive A level results. Head feels that obsessional national emphasis on GCSEs is misguided, but clearly his own reservations do not prevent him from ensuring pupils score top marks. Pupils take 9 GCSEs. Pupil/teacher ratio is 1:12. Years 1 to 3 have 25 maximum class size, narrowing down to a maximum of 24 (more often 20 or fewer) in GCSE year groups, and in sixth form general maximum target is 12. Average age of staff is 40, half of whom have been at school for ten years or more. No statemented pupils in school, although several have dyslexia, which does not, however, prove a barrier to learning or to acceptance into school in the first place.

Games, Options, The Arts: Sport very popular and important. Everywhere you look there's a sports pitch. School has own swimming pool. New sports hall. Lots of sporting activities and matches. Rugby and lacrosse popular – lacrosse teams are given special coaching by US coach. Football was introduced for first year pupils in 2003. Saturday morning practices and fixtures provide opportunity for pupils and staff to build good relationships in less formal context.

Music another strength. About half of pupils learn at least one musical instrument, mostly in school. Lots of choirs, orchestras, bands, performances at Manchester's Bridgewater Hall and on TV. In drama, there are usually three school productions a year. Lower sixth stage own production in the few weeks at the end of the academic year. Art, whilst valued, does not have particularly good facilities. Walls of corridor leading to head's office are testimony nonetheless to high standards.

Background and Atmosphere: Founded in 1487 by Sir Edmond Shaa, for boys, 'to teche allman persons children the science of grammar'. Became co-educational in 1980 (girls insist there's no sense of being add-ons at a boys' school). Continues to have links with The Worshipful Company of Goldsmiths. Atmosphere purposeful but not pedantic. Pupils happy, positive, proud of their school. Friendly, generous spirit pervades. Parents find school accessible. Their views are taken into account and they are kept properly informed on a regular basis.

Pastoral Care and Discipline: Pastoral care primarily the concern of form teachers. No peer support system, though school has instituted 'buddies' – ie sixth formers assigned to new pupils. Pupils rather vague about procedures in the event of bullying – perhaps a sign of its scarcity? Discipline, and self-discipline, important to school, part of its package of traditional values.

Pupils and Parents: Drawn from Greater/ South Manchester and from further south through Cheshire into Derbyshire, as well as from Stockport itself. Year 1 intake represents 50 per cent from own junior school and rest from between 50-75 primary schools. Famous Old Boys/Girls so far: Professor Sir Freddie Williams (inventor of the first stored program computer), John Amaechi (basketball player), Sir Victor Blank (chairman of the Mirror Group) and Gordon Marsden, MP for Blackpool South. Association of Old Boys and Girls (Old Stopfordians) going from strength to strength. Parents reflect solid ethos of the school.

Entrance: By full day examination, encompassing maths, verbal reasoning, English and comprehension. Followed by interviews, which provide opportunity for school to get to know pupils a little and vice versa.

Exit: Almost without exception, to university, often the more prestigious. Pupils tend to do well, achieving upper second and first class degrees. Regularly 16-22 Oxbridge offers.

Money Matters: Fees very good value. No scholarships, but some bursaries available.

Remarks: Safely square, gentle school. A good bet for a solid, traditional style of education in a caring environment. As the school's motto – 'Vincit qui patitur' – suggests, this is a school where the value and the rewards of hard graft are recognised, but not to the exclusion of 'a balanced diet' of interests and activities.

STONAR SCHOOL

Linked to Stonar Preparatory School in the Junior section

Cottles Park, Atworth, Melksham, Wiltshire, SN12 8NT

Tel: 01225 701 740
Fax: 01225 790 830
E-mail: k.ibbott@stonarschool.com
Website: www.stonarschool.com

• Pupils: 400 girls; 200 board, 200 day • Ages: 2-18 • Size of sixth form: 80 • Christian, non-denom • Fees: Senior boarding £5,550, junior boarding £4,750; day £1,600 - £3,125 • Independent • Open days: November

---

Head: From 2006, Mrs Shirley Shayler MA BSc(Hons). Formerly deputy head of Taunton School. She follows Mrs Claire Osborne, head since 2002, who left to become head of Rockport School in Ireland.

Academic Matters: Biology, psychology, English strong overall, also history and geography as well as geology; mod langs popular, with Chinese, Japanese as well as the trad French, German and Spanish; maths strong, as are physics and chemistry at A level. New head of drama from September 2004. Stonar is very proud to count Romola Garai as an ex-pupil. Theatre studies results pathetic at A level but unsurprisingly stronger are art, music, photography, home economics and PE. Much better showing across the board at GCSE. Trad teaching, staff mainly female, but with several senior chaps. Encouragement freely given. No problems with dyslexia, SEN teachers for both one-to-one and withdrawn from class.

Games, Options, The Arts: Super stabling for over 60 horses – 'better than the dorms' according to a mother – good sized covered indoor riding school and a mini Badminton cross-country course. Local pony clubs rent the facilities for camps etc. Famous for holding British Inter-schools One Day Event each year – and, not surprisingly, Stonar girls do extremely well in this. Currently about 150 riders in the school. Top-level riders do BHSAI (horsy qualification). Sports are taken seriously, one or two stars currently in the school, several county hockey and netball players. Fitness centre, sports hall, swimming pool, Astroturf. Lively art and music does well – more play instruments than ride. Dead keen drama, with lots of productions. Imaginative on outings and trips – going as far as New Zealand, South Africa, Canada, USA.

Background and Atmosphere: Elegant Strawberry Hill Gothic house (once the home of the Fuller family), at odds with a motley collection of modern outbuildings; prep school on site (most girls move on to the senior school); separate sixth form house. Good new sixth form study centre. No five star accommodation here but comfortable enough. All dorms have been recently refurbished. Dining hall where each girl must wipe her place clean. Lots of computers – games no longer allowed on them. Girls can help with tinies in the nursery but no official qualification (Norland Nanny College just down the road). New science laboratories in November 2003. Brand new nursery opened in 2002. Parental grouses reach us that there is not enough emphasis on reading – disputed by school. Not overly tidy – relaxed, gentle, cosy. Horse boxes fill the drive at start and end of term.

Pastoral Care and Discipline: Not a problem. Lively school council consisting of girls of all ages and staff. All staff are watchful, a key part of school policy. Non-teaching house staff, 'so they are fresh at the end of the day'.

Pupils and Parents: Mutually supportive friendly girls at ease with themselves and their teachers. Around 30 children from overseas, Europeans and Far Easterners. Londoners, locals and Home Counties' girls. 180 boarders. New green and white tartan uniform popular with girls.

Entrance: Girls have to sit the entrance examinations held in January. Limited spaces for girls with special needs.

Exit: About 80 per cent go on to take degrees – London, Nottingham, lesser lights. Several follow equine careers, some to art college.

Money Matters: Scholarships at 11, 13 and 16, including for music, art, drama, sport and riding. Services bursaries available.

Remarks: Just the place to send your pony-mad daughter, where she will emerge pleasantly confident and probably with some decent exam results too. Needs now to settle down under the new head after an interregnum and a head who did not work out.

STONYHURST COLLEGE

Linked to Saint Mary's Hall in the Junior section

Stonyhurst, Clitheroe, Lancashire, BB7 9PZ

Tel: 01254 827 073
Fax: 01254 827 135
E-mail: admissions@stonyhurst.ac.uk
Website: www.stonyhurst.ac.uk

- Pupils: 438: 305 boys, 113 girls; 281 full boarders • Ages: 13-18 • Size of sixth form: 130 boys, 50 girls • RC but enquiries welcome from other Christian denominations • Fees: Boarding £7,101; weekly boarding £6,075; day £4,152 • Independent • Open days: Early November

Head: Adrian Aylward MA (mid forties), appointed as the second lay headmaster in 1996. Educated at Worth and Oxford, where he read literae humaniores. Spent ten years in the City and industry becoming MD of a plc before entering education. His passion is philosophy and theology, the latter he teaches when he can. He is articulate, engaging and open minded, describing himself as a family man but admits to enjoying fishing when 3 young children permit. His wife joins in school life and 'recruits in local supermarkets!' He seeks to strengthen the clear vision of education set by the Jesuits and sees the school as a community but highly values the individual.

Departing in July 2006.

Academic Matters: Broad curriculum including astronomy (up to GCSE if demand) – own observatory for this. Average class size 17, 10 in the sixth form. Some setting. RE compulsory to GCSE, thereafter theology. Pupils are assigned a personal tutor whom they meet twice weekly to discuss progress. Broad ability intake and thus not the academic powerhouse of city day schools but a genuine wish for each pupil to fulfil their potential. Head did not publish results for league tables – 'it undermines the value of the individual'. Average results over a three-year period show 42 per cent A* and A at GCSE, 59 per cent A and B grades at A level. Maths consistently popular at A level achieving good results. 10 per cent of pupils have special needs and receive extra help – majority of these are dyslexic. Plenty of computers around linked up to the school's intranet and all pupils have their own email address. Pupils do 'a quick GCSE in IT' at 13 years. Terminals in sixth form study bedrooms.

Games, Options, The Arts: A 'sport for all' policy.

Compulsory sport throughout the school achieving notable success in rugby, golf, hockey and netball. Super indoor swimming pool and new all-weather pitch, the latter used by athletes training during the 2002 Commonwealth Games. School is divided vertically into four 'lines' for sporting competitions. Music is highly valued. Free instrumental tuition on an orchestral instrument is available to all pupils and maintained if satisfactory progress is made. Three pupils were recently selected for the Halle youth orchestra. The school is the proud owner of a Steinway, Bosendorfer and Bechstein and other facilities include a keyboard lab and practice rooms looking like mini greenhouses. Good DT department with plenty of scope for those artistically inclined. Outdoor pursuits in abundance – fishing, canoeing, sailing, fell walking, clay pigeon shooting etc. Further afield pupils participate in world challenge trips, this year to Peru, pilgrimages to Lourdes, D of E expeditions, to name but a few. In the second year the cadet corps is compulsory.

Background and Atmosphere: Founded by the Jesuits at St Omer in what is now northern France for English families forced to pursue a Catholic education abroad. After a succession of moves the school was given refuge at its present site in the Catholic part of Lancashire by Thomas Weld, who later donated the property to the school. The magnificent buildings are set in a 2,000-acre estate, most of which is farmed. 'I arrive each morning and cannot believe that this is my school,' comments one pupil. Each year group is termed a 'playroom' with its own common room and boarding facilities, cared for by a married couple. The girls have separate accommodation and are looked after by a housemistress. Recent developments include a magnificently refurbished and equipped library and study centre in the heart of the school and years 9 and 10 boys' dormitories have been transformed. Other parts of the school are truly splendid; huge staircases, wood panelling, polished stone, works of art, brimming with history and tradition. Some formerly hidden treasures are now exhibited in a millennium display for all to enjoy. Shared boarding accommodation (4-5 per room), lower down the school, makes way for smart study bedrooms for the sixth formers. This is essentially a full-time boarding school, 'no mass exodus at weekends' but exeats are readily approved according to pupils. Sunday afternoon appreciated by some as their only free time to do as they please, as much of the weekend is consumed by prep, excursions and church. Religion is taken seriously but is not oppressive. Now co-ed and feels as if it has always been so. Girls' have improved communication at all levels,' says head, as well as 'making the school a more cheerful place'.

Pastoral Care and Discipline: A Family Handbook sets out clear expectations of conduct and behaviour. Cases of bullying are dealt with by playroom staff and general policing by the pupil-run playroom committees. A few suspensions in the past for drug offences but 'not a drugs school'. Discipline not a major problem. The Jesuit school chaplain is singled out for special praise by pupils. Being a former pupil, but widely travelled in the interim, he is highly valued for his pastoral care and general availability.

Pupils and Parents: 'Broad mix,' comments head. More socially mixed than equivalent schools – being in Catholic Lancashire. Catholics make up 70 per cent of the total. Southern parents cite one reason for their choice being the school's lack of consumerism and the social competitiveness of some southern schools. Rich mix of accents – regional and international (25 per cent pupils are non-Brits). International links are highly valued and there has 'never been a problem with racism,' comments head. Confident, articulate and mature pupils praise the community feel of the school, which is enhanced by the playroom system. 'Looking at the whole picture,' comments one pupil, 'the school works extremely well.' Day pupils are encouraged to stay after school for studies and activities – a facility valued by parents – and may feel left out if they choose not to do so. Head disagrees, pointing out that the head boy was a day pupil for 4 years. Alumni include twelve martyrs, seven VCs, also Arthur Conan Doyle, Charles Laughton, General Walters, Paul Johnson, Peter Moorhouse, Bishop Hollis, Bishop Hines, Charles Sturridge, Hugh Woolridge, Jonathon Plowright, Bill Cash MP, Bruce Kent, Mark Thompson, Lords Chitnis and Talbot, Kyran Bracken and Robert Brinkley.

Entrance: From own prep (St Mary's Hall), St John's Beaumont and a variety of other schools, both here and abroad. Broad ability intake – 'for some, 6 GCSEs will be an achievement,' comments head. Academic entrance exam but other factors taken into account, particularly family connections with the school. Six GCSE passes, plus interview, for entry into sixth form. Those unable to attend for interview eg overseas pupils, write a 500 word essay explaining why they wish to come to Stonyhurst

Exit: All over. London popular. Numbers vary to Oxbridge, but average 10 per cent over recent years. 2004 saw 10 per cent enter medical school. Art foundation, management and business courses currently look popular. Plenty of international links and scope for travel through the Jesuit community with many students taking a gap year.

Money Matters: A variety of scholarships; academic, music and art and design to a maximum of 50 per cent of fees. Some bursaries are available up to 50 per cent of fees

for those in need.

Remarks: Distinguished Jesuit boarding school, steeped in history and set in beautiful surroundings, now comfortably co-ed and at capacity. A genuine concern for the individual pervades.

STOVER SCHOOL

Linked to Stover Junior/Preparatory Schools in the Junior section

Stover, Newton Abbot, Devon, TQ12 6QG

Tel: 01626 354 505
Fax: 01626 361 475
E-mail: mail@stover.co.uk
Website: www.stover.co.uk

- Pupils: 510 girls (65 board), 130 boys • Ages: 3-18 • Size of sixth form: 55 girls • Christian • Fees: Day £2,715. Boarding £3,745 - £5,545 • Independent • Open days: One each term

Headmistress: Since 2005, Mrs Sue Bradley BSc CBiol MIBiol PGCE. Mrs Bradley is well known in the Stover community as former head of science, director of studies, deputy head and, most recently, as head of the senior school. She is a very experienced educator and has been involved with all aspects of the school's developments over

many years. BSc CBiol MIBiol.

Academic Matters: 92 per cent of girls gained 5 or more GCSE Grade A*-C, 82 per cent per cent plus gained 8 or more A* to C at GCSE, 97 per cent plus A/E grades at A level. Not the highest performer in the west country but still noticeably good. Offers over 20 subjects at GCSE and 20 at A level. Cambridge Business Skills, RSA CLAIT, EFL popular as additions. Nice sixth form centre with a living-together feel. Daily help available for children with special needs like dyslexics. Freelance educational psychologist utilised in rarer cases.

Games, Options, The Arts: Varied sports programme available with area champions in cross country, netball and hockey; pupils also qualified for the National Prep Schools Athletics. Promising rugby side. Strong international touring netball team, visited Barbados in 2002. Good facilities: athletics track, six all-weather floodlit tennis courts, hockey pitches, rugby/football pitches, cricket, rounders, tennis, badminton, basketball and masses of other sports too.

Varied extra-curricular programme includes the likes of astronomy and science, public speaking, life-saving/first aid, fencing, judo, Italian and skiing. Horse riding, après-school, is particularly popular with links to riding club five miles away. Busy music department with over 170 pupils receiving instrumental tuition. Music exam results consistently merits and distinctions. Enthusiastic teaching from older music scholars rubs off on the younger ensembles. Some pupils still find time to opt for the Duke of Edinburgh or the popular Tens Tors competition on Dartmoor. Stover has supportive links with a school in Moldova. 'Learning about Moldova certainly made us all appreciate what we have,' said a pupil.

Background and Atmosphere: Arriving at Stover is like driving into a period television drama. A long meandering drive brings you to the architecturally breathtaking school building. Founded, in the grounds of Stover estate, by two sisters in 1932, to help girls lead independent lives – still the school's ethos. Once owned by the Duke of Somerset's family, it sits in 60 acres of wildlife-friendly grounds on the edge of Dartmoor, with stunning views.

Radical expansion began in the 1990s – First Steps Nursery opened; Stover Junior School followed in 1996; humanities block and sixth form centre in 1997; and Millennium Art and ICT Centre in 2001 opened by HRH The Princess Royal. September 2005 new science block with four new classrooms as well. Extensive developments in the prep school, new ICT suite and art/technology Room.

Unusual feature of boys and girls taught in separate classes but mixing for extra-curricular activities and break

times. Day boys admitted to senior school from 2005.

Boarding facilities – for girls only – recently modernised to cope with increasing demand – girls like it so much some of the weekly boarders want to stay the weekend as well. 'There's so much going on,' they say.

Girls wear smart grey and green kilt (Devon Tartan) with green jacket. Boys green blazer and black trousers. Friendly atmosphere, pupils extremely enthusiastic and protective about Stover, quick to dismiss any sniff of elitism or pretentiousness although confidence abounds. Strong friendships are made at Stover and the Old Pupils' Portico Association helps them live on through frequent reunions.

Pastoral Care and Discipline: Not much of a problem; rules based on 'code of conduct and common sense.' Anyone who would dare upset the school's clean reputation with drugs or the like would be out. Pupils consider those who break the rules to be 'time wasters'. Sees occasional misdemeanours, 'but what school doesn't?' Older students who admit they have a social life outside of school may blush at the words smoking or alcohol but the majority appear healthy, strong-willed and well turned out young ladies who keep you on your toes with their politeness and good manners. Cantonese girls are made to feel at home with Stover's special Chinese Mid-Autumn Festival.

Pupils and Parents: Day pupils from Newton Abbot, Exeter, South Hams, Torbay, Bovey Tracey, Moreton-hampstead, Plymouth. Boarders from as far as Aberdeen – or overseas. Parents have varied occupations – doctors, lawyers, hoteliers, business owners and members of Hong Kong police force.

Entrance: By examination in English, mathematics and non-verbal reasoning, together with school report and interview.

Exit: 75 per cent stay on for sixth form, the others head for non-fee paying alternatives such as Exeter College and Torquay Girls Grammar, or co-education. Popular university choices: Bath, Sheffield, Warwick, Cardiff, Exeter, York; subject choices include aeronautical engineering, law, mathematics, medical sciences, biochemistry, electrical engineering. All sixth formers go on to university; 10 per cent take gap year first. Stover has host families in many countries – Nepal, Canada, Hong Kong, Australia, Switzerland – for gap pupils.

Money Matters: Academic, music, art and sport scholarships available at most ages, a small number of bursaries for existing pupils.

Remarks: Small class sizes, excellent results and a stunning school in beautiful, safe, surroundings.

STOWE SCHOOL

Stowe, Buckingham, Buckinghamshire, MK18 5EH

Tel: 01280 818 000
Fax: 01280 818 181
E-mail: admissions@stowe.co.uk
Website: www.stowe.co.uk

• Pupils: 615; co-ed from 2005: 23 girls starting in the Lower School, 98 girls in sixth form. 65 day pupils, rest full-time boarders • Ages: 13-18 • Size of sixth form: 305 • C of E • Fees: Day £5,665; boarding £7,660 • Independent • Open days: Minimum 2 per term, see website. Individual visits welcomed

Head: Since 2003, Dr Anthony Wallersteiner MA PhD (early forties), the youngest head since the legendary J F Roxburgh. Educated at King's School, Canterbury, history scholar at Trinity, Cambridge, he read history and theory of art at Kent. Dr Wallersteiner comes to Stowe from Tonbridge where he had been a housemaster, head of history and ran Oxbridge entrance; taught at St Paul's and Sherborne before that. An academic, 'unashamedly academic' he says, with a focus on raising academic standards. Stowe has finally got the head it so richly deserves, 'I want to put back the academic core, it has been missing for a while'. 'Some staff could set tougher targets' he comments, 'we need to stretch the more able'.

An open door head, Dr Wallersteiner has a cupboard full of birthday presents for pupils, hosts the head's essay society and teaches VisEd (aka visual education: an instant architectural gallop round the house and grounds) to third formers 'as much to teach myself as to get to know the boys', and history to GCSE pupils. Loves teaching, 'I don't want to develop a bunker mentality' and has promptly (with the full support of the governors) turned the previous head's building programme upside down, concentrating on art, music, drama and sports facilities.

The main building itself has been shaken (not stirred) and made to work for its living. The original library 'in the heart of the school' previously used for rather grand meetings and debates has become very much a focal point, full of desks, plasma screens and computers, the middle doors flung open, and humming with young. 'More than twice as many books taken out as this time last year' said the librarian, 'and particularly busy during the evenings and at lunch time'. Stowe is going fully co-ed, with the first intake of junior girls in 2005. The two third formers who joined in 2004, trialling the place, were pleased as punch with the experience. Dr Wallersteiner is married to Valerie, and they have three children, two girls and a boy, currently 'up the road' at Winchester House.

Academic Matters: 'We will continue to draw out pupils from a broad academic spectrum' said Dr Wallersteiner as he raised the CE pass mark to 50 per cent. Wide range of academic abilities, streaming in all disciplines. A level and GCSE results well below what they should be – this, as we said above, is the focus of Dr Wallersteiner's attention. Four langs on offer: French, German, Spanish and Italian. Geography, design tech & production design, economics and fine art results stand tall among the weeds. Sciences are relatively unpopular and unsuccessful – particularly strange as we sat through the note-taking session of a chemistry class, with reactive white boards (fascinating, you change the programme by dragging your finger along the screen) and 'fools' chemistry programmes' replicating the various experiments performed in class, on line in every house, there should be no reason for uninspiring marks. The teaching tools are in place: white boards, smart boards, you name it – this is a school geared up to help pupils learn, regular drop in clinics between 5.30 and 6, with 'different teachers on different days' in most subjects where pupils can (officially) get one to one tuition. 'Trouble is', said one pupil 'the staff in charge either make you feel a bit stupid, or the ones you really want to talk to are doing something more important'. Maths, sciences and English assignments are 'usually ok' on line, though some staff 'do want hard copy'. School has wired up (neatly encased in square plastic tubing in the posh bits of the house) all over the main school and in the houses, and has a popular laptop purchase scheme. European (computer) driving licence for all, including staff (Latest results: Complete ECDL passes (7 modules): 8 passes by students – 2 passes by staff) Now piloting a new BCS (British Computer Society) course with a 4th form group. Three-week orders (assessments/progress reports etc). Artist in Residence and regular visiting speakers and seminars on a range of subjects. The skills development centre gives help to pupils with mild to moderate learning difficulties and/or specific needs. All pupils remain integrated in the mainstream curriculum. However, while the specialist teachers in the centre are qualified and able to help with mild to moderate dyslexic and dyspraxic difficulties, they are not able to deal with severe learning difficulties and their associated behavioural and social problems.

Games, Options, The Arts: Art, sports science, and various design technology disciplines all did well at A level with almost half the A level art candidates getting A, and stunning work on the stairs of the art room, but gosh why have four separate classes teaching four different ages the same boring drawing technique at the same time? Some ultra enthusiastic staff, and artists in residence, 3D, ceramics, colour exploration and etching with copper sulphate all on offer. Schemes of co-operation with Alexander Talbot Rice to turn the proposed new art block into an art academy are in the pipeline, and Stoics past and present staged a fund raising art exhibition at Christies in 2004. Head has visions of a Yehudi Menuhin template for the new art centre, turning the school into a centre of excellence with classical training as well as modern forms of painting, drawing, sculpture, graphic arts, etc.

Drama and music poor relations in comparison, though this is improving. School says 'Congreve performances are regarded as training ground for RADA, The Guildhall or the Old Vic.'

Sport is important at Stowe, all the trad games as you might expect, rugby and cricket particularly strong with 3 U18 England cricket players. Girls proud of their hockey prowess. Plus fives (court due for re-vamp), athletics (track due for a re-vamp), polo popular, ditto rowing; one of the few schools to boast its own pack of beagles, about 30 pupils follow each week and much of the husbandry is done by pupils. The beagles are being kept, following the hunting ban, and are being re-trained for drag-hunting. Terrific number of options, fly fishing, martial arts and clay pigeon shooting, but sewing machines, creative textiles and dress design for all.

Thriving evangelical Christian union, D of E, pupils complain 'there are almost too many options available' music rooms, art studios are all open at weekends, and 'if we want to encourage a new activity all we have to do is persuade a member of staff'.

Background and Atmosphere: School founded in 1923. Stowe, home of the Dukes of Buckingham and Chandos, has been described as 'one of the most majestic English houses of the eighteenth century' and has recently undergone (and is still undergoing) a very serious restoration.

Mind boggling millions from Heritage Lottery funding, the fabric of the buildings are now owned by the Stowe House Preservation Trust, the 750 acres of Capability Brown designed grounds and gardens having been long given to The National Trust. During our first visit it was umbrellas in the dining room and buckets in the attic, now the place is let for weddings and bar mitzvahs and open to the public in the holidays. It was also used (as were the pupils) in the last James Bond movie. Slightly strange red carpets adorn the portrait strewn entrance hall, family pics abound, and the head's study, aka the gothic library, is a gem.

Vanbrugh, James Gibbs, William Kent and Robert Adams all had a hand in the main building and would be turning in their collective graves at some of the sixties class room blocks. Two houses in main block much more convenient and romantic, but not quite so user-friendly, certain amount of work-space reorganisation so that boys no longer have to share cross-year common rooms. Boarding being gradually refurbished. All eat in main house, two dining rooms in action, architectural gems, pupils say 'lunch and breakfast OK salad bars and jacket potatoes, but supper pretty boring'.

Pastoral Care and Discipline: PSHE with tutors, head has clamped down quite hard on discipline and school is no longer the choice for kids bombed out of other schools, though there's a fair amount of wickedness still. Out for drugs (Augean stables syndrome notwithstanding) and out for 'continuous smoking', boozing or bullying. Prefects say they are the first line of defence on the bullying front 'but really there isn't that much around'. But housemasters/mistresses, matrons and tutors are all on call. Petty punishments are a thing of the past and are replaced by those designed to the fit the offence: litter patrol, working in the grounds, etc. Out also if pupils 'are not trying and continuously getting into trouble' but not out, say their peers 'if they are trying and making an effort'. Around 60 day boys and girls, but full boarding encouraged no flexi- or weekly on offer.

Pupils and Parents: An eclectic mix, some quite grand with other children at Eton or Winchester, and some first time buyers who occasionally appear a trifle surprised by their choice. The young gel well, 'absolutely friends for life', work together, play together, shoot together. Traditionally a school that fed the army stream, now in the maverick production game. New uniform: blue tweed blazers with gold lining, with grey trousers for the boys and short grey skirts for the girls (or visa versa if they appeal to the Equal Opportunities Commission). Dark suits of the girls' own choice (trouser or skirt) in the sixth form. Around 10 per cent from real abroad and about the same ex-pats, a fair number from Scotland, ditto London. Exeat weekends occur midterm. There is a strict alcohol policy, and housemasters have been issued with breathalysers – so we'll see no more Stoics paralytic in the Kings Road? Fiercely loyal old boys include Richard Branson, George Melly, Sir Peregrine Worsthorne, Lord Sainsbury and a clutch of guitarists/rock musicians/property developers. Amongst those who are no longer with us Sir Leonard Cheshire, David Niven.

Entrance: Common Entrance now 50 per cent, own exam for those from the state sector or ill-prepared and from abroad. Still seen as an excellent bet if you fail to make the grade for Eton. Places competitive for girls, though the odd place still available at odd moments. Waiting lists looming. The Dragon, Papplewick, Haileybury, Cheam all send representatives. Standard A/Bs for both girls and boys joining at sixth form level.

Exit: Occasional creature to Oxbridge (4 last year, but still too few in the head's view); otherwise around 97 per cent to uni: Edinburgh, Newcastle, Bristol and Durham all well represented, plus the odd Cirencester candidate, a number to gap year and then decide.

Money Matters: Expensive, but by no means heading the queue. Two main appeals currently: The Stowe House Preservation Trust, which is more or less up to scratch and The Stowe School Foundation which will be funding the new music school complex and increasing the scholarship and bursarial fund which is currently trailing at nearly a million quid a year. Huge numbers of bursaries, scholarships in almost every discipline, art, music, sport, academia, plus a Stowe/Harvard foundation.

Remarks: As we said last time: back in fashion once more, it's a complete winner for turning out confident young things with enough self-belief to reach great heights. With the added advantage of an academic leader who has tackled the boozing druggy culture that was prevalent head on and makes no bones about his aim for excellence in all things. We look forward to reporting slightly sharper exam success, though hopefully without loosing any of the inherent charm.

STRATHALLAN SCHOOL

Forgandenny, Perth, Perthshire, PH2 9EG

Tel: 01738 812 546
Fax: 01738 812 549
E-mail: admissions@strathallan.co.uk
Website: www.strathallan.co.uk

• Pupils: 260 boys, 195 girls; all board except for 130 • Ages: 10-18 • Size of sixth form: 180 • Non-denom • Fees: Day: junior £2,882; senior £4,396. Boarding: junior £4,629; senior £6,504 • Independent

Head: Since 2000, Mr Bruce Thompson MA (forties) educated at Newcastle High, thence New College where he read literae humaniores (classics to the rest of us) and comes to Strathallan via Cheltenham College, where he was head of classics, and Dollar Academy – he wanted to 'try the Scottish system'. 'Loves Scotland, and loves Strathallan', as does his wife, Fabienne (French, teaches at a local prep school, worked in travel and tourism, expert skier – coaches it). The Thompsons have two young daughters and are delighted to find a young staff with similar-aged children. Head teaches classics and coaches rugby;

the pupils enjoy finding him practising weights alongside them. He has a reputation for calling into houses unannounced for the odd chat with a pupil on their own ground and has lots of informal brain-storming sessions in the evenings. ('Great fun, got to kick 'em out'.) He 'needs pupil stimulation' and finds himself creating oppportunities to meet more pupils on an informal basis.

Academic Matters: Not tremendously academic (school says 'strong academic record') – but you can reach the heights from here. 2005 A level results include over 80 per cent A-B in art, business studies, Eng lit, Chinese, classical civilisation, further maths, Spanish and German. School plays the system, both Scottish and A levels. 60/70 per cent take A levels, the rest do Highers (over two years). School tries to please parents but the choice between A level and Highers is always a contentious one. All pupils do double award science at GCSE. No subject much stronger than others and exam grades are generally good across the board. DT continues to be excellent. Sophisticated computer design equipment, and pupils work here in spare time. Intranet access all over. Four separate computer rooms and computers everywhere. School has always had a reputation for picking up weaker brethren and has a smallish but effective learning support system which had a smashing HMI report in June 2004, with talk of 'systematic identification', 'sensitive support', 'informative advice'. All pupils screened on entry with psycheds brought in where necessary. One-to-one, small groups, plus after school clinics in various disciplines. Two full-time trained staff, plus three others, and a dedicated full-timer for 10-13-year-olds in Riley who has strong links with the senior school. Extra time for exams. Three week assessment orders for all – ie reports (these are becoming more commonplace).

Games, Options, The Arts: Fantastic new state-of-the-art art school over three floors with marvellous light and inspired work. Art/history combined field trips to Venice etc graphics camera and screen printing. Good music (Copeman Hart manual organ) including keen traditional Scottish music group. Popular pipe band. Lots of drama and small theatre, a clever conversion of a former dining hall, the insides cleverly scooped out (theatre doubles as an examination hall). Swimming pool curiously juxtaposed to the theatre. Swimming team developing under new coach. Sport taken seriously (hideous pale green Astroturf), rugby, cricket, own golf course, skiing, CCF (boys and girls, voluntary), flying, sailing. Masses of charity work.

Background and Atmosphere: School was founded in 1913, based in 18th century country house with masses of additions, set in 150 acres. Two fantastic double-deck libraries, one with the (obviously commissioned) carpet reflecting the plaster work in the ceiling. Nice chapel, hideous dining room. Main classrooms 150 yards away beside the old stable building which has been converted into a splendidly cosy junior house, Riley. Riley now boasts a most amazing atrium plus library and music practice rooms etc. Classroom blocks undergoing programme of refurbishment, with latest improvements including three new state-of-the-art chemistry labs. Houses new and newish, boys and girls have own study bedrooms, lots of kitchens, and common room area on each floor. Much general to-ing and fro-ing, but co-ed works very well here; girls' houses out of bounds to boys on Sunday mornings so that girls 'can laze around in their dressing gowns if they want'. School facilities much used by groups during holiday period. Staff live on site in school houses, lots of young and good family feel.

Pastoral Care and Discipline: House parents live on site with two staff on duty in each house every night. Tutors often using the time available for informal chats. Mr Thompson 'aware that things happen' and talks of rustication and drugs testing 'in case of suspicion'. Punishment system for misdemeanours of 'fatigues' – jobs around the buildings and grounds -'no shortage of them'!

Pupils and Parents: A few from the eastern bloc via the HMC placement scheme, plus Hong Kong, Germany etc. A third in all live overseas, mostly expats. School is popular with Scots (regional accents of all kinds) well-placed, an hour from both Edinburgh and Glasgow, plus a small contingent from south of the border. FPs Dominic Diamond (computer games whizzo), Colin Montgomerie (golfer), Sir Jack Shaw,(Bank of Scotland), John Gray (former chairman of the Hong Kong and Shanghai Bank). Not a toffs' school, despite brief showing in the fashion stakes when David Pighills took the school co-ed.

Entrance: At 10 or 11 for the junior house (interview and test) then automatic entry, otherwise by CE – more than one attempt OK. Not a high hurdle, but popular. Later entry if space available.

Exit: More than 95 per cent to a wide range of universities,(Aberdeen popular). Usually 'a few' to Oxbridge.

Money Matters: School financially strong. Junior scholarships, open scholarships and sixth form scholarship plus academic, allrounder, sport, music and art scholarships. Parents can also apply to the Ochil Trust for means-tested help with fees.

Remarks: David Pighills (the last head but one who was all that was wonderful for Strathallan) is back as chairman of the governors and, with a dynamic new head, school should be on the up again.

STREATHAM AND CLAPHAM HIGH SCHOOL

Linked to Streatham & Clapham High School Junior Department in the Junior section

42 Abbotswood Road, Streatham, London, SW16 1AW

Tel: 020 8677 8400
Fax: 0208 677 2001
E-mail: enquiry@shc.gdst.net
Website: www.gdst.net/streathamhigh

• Pupils: 495 girls, all day • Ages: 11-18 • Size of sixth form: 80 • Non-denom • Fees: £3,063 • Independent • Open days: October and November

Head: Since 2002, Mrs Sue Mitchell MA (Oxon) PGCE NPQH (early fifties). Initially a classicist who became an English specialist (once-time head of dept at Bradford Girls Grammar) and who, prior to this appointment, was acting head at Bromley GDST, Mrs Mitchell is instantly likeable, direct and open. A commonsense and capable head, she seems ideally suited to this sound and sensible school – nothing here is showy or pretentious – and the head's practical and positive approach to her school, her staff and her girls seems likely to build on the creative school-building achieved by her predecessor. Mrs Mitchell is backed by a largely new senior management team, though can also draw on the knowledge and experience of other long-term, committed and enthusiastic senior staff members. Head expresses special satisfaction with the value-added benefits of her school, 'we take children who are not in the top-ranking league and they end up with very good GCSE results which is the result of what we have to offer...above all very good teaching'. She accepts that school's popularity is partly due to school's reputation for not over-pressurising girls – homework time has actually been cut in recent years – something one seldom hears! 'My key is that I want the girls to be happy – not that it's playtime but I want them to enjoy coming to school.'

Academic Matters: Results are not starry by top GDST standards or the standards of the highest-flying of the other London independents but they are more than respectable especially when it is remembered that, with tough competition on the doorstep, this school does not get the pick of the brightest each year. 2005 results included 60 per cent A*/A grades at GCSE. Class sizes are small – no A level class is

bigger than 9 – and teacher pupil ratio averages 12:1. At GCSE three separate sciences are available though most take the dual award – thus allowing more scope for other subjects and modern languages are well supported, popular and successful here. Latin thrives until GCSE and survives into the sixth – new head of classics just appointed at time of our visit – classical civilisation is a popular A level choice. Both English lit and a combined English lang and lit A level offered. Business studies a new and highly-favoured A level subject. Psychology and law available as distance learning subjects ie taught by online university but monitored onsite.

Overall, your motivated child will be well taught across the board here and should achieve her full potential – the brightest will fly as high here as anywhere. The school now has a fully qualified SEN to develop Individual Educational Programmes for those who need them.

Games, Options, The Arts: For a school down a leafy suburban side street, this school is astonishingly privileged in most of its provisions and especially its sporting facilities. A superb, vast sports hall (1997) with Olympic floor area – this hoary old editor had not seen its like in comparable urban girls' schools – an inviting adjacent playing field (though with a decidedly decayed pavilion), a designated dance studio (school excels in dance), a gym and fitness centre – few well-endowed boys' schools can offer much more. Football is a popular option and the coach comes from Fulham FC. Athletics, gymnastics, badminton all strong and also some of the options which include all the usuals plus self-defence, cricket, yoga, street dance and kickboxing – a rare and enlightened breadth of approach. A/S PE on offer.

Lots of drama including to A level, a good hall for productions plus recital hall in music block though no drama studio. Art is good and the school displays its artwork everywhere – exceptionally well. Many individual recent prizes for art. Pottery and ceramics especially imaginative and fun. DT and woodwork also well provided for and exciting. New music block is highly attractive and an excellent resource. Eight practice rooms, super recital hall – all encourages musical activity which now has room to grow. Music technology looks set to take off as all girls now learn keyboard and most will move on to GCSE music. School claims it has the 'best equipped music studio in London' and it is clearly a top contender. Main music teaching room in shape of a piano lid – all part of this imaginatively designed, witty building. Good public speaking record. Lots of lunchtime clubs for such esoterica as bag-making, cheerleading, hairbraiding and chess – all led by sixth formers. Has 'Investors in Careers' kitemark.

Background and Atmosphere: School moved into existing buildings – formerly the home of the Battersea Boys' Grammar school – in 1993. Austere, unappealing beige-grey brick 1930s buildings come as a surprise in the quiet, prosperous suburban setting but a greater surprise is how attractive and well designed the buildings are internally. Spacious corridors – a rare boon for any school – large, light classrooms and plenty of them, excellent later extensions – all creates a sense of relaxed space and ease. Even labs not too austere and some have geraniums in pots on the window sills. Library has new librarian and is much in need of restocking. Whole school is networked. IT centre with technicians always on hand to help individuals. Lots of other IT rooms. This is one of the most orderly and tidy schools we have visited – work on walls and posters are imaginative and well-displayed everywhere – and there is a feeling that everyone feels responsible for taking a pride in the school environment. Some attractive small gardens – school inherited boys' school cenotaph and sunken pond.

At end of the main drive, the new music centre adds considerably to overall external appearance and includes sixth form centre – again light, spacious and well-equipped with good kitchen, study rooms and large, attractive common room – few London girls' schools can offer as much. Exterior of bleaker main buildings could be enhanced with some painting of grim Crittall windows. Parents pay tribute to happy atmosphere but comment, 'it's a bit slow' and feel that more of an edge is needed across the board – 'something they can excel in to compete with the other schools in the area', said a parent. 'It's not very dynamic but does now seem to be going the right way.'

Pastoral Care and Discipline: School council, system of head girls and prefects. House points (and minus points), certificates and prizes. School also has subject prefects – a sensible idea in the drive to promote individual subjects. Pastoral care in overall hands of highly capable and experienced senior teacher but devolves to form tutors and anyone from the head herself to the school nurse – whoever girls feel they can talk to. No counsellor. School adheres to GDST drugs policy but current head has yet to have recourse to it. Strong PSHE programme. Relaxed but disciplined atmosphere evidence of a school community at ease with itself. Year 13 girls allowed out over lunch but most seem to prefer to stay in.

Pupils and Parents: Ethnically mixed as one would expect in this area ringed by Brixton, Balham, Norbury and Tulse Hill. A third of the pupils non-white, and to all appearances school is a model of happy co-existence and inter-racial harmony. They come from a wide area of South London and transport connections are good. Many walk or cycle to school. Socio-economic backgrounds also widely various and girls come from a huge number of feeder schools – many state. (School provided us with a list of nearly 100!) School, very helpfully, runs a bus between the junior and senior schools – five minutes apart. Old girls include June Whitfield, Angela Carter, Carol Royle, Hannah Waddingham, Eva Myers, Cordelia Kretzchmar, Nazarnine Moshiri.

Entrance: At 11+ via entrance exam, group interview and school reference. Vast majority of junior school pupils come seamlessly through after a test in year 5 which guarantees them a place if they pass – which all but 3-4 a year do. All sit the entrance exam in year 6 – a formality for all but said 3 or 4 who may, with plenty of warning, be advised to find a fallback school. Perhaps an anomalous, but common, system. Thereafter, for occasional places, via exam and interview. For the sixth form, aptitude test, interview and conditional offer.

Exit: Some at 16 to boarding schools, sixth form colleges, local mixed comps. School tries to discourage this premature exit but is philosophical. At 18, across the board to everywhere to study everything. 2003 destinations included various London University colleges, medical and art schools around the country, one or two to Oxbridge. An impressive list. Some straight to employment.

Money Matters: Scholarships (not means-tested) awarded on academic performance in entrance exams; also for top-class work in middle school and again in the sixth. Bursaries (means-tested) awarded for academic excellence at 11+ and sixth. No sibling discounts. The GDST schools, in general, are exceptional value for money everywhere.

Remarks: One's overall impression is of a large but comfortable, relaxed, uncrowded and sane environment where good but unpressurised work and activities buzz all around. Everyone talks of the huge range and quality of extra-curricular activities on offer (though some parents talk of need for more after-school activities) and there is a genuine sense of enjoyment in this pleasant place. School became a four-form entry only in 1999 so is still expanding but another class of 30 or so still won't fill it up. An unusually orderly place – but not neurotically so – the only relieving signs of disorder acceptably in the DT room – a good, workful place. Pervasive sense that head has things to do and is busy doing them together with an atmosphere of cooperation and cheerful excitement as it happens – though perhaps not fast enough for some. School looks set to challenge its glitzier local rivals in the near future.

STROUD HIGH SCHOOL

Beards Lane, Cainscross Road, Stroud, Gloucestershire,
GL5 4HF

Tel: 01453 764 441

Fax: 01453 756 304

E-mail: admin@stroudhigh.gloucs.sch.uk

Website: www.stroudhigh.gloucs.sch.uk

• Pupils: 901 all day girls • Ages: 11-18 • Size of sixth form: 257 girls in mixed sixth form, Downfield, formed jointly with next door boys' school Marling • Non-denom • State • Open days: September and (for the sixth form) November

Headteacher: Since 1999, Mrs Jo Grills MA (fiftyish). Educated at Pontefract High School and Bristol University, where she read theology. Worked in a number of state comprehensives, deputy head of Worle School in Weston-super-Mare before taking up headship of Stroud High. Married to the Rev Malcolm Grills, with daughter working for BBC local radio and son at Warwick University. Bubbly, refreshingly frank, passionate about her 'magic girls'. Mrs Grills has been seconded as Director of Education for two terms 2005/6 and Joyce Winwood, deputy head, is acting head teacher.

Academic Matters: Across-the-board excellence combined with big efforts to offer flexible choices. Combinations of subjects tailored to individual. Head long resisted idea of becoming a specialist school for languages or sciences – 'we are already a specialist school for the very able' – but has now given in, the school achieved Specialist Science status in July 2003 with many exciting ideas about encouraging more girls to follow scientific and mathematical careers but the school will also maintain excellence across the full range of subjects. Lots of mixing of arts and sciences at both GCSE and A level, with more than 98 per cent pass rate at GCSE at A* to C in most subjects. Double science, with separate sciences offered to the more scientifically minded. At A level, English is extremely popular and grades are consistently high – in 2005 94 per cent of the 127 students who took English language at GCSE achieved A* or A and in history 80 per cent achieved A* or A. At A level, politics, English, mathematics and psychology are very popular choices with good results; science subjects popular with more mixed results. Almost 70 per cent A/B grades overall. One student achieved in the top 5 marks for English and politics. Those entering AEA achieved 3 distinctions and

6 merits. No reports on languages – they seem to have a far lower profile here.

Surprisingly few take music at exam level, despite the popularity of orchestras and performance elsewhere in the school. Existing modular teaching style and huge commitment of girls and staff have brought outstanding early AS results, with both coping admirably with the repeated changes thrown at them by state education reforms. Combined teaching groups with Marling boys in sixth form for last two years have not affected results but have afforded greater subject choice. Further links with nearby comprehensive Archway and Stroud College for vocational courses and media studies A level. Large, busy, lively classes: 32 in years 7-9, 28 in years 10-11 and around 15/20 in the sixth form. Core of longstanding experienced staff combining with enthusiastic, able new recruits. A dozen SEN pupils with dyslexia or physical disabilities, although most of the school is inaccessible to wheelchairs.

Games, Options, The Arts: Lots of sports on offer and superb new sports hall. Tennis courts have recently been totally refurbished thanks to money from the Parents' Association. Stroud High has girls competing for county and country in tennis, hockey and netball, plus a champion skier and basketball player. No houses in school, so sporting competition tends to be external. Many non-competitive and slightly obscure sports, such as new image rugby, dance, stoolball, trampolining, softball and gymnastics. World Challenge expeditions, including Thailand, very popular. Very musical bunch, with more than a third taking individual lessons and enthusiastic support for giving and attending concerts and band performances, both locally and in Europe. Lovely new music centre, with fine performance space and soundproof rooms, finally replacing cramped and noisy old music block.

Old fashioned but well stocked library, three newish computer rooms. No school magazine, although annual supplement contributed to local newspaper. Drama very popular, with a drama club and regular plays, including joint productions with Marling. Regular foreign exchanges, particularly to France but also Germany and Spain, with the chance to complete work experience while there. Big on charity and excellent fund raisers, with thousands of pounds raised in Rag Week each year and many smaller kind gestures. The school recently won the 'Giving Nation' award, presented for fundraising (£25,000 raised in 2003-4) The award was presented in 11 Downing Street and, as a result, 8 students and a member of staff visited a Save the Children Project in India early in 2005.

Background and Atmosphere: Stroud High School

began life in 1904, after a group of local dignitaries agreed to provide for local girls a similar education to that offered to Stroud's boys at Marling School, founded almost 30 years previously. Squeezing into the School of Art in nearby Lansdown, the school moved into its purpose-built home just outside the town centre in 1911. At first sight, its red-brick grandeur and green frontage are impressive. But looking deeper, even the most unobservant visitor cannot miss the poor state of many of the buildings. However a new eight classroom block, every room equipped with an interactive whiteboard, has recently been opened to house English and maths. A new design and technology block, shared with Marling School, has also been recently completed. A new one million pound sixth form block will open in November 2004 to provide much needed study and social space. However, there are still buildings which need to be replaced – girls and staff make enormous efforts to overcome the shortcomings of the structure, with bright displays and lots of colour in every classroom, but their enthusiasm and hard work barely disguise the years of underfunding. It is a credit to the girls and staff that despite the failings of the buildings, the place has a tremendous buzz, a truly happy, supportive and caring atmosphere in which pupils clearly flourish.

Pastoral Care and Discipline: Lots of support schemes in place – communication the main thrust. Pupils failing to thrive are mentored by designated members of staff. Buddying system – older pupil paired with younger girl to talk through any sort of problem – works well. Peer mentoring has also been successfully introduced after a training session for mentors led by Relate. Very active whole school council. All senior pupils are eligible to become termly prefects and sixth form policy is guided by sixth form council, formed and run by students. Very keen to keep pupils in school – pragmatic approach to rare incidents involving soft drugs, with each case judged on merit, guided by realistic view of what happens to excluded pupils: 'they disappear into a black hole', and the fact the school is in Stroud, home to large numbers of first-generation, pot-friendly, hippies.

Pupils and Parents: Largely middle class, white girls, many indulging their high-fashion, flamboyant taste in clothes in the sixth form. But Mrs Grills notes that a number face real hardship at home – school will help where it can. Most are local but some travel from Cirencester, Cheltenham and Gloucester. A few are much further away, with a cluster from Malmesbury and even Swindon – an hour's journey by train.

Entrance: Tough but not impossible. Around 3 applications per place, with acceptance based solely on perform-ance in school's VRQ-based entrance exam. Waiting list leaves some hope – around a third eventually gain places. Many appeals – three dozen this year – but virtually no prospect of success. Additional places available in sixth form, with minimum requirements of 5 A*-C at GCSE.

Exit: Nearly all go on to higher education, in almost every subject under the sun. Traditional universities such as Bristol, Exeter, Manchester and Newcastle popular. But head berates Oxbridge interviewers who, she believes, have appeared to discriminate against state school pupils, including many of her most able girls. Nevertheless, at least one or two and up to half a dozen will get in each year.

Remarks: Lovely warm atmosphere for thoughtful girls with outstanding academic abilities who are happy to turn a blind eye to the décor.

SURBITON HIGH SCHOOL

Linked to Surbiton High Junior Girls' School in the Junior section

Linked to Surbiton Preparatory School in the Junior section

Surbiton Crescent, Kingston Upon Thames, Surrey, KT1 2JT

Tel: 020 8546 5245

Fax: 02085 470 026

E-mail: surbiton.high@church-schools.com

Website: www.surbitonhigh.com

• Pupils: 689 girls, all day • Ages: High School 11-18, Junior Girls' School 4-11 and Boys' Prep 4-11 • Size of sixth form: 188 • Christian ethos (but all denominations accepted) • Fees: £3,199 (Senior school/sixth form only) per term • Independent • Open days: October/November

---

Head: Since 2001 Dr Jennifer Longhurst MA PhD (modern languages, University of Exeter) (fifties), formerly vice-principal, Solihull Sixth Form College. Married with grown-up children. A glamorous figure – 'she dresses like a minor royal,' said one mother. She treats the school as her domain and is a powerful presence around the place; 'gushing' says one Mum 'overpowering at times,' added another. Fiercely proud of the school, she never misses an opportunity to sing the praises of the school and the girls – to the extent that one parent wondered quizzically if Dr L ever thought there were any problems. However, parents are left in no doubt over her 110 per cent commitment to the school. She has overseen huge investment and expansion of the school in the past few years. Very hands-on – even follows up on some pastoral issues personally. Some parents find her manner lacking in empathy, although, all said, the girls like her.

Academic Matters: Academic, but not overwhelmingly so. Local reputation for wider range of abilities than some other more high-pressure girls' independents in the area. Good solid results – 90-ish per cent A*-B at GCSE, 83 per cent grades A/B at A level. Most impressive in art at A level – but no weak subjects. Head values 'all-rounders' and 'nice' girls and is loath to throw anyone out on grounds of under-achievement, even post-GCSE – 'we hang on in there for them.' GCSE results translated into scores, which determine number of A, A/S levels taken – B necessary at GCSE to proceed in any given subject. School claims to emphasise languages and allows girls to study up to four in one year in the lower school. Dyslexia, dyspraxia and ESL are all catered for and charged termly.

Games, Options, The Arts: No on-site sporting grassed areas – currently substantial sports facilities are out at Hinchley Wood (10 minutes by coach) – 33 acres of school-owned games fields offer netball, tennis, athletics and hockey. Rowing at East Molesey boat club. Renowned for school skiing trips and (championship level) school ski team, which may have spawned Chemmy Alcott, Old Girl and Olympic ski-team member.

Nicely furnished music facilities and plenty of individual instrumental lessons. The school is becoming more musical than it might once have been under new director of music. Orchestra, choir and various opportunities to perform. Drama is strong and a popular option, several theatrical productions and competitions a year. Boys borrowed from Tiffin School for male roles. Commitment to high tech evidenced by impressive two-room IT suite, ubiquitous 'smart' electronic whiteboards in every classroom and a video link messaging system with eye-high televisions in the public areas (not operational on day of visit). Design technology and art rooms are well equipped and girls' efforts rewarded in corridor displays. Two timetabled periods a week, as well as lunch time and after school, allow for a full extracurricular programme.

Background and Atmosphere: Main school site is housed in a series of modern buildings, as well as the characterful Surbiton Assembly Rooms. Inside classrooms are orderly, old and new blend nicely. The school has just completed the redevelopment of its main school site – to include 14 spacious classrooms, specialist labs for science & modern languages, a new learning resources centre, administrative area and open plan art school. £15 million of redevelopment has taken place in the last 5 years! The school is expanding – currently six forms enter at 11 (due to enormous pressure on places). Officially, maximum class size is 24. Some parental mutterings about growing number of pupils. School fills one suburban block, bounded by assorted housing stock and wide, parking-choked, avenues. Parking issues in evidence on site, staff cars vie with pupils for outdoor space comprising a couple of tennis/netball courts, a lawn bordered by tired outhouses – 'it is flooded with girls in the summer' – and an environmental garden. There is a lot of walking around to different parts of the school site, which puts off some prospective parents. Pupils must leave the main site to reach the recently purchased and thoroughly refurbished Surbiton Assembly Rooms (C19th century listed building, quirky and not unglamorous once above the sad sixties façade) situated across the road from the main school and which houses 10 classrooms, music practice areas, an ample hall/theatre and refectory. Bridge/tunnel access now abandoned for planning reasons, but the head says the school is going to try again to win over the planners. Girls make short walk several times a day with aid of full-time crossing wardens and pelican lights. The sixth form college is also away from the main site and head has brought with her an expansion project – as sixth form numbers seem bound to grow, given large influxes at the bottom of the school. The already modern building has been doubled in size onto ground purchased behind it – expanded common rooms and 10 more seminar-sized classrooms plus a new all-singing, all-dancing subterranean gym (a new sports hall is planned on the main site for whole school use replacing the ageing gym). Head admits somewhat unexciting grey/green uniforms are due for revision. Sixth formers are smart casual.

Pastoral Care and Discipline: Much emphasis given to Christian ethos, quite churchy assemblies. Approximately 8 per cent of girls are non-Christians but in school are expected to fall in with prevailing faith practices. Charity and good deeds are lodestones, witnessed in links with local community; elderly and disabled groups etc. School prides itself on high levels of pastoral care, local reputation for such sees it used as repository for 'refugees' who have been let down on this front elsewhere.

Large year 7 intake is organised into classes with groups of friends from feeder junior schools. Form tutors report back to heads of year in weekly meetings – problems spotted early. Less than 10 per cent of the full time teaching staff are men but peripatetics bring up the percentage. School lunch compulsory to year 9. Healthy eating policy extends to salad daily and chips on Friday. A school nurse keeps an eye on health and takes messages into the classrooms. Well-disciplined environment backed by exhaustive and stringent drugs/banned substances policy and child protection document. One-day suspensions, detentions and community duties for infractions of school rules. Praise meted out in equal measure with merit mark competitions and commendations.

Pupils and Parents: Close to Surbiton BR for mainline services, 44 per cent of pupils use parent-run and jolly extensive school bus network. Parents appear welcomed and involved; organising the annual pupils' (mixed) ball and other charity events. Many parents are quite devoted in their affection for the place. Pupils genuinely from a mixture of backgrounds with about 40 per cent joining from state primaries at 11. Broad catchment area covers Wimbledon, Putney, Richmond, Twickenham, Kingston and further reaches of the Surrey commuter belt. School occupies comfortable middle ground in terms of community and location, not quite as urban/streetwise as its nearer London neighbours, but less sheltered than the leafy Surrey institutions also on its doorstep.

Entrance: Initially – application form, previous school report and entrance examination. 'Reckon on the top third of state primary girls getting in,' says a parent. Pressure on places may see an end to this, as increased number of 11+ applications is pushing up pass mark for the entry test. No test for joiners at sixth form – GCSE results, school report and interview win entrance.

Exit: Vast majority stays on into sixth form and most of these go to traditional universities; 6 or so to Oxbridge. Fifteen per cent of leavers take a gap year.

Money Matters: At 11 academic scholarships (50 or 25 per cent of fees). Music, art or sport scholarships (33 per cent of fees). Broadly similar reward scheme at sixth form entry. Means-tested bursaries for girls who will 'benefit from what the school has to offer' funded by the Church Schools Foundation. Discounts for daughters of the clergy.

Remarks: Solid, academic, school with determined new head. Suits broader range of abilities than some of the other academic independent schools in the locality and is particularly well thought of for its pastoral care. Very large school now expanding into welcome new space. However, proximity clearly breeds friendliness for which it enjoys an indisputable reputation.

SUTTON GRAMMAR SCHOOL FOR BOYS

Manor Lane, Sutton, Surrey, SM1 4AS

Tel: 020 8642 3821
Fax: 020 8661 4500
E-mail: sgs@suttonlea.org
Website: www.suttongrammar.sutton.sch.uk

• Pupils: 810 boys, all day • Ages: 1-18 • Size of sixth form: 210
• Non-denom • State • Open days: September

Head: Since 1990, Mr Gordon Ironside MA PGCE (fifties). Read physics at Cambridge. Joined the school in 1983 as head of maths, then deputy head in 1987. Comes across as a generally good egg and proud Northerner. Very much a man's man rather than a smooth charmer – no bad thing. His out of school interests include sport, particularly golf and tennis, and Rotarians. 'And, like everyone, family life takes up a lot of my time,' he says. Highly rated by parents who describe him as 'friendly' and 'effective.' 'He's a great role model for the boys and a very strong figure, but friendly rather than frightening,' says one mother. He tends to play good cop to the bad cop (but not unpopular) deputy Mr Gibson – who has more day to day interaction with pupils and is responsible for their pastoral care.

Academic Matters: Very impressive – a selective school with excellent SATS, GCSE and A level results. 'It's not a hothouse like some other state grammars, although the results are on a par,' says one pleased parent. Head says boys are picking up prizes all the time (top GCSE score in geography, design awards and Arkwright scholarships – offered to A level students intending to go on to university to study for careers in engineering). Popular optional GCSEs include history, geography, and business studies, at A level, maths and physics (by a mile). Mathematicians thrive here. At the end of year 8, the maths high achievers are selected to study for their GCSE early and to start their A level work in year 11. Science is another real strength. About 75 per cent (a hefty chunk compared to other schools) of the boys take separate science GCSEs instead of the easier dual award. Plenty of homework, but parents feel the pace is right. 'You probably would not enjoy it here if you just scraped in after being heavily coached as standards are very high,' said one parent.

There are EAL students but their success in passing the entrance test shows that this is not a major issue. The school has a part-time SENCO – as a selective school there is only the occasional statemented pupil, but dyslexia and dyspraxia are more common – though not exactly loads of it – and the school advises staff how to handle these conditions in their classrooms.

Games, Options, The Arts: A high achieving sporty lot. Parents at pains to point out how good the sport is here – several feel the school underplays its sporting card for fear of not being taken so seriously as a strongly academic school. Fantastic sports grounds – 27 acres of playing fields, pitches, cricket squares and athletics track – three miles from school in Cheam and the boys make the 15 minute journey in the school's own coach. On the main school site there is an old faithful, heated, 25m open air swimming pool (in regular use) and a sports hall. 'Lots of football – which makes a nice change as you usually get rugby at selective schools,' says a mother. School also supplies ball boys for Wimbledon – the envy no doubt of many a private school boy.

The old gym is due to become a drama studio – drama gradually getting stronger and will be introduced at A level in 2006. Lots of the music and drama is produced in conjunction with Sutton High School for Girls. Usual mix of Young Enterprise, DofE, and CCF is popular here – we did a double take as boys in camouflage sat in lessons, they wear their CCF uniforms during school hours if they are meeting afterwards.

Background and Atmosphere: School has been around in various incarnations for 100 years and is now on a small compact site, rather hemmed in by the popular Sutton shopping centre which has grown up around it. (Pupils are allowed off-site at lunchtime from year 10, which eases pressure on space and the limited canteen facilities). Main building is circa 1928, and looks it, with associated wood panelling in places and the odd old-fashioned lab still surviving, but lots of new bits have been added as part of a major modernisation programme. A couple of the science rooms have roof gardens housing outdoor experiments. IT facilities are all around the school, with two main classrooms for full-class teaching. Corridors are narrow and warrant a 'one-way' system as the boys navigate the school. Overall facilities are workmanlike rather than flashy – but it's all there. Scruffy in places – these are boys after all. A traditional grammar school environment where the boys appear to work and play hard: 'it's a lovely, lovely, place,' says one mother. Boys we saw were fully engaged in what they were doing. Purposeful atmosphere. 'It's formal and old-fashioned in a good way,' say parents. Long standing staff – over a third have been there more than 10 years and turnover is low.

Pastoral Care and Discipline: 'Very happy and caring' says one mum. 'There's an emphasis on everybody participating in everything,' adds another. Buddy system exists for new boys. School acts quickly if any problems occur. A parent we spoke to was very impressed with the fast and effective way her son's experience as a victim of bullying was handled. Form tutors, heads of year and pages of policy are in place – but in fact all staff take responsibility for the boys' welfare. Parents feel their sons have a healthy respect for the head and his staff and the staff get to know their pupils well. Head says he prefers to inspire self-discipline but he doesn't think twice about imposing it where necessary. A boy was sent home on the day of our visit for arriving with streaks in his hair after a study break. Zero tolerance of smoking, drink or drugs. (School feels a strong line on smoking makes the latter vices less likely.) Strictly upheld standards for uniform, hair and behaviour. Sixth formers dress for business in suits. Basically, you have to toe the line here.

Pupils and Parents: Good cultural mix (over a third of the boys are from non-white ethnic backgrounds), a confident and polite bunch. Majority are local, but others travel from homes along the main transport links to Sutton, including Cheam, Worcester Park, Kingston, Surbiton, Merton and South Wimbledon. Most from state primaries. There are about 60 feeder schools with none sending more than about four boys in any one year. Parents are mostly 'middle class and middle aged,' jokes one mother. Lots of professional parents and supportive PTA. OB network very strong – David Bellamy is one of the better known and is a regular visitor.

Entrance: Mostly in year 7. School sets its own exam covering verbal reasoning, literacy (including a piece of 'free writing') and numeracy. 'I felt it was a fair test,' said one mother 'it's based on what they will have learned in year 5 rather than necessitating lots of extra coaching.' Hugely over-subscribed – generally between 750 and 800 boys take the test (from about 60 feeder schools) for 120 places. The 30 highest scoring boys will get a place wherever they live; the remaining places are allocated among those exceeding the pass mark according to proximity to the school, with some priority for siblings. For the sixth form, the minimum entry standard is four A grades and two Bs at GCSE. Existing pupils take most places, with only a small number (5-10) joining from elsewhere.

Exit: Each year 10-15 boys leave at 16, mostly for FE colleges: some have not made the grade for the sixth form, others are looking for different A level options or more freedom. At 18, most go to university, with approx 10 a year to Oxbridge.

Remarks: A friendly, disciplined school with high academic standards and good pastoral care. Not for free spirits or rule breakers.

SUTTON HIGH SCHOOL

Linked to Sutton High Junior School in the Junior section

55 Cheam Road, Sutton, Surrey, SM1 2AX

Tel: 02086 420 594
Fax: 02086 422 014
E-mail: office@sut.gdst.net
Website: www.gdst.net/suttonhigh

- Pupils: 745 girls, all day • Ages: 4-18 • Size of sixth form: 120
- Non-denom • Fees: Senior school: £2,883; junior school:
£2,243 • Independent

Head: Since 2003, Mr Stephen Callaghan BA NPQH (forties), a linguist, formerly deputy head at Guildford High (also a girls' school). Approachable and down-to-earth, an easy communicator and a great advocate for the girls. Married with two children; his wife is also a teacher.

Academic Matters: Academically strong across the board – a good first division school. 65 per cent plus get straight A*/A at GCSE; 80 plus per cent of A levels A/B. Traditional range of subjects on offer, very good results in English, history and French but most encouraging is take-up and success in less typical areas of study for girls – physical sciences, maths. Much is made of IT as both an examined subject and as a cross-curricular educational tool. State of the art ICT suite and all girls in years 12 and 13 take CLAIT.

The head, as a modern languages specialist, has raised their profile: French, German and Spanish all offered at GCSE, and the last now also introduced in year 7. Extensive and imaginative programme of field trips/exchanges.

Only nine subjects are compulsory at GCSE as head keen to have space for eg further challenges/subjects for stretching the most able, or support for SEN or EAL students – a genuinely bespoke support system. Head doesn't weed out weaker candidates post-GCSE, and his approach of supporting all pupils in their progress through the school is refreshing and praiseworthy, particularly in this academic environment (other heads take note). 'Endless support is there if you need it but you have to want to help yourself too,' acknowledges a sixth former.

Class sizes start off quite large (an average of 24 up to KS3) falling to 15 by A level.

Games, Options, The Arts: Vast, aircraft hangar-type gym and fabulous 25m heated indoor pool. Both facilities much used (also for after school clubs) and help the inclusive feel at the school by being open to pupils and their families at weekends. Outside sport not so much available – a few hard tennis/netball courts (some girls in National Netball squads) and one hockey pitch used by year 7 only, everyone else is bused out.

Large, light and airy hall for performing arts, with staging and lighting equipment. Girls are often joined by boys from Sutton Grammar for drama productions. Lots of music – particularly impressive music technology rooms – active orchestra, chamber choir and mixed choir – again with Sutton Grammar. Large art department, but housed in different buildings, includes ceramics/pottery, photography suite (although has no pretensions to offer such specialties as separate A level subjects) – evidence of talent and hard work on display throughout.

Background and Atmosphere: The original school is a lovely Victorian building which now mainly houses the headmaster's office, reception, etc. The rest of school comprises several large buildings and a few smaller ones (some more attractive than others) built at various stages through 20th century. This gives a cramped first appearance but large open areas at the centre of the site create a more spacious feel than expected. Some grassy areas for girls to enjoy on warm days. Sixth form block (Dene Centre) is a delight with plenty of space and extra facilities (it even has its own gym!) including the much appreciated careers centre with its own dedicated laptops for pupils' research. An ideal place for the sixth formers to spread out and feel independent from rest of school.

Pastoral Care and Discipline: Head (with plenty of support from form tutors, heads of year and school council) places particular emphasis on pastoral care and discipline – it is a great source of pride to the school. Very clear strategies for dealing with anti-social behaviour and for nurturing a feeling of community. Successful 'buddying' arrangement between year 7 and year 13 encourages vertical friendships and a sense of belonging for new pupils (house system in junior school may soon be extended to senior school to develop this further). Strong on discipline with subject detentions held during lunchtime, and headmaster detentions after school followed up with a letter home.

Pupils and Parents: Wide ranging in every sense. Geographically – from Wimbledon to Reigate and everywhere in between. One reason for the geographical spread is the local state grammar schools – many pupils travel in from beyond their catchment areas. (These highly respected state schools also account for loss of some of brightest local pupils from the junior school at 11+). Socially – daughters of local business people and City mix. Lots of first time buyers with ethnic mix representative of the area, especially popular with Korean families. Belying outward appearances typical of their age, girls are polite, mature and well informed; seem to know exactly what they want out of life and where to look for it. OGs of note include novelist Susan Howatch and Sue Littlemore, BBC correspondent.

Entrance: At 11, 60-70 per cent from junior school, others from wide range in both State and independent sectors, including some from international schools. Entry test in January before admission – English, maths, verbal and non-verbal reasoning and interview. Sixth form candidates need 'good GCSE results' and A or A* in chosen A level subjects together with passes in general and verbal reasoning papers. Occasional places do arise at other stages, so definitely worth a try.

Exit: About 90 per cent stay on to sixth form. Loss of some, due to girls having been in same place from age 4, 'so feel time to move on' and to others wanting to take a less traditional range of A levels. Most to top universities to read traditional subjects – wide range of sciences, medicine and law recently popular. Around 10 per cent to Oxbridge. Some opt for the more vocational, for example, QTS courses, physiotherapy and art schools. Careers advice much praised and is taken very seriously, with many outside speakers and an in-house ISCO adviser -'we do feel up to date and well informed about our choices,' comments a sixth former.

Money Matters: Scholarships and bursaries for senior school pupils only. Bursaries are means tested. Scholarships at 11 and 16 for those who excel in entrance exam. Head is able to 'flex amount of money available' and sixth form awards can be made for music, drama, sport as well as academic prowess.

Remarks: Happy, purposeful school with good results and grammar school feeling and strengths. Head keen to continue 'maintaining high standards but the challenge comes with retaining flexibility too.'

SUTTON VALENCE SCHOOL

Linked to Sutton Valence Preparatory School in the Junior section

Sutton Valence, Maidstone, Kent, ME17 3HL

Tel: 01622 845200
Fax: 01622 844 103
E-mail: enquiries@svs.org.uk
Website: www.svs.org.uk

- Pupils: 510; 373 boys, 137 girls. 94 boys and 32 girls board
- Ages: 11-18 • Size of sixth form: 141 • C of E • Fees: From £3,460 junior day to £7,150 senior boarding • Independent
- Open days: September, November and March

Head: Since 2001, Mr Joe Davies (mid forties); educated St John's College, Cambridge – MA in history. Previously a housemaster at Tonbridge, then six years as deputy head of St John's School Leatherhead – many parents were sorry to see him go. Married with 4 children, 1 now attends the school; his wife is also a teacher. Head consults his school council on changes and new developments. Parents commented, 'he is going about his job enthusiastically and has a genuine desire to be inclusive'.

Academic Matters: A school which looks for good for all-rounders who will work to the best of their abilities and benefit from the wide extra-curricular programme; the emphasis is on joining in and getting involved. Selective intake but not hugely. Strong science and maths; 30 per cent enter international maths challenges. Also good English, drama and media studies. Four languages taught and foreign exchanges arranged. Computers everywhere, access at any time, pupils run the school website and newsletters. Peaceful, well stocked library.

Good quality staff, with purposeful approach; average age is 40. School likes to have teachers who have their own families, many of whom live on site. Results are good given the broad intake – most take 8/9 GCSEs, 85 per cent-ish A*- C grades (many take them late, so don't appear in the league tables); most go on to A level. Popular subjects at A level include ICT, psychology, media studies and the sciences; OK results.

Both group and individual teaching is available for mild dyslexia/dyspraxia, the principle being that strong support at the right moment leads to independence. Parents feel that staff have a good awareness of children's difficulties. EFL well-resourced, with specialist teachers on hand to help with language, settling-in and customs; the school gets more applications from foreign students than they can accommodate. A good choice of outings, theatre trips, sports/music tours and foreign travel is arranged for pupils.

Games, Options, The Arts: Sports are strong, main games are rugby, tennis, athletics, netball, and cricket; enormous sports hall, opened in 2002, contains full-sized indoor hockey pitch, sprung floor cricket nets, gym, changing and teaching facilities. Girls have been hockey and netball county champions. School has links with professional cricketers Richie Richardson and Brian Lara; girls' cricket is growing in popularity. Outdoor swimming pool – some parents would like to see this updated. High quality music and drama, a third of the pupils play an instrument, splendid concerts and plays that are welcomed by parents and staff. Also jazz group, concert and chamber orchestras, big band, girls' choir, chapel choir.

The art and DT departments have expanded in recent years to offer wider scope. Now housed in the village a few minutes walk away, art in a converted chapel complete with sculpture and photographic studios and lecture room, DT in a converted gymnasium; everything appears to be on offer from metalwork to pottery. Sixth form DT pupils have the opportunity to enter the 'Audi Young Designer of the Year' competition.

A very busy extra-curricular programme includes many sports, games and arts. Pupils choose between community service and CCF (army, navy or air force – some of these groups interestingly are run by female teachers). Community service pupils get involved with environmental projects, old people's homes, tending graves and helping in local primary schools.

Background and Atmosphere: One of the oldest public schools in the UK, founded by William Lambe in 1576; a portrait of the gentleman hangs in the school, no longer atmospherically draped in cobwebs. The original school building was demolished although some Tudor almshouses still exist now converted into classrooms. Uninspiring but bearable buildings. Extensive grounds with beautifully kept gardens that help to create a tranquil feeling about the site. Part of the Westminster Schools Trust – other members include Emanuel and Westminster City Comprehensive – they still meet for traditional annual inter-school sporting events.

Pastoral Care and Discipline: Solid support, the traditional 'house' system has been replaced by tutor groups – each pupil will attend their tutor group twice a day, and will have access to their tutor at any time if they need it. There is set of clear school rules to follow – fair but firm, detention for persistent offenders. Prefect system. New school council just established. Boarding houses are well kept and homely, particularly the girls' where there is a very friendly matron. Lots of flexi-boarding – aims to meet parents' and pupils' many different needs.

Pupils and Parents: Parents mainly from the professional classes; popular with foreign parents – 12 per cent from abroad, Hong Kong Chinese predominant. Pupils are relaxed and friendly. Alumni Ben Brown TV journalist, Mark Benson cricketer, Stephen Hopkins film director, Prof Allan Hobson professor of psychiatry Harvard, Terence Cuneo painter, Sir Charles Groves conductor.

Entrance: 11+ exam, looking for those who have A level potential; also 13+ and 16+. 40 per cent come from Sutton Valence's prep school, and then a radius of 15/20 miles – Hastings, Sevenoaks and Weald of Kent from both state and independent sector.

Exit: 95 per cent go on to university; popular choices are Leeds, Bristol, Durham, Bath, Oxbridge and Nottingham. 97 per cent gain entry to their first choice university.

Money Matters: A quite well-endowed school; up to 10 scholarships and bursaries each year including music, art, drama, D&T, sport, all rounder, academic and some sixth form. Can also help some pupils with fees whose family circumstances change, at the head's discretion.

Remarks: School gets good results both academically and socially. 'Both my sons left the school confident, feeling they had achieved well in a number of different areas and went on to university. Most of all, I appreciated the fact the they had a sense of reality about the world, something that not all public schools manage to achieve with their leavers'.

SYDENHAM HIGH SCHOOL GDST

Linked to Sydenham High Junior School GDST in the Junior section

19 Westwood Hill, London, SE26 6BL

Tel: 020 8768 8000
Fax: 02087 688 002
E-mail: info@syd.gdst.net
Website: www.gdst.net/sydenhamhigh

• Pupils: 690 girls, all day • Ages: 11-18 • Fees: Junior: £2,383; Senior: £3,063 • Independent • Open days: Early October

Head: Since 2002 Mrs Kathryn Pullen BA MA PGCE (early fifties). Educated at Llanelli Girls' Grammar School. Studied English and American Studies at Warwick followed by a drama PGCE at Phillippa Fawcett College London. Appointed headteacher after spending 12 years as deputy. Says it was beneficial to already know girls and their parents. Recognised and appreciated academic strength but wanted to add a caring dimension too. Changed management systems – sought to empower staff.

Smart and fashionable, an inspirational role model for the girls, worked hard to get to where she is today, still very hands-on. Says work and learning should be a challenge not a pressure and each child should be happy in their own skin. Lovely Welsh lilt exudes genuine warmth, big hit with girls and parents alike.

Academic Matters: An academic school currently soaring up the league tables. All usual suspects on offer with additions of classical civilisation, government and politics, philosophy and theatre studies in sixth form. Languages and sciences ever popular, there's even a Japanese club. Classes average 20 in senior school, much smaller in sixth form. All pass A level with 70-ish per cent graded A or B. GCSE A* to C pass rate a commendable 95 per cent with no subject 'letting the side down.' Excellent well-stocked library. Lots of ICT; many classrooms have interactive whiteboards – 'they make lessons fun, bring things to life, teachers use things from the internet, computer documents and drawings – much better than blackboards.' Mix of traditional and modern teaching styles plus specials such as science week. Emphasis now on how learners learn; believe it's important to teach to learn, not just to pass exams – must look ahead to demands beyond GCSE. Girls say they get very involved in lessons and are encouraged to ask questions; the ones we spoke to were able to intelligently and enthusiastically discuss their work. Even homework was manageable and if it isn't 'you can always talk to the teachers, they're very understanding'.

Separate sixth form block, small classes, dress code: casual smart (former prevalent) – must be ready to meet parents so jeans permitted but not with holes, parents comment on lovely fresh faces. School says no make up but girls we interviewed said, as long as it was discreet like theirs, that was fine – and it looked jolly pretty too. Email links for help with work on tap for sixth form soon to be extended school-wide. Separate careers library plus Connexions and member of Independent Schools Careers Organisation (ISCO).

A few pupils have SEN – dyslexia, dyspraxia – but on the whole mild-moderate. We know of some parents of bright SpLD girls who've cited lack of SEN support as a reason not to choose Sydenham so it's welcome news that a head of learning support (currently working in junior school) has been in place since September 2005. 'Some of our brightest girls have dyslexic tendencies and may be disorganised, occasionally eccentric.' Pupils who need a little extra support can opt to swap Latin for communication studies (mind-mapping, organisational skills, additional literacy etc). Girls take GCSE ICT in year 9, brightest go on to do a further 9 but frees up time for those who'll benefit from extra English or additional study time.

Games, Options, The Arts: Hockey, netball, cross country, trampolining, volleyball, badminton all popular. Modern gym block houses a large sports hall hall, fitness centre and vending machine stocked with mouth-watering

chocolate (school insist this is for lettings but girls say differently). There isn't a swimming pool but there is a decent Astroturf on site with playing fields a coach ride away in lower Sydenham. Girls spoke highly of PE staff – saying department transformed in recent years. Emphasis changed too from one of taking part to one of winning – sport seen as a good area to build in a competitive spirit – 'you need a competitive edge to make it in life.' Expressive arts thrive, plenty of opportunities to perform: wind band, jazz, percussion group, orchestra, choir plus numerous drama productions. Facilities acceptable but head hopes for new theatre and recital room in near future. 'We have the talent and expertise; we want to be able to show it off in our own environment not perform in someone else's facilities.' Indeed a recent leaver was one of only four successful applicants out of 40 accepted for Royal College of Music. Technology areas receiving imminent, welcome refurbishment. Super 2-D and 3-D artwork – the clay fruit looked good enough to eat. Stacks of after school activities: music, sport, D of E, sign language, puppetry, Amnesty, ballet, speech and drama, subject orientated and much more – all timetabled so pupils can plan extra-curricular life carefully. Plenty of trips including link with Rugambwa Girls Secondary School, Tanzania – visit in 2004 reciprocated with return visit to Sydenham in 2005.

Background and Atmosphere: Set in open leafy grounds, the original Victorian mansion was built as the home of a diamond merchant and, despite the many red-brick additions, the splendour of the day still seeps through. Indeed the eclectic mix of traditional and modern is very much a hallmark of the school.

Pastoral Care and Discipline: Pastoral care is supportive and academically enabling, caring but not cosy. 'Girls are presented with opportunities, they must grab them and run.' Much tracking and monitoring takes place to identify girls who are under- performing. Children here are known and valued with parents involved whenever necessary. Excellent pupil planner, full of useful curriculum pointers and targets as well as places to record successes and misdemeanours. Thriving house system revived under current head along with introduction of a student council (in lesson time)- wanted to give girls opportunity to take on responsibilities. Lots of photos of y6 visits displayed on walls – helps new girls feel part of the school prior to entry. Several joint social ventures with local boys' schools. Lunch a mix of healthy and the devilishly tempting, hot food also available before school and at breaks.

Pupils and Parents: Wide catchment area: south-east London as far as Peckham and into Kent. Handful from north of the Thames, especially if brothers go to Dulwich College. Parents a wide social and cultural mix of professional and blue-collar workers, three quarters are first time buyers of independent education. Achieved aim of being academically selective but not elitist makes school an approachable option for first timers. Head candid, says they're in a highly competitive market so have to work hard to get people through the doors. 'Lots of schools get pupils 9 GCSEs so we have to add in something else, give parents value for money.' Famous old girls include Margaret Lockwood, Philippa Halben (scientist), Dame Rosemary Rue (scientist), Winifred Gerin (critic), Elizabeth Anstruther (philosopher), Rachel Joyce (actress), Sandie Powell (Oscar winning costume designer).

Entrance: Entrance for all, including Sydenham junior pupils, is via interview and exams in maths, reading/comprehension and writing, in the January prior to September entry. Part of South London GDST Consortium (Blackheath High, Bromley High, Streatham & Clapham High and Sydenham) – girls sit for whichever schools they choose with all schools sending out offers on the same day and no parent having to confirm acceptance for a further month – gives parents chance to look again at schools before making final decision. Notification also given to those placed on waiting list. Majority of pupils enter at beginning of y7, a few places occur at other times. Sixth form places available, keen to attract more. However, not a bums on seats exercise – if girls don't come up to scratch they won't get a place.

Exit: Lose quite a few post GCSEs – some to co-ed schools; some because they've been at Sydenham for 12 years and want to broaden experience before a move to University; many for financial reasons. School competes for entry with super selective local state schools, girls may not have been offered a place at 11 but do so well at Sydenham that state schools are happy to take them for A levels. Popular moves are to St Olave's and Newstead Wood. Sixth formers to a wide range and mix of universities and courses, traditional and modern. Handful to art colleges, occasional one to Oxbridge.

Remarks: Staff say, 'girls are a pleasure to be with.' Suits capable, compassionate but confident girls who get results but have interests too – heavily coached could come unstuck. May not compete on quite the same terms as some of its flashier rivals but has no problems producing an equally desirable end product.

TALBOT HEATH SCHOOL

Linked to Talbot Heath Junior School in the Junior section

Rothesay Road, Bournemouth, Dorset, BH4 9NJ

Tel: 01202 761 881
Fax: 01202 768 155
E-mail: admissions@talbotheath.org
Website: www.talbotheath.org

- Pupils: 393 girls. Mainly day, but 28 girls board, weekly and full, from age 11 • Ages: 3-18 • Size of sixth form: 83 • C of E
- Fees: Day: kindergarten £920, reception £1,330, junior £1,500 - £2,365; senior £2900. Full boarding £1,930 on top. Weekly boarding £1,800 on top • Independent • Open days: October

Headmistress: Since 1991, Mrs Christine Dipple BA M ès Lettres PGCE (late-forties). Educated at Barnard Castle Grammar School, read French and Italian at Leeds University, followed by a master's degree in France, then PGCE at Oxford. Taught at Millfield, Sherborne School for Girls and St Swithun's (head of modern languages at last two). Married with grown-up stepdaughter. Approachable, energetic, no-nonsense head with clear ideas of standards she expects from girls. Enjoys choral singing, gardening and travel. Took over from Miss Austin-Smith, who was here from 1976.

Academic Matters: Traditional teaching and solid results. ISI report in 2001 said GCSE and A level results 'very good in relation to pupils' abilities'. 60 per cent A/B at A level and A*/A at GCSE. Offers good range of subjects, with maths and science very popular – all take dual award GCSE science and a number go on to study medicine and veterinary science at university. Most girls take nine subjects at GCSE, four at AS level and three or four at A2. Setting by ability for French and maths term after 11 year olds start – 'we give them time to get settled,' says head – and for science at GCSE level. Majority learn two languages and there are exchange trips galore to France, Germany and Spain.

Lots of computers – each subject area has access to IT, every girl has email address and there are three computer rooms for use by all. Textiles and cookery on offer in the newly equipped technology centre. Many long-serving staff – average age of teachers in senior school is 46 – and 66 per cent have been at school for more than 10 years. Head says girls are very motivated and expect staff to deliver. Higher number of male staff than in the past – deputy head is male – but men still few and far between. Class sizes

range from 20 at lower end of school to 15 at GCSE stage. School has EAL teacher and caters for those with dyslexia, dyspraxia and ADHD.

Games, Options, The Arts: Sport is compulsory for all, though number of timetabled sessions decreases as girls progress through school. Particularly strong in netball, tennis, swimming and athletics – with several county champions over the years. Heated outdoor swimming pool used from May till October for lessons and lunchtime clubs. Large sports hall offers everything from aerobics and dance to fencing and trampolining. Own all-weather playing fields, netball and tennis courts.

Art impressive – with wide range of work on display, from self-portraits to stunning black and white still-life photographs. Flourishing music department – cellist Natalie Clein (former Young Musician of the Year) is an old girl as is Kate Royal, winner of the 2004 Kathleen Ferrier Award. 250 girls have instrumental lessons in school and loads of choirs, ensembles and orchestras to join – including the jazz-based Double O'Sax group which has reached the Music for Youth National Festival three times running in recent years. Excellent drama. Between ages of 11 and 14 every form has to produce a play for the annual drama festival. There is a major drama production every autumn and some go on to take theatre studies at AS and A level. Modern drama studio with state of the art sound system and computerised lighting desk.

Background and Atmosphere: Founded as Bournemouth High School in 1886. First head was Mary Broad who believed girls should have same opportunities in education as boys and shocked locals by teaching her pupils cricket and gymnastics. School moved to picturesque 24-acre purpose-built site in Talbot Woods in 1935, when it became known as Talbot Heath – school birthday is still celebrated every May. Senior school is built round two quads and has been vastly added to over the years. Girls encouraged to use grounds – walks in pinewoods, building dens etc – yet kept secure.

School prides itself on helping girls settle into routine when first join. Sparky unofficial handbook written by 11-year-olds advises new girls to 'be ready with a clear 'yes' at registration – unless you are absent!' and not to 'PANIC – unless absolutely necessary!' Tiny number of boarders lives at St Mary's boarding house, a short walk from main school building. Boarding house fairly traditional in appearance, with dormitories for younger girls and cubicles for older ones, but boarders are allowed to keep their own hamsters ('no rats,' says head firmly) and there are skateboards propped up all over the place. (See recent CSCI report on school website). Girls wear simple uniform of navy blazer, skirt, blouse and tie – vast improvement on old-fashioned grey felt hats once worn. Sixth form girls are given more freedom – no uniform (but have to look smart – no flip-flops or pierced tummy buttons on show), more free periods and sixth form common room. After-school and lunchtime clubs entirely voluntary (computers through to hand-bells) – though a puzzled sixth former told us she couldn't imagine any girl going through school without joining something. Once a year each form chooses its own charity and holds a fund-raising week. Many take part in Duke of Edinburgh's award scheme and Young Enterprise. Local employers have praised Talbot Heath girls on work experience post-GCSE for being reliable, competent, able to shoulder responsibility and work as a team.

Pastoral Care and Discipline: Apart from noisy corridors, head says girls generally behave well. No girl has been suspended in recent years but head would not hesitate to do so for smoking, drinking or drugs offences in school or for persistent bullying. School has system of sanctions – order marks, detentions etc – for unsatisfactory work or behaviour. Parents always informed. Each form has two form leaders, voted for by peers each term, and there are two head girls, two deputies and a raft of prefects. In senior school, full assembly held four days a week, led by head, staff, outside speakers and girls themselves.

Pupils and Parents: Girls come from enormous catchment area – some cycle in from close by while other travel from as far afield as Beaulieu to the east and Weymouth and Portland to the west (good train service). Wide range of backgrounds, including first-time buyers of private education. Large proportion of boarders come from overseas, particularly Service families. Very friendly, purposeful, well-mannered girls, proud of their school. Confident and outgoing – but not as alarmingly sophisticated as you find in some schools. School is not snobby – very down-to-earth. Notable old girls include Dame Shirley Williams, Caroline Gledhill (first woman to receive Young Engineer of the year award) and Frances Ashcroft (first woman to receive Fellow of Royal Society award). Natalie Clein and Kate Royal (see above).

Entrance: Senior school holds entrance exam in January for the following September. Most Talbot Heath juniors progress through to senior school but all must pass exam. At 11 girls sit papers in English, maths and verbal reasoning and at 12, 13 and 14 there is a French exam too. Not too horrific a hurdle. Some girls join from state schools, others from preps like Hordle Walhampton, Castle Court, Dumpton and Durlston Court. Entry at sixth form requires a minimum of five A-C grades at GCSE and at least Bs in subjects to be studied at A level.

Exit: Three-quarters of girls stay on for sixth form – those who don't tend to leave for local FE colleges to do subjects not on offer here. Virtually all sixth form go to university – Exeter, Birmingham, Surrey, Bath currently popular choices. 10 per cent of upper sixth to Oxbridge each year.

Money Matters: Offers a wide variety of scholarships (academic, all-rounder, performing arts, music and sport) and bursaries. There are also discounts for children of parents serving in the Services and clergy.

Remarks: A happy, successful school that has moved with the times while firmly maintaining its own unique character and traditions. Suits able girls who want to work hard and get involved.

TASIS - THE AMERICAN SCHOOL IN ENGLAND

Linked to TASIS - The American School in England Lower School in the Junior section

Coldharbour Lane, Thorpe, Egham, Surrey, TW20 8TE

Tel: 01932 565 252

Fax: 01932 564 644

E-mail: mpower@tasis.com

Website: www.tasis.com

• Pupils: 715 boys and girls • Ages: 3-19 • Size of sixth form: 330 (160 are boarders) • Non-denom • Fees: Two terms per year. Per term: nursery £2,600 half-day; Day: pre-K half-day £3,000; K- 3 £6,600; 4-8 £7,150; 9-13 £7,650. Full boarding £11,250. Extras: one time £750 building contribution; bus service £1,100 per semester • Independent
• Open days: Any day

Headmaster: Since 2005, Dr Jim Doran who has degrees in education, educational administration and a doctorate in curriculum and instruction (fifties). After spending 25 years in international education as a teacher and K-12 administrator in Panama, Singapore, Tokyo, Manila, Jeddah, and Tunis, in 2001 he became executive director at the Stetson University Center in Celebration, Florida where, in addition to handling his administrative responsibilities, he taught graduate level courses in educational leadership, research, communications and school finance. Married to Vickie who has joined the staff. They have two adult children.

Academic Matters: International Baccalaureate diploma and American college prep programme, with emphasis on the Advanced Placement curriculum with stunning results – in 2005, 88 per cent of all 131 students taking 284 AP tests in 21 subjects made a passing grade of 3 or better (31 per cent 5s and 36 per cent 4s). Average SATs: 635V/618M. Students are expected to meet the challenge of the tough academic regime and are given great support through frequent advising and daily opportunities to see teachers during the tutorial period. Class sizes are 16 or smaller, taught in seminar or lecture style with a good bit of give and take. Plenty of computers, new 'airport' system so any desktop or laptop connects to the internet anywhere within school boundaries, indoors or out. Outstanding ESL teachers (who also serve as counsellors), with very successful four-year sequence for students who are placed according to proficiency; there are several courses offered in the 'international section,' out of the main stream, to students whose English is still too weak for the more verbal courses in the AP curriculum. Dedicated teachers assess and bolster the learning disability picture.

Games, Options, The Arts: New construction has just beefed up the gym facilities for an already highly successful sports program, particularly basketball, coached by a former pro player; they've won multiple year school championships and have steady participation in National League teams from under-13s through under-18s. Everyone is encouraged to play a sport but it's not compulsory. Lots of extra-curricular sports for lower school children after school and on weekends. The art studios look interesting and busy but something else is going on here. Many schools hang their students' art around in the halls but it is rarely so good you begin asking if it's for sale. It is that good here. All arts programs are performance-based – plays, musicals, art shows, recitals are all student-led and supported. But perhaps best of all, there is an extensive travel study programme, all over England, up and down London, long weekends in Paris or on language exchanges with other students; one- and two-week long travel periods per year offered for different curricula, from France, to Budapest, to Kenya or China, and all seniors go to Greece as a part of the twelfth grade humanities programme.

Background and Atmosphere: You'll think you've wandered onto a Hollywood back lot set for Snow White. The 28-year-old school is housed in an enchanting jumble of crooked shingle roofs, soft-coloured old brick cottages, gardens, leafy paths and manor house, all in a kind of hamlet in the ancient village of Thorpe. Small groups of boarders live in cosy comfortable rooms under thatched eves or low oak-beamed ceilings. Day and boarding students blend seamlessly, feet up watching videos in the tiny 15th century movie theatre (possibly not its original use), off the upper school common area, or spending the tutorial hour reading in the floor-to-ceiling book-lined panelled library or conservatory. Lower school students eat in their own lunchroom, supervised for good manners; upper grades and staff eat notably tasty hot lunches (with very fine salad bar) in the warm, pretty apricot-painted dining room. The additions and changes have been incorporated into and amongst the historic buildings very carefully but have very effectively readied the school for 21st century education.

Pastoral Care and Discipline: First-rate literature-based character education in the lower school curriculum called Core Knowledge builds a base for discussion of values (respect, responsibility, perseverance, courage etc) in class and weekly assemblies, and sets a tone for tolerance and respect for others that is apparent throughout the school. Students 'like and admire teachers so much, you don't want to let them down.' On bullying, 'new kids might try out bullying but then they realise it's different here; you don't need to make fun of people in order to fit in.' Heavy emphasis on community service, from London to Romanian orphanages – teachers travel with students, get to know them and sense problems early; even the cleaning staff and caterers keep an eagle eye out for anything that's not quite right.

Pupils and Parents: Smart, articulate sophisticated kids, polite, lots of eye contact, largely American but also from 44 other countries, some Brits (19 per cent of boarding students' families live in UK); surprisingly sharp-looking for this age, even given the dress code (ties, jackets, girls tailored) – not as much blazer-through-the-mangle look. Students say everyone is so international in outlook, 'this is the best place for kids not used to diversity, because they soon will be, but kids not open to diversity shouldn't come.' They realise that 'at any minute, people could be transferred – there's no time to waste arguing. There's a maturity factor from moving around a lot, you want to be around others like that.'

Parents are often not here long enough for both to get back into a career, so their highly capable attentions are turned full focus on the school and the school is delighted to have them. They volunteer everywhere – as aides in classrooms, in Saturday extra-curricular sports, organising parent seminars and welcome events; there were 200 at a library volunteer coffee morning alone recently. They send their children to TASIS because of its excellence and because of the chance to live in the countryside and still commute to London.

Entrance: Selective, looking for children who know they will be stretched and are seriously concerned about their academic development. About a 20 per cent turnover from year to year, due to a population of corporate and diplomatic families, but not so much during the school year. Most transitional support occurs during the summer (and via email and phone before families ever arrive).

Exit: Unusually perceptive college counselling staff, who stay abreast of American and British schools particularly and are very successful at guiding students and families through a well-thought-out range of schools and appropriate preparation. They feel they, kids and parents, are 'buffered by the ocean' in terms of the feeding frenzy and hype of Ivy League, SAT prep, early admissions etc. Students go to most top and second-tier colleges, from small liberal arts to large state universities, across the US but with a good smattering in the UK. Students in the lower grades stay unless their parents are transferred, and even then may shift over to become boarders if they're ninth grade or older.

Money Matters: School originally owned by private family, now owned and governed by a not-for-profit Swiss foundation, with the executive board located in UK. Fees cover tuition, books, IT, materials, lunch, field trips, weekend excursions and, in the case of boarding students, weekly linen service and autumn travel week as well.

Remarks: Outstanding American and international boarding and day school in a quintessential English village environment; exacting academics (superb AP offerings); small enough for close ties but large enough for a million extra-curriculars, easy to transfer out to any place else but who would want to?

TAUNTON SCHOOL

Linked to Taunton Preparatory School in the Junior section

Linked to Taunton Pre Prep and First Steps in the Junior section

Staplegrove Road, Taunton, Somerset, TA2 6AD

Tel: 01823 349 200

Fax: 01823 349 201

E-mail: enquiries@tauntonschool.co.uk

Website: www.tauntonschool.co.uk

- Pupils: 1,010. 60:40 boys:girls. 245 board – mostly in the senior school • Ages: 2 1/2 - 18 • Size of sixth form: 200
- Inter-denom • Fees: Day £3,940; boarding £6,310
- Independent

Head: Since 2005, Mr John Newton MA PhD FCollP DipMS(Ed). Educated at The Manchester Grammar School and Merton College, Oxford. Has a doctorate in organisational culture in independent schools. A teacher of French and Russian, involved in the CCF, has sung in school choirs, coached rugby, hockey, cricket, fives, rowing and football. Previously director of studies and housemaster at Eastbourne College and head of modern languages at Bradfield. 4 young children, all at Taunton; wife Catherine a trained primary school teacher and musician.

Deputy head: Mr William Duggan MA was head of classics at St Paul's, London, and now has three daughters at the school. An engaging man, he brings a scholarly polish to the place. Female counterpart Mrs Shirley Shaylor BSc MA, was formerly housemistress and 1st XI hockey manager at Millfield.

Academic Matters: Despite reputation as an all-round school, has kept consistently high A level results during past decade – 64 per cent A and B grades. Huge sums spent on ICT development – pupils can access the network from anywhere. Class size 15, max 22. Staff ratio 1:7. Potential Oxbridge candidates identified in lower sixth and prepared. Careers taken seriously – much input from OTs who give 'Horizon Lectures' each Saturday and offer work experience as far afield as Hong Kong. Some help for mild/moderate dyslexia. EFL assistance available. A thriving International Study Centre adjacent to campus brings 55 foreign students and crucial cash flow. 'One's almost setting up a business behind a school', says Mr Whiteley 'you cannot run a school on fees any more!'

Games, Options, The Arts: Use of facilities is maximised – flourishing art department with four studios equipped to art school standard obtains 100 per cent grade As. Artist in residence. Innovative head of dept who trained as sculptor says half of each year group ends up at art foundation courses. Music taught in core curriculum from third form. One third pupils learn an instrument, many two or more. The orchestra, jazz band, wind and madrigal group play regularly outside school (Euro Disney in Paris). Ask for one of four CDs produced in house (by music technology) using many choirs from pre-prep upwards. Drama and public speaking given full rein.

A wealth of sports facilities with a zillion pitches which turn out dozens of county and several international champions in hockey, rugby, swimming, aerobics, tennis, wakeboarding(!), athletics, cross-country and National Schools showjumping. This astonishingly high calibre explained by the school's effort to put county fixtures before school matches – 'inter-school results may suffer but it's worth the pupils getting exit routes for later,' says sports coach (from an England squad.) A reciprocal gap year arrangement with Geelong Grammar (where Prince Charles spent his year at Timbertops) brings 5 gappies to assist resident staff.

Background and Atmosphere: Founded over 150 years ago for sons of dissenters (non-conformists) and moved to its present site on spacious campus (eclectic buildings surrounding a purpose-built one) in 1870 on edge of Taunton, with London train track at bottom of 56-acre sports pitches. For such a friendly and unpretentious school (first names for pupils all through) it sends out a decidedly flash prospectus resembling a Club Med brochure – might infuriate some but marketing man's intention, we're told, is to lure one to look closer.

Warm, un-public-school feel. Pupils calmly confident that staff are on their wavelength. Sixth formers are treated with respect and have their own refurbished centre, 'The Guvvy', bright, light and self-contained.

Pastoral Care and Discipline: Houseparents primarily responsible for each pupil's progress and two tutorial meetings a week to monitor both academic and pastoral. At fourth form, pupils choose a personal tutor. Very approachable chaplain teaches reduced timetable to give more time for pastoral role; sensitive to other faiths. Tremendous rapport between students and staff, thus bullying gets reported instantly and eradicated. Head recognises that a few sometimes experiment with cannabis and acts accordingly but anyone caught dealing or doing hard drugs goes out. Average age of staff 40; 20 of them have been here over a decade. Things 'relaxed but orderly'.

Pupils and Parents: Not a county-set school and glad of it. Recent survey showed that large proportion of OTs use it for second and third generation, also that 94 per cent of pupils would recommend the school. Parents are professionals, farmers, local businessmen. 10 per cent London émigrés. Day pupils arrive from Sidmouth, Exeter, Minehead, Yeovil in school's own buses. 1 in 9 pupils from 20 countries overseas. Old Tauntonians: Mark Getty, Vice Admiral David Blackburn, Sir Robert Malpas (MD of BP), Michael Willacy (advisor to Mrs Thatcher), Nicholas Prettejohn (Chief exec Lloyds), Peter Westmacott, Sir Peter Wallis, Dr Christopher Gibson-Smith, Sir Michael Milroy Franklin.

Entrance: 60-70 per cent get in the easy way via own prep at 13 (very few turned away). Otherwise Common Entrance or entrance assessment but particular attention paid to report from head. 25 enter at 16 on minimum 5 grade A-Cs, again interview more important than academic – 'we always take a sibling'.

Exit: 96 per cent go to universities or colleges (half a dozen to Oxbridge, ditto to medical school.) 10 or so leave at 16 for sixth form colleges or employment.

Money Matters: 88 former Assisted Places have shrunk to 18. Scholarships at 11, 13 and 16 for academic, music, art, sport and an all-rounder.

Remarks: Good value. Getting noticed by a more cosmopolitan crowd and numbers are 'getting close to a waiting list for 13' says the head. A great find for sportsmen or musicians.

TEESSIDE HIGH SCHOOL

Linked to Teesside Preparatory School in the Junior section

The Avenue, Eaglescliffe, Stockton-on-Tees, TS16 9AT

Tel: 01642 782 095
Fax: 01642 791 207
E-mail: info@teessidehigh.co.uk
Website: www.teessidehigh.co.uk

- Pupils: 350 girls in senior school. All day • Ages: 3-18
- Size of sixth form: 80 • Non-denom • Fees: £1,580 - £2,100
- Independent • Open days: September and November

Head: Since 2000, Mrs Hilary French MA MEd NPQH (mid-forties). Educated at Convent of the Sacred Heart Grammar School, Newcastle upon Tyne, St Anne's College, Oxford and Durham (PGCE). A historian, started teaching career at Ousedale Comprehensive School, Newport Pagnell, before moving to Thornhill Comprehensive School, Sunderland and, later, Dame Allan's Girls School, Newcastle upon Tyne. Deputy head at Teesside High 1996-2000. Married to

Durham University lecturer and has one daughter who attends the school. Down-to-earth, warm and approachable (parents and girls alike say this). Knows every girl by name and aims to produce confident girls who achieve their potential in all areas of life.

Academic Matters: Good. 52 per cent of GCSE grades are A*/A, 70 per cent grades A/B at A level. Traditional academic curriculum. Girls get option of studying three separate sciences at GCSE or taking dual award science course. All 11-13 year olds take (inter alia) separate sciences, three languages (French, German and Latin), RE, music, home economics and IT (everyone takes CLAIT in year 9). Free access to IT suite during school hours and each girl has own e-mail address at school. Maximum class size 22 for girls aged 11-16 and 13 in sixth form but, in practice, groups far smaller. Experienced staff – half have been at school for more than 10 years and average age is 48. Some mixed ability teaching for 11 year olds but, from year 8, girls are setted for maths, science and languages.

Homework ranges from 90 minutes a night for 11 year olds through to three hours a night for sixth form. Girls get report of some kind every term with full report sent out at end of year. Special needs co-ordinator – support for dyslexia and dyspraxia. A few girls come from families where English is not the first language but don't usually need support with English as an additional language.

Games, Options, The Arts: Head has introduced more extra-curricular activities. All girls now take part in wide range of activities – these include public speaking, market gardening, chess, sign language and, a very popular recent innovation, football. Most girls take Duke of Edinburgh awards. At time of writing, four girls raising money for World Challenge trip to Malawi to teach disadvantaged children. Music and drama very strong. Most girls play a musical instrument and there are lots of orchestras and choirs. One pupil was recently accepted for National Children's Orchestra. Girls were rehearsing for performance of 'Daisy Pulls it Off' when we visited while recorder group were recording a CD in school hall, padding around in slippers to avoid making a noise in between takes! Large number take Guildhall speech and drama awards. Art is very popular – 50 per cent take it at GCSE and paintings and sculpture on show everywhere. Sport is strong and compulsory for all – several county standard hockey and netball players. Other sports include athletics, tennis, fencing, rowing and badminton.

Background and Atmosphere: School founded in 1970 when Queen Victoria High School and Cleveland School amalgamated. Set in 19 acres bordering the River Tees. Extensive woodland used for forest trails. Site has stunning views of the Cleveland Hills – 'brilliant for teaching perspective' say art teachers, appreciatively. Classrooms are newly decorated, bright and cheerful. Smart new dining room with cafeteria system, trendy blue tables and murals painted by girls, offers choice of hot and cold meals. Even though this is a day school, breakfast and tea are available too if wanted. For years girls have worn slightly old-fashioned brown and pale blue uniform but, following heated debate, new uniform of Black Watch tartan skirt and navy blazer is being introduced. The sixth form used to wear own clothes but after requests from girls themselves they now have uniform of navy skirt or trousers, white blouse and navy top. Sixth form has self-contained building – 'a stepping-stone to university' says the head, with shared studies (girls are given a free rein how they decorate them), kitchens and common room. Atmosphere everywhere is bubbly, enthusiastic and busy. Work is important but emphasis on fun too.

Pastoral Care and Discipline: The school prides itself on being 'a community in which everyone is treated with respect and understanding and where all talents and gifts are nurtured and valued'. Form tutors play very important role in guiding girls. Mrs French sets a lot of store by community projects – Christmas parties for OAPs, charity quizzes, visits to local hospice etc. Dialogue and discussion are strongly encouraged. Head girl and deputy head girl run school council – each year group has three reps and recent innovations include chilled water supply and napkins in dining room! Buddy system introduced to encourage older girls to befriend and help younger girls. There is also open forum for parents to raise issues once a term. Girls' behaviour is good – no vandalism, graffiti or discipline problems, says head, just occasional high spirits in corridors. School has introduced extended day to help working parents – now open from 7.45am till 6pm. Also runs popular Megakids holiday clubs for 3-12 year-olds during school holidays.

Pupils and Parents: Girls come from wide range of economic and social backgrounds and from rural as well as urban areas. 'A lot of parents make real sacrifices to send their daughters here,' says Mrs French. Many travel in by bus from 25-mile radius, from as far afield as south Durham and north Yorkshire. Delightful girls who take pride in their school and brim with enthusiasm. Old girls include broadcasters Shiulie Ghosh (of ITN) and Pam Royle.

Entrance: At 11 all girls (including those from the prep) sit verbal reasoning paper and emotional intelligence questionnaire. Two thirds entering senior school come from prep, a third from primary schools. Girls entering sixth form need at least six GCSE passes (preferably grade B and above).

Exit: About ten per cent leave post-GCSE (drawn by co-ed schools or FE colleges) – not unusual for a girls' school and far, far better than it was a few years ago. Almost all sixth form leavers go to university. Durham, Nottingham and Edinburgh are currently popular choices.

Money Matters: The school offers up to eight means-tested bursaries every year on a first come, first served basis.

Remarks: An attractive, happy, unpretentious school that prides itself on turning out well-educated, confident and compassionate young women. Environment is safe and nurturing yet encourages girls to have a go.

THE THOMAS HARDYE SCHOOL

Queen's Avenue, Dorchester, Dorset, DT1 2ET

Tel: 01305 266064
Fax: 01305 250510
E-mail: admin@thomas-hardye.dorset.sch.uk
Website: www.thomas-hardye.dorset.sch.uk

• Pupils: 2002 boys and girls, all day • Ages: 13-18 • Size of sixth form: 720 • Non-denom • State

Head: Since 1988, Dr Iain Melvin BA PhD OBE (2005) (fifties). Educated at St Francis Grammar School, Hartlepool and read English at the University of Nottingham. Deputy head of the Royal Latin School in Buckinghamshire before taking the reins here. Married, no children. In no doubt about the excellence of his school. When asked how it differed from comprehensives in similar Dorset towns, he beamed, 'our results are much better!' Although he teaches some A level English, Dr Melvin is more a master chef, pulling everything together, than a hands-on head with his fingers in the batter. The school absorbs both his working day and much of his free time ('there are 2002 pupils here – I don't have any outside interests'). Admits that at a cchool of thic size it is impossible to know all the pupils' names, but 'I can guarantee they all know me!' With 218 members of staff, just keeping abreast of all the teachers' names must be a trial. Masterful at weaving together a complex range of pupils, programmes and – especially – funding into a thriving and vibrant web. Inexhaustible supply of ideas – aiming to offer the IB programme as an alternative to A levels from September 2006. Not getting any younger, but as one parent of a sixth former said dismissively, 'oh, there have been rumours of him retiring for

years.' Not going anywhere for now.

Academic Matters: There are some smart cookies here. In 2005, one boy gained 13 A*s in his GCSEs and several others were close behind. Nine pupils scored one of the top five marks in their GCSE subjects in the whole of the UK (two in maths). Maths particularly strong and, far and away, the most popular A level subject here. Head points out that there are more pupils doing A level maths here than in all the schools in the rest of the county combined. Science popular but results a little disappointing for a school that became a science college in 2002. OFSTED report so over the top with gushing praise that it makes embarrassing reading. Has been given every award going: Charter Mark, Schools Curriculum Award, Investor in People, Arts Mark Gold, Leading Edge School, Education Extra Award, School Achievement Awards ... you get the picture.

Being so large allows the school to provide some unusual subjects, including Latin and dance at GCSE, and sociology, dance, electronics, food technology, travel & tourism and accounting at A level. Also offers the CACHE diploma in nursery nursing. On top of all this, Hardye's is a teaching training school, working in partnership with Exeter and other universities. IT a sore point for some pupils: though well-equipped with swarms of new boxes, monitors, interactive whiteboards etc, pupils speak of perpetual printer problems down on the shop floor – while the head's printer purrs like a dream ...Some 180 pupils take advantage of SEN provision here, ranging from moderate learning difficulties (the majority) to a handful of pupils in wheelchairs. The school has a physiotherapy room, a unit for the hearing impaired, two large SEN rooms and several specialist SEN staff. And for pupils who just need a boost, there are after-school homework help sessions – well attended 'and no stigma attached,' said a pupil. A few parents of kids with minor problems (eg poor handwriting, organisational issues) felt the school could do more.

Games, Options, The Arts: Super sports facilities – floodlit Astro, sports hall with climbing wall, fitness suite, verdant playing fields, plus use of the facilities at the Dorchester Rugby Club and neighbouring leisure centre (two swimming pools). Rugby keenly played, along with football (boys and girls), cross-country, netball, athletics, traditional cricket and swimming. Vast numbers of pupils to choose from means the school's 'won' column contentedly exceeds its 'lost'. A good range of minor sports eg water polo and kayaking, plus outward bound activities. Drama, music, art and dance are all buzzing. Music department stands out, with recording studio and music tech room. Music tours, two orchestras, school music festival, lots of rock bands, annual joint concert with Imperial College, steel band, chapel choir – 'you name a cathedral, they've sung in it!' says the head. Drama in own theatre, RSC visits every second year. Small museum area displays some excellent artwork. THTV, the school's in-house television channel, shows pupil-produced programmes on a plasma-screen TV in the heart of the school, know as the Spine. Lots of charity do-gooding and recycling.

Background and Atmosphere: Thomas Hardye founded the first free school in Dorchester in 1569 (the school has nothing to do with Dorset novelist Thomas Hardy who confusingly attended school in Dorchester in the 1850s, in case you are wondering). Doubled in size in 1992 when amalgamated with local girls' school. Is now enormous, heaving, multi-layered campus. Feels more like a small university than a comprehensive – owing partly to the absence of 11 and 12 year-olds, a key element of Hardye's uniqueness. Sixth form immense. 'We think it is the largest of any comprehensive in the country,' says the head, which gives you some idea. Just in case any other school is plotting to eclipse them, Hardye's is in the process of expanding its sixth form further still, until they will be the ... SUPREME ... MASTERS ... OF ... THE ... UNIVERSE. A gigantic sixth form means better funding which 'percolates down through the rest of the school'. It also allows them to offer their good range of A level courses.

School's swish office and reception area immediately radiates a school that has its act together. Lots of new building including £2.7 million English and modern languages block with central glassed-in atrium housing 50 computers (2004). Beauteous sixth form centre, with own mini-canteen, well appreciated by the students. Class sizes pushing the boundaries in the sixth form (AS pupils we spoke to griped about tutor groups of over 30 kids) but kept smallish in the lower school.

Pastoral Care and Discipline: The few local parents who do not choose the school mainly cite pastoral matters (will my child be lost in the vastness? will he suffer peer pressure?). But parents who have taken the plunge are almost all happy here. The head points out that, by breaking the school down by year group, they have created five manageable-sized groups of children. Pupils coming into year 9 keep the same tutor for three years – helps enormously. Appearance a constant source of skirmishes, with the pupils' guerrilla tactics usually overpowering the administration. Girls' skirts worn short with, in some cases, stilettos. Barber shop visits have not greatly troubled the boys. However, the school has outflanked the pupils in the battle of the neckwear, introducing clip-on ties for new pupils in 2005. One set of Dorchester parents explained their decision to send their daughter to an independent school thus, 'she could get a perfectly good education at Hardye's. We are essentially paying £16,000 a year to make sure she wears a kilt below the knee.'

Behaviour otherwise OK, if informal. No uniform in sixth form. Out if caught in possession of drugs but head says he is 'a realist' and there have been no permanent exclusions in the past six years. Area where sixth form pupils store their bags is guarded by CCTV (a good idea). Library well used and quiet – a sea of heads earnestly down. Bullying low on list of concerns – 'it's uncool to fight here,' said a pupil.

Pupils and Parents: School is the pinnacle of Dorchester's Schools Partnership, a cohesive 4-19 educational pyramid. Hardye's has traditionally been able to count on this mainly homogeneous, middle income, non-urban catchment to provide reasonably wholesome kids with a good work ethic. Sadly, some negative aspects of youth culture are reaching even here, and Hardye pupils are not quite the bushy-tailed, fresh-faced youngsters they were when Dr Melvin first came to the school. Negligible sprinkling of ethnic diversity – most with English as their home language.

Entrance: 450 pupils at 13+ mainly from Dorchester's three middle schools. Some fifty pupils come from outside the area, from as far away as Sherborne and Blandford. Handful from local prep, Sunninghill, settle in just fine. Number seeking entry roughly matches places available. All candidates for entry to the sixth form are interviewed, including the school's own pupils. 120 new pupils enter at that stage, a few from Poole and Bournemouth's grammars, attracted here by wide range of A levels, less authoritarian sixth form and lure of the opposite sex.

Exit: At least 80 per cent to higher education. 20 per cent leave after GCSEs, most of these to further education elsewhere. Head says that none are pushed out, but that the less able tend to leave, some looking for more vocational courses. UCAS a Herculean labour here, with Dr Melvin reading every single application. Half a dozen pupils to Oxbridge most years – sometimes more.

Remarks: Bulging metropolis, humming purposefully under efficient head. Exactly what educationalists had in mind when comprehensives were first invented, and going from strength to strength.

THOMAS MILLS HIGH SCHOOL

Saxtead Road, Framlingham, Woodbridge, Suffolk, IP13 9HE

Tel: 01728 723 493
Fax: 01728 621 098
E-mail: inmail@thomasmills.suffolk.sch.uk
Website: www.thomasmills.suffolk.uk

• Pupils: 1,110; 535 boys, 575 girls . All day • Ages: 11-18
• Size of sixth form: 300 • Non-denom • State • Open days: One
in November; two information days for sixth form, also in
November

Head: Since 2005, Mr Colin Hirst, a biologist with considerable teaching and management experience (and knowledge of the area; he taught at East Bergholt High). Previously head of Noadswood School in Southampton.

Academic Matters: Significantly above average results across the board at both GCSE and A level, and superb value-added scores. A specialist school for technology since 1996 – the then new head used the funds to improve provision for science, maths (a whole new block) and IT, which is impressive in every area. Express streams in maths and science take GSCE in y10, and there is setting in maths, science and languages at KS3/4. 'Key players' used to teach the mainly male middle sets, aims to bring boys' performance more in line with girls'.

Humanities and arts subjects also do very well. A language is compulsory at GCSE and all pupils do French and German at KS3. Latin is taught as an optional extra-curricular subject and is increasing in popularity. Some 22 subjects at A level – take-up is variable so some, like languages, have small groups, whereas psychology nets an extraordinary 60 or so at AS level. Not that results seem at all adversely affected by group size – large classes are the norm at all levels. Provision for learning support is excellent, and the department has its own cheerful area.

Games, Options, The Arts: Bought back a lost games field, so facilities are good, and shared by the public after hours. A thriving house system, dating from grammar school days, means that large numbers are involved in competitive sport, much encouraged as part of the school ethos. On Sports Day, there is an 'open mile', in which around 300 children take part.

Art department a haven of creative chaos, producing bold, quite avant-garde results not enough in evidence around the school. Music is superb. Despite a shortage of practice rooms, orchestras, choirs and instrumental groups abound, catering for all tastes and providing frequent concerts. Drama is on the curriculum in years 7/8, and the new performing arts studio with its dramatically sweeping black curtains is every young thespian's dream environment. Every member of staff is involved in one or more of the wide range of extra-curricular activities, visits and foreign exchanges.

Background and Atmosphere: This is one of the 18thC Mills schools, a grammar school from 1902 to 1979. The campus is large, in a semi-rural setting on the outskirts of Framlingham, and consists of a hotch-potch of buildings. The main block is a bit battered- looking, with rather oppressive long corridors, but new building in the last ten years lifts the spirits. A much needed new canteen is next on the agenda, and the more enlightened pupils hope that the current menus will meet the same fate as the inadequate barrack which is the current building. There are some nice touches; two air-raid shelters preserved on site provide a 2nd world war museum and an experience of the blitz, complete with terrifying sound effects. The whole school and grounds are amazingly tidy and litter free and the general atmosphere is exceptionally studious and well disciplined. In the large, very well appointed and modernised, library even when it is full, you could hear a pin drop. Pupils are relaxed but courteous and well behaved. The head is keen to promote a sense of pride and the site is peppered with plaques celebrating this or that achievement or new development.

Pastoral Care and Discipline: The usual system of form tutors appears to work very well, with, additionally, sixth formers involved in befriending and counselling younger pupils, and also helping those with reading problems. Traditional values and individual responsibility. A real feeling about the place that only the highest of standards of behaviour and effort are expected. The house system, which permeates many areas of school life, and is entirely run by the sixth form, promotes a strong sense of pride and belonging.

With so many pupils on a crowded site, noise levels are surprisingly low and unauthorised absences are well below national average, although this is probably to be expected in a school with an essentially problem-free intake and few inherent issues with discipline.

Pupils and Parents: Pupils are all from the surrounding region, and from a broad spectrum of social backgrounds, but there is very little ethnic diversity. Both pupils and parents are highly complimentary about the school and tend only to express minor complaints about, for example, the untrendy design of the girls' trouser option (you have to look hard to see any girls in trousers!). Parents are very supportive and everyone seems extremely proud of the school's outstanding achievements.

Entrance: About 70 per cent come from the catchment area of surrounding villages, plus 30 per cent from out of catchment (quite a few more apply in this category than can be accommodated). There is an influx of 25-30 per cent into the 6th form, from other high schools and even from independent schools.

Exit: The vast majority of students go on to further education and a wide range of courses, including a good number to the top universities. A few to vocational training or directly into employment.

Remarks: One of the best comprehensive schools in the country; a real community school.

THOMAS TELFORD SCHOOL

Old Park, Telford, Shropshire, TF3 4NW

Tel: 01952 200 000
Fax: 01952 293 294
E-mail: admissions@ttsonline.net
Website: www.ttsonline.net

• Pupils: 1,175 boys and girls, all day • Ages: 11-18 • Size of sixth form: 330 • Non-denom • State • Open days: In March 18 months before proposed entry

---

Head: Since 1991, Sir Kevin Satchwell BA (early fifties). OU education degree plus a diploma in educational management. Taught PE, ran his department in two schools, then deputy head in Kirkby and head of Moseley Park in Wolverhampton, before being appointed as TTS's founding head, with the brief 'to raise educational standards in Telford and Wolverhampton'. This he has unequivocally done, hence the superhead gong. The school is very much his creation, and he's proud of it, as he is of fighting his way out of his limited background to current fame. Likes media attention and the range of visitors it brings (many turned away), but keeps closely in touch with pupils (is part of the personal tutor team, holds regular working lunches with students of all ages, runs a football team – on the day of the GSG visit was seen after school boarding a minibus with them for an away match).

A quiet, modestly confident man, down-to-earth and direct in manner. Married, with two children. Sometimes sounds like the head of a successful trad independent grammar school – which indeed the school resembles in many ways. Prides himself on innovative approach to running a school, eg day divided into 2 x 3-hour periods – a long day, especially if pupils stay for a third session (up to 5.40) for sports and activities – but no one seems to complain. Also flat management structure for staff: nine deputy/departmental heads have responsibility for the curriculum and for appointing their own teachers; Sir Kevin claims that this releases cash for everyone else (teachers have a lightish teaching load and get overtime for extra duties).

Academic Matters: Very important (the head's first sentence in the prospectus), and very successful. The claim to be 'England's top comprehensive school' gives rise to lively and intermittent argument about how they do it – and how the exam statistics are worked out – but there is no doubt that drive towards achievement and celebration of success are hot-wired into the place. Some A level students recently wrote to the press in answer to a disparaging criticism of the school (see below): 'Our school and students are competitive and we make no apologies for that. We do not accept mediocrity, and why should we?'

Pass rates at both levels are high and rising (vocational qualifications included in the calculation); science, maths and technology A level are strong (as one might expect), also English literature, history and business studies. Languages feature pretty well at GCSE though few take them in the last two years. Still, this is a wide-ability school, and clearly something in the air makes the pupils work hard and want to do well. 'Students should feel good about being successful.' Sir Kevin would say it's all to do with an ethos of high standards, secure surroundings, staff commitment and strong parental involvement; now where have we heard all that before? Bags of encouragement and reinforcement underpins all this.

The school pioneered the use of IT early in the 1990s, and is still at the leading edge in the production of educational software – so much so that it sells its curriculum and allied material to schools nationally as part of an outreach programme, which brings in a handy £2m a year. The whole curriculum is planned in July for the following year; the claim is that it can be accessed in school or from home at any time. Quite what 'curriculum' means here is not clear – it sounds as if teachers are expendable – perhaps 'schemes of work'; but in context it has to be a bright idea, handing initiative to pupils to learn and releasing teachers from some drudgery. 'It may sound mechanistic', says the head, 'but it's very productive'.

Average class size is 24 below the sixth; groups range from 4 to 23 in years 12 and 13. 44 pupils on the SEN roll, nine of them statemented.

Games, Options, The Arts: Enormous range of games played (Sportsmark Gold with Distinction awarded), much student representation at every level up to national: football (boys have link-up with Wolves, one girl played for England), cricket, hockey, athletics, swimming, etc. etc. Inter-house competitions taken seriously; excellent facilities, including floodlit pitches. Over a hundred pupils currently involved in D of E at all levels. Performing arts are strong, especially dance and music.

Background and Atmosphere: Founded in 1991 with attractive purpose-built campus; the use of space underpins the head's philosophy. As a CTC, the school is sponsored, notably by the Mercers' Company and the Tarmac Group, who have plenty of influence on the governing board. This means the head has great freedom of action – and no anxieties because no fees to garner.

Plenty of open spaces, including open areas where two or three classes are taught simultaneously; an interesting reversion to the old schoolroom idea, which appears to work well, and certainly suits the 3-hour periods. Generally there is an impression of quiet and purposeful study, with elements of both focus and relaxation. Everywhere is carpeted, and noise levels are impressively low (no bells). Reception area could belong to a corporate HQ, with (silent) TV screens giving the latest in news and sport, and a monitor for visitors to access the school's very professional website – and indeed much of the building looks like a modern open-plan office. Neatly uniformed boys and girls (they even have TTS lab coats).

Parents encouraged to become involved in the school's life, through an advisory council and through constant monitoring of their children's progress: they get a report every 3 1/2 weeks, and are invited to comment on eg whether they are satisfied with their child's work. Much contact with personal tutors, who are encouraged to draw the diffident into the educational process; they even visit housebound parents on their own initiative. The very hard-working can be rewarded by becoming Parent of the Year.

Pastoral Care and Discipline: Vertical tutor-group system (like St Paul's London – another Mercer's school), two to three from each year in one 'family'; meets every day for 20 minutes. 'Students can see the headmaster at any time to discuss issues of concern.' Zero tolerance over bullying and use of harmful substances, inside or outside school. Uniform rules strictly enforced.

Pupils and Parents: From Wolverhampton (nine coaches ferry pupils to and fro), or from Telford town. Obviously a wide span of social backgrounds – some families on income support and some middle class parents who, elsewhere, might have avoided comprehensives but can sniff out a successful middle class school. Ideologically-driven observers like Roy Hattersley have sought to explain academic success by accusing the school of a socially skewed selection policy, a charge vigorously countered by Sir Kevin, who points out that all CTCs have to pick in fixed proportions from the standard distribution of ability bands. The argument will doubtless continue.

Entrance: Entrants at 11+ come from a defined catchment area; no preference for siblings. Selection is 'from the full ability range ... in accordance with the criteria embodied in the funding agreement between the school and the Education Secretary', which is different from LEA schools. Within each of the nine ability bands 'places will be allocated as far as practicable over the full range of ability. The headmaster will select students ... and in exercising his professional judgement will take into account the range of ability admitted, geographical dispersal of intake, and competence in science, technology and maths.' So the head has some freedom within broad parameters. (Note carefully: applications have to be in by 30 September for the next September.) Our translation of this for eager parents would be – underlying ability is no barrier or advantage but do interest your child in something technological or mathematical. There will be geographical patches where the chances of success are higher because the level of applications is lower. This is one of the few good schools where moving to a cheaper house will give an advantage? Enthusiasm for the school, a real interest in education, and an obvious willingness to get stuck in should be on display at visits/interviews; this applies to your child too.

There may be a few places after GCSE.

Exit: Increasingly to higher education, mainly in and around the midlands – 80 per cent in 2004, with 7 per cent taking a gap year, the rest to employment or training. About a third of leavers to older universities – four to Oxford. Numbers staying on to the sixth are steadily increasing (now over 90 per cent). The school claims a low drop-out rate at university (two per cent).

Remarks: A remarkable school, proof (for some) of what a comprehensive – albeit a special one – can achieve under strong and visionary leadership. Whatever you think about the overtly competitive drive towards academic success, you can't be unaffected by the pupils' all-round confidence, and their pleasure in belonging to an institution which stimulates them in the classroom and appreciates them for what they can offer outside it; not new values by any means, but all the better for being asserted here. If you're moving to this part of the west midlands, get your form in in good time.

THURSTON COMMUNITY COLLEGE

Thurston, Bury St Edmunds, Suffolk, IP31 3PB

Tel: 01359 230 885
Fax: 01359 230 880
E-mail: admin@thurstoncollege.suffolk.sch.uk
Website: www.thurstoncollege.suffolk.sch.uk

• Pupils: 1,420 boys and girls, all day • Ages: 13-18 • Size of sixth form: 375 • Non-denom • State • Open days: Main school - October; sixth form - November

Principal: Since 2005, Miss Helen Wilson (fortyish) who joined the college as vice principal. She was instrumental in the college's successful bid for Specialist Science Status in 2004. Miss Wilson is not only the youngest principal in the history of the college but is also the first woman to get the job.

Academic Matters: Considerably above national average results at GCSE and A level. At GCSE there is a 69 per cent (A*-C) pass rate with the bulk of pupils scoring B and C grades, but with a good smattering of A and A*s. At A level, 2004 saw a 99 per cent pass rate. Ofsted (inspection just after previous head arrived in 2002) felt that the school had yet to achieve its full potential. A major programme to meet the needs of the most able. There is a broad range of subjects on offer and 'a significant amount of very good and excellent teaching', although inspectors saw some lessons as too teacher dominated. Pupils with special needs are well catered for. Pupils produce bold, exciting work. Average class size is 27, with a maximum of 30. Setting in several subjects. General studies taken by all students in the lower sixth.

Games, Options, The Arts: Games very strong. The school has recently provided an u18 all-England hockey player (boy) and an international kayaker (girl) and an England netball player. A wide variety of musical activities, choirs, bands, orchestra etc and two theatres for lots of concerts and drama. Debating is very popular; in 2002 the school came sixth in an all-England competition (highest state school). As 4 out of 5 of pupils come to school by bus or coach, most activities are fitted into the lunch hour, but there are late buses every Monday.

Background and Atmosphere: Airy, pleasant setting in a largish village. Main buildings were purpose-built in the seventies, with plenty of space and moderately good facilities. A major programme of modernisation is taking place. New science laboratories and 'facilities' for dance and drama. The very pleasant well-stocked library is full to bursting at lunchtime. Brand new state-of-the-art sixth form centre with a super big computer room, largely self-sufficient. Atmosphere relaxed and friendly and, for such a big school, amazingly quiet. Pupils say relations with staff are very easy and it is definitely not uncool to want to do well. Staff and pupils can have breakfast at school every morning.

Pastoral Care and Discipline: Because of its huge size, the school is divided into six houses, each with a team of tutors providing excellent pastoral care and the backbone of the school's discipline. Students have year and house assemblies, and 'thought for the day' every day. There is keen inter-house competition, particularly on the sports' field. Last head tightened up a lot and reversed a decline in attendance. The two earrings per ear of the past are now reduced to one! A system of 'positive discipline' has been introduced, based on rewards, but detentions etc remain and smoking can, at worst, lead to exclusion. Really bad behaviour is rare.

Pupils and Parents: Largely from surrounding rural area, predominantly middle class, with a tiny number from ethnic minorities. Lots of links with the local community, who use the school facilities a great deal. Parents and children like the very informal uniform of pale blue polo shirt, navy sweat shirt and black trousers (girls rarely wear skirts), which is the norm in Suffolk schools.

Entrance: Usually only from the catchment area, as the school is heavily over-subscribed. Three main feeder middle schools, with whom the college maintains constant contact, so that children are largely known on arrival.

Exit: Six out of ten pupils carry on into the sixth form and about half of sixth form go on to higher education.

Remarks: A self-confident, successful rural comprehensive school, which looks set to do even better.

THE TIFFIN GIRLS' SCHOOL

Richmond Road, Kingston Upon Thames, Surrey, KT2 5PL

Tel: 020 8546 0773
Fax: 020 8547 0191
E-mail: tiffin.girls@rbksch.org
Website: www.tiffingirls.kingston.sch.uk

• Pupils: 889 girls, all day • Ages: 11-18 • Size of sixth form: 278 • Non-denom • State • Open days: Autumn

Head: Since 1994, Mrs Pauline Cox BA MA (fifties). Educated at High Storrs Girls' Grammar School in Sheffield, followed by geography at Birmingham and an MA in education at the London Institute of Education. Came to Tiffin from Cranford Community School in Hounslow and previously worked in the British Embassy in Poland before spending three years teaching in Accra and thereafter in the 'plusher parts of London'. Described by Ofsted as having 'a very clear vision, drive and high expectations for all', she is also charming, friendly and great fun. Fairly single-minded, with the ability to switch between subjects and people at will – she runs the school with a couple of deputy heads. Husband is Executive Secretary of the Royal Society; one daughter and one son. Mrs Cox is keen on sport including skiing ('avid but hopeless').

Academic Matters: Ofsted Report (2000) says it all: 'Standards are very high. The overall quality of teaching and learning is excellent. The breadth of curriculum offered is very good with an extensive range of extra-curricular opportunities. Leadership by the head teacher is excellent. The school promotes excellent standards of behaviour; the personal development of the pupils ... excellent. The school provides excellent value for money'. Bit difficult to cap that really, particularly as the word excellent recurs in almost every paragraph (and sometimes twice in a paragraph) throughout the whole report – over 90 times in all.

This is a first-class academic school, the results are outstanding, with trails of As and A*s at GCSE and an impressive collection of As at A level; results fairly evenly spread, with English and the sciences both featuring in the ribbons; maths popular. Girls choose four subjects for AS at the end of lower sixth and can choose their A level subjects at the beginning of upper sixth when they have had the results of their ASs. 'Girls are fickle and their most favourite subject at the beginning of lower sixth may not be their favourite at the end – give them as much choice as possible'.

A few children currently getting help from sixth formers in maths and English ('but they have to be bright to come to us in the first place'), and several getting English 'as an additional language'. 'Big staff turnover', usually they last 'two or three years, but they're good'. The school is regarded as a jumping-off point on the promotional ladder and lost an assistant head to Putney High School. Lack of cash always a problem, and the 'staff have a much higher teaching load than in the private sector', bigger classes, more lessons per week and more homework to mark. 'Dynamic improving staff, no weaknesses at all,' says the head. Super friendly library and a jolly librarian, who collects all those tokens you get in supermarkets, crisp packets etc.

Games, Options, The Arts: Impressive community sports centre used by local community after hours at weekends, Astroturf, tennis courts, two gyms with adjoining doors and sports area outside main building. Girls doing athletics when we visited on a stinking hot day in June. Trails of glory on the sports field with regular finalists and championships (and masses of silver in the front hall).

'Proper' ICT, jewellery making, graphics and drama are strong with annual musical, masses of music – regular concerts in all disciplines, with girls studying music after school. Keyboards computer linked. Art is very exciting, with fabulous textiles (girls make their own costumes for their productions). Masses of trips, skiing in Italy, trips to Iceland and New York. Trips germane to course work (ie geography to Barcelona) and all other jollies must be funded by parents.

Background and Atmosphere: We nearly didn't find the place when we visited in 1999 as the Tiffin boys had replaced the sign for Tiffin Girls with their own and vice versa. But by the time we arrived there were no signs, only one for the community sports ground shared with the school which moved to their rather dreary present building in 1987. Signs replaced since, we are assured. Depressing former secondary modern has been radically transformed with passages and reduced kitchens to form workable warren of classrooms. Very hot on top floor. Separate sixth form room, masses of computers, a lot of revamping, but more paint would not come amiss. Number 65 bus stops outside the school. Most of 1950s laboratories have been modernised at a cost of £300,000 and are now state of the art.

In December 2003, the school was seriously damaged by fire and one third of the school – classrooms and office space – was destroyed. (Also a lot of pupils' work.) The school is temporarily functioning with what the head describes as, 'a village of mobile classrooms.' However, replacement buildings by end of 2006. Exciting new £4 million teaching block of 18 classrooms planned, with large spacious atrium and specialist ICT suite of rooms.

The school evolved courtesy of the brothers Thomas and John Tiffin who, in 1638-1639 left £150 in trust for the education of 'some poor men's sons'. Elizabeth Brown left dwelling houses in St Brides to her son to be conveyed to the town of Kingston and a small yearly income to be paid to 'some honest industrious woman'. Edward Belitha had needlework in his sights for 'honest respectable women' and the consequence was the foundation of the Tiffin Schools in 1880.

Recent innovations have included the setting up of a house system, called after the second, third, fourth and fifth headmistresses. The first, a Miss Fysh, resigned after a spot of financial disagreement with the Board over a matter of a gas bill and promptly set up a rival establishment with her deputy. But Bebbington, Flavell, Watson and Schofield are now part of Tiffin life; girls not entirely sure that 'they were that competitive', but seem more adjusted to the new concept which also gives scope for more girl responsibility.

Pastoral Care and Discipline: No exclusions, occasional 'falling by the wayside' means 'putting on report,' and signing in after every lesson, bullying no problem. Girls have masses of responsibility, with positions running from Easter to Easter so that the summer, exam term, is free. Head girls, deputies, house prefects and deputies, ICT, technical support and music prefects etc, all with assistants and sixth form volunteers do extra coaching for tinies. Good bonding. Professional counsellor on hand for one session each week . Tutorial system and strong PSE in place. School Council – a girl-inspired forum – advises the staff on changes they would like to see put in place, like the (not particularly thrilling) summer dresses and the new style school uniform trousers.

Pupils and Parents: Caring, ambitious, mainly middle class. With lots of ethnic minorities, with clever and hard working parents as role models.

Entrance: Difficult, 120 places for every 1,000 applicants; some leave after GCSE and rather more arrive. Competitive testing. Any one 'who can access the school' can come here (if they pass – for which they probably need to be in the top 7 per cent of the ability range). Places available after GCSE, should have As in subjects to be studied at A level.

Exit: Almost all to higher education but the occasional surprising choice, eg diploma in aromatherapy/massage. Masses to medicine and the arts. More girls now take a gap year before university. 18 or so annually to Oxbridge but the medics prefer London.

Money Matters: Kingston - 'leafy green Kingston' - is apparently the richest borough in London but funds still a problem. Parents good at fund-raising and pay £25 a month by direct debit to boost finances. Last year they raised £80,000 for computers and the like. Local industry also tips in with donations. Fire appeal has raised over £160,000 in 18 months.

Remarks: Super vibrant state girls' grammar school with an excellent record, remains delightfully unassuming and lacking in intellectual arrogance. Humming and, dare we say it, excellent.

TIFFIN SCHOOL

Queen Elizabeth Road, Kingston Upon Thames, Surrey, KT2 6RL

Tel: 02085 464 638

Fax: 02085 466 365

E-mail: office@tiffin.kingston.sch.uk

Website: www.tiffin.kingston.sch.uk

• Pupils: 1,045 boys, all day • Ages: 11-18 • Size of sixth form: 342 • Broadly C of E, all faiths admitted • State • Open days: Early October

---

Head: Since 2004, Mr Sean Heslop MA Hons PGCE (mid-thirties). Read English at Queen's College, Cambridge, where he played football and cricket for the college. After early career in IT poetry publishing joined Queen Elizabeth's, Barnet, 1994 to 1997, thence to St Olave's Grammar School as head of English. In 2000 to Ravens Wood School, Bromley, as deputy head. Clearly very committed to, influential and experienced in, pioneering work in the state sector on all fronts.

Academic Matters: Unashamedly academic, pre-applicants are warned – 'don't sit the tests if you are not up to academic rigour.' However school is also prepared to challenge existing styles of learning and teaching; the opening of the new Dempsey building in 2004 has given the school an opportunity to put innovation into practice. Another open day mantra predicts two hours homework per night – if that doesn't thrill, look elsewhere. In practice, whilst there is plenty of it, homework loads rarely match up to such daunting warnings. Results are solid – almost all pass GCSE at A*-C (65 per cent at A*/A) and 75 per cent get A/B at A level. Predictably, the quintessentially male subjects, maths and the sciences, far and away the most popular at A level. However the school's specialism is the performing arts, based upon its excellence in music, drama and dance. Broader span of success at GCSE with English language and literature eliciting some good grades.

Average class size is 30 in line with other state schools. At A and AS levels less popular subjects generate smaller classes whilst favourites strain at the seams (maths being a case in point). Any child who passes IQ-based entry exams sees automatic acceptance, therefore, broad range of special needs catered for, from Asperger's syndrome to severe physical impairment and usual range of dyslexia/dyspraxia. All benefit from free specialist support within curriculum.

Games, Options, The Arts: Detached sports hall on site, built under the auspices of Sport for All and used by the local community evenings and weekends. A great modern facility with space for 6 badminton courts and full disabled access. Outdoor sports are exiled to own playing fields, Grist's at Hinchley Wood (half an hour by public transport, sometimes coach). Timetabled sport one afternoon a week and plenty of extra-curricular ventures at lunch-time and after classes. School performs well in local independent/state leagues, particularly in rugby, cricket and rowing. Own boathouse is short walk away down at the Thames. Genuine attempts to give boys extra-curricular space to shine beyond the relentless exam machine. Strong house system with sporting and other competitions.

Music department offers individual instrumental tuition (payable termly) with acoustic practice areas; 30 per cent of boys play an instrument across several bands and orchestras. The choir has covetable links with the Royal Opera House. Modern facilities and renowned drama. Have achieved performing arts college status (brings with it D of E grant). School takes its productions to the Edinburgh Festival and on tour internationally. Art and design technology workshops are functional and up-to-date, as are IT suites.

Background and Atmosphere: Inescapably urban location, at the heart of Kingston's notorious one way traffic system. High redbrick walls largely hide it from the outside world and form a fair security/sound barrier. Inside the perimeter, grounds offer a surprising amount of outdoor space; slightly unkempt five-a-side football pitch, several tarmac quads, plus sixth form/staff-only lawns and gardens Main school block built in 1929 is attractive and creeper laden, set just behind a smallish, heavily listed early nineteenth century school house Elmfield currently housing the sixth form common rooms, library and careers suite. Listed buildings, no matter what gravitas and history they lend, are, one senses, the bane of schools choked by LEA budgets. The oodles of funds that it would take to restore Elmfield to any former glory and make its interior space usable and appealing are clearly not forthcoming. Two modern extensions are sympathetic. The Dempsey building, opened in June 2004, links an existing extension to the body of the school and provides lecture theatre, new library and other teaching spaces. Overall, classrooms and facilities are of a good standard, décor is sometimes tired, but there is no sense of neglect. At the bell, well-kitted-out boys fill the corridors with chatter; relationships seem convivial. Canteen housed in worryingly ugly Nissen-hut style accommodation on the edge of the site. The school introduced a 'healthy eating regime' in September 2004 so no chips! It was well patronised at break-time on the day of visit. Options of school or packed lunch – 'food is OK.'

Pastoral Care and Discipline: New head is strict on uniform, behaviour and consistency across the school. Rules are rules, boys kept in line with well-oiled detention (ultimately suspension) system and homework clinics for those whose main misdemeanour is not keeping up. Some find it quite starchy. Conducive working atmosphere is defended at all costs. Good anti-bullying policy and pupils attest to feeling safe and supported. Prefects, form tutors and year heads keep an eye on pastoral problems. Cross three lanes of slow-moving traffic next to the school and you will reach Kaleidoscope needle exchange project with its clients jostling (and worse) on the pavements outside. Perhaps serves as a warning to their impressionable young neighbours as no major infringements of the banned substances policy have recently come to light.

School has a distinctly male vibe though 33 per cent of teaching staff are female. Plenty of social opportunities with the opposite sex, however. Pupils are much in demand for drama and other accompanying roles at local girls' schools, not least Tiffin Girls' (a mile up the road in cosier Kingston suburbs).

Pupils and Parents: Fairly solidly middle class group. Some would almost certainly have opted for the private sector if the Tiffin pass mark had not been attained and about thirty acceptees a year go that way regardless. A percentage of pupils come from low income families and school has forged social links with disadvantaged high-rise estates less than a mile away. Half of the pupils come from primary schools in Kingston borough and, despite being open to all-comers, Tiffin is well regarded as a local asset. Forty per cent of the intake is non-C of E, plenty of respect for other religions and cultures institutionally and at playground level.

Entrance: Highly selective. Catchment stretches wide across south London and Surrey – places are oversubscribed seven to one. At 11: two half-day tests, verbal and non-verbal reasoning in November of year before entry.

Results are 'age-weighted'- August birthdays not disadvantaged. Top 140 are offered places (possibly a few more or if any positions are tied). The rest are put on a waiting list in order of score. Places offered up until September in the year of entry. After this doors are shut to newcomers until sixth form. Leavers are not sufficient over five years to deplete the year group/affect funding. Minimum requirements for incumbents to progress to sixth form (GCSE Grade B or above in given subject and four other passes) mean that, in principle, there could be forced departures. In practice, all measure up. Nonetheless, between 16 and 17 approximately twenty leave of their own accord to other institutions. Empty places, plus fifty new vacancies, are filled by application and a competitive set of GCSE results. Incomers settle well and often progress to be prefects after just a year in school.

Exit: Majority to higher education. Oxford is most attended university with 16 boys gaining places (4 to Cambridge). Nottingham, Warwick and various University of London colleges are also popular.

Money Matters: State funded, free for all. Manages well on limited budgets and is hot on the trail of any opportunities for extra government cash. Newsletters witness constant appeals to parents. Fund raising activities are rife, weekend car-boot sales have become something of an institution in the area. School shop retailing a dizzying range of varying ties and blazers which are used to differentiate houses, lower school, upper school and upper sixth, must turn in a fair profit. Well-supported alumni association also lends financial muscle.

Remarks: Selective state school with excellent local and national reputation. Takes academic high flyers and gets the job done with them in a humane and no nonsense way. Oddballs at primary school, who seemed too nerdy for words, will at least find like-minds here and, at best, end up folk-heroes. The super-sensitive may be happier with the smaller classes and refined atmosphere of the private sector – if they are bright enough for here, they may get a scholarship there.

TONBRIDGE GRAMMAR SCHOOL

Deakin Leas, Tonbridge, Kent, TN9 2JR

Tel: 01732 365 125
Fax: 01732 359 417
E-mail: office@tgs.kent.sch.uk
Website: www.tgs.kent.sch.uk

- Pupils: 1,083, mostly girls; includes about 40 boys in the sixth form; all day • Ages: 11-18 • Size of sixth form: 325 • Non-denom • State • Open days: October or tours once a month (telephone for details)

Head: Since 2005, Mrs Rosemary Joyce BA (Hons) MA, previously deputy head of Nonsuch High School for Girls in Cheam, Sutton. First degree from University of Stirling, PGCE and second degree from University of London Institute of Education. Areas of educational specialism – Religious Studies and history. Previous schools include Clarendon School Trowbridge, Aylesbury High School, Millais School Horsham.

Academic Matters: Much praise from Ofsted 2002. The school is consistently at the top of league tables. Excellent A level results in 2005 and GCSE results in 2004 and a good range of languages including Italian, Latin and Spanish – an exceptional department praised by all, with work experience done in Spain, France and Germany. English – 82 per cent A/A*. Maths teaching excellent, accelerated maths group takes GCSE in year 10. A lot take drama, 93 per cent A/A*, described as 'transformed and uplifted ' by the students – the statistics speak for themselves. Their trump card is the flexible curriculum that allows them to spread their GCSEs and take some early, giving more time for other studies, minimising exam pressure and allowing time for just the learning experience of eg drama for fun. The school is piloting AS levels in year 10 for some students. Girls learn how to be independent and manage their work load early. School now also offers the International Baccalaureate as an alternative pathway for students not wanting to follow the traditional A level route.

Staff profile is a healthy mix of young NQTs and experienced staff; calibre is top notch and kept on their toes with very effective monitoring of stats internally and externally. Any shortcomings quickly surface and mentors always on hand. Setting in maths begins in year 8 and some setting in modern languages. Generally, however, there is no streaming or fixing of labels, as this doesn't tally with the culture of being respectful of others' different and diverse strengths. Very good science, holds science careers conventions, speakers ranging from chemical engineer to a patent agent. ICT integrated into every subject. Pays attention to learning difficulties and the particularly gifted – personalised programme for those who need it including running its own summer school and Saturday enrichment sessions. 'This is certainly not a hot-house for pressurised academic success,' comments a deputy head.

Games, Options, The Arts: Corridors are decked with students' work in a nice higgledy-piggledy way, showing a full range of pupils' abilities. There are increasing amounts of work presented digitally. Technology is rated highly by the girls, teachers give 110 per cent of their time – some contemporary and dazzling garb hanging on models contrasting with a traditional but stylish green/blue tartan uniform.

Artsmark Gold re-awarded in 2004 for outstanding provision in art, dance, drama and music. Music technology studio and spectacular graphics software. Plenty going on, presently 300 students learn a full range of musical instruments, two rock bands, three choirs, two orchestras etc etc. Plenty of students involved in county and national youth orchestras as well as choirs and bands. School seeking final permission to exchange brownfield land at one end of the site for a new three-story teaching block with adjoining sports hall, drama studio and dance studio plus refurbishment of all the facilities for art and music.

Usual games are on offer and the school is well represented at county and national level (particularly at netball and hockey). Sportsmark re-awarded in 2004. One pupil managed to swim for England and still maintain a successful A level programme. There are plenty of playing fields (easily waterlogged and slushy in the winter and wide craters appear in the summer), hard and grass tennis courts, an outdoor pool and limited indoor facilities. Good partnerships with local schools under the School Sports Coordinator programme. Duke of Edinburgh popular at all levels. Developing programme of outreach for students through the school's specialist and leading edge status. Developing programme of international links with schools in Washington DC, Singapore and Sri Lanka. School supports the World Challenge expedition to Peru 2006.

Background and Atmosphere: Main building early 20th century, redbrick, very C grade and the only thing about this school that is. Corridors recently refurbished and the canteen very antiquated. School has expanded by scattering a hotchpotch of classrooms (a little barrack-like) on the hill; there is a newer science and technology block and

'we're thinking big on facilities' says the deputy head. The age of the current buildings does not deter the pupils' natural enthusiasm and pride in their school – they're all too productive to notice wear and tear.

Introduction of boys has proved good news, particularly in debate, 'some of these girls are as ambitious as the chaps, this is a good stepping stone for their later working environment'. The large common room is a very friendly place. Sixth form students play a major role in the running of the school and in contributing to the culture – responsibilities include publicity, environment, one2one, charity work etc.

Pastoral Care and Discipline: Parents really impressed with the confidence and level of maturity the girls achieve. Sixth form students have initiated a peer mentoring, one2one system whereby each student takes responsibility for a topic, eg anorexia; they receive counselling advice and provide confidential support for junior girls. Discipline is hardly an issue as girls are motivated. 'Perhaps one downside of being so selective is that pupils can feel they fail if they achieve a B grade. We work very hard with their self worth and perception,' says the deputy head.

Pupils and Parents: Students come from over 70 schools, both maintained and private, mainly the surrounding areas of Tonbridge, Sevenoaks, Tunbridge Wells, some from Surrey and East Sussex. Majority are very middle class, supportive of the school, friendly and no pretensions. Small numbers from other European countries, middle east, America, Australia – attracted to the school because of its reputation and approach to language teaching. All but 15 have English as their first language. Good Old Girl network – Baroness Sharpe, Hayley Allen (Olympic diver), Rebecca Stephens (Everest mountaineer), Felicity Aston (polar explorer), Sophia Macdougall (novelist)].

Entrance: 140 places via the Kent selection procedure (11+ exam), which is overseen by Kent. Usually oversubscribed. A minimum of 35 'governor places' are reserved for able pupils from outside the area but the same criteria apply as for Kent selection. Entry to sixth form 'where ability is appropriate'. The school welcomes students with special needs. Admissions latest information is available in the prospectus and on the school website.

Exit: Diverse choices – mainly to Higher Education through university, studying anything from the traditional, eg classics, medicine, law, psychology through to film and French, chemistry and forensic science, politics, early childhood studies, textiles and fashion, sports science etc. Increasing numbers to Oxbridge, including choral scholarships. Good tradition of specialist art, music and drama college places.

Money Matters: State-funded. Music bursaries available and awards in sixth form. Some academic bursary-scholarships in the sixth form. The school also co-ordinates a fund, administered exclusively by the head teacher, to assist in cases of financial hardship.

Remarks: The façade may not be (yet) refined and polished oak but the students are top brass and so is the education.

TONBRIDGE SCHOOL

High Street, Tonbridge, Kent, TN9 1JP

Tel: 01732 365 555
Fax: 01732 363 424
E-mail: hmsec@tonbridge-school.org
Website: www.tonbridge-school.co.uk

- Pupils: 755 boys; 435 board, 320 day • Ages: 13-18 • Size of sixth form: 305 • C of E • Fees: Day £5,602; boarding £7,928
- Independent • Open days: Visits and tours arranged individually Monday to Saturday in term-time

Head: Since 2005, Mr Tim Haynes BA (fortyish). Educated at Shrewsbury and Reading, PGCE at Pembroke, Cambridge. Taught at Hampton and for thirteen years at St Paul's, where he became Surmaster. Monmouth (well, its governors) has a tradition of picking, for their first headship, bright young men who then go on up the educational ladder – and here's the latest example. Straightforward, down-to-earth, effective, cheerful. Bags of vitality, evident everywhere. Reported to be a very strong manager who motivates and delegates to a top-class management team. Still teaches some history. Wife Charlotte great support in school. Two young sons. Vintage car buff.

Academic Matters: Has the most wonderful collection of enthusiastic, inspired staff we have encountered anywhere. You just go into most departments (particularly biology and chemistry) and immediately want to sit down and start learning. Staff put in many over-and-above hours including A level reading and revision groups in the holidays in Cornwall, and reading parties for Oxbridge students – 'brilliant,' said a boy.

Ratio of academic staff to pupils 1:8. Some setting (maths, classics and languages). Latin compulsory in the first year, the top four sets combine it with Greek. Maths and French GCSE taken one year early by a substantial number of boys (most pupils take ten in all). 'Boys are really taught how to work and have to work hard,' commented a parent. 'There's no let-up.' Lessons organised on a ten-day cycle. GCSE teaching groups of about 17 boys, down to 8 at A level. Firm emphasis on the critical and analytical approach to study – how to think, reason and argue – starts well before the sixth form. Each department housed in its own area, with offices and (usually) own library. Wonderful warm main library, full of life and with an impressive budget. Exam results very impressive – hard to pick out any particular star in such a galaxy; languages results very fine but, as in most academic boys' schools, not notably popular, but numbers increasing. Of the odd isolated D and E grade, the head says he, 'doesn't know why that should be – probably means they weren't working.' Under the new system almost all take four ASs and over half four A2s. Learning support co-ordinator for able boys with some degree of dyslexia. In 2005, virtually 90 per cent achieved A/B at A level. 30 boys (21 per cent of the upper sixth year-group) won places at Oxford or Cambridge. Unbeatable?

Games, Options, The Arts: A very sporty school, games still compulsory even for sixth form, huge numbers of squads and teams at all levels. Proud of their sporting reputation: powerful cricket, hockey and rugger sides, with 100 acres of pitches. 20+ sports on offer include rackets, fives, sailing, golf (results in matches up and down but still good overall). Marvellous all-weather athletics track with discus, shot putting, high and long jumps; two all-weather pitches. New water-based Astro completed January 2005. Rowing, alas, has been phased out.

Keen and increasingly impressive music. Head of music is an outstanding teacher – Mr Hilary Davan Wetton – who arrived from St Paul's Girls' and is chief conductor of the Milton Keynes orchestra. Fine chapel choir with chorister scholarships for trebles from local prep schools. Excellent crop of grade VII and VIII associated board exams. Drama is keen and has ritzy new theatre and new head of drama from Bedales. Duke of Edinburgh awards, CCF 'encouraged'. Good language exchanges and foreign expeditions are 'particularly well thought out and organised,' commented a parent. Art 'booming' under head of art James Cockburn (ex-Canford), notably excellent exam results (even by this school's standards), and increasingly popular.

Background and Atmosphere: Founded in 1553 as the 'Free Grammar School of Tonbridge'. (Re)built in the 19th century (Gothic style) along the bottle neck which winds into the pretty old part of Tonbridge – non-stop traffic. Boarding and day houses (five of the latter – numbers have been growing) scattered along the road, some in mellow brick, some not so mellow. A copious amount of new building – witness the recent £20 million development plan –

including a school uniform boutique which would not look out of place in Knightsbridge, and a tuck shop like a trendy trattoria, with chairs and tables outside on a terrace at which to eat your bacon butties; food good generally. Also brilliant development of existing buildings, with acres and acres of carpet, beautiful wood panelling and no expense spared.

And as for the Chapel! It was gutted by fire in 1988, while a Mr Burn (yes) was preaching to the school on 'Tongues of fire'. Restored amidst unbelievable brouhaha in a modern style – highly successful, acres of glorious English oak, roof in Canadian hemlock, granite and Italian marble-patterned floor – the very best materials, creating a monument to the twentieth century. Cost – £7 million, including £0.8m for a new sweet-sounding organ built by Marcussen of Denmark, with four manuals, sixty-six stops, which stop people in their tracks. Well worth a detour.

Day boys and boarders keep to separate houses, new day house recently acquired as part of the school's expansion schemes. Slight element of 'we/they' split personality. 'Marvellous for day pupils,' commented a parent. 'They get all the advantages of a big, strong, round-the-clock boarding school.' Flexible weekend leave now allows weekly boarding. Boarding houses are 'twinned' with Benenden houses for occasional social life (now extends to Tonbrige Grammar School too). The school was perceived as tough, ruggy-buggy, but this is no longer the case. There is a benign and friendly atmosphere, kind, tolerant and safe (albeit bouncy). Enthusiasm extends right through the school – not just the academic staff, but the gardeners, groundsmen and maintenance men in their smart uniforms (spotless loos).

Pastoral Care and Discipline: Both in very good shape. Tutors' brief is 'get to know the boys' and they do their best; first year groups of three or four visit the tutor at home. Small group pupil/tutor meetings for sixth formers to discuss/explore intellectual matters. Last head fiercely anti-smoking (jacked up first-time fine to £15; detention, letter home, rustication). 'But you never entirely get rid of it.' Alcohol reported to be 'under control' and (legally aged) upper sixth boys are allowed to local pubs on Saturday evenings. Boys still eat in their own house – a significant pastoral factor. Few (16 per cent) female staff.

Pupils and Parents: A fairly broad cross-section, especially in view of the generous scholarships. Mostly within one and a half hours' drive (including the 'Eastern corridor' now that this is easily accessible), and not socially upper crust. Many sons of the solid middle middle class, not flashy. Boys are open, well informed, look-you-in-the-eye, 'friendly and engaging, quietly confident, courteous and

sometimes disarmingly entertaining, tolerant and concerned for others' said a prospective parent. Old Boys include Lord Cowdrey, E M Forster, Sidney Keyes, Lord Mayhew, Vikram Seth, Frederick Forsyth (note the literary strength – still much in evidence).

Entrance: Reasonably tough. Main feeds are Holmewood House and New Beacon, Yardley Court, Hilden Grange, also Dulwich College Prep School. Otherwise from over 50 prep schools round about, including music scholars from choir schools. Very much at the sharp end of competition with extremely good grammar schools on the doorstep. Two thirds via CE at 13, one third through the scholarship exam (but not all with awards). Head notes (as others do) parents leaving the choice until later. For entry from outside at sixth form (very few) – minimum six GCSEs with A grades in subjects relating most closely to A level choices. Internal hurdle – six GCSE passes at grade B. Potentially embarrassing over-subscription partly met by one-off provision of an extra form, for the 2003 entry.

Exit: All to university, including 21 per cent to Oxbridge. Medicine, science, classics, law, engineering continue to be popular. NB the school does not weed out boys post-GCSE.

Money Matters: Rich, rich - fat fees and large endowment by Sir Andrew Judd administered by the Skinners' Company (who also provide the majority of governors). Over £1.3 million was shelled out in scholarships and bursaries last year (including top-ups to 100 per cent if necessary). 21 academic scholarships, 11/12 music scholarships, five or so art, drama or technology, three for sporting ability and sportsmanship. Also junior scholarships for boys 'who would otherwise leave for the maintained sector at eleven'. Extensive resources for the unexpectedly needy.

Remarks: One of the very best, outstanding in everything that really counts. Good reports; happy parents – ditto pupils. Parents who need social status might not choose it, but otherwise, go and look.

TORMEAD SCHOOL

Linked to Tormead School Junior Department in the
Junior section

27 Cranley Road, Guildford, Surrey, GU1 2JD

Tel: 01483 575 101
Fax: 01483 450 592
E-mail: head@tormeadschool.org.uk
Website: www.tormeadschool.org.uk

• Pupils: 550 girls, all day • Ages: 11-18 • Size of sixth form:
100 • Non-denom • Fees: £1,380 - £2,900 • Independent

Head: Since 2001, Mrs Susan Marks MA Oxon (forties). Prior to headship, she was head of sixth form at the school and before that head of economics and politics at St George's Weybridge. Read PPE at Jesus, Oxford, winning blues in rowing, athletics and (almost) hockey. Worked in the City, latterly in airline lending at Bank of America. Three daughters and a son, her youngest daughter is at Tormead – her eldest daughter died suddenly in 2002 at the age of 17. A hands-on head (although no longer teaches) with very clear views on the running of the school, she's 'passionate about girls' education in girls' schools.' No-nonsense, but encouraging approach ('very gung-ho and go-for-it,' says a parent), she runs the school with a balance of warm humour and a firm hand. Excellent understanding of what makes her pupils tick. Refreshingly open and honest, aware that there are always things that need improving and doesn't duck the tougher issues such as drugs and bullying. Clearly commands respect amongst pupils and parents alike.

Academic Matters: One of the high fliers in Surrey (and way beyond). Excellent academic results across a wide range of subjects – 79 per cent of GCSE passes are A*/A with particularly good performances in maths, English, sciences and languages (mostly As). Plenty of scope for choice in languages at both GCSE and A level including Spanish, German and Greek. Art is exceptionally strong here – 97 per cent of GCSE and 100 per cent of A level students attained A*/A – wonderful examples are on display around the school.

Nine GCSEs is usually the maximum allowed. Head keen to emphasise that academia is not the be-all and end-all – 'children need time to be children,' and parents agree that 'it's not a results factory.' Refreshing to see that risk taking is also encouraged – pupils who are keen to pursue

a subject which may not be their academic forte are still encouraged to follow their dreams. Pupils do not feel unduly under pressure academically ('not as pushy as other schools,' says a parent), and any worries about exams are sensitively handled by the school. Head famously anti league tables but has more time for the new value-added results – school does very well in all the tables. Grade sheet system introduced where pupils are marked for effort as well as attainment throughout the school year, so the less academic still get plenty of credit for trying hard and 'you feel on top of how your daughter is really doing,' says a parent.

SEN provision is there for those who need it on an individual basis and no stigma here for anyone needing extra help. Some parents feel that those with learning difficulties might struggle with the pace – one parent chose to send one of her daughters who has dyslexia elsewhere. Mrs M says 'some of our brightest students are dyslexic including two who are currently at Oxford!'

Games, Options, The Arts: A school known for its gymnasts ('we're hot on gymnastics here,' says one pupil, proudly); there's an excellent complex (one of the newer buildings on site) with sports hall, specialist gymnasts' training hall, strategy area with teachers' rooms leading off and viewing gallery. All sport is played keenly and to a high standard – including hockey, netball, rounders, swimming and tennis. There is enthusiastic uptake of a new system of 'development squads' for the keen but less naturally able players. However 'there should be more fixtures for the B and C teams,' says a parent.

It's a small site and space is at a premium – hockey teams have to practise off site ('it used to take us the whole lesson to get there and back,' says a pupil). Tennis on two on-site all-weather tennis courts but swimming is at the Spectrum Centre in Guildford. Some parents find the sports facilities limited but 'what they do, they do well.' Tormead has sporting success at county level and nationally, especially in swimming, gymnastics biathlon and sports acrobatics – a lack of facilities isn't holding them back.

Big tradition of music – borne out by high number of individual instrument players (325 individual lessons a week), two school orchestras, jazz band (which tours Europe), various ensembles and choirs. There is a programme of events throughout the year, including the Inter-House Music Competition where every girl takes part. Head is the first to admit that provision for drama is lacking (although drama teacher described by pupils as excellent). Currently drama taught in a 'studio' that has seen better days – probably in vogue when flares were in fashion the first time round. It is due to be bulldozed and replaced with a new all-singing, all-dancing performing arts centre.

More extra-curricular opportunities were requested by parents and head responded. Now a huge range of sporting, language, film, art and craft activities – including the more unusual choices of fencing, Japanese, classic movie club, cake decorating, origami, and debating (another school success story). Some are selective (mainly the sports and music clubs) but there is something for everyone and there is a palpable 'have a go' attitude. In addition there is the D of E Award Scheme as well as the opportunity to do community work.

Background and Atmosphere: Founded in 1905 and is now a mish-mash of old and new tacked onto the original and once lovely Victorian building in relatively small grounds. It feels quite small and intimate – and is divided into four sections, each with its own head reporting to Mrs Marks – junior, lower, upper and sixth form – parents commented on how 'sensible' this arrangement is. New areas of the school are quite impressive, old parts rather dark and confusing – cramped corridors and Hogwarts-style staircases seemingly appearing out of nowhere. Daunting names like 'the Maths Corridor' could be a bit off-putting with apparently endless number of classrooms in dark hallways. New pupils 'get lost all the time' but there is always someone to ask.

Well-equipped science labs, design and technology room and super textiles room (inspiring stuff going on in there) as well as the impressive art department. Two libraries, one small and intimate and a larger, brighter one, which is used for some lessons, quiet research etc. You might get trampled in the rush at lunchtime – pupils from

the junior department as well as the seniors use the refectory; luckily lunchtimes are staggered. IT provision is good with plenty of the latest computers and internet connections. The sixth formers have their own department (rather hallowed by the younger girls who clearly see it as the place to aim for) and no uniforms in the sixth form either so girls can let their hair down a bit – and they do, but nothing to frighten the horses. The sixth form common room certainly fulfils the cool quotient with snooker table, comfy chairs, kitchen area and stereo system. There's a warm, family feeling and a sense of belonging in the whole school. The girls have various socials with the Royal Grammar School boys, which are popular. The sixth form curriculum also includes a joint general studies programme with the boys from RGS – 'very popular with the girls, especially ballroom dancing,' says Mrs M. Also quite a social life with other Guildford schools via the daily train journeys but they are 'a nice crowd,' says a parent.

Pastoral Care and Discipline: A strength of the school is the nurturing environment it offers. There are various problem-solving options open to pupils that start with the form tutor. A trained counsellor is also on hand to help girls (appointments made through school nurse). System of 'Aunts' put in place, whereby every new girl has another girl assigned to them to help them through the first few weeks. Good career counselling and advice.

Pastoral care programme unanimously praised by parents as being superb – for some parents this proved the deciding factor in choosing the school. Less confident girls undoubtedly benefit from the caring and positive ethos - 'the greatest gift anyone can get is self confidence' says the head. Pupils leave the school with good social skills, self-confidence, and a dash of worldliness.

Parents 'have no hesitation' in getting in touch with the school on any issues – they are dealt with swiftly and effectively with genuine concern. Personal, social and health education lessons start in the junior department and continue throughout – including moral and social discussions and, by the time the girls are in the sixth form, debates on eg substance abuse, personal safety, relationships and child care. Assembly is an important part of the school day, and there is an emphasis on care and respect for others apparent throughout the school. Tough line on all transgressions including smoking, with expulsion for persistent offenders, and drugs possession would be likely to lead to instant expulsion. Bullying is tackled head-on, with open debate and a school policy drawn up in consultation with pupils – no whitewash here. Pupils and parents are clued up on the reality of bullying – these days via email and text – and

report back accordingly to teachers. When it does happen, 'it's stamped on pretty quickly,' says a pupil.

Pupils and Parents: Pupils are a self-confident lot (without being arrogant), friendly, and sociable – also pleasingly noisy as they wander from lesson to lesson. Neatly dressed on the whole, hair tied back, although a few customised uniforms in evidence. No ties – pupils requested this through the school council and their pleas were heard.

Parents from a mix of backgrounds – old girls, first time buyers, professionals, with a wide catchment of the Surrey stockbroker belt from Esher to Haslemere. Excellent coach service from the outlying towns and villages takes the hassle out of the school run.

Entrance: Entrance exam at 11 – pupils selected on the basis of academic potential (reasoning, maths and English tests) and extra-curricular interests although no interview apart from those applying for scholarships. Places are very competitive as junior department girls get priority – 95 per cent of the juniors sit the entrance exam and go on to the senior school. Only the cream of students from other schools get the remainder of places – main feeders are: Rydes Hill, Rowan, St Hilary's Godalming and Halstead. 'You wouldn't want to scrape in,' commented a parent. Sixth form entrance requirement described by the school as 'modest': 7 GCSEs, A*-C with a minimum of 4 Bs in the subjects to be studied (Tormead students usually far exceed these requirements). Girls entering the sixth form from other schools will also be interviewed.

Exit: Majority of girls stay on for sixth form – on average 18 students a year go elsewhere (three years ago the average was 35). From the sixth form, about five a year to Oxbridge, with other popular university choices Nottingham, Exeter, Durham, Leeds, Birmingham, Cardiff, Bristol, University College, London, also various medical schools. Recent places at London College of Fashion and Wimbledon Art School are a testament to high standard of art.

Money Matters: Several parents remarked on the 'good value' represented by the school. Five each of academic, music and art scholarships, worth up to a third of the tuition fees. Scholarships are also available for sixth form entrance.

Remarks: A school with high standards, superb academic results (without undue pressure) and commendably keen to winkle out any sparks of talent elsewhere – whether it's art, sport, drama, music. Not the ideal place for girls who are bookish without any other strings to their bow, or for the rebel who may find it hard to toe the line (although the all-embracing approach might just win them over).

TORQUAY BOYS' GRAMMAR SCHOOL

Shiphay Manor Drive, Torquay, Devon, TQ2 7EL

Tel: 01803 615 501

Fax: 01803 614 613

E-mail: enquiries@tbgs.torbay.sch.uk

Website: www.tbgs.co.uk

- Pupils: 1,040 boys • Ages: 11-18 • Size of sixth form: 290
- Non-denom • State • Open days: July and September

Head: Since 1987, Roy E Pike BA BEd FRSA (fifties). Initially taught history at old Torquay Boys' Grammar School, founded in 1914. Progressed to head of department, then took over new school as deputy head, until appointed head. Beneath a somewhat austere and authoritarian manner is a warm and personable head. Likes to unwind on his smallholding in the country with his family. Married with six children. Both boys at the school.

Academic Matters: Over 80 per cent grades A – C at A level, 60 per cent A*/A at GCSE. Maths, English and science are the top subjects. Identified by Ofsted in 1997 as being in top 2 per cent of schools of its kind nationally and again in 2003 as a 'particularly successful school'. A language college, offering French, German, Russian, Japanese and Italian. Depending on subject and year, class sizes vary from 6 to 30 pupils, taught by over 70 specialist teachers. Some A level subjects are taught to mixed classes with girls from neighbouring Torquay Grammar School for Girls – optimises available resources and a good way of mixing. Common rooms shared on both sites. Various scholarships and awards won by boys from RAF to National Youth Choir.

Panel for individual needs for pupils who are dyslexic or have problems with numeracy etc. Two students have statements.

Games, Options, The Arts: Lots of sports and lots of enthusiasm. Tradition of distinction in swimming and water-polo with players in under 19 England squad. Rugby, soccer, cross-country, hockey, athletics, cricket and tennis. Every sport has regional or county championship teams and all four Torbay Hockey Club teams are stuffed with students from here. New Astroturf courtesy of Sport England. Ten Tors and Duke of Edinburgh Gold Award, often followed by the more demanding Three Peaks Challenge and the World Challenge Expedition. All students are treated to potholing, canoeing, rock climbing, orienteering and, thanks to special rates with the local sailing club, everyone has the chance to learn to sail. Serious enthusiasts have become National Schools Sailing Champions. Other top acts have included water polo players in under 19 England squad; skiing for Britain's under 16s at international level. Torquay Boys' Grammar School Charitable Trust provided £150,000 for sand-dressed tennis courts that were lost when the sports hall was built.

National chess team consistently reaches the finals of Times Chess Championships. National Bridge champions in 2000. In the last ten years, two films made it to finals of the Disney Young Video Makers of the Year award. One won, with follow-on screenings on Sky's Disney Channel and on Channel 4. Target 2.5 Business Studies national finalists in 2000. The musicians have recorded three CDs. Art ranges from graphics through fine art to sculpture, with exhibitions in the region eg at Cockington Court. One student representing the UK in the British Informatics Olympiad.

Background and Atmosphere: Since its 1983 opening, £2m has been spent improving, expanding and resourcing the school – an impressive hi-tech media suite and new science and technology centre included. A new music department is its latest venture. The 60 classrooms are well arranged, in different subject sections. 40 acres of grounds, 15 minutes above Torquay town centre. An atmosphere of purpose, keeping boys busy. Dedicated teachers prefer being here to past posts. Went grant-maintained in 1993 but now referred to as a 'quasi-independent' foundation school by the head.

The school has a 19-inch Newtonian telescope, one of the largest in the south-west; members of the astronomy club undertake deep sky photography and video imaging of the moon and planets. Not surprisingly, the school's patron is famous astronomer, Sir Patrick Moore.

Pupils rave about the food. School Nutrition Action Group (including community dietician, school nurse, parents and pupils) recently won the Local Authority Caterers Association award two years running for promotion of healthy eating for its students.

Pastoral Care and Discipline: Evident respect and self-discipline among pupils and teachers. School nurse, counselling expertise of 30 staff, school council and consultative approach to rules all encourage participatory and co-operative culture among pupils. Bullying dealt with sensitively, where possible would try to turn the bully around; instant punishment is not the preferred route. School's five houses are linked to community through extensive charity work.

Pupils and Parents: Parents come from a large area stretching from Plymouth across to Exeter; many move to be near the school. Past pupils include former Wimbledon tennis player Mike Sangster, newspaper mogul Sir Ray Tindle, six times British swimming champion Malcolm Windeatt and Professor David Southwood, Director of Science at the European Space Agency. One former languages graduate, Marcus Richardson, now fluent in Serbo-Croat, became the interpreter at the War Crimes Tribunal at the Hague. Chris Lintott, old boy and Cambridge astronomer works alongside Patrick Moore. Not much ethnic diversity here so school has grown links with a school in London through the Beacon initiative.

As long as they have the ability, all types of boys excel here from slightly- built budding masterminds to burly rugby types. Younger pupils seem relaxed and happy, while older ones extremely polite and incredibly mature. All seem modestly proud to be here.

Entrance: Takes from the top 30 per cent of up to 70 primary schools, with some coming in at 13 and some at sixth form. Exam includes NFER verbal reasoning, and maths and English set by the school. Candidates have to pass at least two of the three elements. Numbers have risen from 750 to 1,000+ in the last five years; head trying to resist further demand. No student will be admitted to sixth form with fewer than 6 GCSE successes at B or above, although exceptions may be made in extreme circumstances.

Exit: More than 95 per cent go on to university including a dozen or so to Oxbridge. Other preferences are Cardiff, Bristol, Bath, Southampton. Medicine is popular, 50 students went on to read science, followed by maths, law, business and sports studies.

Remarks: A rich educational environment for career-driven, well presented boys who work and play hard to be high achievers. No thumb twiddling or fashion statements here.

TORQUAY GRAMMAR SCHOOL FOR GIRLS

Shiphay Lane, Torquay, Devon, TQ2 7DY

Tel: 01803 613 215
Fax: 01803 616 724
E-mail: admin@tggs.torbay.sch.uk
Website: www.tggs.torbay.sch.uk

• Pupils: 860 girls • Ages: 11-18 • Size of sixth form: 250
• Non-denom • State

Head: Since 1996, Ms Susan Roberts BSc MBA (fifties). Geography graduate of Aberystwyth. Studied PGCE at Liverpool. Worked at Notre Dame High School, Norwich, then lectured at a Welsh technical college. Took eight year gap to start family. Joined Ivybridge Community College in 1982, then moved to Plymouth High School for Girls in 1988 to become head of geography and careers then deputy head. A scholar through and through. Believes one must be learned to have credibility as a teacher, let alone head. Evident grasp of psychology. Rules the roost as friendly guardian and successful director. Strong belief in ability of teaching staff. Does not teach but in tune with pupils, exuding great philosophical understanding of a fledgling girl developing into young adult. Likes to think her nurturing philosophy is also utilised by teachers.

Academic Matters: Results are consistently well above average across the curriculum, especially in maths and English. More than 50 per cent of GCSEs graded A or A*; with 50 per cent A or B grades at A level. General class size 30; 24 for GCSE. Some A level subjects are taught to mixed classes with boys from neighbouring Torquay Grammar School for Boys. In some subjects, girls have choice of two syllabi – one on-site, the other at the boys' school, and vice versa. Optimises available resources, and a good way of mixing before the real world. Common rooms shared on both sites. Every girl in year 7 and year 9 spends a week at the school's Brittany Residential Centre in France, studying through the French curriculum and receiving some of their tuition in French. Pupils described a majority of their teachers as good and committed. Exchange links with Lohr am Main and Nantes.

Girls taught to recognise and push their own talents, respect moral values and each other. Open and relaxed atmosphere. No stringent rules about late homework; instead, extensions and extra support where necessary.

Girls encouraged to do what they can – not told off for what they can't. Special needs co-ordinator looks after anyone with dyslexia, epilepsy, diabetes etc. Formally organised clinics in maths where older girls help younger girls at lunchtime. Some 30 'seniors' in year 11 appointed as school helpers. Given jobs like looking after microphones/ lighting system for assemblies/concerts.

Games, Options, The Arts: Art, geography, RE, languages and business studies are popular options. Since 1999 Ofsted report, uptake in music at GCSE and A level has markedly improved – new enthusiastic teacher. School now boasts an orchestra, various choirs and bands. At GCSE, contemporary dance is popular for those who enjoy performing to a crowd on stage – a real confidence booster, no boys laughing behind the curtains.

Year 12 students take four AS levels, study RE and PE, and can opt for either a community studies programme award working with members of a local physically and mentally disabled school (and taking them to Brittany Residential Centre), a sports leader award or OCR Curriculum Enrichment Programme. Critical Thinking AS is also available.

Broad programme of fitness/sport available for girls to find what's right for them. Idea is for them to find something they will enjoy for life. Football team exists and the number of other schools with teams is increasing. All-weather pitch through lottery funding with the boys' school and local community groups is now in use and new tennis and netball courts just completed. Uses nearby facilities including English Rivera Fitness Suite for squash and swimming. Duke of Edinburgh popular every year with up to 120 pupils taking part.

Background and Atmosphere: School began in 1915 but moved to present site in 1937 high on a hill on the outskirts of Torquay. Looking much smarter thanks to refurbishment and face-lift in 2000-1. New multi-purpose dining hall and science laboratory 2003/4 and further new buildings ready 2005. Busy but friendly atmosphere.

Pastoral Care and Discipline: Girls taught that to be successful they need to co-operate and negotiate. Head will not humiliate pupils in front of peers but will have a quiet word. Smokers placed on litter duty for a week. Community police visit to frighten girls against taking drugs; apparently working. Parents are notified when peers or teachers say anything negative about their child.

Pupils and Parents: Mainly Torquay-based. Also from Newton Abbot, Paignton, Teignmouth and Exeter. From mixed social backgrounds, pupils collectively appreciate the chance to study for higher grades. Repeatedly commenting – 'friendly, happy atmosphere'. Past pupils have become actors (no hugely famous names), doctors, lawyers, business executives, media moguls, even an underwater photographer in the Red Sea. Parents confident they made the right choice and siblings follow. Some known to move nearer to school to make commuting easier.

Entrance: Takes in 120 pupils each year. Became Foundation school in 2002 – admission purely ability-based – top 11+ results from schools in Torbay Unitary Authority. Exams now tailored more for girls. Parents can now deal directly with school on 11+ matters rather than via LEA (a quicker and more effective system). No other selective girls' school in area. Every year handful of German students enters sixth form to study AS or A level English through Torquay-based agency, which arranges their accommodation.

Exit: Some 90 per cent continue at sixth form; most others move away from area. Alternative choices are South Devon College for NVQs. Sheffield, Nottingham, Warwick and Cardiff are popular choices; 3 or so to Oxbridge.

Remarks: Good teaching philosophy and happy atmosphere which attracts pupils instantly. Definitely worth a look if you live in the south west.

TRURO HIGH SCHOOL

Linked to Truro High School Preparatory Department in the Junior section

Falmouth Road, Truro, Cornwall, TR1 2HU

Tel: 01872 272 830
Fax: 01872 279 393
E-mail: admin@trurohigh.co.uk
Website: www.trurohigh.co.uk

- Pupils: 471 girls • Ages: 3-18 (boys age 3-5 years)
- Size of sixth form: 70 • C of E • Fees: Day £1,700 - £2,728 per term; boarding £4,902 - £5,143 • Independent
- Open days: Early October, but at any time to meet headmaster and have personal tour of school

---

Headmaster: Since 2000, Mr Michael McDowell BA MLitt (mid forties). Previously deputy head at Prior's Field, Godalming. Studied at University College, Swansea, and University of Edinburgh – English language and literature. Loves classical music. Has overseen nearly 20 per cent rise in pupil numbers in last two years. Well-liked by pupils and parents alike. Perhaps his 'approachable' caring and genuine demeanour has earned him brownie points. He's even been known to adopt the role of lollipop lady, when necessary. If it means seeing his girls safe, he's the type of chap who easily bends to the task. Married with one daughter.

Academic Matters: As an ex-direct grant school, has a strong academic tradition and an enviable record of examination success and university entrance. Consistently excellent results in recent years suggest strength within the school. Now a 25-hour week with one hour per lesson. Traditional Latin tuition is a strong point, one of few Cornish schools still teaching the subject. In the sixth form more than 50 per cent study science. Latin and classical civilisation are also popular choices.

Consistently good marks in French, German and Spanish. Traditional 'seventies' teaching style of listening booths with headphones and tape recorder proving fruitful. Foreign trip organised every year to complement studies and enrich experience. Learning difficulties/dyslexia well catered for.

Games, Options, The Arts: Music, art and drama loud and strong. Scholarship pupils are reminded of the privilege through concerts and music tours abroad. For girls showing music talent at audition, free lessons are provided on one instrument for one year if lack of funds would make keeping up studies a problem. Drama and theatre studies block named after and opened by actress Jenny Agutter in October 2000 – an inspiration to aspiring actresses. New art block opened by art historian Anthony Slinn. Planning permission and funding now secured for new sports hall.

Rain never stops play on the extensive all-weather hard surface sports area. Four grass courts and three hard courts available. Heated indoor pool and large gym. Many county titles in netball, hockey, cross country, swimming. D of E encouraged.

Background and Atmosphere: School was founded in 1880 by Bishop Benson before he became Archbishop of Canterbury. It has retained its commitment to providing girls with an academic education in a purposeful, Christian community. Since moving to its present site on Falmouth Road in 1896, the school has seen much investment and improvement. The school provides full, weekly and flexi-boarding facilities – the latter particularly useful for further-flung pupils, given chronic transport problems.

Four competitive house groups. Student guides appointed to help some 22 foreign students feel at home. A 'get-to-know you' weekend arranged every year at youth hostel in Fowey for year 7 pupils and staff, helps to build foundations for strong family atmosphere.

Pastoral Care and Discipline: The whole school meets at least twice-weekly for an act of worship. Boarders attend a local church on Sundays. All girls take part in work experience and have individual career interviews and aptitude tests. As part of PSE, 'issues relating to motherhood and a woman's role in modern society are addressed'. Any breach of rules is acted upon quickly. Possession of drugs is punishable through expulsion. Mr McDowell would, however, look at each case individually and 'try to' avoid ruining a student's career for the sake of a few remaining weeks. He is renowned for his fairness.

Pupils and Parents: Most parents live in or near Cornwall. Varied professions including doctors, solicitors, accountants. Now very few farming families.

Entrance: Largely from 36 Cornish feeders (about 30 per cent from own prep school) via its compulsory 11+ entrance exams in maths, English and verbal reasoning. Those entering sixth form (about 75 per cent of own students) required to have at least 5 GCSE passes at grades A-C.

Exit: Over 95 per cent go to university – about 98 per cent to their first choice. Rich mixture of degree courses pursued indicating strength and depth – both of candidates and teachers eg medicine, dentistry, astrophysics, mechanical engineering, chemical engineering, ocean sciences. Others to speech therapy and caring professions. Falmouth College of Art is a local option for the more creative – LAMDA and RADA too.

Money Matters: Academic, music, art and sports scholarships at entry to year 7. Bursaries too, at any point of entry to senior school, although academic competence must be shown. No fee assistance for nursery or prep school.

Remarks: Strong traditional all-round girls' school with sense of family values and respect between staff and pupils. Pleasantly caring headmaster whose goal is to strengthen the school and further develop its excellent academic and recreational facilities.

TRURO SCHOOL

Linked to Treliske Preparatory School in the Junior section

Trennick Lane, Truro, Cornwall, TR1 1TH

Tel: 01872 272 763

Fax: 01872 223 431

E-mail: enquiries@truroschool.com

Website: www.truroschool.com

- Pupils: 506 boys, 303 girls, including 94 boarders (38 girls, 56 boys); prep 134 boys 77 girls, all day • Ages: 10 -18 • Size of sixth form: 210 • Methodist foundation • Fees: Pre-prep £1,745; prep £2,553 • Independent • Open days: Prep school, September; Truro School, October

Head: Since 2001, Mr Paul K Smith MA MEd (fifties). Read geography at Cambridge (rugby blue, and played cricket). Previously head of Oswestry School in Shropshire and before that at Royal Grammar School, Worcester and St John's, Leatherhead. Took over from the well-liked Mr Guy Dodd, who was here for eight years.

Academic Matters: Consistently good results – the school is doing its averagely selective intake proud. Once a weakness, French results have now improved. Traditional teaching in some subjects especially at A level where maths, physics, biology and chemistry are popular. Sixteen science labs and dedicated teachers ensure budding scientists or doctors can excel here. Excellent technology and IT which is networked. Special needs – trained support is available but generally pupils 'are expected to be able to cope with ordinary lessons'.

Games, Options, The Arts: Creativity adorns the corridors. Chess continues strong, though a minority interest. Participation in Duke of Edinburgh Award substantial. Head believes it instils discipline and enhances character as pupils recognise and work with one another's strengths and weaknesses. Still firmly into Young Enterprise (one company was South West Regional winner in 2004, with MD named Best Young Business Leader in the UK at London Finals.) Varied sports including water polo, golf – 1997 'independent schools' golf champions' – climbing, squash, netball, rugby and hockey. Lots of swimming and sailing going on. Many pupils reach county, South-West or national standard. Girls and boys are currently in British sailing squad and national fencing team. Good on organising expeditions, keen on the great outdoors. Indoor swimming pool, a sports-hall and a gym, and new astroturf.

60-piece orchestra performs to 900-strong audience annually at The Hall for Cornwall; a jazz band gives its own concerts and occasionally tours. Frequent cultural visits to London art galleries, opera, ballet and drama productions.

Background and Atmosphere: Glorious site 'on the ridge' overlooking the River Truro and the cathedral. Grounds overlook splendid old trees and picturesque views. The school, founded in 1880, is slightly older than Pearson's fine Victorian Gothic cathedral, which can also be seen from its vantage point high on the hill to the south of the city. Rather scattered school buildings (need an umbrella if raining between lessons). Impressive new theatre, 2002 and modern languages building, 2004. Truro School is outstanding academically, complemented by a huge amount of extra-curricular activity. Perhaps it is its large pupil numbers that make it reminiscent of a good state school. The Wednesday surf club is popular with many surfboards seen rushing towards the beaches after school. Fully co-ed from 1990, which school believes 'promotes equality in the workplace, understanding and respect between the sexes'.

Pastoral Care and Discipline: Appear to be firmly in place. Christian and spiritual values positively instilled and much goes into the safety nets, which catch bullying and other anti-social behaviour. Prefects, who represent each form, meet weekly to discuss 'their responsibilities'. Over half the lower sixth volunteer to spend two terms training weekly for listening ear scheme for other pupils. Drugs – 'you lose the right to be here but offenders may be re-admitted on condition that they submit to a regime of random testing'. 'Getting-to-know-each-other' programme organised for first years and lower sixth in autumn term.

Christian ethic is encouraged through teaching practices and supported by the ministry of the school chaplain and services. Joint confirmation and church membership services are organised with nearby Methodist and Anglican churches. A small Christian Union room exists for private prayer and contemplation.

Ex-pupils and teaching staff use chapel for marriages and baptisms. Parents also welcomed as congregational members.

Pupils and Parents: Pupils involved in variety of charitable projects, from care for the elderly locally to organising sponsored events for charity, help instil maturity and community spirit. Pupils have raised money to purchase a house for Romanian orphans. OBs include Michael Adams (chess), Olympic sailors Ben Ainslie and Barry Parkin, actors Robert Shaw, Nigel Terry, M & S Chairman Paul Myners. Parents come from across Cornwall – the Scilly Isles to Saltash and of course many from Truro itself. Solicitors, engineers and geologists to doctors, carers and teachers.

Entrance: By 11+ and 13+ exam in January on English, maths and general reasoning – Truro School Prep School pupils make up about 35 per cent of the entry. Mature 10-year-olds sometimes accepted. Grammar school ability is required. About 10 per cent of the sixth form comes from nearby state schools – through GCSE examination and school report.

Exit: Twelve to Oxbridge in 2005; a dozen pupils pursued medical courses at university. Falmouth College of Art is also popular. Final occupations are diverse – civil engineers, lecturers, stockbrokers, solicitors, businessmen, hotel managers, management consultants, not to mention a scuba diving instructor and shark feeder in Nassau. A large number go into teaching – some on the staff.

Money Matters: The Methodist church technically owns the school. 'The school has virtually no endowment for scholarships or bursaries, money has to come from general income'. Good value for money though. Truro School Assisted Places scheme provides a small number of means tested bursaries up to the value of full fees.

Remarks: A good school, made much progress under the previous head, and still in good hands, according to the latest Ofsted inspection.

TUDOR HALL SCHOOL

Wykham Park, Banbury, Oxfordshire, OX16 9UR

Tel: 01295 263 434
Fax: 01295 253 264
E-mail: abrauer@tudorhallschool.com
Website: www.tudorhall.oxon.sch.uk

• Pupils: 275 girls; 220 boarding, 55 day • Ages: 11-18 • Size of sixth form: 80 • Anglican, but makes provision for RCs • Fees: Boarding £6,515; day £4,200 • Independent • Open days: Spring and summer

Head: Since 2004, Miss Wendy Griffiths BSc PGCE (forties). Educated at Queen Elizabeth Grammar School, Carmarthen, followed by University of Wales, where she read zoology. Taught at Tormead School (member of senior management team and head of sixth form), then became director of studies at St Catherine's, Bramley. Married to history teacher and has young daughter – they live in newly-built house in grounds. A powerhouse of energy who leads from the front. Approachable, dynamic and brimming with ideas. Still teaches biology several times a week and says, 'I love teaching – there's nothing quite like it.' Knows every girl by name and takes huge delight in their achievements, great and small.

Academic Matters: Once known as school for toffs' daughters without academic aspirations but this is certainly not the case now. Academic matters taken very, very seriously and school aims 'to get the best out of every girl.' Achieves good results and comes out well in value added data. 60 per cent plus of GCSE grades A*/A, with girls taking average of 10 subjects. Choice of 20 subjects at A level, with English by far the most popular, followed by French, art and history. 70-ish per cent of A2 and AS grades A/B.

Setting by ability for maths, science and French from first year. Majority of girls learn two languages and there are regular exchange trips to France and Germany. About one third of pupils take separate sciences at GCSE, with rest opting for dual award. Gifted and talented co-ordinator recently appointed to stretch most able girls. School has number of pupils with mild dyslexia and/or learning difficulties – they are taken out of prep periods for one-to-one help at cost of £38 per hour. 155 computers dotted throughout school; most subject areas have access to IT, every girl has e-mail address and there are light, airy computer rooms. Library equipped with 7,000 books and £3,000 a year is spent on new books – Philippa Gregory and Mark Haddon most-borrowed authors. Long-serving and supportive staff who light up with enthusiasm for school. Average age of teachers is 41 and 30 per cent have been at school for more than 10 years. Maximum class size is 24 but, in practice, groups are far smaller.

Games, Options, The Arts: Games are very important part of school life. All girls play sport (including sixth form), exuding fresh-faced enthusiasm and energy in their tartan games skirts and cheery red socks. Professional games staff who teach hockey, lacrosse, netball, rounders, athletics etc. Tennis very popular, played in the old walled garden, covered tennis court or summer-only Astro courts. Two squash courts, large sports hall (complete with basketball court, exercise bikes, weights etc), gym and swimming pool (recently covered with bubble roof for swimming in autumn term). Lots of matches at weekends – though nearest comparable games school almost an hour away.

Music school buzzes with activity. Around 75 girls have instrumental lessons in school and there are concerts galore throughout the year, featuring choirs, orchestras, even a samba band. Dynamic art department, with lots of activities at weekends – candle making, photography, jewellery design etc. Art, textiles, design technology and history of art

v popular at A level. Riding, judo, cookery, ballet, tap, word processing. Strong debating and public speaking tradition, with girls taking part in mock United Nations. Lots of community service, including concerts for local OAPs and charity fund-raising. Each year girls form a Young Enterprise company with the help of local businesses. A couple of years ago enterprising pupils set up a knicker company – the most popular product was a pair of knickers emblazoned with 'Good girls go to heaven, bad girls go to Tudor Hall!' Work experience is compulsory for every pupil and there's a World Challenge expedition every two years – recent destinations have included Madagascar, Peru and Tanzania.

Background and Atmosphere: One of the oldest girls' schools in the country, founded in 1850 by the Reverend and Mrs John Todd. Has moved several times but headmistress Nesta Inglis bought stunning Wykham Park at end of World War 2 and school has been there ever since. Main building an imposing country house in honey-coloured stone set in 48 acres of rolling parkland, with maze of interconnecting buildings added on. Each year group lives in separate bit of school, with lucky 11-year-olds ensconced in cosy Todd House, complete with jolly dorms (plastered with pictures of family and sporting heroes like Jonny Wilkinson), swings and garden where they get their own patch to look after. New girls are assigned 'keepers' from year above to help them settle in and as they move up through school they earn much-prized 'privileges.' These range from 13-year-olds who are deemed to be 'well-behaved and responsible' being allowed to go shopping on Saturday afternoons to 15-year-olds getting the chance to wear home clothes all the time.

Impressive sixth form block – lots of light, space and no uniform. Upper sixth boarders can go home every weekend if wish. Mobile phones are banned for girls in the first two years and after that there are strict rules – depending on age. Younger girls wear slightly old-fashioned bottle green cord skirts and striped blouses. The uniform was under review at the time of our visit but lots of girls said they were quite fond of it! Good, wholesome food served in bustling dining room. Lots of weekend activities and visits to Stratford-upon-Avon, Oxford, Horse of the Year Show etc. Once a year the whole school departs en masse for the day to celebrate the school's birthday – Alton Towers a popular venue. A proper 'full' boarding school – with two organised exeats each term.

Pastoral Care and Discipline: Tudor Hall's forte. Firm, clear rules and no major problems re drugs, booze etc. 'You can never be complacent,' says head, 'but they are just not big issues here.' School's motto is Habeo ut Dem – I have that I may give. School puts strong emphasis on courtesy and holds manners meetings twice a term, where each girl is awarded marks for conduct, kindness, helpfulness etc. Grade A denotes 'an outstanding member of the community' whereas grade E is 'unacceptable behaviour.'

Staff in regular email contact with parents and there are meetings each year to discuss girls' progress. Each house has housemistress and assistant housemistress who take charge of pastoral care. Girls can also talk to their form tutor, the school's 'larger than life' chaplain and a newly-appointed counsellor who comes in several hours a week. Revamped house system, with mixed-age houses – they attend chapel and social events together. Head girl is chosen from lower sixth and changes every term.

Pupils and Parents: Very smiley, purposeful, well-mannered girls, proud of their school and not as frighteningly sophisticated as peers elsewhere. Ex-head girl on point of taking A levels wistful at prospect of leaving – 'it's such a way of life here,' she says. Everywhere you go girls confidently leap to open doors and answer questions. Girls come from all over the UK, many from rural areas. Very few overseas pupils. Notable old girls include Serpentine Gallery director Julia Peyton-Jones, writer Sacha Bonsor and sculptress Candida Bond.

Entrance: Register early. Entry at 11, 12 and 13. Selection process includes school report, common entrance and interview with the head, who looks for 'that special spark.' Occasional vacancy in sixth form – minimum of 5 GCSEs, with grades A*-B in subjects to be studied at A level.

Exit: Average of three leave post-GCSE, usually for co-ed schools. After A level most go to university – Newcastle, St Andrews, Edinburgh and Exeter current favourites.

Money Matters: Academic, music, art, drama and sport scholarships, but not for huge amounts, plus bursaries. Not a particularly rich school but manages an impressive building programme out of income.

Remarks: A wholesome, happy, successful boarding school that has moved with the times while still hanging on to its much-loved customs and traditions. Large enough to offer good range of subjects and activities but small enough for everyone to know each other. Girls make lifelong friends and school really feels like one big happy family – evidenced by the fact that so many Old Tudorians choose to send their daughters here.

TWYFORD CHURCH OF ENGLAND HIGH SCHOOL

Twyford Crescent, Acton, Acton, London, W3 9PP

Tel: 020 8752 0141
Fax: 020 8993 7627
E-mail: admin@twyford.ealing.sch.uk

• Pupils: 1,247, boys:girls 160:133 • Ages: 11-18 • Size of sixth form: 293, mixed • C of E • State • Open days: October

Head: Since 2002, Ms Alice Hudson MA (fortyish) educated at Slough Girls' High and Leighton Park, then St Hilda's, Oxford, where she read English. Previously deputy head at Brentside HS, also in Ealing, and prior to that taught at Central Foundation Boys', Islington and Maria Fidelis, Euston. Joined Twyford in 2000, first as deputy then as acting head. Married, three young children. This was a failing school, financially, and seriously underperforming academically and socially, when Ms Hudson arrived and one needs to visit the school to believe the extraordinary turnaround she has achieved in her, so far, brief tenure. It is a unique experience for this particular, hardened, Guide editor to see so much change in every aspect of a school's life, effected with such irresistible enthusiasm, focused and intelligent rethinking, authority, conviction and energy – all articulated in an entirely disarming and infectious manner. Very much faith-inspired vision of what the school should – and could – be.

Our meeting was delayed and then punctuated by fallout from an incident before school – pupils set upon by a child from another school – and Ms Hudson was hot on the case to identify the culprit and ensure via a meeting between perpetrator and victims that it wouldn't be repeated. 'She gets involved.... you see her about.... she makes people take a pride in themselves'. Somehow she manages to teach 9 periods weekly. Her idea of a 'career break' was to have three children in four years and to do a simultaneous MA in education policy. Hm! 'Profoundly', is a key word in her vocabulary. Staff pay tribute – 'she is an absolutely delightful person to work for'. Lucky school.

Academic Matters: Hugely improved results in this, academically, non-selective school. 3 Bs average at A level; maths results exceptional. Choices include economics, music tech, photography (very successful), psychology, sociology. Biggest improvement in sixth form – head's especial baby – 'it's a reliable place for your high-achieving child

... we chase them much more in the sixth form', but the less academic well supported too.

ICT (we saw loads of computers) a developing area though head refreshingly cheery when asked about interactive whiteboards – 'almost nothing.' Head sees wisdom in routeing the less academic to the practical which 'can be studied alongside A level', so double AVCE in ICT popular along with other more vocational subjects. 12 per cent have SLD or SEN (65 have statements) and are well-supported, either by regular staff or from outside. 'They will be valued and survive here,' says head, 'and parents are very well supported – we have very good home-school links.' 280 pupils have EAL – first languages in this very ethnically mixed area Gujarati, Punjabi, Arabic and Urdu – but no-one needs additional help in English. Proactive on modern languages – 'we identify potential linguists in year 7, accelerate them in French and, in year 8, give them a choice of German and Spanish.' RE always a feature of school life and supported by two conferences each year, often with outside speakers on moral or spiritual topics. Curriculum taught on an alternating two-week cycle which some find confusing at first but they get used to it.

Games, Options, The Arts: Remarkable playing fields, well-concealed along this urban high street site. Netball especially strong here but hockey, tennis, football, cricket, basketball too. Dance and athletics popular. Rugby coached by pros from London Wasps. Consistent successes in many sporting areas and representation in borough and regional levels. Thriving art, drama popular and lively though restricted to one well-used studio. Good and well-used music and music tech facilities, especially now with new block and state-of the-art audio-visual recording studio. Good work placement programme. Pupils enthuse about the number and quality of trips and expeditions – everywhere from St Petersburg to the New Forest for every activity imaginable – photography to water skiing. Lots of charity work.

Background and Atmosphere: School tucked behind rare bit of green along the Uxbridge Road. Main building, Grade IIA listed 'The Elms', an elegant, early Georgian house, built 1735, now well-preserved and sensibly painted in blues, houses the admin and offices side of things. A diverse mixture of less distinguished and pretty scruffy later blocks, A, B, unaccountably then D and M, house rest of school – not too much room for growth and development.

Black uniform with white shirts creates somewhat sombre impression but most pupils look tidy (head strides around, unaverse to pointing out, amicably, 'shirt!' to any wearer of stray shirt tails) and overall impression of a good-humoured, confident, mix of the boisterous and the purposeful. No uniform for the sixth. Huge ethnic diversity – 52 per cent from non-white British backgrounds, of whom the largest number from Afro-Caribbean families; Asians make up next biggest group. Christian principles in practice evident in staff's approach to all aspects of this richly diverse community. While Anglicanism predominates, all churches and faiths are celebrated and explored here and everyone feels part of the school.

Two minutes' daily silent reflection before lessons - 'everyone is quiet', said a sixth former. 'Faith has a big profile here', says head, 'we place a high premium on formal acts of worship.' Everyone attends a termly Communion service and there is a weekly voluntary one. Assemblies are inclusive but have an unashamed Christian bias. 'The key to inter-faith issues,' believes head, 'is to be clear about what one's standpoint is.' She talks of the validity of each individual's own 'faith journey'. 'Spiritual matters are neither embarrassing nor taboo here' – a big claim but it feels legitimate. Pupils, though seldom deferential, respect teachers here – there is a good working relationship between staff and pupils at all levels. 'They stretch you as far as you can go – but not beyond what you can do,' reflected one sixth former.

Pastoral Care and Discipline: Well established system of form tutors – first resource though pupils able to talk to which member of staff they choose. Heads of year back up the tutors and pupils have regular meeting with tutors to check on targets, progress, happiness. Chaplaincy team also available. Interaction between ages encouraged – actively by sixth form mentoring to younger pupils and system of form reps. School Council much appreciated – 'it has a lot of power over changes and we can meet the governors,' we were told. Few serious problems – most pupils feeling that offending in school time and on school property 'not worth it' and seemingly a bit immature, though usual crop of minor misdemeanours.

Pupils and Parents: As above, huge ethnic mix, Christianity being the unifying principle though 30 places reserved each year for those from 'other world faiths' and Christianity itself taking in Russian/Serbian/Eastern Orthodox along with other denominations. Pupils come from wide geographic area – Brent, Hounslow, all over Ealing and further into town. Most, though, from Christchurch junior school, half a mile away and nearly 50 other primaries. More boys than girls though this not generally perceptible. Princes and paupers here – all social strata represented and cheerfully interrelate.

Entrance: Hugely oversubscribed and getting ever

more so. 2003 saw 600 applicants for 190 places and school already stretches its capacity. Complex pecking order based on family's attendance at and commitment to church, along with home's distance from school. Worth checking this out in detail before losing your heart to the place. No-one is fooled by rapid conversion when your child is in year six – though it is still – widely and unsuccessfully – tried. 30 places for pupils from other world faiths where the family is committed to the idea and principles in practice of 'faith'. Sixth less stringent – though they must 'have sympathy with the aims of the school' as well as 6 GCSEs at C or above and A/B in A level subjects.

Exit: Vast and creditable range of courses and universities – two to Cambridge in 2003 and everywhere else from Exeter to Newcastle. Pupils encouraged to aim high and have aspirations while remaining realistic and practical.

Remarks: This isn't a smart school and its priorities in the last two years have been to get straight the finances, the staffing, the ethos – this has been triumphantly achieved in startlingly little time but a lot remains for this dynamic regime to accomplish.

UNIVERSITY COLLEGE SCHOOL

Linked to University College School Junior School in the Junior section

Linked to Phoenix School in the Junior section

Frognal, Hampstead, London, NW3 6XH

Tel: 020 7435 2215
Fax: 020 7433 2111
E-mail: seniorschool@ucs.org.uk
Website: www.ucs.org.uk

• Pupils: 735 boys; all day • Ages: 11-18 • Size of sixth form: 220 • Non-denom • Fees: £3,850 - £ 4,165 • Independent • Open days: September and October

Head: Since 1996, Mr Kenneth Durham BA (forties), read PPE at Oxford. Previously director of studies at King's College School, Wimbledon. Has written economics books and resource packs for primary, GCSE and A level studies. Keen on acting, film, books, music etc. Parents commented, 'he's very bright, very sharp, very eloquent.' 'Some people feel he could be more pushy but he's very caring and his door is always open to parents.' 'He has the right priorities. He wants to turn out responsible, free thinking members of society.'

Academic Matters: 'The teachers are amazingly committed,' said a sixth former. Another said, 'if I need help they will give me a private tutorial – for hours if necessary'. Pupils and parents both mentioned a minority of timeservers past their sell-by date, 'but isn't that true of most schools?' mused a pupil. But generally high praise for the teaching standards. Class size: 22 or 23 in the lower forms, 20 or fewer at GCSE level. Setting only for French from year 7 and maths from year 9. The school is unusually flexible about GCSE subjects, 'this choice is as free as possible,' says the prospectus. Everyone takes at least nine, but only English, maths, a science and a modern language are compulsory. Boys can choose the other five from a list including drama, business studies, art, technology and music. 'You're encouraged to do subjects you like and enjoy,' said a pupil. Maths and science are popular A level subjects, along with economics, English and history. Nearly half the leavers in 2000 went off to study one of the social sciences at university. The head feels that this is a reflection on the north London catchment area of homes where discussion and argument are encouraged. Excellent DT and IT facilities, though these subjects show relatively poor results at GCSE. The emphasis is on self-motivation rather than pressure – 'this is not an exam factory,' say sixth formers – with an informal relationship between pupils and teachers. 'They teach you to understand and apply your knowledge.' The lack of pressure means the school is probably best suited to bright, well-motivated boys. A parent commented that the school may not be very helpful if a child is struggling academically, but the head disagrees with this. A sixth former said, 'people are happy to work because they are enjoying themselves.'

Games, Options, The Arts: Excellent games facilities, given the inner London location, with tennis and fives courts, a sports hall, weights room and indoor pool on the premises and playing fields a ten-minute walk away. Everyone spends two afternoons a week playing sport and the soccer and rugby teams win a large proportion of their matches. Older boys can choose from a selection that includes golf, sailing and squash. 'They want you to find a sport you really enjoy,' said a pupil.

Four or five plays a year are performed in the well-equipped school theatre, some in conjunction with the girls of South Hampstead High School, and there are ample opportunities for learning the technical side of theatre production. Music is very strong, with a range of orchestras, groups and choirs. 'At a concert you might hear jazz, rock and chamber music because that's what the boys want to perform,' said a parent, approvingly. A popular recent innovation is lunchtime recitals in the great hall by students and teachers. 'It's great to hear music wafting through the hall as you go about your business,' said a pupil. Artists can try their hand at a wide range of techniques including sculpture, welding and stone carving.

Background and Atmosphere: UCS was founded in 1830 as the 'Godless College' of Gower Street by a group of radicals, dedicated to the principles of toleration and non-discrimination. It moved to Hampstead in 1907 and still prides itself on its liberal outlook, with no religious education, no school bells and a relaxed attitude. Boys are encouraged to follow their interests in running activities. 'You're always being encouraged to take on responsibility,' said a pupil and boys emphasise the friendly and helpful atmosphere. The hub of the school is the panelled and galleried great hall, with organ pipes looming above. The rest is mostly comfortably shabby, though massive investment is evident in the new Slaughter wing (named for the previous head), with computers aplenty, the newly developed library and the smart lecture theatre (which hosts speakers such as OB Alex Garland). Appropriately green and leafy, though a large proportion of the grounds is taken up by the school carpark and playground.

Pastoral Care and Discipline: Non-authoritarian regime. 'The boys feel they're known and respected as individuals,' says the head and pupils agree. The school's statement on bullying emphasises that it includes spiteful comments, racist and sexist taunts and exclusion. Expulsion is the ultimate sanction for drugs but, 'I don't want to destroy the lives of children on the basis of one error of judgement.' 'We feel that the teachers are on our side,' say pupils.

Pupils and Parents: Middle class north London professionals, including a large Jewish element. 'It can be cliquey,' said a parent. 'And some parents put the school under a lot of pressure to achieve the best results – but it does try to steer its own course.' Boys tend to be confident and self-assured. 'They're kids who feel good about themselves,' said a mother. OBs include Sir Chris Bonington, Sir Dirk Bogarde and Alex Garland.

Entrance: Two thirds of 11 year olds come from the UCS prep school in Holly Hill. The other 28 are mostly from state primaries and have taken maths, English and verbal and non-verbal reasoning tests over a morning, with half the 200 or so candidates called back for interview. Those after one of the 27 places at 13+ entry are assessed during the autumn term of year 7, with half invited back for a morning of sport, music, art, drama or technology, 'to see how they relate to other kids and how they work in a group, and to give us a sense of their personality.' Places are confirmed by Common Entrance.

Exit: Nearly all to university, many to do one of the social sciences. Around a quarter go to Oxbridge. Many end up as lawyers, accountants and businessmen, or working in the media.

Money Matters: Used to have 84 Assisted Places. Academic and music scholarships and bursaries are available to those coming in from outside at 11, 13 and 16, and school can help with parental financial crises.

Remarks: High-achieving liberal north London day school in a leafy setting, which 'really encourages boys to develop their individuality,' say parents.

UPPINGHAM COMMUNITY COLLEGE

London Road, Uppingham, Oakham, Rutland, LE15 9TJ

Tel: 01572 823 631
Fax: 01572 821 193
E-mail: principal@ucc.rutland.sch.uk
Website: www.ucc.rutland.sch.uk

- Pupils: 852 boys and girls, roughly split 50:50; all day
- Ages: 11-16 • Non-denom • State

Principal: Since 2000, Mr Malcolm England MA PGCE (mid-forties), educated at the Royal Grammar School, Worcester and Worcester College, Oxford. A linguist, he succeeded the highly respected Peter Macdonald-Pearce,

working closely with him prior to taking up post. Previously head of Testbourne Community School, Hampshire. One of first group to take National Professional Qualification for Headship (1998). Married, with three children. Friendly and approachable. Knows large proportion of pupils by first names.

Academic Matters: School has had specialist technology college since 1995. Most recent Ofsted report (February 2001) describes it as 'a very successful school with many significant strengths and no major weaknesses.' Particularly strong in ICT, maths, science and design technology but prides itself on being just as good in the arts. Was one of the first schools in the country to be awarded the Artsmark for excellence in the provision of arts education and has now achieved Artsmark Gold status. Full network of bang-up-to-date computers, with one computer to every four pupils. Most take ICT at GCSE and the college is currently a pilot school for the new Diploma in Digital Applications course. Good GCSE results in general (65 per cent achieved at least five grades A*-C at GCSE in 2005). Healthy mix of experienced staff – many have been here for more than ten years – and newly qualified teachers. The average class size is 28. Mixed ability classes on entry but by year 8 there is setting in maths and languages (French and German). Homework ranges from 30 minutes a night for the youngest to two and a half hours for GCSE students. Parents are asked to sign their child's homework diary each week. Cheerful 'Additional Needs' room offers help to 160, often one-to-one. Can also cater for pupils needing English 'as an additional language' though there aren't many.

Games, Options, The Arts: School rightfully proud of its 'session six' courses – 40 different activities, from sport, music and dance through to chess, pottery, sign language, film making and fashion design. All students must take at least one session six course each term and some take more. Good on sport – including football, rugby, hockey, cricket, tennis, fitness, gym and dance. Large sports hall, fitness centre and extensive playing fields on school site. College also holds Sportsmark award for strengths in PE. All pupils have two games lessons every week and 25 per cent take PE at GCSE. Very popular sporting exchange link with school in Haacht, Belgium, has been going for 30 years. The college has secured most of the funding for a proposed new full-size artificial playing surface which is likely to be built in early 2006. Music strong though only 150 pupils play a musical instrument and there are lots of orchestras, choirs and bands to join. Fantastic drama studio, with specialised lighting, where assemblies are held too.

Background and Atmosphere: Set on edge of historic town of Uppingham, overlooking rolling countryside. Self-contained site is key attraction for parents. Has been a school on this site since 1920. Original redbrick school building has been vastly added-to and is now a maze of inter-connecting buildings – visitors need a map to make sense of it! More building work – to add three classrooms and extra changing facilities – taking place when we visited. Pupils enthusiastic, friendly and forthcoming. A chirpy year 8 was manning the reception desk – principal says it encourages pride in the school and everyone gets a go. College council with reps from each year group offers forum for airing ideas and suggestions on how to improve school. A recent complaint about the dreariness of the girls' cloakroom led to a group of year 11s being allowed to come in before term to redecorate in zingy greens and yellows! Principal holds 'success assembly' every half term to celebrate students' achievements both in and out of school – not simply a eulogy to the brightest students. The school also acts as a lead school for the international EC Comenius project and has links with schools in Italy, Poland and Germany.

Pastoral Care and Discipline: College logo is 'caring and challenging.' Students can talk to head of year or their form tutor, who remains with them as they progress through the school. College has structured approach of reports and detentions. Bullying is rare and swiftly dealt with in line with a charter developed by students and staff and endorsed by governors. College also has strong links with local community. There is an on-site nursery – where some year 10s choose to do work experience – an adult learning centre and an Extended Schools Centre.

Pupils and Parents: Students come from predominantly rural catchment area – around 300 from town of Uppingham itself. Increasing number from outlying areas of Oakham and Corby. Plain navy/black uniform worn, with older students getting chance to choose a different coloured sweatshirt to the rest of the school. Former pupils include Sally Reddin, shot put gold medallist at the 2000 Paralympics, and businessman John Browett, chief executive of Tesco.com.

Entrance: Comprehensive intake. Regularly oversubscribed. Priority given to pupils from seven designated primary schools in Rutland and Leicestershire and those with siblings already at the school. Parents very impressed with induction arrangements for new pupils.

Exit: Most students (around 85 per cent) continue into further education at 16. The majority go on to local sixth form colleges or FE colleges, a few to independent schools.

Remarks: A popular and thriving community school with dedicated staff and motivated students.

UPPINGHAM SCHOOL

High Street West, Uppingham, Rutland, LE15 9QE

Tel: 01572 822 216
Fax: 01572 821 872
E-mail: admissions@uppingham.co.uk
Website: www.uppingham.co.uk

- Pupils: 748 pupils; 510 boys and 238 girls. Mainly boarding but some day • Ages: 13-18 • Size of sixth form: 348 • C of E
- Fees: £7,500 boarding, £5,250 day • Independent • Open days: Contact the Admissions Department to visit the school

Headmaster: Since 1991, Dr S C Winkley MA (late fifties). Educated at St Edward's Oxford, read classics at Brasenose, doctorate in mediaeval Greek poetry. Was second master at Winchester, in charge of scholars there. Married with two children. Ebullient, thoughtful, impressive intellectual sophisticate who likes to pose philosophical teasers to the new pupils. Popular, 'he goes around looking as if he doesn't know what's going on but he knows everything,' said one pupil, respectfully. He believes the school offers 'a proper childhood' in a fast-moving world. 'There are very few children here with whom I can't do business. We think we're all on the same side, with no "Them and Us".'

Retiring in July 2006. Replacement will be Mr Richard Harman MA PGCE (forties), currently head at Aldenham, educated at The King's School, Worcester, and read English at Cambridge. Tried his hand at the marketing side of publishing for a couple of years, then five years at Marlborough (with a sabbatical to do a PGCE) teaching English and drama, and twelve at Eastbourne College where he progressed from head of English via housemaster of girls' boarding to becoming part of the senior management team. Whilst at Marlborough, he met and married his wife, who currently teaches at South Hampstead High School. One daughter at North London Collegiate. Urbane, charming, film star looks. Gave Aldenham a useful shake-up.

Academic Matters: Confident they deliver the best for the individual, whether less academic or a real high flier. Good results in both arts and sciences. For a major public school, refreshingly unhung-up about league tables and Oxbridge results but get impressive number in every year and give good preparation for entry. Good A-level results, 45 plus-ish per cent A grades; history, business studies, English, art, theatre studies, biology, geography, French and mathematics the popular subjects. IT and life skills classes for all. GCSE retakes possible.

Games, Options, The Arts: Very strong. Music is famously superb – currently 41 music scholars (many ex-cathedral choristers) and, in the last few years, school has gained over 30 organ, choral and instrumental awards, mainly at Oxbridge. There are approximately 700 instrumental lessons given per week; about two thirds of pupils learn an instrument and play in ensembles ranging from jazz groups to full symphony orchestra. Choir is famous with demanding repertoire, has been invited to Christ Church Oxford, King's Cambridge, York Minster, Cologne Cathedral and St Paul's Cathedral in recent years. Has been recorded. Resident teachers and visiting staff include professional musicians.

Wonderful, envy-making art block – building designed by Old Boy, Piers Gough. Immediate impression of exciting and diverse activity. Walls hung with accomplished drawings, paintings, sculptures. There is a film studio and photo lab which everyone can use to develop own photos. Architect Simon Sharp brought in to combine art, architecture, design and technology. Consistently high percentage get A grades at A level. Very well-equipped, newly refurbished computer department. The whole school is comprehensively wired up – 1800 outlets. Also computers in each house and a computer in every pupil's study. Has long-standing relationship with Microsoft (UK) to keep right up-to-date. Drama is very popular. 300-seat theatre, for polished productions of classics, eg 'The Caucasian Chalk Circle', musicals eg 'Cabaret', 'Grease' and 'Bugsy', and recently a play written by a pupil.

Very strong on sport but not obsessive. 'You don't have to be brilliant,' according to pupils. Sixty acres of playing field (the largest playing field in England), Astroturf hockey pitches, reams of tennis and netball courts, swimming pool, diving pool, dedicated 1st XI cricket pitch, squash courts and rifle range. Rugby excellent, links with Leicester Tigers and Northampton Saints RFCs. Great range of sports on offer, water-polo, shooting (Uppinghamians recently represented Great Britain), canoeing, fencing etc. Sailing and windsurfing on nearby Rutland Water. D of E popular. CCF or community service in the fifth and sixth forms. Gap year increasingly popular, useful international network of Old Boys and Girls.

Background and Atmosphere: Founded in 1584, the school with its splendid buildings dominates the pretty market town of Uppingham. Pupils are allowed a reasonable run in the small genteel town but some places out of bounds and there are some tea-rooms which are the privilege of prefects. Relaxed attitude to comings and goings from their own house. 'We trust them to be sensible about where they go.'

There are fifteen boarding-houses in mainly Georgian and Victorian houses around the main school, each with their own flavour. Fourth formers are in dormitories, with own studies, sixth formers have bedsits. Parents and prospective pupils are encouraged to look around and make their own choice. Furthest out is ten minutes walk from the main buildings. Pupils eat within their house – 'not the most economic way to do it but it encourages friendship within a family setting.' 'Vertical' friendships encouraged, ie younger boys and girls will chat confidently to older boys and girls, not just with peers. Also have a chapel service 5 days a week for the whole school. Girls well integrated – have been here since 1975. There is a tuck shop and buttery for all and a bar for upper sixth formers (tightly restricted hours/ consumption). Uniform is dark and undistinguished. Atmosphere strikingly happy, lots of cheerful, lively faces.

Pastoral Care and Discipline: Good pastoral care deriving from small houses run by husband and wife teams (often with own children) and tutor system. Pupils have allocated tutor who also lunches in the house once a week. Chaplain, Revd Harrison, has house just by the main gate open to all comers. Wide choice of possible confidantes for pupils – housemaster/housemistress, matron, tutor, school counsellor etc.

Dr Winkley takes a firm line on drugs (expulsion), drink and smoking. No exeats but parents welcome to visit and, by arrangement, take child out for a meal. Delivering child back to the school 'tanked up with drink' absolutely not acceptable. Passionately anti-bullying. 'I was bullied at school and it's something I will not tolerate.'

Pupils and Parents: Not a grand school – solidly middle-class. The process of going fully co-ed started in 2001. Well-off professionals, farmers, business people. Mainly from East Anglia and middle England counties, although 12 per cent of pupils come from north east England. Some offspring of Brits working for multinationals overseas. And 'metropolitan refugees,' says Dr Winkley, 'who leave London and want their children to grow up more slowly'. A very British school, about 8 per cent foreign nationals.

Very friendly, well-mannered pupils, confident talking to adults. 'It's really friendly,' say new boys. Accepting of each other – 'girls don't have to be pretty to get on here!' About 8 per cent children of Old Boys and Girls. Old Uppinghamians quite diverse – Rick Stein, Stephen Fry, Stephen Dorrell, Tim Melville-Ross (ex-DG of the Institute of Directors), Charles Dunstone and David Ross (Founders, Carphone Warehouse), Jonathan Agnew, Johnny Vaughan, John Suchet, Jenny Willott (MP), Charlie Simpson of Busted, even Boris Karloff.

Entrance: Apply at any time – ideally more than 3 years before proposed entry. Test and interview 2 years before entry, plus reference from present school. Offers made and deposits taken at that stage but offers are conditional on hurdles at 13 – conduct (ie head says he's a good boy) and academic (either a baseline CE mark of 50 per cent, or the Uppingham scholarship exam, or tests/ reports for boys 'not prepared for CE' – ie state school pupils). Much emphasis on broadness of entry requirements. Pupils must get at least six Bs at GCSE to continue into the sixth form. Girls (and a few incoming boys) are offered sixth form places on basis of reports from present school, tests and interviews, and the same GCSE criteria.

Excellent information pack for prospective parents, stuffed with detail, and also contact numbers of parents happy to talk about the school. Impressive parent contentment rating.

Exit: 10-ish to Oxbridge. Loads to Bristol, Durham, Edinburgh, Nottingham, Newcastle, Leeds, London etc.

Money Matters: A couple of dozen academic, music, art and design and all-round scholarships at 13, and some at 16 (not all-rounder). Dr Winkley hoping to set a up a scholarship scheme to provide places for children who could not otherwise afford it.

Remarks: A wholesome, positive, happy school. You feel any child would be safe and happy there, whatever their ability, and the best would be brought out of them. Despite increasing nationally-set demands on the curriculum, loads of extra-curricular fun to stimulate and give ideas of the world beyond – from wine tastings and debates to Burns Night with haggis and reeling.

'Children aren't "sent" to boarding school any more – they come because they wish to,' says Dr Winkley. It shows.

WAKEFIELD GIRLS' HIGH SCHOOL

Linked to Wakefield Girls' High School Junior School in the Junior section

Wentworth Street, Wakefield, West Yorkshire, WF1 2QS

Tel: 01924 372 490
Fax: 01924 231 601
E-mail: office@wghsss.org.uk
Website: www.wgsf.org.uk

• Pupils: 735 girls, all day • Ages: 11-18 • Size of sixth form: 170 • Inter-denom • Fees: £2,632 senior school; £1,912 - £2,087 junior school • Independent • Open days: Early October

Principal: Since 1987, Mrs P A Langham BA MEd (fifties) who was educated at Carlisle and County High School for Girls and read English and Russian at Leeds; previously taught in the state sector before coming here as head – (also principal of Wakefield Girls' Junior School and of Queen Elizabeth Grammar School (QEGS) and Junior School – ie senior partner of the whole caboodle).

Zinging, bubbly and fun, a most eloquent and elegant lady. Over the past sixteen years she has had a 'constant policy of seeking out the best possible staff and can confidently say that, at the moment, she has the best ever'. 'You have to work on the "softly softly catchee monkey" principle.' She manages her dual role with panache and charm and the school has grown both in numbers and academic success under her guidance. Head maintains that the school 'is not an academic hothouse'. Also, 'girls are special and I couldn't do any other job than this'. Girls think she is 'great' and are particularly impressed with her personalised number sports car (but then they would be, wouldn't they). The girls also much enjoyed the Robbie Williams lookalike concert that Mrs L organised a couple of years ago – both pupils and head described the evening in glowing terms and all agreed that it was fun – but then head has a theory that unless things are fun, academia will not thrive.

Academic Matters: Trenchant. Max form size 22. In 2005, GCSE results impressive – 35 per cent of all passes were A*s and 73 per cent at A* or A. At A level, 75 of results were A or B grades. English lit, chemistry and physics results are spectacular, human biology a popular option to straight biology at A level, both dual award and single science on offer at GCSE, again tranches of As and A*s; and

results pretty consistent over the past few years. Latin, Greek and classical civilisation, penny numbers in the latter, but a good showing in the classics. Spanish, German plus the odd success in Chinese and Arabic, often taken out of sync, ie by native speakers.

Boys from QEGS across the road join up for business studies, psychology, PE and some languages. Much to-ing and fro-ing across the cobbled lane. The combined schools have over 30 A levels on offer. Business studies, IT, politics, economics, further maths and RE all make a showing, with psychology the latest recruit. Computers all over the shop, in classrooms as well as a dedicated computer building plus extra sixth form only machines in Sotterley House, the sixth form centre. Laptops not a problem. Good dyslexia provision. Trips abroad in every discipline, though the recent history trip to the States appeared to be more of an adventure in retail therapy than into relics of yesteryear.

Games, Options, The Arts: The art dept is buzzing, with pics and models of every description festooning the building, a fantastic papier-mâché dinosaur presides over the first floor art room. Excellent art in the school mag. Art & design popular at GCSE and A level, with both textiles and food featuring in the home economics programme, only the former last year. Ceramics, screen printing and sewing all on tap, girls can and do design their own clothes. Music is good and strong, girls sing with Wakefield Cathedral Choir, and the school has just celebrated the tenth anniversary of girls being admitted to the choir – oodles of trips to other English cathedrals and abroad. Trad music thriving, the Foundation's director of music is based chez les filles, and there are plans afoot to 'make music with all four schools working together'. Masses of individual lessons, and orchestras and bands of every description, and combined ensembles and groups with QEGS. Fantastic Golden Jubilee Hall, impressive, masses of lunch-time concerts and clubs, recently revamped, plays included Guys and Dolls and Ratz, based on the Pied Piper of Hamelin. Joint drama and music with QEGS is extra-curricular and well-attended. Dance is strong here and we interrupted a lunchtime aerobics class on our wanders. Trad gym, plus new sports pavilion at playing fields and new sports hall which is all singing and dancing, much used for indoor hockey. Outstanding hockey team, Astroturf (girls share the boys facilities 'up the road' with the occasional excitement of police helicopters landing) and school performed at the national championships in athletics. Recent netball, and cross-country successes, older girls not that hot on the tennis court. Joint (with QEGS) hockey and netball tour to Australia and New Zealand in 2003. Very enthusiastic D of E, with a pleasing number of golds. Girls hot on charity, and there is a regular stream visiting the local primary school for paired reading. Important links with a school in Africa where they underwrite the girls' hostel and staff support the teachers.

Background and Atmosphere: Huge uncohesive campus. School originally founded in 1877, 'when Governors bought Wentworth House, just across the road from Queen Elizabeth Grammar School, from Elias Holt, a woollen manufacturer'. The land had a covenant that it 'should not be used for any business, trade or occupation which might be deemed a nuisance' and the school opened on September 16th 1878 with 58 pupils, each of whom paid £10 per annum. The Georgian Wentworth House is still the hub of the school and Mrs Langham is the only head we have met with a fridge in her study, an otherwise elegant room of fine proportions. During the years, the school has bought the adjoining Victorian villas, as well as flowing across Wentworth Road with a spot of new build (the science and IT dept, which share the building with part of the junior school). The houses all keep their original names and most still have their original moulded ceilings, though some have modern external shells joining them to the buildings next door. And more modern links are planned. The recently revamped sixth form centre boasts a café where girls can go for breakfast.

The final phase of the creative arts development was opened in October 2004, incorporating a brand new English block, drama studios, textiles workshops and a recording studio which 'will release space from other departments. No thoughts of increasing numbers, just facilities'. Part of the junior school adjacent is entirely new build and the baby school (for both boys and girls), which looks out on to the sports hall has an Astro playground. Two-storey dining room, which must be interesting to police, with hot food as well as sandwiches and masses of salads, an ice-cream van turns up in the quad each lunchtime and does a roaring trade (well, he did during our visit). A hotchpotch of paths, with benches placed at strategic intervals, link the various buildings; it must take a map, compass and a great deal of patience for newcomers to find their way around. Head would like to acquire the Christian Science church, which the school surrounds, for a car park. WGHS, along with QEGS, moved from direct grant to fee-paying in 1976. Older boys much in evidence, with a fair concentration of pupils round the pedestrian crossing in Northgate.

Pastoral Care and Discipline: No major 'major' problems, no drugs in school – 'girls wouldn't jeopardise their place here'; Mrs Langham takes a tough line. Out for smoking – immediately. No 'physical bullying' as such but girls are more prone to fall out with each other, and great store is set by teaching 'tolerance, care and mutual appreciation'; there are 'strict guidelines and acknowledged parameters, beyond which girls will not go'.

Pupils and Parents: As with QEGS, many siblings, fair number of first-time buyers and huge ethnic mix – chadors OK. Wonderfully close to the motorways and bus and rail stations; huge catchment area. If no suitable bus, then parents organise their own. Not perceived by the head as 'particularly rich' but perhaps climbing further up the middle class ladder, 'some make real sacrifices'.

Entrance: 11+ and grossly oversubscribed. Pre-CE paper, plus interview plus CE; not automatic from junior school – though most come on. Post-GCSE min six GCSEs with As in subjects chosen for A levels; toughly competitive.

Exit: Most to further education: one or two gap years. Newcastle and Northumbria still the choice for those leaving at sixth form, with strong bias towards the sciences, followed by law. Four or five regularly to Oxbridge. Hardly any leave post-GCSE.

Money Matters: Part of the Ogden Trust scheme, which supports 32 former high or grammar schools with bursaries for 'talented children through independent secondary education, regardless of parental ability to pay. Bursaries of up to 100 per cent including travel, uniform and school trips are available at 11 (Peter Ogden Bursaries) and at 16. Children must be in the state sector, high scoring at key stage 2, with parental income of less than £35,000 per annum. Plus Foundation Awards established in 1997, awarded originally to 7 year olds 'It should be understood that a Junior School Foundation Award is not automatically extended to the senior school'. Means tested to under £35,000 per annum, and parents' income will be 'reviewed annually in May each year and as a result adjustments made to the level of award if appropriate'. State 'education maintenance allowance', available nationally to keep pupils in sixth form, school will top up if necessary. At 16, 100 per cent bursary available for a student wishing to take sciences and/or maths at A level. Sprinkling of other scholarships and bursaries.

Remarks: This is a happy school, in good heart, with single-sex education but masses of interaction with QEGS next door.

WALDEGRAVE SCHOOL

Fifth Cross Road, Twickenham, Middlesex, TW2 5LH

Tel: 02088 943 244
Fax: 02088 933 670
E-mail: info@waldegrave.richmond.sch.uk
Website: www.waldegrave.richmond.sch.uk

• Pupils: 1,040 girls, all day • Ages: 11-16 • Non-denom • State

Head: Since 1992, Mrs Heather Flint BSocSc (Soc Admin) PGCE MA (fifties), educated at Birmingham and London universities. Has taught since 1973 in London comprehensive schools, with a break 1987-1992 when she was an adviser on educational issues to ministers in the Employment Department. Married with grown-up step-children. Very welcoming to visitors, bubbling with enthusiasm to show people around the school but with a slightly hurried air as she marches at top speed down the corridors. However, she gives the impression that she would make time for any girl or parent who needed her – she is very approachable. Parents describe her as 'highly respected' and 'very organised' or 'a bit formidable'.

Departing in 2006. Successor will be Mrs Philippa Nunn, currently head of Holt School in Wokingham. Married with two children.

Academic Matters: Academically, the strongest state school in the borough of Richmond – 80 per cent got 5+ GCSE A*-C grades in 2005. Most students sit 9 GCSEs. In 2005, a third of GCSE grades were A*/A. One student got one of the top five marks in the country in English literature. The school feels that it, 'succeeds in setting high standards for its wide range of pupils through interesting, varied and appropriate teaching and the setting of individual challenging targets'. Curriculum adequate but not very wide – only French and German as modern foreign languages, no Latin, and currently only dual award science. Plenty of DT, and PE and IT are both taken at GCSE. For the majority, there are quite enough subjects on offer – 'my child could not cope with three foreign languages and Latin,' said a parent. A very bright pupil might not agree.

School now a specialist science school – hoping to offer single sciences to some and increase the number of girls who go on to science A levels – at present very low. Waldegrave has Beacon status and is a Leading Edge school – brings in extra money but, even so, you feel there is simply not enough for the needs of such a diverse school

population. Priority recently given to ICT (all the computers, old and new, were in use on our visit) but probably what can't be afforded is more staff to increase the breadth of the curriculum and extra-curricular activities and to provide stimulus for the girls for whom an A* at GCSE is a piece of cake.

Pupils are put in sets for maths in year 7 and for science and foreign languages in year 8. Further setting as they move up the school but not for English – school feels it best taught in mixed ability groups. Targeted help for EFL (currently about 10 per cent of pupils) and for any type of special needs through an Individual Learning Department described as 'very strong' by one parent.

Lots of voluntary extra lessons at various times throughout the day to help those who need it (apparently well-attended) – may be part of the reason for the good academic record but it could be to the detriment of extra-curricular activities. For example, all lunch-time clubs currently are extra classes for curriculum subjects, except rehearsals for the school play. After school there is orchestra, choir, drama, IT and sport but also a homework club. School day ends at 3.15pm – you wonder what the girls do for the rest of the day if they have finished their homework by 4.00. Some parental grouses on homework – 'there is an element who do not complete the work assigned......work is not always marked and returned or only very late.' School disputes both vigorously.

Games, Options, The Arts: Opportunities for sport are limited – only one small sports hall and team sports do not apparently appeal to many, eg the twice weekly after school hockey practice is for all age groups at once; only one PE lesson a week for years 7 and 9 (two for year 8). Despite this, school has achieved a Sportsmark award – the situation in other state schools is a lot worse. New dance studio soon to be built and off-site activity courses are made available from time to time. Art is a strength – school has an Artsmark silver award – and more than 50 per cent take it at GCSE. Music department described as 'lacking' by a musical family but Richmond Music Trust (a borough organisation) helps here.

Background and Atmosphere: Buildings fairly scruffy and the newer block is workmanlike rather than smart – however, lots of excellent artwork on the walls to cheer things up. Indoor space is at a premium – school is so full – but some of the outdoor space is under-used and under-maintained; the large athletics pitch doesn't show many signs of regular use. Sensible, workmanlike uniform worn by all, with skirts worn far too short by some (very common in other girls-only schools in the area too).

The only single sex state school in the borough of Richmond – more opportunities for the predominantly female staff to fill leading roles within the school and become good role models for the girls, says the head. She also feels it removes any concerns about girls not feeling 'cool' in front of boys if seen to be working, especially at more 'male' subjects like science. 'All my child's teachers are very enthusiastic and motivating and set her very high targets,' said a parent, 'but sometimes her achievements are not recognised as she does not collect her merit awards.' Perhaps too uncool to do so?

Pastoral Care and Discipline: Tutor groups (classes) keep the same form tutor right through their school career. 'I see this as a positive thing,' said a parent, who felt that his child benefited from the close relationship. Another, though, said that the tutor still did not seem to know her child after a year. Behaviour generally good – usual noise and chatter at the end of class as pupils proceed one way – lack of space – down the corridors but attentive and interested pupils in class. Opportunities to take on responsibility, eg a system of peer mediation – a group of specially trained girls available to talk through disagreements between pupils – designed to cut down on bullying. Every girl at some point takes a turn to man reception for a day and charitable activities a regular feature.

Pupils and Parents: Misses out on some of the brightest girls as the most 'pushy' parents who can't afford private school will attempt to move heaven and earth to get a place at the local grammar. School ethnically mixed and pupils and parents are also a social mix. Local 'posh' private school girls complain of bad language, taunts and smoking on the bus but are they such angels themselves, we wonder?

Entrance: From 50 local primary schools in the boroughs of Richmond and neighbouring Hounslow. Preference for SEN, girls in care, siblings (widely defined), then for girls who have expressed a preference for single sex education. A complicated and changeable system of 'quadrants' decides who get a place, based on distance (by public road or footpath) from the school. The school isn't even the central point of the four quadrants and, although the quadrant areas have not changed since 2000, the chance of success is dependent on how many people have applied from each quadrant. Hence the pattern of successful applications varies from year to year. Understanding the system should be enough to guarantee anyone a place at the school – alas, it is not. Heavily oversubscribed, a handful of girls is awarded a place each year on appeal (10 in 2004) – thus school is always overcrowded. 'The staff has to get used to it', says Mrs Flint, 'only 26 in a class would be ideal.' Most tutor groups have 28.

Exit: Currently no Richmond state schools have a sixth form, so most girls go on to the Richmond sixth form college.

Remarks: Happy atmosphere and professional feel. A girl with drive and independence could do very well here but extras like high level sport or further academic subjects would have to come from outside school.

WALLACE COLLEGE

12 George IV Bridge, Edinburgh, EH1 1EE

Tel: 0131 220 3634
Fax: 0131 220 3633
E-mail: info@wallacecollege.co.uk
Website: www.wallacecollege.co.uk

• Pupils: 30 • Ages: 14 - 18 • Fees: Varies with the course; about £2,000 for a one-year single A level • Independent

Head: Since 1975, Mr Simon Skotzen BSc (fifties), who was educated at Marlborough, and studied engineering at Leicester. Acutely uncomfortable about discussing any personal details, charming and affable, Mr Skotzen is married with two grown-up sons. A beady-eyed realist.

Academic Matters: Founded in 1972. The nucleus of traditional tutorial students, primarily from the independent sector, primarily from Scotland. Vast range of subjects in the tutorial dept. Easter revision courses for Highers A Levels GCSEs and Standard Grades held in Edinburgh and Aberdeen. Two hours per subject per day. Aberdeen the busiest. Pupils in Edinburgh use physics labs at Heriot Watt.

Individual tuition in almost any subject. Wallace is a recognised exam centre, much used by external candidates. Exam results asked for but not forthcoming – the sample is probably too small in any case – 'pupils achieve the best they are capable of achieving' – which may not be the same as parental ambition.

A continuous stream of EFL students come throughout the year, for the 'General English Courses' (five levels), plus 'English for Special Purposes', evening courses and summer holiday courses for juniors.

Background and Atmosphere: Trad Edinburgh town house, sandwiched between bookshop and main library, almost midway between the Royal Mile and Grey Friars Bobby. Surrounded by pubs and sandwich shops (boozing at lunch time apparently not a problem, but staff and students smoke cigs outside the front door), college has own study area, plus six or seven classrooms. Reception area is a combination of student info centre and a permanent reminder of Edinburgh Festivals past and future.

Pastoral Care and Discipline: Pupils come from all over and the College will find host families if there are no responsible family members in Edinburgh, with 'a couple of hundred families on the books for the summer school' it is no great problem placing the odd half dozen pupils during the year. Fees are paid to Wallace direct, who employ the families – on a bed, breakfast and evening meal placement – and will move students if temperaments clash. Wallace sees itself very much as a halfway house between school and university, and while the principal hopes that pupils will be self-motivated, he liaises closely with parents where necessary (absenteeism the real bugbear). Help with UCAS and continuing back-up with clearing if necessary.

Pupils and Parents: Motley collection, Wallace will accept pupils who have been expelled through drugs 'hope they have learnt their lesson and won't be doing it again, give them another chance', as well as school refusers and those who need a more personal regime.

Remarks: Outstanding revision courses, well worth thinking about if you need a crammer in Scotland. Takes skool refusniks from 14-20.

WALLINGTON COUNTY GRAMMAR SCHOOL

Croydon Road, Wallington, Surrey, SM6 7PH

Tel: 020 8647 2235
Fax: 020 8254 7921
E-mail: admissions-wcgs@suttonlea.org
Website: www.wcgs.org.uk

• Pupils: 870 boys, all day • Ages: 11-18 • Size of sixth form: 250 boys and girls • Non-denom • State

---

Head: Since 1990, Dr J Martin Haworth MA BEd BA FRSA (fifties), London School of Theology, Birmingham and Warwick. Only the fourth head in school's history – they are all obviously long stayers. Parents describe him as friendly, charming and altogether approachable. Pupils also find him favourable, if not slightly eccentric and, on the whole, feel able to come to him with any problems they may have. His enthusiasm and dedication to the school is evident for all to see. His office overlooks the front of the school and parents feel they can poke their heads round the door should they need a word at home time, if he is not already outside chatting to parents. 'He is always around,'

says one parent, 'he even answers the school phone if the secretary is away from her desk.' A black belt in karate, which should impress boys and parents alike.

Academic Matters: A top notch, academic, selective state school. Pupils take up to 12 GCSEs; consistently very good results. 70 per cent A/B at A level in 2005; lots clock up four or more straight A grades – English Lit and maths particularly impressive. Inclusion of girls in the sixth form has not distracted the boys from their studies – in fact, one parent claims that it promotes a slight rivalry to do well; one of the relatively few schools where boys get better results than the girls. IT department is extensive (three IT teachers all with master's degrees in the subject – very impressive) and it is a popular option for GCSE. Technology is up to date with interactive white boards in most classrooms, most teachers have laptops. DT dept has been refurbished and enlarged. Now has state-of-art equipment. Class sizes average a hefty 29 in the lower years, and 25 in years 10 and 11. Sixth form classes average 14-17 pupils. No specialist teachers for SEN – it is not really an issue here.

Games, Options, The Arts: Heaps of outdoor space for sports with a large school field for rugby and 30 acres (owned by the school) at the Clockhouse for rugby and hockey. Distinct lack of space for indoor PE. Sport is considered extremely important and there is an extensive fixture list against leading schools in the south east, including athletics, cross country, tennis, cricket, hockey and, in particular, some impressive rugby. Other choices include squash, badminton, basketball and volleyball.

Music and drama taught extensively but again there is a lack of space for music practice (although group performances take place in the school hall). Music has become more emphasised with the arrival of a director of music (who studied at Christ Church, Oxford). She is said to be extremely enthusiastic – a musical production of Grease played for four nights to a packed house. There is also an orchestra, wind band and choir. Excellent artwork is proudly displayed, predominantly in the main hallway outside the head's office. Art is very well catered for, with several spacious art rooms. Average selection of after school clubs, societies and activities including chess, art and drama.

Background and Atmosphere: Redbrick building circa 1935 houses the main body of the school (founded in 1927), which encircles a superb courtyard garden – 'the Quad' -which is used only by teachers; pupils gain access on rare occasions. Inside, wooden floors, a pleasant entrance hall and the impressive oak panelled main hall create an impression not dissimilar to an independent school. Overall, the school is a good size and not overcrowded. Different playgrounds are allocated to various year groups, which must be a relief for new pupils in particular, who have their own separate playground. Largeish cafeteria with a wide range of hot food. Overall, a studious atmosphere yet the pupils seem relaxed, friendly and polite. To quote one parent – 'when we visited, the first thing we all noticed was how lovely the atmosphere was.'

Pastoral Care and Discipline: School has embraced a new buddying system – kindly sixth formers take a small clutch of year 6 pupils under their wings just before the school summer holiday. New pupils get a good feel for the school prior to the start in September and (unlike other schools) this initiation lasts for four days – the newcomers can really get to know their new environment and teachers, as well as their 'buddy' sixth former. They then have the summer holiday to mull it all over, and there is a friendly face to say 'Hello' when they start school. According to Ofsted, this is one of the best induction programmes in the country; at least 7 opportunites for pupils to get together before they arrive plus the 4 induction days when get there. Parents are extremely happy with the results – 'my son settled down really well, he has found the school to be very friendly...a few teachers are on the strict side however! Luckily, he was used to having a lot of homework at his previous (independent) school, so homework was not a problem and the buddying system really helped him feel at home.'

Bullying dealt with swiftly and severely. Smoking is forbidden on the premises for teachers and pupils alike and there are very few instances of smoking, drinking or drugs. House system, a focus for loyalty and competition. Badges and ties awarded for sports and other school achievements.

Pupils and Parents: A big mix, well-integrated. Pupils are smartly turned out in uniform – even the sixth formers (their only concession is to wear a different coloured shirt). Pupils are expected to be involved in sports and drama and with the local community. Parents can be as little or as much involved as they like. Good information-flow from the school.

Entrance: Selective at 11 – entrance exam prepared by the school, English maths and a short verbal reasoning paper. Competition is stiff for the 120 places available with typically over 1,200 applications – of who 830 take the exam and 244 pass. Not surprisingly, private tutors are earning a good living with many children being coached to give them a chance of entry though school discourages this. Wide geographical intake – pupils come from south east London, Croydon, Sutton, and Surrey, from numerous primary schools, including a few independents. With the school's high standard of GCSE results, entry to sixth form

does not pose a problem to most pupils and they are rarely denied their chosen subjects. Each year there are typically 150 external applicants for 20-30 places in the sixth form; they need at least 7 GCSE subjects at grade A and are then selected in rank order according to a criteria such as siblings already in the school etc.

Exit: Many pupils elect to stay on to the sixth form, only a few leave for other further education or sixth form colleges. University choices are varied, many to London universities (7 in 2004 to Oxbridge) and quite a few students studying law and medicine. Very few take a gap year.

Remarks: A friendly and welcoming academic school with excellent results and much praise for the pupil/teacher relationships. A real alternative to private school if your child is bright enough to get in.

WALLINGTON HIGH SCHOOL FOR GIRLS

Woodcote Road, Wallington, Surrey, SM6 0PH

Tel: 020 8647 2380
Fax: 020 8647 2270
E-mail: wallingtongirls@suttonlea.org
Website: www.wallingtongirls.sutton.sch.uk

• Pupils: 1,245 girls, all day • Ages: 11-18
• Size of sixth form: 360 • Non-denom • State

Head: Since 2002, Mrs Barbara Greatorex (fifties) BSc in molecular science from Warwick University MA (in educational management from the Open University). She came to Wallington from Wolverhampton, where she was a deputy head for five years (previously held posts as a science teacher). A relaxed, very friendly and down to earth lady, she likes to teach but doesn't do too much – 'it's not fair to the students as I am away so much.' She describes herself as understanding, patient, supportive and caring. Her compassion is for all to see but she also clearly has vision, aspirations and high expectations for all. Has been driving force behind recent changes as well as fantastic new facilities. She is a head who is not afraid of change – 'I want continuous improvement. I have high expectations.' She strives for 'excellence in everything' and hopes she can pass on a 'life-long love for learning' to her students. Parents describe her as 'very approachable – always surrounded by smiling girls when she walks around the school.'

Academic Matters: Academically impressive – in 2005, 69 per cent A/A* grades at GCSE and 82.5 per cent

A/B grades at A level. Particularly refreshing to see a girls' school so heavily promoting and succeeding in the science subjects. Sciences form the backbone of academia here (and there are remarkable facilities). Pupils take up to 12 GCSEs and, not surprisingly, popular subjects for both GCSE and A level are the sciences, maths, and technology – 70 per cent of girls take at least one science subject for A level. Awarded specialist status in engineering in 2004 – means extra funding for school development. Head chose engineering to steer girls towards problem solving, creating and designing, as well as pushing engineering up to the same status as medicine (an extremely popular career choice at the school, especially among the girls from ethnic minorities). Strong maths department. Amazing IT facilities with three IT rooms equipped with state-of-the-art flat screen monitors. School has been kitted with thirty interactive whiteboards and every teaching member of staff has a laptop (top of the range!). A parent who moved to the school from the private school sector said she was 'amazed to find equipment I had never seen in my daughter's previous school!' Needless to say computers feature heavily in teaching of most subjects – students can easily access topics and their homework from computers at home. Good choice of languages, English and humanities very sound. Much praised teaching throughout the school – but some concern expressed about many staff being mid to late 50s and that younger ones jump ship because of lack of promotion prospects. Head points out that staff movement has been stable for many years but young teachers are coming in. 'Not always great,' she comments, ' we train them for two or three years and they move on to get promotions elsewhere – a lot of the time to the private sector.'

Classrooms are accessed through a warren of corridors displaying girls' work and posters from school trips (Tanzania, Morocco, Vietnam and others). Bang up to date classrooms, buzzing science labs, art rooms and textile rooms. Technology classrooms are equally impressive. Pupils are focused, neat and happy – lots of keen hands in the air. Library is very small but in full action at lunchtime. School's intake of students with dyslexia is very low. SENCO and teaching assistants are on hand. Study support groups are offered on all major subjects.

Games, Options, The Arts: Sport is strong and girls take part in the sports leadership programme where they help out pupils from feeder schools. Attractive grounds offer surprising amount of outdoor space; huge concreted area used for tennis and netball, acres of playing fields. Next on head's wish list is new indoor sports facilities – currently the school hall doubles as sports hall, there is also a very cramped gymnasium: 'we are hoping to have raised funds by 2007, however the school has a Sportsmark Award.'

Very impressive art displayed in classrooms as well as reception – not surprising being an Artsmark Gold status school. Fabulous designs by the textiles students. Drama very impressive – parents 'amazed' at the latest production of Les Miserables and The Pirates of Penzance. The girls do everything from producing, directing, acting and lighting to costume design. One parent happily said, 'if I did not know any better, I would have thought I was in the West End!' Girls who take part in a production are immediately set to train the girls who get involved in the following year's play. Music lessons on offer for groups as well as one to one tuition. Sixth formers introduced to variety of leadership programmes and from year 9 upwards work experience is on the agenda.

Background and Atmosphere: Very large school. Established in 1888 but moved to its current site in 1965. Easily houses the 1,250 girls as well as staff without making you feeling claustrophobic. Archetypical 1960s school-building – however hiding behind a massive, rather hospital like, shabby entrance hall is a surprisingly professional and vibrant school. The head feels that her aspiration to teach her girls 'excellence in everything' can only be attained by providing the girls with a friendly happy atmosphere – 'life is about enjoying what you do and if you do not, then you need to reflect,' (parents feel this depicts Mrs G perfectly). Huge amounts of money have been raised by the school and parents alike, to bring to life the music block (which opened during Mrs G's first year at the school) followed by the major development of the new Link building with six classrooms, two offices and lifts. School day starts at 8:25 and ends at 2:50. Girls can be dropped off as early as 7:30 and after school clubs like drama, sports and chess clubs are run by sixth formers until 4:00. IT suites are also available for use during these times. A breakfast club service is in the pipeline. New independent catering company offering the girls freshly cooked meals, and a 'green' vending machine has proved to be very popular!

Pastoral Care and Discipline: Both very high on the agenda. Very little bullying, some smokers, who are dealt with as they appear. 'You have to be realistic,' says Mrs G. No drugs problems faced. The head feels that punishment does not work in all cases and support can be more productive, she is very much in control of her girls – kind but firm. Anorexia and self-harm (a growing problem in many girls' selective schools – who said that academically bright girls don't have personal issues?) were 'major problems' in the past. Mrs G has since employed full time counsellor –

'no cases since!' she says with a real sense of achievement and care. Counsellor has proved to be a huge success generally – 'my daughter's friend lost her father and the support she received from the counsellor was just amazing.' Parents are kept informed regularly with newsletters, reports and parent/teacher meetings. Mrs G also runs a drop-in session on a monthly basis should anyone wish to see her personally – a super idea, particularly in such a big school.

Pupils and Parents: Lots of ethnic minorities, with parents who want their daughters to achieve highly – particularly those looking to study medicine. Very harmonious and friendly, it is an outgoing place, but quieter, less motivated, souls may struggle a little. Girls are very polite, happy and extremely smart. Hair neat and skirts of a decent length. Sixth formers (who do not wear the school uniform) range from smart dressers to followers of fashion.

Entrance: From over 60 feeder schools – private and state. Highly over-subscribed for entry at 11: about 750 girls compete for 180 places. Entrance is via exam – verbal reasoning and maths papers. 'Apply via common applications process and put us as your school of preference,' stresses Mrs G. In addition she says, 'if you have a sister here – provided you pass the entrance exams, we will take you.' Entry into sixth form – six passes grade B or above, with an A or a B in subject chosen for A level as well as its supporting subjects.

Exit: Between 10 and 12 girls leave after GCSEs. Around 98 per cent go onto higher education after A levels. Surprisingly only 7 – 8 per cent to Oxbridge (6 in 2005) – head admits 'not as many as I would like.' Others to University of London, Reading, Loughborough, Warwick and many more. Popular degree courses are medicine, engineering, law and dentistry.

Money Matters: Fundraising is high on the agenda – 'unless we raise the funds ourselves nothing would improve,' says Mrs G. Parents work very hard to help fund raise and support the school.

Remarks: Vibrant, happy and positive place with top academic results and a switched on head. Ideal for academic, confident girls (particularly for aspiring medics) who have a clear aim and are up for a challenge.

WARWICK SCHOOL

Linked to Warwick Junior School in the Junior section

Myton Road, Warwick, Warwickshire, CV34 6PP

Tel: 01926 776 400/1
Fax: 01926 401 259
E-mail: enquiries@warwickschool.org
Website: www.warwickschool.org

• Pupils: 1075, all boys, of whom 47 board • Ages: 7-18 • Size of sixth form: 255 • C of E but accepts all denoms • Independent

Head: Since 2002, Mr EB Halse BSc FRSA, whose predecessor undertook a major and expensive renovation programme of this venerable school.

Remarks: A large boys' school with a, now tiny, boarding department. All boarders are housed together in 'The Boarding House', though divided into juniors and seniors. Full, weekly, day and ocasional boarding are available. Most boarders from overseas. Most pupils very local and all day pupils from within a 30 mile radius of the school. Breakfast club and extended day schemes give working parents flexibility.

Academically selects roughly top fifth of ability range and does well – 75-ish per cent A/B grades at A level, and 65 per cent A*/A at GCSE. Everyone has a shot at Latin and at least two modern foreign langs in the first two senior years and all do separate sciences to GCSE plus 3 from geography, history, Latin, classical civilisation, German, Greek, RS, Spanish, music, drama, art, D & T and ICT – a good spread and nice to see Greek here. Maths is a starry performer at A level and history, politics, economics and business studies are also impressive. Roughly ten each year to Oxbridge. School proud of its value-added statistics. Rugby is main sport and one feels sorry for their regular opponents who must know they're in for a drubbing when the fixture comes round. School has extensive playing fields on site. Arts are strong and school has onsite Bridge House Theatre with a terrific programme of professional visiting ensembles, both thespian and musical, as well as its own in-house productions – a real asset. Some musicians hit the heights, winning Oxbridge choral schols.

WATFORD GRAMMAR SCHOOL FOR BOYS

Rickmansworth Road, Watford, Hertfordshire, WD18 7JF

Tel: 01923 208 900

Fax: 01923 208 901

E-mail: admin.watfordboys@thegrid.org.uk

Website: www.watfordboys.herts.sch.uk

• Pupils: 1,190 boys • Ages: 11-18 • Size of sixth form: 320
• Non-denom • State

Head: Since 2000, Mr M (Martin) Post MA FRSA (mid-for-ties). Married, one son. Former head boy of Watford Boys in the seventies. Started his career at King's, Rochester, then moved to Mill Hill County High and Richard Hale School in Hertford before joining Watford Boys as deputy head in 1995. Read English and related literature at the University of York, teaches English to GCSE and A level. Very proud of the school's national reputation and keen to continue to build on the school's success under previous head Professor John Holman. 'I think we are a unique school because our level of success puts us in the top five per cent of state schools in the country and we are one of the few in that league who are not 100 per cent selective. But we are not an exam factory. We have boys who could go in for 12 or 13 GCSEs but, if they did, they might not have the opportunity to excel in other areas outside academic life, such as sport or drama. I believe it's important boys get an all-round experience.' Tries to know as many boys as possible but doesn't know them all. Pupils regard him as fair and approachable.

Academic Matters: A very successful school with boys doing well in modern languages and English, often seen as unfashionable subjects for boys. Around 95 per cent of GCSEs A – C grades, 78 per cent A/B at A level. Maths the king subject, as usual in selective boys' schools, with very strong results at all levels. Other popular subjects include economics, the sciences, English and history; the-atre studies too. Class sizes good for the state sector – around 27.

All boys are tested in their first term and monitored closely for special needs. Setting is introduced towards the end of year 7. Most pupils enter for ten GCSEs (about half do separate sciences) but those less able concentrate on seven or eight; no subjects taken early. Boys are allocated French or German in year 7, then take a second language in year 8;

Spanish is available in year 10. 88 per cent stay on for A levels; no GNVQs or general studies.

Games, Options, The Arts: Three major sports – rugby (partnership with Saracens), cricket and hockey – are played at county and national levels and the school proves more than a match for some of the top private schools nearby. Cross-country, athletics and tennis too. Good facilities.

Music strong; 10 per cent of places are awarded on musical ability and some 300 boys learn a musical instru-ment at school. 15 musical groups and choirs. New music centre planned. Plenty of clubs to choose from – chess, debating and young scientists notable. Regular trips and sports tours abroad. Facilities include 280-seat purpose-built theatre.

Background and Atmosphere: The boys' and nearby girls' grammar schools grew from the Free School, a char-ity school for 60 pupils founded by Dame Elizabeth Fuller in 1704 on the ground next to the parish churchyard in the centre of Watford. In 1881 the schools became separate foundations; the boys' school moved to its present site about a mile from the town centre in 1912. The boys' and girls' schools still retain strong links. Looks and feels like a grammar school, with an imposing Edwardian building sur-rounded by 1960s and later additions – some could do with a lick of paint.

Pastoral Care and Discipline: Built on form tutor system and aims to establish close links with parents. Clear system of rewards and sanctions, 'we try to play up the suc-cesses of boys in all areas.' Detentions after school or, in more serious circumstances, on Saturday mornings. Counselling on offer. Head says, 'our boys are not saints – they come from a variety of backgrounds and have a huge number of influences – but in school they behave them-selves.' Two expulsions in the last eight years.

Pupils and Parents: From a wide social and cultural mix which 'adds to the strength of the school'. Pupils mostly live in the Watford area, some from Wembley and Harrow in the south and Kings Langley in the north. Around a quarter of the boys have English as a second language, with about 25 different first languages.

Entrance: Heavily oversubscribed because of its repu-tation as a very good state school but admission rules are complex and if you live outside the catchment area (check your post code starts WD or HA) don't bother applying. Last year 672 boys applied from 52 feeder schools for 180 places. 45 per cent of places are allocated to 'specialist' applicants, 55 per cent to 'community' applicants', and within each category applicants are placed in one of two subcategories based on where they live – the Watford area (60 per cent of places) and the rest of the traditional area determined by post code (40 per cent). Within the community category, siblings get priority; places are then awarded to pupils with brothers who have attended the school in the past or boys with a parent who works at the school. Applicants with sisters at nearby Watford Grammar School for Girls then get the chance of a place followed by those who live closest to the school. Generally all the places are absorbed before distance from the school comes into play, but distance is used to choose between pupils in the criterion that the cut-off point falls within. Within the specialist category, a total of 10 per cent of places are awarded on musical aptitude, then 35 per cent are selected on academic ability with tests in maths and verbal reasoning.

Entrance to the sixth form from within the school is subject to getting 6 B grades or better at GCSE. In addition the school usually receives around 150 external applications for some 40 places – a good number from the Harrow area where there is a break point at 16. The only criterion is GCSE results: the school takes the best, with a cut-off of 6 A-C grades with at least B in subjects to be studied at AS/A2 in subjects to be studied at A level.

Exit: Most boys go on to university with Kings College, UCL, Manchester, Leeds and Birmingham among the most popular. 20 to Oxbridge in 2003.

Remarks: A popular and successful traditional school and parents will move house in a bid to get their son a place. The boys are proud and conscious of their school's reputation in all areas and are prepared to work hard to achieve excellent results.

WATFORD GRAMMAR SCHOOL FOR GIRLS

Lady's Close, Watford, Hertfordshire, WD18 0AE

Tel: 01923 223 403

Fax: 01923 350 721

E-mail: admin.watfordgirls@thegrid.org.uk

Website: www.watfordgirls.herts.sch.uk

- Pupils: 1,250 girls; all day • Ages: 11-18 • Size of sixth form: 335 • Non-denom • State • Open days: October

Helen Hyde: Since 1987, Mrs Helen Hyde MA (fifties). Married to a consultant paediatrician. Two grown-up daughters. Educated to degree level in South Africa and moved to the UK in 1970. Masters at King's College, London. Started teaching career at Acland Burghley, a state secondary in London, then moved to Highgate Wood in Haringey, a mixed state secondary, as the curriculum deputy before taking the headship at Watford Grammar. Teaches French and thinking skills. Accredited trainer for the De Bono thinking skills and the Buzan method of mind mapping. Is proud of the fact that, 'first and foremost we are an academic school. From the outset I tell the girls they must have a "can do" attitude. We push the girls' confidence so that they believe they can succeed and they do.' Looks upon the school as a 'family.' Gives credit to her committed teachers who she expects to give time and energy to out-of-school activities. Admits she doesn't know all the girls by name but says she would spot them anywhere. Is aware of the 'huge' challenge she has of maintaining the school's well-earned reputation and is determined to build on its success.

Academic Matters: Excellent. 98 per cent plus get five or more GCSEs (A* to C) with 85-ish per cent achieving nine or more. The school has a wide religious mix – Muslims, Sikhs, Hindus, Jews and Christians – and for many English is not their first language. Despite this, almost all get A* to C grades at GCSE in English with three quarters getting either an A* or an A. About 80 per cent grades A and B at A level with biology, chemistry and English literature popular (very good science results). Science is taught separately up to GCSE but pupils are examined on the double award. French or German is offered in year 7 then a third language is added in year 8.

Class sizes are standard for a state secondary school – around 30. At A level, classes are big – 20 plus – but pupils don't see this as a disadvantage. No GNVQs; general studies course is followed but not examined. Some of the younger girls feel they get a lot of homework – recommended around 1 hour 30 minutes each night rising to at least six hours per subject per week in the sixth form. Girls are continuously assessed and given individual targets. Internal exams once a year. Advanced Extension examinations available in the upper sixth year.

Games, Options, The Arts: Sport is an important feature of the school and girls do well at district and county level. Two playing fields, an indoor pool, tennis and netball courts, a gym and recently built sports hall. Girls are offered hockey, netball, swimming, gymnastics, dance, rounders, football and basketball. In the sixth form, squash, self-defence, weight training and golf as well.

Music is the soul of the school, according to the head. More than 300 have lessons in the school; two orchestras, a big band, two choirs and various other groups. Girls play in a joint orchestra with Watford Grammar School for Boys. Girls are expected to take part in at least three extra-curricular activities each week from a huge choice ranging from debating and Duke of Edinburgh (very popular) to history and geography clubs. Plenty of trips, including exchange visits, ski trips, sailing parties and cultural and study visits.

Now a well established visual arts specialist school with many opportunities for the girls and the community. School is also a national training school for De Bono thinking skills.

Background and Atmosphere: Founded in 1704 by Mrs Elizabeth Fuller, it originally taught girls to read, knit and sew, as well as recite the Church of England catechism. Mrs Fuller's values – care, dedication, tolerance and service to others – were at the heart of school life then and the head tries to instil the same values today. School motto is Sperate Parati – go forward with preparation. Girls use the following motto – ' I can do it and I will do it'. Strong emphasis on building girls' confidence and self esteem.

Buildings date from 1907, now radically extended. Because of its central location, access is difficult at peak times. Traditional girls' school feel – polished wooden floors greet the visitor, a wooden bench sits outside the headmistress's office and a portrait of the founder hangs on the wall. A bright new sixth form study centre was recently opened where girls can relax and make drinks and prepare food in the kitchen or study in one of the quiet rooms nearby. All year 7s are taught in a nearby separate building, the elegant Lady's Close House, though some of the girls feel this segregates them from the rest of the school.

Pastoral Care and Discipline: Girls stay in the same form group from year 7 to 11 which gives continuity of care.

Bullying is taken very seriously – the head talks to all year 7s and says she will not tolerate any form of teasing; sixth formers act as tutors to younger pupils who have difficulties in various subjects and this enhances pupil relationships through the school. The head is no soft touch on discipline – if she hears a rumour about a girl breaking a school rule she will act to get to the bottom of it and involve the parents from the outset. Girls are treated with respect and bad behaviour does not seem to be much of an issue.

Pupils and Parents: A real ethnic and socio-economic mix. Because of its national reputation it attracts those who are also considering the independent sector – some parents send their children to prep school to give them a better chance of passing Watford Girls' assessment test at 11. Pupils are well behaved and polite although some could smarten up their appearance. Uniform of navy blue skirt or trousers, yellow shirt (white for sixth formers) and navy blue sweatshirt. The girls recognise the school has a strong work ethos and want to do well but don't feel over pressurised. Some sixth formers feel they should have more freedom to come and go, some would like to see more mixing with the nearby boys' school. Parents very supportive and help stage autumn fairs, quiz evenings, fashion shows, dances and discos.

Entrance: Oversubscribed; last year over 600 girls applied for 180 places. There were 38 appeals; four were successful. Admission rules are complex and if you live outside the catchment area (check your post code starts WD or HA) don't bother applying. 45 per cent of places are allocated to 'specialist' applicants, 55 per cent to 'community' applicants' and, within each category, applicants are placed in one of two sub-categories based on where they live – the Watford area (60 per cent of places) and the rest of the traditional area determined by post code (40 per cent). Within the community category, siblings get priority; places are then awarded to pupils with sisters who have attended the school in the past or girls with a parent who works at the school. Applicants with brothers at nearby Watford Grammar School for Boys then get the chance of a place followed by those who live closest to the school. Generally all the places are absorbed before distance from the school comes into play but distance is used to choose between pupils in the category that the cut-off point falls within. Within the specialist category, a total of 10 per cent of places are awarded on musical aptitude, then 25 per cent are selected on academic ability with tests in maths and verbal reasoning.

Entrance to the sixth form from within the school is subject to getting 6 C grades or better at GCSE plus the subject requirements for the courses that they want to follow (the minimum requirement for most A level courses is a grade B). In addition the school usually receives around 30 external applications – a good number from the Harrow area where there is a break point at 16 – who have to meet the same criteria.

Exit: About 25 girls leave post-GCSE (some look for more vocational courses or are tired of being in a single-sex environment) and some 25 new pupils arrive. At 18 the vast majority go on to university – Birmingham, UCL and Manchester. A dozen to Oxbridge.

Remarks: An excellent girls' school offering traditional values with an enviable local and national reputation. Worth moving house for although the assessment test may prove an obstacle for some. The head inspires confidence and is determined to see her girls succeed.

WELLINGTON COLLEGE

Linked to Eagle House School

Crowthorne, Berkshire, RG45 7PU

Tel: 01344 444 012
Fax: 01344 444 004
E-mail: registrar@wellingtoncollege.org.uk
Website: www.wellingtoncollege.org.uk

• Pupils: 705 pupils, 55 girls (all in sixth form). 100 day pupils, the rest board; virtually all the girls board (5 day) • Ages: 13-18 • Size of sixth form: 330 • C of E • Fees: Day £6,132; boarding £7,665 • Independent • Open days: Contact Registrar for details

---

Master: From January 2006, Dr Anthony Seldon MA PhD MBA FRSA FRHistSoc (early fifties), who has been the making of Brighton College since his arrival there in 1997. Educated at Tonbridge School and Worcester College, Oxford. Author of many well-regarded books on British history, including a biographies of John Major and Tony Blair. Capable of rattling off books at a tremendous speed – his history of the Foreign Office was written in three weeks – and ploughs all the profits back into education charities. Charismatic, enthusiastic, strong social conscience; a star. Wife, Joanna (Oxford double first and DPhil) teaches English; three children.

The change of head clearly reflects an underlying unease about the current state of affairs at Wellington. Dr Seldon has the ambition, and the ability, to restore the school to the first division – but it is difficult to know how a school will respond to a new head until he has been in the saddle for a term or two. Has been seeing all current parents at a series of meetings in 2005, setting out his plans. For more on these see below.

Academic Matters: For a school that many parents consider alongside Eton and Radley, exam results are less good than one would expect: Wellington has always emphasised breadth over swotting and takes in a broad ability range. It is one of Dr Seldon's ambitions to move the school into the first division academically (GCSE results are improving anyway). Excellent results in art, German, Latin and the few brave souls who do Greek. Less good in geography and classical civilisation. Biology the most popular A level subject by far, taught by an enthusiast who keeps a tank of enormous snapping piranhas in his classroom. Fantastic biology expeditions to Belize and Sulawesi in conjunction with geography department. Theatre studies a relatively new offering. School now refutes our earlier comment that this isn't really 'the place for dyslexics and the like' – seven per cent are receiving help for mild learning difficulties – 'we keep the help low-key and rather invisible.' Setting from the start in English, French, Latin, maths and science and, later, in virtually every subject. Latin 'almost compulsory' (six out of seven first year sets learn it, with the remainder doing classical civilisation).

Dr Seldon aims to get the A level A/B percentage up to 80 (already there for the girls, but 60 per cent for the boys). This will involve a raising of the Common Entrance hurdle to 60 per cent (as demand allows), but Dr Seldon emphasises that this will be interpreted flexibly for eg pupils with notable talent outside academia, and that no pupil currently in the school will be hoofed out if their GCSEs or AS levels fail to impress (as long as they make the grade in behaviour and effort). The school is now setting minimum standards, however, for taking a subject forward to A2 (at least D grade AS level in that subject). SEN should be well supported – one of Dr Seldon's strong points at Brighton.

Games, Options, The Arts: Spectacular, invincible sportsmen, particularly good at rugby and hockey where they do almost nothing but win, win, win (three U18 international players recently in the school). Everyone is involved in something (the school turns out 23 rugby teams and 17 hockey and cricket teams, plus teams in 17 other sports). Rugby for all in the early years has been an irritation to boys who hate the game and have barely survived six years of being forced to play it at prep school. English school polo champions, good shooting and rackets. Golf course (opened 2001) a thing of wonder and beauty ('better than Eton's!' boasted a staff member and we agree). 400 boys immediately signed up for golf after the course was built. It and the fitness centre are open to the public. The 'Field Gun Run' a popular if eccentric pastime. Girls' sport slightly restricted by small numbers to choose from but at least low numbers does mean that any keen girl can get into a team. Dr Seldon wants the girls' games to become as strong as the boys'. Art better than impressive, energetically taught and housed in beauteous, new building. Keen drama with the school taking a play to the Edinburgh Festival each year. Lots of music going on with standard as you would expect at a keenly sporty boys' boarding school where mum is not around to nag. Orchestra tour to Australia in 2005. A good place to have a go at a music scholarship.

Background and Atmosphere: In 1852, when the Duke died, the existing plan was to erect his statue in every town in England. Felicitously, someone decided to build a school instead on a distant end of the old Windsor estate. Queen remains the school's official Visitor. Immaculate, formal grounds reached via imposing avenue of oaks, Wellingtonias and Andean pines. Five lakes, endless lawns and abundant green space. Six houses 'in college' for gregarious pupils who want to be at the centre of action. Those in the eight outlying houses have a quieter life, more independence and a great opportunity to develop their leg muscles (these are slightly more popular that the central houses). Rooms cheerfully unkempt. Most popular/sporty houses: Benson and Beresford. Most academic: Stanley and Lynedoch. Newly built boarding houses, Talbot, opened 2003, and Beresford, 2005. New Orange 13+ girls' house to open September 2006. An in-college girls' house will open in 2007 to become the third girls' house. Four houses have own catering but the rest eat in formal, grand dining hall. Separate dining room for first year pupils. Beautiful chapel. Delightful library with two full-time librarians and CCTV scanning nooks and crannies. With such abundant loveliness, the dark and nasty Queen's Court teaching block, opened by the Queen in 1974 and described by staff as built in 'neo-brutalism', is an unfortunate sore thumb. It does, however, house a well-equipped theatre (doubles as a cinema). A number of new classrooms, with interactive whiteboards and PC keyboards for all, cost the school a fortune. Eight-day academic cycle, so lessons fall on a different day each week, but children soon get the hang of it. Day pupils may be collected after 7pm.

Dr Seldon wants to make the school distinctive – not clear how yet, but service to the community and sport (long-term Wellingtonian virtues) will feature.

Pastoral Care and Discipline: The 'Basic Courtesies,' published in school diaries, sets the high standard for behaviour (how many schools still have rules like: 'If you are wearing any kind of head-gear, you should raise it – or at least touch the brim – to all adults'? And, our favourite, 'In our culture, it is considered discourteous – and probably a sign of weak character – not to look directly into the eyes of the person who is talking to you'). Girls tucked in own house: Apsley. Many parents and staff feel numbers of girls too low to be genuinely viable but girls we met were not complaining. Girl numbers are being addressed: in 2006, the intake of senior girls is to increase, and 13+ girls will arrive. Atmosphere has loosened up a little since the departure of long-time South African head Jonty Driver. Member of the Round Square since 1995 (international family of schools, associated in this country with Gordonstoun, Kurt Hahn, and bracing fresh air and exercise). The organisation provides endless opportunities for fund-raising for impoverished schools in the southern hemisphere and ready-made destinations for school trips. It also runs team-building weekends, international conferences and exchanges, leadership training course for sixth form. Through these activities and others the school's genuine commitment to community service and helping others is much in evidence.

Some unsettling stories of bullying and similar over the past year or two – Dr Seldon plans an immediate and continuing crackdown, with the introduction of an 'honour code'.

Pupils and Parents: Turns out nice, unsnobbish, decent chaps, popular with their girlfriends' mothers. Similarly for girls and fathers. Four per cent from British families abroad and 5 per cent foreign (17 boys are receiving ESL tuition but the school requires very good English for entry). Around 10 per cent of pupils' fathers were here. Still some Services children, though numbers dwindling. Some well-known sporting families. Girls mainly with pre-existing links to the school (brothers, fathers, uncles). OBs: Sir Harold Nicolson, Robert Morley, Sebastian Faulkes, Rory Bremner, Peter Snow, Sir Nicholas Grimshaw (architect of Eden Project), Pop Idol winner Will Young and 15 winners of the VC.

Entrance: 140 pupils at 13 through scholarship, or CE, or school's own test. Main feeders: Caldicott, Crosfields, Elstree, Feltonfleet, Eagle House (a mile away and owned by Wellington – 70 per cent of its leavers come here), Hall Grove, Lambrook/Haileybury, Papplewick, Shrewsbury House, St John's Beaumont, Thomas's, Twyford and Yateley Manor. 10 boys enter at 14 for GCSE courses; 20 boys and about 40 girls join at sixth form.

Exit: Largest numbers to Newcastle, Edinburgh and Bristol, also University of the West of England. Then Exeter and Oxbridge; much more Ox (classics, history and PPE) than Bridge (sciences). Sixty per cent to gap years.

Money Matters: Reckons to 'get child on to next stage'

when parents have fallen on hard times, though this is not always possible. Numbers of scholarships and exhibitions for academic, sports, arts and all-round talent, and bursaries are available. Brilliantly run endowment fund, according to the master, set up by Frank Fisher in the 1970s. Has also set up a Heritage Fund, to plough in land sales (400 acres in all belonging to the school). College's charter allows for children of deceased Army officers (and, latterly, other Services) to be educated here on a means-tested basis - currently a dozen of these, though numbers fluctuate.

Remarks: We would bet on Anthony Seldon making this a great school again.

WELLS CATHEDRAL SCHOOL

Linked to Wells Cathedral School Junior School in the Junior section

The Liberty, Wells, Somerset, BA5 2ST

Tel: 01749 834 200

Fax: 01749 834 201

E-mail: admissions@wells-cathedral-school.com

Website: www.wells-cathedral-school.com

- Pupils: 481 of whom 197 boarding; boys 256, girls 225 • Ages: 11-18 • Size of sixth form: 183 • C of E • Fees: Day £1,685 - £3,860. Boarding £5,410 - £6,450 per term • Independent
- Open days: Sixth form: September; Senior school: October and February. Junior school: October, February and June. Individual visits arranged at any time

---

Head: Since 2000, Mrs Elizabeth Cairncross (fiftyish), married with three children. Formerly deputy head of Christ's Hospital, Horsham, where she had been a mistress since 1986. The first female head in the history of the school, obviously delighted to be in such truly beautiful surroundings. 'Such a wealth of history and tradition that we can get on and do modern things.' Quietly determined and respected as a manager – 'she has not made great changes but is really tightening things up,' comments a sixth former. Teaches English and religious studies and runs the Latin club, Minimus, in the junior school.

Academic Matters: Academic results consistently high at both GCSE and A level and a good mix of subjects including design, geology, media studies, theatre studies, psychology and Latin. Choristers and specialist musicians are taught in the 'M' form of each year with a curriculum which allows extra time for practice; all other forms are a deliberate mix of ability and status – girl/boy, day/boarder.

All pupils are setted for French and maths on entry to the senior school. Specialist musicians throughout the school have adjusted timetables and curricula to integrate music and, especially, practice. Pupils at this level are grouped in faculty-based tutor groups and therefore have two staff responsible for them – a housemaster/mistress seeing them daily at registration and a tutor responsible for monitoring academic progress and welfare. Innovative teaching includes bringing several classes together in order to debate ethical issues, for example, in science – creating quite a buzz.

Games, Options, The Arts: One of five independent schools in the UK with government-funded specialist music provision. So the music, of course, is fabulous. The prospectus lists over 60 music staff, with departments of strings, keyboard, brass, percussion, woodwind, vocal and choral studies, music technology and composition. All pupils are encouraged to benefit from the musical expertise. There are about 40 choristers (roughly 50/50 boys and girls in separate choirs). Rehearsal is five mornings a week before school and alternate Friday afternoons. They sing in the cathedral on most Sundays during term time, plus evensong every day except one. There is also a strong tradition of drama and fine art and, as would be expected in a school where performance is important, standards are high. Sport does not share the high profile of the arts but is well provided for – rugby, hockey, netball, cricket and tennis. There is a smallish outdoor swimming pool and indoor climbing wall. PE ('the academic side of sport') is popular and can be taken at GCSE and A level. Pupils are encouraged to take part in special weekly service activities including D of E, a community service programme and the CCF.

Background and Atmosphere: The city of Wells has a unique, comfortable feel that permeates the school and provides a solid grounding of tradition and history. After all, the school's link with the cathedral goes back nine centuries and it occupies all but one of the splendid canonical buildings around The Liberty – the large Georgian house containing the main school and most of the boarding facilities. Classrooms, sixth form study centre and library are situated in buildings of the former stable yard; the music department occupies the medieval buildings across the road and includes some of the houses in the lovely Vicar's Close. Modern science block complete with lecture theatre. Junior and senior schools are adjacent, separated by the juniors' playground; the proximity of the smaller children adds to the family atmosphere and also means that siblings can see each other in the day.

A high-energy school that somehow manages to

remain remarkably laid-back. Encouragement to have a go seems to be the key with many layers of prizes and rewards including the highly desirable 'Good Egg' award. A school which manages to look after the extrovert and the introvert. Because so many of the buildings around the cathedral are labelled as Wells Cathedral School it is actually quite difficult to find the main entrance on the first visit – follow the noise and you will end up in the juniors' playground, arguably the heart of any school. Difficult to get through to by phone too – don't worry if you are put on hold when ringing the school, the lovely choral piped music makes it a relative pleasure to wait.

Pastoral Care and Discipline: A busy co-educational school – very happy, friendly and relaxed with few rules due to an established culture of 'mutual consideration, respect and courtesy' (Code of Conduct); a culture based on trust. Wells Cathedral is involved in the governance of the school which is run on Christian principles but without a heavy hand. The cathedral is used for morning service for the whole school, every Wednesday. Alexander Technique tuition is available (15 staff listed!). A designated tutor looks after overseas students with help from senior pupils -'every-one just gets stuck in,' says a sixth former. There are EFL tutors available and Chinese and Japanese feature in the A level results.

Pupils and Parents: Large local catchment area for day pupils, boarders from far and wide but mostly south west. Not a huge cohort from overseas (about 5 per cent) – some for music, some not. School bus routes include villages towards Bristol and Bath (worth investigating which ones). Pupils confident and articulate, interested in each other and in the community of the school, including the juniors. Old Wellensians (or Old Wellies even) include businessman Roger Saul (founder of Mulberry), opera singer Sarah Fryer, portrait painter Justin Mortimer, Bruce Parry of BBC2s 'Tribe' and Olympic gold medallist Danny Nightingale.

Entrance: At 11 and 13; tests are held annually at the school on a Saturday in late January. Also at 14 to begin the two-year GCSE course; applicants are interviewed by the head and written tests may be set. Entry to sixth form subject to interview and at least 6 grade B passes at GCSE including the subjects to be taken at AS level where relevant. Those who wish to be auditioned as specialist musicians should enter for pre-audition before the January (auditions are held in January) of the year of entry. Those gaining music scholarships and bursaries are expected to be successful also in the relevant academic entry tests.

Exit: All expected to go on to higher education and many take a gap year to travel or work overseas. Diverse choices of subjects, approximately 20 per cent with places at music academies although the musicians are also encouraged to look at universities. Regular sprinkling (5-7 per annum) of places at Oxbridge. Very good careers unit in the library.

Money Matters: School is not well-endowed. 70 specialist music places are funded by DfES, awards are subject to parental means test. Choral scholarships but for some reason boys are entitled to up to 45 per cent off fees and girls only 10 per cent. Sons and daughters of clergy may qualify for a 10 per cent bursary. Internal scholarships are offered to current pupils entering years 7, 9 and sixth form.

Remarks: The whole school feels very relaxed and perhaps, rather surprisingly for a place of work, cheerful. A school where you can have a lot of fun without jeopardising academic success.

WELLSWAY SCHOOL

Chandag Road, Keynsham, Bristol, BS31 1PH

Tel: 0117 986 4751
Fax: 0117 916 1039
E-mail: headteacher@wellsway.bathnes.sch.uk
Website: www.wellsway.bathnes.sch.uk/

- Pupils: 1,330 boys and girls • Ages: 11-19 • Size of sixth form: 275 • Christian • State • Open days: October

---

Head: Since 1995, Mr Paul Kent MA MPhil FRSA (fifties) married with 4 grown-up children. Studied English and postgraduate work in Shakespeare at Worcester College, Oxford, did an English degree and was an Oxford blue in Rugby. Previously head at Speedwell School, Bristol. Very much a hands-on head. Teaches, likes to be accessible and has achieved much during his energetic and caring reign. No money wasted on smartening offices and staff rooms. His study is noticeably devoid of computers, instead pupils' art, cartoons and mementoes displayed on vast noticeboard above his desk like a proud parent. Talks calmly but passionately – 'there's no such thing as a write-off with any child. I see my job as ensuring that relationships are open and trusting so young people will be safe and happy, and therefore achieve success.'

Academic Matters: Fine results for a non-selective school in a not solely middle class area. 75 per cent plus get 5 A*-Cs at GCSE. 70 per cent stay on for sixth form and get 50-60 per cent A/B. Investor in Careers awarded 1999. Investors in People awarded 1998 and re-awarded 2000.

Very strong departments led by specialist staff. Sound provision for statemented pupils.

Games, Options, The Arts: Sportsmark Gold in 1997 and re-awarded 2000 and 2004. Heaps of teams in all sports. Annual French trip for year 7, ski trip, water sport trip. World Challenge expeditions have been to Ecuador, South Africa and West Canada. Wellsway Challenge introduced in 2004 to Corsica.

Innovative and fabulous art department with 2 kilns; several looms produce vibrant textiles. Dedicated staff stay long after school hours to keep facilities open. Mad on musicals – staged Return to the Forbidden Planet, Barnum, Grease, Guys & Dolls, Billy, Cabaret, My Fair Lady, Animal Farm.

Background and Atmosphere: A once thriving market town between Bath and Bristol, Keynsham is a town of churches – 5 Anglican, 1 Baptist and 1 Methodist, denoting its past trade wealth. East of the River Chew are the villages of Compton Dando, Corston, Marksbury, Newton St Loe, Priston and Saltford whose residents get a place at Wellsway, formed in 1971 when Keynsham's grammar and secondary modern schools merged.

A spacious campus amongst green fields is cheek by jowl with Chandag Junior & Infant Schools. Highly motivated staff aged 22 to 60 seems far less frantic than most at large comprehensives. 38 of them have own children here and the relationship between staff and pupils is that of a close-knit village school. Christian ethos prevails. Unauthorised absence virtually nil. Bulletin boards bursting with news or press cuttings of ex-pupils making local headlines.

Pastoral Care and Discipline: Policies on everything from asthma to child protection. School rules insist that anyone being bullied report it. Comes down ton-of-bricks on anti-social or violent behaviour and nips any incident in the bud by locating pupil's parent instantly. A counsellor is on staff. Sixth formers become 'buddies' to any year 7 who request one and may coach sports/share lunch and chat/solve bigger problems.

Pupils and Parents: Local business folk, many Old Girls'/Boys' kids, every class and creed. Very loyal. A weekly newsletter keeps parents well-informed and asks parents to monitor homework and control absence. Uniform of black blazer/trousers for boys and bottle-green pullover/skirt or black trousers for girls worn quite tidily. Strong on community service and raising funds for charities.

Entrance: Over-subscribed. Wellsway serves Keynsham (to the east of the River Chew), Chelwood Village, Compton Dando, Corston, Marksbury, Newton St Loe, Priston and Saltford. Children from within this area whose older sibling will be attending the school on the admission date come first, followed by other children from the area, then other siblings. 5 Cs at GCSE preferred for sixth form entrance.

Exit: 70 per cent of GSCE pupils continue on to sixth form here, 7 per cent to education elsewhere. After A levels most to universities eg Cardiff, West of England, Plymouth, Bristol, Cheltenham, Birmingham, Leeds, Loughborough, Manchester, Nottingham, Oxbridge. A few to a gap year or employment and a sprinkle to art foundation or drama school.

Remarks: Confident pupils with high expectations well prepared for life. Loveliest bunch of teachers in the county.

WESTBOURNE SCHOOL

Linked to Westbourne Lower and Upper School in the Junior section

50 Westbourne Road, Sheffield, South Yorkshire, S10 2QQ

Tel: 0114 266 0374
Fax: 0114 267 6518
E-mail: jhicks@westbourneschool.co.uk
Website: www.westbourneschool.co.uk

• Pupils: 296 boys and girls, all day • Ages: 4-16 • Non-denom • Fees: £1,800 - £2,500 • Independent • Open days: Mid October

Head: Since 2004, Mr John Hicks MEd (forties). Educated at Archbishop Holgate Grammar, York and Exeter University before completing his postgraduate Masters at Kingston University. Previously head of Upper Secondary and Head of Campus at the International School of the Regents, Thailand, which taught the UK National Curriculum. Prior to that was deputy head at Durston House in west London and senior master at Parkside. Still teaches maths to seniors and coaches sport. We look forward to seeing at first hand how things settle down under the new regime.

Academic Matters: School is non-selective intake and tinies with learning problems are well looked after. Two in-house dyslexia teachers who work on a 'federal basis' ie the parents pay; otherwise dyslexia support across the board (and free). Will 'never ask a child to leave' but may not take on a child who requires more learning support than that year and class teacher can handle ie if it alters 'the balance of a particular class'. Recent foray into GCSE gave excellent results across the board (bearing in mind the pupil profile) and this year's syllabus will be even wider. Tiny classes: max 16, a 32 strong year group will be divided into two lots of 16. Computers all over the shop – no-one is afraid to put their hand up. Streamed at 11.

Outstanding French language teaching throughout, French starts at reception and by the time children reach the French department in the senior school they are taught French in a French café – complete with little round tables and café-type chairs – no Pernods for authenticity. Spanish at 11. Science from 8/9 and dedicated labs in both buildings, taken either as single subjects or dual awards at GCSE (and labs in senior school smashing – junior school not that bad either). Ten subjects the norm. GCSE early if 'appropriate'. ICT, the humanities, music, drama, DT and PE are options. Longevity in the staff is amazing, but offset by a much younger intake.

Games, Options, The Arts: Two tiny playgrounds, one covered, make do for in-house games, otherwise much use is made of local facilities: Abbeydale, Don Valley, and Rotherham Valley Country Park. Rugby, football, sailing, canoeing etc. The school hires coaches though they have a smaller clutch of their own.

Stunning art in both sectors; excellent drama, and in the recent Midsummer Night's Dream, held in the garden of the senior school (which has a fab outdoor theatre with raised seating above – think Bryanston), eight of the staff – of both sexes – were fairies. Adds a totally new dimension. GCSE music started in 2005 – lots of individual tuition and an orchestra. And masses of noise. Loads of trips everywhere, at most age groups, all over. Excellent use made of local activities and a recent trip to the Bradford Interfaith Centre, with visits to the cathedral, the mosque and both a Sikh and a Hindu temple caused enormous interest, with pupils learning how to play the Indian drums (tablas) with Sukvinder Singh who taught George Harrison.

Background and Atmosphere: School founded around 1885 by a Mrs Whitfield as a boys-only prep school, the actual date is uncertain as Gaffer Johnson who was head in 1941, terrified that Hitler was about to invade, burnt all the school records. (He also used to quell unruly youngsters by taking out his glass eye and polishing it on his hanky.) Took girls in 1998 and went up to 16 in 2000. The original prep school composed of three Victorian buildings – very nooky and cranny, with staircases everywhere, much revamped, with good tinies' wing, and sensible classrooms for every discipline further up. The senior school is a fantastic late Georgian building plumb opposite, with a garden to die for (think grand Philadelphia – well it was an offshoot of the local Botanic Garden – listed garden, so no games). House has been totally rearranged, with brand new staircase leading everywhere (but without a lift, which may prove to be an expensive oversight with the equal opportunities for the disabled legislation – careless). Wish list includes sports hall – this may well happen, and there are designs which we saw, but conservation area equals not a lot of room for inspired architecture. Breakfast for all on arrival – Fridays is bonanza day with a cooked brekky from 8am and late waiting for littles till 6/6.15pm (the end of prep). CHAMPS sports camp throughout the holidays, run by one of the dedicated sports masters – open to all, it shares the uni sports fields and equipment.

Pastoral Care and Discipline: God not top of the list, head is agnostic, but comparative religion taught throughout and, says school, mutual respect reinforced daily. PSHE taught throughout. Strict on behaviour, drugs and smoking. If difficulties and trouble persist, will weigh up previous conduct, if OK, then a spot of leniency, otherwise – out. Drugs equals out anyway.

Pupils and Parents: Mainly middle class, not a huge number of ethnic minorities (Sheffield isn't high in these). No overt facilities for Ramadan, no Halal fare in the dining room. Late waiting for tinies = after-school facilities. Charming uniform for girls plus blazers, boys equally smart in grey jackets. Pupils incredibly polite, stand up, say sir – both sexes.

Entrance: Children taken at any time, at any age but waiting lists now the norm. Absolutely non selective intake into junior school, first come, first served. Assessment into senior school, via CE, child visits school and both child and school assess what they thought of each other. Four fifths of the junior school go through to the senior school, with more joining at 11 or 13. The school is fully booked at pre-prep level until 2007.

Exit: Not all go on to the senior school at 13, though progressively more do; otherwise (as Westbourne started life as a primarily boys' prep school) there is a slight trickle away to Oundle, Uppingham, Repton and Trent. 'Girls are so far staying,' and other girls from local schools joining for senior school. Post-GCSE and still early days here, almost all into further education, Birkdale, Worksop, sixth form or agricultural colleges.

Money Matters: Schols available for years 7 and 9.

Remarks: The prep school ethos is still important here, but the stunning new senior school with its non-selective intake has a niche market in the area. This is a school which 'aspires to educating children for life'.

WESTLANDS SCHOOL AND TECHNOLOGY COLLEGE

Westlands Lane, Torquay, Devon, TQ1 3PE

Tel: 01803 400 660
Fax: 01803 408 897
E-mail: cabarr@westlands.torbay.sch.uk
Website: www.westlandstc.com

• Pupils: 1,400 boys and girls • Ages: 11-18 • Size of sixth form: 250 • Non-denom • State

Head: Since 1995, Mr Michael TH Stewart TD BEd AdvDipEdMan FIMgt FRSA (fifties). A Sussex University graduate. MPhil from East Anglia University; Open University advanced management diploma. Taught in various comprehensives. Positions include head of ICT and maths departments; deputy head and education officer for a spell. Quietly confident, competent and successful. Aims to turn out all-rounders who leave to become 'responsible well-adjusted citizens with a caring attitude to others.' Former member of TA for 27 years. Married with two children; one achieved a first class honours degree after being educated at Westlands.

Academic Matters: Lots of opportunities to develop individual talents. Depending on performance, pupils can migrate between two grammar-stream sets and six non-selective ones. Varied abilities however, are reflected in overall results. Top-stream pupils and parents believe the more relaxed atmosphere leads to higher grades – 'it's a less pressurised environment than some grammar schools where bulimia and anorexia can prevail'. Popular A level choices are English, maths, art, history and geography. Other courses include NVQ business studies, GNVQs, BTEC public services course. Mr Stewart equally proud of university undergraduates leaving with two Es or four As at A level. 'The school places enormous emphasis on the individual, ensuring their education and well-being are closely monitored.'

Dedicated partially-hearing unit with well-qualified staff provides extra tuition where needed. Otherwise, partially-hearing students wear hearing aids and are fully integrated into lessons. 'Teachers really seem to care above and beyond their call of duty,' say parents, and some have voluntarily learnt to sign to improve communication.

Games, Options, The Arts: Facilities to boast of – impressive soundproof media/recording studio, five ICT rooms, two drama practice rooms, dance studio, eight music rooms. Multi-purpose, sports and drama production halls. Large, well-stocked and organised library, ample computers. Uses neighbouring public swimming pool and tennis courts. Extensive sporting and extra-curricular opportunities including DJ skills, first aid, various music clubs, astronomy, aerobics, girls' football, dance. County successes in chess, rugby (Harlequins), athletics. Cricket is definite strength, lots of cup wins. Outstanding success in D of E and Ten Tors. Up and coming orchestra – first UK tour in 2003. Family-to-family exchange arrangement with French school proving popular.

Background and Atmosphere: The school doors open early and shut late. There is always something happening so pupils can and do enjoy school life to the full – important to the pupils and achieved by most. Perhaps not the world's calmest sea but a place replicating a real and normal community, where politeness is usual, and the high standards of bright and exceptionally able students entwine with the talents of slower developers. 'Pupils are proud of their new school and generally care about it,' say parents.

A technology college since September 2002, it began in 1973 with the amalgamation of two high schools. One of four bilateral schools in country. Completed rebuild in 2001, a 'breath of fresh air' say its hardworking and dedicated teachers. Hi-tech security system, with cameras in corridors and classrooms, helps to eradicate any disruptive behaviour that can creep in on occasion (extreme mixes in social backgrounds here). Everyone is screened before entering through electronic doors. Students encouraged to see themselves as part of community by taking school band to elderly people's homes, organising charity fund-raising events, helping in special schools (sixth formers).

Pastoral Care and Discipline: School's teaching ethos includes social training, although tireless efforts are not always rewarded. 'I hated my old school; everyone is friendlier at Westlands and I now enjoy going. The staff and pupils treat you as an individual and with respect.' Westlands' excellent pastoral care has resulted in Investors in People, Healthy School, Investors in Careers and School Achievement awards. In-house education welfare officer helps abate truancy. Few expulsions in current head's reign. An air of leniency and forgiveness for one-off misdemeanours. No smoking on-site for teachers and students alike. 'The dedicated parent telephone line is extremely useful', say parents, 'you can always speak with someone if necessary.'

Pupils and Parents: Two nationally designated 'deprivation wards' situated within Westlands' catchment area means pupils come from both ends of social scale – they mix happily.

Entrance: Foundation school since 2003, therefore responsible for own admissions via common admissions process. Students achieving high enough 11+ scores awarded one of 60 selective (grammar) places; usually from Torbay. 150 comprehensive places filled by students from St Marychurch, Babbacombe and Ellacombe areas of Torquay. Pupils living outside Westlands' catchment area still eligible and parental preference is acceded to wherever possible.

Exit: 10 per cent of sixth form enters from outside. 80 per cent of year 11 continue at Westlands with its 26 available courses, 12 per cent go to South Devon College, others to armed forces, public services or work placements. Up to 80 per cent to university – mainly at Plymouth, Exeter, Swansea, Bristol, Southampton. Popular choices: media, biology, business management, communication.

Remarks: Enormous scope and opportunity. Pupils feel accepted here no matter what their social background.

WESTMINSTER SCHOOL

17 Dean's Yard, London, SW1P 3PB

Tel: 020 7963 1003
Fax: 02079 631 006
E-mail: headmaster@westminster.org.uk
Website: www.westminster.org.uk

• Pupils: 615 boys; 120 girls all in sixth form; 470 day boys, 145 boarders; 85 day girls, 35 boarders • Ages: 13-18 (but a few Westminster Assisted Places from 11, see below)
• Size of sixth form: 367 • C of E • Fees: Day £5,321, sixth form £5,771; boarding £7,316 • Independent • Open days: Autumn for sixth form; 13+ entry tours arranged by appointment throughout the year

Head Master: Since 2005, Dr Stephen Spurr MA DPhil, previously at Clifton. Educated King's, Canterbury and Sydney Grammar School. Studied classics at Sydney and Oxford. Early career as university academic, teaching classics at Oxford, Rome and Australian national universities, followed by 15 years at Eton, becoming housemaster and head of classics. Married with two children. Gently spoken and thoughtful.

Academic Matters: Stunning results (and so they should be). Huge amount of, mostly self-imposed, academic pressure (some students choose to sit extraordinary numbers of high level, high maintenance subjects – and get As).

Hard to pick out individual subjects for special praise, so many get gleaming results. Maths dept stunning but all other depts outstanding with some extraordinary teaching in each; science (school produces doctors by the ward-ful) modern languages, classics – all brilliant. Wacky intellectuals among the staff, with 32 per cent females. Saturday morning school. Fabulous science laboratories, round the corner in former Imperial Tobacco HQ. Several new young staff. Entire school is wired up and fully networked. Glorious library – a series of rooms, where the atmosphere has been transformed from gentleman's club to superb resource.

Games, Options, The Arts: Good art (facilities have just been expanded), also music – new music centre opened in 2005. Good orchestra, operas, musicals, concerts – masses of talent. Terrific drama – 17 productions last year, an average of one every two weeks of the term. Latest acquisition is the Millicent Fawcett Hall nearby, now revamped as a studio theatre – always in use with new productions – house plays, school plays or just individuals with unaccountable spare time putting something on out of enthusiasm. Debating highly successful in national and international competitions, Model United Nations, chess and other intellectual sports perennially popular. Tuesday and Thursday afternoons for sports: water sports and fencing both successful (fencing unbeaten in six years); cricket and football, however, inconsistent. Many other sports, including fives, rock climbing. Big on trips abroad – India, Mexico, Russia, Paris among others.

Background and Atmosphere: Glorious and historic buildings, something of a rabbit warren in parts. Umbilically tied to Westminster Abbey, where school services are held twice a week, and Latin prayers once a week (Wednesdays). Founded in 1560 by Queen Elizabeth I, following her father's provision for forty King's Scholars at the Abbey (whose privileges still include queue-jumping Commons debates). Under the patronage of the Abbey, the Dean is the chairman of the governors, and the school is very much in the glare of the world. Beyond the calm of Dean's Yard lies a warren of buildings, some very ancient, often anything but calm – noisy, scruffy, seething with pupils and staff coming and going, not to mention goggling tourists. Dormitories in boys' houses recently refurbished. Liberal tradition alive and well, without much structure beyond the classroom for boarders (staff disagree). Day pupils leave at 5, 6 or 9pm – but this feels like a boarding school, which it is. No bells. Lunch is a ten-minute affair. Library now an inspirational place to work in.

Pastoral Care and Discipline: Previous head made determined efforts to organise more on the pastoral care front, with tutors meeting tutees every week, over lunch. Bullying given high profile, head hears of every case – 6 or 7 when previous head arrived, now down to 2, creating a culture where boys can talk to housemasters and say, 'I don't like what's going on'. School counsellor on hand. Recent leaver says, 'in other schools you'd get picked on if you're different or if you work or are thought to be a nerd – none of that's an issue here.' High profile break-outs occasionally but, perhaps, par for the course in this high octane establishment.

Pupils and Parents: Some things don't change – boys are street smart; they are highly articulate, quick, sometimes over-confident, often nervously brilliant, with a reputation of being difficult to teach (also to have at home), they can be mocking and irreverent. Also, they can be charming, considerate and sophisticated. Large numbers with one or more parents from abroad; bilinguals in profusion; rich Middle Easterners; heavy middle class intelligentsia – the moneyed and the hopelessly stretched – and the offspring of ambitious yuppies, media and city, all professions, broken homes, also two-income, suburban, plus computer and chess geniuses. Day boys need (but don't always have) supportive solid family. Girls come in from both London day schools – Godolphin and Latymer, St Paul's, Francis Holland etc – and from boarding schools – Wycombe Abbey, Woldingham etc – for subjects, for teaching, for a social life. Tend to be well-heeled, confident, capable, bright and gel quickly. OWs include six prime ministers, the original William Hickey, Warren Hastings, Sir John Gielgud, Peter Brook, Angus Wilson, Stephen Poliakoff, Tony Benn, Ben Jonson, John Locke, A A Milne, Ruth Kelly, Dido etc etc etc.

Entrance: Still one of the most sought after schools in London. Put the name down at 10, boys weeded out at 11; interview and CE (highly competitive, minimum of 65 per cent). Large numbers of bright boys are encouraged to sit for scholarship (the Challenge) even if they don't have a real chance, thereby giving the school a more finely tuned exam to test able boys. 45 per cent come in from the Westminster Under School (same entry requirements apply). Entry at sixth form (for all candidates) – minimum five A grades at GCSE and a pass in at least six subjects, preferably A grades in A level subjects to be studied.

Exit: One and all to university, with around 75 or more – approximately 50 per cent – going to Oxbridge. London, Edinburgh, Bristol, Newcastle, UEA. Increasing number opting for American universities. All manner of subjects and careers. Gap year popular.

Money Matters: Money newly acquired - £1 million from old boy Michael Zilkha - for the benefit of the teaching staff – a terrific fillip. At 11 a number of Westminster Assisted Places tenable at the Under School from 11 and at the senior school to 18. At 13 eight Queen's scholarships per year - 50 per cent of fees, scholars must board - plus five music scholarships of up to half fees. Plus some means-tested bursaries at 13.

Remarks: To many – especially baffled tourists – it is astonishing that, metres away from the Mother of Parliaments, Big Ben, the Abbey and so on, is a school and that its buildings are almost anonymously integrated into the small, uncannily quiet streets around this unique city centre. Not a conventional school in any sense and not a convenient one – everything has to be walked – or run – to as the buildings and facilities are spread around but all possible facilities – above all superb teaching – are here and, for the right child, no better education is available in the country. An immense privilege no-one ever quite forgets.

WESTMINSTER TUTORS

Linked to David Game College

86 Old Brompton Road, South Kensington, London, SW7 3LQ

Tel: 020 7584 1288
Fax: 020 7584 2637
E-mail: info@westminstertutors.co.uk
Website: www.westminstertutors.co.uk

- Pupils: Between 30-100 depending on course and time of year
- Ages: 14-19 • Fees: per subject eg 1 A level is £4,650 per year
- Independent • Open days: Visitors welcome at all times

Head: Since 2000, Mr James Layland, BSc ARCS (early thirties), who shared the post with Mr Peter Brooke (who died Christmas 2001). A charming young man, something of a maverick, he was educated at Bluecoat School, Manchester, going on to study physics at Imperial (he got a first) and music at The Royal College of Music. He still plays the flute. Joined Westminster Tutors straight from Imperial, with which he maintains close links and where he helped to plan a new undergraduate course in maths. Giggly and fun, he makes teaching seem a breeze and learning a doddle.

Entrance: By interview

Remarks: Founded in 1934, this tiny (by London standards) tutorial is a very personal crammer and A level college. All ages and courses catered for, especially Common Entrance, GCSE and A levels. Staff are pulled in to teach the esoteric as well as the mundane. Easter, Christmas and half term revision courses and after school assistance all year round. Max class size seven (usually much smaller), plus lots of one to one and smaller seminars. Hours can be long, from 9am to 9pm if need be. IT training in the evenings (after work for grown-ups too) and intensive crash courses in French, German, Spanish, Italian and Chinese by native speakers. This is a really helpful, friendly crammer. Students from all over, usually, but not exclusively from the independent sector. They have use of the sports centre at Imperial College. No history of drugs or school drop-outs. Jolly bright rooms opposite Christie's, South Ken, with a good library and IT facilities and common rooms with running tea and coffee.

WESTONBIRT SCHOOL

Linked to Querns Westonbirt School in the Junior section

Westonbirt, Tetbury, Gloucestershire, GL8 8QG

Tel: 01666 880 333

Fax: 01666 880 364

E-mail: office@westonbirt.gloucs.sch.uk

Website: www.westonbirt.gloucs.sch.uk

• Pupils: 230 girls; 140 board, 90 day • Ages: 11-18 • Size of sixth form: 70 • C of E • Fees: Day £4,580; boarding £6,635 - £6,860 • Independent • Open days: Early October (Open Morning) & first Bank Holiday in May (Open Day)

Head: Since 1999, Mrs Mary Henderson MA PGCE (late forties). Educated at Berkhamsted as a day girl then read French at St Andrews and played lacrosse for Scotland. PGCE from Durham before teaching modern languages at Cheltenham Ladies' where she became a housemistress; spent four years at co-ed Warminster School before joining Westonbirt in 1996 as head of modern languages. No doubt that single sex education benefits girls. Married to retired senior lecturer from Bath University with whom she sings in local choirs and tours Europe. No children. In seventh heaven here enjoying 'sport, music and beautiful things'. Girls like and respect her as 'traditional without being old fashioned.' Genuine and candid manner; really caring – 'knows what makes girls tick' but prepared to get tough if necessary. Encourages girls to be 'keen' like her. Praises staff; touched by girls who say 'thank you.'

Academic Matters: Makes top 5 per cent in government 'value added' tables; 70-ish per cent A and B grades at A level; cheap comments about academic level should be ignored. More girls opting for science and unusually flexible timetable allows odd subject combinations. Successful art department, English popular too. Good results by smaller numbers in a range of other subjects. History buoyant; theatre studies popular but yet to achieve top grades. Latin still survives to GCSE and sometimes has takers at A level; similarly classical civilisation. RE compulsory through school but few takers for short course GCSE; many girls achieve marketable European Driving Licence qualification in ICT. Innovative Young Enterprise companies. Prep compulsory after supper for an hour and no upper limit for sixth formers who like study slots during day. One parent said school had 'transformed' his daughter and given her academic interest for first time – most parents thrilled at outcome. Cuddly EFL department accepts overseas girls without strong English and is successful at range of qualifications including IELTS for university entrance. Strong learning support includes two full and three part-timers working with a fifth of girls plus self-help access: mainly SpLD but a few dyspraxia and dyscalculia. Separate programme for talented and gifted.

Games, Options, The Arts: Sporty school: fabulous new sports centre including 25m indoor swimming pool, fitness room etc opened September 2005; lacrosse 'superb' and boasts American coach at present; regularly reach top eight nationally; girls have 'whale of a time' on triennial tour to USA; all play up to year 9 plus 50 older girls; similar numbers for tennis with year round coaching available; netball, rounders, squash and trampolining plus own nine hole golf course; hockey historically low key but gaining ground. Elite athlete runs PE and games; swimming, basketball and volleyball getting boost with futuristically designed pool and sports hall. School teams participate in local and national equestrian events – good links with nearby Beaufort polo club results in three teams; school sponsors annual Mini Horse Trials at local pony club; girls ride at local stables but no bringing Dobbin to school.

Handy connection with Leith's helped Westonbirt get in at start of prestigious five term cookery course still offered to only ten schools in UK; hadn't yet covered wine when we visited but at least girls knew that a white would go best with their tuna mousse.

Over half school learning musical instruments. 22 rehearsal rooms in outgrown music department; informal concerts in elegant Camellia House; two pipe organs to accompany élite chapel choir; jazz band and school orchestra perform less frequently. Drama centred around capacious Orangery theatre, dynamic drama department impacts strongly on timetable and extra-curricular activities. Three major productions annually; successes in local Bath festival and in speech and drama awards. We watched year 9 girls perform sensitively with masks under bubbly, imaginative direction.

Computer network points for sixth formers in study bed-rooms. Vast, interconnecting art studios lend themselves to large scale work whilst DT is surprisingly well resourced; seriously impressive furniture being built here alongside feats of small scale engineering. One recent leaver joined formula one racing team having built go-kart at school. Accredited careers department paying far more than lip service with key skills day. Work experience. Sound HE advice for girls – last two head girls getting army university scholarships. Malmesbury bookseller runs browseworthy bookshop. Good library for sixth but state rooms probably rather too daunting for younger readers; budget provides for new and interesting material but Jilly Cooper still popular.

Background and Atmosphere: Magnificent neo-Renaissance pile built for ludicrously wealthy Holford family (who also founded nearby arboretum at Westonbirt) at height of Victorian age. Apparently, Stanley Kubrick had eye on front entrance at one stage but change of mind denied girls sight of Tom Cruise on their doorstep. Fortunately imbued with excellent taste, Robert Holford spared no expense here and since 1928 school has been worthy cus-todian of the grade 1 listed building and ornamental gar-dens plus 250 acres of parkland. Some dorms exquisite with plum billet in Lady Holford's boudoir; individual dress-ing tables as well as wardrobes. Girls' lasting memories tend to be of delightful gardens rather than of marble columns, frescoes, glass ceilings and vast state rooms. De rigueur moans about being 'in middle of nowhere' don't need taking too seriously.

Friendly atmosphere with good balance of female and male staff – much more down to earth than you'd expect. Day girls can 'sleep over' once a week for free and some buy extra nights to be with friends. Delightful guiding tradi-tions survive eg vespers sung whilst stood around edge of Great Hall.

Classrooms huddle around former carriage and sta-bling courtyard making 35 minute lesson changes quicker than in most places. Discrete sixth form house above with two, well-appointed social areas is popular with older girls who customise their study bedrooms, do own laundry, eat and make snacks in ambiguously named 'piggery' plus smaller 'piglet' for coffee. Viewed from Italian garden, former gym is an eyesore waiting to be rebuilt more in keeping with environs. School food not an issue – own chef does good job. Some socialising with other schools. Popular shopping trips to Bath and Cheltenham. Senior girls can have own car at school. Own choice of dress in sixth and sensible worka-day cream blouse, maroon sweater and tartan skirt for remainder. Low church tradition – not dogmatic and lots of Christian giving to charities.

Pastoral Care and Discipline: Parents praise house staff for giving quality time to girls and having 'mature approach.' Counsellor comes regularly to lend confidential support; star of a chaplain whom 'girls really trust;' qualified nursing staff in sanatorium around clock. Fines for smoking offences (some girls are bound to get caught); glass of wine permitted to sixth formers for special occasions but never spirits; tough on drugs. Night-time high jinks avoided by alarmed doors and ex-policeman patrolling grounds with Alsatian. Overall, parents like measured approach to disci-pline which gets girls 'on side.'

Pupils and Parents: No riffraff but many parents having to make sacrifices. Appeal to sporty, creative and willing workers. Sociable, hearty girls; resilient yet sensitive, who look neat, happy and healthy; sit by houses at lunch with staff so no hiding eating disorders; boarders do twenty minutes' housework before breakfast. Draws from further afield in UK than many competitors and not overrun with international students; absence of bitchiness; different age groups and nationalities mix surprisingly well. Famous old girls include socialites Lady Emily Compton, Lady Sybilla and Lady Natasha Rufus-Isaacs as well as Georgia Byng, children's author.

Entrance: Common entrance at 11 and 13; own exam for those outside CE system and for sixth formers outside of GCSE system (otherwise 5+ GCSEs at A*-C are needed). Main feeders Beaudesert Park, Rose Hill, St Margaret's, Calne etc; London preps such as Thomas's and Garden House; provincial preps – Leaden Hall, Godstowe and increasingly from north including Scotland. Own prep and local primaries provide some day girls. Educational psychol-ogist's report required if special needs but only turned away if really unable to cope. 25 per cent overseas – many from Europe. All nationalities fit in remarkably well.

Exit: A few to co-ed boarding schools or day colleges after GCSE. Virtually all sixth form leavers to higher educa-tion. Possibly one or two to Oxbridge annually but generally going for wide range of courses at mixture of trad and new universities.

Money Matters: Scholarships and exhibitions offered at 11, 13 and 16 include academic, art, drama sport and music. 5 per cent sibling reductions; more for services, diplomatic and clergy daughters. Extras range from learning support to ballet.

Remarks: Turns out self-confident and accomplished young women. Few boarding schools (if any) can match set-ting; modern, unshockable head. Lovely atmosphere for treasured daughters.

WHITGIFT SCHOOL

Haling Park, South Croydon, Surrey, CR2 6YT

Tel: 020 8688 9222
Fax: 020 8760 0682
E-mail: hmspa@whitgift.co.uk
Website: www.whitgiftschool.net

- Pupils: 1,195 boys; all day • Ages: 10-18 • Size of sixth form: 275 • Non-denom • Fees: £3,541 • Independent • Open days: Open afternoons every week; open morning on the last Saturday in September

Head: Since 1991, Dr Christopher A Barnett MA DPhil (early fifties). Tip top intellectual credentials – read modern history at Oriel College, Oxford; doctorate also from Oxford. Worked as research assistant for an MP for several years before moving to Brunel University to lecture in economics, and then to school teaching. Head of history at Bradfield for almost a decade, then second master at Dauntsey's. Married to a psychotherapist. Three sons educated at Whitgift, and one daughter. Tall, commanding, serious and … die-hard horseracing aficionado. Races three horses, including 'Whitgift Rose'. Constantly striving to stretch, innovate and improve the school. Has done wonders thus far and has a seemingly inexhaustible stream of ideas waiting in the wings.

Academic Matters: Solidly entrenched in the higher reaches of the A level and GCSE league tables. Intensely high standards but, if you've passed the entrance exam,m you should cope. On top of English and maths, all boys are expected to do two languages and three sciences at GCSE. The excellent modern languages department offers Spanish, Italian, French, German, Mandarin Chinese and Japanese. Whitgift has the largest Japanese department of any British school – 33 GCSE A*s in 2003. There is also an unusual bilingual programme, offered in French and in German, and the school has introduced the International Baccalaureate programme as an optional alternative to A levels. 15 science labs, good DT centre with impressive workshops and welding equipment (more Arkwright Design Technology Scholarships have been won by Whitgift than by any other school). Huge recent investment in IT (2003-4). Class sizes average 18 (10 in the sixth form) with 25 maximum. Staff mostly young(ish), with 40 per cent women. School now tackling special needs more energetically and expertly than in past ('several of the school's ablest boys in this category,' says the head).

Games, Options, The Arts: Sport exceptional as befits a large, strong, competitive semi-London boys' school (with 27 rugby sides – including an 'E' team, 20 cricket teams and 16 hockey teams). Win county and national competitions in rugby, cricket and fencing, and are local honchos in hockey, athletics, swimming and football (two ex-professionals on the staff). Cricket particularly strong, with some expert coaching, and Surrey CC holds a Cricket Festival Week and four-day, first-class game at the school. Riding, golf, water polo and fives (on school's own court) also offered. Fabulous £9m sports complex – for many years a pipe dream – will be open by time of publication ('one of the wonders of the educational world!' says head). Development includes new indoor pool, 4 squash courts, fitness centre, conference room, kitchens, classrooms, plus vast sports hall. Astro pitch across the road.

Very high standards in the music department. Free lessons on a string instrument for all new pupils. Loads of orchestras, choirs, chamber groups, bands plus Whitgift's own 'Corp of Drums'. Some boys attend Saturday lessons at Trinity College of Music or the Royal Academy of Music and are members of the National Youth Orchestra. Whitgift hosts the Croydon Music Festival, one of Britain's largest, and the London Mozart Players have an association with the school, offering masterclasses, commissioning music and providing performance opportunities for pupils. Art less buzzy and inspection report recommended a strengthening of the position of creative subjects. Still, the art, pottery and photographic facilities are super and plenty of excellent work is being done. Next building project will see swimming pool/squash courts transformed into a performing arts centre. Head would like to bring professional actors to work in the school. Overseas expeditions for musicians, linguists, sportsmen and adventurers. CCF, outdoor pursuits and D of E on offer. Many and varied community service projects.

Background and Atmosphere: Founded 1596 by John Whitgift, Elizabeth I's last Archbishop of Canterbury. In 1931 moved to Haling Park, onetime home of Lord Howard of Effingham, Lord High Admiral of the fleet sent against the Armada. 45 acre oasis bordered by graceful upmarket residential area on one side and gritty central Croydon thoroughfare on other. Grounds designated as a 'site of scientific interest' so most of the acreage cannot be developed. Some eccentric touches. Prefects range around in royal purple gowns. Legendary central quad has topiary in shape of red squirrels (their furry counterparts are bred in cages here) and freely rampaging peacocks (soothing to look at until they open their mouths: 'they can be a pain during exams,' said one boy). Junior section nicely separated from main school buildings and eerily silent when we visited with well-behaved hard-working boys. Compact dining room serves the boys who eat in two shifts, many of them bringing packed lunches.

Pastoral Care and Discipline: Zero tolerance of drugs, including cannabis. Head excluded 25 boys in his second year at Whitgift, which sent a clear message. 'Head is big on discipline' said the boys. Bullying, alcohol, dyed hair, 'excessive laziness' – all forbidden. Boys tend to arrive early (breakfast served from 7.30am) and leave at 3.45pm, unless they have sporting commitments at school. Sixth form common room an expanse of exposed steel and grey floors. 'They don't give us that much stuff because we'll just wreck it,' explained a pupil solemnly. Two boys recently expelled for mobile phone theft.

Pupils and Parents: Pretty good social mix thanks to bursary scheme, but funds no longer doled out as liberally as they once were (see Money Matters). Around 25 per cent ethnic minorities but no provision for helping pupils with English as a second language. Most boys fall within the London day school species, homo boffinus – this is not a hive of eccentric creative rebels – and many are notably mature and focussed. Astonishing geographical range for a day school: some from across the road, others via rail (South or East Croydon Station) from Surrey (Brighton!), Kent, West and East Sussex, North London. One bus delivers boys from Epsom. OBs: Cricketer Raman Subba Row, actor Martin Jarvis, Professor Sir Bernard Crick, WWII pilot 'Cats Eyes' Cunningham.

Entrance: Via report, interview and examination, with emphasis on the latter (taken in January in maths, English and verbal reasoning). Five applicants for each place. Commitment matters – places are most likely to go to persistent, keen, bushy-tailed families who make Whitgift their first choice. Takes just under 100 ten-year-olds and the same number of 11-year-olds. Another 30 boys cobbled on at age 13, and there is an intake at 16. Not on radar screens for many trad preps where all boys stay on to 13. Head not a fan of 13+ entrance, 'When they come at 11, they are a long way from public exams and have time to stretch themselves.' Half the pupils come from state primaries, half from preps. Main feeders are Elmhurst, Cumnor House (in Croydon, not the E Sussex prep), Downsend, Homefield, Oakhyrst Grange and several strong local primaries. Dizzyingly large catchment area of more than 1,000 square miles.

Exit: Up to 25 per cent a year to Oxbridge – history and Japanese the top subjects. Then London, Nottingham, Sheffield and Birmingham, in that order. A very few pupils leave after GCSE 'to pursue more career-orientated options'. Handful of the least academic pupils allowed to continue into sixth term 'on probation' with final decision about their viability made after first term in lower sixth.

Money Matters: Once the primary beneficiary of the Whitgift Foundation's largesse, with up to 40 per cent of pupils receiving financial assistance, the school has increasingly had to share with nearby boys' school, Trinity, and more recently, with the girls' academic power house, Old Palace. Bursaries now more limited in number and fraught with competition. Still, thanks to the Whitgift Foundation, Croydon remains an excellent area in which to be clever but poor. Scholarships for candidates of outstanding merit also on offer for boys entering at 10, 11, 12 or 13. All boys automatically entered for scholarship and bursary schemes when they sit entrance test. Awards also for music, art, technology, sport and all-rounders.

Remarks: Superb, academic, cosmopolitan, boys' school, with reasonable prices, and peacocks and red squirrels to boot. Almost makes it worth moving to Croydon.

WIGMORE HIGH SCHOOL

Ford Street, Wigmore, Leominster, Herefordshire, HR6 9UW

Tel: 01568 770 323
Fax: 01568 770 917
E-mail: admin@wigmorehigh.hereford.sch.uk
Website: not applicable

• Pupils: 270 boys, 225 girls; all day • Ages: 11-16 • Non-denom • State

Head: Since 2005, Mr Andrew Shaw BSc PGCE NPQH. Previously worked in Worcester and Gloucester as well as Jersey and Staffordshire. Enjoys all sports but especially football (less so now 'my body can't stand it!') squash and golf, and reading. Has firm belief that all children should have the opportunity to achieve.

Academic Matters: Results are well above the national average for similar schools, with 85+ per cent of the children achieving five or more GCSEs at A* to C. Friendly, committed teachers (very few leave) and a high expectation from the children, with focused, well-run classes. All children tested on entry. Setting from year 8 to year 11. Exemplary special needs support.

Games, Options, The Arts: At a time when the large majority of state schools have thrown in the sponge with organised games and flogged off the pitches for building, Wigmore rightly prides itself on the range and scope of what its children can do and looks instead to extend them. Excellent pitches and hard play area (six tennis courts) adjacent to school, with regular soccer, netball, hockey, tennis, cricket, basketball and athletics matches, and a number go on to play at county level. Wonderful sports hall and attached fitness room. Good art. Well-equipped music school, with 130 receiving tuition in up to 25 different options. Superb drama – zippy musicals involving 150 children and staff. Excellent IT provision with loads of computers. The library is not overstuffed with impressive-looking books that nobody reads but is attractive and simple and is, above all, full of children reading for enjoyment.

Background and Atmosphere: Classic sixties secondary modern, which converted to comprehensive in 1973, and is, with its attached Portakabins, no beauty, but is much redeemed by its position in the pretty village of Wigmore, which nestles in the north Herefordshire hills, and by the state-of-the-art sports hall and brand new science and modern foreign language centre. It has a cheerful, calm and happy atmosphere, combining freedom with a sense of community. Children are proud to succeed and don't mind showing it. They say, 'we can talk to teachers about anything...' 'the teachers trust us...' 'teachers know everyone...' 'the head knows all the kids...' 'people are looked up to for whatever talent they have.' Who wouldn't fit in? Someone who didn't appreciate anyone else and didn't want to do well.

Pastoral Care and Discipline: Form tutors stay with year group for five years and there is a good level of pupil monitoring. Strong emphasis on leadership and a well-run prefectorial system ensures that most children get a shot at it. It engenders, and expects from its children, a high degree of trust – there are no locked doors or lockers – and belongings can be left anywhere. A strong sense of right and wrong, backed by peer pressure, ensures that they stay there. Head sets exacting standards of behaviour but is very supportive of those with problems, and will not give up on any child, however challenging to the system.

Pupils and Parents: Anyone and everyone; the result is a cheerful, homogeneous mix. There is a solid core of children from the predominately farming and agriculture-related community but the school is popular too with the professional classes and it has its share of lawyers, doctors, dentists, estate agents and business people, who give much impetus and know-how to the governing body. Not all the children are sophisticated and, inevitably, there are one or two rough diamonds but generally they are friendly and

courteous. The positive ethos produces confident, articulate young people, who have an excellent attitude to their work and each other.

Entrance: It is truly comprehensive (there are approx. 75 special needs children on the register, of whom approx 25 are statemented) and it takes all who wish to come. It draws children from the whole of north Herefordshire but, unsurprisingly, it is considerably oversubscribed (local estate agent reports that it has put 5 per cent on house prices locally), and those on the fringes of the catchment area where there are other alternatives may be told to look elsewhere.

Exit: The large majority go on to do A/S levels at sixth form college, mainly in Ludlow or Hereford. One or two go on to independent schools. A significant minority will do apprenticeships.

Remarks: Wigmore rightly enjoys its good local reputation. This is a school that really does its best for, and gets the best from, a mixed bunch of kids and affords a range of opportunities that is not normally available in the state system. If all maintained schools were as good as this one, there would be little point in an independent sector.

WILLIAM ELLIS SCHOOL

Highgate Road, London, NW5 1RN

Tel: 020 7267 9346

Fax: 020 7284 1274

E-mail: tanton@williamellis.camden.sch.uk

Website: www.williamellis.camden.sch.uk

- Pupils: 870 boys, all day • Ages: 11-18 • Size of sixth form: 1,250 in a consortium of four schools, 'La Swap' • Non-denom • State

Head: Since 2002, Mr Richard Tanton BA (forties), previously head of Westminster City School. A trainee teacher at William Ellis in the early 1980s, and has since taught at Highbury Grove, Gladesmore and Archbishop Tenison's. Married to Sue, also a teacher, has three children and lives in Potters Bar. A passionate cricket, football and rugby fan, and has run the London marathon six times. A good leader, who has already strengthened some of the weaker areas of the school. 'He has lots of energy,' said a parent. 'And I was impressed that he has no truck with the culture of it not being cool to work. He encourages the boys to excel.'

Academic Matters: National average in value-added and absolute terms (ie quite good for the borough). A large percentage of its lower ability pupils achieved good KS3 SATs levels in 2003. The improvement is not so marked at GCSE, though around half the pupils get at least five A* – C grades – a very creditable result, given the student profile, and above the national average for boys (shows up well in value-added for this stage). Few boys leave the school without qualifications.

Sixth form is the 'La Swap' consortium – value-added not special here, but OK. The La Swap system can result in large classes with a wide range of ability, but it gives students a good choice of subjects, ranging from Health and Social Care GNVQ to Critical Thinking AS level and law A level, and results are at or above the national average.

Maths is a particular strength; 'The top set always does GCSE in year 10 and always does well.' Good English results, too. A specialist language college, but although there are several languages on offer, and a good take-up rate, the results are among the schools' weakest. They are, however, improving, with a stable set of teaching staff in place. Pupils here, unlike those at non-specialist schools, all try two languages and are not allowed to give up both at 14, but may be directed to vocational rather than academic courses. Talented linguists can take one language GCSE in year 10 and another in year 11, and the La Swap consortium offers a good range of languages, including Mandarin, to A level. There is also a range of vocational subjects on offer, and the head is keen to increase these options lower down the school. 'We value the vocational as well as the academic, and some boys will want to do both pathways, ending up with a good mixed portfolio of GCSEs and vocational qualifications. When boys are on a pathway where they know they can succeed they will work harder.'

Mixed ability teaching in year 7, in classes of 25, with setting from year 8 for languages and year 9 for maths and science. 'Setting too early could have a deleterious effect, as SATs results from primary schools can be misleading, so we like to let them settle. But we have some very bright boys who could cope with a fast pace from the start.' 'At the beginning of year 8 we felt our son was very bored,' said a parent. 'But we talked to his form teacher, who was very responsive.'

The Gifted and Talented programme includes summer courses for able year 6s about to join the school, a performance programme for musicians, and extension clubs in maths, sciences and languages. Talented mathematicians can be put up for university summer schools, maths days at colleges and enter Global Maths Challenges. The school devises an alternative curriculum of individual, intensive support programmes for boys who are struggling academ-

ically. 'The younger boys, in particular, can misbehave if they don't have the academic skills to cope with the curriculum. We like to work on that intensively early on.' A recent Ofsted report commented: 'The school does identify and support ... disadvantaged students well'.

Classes keep the same form teacher throughout. There are twice-yearly academic review days where boys, parents and teachers talk about assessments and set targets. 'They are a very dedicated bunch of teachers who have a good grip on each child and what to expect of him,' said a parent. 'I've always had a good sense of their ambitions for my son, and they've always been high.' Other parents comment that while staff expectations vary, 'there are a lot of young, committed male teachers who are very good role models for the boys.'

Games, Options, The Arts: A sporty school, with the usual range of clubs and fixtures and an enviable location on the edge of Hampstead Heath. The new sports hall, on the site of the old gymnasium, includes full-size basketball and badminton courts. The school uses the running track and sports pitches on the Heath, but its own outdoor space is limited to some small tarmac five-a side pitches. The head is negotiating, however, for the use of a sports field directly behind the school, owned by the Corporation of London and at present used purely for exercising police dogs.

Good, well-equipped, very lively music department. Joint orchestra with Parliament Hill girls' school next door, plus jazz and rock bands and singing groups. 'The music tends towards the popular rather than the classical, but it's very buzzy and a lot of fun for the boys,' said a parent. 'I was terribly impressed by the Christmas concert,' said another. The recent highly-praised production of Five Guys Named Mo, in conjunction with the Roundhouse, is one of several in the pipeline. 'There were 35 boys up there singing and dancing and absolutely loving it,' said a parent.

Year 7s visit the school's converted water mill in Surrey for an outdoor pursuits week. It is also the site of biology and geography field studies and extension weekends. Ski trips and plenty of language trips abroad, plus annual study trips to Russia, Spain and China.

Background and Atmosphere: Founded in 1862 in Gospel Oak by businessman William Ellis, who wanted children to be taught 'useful' subjects like science instead of rote learning, the school moved to its present site on the edge of Hampstead Heath in 1937. Recent building work – funded, astonishingly, by £4.5m from the DfES – has produced a new science and technology building plus arts and media studies rooms and sports hall. 'It's very much a community school,' said a parent. 'It's small and very local and the teachers know the boys very well.'

Pastoral Care and Discipline: 'It's quite a tough school,' said a parent. 'But it's a very happy one – the boys really enjoy being there and they feel safe.' Ofsted commented that pastoral support is a major strength of the school. On-call teachers are on hand to deal with disruptions in the class-rooms and there are CCTVs to keep an eye out for trouble-makers elsewhere. 'We do our best to get as much information as possible about the boys from their primary schools,' says the head. 'We ask what strategies worked and didn't work, so we're equipped to deal with them when they start here.' Not much bullying, by all accounts, and the school deals with it well.

The school celebrates effort and achievement with termly presentation assemblies and a prize evening in the summer term. Boys are rewarded with treats such as trips to see Lord of the Rings on its opening day or activity afternoons. 'They have an incentive to work hard and behave well,' commented a parent approvingly.

Pupils and Parents: Pupils come from a staggering 76 countries, including Afghanistan, Zimbabwe, Venezuela, Ecuador, Sierra Leone, Mauritius, Slovakia, Somalia and Kosovo. Mainly from families of neighbouring manual workers, with a few from the liberal middle classes, including some well-known political and legal families. OBs include rock guitarist Mark Bedford, journalist David Aaronovitch, England cricketer Freddie Titmus and scientist David Deitch.

Entrance: Around 550 applicants for 123 places. Admission criteria: (i) a brother in the school (ii) musical ability – there are 12 music places, chosen without audition (iii) a family connection (iv) location – in practice, within about half a mile. Takes eight statemented children a year.

Exit: About 75 per cent stay on to do A levels or vocational courses at La Swap. Of these, about 75 per cent move on to further or higher education, to do a huge range of courses at a huge range of old and new universities, including three or four a year to Oxbridge.

Money Matters: Has done well out of the DfES for building funds, and is voluntary aided by the William Ellis and Birkbeck Schools Trust, but otherwise is as hard up as most other state schools.

Remarks: Small north London comprehensive with a community feel, and bright, dedicated staff who do their best to tailor-make the work for each boy. Committed to rewarding effort and achievement and, despite the best efforts of some disruptive elements, creating a culture that values hard work, enterprise and success.

WIMBLEDON HIGH SCHOOL

Linked to Wimbledon High School Junior School in the Junior section

Mansel Road, London, SW19 4AB

Tel: 020 8971 0900

Fax: 02089 710 901

E-mail: info@wim.gdst.net

Website: www.gdst.net/wimbledon

• Pupils: 567 girls, all day • Ages: 11-18 • Size of sixth form: 150 • Non-denom • Fees: Junior £2,383; senior £3,063 • Independent • Open days: October

Head: Since 2001, Mrs Pamela Wilkes BEd (fifties), did her BEd at Hull University in history and theology. Previous schools include Malvern Girls' and Sutton Coldfield Girls' Grammar, where she was deputy head for 14 years. Came mid academic year after her predecessor, Dr Clough, 'left to pursue her interests as an educationalist and to take on the challenge of running a school that had been put into special measures.' She readily admits it was a difficult time to take over but she now feels well ensconced (as parents would agree). Friendly, open and positive, parents describe her as 'caring and traditional, very concerned with nurturing a caring and respectful environment.' A no-nonsense head who is expected to change the school slowly and subtly. Keen for every girl to fulfil her potential academically and socially – wants the girls to make a difference when they go out into society and to be socially aware. Her aim is to 'remove barriers so that they can all fly.' Runs an 'at home' every fortnight for any parent to drop in without an appointment – nice idea.

Academic Matters: Academic but does cater for wider range of abilities than some other girls' senior schools in the surrounding areas. Continues to turn out good results; 100 per cent GCSE entrants achieving A*-C, over 80 per cent A* or A in English and maths. Girls entering year 10 are expected to study 10 or 11 GCSEs. Offers GCSE in PE since appointing new staff and one of few schools with GCSE option of food technology. Three separate sciences are available at GCSE as well as double award. Languages include French, Spanish, and German plus Latin (30 per cent uptake) and Greek. 1:1 interviews for GCSE selection to encourage breadth and balance.

School requires at least 7 grade Bs at GCSE level to study for A levels (although some departments prefer A grades or above in the subjects chosen at A levels). The head adds, 'over the last few years, all girls have surpassed the entry requirements so none have been asked to leave.' A level results overall very good – particular aptitude for maths and geography. Good provision for special needs with appointment of dedicated part-time member of staff. Class sizes are not small – about 28 up to GCSE (with smaller groups for GCSE and above). 13 full-time male members of staff (12 in the senior school and 1 in the junior school).

Games, Options, The Arts: Nursery Road playing fields (10 minutes walk from school) providing hard and Astroturf surfaces for netball, tennis, athletics and hockey with picturesque changing pavilion (original building used by the All England Tennis Club before it moved to Wimbledon Park Road). Several girls play for Surrey squads in tennis and netball. 25-metre swimming pool and fully equipped sports hall at school site. New sports club for year 10 upwards to include less traditional sports like karate. Excellent art department – arty girls make their way subsequently to Wimbledon Art School to do an art foundation year. IT well funded, keeping apace with technological developments. Thriving drama department with productions in modern and classical languages, some with the boys from King's College School. Numerous instrumental groups and choirs. Community service greatly encouraged and Duke of Edinburgh Awards. Fair selection of after-school clubs, particularly in sport, eg martial arts and trampolining.

Background and Atmosphere: Victorian redbrick buildings front Wimbledon Hill with tube and BR stations less than 10 minutes' walk away. Although quite cramped for space, new buildings are light and airy, trees have been planted and there is grass to sit on and chat. Steady programme of refurbishment. A new technology building opened summer 2005 and new performing arts centre due March 2006. Relaxed atmosphere, girls seem happy, polite and friendly. Strictly non-denominational. Assemblies run as a showcase of achievement.

Pastoral Care and Discipline: A high priority pastoral system ensures even greater care from tutors and year heads – some indications of stressing-out and bullying in the past with luck will be a thing of the past. Headmistress frequently shadows a pupil (randomly selected) for a day. Great idea – how many other heads would have the guts to do likewise? A house system has recently been implemented. Older girls already tutor younger. School rules are established through a referral system, which leads to a detention system – performing a helpful task. Three detentions and parents are involved. Pupils rarely asked to leave;

head believes all behaviour is causal and can therefore be dealt with.

Pupils and Parents: Big mix of parents, multi-cultural and multi-ethnic, but definite emphasis on professional (lawyers/accountants), company directors and academics. Thriving parents' association. Girls wear smart low-key predominantly navy uniform until mock GCSEs completed – then own clothes. Sixth formers mostly jeans and smart casual clothes – not scruffy and few designer labels.

Entrance: Selective at 11: tests involve English, maths and non-verbal reasoning plus interview. Looking for independent thinkers and girls with opinions. About 35 per cent intake from own junior school – remainder from local state primaries such as Bishop Gilpin and Hollymount First School and private schools including The Study and Kensington Prep (GDST primary). For sixth form entry, external applicants sit entrance assessments including data analysis, maths, English and a narrow-gauge IQ test in verbal and non-verbal reasoning. All applicants are interviewed. Places are usually conditional on candidates achieving A grades in their preferred A level subjects and at least C grades in all other subjects.

Exit: Most girls stay on for sixth form, handful leaves for boarding school (usually family tradition) or to other sixth forms (particularly if they have been at the school since their junior days). University choice tends to be quite selective: 10 or 12 usually go to Oxbridge, other universities include Durham, Edinburgh, Exeter, with Warwick becoming more popular, and London universities (particularly for medicine). Gap year very popular.

Money Matters: Some bursaries available per year plus scholarships at 11 and 16, also music scholarship at 11 and sixth form science scholarship from OG's endowment.

Remarks: Academic school with good results, not too pushy, although not a school for the daydreamer or non-motivated. Head looks set to keep the flag flying. Strengths of the school drawn from the atmosphere and friendships.

WINCHESTER COLLEGE

College Street, Winchester, Hampshire, SO23 9NA

Tel: 01962 621 100
Fax: 01962 621 106
E-mail: information@wincoll.ac.uk
Website: winchestercollege.co.uk

• Pupils: 700 boys; 685 boarding, 15 day • Ages: 13 - 18 • Size of sixth form: 286 • C of E • Fees: Boarding £7,833; day £7,442 • Independent • Open days: June

Headman: Since 2005, Dr Ralph (pronounced Rafe) Townsend, early fifties. Previously head of Oundle since 1999 and before that head of Sydney Grammar School, Australia and head of English at Eton. Dr Townsend is a high-flier – he has already been a head for sixteen years. A good and popular headmaster at Oundle, maintains close contact with the sixth form and staff. Some parents find him remote and anonymous, others outward going, friendly and very optimistic about the future of the school; head-magisterial colleagues seem to have a high regard for him and rate him as likely to be able to sort out Winchester's underlying difficulties. The Daily Telegraph's educational guru, John Clare talked of his 'low-key manner and consensual management style' as well as his determination. Tough – but with the housemasters having seen off his predecessor Dr Tate, amid extraordinary scenes of staff infighting, he will need to be.

Academic Matters: Outstanding academic education coupled with excellent teaching. GCSE performance statistics distorted by Winchester's use of IGCSEs, and by some boys bypassing GCSE altogether. GCSE taken on the wing at different moments, cleverest miss out GCSEs in some subjects; AS fitted in here and there, many early A levels, boys go on to take fourth or even fifth or sixth. Endless shadow of exams might daunt lesser mortals but most seem to cope well enough. Aim is less pot-hunting than breadth of learning, though the school regularly features near the top of the league. Japanese and Mandarin popular, now part of modern languages department. Enormous numbers take A level maths. Small but successful Greek sets; popular and excellent science.

Unique and enviable feature is 'div': unexamined general studies, one period a day with the same master ('don'), starting with broadly based European history in any aspect the teacher chooses and moving on in the sixth form to pretty well anything intellectual. Boys encouraged to take charge of discussion, can be any topic from political philosophy to reproductive and genetic ethics. Successive heads keen to promote this area, partly to counter minority utilitarian culture – bright and committed pupils make this possible. IT (criticised by recent inspection) now being completely revamped thanks to £1m legacy. Much of school networked, geography set up as beacon department; all dons have laptops, boys sometimes e-mail essays to staff. Library provision pretty lavish, excellent collections both old and new. Several staff members trained in special needs; EFL teaching on tap (some overseas boys need help). School continues to consider national and international examination systems.

Games, Options, The Arts: The perfect place for a boy who is shaping up to be bolshie about team games. After the first year individuals are allowed to do their own thing and there is a huge number of options. Main games are soccer, cricket and the college's home-grown and robust variety of football – keen inter-house rivalry. Hugely successful cricket and tennis season in summer 2005. Glorious grounds with one of the most beautiful cricket fields in the country, stretching down to the River Itchen, where the school's famous fishing club still flourishes. Basketball good and the school is often national cross-country champion. Long-established sports centre in use for 85 hours a week, by outsiders as well as boys. No large all-weather surface – forbidden by city planners.

Large light art department with a remarkable collection of watercolours (Cotmans, Rowlandsons etc). Music is quite outstanding; college has maintained founder's 14th century provision of sixteen quiristers selected from all over the country and trained by director of chapel music to sing in chapel. Superb results at A level, and the most successful school in England at Oxbridge choral/organ awards. 700 lessons are provided each week by a staff of more than 50 specialist teachers; there are nearly 70 music scholars. £4m music school opened in 2004. Magnificent 1960 concert hall, with panelling by a pupil of Grinling Gibbons (taken from elsewhere in the school). And so on. Drama is strong too, with more than 20 productions per year – many of them directed by boys in the school. Boys are expected to make choices and stick with them. Community service is encouraged (and the college is the third largest employer in Winchester). Charge of exclusiveness countered by boys eg manning night shelter, clearing litter in cathedral grounds. Playing fields are let to Southampton FC youth team.

Background and Atmosphere: Centre of school still the 14th century quad built by William of Wykeham, bishop of Winchester and chancellor to Richard II. Other buildings bolted on at regular intervals, giving a glorious but slightly rabbit-warrenish feeling to the place, where every stone has a history. Chapel has christening robe of Henry VII's son Arthur and some original stained glass. Wonderful grounds – on one side the town, on the other the cathedral close; long acres of playing fields stretching lushly down to water meadows. Architectural gems everywhere, including a 17th century sick house, beside which a contemporary herb garden has been planted. Everywhere, a feast for the eyes and the soul. Several buildings still used for their original purpose.

Boarding houses (mostly rambling red brick) dotted round the town in narrow streets (hard to park). Meals still eaten in houses – one of the last schools to retain this civilised (excellent for pastoral care) custom. Genuine family atmosphere fostered by hard-working housemasters. New post of assistant housemaster recently introduced to ease the burden. New system of personal tutors for years 9-11. Large house has been converted as annexe for nine last-year students.

Academic and intellectual pursuits are what the boys rate highest. In general, 'a sixth form college from age 13'; much free time and responsibility for sorting yourself out. Inevitably a few can't hack it. Scholars live in separate 14th century house – 'College', where – they claim – they are worked extremely hard; a kind of academic praetorian guard.

Housemasters are traditionally very strong – admission to Winchester is by house. Recent heads have aimed to foster an all-school sense; hence new termly cathedral service and some tidying up of disciplinary procedures – part of 'drawing more threads into the middle'.

Pastoral Care and Discipline: Routine discipline is house based; most parents will get to know their son's housemaster very well over five years – though things are changing and they will find themselves talking to the headmaster as well. Pastoral matters taken very seriously, as you would expect. First and second-year boys sleep in small dorms and work in 'toys' (small cubicles = more Winchester private language); older boys have reasonable studies. Winchester town is a druggy place and there are predictable strayings into pubs and clubs on Saturday nights. Housemasters accustomed to dealing independently with everyday misdemeanours. The school is tightening up on drugs. Alcohol considered more pernicious. Little truck with counsellors but expert help is always to hand. Staff expected to deal with most problems.

Pupils and Parents: Bright to brilliant, many from intellectual (upper) middle class; also contingent of clever Hong Kong Chinese and other foreign nationals. Pupils confident, charming, frank, critical, unorthodox. 'You have to be able to laugh at yourself to survive here,' said one sixth former. Irony and self-deprecation the keynote. Winchester is so good in many ways that there can be a tendency to self-absorption too; products of other schools still say that Wykehamists are out of touch with the real world. Enormous roll of distinguished Old Boys, including Willie Whitelaw, Hugh Gaitskell, Richard Crossman, Geoffrey Howe, Jeremy Morse, George Younger, Tim Brooke-Taylor, the Nawab of Pataudi, Peter Jay, Sir Humphrey Appleby. Pianists Ian Fountain and Nic Hodges and actors Hugh Dancy and Charlie Edwards are recent old boys. Another famous OB is Buffy the Vampire Slayer creator, Joss Whedon – American, but spent 3 years at Winchester. As he said in an interview, 'most of the things that I've done that have been truly creative have been extra-curricular. However, stories that I've written have gotten me recommendations, which was nice. At Winchester, they tried to squash a lot of things. Certainly everything I wore or said bothered them but, at the same time, I studied classic literature and drama with some of the greatest teachers out there. You couldn't help but become more creative.' To judge from recent events, Sunnydale has more in common with Winchester than might be wished.

Entrance: Full to bursting. Register after boy's eighth birthday. Interview at 11, with IQ test for selection to take school's own entrance exam at 13. Pupils drawn from 170 prep schools – most popular are Pilgrims' School (on doorstep, quiristers educated there), Horris Hill, Twyford. Efforts made to encourage state school boys. Sixth form entry via exam in prospective A levels plus interview.

Exit: Very few escape university; nearly fifty a year to Oxbridge over the last five years.

Money Matters: Seventy scholars 'in College' and about six exhibitioners a year, plus a bursary or two for Hampshire state school boys, plus a very large number of music exhibitions and two sixth form exhibitions. Hardship cases considered on merits. School working hard to widen access.

Remarks: Among the best, and possibly the sharpest of the public boarding schools in the country, wedded to traditional broad liberal education. Enormous intellectual and financial muscle. Leavers are far more rounded than ten years ago and school is making strong efforts to put familiar charge of ivory-towerishness behind it; certainly little evidence these days of the embryo coldly rational, top civil servant of received myth. For example, the school has produced more than its fair share of actors, musicians and academics in recent years.

WINDERMERE ST ANNE'S SCHOOL

Linked to Elleray Preparatory School and Day Nursery in the Junior section

Browhead, Patterdale Road, Windermere, Cumbria, LA23 1NW

Tel: 01539 446 164
Fax: 01539 488 414
E-mail: office@wsaschool.com
Website: www.wsaschool.com

- Pupils: 145 girls, 129 boys, roughly 50:50 boarding and day
- Ages: 11-18 • C of E • Fees: Day £3,000 - £3,322; boarding £5,040 - £6,000 • Independent • Open days: October, February and May

Head: Since 1999, Miss Wendy Ellis BA (mid-forties). Read history and politics at Lancaster University. Young housemistress at Wycombe Abbey, then deputy head at St Anne's. Took charge at a difficult time for school – 'we're still inventing some systems and consolidating others'. She is overseeing a remarkable change in the school, recovering from near-extinction and introducing coeducation at the same time. No longer a nice, young ladies' academy, but bursting with students and confidence. Miss Ellis is approachable, articulate, clear-sighted ('the honeymoon's over'), and obviously able. Keen hill walker, and supporter of Round Square (see below). In a small, virtually new school staff have a voice in moulding the future, but it's evident who is in the driving seat.

Academic Matters: Hard-working pupils, taught in small classes (15-20 up to GCSE). Intake is broad, so results don't compare with selective schools, though in a good year there have been plenty of top grades and few Ds and Es at A level. Hard to give a definite picture here, as expansion and change to coeducation have in effect created a new school. But the signs are good – committed and well qualified staff (many attracted by size, service ethic and breathtaking locale), cheerful and ambitious students. All the usual subjects offered, plus occasional exotic languages (up to 25 nationalities in school at any time); Chinese often figures, reflecting steady Hong Kong intake. Sciences popular at A level. All do ICT in some form up to 18; computers all over the place, especially in boarding houses. Efficient learning support on hand; integration into classes favoured. Good mix of staff ages; now 50:50 female and male.

Games, Options, The Arts: Extensive use made of beautiful surroundings; school has its own jetty and boats on Windermere, all pupils have RYA sailing qualification by age 14. Also D of E, expeditions, 'Swallows and Amazons weekends'. Games still show girls' school influence (hockey, netball and tennis good), but boys' teams now winning competitions. Excellent facilities for music produce high standards. Vigorous drama, too, backed by visits to Manchester and Stratford. Art impressive; wide range of courses.

Background and Atmosphere: Founded in 1863 as St Anne's High for girls, moved to Windermere site from Lytham in 1924. Much building in 70s and 80s (sports hall, science block, performing arts centre, sixth form house). Ran into trouble in late 90s, rescued by parents' consortium, reinvented itself in 1999. Fine new boys' boarding house opened in 2001; girls' accommodation soon to be similar. Buildings are spread out around original Victorian house on steep wooded site, with occasional glimpses of lake. Spirits can't fail to be lifted, even in Cumbrian rain. Boys and girls, seniors and juniors live in remarkable harmony, making a reality of the 'family atmosphere' cliché. Sixth formers live in single-sex flats with joint common areas. Boarding provision very attractive, and much effort put into making day pupils feel part of the community. Everyone seems keen to make things work smoothly and humanely. Teachers expected to devote a lot of their time to running activities, which is certainly appreciated by the young. Great play made of the Round Square movement, founded by Kurt Hahn of Gordonstoun, dedicated to service and internationalism (Miss Ellis is the UK representative on its board); many community projects and exchanges with E.Europe and the Third World.

Pastoral Care and Discipline: Excellent; small school atmosphere works to pupils' advantage. 'We recognise free spirits,' says Miss Ellis, 'difference is good, though there must also be a clear framework.' Drug use and bullying hardly figure – 'the students don't like it' – but the headmistress would expel for both use and trafficking.

Pupils and Parents: Boarders from the locality, also West Cumbria, Yorkshire, Scotland, Manchester conurbation, abroad – perhaps more evidence of a parental desire for low-temptation and wholesome surroundings. Many parents of day pupils in hotel and tourism business. You're struck by the pupils' unaffected but courteous directness – not unusual in the north – and they are, perhaps, a touch innocent compared with the Thames Valley, but a good thing nevertheless. Parents are appreciative and supportive.

Entrance: Entrance exam not too taxing (wide range accepted), though all applicants vetted by Miss Ellis. Two streams at 11 grow to three at 13.

Exit: A few leave after GCSE, outnumbered by incomers. Leavers go on to the usual range of higher education, including Oxford; some directly into eg police.

Money Matters: Some academic scholarships available, plus awards in sports, music, arts, dance and drama.

Remarks: A genuine phoenix, thriving on the opportunity to reinvent itself. Strong on service, challenge, adventure and internationalism. Not perhaps for the urban sophisticate nor the competitive academic but classroom expectations are on the up and the school scores heavily on positive individual encouragement.

THE WINDSOR BOYS' SCHOOL

1 Maidenhead Road, Windsor, Berkshire, SL4 5EH

Tel: 01753 716 060
Fax: 01753 833 186
E-mail: windsorboys@rbwm.org
Website: www.twbs.org.uk

- Pupils: 967 boys • Ages: 13-18 • Size of sixth form: 282
- Non-denom • State • Open days: contact school for details

Headmaster: Since 1997, Mr Jeffrey Dawkins BA Hons (in Semitic langs) MA MEd, early fifties. Instantly likeable, open, straightforward and friendly, this is clearly a popular and effective head and, seemingly, a round peg in the appropriate hole. Despite thirty years on the wrong side of the border, a vigorous Welsh tang lingers in the speech of Mr Dawkins who has held two previous headships – in Hungerford and in Reading. While at The Prospect school in Reading he oversaw the change to grant maintained status and to specialist technology college status. He remains a prime mover in the specialist schools movement and deeply committed to it. He has a practical and hands-on approach (his hands were, in fact, mostly on the copious litter we met on our tour around his demesne. He is famous for collecting it himself, seemingly regarding it as a normal part of the job). A sense of mutual respect between him, the other staff and the boys was tangible and informed the healthy working atmosphere we felt as we went round. He challenged the odd uniform infringer and minor renegade but in a good-humoured way and was received similarly. Mr Dawkins has a justifiable pride in his school, its achievements and in his pupils, 'they're good boys in the main', and shrugs his shoulders at the neglect of general maintenance over which he has only little control. He has managed, nonetheless, an impressive amount of fund-raising

and much of the new-build and renovation has come about through his efforts. A sensible, feet-on-ground head with drive and imagination – just about anyone's cup of tea.

Academic Matters: In 2002, 60 per cent of pupils gained five or more grades A*-C at GCSE. This was before the school became a Specialist School in the Arts. The last four years has seen this rise to, in 2005, 72 per cent. Similarly, at Advanced level, 78 per cent of all grades were at A, B or C; 53 per cent of grades were A/B – not bad for a full comprehensive in an area where the many well-regarded local grammars – to say nothing of one or two well-known independent boys' schools nearby – cream off the cream. Over 100 students gained their first choice place at university. School now in the top 10 percentile of all schools and colleges in the country. This is now the school of choice for many and not just on account of its famous sporting prowess.

A level subjects are a trad mix plus psychology, sports studies, theatre studies, DT. New computer-controlled, digital language centre with satellite/video links – this is high-level stuff – allows individual and distance learning but French is the only modern language to survive to A level here and few takers. ICT now better-resourced than hitherto and used intelligibly and appropriately. GCSE subjects include PE, electronics and graphics. GNVQ intermediates in IT taken in year 12 and advanced in year 13 with impressive results. When asked about performing arts college status, head says it enables them to 'use performance, music and dance to stimulate achievement across whole school'. SENCO and team of twenty, either onsite or at local 'Achievement centre', where first-rate, creative work in learning support takes place. School being adapted for the less physically able. In general, Ofsted reports well above average results in comparison with similar schools. Parents report good teaching across the curriculum. This is a school where, if you work, you can reach the heights, but there are opportunities for everyone.

Games, Options, The Arts: Famous for sport, above all, rowing. School has a boat house on the nearby Thames and, by 2003, its under 18s had won the coveted Fawley Cup at Henley five times in the previous nine years. Pictures of boats and crews everywhere and a stack of upturned boats in the car park. Similarly impressive rugby teams tour internationally – South Africa and Canada in 2004. Financial help for those who need it. Athletics and cricket also strong and everything else you'd expect played hard here too. As well as rowing. School has 1994 sports pavilion, extensive onsite fields including a large Astroturf pitch. Plays cricket against the MCC! School has a Sportsmark and head feels that sport is, overall, school's strongest suit. Especially rowing.

When not rowing, boys remember that theirs is a specialist arts college and has gained an Artsmark gold award. Drama is famously good and ambitious. Lord of the Flies and Berkoff's Agamemnon among recent productions – some with girls from Windsor Girls' School. Excellent drama studio. New performing arts, exhibition hall and sixth form block in 2004. Imaginative cross-curricular work eg a languages and drama collaboration praised by Ofsted 2003. Music is formidable – every kind of instrumental tuition and bands including a full orchestra, jazz band, close harmony singers and a 'junk band' – instruments made out of old plastic bottles etc. Good recording studio. Annual themed arts week each summer provides opportunities for experimentation of all kinds and visits from celebrity writers and musicians. Art is imaginative and varied, despite somewhat shabby – though light and spacious – art room and boys actually learn to draw here. Lovely, lively and thoughtful work here and around the school – critical Ofsted report clearly bonkers. New completely refurbished and re-equipped art rooms with state-of-the-art ICT facilities will make computer art a new and exciting challenge here from autumn 2004. School has excellent 'artists in residence' scheme and benefits from charismatic and inspiring onsite sculptor in addition to dedicated regular staff. Lots of local, national and international trips – sporting, artistic, linguistic, cultural. Lots of extracurricular options – Young Enterprise, public speaking, debating, clubs for riding, philosophy, chess etc – and then there's always rowing.

Background and Atmosphere: Main, almost handsome, redbrick building dates from school's foundation as a boys' grammar in 1908. Later blocks of various vintages and degrees of attractiveness at rear make for a somewhat cluttered and amorphous site but no building more than two storeys so a human-scale, unthreatening, almost domestic ambiance overall. Subjects taught in all redbrick faculty blocks. School became a comprehensive in 1977. Chronic lack of investment makes for a general interior shabbiness – oh for some floors without chewing gum blots! – and exterior neglect but no more here than in comparable schools elsewhere and made up for by ubiquitous worthwhile displays of work and evidence of achievement. Head is wistful, 'I'd like a laptop, projector and an electronic whiteboard in every room,' he muses. 'I'd like two million to refurbish the whole lot,' and you want to give it to him.

Inescapable distant roar of the motorway at the end of the road punctuated by traffic in and out of Heathrow a couple of miles away, nonetheless, the school feels peace-ful and purposeful. Surrounded by genteel if not affluent Victorian sprawl on the way to Maidenhead, it's easy to ignore the vast regal edifice down the road if you choose to do so. Litter is a feature here but school is used by the local community until late most nights and all weekend so it's a lost battle though still gamely joined by head. House system important in all school activities. About a third of teachers are women.

Pastoral Care and Discipline: Head believes in permanent exclusion for anyone who brings drugs into school in most circumstances – not the fashionable view perhaps but the conviction of a clearly humane man. 'Traditional' is a word he uses and mostly as a term of approbation. Assemblies 'with me in my gown' are used to celebrate school successes but 'if you talk during assembly in our hall you're in detention for an hour.' Would sound familiar to – and go down well with – many parents. Atmosphere is relaxed and civilised – boys look you in the face and smile at their teachers.

Pupils and Parents: Boys come from all over Windsor, Slough and surrounds. Intake is strictly according to catchment area so applying from further afield is a waste of time. Socio-economic backgrounds greatly varied as demographics would suggest. Despite several good local grammars, this is increasingly the school of choice for the less-than-loaded parents of the less-than-brilliant prep school leavers – and there are a lot of prep schools in Berkshire. Parents put a lot into this school – it has a true sense of community and a pride in being what it is – not glitzy, not flash nor trendy. About a fifth of boys from a variety of minority ethnic heritages, predominantly Indian and Pakistani. Very few need substantial EAL help. Pupils mostly from four local middle schools and various preps.

Entrance: Via local authority registration and application. See note above about catchment areas. This school is now seriously over-subscribed. From 2006, 10 per cent of students selected by aptitude in the performing arts.

Exit: After GCSEs school loses 10 per cent to other educational establishments and 20 per cent to employment or training. The rest stay on for sixth form studies. A further 10 per cent of those will leave for employment after one year in the sixth. Of those who complete the sixth, around 90 per cent go on to higher or further education – Oxbridge to vocational courses of all kinds. A good record.

Remarks: 'Success' is a word you read a lot as you go round the school. 'Achievement' is a word the head uses frequently and there is, throughout, a sense of realistic aspiration. Parents put a lot into this school – it has a true sense of community and a pride in being what it is – not glitzy, not flash nor trendy. Quietly, carefully and with dedication this school is, in the head's words, 'building on our traditional strength with an eye to the future' and achieving impressively across the board. And on the river.

WITHINGTON GIRLS' SCHOOL

Linked to Withington Girls' Junior School in the Junior section

Wellington Road, Fallowfield, Manchester, Greater Manchester, M14 6BL

Tel: 0161 224 1077
Fax: 0161 248 5377
E-mail: office@withington.manchester.sch.uk
Website: www.withington.manchester.sch.uk

- Pupils: 650 girls, all day • Ages: 7-18 • Size of sixth form: 160
- Non-denom • Fees: £2,370 Seniors; £1,760 juniors
- Independent • Open days: Late October/Early November

Head: Since 2000, Mrs Janet Pickering BSc (mid fifties). Read biochemistry at Sheffield and came to teaching via research, lectureship, motherhood and scientific publishing. Taught at King's Canterbury (qv) from 1986 where she became housemistress and deputy head during its move to co-education; before spell as head of St Bees in Cumbria (qv), then Withington. Believes in choice in education and described coming to all-girls Withington as 'an eye-opener'. 'The girls think they can do anything, so they do. They grasp opportunities, free from the potential inhibition of being with boys, in all subjects including physics, engineering, computing, cricket and football.' Unpretentious and enthusiastic. A 'people person', likes to know all the pupils and hugely proud of them so is delighted about recent appointment of school's first-ever bursar to shoulder some of budgeting, finances and health and safety work. Married to assistant headteacher at Altrincham Grammar School for Girls (qv), also successful textbook author. Two adult sons.

Academic Matters: Outstanding. Tip top of tables GCSE almost only needs two columns, A* and A for over 90 per cent of papers (94 per cent in 2003, 2004 and 2005). Over three quarters of all girls achieve 9 A and A*s at GCSE. Over 20 girls with top 5 marks nationally each year (36 in 2004, 28 in 2005). At A level well over half of the girls achieve three or more A grades. All take general studies – 'it's good educationally, for breadth,' says head, 'I genuinely don't think we've got any areas of weakness in the curriculum.' Excellent teaching across the board. 26 in a class, 28

max. Streaming in French and maths. Strong science, 'goes back to foundation of school'. Girls regularly feature in science and maths Olympiads and win prizes. Research links with university chemists and physicists. German taught in year 8, Spanish in year 9 and Italian offered as an A level only subject as are theatre studies, politics, economics and psychology. Curriculum revised annually to accommodate girls' choices. Parents impressed by ICT, 'ahead of other similar schools'. Computers available to use before and after school. Head not a fan of AS levels, 'the lower sixth should be an exam-free year when students can take risks, explore other things'.

Games, Options, The Arts: Busy with sport, music, drama, fund-raising. Astroturf pitch for lacrosse and hockey, county and country players in both and county in netball and cricket. Strong lacrosse tradition, reaching national finals, also tennis. Older girls have individual fitness plans. Community service in local schools and old folks' home. Charity efforts, Barnardos favourite, links with Kenya, two schools and a hospital and with The Gambia and Bolivia. Over sixty DofE Bronze each year and increasing numbers of Silver and Gold, Young Enterprise, Ogden Trust business game, Model United Nations and Mock Trial. Fabulous hexagonal theatre in the round for concerts and drama, strong links with Manchester Grammar (qv), joint productions. Three orchestras, wind band, jazz group, several choirs.

Background and Atmosphere: Small, square site in residential Withington, south of city centre. Playing fields and all-weather pitch behind buildings that include new sports hall. Big building project summer 2002 created new drama studio, classrooms and labs. Following a major fire in 2003, the library, sixth form resource centre, mathematics rooms and computer suites were renovated and refurbished. New science block opened in September 2005.

Founded in 1890s by group of far-sighted and eminent Mancunians who wanted the same educational opportunities for their daughters as were already available for their sons. An original philosophy, still upheld, was the absence of academic prizes, with the pleasure of learning being its own reward. Little girls, from seven years old, share corridors with big girls, up to 18, cultivating a nurturing atmosphere, a non-threatening environment. Relaxed sixth form common room where girls are pleased as punch with new microwave and the air hangs heavy with the aroma of popcorn and burnt toast. Laid-back sixth form dress, lower years sport skirts as short as is decently possible. Girls naturally and spontaneously helpful to visitors.

Pastoral Care and Discipline: Via form teachers, form tutors in sixth form and heads of year. PSHCE in form periods. Size of school means staff really know pupils. Older girls in peer support scheme for mentoring younger girls, have NSPCC training. Few written rules except, 'respecting other people and respecting self'. No hint of drugs – girls too sensible. Anorexia no worse than elsewhere and staff always on the lookout. Not unduly pressurised, 'you wouldn't come here if you didn't want to work,' say girls.

Pupils and Parents: Wide mix of ethnic and denominational backgrounds, 'a diversity in which the school rejoices,' says prospectus. Head says this promotes genuine mutual understanding and tolerance, 'after September 11th 2001, Muslim girls volunteered to speak in assembly.' Separate Muslim, Hindu and Jewish assemblies are organised by girls once a week. Intake from huge area, friends far flung – 'it's a problem for the girls' social lives,' say taxi service parents. 'The majority of parents pay full fees but there aren't a lot of very wealthy parents,' says head. 'There seem to be a lot of very wealthy parents,' say many parents. Head describes girls as, 'bright, focused, ambitious, confident, competent and well rounded; with supportive parents.' Old Girls include the first female director of Price Waterhouse in Manchester, C A Lejeune (Mrs Louisa Lejeune was one of school's founders), Judith Chalmers, up and coming opera star Christine Rice and Katherine Stott.

Entrance: Exam in January, two English, two maths papers with drinks and biscuits in between, with head greeting all on arrival and departure. Three applicants for every place, standards are exacting. Followed by 15 min interview for likely candidates, including a few minutes with parents. At least 6 GCSE As needed for sixth form entry with As in chosen A level subjects. Head says, 'because we're so academically successful people think we must be an academic hothouse but we're looking for girls whose eyes light up when presented with a challenge, who'll want to do everything and to give.' Potential is key – importantly, previous educational background is considered.

Exit: Very few leave for sixth form elsewhere, fed up of travelling or wanting co-ed sixth form. All sixth form leave to university. Approx 15 to Oxford or Cambridge. Huge range of courses in top universities across country.

Money Matters: Once upon a time had over 100 Assisted Places. Replaced by up to a dozen means-tested bursary and trust-aided places in each year group, with plans to build on this base. First ever development director appointed 2004 to steer through a major bursary appeal officially launched in October 2005.

Remarks: Reputation and results to die for and deservedly so, producing confident, capable women of note for the future, especially those that sail plainly. A few parents

feel the school doesn't cope well with problems but by far the majority are thrilled to have their daughters here.

WOLDINGHAM SCHOOL

Marden Park, Woldingham, Caterham, Surrey, CR3 7YA

Tel: 01883 349 431

Fax: 01883 348 653

E-mail: registrar@woldingham.surrey.sch.uk

Website: www.woldinghamschool.co.uk

• Pupils: 500 girls; 398 board, 102 day • Ages: 11-18 • Size of sixth form: 140 • RC, but ecumenical community and all denominations welcome • Fees: Day £4,230; boarding £7,080 • Independent • Open days: September/ October; smaller open mornings throughout the year

Head: Since 2000, Miss Diana Vernon BA (early forties). Anthropology at Durham and PGCE from London. Has an unusual background for a head – her early career was spent in publishing and PR, and it shows – there is much more of the real world about her than with most heads. She is not RC, but was brought up as a High Anglican. Previously a housemistress at Downe House teaching biology and business studies (when she left, we hear that some parents considered moving their girls with her). Appointed deputy head at Woldingham in April 2000 and took over headship only a few months later, following some haemorrhaging of pupils and abrupt departure of existing head. Teaches some biology to years 7 and 8 and business studies at A level.

No exaggeration to say that she is hugely popular with parents and girls alike – typical comments from parents are: 'extraordinarily satisfactory'; 'a gift from heaven' (editor's note: this really was said!); 'a wonderful role model'; 'the best head ever'; 'truly inspirational' and '10 out of 10 plus gold star.' Somewhat thrown when we asked her to describe herself, even though she confessed that she frequently asked prospective staff the same question, her secretary came to the rescue by reminding her that she was decisive and then she herself added that she was democratic and approachable (confirmed by the girls). Immensely likeable, feminine, ambitious, humorous, distinctly un-headmistressy, interested in everything going on in the school and in the girls as individuals. Girls say that she is also very keen on recognising achievements obtained out of school. Undoubtedly, a head to watch for the future.

Academic Matters: Impressive, given relatively broad

intake. A parent sums up the academic ethos, 'there is a clear understanding at the school that these girls will have to earn a living. The school is good for a wide range of children, from the very bright downwards.' The school is currently in the top ten per cent in the country for value-added performance. Average number of GCSEs obtained is over 9, with 99+ per cent of grades C or higher – 71 per cent get A* or A. RS compulsory for GCSE, as are maths, English lang and lit. Geography popular and most take double award science. A level results – over 92 per cent obtain grade C or better; average points score per candidate 23-ish. Theology, Eng lit, Economics and maths the most popular at A level. In the past, some very bright pupils have left to be 'stretched' elsewhere – head not aware of this now being the case. Recent introductions for AS and A2 include politics and music technology. 45 pupils receive EAL support. Only 14 girls have SEN (dyslexia) and receive one lesson a week with a qualified dyslexia teacher. Head has no plans at present to introduce the IB but is keeping an open mind about it.

Games, Options, The Arts: New all-weather pitch completed recently. Terrific grounds with every facility, with all major games played. Compulsory sport for all, but sixth formers have more choice. New head of PE has brought energy and dynamism to the department – much-needed at lower end of ability range. For example, introduction of water polo and body combat as well as dance club now run by professional dancers. Three golf courses available nearby and riding at local stables, either with or without your own horse. Smaller animals can be accommodated at Hamster Hall and Guinea Pig Gallery.

New Saturday morning weekend programme (Saturday Active) – run by professionals to a very high standard – includes clay pigeon shooting, yoga and fencing.

Great drama facilities, with splendid studio theatre with computer-controlled sound and lighting systems, dressing rooms and costume workshop of a really professional quality. Frequent theatre visits. Not surprisingly, A level theatre studies results have been good over recent years, with typically 75 per cent of candidates gaining A or B grades. Music teaching accommodation very high standard and choir performs overseas on concert tours. 330 girls learn a musical instrument but few take it for GCSE or A level. Art very good, with art and history of art popular at A level sixth form has allocated desk space in the art building, which also has a sculpture room, kiln and darkroom.

Background and Atmosphere: Splendid rural setting in 700 acres in Area of Outstanding Natural Beauty, much of it let as agricultural land. However, readily accessible from London (Woldingham railway station is within the grounds and a free minibus shuttles girls to and fro – central London 30 minutes by train, East Croydon 7 minutes by train – teachers accompany the girls on the train to Victoria.) Some parents have organised a bus from Reigate and another is under consideration on same basis from Sevenoaks; because the Reigate run works so well, school is happy to leave this to parents. By car, allow at least 10 minutes to get up the two-mile long drive; en route you can buy some free range eggs from a local farmer and arrange for your daughter's horse to be accommodated at the stables (a few girls do this).

Lovely grounds, with flower beds, topiary, striped lawns and pergola walk. Formerly a Convent of the Sacred Heart (has links with other Sacred Heart schools throughout the world and does a week's exchange if desired with some European ones). Mellow chateau-style house with wide sweeping balustraded steps to front door. Overall impression is one of spaciousness, with some truly impressive modern building on site, especially the air-conditioned auditorium used daily for assembly – can house the whole school and boasts a hydraulically raised orchestra pit and state-of-the-art sound and lighting systems. New sports centre has a huge multi-purpose hall with sound system and used for discos, dance studios and squash courts – the gallery is very popular with the girls for playing table football. The separate science and art blocks are also new. Recently renovated chapel used for compulsory Sunday Mass and for 15 minutes prayers one night per week.

School recently 'restructured' to feature three step boarding – girls move through three distinct stages. Marden is, school says, 'home-from-home' and a gentle transition from prep school where girls take positions of responsibility; Main House is more of a senior school where girls are encouraged to make choices and the sixth form is a more adult experience focussed on freedom and independence. Own room from year 10 onwards and in lower sixth at ultra-modern Berwick House, known among the girls as 'The Hilton'. Separate new upper sixth form block, Shanley, recently completed with university-style ensuite study bedrooms. CCTV surveys the site and most buildings have linked TV screens displaying the day's activities, menus etc. Girls speak well of the meals, especially the theme days eg National Sausage Day and Italian Week.

Saturday morning attendance compulsory for boarders but they can then go home for weekends. Day girls can stay overnight, arrive early or stay late, they can also come in on Saturday mornings and some Saturday attendance is compulsory for them. Annual Day of Reflection compulsory (on a Sunday), when the girls go into retreat and contemplate issues such as 'friendship' or 'image'. Typical weekend activities for the boarders are shopping excursions to London or Bluewater (very popular), Millennium Wheel, ice-skating, paint-balling with Worth School and group treasure hunts around London with Worth. Socials at weekends with boys' schools for all years. Great school magazine produced entirely by pupils. The senior girls have the opportunity to earn during term by acting as receptionists – 'comes in handy for buying phone cards,' said a sixth-former. Young Enterprise Scheme where girls can set up their own businesses eg printed T-shirts, profits going to charity and excellent careers advice in dedicated library. Strangely, no pressure from sixth form to wear own clothes (can wear their own dark suits instead of uniform with pastel shirts) – apparently the absence of boys and any nearby town means that girls feel under no pressure to be mega-cool. Both RC and Anglican parents appear to feel comfortable with the religious ethos of the school – one Anglican mother said, 'we are not in any way made to feel second-class citizens.' Alternating C of E and RC confirmation years. Parents consistently praise the very happy atmosphere.

Pastoral Care and Discipline: Parent after parent comment that the pastoral care is the best aspect of the school. One parent told us that the staff are 'a tremendous bunch of dedicated and caring professionals.' The same form tutor generally stays with the girls the whole way through from year 7 to year 11 and then girls can in addition choose their own personal tutor. 'Buddy' scheme run by lower sixth girls to counsel years 7 and 8. Sixth formers can become Ribbons (prefects): they have special responsibility for the well-being of others and for promoting the spirit of the school – election is initially by democratic process. Every upper sixth year publishes a year book recording their particular year's memorable achievement and characters, with photos of all girls, their CV to date and life ambitions. Parents praise the way the school introduces the girls to levels of responsibility, with lots of opportunities for leadership. 'It's really good at teaching the girls how to organise themselves,' according to one mother. Head very anti-smoking and has no hesitation in suspending persistent miscreants. No make-up or nail varnish allowed, use of mobile phones permitted but not during the school day.

Pupils and Parents: 40 per cent of pupils are RC. 12 per cent are boarders from overseas; 30 per cent from London (boarders and day) and 58 per cent from the Home Counties. Parents from professional backgrounds – bankers, company directors, Foreign and Commonwealth Office, lawyers, accountants. Lots of daughters and granddaughters of Old Girls. Famous OGs include dress designer Caroline Charles, writer Victoria Mather, restaurateur and political wife Caroline Waldegrave, Louise Bagshawe (chick-lit novelist), cabaret singer and member of 'Fascinating Aida' Dilly Keane and UK water-skiing champion Sarah Gatty-Saunt.

Entrance: Main entry at 11 with 70 places – boarders mainly come from several London and Home Counties preps and most day girls come from Laverock School in Oxted. At 13, 15-20 are taken, head keen to increase intake at 13 – these would be girls who have attended co-ed prep schools.

Siblings automatically accepted, subject to general overall suitability. Candidates take a series of tests. In the morning – English, maths and verbal reasoning at 11; English, science, maths, general and verbal reasoning at 13. Activities in the afternoon – art, science and music at 11; drama and music at 13. The girls also see the head for a short chat. Followed by CE in spring term or summer for some 13+ candidates. Applicants are required to spend an assessment day at the school during the autumn term prior to entry. After the assessment day, school identifies any high-flyers to sit for the scholarship exam in January. About 15 taken into sixth form at 16. Minimum entry requirement for sixth form is six GCSEs at C or above. Applicants sit the school's own entrance exam.

Exit: Mostly to Russell Group universities, with London, Exeter, Bristol and Edinburgh being the most popular. Wide variety of subjects – some go down the traditional path of medicine and law, also history, philosophy, theology, engineering and languages. Drama courses and art school also very popular. About 15 pupils leave after GCSE, mostly unable to resist the lure of co-ed sixth forms at schools such as Charterhouse, Marlborough, Wellington, Stowe and Uppingham – some of the leavers subsequently regret their departure.

Money Matters: One major academic scholarship(£1,000 per term) two minor academic scholarships (£500 per term), drama, music, art and sport scholarships (each at £500 per term) available at the following entrance levels: 11, 13 and sixth form for a duration of two years, three years and two years respectively.

Remarks: Hugely impressive school really going places under dynamic head – it is back to full speed and more after a temporary blip. Friendly and caring, it caters for wide range of abilities; a parent summed up the school in a nutshell, 'I have two daughters there. One is outgoing and academic and the other is shy and laid-back. The school is absolutely ideal for both of them.'

WOLVERHAMPTON GRAMMAR SCHOOL

Compton Road, Wolverhampton, West Midlands, WV3 9RB

Tel: 01902 421 326
Fax: 01902 421 819
E-mail: wgs@wgs.org.uk
Website: www.wgs.org.uk

• Pupils: 405 boys and 285 girls, all day • Ages: 11-18 • Size of sixth form: 205 • Non-denom • Fees: £2,764 • Independent

Head: Since 1990, Dr Bernard Trafford (forties), married to Katherine, two daughters now both at University. Educated at Downside and St Edmund Hall Oxford, and secured an external doctorate in education from the University of Birmingham in 1996 whilst serving as head. Dr Trafford has spent most of his career here, except for a short spell at the Royal Grammar School in High Wycombe. Arrived in 1981 as head of music, then head of sixth form and finally head. This is a very unusual, perhaps unique, curriculum vitae within the independent school world. He has a fine voice, and continues to take an active part in the musical life of the school; (noted for organising a choir at HMC conferences.) A musician head is remarkably enough; to have achieved such rapid promotion within the same school is virtually unheard of. This says much of Dr Trafford's ability. Dr Trafford's particular educational interests are centred on the issues of inclusion and accountability in schools, where he is an acknowledged authority.

A very civilised and courteous man with, as one might expect, a relaxed approachable style. Yet that should not in any way lead you to underrate his steely purpose and real determination. Dr Trafford is someone who leads from the front and continues to immerse himself fully in the life of the school. He understands fully what the school should achieve and has led Wolverhampton through stormy waters with the advent of co education and the ending of Assisted Places. He believes in offering his pupils a breadth of education and is determined that Wolverhampton Grammar should be a beacon of liberal, tolerant and civilised values. One of the largest new development projects in many years is the creative arts centre, which wholly expresses his educational vision.

Academic Matters: Wolverhampton Grammar School survives and indeed thrives in a very competitive market. Wolverhampton itself is blessed with at least two oversub-scribed comprehensive schools as well as the very selective Wolverhampton Girls' High School as a serious academic rival. The close proximity of the King Edward's schools in Birmingham must also be taken into account. The Grammar School has solid if not spectacular results across the whole curriculum; its results at both GCSE and A level have improved steadily over the years with A level A/B grades at over 70 per cent. Given the fact that the school is not especially selective these figures are extremely impressive and place it amongst the best performing schools in the region. Art is especially strong. Not an academic hothouse. Something of a pack leader in the provision of appropriate help for bright dyslexic children: the head takes a personal interest in the OPAL programme which is specially designed for their needs.

Games, Options, The Arts: There are attractive games fields (including Astroturf) hard by the main school complex as well as a newish sports hall and squash courts as well some rather underused fives courts. The school is a big player in the local and very competitive games scene. Football, netball and cricket special strengths. School offers a wide range of out-of-school activities; these include drama and debating as well as the more sporting alternatives. Outdoor education (trekking, climbing, expeditions etc) is a huge growth area at present. (23 senior students climbed Mt Kilimanjaro summer 2005). Music is an important component – several instrumental and choral groups – more than one might expect. A third of the pupils have instrumental lessons: this is a proportion that the head is endeavouring to increase.

Background and Atmosphere: School founded by the Merchant Taylors' Company in 1512. Moved to its present imposing building in the smarter suburbs of Wolverhampton in 1875. The campus still reflects the social and academic aspirations of its Victorian benefactors: the front of the school would not disgrace a university college or grand public school with all the gloss of neo-gothic antiquity by which no 19th century burgers could fail to be impressed. The atmosphere is both relaxed and purposeful. This has been aided by the development of attractive communal areas where pupils can 'chill out' during lunchtime and after school. Most of the newer building developments are attractive and the school seems to have avoided the municipal brutalism than has been inflicted on so many similar institutions. Despite the elite resonances of the site the whole atmosphere is unpretentious.

Pastoral Care and Discipline: Inclusion, involvement and empowerment are the school's watchwords in dealing with pupils' needs. Pupils are involved and listened to and nowhere is this better illustrated than in a powerful school council which is genuinely consulted on a whole range of issues. The system seems to work seamlessly and the atmosphere of openness and mutual respect that it engenders is evident throughout the school. This approach to pastoral care is genuinely innovative and clearly marks out Wolverhampton from the pack. We were especially impressed by the friendly confidence of the pupils.

Pupils and Parents: The intake is a fair cross-section of wealthier citizens of the Wolverhampton area, with pupils travelling up to 20 miles to attend. Around 30 per cent of the school is from ethnic minorities; the largest single group by far being from the Asian sub-continent. The ending of Assisted Places has narrowed the social base of the parent body – something that concerns the head and a generous scholarship fund goes some way to address. Not a 'posh' school: social pretensions are not something valued, or even tolerated. Modest fee levels appeal to less well-off parents and the school also attracts those who want something special for their children and have rejected many of the Birmingham and Wolverhampton academic and social hothouse alternatives.

Entrance: Mostly from local primary schools with a smattering from prep-schools. The school has its own entrance examination at 11 and 13, and has recently opened the 'Big Six'. This is a year 6 group of 10 to 11 year olds where parents can choose to enter their children early into a genuinely caring academic atmosphere, without having to subject them to all the nonsense of Key Stage 2 testing. It makes much of its experimental 'learning to learn' curriculum, and has proved very popular. A cynic might suggest that this is a clever marketing ploy to grab the cream of local primary school pupils a year early – certainly it is not universally popular with local primary heads. However, it does show the kind of innovative thinking one would expect from a school led by Dr Trafford.

Exit: The vast majority go to university. One in fifteen to Oxbridge. The rest to a wide range of institutions, the largest number to the University of Birmingham. Around 10 per cent read medicine or pharmacy. Few choose 'Mickey Mouse' universities and fewer still 'Minnie Mouse' courses.

Money Matters: The school was badly hit by the ending of Assisted Places (numbers have dropped by 100 since the peak in the mid nineties.) The present size of the school seems more appropriate for the space and available facilities. Fees are competitive and there are some scholarships and bursaries for brighter and needier pupils. Money has been wisely spent on many fine facilities, but there are few of the whizzier additions that one might find in the more expensive and grander alternatives.

Remarks: A fine school with an exceptional and innovative head. Good results but also a balanced and happy environment; especially good for bright dyslexics where the Opal programme is at the top of its class.

WOODBRIDGE SCHOOL

Burkitt Road, Woodbridge, Suffolk, IP12 4JH

Tel: 01394 615 000
Fax: 01394 380 944
E-mail: admissions@woodbridge.suffolk.sch.uk
Website: www.woodbridge.suffolk.sch.uk

• Pupils: 900 boys and girls, all day with some sixth form boarding • Ages: 4-18 • Size of sixth form: 155 • C of E • Fees: Senior school: day £3,282 - £3,458; boarding £6,022. The Abbey £1,881 - £2,854 • Independent • Open days: See website

---

Headmaster: Since 1994, Mr Stephen Cole (early fifties), married with grown-up stepchildren. An Oxford educated scientist, previously taught at Wellington and at Merchant Taylors', where he was housemaster and head of science. Is also an experienced schools' inspector. Has run 14 marathons. When he arrived, governors wanted to close down the boarding house but he has kept it open in order to introduce a bit of multi-culturalism (two thirds of the boarders are from abroad) into an otherwise very Anglo-Saxon, East Anglian community. Charming and approachable, extremely proud of the school, he has resisted the lure of more prestigious job offers.

Academic Matters: Results very sound, with plenty of top grades at GCSE and A level, and a bulge around the B

BY ROSIE HAMILTON

lick of paint here and there, with technology much to the fore (there is, for example, a state-of-the-art language lab).

The library is well-stocked and managed and a pleasant environment. The nine period school day (there is no Saturday school) is quite densely packed, with every pupil involved in extra-curricular activities on a Friday afternoon. About 3 per cent of pupils need learning support, for which there is a full time teacher who likes to integrate her work into mainstream lessons. A charge is made for those needing more concentrated support. There is also a highly resourceful EAL teacher.

Games, Options, The Arts: The school is well supplied with fine games fields and courts, a superb sports hall (best viewed from the inside – outside it looks like an alien spacecraft), and an outdoor swimming pool. Local schools must tremble when Woodbridge features on their fixture list, as school teams regularly trounce the opposition at all levels. There is a wide range of sport and pupils are frequently selected for county teams. On Friday afternoons the entire school stops lessons for the 'Seckford Scheme', with everyone taking part in an amazing carousel of non-academic activities, including work in the community. The CCF figures prominently in the scheme, as does D of E. In addition, the school has a full-time chess coach; teams are county champions at all levels, and pupils take part in competitions at international level.

A huge performing arts centre is under construction, which should provide the means for the drama department to rival the outstanding music department. Over half the pupils learn an instrument and the standard of the vast range of choirs, orchestras, groups and ensembles make the school a magnet (especially in the sixth form) for parents wishing to further their children's musical ambitions. For the last three years, the school has had more pupils in the National Youth Choirs of GB than any other school. A proliferation of links with other countries, with many visits and exchanges. Charity fund-raising is a real feature.

Background and Atmosphere: Founded in the 17th century, the school moved to its very pleasant, beautifully kept 45 acres in the 19th century, and became co-ed and independent in the 1970s. It is part of the Seckford Foundation, which also owns almshouses in the town, and whose members form the governing body of the school. A mix of buildings dates from Victorian times to the present. There is a very good and busy feel about the place and no visible litter. The atmosphere is relaxed, pupils are courteous and friendly and walls are cheerfully covered with artwork and photographic evidence of what goes on outside the classroom.

Pastoral Care and Discipline: Excellent pupil care through both the tutorial and house system. Sixth formers are also involved in the welfare of younger pupils. Boarders have their own large Victorian house and, because there are not many of them, are completely integrated into the school, often, informally, spending weekends with friends. The head doesn't much like a formal prefect system, so sixth formers apply for jobs, the most sought after of which is school charity organiser. Few discipline problems.

Pupils and Parents: Day pupils often come from quite far afield in Essex, Suffolk and even Norfolk, in fleets of buses. Social backgrounds are quite varied (professional, scientific, artistic, musical), as a result of the proximity of BT on one side and Aldeburgh on the other. Foreign students come from far and wide, either for long or short stays. The majority of pupils are still solidly East Anglian in origin.

Entrance: By testing and interview at 11 and 13 and by GCSE results for the sixth form. In y7 about half the intake is from The Abbey, the junior school, the rest from local schools. About three quarters of tested applicants gain a place. Many join the sixth form from nearby independent and state schools.

Exit: Some leave after GSCE for vocational courses elsewhere. Exit after the sixth form is nearly always to university (98 per cent), with a good number to Oxbridge and other top universities.

Money Matters: Academic scholarships worth up to 50 per cent of fees and bursaries for the needy. Music scholarships which include a proportion of the fees and instrumental tuition, an art, sports and even a chess scholarship.

Remarks: A very positive and ebullient school for wide variety of tastes and quite a wide range of ability. Thoroughly solid and sound, but innovative. Even the lunches are good.

WOODFORD COUNTY HIGH SCHOOL

High Road, Woodford Green, Essex, IG8 9LA

Tel: 020 8504 0611
Fax: 020 8506 1880
E-mail: admin.woodfordcountyhigh@redbridge.gov.uk
Website: www.woodford.redbridge.sch.uk

• Pupils: 840 girls, all day • Ages: 11-18 • Size of sixth form: 240 • Non-denom • State

Head: Since 1991, Miss Helen Cleland (mid fifties but looks much younger). Educated at King Edward VI High School for Girls in Birmingham. BA in English from Exeter University and PGCE from Homerton College, Cambridge. She has a grown-up son and daughter who both went to school in north London, where she lives. Her passions are theatre, literature, riding and hill-walking. She says the school has a strong ethos of pupils supporting each other.

Academic Matters: Since this is a selective grammar school you'd expect good exam results and you'd be right. 76 per cent A*/A at GCSE, 77 per cent A/B at A level. Languages offered include French, German, Italian and Latin. Results are equally good in humanities and the sciences. The most popular choices for A level are mathematics, chemistry and biology, with economics, English and history some way behind – quite an unusual profile for a girls' school. Staff training days include special needs issues – not that there are many such here. The school also operates a mentoring system in which sixth formers give academic support to younger girls if needed.

Games, Options, The Arts: Winter sports are netball, at which school was U16 national champion in 1996, and hockey. Summer sports are tennis and rounders. Gymnastics, dance, athletics and trampolining are popular and there are successful extra-curricular girls' football and cricket teams. The school has fairly extensive playing fields but little in the way of indoor facilities. Work begins soon on a sports hall and aerobics/dance studio, funded in part by a successful lottery bid. There are several orchestras and choirs and regular concerts and recitals. House drama competition and an annual school play – 'My Fair Lady', 'Oh What a Lovely War!' and 'Hello, Dolly' all recent productions – all parts played by girls, of course. The Asian Society also puts on an annual drama/musical production. Recent visits include France, Germany and Italy as well as expeditions to Peru and Ecuador.

Background and Atmosphere: The school building was formerly a country manor house, Highams, built in 1768, with landscaped gardens added in 1794 by Humphrey Repton. There's a small Greek open-air theatre in the grounds which, sadly, isn't used much, except that girls sit on the steps to eat their lunch in the summer. It's been a school since 1919 and the school birthday, 29th September, is celebrated every year. It's an attractive setting but the once-white facade of the listed building is in urgent need of a lick of paint and school admits that it is expensive to maintain and they don't have that kind of money. Indeed, shortage of money is the main problem here.

Most classrooms are equipped with computers and some with interactive whiteboards. There are two IT rooms with 20 networked computers apiece but that's not many for 840 girls. Also a shortage of space – the school does feel decidedly crowded. The atmosphere, though, seems happy and supportive. Some pupils report that there's quite a competitive atmosphere; one girl said that there was occasional teasing for being a boffin but added that it 'wasn't too bad because we're all boffins here, really'. Woodford is the only girls' grammar school in Redbridge; there is a brother school, Ilford County High for Boys (qv), and the two schools link up occasionally for debates and discos.

Pastoral Care and Discipline: Discipline provided through form tutors and also a peer support system in which sixth formers help younger girls with problems or worries. They are specially trained for this. It's a pretty well-behaved school. Detentions are held once a week but don't tend to be very crowded – usually only one or two girls. No pupils have been expelled since Miss Cleland took over and there have been only a couple of fixed term exclusions. The school's policy is to nip problems in the bud. Bullying (usually teasing or cold-shouldering rather than physical violence) is dealt with swiftly; the school brings those involved together to talk it out whenever there is friction. Rarely, if ever, is there need for action beyond that.

Pupils and Parents: All pupils are drawn from the borough of Redbridge or very nearby, so that's where you'll have to live if you want your daughter to come here. Cultural diversity contributes to the richness of the school. There is a flourishing Asian Society, Jewish Society and a Christian Union.

Entrance: By 11+ style exam, with verbal reasoning and non-verbal reasoning papers. Competition is intense: 900 candidates for 120 places.

Exit: Nearly all pupils go on to university – 115 out of 120 in 2004. Around 8 a year to Oxbridge.

Remarks: Traditional girls' grammar school and parents love it. One said, 'the best thing is the way the older children look after the younger ones – the academic success is a bonus'. Main drawbacks – lack of space, lack of money and it's fiendishly hard to get into.

WOODSIDE PARK INTERNATIONAL SCHOOL

Linked to Woodside Park International School Kindergarten and Junior in the Junior section

Linked to Woodside Park International School Junior Department in the Junior section

Upper School, Main Office, 6 Friern Barnet Lane, London, N11 3LX

Tel: 020 8920 0600
Fax: 020 8368 3220
E-mail: admissions@wpis.org
Website: www.wpis.org

• Pupils: 470 boys and girls • Ages: 2-7 kindergarten & junior (4-7); 7-11 junior; 11-16 senior; 16-18 IB Diploma Centre • Size of sixth form: 25 • Non-denom • Fees: Kindergarten up to £2,100, Lower School up to £3,200, Upper School £3,550, IB £5,100. Plus lunch. Quest and EAL up to £2,400 (for 5 sessions per week) • Independent • Open days: Open day once a term; private tour upon appointment

Head: Since 2005, Mr David Rose as head of school, former head of The British School of Houston. After working overseas for over 20 years he and his wife Vivienne are enjoying being back in UK and close to their 2 daughters.

Academic Matters: Two form entry, max class size 20 and often much smaller. Most of the teaching is based on 'the defining question, with pupils becoming adept at problem solving, rather than learning by rote.' School has moved forward to true international status and follows the IB discipline. Pupils at the senior department are using the MYP – Middle Years Programme; with the IB Diploma Centre on stream, and the junior department currently waiting for accreditation of the IBO to teach their primary years programme, Woodside will be one of only two schools in the country to undertake the complete IB syllabus. For the moment run on trad lines, with pupils taking nine or ten GCSEs in a vast array of subjects. Results to hand show a scattering of A*s and As, more or less across the board. Design and technology fairly dismal – perhaps the Hall is a road too far?

French, German, Spanish, Italian, Chinese and Turkish on offer as well as the more trad subjects, as you might expect with a quantity of native speakers. Combined sciences. Strong homework ethos. 'No real problem' with staff, but the pay is not that of Inner London and recent appointments have included an Italian (maths) as well as teachers from Singapore, India and an American via Sweden. Computers all over, everywhere, but no timetabled keyboarding.

School has specialist teachers for learning support so dyslexia 'not a problem'; usually one-to-one but various disciplines are employed, including Quest. 'The aim of the Quest programme is to teach students with different learning styles to function successfully and independently in an academically challenging mainstream setting.' One statemented child in school. 'Those with ADD can be considered', but school not keen for those with recognised ADHD. The previous head of special needs at St Christopher's has been appointed as consultant. That has to be a real coup.

The EAL (either English as Alternative or Additional depending, apparently, on the day of the week) offers non-fluent English speakers extra help, in English traditions and culture as well as ABC. Again, often one-to-one. These two add-ons cost extra: cost of Quest programme up to £2,400 for 5 sessions per week. Cost of EAL 'add-ons' up to £1,750 for 5 sessions per week.

Games, Options, The Arts: Games field ten minutes' coach ride away; all the usual suspects, gym in the Hall (not vast by modern standards) and much use of local swimming and other facilities. 'Masses of joining in'.

Interesting art but, when facilities improve, this will too. Not much child-inspired art in evidence around the place. Masses of trips to museums and art galleries in London and further afield. Drama on the up. No music at all until three years ago but gradually making itself heard. Class music for all and plenty of individual tuition. Again, masses of visits to concerts and plays in London. Big blitz in 2003 for the creative arts. Clubs for almost everything, with just as many for the younger pupils as those in the senior school – choirs, handwriting, Scrabble, RE and guitar either at lunch time or after school.

Background and Atmosphere: This is the complicated bit. School operates on four sites. The senior department was originally Friern Barnet Grammar School and still looks and feels like a grammar school – pretty scruffy, with bags in corners and older classrooms running irritatingly off each other. Woodside Park pre-prep, the kindergarten and nursery based in the rather jolly, somewhat expanded

Holmewood site. The IB Diploma centre was formed in 1995 and has just moved into the new Jubilee Hall development. (Got it so far?) Senior, junior departments, and the Jubilee Hall/IB Diploma Centre are all surrounded by uniform bright blue railings; the gates are locked. The sites are really quite far apart but a school bus 'does the loop'.

The school only joined the international circuit in 2000; and the original concept (and funding) came from Dr Steven Spahn – he is on the school board and rang the director during our interview. Dr Spahn, who is American, has been involved with IB for yonks, and founded the original international school of London (no connection with the current IS of L). WPIS is sister school of The Dwight School in New York.

Children in baby school smart in bright blue track suits; pre-prep wear trad school grey trousers for boys, tunics for girls, with pretty patterned dresses for summer – blazers for all, caps for the boys, and felt hats or boaters for girls. Sadly this charming image falls off as you progress up the school, the junior dept look much as you would expect, while the senior pupils are very teenagey and the current fashion appears to be girls wearing their ties some five inches long with skirts barely longer.

IB Diploma centre is a new creation, only six years old, and whilst all singing and dancing is available here, the tradition of leaving at 16 (from the old Grammar School) dies hard, and it was sadly empty when we visited (exam leave). Centre follows recognised IB syllabus including theory of knowledge, creativity, action, service, plus the extended essay and six other subjects. French, German, Italian, Chinese and Spanish on offer, and all must do some form of science. Quest and EAL as one might expect. Laptops for all. All but one of the previous pupils have gone to university and the exception was that of choice. Staff commute between the sites, plus some part-time specialist language teachers. Informal rather grown-up atmosphere, pupils wear mufti/with a dress code.

Slight feeling of 'being out on a limb with so few pupils, and perhaps not enough interaction with the rest of the school – 'more music, drama and art would be a bonus'. Foundation year (at the centre) to get incomers up to speed. Pupils are composed of roughly 50 per cent from the senior department, and 50 per cent incomers. 'They bond well and tend to do things as a group out of school hours'. A bonus for those (most at present) from abroad on contracted 'homestay' arrangements, who are under the aegis of the pastoral director and can be met at the airport etc.

Pastoral Care and Discipline: Excellent; school follows the IB philosophy of value, system and peace, this is tolerance 'put in place'. Bullying firmly sat on, with girls having their own common room – well, they are still the smaller number. No apparent problem with drugs, or fags or booze and the gate of the senior dept (on the busy main road) was being guarded when we arrived at lunchbreak. One recent expulsion for general mischievousness. Fair amount of obvious dossing around after lessons when we visited.

Pupils and Parents: Mostly from a very small catchment area, school organises buses but, that being said, truly international, with 30/35 per cent expats. A preponderance of Japanese but also Indian, Greek, Iranians, Israelis – whatever. Senior dept slightly less international because of its grammar school roots and perceived bias but all this is changing as the school's own babies come through the system. Parents a middle class professional business bunch, quite a lot of first time buyers. International with a small i.

Entrance: 60 per cent come up from the junior dept, otherwise from state or independent local schools. Quite a lot of 'to-ing and fro-ing' with other local independent schools. Entrance by interview and previous school reports. Children arriving from overseas can come immediately if there is space available, or indeed any child moving into the area.

Exit: Some traditionally leave to go to other nearby independents, either straight from junior dept, or at 13; to Haberdashers', City of London, Henrietta Barnett etc. Otherwise at 16 for the IB Diploma centre or to other schools or colleges of further education.

Money Matters: Scholarships fixed percentage of the fees, competitive exam at 11; plus bursaries on appeal. School runs 'a tight ship'; late payers are regularly reminded and will, if necessary, be taken to court.

Remarks: This is a school on the cusp; as the previous head freely admitted, 'there is a fair way to go' but his successor is looking to make it 'the best international school in London'. Time will tell.

Worth School

Paddockhurst Road, Turners Hill, Crawley, West Sussex,
RH10 4SD

Tel: 01342 710 200
Fax: 01342 710 201
E-mail: registry@worth.org.uk
Website: www.worthschool.co.uk

- Pupils: 445 boys; about 70 per cent board • Ages: 11-18
- Size of sixth form: 160 boys • RC but others welcome • Fees:
Junior: day £4,705; boarding £6,349. Senior: day £5,226;
boarding £7,055 • Independent • Open days: October,
November, February, May

Head: Since 2002, Mr Peter Armstrong BEd MA,(fiftyish) joined as deputy in 1996 under the lauded leadership of Father Christopher Jamison who was appointed Abbot in 2002 and is, therefore, still on site as an inspired mentor to the senior management. The head is approachable, very down to earth, compassionate, can be robust. Full of projects for the 12-year development plan: admissions policy, staff development and major refurbishment. Started out at the tough end of education in London but (via Australia and elsewhere) has ended up here.

Passionate about 'how children learn' and this is constantly on the agenda with staff, eg his research showed that visual cues were a priority and thus every class is rigged with smartboards, colourful displays, etc. Rates success of a pupil by his ability to place himself confidently in the world.

Academic Matters: No hothouse but excellent results by any ordinary standards and (considering the reputation for its tender intake) no mean record at gaining university places. Almost all pupils go to university with significant numbers to Oxbridge. Not in value-added tables but we suspect they would show up well. Focuses on individual talent and confidence-building. Has own qualified LSSEN/TEFL staff. Sciences, maths, religious studies, Spanish, history, English, economics and theatre studies popular, Latin, German and art not so. The boys comment that, 'a real strength of the school is the high quality teaching' and the staff are getting younger.

The recently appointed deputy, Dr Dominic Luckett, an academic, taught previously at Harrow and is excited by the buzz of the place. Charged with moving up an academic gear so big changes are afoot here in the form of the International Baccalaureate. Oodles of commitment, staff training, new resources and staff etc – outstanding first set of IB results in 2004. Head of IB studies (also doubles as an inspired head of drama) firmly believes that the IB will predominate over A levels. 'It encourages study in the wider context, more active research and more connection between subjects'. Lots of monitoring – mid year tests (years 7 & 9), ALIS- constant communication via phone/email across departments and all parents given each teacher's/housemaster's personal email and phone no. Very approachable easy access. Learning resource centre being developed as hub of the school.

Games, Options, The Arts: Very games orientated. Rugby a major sport, ex head boy capped for England schoolboys. Very good fencing, both foil and epée – students compete at national level. Eight hole golf course. Large, well equipped sports hall and multi-gym, trampolines etc. Rugby not compulsory – the less hardy (and there are plenty of them) have a multi sports programme of badminton, fencing and squash.

Superlatives are exhausted when discussing drama or music and a large oval handsome theatre to match any commercial one. Many involved in a productive theatre life and any boy wanting to be on the stage gets on stage. Parents claim a strong personal identity was achieved through the theatre, two or three productions per term – many past-pupil plays where students give up their holidays, pay their fares to return and perform – a very lasting effect and semi professional standard. Plenty of debating and drama productions integrated with Burgess Hill. Similarly, excellent music has long enjoyed high standards under directorship of Mr Michael Oakley. Pupils regularly win choral and organ awards to Oxbridge. Art rooms, however, with tall ceilings, rather gloomy, noticeably few taking it and appears mediocre in comparison with drama and music.

Massive funding put into a campus-wide ICT network, all classrooms have smartboards – pupils noticeably confident using IT for research. Duke of Edinburgh awards are done on site.

Background and Atmosphere: Original building by Lord Cowdray, late 19th century house in 500 acres of rolling Sussex parkland – a beautiful place to be. Imposing architecture with new Cotswold stone and a very large 1960s weathered concrete UFO – the abbey. Benedictine monks housed on periphery of extensive gardens; cassock and habit still evident. A Catholic school but open to other denominations. The relationship between the boys is respectful – across the ages – even the staff queue for lunch with everyone else. A good feel to the place.

Some say very social (girls are bused in from Woldingham, Burgess Hill, Ascot and then firmly bused out). 'Time and facilities under-utilised', says one parent, 'and a pity no shop for the boys to wander into', although the boarders venture into nearby Crawley. New sixth form centre and upper sixth form house, 'the Hilton' – individual en-suite study bedrooms, excellent facilities with spacious beechwood warehouse loft conversion, exposed beams etc – (Ikea showroom says one pupil). Very good senior house (Years 9-12) boarding accommodation, recently refurbished at vast expense. Years 9-10 have four or five to a room, year 11 share and year 12 have their own rooms, frescoed cornices and wood panelled/pillared living rooms with views across the countryside. Not impossible that it will go co-ed within the next decade.

Pastoral Care and Discipline: Parents (and inspectors) say this is a major strength – boys allowed to be and accepted as an individual. Chaplaincy team and tutors deal with problems – no reports of bullying have reached us. Daily prayer in all three boarding and two day houses, whole-school assembly weekly. No real discipline issues, boys clear about boundaries, suspension for smoking indoors, zero tolerance drug policy but supportive of testing.

Pupils and Parents: Still has a big appeal to Catholic Europe – Spain, Gibraltar, Italy, Germany and also the Chinese. Parents like the fact that it is only 15 minutes from Gatwick airport and its traditional feel – first-time buyers are not so attracted. Full of middle, professional and caring classes. Pupils a cheerful and open lot, though Worth's isolation can't be relied upon to breed independence.

Entrance: Mainly at 11, 13 and 16. Exams at 11 and 13 involve maths, English, verbal reasoning plus interview. For sixth form interview, report from current school and at least 6 GCSEs grade A*-C, with at least 3 at Grade B or above. Would not turn away a pupil just on exam results – effort and attitude to work is more important.

Exit: Almost all to university, significant proportion to Oxbridge, generally business, science, agriculture, art, the Services. Some leave at 16 – academic reasons, or to join a co-ed.

Money Matters: Academic scholarships up to 40 per cent, music scholarships up to 40 per cent (two instruments, one of these often choral) and art awards – more accolade than monetary.

Remarks: New appointments, new buildings, International Baccalaureate, and strong winks that co-ed is on the cards. Academic upgrade too but still resolutely supportive of a broad intake.

WYCHWOOD SCHOOL

74 Banbury Road, Oxford, Oxfordshire, OX2 6JR

Tel: 01865 557 976
Fax: 01865 556 806
E-mail: admin@wychwood-school.org.uk
Website: www.wychwood-school.org.uk

- Pupils: 150 girls, of whom 50 weekly or full boarders • Ages: 11-18 • Size of sixth form: 40 • Non-denom but Christian foundation • Fees: Day £2,975; weekly boarding £4,600; full boarding £4,800 • Independent • Open days: Early October

Head: Since 1997, Mrs Susan Wingfield Digby MA PGCE (fiftyish). Read Italian and French at Somerville College, Oxford. First job teaching maths (a throw-back to her A level days) at state middle school in Oxford, then number of London schools and North London Tutorial College before returning to Oxford. Has been at Wychwood for 20 years now, progressing from part-time post to head of whole school. Quietly determined and committed to her girls. Clearly efficient and has well-defined goals for this small, single-sex, niche-filling school. Made subtle changes as soon as she got installed – like encouraging staff to see beyond their own subjects and discover what their colleagues are up to. 'I have tried to develop a greater sense of team spirit within both the staff and the girls,' she says.

Promotes merits of well-rounded education and fiercely defends girls who struggle academically. 'Their strengths lie elsewhere,' says head. 'What some may lack in academic areas they more than make up for in other ways. That type of girl is just as valuable to us as the academic high-flyers.' Prides herself in producing 'non-stereotypical individuals' who can take on whatever life throws at them despite (or may be because of) coming from 'a sheltered small school environment'. Still actively teaching as well as mountain of headship duties. No plans to move on yet, though will never say never. Husband, Andrew (vicar) chairs Christians in Sport. Three children, the youngest still at university. Parents and pupils hugely supportive – with good cause.

Academic Matters: Good choice of subjects bearing in mind small size of school. In fact curriculum still growing. All GCSE pupils have to do English, French, Maths, short course ICT and RS, at least one science and a humanity, in addition to three, sometimes four, other subjects which, as well as separate sciences, history and geography, now include music, photography, drama, sports studies, Spanish and textiles. High 90+ per cent A-C grades at GCSE. 'It fluctuates from year to year depending on who's sitting the exams. We don't put them under pressure to do better than anyone else – just to do the best they can as individuals. That's what's important.' A level 97 per cent A/B in 2003 put the school third in the country in this category and fourth in 2004.

Class sizes up to year 10 comparatively large at around 25 but then years split for GCSEs. Small sixth form (or Study as it's called here) means lots of one-to-one with course tutors. Usual crop of subjects includes music, drama, photography, PE, psychology, business studies and history of art. Wide spread of abilities. Learning support available as well as extra English lessons for overseas pupils for whom it's not their first language.

Games, Options, The Arts: Plenty of sport on offer, despite the rather confined North Oxford school location. Hockey played on school field near River Cherwell, rounders and athletics in summer. Tennis and netball on school courts or in school gardens. No swimming pool but use university one. Also use university indoor sports facilities. All girls encouraged to get involved and sports studies increasingly popular GCSE option. New school hall from April 2006 for sport and performing arts.

Arts a thriving branch of school life (as is evident from the strong showing of photography, art and textiles at A level, and the number who pursue arts foundation courses when they leave); the work on show in bright airy studios was of a very high standard. Good array of instruments in music rooms and we're assured most pupils take up music on arrival and a third continue to GCSE. A few take music A level but many continue to learn at least one instrument. Very strong choirs – senior, junior and chamber – which do well in school music competitions and often perform. School orchestra, jazz band and number of chamber groups. From time to time girls make it into county youth orchestra too.

Extra activities include basketball and volleyball, football, modern dance, Duke of Edinburgh Awards, drama, cookery, IT, mask making and film club, to name but a few. Certainly no time to get bored. 'Sometimes girls, boarders in particular, would rather do nothing but we encourage them to get involved and they're always glad they did,' head says. (Library transformed thanks to donation left by former head). Whole school ICT networked – one computer between four pupils.

Background and Atmosphere: Established in 1897 by Miss Margaret Lee, a key Oxford female academic, who wanted to educate 'genuine girls not imitation boys',

Wychwood's mission still today. Occupied numerous sites, outgrowing each one, until finally settling at No 74 Banbury Road in 1918, acquiring and knocking through to No 72 eleven years later to form its current typically redbrick North Oxford home. Gardens behind dominated by tennis/netball court and more recent additions beyond, including fine purpose-built science labs, photography and art studios. Very attractive surroundings even on a miserable day in March. Feeling of cosy security with everything close at hand. Classrooms vary greatly in size but all functional and eyes-front teaching much in evidence. No complaints from pupils we spoke to though. 'I really like it here,' said one 13 year old. 'Because it's small you get to know everyone quickly and there's always loads to do.'

Daily running of school down to school council – an institution of co-operative government that's been in existence for many years. Investigated by the Daily Mail in 1969, it prompted the sensational headline, 'Where The Girls Make Rules for the Teachers'. But head insists, 'that isn't its function.' Made up of staff and elected pupil councillors, it meets weekly to discuss issues and decide such matters as the next charity-related 'home clothes day'. 'It's a great tradition,' says head. 'It gives the girls responsibility and teaches them to listen to the opinion of others as well as giving them the courage to voice their own opinions.' Whole atmosphere pretty relaxed with easy pupil-teacher relationships. Get the feeling head knows her girls well and makes herself available. Pupils show respect without subservience. Close proximity to centre of Oxford a big plus for older girls who are allowed to walk in for shopping trips etc.

Pastoral Care and Discipline: Multi-tiered care starting with year 11 taking responsibility for younger pupils. Unusually no traditional house system, not even for boarders, so class teachers look after pupil well-being as well. Girls allowed to take problems to any member of staff however, not just their own form teacher or progress tutor. 'It may be that they feel closer to another teacher and feel more comfortable confiding in them,' says head. Ultimately pastoral care lies with head and her deputy. Housemistresses for boarders are responsible for them after hours and at weekends.

Sixth formers have own study bedrooms. Younger girls in rooms of about three or four with a mix of ages. One pupil told us, 'it's good to have a break from your classmates at the end of the day. It's a bit like sharing with older and younger sisters and, as we move rooms every term, you can make friends with everyone.' Loads of photos and home property everywhere. 'Just like being at home,' said another girl.

Definitely strict rules in other areas though. No toleration of drugs (haven't been put to the test yet) and smoking not allowed either. Also no alcohol permitted except 'the odd glass of wine' at sixth form dos. Firm anti-bullying policy in place. Girls say there is no bullying but head says, 'that's not right, teasing does go on but nothing gets out of hand and everything is dealt with promptly.'

Discipline and good, caring behaviour maintained through reward rather than punishment. Girls of all ages can become 'citizens' if they're 'kind and considerate, play an active part in school life, have sound opinions and are co-operative with authority'. Extra privileges, like shop visits, bestowed on 'citizens' who are likely to be elected later to school council.

Pupils and Parents: 50-50 split of pupils from state and independent schools. As a result, girls come from wide variety of backgrounds – some well heeled, others whose parents make financial sacrifices to send them there. Intake from overseas, currently stands at about 12 per cent – a large proportion of the boarding population. Uniform a must for all except sixth form who can wear tidy 'work or office style' home clothes (which seemed to be quite loosely interpreted the day we were there). Girls polite and friendly, only too happy to welcome newcomers. Strong supporters of single sex schooling. They tell us they feel 'less inhibited'. Famous old girls include author Joan Aiken and horse-story writers Christine and Diana Pullein-Thompson.

Entrance: By exam, interview, participation and report from current school. Lasts a full day, starting with maths and English test in morning, meeting with head, and rest of day following variety of activities like music and art. Says head, 'we look at the year group as a whole and want to be sure everyone will be happy here. We look at the girl as a whole, not simply in academic terms, so there's no pass mark as such.'

Exit: Vast majority goes on to higher education. Some take gap year first. Most recently art foundation, medicine and English courses seem a winner. But favourites change annually, among them law, accounting, business studies, history and biochemistry. School certainly does not produce a certain type.

Money Matters: Very middle of the road fees. But lunch, mid morning buns and prep charged extra to day pupils. Also photography equipment, photography A level, and individual music tuition. Scholarships and bursaries available for academic, art, music and sixth form students.

Remarks: A small, friendly, quite informal but well-run school that fills a gap in the education market. Its size and single sex status make it attractive to some, but would clearly be an off-put to others. As the head says, 'it's horses for courses. Girls we meet appear to be relaxed and happy and achieve well in many different areas. Would definitely suit the kind of girl who needs careful nurturing to reach her full potential. High self-esteem seen as all-important. Turns out confident, well-adjusted individuals. An extremely welcoming environment – a feel-good school.

WYCLIFFE COLLEGE

Linked to Wycliffe Preparatory School in the Junior section

Bath Road, Stonehouse, Gloucestershire, GL10 2JQ

Tel: 01453 822 432
Fax: 01453 827 634
E-mail: senior@wycliffe.co.uk
Website: www.wycliffe.co.uk

• Pupils: 430, two-thirds boys, one-third girls; two-thirds boarding • Ages: 13-19 • Size of sixth form: 195, plus 30 in 'Development Year' (Year 11) for A level English language preparation • Inter-denominational • Fees: Senior school: day: £4,065 - £4,465; boarding: £6,515 - £7,025 (£7,925 including ESOL) ; prep school: day: from £1,535 in the Nursery to £3,140 (years 6,7 & 8); boarding £3,620 -£4,545 • Independent • Open days: Early October and mid February

Head: Since 2005, as acting head, Mrs Margie Burnet Ward MA (Hons), replacing Dr Tony Collins, who left unexpectedly in March 2005. Mrs Burnet Ward had been second master for three years.

Academic Matters: Standards going up judging by last few years' results. Broad intake (not massively selective) but exam success still steadily rising with 100 per cent passes at A level for first time ever in 2002 and again with 60 per cent A/B grades in 2003, 2004 and 2005. No slackers at GCSEs either. Not quite a clean sweep with recent A*-Cs ranging from a low of 85 per cent to a high of almost 92. Great emphasis placed on value-added results (school in top 10 per cent in its field). Overall GCSE grades nearly half a grade better than predicted – maths, English and art better still. Traditionally strong in sciences, impressive labs block. Outstanding DT facilities, computers on equal footing with work benches, lathes etc. Pupils produce everything from prize-winning cello to beds and chairs. ICT the lifeblood of education here. Around £600,000 spent on it in last three years – now 250 computers around school, 60 staff laptops, 30 white boards, whole campus networked, and more to come. The new advanced learning centre in main school building which houses the latest interactive whiteboard technology as well as provide home for maths, English, media studies, history and special needs opened in 2004, together with the state-of-the-art library which is a multimedia resource centre.

Pupils profiled 'in terms of their preferred learning style.' Life skills programme for all pupils (like PSHE with knobs on) aims to develop skills like team working, problem solving, creative IT, self and social awareness and 'learning how to learn.' 'There's more to education than leaving school with a set of exam certificates'. Immense interest from abroad (see Pupils and Parents). Two English language preparation courses specifically targeted at overseas students – foundation course for 14-16 year olds and development year (DY) for new pre-sixth formers – both designed to get foreign pupils up to speed for English exam system. Mrs Burnet Ward explains, 'the whole point of the courses is that they are tailor-made to the needs of the individual pupils. Flexibility is very important. Those pupils will only sit GCSEs and A levels when they are ready for them, not because they're the right age.' Means some pupils stay on beyond 19. Saturday morning school for years 9, 10 and 11 only. The sixth form can have tutorials, extra lessons, use the library but must take part in games commitments in the afternoon. Masterclasses for gifted pupils.

Games, Options, The Arts: A force to be reckoned with in certain sports. Big in sculling, rowing and, more recently, basketball; very big in squash, both national and international status. Pupils currently use pool at nearby prep school. Playing fields slope gently down to A419 (road to Stroud), include all-weather cricket crease. Floodlit Astroturf hockey pitch and battery of well-used squash courts. Rugby making a comeback, cricket undeniably good (seven county players), and girls' hockey another success story. Plenty of extra activities on offer, with the emphasis on active. As well as the usual D of E and CCF, there's strong scouting tradition here. Focus very much on such 'character building' experiences such as caving, climbing and canoeing. Good debaters too. Freedom of thought and speech encouraged. Drama and theatre arts popular exam choices as well as club. Wycliffe Youth Theatre has featured twice at Edinburgh Fringe. Vibrant music department and 35 per cent of pupils learn instruments. Orchestras and choirs (one with 70 pupils) aplenty, very high standard in exams and performances. Director of music described as 'an absolute star'. House music competitions a highlight of school year – 'everything stops for a week and a half beforehand,' admits Mrs Burnet Ward. 'It's a wonderful opportunity for the kids to show their creative talents.' Same goes for inter-house

drama contest. Pupils' artwork on show in the new atrium space in the new School House learning area and around the school.

Background and Atmosphere: Founded by vegetarian G W Sibly in 1882 who chose Stonehouse because of its rail connections. Soon grew in size, developed strong links with scouting and 'almost an obsession' with vegetarianism – a link not entirely severed (see Money Matters). Set in 60 acres, the original listed building (housing head, admin and the advanced learning centre) has now been joined by newer additions, varied in design and age but not looking totally out of place. Intended for boys only, its single sex-status remained until the 1970s when girls arrived in the sixth form and the following decade they were welcomed throughout the school. Like many independents, took a bad hit in the 1990s recession but has made full recovery with pupil numbers now full to capacity and with a waiting list in some year groups. School council, initiated by head, gives pupils big say in running of school life – from what they wear to what they eat. Pupils had say in design of new day house and sixth form uniform. 'It teaches them they have a voice and can make a difference but it also teaches them that sometimes change can take a long time.'

True spirit of 'can-do' which always seems to have been a heart of school. Back in the 1950s, staff and pupils built and furnished their own chapel (using wood from Isle of Wight pier!). Daily assemblies held here with alternative assemblies offered to non-Christians. Fabulous new dining hall doubles as conference centre. Food, provided by outside caterers, certainly looked and smelled good. Sunday brunch unmissable, say pupils. Even so, it's a subject that invariably crops up at school council meetings – known as PM's question time. New flexi boarding house for day pupils with their own building for prep, changing for games and overnight boarding when it suits them. Sixth form boarding house second to none – boys' section boasts own sauna and jacuzzi. All rooms en-suite. Conditions for other boarders less impressive but lots of focus on personal privacy as well as communal areas. School motto: Bold and Loyal.

Pastoral Care and Discipline: House system for day pupils and boarders, each one led by housemaster/mistress with support from matron, assistant house staff and all-important team of tutors, not to mention responsible sixth formers or prefects. It's a wide but well-woven net which shouldn't let too much slip through. School rules kept to a minimum. Nine straight-forward Don'ts, with one big Do – You must obey the law. No automatic expulsions (except drug-dealing for personal financial gain) – all punishments at head's discretion. 'Taking risks is part of growing up. Kids must be allowed to make mistakes.' Fines (and then suspension for second offence) for smoking. No drugs (pupils can be randomly tested). Well-publicised anti-bullying policy. Pupils not aware of any particular problems. 'We all get on well together,'... 'we look out for each other.'

Pupils and Parents: A well-heeled bunch without a doubt. But nice with it. No artificial airs and graces – simply friendly, polite and polished – and totally unaffected. Professional backgrounds. Very supportive parents who volunteer or get roped in to help in a variety of projects as and when their skills are required. High percentage of overseas pupils – around 35 per cent – from 27 countries, including former Soviet Union, mainland China, Hong Kong and Japan as well as Europe. Also fair number of Services and children of old boys. Famous OBs include TV doctor Mark Porter, horse trainer Mark Pitman, Dome designer Derek Tuke Hastings and Sir Michael Graydon, lately Chief of the Air Staff. Famous OGs? 'There will be.'

Entrance: Bulk of year 9 entry from own prep school but increasingly from other local and further afield prep schools. Pupils there sit scholarships and Wycliffe exam, not Common Entrance. Allows school to sort them into the right sets at senior school. External candidates at 13 will sit either CE, scholarship papers or tailor-made exam. Will accept 50 per cent pass, less in cases where other strengths show. Much hangs on interview and school reports. Entry to sixth form – at least 5 GCSEs grade C or above.

Exit: Over 93 per cent go on to higher education. One or two Oxbridge, others far and wide (many overseas pupils continue studies in home countries). Nottingham, Birmingham, Cardiff and Bournemouth perennially popular. Lots of business and computing type courses. Large number opt for gap year. Regularly lose about 10 post-GCSE to vocational courses and sixth form colleges.

Money Matters: Scholarships available at 13 and 16 for academic excellence, art, music, DT, ICT, drama and sport. Maximum value up to 50 per cent. Some bursaries funded by Wycliffe Endowment Trust and generous Old Wycliffians. Throwback to past is existence of vegetarian scholarships (quirky but not worth much). Candidates need to write good essay on merits of being vegetarian, apparently.

Remarks: Looks good, feels good and past and present pupils seem in no doubt whatsoever that it's done them good. May not be one of the country's academic high-flyers but really puts body and soul into preparing kids for the after-school life. Somehow manages to be a modern thinker without losing any of its traditional values. High international profile might not suit all but definitely worth a long, hard look.

WYCOMBE ABBEY SCHOOL

Abbey Way, High Wycombe, Buckinghamshire, HP11 1PE

Tel: 01494 520 381
Fax: 01494 473 836
E-mail: WycombeAbbey@goodschoolsguide.co.uk
Website: www.wycombeabbey.com

• Pupils: 553 girls, all board except for 26 day girls • Ages: 11-18 • Size of sixth form: 170 • C of E • Fees: Day £5,775; boarding £7,700 • Independent • Open days: Saturday mornings twice a term – but need to book well in advance. Parental tours during the week by appointment

Headmistress: Since 1998, Mrs Pauline Davies BSc PGCE MEd (early fifties). Previously head of Croydon High (GDST) after teaching in various schools. Read botany and zoology at Manchester. Married with two grown-up sons. Superb role model for her girls – hard-working, dedicated, successful, not enough hours in the day; also smart, confident and caring. Aware of Wycombe's reputation and top-of-the-table ranking, but not a laurel in sight to rest on. Big plans for the future – driving school onward into the 21st century. Applauds girls' all-round achievements. 'The girls are ambitious for themselves,' she says. 'All we do is develop and enhance that ambition.'

Academic Matters: Brainy without a doubt. Committed teachers, committed pupils – it's a pretty heady mixture. Teaching staff of about 80 (mostly women but around 12 men) means small class sizes and good staff/ pupil ratio. But self-motivation is the key here. From an early age, girls encouraged to organise own timetable. No fixed prep sessions – every girl knows she has so much to do and simply gets on and does it. All but first year work unsupervised in house study area. Lessons go on until 6pm, after taking a 'break' for games on some afternoons, and on Saturday mornings, but do the girls look wiped out? Not a bit of it.

Exam selection gives Wycombe the crème-de-la-crème – a bunch of hard-workers who love it. Results reflect this with 100 per cent GCSE passes, 95+ per cent A*/A. A levels too are hugely impressive, 95+ per cent A/B grades. Head was reluctant to identify particular strengths. 'I don't think it's fair to set one department against another,' she explained. 'All the teaching here is very good, very enthusiastic. Teachers are committed both to the girls and to their subject specialities.' Cookery on the curriculum for 11 year olds in addition to all the usual subjects, second language at

12 – modern or ancient. Girls recommended to take 9 (maximum 10 for real high-flyers) GCSEs. Large choice includes business and communication systems, drama and music. Over 20 options in sixth form (critical thinking and PE offered as AS only) including Russian and Mandarin as well as more traditional Latin and Greek. Satellite TV link in language labs. Computers everywhere (girls can also use own laptops). Dedicated IT rooms plus internet access in six well-stocked libraries and boarding houses. New laboratories and classroom block with interactive whiteboards, projectors and the latest IT technology. The means and will to work can be found at every turn. Some learning support available, mostly in English.

Games, Options, The Arts: Enthusiasm and talent don't stop at the classroom door. Relatively recent performing arts centre incorporates light and airy art gallery, first-rate fully equipped modern theatre and purpose-built music suite. Outstanding display of wall-mounted photos on show at time of visit. A centre certainly to rival any public facility, overlooking lake and contrasting well with original school buildings. All aspects of stage production can be studied – from acting and costume to lighting and stage design. Music extremely popular with almost 75 per cent of pupils learning at least one instrument, some make the grade to enter National Youth Orchestra. Lots for players and singers alike – two orchestras, string, wind and brass ensembles, choral society and three choirs. Chapel Choir tours overseas every two years – destinations like Prague and Paris. 'It's a real highlight of the year,' commented one member. Art, ceramics, textiles and DT a must for all younger girls which many pursue to exam level. A clean sweep of art As is not uncommon.

A 'state of the art' sports centre opened March 2004 provides pupils with one of the best facilities of any school in the UK; it includes a 25m swimming pool, gym, sports hall, 4 squash courts, fitness suite, climbing wall, fencing gallery, dance studio and café. In sport, lacrosse has long been Wycombe's claim to fame with county, regional and national players among pupils. Once played host to Women's World Cup Championships on all weather pitch. Keenly played, keenly contested between houses. Tennis coaching all-year round on 24 courts, national, regional and county level horse-riding, athletics, cross-country, netball, squash to name a few other options. Extra clubs and activities too numerous to list. One teacher explained, 'if there's enough interest in an activity we don't yet offer, then we'll move heaven and earth to provide it for as long as that interest lasts.'

Background and Atmosphere: Not for the faint-hearted. Main building a rather grey, grim Gothic structure, but the majority of buildings are more modern and the whole school is set in refreshingly green, rolling, substantially wooded grounds of 166 acres on edge of High Wycombe. Rebuilt in 1798 by James Wyatt for first Lord Carrington (present Lord Carrington is council president, ie president of board of governors). School founded in 1896 by Miss Dove, later Dame Frances Dove (a formidable lady if her portrait is anything to go by) whose aims to develop students' talents, foster awareness of God and understand others' needs are still upheld today. Former Carrington family residence now home to three boarding houses, two more in Abbey building, another four in purpose built red terrace known as 'outhouses' (cosy and homely but backing onto busy four-lane main road). Junior house up hill from main school and quite separate as is upper sixth boarding house Clarence (a hall-of-residence style set-up all girls aim for).

First and foremost a boarding school, they would never have more than 30 'day boarders', where work and recreation is on a seven-days-a-week rolling programme. Regular contact (debates, socials) with selected boys' schools like Eton, Radley, Harrow, Abingdon and Wellington. Chapel an important feature of daily life. All faiths welcomed, but short morning service compulsory. Allowances made on Sundays when RC girls can attend Mass in town and Jewish girls have 'teacher'. Much mingling between age groups. Starts in dorms and spills over into other activities. Mobile phones not just allowed but welcomed. 'I think it's the greatest invention of recent years,' said one housemistress. Can only be used at certain times and in certain places though. Fixed overnight exeats but very flexible on Sundays. Parents very supportive and encouraged to get involved and keep in touch. 'We're far more flexible about that kind of thing than we used to be.' TV-watching closely controlled, especially in junior house where girls only allowed to view specially chosen pre-recorded programmes.

Pastoral Care and Discipline: Lower sixth girls responsible for looking after younger ones on 'big sister' basis. Each house also has housemistress and tutor. Houses run on friendly, informal lines. 'After all, this is the first time many of them have been away from home and it can be a pretty frightening prospect.' But security is paramount. Over a page of 'community rules' lay down law in prospectus, the majority aimed at health and safety – like never being outside alone. Junior house girls must be in packs of four, even lower sixth in threes after dark. Every external door security coded. Local police allowed to park private vehicles in school car park 'so that makes us feel pretty safe,' said one girl. Rules seen as sensible rather than extreme though. Girls still allowed out into town and nearby Marlow (with member of staff accompanying younger ones). Strict policy on drinking, smoking, drugs and bullies. Suspension most likely, expulsion probable. 'We have to learn to live together. Rules exist to protect both the individual and the community,' says head.

Pupils and Parents: A shared desire to achieve. One teacher explained, 'girls here work much harder than anybody I have ever come across. They have a very optimistic ambition to be the best.' Delightfully confident without being OTT, poised, polite and purposeful. Pretty exclusively trawled from prep schools for whom private schooling holds no surprises. Come from all over the UK and percentage from overseas. 'It's hard to say exactly how many because a lot of parents have homes in this country as well.' Parents fall easily into the well-heeled category, professional folk mainly at the higher end of the class system. OGs include Elizabeth Butler-Sloss, Rachel Stirling and Elspeth Howe.

Entrance: Entry at 11 and 13 through common entrance (at 12 through school's own exam) and interview (an important part of entry procedure apparently but girls still have to reach around 60 per cent CE pass rate). Places in sixth form extremely limited – school's own exam plus good GCSEs. Stringent selection process designed to let cream float to surface. 'Having brains isn't enough,' said a former pupil. 'You've got to have the energy to throw yourself into everything else that's on offer. For some, it's just a bit too much.'

Exit: A quarter regularly head for Oxbridge, most of the others to top universities like London, Edinburgh, Bristol, Durham and USA Ivy League. Gap year becoming increasingly popular but these are well planned in advance. History and medicine (including veterinary and dentistry) top of the pops, but law, politics, English and engineering come close second. Some bow out before A levels, including a few who feel they can't cope with pressure of work and expectations. 'In those cases we talk to girls and their parents and suggest other schools to which they might be better suited,' said a teacher. 'They leave quite happily knowing it's for the best.' Others opt for sixth form colleges or co-ed independent day schools.

Money Matters: A pricey option for day girls (some excellent alternatives offered on the state just down the road!) but some scholarships and exhibitions up for grabs. Academic and music. Up to 50 per cent off fees. Bursaries for seniors' (Old Girls) daughters and granddaughters and some assistance available for existing pupils whose families fall on hard times

Remarks: Well-known, well respected, traditional girls' boarding school which suits self-starters and undoubtedly

does well by them. Prides itself on turning out individuals not clones. Academically struggling need not apply. 'You need to be academically bright enough to hack it and enthusiastic enough to make the most of it.'

Wymondham College

Golf Links Road, Morley, Wymondham, Norfolk, NR18 9SZ

Tel: 01953 609 000
Fax: 01953 603 313
E-mail: wymadmissions@aol.com
Website: www.wymondhamcollege.co.uk

- Pupils: 975 boys and girls; about 50 per cent board (both sexes) • Ages: 11-18 • Size of sixth form: 320 • Non-denom
- Fees: £2,000 per annum full boarding; £550 day boarding (means all meals taken at school but no overnight stays) • State
- Open days: Six Saturday mornings spread through the year and sixth form open evening in October of each year

Principal: Since 2000, Mrs Victoria Musgrave BEd MEd FRSA (fiftyish). English/drama specialist. Previously deputy head at King Edward VI Grammar, Louth and head at Blenheim High, Epsom. An impressive head, Mrs Musgrave oversees this rare hybrid of a school – usually referred to as 'college' – with dedication, efficiency and pride in its 'one-offness', recent developments and achievements. Running such a large and complex place is no pushover and Mrs Musgrave has the energy, experience and hands-on approach to build on the successes already achieved.

Mrs Musgrave has been seconded to Rosemary Musker School in Thetford and will be returning to Wymondham College in 2006. She is the Executive Principal of Wymondham College and is in attendance at the College at least one day per week. Mr Dominic Findlay is currently Acting Principal until her return.

Academic Matters: GCSE results good – 100 per cent get A*-C in 5+ subjects – the best in the area and now one of the top 3 comprehensives in the country. A levels show a spread across the grades, the best candidates doing as well as anywhere – 2005 saw a 98 per cent pass rate. Technology college, and centre of excellence status in maths, science and technology; commands extra funding and has led to worthwhile links which involve pupils in helping in primary and special schools, University of the Third Age input, and also rigorously demanding academic achievement in school. RS popular and successful at GCSE and A level. Art most popular and successful subject, includes impressive work in multimedia, digital imagery and IT-based projects. Splendid new buildings for DT and humanities. Spacious new science labs. Very well-equipped for all ICT and internet activities throughout site. Sadly, have abandoned plans for new creative and performing arts centre but planning to expand the boarding and classroom provision – plans are with DfES for funding. Small SEN unit supports the few pupils with a range of SENs.

Games, Options, The Arts: Good variety of options, especially at sixth form level, including various vocational courses. Rugby, football, basketball, cricket and hockey college sportsmen and women have strong representation in county teams and champions in many regional finals. Sportsmark Gold awarded in 1997 and 2000 for all-round excellence in results and facilities. 30 per cent learn instrument. Bands and jazz groups, orchestral, choral and instrumental concerts in and out of college.

Background and Atmosphere: Unlike anywhere else. Has many of the advantages of a traditional academic boarding school, many of the advantages of a good, large state co-educational comprehensive and, in the sixth form, the advantages of a well-resourced sixth form college. Recent inspection commented on the 'positive Christian ethos' of the college which head now interprets as an emphasis on a 'strong moral and spiritual dimension' informing daily life. However, attendance at chapel compulsory. Confirmations a regular school event. School officially non-denominational but most pupils C of E or 'nothing in particular', possibly reflecting location as much as anything. Chapel itself the only remaining Nissen hut out of many which formed major part of school site at its inception and now rightly seen as something of a college treasure, being part of its unique history, and lovingly preserved.

Male dominance mitigated by current head who has begun to elevate profile of 'girls' things', to the general benefit, no doubt. Her influence also increasingly obvious on site. 'We don't have the faded elegance of the traditional boarding school but we are beginning to break up the site', she says and evidence for this now building up all around tho cito which, potentially, could compete in ambience with the best purpose-built schools in the country. Humanisation includes excellent adaptation of site for the disabled, and college has to be a serious option for the physically disabled, but otherwise robust, student. Head has 'Principal's Council' – a council of pupils elected by staff and pupils. College keeps its fees so astonishingly low partly by having larger class sizes than in the independent sector, and this must be a factor in the decision making of potential applicants.

The largest state boarding school in Britain and, possibly, in Europe was founded in 1951 on a site which had housed a US air force base. The military (and municipal) background clear on arrival as one faces the uniform, stark 1960s teaching and boarding blocks. However, further penetration into this well-signed site reveals later, more sensitive and imaginative buildings, notably the white 'Tech Block' – a light and exhilarating, open-plan addition in the centre of things which houses art, design, technology, business studies, IT and various vocational courses. Also a new medical centre, and other recent, small-scale buildings and extensions. New sprung floor in vast sports hall which doubles as college hall, accommodating entire school population. Head keen to humanise the site (82 acres of it) and new planting evident everywhere beginning to mitigate the effect of local authority street furniture and hospital-type signing.

Pastoral Care and Discipline: Years 7 and 13 boarders housed in age-grouped accommodation while years 8-12 are in four mixed age houses, 90-100 in each block. Single rooms for upper sixth, doubles for lower sixth, others in larger numbers. 40-50 per cent of sixth form board, many for the first time and seem to like it, seeing it, perhaps, as practice for university. Everyone, day or boarding, in house-based tutor groups, tutors overseeing both academic and extra-curricular activity. Strict code on drugs, drink, cigarettes and solvents strictly adhered to as local authority policy. College given Princess Diana Award for Drugs Education Programme. Peer-mentoring programme. Head has 'Principal's Cabinet' a council of pupils elected by each house to discuss/decide on general school/pupil affairs. Houses accommodate resident academic and non-academic staff and behaviour generally not a problem.

Pupils and Parents: From everywhere – nationally and globally – though preponderance from East Anglia/London. Though MOD presence (officers and ranks) less than hitherto, still accounts for 20 per cent of pupils. Also other overseas postings make up further largish group. 20 per cent overseas British citizens. 10 per cent from HK, Macao, Germany, France. Many pupils with fluent second languages. Mostly 'professional' background, families from all over the world who value education. 'Time poor, money rich', the head says of the clientele. Huge pressure now on day places. Boarding also oversubscribed.

Entrance: Main intake at 11+, a very few annually thereafter. An application can only be made for a day or a boarding place, not both.

Day: through the LEA. This year more than 10 applicants for each place. Admission criteria in order of importance: sibling; excelling in music or sport; distance from school – at present this tends to be no further than 1.5 to 2 miles.

Boarding: through the school's admissions officer. This year 66 places, 133 applicants. Numbers up 470 to 544 in last five years. Admission criteria in order of importance: sibling; boarding need for educational continuity ie for a child with parents who move around because are associated with the MoD; proximity – at present the furthest is 45 miles away.

Sixth form entry. Although the majority of pupils stay for the sixth there is some movement between yrs 11 and 12. 15 or so places and well oversubscribed.

Applications a year in advance.

Exit: Few to employment, most to huge range of institutions and courses. Large numbers to 'modern' subjects – business studies, computer science, leisure, marketing but some, too, to maths at Imperial and law, physics, English at 'older' universities.

Money Matters: College supported by LEA but also raises funds via lettings of buildings - fund for large initiatives. Academic, sporting and music scholarships in the sixth form (half fees). Whichever way you look at it, this school is money well spent.

Remarks: Now has the reputation it has long deserved. A tightening of the school, strong results and glowing Ofsted report. Positive vibes from local parents. Low fees and a state school which gives a let out to those who would like the benefits of a public school education but have problems with the ethics of the system. Perhaps not the place for your potential Oxford classics student or future Cambridge historian but an exciting place to spend seven years for anyone else.

YEHUDI MENUHIN SCHOOL

Linked to Yehudi Menuhin Junior School in the Junior section

Stoke d'Abernon, Cobham, Surrey, KT11 3QQ

Tel: 01932 864 739
Fax: 01932 864 633
E-mail: admin@yehudimenuhinschool.co.uk
Website: www.yehudimenuhinschool.co.uk

• Pupils: 66 boys and girls; mostly boarders • Ages: 8-18 • Size of sixth form: 10 • Non-denom • Fees: per annum - £31,410 boarding; £30,594 day • Independent • Open days: Termly

Headmaster: Since 1988, Mr Nicolas Chisholm (early fifties). Educated at Christ's Hospital and then choral scholar at St John's College, Cambridge, where he read Classics. Formerly head of classics at Hurstpierpoint. Continues to pursue professional singing career and directs choral events at the school. Wife Aurial teaches at local primary school and lives with him on site, seeing to Open Day, staying guests and recital room flowers. No children. Head is academic, deeply aware of the specialness of his situation and professional role; heading an institution which encompasses extreme musical talents, international repute, significant alumni and an illustrious founder.

Academic Matters: Plenty of visiting professors supplement extensive staff list – they almost equal pupil numbers. Maximum of eight to a class, lots of one-to-one, one-to-two etc. Five GCSEs are common. Foreign students with ESL may take fewer and study their native language as soft option. Senior pupils mainly take just two A levels, one being music. Relatively light academic workload coupled with brilliant children and fab teaching ratios means impressive results: near 100 per cent pass GCSE A-C (65 per cent plus A/A*), 80 per cent plus A/B at A level.

Real focus of the school is quite obviously music; at least half of each day is musical studies, with timetabled practice, twice weekly instrumental instruction, lessons in composition, singing and Alexander technique (good posture is key). Everyone plays two instruments: violin, cello or piano. Music practice is the focus of most extra-curricular activity with plenty devoting much of their free time to their craft.

Games, Options, The Arts: Compulsory weekly games eschew contact sports to protect playing hands and other parts. Heated outdoor swimming pool is very popular. Heavy bias to the liberal arts in pupils' choice of exam subjects.

Also reflected in extra-curricular, extra-musical activities, where drama productions and forays into fine art predominate. At time of visit an invited sculptor had put up spectacular outdoor display featuring six-foot tin unicorn and moulded life-size geisha.

Background and Atmosphere: Established in 1963 by Lord (Yehudi) Menuhin who had noticed that musically gifted children struggled to achieve fulfilment within the normal education system. The school remained a pet project until his death in 1999. He is buried in the grounds and his family is still involved. Majority of children board, although currently six come from the locality and are able to live at home. Beautiful leafy grounds in commuter-belt countryside, gravel drives lead to Victorian Gothic 'White House' surrounded by mish-mash of attractive modern boarding, teaching and concert blocks. Generally all appears well-maintained although one set of classrooms was off bounds to visitors because of its smell. 'Probably a rat stuck in the wall, it happened before in the boarders' bit – awful,' remarks a sixth former insouciantly.

Pupils are two to a bedroom and these all house pianos and double as practice areas. Practice locations are at a premium, 'finding somewhere is sometimes a problem'. Shared common rooms are not many or altogether homely, 'when we have the time, we socialise in our bedrooms'. There are book and music libraries, instrumental teaching studios and quite a few biggish classrooms, one is devoted to juniors (8-11s) although it is not very primary schoolish. Modern recital room, all glass and wood beams, is lovely. Sublime lunchtime concerts performed daily by pupils take place here, compulsorily attended by the whole school.

Pastoral Care and Discipline: Boys and girls separate boarding houses with two sets of house parents and matron living in. Easy phone contact with home. 67 per cent of present intake is girls and, therefore, some end up in boys' accommodation. Boy/girlfriend relationships are strictly discouraged and gating arrangements in the premises keep the sexes apart. Smallness guarantees intimate family atmosphere although, with only 65 pupils, making friends of the same gender and age group may not always be easy. This said, children do very obviously share their passion for music and seem generally well-integrated with one another.

Standard rules re bullying, drugs, alcohol, sex: suspension/sacking may result but is relatively rare. Laziness towards studies/instrument equally infrequent but offending pupils may be asked to leave and a very few do so of their own accord. Forty per cent of students from overseas, UK based contingent if concert commitments allow are entitled to exeats on Saturday and Sunday with little ones out on Friday evening. In practice, many stay until the holidays. Despite some organised activities at the weekends, country location is bemoaned and weekly tuck trips to Sainsburys offer greatest diversion. The refectory is generally well-regarded.

Pupils and Parents: Broad cultural mix, genuinely non-denominational, social/moral instruction replaces taught religion. Musically gifted thrive amongst like-minds, parents not necessarily musical themselves, may take a back seat, 'they are happy to leave them to us'. Fair number of household chores, for all but the youngest, serves to keep the highfaluting in check. 'Prima donnas are not encouraged.'

Entrance: Follows rigorous auditions held twice a term. Joiners any age between 8 and 16, average of 5 a year from many applicants.

Exit: Entry to the very best British musical academies and overseas conservatories is pretty much guaranteed at 18. Occasionally, leavers take a gap year.

Money Matters: All UK pupils qualify for an 'Aided Place' under DfES Music and Dance Scheme whereby government settles most of the fees on a sliding scale linked to family income (also available to overseas pupils after 3 years). Other school-run scholarships in place.

Remarks: Rarefied environment for the musically gifted. Window on the real world through exhaustive concert schedule across SE England (and beyond) and outreach to local community attending for lessons and workshops. Won't suit all-comers but, of those talented enough to be offered a place, most would grab it with both lithe, sinewy hands. Amongst many esteemed alumni are Tasmin Little (violin), Nigel Kennedy (violin) and Paul Watkins (cello).

JUNIOR & PREPARATORY SCHOOLS

ABBERLEY HALL

Worcester, Worcestershire, WR6 6DD

Tel: 01299 896 275
Fax: 01299 896 875
E-mail: john.walker@abberleyhall.co.uk
Website: www.abberleyhall.co.uk

• Pupils: 117 boys, 54 girls; 70 per cent board, the rest day. Also pre-prep/nursery with 50 boys, 35 girls • Ages: 7-13, pre-prep 2+ - 7 • C of E • Fees: Boarders £4,950; day £3,965. Pre-prep and nursery £955 - £2,120 • Independent • Open days: October

Head: Since 1996, Mr John Walker BSc (fiftyish) who was educated at Bradfield, and took his degree (in psychology from Surrey) on the wing. He went straight into schoolmastering from school itself, with stints at West Hill Park, Edgeborough and Sunningdale, before going to Pembroke House in Kenya, where he became head of studies (retains strong links – a rugby team was visiting when we were at the school). He also spent four years at Bramcote. His wife, Janie, is 'fully involved with the school, particularly on the pastoral side'; she also supervises the school ponies. A charming and delightful couple, with three grown up children, they love being in the 'people business'. Head comments that the 'golden thing about a small school is small classes – not only can you see the problems but you can always get on top of them'. He teaches maths to scholars and the bottom rung of the CE ladder and monitors work cards – both the good and the bad.

Entrance: Informal interview, no exam as such but children are tested before their interview to give the school some idea of their strengths and weaknesses. All ability intake, a few means-tested awards on offer 'for nice children who need boarding, who will fit in and for whom the school can do something'. This is not a scholarship award and, often as not, will go to a single parent. Main entry in September but can and will take at any time.

Exit: Historical links with Winchester and still sends a regular supply; also to Shrewsbury, Radley, Cheltenham, a few to Eton, Malvern, Marlborough – all over. Girls to Cheltenham Ladies, Malvern Girls, Haberdashers' Monmouth, Cheltenham College, Malvern College, Tudor Hall, Rugby, Marlborough etc. New Malvern day house popular with locals.

Remarks: This is predominantly an English school (check the number of green wellies in the cloakrooms) so

'no need for EFL', despite the 'odd Spaniard or two who come for a couple of terms' (via the Astec agency in Madrid). Mixture of parents, mostly from Shropshire, Hereford, Warwickshire, Worcs and Derbyshire with a trickle from London; trad families and quite a number of first time buyers and, strangely enough, a growing number of ex-pats and Services personnel. Excellent feedback and regular reports to parents. Super parents' book too, with alphabetical lists of subjects of possible concern eg 'Teddies: These are a delightful feature of boarding school life and most pupils' beds are awash with them' (they were). School only offers full boarding with all-in and all-out weekends, plus some optional outs, no weekly boarding then. Top two years have their own bedside lights. Fabulous dorms carved out of stable lofts, the old drama studio, bachelor quarters.

The school is housed in a remarkable Grade II listed Victorian country house, complete with fine crumbling stucco and a ceiling to die for in the main drawing room. Outstanding conversion of existing buildings and sympathetic additions make this one of the most pleasing schools this (incredibly fussy) editor has visited in many years. A delight. School was originally founded in 1889 at Blackheath in south London – then called Lindisfarne after the monastery – and moved to Worcestershire in 1917 under the aegis of the remarkable Ashton family who eventually endowed the place when it became a charitable trust. Mostly quite jolly extensions, enlivened by a giant chess board which slightly suffers from courtyard cricket; plus peacocks and a guinea pig club. Fishing lake, 'the ink pot', popular with children. School digging own bore hole during our visit, sadly out of bounds, could have provided hours of pleasure, rather like the somewhat bizarre clock tower, popularly used for abseiling.

Wide range of abilities, so fairly tight academic standards; no prep; lessons and homework are combined and, after the first two years, school runs on a 29.5 hour week. Reading encouraged, library has £750 worth of books new each term, pupils read in chapel and once a year they prepare and give a speech. Great for self confidence. More than 40 per cent have some sort of learning support in super suite of rooms in the old lofts (there may be an extra charge). French from eight, with newspapers, telly programmes and articles as important as text books, regular study trips to France, with their own chalet near Bourg Saint Maurice in the French Alps. Groups of nine and ten year olds spend three weeks there during the term learning 'to speak French but also to discover the mountains and to learn about the French way of life'. Latin on tap for all, with Greek option for the brightest; school has its own Latin course:

Disce Latinum. Older children must spend 18 months doing German and Spanish – 'no choice'. Tiny classes, 12 the norm, usually streamed and set where necessary. School has abandoned Key Stage 2 tests in English, maths and science – 'they were a waste of time', head asserts, 'they disrupted teaching' – and embraced modern technology plus all the usual suspects, touch typing for all at eight and a huge recent investment in machines and networks. School proud of its interactive white boards. 'We only bought them where they could be of use'. Class names vary according to form teacher.

No problems with staff either on the academic or the pastoral side, 'they like our way of life'. The entire span of British history is taught over three years. Extremely competent academic briefing booklet. Art, design, music and drama all important with stunning new music dept underneath the octagonal Ashton Hall in the former shooting range. Ambitious woodwork, DT and art rooms open each evening. Own kiln and good pottery. This is a keen sporting school, pupils regularly qualify for regional and local championships. Ricochet court (sort of mini-squash – not a lot of 'em around) plus Astroturf, huge sports hall which is used by the local cricket club, climbing wall, super 25 metre indoor swimming pool and a proper manege. This is a terrific child-inspired school, no uniform except for 'formal', lots of visits, with firm discipline, jolly high standards producing self-confident, articulate pupils with a fair number of scholarships and an enviable CE record.

THE ABBEY JUNIOR SCHOOL

Linked to Abbey School Reading (The) in the Senior section

30 Christchurch Road, Reading, Berkshire, RG2 7AR

Tel: 0118 987 2256
Fax: 0118 987 1478
E-mail: office@abbeyjunior.co.uk
Website: www.theabbey.co.uk

• Pupils: 315 girls, all day • Ages: 3-11 • Non-denom • Fees: £2,980 • Independent • Open days: Early May and mid October

Head: Since 1999, Mrs Jane Tuckett BA MA PGCE (mid-fifties). Educated at the euphonious SCEGGS Redlands in Sydney, Australia, then Cambridge (New Hall, languages) and Homerton. Long inningses at Manchester High School for Girls and The Perse School for Girls, Cambridge. Has raised three children herself so she has acquired no small measure of understanding about what children need – par-

ents, too. Exemplifies what she preaches and does lots away from her desk from choral singing to mountain climbing. Shares Mrs Stanley's strong commitment to social responsibility.

Entrance: Own entry test plus interview. Brains and diligence are so highly prized and, thereafter, nurtured, that even 3-year-olds have been known to fail the interview.

Exit: Almost all to the senior school, a tiny handful to free grammars. Those who, it turns out, won't make the senior school are picked up and gently redirected in good time.

Remarks: No curricular eccentricities. The tinies inhabit an Alfred Waterhouse villa surrounded by a fairytale 12-foot yew hedge. The juniors in their own big house. Have just bought the house next door, knocked it down, and are building a common room, music suite, dining hall and classrooms so that the last year, currently taught at the senior school, can come back to the fold. It's all being done to eco-schools standard – sun pipes, wind-powered lights etc. Great care taken to spark up every brain cell, rave Ofsted report on the early years centre, efforts made to inspire intellectual curiosity – encouragements to read, speak in public, lots of trips of all sorts. Wide ranging extra-curricular programme. It's all strong.

While the atmosphere is anything but laid back, these bright-eyed girls are infused with gusto, excited by what they're learning. The social tone is set by the ladies at reception, where everyone gets the same big welcome – all parents remark on this, so do we, it's special, and they say new girls feel at home almost at once. Relationship management canny, clique formation discouraged by mixing classes up. Buddy system, school council. You don't have to be brilliant at everything, so it's sport for all – it has the Activemark Gold imprimatur – and, at concerts, squawkers do their happy bit. One mum summed it up, 'it's just the way you'd want your child to be looked after.' Thoughtful touches like all correspondence on instantly identifiable yellow paper. Thriving PTA, second-hand uniforms, fundraising, social events, gadding off with daughters on trips.

Intensely purposeful, in no way remorseless. Peace of mind for those who get angsty about senior schools: the first part of an attractive 3-18 package.

ABBOTS BROMLEY SCHOOL FOR GIRLS JUNIOR SCHOOL

Linked to Abbots Bromley School for Girls in the Senior section

Abbots Bromley, Rugeley, WS15 3BW

Tel: 01283 840 232
Fax: 01283 840 988
E-mail: registrar@abbotsbromley.net
Website: www.abbotsbromley.staffs.sch.uk

• Pupils: all girls, some board • Ages: 4-11 • Independent

Remarks: See senior school.

ABERLOUR HOUSE THE JUNIOR SCHOOL AT GORDONSTOUN

Linked to Gordonstoun School in the Senior section

Gordonstoun School, Elgin, Moray, IV30 5RF

Tel: 01343 837 829
Fax: 01343 837808
Website: www.gordonstoun.org.uk

• Pupils: Day 38, boarding 45; boys and girls 50/50 • Ages: 8 - 13 • Fees: Junior school - £2,723 day; £4,881 boarding
• Independent • Open days: Nov, March, May - junior school

Head: Robert McVean.

Remarks: Rather jolly, purpose-built, junior school in the grounds of Gordonstoun itself with self-contained classrooms and dorms all in the same building. Children all use the main school facilities and dorms are strategically placed on the second floor with glorious views and somewhat incongruous work-station type beds. Children sleep above and work below, which is splendid in principle but, with low ceilings, dorms looked rather cramped when we visited them. Hopefully a certain amount of re-arranging of these elephantine sleeping areas will make the place feel roomier. Interestingly, although the junior house was originally designed for 80, with 60 boarders (30 of the old guard and 30 anticipated new pupils); the boarding facilities are now nearly full, siblings of children already in the school are flocking in. A new modular building housing extra classrooms and a recreation room built in 2005 due to increased demand. Parents appreciate the convenience of having all their young in the same place.

THE ACADEMY SCHOOL

2 Pilgrims Place, Rosslyn Hill, Hampstead, London, NW3 1NG

Tel: 020 7435 6621

• Pupils: 70 boys and girls, all day • Ages: 6-13 • Fees: £3,950
• Independent

Head: Mr Garth Evans BA (forties), who started the school with Chloe Sandars in 1997. Taught English at Trevor Roberts (qv) for two periods of five years each, as well as private tutoring, and started the Academy School partly at the request of clients. 'They liked the way I taught – their children were inspired and given confidence – and suggested I set up a school along those lines.' Relaxed, informal and completely dedicated; at the end of a phone 24 hours a day, even for pupils who have moved on to secondary school. 'For a whole term I used to ring him up every day,' said a parent. 'He was totally involved.'

Entrance: Most come in at seven or ten years old but applications welcome at any time. Some pupils move on from pre-preps, others transfer from any of the local prep schools, a few from state primaries. Most have failed to thrive in more traditional and inflexible environments. Children spend a morning at the school, taking part in lessons, to see if they will fit into the group socially and educationally.

Exit: Girls usually leave at 11, boys at 13, to selective London day schools ranging from Mill Hill to Westminster, Queen's College to St Paul's Girls.

Remarks: The school was set up to fill the need for a small, nurturing, co-ed environment. 'Children need emotional security and to feel good about themselves. Then work falls into place.' Classes of up to about 14 pupils, but often fewer, meet in small rooms in two adjacent cottages, in the adjoining Unitarian chapel, complete with stained glass windows, and in its hall. The science teacher heats a solution over a portable Bunsen burner to a rapt class in a basement classroom. Another teacher sits on the steps in the sun marking books. 'It feels like going round to your favourite teacher's house for tea, only there happen to be other teachers and children there too,' said a parent. Classes are not strictly by school year – they often encompass an 18 month age range but similar abilities. Specialist teachers for every subject, including French and Latin. Lessons start at 8am, and continue with a short break till (packed) lunch at 1pm. As far as possible, academia takes up the first part of the day, with art, music and sport in the afternoon. The school is mixed-ability, the teaching rigorous and lively. High praise from parents for the dedication of the staff, which includes several charismatic young men. No scholarship classes, though children do sometimes get scholarships. 'We want to make very little of the differences in ability. You can't improve the intellect but you can praise the endeavour. There's lots of praise here.' Parents value the breadth of learning, 'my 10-year-old has astounded us with his general knowledge.' As 11+ and Common Entrance exams approach, the level and pace of learning increases. 'They really work the kids hard – but the teachers work hard too,' said a parent. 'They'll stay till seven at night and give up their holidays if necessary.' Computers are the weakest link. 'All the children have one in their bedroom, so we don't use them overtly. But it would be desirable to teach them to touch type if we could find the time.'

Not a school for a special needs, though it can accommodate mild learning difficulties, and behavioural problems provoked by more rigid environments. Children must be able to sit down and learn at an appropriate level. The small class sizes mean they get plenty of individual attention, with some one-to-one help where necessary. 'But our curriculum is flexible. We can help children catch up and improve their performance skills but they must not disrupt the group and they need to function as part of our community.'

Two afternoons a week of sport plus extra PE periods. Swimming and eg badminton at the nearby Royal Free leisure centre; football and hockey on Hampstead Heath when weather permits; PE in the hall next door. The school does on occasion put together a team to play a match but its small pool of players means success is a bonus. 'We were excited to lose by only 5-4 to Westminster Under School, until we found out we had played their 12th or so team.'

Art, however, is strong, with a specialist pottery teacher and – unlikely as it seems in such a small space – a kiln. Co-proprietor Chloe Sandars was trained at the Royal Academy of Music and teaches singing plus another music lesson every week. Children can also learn the violin, clarinet and saxophone, and there is a small orchestra. Rehearsals for the big school musical take over the school for several weeks of every summer term. 'The standard is phenomenal,' said a parent, 'and we're used to the performances put on by the big senior schools.'

Informal environment; everyone is on first name terms, and rules and regulations are minimal. 'Everything is based on mutual respect. Our children get plenty of freedom but they have to meet their responsibilities. It's a far more sophisticated concept than having a list of rules. You put the mirror up in front of them and let them look at themselves. That's far worse than any punishment.

'The main ethos of the school is that we really care for the individual needs of each child. They feel completely safe and secure emotionally.' Parents concur, 'my son, who felt alienated at his previous school, loved it here from the start. It's small, cosy and very nurturing. They steer a steady course between being too strict and too lax, and they get the most out of every child.'

Families are mostly wealthy, from Hampstead and environs. Most have already tried the more conventional prep schools. 'I just had a gut feeling my son wasn't happy at his old school. As soon as I walked in here I knew he would adore it and he did. It gave him the confidence to feel he could succeed.'

ACS COBHAM INTERNATIONAL SCHOOL JUNIOR SCHOOL

Linked to ACS Cobham International School in the Senior section

Heywood, Portsmouth Road, Cobham, Surrey, KT11 1BL

Tel: 01932 867 251
Fax: 01932 869 789
E-mail: w.green@acs-england.co.uk
Website: www.acs-england.co.uk

• Pupils: girls and boys; all day • Ages: 2 1/2 - 11 • Fees: Day: £4,900- £15,650 • Independent

Remarks: For further information, see senior school.

ACS Egham International School Junior School

Linked to ACS Egham International School in the Senior section

Woodlee, London Road, Egham, Surrey, TW20 0HS

Tel: 01784 430 611
Fax: 01784 430 626
E-mail: w.green@acs-england.co.uk
Website: www.acs-england.co.uk

• Pupils: all day • Ages: 2 1/2 - 11 boys and girls • Fees: £2,360 (Pre-K) • Independent

Remarks: For further information, see senior school.

ACS Hillingdon International School Junior School

Linked to ACS Hillingdon International School in the Senior section

108 Vine Lane, Hillingdon, Hillingdon, Middlesex, UB10 0BE

Tel: 01895 259 771
Fax: 01895 818404
E-mail: w.green@acs-england.co.uk
Website: www.acs-england.co.uk

• Pupils: boys and girls • Ages: 4-11; all day • Fees: £7,250 - £15,000pa • Independent • Open days: October and February

Remarks: For further information, see senior school.

Albyn Lower School

Linked to Albyn School in the Senior section

17-23 Queen's Road, Aberdeen, AB15 4PB

Tel: 01224 322 408
Fax: 01224 209 173
E-mail: information@albynschool.co.uk
Website: www.albynschool.co.uk

• Pupils: 200 girls and boys • Ages: 3-11 • Fees: £1,527 - £2,205 • Independent

Remarks: For further details, see senior school.

Aldenham Preparatory School

Linked to Aldenham School in the Senior section

Elstree, Borehamwood, Hertfordshire, WD6 3AJ

Tel: 01923 851 664
Fax: 01923 854 410
E-mail: prepschool@aldenham.com
Website: www.aldenham.com

• Pupils: 60 in prep, 55 in pre-prep plus 36 in nursery • Ages: nursery 2-5, pre-prep 5-7;prep 7-11 (boys and girls) • Fees: Day: pre-prep £2,560; prep £2,831, junior £3,266, Day boarders: junior £4,098, Boarding: junior £4,892 • Independent • Open days: June & October

Remarks: For further information, see senior school.

ALDRO SCHOOL

Shackleford, Godalming, Surrey, GU8 6AS

Tel: 01483 409020
Fax: 01483 409 010
E-mail: hmsec@aldro.org
Website: www.aldro.org

• Pupils: 221 boys; 55 boarders, 166 day • Ages: 7-13 • C of E •
Fees: Boarders £5,515; day £4,270 • Independent

Head: Since 2001, Mr David Aston (early forties). Formerly, housemaster at Shrewsbury and, before that, taught at Monkton Combe junior school. Educated at Monkton Combe and Durham University where he read geography. PGCE from Cambridge. Likes sport, antiques, antiquarian books and steam railways. Wife, Sue, is a classics teacher and they have two children.

Entrance: Name down in infancy assures a place at 7 or 8. Complicated system of main and reserve lists being replaced (for 2009 entry) with a single entrance list and a waiting list for latecomers. Boarders generally receive priority for places and can occasionally be accommodated up to the last moment. For day places, entry is more competitive. The entrance exam, given in January for the following September, is not a rubber stamp and a few boys do not pass. Boys come from all over (33 different schools in 2005) including a few from overseas (half ex-pats, half overseas nationals). Do let the school know if your son harbours some special, even if offbeat, talent.

Exit: Almost all to traditional public schools, with about ten a year to Charterhouse (five minutes away) closely followed by Wellington, then Radley, Eton, Sherborne, Winchester, Harrow and Cranleigh. Nineteen scholarships won by fifteen boys in 2005 (out of 41 leavers), including three at Eton and two at Winchester.

Remarks: Flourishing boys' day and boarding school quietly lurking in an unknown village on the outskirts of Godalming (five minutes from Guildford). Unashamedly traditional, sometimes eccentric, marching to its own drum of excellence in all things and employing tried and true teaching methods. Set on 30 acres of splendid Surrey countryside in a beautiful country house and surrounding buildings. A teaching block completed in 1999 provides most of the classrooms, including an excellent IT centre, dazzling library and shiny changing rooms. A new dining hall, which also provides new staff accommodation, was completed in

August 2003. Although over half the boys are day pupils, Aldro stands out among other day/boarding preps in functioning as if it were 100 per cent boarding. Written prep is done at school (parents love this), the days are long and full of activity (seven and eight-year olds finish at 5.00pm but 13-year-olds toil on until at least 6.30pm). Saturday school most weeks with matches afterwards.

Academically, the school starts deceptively gently (just as well, while most of the boys are learning how to knot a tie and not wet themselves), but builds to a frenzy of academic intensity in the last few years. Boys are streamed from age nine, but there is to-ing and fro-ing between the streams. The most able are accelerated through the form system, spending two years in the top form, which helps to explain the stunning scholarship results. Exams in every subject twice a year, until boys are so expert at revising that they hardly bat an eyelid. Most boys are snapped up by the school of their choice at 13. Strong classics. All boys learn Latin from age nine or ten and, thanks to fantastic teaching, it is an oddly popular subject (not all boys carry on with Latin during their final year). Despite being a firm chalk and fountain pen school, IT has been thoughtfully woven into most subjects, including maths, English, French and – most creatively – music. Good old-fashioned general knowledge quizzes every few weeks (Aldro's senior general knowledge team came 7th out of 109 schools in 2000 and the junior team came 4th out of 135 in 2001). Help for learning disabilities is available and about 10 per cent of boys take advantage of the support, but this is not the place for a boy with more than mild difficulties.

Very sporty. Rugby, hockey, soccer, cricket and athletics are all played from age seven – terrifying opponents from schools which mollycoddle the tinies with rounders, unihoc and other less-manly pursuits. Recent cricket tours to South Africa and Zimbabwe and the Under 11 rugby team toured Scotland. Five tennis courts, squash, rifle and pistol shooting, riding and rowing (on its own lake). Lovely gymnasium/theatre. Heated outdoor pool (team swimmers train nearby at Godalming Leisure Centre). Brilliant chess – Aldro's name is dreaded by chess-playing schools throughout Surrey and beyond. The school has won seven national championships in the last two years. Boys routinely play chess for the county and five played for England in 2004-5. Three major dramatic productions each year provide opportunities for the less-sporty, less-academic to shine. Attractively housed music department with some excellent teachers and results. Recent upsurge in interest mean that the school now has three choirs. Outstanding art. Gargantuan list of extra-curricular activities, ranging from relatively ordinary (golf, sailing and model railways) to off-beat (bottle excavation, fossil hunting and fly-tying).

Unsurprisingly – in mid-commuter-belt-Surrey – the majority of parents are straightforwardly rich, with their sights set on famous public schools. But there are less affluent parents who scrimp and save to send their sons here. Parents are thrilled to find a confident and bustling school that is not overly bogged down with National Curriculum mumbo jumbo. Several mentioned the remarkable transformation (for the better) in their son's table manners since starting, alone worth the school fees. Parents also keen on 'industry' marks given four times a term according to how hard boys are trying in each subject: sloth is detected and sorted out early and boys who are eager beavers, but not necessarily great brains, receive due credit. Lots of competition among boys and 'squads' (houses) curiously named after bits of the Commonwealth.

Only a very few boarders at seven but over two-thirds of boys board their final year. Aldro provides a homely atmosphere for them and the scene on a summer afternoon with boys swimming, rowing, and playing cricket on the rolling lawns is nothing short of idyllic. Any boy would find a niche here no matter how strange, shy or disorderly. Eccentrics definitely welcomed – 'they fit right in with many of the teachers,' said a parent.

ALLEYN'S JUNIOR SCHOOL

Linked to Alleyn's School in the Senior section

Townley Road, Dulwich, London, SE22 8SU

Tel: 020 8557 1519
Fax: 020 8693 3597
E-mail: juniorschool@alleyns.org.uk
Website: www.alleyns.org.uk

• Pupils: 230; 115 girls, 115 boys • Fees: Junior £2,930 - £3,050 • Independent • Open days: Autumn

Head: Since 2003, Mr Mark O' Donnell BA, PGD Des MSc (Arch) EdM PGD ES (mid-forties). Previously deputy head of Thorpe House School, Gerrards Cross. Educated at Stonyhurst and St Ignatius College, New South Wales. Married to Esther with three sons of junior school age, this is a quietly-spoken but intensely committed and dedicated head who has his finger on every detail of his super school, its management, its assets, its achievements and its plans. Clearly assiduous, though almost disconcertingly earnest, Mr O'Donnell is clearly a prize catch for the school and has

an excellent working relationship with Mr Diggory (head of the senior school) and the other senior staff. He will put himself out to a, perhaps, unique degree to help a child or family with a problem.

Entrance: Around 160 applicants for 16 places in reception. Days are spent assessing hopeful 4-year-olds; immense care is taken and candidates are given a range of developmental exercises. As the school is reluctant to say a final 'no', children are regularly invited back for re-tries. Lots of helpful feedback to parents. The result is a happy, homogeneous bunch of eagerly collaborative, exploring and creative learners in a safe, comfortable and stimulating environment.

Exit: Almost all to the senior school (automatic right of entry, though they all sit the exam). Some go for scholarships elsewhere.

Remarks: The 'two schools within one school' format really works here, for the benefit of all. A 'safe routes' scheme funded by £250,000 of local authority cash, has made a green path for safe travel around the site from the main school to the junior school end. The school is at the far end of the main site, behind the music block but has the benefit of a huge field for outdoor play. It has a special science garden with a wildlife pond and herb, flower and vegetable plots. Two adjoining semis newly acquired will provide an inviting garden entrance just for the tinies – a lovely and imaginatively thought-up way to enter your school.

The building itself, purpose-built in 1992, is a model of what a junior school should be. School day begins with an enlightened 40 minutes of time for chat, admin and 'warm-up' and then a smooth transition into a 'calm and orderly' day. Spaces are big enough to allow a sense of freedom but not overwhelming – bright, stimulating, but not over-busy, classrooms, a first rate IT room with passionately committed specialist staff (when we visited pupils were peacefully absorbed at individual PCs to the sound of evensong from St Paul's Cathedral), excellent library – 'the hub of the school' – and a good, multi-purpose hall/gym. A sense of purposeful, pleasurable work pervades the whole – super textiles and excellent artwork everywhere, rooms have French names, everyone has two years learning a string instrument and around a third take it further. Lots of other music, individual and collaborative. Lots of drama including a major production annually. Plenty of sport and games to suit everyone. SEN have exceptional resources for a junior school – two super little roomlets for individual help, after careful assessment, and bright, dedicated and expert support. As in the main school, loads of clubs – 35+ for chess, gardening, judo, drama and everything else you could imagine.

There are other super junior schools in the area – ones you'd practically reproduce for – but you'd be hard put to find a happier, more secure environment than this and one run with more dedication, vision and enthusiasm.

ALLFARTHING PRIMARY SCHOOL

St Ann's Crescent, Wandsworth, London, SW18 2LR

Tel: 02088 741 301
Fax: 02088 702 128
E-mail: info@allfarthing.wandsworth.sch.uk
Website: www.allfarthing.wandsworth.sch.uk.

• Pupils: 460 boys and girls, all day • Ages: 3-11 • Non-denom
• State • Open days: All through the year

Head: Since 1979, Mrs Veronica Bradbury MBE (for services to education in Wandsworth since 1966) (late fifties); was deputy head for five years before that. Has no plans to retire and she'll be a very hard act to follow – loves the job and will keep going 'as long as she's fit'. Married with two sons. Gained an MA in school and college management from Kingston University in 1996. Has a very strict philosophy on education – believes in 'a rich curriculum' – the three Rs come first 'they are the tools we need'. Energy and enthusiasm pulse through her and her school; 'isn't she great? Don't you just want her to teach your children?' raves a delighted parent. Staunch advocate of state schools – 'some very good ones in London… they should be highlighted'. Enjoys teaching and 'being with the kids' as 'admin is such a thankless task'. Will happily go into a classroom and take over should a member of staff be off sick – no risk your embryo Einstein will be taught by an endless stream of supply teachers here.

Entrance: At 3 to nursery or 4 to the main school. Waiting list. Operates a siblings first policy. Next comes geographical proximity to the school. No tests or interviews and no religious affiliation. Like most inner-city schools where there is a floating population, spaces do become available further up the school. Telephone to find out what's available.

Exit: Very wide choice from good state secondary schools with which the primary has special links ie Southfields community college and Elliott secondary school in Putney to independent schools such as Alleyn's, Dulwich and Latymer where there's an entry at 11. Also to Lady Margaret's in Parson's Green, City of London, Emanuel and Wimbledon.

Remarks: Excellent example of good practice in state education. 'A recent Ofsted commented that all groups do well in all subjects, including the more able and those with SEN, with standards well above average. Class size is a manageable 28 with a classroom assistant in every class. French is taught in year 6 with selected pupils encouraged to attend master-classes at Elliott every week. Homework is taken very seriously – all parents are issued with a homework schedule so there is no chance of little Johnnie protesting, 'we never have maths on Tuesday!' A 'Path to Excellence' document is signed by parent, pupil and teacher at the start of school to encourage interaction between school and family and the resultant PTA is thriving, seriously: book weeks, visiting theatre companies, professional storytellers, illustrators, poetry readings, art competitions all vie for space in this amazing hub of learning. A fully inclusive school for SEN.

Music is strong, with all children in year 3 and 4 learning recorders and over sixty children learning individual musical instruments with many taking Guildhall School of Music exams to a high standard. Drama and the arts are well taught and promoted – each class puts on an end of year production for parents which is linked to the class project for that year; an Allfarthing pupil came 2nd in the Harvey Nichols 'design an apron' competition 2001; another came 1st in the Wandsworth Traders' Christmas card competition. In 1998 it became a Satellite centre of excellence for ICT.

Even after school this buzzing hive of activity continues in the form of endless clubs – choir, card games, netball, football, IT, Spanish, art & design to name but a few – 'what a lovely way to end the school day for all these children, to be with their friends, all doing an activity they want to do and enjoy – and it's free' proclaims an enthusiastic parent. From this fount of knowledge came Louis and Marcel Theroux and jazz pianist Julian Joseph – winner of a 2001 Emmy award. Alun Armstrong (last seen in 'Sparkhouse') sent his sons here as did Peter Marinka of stage and film and television. An excellent primary school but one which owes a great deal to the excellence of its head.

ALTARNUN COMMUNITY PRIMARY SCHOOL

Five Lanes, Altarnun, Launceston, Cornwall, PL15 7RZ

Tel: 01566 86274
Fax: 01566 86274
E-mail: head@altarnun.cornwall.sch.uk
Website: www.altarnun.cornwall.sch.uk

• Pupils: 70 boys and girls; all day • Ages: 4-11 • Non-denom • State

Head: Since 1991, Mr Malcolm Vian (early fifties). Educated at Queen College, Taunton and Chester College. Various teaching posts – a Liverpool comp, Biscovey Junior School, primary school in Dudley. Became deputy head of Bosvigo primary in Truro (six years), then head at Blisland. Seen as focused and hard-working. Enjoys reading, football and keep-fit. Juggles heavy teaching commitment with effective management. Married with two children.

Entrance: Criteria: sibling already or previously at school, other family connection, geographical proximity, medical, psychological or social service recommendation. Any mitigating circumstances considered by head in consultation with governors to be important. Pupils are from mixed social backgrounds, majority are one-car owners from local farming community but this is changing to include middle-class parents moving away from the London rat-race to idyllic Cornish countryside (now 20 per cent). Caters for ten under-fives part-time. Competition includes the newer schools of Lewannick and Tregadillen.

Exit: Virtually 100 per cent to Launceston College.

Remarks: A happy, extremely family-like, school with strength being teaching quality, assisted by volunteer parents. Teachers (who stay a while) communicate and work well together. Pupils taught in three mixed-age classes, with average size of 22. Attainments at end of each key stage in line/above national average with 100 per cent achievement at level 4+ in maths and science at Key Stage 2. English not far behind.

Typically Cornish and under-funded. Sadly lacks canteen – classroom blackboard drawn back to reveal through-hatch to kitchen. However, children seem happy enough to sit with dinner tray at worktable. No main hall on-site – children walk 10 mins to use village hall. Indoor PE constrained due to lack of space but situation compensated by excellent outdoor facilities – activity area and wonderfully large playing field that could give school more building space. Governor recently appointed to achieve such building funds. Hot on netball and football. Swim all year at Launceston Leisure Centre. After-school/lunchtime clubs include chess, gardening, recorder, performing arts, music, netball, football, swimming.

Situated eight miles west of Launceston, Altarnun boasts stunning views of Bodmin Moor (on a clear day) and serves largest catchment area for Cornwall. Founded in 1878, moved from smaller village green premises to existing development in 1935. Three permanent classrooms are stacked in a line next to cramped and inadequate office, administration and storage facilities. One classroom doubles as library/resource, music and staff room. Due to be transformed into £15,000 stimulating hi-tech bridge of Starship Enterprise with more IT. Two additional pre-fab classrooms. Teaching staff are fond of school and pupils. Caters well for children with SEN including physically disabled – 14 per cent of total roll.

School colours are grey/black and red, a watch and stud earrings (only) are acceptable. Parent involvement welcomed and there is a lot. Good communication between home and school which seems to support homework programme with an active PTA.

Parents overall are happy with way their children are helped by the school. Effective discipline system (liked and mostly respected by children); yellow card issued when rule broken, red card if two are broken in same day, resulting in loss of choice play session at week end – computers, drawing, chess, instrument etc.

ALTRINCHAM PREPARATORY SCHOOL

Marlborough Road, Bowdon, Altrincham, Cheshire, WA14 2RR

Tel: 0161 928 3366
Fax: 0161 929 6747
E-mail: admin@altprep.co.uk
Website: www.altprep.co.uk

- Pupils: 320 boys; all day • Ages: 3-11 • Non-denom
- Fees: £4,350 - £4,956 • Independent

Head: Since 2000, Andrew C Potts BSc PGCE. Young-looking, bearded 53 year old came from 17 years as head of biology/deputy head of The British School of Paris – 'a big change'. Keen ecologist, sings and plays trombone semi-professionally, was player, then home referee for the British Rugby Club of Paris. Keen on private education because, 'like private health care, it delivers and has to, to survive,' but says he won't run a crammer or a sweatshop. 'I provide for the boys, the boys don't provide for me'. Married to Marilyn, modern languages teacher at Chetham's School of Music; youngest two of their five children are pupils there.

Entrance: 40 non-selective reception places. Selective higher up as classes rise to 24. Registration fee gives all on over-subscribed waiting list an 'interview' with head. Prospectus says 'parents will immediately be consulted and advised if their child is not able to maintain a certain standard'. Head says, 'education is a moral issue. If I take a boy on he stays unless the parents decide it's the wrong school.' Extra help for dyslexic and other pupils in designated 'support' rooms but head admits, 'we're not selective but selected'.

Exit: Lots to Manchester Grammar. A quarter straight across the road to Altrincham Boys' Grammar; partnership between French departments with plans to fast track APS boys to early GCSE. Some to Cheadle Hulme, North Cestrian and others. Head prides himself that, 'all the boys go to the right school for them'.

Remarks: Relaxed atmosphere for juniors and nursery in super new (1996) buildings with impressive entrance and hall. Infants in Victorian building a mile away; school bus for rare travel between the two. Owned by governors who're also directors. Confident, articulate boys who open doors and stand aside but who're busting to speak when spoken to. Max class size 24. Core subjects in mornings, French from 4, A* school for maths, daily homework. Half classes for IT and DT with jig saws and drill at end of bright art room. Designated teachers for art, DT, IT, sport, geography and music. 'Fantastic music department,' say parents. CD cut in 2003. Three choirs, 75 strong orchestra, 'all welcome, even beginners,' say parents. 'If they can only play three notes we write those notes in for them,' says head. Associated Board exams centre, two thirds of boys learn instruments with peripatetic teachers.

Ten sports, lots of tournaments won, all boys represent school at some time. Assemblies follow church calendar with hymns and prayers and parental input for Jewish, Muslim and Hindu festivals. House point system for reward and punishment. Teachers have sweetie tins (contradicting dental education). School lunches compulsory, fruit and salad optional but not favourite. New school council for democracy. Captain's table for class reps' working lunches with cook and staff. Buddy system for y3 juniors arriving on new site. Lunchtime and after school clubs for chess, Lego robotics, German, gym, drama, short tennis. School buzzing until 4.45pm.

Happy air. Late arrivers seem to settle well. 'It wouldn't suit someone who's lazy but I can't think of any loners in this school,' say boys. 'Its hothouse reputation has changed,' say parents, 'there's pressure before the entrance exams but overall it's quite laid back.' 'I hope the boys are enjoying the happiest days of their lives,' says head.

THE AMERICAN SCHOOL IN LONDON JUNIOR SCHOOL

1 Waverley Place, London, NW8 0NP

Tel: 020 7449 1200
Fax: 020 7449 1350
E-mail: admissions@asl.org
Website: www.asl.org

- Pupils: girls and boys; all day • Ages: 4-10 • Fees: £5,100-ish
- Independent

Remarks: For further information, see senior school.

ARDINGLY COLLEGE JUNIOR SCHOOL

Linked to Ardingly College in the Senior section

Haywards Heath, West Sussex, RH17 6SQ

Tel: 01444 893200 (Jnr Sch)
Fax: 01444 8932001
E-mail: registrar@ardingly.com
Website: www.ardingly.com

- Pupils: 230 in the Junior school and 85 in the Pre prep
- Ages: 7-13 in the Junior school 3-7 in the Pre prep • C of E
- Fees: Pre-prep £950 - £1,900. Juniors - day £2,545 - £3,200; boarding £4,720 • Independent • Open days: Some Saturdays in October, March and May

Head: Mr Mark Groome (Junior school) Mrs Sue Vermeer (Pre preparatory school).

Entrance: Interview with the head and an assessment during a 'taster day'.

Exit: All pupils sit Common Entrance in year 8.

Remarks: Lower school actually in two – pre-prep 'Farmhouse' in old farm buildings takes from 3-7, junior school in wing of main building, from 8-13 – all integrated into one 'college'. Juniors has excellent performing arts studio and strong dance, music and much specialist subject teaching. Uses main school sports, music and other facilities but pretty self-contained otherwise. 20 full time boarders still in 2004 but Saturday school on the way out and casual flexi/weekly boarding on offer from 2005. Daily games, very secure site, parents met at end of day by head. Good, popular after school activities until 5.30 to help busy parents. 'My school,' announced unprompted 11-year old, 'is exceptional. They have helped me hugely even though I'm not sporty and it's very good academically and musically too.' Parents agree, 'they produce all-round individuals rather than hot-housing them.' This school is on the up.

ARDVRECK SCHOOL

Gwydyr Road, Crieff, Perthshire, PH7 4EX

Tel: 01764 653 112
Fax: 01764 654 920
E-mail: office@ardvreck.org.uk
Website: www.ardvreck.org.uk

- Pupils: 147 (split roughly 60/40 boys/girls); 109 board, 38 day. No weekly or flexi boarding; 19 in pre-prep department • Ages: 4-13 (including Little Ardvreck) • Inter-denom • Fees: Boarders £4,795; Day Pupils £3,190 • Independent

Headmaster: Since 2000, Mr Patrick (Paddy) Watson MA PGCE (mid-forties) who comes to Ardvreck from Swanbourne House where he was housemaster and head of English. Educated at Charterhouse, followed by philosophy and theological studies at St Andrews, then PGCE at Reading, Mr Watson started his teaching career at Woodcote House, after a brief spell in the banking world. His wife, Sara, taught French at Swanbourne; they have a son at Gordonstoun and a daughter at Ardvreck – and of course the essential black labradors – this time called Bracken and Waffle.

Bubbly and enthusiastic, Mr Watson, positively buzzes when he talks education, and is delighted to be able to do at least some teaching – sixth and third forms. Children like him – 'he's a nice head but not as much fun as our last one, who was a bit like a used car salesman', was one child's comment.

Entrance: Via nursery or pre-prep but most come at 8. Boarding in the last year no longer compulsory but great majority do. Prospective pupils spend a day in school (or overnight if boarding) and wear school uniform 'so they don't stick out'. Head and wife spend a long time interviewing parents and give all prospective pupils 'an academic assessment, not very difficult, but like to know where children are at'. He occasionally says no.

Exit: Last year's thirty-one leavers went to fourteen public schools – ten south of the border and twenty-one staying in Scotland. About a third go to nearby Glenalmond, a smattering to Gordonstoun and Fettes and, interestingly, Oundle. Beyond that, in ones, to Scottish and English schools – more of this now than a few years ago. The 'steady handful of awards' continues.

Money Matters: Selection of academic scholarships on offer and bursary support available, subject to means test.

Remarks: Numbers steady. School had a bit of a glitch in the late 1990s and is now said 'to be back on form again'. It's about two pupils off being full – register now! Purpose-built Victorian school (1883), with swimming pool (rather grand, but in a polythene tent nonetheless) and a fairly ad hoc collection of classrooms (some a lot better than others) which straggle across the back of the hog, but work well. Little Ardvreck now gathered at one end of the hog, rows of green wellies everywhere.

Ardvreck has just had a mini building boom and Mr Watson inherits a brand new combo-hall, with carpentry below, all singing and dancing above, cunningly perched on really quite a steep slope. Four tennis court/three netball court/hockey pitch Astroturf opened September 2004; two senior houses to prepare boys and girls for public school, with mixed age dorms except for the last term when CE candidates bond – girls can and do their own washing. Dorms filled with climbing boots and rucksacks; school does three mini Barvicks each summer term, very popular. Fixed exeat every third weekend, Friday noon – Sunday 7.30pm, and great misery if the exeat coincides with any dorm's turn for the 'red room' (equal in hideousness of colour and popularity and full of games).

Class sizes 15/16, no streaming though maths is taught in sets. Two sister CE classes in sixth (RTQ = READ THE QUESTION), lots of scholarships and awards, but no honours board. Excellent learning support both for the bright and for those with dyslexia et al, plus three student teachers who help in class. Keyboarding skills on offer and computers for teaching maths and English as well as more trad teaching; French from five, lyrical art room. Seriously strong orchestra – forty play at assembly each Friday. Singing and drama outstanding, school regularly features in the ribbons at the Perth Festival. Outstanding on the games front – all sports, all comers, though parents from other schools have been heard to mutter about trying too hard (still). Games pitches fairly well scattered on the flatter areas.

Head likes to 'discuss naughtiness rather than just punish it' and 'work out what went wrong', 'it's a true family atmosphere'. Parents 'a close-knit group of families', not too many first time buyers, with pupils 'tending to remain friends well into middle age' – and beyond!!

ARNOLD HOUSE SCHOOL

1-3 Loudoun Road, St John's Wood, London, NW8 0LH

Tel: 02072 664 840
Fax: 02072 660 655
E-mail: office@arnoldhouse.co.uk
Website: www.arnoldhouse.co.uk

• Pupils: 252 boys, all day • Ages: 5-13 • C of E, but all are welcome • Fees: £2,950 plus £150 for lunches • Independent

Head: Since 1994, Nicholas Allen BA PGCE (fifties), educated at Bedales – 'it taught me that you look at people as individuals'. Read history and archaeology at Exeter and this is where his interests lie. Formal, pin-striped, very concerned for the welfare and reputation of the school. Not beloved by all the boys but generally agreed to be a highly efficient head. 'He might seem a bit like the Demon Headmaster when you first meet him,' said a parent, 'but he's actually very approachable if you have any concerns.' Still teaching where and when required.

Off to head Newton Prep (qv) in July 2006.

Entrance: Parents should register their son's name after his first birthday and before his second. At rising four, boys come in for a ten minute individual meeting with a senior member of staff. The school takes into account reports from nursery schools as well as looking at how the boys interact, but it's probably more important that parental values are in line with those of the school, plus, 'I'm hoping I've identified those who really want to come here.' Head says he aims to 'produce a balance of parental backgrounds.'

Exit: A large proportion to London day schools especially Westminster, St Paul's and Highgate. Also boarding schools eg Winchester, Eton, Harrow. OBs include Sir Jonathon Porritt, Sir Jonathan Miller, Sir Crispin Tickell, Sir John Tavener, Lord Ackner and Lord Wolfson.

Remarks: An extensive building programme, finished in 2001, has given the school five new classrooms, a six-room music suite, a large ICT room and a new library. Light, airy classrooms, a gym used for assemblies (the school has a larger hall at its sports ground in Canons Park, near Edgware), science lab, sunny art room at the top of the school. Largish (for inner London) playground. The junior school, years 1 and 2, is kept as separate as possible to create a family atmosphere. Class size 16 'which makes it feel almost like one-to-one tuition,' commented a parent, with two classes in each year. The junior forms are balanced by age. Setting from year 6 for maths and Latin. A few of the brightest take up Greek. French from year 2; in year 8 boys spend a week in France. A part-time special needs teacher works with boys who need extra help up to year 6; after that, 'they tend to prefer support outside the school, and we have a network of people we can recommend'. However, one mother commented that she felt the school doesn't tackle dyslexia seriously. Her son has managed to keep up and is very happy – 'which says a lot for the teachers' – but doesn't get enough support.

The school is in a quiet side-turning off the Finchley Road, opposite the American School. Eight acres of playing fields, plus a large hall, at Canons Park. 'It is quite a long trek,' commented a parent. Boys are bused there once or twice a week for football, rugby, hockey and cricket and matches on Saturdays. Gym, basketball, volleyball back at the school. 'It's great if your son's very good at games – not so good if he's just normal,' said a parent – school says most would not agree. Strong on art with plenty of paintings and ceramics on display, including delightful individual plaques designed and made by leavers. Most boys learn at least one instrument; several orchestras and choirs, with entry by audition and invitation. Plenty of drama. Some after-school clubs eg judo, chess, but 'boys in London lead busy lives – it's tempting for families to overload their children,' says the head.

The school code of conduct, written by the head, indicates 'the school's expectations of civilised behaviour in the belief that good manners provide the foundation on which a happy community is built.' The school prefers remonstration to punishment, with 'far more rewards than sanctions. One tries to impress on the boys the value of civilised living.' School dinners still have a good reputation. Newly formed Parents' Association, composed of reps from each form, organises fundraising events, coffee mornings and cocktail parties. Weekly newsletter and termly parent-teacher evenings, though one parent commented that she didn't have much of a feel for what was going on – 'I rather feel that I'm kept at the gate;' head is there for half an hour every morning to greet boys and parents. Head says that parents are encouraged to get in touch swiftly if they feel there is a problem. Many rewards for achievement, and parents of high-flyers sing the school's praises, although a parent of an average-ability child commented, 'there should be more for those who aren't stars.'

School is pretty popular, especially amongst St John's Wood-ites. Parents are mostly upmarket north London professionals; plenty of four wheel drives and Space Wagons around at collection time. Boys lively, very polite, very privileged – 'it's a typical English prep school – it turns out little gentlemen,' said a satisfied parent.

THE ARTS EDUCATIONAL SCHOOL (TRING) JUNIOR DEPARTMENT

Linked to Arts Educational School (The) (Tring) in Senior section

Tring Park, Tring, Hertfordshire, HP23 5LX

Tel: 01442 824 255
Fax: 01442 891 069
E-mail: info@aes-tring.com
Website: www.aes-tring.com

- Pupils: a few girls and boys, can board • Ages: 8-11
- Independent

Remarks: See main school.

ASHDELL PREPARATORY SCHOOL

266 Fulwood Road, Sheffield, South Yorkshire, S10 3BL

Tel: 0114 266 3835
Fax: 0114 267 1762
E-mail: headteacher@ashdell-prep.sheffield.sch.uk
Website: www.ashdell-prep.sheffield.sch.uk

- Pupils: 115 girls, all day • Ages: 4-11 • C of E • Fees: £2,050
- Independent • Open days: Early October

Head: Since 2002, Mrs Sheila Williams (late forties); Diploma in Education from Aberdeen College of Further Education and Certificate in ICT. Has worked as a training officer for two multi-national companies, one based in the Netherlands, as well as teaching, in France and as head of Key Stage Two at Kent College. Very capable, up to date, innovative in a thoughtful way, enthusiastic, involved and easy to talk to. Particularly interested in IT, sport, music and French. Supported by an energetic, multi-talented male deputy head.

Entrance: The school looks for confident, mature girls of at least above average IQ. Initial pre prep entry is by informal assessment; maths and English tests after that.

Exit: Mostly to Sheffield High with the odd girl going to Oakham, Wakefield High or other local schools.

Remarks: Attractively decorated Victorian houses with well-tended small-scale gardens, including a lily pond, and thoughtfully designed asphalt play areas – the pre-prep has three Wendy houses and the prep a climbing wall. Classrooms are spacious, bright, light and well equipped, particularly for practical subjects; plenty of displays of good work and photographs of school activities in the corridors. Well-stocked library; all girls learn to touch type – 'fabulous IT,' commented a parent.

Academic standards are high, classes are small (a maximum of 20, with only 11 in one this year); there is regular testing and an atmosphere of enthusiastic, well disciplined learning in the classrooms; specialist teaching builds up over the years and is offered throughout in ICT, sport and creative/practical subjects. SATS are taken but marked internally and not allowed to dominate the curriculum. The very able receive a separate stimulating programme delivered by staff specialists for half a term/year. Special needs girls receive extra support (no extra charges; all pre prep children are to be screened for dyslexia from this year) and care is taken to nurture every pupil's self esteem – emotional intelligence is taken seriously, as are awareness of different learning styles, encouragement of creativity and independent learning and girls taking responsibility for enterprises. Woodwork, textiles and cookery are timetabled – school dinners (made on the premises) excellent.

Lots of music, in the lunch hour and after school (though girls are mostly encouraged to use the lunch hour for outdoor play): all learn the recorder and keyboard; orchestra for all plus choirs and instrumental groups. Other after school clubs are developing. Girls compete against local schools in a variety of sports; everyone has a chance to play in a team.

Only a few obviously ethnic minority children but girls come from a mixture of cultures/countries and levels of incomes. 3 per cent have bursaries. Pupils confident, happy and enthusiastic. The uniform – dark red blazers, summer boaters and winter grey felt hats, and even red schoolbags – bespeaks its traditional leanings, but the relatively new head is bringing the school tactfully into the 21st century. Teachers know the girls well and talk openly to parents. A protected, very well endowed little world for bright responsive girls, but not so much for those of a less conventional or less tractable turn of mind.

ASHDOWN HOUSE SCHOOL

Forest Row, East Sussex, RH18 5JY

Tel: 01342 822 574
Fax: 01342 824 380
E-mail: headmaster@ashdownhouse.com
Website: www.ashdownhouse.co.uk

• Pupils: around 115 boys, 65 girls; all board except for a few in the early years • Ages: 7-13 • C of E services, but with wide ecumenical base • Fees: £5,700 • Independent • Open days: Visits by appointment

Headmaster: Since 2003, Mr Robert Taylor BA PGCE, mid-thirties. Eleven years at Wellington College, six as housemaster, teaching English. Married to Sarah, formerly deputy head in Eagle House's pre-prep. They make an engaging team, with the earnest enthusiasm and eager freshness of a couple of gap year students and you do get the feeling that they are enjoying a great adventure – along with putting in all the dedication and hard work necessary to maintain the reputation of this doyen among preps. Their two small sons will join the school in due course and are already, though still of pre-school-age, very much part of the school family. A teaching head, he broke our meeting to continue his lunchtime reading of 'Twelfth Night' with his top year – clearly much relished by all. Mr Taylor has a clear focus on what makes Ashdown different – 'we could probably get another 5-10 per cent out of them at CE but we're not "results-driven"'. Relaxed approach – 'we let them climb trees' – and carries his parents with him.

Entrance: At 7 by interview and 'chatting to parents'. There is no testing. Later on, at 10-11, there will be some testing in core subjects but the main assessment is still by interview and the applicant may be invited to spend 24 hours at the school. Everyone boards although the new, younger, children who live locally may spend the first term or two as day pupils – but they miss out on so much they soon want to move in.

Exit: Very, very impressive – extraordinarily so given the lack of academic screening at entry. Head and pupils concur – 'it's fantastic teaching'. We grilled (gently) a number of pupils and not a word of dissent! And the results: 2004 saw 5 each to Ampleforth, Benenden, Marlborough, Stowe; 3 each to Charterhouse and King's Canterbury and 8 to Eton. The total tally of places 1999-2004 is between 10-17 places each at Benenden, Bryanston, Charterhouse,

Harrow, Tonbridge and Winchester; 25 at Marlborough, 32 at King's and 54 at Eton. Ten schols awarded in 2004 including 2nd and 6th to Winchester and music schols to Eton and Marlborough. Notable former pupils are Boris Johnson, Rachel Johnson (Daily Telegraph), Damian Lewis, Nicholas Coleridge and Viscount Linley.

Remarks: You have to know where you're going. You leave the village of Forest Row, just south of east Grinstead, and turn left through farmland – the school is 'landlocked' by the farm and wonderfully secure and unvisited as a result. It could otherwise be a bit of a Mecca for tourists. The house is one of only two in this country designed, in 1793, by the extraordinary Benjamin Henry Latrobe, later the designer of the Capitol and White House, and the Greek revival style evident there is plain in the square grey stone house with its elegant front portico. It looks out over delicious Wealden hills and fields, is surrounded by proud trees, beautiful gardens and birdsong. There are no signs and it feels like a very inviting family home. It's hard to imagine a more privileged place in which to spend your early years.

The main building, into which the school moved in 1893, houses the headmaster's study, the school secretary and the library and leads upstairs into the boarding accommodation. Everywhere are newer buildings – some unremarkable blocks used for subject teaching, other more imaginative ones, built in the last 20 years, include a first-rate theatre (1986) in which they do 8-9 plays a year, science block (2002) and swimming pool. Old farm buildings have been adapted – art happens, excitingly, in the old piggery and The Barn – huge and empty but for rubber floor and nets – is a much prized asset into which Old Boys scurry when on visits, given half a chance. The emphasis, then, is not on 'smart' or 'facilities' to impress parents but on a relaxed atmosphere and freedom. 'We're a bit madcap,' says head, cheerily. 'You won't find all the boots in order on the boot rack. We think of it as homely.' So, there is a little farm in which children can take care of goats, chickens and guinea pigs' and it's not a sanitised place. There's a 'jungle' – a wonderful woody place for making dens – and a pond – 'we don't fence it off because that's not what this place is about' – and lots of space around, despite all the buildings that former pupils wouldn't recognise. There's also space for the houses which the head hopes to build so that more staff can live on site. Lots do – in attractive ordinary houses and it all helps to maintain the homey feeling. Staff here clearly like joining in and off-duty staff will be found at weekends playing games or helping in some way or other. Head's house, in happy white clapperboard, abuts playing field – a 10-second sprint to his study.

In the middle of it all near the main house is the rather grim-looking chapel but, once you're inside you're in something that looks like a charming combination of a wooden dolls' house and a Quaker meeting house with lines of pews facing each other and a super little gallery looking over one side. Prayers for the whole school happen in here and are traditional – Authorised Version and so on. Playing fields all around (though girls visit Astroturf in East Grinstead for hockey.) Very successful sports – especially for girls, who were U13 netball national champs in 2002 and 2003. Brilliant athletics, national polo champs and rugger, soccer, tennis golf all played enthusiastically and successfully. Music of all kinds comes mellifluously out of windows – we heard a recorder group, trumpet and some very good jazz piano on our wanderings. Art is fun – a recycling project involved preparing for a fashion show using old sacks and other recyclables in every possible style.

Exeats are once or twice a term in addition to a week's half-term. Also up to three or four Sundays allowed out per term (after chapel) but – there's so much to do if you stay in. One boy, asked what he did at weekends when others went out, looked breathless at the choices and gulped, 'yesterday I played golf (on their own 9-hole course) for six hours – pretty amazing!' Around a half will be in school on any given weekend and have pretty much free range. Food – we saw it – looked like proper food; lots of variety and properly cooked and very healthy, though there were sausage rolls and sponge puds for the die-hards. Dorms vary in size and bed numbers – from 9 to 4 – but all are reasonably roomy though hardly smart. Older children have bedside tables and no room is worryingly tidy. Good system of pastoral care which begins with the 'dorm captains' – a year 8 pupil is in each dorm – and devolves to the house parents, matron, school sister, teacher or Mrs Taylor as required. Children express immense confidence in it. Sanctions and withdrawal of privileges applied where necessary – the principal crime being cruelty and treated severely. 'I have three rules,' says head, 'Be kind. Be kind. Be kind.'

A third of pupils comes from within a 30 mile radius, a further third from London and the rest from overseas, the majority of those being ex-pats. A few overseas pupils but very few require help with English and school is not busily selling itself in the Far East. Around 30 have some kind of special educational needs and are helped by 3 part-timers and the head of learning support – the extent depending on need. School selling its chateau in Normandy as they are 'keen to extend the range and variety of school trips to include more adventurous training, specific history and geography fieldwork trips that pursue the interests of the staff'. Much lamenting among ex-pupils and their parents (who were allowed to borrow it) over this. Teaching (see above) uniformly praised. Whole school is networked including in the boarding areas so 'they can send emails in their pyjamas' – as you do. New 'webclub' acts as school newspaper and everyone enjoys contributing and, now, adding their own photographs to the pages. Head writes a weekly letter to parents – much enjoyed.

Not many full-boarding co-ed schools around. School is not overfull and feels just pleasantly busy. It's pretty hard to imagine the child who wouldn't think this place paradise.

ASHFOLD SCHOOL

Dorton House, Dorton, Aylesbury, Buckinghamshire/Oxfordshire border, HP18 9NG

Tel: 01844 238 237
Fax: 01844 238 505
E-mail: hmsecretary@ashfoldschool.co.uk
Website: www.ashfoldschool.co.uk

• Pupils: 273 prep and pre-prep; 187 boys, 86 girls. Day and flexible boarding • Ages: 3-13 • Christian • Fees: Day: pre-prep to prep £2,080 - £3,670; weekly boarding £4,160.
• Independent • Open days: November and February

Headmaster: Since 1997, Mr Michael O M Chitty (early forties), married to barrister wife Louise, with two children at public schools. Previously housemaster and economics/politics teacher at Stowe, head-hunted to reverse failing fortunes at Ashfold. Educated at Clifton College, Bristol, read economics at Exeter before following father's and grandfather's footsteps into the Army. During nine years' service, reached rank of captain in Queen's Royal Irish Hussars. Travelled extensively, temporary equerry to Prince Philip, bitten by the teaching bug when posted to Sandhurst as officer instructor. Resigned commission and followed fast track to school headship.

He has already had a huge impact, with pupil numbers rocketing. Boundless energy and enthusiasm, hits floor running when faced with new challenge. Great supporter of co-education (girls now number almost 40 per cent) and benefits of boarding, shamelessly proud of pupils' achievements. No longer teaching but adopts 'hands-on' leadership role wherever possible. Regularly seen on the sporting field as well as in the classroom. Leaves running of pre-prep very much to department head Gill Venn, though 'would hate to think the younger children don't know who I am'.

Commands respect throughout school – well-liked by staff, pupils and parents alike – and enjoys overwhelming support of governors. Runs the school with military efficiency. Clearly loves the place. 'I'm here to stay.'

Entrance: Non-selective. Children invited to visit school for assessment only. 'It's important that the child is placed in the right form and that parents are sure they've made the right choice,' says Chitty. Screening process at age 7 for dyslexia and other learning difficulties in both new intake and existing pupils. Limited specialist provision available so more suitable schools may be recommended in more serious cases. Waiting lists for pre-prep places. Get in early.

Exit: No one school favoured, exit list changes year to year according to pupils' needs. Most popular are St Edward's, Oxford, Magdalen College, Radley, Stowe, Bradfield, Rye St Antony Oxford, Rugby and Oxford High. Local grammars also get a few. Sixth formers consistently successful in winning places at chosen schools, some on scholarships.

Remarks: Visually stunning Jacobean mansion set in 30 acres of well-kept playing fields and rolling Buckinghamshire countryside. Six years ago, school numbers declined to 156 and were still falling. Chitty's arrival stopped the rot. More than half the staff have changed since his appointment and pupil numbers are up to 273 with more registered. Wants to keep school 'small' though and won't go above 280. Now genuinely co-ed with all classes mixed, only competitive sports segregated. Boarding making a bit of a comeback (fiercely promoted by the head). Only weekly boarding available though most stay just one or two nights a week to take full advantage of evening clubs and after school activities like drama, shooting, chess and art. Facilities impressive for a school of this size. Pupils have no excuse for finding themselves at a loose end.

Classes, average size 15, scattered around the site. New nursery and pre prep department due to open in September 2006. All classroom walls covered with children's work, more hanging from ceilings. Real feeling of happiness as well as learning. More pleasing to the eye are the original red-brick out-buildings which have been transformed internally to provide music, art, French, design and technology and ICT rooms. Classrooms have own computer and interactive whiteboards. Library in main school building overhauled, £1000s worth of new books being bought thanks in part to parental fund-raising.

Brightly painted dorms on mansion's first floor, a landing of creaky floorboards separating the boys' from the girls'. Bathrooms refurbished (they needed it). Junior department occupies recently reorganised wing of main house with senior department lessons and science lab in functional single-storey structure near pre-prep. Dreary environment for older pupils more than compensated for by freshness of teaching. Lots of interaction in lessons. Won't be found in any national league tables as pupils don't sit SATs (exams dismissed as 'nonsense' by the head. 'How do you measure confidence, kindness and enthusiasm?'). Instead school sets own tests from year 2 onwards and last inspection found 95 per cent were reaching or exceeding levels expected of them. No Saturday morning lessons.

Sport important to Ashfold, where games are played every afternoon. New changing rooms alongside the large, bracing sports hall. There's rugby, football, cricket and hockey for boys, hockey, netball and rounders for girls, with tennis, athletics and swimming (summer only in smallish outdoor pool) for all. Compete to high standard against rival schools. Chitty says school 'can't compete against the likes of The Dragon and others which are so much bigger' but even so results are surprisingly good. 'Ashfold can more than hold its own on the sports field,' he insists. Also (for many years) national prep school champions in clay pigeon shooting.

Everyone learns recorder (parents have our sympathy) as part of the curriculum, with 75 per cent taking up second or third instruments. Orchestra, two strings groups, junior choir (all-comers welcome), intermediate choir and senior choir (by audition) as well as mixed choir of parents and pupils. Daily school life starts with assembly in the village church or in the wood-panelled saloon (school hall). Strongly C of E, accepts other denominations. All pupils put into one of three houses – Dragons, Gryphons and Lions – for competitive reasons only. Rewards system of credits and debits a big hit with children who get personal pride from a job well done as well as seeing their efforts added to the 'house' total. 'They can see how their behaviour affects others.' Trophy is awarded to house with most credits. Houseparents living in school look after boarders but pastoral care undertaken by form teachers. Younger children also encouraged to turn to prefects who have powers only to report not punish. Bullying taken very seriously by staff but, when asked, pupils said it didn't exist although anti-bullying policy does. 'It starts with making sure children understand it is not acceptable behaviour,' says head.

Ashfold's real strength is breadth of education. Not fiercely academic – 'I don't believe in thrashing children academically,' says head – but balanced across the board. High percentage of sixth formers gain scholarships to their next schools. Director of studies reviews the curriculum to see if changes need to be made. Pupils come from wide variety of backgrounds. Some old money, some new. Chitty says, 'this is a warm, friendly, family, purposeful school that turns out nice, well balanced, confident children.' Kids agree it's 'fun' and 'friendly'.

ASHFORD FRIARS PREPARATORY SCHOOL

Linked to Ashford School in the Senior section

Great Chart, Ashford, Kent, TN23 3DJ

Tel: 01233 620493
Fax: 01233 636579
E-mail: ashfordfriars@ashfordschool.co.uk
Website: www.ashfordschool.co.uk

- Pupils: 335 girls and boys; boarding and day • Ages: 0-11
- Christian, but all faiths welcome • Fees: £1,588 - £2,808
- Independent • Open days: £1,588 - £2,808

Head: Richard Yeates, previously housemaster at King's College, Taunton.

Entrance: All pupils interviewed (not always tested); not hard to get in (the nursery is currently over-subscribed) but getting tougher.

Exit: Automatic entry to the senior school – refreshing. About 20 per cent pupils go elsewhere, mainly to grammar schools, some to other independent schools.

Remarks: Since the move to Great Chart has spacious and comprehensive facilities of its own in addition to those shared with senior school. On-site playing fields, swimming pool with learning pool, sports hall, tennis courts, theatre, science labs, technology lab, music rooms and modern learning resource centre.

Science specialists from year 2 and music/art/dance specialists from year 3. Buzzy art department. ICT is used across the curriculum. Generally a lively feel to the place.

ASHVILLE JUNIOR SCHOOL

Linked to Ashville College in the Senior section

Green Lane, Harrogate, North Yorkshire, HG2 9JP

Tel: 01423 724 800
Fax: 01423 505 142
E-mail: ashville@ashville.co.uk
Website: www.ashville.co.uk

- Pupils: boys and girls; boarding and day • Ages: Pre-prep: 4-7; junior 7-11 • Fees: Day £1,948 - £2,348; boarding £4,758 - £4,845. Pre prep £1,590 • Independent • Open days: October

Head: Mr Chris Britt-Compton. Pre-prep head Miss Louise Savage.

Pupils and Parents: For pupil numbers, see senior school.

Entrance: Entry to pre-prep and junior school is by interview with the head of the school.

Exit: Majority to Ashville College, some to local state schools, handful to other independent schools.

Remarks: A cheerful and cosy environment with a convivial head who's done much to develop the school during his 21-year reign. Art abounds, all y4 learn the violin and recent introduction of interactive whiteboards brings a new dimension to lessons. Pupils taught in form groups but specialist teaching in French, music, science and ICT. Over 20 clubs from dancing and bridge to orienteering and Spanish. School council a role model to others. Recent push on teaching and learning is impacting positively on results but no room for complacency, well aware of competition from local state schools.

Pre prep a purpose-built happy, vibrant environment. Pleasing inspection. Used to be popular with those unable to secure a place in the local high-achieving primary schools but now over-subscribed so book early.

ATHOLL SCHOOL

Linked to Glasgow Academy (The) in the Senior section

Mugdock Road, Milngavie, Glasgow, G62 8NP

Tel: 0141 956 3758
Fax: 0141 337 3473
E-mail: enquiries@tga.org.uk
Website: www.theglasgowacademy.org.uk

- Independent

AUCHTERGAVEN PRIMARY SCHOOL

Prieston Road, Bankfoot, Perth, PH1 4DE

Tel: 01738 787 227
Fax: 01738 787 595
E-mail: headteacher@auchtergaven.pkc.sch.uk

- Pupils: 145 boys and girls; all day • Ages: 3-11 • State

Head: Since 2004, Miss Linda Rogers CertEd, AUPE (which she doesn't use) (fifties – but you would never guess) who was educated at Peterborough, the County Grammar, followed by Bourne Grammar, and Stanford College of FE. Post school she attended the Kesteven Coll of Ed followed by the Associateship of Upper Primary Education. She was head of Airlie Primary School before coming here and previously taught all over the Perthshire/Dundee hinterland. Keen on rubrics, and 'supply teaches'; she also answers the telephone, acts as receptionist, and whizzes all over the school picking up and sticking together. An effervescent and bubbly head, she is enjoying her latest challenge, and talks faster than most heads we have recently interviewed.

Entrance: The school is all-embracing, so children coming up from the nursery – as long as they are in the right catchment area – plus all comers. Slight problems when children arrive in the area and their particular age group is full, but composite classes (ie more than one age group) are OK.

Exit: Usually at 11 to Perth Grammar or Breadalbane Academy (the two are equidistant). A very occasional pupil will head off to the independent sector.

Remarks: A stunning school – an earlier Victorian

building which was much extended in 1999, with new windows and a totally modern feel. Max class size is 24 – but it might be 25 or 33, SEN on board, but currently no problems. The school follows national guidelines. IT is rampant, wireless throughout, with two interactive whiteboards, masses of computers everywhere – even in the nursery – where we found a small girl totally engrossed, with earphones, on a serious computer. Flat screens abound, and there is a trolley of lap tops which motors round the school. The ICT programme includes keyboarding. French from ten, currently Gaelic at six; good sciences, school is piloting the new Perth and Kinross maths initiative. Strong positive personal social development.

Has the occasional glitch with city (ie Perth) pupils being a trifle 'cityish', but bullying firmly sat upon. Weekly assemblies, where God is not totally omnipresent. Good parent back-up. Much involved in charity, collection boxes everywhere. Strong games ethos, with more than the regulation one period a week of PE. The netball team won the rural schools league. Loads of parental support, and a 'jolly supportive school board'. School is keen on eco-education and they are currently building a bog-garden, much use is made of the (very) local Scotswood for environmental studies. Cooked lunch comes in from Stanley, buffet style, good dining room. Loads of care. What more can you ask?

AYSGARTH SCHOOL

Bedale, North Yorkshire, DL8 1TF

Tel: 01677 450 240
Fax: 01677 450 736
E-mail: enquiries@aysgarthschool.co.uk
Website: www.aysgarthschool.co.uk

- Pupils: 123 boys in the prep school, 80 boys and girls in pre-prep and nursery; 90 per cent plus board in the prep school
- Ages: 3-13 • Christian • Fees: Pre-prep £1,625 - £1750 day. Prep £4,015 day, £5,015 boarding • Independent

---

Head: Since 2002, Mr Anthony Goddard (fiftyish); succeeded popular ex-Uppingham housemaster Mr John Hodgkinson (Mr Goddard went from Cambridge to ICI and thence to Accenture – head of chemicals practice). Successful manager and marketing expert; no teaching experience but was an Aysgarth governor for ten years – imaginative appointment and numbers have risen by 20 per cent whilst maintaining the boarding focus. He teaches geography, some games and is very involved on the pas-

toral side. His wife Caroline ran her own Montessori school and is now a special needs teacher; she is very involved on the pastoral side, especially the settling in of new boys, and teaches Religious Studies. Three children, one at university and two working in London. Energetic and charming Mr Philip Southall (married to Louise, two boys on their way through Aysgarth and one at Uppingham) continues as assistant head; much liked and respected by the boys.

Entrance: By interview and assessment, no exam. 'We try not to turn anyone away.' A few scholarships and some bursary help. Siblings' discount.

Exit: Excellent record to public schools. Eton, Harrow, Shrewsbury, Ampleforth, Radley, Sedbergh, Stowe, Uppingham. Good sprinkling of academic and music scholarships.

Remarks: Beautiful rural setting in fifty acres of parkland; purpose-built 19th century school, including splendid tower from whose roof bagpipes may occasionally be heard. Sports facilities to die for especially cricket field and swimming pool. Traditional demanding curriculum (nearly all do Latin), taught by capable and committed staff; all lessons rated 'good or very good' in recent (2000) ISC inspection. Gaps noted by inspectors in DT and PSHE have been filled, with an impressive new creative arts centre just opened. Music outstanding under charismatic director, both instrumentally and chorally; Victorian chapel, with organ, is a gem. New staff and facilities have given a boost to the art, design and technology activities – creative side in general needed a boost. Very thoughtful SEN provision – clear and helpful leaflet for parents.

Sport has high profile – for all but the less sporty are offered various options. Not unusual for seven cricket sides to be fielded on one day. Golf and clay-pigeon shooting on offer. Great rivalry with Bramcote. Parties go regularly to an outdoor centre in the Hebrides run by the exotically named Torquil Johnson-Ferguson (old boy). Pastoral and boarding care excellent – inspected 2005 and met or exceeded all standards assessed; staff know boys well and boys look after each other (these easy relationships praised in ISI report) Plenty to do at weekends, though boys are not forced into multiple activities. Two exeats and a half term every term. Boarding accommodation has been renewed, top quality matrons and school nurse. Very strong parental support, including on governing body. Clientele mainly solid (upper) middle class from the north (including Scotland) and midlands, though a few NCOs' children from Catterick are starting to appear. Governors very active and close to headmaster. Lively Old Aysgarthian association – useful reporting from recent leavers at senior schools and former pupils keep in touch in adult life; a healthy family atmosphere centred on school.

Many of the boys look as though they are about to take Eton in their stride. There's an almost Edwardian ease about the place and few families seem to live in large towns. Some parents new to the game might be put off by this but they would probably be wrong. Aysgarth is a happy, lively place, full of confident, industrious lads, without a trace of snobbishness. And if you want a boys-only boarding school in the north of England, it's the only one there is.

BADMINTON JUNIOR SCHOOL

Linked to Badminton School in the Senior section

Westbury Road, Westbury-on-Trym, Bristol, BS9 3BA

Tel: 0117 905 222
Fax: 0117 962 8963
E-mail: juniorhead@badminton.bristol.sch.uk
Website: www.badminton.bristol.sch.uk

• Pupils: girls; a few board • Ages: 4-11 • Fees: £1,900 - £2,770 day • Independent • Open days: October and May - individual visits preferred

Head: Mrs Ann Lloyd, married, with grown-up children. Mid-fifties but claims to be 10 going on 9 and a half. Whatever her age, with her room full of teddies she is unquestionably on a par with the children. Warm, friendly, jolly and, without doubt, approachable by parents and pupils alike.

Entrance: Classes are small. Early registration is recommended to avoid disappointment, family moves, though, sometimes free-up places. Girls are invited for the day and observed at work and play; no formal assessment but girls need to have above-average ability to get in. Mrs Lloyd and her team will look out for the inquisitive, keen learner.

Exit: Girls are nurtured for automatic entry to the senior school, with boarding for those wanting to get the hang of it before moving up.

Remarks: Well-equipped dedicated classrooms, junior science lab, art and language rooms and well-stocked library. Full use made of the senior sporting facilities including pool. All girls encouraged to play a musical instrument with many playing more than one. Opportunity for the most able to join in with the senior girls' orchestra as well as their own. Healthy, balanced meals cooked in school, taken 'en

famille' with teachers. A traditional prep school where little girls, like the seniors, learn to work hard and play hard, developing talents and interests with a full academic and extra-curricular timetable. Any girl needing extra attention can be helped at the nearby dyslexia centre. Option of breakfast; after-school activities until 6pm, occasional overnight boarding. Parents say they can relax knowing that every aspect is catered for.

BANCROFT'S PREPARATORY SCHOOL

Linked to Bancroft's School in the Senior section

611-627 High Road, Woodford Green, Essex, IG8 0RF

Tel: 020 8506 6751
Fax: 020 8506 6752
E-mail: chris.curl@bancrofts.essex.sch.uk
Website: www.bancrofts.essex.sch.uk

• Pupils: 200 boys and girls, all day • Ages: 7-11 • C of E, but other faiths properly provided for • Fees: £2,322 • Independent • Open days: October, June

Head: Since 2005, Mr Christopher Curl, previously head of Ferndale Prep School in Oxfordshire.

Entrance: No waiting list. All candidates are seen twice individually in January of the year of entry, and there are admission tests 'designed to look for long-term potential more than precocious attainment, and not an intimidating experience'.

Exit: Guaranteed entry to the senior school.

BARNARDISTON HALL PREPARATORY SCHOOL

Barnardiston Hall, Nr. Haverhill, Suffolk, CB9 7TG

Tel: 01440 786 316
Fax: 01440 786 355
E-mail: barnardistonhall@yahoo.co.uk
Website: www.barnardiston.com

• Pupils: 115 girls, 125 boys (50 boys and girls board) • Ages: nursery and pre-prep; 2-7; prep 7-11 • Non-denom • Fees: nursery-pre-prep: £1,100-£2,300; prep: £2,950; boarding: £4,500 • Independent • Open days: None. Prospective parents visit at any time to tour school and meet children

Headmaster: Since 1990, Colonel Keith Boulter (fifties), married to Gail, who is deeply involved in the school; three grown up children, all working in education. Cambridge theology graduate, hockey blue and keen musician, he joined the Royal Army Educational Corps in 1973 and administered five Gurkha schools in Hong Kong, Nepal and Brunei. Also worked at MOD, briefing four star generals.

On leaving the army in 1990, Colonel Boulter bought Barnardiston when there were 52 children and no boarders. In 1995 a £1m pre-prep department was opened, and in 2004 a £1.5m prep extension, including classrooms, language lab and the Bridge (the SEN department). A straightforward, direct person, he is devoted to education and, although he claims not to be much of an administrator, he has more than put the school on the map and is thoroughly acquainted with every last nut and bolt of the organisation. He is very much hands-on, teaching hockey, maths to pupils from 9-13, training the choir, and leading frequent expeditions to the Derbyshire Dales, Ben Nevis and Snowdon. An ISC inspection report described his leadership as enthusiastic and visionary, others call him charismatic. He believes that a flexible approach is the key to bringing out the best in individual pupils and is keen to challenge and stretch them, both physically and mentally. Camping out in the grounds starts early. When the headmaster retires he would like to hand over the school to his own children, one of whom has already taught there.

Entrance: Children spend a day attending lessons and being observed and tested by subject teachers. The school's educational psychologist is used in the case of children with learning difficulties, to assess their particular needs.

Exit: Pupils tend to go on to independent schools of their first choice broadly in the area (there is always a good smattering of scholarships), or (a few) to local state schools.

Remarks: The school is in a lovely rural setting with about 15 acres (including an exciting adventure playground), where children are given a lot of freedom to roam around, build dens and explore. The main house, which is wood panelled and rambling and contains the office and boarding area, is also the Boulter home and has all the comfy domesticity and attractive clutter of a family house. Children, staff and large dogs mill around everywhere and there is clearly little or no distinction between private and public areas. Prospective parents are left to face up to 30 children crammed into the family sitting room, where the latter give an exuberant, no-holds-barred account of the school, which leaves the parents in no doubt as to the brilliance of the sport, the dubious quality of the macaroni cheese, the low tolerance of bullying and the bubbling confidence and happiness of the pupils.

Academically, the school does very well, with the pre-prep scoring well above the national average in maths and English tests. Children are streamed more or less from the word go, then setted for various subjects later on. French is taught from the nursery and Latin from y1 of the prep, with 'A' set French pupils taking Latin on to y6. IT provision is excellent, with a computer to every three children, and there is a fully computerised weather station. Full sets of armour doubtless add a touch of realism to history lessons.

About 50 children in the school, with anything from mild dyslexia, a problem with a specific subject to autism, are looked after by the Bridge. The name is apt, as it is both a long suite of cheerful, well-equipped first floor rooms, and also the department which aims to keep children with problems happily integrated in normal lessons. Up to 12 staff 'man' the Bridge, including 5 classroom assistants, who give help to small groups of children within the classroom, and specialists (two of whom are fully qualified SEN teachers) who deliver one-to-one help outside lessons. Staff at the Bridge have been trained to run a highly successful programme called 'Sound Foundation', which helps children with reading difficulties to make rapid progress. All subject and class teachers are fully briefed about SEN children and armed with teaching strategies. There are several statemented children (with Aspergers, dyslexia, dyspraxia and autism) whose school fees are paid by the state. Children talk openly about their experience of the Bridge, which they clearly love, and there is absolutely no sense of any stigma, as all children see it as part of normal school life. The atmosphere of the Bridge is warm and lovely, as are people who work there. Colonel Boulter won't accept children he knows he cannot help, but the school quite literally 'turned round' more than one child rejected by every other school. The Bridge is also used for TEFL, to cope with some of the 15 per cent or so temporary or full-time pupils from overseas.

Art, music and drama are strong. The art studio, commanding stunning views of the countryside, produces highly colourful and creative work. 80 children play instruments and music plays a key role in the annual drama production. Choirs are regularly asked to perform at functions throughout the county. Sporting competition between houses and with other school is keen and teams do well. A recently erected semi-permanent marquee provides quite a reasonable sports hall until funds can be found for the real thing and, although Astroturf is also on the agenda, children seem to be very happy running about in the mud and rain.

Children wax lyrical about the wealth of extra-curricular activities and expeditions (one will be going soon to the base camp of Mount Everest), and children and their parents raise large sums for charities from Swaziland to Venezuela and Nepal, where a school party visited a school in 2004. The ISC report referred to the very high standard of pastoral care. Parents who choose this school can feel confident that no child will fall through the net in the warm family atmosphere that prevails. There is a 'I just wanted to tell you' letter box for anyone feeling shy about a particular issue, and the fact that several staff have or have had children at the school speaks volumes in itself. Staff say what a wonderfully happy place it is to work, and parents are similarly enthusiastic. This school comes highly recommended.

BASSETT HOUSE SCHOOL

60 Bassett Road, London, W10 6JP

Tel: 02089 690 313
Fax: 020 8960 9624
E-mail: info@bassetths.org.uk
Website: www.bassetths.org.uk

• Pupils: 170 boys and girls, all day • Ages: 3-8 boys, 3-11 girls
• Non-denom • Fees: £1,620 - £3,360; £1,000 deposit on joining the school (refunded when child leaves the school)
• Independent • Open days: Saturday open mornings held in the autumn and spring terms

Head: Since 2003, the glamorous Mrs Andrea Harris BEd Cert Ed CEPLF (forties). Married to another headteacher, with two sons in their twenties, she came directly from 8 years as deputy head at Denmead School in Hampton, with

comprehensive school experience from her pre-motherhood days. Don't be too fazed by the immaculately-coiffed reserve – parents say that she knows every child's name and face. Mrs Harris is articulate, and the general opinion is that she will prove very effective. Determined to expand the school to 11-plus, increasing the class sizes in the early years with scholarships offered to 'bright girls from the maintained sector'. Very keen on rewarding and recognising all levels of success for the children (and teachers) – there is a book with calligraphied weekly achievements in the entrance hall, popular with both children and parents.

Entrance: Only after a visit to the school – as soon as possible after birth. Parents are shown around by headmistress in small groups. Entry into the Den (3 years old) and Lower 1 (4 years old) needs no assessment but the final decision rests with headmistress. Child's first term is in the autumn unless a place becomes available at other times. Places occasionally become available for older children – by assessment; there is usually a waiting list. Places are offered in registration order with priority given to siblings – provided they are registered within one month of birth.

Exit: To day and boarding prep schools: Colet Court, The Dragon, The Hall, The Latymer Preparatory School, St Philip's, Summer Fields, Sussex House, University College, Westminster Cathedral Choir School and Westminster Under School. In due course Bassett House girls will sit exams for senior girls' schools in and outside of London.

Remarks: Just north of the Westway off Ladbroke Grove in a late 19th-century family house. A mother registered the need for the appreciation of individual children's differing levels of achievement and founded the school in 1947 – her three sons are part of the governing body today and her original ethos still prevails. Substantially rebuilt in 2001, the premises now include St Helen's church hall (about 100 yards away and only a side-street to cross) where assemblies are held. The church hall also houses a gymnasium, 3 classrooms, kitchen and a garden – after some shuffling of classrooms in the cosy main house, the Den and Lower 1 are based here – there is a 27-year lease and children are escorted here in a crocodile, holding hands. This split campus is common in London junior schools and the roads that have to be crossed do not cause parents concern. The main school building has a small playground/basketball/netball court and a nearby park provides extra recreational space. A fresh and varied lunch is prepared on site for full-day pupils and staff. A snack is prepared for children staying on for the many after school clubs. Uniform is compulsory from Lower 1 upwards.

Many pupils are walked to the school by ma or pa; a

few are dropped off by a mother driving to the gym or their office. The fluorescent-vested school marshals reckon the school is very friendly; parents often stop for a chat with each other or at least say hello to their child's classmates before the mobile pulls them to a nine o'clock meeting. The uncertain head situation for the two years prior to Mrs Harris's appointment (sudden illness the cause) encouraged strong relationships between parents who pooled advice and their children's social lives. With Mrs Harris at the helm, the parents are enjoying a stable, open-door policy from the school, yet the pressure to get the smartest children into big names schools is marked – as ever, this comes from the parents as much as the school.

An SEN teacher comes in two mornings a week and those pupils for whom English is a second language are looked after (not many, most non-English pupils are Americans and bi or tri-lingual Europeans) – a range of religious festivals are explored and celebrated by all.

The children are welcoming and forthright – from the traditional chorus of 'Good morning Miss...' to opinions about favourite teachers, subjects and food. The most confident do not seem to squash the opinions of the quieter ones for long. Lower school's teaching is based on the Montessori system and incorporates the Early Learning Goals – the little ones normally have a full-time student teacher as well as the usual form teacher. The Den teachers are loved and effective; all of the staff are well-qualified and dedicated. Everyone learns mathematics, reading, writing, drama, PHCSE, art, CDT, music, IT, PE and French; older children history, geography, Latin and science. Class sizes are usually under 20 and there are regular standard and non-standard assessments and the upper school sits SATs.

Each class has access to its own Apple Macintosh with broadband and cyber-patrolled ISP. An e-pal scheme with an Australian school has been set up. Links to the National Grid for Learning and an intranet configured with the sister schools, Orchard House School in Chiswick and Prospect House School in Putney. The early introduction to computer technology is impressive and introduction of laptops for the 'Classroom in a Box' initiative is explained on the school's website. Every classroom is equipped with an interactive whiteboard which has embedded ICT across the curriculum.

Sports skills are developed using the Kensington Memorial Park, Kensington Leisure Centre and the all-weather pitches at the Westway Centre, with matches arranged with the sister schools and other local ones. Individual music lessons are available as well as the group music lessons for each child and the weekly Dalcroze eurhythmics class for the younger children. A music performance at Christmas, a concert in the summer term and numerous after-school clubs – trips to the theatre/Imax and National Curriculum based workshops at a local centre, The Making Place, to encourage the children's creativity.

BEATRIX POTTER PRIMARY SCHOOL

Magdalen Road, Earlsfield, London, SW18 3ER

Tel: 02088 741 482
Fax: 02088 719 416
E-mail: Info@beatrixpotter.wandsworth.sch.uk
Website: www.beatrixpotterschool.com

• Pupils: 230; all day, 50/50 girls and boys • Ages: 3-11 • Non-denom • State

Head: Since 1988, Mr Stephen Neale MA DipEdTec (late forties), educated St Bede's, Guildford. Previously taught at a variety of London primaries, married with one grown-up son. Relaxed, a delightful person to talk to, might appear too easy going but, fear not, he fights hard for his school and knows exactly where he is going. A man with insight in many different areas, well-liked by parents and staff.

Entrance: Always over subscribed, 3+ nursery or 4+ reception, attending the nursery does not guarantee a school place. Very local clientele as priority given to those living closest to the school, sibling policy also only applies to those living in the priority area.

Exit: At 11+, 50/50 to independent/state sector, including Dulwich College, Streatham High, JAGS, Lady Margaret and the Sutton Grammar schools.

Remarks: A popular choice for some years. Took its name from the author (who used to draw on Wandsworth Common) – they have a display area for her works and memorabilia. Purpose-built, 1927, single-level accommodation reminiscent of a village school. Fabulous landscaped garden, imaginative range of play equipment including giant chessboard, pond with great crested newts.

Standard National Curriculum with added value, delivered by mainly long-serving, committed staff. Display boards brimming with colourful art work and an area dedicated to news from schools abroad where they have links: the next trip is to Louisiana. Good sports programme, works with Sport England. A choir and a talented dance teacher who undertakes anything from salsa to modern ballet. Head committed to everyone being involved, parents help in the school, open session every Thursday when pupils show visitors round the school and tell them what it's like to be a pupil there. SEN and EFL are catered for in-house by a specialist teacher. The head has housed The Rainbow Autistic School for the past couple of years which has recently found a permanent larger site.

A variety of after-school clubs are on offer but pupils have to find outside tutors for 11+ preparation. 'Busy children are happy children' atmosphere, there is something for everyone. Sadly, Beatrix Potter is only one class entry, the size of the school is part of its success and consistently high standards. Do not be put off by the prospectus, definitely not a glossy.

BEAUDESERT PARK SCHOOL

Minchinhampton, Gloucestershire, GL6 9AF

Tel: 01453 832 072
Fax: 01453 836 040
E-mail: office@beaudesert.gloucs.sch.uk
Website: www.beaudesert.gloucs.sch.uk

• Pupils: 156 boys (of whom 30 board), 138 girls (of whom 25 board); pre-prep 61 boys, 53 girls • Ages: 4-13 • Mostly C of E
• Fees: Day: pre prep £1,995; prep £2,590 - £3,735. Boarding £4,890 • Independent

Head: Since 1997, Mr James Womersley BA PGCE (forties) (aka Jumbo), educated at The Dragon, St Edwards and Durham where he read 'economics, history and rugby'. Previously at Eagle House, Emanuel (London), and a very popular housemaster at The Dragon where he taught maths and history. Married to Fiona who comes from a prep schooling family. Fiona is very involved in school life and takes a special interest in the girls' welfare. They have three sons, one in the school and two moved on to St Edward's, Oxford. Mr Womersley coaches rugby and athletics, enjoys walking, tennis and golf. Relaxed and very much hands-on.

Entrance: Waiting lists for the pre-prep till 2008, automatic transfer to the main school via a basic assessment, 'not selective in any way'. Pupils mainly local: Gloucestershire, north Wiltshire, Oxfordshire border etc.

Exit: Again, mostly local: Marlborough, Cheltenham and Ladies', Radley, Eton, Winchester, St Edward's, St Mary's Calne, Westonbirt and a wide range of others.

Remarks: School is perched at the top of a hideous (school says 'wiggly') drive up a hill on the edge of Minchinhampton Common surrounded by 30 acres of steeply terraced games fields, including a floodlit Astroturf and use of a further 12 acres on the common. Splendid Victorian Gothic with many additions (sympathetic Cotswold stone at the front) filled with rows of graded green wellies. The school term follows the Badminton set (ie closes down for the Horse Trials).

Three-weekly reports on each child as opposed to just one at the end of term. Children are graded on their individual improvement and marks are not read out for comparison. Great emphasis on self-worth. Certificates of Effort handed out in assembly, when everyone claps. Three forms in each year but pupils setted for maths, lang (French and Latin only) throughout and science in top forms – scholarships are important you see. Consistent learning support both one-to-one and in class throughout school. Music strong and ambitious, art and drama good.

Huge increase in younger staff, with accommodation currently being provided in rented cottages, plans afoot to convert the stables. Computers everywhere, each child has its own email and all sciences computer-linked. Good CDT and fabulous mega-gym with links to swimming pool tiled like a Roman bath. New building with 8 classrooms and art and design studios completed spring 2003, three new state of the art science labs completed October 2005. Performing arts centre planned for 2008.

Day pupils usually opt to board in their senior years, flexi-boarding an option but absolute max is 75 boarders. Uniform throughout, rather a jolly green, with girls in Black Watch kilts.

Friendly, happy school getting good results and turning out tomorrow's embryo Sloanes, not very streetwise.

BEDFORD HIGH SCHOOL JUNIOR SCHOOL

Linked to Bedford High School

Bromham Road, Bedford, MK40 2BS

Tel: 01234 334 205
Fax: 01234 217 118
E-mail: officesec@bedfordhigh.co.uk
Website: www.bedfordhigh.co.uk

• Pupils: all girls, all day • Ages: 7-11 • Christian ethos but respects other faiths • Independent

Remarks: See senior school.

BEDFORD PREPARATORY SCHOOL

Linked to Bedford School in the Senior section

De Parys Avenue, Bedford, Bedfordshire, MK40 2TU

Tel: 01234 362 271
Fax: 01234 362 285
E-mail: prepinfo@bedfordschool.beds.org.uk
Website: www.bedfordschool.org.uk

• Pupils: 458 boys, day and boarding • Ages: 7-13 • Fees: £7,782 - £12,030 pa • Independent • Open days: Late November and early May

Head: Mr Chris Godwin MA

Entrance: Major intake at 7 of 50. 15 at 8 and at 11, few in other years.

Exit: Most boys transfer smoothly to the senior school though all sit the internal entrance test.

Remarks: School shares playing field and many facilities with the senior school, though not teachers or main buildings. 1890s building, for 9-10 year-olds, engagingly known as 'The Inky' – from Incubator for fledgling Bedfordians. Good combination of the old and new here – very attractive new block with super Erskine May Hall used by town's population for musical events etc. Plenty of space, Astroturfed playground, civilised ambience. Good 1990s boarding house, good sport, pastoral care. Strong academic curriculum, good teacher/pupil ratio. A privileged, though not over-privileged, start in life.

BEDGEBURY JUNIOR SCHOOL

Linked to Bedgebury School in the Senior section

Goudhurst, Cranbrook, Kent, TN17 2SH

Tel: 01580 878 143
Fax: 01580 879 136
E-mail: registrar@bedgeburyschool.co.uk
Website: www.bedgeburyschool.co.uk

• Pupils: girls boarding from 9yrs onwards • Ages: Girls 2 1/2- 11 and boys 2 1/2- 7 • Church of England Afiliated • Fees: £6,575 boarding (full & weekly). £4,115 day • Independent • Open days: March and May

Head: Since 2000 Mrs Hilary Moriarty BA Hons, PGCFE, MA, diploma in educational leadership (late fifties, seems younger.) Married with four children – 3 grown up, one in sixth form at Worth. Educated Denbigh grammar school, read English. Previously deputy head of Red Maids' school in Bristol. An ISI Inspector. Has a regular monthly column in Home and Country, the national magazine of the WI and regularly contributes to the educational press. Straight talking, energetic and enthusiastic, wants the best for her students. Has a 'how can we do it better?' approach. Well-liked by the girls who say she has a good sense of humour, is approachable, friendly and understands their needs. Highly professional, runs a tight ship, cares passionately about the school.

Remarks: Modern, purpose-built, well-equipped junior school shares a handful of facilities with senior school: sports hall, chapel, dining hall, swimming and boarding otherwise largely autonomous. Own dedicated outdoor play area. Good disabled access throughout (not so in senior). All children screened annually; learning support available if needed. Close liaison and good communication seen as key. Mostly mixed ability grouping but set for maths from y4. Paired reading scheme operates between Bedgebury sixth formers and the juniors. Recently invited to join Learning through Landscapes project.

BEECHWOOD PARK SCHOOL

Markyate, St Albans, Hertfordshire, AL3 8AW

Tel: 01582 840 333
Fax: 01582 842 372
E-mail: admissions@beechwoodpark.herts.sch.uk
Website: www.beechwoodpark.herts.sch.uk

• Pupils: 500 boys and girls, flexi-boarding and day • Ages: 2 1/2 -13 • Inter-denom • Fees: Day fees £2,350 - 3,214; weekly boarding fees £4,138 • Independent • Open days: Termly

Head: Since 2002, Mr P C E Atkinson BSc MIBiol PGCE (mid forties). BSc and PGCE from Nottingham (a biologist), introduced IB biology at Sevenoaks School, deputy headmaster at the New Beacon School, Sevenoaks, then eleven years as head of Lochinver House School. Married to Claire, an educational psychologist; two children. Believes in breadth.

Took over from Mr D S (David) Macpherson, who was here for 15 years.

Entrance: Assessment and interview. The head stresses every child must qualify but entrance is non-competitive. Priority is given to siblings then date of registration is used. There are no scholarships but there is a bursary fund for those families who have fallen on hard times. Register early.

Exit: Co-ed choices anywhere in the country but most frequently to Rugby, Haileybury, Oundle, Mill Hill, Uppingham and Berkhamsted. Girls tend towards St Albans High, Abbot's Hill, Haberdashers' Aske's and Queenswood; boys also choose St Albans, Haberdashers, Aldenham and Bedford. Regular academic, music, art scholarships – including one recently to Winchester.

Remarks: Once the home of the Saunders Sebright family, set in 37 acres of countryside on the Hertfordshire/ Bedfordshire borders just outside Markyate. The original grade 1 listed building has been carefully maintained with new buildings housing the junior/middle departments, sports hall and performance hall. The stable block has been converted into a music school. There are two well-equipped computer rooms and each pupil has his/her own email address. Impressive,if, perhaps, a bit imposing for a young child, traditional wood-panelled library with modern computer catalogue system. Original parkland designed by Capability Brown and film buffs will recognise the drawing room from The Dirty Dozen.

Montessori nursery for children aged 2 1/2 to 5 years recently acquired. Daily bus and coach services pick up from surrounding towns and villages. Boarding is offered on a flexi-system from one or two days each week to weekly. The average age of teachers is 38. French is taught from reception, maths is set at year 4 and Latin and Greek are offered at year 6. Science is strong; the subject benefits from bright and well-equipped science labs. Pupils are continuously assessed and parents receive termly reports; school exams twice a year. Children are taught in class sizes of 20 with sets generally reducing class sizes. SATS results usually at level 5 for Key Stage 2.

The school takes special needs seriously. All children are screened for learning difficulties and those with special needs (dyslexia, dyspraxia) are given extra help from three SEN teachers. Several boys with dyslexia have gone on to become head of school. The school places equal emphasis on the 'special needs' of the academically gifted and those with outstanding talents. There's a special scholars' group in years 7 and 8 and a 'sparklers group' for academically gifted children lower down the school.

Pupils are taught that bullying is not acceptable via regular talks by the head and a pamphlet which is given to all children. Discipline is enforced via the 'pink card' which lists a pupil's merits and offences and must be signed by his/her parent. Those with rather more offences than others are sent to the head. Star badges are awarded every few weeks for effort rather than attainment. Certificates of merit given every term for special achievement.

Inter-school sporting fixtures on Saturdays. As well as outdoor playing fields, facilities include an indoor sports hall, squash courts, covered and heated swimming pool, tennis courts. Plans are underway for an all-weather pitch. Music, art and drama are strong here. Some 150 children learn a musical instrument. The choir was voted Choir of the Year in 1991 and 1992 and was also a finalist in the National Choir competition in 2000. Several children gain art scholarships and the new theatre stages many drama productions and concerts.

Beechwood comes across as a caring school with a warm, friendly atmosphere. Pupils are polite, happy and confident and achieve high standards.

BEESTON HALL SCHOOL

West Runton, Cromer, Norfolk, NR27 9NQ

Tel: 01263 837 324
Fax: 01263 838 177
E-mail: office@beestonhall.co.uk
Website: www.beestonhall.co.uk

• Pupils: 165. Co-educational (boys:girls 5:3) 95 boarding and 70 day, 'daily boarders' free at weekends • Ages: 7-13 • Mainly C of E, but provision made for RCs • Fees: Boarding £5,025; day £3,755 • Independent • Open days: Twice yearly

Head: Since 1998, Mr Innes MacAskill BEd (late forties). Spent 17 years at Caldicott Prep ultimately as deputy head. Married with three teenage daughters. Clearly a 'hands-on' head, knowing each child well and taking a fatherly interest in their concerns. Keen to keep the size and character of the school as it is, though clearly has both space and resources to expand if he wants to. Pristine yet inviting state of boarding houses testament to his belief that school has to be 'homely and comfortable as this is their home in term time.' A popular head, supported by his wife, Sandy, lively and fun, this is a partnership. Mr MacAskill clearly knows his market well and, through hard work and a twenty-four hours approach, gives parents exactly what they want for their children. A fellow head says he 'has all the best bits of headmastering under his belt and actually likes the children.' – not a universal characteristic.

Entrance: Candidates seen in spring prior to entry and assessed via 'reading and reasoning tasks'. Potential boarders invited to 'try it out'. Boarding numbers slightly down but most children opt to board before they leave. Entry not a foregone conclusion.

Exit: Wide spread of good schools, including Eton, Harrow, Oundle, Uppingham. Largest group go to Gresham's – several with academic and/or music scholarships here as well as to other excellent schools. Large number of awards 2002-3. On average, 30 – 40 per cent of leavers get them – in academic, music, art, all rounder and sporting fields – to schools as diverse as Queen Margaret's, Tudor Hall, Radley, Harrow, Oundle, Downe House and Uppingham. CE results good even for children in lower sets – recently all children have got into their first choice schools.

Money Matters: New means-tested bursaries for talented children and school has own in-house charity for parents who 'fall on hard times'.

Remarks: A very different ethos and atmosphere from, for example, Home Counties preps. Few video games, play stations and, even, TVs in evidence here. Children less sophisticated but open, natural, spontaneously friendly. Head stresses the pleasure children take in outdoor play – in the woods, in the extensive fields around school site, on the nearby beach in West Runton. School benefits from its position a couple of miles from north Norfolk coast, surrounded by farmland, National Trust woods and heathland. Most pupils come from trad country families but also now attracting families from very different backgrounds too. Shooting a popular activity here, as are sailing, golf and archery. School recently bought own fleet of toppers. National champions in several sports at this level in recent years, as well as many children gaining county, regional and national recognition.

Main school building a super Regency hall, sensitively adapted and beautifully maintained, extended and transformed. New buildings fit well into the site, being small scale and inviting. Super music school, new library, DT and IT rooms. Newly refitted labs, wonderfully civilised dining hall with conservatory extension looking onto putting green, surrounded by traditional Norfolk flintstone walls. Everywhere is beautifully decorated and kept in very good condition – remarkable given the age of the residents! Children are encouraged to keep their habitat orderly and given various duties and responsibilities – seen as part of their general education. Attractive boarding houses – recent ones like 'real' houses in scale. Rooms for 10s, 8s and 4s, dependent on age; a senior pupil in each room for younger children acts as a kind of 'room parent', for which they are given extra privileges in compensation. Boarding rooms not huge but colourful and snug with home duvets and toys, photos etc. Recent inspection praised pastoral care.

School rich in activities and clearly scarcely time enough in the day to do everything on offer. Superb, richly imaginative, witty and highly skilled artwork of all kinds, taught by teacher 30 years in post who clearly gets the best out of the children – beyond expectations. Pupils' art is everywhere, deservedly, in the school and a good thing too. Also everywhere are sofas – in the library, in the Common Room etc – giving lovely relaxed, civilised feel. Music also good – 80 per cent learn instruments – a huge variety offered, including bagpipes and harp. Ensembles of all kinds flourish, as does solo work. Strong SEN dept supports 15 per cent of children, mostly with mild dyslexia. Most children, against national trend, come from traditional boarding school families though few parents will have experienced comfort and care on this scale. Parents travel considerable distances to support weekend activities, although most do come from Norfolk or surrounding counties.

One of the very few full-boarding prep schools in East Anglia. Its small size creates rare family atmosphere. It does well by its pupils and turns out friendly, eager, purposeful and confident children who have been taught to take a pride in their school and in themselves.

BELHAVEN HILL SCHOOL

Dunbar, East Lothian, EH42 1NN

Tel: 01368 862 785
Fax: 01368 865 225
E-mail: headmaster@belhavenhill.com
Website: www.belhavenhill.com

- Pupils: 68 boys, 54 girls; 100 board, 22 day • Ages: 7-13
- Non-denom • Fees: Day £3,415; boarding £4,925.
- Independent

Head: Since 1987, Mr Michael Osborne MA (sixties) educated at Radley and Cambridge where he read economics and qualified as an accountant. Separated from his wife, who lives 'amicably' nearby with his two sons and daughter. Popular head, a Pied Piper, children love him – he knows his 32 and 57 times tables – 'well actually any times table'. Charming and enthusiastic, good at advising on senior schools, children keep up with him after they leave (and he writes back). With influx of excellent new staff parents no longer comment that not all staff are up to head's high standard and few mutter about, 'Michael showing his age'. He was very cross about this sentence, until we pointed out that not everyone knows their 57 times table (pupils test him regularly), and he is generally considered to be the best teacher of his generation in Scotland, which takes some living up to. MO (as he refers to himself) has yet to learn how to hold Anno Domini at bay, but has 'no intention of going for at least another ten years'.

Entrance: No test, but register as soon as possible. Children spend a day at Belhaven the term before they come.

Exit: About three a year to Eton, Ampleforth and Queen Margaret's, York, otherwise Glenalmond, Harrow, Loretto, St Mary's Calne, Downe House. Fettes, Gordonstoun, Oundle, Radley, Winchester, Shrewsbury, Uppingham and Stowe.

Remarks: Numbers greater than ever before and waiting lists for the next few years. Successfully co-ed since 1995 and additional, very comfortable girls' house built in

2004. 'Rash of new younger staff recently employed – they really care,' said one mother of three. School now boasts a formidable common room with, says the head, 'brilliant house staff, matrons and learning support teacher'. 'Scotland's school for toffs, which specialises in sending the little darlings to public school in the south. Dubbed 'Hogwarts for Muggles' by the Edinburgh Evening News, MO delights in answering the phone as Hogwarts. Based in late 18th century sandstone house, with imaginative new additions and tower, eight new classrooms built on site. All pupils now on-line, two computer rooms. Streaming after two or three years and class sizes down to 10/14. Scholarship stream; good remedial help on hand.

Occasional Greek on offer, drama and dance now increasingly popular, magnificent sports hall which adapts for school plays, though sadly the air rifles have fallen to PC. Piping much encouraged and very well taught, manicured grounds including two cricket pitches, new cricket nets, six tennis courts, masses of Astroturf, a putting course and an 18-hole golf course 'over the wall'. Bracing sea air. Streams of unbeaten teams, boys' and girls', in almost every discipline, regular trips to Hillend artificial ski slope, children encouraged to have their own bit of garden and staff eat the produce in the holidays ('not true' says MO). Boys' dorms recently had a face lift, bunks out, much 'snazzier' says the head.

Lyrical recent HM Inspector's reports could have been written by Osborne himself. Parents and children incredibly happy, with masses of input from the parents – tranches of farmers/Charlotte Rangers from East Lothian, plus the usual quota of quite grand children and an increasing gang from south of the border – usually with Scottish connections. Girls fully absorbed. School is flourishing.

BELMONT PRIMARY SCHOOL

Belmont Road, Chiswick, London, W4 5UL

Tel: 020 8994 7677
Fax: 020 8742 7866
E-mail: belmontprimary@dingwall.demon.co.uk

- Pupils: 470; boys and girls equally; all day • Ages: 3-11 • Non-denom • State • Open days: Regular - Oct-Feb

Head: Since 2000, Ms Anne Williams BA Dip Sch Management, fiftyish. Mrs Williams was previously head of Hathaway Primary, a borough down the road in Ealing.

Hathaway was a very different place – a tough estate school with a high proportion of children whose first language is not English and a poor level of attendance. However, Belmont in prosperous Chiswick, was no pushover. Ms Williams took on a neglected school with a somewhat disaffected school population and 'got on with it'. Quietly spoken, measured and highly methodical, Ms Williams has transformed her school and parents who have been there for the whole ride pay tribute. 'I thought it was good before,' said one, 'but she has really brought it up. She's terrific'. She manages to teach the lower set in year six – always a good sign in a head. Clearly, she has also known how to mobilise resources of all kinds and the result is an orderly, oversubscribed and popular school.

Entrance: Preference given to those who live within the 'Primary Admissions Area' – that's 'catchment' to you and me. Second come siblings who, in effect, are more-or-less guaranteed a place. Children with SENs and medical/social needs who fit these criteria,come higher on the admission list. A few places each year are offered to those living outside the PAA but very close to the school. After that – don't even try. Very over-subscribed, despite head's telling all-comers from outside the area that, really, there is really no chance. Parents are known to rent property within the area just to qualify and then....... ? However, although the area is largely made up of quiet Victorian streets with large Victorian semis in private ownership, it's not all like that and a sizeable proportion of pupils comes from non-home-owning families, those on temporary contracts and those who need EAL support. School's inclusion policies help to level these differences and there no appreciable differences in achievement between those of such diverse backgrounds – much to the school's credit.

Exit: Around half to two thirds to Chiswick Community School. Some to other local state comprehensives such as Twyford C of E or The Green School. The rest to the local independents eg Godolphin and Latymer, Notting Hill and Ealing, Latymer Upper, City of London. Belmont does nothing extra to prepare children for such schools so many do have outside coaching. However, education levels in school are such that in 2003 one child won a top scholarship with no outside help at all.

Remarks: Belmont is housed in a large, 3-storey, London brick building and celebrated its centenary in 2004. Thanks to a very extensive refurbishment programme initiated by Ms Williams with the support of both public money and funds raised by parents, it looks pretty good for its age. It has a decent amount of outside space too and all ages have their own designated play areas with equipment and surfaces appropriate for their needs and capacities. No green anywhere apart from a small nature garden with pond – certainly no playing fields – but there is no feeling of being cramped or choked here as with so many schools in comparable urban situations. The locality is certainly urban – it's on a crossroads with Sainsbury's and Starbucks opposite, lots of residential streets and light industry all around. It's near the tube and on a bus route but, once inside, the environment feels safe, comfortable and peaceful and the outside world is decidedly outside.

The ground floor is home to the nursery, reception and year 1 children and is remarkably spacious. The nursery in particular – 26 children – has 3 large rooms and a hall. Few chic little independent nurseries provide as much as this. The quality of work, as demonstrated by the classroom displays, is exceptional. In one nursery room we saw 'The Belmont Hospital' with a very expert game of doctors and nurses in progress aided by real X-rays of hands, skulls, chests and ankles suspended over the enthusiastic patient's bed; we saw work on textures, water play, construction toys and individual reading – this with one of the army of parents who help with many aspects of class work. Reception was similar – very orderly classrooms with everyone at a table for 5-6 and working away at a large variety of topics between which they swap during the course of a morning. Parents come and help with cooking – everyone wears a 'Belmont Bites' apron and a deliciously slurpy Strawberry Fool was developing when we visited.

The first floor houses years 2 and 3 and is the 'transition floor'. Again a good hall for PE with £8,000 worth of new equipment paid for by the Parents' Association. A designated music room in which everyone has two class music lessons weekly – singing and 'composition' – and, we are told, few children leave the school unable to read music. We witnessed a year 6 class, all armed with instruments, mostly percussive, and singing away with gusto. 'Music permeates the school,' said Ofsted and, in addition to class music, many learn individually. Annually, year 6 puts on a Shakespeare play – 'Twelfth Night' and 'Macbeth' in recent years – and the 'Dream' was in rehearsal as we visited. Photographs on display suggest a high level of production, again much supported, especially with costumes, make-up etc, by parents, many of whom are, of course, 'in the arts'.

Teaching up to the end of year 2 is mixed ability. Setting in maths and English arrives in year 3. There are two sets – the higher being slightly the larger and having, therefore, around 33 children to the lower set's 27-ish. The upper set has just one teacher, no classroom assistant being needed with these children because, of course, they are motivated and keen to learn. We couldn't see much problem with the lower sets either. Years 3-6 are on the top floor and, again, all classrooms are orderly and full of displays you want to stop and look at – both of the children's own work and of materials from outside. Years 3-6 have 40 minutes French weekly. There are libraries – well-stocked (parents again!) for both infants and juniors and two excellent IT suites – 15 PCs for the younger children and 30 for the older ones – intelligently used by specialist staff and, when we visited, a year 3 class was concentratedly working on a maths programme about 'capacity' – well beyond ours! Interactive whiteboards also now in use and Ofsted's one and only quibble about ICT being under-used now decidedly out-of-date. Everyone has 2 hours of physical activity weekly and it was especially pleasurable to see a dance class with budding Billy Elliots clearly not at all embarrassed to be dancing – quite balletically!

Belmont does very well academically. SATs results in all subjects are at least 10 per cent above local and national averages and are far higher by year 6. The achievement and value-added results from those from ethnic minority groups especially remarkable. SENs of all kinds are well-supported here. Hounslow borough has a well-established language service and those with EAL needs are seen individually or in small groups for up to a year until they are up to the general standard. A SENCO gives three full days to individuals, pairs or groups. A 'reading recovery' teacher sees individuals who, by year 1, are falling behind – with 'fantastic' results. School has children with a large range of physical disabilities – lots of asthma but also cerebral palsy, Downs Syndrome, Cystic Fibrosis and parents clearly grateful for the care and individual attention their children are sure of here. Head pays tribute to her staff – 'they are very highly committed – they go that extra mile – we work as a team.' When we visited there had been no staff changes for two years.

Outside, in the extensive playground areas, there are lots of bike sheds, a covered stage with costume boxes, all kinds of different trails, apparatus, a super climbing wall painted by parents. Inside is cheerily decorated in a rich yellow and aqua blue and it feels cosy and bright. The rooms are all good sizes, the furniture is in good nick and everywhere are thoughtful, orderly displays in a stimulating, orderly environment. The uniform – seemingly strictly adhered to – is attractive, navy and, again, orderly and neat. We saw not one scruffy child. Three male teachers – always a bonus – six staff have been in school for 10+ years and staff covers the whole age range. Two thirds of children bring their own lunch. The local borough delivers the hot

lunches – we saw the menu rather than the real thing – and there is a clear emphasis on starch, though tasty starch, and a sad lack of fresh fruit and veg, though the children are offered a salad bar every day. Everyone eats in the canteen – possibly not the most attractive area in the school – two rooms being given over for lunchbox eaters.

A transformed school. Ms Williams is greatly aided by a posse of 'liberal middle class' parents only too eager to help in all areas of school life including in giving unobtrusive financial support when needed for the disadvantaged pupils who wouldn't otherwise be able to take part in trips etc. She is aided, too, by an excellent governing body entirely made up of new members since her advent, as well as by a good relationship with her local authority. She had, at first, to be tough and there were a number of early exclusions. There had been no exclusions in the two years preceding our visit. There is a proper and well-understood system of sanctions. There is an established homework system with extension work on the school website for those who want to push their offspring further – this school is working on all fronts. 'We got the systems in so pupils could learn,' says this thoroughly professional head. The 2003 Ofsted report concluded, 'the school ensures that all children do as well as they can...the leadership of the headteacher, in partnership with the governing body, is excellent... an imaginative and innovative curriculum promotes high levels of achievement. Partnership with parents is very good. The school provides very good value for money.' Find the 'Primary Admissions Area' and move in.

BELMONT SCHOOL

Linked to Moon Hall School

Feldemore, Holmbury St Mary, Dorking, Surrey, RH5 6LQ

Tel: 01306 730 852
Fax: 01306 731 220
E-mail: enquiries@belmont-school.org
Website: www.belmont-school.org

• Pupils: 190 boys, 90 girls; 35 weekly boarders Mon – Thurs night, 245 day pupils. Includes 80 pupils in pre- prep • Ages: 7-14 main school, 3-7 pre-prep • C of E • Fees: Day: pre-prep £1,730. Years 1 & 2: £1,915. Years 3 - 8: £3,010. Boarders: + £1,380 • Independent

Head: Since 1991, Mr David St Clair Gainer BEd (forties). Educated at Claires Court, Maidenhead and Belmont Abbey in Herefordshire followed by St Mary's, Strawberry Hill,

London, where he studied mathematics and drama. Began career at Llanarth Court Prep School in south Wales then housemaster of junior house at his old school Belmont Abbey, followed by 3 years at Forest Grange prep in Horsham where he was deputy head, before taking up present position. Friendly, jovial and approachable, obviously enjoys running this happy school. Believes in being visible around the place. Married to Cathy who teaches geography and is the school's SENCO. She also organises housekeeping and welfare.

The headmaster is responsible for all drama productions. He also reads to all pre-prep pupils every Friday afternoon. Has two teenage children who attended Belmont until 13. Mr Gainer appointed in 1991, just a month after disastrous fire which seriously damaged Feldemore – the grade II late Victorian mansion – once private home to the Price Waterhouse family. Head's first governors' meeting agenda included 'the closure of the school.' Feldemore has since undergone £2.5m rebuild and pupil numbers increased from 160 to current number.

Entrance: 20 pupils aged 3+ admitted to pre-prep. 20 pupils in each of first 4 years. Numbers increase to 32 in years 3-5, two streams each. Years 6-8 have two forms of 18-20 each, one for more academic Belmont pupils and the other for those from Moon Hall (school for dyslexics on same site-see separate entry). Broad range of ability. Pupils assessed during whole day spent with appropriate teaching group. Short waiting lists for all years. Occasional places available due to pupils moving out of area. Sibling policy but no fee reduction. Some day pupils travel long distances with taxis and minibuses organised by parents.

Exit: To as many as 14 different schools mainly in south eg St John's Leatherhead, Shiplake, Epsom College, Cranleigh, Box Hill, City of London Freeman's, St Bede's Hailsham, King Edward's Witley, Reed's Cobham, Stowe, Bedales, St Teresa's. Some academic awards (typically one per year) and the odd sports, ICT and art awards. More academic pupils sit Common Entrance in year 8. Others, including dyslexics, likely to enter a school of choice following assessment and report only

Remarks: Normal Common Entrance curriculum followed. Caters well for dyslexics who may be supported in English and maths at Moon Hall qv. Individual timetables available. Depending on need, pupils may have between 1 and 16 lessons at Moon Hall each week. 'Phono-Graphix' method forms central part of reading scheme. Study skills and touch typing available at Moon Hall. Two classes for maths and English in years 3-5 (pupil:staff ratio 10:1) and three streamed classes in years 6-8 (ratio 10-12:1). French

not taught to those from Moon Hall. Games, PE, art, music and DT taught by specialist staff. Around 90 learn individual instruments from peripatetic teachers. 2 choirs. Sufficient keyboards for whole class teaching. Major musical production at end of Spring term. Productions at Christmas each year involving all pupils. Sports teams compete against those from local schools.

All-weather pitch and outdoor heated pool. Sports fields rented from local country estate across road as school's 65 acre site is on a steepish hillside. Pupils, closely monitored by staff, allowed to don boiler suits at lunchtime and explore school's woodland. Variety of clubs. Boarders stay in main house with separate wing for girls (currently 10. Open door policy operated by head who advertises his home telephone number in phone book. He is available at any time except when teaching. Informal opportunity for all parents to talk to staff over tea on Friday when collecting pupils. Since last inspection (2001) improved policies and better planning and monitoring of academic work have been implemented.

Generally the pupils at Belmont are polite and happy and appear to have an understanding of each other's needs. Not perhaps a school for high flyers, but suitable for able dyslexics and others who would benefit from small group teaching and a very supportive cosy atmosphere.

BELMONT SCHOOL

Linked to Grimsdell Mill Hill Pre Preparatory School in the Junior section
Linked to Mill Hill School Foundation in the Senior section

The Ridgeway, Mill Hill Village, London, NW7 4ED

Tel: 020 8959 1431
Fax: 020 8906 3519
E-mail: Info@belmontschool.com
Website: www.belmontschool.com

• Pupils: 400. About a third girls, and rising; all day • Ages: 4-13
• Independent

Head: Mrs Lynn Duncan
Exit: Nearly all go on to the senior school.
Remarks: Popular prep with few adverse comments.

BENTLEY CHURCH OF ENGLAND PRIMARY SCHOOL

School Lane, Bentley, Farnham, Surrey, GU10 5JP

Tel: 01420 525 010
Fax: 01420 525 011
E-mail: phil.callaway@bentley.hants.sch.uk
Website: www.bentley.hants.sch.uk

• Pupils: 215 boys and girls, all day • Ages: 4-11 • C of E • State

Head: Since 1991, Mr Phillip Callaway (fifties). Previously 7 years as deputy head at a primary school in Farnborough. Appears very easy going but underneath is determined to fight hard for his school. His enthusiasm for the children and the school is obvious and he encourages everyone to have a go and do their best. A well-liked chap by pupils and parents, he is also highly regarded by the LEA – he was recently seconded to another Hampshire primary for half the week. 'This happens from time to time,' he explains 'but I am confident the school is left in good hands and it brings more vital money into Bentley.'

Entrance: Always oversubscribed, although not hugely so, so not much chance for those outside the immediate Bentley & Froyle area. School is open to discussing the number of applications received as the deadline approaches. Attending local nurseries does not guarantee a place but siblings of out-catchment children have first pick of any places not taken up by catchment children.

Exit: 70 per cent to Eggars (local state secondary) in Alton. Rest to local independents such as Royal Grammar Guildford, Lord Wandsworth, Churchers and Alton Convent.

Remarks: Typical village school full of happy children who want to learn – worth moving to be near, particularly if you are a hands-on parent. Academically very strong and consistently outperforms national and LEA key stage averages – often achieves 100 per cent in English and maths. Average class size 32 in junior and 30 in younger classes but pupils often work in smaller groups. Super ICT facilities with new equipment and interactive whiteboards in all classrooms – very impressive for a state school. About 10 per cent with SEN (but no statements), taught mainly with the class or in groups by one full time SEN teaching assistant. Parents feel much of the strength of the school lies in the (mainly female) staff - 'they are so dedicated.'

The school is housed in an original Victorian building with additional bright, airy – sometimes chilly, according to staff – classrooms. Not much space – very small assembly hall/gym where packed lunches are eaten on a rota basis. School has no facilities to provide hot lunches – several moans from parents. Indoor PE severely constrained, compensated by generous playing fields. More than half the children learn an instrument, lessons are held mainly at lunchtime or after school – 'music tuition is wonderful'. Sport, particularly football, cricket, netball and cross country, is good with regular competitions against other local schools. Swimming at nearby Treloar School; early bird swimming club before school for the keen.

Lots of the usual extra-curricular activities run by staff or privately organised – a veritable hive of activity – 'if we have a failing it's that we take on too much,' says Mr C. All children from year 3 upwards go on a residential trip each year, usually to various nearby outdoor activity centres. Often the first time away from home – 'the children love it especially when they get really wet and muddy,' said one mother. Mr C. feels these trips are vitally important to the children's development and a great opportunity. Pupils are a lively, well behaved bunch. Problems are dealt with efficiently and thoroughly by teachers – Mr C. is confident that there is nothing more serious than playground squabbles, which are quickly resolved, and the children are taught the importance of respect for each other in regular circle time discussions. 'The children are totally absorbed in the life of the school,' comments one parent 'and so are we!'

BERKHAMSTED COLLEGIATE PREPARATORY SCHOOL

Linked to Berkhamsted Collegiate School in the Senior section

King's Road, Berkhamsted, Hertfordshire, HP4 3YP

Tel: 01442 358201
Fax: 01442 358203
E-mail: prepadmin@bcschool.org
Website: www.bcschool.org

• Pupils: 460 girls and boys • Ages: 3-11 • Fees: Day: prep £878 - £2,940; Boarding £5,992 - £6,618 • Independent • Open days: Early October

Remarks: For further information, see senior school

BILTON GRANGE SCHOOL

Rugby Road, Dunchurch, Rugby, Warwickshire, CV22 6QU

Tel: 01788 810 217
Fax: 01788 816 922
E-mail: headmaster@biltongrange.co.uk
Website: www.biltongrange.co.uk

• Pupils: 330 boys and girls including 125 in pre-prep. Around one third of children board – there are full, weekly and some flexi-boarders • Ages: 4-7 pre-prep; 8-13 prep • C of E • Fees: Day £1,790 - £4,050; boarders £4,950 • Independent • Open days: September, March and June

Head: Since 2003, Mr Peter Kirk BSc, FRSA.

Entrance: Early enquiries recommended. Non-selective but there is an entry test and interview. Popularity reflected in 23 per cent rise in numbers since 1995. More boys than girls – roughly 60:40. Starters' scholarships and open awards offered at 8. Children with academic potential encouraged to apply. Artistic, musical, design or sporting talent 'taken into account'.

Exit: Regular tests a way of life here, so pupils shouldn't be fazed by major exams later. Roughly third of pupils leave for senior school at 13 with academic, sport or music scholarships. Rugby takes almost 45 per cent, other favourites include Oundle, Uppingham, Bloxham, Stowe, Oakham and Princethorpe.

Remarks: Stunning setting for this lovely, originally Georgian red-brick, school on raised plateau with far-reaching views across surrounding countryside. Children can explore 2.5 acres of well-kept grounds with enviable freedom, though school occupies 150-acre spread in all. Founded in 1873, was once boys-only with separate school for girls on nearby site. Now fully co-ed with pre-prep, Homefield, in former girls' school. All classes mixed but dormitories very much apart. Boys can never enter girls' dorms and vice versa. 'You must never make the mistake of thinking children are too young,' said the head sagely. Dorms recently decorated, largest has 8 beds (including bunks) with plenty of posters, own possessions on show.

Latin and French compulsory. Extensive range of extras include golf, sailing, scuba diving and fly fishing. 'We really give children a tremendously enriched experience here.' Average class size 14, with years streamed according to ability. Weekly spelling and tables tests for little ones, hour's homework a day when older. Pupils decide when to do it, as long as it's done on time. Supportive of slower learners and proud of achievements but, if more than extra hour a week needed, parents may be advised to seek more suitable school.

Education seen as more than just lessons. Pupils encouraged to be responsible for their actions, to take charge. 'We are genuinely a preparatory school. Our children arrive at their next school running.' Famous Old Boys and Girls include composer Sir Arthur Bliss and Independent columnist and humorist Miles Kington, also a number of Tory MPs.

Little evidence of mixing outside class. Pupils tend to opt for self-segregation at meal-times and so on. Well-stocked library restored to original Pugin splendour (Pugin is the Victorian architect responsible for much of the school's regal interior) complete with computers and CD-ROMs and stacks of new books. Thousands spent on fresh stock each year thanks to healthy budget and money raised from book fairs. Dining room leads into pretty little chapel which has a fine old organ – the one Arthur Bliss first learned to play – which is undergoing massive restoration work. Classrooms bright, airy, functional. Bit of a rabbit warren with narrow corridors, twists and turns. Pre-prep cosier with lots of work on display. Good IT provision with an emphasis on interactive whiteboards in both parts of the school.

Impressive art studio on main site, sports hall and 25-metre pool plus new all-weather outdoor courts. C of E school which welcomes all denominations but no-one gets out of going to chapel to kick start the day. Pupils from all walks of life. 'We're not snooty.' Broad curriculum in which PSHE plays important part. Bullying 'not an issue that concerns me,' says head. But well aware of it and can become a disciplinary matter. Very keen on adventure training. Teaches 'self-reliance, tolerance, ability to cope with each other's weaknesses'. Also leadership training in year sixth gets them thinking about others' needs. As a result pupils come across as confident, not cocky.

Continuing tradition of Saturday school, lessons in morning and sport after lunch. Wednesdays timetabled in same way. Not too many grumbles when children quizzed about this even from day boys/girls. 'That's just the way it is,' said one. As scholarships show, strong academically, but good too for science and design technology, ICT and drama. Children's production has featured more than once at Edinburgh's Fringe. Music department even has composition and recording suite. Teams fare well at most sports, but rugby disappointing since main competitors (like The Dragon) now much bigger.

Real school for real kids. Not just for smart Alecs and

Alices. Would also suit outdoors type as must get chilly up there in the winter. Feeling of real contentment in the wood-panelled halls and, even at this age, pupils know exactly where they're going and what's expected of them. They seem only too happy to oblige.

BIRKDALE SCHOOL
PREPARATORY SCHOOL

Linked to Birkdale School in the Senior section

Clarke House, Clarke Drive, Sheffield, South Yorkshire, S10 3NS

Tel: 0114 267 0407

Fax: 0114 268 2929

E-mail: prepschool@birkdale.sheffield.sch.uk

Website: www.birkdaleschool.org.uk

• Pupils: 263 boys; all day • Ages: 4-11 • Fees: Juniors £2,128; pre-prep £1,799 • Independent • Open days: October/November

Head: Mr Alan Jones BA(Ed) MA(Ed) MA(Theo) CertEd (forties) who was educated at a grammar school in Wolverhampton, followed by Dudley College, Oxford Brookes (twice) and Leeds. Mr Jones has taught in a variety of prep schools during his 24-year teaching career. A lovely Santa Claus of a man, full of kindness and understanding and perfectly in tune with his charges; constant refrain during our visit of, 'pull your socks up'. An independent schools' inspector.

Entrance: At 4, by interview and at 7 by interview and exam held at the start of the Easter term; Eng and maths, and reasoning. Boys come both from the independent and maintained sectors and from as far away as Retford, Doncaster – huge catchment area.

Exit: All but a handful on to senior school, rest to other independents or into the state sector.

Remarks: Elegant, late-Georgian house, overlooking the Botanic Gardens and once home of the Osborn family, he a master cutler. School acquired building in 1988 and did a spot of adapting. Now works well, servants' quarters house the computer room. Hall was probably purpose-built when the buildings housed either the grammar school or the nurses' training establishment, some slightly surprising alterations giving rooms glass windows onto corridors. Gloriously cosy tinies' wing with sand pits and a dedicated play area. All immobile items labelled in large letters – DOOR, PRINTER, COMPUTER, DESK.

NB this is not a school with a nursery and is academic,

starting French at four, science right through, specialist teachers from seven when boys are setted in maths. Sets in English and science at nine. Strong learning support, both withdrawn and dual teaching in class, no problems with dyspraxia, ADHD, ADD, all boys screened. Good library and boys decide which books they would like to read. Christian foundation, act of worship four times a week; about 12 Muslims and Hindus, no-one feels indoctrinated and indeed, non-Christians prefer to be at a school with a 'living faith'. Appropriate religious texts all over. Halal meat on request and vegetarian options, 'we like kids to finish their veg but we don't insist'.

Loads of first-time buyers, not all middle class by any means, 'parents beggar themselves to come here'. IT throughout, oodles of computers, ICT lessons from seven. Computer-linked piano, and masses of music and theory of music, drums and percussion and other instruments (everything except the harp). Good orchestra and choir. Drama vibrant. There is significant liaison between staff at senior and prep schools. Older boys and girls come and help out on a one-to-one basis already and there are future plans for staff from the senior school to visit the term before boys move up and teach the relevant classes to ensure continuity. Uses big school games field. Uses cricket nets at senior school, and shares the extensive playing fields 10 mins from the campus. Hopes to develop building here, with enlarged class rooms, particularly in the pre-prep department. Masses of post-school clubs, late waiting till 5pm and children can be left at 8.30am. Jolly, academic prep school. Zinging.

BISHOP'S STORTFORD
COLLEGE JUNIOR SCHOOL

Linked to Bishop's Stortford College in the Senior section

10 Maze Green Road, Bishop's Stortford, Hertfordshire, CM23 2PJ

Tel: 01279 838607

Fax: 01279 306110

E-mail: jsadmissions@bsc.biblio.net

Website: www.bishops-stortford-college.herts.sch.uk

• Pupils: 35 full-time, flexi and extended day boarders. Pre-prep: 120 boys and girls • Ages: junior school 8-13, pre-prep 4-7 • Independent

Entrance: Entrance to the pre-prep department is by a day's assessment; for the junior school by entrance exam.

Remarks: The junior school shares the same grounds and many of the same facilities as the senior school. Heads work closely together and promote the same work hard/play hard ethos. Junior boarding house offers the same boarding options as the senior school, including flexible boarding. Academic streaming starts in year 4 plus setting for maths. All pupils study Latin from year 5. Saturday school for everyone above pre-prep. Average age of staff is 34 and nine members of staff have been with the school for ten years or more.

BLACKHEATH HIGH SCHOOL (JUNIOR DEPARTMENT)

Linked to Blackheath High School GDST in the Senior section

Wemyss Road, London, SE3 0TF

Tel: 020 8852 1537
Fax: 020 8318 3943
E-mail: info@blj.gdst.net
Website: www.blackheathhighschool.gdst.net

• Pupils: 300 girls, all day • Ages: 3-11 • Non-denominational
• Independent • Open days: November

Head: Mrs Virginia Rickus.

Entrance: By individual assessment.

Remarks: Housed in the original, purpose-built school (1880s) about a mile from the senior school, this establishment has a charm and character to match its delightful building in a quiet residential street. Lovingly preserved parquet hall with splendid, classical-subject frieze, busts, columns and balustraded double staircase. Attractive, inviting classrooms lead off, combining business with orderliness and well-displayed work. New purpose-built nursery. Two new IT suites. Newly refurbished dining room and library. Science laboratory, gymnasium, art room, Design and Technology room. Specialist teaching in English, mathematics and science in Years 5 and 6. French taught throughout the school. Mandarin taught in year 6. Excellent artwork. School orchestra, two choirs, individual instrumental lessons. Wide extra-curricular activities programme. Breakfast club and after school club. Girls are relaxed, chatty, confident and well-behaved. Somewhat stark outside areas overlooked by houses and trees but reasonably spacious. Learning support teacher.

BLUE COAT SCHOOL

Somerset Road, Edgbaston, Birmingham, West Midlands, B17 0HR

Tel: 0121 410 6800
Fax: 0121 454 7757
E-mail: admissions@bluecoat.bham.sch.uk
Website: www.bluecoat.bham.sch.uk

• Pupils: 520 (including pre-prep), 60:40 boys:girls; all day
• Ages: 2-11 • C of E, but respect shown to many other faiths
• Independent

Head: Since 1998, Mr Alan Browning (fifties), succeeding the popular and long-serving Brian Bissell. Married to Helen, who is very much involved in school life; three boys, two at King Edward's School, Birmingham and one still at Blue Coat. Educated Clifton, Trinity Cambridge and Oxford. A musician, started career as a lecturer at Leicester University, thence to Blue Coat as director of music in 1982 and then deputy head and director of studies in 1993. 'He is someone who has lived and breathed the school for most of his professional career,' remarks a parent. This is of course both a strength and a weakness. A devout evangelical Christian, sees his faith as central to his role as headmaster. A man who is deeply committed to the interests of the children. 'This is a school that really cares about its pupils,' says the parent – a reflection of the head's most important priority.

Entrance: Usually at 2 into pre-prep or 7 into prep. Test and interview at 7. Most children sign up at or near birth. The vast majority of the pupils enter the nursery (Buttons) then move through the school. Head keen to ensure that the girl/boy balance is maintained. There are some places (dependent on natural wastage) at all levels but especially so at 7. The vast majority of the children are recruited from the local Edgbaston and Harborne areas but the school is expanding its catchment area.

Exit: Blue Coat copes well and in many ways prospers in the demanding educational environment of Birmingham. The aspiration of most parents is to get their child into one of the super-academic King Edward VI schools or one of the many fine selective maintained schools in the area. Bearing in mind that the intake is an academically wide one, the school does well to get the largest single group into the King Edward schools. Others to schools such as Solihull, Edgbaston High and Old Swinford Hospital. School now ends with the eleven-year-olds, bowing to the realities of now, virtually universal – in this area – exit at that age.

Remarks: The school was founded in 1722 by the Reverend William Higgs as a co-educational charity school (making it one of the oldest co-ed schools in the country), and now occupies a truly beautiful site in 15 acres of playing fields and gardens. The school moved here in 1930 and the buildings, nearly all of which were erected at that time, are clustered around well-manicured lawns, giving the impression of a cloistered antiquity that would not be out of place in a public school. This is a true oasis of peace and tranquillity just outside the bustling heart of inner city Birmingham.

One might suppose that the avowedly Anglican tone of the school might fit uneasily within the modern multi-ethnic West Midlands community. Yet it all seems to work remarkably well and the school has retained its Anglican tradition – though no longer its own full-time chaplain – and lovely collegiate-style school chapel. At the same time it has a school roll of which 30 per cent are from an ethnic minority background, and only some of the rest are in any sense strictly Church of England. The recent ISI Inspection Report (2001) especially praised the school for managing this so well. Whilst there is no doubt that the Anglican voice is the dominant one, the school has gone to great lengths to invite visiting speakers from other Christian denominations and to introduce discussion of the Muslim, Hindu and Sikh traditions. This is a school where tolerance and mutual respect are taken very seriously indeed.

The school has an innovative approach to language teaching, with all the children having the opportunity to taste German, Italian and Spanish before focusing on the main language, French. Science and art both flourish conspicuously, helped by some quite outstanding facilities. The success of so many pupils in the demanding King Edward VI entrance examinations says much for the quality of the teaching of the core academic subjects. As you would expect with a musical headmaster, music is especially strong, and the school has well-established links with Birmingham Cathedral and Birmingham Conservatoire. This is no doubt one reason why Sir Simon Rattle sent his children here. Chapel choir and four other choirs, numerous orchestral ensembles and 220 children learning at least one musical instrument. A notable recent addition is a Steinway Concert Grand piano. Lots of wonderful concerts, most notably special events at Symphony Hall (conducted by Rattle), St Paul's, Hockley and the CBSO Centre.

Whilst the school's selection procedure ensures that it has few if any children with serious educational difficulties,

it does have up to 40 children with some kind of SEN, usually of a mild form. To help these children it has a very effective learning support unit that is highly prized by parents.

Boarding a thing of the recent past. The house system, originally designed for a predominantly boarding population, has been imaginatively reorganised to meet the needs of a day environment. Every prep school child is designated a house, uses the common room facilities of that house, and is under the care of a particular house parent. This ensures that pastoral support is especially strong and each child has a very intense sense of belonging to a small, intimate unit. It also means that the school is able to offer very effective and well organised out of school care until 6.00 pm – a great boon for working parents. Happy, well-motivated children.

A great deal of emphasis is placed on a wide range of games, and the hugely impressive new sports centre (incorporating a 25m pool) enhances this sporting tradition. The school organises its own sporting tournaments, which are enthusiastically attended by preparatory schools from far and wide.

Blue Coat is without doubt the best preparatory school within Birmingham. It has enormous strengths and would be the natural choice for parents looking for a traditional preparatory school education within this city.

THE BOLITHO JUNIOR SCHOOL

Linked to Bolitho School (The) in the Senior section

Polwithen Road, Penzance, Cornwall, TR18 4JR

Tel: 01736 363 271
Fax: 01736 330 960
E-mail: enquiries@bolitho.cornwall.sch.uk
Website: www.bolitho.cornwall.sch.uk

• Ages: infants 5-6, juniors 7-10, middle 11-13 • C of E
• Fees: From £1,500 (infant day) to £5,300 (senior boarding)
• Independent

Remarks: For further information, see senior school.

BOLTON SCHOOL GIRLS' DIVISION JUNIOR SCHOOL

Linked to Bolton School Girls' Division in the Senior section

Chorley New Road, Bolton, Lancashire, BL1 4PB

Tel: 01204 840201
Fax: 01204 434710
E-mail: info@girls.bolton.sch.uk
Website: www.girls.bolton.sch.uk

- Pupils: 206 girls in the main school; Infant dept (Beech House) 200 boys and girls; all day • Ages: nursery 0-4, infants (Beech House) 4-7, juniors 7-11 • Fees: Junior/infants £1,854 (plus £105 for lunches) • Independent • Open days: Mid October

Head: Head of infant school Mrs H Crawforth. Head of junior school Miss J Yardley.

Entrance: Entrance via test at 7, also for children who have been in the prep.

Exit: Most girls transfer to the senior school via tests.

Remarks: Housed mainly in same building as senior school and shares some facilities. Like senior school, wide range of popular lunchtime clubs and activities. Assessment Tests held in January, in English, maths and reasoning. Headteachers' reports from previous school and KS1 results taken into account. After school care until 6pm.

Infant dept (Beech House) on same site as senior school but in attractive Victorian mansion. Entry in September following fourth birthday via short individual interviews during Autumn Term of previous year. No formal skills required but readiness to listen, concentrate and adapt to school life essential. Many go on to junior depts of main school but this is not automatic.

Nice dept with evidence of much industry and happiness – takes traditional harvest festival seriously, with proper little baskets of fruit and vegetables – none of your cash donations and a token tin of baked beans! After-school care until 6pm.

Nursery school a modern, purpose-built nursery close to senior school. Excellent Ofsted report. No automatic transfer to Beech House but majority do. Lively programme of activities.

BOLTON SCHOOL BOYS' DIVISION JUNIOR SCHOOL

Linked to Bolton School Boys' Division in the Senior section

Park Road, Bolton, Lancashire, BL1 4RD

Tel: 01204 52269
Fax: 01204 410 073
E-mail: junior@boys.bolton.sch.uk
Website: www.junior.boys.bolton.sch.uk

- Pupils: 200 boys; plus 200 boys and girls in the pre prep (Beech House); all day • Ages: 7-11, 4-7 in pre-prep (Beech House) • Fees: Junior: £1,854 + £105 for lunches • Independent • Open days: October Saturday, plus conducted tours by appointment

Head: Since 1990, Mr Michael Percik, BA PGCE (forties).

Entrance: Entrance via test, with no automatic entrance from the school's own pre-prep.

Exit: Nearly all progress to senior school at 11.

Remarks: Strong feeder, just across road from senior school.

BOUSFIELD PRIMARY SCHOOL

South Bolton Gardens, Old Brompton Road, London, SW5 0DJ

Tel: 020 7373 6544
Fax: 020 7373 8894
E-mail: info@bousfield.rbkc.sch.uk
Website: www.bousfield.rbkc.sch.uk

- Pupils: 200 boys, 200 girls, all day • Ages: 3-11 • Non-denom • State

Head: Since 1998, Ms Connie Cooling MA DipEd (forties). Studied education management and the teaching of maths, has taught in a number of London schools rising to deputy head of Sherringdale Primary School in Wandsworth before coming to Bousfield.

Entrance: Over-subscribed. Nursery place does not guarantee entry to reception. Priority given to brothers and sisters and to children who live nearest the school. 30 in September, 30 in January: 2 reception classes. 30 children in a class. Lots of European ex-pats. Broad social mix.

Despite location, 25 per cent of children are eligible for free school meals (lots of temporary accommodation in Kensington).

Exit: One quarter goes to a wide variety of private schools – four to the French Lycée in 1999. State favourites are Holland Park and Elliott.

Remarks: Continuously and deservedly popular, much-sought-after primary school in a very useful central London location. Support from the borough. Successful Ofsted inspection in 1999. English is not the first language of about half of the pupils – over 30 mother tongues (Arabic and French chief among them). No school uniform but children are tidy with nice haircuts. Well-run, fun, strong on parental involvement. Draws on parents' skills (actors, artists etc). Bousfield busily fosters the creative arts – music especially good, also art. New (2003)specialist dance teacher.

Head keen on 'achievement across the curriculum', good manners, minds about discipline (not a problem), all classes have homework. Well-used and well-stocked libraries. Offers an early morning maths class but doesn't coach; buys in additional support for learning and behaviour difficulties. Children heading for private schools typically get extra boosting (for a year or more) from outside teachers in maths and English, though school questions this.

Classrooms bursting with colourful and creative project work. School is on the site of Beatrix Potter's childhood home, built in 1956 (and now a listed building), with light airy classrooms – 'too small,' sighs the head – and grass play area, plus very large playground, the envy of private central London schools. Central body of the building consists of two large halls mirroring each other for infants and juniors, used for dance, productions, gym, assemblies etc. Ms Cooling oversees everybody and often 'goes walkabout'.

BRADFORD GIRLS' GRAMMAR SCHOOL PREPARATORY SCHOOL

Linked to Bradford Girls' Grammar School in the Senior section

Duckworth Lane, Bradford, BD9 6RN

Tel: 01274 545395
Fax: 01274 483547
E-mail: headsec@bggs.com
Website: www.bggs.com

• Pupils: 215 boys and girls; all day • Ages: 2-7 boys, 2-11 girls
• C of E • Fees: £1,914 • Independent

Head: Miss J Everington.

Remarks: For more information see senior school.

BRADFORD GRAMMAR JUNIOR SCHOOL (CLOCK HOUSE)

Linked to Bradford Grammar School in the Senior section

Keighley Road, Bradford, West Yorkshire, BD9 4JP

Tel: 01274 553 742
Fax: 01274 553 745
E-mail: chsec@bradfordgrammar.com
Website: www.bgsjuniorschool.co.uk

• Pupils: 203: 154 boys and 49 girls; all day • Ages: 6-11
• Fees: Junior school £1,996 • Independent
• Open days: Mid January

Remarks: For further information, see senior school.

BRAMBLETYE SCHOOL

East Grinstead, West Sussex, RH19 3PD

Tel: 01342 321 004
Fax: 01342 317 562
E-mail: admin@brambletye.com
Website: www.brambletye.com

- Pupils: 255; 166 boys, 89 girls; 30 per cent board • Ages: 7-13, pre-prep 3-7 • C of E • Fees: £1,270 - £5,200
- Independent • Open days: October and March

Headmaster: Since 1997, Mr Hugh Cocke (pronounced Coke) BA CertEd (forties). Previously head of Old Buckenham Hall, prior to that head of history at Cheam School and The Old Malthouse. Two adult daughters. He was appointed with his wife, Lucy, the 'double act' very evident, she takes on a pastoral role and is considered a very positive influence around the boarders – together, a hard-working and buoyant couple. He treats the pupils with unhurried courtesy and has 'noticeably relaxed and come into his own'. Mixed reports, however – contented sounds from parents of able children but some disgruntled cries from parents of children who are less than perfect, either behaviourally or academically, and 'rather aloof with dyslexics.' Evidently au fait with what senior schools offer and able to match a child to an appropriate school (but can seem dismissive of what he considers more second league schools).

Has overseen two major building projects, the latest designer-inspired addition of the new Beeches pre-prep and a spectacular sports hall (financed by grateful parents). Now teaches religious studies (befitting a vicar's son with a daughter who studied theology) and sees his key mission 'to develop the best for each child in and out of the classroom as a preparation for boarding school'. He coaches the U9s rugby, cricket and runs every morning around the large grounds with much loved dog, Monty. (Lucy not in tow).

Entrance: No entrance test but detailed questionnaire completed by pupil's previous headmaster. Entry at all levels but primarily at pre-prep age, then 7-8 years and 11 years. Pupils consist of 3 distinct groups: the majority, who live within 10-15 mile radius; pupils from London (school coach every fortnight for exeat weekends); and from overseas (France, Hong Kong, Nigeria, Russia, Spain). Children who are most likely to pass Common Entrance will be accepted. A good catchment area, close to London and on the edge of East Grinstead, keeps the numbers buoyant.

Exit: To 18 different boarding schools, Eton, Harrow, Charterhouse, Wellington, Radley, Winchester, Uppingham, King's Canterbury, Benenden etc. 19 awards in 2001 – a school record (academic, art, design technology, drama, music). Forum held annually with the heads of senior schools to develop strong links, results in children being placed by Brambletye as much as by parents; lack of fallout suggests parents are happy with the results.

Remarks: A splendid, old, stone country mansion in rolling countryside, with aged oak trees and large lakes, once owned by the Abergavenny family and now by a charitable trust. Built as a hunting lodge, little has changed, with oak panelled reception rooms, hot chestnuts roasting by an open log fire (alas no pheasant, but a very adequate lunch) and a substantial feel to the place. This is a well-established boarding school with a happy bunch of children, being given a resounding thumbs up by parents for the all round pastoral care. Girls were introduced in 2000; they have blended in well and their presence is felt in the junior school. 'The head has bent over backwards to accommodate the girls, eg purchasing trampoline, appointing a dance/jazz teacher,' commented a parent. Boarding facilities are cosy, some compact dormitories (11 to a room), older children cubicled in 2s. Head's wife, matrons and sisters are a stalwart, organised team – Lucy Cocke was 'particularly helpful arranging exeat weekends with other boys', said a grateful overseas parent.

Some rather dowdy colour schemes and linoleum floors. Quiet gripes that day pupils are not on an equal footing, are excluded from the myriad of activities and thus feel pressured to become boarders. 'The evening activities are there for the privilege of the boarders and there is a clear expectation for day pupils to board by year 6,' says the head – 'the pressure to board comes from the children'. Parents divided between those who feel that the pre-prep is accepting too many first time buyers and those who say nothing has changed – 'the majority of parents are company executives, financiers, lawyers, doctors etc – all once educated in the independent sector.'

Academically a broad spectrum of abilities – the school has no delusions of being a hothouse – and accommodates the less academic well. Seems to achieve good results. The headmaster sees appointment of staff as top priority (recently not appointing a post from a strong field of candidates – 'not quite right') and this reflected in a good calibre of dedicated staff. More than 75 per cent live on site and it gives a 'strong sense of family' to the whole school.

All the arts are well-resourced, with fine staff, and

achieve exceptional results and much parental praise. Music very strong, 80 per cent learn, and 17 peripatetic teachers provide tuition on every conceivable instrument including bagpipes, bassoon and a recently acquired harp. Choirs and instrumentalists visit New York, Prague and recently, Johannesburg – musical director John Gowers has recently composed a South African Cantata. Drama an important part of the school, magnificent theatre houses 280 and productions staged every term. Activities on offer, too numerous to mention, range from origami to canoe polo; special expedition last year was a visit to Kenya, including a climb to the top of Mount Kenya and scuba diving in the Indian Ocean.

New fully equipped sports hall featuring internal climbing wall, even a balcony with its own fencing pistes (parry ho!). Heated pool. Every conceivable sport on offer; expertise brought in for eg trampoline, fencing, golf. The teams take their sporting achievements seriously – some gentle braying that a sane approach to winning is not adopted and more could be done to accommodate the more gentlenatured. This, however, is perhaps being naturally addressed by girls creeping up the school, 'making the atmosphere more relaxed', says the head.

Good old-fashioned manners and standards of behaviour prevail; one parent recording that, 'a case of verbal bullying was nipped in the bud and dealt with sensitively by the head. It did not happen again.' Particular mention made of half-term and meetings being organised at helpful times for overseas parents. Finances healthy – no bursaries on offer.

BRAMCOTE SCHOOL, NORTH YORKSHIRE

22-30 Filey Road, Scarborough, North Yorkshire, YO11 2TT

Tel: 01723 373 086
Fax: 01723 364 186
E-mail: headmaster@bramcoteschool.com
Website: www.bramcoteschool.com

- Pupils: 105 (55 boys and 50 girls), 50+ per cent full boarding, with 30 per cent regular boarders and 20 per cent day pupils
- Ages: 7-13 • C of E Foundation • Fees: Boarding £4,770, day £3,425; year one pupils £3,125 • Independent

Head: Since 2003, Mr Andrew G W Lewin BA PGCE (forties). Geography degree from Newcastle then taught at Dunchurch – Winton Hall, Winchester House and Loretto before coming to Bramcote as deputy head in 1999. He and his wife, Debbie, with their young family form the core of the pastoral responsibility, hence the strong family atmosphere. High standards, strong community spirit and a sound Christian understanding continue at Bramcote. Andrew is a keen sportsman who runs the rugby, is an MCC Playing Member and a single figure handicap golfer.

Entrance: By interview and previous school report, no exam. Children from all over the UK and from abroad, mainly Yorkshire, Northumberland and Lincolnshire. Families mostly business and professional, several in Services. Learning difficulties looked after by full-time specialist. EFL available.

Exit: Excellent record of academic and music scholarships, and entrance to wide range of schools. Brightest go regularly to Winchester (long connection), Oundle, Radley, Shrewsbury (popular), Eton, Ampleforth, and Uppingham. Queen Margaret's York and and Wycombe Abbey becoming favourites with girls.

Remarks: Founded 1893 in solidly respectable red-brick buildings away from fish-and-chip part of town in Scarborough's South Cliff area , looking like good class seaside hotel. Extensive and self-contained playing fields, sports hall, steamy swimming bath, pavilion once belonging to North of England Tennis Club (a period piece) come as an agreeable surprise on rear seaward side.

Straightforward no-nonsense preparation for CE: 'extension' work to stretch ablest on offer from year 2, Latin for nearly all, Greek available, but no sense of the rest being sacrificed to academic stars. Teaching mainly traditional. IT support available and children can e-mail parents. Some long-established teaching staff outstanding, especially John Horton (history) and Richard Lytle (English) – intense class reading of 'Journey's End' in darkened room, with hurricane lamp and assorted WW1 gear was unforgettable. Recent changes due to staff retirement have further strengthened the staff team. High quality, highly motivated and dedicated staff has been the school's chief draw for many years. Class size averages out at 12. Staff:pupil ratio 1:7. Much individual tuition and guidance (many staff live in).

Girls fully integrated (since 1996) into life of what was traditional boys' prep. They clearly like it here, judging from mixed break-time footy in playground, scene of much cheerful shin hacking by both sexes. Girls and boys very confident and relaxed with each other.

2003 National Care Standards Commission report noted what the school does well in boarding welfare. There was 'clear evidence based on discussions with the children that they feel able to talk to any member of staff about issues which they are concerned about. Standards of boarding provision at Bramcote are high.' 2003 National Care Standards Commission report noted that what the school does well in boarding welfare The children are cared for by staff who have chosen to work in a boarding environment as a way of life and are therefore committed to the welfare of the children. There was clear evidence based on discussions with the children that they feel able to talk to any member of staff about issues which they are concerned about. All staff of the school have a responsibility to be aware of the children's welfare in addition to their academic needs, and those members of staff spoken to during the inspection demonstrated a very strong personal interest in the welfare and happiness of each child. They also identified no major issues during their inspection to improve the boarding welfare of the children. Standards of boarding provision at Bramcote are high. Dorms are clean and cheery, some with wonderful sea views, 5/6 to a room, own duvets, teddies etc. Pastoral system, in which Mrs Snow (wife of deputy head) takes a major part, is excellent. Boarding arrangements flexible with most day pupils starting to board when they are ready to do so. Two long weekend exeats per term (plus half term) soften absence (at any rate for parents) and give heavily committed staff a break. Parents always welcome to drop in during term, especially at Wednesday and Saturday open house, if only for the famous egg sandwiches.

Games are strong, especially cricket, rugby, football (senior boys recently won big five-a-side tournament). Aysgarth great rivals. Scarborough Town FC use sports field in return for lending school its coach. Girls have own PE teacher (under 11s unbeaten at netball); rounders, swimming, cross-country tennis, riding, hockey, on offer, much of it mixed; 'all on an equal basis', says Mr Lewin, 'with possible exception of rugby'. Music is top class, run by dynamic Mrs Hartley: nearly every child learns at least one instrument, much singing (well-trained choir). Strong drama, too, helped by visits to Alan Ayckbourn's nearby theatre and further afield.

The leavers' programme is famous, including visits to the Somme, a survival night, various science and design projects, trips to the theatre, a day in court and the stockmarket game. Parents are a loyal bunch and tireless advertisers of the school's undoubted virtues. They need to be – geography is against it (everything to the east is sea) – and numbers have dropped since 1998 although this is probably more a reflection of social trends than anything.

BRAMDEAN PREPARATORY SCHOOL, KINDERGARTEN AND PRE-PREP

Linked to Bramdean School in the Senior section

Richmond Lodge, Homefield Road, EX1 2QR, Exeter, EX1 2QR

Tel: 01392 273 387
Fax: 01392 439 330
E-mail: info@bramdeanschool.com
Website: www.bramdeanschool.com

- Pupils: 150 boys and girls; all day • Ages: 2-13 • Inter-denom
- Fees: £3,554 • Independent

Entrance: Children admitted to kindergarten and pre-prep on understanding they remain in prep until aged 13. Must pass common entrance exam at 13 to stay at Bramdean.

Remarks: Gentle transition to full-day pre-prep after at least one/two terms of five mornings in reception class. Very busy; well-stocked and visual rooms. Lunch in dining room at different sitting time to main school.

BRENTWOOD PREPARATORY AND PRE-PREPARATORY SCHOOL

Linked to Brentwood School in the Senior section

Middleton Hall, Middleton Hall Lane, Brentwood, CM15 8EQ

Tel: 01277 243 333
Fax: 01277 243 340
E-mail: prep@brentwood.essex.sch.uk
Website: www.brentwood.essex.sch.uk

- Pupils: 130 boys and girls in pre-prep; 230 in prep. All day
- Ages: 3-11 • C of E • Fees: Nursery £1,379; pre-prep & prep £2,767 • Indopondont

Head: Since 2005, Mr Nigel Helliwell (prep). Mrs Sarah Wilson (pre-prep).

Entrance: Interview for pre-prep, exam for prep.

Remarks: Pre-prep and prep buildings occupy own site over the road from main school and use the seniors' facilities. Super 1995 pre-prep building in style of prep's grand Middleton Hall, plus lots of other small scale buildings and adaptations eg stable block now used for art and science. Bright, lively classrooms and displays, spacious rooms, super walled garden plus pool. Toilet for the physically disabled sensibly placed, new state of the art PC suite in prep plus fabulous library and other rooms with arts and crafts fireplace, stained and leaded glass, stuccoed ceilings – a privileged start to learn in such surroundings. French for everyone, themed days for enjoyable project work, imaginative approach across the curriculum and enough space results in the happily occupied children we saw.

BRIGHTON AND HOVE
HIGH JUNIOR SCHOOL

Linked to Brighton and Hove High School in the Senior section

Radinden Manor Road, Hove, BN3 6NH

Tel: 01273 505004
Fax: 01273 505006
E-mail: enquiries@bhhs.gdst.net
Website: www.gdst.net/bhhs

• Pupils: 275 girls, all day • Ages: 3-11 • Non-denom
• Fees: £1,779 • Independent

Head: Miss Carole Vickers.

Entrance: By varied tests and observation.

Exit: Almost all to Senior School.

Remarks: Situated further into the suburbs and half a mile away from the senior school, on a good sized site with excellent facilities for a junior school: netball courts, full sized Astroturf, grassed areas for eg tomato growing. Light rooms. Miss Carole Vickers has headed the school for 17 yrs, still teaches some music, and elicits varying degrees of support and comments from the parents, ranging from 'professional and communicative' to 'overly firm and inflexible'.

Head is enthusiastic about what the school offers – a good grounding and preparation for the senior school. There are two parallel forms in each year group, unstreamed and often brought together for social events, trips etc. The children are taught by their form teachers who are specifically appointed for their all round strengths including music, art, drama – plenty of craft/art displayed around the whole school. Netball teams do well; PE and French specialists from senior school visit junior school.

The girls do SATS, and understandably shine. Numerous clubs. School menu looked appetizing, all fresh produce cooked on the premises – salad bar, veggie option, very healthy eating. Parents remark how sociable the girls are.

BRIGHTON COLLEGE
JUNIOR SCHOOL
PRE-PREPARATORY

Linked to Brighton College Prep School in the Junior section
Linked to Brighton College in the Senior section

Sutherland Road, Brighton, East Sussex, BN2 2EQ

Tel: 01273 704 200
Fax: 01273 704 204
E-mail: registrar@brightoncollege.net
Website: www.brightoncollege.net

• Pupils: 185 boys and girls • Ages: 3-7 • Non-denom
• Fees: £1,154 - £2,419 • Independent • Open days: One or two mornings and evenings per term

Entrance: By assessment – observed play at 3, peer-group interaction and tests later on.

Exit: Most to the Junior School.

BRIGHTON COLLEGE
PREP SCHOOL

Linked to Brighton College Junior School Pre-preparatory in the Junior section
Linked to Brighton College in the Senior section

Walpole Lodge, Walpole Road, Brighton, East Sussex, BN2 2EU

Tel: 01273 704 210
Fax: 01273 704 286
E-mail: registrar@brightoncollege.net
Website: www.brightoncollege.net

• Pupils: 295 boys and girls, all day • Ages: 8-12 • Non-denom
• Fees: £2,945 - £3,775 • Independent • Open days: One Saturday per term

Entrance: By assessment and observation; the main entry is at 11+ by assessment in maths, English and verbal reasoning. Special arrangements for dyslexic pupils.

Exit: Most to the senior school – but they have to take CE on a par with outsiders.

Remarks: After-school care. Notable dyslexia provision.

Bristol Grammar School Lower School

Linked to Bristol Grammar School in the Senior section

University Road, Bristol, BS8 1SR

Tel: 0117 973 6109
Fax: 0117 974 1941
E-mail: lshead@bgs.bristol.sch.uk
Website: www.bristolgrammarschool.co.uk

• Pupils: 145 boys and 65 girls; all day • Ages: 7-11
• Non-denom • Fees: £1,596 • Independent

Head: Ms Alison Primrose.

Entrance: By examination.

Exit: Many to the senior school – but you have to pass the exam.

Remarks: For further information, see senior school.

Brockhurst and Marlston Schools

Marlston Hermitage, Hermitage, Thatcham, Newbury, Berkshire, RG18 9UL

Tel: 01635 200 293
Fax: 01635 200 190
E-mail: info@brockmarl.org.uk
Website: www.brockmarl.org.uk

• Pupils: 250 boys and girls (split roughly 60/40); flexi-boarding
• Ages: boys 3-13 (Brockhurst), girls 8-13 (Marlston House) • C of E
• Fees: Day £440 - £3,725; boarding £4,950 • Independent •
Open days: Held every term. Please telephone for details

Head: Since 2000, Mr David Fleming MA MSc (early forties). Has been at Brockhurst (the boys' school) quite literally man and boy. A former pupil who now not only heads school but whose family owns it too. Previously bursar, science and geography teacher as well as estate manager. 'I did my apprenticeship.' Unusually two previous heads still work there. Educated at Brockhurst and Radley College, read natural sciences at Trinity College, Oxford, medicine, then land management before going back to square one. Still teaches geography. 'I feel it's a very important thing to do, to keep up that classroom contact with children, otherwise you never get to know them properly.' Nine months into the job, has modest ambition for school 'to be the best'.

Impressive figurehead, but not unapproachable. Boys clearly call him 'Sir' out of respect not fear. But won't stand any nonsense, as group of 'miscreants' were made only too well aware at time of our visit. Married with two daughters in pre-prep, wife Catherine is company secretary at major publishing house.

Head of Marlston House (the girls' school) Caroline Riley MA BEd CertEd (forties), since 1999. Previously ran mixed school in Hazelgrove, which trebled in size during her reign. Has similar plans for Marlston House where girl population lagging behind their brother school. Educated at West Country girls' school. Held several teaching and senior staff posts in single-sex and co-ed schools. Relishes the challenge of boosting pupil numbers. 'What attracted me here was the fact I could start right from scratch in building a school.' Very much her own boss who exudes quiet efficiency. Two grown-up children, husband a helicopter engineer.

Entrance: Many via school's own pre-prep, Ridge House, in main school site. Non-selective but admit aiming for average and above average intelligence. 'We are not a school for special needs,' says Mr Fleming. Hopeful pupils are interviewed, prospective parents also given the once over.

Exit: Huge variety of schools – no particular favourites, it would seem. Boys' list includes Abingdon, Bradfield, Charterhouse, Eton, Marlborough, Radley, Stowe and Wellington. Girls head for Downe House (Newbury), Heathfield, St Helen & St Katharine (Abingdon), Wycombe Abbey, Cheltenham Ladies' College and Marlborough amongst others.

Remarks: Two schools with but a single thought – 'to see Brockhurst and Marlston House recognised as one of the best prep schools in the south of England'. Brockhurst boasts a fine history. Founded as a boys' prep in 1884 in Shropshire, it moved to Hermitage in 1945 after 'the family' bought its current country house premises set in 60 acres of breathtakingly beautiful countryside. Its redbrick, mock-Jacobean style provides the perfect location and layout for youngsters who blindly accept their glorious surroundings. Less than a stone's throw away on the same estate are the pretty listed buildings of Marlston House established in 1995 as Brockhurst's twin school for girls. The classrooms on both sites are large, bright and airy with walls festooned with pupils' work.

To all intents and purposes the two schools are run separately, only coming together 'to foster the social development' of pupils. Even their 'joint' prospectus contains a brochure for each school, though the wording in parts is identical, like their mission statement: '(the school) aims to combine the best features of the single sex and co-educational systems.' Lessons are strictly single-sex, except for music and drama. Segregation and co-education run side by side in happy harmony, according to staff, children and parents alike. 'I don't want boys in my class,' stated one single-minded 8-year-old girl. 'We're better off without the girls,' her male counterpart agreed – though both sides admitted more mixing in less academic areas would be better. Little chance of this, I fear. Fleming says, 'there are no plans to integrate the two schools further.' Both heads are in no doubt they've got it right – and the results would confirm that, with almost 100 per cent of boys and girls getting into their first choice 'big' school. Recent poll of parents gave the system the thumbs up too.

Small classes appeared formal but lively with lots of input from pupils. Bright children given opportunity to flourish in higher forms or scholarship sets while learning support staff offers limited help to slower starters. French for all from three and annual two-week term-time trips to school's own chateau in south west France (parents only have to pay for the return flight) help reinforce what's learned. Greek and Latin high on the agenda further up the school for sound Common Entrance reasons. Impressive ICT facilities. Plays a big part in all aspects of school life including the production of monthly school newsletters. Two new science/geography labs opened September 2002. Plenty of success on the sports fields (Midlands short tennis champs, for one). Horse riding a popular option as children can bring own ponies and stable them at school. There's also a six-hole golf course and fishing in school lake. New indoor swimming pool, art and DT Centre and central reference library opened 2005.

All pupils (day or boarding) put in houses – four for boys and two for girls – where house tutors responsible for pastoral care. Boys' dorms are basic but girls' rooms more homely and given huge lift thanks to stencilling by artistic parent. Boarders have own common room and also allowed mobile phones (only for use in free time). Misbehaviour dealt with swiftly as is excellence. Pupils rewarded with stars and punished by stripes, detention, suspension and ultimately expulsion. Best of the crop chosen to be prefects – particularly useful in the war against bullies, as they can work 'under cover' to root it out, say heads. High uptake of musical instruments with around 80 per cent having individual lessons in addition to class music. Excellent (mixed) choir heard in rehearsals. There's also a mixed orchestra, wood-

wind group and brass ensemble.

Children come from wide variety of backgrounds – from local aristocrats to nouveau riche of Silicon Valley. Bursaries and scholarships available. Also a hardship fund if parents fall into financial difficulties. Would suit academically switched-on child with competitive edge thrown in for good measure. One parent commented, 'it's certainly not the kind of school for everyone but it was perfect for my boys. They're smart and sporty and this school brought out the best in them. The link up with the girls' school can only be a good thing for all involved.' Parents looking for fully co-ed should continue looking – this isn't the school for them.

BROMLEY HIGH SCHOOL (GDST) JUNIOR DEPARTMENT

Linked to Bromley High School (GDST) in the Senior section

Blackbrook Lane, Bickley, Bromley, Kent, BR1 2TW

Tel: 020 8467 6555
Fax: 020 8295 2569
E-mail: b.philpott@bro.gdst.net
Website: www.bromleyhigh.gdst.net

• Pupils: 310 girls; all day • Ages: 4-11 • non denom • Fees: £2,382 • Independent • Open days: First Saturday in October, or by appointment

Head: Marilyn Trask (MA) Lancaster; BEd (Southampton). **Remarks:** For further details, see senior school.

BROOKHAM SCHOOL

Linked to Highfield School in the Junior section

Highfield Lane, Liphook, Hampshire, GU30 7LQ

Tel: 01428 722 005
Fax: 01428 729017
E-mail: office@brookhamschool.co.uk
Website: www.brookhamschool.co.uk

• Pupils: 120 boys and girls; all day • Ages: 3-8 • Independent

Head: Mrs Diane Gardiner MEd CertEd.
Entrance: By registration.
Exit: Majority to Highfield.
Remarks: Highfield's (qv) on-site pre-prep.

BROOMWOOD HALL SCHOOL (NIGHTINGALE LANE)

Linked to Northcote Lodge School in the Junior section

Linked to Broomwood Hall (Ramsden Road)

Linked to Broomwood Hall (Garrads Road)

74 Nightingale Lane, London, SW12 8NR

Tel: 020 8682 8800

Fax: 0208 675 0136

E-mail: broomwood@northwoodschools.com

Website: www.broomwood.co.uk

• Pupils: 480 boys/girls, 140 at Garrads Road and 100 girls at the Upper School in Ramsden Road • Ages: 4-8 Lower School, 8-13 Upper School • Cof E • Fees: £2,825 - £3,760* (2.5per cent discount for first sibling, 5 per cent for second, 20 per cent for third or more) • Independent • Open days: May and October

Headmistress: Since 1984, Mrs Katharine Colquhoun (pronounced cahoon), BEd (fifty). After teaching at prep schools here and in Australia, Mrs Colquhoun was thinking of setting up stall in Notting Hill when her attention was drawn to the more pressing needs of south London. Married to Malcolm Colquhoun, who takes care of the finance and administration as well as the school's expanding portfolio of Wandsworth property. The couple have three children, one still at the school, one recently left for Eton. Mrs C, a soigne and dynamic brunette, takes assembly, teaches literature and remains very much the directing force, but each part of the school now also has it own head. Miss Alison Field, BA Ed QTS and Miss Diana Mardon, Adv Dip Tchg TTC are in charge of the lower school, and Mrs Carole Jenkinson, Bsc, PGCE – a bright and bustling former parent, who read physiology at St Andrews, before having children and re-training as a secondary school biologist – is head of the upper school.

Entrance: 100 children (50 per cent boys, about half siblings) admitted to the pre-prep in the September after their fourth birthday. All must live (roughly) within one mile of the school. Entry is by personal interview, but 'people who are really keen to come usually do.' The school does not select on academic potential ('which is virtually impossible at 3') but does attempt to discover whether the child is 'truly ready for school'. Girls entering the upper school at 8 – where the catchment rule is relaxed – are asked to come in for an assessment day to test maths and English and see whether they'll get on with other girls. Some new entrants, too, after 11, for those who hope to continue at a London prep school until boarding at 13.

Exit: The majority, now as always, to boarding school A handful of boys to traditional preps at 8 – Ludgrove, particularly popular – though about 50 per cent continue to brother day prep Northcote Lodge, where their place is guaranteed. Some girls leave at 11 to London day schools – JAGS, Alleyns, Streatham High – and both at 11 and 13 to top boarding schools – Wycombe Abbey, Heathfield, Woldingham, Benenden, Downe House. The vast majority of children to their first-choice school, plus a good sprinkling of scholarships. Girls (and parents) take the decision in year 5 whether to sit 11+ or 13+ and are then taught in separate classes to focus on the requirements of each exam. They can, however, change their mind.

Remarks: Mrs Colquhoun has seen her school expand from 12 children in a local church hall to nearly 500 in five substantial Victorian Houses sprinkled round the south side of Clapham Common, but her approach and values have remained constant. She firmly believes that a young child does not benefit from long drives across London (hence the catchment rule), that single sex education works best after 8, and that the traditional virtues of self-discipline, a sense of responsibility and good manners are the core of a good education. Beyond that everything is comfort and the best of care, with a homey atmosphere and a genuine family emphasis.

The upper school is unique in London in providing an education for girls specifically aiming for boarding at 13. 'We feel it's much easier to make a good decision at that age,' says Mrs Colquhoun. 'You're dealing with a young lady rather than a little girl.' When both sexes stay till 13, too, boys' and girls' preps can run in tandem, sharing Outward Bound, debating and the annual chateau visit.

The physical arrangement of the school is complex. There are four separate sites: a pre-prep of 140 children at Garrad's Road, another pre-prep of 220 – sub-divided into two neighbouring buildings – at Ramsden Road. And finally, the Upper School – 130 girls aged 8-13 – which has recently been re-housed in the gracious Victorian mansion at 74 Nightingale Lane.

All the buildings are bright and cheery with practical tartan carpets, plenty of chintz, fresh-cut flowers, landscaped gardens and a general air of up-market domestic comfort. Children and parents clearly very attached to the school: many ex-parents continue to work here in a voluntary or paid capacity, while ex-pupils come back in their gap year to teach, as well as popping in to say hello.

Teaching – in small groups (20 in pre-prep, 15 in prep) – strong throughout, but particularly vibrant in the upper school, notably in English and science where girls are stretched and strengths strengthened. Most teachers have a specialist university degree as well as a PGCE. Mixed ability classes, but setting in maths and English. French at 5, Latin at 9. A long day because homework is done at school. Younger ones stay on till 5 o'clock, senior girls till 5.20. After that, a variety of clubs – karate, mini-rugby, chess, pottery – can take you up to 6. 'But then the children can just come home, relax and be part of their family.'

Not a school for severe learning difficulties, but able to provide a 'leg up' for those who have specific difficulties, with a full-time remedial teacher on each site and access to outside specialists who come in and work with the child at school.

Art particularly lively (with a most impressive reproduction of the Bayeux tapestry ornamenting the walls). Strong music, with two music lessons a week and more than half taking up individual instruments. Chamber choir, wind ensemble, brass band. Loads of drama – everyone takes part in two productions a year. Netball, hockey, PE, football, touch rugby, athletics, cricket, rounders and tennis taught on site or nearby (five courts in walking distance), with inter-house competitions and external matches. Swimming at local baths, with swim squad once a week. Very good library (including a section on horses). Sophisticated ICT, with state of the art computers, permanent high-speed internet connection and an email account for every child above class 2.

Unashamedly a Christian school with regular RE, morning assembly with hymns and prayers and church attendance once a week. Happy to welcome all faiths (special arrangements for Catholics to attend Mass and days of obligation), but all pupils must attend all services. Pastoral care extremely well thought through at every level. From class 5 girls have a personal tutor (chosen by themselves), whom they meet weekly to discuss social and personal issues as well as a work. The tutor liaises with parents, helps plan revision, sorts out friendships and writes report, but girls are known well by all the staff and progress is discussed regularly at weekly staff meetings. Social skills as important as academic ones and manners definitely a priority. Loads of positive reinforcement: with a table manners cup, a cheerfulness cup, a friendship cup. 'We have lots of carrots,' says Mrs Jenkinson. 'Most girls get something every two years – it's very rare for someone to slip through the net.'

One compulsory – though much enjoyed – course is the weekly Prue Leith cookery lessons for girls in years 7 and 8, which is examined by the parents when they consume a three-course dinner party cooked unaided by the girls at the end of the year. Lunches – organic and prepared on site – are accompanied by the teachers for the younger children to ensure that table manners are observed and food is finished (stickers for those who eat up nicely).

Very well run school, with a strong philosophy followed through in immaculate detail. A delightful place to start your education which sets firm foundations both academically and socially. Not for those who want ethnic diversity, co-education or their children to be pushed.

BURGESS HILL SCHOOL FOR GIRLS JUNIOR SCHOOL

Linked to Burgess Hill School for Girls in the Senior section

Keymer Road, Burgess Hill, West Sussex, RH15 0EG

Tel: 01444 233167
Fax: 01444 870314
E-mail: registrar@burgesshill-school.com
Website: www.burgesshill-school.com

• Pupils: 230 girls; plus 35 boys and 55 girls in the nursery; all day • Ages: 4-11 junior, 2.5 - 4 nursery • Fees: Juniors school £1,620 - £2,835 • Independent • Open days: October, November, March and May

Head: Miss Fenneke Fulleylove would like to think her pupils are relaxed, hard- working and confident; values self-esteem above academic success.

Entrance: Nursery (boys and girls), flexible entry criteria. Junior school (girls only): school tests and previous head's report.

Exit: Almost automatic entry to the senior school so long as pupils can cope and are comfortable with the work ethos.

Remarks: Occupies a separate house next to the main school, the twain overlapping very occasionally but the facilities of the senior school are available. A few subjects taught by subject specialists from senior school eg French but generally taught within their own age group. No more than 15 to a class. Good IT suite with specialists on hand with smartboards and most classrooms now have this technology. Strong music tradition with 4/5 music periods per week. Orchestras in years 4, 5 and 6 plus flute, clarinet ensembles, choirs – high percentage learn an instrument. Good art clubs and well renowned stamp club – very popular. Happy, happy children on a wet, wet day.

BUTE HOUSE PREPARATORY SCHOOL FOR GIRLS

Bute House, Luxemburg Gardens, London, W6 7EA

Tel: 02076 037 381
Fax: 02073 713 446
E-mail: mail@butehouse.co.uk
Website: www.butehouse.co.uk

• Pupils: 306 girls, all day • Ages: 4-11 • Non-denom, predominantly Christian, currently 15 different religions represented • Fees: £3,076 • Independent • Open days: In the summer term, by invitation only

Head: Since 1993, Mrs Sallie Salvidant BEd (early fifties). Formerly head of Rupert House School. Has a daughter living abroad. Looks set for the usual long reign: only three headmistresses since the school opened in 1932. An energetic, engaging personality who has already transformed the school and has the intention of building further on her achievements – wants the school to be 'perceived as a very open happy place for children and parents. Wants pupils to look back on schooldays as a period of their lives where they were happy and valued'. A new uniform designed to be practical, easily identifiable but without the usual falderals of some private schools; girls joining at reception level and rebuilding 95 per cent of the school without disruption to the pupils are some of the more obvious achievements of her 12 year reign.

Entrance: Still by non-selective ballot at 4 and by competitive (very) exam at 7. Roughly 400 enter the ballot for some 20 places and 150 sit for some 40 places at 7. Siblings are given priority at 4 regardless of their academic ability but not at 7. Meetings and an open morning are held for parents applying for entry at 4 or 7 and they are shown around the school by staff and pupils or are free to roam at will. Head insists that the mix generated by this entry system is integral to the ethos of school to 'educate' not to 'school' girls. 'Our strength is in the fact that we have children with so many talents. Academic success is not the only thing that counts.' Is strongly opposed to the notion of league tables for prep schools.

Exit: St Paul's Girls and Godolphin and Latymer are the two most favoured secondary schools with Bute girls often being offered scholarships and by no means all choose St Paul's. Downe House, St Swithuns, Cheltenham and Wycombe Abbey are the popular boarding options at the moment.

Remarks: Undoubtedly a very academic prep but with an interesting twist. The open ballot genuinely does introduce mixed-ability levels and the staff are happy to handle this. There are currently 4 Learning Enrichment teachers (no extra charge is made for this provision) and girls are withdrawn from class or supported within class if necessary, for extra help but also for extension work in the case of the extremely bright but underachieving child. Head has brought on board a 'gifted and talented' pupil support teacher; one parent of a very bright child reported that she was 'allowed to explore her talent but the school does not have class rankings or streams so she's just one of the girls and developing well socially'. The current teacher ratio is 1:13 and the class size is approx 20.

Sport is good and competitive and all taught on site. Swimming, gym, tennis, pop lacrosse and netball are notable, as are cricket (taught by the MCC) and football taught by Fulham Football Club. Badminton and cross country clubs have been introduced. Debating, Mandarin Chinese, simple bridge (disguised as 'card games') and chess taught by outside experts, reflecting the variety of lunch-time and after-school clubs on offer (another Mrs Salvidant inspiration). Drama is popular and available to all, music flourishes at every level, with orchestras, choirs and ensemble groups, and art is inspiring – visiting artists a regular feature in the year. DT room is worth a visit to be reminded of the meaning of the word craftsmanship.

The new buildings house bright, cheerful, air-conditioned classrooms with a new music and drama wing completed in April 2004, laboratory and a library manned by a full-time children's librarian. All facilities are excellent with plenty of Smartboards and laptop computers available to everyone and a wireless school network improving computer literacy. Touch-typing is an integral part of the curriculum. A forward-looking dynamic prep which well deserves its reputation and attracts 'teachable lively bright little girls'. Parents have included such worthies as Andrew Marr, John Cleese, Peter Blake, Andrew Lloyd Webber, Norman Fowler, Anna Ford, Sue Lawley, David Dimbleby. Anna Pasternak and Lady Helen Windsor are Old Girls.

CALDICOTT SCHOOL

Crown Lane, Farnham Royal, Slough, Buckinghamshire, SL2 3SL

Tel: 01753 649 300

Fax: 01753 649 325

E-mail: office@caldicott.com

Website: www.caldicott.com

• Pupils: 250 boys, 130 board (including all in the last 2 years), the rest day • Ages: 7-13 • C of E • Fees: Day £3,800; boarding £5,068 • Independent

Head: Since 1999, Mr Simon J G Doggart BA (early forties). Educated at Winchester and read history at Cambridge. Head of history at Eton before coming here. Mad keen on cricket and is pictured in school's 2001 South African cricket tour leaflet proudly opening two Caldicott-funded cricket nets in townships. Parents give him thumbs up. Wife, Antonia, looks after their three young children (two sons at Caldicott) and is very involved helping with school and boys.

Entrance: Two forms (15 pupils each) at 7; a further form enters at 8. In the October before September entry, registered boys and parents come to meet the head, be suitably dazzled by superb grounds and facilities, and sit a 35-minute assessment (reading aloud plus small maths and English comprehension papers) – all meant to be very gentle. A place is then offered and a £400 deposit required. Families mainly from Windsor, Henley, Amersham, Beaconsfield, Gerrards Cross, London, abroad (some 20 non-Brits and 10 ex-pats). Many (including head's children) from excellent local (state) infant school, Dropmore.

Exit: Diverse, but not very diverse. About a fifth to Eton (annual carol service is held there), a fifth to St Edward's, Oxford (head is a Caldicott governor), almost as many to Harrow and Radley, then in ones and twos far and wide (esp Wellington, Marlborough, Oundle).

Remarks: Hotshot boys boarding prep. Academic. Sporty. Orderly. Polished. Boys famous for genuinely good manners (staff handbook: 'Essentially rather "old-fashioned" standards of behaviour are expected'). No hands in pockets, untucked shirt-tails or Pop Idol haircuts and boys wear shorts year-round until final year. Excellent inspection report – fancy copies provided with the prospectus.

Academically, a well-oiled machine, good at giving boys all the opportunities and cranking out top-notch public school fodder. Boys bustle purposefully about, all clutching identical box files of pens, paper etc. Average class size 15 and can be much smaller in the final year. Boys streamed from day one, an irritant to some who feel their sons may be pigeonholed prematurely (but the streams are not static). From 9, the geniuses go into the 'scholarship' stream (openly called this – this is not a school for those squeamish about competition). Proto-scholars are given extra subjects (Spanish, Greek) and an extra push. At the other end, the school caters impressively well for some 50 pupils with mild special needs (in many cases, just a bit of extra maths or English). In between, a few boys may travel a rocky road. Cases have reached us of parents disappointed with their boys having to redo the previous year's work after demotion from the scholarship stream to the form below. Some setting from age 10 in science, Latin, French and maths. From fourth year (age 10), one hour nightly prep, done at school. Good system of frequent reports keeps parents up to date on boys' progress before problems can fester.

Art and DT departments beautifully housed and well taught (husband and wife team). Mounds of impressive art projects on display. Excellent, well-thought-out programme of art visits – each year-group visits a major London gallery every year so they have seen six by age 13. Standards rising in the music department and head is keen to celebrate the boys' musical achievements. Music practice timetabled four times a week. Annual concerts given by visiting professional musicians who spend a day at the school. Good drama with a major play and smaller performances each year. Other excitements – everyone must learn a poem for the annual declamations competition, debating in top year, good chess, full-size snooker table, volunteering on Thursday afternoons in the local old-folks' home.

Strong keen rugby school, though head is very gently toning this down. For a traditional school, Caldicott does not do badly at including majority of boys in sport (we've seen a lot worse). Duffers benefit from the same coaches as the top players and virtually every senior boy can have a go on a team if he wishes (especially in rugby where there are six senior XVs). Five senior cricket teams, sports hall with cricket nets and two squash courts (there are several squash leagues), golf area, three tennis courts, heated outdoor pool, tidy and warm changing rooms. No football.

Requirement to board at age 11 puts off some parents who want to keep their options open. But note new weekend regime – junior boarders may go home from 1:00pm on Saturday until Sunday evening provided they tell the school ahead of time; senior boarders (11+) may go out on Sundays. Pupils with parents overseas well-catered for with weekend visits to classmates' homes and school-organised

Sunday outings. Still, they are perhaps the only boys in the school who do not relish the new, more relaxed regime. Nice, cheery dormitories. A senior boy sleeps in each junior dorm to keep the peace. No 7 year olds currently board (head discourages it during the first year, but will accommodate younger brothers and other special cases). Parents of boys who boarded all the way through comment that the experience gets better and better as the boys get older. Oldest boys given many important responsibilities in running the school. No tuck may be brought into school and there is no shop but some sweets are doled out as prizes to boarders on weekends. Lots of pleasant indoor common rooms and a tarmac out front for ball games at play time. Would benefit from a climbing frame etc for the littles. Orderly dining with oldest boys jointly supervising tables with teachers. Charts on the wall document the boys' favourite meals (spag bol and pizza) and horrors (curry). NB nut-free kitchen, nut-free school.

Founded in 1904; a fascinating article by OB in school bumf, points out that it was then mainly a preparatory school for the (Methodist) Leys School in Cambridge. 40-acre grounds include vast expanses of immaculate playing fields, the envy of its competitors (see Papplewick). 700 acres of Burnham Beeches woods opposite. Beautiful views over choice Home Counties countryside with local power plant substantially camouflaged by greenery. Victorian main building with neat, logical additions, including staff housing for 20 teachers. Dated assembly hall/theatre to be replaced for school's centenary in 2004. Most interesting uniform – two different sets – one for autumn/winter, which is very traditional, and one for summer, which isn't.

All in all a good show and for some it is idyllic. Very much a prep aiming to place boys at their chosen schools. Academics and sport tower above all (since 1969 the school has won 3 art scholarships and 25 music scholarships but 159 academic awards) and the happiest boys seem to be those who are very good at at least one of these.

CAMERON HOUSE SCHOOL

4 The Vale, Chelsea, London, SW3 6AH

Tel: 02073 524 040
Fax: 02073 522 349
E-mail: info@cameronhouseschool.org
Website: www.cameronhouseschool.org

• Pupils: 70 girls, 50 boys; all day • Ages: 4-11 • Non-denom but C of E roots • Fees: £3,595 • Independent

Principal/headmistress: Since 1980, when she founded the school, Ms Josie Cameron Ashcroft BSc DipEd CertEd, member of IAPS. Taught at Thomas's and coached children privately before setting up her own school in St Luke's Church, Sydney Street. She is the principal and is in overall charge of the school. She is responsible for the ongoing vision and image of the school and is actively interested and involved with parents and pupils.

Since 1994, Finola Stack BA (Hons) PGCE, has been headmistress, in charge of management on a day to day basis. She teaches in every class. Previously co-founder and co-principal of Finton House. Two of her children have been through the school, with the third still there. Very caring and thoughtful. Pupils clearly like her, addressing her by her first name. She takes great care to see that her pupils get to a school where she knows they will flourish. Her finger is definitely on the pulse where London senior schools are concerned.

Entrance: Register your child at an early age (but not before birth) – a popular school, and places are allocated first come, first served (but siblings tend to get priority). Occasional places across the year groups. Children, twelve at a time, are invited to an assessment six months prior to starting. The emphasis is on informality and the environment is secure – the school do not want the children to perform.

Exit: All the top London schools. Fewer boys are leaving at 8 and tend to move on with the girls at 11 to Colet Court, City of London, Westminster, King's College, Wimbledon, Dulwich, Latymer. Girls to St Paul's, Putney High, Godolphin, Francis Holland, City of London Girls' and a small number to leading boarding schools.

Remarks: On the small side but a serious player in getting children into sought-after London schools. With all its academic success, the school isn't a hothouse and caters for children whose ability ranges from the very high to the ordinary. You get the impression that the children take everything in their stride. They are given the preparation but not the pressure.

The school is spotless, bright and sunny. Walls plastered with artwork, projects thoughtfully displayed in classrooms – high standards. Children look very happy, are settled and at ease with their environment. Class visits to museums and galleries very much part of the curriculum, with parents offering their time to help (a number of them also visit the school regularly to assist with reading.) Class size not more than 18, with each teacher of 4-7 year olds having a qualified assistant. Three support teachers look after SEN – the school has found that children of mixed ages work best in small groups. Staff young and predominantly female.

After school clubs are a thriving part of the school, especially drama, karate, chess and fencing. Children in clubs stay at school and do their homework under supervision before clubs begin. Children are bused to football, netball and tennis in Battersea Park and to Putney for rowing. Chelsea Sports Centre is used for swimming and gym.

Music is a major force in the curriculum with children encouraged to take up an instrument, although it is not obligatory. There are violin and recorder groups and tuition for the piano, trumpet, guitar, clarinet and flute.

Playground well-used by everyone at break and lunch. In addition to the IT suite at the top of the building and the 16 laptops, each classroom has a computer and printer which link into the school's network. Children have access to computers from an early age and their own files and email address from the age of 7.

Once the leavers have taken entrance exams to their next school, they are prepared for the next step through the PSHE programme. Three children recently returned to Cameron House to give a talk to the leavers about their experiences at senior school.

More than anything, Finola wants her pupils to be confident and happy, looking forward to the challenges they face and, all the while, being kind and considerate to their peers. The school provides a friendly environment where the children can do just that.

CARGILFIELD SCHOOL

Barnton Avenue West, Edinburgh, EH4 6HU

Tel: 0131 336 2207
Fax: 0131 336 3179
E-mail: secretary@cargilfield.com
Website: www.cargilfield.com

- Pupils: 7-13 years: 135 girls and boys; 30 two-weekly board (many flexi-board). 3-7 years 85 girls and boys • Ages: 3-13
- Non-denom • Fees: £2,150 to £3,450 for day; £4,400 boarders • Independent • Open days: October

Headmaster: Since 2004, Mr John Elder MA PGCE (fifties), formerly head of Malsis and before that Beeston, he has been headmaster for 20 years. (And he has imported his deputy head from Malsis, his head of outdoor pursuits, and the new head of nursery plus a fair number of pupils from Yorkshire). Educated at Lathallan and Cranleigh, followed by St Andrews and Edinburgh unis (he changed from history at St Andrews to American history at Edinburgh) Mr Elder started off by recycling wine bottles in Docklands – and would probably have been a millionaire by now, had he stuck at it. Charming and charismatic, he has given Cargilfield a much needed boost in continuity and in confidence. Mr Elder's Dutch wife, Hanneke, teaches RS and is heavily involved in Cargilfield: taking Catholic boarders to St Mary's Cathedral on Sundays is a minor part of her duties. Two of the three Elder children are at uni, and the youngest still at Glenalmond (they have a house in Angus and Mr Elder is a Scot).

A giant of a man, Mr Elder teaches 16 hours of maths a week ('strong maths staff are the most difficult to find') and who still 'for my sins' coaches rugby. Very understanding with children when they get through to him – does care, but likes his own way.

Entrance: Nursery and pre-prep popular, and Upper School numbers have grown enormously; places pretty well guaranteed through pre-prep, but tests if learning difficulties suspected.

Exit: All the Scottish public schools, Glenalmond heads the list, but also Merchiston, Fettes, Kilgraston, Gordonstoun, Loretto – much as you would expect. Also down South: Eton, Harrow, Shrewsbury Ampleforth, Downe House and Queen Margaret's (York), popular. 36 'genuine academic awards', in last 6 years, including one at Winchester. Three per cent annually to Edinburgh day schools.

Remarks: The arrival of Mr Elder signals the end of the recent rapid turnover in heads, and the despairing attitude to competition from Fettes. Mr Elder said he would 'focus on Cargilfield virtues as a family school with superb facilities, preparing children for the great schools in Scotland and the South'(and he has). Expect investment in the academic facilities, not the frills (and the stunning recent HMI report is evidence of this). Spanish recently introduced and superb classics results, with 20 doing Greek: Latin for all from eight. Two weekly boarding is now on stream, with day pupils joining boarders for a huge variety of weekend activities (though all must stay for three nights and can't just pick and choose). Huge choice: ranging from kayaking, to international coaching in fishing, shooting, classics and chess. Trips all over, both at weekends, and longer ones 'to abroad' – Spain this year.

Founded in 1873, the school moved to its purpose-built site in 1899 (23 acres then, 15 now: recent sale of land for £4.5 million accounts for superb and much-modernised facilities – notably for IT and boarding, and the new pre-prep and nursery. A new (academic) building is now planned – in the Ash Court – which will house the language department . Girls' dorms are being moved from the slightly cosy servants' quarters to a stunning revamp of about-to-be former classrooms.

Pupils set and streamed, scholarship help (with five 50 per cent plus skols available to those from state primaries with high IQs) as well as learning support on hand – Jan McAuslan runs one of the best learning support departments in Scotland, though the school will now no longer be able to accommodate many of the weaker brethren, unless they are in fact brethren. Masses of options and extracurricular activities – lots of music, and the pipe band is second to none, taster sessions for all in pre-prep, with 147 individual music lessons each term. V popular pop group. A revamped concert hall is on the stocks. Discounts for MoD children (v handy for Scottish Command), a mixed bunch of parents, with a handful of expats, and less first time buyers than previously. School buses whiz up the M74 from Yorkshire after weekends out and come daily from India Street in Edinburgh and Fife – there are plans afoot for a West Lothian bus, but as children often stay till after eight, parents must collect themselves.

CARRDUS SCHOOL

Overthorpe Hall, Blacklocks Hill, Banbury, Oxfordshire, OX17 2BS

Tel: 01295 263 733
Fax: 01295 263 733
E-mail: office@carrdusschool.co.uk
Website: www.carrdusschool.co.uk

- Pupils: 120 girls, 30 boys, all day • Ages: 3-11 (boys 3-8)
- Non-denom • Fees: £2,180-£2,320 • Independent • Open days: May

Head: Since 1985, Miss Susan Carrdus BA (fifties). Educated at The Carrdus School (her mother Kathleen founded school in 1952) and Banbury Grammar School, followed by Southampton University, where she read English. Previously head of English at nearby Tudor Hall. Has a grown-up daughter and two grandchildren.

Warm, approachable and immensely dedicated. Unusually for a head, she spends a third of her time in the classroom and is responsible for all year 5 and 6 English teaching. 'I love it,' she says. 'I really like and enjoy the company of children.' Very child-centred and doesn't miss a trick, whether greeting pupils by name as they race around the garden at break-times, searching out pencil sharpeners in the stationery cupboard or crouching down to help a nursery child put her shoes on the right way round. Throws herself into all school activities, even painting, decorating and sorting out the garden during the holidays. 'I drive a mean dumper truck,' she laughs. Enjoys walking and learning to play the piano in her spare time (not that there's much of it.)

Entrance: No entrance test. Very broad intake. Majority of pupils come from Banbury and surrounding villages, with parents registering children up to three years in advance. Most common entry points are nursery, reception and year 3 but it's worth trying in between too.

Exit: At 11, girls leave for a plethora of schools, including Tudor Hall, King's High, Headington, Rye St Antony, Oxford High, Cheltenham Ladies' College and Bloxham. Good smattering of scholarships over the years. At seven or eight, boys head for prep schools like Winchester House, Warwick Junior, Cothill and Bilton Grange.

Remarks: School moved to present site in 1970, when Kathleen Carrdus (now in her eighties but still taking a huge interest in school activities) bought Overthorpe Hall for the princely sum of £22,500. Became an educational trust in

1991, with 100 per cent of fee income ploughed back into the school. Main building a rambling 1880s hunting lodge set in 11 acres of grounds. Latest ISI report (2004) says school gives pupils 'a very caring and positive education'. Friendly staff pride themselves on making sure children are happy and secure in 'informal yet stimulating' atmosphere. Place feels straight out of a Mary Wesley novel – lots of fresh air, smiley faces, muddy knees and heaps of praise.

Despite relaxed ambience, pupils work hard and academic record is impressive. Hugely experienced staff (average age 48 and around a quarter have been at school for more than ten years.) Maximum class size 24 but in practice more like 18. No setting, but most able get chance to move faster in 'sparkle sessions.' Head of maths holds walk-in surgery first thing every morning for anyone who needs help, including parents puzzled by modern maths! School has number of pupils with dyslexia, dyspraxia and/or learning difficulties and they get support from two specially trained staff. No extra subjects apart from instrument lessons – school ethos is that everyone does everything. Children learn French from reception and take Latin for last two terms of year 6. Homework for all. Reception children take reading books home; year 3 pupils get prep three times a week, year 5 and 6 pupils every night. Thousands of books, all colour-coded for different reading abilities – head reckons school possesses virtually every children's book published since her mum was a girl in the 1920s. At least one computer in each classroom.

Arts strong, with children encouraged to play instruments, speak confidently in public and take part in concerts. Pupil's work on display everywhere you look. African tribal masks dangling from the main staircase, a collage of moles burrowing underground (using real mud!) and a poll of favourite books in the entrance hall – just for the record, year 6 voted for Private Peaceful and Holes while year 3 reckoned Roald Dahl's BFG was tops. Music terrific, with youngest children all playing percussion instruments and everyone from seven upwards learning the recorder. Many older pupils also learn piano, violin, guitar, saxophone or flute. Daily assembly, as well as weekly hymn practice and bible story. Delightful – and short – list of school rules advises pupils 'no sticks, no stones – only climb as high as your friend's head' and 'it's only fun if everybody is enjoying it.' No school uniform, games kit aside. Dress code is 'not smart, not scruffy,' with parents advised to send children in comfy, machine-washable clothes because there's 'lots of mud and trees.' Pupils, mainly kitted out in mini Boden-type leggings and stripy jumpers (no jeans or bare midriffs) approve wholeheartedly. When we visited only one girl said she'd quite like to wear uniform – as long as it was blue.

Sport is compulsory for all. Children do hockey, netball, athletics, gym, tennis, gymnastics, dance, cycling proficiency and swimming (heated outdoor pool set in pretty walled garden.) Cross-country a particular strength – pupils have won every cup going. Lots of school trips, to Stratford-upon-Avon, Oxford's Ashmolean Museum, Roald Dahl Museum etc. All year 6 girls get annual expedition to Normandy – French-speaking only from the minute the coach leaves school.

Nutritious, wholesome lunches cooked on-site and served by friendly dinner ladies who know children well. At break-time youngsters help themselves to cheese, crispbread, raw vegetables and fruit before racing off to play in the garden in virtually all weathers.

Very strong, sociable PTA, with activities ranging from new parents' breakfasts to annual bonfire party, Christmas fair and spring sale. Parents arriving to collect their children in the afternoons gather in the entrance hall, complete with squashy sofas and, in winter, a roaring fire. Way ahead of its time, school launched annual Carrdus At Work day 15 years ago, giving mums and dads the chance to work alongside their children in class for a day during the spring term.

Children have a whale of a time here, while achieving good results. Devoted pupils and parents stay in touch for years after they leave, ringing for advice about everything from university entrance to career choices. Much to head's amusement, old girls frequently implore her, 'can't you start a secondary school like this?'

CASTERTON PREPARATORY SCHOOL

Linked to Casterton School in the Senior section

Kirkby Lonsdale, Carnforth, Lancashire, LA6 2SG

Tel: 01524 279 282
Fax: 01524 279 286
E-mail: admissions@castertonschool.co.uk
Website: www.castertonschool.co.uk

- Pupils: 90; 70 girls, 20 boys; boarding and day • Ages: 3-11
- Fees: Prep: day £1,602 - £3,016 boarding £4,303 - £4,737
- Independent • Open days: October and February

Remarks: For futher details see senior school.

CASTLE COURT

Knoll Lane, Corfe Mullen, Wimborne, Dorset, BH21 3RF

Tel: 01202 694 438
Fax: 01202 659 063
E-mail: hmsec@castlecourt.com
Website: www.castlecourt.com

- Pupils: 350, boys and girls; all day • Ages: 3-13 • C of E
- Fees: £3,700 • Independent • Open days: October and May, but ring for visits at other times

Head: Since 1989, Richard Nicholl BA (enviably youthful early fifties). Shared his schooldays at Stowe with Richard Branson, then diverged. After Durham and Oxford came teaching at Haileybury where he administered English and religious studies to Dom Joly, coached all species of game-splayer and housemastered sixth form girls. Bright-eyed, effective, engaging, thoughtful. Unexpectedly humorous. Innerly lit by his Christian faith, which permeates everything that happens here. His wife, Vicky, is equally beloved by parents and children. As admissions secretary, she will be your first point of contact. She also oversees catering and cleaning. Two daughters, one ex-Oxford, one at Durham. Will stay until 2011.

Entrance: For 3-5 year-olds, first come, first in. Thereafter, informal assessment 'to ensure that children will be comfortable with the pace here'. Mild dyslexia only. They flock from all compass points: Weymouth-Shaftesbury-Burley-Swanage. First choice for Poole-Bournemouth conurbanites. Scholarships from 7+ for those likely to repeat the performance at a senior school. Automatic discounts for brothers and sisters.

Exit: Canford. If not, one of a scattering of premiership independents. Impressive numbers of awards. Around a quarter leave at 12 for the excellent local grammars, or the equally good comps. Golden alumni include Tony Blackburn, pop singer Amy Studt and rugby sevens hero Ben Gollings.

Remarks: Though held in highest esteem, this school is beguilingly unpretentious. Parents span old and new Dorset – farmers to flashy over-achievers/entrepreneurs. Expect no quirks. Castle Court is the product not of evolution but meticulous planning and it all stems from the top. Everything is tickety-boo, but never too good to be true. Beautifully behaved children walk to assembly in marshalled lines, evenly spaced. They sit in rapt silence – contentedly. They listen to the Word as it relates to contemporary events, as it applies to daily lives, the delivery humorous, interactive, thought-inspiring, backed by PowerPoint. The objective lies not in the act of worship but in what they call outworking: being kind to each other, raising money for charity. That's why parents like it – there's no sense whatever of evangelical mind-stealing. Zealous atheists may wince, though.

In the classroom the pace is rapid, for this is a blue-chip school. Slower children will puff a bit but they are supported and almost all subjects are setted. The brightest are not worked to death, yet mop up scholarships by the barrowload. Every lesson we invaded was calm and, yes, orderly, but with masses going on. It's that sort of school. They want the children to work well together, and they do. So do the teachers. Marvellously focussed. Careful as can be. Results are no happy accident because each child is so painstakingly tracked – every building block is put in place before the next block is added. One mum says, 'pupils miss nothing academically, socially or extra-curricularly. A child can enter at 3 and leave at 13 and you can be absolutely confident that there is no chink in what they have learned or experienced.' Those with emergent SENs are pit-stopped and fine-tuned, mostly one-to-one, expertly, and equipped with 'special skills'. The void left by those off to grammar school is instantly filled for those who remain with extra attention from really impressive form teachers.

Does such an environment favour passive conformity? No. At break-time we saw reassuringly semi-feral high spirits in the rough-and-tumble covered playground and the surrounding woods. This really is a school for all sorts where problems are earnestly remedied, never shuffled off. Sport is played with exuberance and winning is prized. Everyone has a go in a team at some level. Pastoral care is attentive and personal. Music is strong, 75 per cent learn an instrument, and there are performance opportunities of all shapes and genres. Art is superb and has wide appeal, including a thriving after-lunch drop-in club where children do their own thing. Children are urged to try their hands at everything, so the IT suite has outward bound posters above the monitors. Juniors have a go at riding and sailing. From year 5 children can stay till 6pm for 'tea and prep' and activities – a good range. Camping weekends for year 3 and up, some at the wonderful Kingcombe environmental centre.

Classrooms and facilities generally sound but not snazzy. Knoll House, the homely Regency mansion, lies at the heart of a roomy 30 acres. Lovely gardens, azalea-smitten in early summer, where we watched weenies playing Grandma's Footsteps before lunch, an Edwardian vision. All-weather pitch. Constantly uplifted IT. Classrooms comely if unremarkable. Building and upgrading under way subject to planning regs.

This is a kind, gentle school which inspires in parents admiration and affection in equal measure. It is as good as they get.

CATERHAM PREPARATORY SCHOOL

Linked to Caterham School in the Senior section

Harestone Valley Road, Harestone Valley Road, Caterham, Surrey, CR3 6YB

Tel: 01883 342 097
Fax: 01883 341 230
E-mail: howard.tuckett@caterhamschool.co.uk
Website: www.caterhamschool.co.uk

• Pupils: 111 girls and boys; all day • Ages: 3-11 • Fees: Nursery £1,034; reception, years 1 and 2 £1,737; years 3 and 4 £2,217; years 5 and 6 £2,665 • Independent

Remarks: Sharing the senior school site in separate large redbrick buildings set in leafy spaces, both schools are inviting and well away from busy roads. Many shared facilities with main school. Nice touches here and there – a huge aquarium in the prep's main corridor, super displays in the pre prep's classrooms, masses of space and good libraries. Charming and enthusiastic head (and parent) Mrs Owen-Hughes. Sensible uniform includes burgundy anoraks.

CATTERAL HALL

Linked to Giggleswick School in the Senior section

Giggleswick, Settle, North Yorkshire, BD24 0DE

Tel: 01729 893100
Fax: 01729 893158
E-mail: R.D.Hunter@giggleswick.org.uk
Website: www.giggleswick.org.uk

• Pupils: 140 girls and boys, including approx 50 boarders
• Ages: 3-13, pre-prep 3-7 (Mill House) • Fees: Catteral Hall, years 7 & 8 boarding £4,910; day £3,835. Catteral Hall years 3-6 boarding £4,140; day £3,400. Mill House pre-prep £1,700
• Independent • Open days: October

Head: R D Hunter MA.
Entrance: Broadly selective. Children from 7 years are offered places provided they have a good basic knowledge of reading and writing. Entrance is via tests, interview with the parent and child and a full report from the previous school. Pupils who are non-native speakers of English may expect to take extra English lessons (EFL) according to need. Children with specific learning difficulties may be accepted provided the school feels able to offer the specialist and general assistance required.

Exit: Majority to Giggleswick.

Remarks: Majority of teaching takes place in the recently completed Partridge building. Facilities include seven bright modern classrooms, library ICT suite, learning support tutorial room, self-contained playground and brand new sports hall. The two heads work closely together, sharing some facilities and teaching expertise. French is introduced in year 3 and Latin in year 6. Younger children spend most of their time with their form teacher but by year 6 all lessons are taught by specialist teachers. Children follow National Curriculum and take SATs. Separate junior boarding house, opportunities for day pupils to board on an occasional basis at any time subject to space. Special year group sleepover weekends organised from time to time. Full activity programme for boarders.

CENTRAL NEWCASTLE HIGH SCHOOL JUNIOR DEPARTMENT

Linked to Central Newcastle High School in the Senior section

West Avenue, Gosforth, Newcastle upon Tyne, Tyne and Wear, NE3 4ES

Tel: 0191 285 1956
Fax: 0191 213 2598
E-mail: cnhsjuniors@cnn.gdst.net
Website: www.newcastlehigh.gdst.net

• Pupils: 325 girls, including 24 girls in the nursery; all day
• Ages: 5-11, nursery 3-5 • Fees: junior £1,674; nursery £1,383
• Independent • Open days: Early November

Head: Mrs Avril Lomas.
Entrance: Assessment and interview.
Remarks: School has recently acquired new premises in Sandiford, a former convent, set in five acres of grounds which is now home to the 8-11 year old group. Younger girls (3-7) are still at the original building in Gosforth.

CHAFYN GROVE SCHOOL

Bourne Avenue, Salisbury, Wiltshire, SP1 1LR

Tel: 01722 333 423
Fax: 01722 323 114
E-mail: admissions@chafyngrove.co.uk
Website: www.chafyngrove.co.uk

• Pupils: 149 boys and 58 girls in prep; 45 boys and 28 girls in nursery and pre prep. 44 boarders – well down on what it used to be • Ages: 3-13 • C of E • Fees: £1,855- £5,115 • Independent • Open days: Early October and May

Head: Since 2004, Mr Eddy Newton MA PGCE (forties). Stonyhurst, Jesus College Cambridge (classics). A decidedly classy career before coming here – head of classics at The Dragon, Oxford, deputy head of Pinewood, near Swindon, director of studies and housemaster at Highfield School, Liphook, then headmaster of Felsted prep, Essex. For all his distinguished ancestry there's an unassumingness about Mr Newton. He listens carefully, his responses reassure and he is clearly wise in the ways of children. His mission is not to change the school, no need for that, but to fine tune it, up the tempo and do it all better, so he's a systems man, not so down-home as his predecessor James Barnes (now head of Lambrook Haileybury), famous for his shirtsleeves and mug of coffee in the playground. He is raising expectations all round and recent academic performance seems to be a beneficiary. Most parents like his style and are glad to get it. Communication, a longstanding grouse, is improving – 'he's direct. You may not get the answer you want but at least you get an answer.' Some, missing the colour of the ancien regime, find him a tad grey but assent that a safe pair of hands is what's needed just now. With a big build under way and no urgent need for any more, his role in the medium term has to be managerial. Wife Alison is much the bubblier, very involved in school on the PR side, superintends the nutritiousness of the food and shows prospective parents round. Two young children.

Entrance: Interview as much to display school to child and parents as for the school to assess them. Known to do a good job by the brightest, the brain range is broad but the climate is quick-witted, so think hard if it looks as if your child may dawdle. Scholarships available at years 3, 5 and 7 for pupils showing promise academically or in sport, music or art. Parents come from a 45-minute radius, mostly, from the city and from Salisbury's satellite villages. They're a mixed bunch, professionals, business, around 15 per cent army. The feel of the school is, say some parents, 'a clever blend of town and country' or, say others, a touch balefully, 'getting townier all the time' but all agree with unanimity of emphasis, 'no, we don't feel we have to dress up when we go to get our children.' Sting's children were here. No PTA but there are year group reps, volunteers or co-opted, who channel niggles to the head and – this is good – introduce new parents and children to old hands before they start, and arrange social jollies for all year group parents. There is a comprehensive parents' survival guide to the school (and, usefully, to the English system of exams) written by parents.

Exit: The usual seepage at 11 to local free grammars – around a quarter. They are supported and prepared. Most stay till 13, moving on to a variety of senior schools including Bryanston, Canford, Dauntseys, King's Bruton, Godolphin, Marlborough and Sherborne and Winchester.

Remarks: There's a 'family atmosphere' says parent after parent and, cliché it may be, that's how they reckon it's best summed up – and we all know what that is. The welcome is warm, the children enjoy chatting to adult strangers and the teachers are pleased to see you – not the case everywhere. It's an evidently agreeable milieu in which children move at speed, bright eyed, fired up, flapping a bit clothing-wise. We were set free with a senior boy and girl, no restriction on our movements – always a sign of a confident school – so we followed our pooled whims and invaded lessons at will. We saw Mr McKay teaching Latin and we shan't forget the hilarity and the inspiration. Marvellous. We had to go and see the art room and agree that what goes on there is excellent. There's even an artist in residence. We enjoyed the names of the houses (they call them Eights) – Wasps, Birds, Frogs, etc – and we approved of the proper old-fashioned playground bell.

For a town school there's plenty of room and, when the new library is built, they'll not want for anything. The imposing Victorian main school building is supplemented by modern, light and bright, purpose-built classrooms. Library buzzing when we saw it, very well run. They work really hard to get the children reading. Large sports hall and performance hall – these facilities are very impressive. Though only 10 minutes' walk from the centre of Salisbury, the school has plenty of grounds with pitches, Astro, hard tennis courts, 2 squash courts, an outdoor pool and lovely views of Salisbury Plain. Sport is big to the exclusion, some complain, of the non-sporty who have spent afternoons in classrooms doing nothing in the rain. Timetabling has, we are assured, been re-jigged to stop this. Boys play rugby, hockey and cricket and girls, hockey, netball and rounders.

Boys only play football in the lower age groups. Music is strong, renaissance to rock, 70 per cent learn one or more instruments, but many wish orchestra were not classed an activity because it means you can't do any activities – which goes to show how popular activities are for, together with prep, they account for the 70-75 children still in school every day at 6 o'clock. Drama has long been a crown jewel but the charismatic teacher has just left, so it's watch this space. Indeed, on the teacher front it's watch these spaces because there's a big new untested intake, including a new deputy head.

Large computer room for ICT and specialist use in some subjects. Everyone is taught to touch-type. Useful onsite stationery, book and uniform, new and secondhand, shops. Learning support given discreetly by assistants in the classroom and specialist learning support is available for individuals from four part-time teachers. Food a source of pride – the children don't rate it, what would they know? – but it's proper and prepared by their own chef, not one of those catering outfits. Form teachers and tutors are available for parents before and after school in the pick up area for quick consultation – 'this cuts out car park gossip and nips any problems in the bud'.

Big efforts are being made to make boarding special. There are excellent people in charge, the dorms are painted in colours that would blind parakeets, and they find the children plenty to do, especially at weekends, when something like half of them are in. Big praise here from the social care inspectors, and justified. Big big praise from parents and children, who definitely love being here. They offer flexi options but expect regularity.

A famously informal school where, all parents agree, their children are very happy.

CHANDLINGS MANOR SCHOOL

Linked to Cothill House School in the Junior section

Bagley Wood, Kennington, Oxford, Oxfordshire, OX1 5ND

Tel: 01865 730 771
Fax: 01865 735 194
E-mail: jogoddard@chandlings.com
Website: www.chandlings.com

- Pupils: 300 boys, 100 girls, all day • Ages: 3-11 • Inter-denom
- Fees: £2,330 - £3,100 • Independent

Head: Since 1999, Judy Forrest, appointed by the Cothill Educational Trust but with complete independence and full responsibility. Headhunted from Upton House, Windsor, much to the dismay of parents and children there. Described as 'a mummy rather than a head,' said one parent, 'you know you've done the right thing when you see little children clutching her hand'.

Entrance: From 3 years of age by informal assessment

Exit: At 11. A few go on to join Cothill as boarders and another handful to the maintained sector while the majority proceed to a variety of prestigious Oxfordshire senior independent day schools.

Remarks: Sixty acres of beautiful playing fields, woodlands and lakes. Early years get a good phonic grounding with plenty of teacher support and specialist help if needed. Older children have a broader-based curriculum and subject teaching with mixed ability settings in the main. French from reception upwards, Latin is optional for the last two years. Leavers can boost their French by taking a trip to a French chateau owned by the Cothill Educational Trust.

Sport for girls and boys timetabled each day. Indoor and outdoor swimming pools, a nine-hole golf course, a riding school and fishing as well as the normal range of sporting facilities. Well-equipped music, art and drama departments where each child is encouraged to exhibit their talents. Excellent ICT department, spreading its tentacles into each of the classrooms. Children say that they feel comfortable and at home at Chandlings and even admit to enjoying school food.

The brainchild of Cothill's head, Adrian Richardson, who previously set up Château de Sauveterre for Cothill boys to perfect their French. Cothill and Chandlings each have their own identity and ethos, but have a close association.

Parents who want to keep their child at home and who like to play an active support role have no doubts that Chandlings is for them. With all that this school has to offer it should not be too long before it becomes oversubscribed.

CHAPTER HOUSE PREPARATORY SCHOOL

Linked to Queen Ethelburga's College in the Senior section

Thorpe Underwood Hall, York, YO26 9SS

Tel: 0870 742 3330
Fax: 0870 742 3310
E-mail: enquiries@ChapterHouseSchool.org.uk
Website: www.chapterhouseschool.org.uk

- Pupils: 115 girls and boys; boarding and day • Ages: 2-11
  • Independent

Remarks: For further details see senior school, Queen Ethelburga's College.

CHEADLE HULME SCHOOL JUNIOR SCHOOL

Linked to Cheadle Hulme School in the Senior section

Claremont Road, Cheadle Hulme, Cheadle, Cheshire, SK8 6EF

Tel: 0161 488 3334
E-mail: registrar@chschool.co.uk
Website: www.cheadlehulmeschool.co.uk

- Pupils: 284 girls and boys; all day • Ages: 4-11 • Fees: Juniors
  £1,968 • Independent

Remarks: For further details, see senior school.

CHEAM SCHOOL

Headley, Newbury, Berkshire, RG19 8LD

Tel: 01635 268 381
Fax: 01635 269 345
E-mail: office@cheamschool.co.uk
Website: www.cheamschool.com

- Pupils: 286; 160 boys, 120 girls; half boarding, half day. Plus pre-prep with 110 boys and girls • Ages: 8-13, pre-prep 3-7
- C of E • Fees: Boarders £5,775; day: £2,445 for Reception - year 2 ; £4,275 for years 8, 7 and 6 • Independent

Head: Since 1998, Mr Mark R Johnson Bed(Hons) (forties). A West Country product – educated at Buckland House, Devon, and Exeter School; got his degree at the College of St Mark and St John, Plymouth. His last post was as deputy headmaster at Summer Fields, where he was hugely popular. Nickname: Mr J (from his initials – M R J). Bursting with enthusiasm and energy, slightly hail-fellow-well-met, describes himself as 'restless – bubbling with ideas for and about the school we 'whizzed' (regularly) all round the place. Does not (currently) teach, because he reckons it is more important for him to be seeing parents, potential and present. 'He's very parent-friendly,' remarked one, warmly, 'an overgrown prep school boy', said another. Married to Jane, a lovely bouncy lady, a classicist, who does a little Latin and Greek teaching (NB Greek back on course). Two daughters, one now at Teddy's, the other in the school.

Entrance: Informal tests – children spend one day at the school four terms before entry. First come, first served (but at the time of writing oversubscribed, so book early). But figures are meaningless here, as not all year groups are full and there is often place for the odd child 'further up the school'. Can come at half term throughout the year if space available. School holds four in-days for up to ten potential pupils on the list under the watchful eye of the former head of the pre-prep who is accustomed to the vagaries of six-year-olds, a gentle assessment, parents come too and meet the head.

Exit: Boys to Marlborough, Sherborne, Stowe, Eton, Radley, St Edward's Oxford, Winchester 'creeping in' plus Wellington and a number of others; Harrow occasionally. Girls (mostly at 13) to Downe House, Marlborough, Cheltenham Ladies, Sherborne Girls, St Mary's Calne, and Ascot, Heathfield, St Edward's Oxford. Most famous Old Boys: HRH The Duke of Edinburgh, HRH The Prince of Wales, Lord Randolph Churchill, William Pitt the Younger.

Remarks: Back on course as a vibrant and strong prep school after several years in the wilderness. Claims to be the oldest of all the prep schools, traces its history back to 1645. Set in gloriously well-kept grounds with an elegant terraced garden, the main house is partly by Detmar Blow, although the expanded new chapel and Taylor building makes the turn-in to the main school somewhat cramped and surprising, some tree pruning would be a great improvement. Lots of new buildings (classroom block and music school 2002, sports centre and additional ICT suite 2003). Plans for further expansion and improvements in the pipeline (art centre and Astroturf). Six years ago the local pre-prep had to close and 'offered to merge'. Numbers have, therefore, shot up and the school is now choc-a-bloc. Day numbers have also increased and presumably will continue to increase as the local pre-prep children grow into the main school, 'but remember, a lot of them insist on boarding in the last two years.' The boarding/day split in the prep school is about 50/50. Boarding accommodation completely renovated over last two years and Cheam's boarding provision was praised highly following a recent CSCI inspection; splendid new boarders' common room. Large London contingent and a few from overseas (one term, one year, EFL an option). Strong on PSHE, tutors for all. Flexi-ish boarding available but pupils and parents must commit, min two nights. Serious weekend programme for those left behind. New and younger staff have been brought in, adding zest to staid older teachers, and planning permission has been granted for ten staff house units in the grounds which will make getting younger staff easier (prices are high round Newbury).

Setting and streaming in most subjects. Latin considerably beefed up with a Latin reading competition now on the menu. Scholarship forms in the top two years; top stream and 'scholars' take Greek in their final year. Strong on outings and trips to provide hands-on teaching eg workshops at archaeological digs, French classes in Bayeux, environmentalists to the Wyld Court Rainforest, plus all the usual museum visits. All children spend a week in France in their penultimate year for a complete immersion in the language in the build-up to CE and scholarships. Help for the gifted and for the SEN pupils, some may come with a statement of needs, others are spotted in their original assessments, currently 40 pupils have some form of serious help either one to one or in small groups. 'Quite a lot' of dual teaching. Two full time and three part time assistants, most problems fall within the dys-strata, couple currently with mild Aspergers. 'Always someone to turn to' if problems hit (more or less at any time) and laptops for most in the SEN stream. (Learning support knocks in at £17 per individual 40 minute lesson, £10 if shared and for EFL £15 per 30 minute lesson, £8 if shared). The school is otherwise completely-friendly.

Music is on the up (school says 'outstanding') – the school boasts four choirs (40 choristers toured New York Christmas 2005); 90 recently performed Fauré's Requiem, helped by adults; 60 perform regularly in school orchestra; numerous ensemble groups and jazz band. Keen drama for all ages (drama now on the curriculum) and very good art displayed all over the school (art scholars embark on a four day art retreat to Paris in the autumn term). Minimum TV watching, reading period (Digest) after lunch; computer games rationed, digital games forbidden here. Cooking for all, sewing machines for girls – who are allowed to be gentle – that having been said, there is a dedicated lax pitch. Popular Scottish country dancing a regular feature. School day starts at 8.15am with daily chapel and all the children must say good morning and make eye contact with the head on the way out. Saturday morning school. Huge numbers (75) of extra-curricular activities, from copper etching to fly fishing. No winter timetable, throughout the year children work all morning, after lunch do more lessons until 3.30pm, then games, floodlighting, though not over all the hundred or so acres.

Games are big here, with matches and competitions at all levels, so practically everyone is in a team – and, by the way, they beat other schools. Competitive on the house front (divisions). Wide range of sports on offer including rugger, football, cricket, hockey, netball and rounders. Polo (courtesy of Lord Lloyd Webber – 20+ players) and fencing popular, the latter with streams of ribbons and mega cupboards full of cups for each house. Notably good tennis. New sports hall, opened by Martin Johnson, now offers plethora of opportunities for games for pre-prep and prep children. Overseas tours in abundance – girls' hockey to Barcelona, boys' cricket to South Africa. Notice-boards everywhere along passages and meeting places, bulging with (computer generated) information, lists, newspaper cuttings, news etc. 'We know where every pupil is at any time and can pull up his or her profile at will'. The first notice to hit you in the eye as you enter the school asks, 'Are You Happy?' Head's stated aim is to have 'blissfully happy children'. Manners well taken care of and the school operates a fierce anti-bullying policy. Magical head, magical school, all things for all children. Terrific, but much better if they get the loppers out.

CHELTENHAM COLLEGE JUNIOR SCHOOL

Linked to Cheltenham College in the Senior section

Thirlestaine Road, Cheltenham, GL53 7AB

Tel: 01242 522 697
Fax: 01242 265 620
E-mail: ccjs@cheltcoll.gloucs.sch.uk
Website: www.cheltcoll.gloucs.sch.uk

- Pupils: 450 girls and boys; boarding and day • Ages: 3 - 13
- Fees: Day: £1,705 - £4,160; boarding £4,125 - £5,400.
- Independent • Open days: October & March

Head: Since 1992, Mr Nigel Archdale BEd MEd (forties). Educated John Lyon School and Bristol and Edinburgh universities. Previously at Edinburgh Academy junior school. Then four years as head of Royal Wolverhampton Junior School before putting down roots in leafy Cheltenham. Only 10th head in school's history. Three children (daughter at university, sons at Cheltenham College) and ex-teacher wife, now head's right arm. 'I couldn't do this job without her,' he insists. Very sporty, keeps trim with daily swim or run. Energy is hallmark of his headship. 'There are so many exciting things coming to fruition,' he says. 'It's a truly dynamic school.'

Entrance: At 3, 4, 7 and 11. Non-selective below age 11 with entry by assessment and interview. More choosy later on as pupils must be able to pass CE at 13. Lots of local interest. Tiny intake from overseas. Popular with Services. Doors opened to girls in 1993. Discount available for third and subsequent siblings, bursary scheme for Services, and 11+ scholarship up to 50 per cent of fees.

Exit: In 2005, 100 per cent of pupils got into their first choice school. Vast majority move across the road to mixed senior school, Cheltenham College. CE entry pass around 50 per cent, other schools vary. Number of girls leave at 11 for Cheltenham Ladies' College, despite efforts to hang onto them for another two years. A few also to good local grammars. Parents advised on best senior option for their child. Famous OBs (head calls them OJs as in Old Juniors) include General Sir Michael Rose and actor Nigel Davenport.

Remarks: Known simply as The Junior. Set in conservation area, large Edwardian red-brick purpose-built (in 1908) school house with seamless (and some not so seamless) additions over the decades. Newest building for lower

school the best yet and overlooking lake. Head's decision to go co-ed caused great ructions but school has never looked back – there were fewer than 240 pupils when he took over, most in years 7 and 8, now there's twice as many.

School day action packed – hardly enough hours in it. Lessons start 8.15am for all but youngest (Kingfishers pre-prep department launched in 1993 in own well-designed extension) and include daily class music. Not at expense of anything else though. Still find time to fit in French from age of 3 alongside staple diet of core subjects. ICT extremely well catered for with annually updated computers, 24-hour internet connection, and school network. Laptops everywhere. Internal e-mail system keeps staff in touch – replaced old-style staff notice-boards. Academically thrusting for a non-selective school but geared up to the individual. Help available (at no extra charge) for mild dyslexics, dyspraxics and other minor learning difficulties. 'We're not a special school,' says head. 'The emphasis is on mild.' But parent with criticisms elsewhere in the school is unstinting in his praise of the help for SEN. Well-run shuttle system boosts youngsters' intake of core subjects in place of occasional French or Latin. Extra charge for EFL lessons. Well-stocked pleasant library, used to be school gym.

Artwork on show quite unbelievable (it was easy to forget you were in a junior school) so it seemed a shame more was not spread around the school. Main exception is outstanding series of murals along one corridor wall, painted in 2000. Justly proud of working scale model fleet of warships (made by past pupils and maintained by current pupils) which are sailed each year on Junior's own shallow lake. Bags more innovative projects emerging from tech department – great merging of design, woodwork and electronics – as big a hit with girls as boys. Super sports hall and indoor pool (shared with senior school, as are science labs). Lovely cricket pitch, good hockey and rugby tradition, hard courts for tennis. Brand new assembly hall, attached sympathetically to old school, is all their own. Has transformed the big event, put drama back on the map and given school a unique venue for major productions, concerts and gatherings. Only non-purpose building is music school, a lovely wood-panelled setting for individual lessons and small group recitals. Four choirs (chapel choir regularly tours).

Boarding not at full capacity but allows for sleepovers. Large airy dorms in old building, shared curtained cubicles for older children, all well kept with enough pictures, toys and own duvets to make it homely. Boarders' privileges extend to use of library, computers, art and DT studios at any time of day. Can also use pool for special supervised sessions. Only pupils to be allowed mobile phones though use strictly controlled. Fabulous grounds and lush green setting provide plenty of scope for outside play. Pupils allocated houses for competitive and pastoral reasons. Strict anti-bullying policy rigidly enforced. 'Bullying is a fact of life,' admits head. Will go to great lengths to resolve difficulties but head has been known to ask repeat offenders to leave.

Weekly chapel on Saturday, Sunday service three or four times a term. Chapel 'essential but not in an over-arching way,' says head. Saturday school a bone of contention with some parents; now being made optional for year 3, still compulsory for all above. Topic constantly raises its head at annual parents forum and three-yearly parental survey – so watch this space.

Plenty of moneyed backgrounds, landed gentry and self-made millionaires (there's soon to be an addition to the fact-packed parents' handbook on landing helicopters at school), but there are ordinary folk too. 'We have a very broad parental constituency.' No parent teacher association. Tried it once, didn't work. No fund-raising for extras either. 'Parents are already paying enough through fees,' says head. 'I don't think it's fair to keep on asking them for more.' Extra activities include twice-weekly dry slope skiing in nearby Gloucester, squash, trampolining, and paddle-boating on lake.

Smashing bunch of children seen around school, no-one apparently at a loose end, and a certain confidence clearly evident from the youngest Kingfisher up. Head sums up school in one word – enthusiasm. The enthusiasm of pupils, staff and 'most parents'. There's an overwhelming feeling here of purpose and activity. Everything is designed 'to produce a child who can make meaningful sense of this incredibly confusing 21st century,' says head. In other words, kids with street cred as well as an appreciation of their privileged circumstances.

CHETHAMS SCHOOL OF MUSIC JUNIOR DEPARTMENT

Long Millgate, Manchester, M3 1SB

Tel: 0161 834 9644
Fax: 0161 839 3609
E-mail: lesleyhaslam@chethams.com
Website: www.chethams.com

• Pupils: boys and girls, some board • Ages: 8-11 • Independent

Remarks: See main school.

CHIGWELL JUNIOR SCHOOL

Linked to Chigwell School in the Senior section

High Road, Chigwell, Essex, IG7 6QF

Tel: 020 8501 5700
Fax: 020 8500 6232
E-mail: hm@chigwell-school.org
Website: www.chigwell-school.org

• Pupils: 260 boys and girls, all day • Ages: 1-11 • C of E but welcomes all • Fees: £2,290-2,894 • Independent • Open days: October

Remarks: In a purpose-built, welcoming home on the main school site, the junior school is integral to the whole and the pupils share most of the seniors' facilities such as the gym and dining room. Their visibility – yet separate playground and classroom block – increase the family feel and lessen the adjustment shock when they move – as virtually all do – into the senior school. As in the senior school, the place feels orderly and is attractive – good, thoughtful displays everywhere. Juniors have their own library and teaching is good. 2004 ISI report had few criticisms (SEN provision was, again, one) and much praise across all academic and extra-curricular areas. In particular, it noted how the school integrates pupils of different cultures, producing 'a harmonious and lively atmosphere in which everyone is accepted and valued'.

CHRIST CHURCH CATHEDRAL SCHOOL

3 Brewer Street, Oxford, Oxfordshire, OX1 1QW

Tel: 01865 242 561
Fax: 01865 202 945
E-mail: schooloffice@cccs.org.uk
Website: www.cccs.org.uk

- Pupils: 135 boys, 85 per cent day, rest boarding choristers
- Ages: 7-13; 4-6 pre-prep; 2-3 yrs nursery (female siblings in nursery only) • C of E • Fees: Nursery £940 to £1,750; pre-prep £1,980; prep £3,135. Boarding choristers £1,930 to £2,130.
- Independent • Open days: Voice trials and open days October - pre prep and prep

Headmaster: Since 2005, Mr Martin Bruce BA, who brings a strong musical background to strong musical school. Was chorister at All Saints', Margaret Street, London, then at Winchester Cathedral. Won major music scholarship to Wellington College, choral scholarship to Durham where he read English. Continues to sing, also plays organ and has written several musicals and choral works. Latterly head of Bickley Park School, Kent, plenty of experience in single sex and mixed schools. On council of IAPS and is independent schools' inspector. Married (wife K.T. a teacher, life coach and artist) with two children, Sophie, soon to start university and Tristan, third year Tonbridge School.

Entrance: At least 90 per cent apply on the recommendation of others and word of mouth approval. Lots of siblings. Ability tests for entry at 7 but most join in nursery or pre-prep and are virtually assured entry to the school. Very occasional places occur across age range. Effectively first come, first served. No scholarships for day pupils. Four choristers per year selected by voice trial and by aptitude and intelligence tests. They pay only 40 per cent of full boarding fee.

Exit: Fine record of winning music and academic scholarships to top schools – most years 100 per cent of choristers win music scholarships or awards. Usually pick up a batch of musical awards from Wellington, Uppingham, Rugby and nearby St Edward's, Radley and Abingdon. Regular academic scholarships from Magdalen College School and St Edward's. Most go on to fee-paying schools but a few switch to Oxford's best state senior schools, such as Cherwell. Most famous OB is William Walton but lots of successful music figures are ex-CCCS.

Remarks: Charming prep-school tucked into a small site in the heart of Oxford. Three distinct buildings on very small site. Principal old building, all dark wood, ageing paint and faint aromas, dates from 1892, although CCCS was actually founded in 1546, to educate eight choristers on Henry VIII's foundation of Christ Church. It houses the beautiful panelled refectory and the boarders' rooms, painted lurid green (the choice of the boys, says the head – the choice of the head, say the boys).

Pianos in every corner and usually with boys attached to them. Also home to fabulous new IT suite, 20 networked computers, kitted out with the latest technology and a terminal for every boy. At right-angles is the new building, where younger pupils begin their school days in airy, bright classrooms on the ground floor, alongside the compact school hall, which doubles as an indoor games area. Upstairs are more classrooms with names like Darwin and Shakespeare to indicate their use. Very lively lessons – French students jumping around pretending to be gorillas to learn pronunciation – and rather more traditional whole class teaching side by side. Strong on languages – French from 7, Latin from 9. Original boarding house – established by Dean Liddell, father of 'Alice in Wonderland' Liddell, in the late nineteenth century – redeveloped to house spacious art and design technology rooms and self-contained nursery with its own garden. Lots of heavy-duty security on the doors between the buildings and security gates guard the way to the outside world – obviously necessary in the heart of a city.

Head at pains to stress this is not a specialist music school, despite awesome reputation of main choir. Boys confirm there is no pressure to take individual music lessons, although 85 per cent do, or sing in choirs. But there are four choirs in school and the day boys' Worcester College Choir is always oversubscribed. Boarding choristers have to be extra-bright and 'personally resilient' – no academic concessions made for three hours of choir practice and performance every day. There are compensations – boys earn royalties from all concerts and recordings, which include the theme music to The Vicar of Dibley. Also parents get 60 per cent off full boarding fee.

Very good support for specific learning difficulties, but 'we don't deal with low ability'. Good manners clearly a top priority – boys stand to attention when anyone enters the room and they are notably confident and courteous from a young age.

Strong belief in education beyond the classroom – oldest boys go on outward bound trips and ski trips, younger children have raised thousands for a school in Zambia.

Extensive range of school clubs now forms part of the curriculum and the school day. These include chess, jigsaws, business, drama, german, squash, models, origami and board/cards. Judo is currently offered as an after school club.

Access and parking can be a problem but pick-ups by parents are down to a fine art. Games, including football, rugby and cricket, mostly take place a five minute walk away on the scenic Christ Church Meadow. Regular matches against 'appropriate' teams from bigger local schools, with nearly all boys making one team or other. Anglican school teaching value of respect for others, with daily assembly, but popular with parents of all faiths whose children happily attend the cathedral with their classmates. Very rare instances of bullying – 'children, like adults, can be unpleasant' – dealt with by all parties talking through the problem together. Not a school for the timid, but for those who are prepared to join in and lead a busy life. Quality education in and lead a busy life. Quality education in a family atmosphere, in which boys are both cherished and encouraged.

Parents struggle to find anything bad to say about school. 'Can't think of any weaknesses at all,' says one. 'There's a real family nurturing atmosphere. The children are very well looked after and we're delighted with his results. Our son's come on immeasurably in the last two years. He loves it!'

CHRIST CHURCH C OF E PRIMARY SCHOOL

1 Robinson Street, London, SW3 4AA

Tel: 02073 525 708
Fax: 02078 233 004
E-mail: info@chch.rbkc.sch.uk
Website: www.chch.rbkc.sch.uk

• Pupils: 210 boys and girls, all day • Ages: 4-11 • C of E voluntary aided • State

Head: Since 1992, Ms Anna Kendall BEd (fifties). Formerly an adviser for the Royal Borough of Kensington and Chelsea, for Camden and Westminster; before that a class teacher.

Entrance: Application by February for the following September as the child is rising 5. All other ages on an ad hoc basis. Priority given to (i) children having siblings in the school; (ii) children of families who are regular worshippers in St Luke's or Christ Church, Chelsea; (iii) children living in the parish; (iv) children of families who are regular worshippers in a neighbouring parish church etc.

Exit: Shene School, Grey Coats, Gunnersbury, Holland Park, Graveney, ADT etc etc and about 20 per cent to private London day schools – Alleyn's, Emanuel, Dulwich etc.

Remarks: Excellent primary school in super location tucked away in a quiet corner of Chelsea, with – by London standards – lots of space, including good-sized playground and extra area of garden/pond etc. Founded 1840, affiliated to local churches (Helen Morgan Edwards is now chair of governors). Cherry-coloured uniform. Bright classrooms. Approximately 50 per cent of pupils from Chelsea, the rest from Wandsworth, Westminster and beyond – mixed intake. Popular with media folk.

Good core and cross curricular provision; all children have experience with computers. Maths and English very good and Spanish on offer after school; swimming for year 3. PE in much-used all-purpose school hall. Keen games and music. Even here parents sending children on to private schools usually opt for a year or two of coaching. Continuing good and happy reports from parents though some would like to see an 11+ class.

CITY OF LONDON FREEMEN'S JUNIOR SCHOOL

Linked to City of London Freemen's School in the Senior section

Ashtead Park, Ashtead, Surrey, KT21 1ET

Tel: 01372 277 933
Fax: 01372 276 165
E-mail: headmaster@clfs.surrey.sch.uk
Website: www.clfs.surrey.sch.uk

• Pupils: 180 boys, 180 girls, all day • Ages: 7-13 • Inter-denom
• Fees: £2,862 - £2,952 • Independent • Open days: October, November, January, March and April

Head: Since 2005, Mr Ian Thorpe (mid thirties) married with two young sons. Previously 4 years as deputy head & head of ICT at Caterham Prep. This is his first headship, but he seems very well suited to the role (has a sporting background and lots of prep school experience). Was able to prepare well prior to arrival with a lengthy induction, and seems very settled in the role and already knows lots of names – 'a fortunate strength of mine,' he jokes. He says the fact he has been able to 'hit the ground running' is testament to the staff and good systems in place within the school. Early days, but looks v promising – already much praised by staff and parents.

Entrance: Selective entrance at 7 and occasionally at 8 & 9 and there is always very tough competition. Selection is made by combination of formal tests in English, maths and non verbal reasoning, an interview with the head or a senior teacher including reading aloud (v important says Mr T) and report from the feeder school. In 2005, there were 90 applications for 60 places – but only 44 made the grade! Mr T stresses the standards are high and it can be difficult to make decisions at 7, hence some are asked to return the following year to sit again.

Exit: 99 per cent of the pupils to the senior school (no entrance test for them).

Remarks: Children are challenged but it is not a grinding academic pace according to staff – not all parents would agree, but most think there is good balance between academia and fun. Outstanding purpose-built facilities in the Kemp House complex on the main CLFS site. Mr T says that while the junior school is seen as operating as a prep school in its own right, it has the additional benefit of being able to take full advantage of senior school facilities and support. Staff work closely with heads of departments in the senior school; from age 11 pupils are increasingly integrated into, and taught by senior school staff in, the main school. KS2 SATs results in English, maths & science were exceptional in 2005 and junior school was in the top 1.5 per cent nationwide.Average class size is smallish – about 20 or less in many cases. Lots of young and enthusiastic staff. 'very dedicated to the children' said one parent. School offers the usual 'curriculum support' with spelling, reading etc and is considering the introduction of screening for dyslexia on entrance. Although assistance is readily available to those who require it, this would not be a first choice for those with SEN if they are not able to keep up with the academic pace. School does v well at sport. Boys play rugby and cricket and the girls hockey and tennis – all swim throughout the year. Very competitive with lots of inter school matches- after school and Sat am – and v successful: boys recently won the Surrey U12 rugby title. More than 60 per cent of pupils play an instrument and they perform weekly recitals and in a concert each term. Musical productions are also popular – all who audition play some part.A lively and fun place throughout the day, and this continues after school with all the usual extracurricular activities. Outside space is superb – an adventure playground complete with timber assault course was built in 2003. Pupils have access to the extensive playing fields shared with the senior school and free play is encouraged. Lots of visits throughout the year including a popular residential activity weekend after SATS week and a ski trip. Informative weekly newsletter revamped by Mr T – thumbs up from parents. Lots of fantastic work is displayed throughout the place and the children are very proud of their school. Mr T is keen on rewarding pupils and has already expanded the merit system. Pupils an extremely well behaved and polite bunch; the strong pastoral system ensures problems are minimal.

CITY OF LONDON SCHOOL FOR GIRLS (PREPARATORY DEPARTMENT)

Linked to City of London School for Girls in the Senior section

St Giles Terrace, Barbican, EC2Y 8BB

Tel: 020 7628 0841
Fax: 020 7638 3212
E-mail: info@clsg.org.uk
Website: www.clsg.org.uk/prepdept.htm

- Pupils: 105 girls; all day • Ages: 7-11 • Fees: £3,528
- Independent • Open days: In autumn and summer terms

Head: Mr Jonathan Brough, BEd (Cantab)NPQH NCSL.

Entrance: Whole day assessment, over-subscribed, put names down early. Umbilically attached to the senior school and a way in (with very rare exceptions), though pupils take same entrance exam as external candidates.

Remarks: Shares some of the facilities (pool, gym, DT) with senior school and has assembly with them twice a week. Particular focus on French and IT; termly music and drama events. A very busy and active little school.

CLAYESMORE PREPARATORY SCHOOL

Linked to Clayesmore School in the Senior section

Iwerne Minster, Blandford Forum, Dorset, DT11 8PH

Tel: 01747 811 707

Fax: 01747 811 692

E-mail: prepadmissions@clayesmore.com

Website: www.clayesmore.com

• Pupils: 265 boys and girls; 65 board. 15 in nursery • Ages: 2-13 • C of E • Fees: Boarders £4,675 - £5,124; day £3,565 - £3,805. Pre-prep (including after school care) £1870 • Independent

Head: Mr Martin Cooke (see senior school).

Entrance: Interview with HM, report from previous school, all come for a trial day and are informally assessed, with an ed psych's report if necessary.

Exit: 'More or less an automatic transfer to senior school – about 85 per cent go on' though Mr Cooke 'makes an effort to see parents again and make them welcome'. Some may return to maintained sector (Poole Grammar popular), Canford and Millfield pick up one or two.

Remarks: A separate school which this year celebrates its seventy-fifth birthday; Mr Cooke, head of the senior school, is currently running both with the aid of a deputy and assistant head in each. Charming, with a delightful combo building on a sort of cruciform shape with dormitories and classrooms dotted around (in a rather more organised fashion than it reads), it is first on Mr Cooke's wish list for improvement. Previously based in Charlton Marshall, the school was sold by its founder to Lt Col Ivor Edwards-Stewart who, when he retired in 1974, 'funded a school of a most modern design' on the senior school campus, with a dedicated play area (hopscotch and climbing frames) – it uses senior school facilities, indeed the old squash court, which has a tremendously grand entrance on the school side and forms part of the senior school music department, is divided, with the nether end currently used for tinies' cooking (a bit under used if the truth be told).

Trails of children (some being carried) skipping back from lunch in the big school dining room (terrific lunch), and good use made of the sports pitches, dining room, music school, chapel and leisure centre. Runs popular Arts Week at the end of the summer term. Similar emphasis to the senior school on good pastoral care and the importance of the individual. A very popular school with parents in the area, also has a sprinkling of expat children, some foreigners; fair number of Forces children plus siblings of those in the senior school, plus a number of first time buyers and ex-London refugees. Seventy-five boarders max, flexi-boarding not a problem (£16.65 per night), and no charge if doing sport or choir or sleeping bags on mattresses. Dedicated team of houseparents, plus matrons who are known as 'the sisters'. All are assessed at five, COPS on the computer, and each child is monitored, and the results held for future referral at all times. A centre of excellence. Pupils have learning support as and when it is required and may spend an hour or two in the unit daily, and then transfer back into the main school for the rest of the day. Senco, plus fully trained Learning Support Assistants (not teachers) and gappers help in the classroom, plus properly qualified teachers. Gym club and OT group, touch typing, speech and lang therapy once a week, sloping desks, special pens, all sorts of tricks brought into play. IEP for every child, some need full time special needs assistant for which parents must pay. Register of gifted and able, staff aim to stretch them. Social and emotional needs are catered for here, as well as individual educational programmes. Three live-in dedicated assistants, plus two part timers. Though if a child has really severe learning problems, this may not be the school for them.

Trad school curriculum, strong tutorial system: tutors are also responsible for PSHE. Maths, German, Spanish (not French) plus study skills though French and Latin. Strong music, as per the rest of the school, drama and good art. For the challenged child this could be just the place, for the less challenged, or those who need challenging, this school is all singing and dancing. Continuation scholarships to senior school.

CLIFTON COLLEGE PREPARATORY SCHOOL (THE PRE) + PRE-PREP

Linked to Clifton College in the Senior section

The Avenue, Clifton, Bristol, BS8 3HE

Tel: 0117 3157 502
Fax: 0117 3157 504
E-mail: admissions@clifton-college.avon.sch.uk
Website: www.cliftoncollegeuk.com

- Pupils: 380 girls and boys; one fifth board • Ages: 3-13
- Pupils come from many different faith backgrounds • Fees: Boarding max £5,240; day max £3,575 • Independent • Open days: Termly

Head: Preparatory school: Since 1993, Dr Bob Acheson. Aims to provide a focused, happy environment in which his bright-as-a-button pupils can thrive. Ably assisted by wife, Jill.

Pre-prep: Butcombe, with its own headmistress, Dr Wendy Bowring, operates separately from the prep but is just down the road.

Remarks: Prep school places particular emphasis on ICT and languages, with new science suite kitted out with new computer terminals, tuition in French from day one and German, Spanish and Mandarin as options in years 7 and 8. Head knows his SEN – even Aspergers – and is thoroughly supportive – though five-and-a-half day week can be overwhelming for some. Rambling club for those who don't enjoy sports.

Most boarders here are from overseas, many from Service families. Succession of artists-in-residence, unusual for prep school. Flexi-boarding, from age 8, very popular and well-used by local parents. Thriving music and choir. Produces easy-going, confident, well-mannered young people and aims at academic success for all.

CLIFTON HALL SCHOOL

Newbridge, Edinburgh, EH28 8LQ

Tel: 0131 333 1359
Fax: 0131 333 4609
E-mail: headmaster@cliftonhallschool.org.uk
Website: www.cliftonhall.org.uk

- Pupils: 115 boys and girls, plus 30 in nursery school. All day.
- Ages: 5-11, nursery 3-5 • Non-denom • Fees: £1,750 - £2,400 • Independent

Headmaster: Since 2005, Mr Rod Grant BA Hons PGCE (fortyish) who, formerly, taught English at Hutcheson's for seven years as 'principal teacher' and had responsibility for literacy. Mr Grant has a young family and enjoys sport, reading and drama.

Entrance: Mainly through the (non-selective entry) nursery – a proper nursery school with many of the children wearing uniform and a member of the Edinburgh City Partnership Scheme. Otherwise by assessment and interview.

Exit: The school follows the Scottish system and children leave at 11 for the big Edinburgh day schools – George Watson's, Merchiston, St George's, Stewart's Melville College & The Mary Erskine School and George Heriot's. 90 per cent plus get into their first-choice school. Almost all of these schools will consider deferred placements until the children are ready to move at 12.

Remarks: This is an 'independent primary school' based in a magical Bryce house (classrooms and passages painted jolly pinks, blues and yellows) in 42 acres of child-inspiring grounds just off the Newbridge roundabout – the junction of A8, M8 and M9. A boon for parents to the west of Edinburgh who can either take advantage of the school bus which leaves Bathgate daily at 8am (and leaves the school at 5pm each evening) or drop their little darlings on the way into work in Edinburgh. The school opens at 8am and children can stay till 6pm for after-school club – two fresh staff who help with homework etc. There are other clubs for judo, ballet, fencing, swimming et al until 6pm. Morning drop-off point for parents very sociable, with coffee on tap, and door to head's study open and school secretary on hand. Weekly menus handed out to all, so that parents don't cook the 'same for their tea'. Lots of parent participation. (Hours from 8.20am to 3.15, or 4.45pm with a fine of a fiver every fifteen minutes if you are late in the evening.) This is childcare made easy.

Previous head started the nursery in 1989; the boarders were thrown out in 1995, since when numbers have risen and risen. Huge growth and conversion of outbuildings has occurred. Great facilities,swimming pool, sports hall networked computers, music classrooms and French from nursery; tiny classes, learning support both withdrawn and dual teaching, and 'learning enrichment' to encourage clever-clogs who might otherwise be bored. Music and drama are particularly strong.

The main catchment area is West Lothian: Livingston, Linlithgow, Bathgate – Silicon Glen – 85 per cent or more first-time buyers, ditto two working parents. Jazzy young staff blend well with the more mature.

Strong theatre, masses of music and peripatetic teachers. Children devised own Golden Rules. Fees include almost all extras; trust fund on hand to pick up financial hiccups 'for a year or two', 'safety net', rather than 'safety blanket'.

'School is going places and it is growing'. Governors very bullish – and so they should be. Complimentary inspection report from HMI 2004. New head should maintain and even increase momentum.

CLIFTON HIGH LOWER SCHOOL

Linked to Clifton High School in the Senior section

Clifton High School, College Road, Clifton, Bristol, BS8 3JD

Tel: 0117 973 8096
Fax: 0117 933 9097
E-mail: enquiries@cliftonhigh.bristol.sch.uk
Website: www.cliftonhigh.bristol.sch.uk

• Pupils: 340 girls and boys; all day • Ages: 3-11 • Fees: From £1,935 • Independent • Open days: Several in October/November

Remarks: For further details, see senior school entry.

COKETHORPE SCHOOL JUNIOR SCHOOL

Witney, Oxon, Oxfordshire, OX29 7PU

Tel: 01993 703921
Fax: 01993 773499
E-mail: admin@cokethorpe.org.uk
Website: www.cokethorpe.org.uk

• Pupils: boys and girls; all day • Ages: 5 - 11 • Fees: £1,890 - £3,350 • Independent • Open days: Early February and May

Remarks: For further details, see senior school.

COLET COURT

Linked to Saint Paul's School in the Senior section

Lonsdale Road, London, SW13 9JT

Tel: 020 8748 3461
Fax: 020 8746 5357
E-mail: hmseccc@stpaulsschool.org.uk
Website: www.coletcourt.org.uk

• Pupils: 430 boys, all day • Ages: 7 to 13 • Colet Court is a Christian foundation, but boys of all faiths are represented at the school • Fees: £3,640 • Independent • Open days: November

Headmaster: Since 1992, Mr Geoffrey Thompson (fifties), who has more qualifications than you ever dreamed of: BA from Newcastle in biology, MEd, CertEd, MIBiol, CBiol, Fellow of the College of Preceptors, Fellow of the Linnaean Society. In other words, the man is formal, professional, experienced. Married to a teacher. Parents say he's sociable but not likely to engage in in-depth conversation. Not surprising, said one, when you consider many parents micro-manage their children's education, beating a path to his door for the slightest triviality. Pupils say, 'we don't see a lot of him but he is kind and patient and he's doing the play; we like that, it's good to see more of him.'

On entering his study your eyes are drawn to the 'sulking boy' and your nose to the fab coffee machine – a gift from an appreciative parent. Then there's the 'doll' bought from a shop in Helmsley, the coffee, Taylor's of Harrogate and very quickly the conversation turns to the head's passion for Yorkshire. 'I escape there as often as possible. We have school trips too. Many drag their parents back to share the beauty.' So a part time job with the Yorkshire tourist board? Not quite, not yet. For now he's settled at the school – still a long time to serve if he's to beat the tenure of many previous heads but he clearly enjoys it here and who wouldn't? His current passion is 'Jones' a musical written by a master at St Paul's that he's producing and directing. He hopes it will be the next Joseph. Not so crazy, when you remember that Joseph was originally written by Lloyd Webber for pupils at Colet Court to sing at their Easter end of term concert.

Entrance: At 7, 8, 10 and 11 – these last two ages are now a good route in for beady parents with kids at state primaries. Name down asap. Heavyweight test changed yearly to confound preparation – looking for those who can take the pace.

Exit: Around 98 per cent to St Paul's (when you sign on at Colet you sign up for St Paul's). Handful to boarding schools: Winchester, Eton, occasional to Charterhouse.

Remarks: This isn't a good school – it's an excellent school – says who? Says the ISI inspection report (gushing, there's a void in the 'could do better' section); say the parents (who admit to feeling a slight thrill the first time they enter the school gates); say the results – among the best, if not the best, in the country – 18 scholarships in 2005, one to Winchester, 17 to St Paul's – and say the pupils, read on.

This is a school for bright young things (IQ 120 plus). All will sail through exams, no need to spoon-feed, encourages lateral, imaginative and creative thinking. The entrance exam is designed to weed out the coached from the innately intelligent and seems to do so successfully. So you have to be intelligent? Definitely. Rich? Well it's not cheap but no child who passes the entrance exam will be turned away because of parents' inability to pay the fees. There are generous bursaries up to 100 per cent of fees, plus help with funding extras such as trips and tours abroad. SEN free? No, a generous handful of boys have a learning difficulty and before you choke on your muesli, Einstein was dyslexic. The reality is some 30 plus boys have a difficulty of some sort, mostly mild dyslexia or dyspraxia but ADD, ADHD (Ritalin okay), and Aspergers are found among the numbers. The lovely (phenomenal said one parent) 'dys lady' – 'dyslexia, dyspraxia, dysgraphia, dispirited' is on hand to help out. Boys may receive one-to-one for up to 1 lesson a week (and never withdrawn from core subjects). There's great communication between staff so problems are quickly spotted, PE will flag up those who present with coordination problems; with handwriting, problems are eased by use of laptops and some self-refer. 'Some of our best and brightest have a difficulty. Ironically the baggage can help. They

have to develop strategies to cope, they think differently and some get to Oxbridge.'

Wonderful facilities. Yes the buildings are 1960s, not monstrosities by any stretch, though definitely not the ivory towers you'd expect from a school with such long-standing traditions. The 40-acre green site, immaculate, classrooms, airy with frequently changing, stimulating displays, vibrant corridors and naturally everything you'd want to find in a prep school (though some facilities are shared with senior school). There's a full size swimming pool, large sports hall, fencing salle, dojo for aikido, racquets court and tennis courts, plus cricket nets, basketball courts, ICT suites, technology workshops, fully equipped science labs, music school, music hall, large assembly hall, separate dining hall, playground with wood, ropes, swings for littlest boys, a great addition. Class sizes on the biggish side: 18-24 pupils. No setting or streaming in first three years, then setted in maths, Latin and French and a scholarship group is selected by the end of that year. All boys study Latin from year 6 and scholars study Greek (small Greek group for non-scholars).

Hotshot music department. Three choirs, full to bursting, with invigorating schedule of appearances. Three orchestras, chamber ensemble, string quartet. Piles of distinctions on music exams. Over 80 per cent of boys learn one or more musical instruments. Art superb, in bright, spacious art classroom overlooking Thames. Excellent chess team (with national players); super well used library, regular additions. Sports abundant. Compulsory rugby in autumn (except 7-year-olds), soccer in spring, cricket in summer. Games for two hours, two afternoons a week, plus a session of PE. Loads of teams – most boys can represent the school at some level. One of the few independent preps to take boys on overseas soccer tours. Cricket tour to Barbados, football to Brazil. Saturday morning games or practice, for boys in teams. Golf off-site.

The biggest draw though is the inspirational and fizzy teaching – excellent. 'We do lots of practical things in all kinds of subjects and staff use the interactive whiteboards, show us things from the net or use special packages.' The boys have a genuine thirst for knowledge, a desire to learn, to discover. The beauty is, that here, it's permitted. There's no laddish culture, no fear of being branded a swot – bliss. So what of the boys? Privileged? Yes but privileged to be at the school. But, and this is a big but, the boys are grounded (yes, the odd trace of arrogance from the odd boy but no more than in the poorest comp), they huddle round with trading cards or top trumps at break, or kick a football; shirts hang out as often as they're found in; they teased us and their masters that they were being paid to say great things about the school (perhaps they were!) They have a wicked sense of humour, great sense of fun, not all geniuses, but hard working and polite – it's the parents one worries about. Many see entry to Colet Court as grasping the Holy Grail itself, when in reality it is just the beginning of their worries. They can now look forward to 11 years of making sure their son makes the grade, at least the many parents' activities promote a sense of 'in it together.' There are down sides for the pupils too. From being top dog at previous schools, many will find they're placed in lower sets but the boys are bright enough to realise that being in a low set here is still a great achievement and all are on course for a glowing array of A-levels, a few years down the line. 'Sometimes it would be nice to have longer to assimilate a new topic, or idea. Some people grasp things instantaneously. I find that a problem in maths but I know I'm the one getting things straight away in science.' That seems to be the key. Every boy is good and virtually every boy, excellent in something, be it music, sport, science. The pace is frenetic but the boys handle it – no let-up (holidays are known in school jargon as 'remedies').

Everything you'd expect from one of the country's top preps and a whole lot more too. But do not be tempted by the designer label unless your son is the genuine article – bright, keen and robust.

COLFE'S PREPARATORY SCHOOL + PRE PREP AND NURSERY

Linked to Colfe's School in the Senior section

Horn Park Lane, Lee, London, SE12 8AW

Tel: 020 8852 0220
Fax: 020 8297 2941
E-mail: prephead@colfes.com
Website: www.colfes.com

• Pupils: boys and girls; all day • Ages: 3-11 • Independent

Head: Mr Neil Murray, deputy head. Mrs Sarah Redman in charge of pre prep

Entrance: Prep school interviews and formal or informal tests depending on child's age; nursery and pre prep by informal assessments.

Exit: Most to the senior school, though you have to take the exam and a couple fail each year.

Remarks: For further details, see senior school.

THE COMPASS SCHOOL

West Road, Haddington, East Lothian, EH41 3RD

Tel: 01620 822 642
Fax: 01620 822 144
E-mail: office@thecompassschool.co.uk
Website: www.thecompassschool.co.uk

• Pupils: 60 boys, 65 girls; all day • Ages: 4-12 • Inter-denom
• Fees: £1,160 - £1,850 • Independent • Open days: First Thursday in November

Headmaster: Since 1997, Mr Mark Becher (pronounced Becker) MA PGCE (thirties), educated at Queen Margaret's Academy Ayr, followed by Dundee University where he read modern history, and PGCE at Craigie College of Education in Ayr (now part of Paisley University). Previously head of sport at The Mary Erskine & Stewart's Melville Junior School, and primary teacher at Edinburgh Academy.An open, engaging head, with a confident manner, he teaches games, Latin, history, and support teaches at all levels throughout the school.

Entrance: Children can come (and do) at any time. School uniform is sold in house. Children can come for an informal assessment on Thursday and start the following Friday.

Exit: Children now regularly stay until the end of their primary education, with more leaving at 11 or 12, either to go to the Edinburgh independent day schools, the state sector, or off to trad prep schools as before. Belhaven, Loretto popular.

Money Matters: Applications for bursaries can be made for candidates entering forms 6, 7 and 8. Sibling discount.

Remarks: The Compass is no longer the sleepy dame school it was. Started in 1963, and run by Mrs Alny Younger for years. French from 4, with formal Latin at 8. Small classes in a still very cramped space, learning support. Stunning new attic development (the previous new-build) houses older children with sag bags and a raft of computers. Lots more games and sport and make use of local authority grass and Astro pitches and Haddington Golf Club. Rugby, cricket and hockey matches a feature. Music and drama on the up, plus all the usual trad subjects.

Lots more first-time buyers, with pupils coming from as far away as Duns and Dalkeith, some from the farming community as well as business folk and landowners. A popular school, good ethos, good manners important with lots of parental input. Staff come from across the Lothians.

CONNAUGHT HOUSE SCHOOL

47 Connaught Square, London, W2 2HL

Tel: 020 7262 8830
Fax: 020 7262 0781
E-mail: office@connaughthouse.wanadoo.co.uk
Website: www.connaughthouseschool.co.uk

- Pupils: 35 boys, 40 girls, all day – working towards 50/50
- Ages: 4-11 but boys leave at 8 • Non-denom • Fees: Reception £2,400; main school £3,450 • Independent • Open days: March

Principals: Since 1991, Mrs Jacqueline Hampton (fifties), took over from her mother Mrs Keane. She and her husband Fred Hampton MA RCA are joint principals; both trained as artists. They have 2 grown-up children who attended the school as did Mrs Hampton. Gentle-mannered artists with a small-is-beautiful approach that has worked and is working well.

Entrance: At 4 all new entrants are invited to attend an informal assessment. Sibling policy. Music scholarships available throughout the school and academic schols are available for girls at 8+. Small intake of girls at 8.

Exit: Boys at 8 go to London day preps, favourites being Westminster Under and Sussex House. Girls at 11 go to all the major London day schools, plus a few to boarding such as Wycombe Abbey. Some get art and/or music scholarships, majority get into their first-choice secondary schools.

Remarks: A small family-run school, founded by Mrs Hampton's mother when the school she was teaching at closed down in 1953. Accommodated since 1956 in a large London house on the corner of Connaught Square. Very much a community school in the heart of London, with no airs and graces. Local clientele mostly come by word of mouth.

Follows a fairly traditional curriculum mixed with excellent arts and IT – as one mother said, 'an excellent grounding for entry into the good London preps. The stairwells and classrooms display an abundance of imaginative and well-crafted works of art. Children have the opportunity to use a vast range of media guided by experts, a great advantage and not always readily available in some larger establishments. Music and drama are also strong, 2 choirs, an orchestra. 70 per cent play an instrument or take singing lessons. Musical assemblies, plays and concerts year round.

No outdoor space: pupils go to Hyde Park et al for play time and sports. Swimming at Francis Holland pool, from 5

years. After school club activities through the week including chess with a lady 'grandmaster'. Lunches cooked on the premises, absolutely delicious, agree both past and present pupils. Full understanding of Specific Learning Difficulties, part time SEN teacher, those who need to may use laptops but school does not pretend to be able to offer a fully-staffed SEN dept – it's just too small. However, many staff have SEN training and school can draw on ed psychs, therapists and optometrists when necessary.

A nice ethos of developing the individual rather than imposing a style. Motivated children who are encouraged to be creative and discover what they can do. School retains its character and quality by remaining small. 'A cosy place to start your education', say parents.

COOMBE HILL INFANT SCHOOL

Coombe Lane West, Kingston upon Thames, Surrey, KT2 7DD

Tel: 02089 429 481
Fax: 02089 497 496
E-mail: CHI@rbksch.org
Website: www.coombehilli.kingston.sch.uk

- Pupils: 270 boys and girls • Ages: 4-7 • Non-denom • State

Head: Since 1991, Mrs. Sarah Hobhouse CertEd DIPSE in school management (early fifties). Comes from Somerset, educated at Sherborne School in Dorset and Surrey University. Tall, elegant, previously deputy head at St. Paul's Chessington. Describes herself as 'user-friendly,' with an open door policy; described by more than one parent as 'fantastic.' Teaches RE and obviously has a great rapport with the children – all clamouring for her attention with 'Mrs Hobhouse look at this' and 'Watch this Mrs Hobhouse.' V. impressive the way she knew every child by name and all wanted to show her something they had done or tell her something about themselves.

Entrance: You need to live almost on the school's posh doorstep to get in. Substantially oversubscribed – more so than any other infant school in the borough: typically 162 applications for 90 places. Priority: to children with sibling attending the school or the associated junior school at the time of admission; pupils with a medical or social need and then those living nearest the school. In practice, about a third of places to siblings. one or two have medical or social needs and the rest tend to live within three-quarters of a mile of the school.

Exit: Majority trot off to the junior school next door. A few to independent schools – Kings College School Wimbledon, Surbiton High School, Wimbledon High School, Putney High School, Rokeby and Shrewsbury House.

Remarks: Top notch school in upmarket area, with winning combination of supportive middle class parents, rich cultural mix and good achievement. Located in one of the most prestigious residential locations in the borough and surrounded by substantial detached houses bristling with security alarms and locked gates to their private roads. A most favourable location for any school, so hugely refreshing that the intake is very ethnically diverse, with 50 per cent of the children having EAL, a third speaking more than one language and some speaking more than two. They get great support – EAL teacher virtually full-time. Many children from European background, together with some Korean and Japanese. School celebrates this rich mix of cultures to the full; highly popular international week and international evenings every year for the whole family – they are invited to wear national dress (even the Brits), have national dancing shows and sample many homemade culinary delights. Three forms of mixed ability entry – 30 per form. KS1 results are v.good, but head points out that with so many children having EAL, the higher grades in literacy are harder to achieve for many pupils. SEN- typical of the national average -21 per cent.

School recently updated to a v. high standard, on a semi-open plan basis with lots of natural light. Amazingly for a state primary school, computerised interactive (and expensive) white boards (we have seen many independent prep schools without these), together with a new IT suite. Lovely grounds with far-reaching views. Shares swimming pool with junior school, used by each class twice a week in summer. Buildings adapted for disabled users. Super school to visit with loads going on and children very absorbed. Great range of after school activities: clubs for gym, drama and music, art and craft, German, French, construction, cooking and a dinosaur club – charge of approx. £3 per session. Lending library for videos, games, reading and maths schemes. Do look at the super website, a lot of it created by the children. Support from the solid middle class parents is tremendous: ' The parents raise a fortune,' says the head, – the school's swimming pool is heated and maintained from proceeds raised by the PTA.

No lunch provided, children have to bring packed lunch from home. Parking problematical, as ever, with busy main road outside. No problems dropping off in the mornings – a quick in and out- not so easy in the afternoon when Head insists parents park in adjacent side roads and walk to col-

lect. School has everything going for it – great head, vibrancy, enviable buildings, grounds, location and catchment area. Deservedly v. popular, worth moving to be near – or should we say very near – to get a place, assuming of course you have the money to buy in its largely upmarket catchment area.

COOMBE HILL JUNIOR SCHOOL

Coombe Lane West, Kingston Upon Thames, Surrey, KT2 7DD

Tel: 02089 491 743
E-mail: CHJ@rbksch.org
Website: www.coombehillj.kingston.sch.uk/

• Pupils: 320 boys and girls, and rising; all day • Ages: 7-11
• Non-denom • State

Head: Since 2004, Mr Chris Hodges.

Entrance: 90 places on offer into three forms, vast majority comes from the infants school next door (with which it is paired). Only a handful of places go to others. NB Having a child at the junior school gives you priority entry for another child into the infants school.

Exit: An impressive number to the Tiffin Schools (girls' and boys' state highly selective grammar schools in Kingston), other popular schools include nearby Coombe Hill Girls' School, also Hollyfield (mixed state, Surbiton). A handful every year to independent schools such as Canbury, Ewell Castle, Hampton, Kings College School at Wimbledon, Kingston Grammar School, Marymount, Moor House, Notre Dame, Reeds, Surbiton High and Wimbledon High. School seems totally at ease that some children go on to state and others to private schools.

Remarks: Super, top notch, state primary school which has the lot, but is now getting too big for some parents, who viewed it as an appealing cosy alternative to private school. Site is most attractive and spacious, with an orchard area which is grassed and used for play and study and ample space for field sports and playgrounds. Many expensive prep schools lack a heated swimming pool like the one here, shared with the infants school. Brand new block and extensive internal works – include disabled access by lift in the new block and something that few state primaries can boast – a new IT suite which has 20 machines plus a laptop trolley with wireless connection, sufficient to accommodate the whole class (IT technician is here for half the week).

The three forms are divided into four sets for English

and maths from year 3 (pupils separately assessed in each subject), science and games are in four sets of mixed ability. Very impressive academic results – particularly as the vibrant ethnic intake of the infants school is repeated here and a significant number above the national average has English as a second language. KS2 results in English are real pat on the back standard, 97 per cent achieve the target level 4 or above (national percentage 75); maths 91 per cent (national percentage 71) and science a tremendous 100 per cent (national percentage is 87). Results are all considerably higher than the Kingston LEA averages, and good in value-added terms too. Unusually, boys' achievement is virtually the same as the girls'.

No school lunches. Several after school clubs, a couple run by private organisations. Difficult to assess the atmosphere of the place because of the building works – in new block, furniture had just been moved in and paint was barely dry. However, the school has a nice feel about it and there is much parental involvement. One parent told us, ' I feel that the school has a strong moral base, although it is not a church school.'

To sum up – a super, state primary which has consistently turned out happy and high achieving youngsters to a wide variety of respected senior schools, both state and private. Was in a state of flux with the arrival of a new head in January 2004, building works and increasing pupil numbers – not an easy combination for any school – not even one of the best.

CORAM HOUSE

Linked to Ackworth School in the Senior section

Ackworth School, Ackworth, Pontefract, West Yorkshire, WF7 7LT

Tel: 01977 612277
Fax: 01977 616225
E-mail: 100021.3420@compuserve.com
Website: www.rmplc.co.uk/eduweb/sites/ackworth/index.html

- Pupils: 180 boys and girls; all day • Ages: 4-11 • Quaker ethos
- Fees: Coram House, day £1,090 • Independent • Open days: A Saturday in early October

Head: Mrs Mary Wilson.

Entrance: Youngest are interviewed, entry from 8+ is via test and interview.

Remarks: School over-subscribed in younger years.

COTHILL HOUSE SCHOOL

Linked to Chandlings Manor School in the Junior section

Cothill, Abingdon, Oxfordshire, OX13 6JL

Tel: 01865 390 800
Fax: 01865 390 205
E-mail: office@cothill.net
Website: www.cothill.net

- Pupils: 235 boys; all board • Ages: 8-13 • C of E • Fees: Fees: £5,800 • Independent

Head: Since 2003, Mr Neil Brooks BA QTS (late thirties). Educated at Magdalen College School, Oxford, and Warwick University, where read PE and geography. Spent eight years as army officer (7th Parachute Regiment, Royal Horse Artillery) before deciding to teach. Wrote 112 letters to schools – 'I knew it was the world I wanted to be in,' he says – and was snapped up by Cothill. Ran senior boarding house for two years, then took over from Mr Adrian Richardson (now principal of the Cothill House Educational Trust) as headmaster. Enthusiastic, approachable and super-energetic. Teaches English to youngest pupils and knows every boy in school by name. At break-times is quite likely to be found in school yard with sleeves rolled up playing cricket with pupils. Study door wedged open by basket overflowing with sports gear – boys come and ask (v politely) to borrow bats and balls. 'I want the boys to be participants, not observers,' he says. Married with two young sons. Tracy, his wife, is responsible for youngest boys and also runs domestic side of school – everything from overseeing catering to cutting boys' toenails! Family live in part of the school and their door is always open. Boys love popping in to chat to Mrs Brooks and make a fuss of springer spaniel Jessie.

Entrance: Best to register as early as possible – 'we get quite busy,' says head modestly. Boys visit a year prior to entry and are then invited for informal assessment (maths, comprehension, etc) and interview in the spring term before they are due to start. Broad range of ability but by the time boys leave head says they are 'competent and confident academically, keen to make a contribution and with something to say.' Pupils come from all over the UK (Scotland to Cornwall), with handful from abroad (Thailand, Russia, US, France, Spain all represented.) A fair number of old boys' sons too.

Exit: Mainly to Eton, Harrow and Radley (scholarships to all three in 2005) but also to many other public schools –

Marlborough, Rugby, Shrewsbury, Winchester etc. 'You've got to get boys into the school that's right for them,' says head.

Remarks: Six miles south of Oxford in pretty country village. School founded in 1870 and moved to present site nine years later – fees in those days were £100 a year, with an extra charge of £1 a term for 'washing.' Main building a large country house set in 26 acres of well-kept grounds and playing fields, complete with 19-metre indoor swimming pool, squash court, six all-weather tennis courts and even a nine-hole golf course (a golf pro visits everyday.) Classes are small (maximum 18 but more likely to be around 14.) Well qualified and committed staff – majority in their thirties and more men than women.

Traditional curriculum, plus Spanish and Mandarin (largely for boys who already speak language.) SEN provision for mild dyslexia and dyspraxia and all pupils regularly screened for early intervention. Weekly reports (academic progress, attitude and behaviour) for all at assembly every Monday morning. The icing on the cake for most boys comes at the age of 11 or 12 when they all spend a term at the Chateau de Sauveterre near Toulouse. There, 800 miles from Cothill, they are totally immersed in French language and culture. 'It's a real rite of passage for them and does wonders for their French,' says head. An appreciative group of boys capture the experience perfectly in the school magazine: 'It is hard to even begin to count the memories that spring to mind when one says the word, Sauveterre. The sun, the rose-coloured bricks, the local people, the sweets and the food! We knew we had been a part of something special.' With Spanish now on the curriculum, the Sauveterre experience may well be repeated in Spain. Watch this space.

In age of nationwide concern about reluctant boy readers, pupils encouraged to read every night before lights out – Anthony Horowitz still sweeps the board with first five places in boys' top ten favourites. Airy new library on top floor of classroom complex is well-stocked (more than 8,000 books) and operates sophisticated thumbprint scanner to keep track of borrowings. Computer room with 17 terminals but boys' access strictly monitored.

All food cooked in-house. Lots of choice and pupils give it the thumbs-up. Staff eat with boys at breakfast and lunch, encouraging good table manners and intelligent conversation. Boys' dorms are wholesome and well-kept. New eight-year-olds ensconced in comfy rooms adjoining head's house in main building. Lots of teddies and walls covered in posters of footballers, dogs and The Simpsons – 'our rule is that they can't put anything on the wall that shocks our cleaning ladies,' says head. Final year pupils live ten min-

utes away from Cothill at Chandlings Manor, gaining more independence in readiness for their public schools. Boys bussed to Cothill every morning for lessons and sport.

Music and drama terrific. All boys try out an instrument and there are more than 180 individual music lessons a week. Lots of music groups – choirs, orchestra, wind ensembles, jazz band etc. Major drama production once a year and new school hall with telescopic seating should be ready in 2006. Art, pottery and DT v popular, with creations on display all over school. Woodwork is amazing. Staff say boys can make anything they like – as long as it will fit through the door to take home at the end of term. Past choices include garden benches and a chicken house big enough for 45 chickens! Heaps of sport. Soccer, rugby and hockey in winter and cricket, tennis and athletics in summer.

School fizzes with activity from dawn till dusk. When lessons end for day, boys rush off to play 40-40 or build dens in the woods. Perhaps unusually in this day and age, pupils aren't allowed to bring GameBoys, iPods, mobile phones etc to school. They don't watch TV either – apart from a film on Saturday night or unmissable sporting events. Boys encouraged to keep abreast of what's happening in outside world by reading newspapers – head's wife posts interesting snippets from papers on notice board everyday too. Parents approve wholeheartedly. 'What the boys need to learn at this stage is how to interact with other people and be part of a community,' says head.

Weekends seem just as busy as weekdays, with lots of sport, clubs and outings to places like Blenheim Palace, Cotswold Wildlife Park and the climbing wall at Oxford Brookes. Boys use grounds to full, building go-karts and whizzing around on scooters and skateboards. On Sunday mornings most go to church (alternative arrangements made for non-C of E) and write letters home – fountain pens a must. Handwriting a strong point. Whole school recently won national handwriting competition.

Sparky lot of boys who are v proud of their school. When we visited, a trio of chirpy eight year-olds showed us everything from the weekly 'grub shop' (boys allowed limited amount to spend on old favourites like sherbet fountains and dip dabs) to the small pets they're allowed to keep (hamsters, frogs, even cockroaches – eek!) Major emphasis on politeness – school handbook gives tips like 'if you see anyone looking lost, offer to help them.'

A traditional, full-boarding prep school where everyone is treated as an individual and pupils' feelings of security, achievement and self-worth are paramount. Boys work hard, learn to be independent and have fun – without growing up too fast. A happy place to be.

COTTESMORE SCHOOL

Buchan Hill, Pease Pottage, West Sussex, RH11 9AU

Tel: 01293 520 648

Fax: 01293 614 784

E-mail: schooloffice@cottesmoreschool.com

Website: www.cottesmoreschool.com

• Pupils: 100 boys, 50 girls; all board • Ages: 8-13 (may start at 7 if 8th birthday falls in the winter term) • C of E • Fees: £5,300 • Independent

Head: Since 2002, Mr Ian Tysoe (forties), who was previously assistant deputy head at Aiglon College in Switzerland and before that head of maths and housemaster at Holmewood House, Kent, where he and his wife, Jane, set up and ran the first girls' boarding house. Jane previously taught at Cottesmore and their young twins joined in September 2004.

Entrance: In September, January or April. Non-selective, 'first come, first served,' says head. Prospective pupils come for short interview and placement test. Children mainly from London day schools. Some 34 children have parents overseas; of these, 16 are non-British (from 9 different countries). 3 have ESL requirements and 'learn English swiftly by receiving extra support and social integration within the school......we try not to have more than one or two from any one country,' says the head.

Exit: All pupils leave at 13 to public schools far and wide. Largest numbers of boys to Charterhouse, Radley, King's, Wellington and Eton; girls and boys to Marlborough, Canford and Millfield and girls to Benenden, Downe House and Wycombe Abbey.

Remarks: A happy camp, set in a turreted Victorian mansion built by Sir Ernest George which became the home of an ostrich-feather magnate (painted ostrich feathers still adorn the ceiling of the main hall). Set in beautiful 30-acre grounds approached via grand drive.

Small classes – 14 average. Most staff live on site. High academic standards. Recently won record 16 scholarships (academic, sport and music) to senior schools. Chess strong, with external coaching and annual Cottesmore Chess Congress. Traditional prep school curriculum, plus Spanish, Mandarin (the latter 2 mainly as boosters for children who already speak them) and Greek 'taster.' Not a school for dyslexics.

The splendid Sopwith Centre for technology and the arts is named after old boy Tommy Sopwith, WWI aircraft engineer and inventor of the Sopwith Camel. The centre houses the main computer suite (ratio of computers to pupils 1:3), art room with views across Sussex, science labs, ceramics studio and a fantastic DT area (pupils attend three DT lessons a week).

Like all the best preps, Cottesmore excels in providing an opportunity for every pupil to shine, 'they're all good at something,' says the head, 'I don't care if it's tiddly-winks.' Sports very strong and most children are involved in teams (bravo!). Excellent swimming in indoor pool. All children swim at least three times a week and Cottesmore wins loads of trophies. Nice, flat playing-fields. Small lake for fishing and boating. 9-hole chip and putt golf course (top golfers may use the adjoining private golf club). Lots of overseas excursions (unusual for a prep school)- recent geography trips to Egypt and Turkey, ski trips, choir to Barcelona 2002, plus annual French trip. Music department features the usual choir and orchestra plus a marching band consisting of 20 children on brass and woodwind instruments, 12 pom-pom girls, a boy on side drum and assorted enthusiastic teachers. Two school plays each year in small, antiquated gymnasium/theatre (plans afoot to rebuild this on a grand scale). Air rifle shooting practised down in the basement (former wine cellar) in a narrow corridor that doubles as a 'bowling alley.' Here one also finds the model railway and Airfix model departments.

Pastoral care all-important, 'we treat every child in the school as if he or she were our own,' says Mr Tysoe. Head's warm, jolly, fear-free relationship with the children much in evidence. Co-education works a treat, controlling problems of bullying/cliquishness that can fester in single-sex preps. Brilliant 'Happiness Charter,' a model document, encouraging children to 'speak out' if they (or anyone they know) are unhappy. Must surely win award for best school food in Britain. Every child we spoke to singled out the food as top notch and there is plenty of it – including a snack before bedtime. Only pupil complaint, 'punishments can be harsh, like having to run around the croquet lawn for 15 minutes during free time.'

Free time a valued commodity. Biggest dorms 10 to a room, but most sleep 4-6, looked after by 4 live-in matrons. Lots of table tennis and pool. Music piped through the school – mostly classical but the head is also partial to Dire Straits. Very traditional, very competitive – form orders published in the school mag for all year groups. Girls' uniform a 1930s marvel – hound's-tooth check pinafore in the winter and sailor-style dress in summer. Several unusual customs eg 30 minutes prep every day after breakfast (older pupils also have 45 minutes in the evening) and an hour mid-morning break for activities, music lessons etc. Some holiday work, particularly for scholarship pupils and those who are struggling. Exeats nearly every second weekend (from 4pm on Friday until 6.30pm on Sunday).

COWORTH-FLEXLANDS SCHOOL

Valley End, Chobham, Surrey, GU24 8TE

Tel: 01276 855 707
Fax: 01276 856 043
E-mail: secretary@coworthflexlands.co.uk
Website: www.coworthflexlands.co.uk

- Pupils: 140 girls 15 boys, including nursery, all day • Ages: 3-11, boys until 7 • Inter-denom • Fees: £1,045 - £2,450 • Independent • Open days: October, November, March

Head: Since 2004, Mrs Sandy Stephen (late fifties) who was head of Coworth Park (from 2003), and when nearby Flexlands school merged with Coworth Park in September 2004, Mrs S was appointed head of the newly combined school Coworth-Flexlands. A widow with two married daughters, she first came to Coworth Park in 1984 as a parent when her children attended the school; she subsequently joined the teaching staff (moving from a secondary school in London). She has risen up the ranks and was deputy head prior to the headship. Her younger daughter taught piano at the school for two years and the family tradition will continue when her granddaughter starts in 2006. A delightful lady, informally dressed and very grandmotherly – a refreshing change from the business-suited heads of many other preps.

Entrance: Non selective. Places are offered following a meeting with the head and a tour and introduction to the school (together with the receipt of registration fee) on a first come first served basis. Children join the nursery in the term they become 3. The merged school is not yet full to capacity, so worth trying for vacancies at other times.

Exit: Papplewick, Lambrook Haileybury and Woodcote House popular destinations for the boys when they leave at 7. Girls depart to a whole variety of places including St Georges, Ascot, The Marist and Luckley Oakfield locally, but some move further afield to Guildford High, St Catherine's Bramley and Cheltenham Ladies' College. On average about 5 or 6 each year win scholarships.

Remarks: A delightful school which has been going

through an unsettled time but, now the merger is complete, they can continue with their vision of developing the 'whole' child – an ethos which has pleased parents, with the good results achieved in a relaxed atmosphere.

Our visit took place a couple of weeks into the opening of the newly merged school on the site of the previous Coworth Park. The school is set in 13 acres of grounds on the edge of Chobham Common and attracts pupils from the local (and very expensive) Surrey/ Berkshire area – Chobham, Ascot, Windlesham and Woking. The school is centred on a large old house with later additions – something of a rabbit warren to find your way around but there are big plans for expansion to provide new classrooms, music rooms, staff room and ICT suite in 2006. Until then, the nursery, kindergarten and some others are housed in temporary classrooms. Excellent library – well-stocked with lots of new books: pupils use the library during lesson time and are also encouraged to visit at lunchtimes when they can sit and read quietly on one of the comfy beanbags!

Average class size is smallish: 18 – 20 or less in some years as the year group has been split into two where space allows. Year group sizes vary as a result of the merger. Several young and enthusiastic staff members and 'some who have been there for a very long time' according to one parent. Mrs S is very proud that this non-selective school achieves good SATS results and that many pupils go on to gain places (and also scholarships) at some top senior schools – she is convinced they do well because they do not pressurise the children. Pupils are encouraged to be enthusiastic and creative and to follow a broad-based curriculum. School offers SEN assistance readily to those who require it. They can cater for dyslexia, dyspraxia, hearing impairment and physical disability and also offer a gifted child programme. There are 2 SEN qualified staff members and the school is happy to discuss individual requirements. Maybe not top of an SEN school list, but the relaxed and happy atmosphere combined with lack of academic pressure could make this a good choice.

Sport is compulsory for all and children are encouraged to take part in a variety of activities including netball, rounders, athletics and swimming once a week in Woking for years 2 – 6. About half the children play an instrument, they have a free choice – piano is very popular as is guitar; others learn cello, clarinet, sax and one is even learning to play the double bass. Music lessons are timetabled mainly before and after school to minimise class disruption, which is a popular move with staff and parents. Pupils take part in the local Chobham music festival and put on a musical production each summer.

Very attractive uniform – blue tartan pinafores or kilts for the girls and the more usual grey shorts or trousers for the boys – the younger ones wear tracksuits in the nursery – very practical commented parents. Lunch is excellent said the staff, and this was confirmed by pupils. All have a hot meal cooked on site, with a choice of salads.

Pupils are encouraged in areas of decision making – two representatives from each year are on the school council and attend weekly meetings chaired by a member of staff. A lively place throughout the day and this continues after school with all the usual extra-curricular activities including clubs for gardening, science and homework (groan!). The school also has its own Rainbow and Brownie packs. Outside space is good – despite the addition of the temporary classrooms – there is a fantastic adventure playground and a separate smaller area for the younger children. Pupils have access to the extensive school grounds and playing fields. Security is tight with key pad entry and plans to enclose the front of the school to increase security.

The six 'golden rules' are displayed all around the place. Lovely family atmosphere and the pupils are friendly and polite. Mrs S is keen to send all her pupils away confident in their own abilities (whatever they may be) and with high self esteem.

CRAIGCLOWAN PREPARATORY SCHOOL

Edinburgh Road, Perth, PH2 8PS

Tel: 01738 626 310
Fax: 01738 440 349
E-mail: mbeale@btconnect.com
Website: www.craigclowan-school.co.uk

• Pupils: 270 boys and girls, plus 50 or so in the nursery (it comes and goes). All day • Ages: 5-13, 3-5 in nursery • Inter-denom • Fees: £2,340 • Independent

Head: Since 1979, Mr M E (Mike) Beale BEd (fifties) educated 'at a grammar school in Dorset', followed by a BEd in Birmingham. Taught at Downside where he was head of economics and politics. The parent of a pupil persuaded him to apply for the headship of Craigclowan and he has been here, happy as Larry, ever since. School has grown enormously under his reign, starting with just fifty children, rising to current size, which has been more or less static for the last ten years. Married to Angela, who acts as bursar,

they have two grown-up daughters. Busy border terrier, Breagh, 'my favourite pupil'.

Mr Beale is a lovely head. Confidential, loving to the children; during our visit trails of tinies came to have their work approved – stickers of mice on a mountain were issued to all, and the children put out their hands, had their hair ruffled and were alternately called 'honey-pot' and sweetie-pie'. 'I make it a rule always to stop and talk to children wherever they find me', and 'if they are happy to come and see me for praise, it is so much easier to come and see me when they have done something wrong – and then we discuss it'. No punishment for a first offence but if it is repeated 'we get Ma and Pa in'. No actual teaching duties, just games, rugby and cricket – Mr Beale also fronts the ski team – trips to America as well as the Highlands.

Entrance: Children from all over the northern central belt; usually within forty minutes travel/thirty mile radius, middle class professionals, plus a toff or two. Large number of first time buyers.

Exit: 70 per cent go relatively locally, Glenalmond, Strathallan, Fettes, Merchiston, St Leonards, Kilgraston. 25 per cent down south; trickle to Eton, quite a few to Downe House ('Emma McKendrick likes our product'), plus Rugby, Stonyhurst, Ampleforth, QM York, Haileybury, Stowe. All to their first choice of school over the last 3 years, 15 or so scholarships a year.

Remarks: Cunning conversion of Victorian mansion set in 13 acres of undulating urban Perth overlooking the M90. Plans well underway to remove the rather tacky temporary classroom and build a mirror block to the rather grand clock-towered classrooms. New Astroturf for tennis and hockey, plus a – very small – artificial ski slope. Tinies work in the main house, lining up either on yellow painted human or webbed feet at the main door. And we are greeted most excellently, by mini-tartaned creatures who escorted us with great aplomb to the head's office. Tartan everywhere.

Two tiny classes throughout, some streaming further up, but basically divided alphabetically, with those whose birthdays fall in the spring or summer term joining the school the summer term before their fifth birthdays. French from nine (though some earlier exposure), traditional teaching. Latin, computers; fantastic sports hall, fine art. Learning support for 'any child who needs help for any reason either for a long or a short term, and for the very able'. Two teachers for every year, plus trained support staff – we saw many children getting one to one attention in little work stages all over the main classroom block. Excellent staff. Part of the Comenius project, lots of foreign contact, as well as regular tours abroad.

This is a vibrant seven day a week co-ed day school, with classes on five days, and a mass of extra-curricular activity. Parents can (and do) leave their young at 7.50am and collect them again at 6pm. Lots of involvement with Perth festival; a film crew was auditioning when we visited. All singing and dancing.

CRAIGHOLME LOWER JUNIOR SCHOOL AND NURSERY

Linked to Craigholme School in the Senior section

204 Nithsdale Road, Glasgow, G41 5EU

Tel: 0141 427 0375
Fax: 0141 427 6396
E-mail: development@craigholme.co.uk
Website: www.craigholme.co.uk

• Pupils: 260 girls; all day • Ages: 3-9 • Fees: £1,960 - £2,500
• Independent

Head: For Lower Junior School Mrs Janet Smart, for Nursery: Mrs Elizabeth Smith.

Remarks: Upper Junior School is located with senior school. The nursery has a separate site at 62 St Andrew's Drive (next to the senior school). For more information on the Lower Junior School, see the entry for the senior school.

CRANLEIGH PREPARATORY SCHOOL

Linked to Cranleigh School in the Senior section

Horseshoe Lane, Cranleigh, GU6 8QH

Tel: 01483 542 051
Fax: 01483 277 136
E-mail: fjmb@cranprep.org
Website: www.cranleighprepschool.org

• Pupils: 165 boys, 105 girls, 200 day, 70 board • Ages: 7-13
• Non-denom • Fees: Day: £3,160 - £3,825; boarding: £4,155 - £4,820 • Independent • Open days: October

Headmaster: Since 2000, Mr Michael Roulston MBE CertEd BPhil MEd (late forties). Married to Janet, who teaches food technology at the school. Previously head-

master of the British School in Tokyo where he transformed the place. He has worked the same magic here, taking a lacklustre boys-only prep and turning it into a 21st century co-ed prep school of huge merit. Lovely man – approachable, humorous, interested and interesting, also somehow remarkably unassuming. 'I love what I do – there's a feel good factor here,' he says. Certainly his enthusiasm knows no bounds and touches everything and everyone around the school. Says that he has been hugely supported by the governing body and has felt he has been allowed to 'run with it'- and run he has. There aren't enough positive epithets in existence to describe the man as far as parents are concerned: 'incredibly dynamic, 'wonderful,' 'inspirational,' 'not your average head,' 'a real leader,' 'fabulous'. One parent going so far as to say 'he walks on water.' That we would like to see.

Entrance: The main entry point is at 7+, and then another at 11+: usually about 50/60 applicants for the available places. Pupils are selected on academic merit, and ability to contribute to the life of the school -'we're looking for girls and boys who love school, are fired by it, and can give as much to the school as we can give them,' says Mr R. At 7+ pupils take written and/or oral assessments in English, maths and non-verbal reasoning as well as assignments in art and sport. At 11+ candidates also sit a general knowledge paper and have an interview with a senior member of staff. A report from the head of the pupil's present school is also sought. Prospective pupils spend a day at the school and are observed for their interaction: it's not just about paper results but more about the whole person, and how the Cranleigh ethos will suit them.

Exit: Around 60 per cent over the road to Cranleigh School - the majority sit CE and CASE. Other pupils go on to Charterhouse, Eton, Marlborough, Winchester, Wellington, Cheltenham Ladies, Heathfield Ascot, Lancing, Royal Grammar Guildford, amongst others.

Remarks: A super go-getting, can-do place, but tempered with a tangible warmth and friendliness. Remarkable transformation of buildings, teaching, extracurricular activities – in fact everything has had the Roulston touch. Academically, it is a challenging atmosphere where children are inspired to learn. Energised approach to education – 'there's no drudgery here – it's a fun atmosphere,' says one parent. 'My children virtually skip in to school – even on a Saturday,' said another. School encourages lateral thinking and asking questions – 'to think outside of the box,' says a parent. Mr R looking at introducing the primary years programme of the IB. Parents feel that the teaching is 'leagues ahead' without huge pressure on the children.

Children start off in mixed ability groups with the majority of time spent with their form teacher, and in the third year are streamed for English and maths. In the upper school every subject is streamed, and there is a scholars' set.

SEN provision v good. Dedicated learning support department and specialist tuition for pupils with dyslexia, dyspraxia and dyscalculia – which parents pay extra for. The school's SENCo has a team of three part time tutors and teachers. Pupils are not specifically tested for learning difficulties: 'our own entry tests may reveal weaknesses,' says the head. School asks for any educational psychologist's assessment, so that the SENCo can advise if the school is right for the child. A multi-sensory approach and teaching is tailored to the child's needs – every pupil has an individual educational plan. One parent commented that her dyslexic daughter's confidence 'had soared.' Another parent said that her very academic child was 'stretched and challenged.'

On a musical note, vast range of activities on offer from singing lessons to electronic music. Lots of individual music lessons (27 specialists teaching 400 pupils a week). Dance teacher gets a pat on the back for getting boys up on their feet – street dance is very popular with the boys here. Impressive drama and art facilities – head of art believes everyone capable of doing amazing things, which is obviously filtering through to pupils as standard is extremely good and children's art is everywhere round the school.

Sport is very definitely for all, regardless of talent, the very unsporty may find this aspect tough but as Mr R says 'Everyone is encouraged to do everything – we'll find what they're good at.' One parent commented on the competitiveness for team places, and resultant disappointments. Whole gamut of usual sports, in addition, options for riding, squash, golf, judo and Eton fives. Extracurricular opportunities abound: pupils are busy, busy, busy all day and beyond – hence encouragement to board so that these can be enjoyed to the full. Boarding is actively on the agenda in the last couple of years of school and the head feels this is important: 'At 12 and 13 the children positively look for opportunities to be independent and boarding gives that opportunity – they can flex their wings in a nurturing environment.' No question that the boarding aspect of the school adds another edge to the prep school atmosphere, but this constant go-getting all day atmosphere is not for everyone: sit down and read a book at home types may feel it is all too much. Saturday school for everyone, every alternate weekend.

Opposite its big sister, Cranleigh, in rolling Surrey countryside. Money has obviously been chucked at the place,

but it has been done with intelligence. Integrity of the original buildings has been kept, whilst transforming the interior into a light, bright and breezy welcoming environment. Reception area is full of squashy sofas, giving impression of a swish hotel. Design and technology block impressive – Mr R has been busy knocking down walls (not personally) to create one huge workshop. Inventions are created on computers and then made in the workshop which is gadget heaven – every possible piece of machinery is available there. Dorms are light and bright – again with really attractive furnishings. One has a funky living room called 'the Ikea Room' – apparently according to matron because some brave soul went to Ikea and bought all the furnishings in one go. Matrons seem lovely – 'you can always talk to them'.

Pupils are a remarkably self-possessed and happy bunch. Parents are mostly local, middle class professionals, but the school is currently riding high and is becoming increasingly popular out of the immediate area.

CRANMORE SCHOOL

West Horsley, Leatherhead, Surrey, KT24 6AT

Tel: 01483 280340
Fax: 01483 280341
E-mail: catherineblack@cranmoreprep.co.uk
Website: www.cranmoreprep.co.uk

• Pupils: 525 boys, including 32 in nursery, all day • Ages: 4-13, nursery 3-4 • RC, but other denominations welcomed • Fees: From January 2006 £1,100 - £2,950 • Independent • Open days: October & March

Head: Since 2001, Mr Anthony Martin BA (in classics) DipEd (Newcastle), MA (Open University) (fifties). Comes from Lancashire, where he attended Morecambe Grammar School, meeting his wife, Elizabeth there; they now live on site. Wide experience – previously taught at St Chad's, Wolverhampton (a grammar school), St Mary's Primary at Morecambe, Whitley Bay High School (a comprehensive) and St Edward's School in Cheltenham, an independent RC prep and senior school where he stayed for 27 years, the last 10 of them as head. The move to leafy Surrey from Cheltenham has not proved to be too much of a culture shock. Very much a family man, he has four adult children and six grandchildren; three of his children have followed him into teaching. He describes himself as 'an enabler and an encourager', with an open-door policy. This has been noticed and confirmed by parents – 'the door is a lot more open, both literally and metaphorically,' says one. Approachable, jovial and welcoming, he teaches some Latin and hopes to increase this.

Retiring July 2006. New head will be Mr Michael Connolly, presently head of Barrow Hills in Godalming.

Entrance: Mainly into the nursery at 3, and into the pre-prep department at 4. Others are taken at 7 subject to an entrance test and at other ages subject to a vacancy being available. Oversubscribed in certain years, when priority may be given to Roman Catholics, although currently they comprise less than half of the total.

Exit: Thirty per cent to the Royal Grammar School, Guildford, where the top 13+ scholarship has been awarded to a Cranmore boy 9 times in last 12 years. The school also collects an assortment of scholarships from other schools. Boys go on to a variety of schools including St George's, Weybridge and St John's, Leatherhead, Charterhouse, Cranleigh, Epsom College, Reed's at Cobham, Tonbridge, Worth and the Oratory (Reading). A few leave at 11 for state schools.

Remarks: Splendidly situated and equipped school, with high academic, sporting and musical attainment, which should get your son off to a flying start in the competitive Surrey set, plus, as one mother says, 'the junior school is also very caring and loving, which I think is probably due to its Catholic ethos'. Some isolated parental rumbling about too much pressure too early but the arrival of the new head should counter that. Maximum class size between 16 and 21. Average age of staff is 46 and staff loyalty is impressive – an amazing 20 (over 50 per cent) of them have been here for more than 15 years. Staff numbers are on the increase, with no corresponding increase in pupil numbers – this will improve the already good pupil:staff ratio of 12:1. Several parents praise the standard of teaching, saying that the school has a good understanding of how boys learn and that the teaching is very well structured.

Each school year is divided into three parallel forms of equal size of around 18 until age 8 when the boys are assessed for assignment either to the scholarship class or to one of the two parallel Common Entrance classes. Some parents find this divisive and would prefer setting to the more rigid division by form. Scholarship candidates and some from the two CE classes study Latin. SEN provision is via the Progress Units, one for juniors and one for seniors (but school only caters for those with mild to moderate specific learning difficulties). Units have two full-time teachers and others assist. Currently 27 receiving help in the senior unit and 58 in the junior unit. One mother comments that she was 'extremely pleased' with the extra support that her

mildly dyslexic son receives. She adds, 'the school works well for those who are bright but other children have been advised to leave because the school was unable to provide the level of support that they had been found to require.' In practice, no demand for English as an additional language. Exceptional IT provision with impressive hardware and software. Some classrooms already equipped with 'smartboards' (interactive computerised boards), and plan is to increase this number.

In a lovely setting in 24 acres of prime countryside between Guildford and Leatherhead, school draws its intake from an enviable catchment area bounded by those two towns, together with Dorking and Woking, but with most living within 5 miles. Some daily school transport is available, with minibuses running from the Worplesdon, Wonersh, Dorking and the Weybridge/Walton areas. Vast majority brought by car – fortunately, extensive car park and one-way service road helps to alleviate congestion at beginning and end of the day. Parents very typical of the area – professionals, businessfolk and company directors. One parent says, 'the size of your house and what car you drive doesn't seem to be important, unlike with many schools in the area.' Strong parents' association – usually a sign of a school where parents feel comfortable.

School moved to its present site (formerly part of St Peter's RC School in Guildford) in 1968, changing its name to Cranmore in the process and remaining independent. Hub of the school is a newly built entrance block with new art, design/technology and library provision. The original late Victorian house has recently been converted into a purpose-built nursery block. The other buildings are all close by and mostly connected. Playgrounds and other areas surveyed by CCTV. Modern and airy with a central atrium and everywhere sparklingly fresh, clean and bright – no bursting at the seams or penny-pinching here. The modern assembly hall (known as the auditorium) has slatted, wooden ceiling, tiered seating for 280 and an organ and Steinway grand piano. Mass is compulsory for all and is held on Catholic festivals. The chapel is smaller, holding around 60 and used for year or form mass and some RE teaching. (The Catholic element is, if anything, underplayed, according to one parent, and some RC parents say that this element of school life could be stronger.)

Half of all pupils have individual instrumental music tuition, some having to miss a timetabled lesson for this, although music teaching does take place at lunchtimes and after school in a specially designed building. Some boys learn two or even three instruments and Associated Board exams taken, some up to grade 6 – very impressive for this age group – many merits and distinctions. School takes part in local music festivals, choirs very popular, two in the junior department and four in the senior department, with an orchestra in each. Some choirs by invitation only; others open to all. Two or three music scholarships to senior schools won annually. Some maternal muttering that the arrangement for teaching music is a little too enthusiastic and, as a result and in spite of the high standard, some boys find the expectations quite demanding.

Given the wonderful grounds – six-hole golf course, athletics track, four squash courts, four hard tennis courts, sports hall and gym, including climbing walls and indoor nets – no surprise to learn that the school is very good at sport – won the National RC Schools 7-a-side Prep School Rugby Championship in 2002. Teams are selected from those boys who attend team practices before school (at 8am), after school and at lunch-times. Up to six teams in each age group for football, rugby and cricket and the official school line is that all boys have the opportunity to be in a team if they want. In practice, it seems that it may not be the case, with some maternal concern and pupil angst about team selection.

'Cranmore is very competitive,' says one mother of a sports-mad but not terribly able child, ' lots of boys who would want to play for the school never get the chance because they are not good enough and there are not enough teams to cater for all abilities.' Some resentment, therefore (not uncommon in prep schools) that some boys are in more than one team while others are in none. Rowing for boys of 9+ takes place mainly on Saturdays at Walton on Thames, where school keeps its own four boats at Walton Rowing Club, and is proving very popular with a recent tour to Ghent in Belgium. Excellent 25-metre indoor swimming pool, also used for water polo and kayaking. Annual ski trip to the Alps; Easter adventure trip to Ross-on-Wye; annual French trip. Cub pack meets after school on Friday and there are camps every year. Numerous clubs operate before school, at lunch-times and after school, mostly run by teachers but some specialist staff eg for golf and tennis olubc.

In all, an impressive, unstuffy, boys' prep with great facilities and very good all-round attainment, underpinned by popular promising new hcad and a Christian foundation, which it wears relatively lightly.

CROYDON HIGH JUNIOR SCHOOL

Linked to Croydon High School in the Senior section

Old Farleigh Road, Selsdon, South Croydon, Surrey, CR2 8YB

Tel: 0208 651 3137
E-mail: Junioradmissions@cry.gdst.net
Website: www.gdst.net/croydonhigh

• Pupils: 270 girls; all day • Ages: 3 - 11 • Fees: Junior Department £2,383 per term, Nursery - full time £1,838 per term
• Independent • Open days: October

Head: Since 1994, Ms Annette Grunberg, previously the deputy head.

Entrance: From 3 into the nursery, then by assessment from 4 and all subsequent year groups.

Exit: Most continue to the senior school, a few to local grammar schools.

Remarks: Excellent local reputation for music, sports and academics, some of the senior school staff also teach in the junior school. Super new ICT suite.

CULFORD PREPARATORY SCHOOL AND PRE PREP

Culford, Bury St Edmunds, Suffolk, IP28 6TX

Tel: 01284 729348
Fax: 01284 728183
E-mail: vseaman@culford.suffolk.sch.uk
Website: www.culford.co.uk

• Pupils: boys and girls; boarding and day • Ages: 2-13
• Independent

Remarks: For further details, see senior school.

CUMNOR HOUSE SCHOOL

Danehill, Haywards Heath, West Sussex, RH17 7HT

Tel: 01825 790 347
Fax: 01825 790 910
E-mail: office@cumnor.co.uk
Website: www.cumnor.co.uk

• Pupils: 311; 181 boys, 150 girls (18 boys, 15 girls currently board) • Ages: 7-13, pre-prep 4-7 • C of E • Fees: Pre prep £2,180; Prep: day £4,110, boarding £4,915 • Independent

Head: Since 2001, Mr Christian Heinrich BA PGCE (mid forties), educated at University of Kent and Westminster College, Oxford. Previously 15 years at Summer Fields as housemaster, then head of junior school (1990) to deputy head (1998). He says, 'although this does not suggest a meteoric rise, I stayed a little longer to see my four children born and looked further afield when the time was educationally right for them.' He feels Summer Fields was a great training experience under an exceptional head. His wife, Belinda, supervises the household staff and teaches French in the pre-prep. A new era dawns as he takes over from the Milner-Gullands, 'who created a wonderful atmosphere' and ran the school as their baby since they founded it on the present site in 1948. He is supported by a good, long-standing senior management team and is making a resounding success of his new post and it is easy to see why. Smartly turned out, articulate, ungushing (appearing almost nonchalant) but most certainly with a finger on the pulse as an effective organiser and manager. A new broom was needed and he is managing to smarten up the school from being delightfully shabby without losing the essentially friendly nature or underlying ethos of the school.

Believes the school is run on three standard constituents: pupils are (a) treated as little individuals and not as a group (b) listened to with respect for their concerns and (c) the return is that they take personal responsibility and make more effort. He coaches u11 cricket, enjoys modern English novels and holds the advanced diploma of wines/spirits. Intends to stay until retirement – good news all round.

Entrance: Non selective at reception – thereafter by interview. Headmaster spends huge amounts of time with prospective parents and pupils 'making sure they are comfortable with the feel and culture of the place'. Pupils are all British nationals (some dual nationality) made up of broad-

ish range, a few first-timers, many city commuters and local country professionals within a 40-minute radius.

Exit: A school where no special type of pupil emerges and thus this year eighteen schools were fed, including Worth, King's Canterbury, Tonbridge, Charterhouse, Eton, Radley, Sevenoaks, Benenden, Cranleigh, Lancing, Brighton College, Eastbourne, Woldingham, Millfield, Wellington and Wycombe Abbey. 'It is very rare indeed for a child not to get into the school of their choice.'

Remarks: Once a family-run school, it has grown in just over a decade from 175 to 311 pupils and is presently extending in every direction – new kitchen/dining area, new indoor swimming pool, new boarding accommodation, CDT rooms and new classrooms. Offers a very aesthetic and safe environment, emphasis on allowing pupils to remain children and 'not to be hot-housed into young adults before their time'. It is genuinely child-centred and happy in its reputation of going straight to the child arriving for interview and then acknowledging the parents – a reputation borne out during my visit when I was politely sidelined while a member of staff finished discussions with pupils – no bad thing.

Set in 62 acres of rich green countryside, the main building is an old redbrick country house with a new attached boarding wing. Many of the outbuildings have been built around a 'stone sculptured water feature', including artisan-restored barns and granaries giving light, spacious beamed new classrooms. Strolling through the grounds, one has sightings of happy children climbing trees, swinging from Tarzan-like ropes into small lake, meandering through coppices, glades and stumbling upon their own outdoor mini amphitheatre! 'O had I but followed the arts!' – yes, Twelfth Night was being rehearsed. Year 8 performs an annual Shakespeare play, no surprise that some established actors and scriptwriters choose this school for their children.

Modern ICT suite with smartboards and IT soon to be thoroughly integrated into each subject on the curriculum. Staff undergoing training to become fully IT literate, bi-annual staff appraisals and target setting undertaken by the new head (often sadly neglected in the private sector).

Flexible streaming begins in year 6 with usual progression to Common Entrance or potential scholarship form. CE papers done every term under exam conditions rather than at the end of the year. Each term a test paper is done in each subject to help the children regard exams as routine, to identify weaknesses sooner not later and to familiarise them with exam techniques. The new head is shaking up and modernising the curriculum to integrate PE, CDT and more music.

Academic standards are very good with some 25 per cent achieving awards or scholarships. Parents feel pre-prep is strong with good age range of staff. No more than 12 pupils in reception classes with a gradual fill to 18 in each form. New policy from 2003 of no more than 16 per form from current year 3 onwards. Year 3 intake has expanded to 3 forms of 14 due to demand this year. Handwriting is taught as a cursive script, winning the Parker Pen prize award from over 30,000 entries. Languages strong, French links with Paris school and a French gap student. Latin also hot favourite with the boys – 'he is a great teacher' – and starts at age 8 with the Minimus scheme. Often considered well ahead of the game in Latin when going on to senior schools. Maths results slightly disappointing recently but being addressed.

The arts are central, good art on display in converted granary and in school magazine; offers pottery, batik and encourages extra art courses. Music is ab fab, the legacy of former head and taken over by new director, Alison Wicks. 85 per cent of pupils learn one instrument and the norm is two. First orchestra performs frequently and also in Siena and France – also a training orchestra, wind band, senior and junior brass, senior and junior chorus and plenty of impromptu coffee concerts in the charming Barn Theatre.

Games are taken seriously, presently doing well on a competitive circuit with their 'aim to win' philosophy with recent tours to Sri Lanka, South Africa, Australia and France. All usual range on offer here with expert coaching in many minority sports, there is also a 6-hole golf course. Girls' sport is on the agenda for improvement – a welcome and perhaps overdue development considering the school has been co-ed since 1971.

Some lively lessons were in progress when we visited, eg RE lesson on Job – good use of visual aids with video and mass for Ascension Day by Palestrina being played in the background (a good ploy and just the tonic needed to spice up the story of Job's sometimes dispirited state).

Considered more of a day school, although a large proportion of year 7 and all year 8 board, 'there was no point in going into direct competition with the surrounding rival boarding schools', although now considering widening its geographical intake and can accommodate more boarders. There are well-qualified and adored matrons, 'first-rate pastoral care' said many parents, facilities are modern with all beds changed recently from iron to Canadian pine giving the place a less Dickensian feel. Matron keeps in constant touch with parents re any personal concerns eg bullying, anorexia alert and in the evening they have 'circle time' to enjoy games and discussion which has a cathartic effect

and relieves them from peer pressure. Head has introduced a tutorial system for senior years when they're most likely to be under pressure.

School stays steadfast to its motto 'Aim high, be kind and dare to be different.' Parents tend to think the children are remarkably courteous to each other and think of the school as slightly off-beat, allowing for the eccentricity factor and not being encouraged to run with the pack. Senior schools comment that a Cumnorian child is confident and unafraid to question. A gem of a school with a hugely able, energetic new headmaster.

DAME ALICE HARPUR JUNIOR SCHOOL

Linked to Dame Alice Harpur School in the Senior section

Cardington Road, Bedford, Bedfordshire, MK42 0BX

E-mail: enquiries@dahs.co.uk
Website: www.dahs.co.uk

• Pupils: 200 girls; all day • Ages: 7-11 • Fees: £2,075
• Independent • Open days: October and May

Head: Susan Braud

Entrance: At 7 girls have a group interview and an assessment day.

Exit: The vast majority of junior school girls transfer to the senior school.

Remarks: Based in Howard House opposite the senior school. A former Barnardo's Home – delightful gardens and brightly decorated accommodation. Strong links with the senior school – girls from the sixth form, for example, often pop over to Howard House to help with reading.

DAME ALLAN'S SCHOOLS JUNIOR DEPARTMENT

Linked to Dame Allan's Girls' School in the Senior section
Linked to Dame Allan's Boys' School in the Senior section

Fowberry Crescent, Fenham, Newcastle upon Tyne, Tyne and Wear, NE4 9YJ

Tel: 0191 275 0608
Fax: 0191 275 1502
E-mail: l.stephenson@dameallans.co.uk
Website: www.dameallans.co.uk

• Pupils: 55 boys, 40 girls; all day • Ages: 8-11 • Christian foundation • Fees: £1,666 • Independent

Head: A J Edge, MA (St Andrews).

Remarks: For further details see Dame Allan's Boys School.

DANES HILL SCHOOL

Oxshott, Leatherhead, Surrey, KT22 0JG

Tel: 01372 842 509
Fax: 01372 844 452
E-mail: registrar@daneshillschool.co.uk
Website: www.daneshillschool.co.uk

• Pupils: 470 boys, 385 girls, all day • Ages: 2 1/2-13 (nursery, pre-prep school (known as Bevendean), middle and upper school) • Christian non-denom • Fees: reception and yr 1 £2393, yr 2 to yr 8 £3375 • Independent

Headmaster: Since 1989, Mr Robin Parfitt MA MSc (late fifties). Two headships prior to Danes Hill, Mr Parfitt has grown and developed the school considerably since he has been at the helm. Married to Angela (director of studies). A very confident, business-like man who is seen by parents as a strong leader. Wants to be at the cutting edge of change and he believes the school is 'very different from smaller local preps.' Demands respect. Lots of very efficient support staff around him.

Entrance: Waiting lists are not generally an issue, but they do exist for some year groups (although they do not operate more than two years ahead) so get names down early. Entry points at nursery (2 1/2 – 3 years), transition (3 – 4 years) reception (4-5 years) and Year 3 (7 – 8 years) when they are tested in English, maths and reading. In such a large school, worth ringing at odd times to see what is available. From September 2007, the school will take fewer new children into transition making spaces available for entry into reception. Some scholarships and bursaries on offer. Extremely approachable registrar, Mrs Shattock, described by one parent as 'fantastic'.

Exit: Boys and girls theoretically both leave at 13 (although about 25 per cent of girls exit at 11). Pupils go on to City of London Freemen's School, Epsom College, Royal Grammar School Guildford, King's Wimbledon and Guildford High School amongst others. Impressive list of school awards particularly academic and sports from a wide range of schools including St John's and Cranleigh.

Remarks: A very large school with traditional values and a strong feeling of discipline and achievement. Academically strong with a broad curriculum and a very good level of general education. Main aim is to prepare children for CE and public school scholarships with a high success rate in both. Some parents feel not as much importance is put on 11+ and that the focus on girls leaving at 11 is lost.

So what about the school's reputation as an academic hot-house? Yes, academia is extremely important, yet there's a real sense of pride in helping the less able to achieve their best. According to the head, as long as your child shows 'enormous compassion and imagination' then their achievements are valued. On average 22 pupils in each class, but children are placed into small sets from year 3 and scholarship streams from year 6. Class groups are mixed at year 3 and 6, so children get the opportunity to make new friends. Classroom layout is traditional with pupils taught at individual desks facing the teacher from an early age. The head is strongly of the view that this method gets the best from his pupils. There is controlled discipline in the classroom – children stand automatically as you enter – and this is well balanced by 'friendly teachers who help to bring fun to the lessons.' Lots of hands-on experimentation and practical work. Computerised white boards in every classroom. Two noticeably impressive computer suites.

Unanimous parental comments that there are no weak teachers. Mr Parfitt says he pays his staff well and expects high standards in return. Languages v strong: all introduced to three languages – more if they study the classics! French in the pre-prep, a 'taster' course in Spanish and German (six months each) in year 3 and then either Spanish or German as their single language in year 4. French is introduced again in year 5. After that, French and Spanish or

German are taught on an equal basis. Works well – a high pass rate for language GCSE at age 13. Lots of exchange trips with very intense language study whilst abroad. Latin, and classical Greek- about twenty 10 year olds studying this option.

Significant learning support unit that works hard to provide additional help. The unit also plucks out the very bright, gifted and talented children and enjoys bringing them on. Some parental feeling that 'there's not such a focus on the average child – who must be self motivated to succeed.'

Great emphasis on the arts, many arts scholarships to senior schools... 3 separate art rooms (3-dimensional, graphic design and general). Some beautiful and very mature 3-D work and an extremely enthusiastic art teacher. Art work adorns the walls in the most unexpected places and children use visual work in all areas of study. Design technology, drama and music equally strong. Drama teachers write their own plays, so parents don't know what to expect. Isolated comment from a parent that 'it's always the same kids who get the lead roles.' A high percentage of pupils learn a musical instrument (up to grade 8) and many play more than one. Practice takes place at home although orchestra and ensembles, as well as choirs, rehearse in timetabled sessions at school. Performances recently at the Royal Albert Hall, Guildford Cathedral and Southwark Cathedral. Pupils also in the National Children's Orchestra and the National Children's Choir.

Sport flourishes helped by the school's extensive grounds, and sporty children really thrive here. Grand display cabinet full of sporting trophies in the reception. Lots of tournaments. Rosslyn Park 7-a-side semi-finalists and finalists, and national biathlon champions. One parent comments 'There's a huge focus on rugby. It's given so much priority each year that football peters out.' Despite this, there's such a variety of sport on offer that any child should find something to suit.

School site is large and wooded with many areas for the children to play and explore. Lovely naturalistic feel, with beautiful sculptures and building names – The Rookery, The Ark. Tidy and litter free. A real feel of history and tradition about the place – the school has only existed since 1947, but the Victorian buildings and choice of décor in reception areas make it appear more long-standing. New buildings have been sympathetically added to the main house, some temporary classrooms. Bevendean is being rebuilt with a new double storey classroom block due for completion Dec 2006.

Head sees himself as 'a facilitator who allows his senior management and heads of department to get on with the job.' There's a feeling of strict order and control. Children don't mill around, but move along with purpose. A large school. 'Without the size', the head says, 'Danes Hill would not be able to offer such a wide and well resourced curriculum with so many specialist teachers'. On the negative side, parents feel that the management structure stops them from talking directly to the head about day-to-day matters. Parental opinions vary from the disgruntled – 'It's hard to see the head. You are referred to the head of year or head of school' to the more positive 'If you want to see the head he'll make time for you'. But it's often better to deal with the head of year because they know your child better.' (Unanimous thumbs up for the head of the upper school: 'He is excellent. He's very in touch with the children' and 'Lots of help when discussing where your child should go next').

Pastoral care is much praised. Children taught to be responsible for their own actions from an early age. 'The school makes children very independent' says one parent, 'They're very responsible. There's sex education and puberty education!' Good home cooking with plenty of healthy choices.

The large number of international children creates a unique atmosphere (there's even a specialist EAL teacher). The school is the only factor that binds all these disparate people together – may explain why there is such a strong sense of community. Parents are corporate chieftains and the like, and mostly rather wealthy. They put in a large amount of effort and commitment to the school and this is strongly encouraged by the head. A few comments that the parents form cliques. Drop-off and pick-up times are a nightmare – the entrance to the school is on the brow of a steep hill. School runs a bus service from and to the immediate surrounding areas (Walton, Weybridge, Esher, Claygate and Bookham).

Suits bright, confident, sporty children happy to get involved in school life and who would not get lost in the crowd.

DEAN CLOSE PREPARATORY SCHOOL

Linked to Dean Close School in the Senior section

Lansdown Road, Cheltenham, Gloucestershire, GL51 6QS

Tel: 01242 512 217
Fax: 01242 258 005
E-mail: dcpsoffice@deanclose.org.uk
Website: www.deanclose.co.uk/prep

- Pupils: 261 boys and girls, 60 board; pre-prep 124 boys and girls • Ages: 7-13; pre-prep 2-7 • C of E • Fees: £1,780 - £4,075 day; boarding £4,195 - £5,295 • Independent • Open days: September, November, March and May

Head: Since 2004, the Reverend Leonard Browne MA, educated at St Catherine's College Cambridge. Previously, Rev Browne was the chaplain and religious education teacher, previously recorded by us saying, 'the brilliant Irish chaplain who doubles as rugby coach is incredibly popular'.

Entrance: Own exam.

Exit: 90 per cent to Dean Close.

Remarks: The pre-prep and preparatory schools share the senior school facilities plus a considerable amount of new-build, which was long over-due. French from the age of four, Latin at 11, classes streamed with maths, French and Latin setted. IT, science, masses of computers. Popular rink for roller-blading and the like, good art, good drama, now with their own theatre.

DOLLAR ACADEMY PREP AND JUNIOR SCHOOL

Linked to Dollar Academy in the Senior section

Dollar, Clackmannanshire, FK14 7DU

Tel: 01259 742 511
Fax: 01259 742 867
E-mail: rector@dollaracademy.org.uk
Website: www.dollaracademy.org.uk

- Pupils: boys and girls; boarding and day • Ages: 5-11 • Fees: Boarding: £5,214 - £5,850; day: £1,932 - £2,568 • Independent • Open days: 'Every day is an Open Day - come and see Dollar at work.'

Remarks: For further details see the senior school.

DOLPHIN SCHOOL

Hurst, Reading, Berkshire, RG10 0BP

Tel: 0118 934 1277
Fax: 0118 934 4110
E-mail: omnes@dolphinschool.com
Website: www.dolphinschool.com

- Pupils: 300, all day – 160 boys, 140 girls • Ages: 3-13
- Humanistic – they dip toes in all religions. Christianity principally as a means to decoding art and architecture
- Fees: Yrs 3-8 £2,830. Yrs 1 & 2 £2,735 • Independent

Head: The founder and owner, Nancy Follett, remains the power in the land, though her role these days is avowedly hands-off – she 'does jobs' she says. Lives next door in the bijou Tudor manor where the school was born. Here she tends her garden, indulges the busy-ness of her mind and entertains the staff to Parnassian luncheon parties. Her life has been a series of prodigious feats of strenuous busy-mindedness. Educated to formidable altitudes, PhD from London in Latin love poetry, inspirer of the school's enduring classical penchant (see e-address).

The school is run by Heather Brough, who dropped in to teach art in the 70s, discovered that if she wanted shelves in the art room she'd have to put them up herself, and has been there ever since. Like many here for whom no other school would be good enough, her pride in the place exceeds the conventional and delights rather than deters. She it is who has overseen the transition from the joyous ad hoc-ery of the early years to the tightly run ship of today. She has pulled off the difficult trick of laying paper trails to delight sniffing inspectors, yet kept the school as it was. In Nancy's grateful words, 'It's the same spirit, but organised.' Heather retires in '07, and her successor, James Wall (classicist), is groomed.

As for Nancy, she could most straightforwardly have made the place over to a charitable trust, but the prospect of a board of owl-eyed governors emanating dullness disquiets her, so she has formed a trust governed by her children whose co-opted members will be former pupils only.

Entrance: Seriously aspirational in the most liberal sense, which is why the school appeals to people interested in education – university types from Reading, enlightened professionals, nice people like George Harrison, Lenny Henry and David Gilmour of Pink Floyd. Your child must be bright but not necessarily stellar. Entry exam, interview, attendant sense of drama, crossed fingers, white knuckles. Special needs run to running repairs only.

Exit: Many stay local, where there are rich pickings for high fliers: the Abbey and Queen Anne's for girls, the Blue Coat and Reading School (grammar) for boys, and Leighton Park for either. The rest smatter all manner of leading independents and state schools. Long link with St Paul's. Mildly depressing to see so many free-range intellects go on to some really geeky places, but that's the tyranny of yer A-stars, innit? Owing to the school's youth its best former pupils are still en route to superstardom. Arguably Matt Allwright, TV presenter and Rogue Trader slayer, has arrived.

Remarks: Began as a Montessori nursery in 1970 on a day of burst pipes and 28 determined but moist children. They got older, refused to go, so the school grew with them. The dynamic endures – this is a complacency-free zone – but pioneering anarchy has evolved into strong purpose and some architecturally commendable new buildings. This is one of the few schools left in Britain that does things radically differently. The educational idea derives from a love of learning for learning's sake combined with an irresistible urge to rush off and see for yourself. Plato definitely up for it. Yes, holistic. Cross-curricular if you prefer. Ask for details of what they do, you'll be dead impressed. Classroom learning culminates in impressively scholarly annual field trips, cost included in fees, when the word is made flesh and children apply their knowledge as skills. Parents come along too. Eight year-olds spend 3 days in East Sussex considering the Norman invasion from the point of view of all (academic, that is) subjects. Finally, 'we went to the battlefield to enact

the Battle of Hastings. My dad was Harold and Sue was William of Normandy.' By age 13 the children are in Italy displaying an astonishingly sophisticated understanding of art and architecture. These trips happen in holidays. The children, present-day creatures all, may greet the prospect with dragging feet but, say parents, 'all that changes when they get there.' This programme is the fruit of years of doing it combined with a degree of collaborative planning among teachers we have seen nowhere else. Trips are compulsory. An attitude shift among Thames Valley parents – all you need is results – means some now try to slide out, thereby missing the point. 'This school,' says Heather, 'demands commitment. Parents must know that we will do what we think is right.' Basta!

The cross-curricular programme attracts high calibre teachers who have to work a lot harder than normal teachers – 'You've got to be better than the norm if you are going to do something different.' A well bonded lot, they go away and confer and freshen up annually – no hunkering down in your specialism here. They are given their head where their enthusiasms lie, and it shows in their demeanour and low turnover. Children learn what all children learn, and more besides. Subject specialist teachers from year 3. French from nursery, Latin in year 5, German, Spanish and Greek in year 7. Philosophy, astronomy, natural history, current affairs. Drama, music and art all exceptional. Maths v strong. Science lab state of the Ark ('it's next on our building list!'), but don't sniff: results are terrific, a reminder that teachers still have a role to play, yes they do, amidst the winking gadgetry. Parents say they do everything well, bar the odd (the sort you get everywhere) niggle.

Homework not the usual nightly worksheet re-hash we can all do in a family way in front of the telly, but calls for reading and research, which parents find testing, too. It all goes to nourish self-motivated study and requires planning, which is why parents say 'At senior school it's the Dolphin pupils who can organise themselves.' Breadth is never sacrificed, so scholars never drop subjects, and key stage results, though incidental, are right up to level 5 for almost all by KS2. A Dolphin education is an investment for life. There's a grown-upness about these children who know about Bernini years before their fellows – natural, not uppish. Nicely mannered, oh yes. The very bright revel, of course, get the full racehorse treatment and win super schols. The less bright, say some parents, could do with being made to feel less far off the leaders. Special needs picked up and dealt with by Inco – individual needs coordinator – who picks up the brightest, too. Not the sort of school where pupils are frogmarched past developmental milestones in line abreast – it's too child centred for that sort of National Curriculum control freakery. Parents say 'It doesn't always come good year after year. Stick with it.'

Sport is an after school thing. Teams in all the usuals at all levels achieve respectable outcomes. Claire Taylor, England wicketkeeper, first donned gloves here. Pastoral care is rated high, problems solved fast and properly. Parents get well involved – many accompany the field trips and the walking trips. It's a vicarious thing: they wish they'd had this. Most aren't a bit keen on lunch eaten with form teacher in the classroom – last vestige of the prefab days. Those who buy into the educational idea of the school worry that convenience shoppers who just want results may dilute its character – 'It must not become more normal.' Difficult to find a senior school which offers anything so humane and broad except top premiership independents but, as we see, many parents are happy to pop their kids into exam factories after Dolphin to be sure they get the best of both worlds. Dolphin will endure long after the next has been forgotten.

Decidedly different. The sort of place where you can march into any classroom and they will gather you in and crack on, always with time to nip down roads less travelled. The warmth of the greeting everywhere is striking and genuine – full of excitement and pride in what's going on. This is a still young, unhidebound school where knowledge is celebrated and fun had. Everyone else does the cross-curricular thing up to a point. Only here do they give it the full Monty.

DOVERCOURT - PORTSMOUTH HIGH JUNIOR SCHOOL

Linked to Portsmouth High School in the Senior section

35 Kent Road, Southsea, Hampshire, PO5 3ES

Tel: 023 9282 6714
Fax: 023 9281 4814
Website: www.gdst.net/portsmouthhigh

• Pupils: 195 girls, all day • Ages: 3 - 11 • Non-denom • Fees: £1,779; nursery £1,470 • Independent • Open days: Open Day in October. Regular 'drop-in' mornings throughout the year and taster days

Head: Mrs A Howarth BEd, MEd.

Remarks: Junior school, Dovercourt, in elegant house two minutes walk down Kent Road. Old fashioned, spacious

feel – complete opposite of the senior school. New early years building and nursery. Four tennis courts (also used by senior school). Grass playground. Virtually all girls move on to the senior school.

THE DOWNS SCHOOL

Charlton House, Wraxall, Bristol, BS48 1PF

Tel: 01275 852 008
Fax: 01275 855 840
E-mail: office@thedownsschool.co.uk
Website: www.thedownsschool.co.uk

• Pupils: 153 boys, 68 girls (6 boys board, 147 day boys) • Ages: 4-13 • Christian ethos • Fees: Boarding: £4,300; day 8+ £3,330; day reception £1,950 • Independent

Head: Since 2001, Mr Marcus Gunn MA(Ed) BA PGCE (late forties). Went to Bloxham then Liverpool followed by South Bank and an OU postgraduate degree in education. A cheery traditionalist who believes in children developing old-fashioned virtues such as 'opening doors for others, shaking hands and looking adults in the eye.' Career began at now defunct Marton Hall before deputy headship at Mowden Hall in Northumberland. Didn't quite realise what he was walking into as fourth head at The Downs within two years. After some much-needed hatchet work in the staffroom precipitated by a critical ISI report in November 2000 and substantial withdrawals by unimpressed parents, he has now managed to turn the school around. Has established a 'happy, talented staff' encouraged by a positive follow-up inspection in October 2002 and seen through some major changes. With wife Valerie looking after the few boarders still at the school and three children (Joshua 16; Olivia 14; Henrietta 12) going through the independent school mill, the Gunns are clearly seen as good news by the parents whom they have gone out of their way to get on side. A former windsurfing buff, Marcus is less athletic these days and when we visited was limping badly following a spot of rugby refereeing; likes to snatch quality time with the family or perhaps dabble in a bit of painting or photography.

Entrance: Candidates above year one are assessed informally for a day and offered places if they are of at least average ability. Low ability candidates are accepted provided school's learning support department can meet their needs. Former nursery, located near the entrance off the B3128, has been off-loaded to a year round, whole day care outfit which meets local demand better. Pre-prep now free to recruit four-year-olds from various local nurseries with encouraging results. 4:1 ratio of boys to girls in prep may be partly attributable to school's long rugby tradition, but girls appear confident and are increasingly making their presence felt. Four or five scholarships offered annually with academic scholarship worth up to 50 per cent of day fee.

Exit: Majority of CE candidates go to Clifton or QEH, though King's College, Taunton and Millfield are currently popular choices as have been Badminton, Bryanston, Malvern and Sherborne. All in recent years have been accepted by first choice school. Impressive scholarship success rate continues. Very few now go off to Bristol day schools after 11+ entrance exams so majority, including girls, stay to 13.

Remarks: Founded in 1894 overlooking Clifton Downs, school 'escaped' from Bristol in 1927 and were tenants on late Lord Wraxall's estate until 2002 when Charlton House along with assortment of other school buildings, 60 acres of playing fields and parkland were bought by governors 'for a song.' 20mph speed limit on mile long drive is a first challenge for visitors; unsympathetically rendered exterior to mansion finally comes as anti-climax. Entering the matrix (Hugo Weaving is an old boy), Victorian gothic interior with magnificent fireplace and spooky staircases more than compensates.

Experienced staff exact high standards in what still feels like trad prep; has woken up to unpopularity of Saturday lessons and scrapped them; boarding ends in July 2006. For parents who don't want their children to leave home before 13, The Downs offers as full a programme as you can find in a day prep. Attracts broad social mix and now that school has accepted the inevitable (though Saturday afternoon matches continue most weekends) demand is likely to rise further. Accessible from quite a wide area, being close to junction 19 on the M5 and only ten minutes' drive from Bristol's western edge.

Pre-prep's classroom accommodation being upgraded to provide a better indoor- outdoor facility. Teenies taught to read phonically with a number of schemes (not just 'Jolly Phonics') in use. Children not hemmed in by formality and come across as lively but respectful. Music at this level includes recorders; plenty of creativity though thematic work would benefit from more imaginative displays.

School is retaining positives from boarding regime with older ones mostly staying for after school clubs (ranging from Warhammer to cookery) or supervised prep until supper at 6.00pm despite formal day ending at 5.10pm. After-school care for pre-prep children also runs until supper. Even second prep and activities session between 6.45 and 8.00pm. is set to continue. Saturday matches every third weekend. Workaday uniform is low key and practical but children don garishly striped blazers (which they refused to have scrapped) for all travel to and from school as well as functions.

The curriculum from year 5 is geared to demands of CE with all subjects, including Latin, French, Spanish and science (separate sciences in years 6, 7 and 8), taught by specialists. There is a new art area but not much provided for DT as yet. New library, which would benefit from a CD-ROM (let alone DVD) facility, is a long overdue bonus.

Sporting tradition is paramount but head has worked at improving creative and performing arts. Music department is particularly strong with 75 per cent being taught one or more instruments; there are junior and senior choirs plus variety of concerts and productions. Boys' and girls' sports teams perform exceptionally well. The Downs has won the prep schools' rugby sevens at Rosslyn Park more than any other school and the girls are currently national rounders champions and runners-up in hockey. There is an imaginative alternative to games for the less sporty known as The Downs Award Scheme which concentrates on more individual and outward bound type activities and in which everyone participates on Thursdays.

Three specialist teachers support pupils with special needs; department has experience of a range of learning disabilities. Targeted support in literacy and numeracy working well to raise pupil performance.

Older pupils still to benefit from own social areas; children in year 8 have at least one school responsibility so no-one gets left out. 'Tiffin' is provided for all mid-morning and afternoon; tasty nosh served up for a fairly formal lunch with staff in the dining-hall which ends in 'pin drop' silence while notices are given. Plenty of places outside to let off steam; good use has been made converting a former walled garden into an area for tennis and other ball games. Floodlit Astroturf in the pipeline. Science laboratories adequate. Definitely not a laptop school and thankfully still a mobile phone free zone. More than adequate sports hall somehow got past planners fifteen or so years ago; bears external scars inflicted by hockey sticks in rowdier days. Heated, outside pool has failed repeated attempts to get it covered but remains popular through summer months.

In a school where manners still matter, we felt that most children would be happy and do well. Not an obvious stomping ground for city slickers but parents from nearby Bristol might be pleasantly surprised at the benefits for children of regular exercise in fresh air.

DOWNSIDE ST OLIVER'S (JUNIOR SCHOOL)

Linked to Downside School in the Senior section

Stratton-on-the-Fosse, Radstock, Somerset, BA3 4RJ

Tel: 01761 235103
Fax: 01761 235105
E-mail: registrar@downside.co.uk

- Pupils: 63 girls and boys; boarding and day • Ages: 9-13
- Fees: boarding £5,186; day £3,408 • Independent • Open days: October, November and March (call Registrar)

Remarks: For further information, see Downside School.

THE DRAGON SCHOOL

Bardwell Road, Oxford, Oxfordshire, OX2 6SS

Tel: 01865 315405
Fax: 01865 311 664
E-mail: admissions@dragonschool.org
Website: www.dragonschool.org

- Pupils: 400 boys, 200 girls; 200 boys and 70 girls board. Plus 140 boys and 75 girls, all day, in the pre-prep – Lynams – on separate site • Ages: 8-13, pre-prep 4-7 • C of E • Fees: Lynams £2,310 - £3,060; Dragon day £4,260; boarders £6,100 • Independent • Open days: Parents can make individual appointments to see the school

Head: Since 2002, Mr John Baugh BEd (forties) who was educated at Aldenham School, followed by St Luke's Exeter, where he read education with geography and still does the odd spot of teaching, 'takes occasional cover lessons when staff are away for some reason'. Taught RS last year. Started his teaching career at Haileybury and was previously head of both Solefield Prep School in Sevenoaks and Edge Grove. An experienced head then. He found the school 'in fantastic shape', 'the children are terrific; getting on with things from day one', and regularly praised 'the wonderful quality of the staff room' and mentioned dozens of times 'the sheer buzz and excitement'; 'I get up in the morning excited to get on with the job'. A 'people person,' said our guide, he has instigated open days for parents 'so that they can find out exactly what (and how

much) the school has to offer'. 'Every single child has to believe that they are part of the school'. Caring, thoughtful, GSOH (thank goodness) he has the support of staff, parents and pupils and is keen on promoting parent-school partnership. Married to Wendy, who is fully involved in the school, they have two daughters, both at Haileybury.

Entrance: By early registration, nothing has changed, though immediate places available in exceptional circs (and in the middle of term for visiting academics to Oxford) – but getting harder and harder to do, school adds 'virtually unheard of now'. A seriously intimidating double A4 sheet of instructions for parents of would-be pupils. No tests for 4+ entry to Lynams but non-competitive assessment for all for entry to the main school. Easier to board than day, takes occasional refugees from London hothouse preps, worth a try at any time. Recent, not altogether welcomed, influx of London day refugees, whose parents are buying up in the neighbourhood. With North Oxford houses now selling for over two million, dons are being pushed even further out. School is keen not to stray too far from the trad parent base (busing under consideration). New boarders have taster sleepovers before they come. 30/40 from abroad, both foreign nationals and ex-pats. One of the selected Eton continuation scholarship schools, where pupils from the state sector are underwritten at prep school before going on, but not many of these recently. Tres chic little prospectus (about to be re-written) in jolly Oxford blue cover with vintage pics of ODs: Sir John Betjeman, Dame Naomi Mitchison, and Sir Jack Smyth VC. Bursaries, and more in the pipeline in memory of Nicholas Knatchbull who was killed with his grandfather Lord Mountbatten. Prince Charles recently unveiled a commemorative plaque.

Exit: To 95 or more different schools over the past few years, but many to St Edward's Oxford and tranches to Eton, Radley, Marlborough and, more recently, Rugby plus Abingdon, Magdalen College School, Headington and Oxford High, otherwise all over the public school shop from Ampleforth to Wrekin. Regularly wins squillions of scholarships for everything, 40 last year.

Remarks: Still one of the best, most exciting and charming academic prep schools in the country. A genuine co-ed; head has tried 'really hard to get girls part of the whole set-up', give them a 'much higher profile' and improve their lot – moving their games programmes alongside the boys has done wonders for their self-esteem. Boys' boarding houses broken down by age, two for the youngest two years, two for ten-year-olds, and three for the top two years. Girls' houses charmingly full of Barbies and ponies, boys' with table football and rugby posters. Excellent houseparents on all fronts. Noticeably easy though respectful pupil/staff relationship – some staff still called by their nicknames – Chips, Pabs, Scotty; female teachers and house mothers called Ma (eg Moira Darlington is Ma Da).

Certain amount of tinkering with the tutorial system in the final two years which 'now involves many more staff', integrating boys and girls, day and boarding in the same two year group. The school projects an image of informality – scruffy cords, the scruffier the better (and only day pupils wear bomber jackets) blazers for best; girlies wear jolly yellow shirts and tartan. Even scruffier casuals after school. All meals taken in main dining room, and food 'much better', bun break and tea still in houses, day pupils have their own houses too.

This laissez faire attitude to outward appearances charms the children who feel that someone somewhere is on their side. Underneath, however the school is very disciplined with rigorous academic timetabling, and absolutely no messing about allowed in class. Max class size 23, average 19. Seven streams in each year after the junior school with pupils moving up and down (within their age group) where necessary, even in the middle of term. Maths, French and Latin setted separately, top two streams do Greek, German or Spanish in their last two years, and much more setting at this time. Japanese and Mandarin available as extras. Strong scholarship streams, 'it is quite common for people to take scholarships whilst still being in the second stream'.

Six state of the art science labs, with six lab technicians (more than many public schools), and five ICT suites. Impressive library, dead efficient with trillions of computers and more scheduled, plasma screens have replaced notice boards throughout the school and duty staff can change them from their lap tops. Laptops around the place too. Classes often taught in the computer suites. Intranet, interactive white boards, and 'computer operated telephoning'; all singing and dancing. 'Learning Support' fully integrated, with seven part time staff, pupils either withdrawn or certain amount of team teaching in class, pupils with problems greater than The Dragon can deal with are encouraged 'to go elsewhere', though siblings are often allowed to come on a trial basis. PSHE increased, and strong anti-bullying ethos in place 'the old culture of sneaking has now gone, it is a child's right to say I am unhappy'. 'Good system of checks and balances in place'.

Superb music, with choirs, orchestras, jazz bands, etc; terrific art and three heavenly art rooms above the swimming pool. Cad Cam in place as well as trad drawing and painting – children crouching on the table to 'get a better angle', when we visited. Good (once state of the art) assembly/multi-purpose hall, with professional sound box and lighting, much used for daily assembly, service on Sunday, regular talks (both during and post school hours) and all sorts of entertainment. Jolly drama, regular hysterically funny trad staff pantomime. No prep on Fridays, school has instituted 'a cultural evening known as 'Spectrum' and has a selection of lectures and performances. Open to day pupils and parents too. Popular.

Masses of options, trips all over, parents often go too. Links with school in Tokyo, with pupils and staff doing regular exchanges and attending school there. Masses of sport and good at it: trad rugby, football, hockey, tennis etc., extra land recently acquired for more tennis courts, Astro-turf everywhere. Children must still swim two lengths of the pool before playing by the river, girls now proficient at sculling and Frances Houghton won silver at the 2004 Olympics. Health and Safety regs mean specialist staff employed for climbing wall and canoeing. Teaching days end at 4.15, but masses of activities both before and after; school will field all day pupils till 6 pm.

Conglomerate of purpose-built blocks mingling with Victorian North Oxford. Planning rules will prevent massive expansion. School runs own very busy pre-prep (Lynams) about a mile away. Lots of Dragon traditions, Christmas fair attracts ODs back for Chrissie pressie buying, and back anyway at regular intervals 'to see what's happened now'. A very exciting school to be at and a place which ODs are proud to have attended.

DUCKS (DULWICH COLLEGE KINDERGARTEN AND INFANTS SCHOOL)

Linked to Dulwich College Junior School in the Junior section
Linked to Dulwich College in the Senior section

Eller Bank, 87 College Road, London, SE21 7HH

Tel: 020 8693 1538
Fax: 020 8693 4853
E-mail: ducks@dulwich.org.uk
Website: www.dulwich.org.uk

• Pupils: 240 boys and girls • Ages: 3 months - 7 years • C of E
• Independent

Head: Mrs Heather Friell.

Entrance: Non-selective. Position on the waiting list is determined by the date of registration.

Exit: At 7+ the majority of boys gain admission to Dulwich College and some to other local schools. Girls sit the entry assessments for the Dulwich Foundation and other schools.

Remarks: DUCKS takes babies at 3 months and keeps children until they leave at seven. It is housed in a splendid Victorian arts and crafts house – Eller Bank – three minutes walk from the main site and is a dream of a start to an educational life. Outside there is every kind of play on safe surfaces and exciting apparatus; inside the rooms are big and bright with good displays and absorbed, happy children working in small groups. 'Learning through play' is the watchword with the younger age groups; older children have imaginative, well-structured activities and lively teaching. French, music and PE are taught by specialists, good IT, good library, all in excellent nick. Full-time learning support in small groups.

DULWICH COLLEGE JUNIOR SCHOOL

Linked to DUCKS (Dulwich College Kindergarten and Infants School) in the Junior section
Linked to Dulwich College in the Senior section

Dulwich Common, London, SE21 7LD

Tel: 020 8693 3601
Fax: 020 8693 6319
E-mail: info@dulwich.org.uk
Website: www.dulwich.org.uk

• Pupils: all boys • Ages: 7-11 • Independent

Remarks: See Dulwich College for more information.

DULWICH COLLEGE PREPARATORY SCHOOL

42 Alleyn Park, Dulwich, London, SE21 8AT

Tel: 02086 703 217
Fax: 02087 667 586
E-mail: registrar@dcpslondon.org
Website: www.dcpslondon.org

• Pupils: 800 boys, mostly day but up to 35 weekly boarders
• Ages: 3-13 • C of E • Fees: £2,351 - £3,808; boarding £1,779 extra • Independent

---

Head: Since 1991 (and looks set to stay a good while longer), Mr George Marsh MA (sixties) – previously head of Edgarley Hall, the junior school to Millfield (qv). Has responded to increased competition from burgeoning south London prep schools by rounding the edges of DCPS. Tactful and beady-eyed and – rarer than you might think in this world – genuinely loves children and enjoys their company. Parents say that they have never heard a boy say a bad word about him.

Entrance: At 3 to the nursery, and at 4, 5, 7 (large intake) and 8. Registrar closes lists when the school is heavily oversubscribed. Informal interview for all 'to assess potential, not what they've been taught. The registration fee is £50.

Exit: Around one third to Dulwich College and to other top boarding and day schools. Scholarship class produces a regular clutch of academic and music scholarships eg to Eton, St Edward's, Winchester, Dulwich College, King's Canterbury, Westminster, Tonbridge, Marlborough.

Remarks: Maintaining its place as one of the top London prep schools. However, this is not the prep for Dulwich College as its misleading name suggests and there is no automatic transfer to that institution. Ongoing impressive building programme has provided new library, ICT suite, art rooms, classrooms and entrance hall, cheering it up no end. Set in the middle of prosperous tree-lined Dulwich, parents are mainly solid (slightly anxious?) professionals with a sprinkling of foreigners here on secondment. The grounds are large (for London) and sport is big, with boys and staff strong on main games – rugby, football and cricket, although competition for teams is stiff. Plenty of other sporting options for the less team-minded. High-quality artwork everywhere and head of art producing some inventive installations – and boys drawing for fun at lunchtimes. Science strong – very enthusiastic head of department runs lots of extra-curricular clubs eg ecology, and regularly wins national science competitions.

Over 80 per cent of boys take at least one musical instrument. Orchestra plus jazz, brass, swing bands and several choirs. English department produces an annual play that is always of an extraordinarily high standard. Games and music tours recently to South Africa, Strasbourg and Italy – regular skiing trips and language groups to France and Germany. Lots of bright, precocious types, full of ideas and used to having their opinions taken seriously – not a place for wimps or special needs cases, although pastoral care taken very seriously and one parent saying 'it's as good as it gets.' Some rumbles that only the brightest and best get to use the facilities fully and have the lion's share of the best teaching. School, deeply hurt, disputes this.

Boys divided into houses (Native American tribal names). Brightlands, the weekly boarding house, set in 5 acres of grounds, provides good practice for boys off to board at 13 – has space for 35 boys – very useful for parents who travel often. The housemaster, who teaches geography, and his wife, a year 3 teacher, have a young family. Parents run minibuses bringing in some boys from Wandsworth area and many other use buses from all over south London run by Foundation Schools' Coach Service. Virtually all boys stay to 13.

DULWICH HAMLET JUNIOR SCHOOL

Dulwich Village, London, SE21 7AL

Tel: 020 7525 9188
Fax: 020 7525 9187
E-mail: office@dulwichhamlet.southwark.sch.uk
Website: www.dulwichhamlet.southwark.sch.uk

• Pupils: 370 boys and girls, all day • Ages: 7-11 • Non-denom
• State

Head: Since 1993, Ms Diana Bell Cert Ed (fifties), educated at Rochester Grammar and Furzedown College of Education. Previously head of Eardly Juniors and deputy head of St John's Angell Town. Ms Bell has worked in primary education all her professional life, dedicated to developing 'well rounded pupils who understand there are certain choices for them in life'. Encourages continuous professional development for all staff including vocational or academic sabbaticals from school. Hugely energetic, committed and extremely highly thought of by staff and parents. 'An absolutely cracking good head,' says a fan.

Entrance: Priority is given to those who apply by the 30th March deadline, statemented children, siblings and those who live closest to the school. Pupils come from many local primaries particularly Dulwich Village Infants. Always oversubscribed.

Exit: At 11, most to the state sector: The Charter, Newstead Wood, St Olave's, a few to local independent schools. Has won music and academic scholarships to James Allen, Dulwich College and Sydenham High School.

Remarks: One of Southwark's most sought-after primary schools. A spacious site accommodates several different Victorian and modern buildings skillfully blended and connected. Boasts a new library with a super silk wallhanging by pupils.

Rigorous and inspiring academic curriculum. Classrooms well-resourced and attractive, interactive whiteboards gradually being introduced. Class sizes the standard (for state schools) 30. Setting for year 5 in maths and year 6 in both maths and literacy. French for years 5 and 6. Specially trained team of teachers run an effective SEN provision; links with speech, occupational and drama therapists for children needing specialist help. ESOL also available.

A host of musical opportunities. Nearly all pupils learn

an instrument and music lessons are part of the curriculum for everyone. A most impressive range of instruments from all over the world. The arts are interwoven into the curriculum, and there's a variety of dance and drama projects. Link with the Globe Theatre, with actors coming into the school. Uses local sports facilities – swimmers awarded best state school in the borough, athletes represented Dulwich in local athletics finals. Young cricketers being coached by members of the Surrey cricket club. Lots of after-school clubs and trips.

Peer mediation program: children trained to become mediators, learn to resolve problems without always relying on an adult to intervene. Cheerful, motivated and responsible pupils are from a wide multi-ethnic and social background, supported by committed and innovative staff of all age groups. Refreshingly friendly office staff, efficient administration. Parents are asked for a small voluntary contribution each term to help support the many activities that supplement curriculum. 'No stone is left unturned here,' say parents proudly.

The only primary school in London this year to be awarded Training School status, entitling the school to extra funding for the training of new teachers and their own staff.

DULWICH PREPARATORY SCHOOL

Coursehorn, Cranbrook, Kent, TN17 3NP

Tel: 01580 712 179
Fax: 01580 715 322
E-mail: registrar@dcpskent.org
Website: www.dcpslondon.org

• Pupils: pupils, 50:50 boys and girls. Mainly day with some (up to 70) weekly and occasional boarding • Ages: 3-13 • Broadly Christian but all denominations welcome • Fees: Reception & Year 1 £2,335. Lower School £3,088. Upper School £3,612. Weekly boarders £5,281 • Independent

Head: Since 2004, Mr Stephen Rigby (early fifties). Educated at Rugby and University of London, has taught in both the maintained and independent sectors. Previously headmaster of Westbourne House for 14 years. Married to Frances, a qualified and experienced teacher; they work closely as a team and have five children between them. Very open and friendly. Teaches Latin and PSHE and is very much in evidence around the school.

Entrance: On a first come first served basis with the only priority being given to siblings. Non competitive assessment tests from age 7+ – it is very rare for a child to fail but school don't want to take someone who can't cope. Intakes in Nursery, Reception, years 3 and 5 (and anywhere else in between if there is a space). Another intake in year 7 when some children leave for the grammar schools and others come from local primary schools to prepare for Cranbrook entrance at 13+.

Exit: Up to half to Cranbrook at 13+. About 10 or 11 per year (of 72) move on to the grammars at 11+ and the school will prepare the children for these exams. Other than those routes, the most popular schools are Tonbridge, King's Canterbury, Sevenoaks, Sutton Valence, Eastbourne, St Leonard's Mayfield and Bethany with a few going further afield to eg Charterhouse, Bedales and Winchester. Variety of scholarships each year ranging from major academic awards to Tonbridge, King's Canterbury and Cranbrook to art, design technology, sport and music scholarships; 30 scholarships in all in 2005.

Remarks: Evacuated from London to Cranbrook in 1939, the school began life as a series of huts. These are long gone and have been replaced over the years by modern buildings. In spite of the historical links, the school is quite separate from Dulwich College, London.

Set in 50 acres of grounds, playing fields etc: has a campus feel to it. Divided into three self-contained sections: Nash House (3-6 year olds), Lower School (6-9 year olds) an Upper School (9-13 year olds). All children from the age of 6 are split into four Tribes: Chippeways, Deerfeet, Mohicans and Ojibwas (seriously non-PC in a decade when US sports team are being persecuted for using 'Native American' names) – lots of inter-house competitions. Whole school has a theme for each term eg 'Look Smart be Smart'.

Nash House is set away from the main school in its own building, all very up to date with interactive whiteboards; climbing frames and sandpit outside. Open door for parents to come in and see how their children are learning. Great emphasis on building children's social confidence; they are encouraged to stand up in front of an audience on a regular basis, whether it be relating their news in Assembly, taking part in form plays or participating in class 'Showing Times' when parents come into the school to hear what the children have been doing (shades of Calvin & Hobbes). Music and PE taught by specialist teachers, a member of the special needs department teaches any children who need extra help. Structured but relaxed atmosphere. Lots of theme days. Every child has work on the wall. Wonderful music. Lower School has specialist teachers for science (taught in a lab), music, PE and French. Classrooms very colourful with children's work all over the walls. Each classroom has its own computer linked to a network system + an IT suite and set of laptops for classroom use. Well used library with its own librarian. Outings, talks and workshop days a major part of the curriculum particularly in history and geography. Upper School feels more like a public school than a prep school – superb facilities. Children are (where possible) set for academic subjects (but not streamed) and there is a separate scholarship form in the final year. The average class size is 18 with a maximum of 20. IT top notch: all class rooms have interactive whiteboards, overhead digital projectors and video-recorders and monitors; separate computer room with 24 computers plus computers in every classroom. Much use of the internet. Education outings a major feature of school life and include theatre trips, visits to sites of historical interest. Geography field study trips, visits to France and an adventure training week for the final year pupils after their exams.Fantastic library – masses of books, and computers linked to network. Authors visits every term. Twice-yearly book fairs. Library competitions. Audio tapes in library for those not so keen on reading.About 20 per cent of children have some sort of learning support individually and in small groups – no extra charge. Provision for the physically disabled, one or two statemented children.Older pupils choose a member of staff to keep an eye on their academic progress and general well being. Strong anti-bullying policy – school intranet can be used for children to email worries in confidence. Democratic structure – no prefects or head boy or girl. Every leaver is a 'senior' with a specific area of responsibility.Regular parents' evenings. A curriculum summary is provided for parents so that they can see the work being done by their child's year group. Each term parents are invited to attend a Subject Evening at which they can sample the lessons given to their children.Strong musical tradition. All children can read music by the time they leave Nash House age 5/6. Separate music department with a director and three full-time music specialists. All children have two or three class music lessons a week. About 280 learn an instrument – 19 peripatetic teachers. Over 15 extracurricular groups including an orchestra, two wind bands, six choirs, a jazz band, pop groups plus a number of smaller chamber groups. Small informal concerts two or three times a term after school and more formal evening concerts twice a year. Lots of music exams + children take part in music tours in Italy, Germany, Holland, Paris and Austria.Drama incorporated into weekly timetable. Drama clubs for the enthusiasts and children can take the English Speaking Board examinations each year. Each section of the school produces plays annually. Wonderful John Leakey Hall with fixed seating which can be moved electronically. Art clubs held after school plus extra tuition for those taking art scholarships (usually win a couple of these each year). Lots of artwork displayed around the school.Strong tradition of cross country running for both boys and girls. All the usual sports, with teams in most: as many children as possible are included – up to four teams per age group and the school tries to have an inter-school or 'Tribe' fixture every week for each age group. Opportunities to have trials for, and play for Kent teams. Good sports facilities.Boarding boys at The Lodge and girls at The Manor. School very accommodating (when they have room) if parents need to go away for a few days or on holiday. School day for boarders ends at the same time as it ends for day children and the boarding houses are very much 'homes from home'.Parents include lots of local business people and farmers as well as City commuters and most children live within about 15 miles of the school. Saturday school for top two years – those not in matches go home at lunchtime.Just about everything you could possibly want here – its size means that the facilities are superb. Some parents who avoid it say children can get lost in the system but, as one parent put it, most children are very happy and do well here but it particularly suits those who are up front, determined and capable.

DUNHURST (BEDALES JUNIOR SCHOOL)

Linked to Bedales School in the Senior section

Petersfield, Hampshire, GU32 2DP

Tel: 01730 300 200
Fax: 01730 300 600
E-mail: jjarman@bedales.org.uk
Website: www.bedales.org.uk

• Pupils: 186 boys and girls in Dunhurst; 41 board; 90 in preprep Dunannie • Ages: 8-13; pre-prep (Dunannie) 3-8 • Fees: Dunhurst: boarding, £6,040; day £5,392. Dunannie: £1,049 - £2,213 • Independent • Open days: Five each year

Head: Since 2004, Ms Penny Fryer (early fifties) previously deputy head at Bedales. Read English at Cardiff University and was head of English at Latymer Upper School and then senior mistress at Whitgift before moving to Bedales. Well-liked, trusted, practical, hands-on, a good organiser – in short a soothing presence after years of turmoil. 'Has managed to get the school back into good working order,' said a father who has been involved with Dunhurst for many years. Is restoring confidence in the school both among parents and staff. Extremely good news.

Head of Dunannie: Since 1987, Miss Sarah Webster (fifties), Froebel trained, MA in psychology from Colorado University. Came here from the Unicorn School in Kew. Likes sailing (sailed from Venezuela to Guatemala during a recent sabbatical), music and travel. Top-class professional, has thought everything out from top to bottom. Dedicated to the school which is very much her own creation, and idolised by parents. We have previously reported that she is scheduled to retire in 2007 but this is far from certain according to Bedales and to her.

Entrance: For entry to Dunhurst children come for a 24 or 48 hour assessment, spending a night or two and getting to know the school. As much an opportunity for the school to sell itself as for the children to be tested and most who come along have a grand time. Entry at 8 but also a large wodge comes in at 11 as a run-in to Bedales. Virtually all pupils are British with a few overseas Brits and one or two foreigners (no ESL provision). 30 pupils with learning difficulties (mild dyslexia). Numbers coming back up under new regime. Dunannie: at age 3, first come first served admission. Older children must spend a trial day at the school for an informal assessment. Dunannie oversubscribed with enormous waiting lists. Since September 2005, the school has run two year 3 classes.

Exit: Almost totally geared to sending pupils to Bedales and almost all will go there. NB Dunhurst pupils must now reach same standards for entry to Bedales as outside applicants and must take the same exams – the perceived (by Bedales management) quality of the pupils coming through to Bedales has been one of the main causes of the breakdown in the (previously pretty independent) relationship between the two schools. About 5 per cent of pupils choose other public school destinations and are prepared accordingly, but Dunhurst does not follow CE curriculum, no formal CE practice, external scholarship mocks etc. Most years one or two do go elsewhere – sometimes to famously academic schools. From Dunannie, majority now going on to Dunhurst again. The rest to Twyford, Pilgrim's, Westbourne House, Highfield.

Remarks: As we pointed out in the last two editions, Dunhurst badly needed to get a grip and we are delighted to report that, at last, it seems that the grip has been got. For years now, heads here have been toppling like skittles at a fun-fair. The instability was lately compounded by dissent over the governors' efforts to eliminate Dunhurst and create

a kind of bber-Dunannie for 3-11 year olds. This issue is now 'dead in the water' and the school will continue in its long-standing form, as a prep school for 8-13 year olds. New head Penny Fryer has told us she is 'not going anywhere.' And we believe her. Parents we spoke to (and who sought us out – mums and dads here are not known for keeping their views under a barrel) were grateful for her steady hand on the tiller. And anyway, after last year's turmoil, no one has the stomach to make trouble just now.

Dunhurst is populated mainly by children of parents seeking to avoid the traditional academic straightjacket that they endured as children – 'it's where I wish I'd gone as a boy,' said one. Pupils include cheerful normal kids plus oddballs, youngsters fleeing bullying at previous schools, the super-confident, the rebellious – all happy here, at least when the school is running well. Most come across as extremely at ease with adults (all of whom they call by their first names, including all teachers and the headmaster). No uniform. Boys lope through the hallways in backward baseball caps. Teachers mostly 'so cool', say pupils. French enthusiastically well taught in the 'French barn' – a charming outbuilding. Latin available as an option. Spanish for all (except those who would really struggle if they had to learn a second language) in year 8. Science lab refurbished (2002). Excellent IT provision. Setting in maths and French in year 8. In the first three years, lessons finish at 4.30, but 6pm thereafter. Dunhurst has a unique timetable in which 'prep' is integrated into the school day in non-teaching periods. Pupils' academic commitments are therefore completed by 6pm, leaving the evenings free for a vast range of extra-curricular activities for both boarding and day pupils.

Music a big deal here. Music school well kitted out with zillions of practice rooms and 90 per cent of children play a musical instrument. There is an annual musical or opera and pupils take part in local music festivals. Art also superb with astonishingly accomplished work produced. Lovely pottery and textiles including tie-dye, batik and weaving. Imaginative events like 'Aztec workshop day' combine variety of art forms. Arts and language trip to Barcelona (Gaudi, Picasso, Dali) in 2003, and an exchange with an Indian school in the foothills of the Himalayas. DT, known as 'workshop', produces lovely stuff, including exquisite stained glass. Sport not worshipped to put it mildly, but some teams and individual children have accomplished great things. Rugby popular. The non-competitive atmosphere means that it is quite easy to get into teams. Uses Bedales' pool, games pitches, sports hall and Astro. Good hall/gym with stage (Bedales' theatre used for most dramatic performances). Boarding numbers recovering: re-opening the Junior

Wing boarding house as from September 2006. Dorms pleasant and mostly three to a room, all refurbished in 2002/03. Walls are a free-for-all: posters up when we were there read 'Oh shit!' and 'Queen of the Bitches' – not standard prep school decoration. In their last two years pupils may sign out in groups of four or more to go to Petersfield – 'to buy tuck!' said a boy. Relationships among pupils and between pupils and adults are genuinely impressive – kind, thoughtful and full of respect.

Dunannie is a joyous tour de force, with academic fare served up alongside hefty dollops of creativity, music, art and sport. More discipline and order than is traditional at Dunhurst – has to be that way at this age. Lots of parent involvement and Bedalians come down to help with gardening (each class has its own) and to perform in weekly music concerts. Learning support teacher for children with special needs. Lots of fresh air and outdoor activity in lovely play area. 'Leavers' spend five days on an organic farm in Dorset and, although there is no school uniform, children must have wellies, tractor suits and windbreakers. Much emphasis on music with individual lessons and recorder and string groups offered in addition to class music lessons. Physically, the school is a colourful wonderland with beautiful classrooms. Huge, airy central open space serves as a library, and is used for 'circle time', assembly, music and drama lessons. New ICT room (2005). Well-laid-out children's work on every wall – much of it done on computers. Part-time PE instructor teaches games, swimming and gymnastics, taking advantage of Dunhurst and Bedales facilities.

DURHAM HIGH SCHOOL FOR GIRLS JUNIOR SCHOOL

Linked to Durham High School for Girls in the Senior section

Farewell Hall, Durham, County Durham, DH1 3TB

Tel: 0191 384 3226
Fax: 0191 386 7381
E-mail: headmistress@dhsfg.org.uk
Website: www.dhsfg.org.uk

• Pupils: girls; all day • Ages: 3 - 11 • Accepts all faiths and none
• Fees: Infants/Juniors £1,770 - £1,900 • Independent

Remarks: For further information see senior school entry.

EATON HOUSE BELGRAVIA

Linked to Eaton House The Vale in the Junior section
Linked to Eaton House The Manor School in the Junior section

3-5 Eaton Gate, Eaton Square, London, SW1W 9BA

Tel: 020 7730 9343
Fax: 020 7730 1798
E-mail: admin@eatonhouseschools.com
Website: www.eatonhouseschools.com

• Pupils: 230 boys, all day • Ages: 4-8 • Non-denom
• Fees: £3,050 • Independent • Open days: Tour with head for parents one or two terms before son joins

Head: Since 1998, the energetic and enthusiastic Miss Lucy Watts (thirties) previously taught at a co-ed Montessori Prep school before moving to Eaton House Belgravia in 1990. Joined as a class teacher, then head of science and deputy head before working her way up to lead the school. She does just that – providing calm, considered and efficient leadership coupled with a sense of fun. Feels strongly that the Eaton House Group of Schools is an inclusive family – pupils, peripatetic and admin staff, cooks and teachers – which is caring and hardworking, with good manners. Very keen on upholding tradition while innovating; open to new suggestions from parents and staff (eg staggered leaving times for seniors and juniors to avoid congestion on stairs) but will weigh pros and cons carefully before implementing. Committed (four God children through friendships formed at Eaton House) and full of good ideas (seniors discuss daily headlines in current affairs group for 15 minutes while lunch queue dies down). Covers absences and currently teaches handwriting to the little ones, maths to the year 3s.

Entrance: Preference for siblings, children of staff, ex-staff and old boys, otherwise first come first served. With a waiting list – most parents put names down at birth. £40 for definite registration, £20 to go on the waiting list. Deposit of term's fees, two terms before pupil starts – credited in full against final term's fees.

Exit: Top London day schools are most popular (85 per cent of leavers): Westminster Under, Colet Court, Westminster Cathedral Choir, Eaton House The Manor, Sussex House. Also boarding schools: Summer Fields, The Dragon, Ludgrove. Westminster Cathedral Choir and Eaton House The Manor run specific open days for this school, also good relationships with heads of feeder preps for Eton, Radley etc.

Remarks: Cheerful, hardworking, well principled pre-prep, with delight in learning obvious as you walk in the door and are faced by a display of photographs documenting the worldwide travels of Percy the school bear. Only two and half buildings just off Sloane Square mean that the school is vertical rather than horizontal (lift available), but colourful art and awards cover all the available wall space. No outside space, so boys are bussed to Hyde or Battersea Park every afternoon to let off energy/play sport, or to the Queen Mother Sports Centre to swim – all made aware of the school sports motto 'Win with grace, lose with dignity'. Inter house competitions encourage 'friendly rivalry'. Indoor hockey, football, cricket and climbing take place in a hall which is also used for assemblies – the whole school troops in daily with the head boy and deputy holding the door open politely!

Manners are taught early here, with prizes for a tidy class, smart pupil and a 'visitor's boy' in each form shakes the hand of any stranger who enters the door...Each pupil is taught peer responsibility, every senior who is not a head of house/monitor has mentor duties for a younger boy. Usual curriculum with great science lab, drama, French and IT – while not neglecting handwriting skills. Class exams get children used to formal tests each term and termly written reports back up more informal contact with class teachers (available in their forms for parents at the beginning of every day). No formal PTA but each class hosts information evening every September and a Christmas newsletter is sent out as well at the annual issue of The Column (covers all the Eaton House Group of Schools news).

Head provides extended help to parents – these are largely local and bankers, lawyers and MPs – when choosing next school. Most parents are confident of their sons' long term prospects and see the future involving schools such as Eton or Radley and then perhaps Harvard. Eaton House is part of the Boys School Coalition whose other members are chiefly from the US and Australia. Exchanges with NY schools particularly popular. Approximately 30 per cent of the boys have one non-British parent but on the whole these boys stay through the school; less transient than neighbouring pre-preps.

Lunch is served in two sittings in the basement, small rooms but a choice of healthy, fresh food daily. The three music rooms are also below street level; an experienced and long lasting part-time music staff teaches the boys piano, violin, guitar, recorder, voice and cello. Performances in assemblies and choirs outside school encourage confidence.

School trips take advantage of all that London has to offer and extracurricular clubs are popular, karate especially.

Guest speakers also visit; the local vicar (St Peters), local policeman, charities and parent volunteers.

'Since we are non-selective we need a good team' and SEN is particularly well supported here – this has been a tradition for Eaton House ever since dyslexia was called 'word blindness'. There is a family feel about this school, each individual, pupil or staff is cared for – encouraged by the Harper family (principals of the Eaton House Group) who began their association when Mrs Harper was a teacher at the school in the 1960s. In the past this pre-prep has been referred to as an academic hot house but there is no doubt that the boys are enjoying themselves enormously as they learn. 'An 'us' school in a 'me' area,' comments a parent. The boys are exuberant – it is the responsibility of both parents and staff to make sure their confidence does not stray into arrogance outside the school door!

EATON HOUSE THE MANOR SCHOOL

Linked to Eaton House The Vale in the Junior section
Linked to Eaton House Belgravia in the Junior section

The Manor House, 58 Clapham Common Northside, London, SW4 9RU

Tel: 020 7924 6000
Fax: 020 7924 1530
E-mail: admin@eatonhouseschools.com
Website: www.eatonhouseschools.com

- Pupils: Prep 200, pre-prep 240, nursery 80; all day • Ages: Prep: 8 -13, pre-prep 4 - 8, nursery 2.5 to 4.5 • Non-denom
- Fees: Prep: £3,680; pre-prep £3,050; nursery: £645-2,060
- Independent • Open days: Annually October/November

Head: Prep: Since 1993, Mr Sebastian Hepher BEd (Hons)(early forties), previously taught at Eaton House near Sloane Square and has taught in both state and private senior schools. Gentle, straightforward, enthusiastic, married with four young children. Keen reader. The Hephers have a house in the south west of France, which they go to 'whenever we can.'

Pre-prep: Since 2001, Mrs Sarah Segrave BA(Ed) MA (early thirties); has taught at the school since 1993.

Nursery: Since 2004 Miss Roosha Clement-Sawle (late twenties).

Entrance: Put names down early (at birth for the nursery) – entry at 4 on a first-come first-served basis. At 7 or 8 by assessment (English and maths are what matter) and school report. No automatic entry from the school's own pre-prep but most go through. Scholarships for 8 year olds in academic, music, sport, art and design and for all rounders.

Exit: At 8 over three quarters move to the prep, the remainder boarding at Ludgrove, Summer Fields, Sunningdale, Windlesham, Cothill and the Dragon. At 13 50 per cent move to day schools and 50 per cent to boarding via CE or scholarship routes – Westminster, St Paul's, Dulwich, City of London; Winchester, Radley, Eton, Harrow and Marlborough.

Remarks: Younger brother school of the older established (1857) Eaton House School Belgravia near Sloane Square (pre-prep only, for boys ages 4-8): boys at the Eaton House schools wear the same holly green and red uniform. Mrs Harper is the principal at both these schools (also Eaton House The Vale, in Elvaston Place is part of their group). Eaton House The Manor schools were set up in 1993 and quickly established themselves. A popular first-choice school, well run and happy, with prep, pre-prep and super nursery school all on site. Distinguished main Georgian house, with Victorian additions plus newly purpose- built block behind, with attractive courtyard. Previously part of South Bank Polytechnic (ie lots of teaching devices already in place) and before that a prep school. Acres of green with Clapham Park just across the road. Children mainly from Wandsworth, Clapham, Stockwell; the school runs a bus service to/from Eaton Gate, another from Parsons Green.

Pre-prep uses the same excellent teaching methods as its older brother school across the Thames – ie children are taught in small groups within the class according to their ability (which is mixed). Pre-prep and nursery (both super) are round at the back of the school, the latter smelling deliciously of baking the day we visited).

At 8, boys are put into sets for English and maths, two parallel classes per year group, Latin for all at 8, specialist subject staff from first year in prep. Small special needs department. Lots of male teachers, average age of staff 35 (several with public school teaching experience). Thorough teaching throughout, big emphasis on reading. Supervised homework option from 4 till 5 pm every day. Light bright classrooms, and good equipment, big gym, theatre. Keen games. Busy extra-curricular programme, with lots of clubs (including air rifle shooting) – this is a work hard, play hard school. Boys appear industrious and cheerful and not over-pressurised – but it is a competitive place. House system, cups galore. Plenty of parental involvement. Popular with parents – 'just the right balance of tradition and spark' according to a father.

EATON HOUSE THE VALE

Linked to Eaton House Belgravia in the Junior section
Linked to Eaton House The Manor School in the Junior section

2 Elvaston Place, London, SW7 5QH

Tel: 020 7584 9515
Fax: 020 7584 8368
E-mail: eatonhse@aol.com
Website: www.eatonhouseschools.com

• Pupils: 60 girls, 40 boys; all day • Ages: 4-11 • Non-denom
• Fees: £3,050 • Independent

Head: Since 1987, Ms Susie Calder CertEd (geography) (early fifties), educated at Putney High School. Miss Calder worked as a teacher at Eaton House before becoming head at the Vale. A calm friendly person who shares her office with the school mascot Angus, a long-haired dachshund. Just the sort of person you would want to entrust your child to.

Entrance: At 4 non-selective first come first served basis. At 8 entry (mainly girls) and occasional places, pupils come for an informal assessment day.

Exit: Boys at 8 go to Sussex House, Colet Court, Westminster Under or Cathedral School. Some to boarding schools. Girls at 11 to all the major London day schools or boarding – Woldingham, Westonbirt, Tudor Hall, St Mary's Calne are popular choices. Some scholarships.

Remarks: Small traditional school with an emphasis on the abilities and talents of each individual, class sizes reflect this. Part of the Eaton House Group of Schools. Accommodated in a large six-storey town house just off Gloucester Road, some of the older children's classrooms are on the small side; well-stocked library, science lab and an ITC room. The staff are committed and mostly long-serving, good mixture of age groups and experience. Classes are mixed ability, no streaming; the curriculum is 'all good solid stuff' commented one parent, along with interesting projects and a range of outings, the premises being ideally located for easy access to all the London museums and galleries. There is no playground – for morning break each class goes for a short walk followed by snack time in the hall, where pupils are encouraged to interact with other age groups. After lunch, pupils are taken to Kensington Gardens for playtime. Lunches are home cooked by a long-serving cook, unanimous vote from pupils was ' pretty yummy!' Interesting drama and music – Miss Calder is keen on children developing self-confidence and learning through drama. Varied choice of individual instruments and music lessons. Regular plays and concerts are performed at nearby Baden-Powell House. Sports in either Kensington or Battersea Parks, swimming and gym also on offer. From 7, pupils are taken on multi-activity weeks so they can try their hands at canoeing, abseiling, raft building and the like. After-school clubs include dance, art and touch-typing – becoming a must for today's generation. Homework club four nights a week.

Sympathetic approach to minor SEN difficulties, individual help can be arranged and children who need to can use a laptop. The school is not able to cope with more severe difficulties.

Active parents' group – many live within walking distance of the school – who run the library, listen to readers and fund-raise for the school and charities. Whilst not for the really rumbustious, the Vale provides a happy learning environment for most.

Ebor School

Rawcliffe Lane, York, North Yorkshire, YO30 6NP

Tel: 01904 655021
Fax: 01904 651666
Website: www.bootham.york.sch.uk

- Pupils: 130 girls and boys; some boarders • Ages: 3-11
- Independent

Remarks: for further information, see senior school: Bootham School.

Ecole André Malraux

Linked to Ecole Charles de Gaulle - Wix in the Junior section
Linked to Lycée Français Charles de Gaulle in the Senior section
Linked to Lycée Français Charles de Gaulle Primary in the Junior section

44 Laurie Road, Hanwell, London, W7 1BL

Tel: 020 8578 3011
Fax: 020 8575 0191
E-mail: secretaire@ecoleamalraux.org.uk
Website: www.ecoleamalraux.org.uk

- Pupils: 260 girls and boys; all day • Ages: 7-13 • Independent

Remarks: For further information see senior school, Lycee Français Charles de Gaulle.

Ecole Charles de Gaulle - Wix

Linked to Ecole André Malraux in the Junior section
Linked to Lycée Français Charles de Gaulle Primary in the Junior section
Linked to Lycée Français Charles de Gaulle in the Senior section

Wix's Lane, Clapham Common North Side, London, SW4 0AJ

Tel: 020 7738 0287
Fax: 020 7223 9128
E-mail: directeur@ecolewix.org.uk
Website: www.lyceefrancais.org.uk

- Pupils: boys and girls, all day • Ages: 7-13 • Independent

Remarks: See senior school.

Edgbaston High School for Girls Preparatory Dept

Linked to Edgbaston High School for Girls in the Senior section

Westbourne Road, Edgbaston, Birmingham, West Midlands, B15 3TS

Tel: 0121 454 2401
E-mail: prep@edgbaston.bham.sch.uk
Website: www.edgbastonhigh.bham.sch.uk

- Pupils: 455 girls; all day • Ages: 3-11 • Independent

Remarks: For further details, see senior school entry.

EDGE GROVE PREPARATORY SCHOOL

Aldenham, Aldenham Village, Hertfordshire, WD25 8NL

Tel: 01923 855 724
Fax: 01923 859 920
E-mail: admissions@edgegrove.indschools.co.uk
Website: www.edgegrove.co.uk

• Pupils: 243 boys and 109 girls; 60 board, the rest day • Ages: 3-13 • C of E • Fees: Pre-prep £1,220 - £2,225. Prep: day £3,040- £3,650; boarding £4,065 - £4,975. Casual boarding £29 per night • Independent • Open days: Oct/Feb/June

Headmaster: Since 2002, Mr Michael Wilson BSc (early forties). Setting about turning this beautiful school into a top-flight co-ed prep. He and his highly capable wife, Carolyn, a SEN specialist, make a dedicated team, clearly fired by the potential of the site, the buildings, grounds and the position – in the country but just outside London. Not driven by lists or leagues but by the possibility of offering the best to each child.

Three boys – one still at the school, two now moved on to Haileybury. Mr Wilson, brought up in Kenya and with experience of schools there, in Thailand as well as over here, wants to create, as he says, an African school in England, by which he means a place of excellence across the board, a total curriculum with academics at its heart and a twenty four hour culture of creative involvement and enjoyment. Judging by the absorbed and relaxed faces we saw, this is already happening.

Entrance: Interviews for children from 3+ along with parents, plus assessment over a day's visit via games and lessons and general observation. Later via tests in English, maths, reasoning, plus interviews. School not aiming to cream off the brightest, 'I want the range,' says head and looks as much for character, personality and the capacity to make the most of what school offers as for academic potential. While not a school with an SEN specialism, school does well by such children and is unashamedly mixed ability. Now very oversubscribed at bottom end.

Exit: Not a place where children will be hot-housed to leave at 7 for some more glitzy establishment. You're in for the whole ride here. A proportion of girls leave at 11 for St Albans Girls School, Haberdashers, Abbots Hill, Queenswood, St Margaret's, Watford Girls' Grammar, The Mount and other good local schools. Boys stay until 13 with

a few leaving at 11. Day pupils go on to St Albans, Merchant Taylor's, Mill Hill, Aldenham, Haberdashers', Watford Boys' Grammar or Queen Elizabeth's, Barnet and boarders make for Harrow, Haileybury, Eton, Sherborne, Uppingham, Oundle, Canford and Rugby among many others. 2005 saw scholarships being awarded to 22 of the 42 leavers, including a King's Scholarship to Eton. The pupils were heading for 19 schools and head works assiduously – visiting schools and chatting with heads – to make links with senior schools everywhere. A head who will take great care in placing your child.

Remarks: Just inside the M25, minutes from junction 5 on the M1, you're on a country estate with a delicious 1751 house at its centre, walled gardens (one with heated pool), plentiful playing fields, flower beds, lake, woods, neighbourly cows. There are twenty-five acres here – only fifteen miles from the centre of London – and it's a bit of a miracle. You arrive down a short drive through fields, just past the pretty village of Aldenham. A quiet, tree-studded, safe-feeling school. Formerly the home of JP Morgan, the house is a gem, magical trails of wisteria hanging over the main entrance porch. Three boys were happily and co-operatively playing croquet on the inviting lawn when we arrived. Wonderful entrance hall – all wood panels, stucco ceiling, glass dome and civilised furnishings – 'you put up your own pictures and nobody breaks anything,' says head – houses admin offices. Onsite pre-prep is Hart House – one storey modern block – bright and cheery with spacious, well-organised rooms and good facilities.

Edge Grove became a school in 1935. Boys only until 1997, it is now co-ed and takes children from 3 – thus has recently expanded rapidly. Still 3:1 boys:girls. Mixed ability classes for 7-9 year-olds but streamed thereafter – though in a flexible structure. Saturday morning school gradually receding – no longer compulsory for 7-10 year-olds – and now consists of activities for 7-10's and mix of activities and lessons for the older ones. Day goes on until 5.00pm. Day pupils may opt to stay until 5.45pm if they wish to complete their prep at school – useful for two working parents. New head immediately set about huge updating and upgrading programme – curriculum, buildings, resources, grounds. 'I was brought up in East Africa where you have to move quickly or someone runs over you!'

Curriculum now runs on a streamlined 'whole school' system. Much done but far more still to be done as part of ambitious ten-year plan. Catchment area suggests no lack of available funds – some of country's richest send their offspring here. So, while some lessons still in upmarket portakabin, changes already in train mean that much of school's teaching accommodation will be new-build or seamless extension in five years time. SENs well identified and then exceptionally well catered for under Mrs Ryder and Mrs Wilson's eye. Carefully structured and graded individual programmes plus in-class support. In 2004/5, 43 pupils having varying levels of support. Extra maths and English given instead of Latin where appropriate. Charges for one-to-one and some small group work additional to fees. Aiming to 'support the less able and stretch the most able', school also has an ABCo – ie teacher extending the range of the brightest. Policy of employing both SENCO and ABCo widely in the school to meet needs everywhere. Head takes particular pleasure in 2005 drama, music, sport and all-rounder scholarships won by pupils in every stream – 'that's what I'm after'. Overall, impressive 63 scholarships to senior schools won in 2000-2005, including – why not say it again? – a King's Scholarship to Eton – third in four years. EAL link with Mill Hill school supports few who need it.

Boarding expanding rapidly. Accommodation, though glamorous in wood-panelled, beautiful rooms, is overcrowded by modern standards and, though well furnished with sofas and books, is not homely. Necessary changes imminent and plans have been submitted. New extensions and rearrangements will mean fewer boarders in lovely, main house, rooms with views and space. Carpet everywhere. Super, reassuring housemistress in relaxed, though secure-feeling, environment. Boarders increasingly from Services families, many based at Northwood but also from everywhere overseas – Hong Kong, Korea, Cyprus etc. Weekly boarding increasingly popular and available. Walkabout phone available so that parents can be carried to children. Good pastoral care throughout in this happy, relaxed and civilised community.

Rapid improvements in teaching accommodation. Average class size 16. Greek taught to scholars. ICT was updated in 2005 and now consists of two fixed labs with wireless technology throughout the school to support a mobile laptop trolley with 20 units. Art among the best anywhere with extraordinarily sophisticated, careful yet free and creative work in many media – most notably in ceramics. (The Indian slippers in painted clay are alone worth a visit!) Drawing to a staggeringly high standard. Visits to galleries, an annual resident artist – all helps but this is seriously good stuff. Good, bright classrooms, good displays for the most part. A gorgeous library in main house – may become a common room which would be a sensible change. Music very strong – 90 per cent learn an instrument – loads of bands, ensembles. Twenty-five plus sports, excellent sports hall – school does well in competitions and sends repre-

sentatives to local and national sides. Head is an ex-Davis cup coach. Cubs, scouts, beavers etc etc etc.

THE EDINBURGH ACADEMY JUNIOR SCHOOL

Linked to Edinburgh Academy (The) in the Senior section

10 Arboretum Road, Edinburgh, EH3 5PL

Tel: 0131 552 3690
Fax: 0131 551 2660
E-mail: juniorschool@edinburghacademy.org.uk
Website: www.edinburghacademy.org.uk

- Pupils: Prep school 305 boys; nursery 50 boys and 1 girl
- Ages: prep 5-11, nursery 3-5 • Non-denom • Fees: Geits (top of Junior school – but based in senior school) £2,150 Junior school £1,950 - £1,440; nursery £1,350 full time, £626 - £1,565 (2+) • Independent

Head: Since 2003, Mrs Caroline Bashford BA PGCE (forties) who was educated at St Leonard's, did modern languages at Edinburgh University and her PGCE in Portsmouth. She taught in the state sector in the south for a year before returning to Scotland, where she taught at St Margaret's, did five years at Stewarts Melville and Mary Erskine, and became senior depute at Heriot's. She is the first female head of this prestigious boys' prep, and comes to the place after a particularly upsetting – though mercifully brief – interregnum. Buzzy and fun, she teaches eight periods of health education across the board, and French to nine- and ten-year-olds. Keen on keeping old-fashioned traditions but translating them into modern teaching methods. 'Thinking skills important'. 'Still very much the new girl on the block' – has changed the management structure, and now has her own deputy. Says 'staff are very loyal' – also young with attractive girls as well as macho males around. But 'it has been quite a challenge since I have been here … sorting it out'. 'Honeymoon period'. 'Supportive parents'. Mrs Bashford is married to a doctor, with three grown-up children, with a strong marketing (schools) background, and boundless enthusiasm; this is a prep school on a roll.

Remarks: Junior school incorporates busy and popular nursery with early birds' breakfast club for all; school open from 8.00 am, and after-school club till 6.00 pm. Head keen to encourage clubs of the non-sporting variety: drama, chess, bridge 'on the horizon'. Various holiday clubs, mostly based at the sports centre. Girls in nursery, but only boys from five. Huge dining hall, with 'proper lunches for all'; staff can cater for any kind of diet and no packed lunches allowed.

Forbidding, perfectly frightful concrete building, with massive modern extensions and charming Denham Green (pre-prep) area for tinies. Computers everywhere. No Latin. Max class size 24. Parallel classes throughout; though setted for maths at eight. School buzzes with energy and enthusiasm despite its utilitarian layout (could be any sixties state school anywhere). Art room gratifyingly exciting, and art all over the place; Ambitious music and plays, lots of games and sports hall; both on site. Junior school, in general, very good, the old gang have more or less gone, and a new influx of whizzy young teachers gladden the eye. Support for learning in place, though not yet team teaching. As in senior school, small ethnic minority, Chinese and Indian pupils put all others to shame with their work ethic.

EDINBURGH RUDOLF STEINER LOWER SCHOOL

Linked to Edinburgh Rudolf Steiner School in the Senior section

60 Spylaw Road, Edinburgh, EH10 5BR

Tel: 01313 373 410
Fax: 01315 386 066
E-mail: bursar@steinerweb.org.uk

• Pupils: girls and boys; all day • Ages: Kindergarten 3.5 - 6yrs
• Fees: Lower school £962 - £1,697 • Independent

Remarks: For further information see senior school.

ELLERAY PREPARATORY SCHOOL AND DAY NURSERY

Linked to Windermere Saint Anne's School in the Senior section

Windermere, Cumbria, LA23 1AP

Tel: 015394 43308
Fax: 015394 46803
E-mail: elleray@wsaschool.com
Website: www.ellerayprepsch.org.uk

• Pupils: 145 girls and boys • Ages: 2-11, boarding from 8+
• C of E • Fees: October, February and May • Independent

Remarks: Down the road towards Windermere in 17 acres.
For further details see senior school, Windermere St Anne's School.

THE ELMS SCHOOL

Colwall, Malvern, Worcestershire, WR13 6EF

Tel: 01684 540 344
Fax: 01684 541 174
E-mail: office@elmsschool.co.uk
Website: www.elmsschool.co.uk

• Pupils: 70 boys, 60 girls; 80 per cent board; plus 70 children in pre prep • Ages: 3-13 • C of E • Fees: Boarding £5,695; day £4,945; pre prep £1,850 - £3,150 • Independent

Head: Since 1985 Clive Ashby BA Cert Ed (fifties), single (unusual in prep schools these days). Educated in a number of schools both in England and Spain; most notably Belmont Abbey in Hereford: now defunct. Degree in science from Nottingham. Interesting background, firstly in commerce, then St Richard's in Bromyard in Herefordshire and finally Sunningdale, where he was hugely influenced by the Dawson twins. Truly gargantuan appetite for work. He not only teaches, mainly maths, but is also his own bursar and even finds time to maintain the beautifully kept school garden. Has an almost obsessive love for all things rural. The school attended the countryside march en masse and the banners are still displayed over the school entrance. This is a man who provokes the most partisan reactions. His energy, focus and determination to succeed do not always make him popular with some of his independent school colleagues but he is highly regarded and even loved by many of his staff, parents and pupils. One especially notes the real affection many parents feel for him. The school has its own working farm and he breeds a string of thoroughbred racehorses. Lucky to have a wonderfully warm enthusiastic and extraordinarily accessible head of boarding in Sarah Wilson, who fulfils many of the traditional functions of headmaster's wife.

Took over a moribund school of 48 children in 1985 and has transformed it into one of the most successful preparatory schools in the Welsh Marches, currently with numbers in excess of 200. He has what are now regarded as rather old fashioned views on education. Hates the pressurised tick box concept of so much modern educational ideology. He is concerned with the breadth of education and the need for every pupil to succeed at something – a philosophy that goes down jolly well in rural Herefordshire! Has a very clear understanding of his potential market and a considerable flair for attracting the 'right' parents – very largely the richer smarter rural set; owners of agricultural estates are not untypical. The school is entirely in his image and its success is an extraordinary testament to the fact that it is still possible for unusual eccentric heads to thrive in the post-modern landscape of modern education.

Entrance: Over-subscribed, but not excessively so. Entrance into pre-prep as early as 3, regular intake at 7 and 8. A few children from local state schools but the majority from very traditional independent school families. Most children from Herefordshire, Gloucestershire, Monmouthshire and Powys but a significant number from other parts of the country – notably London.

Exit: A few girls still leave at 11, but increasingly rare says head. The largest number goes to Malvern College, Shrewsbury School or Malvern Girls' College but, over the last five years, pupils have exited to 23 different schools including Cheltenham College, Eton, Winchester, Marlborough, Monmouth, Uppingham, Rugby, Cheltenham Ladies' College and Tudor Hall. The majority of girls still seem to go on to single sex schools. Respectable scholarship list, seven in 2004; about 25 per cent of leavers get some kind of award but one needs to bear in mind that a number of awards over the last few years have been for art, drama, sport etc reflecting the head's aim to provide a breadth of education. This is not an academic hothouse!

Remarks: The oldest prep school in England, founded by Humphry Walwyn in 1614. In the middle of the attractive village of Colwall just outside Malvern. Not immediately

impressive, the main school buildings abut the main road, yet to walk through the gates is a revelation. The school backs on to 150 acres of pristine gardens, beautifully maintained games fields and a small working farm complete with pigs, cows and horses. Perhaps unique amongst prep schools in having rural studies as part of the curriculum. The animals are not just here for show, one is assured – 'we eventually eat the pigs, chickens and cows' (not the horses!) The farm is a wonderful asset for all the children but especially for the less sporty and the academically challenged, who can get a real sense of achievement in helping in the farm. Riding and shooting are important parts of the school activity programme with children having achieved success at national equestrian events – and school is said to provide, in one way or another, half the Ledbury hunt. Winners of the prep school National shooting competition in 13 out of the last 18 years!

Remarkable number of new buildings including a vast sports hall, indoor swimming pool and brand new changing facilities. There are plans to build a new girls' boarding house and further classroom to start in the next twelve months. There cannot be many small schools with equivalent facilities. Remarkably, so successful has the financial management of the school been, that all this has been achieved without an overdraft. A factor in this is no doubt the somewhat high fees with little distinction made between the charges for boarding or day. The Elms charges the highest termly fee of any prep school in the area but, perhaps, this just adds to its exclusive appeal.

The least impressive part of the school is the children's dormitories (although one is assured that this will be addressed in the new development programme). Every child in the prep school (not pre-prep) has a designated bed; there are rest periods after lunch every day. This means that day children can board when they want, provided it is not more than four nights a week when they must convert to full boarder and stay over the weekend. However, this policy has meant that the dormitories are overcrowded and not very homely.

Academically sound with many long-serving staff (very low staff turnover). Inspection imminent. Traditional curriculum which includes a strong classics department. Follows a traditional prep school policy of moving children through classes as the need appears – this the head describes as the ladder system – which can mean that the brighter sparks might spend the last two years in the top class. However, it is quite clear that the head is very sensitive to parental concerns and there is a certain flexibility in the system. His determination to maintain this structure cocks a snook at current educational theory – it will be interesting to see what the inspectors make of this. Groups are very small and no class is larger than thirteen, the smallest just nine. It seems to work well and both parents and children seem happy with it.

Delightful well-mannered, cared-for children. Head places great emphasis on developing polite, confident children and in this he is very largely successful. Very few foreign pupils, fewer than half a dozen. Very conventional school uniform, boys wear corduroy shorts until they leave at 13. Wonderful cosy family atmosphere, not only the farm animals but lots of friendly dogs wander around the school, children are even encouraged to bring in their own (smaller) animals. Difficult to imagine much problem with homesickness here! The small size of the school means that each child is known as an individual and it is clear that the head knows and understands his charges extremely well. There is a wide range of activities which are well chronicled in very full termly newsletters (nb the school does not have an annual magazine). It is nice to see so many children involved in a wide sporting programme with the emphasis on participation rather than producing a sporting elite. Very strong art and drama but the head is refreshingly honest in admitting music is not especially strong although nearly 60 per cent of pupils learn at least one instrument

An ancient foundation but the resurrected present Elms School is very much in the image of the current head. In many ways an idiosyncratic and very unusual school, offering a traditional prep school experience increasingly rarely found. Not everyone will care for it but those who do have nothing but good to say of it.

ELSTREE SCHOOL

Woolhampton, Reading, Berkshire, RG7 5TD

Tel: 01189 713 302
Fax: 01189 714 280
E-mail: secretary@elstreeschool.org.uk
Website: www.elstreeschool.org.uk

• Pupils: 185 boys plus 65 boys and girls in pre-prep (Home Farm). 80 full boarders, 20 regular flexi-boarders, rest day • Ages: 7-13, pre-prep 3-7 • C of E • Fees: Pre-prep £2,332; prep: day £4,030; boarding £5,460 • Independent • Open days: December, March, May and October

Headmaster: Since 1995, Mr Syd Hill MA (mid fifties). Read geography and education at Cambridge; previously housemaster at Malvern College. Typical headmaster in appearance – tall, ruddy, sporty, slightly shy but knows all boys and is extremely quick to praise. Runs a tight ship with strict rules. Has successfully shaken off Elstree's 'snooty' image. No plans to bow under parental pressure to go co-ed. Firmly believes in single-sex schooling at this age. 'We much prefer to set ourselves up as a first-class boys' school,' he says. Encourages boarding from early age but very flexible. Wife Jane very lively, supportive, with good people skills. 'She's everything a headmaster's wife should be.' A son now following in father's footsteps at Mount House (qv), two daughters at university.

Entrance: Non-selective. 50 per cent move up from Home Farm, rest from far and wide (large proportion from London and Home Counties, around 10 overseas). No test, but prospective pupil assessment. Report from previous head also important 'just to make sure we're the right school' and identify any learning difficulties.

Exit: Clear favourites over last eight years (in descending order) are Bradfield, Eton and Radley closely followed by Marlborough, Harrow and Wellington. Other popular choices include Stowe and Charterhouse. 'We know by age 10 which school a boy would be suited to and we advise parents accordingly,' says head.

Remarks: Prides itself on a traditional character. Established in 1848. At the outbreak of war, staff and 70 boys upped sticks from Elstree, Herts and never went back. Glorious Georgian country house and 150-acre estate set in heart of leafy Berkshire, formerly home to a Polish family (Gurowski). Intricate carvings and floor-to-ceiling wood-panelled walls form welcoming main entrance. Freshly painted dorms in rooms above. Bright, very cheerful and homely with lots of home photos pinned up. 'It's like after the match at Twickenham in here there's so much noise and chatter,' quips the head. Housemaster looks after boarders' welfare while younger boys cared for by housemistress. 'Our pastoral care is second to none,' claims head, and this was clearly identified in recent ISI inspection. There are also resident matrons and a qualified nurse. Parents invited to visit as often as possible. No mobiles permitted. Letters home written weekly. Academic studies obviously important but not be all and end all. Plenty of help for dyslexics/learning difficulties. 'I feel the atmosphere of the school is enhanced by different abilities and strengths,' he says. 'We offer an all-round education; developing self esteem is crucial.'

Few boys fail to get into next school of their choice. Lessons six days a week (for day boys too). Brand new ICT room of networked terminals, plus bank of laptops for use in other classrooms, skills taught to all (starting with top year from Home Farm) and used in all subjects. Streamed classes from age 9 – average size 15. Setting in mathematics. Boys were attentive and responsive in lessons we saw. Not shy to speak up. Big, functional classrooms in newish block. Wide subject range (as curriculum demands), focus on Common Entrance – scholarship hopefuls creamed off early and taught in separate class. Hugely successful. Regularly produce six scholars a year, including awards in art, music and sport – 2002 a bumper year with 15 awards including 6 music scholarships. Awards in 2003 included King's Scholarship to Eton. Class music tuition as well as individual lessons. Violin and piano particularly strong. Two to three even learn bagpipes. Orchestra and bands in abundance. Senior choir performs often at concerts, not just in church every Sunday.

Religion a fundamental part of school life. Scriptures studied closely, boys encouraged to read Bible for themselves and morning prayers held daily. 'I think it's our job to plant the seed,' explains head. 'It also has a major influence on the boys' behaviour.' Certainly what we witnessed was impeccable – excellent table manners, courtesy and respect for others. 'There's absolutely no bullying here,' stressed one boy now in his final year. When pressed, he admitted there's a certain amount of teasing but no worse. 'All boys know precisely what is right and wrong,' says head. Remarkable.

Four school houses (North, South, East and West) for purely competitive reasons. Stars earned by boys go towards house cup. Games played daily (usual rugby, football, hockey, tennis, athletics) to good competitive level but seen more as good experience. 'Every boy has played for the school, that's what's important to us and to him,' head says. Brand spanking new sports hall opened in 2000 by Elstree old boy Field Marshal Lord Bramall (other famous OBs include Sebastian Faulks, an active school governor) – a great improvement on old school hall. 'One of the best gyms I've seen,' commented visiting fencing tutor. New all-weather tennis courts. Superb new library just opened last year in main house. New junior classroom block opened in Summer 2005 as part of ongoing development programme. Good facilities for art and DT – boys happy to show off their work. Large teaching staff – good mix of experience and more youthful enthusiasm. Type of boy, also mixed. Head asserts 'it's a school for all sorts. I'm very keen that parents should not choose Elstree for the wrong reasons just because it has the right social status'. There are not many families here for whom independent education and boarding is a first.' Might this be changing?

Home Farm School (pre-prep): Head since 1999, Mrs Sue Evans CertEd (early fifties), previously taught at Crosfields. Widowed, two daughters – one in fashion industry, the other in gap year. Runs happy, friendly mixed pre-prep in lovely converted 18th century farmhouse and barn a short walk from Elstree. First opened in 1993 with just eight children – now flourishing. Small class sizes. All rooms and corridors exhibit children's work. 'Every child has something up,' says head. 'And it's all their own work – I don't believe in putting teachers' work up on the walls.' Non-selective. Parents register son/daughter before assessment day. Computers in every room. Music taught to all from nursery up with special extra sessions for mothers and toddlers – useful focal point for new parents. Automatic transition to Elstree, no additional test taken, but screened for learning difficulties at 5. Lots of learning through play as well as focus on literacy and numeracy. Really cosy, homely atmosphere. After school club is asset for working parents. Popular with families moving out from London as well as from more immediate locality but it's well worth a car journey.

ELTHAM COLLEGE JUNIOR SCHOOL

Linked to Eltham College in the Senior section

Grove Park Road, Mottingham, London, SE9 4QF

Tel: 020 8857 3457
Fax: 020 8851 7160
E-mail: klj@eltham-college.org.uk
Website: www.eltham-college.org.uk

• Pupils: boys; all day • Ages: 7-10 • Independent

Remarks: For further details see senior school.

ERIDGE HOUSE SCHOOL

1 Fulham Park Road, Fulham, London, SW6 4LJ

Tel: 020 7371 9009
Fax: 020 7371 9009
E-mail: office@eridgehouse.co.uk
Website: www.eridgehouse.co.uk

• Pupils: 95; 50/50 boys/girls; all day • Ages: 2-11 • Fees: Part time (ie ages 2-3 years, mornings only) £1,575; other years £2,850 (sibling discount of £100) • Independent • Open days: contact school

Principal: Since its inception in 2001, Mrs Lucinda Waring (thirties), dynamo, bombshell, sage and mother. Mrs Waring, who also founded and runs two local Montessori nurseries, is a conviction head with very sound convictions indeed. Her aim was to create 'a village school in the middle of Fulham'. Impossible? You'd have thought so and she waited till she found the right property to try out the idea. 'We're not a pretty London school', she claims but isn't, actually, right as her school is very attractive indeed. Determined not to hothouse her charges, Mrs Waring finds plenty of parents who like the approach though, she considers, 'we're not nearly smart enough for some parents.' She has built a devoted staff – 'we work as a team here' – who are of the same mind and they have the new school's privilege of building resources according to need. 'As we grow, we look at what we need and then put it in place,' – and this applies to speech therapy, SEN and EAL provision – now laid on.

Many heads – and parents – claim to be against pressure early on. This is the real thing. 'I'm very anti reading and writing in pre-Reception classes, unless children are ready' she says. 'We don't do SATs and we never will'- a bold pitch in these days of appraisal-obsession. Her approach is to find for all her children the round holes they slot into – no-one is pushed too far too fast. 'We're not laid back – our ethos is to give them a very strong grounding but only with minimal homework. Children should be allowed to be children.' An intelligent, articulate and visionary head with energy, humour and compassion.

Entrance: 'We assess all children from reception upwards', says head – though, as numbers of applicants increase there may have to be a cut-off at some point. Testing is careful and exhaustive – looking for how children react to each other, to a teacher, to different situations and types of play, their motor skills – fine and gross (can they walk up stairs, handle different toys etc?) and so on. Inevitably, now over-subscribed at nursery level and for reception, a few places may be found higher up the school – but for how long? Most currently come from Seahorses, the sister nurseries in Fulham – 10 minutes walk away at Cloncurry Street and Burnthwaite Road.

Exit: No exit to speak of yet. The aim will be to continue the round hole policy rather than to prepare all children for the swankiest or most academic next schools. Expectation is to send leavers to a mix of Colet Court, Thomas', Broomwood Hall, Putney High, Bute House, Godolphin and Latymer, etc.

Remarks: School housed in former lodge to Fulham Palace and a handsome building it now is, having been in local authority use for forty years followed by two years of neglect and dereliction. A generously proportioned Victorian house, comfortably on a corner in leafy, residential Fulham, it has good sized classrooms plus some useful odd little rooms for cloaks, loos (very dinky) and stores and little passages to add interest. The former lodge must have had large and leafy gardens as school has an extraordinary amount of space around it for a large Astroturf pitch (carefully cut round mature trees) and play area plus a good-sized playground with toys and safe surface areas. Few preps in this part of London could compare – no-one is bussed out of here for anything. Displays in classrooms are lively and fun and well-planned. No cramming into tiny rooms here – room to move, to play, to feel relaxed. Super, newly designed library area. Computer room where pupils learn basic skills on maths, language and game programmes. School needs – and has applied to build – a hall as, currently there is little indoor space for drama or for running around in wet weather. 'I'm desperate for a larger place where they can go completely mad' yearns head, cheerily. Building plans also include four new classrooms, plus additional science and art rooms all with disabled access provision. One has to hope the application is accepted and also that head's dream of keeping her girls until 11 will also materialise. Luckily she has the space to go up to 11 without the extention. She points out that only two streets away is Hurlingham Park with tennis, netball and athletics facilities – seems meant, somehow.

In charge of curriculum development is the impressive and warmly approachable Janie Richardson. School cherrypicks the best of three systems – the Montessori, the National Curriculum and the French programme. French pupils – a small but significant number – are taught a carefully planned version of the CNED by school's resident French native speaker and highly experienced teacher and this is co-ordinated into the main curriculum. All children have French twice weekly. Otherwise a good and varied syllabus with much specialist teaching including music, sports and ballet. A well-run tennis class going on when we visited. Lowest class has 'lots of structured play' and we saw intently involved children with wet and sandy arms and others doing some serious dressing up. All children are heard reading each day – some by parent helpers. Excellent assessment and general records kept. Excellent system of communication with busy parents. Parents reps for each year. No school food – everyone brings packed lunches, maybe a mixed blessing for some. Useful after school clubs until 4.30pm with cooking (most popular) gardening and board games. All pupils come from minutes away – many can – not all do – walk to school so the place has a real local feel. It's a bit of a gem. If it can expand while preserving its ethos and if you live in Fulham and are not paranoid about league tables, it could well be for you.

EXETER CATHEDRAL SCHOOL

The Chantry, Palace Gate, Exeter, Devon, EX1 1HX

Tel: 01392 255 298
Fax: 01392 422 718
E-mail: reception@exetercs.org
Website: www.exeter-cathedral.org.uk

- Pupils: 170 boys and girls (including pre-prep); 30+ boarders
- Ages: 3-13 • C of E • Fees: Day £1,430 - £2,440; boarding an additional £1,530 (full), £1,360 (weekly) • Independent

Head: Since 2005, Mr Brian McDowell. Married to Diana, four children. Educated Haberdashers' Aske's and University of London. Taught in preps and primaries before becoming head of St Aubyn's Preparatory School, Devon. Music and outdoor pursuits.

Entrance: Open entry for ages 3-7. Informal assessment for all others on taster day. Voice trials for choristerships.

Exit: Almost all children stay until 13. Many senior school destinations including Christ's Hospital, Sherborne and Eton as well as south west schools: King's Taunton, Exeter's Maynard School and St Margaret's, Torquay Boys' Grammar School, Blundell's. Two thirds commonly win music scholarships. Former pupils include Chris Martin, front man of Coldplay; former Rochester Cathedral Organist Barry Ferguson, 14th century theologian Boniface.

Remarks: Part of Ecclesiastical Charity of the Cathedral church of St Peter in Exeter (better known as Exeter Cathedral). Music taught with a capital M – pianos at every turn including in boarders' rooms and corridors.

Founded in the 12th century, until the 1950s the school existed solely for choristers' education. Housed in several attractive redbrick buildings adjacent to architecturally stunning cathedral, the distance between individual buildings is not too bad but children may get wet when it's raining. Doors all secured with combination locks. University campus feel, neighbouring shops and greenery. Day children began in 1961, Exeter became the second cathedral after Salisbury to have girl choristers in 1994 and the school followed suit with co-education throughout.

Choristers get up to 25 per cent scholarship, plus means-tested bursaries, if necessary – and they really need to board to cope with the extra-curricular commitment. Exceptional director of music, Stephen Tanner – with the school for 16 years. New faces may find the musical talents of older pupils somewhat daunting but anyone would thrive, even the tone deaf – 'no-one is pushed to do anything they don't want to do'. Regular winners of drama competitions. Standard of art is more reminiscent of senior schools – art teacher spoken highly of. Maximum class size 18, average for key stage I is 11.

Children with special needs are considered on an individual basis and accepted at the discretion of the headmaster. The SENCO plus four part-time specialist teachers; moderate dyslexia and other mild learning difficulties, English as a second language.

No playing fields. Four minibuses transport pupils to local facilities within ten minutes eg Astroturf at Exeter University for hockey, rugby – players enjoy seven-minute run to pitch. School uses Bishop's garden for special functions including concerts. Uses the main school's facilities including minibus for swimming on Fridays. Year 8s allowed into city after school to shop – system respected.

Small international department which includes pupils from France, Hong Kong, Japan, South Korea and Russia, for whom English as a Second Language is provided.

Wonderfully popular pre-prep – warm atmosphere, own garden, play area, guinea pigs, climbing apparatus, oodles of educational toys and cosy library (with a piano!)

EXETER JUNIOR SCHOOL

Linked to Exeter School in the Senior section

Victoria Park Road, Exeter, Devon, EX2 4NS

Tel: 01392 258712
Fax: 01392 498144
E-mail: headmistress@exeterschool.org.uk
Website: www.exeterschool.org.uk

• Pupils: 99 boys and 60 girls; all day • Ages: 7-11 • Fees: £2,385 • Independent • Open days: Taster days in November for all entry ages. Open Days in July and October

Head: From 2006, Mrs Alison Turner BA (early forties). Previously assistant head in two maintained primary schools and head of a Devon primary school for 3 years.

Remarks: Modern and bright, well-stocked and plenty of room thanks to major extension. Next to the senior school – the playground is possibly frustratingly close for senior pupils trying to concentrate in the French rooms above. School dinners compulsory.

FAIRFIELD PREPARATORY SCHOOL

Linked to Loughborough High School in the Senior section
Linked to Loughborough Grammar School in the Senior section

Leicester Road, Loughborough, Leicestershire, LE11 2AE

Tel: 01509 215 172
Fax: 01509 238 648
E-mail: admin@fairfield.leics.sch.uk
Website: www.fairfield.leics.sch.uk

• Pupils: 480 girls and boys; all day • Ages: 4-11 • Non-denom • Fees: £1,899 • Independent

Head: Since 2001, Mr Roger Outwin-Flinders. Great sense of humour and a drive for his pupils and staff to succeed.

Entrance: At 4 (selective) and at 7 (tested).

Exit: Most children go on to either Loughborough High School (girls) or Loughborough Grammar School (boys) – but it's competitive and not automatic.

Remarks: A very active, busy school with excellent facilities for science (own lab), music, ICT, art and gym. Run along traditional prep school lines. A happy place; plenty of opportunities for children to excel in academics, music, drama and sport.

FAIRSEAT

Linked to Channing School in the Senior section

Highgate, London, N6 5HF

Tel: 020 8342 9862
Fax: 020 8342 9862
E-mail: fairseat@channing.co.uk
Website: www.channing.co.uk

• Pupils: 160 girls; all day • Ages: 4-11 • Fees: Junior £2,845 • Independent

Head: Since 2003, Mrs Jane Todd, previously deputy head, who took over when Mrs Jo Newman returned to head North London Collegiate Junior School. Some disquiet was felt at Mrs Todd's appointment by parents of daughters who are not academic, but she has in fact instigated something of a renaissance. The library, formerly a dump, has had yards of new bookshelves and books, the quality of teaching has been upgraded and the whole place is becoming more organised. There are more visits and interesting speakers from outside.

Entrance: By interview and tests.

Exit: Around three quarters go on to the senior school.

Remarks: Across Highgate Hill from the main school, takes 160 4-11 year olds. Elegant old buildings in lovely grounds with plenty of grass and trees and outstanding views. Modernised to include a performing arts studio, music rooms and a computer room. Popular local junior school, particularly since it opened a reception class for four year olds. The food is still dire.

FALKNER HOUSE

19 Brechin Place, London, SW7 4QB

Tel: 02073 734 501
Fax: 02078 350 073
E-mail: office@falknerhouse.co.uk
Website: www.falknerhouse.co.uk

• Pupils: 140 girls, all day. Plus co-ed nursery for 48 • Ages: 4-11, nursery 3-4 • Christian non-denom • Fees: £3,600 and pretty all-inclusive • Independent

Principal: Mrs Flavia Nunes, who founded the school in 1954 and who now resides in retirement like a kindly and charming dowager empress on the top storey, taking a keen interest – but no part – in the running of her school.

Since 1999, Mrs Anita Griggs BA PGCE (fiftyish), daughter of Mrs Nunes and formerly head of economics at St Paul's Girls School. Ousted her sister, Mrs Bird – something of an upset at the time. The cheerily formidable Mrs Griggs became headteacher having produced four daughters and run the family property business for fifteen years. 'My job is to bat for the child,' she declares and clearly brings every ounce of redoubtable energy and commitment to this particular wicket. Masses of common sense and sound educational values combine with unashamedly academic aspirations for her girls to make Mrs Griggs a rare bird in what can be the rather precious world of girls' prep schools in this chic and expensive area.

Entrance: Lists now closed for 2006 and 2007. However, it's always worth a call in case someone has left unexpectedly. It's as hard to get into as you'd expect when 100 girls compete for the precious 22 places. All children tested by lower school coordinator but head admits to there being very difficult choices.

Exit: Many to Francis Holland (Graham Terrace), Godolphin & Latymer, St Paul's, fewer to Francis Holland (Clarence Gate), Putney High and other local day schools. Some to board at, principally, Wycombe Abbey, Woldingham, Benenden, Downe House, St Mary's (Calne) and St Mary's Ascot. Two or three academic and music scholarships won annually.

Remarks: Not the school if you want on-site playing fields, spacious classrooms, mixed ability classes and a gentle ride. Decidedly the school for you if you want an atmosphere that is both exciting and orderly, stimulating and caring, creative, civilised and unapologetically ambitious for its bright, responsive girls. This school takes every care to match the capacities and needs of each individual. It will go every inch of the mile for its girls. It is not, though, 'a school for the fragile flower who develops late' says the headteacher, unashamedly, nor is it for the unconfident child with SEN, though dyslexics are supported to the hilt so long as they can stand the pace. Girls cite the warm friendliness of the place and the excellence of their teachers as main assets.

Food is cooked to at least home standards – no restriction on helpings here! No bells and no rules contribute to the naturally self-policing, civilised atmosphere in the busy 'home-at-school' atmosphere, and pupils have an engaging openness, directness and courtesy. 'We like them to have ability and oomph,' says Mrs Griggs, 'but not to be sassy or precocious.' This seems to be exactly the type of girl she produces.

All in two, joined, seven-storey Victorian houses in a quiet side street off Gloucester Road. Walls are decorated by lively, rich displays of girls' work alongside real and reproduced 'serious' pictures and artefacts to give an 'at home' feel and demonstrating the wisdom of surrounding children with good things. Music is strong, lessons are imaginative and fun. A new science lab, good IT facilities, a lovely big bay-windowed room for assemblies and dance while all sports are a ride away, staircases are narrow, classrooms, especially for the larger girls, are a touch cramped, and the playground adjoins the pavement but no-one seems to mind and it's a small price to pay for everything else. Off-site sports keenly supported, school now has link with Fulham FC.

Early and Late Bird systems – a godsend for working parents. Multinational clientele though current oversubscription will favour permanent residents. Parents made welcome; enthusiastic and supportive in return.

FARLEIGH SCHOOL

Red Rice, Andover, Hampshire, SP11 7PW

Tel: 01264 710 766
Fax: 01264 710 070
E-mail: office@farleighschool.co.uk
Website: www.farleighschool.com

• Pupils: 233 boys and 160 girls; 115 boarders (two-thirds boys, one-third girls), more weekly than full, 278 day pupils • Ages: 3-13 • RC • Fees: Boarding £5,325; day £4,075; flexible boarding £27.50 per night; pre-prep £2,240 • Independent • Open days: October

Head: Since 2004, Father Simon Everson, a central figure in the school and still its resident chaplain. Father Simon Everson (rather unusually for an RC priest) resides on site with his wife and two children. The explanation is that he was formerly an Anglican vicar in an inner London parish, who subsequently converted to Catholicism. Fr Simon was ordained in Westminster Cathedral by the Archbishop of Westminster, accompanied by a party of 600 from the school, including parents. He teaches RE and PSHE, which includes sex education within the context of a loving relationship within marriage. Highly regarded by pupils and parents, both RC and otherwise. Took over suddenly as head following the abrupt departure of Mr John Alcott.

Entrance: To kindergarten at 3 and into the pre-prep at 5, both on non-selective basis. Assessment (not too rigorous) at 7 if coming from outside, plus reference from existing school. Oversubscribed in most years so priority given to RCs, boarders, siblings and children of former pupils. Presently 50 per cent RCs, who come from all over the country. Others come from London and local preps and primaries, mostly within a 25-mile radius. Boarding numbers holding steady.

Exit: To wide selection of prestigious schools, including, for the boys, Ampleforth, Eton, Downside, Sherborne, Radley, Harrow, Marlborough, Winchester and, for the girls, St Mary's Shaftesbury, St Mary's Ascot, Downe House, Marlborough, Godolphin and St Swithun's. About 10 per cent leave at 11, some to take up places at sought-after state grammars in nearby Salisbury (boys to Bishop Wordsworth and girls to South Wilts) and also girls to take up places at senior boarding schools. About 10 scholarships won per year.

Remarks: Appealing school with friendly, family atmosphere (lots of children of former pupils and many brothers and sisters) and good academic achievement. Formerly a boys' Catholic prep, now co-ed boarding with strong day element. Based in a lovely Georgian house in the Test Valley, full of light and surrounded by 60 acres of parkland with impressive cedar trees and woodland. Lovely, recently constructed kindergarten and pre-prep department and the former gym now houses a well-equipped theatre with tiered seating. A new art and design block was opened in April 2004 and an indoor heated swimming pool, located alongside the new sports hall, was opened in April 2005. The old outdoor swimming pool is still used by hardier boarders in the summer months.

A new junior boarding house for boys and girls aged 7 to 10. One boarding house for senior boys and one for senior girls, in dormitories, some parts of which have been sub-divided, nothing fancy but homely. Flexible boarding available with many day pupils requesting to board two to three nights per week, as a stepping stone to weekly boarding. Food 'really nice', according to the children, with popular fish and chips every Friday and themed suppers twice a term.

Academically very sound, with children proceeding to very well-respected senior schools. Excellence Board affixed to wall outside head's room to display outstanding work. Children setted according to ability in a gradual process over years 4 and 5. Average class size 16. Latin begins in year 6. Strong learning support with 4 fully qualified staff. Experience of most areas of learning difficulties, which include dyslexia, dyspraxia and mild social/communication difficulties. 68 pupils on the learning support register. Of those, approximately 20 pupils identified as gifted and able, and are catered for. A mature, stable, staff base, up-to-date with current thinking.

Mass is held every Thursday and Sunday morning and parents and locals are welcome in the lovely chapel. Grace said at all mealtimes. Fr Simon wants children at the school to have a strong awareness of their faith, but he stresses that all faiths are welcomed.

A feature of the school is its 5 GAs – the gap year students recruited on to the staff each year from the UK, Australia and South Africa. They act as older cousins to the children, supervising breaks, taking on boarding duties, running clubs and societies. These popular people live on site, together with 23 other resident staff.

Parents generally regard the school as sporty. 'Nearly every' child who wants to play for the school has the opportunity to do so, providing matches can be arranged with enough teams. Lots of emphasis on outdoor activities, not just sport. Making dens in the school woods, cycling, roller blades and scooters are very popular with the children and not something found at your average London prep. For the non-sporty children, there is a chance to excel at activities like public speaking, ICT, art and reading competitions. Mobile phones banned, as are electronic games.

Not many pupils from abroad, but school has traditional links with Spanish children from Madrid and Seville and there are usually a couple of pupils from there and about 10 overseas Brits. No local transport laid on, except for escorted train collections together with deliveries to Waterloo and airports for boarders. Parents mainly professional and managerial (lots with boarding experience themselves) – a very well-heeled, upmarket, bunch. Strong contingent of London parents and some Services families. A growing number are so taken by the Hampshire lifestyle, with its spaciousness and picturesque thatched villages that they sell up and move to the area, commuting to London on the 70-minute train journey from Andover to Waterloo. Good social life for local parents as well as the London ones – the Friends of Farleigh is a purely social association, which organises bonfire nights, fish and chip race evenings, Family Fun Day and so on. When we visited, a charity tennis tournament for parents was in full swing and well supported. Happy mums here, which make for a happy school. Notable Old Boys include the actor Rupert Everett (star of the 2002 film of 'The Importance of Being Earnest'), the journalist Craig Brown, Lords Stafford (pro-chancellor of Keele University), Hesketh (of Formula 1 racing fame) and Grantley, and Hugh Vyvyan, member of the England rugby squad.

FELSTED PREPARATORY SCHOOL

Linked to Felsted School in the Senior section

Felsted, Braintree Road, Felsted, Essex, CM6 3JL

Tel: 01371 822 610
Fax: 01371 821 443
E-mail: rmw@felstedprep.org
Website: www.felsted.org

• Pupils: 375 boys and girls; boarding 11+ • Ages: 4-13 • C of E
• Fees: £1,769 - £3,871 • Independent • Open days: May & October

Head: Since 2004 Mrs Jenny Burrett BA (Hons) (mid-forties). She was educated at Birkenhead High School and Durham University and has a degree in modern languages. Formerly head of department and housemistress at Felsted School. Enthusiastic, friendly and ambitious for the school. Married to city banker, Richard with 3 teenage children.

Entrance: Nursery assessment for reception entry. Standard English, maths and VR testing together with an interview at 7 years and above.

Exit: Of a year group of 60, 50-55 will move on to the senior school.

Remarks: For further details, see senior school.

FELTONFLEET SCHOOL

Byfleet Road, Cobham, Surrey, KT11 1DR

Tel: 01932 862 264
Fax: 01932 860 280
E-mail: office@feltonfleet.co.uk
Website: www.feltonfleet.co.uk

• Pupils: 335 girls and boys. 40 weekly boarders, rest day. Nursery and pre-prep (Calvi House) 70 boys and girls • Ages: 7-13, pre-prep 3-7 • mainly C of E • Fees: Nursery £1,296 (mornings only); pre-prep £2,424; main school £3,553; weekly boarding £4,964 • Independent • Open days: Saturday in October and February; during school day in May

Head: Since 2000, Mr Philip Ward BEd (mid-forties, but looks younger). Educated at Reigate Grammar School and Exeter University. Spent 17 years at Uppingham (he is a huge fan) working his way up the ranks to senior house-master. Married to Sue, who plays an active wife-of-the-headmaster role, as well as running junior department and having overall pastoral responsibility for girls. Two children – both of whom were pupils of Feltonfleet and now at Cranleigh. Clearly passionate about his school; a charis-matic, family man who enjoys a chat. Full of energy, he says he wants 'fizzy-buzzy staff'- fresh faces and fresh approaches. Very approachable, 'cares greatly that this is a place where children feel at ease.'

Entrance: Waiting list for entry into pre-prep on a first come first served basis – get names down early. Most join at age 7 into year 3; 18 from the pre-prep and about 30 from many feeder schools including Milbourne Lodge Junior, Wimbledon College Prep, Grantchester House, Emberhurst, Glenesk, the Hurlingham and Putney Park. Tested in English and maths but it's a 'gentle approach' to pupil evaluation. Head says they're looking for long term commitment and potential, known as 'headmaster's eye test.' Entry possible higher up as odd gaps appear – always worth a try.

Exit: Mainly at 13 after Common Entrance. A few leave at 11. Leavers go all over the place: local schools Reeds Cobham, St George's Weybridge, St John's Leatherhead, Cranleigh and Epsom College get a chunk, but popularity goes in peaks and troughs. Increasingly to co-ed schools and weekly boarding is popular. Number of scholarships increasing – more to all round schools than to real academic hothouses.

Remarks: Family feel, love-of-life atmosphere, an incredibly energetic and sporty school. Suits active kids who like to be busy – as one parent says 'not for the child who needs stillness and down-time as pupils are always on the go.' Has come a long way in recent years and feels like it's still evolving.

Buildings centred on a large Edwardian house, hidden from view behind woodland and high fences. Centenary Building houses 'super-duper' new library and spacious classrooms for geography, history, French and Latin, net-worked wireless laptops and interactive whiteboards. Lots of space outside, well maintained and tidy, but the school is next to the A3 which gives a constant background hum to the otherwise peaceful surroundings.

Academic standards are high, but a broad range of children are accepted and it is not a school for parents who want hot-housing. Staff believe happy kids flourish – every class has a newly introduced 'circle time' to help build their self-esteem. Teachers are young and friendly, although the ever youthful Mr Ward says 'the average age of staff is 40 – we have several wise and energetic ones too.' Progressive

style of teaching – mixture of few desks facing forward and desks in circles. School reckons that a variety of different teaching styles gives children more chances of success.

Average 16 children per class from year 3 upwards; setting in English and maths begins in year 3. From year 5, teaching is by subject specialists, with setting in French (starts in the nursery and very well taught) and science. Scholarship streams in year 7. School fully supports 11+, though one isolated parental comment that 'they do as much as they can to prepare for 11+, but are limited by majority continuing to CE.' Languages are strong. Spanish from year 6 introduced in 2004. Year 8 scholars do some Italian and Greek. Science, ICT and DT are together in a newly refurbished building.

Pupils with moderate learning disabilities welcome – about 38 children have support. School has full-time SENCO and team of peripatetic learning support staff. Also a Gifted and Talented co-ordinator.

Music has seen a revival under a new director. Own computer room where pupils experiment with melodies. Lots of positive changes, and loads of new music clubs including pop bands. 180 children learn a musical instru-ment and there's an annual Party in the Park every May. Drama also strong despite being taught in the old gym, and takes productions to The Edinburgh Festival. Art is on the way up.

Sport is an incredibly important part of a Feltonfleet child's life. There's a well-used covered swimming pool, a large leisure centre with 2 squash courts, a small Astroturf pitch and loads of space for rugby, hockey, cricket etc. Matches every Wednesday in school hours. Girls have a super games mistress who also takes on role of 'big sister'. Lots of overseas tours and national tournaments. Girls strong in netball and hockey, boys in rugby. Squash scholar-ship to Millfield awarded in 2005. Head very involved with sport – he referees, runs golf and senior girls' tennis.

Massive choice of clubs: pupils encouraged to be busy. One parent felt too much is expected of their child – 'I get the impression they spend a lot of time dashing about.' Long school day with flexible finish times. Weekly boarding is part of the ethos – 25 boys and 15 girls. Boys and girls get along very well and mix at 'activity time'. Dorms are cosy and homely. New boarding master has built boarding up to a very high standard and there's a good feeling of close-ness. Flexi-boarding also available for occasional use.

Pupils are a happy, active and lively bunch but boys outnumber girls by almost 3:1 – the effect of local compe-tition. Some see this as an advantage – 'girls get lots of opportunities to play in teams because there are fewer to choose from.' – others do not. Head hopes that plans to extend the pre-prep will mean more girls moving up the school. Uniform guidelines are adhered to but a certain amount of individuality glimmers through.

Pupils get lots of praise and encouragement from staff, especially from the head who opens his doors to a queue of children every morning to show him good work for 'head-master's initials.' Thumbs up from the parents for the school's pastoral care – 'it's a caring, nurturing and supportive environment.' Mix of parents, lots of first time buyers and professionals. Growing number from SW London. The school is perceived as full of moneyed souls – the usual convoy of suburban 4x4s does little to allay the perception. Plenty of parking for drop-off and pick-up but allow time in the morning to battle with the rush-hour congestion. School bus runs from Wimbledon and Cobham with more routes planned.

FERN HILL PRIMARY SCHOOL

Richmond Road, Kingston Upon Thames, Surrey, KT2 5PE

Tel: 02082 470 300
Fax: 02082 470 309
E-mail: FHP@rbksch.org
Website: www.fernhill.kingston.sch.uk

• Pupils: 415 boys and girls in main school, all day (52 half day places in the nursery) • Ages: 3-11 • Non-denom • State

Head: Since the school opened in 1994, Miss Diana Brotherston BEd Hons DipEd Science MA (forties). Previously deputy head at Coombe Hill infant school. A self-contained person, who prefers to talk about her school rather than herself, but she is welcoming and v polite to everyone – acting as a role model for her pupils. Parents say she is straightforward, responds well to problems, knows her stuff and gets parents fully involved in school life.

Entrance: School is hugely popular and heavily over-subscribed. Two-form entry with 30 in each class. Children who attend the nursery do not have priority, but siblings do, then proximity to school comes into play. Children come from a more and more local area – pretty much white middle class. Frantic house moving by parents to get into the perceived catchment area: which road you live in and even which end of the road is becoming more and more important! Parents who live half way between Fern Hill and

the other local in- demand school, Latchmere (qv), may find themselves counting the metres between home and school to work out which school is more likely to offer them a place.

Exit: To a wide variety of schools including all the local state secondary schools. Head is sanguine about children being privately tutored for grammar or independent school entrance, but is quite happy to offer parents her opinion as to whether a child will be able to cope in a highly academic school. Private tutoring (a booming industry in this part of the world) can pay off with pupils going to some of the best local secondary schools including Tiffin Boys and Tiffin Girls and independents, particularly Surbiton High, Kingston Grammar and The Hall, Wimbledon.

Remarks: The school of choice for parents who like a formal atmosphere where it is easy to see learning happening: a private school feel, traditional, conservative, with homework, concern about children's appearances etc etc. A school with structure- in its buildings, organisation and attitudes.

One of the best academic schools in the borough. V good SATS results and pupils look as though they are enjoying their work in an organised environment. They sit still in class in an attentive way (fidgeters and daydreamers could find it rather too ordered). Head says 'we are also developing a more creative way of learning.' Staff v. aware of their able pupils policy -they feel that setting high standards for the brightest raises the achievements of everyone. About 50 children with SEN needs, SEN co-ordinator three days a week, and Mrs B says, 'We constantly self review to evaluate the effectiveness of our approaches and we keep abreast of any new studies and programmes. We adopt a "Dyslexia Friendly approach" (including. brain gym, multi sensory teaching and learning, IT) and we are regularly advised by the excellent support services in the Local Authority. Each pupil presenting with reading difficulties is carefully screened to find out exactly where their difficulties lie.' Only a handful of children with EAL.

Very light, bright and busy place and quiet. Quietness will appeal to some parents; others will feel a lack of vibrancy. Children wear a neat uniform, strong emphasis on politeness and courtesy: this shows itself in a very detailed home-school agreement to be signed by parents, pupils and the school, which is augmented by a seven page behaviour partnership document.

Buildings feel much more spacious than many primary schools and security is strong. Corridors are wide with some open plan areas off them – used for small group activities like reading. Classrooms bright and airy with masses of art-work on display. Super music and drama room (but underused according to one parent), a dedicated SEN area and a computer suite with 15 terminals in addition to the terminals in the classrooms. Classes called after trees and flowers; reflect the importance attached to nature in the school. Classrooms look onto an attractive courtyard, which allows easy access to the outdoors in the summer. Nursery, infant and junior classes are also easily accessible to each other, helping to promote a sense of community. Communication between year groups is encouraged via a buddy system and pairing of classes for certain projects. Lovely gardens where parents and children work regularly- they grow vegetables which are eaten later by pupils.

Grounds are well maintained with reasonable outdoor sports facilities for football and netball. Pupils take part in matches against other schools and after-school sports clubs are available, but not a strong feeling of a competitive sports ethos (no sports photos obviously on show) and swimming is only available in Year 4. You get the impression that academia rules the roost here, and a few parents feel that the school is happy merely to fulfil the requirements of the National Curriculum for sport rather than make use of the good facilities available. Drama is regarded as strength with some kind of production every term. Peripatetic teachers come into school to give individual lessons in a range of musical instruments and all pupils get a chance to learn the recorder. No opportunities for playing in an orchestra or band within the school, despite the large dedicated music and drama room. Again impression that there is potential for more than is actually provided. Annual art exhibition for parents to enjoy.

Praise for the pastoral care, communications with parents are also excellent: the head and/or her deputy (an ebullient soul much praised by the parents) are at the school gates every morning, and parents are encouraged to speak to teachers about any concerns. Parents are hugely loyal to the school: it is judged by many to be the best school in North Kingston (and in the whole borough?) although the Latchmere parents (much undisguised rivalry with this neighbouring school) would ferociously disagree.

FETTES COLLEGE PREPARATORY SCHOOL

Linked to Fettes College in the Senior section

East Fettes Avenue, Edinburgh, EH4 1QZ

Tel: 0131 3222976
Fax: 0131 3224724
E-mail: PrepSchool@fettes.com
Website: www.fettes.com

• Pupils: 90 boys, 60 girls; 40 boys and 15 girls board • Ages: 7 - 13 • Fees: Prep: £3,270 day, £5,120 boarding • Independent • Open days: October, senior and prep; February, prep only

Head: Since 2003, Mr A A Edwards BA London (early forties). Formerly a housemaster at Gresham's School, Norfolk. Married to Jill; three young sons and one young daughter. A history graduate and a talented sportsman.

Entrance: By assessment test and interview.

Exit: Internally set exam for entry to senior school.

Remarks: With 140 pupils during the fifth year of its life, this newest addition to Scotland's prep schools is shaking other prep schools – particularly Edinburgh prep schools – rigid. In a previous incarnation this was a Junior House and before that a Junior School, in each case taking children from 10. Tiny classes, excellent remedial (Catriona Collins who also does the big school), super facilities, and plumb in the centre of Edinburgh. Latin early, computers everywhere. Possible drawback would be the lack of stimulation for children spending 10 years in the same place. 'Edinburgh's best kept secret', huge expansion on the way.

FINTON HOUSE SCHOOL

171 Trinity Road, London, SW17 7HL

Tel: 02086 820 921

Fax: 02087 675 017

E-mail: admissions@fintonhouse.org.uk

Website: www.fintonhouse.org.uk

- Pupils: 125 boys, 185 girls; all day • Ages: 4-11 • Non-denom
- Fees: £2,900 - £3,225 • Independent • Open days: First Wednesday in February

Headmaster: Since 2005, Mr Adrian Floyd. Mr Floyd came from Newton Prep, where he was head of upper school. Previously had taught at Tower House, East Sheen, as head of English. Prior to working in London, taught at Summer Fields, Oxford.

Entrance: Much sought after. Non-selective first come first served – put names down early. Places appear in later years, always worth checking – children very welcoming to newcomers. At least 3 special needs places per year for children with significant but not severe needs. LEA funding may be available for statemented children – very oversubscribed – following Ed Psych assessment places are offered to children with the greatest need that can be met by the school's resources. Siblings have priority. Comprehensive academic ability ranges from gifted and talented to SEN with some children appearing on both registers.

Exit: Some move to 'the country' before 11. A handful of boys leave at 8 for boys' prep schools: King's Wimbledon, Westminster Under, Northcote Lodge, Eaton House, Dulwich Prep, or go on to board at Summer Fields, Windlesham, Ludgrove etc. At 11, guided choice to wide variety of day and boarding schools: Putney High, Wimbledon High, JAGS, Alleyn's, Francis Holland, St Mary's, Ascot, Woldingham, Benenden, Dulwich, Wycombe Abbey etc.

Remarks: Caring, welcoming, environment with parent-friendly atmosphere. Children are local to smart Wandsworth. Smallish school accommodated in two handsome and well-proportioned Victorian houses sensitively adapted for school use. Light rooms – gym (doubles as dining hall), specialist science, art, ICT and DT rooms, purpose-built music block (plenty of extra-curricular music and opportunities to perform), good library, lots of stairs (would be difficult for children with physical disabilities). New, purpose-built reception block opened in autumn 2005. Decent sized playground packed with equipment including Wendy houses,

friendship bench, climbing frame and much used barrels – great for rolling on and in. Plenty of sporting opportunities and regular successes in local competitions – inclusive policy means every child has the opportunity to represent the school in matches. All usual curriculum subjects offered including French from reception and Latin as a club.

School fizzes with enthusiastic youngsters – comfortable with adults, look you in the eye and clearly love school – 'it's fun and we do loads of sport' (fixtures from y1). Respect for teachers (all called by first names prefixed with Miss or Mr) and sensitivity to each other are virtues to the fore. Interactive whiteboards, used by pupils and staff, add a new dimension to already sparky teaching and learning. Even assemblies were deemed great fun – 'especially the trust one where a teacher pretended to be late then ate cat food – which was actually mars bar and jelly.' School walls burst with fantastic displays of work by all pupils reflecting the very inclusive nature of the school. Plenty of theme days (India, Romans, Vikings ...) lots of project based work and trips throughout but especially for y6 once exam pressure removed – 'it's important to educate in the broadest sense not just to pass exams,' insists the head.

This is not a special needs school but the school's team including speech and language, occupational therapists and special needs assistants (a staggering fourteen full-time and eight part-time) means that children with learning difficulties can be helped on site on a one-to-one basis (many schools claim this, few actually deliver). Some help is free but one-to-one specialist support outside the classroom incurs a cost – 'kept to absolute minimum, we don't want to make a profit out of SEN.' The head of special needs is assisted by two SENCOs; one for the 10 per cent of children who arrive with more complex needs, the other for children with specific learning difficulties who may require monitoring or intervention. Cater for wide-ranging SEN: profoundly deaf (must have some form of communication), Downs, Aspergers, speech and language disorders, specific learning difficulties etc. An early intervention programme has been established to identify mainstream pupils who require additional support. Keen to stress all gain from having SEN children in the school and happily co-exist in a non-patronising environment where differences don't matter. Lots of clubs and activities: some such as brain gym target SEN, super siblings the brothers and sisters of children with SEN, others such as chess, football, dance, rugby for all. School stresses even the most able, outgoing and ebullient child needs nurturing and care.

Emphasis on inclusion, individuality and results without pressure is its forte.

FORD HOUSE

Linked to Leeds Girls' High School in the Senior section

Headingley Lane, Leeds, West Yorkshire, LS6 1BN

Tel: 0113 2744000
E-mail: enquiries@lghs.org
Website: www.lghs.org

• Pupils: junior school (Ford House) 219 girls, pre-prep (Rose Court) 166 girls; all day • Ages: junior school 7-11, pre-prep 3-7
• Fees: Ford House (7-11) £1,896; Rose Court (3-7) £1,741
• Independent • Open days: Mid October, early November

Head: Mrs Addison (fifties); taught in maintained sector; at school since 1985, head since 1988; kindly, enthusiastic.

Entrance: Simple tests and interviews. Most join the pre-prep, Rose Court, but some come in at 7 to the prep, Ford House; occasional vacancies at other ages.

Exit: Assessed by last two years' work for entrance to the senior school.

Remarks: Specialist teaching for French and PE; also Spanish club. Access to senior school sports facilities. Good IT provision and library. No SATS – National Curriculum followed plus extra interests. High standard of written work, especially creative writing; excellent work on display. Special needs teaching for both ends of ability range. Happy, involved children in classrooms. Major £2m development completed September 2003 which provides specialist teaching rooms and allows for smaller classes (down from present 25 max to 20). Delightful pre-prep department in lovely old house with very warm head (Miss Pickering). Brightly decorated and furnished classrooms throughout. Lots of teddies, eg in head's office and covering dining room walls.

FOREMARKE HALL (REPTON PREPARATORY SCHOOL)

Linked to Repton School in the Senior section

Milton, Derby, Derbyshire, DE65 6EJ

Tel: 01283 703 269
Fax: 01283 701 185
E-mail: registrar@foremarke.org.uk
Website: www.foremarke.org.uk

• Pupils: 450 boys and girls; boarding and day • Ages: 2 1/2 -13
• C of E, other faiths welcome • Fees: Day £1,850 - £3,570; boarding £4,740 • Independent • Open days: Early October, late January, early May

Head: Since 2000, Mr Paul Brewster (forties), previously head of St Mary's Preparatory School, Lincoln. A mathematics and computing graduate of the University of London. Married to Debbie, three children. Mrs Brewster also works in the school as registrar and oversees domestic affairs and liaising with parents.

Entrance: A day of assessment. Academic scholarships at 11 and 7. Awards for music, art, drama, DT, IT, sport and chess.

Exit: At 13, with roughly 75 per cent going to Repton and the rest to a wide range of other independent schools.

Remarks: For further information, see senior school.

FOREST PREPARATORY SCHOOL

Linked to Forest School in the Senior section

College Place, Snaresbrook, London, E17 3PY

Tel: 020 8520 1744
Fax: 020 8520 3656
E-mail: prep@forest.org.uk
Website: www.forest.org.uk

• Pupils: 220 girls and boys; all day • Ages: 4-11 • C of E foundation with a sizeable proportion of pupils from other faith groups • Fees: Prep £2,258 - £2,761 • Independent • Open days: Main Open Day in September each year followed by a number of Information Mornings

Head: Mr Ian McIntyre (early thirties) - former director of studies at St Cedd's School, Chelmsford. Leaving in 2006.

Entrance: By assessment and exam at 4 and 7.

Remarks: For further information see senior school.

FORRES SANDLE MANOR SCHOOL

Sandle Manor, Fordingbridge, Hampshire, SP6 1NS

Tel: 01425 653 181
Fax: 01425 655 676
E-mail: office@forressandlemanor.hants.sch.uk
Website: www.forressandlemanor.com

• Pupils: 290 boys and girls, 100 board • Ages: 3-13 • Broadly C of E • Fees: £5,280 boarding and £3,880 day • Independent

Head: Since 1988, Mr Dick Moore (late forties). Headed Forres from 1988-93, then oversaw the fusion with Sandle Manor, now FSM in quickspeak. Educated at Cranleigh, where he returned after sociology at Durham to be housemaster and director of rugby. There's nothing recycled about him, though – here's where he learned how it could be done better. Anything but hidebound – 'nothing is set in stone', he says. Change, here, is always afoot, not the sea-change sort, more the fine-tuning variety, but enough, perhaps, to unsettle some parents. Married to Sheena, astrophysicist, hers is the still, small voice to his earthquake, wind and fire. She superintends the children's wellbeing in everything from

food to boarding. An impressive partnership of complementary attributes. Four sons, 20 to 12.

Entrance: Most at age 3 or 8. Boarders at 8 only 'if the headmaster is satisfied that the child wishes to board'. Non-selective and they get the full rainbow. The superb learning centre for those with SENs is a draw. Day children bypass perfectly good schools in a 25-mile radius – Winchester, Poole, Salisbury. A good crowd from the New Forest, Avon valley and environs of Cranborne. Boarders a 50-50 mix of ex-pats, mostly Services and locals. Around 50 per cent of parents first time buyers. Geography is against ethnic mix but there's always a wodge of migratory Norwegians (a quirky historic link) and a handful of Spaniards. Start when you like, if there's room. Lists of day children wishing to convert to boarding run to 2011 and rising. No schols or bursaries, but 10 per cent off for Services' children.

Exit: Canford's a staple. Then comes the full gamut of locals – the Sherbornes, Bryanston, Marlborough, Blundells, Millfield, Wells. For the less conventionally academic, Milton Abbey, Clayesmore, Grenville. Impressive numbers of schols in everything. 80 per cent stay to 13. At 11, 20 per cent to single-sex girls, grammars or comp. Eminent outcomes: Michael Foot (Forres), Alec Guinness (Sandle Manor).

Remarks: It feels good and it looks good – the Jacobean manor, the bosky grounds, the engorged rhododendrons – but reality matches it. The educational idea is simple enough – children thrive when they feel good about themselves. This is the exclusive focus and all achievements are reckoned a by-product. No SATs. Parents don't call for regular benchmarking 'because they trust the school'. Expectations must be high because academic results are boast-worthy and rising. Annual Headmaster's Prize to each year group for the child who has worked the hardest.

The school does not apply a play-safe policy to staff appointments, preferring passion, character and kindness. Teachers must be 'up for it'. Plenty of that. Rob Harvey, avant-garde music teacher, has the children playing fruit – even bicycles. Lots of new young faces and a reassuring leavening of wise ones.

The flagship learning centre for children with information processing difficulties – average to above-average IQs only – has no whiff of casualty about it. The brightest are tweaked there, too, and none are hived off: it is integral to mainstream learning, and the techniques in use have pervaded all classrooms. Teaching methods accord with up-to-the-minute thinking. Impressively led. The children rate attendance enviable.

Boarding is well done and a matter of some vanity. Over half the 7-13s do it. The secret lies in the supervision –

there are always from 7 to 10 adults on duty and 10 sleep in the main building. Rooms are amusingly painted in colours children delight in. Plenty to do, Wednesday fun evenings the biggest hit. Always around 50 in at weekends, and rising. Genuinely humane. Parents say the children look after each other. Sports facilities are adequate. All-weather pitch coming soon. Heated outdoor pool.

For all the equal emphasis on everything, music is transcendent under the inspirational Dave Andrews. Here, democracy of opportunity defers to a little light elitism and the less able are less indulged. They do the lot, from hip-hop to holiness. We heard the jazz band (breath-stopping) and delighted in the number of girls playing sassy brass. More than three quarters learn an instrument and they perform, perform, perform. Ensembles of everything and choirs too. Demand the CD with your prospectus pack.

FSM is an un-snobby, unselfconscious school apparently too busy to bother with narcissistic PR or bigging itself up, which it could frankly do more of. Manners work on a democracy of respect basis, with the staff reciprocally holding doors open for children. Discipline is intelligent – errant year 8 children may be despatched to devise their own punishment. Discipline extends to parents, too. Strict rules of courtesy and self-restraint govern their conduct at sports events. The excellent parents' handbook both informs and requires – with no shred of bossiness or hauteur. The children themselves are delightfully at ease with everyone – we recall three slightly smudged girls out sketching – but live, reassuringly, in a child's world. Parents tell us they always feel welcome and listened to. Those whose children had problems say they were dealt with quickly and expertly.

This is a school where, clearly, most of the children and staff have a lot of fun most of the time but the philosophy of fun is underpinned by strong seriousness and rigour. Parents who prefer FSM do so over schools they reckon 'too precious' – the sort where toil is tightly focused. The prospectus and website give you the flavour of the place and act as an effective filter. Take it from there.

FRAMLINGHAM COLLEGE JUNIOR SCHOOL (BRANDESTON HALL)

Linked to Framlingham College in the Senior section

Brandeston, Suffolk, Brandeston, Suffolk, IP13 7AH

Tel: 01728 685 331
Fax: 01728 685 437
E-mail: office@brandestonhall.co.uk
Website: www.framlingham.suffolk.sch.uk

- Pupils: girls and boys; day and flexi-boarding • Ages: 3-13
- Fees: Day: £1,740 - £3,026 Brandeston Hall • Independent
- Open days: Late Jan, May and early October

Remarks: For further details see senior school.

FRANCIS HOLLAND JUNIOR SCHOOL (SW1)

Linked to Francis Holland School (SW1) in the Senior section

Graham Terrace, London, SW1W 8JF

Tel: 020 7730 2971
Fax: 020 7823 4066
E-mail: education@fhs-sw1.org.uk
Website: www.fhs-sw1.org.uk

- Pupils: 200 girls; all day • Ages: 4-11 • Fees: £3,120 - £3,735
- Independent • Open days: Several

Head: For the last 23 years, Mrs Molly Bown DipEd Cert Ed SRN (fifties) bright-eyed and elegant who clearly loves her school and claims to have 'the happiest staff room I've worked in'. Staff certainly keen to stay. She came late to teaching, her first career being as a ward sister. Wants girls to be polite but not stifled, and to have a sense of humour balanced by discipline.

Entrance: At 4. Children are 'tested' in January for the September term. Mrs Bown and staff see 100 for 24 places (potential is sought).

Exit: Half to two-thirds to the senior school (via London Schools Consortium exam), and the rest to St Paul's, Godolphin, Wycombe Abbey, Cheltenham Ladies College, Downe House, Benenden, St Mary's Ascot and occasionally

Royal Ballet School.

Remarks: Strong, academic pre-prep and prep school near Sloane Square. Remarkable building for Central London the site being shared with the senior school. A quad in the middle serves as playground for all years but plenty of games (either on site or Battersea Park four days a week). Head of ballet recently organised a 'really most impressive' Princess Margaret Classical Ballet Awards Day, though some parents feel that drama and modern dance could be given more of a push. A happy atmosphere and pleasant good manners throughout the school and lots of unspoilt-looking girls.

Parents very social – banking, diplomats, lawyers, media types, some royalty and celebs, although everyone frightfully discreet. Mostly from Chelsea, Fulham, Pimlico. Old Girls include Lady Sarah Chatto, Vanessa Mae and Jemima Khan. Big building programme completed recently and opened by the Duke of Westminster (niece attended the school) has provided new science labs, ICT suite, gym and lovely outdoor amphitheatre. Vigorous science department under buzzy Scottish head who has lots of clubs (doing all the experiments you'd rather they didn't do at home) and an annual 'spaghetti and marshmallow' day where families compete (some fathers taking it very seriously indeed) to build the biggest structure.

The school is keen on trips eg Docklands, Canterbury, York, ENO and making 'full use of being in central London'. Music is strong with at least 80 per cent of girls learning an instrument. Head looked blank at the mention of special needs, but parents say there is super support in the class-rooms for anyone lagging behind. Specialist teachers brought in from the senior school in science, ICT, art, PE and also French which is taught from 8. Strong 'helping others' ethos with girls raising money for charity at home and abroad. Bright and airy library shared with the senior school.

FRENSHAM HEIGHTS LOWER SCHOOL

Linked to Frensham Heights School in the Senior section

Rowledge, Farnham, Surrey, GU10 4EA

Tel: 01252 792561
Fax: 01252 794 335
Website: www.frensham-heights.org.uk

- Pupils: boys and girls; day and boarding 11+ • Ages: 3-13
- Fees: First school: £1,480 - £2,220. Lower school: £2,220 - £3,920 • Independent • Open days: Five each year - see website

Remarks: New, lovely, bright First School houses three- to eight-year-olds. Confident, busy six-year-olds rushing about calling teachers 'Sue' and 'Caron' (still). Seven-year-olds get specialist teachers for French, drama, ICT, music and PE.

For further details, see senior school.

FRIENDS' JUNIOR SCHOOL

Linked to Friends' School in the Senior section

65 Debden Road, Saffron Walden, Essex, CB11 4AL

Tel: 01799 527235
Fax: 01799 520681
E-mail: adminjs@friends.org.uk
Website: www.friends.org.uk

- Pupils: 160 girls and boys; day and boarding • Ages: 3-11
- Quaker ethos • Fees: Day £2,050-£3,590; boarding £5,790
- Independent • Open days: Termly

Head: Andrew Holmes BA BEd
Entrance: By individual assessment.

THE FROEBELIAN SCHOOL

Clarence Road, Horsforth, Leeds, West Yorkshire, LS18 4LB

Tel: 01132 583 047
Fax: 0113 258 0173
E-mail: office@froebelian.co.uk
Website: www.froebelian.co.uk

- Pupils: Around 190 boys and girls; all day • Ages: 3-11
- Christian, non-denom • Fees: £1,040-1,685 • Independent
- Open days: March

Headmaster: Since 1991, Mr John Tranmer MA PGCE (late forties), read history at St John's, Cambridge, PGCE at St Martin's Lancaster. Has had varied career – teaching at Bolton School, HMS Indefatigable (nautical school), Parkside School, Cobham (ran history, RE and games). Two 2-year career breaks, with a building society and at GCHQ. Wife works for a charity and both their children attended the school when younger.

Very articulate, with a firm intellectual grip on what is going on. Easy, unaffected manner, very much at home in a small prep school, sees himself as an enabler, relieving staff of tedious admin tasks (he treats them regularly to cream cakes). A teaching head – one-fifth timetable, mainly history; coaches sport, runs marathons. His office has sweeping views over wooded valley to ruined Kirkstall Abbey.

Entrance: Almost exclusively at 3; first 24 to register are invited to spend two hours in school, where they are informally assessed by staff. One-form entry of 24, perpetual waiting-list of between 20 and 30. Places occasionally available for older children.

Exit: About 80 per cent to Bradford and Leeds independent grammar schools (boys and girls). Harrogate Ladies' College, Ashville and Woodhouse Grove also popular. Occasional entrant to boarding (eg St Peter's, York) or reputable maintained (St Aidan's, Harrogate).

Remarks: Small, intimate, family-atmosphere prep school on a cramped (school says 'compact') site, on the northern fringes of the Leeds-Bradford conurbation. Founded 1913, but no longer any formal connection with the Froebel Institute. A recent extension has provided two large additional classrooms, a multi-purpose studio and a welcome enlargement of the playground.

Serious academic ethos but by no means a sweatshop. Consistently high SATs results. Top-quality, feet-on-ground staff dedicated to helping children enjoy learning. Average class size 24 – but early years always have one or two classroom assistants. Exposure to IT from the start – 4-year-olds manipulate enormous mice, year 5s email and surf the net on their own – and they're taught how to use the conventional library. Much specialist teaching in junior (8-11) department – science, D&T, French, music, IT, games and drama. Teacher/pupil ratio 1:11. All pupils screened for SEN at ages 7 and 8 (eight pupils currently have 1:1 support with a specialist teacher). Plenty of sport on offer, despite limited facilities (school uses nearby fields and pool) with the emphasis on taking part. PE/games co-ordinator, Wendy Staniland, was awarded the 'Sports Teacher of the Year Award, 2003' by the National Council for School Sport. Music and drama very strong – over 90 per cent of juniors learn at least one instrument, school is famous locally for its musicals (Bugsy Malone, Oliver). Also field trips, outings, juniors' week in France. 'Pastoral care', says Mr Tranmer, 'exists in the fabric of the place; given that staff and pupils live in each other's pockets, it can function largely through teachers' intuition.' Very clear school code and anti-bullying policy. Parents happy with all this. Pupils wear neat, bright-red sweaters (staff, too, are encouraged to dress smartly), and go about their daily business calmly and cheerfully. Strong emphasis on children allowing each other to be happy in their school lives – and older boys and girls (amazingly) help supervise tinies' lunch-time. All in all, a happy and successful little school, which turns out well-prepared and confident children ready for local high-reputation day schools (where they do well). Mr Tranmer thinks wistfully of moving to a more spacious site but this must be long term. Not for those who want a stately home in hundreds of acres. Very popular with Leeds-Bradford medical mafia; governors are mostly current and past parents. Excellent value, too.

FULHAM PREP SCHOOL

200 Greyhound Road, London, W14 9RY

Tel: 020 7386 2444
Fax: 020 7386 2449
E-mail: prepadmin@fulhamprep.co.uk
Website: www.fulhamprep.co.uk

- Pupils: 430 boys and girls; all day • Ages: 4-13 • Non-denom
- Fees: £3,150-£3,500 • Independent • Open days: Contact registrar

Head: Since 1996, Mrs Jane Emmett BEd (fifties). Previously at Cameron House; Mr Emmett is the bursar. 2 sons, 4 grandchildren. Jolly. Full of energy and enthusiasm with a 'hands-on' approach. Thought by parents to be 'helming her ship onward and upward'.

Entrance: At 4, non-selective, first come first served basis; siblings of attending pupils get priority. Reception intake of 90 children each September. Selective at 7, 8 and 11. Assessment and interview mornings held in January preceding September of entry. Deadline for registration December 1st preceding September entry.

Exit: To a wide range of day and boarding schools.

Remarks: In order to accommodate an increasing number of children, the prep department has moved into new premises near the Queen's Club, within half a mile of its pre-prep department. Still good sized, friendly, family-run school with a cosy feel to it, still expanding. Mostly local children who walk to school, as parking is tricky. With prep department now based in Greyhound Road, transport from Parsons Green, Chiswick & Fulham. Founded in 1996 by Mrs Emmett with a handful of children in a church hall, today housed in a well-adapted Victorian school plus its own new buildings. Light rooms, lots of stairs but there is a lift in the new building, lovely art displayed throughout. ICT suite, art room and gym/assembly room whilst the reception area has its own wet-play room. Busy children everywhere who are eager to show you their work. Mixed ability classes with an emphasis on developing the individual. Maximum class size is 18. Experienced remedial teachers are available to help with mild dyslexic/dyspraxic type difficulties; those who require more than this may find that a move elsewhere is suggested. Broad curriculum particularly strong on music. French throughout the school. Active after-school clubs. Children are taken swimming and walk to Hurlingham Park for sports. The new 30,000 square foot building has under-gone complete refurbishment and contains three purpose-built science laboratories, a state of the art IT suite, a music technology room, a library, an assembly hall/theatre as well as all the normal subject classrooms. The old reception block has been completely rebuilt to provide a 180-seat dining room with modern catering facilities and planning permission has been obtained for a purpose-built sports hall adjacent to the all-weather sports pitch, all within its own grounds of approximately one acre. The prep department has classes of no more than 18 and specialist teaching in all subjects from year 4. It offers a wide-ranging academic programme and puts great emphasis on the all-round development of each child. Latin and philosophy are added to the curriculum from year 5 and Greek can be provided if required. 'If there is a demand Mrs E will try to meet it,' said one enthusiastic parent. Keen sports teachers often antipodeans, offer Saturday sports. Very popular with Fulham parents, appreciated for understanding pupils' strengths and weaknesses. Good reputation for getting children into suitable senior schools.

GARDEN HOUSE SCHOOL

Turks Row, London, SW3 4TW

Tel: 020 7730 1652
Fax: 020 7589 7708
E-mail: info@gardenhouseschool.co.uk
Website: www.gardenhouseschool.co.uk

- Pupils: 290 girls, 140 boys, all day • Ages: 3-11 • Non-denom
- Fees: £1,875-£4,089 • Independent

Principal: Since 1973, Mrs Jill Oddy BA, owner and administrator. Dynamic and proactive. For past 10 years has also owned two pre-schools in New York.

Head of upper girls: Since 1998, Mrs Janet Webb CertEd who runs school jointly with Mrs Wendy Challen CertEdFroeb, head of the lower girls since 1988. Both very approachable. Mrs Webb teaches 10 maths lessons each week.

Head(s) of boys' school: Since 2000, Mr Magoo Giles (pastoral), charming, enthusiastic, ex army, obviously adores his job. Boys' school opened in 1989.

Entrance: At 3 or 4, very occasionally places later. Pupils come from cosy local nurseries and kindergartens. All live locally in Sloane Ranger land. No room for children of ex-pats on temporary contracts. Entry test one year before entry. Long waiting lists. Names down asap. Sibling policy.

Exit: Girls to Downe House, Wycombe Abbey, St Mary's Ascot, Heathfield, St Paul's, Godolphin & Latymer, Francis Holland and a handful of more gentle girls' schools. Hardly any to co-ed schools, and 70 per cent will board. Boys to Northcote Lodge, Sussex House, Eaton House the Manor, Westminster Under, Colet Court. Approximately 30 per cent will board: Summer Fields, Horris Hill, Ludgrove; occasional scholarships.

Remarks: The whole school moved in 2004 to spacious new premises in a listed building in the Duke of Yorks. New facilities include IT and recital room, new gym and dining room. New building also includes art and science rooms. Boys and Girls are taught separately.

Kindergarten 3-4 years is housed in Sedding St at the back of Holy Trinity church.

Small class sizes ranging from 14/16 in reception to 18/20 at age 11. Parallel classes throughout but setting for maths into three streams from year three using multisensory approach. Otherwise subjects taught traditionally in class with French from 4 years by French national. Exams for all upper girls each summer term. Computer suite for both sexes. Dyslexics and dyspraxics catered for by part-time visiting specialist – two members of staff currently attending special needs courses. Class size about 12-18, female staff in the majority, one classroom assistant per class. Good food.

All school drama productions staged ambitiously at Royal Court Theatre (round the corner). Art copiously displayed throughout. Individual music lessons may commence at 4 years. Very young team of female teaching staff likely to be sharing houses in Fulham. Even classroom assistants are graduates. Some of the staff visit the schools in New York and vice versa. Year 6 girls spend a week in France. Year 5 girls go to Juniper Hall in spring term for geography field trip. Help is given for dyslexia in small group teaching by specialist members of staff. No games facilities on site but short walks to Burton Court and Ranelagh Gardens, minibus transports to Battersea Park for sports day. Swimming is taught throughout the school and fencing (for 8-11 year olds boys and girls).

Clubs run after school including seasonal tennis. Year 3 upwards may stay for supervised (but not assisted) homework club until 5.00pm. School finishes at 1.00pm on Friday for sport including handball, basketball, judo. Football and athletics at Burton Court. Saturday football club in Battersea Park. Annual camping trip for 7 year old boys and activity week in Cornwall for 8 year olds plus ski trip to Switzerland for boys and girls.

Gentle atmosphere suits most, but a more academic child might not be sufficiently stretched.

GATEWAYS PREPARATORY SCHOOL

Linked to Gateways School in the Senior section

Harewood, Leeds, West Yorkshire, LS17 9LE

Tel: 0113 288 6345
Fax: 0113 288 6148
E-mail: gateways@gatewayschool.co.uk
Website: www.gatewaysschool.co.uk

• Pupils: Girls and boys (3-7), girls only 7+ • Ages: 3-11 • C of E foundation, but 'all faiths or none' accepted • Fees: £1,089 - £2,655 • Independent

Remarks: For further details see senior school.

GEORGE HERIOT'S JUNIOR SCHOOL

Linked to George Heriot's School in the Senior section

Lauriston Place, Edinburgh, EH3 9EQ

Tel: 01312 297 263
Fax: 01312 296 363
E-mail: admissions@george-heriots.com
Website: www.george-heriots.com

• Pupils: all boys, all day • Ages: 4-11 • Independent

Remarks: See senior school.

GEORGE WATSON'S COLLEGE JUNIOR SCHOOL

Linked to George Watson's College in the Senior section

Colinton Road, Edinburgh, EH10 5EG

Tel: 0131 447 7931
Fax: 0131 452 8594
E-mail: admissions@gwc.org.uk
Website: www.gwc.org.uk

• Pupils: boys and girls; all day • Ages: 3 - 12 • Fees: £1,723 - £1,940 • Independent

Head: Since 1989, Mr Donald McGougan DipCE (forties), educated at Campbeltown Grammar School and then Moray House. Internally appointed and well liked by staff and pupils.

Entrance: From 3 to the nursery. Early entries by interview but after 7 by English, maths and VR assessment.

Exit: No guarantee of advancement from nursery to main primary school but, once in, majority go on to senior school unless family circumstances dictate otherwise.

Remarks: Learning begins through play in nursery. The Watson's claim is that learning should be fun – even at home; homework given from first year and parents encouraged to support. Specialist subject teaching for the older children but French begins at 6 years old with native speakers. Special catch-up classes run for any latecomers. ICT skills taught and used widely to support other subjects. Mixed ability groups with setting only for maths at the top end of the school. Extensive library, and audio books. And quite a rarity for a primary school, a librarian on hand to help make choices. Good dyslexia support throughout. All for inclusive education, anxious to get away from any image of having 'a school with a unit'.

Lots of opportunities for children to exhibit their dramatic or musical talents on stage. Four choirs, two recorder groups, chamber orchestra, ensembles and pipes. Oodles of extra activities and clubs. Out on the field there's hockey for girls and rugby for the boys and back inside swimming for all. No official scholarships but in line with the ethos of the school, financial help given in unforeseen circumstances. Mostly children from professional parents who are pleased to have the 'extended day' for just a little extra, breakfast and after-school clubs. A big school and, at 23+, biggish classes. But manages its size well, taking advantage of its senior school's facilities. Good teaching and good value for money.

GILBERT INGLEFIELD HOUSE

Linked to Haberdashers' Agincourt School in the Junior section
Linked to Haberdashers' Monmouth School For Girls in the Senior section

Hereford Road, Monmouth, Monmouthshire, NP25 5XT

Tel: 01600 711 100
Fax: 01600 711 233
E-mail: admissions@hmsg.gwent.sch.uk
Website: www.habs-monmouth.org

• Pupils: 110 girls; all day • Ages: 7-11 • Fees: Day: £2,310 in the prep • Independent • Open days: October

Entrance: Exams at 7, 8, 9 and 10.

Exit: Most to senior school after sitting 11+ exam.

Remarks: Lovely, intimate junior school at the heart of main school site. Physical education, science and music lessons taught by specialists, most of rest taught by class tutor. Lots of music, singing and dancing. Separate play area. Newly built mini-amphitheatre provides unusual outdoor performance area. Self-contained facilities, such as art area and well-stocked library, plus ready access to extensive facilities of main school, offer the best of both worlds.

THE GLASGOW ACADEMY PREPARATORY SCHOOL

Linked to Glasgow Academy (The) in the Senior section

Westbourne House, Colebrooke Terrace, Glasgow, G12 8HE

Tel: 0141 334 8558
Fax: 0141 337 3473
Website: www.theglasgowacademy.org.uk

• Pupils: 251 boys, 224 girls; plus nursery 5 boys, 5 girls
• Ages: Prep 5-11, nursery 2-5; all day • Fees: £865 - £2,560
• Independent • Open days: November

Head: Mrs Helen Fortune.

Remarks: For further details, see the senior school.

GLENDOWER PREP SCHOOL

87 Queen's Gate, South Kensington, London, SW7 5JX

Tel: 020 7370 1927
Fax: 020 7244 8308
E-mail: office@glendower.kensington.sch.uk
Website: www.glendower.kensington.sch.uk

- Pupils: 185 girls, all day • Ages: 4-11 • Inter-denom • Fees: £3,230 • Independent • Open days: Open mornings some Fridays every term, by appointment only

Head: Since 2004, Mrs Rosamond Bowman BA Hons PGCE, a modern linguist, forties. Previously taught at Colet Court, ultimately as assistant head, then head of juniors at The Hall, Hampstead and 2 years as head of Willington prep in Wimbledon. Immensely likeable, quietly spoken but transmitting intense enthusiasm and enjoyment, this is a head who makes you want to hand over your daughter on the instant. Mrs Bowman speaks of her girls, her staff and her school with the confidence of a round peg in the right hole. In her brief reign the school has speedily recovered from the hiccup and minor haemorrhage of pupils that occurred towards the end of her long-serving predecessor's tenure – the former regime being felt by some to be autocratic and over-pressurising. Common sense and a genuine concern for each individual now prevail and a relaxed Mrs Bowman presides, supported by a loyal staff and a governing body which includes some of the biggest brains in the city – most current or ex parents. It also includes the head of Godolphin and Latymer which can't hurt. If the governing body is formidable so are the parents and a few are impatient that the rather rigid regime of Mrs Bowman's predecessor has not yet been modernized as quickly and as radically as was hoped. Mrs Bowman, however, has a gentle determination of her own and there can be little doubt that considerable changes are on the way.

Entrance: The applications of 150 tots are taken for the 22 places at the age of 4 but this degree of competition is normal anywhere good in this area and no-one should be deterred from having a go. After that the list is closed. 80 children are assessed by careful observation – mostly for their 'social maturity' – and any parents who think that coaching at this age is a good idea need to forget it now. 'I don't want them coming here reading the FT,' asserts Mrs Bowman. The notional 22 places may, in the event, be diminished by the school's sensible sibling policy. At 7 a fur-

ther 10 places are available and those who were turned away – often with much regret – at 4 are invited to reapply. Assessment is by way of a morning spent reading, writing, on maths and generally socialising. No particular feeder schools. Occasional places occur but school unlikely to fill them after year 5 – the cohesion of the year being seen as paramount. It's worth a call though.

Exit: Unusual not to get into your first choice from here. Most to the top London day schools with biggest contingents to St Paul's and Godolphin and Latymer. Far more offers than the pupils can take up, this school is maybe uniquely successful in placing its girls. Some to board – 2003/2004 saw places taken up at Heathfield, Malvern, Cheltenham, Downe House, Dauntsey's, the St Mary's in Ascot and in Calne, and Wycombe Abbey.

Remarks: An elegant 1830s white building – Cubitt? – on Queen's Gate occupying a large corner plot facing Stanhope Gardens. The 6 storey building is remarkably spacious. An airy, panelled and white-painted entrance hall complete with wonderful large Quentin Blake originals greet the visitor and is also used, with the doors opened to the adjacent library, as an assembly space. Library attractive and well-stocked. Super staircase, excellent displays of work everywhere, lots of up-to-the-minute equipment in all rooms and all rooms remarkably orderly with inviting and interesting-looking work and resources everywhere. A good mix of the formal and instructive with the creative and inspirational. Classes are light and bright but some were pretty airless on our visit and we longed to open windows, notwithstanding the street noise which isn't very great here. Rooms are good sizes and, though some passages are very narrow, this school feels less cramped than some of its local competitors. 1 teacher/assistant to 11 girls and a class maximum of 16 in the upper school.

Not a school for those with serious SENs but school will pick up and support those with mild difficulties and make individual learning plans for those who need them. Up to 5 per cent or so come needing a little extra help with English – many, given the South Kensington population, are French – and EFL is given in small groups or 1-to-1 as needed. French is well-supported with 3 weekly lessons for everyone and taught by native speakers. Year 6 has a 5-day trip to Normandy. Latin from year 6 and one all-purpose lab. The full academic programme includes DT and ICT and, despite having no grounds to speak of the school is famously sporty. They seem to win more than two thirds of their matches and excel in tournaments of all kinds especially in swimming and netball. They are bused everywhere – 'we keep Impact in business', says Mrs Bowman – and sporting activities take place in local parks and sports centres and the timetable is adapted to take traffic problems into account. Many of the academic staff are involved in the sporting side and, somehow, it all seems to work.

Drama is creative, they write and produce their own plays. Lovely, varied and imaginative art taught by professional illustrator/teacher. We saw clocks and mazes and silhouettes and papier-mâché creatures and wanted to get stuck in. Music is busy – lots of individual lessons.

Lunch is unusual. All vegetarian and cooked in the basement kitchen and then 'great big Brazilian students' carry everything – cutlery, crockery, tablecloths, napkins and food – into the classrooms where it is served to the children, after grace – and clear it away again afterwards. 'Crudités' and fresh fruit with every meal and meals have names like 'cowboy stew' (veg bangers and beans). Classroom feeding means that no precious space is taken up by a dining room and it does sound like fun.

Girls come from high-achieving, well-off families as you'd expect in this area. Parents are heavily involved and many live round the corner. A family atmosphere is what Mrs Bowman is after and, therefore, however tempting, expansion is unlikely. 'I don't want to lose sight of our ability to cater for the individual,' she says and she is clear about the sort of girl who will do best here. 'We look for a Glendower girl – with enthusiasm, curiosity, a love of life, a willingness to fit in and be part of the group and we have an ability to build up her self-respect. By building on their individual strengths you can give children a sense of their individual self-worth. We don't have any arrogant girls here.'

School keen to quote ISI inspection report of June 2005: '...small, happy and very caring environment... good standard of attainment across a broad and challenging curriculum which prepares them very well for success in entrance examinations... high level of pastoral care...'. You can read the rest yourself online.

The faces we saw were happy and attentive and it felt harmonious and purposeful. Places here are rightfully prized and not just because of the admirable record of placing pupils in their next schools. Nonetheless, discontent among some few families persists to the extent that one or two choose to remove their daughters early or to send their second daughters elsewhere – perhaps to schools which are felt to be less rigorous and old-fashioned in their approach to teaching methods and to discipline. Also to schools felt to be more friendly to parents – still seen by Glendower staff as the enemy, according to some. Whether or not this proves to be a short-sighted move remains to be seen – Mrs Bowman has yet fully to impress her quietly

articulated but strong and clear-sighted vision of the school on its entire community.

Overall, still an outstanding school in many respects but probably better for Brunnhilde than for Mimi.

GODOLPHIN PREPARATORY SCHOOL

Linked to Godolphin School (The) in the Senior section

Laverstock Road, Salisbury, Wiltshire, SP1 2RB

Tel: 01722 430 652
Fax: 01722 430 651
E-mail: prep@godolphin.wilts.sch.uk
Website: www.godolphinprep.org

• Pupils: 60 girls, all day • Ages: 3-11 • Fees: £1,462 - £2,874
• Independent • Open days: October and February

Head: Since 2005, Mrs Paula White, formerly head of Burghclere Primary School, Hampshire.

Entrance: Assessment day and head's report.

Exit: Girls are prepared for Common Entrance, a range of 11+ examinations and scholarships; about 75 per cent go on to the Godolphin School, a few to the local grammar school, the rest to St Mary's Calne, Wycombe Abbey, Dauntsey's and St Anthony's-Leweston.

Remarks: Has good access to senior school facilities.

GODSTOWE PREP SCHOOL

High Wycombe, Buckinghamshire, HP13 6PR

Tel: 01494 529 273
Fax: 01494 429 009
E-mail: head@godstowe.org
Website: www.godstowe.org

• Pupils: 100 boarders, 210 day girls. Also pre-prep of 100 boys and girls, all day • Ages: 7-13, pre-prep 3-7 • C of E • Fees: £1,660 - £3,565; boarding £5,240 • Independent • Open days: Termly on Fridays, check website for dates

Head: Interregnum. In late June 2005 Mrs Frances Henson, head since 1991, departed precipitately over the course of a weekend. This appears to have been the culmination of long-running disagreements as to the future direction of the school. Not brilliantly handled, putting it mildly. We do not, though, detect any underlying malaise that could not be put right by a good new head (due July 2006). Governors remain committed to Godstowe as it always was – girls only through to 13 – but with better provision for those who want to try for state selectives at 11.

Entrance: Not a selective school, and numbers are down anyway. Entry at 7 for the main school. Academic scholarships at 8 and 11.

Exit: Pre-prep boys usually go to traditional boys' boarding at seven. Girls to major senior schools, including Wycombe Abbey, Cheltenham Ladies' College, Downe House, Haileybury, Rugby, Badminton, Benenden etc etc. Most take CE at 13, with scholarships and exhibitions on all fronts. 30 per cent won scholarships to senior schools in 2003. Small trickle to state sector at 11.

Remarks: The first girls' boarding prep in the country, purpose-built 1900 (with later extensions). Magical new music school (with spectacular views across the valley), serious re-vamp of older buildings, particularly the dining room, and other new building. Brilliant use of very hilly ground on outskirts of High Wycombe, assault course and outdoor activity areas. Masses of activities at weekends, plus free clubs and options – 2 hours per day from 4.30pm. Early drop-off plus breakfast (7.30am) and late pick-up plus supper (7.30pm) for 'a few pounds'. Excellent PSHE in place and girls get lifestyle course after CE which includes lectures from representatives of The Body Shop.

Pre-prep has expanded hugely; now has new separate buildings. French from age four. Latin or Spanish at ten. Classes 'subtly' streamed. Maximum class size 18, scholarship stream. IT, art, marvellous textiles and ceramics; fantastic music (long tradition of this) with masses of girl-inspired concerts. Dyslexia help on hand, with one-to-one help where necessary, regular spelling and reading help available. EFL also available, though only about 5 per cent foreigners (not counting ex-pats). Some MoD parents.

A parent said to us, 'excellent pastoral care, really fantastic homely feel to the boarding houses. All the girls are friendly and caring with good manners. I am really pleased with the high academic standard. My daughter has consistently received a very sound education without feeling at all pressured, despite arriving there in year 6. We have just done the rounds of 13+ interviews to very selective senior schools, and were welcomed at all with a big smile and exclamation of 'Ah ... Godstowe' – acceptance letters poured in soon after! Girls well prepared for interviews, confident and cheerful (and smart).' School is very much on form as a boarding school with a large day element – 'the only good one (ie girls' prep) in the area,' say parents.

That, at least, is what applied until things came unglued. We look to the new head to get it back on the rails fast.

THE GRANGE

Linked to Haberdashers' Agincourt School in the Junior section
Linked to Monmouth School in the Senior section

St James Street, Monmouth, Monmouthshire, NP25 3DL

Tel: 01600 710 408
Fax: 01600 772 701
E-mail: admissions@monmouthschool.org
Website: www.habs-monmouth.org

• Pupils: 105 boys, all day • Ages: 7-11; pre-prep 3-7 • Fees: £2,065 • Independent • Open days: Early October and mid-January

Head: Mrs Elaine Thomas.

Entrance: Entry at 7, though other stages considered if places available.

Exit: Most to Monmouth School – but they have to take the exam on the same terms as outsiders.

Remarks: Co-ed pre-prep Haberdashers' Agincourt School.

GRESHAM'S PREPARATORY SCHOOL

Linked to Gresham's School in the Senior section

Cromer Road, Holt, Norfolk, NR25 6EY

Tel: 01263 714600
Fax: 01263 714060
E-mail: prep@greshams.com
Website: www.greshams.com

• Pupils: roughly 60/40 boys and girls; boarding and day • Ages: 3-13 including pre prep and nursery • Fees: Prep school: boarding: £5,025; day £3,855. Pre-prep: from £1,905-£2,115 • Independent • Open days: First May Bank Holiday Saturday, plus taster days in September, October and November

Head: Since 2003, Mr James Quick BA PGCE (forties), educated at Rendcomb, did his BA and PGCE at Durham, and teaches history as much as possible – 'I do like being in the classroom... you can find out what's really happening'. Previously taught at The Dragon in Oxford, where he was housemaster (and taught this editor's children history) and subsequently at St Edwards. He did a sabbatical at Geelong Grammar in Australia before coming here with his wife, Kim, and their four daughters, all at Gresham's.

Entrance: Either through the pre-prep or via own test.

Exit: Predominantly to the senior school, though one or two may go elsewhere.

Remarks: Jolly little school, autonomous as far as it goes, but within walking distance of Gresham's (mini-bus for smalls) for all the main facilities like games, swimming pool and theatre, though the prep does have its own integrated games pitches and a fab new play area with wizard wooden climbing frames and a somewhat strange pagoda. Stunning art dept – with pottery and ceramics and their own kiln; terrific pupil pics all over the shop. Terrific music too; many jazz, wind, string and rock bands, plus little theatrical performances; they have taken a 'production to the Edinburgh fringe for the last ten years.

Big jolly library, with computers and more computers all over the school. Terrific selection of board games, chess popular and giant chess in the garden, and spit new wooden climbing frame. Dedicated classrooms, langs from seven, Latin from nine. One full-time and three part-time SEN assistants, again extra charge for this, but will take ADHD (which senior school is chary about) and finds no problems with Ritalin. This is a charming school within a school, dedicated boy and girl houses, cheerful bright (dare one say garish?) colours in the dorms, with a happy mixture of full, weekly and flexi boarders. Head reckons that shortly the full and weekly boarders will become as one. School nominally full, but 'could take the odd one at the odd time'. Worth a try.

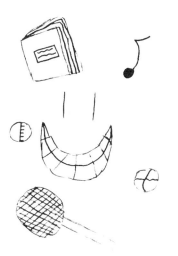

GREYCOTES AND THE SQUIRREL, OXFORD HIGH JUNIOR DEPARTMENT

Linked to Oxford High School GDST in the Senior section

Belbroughton Road, Oxford, Oxfordshire, OX2 6XA

Tel: Greycotes 01865 515647
Fax: Greycotes 01865 510841
E-mail: oxfordhigh@oxf.gdst.net
Website: www.gdst.net

• Pupils: 305 girls in the junior dept (nursery – y6); 43 boys in the junior dept (nursery – y2); all day • Ages: 7-11 at the junior department at Greycotes; 3-7 at the junior department at The Squirrel • Non-denom • Fees: £735 (nursery), £1,779 (junior) • Independent • Open days: October

Remarks: Merger of two popular local schools in 1998 within walking distance Greycotes, which houses the juniors, and The Squirrels for co-ed pre-prep. For further details, see Oxford High School GDST.

GRIMSDELL, MILL HILL PRE-PREPARATORY SCHOOL

Linked to Belmont School in the Junior section
Linked to Mill Hill School Foundation in the Senior section

Winterstoke House, Wills Grove, Mill Hill, London, NW7 1QR

Tel: 020 8959 6884
Fax: 020 8959 4626
E-mail: office@grimsdell.org.uk
Website: www.grimsdell.org.uk

• Pupils: 69 girls and boys; all day • Ages: 3-7 • Independent

Remarks: For further details see senior school.

Guildford High School Junior School

Linked to Guildford High School in the Senior section

London Road, Guildford, Surrey, GU1 1SJ

Tel: 01483 562475
E-mail: jackie.thompson@church-schools.com
Website: www.guildfordhigh.surrey.sch.uk

- Pupils: 300 girls; all day • Ages: 4-11 • Fees: £1,979 - £2,698
- Independent • Open days: Several per term, please see website

Remarks: For further details see senior school.

Haberdashers' Agincourt School

Linked to Gilbert Inglefield House in the Junior section
Linked to Haberdashers' Monmouth School For Girls in the Senior section
Linked to Grange (The) in the Junior section
Linked to Monmouth School in the Senior section

Dixton Lane, Monmouth, Monmouthshire, NP25 3SY

Tel: 01600 713 970
Fax: 01600 714 097
E-mail: enquiries@agincourtschool.org
Website: www.habs-monmouth.org

- Pupils: 95 girls and boys; all day • Ages: 3-7 • Independent

Remarks: For further details see senior school.

Haberdashers' Aske's Prep School

Linked to Haberdashers' Aske's Boys' School in Senior section

Butterfly Lane, Elstree, Borehamwood, Hertfordshire, WD6 3AF

Tel: 020 8266 1779
Fax: 020 8266 1800
E-mail: prep@habsboys.org.uk
Website: www.habsboys.org.uk

- Pupils: 210 boys; all day • Ages: 7-11 • Fees: £3,200
- Independent • Open days: October

Head: Since 1997, Mrs Y M Mercer.

Entrance: Competitive entry exam plus report from previous school and the (long) short-listed boys and their parents are called in for interview.

Exit: Very rare for boys at 11 to be directed elsewhere.

Remarks: A popular choice as a way-in to the senior school, heavily over-subscribed. Pleasant building, light, airy classrooms, lots of outdoor space.

Haberdashers' Aske's School for Girls, Junior School

Linked to Haberdashers' Aske's School for Girls in the Senior section

Aldenham Road, Elstree, Borehamwood, Hertfordshire, WD6 3BT

Tel: 020 8266 2400
Website: www.habsgirls.org.uk

- Pupils: 300 girls; all day • Ages: 4-11 • Fees: £2,508 - £2,990
- Independent • Open days: October & July; Open mornings November

Head: Mrs S Worthington

Entrance: Fiercely competitive entry, via an hour-long playgroup, followed, for the successful, by an interview later.

Remarks: Attached to the main school building and shares all the senior school facilities but has its own science lab, computer suite, art room, maths room, languages room, music room and gym. New two storey building opened September 2005 incorporating larger classrooms.

First primary school in country to have Japanese as part of the curriculum in juniors and infants from September 2003.

HALE PREPARATORY SCHOOL

Broomfield Lane, Hale, Altrincham, Cheshire, WA15 9AS

Tel: 0161 928 2386
Fax: 0161 941 7934
E-mail: administrator@hale-prep-school.demon.co.uk

- Pupils: 182 boys and girls • Ages: 4-11 • Inter-denom • Fees: £4,485 • Independent

Head: Since 1980, Mr John Connor (early sixties). Down to earth, old fashioned, genial disciplinarian. Previously senior teacher at Xaverian College, Manchester and head of Hillcrest Grammar, Stockport. Founded Hale Prep in 1980 to be his own boss; now owns buildings too. Has 'no intention of retiring', two of his four children work at the school. Puts school's success down to high expectations, small classes, help when needed, instilling self discipline and ability to work independently. Ultra-available – head or deputy (head is magistrate one day a week) stands at school gate morning and afternoon and positively encourages parent interaction. Children describe him as funny, 'he can make lessons we don't really like enjoyable', 'we like his jokes and stories', 'he doesn't like dangly earrings or children leaving others out'.

Entrance: Non-selective, strictly by waiting list. Most of 22 places in reception go to those registered before birth but classes grow in juniors and people move so worth signing up. Late entrants do take a 'happiness (IQ) test' to ensure they'll integrate successfully.

Exit: Outstanding for a non-selective intake; almost all to top rate secondary schools. Lots to Manchester Grammar, also Withington Girls School, or the grant-maintained Altrincham Grammars.

Remarks: Beavering, happy but ordered atmosphere with enthusiastic teachers on four floors of Victorian mansion, plus extra classroom block. Most academic teaching in half classes, so maximum size at top of school is 16. 'We do offer a lot of help, a lot of one to one', says head. Over 70 per cent 3s at key stage one, over 90 per cent 5s at key stage two, especially strong in maths and science. Designated rooms and teachers for music, art, IT and science lab.

Specialist teachers too for drama, DT and games. LAMDA exams, after-school dance club, choir, individual instrument lessons during lunch hour and after school. Disproportionately (for size) successful in local netball, football, tennis, rounders and cross country contests; also offers lacrosse, athletics, fencing and cricket. Annual ski trip (first come first served) and outward bound in Wales for all, plus diverse day trips.

School lunches compulsory, infants served, juniors self-serve at later sitting, head presides over both. Salad bar and fresh fruit available; pupils say, 'some lunches are dodgy, some are really nice; we like the doughnuts and fish and chips on Fridays.' Some Jewish and Muslim pupils, daily assembly with prayer, head says, 'my aim is not to confuse them but to make them aware of other religions and give them a code of behaviour that's moral for all.'

Congested road at drop-off and pick-up time. A few parents feel the pressure of homework; maximum expected is one hour a day but pupils want to succeed – 'they want you to do well and try your hardest but they make it fun,' they say.

THE HALL SCHOOL

23 Crossfield Road, Hampstead, London, NW3 4NU

Tel: 020 7722 1700
Fax: 020 7483 0181
E-mail: office@hallschool.co.uk
Website: www.hallschool.co.uk

- Pupils: 440 boys; all day • Ages: 4-13 • Christian foundation, all faiths welcome • Fees: £2,785 - £3,390 • Independent
- Open days: Open evenings for those who have registered their sons

Head: From 2006, returning to hold the fort during an interregnum, popular previously head, Mr Ramage. His successor left to head the junior school of Geelong Grammar. New head due September 2006 – watch the proverbial space.

Entrance: Register before your son is a year old (though it's worth trying for gaps at odd moments and the school often takes four or five new boys into year 4). The school registers and takes a £50 deposit from the first 200 applicants. Around 30 boys come into reception at 4 and 20 or so into year 1 at 5 – parents decide whether or not their son would be better off at nursery for another year. Boys are assessed in groups of six or so: 4+ applicants in the January before they join; 5+ applicants in May of the same year (they join the school 16 months later). 'These are not real academic assessments. We're looking for boys who will make the most of our opportunities.' Parents have already met the head and the head of the junior school in the autumn term. 'We need to like them and feel they will support us and they need to like us. It's important that the boys have got help at home when they need it.' Those accepting a place pay a deposit of £1,000, of which £500 is returned at the end of their son's first term, the rest when he leaves the school.

Exit: Westminster and St Paul's are the most popular destinations (there are apparently more boys from The Hall at Westminster than from any other prep school); also City, UCS, Highgate, Eton, Winchester and Harrow. Seven academic, four music and one art and one sports scholarships in 2004.

Remarks: Highly academic prep school which is extremely effective at getting boys into the top senior schools. Work and play both proceed at a brisk pace, and Life Skills and Study Skills are part of the curriculum. 'The quality of the teaching is fantastic,' said a parent. 'They do a lot more for the boys than just getting good results from them. They have such a broad education.' High praise for most of the staff. 'It feels as if they are really committed to the boys,' said another parent.

French, science, art, PE, music and ICT are taught by specialists from reception onwards, other subjects by class teachers in the junior school. The middle school, years 4 and 5, is a transition between junior and senior schools, with lessons taught by specialist staff but in the boys' own form-rooms. Setting for maths and English in year 6; in year 7, one form is hived off 'to work at a faster pace with a greater degree of challenge'. Most, but not necessarily all, of this group will become the scholarship form in year 8. This, naturally, upsets some of the parents, who complain about their boys being treated as second-class citizens. 'It is an unnecessary elitism,' said a parent whose son is one of the chosen, 'but they do some fantastic things in that class.' 'The parents do create pressures,' agrees the head, 'but I expect them to support what we are doing. All the boys will achieve good results.' Everyone, particularly the scholarship class, works very hard. 'They have a very strong foundation of learning and they are taught to work hard consistently – which is a wonderful asset to them,' said a parent. 'There are some extraordinarily talented children in the school and I think all the boys benefit from this. It gives them an insight into excellence and the hard work it takes to attain it. And they realise that everyone can shine in their own way with a bit of effort.'

A full-time learning support co-ordinator and part-time specialist staff support boys with moderate dyspraxia and dyslexia. Individual programmes in place for the 40 or so children with additional needs, help extends beyond the basics to eg ICT. 'My son had some difficulties with writing, and they've been brilliant at providing extra support,' said a parent. Boys who cannot take the pace may be asked to move elsewhere ' but generally the parents will have formed a good relationship with the teachers and any decision is usually arrived at on an amicable basis,' says the head. Not surprising then, that school doesn't approve of pupils being coached outside of school unless it's for handwriting issues or similar and only with school's agreement. Strongly believe own staff should be addressing issues (hear hear!).

Building work has resulted in the new middle school, opened in 1998, a refurbished senior school, new DT centre, pottery room and library – all light, bright and airy. The junior school, reception and playground have all been refurbished and were completed in 2004.

'There is the most amazing sense of things going on all the time,' said a parent. 'The kids are fired on all cylinders.' Lots of sport – two afternoons' sport a week for middle and senior boys at the school's sports ground at Finchley, pitches in Mill Hill or the athletics track at Parliament Hill; fencing, squash at Lord's and golf are also offered; the senior school has a large-ish playground and a multi-purpose sports hall which doubles as a setting for concerts, plays and assemblies. 'The sport has been fantastic,' said a parent. 'There's lots of opportunities for everyone, not just the first team.' And indeed the school magazine lists zillions of awards for everything from U9 Most Improved Cricketer to Snooker Doubles Shield.

Excellent drama – it is on the timetable throughout and, alongside impressive school productions, there is informal drama for year 5 upwards. 'For a whole term the children are writing their own skits and rehearsing to perform in each other's,' said a parent. 'They get the chance to try their hand at all sorts of different roles and they have wonderful fun.'

Prolific and high quality art and pottery; strong music – about three-quarters of the boys play one or more instruments and are expected to perform in the numerous concerts from year 1 upwards. 'I was surprised when my son told me his favourite music was a piece by Vaughan Williams,' said a parent. 'Then he explained that they hear music and discuss it in assembly every week.'

Numerous outings – ranging from junior school trips to Whipsnade Zoo, Madame Tussaud's and Mountfitchet Castle and middle school outings to Southwark Cathedral, Verulamium and The Ragged School, to senior school trips to Normandy, Holland and Devon.

Parents find, unexpectedly, that the pastoral side is strong. 'My son used to be very shy and sensitive and they have really nurtured him and brought him out,' said a parent. 'When I've had a problem it's always been easy to sort it out with the teachers.' The school is in the process of introducing a new anti-bullying policy, in consultation with boys and parents. 'We keep revisiting pastoral care because it's important to keep looking at your policies. There will always be someone who slips through the net but we do our best.'

The school unashamedly rewards the brightest and best but boys and parents agree that it is also good at spotting, nurturing and rewarding more hidden talents and effort. 'Everyone's got something they're good at and the school really brings it out,' said a pupil.

Parents are a high-powered lot, mostly wealthy, very demanding, inclined to drive local residents mad by thoughtless double-parking but kept under control by Mr Pierson. 'They expect a lot of the boys and drive them very hard,' said a parent. 'But my son is always really keen to go to school – which is fantastic.' Another commented, 'my son has said that his sons will go to The Hall – and you can't get a higher recommendation than that.'

THE HALL SCHOOL WIMBLEDON JUNIOR SCHOOL

Linked to Hall School Wimbledon (The) in the Senior section

Stroud Crescent, Putney Vale, London, SW15 3QE

Tel: 020 8788 2370
Fax: 020 8788 2121
E-mail: principal@hsw.co.uk

• Pupils: 340 boys and girls, all day • Ages: 3-11 • Fees: KS1 £2,323. KS2 £2,656 • Independent

Head: Since 1990, Mr Timothy J Hobbs MA. Educated at Eastbourne College and St Andrew's, founded The Hall in 1990, after teaching at Hill House and becoming disillusioned with the sausage factory approach to teaching and learning. In 1999 his brother Jonathan M Hobbs MA (Education Management from OU) also educated at Eastbourne College and then at the British School of Osteopathy, joined as principal of the school. Jonathan is responsible for the daily running of the junior school, staffing, trouble-shooting and the minutiae that TJH openly

professes to dislike. Not that parents are likely to meet either brother on a visit, admissions are handled by a very capable admissions team but any parent requesting an appointment with head or principal will have their wish granted.

TJH oversees both senior and junior schools, working tirelessly at the sharp end, devoting his energies to preserving the spirit of the schools and looking after the children. Seen by some as a bit of a maverick, not afraid to ruffle feathers for the greater good, there for the children. Thinks outside the box. Fans say he's charming and charismatic, others disagree. TJH is passionate about education in the broadest sense, he wants children to discover themselves, celebrate their individuality yet have due regard and care for others. Says: 'he'd like to feel children leave school not only well educated academically but with practical skills and confidence in all areas in preparation for their future'.

Entrance: Hold a number of open mornings each year. Try to keep a realistic waiting list, must visit school prior to requesting a place. First come first served for reception places. In other years they look to see if a child is compatible with their system. Non-selective but assess all to determine where the child will fit into the school. Parents from wide socio-economic spread, 20 per cent from overseas, several first time buyers.

Exit: Pupils can be prepared for 7-11+ exams and Common Entrance to all major London schools (a minority to boarding). Don't prepare children for scholarships even though some win them. Approximately two thirds to own senior school – automatic entry.

Remarks: Follows the National Curriculum, or rather leads it: all mainstream subjects taught a year ahead of schedule, ensuring children are well-prepared for demands of Common Entrance. Set for maths and English from Y3. Totally committed to hearing every child read daily until they're confident, fluent readers. Strong on history and geography, 150 day/residential field trips and outings annually, with plenty of hands-on learning, both home and abroad. School runs a monitoring and homework system called 'Flints', which: 'enables efficiency and independence in all subjects.' Each child has a folder with weekly Flint sheets to complete. Flints, popular with staff and parents, demonstrates how 'little-and-often produces success.' Extension work is given through a similar system 'Pyrite.'

Classes average 20. Good SEN support, with two full time staff. Provides a wonderful environment for the mild dyslexic or dyspraxic. Recognises that a bright dyslexic child often makes highly valued verbal contributions and is able to engage in lively, informed debate. Can cater for MLD, mild visual impairment, physical difficulties, and mild aspergers – but those who need in-class support for behavioural difficulties should look elsewhere. Say everything should work well for children at the school, believe too much teacher intervention can hinder progress. Provision varies according to needs but must be able to manage mainstream and need no more than a couple of half-hour one to one sessions per week. Will refuse children who need specialist support that school is not able to provide.

This fast developing school opened in April 1990 in Wimbledon Village, moving to current site (former council school) in 1992. Classrooms are light, well equipped and set in a terraced site where children have helped plant trees, make ponds and develop a tranquil, stimulating place to learn. There's an Anderson shelter, an American garden to commemorate 9/11, flags portraying the international flavour of the school, a Shepherd's caravan, a partly constructed Cruck house using resources available in medieval times, chickens (rescued from a battery farm) and rabbits but no pigs (locals got tetchy). School, extended with the most delightful log cabins, backs onto Wimbledon Common so plenty of rural science opportunities and terrific views. One bright-eyed youngster told us: 'sometimes we have sleepovers to badger watch.' Swallows and Amazons eat your heart out; an idyll in this playstation orientated world.

Strong and keen sports, games everyday good facilities: tennis court, basketball court, adventure playground, garden, outdoor climbing wall. All children from 7 years old start the day with circuit training: healthy body, healthy mind, attitude (good wholesome food too). All get to be in teams, not just the best. Emphasise sportsmanship, team skills, fun and joining in, rather than always winning. Lots of after school activities (small additional charge). Art and technology well served, we spied giant Jimmy Choo shoes made by pupils, a whole new take on Cinderella! No dedicated music teacher when we visited but school sang tunefully: in the classrooms, we saw a fine example of cross-curricula work – music mixed with PSHE and literacy, during lunch (rousing rendition of happy birthday complete with parent guests and cake provided by TJH) and at the impressive and energetic Y4 'Oliver' dress rehearsal.

Staff committed to pastoral care, good code of morals and behaviour, anti-bullying policy that works. No formal punishments, persistent offenders can be suspended but head feels pupils benefit more from discussion or counselling (some staff don't always adhere to this policy).

A can-do school with a positive and enlightened outlook on education. Produces confident, caring, tolerant, informed youngsters.

Ann Margaret House. Opened in 1998 to cater for children with a diagnosis of severe Autism. Founded in response to a plea from a former teacher whose quest to find appropriate provision for her autistic granddaughter proved fruitless. Currently run by senior tutor Jackie England (managed by JMH). Provision exists for four children (three with statements, one private) but plans afoot to extend to six (limited by space). Fees of £50,000 a year are based on inclusive provision so all reasonable needs met immediately without recourse to LEA. No yearly intake – places as and when a space arises. Plan to greatly expand provision when new premises become available.

Unit is housed in own well-equipped, secure building within the grounds of the junior school. All children have a workstation in minimally decorated rooms to avoid overstimulation. There's a decked play area built in the style of a castle; well equipped kitchen where pupils help prepare snacks and food purchased as part of a daily trip to Asda (a favourite part of the day according to one pupil); a large classroom for group activities such as role play and a sensory room for the daily kinder kinetics session (a cross between physio and occupational therapy), working on muscle development, balance, coordination fine and gross motor skills. A speech and language therapist visits weekly and designs programmes that promote speech 'in context'. Use PECS with all. Each child has visual timetable with photo's or symbols.

Believe having a small unit and being able to work so closely with each individual on communication, social and independent skills, really helps, recognise: 'children with autism don't always follow natural path of development, behaviours can be hard to break, they like their own company.' The children have varying levels of ability, some are learning to read, write and do basic calculations, others concentrate on social and life skills and working with distractions. New concepts taught on an individual basis moving to paired or group work when appropriate. IEPs set out targets that are reviewed regularly in partnership with parents and relevant professionals.

All follow key curriculum elements of language and communication, reading, writing, PSHE & citizenship, maths, science, PE, ICT, humanities and creative and expressive arts. Challenging behaviour impedes learning so address and control with lots of positive reinforcement, praise, and by encouraging 'good learning'. Realise children with autism rely heavily on adult support but recognise need to encourage independent work. If a child can cope with time in mainstream they will look at ways to include. All integrate for weekly PE when small group of children from mainstream come and take part in PE skills at the unit (works well, helps children socialise and follow examples of others). Top year group from junior school visit daily during break times and play with children, say: 'need right role models as autistic children aren't great for each other.' Add 'children in mainstream are fantastic, they love to come over and are tolerant and accepting.' Mainstream children are naturally curious too and ask questions such as: Can they speak? Why can't they? What is autism? Do they live at home, go on holiday etc?Do production with mainstream including sing-along, dance performance etc. Children swim twice a week and trampoline at the senior school. Plenty of trips supplement the curriculum, recent outings to London Aquarium and the science museum using public transport – a skill they need to learn to cope with. Twice yearly, short field trips to the Queen Elizabeth Jubilee activity centre (for SEN), horse riding, climbing, canoeing, caving, all popular.A lovely unit for a handful of children lucky enough to be supported by enlightened, professional, caring staff in a tolerant and inclusive setting.

THE HAMPSHIRE SCHOOL (ENNISMORE GARDENS)

Linked to Hampshire School (Queensborough Terrace) (The)
Linked to Hampshire School (Wetherby Place) (The)

63 Ennismore Gardens, Knightsbridge, London, SW7 1NH

Tel: 02075 843 297
Fax: 02075 849 733
E-mail: hampshire@indschool.org
Website: www.ths.westminster.sch.uk

• Pupils: 220 all day, 50/50 girls and boys, spread over the three sites • Ages: 3-13 • Non-denom • Fees: £2,080 - £3,330 • Independent

Principal: Since 1986, Mr Arthur Bray CertEd MISA (fifties). Came from Millfield Junior where he and his wife were senior house parents. Mrs Bray is school bursar; 2 adult children, both attended The Hampshire. Mr Bray has a balanced approach to pupils' welfare and academics that, combined with Mrs Bray's tip top administration, make a good team, parents feel.

Entrance: From 3, an informal interview, older children attend an assessment day, nothing too daunting.

Exit: Handful of boys leaves at 8, majority at 13, most girls at 11, very few to boarding schools, majority to London day schools. Favourites with the girls are Godolphin & Latymer and St Paul's; for boys Latymer Upper, St Paul's and Westminster. Mr Bray offers excellent individual advice on senior school selection.

Remarks: Founded as a dance school 1928 by June Hampshire; on moving to London in the early 1930s became mainstream. Her daughter Jane Box Grainger took over as head in the 1960s; another daughter is the well known actress Susan Hampshire. Now part of the Nord Anglia Education Group, has grown from 150 to 220 pupils since the Brays' arrival. On three sites – 63 Ennismore Gardens, London SW7 1NH; 5 Wetherby Place, SW7 4NX; and 9 Queensborough Terrace, W2 3BT – all large converted town houses, classrooms tend to be on the small side, ditto class sizes.

Family-based, community-spirited atmosphere; pupils are friendly and encouraged to look after each other, they work hard and are much praised. A wide curriculum, including four languages – every child from 8 years old and up goes on an annual study trip to France. ICT a great strength, all the IT suites have been recently refurbished and updated, everyone has the opportunity to learn touch-typing – something that is missing from far too many schools. Children become highly competent with technology. Mr Harman, the long-serving history, mathematics and Latin teacher is particularly praised by both pupils and parents. Full-time special needs teacher and visiting speech therapists. EFL catered for in-house.

Good inclusive arts programme: everyone is in an annual drama production, often a musical, busy choir and orchestra (more than half the school play an instrument.) No playgrounds, children are bused to local parks and have sports periods four days a week. Lots of sports options which change each term, pupils use a variety of different sports centres and gyms, and even the nursery children are taken swimming.

Enthusiastic noises from parents.

HAMPTON COURT HOUSE

Linked to Hampton Court House budding senior school in the Senior section

Hampton Court House, The Green, Hampton Court Road, East Molesey, Surrey, KT8 9BS

Tel: 020 8943 0889
Fax: 020 8977 5357
E-mail: office@hamptoncourthouse.co.uk
Website: www.hamptoncourthouse.co.uk

• Pupils: 100, slightly more boys than girls, day but weekly boarding available • Ages: 3-14, but rising to 18 • Non-denom
• Fees: £2,390 to £2,725; weekly boarding £1,650 extra
• Independent

Headmistress: Since 2001, when school opened, Lady Eliana Houstoun-Boswall ISIT (Paris) (fifties). Founded the school (having previously founded the Harrodian – the story of her time there may interest inquisitive parents); children and staff alike call her 'Eliana'. Very beautiful, not at all grand despite the grandeur of the school. Never stops talking, looking deep into your eyes, with an infectious enthusiasm about herself, the children and the architecture. 'Makes you feel as though your own child is the most important in the world' – though some parents feel she's 'on a mission.' Believes that all education should be as she offers - 'to light a spark in every child.' A linguist by training, teaches French with a perfect French accent.

Entrance: Into the nursery at three and a half- children are offered a trial session to make sure they are happy – but no test at this stage: 'it's more important that there is a meeting of minds between the parent and the school'. 'Children usually pass effortlessly into the school's preparatory section' – ie a few do not. Potential pupils older than nursery age are tested and interviewed at length – interview matters most, school is looking for interesting pupils. A father described the family's two hour interview as a two-way process – parents able to evaluate the school, as the school evaluates the children (and the parents). A few scholarships available – academic, music and chess; helps to create a social mix.

Currently the oldest pupils are 13/14, but the school intends build up a senior department running up to 18 (and offering the IB).

Exit: Some bright pupils prepared for scholarships to academic day or boarding schools eg St Paul's Girls and

Eton, but the thrust of the school's teaching is aimed at 11+ exit. As yet no pattern where other pupils might go, though Eliana is a fan of Kingston Grammar.

Remarks: Liberal school with very traditional teaching in a stunning environment. House quite exceptionally beautiful – classrooms rather like drawing rooms with enormous sash windows opening onto Bushy Park with rabbits playing and deer grazing below. Is the temptation to stare out of the window too great for some children? 'Not if the teaching is capturing their interest,' replies Eliana. Dining room a massive conservatory; home-cooked food served to pupils and staff together. Grounds a child's paradise of woods and meadows, with play equipment; one football pitch on site (and one off site for matches against other schools).

At least while numbers are below capacity, children are taught in a group appropriate to needs – whatever their age. Eliana assesses those needs and is v flexible in her approach as to how they are met – children regularly moved between teaching groups and specialist help is brought in where necessary. 'Eliana sees each child as a different being, and works on their strengths,' remarked a mother. Aim of the teaching – to be inspirational and civilizing, though with entrance exams and Common Entrance in mind.

In English, great classic authors are studied with lots of interesting and child-oriented information about their lives – to help fire the imagination. 'My children age 10 are very hot on their Shakespeare, even if they're not reading Molière quite yet,' said one mother. 'My eight year old and her friend were telling each other stories from Chaucer in the car the other day – including the rude bits,' said another. The director of studies, known to all as Guy – a very approachable chap – organises the curriculum. He described the sort of question asked in a year 6 SATS paper as 'child abuse,' and simple poetry, which a child might read in a Common Entrance paper as 'junk – when they could choose from 'the sensuality of Keats or the wit of Pope.' Cartoon stories used to introduce Latin to children are in his opinion a waste of time – they don't actually learn any grammar from them. In French too, grammar must be fully understood as well as the accent perfect, and there's lots of hand-writing practice from an early age.

Exceptionally high-quality music (European classical) teaching by specialist teachers and masses of drama culminating in a termly production of adult plays in an absolute gem of a theatre. 'My son is the lighting technician for this term's production,' said a parent, 'and I'm sure that on the night it will be completely his responsibility.' School believes in giving responsibility at an early age – the boy in question is only eight. Art teacher has just joined the teaching staff. IT is in the curriculum, all children learn to touch-type in the computer room and there is small science room (while awaiting planning permission to put one in a new block). 'Plenty of explosions,' reported a parent. Not an obviously sporty school – numbers can restrict team sports. Opportunities for judo and swimming.

Liberal attitude to school life shows in lack of bells – it doesn't seem to matter if a class starts or finishes five minutes late. 'It can take half an hour to get out of school in the afternoon,' said a mother with a smile, 'the children always want to do something else.' 'My children see school as a second home,' enthused another. 'Teachers often spend ten minutes at the end of the day updating me on my child's progress. It will be a challenge for the school as it grows to keep up this level of individual input,' added a third. No fixed uniform, but guidelines for sensible clothes. Most staff known by their first names and chat to the children on a basis of equality – 'Teachers really respect the children,' a mother said. Children often seen hugging Eliana. Behaviour problems dealt with through discussions between the children involved and a teacher, rather than punishment, and children go in or out of staff rooms freely.

Classes reasonably ordered though not silent – with such (for now) small classes there is plenty of opportunity for question and answer. Children skip happily down the corridors; with so much space no one has to tell them to slow down or go quietly. Staff spoke of the delight of not being restrained by requirements of literacy/numeracy hours. Maybe like some of the pupils, they too would not quite fit into a 'normal' school.

Pupils welcome at any stage of the school year (though this may become harder as numbers build up). From Central London, as well as local areas and the suburbs: well-placed for train and buses. At present, the majority of pupils are either bright, or for some reason have not fitted in at their previous school. 'My daughter was becoming badly behaved at her primary school, but now she is Miss Goody-Two-Shoes,' a mother remarked. A slightly rarefied world with a 'creative atmosphere' which will not suit everybody: 'not for all future lawyers and accountants,' said a parent. May prove hard for some children to adjust to the social and cultural norms (pop music, playstations and David Beckham) at some senior schools.

HANFORD SCHOOL

Childe Okeford, Blandford Forum, Dorset, DT11 8HN

Tel: 01258 860 219
Fax: 01258 861 255
E-mail: hanfordsch@aol.com
Website: www.hanford.dorset.sch.uk

• Pupils: 110 girls; all board • Ages: 7-13 • C of E • Fees: Day £3,900; full boarding £4,900 • Independent

Head: Since 2003, Mr Nigel Stuart Mackay (mid forties), mathematician, formerly head of Ruzawi School in Zimbabwe. Born and educated in Zimbabwe, has taught there since then. Married to Sarah, the director of music at Ruzawi, before which she was at Sunningdale. The Mackays have four young children.

Miss Sarah Canning MA (seventies), the source of Hanford's spirit, has at last retired. Her parents, the Reverend and Mrs Clifford Canning, started the school in 1947. We wait to see how the school changes in her absence, and will re-visit soon.

Entrance: Some at 7, but the largest number come as 8 or 9 year olds. On the whole, pupils are very British (and posh British at that) but odd Europeans, usually Spanish, tip up for the occasional half term to boost their English. Otherwise a combination of locals, Wessex girls, Londoners and numerous families posted abroad. Not too many first-time buyers. Some bursaries. Girls can come at any time, if space available and, if the numbers are anything like when we visited, they will be dead pushed to squeeze in a mouse (except perhaps in the Cabin under the eaves).

Exit: Mainly to Sherborne, Bryanston, Marlborough, plus all over; Stonar and Westonbirt (very much on the up at the moment) for the less academic. School strives to find the right niche for each child – truly there is no other school like it and certainly not in the senior department. Huge range of scholarships, academic, art, games and music. Tendency for the majority of girls to stay till 13.

Remarks: Tiny classes, with remedial help on hand and extra tuition in maths and English. Children are streamed with the weaker vessels having the smaller number. French from 8, pupils are usually way past the standard of their senior school by the time they leave, and all articulate with good pronunciation. A heated discussion was in place when we visited as to which of the 'Il était une petite Grenouille' books was more fun. 'Native foreign speakers' are encouraged to continue plus the daughter of a British diplomat based in Moscow and such-like. Separate sciences at nine; all singing and dancing. In the IT department, e-mail whenever. Classrooms are incredible – some in the converted stables, you go in and out of the window (promise) and some in the most ramshackle collection of what might, in a real world, be temporary buildings – they appear to have been put down at random. Gym and dancing hall in Fan's house.

Set in 45 acres of rolling countryside on the edge of the Stour valley and surrounded by iron age barrows and Roman fort remains, Hanford House was built in 1620 for Sir Robert Seymer (later Kerr-Seymer). Basically Jacobean with Victorian overtones, it has been splendidly adapted to scholastic life. The magnificent glazed-in internal courtyard is now the dining room. Pupils still climb the famous cedar tree, regularly pruned by tree surgeons, under the gaze of watching staff and play games on the lawn below, adjacent to the outdoor swimming pool. Extra classrooms are pulled into play in the summer months, when lessons and free periods are spent in the fabulous box-garden with box hedges up to the shoulder (and above most girls' heads). The gardens are truly wonderful with a small collection of girl-inspired plots and a magnificent walled garden. They provide all the flowers for the house and all the veggies, with the exception of potatoes.

Younger pupils sleep in various dilapidated dorms on the top two floors – paint peeling, that sort of thing (though a parent rebuked us with the information that 'the fabric is in stunning order, we did up the whole building last year'). Posters, fluffy toys, bedspreads, 'which you can wrap yourself in if there is a fire' said my guides. Dorms appear more cramped since the old white painted iron bedsteads were replaced by slightly larger pine beds and bunks. Very spartan but some weird and wonderful coloured walls and hardly a carpet in sight. We liked the loo roll holder – bailer twine attached to the window.

Great store put on 'not changing anything'. There was general dismay when it was discovered that the first floor shower room HAD NEW TILES AND BEEN REPAINTED (blue and white) – 'it was much cooler before', despite the fact that the grotty brown tiles leaked ('not very often') into the kitchen. Woodwork certainly needs help. 'Faded Dorset feel,' said member of staff, 'a heavenly place to grow up in'. Certainly, as we said before, 'this is one of the nicest, if not the nicest, girls' boarding school in the country, with a gentle, kind, friendly, enthusiastic gloriously happy-go-lucky genuine family atmosphere. 'A place you can feel absolutely confident leaving your ewe lamb in with the knowledge that the school will probably do a better job of looking after her than you would yourself and, almost as a side issue, give her a thorough grounding in CE subjects and a fun time with it.' No uniform, girls sit happily in class in their riding togs, their (seriously padded) crash helmets on the desk in front of them, working as hard as they can, because the next lesson has four legs. Ponies are important here – the school has 'around' 20 – and when we visited there were three private ponies used by the school, but basically there for the tetrathlon which had been held the previous week at Sandroyd. All the animals have some sort of walk-on parts in the school plays, marvellous wardrobe room, tap dancing, ballet, everything a growing gal could want. 13 year olds live in Fan's house, which lies uneasily with the charming chapel to St Michael and All Angels (Mrs Canning commissioned the chairs which were later copied for St Paul's Cathedral Choir School).

Music very important, girls are auditioned for the chapel choir (only), bands for everything, woodwind, string, recorder and orchestra. Loads of local participation. Masses of music awards. Incredibly ambitious art, really really good, with ceramics that would not disgrace any senior school; regular masterclasses. Fantastic teapots, masques. Huge number of options.

Excellent pastoral care, strong emphasis on manners; there are no punishments, but SYRs (serve you rights) when miscreants have to do 'terribly boring' things, like spending half an hour on the balcony WITHOUT TALKING or writing out a long dull poem. Sweets the current bribe (currency is the buzz word). Half term is fixed but no exeats as such, girls can more or less come and go any weekend and those whose parents do not live close enough go out regularly with chums – 'but' said our informant, 'we all love the school so much, that we often don't want to go home – it's more fun here'.

Sarah's final exit may well, we feel, lead to a change in style and direction. But we are not yet clear what that might be. Parents still making happy noises.

Harrodian Preparatory and Pre-preparatory Schools

Linked to Harrodian School (The) in the Senior section

Lonsdale Road, London, SW13 9QN

Tel: 020 8748 6117
Fax: 020 8563 7327
E-mail: admin@harrodian.com
Website: www.harrodian.com

• Pupils: Girls and boys; all day • Ages: 4-11 • Fees: Pre-prep £2,944; prep £3,306 • Independent • Open days: Regular small group tours. Phone for appointment

Remarks: For further details see senior school entry.

Hazlegrove School

Linked to King's Bruton in the Senior section

Hazlegrove House, Sparkford, Yeovil, Somerset, BA22 7JA

Tel: 01963 440 314
Fax: 01963 440 569
E-mail: office@hazlegrove.co.uk
Website: www.hazlegrove.co.uk

• Pupils: 180 boys, 120 girls. 40 boys and 15 girls board. 30 boys and 25 girls, all day, in the pre-prep • Ages: 3-13 • Christian • Fees: Boarders £4,550 - £5,155; day £2,945 - £3,755; pre-prep £1,850 • Independent • Open days: 8 per year – ring and ask

Head: Since 2002, Mr Richard Fenwick MA (forties). Educated at Bishop's Stortford College. Had a misguided shot at banking till his vocation dawned. After that, a rapid rise through the ranks of a number of preps till he reached the summit of St Andrew's Turi, Kenya. Not by any means an everyday sort of head from whom you expect the customary, ever-lulling stream of blah, Mr Fenwick can be intriguingly enigmatic, deceptively sphinx-y. Sentences, at the ends of which seem to hover ghostly question marks, sometimes trail off half-said. Don't be fazed, there's no dark purpose. It's because he's a wonderer. He genuinely wonders what you think. Not a lot of heads, when you come to think of it, wonder what you think. His utterances can be oblique, runic, playful, can raise eyebrows, but stem actually from constant cogitation and a passion for what he's about. It's very simple – he wants every day to be the best of every child's life and he wants everything they learn to be useful in their later lives. When he talks about what the school does and how, he often tags on the words 'for the benefit of the children', and you can see it's not for the benefit of the shop window, that's incidental. Here is a man whose mind and spirit have, as he avows, expanded under wide African skies. There's steel here, he's an effective force, tremendously ambitious for every child. Parents and pupils cheer him to the echo. Wife Katie deeply implicated, in charge of the boarders. Three teenage children.

Entrance: No academic hurdle to worry about unduly, there's the full academic rainbow here, but the waiting list is filling.

Exit: The brightest win awards everywhere, and every year brings an estimable hatful. No channelling to the senior school, King's Bruton, on to which go around a half. Sherborne and Sherborne Girls are popular. So are any number of others.

Remarks: 'Academically they know what they're about,' says one mum – she's a teacher somewhere else, so there's verification – 'it's a tight ship.' Achievement speaks well of the school, parents declare themselves pleased. The head says, 'amid all the romantic fun there must be results. Our education must be sound.' They do well by their best – 'there are children winning scholarships who wouldn't have two years ago' – and also by their pretty long tail. The secret lies in the delivery thing, of course, and you'll find no National Curriculum apparatchiks here. The head wants only passionate teachers who like children (that's two rare breeds already) and he gets them – almost half the staff are his appointments. Any applicant who asks at interview about salaries is out on their ear – 'they've got to want desperately to work here.' You meet big-heartedness wherever you go. Some of the best have been here for years and the new crop are top drawer. Perhaps the person who exemplifies them is Mr Carnegie, make sure you meet him, he'd make the Pied Piper feel like an also-ran. They call him Killer – for an immemorial reason no one can recall. We met him in a scene from a Jennings story. Children were rushing up to him bearing bits of woodland, having scores marked on a chart. They were the codebreaking club, some of the school's brightest, having their minds laterally stretched in the trickiest, most joyous way. He teaches beekeeping, too. Kite making. All sorts. English. One lit-up little girl rushed up and told her father, 'we've been building a hut with Killer' – and little girls, when you think of it, aren't necessarily the sort who like building huts. He expresses the spirit of the place – says the head, 'we like to take children to the edge of their experience' – and it's invidious to single him out.

There's a gifted and talented programme; they work jolly hard to prepare their scholarship candidates. There's an established, highly-rated learning support unit. Diagnostic test on entry, remediation as necessary only for as long as – no dependency creation here. It's cool to go and at the end of every term the pupil who makes the most progress wins the cockerel (don't ask).

'If a child isn't very good at something, focus on what they can do,' says the head, and there is praise from parents for the way they work out the best way forward for every child, radically if necessary; nothing here is formulaic, giving some their first cloudless experience of school. All individual achievement is pursued and celebrated – if there's any chance of winning whatever, they go for it. Creativity expresses itself in excellent art and design, and 'fantastic music' – this from a violin-maker father. Fifteen ensembles bear witness. Drama is strong, taught to all from year 3, purpose-built theatre. Sport is win-win, played hard in the right spirit, productive of county and national players. Sports hall, swimming pool, squash courts, Astro – this really is a well-resourced school. Outdoor ed is big, taught to all in years 5 and 6, and there's camping out in the grounds for the littlest. Pre-prep purpose built, set apart, shipshape. Parents hugely approve of the nursery.

The school day ends at four when there are clubs and activities and prep, popular for parents who value family life unclouded by homework, so around half the children are still there at six as, most days, are all the teachers. You can come for breakfast, stay for tea. They'll take your fraught work schedules in their stride right up to the last minute.

The setting is drop-dead gorgeous, early 18th century house fronted by the newly restored Williamite Court set in lord-of-all-you-survey grounds at the end of a drive halfway up which time stands still. No wonder former pupils remain so fond, 163 of them at the last reunion, some dating back to 1947. Indeed, a lot of present parents did time here. These days children come in minibuses from as far away as Crewkerne; many are brought by their parents 'so we can pick up on what's going on.' Some reckon the school takes a fair bit of motoring to get to but, nestling as it does on the banks of the A303, these are quick miles. Parents a mixed bag, some Services (esp boarders), local farmers and business people, old money, a sprinkling of those metro exiles and quality-of-lifers who are beginning to colonise this part of Somerset. What sort of child wouldn't be happy here? 'An arrogant child,' says the head, and you can see he'll have

none of that.

Discipline in this child-centred school is all about good manners and consideration for others and there's no hiding place for those who don't see it that way. Values are Christian values. Parents rate the pastoral care and we stayed on till lights out to check out the boarding. Excellent staff, very well done. Had to tear ourselves away, actually.

There's something good going on here and it's getting them talked about.

HEADINGTON PREPARATORY SCHOOL

Linked to Headington School in the Senior section

26 London Road, Oxford, Oxfordshire, OX3 7PB

Tel: 01865 759400
Fax: 01865 761774
E-mail: enquiries@headingtonprep.org
Website: www.headingtonprep.org

• Pupils: Mostly girls; all day • Ages: 3-11 girls, 3-4 boys • Fees: Prep school £1,575 - £2,360 • Independent • Open days: October

Head: Since 1998, Mrs Rachel Faulkner, MEd, CertEd. Very experienced, previously head of E Block at The Dragon. Firmly believes that 'learning should be fun.' From September 2006 Miss Andrea Bartlett, currently deputy head of Bute House qv, will take over.

Entrance: By test and interview from age of 7. Before that, first come, first served – many parents register children up to three or four years in advance. Priority given to siblings of children already in school.

Exit: Vast majority to senior school with good smattering of scholarships every year.

Remarks: Friendly school housed in converted Victorian house a five-minute walk from senior school. Set in four acres of pretty, child-friendly grounds, which are used to the full. New library and new classroom block for foundation stage children (complete with own play area, guinea pigs and fence made of giant pencils) opened in 2004 and new science block followed in 2005. Children happy and confident. School very busy when we visited – oldest girls rehearsing Midsummer Night's Dream 1970s-style in one classroom while tiny ballerinas concentrating on being snowflakes in another. Lots of clubs at break, lunchtime and after school and very popular after-school care till 5.45pm every day.

HIGH SCHOOL OF DUNDEE JUNIOR SCHOOL

Linked to High School of Dundee in the Senior section

Euclid Crescent, Dundee, DD1 1HU

Tel: 01382 202 921
Fax: 01382 229 822
E-mail: admissions@highschoolofdundee.co.uk
Website: www.highschoolofdundee.co.uk

- Pupils: 320 girls and boys; all day • Ages: 5-11 • Non-denom
- Fees: £1,740 - £2,475 • Independent • Open days: November

Head: Since 1993, Mrs Maggie Woodman DipCE IE LCP (fifties) who came from Dollar, Lomond and 'all over'. She has been in situ for 11 years, brought her children (now grown up) with her and fronts this very jolly not so little school scattered around Bell Street (internally) with a raft of pretty gassy young teachers who take the tinies up to senior school.

Remarks: Junior school has its own dining area, gym and games zone. French from P6; P6 and P7 move to main school for a number of lessons, computer, art, labs etc. Representatives from P3-P7 on junior school council. Computers in classrooms, but juniors use computer suites in main building. Huge number of clubs, plus gardening in the greenhouse attached to the biology lab, dance, drama, first aid. IT for early birds and at lunchtime taken by IT trained primary teacher. Cunning friendship club held under staff supervision for children who either feel vulnerable or need extra cosseting – good for spotting maverick problems in the making, and nipping them in the bud. Classes held at low twenties, occasional pupil could be squeezed in, fair amount of juggling to help lesser brethren, but space here is tight. Before and after school care from 8-8.30 am and 4-6pm costs extra, but free up to 4pm when the school buses leave.

A splendid hotchpotch of interlinked brightly coloured rooms for tinies with some spectacular ceilings from the former bank, the gents jute club and magnificent stained glass windows – the lady with the yellow yoyo gives younger pupils much pleasure. The music department is above. Junior school has waiting lists (expected to increase following the closure of one of the smaller Angus primary schools) and it could be that some of the rest of Bell Street will undergo a rapid conversion.

HIGH SCHOOL OF GLASGOW JUNIOR

Linked to High School of Glasgow (The) in the Senior section

27 Ledcameroch Road, Bearsden, Glasgow, G61 4AE

Tel: 01419 420 158
Fax: 0141 570 0020
E-mail: rector@hsog.co.uk
Website: www.glasgowhigh.co.uk

- Pupils: 380 boys and girls in the junior school, 55 in the nursery. All day • Ages: 4-10; plus nursery (kindergarten) 3-4
- Non-denom • Fees: Primary £1,527 - £2,151; nursery £813
- Independent

Head: Since 2001, Mrs Karen Waugh BA DipPrimEd (forties) who was educated at Hutcheson's Girls' Grammar, followed by a DipEd at Jordanhill College and took her BA via the Open University. Married, with a flexible husband, her children are in the school. Enthusiastic and fun, as well as very pretty, she brings a wealth of experience to this much sought after school. She was previously head of Mearns Primary (700 pupils), depute head of Carolside Primary (800 pupils) and then acting head; and before that she taught at Carlibar, team-taught at Crookfur and taught at the open plan Torrance Primary. Her current appointment is her first in the independent sector. The rector much in evidence during our visit – he carries out regular monthly assemblies here – and does a 'state visit' on Fridays, 'when Karen and I have a blether'. New staff appointments very much a joint activity. School has moved seamlessly forward under new head.

Entrance: 80/100 applicants at kindergarten level (max 54), though this is now 'capped at 50 to allow for the odd beginner at primary 1'. But get in early. School 100 per cent oversubscribed for entrance thereafter. Parents have coffee and cakes and the children are taken to the kindergarten and assessed individually. Social interaction and 'emotional readiness' rather than crammed academics is the yardstick, so children with a reading age of six will not necessarily come up trumps. Interviews are held annually, if you don't get a place the first time round, you may be kept 'on hold' and may be accepted – so don't give up. Recently there have been 63 applications for two places between primaries 1 and 6. Priorities to siblings, FPs' children and the rest of the field.

Exit: Automatic transfer to senior school and usually all do.

Remarks: The Glasgow prep they all – with good reason – fight to get into. Still holds true. Huge number of pupils shoe-horned with enormous skill into tiniest site imaginable; (rector doesn't like this description: he would prefer 'restricted site'). But think Victorian villa, think stained glass windows, think very steep site, think 380 odd children, think the impossible. Massive new build since our last visit, positively Swiss engineering to construct a magical new basement, fantastic kindergarten (with its own entrance); masses of light, this is imaginative architecture at its most productive. (Step forward Dr Easton, rector and architect manqué).

Junior school shares senior school facilities, bused to Anniesland for rugby and hockey, swimming at the Allander centre, not a huge amount of playground on site (a couple of converted tennis courts) but each age group has their own. Small gym (ie not a sports hall) and impressive convertible hall/theatre. Excellent and imaginative drama. Superb music, three choirs, orchestra, wind, guitar, chamber, chanter – you name it. Specialist art teacher, the entire complex (building is too simple a word) is covered in child-paintings and models.

One (only) male teacher, dedicated French, drama, music, art and PE teachers, otherwise form teacher throughout. Two parallel classes for each year group, with 'group teaching where appropriate'. Support for learning at both ends of the spectrum with specialised learning support (as in dyslexia, dyspraxia, and those whom the rector would prefer us to call 'slow learners') upstairs in main building. No 'problem' with ADHD or children on Ritalin (none in the school at the moment). Sixth formers at senior school act as buddies when pupils move up to senior school. Class size 27 and down, French from the age of eight, IT from the start – IT Works, spread sheets, word processing, data bases. Dedicated computer lab. The works.

Same ethos as senior school, positive relationships and anti-bullying plans. Elected junior school council – who have a serious input and recently quizzed the catering manager about the lunch supplied. Trips for everything everywhere. This is a busy school, own tartan for children. Mainly middle class parents, some from far away, children can be left early and collected late. Buses which link up with senior school runs. Kindergarten super with dedicated area, children on the academic ladder at four – play learning at its best. All wear badges with their name on it – automatic for the first few weeks, but then, 'the children love wearing them'. Charming, convenient, couldn't do better.

HIGHFIELD PREP SCHOOL

Linked to Harrogate Ladies' College in the Senior section

Clarence Drive, Harrogate, North Yorkshire, HG1 2QG

Tel: 01423 504 543
Fax: 01423 568 893
E-mail: enquire@hlc.org.uk
Website: www.highfieldprep.org.uk

• Independent

HIGHFIELD SCHOOL

Linked to Brookham School in the Junior section

Highfield Lane, Liphook, Hampshire, GU30 7LQ

Tel: 01428 728 000
Fax: 01428 728 001
E-mail: office@highfieldschool.org.uk
Website: www.highfieldschool.org.uk

• Pupils: 110 boys, 105 girls; 80 boarders, 135 day • Ages: 8-13 • C of E • Fees: Day £3,600 - £4,700; boarding £3,725 - £5,350 • Independent • Open days: Last Saturday in September

Head: Since 1999, Mr Phillip Evitt MA (early forties). Educated at Kimbolton School and Cambridge (history and PGCE). Taught at Monmouth School and then at Dulwich College for fourteen years. Firing on all cylinders as if he were leading a public school rather than a little country prep and the thriving results attest to his achievement. Teaches history. Speaking voice disarmingly similar to Tony Blair's. Married to Joanna, solicitor and homeopath; four young children at Brookham and Highfield. Succeeded Mr Nigel Ramage, now teaching English and drama at Papplewick. Since his arrival, Mr Evitt has undertaken a major staff reshuffle, bringing in much new blood to key positions. Highfield and Brookham (the on-site pre-prep) both owned by William Mills, grandson of school's identically named founder.

Entrance: By registration, interview and NFER tests in maths, spelling and reading. Non-selective intake but must be of at least average ability in maths, reading and writing. Most pupils live quite locally (starting off as day pupils, or numbering among the 30 or so 8-year-olds who come up from Brookham pre-prep located in Highfield's grounds).

Increasingly from farther afield including quite a few ex-pats and Services/diplomatic children.

Exit: Many to Downe House, Wycombe Abbey, Charterhouse, St Swithun's, Winchester, Eton, Canford, Sherborne, Marlborough and Bryanston. At least four or five awards won most years (eight in 2003 and 2004, nine in 2005) to these and other schools. OBs: Ludovic Kennedy and Terence Conran.

Remarks: Charming country prep in sumptuous 175 acre grounds where children can be children. Has got almost everything right – from academics to roller-blading – all in an amazingly happy, humane environment. In the past, the school was sometimes faulted for being cheerful but not always challenging. Mr Evitt has gently raised standards throughout the school – so far without unpleasantly cranking up the pressure. Three forms in each year. No streaming to avoid labels of 'boffin' and 'thicko'. Setting in English and maths from age 9 and French and science from 11. Approximately 25 children (10 per cent of pupils) receiving some one-to-one learning support each week but outstanding Common Entrance results. A few parents expressed concerns that increased popularity and academic success could tempt the school to adopt a more selective entrance policy and increase pressure to win scholarships etc but this has not happened.

Sport for all. Virtually 100 per cent of pupils represent the school in a sports team at some level. A parent whose children were previously at a school where sporting success was all, commented that 'at Highfield you have to get used to not winning everything'. But the school does jolly well, usually winning more than it loses (1st XI hockey team unbeaten for five years).

Glorious art block (1995) would not be out of place in a major public school. Wonderful art teaching and huge range of projects. Superb new indoor swimming pool. New music school opening in spring 2006 will provide a music technology room and a magnificent music room as well as ten practice rooms. Department working hard to push back the frontiers of musical achievement – an increasing number of Grade 5s and above in music exams and awards to leading senior schools. Well over three quarters of children learn at least one instrument, there are three strong choirs and the annual spring concert involves every pupil. Strong range of extra-curricular activities including riding, dance, judo, pet club (boarders may bring own pets), golf club, squash, fencing, archery. In the summer, children can sign out in groups to play in the woods (patrolled by duty staff) and build camps, also an excellent mountain bike track. Little 8-hole golf course on site, with members of school golf club taken

out to proper course. Lots to keep everyone busy – photo competition, general knowledge quizzes, poetry recitation, dorm decorating competitions etc.

Lovely relationships between pupils and teachers. Pupils speak of teachers as 'nice', not frightening. Booklet for new pupils immediately sets the welcoming, reassuring tone eg 'even the headmaster had to ask for help when he started at Highfield, so don't panic!' Lunch we witnessed brought out all the best qualities in the school, beginning with a teacher cheerfully barking reminders about table manners – 'elbows off! Don't fiddle with the cutlery!' then silence as staff served children at their tables, then the din of happily chattering voices for the rest of the meal. Boarding no longer compulsory at 11. Head says, 'we constantly work to make boarding so enjoyable that the children want to board'. Seems to be working as the boarding numbers are quite stable and girls are starting to board at an earlier age than in the past. Dorms are works of art, imaginatively named (Stevenson, Shakespeare, Fonteyn) and painted with the most fabulous themed murals. Dormitory hallways also decorated, including a circus theme complete with fun-house mirror. Junior boarding house with 15-18 youngsters is particularly well cared for and has a comforting family feel and a fantastic common room. Boarders offered a wide range of activities each evening which prevents them lolling around in front of the TV as often as you find at similar schools. In addition games rooms available to all – offering table-tennis, table football and pool. Boarders may bring bicycles to school and anyone can bring skateboards, scooters or rollerblades to use in breaks. Uniform allows for limited individuality. Girls choose from loads of different kilt patterns and summer polo shirts can be one of a wide range of colours.

Well-designed, bright classrooms with creative displays of work throughout. New classroom block with science labs, maths rooms and IT room. Overall exceptionally good IT facilities (two IT rooms and 12 interactive whiteboards in the school) and each pupil has an email address. Pupils have evening access to IT and art rooms. Splendid chapel attended three times a week by older children and four times a week by younger. There is still (a little) room for improvement. Refurbishment of theatre is on the drawing board. The sports hall has been transformed by redecoration during 2005 and heating is, we are told, 'on the way'. School day finishes for all at 4.30pm but extensive activities programme open to all runs until 5.20 when day children leave. Boarders then do music practice or quiet reading before prep, which is followed by tea (hot evening meal served at 6.30pm). Saturday school until 4pm with matches or games for everyone.

All in all a delight and one of the most innovative and successful boarding preps going.

HIGHGATE JUNIOR SCHOOL

Linked to Highgate Pre-Preparatory School in the Junior section
Linked to Highgate School in the Senior section

3 Bishopswood Road, Highgate, London, N6 4PL

Tel: 02083 409 193
Fax: 020 8342 7273
E-mail: admissions@highgateschool.org.uk
Website: www.highgateschool.org.uk

• Pupils: 390 girls and boys; all day • Ages: 7-13 • Fees: £1,777 nursery (half day); £3,565 pre-prep; £3,820 junior • Independent • Open days: Call school office

Head: Since 2002, Mr Mark James BA MA PGCE (forties), previously deputy head at King's College Junior School, Wimbledon, and before that head of liberal studies in the sixth form at Dulwich College. 'My wife, who is a trained junior school teacher, persuaded me to move to the junior age range. And I love it – the children are so refreshing and optimistic.' He teaches RE throughout the school. Two daughters in Highgate pre-prep.

Much praised by parents. 'As well as being extremely energetic, attractive and charming, he is very effective.' 'He's good at investigating parental concerns and at making the children feel special.' 'He's a breath of fresh air.'

Entrance: Junior: there are now four year 3 classes, with around 40 children coming in at seven to join the 30 or so who move up from the pre-prep. Nearly half of these are girls. There are around 200 applicants for these places. The principal interviews all the children in pairs, including some reading, chatting and mental maths. 'The idea is to keep it within their zone of confidence.' Another 30 or so – from around 150 applicants – come in at 11, nearly all from state primary schools. They are tested in maths, English, verbal and non-verbal reasoning, and nearly all are interviewed by the principal. At present, there are a few places at eight and nine but these are being phased out.

Pre-prep: apply immediately after your child's first birthday. There are usually over 400 applicants for 32 places, and the head sees over 100 of these, not on a first-come-first-served basis. A connection with the school helps

– 'we ask parents why they want a place and try to match their aspirations with what we are offering.'

Exit: Junior: nearly all transfer to the senior school; a few with learning difficulties or a yen for boarding school move elsewhere.

Pre-prep: most move on to the junior school; one or two a year do not make the grade.

Remarks: Wonderful setting in a quiet side road near the top of Highgate, with playing fields on both sides, sports centre across the road and the senior school buildings a short stroll away. Many of the houses nearby are owned by the school and occupied by staff, which does wonders for recruitment. Being transformed by the gradual influx of girls, which has upped the academic stakes. 'Highgate has always been viewed as sporty,' says the principal. 'I hope that taking in girls will broaden its cultural strengths.' The senior school head emphasises that Highgate should be viewed as a single foundation in three parts, with virtually all those coming in to the pre-prep at three staying at the school until the sixth form. Plans in the future to move years 7 and 8 to the senior school, so the junior school will be for 7 – 11 year olds, and 11-year-old entrants will join the bottom of the senior school rather than the top of the junior school.

The school has converted one of its buildings into a centre of excellence for art, design and technology for the whole foundation. It is called the Mills Centre. Field House has already been redecorated in fetching shades and purple and green, with the ground floor given over to the library and ICT resources centre for topic and project work.

There is no longer one elite class in years 7 and 8; instead, children are divided into four sets for maths, science and French, including a 'new students' French set for those coming in at 11 who have not studied it before (Highgate teaches French from year 4). Latin now starts in year 7, so newcomers can begin with everyone else. There is some learning support for those who are struggling, though the school cannot cope with severe difficulties. At the other end of the spectrum, high fliers in the top classes have enrichment group activities such as French conversation classes with native speakers. Praise from parents for 'hugely stimulating, informative and creative' teaching without overt pressure. The principal acknowledges an advantage of being part of a 3 – 18 school – 'we're not driven by the huge pressures of Common Entrance. We have the space for a broader, more enriched curriculum than the average free-standing prep school.'

Another advantage is sharing the extensive playing fields and splendid sports centre. The school has three full time sports coaches; there are sufficient teams to include the keen along with the elite. All the usual sports are available; the fencing teacher coached James Bond in Die Another Day, and the Fives teams seldom lose. The range of activities now includes dance and other female-orientated games such as netball.

Plenty of exciting artwork on display. Years 3 and 4 learn ceramics from their own specialist art teacher. Strong DT. Around three-quarters of pupils learn a musical instrument; there are many choirs and musical groups as well as the school orchestra. Each year group puts on an informal concert every term. Drama is taught throughout the school, and one of the two plays each year is usually a musical with songs written by year 5 teacher Sarah Roberts.

Every member of staff now runs an after-school club – ranging from drama, squash and computers to ceramics. School trips include visits to the school's field centre in Snowdonia, orchestra and sports tours and ski-ing. Fundraising encompasses talent shows and charity basketball matches. Some joint activities, eg breakfast enrichment maths club and music-making, with nearby St Michael's primary school.

Some bursaries, six or seven scholarships and several music awards up to 50 per cent of fees at 11.

Parents remark on the school's 'combination of kindliness and discipline'. 'They make sure you know about your child's successes,' said one. House points and awards for good work. One of the deputy heads is in charge of pastoral care and has introduced meetings for parents on coping with teenagers and a highly-praised talk on drugs by an ex-addict. Nearly two pages of the parents' handbook cover bullying. Families are welcome to call in for breakfast any morning. 'They really care about the children,' said a parent.

Pre-prep: all nursery places are part time, then full time from reception onwards. Two parallel classes of 16. Excellent, creative teaching which includes plenty of topic work. The learning support department helps those with difficulties and very able children. Violin and cello taught from reception onwards; cookery, drama, IT and ceramics are all part of the curriculum. Shares the sporting facilities of the rest of the school. Friendly, family feel.

Victorian building with a glass mosaic of birds and animals in the stairwell, large windows overlooking the playing fields, walls and ceilings festooned with artwork. The playground has a separate nursery area, a water feature and a 'friendship bench' where lonely children can sit.

'My rather reserved daughter has blossomed here,' said a parent.

HIGHGATE PRE-PREPARATORY SCHOOL

Linked to Highgate Junior School in the Junior section
Linked to Highgate School in the Senior section

7 Bishopswood Road, London, N6 4PH

Tel: 020 8340 9196
Fax: 020 8340 3442
E-mail: admissions@highgateschool.org.uk

• Pupils: 130 girls and boys; all day • Ages: 3-7 • Fees: £1,777 nursery (half day); £3,565 pre-prep • Independent

Remarks: For further details see prep school and senior school.

HILL HOUSE ST MARY'S, NURSERY AND MIDDLE SCHOOL

Rutland Street, Thorne Road, Doncaster, South Yorkshire, DN1 2JD

Tel: 01302 323 563
Fax: 01302 761 098
E-mail: info@hillhousestmarys.co.uk
Website: www.hillhousestmarys.co.uk

• Pupils: 460 girls and boys; all day • Ages: 21/2 - 11 • Fees: £1,850 - £2,643 • Independent

HILL HOUSE SCHOOL

17 Hans Place, Knightsbridge, London, SW1X 0EP

Tel: 020 7584 1331
Fax: 020 7591 3938
E-mail: hillhouse@goodschoolsguide.co.uk

- Pupils: 1,030, 60:40 boys:girls; all day • Ages: 4-13 • Non-denom • Fees: School quotes fees by the quarter. Per term equivalent £2,315 - £2,805. Boys more than girls at some stages • Independent • Open days: any morning

Principals: Since 2003, Mr Richard Townend FLSM, a musician, and his wife, Mrs Janet Townend Cert Ed. Mr Townend is principal and headmaster and Mrs Townend is principal and director of admissions. The school was founded by Mr Townend's father, Lt Col H Stuart Townend, a legend in his lifetime and since, and his image, influence and inspiration are still all-pervasive. Mr Townend, a quiet musician, whom we did not meet, is regarded as mild and likeable and, along with being i/c music, about which he is passionate, also does much of the admin. Mrs Townend is the more visible partner and is regarded by parents as running the school. She does no teaching and sees her role as administrative – a demanding role running a large school on several sites in a busy part of London. She is brisk and busy and spends much time going between the sites, sometimes chauffeured in the Colonel's venerable Bentley. Each part of the school has its own head. Another key figure is Mr Donal Brennan, the undermaster. Mr Brennan takes assemblies, is voluble and high profile. Some pupils apparently think he is the headmaster.

Entrance: First come, first served at four but the school, famously, will fit people in if they possibly can and if they like them. At six there is a test in maths and English. Prospective parents are invited to turn up for a tour of the school on any morning without appointments. They will be greeted by eager children who sit on the entrance hall stairs hoping for custom. Places do occur at all ages as, inevitably, people move in and out of the area.

Exit: Girls mostly go, at 11, to London day schools though a few to board at Benenden, Millfield and Wycombe Abbey. Chief destinations are Godolphin and Latymer, JAGS, Queen's College, Queen's Gate, the two Francis Hollands, More House and St Paul's Girls. Boys mostly leave at 13, about half to London day schools and the other to board. A few leave at 11 and get schols – in 2004, one each to Alleyn's, Dulwich College and Latymer Upper. Chief day destinations are Latymer Upper, City of London and a few to St Paul's, Westminster, Dulwich College and Highgate. No special boarding favourites but a spread of top schools which includes Eton, Stowe, Charterhouse, Bedales, Winchester, Worth and Haileybury. 6 schols were won in 2004, most pupils get to their first choice of school. School does not expect pupils to leave at 7 and won't prepare them to sit exams for other places – a pretty universal and understandable attitude.

Remarks: A school with a notable and inescapable past which booms at a visitor from every wood-panelled wall, display board and cabinet. It was founded by the late Colonel, firstly in Switzerland in 1949 and two years later in Hans Place. Its aim from the first was to be 'international' and to nurture each individual child's talents. The classes are unusually small, averaging 12 – just as well, as most rooms are too small for many more and some of the larger children in bigger classes are pretty cramped. The Swiss connection has faded for various reasons – though the school retains the Glion house and every pupil will still have at least one trip – and is, perhaps, less significant in the life of the school and its pupils than it was – a reality lamented by many. However, school maintains that, whereas hitherto pupils went just because they had reached a certain form in the school, now they are invited because of their aptitude for the particular course on offer and some parents prefer this approach because the courses are more focused. Whereas before, some 160 children went each year, now 130-140 do.

Photographs of fabulous landscapes, many mountainous but also many seascapes and island paradises, take their place on the walls amid the huge boards celebrating 'top boy', 'top house' 'monitors' and 'house captains' and gladden the heart. The outside world and activities to be enjoyed there are fundamental to the school's ethos, despite the irremediably urban setting. Urban in this case is remarkably tranquil considering it's two minutes from Harrods and three from Sloane Square. Six-storey, Victorian redbrick elegance around a quiet oval 'square' of similar domestic grandeur houses the main school – embellished with stylish bow windows and barley twist chimneys. Professional dog-walkers, window cleaners, maids and cleaners, gardeners and handymen abound in the square, busily making life comfortable for the residents. No PE or sport on site -'we need a gym,' admits Mrs Townend and a fund has been established to that end. Games take place in Battersea and Hyde Parks and various local halls, pools and gyms provide facilities for a good range of physical activity – 24 sports, we're told. The school has six buses which do the ferrying.

Parents commend the collaborative rather than competitive attitude to games.

Specialist music and art teachers contribute appreciably to the general ethos. Music is central and much aided by a specially commissioned 456 pipe organ in the beautiful bow-fronted 'organ room' used for class music lessons. The school possesses more than 300 instruments on loan for individual use – a rare and special asset. There are 32 choral scholarships available to existing school choristers which enable them to attend residential music courses, often abroad. During our visit, industrious papier-maché making was cheerfully going on in the science room – 'the only room we can make a mess in'. There is little pupil art on the walls of the main school and what there was, was mostly from 2-3 years before – far more, well-mounted and displayed, in the Cadogan Gardens building which houses the upper school – the 7-10 year-olds. However, the new Pont Street building includes an art gallery – a major addition. Main school artroom displays work of established artists and, indeed, the example of others in all areas of endeavour pervades this building – rooms have names eg Churchill, Newton, Shakespeare, numerous display boards show photographs of bygone pupils enjoying the outdoor life but it is hard to see what, now, is gained from fading photos from 1976 of happy smiling children which current pupils frankly admit they never look at.

Upper school, in a similar super building, is brighter and more spacious. 'Small school' in Flood Street, for the 190 four-year-olds, is in a chapel-like 'Hall of Remembrance'. Two thirds of the children learn in smallish individual classrooms, the rest are in the subdivided main hall in small groups. The atmosphere is relaxed, cheery, purposeful – if rather noisy. Main school opened a new extension (on the site of the boys' dept of Garden House which has decamped elsewhere) in 2005 which adds appreciably to the available teaching and eating space. Main, middle and upper schools have small but well-stocked, well-used libraries and school has made major recent expenditures in this area. The staff is young but turnover is low. Many staff from South Africa or the antipodes. Most look bright-eyed and keen.

The uniform -'not going to change' – is famously conspicuous – knickerbockers, split skirts, chunky honey-coloured jumpers etc – but it's also comfortable and practical and the children like it, though some would rather not wear it on the bus. The start and end times of the school day are staggered to help parents with children at more than one site. Children can also stay until 6.00 pm (Monday to Thursday) and 5.00 pm on Fridays and relish the tea available. Many can walk to school and school has won an award

for having more children walking to school than any other in the borough. The rest mostly from Fulham and Kensington. This is a local school. Additionally, school has a 'green travel plan'. The six school buses make a morning collection and evening return to many areas north of the Thames. Parents also good at car-sharing. Clientele much as you'd expect – largely moneyed professionals but others too and everyone blends successfully. It is also truly international in that it takes children from more than 30 countries. No appreciable EFL needed or provided though small class sizes allow for individual help when needed, we are assured. No SEN to speak of either – nothing more than mild dyslexia catered for here and you would be advised to look elsewhere if this is likely to be a problem.

It is hard to believe the school is as big as it is – the splitting between, now, three sites, obscures the fact that 1,000 children are educated here – a 'small school' intimacy and friendliness prevails amid the august surroundings. Hill House is in transition. The Colonel and his legacy are a rich inheritance but also an encumbrance. IT has arrived in the two years since his death and, we are promised, a website and email address are on their way. It is, beyond doubt, a happy school but one now which seems to lack visible leadership – clearly neither Townend is the charismatic and extrovert figurehead the Colonel was. 'A bit rudderless, perhaps, ' thought one parent. Apparently the two Townend sons will one day take over – both currently pursuing careers in other fields elsewhere. It appears well-run though communication with parents and the outside world seems pretty minimal – a good thing, you might feel – and there is no proper prospectus. 'Hill House is a place you have to visit and experience so you will never get a glossy brochure out of me,' says Mr Townend, rather touchingly. But, despite the school motto – 'A child is not a vessel to be filled but a fire to be kindled' – the learning is decidedly teacher-directed and, some feel, dependent on photocopied sheets and copying. An alert, forward-looking, overall educational drive seems lacking. Hill House should have a future as robust as its past but work is needed.

HOLMEWOOD HOUSE SCHOOL

Langton Green, Tunbridge Wells, Kent, TN3 0EB

Tel: 01892 860 000
Fax: 01892 863 970
E-mail: registrar@holmewood.kent.sch.uk
Website: www.holmewood.kent.sch.uk

- Pupils: 515; 322 boys, 193 girls; 6 weekly boarders, the rest day • Ages: 3-13 • Inter-denom • Fees: Weekly boarding £5,400; day £2,750 - £4,285; nursery £1,250 (half-day) - £1,875 (full day) • Independent • Open days: None. Individual attention on private tours of the school

Head: Since 1998, Mr Andrew S R Corbett MA PGCE (mid-fifties). Educated at Marlborough and at Edinburgh where he read history of European art and architecture. PGCE at London University. Came here from King's College School, Cambridge where he was headmaster for 5 years. Prior to that, head of history, director of studies and girls' houseparent at Port Regis and before that head of history and housemaster at The Hall, Hampstead. Very approachable, open and kind – diplomatic but firm with some demanding parents. Wife is a very popular full-time teacher here and they have two daughters who were at Holmewood but who now attend King's, Canterbury. Very keen on golf and takes pupils to inter-school competitions. Took over from Mr David Ives, who was head from 1980.

Entrance: Some at 3 into school's own newly built nursery (with 36 places), some into reception and some into year 3, although children can and do join at any age. All pupils assessed (extra time, laptops etc permitted for those with special needs if recommended by EP). Won't shy away from trying to accommodate pupils with physical or learning difficulties provided they have ability to cope with demands of the curriculum and the school. Majority stay until 13 but some leave at 11 to local grammar schools and girls' secondary schools.

Exit: Many pupils to Tonbridge, also Sevenoaks, Eastbourne, King's Canterbury, Cranbrook, Lancing, St Leonards-Mayfield, Marlborough and various other top independent schools. Very much the exception for pupils not to pass into their first choice school. Many prestigious scholarships won.

Remarks: Top prep school, top fees but with such extensive facilities you would expect this. Exceptionally aca-demic; considering the non-selective procedures, the children achieve some wonderful results which reflect the quality and enthusiasm of the teachers. Also very focused on sport. The school tries to put out as many teams as possible in each age group so that all pupils have the opportunity to represent their school. 1st XV rugby team unbeaten last season. Under 11 IAPS national netball champions. Regular gymnastics success at national level. Stunning indoor 25-metre swimming pool built in 2001 – swimming teams national champions four years in succession; full-time swimming coach. Apart from usual team games, squash, athletics, tennis, golf and shooting too.

Extremely active music department – over 70 per cent of pupils learn an instrument – five choirs, two orchestras, a swing band, pop group and two jazz groups to name a few; over last 5 years they have had 20 major music scholarships to various schools. Music department also has its own computerised keyboard room where pupils can compose. Art equally impressive with two very dedicated and enthusiastic teachers. In 2003, they won two awards given by Artworks – Young Artists of the Year Awards. The award-winning work by the children was featured in a virtual reality exhibition at Tate Modern. Well-equipped DT workshop producing some impressive work. Drama popular as an afternoon and after-school activity in fully equipped theatre.

Lovely fully computerised library with full-time librarian; library lessons also given. Computers in evidence all round the school – all pupils have their own email address – and there are over 30 interactive white boards. Pre prep and nursery in separate blocks with their own head; very well organised; they have full use of all main school facilities. Separate junior department for years 3 and 4. An accelerated band is introduced in year 3 and further setting is carried out in later years. Excellent special needs department – problems are spotted very early on (all children screened in year 3) and help is given. Boarding offered only on weekly basis; some flexi-boarding by younger pupils. Dorms very light, airy, cosy and tidy.

Its reputation as a highly competitive school doesn't seem to phase the children, who are confident, bubbly, honest and well-mannered.

HOLY CROSS PREPARATORY SCHOOL

George Road, Kingston Hill, Kingston-upon-Thames, Surrey, KT2 7NU

Tel: 020 8942 0729
Fax: 020 8336 0764
E-mail: admissions@holycrossprep.co.uk
Website: www.holycrossprep.co.uk

• Pupils: 265 girls, all day • Ages: 4-11 • RC, but other denominations and faiths welcome • Fees: £2,255
• Independent • Open days: October (weekday) and May (Saturday morning)

Head: Since 1992, Mrs Kathleen Hayes BEd MA (fifties), studied education at St. Mary's (University of London) and at Roehampton. First lay head of the school (the Sisters of the Holy Cross own it), blonde, petite, very down to earth and very well-liked by parents, many describing her as 'very caring.' 'Very switched on, with a relationship with the girls that I would call one of quiet respect on both sides,' says another. A dynamo, she considers herself to be 'an ideas person' and greatly fond of children.

Entrance: Oversubscribed by about 2:1 for main intake at age 4: 40 places available to fill two parallel classes – pupils come from about twelve local nursery schools. Apply to the school as early as you can and by September 30 in the year prior to entry. In effect there is a test for admission – children attend an introductory session on a Saturday in November for what the head describes as 'a holistic look' at the child, focusing on attitude and concentration, social and personal skills. Spaces occur periodically in other years and are filled on an ad hoc basis. No scholarships.

Exit: Impressive record of success to the best local senior schools (with a handful of academic scholarship won every year): Surbiton High, Putney High, Lady Eleanor Holles, also Tiffin Girls' School (state grammar), and state girls schools Holy Cross in New Malden and Coombe Girls' in Kingston. Occasionally to some of the swanky boarding schools such as Benenden and St. Mary's, Ascot.

Remarks: Lovely inclusive school in smart location with friendly atmosphere and excellent academic results. School is housed in a wonderful Victorian house complete with sweeping carriage drive and specimen trees, high up on the upmarket private residential Coombe Estate – in arguably the most prestigious road. Formerly the home of novelist John Galsworthy of 'Forsyte Saga' fame. Library is a wood panelled room; it is easy to imagine Galsworthy, sitting there, pen in hand, gazing out over the 8 acres of well-maintained grounds. Modern block houses reception class and years 1 and 2 – everything bright and cheery, with loads going on. Up-to-date IT.

Academically the school shines, with sky-high KS2 results across the board. Mild to moderate SEN catered for and an independent teacher provides assistance – extra fees are paid direct to her. Occasional girl has EAL and one member of staff is the nominated support teacher. Class sizes maximum 20.

Sister Ursula, the present deputy head, is now the only sister on the staff, she is hugely popular. 'Every child should have a Sister Ursula; she is quite wonderful with the girls' said one mother. The RE programme embraces all faiths – 45 per cent of the girls are RC, the remainder being mostly C of E, with a few Muslims and Hindus. Non-RC parents frequently talk to the girls about their faiths and practices – particularly appreciated by RC parents, one of whom commented that he 'would not feel nearly so comfortable with a conventional convent school.'

Terrific artwork on display everywhere, particularly involving textiles. Music important; choir and orchestra open to all, although naturally the orchestra tends to attract those with music exam grades. Unusual clubs include pottery, ecology, and German (although not on syllabus).

All sports on site, except swimming. There's a feeling among parents that grounds could be used for more sport – but only one PE teacher for the whole school. Sports teams are selected on merit and girls can be in more than one team; those who don't make the team are encouraged to join the relevant club.

Girls are polite and courteous, individually greeting visitors in the corridors and chorusing 'Good morning, Mrs.T' unprompted in class. Top two parallel classes write letters of welcome to the prospective little newcomers into the reception class and become their mentors for the following year. Girls we spoke to assert that bullying does not exist and that relationships with staff and pupils are tremendous. One said: 'It's a very enthusiastic school, which does lots of exciting things. We laugh with the teachers, but we also respect them.' Parents heap praise on the pastoral care at the school, said to be very concerned for each and every girl's moral welfare.

HONEYWELL INFANT SCHOOL

Honeywell Road, Battersea, London, SW11 6EF

Tel: 02072 286 811
Fax: 02077 389 101
E-mail: office@honeywell.wandsworth.sch.uk

• Pupils: 334 boys and girls • Ages: 3-7 • Non-denom • State

Head: Deputy head since 1994, Jane Neal is now acting head.

Entrance: At 3 to nursery but this does not guarantee a place in the school at 4. Criteria are broadly siblings first, then proximity to the school, but there is a category for special medical or social applications and children in LEA care. Everyone transfers automatically into the junior school.

Exit: All to Junior School.

Remarks: Infants and juniors share a site, each with their own accommodation and head teachers enabling them to specialize in each age group. Class sizes 30 max. School Achievement Award for improving SATs results, also Wandsworth quality award for organization and management development (self-review and evaluation). New library, enlarged and improved the playgrounds and environmental gardens.

SEN specialist support runs for groups and individuals. Discipline is good with a sensible set of rules but no uniform can make the children look a bit scruffy. A happy, positive and hands-on atmosphere prevails. A super state primary, and much sought after.

HONEYWELL JUNIOR SCHOOL

Honeywell Road, Battersea, London, SW11 6EF

Tel: 02072 235 185
Fax: 02077 389 101
E-mail: office@honeywell.wandsworth.sch.uk
Website: www.honeywelljuniorschool.com

• Pupils: 360 boys and girls; all day • Ages: 7-11 • Non-denom
• State • Open days: November. Please contact the school

Head: Since 1999, Mr Duncan Roberts BEd NPQH (mid forties), married, previously deputy head. Well liked by staff, pupils and parents; straightforward and approachable with a great sense of fair play. A keen sportsman.

Entrance: Most from the infants school. A few other places at 7, then casual vacancies as they occur.

Exit: Two thirds to state sector – Sutton Grammar, Wilson's, Wallington High, Lady Margaret, Elliott, Graveney and Burntwood. One third to independent – Streatham and Clapham High, Dulwich College, Emanuel, Alleyn's.

Remarks: Long reputation for being one of the best in south London set in the heart of Wandsworth. Infants and Juniors share a site, each with their own accommodation and head teachers enabling them to specialize in each age group. Class sizes 30 max. After outstanding OFSTED report in December 2002, Mr Roberts chosen to meet HRH Prince Charles as headteacher of one of the most successful primary schools in England. Mr Roberts has raised funds to improve the school's facilities and they are now able to boast an on-site all-weather pitch and ICT suite which he, with the help of parents, decorated. 'So there is more money for equipment and teachers – clever man,' say parents.

Variety of sports, matches with other schools, even lacrosse and cross country and Gold Active Mark for Sports awarded by Sport England. French now taught throughout the school as part of the curriculum. Good music, choir, orchestra and string sections, individual tuition on the cello, violin or flute, big spring concert. Annual sell-out drama and music show produced at the Clapham Grand Theatre. Many choices of lunch-time or after-school clubs include drama, guitar and French. Clientele is a good social mix. 'Open-door' policy – parents encouraged to support the school through PTFA, with fund-raising, as reading partners, library partners or helping in the classrooms.

SEN specialist support runs for groups and individuals,

laptops for pupils who need to use them. Discipline is good with a sensible set of rules but no uniform can make the children look a bit scruffy. A happy, positive and hands-on atmosphere prevails in both schools. If you are looking for added value and strong leadership, it's definitely here. A super state primary and much sought after.

Hordle Walhampton School

Walhampton, Lymington, Hampshire, SO41 5ZG

Tel: 01590 672 013
Fax: 01590 678 498
E-mail: office@hordlewalhampton.co.uk
Website: www.hordlewalhampton.co.uk

• Pupils: 330 (more boys than girls), 200 in the main school (inc 50 boarders), 130 in pre-prep • Ages: 7-13; pre-prep 2-7 • C of E • Fees: Boarding £4,750 ; day £1,805 - £3,610 • Independent • Open days: Near the start of each term

Head: Since 1998, Mr Henry Phillips BA (fifties), educated at Harrow, worked as a stockbroker before doing an Open University degree in English. Deputy head at Summer Fields, then head of Hordle House, which subsequently amalgamated with Walhampton (see below). 'He's larger than life,' said a parent. 'He says what he thinks and doesn't tolerate fools,' said another. 'He's got a wicked sense of humour and the children think he's fantastic. Every year he hosts a grandparents' lunch and they all adore him.' His 'wonderful' wife, Jackie, helps out with the boarders, teaches and works hard around the school. Three children.

Entrance: First-come-first-served entry at 2 into the very popular pre-prep, with preference for siblings. Nearly everyone goes through to the prep at seven; more join at that point. There is a fair amount of to-ing and fro-ing; a few leave the pre-prep for state primaries, some come in from abroad for a term or two to improve their English, others move into or out of the area. Always worth trying for a place; those coming in higher up are assessed. 'We're comfortably full but will always take a good child at the last minute.' That doesn't necessarily mean academically gifted. 'All children have something to offer, whether on the games field or in the concert hall. We're a school for good all-rounders.'

Exit: A few leave at 11, for eg King Edward VI in Southampton, but most stay till 13, moving on to a wide variety of secondaries, particularly co-ed Wessex boarding schools such as Bryanston, Marlborough, Canford, but also Eton, Harrow, Winchester, St Swithuns, Downe House. Very few to selective state schools.

Remarks: Has put behind it the traumas of the merger between Hordle House and Walhampton in 1997. Splendid Queen Anne/Victorian building with panelled, galleried entrance hall and chapel in what was once the music room, with original cornices. Glorious 100 acre grounds on the edge of the New Forest with lakes for ducks and sailing, extensive playing fields, outdoor swimming pool backed by Italianate colonnade and shell grotto, stables (bring your own pony), pet shed, new sports hall and performing arts centre. Non-selective. French from 4, Latin from 9, German club. Years 3 and 4 have two parallel classes; years 5 – 7 are divided by ability into two classes; about a third of year 8 form a scholarship class. The latest Independent Schools Inspectorate report commented that work set in years 3 – 5 tended to aim at the middle range; the school has addressed this by setting for maths and English and differentiating work in other subjects. 'We're not an academic hot-house, but children fulfil their potential.' 'They teach the children to their own level but don't cram them,' agreed a parent approvingly. Having said that, in 2005 six children gained entrance to Winchester, three gained academic scholarships, two gained sports scholarships, one gained an all-rounder scholarship (for prowess in art, music and sports) and one a music scholarship – a school record.

Has an excellent SEN department (individual and shared teaching at extra charge, plus extra help in class). Good at spotting problems. Will cater for mild Aspergers, ADD, specific learning difficulties (Dyslexia unit is registered with CReSTeD). Children with behavioural or severe learning problems may be turned away. Hot on spotting SpLDs and will arrange EP assessments. Go back to basics if necessary – fill in gaps. Very bright boys get help too, if they need it. Children view one-to-one as a real treat, no stigma. Make great strides not just academically but socially too. Only grumble: parents say sometimes they wish school would tell them a little more be a bit more open – tend to say doing fine, don't worry, but parents do worry.

IT is now particularly strong; art and DT good too; plenty of drama. Music, say parents, is more patchy but about 80 per cent of pupils learn an instrument. There is now a school orchestra, a number choirs and specific music groups (including a steel band) and a couple of rock bands. 'We have a very cool guitar teacher. Activities range from cookery to canasta to camp craft. 'My son learned bee keeping and we now have our own hive,' said a parent. Games features very strongly. Individual sports such as archery cater for those who aren't team players. Some mutterings that girls' sport is perhaps slightly less strong than boys' – 'I have appointed an experienced coach to bolster that area and results this year have been pretty good,' says the head. 'We love sport, and are not afraid of competition.' Planning permission for a new Astroturf has just been approved to back this up. School teams win medals for tetrathon and sailing as well as the more usual swimming, tennis, rounders and so on. In 2003, rugby and hockey teams toured South Africa.

Towards the end of the summer term the whole school goes off on expeditions, which include a year 7 leadership skills week at the school's own base on the Isle of Mull. This week, which features highly in children's fond memories of the school, helps staff to choose the head boy and girl, prefects and patrol leaders. The school's four houses are divided into mixed aged patrols, whose leaders look after the younger children. 'My children revere their patrol leaders,' says a year 3 teacher.

Excellent pastoral care; staff and parents emphasise that it is a very happy school. 'Parents are amazed at the staff's depth of knowledge of their children.' It takes a no-blame approach to bullying. 'We're very vigilant and try to knock it on the head as fast as we can. Usually a word here and there sorts it out.' Mentors are allocated to new children and there are flexible behaviour strategies for individuals if necessary. Strongly Christian ethos. Assembly takes place in the chapel every morning and there is a service on Friday evenings. 'It is an important part of communal living.' 'Everyone is encouraged to board in the last two years and a few do so lower down – weekly and flexi-boarding available. The school runs a boarding timetable, with sports and activities every afternoon until 6.15pm (except for year 3, who leave at 3.45). There are also Saturday morning activities and afternoon sports matches, and special outings on Sunday for boarders.

Links with local state primaries, whose pupils come up for multi-activity days. 'We're very keen not to be seen as that snobby school on the hill.' Pupils come from the Channel Islands and the Isle of Wight as well as mainland Hampshire and Dorset. Popular with army and civil service families.

Probably not the school for children whose favourite activity is sitting in the corner with a book. '"Robust" conjures up our outlook,' says the head. There is a wide enough range of activities for everyone to shine at something, whether clocking up runs for the 3rd XI, singing in the chapel choir or performing in Bugsy Malone. 'We chose the school because it had so many different activities on offer and we haven't been disappointed,' said a parent. 'My boys have always wanted to go to school every day.'

HORNSBY HOUSE SCHOOL

Hearnville Road, London, SW12 8RS

Tel: 020 8673 7573
Fax: 020 8673 6722
E-mail: school@hornsby-house.co.uk
Website: www.hornsby-house.co.uk

● Pupils: 320 girls and boys, 50/50; all day ● Ages: 4-6 infants, 7-11 juniors ● Non-denom ● Fees: £2,800-£3,048
● Independent

Head: Since 1998, Mrs Jenny Strong BEd (fifties). Married with 4 grown-up children, she was brought up in Scotland and educated at St George's Edinburgh. Formerly the deputy head at Alleyn's Junior School also taught at JAPS. Mrs Strong has an interest in maths and science. Very much a hands-on head with a firm belief in co-education. Retiring July 2006.

Entrance: Non selective at 4-6 years. From 7 and for occasional places in the junior school an assessment test and interview with the head. Places are allocated on a first-come-first-served basis, so it is worth putting your child's name down in advance. Sibling priority.

Exit: At 11 years to a range of London day schools including Wimbledon and Streatham & Clapham Girls High Schools, Dulwich College, King's College, Emanuel, Alleyn's, James Allen and The Hall. Handful to boarding schools such as Woldingham, Windlesham House, Wycombe Abbey and Heathfield.

Remarks: Hornsby House was founded in 1988 by Professor Beve Hornsby. The school opened with 20 pupils in a church hall premises, they moved to a permanent site in 1993 and have gone from strength to strength ever since. New buildings were opened in September 2000 and 2003 providing further classrooms, a science room, music rooms, art room, library and a state-of-the-art ICT suite complete with all the new technology a good prep school needs.

Has a good reputation for being a friendly, welcoming school where everyone knows each other as it has not grown too large. The staff are mostly long serving. The pupils are predominantly local, especially in the younger age groups. The school is now housed on a well-modernised Victorian (ex local authority) primary school site; spacious light classrooms, a large gym/assembly hall, two playground areas, a well-stocked library, art room. Displays of the children's work everywhere.

Reception classes in a separate building – a cosy and secure atmosphere for the 4-6 year olds, with their own small hall and playground. Class sizes are between 18-22, all classes are mixed ability, have a teacher and an assistant teacher some of whom are graduates. No meals are provided, all bring packed lunches. Good music, drama and sport – the school produces some very colourful shows each term and also has theatre groups to visit. Three choirs, orchestra and a wide choice of individual instrumental tuition. An enthusiastic new sports master arrived recently, the children use the nearby Trinity Fields. A strong parents' group, 'Friends of Hornsby House', runs social events, fetes etc for school and charity fund-raising.

Children with known specific learning difficulties entering the school will be asked to have a full assessment. There is a full time SEN co-ordinator and three part-time dyslexia therapists who work with children on maths and English. The school is also able to accommodate some children with physical disabilities. Where necessary, pupils use laptops, and the school has good links with touch-typing tutors. A parent comments, 'having moved my children to Hornsby from another school this was a good decision, it is much more relaxed.'

HORRIS HILL SCHOOL

Newtown, Newbury, Berkshire, RG20 9DJ

Tel: 01635 40594
Fax: 01635 35241
E-mail: enquiries@horrishill.com
Website: www.horrishill.com

• Pupils: around 120 boys 115 boarders (compulsory in last two years) • Ages: 8-13 • C of E • Fees: Day £4,650, boarding £5,650 • Independent

Head: Since 1996, Mr Nigel Chapman BA (fifties), previously senior-head at Lockers Park and before that taught for 20 years at Summer Fields. Educated at Felsted and London University. Fanatical Arsenal supporter. Married to Lindsay, three children (a daughter at Marlborough and 2 sons who attended Shrewsbury). Mrs Chapman is fully involved in the school on the boarding and domestic side. Took over from Mr M J Innes who taught here for a record thirty-five years, eighteen of them as headmaster. Retiring in July 2006.

Entrance: By registration and informal one-on-one test. Take in around 25 boys each year. Brainboxes may sit competitive exam, on the basis of which up to four concessions on fees may be awarded. Around a quarter of boys are local, with further quarters from London, the rest of the UK and abroad (half expats, half foreign). Cheam Hawtreys, close by, takes the local, co-ed, day contingent.

Exit: More to Eton and Winchester than anywhere else and many families choose the school for these strong ties. Then Radley, Harrow and on down the list of usual suspects. Recent surge in popularity of Shrewsbury and Marlborough. Number of scholarships won bobs up and down and head is not keen on entering boys who he knows have little chance. No boys entered 2002-3 but 7 entered in 2004.

Remarks: Famous country prep school (nicknamed by boys 'Horrid Hell') founded in 1888 by an ex-master at Winchester to train up boys for entry to that school. A super place. Scruffy and relaxed, with a curious lack of polish that exerts a refreshing, strong appeal. Lovely down-to-earth boys with good, but not slick, manners. Combs obviously not compulsory. Boys can wear any ties they like and we particularly admire some of the eight-year-olds' choices. Staff members' dogs wander in and out of classrooms, including one nestled under the sickbed in the nursing sister's quarters.

Main entrance non-existent, so Mr Chapman must come out and personally whisk visitors from the car park if they are to find their way to his study (this happy state of affairs set to change as the school is planning a new entrance). Central building a square of narrow corridors painted a dingy prison-cell-pink. Swish new classroom block (2000) with rooms named after schools to which boys move on (Eton, Radley etc). The grounds comprise more than 70 acres and boys we spoke to singled out Saturday night camping in the woods as a favourite activity. Youngest boys play in the 'junior wood' next to the main building while older boys roam far and wide.

Brilliant school magazine, the best in the business, with lots of pupil input and hilarious schoolboy humour (eg boys' report on having to learn ballet for a school play and series of mock newspaper front pages). Packed with photos taken and developed by the boys. School prizes for sports and academics but also less mainstream accomplishments, eg general knowledge, current affairs and gardening. A few unusual rooms tucked away include the 'old gym' crammed with table tennis, snooker and drum kits; the photo lab; the model railway room and the modelling room (Airfix and Warhammer model-building a big deal here – our guide named Airfix as his winter game).

Eccentric form system. No year groups – boys are moved up as and when they are ready. On average, boys spend 2 terms in each form but this can be lengthened to three terms or shortened to one, according to the boy's ability. This 'ladder' system ends in the final year when most 12-year-olds go into one of two CE forms. Scholarship candidates – if there are any – will have moved swiftly up the ladder to spend the final year in a separate top form. Class sizes average 11-12 with a maximum of 15, and some of only six or seven. Half-hour prep done at school, increasing to an hour further along in the school. Four boys currently benefit from EFL instruction; limited SEN provision.

Keen sports. Everybody plays and boys get a good grounding. Match results vary widely. Gamesy boys play up to five times a week, the less enthusiastic can get away with twice. Long tradition as a football school but rugby was introduced in 1998 and the first XV is now able to compete without embarrassment though 'we can't quite win yet,' says the head. Good record at cricket. Nine-hole pitch and putt golf course and visiting golf pro. Two squash courts.

Double lesson of art for all. Very good drama and every boy takes part in a play (as actor or behind scenes) each year. Energetic and innovative music department stresses performance, performance and performance. Music exam results not setting the world on fire and preparing boys for music scholarships has not troubled the school greatly over the years. Still, we reckon boys at Horris Hill do more music – and have more fun with it – than those at most preps. A form class we visited was comparing Glen Miller to Shostakovich, noting that they worked at the same period of the twentieth century. Ninety per cent of boys learn an instrument, including class violin lessons for youngest boys. Drums and guitar popular and there is a jazz piano class, three choirs and loads of string, wind and brass ensembles. Head of music takes boys on many outings (from Mozart to the Blues Brothers) and doubles as leader of outward-bound expeditions. NB Pop Idol winner Will Young is the school's most famous old boy.

Lovely dorms, especially those for the youngest boys, tucked up a little, narrow staircase above the Chapmans' home. These boys are looked after personally by the head and his wife and parents speak warmly of their confidence in the care – head says 'we mollycoddle them'. Middle-aged boys live above the main part of the school. The oldest boys live in public school-style houses two or three minutes walk from the classroom blocks, each with its own married house master and assistant. After the first weekend of each term, boys may go home after commitments on Saturday until Sunday evening but over half the boys are in school on any given weekend, lured to remain by brilliant range of Sunday activities. At the time we visited, junior boarders had just finished designing and sewing 'pillow people' and the marvellous results were much in evidence in the dorms. 'Grub' (sweets) handed out after lunch three days a week (range has widened after successful lobbying by student council which also wangled Sky TV!). Food good and plentiful, biscuits and hot chocolate available three times a day. Bullying taken seriously – one boy was excluded for this a few years ago and school maintains that any witness to bullying must tell someone or they will be considered part of the bullying group. Chapel not a thing of beauty but provides good opportunity for the oldest boys to take turns leading the Sunday evening services (idea came from the Dragon). Oldest boys also serve as school prefects.

A glorious example of a dying breed – the small, informal, boys-only, country, boarding prep. Serenely marching on into the new millennium to the beat of its own drum.

HOTHAM PRIMARY SCHOOL

Charlwood Road, Putney, London, SW15 1PN

Tel: 02087 886 468
Fax: 02087 898 732
E-mail: info@hotham.wandsworth.sch.uk
Website: www.hotham.wandsworth.sch.uk

• Pupils: 245; 50/50 boys and girls; all day • Ages: 3-11 • Non-denom • State

Head: Since 1997, Ms Pam Young BA (forties) originally from New Zealand where she trained in 'early years'; has been teaching in the UK for the last 17 years. An enthusiastic and dedicated head much appreciated by staff and parents alike.

Entrance: At 3 to the nursery or 4 into reception; some occasional places in the older age groups. Criteria for admission are siblings and those living closest to the school – Putney, a few from Roehampton.

Exit: To a range of 'good' local state schools – Elliot, Lady Margaret and ADT College. Some to fee paying schools – Ibstock Place, Emanuel and the GDST and grammar schools in Sutton.

Remarks: A large Victorian building with lots of space as well as stairs. Well-maintained with imaginative displays of awards, competitions, photographs and art throughout the corridors. The school employs a number of specialist teachers/coaches. A specialist art teacher takes all classes for 7-11 year olds, a sports coach takes children in years

3 & 4 and a music teacher takes all children from nursery to year 6. There are 3 playgrounds so younger pupils have their own areas, whilst older ones have plenty of room for ball games or adventures in the school boat (dry-dock!). The school has developed its Key Stage 2 playground where there is now a defined ball area with football, basketball and short tennis courts, activity trail, climbing walls, running track etc. The children are cheerful, polite and obviously enjoying themselves as well as working; this is an active school with much going on. Also keeps up to date with current research – the handwriting policy has been reviewed to incorporate new evidence on the advantages of teaching cursive style from school entry. During 2003/4, the school looked at different learning styles and has introduced 'Brain Gym'.Has a strong focus on science and has been made a Wandsworth Borough Centre for Excellence. KS2 results are well above average; extension work is provided for more able year 6 pupils. Parents are encouraged to help with listening to reading. Computer suite as well as computers in all the classrooms. SEN is well covered by an individual member of staff and other specialist help is brought in when and if required. 'Secret Garden' project, for which the school raised £17,000 in a joint venture with the local Adult College, transformed a piece of wasteland into an environmental garden with a mini-beast area, wild flowers, a Victorian hedgerow, a human sundial and an art and nature studio. A real treat.Sport is also strong, particularly for a state primary; netball, football and cricket and matches against other schools too. Cross-country and athletics competitions, also swimming galas. After-school clubs, some of which are run by the teachers, include gymnastics, science, photography, jazz ballet, drama, French and art. Subsidised violin and keyboard tuition is on offer, also good drama – the school performs 2 shows each year, usually musicals, eg Oliver or The Wizard of Oz. Hotham boasts many awards: Wandsworth Pupil Achievement 2000, 2001, 2002 and 2003, Primary Teacher of Science 1999, BT Science Teacher of the Year Award 2002, DfES school excellence and environmental awards etc. Quite a few teachers have been students here and stayed on. Committed, enthusiastic and, mostly, long-serving staff, help make this school the success it is. Pupils mostly local, come from a range of different backgrounds making up a good social mix.A solid primary serving its community well, with pupils and parents responding enthusiastically. A real plus to see so many of the staff involved in extra-curricular activities. A parent commented, 'although we have moved away from Putney our children still attend Hotham, as we were not able to find anything to match its scope.'

HOWELL'S SCHOOL JUNIOR SCHOOL, LANDAFF

Linked to Howell's School, Llandaff in the Senior section

Cardiff Road, Landaff, Cardiff, South Glamorgan, CF5 2YD

Tel: 0290 562 019

- Pupils: 300 girls; all day • Ages: 4-11 • Non-denom
- Fees: £1,293 to £1,565 • Independent

Head: Mrs Marissa Davies who positively beams and sparkles and is quite passionate about childhood and creativity. Feels 'childhood should be celebrated' and wants to be a part of their growing into confident, problem-solving, balanced individuals with a positive attitude to life. 'Education sets the tone'.

Remarks: Happy atmosphere. Amazing new 'S' bend, zany, modern build with aluminium roof, non-square classrooms, dedicated art room 'reflects our creative philosophy', says the head. Distant enough from the main school to give the junior school an independent feel. Close by is the nursery in Cumberland Lodge (which is Roald Dahl's childhood home).

HURST LODGE JUNIOR SCHOOL (PLUS PREP AND KINDERGARTEN)

Bagshot Road, Ascot, SL5 9JU

Tel: 01344 622 154
Fax: 01344 627 049
E-mail: admissions@hurstlodgesch.co.uk
Website: www.hurstlodge.co.uk

- Pupils: girls (boys from 2.5-7); day and boarding from 9+
- Ages: 2.5 - 11 • Independent

Remarks: See senior school for further detail.

HURSTPIERPOINT COLLEGE PREPARATORY SCHOOL

Linked to Hurstpierpoint College in the Senior section

Hurstpierpoint, Hassocks, BN6 9JS

Tel: 01273 834 975
Fax: 01273 833 957
E-mail: hurstprep@hppc.co.uk
Website: www.hppc.co.uk

• Independent

HUTCHESONS' JUNIOR SCHOOL

Linked to Hutchesons' Grammar School in the Senior section
Linked to Hutchesons' Junior School in the Junior section

4 Lilybank Terrace, Glasgow, G12 8RX

Tel: 0141 423 2933
Fax: 0141 424 0251
E-mail: rector@hutchesons.org
Website: www.hutchesons.org

• Pupils: 360 girls and boys • Ages: 3-11 • Non-denom
• Independent

Remarks: See senior school.

HUTCHESONS' JUNIOR SCHOOL

Linked to Hutchesons' Grammar School in the Senior section
Linked to Hutchesons' Junior School in the Junior section

44 Kingarth Street, Glasgow, G42 7RN

Tel: 0141 423 2933
Fax: 0141 424 0251
E-mail: rector@hutchesons.org
Website: www.hutchesons.org

• Pupils: 800 boys and girls; all day • Ages: 4-11 • Non-denom
• Fees: £1,615 - £2,289 • Independent • Open days: Late
October/early November

Entrance: One intake a year (but see senior school above), all children assessed, 120/150 apply for 81 places.

Exit: Most children go on to senior school, having learnt how to work (with a vengeance).

Remarks: An enormous junior school, in the most fabulous original Victorian academy, think green and cream tiles, think fabulous carved oak assembly hall, think huge sunlit classrooms (three of the old ones now converted into two), spacious, full of light.

HYMERS COLLEGE JUNIOR SCHOOL

Linked to Hymers College in the Senior section

Hymers Avenue, Hull, HU3 1LW

Tel: 01482 441 211
Fax: 01482 472 854
E-mail: enquiries@hymers.hull.sch.uk
Website: www.hymerscollege.co.uk

• Pupils: 445 girls and boys; all day • Ages: 8-13 • Non-denom
• Fees: £1,965 - £2,235 • Independent

Remarks: See senior school for details.

IBSTOCK PLACE SCHOOL, JUNIOR AND KINDERGARTEN

Linked to Ibstock Place School in the Senior section

Clarence Lane, Roehampton, London, SW15 5PY

Tel: 020 8876 9991
Fax: 020 8878 4897
E-mail: registrar@ibstockplaceschool.co.uk
Website: www.ibstockplaceschool.co.uk

• Pupils: boys and girls • Ages: 3 -11 • Inter denom
• Fees: £2,989 up to year 2; £3,040 up to year 6 • Independent
• Open days: Throughout the year

Remarks: For details see senior school.

INTERNATIONAL SCHOOL OF ABERDEEN, PRESCHOOL AND ELEMENTARY

Linked to International School of Aberdeen in the Senior section

296 North Deeside Road, Milltimber, Aberdeen, AB13 0AB

Tel: 01224 732 267
Fax: 01224 735648
E-mail: admin@isa.aberdeen.sch.uk
Website: www.isa.aberdeen.sch.uk

• Pupils: 165 boys and girls; 30 in pre-school • Ages: Elementary (5-11); pre-school (3-4) • Fees: Underwritten by the oil companies 'who meet the tuition fees for their employees'. Some non-oil pupils: £500 registration; £2000 capital fee; £4,375 to £4,900 • Independent

Remarks: For details see senior school.

INTERNATIONAL SCHOOL OF LONDON JUNIOR SCHOOL

Linked to International School of London in the Senior section

139 Gunnersbury Avenue, London, W3 8LG

Tel: 020 8992 5823
Fax: 020 8993 7012
E-mail: mail@ISLondon.com
Website: www.ISLondon.com

• Pupils: 120 Juniors, boys and girls • Ages: 3-11 • Non-denom • Fees: £3,416 - £4,583 • Independent • Open days: Early October

IPSWICH HIGH SCHOOL JUNIOR DEPARTMENT

Linked to Ipswich High School in the Senior section

Woolverstone, Ipswich, Suffolk, IP9 1AZ

Tel: 01473 780 201
Fax: 01473 780 985
E-mail: admissions@ihs.gdst.net
Website: www.ipswichhigh.gdst.net

• Pupils: 100 girls; all day • Ages: 3-11 • Non-denom • Fees: £1,470 - £1,779 • Independent • Open days: In autumn and summer terms

Head: Since 1993, Miss Valerie MacCuish BA (mid-fifties). Educated at Lady Edridge Girls' Grammar and Westfield, London University. Modern linguist. Formerly deputy head at Surbiton High then head, Tunbridge Wells Girls' Grammar. A twinkly, approachable head, with a shrewd and pragmatic approach to her rather special school and its girls.

Retiring July 2006.

Entrance: At 3, assessed in informal play session. Later, at 7, 8 and 9, via written assessments in basic skills. Occasional spaces at other ages.

Remarks: One/two-storey school, bright, modern if not the most attractive building on site. Two parallel classes from year 3, 24 to a class. Well-equipped, good extra-curricular activities especially music, some homework. A lovely safe setting for early school years – space, trees and resident sheep 'an educational thing', according to head, must be special for any but girls from farming backgrounds.

IPSWICH PREPARATORY SCHOOL

Linked to Ipswich School in the Senior section

Henley Road, Ipswich, Suffolk, IP1 3SQ

Tel: 01473 281 302
Fax: 01473 400 068
E-mail: prepregistrar@ipswich.suffolk.sch.uk
Website: www.ipswich.suffolk.sch.uk

• Pupils: 303 boys and girls, all day • Ages: 3-11 • Fees: £1,953 - £2,221 • Independent

Head: Mrs Jenny Jones BA ARCM NPQH PGCE.

Entrance: Via tests in February in maths, English and reading plus report from current head.

Exit: Most to the senior school – but they have to pass the test with the rest of them.

Remarks: Nursery and pre-prep in purpose-built accommodation adjacent to main school. Prep shares many of senior school facilities including playing fields, indoor pool, sports hall, theatre. Unusual in that the prep has been going since 1883 – not just a modern addition to pull 'em in early. A well-organised, welcoming school.

JAMES ALLEN'S PREPARATORY SCHOOL (JAPS)

Linked to James Allen's Girls' School (JAGS) in the Senior section

East Dulwich Grove, London, SE22 8TE

Tel: 02086 930 374
Fax: 02086 938 031
E-mail: Japsadmissions@jags.org.uk
Website: www.japs.org.uk

• Pupils: 105 boys and girls in pre-prep, 190 girls in middle school, all day • Ages: 4-7 pre-prep, 7-11 middle school • C of E Foundation, but all are welcome • Fees: £2,766 • Independent
• Open days: September, October and November

Head: Since 1992, Mr Piers Heyworth MA PGCE (early fifties) Marlborough and Christ Church, Oxford, where he read English and founded the Oxford Survival Society (keen on environment). Previously celebrated head of English at JAGS, and appointment here an unusual and inspired choice – there's even more scope for his enthusiasm. Comments that the school takes 'a hundred and ten per cent of my time'. Married in 1998 Sarah Russell, who teaches at neighbouring Alleyn's Junior School. Two young children. As school recently expanded to double the size, most of the staff are his own appointments.

Entrance: From 'a hundred different nurseries', mainly in Dulwich and Clapham. Selective entry test in December and January for September, teachers watch out for 'adventurousness of spirit'. Followed by interviews.

Exit: Girls get sackfuls of scholarships. Boys at 7 go on to Dulwich, Dulwich College Preparatory School, Alleyn's junior school, etc.

Remarks: God's gift to the people of Dulwich. Part of the same foundation as JAGS, etc, and consequently very well funded. As the prep department of JAGS, has now spread its wings, with IAPS membership and co-education up to 7. On two sites – littles in Edwardian mansion down the road, 'middle school' tucked beside JAGS, with large extension opened in 1993 to include large sports hall, and super user-friendly library with own librarian – light and much used. Separate IT room, IT is being 'firmly incorporated in all subjects'. Timetabled computing for all, large sunny science room.

Specialist staff in a wide range of subjects – a tremendous strength. Brilliant 'immersion' French from age 4, with Mm Helène Gilbert, who speaks entirely in French and so far children have not cottoned on to the fact she speaks English as well – lots of fun games, impeccable accents and, by the time these children leave the school they will need special fast stream to keep up the good work. French taught in half classes in the middle school by another French specialist who produces an annual play en francais. Chosen by the French Embassy to represent the UK in the Parlement des Enfants in the Assemblée Nationale in Paris 2004. Eighteen per class in pre prep, rising to 24 in middle school, though most classes have two members of staff and can be split. Consequently 'we feel no need for setting or streaming'. Year 6 pupils take the National Curriculum key stage 2 and come out considerably above other IAPS schools. According to Sunday Times in 2005, JAPS 5th best in the UK.

Brilliant art and music. Drama strong (head keen and experienced). Fifty-five clubs after school and a staggering 420 pupils – from JAPS and 60 other local schools – turn up for 'Saturday school' – brain child of staff member, Miss Beverly Sizer – music, drama, dance from 8.30am till

2.30pm – wonderful way for pupils to work off excess energy and parents to get to Tescos in peace. Share new £4m JAGS' swimming pool – JAPS' pupils always in Bazuka national swimming finals. Active parents' committee organising social events etc. Two part-time qualified specialists provide one-to-one tuition for the small proportion of children – 'often the brightest' – needing it – special rooms set aside for this. Also 2 f/t and 1 p/t learning support staff. School absolutely full of fizz, top-class staff, strong all round. Has to be contender for one of the two best London preps south of the Thames.

JORDANHILL SCHOOL PRIMARY

Linked to Jordanhill School in the Senior section

45 Chamberlain Rd, Glasgow, G13 1SP

Tel: 0141 576 2500
Fax: 0141 950 2587
E-mail: info@jordanhill.glasgow.sch.uk
Website: www.jordanhill.glasgow.sch.uk

• Pupils: 460 girls and boys; all day • Ages: 4.5-11 • State

Remarks: For details, see Jordanhill School.

JOSCA'S PREPARATORY SCHOOL/ABINGDON JUNIOR SCHOOL

Linked to Abingdon School in the Senior section

Kingston Road, Frilford, Abingdon, Oxfordshire, OX13 5NX

Tel: 01865 391 570
Fax: 01865 391 042
E-mail: enquiries@joscas.org.uk
Website: www.joscas.org.uk

• Pupils: 200 girls and boys; all day • Ages: 4-13 • Independent

Remarks: For further details, see senior school: Abingdon School.

KELLY COLLEGE PREPARATORY SCHOOL

Hazeldon, Parkwood Road, Tavistock, Devon, PL19 0JS

Tel: 01822 612 919
Fax: 01822 612 919
E-mail: admin@kellycollegeprep.com
Website: www.kellycollegeprep.com

• Pupils: 90 boys, 70 girls; 10 board, rest day • Ages: 2-11
• Anglican foundation but all faiths and denominations welcome
• Independent

Remarks: Lively head. High academic standards; predominantly feeding Kelly. Broad range of extra-curricular clubs from chess to fencing. Boasting an undefeated football team and victorious netball team. Choir has won numerous certificates and trophies at Exeter Music Festival. Nursery has 25 pupils from age 30 months. Boarding from year 5.

KELVINSIDE ACADEMY JUNIOR SCHOOL

Linked to Kelvinside Academy in the Senior section

33 Kirklee Road, Glasgow, G12 0SW

Tel: 01413 573 376
Fax: 01413 575 401
E-mail: rector@kelvinsideacademy.org.uk
Website: www.kelvinsideacademy.org.uk

• Pupils: boys and girls; all day • Ages: 3-11 • Inter-denom
• Fees: nursery £700-£1748; Primary £1500-£2320
• Independent • Open days: November x 2

Remarks: For details, see senior school.

KENSINGTON PREP SCHOOL

596 Fulham Road, London, SW6 5PA

Tel: 02077 319 300
Fax: 02077 319 301
E-mail: enquiries@kenprep.gdst.net
Website: www.gdst.net/kensingtonprep

• Pupils: 275 girls; all day • Ages: 4-11 • Non-denom • Fees: £2,917 • Independent • Open days: Summer term 18 months before joining

Head: Since 2003, Mrs Prudence Lynch MA PGCE (fifties) who hails from Guernsey, did her MA in psychology at St Andrews and her PGCE at Goldsmiths. A thoroughly experienced and fun pair of hands, she comes to Ken Prep out of that breeding ground of head teachers, Colet Court, via a six year stint as head of juniors at the GDST Notting Hill and Ealing High School. 'It would have been quite difficult to come here if you didn't understand what the Trust is about,' she admitted. Mrs Lynch is 'having a ball', teaching only the top end at the moment, but she is hoping to develop 'philosophy and thinking skills throughout the school'. Enormously enthusiastic and bubbling with ideas, she is obviously keen on her girls – she also cheered up a very concerned six-year-old who found the idea of writing a poem about the month in which you were born quite beyond her. Expect to see the school doors changed from deep pink to turquoise green asap. Mrs Lynch inherited 'a brilliant' senior management team and has nothing but praise for her deputy, whom she appointed from within the school. Married, with two grown up sons, her husband works for the Beeb.

Entrance: Register child's name up to June in the year before entry. Four-year-olds are tested in early spring of the year they start school; girls observed in groups of four, 'then we home in on one at a time.' There is also an official entry point for a small number of girls at age seven (when Sloane parents reckon they have saved up enough to buy the Old Rectory and abandon Fulham for the good life etc – 'sometimes they come back'), Occasional places do become available in other year groups (keep trying). All are tested. No sibling bias.

Exit: The majority as ever to London day schools: Godolphin & Latymer, St Paul's Girls, Putney High the most popular, followed by the Francis Hollands (regular string of scholarships) plus an ever increasing number of boarders: Wycombe Abbey, Cheltenham Ladies' and Downe House the faves.

Remarks: 130 years old. Moved to the former Marist Convent in 1997 and now has a whole new catchment. Glorious Georgian coach house (with the dinkiest windows in the staff loos) and hideous sixties concrete additions – about to be swept away and replaced with larger teaching blocks and an extended hall. Terrific dedicated facilities, two netball pitches, music suite (nuns' cells equal practice rooms) and dedicated drama room. Faintly dated science lab, good IT area, computers in all classrooms, and serious amount of dosh about to be spent again – wireless access throughout and tablets for use everywhere. Touch-typing for all. Smartboards all over the shop. DT imaginative; both computers and microwaves in evidence, room also doubles as a dark room. Library in converted chapel (sadly no stained glass).

All staff teach with their doors wide open, lots of jolly pics and models on walls, and each form has their own set of rules somewhere on view (as decided by the pupils). French from five, Latin at the top end for half a year or so – taster only. Max class size 22, going down as age goes up with parallel classes throughout, fluid setting final two years for maths. Support (as a paid extra in KS2) for those with mild learning difficulties 'sometimes quite difficult to spot at assessment' – 'this is, in the end, a school with high academic expectations, it isn't the right place for everybody, but we do our best to provide for those pupils we identify' – ie once you have made a commitment to them they commit to your child. Resident SENCO, masses of teaching assistants and one permanent 'floating teacher' three days a week. Extra help for bored geniuses (by extension work and differentiation) as well as explanations for the needy.

A buzzy school with buzzy pupils. Staff young and beautiful, good role models. Art room about to be re-organised, currently boasts three new windows in the roof and an awful lot of storage space. Masses of ensembles and regular impromptu concerts at assembly as well as parental entertainment. Mrs Lynch talks wistfully 'of sharing music with local state primaries' but this is a way off. Huge dining room in the basement (with pillars holding the school up) – compulsory grub for all – no lunch boxes – but diet restrictions 'not a problem'; tinies have their grub doshed out, whilst the senior girls can pick and choose. Salad bar. Fairly uninspired uniform.

School makes much use of London facilities but is no longer the trad dame school it once was: autres temps, autres moeurs. And, do you know, it feels like a country school. Mrs Lynch would agree – 'the girls are not terribly street-wise – they have a certain amount of innocence' – and some of the best spelling and handwriting we have seen in a long time.

KILGRASTON JUNIOR SCHOOL

Linked to Kilgraston School in the Senior section

Bridge of Earn, Perthshire, PH2 9BQ

Tel: 01738 812 257
Fax: 01738 813 410
E-mail: registrar@kilgraston.pkc.sch.uk
Website: www.kilgraston.com

• Pupils: 86 boys and girls in the junior school and 25 in the nursery school • Ages: junior school 5-13 (boys to 8), nursery 2.5-5 • Fees: Junior school from £2,020 day to £4,950 for boarding • Independent • Open days: May and October

Head: Mrs Audrey Kellaway.
Exit: To Kilgraston and other senior schools in Scotland and England.
Remarks: Based in the converted stables. Delightful. All girls learn French from seven, physics from 11 and progress automatically up the senior school. All use the senior school facilities, and 11+ year olds share senior specialist staff and visit main school for lessons.

Pupils from the age of 5, with boys to 8. School shares main school facilities and is based in the stable block, which also shares with the nursery. The nursery includes local children of whom 24 are currently paid for by County Council.

KING ALFRED LOWER SCHOOL

Linked to King Alfred School in the Senior section

Manor Wood, 149 North End Road, Golders Green, London, NW11 7HY

Tel: 020 8457 5200
Fax: 020 8457 5249
E-mail: pressoffice@kingalfred.barnet.sch.uk
Website: www.kingalfred.barnet.sch.uk

• Pupils: boys and girls • Ages: 4-11 • Fees: £3,000 - £3,780 + optional lunch • Independent • Open days: July

Head: Ms Dawn Moore BSc MA PGCE (early forties)
Remarks: For details see senior school.

KING EDWARD'S JUNIOR SCHOOL (BATH)

Linked to King Edward's School (Bath) in the Senior section

North Road, Bath, BA2 6HU

Tel: 01225 463 218
Fax: 01225 442 178
E-mail: juniorschhead@kesbath.biblio.net
Website: www.kesbath.com

• Pupils: 185 in junior school (55 girls, 130boys), 100 in pre-prep; all day • Ages: junior school 7-11, pre-prep 3-6 • Non-denom • Fees: Pre-prep: £2,175; junior: £2,318 • Independent • Open days: Late September

Head: Since 1998, Mr John Croker BA PGCE (rising fifty) who played football for the public schools' XI whilst at Bradfield and still looks as if he could put in a useful shot or two. Read economics then PGCE at Manchester before two years in a state middle school in Redditch. Took off backpacking in South America and Far East – 'I learnt so much about life and myself in those years,' – before resuming teaching in Hong Kong where he met wife, Louise. Moved to Germany for eight years becoming deputy in a Services school and returning to UK in 1993 to headship of a 'failing' state primary in Wiltshire, seeing it through to grant maintained status. Has six children of his own and lives near

Warminster. Clearly has his finger on the pulse and is liked by pupils. Thoroughly enjoys the level of all-round commitment at KES and considers himself 'an extremely fortunate man.'

Entrance: Non-selective into pre-prep then Durham tests used to screen out any pupils unsuited (less than 10 per cent) to academic pace of junior school. Admits 36 pupils annually into year 3 with verbally administered tests, small numbers into years 4 and 6, but up to 20 into year 5. Tests in English, maths, reading and non-verbal reasoning plus writing a 20 minute story. Flexibility over points of entry has proved popular with increasing number of parents choosing to move to Bath from London.

Exit: Nearly all pupils proceed to King Edward's senior school via entry examination at 11.

Remarks: Outstanding nursery and good pre-preparatory provision with experienced, committed leadership. Generous staffing ratio of 1:8 at this level with loads of stimulating display work and groovy outside apparatus. Staff well aware of different learning styles and teaching strategies though we thought auditory learners would fare best. Good use of phonics, plenty of reading material and stimulating maths teaching with and without computers. Little ones seemed to clamber up and down the Victorian stairs well. Impressive ICT and art resources at this self-contained site on the western perimeter of Bath which was formerly a prep. Staff clearly enjoy their work and are seen as good at 'switching on' late developers. The whole place buzzes with creativity and industry. Consistently high results at Key Stage 1 despite mixed ability intake.

King's College Junior School (Wimbledon)

Linked to King's College School (Wimbledon) in the Senior section

Southside, Wimbledon Common, London, SW19 4TT

Tel: 02082 555 335
Fax: 02082 555 330
E-mail: jsadmissions@kcs.org.uk
Website: www.kcs.org.uk

• Pupils: boys • Ages: 7-13 • C of E (but other faiths welcome)
• Fees: £3,285 - £3,695 • Independent • Open days: Late September

Head: Since 1998, Mr John A Evans BA (mid fifties). Educated Priory Grammar School, Shrewsbury and at university at Bangor, Sorbonne and Cambridge. Promoted from the senior school. Taught modern languages: French and German. Senior housemaster then senior master in 1992. No longer married, two children. Interests – music, reading, France and Germany, theatre etc.

Retiring in July 2006.

Entrance: Difficult. Takes 45 boys at 7 and a further 15 at 8, some at 9, 10 and up to 15 at 11. All boys interviewed. Weed out boys who have been over-coached. There are some bursaries at 11. Boys come from mainly local private (eg Rowans, its own pre-prep, and WCPS) and state (eg Bishop Gilpin) schools and there are coaches from all over SW London.

Exit: Boys almost always go on to the senior school, gaining a good number of the scholarships, academic, art and musical, although two or three per year may go elsewhere.

Remarks: A busy, bustling school. On the same site as the senior school, neatly tucked at one side. Heart of its main building was once Tudory Victorian, brutally destroyed and built over in the 1960s, but softened, face-lifted and altogether improved in the 1980s and 1990s. Corridors are enlivened by pupils' work/paintings/maps, posters. Good library and quite terrific emphasis on reading (lists galore). All subjects taught in subject rooms. Some facilities (art, music, sport, dining hall) are shared with the senior school. Indeed some staff, unusually, teach both age groups.

Acquired Rushmere in 1992, the large handsome Georgian house which backs on to the main junior school building (divided by a garden and now a jolly playground), bought from the sculptor David Wynne, and the home base for the 7- and 8-year-olds who have a quiet, low-key start with cosy classrooms and their own dining room which doubles as the hall. At 9 life gets much busier. From 10 onwards boys are setted in French, maths and Latin. Music is extremely strong. Touch-typing in the IT room for 7 and 8 year olds. Maximum class size 24.

Lots of clubs; chess and debating keen. Some nice art and wonderful creative writing. Drama hall (shared with senior school) has tiered seats that fold and run to the wall at the press of a button so that six ping-pong tables come into their own at lunchtime. School does consistently well in tennis and cricket. Recent first XI tour to South Africa was hugely fun. The school holds workshops for parents to discuss any relevant issues. Broad social and ethnic mix. Bright-red blazers. An outstanding prep school.

KING'S COLLEGE SCHOOL (CAMBRIDGE)

West Road, Cambridge, Cambridgeshire, CB3 9DN

Tel: 01223 365 814
Fax: 01223 461 388
E-mail: office@kingscam.demon.co.uk
Website: www.kcs.cambs.sch.uk

• Pupils: 30 boys and 35 girls in the pre-prep; 170 boys and 90 girls in the prep. All day except for 34 boarders (including 16 choristers and 8 probationers) • Ages: 4-13 • C of E - other faiths welcome • Fees: Boarding (boys only) £5,050; choristers £1,685; day £3,260; pre-prep £2,535 • Independent

Head: Since 1998, Mr Nicholas Robinson BA (forties). Educated at Worth, read English at Anglia Polytechnic, PGCE in maths at Goldsmith's College. Master and subsequently housemaster for twelve years at Worth, where he gained a well- deserved reputation for raising money and getting things moving. A bachelor, a charming man – keen sportsman (skiing his especial forte), seriously musical (conducts). Very energetic and has a nice sense of humour. Has radically restructured the management of the whole place. He has two deputies and has increased the emphasis on the pastoral side. Popular with staff, boys and parents – quite a rarity.

Entrance: At 4, children are invited to spend an afternoon in the reception class; at 7, via assessments in English, maths and verbal reasoning and, occasionally, at other ages via assessment. A fairly broad intake. Annual choir auditions – lots apply. Pre-prep, opened 1992, and the Learning Support Centre (mild Aspergers, ADD, dyslexia, fine) – both oversubscribed. Children of local farmers, business people and academics.

Exit: Half to The Perse (boys and girls). Also The Leys, King's Ely, Harrow, Eton, King's Canterbury, Uppingham, Oundle, Queenswood, Tonbridge, Rugby, Kimbolton. As you would expect, masses of music scholarships awarded. (NB Girls leave at 11 and 13). Old Boys include Orlando Gibbons, Michael Ramsey, Christopher Tugendhat, John Pardoe, Professor Andrew Wiles (who solved Fermat's Last Theorem).

Remarks: One of the top Cambridge prep schools and the smallest by far of the three – St John's and St Faith's being the others – and the only one to operate a sibling policy. Dates back to the 15th century, though buildings are largely 19th and 20th century, away from the centre of Cambridge. Originally boys only, the school went co-ed 25 years ago, then sprouted a highly popular pre-prep and has inevitably evolved from being a boarding plus day prep to become a day school with not many boarders. All choristers must be full boarders, the rest are weekly boarders. Choristers are all boys. King's choristers are of world renown, well used to being in the public eye (gowns, top hats and stiff collars). In 2003, for instance, they gave 11 concerts on a world tour that included Hong Kong, Tokyo, New York, Chicago and their diary reports that, 'we went through 6 time changes and arrived in New York before we left Tokyo'. Which said, the choristers are extremely well-integrated with the rest of the school – 'sometimes the children don't know who is a chorister', said a parent – and it is not unheard of for a chorister to be an academic scholar as well, or an outstanding cricketer.

Three classes of 15 for 7-year-olds and up. Children taught in small groups within each class. Scholarship class for the top year. Classics getting a boost now ('much needed,' say parents). High standards of teaching in all areas. Staff, half male, half female, include a useful recent injection of young blood, also some of long-standing, for example Mr David Higginbottom, deputy headmaster for decades, now the registrar, and official school listener, a real Mr Chips. DT is excellent, art is imaginative. Spacious new library. School inspectors commented positively on the readability of all the books here, though we did not find children here to be particularly enthusiastic readers. 'They don't have enough time to read,' complained a mother. However, enormously enthusiastic on other fronts.

The school has a very good learning support department run by Mrs Karen Richardson who works alongside four part timers – all qualified to deal with specific learning difficulties. There are another three part time teachers who help those who don't have a specific educational need but would benefit from additional support in English. Kings will take children who have been identified as having mild SEN (but can cope intellectually) and recognises that needs can crop up after entry. In these cases in-house assessments are made (prior to a referal to an educational psychologist if necessary) and there are useful contacts with educational psychologists. Support in the lower school is given in the classroom or in the learning support department. In the upper school it happens outside lesson times (first thing in the morning, break, lunch) except in cases where French or Latin has been dropped. Times don't vary 'otherwise the children would get muddled'. Additional charges are made for the thirty minute sessions.

Open door policy. A professionally run department – individual learning programs, learning strategies, liaison with class teachers, comments with the termly reports plus a yearly overview. Once a term there's a themed open evening for parents of children who use the unit – topics include paired reading and home support.

Good keen sport, some on site, some five minutes walk away at the athletics ground; full-time tennis coaching throughout the year (only this and individual instrument lessons at extra cost). Classes end at 4.20pm but children regularly stay on until 6pm. Outstanding music – of course – with 270 children learning an instrument, and many learning two or even three. Thirty-seven chamber groups (a prep school record?) and all manner of orchestras. Head of music is Mr Simon Brown, previously head of the academic side of music at the Purcell School. New music centre (rather, the old one cleverly re-jigged) opened summer 2001 by Sir David Willcocks. Space everywhere carefully used – the headmaster skilfully turned the building programme on its head on arrival. This traditional, liberal prep school is in fine fettle, somewhat bursting at the seams, and bursting with energy, producing friendly, cheerful and happy children.

King's Hall

Linked to King's College (Taunton) in the Senior section

Pyrland, Kingston Road, Taunton, Somerset, TA2 8AA

Tel: 01823 285 920
Fax: 01823 285 922
E-mail: kingshall@aol.com
Website: www.kingshalltaunton.co.uk

- Pupils: Prep: 60 boarders, 245 day pupils (50/50 girls and boys). Pre-prep: 120 day pupils • Ages: 3-13 • C of E • Fees: Day £1,200 nursery; £1,770 year 4; £3,365 year 8. Weekly boarding £3,650 - £4,750; full boarding £3,650 - £4,750
- Independent • Open days: Early May (usually the first Friday and Saturday but please phone for confirmation)

Headmaster: Since 1999, Mr James Macpherson (fifties)

Entrance: Assessment in English and maths, report from present school and informal interview.

Exit: Two thirds transfer to King's College, Taunton at 13, the remainder to other senior schools both in the west country and further afield.

Money Matters: Generous discounts for Services families. Scholarships available at various ages, notably those awarded at 11 continue through King's College as well

(subject to annual review).

Remarks: The junior school for King's College (Taunton). Set in country surrounding National Trust farmland on edge of the Quantocks, the original house (1780s) has had recent additions – a new theatre, sports hall and classroom complex.

King's Hawford School

Linked to King's St Alban's Junior School in the Junior section
Linked to King's School Worcester in the Senior section

Worcester, Worcester, WR3 7SE

Tel: 01905 451 292
Fax: 01905 756 502
E-mail: info@ksw.org.uk
Website: www.ksw.org.uk

- Pupils: 209 girls and boys; all day • Ages: 3-11
- Fees: £1,575 - £2,785 • Independent

Remarks: For further details, see senior school, The King's School (Worcester)

King's House School

68 King's Road, Richmond, Surrey, TW10 6ES

Tel: 020 8940 1878
Fax: 020 8939 2501
E-mail: secretary1@kingshouse.richmond.sch.uk
Website: www.kingshouse.org.uk

- Pupils: 370 boys; all day • Ages: 4-13 • C of E • Fees: £2,200 - £2,970 • Independent

Head: Since 2002, Mrs Stephanie Piper MA BA (forties), formerly at Durston House in Ealing, Notting Hill & Ealing High School and St. Helen's in Northwood. A modern languages expert married to a teacher at Francis Holland with two teenage boys at Latymer and a girl at the Old Vicarage. The third female to be appointed head of an independent boys' prep in Britain, which is quite a coup considering previous King's House heads were from a very traditional mould – male, bearded, sporting tweed jackets; 'the feminine touch' is generally viewed as a good thing. Having survived the 'Kevin' stage of her own sons, King's House boys hold no fears for her. Since arriving, she has renovated the front of house area ('was rather gloomy'), improved security, invested greatly in IT both in admin and the classroom (interactive whiteboards throughout) and has introduced more streaming so that all levels of ability are catered for. She is happy and proud to maintain the tradition of a mixed ability school serving local London day schools and nearby boarding schools. Ran a senior schools' fair for some twenty three independent senior schools – those not invited were said to be quite miffed.

Entrance: Most boys enter at 4+ – places are offered a year before entry in order of registration; word is spreading re great new head so places are slightly harder to come by that they used to be. Some casual vacancies later, and a small 8+ entry following a test. Most boys are from the local area; Richmond, Barnes, Kew, Wimbledon, Chiswick. Parents are middle class, professional, university educated.

Exit: It is a given that all boys stay until 13. Twenty five per cent go to boarding schools within the M25. Epsom College (weekly boarding) is popular. Cranleigh, Wellington, Bradfield, Charterhouse are the other usual choices. Good relationships with London day schools (Hampton, St. Paul's, Latymer, Westminster, King's Wimbledon, Emanuel, Kingston) – high success rates at screening.

Remarks: What was a rather dull, plodding boys' prep, albeit with a good local reputation, has been rejuvenated. Within the somewhat limited facilities the buildings can offer, innovations support and inspire staff. The new purpose built theatre with its state of the art equipment can seat 200 – drama department has spread its wings, and all can take part.

Sport is an evident strength; mainly rugby, football and cricket. Head of PE encourages everyone, 'not just the firsts', and A to E teams play regularly and enjoy considerable success. Mrs. P herself turns up at rugby matches – it helps that she knows the rules and understands the game. Everyone has a music lesson a week and nearly three quarters learn an instrument. Miss Ficek, head of music, travels all over with the various music groups giving them loads of opportunities to perform. Described as 'driven', her own high standards demand the best from her pupils. Wind instruments are exceptionally good providing jazz and blues ensembles.

On the academic and pastoral side, there is the legendary and inimitable Mr. Sharrock, senior master, history teacher: 'The core of the school; the heart and soul of King's House' says the head. How many parents must re-live their own school history lessons on hearing their sons relate the latest battle played out on Mr. Sharrock's blackboard, whether it's between the Roundheads and the Cavaliers or the Persians and the Greeks?

Links with parents are excellent – a weekly newsletter ensures good communications between school and parents and there is a thriving Friends' association which raises money for equipment and charity. Every class has a representative to organise social events within each age group. A lively, happy, flourishing prep school.

KING'S JUNIOR SCHOOL

Linked to King's School Chester in the Senior section

Wrexham Road, Chester, Cheshire, CH4 7QL

Tel: 01244 680455
Fax: 01244 689518
E-mail: junior@kingschester.co.uk
Website: www.kingschester.co.uk

- Pupils: 222 girls and boys; all day • Ages: 7-11 • cathedral foundation • Fees: Junior £2,010; plus lunch • Independent • Open days: Second or third Saturday in November

Head: Mr S A Malone BEd.

Entrance: Selective entry and waiting lists, entry to senior school is likely but not guaranteed, being dependent on same entrance exam as outsiders.

Exit: By examination related to Key Stage 1 requirements, designed to assess potential as well as achievement. Tests in maths, written English, reading and reasoning as well as a talk with staff and play activity. Past papers not available, although summary details of the content of the tests may be had from the school.

Remarks: For further details see senior school.

KING'S PREPARATORY SCHOOL

Linked to King's School Rochester in the Senior section

St Nicholas House, King Edward Road, Rochester, Kent, ME1 1UB

Tel: 01634 888 577
Fax: 01634 888 507
E-mail: prep@kings-school-rochester.co.uk
Website: www.kings-school-rochester.co.uk

- Pupils: Nursery (3+) 26; pre-prep (4+) 128; prep (8+) 228
- Ages: Pre-Preparatory & Nursery: 3 - 7 yrs, Preparatory School: 8 - 12 yrs • C of E • Fees: Day: pre-prep/prep £2,375 - £3,460; Boarding: prep £5,335 • Independent • Open days: Second Saturday in October

Head: Prep Mr Roger P Overend, who came here from Westminster Cathedral Choir School. Pre-prep Mrs Anita M Parkins.

Entrance: Entry to pre-prep at 4+ (super headmistress, Anita Parkins) via interview with parents and discussion/assessment. Prep school tests for maths, English and non verbal reasoning at 8. More children join at 11 via similar method.

Exit: Transfer from prep to senior school is not automatic – children must meet the entry criteria, although refusals are rare.

Remarks: For further details, see senior school.

KING'S ST ALBAN'S JUNIOR SCHOOL

Linked to King's Hawford School in the Junior section
Linked to King's School Worcester in the Senior section

Mill Street, Worcester, Worcestershire, WR1 2NJ

Tel: 01905 354 906
Fax: 01905 763 075
E-mail: ksa@ksw.org.uk
Website: www.ksw.org.uk

- Independent

KING'S SCHOOL ELY, JUNIOR SCHOOL

Linked to King's School Ely in the Senior section

Barton Road, Ely, Cambridgeshire, CB7 4DB

Tel: 01353 660732
Fax: 01353 665281
E-mail: MaryMorgan@kings-ely.cambs.sch.uk
Website: www.kings-ely.cambs.sch.uk

- Pupils: 165 day boys, 105 day girls; 35 boarder boys, 5 boarder girls. Plus Acremont House pre-prep with 160 and nursery with 45 • Fees: Day: pre-prep £2,100; years 3 & 4 £2,965; years 5-8 £3,235; years 9-13 £4,470. Boarding: year 4 £4,725; years 5-8 £4,990; years 9-13 £6,470 • Independent • Open days: Whole school open morning September; but tours/visits available all year

Head: Tony Duncan BA BEd CertEd.

Remarks: Very active and busy school with incredibly enthusiastic staff and pupils. Very strong music department and own orchestra and choir. The art department is excellent with a huge variety of work: painting, sculpture, textiles etc. French and IT begin in year 4 and Latin from year 6. Specialist teaching rooms for science, art, design & technology, IT, drama and music. Lots of after-school activities: dance, drama, chess club, football and other sports etc. A very happy bunch of children and teachers.

The King's School in Macclesfield Junior Division

Cumberland Street, Macclesfield, Cheshire, SK10 1DA

E-mail: mail@kingsmac.co.uk
Website: www.kingsmac.co.uk

• Pupils: 350 girls and boys; all day • Ages: 3-11 • C of E • Fees: Infants £1,665; juniors £1,925 • Independent • Open days: Autumn and spring term plus weekly tours all year round

Principal: G J Shaw.

Entrance: Entrance to the infants is non selective, to the juniors by assessment.

Remarks: Occupies a site integral to the girls' division. Juniors and infants housed in separate buildings. Bright classrooms with every inch of wall space covered by ever changing colourful displays. Pupils have the use of the girls' sports facilities, assembly hall but have their own playground. A happy atmosphere.

Knighton House School

Durweston, Blandford Forum, Dorset, DT11 0PY

Tel: 01258 452 065
Fax: 01258 450 744
E-mail: enquiries@knighton-house.co.uk
Website: www.knightonhouse.dorset.sch.uk

• Pupils: 90 girls, of whom 75 board. Pre-prep with 33 children including 20 boys, and around 10 at any given moment in the nursery • Ages: 7-13; pre-prep 4-7; nursery 2+ - 3+ • C of E • Fees: Pre prep £1,844. Prep: day £3,644; boarding £4,850 • Independent

Head: Since 2004, Mrs Claire Renton MA DipRE, a classicist. Mrs Renton took over after three years as deputy head at Perrott Hill in Somerset where she tutored the scholars and headed the classics and RS depts. Nominated in 2005 Tatler schools award for the best girls' prep school head. Classics remain her first love and she teaches both Latin and Greek to the senior pupils.

Entrance: Via own pre-prep or at seven or eight, informal interview plus report from previous school. Rather tougher quarantine period for ponies, who may be sent home after a trial period, 'mine was expelled after three weeks for kicking', said one pupil. Any child can come – more or less at any time – providing space is available.

Exit: Usually now at 13, to Sherborne, Bryanston, St Mary's Shaftesbury (popular with Catholics), but girls go anywhere and everywhere: all the top girls' schools feature in the list. Pre-prep boys go on to – mainly – Sandroyd, Claysmore and the Old Malthouse – tranches of scholarships, though surprisingly, the boards only go back to the 1980s, which is a bit sad if children want to look up their parents or grandparents.

Remarks: Founded in 1950, by Christopher Booker's parents, this delightful, happy, unassuming school, is perched on a windy hilltop beside Bryanston's western gate surrounded by paddocks and games fields. Breezy garden with an orchard full of apples, greengages and plums. Rather boring old-rectory type house – said to be the dower house for Bryanston, but it seems unlikely – with usual carbuncular collection of add-ons. However, a new building containing two classrooms and a preparation room for the science lab has just been opened. This is phase one – more new classrooms are planned. Perched on the edge of Bryanston's west drive, the school makes much use of the Bryanston connection, not only because of the Booker association but the school uses their Astroturf hockey pitches and swimming pool, as well as riding through their grounds.

Forget the elitist past, this school is now thoroughly integrated into the locality, with a raft of day girls, as well as pre-prep and nursery. Flexi-boarding available if required though twice the price of Sandroyd's up the road. Buses to Wareham and Shaftesbury area, most pupils come from a 20-mile catchment area. Certain proportion of non-Brits – never more than one or two per form. Good dyslexia provision, plus SEN, excellent, plus EFL as required. French from six, Latin from ten, Greek an option – if good at Latin, plus a whole raft of extras as you might expect.

Tiny classes, max 16/18, with some setting as required in maths; French from the early years and Latin. Regular half-termly assessments. Two libraries: reference and fiction. State-of-the-art IT, girls all have their own e-mail, Spanish is a club; home economics is part of the curriculum (and posh it is too – with very low sinks, what do they do, the poor dears, when they try and cook at home?), dressmaking (at last!) and touch-typing (ditto) the norm.

Difficult to decide which is the more important – the horsy factor or the music. The latter has (again rather boring) dedicated red-brick buildings, with recital room and masses of individual practice rooms. This is a school with a musical heritage (and should probably be a feeder for the Yehudi Menuhin School but that name has, surprisingly, not cropped up); squillions of different bands, and groups and an orchestra that 'sounds like an orchestra', says the head. Certainly, as we arrived, there was a flautist sounding like one but there was also a ride going out, with nary a pelham between them, and only one leading rein.

The much-loved red dungarees were disastrously changed from cotton to rather a nasty polyester – they hang very badly and don't fade. Now revamped 'best uniform' – red knitted jersey, checked blouse with Peter Pan collar and dark grey kilt. Cotton dungarees and grey cloaks are back.

This is a school which has weathered and adapted to the changes of a turned millennium; all the pupils, and girls in particular, are friendly, mutually supportive, many from the country. This is a school where they can stay relatively unsophisticated until they go to public school, though whether this is what the girls themselves want, in this, the 21st century, is anyone's guess. But a jolly useful school nonetheless, well-integrated with the local community.

THE LADY ELEANOR HOLLES SCHOOL, JUNIOR DEPARTMENT

Linked to Lady Eleanor Holles School (The) in the Senior section

Burlington House, 177 Uxbridge Road, Hampton Hill, Middx, TW12 1BD

Tel: 020 8979 2173
Fax: 020 8783 1962
E-mail: junior-office@lehs.org.uk
Website: www.lehs.org.uk

• Pupils: 175 girls • Ages: 7-11 • C of E • Fees: £2,565
• Independent • Open days: Contact the Registrar

Head: Since 2004, Mrs Gillian Low MA Oxon PGCE Cantab (mid forties) formerly head of Francis Holland NW1. Educated at North London Collegiate School, read English at Oxford, taught at various comprehensive schools, former deputy head of Godolphin and Latymer School. Approachable, down-to-earth. 'She's very warm and caring,' said a FH parent. Another commented that she will deal immediately with any concerns. Three children, all at independent schools.

Entrance: Entrance by examination and interview; at 7, 40 places available and another 8 are taken in at 8. They are examined in maths, English and spelling.

Exit: Vast majority transfer to the senior school but subject to exam, and entry not guaranteed.

Remarks: Under the aegis of head of senior school but with its own departmental head. In adjacent Victorian Burlington House, which has recently undergone complete internal rebuilding and refurbishment. There are now three floors of light, bright classrooms and specialist rooms for art, science, DT and ICT. Shares the facilities of the main school; not a lot of contact between the two parts of the school otherwise.

LAMBROOK HAILEYBURY SCHOOL

Winkfield Row, Bracknell, Berkshire, RG42 6LU

Tel: 01344 882 717
Fax: 01344 891 114
E-mail: info@lambrook.berks.sch.uk
Website: www.lambrook.berks.sch.uk

• Pupils: prep: 202 boys and 93 girls, 20 weekly board; pre-prep 103 boys and 47 girls • Ages: 7 -13. Pre-prep 4-7 • C of E
• Fees: Day: pre-prep £2,330 - £2,435; prep £3,585 - £3,900. Boarding £4,760 - £5,325 • Independent • Open days: October and May

Headmaster: Since 2005, Mr James Barnes (late forties), headmaster of Chafyn Grove until the summer of 2004 when he left to manage schools for GEMS – a job he left with some rapidity. Married with three children at Bryanston. We remember him from Chafyn as approachable, charming and effective. Lists his interests as squash, running, cricket, rugby, golf, First World War history, political biography, music, classic cars and food!

Entrance: From local primaries, Montessori schools and own popular pre-prep. Numbers have increased from 295 to 325 last year and 425 this, so presumably a spot of poaching as well; children can and do come at any time, half term, relocation, whatever, 'as long as there is space'. High percentage of first time buyers.

Exit: Impressive collection of scholarships to Eton, St Paul's, Charterhouse, Wellington, Bradfield, Haileybury and Reading Bluecoats, Harrow, Rugby, Marlborough. 'Bright children and well taught' girls' school, St George's Ascot, is a favourite and a first scholarship this year. Noticeable trend at the bottom of the school for brother and sister to be down for the same co-ed senior school (Marlborough tops).

Remarks: What a transformation. When we last visited this was a dreary little school, a Marie Celeste with falling numbers (and we took with us an Old Boy who hadn't been back for over forty-five years and 'didn't see much difference'). Lambrook and Haileybury prep school amalgamated in 1997 when school moved 'seamlessly' to the 40 acre Winkfield Row, and the Haileybury site on the edge of Windsor was put on the market – Persimmon are now building little boxes. The cash-rich combined school is flourishing, numbers have increased enormously, facilities have improved, the new science and IT centre is up and running, as is the new baby house, the leisure centre is in pipeline and there is still money in the pot. Girls are pouring in through the pre-prep, and working their way up the school but this is a softly-softly operation. Tiny classes, average 16 (maximum 18) with three parallel classes in pre-prep rising to four parallel in most classes – the projection was 450 children by 2003/4 so hasn't been reached yet by quite a way. Could take 80/100 boarders. The grounds are terrific, boy-inspiring woods for camping, plus squash, tennis, swimming, golf – could be a country club rather than a prep school. The most vicious sleeping policemen we've seen anywhere.

Academically impressive, computers everywhere, revision on computers. Very comprehensive learning support division with double teaching where necessary from Australian stooges. Greek for the gifted, public speaking practices and lots of options. Drama timetabled and masses of music. At least three quarters of the children play at least one instrument and the choir is seriously good; they provide trebles for Eton and have produced their own CD; lots of rehearsals but lots of trips and jollies too. Original school buildings have had a lick and a promise and the dorms have been painted and carpeted but they really need radical surgery to get the place totally up to scratch. Food looked jolly good but the painted panelled walls of the dining room looked too old fashioned for words despite being covered in pupil paintings. The older library and chapel were far more the thing.

Thriving boys' school with a fast increasing number of girls, on the up but not there yet.

LANESBOROUGH SCHOOL

Linked to Royal Grammar School (Guildford) in the Senior section

Maori Road, Guildford, Surrey, GU1 2EL

Tel: 01483 880 650
Fax: 01483 880 651
E-mail: secretary@lanesborough.surrey.sch.uk
Website: www.lanesborough.surrey.sch.uk

- Pupils: 350 boys, all day • Ages: 3-13 • C of E • Independent
- Open days: One Saturday morning in mid October

Headmaster: Mr K S Crombie

Exit: Around half the boys go on to the Royal Grammar School, which is more that twice as many as from any other feeder, but far from an automatic guarantee. Others to St John's, Charterhouse, Reed's, Cranleigh and several other good schools.

Remarks: The preparatory department of the Royal Grammar School (Guildford). Edwardian house plus many extensions set on the green north east edge of Guildford (not particularly close to RGS). Provides the choristers for Guildford Cathedral and offers choral scholarships. Excellent music all round and strong, but not towering, academics. Some pressure and parental panic unavoidable as boys near age at which they will be competing for a place at the senior school.

LATCHMERE INFANT SCHOOL

Latchmere Road, Kingston upon Thames, Surrey, KT2 5TT

Tel: 020 8546 6507
Fax: 020 8547 0187
E-mail: lti@rbksch.org

- Pupils: 268 boys and girls, all day • Ages: 3-7 • Non-denom
- State

Head: Mrs Anne Delaney BEd (Hons) MA no personal details – 'let's concentrate on the school,' she said. Not as touchy feely as some infant school heads, but a highly efficient operator (her professionalism would do credit to a senior school head) with great pride in her school and a welcoming smile on her face. 'She is very approachable,' said one parent.

Entrance: Latchmere and Fern Hill (qv) are the two top-notch, over-subscribed schools in N Kingston. For those who live equidistant between the two schools, it must be an agonising decision which to choose – 'I had to keep ringing both schools to find out how many parents had applied from which roads so that I could decide which one to put down as my first choice,' said one prospective parent. We're talking 'savvy' parents in this area, many could afford independent schooling at a pinch, but instead 'I want my child to be part of the local community.' Worth putting all your energies into getting a child into the nursery.

Exit: To Latchmere Junior – transition between the infant and junior school well organised through visits and a buddy system with year 5 children.

Remarks: A super infant school – the atmosphere of 'welcome' hits you even before you read the word in various different languages around the entrance hall. 'We chose the school because it's so open and friendly,' said one parent who's had three children there. Partnership with the school starts before the child does – 'our initial tour was very detailed so that we felt we were already part of the school,' said one new parent.

Key Stage 1 SATS results have fluctuated over the last few years but recently children have done well – many above the national average. However, head hates the divisive effect of league tables. Assessment procedures are very strong in the school and she believes they know the needs of their pupils.

Children enjoy lessons and are able to work independently and quietly from an early stage. 'High quality teaching is a strength throughout the curriculum,' said one mother. Opportunities for grouping by ability are timetabled into the day, so that all abilities can be dealt with including the very able and those with special needs. Good expertise in SEN. Full time SENCO and both the head and the SENCO have advanced qualifications in SEN which includes dyslexia. Within the school there is also considerable expertise in dyspraxia, ADHD, and autistic spectrum disorder. Very few children need one-to-one support, but group support is much more widely employed. Approximately 24 children currently receive speech and language support from trained staff. All year 1 and 2 grouped by ability in English and maths, so most able are stretched and those experiencing problems helped in small group settings.

Particular curriculum strengths are art, music and sport. Dedicated art area and super art teaching – stunning artwork for all to see (which often wins awards). Music

teacher comes in twice a week and runs a choir for year 2 – regular performances. School shares a covered swimming pool with the juniors.

Social education (to teach children how to be part of a community) starts in the nursery and is given much prominence. Pupils delightfully self-confident. Pastoral care is felt to be strength – 'my child's class teacher will tell me exactly what action has been taken if there is a problem,' remarked one mother.

Nursery in an attractive new building. Play areas packed full of every type of climbing equipment, quiet areas and games. School promotes healthy eating; children have the opportunity of cooking and eating a wide range of dishes to widen their experiences of different food – chips with everything is definitely not on the culinary menu here.

After school club offers childcare and curriculum extension activities exclusively for full time infants and their siblings who attend the junior school. You get the feeling that the school would suffer financially – and thereby educationally – without the help of the parents. Loads of parents help in the school, while the parents' association concentrates on (hugely successful) fund-raising – a staggering £60,000 was raised to renovate the swimming pool with professional fund-raising help given for free.

LATCHMERE JUNIOR SCHOOL

Latchmere Road, Kingston Upon Thames, Surrey, KT2 5TT

Tel: 020 8546 7181
Fax: 020 8549 9182
E-mail: LTJ@rbksch.org
Website: www.latchmerej.kingston.sch.uk

• Pupils: 360 boys and girls, all day • Ages: 7-11 • Non-denom
• State

Head: Since 2003, Mrs Valerie Al-Jawad MA (forties), previously deputy head and has taught at the school for 17 years. SEN specialist. Married with two grown-up daughters. Clearly loves the school and is enormously proud of it, without in any way resting on her laurels.

Entrance: From infant school on same site. Three classes per year. Since maximum class sizes were introduced for Key Stage 1, school has decided to keep classes at 30 pupils, if possible.

Exit: About 50 per cent of children to Grey Court School in Ham, the nearest state secondary school, with others to various Kingston state secondary schools. Sizeable number (up to 20) accepted each year at the highly selective Tiffin grammar schools. Handful to local independent day schools (mostly Kingston Grammar and Surbiton High).

Remarks: Latchmere and Fern Hill (qv) are the shining stars in North Kingston and beyond. Both achieve excellent results and have ferociously loyal parents, who will not hear a word said against their particular school. Two things make Latchmere stand out from other primary schools: exceptionally wide-ranging curriculum and emphasis on social skills in a broad sense.

Breadth of learning, according to the head, is what enables the school to achieve highly in the SATS tests: well above national average. Specialist teachers for art, music, social skills and French; more able linguists offered either German or Spanish. French taught from year 3; annual trips to European schools ensure a much higher standard of linguistic ability and awareness than amongst most primary school children. However, 'Let's not pretend they become great linguists,' says one dad. Parents generally are impressed by the professionalism and teamwork shown by the staff – several male teachers – and they feel that on the whole they can talk to the class teacher about individual problems. One parent described how the brighter children are given extra challenges: head gives examples of science days, citizenship conferences, maths master classes at Tiffin Girls' and Science at Greycourt.

Currently, about 50 children with special needs. These needs range from dyslexia, dyspraxia, autistic spectrum disorder to global delay. Eleven teaching assistants, including two 'higher level', who help children, together with the SEN teacher. Ten children with EAL have special provision two sessions per week.

Specialist art teacher and art room produce outstanding work, of a standard normally expected from pupils several years older. Numerous opportunities for music: through class teaching from the specialist teacher and instrumental tuition from peripatetic teachers. The school boasts two choirs and an orchestra.

Sport is strength, overseen by one of the few advanced skills teachers for PE. Heated indoor swimming pool (shared with the infants) in use from spring to autumn, large grass playing fields across the road, in addition to own playground space for hard courts. Regularly wins sporting competitions in the borough- many cups proudly displayed in the hallway. Sports day is a major event – every child's achievements earning points towards the team. More than 25 after school clubs, also plenty of after school sports which are heavily oversubscribed. Indoor sports hall planned, to be shared with the community.

Social skills programme very evident in the school: friendship bench in the playground 'it must feel good for a child feeling upset at playtime to have somewhere to go and someone to talk to,' one parent remarked – and pupil-written rules in the classrooms. Positive discipline promoted by pupils learning to take responsibility for their own actions through social skills programme. Makes a real difference, as much for the older child learning to mediate as for the child being helped. School council treated as important body – pupils want to gain a place.

No one could say that the buildings are particularly smart (but there is a programme of improvement). Outdoor play space divided into areas for different activities, both quiet and sporty, lovely signposts pointing children in the right direction: eg 'the enchanted wood' – an area of trees, paths and benches with a playhouse nestling at the end, there is also a vegetable garden, an area for ball games as well as good climbing equipment.

Unusually for the borough of Kingston, hot lunches are available – and of a surprisingly high quality. 'They actually seem to care about food here,' a father said in a surprised tone of voice. General communication with parents excellent and they are made to feel a vital part of the school. The head produces a newsletter every week, and governors' annual report written in an informative but informal style. Breakfast club, for parents with early morning commitments and a holiday club which is open to all the local schools and very well attended.

LATHALLAN SCHOOL

Linked to Lathallan budding senior school in the Senior section

Brotherton Castle, By Johnshaven, Montrose, DD10 0HN

Tel: 01561 362 220
Fax: 01561 361 695
E-mail: office@lathallan.com
Website: www.lathallan.com

- Pupils: 95 boys, 60 girls; 100 day, 25 weekly board + flexi-boarding (62 max); plus pre-prep with 50, plus nursery with 35
- Ages: 8-13, prep 5-8, nursery 7 weeks to 5 years. Plus from 2005 adding a senior school to 18, growing from the base year by year • Non-denom • Fees: Day £2,279-£3,267; weekly boarding add £950 per term; £22 overnight • Independent
- Open days: No open day as such, visit at any time

Head: Since 2003, Mr Andrew P Giles (Andy) BSc PGCE (thirties) who comes with his wife Jacqueline (Jackie) and her two grown up children. Mr Giles went to Wellington School, took his A levels at Richard Huish College in Taunton, his BSc in PE and maths at Chester and his PGCE in Swansea. (He still has his slight south west burr). Despite what we said in the last edition, he has not yet completed his masters – 'still working on his dissertation' – as is his wife, on hers).

First taught at King Edward's, Bath, where he became head of sport, and comes to Lathallan from Kingswood School in Bath, where he and his wife masterminded the birth of a new junior boarding house. Mr Giles also started a company running summer clubs on the side (this he closed down last year); but held a successful summer club at Lathallan in 2003 and proposes two one week courses this summer, 'not necessarily for pupils from the school'. Last year's three day (geology) course was a sell-out; this year geology and goodness knows what are on the cards. A relaxed character, he was most upset by the inaccuracies of the previous entry, and we look forward to putting MEd back in next time. He is married to Jacqueline, who has two grown up children – and looks ridiculously young. She teaches maths and they have introduced a new curriculum subject LEAPP, her speciality, which teaches cognitive skills and thinking about thinking to all. The Gileses have also re-introduced the early nursery facility, so brutally removed by previous heads. Despite Mr G's stated aims to train with the Independent Schools Inspectorate and learn the pipes, he has progressed no further than the chanter, though he has

persuaded local senior schools to introduce piping scholarships.

Entrance: From local primaries and own kindergarten, no longer ex-pats with handy grannies; weekly boarding only.

Exit: Mostly to Scottish public schools, Glenalmond tops, plus Strathallan, Fettes, Merchiston, Gordonstoun, Loretto, St Leonards, Robert Gordon's and local state schools, a tiny dribble to the South, St Margaret's, Escrick. Magnificent record of scholarships across the board last year. 75 per cent of sixth form got some form of scholarship in 2003, be it academic or all-rounder. Interestingly, there appear to be 'no' exits at eight, when one might expect a dribble off to other – possibly better known – prep schools in the south.

Remarks: Pupil profile has changed radically. Weekly boarding only. 'Good all round school', small classes (14 the norm), high staff pupil ratio (1:7), boys sleep in main castle block, with girls cosily ensconced above the servants' quarters. Great improvement here, with better heating throughout, and dorms undergoing decoration again. Stunning HM welfare report. Classroom block in the old stables which also houses the kindergarten has been revamped and more staff, particularly sports specialists, employed (Rob Wainwright an old boy). New dedicated learning support and accelerated learning department. Impressive art and IT, new Dell computers all over the shop, library now a resource centre.

Learning support in place (withdrawn from class once or twice a week). French from seven, classical studies from nine, moving to Latin. Streaming for maths from 10, and streamed into tiny scholarship classes for maths, English, science and French at 12. New student council chaired by sixth former with year reps comes up with all sorts of new ideas. Loads of music, more than 85 per cent learn at least one musical instrument, pipe band flourishing (and much in demand for charity groups), over 20 after-school clubs, drama strong. Good links with parents and popular parent group. Daily mini bus from Stonehaven and Aberdeen (45 miles away); return bus at 5pm. Weekly boarding is now a popular option; there is no school on Saturday mornings, though there are matches. Children from a wide variety of backgrounds, the Aberdeen business community still in evidence, plus local farmers, commuters and the like.

Lathallan Foundation established in 2001 to fund new arts block. Set in own 62 acres of woodland, with ten acres of playing field overlooking the North Sea and own beach (bracing) masses of play areas. All 7-13 year olds play sport daily. Tennis courts double up for netball; fab enclosed adventure playground for tinies. Keen games, but no longer thrashing all-comers; jolly rugby trip to Ireland recently. Lots of trips and links abroad at this popular and good local prep and pre-prep where 'joining in is de rigueur'; we only wonder whether the children might just be a teeny bit over-stretched or bamboozled by the number of clubs and option, but at least they are unlikely to be bored.

From September 2005 setting out to become a 0 to 18 school, taking on a class of 14-year-olds and adding years as they move up the school. USP is the provision of co-ed flexiboarding – nearest alternative is 60 miles away by crow. Senior school destined to be under aegis of James Ferrier, and will be based in the music centre to start with.

Nursery currently being revamped, to make provision for tinies from six weeks; this was mooted during our earlier visit, and was indeed in place several heads ago.

LATYMER PREP SCHOOL

Linked to Latymer Upper School in the Senior section

36 Upper Mall, Hammersmith, London, W6 9TA

Tel: 02087 480 303
Fax: 02087 414 916
E-mail: mlp@latymerprep.org
Website: www.latymerprep.org

• Pupils: 160 girls and boys; all day • Ages: 7-11 • Non-denom
• Fees: Prep £3,625 • Independent • Open days: September and November

Head: Mr S P Dorrian BA (previously head of English and head of Years 7 and 8 in the senior school).

Entrance: Maths, English and verbal reasoning exams at 7 plus interview.

Exit: Virtually all go on to the senior school. Very occasionally parents advised to move their child to a less academic establishment.

Remarks: Beautifully-situated building with views over the Thames from one side and lawns from the other side, plus all the senior school facilities. Has broadened the activities available since going co-ed eg circus skills as well as football at playtime. 'We have some very unsporty boys who spend all their time on stilts.' Mixed teams for all sports, dance also available – 'the boys love it'. Curriculum enriched by eg looking at famous women in history. Italian from year 3 and French in year 6. Broad curriculum benefits from not having to work towards Common Entrance.

SEN department liaise closely with the senior school;

currently ten boys with statements of needs plus ten more, any pupils with suspected problems are given 'a battery of tests' to suss out their problems, school can deal with mild to moderate dyslexia et al, but if pupil has 'severe' dyslexia then parents are advised to get external help (school has neither the staff nor the time to spare). Not frightened of Aspergers – one boy currently with full time mentor part paid for by the school and part by the parents, and can deal with moderate physical problems, CP, ADHD, profoundly deaf etc. Chaps who come armed with edpsych's reports get 25 per cent extra time in their entrance exam. Two fully trained and dedicated staff, one to one help, school will 'pick up and run' with pupils, but must be able to access mainstream.

JUNIOR LAVANT HOUSE

Linked to Lavant House in the Senior section

West Lavant, Chichester, West Sussex, PO18 9AB

Tel: 01243 527 211
Fax: 01243 530 490
E-mail: office@lavanthouse.org.uk
Website: www.lavanthouse.org.uk

• Pupils: girls • Ages: 3 - 11; boarding from 8+ • C of E
• Fees: Day: junior £1,670-£2,800; boarding: junior £4,445
• Independent • Open days: October

Head: Teacher in charge since 2001, Mrs Meg Gardner.

Remarks: On the same site, next door to the main school. Small classes, some run with mixed age groups. Cosy atmosphere. For more details see Lavant House School.

LAXTON JUNIOR SCHOOL

Linked to Oundle School in the Senior section

East Road, Oundle, Peterborough, Cambridgeshire, PE8 4BX

Tel: 01832 277 275
Fax: 01832 277 271
E-mail: laxtonjunior@oundle.co.uk
Website: www.laxtonjunior.org.uk

• Pupils: 280 boys and girls • Ages: 4-11 • C of E
• Fees: £2,455 • Independent

Headmistress: Miss S C A Thomas CertEd. Pleasant.

Entrance: Most children enter the school in the September after they are four years old on a non-selective admissions list basis, although all children entering the school are assessed in order to establish their current abilities and aptitudes.

Exit: Attending the Junior School in no way guarantees automatic passage into Laxton School, as an entrance examination has to be passed. Parents of children, for whom Laxton School is considered inappropriate to their needs, are advised early that alternative senior education should be considered.

Remarks: Fantastic building with excellent facilities. Focused on entry to the senior school. Might be tough for the sensitive child.

LEEDS GRAMMAR SCHOOL JUNIOR SCHOOL

Alwoodley Gates, Harrogate Road, Leeds, West Yorkshire, LS17 8GS

Tel: 0113 229 1552
E-mail: juniorschool@lgs.leeds.sch.uk
Website: www.leedsgrammar.com

• Pupils: 314 boys • Ages: 4-10 • Non-denom • Fees: Junior school £1,683 - £2,280 • Independent • Open days: October, November, January and June. See school website for dates

Head: Ably and sympathetically led by historian John Davies, at LGS since 1976.

Entrance: Selective, by observed activities and tests appropriate to the child's age. Main entry at 4 (36) and 7 (20) but applications considered at all stages.

Exit: All pupils transfer at 10+ to senior school unless they are obviously going to struggle; parents consulted well in advance.

Remarks: On same site, sharing senior school facilities yet sufficiently distinct from it to allow younger boys to grow up in secure surroundings. Atmosphere is happy, positive and purposeful, commended by ISI: 'pupils show strong motivation and an ability to concentrate on the task in hand'. Year 5 on average one chronological year ahead. French or German studied from Year 4. Unusually for this age-group, half staff are male. Pre-prep (age 4 – 7) successfully introduced in 1997. Parents have open access as classroom helpers.

LINCOLN MINSTER PREPARATORY SCHOOL

Linked to Lincoln Minster School in the Senior section

Eastgate, Lincoln, Lincolnshire, LN2 1QG

Tel: 01522 523769
Fax: 01522 514778
E-mail: enquiries.lincoln@church-schools.com
Website: www.lincolnminsterschool.co.uk

• Pupils: boys and girls • Ages: 2-11 • Independent

Head: Mrs Anne Wood.

Remarks: For details see senior school.

LINDEN SCHOOL

Linked to Dame Allan's Boys' School in the Senior section
Linked to Dame Allan's Girls' School in the Senior section

72 Station Road, Forest Hall, Newcastle upon Tyne, Tyne and Wear, NE12 9BQ

Tel: 0191 266 2943
E-mail: linden@dameallans.co.uk

• Pupils: 120 boys and girls • Ages: 3-11 • Christian foundation
• Independent

Remarks: A prep and pre-prep for Dame Allan's (qv).

LITTLE ST HELEN'S AND ST HELEN'S JUNIOR SCHOOL

Eastbury Road, Northwood, Middlesex, HA6 3AS

Website: www.sthelensnorthwood.co.uk

- Pupils: Little St Helen's 225; Junior School 235; all girls
- Ages: Little St Helen's 3-7; Junior school 7-11 • C of E, but all faiths welcome • Fees: Nursery £2,115; Little St Helen's £2,332; Junior school £2,529 • Independent • Open days: June and October

Entrance: At 3 or 4 by observation and interview. At 7 by tests in English, maths and non-VR, and interview.

Exit: Usually a smooth transition from LSH to the juniors (via exam) and from juniors to seniors but head is clear. 'We do it very carefully. If I genuinely thought a girl was going to struggle, we talk to the parents well in advance -usually by year 4 – and help them look at alternatives.' Very few to local state grammars, boarding or competition.

Remarks: The nursery, Little St Helen's and the junior school are all housed in buildings around this beautiful site and share many of the facilities of the main school. Some buildings have more inviting exteriors than others, however each has bright, airy classrooms, excellent, thoughtful displays and exhibited artwork, libraries, gyms, good-sized halls or studios and is well-resourced. Heartening posters greet one eg 'Enter with an Open Mind' and we saw an exciting display about pirates complete with huge paper schooner. Lots of ICT, good DT and everyone tries out three languages before they move up to the senior school. All do ballet, PE, music and speech and drama as part of the curriculum. Happy atmosphere, lovely bright uniform, civilised loos and teachers who say, 'Ladies will you please take off your shoes now', to a crocodile of receptive six-year-olds. A teacher, teaching assistant and gapper to each class in Little Saints, some teaching assistants in Junior school. 'I think these girls are so lucky,' sighed the registrar wistfully as we strolled. 'We are the lucky ones', replied a passing teacher.

LOCKERS PARK SCHOOL

Lockers Park Lane, Hemel Hempstead, Hertfordshire, HP1 1TL

Tel: 01442 251 712

Fax: 01442 234 150

E-mail: secretary@lockerspark.herts.sch.uk

Website: www.lockerspark.herts.sch.uk

- Pupils: 141 boys; 40 full boarders, 30 flexi and the rest day
- Ages: 7-13 • C of E • Fees: £3,065 - £3,965 day; £4,900 boarding • Independent • Open days: Mid October and mid March

Head: Since 1996, Mr David Lees-Jones GRSM ARCM (mid fifties). Educated at Stowe, Manchester University and Royal College of Music. Postgraduate at Reading. First teaching job at Bramcote where he developed a passion for the great outdoors (skiing, adventure trips and so on), continued up educational ladder with posts at Epsom College (director of music, housemaster and officer commanding compulsory CCF with much emphasis on outward-bounding) and Marlborough House where he was head for eight years. Saw his appointment to Lockers Park as 'the perfect opportunity. I always wanted to return to a boys-only school and I felt there was a lot to be done here.' Has succeeded in boosting school roll in last five years. Lively, energetic approach to school leadership, very much hands-on, likes to be involved at all levels and still spends a third of each week teaching Latin to year 6 boys. Is also bursar and recently appointed himself assistant director of music. Very accessible, door always open. Physiotherapist wife Katharine teaches French and maths and is much involved in pastoral care. One son, two daughters.

Second headmaster: Mr Roger Stephens BA (fifties). Educated Repton and Durham. A jolly beaming bachelor with 30+ years teaching at Lockers to his credit. Seen as head's right-hand man, his 'tower of strength', responsible for daily running of school as well as teaching maths.

Academic Matters: Lockers is proud of its academic record; its success in both CE and scholarship exams to 45 different schools over the past ten years reflects this well. (Total of 10 scholarships in 2004 including academic, music, art and technology). Average class size is 14 and teacher/pupil ratio a healthy 1:7. The music dept is well known and encouragement is given to every boy to find an instrument which he will enjoy and most gain proficiency in at least one. Drama also plays a large part in the school with one major and several minor productions each year.

Games, Options, The Arts: An excellent record with a wide variety of games/sports played. Main sports are soccer, rugby, cricket and hockey. There is a fully fitted modern sports hall, heated swimming pool, an all-weather sports surface and cricket nets, two tennis and squash courts, a nine hole golf course and shooting range.

Entrance: No pre-prep but take a fair number from local schools at 7 and 8. Space allowing, boys can also enter at 9, 10 or 11. Basically non-selective, interview and simple test looking for 'potential' either academically or as sportsman, actor or musician. Currently oversubscribed, many parents keen to get sons' names down early. Most recent visitor was just six weeks old. Limited special needs help.

Exit: Far and wide, but Harrow a clear favourite over last 10 years. Shrewsbury, Stowe, Haileybury, Charterhouse and Rugby all popular.

Remarks: 'Two heads are better than one' is debatable and certainly Lockers' two-head status has its roots in history rather than need. But with roles clearly defined, it appears to work. A rather lovely, warm and welcoming school. Purpose-built in 1874, the red-brick buildings are set in 23 rolling acres of playing fields and grounds. Drab, crumbling fabric completely refurbished after head's arrival. He has spent £650,000 on variety of projects to return school to former glory as well as bring it into 21st century. Presently at full capacity which includes the boarding house; 'I'm sure part of it is thanks to Harry Potter,' says head. Matrons and resident boarding staff look after them in recently refurbished and surprisingly tidy but fairly basic dorms. Washing/bath facilities pretty basic but it's doubtful that the boys complain.

Lack of formal school uniform adds to homely atmosphere. Boys wear navy cord trousers and lumberjack-style shirts (of their own choosing) around school with the school sweatshirt to keep out the Hertfordshire hillside chill. For more dressy occasions, pupils' own choice of sports jacket, grey flannel trousers, blue shirt and tie is called for. Lack of formality in attire not reflected in attitude though. There were 'Sirs' a-plenty when the head asked boys direct questions, demonstrating complete knowledge of first names, and although younger ones seemed slightly in awe of him, the relationship with 'seniors', while still respectful, was decidedly more relaxed. Head commented, 'in a school of this size, everyone knows everyone else. The relationship between pupils and staff is second to none – it's the jewel in our crown.' School day can last up to 12 hours (including supper and supervised prep) plus Saturday lessons till lunch.

1980s teaching block a relatively new addition with large, airy, well-lit classrooms and loads of work on walls and tabletops. Younger boys taught in enormous high-ceilinged rooms in original school building now redecorated in trendy greens, blues and yellows. Poor DT workshop on gloomy north side of school but plans afoot to move and modernise it soon.

School library recently refurbished, fresh stock hitting shelves all the time with bank of computers along one wall – in fact an absolute hive of activity when we saw it. Undoubtedly the busiest room in the school. Over 20 new computers also installed two years ago in IT room. Computer skills taught as stand-alone subject but also cut across all areas of schoolwork. Other recently completed projects include sports hall and chapel face-lifts and an all-weather sports pitch. All thanks to 125th anniversary fund-raising appeal which was phenomenally successful. Boys are very strong on sporting field, more than often beating teams from larger preps. Chapel choir has fine reputation. Good orchestra/wind band and even managed to muster enough young musicians to make trip to Philadelphia worthwhile two years ago and another to Barcelona in 2004. Other departments also regularly take foreign trips – 2003 saw a classics trip to Italy and a French trip to Burgundy in addition to the annual ski trip to Austria and the leavers' trip to Normandy.

Religion is central to school's ethos – Christian values – how we treat each other, tolerance, patience and support have particular significance in matters of discipline and behaviour. School has few rules as such; success and good citizenship are rewarded. Community service, like washing out the minibuses or picking up litter, is meted out to transgressors. Two expulsions since the head's arrival for repeated bad behaviour and only after several warnings. Boys come from rich mix of backgrounds – many live locally, around six from abroad – ranging from well-heeled Ferrari set to less affluent (bursaries available for needy cases). On the whole, school enjoys parental support and there seems little pressure for major change, particularly of late. Nicely old-fashioned school in many respects with own terminology eg 'sets' instead of houses and 'slatter' for tuck or sweets, with fine alumni including Lord Mountbatten, former politicians Keith Joseph and Paul Channon and the Nawab of Pataudi.

Head sets the tone for the whole place. As a doer himself he runs a school for boys 'who want to have a go'. Extras include shooting, golf, riding and dry slope skiing. 'We look to produce individuals,' he says. 'As long as you've got energy, enthusiasm and want to join in, then it's the school for you. I'm here to make sure the boys make the most of their intellect, underpinned by an absolute balance of other activities.'

LOMOND SCHOOL JUNIOR DEPARTMENT

Linked to Lomond School in the Senior section

10 Stafford Street, Helensburgh, G84 9JX

Tel: 01436 672 476
Fax: 01436 678 320
E-mail: admin@lomond-school.demon.co.uk
Website: www.lomond-school.org

• Pupils: 120 boys and girls, plus nursery • Ages: Prep: 5-10, Nursery: 3-5 • Non-denom • Fees: Nursery £700; junior £1,230 • Independent • Open days: Early November

Remarks: For details, see senior school.

THE LONDON ORATORY SCHOOL JUNIOR HOUSE

Linked to London Oratory School (The) in the Senior section

Seagrave Road, London, SW6 1RX

E-mail: admin@los.ac
Website: www.london-oratory.org

• Pupils: 80 boys; all day • Ages: 7-11 • State • Open days: September and November

Head: John McIntosh OBE.
Remarks: The Junior House was opened in 1996, specialising in musical training. Most pupils play two instruments and learn Italian, many sing as well in the Schola (for the top 25 per cent of voices) which performs every Saturday evening at the Brompton Oratory and performs in Rome, Paris and USA.

For more details see senior school entry.

LORETTO JUNIOR SCHOOL AKA THE NIPPERS

Linked to Loretto School in the Senior section

North Esk Lodge, North High Street, Musselburgh, East Lothian, EH21 6JA

Tel: 0131 653 4570
Fax: 0131 653 4571
E-mail: juniorschool@loretto.com
Website: www.loretto.com

• Pupils: 190 girls and boys; boarding and day • Ages: 3-12 • Non-denom • Fees: £4,955 - £5,286 boarding; £1,748 - £3,507 day • Independent • Open days: One each term; see school website

Head: Since 2001, Mr Richard Selley, BEd (Exeter).
Remarks: Super school just across the river Esk. Newly refurbished and spacious co-ed boarding house, bright and cosy dorms. Parents can drop children from around 8am and collect around 6pm – very popular. Generously staffed, science lab and computer room, linked via cable to the communications and resource centre in the senior school and share main school facilities – the Astroturf (which to be honest is quite a long hike for smaller legs), swimming pool and theatre. Plus nursery.

LUDGROVE

Wixenford, Wokingham, Berkshire, RG40 3AB

Tel: 01189 789 881
Fax: 0118 979 2973
E-mail: office@ludgroveschool.co.uk
Website: www.ludgrove.net

• Pupils: 195 boys; all board • Ages: 8-13 • C of E • Fees: £5,550 • Independent

Heads: From 1973 the school was run by two heads, Mr Gerald Barber and Mr Nichol Marston, both with MAs from Oxford and both in their late fifties/early sixties; Mr Marston retired in 2004. One of the Barbers' three children, Simon, aged 32, joined the school in 2002 (formerly teaching at Ashdown House in Sussex) with a view to continuing the family tradition; the fourth generation of his family to do so;

he is now joint deputy head with Andrew Inglis, who has taught at Ludgrove for 10 years. All are great believers in the committed schoolteacher, one who'll turn their hand to anything. The Barbers live on site with their two springer spaniels (waggy and friendly). Mr B oversees the gardens while Mrs B manages the house and 'wonderful staff'. Charlie the chef has been there for 18 years.

Entrance: 40 boys join each year. Names down at birth. No entrance exam but take note, this is a competitive school with high academic standards. Siblings are still given preference if that is the parents' wish. Boys don't particularly come from local or London pre-preps; they come from all over the UK and some from further afield but the majority of parents are within a 2-hour car journey.

Exit: Fifty-five per cent to Eton, most of the rest to Radley and Harrow and a smattering elsewhere to Winchester, Marlborough, Stowe. The very high success rate for Eton candidates is a reflection of the academic level and disciplined structure. Not the place for slackers.

Remarks: Set in a flat Berkshire landscape, the school is housed in a half-timbered farmhouse-style building, covered in wisteria and creepers, surrounded by 130 acres of gardens and woodland. It boasts a nine-hole golf course, 2 squash courts, huge sports hall, 2 Eton fives courts, its own chapel, myriad playing fields. A new indoor heated swimming pool opened in 2002; within the grounds there are no out-of-bounds so boys are free to build dens, make camps, cultivate the gardens – but not climb trees. The old milking parlour has a new lease of life as an art room busy with boys being creative in pottery and woodwork – 'boys all absolutely adore this'.

Smashing choir, lots of instruments played, three drama productions a year, trips to France. Rugby, football, cricket, golf, tennis, squash, fives, fencing, athletics are on offer. Judo recently introduced. Boys are encouraged to participate in activities, which parents can come and watch – not just the first XI. Weekends are deliberately full – games and matches every Saturday afternoon, letters home (handwritten!) and assembly and Chapel every Sunday followed by inter-house activities. Pleasantly shambolic atmosphere with the feel of a country farmhouse.

Parents very involved and supportive and there are more weekends at home these days. Tremendous trust between parents and school; emails and the telephone (mobiles not allowed) have dramatically changed communications, 'dads especially like emails as they can email their sons from the office, keep in touch (whole school is now networked), see who's been selected to play in the match, how many goals were scored.' A school with excellent pastoral care and wonderfully enthusiastic teachers offering a wide range of 'Boys' Own' type activities plus high standards of behaviour – 'Manners (with a capital M stresses school!) hugely important and kindness to each other. These things don't change.' It's a winning combination that continues to appeal.

LYCÉE FRANÇAIS CHARLES DE GAULLE PRIMARY

Linked to Lycée Français Charles de Gaulle in the Senior section
Linked to Ecole Charles de Gaulle - Wix in the Junior section
Linked to Ecole André Malraux in the Junior section

London,

Tel: 02075 846 322
Fax: 02078 237 684
E-mail: lyceefrlondres@lyceefrancais.org.uk
Website: www.lyceefrancais.org.uk

• Ages: boys and girls: all day • No religious affiliation
• Independent

Remarks: Two outlying annexes: Ecole Charles de Gaulle – Wix on Clapham Common North Side, and Ecole André Malraux in Ealing. Wix shares a building with a state primary school – 'permet de nombreux et fructueux échanges bi-culturels qui sont une source d'enrichissement réciproque pour les élèves et leurs enseignants,' dit the school.

THE LYCEUM

Kayham House, 6 Paul Street, London, EC2A 4JH

Tel: 020 7247 1588
Fax: 020 7655 0951
E-mail: lyceumschool@aol.com

• Pupils: 100 boys and girls (including nursery); all day • Ages: 3-11 • Non-denom • Fees: £2,400 • Independent • Open days: The first Thursday of every month, by appointment

Heads: The school was set up in 1996 by joint heads and owners Jeremy D Rowe (managing director) and Lynn Hannay (director of curriculum). Both were previously primary school teachers and spent many years as head and deputy head, respectively, of a Hackney primary school. He is chair of the National Association for Primary Education – the first ever independent school head in that role. He is passionate about the role of the arts, especially music, in education for all. He is also programme director of the Wagner Society. She is particularly interested in environmental studies and is an active member of NAFSO.

Entrance: No entrance test except for those who may have special needs. Come to an open morning and have a look round; then you can register, pay a deposit of £75, and are offered a place or a waiting list place for the reception class, with the option of a part- or full-time nursery place. At that point you go onto the mailing list and get newsletters and invitations to school events, 'so you get a feeling for what's going on.' About a year before entry, you are invited in for a talk with one of the heads, 'to confirm that everyone feels comfortable with the decision.' Then you are asked for a £750 deposit, credited against the last term's fees.

Exit: Not really geared up for 7+ exams. To various independent London day schools at 11+ eg City Boys' and Girls', Francis Holland, Forest School, Alleyn's, Channing, Bancroft's. Queen's College is particularly popular with girls and Dulwich College with boys. 'A lot of our parents want a liberal, creative senior school that isn't too pressured'.

Remarks: Just off City Road, a short walk from Liverpool Street and Moorgate, this school is aimed particularly at the children of City workers. 'The future of education is to do with linking it into the way people work,' says JR. 'So for parents who work in the City, commuting here with their child enables them to have a strong relationship with the school.' The school opens at 8.30am and runs after-school clubs (eg ballet, chess, jazz band) until 6.00pm, plus holiday courses (eg art and the environment, music theatre). School functions often take place at lunch-time and parents are welcome to drop in and have a sandwich with their children any day. They are also encouraged to stay for Friday morning assemblies, and watch their children show off their work or musical skills.

The school ethos is strongly arts-based. Mornings are given over to academe, the afternoons to art, music and sport. JR emphasises that this is not a crammer; its aim is to give a creative, rounded education. Work concentrates on a different topic each term in great depth, with outings scheduled accordingly. Classes are mostly 16, and taught almost entirely by class teachers, though a French teacher comes in one morning a week to give lessons to the entire school. Unusually, the top two forms learn Latin. Interactive, mostly whole-class teaching – 'we will start a topic, then identify anyone who needs help as an individual or in a small group.' As well as classroom assistants, the school has its own part-time therapist who helps with emotional difficulties and a part-timer who helps with basic skills. The school will take children with mild special needs, though not behavioural difficulties, but tries to limit them to one per class, 'though if things emerge from the woodwork later on we'll deal with them as they come up. We can manage this because our classes are so small.'

The school building was originally a print workshop, then a distribution centre for the TV Times. Although almost entirely windowless, it has a light, airy feel. Whitewashed classrooms are in the large lower ground floor, partially divided by plastic partitions, with a central space for coat-racks and pipes wending their way round the ceiling. 'I always wanted an open-plan school,' says JR. 'I like a through-flow of children; everyone knows what's going on and you get a sense of community.' This has the potential for considerable noise problems, but the classes seem orderly. 'We think children learn best when they are focused. They're trained to get on with their work even without a teacher there.' Since both heads teach, classes may indeed be left to get on if an unexpected visitor turns up; and get on they do.

Upstairs, the nursery and reception space is separated from the street by a wall of glass blocks. There's also a large white hall with pale wood flooring, a grand piano and a selection of other musical instruments, used for assemblies, plays, concerts and clubs, with music practice rooms leading off. Next door is the small indoor playground, with a basketball net and playhouse. The school is applying for planning permission to convert the flat roof into a playground.

There is no outdoor space, but the children have a physical activity every day. They play sports at the nearby Artillery playing fields and use the tennis courts and swimming pool at Golden Lane. They also use Finsbury Square as a playground, and visit the Broadgate ice rink in winter.

Art – plenty is displayed round the hall – is 'based on a strong belief in observational drawing', and pupils graduate from using pencil and watercolour to oil paints. They have frequent trips out to paint and study paintings; year 6 visits Amsterdam, to see the Van Gogh museum and Anne Frank's house, and Paris, where they paint the lily pond at Giverney. Classes can walk to lunch-time concerts at the Barbican, to the Museum of London, to Tate Modern and the Globe. 'We have a hidden curriculum of going out and looking after yourself and we virtually pioneered many of the new government rules on school journeys.'

Everyone goes to stay at Kench Hill study centre – 7 year olds stay overnight, 10 year olds for a week – doing environmental studies, drawing, field studies and sports. Music is a big deal. All the children learn to play the recorder and most learn at least one more instrument. 'All our music teachers are professional musicians, so if you learn piano you will be taught by a concert pianist. We can offer virtually any instrument – except bagpipes.' The school mounts three productions a year of drama, dance and music, such as an hour-long modern dance show at Sadler's Wells, and a Christmas musical presentation at the Geffrye museum. These usually happen at lunch-time to fit in with working hours.

Families mostly come from Islington and the NE London fringes, with parents who want a school that fits in with their working life, and offers plenty of art, sport and opportunities to get out-and-about, rather than a hothouse atmosphere.

LYTTON HOUSE

Linked to Putney High School in the Senior section

35 Putney Hill, London, SW15 6BH

Tel: 020 8788 6523
Fax: 020 8780 3488
E-mail: putneyhigh@put.gdst.net
Website: www.gdst.net/putneyhigh

• Pupils: girls; all day • Ages: 4 - 11 • Non-denom • Fees: Junior £2,383 • Independent • Open days: Late October or early November

Entrance: By assessment.

Exit: No automatic entry to senior department but high standards in the three Rs mean most of the junior girls are well prepared to pass the 11+ entrance in open competition with outsiders. 'While there are occasions when we advise against transfer for a girl from our junior department to the senior department if we feel that this is in the best interests of a child, in practice this is very rare. Indeed it has been two years since this last happened', says the school.

Remarks: Independent facilities on site. School is very popular and has been expanding to cope with demand. Shared dining hall in the senior department allows for extra junior lunches. 'School is lots of fun,' says a parent and clearly there is academic input too. Sporting and musical successes and consistent achievements in national chess and handwriting competitions.

MAGDALEN COLLEGE JUNIOR SCHOOL

Linked to Magdalen College School in the Senior section

Cowley Place, Oxford, Oxfordshire, OX4 1DZ

Tel: 01865 242191
Fax: 01865 240379
E-mail: registrar@mcsoxford.org
Website: www.mcsoxford.org

• Pupils: 100 boys; day • Ages: 7 - 11 • Fees: £2,672 years 3/4; £3,294 years 5-13. Plus lunch • Independent • Open days: Late September and early January

Head: Mr A D Halls.
Remarks: For details see senior school.

THE MALL SCHOOL

185 Hampton Road, Twickenham, Middlesex, TW2 5NQ

Tel: 020 8977 2523
Fax: 020 8977 8771
E-mail: admissions@mall.richmond.sch.uk
Website: www.mall.richmond.sch.uk

• Pupils: 300 boys; all day • Ages: 4-13 • C of E • Fees: £2,517 • Independent • Open days: October

Head: Since 2004, Dr Jeremy Jeanes MA DPhil FRSA, previously head of lower school (years 7 and 8) at Latymer Upper in Hammersmith. Modern linguist (French, German and Spanish) who stresses the needs of the individual child.

Entrance: First come, first served with the main unselective entry at 4 into reception in September – there is a waiting list so book early. Thereafter, including at 7 and 8, subject to test. Feeds include Jack and Jill, Pavilion Montessori, Sunflower Montessori, Lebanon Park Nursery, The Falcons, Athelstan House – the list changes year by year.

Exit: Wide selection, mainly day, in particular King's College Wimbledon, Hampton, St Paul's and Kingston; also eight or so to high-powered schools outside the area eg Winchester, Eton, Wellington, Harrow. Gets an average of eight academic awards per year.

Remarks: Traditional prep school ('Mall' pronounced short as in 'shall') with unusually informal and friendly atmosphere. Average class size 20 but in the final year boys are in three or four sets (smallest grouping for those who need most attention), and the scholarship class where they spend two years. Little ones are 'mothered' for three years, 6-year-olds' computer is programmed for them and there is a multi-media computer in all junior classes (5-year-olds know how to use it quicker than their teacher); senior department networked (broadband), all have email and internet access. Reception class bakes, sews and learns joined-up writing.

Cosy plus trad in a nice balance all through the school. Learning support available. Strong sport now, especially swimming, football and rugby; music also good (two choirs, two orchestras). Lots of plays. Lively. Good on clubs and projects – with boys queuing up before 8am (Daddy drops them off) to get stuck into their activities (table tennis is popular). Judo, fencing, chess, computing, carpentry all on offer. Considerable amount of new building in the last three years has greatly improved the facilities, classrooms and space; new science and music block opened in 1997, swimming pool in 1999, junior department in 2002. As we have said before, there is notably strong rapport between parents and staff, intimacy and warmth the keynote of the school. Happy reports from parents. And, 'nothing else like it around,' comment parents clamouring to get boys in. Very hard working – academic but 'not a hot-house,' says head.

MALSIS SCHOOL

Cross Hills, North Yorkshire, BD20 8DT

Tel: 01535 633 027
Fax: 01535 630 571
E-mail: admin@malsis.com
Website: www.malsis.com

● Pupils: 90 boys, 40 girls. 40 board, the rest day. Plus pre-prep with 55 pupils ● Ages: 7-13, pre-prep 3-7 ● Inter-denom: C of E and RC ● Fees: Boarding £4,700, day £3,600; Garden House pre-prep £1,920 ● Independent ● Open days: Termly

Head: Since 2004, Mr Christopher Lush MA. History at Cambridge. Married to Ingrid, two children both at Malsis. Formerly a housemaster at St Edward's Oxford, having joined the teaching staff at St Edward's in 1995 to run the history department. Before that he was an assistant housemaster at Cranleigh. A keen cricketer and hockey player,

captained Eastbourne College at both sports and represented Sussex at junior level. Earlier in his career he taught at St Andrew's Prep School in Eastbourne. A caring and compassionate head – a parent who suggested that, as head was referee for a rugby match, Malsis had an advantage, received a chorus of, 'Oh no he's far too fair'.

One of the teachers (a very good one) felt some of head's changes, eg greater frequency of reports, parents' consultations etc put more work on staff but were benefiting all. Parents agree: 'the frequent ability grades as opposed to just effort are making my son raise his game – and I find the comments useful.' Lots of happy children, but not all changes welcomed by all; some staff (and a couple of pupils) voted with their feet and followed the previous head.

Entrance: Spend at least one day in school and do tests in maths and English. No longer the Yorkshire mafia, now come from Cheshire, Lancashire to Somerset and the west of Glasgow. Trickle of Services families.

Exit: The usual suspects: Oundle, Glenalmond, Shrewsbury, Giggleswick, one or two to Sedbergh, Uppingham, Eton (steady one or two), Rugby and Ampleforth. Plus Radley and Stowe. Regular stream of scholarships to all over, including music, sport and art.

Remarks: School founded in 1920 by a teacher from Giggleswick in a glorious over-the-top Victorian mansion with incredible ceilings re-painted and gilded and shining bright, set in 40 acres of games pitches and fields. Worth every inch the £500,000 that it cost for a total facelift, which extended into the many additions. Old style spiral bound prospectus comes with a series of jolly pics of children having fun and getting dirty, check out the very good web site too, even has really useful recommended reading lists for children of all ages.

Busy little cheerful faces in striped shirts trot purposefully round jolly classrooms, stand up when you go into the room, hold the door open, and say Sir. Refreshing. Marvellous John Piper War Memorial Windows in the Chapel, plus the flags which used to hang on the Cenotaph in London. Chapel converts into hall theatre. School holds services on Saturday, rather than Sunday, so Sundays are 'free for activities'. Chess incredibly popular, giant-sized sets all over the place, including the library, very child-orientated. Huge range of country-type activities as well as the trad prep school type things, essential (school) equipment includes mountain bikes (Insurance cover OK if parents sign a form), fly-tying, hill-walking, canoeing, camping – including camp cooking. Swimming pool, shooting range, cross-country, nine hole golf course – remember this is not a country club. This is a busy boarding school. Day pupils have to be in school by 8.30am and stay till 6.15pm – though most stay later for clubs (over 50 of them) – they can in any case stay for supper if they want, there is no evening prep. 'Most' 10/13 year olds do board, and one or two younger ones.

Strong academically, head sees all good work. French from 7 (regular trips to France), nativity play in French. Latin from 8 and Greek club from 10 – and surprisingly popular. Regular scholarships to top schools. Small classes, average 12, with dedicated staff.

Excellent learning support; 20 pupils currently mostly dyslexia /dyspraxia but range of others considered if they think they can help and child will cope. IEP's for those with needs, one to one help, regular additional reading (often with parent volunteers), small group work and setting (including holding back the weakest or advancing the brightest a year so they get to spend extra time on scholarship work for common entrance). SEN not seen as a barrier, possible to be getting extra support and work in scholarship classes. All staff informed and involved with SEN. Needs across curriculum recognised: lots of different sports and opportunities for all to represent the school, DT club provides extra time and one to one opportunities for those needing additional help, extra English, calligraphy and finding something child is good at, all feature. Children respond positively to those who have additional needs: great applause when tie, usually awarded for completing gruelling 3 peaks walk in one go, awarded to pupil with physical difficulties who managed a peak a year over 3 years.

Whizzy CDT, video editing, digital cameras, vibrant art room, masses of music, loads of visits to local hot spots: Manchester, Bradford, Halifax, Leeds all have orchestras and theatres. Civilised dining room with table napkins. Famous Old Boys include Simon Beaufoy who wrote The Full Monty, Martin Taylor ex of Barclays Bank and Lord Robinson (of rentals?).

MALTMAN'S GREEN SCHOOL

Maltman's Lane, Chalfont St Peter, Gerrards Cross, Buckinghamshire, SL9 8RR

Tel: 01753 883 022
Fax: 01753 891 237
E-mail: office@maltmansgreenschool.bucks.sch.uk

• Pupils: 385 girls, all day • Ages: 3-11 • Non-denom • Fees: Nursery £870 - £1,570; main school £1,695 - £2,555
• Independent

Head: Since 2005, Mrs Joanna Pardon, MA PGCE BSc (Hons).

Entrance: By assessment/visit – a very mobile local population results in vacancies popping up all the time. Children (with very rare exception) automatically move up the school.

Exit: A good area for grammar schools with eg Dr Challoner's and Beaconsfield High. Also to a number of top boarding schools, seemingly different ones each year, eg Wycombe Abbey, Queenswood, St George's Ascot, Queen Anne's Caversham, Downe House, Cheltenham Ladies'. All girls leave at 11+.

Remarks: Very popular all day school. Housed in what looks like just another grand stockbroker's pile in ritzy suburban belt of Gerrards Cross, tiled floors gleaming with polish. Subject teachers for everything from 8. Good design technology which has been flourishing for some time, smart science and technology building and ICT room. Enthusiastic gymnastics, with girls winning all manner of medals. Art department an Aladdin's cave. Some help for mild dyslexia. Average 14-20 in a class.

Busy, happy, bright place, ditto children, who are confident and outward going, zooming about in their purple uniform. Good food. Good on trips and outings. Eleven well-kept acres, with brand new, indoor 6 lane 25m pool, adventure playground etc. Girls can come in early for breakfast and stay late for tea if it suits their families.

MALVERN COLLEGE PREPARATORY SCHOOL AND PRE-PREP

Linked to Malvern College in the Senior section

College Road, Malvern, Worcestershire, WR14 3DF

Tel: 01684 581600
Fax: 01684 581 601
E-mail: prep@malcol.org
Website: www.malcol.org

- Pupils: 188 girls and boys; boarding and day • Ages: 2-13
- C of E but ecumenical • Independent • Open days: Early in the Autumn term and May day

Head: Mr Peter Moody MA, assisted by his wife, who is also a housemistress.

Exit: Have to sit CE in the same way as othyer aspirants for the senior school. About 90 per cent move up, some move by choice to other local schools. Occasional pupil does not make the academic grade. Pupils' progress is monitored closely and parents would be told at an early stage if it is thought their child will not do well enough to move up.

Remarks: Useful little trad co-ed day/boarding prep which feeds both Malvern and elsewhere. Join at any time, some financial support available. Small classes, children streamed at top end, good languages, science etc. Shares swimming pool etc with senior school, popular locally and particularly with foreigners who tend to come at 11 to top up their English. Good local bus service, after-school club and holiday club. Can't fault it.

MANCHESTER HIGH PREPARATORY DEPARTMENT

Linked to Manchester High School for Girls in the Senior section

Grangethorpe Road, Manchester, Lancashire, M14 6HS

Tel: 0161 224 0447
Fax: 0161 224 6192
E-mail: administration@mhsg.manchester.sch.uk
Website: www.manchesterhigh.co.uk

- Pupils: 200 girls; all day • Ages: 4-11 • Secular
- Fees: £1,718 - £2,412 • Independent • Open days: October/November

Head: Miss S E Coulter BEd.

Entrance: By one-to-one assessment for Key Stage 1. By entrance examination for Key Stage 2, with tests in mathematics, English and reasoning.

Exit: Most girls pass entrance exam to senior school and transfer to it.

Remarks: Close links with senior school, particularly at transition from Key Stage 2 to 3. For practical purposes the junior school is kept fairly separate – infants have their own playground, likewise juniors, and both use a different entrance to the school to the senior school's one. Classrooms informal and bright, equipment excellent. Lots of clubs and other extra-curricular activities. Before-school supervision and after-school club available. Excellent inspection report in 2005. Computer facilities recently upgraded and extended.

MANOR HOUSE SCHOOL JUNIOR DEPARTMENT

Manor House Lane, Little Bookham, Leatherhead, Surrey, KT23 4EN

Tel: 01372 458538
Fax: 01372 450514
E-mail: admin@manorhouse.surrey.sch.uk
Website: www.manorhouse.surrey.sch.uk

- Pupils: 200 girls; all day • Ages: 2-11 • Christian non-denom
- Fees: Prep/junior £1,805 - £2,725 • Independent • Open days: Late October, late March and late May

Head: Mrs Julie Baker.

Entrance: Entry into nursery is from 2. Entry into junior school is by exam – not too onerous (scholarships available) at 7, plus reference from previous school.

Exit: Automatic transfer from junior to senior school with very rare exceptions (no eviction here for the less academic souls). Rarely do girls leave at 7 – an insignificant number move on to more academically challenging schools.

Remarks: The young girls in the junior section enjoy being surrounded and taken care of by the senior girls. 'At break, young girls don wellies and play in the grounds, hide and seek and the like, which does give a happy informal feel,' says one parent. The new building will provide a new nursery and prep section and much larger space for the girls. An ideal place to instil a feeling of security and confidence in a little girl.

MARLBOROUGH HOUSE SCHOOL

Hawkhurst, Cranbrook, Kent, TN18 4PY

Tel: 01580 753 555
Fax: 01580 754 281
E-mail: registrar@marlbhouse.demon.co.uk
Website: www.marlboroughhouse.kent.sch.uk

• Pupils: 210 boys and girls in prep school and 95 in pre-prep; 25 in the nursery; day and boarding • Ages: 3-13 • C of E
• Fees: Nursery £1,060; reception £1,840; years 1 and 2 £2,175; prep school £3,680 • Independent • Open days: October and May

Head: Since 1995, Mr David Hopkins MA PGCE (mid forties). Educated at King's Canterbury and Oxford where he was a scholar. Previously headmaster of Street Court (his old prep school). Married with 3 teenage children. His wife, Emma, is actively involved with the school, particularly with pastoral care and on the boarding side. A diffident and unassuming man but very popular with the children and parents alike; approachable and a good listener. Teaches Latin to the top three years and referees football and hockey.

Entrance: It is worth registering as soon as possible – over-subscribed – but people who really want a place usually get one. Anyone with mild learning difficulties is assessed to make sure the school can cater for his/her needs. Most children arrive in the nursery and stay right through until 13 but a few move on to boarding prep schools at 8. 24 children in the nursery (age 3-4) which rises to 32 per year in the pre prep (2 forms of 16) and 36 in the main school (2 forms of 18).

Exit: Mainly to fairly local schools; up to 40 per cent to Cranbrook, then Tonbridge, King's Canterbury, Bethany, Eastbourne and Benenden. Occasionally sends them further afield to eg Winchester, Eton and Harrow. Some academic scholarships to senior schools + art awards – the top academic scholarship to Eastbourne in 2004 plus a major art scholarship to Benenden. Good art department.

Remarks: Founded in 1874, moved in 1930 to a Georgian house and 35 acres of landscaped grounds on the edge of Hawkhurst. The school now boasts a fine pre-prep building and a large sports hall; the nursery has its own house close to the main school.

No streaming but children are setted in some subjects

from the age of 7. No special scholarship class; gifted children are given extra attention within their year group. Good back-up for mild dyslexia.

An exceptionally friendly school. The Friends of Marlborough House, a parents' group, is very active in welcoming new parents at coffee mornings etc and making them feel part of the school. They also organise social events throughout the year – quiz nights, various parent/teacher friendlies, bonfire night and the annual summer ball.

No full boarding and few weekly boarders but flexi-boarding is a very popular option and most children do a bit of this. Own catering staff, best food in the area. Very good match teas.

The main sports are football, rugby, hockey and cricket for the boys and netball, hockey and rounders for the girls. Plus tennis, Astroturf, .22 rifle range and keen golfers can be ferried to the local golf course for lessons. Taking part is more important than winning; most children are given a chance to play in a team. There is a long list of thriving after-school activity clubs and older children are allowed to stay on at school for supper and prep – a popular option with parents. Strong anti-bullying policy and there is always someone on hand for the children to talk to. Low staff turnover – dedicated team who are happy and committed

Over half of pupils learn a musical instrument, informal concerts throughout the year. Thriving art and IT departments and all children get involved in dramatic productions during the year. One big school play once a year and a fashion show by the girls. Famous Old Boys include cricketer David Gower.

A very happy, caring and gentle school where every child is treated as an individual. The children are encouraged to learn but are not 'hothoused'.

THE MARY ERSKINE AND STEWART'S MELVILLE JUNIOR SCHOOL

Linked to Stewart's Melville College in the Senior section
Linked to Mary Erskine School (The) in the Senior section

Queensferry Road, Edinburgh, EH4 3EZ

Tel: 0131 311 1111
Fax: 0131 311 1199
E-mail: jssecretary@esmgc.com
Website: www.esms.edin.sch.uk

• Pupils: 1,184 boys and girls • Ages: 3 – 11; almost all day
• Non-denom • Fees: Day £1,650 - £2,139; boarding £4,456 - £4,511 • Independent

Principal: Since 1989, Mr Bryan Lewis MA (fifties) educated at Dublin High School, followed by Trinity College, Dublin where he read classics. Married, with three daughters, two still in the school, and one of our very favourite heads (we are always slightly surprised – and thrilled – to find him still here). He first came to the senior school in 1974. Potty about drama, he fronts all the spectaculars that the junior school puts on (Cameron MacIntosh, Lloyd Webber and all that). We spent much of our interview looking at a video of the recent spectacular performance of Noye's Fludde, followed by Whistle Down the Wind, and only brought him back to the real world with the greatest difficulty. He no longer teaches – which is a pity – with his enthusiasm he could be breeding an entire city full of classicists. Charismatic, giggly, fun (resplendent in his Mister Man tie) – he loves hill walking and golf 'but given the choice of doing three Monros on my own, or taking kids and doing even half of one – there wouldn't be a choice: I just love children'. A recent two week production at the Edinburgh Festival Theatre saw him at the theatre almost every night; 'which is more than any parent'.

Very very keen on children's self esteem. 'Every child has a right to make mistakes, every child has a right to be happy'. 'Be proud to be good'.

Entrance: Automatic from nursery (where you should register at birth), otherwise by assessment, oversubscribed. 107 applications for 21 places at Primary 1, and 45 for 24 places at Primary 4; 80 for 60 places at Primary 6. Priority to siblings – as always. But occasional places available at every level. 'Tougher to get into than Eton,' says Mr Lewis.

Exit: To senior school, minimal trickle leave to go elsewhere.

Remarks: This is a super school with a young staff room – the school all other Edinburgh preps look up to. Despite the divided campuses, the various parts of the junior school operate as one and, perhaps because of the divided campuses, children are not overwhelmed by the numbers.

The nursery (Primary Start) leads automatically into P1 and based in the purpose-built Easter Ravelston (tiny classes, can arrive early, stay late). P1 (only) have rather dashing blue bags which are too bulky to fit into the dedicated lockers. At age 5/6 all move into the Mary Erskine site – a very specially constructed part of Mary Erskine, with charming classrooms all opening onto a dedicated playground.

The school runs an educare system called e-Plus, to deal with wrap-around care throughout the entire junior school, which includes early birds, lunch club, after school, and holiday clubs. There are also parent workshops and use of Ravelston Sports Club for all the family. Also coaches to and from school. School is based at Ravelston (Easter Ravelston plus the real thing) until the age of seven, when all move to 'big school' at Stewart's Melville. They remain here until P7 (aged 11/12) when girls return to Mary Erskine proper and boys go up to the senior school. Strong anti-bullying programme Every child made to feel loved – the Lewis touch again.

Emphasis on academia, mainly French from Primary 5, technology, home economics, science from Primary 6 and 7 – all with dedicated teachers. Max class size 25, 20 for practical subjects. From Primary 4 (7/8 year olds) pupils are taught in fairly fluid dedicated ability groups, particularly in maths and language, moving to a subject-based curriculum at the top of the junior school in preparation for senior school. Lots of input from sixth form pupils who help with reading and classroom support (and the boys are as much a part of this programme as the girls). Computers all over; excellent library facilities, plus all the other accoutrements you would expect in the junior department of a truly great school – climbing wall, swimming pool, super gyms, massive games options, plus inspired expeditions and the like.

Magical drama (Mr Lewis again), and, of course music, with over 120 children playing in orchestras and over 300 instrumental music lessons weekly. Specialist choirs from Primary 3. Fab art, with a great millennium staircase decorated by all the pupils – Mr Lewis was cross when we used the word pupils' – 'never use the word "pupils" – "pupils" are things you teach – "children" are real boys and girls.'

(The fire brigade are cross too, so it is about to be sprayed with noxious fire-retardant fluid).

Currently streaks ahead of any other Edinburgh prep school.

THE MAYNARD JUNIOR DEPARTMENT

Linked to Maynard School (The) in the Senior section

Denmark Road, Exeter, EX1 1SJ

Tel: 01392 273 417
Fax: 01392 355 999
E-mail: office@maynard.co.uk
Website: www.maynard.co.uk

• Pupils: 110 girls, all day • Ages: 7-10 • Fees: £2,156
• Independent

Entrance: Tests in English, mathematics, reasoning and reading.

Exit: Majority of pupils migrate to senior school.

Remarks: Housed in its own building on school site. Above National Curriculum levels in most areas, especially English and science. Various junior groups run by older pupils – drama, dance, art, netball, trampolining, gym. Pupils mature, supportive of one another, polite and well-behaved. LAMDA exams in speech and drama available; several girls take part in Exeter Competitive Festival each spring. Caring atmosphere. School ends at 3.55pm, with a late room available until 5pm.

MAYVILLE HIGH SCHOOL JUNIOR DEPARTMENT

Linked to Mayville High School in the Senior section

35-37 St Simon's Road, Southsea, Hampshire, PO5 2PE

Tel: 023 9273 4847
Fax: 023 9229 3649
E-mail: mayvillehighschoolpr@talk21.com
Website: www.mayvillehighschool.com

- Pupils: 191 girls and boys; all day • Ages: 0-11 • C of E, all creeds welcome • Fees: Pre-prep £900; junior £1,675
- Independent • Open days: Tours daily, taster days by appointment

Remarks: For details see senior school.

MERLIN SCHOOL

4 Carlton Drive, Putney, London, SW15 2BZ

Tel: 020 8788 2769
Fax: 020 8789 5227
E-mail: secretary@merlinschool.net

- Pupils: 65 boys, 35 girls; all day • Ages: 4-8 • Fees: £2,543
- Independent • Open days: lots

Head: Since 2003, Mrs Kate Prest BA Music/Ed PGCE (thirties), educated at Oxford Brooks. Formerly head of pre-prep at The Harrodian, and before that teacher and music specialist at Oratory Primary, Chelsea. Married with two young boys – the elder one currently attends the school. Very chatty and enthusiastic, eager to show off the school and seems justifiably proud of school and pupils. Knows all the children well. Parents can discuss any problems easily, and have found her to be 'very approachable.' Sees herself as very open-minded, easy to communicate with and 'always has the children's best interests as heart'.

Entrance: Following a tour of the school, places are offered on receipt of registration (unless there is a waiting list) on a first come first served basis, with priority given to siblings. Currently spaces available – the head says the school not being full 'is a blip and that registrations are healthy for the future.'

Exit: To some top-notch preps and junior schools including Westminster, Bute House, Kensington Prep,

Latymer, and The Harrodian -which has the same owner. The Merlin is not a feeder school for The Harrodian although it does have a link at 8+ if The Harrodian is an option for Merlin parents. (Instead of the normal January 8+ exam for The Harrodian, Merlin children have an informal interview plus a report from the Merlin head in November.) Pupils also go off to Colet Court and King's College Wimbledon, as well as other local independent schools. An occasional few to boarding school.

Remarks: Welcoming and friendly school, which caters for a wide range of abilities but still manages to get places at some of the best London preps. 'It has never been a hothouse, but the children are greatly encouraged,' says a parent. On first appearances, the school is fairly homely (carpeted in most areas) and quite plain, but the classrooms are well equipped with children's work proudly displayed. Good use made of all available space; playground is adequate.

Teachers very keen for each child to reach their best of their ability, without cramming- whilst still preparing them for the 7+ and 8+ entrance exams. Smallish classes – average 16. Computers in each classroom and children are encouraged to use them alongside lessons. French is taught from reception. Separate science lab used by all classes. Classes divided into small teams for maths and English according to ability, but these are not fixed teams, children move regularly within various groups to provide support as and when required. 'The children here really do strive to do the best they can,' says a parent 'even if they are not academically minded, they are helped along without being made to feel different.' Support teacher for English and maths for those who need it, and there is an SEN teacher for dyslexia and dyspraxia at an extra cost to parents.

Sports OK. Much emphasis on music, singing, drama and art – excellent brand new art and music building and Merlin children have recently won local poetry and art competitions. In addition to class music teaching, all children are given the opportunity to learn the piano and violin with peripatetic teachers; years 2 and 3 children learn recorders. Drama and music based productions are part of the school year.

Laid back, cosy atmosphere (some teachers are called by their first name and still command respect), quite a large number of male teachers, unusual in a prep school. Children smart in dark blue uniform and very well behaved. Has always had a tendency to be boy heavy, 'but the girls are very much in evidence' says head. Parents tend to be middle class professionals.

Not for those who want acres of outside space to let off steam, but a real home from home.

MICHAEL HALL LOWER SCHOOL

Linked to Michael Hall School in the Senior section

Kidbrooke Park, Forest Row, East Sussex, RH18 5JA

Tel: 01342 822275
Fax: 01342 826593
E-mail: info@michaelhall.co.uk
Website: www.michaelhall.co.uk

• Pupils: boys and girls • Ages: 0-11 • Non-denom: Steiner Waldorf Schools Fellowship • Fees: Annual Early Years £3,735, Annual Lower School £5,310 - £6,090 • Independent • Open days: Two a term

Chairperson of the College of Teachers: There is no head teacher. Steiner schools are self-governing communities and a 'college of teachers' administers and manages pedagogical issues without a traditional hierarchy supported by the Council of Management (trustees).

Remarks: For details see senior school.

MILBOURNE LODGE SENIOR SCHOOL

43 Arbrook Lane, Esher, Surrey, KT10 9EG

Tel: 01372 462 737
Fax: 01372 471 164
E-mail: admin@milbournelodge.co.uk
Website: www.milbournelodge.co.uk

• Pupils: 190; 160 boys and 30 girls (mostly sisters), numbers have been slightly reduced to meet target of 190ish; all day • Ages: 8-13 • C of E • Fees: 1st and 2nd years £2,650, 3rd, 4th and 5th years £2,700 • Independent

Head: Since 2002, Mr Patrick MacLarnon MA (early forties), educated at Loughborough Grammar School and Oxford University where he read geology. Has only taught at Milbourne Lodge – 'there's nowhere else such fun to teach,' he says and his mostly long-serving staff appear to agree. He is almost fanatically enthusiastic about the regime at the school, hardly ever keeping quiet for long enough to allow questions, and uses his charm and candour to market the school well. 'The essential feature of marketing the school is that we tell parents the truth about what we do and what we do not do. It would be pointless to use "charm" to entice parents who would be better suited to other schools.' He is often in email contact with parents – he still teaches some maths and English – but seems to have time for individuals, in between visits to target public schools. Takes great personal interest in each child, and clearly knows some of the parents very well too, though he is not always completely complimentary about all of them. Has an easy, rather than warm, relationship with pupils and staff – though he says when his staff read this comment they did not feel it was correct – warmth is apparently on the agenda.

The driving force behind the school's ethos, Mr Norman Hale, is now in his eighties, but still takes an interest in the place. His highly traditional and, some would say unique, regime is now over but his influence has not completely waned.

Entrance: About 50 per cent of the children come from nearby Milbourne Lodge Junior School, though there is no affiliation. The rest from other local pre-prep schools, with a handful travelling out from Fulham or Barnes, looking for country-style prep schooling. 'I breathe a sigh of relief as I turn towards Putney Bridge in the morning instead of heading up the Kings Road,' one mother mused, though, in fact, there is a school bus from Putney to relieve her journey. Entry is selective, mostly at 8 (with a few places available at other times), via a maths and English test and a 'chat'. Academic potential (with a view to scholarships) is what interests the school and they take into account previous education. Although co-ed, no plans to increase the number of girls from about 15 per cent (head questions parents very closely if they want to send a girl here who does not have a brother in the school – their choice of best friend is going to be very limited) and it is certainly not the place for a wee, sleekit, cowran, tim'rous beastie (of either sex).

Exit: The scholarship board in the hall seems to groan under the weight of names of pupils and prestigious public schools. St Paul's appears regularly and, more recently, King's Wimbledon, but otherwise it's the boarding schools: Eton, Harrow, Winchester, Charterhouse and other highly academic institutions. The head adds, 'Westminster is becoming increasingly prominent amongst the day schools and Harrow has become a less frequent destination, for no other apparent reason than the awkward journey – parents of boarders seem to like a boarding school around the corner these days.' For girls, Wycombe Abbey and Marlborough. Very few girls leave at 11, so few go on to day schools. The atmosphere amongst the, reportedly very competitive, parents must be frantic at Common Entrance results time!

Remarks: A traditional, academically aggressive school with very high expectations of its pupils, matched only by the possibly even higher expectations of the parents. Main building is a large converted, slightly shabby Gothic style redbrick house and most classrooms are in elderly wooden buildings in the gardens. One parent said that she found this scruffiness reassuring, 'I like my son being taught in a hut, it shows the school is concerned with teaching, not impressing the parents,' while others might wonder where their fees are going. 'It is made very clear to prospective parents that the fees are not spent on glittering playschool-style facilities,' comments the head.

On a sunny day it feels lovely, with roses in bloom and vistas over woods and neighbouring farmers' fields. When the wind howls and the rain splashes, you get wet and freezing as you move around between buildings. Inside the classrooms, pupils work hard and quietly, with only pencils and exercise books on the desks. The teacher needs only the blackboard and rather old text books – no 'classrooms of the future' here. Reference books look as though they've seen better days but beautiful neat work can be seen in the work books. This is traditional teaching by traditional staff (perhaps even eccentric in one or two cases) for bright, motivated and energetic pupils in pursuit of excellence. One parent, who is particularly pleased with the teaching, felt that, 'the teachers make sure my son really understands the foundations before moving on.' She added, 'this might constrict the range of what they learn, but at least it means they can do the homework!' Another said that the children were given the facts, tested on them, and later revised them which ensured a 'sound grounding.' The 'A' stream, especially in the older classes, is given opportunities to think and write around subjects and one parent described a history lesson as 'inspirational'.

The teaching, however, is not without parental criticism. 'Most of the teachers are devoted but there are one or two duds,' said one parent. Another commented, ' maybe not all the teaching is that good – some teachers haven't heard of positive encouragement and can be far too severe.' Certainly, no child would want to be on the receiving end of the sergeant-major style shout heard through the window on our visit – parents confirm that this style of schoolmastering lives on here. The head has apparently heard these critical comments before and replies, 'it seems very likely that the 'duds' are the teachers who have been removed recently, and the 'sergeant-major style shout' was undoubtedly made by one of these teachers. There has been a coor-

dinated effort to instil discipline by quieter, more sympathetic methods, and there is strong staff approval for the way this has worked.'

The school feels no need to follow the National Curriculum but, instead, adheres to the requirements of Common Entrance and the passions of the staff. Pupils are streamed from day 1 into 'A' and 'B' – scholarship stream and Common Entrance stream – but there is movement between the two as necessary. Pupils are made aware of their place within the class for each subject and strive to improve it but they also have rankings for effort. One result of this is that some parents insist on extra outside tutoring when the results are not as high as they think they should be – a tough life for some children with pressure heaped upon them from all sides. In addition to the main subjects, there is Latin for all and Greek for the scholarship stream. One major improvement is the introduction of help for dyslexics and others with particular needs. There is science, of course, but the outdated science lab has to double as a DT room. The head admits that 'the lab is not shiny plastic but it has everything we need.'

Art is a strength, with the school winning the Royal College of Art Best School award, and there is an annual art exhibition. All sorts of music tuition are available, with opportunities to play in an orchestra or group, but there's a very small music room and instruments are stored on odd bits of landing. Art, music and IT are housed in the attic of the main house up a very steep staircase and IT is treated as a skill that must be learnt rather than an integral part of the curriculum (there are no computers in the classrooms).

The garden is used for teaching, eg drama, when the weather allows. Many children learn chess and all pupils research general knowledge questions every week). The general knowledge team recently won the 2004 UK Schools' Challenge (the equivalent of University Challenge for U13s), which is open to all schools in the UK, not just prep schools. After Common Entrance, there are lots of trips and activities.

Sport is played every afternoon, outside in all weathers (no indoor sports hall) with much success competitively. You might expect 'mens sana in corpore sano' (a healthy mind in a healthy body) to be the motto of the school. At break time, pupils are busy, getting out the table tennis or practising cricket – no 'mooching around' here. Outdoor pool is heated and apparently much used as is the enormous playing field. Whilst older boys and girls do cross-country runs, younger ones play a wonderful 'ambush' game in the woods, which they love. A number of pupils do sport to a very high level and many do extra sport outside school. The school day doesn't finish until after five or even six o'clock, you wonder how they find the time, especially since there is plenty of homework every night. 'The homework load can be ghastly,' remarked one parent, 'if only it was always learning Latin vocabulary it would be OK, but when they ask an 8 year old to prhécis some bit about the Celts, it's ridiculous.' Communication with parents is encouraged at the beginning and end of the school day – the parents generally are an ambitious, demanding (both of the school and their offspring) bunch.

Milbourne is a school that attracts vociferous praise from some and vociferous criticism from others. The head is aware of the school's critics but says, 'the healthy, happy, alive-looking children represent our best defence.' The question to ask is whether this mentally and physically action-packed regime will suit both you and your child. Do you both have the energy? Is it hot-housing or is it what a really bright boy or girl needs for inspiration? Not for the faint-hearted or the progressive.

MILLFIELD PREPARATORY SCHOOL

Linked to Millfield School in the Senior section

Edgarley Hall, Glastonbury, Somerset, BA6 8LD

Tel: 01458 832446
Fax: 01458 833 679
E-mail: admissions@millfieldprep.com
Website: www.millfieldprep.com

- Pupils: 500 boys and girls; boarding and day • Ages: 2 - 13
- Inter-denominational • Fees: Available on application
- Independent • Open days: May and October

Head: Since 2001, Mr Kevin Cheney BA, PGCE (fifties). Educated at St George's College, Weybridge did geography at Exeter University and began his teaching career in the Royal Army Educational Corps (where he was promoted to Captain). He first joined Millfield in 1980 with his wife, Hilary, a qualified teacher, where he ran a house for five years; became head of Trinity School, Teignmouth for six years, and head of Cranmore School in 1992. Hilary provides very visible hands-on support at the school; four sons, three post-A levels, youngest at Millfield. Mr Cheney, a sporty, former county hurdler and high jumper is kind, enthusiastic and fiercely proud of his pupils. He was visibly tired and looking forward to half term during our visit,

though when we left, there were parents 'who had done the tour' waiting for him and he was keen 'to get ready to go to Hong Kong tomorrow'.

Entrance: Variety of ways in. Many come via interview and report from previous head, from prep schools finishing at 11, pre-preps, overseas and local primaries. Others sit school exam in January for September entry. Can be flexible – Millfield prep will always make the effort to take pupils and has been a sanctuary for pupils unhappy or failing to thrive elsewhere. 'IQ not the only arbiter, need to see the child, not just a collection of data'. Can and will take when space available.

Exit: Vast majority go to Millfield. Transfer not automatic, with good behaviour and a satisfactory academic standard necessities. A small number move elsewhere, almost always to other independent schools.

Remarks: Extensive site spread round a bend in the road outside Glastonbury, facing the school golf course and a boarding house at the foot of the famous Tor across the road (better view if you move a tree or two). Quite difficult to find Reception, the sign posts are in just the wrong place and having started in the wrong place it is quite difficult to find reception itself. An external car park services the stunning games complex and a certain amount of titivation is being done to the two buildings nearest the road, whilst in the main house, serious chunks are being hauled down, and scaffolding obscures much of the playground. Appearance of school functional rather than beautiful, with limited attempts to co-ordinate or blend in new and less new with the Gothic Victorian pile at its heart where the head is based, and quite a lot of stuff (as in mantle pieces and the like) looks as though it has come from the Abbey itself. The previous owners used to own both. Lots of unusual touches, though – a huge outdoor chess set has moved from outside the girls' houses at the senior school (where we last saw them) to just in front of the main building, and the multi-coloured climbing wall on the outside of one building gives it the personality much of the architecture lacks, a Scandinavian style science block is on the stocks. Architecturally the place needs a Bowen Jones make-over, an enormous (three storey – why? – in the country?) cruciform class room block was deeply muddling to this (experienced) editor, but the children seemed quite content, scurrying around like worker bees under the queen's command – well, it was end of school day and it was daylight and there were golf clubs everywhere and we do mean everywhere. Golf is the current passion.

Two new boarding houses opened in September 2003 and a pre-preparatory department, catering for pupils aged

2-7, is now based on campus in the former kitchen garden – stunning specially made Story Chair and super cosy library. Children coming into the pre-prep are automatically assessed, one-to-one groups and up to three specialist lessons a week for those who need help. The LDC is a centre of excellence, currently with more than 180 pupils in this deceptively small building, with ten tutors, five part time and strong liaison throughout. This the school which all other prep schools recommend when they can't cope (and here this editor speaks from experience – though in the end her son did not go here).

The Language Development Centre is second to none. And I quote from their MAP OF SPECIAL NEEDS PROVISION: 'Pupils from pre-prep are assigned to a class in the Preparatory School taking into account their need for extra support/access to LDC'. Study skills important. Pupils come with a range of problems from ADHD to 'mild cerebral palsy'. Pupils in the pre-prep transfer here with a 'record of phonic skills using Jolly Phonics and Sound Discovery resources as well as the pre-prep yellow files containing IEPs and records of parent discussions'. This also goes for children arriving at the school, whose edpsyched reports and problems are taken into consideration. Detailed assessments are 'carried out in the main body of the school', with ensuing discussions between the department and the heads of year groups regarding individual pupils. If their reading or spelling is more than a year behind their chronological age this is flagged 'but data is not the only aspect taken into account when determining a pupil's current needs'. It can vary from day to day. Each pupil on the SEN register has a Pupil Diagnostic Profile, which includes Lucid Rapid, Lucid Lass Junior, Lass Secondary, Diagnostic Reading Assessments, Spelling Tests (Young's Parents), Phonological Assessment Battery (PhAB), Aspects of The Institute of Neuro-Phylogical Psychology Assessment, Aspects of the Aston Index and they are considering a trial of the InCAS (Interactive Computerised Assessment System of the University of Durham. Brain Gym popular. The head of LDC, who is a CReSTed examiner, is also qualified in Neuro-Developmental Delay with the Institute of Neuro-Physiological Psychology: if the programme is thought beneficial for a pupil and after a positive assessment (co-ordination, balance, visual development, laterality and spatial awareness) then a 'five-ten minute a day programme using no special equipment and replicating movements from the first year of life is then implemented which gives the brain a 'second chance' to develop the reflexes needed to provide a firm foundation for learning'. This programme usually lasts about a year. (NB the much vaunted DDAT Dore programme – said by many to have a very good PR set-up – whilst based on repetitive exercise, does not replicate the first year of life – as we understand it, prescribed excercises are based on cerebellum inactivity and tested via electrodes during an assessment session). Over 120 pupils of all ages are currently attending the LDC on a regular basis, plus some 50 pupils getting additional help, with 15 on a one-to-one basis, and four doing speech and language and occupational therapy. There is also an LDC Link Tutor for those who do not qualify for total LDC immersion; these pupils may be assessed and info put on the staff internet for follow-up. Good tie-up with houseparents when children may need extra help. All areas of life here based on efforts to find an aptitude, build self-esteem and develop the potential of every child. Special programme (Potential Academic Curriculum Excellence or PACE) undertaken by superbright. Help at both ends of the spectrum included in fees.

Pupils follow broad curriculum with setting for maths and languages in all but first year with French taught from the first term and Spanish and Latin added by the age of 10. Plenty of exciting trips out to bolster learning, from nearby basketworks and Hinckley Point power station to London galleries and France. Class sizes small, normal maximum 16. Each child watched over by group tutor, responsible for welfare and progress, and first port of call for anxious parents. Reports are termly, with grades for effort as well as attainment. Scholarships for chess as well as academic, music, sporting and art.

Set in acres of manicured greenery, with a bubble over the tennis court in winter (some houses have their own – as opposed to the school's one). Sport as important as expected, a second sports hall was opened in 2005, an equestrian centre with two maneges (school's preferred word is arena) was built at the same time, a nine-hole golf course just for Millfield prep, a fine 25-metre pool (ditto) and all sorts of courts, pitches and fields to cater for every conceivable sport and activity. Underpinning the school's ethos, finding talent in whatever area and inspiring confidence in its wake, the games' list includes Airfix modelling and touch-typing, as well as sports from pop lacrosse and indoor go-karting to squad training for swimming, rugby and soccer. Music is particularly well-supported, with a wide range of instruments, 350 individual lessons, 29 music ensembles and 18 annual concerts. Facilities include 28 music rooms and a light and airy recital hall (currently under wraps), but junior baroque chamber orchestra plus the expected choirs et al. Art of all kinds very popular, from printmaking to ceramics via ICT, with critical discussion an integral part of its teaching.

Pupils are chatty, bubbly, confident and clearly have a fun time – head very keen that they – not he – do all the talking for the school. He does say that the school makes great efforts to preserve pupils' childhood for as long as possible and there is a welcome air of separation between the school and the town beyond. Boarding houses are particularly cosy, with great efforts made to create homes from home, with bright colours, football team duvet covers and jazzy pinboards a feature of the bedrooms. Welcoming, cheerful school with pupils treasured – whatever their special talent, be it rugby or brass-rubbing. Wonderful facilities in every sphere. Genuinely turning out well-rounded individuals and a centre of excellence for those with serious problems. Couldn't do better.

MOIRA HOUSE JUNIOR SCHOOL

Linked to Moira House Girls School in the Senior section

Upper Carlisle Road, Eastbourne, East Sussex, BN20 7TE

Tel: 01323 636800
Fax: 01323 649720
E-mail: info@moirahouse.co.uk
Website: www.moirahouse.co.uk

- Pupils: 130; a few boarders, rest day • Ages: 3-11 • C of E
- Fees: Day £1,660 - £3,850; weekly boarding £4,725 - £5,900; full boarding £5,175 - £6,625 • Independent
- Open days: Any day

Head: Mrs Linda Young CertEd NPQH, who spent many years teaching in Thailand.

Entrance: Interview, maths and English test from 7.

Exit: 95 per cent to senior school.

Remarks: For further details, see senior school entry.

MOOR PARK SCHOOL

Moor Park, Richards Castle, Ludlow, Shropshire, SY8 4DZ

Tel: 01584 876 061
Fax: 01584 877 311
E-mail: head@moorpark.org.uk
Website: www.moorpark.org.uk

- Pupils: 250 boys and girls (55/45); 70 boarding beds: full time boarding, weekly boarding and flexi boarding, plus weekend tasters • Ages: 2 1/2 - 13 • RC but inter-denom • Fees: Pre Prep £1,365 - £1,710; Prep £2,535 - £3,360; boarding £3,770 - £4,590 • Independent • Open days: 'Every day is an open day'

Head: Since 2002, Mr Mike Piercy BA (forties) who had been working 'with' the school since 2001, and takes over after a turbulent time, including a couple of interregna and a new governing body. Mr Piercy, who was educated at Gresham's, read English at Leicester, worked his way up the prep school ladder via West Downs, Bishops Stortford (which he hated), Great Ballard where he was head of English and boarding, Forres Sandle Manor where he was director of studies and deputy head and finally head of Dunhurst before he came here. A bubbly, experienced head: he came clattering down the uncarpeted stairs with the energy of a 12 year old and we bounced round the school enthusing and chatting interspersed with quite long pauses to watch a (not very needle) rugby game against a neighbouring school.

Moor Park won, most of their scrum wearing head protectors, which must have terrified the opposition (school has a reputation for 'the best teas ever'). Loads of staff changes during the debacle, not a lot recently. Working on restoring confidence, and thrilled by 'super supportive staff'. Some new staff appointed with his blessing during his 'consultative' first year' (ie when he was working out his notice). Mr Piercy would like more staff houses in the grounds.

Entrance: Can take at any time if space available. At any age. All children screened at four for learning support, incoming pupils come for a day 'to see what it is all about' and are given 'standardised test'. If school concerned about learning problems they work on a suck and see policy and can give extra support where needed. One or two Aspergers children in school. The odd 'real' foreigner, ditto Services, quite a lot of grannie-ed children, plus refugees from London whose parents have bought houses locally (Gloucestershire is full).

Exit: Not many recently to Ampleforth, but Downside, Cheltenham Ladies' Coll (scholarship last year) St Mary's Ascot (recent scholarship) Winchester (scholarship). Lots to Shrewsbury, Malvern, Uppingham, Oakham (who are getting sniffier about IQs) Rugby et al. A few girls leave at 11+, most stay to 13. Several art and academic scholarships a year. Over 60 per cent won awards last year: academic, art, sport, music, all-round.

Remarks: Founded in 1964. Enormously happy little local school offering everything from baby care upwards. Taken as read, immaculate baby, nursery care till 6 pm, then add jolly pre-prep with computers and early exposure to languages and then add proper prep school with full boarding if you want it, weekly boarding, and flexi boarding (though the latter is filling up rapidly). The demand is so high for boarding that they are converting another dorm, and unless you book Thursdays and Fridays early you may not get flexi and have to go all the way. Buses for day pupils up to a radius of 45 minutes, ie. Hereford and Kidderminster.

This is a gem of a school and the new head is rapidly stepping into the shoes of the much loved head but one who was ousted by a demented (to put it kindly) board of governors and was a legend in the prep school world. Trillions of options, real science at 7 (and some in the pre-prep) Latin at 10, Greek for scholars (and loads of those); max class size 18, but usually 14. Children setted at 9 in maths, but hardly notice it. Computers everywhere and subject taught.

Music department a bit shabby and head's wish list includes new music centre and new CDT centre: Henderson Hall looks functional, but sad compared to the rest of the school, much used by locals, with an out of this world grand piano just sitting there. Sports hall, and swimming pool, boarders can swim quite late in the evening. Magical art department would do credit to a senior school, entertaining ceramics and carved breeze block sculptures on show. Head of art's influence all over the shop: boys' dorms a bit severe still, but their bathrooms need to go in a glossy, ditto the girls' dorms and their bathrooms. Jaws for the boys, OTT pretty for the girls.

Fantastic regular essentially boarding weekends in school where all can do a taster sport; or, like the weekend after we visited, proper live telly production with parents invited to watch the finished product in the dining room. Pupils are already devising sets. Great pressure on parents from children having so much fun they don't want to go home (and some of those who board live less than a mile away). Last year's art weekend produced the most amazing peacocks from recycled materials which decorate the cricket pavilion, watched overall by a weird collection of totem poles.

All singing and dancing on the scholastic front, plus new classrooms (member of governors is senior builder and supplies the kits at cost with in-house management so not that expensive), more to come. All children tested on entry. Head of learning support, AMBDA qualified does all the testing, if a child is below the 'base line', they might be referred to an ed psych. There is an occasional (very rare) child who may not be 'up to the school', 'can't be everything for everyone' said the head, but 'in reality very few are turned away'. Border line children are invited for a trial day and skool tests (usually unsuspected) find out 'as much data as possible'. A fifth of the school 'have some kind of support' be it for dyslexia et al, organisational skills, mild Aspergers or just plain gifted. One mildly aspergeral pupil whom we met during our visit recently got a scholarship to Stonyhurst. One full time and one part time teacher, pupils either withdrawn from class or taught in pairs or tiny groups, no in class teaching. A couple of children on the SEN spectrum don't do French, and they 'might have a child who doesn't do Latin'.

Good child play area, woods (all checked by arborists for falling branches) and children allowed to go only so far – three girls who recently went further are now temporarily banned from the woods. Tough. Ginormous bonfire in place for November 5th. Stunning Queen Anne house with various add-ons, stunning Robert Adamesque chapel in the ballroom, and terrific entrance hall with leather covered walls. V elegant, even if used for 'Blot on the landscape'.

Moreton First

Linked to Moreton Hall School in the Senior section

Weston Rhyn, Oswestry, Shropshire, SY11 3EW

Tel: 01691 773671
Fax: 01691 778552
E-mail: nortonroberts@moretonhall.com
Website: www.moretonhall.org

• Pupils: girls: boarding and day • Ages: 4 - 11 • C of E • Fees: Moreton First: £1,900 - £2,600 • Independent • Open days: November, May

Remarks: For details see senior school: Moreton Hall School, Oswestry.

MORRISON'S ACADEMY JUNIOR SCHOOL

Linked to Morrison's Academy in the Senior section

Ferntower Road, Crieff, Perthshire, PH7 3AN

Tel: 01764 653 885
Fax: 01764 655 411
E-mail: principal@morrisonsacademy.org
Website: www.morrisonsacademy.org

- Pupils: 85 boys, 75 girls; including nursery: 20 boys and girls
- Ages: junior school 5-11, nursery 3-5 • Inter-denom • Fees: Day £850 - £2,573; full boarding £5,956 - £6,274; weekly boarding £4,586 - £4,904 • Independent • Open days: October and February

Head: Mr Alasdair Robertson.
Remarks: See senior school.

MOUNT HOUSE SCHOOL

Mount Tavy, Tavistock, Devon, PL19 9JL

Tel: 01822 612 244
Fax: 01822 610 042
E-mail: office@mounthouse.com
Website: www.mounthouse.devon.sch.uk

- Pupils: 121 boys, 61 girls (84 full boarders) in main school; 49 in pre-prep • Ages: 7-13; pre-prep 3-7 • C of E • Fees: Boarding £4,800; day £2,460 - £3,600 • Independent

Head: Since 2002, Mr J Massey BSc (late thirties). Educated at Oundle and Reading University. Previously housemaster at Oundle and teacher of economics. Keen sportsman. A passionate (and qualified) squash, rugby and cricket coach. Honest, kind and gentle demeanour, easy to talk to. Childhood comes first, above regimented rules and academic tasks – 'children learn best when happy'. Married to Jo, a structural engineer, who fits in wherever needed. Two children at Mount House.

Entrance: Not academically selective although average pupils are chivvied along by brighter ones. Full-fee sports, art and music awards for gifted local children for years 7-8. Thriving Pre-prep.

Exit: Steady stream to country's elite independents –

Eton, Winchester, Harrow, Cheltenham Ladies College, Radley, plus Sherborne, Canford, Marlborough, Bryanston, King's College Taunton and locally to Kelly College. One in three wins awards.

Remarks: Enthusiastic and specialist teaching (from year 5) combined with plenty of physical activities will ensure children's passions remain alive. 'I've never heard anything negative about this school. Even if there's an incidence of bullying, it's dealt with quickly'. 'Strength of care' here is unequivocally rated by parents. Pupils swim in the rain or get muddy whilst exploring. 'If there's snow on the ground the first lesson will be cancelled,' declares Mr Massey. Pupils' fascinations and talents will be found – a sudden interest in fishing was harnessed by a boy who caught a trout in the river on-site (school has riparian rights), cooked by the school chef, he ate it that day. The great outdoors is seized as a teaching tool and confidence-builder – from canoeing and mountain climbing, to camp craft for the Shackleton award scheme with skinning and cooking a rabbit on the agenda.

Main building is a glorious old manor house set in 60 acres of greenery with magnificent views stretching (rain permitting) to Cornwall. Sport taken seriously – will cross half the country for a match. Heated outdoor pool, smart sports hall with full-size indoor tennis courts, two squash courts, indoor and outdoor cricket nets, tennis court, numerous games pitches, a nine-hole golf course and an Astroturf. Pupils integrate with local clubs like Tavistock Cricket Club. Music much encouraged within splendid new department. Most play an instrument.

Full boarding with two exeats each term as well as half term. Junior (years 3 & 4) boarders may go home on Friday after school but nearly all choose to stay for Saturday morning clubs. Senior boarders are allowed home on Saturday after sport but many stay for highly popular and organised Sunday activities (canoeing down the Tamar, archaeology trips, bonfire and path-building, beach and barbecue trips. Head not over-prescriptive on teaching strategies so long as pupils are academically up to speed. Class size averages 16; two or three streams a year in English and maths, science and French. Strengths are the intangible unquantifiable qualities – politeness, friendliness, the children look you in the eye, hold their heads up – confident without being cocky. A particularly safe, kind and very special place. 'The best traditional boarding prep school in the West Country, with none of that flexi-boarding,' say parents whose children are on a path for Eton. Parents largely professional, academics, docs from Derriford Hospital plus newcomers abandoning London for work on the web in the West

Country. Escort service available to and from London and the airports). OBs: Ed Bye (producer of Jasper Carrott etc), Philip de Glanville, David Owen.

MOWDEN HALL SCHOOL

Newton, Stocksfield, Northumberland, NE43 7TP

Tel: 01661 842 147

Fax: 01661 842 529

E-mail: lb@mowdenhall.co.uk

Website: www.mowdenhall.co.uk

- Pupils: 83 boys, 63 girls; 100 boarders, 46 day • Ages: 8-13. Plus pre-prep and nursery with 85 boys and girls, 3-8 • C of E
- Fees: Day £1,890 - £3,300; boarding £4,550 • Independent

Head: Since 2004, Mr Philip Meadows MA (mid forties), educated in Devon, and St John's College, Cambridge. A chemist, he teaches all ages in the school maths and science. A very keen sportsman – county Rugby – 'some time ago', he claims modestly. Taught at Strathallan and Loretto, was a housemaster at Sedbergh before coming here. Sylvia, his wife, participates on all the school's fronts. They have three children, all of whom attend the school.

Entrance: Wide ability range, no exam or test, three term entry. Children from all over Northumberland, Scottish borders, also Cumbria and Yorkshire.

Exit: Largest numbers to Sedbergh, RGS Newcastle, Oundle, Uppingham, Shrewsbury and Gordonstoun, though Eton, Harrow, Rugby etc feature. Thirty-two awards in last three years.

Remarks: Good and traditional prep school with lots going on, efficiently run in an old country house with many additions and conversions. Splendid setting with fine views, up a long drive with sleeping policemen. Not a rich school but, as a result of energetic fund-raising and good management, it has good facilities. The latest acquisition, and a wild success, is a part share in Sauveterre, a chateau near Toulouse, originally bought by Cothill (see entry under Cothill) – 11/12-year-olds go for a full term. Boarding still very popular and head notes 'high proportion of parents who start their children at the school with no thought that they will become boarders but who then allow them to board at Mowden and go on to send them to boarding public schools.' All children (however local) encouraged to board early and particularly for their final two years.

Jolly atmosphere, a family school with a nice balance of discipline and freedom. Good food in the agreeable dining room with staff seated at each table, children on rotas to clear plates. Pre-prep unstreamed, eighteen per year; first year of main school two streams of thirteen; from then on three streams of twelve, the top being the scholarship stream. Good and imaginative teaching at all levels. Light bright classrooms, with loads of work on display, and heaps of encouragement on hand. Scholars at the top end only, younger ones may do two years. Good library, with a pupil-written (all ages) suggestions book. Brilliantly converted science, art and technology centre in the stable yard (very busy at club time in evenings and over weekends) and super art. Keenly sporting – particularly successful at rugby and girls' hockey. Many matches are played on tour as the school is fairly isolated. New swimming pool, a covered heated version (no diving) takes over from the old outdoor pool. Weekend life is kept busy and full, with lots of expeditions, outdoor pursuits of all kinds (madly popular), lots of staff on hand (rather ugly staff accommodation dotted about the grounds). Three-weekly exeats (Thursday evening till Monday evening), but no half term in Lent.

Nursery has been tacked on by parental demand and moved here from another venue. Pre-prep continues to flourish.

All round, the school is in good heart and doing well; jolly good parental noises. Not a concentratedly academic place – its ambitions and the abilities of its children are both wider than that.

THE NEW BEACON SCHOOL

Brittains Lane, Sevenoaks, Kent, TN13 2PB

Tel: 01732 452 131

Fax: 01732 459 509

E-mail: admin@newbeacon.kent.sch.uk

Website: www.newbeacon.kent.sch.uk

- Pupils: 400 boys, mainly day with some weekly/flexi boarding
- Ages: 4-13 • Non-denom • Fees: £2,400 to £3,100
- Independent

Headmaster: Since 1976, Mr Rowland Constantine (fifties). Educated at Sheffield Grammar School and Cambridge where he read modern languages. After a short period at the Leys in Cambridge he became headmaster of The New Beacon where he has been for nearly 29 years – sees himself as a head with some standing. Constantly seeking to improve the school. Teaches French to the scholarship boys. An ISI Inspector. Sally, his wife of 34 years, is very involved in the school both socially and with parents. They live on site and have three children, two grown up and one who is in the sixth form at Sevenoaks. 'Leads from the front and keeps his cards close to his chest' according to one parent.

Entrance: About two thirds of children join the school in reception or year 1. First come first served, always over-subscribed. Non-selective on principle but there is probably an element of self-selection as the school has a reputation locally for being very academic.

Exit: About 20 per cent leave at 11+ to go to the grammars, and the school prepares them for this: about 90 per cent pass the 11+. Most of the others go on to Tonbridge or Sevenoaks, the less academic to Sutton Valence, King's Rochester or Haileybury. A few to the grammars at 13. Several major scholarships every year, both academic and musical.

Remarks: A very ordered and efficient school, busy and full of energy, set in 21 acres. Has a reputation for being one of the more high achieving schools in the area but parents say that their children are not 'hothoused' and do not feel under pressure. Founded in 1882 by John Stewart Norman and was one of the first prep schools in the country – the Norman family ran the school for nearly 100 years. Moved in 1900 to its present site and renamed The New Beacon.

Divided into three sections: Junior School (3 1/2 -9), Middle School (9-11) and Senior School (age 11-13). House system -known as companies: Drake, Marlborough, Nelson and Wellington – provides opportunities for 'initiative, competition, responsibility and leadership.' The three pillars of the school are academic, sporting and musical achievement with a strong emphasis on self reliance and the development of confidence and self esteem. Older boys carry brief cases as if off to the office.

Light and airy Junior School where the teaching is generally traditional and pays due regard to the requirements of the National Curriculum. Boys take Key Stage tests at age 7 and 11. Provides a very good grounding especially in music and maths. No streaming or setting in Junior School – head philosophically opposed. In the Middle School one set streamed to nurture potential scholars, the other 3 classes are mixed ability. Senior School has a scholarship class plus setting in maths and French for the others. Average class size 16. Modern well-equipped class rooms with digital whiteboards. High expectations and good teaching. Lots of computers and art-filled passages. Cooking very popular. Lots of trips.

Music very strong and a major part of school life. Lots of opportunities to perform in ensembles, jazz band, big band and orchestra. There is also the chapel choir and staff and parents choir. 3 plays a year plus entertainment, 2 large concerts plus many informal ones. Fine theatre with fixed seating.

Major sports: soccer, rugby and cricket. They field enough teams for everyone to play in matches if they want to. County level tennis and table tennis. National level at athletics and swimming. Excellent facilities.

About 10 per cent of children have some sort of learning support, but not referred to as special needs. 3 learning support teachers help in mainstream lessons from the start, and provide formal learning support outside class from about age 7.

Boarding house run by Andrew Snowdon and two matrons (Tuesday to Friday night only) has more the feel of a cosy family home than a boarding school. Only 14 boys live here in great comfort, but the headmaster is very keen to keep the boarding side going.

Parents tend to be local professionals and commuters, and to have high expectations for their children (they get notes home if they are thought to be overworking their children). The Governors are all former parents. Very active Friends of New Beacon who run various social and fundraising events during the year including a ball, murder mystery evening and a quiz.

NEW COLLEGE SCHOOL

2 Savile Road, Oxford, Oxfordshire, OX1 3UA

Tel: 01865 243 657
Fax: 01865 201277
E-mail: jo.asquith@new.ox.ac.uk
Website: www.newcollege.oxon.sch.uk

• Pupils: 155 boys, all day • Ages: 4-13 • C of E • Fees: £1,810 - £2,925. Choristers £1,020 • Independent • Open days: November. Chorister open day in September

Principal: Mrs Penny F Hindle MA (Oxon) PGCE. Previously deputy head, and at the school since 1993. Not the easiest person in the world to deal with, but completely committed to school and boys. Well thought of by parents. She started the pre-prep department in 2001. Governors – the Warden and Fellows of New College.

Entrance: Pre-prep department with entry from age 4. Boys are admitted to lower school at age 7 by fairly lengthy assessment and report. Potential choristers attend voice trials between the ages of 7 and 8. Auditions held on selected days in November, or by special arrangement. Academically (as well as musically) selective. School will consider entry at any age if vacancy arises. Keen to support families relocating to Oxford.

Exit: Magdalen College School, Abingdon, St Edwards (Oxford) are still by far the most popular choices. Sometimes Winchester, Eton, Stowe, Bloxham. Scholarships (academic, music, all-rounder, sport) awarded to about two-thirds of the leavers. OBs = Richard Seal, Ian Partridge, Andrew Lumsden, Howard Goodall (composer – Black Adder, Red Dwarf, etc), Ian Fountain (pianist).

Remarks: The school owes its existence to its foundation as the choir school for New College, of which it still forms an integral part, although choristers now make up only 13 per cent of the prep's pupils. Founded by William of Wykeham (of Winchester College fame, though New College School pre-dates its grander Hampshire cousin by 3 years) in 1379, this is a tiny school in the heart of collegiate Oxford – 'the best-kept secret in Oxford', says Mrs Hindle – and every scrap of space is used. The pre-prep, opened in 2001, has been neatly incorporated: part of the wholesale reorganisation of the school and its site under the present principal.

Mrs Hindle, a brisk, purposeful head, had a lengthy career teaching and as a head in the Sudan and Libya before returning to Oxford. She joined the school in 1993, became acting head in 2000 and principal in 2001. She inherited a quirky, very much arts-based school with an approach characterised by some as lackadaisical and chaotic and by others as relaxed and as offering something more individual than its local competitors. Mrs Hindle set about a vigorous remodelling of school, timetable and curriculum. Saturday morning school – previously an arts-fest – has now disappeared except for senior musical activities. This means a crowded working week – as in other choir schools, chapel practice and music lessons have to fit in to a packed timetable. Great care is given to the welfare of choristers and their demanding lives, under the musical direction of the reputedly formidable Dr Edward Higginbottom, are efficiently patrolled. Here, as in all the best choir schools, choristers lead rich musical lives, including recording with top soloists, regular concerts and tours, in addition to their daily chapel duties. 70-plus recordings to date. There's more to it than just the choir, though – v strong musically for all pupils. Younger boys do class singing, learn percussion and many join junior choir and string groups. Older boys also have concert choir, orchestra and ensembles. 'People hear about the school because its choir is so famous,' said a parent. 'But there's so much the other boys can get involved in. No-one should feel left out.'

The school's clientele is largely academic and musical but parents drive in from a 30 mile radius (which, considering Oxford traffic, requires true commitment) to deposit their sons in this peaceful pocket in the city's centre. There is an air of quiet studiousness.

Don't expect space or smart facilities but in recent times reorganisation has led to better use of compact site. Underused areas (like day room) moved to make way for more library space. Everything tucked into corners; well-equipped IT room used for interactive language work and music technology; one large, multipurpose lab; attractive, wood-lined hall, full of natural light. The school's size makes for a good collaborative atmosphere. Principal stresses importance of fitness, especially when children spend so much time sitting at desks: they use the surprisingly large, recently refurbished playground(with space for non-ball activities) and, for football, hockey, cricket, the New College playing field minutes away. Two afternoons dedicated to games, matches on Saturdays, but parents admit it's not the school's sporting record which attracts them. Lots of activities and trips: chess is an especial strength and pupils keen and successful. Other gentle and popular activities include gardening and cookery. The school makes good use of its Oxford surroundings including the superb Ashmolean museum.

Altogether, strong academically, 'running 1 -11/2 years ahead of National Curriculum,' claims principal, but not for the intellectually idle. 'We do well if a child is prepared to work but we can't work with a child who can't be bothered.' Pre-prep classes are small whereas prep class size averages 21. The top year is divided into a small scholarship group and the rest 'to the benefit of both', asserts principal. Good staff. Not the place for a child with severe SEN though learning support teacher comes in when needed. Despite deserved reputation for musical and academic excellence, school remains small and friendly. At time of going to press, new website www.newcollege.oxon.sch.uk under construction but links to online prospectus.

NEWCASTLE PREPARATORY SCHOOL

6 Eslington Road, Jesmond, Newcastle upon Tyne, Tyne and Wear, NE2 4RH

Tel: 0191 281 1769
Fax: 0191 281 5668
E-mail: enquiries@newcastleprepschool.org.uk

- Pupils: 275 day boys and girls (roughly two thirds boys), plus 30 in nursery • Ages: 5-13, kindergarten 3-4 • Non-denom • Fees: Reception £1,928; years 1 - 3 £2,066, years 4 - 8 £2,200
- Independent

Head: Since 2002, Mrs Margaret Coates (early forties), previously head of infants and juniors at Durham High, before that at RGS Newcastle. Studied English at Westminster College, Oxford. Married with one son in the school. Confident, smart, articulate, obviously loves children; insistent on handing over much responsibility to children for creation of their school world and as a counter to potential over-protectiveness; all within a clear disciplinary framework.

Entrance: At ages 4 and 8; no test but children spend a morning in school and are informally assessed.

Exit: Boys go on at 11 (mostly) and 13 to: Royal Grammar School (where co-education is planned), Dame Allan's, Durham, King's Tynemouth. Girls leave at 11 for Central Newcastle High, Dame Allan's, Newcastle Church High and Westfield.

Remarks: Fairly traditional prep school with nursery attached, long established in city (1885). Firmly entrenched as first choice for parents wanting the two main secondary schools, and successful with it. Three-and-a-half terraced houses in Jesmond near city centre, ingeniously interconnected at various levels, every room crammed with lively work and displays. Cosy feel, inevitably lacks a sense of space, air and greenery; makes up for this by busy sense of purpose. Broad intake, with two parallel classes of 16-20, no streaming or setting. French starts at age 3, and is very well taught, Latin at 10. ICT and library provision in line for improvement. Many opportunities in and out of classroom, including 11-year-olds' philosophy club. Music excellent (professionally run): choirs, orchestra, jazz band, rock group. Provision for learning difficulties. Small playing field and new sports hall on site, otherwise facilities aren't far off, and sport is taken very seriously. Chirpy yellow and dark grey uniform, and cheerful and courteous children.

Parents are as you would expect in a large city: aspirational, many professionals and first time buyers. Lively and supportive Friends' society.

NEWTON PREPARATORY SCHOOL

149 Battersea Park Road, London, SW8 4BX

Tel: 020 7720 4091
Fax: 020 7498 9052
E-mail: HMPA@newtonprep.london.sch.uk
Website: www.newtonprep.co.uk

- Pupils: 292 boys, 283 girls; all day • Ages: 3-13 • Non-denom
- Fees: Nursery (mornings only) £1,750; lower school £3,050; upper school £3,510 • Independent • Open days: October, November. See prospectus for details

Headmaster: Since 1993, Mr Richard Dell MA (fifties). Came late to teaching. Left school at 16, discovered books at 21, attended an adult education college in early 20s, went up to read PPE at St John's, Oxford when he was 27. Former head of Penrhos in North Wales. Approachable, down-to-earth and extremely popular with parents. Teaches philosophy to all children from year 5. Retiring July 2006.

New head will be Mr Nicholas Allen BA PGCE (fifties), head of Arnold House since 1994. Educated at Bedales – 'it taught me that you look at people as individuals'. Read history and archaeology at Exeter and this is where his interests lie. We record him as formal, pin-striped, very concerned for the welfare and reputation of the school. Not beloved by all the boys but generally agreed to be a highly efficient head. 'He might seem a bit like the Demon Headmaster when you first meet him,' said a parent, 'but he's actually very approachable if you have any concerns.'

Entrance: Selective at 3 and 4. All applicants sent to educational psychologist at parents' own expense. Reception year places offered to top IQ scores. Operates a 'sibling policy' – they are admitted if at all sensible. School becoming increasingly popular so average IQ rises each year. From year 1, psychologist's report and in-school trial period assessment. Scholarships available from year 3.

Exit: To Dulwich College, Charterhouse, St Paul's, St Paul's Girls, City of London, Westminster, Trinity, Emanuel, Benenden, Roedean, Heathfield, Wellington College, Francis Holland (both), Alleyn's, JAGS, Latymer Upper and a range of other schools. Success with arts, music, sports and academic scholarships as well as places at 11 and 13.

Remarks: Markets itself as the school for high-ability children. Initial rocky beginning when staff jumped ship en masse to the now-defunct Octagon School in 1994. Everything has now calmed down and the school is flourishing. Large Victorian purpose-built building (high ceilings, long corridors) situated in the no-man's-land between Battersea and Nine Elms, almost opposite Battersea Dogs Home. New additions are light and spacious, including 2 new gyms, state-of-the-art auditorium, art studios and humanities suite.

Emphasis on academics. Maximum class size of 20. French from nursery. Maths setting from year 1, English setting from year 2, specialist teachers from year 4, Latin and philosophy from year 5. Teachers are enthusiastic and some teaching is inspiring. Special resource unit run by SENCO for children of high ability with dyslexia, there is also a High Ability Co-ordinator. Tremendous art. Lots of wonderful brightly coloured papier-mâché figures floating around the school. Good library, generous book allowance. Trying hard with sport; some games on site (football, netball, tennis, cricket, rounders, hockey). Games teachers are an ex-rugby international and an ex-British gymnast.

Wide geographic mix produces larger social mix than other SW London schools. School catchment area stretches into the far reaches of Streatham and beyond. Lots of media types. Attracts first-time buyers. Scholarships available, unusual for a junior school. Children appear happy and keen to learn. A popular school with parents, though some worry that their child has only proven to be above average, not brilliant, and so may suffer in the class as a result.

NORLAND PLACE SCHOOL

162-166 Holland Park Avenue, London, W11 4UH

Tel: 02076 039 103
Fax: 02076 030 648
E-mail: office@norlandplace.com
Website: www.norlandplace.com

• Pupils: 150 girls, 90 boys (to age 8 only) • Ages: 4 - 11 • Non-denom • Fees: £2,771 - £3,497 • Independent

Head: Since 2002, Mr Patrick Mattar LRAM MA PGCE (thirties) who looks ridiculously young. Educated at Solihull School and did his LRAM at the Royal Academy of Music, from whence he joined Norland as director of music. He then spent six years at Wetherby, during which time he did an MA in educational management. Having joined as direc-

tor of music, he rose to become deputy head. A thoughtful head, he was careful in his answers and is obviously enjoying the challenge though he finds the task of finding specialist teachers daunting and 'would rather wait for the right candidate. On one occasion I had to advertise three times for the right person'. Keen that children should leave the place with confidence, independence and self-esteem. Married to Andrea, they have two sons, both at Norland.

Entrance: At four years old – put babies' names down at birth; first come, first served. No tests, but special cases for children of Old Girls and Boys, also siblings ('an amazing number of siblings'). Occasional places available with movement – always worth a try but head has no problems with parents who put their child's name down and then get offered a place elsewhere.

Exit: Mostly to London day schools, academic or otherwise, a good number to the top schools and recently girls have got exhibitions to Wycombe Abbey, scholarships to St Mary's Ascot and Cheltenham Ladies College and a music scholarship to Downe House. Head keen on boarding – 'breadth of opportunity is important'. Boys either to London or trad preps.

Remarks: Founded in 1876, this is a popular Holland Park pre-prep and prep choice. A former head, Mrs Garnsey, is still the owner but has moved to the country and 'keeps in touch regularly'. Most parents live locally – Holland Park, Brook Green – most parents within walking distance; not too many first time buyers. A fairly trad mix.

Good collection of staff – probably not quite enough men around for the 'male role model' (recently appointed male IT co-ordinator has helped redress balance); assistants help out in reception and years one and two, thereafter the teachers are on their own. Thoughtful dyslexia provision, pupils are sussed out early and 'structures are in place to identify and support such pupils' – though the school cannot cope with serious dyslexics who may have to 'go elsewhere' eg Fairley House et al. A dedicated special needs co-ordinator on staff, with visiting experts if necessary. Causes for concern sheet (IEPS) in every class. Good back-up here. (NB extra charge).

Summer babies and winter babies in different groups – two parallel classes; then in year three boys and girls segregate while boys prepare for prep school entrance. Girls charge ahead, same syllabus, different emphasis. No-nonsense approach to teaching and homework. French (only) from four but watch this space. Specialist teachers for English, maths and science in last three years; vague streaming but nothing to write home about. See-through pencil cases and left handed rulers provided. Wow.

God is ecumenical here with a slight lip-service to C of E (and use of local church). Art and music inspirational with masses of orchestras and choirs (head accompanies the chamber choir) – junior and senior choir compulsory for all; ditto orchestras if pupils play at all. School entertains local old folks' home at Christmas and throughout the year – strawberry teas in summer. Instruments hired locally if family does not have one – though there are one or two available in the school itself.

Art all over the walls (kiln in dedicated science lab) and computer-linked – designing cereal boxes the current activity. Massive IT input recently, with all infant classrooms sporting a computer – the tinies are often more street-wise on programmes than their teacher. All staff have laptops, internet-linked in the library.

Three interlinking buildings, tiny doors in-between, classrooms often approached from two different angles – complicated. Good, supervised play area, year 2 have compulsory wellies for walks in nearby St James' Gardens, otherwise a complicated rota of play and work. Meals in house, with vegetarian option. Gym doubles as dining hall. Children can be dropped off at 8.15 am, keen clubs (recorder, violin, IT, cooking and chess, games) after school ends, except on Friday, when estate cars piled high with dogs, au pairs and provisions scoop children up and head off towards the M40 and M3.

NORTH BRIDGE HOUSE JUNIOR SCHOOL

Linked to North Bridge House Senior School in the Senior section

Linked to North Bridge House Nursery School

8 Netherhall Gardens, London, NW3 5RR

Tel: 020 7435 2884
E-mail: junior@northbridgehouseschools.co.uk

• Pupils: boys and girls; all day • Ages: 6-8 • Independent

Remarks: See Senior School.

NORTH LONDON COLLEGIATE SCHOOL JUNIOR SCHOOL

Linked to North London Collegiate School in the Senior section

Canons Drive, Edgware, Middlesex, HA8 7RJ

Tel: 020 8952 1276
Fax: 020 8951 1293
E-mail: office@nlcs.org.uk
Website: www.nlcs.org.uk

• Pupils: 320 girls in the junior and first schools • Ages: 4-11
• Christian foundation, but all faiths welcomed • Fees: £2,832 - £3,339 • Independent • Open days: Two in the autumn term. See website for information

Head: From September 2003, Mrs Jo Newman BEd (Cantab), once head of NLCS First School, who has in the meantime revolutionised Fairseat, Channing's junior school.

Entrance: Group and individual assessments at 3 for entry into the First School at 4 (no reading or writing skills required); maths and English tests for 7+ entry into the Junior School. Highly competitive, with anything up to 10 girls trying for every place.

Exit: Virtually everyone goes through to the senior school. 'There is maybe one girl a year I feel shouldn't go through and she is often the kind who gets anxious and unhappy about falling behind. You shouldn't go through school feeling bad about yourself.'

Remarks: Nice, light building with the advantage of the senior school grounds and sports facilities. Exciting, challenging, creative teaching. Clubs include Latin ('which filled up first'), Mandarin Chinese, knitting and chess. 'I hope we equip them well for the transition to senior life but first of all they must have fun.'

NORTHCOTE LODGE SCHOOL

Linked to Broomwood Hall (Ramsden Road)
Linked to Broomwood Hall (Garrads Road)
Linked to Broomwood Hall School (Nightingale Lane) in the Junior section

26 Bolingbroke Grove, London, SW11 6EL

Tel: 020-8682-8888
Fax: 020-8682-8879
E-mail: northcote@northwoodschools.com
Website: www.northcotelodge.co.uk

• Pupils: 180 boys, all day • Ages: 8-13 • Christian non-denom
• Fees: £3,520 - £3,775 • Independent
• Open days: May and October

Headmaster: Since 1998, Mr Paul Cheeseman BA Dipd'EtFr (mid fifties); used to teach French but got rather bored so turned his hand to teaching maths and Latin instead. Spent 12 years in various boarding schools but then moved to London in 1985 as deputy head of The Hall, Hampstead, for 6 years. After that he ran an educational consultancy. Believes 'children should have a chance to be children' and thinks he's 'pretty old fashioned ... manners, courtesy are important' but doesn't like prissy children, 'it's a tough world out there'. Charming. Some recent parental disquiet.

Entrance: About 50 per cent from Broomwood Hall, whose pupils have an automatic right of entry without any tests or assessments. The rest come from good London pre-preps, Garden House, Eaton House, Redcliffe or the better local state primaries such as Allfarthing or Honeywell. These have a test and interview in November prior to acceptance. There is a current waiting list as the school is rather oversubscribed. It is important that the parents are sympathetic to the ethos of the school.

Exit: Most go on to boarding schools with Marlborough, Eton, Harrow, Wellington and Charterhouse being the current favourites. About twenty per cent go to London day schools – Westminster, Emanuel, Alleyn's, King's Wimbledon, St Paul's. Parents tend to say 'which is the right school for my boy' not 'I want him to go to such and such a school'.

Remarks: Run like a country boarding prep and has the atmosphere of one. Games four days a week – football, hockey, rugby, cricket, tennis. Matches played regularly with plenty of teams so even the D players have a chance. Definitely not for those who hate sport. Everyone does karate for the first two years and the school has earned a justifiably good reputation in the sport. One former pupil has gone on to become keeper of karate at Eton. Another great bonus of the school is the system for laundering PE kit – it stays at school all term – a huge plus for parents, 'no more lost football boots – bliss!' sighs one.

The school day runs from 8.15am to 6.20pm. Tea and prep begin at 4pm and then it's after school clubs between 5.30 and 6.20pm ranging from cookery to computing. Music flourishes with an excellent choir, a strong choral tradition and imaginative musical productions; amazing sets 'bit of an extravagance really but wonderful to look at.' Busy and frenetic art room at the top of the school. New building opened two years ago providing new dining room and kitchen, four classrooms and junior library. Old classrooms converted into a dedicated music school. Visitors to the school praise the boys' easy, pleasant, relaxed manner but, none-the-less, probably not the place for a delicate flower or someone with special needs. Class size is 15 on average and the head promotes classroom-based teaching 'less carting around of work.' Hundred per cent success rate though 'we never cram children' – all get into their preferred schools. Worth considering for parents who live in the area and prefer not to send their boys off to board until thirteen.

NORWICH HIGH SCHOOL FOR GIRLS JUNIOR DEPARTMENT

Stafford House, 93 Newmarket Road, Norwich, Norfolk, NR2 2HU

Tel: 01603 453265
Fax: 01603 259891
E-mail: admissions@nor.gdst.net
Website: www.gdst.net/norwich

• Pupils: 260 girls, all day • Ages: 4-11 • Non-denom • Fees: Junior £1,779; plus lunch • Independent • Open days: October

Head: Mrs J Marchant.

Entrance: Apply to the main school for information on entry. Entrance is via tests and interview.

Exit: Virtually all go on to senior school; parents warned in plenty of time if school doesn't think this would suit their daughter.

Remarks: A branch of the senior school, with own

building, and own head. Designated art and DT rooms, sowing seeds for outstanding design tech in senior school. Shares hall, dining room, pool and sports facilities with seniors. Tumble trail in grounds. Spanish, German and French taught. Setting in maths, IT suite, touch-typing club. Max class size 20-25, in light and airy Stafford House, which still has marble fireplaces, around which pupils enjoy story telling. Wide-eyed and eager girls, keen as mustard. Jolly red shirts under tartan pinafores, and pretty cotton summer frocks.

NOTRE DAME PREPARATORY SCHOOL

Linked to Notre Dame Senior School in the Senior section

Burwood House, Cobham, Surrey, KT11 1HA

Tel: 01932 869 991
Fax: 01932 868 042
E-mail: headmaster@notredame.co.uk
Website: www.notredame.co.uk

• Pupils: 350 girls, all day – plus 50 in the nursery including a few boys • Ages: 2-11 • RC • Fees: Nursery £1,035; reception £2,410; years 1 & 2 £2,500; years 3 to 6 £2,690 • Independent • Open days: June, October, November, and March

Head: Since 2001, Mr David Plummer BEd (forties). Previously principal at Latymer Prep. Married with two daughters, both at the school, his wife runs IT department. A self assured, ambitious Welshman from a boys' school seems an unlikely choice of head in a convent setting, but he's very popular with both parents and pupils.

Entrance: Non selective by assessment (spend a day at school) backed up by report from feeder school. Girls come from the school's own pre-prep, plus around 20 different feeders including St Georges Weybridge, Danesfield Manor, Emberhurst School, Weston Green and local state schools.

Exit: 80-90 per cent move on to senior school. Rumblings amongst some parents that the assumed place at senior school no longer a certainty, and that a gap is forming between the academic standards of year 6 prep school girls and the expected entry level for year 7 senior school girls. Mr P does not accept this criticism and says 'The entrance to senior school is by formal examination, not the non-selective setting of the prep school. Nonetheless standards remain high, with the majority of leavers accept-ing scholarships to Guildford High, Sir William Perkins's, Surbiton High or Tiffin Girls'.

Remarks: Nurturing atmosphere and children seem to settle in well; the head is also keen to mention the 'beautiful grounds'. Enthusiasm for maths, science and IT – following the lead of the senior school. Great IT department, computers used as a teaching aid and pupils taught to touch type in year 5. Girls set for maths in year 3, set again in English and science in years 5 and 6. Sets taught by subject specialist teachers. Average class size 16, although some can get quite a lot bigger – worth checking out when you visit. Lots of new methods of teaching and learning – Yoga classes set up to help girls with emotional needs. Head has taken on five male teachers (he used to be the only one) and he believes the school is now 'not just cosy, but academically exciting with strong pastoral provision.' Girls are prepared well for 11+, but class work is balanced with plenty of extra curricular activities. Music strong and the music room is v. well equipped. There's loads of opportunity for every girl to learn an instrument or sing in a choir, there's even a private room away from the main school housing a drum kit for really noisy practices! Head v. sporty -there is an impressive sports hall- and he encourages all to take part. He's introduced loads of new sports and parents see this as a real plus.

NOTTING HILL AND EALING HIGH SCHOOL JUNIOR SCHOOL

Linked to Notting Hill and Ealing High School in Senior section

26 St Stephen's Road, Ealing, London, W13 8HH

Tel: 020 8799 8484
Fax: 020 8810 9947
E-mail: enquiries@nhehs.gdst.net
Website: www.gdst.net

• Pupils: 270 girls, all day • Non-denom • Fees: £2,383 • Independent

Head: Mrs G Solti.

Entrance: At 5, by assessment involving playing and talking. A few more come in at 7, when class sizes rise from 20 to 22 or 24. Occasional vacancies at other times.

Exit: Nearly all to the senior school.

Remarks: Bright, airy building separated from the senior school by netball courts, pond (well fenced) and its own newly-refurbished playground which includes a wonderful yellow umbrella, murals painted by senior girls and climbing and balancing equipment. Girls who are facing difficulties can have private maths and English tuition at parental expense. Happy girls whose parents value the relaxed atmosphere.

NOTTING HILL PREPARATORY SCHOOL

95 Lancaster Road, London, W11 1QQ

Tel: 020 7221 0727
Fax: 020 7221 0332
E-mail: admin@nottinghillprep.com
Website: www.nottinghillprep.com

• Pupils: 70 boys and girls at present, full capacity will be 260, all day • Ages: 5-13 • Non-denom • Fees: £3,450 • Independent

Head: Since September 2003, Mrs Jane Cameron BEd (early fifties) who ran the Acorn Nursery in Lansdowne Crescent for 25 years. She had long nourished the idea of taking pupils in Notting Hill (though not exclusively) up to CE. Married, with three grown-up children, Jane Cameron is approachable, realistic and respected by parents and pupils alike. She is also persistent and fun. Deputy head, David Gee BEd, was previously director of studies at Hazelwood School in Surrey.

Entrance: Already over-subscribed for tinies – waiting lists to 2010. School more or less filling up from the bottom with Jane Cameron running a twice-yearly ballot for reception and year 1; (anxious to avoid fathers with sleepless post-labour eyes racing in asking 'am I in time?') Siblings' entrance is automatic if places available. Mrs C is still principal of the Acorn – many pupils coming on but not automatic. Applicants now come from a range of nursery schools. Advertising has been word of mouth. Assessment prior to entry for seven-year-olds plus English, maths and a chat with the head. The school aiming to balance boy/girl ratio. Currently some places for older children.

Exit: To date pupils have opted for the London day schools. Parental meetings with headmistress and staff are offered well in advance of final registration dates for senior schools. Jane Cameron and David Gee are updating their knowledge of both the boarding sector and London senior schools.

Remarks: School grew from local demand – with the impetus coming from experienced teachers and local par-

ents – partnership between parents and teachers is particularly strong. Parent profile mimics that of the Acorn – mostly creative, fashionable and successful. NHP is housed in a former school building (just south of the Westway, corner of Lancaster Road and Ladbroke Grove), purpose-built in 1902, but recently used by Camden Charities and now totally revamped with a playground at the front where parents gather and chat. The bleached-blond deputy head stands in his blazer and tie at the security gate to the playground at the beginning of each day. Parents either walk with their children, each wearing a blue rucksack marked with the pink NHP logo, across the busy intersection, or pile 'em out of four by fours.

School opens at 8.20 am and pupils can stay till 4 pm for free, followed by clubs till 5 pm. The school is a warren of large bright rooms but no kitchen on site – organic hot scoff provided by outside caterer in the Youth Centre en face, children can bring their own packed lunch. School gym plus Youth Centre playground (nowhere near as intimidating during the day as it is at night) plus Perkes Field, Westway Sports Centre, Avondale Park and Kensington Leisure Centre available for gym and games though parents of particularly sporty children are worried about the lack of dedicated sports facilities. General sports programme from reception, team games and climbing from year 3 as well as after-school clubs for keen ones.

Dynamic head of music plays the clarinet for the school with his band, The Burning Bush, and then at the Royal Festival Hall – composes a new school song with the children every term. Art and drama from reception, regular plays and performances in assembly give the children performance confidence and weekly certificates and points are awarded to individuals in each house. These merit marks are popular and not restricted to academic skills – witness a little girl knocking on the head's door to make sure that her points were being registered! School divided into four houses (named after local roads). Heads of houses foster a 'buddy' support system. Worry box as well as the anti-bullying policy and procedure, the former has not been put into practice yet.

School follows RML (Ruth Miskin Literacy which is magical – and we mean magical) – based on 44 phonological sounds and graphemes (or Fred and Graeme sounds) – 'my turn, your turn' policy, partner work and small groups. Phenomenal. Class teachers in lower school for literacy and numeracy; max class size 20, no streaming but maths setted from nine. Specialists for those in middle and upper school; science lab now on course, Latin for all at ten, and Greek on offer. Tiny classes at the top end, so really all at scholarship level. School follows nat curriculum. Computers from reception, terrific emphasis on problem solving and reasoning and study skills. Exam technique taught early and regular exams to practise on, ditto practice CEs, good contact between head and senior schools, though fairly steep learning curve for Mrs Cameron. Regular detailed reports home. Homework important and strong parental links – parents and children feel comfortable about 'dropping in on the head unannounced'.

Extensive 'multi-sensory' remedial help on hand from dedicated SENCO. SENCO fronts a 'three-pronged approach' one-to-one, small groups, dual teaching in class plus strategies for teaching staff in particular subjects for particular pupils. Friendly jazzy room in the attics (big enuff to hold small groups) skool can cope with the mild wild (or moderate ADHD) and the dys-strata. (The school prefers 'Specific learning difficulties'). One-to-one support costs extra. Not brill for the physically handicapped but ok if 'they can accommodate their needs'. No wheelchair access above ground level. A statemented pupil in the school part time has a personal mentor who works across borough boundaries. Other LEAs please mark, note and act accordingly. Support, too, for pupils who 'transfer from a different education system'. No EFL.

Non-denom but major Christian and other festivals celebrated, carol service in local church. School uses all that London has to offer, oodles of visits, Nat Hist, Maritime, Museums, V & A, plus residential field trips for older pupils to Calshot activity centre in Hampshire but no lang trips abroad or exchanges as yet. School bedding down nicely, 'feels like a village school' in the centre of Notting Hill. Active parents committee and popular fairs, concerts and fund raising initiatives. Expansion in the air. The unproven record for older children does not seem to deter prospective parents, instead there is a confidence that Mrs Cameron's years of success in shaping confident, happy, creative nursery children will be extended to the older age group and, so far, it is not misplaced.

NOTTINGHAM HIGH JUNIOR SCHOOL

Linked to Nottingham High School in the Senior section

Waverley Mount, Nottingham, Nottinghamshire, NG7 4ED

Tel: 0115 845214
E-mail: juniorinfo@notthigh.rmplc.co.uk
Website: www.nottinghamhigh.co.uk

- Pupils: boys, all day • Ages: 7-11 • Fees: £2,271
- Independent • Open days: Mid November

Head: Since 1987 Mr Phillip Pallant Cert Ed (fifties) married to Jean a primary school teacher, two grown up children – one acting with the RSC in London, the other a keen singer. Used to direct plays and is a member of a local amateur dramatics group. Says school is a place for opportunity, it's about enthusiasm and a positive attitude. Thrives on fact that boys are lively, buoyant and challenging in the right sort of way – 'they ask questions and throw in the one that makes a lesson absolutely brilliant – have a mind that's gone beyond yours.' Boys say he is funny, has a good sense of humour and that he 'gets the message across when we've done wrong but isn't mean.' Head adds governors are gloriously generous and seldom refuse anything requested.

Entrance: Majority by assessment in maths and English at 7 and 8 but some join at 9 and 10. Need aptitude, school selective want children who have a great attitude to life and to working together. Get very bright kids but Joe Soaps too.

Exit: Mainly to senior school. Occasional one or two fail to make the grade so move elsewhere at 11.

Remarks: Modern brick building on 2 floors, separate DT/art room (with kiln), science lab, library, recently improved ICT room, chess room (a big thing here lots of county players, trophy winners and even a few international players) hall doubles for assembly and music. All belong to a house – keep house colour when move to senior school. From y4 do most of lessons outside of form rooms. Lots of earnest faces say learning is fun and teachers are helpful. Learning support display highlights importance of understanding difficulties some children face. Children speak openly about benefit of having extra help and staff interested in how children learn. Bright displays show emphasis given to investigative learning and theme days such as architecture day – want learning to come alive. Reading a big thing – aware of problems with boys and reading so introduced an incentive scheme – not only are boys rediscovering the joy of reading but it's helped identify those with problems and extend the gifted and talented.

Music and sport are passions of the school, giving life and colour. All y3 play a stringed instrument (no additional charge for tuition.) The equivalent of a working day a week is devoted to sport. Plenty on offer: football, fencing, rugby, tennis, swimming etc only downside is that sharing a large site sometimes means having to queue to use facilities. Challenges boys to play with good spirit, play to win but lose with good grace.

Enquiring minds couldn't ask for a better start.

NOTTINGHAM HIGH SCHOOL FOR GIRLS JUNIOR SCHOOL GDST

Linked to Nottingham High School for Girls GDST in the Senior section

9 Arboretum Street, Nottingham, Nottinghamshire, NG1 4JB

Tel: 0115 9500423
Fax: 0115 9240757
E-mail: enquiries@not.gdst.net
Website: www.gdst.net

• Pupils: 300 girls, all day • Ages: 4-11 • Non-denom • Fees: £1,779 • Independent • Open days: November

Head: Since 1997, Mrs Margaret Renshaw BSc PGCE (fifties), educated at Sheffield High School; studied biochemistry at Bristol University. Previously head of Kingsley School (junior department), Leamington Spa. Married with 3 grown-up children. Approachable, kind, has high expectations of behaviour and consideration, enjoys encouraging independence of thought.

Entrance: Majority at 4 and 7, a few places at 9. At 4 letter sent to each child prior to 45-minute interview and additional group assessment. Head says, 'not interested in what they've done academically, looking to see what we can teach a child rather than what she has already been taught'. At 7 children take tests in numeracy and literacy – designed to assess potential not simply what they have been taught. NB – this is a school where things move quickly, and those needing the security of constant instruction and repetition wouldn't be happy here.

Exit: Majority to the senior school. Odd one guided to alternative schools.

Remarks: School split between a modern purpose-built block and converted house. Good facilities: bright classrooms, hall, gym, science room, ICT suite, art room, new multi-activity playground designed this year. Take SATs, all get minimum level 4 with 100 per cent gaining a level 5 in science last year, but don't teach to SATs – see them as just one indicator of pupil performance. Enjoy celebrating excellence, have a special achievers' board. Performing arts important and integrated into curriculum. All take part in at least one annual performance. In recent production of Hiawatha, pupils made own costumes and scenery. 80 per cent of pupils learn an instrument; extra-curricular opportunities include country dancing, gym, steel band and chess – school says they go to matches for the cakes but do have county and national players. Hold regular creative arts weeks where pupils abandon normal lessons and take part in problem-solving activities. Super examples throughout of pupils challenged to think 'outside the box', such as exploration sessions and open homework weeks.

Some help for those with specific learning difficulties – find many dyslexics blossom in y5 when support strategies come to fruition. Say these girls are often hugely intelligent – they just develop in a different way, so it's a disaster to pressure.

A happy, encouraging, child-friendly, environment for able girls.

OLD BUCKENHAM HALL SCHOOL

Brettenham Park, Ipswich, Suffolk, IP7 7PH

Tel: 01449 740 252
Fax: 01449 740 955
E-mail: registrar@obh.co.uk
Website: www.obh.co.uk

• Pupils: 210; 75 girls, 135 boys; majority board (some weekly). Plus attached pre-prep of 55 pupils; and nursery • Ages: 7-13; pre-prep and nursery 2-7 • C of E • Fees: Day: £2,020 (pre-prep) - £4,250. Boarding £5,300, Day £4,250, year 3 (day) £3,475 • Independent • Open days: November and February

Head: Since 1997, Mr Martin Ives BEd (forties). Taught at Papplewick for 12 years where he became head of the lower school. Has spent all his life living and breathing prep schools. Father, David Ives, was head of Holmewood House in Kent and still serves as a prep school governor. Read English at Exeter, where he met wife, Deborah. Two children, both educated at OBH. Deborah is in charge of the non-academic side of the school – matrons, menus, cleaners – and plays a big role in looking after the children in the dormitories.

Entrance: Interview and report from previous school. No entrance exam, no academic selection (although parents suspect this could change as OBH becomes increasingly popular). A few children of overseas Brits and a few foreigners (a couple of Spanish pupils come each year) but most from East Anglia, many parents commuting into London. Ten per cent of children have special educational needs and the school provides good dyslexia support for a limited numbers of pupils. Stopped giving scholarships when it saw that often they were not going to the talented-but-needy, but to the talented-but-quite-comfortably-off-thank-you-very-much. Instead, provides a fund for families experiencing hard times. Pressure on places in the pre-prep so names down early.

Exit: All leave at 13. Majority to nearish schools – Uppingham – the most popular destination by far, Oundle, Framlingham, Felsted , Ipswich, Culford – then at top schools dotted around the country, including Harrow, Winchester, Eton and Radley. Girls throughout the school, heading for trad boarding eg Tudor Hall, Downe House, Benenden, Roedean, St Mary's Ascot.

Remarks: A virtually perfect country prep going from strength to strength. Prospective parents come for a look and rarely bother to search further. Located in nowhereland, Suffolk, and set in a 75-acre park, this is as tranquil and unsullied as England gets. Founded as South Lodge in Lowestoft in 1862, the school moved several times (fires, wars) before settling in 1956 at Brettenham Park, south east of Bury St Edmunds. If coming to visit, treat map provided by OBH as modern art, but do pay close attention to the printed directions if you do not want to end up lost forever among tractors, pheasants and organic chicken farms.

Went co-ed in 1998. Before that, well-heeled locals tended to send boys to OBH and girls to Riddlesworth Hall. Lovely old house, with some splendid showpieces (gilded sitting room where parents come for coffee and wood-panelled hallways), quirky features (prefects have their own staircase up to dormitories) and one or two gloomy corners (the gym/theatre and scattered huts).

Superb girls' boarding house built atop new IT centre. The latter heavily used outside lessons for computer games (provided by school – children cannot bring their own) and emailing home. Lovely art and DT rooms – both open in the evenings. Separate music block with good facilities (most famous OB: Benjamin Britten). Wonderful adventure playground, Rory's Place, named after a pupil who died in a (non-school) skiing accident. 'The Ark' houses the children's pets. In their last year, pupils may bring bicycles to school. Plenty of flat playing fields, hard and Astroturf tennis courts, two squash courts, all-weather netball courts, nine-hole golf course, outdoor pool. Sailing takes place on local lake.

School is expanding. As from 2002, three forms entered at 8 (previously only two) and they will gradually work up through the school, eventually making three forms in all years. More boys than girls, particularly at the top of the school, but this should slowly even out. Head is adamant that girls should stay until 13 and, well, we wish him luck. Pupils start in mixed ability forms but are later streamed. Some setting in individual subjects during last two years. Like most traditional preps, potential scholars can skip a year, spending two years in the top form, consolidating their genius. Less academic pupils also given careful nurturing and do well. Written assessments given every three weeks, plus detailed end of term reports. Usual prep school curriculum including Latin, plus German offered from age 11. Exams twice a year – February and summer. Good reports on academic standards from parents with children now at senior schools.

Brilliant sport, with a real effort (not wholly successful) to draw everyone in (when we were there, a talented girl was playing on the boys' hockey team). School claims that, at any time, 80 per cent of pupils are on a school team – the challenge will be to sustain this as the school expands. Games five times a week plus individual tuition in golf, squash, tennis, sailing, riding and clay pigeon shooting.

No flexi-boarding. Weekly boarding available until age 11. Thereafter, pupils are encouraged to be full boarders. One or two local children continue as day pupils all the way through. Girls housed six to a room in extremely pleasant dorms, with lovely common area. Older girls in rooms of four with ensuite shower room ('like a hotel!'). Boys' rooms also nice. Older pupils take turns sleeping in the younger pupils' dorms, keeping the peace. Exeats every third weekend from 3.30pm Friday until bedtime on Sunday. Day pupils' day ends at 6.15pm on weekdays and 4pm on Saturdays (7 year olds: 5pm/12.10pm). Phasing out form tutors in favour of small tutor groups which meet weekly and can really get to know the children. Politeness and good manners strongly emphasised with good results.

Many homely touches. School operates a catering 'dislikes' list – children may register loathing of a particular dish (eg curry, lemon meringue pie, prunes) excusing them from the ordeal of having it plopped onto their plate. At Christmas, there is a dorm decorating competition and the school organises fireside entertainment with songs, pupils' skits and general hilarity. Organised activities on Sundays include Scottish reeling and discos, archery, horseriding, clay pigeon shooting, plus outings. Lots of evening activities (knitting very popular). Limited tuck – children are allowed to spend the princely sum of 28p in the tuck shop twice a week. Glorious feeling of freedom not found at many other preps – 75 acres, bicycles, adventure playground, unfenced lily pond, cavorting pheasants.

Pre-prep and nursery housed in beautiful new building with main house's charming old walled garden as their play area. The pre-prep practically screams with 'enrichment' – cookery, French, gym, drama, music and movement – all the while producing a very high standard of academic work. Big cheery room for the nursery.

THE OLD MALTHOUSE SCHOOL

Langton Matravers, Swanage, Dorset, BH19 3HB

Tel: 01929 422 302
Fax: 01929 422 154
E-mail: office@oldmalthouseschool.co.uk
Website: www.oldmalthouseschool.co.uk

• Pupils: 105; 75 boys & girls in prep school; 30 board, 45 day; 30 in pre-prep • Ages: 3-13 • C of E • Fees: Boarders £4,535; day £1,305 to £3,435 • Independent

Head: Since 2004, Mr Richard Keeble, educated Douai and Durham (BEd English). Marinaded in good prep schools – Clifton, Farleigh and the Dragon. Ex-Hampshire cricketer. Very games-ey. Teaches English. A man with an open stance who watches the ball onto the bat and plays it straight. Dissection reveals deepdown kindness and downbeat candour. No spin. Not one to rush about with rescue remedies, despite general parlousness. He is doing more than meets the eye, yet will safeguard the spirit of this place at all costs. Parents like that – and they like him. They like his wife, Ruth, too – 'a brilliant asset, such a lovely person.' Two daughters, one at Bryanston, the other at OMH, as the Old Malthouse's aficionados style it.

Entrance: Come one, come all – so long as you pass the entry test designed to deflect deep-seated SENs. The parental mix is eclectic, no doubt about it, inclining to wellie rather than Gucci – OMH has always been a school of choice for the lost manor houses of Dorset. Minibus from Dorchester, Wool, Wareham and Swanage. Plans afoot to ship children in from Poole on the clinkety-clankety Sandbanks ferry. Perhaps the blissfullest way of getting to school this side of heaven.

Exit: There's a nostalgic link with Winchester. Nowadays, anywhere – any of the top trad schools, Wessex ones in particular, of course – Bryanston, Sherborne, Milton Abbey.

Remarks: Here's a school which snootily dropped anchor in a changing market – and almost went down, taking with it some of the best teachers and the nicest children you'll find anywhere. It's a chilling reminder of the vital importance of good governors and OMH's have now got their act together. They've shed a few, renounced nostalgia and drafted in some movers and shakers. High time. All praise to the exceptional bursar, whose wizardry with figures has seen it through – she gives you max value for fees. Can we recommend it in the year in which pupil numbers in the main school have fallen to just 66? Yes we can. Maximum kindness has been re-installed. There's a strong hand on the tiller. Numbers are rising for the first time in years. We see a sprightly bow-wave.

OMH really is a charming little school. It's the first thing you feel. Look about you. The children have an organic, free-range, look about them. The sun shines and the wind blows freshly up from the sea. You sense, not enervated routine, but open-eyed energy. Here's a school whose clothing list in the 1940s required children to pack an axe, the better to chop sticks for camps. Tree climbing has been pruned in forced deference to nanny laws, but knees still grip bark and conkers still conquer. These children retain their axe-memory.

Small school means small scale, so expect nothing grand about OMH. It's terrifically houseproud, though. There's the old house, dining room, library and excellent IT downstairs, dorms atop. It's a lovely old house. Stand in the dining room, full or empty. Feel the vibe. Then you'll understand the place. It doubles as a chapel for assemblies – they pop a cross in the food hatch. Outside, there's a cluster of wooden hut-classrooms. There's the playroom, indestructible, re-varnished every holiday, resounding to the pounding of rollerblades and the hoots of jolly romping. There's a very decent sports-hall-cum-theatre with swanky classrooms on the end of it. And then there are the sports fields (all-weather pitch) and the open air pool and the tennis courts. And in the distance the sea and in the distant distance the Isle of Wight.

Two dedicated staff, one (the SENCO) is an English

whizzo, plus fully trained maths special needs teacher. All children assessed on entry, roughly five per cent of children need some form of help, 'always one to one or small groups', no dual teaching. Small enough school to deal with most problems as they arise.

Small schools are an affair of the heart. What they lack in pediments they make up for in personality. That's the point of them. OMH teachers are as delectably characterful as teachers from way back, and you'd be forgiven for remarking on traits of mild eccentricity. But they're quality. They cut the mustard in the classroom – they bring out the best in the best and they bring on the rest. Their results stand by them. And they do so much. Take Annie Campbell. She's a collectable artist. She teaches it. She plays in the orchestra and conducts the carol service, baton in one hand, fainted chorister in the other, unfazed. There's more where she came from. Old fashioned enthusiasts. They are the school and without them OMH would be nowhere of note, so make sure you meet them. They are the reason the children are so unaffectedly courteous, easy in the company of adults. Learning support rises to three 1:1 rotated lessons a week in English, maths and study skills. All but SENs learn Latin from year 5.

In a little pond, all fishes are big. Small schools can attend to, accommodate and animate individuality. OMH is back on track here. It is freshly co-ed and the girls already look as if they've been there forever. It has modernised its boarding policy to incorporate all the flexi-options from weekly through dinner-party to last minute. The boarding tradition is strong and the head is a boarding man. Vitally needed improvements in quality of kindly care have been carried through, together with an overhaul of the diet. Day pupils are just as welcome in the new market-friendly climate. They can come for breakfast at 7.30, stay for prep, for supper and for the many evening activities – which include carving the local stone – until 8.00pm. Saturday morning school endures forever. Sport is valiantly contested and properly coached. Strong cross-country tradition. Sailing at Swanage.

OMH is a school which inspires passionate loyalty but its reputation locally has suffered in recent years from bad-mouthing by some disgruntled parents. Since the new regime was installed there has been nothing to complain of – indeed, everything to praise. The observable difference, in words of a parent, is that 'the teachers are all smiles again – the gloom has lifted.' Here once more – welcome back! – is a super little school where pupils flourish in their own space.

OLD PALACE SCHOOL OF JOHN WHITGIFT JUNIOR DEPARTMENT

Linked to Old Palace School of John Whitgift in the Senior section

Old Palace Road, Croydon, Surrey, CR0 1AX

Tel: 020 8688 2027
Fax: 02086 805 877
E-mail: info@oldpalace.croydon.sch.uk
Website: www.oldpalace.croydon.sch.uk

• Pupils: girls; all day • Ages: 4-11 • C of E • Fees: Junior Department £2,018 • Independent • Open days: October

Head: Ms Judy Harris.
Remarks: For details, see senior school.

ORCHARD CLOSE

Linked to Sibford School in the Senior section

Sibford Ferris, Banbury, Oxfordshire, OX15 5QL

Tel: 01295 781200
Fax: 01295 781204
E-mail: admissions@sibford.oxon.sch.uk
Website: www.sibford.oxon.sch.uk

• Pupils: 60 boys and girls; all day • Ages: 4-11 • Quaker • Fees: £1,879 - £2,986 • Independent • Open days: Twice a term

Head: Lesley Nell.
Remarks: For details, see senior school: Sibford School, Banbury.

ORWELL PARK SCHOOL

Nacton, Ipswich, Suffolk, IP10 0ER

Tel: 01473 659 225
Fax: 01473 659 822
E-mail: headmaster@orwellpark.co.uk
Website: www.orwellpark.co.uk

• Pupils: 163 boys, 59 girls; 75 full boarders, 81 flexible boarders; junior school 48 boys, 34girls • Ages: Main school 7-13, Junior school 3-7 • Inter-denom • Fees: Weekly boarding £4,915 - £5,465; day £1,505 - £4,260 • Independent

Head: Since 1994, Mr Andrew Auster BA DipEd Hon FLCM FRSA (early fifties), previously head of The Downs School, Colwall and before that director of music at King's School, Gloucester, and then Shrewsbury. Also once head of music for five years at Portslade Community College (a large comprehensive). Keen rugby player (played for English Universities, Durham, Cambridge and Gloucester RFC), accomplished musician. Wife, Liz, greatly involved in school. Three children, two of whom were pupils. Very relaxed and smiles a lot but at the same time gives the impression of being thoroughly in control. Very keen to inculcate strong moral values.

Entrance: By registration and standard assessment tests.

Exit: Impossible to list all the schools nowadays; in fact girls and boys go on to nearly all the major public schools. 2002 saw the highest number of awards and scholarships in the school's history – 19.

Remarks: A lovely place. Glorious setting, the main building is gorgeous late Georgian with Victorian additions and the facilities superb. The place has a warm, happy feel to it but still manages to look business-like and elegant. Visitors and parents can tour the 110 acres in the school's very own working fire engine. Pupils are mainly drawn from East Anglia and many have strong London connections. A nice mixture of politeness, informality and willingness to chat in both boys and girls; they are buzzing with keenness and amazingly tidy. Emphasis on academic standards is strong, with frequent internal assessments, but the head likes to think that the pupils are done slowly in the Aga rather than microwaved and this is certainly borne out by the relaxed atmosphere in the classrooms. Streaming throughout the main school, particularly in the final CE year. Plenty of quiet time – eg every day begins with a twenty-minute reading slot. Maximum class size in the main school is 16, average 12; in the junior school numbers range from 12-16.

Terrifically busy special needs dept with SENCO overseeing a team of five or six. Strong support for those with dyslexia, dyspraxia, dyscalculia, mild Aspergers, ADHD but nothing too serious; must be able to access mainstream. Children with known problems before they come to the school are assessed to see if they can cope and problems for those in school are dealt with as they arise: spelling, handwriting, paired reading, maths and prep support. Study skills for couple of years during run-up to CE. One-to-one, one to two, small groups, dual teaching in class. Around seventy children get some form of help; one lesson each week is free; subsequent lessons cost extra. Outside agencies co-opted if necessary, OTs, SALT and physios.

Plenty of adults around – each class in the junior school has a qualified teacher and an assistant – and there are six gap-year student helpers, including some from eastern Europe – the school has links here through an HMC scheme. Some exciting exchanges and events have come out of this, such as a year's stay by a young Russian concert pianist.

The spirit of competition is far from dead. Children encouraged to take part in verse, public speaking and solo singing competitions and so on and the list of school, regional and national sporting events that boys' and girls' teams compete in (and win) is endless. The head's musical bent is reflected in a breathtaking variety of activities, involving lots of the children, from concerts in St John's, Smith Square, to musicals and celebrity recitals. A concert or lecture every week, with pupils either participating or just attending. Two thirds of the pupils play an instrument, many to grade 5 and above; plenty of orchestras, bands and choirs. Forty music practice rooms in the basement, now equipped with good pianos. Unsurprisingly with all this activity, quite a few music scholarships to public schools every year. Children are kept very busy with a wide variety of activities, from sailing (the school has 10 toppers) to theatre trips, via ten-pin bowling and some very worthy charity fund-raising. The school has its own observatory (manned by a local astronomy group) with a 10-inch refractor telescope and radio station. A very flexible boarding system enables children to choose freely what they want to do. Library and IT room are open at all times and there are no silence rules. Dormitories are airy and bright. Junior school has formal family meals, main school has a cafeteria system. The junior school has expanded hugely lately, largely thanks to an enthusiastic head. They have to manage for the time being in Portakabins but these are beautifully got up, colourful and comfortable. The next major school project is the construction of a full size Astroturf pitch.

OUR LADY OF VICTORIES CATHOLIC PRIMARY SCHOOL

1 Clarendon Drive, London, SW15 1AW

Tel: 02087 887 957
Fax: 02087 850 450
E-mail: admin@ourladyofvictories.wandsworth.sch.uk
Website: www.ourladyofvictories.wandsworth.sch.uk

• Pupils: 190 boys and girls, all day • Ages: 4-11 • RC • State

Head: Since 1990, Mrs Margaret Ryall, previously deputy at Honeywell Junior School in Wandsworth. A no-nonsense head, very proud of her pupils and staff, will not suffer time-wasters. Sceptical of unproven fads in education, happier to fall back on her extensive experience – however not anti-change, just realistic about the constraints of admission, funding and space on her school.

Entrance: No dedicated feeder nursery although there are 19 places for RC at the ecumenical nursery at All Saints School Putney Common. Heavily over-subscribed so first places go to those who live within the Parish of Our Lady of Pity and St Simon Stock and worship there weekly or more often – and have done so for the past three years. Priority given to siblings, then shortest walking distance from school. Admissions are a nightmare for head each year, so criteria and notes are published. Some children (parents working international company placements in London for a couple of years) enter the school near the top when demand is lower, meaning even non-Catholics get a look in.

Exit: To a huge range of independent and state schools, although very rarely in Wandsworth, eg Cardinal Vaughan Memorial School, Gumley House RC Convent School, Lady Margaret, Lady Eleanor Holles School, London Oratory, St Pauls and Tower House School.

Remarks: Founded by Mr Simon Harworth in 1923 and given in charge to the Religious Institute of the Poor Servants of the Mother of God. The Sisters handed the school over to the Diocese of Southwark in 1978. In the web of residential streets to the west of Putney High Street; housed in a Victorian ex-convent and modern extension, where the assembly hall, library and ICT room lie. Two play-grounds, the smallest just for Reception, rostered play times for the rest of the school. The head would love more space and has a potential building in her sights over the road. The present set up is not very good for disabled access, adaptation is being considered.

A happy and colourfully decorated school, renowned for its music – all children learn notation, music making, appraising, singing and recorder. Violin is optional but many play, and other specialist lessons take place at the Wandsworth Centre. There are at least two school productions each year, in the summer and at Christmas, well attended by parents and friends – collections at the end of the production go to charities. The community is really that of the parish – 90 per cent of the parents are regular church goers. On a social level, they meet after service (the school choir sings up there on special occasions or feast days) and the kids play in the garden attached to the church. Father Richard, the parish priest, pops into school twice a month providing an alternative male role model to that of the PE teachers at Putney sports centre and fathers – the teaching staff at OLV is all female.

Food has improved recently, after the Jamie Oliver campaign, and now there is a three way split between lunches cooked on the premises, DIY packed ones and a parent-run enterprise which delivers named bags late morning for signed up kids and teachers. Very low staff mobility, although pupils do move on; when parents need an extra bedroom, Putney property prices make a move out of borough more attractive. A lot of French children (no formal EAL teaching) with parents on short term postings mean that French classes have particularly good role models for accents! Further developments include an exchange day with the French Lycée in Kensington. The SENCO is in 3.5 days a week to provide literacy and numeracy help in small groups – this level of support boosts the bottom tier in each class even if nationwide they would not be deemed to need SEN teaching.

Most children walk to school – if they do it for a month on the trot they get a WOW badge; a pupil at OLV has just designed the new logo to be used to encourage walking nationwide. They walk to the swimming pool or take a coach to the playing fields at Roehampton. Relationships within the school are particularly nice – there is a yellow concerns box on a landing for anonymous complaints, but it has not seen much action since the novelty wore off!

Our Lady of Victories RC Primary School

Clareville Street, London, SW7 5AQ

Tel: 02073 734 491

Fax: 02072 440 591

E-mail: madeline.brading@olov.rbkc.sch.uk

Website: www.ourladyvictories.kensington-chelsea.sch.uk

• Pupils: 210, roughly 50/50 boys/girls; nursery 30 • Ages: 3-11
• RC • State

Head: Since 1995, Mrs Madeline Brading BEd MA (mid fifties). Born in north Wales and educated in Liverpool. She has made many improvements to school life and premises during her ten years at the school. Her MA in Staff Development is evident in the school and in the way she has involved both staff and parents in the school's development. A wizard with her budget – she has managed to make sure her pupils are provided with much more than the average state school offers.

Entrance: From practising Catholic families living in the parishes of Our Lady of Victories, Our Lady of Mount Carmel and Saint Simon Stock, which cover some parts of Earl's Court and Kensington. Attending the nursery does not guarantee you a place at 4. Unsurprisingly, the school is always oversubscribed, although there are occasional vacancies in the older age groups, so if interested, keep telephoning.

Exit: Mainly to the popular and more selective state schools; boys to The London Oratory and Cardinal Vaughan, girls to Lady Margaret and The Sacred Heart; a small percentage going into the independent sector. Scholarships have been won to James Allen, City of London and Tiffin Boys and Girls.

Remarks: One of Kensington & Chelsea's best performing primaries since the start of the league tables; awarded 'School of the Year' for 2000 by The Evening Standard, typically gets almost all to level 4 in the SATs – most to level 5 – impressive considering they have pupils speaking 18 different languages. Very high standards are expected in all areas of the curriculum and behaviour. SEN support, 5 fully statemented children. Extension programme for bright pupils. Lessons well planned and delivered by enthusiastic dedicated staff (mostly long staying) who share a good range of specialist subjects between them. Class sizes are 30 max. Parents come in and help with reading and art, and are provided with training. A dip in 2003/4 due to the retirement of the excellent year 6 teacher. Follows the National Curriculum with lots of added value but what really sets O L of V apart is that French and music are taught to all classes and Latin from 8 years. Interesting and well-stocked children's library, a huge improvement on some fee-paying schools. Very well-equipped music room, all pupils taught music theory and children learn to play the recorder and percussion. Last year the children played at Chelsea Festival with Piers Adams. Also a choir. The school also has an art room, a science room (a rarity in state primaries), computers in all classrooms and a computer suite. The head takes year 6 to Cannes on school journey each year. The music department now has key boards and runs an after school keyboard club because some of the children are so keen. In 2004 the choir took part in the Chelsea music festival working with Harvey Brusk the composer. After-school clubs include ballet, chess, art, Italian and Portuguese. Good sport, with a large gym, a plus as the playground is small. Cricket coach from Middlesex Colts, football coach from Queens Park Rangers. In the summer, Battersea Park for athletics, all classes swim. Children appear happy and well occupied. Discipline is strict, very zero tolerance attitude. We imagine Mrs Brading to be quite alarming when riled! That said, the school really wants to see its pupils doing well and offers them new challenges and opportunities, not just the bare minimum. An active home-school-parish partnership is encouraged, school chaplain visits, daily prayers and school/family masses. Very Catholic maroon and grey uniform. One parent commented, 'ever since my children started here, I have felt so fortunate knowing that they will be well looked after and get a good start to their education with no corners cut. It really is an excellent school.'

PACKWOOD HAUGH SCHOOL

Ruyton XI Towns, Shrewsbury, Shropshire, SY4 1HX

Tel: 01939 260 217
Fax: 01939 262077
E-mail: hm@packwood-haugh.co.uk
Website: www.packwood-haugh.co.uk

- Pupils: 159 boys, 111 girls; Main school – 130 boarders, 98 day; Pre-prep – 42 • Ages: 7-13. Plus small pre-prep department ages 4-7 • C of E • Fees: Day: pre-prep £1,645, year 3 £2,895, prep school £3,825. Boarding: £4,780 • Independent
- Open days: Autumn and spring terms

Head: Since 2000, Mr Nigel Westlake LLB PGCE (forties). Studied law at Exeter, qualified as a solicitor, then taught at Sunningdale until 1990 when he took his PGCE at Exeter. Taught at The Old Malthouse (qv, deputy head, head of English), and Aldro School, Surrey before coming to Packwood as deputy head in 1998. Kind and committed. Teaches English, French and drama; coaches rugby, cricket, squash (strong sporting interests). Unmarried. Active in broadening the clubs and weekend programmes and classroom reorganisation. Says that, 'life at Packwood must be flexible and varied enough to enable each child to flourish', and that each child should leave Packwood 'with a strong sense of Christian values and the courage to stand up for what is right'. Took over from Mr P J F Jordan, who was head from 1988.

Entrance: Short informal assessment – maths and English; academic, sports, music and art scholarships sometimes awarded. Help for the needy. Children from Shropshire, Cheshire, Wales, London and also abroad.

Exit: Boys mainly to Shrewsbury, with good numbers to Eton, Harrow, Malvern, Oundle, Radley, Repton, Rugby and Uppingham and some to Ellesmere (the local school of choice for the less academic). Girls principally to Rugby, Cheltenham Ladies' and Moreton Hall; ones and twos to a wide range of other schools. Good track record of gaining serious awards – academic, music and art – at good schools (average of 16 per year over last 5 years, including top scholarships to Cheltenham Ladies' College, Moreton Hall, Shrewsbury, Rugby and Winchester).

Remarks: Academic but unpressurised, traditional country prep school. Boarding numbers, which had dropped dramatically, back up at record levels. Boys and girls work hard –

they can be found doing so in their free time in small happy groups all round the school – and play hard too. Good learning support department. Careful streaming. High standards but no sense of pressure cooking. Staff very prep-schoolish, several good old hands. Pupils openly nice to each other; a refugee from a London prep commented she couldn't believe how kind and caring and gentle it was, after London.

The outlook is broad – something for everyone to shine at, and a good choice (50 plus) of options and activities, ballroom dancing is the most popular. Sensible use of free time. Keenly sporting – boys and girls do well in wide variety of sports; pupils allocated to 'Sixes' for school competitions. Astroturf pitch floodlit for after-dark games. Covered swimming pool. Music and art much in evidence; IT, art and drama playing their part within other subjects. From September 2003, outstanding new £1 million theatre (seating for 270, air-conditioned, large stage) built for plays , concerts, assemblies, debates, speakers etc. New classroom block from September 2005 to accommodate steady growth in numbers. School mag unusually well written and presented – a must-read.

Original sandstone house and farm buildings encrusted with additions and corridors; the 1960s buildings seriously unhandsome, but recent ones (eg handsome purpose-built boarding house for the girls, run by charming former head of science plus wife) much nicer. Boys' dorms in the main building with a cuddly matron on each landing. Grounds sweep away down the hill – a fine setting. Flourishing pre-prep.

PAPPLEWICK SCHOOL

Ascot, Berkshire, SL5 7LH

Tel: 01344 621 488
Fax: 01344 874 639
E-mail: Saraht@papplewick.org.uk
Website: www.papplewick.org.uk

- Pupils: 200 boys; 125-150 boarders, 75-50 day, boarding compulsory last two years and previous summer term • Ages: 7-13 • C of E • Fees: Boarding £5,925; day £4,550 • Independent
- Open days: None

Head: Since 2004, Mr Tom Bunbury BA PGCE (fortyish), who was previously deputy head and has been at the school since 1993. Educated at Woodcote and Millfield, he read law at Durham and worked for four years before turning to teaching. He first taught at Woodcote before attending Homerton College, Cambridge, and has been both housemaster and head of maths at Papplewick. He is 'thrilled at the chance to lead the staff that had evolved during the ten years that I'd been at Papplewick'; not a weak link in the team, the staff (the previous head) appointed are of a consistently high quality. No immediate staff changes in the pipeline.

Thoughtful, quietly confident and with a laid-back sense of humour, the head runs the school with two deputies, leads a remarkably young common room, and thinks he has 'made the transition' out of the common room into the driving seat. He still teaches four periods a week, 'get to know the little chaps', 'having a lovely time'. He and his wife, Sallie, live on site with three small children, the middle one, Mollie, we met. Two thirds of the staff live on site, and other young abound, though we understand that only Lily's pram goes into the school dining room and baby sitting is high on the boys' list of priorities. Mrs Bunbury holds birthday breakfasts for all chaps (staff sometimes included) whose birthdays fall within the previous week, each birthday boy can bring a friend, and the Bunbury front door was festooned with balloons when we visited. All very jolly and fun.

Entrance: Huge 'bottom entry' at seven, thereafter penny numbers. Waiting lists but suck it and see. First come first served, boys informally screened for setting purposes only and remedial problems often picked up then (in which case they are referred to an 'outside expert' and ed-psyched if need be). One or two from the state sector but most either from the local preps – Upton House and Coworth Park, plus quite a growing number come DAILY from London and school is putting on a daily bus to Chiswick next year (wow); pupils also from Maidenhead, Henley and points north. One or two refugees from Lambrook-Haileybury recently. About 10 per cent ex-pats and ditto foreigners, EFL on hand. Dyslexia and EFL cost extra. Five scholarships – academic, music, art, sport, all-rounder available each year. School fields Eton continuation scholarships on a regular basis. Noticeable change of parent base, an increasing number of first time buyers.

Exit: Streams to Eton, Harrow, Wellington. Stowe, Marlborough, Bradfield, Winchester following and superb record of scholarships in every discipline to top schools.

Remarks: Work is important but fun here, boys happily interacting with staff and visitor alike, male staff called 'sir'. We were treated to a serious display of snake charming in the gruesome biology lab with creepy crawlies, snakes, crickets and fish (and made to wash our hands afterwards). Super boy stuff, with the odd rugby ball which mysteriously moved up and down the classroom staircase throughout

our visit. Old pound weights used as door stops. Class sizes average 13, max 20, three forms from ten up, fiercely setted and streamed, boys move up and down as needed. Top form equals scholarship but Latin for all and Greek for scholars for three years.

Brimful of computers, their keys 'blanked out' until boys 'have passed their test', lessons as much on computers as by trad methods. Interactive white- boards. Artist in residence. Whizzy art everywhere and incredible murals all over the school, 3D fish float up the wall by the swimming pool and mosaics on hand for next installation. Ceramics etc. Good strong music – electric guitars drums, music technology suite (senior stuff this) and strong choral tradition. Head plays the piano. Keen drama, inspired teaching; peculiar combo assembly hall-cum-chapel arrangement which offers endless scope: (serious re-organisation on wish list).

Teams for all for everything, plus under-eight fixtures in trad sports – football as well as rugby. Riding popular and school fields a polo team. 15 acre school site plumb opposite Ascot number 7 car park (which the school are hoping to lease for practice grounds out of season) crammed with boy-inspired activities; chaps scoot madly round the new hard-standing at break time with a great feeling of purposefulness. Latest addition – installation of new indoor pool facility so swimming all year round.

New staff flats in the making, plus even more boarding accommodation. All pupils must board their last two years and this has now been increased to include the previous summer term. Very buzzy boarding, superb junior house parents, regular trail of cocoa and buns. Dorms re-vamped, jolly bunks, pine furniture, absolutely no work allowed upstairs, still the biggest and best dorm in the business, though no longer arranged for round the world. Mobile phones allowed between prep and bed time only. Junior boarders (years 3,4 and 5) now allowed home on Saturdays after matches until Sunday evening, on all but the two 'closed Sundays' per term and day boys allowed the odd taster (and as often as you like odd taster) aka 'the big sleepover'. Day boys stay till 5.15 pm, boarders out post chapel at 11.00am on Sundays till bed time.

Salad option or set meal each day, boys sit in houses, fruit, and biscuits handed out at break time and fruit constantly available. Bullying stamped on at birth – 'it's usually only name calling, but that's enough', top school award basically for niceness. Positive PSHE in operation. Tuck shop two or three times a week and regular 'socials' for oldest boys when they join forces with Heathfield and Downe House. Strong teaching, good ethos, smashing little school with trails of glory on the scholarship field.

The Paragon School

Lyncombe House, Lyncombe Vale, Bath, BA2 4LT

Tel: 01225 310 837
Fax: 01225 427 980
E-mail: office@paragonschool.co.uk
Website: www.paragonschool.co.uk

- Pupils: 135 in junior school (55 girls, 80 boys), 90 in pre-prep (45 girls, 45 boys) • Ages: junior school 7-11, pre-prep 3-7
- Non-denom • Fees: Pre-prep: £1,614, junior: £1,694
- Independent • Open days: Throughout the year

Head: Since 1994, Mr David Martin M Ed (late fifties) whose own schooling 'suffered from frequent family moves'; qualified as a teacher at Bishop Otter College, Sussex. Long- serving state primary headteacher in Somerset prior to joining Paragon; obtained advanced diploma then M Ed from Bristol. Wife, Christine teaches at prep department of Millfield where their three children went to school. Commutes daily from South Somerset to put in long hours at school. Exasperation with 'restrictions imposed by National Curriculum' led to seeking this appointment; prior association with independent schools through Somerset county cricket coaching. Loves sport and encourages it at all levels. Unassuming, involved head who 'has wholehearted respect of pupils' but for whom some parents probably present more of a challenge.

Entrance: Informal assessment for a morning (nursery) or day (pre-prep upwards) plus school report enables school to 'ensure children's needs can be met'.

Exit: Pupils leave for to a variety of senior schools at 11+. Majority in recent years have gone to Prior Park but King Edward's, Bath is an increasingly popular choice. Some go to state schools and a few to other local independents.

Remarks: Lyncombe House is secreted in Bath's most beautiful vale; its seven and a half acre grounds include natural springs and border the defunct railway tunnel which brought erstwhile Somerset and Dorset ('slow and dirty') trains in and out of the city. Lyncombe House School on this site was originally a convent whilst The Paragon was an educational gymnasium started in 1911 at 12, The Paragon in the city centre. The schools amalgamated in 1983, a charitable trust was formed and the facilities were improved. Conservation area restrictions seriously limit further expansion on this site however.

Happy, normal kids sport variations of an unprepossessing uniform. We didn't witness the arrival or collection of children by parents but potential gridlock on the narrow approach roads is apparently avoided by a staggered end to the day; a one-way system operates well through the grounds.

Nursery on ground floor of main building makes a clear initial statement about priorities here. Many children funded under state voucher scheme; creative and highly praised Foundation Stage work continues in reception class, located in converted stables at the bottom of the sloping site. Included an 'Antarctic base camp' when we visited. Phonic approach to word building and lots of practical number work.

Family atmosphere here, with juniors helping when they are free. Lively, busy classrooms throughout pre-prep with a variety of learning schemes alongside thematic approaches. Pre-prep numbers build up slowly so the children have plenty of room and lots of attention, adding new skills including French (from year 2) and ICT which like music and games are taught by specialists.

Preparatory classes are spread between various buildings with specialist areas for ICT, science, languages (Italian as well as French from year 4) and music. Year 2 recorder club, regular performances by chamber choir and full school orchestra – majority learning an instrument. Library is small but well resourced and inviting. Art room feels creative but is cramped in a garret with little space for large scale DT work. Assembly hall at heart of school provides a good space for performances as well as an airy dining area with healthy choices on the menu. Good, level outside play area used alternately by different age groups plus a mini football pitch on the one area of grass. Pupils have to travel to Prior Park College for swimming and games but the arrangement has worked well for both schools. Lots of inter-school matches including Saturday fixtures. All year six pupils are prefects and share responsibilities.

Small, friendly staff with lots of shared sound practice rather than gimmickry. Part-timers, peripatetics and sports coaches give breadth. All pupils get an hour of ICT per week in computer suite using IMacs for creative writing, digital video editing, web site design etc. Plenty of visits including stay in France plus popular theme days when children dress up as Greeks, Romans or Vikings as part of their studies.

School knows its limits with SpLD pupils; friendly atmosphere conducive for bringing on slow starters who will not be made to feel failures here but one parent suggested that more extreme cases are 'bumped off' elsewhere. Site is inappropriate for physically challenged.

Marked improvement in academic standards at Key Stage 2 recently, particularly in maths. Parents like school's 'measured approach'. Head nearing retirement so future direction will be interesting to watch. Only free standing prep school in Bath gives it unique status but has been under marketed to date compared with competitors.

PARKSIDE SCHOOL

The Manor, Stoke D'Abernon, Cobham, Surrey, KT11 3PX

Tel: 01932 862 749
Fax: 01932 860 251
E-mail: enquiries@parkside-school.co.uk
Website: www.parkside-school.co.uk

- Pupils: 300 boys; the nursery has 90 pupils, including girls; all day • Ages: 2-13 • Non-denom • Fees: £2,290 to £3,290 • Independent • Open days: One each term

Head: Since 1999, Mr David Aylward BEd MA FRSA (late forties). Almost an institution, Mr Aylward (affectionately known by everyone as DA) has been involved with the school for 22 years. Down-to-earth, good-humoured and popular, he runs a tight ship without any overt authoritarianism. Educated at Portsmouth Grammar and Kingston University, this is his first headship. He does not give the impression of a tough go-getter, far more of a laid back, relaxed, chap – which must be v refreshing for those Surrey parents more used to heads keen to hothouse their children. Has a genuine fondness for his pupils and does much to ensure a warm and pleasant atmosphere throughout the school. Hands-on approach means he is very visible around the school.

Entrance: Usually boys come via the nursery, but places do come up later. Anyone joining at five or older has an assessment day to check academic ability and to see if they fit with the school. Worth checking for an odd place at unconventional times.

Exit: Popular choices locally include Royal Grammar School Guildford, St John's Leatherhead, Hampton, King's College Wimbledon, Kingston Grammar and Reed's Cobham with boarders going on to Cranleigh and Charterhouse. A handful to other public schools such as Wellington, Winchester, Harrow and Millfield. On average 22 per cent of boys win scholarships – to academic and not so academic senior schools.

Remarks: Happy laid back school providing a good all round education. DA says 'The way we operate is much more low pressure than other schools in the area, but our boys are going on to the same schools as the competition.'

Lovely old building set in bosky Surrey countryside with river frontage. Main house known as the Manor is lovely in a faded grandeur kind of way – dining hall atmospheric ('like something out of Harry Potter' says head) with the beautiful salon providing the location for the twice weekly assemblies. New classroom block known as the Crescent contains well designed airy classrooms. New spacious library is a source of much pride. Plans to extend and upgrade the art room and build a new, second IT suite imminently.

Pupils seem to be a happy bunch and enjoy lessons. 'They're encouraged to have an opinion,' said one mum. Boys are setted from age 9 into three sets. French and Latin are on offer, and every boy will do music, art, PE and DT whether or not they are in the scholarship set. Class sizes on average 16-20. DA comments that 'we're big enough to be flexible with setting and streaming and small enough to be able to value the individual.' Refreshing approach to study – 'I firmly believe setting loads of homework is counter-productive.' This more relaxed style doesn't suit all parents and the head admits that some parents think that the school does not give out enough homework. 'It's not regimented enough for some,' commented a parent. 'Parkside is definitely not a place for pushy parents,' said another.

Excellent approach to SEN – very switched-on team providing across the board support with a wide range of experience. About 20 per cent of boys receive learning support. Head says older boys who join are tested on entry, and the school 'will only take them if we can help them.' Must be able to follow the CE course. One parent described how her son's mild dyslexia was 'picked up on quickly and dealt with.' Another said 'The school's view is that it shouldn't hold you back and that it's not a problem.'

School has an enviable reputation in sport but 'this can be a bit of a drawback' says DA 'as that is all people see.' Super sports facilities with playing fields stretching away as far as the eye can see and top notch indoor pool. Not particularly rugby focused, this is more of a football school which head says is a bit easier and therefore more inclusive. Sport compulsory, but 'there are other things,' says the head if sport is not a boy's favourite past time. Four football teams so there is room for every keen player regardless of talent. Major sporting successes include the national championship for under 11's cricket, and under 11's swimming. Music is strong and important – well over a third of boys learn an instrument, and there is a choir, an orchestra and various ensemble groups. After school clubs include judo, golf, gardening, riding, chess and kayaking which takes place on the river and in the pool.

Strong pastoral care system: there is room for every kind of talent and personality here – each boy is appreciated for his individual character. Boys in their final year wear white shirts so that the younger boys know who to talk to if they want help. Code of conduct drawn up by a committee of pupils encompasses such values as respect, helpfulness, and sharing. Each half term, a pupil from each class is nominated by his peers to be the keeper of the code, embracing the values of the code 'without being a goody-goody' says the head. Discipline has improved as a result of these measures -'the boys feel as if they have ownership of the rules rather than them being imposed.' Zero tolerance for bullying.

A vibrant, happy, atmosphere. Boys polite and well mannered. Parents from a mixture of backgrounds, though most not short of money.

THE PELICAN PRE-PREPARATORY SCHOOL

Linked to Perse Preparatory School (The) in the Junior section
Linked to Perse School (The) in the Senior section

92 Glebe Road, Cambridge, CB1 4TA

Tel: 01223 568 315
Fax: 01223 568 316
E-mail: pelican@perse.co.uk
Website: www.pelicanschool.co.uk

• Pupils: boys and girls • Ages: 3-7 • Independent
• Open days: contact school: usually late Sept/early Oct

Remarks: Parents cannot speak too highly of the Pelican. Deserves its reputation as one of the hardest schools to get into for the best possible reasons. Lovely, affectionate and happy environment.

PEMBRIDGE HALL SCHOOL

18 Pembridge Square, London, W2 4EH

Tel: 02072 290 121
Fax: 02077 921 086
E-mail: contact@pembridgehall.co.uk

• Pupils: 353 girls, all day • Ages: 4-11 • Non-denom
• Fees: £3,667 • Independent

Head: Since 2001, Mrs E Marsden BA (fifties). Was previously head of Combe Bank prep in Kent for ten years and head of two other senior schools for twelve years prior to that. Married with three children. Felt that being head of a London day prep was something she would like to experience. Commutes one hour daily from her home in Kent and uses the time to switch from home to school 'no telephones'. Very focused and very ambitious; fears becoming jaded – 'such a privilege to work with children at this age … you can't afford a bad hair day'. Brings all her past and varied experience (such as opening and running a school in a glorified mud hut when her husband's work took them to Somalia for two years) to this new challenge. Planning sheets cover her study walls – she knows exactly what each teacher is teaching to each class in which room at any time of the day – these are duplicated in the classrooms so that parents share that knowledge. For official school business she dons her black academic gown and looks extremely imposing but has been known to race her girls to the top of the stairs much to the astonishment of the member of staff waiting there to tick them off. A woman of strong views who knows where she wants the school to go and is going to make sure it gets there.

Entrance: Names down at birth (ditto for boys at neighbouring Wetherby's, with whom Mrs Marsden has an excellent relationship sensibly ensuring the schools share the same holiday dates). Otherwise long waiting lists. Girls join at rising 5 with no academic assessment though assessments take place in the first year so parents get an early warning of potential problems and appropriate support/ action can be taken. This is not a school for children with learning difficulties.

Exit: About a third to boarding schools such as Cheltenham, Woldingham, Downe House, Wycombe Abbey; another third to St Paul's and Godolphin and Latymer and the rest to other London day schools with Francis Holland seemingly the current favourite.

Remarks: What was a very good school with an excellent local reputation is set to become a fantastic school. New desks, repainted classrooms, relocations of IT and the brand new library, French from kindergarten ('gone down a storm with parents'), pottery, revitalised after-school clubs, bank of laptops – all these are in the pipeline in order to escape 'the magnolia syndrome ... and create sleek classrooms with a business-like air'. Attracts professionals who live locally, also some French and American nationals; if any parents belong to the great and the good, Mrs Marsden is not prepared to name them – 'to me they are the parents of my pupils, nothing more'. Music, drama, sport, IT – all taught by specialists. Good use made of local facilities such as Kensington leisure centre. Lunch break takes place in the Square gardens. Distinctive red and grey uniform with sweet little pixie hats in winter. Successful, happy, thriving school – gets the good results it deserves.

THE PERSE PREPARATORY SCHOOL

Linked to Pelican Pre-Preparatory School (The) in the Junior section
Linked to Perse School (The) in the Senior section

Trumpington Road, Cambridge, CB2 2EX

Tel: 01223 568 270
Fax: 01223 568 273
E-mail: prep@perse.co.uk
Website: www.perse.co.uk/prep

- Pupils: 175 boys, all day • Ages: 3-11 • Non-denom
- Fees: £3,465 • Independent • Open days: Usually late Sept/early Oct

Entrance: By exam.
Exit: A sure way into the senior school.
Remarks: For details, see senior school.

THE PERSE SCHOOL FOR GIRLS JUNIOR SCHOOL

St Eligius Street, Cambridge, Cambridgeshire, CB2 1HX

Tel: 01223 346140
Fax: 01223 346141
E-mail: office@admin.perse.cambs.sch.uk
Website: www.perse.cambs.sch.uk

- Pupils: 170 girls • Ages: 7-11 • Non-denom • Fees: £2,810 - £3,300 • Independent • Open days: One morning in October

Entrance: By tests at the beginning of the year.
Remarks: Class sizes 15-24. For more details see senior school.

PHOENIX SCHOOL

Linked to University College School Junior School in the Junior section
Linked to University College School in the Senior section

36 College Crescent, London, NW3 5LF

Tel: 02077 224 433
Fax: 020 7722 4601
E-mail: info@ucsphoenix.org.uk
Website: www.ucsphoenix.org.uk

- Pupils: Up to 140 girls and boys • Ages: 3 - 7 • Non-denom
- Independent

Head: Since 2003, Miss Jane Humble, previously head of KS1 at South Hampstead High nearby.
Entrance: At 3 and 4; occasional vacancies higher up. Register a year in advance. Assessments by interview/group play according to age. Priority to siblings and those with a connection to University College School.
Exit: The school is now a member of the UC (University College) Foundation of Schools, and boys are encouraged to sit the entrance exam for transfer to the junior branch at 7+. Girls move on to a range of independent junior schools.
Remarks: Pre-prep for University College School (qv).

THE PILGRIMS SCHOOL

3 The Close, Winchester, Hampshire, SO23 9LT

Tel: 01962 854 189
Fax: 01962 843 610
E-mail: info@pilgrims-school.co.uk
Website: www.pilgrims-school.co.uk

• Pupils: around 200 boys. About 75 full/weekly board, the rest day and day boarding • Ages: 7/8-13 • C of E, but all welcome • Independent

Head: Since 1997, The Reverend Dr Brian A Rees BA BD DipMin PhD (early fifties). A Canadian, left school to go banking, to university (McGill) to study child psychology, computing and religious studies, then a master's degree and doctorate in divinity at St Andrews, Scotland. Trained as a priest in Canada, doctorate in Church history, curacy in Canada, then to Bedford School as chaplain, then housemaster, then head of Bedford Preparatory School, where his charm and enthusiasm for PR wowed potential parents. Soft spoken, clear eyed, still very much a priest. Married to Susan. Has made substantial changes to the fabric of the school (see below). Wants boys to feel glad each morning, and to have a sense of accomplishment each evening. School owned by the Chapter of Winchester Cathedral, and governed by them and Winchester College.

Entrance: Voice auditions for choristers (who sing in the Cathedral) and quiristers (who sing in the Chapel) in November or by individual appointment at other times, aged 7-and-a bit to under 9. One audition for both; parental views on the different musical and life styles (public and committed for Cathedral, private for College), and different vocal requirements (bigger, purer for Cathedral, top line in full for College), usually decide who goes where; no difference in kudos. 'It is expected that successful candidates will stay at the school until 13; the first year is regarded as probationary.' Half boarding fees for these, plus means-tested bursaries if needed. Test at 7 for ordinary mortals, in English, maths, perceptual and verbal reasoning, and 'other such tests and activities as may prove helpful in determining readiness to begin at The Pilgrims' ... a 'fun morning for the candidate'! School looks for all-rounders as much as scholars. Day places oversubscribed. Put name down a couple of years early, at least.

Exit: Up to half to Winchester (40 awards here in nine years). Otherwise hither and yon, to eg Sherborne, Eton, Charterhouse, Canford, Marlborough, – in particular to schools offering music scholarships – 56 of these in the last nine years.

Remarks: Traditional little prep school in the most glorious site in the shadow of Winchester Cathedral (tourists milling round). School (and its previous incarnations) originally for the 22 choristers who sing in the Cathedral. Present incarnation of school founded in 1931 to add 'commoners' and turn what had been a choir school into a 'proper' prep; the 16 quiristers (pronounced kwiristers) who have sung in Winchester College Chapel since 1383, joined the school in 1965.

Music understandably strong – 185 boys learn at least one instrument, and music scholarships are regularly won. Two choirs of its own. 'They emerge', said a mother, 'as little professionals.'

French from year 3, Latin from year 6. Streaming, setting and differentiation within years and subjects. Timetabled computing, satellite French. An impressive staff room – a good many young and female, good teaching; large numbers of Oxbridge graduates teach in the school, head wants teachers to be the best in the UK at their disciplines. Some have used the words 'pressured' and 'overfocused' of the boys (but not in the head's presence unless they wish to provoke a sense-of-humour failure); we don't think that this is any longer the case. Careful not to overcook those not headed for Winchester or Eton. Assessment card filled in for each pupil every three weeks – keeps close tabs on progress, has Ed Psych's reports on many.

School has a bit of a 'split' feeling as choristers go in one direction, quiristers to Dr Christopher Tolley in another, and the rest eg to assembly. School day for day pupils = 8.15am – 4.40pm, then, after first two years, hobbies (known as 'Commoners' Hour – as the singers are singing at this point) till 6.15pm, supper 6.25pm, then prep. Choristers begin at 7.15am – singing with the larks. Maximum class size 18.' Very keen games – 12 sports teams out on the average weekend.

Uniform Lovat-green sweaters, grey trousers. Choristers wear red, quiristers blue. Buildings an interesting squashed hodgepodge from wonderful medieval Pilgrims' Hall, in which pilgrims were thought to rest from their exertions at St Swithun's shrine (now the school hall – note the ancient hammerbeam roof) to impressive new buildings put up to house classrooms, labs, IT etc. Swimming pool 'The Puddle' next to courtyard. New small concert hall, where pupils put on concerts at their own initiative. As you might expect from the head's background, IT, internet, email and music technology all now top notch.

Dormitories in middle of school, no longer spartan – lots of furry animals, the nicest showers we can remember seeing. Twenty-eight also sleep in the 'quiristers' house' that is just down the road. Music rooms and practice cells in what was probably the stables – incredible old oak. River in the grounds – senior boys have fishing rights.

Boys bright-eyed, lively, smart and courteous. A fine school all round.

PINEWOOD SCHOOL

Bourton, nr Shrivenham, Wiltshire, SN6 8HZ

Tel: 01793 782 205
Fax: 01793 783 476
E-mail: office@pinewoodschool.co.uk
Website: www.pinewood.oxon.sch.uk

• Pupils: 200 boys and girls (55/45) of whom 85 board, 30 weekly (but see below) and 55 flexi (but they must commit to particular days throughout the term), rest day. Plus pre-prep and nursery: 115 boys and girls, all day • Ages: 3-13 • C of E • Fees: Nursery: full day from £1,815. Pre-prep: £1,925. Prep: day from £3,245 - £3,690. Full boarding £477; weekly £4,600; flexi-boarding £28 per night; weekend option £45 • Independent

Head: Since 2002, Mr Philip Hoyland BEd (forties) who was educated at The Downs in Malvern (a prep school started by his grandfather, which he owned whilst there as a ten year old!) followed by Cheltenham College. He read English and education at Exeter and teaches the top set English, the little ones French and coaches hockey. Previously housemaster, then a deputy head at The Dragon, he started his teaching career at Ludgrove where he met and married Henrietta (predictably she was under matron at the time). They have three children, two boys and a girl, the younger two currently at Cheltenham, plus a 'black lab and a mad springer spaniel'. Henrietta is head of girls.

Outgoing and charming, do not be fooled by Mr Hoyland's casual red jersey and socks approach. This is a school with firm discipline, but following his Quaker great grandfather George Cadbury's belief, Philip Hoyland is keen 'to allow each child to be an individual'. Mr Hoyland arrived at Pinewood following a period of turmoil, the school was failing, with a distinct lack of confidence and pupils. Governors were considering ditching the boarding side. Bricks and mortar were in place, but love, furniture and children remarkably absent. Place now buzzing (and difficult to get Mr H out of the pre-prep as a profusion of children hung

onto any limb available). Collecting mothers equally insistent on attention in the car park (though fortunately not quite so keen on limbs).

Entrance: More or less ad hoc, though waiting lists at some stages: name down, plus formal academic assessment. 'Subject to there being no obvious academic or behavioural problems a firm offer of a place can be made.' Fair number of children comes up via the nursery and pre-prep, but that having been said, school takes a quantity of Shrivenham children (ie parent doing officer training at JSTC down the road) and early numbers are subject to variation. Occasional refugees from other, larger, nearby prep-schools.

Exit: School lists 36 schools, but primarily Marlborough, Radley, Teddies (St Edwards Oxford), Cheltenham, 'the odd Etonian'. Clifton, St Mary's Calne, Tudor Hall, CLC, Downe House, Heathfield and Dean Close (doing jolly well). Not a hot house. Number of skols – 12 in 2005. School most proud of all- rounder scholarships: two or three a year.

Remarks: Founded in 1875, school moved to this stunning Victorian Cotswold stone house, Rab Butler's cousin's former home, in 1946. A delightful conversion, with vast hall for team teas (important here, and open to all whether their children are in a match or not). Elegant 84 acres of grounds, with terraces and child-proof woods to hide in. Nursery and pre-prep in stable block with fantastic play area for tinies in old walled garden (a space they occasionally share with Basil the goat – visiting the miniature Shetlands at the gate when we saw the school). NB Ask about the Basil factor. Family chapel in grounds can only accommodate four year groups so school uses local Bourton church 'as much as possible' to help the infra-structure of the village; Mr H is on the St. James Church PCC and Chairman of the Almshouses. Selection of staff accommodation available round the back, and a fairly grizzly gym. Cheerful dorms with teddies and posters, boys on top floor, girls the one below.

The Hoylands have jazzed up the fabric of the school and changed the school uniform to blue jerseys with (wash-able and tumble dry-able) tartan skirts for girls (who can wear pink bobbly hairbands if they want, though Mrs H would prefer they stuck to blue!). Splendid, if aseptic modern teaching block attached to main school, with lots of nooks and crannies, each year group cunningly separated, plus classrooms scattered throughout the school. Stunning new computer room, open all hours, with octagonal computer tables. Stately drawing room + widescreen TV (which children can watch in the evenings) doubles as a conference/class room. Library now rehoused in renovated Orangery – lots of new books. Wish list includes a new changing block for games, plus a performing arts complex: the art room itself is a 'bit gaunt'. But strong music, drama and art nonetheless. Pupils grow their own organic veggies, and much fuss is made when they are served at lunch; dining room now does three sittings, and benches augment the original individual carved chairs: family feeding and strict eye kept on diet. Huge number of options on offer on Thursday afternoons. Strong on sport with new Astroturf and extended pitches.

Jolly useful local-ish school: popular down the M4 corridor with collection of London refugees plus Shrivenham, plus Lambourn and the racing crowd. The Wiltshire green wellie brigade, bussing from Marlborough in the mornings. School's reputation is growing apace, the occasional first time buyer. Firm on discipline, but currently no theft, vandalism or bullying (bullying = blow-ups). 'Three strikes and you are out' and yes, they have been sent home 'for a few days'. Mr H keeps an open door, much to the secretaries' chagrin ('but they are learning – the secretaries that is).

This is a school where good manners, courtesy and kindness matter; a 'gentle non-materialistic' environment where '12 year old girls regard going roly-poly down the bank as the height of fun', and it is 'important not to fall out of the trees when you climb them'. Most children in the top year have some form of responsibility, keeper of ducks, keeper of chickens etc., and all wear a different tie (the same tie for all 36, and not, as this editor thought, 36 different ties). Deceptively relaxed attitude to academia and discipline: French from four, Latin from nine, Greek and philosophy for scholars. Year groups up to 36, streamed 'most years', three sets 'for academia'. Recent change-over in staff means new director of studies, new heads of classics and music and a new deputy head winter 2006.

God is 'quietly there', but ecumenical in outlook. Slight hesitation when we asked about dyslexia; Mr Hoyland 'anxious to protect the academic nature of the school' though OK on the sibling front. Highly qualified head of dyslexia, two full time and two part-timers but, surprisingly, no current online link for dyslexic assistance – apparently 'in the pipe line'. Dyslexia lessons = extra charge; ditto EFL, but no need for the latter at the moment. Extra charge too for extras like music, ballet, fencing and polo, though trips during the working week are included.

School operates a fortnightly system, where every other weekend is closed. Those weekends when the school is open are crammed full of activities: caving, trips to the local water world (and day children can join as well – it makes

coach travel cheaper) etc etc. But this is not a school for boarding children without grannies or guardians in the area, though school will step in if need be. School works well, pupils and locals happy. Popular, and growing ever more so, the Hoylands have no intention of expanding beyond the current numbers, they want to know each child individually and to treat them as such.

POLAM HALL JUNIOR SCHOOL

Linked to Polam Hall School in the Senior section

Grange Road, Darlington, County Durham, DL1 5PA

Tel: 01325 463 383
Fax: 01325 383 539
E-mail: information@polamhall.com
Website: www.polamhall.com

- Pupils: girls but with co-ed nursery; boarding from 8+
- Ages: Early Steps 2.5 onwards, Infants 4 - 7, Juniors 8 - 11
- Inter-denominational • Fees: £1,320 - £1,955 • Independent
- Open days: See website

Head: Mrs A P J Foster.
Remarks: For details see senior school.

PORT REGIS PREPARATORY SCHOOL

Motcombe Park, Shaftesbury, Dorset, SP7 9QA

Tel: 01747 852 566
Fax: 01747 854 684
E-mail: office@portregis.com
Website: www.portregis.com

- Pupils: Pupils: 350 boys and girls (57 per cent boys), 265 board, 80 day • Ages: 7-13. Plus pre-prep (around 50 boys and girls ages 3-7) and nursery with 20 children • C of E • Fees: Day £4,795; boarding £6,155 • Independent

Head: Since 1994, Mr Peter Dix MA BA (Natal University) (fifties) who went into the stock exchange when he left Cambridge (Jesus, classics), then decided he would rather have less dosh and more fun, so went to teach at King's, Canterbury – for sixteen years. It is always an interesting transition to move from a senior school – albeit a senior housemastership – to a prep school and, in this case it has worked superbly. His wife, Liz, BA in fashion and textiles, which she teaches at the school, is very much part of the double act. Amused and amazed that we should previously have referred to him as 'a sensitive soul hiding behind a bland exterior' – Mr Dix would have preferred to have been called anything but 'bland'. Keenly aware that people are the most important aspect of school, he strongly believes in teamwork. Hot on emphasising the positive, heaps enthusiastic praise and encouragement on children. Teaches Latin five or six periods a week and would love to teach Greek, 'but the head of classics won't let me'. Two grown-up children.

Reckons he has been 'here long enough to feel the school is ours now' and 'that it is my staff'. When he reckons that staff are underperforming, he suggests they teach something else within the school. 'Getting staff motivated is the real key; if they are happy then they inspire the children'. He has – to date – resisted all approaches from the head-hunting fraternity. Hosts the new prep school heads (IAPS) conference every two years and is pretty well forming up to be the headmaster to whom all the other heads pay heed. Usual credo about wanting children to have really good self-esteem, confidence and self-worth. Keen on pushing the academic side but not at the expense of all-rounders.

Entrance: The comments about academia above notwithstanding, the school maintains it is not 'academically selective'. Name down early, school three times over-subscribed; interview and reports from previous school where appropriate (as much for the parents as for the child). Can come at any time if space available. Can meet the requirements of those with mild to moderate learning difficulties (dyslexia, dyspraxia, dyscalculia, ADHD and Asperger's) who can be catered for within the normal school curriculum and who do not require a specialist school. All new parents are asked to fill in an educational history questionnaire and to supply relevant background information including specialist reports. Stress this isn't part of the selection process merely ensures school does its best for each child.

Exit: Bryanston, Marlborough still the flavour of the month, plus Canford, both Sherbornes (boys' school whizzing up the popularity ladder) plus a whole raft of others – head says that pupils have gone to over 70 different schools during his tenure. Impressive and regular collection of scholarships in every discipline, art, sport, music and academic.

Remarks: Not quite sure where to start here. This is undoubtedly the best-equipped school we have seen in our time with the guide (all ten editions of it); with the exception of the prospectus which is word-light, glossy picture heavy. That aside, the school has had a peripatetic career; founded in London by Dr Praetorius in 1881, then via Folkestone, Broadstairs (where there was an arch commemorating the landing of Charles II in 1683 – hence Port Regis, gateway of the king) Bryanston, Hertfordshire, and back to Wessex, arriving at Motcombe Park in 1947. Slightly younger than the school, the house itself dates from 1894, Victoriana at its most exuberant, with oak panelling and a charming galleried hall – looks like a wasted space, but is much used by all. Pretty hideous really, it was built (all eighty rooms of it) for Baron Stalbridge, younger brother of the first Duke of Westminster.

Fabulous library and grand reception rooms, the fabric is in fantastic condition, as indeed are the 150 acres of grounds, groomed and immaculate: it could be a film set. The adjoining new dining hall is sumptuous, staff (green chairs for staff) and children still sit together; table napkins and 'seriously good food'; fruit available at all times, meals are a civilised experience.

The porch of the main building is filled, rather charmingly, with roller blades; pupils spend their free time merrily roller-blading on the carriage-drive in front of the house (recent traffic management scheme prevents anyone driving straight through). Younger children live in dorms on either side of the main stairway, boys to the right, girls to the left, with older pupils living in imaginatively designed cabin-type dorms, each cabin with a bed, a sink (as the young call them) and clothes and study space. The cabins can be divided but school prefers them not to be. Flexi-boarding on offer at weekends when there is often extra space – no set exeats (there is no space during the week except for the occasional 'taster' sleepover).

Parents a mixed bunch, army, ex-pats plus foreigners, lots from Wessex and a fair number from further east; quantity of first-time buyers. All singing and dancing on the academic front – French from the pre-prep and Latin early, Greek for the top stream, plus German, Spanish, Italian, Mandarin and Hebrew options in the evening – Spanish is a mainstream alternative to French for weaker brethren. (Indeed loads of options in the evening.) Central library recently upgraded and 'book shop' every week so 'children can order what they want and put it down on the bill' – with parents' consent. (What are libraries for? we ask ourselves.) Remedial help on hand for the weaker souls but not too weak, you understand, getting much more academic. EFL for foreigners but not many of them. Computers all over the shop – very modern, flat screen jobs; and timetabled touch-typing. Impressive CDT, art (terrific) and science block which is better equipped than many senior schools we have visited. Children start with techno-lego and move on via electronics to drawing in perspective (they really ought to do their GCSEs in CDT at Port Regis). CAD/CAM, etc, They also have e-mail access for all.

Well-resourced educational support unit (ESU) staffed by eight experienced and qualified teachers trained in dyslexia and other special needs. Additionally, specialist staff provide extra tuition in mathematics, science, French and other modern languages, as well as EAL if needed. All pupils are assessed and any significant discrepancies between tests, or evidence of poor performance, will be investigated further. Likewise any child whom teachers, tutors or parents are concerned about will be given more detailed assessment. School happy to provide names of educational psychologists (EPs) on request; EP recommendations passed on to teachers and tuition arranged. Each pupil has own individual programme, devised in consultation with the head of the ESU and tutor; extra tuition can be requested without formal assessment. Some tuition takes place in small groups, typically of two to four children: curriculum flexes so those with more severe learning difficulties do basic skills instead of French (charged as extra). Extra lessons in certain subjects will be discussed with parents of any pupil who lacks either confidence or educational background or has difficulty with the curriculum.

Music is important here, with all 8-year-olds learning the recorder and 9-year-olds the violin. 344 individual music lessons a week, more than half learn the piano. Serious orchestras and choirs, all taking good advantage of the new music school built the edge of the (tiny) lake with a recital room overlooking the water. Boys can fish in the lake (mainly carp) with permission. Drama for every child every week, with a full-time drama coach. Wind in the Willows the latest offering – the National version, of course.

The facilities are outstanding: shooting range, nine hole golf course (locals can be members and can also use all the other facilities – at no charge for the local school); so are the various gyms one huge sports hall, and one dedicated gym, used as the National Centre for Junior Gymnastics. Plus 25-metre swimming pool, Astroturfs, squash courts, judo and karate hall plus 12 specialist coaches – natty in maroon polo shirts. Masses of county championships. Pets welcome and there is a lot of extra help from parents who run cookery classes and the like (checking up on the choccie content of the school larder before making brownies that afternoon when we visited).

This is school founded on 'core Christian values', they worship at the local church, pastoral care outstanding, 'bullying is any word or act which repeatedly or deliberately sets out to hurt another' and 'breeds on boredom and disaffection and an overtly authoritarian atmosphere'. No chance of that here.

THE PORTSMOUTH GRAMMAR JUNIOR SCHOOL

Linked to Portsmouth Grammar School (The) in the Senior section

High Street, Portsmouth, Hampshire, PO1 2LN

Tel: 023 9236 4219
E-mail: js@pgs.org.uk
Website: www.pgs.org.uk

• Pupils: 512, two thirds boys, all day • Ages: 2-11
• Christian non-denom • Fees: £1,826 - £2,024 • Independent
• Open days: Late September. Open afternoons, November, January, March

Head: Pippa Foster.

Entrance: At 4, children spend a morning playing at the school while the head of the junior school surreptitiously assesses them using test compiled by educational psychologist to identify academic potential – not how many letters junior has learned from his Letterland workbook. 60 places. January entrance tests at 7 (20 places) in maths (no calculators), English and verbal reasoning, plus interview. A few places at 8.

Remarks: Reception to year 4 tucked into one end of senior school grounds. Years 5-6 in cheery separate building outside main school and over two zebra crossings (home to the entire grammar school once upon a time). No grass but unusually pleasant tarmac. Saturday morning sport available to all. Fantastic technology programme for this age, comprising food technology, textiles, Lego and more traditional DT. Badges/lines on jacket awarded for just about everything. Lovely art and science rooms, library, ICT room with interactive whiteboard. Many extra-curricular activities including girls' football. Energetic head of junior school, knows all the children, full of ideas.

PREBENDAL SCHOOL

Chichester, West Sussex, PO19 1RT

Tel: 01243 782 026
Fax: 01243 771 821
E-mail: secretary.prebendal@btconnect.com
Website: www.prebendal.w-sussex.sch.uk

- Pupils: 240: 130 boys (27 boarding), 110 girls (6 boarding)
- Ages: 3-7 Pre-prep; 7-13 prep • C of E • Fees: £760 - £3,012;
- Independent

Head: Since 2005, Mr T R Cannell, of whom promising early reports.

Entrance: By registration, mainly at 3 into the pre-prep, where children are continuously assessed and enter the prep school automatically. Children from outside interviewed and take an assessment test. The main entry to the prep is at 7.

Exit: The majority leaves at 13, a few at 11. Ardingly, Bedales, Bryanston, Cheltenham Ladies' College, Downe House, Eton, Harrow, Milton Abbey, St Swithun's Winchester, Portsmouth Grammar, Lancing, Winchester, to name but a few. Most pupils get into their first-choice school.

Remarks: The Prebendal School is the oldest school in Sussex and probably dates back to the foundation of Chichester Cathedral in the eleventh century, when it would have been a 'song school'. Girls were introduced into the school in 1972, and a pre-prep was added in 1996.

The main school building, the thirteenth century schoolhouse, is a rabbit warren of passages and stairs. The classrooms are not particularly enticing, – a bit of the old-fashioned boarding school feel to it. However, the new Highleigh building has provided new light and airy classrooms for pupils in forms one and two. The school also has an assembly hall, and an art, design & technology room, a modern science laboratory and an ICT room. The atmosphere around the school is friendly and nurturing, all the pupils play together. A friendly and close-knit community, partly because it is a small school, partly because activities are mixed year group. The school gets the best out of its children without undue pressure or anxiety, and they enjoy their work. Class sizes average 16, 20 max. Streaming from year 3 in French and from year 4 in maths, English and Latin. Teaching standards high – most children seem to leave the school about 18 months ahead of their peer group. The many staff changes in the last few years were a

bit unsettling but now there is a good core of young dynamic staff and a few experienced long-standing staff. Special needs teaching has not been a strong point in the past but now all who have contact with the SEN department describe it as outstanding. Over 25 per cent of the school on the SEN register. Mainly the needs are dyslexia, dysphasic spectrum and some Aspergers syndrome. Very qualified staff with varying specialities; all SEN teachers also teach to GCSE. SEN staff are fully supported by the school; good communication – all departments are aware of individuals' needs. Communication with parents, on the other hand, has not been especially good, but is being addressed. Links with the cathedral remain very strong, and although pupils of all faiths are welcomed into the school, during the daily life of the school there is an emphasis on Christianity with school assemblies held every morning and two days a week in the cathedral. Cathedral choristers are all educated at the school, having entered on scholarships. Music is very strong, with two thirds of the pupils learning one or two instruments; but no-one feels left out or pushed into musical activities. Wonderfully dynamic and entertaining new director of music has set everything zinging in all areas. Extra-curricular activities include fencing, model railway, tennis, chess and swimming. Good flexi system of boarding; only the choristers have to board full time, although many higher up the school choose to do so. Meals in a canteen, the children say the food is not very good but there is a choice of hot dinners and also a salad bar. Pre-prep department is on a separate site 5 minutes' walk from the main school. Headmistress is a delightful, kind, switched-on and very approachable lady, leading an enthusiastic staff. Small, cosy, nurturing set up, wonderful for the littles, but the bigger children, especially the boys, do seem to grow out of the space. Own, small, play area, nearby park sometimes used. Links with the main school are good, including joining in the cathedral-based assemblies, the bigger children go swimming and have various other activities in the main school. Some of the prep teachers come down to teach the top year in pre-prep, helping to make the transition a smooth one. The parental buzz is of a happy pleasant atmosphere with perky, chirpy children. One visiting peripatetic teacher, whilst teaching at many schools, still describes this as 'the favourite' due to the pupils being 'well balanced and upbeat'. New head has much to do in this rather special nook and we watch with interest.

PRINGLE, MERCHISTON'S JUNIOR SCHOOL

Linked to Merchiston Castle School in the Senior section

Colinton Road, Edinburgh, EH13 0PU

Tel: 0131 312 2200
E-mail: admissions@merchiston.co.uk
Website: www.merchiston.co.uk

• Pupils: 100 boys • Ages: 8-13 • Non-denom • Independent
• Open days: Information mornings (ie a morning in the life of the school): March, May, October

Head: Mr Peter Hall.
Remarks: See the senior school, Merchiston Castle School, for details.

PURCELL SCHOOL JUNIOR DEPARTMENT

Linked to Purcell School in the Senior section

Aldenham Road, Bushey, Hertfordshire, WD23 2TS

Tel: 01923 331100
Fax: 01923 331166
E-mail: info@purcell-school.org
Website: www.purcell-school.org

• Ages: boys and girls: Two thirds board • Non-denom • Fees: Day £6,434; boarding £8,229 • Independent • Open days: September

Head: Cherry Trotter BEd Hons (University of Lancs) PGCE.
Remarks: For details, see senior school.

QUEEN ELIZABETH GRAMMAR JUNIOR SCHOOL (WAKEFIELD)

Linked to Queen Elizabeth Grammar School (Wakefield) in the Senior section

Northgate, Wakefield, West Yorkshire, WF1 3QY

Tel: 01924 373 821
Fax: 01924 231 604
E-mail: headmaster@qegsjs.org.uk
Website: www.wgsf.org.uk

• Pupils: 265 boys • Ages: 7-11 • Inter-denom • Fees: £1,975 - £2,087 • Independent • Open days: Early October

Head: Mr Moray Bissett from Stirling.
Remarks: See senior school.

QUEEN ELIZABETH'S GRAMMAR JUNIOR SCHOOL

Linked to Queen Elizabeth's Grammar School in the Senior section

West Park Road, Blackburn, Lancashire, BB2 6DF

Tel: 01254 686 300
Fax: 01254 692 314
E-mail: headmaster@qegs.blackburn.sch.uk
Website: www.qegs.blackburn.sch.uk

• Pupils: 150 girls and boys; all day • Ages: 3-11 • Inter-denom on C of E foundations • Fees: £1,449 - £2,567 • Independent
• Open days: October and January

Head: Miss Alison Wharmby.
Remarks: School housed in separate building on main QEGS site (known as Horncliffe) but uses many senior school facilities – dining hall, swimming pool etc. Early Years dept for children aged 4-6 opened in September 2002, subsequently extended to cater for children aged 3-6 from September 2005. Headed by Mrs Kym Marshall, department had only been open for five weeks when we visited but place buzzed with activity.

Queen Mary's Prep School

Linked to Queen Mary's School in the Senior section

Baldersby Park, Topcliffe, Thirsk, North Yorkshire, YO7 3BZ

Tel: 01845 575 000
Fax: 01845 575 001
E-mail: admin@queenmarys.org
Website: www.queenmarys.org

- Pupils: girls, variable boarding arrangements • Ages: 3-11
- C of E (Woodard school) • Fees: Reception £1,620. Pre-prep £1,950. Senior prep day from £2,990; boarding from £4,380
- Independent • Open days: October and April

Remarks: For details see senior school entry.

The Queen's Church of England Primary School

Cumberland Road, Kew, Richmond, Surrey, TW9 3HJ

Tel: 02089 403 580
Fax: 02089 481 796
E-mail: info@queens.richmond.sch.uk
Website: www.queens.richmond.sch.uk

- Pupils: 420 boys and girls • Ages: 4-11 • C of E • State

Head: Since 1996, Mrs Jane Goodlace (early fifties), has a degree in educational psychology, then trained to teach in both primary and secondary schools, gaining her experience in a variety of schools in South West London. Elegant and charming, with masses of enthusiasm for her job and her school, v approachable and pleased to see visitors. 'She runs a tight ship – always knows exactly what's going on', 'I'd have no hesitation in going to see her with a problem', 'the children have great respect for her too' -are some of the comments from pleased parents.

Entrance: Regularly over-subscribed (even though a new non-denominational primary school has opened close by). Siblings get first priority, then one or both parents must be a member of one of the three Kew C of E parishes – applications must be accompanied by a reference from the vicar (word on the ground is that the number of siblings per year effects how important the vicar's reference is), then it depends where you live. No nursery on site so children come from a range of local nurseries including Windham, The Studio, Kew Montessori and The Barn. Worth trying for an odd place further up the school, as there is a mobile business community in the area.

Exit: A jaw-dropping more than 50 per cent of pupils regularly go on to independent schools, and not just any old independent. You are talking tip-top academic schools including The Lady Eleanor Holles, Godolphin and Latymer, St Paul's, Surbiton High, Kingston Grammar, Latymer Upper, Notting Hill and Ealing High, Putney High, Hampton and King's Wimbledon. Even more astounding – there are a few academic and art scholarships each year to these schools (no scholarship board, it's not really politically correct in a state school). Equally impressive each year a handful goes to Tiffin Boys or Girls (top-notch grammar schools in Kingston). Waldegrave Girls Twickenham also attracts five or six each year (but its catchment area regularly changes so it's a risky school to rely on). Christ's C of E School (the most improving state secondary locally) in Richmond is the top choice for the rest.

Remarks: A huge favourite of the well-heeled chattering classes, who want to send their children on to the best senior schools. Yet Queen's feels like a completely normal happy, friendly, state primary school – it is rather scruffy (though in pretty and spacious grounds), doesn't boast exceptional facilities and is in an international area – 20 different second languages are spoken.

The secret of its appeal (to the many who would be willing to pay for primary education if they felt it necessary) is the common desire of the whole school community, particularly the parents, for the children to do well in a wide range of areas, be it academically, in sport, art, computing or socially. Add in the remarkable array of senior schools that the children go on to, and it is no wonder that Queen's is the most talked about school in this area.

The large number of pupils aiming for top notch senior schools does effect the character of the place – one mother described it as her 'free prep school', but this is wide of the mark. There are 30 pupils in most classes and the light homework load differentiates the school from the prep over the road and from any other. In reality, Queen's is a state school where the curriculum is soundly taught by dedicated staff, with lots and lots of parental input – which includes paying out for private tuition to get the children into those sought after senior schools.

The head insists that pupils do not all get extra coaching for entrance exams – doubtless true for the exceptionally bright, but in one year 5, parental chit-chat reckons 80 per cent received private tuition. The head is commendably switched on to her market, and has made it her business to be as up-to-date on the independent sector as the state sector, and offers individual advice interviews to all parents of transferring children (not a normal feature of a primary school). Much praise also for the school staff – despite the class sizes, 'all children seem to get at least some individual attention' said one mum. 'The staff stay a nice long time,' remarked another. 'Of course you get occasional less good teachers,' but most parents are so happy that they even want to join the ranks. It is quite normal for current and past parents to apply for jobs at the school, which Mrs G greatly welcomes.

Mrs G is particularly proud of the thinking skills programme, which she feels improves every part of the curriculum. 'I've no idea what it means in practice', said a parent and a pupil looked blank when asked about it. However, 'There's always been plenty of support for special needs' said a mum. Mrs G is justifiably pleased with 'a wealth of experience in teaching across the autistic spectrum', and groups of children receiving special teaching outside the classroom are in evidence in all parts of the school. At the top of the educational ladder, one mum remarked that 'recently special work for more able children seems to be available from a younger age.' If your child is more middle of the road, they could risk getting a bit lost in an ocean of clever middle-class pupils – 'there hasn't been much special help for my son – he just survives,' was one slight moan – perhaps somewhat harsh.

Music is a strength – how many primary schools can boast two orchestras? Sport is played competitively and with some success. Everyone in the school – staff, children and various parent helpers -are cheerful and busy, with loads of work on display, an enormous world map in the hall, dotted with multi-coloured pins showing the countries of origin of its pupils. A school uniform of school sweat-shirt and grey skirt or trousers is being phased in starting with the younger ones, resulting in the unexpected sight of half the pupils in 'mufti' and half in uniform. This phasing-in was done in consultation with the parents over a long period to achieve maximum consensus, something the head puts great store by. Consensus with the children is also much prized – an enthusiastic school council, discussing matters such as how to deal with bullying resulted in friendship benches in the playground. Discipline doesn't appear to need discussion - there is a foregone conclusion that it is good.

Not a school for parents who just want to sit back and let the school take the strain of educating their little dears. 'There are always loads of parents at curriculum evenings,' one mother said. No doubt, this helps them to monitor whether their children are receiving the rounded education they want. And rounded means parents literally mucking in. There are two orchestras, a choir, recorder groups, drama, song and dance, touch typing, netball, football, basketball, cricket and rugby all going on before and after school, with many parents helping in the classrooms or with outdoor activities during the day. Weekly newsletter to parents is full of information, and with many requests for parental help for various activities, both sporting and charitable. The website is one of the best we have seen – and it appears to be kept up to date.

QUEEN'S COLLEGE JUNIOR SCHOOL

Linked to Queen's College in the Senior section

Trull Rd, Taunton, Somerset, TA1 4QS

Tel: 01823 272990
Fax: 01823 323811
E-mail: junior.head@queenscollege.org.uk
Website: www.queenscollege.org.uk

• Pupils: girls and boys; (16 boarders, 186 day) • Ages: 3-11 • Methodist foundation • Fees: Junior day £1,377 - £3,342 boarding £2,629 - £4,929 • Independent • Open days: A whole college open day in October and 2 further days for junior school

Remarks: Nursery and pre-prep (ages 3-7) use teaching styles that allow everyone to learn in the way that best suits them. This could be visual, auditory or kinesthetic. This multi-sensory approach, proven to enrich their learning, is continued throughout their education at Queens. Pupils move from pre-prep into the junior school having passed an entrance test. Up to two boarding scholarships for juniors. Junior school pupils move up to the senior school without being required to sit a further exam, though parents may wish them to be candidates, with others, for an award at 11.

QUEEN'S COLLEGE PREP SCHOOL

Linked to Queen's College London in the Senior section

59-61 Portland Place, London, W1B 1QP

Tel: 020 7291 0660
Fax: 020 7291 0669
E-mail: queensprep@qcl.org.uk
Website: www.qcps.org.uk

- Pupils: 145 girls; all day • Ages: 3-11 • C of E
- Fees: £3,000 - £3,250 • Independent
- Open days: by appointment throughout the year

Head: From the school's foundation in 2002, Mrs Judith Davies BA, MA (London), Cert Ed, FRSA (fifties). Experienced English teacher, ISI inspector, deputy head of Bromley High from 1991 – 96, then head of Lady Eden's School. Warm, open, competent, deeply involved in every aspect of managing the school. 'She is charming and experienced and very strong at placing girls in the right senior school,' said a parent.

Entrance: Non-selective into the kindergarten, which is more-or-less first come first served. Head interviews all parents individually – 'by the time I've chatted to them I can usually tell if it's going to work out.' Guaranteed places offered two years in advance; those accepting pay a £1,000 deposit. Children after a place in year 1 or 2 come in for a morning to see if they can cope; year 3 entrants upwards sit a formal test. 'Parents are very anxious to get their children into the top quality schools, so we have to go at a fair pace.'

Exit: About a third to boarding schools eg Cheltenham Ladies College (two academic scholarships in 2004), Downe House, St Mary's Ascot, Wycombe Abbey; a third to Queen's College; a third to other London day schools eg Godolphin & Latymer, both Francis Hollands, St Paul's Girls, South Hampstead.

Remarks: A small, traditional girls' prep in a tall, elegant Adam building two blocks from Regent's Park. Shares a board of governors and services with Queens' College but is not a junior department – those wanting to move on to the senior school must sit the North London Consortium exam in the usual way. 'They need to move on to a senior school feeling they've earned their place.'

Good, solid preparation for 11+ and Common Entrance, with specialist teachers in the upper forms. A tutor from the Dyslexic Teaching Centre comes in to help the few girls with dyslexia. The lower classes all have teaching assistants and the higher ones are often taught in half groups. French from kindergarten and Latin in the top two years. 'It's not a hothouse,' said a parent, 'but they do very well.'

Big, bright science lab; ICT room with 12 computers used by half a class at a time. Smallish hall, with pillars and cornices, can squeeze in the whole school for assemblies. New dining room and new gym/hall which can accommodate the whole school quite easily. Dedicated rooms for art, drama, French, music and a handsome new library. Tiny playground with Wendy house, sandpit and netball posts; the younger girls also visit a children's playground in Regent's Park. Physical activity every day includes netball in the park, dance/ballet in the hall and swimming and skating for the older girls, though the difficulties associated with booking and using public facilities have made organised sport one of the weaker areas – school disputes this. Music, however, is a strength, with choirs, orchestra and instrumental groups and teaching in most instruments except brass.

Plenty of competition – the four houses compete at netball, singing, general knowledge and so on; the school also runs poetry recital, singing and handwriting competitions. Everyone enters English Speaking Board exams, and there are lots of concerts, dance and drama performances – 'you need to have plenty of highlights to look forward to'.

Staff members run after-school club for part of each term – art, art history, drama, chess, guitar group and first aid have all been available and there are special clubs for younger girls. Door-to-door school coaches. Trips include ski-ing and a year 5 PGL adventure course, plus numerous visits to London's museums and galleries and further afield.

This is a C of E foundation and, although other faiths are welcomed, assemblies and RE are Christian and all the girls go to church and celebrate Christmas and Easter. The school prides itself on its traditional values, and there is a great emphasis on courtesy and good manners. 'They are very nice, very well-mannered girls and my daughter is extremely happy there,' said a satisfied parent.

Queen's Gate Junior School

Linked to Queen's Gate School in the Senior section

133 Queen's Gate, London, SW7 5LE

Tel: 020 7589 3587
Fax: 020 7584 7691
E-mail: registrar@queensgate.org.uk
Website: www.queensgate.org.uk

- Pupils: 130 girls, all day • Ages: 4-11 • Non-denom
- Fees: £2,900 - £3,050 • Independent • Open days: October

Head: Since 1998, Mrs Nia Webb BA PGCE (fifties) who was educated in Wales, read modern history at Wales University, did her PGCE at King's London and has been at Queens Gate for the last 20 years. She previously taught history to the sixth form. Which is a bit of a transformation. Lovely and cuddly, with a Celtic twinkle in her eye, she is enjoying the challenge of working with a younger group.

Entrance: Put names down early (preference given to grand-daughters/daughters/sisters/nieces of Old Girls). Massively oversubscribed, the school 'looks at everyone'; they visit, a year in advance, 15 at a time, with eight staff on duty for organised 'playtime' and story time. Social skills are important, so it is no use boning little Annie up on her reading practice.

Exit: Massive exodus to senior school, otherwise to other (more academic) London day schools, St Paul's, Godolphin & Latymer, or to boarding schools.

Remarks: Shoe-horned, along with the senior school, into the Queen's Gate School complex, three large converted Victorian mansions imaginatively converted. But they have their own entrance and take up a large part of the ground floor, with older pupils above. Walls bulge with pupils' work, and every available space is used, including press-ganging the entrance hall for reading practice when needed. Free access to the big school facilities, six-year-olds were having music and dance in the surprisingly large music room when we visited, and they use the labs (from eight), libraries, gym and dining room. Best of all worlds really.

One class entry, about 20 per form, with good reading provision, and dual teaching in the class room, with every child, and not just those who need remedial help, getting individual attention so no-one feels too special. Sparky teaching, computers everywhere, touch-typing at eight,

French from four, Latin and some Greek during the last half of the summer term. Much use is made of nearby museums and galleries, 'the girls must realise there is a classroom beyond the school'. Lunchtime clubs for (almost) everything, from stamp collecting to chess, needlework and cookery. Tinies have tiny-sized desks and play areas, and there is a charming little outdoor climbing-framed roof terrace, as well as gardening club for the older ones on a second terrace. Games, and enthusiastic gym, dance and music. Drama important, the recent highly acclaimed Pirates of Penzance was performed in the school hall.

School flowers brought in by class rota. Lots of daily walks in crocodile, holding hands to cross the road, all neat in navy blue Harris tweed coats, with knitted wool hats, blazers and boaters in summer. Good pastoral care, PSHE starts early, with circle time, and popular bonding weeks at 'field study centres' – school a bit sniffy about us calling them adventure parks – from the age of eight. Strong PTA and parental links, many mums and grandmums were here. Day officially 8.40-3.15 (noon on Fridays for tinies), but late waiting until 4.00 or 4.30 is OK in a crisis. Collection time a real bore for passing traffic, double parking all over the shop. Super, not so little, cosy and popular girls' prep school, where all the girls feel cherished, and do surprisingly well.

The Queen's Lower School

Linked to Queen's School (The) in the Senior section

55 Liverpool Road, Chester, Cheshire, CH2 1AW

Tel: 01244 382843
Fax: 01244 381152
Website: www.queens.cheshire.sch.uk

- Pupils: 160 girls; all day • Ages: 4-11 • Non-denom • Fees: lower school £1,755 • Independent • Open days: Oct and Nov

Entrance: Entrance by test, always a waiting list.

Exit: Most move up to seniors.

Remarks: Two Victorian houses with modern extensions in landscaped gardens a mile (busy at peak times) from the senior school. 158 girls, max class size of 24 beavering in studious atmosphere amongst burgeoning creativity on every wall. Dedicated music and PE teachers. Indoor heated pool (shared by seniors), own playing field, supervised play park and friendship garden on site. Christian assemblies. After-school provision until 6pm.

QUERNS WESTONBIRT SCHOOL

Linked to Westonbirt School in the Senior section

Tetbury, Gloucestershire, GL8 8QG

Tel: 01666 881 390
Fax: 01666 881 391
E-mail: querns@westonbirt.gloucs.sch.uk
Website: www.querns.gloucs.sch.uk

• Pupils: 80 boys and girls, all day • Ages: 4-11 • C of E • Fees: £1,705 - £2,350 • Independent

Head: Since 2005, Miss Vanessa James BA PGCE (mid forties). Experienced educator with plans for developing fully fledged co-educational prep school on site adjacent to senior school. Has lots of sports qualifications including rugby football!

Entrance: Unstressful.

Exit: To a wide range of independent and state schools. Regular scholarships to independent schools plus entries to Gloucestershire selective schools. Girls will not have an automatic right of entry to Westonbirt – though 'we would expect any girl who has completed her education at Querns to be of a suitably high standard to meet Westonbirt's entry requirements'.

Remarks: Undergoing rapid development under new head; school moved from Cirencester in 2002 onto Westonbirt campus with access to superb sports and other facilities.

REDLAND HIGH JUNIOR SCHOOL

Linked to Redland High School in the Senior section

1 Grove Park, Redland, Bristol, BS6 6PP

Tel: 0117 924 5796
Fax: 0117 924 1127
Website: www.redland.bristol.sch.uk

• Pupils: girls; all day • Ages: 3-11 • Non-denom • Fees: £1,625- £1,915 • Independent • Open days: October

Head: Since 2003, Mrs Judith Ashill BEd SRN (late thirties) still lives in Caerleon with publican husband, Adrian and young daughters Olivia and Amelia. Went to local comprehensive before training first as a nurse and then as a teacher in Swansea and Newport respectively. Joined Redland High after four years' nursing and built reputation as excellent year 6 teacher before promotion to present post. Modest, shy but committed; parents see her as 'calm' and 'popular with girls'.

Entrance: Non-selective into pre-prep then NFER tests used to monitor progress. Numbers practically double from year 4 as state school parents wake up to advantages of getting daughters into senior school via this route. Early warning given if any girls unlikely to make grade.

Exit: Nearly all pupils proceed to senior school via entry examination at 11+.

Remarks: Safe, caring environment turns out friendly, polite girls; purposeful classroom atmosphere. Grove Park, two linked Victorian houses situated on one of leafier roads in this elegant Bristol suburb, for girls up to year 4. Nearby Redland View houses years 5 and 6 and includes multi-purpose hall used for music and some PE.

Outside play area getting an overdue revamp with new equipment. Inside, plenty of room for movement between activities; girls count well and displays include numerals, patterns and heights measured in handprints. We saw phonic work on letter X and some impressive writing in reception class plus displays from recent 'fairy week'. Key Stage One tests considered unnecessary. Good creative writing in prep – year 4 pupils seen discussing own play scripts; library areas struck as cramped and uninviting; year 6 teacher waxed lyrical whilst dissecting bluebells: girls generally do best at science at Key Stage Two and when they get to senior school.

Own art room with colourful displays; lots of music – orchestra, choir and instrumental lessons. Often outplayed on sports field against tougher local opponents who probably get more practice. Annual stay at outdoor activity centre in Devon includes abseiling and caving. Two male teachers a welcome sight alongside female staff. SENCO works with individuals and follows through to seniors: mainly helping dyslexics. Girls from year 3 upwards use senior school facilities for some specialist subjects and games; all but teenies have lunch there. Successful after school care (popcorn and video on Fridays makes it girls' favourite) and holiday schemes run by a classroom assistant.

Pleasant atmosphere and committed staff; provides good academic grounding and increasingly wide access to better facilities at senior school. Obvious enough way of getting your daughter into Redland High system early if you don't have to save your money for later.

RENDCOMB COLLEGE JUNIOR SCHOOL

Linked to Rendcomb College in the Senior section

Rendcomb, Cirencester, Gloustershire, GL7 7HA

Tel: 01285 832310
Fax: 01285 832 311
E-mail: juniorschool.sec@rendcomb.gloucs.sch.uk
Website: www.rendcombcollege.co.uk

- Pupils: girls and boys; some boarding • Ages: 3-11 • Fees: Nursery £1,500; junior £1,510 - £2,345 • Independent • Open days: Late September, February and early May

Head: Mr Martin Watson.

Entrance: By interview for age 3 for the nursery and ages 4-6, by examination (verbal reasoning test and write a story) plus school reference for ages 7-10.

Exit: 90 per cent to the senior school.

Remarks: For further details see senior school.

RGS THE GRANGE

Linked to Royal Grammar School (Worcester) in Senior section

Grange Lane, Claines, Worcester, Worcestershire, WR3 7NN

Tel: 01905 451 205
E-mail: grange@rgsw.org.uk
Website: www.rgsw.org.uk

- Pupils: 370 girls and boys; all day • Ages: 2-11
- Non-denom • Fees: £1,410 - £2,352 • Independent
- Open days: Prep Oct/Jan; Pre-prep Oct/Jan

Head: Mr Richard Hunt, previously head of the prep division of the senior school.

Entrance: Interview and assessment as appropriate to the age of the child. For example, entry to year one would involve a morning spent working in class with some reading and sums. Into year five there would be a more formal entrance examination with standardised tests in mathematics and English plus both verbal and non-verbal reasoning questionnaires.

Remarks: For further details see senior school, Royal Grammar School (Worcester).

RICHMOND HOUSE SCHOOL

170 Otley Road, Far Headingley, Leeds, West Yorkshire, LS16 5LG

Tel: 01132 752 670
Fax: 01132 304 868
E-mail: milneleeds@tiscali.co.uk
Website: www.rhschool.org

- Pupils: 285 boys and girls; day • Ages: 3-11 • Non-denominational though with a strong Christian base • Fees: £1,104 (nursery, half days) - £1,732 • Independent

Head: Since 1997, Mr Gordon Milne BEd CertEd originally from Aberdeen, married with three children. Studied history at Leicester; keen racquet sports player; wife teaches PE in the school. Pleasant and welcoming head who clearly knows his school and children extremely well; very hands-on approach, is accessible to parents and believes that, in his school, 'all children find their niche in something'. Communicates with parents via weekly newsletter.

Broadened the school's curriculum by encouraging extra involvement in music, art, design technology and sport and expanded extra-curricular choice (adding judo, chess, music, badminton, basketball, IT, Spanish amongst others) – without prejudicing academic standards.

Entrance: 36 children enter nursery each September; then two classes of 18 per year group throughout. Children assessed (albeit informally at 3) before being offered a place, usually in January prior to joining following September. Over-subscribed; most children remain in the school from the age of three, very few additional places available later.

Exit: Pupils tend to remain within private sector from 11, many aiming for scholarships at local favoured schools: Ashville, Harrogate Ladies', Bradford Grammar, Leeds Grammar, Leeds Girls' High, Fulneck, Gateways, Woodhouse Grove.

Remarks: Opened on present site in 1935, housed in large stone Victorian villa, typical of area. Became charitable trust in 1979, further buildings and land added since. Main building houses core classrooms, some a little small but all imaginatively decorated, children's work in evidence and impressive murals distract from steep staircases. Feels small, yet is tardis-like as additional accommodation materialises around site. In main building everything appears rather under-sized (child-sized?) note the diminutive doorways between classrooms – does nothing to help generate feeling of spaciousness but does create safe and comforting environment for pupils who all appear happy and focused.

Children busy with excellent range of extra-curricular activities, choir and orchestra flourishing; pupils form basis of school council and organise charity events. Reward/buddy schemes are part of a proactive approach to pastoral care; problems are dealt with promptly; 'buddy stops', like miniature bus stops, feature prominently in the playground as a safety zone/stop-off point for children short of a friend; it was very gratifying to see children hovering timidly near them at playtime being quickly picked up and drawn into other children's games.

Attractive sports pavilion, 10 acres of sports grounds, tennis, and this has to be one of the very few schools with its own crown bowling green (a Yorkshire marketing niche?); proximity of Carnegie College provides access to additional sporting facilities.

Many restrictions on site as this is a residential area on busy main route into Leeds; some parents may find the lack of a car park problematic. However others (predominantly Leeds doctors, lawyers, financiers, business people, college/university staff) find both location and before and after

school care convenient. Parents demand (and get) high academic standards and, although head baulks at term 'hothouse', undoubtedly a highly competitive and industrious environment, with high expectations; excellent results in end of key stage tests (SATs). No scholarships available, uncommon minimal differential between fee levels at various ages – a consequence of this is that it discourages parents from 'using' the nursery without the intention of continuing through school. Occasional short-term bursaries to support existing parents suffering from hard times.

Enduring reputation of enabling children to get into good schools at 11 and in the face of stiff local competition within private sector; this reputation is of vital importance to whole school community. Many choose this school with the next stage very much in mind; it is a means to an end and it delivers.

RIDDLESWORTH HALL PREPARATORY SCHOOL

Diss, Norfolk, IP22 2TA

Tel: 01953 681 246
Fax: 01953 688 124
E-mail: enquiries@riddlesworthhall.com
Website: www.riddlesworthhall.com

• Pupils: Nursery, prep/pre-prep – largely girls, but boys now progressing from the nursery and pre-prep ; boarding from 7yrs (half of over-7s board) • Ages: main school 4-13; nursery 2-4 • C of E • Fees: Day, £1,950 - £2,835 Boarding £4,620 - £4,935 • Independent • Open days: Autumn and spring terms

Head: Since 2000, Mr Colin Campbell BA (fifties), educated at King George V School and read philosophy at Sussex. Previously deputy head of Belmont School in Surrey where he helped build up decimated school numbers from 90 to 200 pupils. Kind, warm, dedicated and pleasantly dreamy. Enjoys mountaineering and sailing and is introducing outdoor pursuits like scuba diving, sailing and mountain biking to the school. Wonderfully energetic wife, Julia, is head of early years department and also takes charge of special needs. She is full of fun and drive, clearly an equal partner in the Riddlesworth enterprise. Two daughters – one at St Andrew's University, the other at nearby Culford School.

Entrance: By assessment and interview. Most come from East Anglia but a school bus brings girls up from London each Sunday evening and returns them on Friday night (also daily buses to Diss and Bury). Academic scholarships for boys up to age 8 and girls up to 12 (maximum of 50 per cent of fees) and small music and art scholarships.

Exit: Most at 13, some at 11, to a wide range of jolly nice schools. Over the last three years, girls have gone on to Benenden, Gresham's, Millfield, Oundle, St George's Ascot, Badminton, Heathfield, St Mary's Wantage, Culford, Gordonstoun and Tudor Hall, to name a few. Regular schols too.

Remarks: Riddlesworth Hall made headlines in 2000 when, owing to falling numbers, the Allied Schools decided to close it. White knights, Colonel Keith Boulter (owner and head of the co-ed prep Barnardiston Hall, Haverhill) and the Reverend David Blackledge, rode in at the final hour, but not before many more parents had yanked their kids out. The new head is rebuilding the school from the bottom up (reception class is full, and numbers generally are rising strongly). He is also improving special needs provision, running more short courses for foreign youngsters (he hopes these will be reciprocal), increasing parent involvement and admitting more boys into nursery and pre-prep. An International Study Centre is being developed in the former nursery – now relocated to the main school.

Main school is housed in beautiful Georgian-style listed stately home, set in rolling lawns deep in farming country. Facilities are good for a school this size – luxuriously warm indoor swimming pool, three tennis courts, an adventure playground, hutches for pupils' pets – 'Pets' Corner' – and a wonderful feel of fresh air and open skies. Rosy cheeked, unspoilt girls walk arm in arm, and 13 year olds still happily play with their guinea pigs. Inside, besides classrooms and pretty dormitories, lurks a good library, a decent science lab, Harry Potteresque stairways leading to mysterious rooms and passages, lots of music practice rooms, a small games room with pool table and a spectacular common room (newly revamped with glorious stuffed sofas so it looks like what it is – the sitting room of a great country house). School grub dished up in quaintly old-fashioned basement dining room (though parents speak of international days when ethnic cuisine emerges from those institutional kitchens). Academically, the school is very, very sound, shattering a decades-old reputation as a school for nice but thick country lasses. The small class sizes, dedicated teachers and individual attention have produced superb exam results (four scholarships won by recent leavers). Girls who might just drift along at other schools become high-flyers here.

Lots of games – these are competitive girls and, despite the low numbers, go on winning. Nor have low numbers hurt the range of extra-curricular options: dance, speech and drama, swimming, gym, tennis, martial arts, archery, riding four times a week and a highly successful equestrian team -pupils stable their own ponies at school - singing and tuition in a range of musical instruments are all available. 'Nearly every' girl is learning a musical instrument, says the head. The school offers brilliant flexibility – any eccentricity or interest can be accommodated and day children can stay from pre-breakfast to 8.30pm or even overnight. The school's 'family feel', individual attention and full weekend programme for boarders (including 'boarders' Friday night outings') would also suit ex-pat families (there are special scholarships for military and diplomatic offspring). 'All the day pupils are dying to be boarders,' said one local mother.

Ages 4-7 housed in pretty former stable block opening onto own playground next to main building. Reading is brilliantly taught using the Phonographix method. Everyone can read by the end of reception year (this is a school where it is common to find 3-year-olds reading).

The school is heading in a promising direction and is well worth a look. Five years from now we can foresee it being a happy, co-ed, multinational school for 2-11 year olds. One of our favourite Riddlesworth Hall rules is, 'Be happy and cheerful'. The children seem to have no trouble following it.

RIPON CATHEDRAL CHOIR SCHOOL

Whitcliffe Lane, Ripon, North Yorkshire, HG4 2LA

Tel: 01765 602 134
Fax: 01765 608 760
E-mail: admin@choirschool.demon.co.uk
Website: www.choirschool.demon.co.uk

- Pupils: 50 girls, 60 boys; 25 board 85 day • Ages: 3-11
- C of E • Fees: Full boarders: £3,770; weekly boarders £3,479; day from £1,742 to £2,782 • Independent

Head: Since 2001, Mr Richard Pepys BA Cert Ed (fifties). Educated at Winchester, has a degree in science and history from the OU. Spent four years at Mandeville County secondary modern, Aylesbury and 23 years at Highfield School, Liphook where he was latterly deputy head. Married to Jane who looks after catering, housekeeping and health of pupils. Three children, youngest at Cheltenham Ladies' College. Contracted 'till 2012. Enjoys, cooking going to the pub, trips to France, and laments the passing of his motor biking days. A Christian who makes a conscious effort to live by Christian values but doesn't want to stuff Christianity down the children's throats. Says he values links with the Cathedral and wants children to leave having had a wonderful time and regarding the school with affection.

Entrance: By assessment and parental interview. Not a school just for choristers or musicians, those without a musical bent still enjoy their time here in part because of the strong emphasis on sport. Not a soft option for male choristers who are selected through voice trials, receive a 50 per cent fees remission but must become full boarders working an extended school year (including Easter and Christmas) to fulfil Cathedral service requirements. One girl chorister is a full boarder, but can't cater for non-chorister full boarders. All others choose from weekly, occasional boarding or day options.

Exit: Roughly 40 per cent leave at 11 plus, the rest at 13 plus. Have considerable musical success in scholarships to senior schools every year. Popular leaver destinations include: Uppingham, Winchester, Ripon Grammar School, Sedbergh, Queen Margaret's and St Peters.

Remarks: Usual facilities: large hall for assembly, gym and musical productions (of which there are many), with separate dining hall doubling for exams and similar; classrooms, housed in a wooden block resembling stables, err on the small side with only a canopied walkway between, so expect to get wet on rainy days. School hope for a rebuild (currently seeking planning permission).

Subjects taught discretely from year 4, with music school and specialist rooms for ICT, CDT, art, humanities, English and the ever popular science. School say ISI recommended non-fiction books be housed in specialist classrooms with fiction in the English room which doubles as the only lending library. Study all usual subjects plus French, Latin, music and dance. Smallish classes, average 12. All take SATs but school refused to let us see results so do ask when you visit, said their value added was fine but again didn't produce any evidence to support that so we had to take their word for it (school add it's IAPS policy not to disclose SATs info to publications).

Staff run catch-up clinics for those needing extra support and there's one to one help available for mild dyslexia or dyspraxia (extra charge). More severe cases are advised to look elsewhere. Trying to introduce individual education plans for all children to indicate strengths and weaknesses to be addressed, keen to ensure very able are stretched too. No Saturday school though pupils expected to turn up for any school-related events. Choristers have a busy weekend programme with limited free time. School recognise demands and responsibilities placed on choristers and the need to keep a careful eye on them. Say full boarding tends to suit those children who are happiest at home as those with problems at home tend to fret more in school too. Choristers spend a term or so on probation – doesn't always work out.

Fantastic musical productions; 90 per cent of children play at least one instrument over 60 per cent two, with a handful playing three to grade 7 or 8 standard. Masses of orchestras, bands, and choirs. We saw impressive rehearsals with pupils not only singing and playing but accompanying too. Lots of successes in regional and national music competitions. Half of all pupils involved with LAMBDA speech and drama as well as school productions. Well-endowed with sports fields plus adventure playground, aerial runway and separate play area for very youngest. Sport popular, plenty on offer all usual, plus tennis, golf, athletics, dance etc. Play competitively and with success against other preps and schools in locality. Extracurricular clubs include chess, sewing, cookery, ICT and art.

Dorms functional with boys in better nick than girls. Boys are housed in big, light, airy rooms with great views, girls have somewhat shabby attic rooms, clean but with only a sky light, not quite Jane Eyre but... Fortunately proposed rebuild includes boarding. Brand new common room on ground floor provides a pleasant area for boys and girls to relax, watch TV, play games and will eventually have facilities for tea and toast.

Undoubtedly children enjoy their time here and most get the opportunity to shine at something with some, such as the Ripon Young Musician of the Year, positively glowing. Pupils say they have great relationships with teachers and that everyone knows everybody, a real family feel. Not the place for those who don't like being with others and joining in.

You don't have to sing for your supper to come here, but those who do do so in fine voice and good spirit.

ROBERT GORDON'S COLLEGE JUNIOR SCHOOL

Linked to Robert Gordon's College in the Senior section

Schoolhill, Aberdeen, AB10 1FE

Tel: 01224 646758
Fax: 01224 630301
E-mail: d.hardie@rgc.aberdeen.sch.uk
Website: www.rgc.aberdeen.sch.uk

- Ages: boys and girls: all day • Inter-denom
- Fees: Junior £1,460 - £1,990 • Independent
- Open days: November and May

Head: Mrs Mollie Mennie.
Remarks: For details, see senior school.

THE ROCHE SCHOOL

11 Frogmore, Wandsworth, London, SW18 1HW

Tel: 020 8877 0823
Fax: 020 8875 1156
E-mail: office@therocheschool.co.uk
Website: www.therocheschool.co.uk

- Pupils: 205 boys and girls, all day • Ages: 3-11 • Fees: Ages 4-6 £2,560. Ages 7-10 £2,830 • Independent • Open days: November, January, February, March

Principal: Since 1988 Dr James Roche BSc PhD (sixties). Educated at St Paul's, read physics at Bristol and has a PhD in general relativity from Manchester. Taught for 2 years in a London state school then spent 19 years teaching A level physics at Collingham College, Kensington, where his wife Carmen taught languages. She founded the school in 1988. He teaches maths, history and RE. They have two daughters. We caught him on a bad day recovering from flu and looking quite grey (think Jon Pertwee as Dr Who) but he was a joy to chat to. Very bright, has a quote for everything. Apparently Bernard Levin said, 'institutions are best if you don't have quite enough room to run them.' So it's a compact school, but it isn't overcrowded. Handwrites everything even the children's homework indeed (thanks spy) – when he was absent from a lesson a bright pupil (dyspraxic but a maths whiz kid) insisted on setting homework in the doc's

style, handwritten and complete with hints and tips! Parents say, 'he can appear to be completely off the wall (think mad professor) but he's wonderful with the children and the children adore him though he's not so at ease with parents. Children not parents are his priority, which is great.'

Entrance: Majority join in the September of their nursery or reception year but handful of occasional places crops up so always worth checking. Visit on an open morning or request an individual tour. All new entrants spend a familiarisation afternoon in school. For some reason, parents get the idea this is a special needs school – it's not, but, on the other hand, if your child has a difficulty they'll be helped. To set the record straight they have a mixed-ability intake – lots of very bright children (couple of scholars – one boy was offered four scholarships last year) some with SEN lots without. Can cater for dyslexia, dyspraxia, Aspergers, Down's syndrome, speech & language difficulties, ASD, ADD and those with EFL needs as long as they have the ability to catch up with their year group (also recognise that many children with SEN will be academically very able). Smallish site, so can only have odd one or two who require constant learning support assistance. Have flexibility, too, so if it's better for a child to be out of their chronological age group that's what they'll do. Lift (in pipeline) will improve wheelchair access. Look at the child, their profile, strengths and difficulties but it's not the place for those needing a totally different programme. Wants children who'll fit in, be integrated and included.

Exit: Some to boarding schools, majority to London day schools. At 8+ to The Harrodian, Putney High and Northcote. At 11+ to St Paul's, Lady Margaret's, Dulwich, The Hall, Ibstock Place, Wimbledon High, JAGS, Royal Russell, Kings, Bedales etc.

Remarks: Average class size of 16 ensures plenty of individual attention. Very recently praised by Ofsted, no weaknesses, couple of minor considerations. All take SATs – good results – above national norms. Most take 8+ or 11+ for next schools too so get lots of exam practice to lessen the stress. Specialist teachers for French, gym, art and music. Sets for maths and English from y1 or y2 to allow slower children to get a secure understanding and the high fliers to soar.

A parent of a child with dyslexia said she couldn't praise the school enough; they bend over backwards to help. If your child needs it they can have as much SEN help as necessary (though you'll be charged extra for one-to-one, and there may come a time when a specialist school is suggested if no real progress). The gifted and talented needing extension work will also be given some one-to-one help.

IEPs disseminated to all staff and reviewed regularly. Team to help with dyslexia, dyspraxia and speech and language problems (have therapist). Run social skills and friendships groups if need arises. Strong belief that children with SEN enrich the school, teaching others to be kind, considerate and thoughtful.

Lessons are lively affairs that hold the children's interests – then again work's much more fun when you understand it. Have a good sprinkling of investigative and practical work with trips and visits supplementing the diet. Say it's really important to ensure children do as well here as they would anywhere.

Lots happening outside the classroom, parents wax lyrical about the amazing productions, 'my nine year old was in 'As You Like It'. I was cynical but she learned her lines, understood it and it's given her a taste for Shakespeare – I felt so proud.' We caught the final throes of a West Side Story rehearsal not going quite as well as hoped. Productions are very inclusive – everyone gets to perform and share the limelight. Music's popular too – lots learn instruments or sing, all have a couple of music lessons a week and there's a choir and band. We had the privilege of being shown round by the head boy and head girl – took their duties very seriously, even showing us the paper store – and fine though the facilities are we were more impressed by the children. They've a keen awareness of others, a confidence to discuss strengths and weaknesses, they're lively, interested and, try as we might to find at least one child who couldn't explain their work, we failed.

Good sized (for inner London) playground – which children would like grassed (nice idea but with the British weather probably best left), dedicated art room (impressive art work everywhere), well-stocked library, ICT suite, science lab with apparently (according to kids) brilliant interactive white-board, good sized hall for PE, assemblies, productions, lunches. All do sport and, although school wouldn't suit aspirant athletes or potential polo players, for vast bulk of youngsters who're content with archetypal primary school sport it's just fine – usual on offer with fixtures against other schools, after school clubs (most attend at least one extra-curricular club per week) etc.

Not posh, or much patronised by the posh. Not the smartest place either (odd holey jumper and shirts hanging out brought back happy memories for this editor.) Children can be children here and they still get into all the top schools. What's more they're well-mannered and polite without a whiff of arrogance or priggishness. All children, from the non-academic through to the very brightest, are kept happy and there's a genuine belief that everyone has

strengths. Older children look after younger. Mixed age tables at lunchtime (packed lunch only; no chocolate, nuts or fizzy drinks) and all of the 11+ class have a role or responsibility. Not a school where staff hide away – they're chatty and helpful just like the children.

ROKEBY SCHOOL

George Road, Kingston-upon-Thames, Surrey, KT2 7PB

Tel: 020 8942 2247

Fax: 020 8942 5707

E-mail: hmsec@rokeby.org.uk

Website: www.rokebyschool.net

- Pupils: 370 boys, all day • Ages: 4-13 • Non-denom • Fees: £1,660; £2,386 in years 5-8 • Independent

Head: Since 1999, Mr Michael Seigel MA (early fifties), educated at St Paul's and New College, Oxford, where he read classics. Married with two teenage children, lives in Kingston by the river – 'within walking distance but I don't often do it,' he says. Author of four Latin textbooks, he teaches Latin, PHSE and also about Ancient Greece to the new intake of 7-year-olds. Cherishes hopes of one day having time to write a novel but nowadays could be mistaken for a City gent with a Guards background – tall, moustache, upright bearing and very much in control of the whole operation. He describes himself as 'sensitive to the needs of others' – some parents feel, however, that he is not averse to ruffling a few parental feathers. Departure of the previous head still regretted by some, feeling that it coincided with a certain loss of tradition but others say that Mr Seigel is dragging the school into the 21st century with success. Whichever way – he is a chap who evokes a plethora of differing comments.

Entrance: For entry at age 4 into pre-prep (known as Junior Rokeby), register ASAP from birth for a non-refundable fee of £25. Waiting list maintained on a 'first come, first served' basis, taking into account the month of birth. In the January before the year of entry (ie 20 months prior to entry date), first 100 boys are invited to an informal assessment – structured play session which has 'a formal element' – it may appear a bit harsh on such little mites (perhaps a taste of what is to come) but their parents queue up for the privilege. Subsequently, 44 boys offered places and the rest go onto another waiting list.

For entry at age 7, again put names down early – 48 places available, entrance exam – maths, English, reading and comprehension – in November, for entry the following September. No automatic transfer from Junior Rokeby, those unlikely to pass the exam are given prior warning. External candidates pay £200 (refunded if a place not awarded, but not if awarded and not taken up), set against subsequent fees. Boys come from a wide variety of pre-prep and state schools but particularly Wimbledon Common Prep and Putney Park. All parents have to dig deep into their wallets to make a £500 interest-free loan to the school, payable for each child, and refunded when the boy leaves. Three generous scholarships per year for boys aged 7/8, competed for by a separate exam in November and worth 45 per cent of fees – can be topped up in case of need. Based on academic ability but with one for potential in each of music, sport or art.

Exit: At 13, to all the top-notch schools, the main exodus to King's College School, Wimbledon, followed by St Paul's, Charterhouse, Epsom, Eton, Harrow and many others of first and upper second league. Occasionally to Tiffin's (state grammar in Kingston) and head relaxed about such boys exiting at 11.

Impressive record of academic, music and art scholarships to the favoured senior schools: recently scholarships to, amongst others, St Paul's and Wellington, an exhibition and a music scholarship to King's College and an art scholarship to St John's, Leatherhead.

Remarks: A school for seriously Surrey parents with seriously hard-working sons wanting seriously splendid academic results – and no messing. Founded in 1877, school is in a very leafy part of town off Kingston Hill and on the very swanky private residential Coombe Estate. Mainly housed in a large Victorian house which, like its neighbour, Holy Cross Preparatory School, was the home of author John Galsworthy (the Galsworthys owned several houses in the area). Site is largely built upon, there is little open space not occupied by tennis courts or an Astroturf pitch, although the junior school does have its own adventure playground. Open space at the front is crammed with staff cars and is a little weedy (literally) – some judicious gardening instead of detention for errant boys would not go amiss.

Some of the classrooms in the original house are a bit on the cramped side, but the modern additions are airy and spacious, particularly the art room and the well-equipped labs. Computer suite has 24 machines and smart board and the art department has a nice touch of a pottery room.

Academically, a school for the robust – weaklings and worriers will not enjoy it. A great deal is demanded and, if he can cope, your son will flourish and probably obtain a coveted place at one of the prestigious senior schools to which most of the pupils gravitate. If he is not up to it, he (or rather, you) will receive adequate, if unwelcome, warning that your time is up and you should move on to academic pastures new.

Average class size 16. Two parallel classes in each year until year 5, when boys are setted separately for maths and English, and then again in year 6 for French and Latin. Major change takes place in year 7, classes divided into two CE classes and what the head prefers to term a 'potential scholarship' class. All take Latin between years 5 and 8 and all in the scholarship class do Greek in their final year, with some being examined in it.

No pupils have EAL requirements but a few have mild to considerable dyslexia or dyspraxia. Parental comments that SEN provision is admirable – one mother said, 'they have done very well for my [dyslexic] son, who is a good all-rounder, managing well academically.' Another praises the school for 'picking up my son's problem very quickly'. However, such good SEN screening means some boys do not necessarily make it into senior Rokeby, which apparently has caused some parental concern.

Rokeby does nothing half-heartedly – be it academics or sport. On site, they have the all-weather pitch, which is mainly for junior Rokeby for football, rugby, rounders, cricket, short tennis and athletics in the summer. No space for senior field sports on site (land has been sold off in the past), and senior Rokeby boys are bused to Wimbledon Wanderers' Football Club grounds near the Robin Hood roundabout for football in the autumn and rugby in the winter. School is in negotiation, as we write, for the purchase of its own grounds in Worcester Park, but busing will still be necessary. No swimming pool – years 3 and 4 swim in Kingston. Head tells us that teams are not selected solely on merit – increasingly boys get the opportunity to play for the school at some stage in their career. However, as with virtually every boys' prep we see, sport is a bone of parental contention – some parents complain pupils not in the top teams can get more junior teachers and gap year students, however keen the boys may be; also a feeling that more encouragement could be given to less able but still sporty boys.

Parents speak very highly of the music tuition, describing the music teacher as 'fantastic.' All learn the violin in small groups as part of the music curriculum (hire of instrument is extra). Almost 50 per cent go on to take individual music lessons. Choir open to all. Annual Christmas music and drama production.

School has a purposeful atmosphere – you feel it is a veritable seat of learning. Uniform not especially smartly worn, but that's boys for you. Famous former pupils include actor Richard Briers and Labour historian and biographer, Professor Ben Pimlott.

Transport provision is good and very popular with parents, serving Sheen/Putney Heath areas and around Wimbledon. Shared school runs also comes into their own here (many siblings attend Holy Cross next door which eases the ferrying around). Parking near the school is problematical and has been a source of contention with local, highly articulate residents, resulting in detailed instructions issued to parents to avoid potentially inflammatory situations.

Junior Rokeby has own (teaching) head, who is responsible to Mr Seigel. Lots going on and boisterous boys – 22 maximum in class. Separate assembly hall and gym and general impression of metaphorical self-containment from main school (although share certain facilities eg canteen). Own playground in addition to adventure playground.

Rokeby is a school where parents either love the regime or moan about it (and perhaps take off to more gentle pastures) – hence the mixed reports we receive about the school. However, it cannot be denied that Rokeby comes up with the goods – excellent academic results from splendid all-rounders.

ROSEMEAD PREPARATORY SCHOOL

70 Thurlow Park Road, London, SE21 8HZ

Tel: 020 8670 5865
Fax: 020 6761 9159
E-mail: admin@rosemeadprepschool.org.uk
Website: www.rosemeadprepschool.org.uk

• Pupils: 383, 60/40 girls/boys, all day • Ages: 3-11
• Inter-denom • Fees: £1,873- £2,132 • Independent

Head: Since 2003, Mrs Catherine Brown, from a large co-ed prep in Harrow, previously ten years at Dulwich College prep.

Entrance: Main entry of 32 pupils at 3 assessed for language development and co-operation plus parental support. Additional entry at 4 for 7-10 pupils by comprehensive assessment – heavily oversubscribed. No automatic sibling policy. Head has seen catchment area diminish with increasing numbers now walking to school.

Exit: Large variety of schools including Dulwich College, JAGS, Alleyn's, Royal Russell and some highly selective state grammar schools eg Wallington GS, Wilson's GS, Newstead Wood GS and St Olave's GS. Almost 60 per cent of leavers achieved academic awards in 2001. Music, art and sport awards are also won.

Remarks: Broad social mix and wide range of ability – more like a state primary. Class sizes diminish up the school; numbers are not replenished as pupils move away. Constriction imposed by very full, compact site with some tiny classrooms and one playground only. Largest class size 20, year 6 classes have 16, smallest class only 12 – in year 4. Lunch and play times staggered to cope with lack of space. No setting for maths but pupils loosely streamed by class from year 3. Low turnover of 20 staff (mainly female) plus three nursery assistants and one gap year student. Designated music and PE teachers for all levels.

Full range of sporting facilities and professional coaching provided at local sports clubs for year 2 upwards on one afternoon each week – teams compete successfully against other local preps. Swimming also professionally coached at local pools. This recent increase in sports facilities – in response to parents' comments – has plugged the previous leakage of 7 year old boys. Extra help on site for dyslexia/dyspraxia by part-time specialist member of staff.

Art displayed throughout school with occasional imaginative whole-school projects, although there is no designated art room. New ICT suite recently provided. Major drama production in summer term with majority of junior school pupils involved. At Christmas, the nursery and infants take part in the nativity play while all juniors are in the show with year 6 pupils each taking a speaking part. Individual instrumental tuition by visiting peripatetic music staff who also organise string groups and orchestra after school. Some brass, woodwind and recorder groups plus choir. Stiff competition from traffic on South Circular.

Large variety of clubs available at lunch time and after school. The chess club has recently gained bronze awards at under 9 and 11 English National Primary Schools' Championship. Ballet and modern dance very popular with recent participation by several pupils in professional productions. Each class visits theatres and other places of interest at least once a term. Also many visiting guests eg theatre groups, authors, charities and musicians. Previous head aimsed to broaden curriculum to compensate for limited on-site facilities. School achieves level 5 for two thirds of pupils at Key Stage 2. Maths has always made a strong showing.

Rosemead was founded in Streatham by Miss D E Plumridge in 1942 and was moved to its present location in 1974 when the owner retired. The school now belongs to the Thurlow Educational Trust, a non-profit-making charitable organisation administered by a board of governors elected annually by members of the company – which includes all parents. Thus they participate in the company's affairs and help run the school as a business. Two members of staff attend all governors' meetings as observers. Head retains management of the education side. Fees are set by parents and are considerably lower than other prep schools in the locality. Not a wealthy school – special projects and developments require careful budgeting and planning that can include scheduled rise in fees. Active School Association aids fund-raising on regular basis through social activities.

School has humane approach and head will put herself out to help deserving cases. A lively, well-run school which produces happy motivated children, well placed to make the most of their next school.

ROSSALL JUNIOR SCHOOL

Linked to Rossall School in the Senior section

Broadway, Fleetwood, Lancashire, FY7 8JW

Tel: 01253 774222
Fax: 01253 772052
E-mail: enquiries@rossallcorporation.co.uk
Website: www.rossall.co.uk

- Pupils: girls and boys; 88 in junior school (7 board), 105 in infants • Ages: 7-11 in prep, 2-7 in pre-prep • C of E
- Independent • Open days: October, January and April

Remarks: For further information, see senior school entry.

ROWAN PREP SCHOOL

6 Fitzalan Road, Claygate, Surrey, KT10 0LX

Tel: 01372 462 627
Fax: 01372 470 782
E-mail: office@rowan.surrey.sch.uk
Website: www.rowan.surrey.sch.uk

- Pupils: 270 girls; includes nursery and kindergarten (45), all day
- Ages: 2-11 • Non-denom • Fees: £2,985 prep - £2,655 pre-prep, nursery fees based on usage • Independent

Head: Since 2004, Mrs Kathy Kershaw Cert Ed (fifties). Her fourth headship, previously head of nursery and pre-prep at Colfe's School (qv). A gushing enthusiast, she has quickly got her feet under the table and established herself as an instigator of change – academic, pastoral and cosmetic. She's a terrific advocate for the school with a warm manner and very keen to please, 'though perhaps too many people all the time,' comments a parent. She undoubtedly talks the talk, but she will also have to come up with the promised goods to please the parents – some of whom can be more vocal than most. However, her more approachable style of management has so far generally won approval among parents as a 'breath of fresh air.' The girls also are on board – Mrs K says, 'my approach is more user friendly. However the girls respect this and seem to relate to this more positively.' Lots of exciting plans for school's future, not least to challenge its competitive ethos. She feels it's, 'important to do your best rather than just be a winner.' However, she has to tread a fine line -'it is important that parents feel comfortable that the changes will not affect the high academic standards the school is renowned for.'

Entrance: Sept 2005 new nursery department opened (in Rowan Brae) and it is expected that priority in kindergarten is given to those girls moving up from nursery (other places on first-come-first-served basis). Then automatic transfer to pre-prep at 4, followed by prep department at 7. There is usually also a small intake at 7, places permitting. Selection to prep takes form of informal 'activity day', its purpose seemingly to meet the girls and weed out any glaring unsuitables. In reality, not truly selective though this may change once school numbers are back to capacity. (Greater local competition is official reason for lower numbers but, as with every school, a change of head does bring an exodus of some parents). Always worth trying for occasional places at odd times.

Exit: To top local independent schools – every year, large numbers to Lady Eleanor Holles, Tormead, Guildford High, St Catherine's Bramley. Regularly some to Surbiton High and a couple to board, usually Benenden. Consistently one or two to highly sought after state Tiffin Girls' in Kingston. 2005 saw 5 academic scholarships (in addition to another 6 music) to LEH, Guildford High and Benenden. Interestingly, no girls to co-ed senior schools – parents and girls clearly pleased with way Rowan continues to demonstrate virtues of single-sex education.

Remarks: Interesting times ahead as new head continues to implement her vision for the school. The question is – how she will marry a softer, more gentle, approach, with the tip-top academic results parents have come to expect? Most parents seem to be on board so far – 'too early to tell' and happy to 'wait and see' are typical parental comments. But Rowan parents are traditionally a competitive bunch, so the pressure is on the new head to prove that the new regime can be all things to all academic abilities.

Academically, the impressive list of next schools at 11, from an unselected start, is a reflection of the previous rigorous academic structure – often the reason parents chose the school. But it does not suit all – in the past there were clashes with some parents who felt the need for a more nurturing atmosphere (and they often departed to pastures new). With the change of head, school is keen to emphasise that it 'remains consistent in preparing the girls for the senior school of their choice and will not compromise the academic rigour necessary to ensure success for every girl.' A relief, however, to find no evidence of the controversial 'stretch club' for most able pupils we previously encountered – they seem well catered for in mainstream classroom. Mrs K adds, 'we also have a designated teacher who is actively involved in teaching the staff and providing reinforcement and help related to the talented and gifted girls in the school.' Setting no longer from year 3 (now year 4), form time and PHSE now timetabled for more pastoral support.

Class sizes run at around 18, with a maximum of 22. Head seems to have team of excellent supportive staff – school lost several initially but this felt to be natural consequence of change rather than any mass walkout. There is now more of an SEN infrastructure and SEN markedly improved recently. New, though not glamorous, portable classroom at Rowan Hill provides facility for one full time learning support specialist with extra dyslexia and maths help as required. Cost depending on need.

The school is split physically and administratively into Rowan Brae, the pre-prep, and Rowan Hill, the prep. They are a few minutes walk from each other, but both under the aegis of Mrs Kershaw from her office at the Hill. Much effort is being made to achieve a closer relationship between the two departments on a curriculum level, although the whole school seems rarely to come together under one roof.

Rowan Brae, which houses the nursery to year 2, is overseen by its own head, Miss Vicky Goodson. New, young (previously from Tower House) and brimming with ideas, a real bright spark and one to watch for the future. Both premises are converted Edwardian redbrick houses(that blend seamlessly with surrounding imposing properties) – hence a combination of slightly odd shaped classrooms in the original buildings with more spacious later additions. The whole school has nearly completed a huge face-lift, with funding clearly not an issue. Immaculate inside and out, feels very well looked after.

In Rowan Brae, lovely bright, airy classrooms. Lots of it is purpose-built, so layout really works and rooms have their own direct access to playground. Strong on presentation and handwriting, some outstanding yr1 samples. Wonderful, imaginative topics and artwork – year 2 'Healthy Living' project involves participation in Adopt-A-Chef scheme – they visit a commercial kitchen, at House of Commons! Children and parents seem particularly thrilled with this part of the school.

As girls progress through Rowan Hill, they move around the school to be taught in excellently equipped, bright classrooms with evidence of much hard work and inspired teaching adorning walls and corridors. Fab new parent-funded IT suite, doubling as year 5 classroom. New 'smartboards' everywhere. Mrs K has left no stone unturned in a bid to update and enhance the environment for all. It's not only the bits that show which make a glossy impression to parents, but staff also appreciate what she's doing ie centralising resources, improving access to facilities, etc – 'her standards are very high,' approves one.

The grounds at both sites have not escaped the head's beady eye. Extensive landscaping was well underway when we visited, bark chippings even laid in the spinney, an ever popular wooded play area previously inclined to mud! New outdoor games available from specially designed sheds where girls help themselves – and very diligent in returning it all.

Sports facilities at Rowan Brae rather limited although there is a gym and lovely, large, bright playground with areas segregated by picket fencing for different age groups – loads of toys. At Rowan Hill there is a netball court which becomes a playground and a hard tennis court. Girls are bused out to Reed's School for swimming and to the local community recreation ground for athletics.

Excellent music, class and instrumental, backed up by lots of scholarships for leavers. Three quarters of girls at Hill learn an instrument with their practice sessions timetabled into school day. All the usual ones played plus development of some more adventurous ideas, percussion club with samba drum workshops currently proving popular. Participation in orchestra and ensembles actively encouraged. Good choir, lots of concerts throughout year, performed at Albert Hall in 2003.

Head has strong community conscience and has begun to involve the school in lots of schemes, sponsored events eg planting bulbs on traffic island. She feels the need for school to have 'less arrogance and more humility than before,' for girls to be 'better equipped for life beyond it '. To keep up this momentum after leavers' exams in year 6 , new 'life skills programme' has been devised, ranging from community work and cycling profiency to shared social events with Shrewsbury House (qv).

Very polite, natural and open, happy-looking girls. Nice, relaxed atmosphere – gentle hum of activity... not overly quiet or noisy. Distinctive, attractive uniform based on school tartan. No uniform in kindergarten, only aprons for art and lunch.

Rowan is a school very much reflecting its locality – the school of choice for socially mobile, mainly professional parents (lots of first-time buyers) living in the affluent environs of the gated private estates close by. Parental parking at each site is limited to the roadside, creating its share of issues with residents – especially at Rowan Hill which is situated on a private unmade road – at last a use for all those 4x4s!

ROWLEDGE CHURCH OF ENGLAND PRIMARY SCHOOL

School Road, Rowledge, Farnham, Surrey, GU10 4BW

Tel: 01252 792 346
Fax: 01252 795 750
E-mail: admin@rowledge.hants.sch.uk
Website: www.rowledge.hants.sch.uk

• Pupils: 95 boys 110 girls, all day • Ages: 4-11 • C of E • State

Head: Since 2000, Mrs Clare Painter (late thirties), married with a young daughter. Lives locally and previously 3 years as deputy head & SEN coordinator at South Farnham – another top local primary. Friendly but business like, an enthusiastic innovative head who is passionate about her school. Much appreciated by staff, parents and pupils.

Entrance: Non selective and always oversubscribed (although the numbers vary). In 2005 there were 40 applications for 30 places – (50 in 2004). Proximity to the school is key, so consider moving into the village to get the best chance of a place and check the map on the school website. Attending local nurseries in the village does not guarantee a place, despite what you might be told. Usual state criteria apply with priority given to those living closest to the school and then siblings. The entire new intake has a visit at home from the year R teacher before they start. Mrs P says this helps them settle in and the parents really enjoy it!

Exit: Almost all to two local state secondary schools – Eggars in Alton or Weydon in Farnham. A handful of leavers to local independents.

Remarks: A super village school where children enjoy learning – they put a lot into their school life and Mrs P and her staff ensure they get a lot out. Academically standards are good. All Year 5 take an English speaking board exam to assess their reading and public speaking ability. 'It does wonders for their confidence,' said one mother.

Average class size 30 with learning support assistants in every class. Very well staffed, mainly female, several student teachers, parish youth worker and parent volunteers. Mrs P believes in making the school a pleasant place to work, low staff turnover in recent times – one lunchtime supervisor has just completed 43 years service! A pat on the back for teaching skills – the school provides teaching practice for Winchester College. One member of staff with advanced teaching skills also spends one day a week at another school – to widen her experience and share resources: 'very important to help raise standards,' says Mrs P. School caters well for SEN: about 15 per cent receive help, taught mainly with the class or in groups by one part time SEN teacher – school is fully accessible for the disabled. Equal emphasis on 'special needs' of those at the other end of the academic spectrum with assistance from an Able Child Coordinator who visits once a week.

On a quiet lane in an affluent village on the Surrey/Hampshire border, the original Victorian building has been extended and refurbished over the years with additional spacious classrooms and a fab multi use hall. Well equipped ICT, all classrooms to have interactive whiteboards and projectors by the end of 2005/2006. The whole place is immaculately maintained – a refreshing change; a well loved feel about the place. Lots of fantastic work displayed and the children are very proud of their school. Superb outside space: refurbished playground, extensive playing fields (complete with trim trail), the school has its own private access to the adjacent Alice Holt Forest used for lots of activities and assemblies in the summer.

Choir and orchestra, lots learn an instrument. Sport, particularly football, rounders and netball is good, with regular competitions against other local schools. Mrs P is a keen netball player and coaches the school team with great success. A buzzing hive of activity throughout the day and this continues after school with the usual extracurricular activities run by staff or privately organised. Residential and day trips. V. informative, award winning website, 'all the usual news and kept up to date' said a parent. Also includes pages of jokes, quizzes and articles posted by pupil webmasters. 'It's really cool!' said one pupil.

Pupils are an extremely well behaved bunch and few problems arise – 'the children lead very busy lives,' said one parent 'but they love it.' An anti bullying week ensures that all are aware of, and signed up to, the zero tolerance policy in the school. Mrs P is v keen to teach children to take responsibility for themselves. Young governors scheme involves pupils in the running of the school and teaches them about decision-making including whether to allow girls to wear trousers to school!

ROYAL GRAMMAR SCHOOL JUNIOR SCHOOL (NEWCASTLE)

Linked to Royal Grammar School (Newcastle) in Senior section

Lambton Road, Jesmond, Newcastle upon Tyne, Tyne and Wear, NE2 4RX

Tel: 0191 281 5711
Website: www.rgs.newcastle.sch.uk

• Pupils: all day • Ages: 7 - 11 • Non-denom • Fees: Junior school £5,739 pa • Independent • Open days: A Saturday in mid-November

Head: Mr Roland Craig.

Entrance: Test and interview at 8. Year 7 entry available from Sept 2006.

Exit: All to the senior school (provided that internal assessments confirm suitability).

Remarks: Self-contained, purpose-built junior school. Shares facilities with the senior school.

ROYAL HIGH SCHOOL, BATH, JUNIOR SCHOOL GDST

Linked to Royal High School, Bath GDST in the Senior section

Hope House, Lansdown Road, Bath, BA1 5ES

Tel: 01225 422 931
Fax: 01225 484 378
Website: www.gdst.net/royalhighbath

• Pupils: 260 girls, plus nursery; all day • Ages: 3-11 • Non-denom • Fees: £1,779 • Independent • Open days: Usually a Saturday in early November and a Thursday in late April

Head: Miss Lynda Bevan.

Entrance: By assessment and interview with head; children at the nursery are assessed at entry to the reception class and take up the first available places.

Remarks: On the site of the former high school a short walk or drive down the hill from the current senior department. There is little regular overlap, although the juniors use the sports and drama facilities, and there are some shared staff. Big, sunny classrooms in fine Georgian buildings with magnificent views. Grounds are on a steep hillside but somehow children are not seen careering out of sight at playtimes. Rolling is only allowed occasionally. Everywhere there is something thought-provoking to look at, inside and out. A huge mosaic and a fading mural enhance the concreted areas. Another nice touch is the provision of laminated games tables (chess, ludo, snakes and ladders) in part of the playground.

Definitely a more stimulating and buzzy atmosphere than up the hill. Girls look you in the eye and have things to say. The head since 1997, Miss Lynda Bevan, is bright and breezy, and knows every child in the school. She is proud of her girls and quick to make the most of parental input. The girls were able to make a huge copy of a Gainsborough painting, when it was donated by a parent from the school to a Bath Museum.

Fairly traditional timetable concentrating on English and maths and using as a base the core requirements of the National Curriculum. French and music are taught to all children from nursery up. Computers play an important part, and there is a fully equipped ICT room with 30 computers linked to the internet. Loads of clubs. The school is very good at providing basic skills (tables, handwriting etc) necessary for coping with secondary school, so much so that those that take the entrance exam for the senior school are pretty unphased by the process and almost all go on. This pleases parents. Those who are not going to make it through the tests are gently weeded out ('but in a nice way' comments one parent) in advance.

Small nursery school within the grounds, has separate facilities, but children participate in school assembly and eat lunch (if staying) with the big girls. Everyone has school dinner, 'no packed lunches, for health reasons – we believe in providing a substantial midday meal'.

Cheerful, enclosed and safe, a perfect environment for the girls to do what the GDST does best, expand into themselves.

RUDOLF STEINER JUNIOR SCHOOL

Linked to Rudolf Steiner School in the Senior section

Hood Manor, Dartington, Totnes, Devon, TQ9 6AB

Tel: 01803 762 528
Fax: 01803 762 528
E-mail: enquiries@steiner-south-devon.org
Website: www.steiner-south-devon.org

• Pupils: boys and girls • Ages: 3-11 • Christian foundation
• Fees: £810-£1,150 • Independent

Remarks: Learning delivered via a four-week theme through two-hour lessons daily. Specialist teachers for foreign languages, music, sports and crafts. Parent and toddler group for tinies, a nursery group for ages 3-4 and a kindergarten for ages 4-6 where play is orientated toward promoting fine motor skills and manual dexterity. For futher details, see senior school entry.

THE RUSSELL PRIMARY SCHOOL

Petersham Road, Petersham, Richmond, Surrey, TW10 7AH

Tel: 02089 401 446
Fax: 02083 320 985
E-mail: info@russell.richmond.sch.uk
Website: www.russell.richmond.sch.uk

• Pupils: 240; 120 boys and 120 girls in main school plus 52 in nursery; all day • Ages: 3-11 • Non-denom • State

Head: Since 2005, Mr Darren Harrison who worked in the London borough of Richmond for the previous 11 years. He comes from Cumbria but now lives locally with his wife. His interests include travelling, sport and mathematics.

Entrance: Over-subscribed every year: 34 places and 50 plus applicants. Nursery place does not guarantee place in reception class. Siblings of existing pupils have priority and then children who live closest to school. Medical and social circumstances may be taken into account. A few vacancies at seven when some transfer next door to The German School.

Exit: Two thirds to state secondary Grey Court in

Richmond. Others to independent schools such as Christ's Hospital in Horsham, Hampton, Reed's (Cobham), state grammars Tiffin and Tiffin Girls' in Kingston and also to Waldegrave (Twickenham).

Remarks: Vibrant primary school with great package of family friendly, wrap-around care, providing the best of state education for those fortunate enough to obtain a place. SATS results show school compares equally with national percentages at Key Stage 1 and significantly better than national average at Key Stage 2.

School named after Lord John Russell (twice Prime Minister from 1846) who has links with Petersham. Built in 1950s (buildings a bit dated) and blessed with 3 acres of grounds, including two natural ponds full of frogs and newts, an outdoor summer 'classroom' consisting of an area bounded by young trees and an orchard with apples, plums and damsons, all avidly consumed when they crop by the children. Badgers and foxes on site, a 'tame-ish' woodpecker and boxes for nesting birds and bats.

Swanky location, but head says that pupils nevertheless represent the entire social range, their homes varying from those of millionaires to social housing and from a variety of national backgrounds, some with English as an additional language. One mother commented that when her family arrived from Italy, the children were given great support with learning English and were correcting their mother in no time at all! Site rather open and security might be a bit of a worry, apart from nursery playground, which is fenced and secured.

DfES recognition of 'a successful school' means funding has been granted for an additional infant teacher and a building extension, resulting in infant class size below government maximum of 30, with flexible system for teaching groups of between 17 and 25. However, junior class size is 34. Additional facilities include a multi-sensory room which is be available to all children, containing tactile objects, aural and visual experiences with fibre optics and bubbles and the like. An art room is presently being developed. ' The school is very forward thinking and constantly looking for ways to improve,' says one enthusiastic parent. Inspiring work, quotations and maxims exhibited everywhere. Pupils are encouraged to drink water from their bottles throughout the day and to eat a piece of fruit from home during circle time (for those unaware of the idiosyncrasies of the state system, circle time is when the children sit with teacher (in a circle!) and discuss issues such as 'what makes me happy?', 'what is a friend?'; the children take it in turn to speak if they want to and they can speak without interruption). Delightful practice of classes being renamed every

year after, eg birds (Robin, Owl), eco-systems (Swamp, Rainforest), wild flowers or artists; each class preparing a presentation on its name at start of year.

Parents receive a curriculum information sheet for every half term, advising of the topic for period, eg 'What do we do with our rubbish?' or 'The Victorians'; it sets out what the class will be doing in each subject, when and what homework will be given out, what visits are to be made, when weekly tests will take place and how parents can help. A great idea which other primaries – state and independent – would do well to take on board.

Computers placed in clusters all over rather than in a dedicated suite, which head feels better reflects current office practice and thinking. All children have internet access and there is one computer between five, improving on the government target of one computer between ten. The school is currently working with Microsoft on developing the skills of their teachers and improving their IT capability. They will then be used by the local authority as a key school for the training of teachers.

Super pre- and after-hours provision for children from the age of 6 months and 11 years (including meals) – nominal charges and reduction for siblings. Russell Rays is a community facility offering child care from 7.30am until 6.00pm. The Club can even collect children from nearby schools. Also operates during school holidays. Two residential school trips every year: year 5 to Cranleigh, near Guildford and year 6 to the Isle of Wight. Infant swimming at neighbouring German School and junior swimming at Richmond. School continues to be hive of activity at lunchtimes and after school, with plethora of clubs for football (Brentford Football Club helps), cricket (MCC helps), rugby (Middlesex Rugby Club helps), tennis, netball and others ranging from choir to computers to pottery, some with small charge for materials, but no child excluded from any school activity if parents unable to contribute. Popular and well-supported evening talent shows where the children perform – acting, dancing, singing, telling jokes etc.

Exceptional unit for up to eight children of infant age with moderate to severe SEN. Dedicated learning support teacher, together with nursery nurse and special needs assistants. Has own supervised playground but some pupils can play in main playground at lunchtime and be supervised there by one of the lunchtime assistants. Regular integration sessions with mainstream classes, with full support by special assistant. Assessments take place through year. SEN pupils swim at Strathmore School and ride at a centre in Vauxhall. Clubs also open to SEN children.

One of first schools in the country to establish practice

of producing self-evaluation report for staff, and head frequently asked to lecture about it – 'the idea is not to wait for someone to tell you how or why to improve.' Another of the head's innovations that has received great acclaim within the profession is ' The Gold Book', a workbook provided for each child which will contain all that child's work done in one week every term. Work is then marked and sent home for parents to see. Useful basis for parents' evening discussions (every term), as well as a keepsake for each term. Polite, well-behaved and motivated children confirmed by Ofsted report of 2000: ' The Russell is a popular school with a good reputation for advancing its pupils' academic, social and personal development.'

Nursery and reception class provision regarded locally as outstanding. Nursery takes 52 children, 26 in each of two sessions. Overseen generally by reception class teacher. Morning attenders can stay on to play for the afternoon and then, for those who want it, there is the Russell Rays Club for nominal charge.

RYDE SCHOOL WITH UPPER CHINE, JUNIOR SCHOOL

Linked to Ryde School with Upper Chine in the Senior section

Queen's Road, Ryde, Isle of Wight, PO33 3BE

Tel: 01983 612901
Fax: 01983 564714
Website: www.rydeschool.org.uk

• Pupils: boys and girls; day and boarding • Ages: 3-11 • C of E
• Independent

Head: Mr Howard Edward BSc PGCE.

Remarks: In a converted house on the same campus as the senior school but operates almost completely separately, with few staff in common, except those in learning support. Traditional feel, with desks in rows, but bright and cheerful. 'We have a policy that all the children's work goes up on the walls.' Open till 5 every day with after-school arts, crafts, sports and homework clubs. Science lab with parachutes and planets suspended from the ceiling and models of dinosaurs abounding – the Island is a fertile site for dinosaur bones and houses two dinosaur museums. Most pupils go on to the senior school.

ST ALOYSIUS' COLLEGE JUNIOR SCHOOL

Linked to Saint Aloysius' College in the Senior section

45 Hill Street, Garnethill, Glasgow, G3 6RJ

Tel: 0141 331 9200
Fax: 0141 353 0426
E-mail: mail@staloysius.org
Website: www.staloysius.org

• Pupils: 400 all day; 50 boys and girls in kindergarten
• Ages: 5-11; kindergarten 3-5 • RC • Fees: £2,140 - £2,313
• Independent

Remarks: For details, see senior school entry.

ST ANSELM'S SCHOOL

Bakewell, Derbyshire, DE45 1DP

Tel: 01629 812 734
Fax: 01629 814 742
E-mail: headmaster@anselms.co.uk
Website: www.sanselms.co.uk

• Pupils: 195, including one-third girls. About two thirds board. 50 in pre-prep and 25 in nursery • Ages: 7-13, pre-prep 3-7
• C of E • Fees: Day: pre-prep £2160; £3,340 - £4200. Boarding: £4,930 • Independent • Open days: Richard Foster believes every day is an Open Day - prospective parents are encouraged to visit on a normal working day

Head: Since 1994, Mr Richard Foster (mid forties), energetic, friendly and very focused. Came to the school after a lifetime within the independent sector. Educated in a Kenyan prep school, Clifton College and then a BEd in history and PE at St Luke's in Exeter. Since then taught back in Kenya – including 9 years as head of Pembroke House School, 'a very English prep school'. Married to Rachel, also a qualified teacher, who helps in the pre-prep and in headmaster's wife role throughout the school. Their youngest child has just left the school, to follow the other two to Oundle. The head has no plans to leave the school and is on an open contract.

Entrance: No exam, children admitted at all ages providing there is space.

Exit: Recent scholarships include all three major academic scholarships to Oundle in 2003, when leavers gained 20 awards to schools such as Uppingham, Repton, Westonbirt, Oakham. Others in previous 5 years to Eton, Roedean, Rugby, Malvern, Stowe, Ampleforth, Shrewsbury, Oundle, Downe House and Moreton Hall. Non-scholarships go to a wide range of schools around the country.

Remarks: Tucked away on the edge of the attractive town of Bakewell, St Anselm's modest location belies its achievements. Superbly resourced, with a team of dedicated and enthusiastic staff, pupils appear beamingly happy. Prides itself on stretching each pupil to the limit of their potential. Visitors and staff are greeted politely as they pass and pupils show great courtesy at all times. 'I'm a bit of a stickler for manners,' says Foster.

Academically aims high, despite having no entrance exam. Around 30 pupils in each year – two classes in the transition year and three classes in the others. Setting from the age of 9 onwards (8 for maths).

Dedicated learning support team with one full-time and three peripatetic staff; about 1 in 10 take advantage of it. Follows the National Curriculum but with extras – we saw a very vigorous English lesson with 9-year-olds acting one of Shakespeare's bloodiest scenes. 'Sir, please, Sir, Can I be Hamlet next time?' Fabulous, exuberant classics master seen coaching small boy in Latin. Much emphasis on finding 'what makes the child buzz, then we can develop and nurture it.' Lots of schemes where effort is rewarded – certificates, prizes, house points, visit to Mr Foster to be congratulated after a particularly good piece of work. Parents get a grade slip every two and a half weeks, to keep them abreast.

Keen on sport (four times a week), but 'we are mindful of children who are musical or artistic.' Two thirds play an instrument and all eight-year-olds play the violin. New building – as ever – and lots of extras.

Homely boarding houses scattered about the site. Boys' dorms suitably boyish in decor, girls' are pretty and pink. New pupils have a guide in the same year and a senior mentor from the top year. One large dining-room for everyone (good).

Superb staff; blissful, confident children fizzing with energy and enthusiasm.

St Anthony's Preparatory School

90 Fitzjohns Ave, Hampstead, London, NW3 6NP

Tel: 020 7431 1066 / 7435 0316
Fax: 020 7435 9223
E-mail: judith@stanthonysprep.org.uk
Website: www.stanthonysprep.org.uk

• Pupils: 280 boys; all day • Ages: 5-13 • RC • Fees: £3,335 - £3,430 • Independent • Open days: Contact the school

Head: Since 2005, Mr Chris McGovern. Previously head of the junior house and director of studies. When the National Curriculum was written he was chosen by the government to represent independent schools and he has been called to 10 Downing Street on more than one occasion to offer advice on educational matters – so we can blame him, then. A historian with a couple of Paxman interviews to his credit. Sees St Anthony's strengths as 'Catholic but inclusive, academic but not narrowly so, informal but with the highest expectations'.

Entrance: If you phone up early – but not before birth – you should get a place for an assessment. A few places are reserved for Catholic families who apply late. The assessment is gentle and friendly and not a competition with other applicants. Boys need to demonstrate that they can reach a baseline rather than be better than other applicants. Roughly two thirds of those assessed are offered places.

Exit: Most boys leave at 13 and go on to eg City of London, Highgate, Mill Hill, St Paul's, UCS, Westminster. Some travel further afield – Ampleforth, Eton, Harrow, Marlborough etc. A sprinkling will go on to Catholic maintained schools in London – Cardinal Vaughan and the London Oratory.

Remarks: Informality remains important. Staff, pupils and parents are on first-name terms but the school is a little less bohemian than in the past. Universal parental praise for its friendly, caring attitudes; general happiness with the academic standards, despite the gentleness of the selection process. The arts have been criticised by parents – school says 'on the up'. Not an educational hothouse but 'they seem to get the results without pushing them over-much,' said a parent.

Maximum class size 22, smaller at the top and bottom ends. Setting in maths from year 3 and higher up for French. Very good in-house learning support at both ends of the academic spectrum. Difficulties such as dyspraxia are often picked up early by an educational physiotherapist who takes each year 2 class for six sessions. 'When my son turned out to have dyslexia they were very supportive,' said a parent.

The school is on two sites separated by Fitzjohn's Avenue. 'But although we're in two houses we're very much one school, with the same philosophy and ethos.' Major building work at the senior house has seen a new science block built in the garden plus refurbishments to the main building. Computer suites in both houses.

PE and the arts are taught in small groups. There's a smallish swimming pool and a small playground outside the senior house. The junior house has a large playground plus a vaulted hall used for PE as well as music lessons, assemblies and dining room for the whole school. From year 2 upwards, boys travel by coach to Brondesbury cricket club for games; sporting results improving. Majority of boys play a musical instrument and the school's tradition of rock bands has produced Johnny Borrell's 'Razorlight' which played at the G8 concert in Hyde Park.

After-school hobbies programme for year 3 upward which always includes chess and rock band plus other subjects according to the interests of boys and teachers. 'It's an opportunity for teachers and pupils to spend time together in a relaxed atmosphere.' 'They spend a lot of time developing all aspects of the children,' said a parent. 'My son is keen on science but he's been writing and performing plays too.' The new head is keen to develop further the artistic side amidst the increasing demands for a broad academic curriculum.

The school is well-known for its good pastoral care. 'We have a strong relationship with the children – the fact we're all on first-name terms helps.' 'The boys are all made to feel important – no-one is allowed to get lost,' said a parent. 'It's a very friendly, relaxed, caring school,' said another. 'I wish there was a girls' school like it.'

ST AUBYN'S SCHOOL

Linked to Blundell's School in the Senior section

Milestones House, Blundells Road, Tiverton, Devon, EX16 4NA

Tel: 01884 252 393
Fax: 01884 232 333
E-mail: staubyns@blundells.org
Website: www.blundells.org

- Pupils: 360 boys and girls (incl day care centre from 3 months) 260 pupils from 3-11 • Ages: 3 months-11 • C of E
- Fees: £465-2,345 • Independent • Open days: Autumn

Head: Since 2000, Mr Nick Folland, previously 11 years at Blundell's, inc 6 years as housemaster. Speciality: PE and geography. Former master i/c cricket and sports coach. Member of Blundell's senior management team.

Entrance: Extremely popular nursery from 3 years. Some spaces are available.

Exit: Some 85 per cent of pupils join Blundell's (60 per cent under previous ownership) although St Aubyn's stands firm as a separate entity.

Remarks: Blundell's School bought St Aubyn's School and pre-prep in Tiverton in 2000 and built it on its present site. The school links with some Blundell's facilities but the school is autonomous and run separately.

ST BEDE'S COLLEGE PREP SCHOOL

Linked to Saint Bede's College in the Senior section

Alexandra Park, Manchester, Lancashire, M16 8HX

Tel: 0161 226 7156
E-mail: prep@stbedescollege.co.uk
Website: www.stbedescollege.co.uk

- Pupils: 231 girls and boys; boarding and day • Ages: 4-11
- RC • Fees: Day: prep £1,412, additional boarding fees £1,572
- Independent • Open days: Mid September to early November

Head: Mr Peter Hales.

Entrance: By assessment.

Exit: No automatic right of transfer to the senior school though the vast majority do so.

Remarks: Housed in a new building on the same site

as the senior school. Bright, colourful classrooms. Shares facilities with the main school.

St Bede's School-Eastbourne

Linked to Saint Bede's School in the Senior section

Duke's Drive, Eastbourne, East Sussex, BN20 7XL

Tel: 01323 734 222
Fax: 01323 746 438
E-mail: prep.school@stbedesschool.org
Website: www.stbedesschool.org

- Pupils: 420 boys and girls • Ages: 2 1/2 - 13 • Inter-denom
- Independent • Open days: Open morning in early May

Head: Mr Christopher Pyemont.
Remarks: For further details please see senior school.

St Catherine's Preparatory School

Linked to Saint Catherine's School in the Senior section

Station Road, Bramley, Guildford, Surrey, GU5 0DF

Tel: 01483 899665
Fax: 01483 899669
E-mail: schooloffice@stcatherines.info
Website: www.stcatherines.info

- Pupils: 220 girls, all day • Ages: 4-11 • C of E • Fees: £1,830 - £3,010 • Independent

Head: Since 2001, Mrs Kathy Jefferies BSc (forties), born and educated in the USA. Married with 4 children, she is very enthusiastic and driven and believes every child should be happy at the school. The children adore her.

Entrance: Selective entrance, mainly at 4 occasionally at 7, by test, interview and taster day. Girls come from a variety of local nurseries – both state and private.

Exit: To senior school across the road, not automatic, but only a small minority go elsewhere.

Remarks: A thriving, happy, academic school with strong competition for places and high expectations of its pupils. Final phase of £3m building and refurb programme provides very attractive and spacious accommodation,

although lunch, some sports and chapel services still take place in the senior school across the road.

Academically very strong but not too pressured according to parents. Pupils are 'stretched' but there is a balance, and the school's aim is to bring out qualities in all. Average class size 18 (smaller class sizes in pre prep), and pupils are also grouped vertically through the school for tutoring – 12 to 14 girls in each group. The school feels these groupings are very influential – parents not so sure. Super ICT suite in the new building and interactive whiteboards, internet etc in all classrooms.

Music and sport are encouraged. Instruments are introduced in year 2 and almost 75 per cent continue to learn up to grade 5. Excellent brass and strings groups and several pupils have gained music scholarships to the senior school. Parents comment that the 'music tuition is wonderful'. Sport, which includes netball, swimming and gymnastics, is very important with many pupils representing the school in local competitions and at higher levels. All the usual extra-curricular activities – swimming, gym, chess (very popular) and some more unusual, including Spanish and tap dancing. Main problem seems to be what to choose.

Staff are mainly female although there are two very popular male teachers. Any problems are dealt with efficiently and thoroughly by teachers and senior management team. Village location not far from Guildford equals the usual parking problems especially in the morning. Head has introduced a drop-off system for parents to ease the traffic flow, and many use the school transport organised by parents, although this seems to be geared primarily to the needs of the senior girls.

St Christopher School Junior School

Linked to Saint Christopher School in the Senior section

Barrington Road, Letchworth, Hertfordshire, SG6 3JZ

Tel: 01462 650 962
Fax: 01462 481578
E-mail: admissions@stchris.co.uk
Website: www.stchris.co.uk

- Pupils: 170 boys and girls plus Montessori nursery with 35 children • Ages: 4-11, Montessori 2-4; boarding from 8+
- Non-denom • Fees: £2,415 - £3,000 • Independent

Head: Mr Richard Palmer BEd.

Entrance: Some come up from the Montessori nursery, others join the reception class, more join year 3 or 4. Will take a broad range of ability, 'but our community exists on self-discipline, and they must be able to cope'.

Exit: Most to the senior school.

Remarks: Lovely, light buildings adjacent to the senior school, full of paintings and projects. Much of the work is project-based (which can upset inspectors from traditional prep schools). 'The teachers know each child's strengths and weaknesses. It is most important to push their strengths and enrich those areas they find difficult. Being kind and having high expectations are not mutually exclusive.' Play areas include an orchard – children are encouraged to climb the trees and pick the apples. 'Childhood should be celebrated. We try to preserve it as long as possible.'

For further details, see the senior school entry.

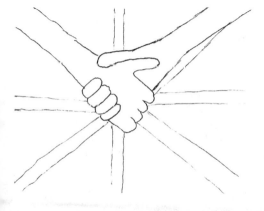

St Christopher's School

32 Belsize Lane, Hampstead, London, NW3 5AE

Tel: 02074 351 521
Fax: 02074 316 694
E-mail: admissions@st-christophers.hampstead.sch.uk
Website: www.st-christophers.hampstead.sch.uk

- Pupils: around 235 girls; all day • Ages: 4-11 • Non-denom
- Fees: £3,193, inclusive of lunch and non-residential trips
- Independent

Headmistress: From 2003, Mrs Susan (Susie) West BA Hons PGCE MA Educational Management (fifties). Educated at Howell's, University of Newcastle, Oxford (PGCE) and OU. Began teaching career at Oakham School with 11-18 year olds and to say she has had a wide range of jobs since would be an understatement. Highlights include head of St Bede's, Eastbourne pre-prep, head of English at a school in Kuala Lumpur, housemistress at Sherborne School for Girls, year 4 teacher at Sussex House, plus a few spells in business. Most recently was deputy head at Kensington Prep. Divorced with grown son, daughter in university. A breath of fresh air in the intimidating world of London preps – down to earth, straight-talking, no hint of snobbery. Always puts the girls first, occasionally exasperating some mums. Cycles to school every day from Pimlico.

Entrance: Unique, we think, and hinges entirely on the fact that the school possesses 13 classrooms rather than 14. With two classes per year group, this leaves only one room (capacity 18 girls) for reception. Now read carefully: girls born in September to February enter reception at four-and-a-half and spend seven years at the school. Those with March to August birthdays stay at nursery an extra year and start in year 1 at 5+, spending six years at the school. Name down at birth – 'we have had calls from the maternity ward'. The school closes the register at 200 names (for 38 slots) but tries to make allowances for people who have suddenly moved to the area. All places awarded on the results of assessments (of potential, not accomplishment) and play. Looking for bright berries, but also a mixture of personalities – 'some leaders, some quieter girls, the odd eccentric.' Sisters accepted automatically unless they are screamingly unsuited to the place. Vacancies arise from time to time, mainly at the end of year two. Over a third of pupils live within walking distance. Rest mainly from, Highgate, St

John's Wood, Maida Vale and Islington.

Exit: Lots to South Hampstead High and Francis Holland. A few to St Paul's, Haberdashers' Aske's, City of London, Channing, North London Collegiate. Handful to boarding schools: Queenswood, Wycombe Abbey, Downe House, Badminton. Sometimes one to Henrietta Barnett.

Remarks: High-achieving, girls' prep in large, airy Victorian dwelling in leafy back road. Dates back, in a convoluted way, to 1883, but was established in its current form in 1950 by the writer Rosemary Manning. Strong family feel, sheltered, cosy, but not twee. Stairs central to proceedings, with throngs of confident little girls making their way up and down, oblivious to headmistress and teachers battling through the crowd. New uniform 100 per cent cotton – 'good for the skin but hell to launder,' said a mum. When we visited, girls were dressed in a mixture of summer and winter wear, shorts and tracksuit trousers, dresses and tunics, shoes and trainers – somehow all gelling into an attractive and comfy uniform. No specific school rules, just the word 'respect'. 'The school has a feeling of controlled but bubbling energy,' said a mother.

Years 4-6 tucked into horrific concrete classroom block out back (plans afoot for a rebuild) – lovely inside though, with super rooms for DT, science, art etc. Library and computer building designed in Scandinavian style with light wood and big windows. Unusually broad range of subjects on offer. French and Spanish both taught, plus Mandarin club, and head dreams of 'putting Latin back' in the programme. Chess part of the curriculum years 2-6. Reading taught mainly through Jolly Phonics, with other methods as back-up. No scholarship class and no setting, with exception of one investigative maths lesson per week in years 4-6. Practice tests every Friday at the beginning of year 6 help to insure that girls shine in senior school entrance exams. Homework burden can get a bit intense as girls progress up the school. Parents gush about special needs help (with no stigma attached) for the few girls – mostly younger siblings – who need support. 'They've done everything they can to help my daughter,' said one grateful parent. Another, whose daughter was attending a special programme for her disability out of school, was impressed that her form teacher had volunteered to attend a course to help her continue the programme in class. Similarly, school takes pains to integrate loners and to thwart cliquishness.

In keeping with the tradition started by Miss Manning, the school excels in music. Over 50 per cent of girls learn at least one instrument at school (plus loads outside). Four music competitions each year (wind, strings, piano and ensemble) plus senior, junior and chamber choirs, two orchestras, and – our favourite – junior and senior piano clubs to take the isolation out of learning that lonely instrument. Recently held joint concert with nearby boys' prep, The Hall, and keen to do more in this vein. High quality artwork displayed throughout school and art history taught as a separate subject in its own room. Less emphasis on PE. Cramped site allows netball, short tennis, rounders. Also some unihoc, tag rugby, cricket, pop lacrosse etc. Gymnastics in school hall which doubles as canteen. Tarmacked playground heavily used, plus small play area out back – somehow sufficient. Huge range of school trips to theatre and museums, taking advantage of London on the doorstep. Interesting parents – media, City, entertainment – with strong opinions. Extremely useful eg in helping to organise themed special studies days in the summer term with visiting speakers. Multi-cultural, though not particularly multi-ethnic. No beef, pork, ham, bacon, shellfish or nuts on menu – we suspect you're out of luck if you don't like chicken. Assembly every Monday, hymns sung, but tone is non-denominational – many children out of school on Jewish holidays.

Not traditional, not high-tech (one interactive whiteboard for 240 girls, though more to come), not woolly. But a well-thought-out and jolly nice school.

St Columba's Junior School

Linked to Saint Columba's School in the Senior section

Knockbuckle Road, Kilmacolm, PA13 4AU

Tel: 01505 872768
Fax: 01505 873995
E-mail: juniorsecretary@st-columbas.org
Website: www.st-columbas.org

- Pupils: 340 boys and girls • Ages: 3-11 • Non-denom
- Fees: From nursery £654 - senior VI £2,490 • Independent
- Open days: November

Head: Mrs D L Cook, DCE ITQ DipAdPrStudies DipEdMan.

Entrance: By assessment and test.

Exit: Automatic transfer to senior school.

Remarks: Positively buzzing, with fabulous new facilities. Two parallel classes throughout, 24 pupils in each.

St Dunstan's Abbey, The Plymouth College Junior School

Linked to Plymouth College in the Senior section

The Millfields, Plymouth, Devon, PL1 3JL

Tel: 01752 201352
E-mail: juniorschool@plymouthcollege.com
Website: www.plymouthcollege.com

• Pupils: 270 girls and boys; all day • Ages: 3-11 • C of E
• Fees: Pre-prep: £1,779, years 1-2: £1,867, years 3-6 £2,000
• Independent • Open days: September

Head: Since 2004, Richard Jeynes, forties.

Entrance: On application.

Exit: Majority of students automatically migrate to Plymouth College, no examination or interview is required. Others leave for eg the Devonport High Schools.

Remarks: Former pupils of St Dunstan's Abbey, now renamed The Plymouth College Junior School, moved into its £2 million newly refurbished premises on the former St Dunstan's site in 2004. Richard Jeynes said, 'to have the opportunity to design a school from scratch has been an exciting project that has given us the chance to create a school exactly as we wanted. It has been a huge challenge but the support of all the staff, parents and pupils has been outstanding and we are all very pleased with the end result.'

St Elizabeth's Catholic Primary School

Queen's Road, Richmond, Surrey, TW10 6HN

Tel: 02089 403 015
Fax: 02083 320 986
E-mail: info@st-elizabeths.richmond.sch.uk
Website: www.st-elizabeths.richmond.sch.uk

• Pupils: 215 boys and girls (plus 28 boys and girls in nursery), all day • Ages: 4-11, nursery 3 • Catholic • State

Head: Since 1988, Ms Christine Brett MEd (in English) BEd (in English) DipMathsEd (describes herself as 'over 21'). Educated at The Ursuline Convent, St Mary's University College (formerly part of University of London and now part of University of Surrey), where she is now a governor and King's College, London. Lives locally in Barnes and taught previously at the Catholic primaries of St Augustine's in Hammersmith and St Mary Magdalen in Mortlake; then deputy head of St Mary's, Clapham. Interests include the theatre, art, foreign travel (providing no aeroplanes involved!), reading and swimming. Likeable and sweet-natured in a way rarely encountered in the 21st century, but 'enormously efficient', according to one mother, and very on the ball educationally. Only the seventh head in the history of the school since its foundation in 1840. Teaches the strongest mathematicians once a week. Parents speak highly of her, particularly her fierce loyalty to the school, her commitment to the Catholic faith and her achievements in promoting the family atmosphere of the school. One mother said, 'she gives lots of encouragement and praise and everyone is made to feel good about something.' Another commented that she cares for each and every pupil as though her own child, but is held in some awe by the pupils.

Entrance: Oversubscribed (72 applicants for 30 places), which means that the intake is effectively 100 per cent Catholic. Realistically, don't even think about applying unless your child is baptised and in a regular or occasionally practising Catholic family within Richmond, Kew, Ham or East Sheen. Regular attenders get priority over the occasional ones. Priority is then given to those living nearest the school and to siblings of present pupils. Extent of practising Catholicism must be certified by the priest: result is large and enthusiastic attendance at local Sunday services. NB head very opposed to parents withdrawing children from school at seven to take up places in prep schools and will require an undertaking in this respect – 'if that's what parents want, they should choose it at 4.' Feels strongly that children need continuity and stability rather than a parking place for three years.

Exit: To up to 20 schools, including the state Catholic schools of Gumley House Convent, Wimbledon College, The Ursuline Convent, Sacred Heart, Cardinal Vaughan and the London Oratory; to local Richmond schools such as Waldegrave Girls, to Kingston schools Tiffin and Richard Challoner and to independent schools such as Lady Eleanor Holles, Surbiton High School, Hampton and Latymer Upper School. One mother said that 'pupils intended for independent schools tend to go to local tutors during the year before entrance exams.'

Remarks: Hugely popular state school, well regarded and chosen by many parents who could easily afford the private sector. Good SATs results – for 11 year olds they are 'well above average' in English and science and even more so for maths when compared with schools of similar socio-economic intake. School built on present site in 1969 to unusual and appealing design incorporating semi-open-plan layout. The building floods with light – hexagonal rooms open out to the grounds and partially glazed ceilings result in conservatory-like environment – very 'Homes & Gardens' and rather appropriate in midst of local ritzy housing. Surrounded by reassuring, impressive security – locked gates during school day with entry phone access both to the site and at main entrance. Head believes that building style also leads to greater openness, willingness to share and consideration for others. Certainly we detected a noticeably caring atmosphere and the pupils are polite, well behaved and neatly attired in traditional uniform. Older children are assigned to look after younger ones who have hurt themselves. Assemblies or prayers are held each day for each class and parents are welcome to assembly on Wednesdays. Religious education report (required by Ofsted in respect of denominational education) in 2001 is extremely complimentary. Family-friendly policy continued with the 'Cam-kids' after-school care scheme run jointly with two other schools – children up to age 11 collected and walked from school to nearby Cambrian Centre until 6pm if required. Currently, one computer to 10 children but a new ICT suite has just been built enabling 30 children at a time to be taught ICT skills. Notable annual arts week when specialists are brought in for clay modelling, tie-dying etc. Recent additions have been a super library, a light and airy group room, the ICT suite, an SEN room and an environmental room, which has French windows to the pond.

Parents include the whole spectrum of society as the catchment area is so wide. 45 children – mostly of white European heritage – have English as an additional language, and 32 have SEN (SEN co-ordinator 4 days per week). School premises are adapted for physical disability, with access ramps and special loo facilities. One third of the 14 staff has been here for more than 5 years. Football, netball, swimming and athletics are all compulsory; school recently very successful locally at swimming and reports that parental worries about inadequate sports now less audible. Unfortunately, there is no playing field, only hard-surface provision which is basically the junior playground, with benching. However, school uses the outdoor facilities of a secondary school two minutes walk away. Infant play area is artificial grass most attractively landscaped and equipped. About 60 learn a musical instrument. There are extra-curricular clubs but some parents would like to see more. Interesting extras include a Latin club run after school by an Oxford classicist mum, another runs a chess club and the Italian embassy provides a teacher to teach Italian for one day a week (timetabled) to ages 7-10. School keen on charitable activities – supports MacMillan Cancer Care and Catholic Children's Society, among others. Nativity play presented at The Royal Star & Garter Home, and carol singing at Richmond railway station. Very active and supportive PTA which raises impressive amount of funds every year. Parental involvement in school high and encouraged. Head says school receives 'huge support', from the governors – because of the needs of the Catholic community governors tend to stay on for longer than the period of their child's education at the school. Nursery is separate unit on site in premises due for upgrade. Fee-paying, although in effect most children over three and a half are funded by government scheme. Same admissions criteria as the school. Some children stay all day and some are part-time – aims to be family-friendly and flexible. Ofsted report of 2000 says: 'The very first thing that strikes a visitor to St Elizabeth's ... is how eager the pupils are to learn and how committed the staff are to achieving the highest possible standards.' As they join the queue for a place, parents obviously agree.

St Faith's

Linked to Leys School (The) in the Senior section

Trumpington Road, Cambridge, Cambridgeshire, CB2 2AG

Tel: 01223 352 073
Fax: 01223 314 757
E-mail: admissions@stfaiths.co.uk
Website: www.stfaiths.co.uk

- Pupils: 510 boys and girls; all day • Ages: 4-13 • Inter-denom
- Independent

Head: Mr C S S Drew MA.
Entrance: By assessment and interview.
Remarks: Junior school for The Leys (qv).

Saint Felix Schools, Preparatory School

Linked to Saint Felix Schools in the Senior section

Halesworth Road, Reydon, Southwold, Suffolk, IP18 6SD

Website: www.stfelix.co.uk

- Pupils: 140 girls and boys in prep/pre-prep, 54 in nursery
- Ages: 1-11 girls and boys • Non-denom • Fees: Prep/pre prep £1,200 - £2,200 • Independent • Open days: Saturdays in May and October

Remarks: For details see senior school entry.

St George's Junior School

Linked to Saint George's School Edinburgh in the Senior section

Garscube Terrace, Edinburgh, EH12 6BG

Tel: 0131 311 8000
Fax: 0131 311 8120
E-mail: office@st-georges.edin.sch.uk
Website: www.st-georges.edin.sch.uk

- Pupils: girls (boys in nursery) • Ages: 2-11
- Fees: £1,830 - £2,335 • Independent

Remarks: See main school for details.

St Hilary's School

Holloway Hill, Godalming, Surrey, GU7 1RZ

Tel: 01483 416 551
Fax: 01483 418 325
E-mail: admin@sthilarysschool.com
Website: www.sthilarysschool.com

- Pupils: 65 boys, 180 girls (nursery 45 boys, 40 girls)
- Ages: 2.5 - 11 (girls), 2.5 -7 (boys) • Non-denom • Fees: £2,090 - £3020 • Independent • Open days: During autumn term and first Saturday after half term in spring term

Head: Since 1999, Mrs Susan Bailes BA MA PGCE (early fifties). Married to long serving history teacher and archivist at St Paul's Girls' School and has two sons (one went to St Hilary's before she took up post). Has a solid gold pedigree in education – formerly deputy head and head of English at Bute House (where she was 'very, very popular and much lamented' according to one in the know), and prior to that, posts at Durston House, Falkner House, and the secondary departments at Guildford High and St Catherine's Bramley. A clued- up, approachable, caring lady, with an extremely realistic approach to education and has a hands-on involvement with the school at all levels, 'I'm not in an ivory tower.' An experienced ISI inspector, she teaches English to years 5 and 6 – she can get to know the girls individually and better advise on senior schools (she maintains very close links with all the local senior schools – 'it's a very important part of the job'). On a lighter note, she is in charge of the school play every summer – she writes it, directs it, and produces it – the whole shebang. 'Mrs Bailes is a major selling point for the school,' says one mother, who has the head summed up in a nutshell.

Entrance: A non-selective school and very popular locally. Best bet for entrance is through the nursery (en passant – nursery is 'fabulous' say all – a well-equipped space with a magical feel – entrance via Winnie the Pooh tree mural in the corridor!). Places do come up later on ('there's always some movement', says head, due to parents' relocation) and there's another opportunity in year 3 for girls (as the year 2 boys move out). Pupils are invited to spend the day in the appropriate year group, staff assess how they will cope and look at the most recent school report. Scholarships available for girls going into year 3.

Exit: Boys leave at 7 and move on to one of the local boys' day schools – Aldro is popular, then Lanesborough, Cranleigh, St Edmund's. Girls leave at 11 either for one of the Guildford academic powerhouses of Tormead, Guildford High or St Catherine's or more locally to Prior's Field in Godalming. Also a few to Cranleigh, Frensham Heights, St Swithun's, Downe House, Wycombe Abbey and The Royal, Haslemere. 'The girls really couldn't be better prepared for the next school,' says an enthusiastic parent. Academic, art, music drama and dance scholarships recently to Prior's Field, Frensham Heights, Tormead, St Catherine's, The Royal and Feltonfleet – on average ten scholarships a year.

Remarks: A thriving, buzzy, place with a warm and happy atmosphere and very impressive academic achievements for a non-selective school. Founded in 1927 by local worthy Miss Marjorie Hiorns, the school holds its traditions and family values dear, whilst embracing the new. Mrs B aims to nurture a love of learning and for the school experience to be 'an appetiser for life'. Keen to stress the 'pressure off' approach and the school certainly does not come across as a hothouse. Small class sizes – you can see their little brains buzzing with all the stimulation. All classes seemed happy, involved, confident and enjoying their lessons. Pupils take SATs and are geared up slowly but surely for the myriad of entrance exams. A parent says, 'they are eased into school life gently in the lower school but, once they get to the upper school, the brakes are off.' The school follows the National Curriculum, and in the lower school (years 1 and 2) most classes are taught by the class teacher. More specialist teaching from then on.

Excellent SEN provision – a lot of thought and care has gone into it. SEN department carries out an initial detailed assessment in consultation with parents. Mrs B says 'Each year we have one or two pupils with severe problems, but the majority of pupils needing SEN support have mild dyslexia or dyspraxia.' Those who need extra help spend time in one to one sessions with dedicated teachers in a well-equipped room. Sessions are during normal lesson time, but pupils are not taken out of core subject lessons. 'Children on our SEN register are regularly discussed so that pastoral care and discipline are seen to be fair and a child with poor organisational skills is not punished but encouraged.' SEN pupils are given (cost inclusive) support in the nursery and lower school, and at additional cost in the upper school.

Music, drama and dance are particular strengths of the school (scholarships abound to top-flight senior schools) – quite wonderful and inspirational music teacher was getting excellent performances out of the year 5 class (every single pupil sang a solo – perhaps for our benefit – but impressive nevertheless). Also much praised speech and drama teacher. Ex-pupils in the drama genre include Jenny Seagrove and David Farr.

School buildings, a Victorian house with later additions, are atmospheric. 'It's a bit of a rabbit warren,' admits Mrs B. Classrooms are bright and generally well equipped with the increasingly popular whiteboards – pupils rather more adept at using them than teachers in some cases. Recent addition of superb ICT suite enhances all pupils' learning. Lovely ICT room where pupils can research using the internet. Design & Technology is housed in one of the less gorgeous portable style classrooms on site but there are some wonderful and imaginative activities going on in there. Super art studio that looks like Hansel and Gretel's cottage filled to the brim with examples of imaginative art. Art projects link to topics in other lessons -some beautiful knot garden collages made after a visit to Hampton Court. Music room small but well equipped (grand piano and keyboards), science lab also well laid out. Good sized library.Small site – part of the reason why boys are off at age 7 to pastures new to let off steam and participate more in competitive sport. The lack of space doesn't detract too much and is the only giveaway that you are in a school almost in central Godalming. 'It would be fantastic if they had their own pool,' said one mum, but this seems to be the only downside for parents. New all-weather courts maximise the space – hockey, netball, tennis can now be played on site throughout the year. Sporting activities are wide ranging and 'very inclusive' so that all can enjoy, regardless of talent and 'there are fixtures for all the teams left right and centre,' says a mum. Mrs B has been instrumental in introducing a wider range of extra-curricular clubs and activities including gardening, golf, judo, archery and chess.Nurturing atmosphere. The head has a communication box in which anonymous messages can be left to alert her to any problems. Any bullying dealt with through class teachers or through 'our lovely matron' – children are encouraged to write down events and talk about them. Exemplary weekly newsletter from Mrs B, well laid out and full of information in an easy to digest format.St H has something of a reputation amongst parents at other local schools as being rather prissy and precious, particularly for boys (there are some boys from all-boy families in attendance – parents like the gentle start to formal school life – but boys in the main usually have sisters at the school). Doesn't feel like this to us – our ten year old guides were assertive, jolly, fun, and interesting. Even so, perhaps not the ideal place for a boisterous, 5-year-old.Uniform is a slightly scary combination of brown and yellow ('I was horrified when I first saw it,' says Mrs B) but it's very distinctive to say the least. Summer dresses are pretty gingham, with new addition of attractive winter tartan skirts and bright yellow fleeces which add to the maximum bumble bee effect. Boys have the pleasure of wearing brown jumpers and shorts with yellow shirts, also with optional yellow fleece.Wide catchment of much of south Surrey including Farnham, Haslemere and Cranleigh and villages in between. Parents are generally professionals, many have moved out of London for better quality of life for their children. Old Hilarians (yes, really) are very loyal to the school – there are children and grandchildren of old boys and girls at the school, and ex-pupils stay in touch.

St Hughs School

Cromwell Avenue, Woodhall Spa, Lincolnshire, LN10 6TQ

Tel: 01526 352 169
Fax: 01526 351 520
E-mail: sthughs-schooloffice@btconnect.com
Website: www.st-hughs.lincs.sch.uk

• Pupils: 160; 90 boys and 70 girls, boarding and day
• Ages: 4 - 13 • C of E • Fees: Day £1,685 - £3,115 and boarding £4,115 - £4,195 • Independent

Head: Since 1997, Mr Stephen Greenish. Previously deputy head of Crosfields, Reading. Teaching is in his blood with both father and grandfather being headmasters of prep schools. Came to St Hugh's with dwindling numbers and has had a huge impact turning it, and its reputation, around. A good, solid chap. His wife is very involved and as a team, they sell St Hugh's as a family orientated school.

Entrance: Majority of the children rise through the ranks of the school's pre-prep. Prospective pupils spend a day at the school for assessment.

Exit: 75 per cent of the children go on to independent senior schools in the A1 corridor, Uppingham, Oundle, Oakham, Repton, Queen Margaret's. The remaining 25 per cent get places at local grammar schools at 13.

Remarks: Set in a leafy residential road in this sleepy Victorian town, with a good acreage of well-maintained grounds. Strong sense of family, excellent facilities – not surprising that it is popular, drawing children from a relatively local area. About 30 per cent of the children are from Services families, many from the RAF bases nearby.

The headmaster doesn't have to sell boarding as the children seem to make that decision for themselves and become weekly boarders in their last years. There are full-time boarders who are well-looked after at weekends and kept busy. Everyone (children, teachers and parents) agrees that the food is 'fantastic' (their words), with plenty of choice. The place is absolutely spotless throughout the boarding and school side.

Classes are grouped according to ability from year 5 with an average of 14 in a class. If a child has the ability, the school is prepared to push but generally, the teaching is taken at a gentle pace. Some of the children are statemented and the SEN department is well-staffed, with one-to-one lessons available. Staff are on average in their 40s and the headmaster is 'proactive in helping with career moves'.

Everyone is given the opportunity to contribute to the school either on the games field, musically or in drama but it's sport that rules the roost. Matches are played at all levels, involving as many as possible. The school is prepared to travel up to two hours for matches and the calendar is full of fixtures, taking the teams hither and thither. No-one is left out.

St Hugh's is a local prep school turning out well-rounded children who are polite and have discreet self-confidence. Happy parents – and children.

St James Independent School for Boys (Junior)

Earsby Street, Olympia, London, W14 8SH

Tel: 02073 481 777
Fax: 020 7348 1790
E-mail: juniorschools@stjamesschools.co.uk
Website: www.stjamesschools.co.uk

• Pupils: 125 boys, all day • Ages: 4-10 • Inter-denom (but see below) • Fees: £2,350 - £2,560 • Independent • Open days: Regular weekly showrounds of the school, by appointment only

Headmaster: Since 1993, Mr Paul Moss Cert Ed (fifties). Grammar school educated, taught for 11 years in the state sector before moving to Thomas's where he taught in all their schools, became deputy head, then head of the Battersea branch. Very hands-on teacher in the girls' and boys' schools. Chairman of ISA from January 1st 2004.

Entrance: First come, first served, but siblings given priority. Special provision for sons of Old Boys and Girls. No formal testing for children joining aged 4 and 5 but there is an informal assessement and a nursery report is required where appropriate. Formal testing for children applying to enter at a later stage.

Exit: All but a few go on to the senior branch – NB in year 6.

Money Matters: A few bursaries are available.

Remarks: School is associated with the School of Economic Science – www.schooleconomicscience.org. The boys' and girls' schools share the same premises but in separate parts and they are run independently. Some shared teaching and activities, they come together for special occasions eg concerts, Speech Day. Both schools moved here from Queensgate, SW7. They share the site

with the girls' senior school (qv). Large pleasant redbrick E-shaped building with arcaded courtyard at the front and a good big playground behind. Light and airy classrooms and fine facilities.

Sanskrit from the age of 5 and philosophy for all children – no National Curriculum, children are 'fed the finest material available – Shakespeare, Mozart.' Same teacher stays with the children from the age of 5 until they leave the school. All children screened at various stages for learning difficulties.

Terrifically strong contacts with parents, who flood into the school each morning. Staff – young and old – spend a residential fortnight each year in the country honing their teaching skills and furthering their understanding about education and the inter-relatedness of all subjects. Strong emphasis on the whole child – and this is not just lip service in the prospectus – the junior schools share the same philosophy as the senior school of nurturing, discipline, caring for your neighbour and work hard, play hard.

Uniform is royal blue. Very good food. Inspiring music, sports given high priority. Happy and blooming children in both schools.

St James Independent School for Girls (Junior Department)

Earsby Street, Olympia, London, W14 8SH

Tel: 020 7348 1777
Fax: 020 7348 1790
E-mail: juniorschools@stjamesschools.co.uk
Website: www.stjamesschools.co.uk

• Pupils: 150 • Ages: 4-10 girls, all day • Inter-denom (but see below) • Fees: £2,350 - £2,560 • Independent • Open days: Regular weekly showrounds by appointment only

Headmaster: Since 1993, Mr Paul Moss Cert Ed (fifties). Grammar school educated, taught for 11 years in the state sector, before moving to Thomas's where he taught in all their schools, became deputy head then head at the Battersea branch. Very hands-on teacher in the girls' and boys' schools. Chairman of ISA from January 1st 2004.

Entrance: First come, first served – but siblings given priority. Special provision for daughters of Old Boys and Girls. No formal testing for children joining at ages 4 and 5, but we have an informal assessment and request a nursery report where appropriate. There is formal testing for children applying to enter at a later stage.

Exit: All but a few go on to the senior branch – NB at year 6.

Remarks: Both the boys' and the girls' schools are on the same premises but in separate parts and are run independently – some shared teaching or activities at, they come together for special occasions (eg concerts, speech day). Both schools moved here (formerly in Queensgate, SW7). They share the site with the senior girls' school (qv). Large pleasant redbrick E-shaped building with arcaded courtyard at the front and a good big playground behind. Light and airy classrooms and fine facilities.

Sanskrit from the age of 5 and philosophy for all children – no National Curriculum, but 'children are fed the finest material available, eg Mozart, Shakespeare.' School is associated with the School of Economic Science – www.school economicscience.org. Same teacher stays with the children from the age of five until they leave the school. All children screened at various stages for learning difficulties.

Terrifically strong contacts with parents, who flood into school each morning. Staff – young and old – spend a residential fortnight each year in the country honing teaching skills and furthering their understanding about education and the inter-relatedness of all subjects. Strong emphasis on the whole child – and this is not just lip service in the prospectus: the junior schools share the same philosophy as the senior school of nurturing, discipline, caring for your neighbour and work hard, play hard.

Uniform is royal blue. Very good food. Inspiring music, sports given high priority. A few bursaries are available. Happy and blooming children in both schools.

St James's Catholic Primary School

260 Stanley Road, Twickenham, Middlesex, TW2 5NP

Tel: 02088 984 670
Fax: 02088 933 038
E-mail: info@st-james.richmond.sch.uk
Website: www.st-james.richmond.sch.uk

• Pupils: 280 boys and 270 girls (including 50 in the nursery), all day • Ages: 3-11 • RC only • State

Head: Since 2000, Mrs Veronica Heffernan, BD MA (late forties). Married (to another head teacher) with two grown-up children. Previously head for 7 years at St Mary's, Chiswick. Neat and petite, she comes across as calm and very capable – completely on top of her brief of running this expanding school, while still managing to fit in some regular teaching and Friday choir practice. 'She is fantastic – and very approachable,' says one mother. 'I think the children are in awe of her and eager to please, but in a positive way.' She knows most children by name and regularly paces corridors, classrooms and playground. 'Visionary,' says another parent. 'She has fantastic ideas and is very friendly and happy.' She is strict and takes no nonsense from the children or their parents. 'I have heard her say that she won't entertain playground gossip, but if there is a genuine issue over anything you can get to see her quickly and she is very very fair,' said another mother. 'She goes by the book and I have nothing but praise for her.'

Entrance: At 3 to nursery, and 4 to the main school. Non-selective academically, children must be baptised Catholics and then admission is based on proximity to the school. Serving four parishes in Twickenham and Hampton, the school changed to 3-form entry to cope with over-subscription in 2002. But the school is still over-subscribed – 2004 saw 110 applications for 52 nursery places and 150 applications for the 90 reception places. Getting into the nursery does not guarantee a reception place but, in practice, most do go on to the main school as criteria are similar. If you want a place get to church and move nearby.

Exit: Popular choices are Hampton and The London Oratory for boys and Gumley House for girls. Recent scholarships to Kingston Grammar and also to St George's, Weybridge (for music) and St David's, Ashford (for PE).

Remarks: Brand new, state of the art accommodation, a gift for local Catholic families. Its very strong Catholic ethos and excellent academic results make it a popular choice around these parts. The school's expansion into a new building on the same site has been welcomed by parents. 'The whole place seems to have been rejuvenated,' says one happy parent. The building is attractive and the school staff worked with the architect to get things right. A good example of being 'built for the purpose' is the ICT suite – where all the computer workstations face front for whole class teaching, rather than the more usual arrangement where they face the wall. Interactive whiteboards are in every classroom – including the nursery. The front of the school is one storey, rising to two storeys at the back (with a lift as well as stairs). Nursery children enjoy an additional outside classroom. Sunny yellow decoration gives a warm, almost Mediterranean feel to the place (indeed Italian is taught from year 3, and to any interested parents after school, as part of an initiative with the Italian embassy). Great use of space outside as well, with covered ways to provide some shelter, tables for lunch in good weather, and a huge climbing frame.

St James's has been up and running since the 1960s, gradually expanding from a single entry school to the current 3-form entry, but retaining its good local reputation throughout. 'We heard fantastic reports of it and moved nearby to be sure of a place,' said one parent. 'We feel it has given our children a really good foundation and that they will get into a good secondary school after this.' Certainly there is a purposeful buzz about the place. Classrooms have a bright and industrious air and the children – all very smart and wearing proper ties – seem engaged in what they are doing.

Expect your child to work hard. There is a structured approach to teaching and a lot of homework (for a state school). 'I was shocked at the amount of homework – 1 1/2 to 2 hours three nights a week when my daughter was in year 4,' said one mother. Mainly literacy and numeracy, there are spellings to learn and reading 'without fail'. The head agrees with the parents we spoke to: she says, 'It's a big commitment which means a lot of parental involvement, especially with the younger children. We expect high standards of academic excellence and behaviour here.'

But it's not all work. 'They play hard too,' said another parent. 'My kids have lots of fun and are very happy.' And don't be discouraged if your child is not an academic high-flier. Parents of children whose talents lay elsewhere seem just as pleased. 'I feel my daughter, who is not so academic, has fared very well here,' says one mother. 'She is young in her year, but got lots of extra help and has gained tremendous confidence. She is good at art and I feel this has been

encouraged. The teachers seem to nourish talent, wherever it lies.' There is an SEN co-ordinator and support teacher – and facilities have been enhanced by the move to the new building, which has more quiet rooms for group and individual work and assessment. St James's also houses The George Tancred Centre for autistic children. 10 places are available here and are open to non-Catholic children. Fantastic facilities include partitioned work areas so the children can control their immediate environment and a 'time-out' room filled with soft play equipment. The playground is separated from, but adjacent to, that of the main school and a regulated number of children from the main school are allowed to go in and play with the George Tancred children at break time – and compete to do so.

Plenty of praise for a delightful and stable staff – a mix of ages, but not gender, with just one male classroom assistant. School is very good at netball (Middlesex and Surrey champions) and chess, but does not really excel in other sporting pursuits. 'There is plenty of sport played and we take part in lots of things – but we don't actually win much,' one parent reports. Musical abilities are nicely encouraged – with a dedicated teacher and practice room and annual presentations of a music cup and another for 'Most Promising' musician.

Located in a cul de sac, opposite another school, access by car in the morning is not the best. Helping to overcome this, the school is heavily involved in a 'green transport policy', running several 'walking buses' and encouraging children to ride bikes and scooters to school, where 'parking' is provided. A very Catholic school – prayers are said three times a day in classrooms and whole school gathers for mass on holy days.

St John's Beaumont School

Old Windsor, Windsor, Berkshire, SL4 2JN

Tel: 01784 432 428
Fax: 01784 494 048
E-mail: admissions@stjohnsbeaumont.co.uk
Website: www.stjohnsbeaumont.org.uk

• Pupils: 325 boys; 60 board, 265 day • Ages: 4-13 • RC (owned by Jesuits) • Fees: Day: pre-prep £1,999, prep £2,586 - £3,682. Boarding: weekly £4,860, full £5,762 • Independent

Head: Interregnum. The remarkable, stylish and long-serving head, Mr Dermot St John Gogarty, died in a car crash in November 2005. His passionate advocacy of the Jesuit principles of service and justice, his distaste for humbug and his insistence on the importance of old-fashioned virtues like trust and honesty, show throughout the school.

Entrance: First come first served, rigorously adhered to – though some turned down after educational psychologist's report, 'if we can't help them'; long waiting list. Most enter at age 4 but places are kept open for another small intake at year 3.

Exit: Eton, Ampleforth, Stonyhurst, Hampton, Harrow, Wellington, Winchester, The Oratory, Bradfield, Milton Abbey, ie the whole range, but skewed towards the more demanding senior schools.

Remarks: Fine 1888 buildings on a hilltop, by the architect of Westminster Cathedral. Lovely Gothic chapel, brand new music and drama block (there is a strong musical tradition), cheerful new junior classrooms. Everywhere inside is bright and wholesome (cleaners on constant duty), including dorms and loos. Extensive rolling grounds, bordering on Windsor Great Park, including 'one of the finest cricket squares to be found in an English prep school' and acres of woodland – one resident priest is fascinated by forestry. Following shortcomings in IT provision and library accessibility noted in recent ISI report the school has erected a purpose-built IT centre for learning and two new libraries. Usual broad curriculum, including Latin and Spanish options from year 5 and Greek for some. Streaming operates from year 5; boys and parents seem happy about this. There is a strong academic drive about the school, without the less gifted being neglected; high standards for all. A very structured, hard-working place. Class size averages 14; EAL help available, and the Campion Unit has teachers in all fields of SEN requirements.

It's a pretty sporty place – games every day and typical RC emphasis on rugby (recent tour of South Africa); swimming also very good. Pupils are kept busy right through the day; school ends for all at 6+ pm. All staff expected to offer at least one extra-curricular activity – aeromodelling to origami and cooking. The sixty full boarders have full weekend programmes, including cultural visits and relaxation time. They sleep in long, old-fashioned dorms, divided into sacrosanct cubicles; plenty of resident staff. Staff are a healthy mixture of young and long-serving and clearly relish the school's success and sense of purpose. When you sidle into a classroom they will march over and shake you by the hand, without apparently losing disciplinary hold or pedagogic flow.

Most pupils come from London and the south east; some from as far as Mexico, Korea, Japan. About 25 per cent are non-Catholic – head boy in 2004/05 was a Muslim – all denominations 'positively welcomed'. Non-Christians are invited to share as far as they feel comfortable in the school's religious life; this seemingly difficult balancing trick is managed with some ease. Parents are issued with an amazingly detailed handbook which covers everything from a mission statement to what 7 year olds are doing at 4.05pm on Thursday. Some financial help available for deserving cases.

A famously prescriptive school, expects high standards of discipline. Successful, with a strong sense of community. 'Glammy Berkshire – turn up in the Rolls,' advises one parent. Pupils are confident, at ease with themselves and with others – much respect both ways between boys and staff; ambitious and socially alert. Everyone seems to enjoy being there.

ST JOHN'S COLLEGE
SCHOOL

Grange Road, Cambridge, Cambridgeshire, CB3 9AB

Tel: 01223 353 532
Fax: 01223 355 846
E-mail: admissions@sjcs.co.uk
Website: www.sjcs.co.uk

• Pupils: around 250 boys, 200 girls. 50 boy and girl boarders, 400 day • Ages: 4-13 • C of E • Fees: Day £2,345 - £3,180; boarding £5,023. Choristers £1,674 • Independent

Head: Since 1990, Mr Kevin Jones (mid forties) MA, plus unfinished thesis on how best to acquire knowledge and preserve creativity. Educated Woolverstone Hall (state boarding) and Caius, Cambridge. Previous post – deputy head in the school and before that head of drama and English at the Yehudi Menuhin School. Married with one son formerly in the school and one in the senior department. A thinker, good with children. Nice sense of humour. Comments, a propos parental observation that the school is a high pressure zone, that this is not so, he thinks, and that 'the most precious thing we can give to our children is their childhood'.

Entrance: Getting in is Cambridge prep Valhalla. Name down embryo on. No testing at 3 - 'ridiculous' – but test at 7. Yearly scholarships for up to five boy choristers a year. Means-tested scholarships and bursaries at 11 for outstanding academic, music, artistic or all-round ability.

Exit: Every year gets clutch of scholarships to strong music schools – Eton, Tonbridge, Uppingham, Winchester. Gets even more academic scholarships, not to mention art, IT, DT and sports awards (about 50 per cent of leavers gain an award). Sends up to one third of boys to The Perse School in Cambridge, also to Oakham, Westminster, Rugby, Radley, Oundle, King's Canterbury etc, and one or two to East Anglian schools. A very few girls leave at 11 usually for The Perse Girls' and St Mary's Cambridge, the rest generally opt for co-educational boarding at 13.

Remarks: Wonderful prep school in a dreamy city – well worth bustling about to get in. Feels like a honeycomb of schools – kindergarten department in separate house, 'so it feels like home'; 5 to 8 year olds are in a wing of the smart tailor-made Byron House, which provides not only classrooms but smart hall/gym, drama studio, DT, computer room, music department etc for tinies. Older pupils in a

house down the road; boarders live above the shop with their own private recently refurbished and upgraded quarters – part of the £2.5 million building development (you name it, they've got it, from indoor swimming pool to junior library and new music school with individual practice rooms, song school and concert room). Adjacent property acquired and recently redeveloped provides gardens, an arts facility and a lecture theatre; space released in old buildings used to expand ICT etc.

Claims to have (and we would not dispute it) best computer facilities of any prep school – whole school networked in 1998; two computer labs and two networks of PCs for the 4-9 year olds plus laptops. More importantly, the school has the staff to go with them – all teachers and classroom assistants are trained in IT in-house to the skill level achieved by leaving pupils ie very high. Recognised as the National Expert Centre for all prep schools for DT and IT. Head's aim is to 'meet individual needs of each child, so the most (and least) able children get what they need' and, with that in mind, he has come up with a number of developments – study skills (teaching children the skills of individual learning) now an integral part of the curriculum; advanced tutorial system, with one member of staff responsible for 'knowing all there is to know' about no more than ten children and their families; reporting system that allows parents to be 'fully involved' in their children's education. Also 'individual needs department' – qualified specialists backed by educational psychologist on staff. Approximately 20 per cent of pupils at any one time receive help with a 'learning difficulty'. Head hopes that a parent's comment that, 'the school's fine if you can cope but no fun for the strugglers', no longer applies – places immense emphasis on children's happiness, the need for fun and laughter and training teachers (wish more did this).

Jolly red uniform. High calibre of teachers who draw all that is best and most original from pupils. Class size never more than 20 and these are subdivided in senior years to make classes of 12-18. Terms now fit in with other schools and not university terms as hitherto. Most helpful, flexible school day/week includes weekly boarding, 'day' boarding (ie until 8.15pm) and 'staying on' (until 5.15pm) – a miracle for working parents. No longer Saturday morning school but sports coaching and optional activities. Although this is not a 'professional' games school, it has lots of sporting options with good coaching including real tennis and rowing (has produced national real tennis champions). Also the usual sports – rugby, hockey (for the girls) etc and head points out the school has produced county players in these sports plus netball, cricket, raquets, athletics and swimming.

Says a past parent, 'there seems to be some sort of magic that infuses everyone with confidence, happiness and generosity. In this atmosphere academic work prospers effortlessly and discipline appears to take care of itself while the children are so good to each other it brings a lump to your throat. In fact, at any school event it's difficult to know who is having more fun – the children, staff or parents. The head, Kevin Jones, is absolutely inspirational and has a staff of delightful characters who are adored almost without exception by the children. I must confess I'm a bit baffled by the whole thing – how can a school be this wonderful when so many others are tense, inhibited and uninspiring?' Quite.

St John's School

Broadway, Sidmouth, Devon, EX10 8RG

Tel: 01395 513 984
Fax: 01395 514 539
E-mail: nrp@stjohndevon.demon.co.uk
Website: www.st-johns.devon.sch.uk

• Pupils: 220 girls and boys (including 47 in Early Birds nursery)
• Ages: 2-13 • RC/Anglican • Fees: Day £1,460 - £2,225; boarding £3,585 - £4,069 • Independent • Open days: Every day

Head: Since 2005, Mrs Tessa Smith BA (Hons) PGCE DipM ACIM.

Entrance: About 60 per cent migrate from nursery. Non-selective although early registration is prudent. Reduction in fees for concurrent siblings. Children invited to spend familiarisation day prior to starting. Foreign intake usually 12 per cent. Day pupils come from 25-mile radius. Parents are typical middle-class professionals. Colourful and well-stocked Early Birds nursery has six-month waiting list for 12 places.

Exit: Popular destinations are King's College, Taunton and Exeter School. Others are Blundell's, Maynards, St Margaret's, Stover or Colyton Grammar School.

Remarks: Attractive former convent with stained glass windows. Stands on hill, bordered by countryside and stunning sea view. Excellent facilities. General administration may seem muddled (school prefers 'relaxed') but parents excuse this as part and parcel of the homey atmosphere.

Main course of study is based on the Common Entrance syllabus. National Curriculum SATS at Key Stage 1 & 2 also taken. Children from year 5 are setted by ability in all subjects. Maths is a particular strength with a good number of pupils gaining gold medals in the UK maths challenge each year. Able pupils are given extension work in the 'Endeavourers' group to extend and broaden their thinking skills in preparation for scholarship work. Major field games played – rugby, football, hockey, cricket (boys) and hockey, netball and rounders (girls). Other games or sports include athletics (8 children at National Championships 2004), swimming, tennis, basketball, cross country running and badminton. Cricket team champions of Devon and the Western Counties (4th in National Championships 2003). Indoor sports centre encourages children to participate in a wide range of sports. Discipline centres on rewards for good work and behaviour with the headmaster awarding special 'tokens' for work deemed to be excellent. Children thrive in the atmosphere of stressing the positive with children keen to gain stars (points) for their house. Successes are celebrated in the weekly assembly and the children thrive in the positive atmosphere that promotes positive behaviour of every kind. Prefects are assigned to each form so that the youngest children are encouraged to behave well by the older children whom they learn to respect and have confidence in. Good pastoral care; peaceful, family environment. Boarders well cared for in fun and colourful dorms painted by the last head and family. Homesickness rapidly resolved. Day parents supportive of boarding community – frequently have boarders staying weekends; ferry them to and from birthday parties etc. After usual settling in period, children may forget to phone home! Children in general confident, self-assured and gregarious individuals. Linked to school in St Petersburg, its pupils visit St John's to improve their English. Average 14 pupils per class. Two full-time SEN tutors and another who teaches English as a second language for foreign pupils. Careful timetabling to ensure dyslexics receive one-to-one tuition. Some pupils arrive here unable to communicate in English but that soon changes; a pupil who speaks their mother tongue is appointed as their special guardian. Every classroom and dormitory has computers; all pupils have own email address (internet is free 8am to 6pm five days a week). Mrs Smith takes over a happy school and we await developments!

ST LEONARDS - NEW PARK

Linked to Saint Leonards School & Sixth Form College in the Senior section

The Pends, St Andrews, Fife, KY16 9QJ

Tel: 01334 472 126
Fax: 01334 476 152
E-mail: info@stleonards-fife.org
Website: www.stleonards-fife.org

• Pupils: girls and boys; all day • Ages: 3-12 • Independent

Remarks: For further details see senior school.

ST MARGARET'S JUNIOR SCHOOL (EDINBURGH)

Linked to Saint Margaret's School (Edinburgh) in the Senior section

East Suffolk Road, Edinburgh, EH16 5PJ

Tel: 0131 668 1986
Fax: 0131 667 9814
E-mail: pcurran@st-margarets.edin.sch.uk
Website: www.st-margarets.edin.sch.uk

• Pupils: 225 girls and boys • Ages: 3 months to 11 years (boys - 3 months to 8 years) • Non-denom • Fees: £1,454 - £2,525 • Independent

Head: Miss Patsy Curran.

Entrance: Mostly at 5. Interview with head and short assessment.

Exit: A few leave to go to trad prep schools, or to public schools, most to senior school.

Remarks: For further details, see the senior school entry.

ST MARGARET'S JUNIOR SCHOOL (EXETER)

Linked to Saint Margaret's School (Exeter) in the Senior section

147 Magdalen Road, Exeter, Devon, EX2 4TS

Tel: 01392 273 197
Fax: 01392 251 402
Website: www.stmargarets-school.co.uk

• Pupils: 70 girls, all day • Ages: 7-11 • C of E • Fees: £2,128 • Independent • Open days: Autumn and summer

Head: Since 1997, Sarah Agg-Manning BA (early fifties). Drama and art degree and PGCE from Exeter University. Studied drama and education at Rolle College and has taught all curriculum subjects in a wide selection of primary and preparatory schools in Somerset, Devon and the Bath, where she lived for 12 years. Married with three daughters who all attended St Margaret's at various stages.

Entrance: By application, entrance test and interview.

Exit: Transfer to senior school unconditional although all sit entrance exam.

Remarks: Self-contained building. Year 6 pupils taught by specialist senior teachers helping to make transition to senior school easier. Academic work closely monitored. Average class size: 15. At least one third scores above national average at level 6. Happy and caring environment. Children allowed to talk during change of class etc. Homely cottage garden with resident mini beasts, grass area and separate hard surface playground provide ample and interesting playing space. Opportunities abound from joining the Junior Choir to classics, Chinese, netball, dance, arts and crafts clubs.

St Margaret's School for Girls Junior Department

Linked to Saint Margaret's School for Girls in the Senior section

17 Albyn Place, Aberdeen, AB10 1RU

Tel: 01224 584 466
Fax: 01224 585 600
E-mail: info@st-margaret.aberdeen.sch.uk
Website: www.st-margaret.aberdeen.sch.uk

- Pupils: all girls, all day • Ages: 3-12 • Non-denom • Fees: £1,381 to £2,189 • Independent

Head: Mrs Tanja van Schie MEd NPQH TEFL.
Remarks: For details, see senior school entry.

St Martin's Ampleforth School

Linked to Ampleforth College in the Senior section

Gilling Castle, Gilling East, York, North Yorkshire, YO62 4HP

Tel: 0143 9766600
Fax: 01439 788 538
E-mail: headmaster@stmartins.ampleforth.org.uk
Website: www.stmartins.ampleforth.org.uk

- Pupils: 200 boys and girls • Ages: 3-13 • RC - accepts pupils of other denominations but they must be prepared to be a full participant in the religious life of the school • Fees: Pre-prep £1,445; thereafter: day £2,685, boarding £4,885 • Independent

Head: Since 2004, Mr Nicholas Higham.
Entrance: By test and interview.
Exit: Most children to Ampleforth, but also to other public schools.
Remarks: In Grade I-listed Gilling Castle – 3,000 acres of woods, lakes and gardens.

St Mary's Hall

Linked to Stonyhurst College in the Senior section

Stonyhurst, Lancashire, BB7 9PU

Tel: 01254 826 242
Fax: 01254 826 382
E-mail: saintmaryshall@stonyhurst.ac.uk
Website: www.saintmaryshall.com

- Pupils: 250; two-thirds boys; one fifth boarders • Ages: 3-13
- Roman Catholic in the Jesuit tradition • Fees: £1,613 - £2,244 (day); £4677 (boarding) • Independent • Open days: November

Head: Since 2004, Mr Lawrence Crouch BA MA PGCE (forties), married with four children. After studying English at Nottingham, an action-packed gap year and a spell teaching English in a comprehensive school, returned to his alma mater in 1982 as head of drama, later appointed head of English. A keen sportsman, a rugby, cricket and golf fan, also the current Stonyhurst campus squash champion; plays piano and oboe and as a singer is renowned for a definitive performance of 'Great Balls of Fire'. Warm, thoughtful, caring, approachable and, despite his impressive achievements, extremely modest; new to the role of prep school headmaster but clearly enjoying it enormously, his enthusiasm is infectious.

Entrance: Pupils enter all years but most commonly at 3, 5, 8 and 11. Admission to nursery and Reception via interview with the head and head of pre-prep, older children admitted following an interview and on receipt of a school report. Ages 10-12 require additional tests in maths, English and verbal reasoning. Two academic scholarships and one for music awarded for entry at 11+.

Exit: Straight on to Stonyhurst College. It is rare for a pupil to stray elsewhere, however school will advise appropriately if it feels Stonyhurst would be unsuitable.

Remarks: Set in glorious countryside amongst rolling fields, the inspiration is clear. However you and your children may have to learn a whole new vocabulary to enter the world of Jesuit traditions and beliefs in this 400-year-old school. For starters 'lines' are school houses, 'playrooms' are common rooms, 'playroom masters' are housemasters and then there is the Latin ... And yet the school is forward-thinking enough to pick up on the whims of modern children, issuing a 'credit card' for consistent good work that allows you jump the lunch queue, MSN offering an active forum for after-school chat and the top year producing their own web page. Traditional in that scholarship classes exist to 'push' the brightest; German taught from four and French from seven; school performances are enjoyed in the theatre; sport is popular as the usual carousel of after school activities and the ARK with goats, ponies, sheep et al is a joy for those children who are animal lovers.

A long school day but children cope and parents are grateful; strong boarding ethos with a mix of local children and others from Mexico, Hong Kong, Spain, Germany, Korea and beyond; Saturday school until lunchtime for day pupils. Charitable giving is important; the school has its own charity and a link with a school near Harare supporting the culture of 'men and women for others'. Parents are a mixed bag of old boys and local professionals, 70 per cent Catholic, other denominations accepting the liturgy also welcome. The nursery and pre-prep are lovely, in attractive modern surroundings with delightful teaching areas and a multi-sensory approach to learning; by contrast the prep school displays more formal teaching in higgledy-piggledy but nevertheless much-loved old buildings. Pupils appear confident and are hugely loyal, dreading the day when they must leave the security of these warm and supportive surroundings.

St Mary's Junior School (Shaftesbury)

Linked to Saint Mary's School Shaftesbury in the Senior section

Donhead St. Mary, Shaftesbury, Dorset, SP7 9LP

Tel: 01747 852 416
Fax: 01747 851 557
Website: www.st-marys-shaftesbury.co.uk

- Pupils: girls, boarding and day • Ages: 9-11 • RC
- Independent

Remarks: For further details, see the senior school entry.

St Mary's Music School Junior School

Linked to Saint Mary's Music School in the Senior section

Coates Hall, 25 Grosvenor Crescent, Edinburgh, EH12 5EL

Tel: 0131 538 7766
Fax: 0131 467 7289
E-mail: info@st-marys-music-school.co.uk
Website: www.st-marys-music-school.co.uk

- Pupils: girls and boys, some boarders • Ages: 9-11
- Non-denom • Fees: individually assessed • Independent
- Open days: October

Remarks: For details, see senior school entry.

St Mary's School (Melrose)

Abbey Park, Melrose, TD6 9LN

Tel: 01896 822 517
Fax: 01896 823 550
E-mail: enquiries@stmarys.newnet.co.uk
Website: www.stmarysmelrose.org.uk

- Pupils: 130 boys and girls in main school (40/60), 40 in nursery (kindergarten); 25 boarders max • Ages: main school 4-13; nursery 2.5-4 • Non-denom • Fees: Weekly boarding £3,990; day 3-8 £3,400; reception - upper transition £2,450; lower and upper kindergarten £20 per morning, £30. per day;
- Independent • Open days: In the summer term

Head: Since 1998, Mr John Brett MA CertMusEd, MCollP GCLCM (forties) who was educated at King's Bruton but did his A levels at Yeovil College ('fantastic music A level'). Studied music at Leeds and London and trails more letters after his name than most. He came from Thomas's (Battersea) where he was head of music, and before that taught at King's Hall in Somerset. An urbane, enterprising head, he oozes confidence (and well he might) and happily chatted up children and staff on our way round. After his appointment he discovered a school firmly entrenched in the trad-boys-prep school mind-set with a newly-built, barely-used, boys' dormitory (hungry builder governor) and rooms shut up all over the place. With sixty children and 'only three in the top year group', St Mary's was a school with a problem and Mr Brett happily admits that 'the first two or three years were a rocky ride'.

His first move was 'to stop the rot', literally. Fundraising helped too, and the school is financially sound. Armed with a strong nucleus of experienced teachers (now supplemented by younger models – more professional, with loads of specialist teachers) he went out and created a new market. 'Lots of input, lots of goodwill' 'Fantastic new board of governors, senior management and structure in place', and lives on the site with his wife Clare, who teaches drama, and their two small children. Mr Brett himself, despite all his musical trail of glory, actually teaches global citizenship to the top three year groups. 'But,' he says, 'children are always popping in (to his book-lined study) to see me so that I can hear them read'.

Entrance: All things to all men. The only independent school in the borders, children come from within a 20/30 mile radius, can come mid-term at any time if space available, otherwise automatically up from kindergarten. The odd state child has been known simply to come for an 'eighteen-month blast' before going back into the maintained sector again. And some come at 11 to do CE.

Exit: 'Most but not all' stay on until they go to their senior school which may be at 11, 12, or 13, depending whether they are going to continue in the independent vein in which case it is Glenalmond, Fettes, Merchiston, Loretto, St Georges in Edinburgh as well as Longridge Towers in Berwick, Queen Margaret's York or dive back into the state sector and Earlston High School.

Money Matters: Scale of sibling reductions.

Remarks: Jolly useful little school, incredibly flexible, with flexi, weekly and day pupils; one or two toffs, but mostly farmers and local professionals who stay to the bitter end, plus 'masses of' first time buyers. Tiny classes, max 18 but usually much less, only one stream but scholars will be 'hived off' and setted at 10 if necessary. Latin and Greek from eight, 'fantastically popular teacher'. Languages from five, taster term of German, French, Spanish then specialise in French for Common Entrance. Science taught separately for the last four years, and pupils move round the staff. 'Excellent' dyslexia department, and good support for the very bright as well. Withdrawn help and staff will go into class as well – 'pretty flexible' (might be the school motto). Keen on handwriting.

Art mistress comes three times a week, and obviously pretty busy if the amount of art on display is anything to go by. Drama strong and timetabled, the school has links with local theatrical costumiers. Good music, rehearsals and lessons in functional school hall, whilst pre-prep have own gym, with Noah and his ark drawn by the young, main school has to use the hall. Somewhat surprising cloistered classroom corridor and incredible conversions and add-ons (or subtractions) on the classroom side, very rabbit warreny. Charming little Foyle library, with computers all over the place and dedicated resource centre for every age group.

Day children can stay from 7.30 am (and breakfast in school) right through to 7.30 pm, by which time they will have done their prep and had supper. Kindergarten can stay till 4 pm, tinies wear delightful green and white check tabliers, and girls evolve from tartan gym slips to kilts. Jolly dorms upstairs, all brightly painted with splendid (unironed) stripy duvet covers. Dining room with proper menu (beware the 'sandwitch') and over-high benches for littlies to sit at the table. Brown bread only, and lots of sugar-free puds, and mainly organic as far as possible. Robert the chef comes complete with starched chef's hat and sparkling white uniform. Cor. He also makes rather natty millionaire's shortbread for the head's guests – not sugar-free at all.

Squads and teams triumph all over the place. Swimming off-site in Gala(shiels) and main games pitches just across some National Trust land. Smashing little school.

ST OLAVE'S SCHOOL (PRONOUNCED OLIVE'S)

Linked to Saint Peter's School in the Senior section

St Olave's School, York, North Yorkshire, YO30 6AB

Tel: 01904 527 416
Fax: 01904 527 303
E-mail: enquiries@st-olaves.york.sch.uk
Website: www.st-olaves.york.sch.uk

• Pupils: girls and boys; day and boarding from 8+ • Ages: 3 - 8 Clifton pre-prep; 8-13 St Olave's • Fees: St Olaves: Day £2,163 - £2,809. Boarders £4,323 - £4,931 • Independent • Open days: September, October and May

Head: Mr Andy Falconer.

Entrance: Selective. Automatic entry from Clifton pre-prep otherwise by assessment, interview and report from current school.

Exit: Majority to St Peter's.

Remarks: For further details see senior school, St Peter's School, York.

St Paul's Cathedral School

2 New Change, London, EC4M 9AD

Tel: 02072 485 156

Fax: 02073 296 568

E-mail: admissions@spcs.london.sch.uk

Website: www.stpauls.co.uk/school

- Pupils: 205 boys and girls, including 40 boy choristers; choristers board, the rest day • Ages: 4-13 • C of E, but other faiths welcome, though choristers mostly Christian • Fees: Day children £2,772 - £2,988; choristers £1,733 for boarding and musical instrument tuition • Independent • Open days: In the autumn term

Head: Since 2000, Mr Andrew Dobbin (fifties). Educated at Uppingham and Emmanuel College, Cambridge, where he read English, architecture and fine art, then 'got way-laid into teaching'. Taught at prep schools then King's Canterbury (qv), where he was a housemaster and head of drama. He is the only non-musician on the staff (even the chef is an organist), but he is passionate about the arts, and 'the artistic temperament is not unknown to me'. Has, by all accounts, done a fair amount of cutting out of dead wood. 'He's revolutionised the place,' said a parent. 'He's recruited some very good, punchy, young teachers who are great role models for the boys.'

Entrance: Sign up for the pre-prep by the time your child is one-ish; registration closes at 50, though there is a waiting list. Children are assessed informally at three for the 20 pre-prep places, mostly to ensure they will fit in with the school. 'Our children are mostly bouncy and extrovert; but we're fairly structured, so very free spirits may be better off elsewhere.' Another seven or eight come in at 7+, having spent a day at the school, which includes an hour's test – taken also by those already in the pre-prep. 'We're not a hothouse but we want to make sure they can keep up with the work.' Occasionally, pre-prep parents are told their child might be better off elsewhere, 'but we will already have flagged up possible problems and we feel a moral obligation to keep children on if possible.' Potential choristers have voice trials at seven or eight.

Exit: Both boys and girls are now encouraged to stay on till 13 – the head is keen on co-ed country boarding schools – but inevitably some do leave at 10 or 11. The prep school starting admitting girls in 2001, so they are making their way to the upper forms. Choristers and day pupils often get music scholarships to schools such as King's Canterbury (increasingly popular), Bedford, Charterhouse, Haileybury, Eton and Westminster. The head is keen to increase academic scholarships.

Money Matters: Bursaries up to full fees available for choristers.

Remarks: 'There was a misconception that everything revolves around the choristers,' says the head. 'Actually, everything revolves around the children.' The rhythm of school life – including a long Easter break that does not necessarily coincide with other schools – is inevitably structured round the choristers' commitments. These include before- and after-school music rehearsals, evensong four days a week, Saturday morning rehearsal and services on Sunday, plus nipping off to sing in Jubilee concerts and the like. The school is overshadowed, literally, by St Paul's Cathedral; it is owned by the Dean and Chapter of the cathedral, who also serve as governors, are members of the school council and funded the recent refurbishment programme. Some chorister arrogance has been reported in the past but the head has ensured that day children now play a part in cathedral services, reading lessons and poetry, and honours are more fairly shared. 'I'm adamant that the choristers are not special people – they're treated perfectly normally.' Non-chorister parents concur that their children don't feel like second class citizens.

This is not a hothouse; it is fairly unselective and, while some pupils do gain scholarships to the top academic schools, it is not the raison d'être. Having said that, standards are on the up, with particular praise for the pre-prep and for the English, geography and science teaching (there's a big science lab). 'The standard of creative writing is amazing,' said a parent. 'There are some fantastic teachers here and the staff really seem to be enjoying themselves.' Languages – pupils start French at four and Latin at eight – are probably the weakest link; IT is improving. Music is streamed at the top of the school; the top four years are streamed for maths. No special needs department; there is learning support, particularly lower down the school but 'help has been patchy,' commented a parent.

Tutor groups meet weekly to discuss the pupils' report cards. Pupils also write their own report, 'which keeps the staff on their toes.'

Music is, naturally, a strong point, with two school orchestras, brass ensembles, clarinet and jazz groups alongside the choirs. Nearly everyone learns at least one instrument, 'anything except bagpipes' and the choristers all learn two. Pupils no longer take music GCSE at 13 ('it's infuriating for the secondary school, who don't know what to do with them after that') though they are often composing beyond GCSE standard by then. 'But it's my job to counterbalance all the music,' says the head, who encourages as much sport and drama as possible. The school's outside space consists of a (mostly tarmac) garden with climbing frame for the pre-prep, and a smallish playgrounds for the main school, but pupils play football, hockey and cricket in Coram Fields and Regents Park and go swimming at City of London School pool and Golden Lane. 'There are only 13 boys in my son's class, so virtually everyone has to be in the teams,' said a parent. 'But they don't do badly. And the jolly, young teachers organise plenty of sporty outings.' There a ski trip every year and year 8 has a week in Snowdonia after common entrance. Good drama in the pre-prep rather tails off higher up. 'I try like mad to encourage it,' says the head, 'but there isn't the time.'

Clubs after school in Thursday (the one day choristers don't rehearse) include fencing, IT and skating at Broadgate ice rink. Nice, light art room with a kiln for firing pottery and a school location which means that pupils can stroll down to Tate Modern during double art, but no facilities for DT.

The boarders sleep in compact bunk rooms in St Augustine's tower overlooking the pre-prep garden, but eat, relax and do homework and music practice in the main school. This is mostly refurbished including carpets throughout, which 'have made a big difference to behaviour', to include a 'quiet' room with chess set and computer, next to the head's office; the common room and TV room are badly in need of their planned revamp.

The school, opened in Carter Lane in 1874, moved to its purpose-built premises in 1967. Day pupils were admitted in 1989; they come mostly from Islington, Hackney, the Barbican and Docklands. Girls first joined the pre-prep in 1998, and the main school in 2001. Mostly professional parents eg solicitors and barristers, many of whom work locally.

'It's a happy school,' said one mother. 'My son, who is quite timid, has felt quite comfortable there.' 'It's a nice, well-balanced school with ethereal music,' said another.

ST PAUL'S CATHOLIC PRIMARY SCHOOL, THAMES DITTON

Hampton Court Way, Thames Ditton, Surrey, KT7 0LP

Tel: 020 8398 6791
Fax: 020 8398 4275
E-mail: info@stpauls-thamesditton.surrey.sch.uk

- Pupils: 140 girls and 150 boys , all day • Ages: 4-11 • RC
- State • Open days: June and October

Head: Since 1990, Mrs Fionnuala Johnson, BEd (late forties), married with two children, the younger one is at the school. Garners huge respect from parents, who regard her as the architect of the school's (and their children's) success. Descriptions of her vary along the spectrum from 'strong impressive leader', through 'powerful personality' to 'formidable' (we'll vouch for that) – but most also mention her caring side. 'The children adore her – tempered by due reverence,' said one mother. 'I've seen children run across the playground to hug her,' said another.

Has plenty to say about the school – of which she is fiercely proud – and is full of plans and ideas for the future. She knows all the children by name – and promises to keep this up even when the school has doubled in size. As it is, parents wonder at her grasp of all the smallest details of their lives and the praise continues – 'She's fantastic – the school is as good as it is because of her. She talks to the children quietly and they all listen – she never needs to raise her voice. They want to please her – and if ever they are in trouble and sent to see her they are not frightened, but sorry they have incurred her disapproval.'

Entrance: Heavy over-subscription has allowed funding for expansion from single to two-form entry. From 2002, the school has accepted 60 children per year (instead of 30) and the pressure has eased up a little – but Catholic families whose children have been baptised (and you need the certificates to prove it) still take 99 per cent of the places. The school serves the parishes of Cobham, Esher and Thames Ditton, a mostly white middle-class lot. It is non-selective academically – regular church attendance will get you a long way.

Exit: Where to go next is the most vexing question for parents. In 2004, the 30 year 6 pupils headed in all directions – to 14 different secondary schools. 'I just wish this school had a secondary equivalent,' sighed one mother, echoing the view of many. St Paul's pupils are guaranteed entry to the RC Salesian School in Chertsey, but few choose it. Among the more popular choices of secondary school are Wimbledon College, Ursuline High, Tiffin School and Tiffin Girls School in Kingston.

Remarks: An academically strong school with a solid Catholic ethos. Set back from a busy dual carriageway, in functional rather than beautiful accommodation, purpose-built in the mid-1960s. There is plenty of space, including a large playground and a grass playing field. The smart new block built to provide the necessary seven extra classrooms does make the older classrooms look a little tired, but good art displays line the walls and lift the spirits. A well-resourced school, with a shiny IT suite and three well-stocked libraries. All classrooms are spacious and light; and each is named after a saint – reflecting the importance of Catholic teaching at the school.

The Catholic Church schools' 'Search for Excellence' theme is seen as key here – both in the spiritual and academic development of the children. Academic standards are high. At Key Stage 2, 93 per cent gained level 4 and above in English, and 100 per cent in maths and science – there were more level 5s than 4s in all three subject areas. Many parents tell us that this is a school for academic girls rather than non-academic boys. Even parents who are not quite so dogmatic believe the environment is more suited to the academically inclined. 'It is not a hot-house, but there is just a general expectation of achievement,' said one mother. Mrs Johnson disagrees strongly – so does Ofsted, who also single out the SEN teaching for praise. There is an SEN teacher with two assistants on hand and the school also brings in outside specialists.

High praise from parents for an able and effective teaching staff. 'Every time we change classes we say we wish we could have that teacher again – and then the next one is just another delight,' said a mother who has had had children at the school for many years. 'Discipline is strong, the children know their boundaries and understand them,' said another. There is plenty of praise and reward, with a system of highly-prized stickers and certificates, not just for academic work but also for helpfulness, cheerfulness and so on. Prayers are said at the end of each day, and children attend mass regularly. The religious teaching really kicks in at year 3 as the children are preparing for Holy Communion.

All the parents we spoke to agree their children are happy at the school which they describe time and time again as 'very caring'. Pupils are respectful and polite – and also extremely smart – with even the reception children

wearing neat ties. 'The fact they can get a four-year-old to tie a tie says a lot about this school,' enthused one mother. Mixed feelings abound over sports provision with some parents feeling it is not a particular strength, especially among the boys – though the school does well in the borough in netball and cross-country.

A real sense of community, which staff and parents are keen to maintain as the school expands. Some parents have expressed concerns that the strong sense of community they have enjoyed may be eroded as the school grows. However, the niggles are few and far between, and overall the positive comments far outweigh the negatives. It is still a first choice for parents seeking a good education for their child in a distinctively Catholic environment.

St Peter's Eaton Square CofE Primary School

Lower Belgrave Street, London, SW1W 0NL

Tel: 020 7641 4230
Fax: 020 7641 4235
E-mail: office.st-peters-eaton-square.westminster@lgfl.net

• Pupils: 266 primary and 50 nursery (intake 10 per term to the nursery and 40 per year to the reception class). All day • Ages: 3-11 • C of E • State • Open days: February

Head: Since 1992, Mr John Wright BEd., MBA (in School Leadership) (fifties). Previous career in state system in London Borough of Merton and in Beaconsfield. Keen on music, especially opera, gardening, also travel planning. Fantastically thorough and efficient and makes a real point of knowing his pupils, his staff and the parents well. Keen on 'the corporate ethos' and has a real talent for 'getting us to work as a team,' said one teacher, not to mention encouraging parents to help. Comments dryly that the school's overall intake 'helps provide an environment well-matched to the society our young people will enter when they leave school'.

Entrance: Register in the academic year before the date of entry (part of the pan-London system). Two points of entry (September and January) for reception children. Nursery moves to two points of entry from the start of the 2006/7 school year. Visit school. Priority given to children whose parents attend St Peter's Church; those who attend church regularly; children with siblings in the school; children whose parents attended the school; children baptised as Anglicans etc etc. Always oversubscribed at early levels, and there is no automatic transfer (but some priority) from nursery to reception classes. Offers are made in the May preceding the year of entry.

Exit: To local state schools, particularly Greycoat Hospital, St Marylebone, Lady Margaret, Pimlico, London Nautical etc. Thirty per cent to private schools – Christ's Hospital, JAGS, City of London, Godolphin & Latymer, Clapham Hill and Streatham High etc.

Remarks: Super central London primary school which got a deservedly glowing Ofsted report. Good social mix – 'everything from duchesses to dustmen and politicians', in the words of the previous head; 'a very broad spectrum of socioeconomic backgrounds', comments the present head. Loyal parents and PTA (good fund-raisers, these), exceptionally committed and dedicated professional staff. Terrific swimming school (all except nursery and reception use nearby Queen Mother's Sports Centre pool every week). Local district swimming competitions abandoned as other schools do not commit to similar regular swimming programmes through the year. Good music and getting better all the time. Keen computers – and new computer centre opened 2000 and IT timetabled. Competent special needs provision, according to parents; school by turns forthcoming and clam-like about what's on offer. All classrooms equipped with interactive whiteboards.

Maximum class size 30 (several classes less than this). Setting for maths in junior classes. French and Mandarin now an 'option' – with parent-organised club after school on Tuesdays and Fridays, staffed by members of the Les Petites Marionettes – a start. Food reported to have improved (was ghastly). Maintenance of school supported by London Diocesan Board. Every inch of the school is used, with cunning timetabling and doubling up of rooms for various purposes. Jolly shouts from the playground (playtimes are staggered – a clever move), with a regular supply of 'midday supervisors' overseeing fair play. Library recently refurbished by active and enthusiastic parents.

School first mentioned in survey carried out by the National Society for Promoting Religious Education in 1864-7, sited in Eccleston Place. Moved to present building in 1872 on a site given by the Marquess of Westminster. Assumed its present form in 1949. Visited by HM Queen in 1972 (centenary year) and by HM Queen Mum in 1995. Strong links with St Peter's Church, and the clergy pop in and out (Church very high Anglican – so high, in fact, that a passing arsonist mistook it for Roman Catholic and burned it down not so long ago). Lots of parental involvement.

Super nursery opened in 1992 in the crypt of the Church, now on site. Morning or afternoon sessions, with groups of 25. New nursery teacher who is well respected by the parents and has made an early, very positive mark, a nursery nurse and two helpers. Has an indoor/outdoor area for structured play and opportunities for development of gross motor skills. Drawback of the main school is that it is very cramped for space (though NB, many local private schools are even more cramped) and playground can be horrifically noisy and bursting at seams at break time. Children are not 'hot-housed'- but with two-thirds of pupils reaching level 5 in year 6 they are well well ahead of national expectations.

Late 2003, school wrote to parents appealing for funds and blaming the government for financial difficulties (including a £14,000 deficit. Balance in credit during the 2003/4 school year without the need for parental donations). School requested £15 per child or £25 per family. 'In Westminster, St Peter's is consistently top in achievement but bottom in funding,' head wrote. Here is a school whose parents could, for the most part, well afford to help.

ST PHILIP'S SCHOOL

6 Wetherby Place, London, SW7 4NE

Tel: 02073 733 944
Fax: 02072 449 766
E-mail: info@stphilipschool.co.uk
Website: www.stphilipschool.co.uk

• Pupils: 110 boys, all day • Ages: 7-13 • RC • Fees: £3,100
• Independent

Head: Since 1990, Mr H Biggs-Davison MA (early forties), educated St Philip's, Downside, Fitzwilliam College, Cambridge, where he read geography – and came straight back to St Philip's to teach in 1978. Aims to run an 'even more excellent little prep school and develop it, not in terms of expansion but as a place'. Seriously good looking. Good at recruiting and good with children. Open. Recently won the school's annual Conker Competition. Wife is the one with ideas.

Entrance: Standard not difficult but oversubscribed like everywhere else. Several tests, but priority is given to Catholics.

Exit: A variety of schools including the London Oratory, St Benedict's Ealing, Westminster, St Paul's, Dulwich, and out-of-London boarding schools eg Ampleforth, Harrow, Worth and The Oratory (Reading).

Remarks: Central London Catholic prep school – could

be a solution. Housed in large red-brick Kensington building. Cramped classrooms but wonderful leafy and paved playground which runs the whole length of the block. Maximum class size 20; top form streamed. Kensington Dyslexia Centre provides teachers for dyslexics/dyspraxics (school will accept pupils with learning difficulties). Pupils a riot of different nationalities.

SAINT RONAN'S SCHOOL

Water Lane, Hawkhurst, Kent, TN18 5DJ

Tel: 01580 752 271
Fax: 01580 754 882
E-mail: info@saintronans.co.uk
Website: www.saintronans.co.uk

- Pupils: 280 boys and girls. Mainly day with flexi boarding
- Ages: Nursery 2.5 to reception age; pre-prep to rising 7; prep school from 7 to 13 • C of E • Fees: Nursery £314 per day of the week; pre-prep £1,995; prep £3,485. Boarding £21.50 per night
- Independent • Open days: Two per term

Head: Since 2003, Mr William Trelawny-Vernon (early forties). Exeter university, briefly a fund manger in the City before moving to Stowe to teach biology. Formerly 7 years as housemaster of Chatham House, Stowe. Married to Emma who teaches divinity, four young children. Very enthusiastic and energetic – has managed to bring the school into the 21st century without losing its old fashioned charm.

Entrance: By interview. No exam; children need to be of a fairly good standard but nonetheless cover a wide ability range. Pre-prep in the capable hands of Joceline Mawdsley since 2003.

Exit: About two thirds of pupils go on to public schools, of which Tonbridge, King's Canterbury, Benenden and Eton are currently the most popular. Harrow, Sevenoaks, Eastbourne and Stowe also in evidence. One or two major scholarships most years. One third go on to local grammar schools, principally Cranbrook.

Remarks: Spiritually a home from home, a relaxed and informal school where teachers are approachable and mud is unremarkable. Saint Ronan's is a quirky and unusual school with a happy and busy feel to it. Aims to develop each individual rather than impose a style, bringing out self confidence, academically as well as socially, and independence. Academic achievement valued – it is cool to be clever for boys as well as girls. Maximum class size is 18 and average

12-14. Latin as a major subject from early on, Greek an option for the academic children in the last two years. Children streamed within their year group according to ability. Very able children can be accelerated to the year above their age group, reaching the top of the school a year early to prepare for scholarship entry to senior schools.

No longer offers full boarding but flexi-boarding is a popular option and most children ask to do this at some stage. As a result there is no longer a Sunday chapel service but visiting speakers are often invited to the Friday evensong. The chapel, which features every leaver's name and destination enrolled on boards, is used every morning for 10 minutes. The school day is a long one as the older children (9+) do not finish school until 6.30pm, but all prep is done at school and it does mean that there is plenty of time for play and fun during the day.

Sport is a major feature of the school day; games are played every afternoon, and the appointment of two sports' specialists has raised the already good standard. Major sports for the boys are football, hockey and cricket – rugby too now – and the girls play netball, hockey, rounders and tennis. There is a strong tradition of cross country running – marvellous practice running round all those acres. Minor sports include shooting, golf (on the school's own small course), judo, gymnastics and archery. The children also seem to find time for modelling and craft as well as tending their gardens.

The school was founded in 1883 in Worthing and moved in 1946 to this rambling Victorian mansion built by an OXO magnate in 247 acres – it has its own 100 acre wood, lakes and a pinetum. There is a splendid one-time ball room (with sprung floor and painted ceiling) known as The Great Space – used as a theatre, indoor football pitch, gymnasium etc – and much loved. The children spend a lot of time outside and a favourite pastime is damming a stream called the Gulch – Wellington boots and old tracksuits essential. A school where children can be children for longer.

The stable block has recently been converted and now houses a fine science lab, an ICT department with new plasma screens, music and art departments and a well-equipped kitchen – cooking is a popular option for both boys and girls. Staff and children eat together in the new dining room where an eye can be kept on table manners.

Lots of music in the school – over two thirds learn a musical instrument, several ensembles, lunchtime concerts throughout the term. Drama part of the curriculum, two major productions a year as well as more informal reviews and mini plays and an art and music festival in the summer term.

Parents very involved in the life of the school – many help with reading for the younger children and others have formed a group to teach them Scottish dancing and there is a thriving Friends of St Ronan's parents' group who organise summer balls, parents' quizzes, Burns Night parties etc. Old Boys include artist Piers de Laszlo and cartoonist Sir Osbert Lancaster, whose Latin master used to tear up his sketches and demand prep instead. Also Charles Saumarez-Smith, Director of the National Gallery.

St Swithun's Junior School

Linked to Saint Swithun's School in the Senior section

Alresford Road, Winchester, Hampshire, SO21 1HA

Tel: 01962 835 750
Fax: 01962 835 781
Website: www.stswithuns.com

• Pupils: girls to 11, boys to 8; all day • Ages: 3-11: girls to 11, boys to 8 • C of E • Fees: Junior: nursery £1,000; reception - y2 £1,985; years 3-6 £2,550 • Independent

Head: Miss Elaine Krispinussen.

Exit: Boys go on at eight to local prep schools eg the Pilgrim's School, Farleigh. A fair number of girls go on to the senior school but also to other girls' boarding schools, Downe House, St Mary's Calne etc. No automatic entry to senior school.

Remarks: In the grounds of the main school, but autonomous. For greater detail, see senior school entry.

St Vincent de Paul RC Primary School

Morpeth Terrace, London, SW1P 1EP

Tel: 020 7641 5990
Fax: 020 7641 5901
E-mail: office.st-vincentdepaul.westminster@lgfl.net

• Pupils: 250 boys and girls, all day • Ages: 3-11 • RC • State

Head: Since 2002 Mr Jack O'Neill STB/MA early forties, single. The enthusiastic, effective and guitar-playing Mr O'Neill came on a fast track to this post – a class teacher for 4 years in Hammersmith and Fulham, then was deputy at St Vincent de Paul before being promoted. He is resourceful and keen to squeeze a lot out of slim funding – they did without a deputy head for a year because of a budget cut. Keen on improvement and feedback: got a 61 per cent return on parents questionnaire.

Entrance: Well oversubscribed and no guaranteed transfer from nursery to main school so priority given to practising Roman Catholics living in parishes of Westminster or Pimlico. Within this category, first siblings, then ex-nursery tiddlers, then children of staff or governors. Next favoured group is Roman Catholics from other parishes, then other baptised Catholics.

Exit: Usually to first choice secondary schools; popular ones are St Thomas More, Greycoat Hospital, Sacred Heart, Salesian College and the London Oratory.

Remarks: Founded in 1859 by the Sisters of Charity of St Vincent de Paul. Sited in the shadow of Westminster Cathedral, and a family mass is held there every month which many parents and pupils attend, some are altar servers there or at other neighbouring RC churches. Principles of the religious community pervades the school, but not in an exclusive or heavy-handed way. There are prayer corners in the corner of every classroom and the school chaplain takes one assembly per week. Also regular other faith weeks – I attended an astounding assembly on Hinduism with hip wiggling dancing, Hindu vocab cards and discussion of blue-skinned gods and goddesses.

School on three levels with disabled access at the rear, 20 CCTV cameras and new boundary railings mean security is effective. A new chapel is being built just inside the entrance but at present the central point of the school is the double height sports hall. This is also used for assemblies, meals and all of the class areas are accessed from it. The form rooms are well decorated with quiet areas in between – beanbagged for reading and rainy day play. Outside, both a nursery playground and a bigger one that is borrowed by 2 other schools, with a child and parent maintained garden. Playground, dining hall and corridor rules are written by the elected school council, whose influence has extended to Mr Soapy Soap in all bathrooms and renewal of a water fountain.

Huge social mix with no one dominant racial or cultural grouping; EAL for 80 per cent and over 15 languages spoken. EAL teacher is in school for 3 days per week on an individual or group basis as needed. The teaching is of exceptional quality with 2 of the staff lead teachers for Westminster in English and Literacy. Very low mobility since professional development is important here. Student teachers, parents and volunteers from BAA, DfES and the Home Office help with the nursery, reading and walking pupils to swim at the nearby Queen Mother Sports Centre, freeing up teachers for specialist SEN courses and the like. The school's record on SEN is quite low since pupils seem to be making too much progress to get statements – here classroom assistants pick up on SEN kids early. A dedicated learning mentor (funded through Excellence in Cities) is the link for the Education Welfare Officer and the joint Child Protection officer with the head. She runs the late book and so is a daily point of contact with the parents and carers. School focuses on targeting social, emotional and behavioural issues; circle time and an anonymous comments box are well used. Buddy friendship scheme and charity initiatives such as a Childline skip-a-thon encourage a caring outlook.

Kids are known for their good behaviour and ongoing participation in events in the Royal Albert Hall, Westminster Archive Centre, Wallace Collection and throughout the West End; if 'there is something going on we'll get involved'. Head is very proud of zero unauthorised attendance record and only having to see 2 children a week for misdemeanours such as pushing. During his time has explained the ethos behind his rules and curriculum to parents and been rewarded by low pupil mobility and huge continuous support – half the cost of the interactive whiteboards in every class was covered by PTFA fundraising, the whole of the inside of the school was decorated by volunteers. The PTFA is dynamic and the weekly newsletter from the head helps the non-school gate parents feel in touch. Priority is 'children's individual success' – head aims to help them gain what they are expected to and more, while not being focussed towards one area of the curriculum. A fantastically happy, disciplined and effective school.

SALISBURY CATHEDRAL SCHOOL

The Old Palace, 1 The Close, Salisbury, Wiltshire, SP1 2EQ

Tel: 01722 555 300
Fax: 01722 410 910
E-mail: info@salisburycathedralschool.com
Website: www.salisburycathedralschool.com

- Pupils: 85 girls, 126 boys; 203 day. Includes pre-prep with 76 children and 45 boarders • Ages: 7-13, pre-prep 3-7 • C of E choir school • Fees: Boarding £5,060; day £3,460; year 3 £2,720; years 1, 2 & reception £1,760; nursery £1,140 (5 mornings) £1,090 • Independent • Open days: November and May

Head Master: Since 1998, Mr Robert Thackray BSc PGCE (early fifties). Educated at Highgate School and London University. Previously taught at St Marylebone Grammar School and Bottisham Village College, Cambs. Was deputy and then head at St James CEVA Middle School, Bury St Edmunds. Married with 2 older children. His wife, Trisha, also a teacher, helps with the boarding house and teaches in the pre-prep. His musical interests are choral singing and playing the double bass but his main passion is vintage cars – has a 1932 Talbot and takes part in competitions.

Quiet and unassuming, he has the reputation of caring for each child and is clearly liked by the children who greet him cheerfully without any flattening against walls. Parents say that he is very approachable. He hopes to have a good 7 years left at the school and aims to develop an ethos for the future which will leave the school on a firm footing. Points out that it can be tricky to define a school which exists primarily for the choristers but would like to encourage a wider spread of children and aims to keep the choristers' feet firmly on the ground. Sums up his philosophy as 'balance in everything'.

Entrance: Many come up from the pre-prep, otherwise at all stages. Chorister places (usually at 8) are offered as a result of a voice trial (January for boys, February for girls), academic assessment and interview. For others there is an informal test. Scholarships are available for music and academic ability at 7 and 11. Sports and arts scholarships at 11. Day children predominately come from rural areas around Salisbury and some from the city. Boarders come from a wide area; quite a few Services children plus many 'first time buyers' from 'a variety of backgrounds....choristership knows few boundaries'. One foreign pupil at present (Chinese). There is provision for mild learning difficulties (52 pupils at present).

Exit: The majority at 13 to a wide range of senior schools, especially local schools such as Bryanston and Canford – many with music awards (94 in the last 8 years). A small selection at 11 to the excellent local grammars.

Remarks: Stunning setting – 24 acres around Salisbury Cathedral. The children probably don't notice the magnificence of their location but the parents certainly do. A safe place to grow up in, with a lot of grounds but encircled by the medieval walls of the Cathedral close.

The school buildings range from a thirteenth century hall to 1960s classroom blocks. A busy, thriving place with a family atmosphere helped by the presence of the pre-prep department and an open door policy for parents. Very popular with local parents especially with those who are keen on the idea of music for their children. 180 music lessons are taught every week to 150 children and very high standards are reached. There is a school orchestra, concert band, 17 different music ensembles and 2 school choirs as well as the 2 cathedral choirs. Despite the obvious emphasis on music, there is a relaxed atmosphere in the boarding house with instruments lying around mixed in with sports things, the odd Gameboy and Playstation and all the other paraphernalia of this age group. The head is anxious to emphasise that the 48 choristers are treated the same as the rest of the school although they clearly have an extra workload with choir practices etc. You don't have to be interested in music to go there but it would be difficult not to develop an interest in such surroundings.

The school has extended its Astroturf to hockey pitch size and sports scholarships have been introduced. Sports are compulsory in the prep school -rugby, football, hockey and cricket for the boys, hockey, netball and rounders for the girls, plus health and fitness training for years 4-8. The enthusiastic games staff are moving the standard of sport ever upwards but no-one would pretend this is the top choice for those for whom sport is all-in-all. However, matches against other prep schools in the area are increasingly successful.

Sound teaching on all fronts. Plenty of computers in evidence and separate IT classes up to year 6, after which IT is integrated into the main curriculum subjects. Latin from year 6 (can be dropped for extra literary skills), Greek and German on offer as extra subjects. Science and technology are strong and a lot of art work in evidence. One of the head's first moves on arriving was to abolish Saturday school at the request of many parents. However there are a lot of Saturday morning activities for boarders and day pupils – coaching in the major sports, archery, cooking, art, horse riding and model making. Supervised shopping trips into Salisbury for boarders on Saturday afternoons (with a limited amount of pocket money tailored to the age group). On Sundays there are outings for boarders to local attractions. As there are always two choirs in residence over the weekend for cathedral services, there are usually plenty of boarders around. New boarding house in the close.

A small caring school in a unique situation where children are free to express themselves and have the space to make mistakes but are well supported throughout. Excellent all round education preparing children for senior school. Judging by the strength of the ex-alumni association and the lasting friendships between former pupils, a happy place to spend your early school years.

SANDROYD SCHOOL

Rushmore, Tollard Royal, Salisbury, Wiltshire, SP5 5QD

Tel: 01725 516 264
Fax: 01725 516 441
E-mail: office@sandroyd.com
Website: www.sandroyd.org

● Pupils: 158: 13 girls, 145 boys (88 full boarding, including 3 girls). Pre-prep: 22 girls and boys ● Ages: 4-13 ● C of E ● Fees: Year 4 and above: boarding £5,450 day; day £4,550 (until 6.30pm). Year 3: boarding £4,400; day £3,350 ● Independent ● Open days: October

---

Head: Since 2003, Martin Harris BSc (Hons) PGCE (forty-ish). Educated at The Skinners School and read geography at Loughborough University. Began teaching at Sevenoaks Prep but has spent most of career at Ashdown House in East Sussex eventually rising to deputy head and then acting head. Keen sportsman, plays cricket, golf and tennis. Married to Catherine (a chartered physiotherapist) who plays a pastoral role in the school. Two young sons, the eldest now in the school's pre-prep. Has overseen big changes since arriving: the opening of The Walled Garden pre-prep, the introduction of girls in the main school, the debut of football(!).

Entrance: Not selective but all children are assessed and then interviewed by the head. Pupils can start at The Walled Garden from 4, at the main school generally at 7 or 8, but pupils start at all ages. Some enter at age 10 or 11, specifically for the boarding. Flexi-boarding available, but all pupils must properly board in the last two years. 70 per cent come from Wiltshire and Dorset, a few from London – a top drawer lot, with the school roll a festival of double-barrelled surnames. 16 boys from overseas, half British expats, half foreign, some of the latter receiving extra English tuition. Minibuses from Gillingham, Blandford, and now Salisbury.

Exit: Virtually all leave at 13, very occasionally one at 11 – girls now entering the school intend to stay all the way through. Sherborne the favourite destination by far but quite a few to Radley and Bryanston and several to Eton and Marlborough. Otherwise all over, far and wide. Strangely few to Canford and Dauntsey's. A couple to good state schools most years.

Remarks: A happy school, bursting with all the extras. Founded in 1888 by the Revd L H Wellesley Wesley as a 'small coaching establishment' in his own home, for 'sons of friends who were due to go to Eton'. The school was evacuated here during the war and later bought the Pitt-Rivers' family house plus paddocks, playing fields and houses for many of the staff. Still a relatively formal and traditional prep in its second year of co-education. School currently owns 55 acres within the 400 acre Rushmore estate, next door to the Rushmore Golf Course (pupils and staff play for free). The park teems with wild life and the school was undergoing something of a pheasant infestation when we visited. Slightly isolated feel, a bit of a world unto itself. The main building has elegance in its bones but a tired feeling within. Grand wood-panelled hall, with classrooms off it. Has been much added to – all very practical but not inspirational. Entire school – classrooms, dormitories, swimming pool, chapel etc under one roof, connected by a warren of corridors. Handy, as the wind can rip through the grounds as we discovered. Children terribly polite – say 'Sir', and stand up as soon as you appear. Dress code rather than uniform on school days: any check shirt, no tie, any brown shoes, green or blue cords – looks great. Girls wear a blue kilt or navy cords, blue blouse, Sandroyd sweatshirt and black shoes. Smarter wear for chapel and outings.

Still strong on traditional teaching: French from seven, Latin from nine, Greek for those who want it, plus a non-timetabled Spanish/German option. Head was keen on sharpening up the academic side when he arrived and he has been rewarded with a clutch of good awards to senior schools in recent years. Max class size 16 but average is 12 (and many are smaller). 30 children receive extra lessons – mainly for dyslexia and extra maths. Up to four sessions a week, if needed, with times varying so pupils miss different lessons or activities. Low tech IT – no interactive white-boards, old computers – but sufficient. Four gap students, fill in here and there, read with the younger children every day. Parents given lots of feedback: termly reports, weekly assessments for effort, twice termly assessments for achievement . Exams every term in the top two years to iron out exam technique and quell any nerves.

Big on sport, especially rugger – the school reached the National Prep School 7s final at Rosslyn Park in 2004 and won the Wiltshire U13 Rugby Cup and there is an annual rugby tour. Every boy represents the school in a rugby match and there are four IVs at the top of the school. Cricket also very strong. Girls have recently begun to play hockey against other schools – there are almost enough of them to make a team – and some have played in boys' teams. Sport every day, though some peel off to attend special lessons – roughly half the pupils do tennis coaching as an extra; many learn squash with pro who visits three times a week. Still offers pistol shooting. A quarter of the school ride – on school's own horses, or you can bring your own. School contines to host an annual National Tetrathlon with 160 children competing. Glass-like cricket pitch, three quarter size Astroturf, rifle range, pets area (with few lodgers), indoor pool (18 and a half metres!), gym 'held together by Sellotape but well-loved'. Adventure playground for use by the youngest.

On Saturdays and Wednesday afternoons, less gamesy older children may seek refuge in the DT room, which is also open on winter evenings. Pupils make their own tuck boxes and decorate them in the holidays. The school still has general knowledge quizzes, with notable national success. Lots of activities on offer, and this is a key facet of the school. Something for everyone, from the nerdy (magic tricks, electronics, Russian) to the sporty (clay pigeon shooting, golf, fencing). God important and children attend the lovely chapel four days a week. Lively music, especially the choir, and the orchestra is 'improving'. 108 pupils learn an instrument – two of them bagpipe. 'We'll teach anything,' says the head. Violin tuition given by a house parent who used to play in The Royal Philharmonic Orchestra (and in a backing band for Elton John!). Busy art in big, airy room, with outstanding ceramics. Drama offered through class lessons and a drama club. The school has drawn up plans for a theatre, which would be a super addition, and has purchased equipment for a film-making club. Cookery in a dedicated room, organised by the mums.

Brilliant boarding with good care throughout. 7 – 9 boys in dorms in younger years – perfectly pleasant. Smaller dormitories of 3-4 boys in top year, and prep at this age is done in dorm – unusual for a prep school. Common room with telly, play station, table football – a stepping stone to public school. No mobile phones, except for overseas boys who keep them in the office. Good food served family style in bright and airy dining room. Fruit available all day. Snacks galore. Top year can make toast and cocoa. Exeats every third weekend. Two Sundays a term pupils must stay in school but school enthusiastically woos them to stay more – and most do. Regular Sunday outings on horseback or cycling. Swallows and Amazons camping weekend for year 4. School does all the boys' laundry, even for the day boys (it was at this point that we were sold on the place). OBs include the Lords Avon, Carrington, Snowdon, Wilberforce, Gladwyn, Sainsbury plus Archbishop Ramsay of Canterbury, Ian Gow, Max Aitken, Sir Terence Rattigan, Sir Anthony Eden, Sir Ranulph Fiennes.

The Walled Garden pre-prep opened in 2004. Still less than half full but numbers growing. Beautiful curving design, light bright and cheery – all built to child size including mini whiteboards and beautiful loos. The children play and learn confidently in their bright purple sweatshirts – very focused. Spacious outdoor play area and these littlies use the main school's swimming pool and computers. One third of them have older siblings in the school. Their day finishes at 3:30pm but many stay for a late club until 5:15 where they can take part in activities like football or pony club.

SARUM HALL SCHOOL

15 Eton Avenue, London, NW3 3EL

Tel: 02077 942 261
Fax: 02074 317 501
E-mail: office@sarumhallschool.co.uk
Website: www.sarumhallschool.co.uk

• Pupils: 170 girls (including nursery); all day • Ages: 3-11
• C of E • Fees: £1,920 - £3,195 • Independent

Head: Since 2000, Mrs Jane Scott (forties), previously deputy head of St Paul's Cathedral School. Has taught at various London junior schools including Arnold House. Child at King's School in Canterbury. Took over from Lady Smith-Gordon, head since 1984 – a happy, creative and caring environment in which 'each girl is encouraged to work hard to fulfil her potential and recognise her talents.' Parents find her 'surprisingly easy to talk to'. Others pay tribute to the enthusiasm of the staff.

Entrance: No tests (which is very popular with parents). Places offered 15 months in advance of entry to the nursery after interviews with parents. Siblings get first preference, 'we like to create a family environment'; geography is taken into account – 'I don't think three-year-olds should be travelling great distances'; plus a view on whether or not the family will fit in with the school ethos – 'it is vital that the parents and I are in sympathy'. Few places higher up the school and those are tested.

Exit: Mainly to north London day schools eg South Hampstead, City of London, Francis Holland, Channing, Queen's College, North London Collegiate School. A few to boarding school including Wycombe Abbey, Downe House and Queenswood. 'We aim to send them to a senior school where they will thrive, which is not necessarily the top academic school.'

Remarks: Amidst wall-to-wall prep schools crammed into redbrick Edwardiana, this light, airy building is probably the only new, purpose-built, girls' prep in London, and won awards for its design. A guide to recent London architecture talks of the 'sympathetic complexion of the two-storey, barn-like construction with its steep-pitched slate roof'. The three lowest form rooms open out onto the terrace and all the rooms are light and cheerful, with plenty of work on display. The top floor art room has huge north windows; there's also a science lab, well-equipped library and computer room with new Dell computers. Good, solid, traditional teaching.

Specialist teaching is introduced gradually. Years 5 and 6 are completely subject taught with half classes for English, maths and science. 'I think we have excellent teachers who ensure that all the girls – and not just the most academic – are getting a balanced education.' Pressure minimal at the bottom of the school, though it does increase higher up as the 11+ approaches.' The class size no more than 22, but year 6 is split into two classes of 10-11. Its non-selective ethos means the ability range within each year group varies, 'but we're a well-staffed school,' says the head, 'with plenty of teaching assistants to help lower down.' The school employs a learning support teacher who works with small groups of girls or individuals needing extra help.

'The art teacher is wonderful,' said a parent. 'She's very good at working with topics they're doing in other subjects and they use lots of different media.' Music is another important feature, with an orchestra, two choirs, optional theory classes and ensemble groups. Over 75 per cent of girls take instrumental lessons in piano, violin, cello, woodwind or singing. Year 6 puts on a major musical play in the summer term, and lower forms produce plays at other times of year. Physical education every day: dance, gym (everyone does BAGA awards) or games which include netball, hockey skills, touch rugby, cricket, short tennis, rounders and athletics – all on site. Football, Stage Combat, netball, maths games are some of the optional after-school activities. As well as a garden play area with rubber flooring, there is a netball court doubling as four short tennis courts. The top two forms go on an outdoor pursuits course and a field studies course. There are plenty of outings, and workshops on subjects ranging from opera to the Vikings.

A small, cosy, traditional school with good groundings in all the basics and a wonderful building. Parents tend to be well-heeled Hampstead/Highgate types, the girls neat and well-behaved. One parent commented that she wished the social mix was slightly wider. 'But my daughter has certainly been very happy here.'

THE SCHOOL OF ST HELEN AND ST KATHARINE JUNIOR SCHOOL

Linked to School of Saint Helen and Saint Katharine (The) in the Senior section

Faringdon Road, Abingdon, Oxfordshire, OX14 1BE

Tel: 01235 520173
Fax: 01235 532934
E-mail: info@shsk.org.uk
Website: www.shsk.org.uk

• Pupils: all girls, all day • Ages: 9-11 • Anglican foundation
• Fees: £2,837 • Independent

Remarks: For further details, see senior school entry.

SEDBERGH JUNIOR SCHOOL

Linked to Sedbergh School in the Senior section

Low Bentham, Lancaster, North Yorkshire, LA2 7DB

Tel: 015242 61275
Fax: 015242 62944
E-mail: hmsjs@sedberghschool.org
Website: www.sedberghschool.org

• Pupils: 80 girls and boys; boarding and day • Ages: 4-13
• Fees: Junior/prep: day from £2,720; weekly boarding £3,990; boarding £4,295. Pre-prep £1,820. Reception £1,590
• Independent • Open days: Junior School - September, March, June

Head: Paul Reynolds BA(Hons) MEd.
Entrance: Ages 4-9 by assessment, thereafter by written exam.
Exit: Almost exclusively to the senior school at 13 provided entrance examinations/scholarships met satisfactorily.
Remarks: Newly opened September 2002 at Low Bentham. 30 minutes' drive from Sedbergh School.

SHEEN MOUNT PRIMARY SCHOOL

West Temple, Sheen, London, SW14 7RT

Tel: 020 8876 8394
Fax: 020 8878 6568
E-mail: info@sheenmount.richmond.sch.uk
Website: www.sheenmount.richmond.sch.uk

• Pupils: 450 (roughly equal numbers of boys and girls), all day
• Ages: 4-11 • Non-denom • State

Head: Since 1999, Mrs Elaine England (early fifties), has thirty years teaching experience, and was previously head at Stanley Infant School in Teddington. Not an obviously touchy-feely 'my door is always open' type of head, but very much a strong leader. Parents describe her as 'efficient', 'well-respected', 'dynamic', 'a good motivator' and 'very involved.' She thinks long-term and is currently planning major building works for the next ten years.

Entrance: Over-subscribed every year. Priority to very special needs then siblings. After that, it's location, location, location – not just the road you live in but the house number in that road can determine whether your child gets a place. 90 per cent of the children have been to one of the many local nurseries – too numerous to list. Unlike other local state primaries, places only rarely become available higher up the school – hardly anyone leaves Sheen Mount at 7 to go to the local prep schools, it's more likely to happen the other way round.

Exit: Mention any local independent school and someone from Sheen Mount has gone there and we're talking top academic schools: St Paul's, Lady Eleanor Holles, Putney High, Kingston Grammar, Latymer Upper, Godolphin, Hampton as well as St Catherine's, Surbiton or Halliford. Obviously lots of private tutoring goes on for the entrance exams but Mrs E feels it is unnecessary – 'we get them to the required level anyway,' but not all parents are quite that confident. Head does not try to advise parents on the choice of independent school – she admits that she doesn't know enough about them. She concentrates instead on the local state schools: Christ's, Waldegrave and Shene. Christ's is the most popular, with Waldegrave hard to get a place in from this side of the borough. With such a choice of exit schools, there is never more than a handful of pupils going on to each.

Remarks: The best primary school in the area according to parents in the know, and we are not going to argue. If you have the money, it is worth moving to be on its middle class doorstep – many see it as a real alternative to the local preps.

A sea of scooters greets you at the school gates – somehow symbolic of children who want to be at school – and as quickly as possible. Everywhere you see groups of eager, self-confident, happy children who enjoying their learning and teachers enjoying their teaching. Reception is regarded as particularly strong – described by mothers as 'a really secure and happy start', 'gets children well-socialised', though children don't all start full-time together – 'a bit divisive' say some.

'A vibrant and lively education,' say one mum, who sums up the feeling of many; parents agree that the curriculum is well-taught with lots of visits to help bring subjects to life, but some mutter that SATS results ought to be higher given the intake. Class sizes are typical of state primary schools – average about 30. Despite the high cost of local housing, staff turnover is low and there are four male teachers including a male deputy head. Parents are very welcome in school, they take an interest in what their children are learning and buy appropriate books or visit museums. At least one child was taken to Egypt because she was studying the Egyptians.

The school prides itself on the help given to children with special needs – there is a small dedicated special needs room and the SENCO is highly experienced with children with specific learning difficulties. Some parental grumbles that more minor problems in children's learning are ignored.

Music, drama and the arts are strengths – two music rooms, with mountains of individual instruments piled up on the floor reflecting the range of individual music lessons and the myriad musical groups practising each lunchtime. In the summer term there's a musical drama production and an art show, and last year the choir sang at the Royal Albert Hall.

Children introduced to a wide range of sports, rather than concentrating on winning in a few. Sports facilities are nothing special. Loads of extra-curricular activities – produces mini chess champions, as well as budding Jamie Olivers through its cookery club. 'I wouldn't eat the school lunches though,' one little girl said ruefully. 'They are inedible,' confirmed a very unfussy mother, 'its lucky children don't have to rely on them.'

Buildings pretty standard for a primary school – fairly scruffy but with loads of artwork on display. A nice computer suite is well-used and Key Stage 2 classrooms all have interactive whiteboards. All sorts of use made of the spacious grounds – reading circles, weather stations, nature trails to name but a few. The hall is being rebuilt to double it in size which should make a real difference to its usefulness for the school and the community. Parents have raised £125,000 towards the hall and more money will come to equip it! The summer fete alone raised a phenomenal £18,000. Leafy and suburban catchment, predominately middle-class parents with a smattering of film stars and media types. Some of the school's success is due to these highly committed, well-off, parents – they undoubtedly know how to give generously, but some less affluent souls aren't so happy at being regularly asked for money – 'they say it will only cost me the same as a daily cappuccino – well I can only afford a cup of instant!'

SHEFFIELD HIGH SCHOOL JUNIOR DEPARTMENT

Linked to Sheffield High School in the Senior section

5 Melbourne Avenue, Sheffield, South Yorkshire, S10 2QH

Tel: 0114 266 1435
Fax: 0114 267 8520
E-mail: enquiries@she.gdst.net
Website: www.sheffieldhighschool.org.uk

• Pupils: girls; all day • Ages: 3-11 • Non-denom • Fees: £1,674
• Independent • Open days: October

Head: Mrs Jones (forties); has taught in the maintained sector and has been at the school since 1993; head since 2002; has introduced touch-typing and designing web pages.

Entrance: Entry to the junior school is through observation during a child-friendly day – they are looking for bright, lively girls who are ready for school.

Exit: All proceed from the junior school as less able girls are counselled out by end of year 5.

Remarks: Specialist teaching for almost all subjects in years 5 and 6; French taught from Reception; specialist PE teaching and access to senior school sports facilities. 18 in infants classes; 19-25 in years 3-6. Visiting teacher from the Dyslexia Institute. Good IT provision. The library is small and has recently been upgraded. New outdoor play areas. Mostly bright, light classrooms. The National Curriculum is followed selectively; good art work on display. More space is badly needed – there are advanced plans to acquire an extra building.

SHREWSBURY HIGH SCHOOL JUNIOR DEPARTMENT

Linked to Shrewsbury High School in the Senior section

33 Kennedy Road, Shrewsbury, Shropshire, SY3 7AA

Tel: 01743 271149
Fax: 01743 260806
E-mail: enquiries@shrj.gdst.net
Website: www.gdst.net/shrewsburyhigh

• Pupils: 190 girls. All day • Ages: 4-11, nursery (boys too) 3-4
• Non-denom • Fees: £1,779 • Independent • Open days: October and November

Exit: To senior school following entrance examination.
Remarks: For details, see senior school entry.

SHREWSBURY HOUSE SCHOOL

107 Ditton Road, Surbiton, Surrey, KT6 6RL

Tel: 02083 993 066
Fax: 02083 399 529
E-mail: office@shspost.co.uk
Website: www.shrewsburyhouse.net

• Pupils: 290 boys, all day • Ages: 7-13 • C of E • Fees: £2,745
• Independent

Head: Since 1988, Mr Mark Ross BA HDipEd (early fifties). Educated at Campbell College, Belfast, degree in English, history and philosophy and higher diploma in education, all from Trinity College, Dublin, where he met his wife, Anthea. She has a BA in modern languages and teaches in the junior department of the school. They have two adult children and one young grandchild. Ebullient and engagingly loquacious, with much native Irish charm, he teaches history to the 9-year-olds and is said to be a great mixer with parents, although he can also be autocratic. 'He runs a tight ship, is friendly to the boys although quite strict,' is how one parent describes him. A keen golfer, he participates in the twice yearly Parents' Association golf days and was the prime mover in the establishment of the 9 hole putting green on site, where the boys use his old golf balls to play at break and lunchtimes. He and his wife live 'just down the road'.

Entrance: Up to 50 places available annually for boys age 7. A few occasional places may be offered at other ages. Two types of entry test: competitive test held in the autumn preceding anticipated entry and offer of places made to those attaining the highest marks. Alternatively, a guaranteed place test (in the autumn before anticipated entry) can be taken by some whose parents make the school their first choice. Head says, 'these parents will have the assurance of knowing that their son joining the school is not dependent on performance in a competitive test' – most do enter via this route and a hefty deposit is required prior to a child sitting the test. School can afford to be picky – three applicants for every place. Head says that his aim is to 'pick' only parents who believe in the school's philosophy. Boys come mainly from pre-prep schools but with about 30 per cent from state primaries. Head says that children have to be 'a good average at least' to get in.

Exit: Almost unknown for a boy not to attain a place at his first choice senior school and these include St John's Leatherhead, Hampton, Epsom College, Kingston Grammar School, St Paul's and King's College School, Wimbledon. Some to boarding schools including Charterhouse, Winchester, Eton and Wellington College. About a quarter of the boys win scholarships to their chosen schools. Head will not accept pupils who do not intend to stay until 13 and is supported in this stance by heads of local senior schools. If a boy takes an assessment to leave at an age other than 13+, it is understood that he will leave at the end of the academic year, regardless of the result.

Remarks: Popular, high-achieving school, which should suit boys of wider ranging academic ability than some of the more hothouse preps. Located in imposing Victorian house in classy residential area within reach of west London and Kingston area generally – very accessible from the A3. Founded in 1865, it had gone through a rocky period prior to head's appointment, nearly closing in 1979; however, a group of parents managed to raise sufficient funds to keep it going. Only 190 on the roll when head took over, 290 now, so he has clearly been successful. Staff numbers have increased from 13 to 40 and class sizes down from an average of over 20 to around 15, with maximum of 19. Staff are 'friendly and accessible,' according to one parent. Head believes very strongly that only someone with expertise in their chosen subject should teach pupils – half of the sports staff, for example, have been outstanding in their particular sport even though they may lack formal teaching qualifications. All academic staff are fully qualified.

Boys placed in sets according to ability from 8+ for maths and English and additionally from 10+ for French. There is at least one scholarship stream from 11+. Some parents have expressed concern over the intensive internal exam timetable – up to three exams are sat in one day – but others say that, as a result, their sons are now not in the least bit fazed by exams. All boys learn Latin and some Greek and Spanish taught 'for fun' for a short time after exams. There is no provision for SEN, but the school does identify those in need of support and recommends appropriate action to parents, any specialist help being the responsibility of the parents and to be obtained out of school hours. Head says, 'parents need to be aware of our limitations; the child has to be intelligent and the parents need the right attitude – understanding, but not too protective nor too harsh.' A mother adds, 'the school realised after only one term that my son had a problem – we hadn't realised at all. He was subsequently diagnosed as mildly dyspraxic and the school has been wonderful, doing everything in its power to help.' All boys learn to touch type and some SEN boys have their own laptops in class. Longer than usual school day – boys can be dropped off at 8am for an 8.30am start and finish at 4.15pm, but they can stay to 6pm to do club activities and their prep. No packed lunches allowed – not easy for those who don't like school meals, but sandwiches and fruit may be brought in to be eaten at times other than lunch hour.

The main building has been adapted to form generally smallish classrooms, all of which have projectors linked to the teachers' laptop computers. The old prefabricated classrooms in the junior school department have been demolished to be replaced by the long awaited £1.5 million block which houses the library (also incorporating a resources centre), the assembly hall/theatre, kitchens and canteen. It also includes 9 new classrooms, a music room, art room and 10 practice rooms – all have greatly improved the standard of the previous accommodation.

There is a heated swimming pool covered by a prefabricated rigid shell (bit on the basic side), hard tennis court, together with an adventure playground. School very fortunate (considering its location) to have playing fields within school grounds but also owns some of equally high standard at nearby Chessington, where boys are transported by minibus mainly for matches.

School very sporty, on which head places great emphasis, 'non-academic pursuits are very important,' and many parents say that the sporting prowess played a large part in their choice of the school. Successful in numerous sporting tournaments both locally and nationally. Parents and boys alike will be pleased to learn that every boy can be in a school football team if he wishes (unlike in many other preps), and the vast majority who wish are able to play in a cricket or rugby team, although head points out that it is not so easy to get matches with other schools for weaker teams in these sports. Regular sports tours and many trips abroad including ski trips and a recent visit to Pompeii. Lots of extra activities on offer eg on-site shooting range for air rifles, scuba diving club and magic club and many more. Drama very strong and popular, with no fewer than 6 plays produced every year, so that every boy who wishes may participate. 'Even if a boy is not sporty, the school does its best to find him a niche in which he can shine,' says one mother.

Music is a strength – over 70 per cent of pupils learn a musical instrument, some with really impressive grades (grade 7) for this age group. Pupils have to miss a regular lesson for their music session. A musical dinner is held every year for the heads of other local schools – a black tie occasion, with the guests being entertained by the numerous musical groups in the school. School magazine states that one head of music at a senior school described it as 'at least as good as, and probably better than, schools who specialise in music.' Regular concerts for parents, which one described as 'truly inspiring.'

Parents are largely prosperous, professional, southwest London and Surrey types, British and a smattering of other nationalities, some who live in immediate locality with others ferried in from (much) further afield – fleet of minibuses transport the boys up and down the A3 and elsewhere, wherever there is the demand. As with all schools in a built-up area, parents' parking was seen as problematical by some locals – however, pick-up facilities supervised by staff has much improved this and has been appreciated.

In all, a traditional all-round school, not one for wild anarchists – those kicking against the system would not go down well here. A strong emphasis on sport – 'the boys all play to win,' says one parent – but music and academia are equally important.

SIDCOT JUNIOR SCHOOL

Linked to Sidcot School in the Senior section

Oakridge Lane, Winscombe, North Somerset, BS25 1PD

Tel: 01934 845 200
Fax: 01934 844 964
E-mail: juniors@sidcot.org.uk
Website: www.sidcot.org.uk

• Pupils: 150 boys and girls • Ages: 3-11 • Quaker
• Independent

Head: Since 2002, Ms Rosie Craig BEd DGE.

Exit: Most proceed to senior school.

Remarks: Previously known as The Hall School (pre-prep department) in Wedmore was acquired by Sidcot and moved in 1990 to the grounds of main school and more recently known as Sidcot Junior School. The junior school has provided a consistent caring environment for pre-prep children who have grown through Sidcot sixth form on to university. French taught from year 1. Access to all main school facilities. Lunch-time activities include riding, pets corner, dance and chess. Early years department housed in smaller building with cosy and colourful rooms. A new junior school building, for nursery to year 6, opened in November 2005.

SOUTH FARNHAM COMMUNITY JUNIOR SCHOOL

Menin Way, Farnham, Surrey, GU9 8DY

Tel: 01252 716 155
Fax: 01252 718 260
E-mail: info@south-farnham.surrey.sch.uk
Website: www.south-farnham.surrey.sch.uk

• Pupils: 480 boys and girls • Ages: 7-11 • Non denom • State

Head: Since 1988, Mr Andrew Carter BEd OBE (mid fifties). Married (his wife Mary also teaches at the school) with three grown-up children. Avuncular and urbane, he is intensely proud of the school which one parent described as 'his invention.' Others describe him as 'visionary,' 'dynamic' and 'dedicated.' Supportive yet demanding of his staff. 'He simply believes that however well the school is doing there is a constant need to improve things,' said one parent. His conversation is peppered with literary quotes and commercial references, leaving parents in little doubt that he knows what he's about. In 2001, he featured in a BBC2 TV programme – he exchanged places with a head of a Birmingham school which was at the bottom end of the league tables.

Entrance: Non-selective and oversubscribed – 153 applications for 120 places last time around – proximity to the school is the key to getting a place. So many families are attracted to the area by the school that its website has a direct link to an estate agent! Four form entry and usual state criteria apply, with siblings first and then other children living in the 'Admission Priority Area.' In practice, most children come from neighbouring infant schools including Bourne, St Andrews, St Mary's, Frensham and All Saints, Tilford.

Exit: Most to the local Weydon Comprehensive School in Farnham. About 40 per cent to the private sector – to the impressive big name schools such as Royal Grammar, Guildford High, Tormead and St Catherine's Bramley.

Remarks: An absolute star in the State system and it stands head and shoulders above many private schools. Academically at the very top of the tables but not at the expense of a really rounded curriculum. 100 per cent of pupils at grade 4 and above for KS2 SATs in maths, science, and English. More than 50 per cent level 5.

Class sizes average 30. All children are tested on entry to year 3 and given targets accordingly. Teaching style is where possible 'to gather at the master's feet,' with children all sitting on the floor in front of the teacher, returning to their desks to complete the task. Pupils who look like falling short of level 4 are taken out of class to work in 'focus' groups of eight, covering the same work as the rest of the class but at a different pace. 90 pupils on the special needs register and, at the other end of the spectrum, there is provision for the most able pupils – the school is a member of the National Association for Able Children in Education and one of the staff has special responsibility in this area.

Yet when parents describe what they like best about the school, this academic excellence appears to be almost taken for granted. Instead parents stress how happy their children are and talk about the 'fantastic' shows. Every child takes some part in the famed Christmas production – 'all the children get tremendous confidence from this,' says the head. A large number of pupils learn a musical instrument and sport is similarly encouraged with trophies lining the corridors. South Farnham has the Sportsmark Gold award and its netball team is current league champion. Football strong. Two of the female teachers are trained football referees, which encourages an unusually keen interest in football among the girls. High praise also for a thriving and varied range of free after-school clubs including sports, pottery, chess and even circus skills.

Facilities above average for a state school. Classrooms are large, bright and airy. Playground mapped into separate areas for football and other sports, leaving room for children who prefer to sit quietly. Children are very visibly valued – there are vases of flowers in their toilets and 150 spare coat pegs so they have room for all their extra bits and pieces. Such touches reinforce the school's belief that you don't improve maths teaching simply by teaching more maths – you have to get other things right so that the whole atmosphere is conducive to learning. Certainly pupils appear confident and happy and are all neatly turned out. 'There is such a warm friendly atmosphere at the school,' said one mother. 'Every child has the opportunity to do their very best – the ethos is that we want to achieve things.'

Staff largely female – just three men at the last count – and includes four 'leading practitioners'. All are closely monitored, with each teacher watched in action by a superior once a week. Staff training is a priority and the school rents out its training facilities to generate income. Lots of staff promotion both internally and to external posts, which does mean a fair turnover – just one member of staff has been at the school for more than 10 years. Mr Carter and staff are at the school gate morning and night and appear to know most of the parents by name. Easy to get to see a teacher, problems are dealt with promptly. 'The only child I could imagine not thriving here would be a bully,' said one mother.

Expect to be involved. The school asks as many parents as possible to come in and discuss their jobs and give children ideas about possible applications for their skills. Parents are also welcome to join their children for lunch in the canteen.

Said a parent who left the private system in favour of South Farnham, 'my daughter simply cannot get there fast enough in the mornings. You don't need to pay for a private school with this on your doorstep.'

SOUTH HAMPSTEAD HIGH SCHOOL JUNIOR DEPARTMENT

Linked to South Hampstead High School in the Senior section

5 Netherhall Gardens, London, NW3 5RN

Tel: 020 7794 7198
Fax: 020 7431 2750
E-mail: junior@shhs.gdst.net
Website: www.gdst.net/shhs/main.html

• Pupils: 245 girls, all day • Ages: 4-11 • Non-denom • Fees: £2,383 • Independent

Head: Since 2002, Mrs Maureen Young, who has been a deputy head and head in primary schools and worked extensively as an educational consultant. She's married, with a school-age daughter, has an MA in education and has been a senior LEA inspector.

Entrance: Entrance at 4 and 7 via telling testettes (no longer at 5+). NB if you flunk first time you can now resit at 7. Register two years before date of entry.

Exit: No examination needed to transfer to the senior school but some are advised to move to less academic secondaries – school insists they are warned of the possibility at least a year in advance.

Remarks: Very pressured indeed – though school disputes this and so do some parents. Bright and busy and very active. In a cul de sac – good selling point for London.

SOUTHBANK INTERNATIONAL SCHOOL (NW3)

Linked to Southbank International School (W11) in the Junior section
Linked to Southbank International School (W1) in the Senior section

16 Netherhall Gardens, Hampstead, London, NW3 5TH

Tel: 020 7243 3803
Fax: 020 7727 3290
E-mail: admissions@southbank.org
Website: www.southbank.org

• Pupils: 190 boys and girls • Ages: 3-14 • Independent

Remarks: For information see W1 branch.

SOUTHBANK INTERNATIONAL SCHOOL (W11)

Linked to Southbank International School (NW3) in the Junior section
Linked to Southbank International School (W1) in the Senior section

36-38 Kensington Park Road, London, W11 3BU

Tel: 020 7243 3803
Fax: 020 7727 3290
E-mail: admissions@southbank.org
Website: www.southbank.org

• Pupils: 195 boys/girls; all day • Ages: 3-10 • Independent

Remarks: For further information, see W1 branch.

St Dunstan's College Junior School

Linked to Saint Dunstan's College in the Senior section

Stanstead Road, Catford, London, SE6 4TY

Tel: 020 8516 7225
E-mail: admissions@sdmail.org.uk
Website: www.stdunstans.org.uk

• Pupils: boys and girls, all day • Ages: 3-11 boys and girls
• Anglican foundation • Independent

Remarks: For details see the senior school's entry.

Stamford Junior School

Linked to Stamford High School in the Senior section
Linked to Stamford School in the Senior section

Kettering Road, Stamford, Lincolnshire, PE9 2LR

Tel: 01780 484 400
Fax: 01780 484 401
E-mail: headsjs@ses.lincs.sch.uk
Website: www.ses.lincs.sch.uk

• Pupils: 170 boys, 165 girls; 10 board • Ages: 2-10 • C of E
• Fees: Day £2,076; boarding £4,320 • Independent

Head: A very lively school run with great enthusiasm by Miss Libby Craig (fifty) who took over the reins in 1997 although she has been with The Stamford Endowed Schools for 23 years.

Entrance: By exam.

Remarks: Children are selected with nationally standardized exam between 6+ and 10+ and are then geared up for direct entry into the senior Stamford Endowed Schools. Class sizes vary between 16 and 24 and all pupils' benefit from the staff's caring attitude. SATS results have been outstanding since Miss Craig became head with Level 5 figures in 2002 for English at 85 per cent and 60 per cent for maths and science putting the school in the top 5 per cent nationally.

Plenty of extra curricular activities including music, speech and drama, dancing, chess, gardening and language clubs. 90 per cent of KS2 children play a musical instrument and are able to join the junior school orchestra. Children are also able to join the Saturday morning activities, many of which take place along side senior school pupils.

Sport, which includes rugby, hockey, tennis, swimming and netball is very important with many pupils competing nationally, with success in all areas. Although a highly selective junior school, children come from all walks of life and are made welcome by everyone. The school is a very lively, happy place for children to develop a natural interest in all subjects which prepare them well for the senior school.

Stockport Grammar School Junior School

Linked to Stockport Grammar School in the Senior section

Buxton Road, Stockport, SK2 7AF

Tel: 0161 419 2405
Fax: 0161 419 2407
E-mail: francet@stockportgrammar.co.uk
Website: www.stockportgrammar.co.uk

• Pupils: 430 boys and girls • Ages: 4-11 • Independent

Head: Since 2000, Mr L Fairclough BA.

Remarks: Junior school is on own site, adjoining senior school. Shares dining hall some sports facilities with senior school. Curriculum is geared to senior school entrance examination, which vast majority pass. Lovely, light classrooms and happy, busy atmosphere. Evidence of projects and artwork bursting out to cover all available space. Staff dedicated. As with senior school, traditional values are centre stage, but lots of scope for exploration and fun.

STONAR PREPARATORY SCHOOL

Linked to Stonar School in the Senior section

Cottles Park, Atworth, Melksham, SN12 8NT

Tel: 01225 701 762
Fax: 01225 790 830
E-mail: prep@stonarschool.com
Website: www.stonarschool.com

- Pupils: 85 girls, of whom 10 board, in the prep school. Plus nursery for girls and boys – boys can stay on until they are 7
- Ages: 2-11 • Independent

Remarks: See senior school.

STOVER JUNIOR/ PREPARATORY SCHOOLS

Linked to Stover School in the Senior section

Stover, Newton Abbot, TQ12 6QG

Tel: 01626 354 505
Fax: 01626 361 475
E-mail: mail@stover.co.uk
Website: www.stover.co.uk

- Pupils: Nursery: 30 girls and boys. Junior: 90 girls (5 board). Preparatory: 90 boys • Ages: 3-10 • Christian • Fees: £1,720 to £2,095 • Independent

Head: Since 2002, Mrs Julie Fairbrother BA MA PGCE.

Entrance: 7 and under – interview and report; 7+ – exam, report and interview.

Exit: About 33 per cent of nursery pupils move on to the prep school; most junior girls and boys move up to the senior school.

Remarks: Own purpose-developed area on same site. Traditional standards and expectations, small classes with bright and cheerful atmosphere. Pinafores for the girls; grey trousers, green blazer for the boys. Separate lessons but co-ed play.

STREATHAM & CLAPHAM HIGH SCHOOL JUNIOR DEPARTMENT

Linked to Streatham and Clapham High School in the Senior section

Wavertree Road, Streatham Hill, London, SW2 3SR

Tel: 020 8674 6912
Fax: 020 8674 0175
E-mail: enquiry@shj.gdst.net
Website: www.gdst.net/streathamhigh

- Pupils: 280 girls, all day • Ages: 4-11 • Non-denom • Fees: Nursery £1,838 (full time), £919 (part time); junior dept £2,383
- Independent

Head: Since 2005, Ms Louisa Burke BEd Dip Psych MA. Came from a British school in Portugal. She has a background in child development and learning.

Entrance: Mostly at the Foundation stage and other occasional places via age appropriate assessment.

Exit: Most girls progress to the senior department at 11.

Remarks: School occupies huge Wavertree site – formerly the home of the senior school – and the school feels like a senior school only with smaller children. Masses of assets unusual for juniors including massive sports hall, ICT centre, library, dance studio, art room with terrific views over London. Very well-staffed and well-resourced but 'not a lot happening yet', says a parent. Good SEN and Gifted & Talented provision. Super adventure playground. Parents report very happy children. Nursery in separate building close by.

THE STUDY PREPARATORY SCHOOL

Wilberforce House, Camp Road, Wimbledon Common, London, SW19 4UN

Tel: 020 8947 6969
Fax: 020 8944 5975
E-mail: wilberforce@thestudyprep.co.uk
Website: www.thestudyprep.co.uk

• Pupils: 320 girls, all day • Ages: 4-11 • Non denom • Fees: £2,795 • Independent • Open days: November and March

Headmistress: Since 2003, Ms Joyce Nicol MA Cert Ed (late forties). Took over from the popular Lindsay Bond; formerly head at Wilmslow Prep, Cheshire and Longacre School, Surrey. Parents say she is organized, unflappable and always ready to listen. Joanna Gay is deputy head, she and Mrs Nicol alternate their time between sites.

Entrance: Non-selective entry at 4+ by ballot; priority given to siblings. Thereafter girls have an informal assessment and interview for occasional places. Girls mainly local, Wimbledon and the surrounding areas of Roehampton, Kingston, Barnes and Putney.

Exit: Regularly get both music and academic scholarships at 11+. Majority go to day schools: Wimbledon, Putney and Surbiton High Schools, Lady Eleanor Holles, Kingston Grammar, Notre Dame. Some to boarding schools Woldingham, Godolphin, St Mary's Calne, odd one to the state sector.

Remarks: Lively prep school founded in 1893 by a governess, now on two sites bordering Wimbledon Common. Pre-prep girls at Wilberforce House in large purpose-built ex local authority premises, surrounded by well maintained gardens and play areas. Year 4 upwards on the original site, Spencer House, which was acquired in 1903 and has a small playground.

Both buildings have been redecorated and modernized recently. Classes are mixed ability although there is some setting for maths and English; a committed band of staff. Girls are taught to enjoy learning; certainly not a hothouse say parents, but all the girls are 'encouraged to reach their potential'. Produces confident, friendly and well adjusted girls, without pressure. Mrs Nicol is strong on staff development too. Science lab particularly well designed and the teaching is very high standard. A learning support team assists girls with specific difficulties and EFL.

A good choice of clubs, with sports being very popular; girls have been selected for SW London athletic squads and swimming teams. No sports field: makes use of the many public sports facilities in the area. Drama and public speaking also thriving – many do LAMDA exams. The head says she likes to encourage girls to try out different activities before thinking of specializing. The jewel in the crown is undoubtedly music; 4 choirs, an orchestra, and smaller strings groups that provide music for assemblies. The school also boasts a parent and pupil choir whose most recent performance was Mozart's Requiem. A new enthusiastic director of music appointed this term. There is always a waiting list for individual instrumental tuition, so put your name down early.

SUMMER FIELDS SCHOOL

Mayfield Road, Summer Fields, Oxford, Oxfordshire, OX2 7EN

Tel: 01865 454 433
Fax: 01865 459 200
E-mail: schoolsec@summerfields.org.uk
Website: www.summerfields.oxon.sch.uk

• Pupils: 250 boys; 240 boarders, 10 day • Ages: 8-13 • C of E
• Fees: Boarders £5,325; day £4,010 • Independent

Head: Since 1997, Mr Robin Badham-Thornhill BA PGCE (forties) who was educated at Cheam and Cheltenham and read history and economics at Exeter. He was previously at Lambrook and before that taught at King's School, Bruton. His pretty wife, Angela, is much involved in the school, and they have two daughters, currently at The Dragon, and Headington. The BTs, as they are called, have nine boys living with them in Beech Lodge (and this is a permanent arrangement, popular with the boys, who almost kill to get a coveted place, writing begging letters in the spring term 'I hear you make the nicest cocoa, please can I come').

Mr BT (it is easier to fall into the mould) was the first head appointed from outside the school, and staff say the place is 'more relaxed', certainly the boys look a trifle scruffier – but happy. The head believes in breadth of education – 'interests and disciplines learnt at prep school are with you into adult life' and excellence in everything – 'if the boys are going to do something, they should aim to do it well'. He denies that the school is known as an academic hothouse, and certainly the scholarship level (and here Eton is the main marker) is not as high as it was in the 1990s, but there is a strong scholarship stream, and parents will not be disappointed. 'A third of our boys are very bright and capable, two-thirds are average and taught well'. Staff are crucial, and at Summer Fields (North Oxford you see) they get the pick of the bunch. Under the previous regime, staff were encouraged to stay (and stay), Mr BT believes in encouraging them to move on – and up: three former deputy heads are now running their own schools.

Entrance: Names down early, the school is full, and though there is no thought of taking more than 250 boys, another boarding house (or lodge) has just been built. Boys come for assessment two terms before they are due to join, and though traditionally this is an upper class place, parents are now less stereotyped, with about half coming from London (mainly lawyers and bankers). One or two real foreigners, and some EFL on offer, but school has no need to trawl for customers.

Exit: Eton feed, about half go there, with roughly 20 per cent each to Harrow and Radley and trickles to elsewhere. A dozen or so awards.

Remarks: Founded in 1864 and set in 60 acres of suburban North Oxford, with elegantly manicured lawns, rhodies and playing fields down to the river (local farmer leases two surplus fields) the school is a delight. (You turn off the Banbury Road between M&S and the Oxfam shop.) The large bow-fronted main building houses an enormous conglomerate of add-ons, super new gym complex with squash courts, fives courts and a climbing wall. Swimming pool (and an outdoor one too), fabulous art department (The Wavell Centre) with pottery and IT, computers everywhere and boys can use the e-mail more or less at will during their free time. Terrific theatre conversion from an expanded old gym umbilically linked to the music department. Outdoor theatre too. Masses of plays and musicals, choir strong, with regular trips to Paris and Germany. Plus oodles of trad classrooms, nattily equipped with green plastic adjustable desks and matching chairs. Long passages with boys in blue guernseys (sleeves usually over their hands) scurrying everywhere. Boys are hotshots on general knowledge; with weekly quizzes at school and regularly beating all-comers in the prep school world. Max class size 17, one-to-one support for those with dyslexia; gappies (Australians, New Zealanders, South Africans) help with reading and odd classes as well as doing more mundane housekeeping and sporting activities. Almost invisible streaming from the start, with scholarship stream for the last two years. Greek on offer for the really bright. Impressive library, reading is important here, with two reading periods a day, one after lunch, overseen by hovering masters, and the second before lights out. School now has a more feminine touch, and even some female teachers, some of whom are also lodge mothers. Most staff live on site, in subsidised houses (obviously anonymously, for there is no list of staff in the prospectus). Lovely chapel, with impressive stained glass, which can extend (into the table tennis room) to accommodate parents when the need arises. Organ popular, and keen organists pop in to practise whenever they can. The altar cloth is embroidered with what could be the school's motto, 'A good seed brings forth good fruit'. School uses French-staffed chateau in Normandy where boys have regular visits, ten days in their third year and two week in the fourth, where they not only learn French as she is spoke, but also experience life in rural France. Strong and enthusiastic sport, boys can swim every single day, nine-hole golf course and popular adventure playground. 'You name it, it's there and the boys do it full throttle', said one parent who knows his son finds holiday and home offer rather less. Clay pigeon shooting in outfields. Unlike The Dragon, with whom Summer Fields have a good natured rivalry, the school does not major in boating activities. Senior boys are allowed into Summertown, but the school shop is brill, selling toys and whoopee cushions as well as mundane rubbers and pencils. Fantastic new cinema in the day room in the main school – with surround sound. Huge dining room lined with the portraits of the great and the good, mostly Old Boys, including Macmillan and Lord Wavell. We joined them for 'little tea'. Day boys, whose numbers won't increase, are often dons' sons. Seven lodges (plus Beech Lodge), arranged horizontally, with younger boys in two-year blocks. Cosy dorms, some bunks, some low horsebox arrangements, with each boy having his own bedside light – which can be turned off at the door. This is a fizzy boarding prep school, all singing and dancing, and undoubtedly for the boys, this is where networking begins.

SUNNINGDALE SCHOOL

Dry Arch Road, Sunningdale, Ascot, Berkshire, SL5 9PY

Tel: 01344 620 159
Fax: 01344 873 304
E-mail: headmaster@sunningdaleschool.co.uk
Website: www.sunningdaleschool.co.uk

• Pupils: 100 boys, all board except a handful • Ages: 8-13
• C of E • Fees: Boarding £4,570 • Independent • Open days:
Parents visit by appointment

Headmaster: Since 2005, Mr Tom Dawson, who took over the reins from his father and uncle. Mr Dawson was educated at Eton and taught at Harrow before joining the staff at Sunningdale in 2002. He is married to Elisabeth – their first child due January 2006.

Academic Matters: Very good results at Common Entrance and scholarships won on a regular basis.

Entrance: At 8 – 'they settle in better at this age' – from a wide variety of pre-preps all over the country including Scotland. Some from London but not as many as expected given the proximity to the London SW postcodes. Also happy to take boys at 10 or 11 from day schools.

Exit: 50 per cent to Eton, 25 per cent to Harrow, 5 per cent to Stowe. One or two to Marlborough, Radley, Charterhouse, Wellington and Milton Abbey.

Remarks: Small, cosy, old-fashioned prep school. A large country house with lots of add-ons including new-fashioned classroom blocks, one furnished with old-fashioned wooden 'lift-up lid' desks. Attention given to individual academic needs. Much movement between classes. A brighter boy may end up doing two years in a top class which gives him a tremendous advantage at Common Entrance. Well-behaved boys juxtaposed with seemingly informal teaching staff.

74 per cent learn a musical instrument. Active chess club with a part-time chess teacher. Lots of sport including Eton fives. Full boarding although boys may weekly board in their first year. Pastoral care has improved dramatically. Present matron is kind and cosy. Carpeted dorms for younger ones (piles of teddies on the beds), cubicles for the older boys, hot chocolate offered as a reward for tidiness. A large communal bathroom with eight miniature-sized cast iron baths with claw feet – new shower block too. House in Normandy used by the week. Boys allowed to walk the Dawsons' dogs in the grounds (wonderful at cheering up a homesick child). Excellent food. Boys have happy, cheery faces with sparkling eyes. Excellent manners and well disciplined. Lots of praise too.

SUNNY HILL PREPARATORY SCHOOL

Linked to Bruton School for Girls in the Senior section

Sunny Hill, Bruton, Somerset, BA10 0NT

Tel: 01749 814427
Fax: 01749 813202
E-mail: sunnyhillprep@brutonschool.co.uk
Website: www.brutonschool.co.uk

• Pupils: girls; boys welcome in nursery and pre-prep until 7
• Ages: 3 - 11; day and boarding from 7 • Fees: Day £1,825 -
£3,225; boarding £4,300- £5,830 • Independent • Open days:
October, November, February

Head: Since 2001, Mr David Marsden.

Entrance: Policy of 'open-entry' into pre-prep at two and a half.

Exit: Seamless entry at 11.

Remarks: After-school care until 6pm (and 30 activities) makes it popular with working mothers. 'Tasters' for boarding on offer. Enjoys most facilities with senior school.

SURBITON HIGH JUNIOR GIRLS' SCHOOL

Linked to Surbiton High School in the Senior section
Linked to Surbiton Preparatory School in the Junior section

95-97 Surbiton Road, Kingston Upon Thames, Surrey, KT1 2HW

Tel: 020 8546 9756
Fax: 020 8974 6293
E-mail: surbiton.juniorgirls@church-schools.com
Website: www.surbitonhigh.com

• Pupils: 242 girls, all day • Ages: 4-11 • Christian ethos but all denominations accepted • Fees: £1,929 (reception and years 1-2); £2,628 (years 3-6) per term • Independent

Head: Since late 1990s, Miss Celia Budge BA PGCE (mid fifties). 'I'm a big fan,' said one father, 'she has set objectives in mind and knows exactly where she wants to take the children.' Other parents describe her as 'fantastic' and 'very good'. 'She is clever and has a great knack of controlling the children without shouting,' said another. 'You get the feeling that these are her girls and she is very protective of them and of her staff.'

Entrance: At 4, by informal assessment during a monitored visit and at 7 by assessments in maths and English. At other times, subject to availability and assessment.

Exit: Girls are groomed for Surbiton High Senior School – and while nearly all will get in, it is not a foregone conclusion and there is an exam to pass.

Remarks: Very much a local school – several parents say that location alone influenced their choice; it's a plus that the girls are likely to make friends near their doorsteps. (The head points to a number of girls who come from further afield). Academic achievement strong. Girls follow the National Curriculum closely (but not exclusively) and sit SATS. In 2005, at Key Stage 1, 100 per cent of the pupils achieved the national target level 2, with many reaching the higher level 3 – 82 per cent in English and 88 per cent in maths. Similarly, school achieved a 100 per cent success rate hitting the national target level 4 at Key Stage 2, with many at level 5 – 94 per cent in English, 83 per cent in maths and 94 per cent in science. 'It's a good mix,' said a parent 'academic standards are high but not at the expense of a balanced curriculum.' From the start there is specialist teaching for music, French and PE; years 5 and 6 move completely to a departmental style of teaching.

The head says the school encourages thinking skills and free thinkers and that 'girly-girls does not describe our children who throw themselves down ski slopes etc with such enthusiasm.' Some parents disagree, 'you do get the impression that they are focused on turning out 'nice' girls for the senior school,' said one mother. 'They like girly-girls who do exactly what they are told and cannot cope so well with a more challenging pupil. But although I would say free-thinkers are not encouraged, you have to judge the school on the girls it produces and by year 6 you have lovely, confident, well-groomed girls with a good set of results. They are the best advert for the school.'

Plenty of PE and sport on offer both via the timetable and through a wide range of after-school clubs, including an award-winning ski team. Like the seniors and prep boys, juniors are bused over to impressive sports facilities at Hinchley Wood, some three-miles away (but unlike the other parts of the school, the girls stay on site for lunch and PE). Housed in a modern, purpose-built building on a main road, junior school has lots of facilities, including ICT suite, drama studio and science rooms, and each classroom has an electronic whiteboard. Average 24 children in a class – school is pushed for space, you get the impression there are girls squeezed in every nook and cranny and according to one parent 'it is desperately hot'. (Head does not accept the school is cramped.) Outside space is limited. Atmosphere is 'friendly' and 'quite formal'. Reflecting the catchment area, pupils are predominantly from English middle-class families, and there is a strong, well-established parents' association.

Overall, parents seem to be getting exactly what they want from the school – a nicely rounded education for their daughters with a direct path to a high achieving senior school.

SURBITON PREPARATORY SCHOOL

Linked to Surbiton High Junior Girls' School in the Junior section

Linked to Surbiton High School in the Senior section

3 Avenue Elmers, Surbiton, Surrey, KT6 4SP

Tel: 02083 906 640

Fax: 020 8255 3049

E-mail: surbiton.prep@church-schools.com

Website: www.surbitonhigh.com

- Pupils: 138 boys, all day • Ages: 4-11 • Christian ethos but all denominations accepted • Fees: £1,929 (reception, years 1-2); £2,628 (years 3-6) • Independent • Open days: November

Head: Stephen Pryce MA BA CertEd FRSA (early fifties), with more than 30 years experience and grown-up children of his own. Roundly praised by parents. 'He is the reason I chose the school,' said one, echoed by others. 'He is absolutely wonderful, knows all the boys by name and character, very firm but very kind.' Operates an open door policy and once a week invites six pupils to 'take tea' with him (actually squash and doughnuts). 'He runs a very happy ship,' said one father.

Entrance: At 4: informal assessment in January for 20 reception places. At other times subject to availability. No need to register at birth – easier to get into than the girls' school.

Exit: With no in-house repository at 11, school achieves a very creditable set of places/scholarships at local independent schools including Hampton, Kingston Grammar, Reed's and St George's College.

Remarks: Good academically but with limited space particularly outdoors. Surbiton Prep is the junior boys' school of Surbiton High School and shares many of its facilities including dining rooms and gym (100 metres down the road, so the boys get plenty of short walks each day) and sports fields (impressive, though a three mile bus journey away). The Prep building has been a school since 1862 (it became part of Surbiton High in 1987) and, while this gives the place a certain homely charm, the downside is that physical surroundings are not great and space is at a premium. 'Reception classroom is small and hot and the toilets need doing,' said one parent. Several others voiced concerns about the playground – 'too small – no space for the boys to have a good run about,' said one. 'Not enough equipment,' said another.

Does not follow the National Curriculum to the letter (boys additionally take French from reception),- but pupils sit SATs at Key Stages 1 and 2. In 2005 at Key Stage 1, 100 per cent reached level 2 (the national target) and more than half reached level 3 – 45 per cent in English, 89 per cent in maths. At Key Stage 2, 100 per cent of pupils reached the national target level 4 in English and science, and 96 per cent did in maths. Again many bettered this: level 5s by 59 per cent of the boys in English, 81 per cent in maths and 68 per cent science. All classrooms have electronic whiteboards. Lots of opportunities for arty children – regular drama productions and a good range of music tuition available as an extra. Plenty of after-school clubs.

Pastoral care and discipline generally considered good. 'It's a very close community where the boys all know each other and the teachers all know them,' said a mother of two boys at the school. 'It's a safe and supportive environment where the children feel secure.' Any issues over behaviour problems are considered well-handled – with the occasional miracle turnaround of a difficult child. Relaxed atmosphere, boys are polite and well turned out. Parents mostly English professional couples – both working, with a sprinkling from overseas. Strong parent association with plenty going on – more social than fund-raising. 'Friendly, not snooty,' said one.

Generally a feel that the prep is a bit of a poor relation of the main school, but 'there's a happy atmosphere and they turn out a good product,' said a father – 'makes you wonder what they could do if the facilities were slightly better.'

SUSSEX HOUSE SCHOOL

68 Cadogan Square, London, SW1X 0EA

Tel: 02075 841 741

Fax: 02075 892 300

E-mail: registrar@sussexhouseschool.co.uk

- Pupils: 180 boys; all day • Ages: 8-13 • C of E • Fees: £3,595
- Independent

Head: Since 1994, Mr Nicholas Kaye MA ACP (early fifties). Was deputy head here before. A reticent man at first, he quickly becomes animated while talking about the school. Very complimentary about his staff, depends upon them greatly. Keeps numbers of boys to 180 and has no desire to expand – 'enables every boy to have a real achievement during their time here'. Very keen on music – is a conductor himself and writes on nineteenth century music. Since becoming head he has restored the Norman Shaw designed building to its former glory exposing panelling and friezes. William Morris wallpaper now adorns the walls (throughout) and the full beauty of the house's original ballroom, with its de Morgan tiles and opulent fireplace, can be appreciated. His aim is to create the 'atmosphere of a boys' boarding prep... a family setting, not institutionalised'. Walking in off the street you wonder whether you're in the right place – only the fabulous 3D artwork dotted around the entrance hall gives an indication that this is not a private house. Apparently tradesmen arriving with deliveries frequently query 'Is this a school or what?'

Entrance: 36 intake per year: about 160 sit the academic, tough exam plus interview in January. Registration can take place up to the day before. Siblings are no longer given preference. £500 deposit payable on acceptance of a place. Most come from local pre-preps: Wetherby's, Eaton House, Garden House and Norland Place.

Exit: Over the past seven years, every boy has achieved his chosen school. Half go to boarding school: Eton, Charterhouse, Radley, Marlborough etc. The London half to Westminster, St Paul's, City of London, Dulwich etc. Weekly clinics give parents sound advice on their choice of senior school; 'let you know if your ambitions are unrealistic'. In 2004, two Eton schols – one was placed second overall.

Remarks: Small, forthright, down-to-earth London prep. Does a very good job and gets results. Homely, happy atmosphere designed to instil confidence. Elegant house on Cadogan Square with annexe in Cadogan Street housing a gym and music facilities. Sport is taken very seriously indeed, even the early morning training sessions are popular. Famous for prowess in fencing – U12 and U14 national champs; is now making a name for itself on the football field with the 1st XI unbeaten in the 2001-02 season. With a musical head, it is not surprising to find that the standard is high (75 per cent play a musical instrument) and it's ambitious and it's adventurous. Celebrated full-scale theatrical performances eg Smike at the West End's Criterion Theatre. Art is everywhere and is prominent, exciting, eye-catching, awe-inspiring. Fitting, really, for a school housed in a building designed by one of the foremost architects in the Arts and Crafts movement and in keeping with 'the strong creative bias associated with Chelsea'.

Greek has recently been introduced and proves very popular with parents and boys alike. There is no PTA as such but an enthusiastic, supportive activities committee. Many Old Boys fall into the writer/journalist/actor category. Would suit parents who are ambitious for academic success but like to keep their options open. Has a structured, fairly formal approach making it a good springboard for a traditional senior school.

SUTTON HIGH JUNIOR SCHOOL

Linked to Sutton High School in the Senior section

55 Cheam Road, Sutton, Surrey, SM1 2AX

Tel: 02086 420 594
Fax: 02086 422 014
E-mail: office@sut.gdst.net
Website: www.gdst.net/suttonhigh

• Ages: 4-11girls, all day • Non-denom • Fees: junior school: £2,243 • Independent

Remarks: For details, see the senior school entry.

SUTTON VALENCE PREPARATORY SCHOOL

Linked to Sutton Valence School in the Senior section

Underhill, Church Road, Chart Sutton, Maidstone, Kent, ME17 3RF

Tel: 01622 842 117
Fax: 01622 844 201
E-mail: anne@svprep.svs.org.uk
Website: www.svs.org.uk

• Pupils: 146 girls and boys; day and boarding from 9+ • Ages: 3-11 • Fees: From £3,230 • Independent • Open days: September, November and March

Head: Mr Tony Brooke, previously head at Yardley Court, Tonbridge.

Entrance: Test.

Exit: Mostly to Sutton Valence School and to local grammar schools.

Remarks: Entry from 3 into kindergarten and pre-prep (Underhill House). Boarding from 9 years. Set in a wonderful 22 acres of grounds in the nearby village of Chart Sutton. Small classes, high standards and same commitment to extra-curricular activities as senior school.

SYDENHAM HIGH JUNIOR SCHOOL GDST

Linked to Sydenham High School GDST in the Senior section

19 Westwood Hill, London, SE26 6BL

Tel: 020 8778 9558
Fax: 020 8778 0206
E-mail: info@syd.gdst.net
Website: www.gdst.net/sydenhamhigh

• Pupils: 255 girls, all day • Ages: 5-11 • Fees: Junior: £2,383
• Independent • Open days: Early October

Head: Mrs Barbara Risk Cert Ed MA. Friendly, chatty, open. Pupils really like the fact she always calls them 'my girls' makes them feel part of a big happy family. Enjoys a good working and personal relationship with head of senior school (who's in overall charge).

Entrance: Informal entry assessment at 31/2 – 'gives us edge over some of our competitors who do formal assessment – children skip out of here, find experience enjoyable, even fun.' 'Weed out the stroppy and difficult' so hope it doesn't fall on a day when your child's in a bad mood!

Exit: Between 60 and 70 per cent to senior school, rest to a range of schools: JAGS, Alleyn's, St Dunstan's College, Royal Russell, some boarding, some state, some to other GDSTs because they're nearer to where a girl is living. School helps find places elsewhere for those who don't make it to the senior school (no automatic entry).

Remarks: Good facilities, new library, and IT suite, classrooms brimming with lively displays. French for all from four, emphasis on music, sport and drama. Close links with senior school – head spends an afternoon a week in the junior school, takes assembly which girls love and say is a very special time. Y6 girls permitted to wear senior uniform and dine in senior school.

Currently caters for range of mild SEN: dyspraxia, dyslexia, dyscalculia, Aspergers, autism, ADD, ADHD and EBD, but all must be able to manage the curriculum. Some specialist support available. Gifted and talented coordinator for most able works with senior girls too.

A very welcoming environment.

TALBOT HEATH JUNIOR SCHOOL

Linked to Talbot Heath School in the Senior section

Rothesay Road, Bournemouth, Dorset, BH8 9LJ

Tel: 01202 763 360
Fax: 01202 768155
E-mail: office@talbotheath.org.uk
Website: talbotheath.org.uk

• Pupils: 127 girls in junior school and 98 pupils in pre-prep, including 10 boys • Ages: 3 - 11 • C of E • Fees: Day: kindergarten £920, reception £1,330, junior £1,500 - £2,365
• Independent • Open days: October

Head: Since 1987, Mrs Karen Leahy.

Entrance: By assessment according to age.

Remarks: Junior school used to occupy part of main school but moved to separate buildings in 1980 (junior department) and 1993 (pre-prep). Own dining rooms, computer suite and play areas as well as purpose-built Jubilee Hall for assemblies, drama and music. Some subjects – eg music and PE – taught by specialist subject staff from senior school. The pre-prep has a handful of boys (usually siblings of girls already at school), who leave for local preps at 7.

TASIS - The American School in England Lower School

Linked to TASIS - The American School in England in Senior section

Coldharbour Lane, Thorpe, Egham, Surrey, TW20 8TE

Tel: 01932 582427
Fax: 01932 560493
Website: www.tasis.com

- Ages: 3-11 boys and girls, boarding and day • Non-denom
- Fees: Two terms per year. Per term: nursery £2,600 half-day; Day: pre-K half-day £3,000; K- 3 £6,600; 4-8 £7,150; 9-13 £7,650. Full boarding £11,250. Extras: one time £750 building contribution; bus service £1,100 per semester • Independent
- Open days: Any day

Remarks: For details, see the senior school entry.

Taunton Pre Prep and First Steps

Linked to Taunton School in the Senior section

Taunton School, Taunton, Somerset, TA2 6AE

Tel: 01823 349209
Fax: 01823 349202
Website: www.tauntonschool.co.uk

- Ages: 2-7 • Inter-denom • Independent

Remarks: For details, see senior school entry.

Taunton Preparatory School

Linked to Taunton School in the Senior section

Staplegrove Road, Taunton, Somerset, TA2 6AE

Tel: 01823 349209
Fax: 01823 349202
Website: www.tauntonschool.co.uk

- Ages: 7-13 boys and girls, boarding and day
- Inter-denominational • Independent

Head: Mr M Anderson.
Remarks: For details, see senior school entry.

Teesside Preparatory School

Linked to Teesside High School in the Senior section

The Avenue, Eaglescliffe, Stockton-on-Tees, TS16 9AT

Tel: 01642 782 095
Fax: 01642 791 207
E-mail: info@teessidehigh.co.uk
Website: www.teessidehigh.co.uk

- Pupils: 135 girls, all day • Ages: 3-11 • Non-denom
- Independent

Head: Since 2005, Mrs Julie Richardson is head of pre-prep and Mrs Faith Potter head of prep.
Entrance: Informal assessment in English and maths during a day spent in school.
Remarks: Has its own building and play area next to the senior school. Bustling and cheerful atmosphere. French taught from eight and IT throughout. Girls very proud of their school. Two ten-year-olds who took us round insisted on showing us everything from the staff room to the contents of every cupboard!

THE GRANGE JUNIOR SCHOOL

Linked to Grange School (The) in the Senior section

Beechwood Avenue, Hartford, Northwich, Cheshire, CW8 3AU

Tel: 01606 77447
Fax: 01606 784581
E-mail: office@grange.org.uk
Website: www.grange.org.uk

• Pupils: 175 pupils in kindergarten to prep 2; 290 in prep 3 to 6; all day • Ages: 4-11 • Fees: £1,765 - £1,905 • Independent

Head: Since 2005, Mr Stephen Bennett. Previously principal of Saudia SAS School in Jeddah, Saudi Arabia.

Entrance: Main entry point is at 4. Informal assessment in small groups.

Exit: Majority, but not all, go on to the senior school.

Remarks: Idyllic setting for friendly, homely junior school. Very much a rural, rather than a street-wise/urban feel. 'Early birds' and 'Sundown' clubs provide before-and after-care for pupils. Relaxed but watchful staff.

THOMAS'S LONDON DAY SCHOOL (KENSINGTON)

Linked to Thomas's Preparatory School (Clapham) in the Junior section
Linked to Thomas's London Day Schools (Battersea) in the Junior section

17-19 Cottesmore Gardens, London, W8 5PR

Tel: 020 7361 6500
Fax: 020 7361 6501
E-mail: kensington@thomas-s.co.uk
Website: www.thomas-s.co.uk

• Pupils: 311 girls and boys • Ages: 4-11 • C of E • Fees: £3,675 - £3,998 • Independent

Headmistress: Since 2001, Mrs Diana Maine MA BEd NPQH (forties). Formerly head of biology and director of sixth form at St Marylebone CE School, sixth form consortium co-ordinator for Greenwich, and deputy head at Blackheath High School (junior department). She was also author and con-sultant on a number of science books for Dorling Kindersley. Married with a teenage daughter and son.

It is hard to imagine a more perfect head for a Kensington school – bright-eyed, well-presented, a totally professional person, inspiring immediate confidence in her management.

Entrance: Parents local. Apply directly. Very over-subscribed – main list up to 2007 is closed. Names down before one year; siblings have priority but are not guaranteed a place. Assessments take place at age 3 in February of year of entry. Applicants need to have 'a measure of confidence, be responsive, sociable, with a light in their eyes.' Children are interviewed in groups. A week later parents receive a letter with an offer of a firm place or a reserve place or no place.

Exit: Aimed at the age-11 entry for the top London day schools, with a good number going on to boarding schools too (often via two years at Thomas's Battersea or a boarding prep).

Remarks: A busy school. Not for the withdrawn type. Loads of music, art, drama and PE from the first day at school. 20 per cent of the timetable is given over to sport after age 8 – rugby, football, cricket, netball, hockey and rounders. Drama is huge – the founder Mrs Thomas was an actor on the West End stage so, not surprisingly, the school is a bit crazy about drama. At the top end it really is quite something, productions are big scale and taken very seriously. 70-ish per cent of pupils learn a musical instrument and there are numerous choirs, string groups, orchestras with music trips to eg Genoa, Stockholm and Paris. Very active PTA. Ballet is popular – though very few boys carry on past age 7.

Drama apart, the other notable characteristics of all the Thomas's schools are the specialist subject teaching (from an early age), the emphasis on 11/13 as the leaving age (no provision whatsoever is made for those wanting to leave at 8), the state-of-the-art ICT room and plasma screens in classrooms (all leave able to use a computer and touch type), a lack of stuffiness and the clearly proprietorial style (no governors, parent reps chosen by the head and form teachers). Thomas's schools are not academically selective – very few siblings are turned away – and there's good SEN provision for the milder end of the spectrum. They seem to be settling into a maturity after their hectic early years, with common strengths and individual characteristics that flow from their parents as much as from their heads.

Kensington is a town-house school, with all the warrenous nature that that implies. Ravished Lady Eden's in 2002, doubling in size as a result (though many of the maidens fled to form Queen's College junior school). The brightest and best decorated of the three (and smells best too), between the other two in style.

THOMAS'S BATTERSEA

Linked to Thomas's Preparatory School (Clapham) in the Junior section

Linked to Thomas's London Day School (Kensington) in the Junior section

28-40 Battersea High Street, London, SW11 3JB

Tel: 020 7978 0900

Fax: 020 7978 0901

E-mail: patohead@thomas-s.co.uk

Website: www.thomas-s.co.uk

• Pupils: 500 boys and girls. All day • Ages: 4-13 • C of E • Fees: £2,764 - £3,905 depending on age and the number of siblings • Independent • Open days: Wednesdays

Principal: Mr Ben Thomas MA (thirties). Educated at Eton, Durham and the Institute of Education. Married with three children, 2 of whom attend the school. Mr Thomas is one of four principals: the two founding principals are David and Joanna Thomas (she originally started the school in 1971), the fourth is Tobyn Thomas who is in charge of all administration – quite something with six different sites (there are two kindergartens) to oversee, not to mention the fleet of school buses, a familiar sight ferrying pupils around southwest London. Before joining the school as head of the Kensington branch in 1995, Ben Thomas was a merchant banker with the now defunct Barings (he left well before the scandal). Teaches English to the scholarship class and the struggling class so 'gets to see the top and the bottom. It's the most important part of my week'. Very approachable, not a headmasterly type – every child hails him with a cheery 'good morning Mr Thomas'. A consensus-seeker. Believes that school should be about fun in the early years, becoming steadily more serious as the children grow up; pupils noticeably more laid-back and relaxed than at the other two schools, and rather more chaotic too.

Entrance: Parents from all over – Notting Hill to Streatham. Apply directly. Very oversubscribed – main list up to 2005 is closed. Names down before one year; siblings have priority but are not guaranteed a place. Assessments take place at age 3 in February of year of entry. Applicants need to have 'a measure of confidence, be responsive, sociable, with a light in their eyes' says the head. Three chil-

dren are interviewed in groups for each place. A week later parents receive a letter with an offer of a firm place or a reserve place or no place.

Exit: 'End goal is 13+' but some leave for London independent day schools and competitive state schools (eg Tiffin) at 11. Not a feeder to any particular school; a wide range of smart London schools (St Paul's much more than Westminster), all the top girls' schools, ditto boys' but no recent Wykehamists.

Remarks: A big, busy school. Not for the withdrawn type. Loads of music, art, drama and PE from the first day at school. 25 per cent of the timetable is given over to sport after age 8 – rugby, football, cricket, netball, hockey and rounders. In years 7 and 8, sculling has become a very popular option. Drama is huge – the founding Mrs Thomas was an actor on the West End stage so, not surprisingly, the school is a bit crazy about drama. At the top end it really is quite something, productions are big scale and taken very seriously. 70-ish per cent of pupils learn a musical instrument and there are numerous choirs, jazz groups, string groups, orchestras with music trips to eg Austria, Finland and Estonia. Entertainments such as Glyndebourne-style evenings or Last Night at the Proms are regularly offered to parents. Ballet is popular – though very few boys carry on past age 7.

Drama apart, the other notable characteristics of all the Thomas's schools are the specialist subject teaching (from an early age), the emphasis on 11/13 as the leaving age (no provision whatsoever is made for those wanting to leave at 8) the lack of electronic clutter (though all leave able to use a computer and touch type), a lack of stuffiness and the clearly proprietorial style (no governors, parent reps chosen by the head and form teachers). Thomas's schools are not academically selective – very few siblings are turned away – and there's good SEN provision for the milder end of the spectrum. They seem to be settling into a maturity after their hectic early years, with common strengths and individual characteristics that flow from their parents as much as from their heads.

Battersea is the most cosmopolitan and laid back of the three, in a fine old building with modern additions. Fabulously imaginative rooftop playground for the younger ones. A lively, likeable school.

THOMAS'S CLAPHAM

Linked to Thomas's London Day School (Kensington) in the Junior section

Linked to Thomas's London Day Schools (Battersea) in the Junior section

Broomwood Road, Wandsworth, London, SW11 6JZ

Tel: 020 7326 9300
Fax: 020 7326 9301
E-mail: Clapham@thomas-s.co.uk
Website: www.thomas-s.co.uk

- Pupils: 520 girls and boys; all day • Ages: 4-13 • C of E
- Fees: £2,620 - £3,705 • Independent

Headmistress: Since 1993 Mrs Carol Evelegh DipCE DipSpLD (forties). Joined Thomas's in 1979 and has risen. Two children, both were at the school and now at Tonbridge and Benenden. A decisive, tidy, organised head. Children jump to attention and intone 'good morning Mrs Evelegh' at her entrance; staff jump too. Likes her teachers young and has no wish to hang on into her grey years herself (though should be good for another five). Special needs trained.

Entrance: Parents pretty local. Apply directly. Very oversubscribed. Names down before one year; siblings have priority but are not guaranteed a place. Assessments take place at age 3 in February of year of entry. Applicants need to have 'a measure of confidence, be responsive, sociable, with a light in their eyes,' says the head. Three children are interviewed in groups for each place. A week later parents receive a letter with an offer of a firm place or a reserve place or no place.

Exit: 'End goal is 13' but a lot leave for London independent day schools at 11. Not a feeder to any particular school; a wide range of smart London schools and boarding schools.

Remarks: A big, busy school. Not for the withdrawn type. Loads of music, art, drama and PE from the first day at school. 25 per cent of the timetable is given over to sport after age 8 – rugby, football, cricket, netball, hockey and rounders. In years 7 and 8 sculling has become a very popular option. Drama is huge – the founding Mrs Thomas was an actor on the West End stage so, not surprisingly, the school is a bit crazy about drama. At the top end it really is quite something, productions are big scale and taken very seriously. 70-ish per cent of pupils learn a musical instrument and there are numerous choirs, jazz groups, string groups, orchestras with music trips to eg Austria, Finland and Estonia. Entertainments such as Glyndebourne-style evenings or Last Night at the Proms are regularly offered to parents. Ballet is popular – though very few boys carry on past age 7.

Drama apart, the other notable characteristics of all the Thomas's schools are the specialist subject teaching (from an early age), the emphasis on 11/13 as the leaving age (no provision whatsoever is made for those wanting to leave at 8) the lack of electronic clutter (though all leave able to use a computer and touch type), a lack of stuffiness and the clearly proprietorial style (no governors, parent reps chosen by the head and form teachers). Thomas's schools are not academically selective – very few siblings are turned away – and there's good SEN provision for the milder end of the spectrum. They seem to be settling into a maturity after their hectic early years, with common strengths and individual characteristics that flow from their parents as much as from their heads.

Clapham is the most disciplined of the three, in a tall old school building with modern additions. Decor on the impersonal side. An efficient and effective school.

TORMEAD SCHOOL JUNIOR DEPARTMENT

Linked to Tormead School in the Senior section

Cranley Road, Guildford, Surrey, GU1 2JD

Tel: 01483 575101
Fax: 01483 450592
Website: www.tormeadschool.org.uk

- Pupils: 190 girls, all day • Ages: 4-11 • Non-denom
- Fees: £1,380 - £2,900 • Independent

Head: Since 2001, Mrs Susan Marks, MA – also head of senior school – who has brought a more cohesive approach to the running of the school (junior section is one of four sections in Tormead and communications between the four are obviously good). Day to day running of the school is by head of the junior department, Miss Paula Roberts – a Tormead stalwart of some 30 years, and head of the junior department for 18 of those; she also teaches Latin. She says that she is certainly allowed to 'get on with it' under the aegis of Mrs Marks. Warm, approachable and straightforward, Miss Roberts has an obvious rapport with pupils.

Entrance: Selective entrance at 4 by a basic assessment test and interview.

Exit: All the junior girls sit the entrance exam for the senior school and have priority on places over external candidates who fight it out for the remainder of places. 95 per cent of junior girls go on to the senior school – those who don't make the grade (although very few fail) are handled sensitively and are advised on 'a senior school better suited to their educational needs.'

Remarks: Traditional, high-achieving girls' school, situated opposite the senior school. Academically the pupils enjoy a wide curriculum very much reflecting the senior school – there is a gradual stepping up of subjects – more are added each year – and by year 5, speech and drama plus Latin are taught as well as the usual subjects, including French and ICT. Girls are gradually prepped for the entrance exam to senior school, although everyone is keen to stress the lack of pressure – pupils included. SEN provision is on an individual need basis. School has three visiting specialists, one a dyslexia expert. Extra help given at lunchtimes, after school etc, room set aside for this purpose in junior department. Certainly not an issue for the school, and no stigma attached – pupils all very open about it.

Facilities impressive. Outside space a little lacking but no complaints from girls. Sport high on the agenda – athletics, dance, gymnastics (very big at Tormead), hockey, netball, rounders and tennis. Sports facilities are shared with the senior school (including impressive gymnasium) although space is tight at the senior school, hence no on-site pool. Lunch is also at the senior school so the girls get a taste of life over the road and feel less daunted about the transfer.

The aim is for an all-round education – 'we work hard and play hard' as Miss Roberts puts it and expectations are high. Everyone is encouraged to find their niche over and above the purely academic; whether it's music, sport, art or other activity, and extra-curricular activities are particularly encouraged. A wide range available – some are selective eg chamber choir and gymnastics but all pupils are encouraged to have a go if keen, regardless of talent. The majority of girls play a musical instrument or are part of the choir.

Girls appointed prefect, librarian, games captain etc by staff and everyone gets a chance to prove themselves in these roles. Pupils don't feel intimidated by their teachers yet have a respectful attitude. Guided tour given to us by confident, articulate and bubbly pupils with obvious pride in their surroundings. All in all, an excellent academic preparation for the senior school.

TOWER HOUSE
PREPARATORY SCHOOL

188 Sheen Lane, London, SW14 8LF

Tel: 020 8876 3323
Fax: 020 8876 3321
E-mail: head@towerhouse.richmond.sch.uk

- Pupils: 175 boys, all day • Ages: 4-13 • Non-denom • Fees: junior school £2,770, senior school £2,845 • Independent

Head: Since 2002, Mrs Jackie Compton-Howlett (fiftyish). Initially a professional musician at Royal Academy of Music, thereafter trained and taught deaf and partially hearing children. Was previously head of Wimbledon High Junior School. Studying for doctorate in educational leadership – so brings lots of new ideas including encouraging children to 'be responsible for their own learning' and attaches great value to their views. Talks enthusiastically – 'we need everyone to turn their hands to everything, matches, and plays ... nobody escapes!' Some parents are still getting used to her new style of management. Business-like, she admits she is 'not a standing in the playground all day' type of head but adds, 'I am always here and can and do see people at the drop of a hat all day long.'

Entrance: From lots of different nursery schools mainly within couple of miles radius. Early (before 1st birthday) registration to guarantee place at 4+. Late applicants held on waiting list, many get in this way, 'people do move around here'. A few places can become available at 8+ and often taken by those from Falcons, Putney Park and Orchard House. Non-selective entry at 4. Short assessment in maths, English and non verbal reasoning for those joining later.

Exit: Academically wide-ranging, reflecting intake. St Paul's, King's College, Epsom College, Ibstock, Hampton, Kingston Grammar, Harrodian, Latymer Upper popular among day schools with a few to board further afield at Marlborough and Charterhouse. 2004 academic scholarships to St Paul's and Bradfield with 4 other music and art scholarships to King's, Latymer, Emmanuel, Harrow. Discussions about destination schools begin 'earlier and earlier out of necessity with more schools pre-testing at 11,' says head, 'we now start the process in y4'. Lots of support and advice given by a head who is trying to build contacts with heads and housemasters for the next stage.

Remarks: Small, gentle, essentially traditional (though perhaps becoming more progressive with new head) all-round prep school which has always had a cosy environment and strong sense of purpose.

Split academically and physically into junior and senior schools linked by shared, rather bijou, playground. Pressure on playground space is clearly an issue for nearly two hundred boys but they appear to make the most of it. Small area with climbing frames available for littlies and older boys encouraged to play 'gently', no bats/batons allowed. Junior school houses boys to y3 where every inch is maximised to give bright, quirkily-shaped classrooms each adorned with 2 state-of-the-art computers. Boys are taught in classes of about 18 by a class teacher and assistant. Great importance attached to 3Rs and school is noted particularly for innovative ideas to get them all reading, eg paired reading schemes with senior boys very popular. Senior school housed in similarly attractive, late-Victorian building. Again, space is at a premium but there is what the head describes as, 'a lovely science lab', an extensive and much-used library, amazingly large, well equipped new ICT suite, light airy loft-style art room. Except for these sessions, boys remain in their own classrooms for lessons, specialist teachers coming to them.

Academically, school does well for broad spectrum of needs. Strong science and maths (setting from y3), streaming in y8 where class splits into two groups, top CE/scholarship and other CE candidates. In-house exams held every year. In y4 Richmond Skills and y5 CAT tests – a thorough assessment of where children are at and what can be expected of them. Incentive scheme for both work and behaviour by system of house plus and minus points, 'life's a mirror' type chat with head v productive for ironing out any concerns. Learning support for dyslexia, dyspraxia, Asperger's and ADHD from experienced SEN specialist 4 days a week. No extra cost.

Lack of on-site sports facilities, so boys bused to fabulous Bank of England Sports Ground in Roehampton to play a range of sports that would impress many a bigger school – football, hockey, rugby, cricket, tennis, athletics and swimming(for ages 5-10 yrs). Arrival of new head has put more focus on music with 60 per cent now learning an instrument up to grade 6, although no practice sessions are timetabled. Two active choirs and orchestra practise weekly after school.

School day is longer for seniors and goes on to include after school clubs – these vary according to current pupil and staff interests and can include fencing, squash, 5-a-side football, drama, and chess. Child-care provision after school; the school is keen to be working-parent friendly. Lots of charity fundraisings, many driven by the boys – the head is particularly keen on responsibility coming with privilege and community awareness.

TREGELLES

Linked to Mount School (The) in the Senior section

Dalton Terrace, York, YO24 4DD

Tel: 01904 667 513
Fax: 01904 667 538
E-mail: tregelles@mount.n-yorks.sch.uk
Website: www.mount.n-yorks.sch.uk

• Pupils: 190 girls and boys • Ages: 3-11 • Quaker • Fees: juniors £2,150; infants £1,405 • Independent • Open days: January, May and October

Head: Mr Martyn Andrews.

Entrance: Entrance by observation (looking for potential), supplemented at 6 by informal examination.

Exit: Most girls move up to The Mount School at the end of year 6.

Remarks: Has the benefit of the facilities and involvement of the senior school, from academic staff (three foreign languages are offered), music and food to mentoring by older girls. Before- and after-school care: from 8.00am to 5.30pm, for an additional charge.

TRELISKE PREPARATORY SCHOOL (TRURO SCHOOL PREP)

Linked to Truro School in the Senior section

Treliske Lane, Hightertown, Truro, Cornwall, TR1 3QN

Tel: 01872 243120
Fax: 01872 222 377
E-mail: enquiries@truroprep.com
Website: www.truroprep.com

• Pupils: 200; 130 boys and 70 girls; all day • Ages: prep 7-11, nursery and pre-prep 3-7 • Methodist • Fees: £2,309 • Independent

Head: Since 2004, Mr Matthew Lovett BA (Ed) Hons.

Entrance: Admission to Willday House nursery via application. External admissions into prep by examination (assessment and report, plus interview and day spent in the school) at age 7, automatic admission from nursery.

Exit: Almost all go on to Truro school, although pupils win scholarships to other schools eg Bristol Cathedral and Bath High (as was).

Remarks: Pleasant light building, good pastoral care. Super enthusiastic place (even had a witty poem dedicated to the 'Toilets in Dinan' in the school magazine). Boarding and day (draws from a wide area). One of the very few prep schools in the area. Prep school for Truro School, two miles away. Set in 10 acres of land with good facilities including sports hall and swimming pool. Scholarships and bursaries available. Remedial help available. Strong pastoral care and inclusive approach to a diverse range of activities and sport.

TREVOR-ROBERTS'

55-57 Eton Avenue, London, NW3 3ET

Tel: 020 7586 1444
Fax: 020 7722 0114
E-mail: trsenior@btconnect.com

• Pupils: 100 boys, 80 girls; all day • Ages: 5-13 • C of E
• Fees: £2,640 - £3,390 • Independent

Senior Head: Since 1999, Mr Simon Trevor-Roberts BA (forties), son of founder Christopher Trevor-Roberts LVO, who moved the school to its present site from the Vale of Health in 1981, and is still principal and teaches in the school. Educated at Westminster, formerly headmaster of the junior school. His son and daughter were both at the school ('which shows confidence in the place,' said a parent). Personable and keen on producing self-esteem and confidence in his pupils. A parent finds him 'slightly shy, but the children are very fond of him.' Head of the junior school is his sister, Amanda Trevor-Roberts MPhil (early forties).

Entrance: Main entry at rising 5 (birthdays between beginning of January and end of December). Soon after the birth, parents do a tour of the school then write confirming they'd like a place (any later is liable to be too late). The first 50 children, in chronological order, are seen a year before entry, and nine boys and nine girls offered places. 'Ability comes into it, but we're trying to get a mix of characters. The most interesting children are often those who are not focussed on learning their letters and numbers at an early age.' Some places higher up, particularly for girls at 11 (keep ringing up if you don't get in straight away, advises a parent).

Exit: A wide range of day and boarding schools. Girls often leave at 11, though the school is keen on co-ed boarding schools, and some are encouraged to stay on with the boys until 13. 'The 11-plus doesn't always show children to their best advantage, particularly if they're lacking in confidence. They're likely to make more of themselves at 13,' says the head.

Remarks: 'It's got such a friendly atmosphere it's hardly like a school,' said a parent. Non-competitive, with no public marks ('a child's work is his own business') and no streaming, though extra tuition for those trying for scholarships and children coming in higher up who need help with certain subjects. Head believes that 'children learn better from seeing other people's strengths and weaknesses' and that even the brightest children can become over-anxious in a hothouse atmosphere. He also believes strongly in co-education – 'you can use the different personalities to bring out the best sides of each. There is more humour in a co-ed class, and humour is very important.' The school aims to give the children confidence and self-motivation – 'I like the teachers to be positive rather than negative.' French from 5 and Latin from 9.

The juniors – aged 5 to 8 – have form teachers for English and maths but specialists for other subjects; the seniors have specialists for every subject. 'The teaching is very high quality,' said a parent, 'and they make it so much fun. It's much more stimulating and interesting than at my daughter's previous school, where they just pushed English and maths for the 11-plus.' 'It's a very flexible school,' said another. 'It takes each child as an individual and gets the best out of them.' But not an easy ride – an hour's homework a night for the seniors, with more as the Common Entrance approaches – 'the purpose of it is to give them the confidence that they can do something for themselves. The homework should be accessible and attainable.'

Large, sunny Edwardian houses, with junior and senior science labs, a computer room, two libraries (the junior one roughly the size of a broom cupboard), music rooms and an airy top-floor art room. 'They're passionate about music,' said a parent, and indeed Christopher Trevor-Roberts was an opera singer before taking up teaching, and still conducts the senior choir. Classical music is played in assembly, and about a third of the pupils learn an instrument during school time. 'It gives us immense satisfaction to bring music to the children,' says the junior head, who admits a secret desire to turn the school into a music school. There is a brass ensemble and a school orchestra which encompasses grade 8 musicians and those just approaching grade 1 – 'I want them to experience playing together even if they can barely keep up. I don't want it to become an elite group.' Past pupils have won music scholarships to Eton and gone on to musical careers, and there is a strong connection with the Mcnuhin family. The school won the Artworks national children's art award in 2000 and 2001.

Plenty of drama, with plays at Christmas and outside in the summer – 'on a completely different level to what we'd seen at my daughter's previous school,' said a parent. Sport is limited by the premises – the smallish rubberised playground is used for games such as basketball and netball. Swimming from 7 upwards and football on Primrose Hill. Occasional inter-school matches, plus football, netball, rowing and fencing clubs. A parent mentions break-time

physical jerks, 'with the head in pinstripes doing star-jumps'. 'They get plenty of exercise,' said another parent, 'but it's not the place for a boy who's longing to be in the school football team.'

Informal atmosphere. 'The staff treat the pupils as equals,' said a parent, 'and the children behave well because they are respected.' The head comments that children coming from other schools are surprised by the lack of an 'us and them' atmosphere. 'It's a very kind school,' said a parent. 'There's almost no bullying.' Semi-uniform of sweatshirt and aertex shirt.

Parents seem unanimously in favour – 'I'm sure my children will look back on it as a very happy bit of their lives,' said one.' It's a unique school,' said another. 'I can't speak too highly of it.'

Truro High School Preparatory Department

Linked to Truro High School in the Senior section

Falmouth Road, Truro, Cornwall, TR1 2HU

Tel: 01872 272830
Fax: 01872 279393
E-mail: admin@trurohigh.co.uk
Website: www.trurohigh.co.uk

- Pupils: 120 girls, and nursery with 15 girls and 5 boys; day and boarding from 8+ • Ages: 3-11 • C of E • Fees: Day £1,700 - £2,728 per term; boarding £4,902 - £5,143 • Independent
- Open days: Early October, but at any time to meet headmaster and have personal tour of school

Head: Since 2002, Ms Alison Miller (early forties), married with two boys. 12 years teaching experience in state and independent schools, co-ed and single sex. Previously in business.

Entrance: Via application form, followed by informal meeting with headmaster/head of prep. Thereafter taster day for informal assessment.

Exit: Most girls (over 90 per cent) choose to move across the corridor to the senior school. All sit 11+ entrance exams alongside local feeder schools. Remainder leaves for other local schools or some to boarding schools out of county.

Remarks: Parents encouraged to become closely involved.

TWICKENHAM
PREPARATORY SCHOOL

Beveree, 43 High Street, Hampton, Middlesex, TW12 2SA

Tel: 020 8979 6216

Fax: 020 8979 1596

E-mail: office@twickenham-prep.richmond.sch.uk

• Pupils: 250 – equal numbers of boys and girls, all day • Ages: 4-13 • Families do not have to be practising Christians, but the school has a strong Christian ethos • Fees: Reception and year 1 £2,140; years 2- 8 £2,290 • Independent

Head: Since 2005, Mr David Malam, BA Hons, Southampton (History), PGCE, King Alfred's College, Winchester. Taught in junior and first schools in the Southampton area before working at Lagos International School, Cyprus teaching age 7-16. Married with four young children, two of whom are at the school. Enjoys all sports especially football and squash and has played chess at high level.

Entrance: At three and a half for a supervised 'play' in small groups, while parents have a tour and a chat with the head. School looks for children who are developing normally, who will be able to cope with normal school life, rather than showing signs of genius. Places are then offered on a first come, first served basis – there's a waiting list. Can usually offer roughly the number of places required.

Exit: Vast majority to a variety of local independent day schools and only occasionally to boarding schools (eg Sherborne). Boys mostly stay to 13 and many go to Hampton, Kingston Grammar, St James's Twickenham or St George's, Weybridge. Girls leave at 11, many for Lady Eleanor Holles, Surbiton High, Kingston Grammar and increasingly Sir William Perkins's. Occasional scholarships.

Remarks: Not a hothouse for the bright but a place where everyone is encouraged and helped to do their best. An all-round school, which aims to give every child a chance to take part in as many activities as possible, rather than dividing children according to ability (except where necessary).

Main school is housed (since 1992) in a handsome building which has been adapted well though some areas look as if they could do with a coat of paint. Pre-prep is a lovely modern purpose-built building with small but charming outdoor areas set apart for the young ones. What a pleasant change to see the youngest pupils housed in the smartest buildings, instead of in tacky temporary ones. Classrooms are just big enough and there is adequate space and facilities for art and science. Outdoor space for the main school is limited, but they have walking access to a large sports field for football etc.

Curriculum is as expected in a prep school, and provides specialist teaching for each subject as soon as children leave the pre-prep department. 'Standards are constantly improving,' said one parent, 'though they don't rest on their laurels.' RE is taught from the Bible without much learning about other faiths, though this point is being addressed, especially with a growing ethnic mix amongst the pupils. Classes are fairly small (18) and are mixed gender and ability, apart from setting for maths. Year 8 and 9 are assessed to see if they would benefit from two streams – only recently have numbers been large enough for this system, so no pattern as yet.

School has no website, which seems to suggest it is behind the times, but IT is very strongly used across the curriculum as evidenced by work on display. Computer suite has one terminal per child and they begin to learn computer skills in reception and continue to have timetabled lessons throughout the school. Music is strength 'it has come on in leaps and bounds,' a long- standing parent said, with lots of individual tuition going on in separate buildings. In line with the ethos of the school, the annual concert is not just for these children – everyone takes part. Similarly, school or class plays have a role for all.

Sports teams play competitively but there will always be a C or D team so everyone can represent the school at some time (wish more prep schools followed this example). In such a small school, sport organised in this way is not going to lead to winning competitions, 'but when I see them playing cricket on Hampton Green, I'm still very proud,' a mother remarked. Extra-curricular sport is offered in after-school clubs as is a range of other activities – most successful is chess, Twickenham Prep's name regularly appears in the local paper in connection with winning chess tournaments. One mother mentioned how disappointed her daughter was when she couldn't join the oversubscribed maths club run by a particularly strong teacher, 'but there are clubs every day except Friday even for the little ones,' she added.

Children seem well-behaved in the school and 'on task' in the classroom. Welcoming atmosphere of the place almost tangible – starting with the initial phone call to the school. 'The community feeling is what attracted us,' one parent said. 'It's very family orientated,' said another who added, 'I feel that I can go and discuss anything with my son's teacher.' At a recent governors' meeting (nice to know there is a governing body) parents were invited to attend and voice any concerns but none turned up. When asked why, they reportedly said that they didn't have any.

There is a strong sense in the school that everyone is trying hard to do well and will be helped to achieve, but if an Eton scholarship is what you have in mind this may not be the place for you- you'll be the only one heading in that direction. On the other hand, if you are looking for the small classes and the extras that no state primary school can give you, but still want the non-competitive atmosphere of an all round, local, mixed, school – Twickenham Prep might suit very well.

TWYFORD SCHOOL

High Street, Twyford, Winchester, Hampshire, SO21 1NW

Tel: 01962 712 269
Fax: 01962 712 100
E-mail: registrar@twyfordschool.com
Website: www.twyfordschool.com

- Pupils: 193 in prep school, of whom about one third girls; mostly day with some weekly- and flexi-boarding. 100 in pre-prep, over half girls • Ages: pre-prep 3-8; prep 8-13 • C of E
- Fees: Day £1,090 - £3,955; boarding £5,115 • Independent
- Open days: None; phone for an appointment to visit

Head: Since 2003, Dr David Livingstone BSc PhD NPQH (fiftyish) formerly deputy headmaster of Rugby and a housemaster and geography teacher there. Educated at Gillingham Grammar School in Kent. Doctorate in environmental sciences (East Anglia), followed by three years as a botany researcher at Durham. A hockey coach, expedition leader and long-distance runner (had run the London Marathon a few weeks before we met him). Married to Janet, one son at the school and three older brothers. Keen that children should be able to pursue all their interests at this age and calls himself 'chief plate spinner'. Mums and dads thrilled with him, praising his 'total dedication' and focus. One gushing parent trying to make a point about his painstaking attention to detail called him 'an old woman in the best possible way!'

Entrance: Children come for a half day informal assessment in the November before they are due to enter the school. Threshold for passing this not too high – 'academically average and above.' Will always try to accommodate siblings. Most pupils live within a 30 mile drive of the school.

Exit: Half (school says a third) to Winchester College, St Swithun's and King Edward VI (Southampton). The rest all over, but mainly to Bedales, Bradfield, Canford, Harrow, Marlborough, Radley, Sherborne, Sherborne Girls', Wellington, Wycombe Abbey and Winchester state schools. Good news on the scholarship front, especially for academics and music.

Remarks: Happy, high-achieving school – 'calm but whizzy,' says the head – but no longer offering full boarding. 'We were a seven-day-a-week boarding school with very few seven-day-a-week boarders,' says the head. In September 2005 Twyford bit the bullet and moved to weekly and flexi-boarding only. The school retains its boarding ethos and continues, in the main, to behave like a boarding animal, with most pupils doing some boarding in the final two years. Best things about boarding according to the children – 'being with friends and Wednesday evening barbecues in the summer!' Worst – 'having to get up earlier than I did when I lived 20 minutes away!' No mobile phones. Taffies (tuck) twice a week. Boarding accommodation lacks personality but the school is working on this. Overseas pupils and children of expats will now be housed with guardians on Saturday and Sunday nights.

Interesting place – goes back to the middle of the seventeenth century and lays claim to being the oldest 'proper' prep school in the country. Converted to its current C of E foundation for the 'sons of Middle Class Persons' in 1809. Wonderful list of OBs, including composer Hubert Parry, Douglas Hurd and Thomas Hughes, author of Tom Brown's Schooldays. Alexander Pope (who wrote The Rape of the Lock) spent a year at Twyford, where he wrote 'a satire on some faults of his master,' which led to his being 'whipped and ill-used...and taken from thence on that account.' Pupils from a relatively wide social mix. 'Not everyone is stinking rich,' said one mum, explaining the financial advantage of the school being weekly boarding only now.

Inscrutably complex setting/streaming system. Evening tutorials for serious scholarship hopefuls – discussing unfathomables like ethics and evolution. Class sizes average 14 – 17. Science taken seriously, Latin for all from year 5. French from the start but German and Mandarin available as extras. The school is 'not set up for lower ability children.' Some 20 pupils receive extra tuition – for mild dyslexia, revision technique, maths struggles. Two or three with moderate SpLD requirements. One parent of a girl with an unusual special need told us that the SEN provision, though good, was a little too one-size-fits-all. Prep done at school; day pupils home at 6pm. Much investment in IT.

Top-class art department and evidence of pupils' work

on walls all over the school. Small art display room – a lovely space and unusual for a prep. Drama less vigorous and children long for a major school play. Music exceptionally strong – two children have reached grade 8 on their instruments in each of the last few years and many more have reached grade 7. 83 per cent of pupils learn at least one instrument and there are three choirs, a jazz band, orchestra, many ensembles, 20 concerts a year, unusual instruments taught (harp!). Large, light music room with soundproof studio, overlooking playing fields, below which squats an open-air amphitheatre. Pleasant 20-acre country site close to Winchester, which includes the original old school hall (wood panelling and echoes of centuries of schoolboys). Religion informal, with parents employed as visiting speakers in the charming chapel. Dining hall with long tables and benches – anyone can sit anywhere but pupils must ask to leave table.

Everyone plays on a team in year 4, but less able pupils gradually ebb away to minor sports. The A teams are chosen by the sports coach based on merit, end of story – 'even I can't change the selection!' says the head. Very bad behaviour = being dropped from the team = 'leads to some interesting scenes in the car park.' Excellent swimming pool and sports hall. School currently raising funds to lay an Astroturf pitch and hopes to reintroduce hockey for boys (girls currently use an off-site Astro). Strong on boys' games, especially cricket. 'Court cricket', Twyford's very own invention, is a summer obsession. Girls' sport also humming with two age groups reaching the national netball finals in 2004 and 2005. Ballet/dance offered as an extra. Chess ailing (though showing signs of new life, says school). Shooting long-dead. Gardening club still going but less robust than in past, like several other features of boarding life.

Pastoral care 'amazing' say parents and the matron 'deserves a knighthood.' Eternal vigilance on bullying. Revamped house system with lots of competitions (sport, music, public speaking, Easter egg decorating, boat building). Pupils cheerful, bouncy and informally attired. Parents emphasize the importance of staying to age 13 – 'you're not the finished product unless you finish the cycle.' Even the mighty St Swithun's – who used to scare parents into removing their daughters at 11 – has learned to accept this. A well-thought-out school from tip to toe.

Pre prep with its own identity and not all children go on to Twyford (St Swithun's gobbles a few of the girls). Children may start from the September following their third birthday. One class of 16-17 children per year group until year three when there are two. Pleasant classrooms and own hall for assemblies, ballet etc. Large play area, very nice if you don't

mind the traffic noise. Learning support teacher helps the 'most and least able'.

UNICORN SCHOOL

238 Kew Road, Richmond, Surrey, TW9 3JX

Tel: 020 8948 3926

Fax: 020 8332 6814

E-mail: enquiries@unicornschool.org.uk

Website: www.unicornschool.org.uk

- Pupils: 175, all day, roughly 50:50 boys and girls (including 22 part-time places in nursery) • Ages: 3-11 • Non-denom • Fees: Nursery (mornings only) £1,370; main school £2,235 - £2,505
- Independent

Head: Since 2004, Mrs Roberta Linehan BA PGCE (forties). She came to the school (highly recommended both formally and informally according to one parent) from Danes Hill Prep in Oxshott where she was a deputy head and she has also worked in an international school in Hong Kong, Lady Eleanor Holles and Tiffin Girls. Very smiley and welcoming, she comes across as open and capable – but she has big shoes to fill. Previous head was associated with the school for 30 years and evidently completely charmed the parents who describe her as 'legendary.' No one (parents, pupils, staff) has a bad word to say about Mrs Linehan, but it is early days and the parental jury is still out. 'She has promised to tread gently and not make big changes,' said one parent. 'So far everything is ticking along nicely but I am sure there will be huge tests of her leadership to come.' Teaches year 6 once a week, visits every class on Monday morning and greets parents and children at the front door of the school most days.

Entrance: Very popular school so names down at birth for entrance at age 3, at other times from the long waiting list according to availability. Siblings take priority, often leaving just a relatively small number of places for new families, which will be allocated 'at the discretion of the headmistress.' One mother advised, 'my top tip would be to persist – keep ringing and asking – at the last minute we got a place.' Non-selective at nursery but for entry at 7 children will have an interview and/or informal tests.

Exit: To all the major London day schools including Godolphin & Latymer, Hampton, King's Wimbledon, Lady Eleanor Holles and Colet Court. Also boarding schools such as Headington. 20-ish per cent of leavers gain scholarships.

Remarks: A favourite with the (dinner party) chattering

classes of south west London, the school comes up with the goods academically but with the trump card of a nurturing and creative atmosphere. Bang opposite Kew Gardens, Unicorn was founded in 1970 by a group of parents who couldn't find the type of education they were looking for elsewhere. Now run as a non-profit making company – one parent from each family becomes a member when their child joins the school. 'We could get a horrible shock if the roof fell in, as fees are adjusted according to spend,' said one father. But generally it is not an issue. Parents also loan the school £2,500 per family (regardless of how many children they have there) payable the term before admission.

Realistically, you will not get much (if any) negative feedback from parents who own a school. 'It is a wonderful school where the children are well- motivated and made interested in what they are learning,' says one mother. Another equally positive soul adds, 'it is friendly, fun and creatively stimulating with a really caring ethos.'

Occupies a large three-storey Victorian house and a separate coach house, linked by a small, but well-equipped, playground. Newly acquired and landscaped 'quiet garden' has almost doubled the outdoor space, although overall the site remains small and more boisterous children might struggle to let off steam. Unicorn is homely rather than flashy and in need of a lick of paint here and there. Visitors won't be bowled over by the facilities – 'but it is all there, they have everything they need – it is just not as pretty and impressive as some of the competition,' says one parent. Classrooms are small but visually stimulating with lovely displays all around. Less impressive is a new, rather narrow, design & technology room.Academically impressive – children do well but are not pressured. 80 per cent level 5s at Key Stage 2, with 90 per cent in English. Yet despite very creditable results, several parents said that they had chosen the school because it is not massively academic. 'I don't think it is for real high-fliers,' said one mother. The head disagrees (as you would expect). Another parent added, 'too many schools view results as the be-all and end-all – here you get a richer, more rounded education.' Staff are described as 'spot-on' with one mother commenting, 'you feel they have a good handle on your child from day one.' Pupils are attentive in class, working at different speeds and frequently assessed. Average class size 22 and the school is very keen on equipping them with learning strategies and thinking skills. French from age 5. Parents praise special needs provision.Not the school for a seriously sporty child (the head does not agree -'there are seriously sporty children at the school who thrive') – there are no playing fields and team performances in traditional sports are not top of the league table stuff. 'Newsletters contain reports of plucky rather than winning performances,' laughs one mother. However the children are bused five minutes down the road to the Old Deer Park in Richmond for sports – mainly football and netball in the winter and the usual summer sports. And every Thursday afternoon the junior children go to clubs – badminton, golf and horse riding among lots of other choices. A rather arty cohort of parents is attracted by the strong focus on arts and music, which is roundly described as 'fantastic.' There are regular and impressive assemblies, drama productions and music concerts. All juniors start by learning the recorder and almost two thirds of them go on to learn at least one other instrument, some very successfully including a recent music scholarship to St Paul's Girls'. Gorgeous artwork displays line the walls and on the day of our visit, some of the infant children were literally hurling paint to create a giant firework picture.Older children have lots of involvement with the younger ones – partly because the school is small and everyone is rather thrust together, but also purposely, with year 6 children coming into the infant classes to read stories and act as monitors. 'The children get to know each other very well, very quickly,' said a mother 'and they are all taught to be concerned about each other – it creates a really lovely caring atmosphere.' There are currently 11 second generation 'Unicorns' in the school as former pupils choose it for their own children. One mother summed up the appeal of the place – 'When I first toured the school my over-riding impression was of how nice the children were and I thought I would be really proud and happy for my children to be like them.' The school benefits from lots of parental involvement. 'Actors, directors, choreographers, writers and producers all share their experiences with the children, making everyday life so much more alive and interesting,' said one mother. On a more pedestrian level, there are also plenty of the usual opportunities to get involved in helping in class and at clubs. 'You could be there all day if you wanted to,' said one slightly weary-sounding mother. Rotas posted outside all the classrooms – 'you are always being asked for something and it can be hard on working mums.'Happy, confident children with good social skills (as well as impressive academic results). Good first impressions of the new head. Not a place for the parent who wants to remain detached from their children's education or for the boisterous child who wants acres of space to let off steam.

UNIVERSITY COLLEGE SCHOOL JUNIOR SCHOOL

Linked to Phoenix School in the Junior section
Linked to University College School in the Senior section

11 Holly Hill, London, NW3 6QN

Tel: 020 7435 3068
Fax: 020 7435 7332
E-mail: info@ucsjb.org.uk
Website: www.ucs.org.uk

• Pupils: 225 boys; all day • Ages: 7-11; pre-prep 3-7 (The
Phoenix School, a separate entity) • Non-denom • Independent
• Open days: September and October

Head: Mr Kevin J Douglas BA Cert Ed.

Entrance: Gives a good grounding, with boys taught to think for themselves from an early age. Good facilities, plus use of the senior school's sports hall and swimming pool.

Exit: Almost all go on to the senior school. Not the place if you are aiming for a different senior school at 13.

Remarks: Gives a good grounding, with boys taught to think for themselves from an early age. Good facilities, plus use of the senior school's sports hall and swimming pool.

VINEHALL SCHOOL

Mountfield, Robertsbridge, East Sussex, TN32 5JL

Tel: 01580 880 413
Fax: 01580 882 119
E-mail: office@vinehallschool.com
Website: www. vinehallschool.com

• Pupils: 400 pupils of whom 130 in nursery and pre-prep and
270 in prep. Boy/girl ratio roughly 60/40 • Ages: 2-13
• Non-denom • Fees: Boarding £4,612; day: £3,546 in the prep;
£2,008 in the pre-prep • Independent

Head: Since 2002, Ms Julie Robinson (mid thirties). Previously head of Ardingly Prep School. Husband organises prefects' training and school trips, and is head of boarding and director of studies – was previously a housemaster in the senior school at Ardingly. A daughter in the school. Head hides her personality behind her professionalism – she was wearing a black trouser suit and looked very much the young businesswoman. Well liked by the parents although she had a hard time from some when she first arrived – not surprising as the previous head had been there for 25 years. 'Very conscientious about following things up', 'perhaps almost trying too hard to please' – two parental comments that could well be describing the same incident.

Entrance: Most children either join the nursery in their third year or reception two years later – partly selective as they want children who can cope with Common Entrance and, we suspect, who 'fit the bill' – Vinehall requires a fair bit of conformism. Small intake at age 9 and occasionally some spaces higher up the school – have to sit a test.

Exit: To a wide range of local schools, the most popular being Tonbridge, Eastbourne, Benenden, King's Canterbury, St Leonard's Mayfield, Sevenoaks and Battle Abbey. A few girls leave at 11 but this is not encouraged.

Remarks: Set in the East Sussex countryside, the school has a very light and airy and professional feel to it. The front hall is lined with the shields of every child who has attended the school and these are now escaping up the stairs and along the passage. Much silverware and children's artwork also in evidence. A very glossy and shiny school with every facility imaginable and takes itself very seriously.

Proud of its scholarship record – art and music as well as academic. Setting in some subjects but the scholars are catered for within their own year group – the school caters for the all-round child with a great emphasis on happiness. Staff a stable team – no trouble attracting good teachers. Top ICT: computers, smartboards, interactive whiteboards, intranet, and the library bristles with new computers. The school can cater for mild special needs but would not suit someone who struggles academically unless they are very gifted at music, art or sport.

Sport bulks large. Girls play netball, hockey lacrosse (as a club option) and rounders and the boys play rugby, cricket hockey and soccer. All can do swimming, athletics, gymnastics cross country running, judo archery and riding – virtually everyone who wants to can play in a team.

Music strong – most play an instrument, two orchestras and several smaller ensemble groups. Lots of musical evenings. Very well-equipped art department plus design technology, carpentry, textiles, pottery etc. Drama is also a major feature of school life – five or six productions each year. Plenty of opportunities for children to learn to speak in public by reading in assembly and chapel as well as music and poetry evenings. All regularly prepare English Speaking Board presentations.

Happy parents – a broad mix, many from the media and medicine and a number of first time buyers. Mostly local, some Services children and some high achieving foreign nationals. Parental involvement very much encouraged, various social activities organised by the parents. Old boys include Tim Smit of Eden Project fame.

No weekly or flexi-boarding though temporary boarding can be accommodated if there are spaces. 65 full boarders – would like more – and the numbers go up at the top of the school in preparation for senior schools. Special clubs for the boarders and they have very structured weekends. Exeat every third weekend.

Day children start at 8.20am, after-school clubs end at 5.30pm. Saturday morning school ends at 12.35pm – matches on two Saturdays per term but most of them are on Wednesdays.

WAKEFIELD GIRLS' HIGH SCHOOL JUNIOR SCHOOL

Linked to Wakefield Girls' High School in the Senior section

2 St. John's Square, Wakefield, WF1 2QX

Tel: 01924 374 577
Fax: 01924 231 602
E-mail: headmistress@wghsjs.org.uk
Website: www.wgsf.org.uk

- Pupils: 475 girls and (up to age 7) boys; all day • Ages: 3-11
- Inter-denom • Fees: £1,912 - £2,087 junior school
- Independent • Open days: Early October

Remarks: Pre-prep Mulberry House (as in 'Here we go round the mulberry bush', the original mulberry tree is in the pre-prep garden).

For further details see senior school entry.

WARWICK JUNIOR SCHOOL

Linked to Warwick School in the Senior section

Myton Road, Warwick, Warwickshire, CV34 6PP

E-mail: enquiries@warwickschool.org
Website: www.warwickschool.org

- Pupils: 235 boys, some boarding • Ages: 7-13
- C of E but accepts all denoms • Independent

Remarks: See senior school.

WELLESLEY HOUSE SCHOOL

Broadstairs, Kent, CT10 2DG

Tel: 01843 862 991
Fax: 01843 602 068
E-mail: office@wellesleyhouse.org
Website: www.wellesleyhouse.org

- Pupils: 80 boys, 45 girls; 80 per cent boarding • Ages: 7-13
- C of E • Independent

Head: Since 1990, Mr Richard Steel BSc, previously head of York House Day Preparatory School. He has three children, one son at King's Canterbury, one daughter at university and one actress daughter. Conventional, very kind man, gives impression of keeping his cards close to chest. Enjoys his role 'as setting the tone for the school', thinks of himself as a people person keeping regular contact with the staff, pupils, parents. He teaches RE to top two years and runs the school on Christian principles hoping that some will subconsciously rub off on the children. 'This is an impressionable age – we are aware that we are establishing their future life skills now.' Strongly supported by a vivacious, attractive, fit wife, Judith (swims daily and runs up main stairs in a blink) – contrasting qualities of husband and wife prove a good double act for the school.

Retiring in July 2007.

Entrance: By interview, broad range of abilities accepted. Will take special needs provided they need no more than 2 half-hour lessons per week (approx 20 such pupils now). An assessment is given to pupils entering at age 10 and over.

Exit: Majority to King's Canterbury, Eton, Benenden, Tonbridge, Harrow, Marlborough and Stowe. Handful of scholarships over the last few years but intake is broad and, as they mainly exit to major league schools, these are competitive and coveted places. 3rd Scholarship to Eton in 2003. 2004 scholarships to Radley, Benenden and Tonbridge. Exhibition to King's Canterbury (academic); to Harrow (music); chemistry Prize in CE to Rugby; geography prize in CE to Benenden. Music scholarship to Eton in 2005.

Remarks: An attractive red-brick building a short leap from the sea situated away from the city hubbub – a rambling building that houses both classrooms and boys' dorms. Mix of old with the new. A predominantly traditional boarding school, family feel pervades, also respect, order, sound principles rooted into the brickwork. Head is keen to promote new style boarding ie interactive and family centred – being blessed with unformidable, very experienced, pleasant matrons and plenty of domestic staff. 'Children are meticulously cared for and boarding is thoroughly planned,' says the head and the pastoral side is a real strength of the school, agreed by parents and inspectors alike.

Dorms are fastidiously clean and tidy – perfectly pressed clothes on the end of the new pine beds, towels and flannels hanging just so – all in light airy rooms. Junior boys sleep, work, eat and play in the junior house. Junior house girls sleep at The Orchard girls' house. Senior dorms upstairs (10-13 years) varying from 5 to 10 in a room. A Captain sleeps in each senior dorm as a responsible vigilante. Judith oversees all health/domestic matters – even holding hands for hospital visits. 'We are conscious of children growing up before their time in boarding life – we guard against that'. All girls board at Orchard House which is situated across the playing fields through an orchard of apple trees, hence the dorms named Blenheim, Russet etc. and run by geography master, Mr Nichol, and his Spanish wife – 'essential they can be feminine and have girlie time,' said a petite and efficient Mrs Nichol. There is constant communication with parents and a sound anti-bullying policy. Food is 'not great' say the pupils, vegetarian option.

2001 inspection must have come as a shock and has led to widespread improvements. Some good news – geography, English and history recognised as good (Townsend Warner winner 1998), Latin and games commended – testimony to this is that eight pupils have read classics in Oxbridge over the last five years and three old boys recently took the classics master out to dinner to thank him for sparking their interest in the subject. Good languages department offering German, Greek and Spanish has developed good links with English-speaking institute in Madrid. We witnessed an especially good English lesson where the deputy head interacted and elicited profound insights from a text, often bursting into dramatic characterisations. Pastoral and social responsibilities also highly regarded.

On the down side (and it is most encouraging to see ISI becoming more critical and objective) the inspectors reported unevenly balanced curriculum, inadequate monitoring of child and staff performance and a 'significant proportion' of below-par teaching, particularly in music and French and at Key Stage 2. This unnerved some parents and staff and served as a wake-up call to bring a refreshing breeze of modernity to the curriculum. Much has now been done to bring the curriculum up to speed. Recent reported visit from an Inspector was very complimentary about teaching and progress. New director of studies, appointed in 2004, monitoring and developing the curriculum. Inset training is also being addressed (very important when there is not much turnover of staff to keep them up to date with new methods in education).

Good, large and comfortable library; ICT room well equipped and plans include networking all departments. Children's art not much in evidence on our visit but head assured us now that corridors always full of it. Art is two lessons a week with drama and design technology timetabled on a rotational basis. Music picking up and results are good. Children are streamed further up the school and because the school is small, it can tailor to individual needs. A real 'fast tracker' will progress up the school unhindered by constraints of curriculum.

Sport is very strong – enviable record as long as your arm of past and present achievements, frequently winning national and county events in hockey, rounders and cricket (only school to have produced two captains of England – Mann and Cowdrey). National winners of JET cricket 2003. Does exceptionally well in golf – greatly benefiting from their own beautiful putting green, also being neighbours with Royal St George's with first rate professionals. School has a well-equipped sports hall, sunny, heated indoor swimming pool, tennis courts, squash courts and a shooting range tucked snugly off a corner of well-manicured playing fields (.22 rifle team regularly achieve success). National winners of JET Rounders U13 competition in 2005.

Culturally, plenty going on – annual dramatic productions, general knowledge team reaching semi-finals recently at national IAPS level, chess, regular debates and fashion shows for the girls. 2002 contributed a school float for the Lord Mayor's parade – he himself an Old Boy. Children given choice with some aspects of uniform but formal wear should conform to any sports jacket, trousers, schools tie and shorts.

A classy school that is steeped in tradition and, considering boarding schools are a dying breed, surviving well (if a little below capacity); little drop-out, and, for the most part, happy parents. The school has responded robustly to 'resting on laurels' and 'lacking fizz factor'. A great deal has been achieved since the ISI report in 2001.

WELLS CATHEDRAL SCHOOL JUNIOR SCHOOL

Linked to Wells Cathedral School in the Senior section

8 New Street, Wells, Somerset, BA5 2LQ

Tel: 01749 834400
Fax: 01749 834401
E-mail: juniorschool@wells-cathedral-school.com
Website: www.wells-cathedral-school.com

- Pupils: 171 boys and girls of whom 8 board • Ages: 3-11
- C of E • Fees: Day £1,685 - £3,860. Boarding £5,410 - £6,450 per term • Independent • Open days: Junior school: October, February and June. Individual visits arranged at any time

Head: Since 1995, Mr Nick Wilson BA (fifties). Extremely popular with both parents and pupils and driving force behind the superior quality of performing arts in the school.

Entrance: No tests for pre-prep but 'friendly' tests for all, for the junior school. On the edge of full most of the time.

Exit: The majority of pupils go on to the Wells' lower school and thence to the senior school.

Remarks: Sunny bright buildings with lovely gardens, well maintained and used frequently as outdoor classroom. A lush conservatory is also used as teaching resource – hot though. Enthusiastic staff, many of whom have been with the school for a long time – some (eg deputy head, who arrived 15 years ago and never left) have never taught anywhere else. Pre-prep includes small, cheery nursery, reception class and years 1 and 2 in very brightly coloured classrooms. There are four year groups and classes are small – 10-18. Every other year a cast of 50 performs to sell-out audiences at the Edinburgh Fringe.

WESTBOURNE HOUSE SCHOOL

Shopwyke, Chichester, West Sussex, PO20 2BH

Tel: 01243 782 739
Fax: 01243 770 757
E-mail: whouseoffice@rmplc.co.uk
Website: www.westbournehouse.org

- Pupils: 365 (200 boys, 165 girls); 50 boys and 25 girls board
- Ages: 3-7 pre-prep; 7-13 prep • C of E • Fees: Full board £4,290; day £1,800 in the pre-prep rising to £3,450
- Independent • Open days: None.

The headmaster wants to see you

Headmaster: Since 2003, Mr Brendan Law (late thirties). Born and educated in South Africa where he taught at their first-ever multiracial school. Came by way of Sweden to Bedford School 1995, where he was meteorically made senior housemaster. Sports mad – coaches the lot. Dyed in the wool boarder. The great Colin Sharman, head for 28 years and father of today's school, says feelingly and with understatement, 'we were very lucky to get him.' Brendan (he's a first name man) is clearly an effective force and affectingly anxious to head a kind, happy, achieving school. Early changes spooked some teachers but the force is with him. Parents like him exceedingly and say his door really is always open. His wife, Linda, is seen by parents as a 'huge asset'. She does a bundle of liaison and coordination things – she's the school mum. Two children, one of each, both at the school. Golden retriever, just as there ought to be.

Entrance: Most from a 15-mile radius. Unfiltered for nursery and pre-prep, assessment for entry to year 3. Because this is a local school the mesh is not fine, but big SENs are urged to think again. Best get in early – roughly 36 go on from the pre-prep to be joined by 18 or so brand new year 3s. Very few chinks higher up. Scholarship: 50 per cent for music. Sundry bursaries for those who fall on hard times and 5 per cent off for brothers and sisters. Racial mix reflects the local community: almost none – but there is a charming smattering of Germans from nearby Rolls Royce. Website a touch stuffy but fully informative.

Exit: Almost all stay to year 8, then fly to the full rainbow of independent seniors of which the most flavoursome are Marlborough, Canford, Sherborne, Charterhouse, Eton, Winchester, Radley, Harrow, Wellington, Cranleigh, Portsmouth Grammar, Bryanston, Bedales, Lancing,

Benenden, St Swithun's, St Mary's Ascot, Downe House. Scholarship hit rate an arrestingly high 35 per cent of all leavers (39 per cent in 2004). Eminent outgoers include R4's Marcus Brigstocke (funny) and Nick Clarke (news); and Monarch of the Glen, Alastair McKenzie.

Remarks: Here's a school which has responded nimbly to a changing market with no sense of reactive incoherence. Until 1990 it was all boys, all boarding. Now it serves a prosperous local community which prefers day early on with some weekly boarding in the last two years as a rehearsal for a boarding senior. Saturday morning school survives impregnable. Parents say the school has done the transition from the old to the now brilliantly.

Blessed with a high acre:pupil ratio, this is a spacious place with a campus-y feel and all the playing fields you can count. In the midst is the late Georgian (1840) house and, liberally disposed, the usual school buildings, some characterful, some not. They've spent well over £2 million in the last five years – including good science labs, IT, dining, classrooms and theatre – and are inordinately and justly proud that the lion's share of that came from prudently husbanded fee income. Indoor swimming pool, sports hall, separate music and art.

Academically the range is wide. Those scholarships tell it all for top-notch teaching, but parents say strugglers are well supported too because all are lauded for what they're good at: 'the teachers really care'. The accent in all things is on making children feel good about themselves. There are extension lessons for the bright and reinforcement lessons for the not-so. Emergent special needs are swiftly spotted and fixed by the superb SEN department where the emphasis is on not creating dependence: 'Our job,' says Lynda Butt, a school hero, 'is to make ourselves redundant.' Children come only if they choose and include a sprinkling of prospective scholars. She does what SENCos do best – get the other teachers talking to each other. All do SATS and results feed internal monitoring systems. Talking about the right senior school starts in year 2.

Art and ceramics flourish luxuriantly and joyously in an inspirational environment where colour blazes and craft skills are taught to the accompaniment of the romping of the imagination. Music is eye-blinkingly good. An unusual number play at grades 6-8, and 80 per cent of the children learn an instrument. Every year, fantastic scholarships and super concerts, but the rigour can be chilling. We are promised that more fun is afoot, and a broader range. Vital.

Sport is played with full fervour and results to match. Observable at every level is a high level of coaching. Whatever they teach you here they teach you to do it well.

Matches well supported by parents, with lots of bonding and dogs on the many touchlines. Picnics in the grounds after Saturday lessons all year round.

Boarding is the tradition and it lives on, most popularly in years 7 and 8. No sloppy sleepover stuff, and 'although we are always open for business over weekends' almost all go home. Most sleep in the main house with some boys in outhouses, looked after by houseparents. It's not much to look at, not as fluffy as some – but the pastoral care is in place and misses little. A key feature, now copied elsewhere, is their system of Friends, trained year 8 counsellors – impressively successful and testimony to strong seriousness. Lots to do after school, it's on the up, and the point is this – the children love it.

Here is a school which does more than it says on the tin. We have never met so many parents who never thought to look elsewhere. The boys and girls are chummy, charming and bright-eyed. In an environment of humanity and hard work parents get what they want: happy, confident children who do the best they can.

WESTBOURNE LOWER AND UPPER SCHOOL

Linked to Westbourne School in the Senior section

50 - 54 Westbourne Road, Sheffield, South Yorkshire, S10 2QQ

Tel: 0114 266 0374
Fax: 0114 267 6518
Website: www.westbourneschool.co.uk

• Ages: 4-13 boys and girls, all day • Non-denom • Fees: £1,800 - £2,500 • Independent • Open days: Mid October

---

Remarks: For further details, see senior school entry.

WESTMINSTER ABBEY CHOIR SCHOOL

Dean's Yard, Westminster Abbey, London, SW1P 3NY

Tel: 020 7222 6151
Fax: 020 7222 1548
E-mail: headmaster@westminster.abbey.org
Website: www.westminster-abbey.org

• Pupils: 32 boys, all boarders, 1st year (probationers) weekly boarders • Ages: 8–13 • C of E • Fees: £1,575 per term (after Dean and Chapter of Westminster's subsidy) • Independent

Head: Since 2002, Mr Jonathan Milton BEd (forties), single, sailor, ex-head of The Abbey School in Tewkesbury, has spent his career associated with choir schools. Sang in a parish choir as a boy and continued ever since, was a choral scholar at York although specialised in English, now teaches geography. Caring and approachable, the littlest boys jump up to see through the half-glazed door into his office before knocking. Believes passionately in choir schools and that the size of this one creates a unique community; timetables can be adjusted easily and all the school family will fit into two minibuses.

Entrance: Informal voice trial followed by recommendation for formal voice trial. The second trial includes a day spent at the school meeting the pupils and staff, with simple tests in English, maths and verbal reasoning. Prospective pupils do not visit all on one day, but a couple at a time. Applicants need not be brilliant musicians already, but must have a good ear and voice and be judged likely to love the school and way of life there. As many as 60 requests for prospectuses – although each year group only has 6 boys in it.

Exit: Usually by music scholarship to a wide range of independent schools: Rugby, Latymer, Eton, King's College School Wimbledon, Worth, Durham, Radley, Stowe, Harrow etc. Head visits about eight senior schools per year and shares experience with parents, offers guidance on preparing and applying for music scholarships.

Remarks: Only dedicated choral school in Britain – however 'it is not just about singing even though that is the core'. There are passionate sportsmen here who climb (in King's Cross), sail (in the Docklands), swim (in the Queen Mother Sports Centre) but their team sport is singing. James O'Donnell, the organist and master of the choristers, treats the boys like young professionals who are part of the abbey.

Lots of musicians on the staff which means music is almost taken for granted; like worship, it permeates much what of the boys do daily.

Current parents hail mostly from within the M25 (although applications are received from all over the country) and like to be part of the Abbey's life too, attend evensong and other fancier events. The choir's participation in the services means that the boys learn to perform, record and are televised – they rub shoulders with the great and the good and ideally develop confidence rather than arrogance. Days begin at 7am for 'the Billy Elliots of the singing world' and the littlest ones are in pyjamas at 7.30pm – in between there is choral practice, two sessions of instrumental practice, specialist lessons, core subjects and prep – and still time for sport, TV, reading, art, Warhammer, table football and train sets. Four residential staff, one female (not including the head and two matrons) mean that tiredness and problems are spotted immediately and dealt with caringly.

The whole school eats together in a basement dining room; George the chef produces food that entices the Dean and Canon of Westminster in for lunch. Few of the pupils would have chosen a boarding school if not choristers. There is a senior chorister and a second chorister as well as a head of school, friendships across the years and brothers – this coupled with circle time in forms encourages a close knit and friendly atmosphere. Pianos everywhere, even keyboards with headphones in the blue painted dormitories. Rooms dedicated to music practice are at the top of the school and boys are encouraged to make it a part of their routine while allowing themselves enough time for other pursuits – either inside or in the Dean's Yard which they have practically to themselves in the evenings (the rabbit warren of Westminster School is across the grass.

There's a Christmas party with Westminster Cathedral Choir School and their arch rivals are St Paul's Cathedral School. Contact with parents is via email and two phone booths, there are no mobile phones allowed. All the academic staff have wireless laptops and projectors or interactive white boards are coming for each form room. The boys' private space is limited to their own bunk bed areas which they can paper with posters, their desks and a cubby-hole for post. The building itself is tall and thin, but the stairs are carpeted and most classrooms have windows on both sides, either to the outside world or to the corridor. French is the only modern foreign language taught from year 4, with Latin being introduced in year 6. The boys undoubtedly look like Harry Potters when heading to the abbey in their cloaks in the winter, but the school has a much more realistic approach to learning than Hogwarts does, both the size of the school and the location mean that it is able to take advantage of the full cultural life that London offers.

WESTMINSTER CATHEDRAL CHOIR SCHOOL

Ambrosden Avenue, London, SW1P 1QH

Tel: 020 7798 9081
Fax: 020 7630 7209
E-mail: office@choirschool.com
Website: www.choirschool.com

- Pupils: 150; 30 boarding choristers, 120 day boys • Ages: 8-13
- RC for choristers, rest ecumenical • Fees: Choristers £2,010; day boys £3,950 • Independent • Open days: Wednesdays during the Michaelmas Term

Headmaster: Since 2000, Mr John Browne BA LLB FRCO FRSA, mid-thirties but with the bubbly, voluble enthusiasm and boyish, wide-eyed energy of your typical polymathic and inexhaustible chorister. Mr Browne, a musician, planned a law career but teaching grabbed him when he wasn't looking – lucky for Westminster. He began his career here in the music dept, then had spells at Latymer – the one in Edmonton – and Berkhamsted Collegiate School. So involved with every aspect of his school and the community of which it is the core is Mr Browne that he literally does not stop talking about it. This is not uncommon but what is truly rare is the way he talks about his individual boys by name – just as any proud father would do – and he is up to speed on every detail of each boy's circumstances, needs and aspirations. He has accomplished a huge amount in his, so far, brief tenure and has an ambitious ten year plan which will continue the transformation. Realistic – 'we can't expand any more' – he knows no limits in respect of what the school experience can be about – 'it's about passion – boys have a passion for things' – and he certainly sets them a quietly driven and inspiring example. Married with a young son, destined, no doubt eagerly, to join the school family.

Entrance: At 8, around 20-30 applicants for chorister places, around 80-100 apply for 24 day places. Assessment is painstaking and thorough. Boys are observed in activities including drama. Verbal and non-verbal reasoning, English and maths are all tested along with a voice trial for would-be choristers and, as important as the rest, attention is paid to the social side – would this boy comfortably fit in? Choristers have to be Roman Catholic, day boys are

mostly RC or C of E though school accepts boys from others faiths who 'like our ethos and style'. Strong sibling policy and many pairs of brothers notably among choristers. Day boys mostly local – from Eaton House, Garden House, Hawkesdown House, the Falcons, Norland Place, The Vale, Wetherby et al, boarders from everywhere. Significant numbers of French and Italian boys.

Exit: Careful work and thought in partnership with parents go into finding the best school for each boy. Mr Browne has close links with many schools and their heads and is busy forging new relationships to have the widest choice of schools. Day boys leave in some numbers for St Paul's and, less so, for Westminster, as well as for solid but less challenging places when appropriate. Boarders like Ampleforth (its Abbot is a governor here), Harrow, Marlborough, Worth and a range of others. Major scholarships not rarities.

Remarks: You could be forgiven for living in the street and not knowing the school is there. One low-key board outside and a more-or-less invisible entrance conspire to keep this school a secret the cognoscenti gratefully keep to themselves. Being so young, the boys are not allowed out in the big world outside on their own so little is seen of them, except, for the day boys at the start and end of the day. The school is tucked away behind the red and white brick splendour of Westminster Cathedral, to which it is physically, and in every other way, attached. The road is a line of august Victorian residences off hectic Victoria Street but the tranquillity, once one reaches the school, is palpable. Once inside, one has a sense – weirdly and remotely reminiscent of a mini Vatican City – of a self-sufficient Roman Catholic community of size and importance housed in deceptively inconspicuous buildings in the middle of a busy secular world but containing immense significance and control. 'We're a tiny school,' says head, 'but part of the organization of the Diocese of Westminster which is based here. We get great support from the diocese – including from the finance and maintenance departments!' 'Family' and 'community' are key words here.

Any idea that the school premises are another example of the cramped inner London prep school type is quickly dispelled at the sight of the large tarmaced playground around which school and diocesan buildings stand. This is a big space for so few boys and in such an area. Cricket nets, a bowling machine and new furniture abut the main area – all of which is over a car park for staff. The classrooms in the various buildings and floors are also good sizes – no-one need feel hemmed-in here. School was purpose built in 1906 which explains the appropriateness of the spaces. Even the two dorms – with, daunting perhaps for some, 12 and 16 beds respectively – don't feel crowded and boarding got an enthusiastic report in a recent inspection. There is a large and inviting common room for boarders with snooker table, PCs – for games! – piano, table football, sofa and huge TV. A small oratory with two chairs invites quiet reflection. Food is superb – lamb navarin and roasted mediterranean vegetables when we visited – followed blissfully by treacle tart – served in attractive refectory planned for impressive redevelopment by the head.

Head had much to do on arrival. ICT now embedded – all staff have laptops and most rooms have data projectors – we saw imaginative use of one in a French lesson. Good IT room with 16 PCs. All rooms have been refurbished and school benefits from galleried library with collection of ancient books – 'our formal grand space', says head and it is used for assemblies, and events. It adjoins the Cardinal's house and school can use the grand reception rooms therein for special occasions. The Cardinal himself is very much in evidence – coming to Old Boys' day and prize giving as well as 'anything you invite him to'. Boys can have access to unique Cathedral treasures for special projects – Mary Tudor's prayer book and Recusant Chalices among them. Edward the Confessor's shroud is also there.

Academics are strong and we met inspiring and endearing teachers with enthusiasm undimmed by long service. Head has redesigned structure to create two-form entry, further dividing into three forms in last two years – to tailor curriculum to needs, aptitudes and destinations of boys. Everyone is screened on entry and twice more in the first year – providing a meticulous profile and also picking up on special needs. For 20-25 per cent, English is the second language, the few dyslexics use laptops – all have good support. Specialist teachers for all subjects after the first year.

Music is, of course, central – two orchestras, regular chamber concerts, masses of instrumental lessons, a good day boy choir, concerts, tours, CDs. Choirmaster is the famed Martin Baker who took over from brilliant James O'Donnell who really put the music here on the map before sauntering down the road to the Abbey. Annually, Cathedral orchestras join with Abbey and St Paul's for a big concert. Art room is big and workful with kiln and plastic moulding machine though no woodwork. Sport is played enthusiastically in various venues including Battersea Park, Queen Mother Sports Centre and Vincent Square. Football, rugby and cricket are main sports. Lots of clubs and much use made of parents and friends as visiting speakers. School can draw on cream of London intelligentsia – bankers, QCs, writers, artists, journalists, MPs and diplomats send their

boys here. They even had cosmonaut Yuri Usachev with 670 days in space under his belt – 'a real-life Captain Kirk', says head.

This is a special place. Special in that, at its foundation, the choir and clergy were granted the right by the Holy See to wear the papal livery of magenta and scarlet, designed for the Lateran basilica in Rome. And splendid they are. But the place oozes specialness in its sense of community and caring. 'What we do is put the round pegs in the round holes,' says head. Every boy we saw looked like a contented peg.

WESTMINSTER UNDER SCHOOL

Adrian House, 27 Vincent Square, London, SW1P 2NN

Tel: 0207 821 5788
Fax: 0207 821 0458
E-mail: under.school@westminster.org.uk
Website: www.westminsterunder.org.uk

• Pupils: 264 boys; all day • Ages: 7-13 • C of E • Fees: £3,697
• Independent • Open days: September/October

Master: Since 2000, Mr Jeremy Edwards BA MA (forties), previously deputy head at Emanuel School in Battersea. An English specialist, still teaches as needed, plus doing PSE with years 4 and 5. Married with three children. Enthusiastic, engaging, unassuming. No easy job taking over from the previous much-loved head, Mr Ashton, who died suddenly in 1999, 'but he has really grown into the role,' said a father. 'He genuinely cares about the children and he always seems to give advice that suits the boy rather than benefits the school. We're very impressed by him.'

Entrance: Three points of entry now, at 7, 8 and 11, with at least five applicants for every place. Tests in maths, English and reasoning. At 7 and 8, the test day is intended to be gentle, with 'lots of fun activities'. About half are invited back in groups of 20 for a lesson and a chat. 'We observe how they react, how they respond to tasks. We like to give them challenges where bright boys who haven't been tutored will shine.' 'They take the time to find out a child's potential,' said a parent. At 11, about half the applicants – and about half those offered places – are from state primaries. 'They are a breath of fresh air and they add breadth to the school because often they question things that prep school boys take for granted.' Bursaries and music scholarships (the amount depending on income) are available at this stage. Successful musicians tend to be at least grade 5.

Exit: About 75 per cent to Westminster School, the rest to Eton, Winchester, Marlborough etc. Although there are only 60 boys in the year group, each year around 10 gain major scholarships. 2005 proved particularly successful with 14 scholarships in total – 7 academic awards to Westminster (including the top Queen's Scholar, 1 to Eton, 1 to Winchester and 5 music awards. Boys coming in at 11 are given a conditional place at the senior school and nearly all go through, but this depends on progress.

Remarks: One of the top central London boys' academic prep schools, with top class teaching throughout. Recent rebuilding work has transformed what used to be rather dingy, cramped facilities into a light and airy space, including a large hall for assemblies, PE and drama, IT room 'with great programs,' said a pupil, extra classrooms and art rooms. The science labs have been refurbished and the music department redesigned to include a music technology room as well as ensemble and practice rooms. Pretty much universal praise for the teaching. 'Many of the teachers really inspire the boys,' said a parent. 'The high standards come from the children wanting to do the work because they're inspired by it. They're genuinely encouraged to think for themselves.' French from year 4, Latin from year 6. (Those accepting 11+ places must attend 10 Saturday morning French and Latin classes over the spring and summer before they join the school to catch up.) English particularly strong with plenty of emphasis on reading and public speaking. Setting for maths and Latin in year 7; in year 8 boys are divided into two scholarship and two non-scholarship classes. 'Some parents become over-anxious about this. We try to persuade them that it is not about success or failure but about choosing an appropriate course for their son. Of course not everyone in the scholarship classes will get scholarships but we choose boys who will benefit from learning to think in unconventional ways. But we're working as hard as we can to make as few divisions as possible between the scholarship and non-scholarship boys.' Ancient Greek, for example, is now taught to everyone in year 8. A part-time study skills co-ordinator gives boys with mild dyslexia or dyspraxia one-to-one help out of the classroom. 'Our son has dyspraxic difficulties and they've helped him to cope very well,' said a parent.

Very high standard of music under the 'brilliant' director, Jeremy Walker. Most boys learn an instrument or sing; all new boys in years 3 and 4 are offered free tuition in stringed instruments for a year. There are 20 peripatetic music teachers offering most instruments. Jazz band, string and brass groups, lots of concerts, including the 'wonderful'

two-day music competition at the end of the summer term. The summer concert in St John's, Smith Square, with its eclectic mix of styles, is 'a source of great pride for the school'. The senior choir does biannual tours abroad – 'one of my most pleasurable duties as head was to see the boys perform for a thousand enthusiastic Brazilians in the historic Church of Saint Benedict in Rio de Janeiro in April 2005. It was a very moving experience.'

Other school trips include an annual Classics holiday to Italy, a ski trip to the Alps, a French Exchange, and every year group has residential trips away (France, New Forest, Devon). 'It's important for London boys to see some of the rest of the world. We value these trips hugely because you see the boys on a different level when you're away with them.' The new art studios include a darkroom and kiln room, though, to the head's regret, no facilities for woodwork or metalwork. There's a newly formed photography club and an annual photography competition – one of the many school house competitions which include chess, reading, model making and Scrabble and involve a large proportion of the boys competing for house points. Chess has been revitalised since the appointment of new head of French in 2004. 'If you don't like competitions don't go there,' said one parent, but another commented, 'my boys are not particularly competitive but they do rise to challenges.'

Drama, once low key, is expanding, with three school productions a year. The school hosts a Latin play competition and there is a tradition of form plays. 'We're keen to establish a booking in the new senior school theatre each year.' The school has an enviable location overlooking the Westminster playing fields in Vincent Square, which it uses three times a week. Cricket and football are the main sports, plus athletics and tennis, with occasional games of hockey and rugby, and teams down to the 9th XI competing in interschool tournaments. Boys also have weekly swimming lessons, 'rather a long walk away,' commented one, and can use the Vincent Square assault course and basketball courts at playtime.

Appears to deal well with bullying. 'When any incidents have happened and we've talked to the school, they've dealt with the situation in an exemplary way.' Parents a mixed bunch, with plenty of wealthy banking folk plus a wide selection of other professions, 'all extremely friendly'. 'It's a very warm and unusual school,' said a father, 'there's a terrific rapport between the children and teachers. The teachers really care about the children and want them to succeed.'

'It's best for self-confident kids with high self-esteem,' said one parent. But another added, 'both of my boys have, unprompted, said that the school has given them so much confidence. If you've got an enquiring mind it's a wonderful place to be.' Pupils walking in over Vauxhall Bridge to avoid the congestion charge.

WETHERBY SCHOOL

Linked to Wetherby Preparatory School

11 Pembridge Square, London, W2 4ED

Tel: 020 7727 9581
Fax: 020 7221 8827
E-mail: learn@wetherbyschool.co.uk
Website: www.wetherbyschool.co.uk

• Pupils: 190 boys (rising to 240 as 3 form entry works through the school) • Ages: 4-8 • Non-denom • Fees: £3,200 • Independent • Open days: Individual visits

Head: Since 1998, Mrs Jenny Aviss MA Psych (fortyish). Studied music at Trinity College, joined Eaton House as head of music and rose to be head six years later; moved here for a change of air – and has been a breath of fresh air for Wetherby. Her MA was gained studying special educational needs at the London Institute. Easy company, dedicated to the children.

Entrance: First come, first served – so within 4 weeks of birth please if you want to be in with a real chance. Casual vacancies arise thereafter.

Exit: To London day schools with competitive entry at 7 and 8: Colet Court, Westminster Under, Sussex House, St Philip's, Westminster Cathedral Choir School, The Harrodian, Trevor Roberts; boarding preps eg Summer Fields, Ludgrove. Wetherby opened its own preparatory school in September 2004. Parents now have the choice of a place at the prep school or to be prepared by examination for other London day schools.

Remarks: Traditional boys' pre-prep focused from day one on the competition for places at 8 in the London day schools. Rows of well-behaved boys but managing to be a caring and happy place too. Children unstressed but attentive, at ease, look you in the eye and talk easily about what they are doing.

'Gets boys where they should be,' says the head. Fights to tune parents' ambitions to the reality of their boys' abilities and then fights to get them in (which she is very good at). Good SEN provision – head has made sure that all teachers know what to look for and how to deal with it in class, and there are several peripatetic SEN staff who give specialist support.

Owned by Alpha Plus who run 12 other educational enterprises (& expanding). Has grown to three-class entry and added dedicated art, music, SEN etc rooms. Rooms airy, light, crowded (school says 'busy'), filled with work and things to look at – pleasant places to be. Smells nice too. Boys say the food is good – lasagne, risotto, fresh salmon. Not the place for the very slow developer or a boy who can't behave, but does very well by the many that it suits. Manners are everything. More of a parents-in-pearls than a parents-in-curlers school.

WHEATHAMPSTEAD HOUSE

Linked to Saint Albans High School for Girls in the Senior section

Codicote Road, Wheathampstead, Herts, AL4 8DJ

Tel: 01582 83270
E-mail: admissions@stalbans-high.herts.sch.uk
Website: www.sahs.org.uk

• Pupils: 315 girls, all day • Ages: 4-11 • Christian • Fees: £2,325 - £2,455 • Independent

Head: Mrs S M Dunkerley MA, BEd.
Remarks: See St Albans High School for Girls.

WIMBLEDON CHASE PRIMARY SCHOOL

Merton Hall Road, London, SW19 3QB

Tel: 020 8542 1413
Fax: 020 8542 1668
E-mail: senior.admin@wimbledonchase.merton.sch.uk
Website: www.wimbledonchase.merton.sch.uk

• Pupils: 500 boys and girls (including 105 in the nursery), all day • Ages: 3-11 • Non-denom • State

Head: Since 2001, Mrs Sue Tomes BEd (fifties), has been at the school for 30 years, moving up the ranks from head of French, senior mistress and then deputy head for 15 years. Married, a self-confessed workaholic and perfectionist, she freely admits that the school plays a major part in her life. Her lovely, large office is very homely, but when she can be prised away from work, she enjoys reading, music, travelling and collecting antiques. Mrs T also tries to maintain her links with France and is keen to support the teaching of primary modern foreign languages across the borough. A modest and unassuming woman, she is popular with pupils (knows all their names) and parents. 'She is pretty amazing,' sums up one mother. Generally seen as v. approachable and open to suggestion and famed for her huge attention to detail. 'We have to sit on her a bit sometimes or she would be ordering the jammy dodgers for the school fair,' jokes one of her many fans.

Entrance: At 3+ to nursery, and 4+ to the main school. Non-selective academically. Applicants must list the school as their first preference, with special needs taking priority, followed by the usual sibling, then proximity criteria. Families need to move close to the school to be sure of a place.

Exit: A regular trickle to selective grammars: both of the Tiffin schools, Sutton Grammar and Nonsuch, while majority move locally to Ricards Lodge, Rutlish Secondary and Raynes Park Secondary School.

Remarks: A school with a heartbeat – lively and like-able; we didn't find anyone with a bad word to say about this happy place. In fact, quite the opposite: 'My children absolutely love going to school,' says one mother. 'It's an amazing place – the opportunities it offers and the way the kids are catered for, are as near to a private school as I could get without opening a cheque book.'

At first sight it's a bit like visiting a senior school with very small pupils. Despite its location near the centre of Wimbledon, the school enjoys the size, site and facilities rarely found at primary level. Buildings date back to 1924 (when they were home to the local senior girls school) consequently there is lots of wood-panelling (slightly Harry Potterish feel to some of it), but more importantly, lots of dedicated space. In 2001, and overseen by Mrs T, the school began its conversion from middle to a primary school with its first intake of reception children and the addition of a big bright nursery. 'Its transition seemed daunting at the time, but we're out the other side and it's great,' said one mother.

Academically all is more than sound -all well above national averages at the relevant Key Stages. What makes this school really stand above other primaries is the sheer range and variety of experiences over and above the National Curriculum. The philosophy is to give children a chance to try things and to make learning fun. So there are lots of themed days and weeks (everything from maths to black history) – the highlight of which is the well-planned 'Enrichment Week' where the afternoon timetable is suspended entirely in favour of workshops on all sorts from boxing to jewellery making. 'We want to find and foster talents wherever they may lie,' says Mrs T. Talent is also nurtured through the inspiring

extracurricular activities after school and at lunchtimes – most of them free. Simple but easily lost skills like skipping, knitting and story telling are promoted via clubs, alongside the more usual sports, dancing (including tap), drama and French.(The children learn French from reception including a residential stay in France for year 5). Lots of days out and trips. Pupils and parents are hugely appreciative of the range and quality of what's on offer.

A very inclusive place (lots of Koreans, Tamil speakers make up the second largest section) – 73 pupils speak 23 different languages. With the mix of languages comes a mix of abilities – but the school does well by them all. Every EAL pupil, except a few SEN children, attained at least a level 4 in their SATS. Similarly, provision for SEN is of high quality. There is a dedicated SENCO, early identification of special needs (including a gifted and talented register) and lots of additional support and catch up programmes. Additionally, the school has a unit for children with additional learning needs (ALN), currently aimed at moderate needs, but by 2006 this is changing to cater for children with language and communication disorders. It will offer 14 places – with top priority for entrance to the school. Currently the ALN children learn in the unit in the morning (their own adapted curriculum, mostly maths and English) and join their class in the main school for the afternoon session, with support staff. There are also facilities for physically disabled children such as ramps and purpose-built toilets. Head feels this mix is good for all the children. Certainly the place is buzzing: from the front hall, packed with trophies, certificates and photographs extolling the achievements of pupils and staff, to the back door leading to beautiful grounds (well used – especially for sports and science); there's lots going on.

A happy school – it's not silent or regimented, but still has a slightly traditional feel and pupils quite smartly dressed. There is a 'positive behaviour management system'- largely stickers and crystals (full jar of gems equals golden time). All the teachers use – and encourage the children to use – 'language of choice', as in 'Is this (behaviour) a good choice? What are the consequences if I do this?' Parents encouraged to use the idea at home. The school also has a worry box, peer mediators, strong school council, buddy bus stop in the playground – all geared for children to sort out any problems. A boon for working parent is the wrap-around care on offer (breakfast and after-school) – another benefit of having the space. Even the half-day nursery children can be accommodated for the rest of the day. Hugely supportive parents are keen to help in the classroom and by raising impressive sums of money. The school returns the favour by providing a dedicated parents' room in school where helpers have somewhere to keep their things and (most importantly) get tea and biscuits!

WIMBLEDON HIGH SCHOOL JUNIOR SCHOOL

Linked to Wimbledon High School in the Senior section

Mansel Road, London, SW19 4AB

Tel: 020 9071 0902
Fax: 020 8971 0903
E-mail: info.juniors@wim.gdst.net
Website: www.gdst.net/wimbledon

• Pupils: 317 girls, all day • Ages: 4 - 10 • Non-denom • Fees: £2,383 • Independent • Open days: October

Head: Since 2003, Miss Catherine Mitchell, formerly deputy head at Alleyn's Junior School, Dulwich.

Entrance: Entry is mainly at 4, school is popular and there is a waiting list.

Exit: Parents are warned in year 5 if their daughter might not make it to the senior school; usually 90 per cent of junior girls are offered places.

Remarks: For further details see senior school entry.

WINCHESTER HOUSE SCHOOL

44 High Street, Brackley, Northamptonshire, NN13 7AZ

Tel: 01280 702 483
Fax: 01280 706 400
E-mail: office@winchester-house.org
Website: www.winchester-house.org

• Pupils: 368 boys and girls; 80 boarders (55 of whom are weekly) • Ages: 7-13, plus pre-prep 3-7 • C of E • Fees: Day: pre-prep £1,765 - £2,225; prep £3,060-3,825. Weekly and full boarding: £4,050 - £5,065 • Independent • Open days: One each in Michaelmas, Lent and Summer terms

Head: Since 2003, Mr Mark Seymour BA CertEd (fiftyish), an historian and previously head of Cargilfield (qv) from 2000 and senior housemaster at Haileybury. Keen cricketer. His wife Andrea has an honours degree in literature and media and has been involved in school PR. Three school-age children. Interests include playing the drums, power-boating.

Entrance: Preferably in September but now completely full with waiting lists in most year groups. Quite the reverse problem to only a couple of years ago and blamed on new head. Day pupils move up via hugely popular pre-prep (Tel: 01280 703 070), others come for an informal test. Most boarders come from within 50 mile radius.

Exit: Mostly to schools within a 60-mile radius – Rugby, St Edwards, Oundle, Uppingham, Stowe, Bloxham, etc. Girls to Tudor Hall, Downe House, Malvern Girls', Wycombe Abbey etc. Has had a good collection of awards over the years. In 2005, of the 27 pupils, a third got schols.

Remarks: Traditional co-ed prep school, now with occasional, weekly and full boarding, based in a converted Victorian hunting lodge. The school was founded in 1876, and moved to its present site in Brackley in 1923. Very much a local school, and popular as such. Keen games, athletics meetings here a great favourite. Thriving well-run pre-prep and nursery over the road, with the playing fields, sports hall and tennis courts. Library block and IT centre attached to the main building.

Sound teaching on all fronts, including Greek for the brightest, strong classics and maths for scholars. Some remedial help for dyslexia – co-ordinator is director of studies (but also trained in special needs). Maximum class size twenty, average around fifteen. New head has introduced various initiatives including, All-A-Board and Learn to Lead (leadership programme for all in upper school.

WINDLESHAM HOUSE SCHOOL

Washington, Pulborough, West Sussex, RH20 4AY

Tel: 01903 874 700
Fax: 01903 874 702
E-mail: office@windlesham.com
Website: www.windlesham.com

- Pupils: 160 boys, 105 girls; all board except for staff's children; Plus pre-prep with 35 boys and girls (who can spend one year in the main school as day children but must board from 9) • Ages: 8 - 13, pre-prep 4 - 7 • C of E • Fees: Little Windlesham Reception and year 1: £1,940, years 2/3: £2,250; Main prep school: 'determined at the time of entry' • Independent • Open days: October and/or March for Little Windlesham; older children and parents by appointment at any time

Head: Since 1996, Mr Philip Lough (pronounced Lock) MA PGCE (fifties), married to Mrs Christine Lough MA PGCE (fifty) who is assistant head. Both are linguists; Mr Lough was educated at Sherborne, followed by Trinity College, Oxford and Mrs Lough went to Madras College in St Andrews, followed by Aberdeen University. This is very much a joint appointment ('But – he's the boss'). The Loughs, who have three grown up children, met and married whilst doing their respective PGCEs at Durham. Both of them teach French – he to the scholars at the top end plus RE, and she to the tinies as well as preparing older children for their next step. 'Drugs, drink, relationships (including sex) and how to deal with peer pressure.' 'Learn to say no, consider the consequences'. PSHE is on-going throughout the school and Mrs Lough masterminds the programme in conjunction with tutors 'so that children go on to their senior schools confident in their own abilities'. She also supervises the anti-bullying initiative. We had a very jolly tour round the school with Mrs Lough greeting each child by name and showing genuine interest in their various activities. The Loughs do a birthday box for pupils and ten mates, either in their flat or in the garden if the weather is OK – no balloons though, just a cake and fizz (the non-alcoholic kind). Mr Lough was previously housemaster at Marlborough and spent seventeen years there 'in various capacities', including a two year exchange with Melbourne Grammar. Before that he taught at Chafyn Grove. Thoughtful and fun, they are obviously enjoying their time at Windlesham and glowing reports come in from

happy parents of children who find themselves 'watching telly and eating crisps' in the Loughs' flat to overcome a temporary blip of homesickness.

Smashing new (if made of somewhat garishly coloured paper) handbook for all pupils (no pics though) full of handy hints, school policies, individual timetables and pages for attainments and staff comments – highly praised by the inspection team (who must be colour blind).

The Loughs started The Rolling Heads, where the heads of Brambletye, Cheam, Summerfields, Beaudesert and St Andrews Eastbourne meet twice a year with their wives to discuss the vicissitudes of prep-school headmastering and how to cope with the latest government initiatives as well as sharing their better schemes and wheezes. The directors of studies, as well as heads of departments and senior management, now also have barn-storming sessions. After nine years, Mr Lough has got the situation here pretty well sussed but still complains about the problems of getting staff, 'it's not always easy but all you need is one good applicant', though at the moment they 'have a brilliant crew', many of them young and zinging (the classics master – think policemen – was organizing a basketball match during our visit and speaks Mandarin into the bargain) and the school has recently appointed a whizzo new head of DT who has transformed the outward bound type activities. Splendid staff accommodation on site with 33 'units' – everything from bachelor flats to 'proper' houses but nothing 'too grand' makes staff appointments easier.

Entrance: Via registration, interview at ages eight to 10, and testing at 11. Loads from London and the south east, about a third local, and 'around 90' from overseas, mainly ex-pats, 30 Foreign Office children, fewer than before, but still (2005) more than any other school, plus 20 Services and a collection of 15 or so non-nationals. Quite a gang of French and Spanish children coming for a term or a year or so, all by word of mouth, the Domecq family 'are a strong influence', EFL on hand. Three term entry but mainly in September, though half term or even in between if space available. Wide ability range. All prospective pupils spend a day and a night in school, attending lessons et al, to see how it works out.

Exit: To a huge range of schools, 70 per cent to co-ed and almost all to boarding schools, occasional dribble back to state sector. Good record of scholarships, nine last year with four pure academic (Downe House, Marlborough, Benenden and Sevenoaks) but only one boy. Most frequent destinations as before: Marlborough, Harrow, Stowe, Bryanston, Eton, Millfield, King's Canterbury, Sevenoaks, St Edwards, Cranleigh, Rugby. Also to Winchester (none last year), Wellington, Charterhouse, Canford etc as well as locally to Brighton, Eastbourne and Bedales.

Remarks: Broad intake, so pupils setted for English, maths, French and science; most classes 15/16, max 20. Extensive learning support based in the snazzily decorated attic but the school is not good for physical handicap, though 'one of our best rugby players' is profoundly deaf. Stunning ISI report in May 2005: 'Pupils with a wide range of needs are very well catered for. Boys and girls make good and, at times, very good progress'. Pupils both withdrawn from class (usually Latin) for individual or small groups and French taught by inspired re-working of the syllabus (Mrs L says she has learnt much about teaching French from the SEN support staff). Six jolly bright dedicated rooms in the attics, with computers accessing the school network, pupils often have their own laptops. 35 per cent of pupils on some form of support, either for the brightest or the less able, usually on the dys-strata plus the odd ADHD child – but only those with organizational dysfunction rather than behavioural problems. Not a good school for those with an IQ of less than 100, though there are the odd siblings; unit is staffed by two full time and five part time teachers, one of whom is a maths specialist. Currently there are two children in the school who have their own teaching assistants. Language therapy (helpful for EFL too) and experienced counsellor on hand (the latter also visits other schools and brings a wider brief to the school). Weekly staff conferences to discuss various strategies and pupil profiles. In all cases parents pay, though there may be help available from their local authorities and an individual mentor may be partially supported by the school when they also help out in class.

All pupils must board, Little Windlesham pupils after their first year (ie aged 9+). Six houses, with boys resident in one building and girls in another; bright jolly dorms, with each girl having their own bedside light (wow!) Both boys and girls have a special 'chill out' common room, where they can have supervised quiet time. Tutorial system as well as houseparents, counsellor in the school. School prides itself on its pastoral care, which is much praised by the official reports. Pastoral board in the staff room where comments, both good and bad, are logged for all to see. Lots of project work, good links with Europe, all pupils learn Spanish for two years, German is an option as an 'activity'. Latin at ten for the brighter pupils, who follow a three year course. Greek another option. New IT system in place which links up all staff houses, plus computers all over the shop, as well as a mass of interactive white boards. Own lap tops too, 'for children recommended to have one either by us or an Ed Psych'. Impressive art and design, school likes to have a

regular presence in London, with exhibitions, concerts and the like every two years. Fantastic array of options, wizard glass fusing (really professional stuff) plus pottery, film making, kayaking, pistol shooting, as well as clays, plus karate, judo, chess coaching and extra tennis and riding (these latter cost extra and equestrians, who can ride up to five times a week could bankrupt their parents at a cost of £20 or so a lesson – but the stables are just a stones throw away and the schools hosts a horse show each May). Some of the most fantastic textiles, and screen painting (the batik is to die for), impressive new kitchens and cookery particularly popular with the boys – perhaps it is the sugar craft? Windlesham has the most stunning music we have ever come across, with outstanding musical director producing and recording works of his own compilation. Last time we said that 'time listening in the cupboard was well worth while' and yes, we had a session in the cupboard again – some superb choral work, plus music for the school's latest offering of Honk deftly re-worked by the head of drama to include some eighty children with two casts. This music/drama combination is terrific, bags of enthusiasm, the place positively buzzes. Huge number of individual lessons (600 or so) any instrument can be learnt, including the pipes, the mandolin and the Jew's harp. Outstanding sport, rugby team had just come back from Scotland and the girls' hockey had spent the same weekend in the Isle of Wight, and recently three boys linked up with a Saudi Arabian school for an Arctic adventure.

Science labs recently revamped and masses of TLC expended on the buildings which no longer look a little neglected, swimming pool windows now replaced with ballproof (jolly expensive) glass and the whole place gleaming like a new pin, new security doors being fitted, though funds are not yet in hand to start the major new build which has been in the pipeline (planning permission received) to attach a dining hall, kitchen, indoor sports hall and extra-curricular centre to the Malden Theatre. The trad dining room has a new child-height servery, with jolly plastic plates and a huge range of salads and Jamie Oliver type dishes. Masses of fruit, and a trendy machine for dishing out baked potatoes.

The main house is a splendid and distinguished old redbrick Queen Anne house on the Downs near the south coast. Last time we visited the school was installing a new sewage plant and water main; and the 60 acres of grounds, with games pitches, tennis courts, a nine-hole golf course and child-inspired woods for making dens are back to their manicured splendour, and now boast a (tiny) observatory courtesy of the Worthing Astronomical society. A small patch of garden is dedicated for pupils' plots, usually taken up by those whose parents live abroad, and who still write regularly to the (now retired) school gardener for years after they have left enquiring about their veggie plots. Loughs keen on home comforts, a fire burns in the hall from mid October till Easter. Regular bus from Putney on Sunday evenings, all pupils must stay in school for two fixed weekends but with so many from real abroad there is no general exodus and children of the same age are grouped together and taken on jollies elsewhere. School founded (elsewhere at the request of Dr Arnold of Rugby) in 1837 by the Malden family who owned and ran it until a few years ago when it became a charitable foundation, The Malden Trust. Charles Malden retired in 1994 and died several years ago, his daughter is still a governor. Efficient, caring country school – less obviously green wellie than some (good showing of pheasants in the policies though) – with purposeful children beavering away at all levels. Windlesham is a happy school, with children getting the kind of care and attention you would expect from a much smaller establishment.

WITHAM HALL
PREPARATORY SCHOOL

Witham-on-the-Hill, Bourne, Lincolnshire, PE10 0JJ

Tel: 01778 590 222
Fax: 01778 590 606
E-mail: secretary@withamhall.com
Website: www.withamhall.com

• Pupils: 241: 119 boys, 122 girls • Ages: Pre prep 3 – 8; prep 8 – 13 • C of E • Fees: Day £3,160; boarding £4,330 • Independent

Head: Since 1997, joint heads, David and Sarah Telfer, combining the best of their attributes to make a round whole. He is a dynamic and determined Scot and Mrs Telfer provides the softer touch. He was head of Broadwater Manor in Worthing previously and turned that round, with a high rate of scholarships for those exiting to public schools. The Telfers are repeating their success at Witham.

Entrance: There are no entry requirements, the majority joining from the pre-prep.

Exit: 12 scholarships out of 27 leavers in 2005. Going on to schools that are reasonably local eg Oundle, Oakham, Uppingham, Repton, Stamford and further afield Queen Margaret's and Ampleforth. A few to Eton, Shrewsbury, Harrow.

Remarks: Considering its academic achievements, it is surprising that the school has a fairly low profile on the UK scene, attracting mainly only local families. It should really be broadcasting its successes in the classroom, the arts and sport more widely. For a small school, they are certainly at the top of their tree. With every year that passes, greater goals are being reached.

The Telfers have undertaken a major building project every two years, all funded from within. Teaching blocks, sympathetically built, complement the comfortable Queen Anne manor that houses the boarding side. Everything has a ring of quality.

The school moves with the times, offering flexi-boarding. Children fit in to this side of the school very easily alongside the weekly boarders. The excellent food is prepared on site and they like to think they were years ahead of Jamie's Dinners; milk is on tap all day with bowls of fruit being refilled on demand. Class representatives from both the pre-prep and prep have weekly meetings with the head cook to discuss menus.

Academically, the school is hitting the right buttons. Staff are in their 30s and 40s, with five teaching special needs. Average class size in the prep is 14.8 and in pre-prep 10.1. The computerised Accelerated Reading Programme has made a big improvement in boys' reading. The school is in the enviable position of having to throw books away – from over use. Art deserves a special mention, not only the scholarships awarded in this medium. There is achievement at all levels. The pictures that cover the walls are eye-catching, well-conceived with a great use of colour and finished to a high standard. Some of the scholarship pupils work on large sculptures, giving them the opportunity to break free of size boundaries that can so often limit talent. Lots of music is being taught and at the last speech day, there were 144 children performing together on stage. LAMDA classes are very popular with a waiting list.

The prowess of the school also filters into sport, where they adopt a sport-for-all policy. Reaching national finals in rounders and travelling to other matches all over, sees the school well-represented.

The school is solid and unflashy with a real warmth about it.

WITHINGTON GIRLS' JUNIOR SCHOOL

Linked to Withington Girls' School in the Senior section

Wellington Road, Fallowfield, Manchester, Greater Manchester, M14 6BL

E-mail: office@withington.manchester.sch.uk
Website: www.withington.manchester.sch.uk

- Pupils: 90 girls; all day • Ages: 7-11 • Non-denom
- Fees: £1,760 juniors • Independent
- Open days: Late October/Early November

Head: Since 2005, Mrs Kathryn Burrows.

Entrance: Own entrance examination held on same day as senior school in January. Very gentle, English and maths, in small rooms with prospective form teacher.

Exit: Almost all to Withington senior school.

Remarks: Happy and busy atmosphere, very close integration with senior school, use of sports, science, music, IT and DT facilities. Girls taught science, music, geography, French, German, Spanish and Italian, RS and DT by senior school specialists and junior school staff teach in the senior school.

WOODCOTE HOUSE SCHOOL

Windlesham, Surrey, GU20 6PF

Tel: 01276 472 115
Fax: 01276 472 890
E-mail: info@woodcotehouseschool.co.uk
Website: www.woodcotehouseschool.co.uk

- Pupils: 105 boys, most board • Ages: 8-13 • Inter-denom
- Fees: Day £3,275; boarding £4,575 • Independent

Head: Since 1989, Mr Nick Paterson BA (fiftyish), educated at Westminster and Exeter University. Called 'Mr Nick' by one and all. Mr Nick's grandfather bought the school in 1931 when it was going 'but only just'. It is now a private limited company. Super wife, with older children, and they have one son at university. Mr Nick comments (in answer to our question) that his biggest challenge is continuing to

instil a code of good manners, fair play and unselfishness in the face of a deteriorating situation nationally.

Entrance: Send for what is still one of the smallest prospectuses in the country (though Ludgrove and Sunningdale come close), small 'because it is vital they (the parents) come and see us with the boy and really we must get on pretty well'. Always prepared to talk to parents right up to the last moment. Takes new boys in at the beginning of all three terms.

Exit: Biggest numbers to Sherborne, Radley, Bradfield, Harrow, Shiplake, Charterhouse, Wellington, plus a dozen others.

Remarks: Super little school where each boy is carefully cocooned so that the shock of leaving 'nursery environment' will not be too much. Main problem might be the shock of leaving Woodcote for their public school. 'Generous' exeats every third week (Friday – Monday), and Mrs Nick will always make arrangements for 'abroad' boys with other families. Lots of other activities/outings on in-school weekends when parents are welcome to join in but not take out. Minuscule but extremely informative, yearly magazine which kicked off last year on the very first page: 'Food. Always the most interesting part of any small boy's day'. Keen chess, bridge, fishing, calligraphy and nice old-fashioned boy things, such as making model aeroplanes, and less old-fashioned things such as 'Warhammer' (the head is appalled at the cost). Set in its own thirty acres, which includes some attractive woods, the main building is Regency and elegant but delightfully worn at the edges, with additional modestly built classroom blocks round the back and charming little chapel across the lawn, made of corrugated iron (painted black) and wooden inside. ('Buildings like hen houses,' said one visiting parent disappointedly.) Barbour and/or Husky part of the uniform, corduroy trousers and a rather dreary brown sweater or school sweatshirt; school now runs its own clothes shop and several changes have recently been made to the uniform.

Lots of golf played on site and cricket, squash (uses courts up the road), rugger and shooting. Several parents join large ski party in early January. Head concentrates on placing boys in the school of their parents' choice rather than on getting scholarships – though they got seven in 2005. Small and very competent remedial unit – recommended by special needs organisations for dyslexia and dyspraxia. Fully-qualified teacher who works in a small unit – some 15 per cent of the boys receive help – also experienced EFL teacher.

One or two gems among the staff including the super dynamic head of science, and the archetypal schoolmaster,

Colin Holman, who has been here for yonks and lives in the lodge and, amongst other things, looks after the grounds lovingly. Development programme means school now has science lab, computer centre, art and music block. Music strong – head and brilliant young head of music co-write musicals. Eighty per cent learn at least one instrument. Choir tours to Holland. New changing rooms (not before time, some might say), also Astroturf hockey pitch/tennis courts and telescopic swimming pool enclosure. About one-third are sons of soldiers or ex-pats, one-third London or local and a third from 'far afield'. One or two Thais (long-standing tie with Thailand), a few 'Europeans' (mainly Spanish). One of a dying breed – the family-owned school – and, unlike some, by and large it works. Continuing good reports.

WOODSIDE PARK INTERNATIONAL SCHOOL JUNIOR DEPARTMENT

Linked to Woodside Park International School Kindergarten and Junior in the Junior section

Linked to Woodside Park International School in the Senior section

49 Woodside Avenue, London, N12 8SY

Tel: 0208 8920 0600
Fax: 0208 445 0835
E-mail: admissions@wpis.org
Website: www.wpis.org

• Pupils: 125 boys and girls • Ages: 7-11 • Fees: £2,860 • Independent

Director: Since 2005, Ms Barbara Moroney, who has extensive experience overseas including Saudi Arabia, Spain, Togo and Milan. Responsible for PYP accreditation.

Dean of nursery and kindergarten (4-7): since 2000, Mrs Gabriele Weber CertEd (forties) who first came to the school in 1988. She was educated in Germany and studied primary education at Karlsruhe University. Previously taught in Golders Hill School in Golders Green. Charming, caring, obviously adored by her charges, she still teaches. Again, enthusiastic about the PYP.

Exit: Most go on to senior but trickle elsewhere to state or independent sector.

Remarks: Lower school – truly international. School celebrates all sorts of different religious festivals. Smashing little school, glorious building, light and sunny with fab nat-

ural lighting, filled with child-inspired batiks, pottery, and art and surrounded by probably not enough playground for boisterous children. But much use made of the park nearby for cross country runs as well as for scientific experiments. Again, much use made of local facilities for swimming and the like. Super gym which converts to dining room, with hot meals being transferred to those who want it in the pre-prep, five minutes' drive away. Music, drama and exceptional art. London and other visits in all disciplines.

Media & Resource Centre, French from 3, and regular trip to France for the top years. Two parallel classes. Max class size 20. Children keep their bags in smart multi-coloured boxes dotted around the school and are classroom based to start with. All lessons in each half term tend to concentrate on one aspect of the IB curriculum. Computers in every class, as well as a dedicated computer suite. Homework important and children keep a homework diary; can stay at school until 5 pm and can arrive around 8 am. Strong emphasis on pastoral care, very good provision for children with special needs – Quest again; and EAL much used. 90 per cent of the children come up from the pre-prep. Kindergarten: positively buzzing with child pictures, all that a pre-prep ought to be. Children work mainly at hexagonal tables to encourage interaction, computers everywhere, French from five. Max class size 20, but children work in small ability groups, often with second teacher in the room. Dyslexia screened for, with outside agencies if need be, EAL on tap, children can usually pick up more or less fluent English within the year (32 different countries). Regular morning assembly. The IB curriculum is geared to a broad philosophy and children are expected to learn to question and to communicate. Tinies in temporary buildings, revamped in 2002, and playground full of utterly desirable climbing frames (and admirably well-supervised); the surface of the playground is bungee, apparently made from reconditioned car tyres. Open 7.45am (breakfast club) to 6pm (after school care). Normal day is 8.30am to 3.30pm. Parents send fruit into school with their children for break. The pre-prep is bulging; if these numbers continue to increase and stay in the system, then the school will easily reach the target of 600 pupils.

WOODSIDE PARK INTERNATIONAL SCHOOL KINDERGARTEN AND JUNIOR

Linked to Woodside Park International School Junior Department
in the Junior section

Linked to Woodside Park International School in the Senior
section

88 Woodside Park Road, London, N12 8SH

Tel: 020 8920 0600
Fax: 0208 445 9678
E-mail: admissions@wpis.org
Website: www.wpis.org

• Pupils: 130 boys and girls • Ages: 2-7 • Independent

Remarks: See Junior department.

WYCLIFFE PREPARATORY SCHOOL

Linked to Wycliffe College in the Senior section

Ryeford Hall, Stonehouse, Gloucestershire, GL10 2LD

Tel: 01453 820470
Fax: 01453 825604
E-mail: prep@wycliffe.co.uk
Website: www.wycliffe.co.uk

• Pupils: 370 boys and girls, some board • Ages: 2 - 13 • Fees:
Prep school, day: from £1,535 in the nursery to £3,140 (years
6,7 & 8); boarding £3,620 -£4,545 • Independent • Open days:
Early October and mid February

Head: Since 2003, Mr Adrian Palmer BA (responsible for
day-to-day running, reports back to senior school head).
Formerly head at Rendcomb Junior School.

Entrance: By interview, report from previous school or
by scholarship at 11. New pupils can join at any time during
school year if places free. Scholarships awarded at 11,
reassessed at 13 for entry to big school. Also awards in
music, drama, dance, sport, art and IT.

Exit: 98 per cent to the senior school. All year 8s sit
Wycliffe's own exams in all subjects 'so we can get a sense

of their ability.' Small loss to local grammar schools at 11.

Remarks: 400 metres away from the senior school,
which allows for shared use of facilities. Small classes,
caring environment where children treated as individuals
and developing talents nurtured. Mixed nursery (Windmills)
for under 3s and kindergarten, pre-prep and prep. Very
much part of Wycliffe life.

YARLET SCHOOL

Yarlet, Near Stafford, Stafford, Staffordshire, ST18 9SU

Tel: 01785 286 568
Fax: 01785 286 569
E-mail: headmaster@yarletschool.co.uk
Website: www.yarletschool.co.uk

• Pupils: 86 ie 63 boys, 23 girls; 65 in the pre-prep; 11 in the
nursery • Ages: 2 - 3 nursery, 3 - 7 pre-prep, 7 - 13 main school
• C of E / inter-denom • Fees: Day: pre-prep £1,665-1,925; prep
£2,300 - 2,595. Boarding: £27 per night • Independent • Open
days: Termly

Head: Since 1989, Mr Richard S Plant MA (early fifties).
Potteries born and bred. Studied English at Pembroke,
Cambridge; worked for a couple of years at Wedgwood and
then joined Yarlet. Cheerful, enthusiastic, still a schoolboy;
clearly loves the job, the place and the children; likely to
be here until retirement. Teaches history to the top three
forms and leads the choir in song. Married to Sue, an elegant lady of perfect taste and sanity, who is much involved
in the life of the school; three grown-up children and now
granchildren.

Entrance: By personal interview with head and his
wife.

Exit: Boys and girls to Repton, Denstone and
Newcastle. Boys to Shrewsbury, Radley, Rugby, Wrekin. Girls
to The Cheltenham Ladies' College. Scholarships/Awards
2004: 4 academic, 2 art, 1 sport.

Remarks: Founded 1873, occupying a grand old
house with fine views to the east and the A34 roaring away
to the west, with various later additions and a dear little
green tin chapel (God important). Dormitories bright and
airy, plenty of furry animals; schoolrooms full of pupils' work
and other decoration; a well-used feel; colours cheerful and
well chosen.

Yarlet became co-educational in 1983 and has become
totally focused on its local day market. Flexi-boarding for
main school children on Thursday/Friday nights is offered

and well looked after by staff. Nursery and pre-prep full to bursting, features the Perkins Cup for Effort; pre-prep building opened in 1999 by Baroness Trumpington and thus assured of great success.

A very sporting school – six days a week for all main school children (early Saturday finish for those not involved in matches) – so Sunday is the only day off. Good pitches including an Astro. Indoors facilities improved through the construction of a new sports hall, which is now in use. Boys' cricket and football strong, also girls' netball, hockey and rounders. Recent successes include winning the Staffordshire County cricket finals at both U12 and U11 ages with sides that included two ten/nine-years-olds. Yarlet boys representing Staffordshire in 2003 at under 13,(Captain), under 12 and under 11. Good athletics, cross-country and gymnastics.

Shows a proper disregard for turning the heating on for cold days in autumn – staff huddled round the fire at break, hands clasped round coffee mugs; boarders sleeping in their dressing gowns however, warm as toast, we are assured!

One form a year, so mixed teaching, with a scholarship stream for academically bright pupils. A dedicated learning support department established in 2003, supported by the Dyslexia Unit in Stone (neighbouring town)- copes with a wide range of SENs. Pupils friendly, articulate, active. Staff a chirpier lot than usual; good art and lively English (there's a poetry reciting competition every year for all – proper poetry too). Drama present and strong, but not overly so; ditto music. Well-stocked computer room totally refurbished in 2004, providing modern technology. Internet access for everyone.

Yateley Manor

51 Reading Road, Yateley, Hampshire, GU46 7UQ

Tel: 01252 405 500
Fax: 01252 405 504
E-mail: office@yateleymanor.com
Website: www.yateleymanor.com

• Pupils: 525 boys and girls, all day • Ages: pre-prep (Wyndhams) 3-7; prep 7-13 • C of E roots • Fees: £2,061 - £2,945 cover everything a child needs or does from 8.15am - 6.30pm plus all school trips and study tours • Independent

Head: Since, yes, 1968, Francis Howard (late fifties). He took the school over from his grandmother and established it as a charitable trust in 1970. Educated at Yateley, Millfield, Cantab and Oxon. Teaches English. Steeped in the past? Not a bit of it. As up-to-the-minute as they come. Calm, effective, singularly kind and, it seems, new every morning. The children pick up on this, light up when they see him and tell him about everything. They say, 'he's always happy, and he always listens.' He gives this place its dynamic and puts it at its ease, a difficult trick to pull off. His wife Delphina is the bursar. Two grown-up sons. No talk of retirement.

Entrance: 'Moderately selective' they say – informal interview and assessment. Mild special educational needs only. Generous scholarships: academic up to 50 per cent of fees – music 35 per cent – sport 25 per cent – chess 15 per cent – all-rounders 15 per cent. Discount for brothers and sisters. Galloping popularity means early registration a must.

Exit: Royal Grammar School Guildford, The Abbey Reading, Lord Wandsworth, Wellington, Bradfield, Leighton Park (increasingly), then a smattering of other nearby top independents. Around 30 out of a typical year group of 76 leave aged 11 for local independents and grammars: Farnborough Hill, Guildford High, Reading Grammar, Kendricks.

Remarks: A tight ship – five hundred children in eight acres. It ticks like a Swiss watch, but efficiency banishes stress – cheeriness is general. The day starts at 8 if you want breakfast, and can finish as late as 6.30pm if you want supervised homework. Academically brisk, success is prized, scholarships are mopped up a-plenty, yet headmaster's commendations reward effort, and charmingly so – for 'being brave this week', for 'telling a lovely story'. Oh, yes, this is a humane place. Everyone learns Latin. And, in years 3 and 4, cooking. Learning support is established and growing – specialist fine tuning in class for problems as they arise, individual tuition charged for. Chess is unusually big, taught by an International Master, and more than twenty children play for Hants and Berks.

We were shown round by a boy and a girl, picked at random, licensed to take us anywhere. What confidence! We went everywhere. The IT is amazing. Message screens stand at junctions and bring the latest news. All pause and peer. Everyone does email – to each other, to their teachers. Interactive whiteboards abound. It's slick but it serves. We had to go see matron because she's so nice. Much new building, all of it excellent, and a painted rainbow along one wall to guide the weenies. Homework is posted daily on the superb website, which keeps parents up to speed with everything. Reporting is meticulous and monthly – pupils are monitored not quizzically but with care. Their record book goes home daily, in which parents can have their say and, every week, their child makes a new resolution.

Music is a matter of pride. More than half the school learn an instrument – all have a go at the recorder in year 3. Art is good, ceramics especially. There's an alluring variety of after-school activities – and, in the holidays, activity weeks, arty ones and sporty ones. Sport is hot and well done, cricket especially. Some parents say they'd like to see more coaching. All can play in a team if they want in many years. Socially, the climate is warm and sunny, the children notably natural and affectionate. Seniors take turns at being team leaders to supervise things, and patrol at break with snazzy walkie-talkies. There's a school council and a food committee with truly democratic elections. Communications are superb. Every week there's a bustling newsletter which comes home. Thriving PTA. For parents there is a strong sense of transparency and partnership, and much praise for the pastoral head, who solves problems thoroughly. Some feel that intimacy has lost out in the recent expansion, and it can sometimes be hard to talk to your child's teacher in person.

This is a fast-moving, high-achieving school dedicated to best possible results. It keeps relentlessness at bay because it places such high value on courtesy, right conduct and happiness. There is something very rooted and very modern going on here.

YEHUDI MENUHIN JUNIOR SCHOOL

Linked to Yehudi Menuhin School in the Senior section

Stoke d'Abernon, Cobham, Surrey, KT11 3QQ

Tel: 01932 864 739
Fax: 01932 864 633
E-mail: admin@yehudimenuhinschool.co.uk
Website: www.yehudimenuhinschool.co.uk

- Pupils: 65 boys and girls (entire school); mostly boarders
- Ages: 8 - 13 • Non-denom • Fees: £9,924 per term for those not on music and dance scheme • Independent
- Open days: Termly

Remarks: See senior school for details.

MAPS

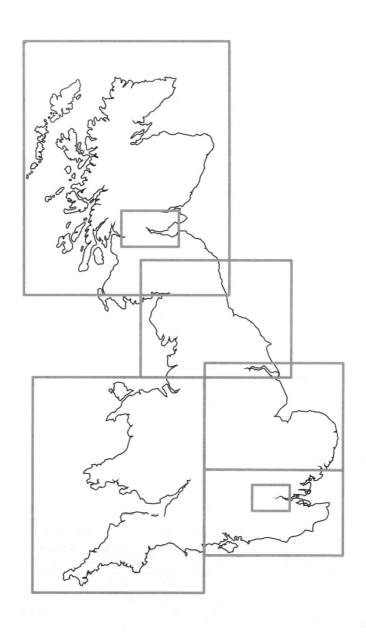

West of England & Wales

West Midlands
1. Blue Coat School
2. Edgbaston High School for Girls
3. Elmhurst, The School for Dance
4. King Edward VI High School for Girls
5. King Edward's School (Birmingham)
6. Thomas Telford School
7. Wolverhampton Grammar School

Somerset
1. Beechen Cliff School
2. Blue School (The)
3. Bruton School for Girls
4. Brymore School
5. Downside School
6. Hazlegrove School
7. Huish Episcopi School
8. King Edward's School (Bath)
9. King's Bruton
10. King's College (Taunton)
11. Millfield Preparatory School
12. Millfield School
13. Paragon School (The)
14. Prior Park College
15. Queen's College
16. Royal High School, Bath GDST
17. Saint Gregory's Catholic College
18. Sexey's School
19. Sidcot School
20. Taunton School
21. Wells Cathedral School

Bristol
1. Backwell School
2. Badminton School
3. Bristol Grammar School
4. Chew Valley School
5. Clifton College
6. Clifton High School
7. Downs School (The)
8. Queen Elizabeth's Hospital
9. Red Maids School (The)
10. Redland High School
11. Ridings High School (The)
12. Saint Mary Redcliffe and Temple School
13. Wellsway School

Dorset
1. Bournemouth School
2. Bournemouth School for Girls
3. Bryanston School
4. Canford School
5. Castle Court
6. Claymoore School
7. Gryphon School (The)
8. Hanford School

9. International College, Sherborne School
10. Knighton House School
11. Milton Abbey School
12. Old Malthouse School (The)
13. Parkstone Grammar School
14. Poole Grammar School
15. Port Regis Preparatory School
16. Saint Antony's Leweston School
17. Talbot Heath School
18. Saint Mary's School (Shaftesbury)
19. Sherborne School
20. Sherborne School for Girls
21. Thomas Hardye School (The)

Gloucestershire
1. Balcarras School
2. Beaudesert Park School
3. Cheltenham College
4. Cheltenham Ladies' College (The)
5. Dean Close School
6. Cirencester Deer Park School
7. Pate's Grammar School
8. Stroud High School
9. Westonbirt School
10. Wycliffe College
11. Rendcomb College
12. Farmor's School

Worcester
1. Abberley Hall
2. Elms School (The)
3. King's School (The) (Worcester)
4. Malvern College
5. Malvern Girls' College
6. Royal Grammar School (Worcester)

Cornwall
1. Altarnun Community Primary School
2. Bolitho School (The)
3. Truro High School
4. Truro School

Shropshire
1. Concord College
2. Moor Park School
3. Moreton Hall School
4. Packwood Haugh School
5. Shrewsbury High School
6. Shrewsbury School

Greater Manchester
1. Altrincham Grammar School for Boys
2. Altrincham Grammar School for Girls
3. Altrincham Preparatory School
4. Bolton School Boys' Division
5. Bolton School Girls' Division
6. Cheadle Hulme School
7. Chethams School of Music
8. Hale Perparatory School

9. Lymm High Voluntary Controlled School
10. Manchester Grammar School (The)
11. Manchester High School for Girls
12. North Cestrian Grammar School
13. Parrs Wood Technology College
14. Saint Bede's College
15. Stockport Grammar School
16. Withington Girls' School

Herefordshire
1. Wigmore High School

Wales
1. Atlantic College
2. Christ College, Brecon
3. Haberdashers' Monmouth School For Girls
4. Howell's School, Llandaff
5. Monmouth School
6. Saint David's College, Llandudno

Cheshire
1. Grange School (The)
2. King's School (The) (Chester)
3. King's School (The) (Macclesfield)
4. Queen's School (The)

Devon
1. Blackawton Primary School
2. Blundell's School
3. Bramdean School
4. Churston Ferrers Grammar School
5. Colyton Grammar School
6. Devonport High School for Boys
7. Devonport High School for Girls
8. Exeter Cathedral School
9. Exeter School
10. Kelly College
11. Maynard School (The)
12. Mount House School
13. Plymouth College
14. Plymstock School
15. Rudolf Steiner School
16. Saint John's School
17. Saint Margaret's School (Exeter)
18. Stover School
19. Torquay Boys' Grammar School
20. Torquay Grammar School for Girls
21. Westlands School and Technology College

Wiltshire
1. Bishop Wordsworth's Grammar School
2. Chafyn Grove School
3. Dauntsey's School
4. Godolphin School (The)
5. Marlborough College
6. Saint Laurence School

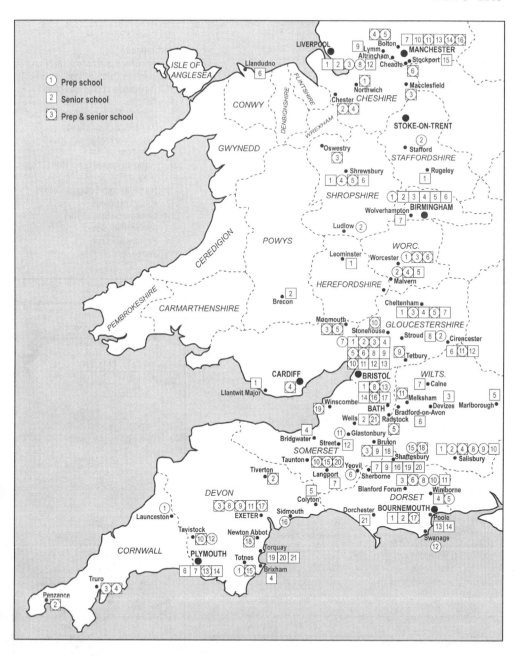

7   Saint Mary's School (Calne)
8   Salisbury Cathedral School
9   Sandroyd School
10   South Wilts Grammar School for Girls
11   Stonar School

Staffordshire

1   Abbots Bromley School for Girls
2   Yarlet School (The)

SOUTH EAST ENGLAND

Brighton & Hove
1 Brighton and Hove High School
2 Brighton College
3 Roedean School

West Sussex
1 Ardingly College
2 Bishop Luffa Church of England School, Chichester
3 Brambletye School
4 Burgess Hill School for Girls
5 Christ's Hospital
6 Cottesmore School
7 Cumnor House School
8 Hurstpierpoint College
9 Lancing College
10 Lavant House
11 Millais School
12 Prebendal School
13 Seaford College
14 Westbourne House School
15 Windlesham House School
16 Worth School

East Sussex
1 Ashdown House School
2 Eastbourne College
3 Michael Hall School
4 Moira House Girls School
5 Newlands Manor School
6 Saint Bede's School
7 Saint Bede's School-Eastbourne
8 Saint Leonards-Mayfield School
9 Vinehall School

Oxfordshire
1 Abingdon School
2 Bloxham School
3 Burford School
4 Carrdus School
5 Chandlings Manor School
6 Cherwell School (The)
7 Christ Church Cathedral School
8 Cokethorpe School
9 Cothill House School
10 d'Overbroeck's College
11 Dragon School (The)
12 Headington School
13 Lord Williams's School
14 Magdalen College School
15 New College School
16 Oxford High School GDST
17 Pinewood School
18 Radley College
19 Saint Clare's, Oxford
20 Saint Edward's Oxford
21 Saint Mary's School, Wantage

22 School of Saint Helen and Saint Katharine (The)
23 Shiplake College
24 Sibford School
25 Summer Fields School
26 Tudor Hall School
27 Wychwood School

Kent
1 Ashford School
2 Bedgebury School
3 Benenden School
4 Bromley High School (GDST)
5 Cobham Hall
6 Cranbrook School
7 Dulwich Preparatory School
8 Holmewood House School
9 Judd School (The)
10 King's School Canterbury (The)
11 King's School, Rochester
12 Marlborough House School
13 New Beacon School (The)
14 Newstead Wood School for Girls
15 Rowan Prep School
16 Saint Olave's and Saint Saviour's Grammar School
17 Saint Ronan's School
18 Sevenoaks School
19 Sutton Valence School
20 Tonbridge Grammar School
21 Tonbridge School
22 Wellesley House School

Berkshire
1 Abbey School Reading (The)
2 Bradfield College
3 Brockhurst and Marlston Schools
4 Caldicott School
5 Cheam School
6 Dolphin School
7 Downe House School
8 Elstree School
9 Eton College
10 Heathfield School
11 Horris Hill School
12 Hurst Lodge School
13 Lambrook Haileybury School
14 Leighton Park School
15 Ludgrove
16 Oratory School (The)
17 Papplewick School
18 Queen Anne's School
19 Saint George's School (Ascot)
20 Saint John's Beaumont School
21 Saint Mary's School Ascot
22 Slough Grammar School
23 Sunningdale School

24 Wellington College
25 Windsor Boys' School (The)

Hertfordshire
1 Arts Educational School (The) (Tring)
2 Beechwood Park School
3 Berkhamsted Collegiate School
4 Bishop's Stortford College
5 Bishop's Stortford High School (The)
6 Dame Alice Owen's School
7 Edge Grove Preparatory School
8 Haileybury
9 Hertfordshire and Essex High School (The)
10 Hockerill Anglo-European College
11 Immanuel College
12 Leventhorpe School (The)
13 Lockers Park School
14 Parmiter's School
15 Purcell School

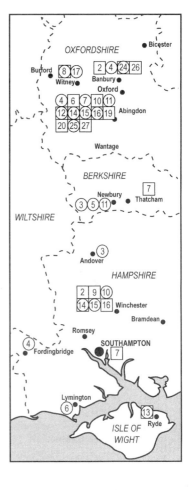

16 Queenswood School
17 Saint Albans Girls' School
18 Saint Albans High School for Girls
19 Saint Albans School
20 Saint Christopher School
21 Saint George's School (Harpenden)
22 Saint Mary's Catholic School
23 Watford Grammar School for Boys
24 Watford Grammar School for Girls

Hampshire & IOW
1 Bedales School
2 Brockwood Park School
3 Farleigh School
4 Forres Sandle Manor School
5 Highfield School
6 Hordle Walhampton School
7 King Edward VI School
8 Mayville High School
9 Peter Symonds College

10 Pilgrims School (The)
11 Portsmouth Grammar School (The)
12 Portsmouth High School
13 Ryde School with Upper Chine
14 Saint Swithun's School
15 Twyford School
16 Winchester College
17 Yateley Manor

Buckinghamshire
1 Ashfold School
2 Aylesbury Grammar School
3 Dr Challoner's Grammar School
4 Dr Challoner's High School
5 Godstowe Prep School
6 Maltman's Green School
7 Royal Grammar School, High Wycombe (The)
8 Sir William Borlase's Grammar School
9 Stowe School

10 Wycombe Abbey School

Surrey
1 ACS Cobham International School
2 ACS Egham International School
3 Aldro School
4 Belmont School
5 Bentley Church of England Primary School
6 Box Hill School
7 Caterham School
8 Charterhouse
9 City of London Freemen's School
10 Coworth-Flexlands School
11 Cranleigh School
12 Cranmore School
13 Danes Hill School
14 Epsom College
15 Feltonfleet School
16 Frensham Heights School

Prep school

Senior school

Prep & senior school

SOUTH EAST ENGLAND CONT.

Essex

MIDLANDS & EAST ENGLAND

Cambridgeshire
1. Barnardiston Hall Preparatory School
2. Hills Road Sixth Form College
3. Impington Village College
4. King's College School (Cambridge)
5. King's School Ely
6. Leys School (The)
7. Oundle School
8. Perse School (The)
9. Perse School for Girls
10. Saint John's College School
11. Saint Mary's School (Cambridge)
12. Stamford High School
13. Stamford School

Suffolk
1. Culford School
2. Framlingham College
3. Ipswich High School
4. Ipswich School
5. Old Buckenham Hall School
6. Orwell Park School
7. Saint Felix Schools
8. Thomas Mills High School
9. Thurston Community College
10. Woodbridge School

Leicestershire
1. Loughborough Grammar School
2. Loughborough High School

Lincolnshire
1. Caistor Grammar School
2. Lincoln Minster School
3. Saint Hughs School
4. Witham Hall School

Warwickshire
1. Bilton Grange School
2. Rugby School
3. Warwick School

Derbyshire
1. Repton School
2. Saint Anselm's School

Norfolk
1. Beeston Hall School
2. Gresham's School
3. Norwich High School for Girls
4. Riddlesworth Hall School
5. Wymondham College

Northamptonshire
1. Winchester House School

Nottinghamshire
1. Nottingham High School
2. Nottingham High School for Girls GDST

Rutland
1. Oakham School
2. Uppingham Community College
3. Uppingham School

Bedfordshire
1. Bedford High School
2. Bedford School
3. Dame Alice Harpur School

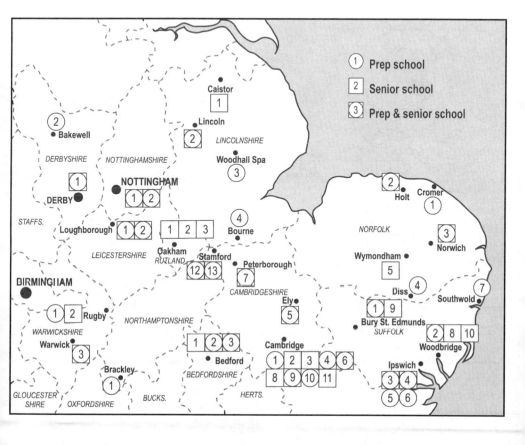

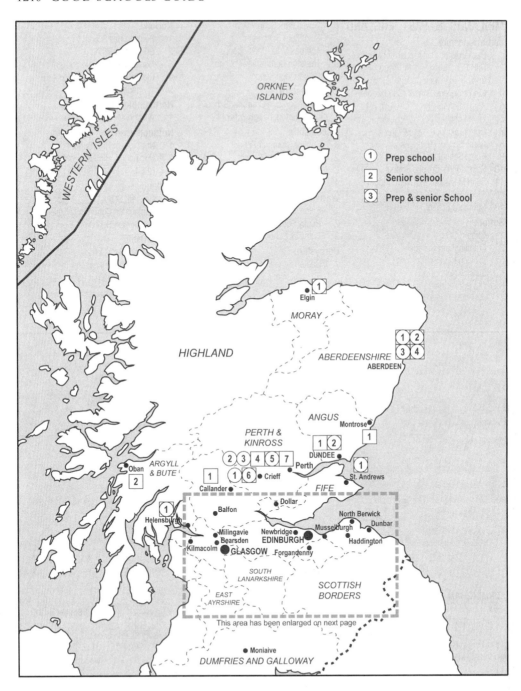

SCOTLAND

Dundee
1 Harris Academy
2 High School of Dundee

Edinburgh
1 Basil Paterson Tutorial College
2 Cargilfield School
3 Clifton Hall School
4 Edinburgh Academy (The)
5 Edinburgh Rudolf Steiner School
6 Fettes College
7 George Heriot's School
8 George Watson's College
9 James Gillespie's High School
10 Mary Erskine School (The)
11 Merchiston Castle School
12 Royal High School (The) (Edinburgh)
13 Saint George's School
14 Saint Margaret's School (Edinburgh)
15 Saint Mary's Music School
16 Stewart's Melville College
17 Wallace College

Clackmannanshire
1 Dollar Academy

Stirling
1 Mclaren High School

Glasgow
1 Balfron High School
2 Craigholme School
3 Fernhill School
4 Glasgow Academy (The)
5 High School of Glasgow (The)
6 Hutchesons' Grammar School
7 Jordanhill School
8 Kelvinside Academy
9 Saint Aloysius' College

Moray
1 Gordonstoun School

Aberdeenshire
1 Albyn School
2 International School of Aberdeen
3 Robert Gordon's College
4 Saint Margaret's School for Girls

Angus
1 Lathallan School

East Lothian
1 Belhaven Hill School
2 Compass School (The)
3 Loretto School

4 North Berwick High School

Perth & Kinross
1 Ardvreck School
2 Auchtergaven Primary School
3 Craigclowan Preparatory School
4 Glenalmond College
5 Kilgraston School
6 Morrison's Academy
7 Strathallan School

Scottish Borders
1 Saint Mary's School (Melrose)

East Dunbartonshire
1 Bearsden Academy
2 Douglas Academy

Argyll & Bute
1 Lomond School
2 Oban High School

Inverclyde
1 Saint Columba's School

Fife
1 Saint Leonards School & Sixth Form College

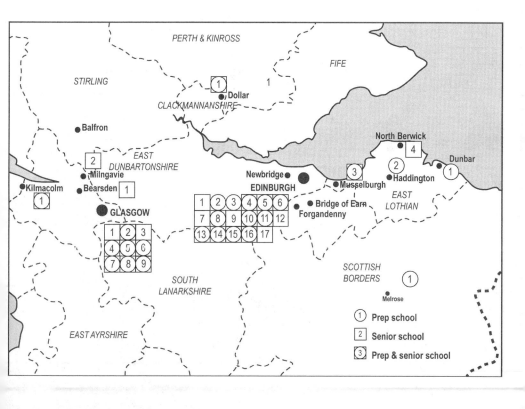

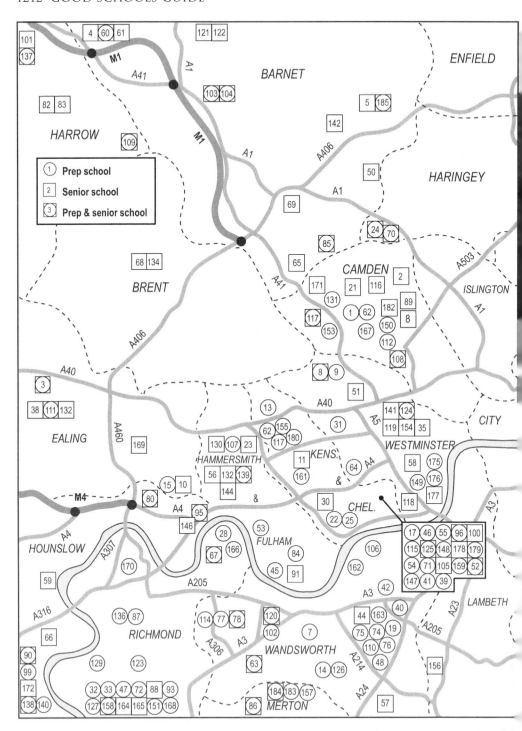

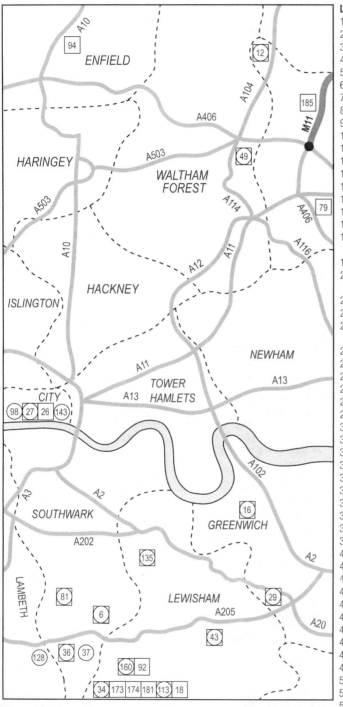

LONDON

1   Academy School (The)
2   Acland Burghley School
3   ACS Hillingdon International School
4   Aldenham School
5   Alexandra Park School
6   Alleyn's School
7   Allfarthing Primary School
8   American School in London (The)
9   Arnold House School
10 Arts Educational School (The) (London)
11 Ashbourne Independent School
12 Bancroft's School
13 Bassett House School
14 Beatrix Potter Primary School
15 Belmont Primary School
16 Blackheath High School GDST
17 Bousfield Primary School
18 BRIT School for Performing Arts and
    Technology
19 Broomwood Hall School
20 Bute House Preparatory School for
    Girls
21 Camden School for Girls (The)
22 Cameron House School
23 Cardinal Vaughan Memorial RC School
    (The)
24 Channing School
25 Christ Church CofE Primary School
26 City of London School
27 City of London School for Girls
28 Colet Court
29 Colfe's School
30 Collingham
31 Connaught House School
32 Coombe Hill Infant School
33 Coombe Hill Junior School
34 Croydon High School
35 Davies Laing and Dick College
36 Dulwich College
37 Dulwich Hamlet Junior School
38 Ealing Independent College
39 Eaton House Belgravia
40 Eaton House The Manor School
41 Eaton House The Vale
42 Ecole Charles de Gaulle   Wix
43 Eltham College
44 Emanuel School
45 Eridge House School
46 Falkner House
47 Fern Hill Primary School
48 Finton House School
49 Forest School
50 Fortismere School
51 Francis Holland School (NW1)
52 Francis Holland School (SW1)

LONDON CONT.

NORTH ENGLAND

Cumbria
1 Keswick School
2 Queen Elizabeth Grammar School
3 Saint Bees School
4 Sedbergh School
5 Windermere Saint Anne's School

Stockton-on-Tees
1 Teeside Preparatory and High School

Northumberland
1 Mowden Hall School

North Yorkshire
1 Ampleforth College
2 Ashville College
3 Aysgarth School
4 Bootham School
5 Bramcote School, North Yorkshire
6 Caedmon School
7 Ermysted's Grammar School
8 Filey School
9 Giggleswick School
10 Harrogate Ladies' College
11 Lady Lumley's School
12 Mount School (The)
13 Polam Hall School
14 Queen Ethelburga's College
15 Queen Margaret's School
16 Queen Mary's School
17 Ripon Cathedral Choir School
18 Ripon Grammar School
19 Ryedale School
20 Saint Aidan's Church of England High School
21 Saint John Fisher Catholic High School
22 Saint Peter's School
23 Skipton Girls' High School

Lancashire
1 Casterton School
2 Lancaster Girls' Grammar School
3 Lancaster Royal Grammar School
4 Queen Elizabeth's Grammar School
5 Rossall School
6 Stonyhurst College

East Riding of Yorkshire
1 Beverley Grammar School
2 Beverley High School
3 Driffield School
4 Hymers College

Durham
1 Durham High School for Girls

West Yorkshire
1 Ackworth School
2 Bradford Girls' Grammar School
3 Bradford Grammar School
4 Froebelian School (The)
5 Gateways School
6 Greenhead College
7 Leeds Girls' High School
8 Leeds Grammar School
9 Malsis School
10 Queen Elizabeth Grammar School (Wakefield)
11 Richmond House School
12 Wakefield Girls' High School

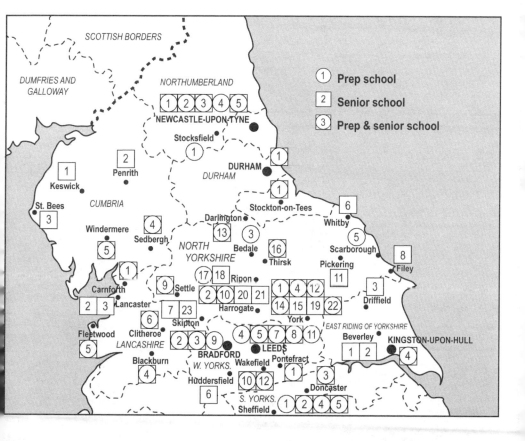

NORTH ENGLAND CONT.

Tyne & Wear
1   Central Newcastle High School
2   Dame Allan's Boys' School
3   Dame Allan's Girls' School
4   Newcastle Preparatory School
5   Royal Grammar School (Newcastle)

South Yorkshire
1   Ashdell Preparatory School
2   Birkdale School
3   Hill House Saint Mary's
4   Sheffield High School
5   Westbourne School

11+ English:
A Parent's Toolkit

Katherine Hamlyn

11+ English:
A Parent's Toolkit

Katherine Hamlyn

www.11PlusEnglish.com

Help your child get up to speed in English for secondary school.

Is this your child?:

*'Her class teacher just
doesn't have time to help her with the basics.'*
○
'He just can't seem to get started with story writing.'
○
'Her stories are lovely but she can't manage a time limit!'
○
*'I would like him to go to a selective school, but I'm
worried that his English is not good enough.'*
○
'She hasn't a clue about comprehensions.'

**If you share any of these concerns then this is the book for
you. It has been written to help parents and children work
together on all aspects of English around the transition to
senior schools, and specifically for children who are going to
take entrance examinations for grammar schools or selective
independent schools.**

*11+ English: a Parent's Toolkit has been distilled from Katherine Hamlyn's 25
years of experience of teaching at this level. This highly readable guide pinpoints
common problems and, using child-centred techniques and games concentrating
on relaxed child/parent collaboration, takes you through essential English with
common sense, clarity and humour.*

UNI IN THE USA

BY ALICE FISHBURN

THE UK GUIDE TO US UNIVERSITIES

WITH
ANTHONY NEMECEK
DIRECTOR OF THE EDUCATIONAL ADVISORY SERVICE OF THE US-UK FULBRIGHT COMMISSION

FOREWORD BY
STEPHEN BALDOCK
HIGH MASTER OF ST PAUL'S SCHOOL, LONDON 1992–2004

THE GOOD SCHOOLS GUIDE

UNI IN THE USA

Alice Fishburn
with Anthony Nemecek

www.UniintheUSA.com

Myths about universities in the USA abound: the cost is astronomical; you won't get in with British qualifications; the cultural chasm is unbridgeable.

Yet, in increasing numbers, British students are looking at the pleasures and possibilities that await them across the pond. And reports are favourable: once you've seen what's on offer in America, you may never look at a UCAS form again.

Choosing a university thousands of miles away is a daunting task; *Uni in the USA* is an invaluable and accurate guide to what you need to know, from formalities such as the SAT (different from SATs) and scholarships to the world of fraternities, dating etiquette and life on campus. American universities vary hugely in character, and *Uni in the USA* also provides a low-down on over two dozen of the best, from the cosy intimacy of Amherst to the high-pressure energy of Yale, via the sun-drenched sprawl of UCLA and the urban edginess of Columbia.

As a recent graduate of Harvard, British Alice Fishburn writes entertainingly and informatively from the inside on what it's like to be a Brit on American turf: the academic expectations, the social mores, the fun and frustrations.

Anthony Nemecek is director of the educational advisory service of the US–UK Fulbright Commission, the only official and independent source of information on US education in the UK. He has twenty years' experience teaching, managing and examining on both sides of the Atlantic.

'There is little doubt that four years at an American college bring a fuller educational experience with greater cultural and social coherence...very few, if any, of those British pupils whom I have seen make their way to American universities have regretted their decision.'

Stephen Baldock,
former High Master of St Paul's, London

GOOD
SCHOOLS GUIDE –
SPECIAL
EDUCATIONAL
NEEDS

The *insightful* and independent guide to special educational needs and schools

2006

The Good Schools Guide for Special Educational Needs

Sandra Hutchinson

www.goodschoolsguide.co.uk

Special Educational Needs (SEN) are much more common than is generally supposed. Upwards of 20 per cent of children in school need specialised help at any one time. SEN might entail anything from mild dyslexia to severe autism, from help with reading, writing and personal organisation, to specialised therapy sessions or behavioural adjustment.

In compiling this guide we've worked with parents, charities and professionals specialising in SEN. We've discovered innovative and inspirational teaching, dedicated practitioners and amazing children. But we've also found worrying gaps, lack of understanding and phenomenal oversubscriptions for places or help.

Whether you just suspect that your child has special needs that are not being met, or are battle-weary from the complexities and shortfalls of a system that seems more bound up in red tape than in finding solutions, this book will help. As well as details of hundreds of schools state and independent, mainstream and special which provide terrific support at various levels, it includes enlightening contributions from educational psychologists, therapists and other professionals, and parents who have been through it all. There is also invaluable advice on statementing, the law and resources to draw on.

'Practical, fearless, frank, sympathetic and lively, this guide is exactly what has been needed for a very long time.'

Nick Hornby

Publication 6th April 2006